International Civil Litigation
in United States Courts
Commentary & Materials

THIRD EDITION

International Civil Litigation in United States Courts

Commentary & Materials

THIRD EDITION

Gary B. Born

Kluwer Law International

The Hague • Boston • London

Kluwer Law International
P.O. Box 85889
2508 CN The Hague
The Netherlands

Tel. 31-70-308-1560
Fax. 31-70-308-1515

Distribution in the USA and Canada
675 Massachusetts Avenue
Cambridge, MA 02139
USA

Tel. 617-354-0140
Fax. 617-354-8595
Internet: sales@kli.com

Library of Congress Cataloging-in-Publication Data
is available for this title

ISBN 90-411-0973-0 (PB)
ISBN 90-411-0972-2 (HB)

Acknowledgments

I am indebted to my colleagues, students, reviewers, and others for invaluable contributions to this book. I am particularly grateful for the wise counsel and generous assistance that David Westin has provided over the years. In addition, present and past colleagues and students at the University of Arizona College of Law, Harvard Law School, Georgetown University Law Center, Pepperdine University Law College, University of Trier, and University College London have made valuable suggestions and criticisms. My editor, John Berger, has also provided continuous assistance and encouragement.

I acknowledge my indebtedness to the following authors and publishers who granted permission to reprint copyrighted material: The American Law Institute, for permission to reprint from the Restatement (Third) Foreign Relations Law of the United States §§111, 402, 403, 421, 441, 442 (1987), Copyright 1987 by the American Law Institute, the Restatement (Second) Foreign Relations Law of the United States §§17, 18, 30, 33, 39, 40 (1965), Copyright 1965 by the American Law Institute, the Restatement (Second) Conflict of Laws §§6, 9, 10, 84, comment f, 92, 94, 98, 122, 145, 146, 156, 187, 188, 202, 204, 206 (1971), Copyright 1971 by the American Law Institute, the Restatement of Conflict of Laws §§1, 6, 47, 55, 63, 65, 332, 358, 377, 378, 384, 585, 610, 611, 612 (1934), Copyright 1934 by the American Law Institute; and the Duke Law Journal, for permission to reprint from Currie, Notes on Methods and Objectives in the Conflict of Laws [1959] Duke L. J. 171.

Gary Born
London, England
February 21, 1996

This book is for
Beatrix, Natascha, and Jedidiah

Table of Contents

PART ONE:
JUDICIAL JURISDICTION

The courts of many nations will not adjudicate civil disputes unless the parties (or their property) and their claims are subject to the forum's "judicial jurisdiction" or "jurisdiction to adjudicate." As discussed below, judicial jurisdiction includes both (a) the power of a court to render a judgment against particular persons or things, and (b) the power or competence of a court to adjudicate particular categories of claims.[1]

Judicial jurisdiction is distinguished from "legislative" or "prescriptive" jurisdiction, which refers to the authority of a state to make its laws generally applicable to persons or activities.[2] Judicial jurisdiction is also distinguished from "enforcement jurisdiction" — the authority of a state to induce or compel compliance, or punish noncompliance, with its laws.[3]

In the United States, a court cannot hear a dispute unless it possesses both "personal" jurisdiction over the parties and "subject matter" jurisdiction over their claims.[4] Subject matter jurisdiction is the power of a court to entertain specified classes of cases, such as any action between parties of differing citizenships.[5]

---

1. *Restatement (Third) Foreign Relations Law* Part IV Intro. Note & §401 (1987); *Restatement (Second) Conflict of Laws* Ch. 3, Intro. Note (1971); Akehurst, *Jurisdiction in International Law*, 46 Brit. Y.B. Int'l L. 145 (1972-73).

2. *See infra* pp. 491-92; *Restatement (Third) Foreign Relations Law* Part IV Intro. Note & §401 (1987) ("make its law applicable to the activities, relations, or status of persons, or the interests of persons in things, whether by legislation, by executive act or order, by administrative rule or regulation, or by determination of a court"); *Restatement (Second) Conflict of Laws* Ch. 3, Intro. Note (1971); Akehurst, *Jurisdiction in International Law*, 46 Brit. Y.B. Int'l L. 145, 179-212 (1972-73). Chapters 7 and 8 *infra* provide a detailed examination of legislative jurisdiction in the international context.

3. *Restatement (Third) Foreign Relations Law* Part IV Intro. Note & §401 (1987). Examples of the exercise of jurisdiction to enforce include execution upon property, seizure of goods and arrest. These materials do not directly address international law limits on national enforcement jurisdiction.

4. *Insurance Corp. of Ireland v. Compagnie des Bauxites de Guinee*, 456 U.S. 694, 701 (1982) ("The validity of an order of a federal court depends upon that court's having jurisdiction over both the subject matter and the parties."); *Still v. Gottlieb*, 305 U.S. 165, 171-72 (1938).

5. *See Verlinden BV v. Central Bank of Nigeria*, 461 U.S. 480 (1983); C. Wright & A. Miller, *Federal Practice and Procedure* §§1350-51, 3522 (1969); *Restatement (Third) Foreign Relations Law* §401, comment c (1987).

Although subject matter and legislative jurisdiction are sometimes confused, there is a fundamental distinction under U.S. law between the two categories. Subject matter jurisdiction is a court's power to hear a category of disputes without necessary regard to the substantive rules that are applied.[6] In contrast, legislative jurisdiction deals with the power of a state to prescribe substantive law, without necessary regard to the forum in which that law is applied.[7]

There is also a fundamental distinction under U.S. law between subject matter jurisdiction and personal jurisdiction.[8] Personal jurisdiction involves the power of a court to adjudicate a claim against the defendant's person and to render a judgment enforceable against the defendant and any of its assets.[9] In contrast, subject matter jurisdiction refers to a court's power to hear categories of claims, without necessarily considering the relationship of the parties to particular cases to the forum.[10]

This Part considers the judicial jurisdiction of U.S. courts in international civil litigation. Chapter 1 examines the subject matter jurisdiction of federal courts in international disputes. Chapter 2 considers the personal jurisdiction of U.S. courts over parties to international litigation. Chapter 3 explores the subject matter and

---

6. For example, the federal district courts enjoy "diversity jurisdiction" and "alienage jurisdiction" over all civil actions between citizens of different states, or suits between U.S. and foreign nationals, where the amount in controversy exceeds $50,000. *See* 28 U.S.C. §1332(a); U.S. Const. Art. III, §2. In conferring this jurisdiction, Congress did not generally prescribe rules of substantive law, but left federal courts to apply the substantive law that would be applied by a state court in the state where the federal court sits. *Erie R.R. v. Tompkins*, 304 U.S. 64 (1938); *infra* pp. 13-14. Much the same approach was taken with respect to claims against foreign states. *See* Chapter 3 *infra.*

7. *See infra* pp. 491-92; *Restatement (Third) Foreign Relations Law* §401 comment c (1987). Despite this distinction, there is often an important relation in the United States between subject matter and legislative jurisdiction. In many cases, Congress's prescription of a substantive rule of law is accompanied by a grant of subject matter jurisdiction to the federal courts for cases arising under those substantive rules. The federal antitrust and securities laws are prime examples of the simultaneous exercise of prescriptive jurisdiction and grant of subject matter jurisdiction. *See infra* pp. 34-35, 69-70 & 605; 15 U.S.C. §§1, 2 & 15 (1982) (antitrust); 15 U.S.C. §§77(g), 77l(2), 78aa, 78j (1982) (securities).

8. *Insurance Corp. of Ireland v. Compagnie des Bauxites de Guinee*, 456 U.S. 694, 701 (1982); *Verlinden BV v. Central Bank of Nigeria*, 461 U.S. 480 (1983).

9. *See infra* p. 67; *Restatement (Second) Conflict of Laws* Ch. 3, Intro. Note (1971); *Shaffer v. Heitner*, 433 U.S. 186, 199 (1977). U.S. law distinguishes between *in personam* (or personal) jurisdiction, *in rem* jurisdiction, and *quasi in rem* jurisdiction. *In rem* jurisdiction involves the adjudication of preexisting claims of ownership or other rights in specific property (*e.g.*, a ship or a bank deposit); although judgments rendered on the basis of *in rem* jurisdiction extend only to the specific assets that are before the court, they are binding on the interests of all persons in such property. *Quasi in rem* jurisdiction most often involves the seizure of specific items of property for the purpose of providing security pending the adjudication of unrelated claims against the owner of the property. *Restatement (Second) Conflict of Laws* Ch. 3, Intro. Note (1971); *Shaffer v. Heitner*, 433 U.S. 186, 199 (1977).

10. *See Insurance Corp. of Ireland v. Compagnie des Bauxites de Guinee*, 456 U.S. 694, 701 (1982). Again, there is sometimes an important practical relation between subject matter and personal jurisdiction. As discussed below, the Foreign Sovereign Immunities Act makes federal court subject matter and personal jurisdiction coextensive. *See infra* pp. 210-12 & 226-27.

personal jurisdiction of U.S. courts over foreign states and their state-related entities.[11]

Judicial jurisdiction has substantial practical importance in international litigation. That importance derives from the role of judicial jurisdiction in determining the forum (or forums) in which an international dispute can be litigated. As discussed below, forum selection has vital consequences for the resolution of many international disputes, thus giving jurisdictional issues central importance in many cases.

For a variety of reasons, the same dispute can often be resolved in significantly different ways in different forums. Procedural, choice-of-law, substantive and statute of limitations vary from one forum to another.[12] The identity, character, competence, and neutrality of the tribunal that decides civil disputes can also differ substantially depending on the forum where adjudication occurs. Some forums may be unfavorable to one party to a dispute: for reasons of convenience, local bias, and otherwise, parties are sometimes particularly reluctant to litigate in the courts of their adversary. As one commentator has correctly observed, "[t]he choice of forum has ... become a key strategic battle fought to increase the chances of prevailing on the merits."[13]

Forum selection is especially important in the international context. Procedural, substantive, and choice-of-law rules differ far more significantly from country to country than they do from state to state within the United States.[14] Differences in political, economic, social, and other attitudes of courts and lawyers are more pronounced in international matters than domestic ones. Inconvenience, forum bias, and the risk of multiple proceedings will often be more important factors in international than in domestic litigation.[15] Obtaining effective enforcement of judgments in foreign countries can also often be unusually difficult.[16]

Forum selection for an international dispute can be particularly important where one potential forum is the United States. This is because litigation in U.S. courts often differs dramatically from that in other countries, including with respect to its procedures, risks, expenses, and potential rewards. A number of factors con-

---

11. A number of other significant means of influencing forum selection are discussed in Chapters 4, 5 & 6 below, including the *forum non conveniens* doctrine, forum selection agreements, *lis pendens*, and venue.

12. *See generally* M. Glendon, M. Gordon & C. Osakwe, *Comparative Legal Traditions* (1985); G. Gloss, *Comparative Law* (1979); J. Merryman, *The Civil Law Tradition: An Introduction to the Legal Systems of Western Europe and Latin America* (2d ed. 1985).

13. Stein, *Forum Non Conveniens and the Redundancy of Court-Access Doctrine*, 133 U. Pa. L. Rev. 781, 783 (1985).

14. *See* Born, *Reflections on Judicial Jurisdiction in International Cases*, 17 Ga. J. Int'l & Comp. L. 1, 25 (1987).

15. *See Asahi Metal Industry Co. v. Superior Court*, 480 U.S. 102, 114 (1987) (noting "[t]he unique burdens placed upon one who must defend oneself in a foreign legal system"); Born, *Reflections on Judicial Jurisdiction in International Cases*, 17 Ga. J. Int'l & Comp. L. 1, 24-25 (1987).

16. *See infra* Chapter 12 at pp. 935-86.

tribute to make U.S. litigation unusual. In general, as detailed below, these factors make the United States a particularly attractive forum for plaintiffs: "As a moth is drawn to the light, so is a litigant drawn to the United States. If he can only get his case into their courts, he stands to win a fortune."[17]

First, civil suits in the United States are ordinarily decided by juries of lay men and women, who have very different backgrounds and sympathies from many judges. Although there are regional, economic, social, and other variations, U.S. juries can be remarkably pro-plaintiff. That is particularly true when compared to jurisdictions where judges are government lawyers or career bureaucrats. As one eminent foreign judge has remarked, "[t]here is in the United States a right to trial by jury. These are prone to award fabulous damages. They are notoriously sympathetic [to plaintiffs]."[18]

Second, several procedural aspects of U.S. litigation tend to favor plaintiffs. Plaintiffs in U.S. courts can enter into contingent fee agreements, which is often forbidden in foreign courts. Unsuccessful U.S. litigants are not ordinarily liable for their adversary's attorneys' fees, although they are in many foreign jurisdictions.[19] Discovery in U.S. proceedings is extremely broad, by international standards, and provides means for plaintiffs both to prove their substantive claims from the defendants' own files, and to impose unrecoverable costs on a defendant.[20] U.S. pleading requirements often permit fairly loosely-formulated claims to be advanced, sometimes enabling plaintiffs with weak cases to survive all efforts to obtain summary disposition.[21] The cumulative effect of these procedural features of U.S. litigation is often to improve a plaintiff's prospects of successful recovery (including by providing substantial leverage in negotiating settlement of marginal or unwinnable suits).

Third, and at the bottom line, is the simple fact that U.S. damage awards tend to be dramatically larger than those in other countries.[22] U.S. juries are often both sympathetic and generous, at least from an injured plaintiff's perspective. U.S. substantive laws are sometimes unusually favorable: American product liability and other tort doctrines, and U.S. antitrust and securities fraud statutes, often grant plaintiffs

---

17. *Smith Kline & French Labs. v. Bloch* [1983] 2 All E.R. 72, 74 (Denning, MR).

18. *Smith Kline & French Labs. v. Bloch* [1983] 2 All E.R. 72, 74 (Denning, MR) ("At no cost to himself, and at no risk of having to pay anything to the other side, the lawyers there will conduct the case 'on spec' as we say, or on a 'contingency fee' as they say.").

19. *See* Symposium, *Attorney Fee Shifting*, 47 Law & Contemp. Probs. 1 (1984).

20. *Societe Nationale Industrielle Aerospatiale v. U.S. District Court*, 482 U.S. 522 (1987); *Hickman v. Taylor*, 329 U.S. 495, 500-07 (1947). The scope of U.S. pretrial discovery is discussed below at *infra* pp. 843-45.

21. *See* C. Wright & A. Miller, *Federal Practice and Procedure* §1202, 1215-25, 1286, 1375 (1987).

22. In one foreign judge's terse summary, "in the United States the scale of damages for injuries of the magnitude sustained by the plaintiff is something in the region of ten times what is regarded as appropriate by ... the courts of [England]." *Castanho v. Brown & Root (U.K.) Ltd.* [1980] 1 W.L.R. 833, 859, *aff'd*, 1981 A.C. 557 (Shaw, J.).

very generous avenues of recovery.[23] Moreover, many U.S. state and federal statutes provide for mandatory awards of multiple damages, while state common law often permits jury awards of punitive damages based on vague, discretionary standards.

At the same time, aspects of U.S. litigation can make it distinctly unattractive to some foreign (and domestic) plaintiffs. Few litigants welcome the prospect of participating in any proceeding, far from home, in an unfamiliar forum that may be inconvenient, parochial, and worse. In the United States, legal proceedings can be uniquely expensive and, compared to at least some foreign alternatives, relatively slow. The availability of broad discovery can be a threat, as well as an inducement, for potential plaintiffs, as can the extensive public, press, and governmental access to U.S. judicial proceedings and discovery materials. And the possibility of large damages awards, by potentially unpredictable local lay juries, can be a disincentive where counterclaims are likely.

For all the foregoing reasons, it is critically important in international commercial disputes for a litigant to have its claims adjudicated in the best available forum, especially where one potential forum is the United States. Plaintiffs therefore often devote substantial effort and ingenuity to finding the most advantageous forum in which to proceed with their claims. Chief Justice Rehnquist has commented on the "litigation strategy of countless plaintiffs who seek a forum with favorable substantive or procedural rules or sympathetic local populations."[24] The issues of judicial jurisdiction discussed in this part are important aspects of these disputes over forum selection.

---

23. *E.g., British Airways Bd. v. Laker Airways* [1984] W.L.R. 413 (H.L.) (English plaintiffs sues English and other European defendants in United States, to take advantage of U.S. antitrust laws, which were more favorable than applicable English law); *Virgin Atlantic Airways Ltd. v. British Airways plc*, 872 F.Supp. 52 (S.D.N.Y. 1994) (same).

24. *Keeton v. Huster Magazine, Inc.*, 465 U.S. 770, 779 (1984).

1/Subject Matter Jurisdiction of U.S. Courts in International Disputes

A U.S. court cannot adjudicate a case unless it has "subject matter" jurisdiction over the action. Subject matter jurisdiction (also referred to as "competence") is the power of a court to entertain specified classes of cases, such as any claim in excess of $50,000 or any action between parties of differing citizenships.[1] This Chapter considers the subject matter jurisdiction of U.S. courts in international cases, focussing on the federal courts.

A. Introduction and Institutional Overview

1. Plenary State Subject Matter and Legislative Jurisdiction

For the most part, there are few restrictions on the subject matter jurisdiction of U.S. state courts: state trial courts ordinarily possess general jurisdiction over all but a few specialized categories of claims. Those exceptions that are of importance to international litigation are relatively scarce.[2] The same generalization is true with respect to state substantive law in the United States. States generally are subject to few significant internal limitations on their powers to exercise legislative jurisdiction.[3]

---

1. *See Verlinden BV v. Central Bank of Nigeria*, 461 U.S. 480 (1983); C. Wright & A. Miller, *Federal Practice and Procedure* §§1350-51, 3522 (1969); *Restatement (Third) Foreign Relations Law* §401 comment c (1987).

2. Claims under some federal statutes, including the federal securities laws, may be brought exclusively in federal court. *See* 15 U.S.C. §§77(l)(2) & 78aa.

3. The U.S. Constitution limits the legislative jurisdiction of the several states, *see infra* pp. 15-20 & 518-44, and valid federal statutes or U.S. treaties may preempt state law, *see infra* pp. 8-9. In addition, customary international law may also preempt state substantive law. *See infra* pp. 21, 49-56.

2. Limited Federal Legislative and Subject Matter Jurisdiction

a. Limited Federal Legislative Authority Under Article I

Article I of the U.S. Constitution endows Congress with only limited legislative powers; those powers not granted to Congress are expressly reserved to the several states.[4] This arrangement reflects the Framers' judgment that the national government's authority should be restricted, both to prevent abuse of its powers and to avoid invading the prerogatives of the several states.

Congress's principal enumerated powers include the authority to regulate interstate and foreign commerce, to levy taxes, and to appropriate funds.[5] These powers have proved both overwhelmingly important and difficult to restrain. The Supreme Court has interpreted congressional authority expansively in the last four decades and, until recently, had abandoned meaningful judicial efforts to limit Congress's legislative powers over commercial matters.[6] There continue to be very few aspects of national commercial matters that Congress cannot regulate.

Congress's powers over U.S. foreign relations are particularly extensive. Among other things, Article I of the Constitution grants Congress the power to declare war, maintain an army and navy, and define and punish piracy and violations of the law of nations,[7] while the Senate is vested with the power to advise on and consent to treaties and the appointment of ambassadors.[8] The Supreme Court has said that the "supremacy of the national power in the general field of foreign affairs ... is made clear by the Constitution ..., and has since been given continuous recognition by this Court."[9] The Court has also repeatedly said that the states have only the most limited of roles in international relations, declaring that the Constitution prohibits any "intrusion by the State into the field of foreign affairs which the Constitution entrusts to the President and the Congress."[10] Invoking this constitutional authority, Congress and the President have frequently preempted state laws in the area of foreign relations.[11]

---

4. Article I, §1, provides Congress with only the "legislative [p]owers herein granted." In addition, the tenth amendment provides that "The powers not delegated to the United States by the Constitution, nor prohibited by it to the States, are reserved to the States respectively, or to the people." *See* Hart, *The Relations Between Federal and State Law*, 54 Colum. L. Rev. 489 (1954).

5. U.S. Const. Art. 1, §8, cl. 1, 3.

6. *United States v. Lopez*, 115 S.Ct. 1624 (1995); *South Carolina v. Baker*, 485 U.S. 505 (1988); *Garcia v. San Antonio Metro. Transit Auth.*, 469 U.S. 528 (1985), overruling, *National League of Cities v. Usery*, 426 U.S. 833 (1976).

7. U.S. Const. Art. I, §8.

8. U.S. Const. Art. II, §2.

9. *Hines v. Davidowitz*, 312 U.S. 52, 62 (1941).

10. *Zschernig v. Miller*, 389 U.S. 429, 439 (1968). *See also* Henkin, *The Foreign Affairs Power of the Federal Courts*: Sabbatino, 64 Colum. L. Rev. 805 (1964); Moore, *Federalism and Foreign Relations*, 1965 Duke L.J. 248. Or, as the Court remarked elsewhere, "in respect of our foreign relations generally, state lines disappear. As to such purposes the State ... does not exist." *United States v. Belmont*, 301 U.S. 324, 331 (1937).

11. *E.g., Dames & Moore v. Regan*, 453 U.S. 654 (1981); *Hines v. Davidowitz*, 312 U.S. 52 (1941); *United States v. Pink*, 315 U.S. 203 (1942); *United States v. Belmont*, 301 U.S. 324 (1937).

The Constitution also provides for broad federal legislative power over international trade, conferred principally by Article I, §8's "foreign commerce" clause.[12] In the Court's words, "[f]oreign commerce is preeminently a matter of national concern."[13] The Court has held that federal power over foreign commerce is broader than that over interstate commerce, and that the "dormant" foreign commerce clause requires greater scrutiny of state restrictions on foreign commerce than for purely domestic commerce.[14]

Congress has frequently exercised its constitutional authority over foreign commerce, particularly in recent decades. Thus, federal legislation exhaustively regulates the fields of foreign sovereign immunity and international arbitration, as well as international trade practices, international transportation and telecommunications, tariffs and customs, and export controls. Notwithstanding its broad legislative powers, there remain numerous areas in the international field where Congress has not chosen to exercise its authority. Thus, federal legislation is generally silent in the international context with respect to substantive contract and tort law, as well as with respect to rules regarding agency, damages, contribution, choice of law, and recognition of foreign judgments. In all of these fields, state law generally provides the applicable rule of decision.[15]

b. Limited Federal Judicial Authority Under Article III

Just as the Constitution granted Congress only enumerated powers, the federal judiciary was established with only limited subject matter jurisdiction.[16] A federal court cannot exercise subject matter jurisdiction unless both the U.S. Constitution and valid federal legislation grant such jurisdiction.[17] Article III of the U.S. Constitution defines the limits of the "judicial Power" — or subject matter jurisdiction — of the federal courts. A federal statute cannot validly confer subject matter jurisdiction on a federal court except within the limits of Article III's grants.[18]

---

12. *See Container Corp. of America v. Franchise Tax Bd.*, 463 U.S. 159 (1983); *Japan Line v. County of Los Angeles*, 441 U.S. 434, 447 (1979); *Michelin Tire Corp. v. Wages*, 423 U.S. 276 (1976); Abel, *The Commerce Clause in the Constitutional Convention and in Contemporary Comment*, 25 Minn. L. Rev. 432 (1941). Article I also grants Congress the power to impose import and export duties and to regulate immigration. U.S. Const. Art. I, §§8 & 9.

13. *Japan Line, Ltd. v. County of Los Angeles*, 441 U.S. 134, 448 (1979).

14. *Japan Line, Ltd. v. County of Los Angeles*, 441 U.S. 434, 448 & n.12 (1979) ("Although the Constitution, art. I, §8, cl. 3, grants Congress power to regulate commerce 'with foreign Nations' and 'among the several states' in parallel phrases, there is evidence that the founders intended the scope of the foreign commerce power to be the greater."). *See infra* pp. 537-44.

15. *See infra* pp. 13-16.

16. *Insurance Corp. of Ireland v. Compagnie des Bauxites de Guinee*, 456 U.S. 694, 701 (1982) ("Federal courts are courts of limited jurisdiction.").

17. *Verlinden BV v. Central Bank of Nigeria*, 461 U.S. 480 (1983); *Hodgson & Thompson v. Bowerbank*, 9 U.S. 303 (1809); C. Wright & A. Miller, *Federal Practice and Procedure* §3522 (1984).

18. *Verlinden BV v. Central Bank of Nigeria*, 461 U.S. 480 (1983) ("Congress may not expand the jurisdiction of the federal courts beyond the bounds established by the Constitution").

Conversely, without a federal statutory grant of jurisdiction, federal courts cannot exercise subject matter jurisdiction contemplated by Article III.[19]

Federal subject matter jurisdiction is generally a non-waivable requirement, and cannot ordinarily be conferred by the parties' consent.[20] It is permitted — indeed, affirmatively required — for a federal court to raise the lack of subject matter jurisdiction on its own motion.[21] In both respects, subject matter jurisdiction differs from personal jurisdiction.[22]

3. Overview of Federal Subject Matter Jurisdiction in International Cases

a. *Article III's Grants of Subject Matter Jurisdiction*

Three of Article III's grants of judicial power are especially important for international cases. First, the federal courts are granted "federal question" (or "arising under") jurisdiction over "all Cases, in Law and Equity, arising under this Constitution, the Laws of the United States, and Treaties made or which shall be made, under their Authority."[23] Second, Article III grants so-called "alienage jurisdiction" over all cases "between a State, or the Citizens thereof, and foreign States, Citizens or Subjects."[24] Third, federal jurisdiction extends to a variety of specialized cases that may raise international issues.[25]

It is not coincidental that Article III contains several grants of federal subject matter jurisdiction specifically applicable in international contexts. In drafting the Constitution, one of the Framers' central concerns was to ensure that the federal government would enjoy broad control over the foreign affairs and trade of the new Republic. The Founding Fathers were convinced that, in these matters, the United States must speak with a single voice. As Thomas Jefferson wrote to James Madison in 1786: "The politics of Europe rendered it indispensably necessary that with respect to everything external we be one nation firmly hooped together; interior government is what each State should keep to itself."[26] Thus, the Supreme Court has said that the

---

19. *Argentine Republic v. Amerada Hess Shipping Corp.*, 488 U.S. 428, 433 (1989); *Insurance Corp. of Ireland v. Compagnie des Bauxites de Guinee*, 456 U.S. 694, 701 (1982) (federal subject matter jurisdiction is "limited to those subjects encompassed within the statutory grant of jurisdiction").

20. *Insurance Corp. of Ireland v. Compagnie des Bauxites de Guinee*, 456 U.S. 694, 702 (1982); *California v. LaRue*, 409 U.S. 109 (1972).

21. *Insurance Corp. of Ireland v. Compagnie des Bauxites de Guinee*, 456 U.S. 694, 702 (1982).

22. *Insurance Corp. of Ireland v. Compagnie des Bauxites de Guinee*, 456 U.S. 694, 702 (1982); *Leroy v. Great W. United Corp.*, 443 U.S. 173, 180 (1979) ("neither personal jurisdiction nor venue is fundamentally preliminary in the sense that subject matter jurisdiction is, for both are personal privileges of the defendant, rather than absolute strictures on the court, and both may be waived by the parties").

23. Art. III, §2. *See infra* pp. 33-66.

24. Art. III, §2. *See infra* pp. 25-32.

25. Article III authorizes federal jurisdiction over "all Cases affecting Ambassadors, other public ministers and Consuls," and "all cases of admiralty and maritime jurisdiction."" U.S. Const. Art. III, §2. As to the former, Article III grants the Supreme Court original jurisdiction.

26. Letter dated October 1786 (quoted in C. Warren, *The Making of the Constitution* 46 (1937)).

Federalist Papers demonstrate the "importance of national power in all matters relating to foreign affairs and the inherent danger of state action in this field."[27]

The perceived importance of federal control over matters affecting U.S. foreign relations and commerce shaped Article III's provisions regarding the subject matter jurisdiction of the federal courts. The Framers repeatedly said that it was vital for Article III to grant federal courts jurisdiction over most international disputes. Alexander Hamilton said:

> [T]he peace of the WHOLE ought not to be left at the disposal of a PART. The Union will undoubtedly be answerable to foreign powers for the conduct of its members. And the responsibility for an injury ought ever to be accompanied with the faculty of preventing it. As the denial or perversion of justice by the sentences of courts, as well as in any other manner, is with reason classed among the just causes of war, it will follow that the federal judiciary ought to have cognizance of all causes in which the citizens of other countries are concerned.[28]

This rationale was used by Hamilton to justify Article III's grants of admiralty jurisdiction,[29] federal question jurisdiction,[30] and "alienage jurisdiction."[31]

b. Statutory Grants of Federal Subject Matter Jurisdiction

Pursuant to these Article III authorizations, Congress has made numerous statutory grants of subject matter jurisdiction to the lower federal courts which are of importance in international civil litigation. Two such statutory authorizations are principally applicable in domestic cases, but are also significant in international disputes: (1) cases involving "federal questions" arising under the U.S. Constitution, statutes, and regulations;[32] and (2) diversity of citizenship cases, between citizens of different U.S. states.[33] Several other statutory grants of federal subject matter jurisdiction are generally applicable only in international disputes. These include: (3) alienage jurisdiction, over actions between U.S. and foreign parties;[34] (4) jurisdiction

---

27. *Hines v. Davidowitz*, 312 U.S. 52, 62 n.9 (1941).

28. A. Hamilton, J. Madison & J. Jay, *The Federalist Papers*, No. 80 at 476 (C. Rossiter ed. 1961).

29. Admiralty disputes typically involved foreign parties and transactions. This was cited at the Constitutional Convention as a primary reason justifying federal jurisdiction. 1 M. Farrand, *Records of the Federal Convention of 1787* 124 (1937).

30. In particular, it was thought necessary that federal courts decide cases arising under U.S. treaties. *See infra* pp. 33-35 & 53-54.

31. Frequent comments were made during the debates surrounding the Constitution regarding the importance of federal subject matter jurisdiction in disputes involving foreigners. *See infra* pp. 33-34 & 49-50.

32. 28 U.S.C. §1331. Pursuant to the Constitution's authorization for federal question jurisdiction, Congress has granted the federal courts jurisdiction to hear claims arising under a number of substantive federal statutes, including the antitrust and securities laws. *See infra* pp. 34-35.

33. 28 U.S.C. §1332(a)(1). Diversity-of-citizenship jurisdiction encompasses disputes between parties from different states where the amount in controversy exceeds $50,000.

34. 28 U.S.C. §1332(a)(2) & (3); *infra* pp. 25-32.

under the Alien Tort Statute;[35] and (5) jurisdiction over actions against foreign states under the Foreign Sovereign Immunities Act.[36]

c. Removal

If both a constitutional and statutory basis for federal subject matter jurisdiction exist, then a plaintiff can commence an action in U.S. district court.[37] When plaintiffs instead choose to commence such litigation against foreign defendants in state court, federal law may permit the defendant to "remove" the case from state to federal court. Section 1441 of Title 28 permits removal of any action that could originally have been brought in federal court. If diversity of citizenship or alienage provides the basis for federal jurisdiction, §1441(b) requires that none of the defendants be a citizen of the state where the action was brought.[38] If federal question jurisdiction is asserted, the case is removable "without regard to the citizenship or residence of the parties."[39]

d. Practical Considerations Relevant to Federal Subject Matter Jurisdiction

Although these bases for federal jurisdiction can raise complex legal issues, discussed below, they also involve important practical considerations. Litigation in federal court can differ in significant ways from litigation in state court, particularly for foreign parties. In some cases, these differences can be outcome-determinative, leading to vigorous disputes over the availability of federal subject matter jurisdiction.

Federal courts are frequently said to possess greater detachment from local political, economic, and social concerns than their state counterparts. Differences in perspective are attributed to the fact that federal judges are appointed with life tenure, while state judges are frequently elected for limited terms, and to the different pools from which federal and state judges and jurors are traditionally drawn. In disputes between a local resident and a foreigner, this detachment may be of considerable significance. Federal judges are also sometimes more experienced in handling complex commercial disputes, particularly involving international matters.

Equally important, federal courts may apply "procedural" rules that can differ materially from those in state courts. These include the forum non conveniens doctrine, principles governing the enforceability of forum selection clauses, lis pendens, and discovery rules. Differences between federal and state procedural rules may be dispositive in particular cases.[40]

For these and other reasons, foreign parties facing legal action in the United

---

35. 28 U.S.C. §1350; *infra* pp. 36-49.

36. 28 U.S.C. §1330(a); *infra* pp. 56-66.

37. As discussed below, the plaintiff will also be required to establish personal jurisdiction over the defendant, valid service of process, and proper venue. *See infra* pp. 67-70, 367-69 & 761-63.

38. 18 U.S.C. §1441(b). *See* C. Wright, A. Miller & E. Cooper, *Federal Practice and Procedure* §§3721-40 (1985).

39. 28 U.S.C. §1441(b).

40. *See especially Dow Chemical Co. v. Castro Alfaro*, 786 S.W.2d 674 (Tex. 1990), *infra* pp. 305-13, and *Sequihua v. Texaco, Inc.*, 847 F.Supp. 61 (S.D. Tex. 1994), *infra* pp. 51-52.

States often prefer to litigate in federal courts. This preference may generally be sound, but it is necessary to consider the actual differences between specific federal and state forums in particular cases. State courts, judges, and procedural rules differ significantly from state to state, and in some cases may be more hospitable to foreign litigants than a federal forum.

4. Relationship Between U.S. State and Federal Law[41]

a. The Erie Doctrine

The relationship between state and federal law in federal courts gives rise to complex issues in both domestic and international cases. These issues are subject to the so-called "*Erie* doctrine."

Until the 1930s, the federal courts had followed the rule of *Swift v. Tyson* and applied a general federal common law in diversity cases.[42] Under *Swift v. Tyson*, federal courts were generally free to apply general federal common law, while state courts were at liberty to apply state common law (without preemptive effect from inconsistent federal common law decisions).[43] In *Erie Railroad Co. v. Tompkins*, however, the Supreme Court narrowly limited the federal courts' authority to fashion general common law rules.[44] Declaring that "[t]here is no federal *general* common law,"[45] the Court held that, in the absence of valid federal legislation, federal courts must ordinarily apply state substantive law, including state common law rules fashioned by state courts. The Court based its decision in large part on the perceived "mischievous results" that flowed from permitting federal courts to apply federal law, and state courts to apply state law, to the same issues:

> [*Swift v. Tyson*] made rights ... vary according to whether enforcement was sought in the state or in the federal court; and the privilege of selecting the court in which the right should be determined was conferred upon the noncitizen. Thus, the doctrine rendered impossible equal protection of the law. In attempting to promote uniformity of law throughout the United States, the doctrine had prevented uniformity in the administration of the law of the state.[46]

To redress these perceived defects, *Erie* established fundamentally new principles governing the relationship between state and federal law. It is, of course, fundamen-

---

41. *See generally* P. Bator, P. Mishkin, D. Meltzer & D. Shapiro, *Hart & Wechsler's The Federal Courts and the Federal System* 771-83 (3d ed. 1988); C. Wright & A. Miller, *Federal Practice and Procedure* §4504-11 (1987); Westen & Lehman, *Is There Life for Erie After the Death of Diversity?*, 78 Mich. L. Rev. 311 (1980).

42. *See Swift v. Tyson*, 41 U.S. 1 (1842); Friendly, *In Praise of Erie — And of the New Federal Common Law*, 39 N.Y.U.L. Rev. 383 (1964); P. Bator, P. Mishkin, D. Meltzer & D. Shapiro, *Hart & Wechsler's The Federal Courts and the Federal System* 771-83 (3d ed. 1988).

43. *Swift v. Tyson*, 41 U.S. 1 (1842).

44. 304 U.S. 64 (1938).

45. 304 U.S. at 78 (emphasis added).

46. 304 U.S. at 74-75.

tal under *Erie* and its progeny that a valid federal statute, treaty, or regulation pre-empts inconsistent state laws, and must be applied by both state courts and federal diversity and alienage courts.[47] If no valid federal substantive law applies, however, the *Erie* doctrine provides generally that "procedural" issues in federal diversity actions are governed by federal procedural law, while "substantive" issues are governed by state substantive law.[48] Federal "procedural" law applies only in federal courts, not in state courts.[49]

In areas not governed by federal statute or rule of procedure, the Court has generally been reluctant to ignore state law rules. For example, the Court has held that statutes of limitations and choice of law rules are "substantive" and therefore governed by state law.[50] Moreover, as noted earlier, state substantive law provides the basic rules of contract, tort, agency, damages, contribution, and the like.

Conversely, *Erie's* "procedural" category is limited. It generally includes all subjects dealt with by the Federal Rules of Civil Procedure.[51] In addition, even absent an applicable Federal Rule, a few common law doctrines fashioned by the federal courts are characterized as "procedural," rather than "substantive";[52] these federal procedural rules govern in federal courts, but not in state courts, and they do not preempt state law. In defining the scope of federal procedural law, the Supreme Court has sought to avoid relying exclusively on the "substance" and "procedure" labels. Instead, the Court has categorized issues in order to further what it has described as two central purposes of the *Erie* doctrine: (1) the "discouragement of forum shopping" between state and federal courts that could result from divergent state and federal laws, and (2) "avoidance of inequitable administration of the laws."[53]

---

47. *See* U.S. Const. Art. VI, cl. 2; *Hines v. Davidowitz*, 312 U.S. 52 (1941); *Jones v. Rath Packing Co.*, 430 U.S. 519 (1977); *Stewart Organization Inc. v. Ricoh Corp.*, 487 U.S. 22 (1988); *Walker v. Armco Steel Corp.*, 446 U.S. 740, 749-52 (1980) ("The first question [is] whether the scope of the federal rule in fact is sufficiently broad to control the issue before the Court.").

48. *Stewart Organization, Inc. v. Ricoh Corp.*, 487 U.S. 22 (1988); *Guaranty Trust Co. v. York*, 326 U.S. 99 (1945); *Erie Railroad Co. v. Tompkins*, 304 U.S. 64, 74 (1938); C. Wright & A. Miller, *Federal Practice and Procedure* §4504-08 (1987). The same general rule applies in federal question cases, although federal substantive law will generally preempt state law in many respects. *See* C. Wright & A. Miller, *Federal Practice and Procedure* §4515 (1987); Westen & Lehman, *Is There Life for Erie After the Death of Diversity?*, 78 Mich. L. Rev. 311 (1980).

49. *See American Dredging Co. v. Miller*, 114 S.Ct. 981 (1994); *Hanna v. Plumer*, 380 U.S. 460 (1965).

50. *Klaxon Co. v. Stentor Elec. Mfg. Co.*, 313 U.S. 487 (1941); *Walker v. Armco Steel Corp.*, 446 U.S. 740 (1980).

51. *Hanna v. Plumer*, 380 U.S. 460 (1965); C. Wright & A. Miller, *Federal Practice and Procedure* §4508-10 (1987). In unusual circumstances, a purportedly "procedural" provision of the Federal Rules of Civil Procedure might be found to exceed either the rulemaking powers delegated to the Supreme Court by the Rules Enabling Act, 28 U.S.C. §2072, or Congress's constitutional authority. *See Walker v. Armco Steel Corp.*, 446 U.S. 740, 752 n.14 (1980); C. Wright & A. Miller, *Federal Practice and Procedure* §4505 (1987).

52. *See American Dredging Co. v. Miller*, 114 S.Ct. 981 (1994) (forum non conveniens doctrine in domestic admiralty actions is governed by federal procedural law); *Byrd v. Blue Ridge Rural Electric Coop., Inc.*, 356 U.S. 525 (1958) (federal procedural law determines what issues are to be submitted to jury).

53. *Hanna v. Plumer*, 380 U.S. 460, 468 (1965); *Walker v. Armco Steel Corp.*, 446 U.S. 740, 747 (1980).

b. Substantive Federal Common Law

Although *Erie* made it clear that "there is no federal *general* common law,"[54] the Supreme Court has sanctioned the judicial development of a limited number of substantive rules of "federal common law," even in the absence of a valid federal statute, treaty, or regulation.[55] Unlike federal procedural rules, these federal common law rules are substantive federal law, applicable in both federal and state courts, that preempt inconsistent state law. As the Supreme Court recently declared, "a few areas, involving 'uniquely federal interests' ... are so committed by the Constitution and laws of the United States to federal control that state law is preempted and replaced, where necessary, by federal law of a content prescribed (absent explicit statutory directive) by the courts — so-called 'federal common law.'"[56]

Substantive federal common law rules will be fashioned only in "few and restricted" cases[57] and only if rigorous standards are satisfied. First, the proposed rule must arise in an area involving "uniquely federal interests."[58] Examples of such federal interests have included the division of interstate waters,[59] the conduct of U.S. foreign relations,[60] the design and manufacture of U.S. military equipment,[61] the civil liability of federal officials for actions taken in the course of their duty,[62] and the rights and duties of the United States under its contracts.[63]

Second, even in such "uniquely federal" areas, federal common law will be fashioned only where necessary to prevent "significant conflict" between state laws and federal policies and interests.[64] If state law does not conflict with federal policies, it will not necessarily be preempted; even a conflict exists, preemptive federal common law will be fashioned only to the extent necessary to eliminate the conflict.[65]

---

54. 304 U.S. at 74 (emphasis added).

55. *Boyle v. United Technologies Corp.*, 487 U.S. 500 (1988); *United States v. Little Lake Misere Land Co.*, 412 U.S. 580 (1973).

56. *Boyle v. United Technologies Corp.*, 487 U.S. 500, 504 (1988).

57. *Wheeldin v. Wheeler*, 373 U.S. 647, 651 (1963). *See Texas Industries, Inc. v. Radcliff Materials, Inc.*, 451 U.S. 630, 641 (1981) ("Against some congressional authorization to formulate substantive rules of decision, federal common law exists only in such narrow areas as those concerned with the rights and obligations of the United States, interstate and international disputes implicating conflicting rights of states or our relations with foreign nations, and admiralty cases"); *Milwaukee v. Illinois*, 451 U.S. 304, 312-13 (1981) ("The enactment of a federal rule in an area of national concern, and the decision whether to displace state law in doing so, is generally made not by the federal judiciary, purposefully insulated from democratic pressures but by the people through their elected representatives in Congress").

58. *Boyle v. United Technologies Corp.*, 487 U.S. 500, 504 (1988); *United States v. Little Lake Misere Land Co.*, 412 U.S. 580 (1973).

59. *Hinderlider v. La Plata River & Cherry Creek Ditch Co.*, 304 U.S. 92 (1938).

60. *Zschernig v. Miller*, 389 U.S. 429 (1968); *Banco Nacional de Cuba v. Sabbatino*, 376 U.S. 398 (1964).

61. *Boyle v. United Technologies Corp.*, 487 U.S. 500, 505-07 (1988).

62. *Westfall v. Erwin*, 484 U.S. 292 (1988); *Howard v. Lyons*, 360 U.S. 593 (1959).

63. *United States v. Little Lake Misere Land Co.*, 412 U.S. 580 (1973); *Priebe & Sons, Inc. v. United States*, 332 U.S. 407 (1947).

64. *Boyle v. United Technologies Corp.*, 487 U.S. at 507-08.

65. *Boyle v. United Technologies Corp.*, 487 U.S. at 507-08.

Federal common law can play a potentially significant role in international litigation. International disputes frequently implicate federal interests in U.S. foreign relations and foreign commerce. As noted above, both fields fall squarely with the constitutional powers of Congress and the President, and can clearly involve uniquely federal interests.[66] Several Supreme Court decisions, fashioning rules of federal common law in international disputes, are illustrative.

In *Banco Nacional de Cuba v. Sabbatino*,[67] the Supreme Court announced a federal "act of state" doctrine that forbade U.S. courts from adjudicating the validity of certain foreign governmental acts. Relying on federal authority over foreign relations and foreign commerce, the Court declared that the act of state doctrine was a principle of federal common law that was equally binding on both state and federal courts:[68]

> it is plain that the problems involved are uniquely federal in nature. If federal authority, in this instance this Court, orders the field of judicial competence in this area for the federal courts, and the state courts are left free to formulate their own rules, the purposes behind the doctrine could be as effectively undermined as if there had been no federal pronouncement on the subject.

Likewise, in *First National City Bank v. Banco Para El Comercio Exterior de Cuba*[69] the Supreme Court adopted a federal common law standard governing the circumstances in which the separate legal identity of foreign state-related entities will be disregarded. Citing *Sabbatino*, the Court emphasized the need for a uniform federal standard in matters affecting U.S. relations with foreign states.[70]

Finally, in *Zschernig v. Miller*,[71] the Supreme Court held unconstitutional an Oregon statute that forbade foreign heirs or legatees from receiving property from Oregon estates if the property would be confiscated by foreign governments or if U.S. heirs or legatees could not reciprocally receive property from abroad. The Supreme Court held that this "kind of state involvement in foreign affairs and international relations — matters which the Constitution entrusts solely to the Federal Government" — threatens U.S. foreign relations and is unconstitutional.[72]

---

66. See Jessup, *The Doctrine of Erie Railroad v. Tompkins Applied to International Law*, 33 Am. J. Int'l L. 740 (1939); Edwards, *The Erie Doctrine in Foreign Affairs Cases*, 42 N.Y.U. L. Rev. 674 (1967); Henkin, *The Foreign Affairs Powers of the Federal Courts: Sabbatino*, 64 Colum. L. Rev. 805 (1964); Hill, *The Law Making Power of the Federal Courts: Constitutional Preemption*, 67 Colum. L. Rev. 1024 (1967); Moore, *Federalism and Foreign Relations*, 1965 Duke L.J. 248.

67. 376 U.S. 398 (1964). *See infra* pp. 691-705 for a more detailed discussion.

68. 376 U.S. at 424.

69. 462 U.S. 611 (1983). *See infra* pp. 217-25 for a more detailed discussion.

70. 462 U.S. at 623 ("the principles governing this case are common to both international law and federal common law, which in these circumstances is necessarily informed both by international law principles and by articulated congressional policies.").

71. 389 U.S. 429 (1968). *See infra* pp. 537-44 for a more detailed discussion.

72. 389 U.S. at 436.

5. Relationship Between International Law and U.S. Law

International law can play an important role in deciding international cases in U.S. courts. In theory, the relationship between domestic U.S. law and international law is simple: "International law is part of our law, and must be ascertained and administered by the courts of justice of appropriate jurisdiction, as often as questions of right depending upon it are duly presented for their determination."[73] In reality, the role of international law in U.S. litigation is more complex. A brief summary of the applicable principles is all that space permits.[74]

a. International Law

International law scholars and practitioners distinguish between "public" and "private" international law (also sometimes referred to as "conflict of laws").[75] Definitions of "private" international law vary considerably, but they generally refer to the body of national law applicable to disputes between private persons, in domestic courts or private arbitral forums, arising from activities having connections to two or more nations.[76] Topics falling within the private international law category typically include judicial jurisdiction, choice of forum, choice of law, taking evidence abroad, service of process abroad, and recognition of foreign judgments. In the United States, these topics are dealt with by "Conflict of Laws" treatises and the American Law Institute's *Restatement (Second) Conflict of Laws*.[77]

In contrast, "public international law" refers to the international legal principles that govern relations between sovereign nation-states.[78] In the words of the *Restatement (Third) Foreign Relations Law*, "[i]nternational law is the law of the international community of states. It deals with the conduct of nation-states and their relations with other states, and to some extent also with their relations with individuals, business organizations and other legal entities."[79] Subjects traditionally governed by public international law include the law of the sea, the law of treaties,

---

73. *The Paquete Habana*, 175 U.S. 677, 700 (1900); *Restatement (Third) Foreign Relations Law* §111(1) (1987).

74. For more detailed discussions, *see* L. Henkin, R. Pugh, O. Schachter & H. Smit, *International Law* (1980); *Restatement (Third) Foreign Relations Law* (1987); *Restatement (Second) Foreign Relations Law* (1965).

75. Lowenfeld, *Public Law in the International Arena, Conflict of Laws, International Law, and Some Suggestions for Their Interaction*, 163 Recueil Des Cours 311 (1979); Starke, *The Relation Between Private and Public International Law*, 207 Law Q. Rev. 395 (1936); Stevenson, *The Relationship of Private International Law to Public International Law*, 52 Colum. L. Rev. 561 (1952).

76. *See Restatement (Second) Conflict of Laws* §2 (1971).

77. Leading U.S. conflict of laws treatises include, *e.g.*, L. Brilmayer, *Conflict of Laws* (4th ed. 1995); E. Scoles & P. Hay, *Conflict of Laws* (1982); R. Weintraub, *Commentary on the Conflict of Laws* (3d ed. 1986).

The *Restatement (First) Conflict of Laws* (1934) also dealt with private international law issues, as well as selected jurisdictional principles of public international law. *See infra* pp. 497-509.

78. *See* J. Brierly, *The Law of Nations* 1-3 (6th ed. 1963); W. Bishop, *International Law: Cases and Materials* 3-6 (3d ed. 1971).

79. *Restatement (Third) Foreign Relations Law* Part I, Ch. 1, Intro. Note at 16 & §101 (1987).

limits on national jurisdiction, the use of force, foreign sovereign immunity, responsibility towards aliens, recognition, and state succession. In the United States, these subjects have in recent decades been dealt with by the ALI's Second and Third *Restatements of Foreign Relations Law* and by public international law treatises.[80]

This distinction between "public" and "private" international law is apparently of recent origin. During the early 19th century, subjects of transnational concern were generally subject to the "law of nations," which was understood as broadly encompassing legal relations between sovereign states, conflict of laws rules, maritime law, and the law merchant.[81] It was only at the beginning of the 20th century that "public" and "private" international law came to be regarded as distinct subjects.[82]

Contemporary public international law is generally the creation of sovereign nations: it is fundamental that public international law is based on the consent of the states that comprise the international community. "Modern international law is rooted in acceptance by states which constitute the system."[83] Thus, a state is not ordinarily bound by rules of international law to which it has not expressly or implicitly agreed.[84]

There are several means by which the consent of states to particular rules of international law is expressed: (1) international agreements; (2) customary international law; and (3) general principles of law.[85] In theory, these sources are of equal weight in the formation of public international law. In practice, however, the best-accepted sources of international law are international agreements.[86]

International agreements between states can take many forms, including treaties, conventions, concordats, and exchanges of notes. Whatever their form, international agreements are analogous to contracts between private parties; in general, they deal with whatever matters the parties choose to address and they create law only for the states that are party to the agreements.[87] There are only a very limited number of fundamental norms of international law ("*jus cogens*"), from which states may not derogate, by agreement or otherwise.[88] A considerable body of inter-

---

80. *See supra* note 74.

81. Dickinson, *The Law of Nations as Part of the National Law of the United States*, 101 U. Pa. L. Rev. 26, 26-29 (1952); Jay, *Origins of Federal Common Law: Part Two*, 133 U. Pa. L. Rev. 1231, 1263-64 (1985); Rheinstein, *The Constitutional Bases of Jurisdiction*, 22 U. Chi. L. Rev. 775, 805 (1955).

82. Nussbaum, *Rise and Decline of the Law-of-Nations Doctrine in the Conflict of Laws*, 42 Colum. L. Rev. 189 (1942); Cheatham, *Sources of Rules for Conflict of Laws*, 89 U. Pa. L. Rev. 430 (1941); Wortley, *The Interaction of Public and Private International Laws Today*, 85 Recueil des Cours 245 (1954).

83. *Restatement (Third) Foreign Relations Law* Part I, Ch. 1, Intro. Note at 18 (1987).

84. *Restatement (Third) Foreign Relations Law* §102 comment d (1987).

85. *See* Statute of the International Court of Justice Art. 38(1); Parry, *The Sources and Evidences of International Law* (1965); Akehurst, *The Hierarchy of the Sources of International Law*, 47 Brit. Y. B. Int'l L. 273 (1974).

86. For commentary concerning the relative weights of the sources of international law, *see* M. Villiger, *Customary International Law and Treaties* (1985); A. D'Amato, *The Concept of Custom in International Law* (1971); Akehurst, *Custom as a Source of International Law*, 48 Brit. Y.B. Int'l L. 1 (1974-75).

87. *Restatement (Third) Foreign Relations Law* §321 (1987).

88. *Restatement (Third) Foreign Relations Law* §§102 comment k, 331, & 702 comment n (1987).

national law exists governing the making, interpretation, application, and termination of international agreements.[89]

A second source of international law is customary international law.[90] Customary international law is not based on express agreements among nations, but instead results from the ongoing practice (or "custom") of states. There is no precise formula for determining how many states must follow a particular custom, nor how long the practice must be followed before it crystallizes into law. Most authorities require the existence of a general, consistent practice of substantially all concerned states, followed out of a sense of legal obligation.[91] Evidence of state practice is derived from the actions of states, their official statements (*e.g.*, in diplomatic notes), and the international agreements they enter into. A rule of customary international law is not binding on a state that declares its disagreement during the rule's formation.[92]

Finally, general principles of international law can be derived from the rules prevailing in major legal systems.[93] "General principles of law" are typically regarded as a secondary source of international law, available only interstitially where no international agreement or customary international law exists. General principles are usually based on domestic laws common to nations with well-developed legal systems.

b. Relationship Between International Agreements and U.S. Law

International law has a complex relationship to U.S. law. At the outset, it is important to distinguish between the status in U.S. courts of: (i) treaties (or other international agreements) and (ii) customary international law.

There is a considerable body of U.S. law dealing with the appropriate domestic mechanism, under the U.S. Constitution, by which the United States enters into international agreements.[94] The U.S. Constitution permits entry by the United States into "treaties," which require the approval of the President and two-thirds of the Senate.[95] In determining the legal effects of a treaty under U.S. law, U.S. courts distinguish sharply between "non-self-executing" and "self-executing" treaties. A self-executing treaty is intended to have immediate legal effects within the contracting states, without the need for implementing legislation or regulations; a non-self-executing treaty is not intended to have direct legal effect, but instead contemplates

---

89. *See* Vienna Convention on the Law of Treaties, 8 Int'l Leg. Mat. 679 (1969); I. Sinclair, *The Vienna Convention on the Law of Treaties* (2d ed. 1984).

90. *Restatement (Third) Foreign Relations Law* §102(1)(a) (1987).

91. *North Sea Continental Shelf Cases* [1969] I.C.J. Rep. 3; *Asylum Case* [1950] I.C.J. Rep. 266; A. D'Amato, *The Concept of Custom in International Law* (1971).

92. *Fisheries Case (United Kingdom v. Norway)* [1951] I.C.J. Rep. 116.

93. *Restatement (Third) Foreign Relations Law* §102(1)(c), §102(4), & Reporters' Note 7 (1987).

94. *See generally* L. Henkin, *Foreign Affairs and the Constitution* 173-76 (1972); Treaties and Other International Agreements: The Role of the United States Senate, S. Rep. No. 205, 98th Cong., 2d Sess. (1984).

95. U.S. Const. Art. II, §2.

domestic implementing legislation.[96] Whether a treaty is self-executing or non-self-executing under U.S. law depends on the intentions of the United States in ratifying the treaty.[97]

Article VI of the U.S. Constitution declares that self-executing treaties are the "supreme Law of the Land." Even without implementing legislation, self-executing treaties are federal law that enjoy essentially the same status in U.S. courts as federal statutes.[98] Self-executing treaties create enforceable rights in U.S. courts and preempt inconsistent state law.[99] In the case of conflicts between treaties and federal statutes, a "last-in-time" rule applies: a federal statute supersedes prior inconsistent treaties, and conversely, a treaty supersedes prior inconsistent federal statutes.[100]

In contrast, non-self-executing treaties lack binding force in U.S. courts until implemented by congressional statute.[101] As a result, federal law ordinarily prevails over inconsistent non-self-executing treaties.[102] The same result apparently also applies with respect to state statutes and state common law.[103]

It is common for the United States to enter into international agreements in other forms than "treaties." So-called "Congressional-Executive" agreements must be approved by both the President and a majority of each House of Congress (rather than, as for treaties, by the President and two-thirds of the Senate.)[104] In general, a valid Congressional-Executive agreement has the same legal effect as a treaty — it is federal law that preempts inconsistent state law, supersedes prior federal statutes, and is superseded by subsequent federal statutes.[105]

Sole Executive agreements, made by the President, are frequently entered into in areas within the President's constitutional powers.[106] Within these fields, an Executive agreement generally has the same legal effects as a treaty.[107]

---

96. *Asakura v. Seattle*, 265 U.S, 332, 341 (1924); *Fairfax's Devisee v. Hunter's Lessee*, 11 U.S. 603 (1813); *Restatement (Third) Foreign Relations Law* §111(3) & (4) & comment h (1987).

97. *Restatement (Third) Foreign Relations Law* §111(4) & Reporters' Note 5 (1987); *People of Saipan v. Department of Interior*, 502 F.2d 90, 97 (9th Cir. 1974), *cert. denied*, 420 U.S. 1003 (1975).

98. *Restatement (Third) Foreign Relations Law* §115(1) & (2) (1987).

99. *See United States v. Belmont*, 301 U.S. 324, 331 (1937); *Asakura v. Seattle*, 265 U.S, 332, 341 (1924); *Fairfax's Devisee v. Hunter's Lessee*, 11 U.S. 603 (1813); *Ware v. Hylton*, 3 U.S. 199, 244-45 (1796).

100. *See United States v. Dior*, 476 U.S. 734, 738 (1986); *The Chinese Exclusion Case*, 130 U.S. 581, 600-01 (1888); *Head Money Cases*, 112 U.S. 580 (1884).

101. *Restatement (Third) Foreign Relations Law* §111(3) (1987) ("a 'non-self-executing' agreement will not be given effect as law in the absence of necessary implementation").

102. *Foster v. Neilson*, 27 U.S. 253 (1828); *Cameron Septic Tank Co. v. Knoxville*, 227 U.S. 39 (1913).

103. *Sei Fujii v. California*, 242 P.2d 617 (1952).

104. *See Restatement (Third) Foreign Relations Law* §303 (1987); *United States v. Belmont*, 301 U.S. 324 (1937); *B. Altman Co. v. United States*, 224 U.S. 583 (1912).

105. *Restatement (Third) Foreign Relations Law* §111(3) & comment h (1987). Like treaties, Congressional-Executive agreements can be either self-executing or non-self-executing.

106. *Restatement (Third) Foreign Relations Law* §303(4) (1987).

107. *Restatement (Third) Foreign Relations Law* §303(4) & Reporters' Note 11 (1987); *United States v. Pink*, 315 U.S. 203 (1942); *United States v. Guy W. Capps, Inc.*, 204 F.2d 655 (4th Cir. 1953), *aff'd on other grounds*, 348 U.S. 296 (1955).

c. Relationship Between Customary International Law and U.S. Law

The status of customary international law in U.S. courts is less clear than that of treaties and other international agreements. In practice, the direct application of customary international law occurs in relatively few cases, owing principally to the comprehensive character of U.S. law and the fragmentary coverage of international law.[108]

In the absence of any federal law on an issue, U.S. courts will generally give effect to customary international law.[109] "In appropriate cases [U.S. courts] apply international law ... without the need of enactment by Congress or proclamation by the President."[110] As discussed below, customary international law — like international agreements — is often said to be federal law.[111]

If a subsequent federal statute requires a result contrary to preexisting principles of customary international law, then U.S. courts must give Congress's legislation priority.[112] They must do so even though this will place the United States in violation of international law. "Federal courts must give effect to a valid unambiguous congressional mandate, even if such effect would conflict with another nation's laws or violate international law."[113] Moreover, even when a preexisting federal statute is said to be inconsistent with subsequent international practice (but not an international agreement), the prior statute will probably prevail.[114] The same result should apply in conflicts between customary international law and rules of federal common law.

The effect of a conflict between customary international law and state law is less clear. Because customary international law is federal law, it should in principle preempt both prior *and subsequent* state law.[115] Parties have rarely argued that customary international law preempts state law, however, and there is little judicial precedent on the issue.[116]

---

108. Trimble, *A Revisionist View of Customary International Law*, 33 UCLA L. Rev. 665 (1986).

109. *The Paquete Habana*, 175 U.S. 677 (1900); *Restatement (Third) Foreign Relations Law* §115, comment d (1987).

110. *Restatement (Third) Foreign Relations Law* §111, comment c (1987). *See* Paust, *Rediscovering the Relationship Between Congressional Power and International Law: Exceptions to the Last in Time Rule and the Primacy of Custom*, 28 Va. J. Int'l L. 393, 418-43 (1988).

111. *Restatement (Third) Foreign Relations Law* §111 (1987); *infra* pp. 49-56.

112. *See Head Money Cases*, 112 U.S. 580, 598-99 (1884); *Whitney v. Robertson*, 124 U.S. 190, 194 (1888); *Restatement (Third) Foreign Relations Law* §115(1) & §403, comment g (1987).

113. *CFTC v. Nahas*, 738 F.2d 487, 495 (D.C. Cir. 1984). *See United States v. Alcoa*, 148 F.2d 416, 443 (2d Cir. 1945) ("We are concerned only with whether Congress chose to attach liability to the conduct outside the United States. ... as a court of the United States, we cannot look beyond our own law.").

114. *Cf. Restatement (Third) Foreign Relations Law* §115 Reporters' Note 4 (1987) ("Courts in the United States will hesitate to conclude that a principle has become a rule of customary international law if they are required to give it effect in the face of an earlier inconsistent statute."); Henkin, *International Law and Law in the United States*, 82 Mich. L. Rev. 1555 (1984). *Compare* Goldklang, *Back on Board the Paquete Habana: Resolving the Conflict Between Statutes and Customary International Law*, 25 Va. J. Int'l L. 143 (1984).

115. *Restatement (Third) Foreign Relations Law* §115, comment e (1987).

116. *See infra* pp. 49-56.

d. Presumption That Congressional Legislation is Consistent With International Law

Few cases involve irreconcilable conflict between domestic and international law. Much more common are cases in which a measure of uncertainty surrounds the content of both U.S. law and international law. In these circumstances, U.S. courts have sought to minimize conflict between international law and domestic U.S. law.

U.S. courts generally apply a canon of statutory construction dictating that, in the absence of an express legislative statement to the contrary, Congress will not be assumed to have enacted a statute that violates international law. As the Supreme Court remarked in 1804, "[a]n act of Congress ought never to be construed to violate the law of nations, if any other possible construction remains."[117] The *Restatement (Third) Foreign Relations Law* adopts the same approach: "[w]here fairly possible, a United States statute is to be construed so as not to conflict with international law or with an international agreement of the United States."[118] Not infrequently, the meanings of federal statutes have been significantly affected by this presumption.[119]

6. Separation of Powers Considerations

An essential feature of the constitutional structure of the U.S. federal government is the separation of power into three distinct branches.[120] This allocation of governmental authority was motivated by a desire to guard against tyranny and rash decision-making by diffusing power among largely independent legislative, executive, and judicial branches.[121] Nonetheless, the international field has long been thought to raise special separation of powers concerns. As a result, the Framers endowed the national executive and legislative branches with expansive authority in the field of foreign relations.

The central figure in U.S. foreign relations is the President. Despite fairly modest textual foundation in the Constitution,[122] successive Presidents have wielded broad authority over the nation's foreign affairs. Thus, although its expansive formulation has been criticized, the Supreme Court has acknowledged "the very delicate, plenary

---

117. *Murray v. The Schooner Charming Betsy*, 6 U.S. 64, 118 (1804). *See also Chew Heong v. United States*, 112 U.S. 536, 539-40 (1884); *MacLeod v. United States*, 229 U.S. 416, 434 (1913).

118. *Restatement (Third) Foreign Relations Law* §114 (1987).

119. *INS v. Cardoza-Fonseca*, 480 U.S. 421 (1987); *Weinberger v. Rossi*, 456 U.S. 25, 32 (1982). The presumption is discussed in greater detail below, *see infra* pp. 549-50, 780-92.

120. *Bowsher v. Synar*, 478 U.S. 714 (1986); *INS v. Chadha*, 462 U.S. 919 (1983); L. Henkin, *Foreign Affairs and the Constitution* 31-35 (1972).

121. *Myers v. United States*, 272 U.S. 52, 293 (1926) (Brandeis, J., dissenting); A. Hamilton, J. Madison & J. Jay, *The Federalist Papers*, Nos. 47 & 51 (C. Rossiter ed. 1961).

122. The Constitution's grants of foreign affairs authority to the president are not especially impressive at first glance: The chief executive is the "Commander-in-Chief" of the armed forces and is solely responsible for "making treaties" and receiving foreign "Ambassadors and other public Ministers." In addition, the President is obliged to execute the laws of the nation and is arguably vested with an unenumerated "executive" power. U.S. Const. Art. II.

and exclusive power of the President as the sole organ of the federal government in the field of international relations."[123]

As discussed above, Congress also enjoys substantial "international" powers, particularly in the foreign commerce field.[124] The allocation of authority between the executive and the legislative branches in the foreign affairs field is imprecise and overlapping. As a result, throughout the nation's history the President and Congress have struggled for control over the conduct of U.S. foreign relations.[125] Particularly in recent decades, Congress has become increasingly assertive, enacting legislation that to restricts presidential foreign relations authority or furthers congressional policies.[126]

Notwithstanding this legislative-executive competition, it is clear that Congress and the President together enjoy largely exclusive control over national foreign affairs. As the Supreme Court remarked in *Oetjen v. Central Leather Co.*, "[t]he conduct of the foreign relations of our Government is committed by the Constitution to the Executive and Legislative — the political — Departments of the Government."[127]

One consequence of the political branches' preeminence in the field of foreign relations has been a marked reluctance on the part of the federal courts to interfere in the conduct of foreign relations. It has long been recognized that international civil litigation can affect foreign governmental and private interests.[128] As a consequence, international cases in U.S. courts have the potential to interfere with U.S. foreign relations and commerce. In the words of *Federalist Paper No. 80*, "the denial or perversion of justice by the sentences of courts ... is with reason classed among the just causes of war."[129]

In several contexts, U.S. courts have fashioned prudential doctrines designed to forestall judicial disruption of national foreign relations. The classic example is the act of state doctrine, noted above, which precludes U.S. courts from adjudicating the validity of acts of foreign states on their own territory. The Court has attributed the

---

123. *United States v. Curtiss-Wright Export Corp.*, 299 U.S. 304, 320 (1936). More recently, the Court has embraced more restrictive, but nonetheless broad, views of presidential foreign affairs powers. *See Dames & Moore v. Regan*, 453 U.S. 654, 669 (1981) (presidential authority in foreign affairs field varies depending on legislative approval "along a spectrum running from explicit congressional authorization to explicit congressional prohibition"); *Youngstown Sheet & Tube Co. v. Sawyer*, 343 U.S. 579, 637 (1952) (Jackson, J., concurring).

124. *See supra* pp. 8-9.

125. *See Goldwater v. Carter*, 444 U.S. 996 (1979); *Youngstown Sheet & Tube Co. v. Sawyer*, 343 U.S. 579 (1952). *See* Bestor, *Separation of Powers in the Domain of Foreign Affairs: The Intent of the Constitution Historically Examined*, 5 Seton Hall L. Rev. 527, 590 (1974).

126. *See* T. Franck & E. Weisband, *Foreign Policy by Congress* (1979); L. Henkin, *Foreign Affairs and the Constitution* 89-123 (1972).

127. 246 U.S. 297, 302 (1918).

128. *See, e.g., Verlinden BV v. Central Bank of Nigeria*, 461 U.S. 480, 493 (1983) ("Actions against foreign sovereigns in our courts raise sensitive issues concerning the foreign relations of the United States, and the primacy of federal concerns is evident."); *Asahi Metal Indus. Co. v. Superior Court*, 480 U.S. 102 (1987).

129. A. Hamilton, J. Madison & J. Jay, *The Federalist Papers* No. 80, at 476 (C. Rossiter ed. 1961).

act of state doctrine, at least in part, to "the strong sense of the Judicial Branch that its engagement in the task of passing on the validity of foreign acts of state may hinder rather than further this country's pursuit of goals ... in the international sphere."[130] Other examples of judicial deference to the political branches' handling of international matters include cases that are dismissed on grounds of "comity,"[131] cases involving foreign sovereign or head of state immunity,[132] cases involving the boundaries of foreign states,[133] and cases involving settlement of foreign claims.[134]

---

130. *Banco Nacional de Cuba v. Sabbatino*, 376 U.S. 398, 423 (1964). *See also infra* pp. 702, 729-32.

131. *See infra* pp. 51-56; *Sequihua v. Texaco, Inc.*, 847 F.Supp. 61 (S.D. Tex. 1994).

132. *See infra* pp. 199-210 & 284-85; *Lafontant v. Aristide*, 1994 U.S. Dist. Lexis 641 (E.D.N.Y. 1994).

133. *See Occidental of Umm al Qaywayn, Inc. v. A Certain Cargo of Petroleum*, 577 F.2d 1196 (5th Cir. 1978).

134. *E.g., Dames & Moore v. Regan*, 453 U.S. 654 (1981); *United States v. Pink*, 315 U.S. 203 (1942).

B. Alienage Jurisdiction of Federal Courts[135]

1. Introduction and Historical Background

Article III's grant of "alienage jurisdiction" conferred judicial power on the federal courts over cases "between a State, or the Citizens thereof, and foreign States, Citizens or Subjects." This grant was thought vital to ensure that U.S. courts would speak with a single, unitary voice on matters affecting foreign parties. Federal courts were also thought less likely than state courts to treat foreign nationals unfairly,[136] thereby prejudicing the Nation's foreign relations and foreign commence.[137] In explaining why federal subject matter jurisdiction should extend to cases involving aliens, Alexander Hamilton reasoned that "an unjust sentence against a foreigner ... would ... if unredressed, be an aggression upon his sovereign, as well as one which violated the stipulations in a treaty or the general laws of nations."[138] At the same time, disputes involving aliens were thought likely to involve legal and other issues of national importance, which the federal courts were deemed best able to decide.[139]

The First Congress immediately implemented the Constitution's grant of alienage jurisdiction in the first Judiciary Act of 1789. Consistent with the broad language used by Alexander Hamilton and others in justifying Article III's grant of alienage jurisdiction, §11 of the Act empowered the federal courts to hear any case in which "an alien is a party."[140]

Dispute almost immediately arose over the scope of §11: in particular, did the section reach all cases involving foreigners — including those where one alien litigated against another alien — or was it limited to suits where a U.S. citizen litigated against an alien? After some uncertainty,[141] the Supreme Court held in 1809 that the federal courts' Article III alienage jurisdiction was limited to suits involving an alien

---

135. Commentary on alienage jurisdiction includes, *e.g.*, Rubenstein, *Alienage Jurisdiction in the Federal Courts*, 17 Int'l Law. 283 (1983); Mahoney, *A Historical Note on* Hodgson v. Bowerbank, 49 U. Chi. L. Rev. 725 (1982); Note, *Alien Corporations and Federal Diversity Jurisdiction*, 84 Colum. L. Rev. 177 (1984); Note, *Federal Jurisdiction Over Suits Between Diverse United States Citizens with Aliens Joined to Both Sides of the Controversy Under 28 U.S.C. §1332(a)(3)*, 38 Rutgers L. Rev. 71 (1985).

136. *See infra* pp. 30-31; Note, *Diversity Jurisdiction: The Dilemma of Dual Citizenship and Alien Corporations*, 77 Nw. U.L. Rev. 565, 568-75 (1982). *See also* Dickinson, *The Law of United States (Pt. 1)*, 101 U. Pa. L. Rev. 26, 34-55 (1952).

137. *See infra* pp. 30-31; A. Hamilton, J. Madison & J. Jay, *The Federalist Papers*, No. 80 at 476 (C. Rossiter ed. 1961); 3 Elliot, *The Debates in the Several State Conventions on the Adoption of the Federal Constitution* 533-34, 583 (2d ed. 1941) (James Madison); A. Prescott, *Drafting the Federal Constitution* 673-74 (1941).

138. A. Hamilton, J. Madison & J. Jay, *The Federalist Papers*, No. 80, at 476 (C. Rossiter ed. 1961).

139. A. Hamilton, J. Madison & J. Jay, *The Federalist Papers* No. 80, at 476 (C. Rossiter ed. 1961) ("So great a proportion of the cases in which foreigners are parties involve national questions that it is by far most safe and most expedient to refer all those in which they are concerned to the national tribunals.").

140. Judiciary Act of 1789, ch. 20, §11, 1 Stat. 73; Mahoney, *A Historical Note on* Hodgson v. Bowerbank, 49 U. Chi. L. Rev. 725, 731-32 (1982).

141. *Mason v. The Ship Blaireau*, 6 U.S. 240 (1804); *Mossman v. Higginson*, 4 U.S. 12 (1800).

and a U.S. citizen. Despite the broader terms of the Judiciary Act, the Court conclud-ed in *Hodgson & Thompson v. Bowerbank* that Article III's grant of alienage jurisdic-tion did not extend to suits solely between aliens; it was confined to cases between a U.S. citizen and an alien.[142] Absent constitutional authorization, the grant of subject matter jurisdiction over suits between aliens in §11 of the Judiciary Act was invalid.

2. Contemporary Statutory Grants of Alienage Jurisdiction

Although federal statutes defining alienage jurisdiction have evolved over time, the basic questions addressed in the early years of the Republic about the scope of alienage jurisdiction continue to arise. At present, statutory provisions dealing with alienage jurisdiction are found in 28 U.S.C. §1332(a)(2) and §1332(a)(3).

a. Section 1332(a)(2)

Section 1332(a)(2) provides the district courts with original jurisdiction over civil actions where more than $50,000 is at stake and the controversy is between "cit-izens of a State and citizens or subjects of a foreign state." Some applications of §1332(a)(2) are straightforward. The clearest case of alienage jurisdiction under §1332(a)(2) is a suit by a single U.S. plaintiff against a single foreign defendant (or vice versa).[143] Similarly, §1332(a)(2) applies if two or more U.S. plaintiffs sue an alien (or vice versa).[144]

Conversely, it is equally clear that alienage jurisdiction under §1332(a)(2) does *not* extend to a suit by one alien against another alien.[145] This is a constitutional requirement, imposed by Article III, as well as a limitation of §1332(a)(2).[146]

Other cases are more difficult, especially in multiparty disputes. The require-ment of "complete diversity" between all adverse parties (*e.g.*, Florida and New York versus Arizona and Pennsylvania and *not* Florida and New York versus Florida and Arizona) is well established as a statutory requirement in domestic diversity of citi-zenship cases.[147] Particularly with this historical background, the language of §1332(a)(2), requiring a dispute "between ... citizens of *a State* and citizens or sub-jects of *a foreign state*," has been susceptible of a "complete diversity" reading. This reading has generally precluded alienage jurisdiction under §1332(a)(2) in cases with aliens appearing on both sides of the dispute (*e.g.*, France and New York versus

---

142. *Hodgson & Thompson v. Bowerbank*, 9 U.S. 303 (1809).

143. *E.g.*, *Maciak v. Olejniczak*, 79 F. Supp. 817 (E.D. Mich. 1948).

144. *E.g.*, *Romero v. International Terminal Operating Co.*, 358 U.S. 354 (1959); *De Korwin v. First Nat'l Bank*, 156 F.2d 858 (7th Cir.), *cert. denied*, 329 U.S. 795 (1946).

145. *E.g.*, *Joseph Muller Corp. v. Société Anonyme de Gerance et d'Armement*, 451 F.2d 727, 729 (2d Cir. 1971), *cert. denied*, 406 U.S. 906 (1972); *Koupetoris v. Konkar Intrepid Corp.*, 402 F. Supp. 951 (S.D.N.Y. 1975), *aff'd*, 535 F.2d 1392 (2d Cir. 1976); *Bergen Shipping Co. v. Japan Marine Serv., Ltd.*, 386 F. Supp. 430, 432 (S.D.N.Y. 1974).

146. *See Verlinden BV v. Central Bank of Nigeria*, 461 U.S. 480, 491-92 & n.18 (1983).

147. *See Strawbridge v. Curtiss*, 7 U.S. 267 (1806) (Marshall, C.J.).

Germany and Pennsylvania).[148] The same result applies in cases where a U.S. citizen, joined by an alien, attempts to litigate against another alien.[149]

b. Section 1332(a)(3)

In recent years, the Supreme Court has said that *Strawbridge's* complete diversity requirement is not constitutionally mandated.[150] It instead flows from the language of Congress's jurisdictional statutes, which could be amended without constitutional obstacle to permit jurisdiction based on minimal diversity. This interpretation of Article III clearly extends to alienage diversity, thus permitting Congress to authorize federal jurisdiction where aliens appear on both sides of a suit that also involves a U.S. party.[151]

In 1948, Congress enacted §1332(a)(3), which authorizes federal jurisdiction in actions between "citizens of different States and in which citizens or subjects of a foreign state are additional parties." The apparent purpose of §1332(a)(3) was to grant jurisdiction where a citizen of one U.S. state and a foreign citizen were aligned against the citizen of a second U.S. state (*e.g.*, New York and France versus Pennsylvania). It was thought that *domestic* diversity existed in these cases (*e.g.*, New York versus Pennsylvania), and that the presence of an alien on one side of the dispute should not deprive a domestic litigant of its federal diversity forum. Section 1332(a)(3) has frequently been applied in cases with this alignment.[152]

The literal language of §1332(a)(3), in contrast to that of §1332(a)(2), arguably also allows jurisdiction where a citizen of a U.S. state and an alien are aligned against the citizen of a second U.S. state and an alien (*e.g.*, Germany and Pennsylvania versus France and New York). Some lower courts have held that §1332(a)(3) grants federal alienage jurisdiction in these minimally diverse circumstances.[153] These decisions have reasoned that "[i]t would be inconsistent with the intent of the provision to

---

148. *E.g., Cabalceta v. Standard Fruit Co.*, 883 F.2d 1553, 1557 (11th Cir. 1989); *Faysound Ltd. v. United Coconut Chem. Inc.*, 878 F.2d 290 (9th Cir. 1989); *Cheng v. Boeing Co.*, 708 F.2d 1406 (9th Cir.), *cert. denied*, 464 U.S. 1017 (1983); *Field v. Volkswagenwerk*, 626 F.2d 293 (3d Cir. 1980); *IIT v. Vencap, Ltd.*, 519 F.2d 1001 (2d Cir. 1975); *Ed & Fred, Inc. v. Puritan Marine Ins. Underwriters Corp.*, 506 F.2d 757 (5th Cir. 1975).

149. *E.g., Eze v. Yellow Cab Co.*, 782 F.2d 1064 (D.C. Cir. 1986); *Ed & Fred, Inc. v. Puritan Marine Ins. Underwriters Corp.*, 506 F.2d 747 (5th Cir. 1975).

150. *See Verlinden BV v. Central Bank of Nigeria*, 461 U.S. 480, 492 n.18 (1983); *Owen Equip. & Erection Co. v. Kroger*, 437 U.S. 365, 373 n.13 (1978).

151. *Verlinden BV v. Central Bank of Nigeria*, 461 U.S. 480, 492 n.18 (1983).

152. *E.g., Tuck v. Pan American Health Org.*, 668 F.2d 547, 550 (D.C. Cir. 1981); *Turton v. Turton*, 644 F.2d 344, 346 n.1 (5th Cir. 1981); *Weight v. Kawasaki Heavy Indus.*, 597 F. Supp. 1082, 1084 (E.D. Va. 1984); *American Nat'l Bank & Tr. Co. v. Hamilton Indus. Int'l*, 583 F. Supp. 164 (N.D. Ill. 1984).

153. *See Transure, Inc. v. Marsh & McLennan, Inc.*, 766 F.2d 1297 (9th Cir. 1985) (California and England versus Delaware and South Africa); *Timco Engineering, Inc. v. Rex & Co.*, 603 F. Supp. 925 (E.D. Pa. 1985) (Florida and Hong Kong versus Texas and Hong Kong); *K&H Business Consultants Ltd. v. Cheltonian, Ltd.*, 567 F. Supp. 420 (D.N.J. 1983) (England and Delaware versus England and Texas); *Samincorp, Inc. v. Southwire Co.*, 531 F. Supp. 1, 2 (N.D. Ga. 1980) (New York versus Georgia and Venezuela; dicta that "diversity is [not] destroyed if citizens of foreign states are both plaintiffs and defendants").

deny a federal forum to diverse [U.S.] citizens because aliens were present on both sides of the controversy."[154] Nevertheless, other courts have continued to require complete diversity (denying jurisdiction if aliens appear both as plaintiffs and defendants).[155]

Significant limitations still exist on alienage jurisdiction under §1332(a)(3). Suppose, for example, a New York plaintiff and a German plaintiff sue New York and Spanish defendants. Because §1332(a)(3) requires a suit between "citizens of different States," which means different U.S. sister states, §1332(a)(3) would not apply. Similarly, §1332(a)(3) would appear inapplicable to a suit by an alien plaintiff against a U.S. citizen and another alien.[156] This result follows from the absence of diverse U.S. parties on both sides of the action, which is the necessary predicate for §1332(a)(3) jurisdiction.

It is less clear how §1332(a)(3) should be applied to cases involving adverse foreign parties from the same foreign nation, together with diverse U.S. parties (*e.g.*, Germany and New York versus Germany and New Jersey). Some authorities have concluded that §1332(a)(3) does not reach this situation, even if it does not require complete diversity.[157] Other commentators, and most of the courts that do not require complete diversity under §1332(a)(3), reject this view.[158]

3. Selected Materials on Alienage Jurisdiction

Excerpted below is *Hercules Inc. v. Dynamic Export Corp.*, which illustrates some of the complexities that can arise in applying §§1332(a)(2) and 1332(a)(3) in the context of multiparty litigation. It also provides the basis for considering the purposes served by alienage jurisdiction, and the limitations on the scope of such jurisdiction.

HERCULES INC. v. DYNAMIC EXPORT CORP.

71 F.R.D. 101 (S.D.N.Y. 1976)

CANNELLA, DISTRICT JUDGE. [Hercules Inc. ("Hercules"), a Delaware corporation, appointed Dynamic Export Corp. ("Dynamic"), a New York corporation, as its distributor for certain chemical products in Iran. These products were to be sold to Dynamic by HITCO, a Hercules affiliate incorporated in the Bahamas. After

---

154. *K&H Business Consultants v. Cheltonian, Ltd.*, 567 F. Supp. 420, 423 (D.N.J. 1983).

155. *Hercules Inc. v. Dynamic Export Corp.*, 71 F.R.D. 101 (S.D.N.Y. 1976).

156. *E.g.*, *Eze v. Yellow Cab Co.*, 782 F.2d 1064 (D.C. Cir. 1986) (no §1332(a)(2) or (a)(3) jurisdiction in suit by Nigerian plaintiffs against Virginian and Ghanaian defendants); *Ed & Fred, Inc. v. Puritan Marine Ins. Underwriters Corp.*, 506 F.2d 757 (5th Cir. 1975).

157. *E.g.*, *DeWit v. KLM Royal Dutch Airlines*, 570 F. Supp. 613, 617 (S.D.N.Y. 1983); Currie, *The Federal Courts and the American Law Institute*, 36 U. Chi. L. Rev. 1, 20 (1968).

158. *E.g.*, *K&H Business Consultants v. Cheltonian, Ltd.*, 567 F. Supp. 420 (D.N.J. 1983); *Jet Traders Inv. Corp. v. Tekair, Ltd.*, 89 F.R.D. 560 (D. Del. 1981); *Samincorp v. Southwire Co.*, 531 F. Supp. 1 (N.D. Ga. 1980); H. Friendly, *Federal Jurisdiction: A General View* 150 n.42 (1973).

disagreements between the parties arose, Hercules and HITCO sued Dynamic for some $200,000 allegedly owed to them by Dynamic for chemical products sold and delivered to Dynamic. Dynamic defended by alleging that it was acting on behalf of H. Mottahedan & Co. ("HMC"), an Iranian company, and joined HMC in a counterclaim seeking damages from Hercules and HITCO for breaching their contract to deliver a larger amount of the chemical involved. The court first concluded that Dynamic could pursue its counterclaims against Hercules and HITCO as agent for HMC, and that HMC could be joined under Federal Rules of Civil Procedure, Rule 20 as a plaintiff on these counterclaims. The Court then considered whether the joinder of HMC as a plaintiff on the counterclaims destroyed diversity jurisdiction over the action.]

HMC, counterclaim-plaintiff, and HITCO, counterclaim-defendant, are both aliens. The presence of aliens on both sides of a controversy will defeat diversity jurisdiction. *E.g., Merchants' Cotton Press and Storage Co. v. Ins. Co. of North America*, 151 U.S. 368, 385-86 (1894). In the face of this doctrine, counterclaimants Dynamic and HMC present an ingenious argument. They assert that 28 U.S.C. §1332(c), deeming a corporation "a citizen of any State by which it has been incorporated and of the State where it has its principal place of business," is applicable to foreign corporations which have their principal place of business within the United States. This being the case, HITCO should be considered a citizen of Delaware, where it has its principal place of business, and not the Bahamas, where it is incorporated. The alignment of the parties on the counterclaims would then be an alien, HMC, and a citizen of New York, Dynamic, versus two citizens of Delaware, Hercules and HITCO. Although this argument may have surface appeal, it is neither supported by the case law nor consistent with the purpose of §1332(c).

Prior to 1958 an alien corporation, for purposes of diversity jurisdiction, was considered a citizen solely of the foreign state in which it was incorporated. *E.g., Barrow S.S. Co. v. Kane*, 170 U.S. 100 (1898). Since the enactment of §1332(c) in 1958 most federal courts have held it inapplicable to foreign corporations, leaving the traditional rule in effect. ... On the other hand, courts confronting the issue more recently have found §1332(c) applicable to foreign corporations whose principal place of business is located in the United States. ... [These decisions have] applied the section to defeat diversity jurisdiction between a citizen of a state and an alien corporation with its principal place of business in that state. This application of the subsection is in consonance with its avowed purpose, the restriction of diversity jurisdiction. S. Rep. No. 1830, 85th Cong., 2d Sess. (1958). ...

For the purposes of the case at bar, however, we need not determine whether §1332(c) is, in fact, applicable to a foreign corporation. For even assuming that it is, it cannot be read to deem such a corporation a citizen of either the jurisdiction in which it is incorporated or the state in which it has its principal place of business, whichever it may choose. The statute creates a principle of dual citizenship, not one of alternative citizenship. Thus, where a corporation is incorporated in state A and has its principal place of business in state B and the adverse party is a citizen of either A or B, diversity is lacking. Likewise, assuming *arguendo* §1332(c) is applicable to alien corporations, when an alien corporation with its principal place of business in state A is adverse to either an alien or a citizen of state A, diversity would be lacking.

...

Notes on Hercules v. Dynamic

1. *Historic rationale for alienage jurisdiction.* Consider the rationale for granting federal subject matter jurisdiction over disputes between aliens and Americans. As discussed above, these lawsuits were thought to carry a significant risk of offending foreign states, and hence of interfering with U.S. foreign relations and foreign commerce; the federal courts were thought to have greater institutional competence to resolve disputes involving aliens in ways that would be fair and internationally acceptable. In Alexander Hamilton's words:

> [T]he peace of the WHOLE ought not to be left at the disposal of a PART. The Union will undoubtedly be answerable to foreign powers for the conduct of its members. And the responsibility for an injury ought ever to be accompanied with the faculty of preventing it. As the denial or perversion of justice by the sentences of courts, as well as in any other manner, is with reason classed among the just causes of war, it will follow that the federal judiciary ought to have cognizance of all causes in which the citizens of other countries are concerned.

A. Hamilton, J. Madison & J. Jay, *The Federalist Papers,* No. 80 at 476 (C. Rossiter ed. 1961). Many comments made during the debates surrounding the Constitution reflected the importance of alienage jurisdiction, often describing it in broad terms. Letter from James Madison to Edmund Randolph (April 8, 1787), reprinted in 9 *The Papers of James Madison* 368, 370 (R. Rutland & W. Rachal ed. 1975) ("all cases which concern foreigners"); 3 *The Debates in the Several State Conventions on the Adoption of the Federal Constitution* 530 (J. Elliot ed. 1836) (remarks of J. Madison) ("all occasions of having disputes with foreign powers"); *The Federalist Papers,* No. 80, at 501 (A. Hamilton) (C. Rossiter ed. 1961) ("all causes in which the citizens of other countries are concerned. ..."). Is federal jurisdiction in fact desirable for alienage cases? Why?

2. *Contemporary relevance of historic rationale for alienage jurisdiction.* Is the historic rationale for alienage jurisdiction relevant in today's international and domestic environment?

(a) *Impact of U.S. civil litigation on U.S. foreign relations and commerce.* Is there now really a risk, as Alexander Hamilton could warn, that some European power will regard a U.S. judgment as a "just cause[]" for war"? On the other hand, consider the political, diplomatic, and commercial impact of such cases as Harry Wu's trial in China, the punishments of some foreign courts, foreign judicial decisions imposing expropriatory penalties on U.S. companies, and the extraterritorial application of various U.S. laws in U.S. civil proceedings. Can judicial decisions in these sorts of cases not have significant impacts upon U.S. foreign relations? *See, e.g., Verlinden BV v. Central Bank of Nigeria,* 461 U.S. 480, 493 (1983) ("Actions against foreign sovereigns in our courts raise sensitive issues concerning the foreign relations of the United States, and the primacy of federal concerns is evident."); *Republica v. De Longchamps,* 1 U.S. 111 (1784).

Sophisticated businesses carefully consider the legal environment in nations where they are considering investments. Judicial decisions are an important aspect of this subject. James Madison's observation, 200 years ago, still has a substantial measure of truth: "if foreigners cannot get justice done them in these courts, [this will] prevent[] many wealthy gentlemen from trading or residing among us." 3 Elliot, *The Debates in the Several State Conventions on the Adoption of the Federal Constitution* 533-34, 583 (2d ed. 1941) (James Madison). The quality of U.S. justice in international cases, affecting foreign parties, will have a direct impact upon their willingness to trade with and invest in the United States. It may also affect the quality of justice received by U.S. parties abroad.

(b) *Federal courts' relative competence to decide alienage disputes.* Even if disputes with aliens can affect U.S. foreign relations and commerce, are federal courts any better suited to resolve such disputes than contemporary state courts? Even determined opponents of diversity jurisdiction generally concede that federal courts should retain jurisdiction over suits involving aliens. In the late Judge Friendly's words: "I would retain two, and only two, pieces of the present diversity jurisdiction. One is for suits between a citizen and foreign states or citizens or subjects thereof." H. Friendly, *Federal Jurisdiction: A General View* 149-50 (1973). Why?

Alienage jurisdiction is a fundamentally radical concept: local judges and jurors (*i.e.*, state courts) are denied the power to decide disputes, involving local residents, that are otherwise within their jurisdiction. Principally in order to avoid foreign diplomatic displeasure and to attract foreign trade and investment, the state courts are replaced with specialized tribunals that are thought to be more sympathetic to foreign concerns. Is this not an unusual arrangement? Is it any more unusual than domestic diversity jurisdiction?

3. *Constitutional limits on alienage jurisdiction.* Article III grants federal judicial power over cases "between a State, or the Citizens thereof, and foreign States, Citizens or Subjects." The Supreme Court has not read this provision expansively.

(a) *No Article III jurisdiction over suits by one alien against another.* In 1809, the Supreme Court held that the federal court's alienage jurisdiction was limited to suits involving an alien and a U.S. citizen. *Hodgson & Thompson v. Bowerbank*, 9 U.S. 303 (1809); *supra* pp. 26-27. Despite the broader terms of the Judiciary Act and expansive comments by the Framers in the Federalist Papers and elsewhere, *supra* pp. 25-26, 30, the Court concluded that the Constitution's grant of alienage jurisdiction did not extend to suits solely between aliens. This continues to be the rule today. *See Verlinden BV v. Central Bank of Nigeria*, 461 U.S. 480, 491-92 & n.18 (1983).

Some commentators have questioned the Court's holding that §11 of the Judiciary Act was unconstitutional, observing that the Judiciary Act of 1789 was enacted largely by those who drafted the Constitution. Warren, *New Light on the History of the Federal Judiciary Act of 1789*, 37 Harv. L. Rev. 49, 57 (1923). Are the purposes of the Constitution's authorization of alienage jurisdiction served by a narrow interpretation of the grant?

(b) *Complete diversity.* The requirement of "complete diversity" between adverse parties (*e.g.*, Florida and New York versus Arizona and Pennsylvania) is well established as a statutory requirement in domestic diversity of citizenship cases. *See Strawbridge v. Curtiss*, 7 U.S. 267 (1806). It also appears settled that complete diversity is not constitutionally required in the alienage context. *See supra* pp. 26-27. Should complete diversity be *constitutionally* required in alienage cases? Consider the Framers' purposes.

4. *Alienage jurisdiction under §1332(a)(2).* Section 1332(a)(2) grants federal subject matter jurisdiction over disputes "between ... citizens of *a State* and citizens or subjects of *a foreign state*." The "complete diversity" rule has been extended to alienage jurisdiction under 28 U.S.C. §1332(a)(2), where it has precluded alienage jurisdiction in cases with aliens appearing on both sides of the dispute. *See supra* pp. 26-27. Should §1332(a)(2) require complete diversity? That is, should the section reach cases in which there are aliens as both plaintiffs and defendants (*e.g.*, Texas and Tanzania v. Minnesota and Malawi)? Are cases with aliens on both sides less likely to involve the threat of parochial bias and interference with U.S. trade and diplomacy than cases with aliens on one side? Does it matter whether the aliens are from the same foreign state?

5. *Alienage jurisdiction under §1332(a)(3).* In 1948, Congress enacted §1332(a)(3), which grants federal jurisdiction in actions between "citizens of different States and in which citizens or subjects of a foreign state are additional parties." Like §1332(a)(2), the new provision has raised the question whether complete diversity is required. What answer does *Hercules* provide to this question? Is the *Hercules* result consistent with one of the basic purposes underlying alienage jurisdiction — namely, to ensure that state courts are not the only available tribunals in cases where they may be inclined to favor a U.S. litigant over a foreign litigant? Is it consistent with the goal of ensuring a federal forum for disputes that implicate U.S. foreign relations?

6. *Citizenship of contemporary multinational corporations.* Contemporary multinational enterprises often consist of numerous corporate vehicles, each with a different place of incorporation; shareholdings are often diffused among citizens of many different states. Management is also "multinational" in composition. In these circumstances, what should be regarded as a company's citizenship? Do major multinationals — like IBM, Shell, or Unilever — in fact have a citizenship" in the traditional sense?

Section 1332(c) provides that a corporation is "a citizen of any State by which it has been incorporated and of the State where it has its principal place of business." Should this provision be read as expanding, or as limiting, alienage jurisdiction? How does *Hercules* read the provision?

7. *Appropriate scope of federal subject matter jurisdiction in international cases.* Given the historic purposes of alienage jurisdiction, is it sufficient to focus strictly on the presence of foreign and U.S. nationals in litigation? Suits only involving aliens can implicate U.S. foreign relations, even if no American

is a party and no question of parochial bias is involved. *Cf. Verlinden BV v. Central Bank of Nigeria*, 461 U.S. 480 (1983) (suit by foreign company against foreign central banks); *Republic of Philippines v. Marcos*, 806 F.2d 344 (2d Cir. 1986) (suit by foreign nation against former foreign head of state). In these circumstances, the parties' formal citizenship is often not a dispositive indicator of a case's likely impact on U.S. diplomatic or trade relations. Given this, would it be wiser for federal courts to be granted substantially wider subject matter jurisdiction over all "international cases"? Would Article III permit this?

8. *Relationship between alienage jurisdiction and applicable law.* There is a distinction between a court's jurisdiction to adjudicate a specific dispute, and the substantive law that governs that dispute. *See supra* pp. 2, 8-13. Sections 1332(a)(2) and 1332(a)(3) grant subject matter jurisdiction to federal courts, but do not directly address what substantive law applies in alienage actions.

(a) *Application of Erie doctrine in alienage cases.* As discussed above, it is fundamental that state substantive law applies in federal diversity actions, except where valid federal statutory or other law preempts state law. *Erie Railroad Co. v. Tompkins*, 304 U.S. 64, 74 (1938); *supra* pp. 8-10. It is orthodox teaching that the same principle generally applies outside the diversity context, including in alienage cases. C. Wright, A. Miller & E. Cooper, *Federal Practice and Procedure* §4515 (1982).

(b) *Arguments for applying federal substantive law in alienage cases.* Are the purposes of alienage jurisdiction served merely by granting federal jurisdiction over alienage disputes? Consider the following argument, also made by Alexander Hamilton in support of Article III's grant of alienage jurisdiction: "So great a proportion of the cases in which foreigners are parties involve national questions that it is by far most safe and most expedient to refer all those in which they are concerned to the national tribunals." A. Hamilton, J. Madison & J. Jay, *The Federalist Papers,* No. 80 at 476 (C. Rossiter ed. 1961). In order to accomplish the purposes of alienage jurisdiction, must federal substantive law apply in alienage cases? Consider the problems that would arise from such a proposal. Where would federal substantive common law be derived from, in such fields as contract, tort, agency, and damages? Would it be thinkable for disputes involving foreigners to be subject to a different set of substantive rules than those involving U.S. nationals? Is this any different from subjecting disputes involving foreigners to a different set of courts than those involving most U.S. nationals?

9. *Federal subject matter jurisdiction distinguished from international competence.* It is often said that international law does not address a nation's allocation of jurisdiction among its domestic courts — provided that the nation itself may properly exercise jurisdiction under international law. *See Restatement (Third) Foreign Relations Law* §421, comment f (1987). As discussed below, both international and U.S. law restrict: (a) the personal jurisdiction of U.S. courts to adjudicate claims against foreign parties that lack meaningful contacts with the United States; and (b) the legislative jurisdiction of Congress (and state legislatures) to make U.S. law applicable to foreign conduct that lacks meaningful connection to the United States. *See infra* pp. 67-94 & 493-544. In addition, international law could also forbid U.S. courts from hearing certain disputes — even where the parties are subject to U.S. personal jurisdiction and even though non-U.S. law is applied. International law could be interpreted to restrict the "competence" or "subject matter jurisdiction" of a nation's courts to resolve certain cases, regardless of personal and legislative jurisdiction, because the subject matter of the dispute lacked any connection to that nation. There is little authority for such a rule in common law jurisdictions. Would it be sensible for such a doctrine to exist? Give some examples of its application.

C. Federal Question Jurisdiction in International Cases[159]

The single most significant aspect of the federal courts' subject matter jurisdiction involves actions arising under federal law.[160] This "federal question" jurisdiction derives from Article III's grant of jurisdiction over "[c]ases ... arising under this Constitution, the Laws of the United States, and Treaties made, or which shall be made, under their authority."[161]

1. Introduction and Historical Background

a. Article III's Grant of Federal Question Jurisdiction

Article III's grant of federal question jurisdiction was one of the principal reasons that the Framers provided for the establishment of a federal court system.[162] From almost the beginning of the Constitutional Convention, it was accepted that federal courts should have jurisdiction over actions arising under federal statutes.[163] Cases arising under the Constitution and U.S. "Treaties" were added later in the Convention.[164] The Framers explained the constitutional grant of federal question jurisdiction as a safeguard against state court subvention of federal law,[165] a basis for achieving national uniformity of federal law,[166] and a means of obtaining neutral arbiters detached from local prejudice.[167]

Particular importance was attached to Article III's grant of federal question jurisdiction in cases arising under U.S. treaties. The Framers emphasized that such

---

159. Commentary on federal question jurisdiction in international cases includes, *e.g.*, Randall, *Federal Jurisdiction Over International Law Claims: Inquiries Into the Alien Tort Statute*, 18 N.Y.U.J. Int'l L. & Pol'y 1 (1985); Rogers, *The Alien Tort Statute and How Individuals Violate International Law*, 21 Vand. J. Transnat'l L. 47 (1988); Henkin, *International Law as Law in the United States*, 82 Mich. L. Rev. 1555 (1984); Moore, *Federalism and Foreign Relations*, 1965 Duke L. J. 248, 291-97.

160. *See* C. Wright & A. Miller, *Federal Practice and Procedure* §3522 (1984).

161. U.S. Const. Art. III, §2.

162. The first of Article III's jurisdictional grants is federal question jurisdiction. *See* A. Hamilton, J. Madison & J. Jay, *The Federalist Papers* No. 16 (1961 C. Rossiter ed.) (A. Hamilton) ("The majesty of the national authority must be manifested through the medium of the courts of justice").

163. 1 M. Farrand, *Records of the Federal Convention of 1787* 22, 211-12, 220, 244 (1937); 2 *Id.* 46-47, 186-87. After considering the report of the Committee of the whole, Madison proposed that federal "jurisdiction shall extend to all cases arising under the National laws: And to such other questions as may involve the National peace and harmony." 2 M. Farrand, *Records of the Federal Convention of 1787* 46 (1937). The suggestion was agreed.

164. 2 M. Farrand, *Records of the Federal Convention of 1787* 423-24, 430-31 (1937).

165. A. Hamilton, J. Madison & J. Jay, *The Federalist Paper* No. 80 (1961 C. Rossiter ed.) (A. Hamilton) ("No man of sense will believe, that such prohibitions [on state authority] would be scrupulously regarded, without some effectual power in the government to restrain or correct the infractions of them").

166. *Id.* at 500 ("The mere necessity in the interpretation of the national laws, decides the question").

167. *Id.* at 502 ("tribunal which, having no local attachments, will be likely to be impartial between the different States and their citizens, and which, owing its official existence to the Union, will never be likely to feel any bias inauspicious to the principles on which it is founded.").

cases have "an evident connection with the preservation of the national peace."[168] The same rationales that justified alienage jurisdiction were advanced for federal question jurisdiction over treaties: because such cases were sensitive, and engaged national obligations towards foreign states, federal courts ought to have responsibility for them.[169]

b. Statutory Grants of Federal Question Jurisdiction

Notwithstanding the importance attributed to it, Article III's grant of federal question jurisdiction was not generally implemented until 1875. Neither the First Judiciary Act, nor any legislation for another 80 years, contained any general authorization for federal courts to hear cases arising under federal statutes.[170] In contrast, however, the First Judiciary Act contained several specialized grants of federal question jurisdiction directed specifically towards international disputes.

First, the Judiciary Act of 1789 included a grant of subject matter jurisdiction to the federal courts over "all causes where an alien sues for a tort only, [committed] in violation of the law of nations or a treaty of the United States."[171] Although no legislative history or other evidence specifically explains the reasons for this grant of federal question jurisdiction — today called the "Alien Tort Statute" — it graphically illustrates the importance that was attributed to international disputes at the time.[172] Although Article III would have permitted jurisdiction in any case arising under the U.S. Constitution, statutes, or Treaties, Congress's implementation of Article III's federal question jurisdiction was limited principally to claims under U.S. Treaties and "the Law of Nations" — presumably those subjects where federal jurisdiction was deemed most necessary.[173]

Second, in 1875, Congress substantially enlarged the federal question jurisdiction of federal courts. With little debate, Congress granted federal district courts original jurisdiction over cases arising under federal laws.[174] That legislation has been preserved substantially unchanged, and is currently codified in 28 U.S.C. §1331:

---

168. *Id.* at 504. The Framers emphasized that the "national peace and harmony" was affected by cases involving "the security of foreigners where treaties are in their favor." 1 M. Farrand, *Records of the Federal Convention of 1787* 238 (1937).

169. A. Hamilton, J. Madison & J. Jay, *The Federalist Paper* No. 80 (1961 C. Rossiter ed.) (A. Hamilton).

170. C. Wright & A. Miller, *Federal Practice and Procedure* §3561 (1984).

171. Judiciary Act of 1789, ch. 20 §9(b), 1 Stat. 73, 77, codified at 28 U.S.C. §1350 (1982) ("[t]he district courts shall have original jurisdiction of any civil action by an alien for a tort only, committed in violation of the law of nations or a treaty of the United States").

172. P. Bator, D. Meltzer, P. Mishkin & D. Shapiro, *Hart and Wechsler's, The Federal Courts and The Federal System* 961 (3d ed. 1988).

173. The Alien Tort Statute is discussed in detail below. *See infra* pp. 36-49. The First Congress also granted federal subject matter jurisdiction over admiralty and maritime cases and cases involving foreign consuls. C. Wright & A. Miller, *Federal Practice and Procedure* §§3662 & 3671 (1984).

174. Act of March 3, 1875, §1, 18 Stat. 470.

"district courts shall have original jurisdiction of all civil actions arising under the Constitution, laws, or treaties of the United States."[175]

Most actions under §1331 are based on specific federal substantive statutes. Typical examples are cases in which a plaintiff files a complaint in federal court alleging violations of the federal antitrust laws, RICO, or securities laws.[176] These actions "arise under" federal law, and are within the scope of §1331. (They do not raise specifically international issues, and are not further considered here).

Determining whether an action "arises under" federal law within the meaning of §1331 can present difficult issues in both domestic and international contexts.[177] As a matter of statutory interpretation under §1331, the issue is typically decided by applying the "well-pleaded complaint" rule, which requires examining the plaintiff's complaint to determine whether it asserts claims created by federal, rather than state, law.[178] In general, an action does not arise under federal law for purposes of §1331 if the federal law at issue in a case is merely a defense to a nonfederal claim.[179] Federal question jurisdiction will exist, however, even if state (or foreign) law creates the plaintiff's cause of action, provided that a substantial, disputed issue of federal law is a necessary element of the plaintiff's state claim.[180]

Third, in 1976, Congress enacted the Foreign Sovereign Immunities Act ("FSIA").[181] The FSIA grants federal district courts concurrent jurisdiction over civil actions against foreign states and state-related entities.[182] The FSIA's grant of federal subject matter jurisdiction is consistent with Congress's history of providing federal jurisdiction over international disputes. Nevertheless, as discussed below, it has given rise to difficult issues under Article III.[183]

The following sections examine each of the foregoing grants of federal question jurisdiction, focussing on the application of these grants in international litigation.

---

175. In addition, a number of federal substantive statutes (such as the antitrust and securities laws) contain specialized grants of federal subject matter jurisdiction relating to particular federal substantive statutes. *See supra* p. 11.

176. These exercises of both legislative jurisdiction and subject matter jurisdiction are discussed below at *infra* pp. 69-70, & 605-06.

177. *See Franchise Tax Bd. v. Construction Laborers Vacation Tr.*, 463 U.S. 1 (1983); P. Bator, P. Mishkin, D. Meltzer & D. Shapiro, *Hart & Wechsler's The Federal Courts and the Federal System* 960-1039 (3d ed. 1988).

178. *Louisville & Nashville R.R. v. Mottley*, 211 U.S. 149 (1908). As discussed below, Article III's constitutional grant of jurisdiction over claims "arising under" federal law is broader than §1331's statutory grant of jurisdiction "arising under" federal law. *See infra* pp. 62-63 & 65. Congress could therefore grant federal courts broader federal question jurisdiction than that permitted under §1331's "well-pleaded complaint" rule. Congress did so in enacting the Foreign Sovereign Immunities Act, and the Court held that Article III had not been overstepped. *Verlinden BV v. Central Bank of Nigeria*, 461 U.S. 480 (1983); *infra* pp. 56-66.

179. *Franchise Tax Bd. v. Construction Laborers Vacation Tr.*, 463 U.S. 1 (1983); *Louisville & Nashville R.R. v. Mottley*, 211 U.S. 149 (1908); C. Wright & A. Miller, *Federal Practice and Procedure* §§3522, 3562 (1984).

180. *Franchise Tax Board v. Construction Laborers Vacation Trust*, 463 U.S. 1 (1983).

181. 28 U.S.C. §§1330, 1601-11.

182. *See infra* pp. 210-12.

183. *See infra* pp. 56-66; *Verlinden BV v. Central Bank of Nigeria*, 461 U.S. 480 (1983).

2. Jurisdiction of Federal Courts Under Alien Tort Statute

a. The Alien Tort Statute

As described above, the First Judiciary Act granted federal courts jurisdiction over "all causes where an alien sues for a tort only, [committed] in violation of the law of nations or a treaty of the United States."[184] The Alien Tort Statute's grant of jurisdiction was[185] and remains concurrent with the state courts.[186]

For much of two centuries, the Alien Tort Statute was largely ignored. Indeed, commenting in 1975 on the statute's allegedly obscure origins, Judge Friendly dubbed the provision a "Legal Lohengrin" (after the mysterious, shadowy character in a Wagner opera), and remarked that "no one seems to know from whence it came."[187] Before 1980, it was also true that no one seemed to care very much where the Alien Tort Statute might go: jurisdiction under the Act was seldom pleaded and had apparently been upheld on only two occasions.[188] In the comparatively small number of other cases where §1350 jurisdiction was claimed, but denied, courts generally concluded that the defendant's alleged conduct did not violate the law of nations.[189]

b. Filartiga and Tel-Oren

In 1980, the Alien Tort Statute left the shadows and, at least for a time, took center stage. In a controversial opinion titled *Filartiga v. Pena-Irala*,[190] which is excerpted below, the Second Circuit held that the Alien Tort Statute provided the basis for federal jurisdiction in a suit against a former Paraguayan police official for the alleged torture and murder of the plaintiff's deceased Paraguayan relative. According to the court, customary international law prohibits official torture, and §1350 provides a jurisdictional basis for suits in federal courts for violations of this "law of nations" prohibition.

---

184. Judiciary Act of 1789, ch. 20 §9(b), 1 Stat. 73, 77.

185. Judiciary Act of 1789, ch. 20 §9, 1 Stat. 73, 77.

186. 28 U.S.C. §1350.

187. *ITT v. Vencap, Ltd.*, 519 F.2d 1001, 1015 (2d Cir. 1975). For analysis of the origins of the Alien Tort Statute, *see* Randall, *Federal Jurisdiction Over International Law Claims: Inquiries Into the Alien Tort Statute*, 18 N.Y.U.J. Int'l L. & Pol'y 1 (1985); Rogers, *The Alien Tort Statute and How Individuals Violate International Law*, 21 Vand. J. Transnat'l L. 47 (1988).

188. *See Adra v. Clift*, 195 F. Supp. 857 (D. Md. 1961) (use of passport under false pretenses); *Bolchos v. Darrel*, 3 F. Cas. 810 (D.S.C. 1795) (no. 1607) (seizure of neutral vessel). *See also* 1 Op. Att'y Gen. 57 (1795) (raid on neutral settlement); 26 Op. Att'y Gen. 250 (1907) (diversion of international waterway).

189. *See, e.g., Huynh Thi Anh v. Levi*, 586 F.2d 625 (6th Cir. 1978); *Benjamins v. British European Airways*, 572 F.2d 913 (2d Cir. 1978); *Dreyfus v. Von Finck*, 534 F.2d 24 (2d Cir.), *cert. denied*, 429 U.S. 835 (1976); *IIT v. Vencap, Ltd.*, 519 F.2d 1001 (2d Cir. 1975); *Akbar v. New York Magazine Co.*, 490 F. Supp. 60 (D.D.C. 1980) (libel is not violation of law nations); *Valanga v. Metropolitan Life Ins. Co.*, 259 F. Supp. 324 (E.D.N.Y. 1966). *See also Hamid v. Price Waterhouse*, 51 F.3d 1411, 1418 (9th Cir. 1995) ("garden variety violations of statutes, banking regulations, and common law" not violations of international law); *Cohen v. Hartman*, 634 F.2d 318 (11th Cir. 1981) (conversion by private individual is not violation of law of nations); *Jones v. Petty Ray Geophysical Geosource, Inc.*, 722 F. Supp. 343 (S.D. Tex. 1989) (negligent police protection is not violation of law of nations); *Guinto v. Marcos*, 654 F. Supp. 276 (S.D. Calif. 1986) (interference with free speech rights is not violation of law of nations).

190. 630 F.2d 876 (2d Cir. 1980).

The Second Circuit's decision in *Filartiga v. Pena-Irala* provoked extensive commentary, both approving and disapproving.[191] *Filartiga* has also provided the impetus for a flurry of litigation under the Alien Tort Statute. It is often invoked by plaintiffs with human rights grievances against foreign officials.[192] This litigation has prompted expressions of concern from both courts and commentators, on the grounds that adjudication of sensitive claims of human rights abuses by U.S. courts will interfere with the conduct of U.S. foreign relations by Congress and the President.[193]

One of the more thoughtful discussions of these issues was in *Tel-Oren v. Libyan Arab Republic.*[194] The *Tel-Oren* plaintiffs' claim arose out of an incident in which alleged members of the Palestine Liberation Organization ("PLO") and other groups murdered a number of civilians during a terrorist attack in Israel. The victims — citizens of Israel, the United States, and the Netherlands — filed an action in federal district court against the PLO and Libya, asserting jurisdiction under the Alien Tort Statute. The district court dismissed, among other things, for lack of subject matter jurisdiction. The Court of Appeals for the D.C. Circuit unanimously affirmed, but all three members of the panel wrote separately.

Two members of the panel, Judges Robb and Bork, rejected the *Filartiga* construction of the Alien Tort Statute, although for different reasons. Judge Robb argued that human rights disputes, such as those in *Filartiga* and *Tel-Oren*, were nonjusticiable political questions, because they involved sensitive matters that touch on American foreign relations.[195] He thought that *Filartiga* failed to "consider the possibility that ad hoc intervention by courts into international affairs may very well redound to the decisive disadvantage of the nation."[196] "[T]he political questions doctrine is designed to prevent just this sort of judicial gambling."[197]

---

191. For commentary approving the result in *Filartiga, see, e.g.,* Cole, Lobel & Koh, *Interpreting the Alien Tort Statute: Amicus Curiae Memorandum of International Law Scholars and Practitioners in Trajano v. Marcos,* 12 Hastings Int'l & Comp. L. Rev. 1 (1988); Blum & Steinhardt, *Federal Jurisdiction Over International Human Rights Claims: The Alien Tort Claims Act After Filartiga,* 22 Harv. Int'l L.J. 53 (1981); Paust, *Litigating Human Rights: A Commentary on the Comments,* 4 Hous. J. Int'l L. 8 (1981); For criticism of *Filartiga, see, e.g.,* Oliver, *Problems of Cognition and Interpretation in Applying Norms of the Customary International Law of Human Rights in United States Courts,* 4 Hous. J. Int'l L. 59 (1981); Rusk, *A Comment on* Filartiga v. Pena-Irala, 11 Ga. J. Int'l & Comp. L. 311 (1981).

192. *E.g., Kadic v. Karadzic,* 1995 WL 604585 (2d Cir. 1995); *In re Estate of Ferdinand E. Marcos Human Rights Litigation,* 978 F.2d 493 (9th Cir. 1992); *Trajano v. Marcos,* 878 F.2d 1439 (9th Cir. 1989); *Siderman de Blake v. Republic of Argentina,* 965 F.2d 699 (9th Cir, 1992); *Tel-Oren v. Libyan Arab Republic,* 726 F.2d 774 (D.C. Cir. 1984); *Fernandez v. Wilkinson,* 505 F. Supp. 787 (D. Kan. 1980), *aff'd,* 654 F.2d 1382 (10th Cir. 1981); *Von Dardel v. USSR,* 623 F. Supp. 426 (D.D.C. 1985); *Sanchez-Espinoza v. Reagan,* 568 F. Supp. 598 (D.D.C. 1983); *Trajano v. Marcos,* No. 86-0207 (D. Ha. July 18, 1987); *Guinto v. Marcos,* 654 F. Supp. 276 (S.D. Cal. 1986). *See* Lillich, *Invoking International Human Rights Law in Domestic Courts,* 54 Cinn. L. Rev. 367 (1985).

193. *E.g., Tel-Oren v. Libyan Arab Republic,* 726 F.2d 774 (D.C. Cir. 1984).

194. 726 F.2d 774 (D.C. Cir. 1984).

195. 726 F.2d at 823.

196. 726 F.2d at 826 n.5.

197. 726 F.2d at 827 n.5.

Judge Bork said it was not necessary to determine whether the political question doctrine barred the plaintiffs' claim.[198] But, like Judge Robb, he believed that the *Filartiga* interpretation of the Alien Tort Statute would thrust the judiciary into foreign affairs and he therefore adopted a narrow construction of the Alien Tort Statute.[199] According to Judge Bork, §1350 was merely jurisdictional and did not itself grant plaintiffs a private "cause of action."[200] Judge Bork also reasoned that the separation of powers principles underpinning the act of state and political question doctrines counseled against implying a cause of action. Finally, he would have held that the human rights conventions and principles of customary international law on which the *Tel-Oren* plaintiffs relied did not create a private cause of action, and therefore that the plaintiffs' claims should be dismissed.[201]

Judge Edwards was the only member of the *Tel-Oren* panel to accept the *Filartiga* reading of the Alien Tort Statute. In so doing, he rejected Judge Bork's contention that §1350 plaintiffs were required to show a private right to sue independent of the Alien Tort Statute, apparently concluding that both §1350 and other sources of national law provided a cause of action.[202] Judge Edwards nonetheless rejected Alien Tort Statute jurisdiction over the *Tel-Oren* plaintiffs' claims, because no tort in violation of the "law of nations" had occurred.[203] He observed that the PLO was not a state recognized by the United States, and reasoned that, because the law of nations ordinarily does not impose responsibility or liability on nonstate actors, the PLO could not commit "a tort in violation of the law of the nations."[204]

c. The Torture Victim Protection Act

Partially in response to *Tel-Oren*, Congress enacted the Torture Victim Protection Act ("TVPA") in 1992.[205] The Act creates a federal civil action against individuals who, under the actual or apparent authority or color of law of any foreign state, subject a person to "torture" or extrajudicial killing.[206] The TVPA was enacted to implement the Convention Against Torture and Other Cruel, Inhuman or

---

198. 726 F.2d at 798, 803.

199. 726 F.2d at 803.

200. 726 F.2d at 811.

201. 726 F.2d at 808-19.

202. 726 F.2d at 777-82, 782-89.

203. 726 F.2d at 791-96.

204. 726 F.2d at 796. *Compare Kadic v. Karadzic*, 1995 WL 604585 (2d Cir. 1995) (certain forms of conduct violate the law of nations whether undertaken by those acting under the auspices of a state or only as private individuals).

205. Pub. L. No. 102-256, 106 Stat. 73 (1992), *codified at* 28 U.S.C. §1350 (note).

206. Torture is defined to include the intentional infliction of severe pain or suffering, whether physical or mental, for the purposes of obtaining a confession, punishment, or coercion. "Extrajudicial killing" is defined as "a deliberate killing not authorized by a previous judgment pronounced by a regularly constituted court affording all judicial guarantees which are recognized as indispensable by civilized peoples." Because of the requirement that the conduct at issue be "under actual or apparent authority, or color of law," plaintiffs are required to demonstrate governmental involvement in the tortious activity underlying the claim.

Degrading Treatment or Punishment,[207] which the United States has ratified. Article 14 of the Convention requires member states to adopt measures to ensure that torturers within their territory are held accountable for their acts.[208] According to the TVPA's legislative history, "[t]his legislation will do precisely that — by making sure that torturers and death squads will no longer have a safe haven in the United States."[209]

Excerpted below is the Second Circuit's decision in *Filartiga v. Pena-Irala*. In reading the decision, consider whether it is sound policy to grant federal courts jurisdiction over the types of misconduct alleged in the case. Consider also how separation of powers considerations affect the answer to this question and the interpretation of the Alien Tort Statute and the TVPA.

FILARTIGA v. PENA-IRALA

630 F.2d 876 (2d Cir. 1980)

KAUFMAN, CIRCUIT JUDGE. [Plaintiffs are a Paraguayan man and his daughter living in the United States. The son/brother of the plaintiffs was brutally tortured and killed by defendant when the latter was inspector general of police in a Paraguayan city. After unsuccessfully seeking relief from the Paraguayan courts, plaintiffs discovered defendant living in the United States, where he was served with process. The district court dismissed the complaint, ruling that the alleged tort was not in violation of the "law of nations" and therefore that 28 U.S.C. §1350 did not apply. The plaintiffs appealed.]

Appellants rest their principal argument in support of federal jurisdiction upon the Alien Tort Statute, 28 U.S.C. §1350, which provides: "The district courts shall have original jurisdiction of any civil action by an alien for a tort only, committed in violation of the law of nations or a treaty of the United States." Since appellants do not contend that their action arises directly under a treaty of the United States, a threshold question on the jurisdictional issue is whether the conduct alleged violates the law of nations.... . [W]e find that an act of torture committed by a state official against one held in detention violates established norms of the international law of human rights, and hence the law of nations. [The Court initially conducted an exhaustive survey of the public international law treatment of torture, concluding that international law forbids torture by state officials. In doing so, the Court relied heavily on a number of multilateral international documents, including the U.N. Charter and various human rights conventions.]

---

207. G.A. Res. 39/46, 39 U.N. GAOR Supp. No. 51, at 197, U.N. Doc. A/RES/39/708 (1984), *reprinted in*, 23 I.L.M. 1027 (1984).

208. *See* S. Rep. No. 249, 102d Cong., 1st Sess. 3 (1991).

209. S. Rep. No. 249, 102d Cong., 1st Sess. 3 (1991). *See Kadic v. Karadzic*, 1995 WL 604585 (2d Cir. 1995) ("Congress enacted the [TVPA] to codify the cause of action recognized by this Circuit in *Filartiga* and further to extend that cause of action to ... U.S. citizens").

Having examined the sources from which customary international law is derived — the usage of nations, judicial opinions and the works of jurists — we conclude that official torture is now prohibited by the law of nations. The prohibition is clear and unambiguous, and admits of no distinction between treatment of aliens and citizens. Accordingly, we must conclude that the dictum in *Dreyfus v. von Finck*, [534 F.2d 24, 31 (2d Cir.), *cert. denied*, 429 U.S. 835 (1976),] to the effect that "violations of international law do not occur when the aggrieved parties are nationals of the acting state," is clearly out of tune with the current usage and practice of international law. The treaties and accords cited above, as well as the express foreign policy of our own government, all make it clear that international law confers fundamental rights upon all people vis-a-vis their own governments. While the ultimate scope of those rights will be a subject for continuing refinement and elaboration, we hold that the right to be free from torture is now among them.

Appellee submits that even if the tort alleged is a violation of modern international law, federal jurisdiction may not be exercised consistent with the dictates of Article III of the Constitution. The claim is without merit. Common law courts of general jurisdiction regularly adjudicate transitory tort claims between individuals over whom they exercise personal jurisdiction, wherever the tort occurred. Moreover, as part of an articulated scheme of federal control over external affairs, Congress provided, in the first Judiciary Act, §9(b), 1 Stat. 73, 77 (1789), for federal jurisdiction over suits by aliens where principles of international law are in issue. The constitutional basis for the Alien Tort Statute is the law of nations, which has always been part of the federal common law.

It is not extraordinary for a court to adjudicate a tort claim arising outside of its territorial jurisdiction. A state or nation has a legitimate interest in the orderly resolution of disputes among those within its borders, and where the *lex loci delicti commissi* is applied, it is an expression of comity to give effect to the laws of the state where the wrong occurred. Thus, Lord Mansfield in *Mostyn v. Fabrigas*, 1 Cowp. 161 (1774), *quoted in McKenna v. Fisk*, 42 U.S. 241, 248 (1843) said:

> [I]f A becomes indebted to B, or commits a tort upon his person or upon his personal property in Paris, an action in either case may be maintained against A in England, if he is there found... . [A]s to transitory actions, there is not a colour of doubt but that any action which is transitory may be laid in any county in England, though the matter arises beyond the seas.

Mostyn came into our law as the original basis for state court jurisdiction over out-of-state torts, *McKenna v. Fisk*, 42 U.S. 241 (personal injury suits held transitory), and it has not lost its force in suits to recover for a wrongful death occurring upon foreign soil, *Slater v. Mexican National Railroad Co.*, 194 U.S. 120 (1904), as long as the conduct complained of was unlawful where performed. *Restatement (Second) of Foreign Relations Law* §19 (1965). Here, where *in personam* jurisdiction has been obtained over the defendant, the parties agree that the acts alleged would violate Paraguayan law, and the policies of the forum are consistent with the foreign law... .

Recalling that *Mostyn* was freshly decided at the time the Constitution was ratified, we proceed to consider whether the First Congress acted constitutionally in vesting jurisdiction over "foreign suits," *Slater*, 194 U.S. at 124, alleging torts committed in violation of the law of nations. A case properly "aris[es] under the ... laws of the United States" for Article III purposes if grounded upon statutes enacted by Congress or upon the common law of the United States. *See Illinois v. City of Milwaukee*, 406 U.S. 91, 99-100 (1972)... . The law of nations forms an integral part of the common law, and a review of the history surrounding the adoption of the Constitution demonstrates that it became a part of the common law *of the United States* upon the adoption of the Constitution. Therefore, the enactment of the Alien Tort Statute was authorized by Article III.

During the eighteenth century, it was taken for granted on both sides of the Atlantic that the law of nations forms a part of the common law. Under the Articles of Confederation, the Pennsylvania Court of Oyer and Terminer at Philadelphia, *per* McKean, Chief Justice, applied the law of nations to the criminal prosecution of the Chevalier de Longchamps for his assault upon the person of the French Consul-General to the United States, noting that "[t]his law, in its full extent, is a part of the law of this state... ." *Respublica v. DeLongchamps*, 1 U.S. 113, 119 (1784)... . As ratified, the judiciary article contained no express reference to cases arising under the law of nations. Indeed, the only express reference to that body of law is contained in Article I, sec. 8, cl. 10, which grants to the Congress the power to "define and punish ... offenses against the law of nations." Appellees seize upon this circumstance and advance the proposition that the law of nations forms a part of the laws of the United States only to the extent that Congress has acted to define it. This extravagant claim is amply refuted by the numerous decisions applying rules of international law uncodified in any act of Congress. *E.g.*, *Ware v. Hylton*, 3 U.S. 198 (1796); *The Paquete Habana*; *Sabbatino*... . Thus, it was hardly a radical initiative for Chief Justice Marshall to state in *The Nereide*, 13 U.S. 388, 422 (1815), that in the absence of a congressional enactment, United States courts are "bound by the law of nations, which is a part of the law of the land." These words were echoed in *The Paquete Habana*: "[i]nternational law is part of our law, and must be ascertained and administered by the courts of justice of appropriate jurisdiction, as often as questions of right depending upon it are duly presented for their determination."

The Filartigas urge that 28 U.S.C. §1350 be treated as an exercise of Congress's power to define offenses against the law of nations. While such a reading is possible, *see Lincoln Mills v. Textile Workers*, 353 U.S. 488 (1957) (jurisdictional statute authorizes judicial explication of federal common law), we believe it is sufficient here to construe the Alien Tort Statute, not as granting new rights to aliens, but simply as opening the federal courts for adjudication of the rights already recognized by international law. The statute nonetheless does inform our analysis of Article III, for we recognize that questions of jurisdiction "must be considered part of an organic growth — part of an evolutionary process," and that the history of the judiciary article gives meaning to its pithy phrases. *Romero v. International Terminal Operating Co.*, 358 U.S. 354, 360 (1959). The Framers' overarching concern that control over international affairs be vested in the new national government to safeguard the standing of the United States among the nations of the world therefore reinforces the result we reach today.

Although the Alien Tort Statute has rarely been the basis for jurisdiction during its long history, in light of the foregoing discussion, there can be little doubt that this action is properly brought in federal court.[210] This is undeniably an action by an alien, for a tort only, committed in violation of the law of nations. The paucity of suits successfully maintained under the section is readily attributable to the statute's requirement of alleging a *"violation of the law of nations"* (emphasis supplied) at the jurisdictional threshold. Courts have, accordingly, engaged in a more searching preliminary review of the merits than is required, for example, under the more flexible "arising under" formulation. *Compare O'Reilly de Camara v. Brooke*, 209 U.S. 45, 52 (1907) (question of Alien Tort Statute jurisdiction disposed of "on the merits") (Holmes, J.) *with Bell v. Hood*, 327 U.S. 678 (1946) (general federal question jurisdiction not defeated by the possibility that the averments in the complaint may fail to state a cause of action). Thus, the narrowing construction that the Alien Tort Statute has previously received reflects the fact that earlier cases did not involve such well-established, universally recognized norms of international law that are here at issue.

For example, the statute does not confer jurisdiction over an action by a Luxembourgeois international investment trust's suit for fraud, conversion and corporate waste. *IIT v. Vencap*, 519 F.2d 1001, 1015 (1975). In *IIT*, Judge Friendly astutely noted that the mere fact that every nation's municipal law may prohibit theft does not incorporate "the Eighth Commandment, 'Thou Shalt not steal' ... [into] the law of nations." It is only where the nations of the world have demonstrated that the wrong is of mutual, and not merely several, concern, by means of express international accords, that a wrong generally recognized becomes an international law violation within the meaning of the statute. Other recent §1350 cases are similarly distinguishable... .

Since federal jurisdiction may properly be exercised over the Filartigas' claim, the action must be remanded for further proceedings. Appellee Pena, however, advances several additional points that lie beyond the scope of our holding on jurisdiction. Both to emphasize the boundaries of our holding, and to clarify some of the issues reserved for the district court on remand, we will address these contentions briefly.

---

210. We recognize that our reasoning might also sustain jurisdiction under the general federal question provision, 28 U.S.C. §1331. We prefer, however, to rest our decision upon the Alien Tort Statute, in light of that provision's close coincidence with the jurisdictional facts presented in this case. *See Romero v. International Terminal Operating Co.*, 358 U.S. 354 (1959).

Pena argues that the customary law of nations, as reflected in treaties and declarations that are not self-executing, should not be applied as rules of decision in this case. In doing so, he confuses the question of federal jurisdiction under the Alien Tort Statute, which requires consideration of the law of nations, with the issue of the choice of law to be applied, which will be addressed at a later stage in the proceedings. The two issues are distinct. Our holding on subject matter jurisdiction decides only whether Congress intended to confer judicial power, and whether it is authorized to do so by Article III. The choice of law inquiry is a much broader one, primarily concerned with fairness; consequently, it looks to wholly different considerations. Should the district court decide that [a choice of law] analysis requires it to apply Paraguayan law, our courts will not have occasion to consider what law would govern a suit under the Alien Tort Statute where the challenged conduct is actionable under the law of the forum and the law of nations, but not the law of the jurisdiction in which the tort occurred.

TORTURE VICTIM PROTECTION ACT

28 U.S.C. §1350 (note)

Section 1. This Act may be cited as the "Torture Victim Protection Act of 1991."

Section 2. (a) Liability. An individual who, under actual or apparent authority, or color of law, of any foreign nation -

> (1) subjects an individual to torture shall, in a civil action, be liable for damages to that individual; or
>
> (2) subjects an individual to extrajudicial killing shall, in a civil action, be liable for damages to the individual's legal representative, or to any person who may be a claimant in an action for wrongful death.

(b) Exhaustion of remedies. A court shall decline to hear a claim under this section if the claimant has not exhausted adequate and available remedies in the place in which the conduct giving rise to the claim occurred.

(c) Statute of limitations. No action shall be maintained under this section unless it is commenced within 10 years after the cause of action arose.

Section 3. (a) Extrajudicial killing. For the purposes of this Act, the term 'extrajudicial killing' means a deliberated killing not authorized by a previous judgment pronounced by a regularly constituted court affording all the judicial guarantees which are recognized as indispensable by civilized peoples. Such term, however, does not include any such killing that, under international law, is lawfully carried out under the authority of a foreign nation.

(b) Torture. For the purposes of this Act -

> (1) the term 'torture' means any act, directed against an individual in the offender's custody of physical control, by which severe pain or suffering (other than pain or suffering arising only from or inherent in, or incidental to, lawful sanctions), whether physical or mental, is intentionally inflicted

on that individual for such purposes as obtaining from that individual or a third person information or a confession, punishing that individual for an act that individual or a third person has committed or is suspected of having committed, intimidating or coercing that individual or a third person, or for any reason based on discrimination of any kind; and

(2) mental pain or suffering refers to prolonged mental harm caused by or resulting from —

> (A) the intentional inflection or threatened infliction of severe physical pain or suffering;
>
> (B) the administration or application, or threatened administration or application, of mind altering substances or other procedures calculated to disrupt profoundly the senses or the personality;
>
> (C) the threat of imminent death; or
>
> (D) the threat that another individual will imminently be subjected to death, severe physical pain or suffering, or the administration or application of mind altering substances or other procedures calculated to disrupt profoundly the sense or personality.

Notes on Filartiga and Torture Victim Protection Act

1. *Section 1350 applies only to suits by an "alien."* *Filartiga* involved a suit by foreign nationals against other foreign nationals. If the Filartigas had been U.S. citizens, they could not have sued under §1350, because the Alien Tort Statute only applies to suits by *aliens*. *E.g., Jones v. Petty Ray Geophysical Geosource, Inc.*, 722 F. Supp. 343 (S.D. Tex. 1989). Why should Congress want federal courts to protect foreign victims, but not U.S. plaintiffs that complain of identical abuses?

Alienage jurisdiction would permit U.S. plaintiffs to bring suits against foreign defendants in federal courts. *See supra* pp. 25-32. Alternatively, the U.S. government could espouse claims of U.S. citizens against foreign states diplomatically, whereas it could generally not do so on behalf of foreign nationals (who are only entitled to the diplomatic protection of their home state). Finally, §1350 only concerns the jurisdiction of *federal* courts, not *state* courts. Because §1350 does not confer exclusive jurisdiction, U.S. citizens could pursue claims against foreign defendants in state court. Still, why should they not have a federal forum for international law violations?

2. *Section 1350 permits suits for torts in violation of the "law of nations."* The touchstone for jurisdiction under §1350 is a tort in violation of the "law of nations." What is the "law of nations"? *See supra* pp. 17-18. Is the "law of nations" a clear and specific set of legal rules? Consider the following: "The *Filartiga* formulation is not flawless. ... [W]hile its approach is consistent with the language of §1350, it places an awesome duty on federal district courts to derive from an amorphous entity — *i.e.*, the 'law of nations' — standards of liability applicable in concrete situations." *Tel-Oren*, 726 F.2d at 781 (Edwards, J., concurring). Is it wise for the federal courts to be granted open-ended jurisdiction over an ill-defined field such as this?

3. *Expanding scope of "law of nations."* *Filartiga* had little difficulty concluding that §1350 incorporated the "law of nations" as it evolved over time and not simply as it existed when the Alien Tort Statute was enacted in 1789. Most other authorities have agreed. *See Kadic v. Karadzic*, 1995 WL 604585 (2d Cir. 1995); *Tel-Oren v. Libyan Arab Republic*, 726 F.2d 774, 777, 820 (D.C. Cir. 1984), *cert. denied*, 470 U.S. 1003 (1985). *But see Amerada Hess Shipping Co. v. Argentine Republic*, 830 F.2d at 429 (Kearse, J., dissenting). This conclusion has important consequences. International law has significantly expanded since 1789, particularly with respect to the protections afforded to individuals from governmental action. *See Restatement (Third) Foreign Relations Law* §§701-13 (1987); Lillich, *Invoking International Human Rights Law in Domestic Courts*, 54 Cinn. L. Rev. 367 (1985). As a result, the scope of §1350's jurisdictional grant has also expanded, permitting a wider range of actions under §1350 than would have been possible in 1789.

Is it wise to read an obscure, seldom-used statute like the Alien Tort Statute to permit expansive federal court jurisdiction over sensitive international matters? Consider how Judge Bork described the matter in *Tel-Oren*:

> It will not do simply to assert that the statutory phrase, the "law of nations," whatever it may have meant in 1789, must be read today as incorporating all the modern rules of international law and giving aliens private causes of action for violations of those rules. It will not do because the result is contrary not only to what we know of the Framers' general purposes in this area but contrary as well to the appropriate, indeed the constitutional, role of courts with respect to foreign affairs. ... [I]n 1789 there was no concept of international human rights; neither was there, under the traditional version of customary international law, any recognition of a right of private parties to recover. 726 F.2d at 812-13.

Is it likely that Congress intended federal courts to apply evolving principles of international law in highly sensitive cases between foreign parties? If such cases were going to be brought, however, would Congress have wanted federal courts, rather than state courts, to hear them? Note that Judge Bork's principal concern is with reading §1350 as granting a private cause of action — not with granting federal subject matter jurisdiction. Does anything stop state courts from granting such private causes of action? *See infra* p. 46.

4. *Diminishing scope of "law of nations."* In contrast to the frequent observations that international law has expanded significantly in recent decades, *see supra* p. 44, some historical scholarship indicates that the "law of nations" has in fact diminished in scope. As discussed above, during much of this century, public international law has been distinguished from private international law. *See supra* pp. 17-18. During the 19th century, however, all subjects of transnational concern were governed generally by the law of nations, which was understood as encompassing legal relations between sovereign states, conflict of law rules, maritime law, and the law merchant. Dickinson, *The Law of Nations as Part of the Law of the United States*, 101 U. Pa. L. Rev. 26, 26-29 (1952); Jay, *Origins of Federal Common Law: Part Two*, 133 U. Pa. L. Rev. 1231, 1263-64 (1985). The distinction between "public" and "private" international law only arose at the end of the 19th century. Nussbaum, *Rise and Decline of the Law-of-Nations Doctrine in the Conflict of Laws*, 42 Colum. L. Rev. 189 (1942); Cheatham, *Sources of Rules for Conflict of Laws*, 89 U. Pa. L. Rev. 430 (1941).

Thus, the First Congress's grant of jurisdiction over cases arising under the "law of nations" arguably would have been substantially broader in 1800 than is suggested by contemporary interpretations. In 1800, §1350 would not have been limited to violations of public international law, but would have included violations of a broader body of international law. Note that this would be consistent with the broad rationales for federal subject matter jurisdiction in *The Federalist Papers No. 80. See supra* pp. 10-12, 25-32, 34-35. Would it be appropriate for §1350 to be given expanded scope today, covering all claims of tort under either public or private international law?

5. *Relevance of foreign relations and separation of powers considerations to interpretation of §1350.* *Filartiga's* interpretation of §1350 would frequently require U.S. courts to adjudicate cases involving human rights claims against foreign officials. These cases can have significant effects on U.S. foreign relations. As discussed above, concern about these effects led Judge Bork in *Tel-Oren* to conclude that §1350 should be narrowly construed. In reaching this conclusion, Judge Bork relied on constitutional separation of powers: "[t]he conduct of the foreign relations of our Government is committed by the Constitution to the Executive and Legislative — 'the political' — Departments." 726 F.2d. at 801 (quoting *Oetjen v. Central Leather Co.*, 246 U.S. 297, 302 (1918)).

After *Filartiga*, §1350 manifestly will implicate substantial U.S. foreign relations concerns. Subsequent decisions under the Alien Tort Statute have concerned serious charges of misconduct against senior foreign government officials. *E.g., In re Estate of Ferdinand E. Marcos Human Rights Litigation*, 978 F.2d 493 (9th Cir. 1992) (kidnap, torture, and murder); *Lafontant v. Aristide*, 844 F.Supp. 128 (E.D.N.Y. 1994) (murder by Haitian head of state); *Forti v. Suarez-Mason*, 672 F.Supp. 1531 (N.D. Calif. 1987) (torture). Does this argue, however, for Judge Bork's narrow interpretation of §1350? Section 1350 merely concerns the subject matter jurisdiction of *federal* courts. If §1350 is interpreted narrowly, to exclude unduly sensitive foreign cases, that does not necessarily mean that state courts cannot hear such disputes, provided that state law permits. Do the authorities cited by Judge Bork, such as *Oetjen*, suggest that the Framers would have preferred state courts to hear such sensitive cases?

6. *Possible constitutional limits on state court jurisdiction — an initial view.* In *Tel-Oren*, Judge Bork suggested that whatever limits were imposed on federal court applications of §1350 by separation of powers concerns would be equally applicable to state courts. "A state-court suit that involved a determination of international law would require consideration of much that I discuss here as well as the principle that foreign relations are constitutionally relegated to the federal government and not the states." 726 F.2d at 814 n.11. What is the basis for this suggestion? Recall the discussion above of *Zschernig* and *Sabbatino*, *supra* pp. 15-16. *See also infra* pp. 537-44.

7. *Limiting the Alien Tort Statute.* Once awakened by *Filártiga*, it is difficult to discern clear limits to the scope of the Alien Tort Statute.

(a) *"Universally recognized" norms of international law.* Various authorities have sought to limit the potentially sweeping scope of §1350. *Filartiga*, for example, would limit §1350 jurisdiction to "well-established, universally recognized norms of international law." Other authorities have also confined §1350 to universally recognized violations of international law. *E.g., In re Estate of Ferdinand E. Marcos Litigation*, 978 F.2d 493 (9th Cir. 1992); *Tel-Oren v. Libyan Arab Republic*, 726 F.2d 774, 781 (D.C. Cir. 1984) (Edwards, J., concurring); *Zapata v. Quinn*, 707 F.2d 691, 692 (2d Cir. 1982); *Huynh Thi Anh v. Levi*, 586 F.2d 625, 629 (6th Cir. 1978). For one listing of universally acknowledged international law violations that meet these descriptions, *see Restatement (Third) Foreign Relations Law* §702 (1987) (genocide, slavery, murder, torture, prolonged arbitrary detention, systematic racial discrimination).

Is there any indication in the language of the Alien Tort Statute that it should be limited to violations of "universally" recognized rules of international law? Is that the sort of limitation that Congress would likely have intended? Would the First Congress have wanted state courts to decide cases where international law was unsettled? Aren't such cases even more likely to be contentious? *Cf. Sabbatino v. Banco Nacional de Cuba*, 376 U.S. 398 (1964) ("It should be apparent that the greater the degree of codification or consensus concerning a particular area of international law, the more appropriate it is for the judiciary to render decisions regarding it. ..."). Is there not a need for even greater federal court involvement in such areas, in order to facilitate the consistent development of international law?

(b) *Territorial limitation. Filartiga* rejected the defendant's argument that the Alien Tort Statute should not apply to "a tort claim arising outside [U.S.] territorial jurisdiction." *See also In re Estate of Ferdinand E. Marcos Litigation*, 978 F.2d 493 (9th Cir. 1992) (rejecting territoriality limit). Other authorities have suggested that the Alien Tort Statute was intended to be limited to torts committed on U.S. territory. *E.g.*, Rogers, *The Alien Tort Statute and How Individuals "Violate" International Law*, 21 Vand. J. Transnat'l L. 47 (1988). Is there anything in the language of the Alien Tort Statute to support this construction?

As discussed elsewhere, U.S. courts have long applied a territoriality presumption, which requires a clear, affirmative statement that legislation was intended to apply to conduct outside the United States before reaching such a conclusion. *See infra* pp. 546-52. This would at least arguably permit construing the Alien Tort Statute to apply only to torts within the United States. Would this be desirable? Does the answer depend on whether state courts could hear such claims?

Consider the grounds for *Filartiga's* conclusion that the First Congress intended to grant U.S. courts jurisdiction over torts committed abroad. Is it persuasive? How does the court deal with the territoriality presumption? Does the territoriality presumption (which concerns legislative jurisdiction) apply to the Alien Tort Statute's grant of subject matter jurisdiction? *See* the discussion of tag jurisdiction below, *infra* pp. 116-23. What about the Statute's asserted creation of a private cause of action?

8. *The "cause of action" requirement.* The *Filartiga* defendants argued that customary international law does not grant individuals private "causes of action" to redress violations of human rights protections. Absent a cause of action, no suit could be pursued (in either federal or state court). The defendant also reasoned that the proper mechanism for redressing most international human rights grievances would be in state-to-state discussions (as historically occurred).

(a) *Filartiga's treatment of cause of action requirement. Filartiga* reasoned that the existence of a private right of action was a choice of law issue, not a question of federal jurisdiction. Under this reasoning, §1350 gives federal courts subject matter jurisdiction over cases involving torts in violation of international law, but the substantive law applicable to, and providing the basis for, such tort claims need not be either international law or federal law; just as in diversity cases, state (or foreign) law can provide the substantive cause of action. *See supra* pp. 41-43. Is that a persuasive interpretation of §1350?

(b) *Judge Bork and other critics of Filartiga's cause of action analysis.* A number of authorities have disagreed with *Filartiga's* cause of action analysis. They would require that plaintiffs under §1350 show either that a particular rule of international law expressly establishes an individual right of action or that a self-executing treaty provides similar access to the courts. *Tel-Oren*, 726 F.2d at 804, 808. This interpretation begins with the proposition that §1350, by its terms, does nothing more than grant subject matter jurisdiction, and does not provide a substantive cause of action. 726 F.2d at 811 ("The Judicial Code, in vesting jurisdiction in the District Courts, does not create causes of action, but only confers jurisdiction to adjudicate those arising from other sources which satisfy its limiting provisions.") (quoting *Montana-Dakota Utilities Co. v. Northwestern Public Service Co.*, 341 U.S. 246, 249 (1951)). Critics of *Filartiga* go on to emphasize the fact that most rules of customary international law were historically not enforceable by individuals, but only by states. Moreover, the argument runs, reading §1350 as *itself* granting a private cause of action would permit private actions under *all* U.S. treaties, non-self-executing as well as self-executing. Such result would be inconsistent with the distinction between the two classes of treaties. 726 F.2d at 816-19.

(c) *Responses to criticism of Filartiga's cause of action analysis.* Replies to Judge Bork's "cause of action" criticism generally advance three theories as to why the cause of action requirement does not prevent international human rights claims from being cognizable under §1350. First, it is argued that §1350 itself grants a private cause of action for violations of international law. 726 F.2d at 779-80 ("§1350 provides both a right to sue and a forum") (Edwards, J., concurring); *Kadic v. Karadzic*, 1995 WL 604585 (2d Cir. 1995); *Paul v. Avril*, 812 F.Supp. 207 (S.D. Fla. 1993); *Forti v. Suarez-Mason*, 762 F.Supp. 1531, 1540 (N.D. Calif. 1987); *Handel v. Artukovic*, 601 F.Supp. 1421, 1426-27 (C.D. Calif. 1985); Note, *Enforcing the Customary International Law of Human Rights in Federal Court*, 74 Cal. L. Rev. 127, 157-70 (1986). Is there anything in the language of §1350 that suggests that it independently creates a federal cause of action when international law does not? In the Statute's purposes?

Second, some authorities have argued that international law does in fact provide private causes of action in certain circumstances, and that, in these cases, §1350 permits federal courts to entertain suits by aliens. *See* Memorandum for the United States as Amicus Curiae, *Filartiga v. Pena-Irala*, 630 F.2d 876 (2d Cir. 1980), *reprinted in* 19 Int'l Leg. Mat. 585 (1980). This, of course, requires considering the content of international law rules regarding private causes of action in particular cases.

Finally, a few authorities have reasoned that, if a particular act violates international law, then *domestic* U.S. tort law (or foreign municipal tort law) can provide the necessary private cause of action even if international law does not. *E.g., Tel-Oren*, 726 F.2d at 788 (Edwards, J., concurring); Note, *A Legal Lohengrin: Federal Jurisdiction Under the Alien Tort Claims Act of 1789*, 14 U.S.F.L. Rev. 105, 123 (1979). Which of the foregoing analyses is most persuasive?

9. *Justiciability limits under Article III.* As noted above, Judge Robb reasoned in *Tel-Oren* that *Filartiga* failed to "consider the possibility that ad hoc intervention by courts into international affairs may very well redound to the decisive disadvantage of the nation." 726 F.2d at 826 n.5. He would have invoked the "political question" doctrine in holding that the case fell outside Article III's grant to federal courts of jurisdiction over "cases" or "controversies."

(a) *Political question doctrine.* The political question doctrine is a rarely-applied constitutional limitation on Article III's judicial power, which bars federal courts from resolving cases that raise issues more appropriately committed to other branches of government. *See Baker v. Carr*, 369 U.S. 186 (1962); *Goldwater v. Carter*, 444 U.S. 996 (1979). Among the factors relevant to determining whether a case presents a political question are a "textually demonstrable commitment" of an issue to the executive or legislative branches, the lack of "judicially discoverable and manageable standards" for resolving an issue, or the existence of prudential considerations counselling for judicial abstention. *Goldwater v. Carter*, 444 U.S. at 997-98 (Powell, J., concurring).

(b) *Lower court applications of political question doctrine in international cases.* A number of lower courts have considered the applicability of the political question doctrine in international cases. In general, these decisions weigh the same factors as in domestic political question cases. *E.g., Occidental of Umm al Qaywayn, Inc. v. A Certain Cargo of Petroleum*, 577 F.2d 1196 (5th Cir. 1978) (dismissing antitrust suit based on charges of bribery and foreign border alterations); *Linder v. Calero*, 747 F. Supp. 1452 (S.D. Fla. 1990) (dismissing action against U.S.-backed contras for war-time death in Central America), *rev'd in part*, 963 F.2d 332 (11th Cir. 1992); *Sanchez-Espinoza v. Reagan*, 568 F. Supp. 596 (D.D.C. 1984), *aff'd on other grounds*, 770 F.2d 202 (D.C. Cir. 1985) (political question doctrine bars claims against U.S. government and others for contra activities).

Other international cases have refused to apply the political question doctrine. *E.g., Klinghoffer v. Achille Lauro SNC*, 937 F.2d 44 (2d Cir. 1991) (political question doctrine does not bar suit against PLO for hijacking and murder); *Ramirez de Arellano v. Weinberger*, 745 F.2d 1500, 1511-15 (D.C. Cir. 1984), *vacated*, 471 U.S. 1113 (1985) (political question doctrine does not bar suit against U.S. government for occupation of plaintiff's ranch in Honduras by U.S.-backed military forces); *Sharon v. Time, Inc.*, 599 F. Supp. 538 (S.D.N.Y. 1984) (political question doctrine does not bar libel suit by Israeli general).

(c) *Political question doctrine in Filartiga.* Consider the dispute in *Filartiga*, which clearly involved foreign governmental conduct and U.S. foreign relations. Does the political question doctrine permit U.S. courts to hear such disputes? Would it be better for the conduct of U.S. foreign relations by the political branches if U.S. courts (both federal and state) did not hear such claims? Was Judge Robb right in *Tel-Oren* when he said that cases of this sort are political questions?

(d) *Political question doctrine in state courts.* The political question doctrine is derived from Article III, which generally applies only to the judicial power of federal courts, not state courts. Does that mean that a state court is free, under the U.S. Constitution, to hear disputes that Article III prevents federal courts from considering because they involve matters committed to the political branches' discretion? *See* Judge Bork's comment above, *supra* p. 46, and the discussion below, *infra* pp. 56, 358-66, 537-44.

10. *Alien Tort Statute and foreign sovereign immunity. Filartiga* involved a suit against a former foreign governmental employee in his individual capacity, and not against the foreign state itself. No issue of foreign sovereign immunity was raised. *But see infra* pp. 284-85 (describing circumstances where foreign state official can qualify for immunity under FSIA or common law). Nonetheless, because the international law rules that §1350 incorporates almost always apply to the actions of nation-states, the availability of a sovereign immunity defense under §1350 is significant. As discussed below, the Supreme Court has held that the Alien Tort Statute cannot be used as a jurisdictional base for suits against foreign states: the FSIA provides the exclusive jurisdictional base for such actions. *Argentine Republic v. Amerada Hess Shipping Corp.*, 488 U.S. 428 (1988); *infra* p. 226.

11. *Torture Victim Protection Act.* How does the TVPA differ from the Alien Tort Statute? Does it create federal subject matter jurisdiction? Who may assert claims under the TVPA? Who may be a defendant under the TVPA? If Singapore officials torture Singapore citizens, should that be the concern of U.S. courts? What if they torture Americans?

12. *TVPA and §1350's cause of action requirement.* The TVPA complements *Filartiga* by specifically providing a federal cause of action for claims of official torture. S. Rep. No. 249, 102d Cong., 1st Sess. 3-4 (1991) (noting that Judge Bork "questioned the existence of a private right of action under the Alien Tort Claims Act," and declaring that "[t]he TVPA would provide such a grant."). Does Congress's creation of a private cause of action for one defined set of international claims — and not others — suggest anything about the existence of private causes of action for violations of international law more generally?

13. *Federal subject matter jurisdiction under the TVPA.* Can claims under the TVPA be brought in federal court? How? The TVPA's legislative history says that the Act "specifically provides Federal districts [sic] courts with jurisdiction over ... suits" involving official torture. S. Rep. No. 249, 102d Cong., 1st Sess. 5 n.6 (1991). Is this accurate? What provision of the TVPA grants subject matter jurisdiction? Doesn't the Act merely create a federal cause of action, not federal subject matter jurisdiction? Will the Alien Tort Statute and §1331's general grant of federal question jurisdiction provide jurisdiction in most TVPA cases? *See Kadic v. Karadzic*, 1995 WL 604585 (2d Cir. 1995); *Xuncax v. Gramajo*, 886 F.Supp. 162 (D. Mass. 1995).

14. *TVPA and separation of powers concerns.* The TVPA was opposed by the Justice Department and others on the grounds that it would interfere with U.S. foreign policy:

> The executive branch, through the Department of Justice, has expressed a most serious concern with [the TVPA], which we share. [The TVPA] could create difficulties in the management of foreign policy. For example, under this bill, individual aliens could determine the timing and manner of the making of allegations in a U.S. court about a foreign country's alleged abuses of human rights. There is no more complex and sensitive issue between countries than human rights. The risk that would be run if an alien could have a foreign country judged by a U.S. court is too great. Judges of U.S. courts would, in a sense, conduct some of our Nation's

foreign policy. The executive branch is and should remain, we believe, left with substantial foreign policy control. In addition, the Justice Department properly notes that our passage of this bill could encourage hostile foreign countries to retaliate by trying to assert jurisdiction for acts committed in the United States by the U.S. Government against U.S. citizens.

S. Rep. No. 249, 102d Cong., 1st Sess. 13 (1991) (Minority views of Messrs. Simpson and Grassley). Are these a persuasive concerns? Should the TVPA have been enacted? What about the concern that foreign states will retaliate against U.S. officials? Is it constitutional, or does it require the Judiciary to decide political questions?

15. *Appropriate defendants under TVPA.* Who may be sued under the TVPA? The TVPA authorizes claims against individuals only, not foreign states. The legislative history makes clear that sovereign immunity will not generally be available as a defense in suits brought against individuals under this Act. Nevertheless, diplomatic immunity and head of state immunity may provide a defense to TVPA actions. *E.g.,* *Lafontant v. Aristide,* 844 F.Supp. 128 (E.D.N.Y. 1994). Why did Congress permit actions against individuals, but not states? Suppose a foreign state engages in torture as government policy.

16. *International competence revisited.* Recall the suggestion above that international law may limit the "competence" of national courts over foreign disputes — even where the parties are subject to personal jurisdiction and where restrictions on legislative jurisdiction are observed. *See supra* p. 32. The dispute in *Filartiga* had nothing to do with the United States, except for the fact that the plaintiff served the defendant there. Given the lack of any U.S. connection to the dispute, should international law permit a U.S. court to exercise competence over the action? Note that the plaintiff's claims were based on torture, an offense generally regarded as subject to so-called "universal jurisdiction," which any state may punish. *Cf. Restatement (Third) Foreign Relations Law* §423 (1987).

3. Federal Question Jurisdiction in Cases Arising Under International Law and Federal Common Law

Filartiga illustrates that U.S. courts often confront issues arising under international law, derived from a variety of different sources, including formal international agreements and customary international law. Even apart from the Alien Tort Statute, many such cases fall within the federal courts' federal question jurisdiction. Jurisdiction in cases arising under international law is based on Article III's grant of jurisdiction over "Cases ... arising under this Constitution, the Laws of the United States, and Treaties ..." In turn, the general federal question statute, 28 U.S.C. §1331, provides federal subject matter jurisdiction over "all civil actions arising under the Constitution, laws, or treaties of the United States."[211] The application of both Article III and §1331 to claims arising under international law is examined below.

a. International Law Regarded as Federal Law

Article VI of the U.S. Constitution provides that U.S. "Treaties" (like the Constitution and federal statutes) are federal law — specifically, the "supreme Law of the Land." As discussed above, valid treaties preempt inconsistent state laws, supersede prior federal statutes, and can be superseded by subsequent federal statutes.[212]

---

211. 28 U.S.C. §1331; *supra* pp. 34-35.
212. *See supra* pp. 17-20.

The same is generally true of international agreements other than treaties and customary international law.[213]

Article III specifically provides that cases arising under U.S. "Treaties" arise under federal law for the purposes of federal judicial power. Thus, U.S. courts have naturally held that claims arising under U.S. treaties are within the federal question jurisdiction of both §1331 and Article III.[214] The same rule applies to Congressional-Executive and sole Executive agreements.[215] And, because customary international law is regarded as federal law, actions arising under customary international law are also said to "arise under" federal law, and therefore to fall within §1331. That has been the holding of several recent lower court decisions,[216] and it is the rule adopted in the *Restatement (Third) Foreign Relations Law.*[217]

b. Selected Materials on Federal Question Jurisdiction Over Claims Based on International Law

Excerpted below are selected materials on the scope of federal question jurisdiction in cases involving international law and federal common law. First, consider §111 of the *Restatement (Third) Foreign Relations Law*, which states the general principles of federal subject matter jurisdiction in the field. Second, in light of these principles, reread *Filartiga*, considering the issues that the court's opinion raises under both §1331 and Article III. Finally, the district court's decision in *Sequihua v. Texaco, Inc.*, also excerpted below, illustrates the application of these principles in cases involving customary international law or federal common law rules.

RESTATEMENT (THIRD) FOREIGN RELATIONS LAW OF THE UNITED STATES §111 (1987)

§111.(1) International law and international agreements of the United States are law of the United States and supreme over the law of the several States.

---

213. *See supra* pp. 19-22; *Restatement (Third) Foreign Relations Law* §111(1) & comment d (1987) ("Customary international law is considered to be like common law in the United States, but it is federal law. A determination of international law by the Supreme Court is binding on the States and on State courts."); Henkin, *International Law as Law in the United States*, 82 Mich. L. Rev. 1555 (1984); *Forti v. Suarez-Mason*, 672 F. Supp. 1531, 1543-44 (N.D. Calif. 1987).

214. *In re Air Disaster at Lockerbie, Scotland on Dec. 21, 1988*, 928 F.2d 1267 (2d Cir.), *cert. denied*, 502 U.S. 920 (1991); *Boehringer-Mannheim Diagnostics, Inc. v. Pan American World Airways, Inc.*, 737 F.2d 456 (5th Cir. 1984), *cert. denied*, 469 U.S. 1186 (1985); *Benjamins v. British European Airways*, 572 F.2d 913 (2d Cir. 1978).

215. *Restatement (Third) Foreign Relations Law* §111(2) & comment e (1987).

216. *In re Estate of Ferdinand E. Marcos Litigation*, 978 F.2d 493 (9th Cir. 1992); *Filartiga v. Pena-Irala*, 630 F.2d 876 (2d Cir. 1980); *Republic of the Philippines v. Marcos*, 806 F.2d 344 (2d Cir. 1986); *Grynberg v. British Gas plc*, 817 F.Supp. 1338 (E.D. Tex. 1993); *Sequihua v. Texaco, Inc.*, 847 F.Supp. 61 (S.D. Tex. 1994).

217. *Restatement (Third) Foreign Relations Law* §111(2) (1987).

(2) Cases arising under international law or international agreements of the United States are within the Judicial Power of the United States and, subject to Constitutional and statutory limitations and requirements of justiciability, are within the jurisdiction of the federal courts.

FILARTIGA v. PENA-IRALA

630 F.2d 876 (2d Cir. 1980) [excerpted at *supra* pp. 39-43]

SEQUIHUA v. TEXACO, INC.

847 F. Supp. 61 (S.D. Tex. 1994)

NORMAN W. BLACK, CHIEF JUDGE. Plaintiffs, residents of Ecuador and a community in that country, filed this action in state court asserting a variety of causes of action arising out of the alleged contamination of the air, ground and water in Ecuador. In addition to monetary relief, Plaintiffs seek an injunction requiring Defendants to return the land to its former condition and the imposition of a "trust fund" to be administered by the Court. The case was removed [and] ... is before the Court on ... Plaintiffs' Motion to Remand and Defendants' motions to dismiss or for summary judgment...

Removal of this case from state court was based on both diversity and federal question jurisdiction. Plaintiffs moved to remand, asserting that this Court lacks jurisdiction. Defendants ... argue that the Court has federal question jurisdiction because the lawsuit "not only raises questions of international law, but threatens to create an international incident." In this regard, the Court notes that the Republic of Ecuador has officially protested this litigation, asserting that it will do "violence" to the international legal system, and has asked that the case be dismissed. Clearly, such issues of international relations are incorporated into federal common law, which presents a federal question under §1331. See *Banco Nacional de Cuba v. Sabbatino* [excerpted at *infra* pp. 691-700]; *Republic of the Philippines v. Marcos*, 806 F.2d 344 (2d Cir. 1986); *Grynberg v. British Gas plc.*, 817 F.Supp. 1338 (E.D. Tex. 1993). Plaintiffs in their complaint assert injuries that arose solely in Ecuador to as many as 500,000 Ecuadorans in an area that covers 1/3 of Ecuador. Plaintiffs complain about conduct which is regulated by the government in Ecuador, which is a country with its own environmental laws and regulations, a nation that owns the land at issue, and that treats all petroleum exploration and development as a "public utility" controlled by the government. Such matters affecting international law and the relationship between the United States and foreign governments give rise to federal question jurisdiction. *Texas Industries, Inc. v. Radcliff Materials*, 451 U.S. 630 (1981); *Sabbatino*.

Additionally, there are essential elements of Plaintiffs' claims which, if "well-pleaded," require the application and resolution of the federal common law regarding foreign relations. Plaintiffs' claims of nuisance and for injunctive relief require them as part of their prima facie case to challenge the policies and regulations of Ecuador, as well as the approvals from Ecuador that Defendants received, in order to show that the conduct was improper on land owned by Ecuador. Federal question jurisdiction clearly exists where, as here, the essential elements of Plaintiff's prima facie case necessarily involve federal international relations, such as the international law relating to the control by a foreign country over its own resources.

Lastly, Plaintiffs' request for a trust fund asks this Court to step into the shoes of the Ecuadoran Health Ministry and supervise a medical monitoring scheme of unknown cost, scope or duration for as many as 500,000 Ecuadoran citizens over the protest of the government of Ecuador. It is incomprehensible that Plaintiffs could argue this does not fully and completely involve the relationship between the United States through this Court and the Republic of Ecuador.

Based upon the important foreign policy implications of this case, upon the international legal principle that each country has the right to control its own natural resources, and the strong opposition expressed by the Republic of Ecuador to this litigation, the Court finds without reservation that Plaintiffs' state law claims, if well-pleaded, raise issues of international relations which implicate federal common law. Consequently, this Court has federal question jurisdiction and the motion to remand must be denied.

Defendants have moved to dismiss on a number of grounds. ... Under the doctrine known as comity of nations, a court should decline to exercise jurisdiction under certain circumstances in deference to the laws and interests of another foreign country. See *Societe Nationale Industrielle Aerospatiale v. United States District Court*, 482 U.S. 522, 543 n.27 (1987) [excerpted at *infra* pp. 903-12]. ... Consideration of these factors leads to the inescapable conclusion that the Court should decline to exercise jurisdiction over this case. The challenged activity and the alleged harm occurred entirely in Ecuador; Plaintiffs are all residents of Ecuador; Defendants are not residents of Texas; enforcement in Ecuador of any judgment issued by this Court is questionable at best; the challenged conduct is regulated by the Republic of Ecuador and exercise of jurisdiction by this Court would interfere with Ecuador's sovereign right to control its own environment and resources; and the Republic of Ecuador has expressed its strenuous objection to the exercise of jurisdiction by this Court. Indeed, none of the factors favor the exercise of jurisdiction. Accordingly, the case should be dismissed under the doctrine of comity of nations.

Defendants have also moved to dismiss on the basis of *forum non conveniens*, asserting that the convenience of the parties and the Court and the interests of justice require that the case be tried in Ecuador. See *Piper Aircraft Co. v. Reyno*, 454 U.S. 235 (1981) [excerpted at *infra* pp. 299-305.]. ... The Court finds without reservation that dismissal on the basis of *forum non conveniens* will "best serve the convenience of the parties and the ends of justice."

Notes on Third Restatement §111, Filartiga, and Sequihua

1. *Treaties and international agreements as federal law.* Section 111 of the *Third Restatement* provides that U.S. treaties enjoy the status of federal law — which is the "supreme Law of the Land" and which therefore preempts inconsistent state law. What in Article VI's language and purposes requires that treaties be treated as federal law — beyond the powers of alteration by individual states? Note that federal statutes can override prior U.S. treaties. *See supra* pp. 19-20. Why didn't the Framers permit the individual states to do the same?

Although Article VI deals only with "Treaties," §111 also categorizes "international agreements" as federal law. The reason for according this status to international agreements has been explained as follows:

> Plainly, the external powers of the United States are to be exercised without regard to state laws or policies. ... And while this rule in respect of treaties is established by the express language of cl. 2, Art. VI, of the Constitution, the same rule would result in the case of all international compacts and agreements from the very fact that complete power over international affairs is in the national government and is not and cannot be subject to any curtailment or interference on the part of the several states. ... In respect of all international negotiations and compacts, and in respect of our foreign relations generally, state lines disappear.

United States v. Belmont, 301 U.S. 324, 331 (1937). Is this rationale entirely persuasive?

2. *Authorities concluding that customary international law is federal law.* Section 111(1), *Filartiga*, *Sequihua*, and other authorities also declare that customary international law is federal law. The view rests on the oft-cited passage in *The Paquete Habana*, 175 U.S. 677 (1900):

> International law is part of our law, and must be ascertained and administered by the courts of justice of appropriate jurisdiction, as often as questions of right depending upon it are duly presented for their determination.

See also Respublica v. DeLongchamps, 1 U.S. 113, 119 (1784); *The Nereide*, 13 U.S. 388, 422 (1815). Is it clear that §111(1) is correct that international law is *federal* law? Note that *Paquete Habana* only says "our" law, which presumably does not resolve internal U.S. issues of federalism. Consider the differences between international agreements — made by the federal political branches — and customary international law — "made" by U.S. judges and academics. Do these differences suggest that customary international law should *not* be regarded as federal law? What are the consequences of treating customary international law as federal law?

3. *Authorities concluding that customary international law is not federal law.* Until the second half of the 20th century, customary international law was *not* regarded as federal law. *York Life Ins. Co. v. Hendren*, 92 U.S. 286 (1875); *Oliver American Trading Co. v. Mexico*, 264 U.S. 440 (1924). Consider also the following excerpt from a case in which a foreign diplomat claimed immunity from service in the United States:

> since the defendant was served while the cause was in the state court, the law of New York determines its validity, and although the courts of that state look to international law as a source of New York law, their interpretation of international law is controlling upon us, and we have to follow them so far as they have declared themselves. Whether an avowed refusal to accept a well-established doctrine of international law, or a plain misapprehension of it, would present a federal question we need not consider, for neither is present here. *Bergman v. De Sieyes*, 170 F.2d 360, 361 (2d Cir. 1948).

Why cannot state courts continue to be left to interpret customary international law? If customary international law is not federal law, then how would inconsistent decisions by U.S. state courts be reviewed? Would it be acceptable for different U.S. states to hold different views of international law (both from each other and from the federal courts)? If international law is not federal law, would it be subject to the *Erie* doctrine — requiring federal courts to follow state court decisions?

4. *Article III federal question jurisdiction over cases arising under U.S. "Treaties."* Article III grants federal courts subject matter jurisdiction over cases arising under "Treaties made, or which shall be made, under [the] authority [of the United States]." As with alienage jurisdiction, this was a class of disputes thought to require the institutional attributes of the federal courts. Chief Justice Jay explained that, because the "United States were responsible to foreign nations for the conduct of each State, relative to the

laws of nations, and the performance of treaties, ... the inexpediency of referring all such questions to State Courts, and particularly to the Courts of delinquent States became apparent." *Chisholm v. Georgia*, 2 U.S. 419, 474 (1793). Why was it "inexpedient" to refer cases involving treaties to state courts? Is this still true?

5. Federal subject matter jurisdiction in cases arising under U.S. "Treaties." Article III's grant of subject matter jurisdiction is implemented by the general grant of federal question jurisdiction in 28 U.S.C. §1331 over "all civil actions arising under the Constitution, laws, or treaties of the United States." If you were drafting §1331 today, would you include treaties? Why?

6. Federal subject matter jurisdiction in cases arising under international agreements other than treaties. As noted above, the United States frequently enters into international agreements with foreign states in forms other than treaties. In particular, international agreements are often concluded as "Congressional-Executive" agreements (authorized, ratified, or approved by Congress and the President) and "sole Executive" agreements (made solely by the President). *See supra* pp. 18-20. Courts have generally held that cases arising under such international agreements arise under federal law for purposes of Article III and §1331. *E.g., B. Altman & Co. v. United States*, 224 U.S. 583, 601 (1912); *Restatement (Third) Foreign Relations Law* §111(2) (1987). Why is this? Consider the language of both Article III and §1331. Is an international agreement a "treaty" or a "law of the United States"?

7. Federal subject matter jurisdiction in cases arising under customary international law. *Filartiga, Sequihua,* and §111(2) provide that cases arising under international law are within the grant of federal subject matter jurisdiction in Article III and §1331. This view extends to customary international law, and is not limited to actions arising under U.S. treaties or other international agreements. Indeed, *Filartiga* and *Sequihua* involved principles of customary international law: "the modern view is that customary international law in the United States is federal law." *Restatement (Third) Foreign Relations Law* §111 Reporters' Note 3 (1986). "Matters arising under customary international law also arise under 'the laws of the United States,' since international law is 'part of our law.'" *Id.* at Reporters' Note 4 (quoting *The Paquete Habana*). Is this persuasive? Under Article III and §1331, is customary international law categorized as a "Treaty" or a "law of the United States"? Should federal courts have federal question jurisdiction over all cases arising under international law, including customary international law? Why should the Texas courts not have been permitted to decide *Sequihua*?

8. Rules of customary international law that are likely to arise in U.S. civil litigation. What rules of customary international law are likely to arise in U.S. litigation? Possibilities include: (a) prohibitions against uncompensated expropriation; (b) denials of justice; (c) violation of international boundaries; (d) assertions of jurisdiction beyond the limits permitted by international law; and (e) human rights violations. Should these sorts of international law rules be treated as federal law, subject to federal court jurisdiction?

Recall that international law is generally categorized into two categories — public and private international law. As discussed above, this was not always the case. Until this century, the "law of nations" and "international" law were generally regarded as encompassing the subjects that are presently divided into public and private international law. *See supra* pp. 17-18. Given this, should actions arising under private international law be subject to federal question jurisdiction? Would this be consistent with the Framers' purposes? What sorts of cases would it extend to?

9. Federal question jurisdiction over customary international law claims. *Filartiga* suggested that §1331 would provide a basis for actions based on customary international law. The rationale for this result is, like §111, that international law is *federal* common law, and therefore that an action based on international law arises under federal law for purpose of §1331. What obstacles would plaintiffs encounter under §1331 that they would not face under §1350? Would a court, applying §1331, be able to leave open the question of what law provides the plaintiff's substantive cause of action? Recall that this is what *Filartiga* did. *Cf. Tel-Oren v. Libyan Arab Republic*, 726 F.2d 774, 779-80 n.4 (D.C. Cir. 1984) (Edwards, J., concurring) (§1331, unlike §1350, requires proof of a private cause of action under international law); *Handel v. Artukovic*, 601 F. Supp. 1412, 1421 (C.D. Cal. 1985) (same). If international law did not itself provide a cause of action, would a suit arise under international law? Conversely, note that §1331 would permit suit by U.S. citizens as well as by "aliens."

A number of lower courts have upheld §1331 jurisdiction in cases based upon international law. *See Kadic v. Karadzic*, 1995 WL 604585 (2d Cir. 1995) ("we need not rule definitively on whether any causes of action not specifically authorized by statute may be implied by international law standard as incorporated into United States law and grounded on §1331 jurisdiction"); *Xuncax v. Gramajo*, 886 F.Supp. 162 (D. Mass. 1995); *Abebe-Jiri v. Negavo, Negewo*, No. 90-CV2010 (N.D. Ga. 1993); *Martinez-Baca v. Suarez-Mason*, No. C-87-2057-SC (N.D. Calif. 1988); *Forti v. Suarez-Mason*, 672 F.Supp. 1531, 1544 (N.D. Calif. 1987).

10. *Article III and Alien Tort Statute.* As discussed above, a federal court may not exercise subject matter jurisdiction unless both Article III and a valid federal statute confer such jurisdiction. What was the *constitutional* foundation for subject matter jurisdiction in *Filartiga*?

(a) *No Article III alienage jurisdiction.* Because *Filartiga* was a case between two aliens, there could be no Article III basis for alienage jurisdiction. *See supra* pp. 25-26.

(b) *Article III federal question jurisdiction.* What was the rationale adopted by *Filartiga* sustaining Article III jurisdiction? Consider its argument that federal question jurisdiction exists over substantive federal common law claims, and that international law is federal law: "The law of nations forms an integral part of the common law, and a review of the history surrounding the adoption of the Constitution demonstrates that it became a part of the common law *of the United States* upon the adoption of the Constitution." Simply put, torts in violation of the law of nations were subject to common law rules in the United States at the time of adoption of the Constitution, and became federal common law at that time. Is this persuasive? Accepting that international law was regarded as part of the common law in 1789, the basic holding of *Erie* was that there is "no federal general common law." Does this preclude Judge Kaufman's "incorporation" argument, declaring that there was a federal common law of international law? Why could international law not have remained part of the common law of the several states? Is international law different from other types of common law, because, for example, there are greater needs for national uniformity and reliability?

Consider also the following excerpt from *In re Estate of Ferdinand E. Marcos Human Rights Litigation*, 978 F.2d 493 (9th Cir. 1992):

> There is ample indication that the "Arising Under" Clause was meant to extend the judicial power of the federal courts, as James Madison put it, to "all cases which concern foreigners," Letter from James Madison to Edmund Randolph (April 8, 1787), reprinted in 9 *The Papers of James Madison* 368, 370 (R. Rutland & W. Rachal ed. 1975), and "all occasions of having disputes with foreign powers," 3 *The Debates in the Several State Conventions on the Adoption of the Federal Constitution* 530 (J. Elliot ed. 1836) (remarks of J. Madison), and, as Alexander Hamilton wrote, to "all those [cases] in which [foreigners] are concerned. ..." *The Federalist No. 80*, at 536 (A. Hamilton) (J. Cooke ed. 1961). It is also well settled that the law of nations is part of federal common law.

Is this persuasive? Does it suggest that *any* international case — any cases concerning foreigners — falls within Article III? Is that what the Framers intended? Is it consistent with the language of Article III? Is it consistent with early readings of Article III's grant of alienage jurisdiction in *Hodgson v. Bowerbank*, 9 U.S. 303 (1809), *supra* pp. 25-26?

(c) *Cause of action requirement and Article III.* If one concludes that *neither* §1350 nor international law grant a federal cause of action, then the only basis for a private cause of action under §1350 would be state or foreign law. *See supra* p. 47. If state or foreign law must be relied upon for a private cause of action, can one still reason that the case arises under federal law for purposes of Article III? Is it sufficient that federal law provides a specialized jurisdictional grant in an area of federal concern? Consider the Court's analysis of Article III in *Verlinden BV v. Central Bank of Nigeria*, 461 U.S. 480 (1983). *See infra* pp. 56-66.

11. *Federal subject matter jurisdiction in cases arising under substantive federal common law.* *Sequihua* held that federal subject matter jurisdiction under Article III and §1331 extends to cases arising under substantive federal common law. Substantial precedent supports this view. In *Illinois v. Milwaukee*, 406 U.S. 91 (1972), the Supreme Court held that "§1331 jurisdiction will support claims founded upon federal common law as well as those of statutory origin." *See also National Farmers Union Ins. Co. v. Crow Tribe of Indians*, 471 U.S. 845, 850 (1985); *Romero v. International Terminal Operating Co.*, 358 U.S. 354, 393 (1959) (Brennan, J., dissenting).

Was *Sequihua* correctly decided? What was the basis for concluding that federal common law displaced state law?

12. *"Well-pleaded complaint" requirement.* As discussed above, federal question jurisdiction does not exist under §1331 unless a "well-pleaded complaint" asserts a claim based upon federal law. It is not

sufficient that federal law provide a defense to a state law claim. *See supra* pp. 34-35. What rule of international law (or federal common law) did the *Sequihua* complaint arise under? Was international law only relevant as a defense? Even if §1331 did not provide a proper jurisdictional base, would §1350 be available? Does the well-pleaded complaint rule apply under §1350? Note that the well-pleaded complaint rule is a *statutory* requirement. *Verlinden BV v. Central Bank of Nigeria*, 461 U.S. 480, 494-95 (1983). Would Article III permit the use of §1350 in *Sequihua*?

13. *Practical importance of federal jurisdiction.* Why did the plaintiffs in *Sequihua* want to be in Texas state court? Why did the defendants want to be in federal court? Note the district court's disposition of the case — dismissal on grounds of comity and forum non conveniens. Would those grounds be available in a Texas state court? We consider this below. *See infra* pp. 358-66.

4. Sovereign Immunity and Subject Matter Jurisdiction Under the Foreign Sovereign Immunities Act

Foreign states have long enjoyed various jurisdictional immunities under international and national law. Foreign sovereign immunity is governed in the United States by the Foreign Sovereign Immunities Act of 1976 ("FSIA"), discussed in Chapter 3 below. This section examines federal subject matter jurisdiction under the FSIA and Article III.

Section 1604 of the FSIA provides foreign states (as defined) with a basic grant of sovereign immunity from the judicial jurisdiction of U.S. courts (both state and federal).[218] Section 1605 then sets forth a number of significant exceptions to this grant of immunity, specifying in detail the circumstances in which foreign states will not enjoy immunity from U.S. judicial jurisdiction. These include, for example, cases where foreign states have waived their immunity, engaged in commercial conduct having a U.S. nexus, or committed noncommercial torts in the United States.[219]

Under the FSIA, issues of sovereign immunity are inextricably linked with both the personal and subject matter jurisdiction of U.S. courts. Thus, the FSIA affirmatively grants both subject matter and personal jurisdiction to federal district courts in all those cases where a foreign state is denied immunity by §1605. Section 1330(a) grants U.S. district courts

> original jurisdiction without regard to amount in controversy of any non-jury civil action against a foreign state ... to any claim for relief in personam with respect to which the foreign state is not entitled to immunity either under §§1605-07 of this title or under any applicable international agreement.[220]

Similarly, §1330(b) provides that "[p]ersonal jurisdiction over a foreign state shall exist as to every claim for relief over which the district courts have jurisdiction under [§1330(a)] where service has been made under §1608 of this title."[221]

Excerpted below is the Supreme Court's opinion in *Verlinden BV v. Central Bank of Nigeria*. The decision considers the application of the FSIA's jurisdictional

---

218. *See infra* pp. 210-12 & 226-27.
219. *See* 28 U.S.C. §1605(a)(1), (2) & (5); *infra* pp. 226-85.
220. 28 U.S.C. §1330(a).
221. 28 U.S.C. §1330(b).

provisions in cases where a foreign plaintiff sues a foreign sovereign, and the extent to which the statute's jurisdictional grant is consistent with Article III.

VERLINDEN BV v. CENTRAL BANK OF NIGERIA
461 U.S. 480 (1983)

CHIEF JUSTICE BURGER. We granted certiorari to consider whether the [FSIA], by authorizing a foreign plaintiff to sue a foreign state in a United States District Court on a non-federal cause of action, violates Article III of the Constitution.

I. On April 21, 1975, the Federal Republic of Nigeria and petitioner Verlinden BV, a Dutch corporation with its principal offices in Amsterdam, The Netherlands, entered into a contract providing for the purchase of 240,000 metric tons of cement by Nigeria. The parties agreed that the contract would be governed by the laws of the Netherlands and that disputes would be resolved by arbitration before the International Chamber of Commerce, Paris, France. The contract provided that the Nigerian government was to establish an irrevocable, confirmed letter of credit for the total purchase price through Slavenburg's Bank in Amsterdam. According to petitioner's amended complaint, however, respondent Central Bank of Nigeria, an instrumentality of Nigeria, improperly established an unconfirmed letter of credit payable through Morgan Guaranty Trust Company in New York.

In August 1975, Verlinden subcontracted with a Liechtenstein corporation, Interbuco, to purchase the cement needed to fulfill the contract. Meanwhile, the ports of Nigeria had become clogged with hundreds of ships carrying cement, sent by numerous other cement suppliers with whom Nigeria also had entered contracts. In mid-September, Central Bank unilaterally directed its correspondent banks, including Morgan Guaranty, to adopt a series of amendments to all letters of credit issued in connection with the cement contracts. Central Bank also directly notified the suppliers that payment would be made only for those shipments approved by Central Bank two months before their arrival in Nigerian waters.[222]

Verlinden then sued Central Bank in United States District Court for the Southern District of New York, alleging that Central Bank's actions constituted an anticipatory breach of the letter of credit. Verlinden alleged jurisdiction under §2 of the FSIA, 28 U.S.C. §1330. Respondent moved to dismiss for, among other reasons, lack of subject matter and personal jurisdiction.

The District Court first held that a federal court may exercise subject matter jurisdiction over a suit brought by a foreign corporation against a foreign sovereign. Although the legislative history of the FSIA does not clearly reveal whether Congress intended the Act to extend to actions brought by foreign plaintiffs, Judge Weinfeld

---

222. The parties do not seriously dispute the fact that these unilateral amendments constituted violations of Article 3 of the Uniform Customs and Practice for Documentary Credits (Int'l Chamber of Comm. Brochure No. 222) (1962 Revision), which, by stipulation of the parties, is applicable.

reasoned that the language of the Act is "broad and embracing. It confers jurisdiction over 'any nonjury civil action' against a foreign state." ... The District Court also held that Article III subject matter jurisdiction extends to suits by foreign corporations against foreign sovereigns, stating: "even though the plaintiff's claim is one grounded upon common law, the case is one that 'arises under' a federal law because the complaint compels the application of the uniform federal standard governing assertions of sovereign immunity. ..." The District Court nevertheless dismissed the complaint, holding that a foreign instrumentality is entitled to sovereign immunity unless one of the exceptions specified in the Act applies [and that none did.].[223]

arises under federal law

The ... Second Circuit affirmed, but on different grounds. The court agreed with the District Court that the Act was properly construed to permit actions brought by foreign plaintiffs. The court held, however, that the Act exceeded the scope of Article III of the Constitution. In the view of the Court of Appeals, neither the diversity clause[224] nor the "arising under" clause of Article III is broad enough to support jurisdiction over actions by foreign plaintiffs against foreign sovereigns; accordingly it concluded that Congress was without power to grant federal courts jurisdiction in this case, and affirmed the District Court's dismissal of the action. ...

II. For more than a century and a half, the United States generally granted foreign sovereigns complete immunity from suit in the courts of this country. In *The Schooner Exchange v. M'Faddon*, Chief Justice Marshall concluded that, while the jurisdiction of a nation within its own territory "is susceptible of no limitation not imposed by itself," the United States had impliedly waived jurisdiction over certain activities of foreign sovereigns. ... As *The Schooner Exchange* made clear, however, foreign sovereign immunity is a matter of grace and comity on the part of the United States, and not a restriction imposed by the Constitution. Accordingly, this Court consistently has deferred to the decisions of the political branches — in particular, those of the Executive Branch — on whether to take jurisdiction over actions against foreign sovereigns and their instrumentalities. ... [I]n the so-called Tate Letter, the State Department announced its adoption of the "restrictive" theory of foreign sovereign immunity. Under this theory, immunity is confined to suits involving the for-

---

223. The District Court dismissed "for lack of personal jurisdiction." Under the Act, however, both statutory subject matter jurisdiction (otherwise known as "competence") and personal jurisdiction turn on application of the substantive provisions of the Act. Under §1330(a), federal district courts are provided subject matter jurisdiction if a foreign state is "not entitled to immunity either under §§1605-1607 ... or under any applicable international agreement;" §1330(b) provides personal jurisdiction wherever subject matter jurisdiction exists under subsection (a) and service of process has been made under §1608 of the Act. Thus, if none of the exceptions to sovereign immunity set forth in the Act applies, the District Court lacks both statutory subject matter jurisdiction and personal jurisdiction. The District Court's conclusion that none of the exceptions to the Act applied therefore signified an absence of both competence and personal jurisdiction.

224. The foreign diversity clause provides that the judicial power extends "to Controversies ... between a State, or the Citizens thereof, and foreign States, Citizens or Subjects." U.S. Const., Art. III, §2, cl. 1.

eign sovereign's public acts, and does not extend to cases arising out of a foreign state's strictly commercial acts.

The restrictive theory was not initially enacted into law, however, and its application proved troublesome. As in the past, initial responsibility for deciding questions of sovereign immunity fell primarily upon the Executive acting through the State Department, and the courts abided by "suggestions of immunity" from the State Department. As a consequence, foreign nations often placed diplomatic pressure on the State Department in seeking immunity. On occasion, political considerations led to suggestions of immunity in cases where immunity would not have been available under the restrictive theory. An additional complication was posed by the fact that foreign nations did not always make requests to the State Department. In such cases, the responsibility fell to the courts to determine whether sovereign immunity existed, generally by reference to prior State Department decisions. Thus, sovereign immunity determinations were made in two different branches, subject to a variety of factors, sometimes including diplomatic considerations. Not surprisingly, the governing standards were neither clear nor uniformly applied.

In 1976, Congress passed the FSIA in order to free the Government from the case-by-case diplomatic pressures, to clarify the governing standards, and to "assur[e] litigants that ... decisions are made on purely legal grounds and under procedures that insure due process," H.R. Rep. No. 94-1487, p. 7 (1976), *reprinted in* [1976] U.S. Code Cong. & Ad. News 6604. To accomplish these objectives, the Act contains a comprehensive set of legal standards governing claims of immunity in every civil action against a foreign state or its political subdivisions, agencies or instrumentalities.

For the most part, the Act codifies, as a matter of federal law, the restrictive theory of sovereign immunity. A foreign state is normally immune from the jurisdiction of federal and state courts, 28 U.S.C. §1604, subject to a set of exceptions specified in §§1605 and 1607. Those exceptions include actions in which the foreign state has explicitly or impliedly waived its immunity, and actions based upon commercial activities of the foreign sovereign carried on in the United States or causing a direct effect in the United States. When one of these or the other specified exceptions applies, "the foreign state shall be liable in the same manner and to the same extent as a private individual under like circumstances," 28 U.S.C. §1606.[225]

The Act expressly provides that its standards control in "the courts of the United States and of the States," §1604, and thus clearly contemplates that such suits may be brought in either federal or state courts. However, "[i]n view of the potential sensitivity of actions against foreign states and the importance of developing a uniform body of law in this area," H.R. Rep. No. 94-1487, at 32, the Act guarantees foreign states the right to remove any civil action from a state court to a federal court,

---

225. Section 1606 somewhat modifies this standard of liability with respect to punitive damages and wrongful death actions.

§1441(d). The Act also provides that any claim permitted under the Act may be brought from the outset in federal court, §1330(a).[226] If one of the specified exceptions to sovereign immunity applies, a federal district court may exercise subject matter jurisdiction under §1330(a); but if the claim does not fall within one of the exceptions, federal courts lack subject matter jurisdiction.[227] In such a case, the foreign state is also ensured immunity from the jurisdiction of state courts by §1604.

III. The District Court and the Court of Appeals both held that the FSIA purports to allow a foreign plaintiff to sue a foreign sovereign in the courts of the United States, provided the substantive requirements of the Act are satisfied. We agree.

On its face, the language of the statute is unambiguous. The statute grants jurisdiction over "any non-jury civil action against a foreign state ... with respect to which the foreign state is not entitled to immunity," 28 U.S.C. §1330(a). The Act contains no indication of any limitation based on the citizenship of the plaintiff. The legislative history is less clear in this regard. The House Report recites that the Act would provide jurisdiction for "*any* claim with respect to which the foreign state is not entitled to immunity under §§1605-1607," H.R. Rep. No. 94-1487, at 13 (emphasis added), and also states that its purpose was "to provide when and how *parties* can maintain a lawsuit against a foreign state or its entities," *id.* at p. 6 (emphasis added). At another point, however, the Report refers to the growing number of disputes between "American citizens" and foreign states, *id.* at 6-7, and expresses the desire to ensure "*our* citizens ... access to the courts," *id.* at 6 (emphasis added).

Notwithstanding this reference to "our citizens," we conclude that, when considered as a whole, the legislative history reveals an intent not to limit jurisdiction under the Act to actions brought by American citizens. Congress was aware of concern that "our courts [might be] turned into small 'international courts of claims[,]' ... open ... to all comers to litigate any dispute which any private party may have with a foreign state anywhere in the world." Testimony of Bruno A. Ristau, Hearings on H.R. 11315, at 31. As the language of the statute reveals, Congress protected against this danger not by restricting the class of potential plaintiffs, but rather by enacting substantive provisions requiring some form of substantial contact with the United States. If an action satisfies the substantive standards of the Act, it may be brought in federal court regardless of the citizenship of the plaintiff.[228]

IV. We now turn to the core question presented by this case: whether Congress

---

226. "[T]o encourage the bringing of actions against foreign states in Federal courts," H.R. Rep. No. 94-1487, at 13, the Act specifies that federal district courts shall have original jurisdiction "without regard to amount in controversy." 28 U.S.C. §1330(a).

227. In such a situation, the federal court will also lack personal jurisdiction. *See* n.223 *supra.*

228. Prior to passage of FSIA, which Congress clearly intended to govern all actions against foreign sovereigns, state courts on occasion had exercised jurisdiction over suits between foreign plaintiffs and foreign sovereigns, *see, e.g., J. Zeevi & Sons v. Grindlays Bank,* 371 N.Y.S.2d 892, *cert. denied,* 423 U.S. 866 (1975). Congress did not prohibit such actions when it enacted the FSIA, but sought to ensure that any action that might be brought against a foreign sovereign in state court could also be brought in or removed to federal court.

exceeded the scope of Article III of the Constitution by granting federal courts sub-ject matter jurisdiction over certain civil actions by foreign plaintiffs against foreign sovereigns where the rule of decision may be provided by state law. This Court's cases firmly establish that Congress may not expand the jurisdiction of the federal courts beyond the bounds established by the Constitution. *See, e.g., Hodgson v. Bowerbank,* 5 Cranch 303 (1809). Within Article III of the Constitution, we find two sources authorizing the grant of jurisdiction in the FSIA: the diversity clause and the "arising under" clause. The diversity clause, which provides that the judicial power extends to controversies between "a State, or the Citizens thereof, and foreign States," covers actions by citizens of states. Yet diversity jurisdiction is not sufficiently broad to support a grant of jurisdiction over actions by foreign plaintiffs, since a for-eign plaintiff is not "a State, or [a] Citize[n] thereof." *See Mossman v. Higginson,* 4 Dall. 12 (1800).[229] We conclude, however, that the "arising under" clause of Article III provides an appropriate basis for the statutory grant of subject matter jurisdiction to actions by foreign plaintiffs under the Act.

The controlling decision on the scope of Article III "arising under" jurisdiction is Chief Justice Marshall's opinion for the Court in *Osborn v. Bank of the United States,* 9 Wheat. 738 (1824). In *Osborn,* the Court upheld the constitutionality of a statute that granted the Bank of the United States the right to sue in federal court on causes of action based upon state law. There, the Court concluded that the "judicial department may receive ... the power of construing every ... law" that "the Legislature may constitutionally make." The rule was laid down that: "[I]t is a sufficient founda-tion for jurisdiction, that the title or right set up by the party, may be defeated by one construction of the constitution or laws of the United States, and sustained by the opposite construction."

Osborn thus reflects a broad conception of "arising under" jurisdiction, accord-ing to which Congress may confer on the federal courts jurisdiction over any case or controversy that might call for the application of federal law. The breadth of that conclusion has been questioned. It has been observed that, taken at its broadest, *Osborn* might be read as permitting "assertion of original federal jurisdiction on the remote possibility of presentation of a federal question." *Textile Workers Union v. Lincoln Mills,* 353 U.S. 448, 482 (1957) (Frankfurter, J., dissenting). We need not now resolve that issue or decide the precise boundaries of Article III jurisdiction, however, since the present case does not involve a mere speculative possibility that a federal question may arise at some point in the proceeding. Rather, a suit against a foreign state under this Act necessarily raises questions of substantive federal law at the very outset, and hence clearly "arises under" federal law, as that term is used in Article III.

---

229. Since Article III requires only "minimal diversity," *see State Farm Fire & Casualty Co. v. Tashire,* 386 U.S. 523, 530 (1967), diversity jurisdiction would be a sufficient basis for jurisdiction where at least one of the plaintiffs is a citizen of a State.

By reason of its authority over foreign commerce and foreign relations, Congress has the undisputed power to decide, as a matter of federal law, whether and under what circumstances foreign nations should be amenable to suit in the United States. Actions against foreign sovereigns in our courts raise sensitive issues concerning the foreign relations of the United States, and the primacy of federal concerns is evident. *See, e.g., Banco Nacional de Cuba v. Sabbatino; Zschernig v. Miller.* To promote these federal interests, Congress exercised its Article I powers[230] by enacting a statute comprehensively regulating the amenability of foreign nations to suit in the United States. The statute must be applied by the District Courts in every action against a foreign sovereign, since subject matter jurisdiction in any such action depends on the existence of one of the specified exceptions to foreign sovereign immunity, 28 U.S.C. §1330(a).[231] At the threshold of every action in a District Court against a foreign state, therefore, the court must satisfy itself that one of the exceptions applies — and in doing so it must apply the detailed federal law standards set forth in the Act. Accordingly, an action against a foreign sovereign arises under federal law, for purposes of Article III jurisdiction.

In reaching a contrary conclusion, the Court of Appeals relied heavily upon decisions construing 28 U.S.C. §1331, the statute which grants district courts general federal question jurisdiction over any case that "arises under" the laws of the United States. The court placed particular emphasis on the so-called "well-pleaded complaint" rule, which provides, for purposes of statutory "arising under" jurisdiction, that the federal question must appear on the face of a well-pleaded complaint and may not enter in anticipation of a defense. *See, e.g., Louisville & Nashville R. Co. v. Mottley,* 211 U.S. 149 (1908). In the view of the Court of Appeals, the question of foreign sovereign immunity in this case arose solely as a defense, and not on the face of Verlinden's well-pleaded complaint.

Although the language of §1331 parallels that of the "arising under" clause of Article III, this Court never has held that statutory "arising under" jurisdiction is identical to Article III "arising under" jurisdiction. Quite the contrary is true. Section 1331, the general federal question statute, although broadly phrased, "has been continuously construed and limited in the light of the history that produced it, the demands of reason and coherence, and the dictates of sound judicial policy which have emerged from the [statute's] function as a provision in the mosaic of federal judiciary legislation. *It is a statute, not a Constitution, we are expounding.*" *Romero v.*

---

230. In enacting the legislation, Congress relied specifically on its powers to prescribe the jurisdiction of Federal courts, Art. I, §8, cl. 9; to define offenses against the "Law of Nations," Art. I, §8, cl. 10; to regulate commerce with foreign nations, Art. I, §8, cl. 3; and to make all laws necessary and proper to execute the Government's powers, Art. I, §8, cl. 18.

231. The House Report on the Act states that "sovereign immunity is an affirmative defense that must be specially pleaded," H.R. Rep. No. 94-1487, at 17. Under the Act, however, subject matter jurisdiction turns on the existence of an exception to foreign sovereign immunity, 28 U.S.C. §1330(a). Accordingly, even if the foreign state does not enter an appearance to assert an immunity defense, a District Court still must determine that immunity is unavailable under the Act.

International Terminal Operating Co., 358 U.S. 354, 379 (1959) (emphasis added). In an accompanying footnote, the Court further observed, "Of course the many limitations which have been placed on jurisdiction under §1331 are not limitations on the constitutional power of Congress to confer jurisdiction on the federal courts." As th[is and other] decisions make clear, Article III "arising under" jurisdiction is broader than federal question jurisdiction under §1331, and the Court of Appeals' heavy reliance on decisions construing that statute was misplaced.

In rejecting "arising under" jurisdiction, the Court of Appeals also noted that §2 of the FSIA, 28 U.S.C §1330, is a jurisdictional provision.[232] Because of this, the court felt its conclusion compelled by prior cases in which this Court has rejected Congressional attempts to confer jurisdiction on federal courts simply by enacting jurisdictional statutes. In *Mossman v. Higginson,* 4 Dall. 12 (1800), for example, this Court found that a statute purporting to confer jurisdiction over actions "where an alien is a party" would exceed the scope of Article III if construed to allow an action solely between two aliens. And in *The Propeller Genesee Chief v. Fitzhugh,* 12 How. 443, 451-453 (1852), the Court, while upholding a statute granting jurisdiction over vessels on the Great Lakes as an exercise of maritime jurisdiction, rejected the view that the jurisdictional statute itself constituted a federal regulation of commerce upon which "arising under" jurisdiction could be based.

From these cases, the Court of Appeals apparently concluded that a jurisdictional statute can never constitute the federal law under which the action arises, for Article III purposes. Yet the statutes at issue in these prior cases sought to do nothing more than grant jurisdiction over a particular class of cases. As the Court stated in *The Propeller Genesee Chief,* "The law ... contains no regulations of commerce. ... *It merely confers a new jurisdiction on the district courts; and this is its only object and purpose.* ... It is evident ... that Congress, in passing [the law], did not intend to exercise their power to regulate commerce. ..." 12 How. at 451 (emphasis added).

In contrast, in enacting the FSIA, Congress expressly exercised its power to regulate foreign commerce, along with other specified Article I powers. *See* n.230 *supra.* As the House Report clearly indicates, the primary purpose of the Act was to "se[t] forth comprehensive rules governing sovereign immunity," H.R. Rep. No. 94-1487, at p. 12; the jurisdictional provisions of the Act are simply one part of this comprehensive scheme. The Act thus does not merely concern access to the federal courts. Rather, it governs the types of actions for which foreign sovereigns may be held liable

---

232. Although a major function of the Act as a whole is to regulate jurisdiction of federal courts over cases involving foreign states, the Act's purpose is to set forth "comprehensive rules governing sovereign immunity." H.R. Rep. No. 94-1487, at 12. The Act also prescribes procedures for commencing lawsuits against foreign states in federal and state courts and specifies the circumstances under which attachment and execution may be obtained against the property of foreign states. In addition, the Act defines "Extent of Liability," setting out a general rule that the foreign sovereign is "liable in the same manner and to the same extent as a private individual," subject to certain specified exceptions, 28 U.S.C. §1606. In view of our resolution of this case, we need not consider petitioner's claim that §1606 itself renders every claim against a foreign sovereign a federal cause of action.

in a court in the United States, federal or state. The Act codifies the standards governing foreign sovereign immunity as an aspect of substantive federal law, and applying those standards will generally require interpretation of numerous points of federal law. Finally, if a court determines that none of the exceptions to sovereign immunity applies, the plaintiff will be barred from raising his claim in any court in the United States — manifestly, "the title or right set up by the party, may be defeated by one construction of the ... laws of the United States, and sustained by the opposite construction." *Osborn v. Bank of the United States,* 9 Wheat. at 822. That the inquiry into foreign sovereign immunity is labeled under the Act as a matter of jurisdiction does not affect the constitutionality of Congress' action in granting federal courts jurisdiction over cases calling for application of this comprehensive regulatory statute.

Congress, pursuant to its unquestioned Article I powers, has enacted a broad statutory framework governing assertions of foreign sovereign immunity. In so doing, Congress deliberately sought to channel cases against foreign sovereigns away from the state courts and into federal courts, thereby reducing the potential for a multiplicity of conflicting results among the courts of the 50 states. The resulting jurisdictional grant is within the bounds of Article III, since every action against a foreign sovereign necessarily involves application of a body of substantive federal law, and accordingly "arises under" federal law, within the meaning of Article III. ...

Notes on Verlinden

1. *Subject matter jurisdiction under the FSIA in cases brought by foreign plaintiffs against foreign states.* All three courts in *Verlinden* concluded that the FSIA's statutory language granted federal courts subject matter jurisdiction over actions brought by foreign plaintiffs against foreign states. Is that correct? Note the numerous references in the legislative history to "U.S. citizens" and "Americans." *See also Verlinden BV v. Central Bank of Nigeria,* 647 F.2d 320, 323-24 (2d Cir. 1981) (citing many other examples). As a consequence, the Second Circuit concluded in *Verlinden* that, "[f]rom this murky and confused legislative history, only one conclusion emerges: Congress formed no clear intent as to the citizenship of plaintiffs under the Act. It probably did not even consider the question." 647 F.2d at 324.

Why should Congress have intended to open U.S. courts, or provide the public resources of those courts, for such actions? Moreover, given the foreign relations and other international implications of suits against foreign states, why should the United States bear the costs of rendering judgments against foreign sovereigns in favor of foreign nationals? In cases of doubt as to Congress's intent to grant jurisdiction over foreign states, should not ambiguity be resolved *against* unintended assertions of jurisdiction? Consider Judge Bork's discussion in *Filartiga* of separation of powers concerns and their requirement that §1350 be narrowly construed. *See supra* pp. 45-46.

2. *Foreign states' general right of access to U.S. courts.* U.S. courts have long held that there is no general bar forbidding foreign states from suing in U.S. courts. In reaching this conclusion, courts have frequently relied on principles of international law and comity. Consider the following excerpt from *Pfizer, Inc. v. Government of India,* 434 U.S. 308, 319 (1978):

> [Holding that foreign states may sue for relief under the Sherman Act] does not involve any novel concept of the jurisdiction of the federal courts. This Court has long recognized the rule that a foreign nation is generally entitled to prosecute any civil claim in the courts of the United States upon the same basis as a domestic corporation or individual might do. "To deny him this privilege would manifest a want of comity and friendly feeling." *The Sapphire,* 11 Wall. 164, 167; *Monaco v. Mississippi,* 292 U.S. 313, 323 n.2; *Banco Nacional de Cuba v. Sabbatino; see* U.S. Const., Art. III, §2, cl. 1. To allow a foreign sovereign to sue in our courts

for treble damages to the same extent as any other person injured by an antitrust violation is thus no more than a specific application of a long-settled general rule. To exclude foreign nations from the protections of our antitrust laws would, on the other hand, create a conspicuous exception to this rule, an exception that could not be justified in the absence of clear legislative intent.

Pfizer relied on a presumption — derived from international law and comity — that foreign states are entitled to access to U.S. courts. This presumption is an application of the more general presumption, discussed above, that statutes will not be interpreted to violate international law unless they clearly require such a result. *See supra* p. 22 and *infra* pp. 549-50, 780-92.

3. *Foreign nationals' general right of access to U.S. courts.* It has long been established that neither foreign citizens nor foreign residents are generally barred from access to U.S. courts. Joseph Story explained:

all foreigners, sui juris, and not otherwise specially disabled by the law of the place where the suit is brought, may there maintain suits to vindicate their rights and redress their wrongs. The same doctrine applies to foreign sovereigns and to foreign corporations.

J. Story, *Commentaries on the Conflict of Laws* §565 (2d ed. 1841). This rule rested on international law and the law of nations. It was acknowledged by U.S. and foreign commentators and applied by state and federal U.S. courts. *E.g.*, H. Wheaton, *Elements of International Law* §140-1 (8th ed. 1866); 3 G. Hackworth, *Digest of International Law* 562 (1941); 4 J. Moore, *Digest of International Law* 2 (1906); Wilson, *Access-to-Court Provisions in United States Commercial Treaties*, 47 Am. J. Int'l L. 20, 26, 30 (1953) ("quite apart from treaty provisions, the alien has had, from the beginning of the National Government in the United States, freedom of access to Federal courts on practically the same footing as citizens"). Is this presumption relevant to the interpretation of the FSIA in *Verlinden*? Compare the reliance in *Pfizer* on the presumption that foreign states have access to national courts.

4. *Constitutional and policy bases for FSIA.* What is the constitutional basis under Article I for Congress's legislative enactment of the FSIA? What are the federal interests in enacting a statute dealing comprehensively with foreign sovereign immunity? Why did Congress deem it advisable to enact the FSIA?

5. *Article III's "arising under" clause.* Even though the FSIA granted federal courts jurisdiction over suits by foreign plaintiffs against foreign states, this authorization would not be effective unless it was within Article III's provisions concerning the judicial power. Article III's alienage clause was inapplicable because *Verlinden* (like *Filartiga*) only involved aliens. *See supra* pp. 25-32. Moreover, the applicable law governing the merits of the parties' contract dispute was either state or foreign law — not federal law. Given this, why is it, according to Chief Justice Burger, that suits against foreign states under the FSIA "arise under" federal law?

Note that foreign sovereign immunity is immunity *from the judicial jurisdiction* of U.S. courts. *See supra* pp. 56-57. Could Congress enact a statute comprehensively granting the federal courts jurisdiction (both subject matter and personal) over all suits against aliens in U.S. courts? Suppose that the statute paralleled the FSIA, permitting state courts concurrent jurisdiction over aliens but forbidding them from hearing claims against aliens not authorized by the federal legislation. Consider the Second Circuit's analysis in *Verlinden*: "There is no intent here [in the FSIA] to create new federal causes of action; the purpose of the Act instead is to provide 'access to the courts in order to resolve ordinary legal disputes.' The House Report states flatly: 'the bill is not intended to affect the substantive law of liability.'" 647 F.2d 325 (quoting House Report at 6605 & 6610). Compare the Court's reply in *Verlinden*:

The Act does not merely concern access to the federal courts. Rather, it governs the types of actions for which foreign sovereigns may be held liable in a court in the United States, federal or state. The Act codifies the standards governing foreign sovereign immunity as an aspect of substantive federal law; and applying these standards will generally require interpretation of numerous points of federal law.

Does this answer the Second Circuit satisfactorily? Would this observation not also apply to the hypothetical statute governing jurisdiction over alien private defendants described above? Should Congress enact a comprehensive statute of this type?

6. *"Federal question" jurisdiction and the due process clause.* As discussed below, foreign defendants

cannot be subject to suit in a U.S. court unless they are within its personal jurisdiction. In many cases, personal jurisdiction over foreign defendants is defined by the Constitution's due process clause. *See infra* pp. 68-70. Why does it not follow that actions against foreign defendants "arise under" federal law for purposes of Article III and §1331? Recall that the Supreme Court has held that federal question jurisdiction exists under §1331 even if state (or foreign) law creates the plaintiff's cause of action, provided that a substantial disputed issue of federal law is a necessary element of the state law claim. *Franchise Tax Board v. Construction Laborers Vacation Trust*, 464 U.S. 1 (1983).

7. *Federal uniformity under the FSIA.* *Verlinden* emphasized that "Congress deliberately sought to channel cases against foreign sovereigns away from the state courts and into federal courts, thereby reducing the potential for a multiplicity of conflicting results among the courts of the 50 States." Why did Congress think that this was appropriate? In many international disputes, state law plays a substantial role in defining both the jurisdiction of U.S. courts and the substantive rules of decision. *See supra* pp. 7-9, 13-22 & 68-70. Why should cases involving foreign states be treated any differently?

8. *FSIA's simultaneous grant of personal and subject matter jurisdiction.* As described above, the FSIA makes issues of sovereign immunity and jurisdiction identical: if there is immunity, there is no subject matter or personal jurisdiction, and if there is no immunity, there is affirmative subject matter and personal jurisdiction. Is it wise to make questions of subject matter and personal jurisdiction identical? *See supra* pp. 56-57. Consider the following remarks:

> In structure, the FSIA is a marvel of compression. Within the bounds of a few tersely-worded sections, it purports to provide answers to three crucial questions in a suit against a foreign state: the availability of sovereign immunity as a defense, the presence of subject matter jurisdiction over the claim, and the propriety of personal jurisdiction over the defendant. ... Through a series of intricately coordinated provisions, the FSIA seems at first glance to make the answer to one of the questions, subject matter jurisdiction, dispositive of all three. This economy of decision has come, however, at the price of considerable confusion in the district courts. *Texas Trading & Milling Corp. v. Federal Republic of Nigeria*, 647 F.2d 300, 306-07 (2d Cir. 1981).

> The effect of this construction is to conceal distinctions that need to be drawn in careful analysis. *Harris v. VAO Intourist*, 481 F.Supp. 1056, 1062 (E.D.N.Y. 1979).

Are the criticisms warranted? Are there any practical consequences of treating sovereign immunity as either a matter of subject matter or personal jurisdiction. Note that §1605(a)(1) denies sovereign immunity to foreign states that waive their immunity. As a result, §1330(a) can grant subject matter jurisdiction based on a party's consent; this runs contrary to well-established rules that subject matter jurisdiction cannot be waived or created by agreement.

2/Jurisdiction of U.S. Courts Over Parties to International Disputes[1]

A U.S. court cannot adjudicate a case unless it has "personal" jurisdiction over the parties to the action. Personal jurisdiction involves the power of a court to adjudicate a claim against the defendant's person and to render a judgment enforceable against the defendant and any of its assets.[2] This Chapter considers the personal jurisdiction of U.S. courts over both foreign and domestic parties to international disputes.[3]

A. Introduction and Historical Background

1. Statutory and Constitutional Requirements for Exercise of Personal Jurisdiction

In determining whether a U.S. court has personal jurisdiction over a party, it is critical to distinguish between two separate requirements. First, there must be a legislative authorization granting the forum's courts the power to exercise jurisdiction over the defendant. Second, the exercise of jurisdiction pursuant to any legislative authorization must be consistent with the due process clause of the U.S.

---

1. Commentary on judicial jurisdiction in international litigation includes, *e.g.*, R. Casad, *Jurisdiction in Civil Actions* (2d ed. 1990); Born, *Reflections on Judicial Jurisdiction in International Cases*, 17 Ga. J. Int'l & Comp. L. 1 (1987); Brilmayer, *How Contacts Count: Due Process Limitations on State Court Jurisdiction*, 1980 Sup. Ct. Rev. 77; Kurland, *The Supreme Court, the Due Process Clause and the In Personam Jurisdiction of State Courts*, 25 U. Chi. L. Rev. 569 (1958); Stein, *Styles of Argument and Interstate Federalism in the Law of Personal Jurisdiction*, 65 Tex. L. Rev. 689 (1987); von Mehren & Trautman, *Jurisdiction to Adjudicate: A Suggested Analysis*, 79 Harv. L. Rev. 1121 (1966).

2. *Restatement (Second) Conflict of Laws* Chap. 3, Intro. Note (1971); *Shaffer v. Heitner*, 433 U.S. 186, 199 (1977).

3. This Chapter does not consider subject matter jurisdiction, venue, or service of process. These topics are dealt with in Chapters 1, 4, and 10 respectively.

Constitution. Only if both requirements are satisfied may the U.S. forum's courts exercise personal jurisdiction.[4]

a. Statutory Authorization for the Exercise of Judicial Jurisdiction

(1) State Long-Arm Statutes

All the states of the Union have enacted statutes (or rules of court) defining the personal jurisdiction of state courts over non-resident defendants, including foreign defendants.[5] Most such statutes provide for "long-arm" jurisdiction over, and service of process upon, defendants who are located outside of the state's territory but have specified contacts with the state. State long-arm statutes are typically used to obtain jurisdiction over defendants located in other U.S. states, but are also generally applicable to defendants located outside the country.[6]

Although long-arm statutes differ from state to state, there are now two basic legislative approaches. First, some state laws incorporate the due process limits of the fourteenth amendment. For example, they may grant jurisdiction to the "fullest extent permitted by the due process clause of the Fourteenth Amendment to the United States Constitution."[7] Slightly different are state long-arm statutes that authorize jurisdiction to the extent permitted by both federal and state constitutions. Thus, California's long-arm statute provides that "[a] court of this state may exercise jurisdiction on any basis not inconsistent with the constitution of this state or of the United States."[8] Examples of such long-arm statutes are excerpted in Appendix A. The trend among the several states in recent years has been towards long-arm statutes that expressly permit jurisdiction to the Constitution's limits.

Second, a number of states have enacted long-arm statutes that catalogue with greater or lesser detail the circumstances in which state courts may assert personal jurisdiction over foreign defendants.[9] The Illinois long-arm statute was one of the earliest examples of such legislation, although even it was recently amended to include a catch-all provision authorizing jurisdiction to the limits of the due process clause.[10] The Uniform Interstate and International Procedure Act, reproduced in Appendix B, provides a representative example of the "laundry-list" approach.

---

4. See *Omni Capital Int'l v. Rudolf Wolff & Co.*, 484 U.S. 97, 104 (1987); C. Wright & A. Miller, *Federal Practice and Procedure* §1063 (1987).

5. See R. Casad, *Jurisdiction in Civil Actions* §4.01 (2d ed. 1991) (describing and reproducing state long-arm statutes).

6. In addition, state statutes ordinarily provide for service of process within the state on agents or officers of non-resident defendants, *see infra* pp. 763-65, as well as for jurisdiction over residents or domiciliaries of the State and companies with sufficiently close connections to the State, *see infra* pp. 95-100.

7. *E.g.*, Iowa Rules of Ct. 56.2 (West 1987).

8. *E.g.*, Cal. Code Civ. Proc. §410.10 (1973).

9. Some state long-arm statutes enumerate the bases for personal jurisdiction over non-resident defendants. *E.g.*, Fla. Stat. Ann. §48.193 (West 1968); N.Y. Civ. Prac. Law §302(a) (McKinney 1972 & Supp. 1988). Other state long-arm statutes contain less detailed formulae specifying when jurisdiction may be asserted over non-residents. *E.g.*, Tex. Civ. Prac. & Rem. Code Ann. §17.043 (Vernon 1986).

10. Ill. Rev. Stat. Ch. 110, §2-209 (Smith-Hurd Supp. 1989). See Currie, *The Growth of the Long Arm: Eight Years of Extended Jurisdiction in Illinois*, 1963 U. Ill. L.F. 533.

In interpreting state long-arm statutes, decisions of the relevant state's courts are generally dispositive.[11] State courts often interpret state long-arm legislation expansively — even when this is not apparent from a statute's language. Many state courts have interpreted their long-arm statutes as conferring jurisdiction to the limits permitted by the U.S. Constitution.[12] In these circumstances, many courts have concluded that jurisdiction depends on only a single inquiry — whether a "trial court's exercise of jurisdiction over [a foreign defendant is] ... consistent with the requirements of due process of law under the Constitution of the United States."[13]

Other courts have rejected this "one-step" approach to jurisdictional analysis on the grounds that particular state long-arm statutes were intended to confer jurisdiction to the constitutional limits only as to those specific categories listed in the statute, and not as to unspecified categories.[14] In addition, not all state long-arm statutes have been interpreted as extending to the limits of the due process clause, even with respect to specified categories of cases.[15] In these circumstances, it is important to distinguish between statutory interpretation and constitutional analysis.

(2) Federal Long-Arm Statutes and Rules

There are important differences between the exercise of judicial jurisdiction by state courts and by federal courts.[16] In contrast to the universal adoption of state long-arm statutes, Congress has not enacted a general federal long-arm statute for the federal courts.[17] Instead, the judicial jurisdiction of federal courts is governed in the first instance by Federal Rule of Civil Procedure 4. Rule 4 was extensively revised in 1993; the current text is reproduced in Appendix C.

Rule 4 provides federal courts with three basic grants of jurisdiction. First, it authorizes federal courts to "borrow" the long-arm statute of the state in which the federal court is located.[18] Second, Rule 4 makes it clear that a federal court can exercise grants of personal jurisdiction contained in any applicable federal statute — such as the federal antitrust and securities laws.[19] Third, recently-adopted Rule

---

11. *E.g., DeMelo v. Toche Marine*, 711 F.2d 1260 (5th Cir. 1983); *Wells Fargo & Co. v. Wells Fargo Express Co.*, 556 F.2d 406 (9th Cir. 1977).

12. R. Casad, *Jurisdiction in Civil Actions* §4.01[1][b] & n.18 (2d ed. 1991) (exhaustively collecting lower state court decisions).

13. *Hall v. Helicopteros Nacionales de Colombia, SA*, 638 S.W.2d 870, 871 (Tex. 1982), *rev'd on other grounds*, 466 U.S. 408 (1984).

14. *E.g., Deluxe Ice Cream Co. v. R.C.H. Tool Corp.*, 726 F.2d 1209 (7th Cir. 1984); *Brown v. American Broadcasting Co.*, 704 F.2d 1296 (4th Cir. 1983).

15. *E.g., Banco Ambrosiano v. Artoc Bank & Trust, Ltd.*, 476 N.Y.S.2d 64 (1984) (N.Y. C.P.L.R. §302 not intended to extend to due process limits); *Fowler Prods. Co. v. Coca-Cola Bottling Co.*, 413 F.Supp. 1339 (M.D. Ga. 1976); *Bank of Wessington v. Winters Gov't Sec. Corp.*, 361 So.2d 757 (Fla. Dist. Ct. App. 1978).

16. *See infra* pp. 171-97.

17. *Omni Cap. Int'l v. Rudolf Wolff & Co.*, 484 U.S. 97 (1987); *infra* pp. 172-73.

18. Fed. R. Civ. P. 4(k)(1)(A); *infra* pp. 183-95.

19. Fed. R. Civ. P. 4(k)(1)(D); *infra* pp. 174-82.

4(k)(2) provides what amounts to a federal long-arm authorization, to the limits of the due process clause, in certain federal question cases.[20]

Although there is no general federal long-arm statute, a number of federal statutes contain specialized provisions dealing with service of process and personal jurisdiction in actions brought under the statute.[21] When such a statute is applicable, federal courts may generally exercise jurisdiction either as authorized by the federal statute (incorporated by Rule 4(k)(1)(D)) or as provided for by the state long-arm statute in the state where the federal court is located (incorporated by Rule 4(k)(1)(A)). Like state long-arm statutes, many federal jurisdictional grants have been interpreted as extending to the limits of the due process clause.[22]

Rule 4's provisions regarding personal jurisdiction are generally exclusive. If a borrowed state long-arm statute, federal jurisdictional grant, or Rule 4(k)(2) does not provide a basis for personal jurisdiction, then the federal courts will not fashion a federal common law basis for jurisdiction.[23]

b. Due Process Limits on Judicial Jurisdiction: Historical Overview and Vocabulary

The due process clauses of the fifth and fourteenth amendments play a vital role in defining the judicial jurisdiction of U.S. courts over foreign defendants.[24] First, even if a state or federal long-arm statute authorizes jurisdiction over a foreign defendant, there will be circumstances in which due process forbids the assertion of jurisdiction. Second, because most state and federal long-arm statutes extend to the Constitution's limits, the due process clause often effectively defines the personal jurisdiction of U.S. courts.

(1) Territorial Sovereignty and Pennoyer v. Neff

From the earliest days of the Republic, American courts and commentators relied on principles of territorial sovereignty and international law to limit judicial jurisdiction.[25] Here, as in other contexts, Joseph Story's classic *Commentaries on the Conflict of Laws* were central to American thinking.[26] With respect to judicial jurisdiction, Story offered an uncompromising statement of the territoriality doctrine:

---

20. Fed. R. Civ. P. 4(k)(2); *infra* pp. 195-97.

21. *See infra* pp. 174-75; 15 U.S.C. §22 (1982) (federal antitrust laws); 15 U.S.C. §77v (1982) (federal securities laws); 15 U.S.C. §78aa (1982) (federal securities laws).

22. *See infra* pp. 181-82.

23. *Omni Cap. Int'l v. Rudolf Wolff & Co.*, 484 U.S. 97 (1987); *infra* pp. 172-73.

24. The fourteenth amendment to the U.S. Constitution provides that no state shall "deprive any person of life, liberty, or property, without due process of law." The fifth amendment contains nearly identical language, applicable to the federal government. *See infra* pp. 173-74.

25. *Rose v. Himely*, 8 U.S. 241 (1808). *See also Mason v. The Ship Blaireau*, 6 U.S. 240 (1804); *The Bee*, 3 Fed. Cas. 41, No. 1219 (D. Me. 1836) ("established principles of the jus gentium").

26. *See* de Nova, *The First American Book on Conflict of Laws*, 8 Am. J. Leg. Hist. 135 (1964); Lorenzen, *Selected Articles on the Conflict of Laws* 193-94 (1947) ("Story's *Commentaries* were without question the most remarkable and outstanding work on the conflict of laws which had appeared since the thirteenth century in any country and in any language"); Yntema, *The Historic Bases of Private International Law*, 2 Am. J. Comp. L. 297, 307 (1953). *See also infra* pp. 493-509 & 544-51.

Considered in an international point of view, jurisdiction, to be rightfully exercised, must be founded either upon the person being within the territory, or upon the thing being within the territory; for, otherwise, there can be no sovereignty exerted, upon the known maxim; *Extra territorium jus dicenti impune non paretur* ... no sovereignty can extend its process beyond its own territorial limits, to subject either persons or property to its judicial decisions.[27]

Story's views were consistently reflected in 19th century U.S. judicial decisions. In 1808, the Supreme Court refused to recognize a foreign prize court's judgment on the grounds that the foreign court had lacked judicial jurisdiction.[28] The case, *Rose v. Himely*, involved a vessel that had been seized outside of the foreign sovereign's territorial waters. Holding that the foreign court could not have asserted jurisdiction over the vessel consistent with international law, the Court reasoned that:

[if a foreign court] exercises a jurisdiction which, according to the law of nations, its sovereign could not confer ... [its judgments] are not regarded by foreign courts ... [T]he law of nations is the law of all tribunals in the society of nations, and is supposed to be equally understood by all.[29]

Similarly, in 1811, in *Mills v. Duryee*, a dissenting opinion of Justice Johnson cited "certain eternal principles of justice," one of which was "that jurisdiction cannot be justly exercised by a state over property not within the reach of its process, or over persons ... not subjected to their jurisdiction, by being found within their limits."[30] And in *D'Arcy v. Ketchum*,[31] the Court held that the full faith and credit clause did not require a state court to enforce a judgment rendered by another state court that lacked valid personal jurisdiction over the judgment-debtor. Among other things, the Court observed:

That countries foreign to our own disregard a judgment merely against the person, where he has not been served with process nor had a day in court is the familiar rule; national comity is never thus extended. The proceeding is deemed an illegitimate assumption of power, and resisted as mere abuse. ... We deem it free from controversy that these adjudications are in conformity to the well-established rules of international law.[32]

---

27. J. Story, *Commentaries on the Conflict of Laws* §539 (2d ed. 1841). Story's territorial view of national jurisdiction also applied to legislative jurisdiction, which is discussed in detail below. *See infra* pp. 493-509 & 544-51.

28. *Rose v. Himely*, 8 U.S. 241, 277 (1808).

29. 8 U.S. at 276-77. Writing for the Court, Chief Justice Marshall also said that a U.S. court must inquire into "the right of the foreign court to take jurisdiction of the thing ... [under] the law of nations and [any applicable] treaties." 8 U.S. at 271. *See also The Schooner Exchange v. McFaddon*, 11 U.S. 116 (1812) (relying on international law for rule limiting U.S. judicial jurisdiction against foreign states).

30. 11 U.S. 481, 486 (1813) (Johnson, J., dissenting).

31. 52 U.S. 165 (1850).

32. 52 U.S. at 174.

The Court went on to hold that the judicial jurisdiction of the several states was restricted by international law, and that the judgment in *D'Arcy* need not be recognized because it was based on a jurisdictional assertion that violated international law.[33]

The Supreme Court's reliance on international law to sustain territorial limits on judicial jurisdiction culminated in its classic decision in *Pennoyer v. Neff*.[34] In *Pennoyer*, the Court expressly relied on what it termed "well-established principles of public law respecting the jurisdiction of an independent State."[35] In ascertaining what international law required, the Court cited leading contemporary international law commentaries and particularly Story's classic *Commentaries on the Conflict of Laws*.[36]

From these authorities *Pennoyer* derived three principles of international law: (1) "every State possesses exclusive jurisdiction and sovereignty over persons and property within its territory";[37] (2) "no State can exercise direct jurisdiction and authority over persons and property without its territory";[38] and (3) "process from the tribunals of one State cannot run into another state."[39] These principles required that the defendant "must be brought within [the forum court's] jurisdiction by service of process within the State" or voluntarily appear.[40] According to the Court in *Pennoyer*, these principles of international law were applicable in domestic American disputes, limiting the jurisdiction of the courts of the several States.[41]

Pennoyer's strict territorial view of judicial jurisdiction found wide support among 19th century American commentators.[42] It paralleled equally strict 19th century territorial limits on legislative jurisdiction.[43] Moreover, Story's conception of territorial sovereignty provided the basis for early American principles of foreign sovereign immunity.[44]

---

33. 52 U.S. at 175-76 ("[T]he international law as it existed among the States in 1790 was, that a judgment rendered in one State, assuming to bind the person of a citizen of another, was void within the foreign States, when the defendant had not been served with process or voluntarily made defence, because neither the legislative jurisdiction, nor that of courts of justice had binding force.").

34. 95 U.S. 714 (1877).

35. In stating these principles, the Court cited its earlier reliance in *D'Arcy v. Ketchum*, 52 U.S. 165, 175-76 (1850), on "international law as it existed among the states in 1790."

36. 95 U.S. at 722 (citing J. Story, *Commentaries on the Conflict of Laws* [no edition specified]; H. Wheaton, *International Law* [no edition specified]). These treatises relied, in turn, on Ulrich Huber's *De Conflictu Legum*. *See* Weinstein, *The Dutch Influence on the Conception of Judicial Jurisdiction in 19th Century America*, 38 Am. J. Comp. L. 73 (1990).

37. 95 U.S. at 722.

38. 95 U.S. at 722.

39. 95 U.S. at 727.

40. 95 U.S. at 733.

41. 95 U.S. at 722.

42. J. Story, *Commentaries on the Conflict of Laws* §539 (2d ed. 1841); H. Wheaton, *Elements of International Law* §§77, 111-14, 134-51 (8th ed. 1866); F. Wharton, *Conflict of Laws* §§646, 649, 715 (3d ed. 1905); T. Cooley, *Constitutional Limitations* 447-48 (2d ed. 1871).

43. *See infra* pp. 493-509 & 544-51.

44. *The Schooner Exchange v. McFaddon*, 11 U.S. 116 (1812); *infra* pp. 199-210.

Territorial limits on judicial jurisdiction were also relied upon by the United States in its foreign relations. During the 19th century, the United States fairly consistently opposed efforts by more established world powers to assert judicial (and legislative)[45] jurisdiction beyond their borders. The U.S. Department of State lodged numerous diplomatic protests with foreign governments, challenging assertions of judicial jurisdiction over U.S. nationals as inconsistent with international law.[46] As one U.S. diplomatic note opined, it is the "uniform declaration of writers on public law" that "in an international point of view, either the thing or the person made the subject of jurisdiction must be within the territory, for no sovereignty can extend its process beyond its own territorial limits."[47]

(2) International Shoe and "Minimum Contacts"

Pennoyer's territorial limits on judicial jurisdiction in domestic cases came under growing pressure as the industrial era progressed. Manufacturing and commerce were increasingly operated and organized in corporate forms without regard to interstate and international boundaries. States affected by foreign corporations' conduct sought to regulate those activities, often by way of judicial proceedings. Those regulatory efforts inevitably confronted *Pennoyer's* rule that a state court could exercise jurisdiction only over persons served with process within the state. The perception that state regulatory needs required less rigid limits on personal jurisdiction made change irresistible.

In 1945, after many decisions foreshadowing the change, the Supreme Court modified *Pennoyer's* territorial approach to judicial jurisdiction. *International Shoe Co. v. Washington* held that the due process clause permitted a state court to exercise personal jurisdiction over persons located outside the state:[48]

> due process requires only that in order to subject a defendant to a judgment *in personam*, if he be not present within the territory of the forum, he have certain minimum contacts with it "such that the maintenance of the suit does not offend 'traditional notions of fair play and substantial justice.'"[49]

Applying this now-classic "minimum contacts" test, the Court concluded that International Shoe, which was headquartered in Missouri, could be subjected to the jurisdiction of Washington's courts in an action to collect contributions to a state

---

45. *See also infra* pp. 493-97.

46. *Case of Lund v. Ogden*, 6 Op. Att'y Gen. 75, 76-77 (1853) (holding that exercise of judicial jurisdiction over United States resident by Texas would be "in violation of international comity and a usurpation of general sovereignty, in derogation of the rights of co-equal States"); Letters from Secretary of State Fish to General Schenck dated Nov. 8, 1873 and Mar. 12, 1875, reprinted in *Foreign Relations to the United States* 490 (1874) and *id.* at 592, 633 (1875) (protesting that exercise of judicial jurisdiction by British courts over civil disputes arising on high seas between sailors on United States vessels violates "rules of comity between nations and the principles of international law").

47. Letter Concerning the Schooner Daylight from Secretary of State Frelinghuysen to Mr. Morgan, dated May 17, 1884, reprinted in *Foreign Relations of the United States* 358 (1884).

48. 326 U.S. 310 (1945).

49. 326 U.S. at 316.

unemployment compensation fund. The Court relied on the fact that International Shoe had maintained a dozen commissioned salesmen in Washington to solicit orders for its products. This ongoing solicitation satisfied the "minimum contacts" test, notwithstanding the fact that International Shoe had no office in Washington and had entered into no contracts within the state.[50]

International Shoe did not entirely abandon `Pennoyer's* emphasis on territorial sovereignty. The Court cited *Pennoyer* with approval for the proposition that the due process clause "does not contemplate that a state may make binding a judgment *in personam* against an individual or corporate defendant with which the state has no contacts, ties, or relations."[51] Rather, *International Shoe's* minimum contacts test modified the content of the territoriality doctrine: state sovereignty continued to limit judicial jurisdiction, but its constraints were less restrictive—*Pennoyer's* strict territorial limits were replaced by a requirement of some minimum connection with the forum's territory.

International Shoe remains a precedent of almost mystical import for due process analysis. Nevertheless, after the Supreme Court modified *Pennoyer's* territoriality doctrine, it was often unclear precisely what limitations the due process clause imposed on personal jurisdiction. The Supreme Court has issued a number of decisions seeking to clarify the "minimum contacts" formula,[52] but without notable success.[53] As the Court has conceded, "few answers [to due process inquiries] will be written 'in black and white. The greys are dominant and even among them the shades are innumerable.'"[54]

(3) Hanson v. Denckla and "Purposeful Availment"

Decisions following *International Shoe* confirmed that *Pennoyer's* territorial restrictions had been significantly relaxed. In 1957, *McGee v. International Life Ins. Co.*[55] held that nothing in the Constitution precluded a California court from exercising personal jurisdiction over a Texas insurance company based solely upon its use of interstate mail to sell a single insurance policy to a California resident. The

---

50. 326 U.S. at 321-22.

51. 326 U.S. at 319.

52. *E.g., Burnham v. Superior Court*, 495 U.S. 604 (1990); *Asahi Metal Indus. v. Superior Court*, 480 U.S. 102 (1987); *Phillips Petroleum Co. v. Shutts*, 472 U.S. 797 (1985); *Burger King Corp. v. Rudzewicz*, 471 U.S. 462 (1985); *Helicopteros Nacionales de Colombia, SA v. Hall*, 466 U.S. 408 (1984); *Calder v. Jones*, 465 U.S. 783 (1984); *Keeton v. Hustler Magazine*, 465 U.S. 770 (1984); *Insurance Corp. of Ireland v. Compagnie des Bauxites de Guinee*, 456 U.S. 694 (1982); *Rush v. Savchuk*, 444 U.S. 320 (1980); *World-Wide Volkswagen Corp. v. Woodson*, 444 U.S. 286 (1980); *Kulko v. Superior Court*, 436 U.S. 84 (1978).

53. A number of authorities have criticized the Court's jurisdictional analysis on the grounds that it provides inadequate guidance for courts, litigants, and businesses. *E.g.,* Abrams, *Power, Convenience and the Elimination of Personal Jurisdiction in the Federal Courts*, 58 Ind. L.J. 1 (1982); Weintraub, *An Objective Basis for Rejecting Transient Jurisdiction*, 22 Rutgers L.J. 611, 625 (1991) ("Jurisdictional doctrine is in chaos."); *Lakeside Bridge & Steel Co. v. Mountain State Constr. Co.*, 445 U.S. 907 (1980) (White, J., dissenting from denial of certiorari).

54. *Kulko v. Superior Court*, 436 U.S. 84, 92 (1978).

55. 355 U.S. 220 (1957).

Court cited technological changes in transportation and communications, and an increasingly national economy, as justifications for diminished due process restrictions on judicial jurisdiction:

> Today many commercial transactions touch two or more States and may involve parties separated by the full continent. With this increasing nationalization of commerce has come a great increase in the amount of business conducted by mail across state lines. At the same time modern transportation and communication have made it much less burdensome for a party sued to defend himself in a State where he engages in economic activity.[56]

Notwithstanding these developments, the Court soon made it clear that the due process clause continued to impose significant limits on assertions of personal jurisdiction. In *Hanson v. Denckla*,[57] the Court emphasized that, no matter how trivial the burden upon a party of defending in a particular forum, the due process clause required a showing that the defendant had deliberately engaged in activities that created contacts with the forum. Adopting what would become another touchstone of due process analysis, the Court declared that the Constitution requires "some act by which the defendant *purposefully avails* itself of the privilege of conducting activities within the forum state, thus invoking the benefits and protections of its laws."[58]

Beginning in the 1970s, the Court's due process decisions increasingly came to reflect an on-going and profound disagreement between various Justices. Some members of the Court (notably Justices Brennan and Marshall) attached increasingly little importance to notions of territorial sovereignty, and emphasized a general "reasonableness" or "fairness" analysis; other members of the Court (notably Justices O'Connor and Scalia) continued to stress the role of state territorial sovereignty in due process analysis.

Opinions for the Court, written by different Justices, came to reflect this tension. Thus, in *Hanson v. Denkla*, the Court declared that restrictions on state jurisdiction "are more than a guarantee of immunity from inconvenient or distant litigation. They are a consequence of territorial limitations on the power of the respective States."[59] Yet, in *Shaffer v. Heitner*, the Court characterized *Hanson* as "simply mak[ing] the point that the States are defined by their geographical territory," and went on to emphasize the primacy of reasonableness.[60] Moreover, the Court was increasingly unable to produce majority opinions, with important cases decided by sharply-divided pluralities.[61]

---

56. 355 U.S. at 222-23.

57. 357 U.S. 235 (1958).

58. 357 U.S. at 253 (emphasis added).

59. 357 U.S. at 257.

60. 433 U.S. 186, 204 n.20 (1977). *See also* the Court's contradicting comments about territorial sovereignty in *World-Wide Volkswagen Corp. v. Woodson*, 444 U.S. 286 (1980), and *Insurance Corp. of Ireland v. Compagnie des Bauxites des Guinee*, 456 U.S. 694, 702 n.10 (1982), discussed at *infra* p. 88.

61. *E.g., Asahi Metal Indus. v. Superior Court*, 480 U.S. 102 (1987); *Burnham v. Superior Court*, 495 U.S. 604 (1990).

(4) World-Wide Volkswagen and Contemporary Due Process Analysis: "Purposeful Contacts" and "Reasonableness"

Contemporary due process analysis has been significantly influenced by the Supreme Court's 1980 decision in *World-Wide Volkswagen Corp. v. Woodson*.[62] There, the due process clause was held to preclude an Oklahoma court's exercise of personal jurisdiction over a regional automobile distributor. Reaffirming the "purposeful availment" requirement, the Court remarked that "'foreseeability' alone has never been a sufficient benchmark for personal jurisdiction under the Due Process Clause."[63] The Court went on to articulate a two-prong due process analysis. First, the Court required purposefully-created minimum contacts between the defendant and the forum[64] — perhaps most accurately characterized as "purposeful contacts." Second, the Court held that jurisdiction could not be exercised unless doing so would be "reasonable."[65]

Five years later, in *Burger King Corp. v. Rudzewicz*,[66] the Court revisited this two-prong analysis. It held that the due process clause permitted Burger King, a franchisor based in Florida, to proceed with a Florida suit against a franchisee based in Michigan. Justice Brennan's opinion in *Burger King* reflected the on-going tension between various members of the Court, treating "reasonableness" as the predominant aspect of due process analysis.[67]

(5) The Reemergence of Territorial Sovereignty: Asahi and Burnham

The Supreme Court's sustained departure from *Pennoyer*'s strict doctrine of territorial sovereignty towards Justice Brennan's reasonableness analysis came to a decisive halt during the 1980s. In *Asahi Metal Indus. Co. v. Superior Court*,[68] a plurality of the Court firmly rejected a pure reasonableness approach to personal jurisdiction, and emphasized the continuing importance of the "purposeful availment" requirement. Justice O'Connor's plurality opinion held that a foreign component manufacturer lacked "minimum contacts" with California because its "awareness that the stream of commerce may or will sweep the product into the forum State does not convert the mere act of placing the product into the stream into an act purposefully

---

62. 444 U.S. 286 (1980) (excerpted below at *infra* pp. 82-85).
63. 444 U.S. at 295.
64. 444 U.S. at 299.
65. 444 U.S. at 292.
66. 471 U.S. 462 (1985).
67. Justice Brennan's opinion in *Burger King* purported to apply the two-prong test set forth in *World-Wide Volkswagen*. In fact, his opinion reflected an increasing focus on "reasonableness" considerations. Thus, it defined "purposeful availment" as requiring relatively few contacts with the forum state. 471 U.S. at 473-75. Justice Brennan also commented that considerations of convenience and "fairness" sometimes serve to establish the reasonableness of jurisdiction upon a "lesser showing of minimum contacts than would otherwise be required." 471 U.S. at 477.
68. 480 U.S. 102 (1987).

directed toward the forum state."[69] Separately, Justice O'Connor denied jurisdiction on reasonableness grounds under *World-Wide Volkswagen*'s two-prong analysis.[70]

Most recently, *Burnham v. Superior Court* unanimously upheld a California court's assertion of jurisdiction based solely on tag service on the defendant while he was present within California.[71] Justice Scalia's plurality opinion held that the mere fact of tag service within the forum's territory satisfied the due process clause — and that considerations of reasonableness were irrelevant.[72] "Jurisdiction based on physical presence alone constitutes due process," without regard to questions of "fairness" or "reasonableness."[73]

As in *Asahi*, Justice Brennan concurred. His plurality opinion acknowledged that the due process clause "generally permits a state court to exercise jurisdiction over a defendant if he is served while voluntarily present in the forum State."[74] But, in contrast to Justice Scalia, Justice Brennan demanded that "*every* assertion of state-court jurisdiction ... must comport with contemporary notions of due process," which incorporated principles of reasonableness and fairness.[75]

c. *"General" and "Specific" Jurisdiction*

The U.S. Supreme Court's due process analysis has increasingly come to distinguish between two types of personal jurisdiction: (1) "general" jurisdiction, and (2) "limited" or "specific" jurisdiction.[76] These categories of personal jurisdiction differ both in the showings required to establish jurisdiction and the consequences of concluding that jurisdiction may be exercised. They are vital to contemporary due process analysis.

"General jurisdiction" permits a court to adjudicate *any* claim against a defendant.[77] As the following materials illustrate, the due process clause typically allows exercise of general jurisdiction over a defendant that has any of several relatively close and enduring relationships with the forum — such as nationality, domicile, or incorporation. Once one of these showings has been made, a U.S. court is constitutionally permitted to assert general jurisdiction over the defendant with respect to *all*

---

69. 480 U.S. at 112.

70. 480 U.S. at 113-16. Seven Justices joined Justice O'Connor's "reasonableness" analysis. Justice Brennan concurred in the judgment, on the grounds that the exercise of jurisdiction would be unreasonable. He wrote separately, however, to reject Justice O'Connor's purposeful availment analysis: "A defendant who has placed goods in the stream of commerce benefits economically from the retail sale of the final product in the forum state." 480 U.S. at 117.

71. 495 U.S. 604 (1990).

72. 495 U.S. at 619.

73. 495 U.S. at 610 & 619.

74. 495 U.S. at 628-29.

75. 495 U.S. at 632.

76. *See Helicopteros Nacionales de Colombia, SA v. Hall*, 466 U.S. 408, 414 (1984); *Calder v. Jones*, 465 U.S. 783, 786 (1984). The terms were first coined by Professors von Mehren and Trautman in von Mehren & Trautman, *Jurisdiction to Adjudicate: A Suggested Analysis*, 79 Harv. L. Rev. 1121, 1136-64 (1966).

77. *See infra* pp. 95-123. Compare Twitchell, *The Myth of General Jurisdiction*, 101 Harv. L. Rev. 610 (1988).

claims arising from *any* of the defendant's activities, including activities entirely unrelated to the forum state.[78]

In contrast, "specific jurisdiction" permits only the adjudication of claims that are related to or arise out of a defendant's contacts with the forum state.[79] A defendant whose only contacts with the forum were, for example, the advertising and sale of product X within the forum, might be subject to the personal jurisdiction of the forum's courts with respect to claims arising out of these sales of product X. But if only specific jurisdiction over the defendant existed, the defendant would not be subject to the personal jurisdiction of the forum's courts with respect to claims based on its other activities outside the forum (such as sales of product Y outside the forum).

Specific jurisdiction may be exercised when the activities of a defendant that relate to the plaintiff's suit have sufficient purposeful contacts with the forum to satisfy the due process standard articulated in *World-Wide Volkswagen* and subsequent cases.[80] The level of contacts required to sustain specific jurisdiction is substantially less than that required for general jurisdiction.[81]

2. Selected Materials on the Foundations of Personal Jurisdiction

The following materials introduce the fundamental principles of personal jurisdiction in the United States. *Pennoyer v. Neff*, §47 of the *Restatement (First) Conflict of Laws*, and *World-Wide Volkswagen* document the historical development of due process analysis. Section 421 of the *Restatement (Third) Foreign Relations Law* purports to state, from a U.S. perspective, the limitations that contemporary international law imposes upon judicial jurisdiction. Finally, Article 14 of the French Civil Code, Articles 636 and 638 of the Belgian Judicial Code, and the Brussels Convention, reprinted as Appendix D, illustrate foreign approaches to personal jurisdiction.

PENNOYER v. NEFF

95 U.S. 714 (1878)

MR. JUSTICE FIELD. [The case involved a dispute over the ownership of real estate located in Oregon. The outcome of the case turned upon the validity of the defendant's claim to the property. That claim was based upon a sheriff's sale of the property, following execution of a default judgment by an Oregon court against the

---

78. *See infra* p. 95.

79. *Helicopteros Nacionales de Colombia, SA v. Hall*, 466 U.S. 408, 414-15 & nn. 8 & 10 (1984); von Mehren & Trautman, *Jurisdiction to Adjudicate: A Suggested Analysis*, 79 Harv. L. Rev. 1121, 1144-64 (1966).

80. *See infra* pp. 114-15, 124 & 149-50.

81. *E.g., In re Damodar Bulk Carriers, Ltd.*, 903 F.2d 675 (9th Cir. 1990); *Donatelli v. National Hockey League*, 893 F.2d 459, 462-63 (1st Cir. 1990); *Brand v. Menlove Dodge*, 796 F.2d 1070 (9th Cir. 1986); *infra* pp. 103-04.

plaintiff. At the time of the proceedings leading to the default judgment, the plaintiff resided outside of Oregon; he was not personally served and did not appear or participate in the proceedings. Constructive service was purportedly made upon him under Oregon law by publication. At issue in the Supreme Court was the validity of that service, and hence of the default judgment against the plaintiff.]

[An Oregon statutory provision] declares that no natural person is subject to the jurisdiction of a court of the State, "unless he appear in the court, or be found within the State, or be a resident thereof, or have property therein; and, in the last case, only to the extent of such property at the time the jurisdiction attached." Construing this latter provision to mean, that, in an action for money or damages where a defendant does not appear in the court, and is not found within the State, and is not a resident thereof, but has property therein, the jurisdiction of the court extends only over such property, the declaration expresses a principle of general, if not universal, law. The authority of every tribunal is necessarily restricted by the territorial limits of the State in which it is established. Any attempt to exercise authority beyond those limits would be deemed in every other forum, as has been said by this court, an illegitimate assumption of power, and be resisted as mere abuse. *D'Arcy v. Ketchum*, 52 U.S. 165 (1850). ...

[It] is insisted upon here, that the [default] judgment in the State court against the plaintiff was void for want of personal service of process on him, or of his appearance in the action in which it was rendered. ... If these positions are sound, the ruling of the Circuit Court as to the invalidity of that judgment must be sustained. ... And that they are sound would seem to follow from two well-established principles of public law respecting the jurisdiction of an independent State over persons and property. The several States of the Union are not, it is true, in every respect independent, many of the right and powers which originally belonged to them being now vested in the government created by the Constitution. But, except as restrained and limited by that instrument, they possess and exercise the authority of independent States, and the principles of public law to which we have referred are applicable to them. One of these principles is, that every State possesses exclusive jurisdiction and sovereignty over persons and property within its territory. As a consequence, every State has the power to determine for itself the civil status and capacities of its inhabitants; to prescribe the subjects upon which they may contract, the forms and solemnities with which their contracts shall be executed, the rights and obligations arising from them, and the mode in which their validity shall be determined and their obligations enforced; and also the regulate the manner and conditions upon which property situated within such territory, both personal and real, may be acquired, enjoyed, and transferred. The other principle of public law referred to follows from the one mentioned; that is, that no State can exercise direct jurisdiction and authority over persons or property without its territory. [Joseph] Story, *Conflict of Laws*, c. 2; [Henry] Wheaton, *International Law*, pt. 2, c. 2. The several States are of equal dignity and authority, and the independence of one implies the exclusion of power from all others. And so it is laid down by jurists, as an elementary principle, that the laws of one State have no operation outside of its territory, except so far as is allowed by comity; and that no tribunal established by it can extend its process beyond that territory so as to subject either persons or property to its decisions. "Any exertion of authority of this sort beyond this limit," says Story, "is a mere nullity, and incapable of binding such persons or property in any other tribunals." [Joseph] Story, *Conflict of Laws*, §539.

But as contracts made in one State may be enforceable only in another State, and property may be held by non-residents, the exercise of the jurisdiction which every State is admitted to possess over persons and property within its own territory will often affect persons and property without it. To any influence exerted in this way by a State affecting persons resident or property situated elsewhere, no objection can be justly taken; whilst any direct exertion of authority upon them, in an attempt to give ex-territorial operation to its laws, or to enforce an ex-territorial jurisdiction by its tribunals, would be deemed an encroachment upon the independence of the State in which the persons are domiciled or the property is situated, and be resisted as usurpation.

Thus the State, through its tribunals, may compel persons domiciled within its limits to execute, in pursuance of their contracts respecting property elsewhere situated, instruments in such form and with such solemnities as to transfer the title, so far as such formalities can be complied with; and the exercise of this jurisdiction in no manner interferes with the supreme control over the property by the State within which it is situated. So the State, through its tribunals, may subject property situated within its limits owned by non-residents to the payment of the demand of its own citizens against them; and the exercise of this jurisdiction in no respect infringes upon the sovereignty of the State where the owners are domiciled. ...

These views are not new. They have been frequently expressed, with more or less distinctness, in opinions of eminent judges, and have been carried into adjudications in numerous cases. Thus, in *Picquet v. Swan*, 5 Mass. 35, Mr. Justice Story said:

> Where a party is within a territory, he may justly be subjected to its process, and bound personally by the judgment pronounced on such process against him. Where he is not within such territory, and is not personally subject to its laws, if, on account of his supposed or actual property being within the territory, process by the local laws may, by attachment, go to compel his appearance, and for his default to appear judgment may be pronounced against him, such a judgment must, upon general principles, be deemed only to bind him to the extent of such property, and cannot have the effect of a conclusive judgment in personam, for the plain reason, that, except so far as the property is concerned, it is a judgment coram non judice. ...

[This] is the only doctrine consistent with proper protection to citizens of other States. If, without personal service, judgments in personam, obtained ex parte against non-residents and absent parties, upon mere publication of process, which, in the great majority of cases, would never be seen by the parties interested, could be upheld and enforced, they would be the constant instruments of fraud and oppression. Judgments for all sorts of claims upon contracts and for torts, real or pretended, would be thus obtained, under which property would be seized, when the evidence of the transactions upon which they were founded, if they ever had any existence, had perished. ... [Although substituted or constructive service may sometimes be effective,] where the entire object of the action is to determine the personal rights and obligations of the defendants, that is, where the suit is merely in personam, constructive service in this form upon a non-resident is ineffectual for any purpose. Process from the tribunals of one State cannot run into another State, and summon parties there domiciled to leave its territory and respond to proceedings against them. ...

Since the adoption of the Fourteenth Amendment to the Federal Constitution, the validity of such judgments may be directly questioned, and their enforcement in the State resisted, on the ground that proceedings in a court of justice to determine the personal rights and obligations of parties over whom that court has no jurisdiction do not constitute due process of law. Whatever difficulty may be experienced in giving to those terms a definition which will embrace every permissible exertion of power affecting private rights, and exclude such as is forbidden, there can be no doubt of their meaning when applied to judicial proceedings. They then mean a course of legal proceedings according to those rules and principles which have been established in our systems of jurisprudence for the protection and enforcement of private rights. To give such proceedings any validity, there must be a tribunal competent by its constitution — that is, by the law of its creation — to pass upon the subject-matter of the suit; and, if that involves merely a determination of the personal liability of the defendant, he must be brought within its jurisdiction by service of process within the State, or his voluntary appearance. ...

To prevent any misapplication of the views expressed in this opinion, it is proper to observe that we do not mean to assert, by any thing we have said, that a State may not authorize proceedings to determine the status of one of its citizens towards a non-resident, which would be binding within the State, though made without service of process or personal notice to the non-resident. The jurisdiction which every State possesses to determine the civil status and capacities of all its inhabitants involves authority to prescribe the conditions on which proceedings affecting them may be commenced and carried on within its territory. ... Neither do we mean to assert that a State may not require a non-resident entering into a partnership or association within its limits, or making contracts enforceable there, to appoint an agent or representative in the State to receive service of process and notice in legal proceedings instituted with respect to such partnership, association, or contracts, or to designate a place where such service may be made and notice given, and provide, upon their failure, to make such appointment or to designate such place that service may be made upon a public officer designated for that purpose, or in some other prescribed way, and that judgments rendered upon such service may not be binding upon the non-residents both within and without the State. ...

RESTATEMENT (FIRST) CONFLICT OF LAWS (1934)

§47

§47. (1) A state has jurisdiction over a person: (a) if he is within the territory of the state, (b) if he is domiciled in the state although not present there, (c) if he has consented or subjected himself to the exercise of jurisdiction over him either before or after the exercise of jurisdiction.

(2) A nation recognized as such by the law of nations, has jurisdiction over its nationals although not present within the territorial limits of the nation.

WORLD-WIDE VOLKSWAGEN CORP. v. WOODSON

444 U.S. 286 (1980)

JUSTICE WHITE. Respondents Harry and Kay Robinson purchased a new Audi automobile from petitioner Seaway Volkswagen, Inc. ("Seaway"), in Massena, N.Y., in 1976. The following year the Robinson family, who resided in New York, left that State for a new home in Arizona. As they passed through the State of Oklahoma, another car struck their Audi in the rear, causing a fire which severely burned Kay Robinson and her two children. The Robinsons subsequently brought a products-liability action in Oklahoma District Court, claiming that their injuries resulted from defective design of the Audi's gas tank. They joined as defendants the automobile's ... regional distributor, petitioner World-Wide Corp. ("World-Wide"); and its retail dealer, petitioner Seaway. ... World-Wide is incorporated and has its business office in New York. It distributes vehicles, parts, and accessories to retail dealers in New York, New Jersey, and Connecticut. Seaway, one of these retail dealers, is incorporated and has its place of business in New York. Insofar as the record reveals, Seaway and World-Wide are fully independent corporations whose relations with each other and with [the automobile's manufacturers] are contractual only. Respondents adduced no evidence that either World-Wide or Seaway does any business in Oklahoma, ships or sells any products to or in that State, has an agent to receive process there, or purchases advertisements in any media calculated to reach Oklahoma. ... Indeed there was no showing that any automobile sold by World-Wide or Seaway has ever entered Oklahoma with the single exception of the vehicle involved in the present case. The Supreme Court of Oklahoma rejected challenges by World-Wide and Seaway to the personal jurisdiction of the Oklahoma courts.

As has long been settled, and as we reaffirm today, a state court may exercise personal jurisdiction over a nonresident defendant only so long as there exist "minimum contacts" between the defendant and the forum State. The concept of minimum contacts, in turn, can be seen to perform two related, but distinguishable, functions. It protects the defendant against the burdens of litigating in a distant or inconvenient forum. And it acts to ensure that the States, through their Courts, do not reach out beyond the limits imposed on them by their status as coequal sovereigns in a federal system.

The protection against inconvenient litigation is typically described in terms of "reasonableness" or "fairness." We have said that the defendant's contacts with the forum State must be such that maintenance of the suit "does not offend 'traditional notions of fair play and substantial justice.'" ... Implicit in this emphasis on reasonableness is the understanding that the burden on the defendant, while always a primary concern, will in an appropriate case be considered in light of other relevant factors, including the forum State's interest in adjudicating the dispute; the plaintiff's interest in obtaining convenient and effective relief, at least when that interest is not adequately protected by the plaintiff's power to choose the forum; the interstate judicial system's interest in obtaining the most efficient resolution of controversies; and the shared interest of the several States in furthering fundamental substantive social policies.

The limits imposed on state jurisdiction by the Due Process Clause, in its role as a guarantor against inconvenient litigation, have been substantially relaxed over the years. ... Nevertheless, we have never accepted the proposition that state lines are irrelevant for jurisdictional purposes, nor could we, and remain faithful to the principles of interstate federalism embodied in the Constitution. The economic interdependence of the States was foreseen and desired by the Framers. In the Commerce Clause, they provided that the Nation was to be a common market, a "free trade unit" in which the States are debarred from acting as separable economic entities. But the Framers also intended that the States retain many essential attributes of sovereignty, including, in particular, the sovereign power to try causes in their courts. The sovereignty of each State, in turn, implied a limitation on the sovereignty of all of its sister States — a limitation express or implicit in both the original scheme of the Constitution and the Fourteenth Amendment.

Hence, even while abandoning the shibboleth that "[t]he authority of every tribunal is necessarily restricted by the territorial limits of the State in which it is established," *Pennoyer v. Neff*, we emphasized that the reasonableness of asserting jurisdiction over the defendant must be assessed "in the context of our federal system of government," *International Shoe*, and stressed that the Due Process Clause ensures not only fairness, but also the "orderly administration of the laws." ... Thus, the Due Process Clause "does not contemplate that a state may make binding a judgment *in personam* against an individual or corporate defendant with which the state has no contacts, ties, or relations." Even if the defendant would suffer minimal or no inconvenience from being forced to litigate before the tribunals of another State; even if the forum State has a strong interest in applying its law to the controversy; even if the forum State is the most convenient location for litigation, the Due Process Clause, acting as an instrument of interstate federalism, may sometimes act to divest the State of its power to render a valid judgment.

Applying these principles to the case at hand, we find ... a total absence of those affiliating circumstances that are a necessary predicate to any exercise of state-court jurisdiction. Petitioners carry on no activity whatsoever in Oklahoma. They close no sales and perform no services there. They avail themselves of none of the privileges and benefits of Oklahoma law. They solicit no business there either through salespersons or through advertising reasonably calculated to reach the State. Nor does the record show that they regularly sell cars at wholesale or retail to Oklahoma customers or residents or that they indirectly, through others, serve or seek to serve the Oklahoma market. In short, respondents seek to base jurisdiction on one, isolated occurrence and whatever inferences can be drawn therefrom: the fortuitous circumstance that a single Audi automobile, sold in New York to New York residents, happened to suffer an accident while passing through Oklahoma.

It is argued, however, that because an automobile is mobile by its very design and purpose it was "foreseeable" that the Robinsons' Audi would cause injury in Oklahoma. Yet "foreseeability" alone has never been a sufficient benchmark for personal jurisdiction under the Due Process Clause. ... If foreseeability were the criterion, ... [e]very seller of chattels would in effect appoint the chattel his agent for service of process. His amenability to suit would travel with the chattel. ...

This is not to say, of course, that foreseeability is wholly irrelevant. But the foreseeability that is critical to due process analysis is not the mere likelihood that a product will find its way into the forum State. Rather, it is that the defendant's conduct and connection with the forum State are such that he should reasonably anticipate being haled into court there. The Due Process Clause, by ensuring the "orderly administration of the laws," *International Shoe Co.*, gives a degree of predictability to the legal system that allows potential defendants to structure their primary conduct with some minimum assurance as to where that conduct will and will not render them liable to suit.

When a corporation "purposefully avails itself of the privilege of conducting activities within the forum State," *Hanson v. Denckla*, it has clear notice that it is subject to suit there, and can act to alleviate the risk of burdensome litigation by procuring insurance, passing the expected costs on to customers, or, if the risks are too great, severing its connection with the State. Hence if the sale of a product of a manufacturer or distributor such as Audi or Volkswagen is not simply an isolated occurrence, but arises from the efforts of the manufacturer or distributor to serve, directly or indirectly, the market for its product in other States, it is not unreasonable to subject it to suit in one of those States if its allegedly defective merchandise has there been the source of injury to its owner or to others. The forum State does not exceed its power under the Due Process Clause if it asserts personal jurisdiction over a corporation that delivers its products into the stream of commerce with the expectation that they will be purchased by consumers in the forum State. *Cf. Gray v. American Radiator & Standard Sanitary Corp.*, 176 N.E.2d 761 (1961).

But there is no such or similar basis for Oklahoma jurisdiction over World-Wide or Seaway in this case. Seaway's sales are made in Massena, N.Y. World-Wide's market, although substantially larger, is limited to dealers in New York, New Jersey, and Connecticut. There is no evidence of record that any automobiles distributed by World-Wide are sold to retail customers outside this tristate area. It is foreseeable that the purchasers of automobiles sold by World-Wide and Seaway may take them to Oklahoma. But the mere "unilateral activity of those who claim some relationship with a nonresident defendant cannot satisfy the requirement of contact with the forum State." Because we find that petitioners have no "contacts, ties, or relations" with the State of Oklahoma, *International Shoe Co.*, the judgment of the Supreme Court of Oklahoma is reversed.

RESTATEMENT (THIRD) FOREIGN RELATIONS LAW OF THE UNITED STATES §421 (1987)

§421.(1) A state may exercise jurisdiction through its courts to adjudicate with respect to a person or thing if the relationship of the state to the person or thing is such as to make the exercise of jurisdiction reasonable.

(2) In general, a state's exercise of jurisdiction to adjudicate with respect to a person or thing is reasonable if, at the time jurisdiction is asserted:

(a) the person or thing is present in the territory of the state, other than transitorily;

(b) the person, if a natural person, is domiciled in the state;

(c) the person, if a natural person, is resident in the state;

(d) the person, if a natural person, is a national of the state;

(e) the person, if a corporation or comparable juridical person, is organized pursuant to the law of the state;

(f) a ship, aircraft or other vehicle to which the adjudication relates is registered under the laws of the state;

(g) the person, whether natural or juridical, has consented to the exercise of jurisdiction;

(h) the person, whether natural or juridical, regularly carries on business in the state;

(i) the person, whether natural or juridical, had carried on activity in the state, but only in respect of such activity;

(j) the person, whether natural or juridical, had carried on outside the state an activity having a substantial, direct, and foreseeable effect within the state, but only in respect of such activity; or

(k) the thing that is the subject of adjudication is owned, possessed, or used in the state, but only in respect of a claim reasonably connected with that thing.

(3) A defense of lack of jurisdiction is generally waived by any appearance by or on behalf of a person or thing (whether as plaintiff, defendant, or third party), if the appearance is for a purpose that does not include a challenge to the exercise of jurisdiction.

FRENCH CIVIL CODE ARTICLE 14

14. An alien, even not residing in France, may be summoned before the French courts for the fulfilment of obligations contracted by him in France toward a French person; he may be brought before the French courts for obligations contracted by him in a foreign country toward French persons.

BELGIAN JUDICIAL CODE ARTICLES 636 & 638

636. In cases not provided for in Article 635, a foreigner may refuse the jurisdiction of the Belgian courts, if the same right exists for a Belgian in the country of the foreigner. However, if the foreigner fails to do so in its first submissions, the court shall retain the action and rule on the merits. Reciprocity is established either by treaties between the two countries, or by the presentation of laws or other legal acts, which would prove its existence. ...

638. If the grounds for jurisdiction indicated in this title are insufficient to determine the competence of the Belgian courts regarding foreigners, the plaintiff may bring the action before the judge of the place where the plaintiff has its registered address or where he has his residence.

CONVENTION ON JURISDICTION AND ENFORCEMENT OF JUDGMENTS IN CIVIL AND COMMERCIAL MATTERS ("BRUSSELS CONVENTION")

O.J. Eur. Comm. (No. L 304 77)
[reprinted in Appendix D]

Notes on Pennoyer, World-Wide Volkswagen, §421, and Selected Foreign Materials

1. *Lack of textual basis for territorial limits on judicial jurisdiction.* The due process clause of the fourteenth amendment provides: "nor shall any State deprive any person of life, liberty, or property, without due process of law." That provision does not, as *Pennoyer* appeared to acknowledge, contain express limitations on the judicial jurisdiction of state courts. *See* Redish, *Due Process, Federalism, and Personal Jurisdiction: A Theoretical Evaluation*, 75 Nw. U. L. Rev. 1112, 1136-37 (1981) ("without any supporting reference to the language, policy, or history of the fourteenth amendment or to the general concept of due process, the Supreme Court has consistently appended considerations of federalism to its due process analysis of personal jurisdiction"). How does *Pennoyer* overcome this difficulty?

2. *Role of international law in* Pennoyer's *due process analysis.* In articulating what it treated as due process limits on jurisdiction, *Pennoyer* invoked principles of international "public law" applicable to independent nation states: "The several States of the Union possess and exercise the authority of independent States, and the principles of public law to which we have referred are applicable to them." The Court also relied on earlier decisions invoking "well-established rules of international law." *See D'Arcy v. Ketchum*, 52 U.S. 165 (1850); *Rose v. Himely*, 8 U.S. 241 (1808); *supra* pp. 70-73. What is the relevance of international law to the interpretation of a due process clause, particularly as applied in a purely domestic case? Was *Pennoyer* correct in analogizing Oregon-Texas relations to United States-France relations? Note in particular that both Oregon and Texas are bound by the full faith and credit clause, and subject to the plenary legislative powers of Congress, while the United States and France are not.

3. *19th century territorial limits on judicial jurisdiction.* When they looked to international law, *Pennoyer, D'Arcy,* and similar 19th century decisions perceived what the Court characterized as universal-

ly-accepted principles of territorial sovereignty. Under these rules, an attempt "to enforce an ex-territorial jurisdiction by its tribunals ... would be deemed an encroachment upon the independence of the State in which the persons are domiciled or the property is situated, and be resisted as usurpation."

Territorial sovereignty was central to defining national jurisdiction in 19th century American understandings of international law. It defined U.S. judicial jurisdiction for much of the next century. *See supra* pp. 70-73 & *infra* pp. 116-23. There was also broad consensus among American authorities that international law imposed territorial limits on the legislative jurisdiction of nations, *see infra* pp. 493-509, while the territoriality doctrine dominated 19th century American choice of law thinking, *see infra* pp. 546-52. Similarly, territorial sovereignty was central to 19th century sovereign immunity, the act of state doctrine, and recognition of foreign judgments. *See infra* pp. 199-200, 685-88 & 939-42.

4. *Rationale for territorial limits on judicial jurisdiction.* What was the rationale for 19th century territorial limits on judicial jurisdiction? *Pennoyer* relied on principles of sovereign equality and territorial sovereignty, derived from Joseph Story's *Commentaries on the Conflict of Laws.* Consider:

> The several States are of equal dignity and authority, and the independence of one implies the exclusion of power from all others. And so it is laid down by jurists, as an elementary principle, that the laws of one State have no operation outside of its own territory, except so far as it is allowed by comity; and that no tribunal established by it can extend its process beyond that territory so as to subject either persons or property to its decisions. 95 U.S. at 722.

Why does one state's assertion of judicial jurisdiction over a person in the territory of another state infringe upon the "sovereignty" of the second state? What if jurisdiction is sought to be exercised over a national of the first state? In respect of actions occurring solely within the first state?

What interests were served by *Pennoyer*'s territorial limits on judicial jurisdiction? Were these limits intended only to protect state sovereignty? Or did they also seek to protect individuals from unforeseeable, unreasonable assertions of judicial jurisdiction? Is there any support in *Pennoyer* for the latter purpose?

5. *Early erosion of territorial limits on judicial jurisdiction.* There were difficulties in maintaining a conceptually pure territoriality doctrine even in *Pennoyer.* Note the Court's efforts to explain how a court in one state may "indirectly" affect property located in another state, by means of an *in personam* judgment against the owner of the property. Note also, in the final paragraph of the Court's opinion, that the territoriality doctrine was thought to permit jurisdiction where a party consented, or could be deemed to have consented, to a state's adjudication of its rights. *See supra* pp. 81-82. In the decades following *Pennoyer,* this caveat to the territoriality doctrine provided the basis for increasingly broad assertions of jurisdiction over non-resident defendants, on the theory that their in-state conduct had constituted implied consent to personal jurisdiction. Kurland, *The Supreme Court, the Due Process and the In Personam Jurisdiction of State Courts — From Pennoyer to Denckla: A Review,* 25 U. Chi. L. Rev. 569, 577-86 (1958). Finally, as discussed below, it was generally accepted that international law permitted a state to exercise personal jurisdiction over absent nationals. *See infra* pp. 95-100.

6. *Due process analysis in* **World-Wide Volkswagen** *and* **Pennoyer.** Is the analysis in *World-Wide Volkswagen* more clearly rooted in the text of the due process clause (or other provisions of the Constitution) than that in *Pennoyer?* What is the rationale for *World-Wide Volkswagen* — international law, federalism, protection against unfairness, individual liberty, or something else?

(a) *Role of territorial sovereignty in* World-Wide Volkswagen. Does *World-Wide Volkswagen* entirely abandon *Pennoyer*'s territorial approach to issues of judicial jurisdiction? Note Justice White's discussion of principles of federalism, including his observation that: "The sovereignty of each State, in turn, implied a limitation on the sovereignty of all its sister States — a limitation express or implicit in both the original scheme of the Constitution and the Fourteenth Amendment." Is it appropriate for the Court to elevate a limitation "implicit" in the "original scheme of the Constitution" into a limitation on state court personal jurisdiction?

(b) *Importance of international law.* What is the relative importance of international law in *Pennoyer* and *World-Wide Volkswagen?* Note the emphasis on federalism principles, instead of international law, in *World-Wide Volkswagen.* Where should one look for guidance on the content of federalism principles? Is there anywhere else, except for international law, that can be consulted? What about the manner is which other federal states — like Canada, the Federal Republic of Germany, Russia, and India — deal with comparable federalism issues?

(c) *Relative significance of "territorial sovereignty" and "reasonableness."* Contemporary due process analysis has seen an ongoing debate over the relative significance of "territorial sovereignty" and "reasonableness." *See supra* pp. 74-77. *World-Wide Volkswagen* emphatically concluded that territoriality remained a critical element of due process analysis. Other Supreme Court decisions, like *Burger King Corp. v. Rudzewicz*, 471 U.S. 462 (1985), accorded greater weight to considerations of reasonableness. *See supra* p. 76. What should the respective roles of territoriality and reasonableness be?

(d) *Role of territorial sovereignty in* Compagnie des Bauxites. Consider whether *World-Wide Volkswagen*'s reliance on territorial sovereignty retains vitality after the following remarks — also by Justice White, the author of *World-Wide Volkswagen* — in *Insurance Corp. v. Compagnie des Bauxites de Guinee*, 456 U.S. 694, 702 n.10 (1982):

> It is true that we have stated that the requirement of personal jurisdiction, as applied to state courts, reflects an element of federalism and the character of state sovereignty vis-a-vis other States. ... The restriction on sovereign power described in *World-Wide Volkswagen Corp.*, however, must be seen as ultimately a function of the individual liberty interest preserved by the Due Process Clause. The clause is the only source of the personal jurisdiction requirement and the clause itself makes no mention of federalism concerns. Furthermore, if the federalism concept operated as an independent restriction on the sovereign power of the court, it would not be possible to waive the personal jurisdiction requirement: Individual actions cannot change the powers of sovereignty, although the individual can subject himself to powers from which he may otherwise be protected.

Justice Powell, concurring in the same case, said:

> Before today, of course, our cases had linked minimum contacts and fair play as *jointly* defining the 'sovereign' limits on state assertions of personal jurisdiction over unconsenting defendants. ... The court appears to abandon the rationale of these cases in a footnote. ... For the first time it defines personal jurisdiction *solely by reference to abstract notions of fair play*. *Id.* at 714 (emphasis added).

In the words of one commentator, "these passages suggest that the Court has shifted its position [on the role of territorial sovereignty in personal jurisdiction analysis], but just what its current position is remains obscure." R. Casad, *Jurisdiction in Civil Actions* §2.04[2][e][ii], at 2-61 n.177 (2d ed. 1991).

7. *Role of territorial sovereignty in international cases.* Putting aside interstate cases, what role should territorial sovereignty play in international cases? Unlike assertions of jurisdiction over U.S. citizens resident in other states, a state court's assertion of jurisdiction over a foreign defendant, who resides and conducts his affairs abroad, generally does not infringe on the sovereignty of other *U.S.* states. Assertions of judicial jurisdiction over foreign defendants can, however, implicate the sovereignty of *foreign nations. See Asahi Metal Industry Co. v. Superior Court*, 480 U.S. 102, 115 (1987) (due process requires a court to "consider the procedural and substantive policies of other nations whose interests are affected by the assertion of jurisdiction by the [U.S.] court"). What role should the sovereignty of foreign nations play in due process analysis? Is foreign sovereignty more or less important, for due process purposes, than the sovereignty of a sister state? Put more concretely, should the Court in *World-Wide Volkswagen* have treated the jurisdiction of an Oklahoma court over a New York automobile distributor differently than its jurisdiction over a Mexican automobile distributor?

8. *Restatement §421 and international law limits on judicial jurisdiction.* Section 421 of the *Third Restatement* purports to state principles of international law. Its authors characterize these as "some international rules and guidelines for the exercise of jurisdiction to adjudicate in cases having international implications, applicable to courts both in the United States and in other states." *Restatement (Third) Foreign Relations Law* at 305 (1987).

(a) *Section 421's "reasonableness requirement."* The Restatement adopts what its authors describe as a "reasonableness" principle, set forth in §421(1). Section 421(2) particularizes this "reasonableness" requirement, providing a number of circumstances in which judicial jurisdiction can ordinarily be exercised. Compare these jurisdictional bases with those in the Uniform Interstate and International Procedure Act, reproduced in Appendix B, and to those in the Brussels Convention, reproduced in Appendix D.

(b) *Sources and evidence of international law limits on judicial jurisdiction.* As discussed above, international law limits on judicial jurisdiction can arise from several sources: (a) international agreements binding on the United States; (b) customary international law; and (c) general principles of law. *See supra* pp. 17-19.

The United States is party to virtually no treaties dealing even indirectly with judicial jurisdiction. The only arguable exceptions involve specialized treaty regimes governing particular industries, such as civil air transport; some such treaties designate permissible forums for claims relating to the subject matter of the agreement, thereby affecting judicial jurisdiction. *See, e.g.*, Convention for the Unification of Certain Rules Relating to International Transportation by Air (Warsaw Convention), Art. 28, 49 Stat. 3000, T.S. No. 876.

In contrast, other countries have entered into a variety of international agreements dealing with the judicial jurisdiction. These arrangements are either bilateral or regional; there is no generalized, global treaty regime dealing with judicial jurisdiction. The leading example of a regional international agreement dealing with judicial jurisdiction is the Brussels Convention, which is discussed below. *See infra* p. 90. A leading example of a bilateral jurisdiction agreement is the Franco-Swiss Convention on Jurisdiction and Execution of Judgments of June 15, 1809; it provides that nationals of each signatory state must be sued in their own country (i.e., a French plaintiff must sue a Swiss defendant in Switzerland, not France).

(c) *Evidence of customary international law limits on judicial jurisdiction.* Customary international law also arguably limits the jurisdiction of national courts. In defining customary international law, "substantial weight is accorded to (a) judgments and opinions of international judicial and arbitral tribunals; (b) judgments and opinions of national judicial tribunals; (c) the writings of scholars; (d) pronouncements by states that undertake to state a rule of international law, when such pronouncements are not seriously challenged by other states." *Restatement (Third) Foreign Relations Law* §103(2) (1987).

Accordingly, decisions like *Pennoyer*, discussing international law limits, are potentially relevant to defining public international law. More clearly relevant are decisions by U.S. and foreign courts in cases against foreign defendants. *See Asahi Metal Indus. Co. v. Superior Court*, 480 U.S. 102 (1987); *Helicopteros Nacionales de Colombia, SA v. Hall*, 466 U.S. 408 (1984). Most clearly relevant are decisions that deal expressly with international law in cases involving foreign defendants (as to which there are few 20th century Supreme Court examples).

Finally, diplomatic protests and other governmental communications purporting to state international law positions are also relevant. Recall the diplomatic protests made by the United States during the 19th and early 20th centuries, typically invoking fairly strict versions of the territoriality doctrine. *See supra* p. 73. During this century, however, there have been few diplomatic protests concerning judicial jurisdiction. *See Restatement (Third) Foreign Relations Law* Intro. Note Chap. 2, at 304 (1987) ("The jurisdiction of courts in relation to private controversies was not an important concern of public international law. ...."). For some exceptions, *see* Note from the United States Department of State to Embassy of Greece, dated June 18, 1973, *reprinted in* Department of State, *Digest of United States Practice in International Law* 197-98 (1973); G. Hackworth, II *Digest of International Law* 172-73 (1941) (U.S. protest that Panama's exercise of judicial jurisdiction over Canal Zone residents violates U.S. sovereignty).

(d) *Does international law limit judicial jurisdiction?* The *Third Restatement's* claim that contemporary international law limits judicial jurisdiction is not universally accepted. Some authors have suggested that no mandatory limits are sufficiently widely accepted to achieve the status of international law, particularly as to litigation between private parties. Consider the following conclusions, by an eminent English commentator:

> [W]hen one examines the practice of States ... one finds that States claim jurisdiction over all sorts of cases and parties having no real connection with them and that this practice has seldom if ever given rise to diplomatic protests. ... The acid test of the limits of jurisdiction in international law is the presence or absence of diplomatic protests. Protests in civil cases are not as frequent or as well known as they are in criminal cases, but they do exist. However, when they are examined closely it will be seen that some of them are isolated protests against practices which are so general that the law must be taken to follow the general practice rather than the isolated protest. ... In practice the assumption of jurisdiction by a State does not seem to be subject to any requirement that the defendant or the facts of the case need have any connection with that State; and this practice seems to have met with acquiescence by other States. ... It is hard to resist the conclusion that ... customary international law imposes no limits on the jurisdiction of municipal courts in civil trials. Akehurst, *Jurisdiction in International Law,* 46 Brit. Y.B. Int'l L. 145, 174-77, 212-14, 226-27 (1972-73).

Is this persuasive? When long-established jurisdictional limits rest on fundamental principles of national sovereignty, is detailed evidence of state practice necessary? Note also that states generally refuse to enforce foreign judgments that were based upon assertions of judicial jurisdiction in violation of the enforcing state's views of international law. *See infra* pp. 968-74. Is this practice not more relevant than the number of diplomatic protests? The weight of authority agrees with the *Third Restatement* in supporting the existence of some international law limits on national assertions of judicial jurisdiction. *E.g.,* Born, *Reflections on Judicial Jurisdiction in International Cases,* 17 Ga. J. Int'l & Comp. L. 1, 18-20 (1987); Mann, *The Doctrine of Jurisdiction in International Law,* 111 Recueil Des Cours 1, 73-81 (1964).

(e) *Why should international law limit judicial jurisdiction?* Articulate why it is that international law would limit judicial jurisdiction. How does a state's exercise of judicial jurisdiction over an individual infringe the "sovereignty" of foreign states? Is it because jurisdiction is asserted over the national of a foreign state, because jurisdiction is asserted over an individual in respect of its conduct in a foreign state's territory, or for some other reason? Would international law prevent the foreign individual from voluntarily consenting to another state's jurisdiction? Does international law only protect the sovereignty of states, or does it also concern itself with fairness to individuals?

(f) *Does international law impose "reasonableness" limits on judicial jurisdiction?* Assuming that international law does limit assertions of judicial jurisdiction, what limits does it impose? Consider §421's "reasonableness" requirement. Does "reasonableness" provide meaningful restraints on national assertions of judicial jurisdiction? In a world of 160 independent states, with vastly differing legal, economic, and political traditions, what does "reasonableness" mean? Does it mean anything at all? What relevance do jurisdictional allocations between the United States and Canada have to those between Ethiopia and Somalia?

9. *The Brussels Convention.* The most important international agreement dealing with judicial jurisdiction is the Convention on Jurisdiction and Enforcement of Judgments in Civil and Commercial Matters, O.J. Eur. Comm. (No. L 304 77) (1978), Common Market Reporter (CCH) paras. 6003-96 (1978), also known as the Brussels Convention. The Convention is reproduced in Appendix D. As its formal title suggests, the Brussels Convention deals with both the recognition of foreign judgments and the permissible bases for judicial jurisdiction in member states of the European Union ("EU"). *See infra* pp. 949-50 for a discussion of the Convention's treatment of foreign judgments.

The Brussels Convention regulates jurisdiction in two ways. First, it prescribes the permissible bases for jurisdiction. Article 2 states the general rule that "persons domiciled in a Contracting State shall, whatever their nationality, be sued in the Courts of that State." Articles 5 and 6 of the Convention set forth additional jurisdictional bases, which may also be used against member state domiciliaries. Among other things, contract claims may be brought in "the place of performance of the obligation in question," Article 5(1); tort claims may be brought in "the place where the harmful event occurred," Article 5(3); and, if multiple defendants are involved, "where any one of them is domiciled," Article 6(1).

Second, the Brussels Convention specifically forbids the use of particular "exorbitant" jurisdictional bases against persons domiciled in a member state. Article 3 provides that French courts may not assert jurisdiction based upon Articles 14 and 15 of the French Civil Code (giving French courts jurisdiction over any case involving a French national); that German courts may not assert jurisdiction based upon Section 23 of the German Code of Civil Procedure (giving German courts jurisdiction over the owners of property located in Germany); and that Belgian courts may not assert jurisdiction based upon Article 638 of the Belgian Code of Civil Procedure (giving Belgian courts jurisdiction over suits by domiciliaries against non-domiciliaries). Compare the bases of jurisdiction that are permitted under the Brussels Convention with those that are permitted by §421 and the due process clause.

10. *Evolution of international law from territoriality to reasonableness.* Contrast the 19th century's territoriality doctrine with §421's reasonableness requirement. What explains the dramatic transformation of U.S. views regarding international law limits on judicial jurisdiction? Consider the quotation from *McGee v. International Life Insurance Co.,* excerpted at page 75 above. Are technological advances in transportation and communications a sufficient explanation for declining importance of territorial sovereignty? Consider the possible change in U.S. interests internationally between 1850 and 1950. As discussed above, 19th century American diplomats relied on territorial jurisdictional limits against more powerful, expansive European states. *See supra* pp. 72-73. After WWII, however, the United States frequently sought to extend U.S. regulatory regimes to international activities, often requiring more expansive assertions of judicial jurisdiction than were historically permitted. Compare the evolution of international law in the context of legislative jurisdiction, *see infra* pp. 493-509.

11. World-Wide Volkswagen — *"purposeful availment" and "reasonableness."* Compare the two-prong approach to judicial jurisdiction adopted in *World-Wide Volkswagen* with the generalized reasonableness requirement adopted in §421 of the *Third Restatement*. Compare it also with *Pennoyer's* focus on territorial sovereignty. Which standard is wiser?

12. *The "purposeful availment" requirement.* *World-Wide Volkswagen's* purposeful availment test is circular: the defendant must have purposefully availed himself of the forum's protections in a manner "such that he should reasonably anticipate being haled into Court there." But expectations about personal jurisdiction will inevitably be determined in significant part by the personal jurisdiction standards that are announced by the Court. Despite this ambiguity, several basic principles are clear under the "purposeful availment" test.

(a) *No requirement that defendant have been physically present in forum's territory.* In *Pennoyer*, personal jurisdiction required service of process on the defendant within the forum's territory. In contrast, contemporary due process analysis permits jurisdiction even if the defendant has never been on the forum's territory — either at the time of service or before:

> Although territorial presence frequently will enhance a potential defendant's affiliation with a State and reinforce the reasonable foreseeability of suit there, it is an inescapable fact of modern commercial life that a substantial amount of business is transacted solely by mail and wire communication across state lines, thus obviating the need for physical presence within a State in which business is conducted.

Burger King Corp. v. Rudzewicz, 471 U.S. 462, 476 (1985).

(b) *Acts outside the forum causing "effects" within the forum.* In some circumstances, the due process clause will permit jurisdiction over a foreign defendant based on the effects its conduct has had within the forum. One influential formulation of the "effects" doctrine for purposes of judicial jurisdiction is §37 of the *Restatement (Second) Conflict of Laws* (1971):

> A state has power to exercise judicial jurisdiction over an individual who causes effects in the state by an act done elsewhere with respect to any cause of action arising from these effects unless the nature of the effects and of the individual's relationship to the state make the exercise of such jurisdiction unreasonable.

Compare §37 with §421(2)(j) of the *Third Restatement* and with Article 5(3) of the Brussels Convention. Do either §37 or §421(2)(j) permit jurisdiction based simply on effects, without regard to the actor's state of mind?

(c) *"Stream of commerce" doctrine.* *World-Wide Volkswagen* appeared to endorse, albeit in dicta, the so-called "stream of commerce" doctrine:

> The forum State does not exceed its power under the Due Process Clause if it asserts personal jurisdiction over a corporation that delivers its products into the stream of commerce with the expectation that they will be purchased by consumers in the forum State.

Suppose D, a Brazilian manufacturer, sells its products to an unrelated Brazilian distribution company, with title and risk of loss passing in Brazil. The products are then distributed to wholesalers and retailers in a large number of countries (and U.S. states), who in turn sell about 100,000 of D's products each year in Iowa. D is aware that its products are sold in many countries, including the United States, but has no specific knowledge that its products are sold in Iowa; D could obtain this information with minimal effort. D encourages the Brazilian distribution company to maximize sales of its products, particularly in the United States. D has no other contacts with the United States or Iowa. After *World-Wide Volkswagen*, could an injured customer in Iowa obtain personal jurisdiction over D in Iowa's courts? What result if D does know specifically of the sales in Iowa? in the United States? Suppose D affirmatively encourages distribution there, for example, by requiring distributors to perform market research or advertising. What result?

(d) *Mere foreseeability of effects in forum does not constitute minimum contacts.* As *World-Wide Volkswagen* illustrates, the mere foreseeability that the defendant's products will have effects in the forum does not establish minimum contacts: "'foreseeability' alone has never been a sufficient benchmark for personal jurisdiction under the Due Process Clause." Rather, the defendant must "purposefully" engage in conduct that creates minimum contacts with the forum. What more than foreseeability that one's products or acts will have some consequence within the forum should the "purposeful availment" standard require? *See infra* pp. 124-43. What purposes are served by requiring "purposeful availment"? Does this safeguard foreign states' territorial sovereignty?

13. *The "reasonableness" requirement.* The second prong of *World-Wide Volkswagen*'s due process analysis requires that any assertion of personal jurisdiction be "reasonable." Deciding whether an assertion of jurisdiction is "reasonable" requires considering a number of factors, set forth above at *supra* p. 83. Compare the role of "reasonableness" in *World-Wide Volkswagen* with that in §421. Which approach is preferable?

14. *Applicability of due process clause to foreign defendants.* In *Afram Export Corp. v. Metallurgiki Halyps, SA*, 772 F.2d 1358 (7th Cir. 1985), excerpted at *infra* pp. 144-47 below, Judge Posner queried the soundness of affording foreign defendants due process protection against the exercise of U.S. personal jurisdiction but suggested that this approach is probably too "solidly entrenched" to be altered. Should foreign defendants be entitled to due process protections in the personal jurisdiction context? the same protections as U.S. defendants? Why?

(a) *Authorities applying due process clause to aliens.* A number of courts and commentators have considered whether the due process clause applies to assertions of judicial jurisdiction over foreigners, concluding it should. *E.g., Asahi Metal Indus. Co. v. Superior Court*, 480 U.S. 102, 108-09, 113 n.* & 114-15 (1987) (excerpted below); *infra* pp. 137-38. As a matter of constitutional interpretation and policy, should the due process clause protect foreigners from U.S. judicial jurisdiction? *World-Wide Volkswagen* focused on safeguarding the territorial sovereignty of U.S. states from jurisdictional claims by their sister states. *See supra* pp. 83-84. What application does this rationale have in international cases? When assertions of judicial jurisdiction arguably infringe the territorial sovereignty of foreign states, is it a matter for U.S. foreign relations? not due process?

World-Wide Volkswagen also sought to protect individuals from unfair jurisdictional claims. Does this rationale not apply in cases involving foreign defendants? Note that several Supreme Court decisions have held that nonresident aliens seeking admittance to the United States may not invoke the procedural protections of the due process clause. *Shaughnessy v. United States ex rel Mezei*, 345 U.S. 206, 212 (1953); *Fong Yue Ting v. United States*, 149 U.S. 698 (1893). Nevertheless, would it not "be unfair and ironic to hale an alien into an unfamiliar United States court, forcing him to litigate according to our procedures and laws, yet deny him the protections of the Due Process Clause on the grounds that he is an alien"? Born, *Reflections on Judicial Jurisdiction in International Cases*, 17 Ga. J. Int'l & Comp. L. 1, 22 (1987). *See also Home Insurance Co. v. Dick*, 281 U.S. 397 (1930) (due process clause applies to state court's choice of law in case involving foreign party).

(b) *Verdugo-Urquidez's interpretation of fourth amendment.* *United States v. Verdugo-Urquidez*, 494 U.S. 259 (1990), held that the fourth amendment does not apply to searches and seizures conducted by U.S. government agents outside of U.S. territory of foreign nationals. The fourth amendment provides, *inter alia*, that "[t]he right of the people to be secure in their persons, houses, papers, and effects, against unreasonable searches and seizures, shall not be violated..." The Court reasoned that the fourth amendment applied only to "the people," a phrase that it interpreted to protect only U.S. citizens and residents. Does this interpretation have any implications for due process analysis? Note that the due process clause does not refer to "the people," but to "persons."

15. *Brussels Convention's treatment of non-EU domiciliaries.* Recall how the Brussels Convention protects EU domiciliaries from exorbitant assertions of personal jurisdiction by member state courts. *See supra* p. 90. How would the due process clause apply to a Texas court's assertion of jurisdiction over a French defendant if the United States followed the Brussels Convention's example in its treatment of foreign defendants? Articles 3 and 4 of the Brussels Convention expressly provide that the Convention's jurisdictional limitations protect *only* persons domiciled in a Contracting State. Persons domiciled in the United States, or other non-EU nations, are not protected, and may be subjected to any available basis of jurisdiction under local law. Indeed, Articles 4 and 31 of the Convention require the Europe-wide enforcement of judgments based upon exorbitant jurisdiction. *See infra* pp. 949-50. Is this a wise approach? Why should not the due process clause serve only to protect U.S. domiciliaries? Why should not, for example, Florida be barred from exorbitant jurisdiction over Georgia residents, but not over Russian residents? *See* Nadelmann, *Jurisdictionally Improper Fora in Treaties on Recognition of Judgments: The Common Market Draft*, 67 Colum. L. Rev. 1995, 1001 (1967) (Brussels Convention "challenge[s] the friendly relations between nations built on respect for due process of law"); von Mehren, *Recognition and Enforcement of Foreign Judgments*, 167 Recueil des Cours 13, 101 (1981) (Article 4 of Brussels Convention is the "single

most regressive step that has occurred in international recognition and enforcement practice in this century"). Are these criticisms of the Convention warranted?

16. **Jurisdiction of foreign courts.** Consider Article 14 of the French Civil Code. French courts have interpreted Article 14 as permitting jurisdiction over a foreign defendant in any case brought by a French plaintiff, including cases based on contract and tort. *See Weiss v. Soc. Atlantic Electric*, Revue Critique de Droit International Prive 113 (1971). Consider also Article 638 of the Belgian Judicial Code, allowing Belgium plaintiffs to sue foreigners in Belgium. Are the French and Belgian statutes consistent with §421 of the *Third Restatement?*

17. *Relevance of reciprocity to judicial jurisdiction in international cases.* Recall the critical influence of international law on due process analysis. Why should a U.S. court be limited to *U.S.* conceptions of judicial jurisdiction? If France believes international law permits French courts to decide all cases brought against U.S. defendants by French plaintiffs, why shouldn't U.S. courts give U.S. plaintiffs the same rights when they sue French defendants? Note that Article 636 of the Belgian Judicial Code adopts this "reciprocity" approach. Is this not sensible? Given *Pennoyer's* basic approach due process analysis, is it not also a reasonable interpretation of that clause?

18. *Relevance of defendant's foreign identity to due process analysis.* Assertions of jurisdiction over foreign defendants often raise different issues than assertions of jurisdiction over U.S. defendants from other states of the Union. The inconvenience that results from requiring a defendant (or plaintiff) to litigate in a foreign country is often greater than that resulting from requiring an American to litigate in another part of the United States. Major differences in procedural and substantive rules — such as the scope of discovery, the existence of fee-shifting provisions or contingent fee arrangements, and the right to a jury trial — are also more likely in the international context. Moreover, a state court's assertion of judicial jurisdiction over residents of another U.S. state virtually never provokes retaliatory measures; in contrast, assertions of jurisdiction over *foreign* defendants can result in retaliation from foreign nations. *See* Born, *Reflections on Judicial Jurisdiction in International Cases*, 17 Ga. J. Int'l & Comp. L. 1, 21-34 (1987).

Should these differences between assertions of jurisdiction over foreign, as compared to domestic, defendants produce any differences in due process analysis? Should due process standards make it easier or harder to obtain jurisdiction over a foreigner? *Compare Restatement (Third) Foreign Relations Law* §421 Reporters' Note 1 (1987) ("the criteria for exercise of judicial jurisdiction are basically the same for claims arising out of international transactions or involving a non-resident alien as a party" as the criteria for domestic cases) *and Deutsch v. West Coast Machinery Co.*, 497 P.2d 1311 (Wash. 1972) (rejecting argument that "a different rule must be applied when [taking jurisdiction] involves the manufacturer in a foreign country") *with Asahi Metal Indus. Ltd. v. Superior Court*, 480 U.S. 102 (1987) ("Great care and reserve should be exercised when extending our notions of personal jurisdiction into the international field."). Which of these various approaches is most sensible?

19. *Relationship between judicial jurisdiction and enforcement of judgments.* Jurisdictional disputes usually arise at the *outset* of litigation, as in *World-Wide Volkswagen*, when one party resists a court's purported assertion of jurisdiction over it. In addition, however, jurisdiction can also be relevant at the *end* of litigation — as in *Pennoyer.* Even if a court asserts jurisdiction, and subsequently renders a judgment in the plaintiff's favor, the defendant may continue to resist. If the defendant has assets within the forum, then it will usually be fairly easy for the plaintiff to enforce the judgment against them. But if the defendant's assets are in another forum, jurisdiction will often be relitigated (or, in the case of a default judgment, litigated for the first time).

It is important to consider at the outset of litigation possible jurisdictional obstacles to the enforceability of any judgment that might be obtained. Foreign defendants often have only minimal assets within the forum state, and enforcement of a judgment will then require litigation in either their home jurisdiction or another foreign country. As described below, *infra* pp. 942-43, the willingness of foreign states to enforce U.S. judgments varies substantially from country to country. Even where a U.S. judgment is, in principle, enforceable, it will often be necessary to satisfy local requirements regarding the jurisdiction of the rendering court. *See infra* pp. 968-74. Counsel in international cases must consider these requirements when suing foreign parties against whom it may be necessary to seek enforcement abroad. If they do not, their clients may be left holding judgments, obtained at considerable expense, that are unenforceable.

20. *Possibility of personal jurisdiction in multiple fora.* Both due process and international law can permit more than one forum to exercise jurisdiction over a defendant in respect of the same dispute. This was true even under *Pennoyer*, where a defendant could be subject to personal jurisdiction in each forum

in which he could be served or to whose jurisdiction he had consented. It is even more likely under *World-Wide Volkswagen* and Restatement §421.

Should either the due process clause or international law seek to confine personal jurisdiction to only one forum — for example, by picking the most appropriate of several theoretically available fora in particular cases? If this is not done, won't infringements on territorial sovereignty and unfairness to individual litigants inevitably result? Consider Article 21 of the Brussels Convention, providing for stays of jurisdiction in all courts of EU member states that might otherwise have jurisdiction once an action has been filed in a forum within one EU member state. Is this a sensible approach? Should U.S. courts adopt it in international cases?

21. *Primary importance of defendant's contacts and inconvenience.* As *Pennoyer, World-Wide Volkswagen,* and §421 all reflect, due process analysis focuses on the *defendant's* contacts with the forum and the inconvenience and burden imposed on the *defendant.* The *plaintiff's* contacts with the forum are of little importance (except as one factor in "reasonableness" analysis). *See Keeton v. Hustler Magazine,* 465 U.S. 770 (1984) (holding that plaintiff's lack of contacts with forum was not a basis for denying jurisdiction under due process clause). Is this focus on the defendant appropriate? Would it not be more appropriate to look broadly to the relations of both parties, and their conduct, to the potential forum?

Several rationales are advanced for the due process clause's focus on the defendant. Some commentators invoke "the old rule of *dubrio prop reo*: the fault of the defendant has still to be proved." De Winter, *Excessive Jurisdiction in Private International Law,* 17 Int'l & Comp. L.Q. 706, 717 (1968). Others reason that:

> The defendant's jurisdictional preference rests on the advantages that a plaintiff typically enjoys in selecting among several forums and on the proposition that, other things being equal, burdens that must rest on either the challenger or the challenged are to be borne by him who seeks to change the status quo.

von Mehren, *Adjudicatory Jurisdiction: General Theories Compared and Evaluated,* 63 B.U. L. Rev. 279, 321-22 (1983). Finally, by focusing on the defendant's reasonable expectations, due process analysis seeks to provide "a degree of predictability to the legal system that allows potential defendants to structure their primary conduct with some minimum assurance as to where that conduct will and will not render them liable to suit." *World-Wide Volkswagen Corp.,* 444 U.S. at 297. Are these explanations sufficient?

B. General Jurisdiction of U.S. Courts in International Cases

As outlined above, the due process clause has been interpreted to distinguish between "general" and "specific" jurisdiction. General jurisdiction allows a forum court to adjudicate *any* claim against the defendant, regardless whether the claim has any connection to the forum.[82] Because general jurisdiction is an unusually expansive basis for judicial authority, it can only be exercised in narrow circumstances. Due process typically permits general jurisdiction over defendants only if they have significant, permanent connections with the forum. This section examines the principal bases for general jurisdiction under the due process clause: (1) nationality, domicile, or residence; (2) incorporation or registration to do business; (3) consent or waiver; (4) "continuous and systematic" business activities within the forum (also termed "presence" or "doing business"); and (5) tag service.

1. General Jurisdiction Based on Nationality, Domicile, or Residence

A natural person who is a citizen or national of a state may generally be subjected to that state's judicial jurisdiction without offending either the due process clause or international law.[83] According to §421 of the *Restatement (Third) Foreign Relations Law*: "In general, a state's exercise of jurisdiction to adjudicate with respect to a person ... is reasonable if, at the time jurisdiction is asserted, ... the person, if a natural person, is a national of the state."[84]

Nationality as a basis for personal jurisdiction under the due process clause was approved by the Supreme Court in *Blackmer v. United States. Blackmer* arose when a federal court, acting pursuant to the so-called Walsh Act,[85] ordered a U.S. citizen residing in Europe to return to the United States to give testimony in pending U.S. criminal proceedings. The Court's opinion is excerpted below.

---

82. *Helicopteros Nacionales de Colombia, SA v. Hall*, 466 U.S. 408, 414 & n.9 (1984); *Perkins v. Benguet Consol. Mining Co.*, 342 U.S. 437 (1952); Brilmayer, *How Contacts Count: Due Process Limitations on State Court Jurisdiction*, 1980 Sup. Ct. Rev. 77, 81.

83. *Restatement (Second) Conflict of Laws* §31 (1971); *Restatement (First) Conflict of Laws* §47 (1934); *Blackmer v. United States*, 284 U.S. 421 (1932). It is said that "[n]ationality was not generally recognized as a basis of judicial jurisdiction at common law." *Restatement (Second) Conflict of Laws* §31, comment d (1971). As discussed below, however, both Joseph Story's *Commentaries on the Conflict of Laws* and *Pennoyer* recognized the principle, at least to a point. Moreover, when the issue arose, U.S. courts often concluded that nationality or citizenship was an adequate jurisdictional basis. *E.g., Henderson v. Staniford*, 105 Mass. 504 (1870); *Matter of Dennick*, 36 N.Y. Supp. 518 (4th Dep't 1895). *Compare Grubel v. Nassauer*, 103 N.E. 1113 (N.Y. 1913) (refusing jurisdiction over German national because he was domiciled in New York, not Germany).

84. *Restatement (Third) Foreign Relations Law* §421(2)(d) (1987).

85. 28 U.S.C. §§1783-84. The Walsh Act authorizes U.S. court to issue and serve subpoenas on U.S. citizens, located outside the United States, in limited circumstances. *See infra* p. 866.

BLACKMER v. UNITED STATES

284 U.S. 421 (1932)

CHIEF JUSTICE HUGHES. The petitioner, Harry M. Blackmer, a citizen of the United States resident in Paris, France, was adjudged guilty of contempt of the Supreme Court of the District of Columbia for failure to respond to [two] subpoenas served upon him in France and requiring him to appear as a witness on behalf of the United States at a criminal trial in that court. ... [A] fine of $30,000 with costs was imposed in each case, to be satisfied out of the property of the petitioner which had been seized by order of the court.

The subpoenas were issued and served, and the proceedings to punish for contempt were taken, under the provisions of the Act of July 3, 1926 [now codified as 28 U.S.C. §1783, also known as the "Walsh Act."] The statute provided that whenever the attendance at the trial of a criminal action of a witness abroad, who is "a citizen of the United States or domiciled therein," is desired by the Attorney General ... the judge of the court in which the action is pending may order a subpoena to issue, to be addressed to a consul of the United States and to be served by him personally upon the witness with a tender of travelling expenses. [Failure to comply with a subpoena is punishable as contempt, by fines not to exceed $100,000.]

This statute and the proceedings against the petitioner are assailed as being repugnant to ... the due process clause of the Fifth Amendment. These contentions [include the claim that] ... the Act does not provide "a valid method of acquiring judicial jurisdiction to render personal judgment against defendant and judgment against his property." ...

While it appears that the petitioner removed his residence to France in the year 1924, it is undisputed that he was, and continued to be, a citizen of the United States. He continued to owe allegiance to the United States. By virtue of the obligations of citizenship, the United States retained its authority over him, and he was bound by its laws made applicable to him in a foreign country. Thus, although resident abroad, the petitioner remained subject to the taxing power of the United States. *Cook v. Tait*, 265 U.S. 47, 54, 56 (1924). For disobedience to its laws through conduct abroad, he was subject to punishment in the courts of the United States. *United States v. Bowman*, 260 U.S. 94, 102 (1922). With respect to such an exercise of authority, there is no question of international law,[86] but solely of the purport of the municipal law which establishes the duties of the citizen in relation to his own gov-

---

86. "The law of Nations does not prevent a State from exercising jurisdiction over its subjects travelling or residing abroad, since they remain under its personal supremacy." 1 Oppenheim, *International Law* §145, p. 281 (4th ed.); Story, *Conflict of Laws* §540, p. 755 (8th ed.); 2 *Moore's International Law Digest* 255-56; 1 Hyde, *International Law*, §240, p. 424; Borchard, *Diplomatic Protection of Citizens Abroad*, §13, pp. 21, 22.

ernment.[87] While the legislation of the Congress, unless the contrary intent appears, is construed to apply only within the territorial jurisdiction of the United States, the question of its application, so far as citizens of the United States in foreign countries are concerned, is one of construction, not of legislative power. *American Banana Co. v. United Fruit Co.*, 213 U.S. 347, 357 (1909) [excerpted below at pp. 552-55]; *United States v. Bowman*. Nor can it be doubted that the United States possesses the power inherent in sovereignty to require the return to this country of a citizen, resident elsewhere, whenever the public interest requires it, and to penalize him in case of refusal. What in England was the prerogative of the sovereign in this respect pertains under our constitutional system to the national authority which may be exercised by the Congress by virtue of the legislative power to prescribe the duties of the citizens of the United States. It is also beyond controversy that one of the duties which the citizen owes to his government is to support the administration of justice by attending its courts and giving his testimony whenever he is properly summoned. ...

In the present instance, the question concerns only the method of enforcing the obligation. The jurisdiction of the United States over its absent citizen, so far as the binding effect of its legislation is concerned, is a jurisdiction in personam, as he is personally bound to take notice of the laws that are applicable to him and to obey them. But for the exercise of judicial jurisdiction in personam, there must be due process, which requires appropriate notice of the judicial action and an opportunity to be heard. ... The question of the validity of the provision for actual service of the subpoena in a foreign country is one that arises solely between the government of the United States and the citizen. The mere giving of such a notice to the citizen in the foreign country of the requirement of his government that he shall return is in no sense an invasion of any right of the foreign government and the citizen has no standing to invoke any such supposed right. While consular privileges in foreign countries are the appropriate subjects of treaties, it does not follow that every act of a consul, as, *e.g.*, in communicating with citizens of his own country, must be predicated upon a specific provision of a treaty. The intercourse of friendly nations, permitting travel and residence of the citizens of each in the territory of the other, presupposes and facilitates such communications. ...

Notes on Blackmer v. United States

1. *Role of international law analysis in due process analysis.* Consider *Blackmer*'s reliance on principles of international law. Compare this due process analysis with that in *Pennoyer, see supra* pp. 70-73 & 78-82. Why is international law relevant to the due process clause's limits on judicial jurisdiction? In international cases, what other sources might define due process limits?

---

87. *Compare The Nereide*, 13 U.S. 388, 422, 423 (1815); *Rose v. Himely*, 8 U.S. 241, 279 (1808); *The Apollon*, 22 U.S. 362, 370 (1824); *Schibsby v. Westenholz*, L. R. 6 Q. R. 155, 161. Illustrations of acts of the Congress applicable to citizens abroad are the provisions found in the chapter of the Criminal Code relating to "Offenses against operations of government" 18 U.S.C.A. §§71-151; *United States v. Bowman*, 260 U.S. 94, 98-102 (1822) and the provisions relating to criminal correspondence with foreign governments, Act of January 30, 1799, 1 Stat. 613, 18 U.S.C. §5.

2. *Nationality principle under international law.* As *Blackmer* suggests, international law has long permitted states to exercise a measure of jurisdiction over their nationals, even when they are outside of national territory. Joseph Story recognized the nationality principle, at least to a point:

> [A]s to citizens of a country domiciled abroad, the extent of jurisdiction, which may be lawfully exercised over them *in personam*, is not so clear upon acknowledged principles. It is true, that nations generally assert a claim to regulate the rights, and duties, and obligations, and acts of their own citizens, wherever they may be domiciled. And, so far as these rights, duties, obligations, and acts afterwards come under the cognizance of the tribunals of the sovereign power of their own country, either for enforcement, or for protection, or for remedy, there may be no just ground to exclude this claim. But when such rights, duties, obligations, and acts, come under the consideration of other countries, and specially of the foreign country, where such citizens are domiciled, the duty of recognising and enforcing such a claim of sovereignty, is neither clear, nor generally admitted. J. Story, *Commentaries on the Conflict of Laws* §540 (2d ed. 1841).

International law also recognised the nationality principle as a basis for legislative jurisdiction. *See infra* pp. 506-07. What was the rationale for the nationality principle as a basis for judicial jurisdiction under international law? Does *Pennoyer*'s territoriality doctrine allow for judicial jurisdiction based on nationality? Should international law permit jurisdiction based on nationality?

3. *Rationale for general jurisdiction.* What is the rationale for *any* assertion of general jurisdiction? Why should a nation's courts ever consider claims that have nothing to do with that nation? Consider the following:

> domicile, place of incorporation, and principal place of business [are] the paradigm bases for general adjudicative jurisdiction. ... These are relationships so direct that they make fair the assertion of state adjudicative power. ... They are unique affiliations that an individual or legal entity normally will have with only one state. Brilmayer et al., *A General Look at General Jurisdiction,* 66 Tex. L. Rev. 720, 782 (1988).

> Justice requires a certain and predictable place where a person can be reached by those having claims against him. ... For an individual, the sole community where it is fair to require him to litigate any cause of action is his habitual residence; for a corporation, it is the corporate headquarters — presumably both the place of incorporation and the principal place of business, where these differ. von Mehren & Trautman, *Jurisdiction to Adjudicate: A Suggested Analysis,* 79 Harv. L. Rev. 1121, 1137, 1179 (1966).

Are these explanations persuasive? Consider the two basic purposes of limits on judicial jurisdiction — safeguarding territorial sovereignty and preventing unfairness to individuals. Do the foregoing explanations for general jurisdiction address both purposes?

4. *Role of reasonableness in* Blackmer. What role does the "reasonableness" prong of *World-Wide Volkswagen* play in *Blackmer*? Does the opinion in *Blackmer* leave any room for even a compelling showing of unreasonableness to overcome personal jurisdiction based on nationality? Suppose that the desired testimony concerned matters occurring wholly outside the United States, that foreign law forbid the defendant's return to the United States to give testimony, and that the defendant had resided outside the United States for 30 years.

5. *Conflicts between jurisdiction based on territoriality and jurisdiction based on nationality.* Nationality-based general jurisdiction makes it inevitable that cases will arise in which two or more fora have personal jurisdiction over a defendant in respect of the same claims. For example, when a national of State A commits a tort in State B, both States A and B will generally be able to assert personal jurisdiction based on nationality and territoriality bases. Is this desirable? Should the due process clause or international law provide a basis for choosing one of several potential fora? *See supra* pp. 93-94.

6. *Definition of nationality under international law.* If judicial jurisdiction can be based on nationality, then the definition of nationality is critical. International law has been invoked to restrict exorbitant definitions of nationality. Section 211 of the Third Restatement provides: "For purposes of international law, an individual has the nationality of a state that confers it, but other states need not accept that nationality when it is not based on a genuine link between the state and the individual." *Restatement (Third) Foreign Relations Law* §211 (1987). *See Nottebohm Case (Liechtenstein v. Guatemala),* [1955] I.C.J. Rep. 4.

7. *Nationality under state and federal long-arm statutes.* State long-arm statutes do not generally contain specific authorizations for personal jurisdiction based upon nationality. Rather, most long-arm statutes refer to persons "domiciled" or "resident" in the state. *See* Uniform Interstate and International Procedure Act §1.02. As a result, nationality generally will be available as a statutory jurisdictional base only when the state long-arm statute extends expressly or impliedly to the limits of the Constitution. In practice, nationality has not frequently been invoked as a basis for jurisdiction by state courts.

Federal long-arm statutes also generally do not expressly provide for jurisdiction based on nationality. "In actions between private persons, the Congress of the United States has never authorized the federal courts to exercise jurisdiction on the basis of citizenship over citizens of the United States who are domiciled abroad." *Restatement (Second) Conflict of Laws* §31, comment b (1971). The Walsh Act, at issue in *Blackmer*, was a rare exception.

8. *U.S. judicial refusals to recognize foreign assertions of nationality.* Nationality is sometimes invoked as a basis for enforcement of a foreign court's judgment against one of its nationals. U.S. courts did not always accepted foreign claims of nationality. *E.g., Grubel v. Nassauer*, 103 N.E. 1113 (N.Y. 1913) (refusing to recognize German judgment against German national who had emigrated to the United States before the Austrian action had begun); *Smith v. Grady*, 31 N.W. 477 (Wisc. 1887) (refusing to enforce judgment against Canadian national because of his absence for prolonged period from country of nationality and acquisition of U.S. domicile).

9. *Domicile as a basis for general jurisdiction.* Closely related to nationality as a jurisdictional basis is domicile. It is now widely accepted that an individual may constitutionally be subject to general jurisdiction in the state in which he or she is domiciled. *E.g., Restatement (Second) Conflict of Laws* §29 (1971); *Restatement (Third) Foreign Relations Law* §421(2)(b) (1987).

Why is it that domicile subjects one to general jurisdiction? The leading precedent is *Milliken v. Meyer*, 311 U.S. 457 (1940), where the Court declared:

> Domicile in the state is alone sufficient to bring an absent defendant within the reach of the state's jurisdiction for purposes of a personal judgment by means of appropriate substituted service. ... As in case of the authority of the United States over its absent citizens (*Blackmer v. United States*), the authority of a state over one of its citizens is not terminated by the mere fact of his absence from the state. The state which accords him privileges and affords protection to him and his property by virtue of his domicile may also exact reciprocal duties. "Enjoyment of the privileges of residence within the state, and the attendant right to invoke the protection of its laws, are inseparable" from the various incidences of state citizenship. The responsibilities of that citizenship arise out of the relationship to the state which domicile creates. That relationship is not dissolved by mere absence from the state. The attendant duties, like the rights and privileges incident to domicile, are not dependent on continuous presence in the state. ... 311 U.S. at 462-63.

Is this persuasive? Does it explain the basis for jurisdiction based on nationality? One's domicile can be different from one's nationality. Is it desirable to have two places in which an individual is subject to general jurisdiction?

10. *Residence as a basis for general jurisdiction.* Closely related to domicile as a basis for general jurisdiction is the defendant's "residence" at the time an action is commenced. "Residence" is often defined as a place where a person has an abode in which he spends considerable periods of time. *Restatement (Second) Conflict of Laws* §30, comment a (1971). Residence within the forum can provide the basis for general jurisdiction. *Restatement (Third) Foreign Relations Law* §421(2)(c) (1987). Compare "residence" as a jurisdictional base with "nationality" and "domicile."

11. *Service in a foreign state.* In addition to challenging U.S. judicial jurisdiction, Mr. Blackmer argued that subpoena service on him in France could not properly be effected by a U.S. consul without infringing French sovereignty. The Court rejected the argument: "The mere giving of such a notice to the citizen in the foreign country of the requirement of his government that he shall return is in no sense an invasion of any right of the foreign government and the citizen has no standing to invoke any such supposed right." Is that persuasive? Why isn't service of U.S. process on a foreign state's territory at least arguably a violation of its territorial sovereignty? *See supra* pp. 86-88. We return to the subject of service abroad below. *See infra* pp. 774-94.

12. *Territoriality presumption — an initial view.* Note *Blackmer*'s reference to the presumption that

legislation, "unless the contrary intent appears, is construed to apply only within the territorial jurisdiction of the United States." As discussed in detail below, this "territoriality presumption" has played a vital role in defining U.S. legislative jurisdiction, *see infra* pp. 493-509, and in shaping choice of law rules, *see infra* pp. 546-52. Compare this rule of statutory interpretation to the apparent view in *Pennoyer* that international law, incorporated by the Constitution, forbid the extraterritorial exercise of jurisdiction.

2. General Jurisdiction Based on Incorporation or Registration to do Business

a. Incorporation

Business entities may ordinarily be subjected to general jurisdiction if they have a sufficiently permanent and substantial connection with the forum. It is now widely accepted that a corporation may be subjected to general jurisdiction in the state where it is incorporated.[88] One commentator has explained:

> A corporation is subject to jurisdiction in the state of its incorporation for any cause of action. Being incorporated in a state is a sufficiently substantial connection to support unlimited general jurisdiction.[89]

Although they have not frequently considered the question, lower courts have reached the same result.[90] Similarly, §421(2)(e) of the *Restatement (Third) Foreign Relations Law* permits a state to exercise jurisdiction over an entity if, at the time jurisdiction is asserted, "the person, if a corporation or comparable juridical person, is organized pursuant to the law of the state."

b. Registration or Qualification to Do Business

Companies incorporated outside of the forum state may be subject to general jurisdiction there if they register or qualify to do business within the forum. Virtually all states require foreign corporations to appoint a registered agent as a condition of "transacting business" or "doing business" within the state.[91] In this context, both "transacting business" and "doing business" are usually defined as requiring substantial, on-going business relations with the forum.[92]

In some states, such as Delaware, statutory registered agents are authorized by state law to accept service of process in *any* action, regardless whether it arises from activities within the state.[93] Other states have limited the process that may be served

---

88. *Restatement (Second) Conflict of Laws* §41 (1971); *Restatement (Third) Foreign Relations Law* §421(2)(e) (1987). In the early 1800's, corporations were treated as artificial persons that could only be sued in the state that created them. *Bank of Augusta v. Earle*, 38 U.S. 519, 588 (1839).

89. R. Casad, *Jurisdiction in Civil Actions* §3.02[1], at 3-130 (2d ed. 1991).

90. *E.g., Applied Biosystems, Inc. v. Cruachem, Ltd.*, 772 F.Supp. 1458, 1461 (D. Del. 1991) ("Because [defendant] is a Delaware corporation, there is no question that this Court can exercise personal jurisdiction over [it].").

91. *See* R. Casad, *Jurisdiction in Civil Actions* §3.02[2][a] & §4.02[1] (2d ed. 1991); Model Business Corp. Act Ann. §15.10 (Supp. 1988).

92. *See* R. Casad, *Jurisdiction in Civil Actions* §4.02[1] (2d ed. 1991); *Kachemak Seafoods, Inc. v. Century Airlines, Inc.*, 641 P.2d 213 (Alaska 1982).

93. *E.g. Sternberg v. O'Neill*, 550 A.2d 1105 (Del. 1988).

upon statutory agents to suits arising from in-state activities.[94] Where state law authorizes statutory agents to accept *any* service of process, lower courts have been required to consider whether the due process clause permits general jurisdiction based upon service on such agents. Lower courts are divided, with some having answered affirmatively,[95] and others having disagreed.[96]

3. General Jurisdiction Based on Consent or Waiver

It is well-settled that a private party may consent, or waive its objections, to personal jurisdiction in a U.S. court. *Pennoyer* expressly acknowledged that the due process clause permitted extraterritorial jurisdiction based upon consent.[97] More recently, the Supreme Court said: "Because the requirement of personal jurisdiction represents first of all an individual right, it can, like other such rights, be waived."[98] Consent or waiver can take many forms, both express and implied. Whatever their form, disputes can arise as to the interpretation and enforceability of purported consents or waivers.

a. *Prorogation Agreements or Nonexclusive Forum Selection Agreements*

International commercial contracts commonly include a provision in which one or more parties submit to the personal jurisdiction of a designated court.[99] Provisions of this sort are sometimes referred to as "prorogation" agreements, or "non-exclusive" forum selection clauses. Such agreements differ from "exclusive" forum selection agreements, discussed below, in that they *permit* jurisdiction in the contractual forum without *excluding* litigation in other potential fora.[100]

In order to provide an effective grant of personal jurisdiction, a prorogation agreement must satisfy both applicable statutory requirements and the due process

---

94. *E.g., Pearrow v. National Life & Accident Ins. Co.*, 703 F.2d 1067, 1069 (8th Cir. 1983) (Arkansas registration statute interpreted "at its broadest, to cover only causes of action arising out of ... transactions in Arkansas").

95. *E.g., Speed v. Pelican Resort NV*, 1992 U.S. Dist. Lexis 8278 (S.D.N.Y. 1992) ("Both this Court and the New York State courts have consistently held that a foreign corporation which registers [to do business] under BCL §1304 and establishes the Secretary of State as its agent upon whom process may be served under BCL §304, has consented to personal jurisdiction in the State of New York"); *Restatement (Second) Conflict of Laws* §44 (1971) ("A state has power to exercise judicial jurisdiction over a foreign corporation which has authorized an agent or a public official to accept service of process in actions brought against the corporation in the state as to all causes of action to which the authority of the agent or official to accept service extends.").

96. *E.g., Siemer v. Learjet Acquisition Corp.*, 966 F.2d 179 (5th Cir. 1992) ("being qualified to do business ... is of no special weight in evaluating general personal jurisdiction"); *Jones v. Family Inns, Inc.*, 1989 WL 57130 (E.D. La. 1989) ("defendant's sole contact with the State of Louisiana is an appointed agent for service of process," which does not satisfy *International Shoe*).

97. 95 U.S. at 735-36.

98. *Insurance Corporation of Ireland v. Compagnie des Bauxites de Guinee*, 456 U.S. 694, 703 (1982). *See also D.H. Overmyer Co. v. Frick Co.*, 405 U.S. 174 (1972).

99. Consent to personal jurisdiction in a pending action (for example, by entering a general appearance) is virtually always regarded as satisfying both statutory and constitutional requirements. *See* R. Casad, *Jurisdiction in Civil Actions* §3.01[5][c][i] (2d ed. 1991).

100. *See infra* pp. 371-72.

clause. In most U.S. states, local law will enforce prorogation agreements as a basis for personal jurisdiction, even where the parties' transaction has no connection with the forum.[101] There are exceptions, but these are anomalies.[102]

If state law will enforce an express contractual submission to jurisdiction, the due process clause generally will not preclude jurisdiction. The Supreme Court declared, in *National Equipment Rental, Ltd. v. Szukhent*, that "parties to a contract may agree in advance to submit to the jurisdiction of a given court, to permit notice to be served by the opposing party, or even to waive notice altogether."[103] In general, if a submission agreement is the result of fraud, duress, adhesion, or similar circumstances, neither the due process clause nor state law will permit enforcement. We examine these defenses to the enforceability of forum selection agreements in detail below.[104]

b. Implied Waivers

Implied submissions to the forum's jurisdiction are common, and generally enforceable, in the United States. As with prorogation agreements, both applicable local legislative authorizations and the due process clause must be satisfied before a purported waiver will confer jurisdiction. The most frequent instances of waiver involve a party's failing to raise jurisdictional defenses at an appropriate time during litigation; in the first instance, the jurisdictional consequences of this are subject to the forum's procedural rules, which differ widely between states.[105]

There is little due process precedent dealing with implied waivers. In *Insurance Corp. v. Compagnie des Bauxites de Guinee*,[106] the Supreme Court held that the due process clause did not preclude finding that a defendant's refusal to make jurisdictional discovery constituted an implied waiver of jurisdictional objections. According to the Court, the defendants' "refusal to produce evidence material to the administration of due process was but an admission of the want of merit in the asserted defense."[107]

---

101. *E.g., Vanier v. Ponsoldt*, 833 P.2d 949 (Kansas 1992); *Transway Shipping Ltd. v. Underwriters at Lloyd's*, 717 F.Supp. 82 (S.D.N.Y. 1989); *Alpa SA v. Acli Int'l, Inc.*, 573 F.Supp. 592 (W.D. Pa. 1983); R. Casad, *Jurisdiction in Civil Actions* §3.01[5][c][iii] (2d ed. 1991).

102. *E.g., McRae v. J.D./M.D., Inc.*, 511 So.2d 540 (Fla. 1987) ("Conspicuously absent from the long arm statute is any provision for submission to in personam jurisdiction merely by contractual agreement."); *Keelean v. Central Bank of the South*, 544 So.2d 153 (Ala. 1989); Mich. Comp. Law. Ann. §600.745(2) (West 1981).

103. 375 U.S. 311, 315-16 (1964). *See also Hoffman v. National Equip. Rental Ltd.*, 643 F.2d 987 (4th Cir. 1981); *Gaskin v. Stumm Handel, GmbH*, 390 F.Supp. 361 (S.D.N.Y. 1975); *Restatement (Third) Foreign Relations Law* §421(2)(g) (1987); *infra* pp. 374-77.

104. *See infra* pp. 395-430.

105. R. Casad, *Jurisdiction in Civil Actions* §3.01[5][b] (2d ed. 1991); *Restatement (Third) Foreign Relations Law* §421(3) (1987).

106. 456 U.S. 694 (1982).

107. 456 U.S. at 709 (citing *Hammond Packing Co. v. Arkansas*, 212 U.S. 322, 351 (1909)).

4. General Jurisdiction Based on "Presence" or "Continuous and Systematic Business" Activities Within the Forum

Another basis for assertions of general jurisdiction is "continuous and systematic" business activity by the defendant within the forum,[108] also referred to as the "presence" or "doing business" standard.[109] If a defendant is found to have continuously and systematically engaged in business activities within the forum, then many state long-arm statutes and the due process clause will expose it to the forum's general jurisdiction.

a. Legislative Authorization

In order for a court to exercise general jurisdiction based on continuous and systematic contacts, a legislative authorization for jurisdiction must exist.[110] Many states recognize this basis for general jurisdiction, often by means of catch-all provisions that have been interpreted as granting jurisdiction to the limits of the Constitution.[111] As discussed below, new Rule 4(k)(2) also appears to authorize general jurisdiction based on continuous and systematic business contacts.[112]

b. Due Process Clause

General jurisdiction based on "presence" or "continuous and systematic" contacts is a potent litigation tool. As we have seen, general jurisdiction permits a plaintiff to assert any claim against the defendant, including claims that have nothing whatsoever to do with the forum.[113] This gives a plaintiff substantially increased opportunities to select a favorable forum for its claims. Reflecting this, most bases for general jurisdiction are commensurately unique and demanding — such as nationality, domicile, incorporation, and consent. As the following discussion illustrates, however, "presence" is a markedly less precise formula, which permits more expansive assertions of jurisdiction.

Due process has long been interpreted as permitting the assertion of general jurisdiction based on a defendant's continuous and systematic connections with the

---

108. *See Helicopteros Nacionales de Colombia, SA v. Hall,* 466 U.S. 408 (1984); *Perkins v. Benguet Consol. Mining Co.,* 342 U.S. 437 (1952).

109. *See Rosenberg Brothers & Co. v. Curtis Brown Co.,* 260 U.S. 516 (1923); *McGowan v. Smith,* 437 N.Y.S.2d 643, 645 (1981) (general jurisdiction requires showing that defendant is "'engaged in such a continuous and systematic course of "doing business" here as to warrant a finding of its "presence" in this jurisdiction.'"); *Deluxe Ice Cream Co. v. R.C.H. Tool Corp.,* 726 F.2d 1209 (7th Cir. 1984); *Broadcasting Rights Int'l Corp. v. Societe du Tour de France, SARL,* 675 F.Supp. 1439 (S.D.N.Y. 1987).

110. *E.g., Provident National Bank v. California Federal S. & L. Ass'n,* 819 F.2d 434, 436 (3d Cir. 1987); *Landoil Resources Corp. v. Alexander & Alexander Services,* 918 F.2d 1039 (2d Cir. 1990); *Complaint of Damodar Bulk Carriers Ltd.,* 903 F.2d 675 (9th Cir. 1990).

111. *E.g.,* N.Y. C.P.L.R. §301 ("A court may exercise such jurisdiction over persons, property, or status as might have been exercised" at common law); *Landoil Resources Corp. v. Alexander & Alexander Serv., Inc.,* 918 F.2d 1039 (2d Cir. 1990).

112. *See infra* p. 196.

113. *See supra* pp. 77-78.

forum.[114] *Perkins v. Benguet Consolidated Mining Co.* is the leading modern Supreme Court decision finding jurisdiction based on this rationale.[115] In *Perkins*, a mining company organized under Philippine law, with its properties in the Philippines, was operated during Japan's World War II occupation of the Philippines from an office in Ohio. The company's president maintained corporate records in Ohio, held board meetings there, paid salaries from an Ohio bank, and otherwise managed the company from Ohio. While not using the term "general jurisdiction," the Supreme Court held that the Philippine company could be sued in Ohio courts in an action arising out of activities unrelated to Ohio; the Court relied on the fact that the company had been "carrying on in Ohio a continuous and systematic, but limited part of its general business."[116]

Defining what sorts of activities will satisfy the "continuous and systematic" business contacts or "presence" test has proven difficult.[117] In one court's words:

> The problem of what contacts with the forum state will suffice to subject a foreign corporation to suit there on an unrelated cause of action is such that the formulation of useful general standards is almost impossible and even an examination of the multitude of decided cases can give little assistance.[118]

It is clear, however, that the "presence" or "doing business" tests require a much more demanding showing than that for specific jurisdiction.[119] Indeed, some courts have concluded that *Perkins* was an unusual case and that general jurisdiction based on the continuous business contacts of a non-resident defendant is seldom available.[120]

c. Selected Materials on "Presence" as a Basis for General Jurisdiction

The Supreme Court's only recent treatment of the "continuous and systematic" business activities test is in *Helicopteros Nacionales de Colombia v. Hall*, excerpted

---

114. *International Shoe Co. v. Washington*, 326 U.S. 310, 318 (1945).

115. 342 U.S. 437 (1952).

116. 342 U.S. at 438.

117. *E.g., Complaint of Damodar Bulk Carriers Ltd.*, 903 F.2d 675 (9th Cir. 1990); *Borg-Warner Acceptance Corp. v. Lovett & Tharpe, Inc.*, 786 F.2d 1055, 1057 (11th Cir. 1986); *Reliance Steel Prods. Co. v. Watson, Ess. Marshall & Enggas*, 675 F.2d 587 (3d Cir. 1982) ("'continuous and substantial' forum affiliations"). *See infra* pp. 111-13.

118. *Aquascutum of London, Inc. v. S.S. American Champion*, 426 F.2d 205, 211 (2d Cir. 1970).

119. *E.g., Provident National Bank v. California Federal Savings & Loan Ass'n*, 819 F.2d 434 (3d Cir. 1987); *Romero v. Aerolineas Argentinas*, 834 F.Supp. 673 (D.N.J. 1993) ("General jurisdiction requires a plaintiff to show significantly more than mere minimum contacts"); *Rolls-Royce Motors, Inc. v. Charles Schmitt & Co.*, 657 F.Supp. 1040, 1044 (S.D.N.Y. 1987)(general jurisdiction requires a corporation to be present not merely "'occasionally or casually, but with a fair measure of permanence and continuity.'").

120. *E.g., Congoleum Corp. v. DLW, AG*, 729 F.2d 1240, 1242 (9th Cir. 1984) (*Perkins* is "limited to its unusual facts"); *Cubbage v. Merchent*, 744 F.2d 665, 667-68 (9th Cir. 1984), *cert. denied*, 470 U.S. 1005 (1985).

below. *Helicopteros* raised as many questions as it answered, as is illustrated by *United Rope Distributors, Inc. v. Kim-Sail Ltd.*, also excerpted below.

HELICOPTEROS NACIONALES DE COLOMBIA v. HALL
466 U.S. 408 (1984)

JUSTICE BLACKMUN. [Petitioner Helicopteros Nacionales de Colombia, S.A. ("Helicol"), is a Colombian corporation that provides helicopter transportation for oil and construction companies in South America. In 1976, a helicopter owned by Helicol crashed in Peru, killing four United States citizens. Respondents are the survivors and representatives of the four decedents. Respondents' four decedents were employed by Consorcio, a Peruvian consortium, which was the alter ego of a joint venture named Williams-Sedco-Horn ("WSH"), headquartered in Houston, Texas. Consorcio was engaged in the construction of a pipeline running from the interior of Peru westward to the Pacific Ocean.

In 1974, on request of Consorcio/WSH, the chief executive officer of Helicol, Francisco Restrepo, flew to Houston and met with the three joint venturers about Consorcio/WSH's need for helicopter transportation on the Peruvian pipeline project. At the meeting, Consorcio/WSH accepted a contract for the supply of helicopters proposed by Helicol. When finalized, the contract was written in Spanish on official Peruvian government stationery. It provided that the residence of all the parties would be Lima, Peru, and that controversies arising out of the contract would be submitted to the Peruvian courts. The contract also provided that Consorcio/WSH would make payments to Helicol's account in New York City.

Helicol had a variety of other contacts with Texas. It purchased approximately 80 percent of its helicopter fleet, as well as spare parts and accessories from Bell Helicopter Company in Fort Worth. Helicol also sent prospective pilots and other personnel to Fort Worth for training and to ferry the helicopters it purchased to South America. Helicol received into its New York City and Panama City, Fla., bank accounts over $5 million in payments from Consorcio/WSH drawn on First City National Bank of Houston. Nonetheless, Helicol was never authorized to do business in Texas and never had an agent for the service of process within the State. It never performed helicopter operations in Texas or sold any product that reached Texas, never solicited business in Texas, never signed any contract in Texas, never had any employee based there, and never recruited an employee in Texas. In addition, Helicol never owned property in Texas and never maintained an office there. Helicol maintained no records in Texas and had no shareholders in that state.[121] None of the

---

121. The Colombian national airline, Aerovias Nacionales de Colombia, owns approximately 94 percent of Helicol's capital stock. The remainder is held by Aerovias Corporacion de Viajes and four South American individuals.

respondents or their decedents were domiciled in Texas.[122] All of the decedents were hired in Houston by Consorcio/WSH to work on the Petro Peru pipeline project.

Respondents instituted wrongful-death actions in Texas state court against Consorcio/WSH, Bell Helicopter Company, and Helicol. Helicol filed special appearances and unsuccessfully moved to dismiss the actions for lack of *in personam* jurisdiction over it. After a jury trial, judgment was entered against Helicol on a jury verdict of $1,141,200 in favor of the four respondents. On appeal, the Supreme Court of Texas held that the state's long-arm statute reaches as far as the due process clause of the fourteenth amendment permits and that it was consistent with the due process clause for Texas courts to assert *in personam* jurisdiction over Helicol.]

The Due Process Clause of the Fourteenth Amendment [is] satisfied when *in personam* jurisdiction is asserted over a nonresident corporate defendant that has "certain minimum contacts with [the forum] such that the maintenance of the suit does not offend 'traditional notions of fair play and substantial justice.'" When a controversy is related to or "arises out of" a defendant's contacts with the forum, the Court has said that a "relationship among the defendant, the forum, and the litigation" is the essential foundation of *in personam* jurisdiction.[123]

Even when the cause of action does not arise out of or relate to the foreign corporation's activities in the forum State,[124] due process is not offended by a State's subjecting the corporation to its *in personam* jurisdiction when there are sufficient contacts between the state and the foreign corporation. *Perkins v. Benguet Consolidated Mining Co.* In *Perkins*, the Court addressed a situation in which state courts had asserted general jurisdiction over a defendant foreign corporation. During the Japanese occupation of the Philippine Islands, the president and general manager of a Philippine mining corporation maintained an office in Ohio from which he conducted activities on behalf of the company. He kept company files and held directors' meetings in the office, carried on correspondence relating to the business, distributed salary checks drawn on two active Ohio bank accounts, engaged an Ohio bank to act as the transfer agent, and supervised policies dealing with rehabilitation of the corporation's properties in the Philippines. In short, the foreign corporation, through its president, "ha[d] been carrying on in Ohio a continuous and systematic, but limited,

---

122. Respondents' lack of residential or other contacts with Texas of itself does not defeat otherwise proper jurisdiction. *Keeton v. Hustler Magazine, Inc.*, 465 U.S. 770, 780 (1984); *Calder v. Jones*, 465 U.S. 783, 788 (1984). We mention respondents' lack of contacts merely to show that nothing in the nature of the relationship between respondents and Helicol could possibly enhance Helicol's contacts in Texas. The harm suffered by respondents did not occur in Texas. Nor is it alleged that any negligence on the part of Helicol took place in Texas.

123. It has been said that when a State exercises personal jurisdiction over a defendant in a suit arising out of or related to the defendant's contacts with the forum, the State is exercising "specific jurisdiction" over the defendant.

124. When a State exercises personal jurisdiction over a defendant in a suit not arising out of or related to the defendant's contacts with the forum, the State has been said to be exercising "general jurisdiction" over the defendant.

part of its general business," and the exercise of general jurisdiction over the Philippine corporation by an Ohio court was "reasonable and just."

All parties to the present case concede that respondents' claims against Helicol did not "arise out of," and are not related to, Helicol's activities within Texas.[125] We thus must explore the nature of Helicol's contacts with the State of Texas to determine whether they constitute the kind of continuous and systematic general business contacts the Court found to exist in *Perkins*. We hold that they do not.

It is undisputed that Helicol does not have a place of business in Texas and never has been licensed to do business in the State. Basically, Helicol's contacts with Texas consisted of sending its chief executive officer to Houston for a contract negotiation session; accepting into its New York bank account checks drawn on a Houston bank; purchasing helicopters, equipment, and training services from Bell Helicopter for substantial sums; and sending personnel to Bell's facilities in Fort Worth for training.

The one trip to Houston by Helicol's chief executive officer for the purpose of negotiating the transportation services contract with Consorcio/WSH cannot be described or regarded as a contact of a "continuous and systematic" nature, as *Perkins* described it, and thus cannot support an assertion of *in personam* jurisdiction over Helicol by a Texas court. Similarly, Helicol's acceptance from Consorcio/WSH of checks drawn on a Texas bank is of negligible significance for purposes of determining whether Helicol had sufficient contacts in Texas. There is no indication that Helicol ever requested that the checks be drawn on a Texas bank or that there was any negotiation between Helicol and Consorcio/WSH with respect to the location or identity of the bank on which checks would be drawn. Common sense and everyday experience suggest that, absent unusual circumstances, the bank on which a check is drawn is generally of little consequence to the payee and is a matter left to the discretion of the drawer. Such unilateral activity of another party or a third person is not an appropriate consideration when determining whether a defendant has sufficient contacts with a forum State to justify an assertion of jurisdiction.

The Texas Supreme Court focused on the purchases and the related training trips in finding contacts sufficient to support an assertion of jurisdiction. We do not agree with that assessment, for the Court's opinion in *Rosenberg Bros. & Co. v. Curtis Brown Co.*, 260 U.S. 516 ..., makes clear that purchases and related trips, standing alone, are not a sufficient basis for a State's assertion of jurisdiction. The defendant in *Rosenberg* was a small retailer in Tulsa, Okla., who dealt in men's clothing and fur-

---

125. ... Respondents have made no argument that their cause of action either arose out of or is related to Helicol's contacts with the State of Texas. Absent any briefing on the issue, we decline to reach the questions (1) whether the terms "arising out of" and "related to" describe different connections between a cause of action and a defendant's contacts with a forum, and (2) what sort of tie between a cause of action and a defendant's contacts with a forum is necessary to a determination that either connection exists. Nor do we reach the question whether, if the two types of relationship differ, a forum's exercise of personal jurisdiction in a situation where the cause of action "relates to," but does not "arise out of," the defendant's contacts with the forum should be analyzed as an assertion of specific jurisdiction.

nishings. ... Its only connection with New York was that it purchased from New York wholesalers a large portion of the merchandise sold in its Tulsa store. The purchases sometimes were made by correspondence and sometimes through visits to New York by an officer of the defendant. The Court concluded: "Visits on such business, even if occurring at regular intervals, would not warrant the inference that the corporation was present within the jurisdiction of [New York]."

This Court in *International Shoe* acknowledged and did not repudiate its holding in *Rosenberg*. In accordance with *Rosenberg*, we hold that mere purchases, even if occurring at regular intervals, are not enough to warrant a State's assertion of *in personam* jurisdiction over a nonresident corporation in a cause of action not related to those purchase transactions.[126]

Nor can we conclude that the fact that Helicol sent personnel into Texas for training in connection with the purchase of helicopters and equipment in that State in any way enhanced the nature of Helicol's contacts with Texas. The training was a part of the package of goods and services purchased by Helicol from Bell Helicopter. The brief presence of Helicol employees in Texas for the purpose of attending the training sessions is no more a significant contact than were the trips to New York made by the buyer for the retail store in *Rosenberg*. ... We hold that Helicol's contacts with the State of Texas were insufficient to satisfy the requirements of the Due Process Clause of the Fourteenth Amendment. ...[127]

UNITED ROPE DISTRIBUTORS, INC. v. KIM-SAIL, LTD.

770 F.Supp. 128 (S.D.N.Y. 1991)

CEDARBAUM, DISTRICT JUDGE. Seatriumph Marine Corporation ("Seatriumph") moves to dismiss the third-party complaint for lack of personal jurisdiction. Plaintiff United Rope Distributors is a Delaware corporation with its principal place of business in Minnesota. Defendant and third-party plaintiff Kim-

---

126. This Court in *International Shoe* cited *Rosenberg* for the proposition that "the commission of some single or occasional acts of the corporate agent in a state sufficient to impose an obligation or liability on the corporation has not been thought to confer upon the state authority to enforce it." 326 U.S. at 318. Arguably, therefore, *Rosenberg* also stands for the proposition that mere purchases are not a sufficient basis for either general or specific jurisdiction. Because the case before us is one in which there has been an assertion of general jurisdiction over a foreign defendant, we need not decide the continuing validity of *Rosenberg* with respect to an assertion of specific jurisdiction, *i.e.*, where the cause of action arises out of or relates to the purchases by the defendant in the forum State.

127. As an alternative to traditional minimum-contacts analysis, respondents suggest that the Court hold that the State of Texas had personal jurisdiction over Helicol under a doctrine of "jurisdiction by necessity." *See Shaffer v. Heitner*, 433 U.S. 186, 211 n.37 (1977). We conclude, however, that respondents failed to carry their burden of showing that all three defendants could not be sued together in a single forum. It is not clear from the records, for example, whether suit could have been brought against all three defendants in either Colombia or Peru. We decline to consider adoption of a doctrine of jurisdiction by necessity — a potentially far-reaching modification of existing law — in the absence of a more complete record.

Sail, Ltd. ("Kim-Sail") is a Cayman Islands corporation with its principal place of business in New York City. Third-party defendant Seatriumph is a Liberian corporation with its principal place of business in Greece.

At the time of the events giving rise to this action, Seatriumph was the owner of the M.V. Katia. Seatriumph had chartered the Katia to a Danish company, Copenship A/S, under a head charter in January 1988. Copenship A/S had in turn sub-chartered the vessel to Kim-Sail in October 1988. In November of 1988, Kim-Sail, through its general agent in New York, Kersten Shipping Agency, Inc., accepted 300,000 bales of twine from Sisalana, SA of Salvador, Brazil, for shipment to United Rope Distributors in Superior, Wisconsin. The twine was loaded onto the Katia beginning on November 5, 1988 in Salvador, Brazil. The cargo was never delivered because the Katia sank on or about November 25, 1988.

United Rope Distributors brought this admiralty action against Kim-Sail for damages arising from the loss of the cargo. Kim-Sail impleaded Seatriumph, seeking indemnity or contribution for any liability Kim-Sail is found to have to United Rope Distributors. Seatriumph moves to dismiss the third-party complaint on the ground that this court lacks personal jurisdiction over it. ... Kim-Sail argues that this court has personal jurisdiction over Seatriumph under §§301 and 302(a)(3) of the New York Civil Practice Law and Rules ("CPLR") and because Seatriumph has consented to be sued in this forum. ... All pleadings and affidavits must be construed in the light most favorable to Kim-Sail and all doubts resolved in its favor.

In order to be subject to personal jurisdiction under CPLR §301, a non-resident defendant must be "engaged in such a continuous and systematic course of 'doing business' [in New York] as to warrant a finding of its 'presence' in this jurisdiction." *Frummer v. Hilton Hotels International, Inc.*, 281 N.Y.S.2d 41, 43, *cert. denied*, 389 U.S. 923 (1967). A foreign corporation may be subject to jurisdiction in New York under §301 when a separate corporation, acting with its authority and for its substantial benefit, carries out activities in New York that are "sufficiently important to the foreign corporation that if it did not have a representative to perform them, the corporation's own officials would undertake to perform substantially similar services." *Gelfand v. Tanner Motor Tours, Ltd.*, 385 F.2d 116, 121 (2d Cir. 1967), *cert. denied*, 390 U.S. 996 (1968). [The court concluded that a company named Richmond Investments acted as an agent of, and at the direction of Seatriumph, and therefore that its contacts with New York, including its New York bank account, were attributable to Seatriumph.] ...

The only business of Seatriumph was owning and operating the Katia. When it sank, the Katia had been under a time charter to Copenship since January of 1988. Thus, most of Seatriumph's activity ... consisted of paying the expenses of the Katia and receiving its hire. These activities were carried out in New York by Richmond on behalf of Seatriumph. The Katia's hire constituted substantially all of Seatriumph's profits. Seatriumph required in its head charter with Copenship that all hire be paid in New York City. Indeed, Seatriumph normally required all charterers to pay hire and freight to it via Richmond's account in New York City. Thus, Seatriumph, in operating the Katia, arranged through its charters to receive virtually all of its income in New York City. This arrangement, combined with Seatriumph's use of Richmond's bank account to make payments for most of the expenses of the Katia, constitutes activity within New York sufficient to make Seatriumph subject to personal jurisdiction as a corporation doing business in New York.

Personal jurisdiction over Seatriumph is also supported by *Arpad Szabo v. Smedvig Tankrederi*, 95 F.Supp. 519 (S.D.N.Y. 1951), in which an injured seaman brought suit against the shipowner, a Norwegian corporation with no office in New York. The shipowner had time-chartered the ship for five years through a New York broker, Winchester. The court found personal jurisdiction over the shipowner because of the services that Winchester had continuously performed in New York for the defendant. "The charges for hire of the vessel of approximately $23,000 monthly are paid directly by the charterer to Winchester in New York City and deposited in a New York City bank." The bills incurred for the ship's necessities "are sent on to Winchester in New York City, who pays them against the monies received monthly from the charterer and remits that balance to the defendant in Norway." The court held that these activities "indicate a form of continuous activity here."

Seatriumph argues that having a New York bank account does not by itself constitute doing business in New York, an unexceptionable proposition. The cases on which Seatriumph relies, however, did not involve bank accounts for the receipt of substantially all of the income of a foreign corporation. ... Neither does the recent case of *Landoil Resource v. Alexander*, 563 N.Y.S.2d 739 (1990), control. In that case, the New York Court of Appeals held that Syndicate 317, a London underwriter and member of Lloyd's, was not "doing business" in New York simply because Lloyd's held a $9 billion trust fund at Citibank in New York City. The court noted that Syndicate 317 could not deposit or withdraw money from the fund, and that the fund's location in New York was fortuitous. Here, Seatriumph had control over its money held in Richmond's account in New York. In addition, Seatriumph purposefully chose New York as the location to receive its hire.

Seatriumph also argues that even if these facts establish that it was doing business in New York, all activity in New York had ceased by March 15, 1989, when the third-party complaint was filed. Hire was last paid to Seatriumph in the New York account on November 10, 1988, and money was last paid out of that account on behalf of Seatriumph on February 22, 1989, three weeks before the third-party complaint was filed. However, Richmond maintained the account until March 20, 1989, five days after the third-party complaint was filed. On March 30, 1989, under the signature of Petropoulos, Richmond's account was transferred to an account in the same New York bank, in the name of Med Investments, of which Petropoulos was also a principal. Under these circumstances, I find that Seatriumph's ties to New York still existed as of the date of the filing of the third-party complaint.

Finally, requiring Seatriumph to defend this suit in New York does not "offend 'traditional notions of fair play and substantial justice.'"

Notes on Helicopteros Nacionales and United Rope

1. *Practical significance of a U.S. forum.* The four plaintiffs in *Helicopteros* were awarded approximately $1.1 million by a Texas jury. That figure is not unusual by U.S. standards. But in Bogota, Lima, and many other places, a recovery of this magnitude would be inconceivable. Mrs. Hall could realistically have expected no more than 5% of her Texas verdict had she proceeded in Columbia or Peru; and that amount would have been subject to local taxes, foreign exchange controls, and other restrictions. What significance should such factors have in due process analysis? Is it relevant to the "purposeful availment" prong? to the "reasonableness" prong? to neither?

2. *Relevance of defendant's foreign identity in* Helicopteros. As described above, jurisdiction over foreign defendants differs in important ways from jurisdiction over U.S. defendants. What importance did *Helicopteros* assign to the fact that the defendant was a Colombian corporation? Suppose that Helicol had been a Californian corporation, operating in Arizona, and the fatal crash had occurred in Arizona. Would Helicol have been subject to suit in Texas? Is the argument for Texas jurisdiction stronger or weaker in the California-Arizona hypothetical, or in the actual *Helicopteros* case? Why? What relevance should be assigned to the unusual hardships a U.S. plaintiff may encounter in a Colombian forum (as compared to a Californian one)? *See supra* pp. 3-5 & *infra* p. 115. What is the relevance of the burdens that a foreign defendant may face in a U.S. forum?

3. *Relevance of plaintiff's foreign identity in* United Rope. In *United Rope*, the third-party plaintiff was a foreign corporation without significant U.S. connections. What relevance should the plaintiff's nationality have for due process analysis? Note that in *Helicopteros*, the plaintiffs were Texas citizens. Does that make for a stronger due process argument than would have been the case if the plaintiffs were Colombian or Peruvian nationals? What about Arizona or New York citizens?

4. *"Continuous and systematic" presence in* Helicopteros. *Helicopteros* held that general jurisdiction requires "the kind of continuous and systematic general business contacts ... found to exist in *Perkins [v. Benguet Consolidated Mining]*." Why didn't Helicol have this sort of contacts with Texas? It is clear that the "continuous and systematic" contacts test imposes a substantially more rigorous standard than the due process "minimum contacts" test applicable in the specific jurisdiction context. *See supra* pp. 77-78. Consider, however, the following excerpt from the dissenting opinion in *Helicopteros*:

> As a foreign corporation that has actively and purposefully engaged in numerous and frequent commercial transactions in the State of Texas, Helicol clearly falls within the category of non-resident defendants that may be subject to that forum's general jurisdiction. Helicol not only purchased helicopters and other equipment in the State for many years, but also sent pilots and management personnel into Texas to be trained in the use of this equipment and to consult with the seller on technical matters. Moreover, negotiations for the contract under which Helicol provided transportation services to the joint venture that employed the respondents' decedents also took place in the State of Texas. Taken together, these contacts [permit the assertion of general jurisdiction.] 466 U.S. at 423-24.

Are you persuaded? If so, would Texas courts have jurisdiction over a suit by a Peruvian bank to recover money loaned to Helicol in Peru? a suit by a Peruvian secretary for unfair dismissal from her position at Helicol's Peruvian office? a tort suit by the survivors of a Peruvian oil pipeline worker killed in an accident in rural Peru?

5. *United Rope — expansive exercise of general jurisdiction.* Notwithstanding the demanding character of the "presence" test for general jurisdiction, some lower courts have found "continuous and systematic" contacts based on surprisingly little. *United Rope*, for example, held that Seatriumph was subject to general jurisdiction in New York, based on its "systematic" use of a New York bank account in the name of another company. Was *United Rope* correctly decided? Is *United Rope* consistent with *Helicoperos*? with §421 of the Restatement?

Suppose that a developing nation asserted general jurisdiction over a U.S. company because one of its wholly-owned subsidiaries maintained a local bank account which it used to conduct substantial business. Could the United States legitimately protest against this jurisdictional assertion? Should it be able to?

Suppose the developing nation's courts purported to decide claims brought by U.S. nationals against the U.S. company arising from wholly domestic U.S. activities.

    6. Factors relevant to application of "continuous and systematic" contacts test. A variety of factors can be relevant to the "doing business" test:

> Although this test is highly fact-sensitive, New York courts typically have focused on the following factors in determining whether a nonresident corporation is "doing business" in New York: "the existence of an office in New York; the solicitation of business in New York; the presence of bank accounts or other property in New York; the presence of employees or agents in New York." *Revlon, Inc. v. United Overseas Ltd.,* 1994 WL 9657 (S.D.N.Y. 1994).

    (a) *Solicitation.* Lower courts have frequently held that "mere solicitation" by a foreign corporation does not constitute "doing business." *E.g., Pizarro v. Hoteles Concorde Int'l CA,* 907 F.2d 1256 (1st Cir. 1990) (placing nine ads in forum newspaper does not sustain general jurisdiction over foreign hotel); *Congoleum Corp. v. DLW AG,* 729 F.2d 1240, 1242-43 (9th Cir. 1984) (foreign company's solicitation of orders, and showroom promotional efforts, plus attendance of employees at trade fairs and meetings in forum, not sufficient for general jurisdiction). On the other hand, some courts have suggested that solicitation provides a substantial basis for general jurisdiction, provided that some other forum contacts also exist. *E.g., H. Heller & Co. v. Novacor Chem. Ltd.,* 726 F.Supp. 49 (S.D.N.Y. 1988) ("once solicitation is found in any substantial degree courts have required very little more to support a conclusion of 'doing business'"). Is this appropriate? If taken seriously, does it not permit general jurisdiction in a broad range of cases?

    (b) *Shipment of products into the forum.* The shipment of products into the forum, without more, will not ordinarily permit general jurisdiction. *E.g., Bearry v. Beech Aircraft Corp.,* 818 F.2d 370 (5th Cir. 1987) ($50 million in annual sales, over a number of years, to 17 distributors within forum not sufficient for general jurisdiction). However, in a few cases, general jurisdiction has been found by lower courts based on substantial sales to forum purchasers. *E.g., Howse v. Zimmer Mfg. Co.,* 757 F.2d 448 (1st Cir. 1985) (out-of-state manufacturer subject to general jurisdiction because it frequently sent agents into forum, had "sizeable sales volume" in forum, and received payments directly from forum customers). In *Keeton v. Hustler Magazine, Inc.,* 465 U.S. 770, 779-80 & n.11 (1984), the Court strongly suggested that the monthly distribution of 10-15,000 magazines by defendant to forum residents was not "so substantial as to support jurisdiction over a cause of action unrelated to those activities." The Court distinguished *Perkins* on the grounds that there "Ohio was the corporation's principal, if temporary, place of business." 465 U.S. at 780 n.11. Is it appropriate to impose such a demanding standard for general jurisdiction?

    (c) *Purchase of products from forum.* The Supreme Court held in *Rosenberg,* and reaffirmed in *Helicopteros,* that the purchase of products from the forum usually does not confer general jurisdiction. Lower courts have virtually never upheld general jurisdiction based on purchases from the forum. *E.g., Rolls-Royce Motors, Inc. v. Charles Schmitt & Co.,* 657 F.Supp. 1040, 1046 (S.D.N.Y. 1987) (foreign corporation's purchase of a "major share of the merchandise to be sold at its place of business outside the state, even if systematic and made upon visits occurring at regular intervals, do not warrant a finding that the defendant was present" in New York). *Compare In re Ocean Ranger Sinking,* 589 F.Supp. 302, 312 (E.D. La. 1984) (general jurisdiction upheld based on $124 million in purchases from forum vendors over 4 year period). Why are purchases of products virtually never a basis for general jurisdiction?

    (d) *Ownership of property in forum.* In most cases, a foreign corporation's ownership and use of property in the forum is not a sufficient basis for general jurisdiction. Most of the cases to consider this point have involved bank accounts. *E.g., Landoil Resources Corp. v. Alexander & Alexander Services, Inc.,* 563 N.Y.S.2d 739 (1990) (foreign company's $9 billion trust fund in New York not a basis for general jurisdiction); *Vendetti v. Fiat Auto SpA,* 802 F.Supp. 886 (W.D.N.Y. 1992) (foreign auto maker's maintenance of incidental bank accounts in New York, plus making of payments to New York marketing entities and communications with dealers not sufficient for general jurisdiction). However, as *United Rope* illustrates, if a foreign corporation makes sufficiently continuous and substantial use of a forum bank account, that may provide an independent basis for general jurisdiction. *E.g., Provident National Bank v. California Federal Savings & Loan Ass'n,* 819 F.2d 434 (3d Cir. 1987) (maintaining bank account, used on a daily basis as a "central" part of defendant's business, is sufficient basis for general jurisdiction).

    (e) *Visits to forum by employees or agents.* Lower courts have generally held that visits to the forum by a company's employees or agents do not create general jurisdiction. *E.g., Complaint of Damodar Bulk*

Carriers, Ltd., 903 F.2d 675 (9th Cir. 1990) (several bunkering calls by defendant's vessel to forum do not permit general jurisdiction); *Huff v. Chandris SA*, 1994 WL 414467 (S.D.N.Y. 1994) (no general jurisdiction over food concessionaire on cruise line whose ships call frequently in New York and serve numerous New York residents).

(f) *Unincorporated branch office.* The presence of an unincorporated branch office within the forum will ordinarily permit general jurisdiction. E.g., *Revlon, Inc. v. United Overseas Ltd.*, 1994 WL 9657 (S.D.N.Y. 1994) ("The maintenance of even a relatively minor office in New York alone justifies an assertion of jurisdiction over a foreign corporation..."); *Ciprari v. Servios Aeros Cruzeiro do Sul, SA*, 232 F.Supp. 433 (S.D.N.Y. 1964) (Brazilian air carrier, that served only Latin American points, held subject to general jurisdiction because of "purchasing office" in New York, employing 2 persons and using 2 substantial bank accounts to buy spare parts for Brazilian aircraft fleet: "defendant carries on with regularity a function vital to its operation from a permanent location in New York"). *Compare Speed v. Pelican Resort NV*, 1992 U.S. Dist. Lexis 8278 (S.D.N.Y. 1992) ("the maintenance of mere telephone lines and listings does not constitute 'presence' or 'doing business'"). Is this appropriate? Why should jurisdiction not be limited to the activities and business of the branch office?

(g) *Entering into contracts with forum residents.* Lower courts have usually refused to find general jurisdiction based upon the fact that the defendant has entered into a number of contracts with forum residents over a significant period of time. E.g., *Golden Gulf Corp. v. Jordache Enterprises, Inc.*, 1994 WL 62384 (S.D.N.Y. 1994) (no general jurisdiction based upon foreign corporation's entry into licensing agreement providing for payment of fees to New York company, provision of materials and information to New York company, and arbitration in New York). In a few cases, however, general jurisdiction has been based principally on contractual arrangements with forum residents, although other factors have also usually been present. E.g., *Elliott v. Faber and Schleicher AG*, 1994 WL 322975 (E.D. Pa. 1994) (asserting general jurisdiction over foreign manufacturer because it appointed exclusive U.S. distributor); *La Nuova D & B, SpA v. Bower Co.*, 513 A.2d 764 (Del. 1986) (general jurisdiction in Delaware over Italian manufacturer that appointed New Jersey regional distributor, empowered to deliver warranty binding manufacturer, which made two significant sales in Delaware and was empowered to deliver additional warranties in Delaware).

7. **Rationale for general jurisdiction based on continuous and systematic contacts.** In both *Helicopteros* and *Perkins*, the Court recognized that jurisdiction could be asserted against a defendant with respect to causes of action not "arising out of" the defendant's activities in the forum state. Is this sensible? Why should a defendant ever be subject to suit in the forum on claims entirely unrelated to activities within or affecting the forum? What interest does the forum state have in adjudicating such claims? Does general jurisdiction pose special threats to the territorial sovereignty of foreign states? to the fair treatment of private parties?

Reconsider the justifications for general jurisdiction set forth above: the desirability of having one forum where a defendant will clearly be subject to jurisdiction on all claims, without the need for expensive litigation over "minimum contacts" or "reasonableness," and the perception that defendants will be neither inconvenienced nor surprised if subjected to general jurisdiction in their "backyard." See supra p. 98. Is this rationale persuasive?

Even accepting the foregoing rationale for general jurisdiction, does it not extend only to jurisdiction based on domicile or incorporation, and not to jurisdiction based upon "continuous and systematic" business activities? Is there a significant risk of unfairness in permitting suit against the defendant at a place where it is continuously and systematically present? Is general jurisdiction based on "continuous and systematic" business contacts necessary in order that the defendant undeniably be subject to personal jurisdiction in at least one forum? Note that permitting general jurisdiction based on comparatively "easy" showings significantly increases a plaintiff's choice of potential forums — and hence its litigation advantages. See supra p. 94.

8. *Effect of* Burnham *on general jurisdiction.* Perkins is the only contemporary Supreme Court decision affirming an assertion of general jurisdiction (other than *Burnham* discussed below at pp. 121-22). In *Perkins*, the defendant corporation was a Philippines company doing substantially all its business in Ohio while World War II and its aftermath made operations in the Philippines impossible. See supra pp. 103-04. Is this a compelling precedent for general jurisdiction based on "continuous and systematic" contacts in cases where suit against a defendant is possible in the place it is incorporated? Should the "continuous and systematic" contacts test for general jurisdiction be confined to cases like *Perkins*, where the defendant

cannot be sued in its place of incorporation? Is *Perkins* even a general jurisdiction case? or did the claim "arise from" the defendant corporation's Ohio contacts?

The plurality opinion in *Burnham v. Superior Court*, 495 U.S. 604 (1990), appears to question — albeit indirectly and in dicta — general jurisdiction based upon continuous and systematic contacts. Justice Scalia wrote:

> We have said that "[e]ven when the cause of action does not arise out of or relate to the foreign corporation's activities in the forum State, due process is not offended by a State's subjecting the corporation to its *in personam* jurisdiction when there are sufficient contacts between the State and the foreign corporation." *Helicopteros Nacionales de Colombia v. Hall*, 466 U.S. at 414. Our only holding supporting that statement, however, involved "regular service of summons upon [the corporation's] president while he was in [the forum State] acting in that capacity." *See Perkins v. Benguet Consolidated Mining Co.* It may be that whatever special rule exists permitting "continuous and systematic" contacts to support jurisdiction with respect to matters unrelated to activity in the forum applies *only* to corporations, which have never fitted comfortably in a jurisdictional regime based primarily upon "de facto power over the defendant's person." *International Shoe Co. v. Washington.* We express no views on these matters. *Burnham v. Superior Court*, 495 U.S. 604, 610 n.1 (1990).

What is it about which Justice Scalia expresses no views? That *Helicopteros* was wrong in indicating that general jurisdiction could be based upon "continuous and systematic" forum contacts? That the "continuous and systematic" contacts rule applies only to companies? What is the rationale for either such result?

9. *General jurisdiction and reasonableness.* Are assertions of general jurisdiction based upon "continuous and systematic" contacts subject to the "reasonableness" requirement of *World-Wide Volkswagen's* two-prong due process test? Lower courts have not frequently addressed the issue, but generally appear to have assumed that they are. *E.g., Amoco Egypt Oil Co. v. Leonis Navigation Co.*, 1 F.3d 848 (9th Cir. 1993) (holding that "reasonableness" test is applicable to general jurisdiction); *de Reyes v. Marine Management & Consulting, Ltd.*, 586 So.2d 103 (La. 1991) (applying reasonableness in "continuous and systematic" contacts case). What impact does the Court's analysis in *Burnham* have on this result? *See infra* p. 121. Compare the Court's analysis in *Blackmer. See supra* pp. 95-100.

10. *"Continuous and systematic" contacts and international law.* Are U.S. assertions of jurisdiction over foreign companies based upon their "continuous and systematic" activities in the forum consistent with international law? Note that the *Third Restatement* §421(2)(a) & (h) provide for general jurisdiction where a person is "present" in the forum's territory or "regularly carries on business in the state." Does the Brussels Convention permit general jurisdiction? Should international law permit it?

Recall the discussion above, *supra* pp. 32 & 49, concerning the possibility of international law limits on the competence of national courts. Are the limits that specific jurisdiction imposes on the claims that may be asserted against a defendant analogous to limits on competence?

11. *Relationship between plaintiff's claims and defendant's forum contacts in Helicopteros.* According to *Helicopteros*, the plaintiffs' claims against Helicol did not "arise out of" and were not "related to" Helicol's activities within Texas. The Court relied on the plaintiffs' apparent concession to that effect. 466 U.S. at 415 n.10. The dissent in *Helicopteros* and a number of commentators have urged that the plaintiffs' claims did in fact "relate to" Helicol's activities in Texas because the ill-fated helicopter was purchased in Texas and because training for the helicopter pilots was provided in Texas. Consider the dissenting opinion in *Helicopteros*:

> [A]lthough I agree that the respondent's cause of action did not formally "arise out of" specific activities initiated by Helicol in the State of Texas, I believe that the wrongful-death claim filed by the respondents is significantly related to the undisputed contacts between Helicol and the forum. On that basis, I would conclude that the Due Process Clause allows the Texas courts to assert specific jurisdiction over this particular action. The wrongful-death actions filed by the respondents were premised on a fatal helicopter crash that occurred in Peru. Helicol was joined as a defendant in the lawsuits because it provided transportation services, including the particular helicopter and pilot involved in the crash, to the joint venture that employed the decedents. Viewed in light of these allegations, the contacts between Helicol and the State of Texas are directly and significantly related to the underlying claim filed by the respondents. The negotiations that took place in Texas led to the contract in which Helicol agreed to pro-

vide the precise transportation services that were being used at the time of the crash. Moreover, the helicopter involved in the crash was purchased by Helicol in Texas, and the pilot whose negligence was alleged to have caused the crash was actually trained in Texas. This is simply not a case, therefore, in which a state court has asserted jurisdiction over a nonresident defendant on the basis of wholly unrelated contacts with the forum. 466 U.S. at 425-26.

Note that the *Helicopteros* majority refuses to address the dissent's argument that specific jurisdiction can be asserted over all claims "relating to" the defendant's forum contacts and that this is a broader category of claims than those "arising out" of such contacts. The Court also refused to decide whether a hypothetically broader "relating to" category of claims would be treated as an assertion of specific jurisdiction.

As discussed below, some lower courts have adopted a "but for" test for specific jurisdiction, while other courts have adopted more restrictive standards, including "proximate cause" requirements. *See infra* pp. 149-50. How would *Helicopteros* be decided under these tests? Which of the following claims against Helicol would be within the specific jurisdiction of a Texas court under both a "but for" and a proximate cause test?

(a) Helicol pilots attempt to ferry a Bell helicopter from Texas to Peru, and it crashes en route in Mexico. The pilots' survivors bring suit in Texas.

(b) Helicol pilots, hired in Texas, are fired without cause or notice while in Peru. They bring suit for unfair dismissal in Texas. Suppose the pilots were hired in Peru.

(c) Helicol fails to pay Bell for helicopters purchased in Texas. Bell brings suit for the unpaid purchase price in Texas.

(d) Helicol's helicopters crash in Peru, killing Peruvians. Their survivors bring suit for wrongful death in Texas.

12. *Jurisdiction by necessity.* *Helicopteros* refused to consider the plaintiffs' argument that Colombian courts did not provide an adequate alternative forum, and therefore that Texas courts properly could exercise "jurisdiction by necessity." 466 U.S. at 419 n.13. *See also Shaffer v. Heitner*, 433 U.S. 186, 211 n.37 (1977). The doctrine of jurisdiction by necessity would permit the exercise of jurisdiction in the absence of minimum contacts (or other reasonable relationship) with the forum, if no other forum for the plaintiff's claim exists. *Helicopteros* characterized the doctrine as a "potentially far-reaching modification of existing law."

Suppose *Helicopteros* had adopted some version of jurisdiction by necessity. What weight should be given to the following facts in determining whether Colombian courts provide an alternative forum? In Colombian courts: (a) lawyers may not enter into contingent fee arrangements; (b) discovery is very limited; (c) there are no jury trials; (d) damage awards are relatively modest, on the order of 5% of U.S. awards; (e) awards will be in local currency and may be subject to exchange controls; and (f) substantive tort law is far less favorable to plaintiffs than U.S. law would be.

13. *U.S. government amicus brief.* The U.S. government submitted an *amicus curiae* brief in *Helicopteros* arguing that general jurisdiction should not ordinarily be based on a foreign defendant's *purchase* of goods in the United States:

> The United States Trade Representative has informed us that while many American export transactions do not require the seller to provide training to the personnel of the buyer, the purchase-training agreement between Helicol and Bell Helicopter in the instant case is typical in certain sectors of the economy. The Trade Representative has advised us that the provision of training by the seller is especially important in the export of high technology, turnkey projects such as nuclear power plants; in such transactions, the seller, as part of the sale transaction, customarily provides training for local personnel involved in the maintenance, overhaul and operation of the plant. The training often takes place at the manufacturer's facilities (i.e., in the United States) because of the specialized and complex nature of the training equipment and procedures. The Trade Representative has advised Congress that services of this nature "are critical to exports of high technology and capital goods." ... [T]o the extent that the decision below relies on Helicol's purchase of its helicopter fleet in Texas, coupled with the presence of Helicol employees in Texas to receive training on the operation and maintenance of the helicopters, it has a significant potential for discouraging foreign firms from purchasing American products. This would thwart positive efforts of Congress and the Executive Branch to make American firms and products more competitive internationally.

Brief for the United States as Amicus Curiae at 6, 9-12 *Helicopteros Nacionales de Colombia, SA v. Hall,* 466 U.S. 408 (1984). Are these factors relevant to due process analysis?

Recall *Pennoyer*'s reliance on international law in defining the due process clause's jurisdictional limitations. *See supra* pp. 70-73. What is the difference between *Pennoyer*'s analysis and that of the U.S. government's *amicus curiae* brief in *Helicopteros?* Suppose the brief had adduced evidence that an assertion of general jurisdiction in *Helicopteros* would have been out-of-step with the jurisdictional claims of other developed trading nations and with contemporary international law. Is this relevant to due process analysis?

How important is either U.S. export competitiveness or international law to due process analysis? Reconsider the hypothetical, posed above, in which *Helicopteros* was a purely domestic case, with the helicopter accident occurring in Arizona. Should due process analysis be affected at all because a Peruvian accident and Colombian defendant were involved?

14. **Distinction between sales and purchases.** *Helicopteros* held that a foreign purchaser's contacts with the forum were less significant for general jurisdiction than a foreign seller's contacts. Should this reasoning apply to specific jurisdiction as well as to general jurisdiction? Note that the Supreme Court leaves the issue unresolved. 466 U.S. at 418 n.12. Many lower courts have also reflected unwillingness to base personal jurisdiction on contacts resulting from an out-of-state person's purchase of products from the forum state. *E.g., Revlon, Inc. v. United Overseas Ltd.,* 1994 WL 9657 (S.D.N.Y. 1994)("well-settled distinction between sales activity and purchasing activity"); *infra* p. 147. What is the rationale for distinguishing between sales and purchases?

5. General Jurisdiction Based on Personal Service During the Transitory Presence of the Defendant Within the Forum

Consistent with 19th century notions of territorial sovereignty, the historic American basis for judicial jurisdiction was the defendant's presence before the court.[128] In Justice Holmes' classic phrase, "the foundation of jurisdiction is physical power."[129] Against this background, U.S. courts long held that service of process on an individual while he was physically within the forum state provided a sufficient basis for general jurisdiction.[130]

The rule that service during the defendant's transitory or transient presence within the forum provided a basis for general jurisdiction reached its most extreme application in the frequently-cited case of *Grace v. MacArthur.*[131] *Grace* upheld tag service on the defendant while he was a passenger in an aircraft in flight through the airspace of the forum state. The transitory jurisdiction rule, particularly in its more extreme applications, has been the subject of substantial criticism. The *Third Restatement* treats it as an illegitimate basis of jurisdiction under international law,[132] and many commentators and lower courts have rejected it under the due process clause.[133]

---

128. *Burnham v. Superior Court,* 495 U.S. 604 (1990). *But see* Ehrenzweig, *The Transient Rule of Personal Jurisdiction: The "Power" Myth and Forum Conveniens,* 65 Yale L.J. 289, 292-303 (1956) (arguing that jurisdiction based on mere presence was a "myth" that began with *Pennoyer*).

129. *McDonald v. Mabee,* 243 U.S. 90, 91 (1917).

130. *Restatement (Second) Conflict of Laws* §28 (1971); *Pennoyer v. Neff,* 95 U.S. 714 (1878); *Burnham v. Superior Court,* 495 U.S. 604 (1990).

131. 170 F. Supp. 442 (E.D. Ark. 1959).

132. *Restatement (Third) Foreign Relations Law* §421, Reporters' Note 4 (1987).

133. *E.g.,* Ehrenzweig, *The Transient Rule of Personal Jurisdiction: The "Power" Myth and Forum Conveniens,* 65 Yale L.J. 289 (1956); Weintraub, *An Objective Basis for Rejecting Transient Jurisdiction,* 22 Rutgers L. J. 611 (1991).

Nonetheless, transitory jurisdiction continues to be important in many U.S. jurisdictions and has significant practical implications for non-residents who are potential defendants. Despite the ease of international communications — by telephone, facsimile, and otherwise — business transactions inevitably involve face-to-face meetings. Indeed, the ease of international transportation makes such meetings (or simple touristic travel) a more common occurrence than hitherto was the case. For this and other reasons, "tag service" on a foreign party who has come to the United States is often possible.

The legal effect of tag service, however, remains uncertain. As described below, the Supreme Court's decision in *Burnham v. Superior Court*,[134] made it clear that tag service has substantial jurisdictional consequences. Nevertheless, the Justices' inability to agree on a majority opinion left the precise character of these consequences unclear. The decision in *Amusement Equipment, Inc. v. Mordelt*, excerpted below, illustrates one treatment of tag service in international cases.

AMUSEMENT EQUIPMENT, INC. V. MORDELT
779 F.2d 264 (5th Cir. 1985)

GOLDBERG, CIRCUIT JUDGE. It all started out innocently enough with a contract to deliver a mechanical display elephant and four control cars. The German engineering of appellee Heimo Heinz Mordelt GMBH & Co. K.G. ("Heimo") would boost the efforts of Florida's Amusement Equipment, Inc. ("Amusement") to amuse and entertain for profit. But where Hannibal's elephants managed to cross the snowy Alps with relative ease, this elephant and its vehicular entourage had an unexpected layover in a London airport on the way to their new world. Thus, for want of a transatlantic flight, Amusement's waiting truck left Florida for New Orleans without its prized quarry, which Amusement had hoped to display there at the convention of the International Association of Amusement Parks and Attractions ("IAAPA"), an Illinois corporation.

Heimo, however, is a member in good standing of the IAAPA, and its general manager, appellee Karl Heinz Mordelt ("Mordelt") attended the convention. Perhaps with visions of *Grace v. MacArthur* dancing through its corporate head, Amusement hunted Mordelt down, found him at the Marriott Hotel, served him and Heimo with process, and plunged the district court and us into the purgatory of transient jurisdiction. Finding that the rule of transient jurisdiction has suffered a fate akin to that of the once proud but now extinct dinosaurs, the district court dismissed as to both defendants. Because we are unwilling, absent explicit instructions from above, to ferry this rule across the river Styx, we reverse and remand as to Mordelt. ...

During September of 1983, the owner of Amusement, John Bond, visited

---

134. 495 U.S. 604 (1990); *infra* pp. 121-22.

Heimo's factory in West Germany and ... discussed with representatives of Heimo the possibility of acquiring certain of Heimo's products for exhibition at the Sixty-Fifth Annual Convention and Trade Show of the IAAPA, to be held in New Orleans from November 17 through 20, 1983. ... Bond [later] contacted Mordelt by telephone to procure [the] additional products for exhibition at the New Orleans trade show. Amusement Equipment agreed to purchase from Heimo one animated display elephant, four remote controlled automobiles, and certain accessory equipment for U.S. $14,295.00. Heimo understood that Amusement intended to display the products at the New Orleans trade show scheduled to begin on November 17, 1983. Amusement needed the products delivered to Miami in sufficient time before the trade show so that they could be transported by its truck to New Orleans. Accordingly, Bond demanded that the products be delivered to Miami by November 12, 1983. [Heimo agreed, but the products were delayed in transit and did not arrive in time for the trade show.] ...

Heimo is a member of the International Association of Amusement Parks and Attractions, the sponsor of the New Orleans trade show. Consequently, on November 20, 1983, Mordelt arrived in New Orleans to attend the show. Amusement alleges that Mordelt attended the show as a representative of Heimo. Thus, on November 21, 1983, Mordelt was personally served in New Orleans for himself and for his employer, Heimo. Other than their presence at the trade show and their knowledge that Amusement needed the goods for display at the show, Mordelt and Heimo had no prior connection to New Orleans or Louisiana. They have no representatives of any sort in Louisiana nor have they ever paid taxes to Louisiana. They have no assets in Louisiana, they have not advertised in any Louisiana news media, they are not listed in any Louisiana telephone directory, and they did not display any products at the trade show. ...

It is an historical truism that the transitory presence of an individual in a state to which he had no attachment or connection other than a momentary pause in his movement to other places sufficed to justify a state's exercise of personal jurisdiction. This notion developed in the days when travel was difficult and a plaintiff seeking to sue a defendant had to choose between travelling to the defendant's state or waiting to catch his prey in the unlikely chance that he wandered into the plaintiff's state. We find it somewhat ironic that we are asked today to discard the rule in these modern times of elastic, expansive, and inexpensive travel. Nonetheless, while changes in the technological landscape have lessened the rule's harsh impact, the legal landscape has changed as well. Theories of jurisdiction grounded on notions of state sovereignty, which undergirded the rule, have been eroded by theories premised on defendants' due process rights.

The transient rule of personal jurisdiction has been much maligned by the commentators. After *Shaffer v. Heitner*, in which the Supreme Court extended the due process requirements of *International Shoe* to the exercise of *quasi in rem* jurisdiction, commentators sounded the rule's death knell. Even those commentators who had supported the rule expressed considerable doubt as to its continuing viability. The source of the commentators' gloom rests principally on the following statement in *Shaffer*. "We therefore conclude that *all* assertions of state-court jurisdiction must be evaluated according to the standards set forth in *International Shoe* and its progeny." We concede that this sweeping assertion undermines the correspondingly categorical claim that "[i]t has long been black letter law that personal service within its geographical area establishes a court's personal jurisdiction over the defendant." *Donald Manter Company, Inc. v. Davis*, 543 F.2d 419, 420 (1st Cir. 1976). However, while *Shaffer* may have rendered the black letter gray, we do not think the letter of the law has become so pale that it can be read only with conjurer's glasses.

If we look to *International Shoe*, as *Shaffer* instructs us to do, we find that:

> due process requires only that in order to subject a defendant to a judgment *in personam, if he be not present within the territory of the forum*, he have certain minimum contacts with it such that the maintenance of the suit does not offend "traditional notions of fair play and substantial justice." 326 U.S. at 316 (emphasis added).

Thus, *International Shoe* itself creates an exception to minimum contacts analysis where the defendant is present within the forum state. ... Recognizing [the *International Shoe*] test as our guidepost, we conclude that there was nothing unfair or unjust in Amusement's play. Mordelt was properly served while present in New Orleans. When the defendant is present within the forum state, notice of the suit through proper service of process is all the process to which he is due. In this case, Mordelt's presence in New Orleans gave rise to a risk of his being haled into court, which, particularly in light of his knowledge that Amusement had intended to display Heimo's goods at the convention, was not so unpredictable as to be unfairly burdensome.[135] By entering Louisiana, he subjected himself to sovereign powers from which, had he remained outside the state, he was otherwise protected.

Given that a traditional notion of fair play and substantial justice has been that presence alone is sufficient to support personal jurisdiction, the facts of Mordelt's presence and proper service are decisive. *Shaffer v. Heitner's* admonition that "'traditional notions of fair play and substantial justice' can be as readily offended by the perpetuation of ancient forms that are no longer justified as by the adoption of new procedures that are inconsistent with the basic values of our constitutional heritage," does not cause us to reach a contrary conclusion. Insofar as the due process clause "does not contemplate that a state may make binding a judgment ... against an indi-

---

135. As Justice Stevens noted in *Shaffer*,

If I visit another State ..., I knowingly assume some risk that the State will exercise its power over ... my person while there. My contact with the State, though minimum, gives rise to predictable risks.

433 U.S. at 218 (concurring in the judgment).

vidual or corporate defendant with which the state has no contacts, ties, or relations," our holding is clearly not to the contrary.[136]

It could be argued that these facts are merely fortuitous, and that substantively, this case is no different from one in which Mordelt leaves Louisiana and subsequently receives service by mail. Analytically, however, there is a significant difference. While the due process clause necessarily restricts the state's sovereign power, no case has yet held that it eliminates that power altogether. That the requirement of personal jurisdiction rests in all cases on the due process clause does not weaken the proposition that the exercise of jurisdiction, as distinguished from its limitation, is a sovereign act. If there is anything that characterizes sovereignty, it is the state's dominion over its territory and those within it. Fairness does not operate in a vacuum. To abstract it from context and elevate it blindly over sovereign prerogatives is ultimately to free the individual from the obligations inherent in a statist system.

Wholly apart from the significance of the service of process, other factors strengthen our view that personal jurisdiction here is just and fair. First, defendant's presence within the forum state was purposefully related to his business existence. This is not a case in which Mordelt, in a purely personal capacity, visited New Orleans just to see relatives or to enjoy the cooking of Antoine's. Rather, the conclusion is undeniable that Mordelt was present in New Orleans on business for the purpose of representing Heimo and drumming up business for it at the convention of IAAPA, of which Heimo was a member.

Second, we note that had this suit been brought in Florida, a strong case could be made that jurisdiction would have been proper ... since the cause of action apparently arose out of business transacted with persons in Florida. The fact that the risk of being haled into a Louisiana court was significantly less than the risk of defending this suit in a Florida court takes on far less importance when the international nature of the transaction is considered. If Mordelt is to be subjected to the jurisdiction of a United States court, it matters little in weighing the burdens and inconveniences to Mordelt that the court is in Louisiana rather than Florida.

Finally, Mordelt is not without protection against the inconveniences and burdens of litigating several blocks from the French Quarter. These protections include *forum non conveniens,* change of venue, and choice of law rules. ... We hold today that the rule of transient jurisdiction has life left in it yet. ... We have asked ourselves whether Mordelt was in a relationship to the forum state that makes it ethical, not onerous, and fair, not oppressive, to subject him to the judicial arm of that state. Having answered in the affirmative, we reverse and remand. [The court also held that state law did not provide a basis for jurisdiction over Heimo GmbH.]

---

136. We do not imply that proper service, without more, is in all cases sufficient. In *Burger King* the Supreme Court explicitly rejected "any talismanic jurisdictional formulas; 'the facts of each case must [always) be weighed in determining whether personal jurisdiction would comport with 'fair play and substantial justice.'" 105 S.Ct. at 2189 (citation omitted).

Notes on Amusement Equipment

1. *Effect of* Burnham *on tag service.* A divided Supreme Court held, in *Burnham v. Superior Court of California*, 495 U.S. 604 (1990), that, where a non-resident defendant is served with process while he is physically present within the forum state, the due process clause will generally not preclude the forum court's assertion of general personal jurisdiction. *Burnham* arose after the break-up of Mr. and Mrs. Burnham's marriage. Mrs. Burnham left the couple's home in New Jersey, and moved to California, with the family's children, while Mr. Burnham remained in New Jersey. Some time later, Mr. Burnham travelled to California on business, and took the opportunity to visit his children. In turn, Mrs. Burnham arranged to have a complaint in a California state court divorce action served on her husband while he was in California. He resisted the suit, arguing that he had no meaningful connection to California, and therefore that the California courts lacked personal jurisdiction over him. The California courts rejected the argument, basing jurisdiction over Burnham entirely on the fact that he had been served with process while present within California territory.

The Supreme Court unanimously upheld the California courts' general jurisdiction over Burnham. Moreover, all members of the Court agreed that service on Mr. Burnham while he was physically present within California was highly significant to due process analysis. But the Court splintered badly, without producing a majority opinion, on the precise importance to be accorded to "tag service."

Justice Scalia, joined by three other Justices, concluded that "jurisdiction based on physical presence alone constitutes due process," without any regard to questions of "fairness" or "reasonableness." 495 U.S. at 610, 619, 622 & 628. The plurality opinion would have held that the due process clause permits "jurisdiction over a non-resident, who was personally served with process while temporarily in that State, in a suit unrelated to his activities in the State." 495 U.S. at 607. In reaching this result, Justice Scalia relied principally upon his historical conclusion that tag service was widely approved in the 1870's when the due process clause of the fourteenth amendment was adopted, and his view that this was dispositive for purposes of analyzing the due process clause. 495 U.S. at 608-16. Justice Scalia also noted that many States continue today to accept tag service as a jurisdictional base. 495 U.S. at 615-16.

Justice Brennan, joined by three other Justices, agreed that the due process clause "generally permits a state court to exercise jurisdiction over a defendant if he is served with process while voluntarily present in the forum State." 495 U.S. at 628-29. But, unlike Justice Scalia, Justice Brennan would have held that "*every* assertion of state-court jurisdiction ... must comport with contemporary notions of due process." 495 U.S. at 632. Justice Brennan apparently endorsed the formulation of §28 of the *Restatement (Second) Conflict of Laws*: "[a] state has power to exercise judicial jurisdiction over an individual who is present in its territory unless the individual's relationship to the state is so attenuated as to make the exercise of such jurisdiction unreasonable." 495 U.S. at 637.

Finally, Justice Stevens refused to join either Justice Scalia's or Justice Brennan's opinion. He reasoned that "the historical evidence and consensus ..., the considerations of fairness [and] commonsense ... all combine to demonstrate that this is, indeed, a very easy case." 495 U.S. at 640.

2. *Critique of the* Burnham *opinions.* Which view of the due process clause — that of Justice Scalia or Justice Brennan — is more consistent with *Pennoyer, World-Wide Volkswagen*, and the Court's other due process decisions? Does Justice Scalia's view that "reasonableness" and "fairness" are irrelevant to due process analysis of tag service find support in the Court's decisions? Should it? Under the two-prong analysis in *World-Wide Volkswagen*, the due process clause forbids unreasonable assertions of jurisdiction even where minimum contacts exist; would the same rationale not preclude jurisdiction in some circumstances, even where service within the forum territory had been effected? How does Justice Scalia reply?

3. *Effects of* Burnham *on* Amusement Equipment *analysis.* How would *Amusement Equipment* have been decided if it had arisen after *Burnham* was handed down? Would the opinions resulting from the Court's 4-4 split in *Burnham* have clarified Judge Goldberg's uncertainty about the validity of tag service?

4. *Territorial sovereignty as rationale for transitory presence rule.* Proponents of tag service rely almost entirely on territorial sovereignty. According to *Amusement Equipment*: "If there is anything that characterizes sovereignty, it is the state's dominion over its territory and those within it." The *Burnham* plurality offered a similar rationale: "[a]mong the most firmly established principles of personal jurisdiction in American tradition is that the courts of a State have jurisdiction over nonresidents who are physically present in the State."

Are these arguments persuasive? Most importantly, does a rule of *tag service* inevitably follow from an acknowledgement of *territorial sovereignty*? Why does the *act of service* on the defendant within the forum's territory — as opposed, for example, to the act of mailing a complaint within the forum's territory — have such significance? Is that significance logically compelled by the doctrine of territorial sovereignty?

Judge Goldberg noted that the "notion [of tag service] developed in the days when travel was difficult and a plaintiff seeking to sue a defendant had to choose between travelling to the defendant's state or waiting to catch his prey in the unlikely chance that he wandered into the plaintiff's state." Does the replacement of the stagecoach with the Concorde, and the carrier pigeon with the telephone, affect the rationale for tag service? What about the considerable expansion of judicial jurisdiction during this century? *See supra* pp. 73-77.

5. *Criticism of transitory presence rule.* Consider the following remarks about the tag service rule:

> Sitting in the lounge of his plane on a nonstop flight over New York, a citizen of California is handed a summons. For many years to come, to his great expense and greater annoyance, he will have to defend a law suit in a New York court three thousand miles away from his home, even though the plaintiff may be a spiteful competitor alleging a fanciful claim dating back many years to a trip abroad. ... The inadequacy of [the transient presence] rule, and its contrast with the law prevailing elsewhere in the world, have often been stressed. ... [A] recent author can find "nothing so irrational as the doctrine of local and transitory actions conventionally applied in the interstate field"; and another would reject wholesale the current "archaic legal techniques" of jurisdiction. ... The *Pennoyer* rule is on the way out, having reached the end of its brief usefulness. ... And pseudomedieval formulas established and perpetuated by nineteenth century conceptualism, which for decades have obstructed the free flow of legal progress, will have been replaced by what may become known as the new and old American common law of interstate venue in the forum conveniens.

Ehrenzweig, *The Transient Rule of Personal Jurisdiction: The "Power" Myth and Forum Conveniens*, 65 Yale L.J. 289 (1959) (citations omitted). Consider also:

> It can hardly be claimed that the interests of our own citizens, or friendly intercourse with other nations, will be served by encouraging the establishment of a sort of international syndicate for promoting the collection of home debts through foreign courts, so that each traveller shall be compelled to run the gauntlet of such litigation under threat of snap judgments, upon which his own government must issue execution on his return. Such a policy would offer premiums to scavengers of sham and stale claims at every center of travel, breeding a class of process servers to lie in wait for their game at docks and railway stations.

Fisher v. Fielding, 34 A. 714, 729 (Conn. 1895) (Hamersley, J., dissenting); *cf.* R. Minor, *Conflict of Laws* §124, at 285 (1901) (seizing chattel passing through jurisdiction "closer akin to robbery than to justice").

Are you persuaded by these criticisms of the transient presence rule? Are the alleged injustices and inconveniences cited by Professor Ehrenzweig all that oppressive? Recall Justice Stevens' common-sense observation that visitors to a state "knowingly assume some risk" that it will assert its power over them. Is that why Professor Ehrenzweig has to reach for the relatively odd example of service in the first class lounge on a transcontinental aircraft flight?

Criticism of tag jurisdiction is often coupled with doubts about the importance of territoriality in due process analysis. Professor Ehrenzweig derides "pseudomedieval formulas established and perpetuated by nineteenth century conceptualism." What relevance do these criticisms have for Justice Scalia's due process analysis in *Burnham*? Is there any plausible alternative to a territoriality-based approach to jurisdiction? Consider Judge Goldberg's observation that "[f]airness does not operate in a vacuum." *See supra* p. 120.

6. *International law challenges to tag jurisdiction.* The *Third Restatement* declared that tag jurisdiction violates contemporary international law. "Jurisdiction based on service of process on one only transitorily present in a state is no longer acceptable under international law if that is the only basis for jurisdiction and the action in question is unrelated to that state." *Restatement (Third) Foreign Relations Law* §421 & Reporters' Note 5 (1987). The Restatement does not, however, cite any authority for that conclusion — beyond reliance upon the Brussels Convention. Consider Article 3 of the Convention, which forbids U.K. courts from asserting jurisdiction on EU domiciliaries based solely on tag service. Does that support the

Restatement's position? Does it matter that (in an Article not cited by the Restatement's Reporters' Note) the Convention specifically preserves England's right to exercise tag jurisdiction over non-domiciliaries of EU Member States (*e.g.*, U.S. domiciliaries)? *See supra* p. 92.

7. *Moderation of transitory presence rule.* Did *Amusement Equipment* abandon entirely the "transitory jurisdiction" rule? Did it hold that the due process clause is invariably satisfied by service on the defendant within the forum state? Is the *Amusement Equipment* analysis more similar to that of Justice Scalia or Justice Brennan?

8. *Exceptions to transitory presence rule — fraud, litigation, and settlement negotiations.* The perceived harshness of the transitory jurisdiction rule has been mitigated somewhat by judicially fashioned exceptions. In general, tag service will not confer personal jurisdiction if the defendant's presence was procured by the plaintiff's fraud or force. *See* Annotation, *Attack on Personal Service as Having Been Obtained by Fraud or Trickery*, 98 A.L.R.2d 551 (1964). Another exception has arisen for persons entering a state solely for the purpose of litigation. *Restatement (Second) Conflict of Laws* §83 (1971). A related exception has been recognized, in some cases, for persons who enter the forum state to negotiate settlement of a dispute. *Henkel Corp. v. Degremont, SA*, 1991 WL 62453 (E.D. Pa. April 19, 1991).

Are the fraud, force, and other exceptions consistent with the territoriality principle underlying the rule of transitory jurisdiction? Are they consistent with the reasonableness prong of due process analysis? Would Justice Scalia really permit jurisdiction where tag service was effected by fraud?

9. *Tag service on corporate officers. Amusement Equipment* held that, under Louisiana law, tag service on Mr. Mordelt did not provide jurisdiction over Heimo GmbH — even though Mordelt was the general manager of the company.

(a) *Lower court decisions dealing with tag service on corporate officers.* The few lower courts to have considered whether tag service on a corporate officer provides jurisdiction over the corporation are divided. *Compare Scholz Research and Development, Inc. v. Kurzke*, 720 F.Supp. 710 (N.D. Ill. 1989) (due process clause does not permit jurisdiction over company based upon tag service on corporate officer); *Easterling v. Cooper Motors, Inc.*, 26 F.R.D. 1 (M.D.N.C. 1960) ("the mere fact that there is personal service upon an officer of a foreign corporation who is present in the State is insufficient to subject a foreign corporation to the jurisdiction of the court") *with Aluminal Indus., Inc. v. Newtown Commercial Assoc.*, 89 F.R.D. 326 (S.D.N.Y. 1980) (limited partnership subject to general jurisdiction based solely on tag service on general partner in New York).

(b) Burnham *dicta dealing with tag service on corporate officers.* In *Burnham*, a plurality subscribed to a footnote that purported to explain the result in *Perkins v. Benquet Consolidated Mining Co.*: Our holding "involved 'regular service of summons upon [the corporation's] president while he was in [the forum State] acting in that capacity.'" *Burnham v. Superior Court*, 495 U.S. 604, 610 n.1 (1990) (quoting *Perkins*). The apparent suggestion is that general jurisdiction was appropriate in *Perkins* only (or principally) because the company's president had been served while within the forum. That suggests that tag service on a corporate officer has at least some jurisdictional consequences for his corporation. *Perkins* itself makes clear, however, that tag service was not the basis of (or even a material factor supporting) jurisdiction. Moreover, the Court had earlier held that tag service upon a corporate officer did not provide a constitutionally adequate basis for jurisdiction over the company. *E.g.*, *James-Dickinson Farm Mortgage Co. v. Harry*, 273 U.S. 113 (1927).

10. *Transitory presence and specific jurisdiction.* Was *Amusement Equipment* the difficult general jurisdiction case that the court's opinion suggests? Note that the foreign defendants knew that the plaintiffs intended to use their products at the IAAPA convention in Louisiana and that process was served on the defendants at the convention. Would *Amusement Equipment* have been decided differently if, for example, the defendants had been served during a U.S. business trip in a state that was unrelated to the plaintiff's agreement with the defendant? during a tourist visit?

11. *Practical implications of tag service.* Although the transitory jurisdiction rule is invoked rather infrequently, lawyers should be aware of its existence in counselling clients both before and after litigation is initiated. Personal service within the forum on the defendant, or a proper agent of the defendant, might foreclose or seriously weaken jurisdictional defenses that could otherwise be available. Counsel should take care that potential defendants and their agents avoid or minimize travel to the forum in these circumstances.

C. Specific Jurisdiction of U.S. Courts Over Foreign Defendants

As described above, contemporary due process analysis distinguishes between general and specific personal jurisdiction. While general jurisdiction permits adjudication of any claim against a defendant, specific jurisdiction permits the adjudication only of claims that "arise out of" or "relate to" a defendant's activities within the forum state.[137]

1. Specific Jurisdiction in International Product Liability and Tort Cases

Vast quantities of products are imported into the United States from foreign sources each day. Inevitably, some of these products cause injury to American individuals or companies, leading to efforts by the injured parties to obtain compensation from all those involved in the design, manufacture, and distribution of the products. These efforts have resulted in countless lower court decisions considering the extent to which foreign parties are subject to U.S. jurisdiction in product liability actions. Unfortunately, this litigation has produced few clear rules.

a. Purposeful Contacts and The Stream of Commerce Doctrine

The "stream of commerce" doctrine has played a central role in international product liability and tort cases. That theory is generally traced to *Gray v. American Radiator & Standard Sanitary Corp.*,[138] a frequently-cited 1961 decision of the Illinois Supreme Court. In *Gray*, the court asserted specific jurisdiction in a product liability suit over an out-of-state manufacturer of components that were incorporated by another out-of-state company into water heaters. The water heaters were then distributed on an interstate basis, including into Illinois, where one of them malfunctioned. Apparently relying entirely on the fact that the component manufacturer had knowingly placed its product in the interstate "stream of commerce," the Illinois court upheld personal jurisdiction. *Gray* was widely followed in other jurisdictions, including in international cases like *McCombs v. Cerco Rentals*,[139] which is excerpted below.

The Supreme Court's decision in *World-Wide Volkswagen* provides the contemporary foundation for dealing with issues of specific jurisdiction in international product liability and tort cases. As discussed above,[140] the Court set out a two-part test under which jurisdiction cannot be asserted unless both: (i) the defendant has "minimum contacts" with the forum as a result of "purposefully availing" itself of the benefits and protections of the forum's laws; and (ii) the exercise of jurisdiction would be "reasonable." *World-Wide Volkswagen* emphasized that the mere "foresee-

---

137. *E.g.*, *Helicopteros Nacionales de Colombia, SA v. Hall*, 466 U.S. 408, 414-15 (1984); *Restatement (Third) Foreign Relations Law* §421(2)(i), (j) & (k) (1987); *supra* pp. 77-78 & 114-15.

138. 176 N.E.2d 761 (Ill. 1961).

139. 622 S.W.2d 822 (Tenn. Ct. App. 1981).

140. *See supra* pp. 73-77, 82-85 & 91-92.

ability" that a defendant's conduct would have effects within a forum did not satisfy the "purposeful availment" test.[141]

Nevertheless, *World-Wide Volkswagen* also accepted at least some formulations of the stream of commerce doctrine. The Court said that due process does not preclude "personal jurisdiction over a corporation that delivers its products into the stream of commerce with the expectation that they will be purchased by consumers in the forum State."[142] It also referred to *Gray*'s stream of commerce analysis, but without specifying approval.[143]

In *Asahi Metal Indus. Co. v. Superior Court*, the Court reconsidered the "stream of commerce" theory, producing a splintered decision.[144] Although 8 members of the Court agreed that assertion of jurisdiction over the Japanese defendant in that case would be "unreasonable," the Court split 4-4-1 on the question whether the due process clause's "purposeful contacts" requirement was satisfied. Four Justices thought that it was not. They joined an opinion by Justice O'Connor reasoning that a defendant's mere awareness that the stream of commerce might carry its product into the forum did not constitute purposeful availment.[145]

Four other Justices thought that purposeful contacts did exist. They joined an opinion by Justice Brennan finding jurisdiction because the defendant had purposefully placed its components in the international stream of commerce knowing that they were regularly sold in the forum.[146] As in *Burnham*, Justice Stevens joined neither opinion, but concluded that purposeful contacts existed.[147] Not surprisingly, post-*Asahi* lower court decisions reflect considerable uncertainty over the present status of the stream of commerce doctrine. The decision in *Gould v. P.T. Krakatau Steel*,[148] excerpted below, is one post-*Asahi* attempt to apply the stream of commerce doctrine.

b. Reasonableness

The reasonableness prong of *World-Wide Volkswagen*'s due process analysis also plays a significant role in product liability cases. As described above, "reasonable-

---

141. *See supra* pp. 91-92.

142. 444 U.S. at 297-98.

143. The *World-Wide Volkswagen* Court wrote:

The forum State does not exceed its power under the Due Process Clause if it asserts personal jurisdiction over a corporation that delivers its products into the stream of commerce with the expectation that they will be purchased by consumers in the forum State. *Cf. Gray v. American Radiator & Standard Sanitary Corp.*, 176 N.E.2d 761 (1961). 444 U.S. at 297-98.

The "*cf.*" citation is capable of ambiguity and ordinarily requires an explanatory parenthetical. According to The Bluebook, a "*cf.*" citation means that the "[c]ited authority supports a proposition different from the main proposition but sufficiently analogous to lend support." *The Bluebook* 23 (15th ed. 1991).

144. 480 U.S. 102 (1987).

145. 480 U.S. at 111.

146. 480 U.S. at 117.

147. 480 U.S. at 111.

148. 957 F.2d 573 (8th Cir. 1992).

ness" encompasses a range of factors, including the burden on the defendant, the plaintiff's interests, the forum state's interests, and the interests of other states.[149]

The reasonableness analysis raises special issues in international cases. The hardship resulting from U.S. jurisdiction is usually greater for defendants in international cases than in domestic ones. International cases also usually affect both foreign nations, and U.S. international relations, in ways that domestic cases do not. These factors often pull in different directions, and give rise to difficult questions under the due process clause's reasonableness prong. Some guidance is provided in *Asahi*, which applies the reasonableness requirement to deny jurisdiction. But lower courts continue to grapple with these issues, reaching inconsistent results.[150]

c. Defining the Forum "State": A Preliminary View

Finally, all three of the following decisions invite reflection upon the appropriate geographic unit for purposes of applying the due process clause's "purposeful contacts" test in international cases. In *World-Wide Volkswagen, Helicopteros, United Rope*, and *Amusement Equipment*, the issue was nominally whether the defendant had constitutionally-sufficient contacts with the particular U.S. state where the forum court was located (*e.g.*, Texas or Louisiana). That is, of course, consistent with the due process clause's focus on state action, as well as the emphasis in *Pennoyer* and *World-Wide Volkswagen* on state sovereignty. Consider, however, whether this focus on state contacts makes sense in international cases. For example, should the due process clause force a district court in Pennsylvania to ignore a French defendant's contacts with New Jersey, Delaware, New York, and Maryland? Consider this issue as you read *McCombs* and *Krakatau*.

McCOMBS v. CERCO RENTALS

622 S.W.2d 822 (Tenn. Ct. App. 1981)

GODDARD, JUDGE. ... Potain, SA, a French manufacturer, insists that the Law Court of Sullivan County erred in denying its motion to dismiss the claim filed by [the McCombs], premised upon want of personal jurisdiction. Potain, SA, a French corporation, manufactured a tower crane, Model 776, in France and exported it to the United States, whereupon it was sold on September 5, 1973, to H.B. Owsley & Sons, Inc., [an unrelated] North Carolina corporation, through Potain, Inc., a wholly-owned subsidiary of Potain, SA and its exclusive North American distributor. On July 15, 1976, H.B. Owsley & Sons, Inc. and Potain, SA entered a contract, which

---

149. *See supra* pp. 83 & 92.

150. *See infra* 139-43; *Barone v. Rich Bros. Interstate Display Fireworks Co.*, 25 F.3d 610 (8th Cir. 1994); *Beverly Hills Fan Co. v. Royal Sovereign Corp.*, 21 F.3d 1558 (Fed. Cir. 1994); *Amoco Egypt Oil Co. v. Leonis Navigation Co.*, 1 F.3d 848 (9th Cir. 1993); *Vermeulen v. Renault, U.S.A., Inc.*, 965 F.2d 1014 (11th Cir. 1992), *modified*, 985 F.2d 1534 (1993); *FDIC v. British-American Ins. Co.*, 828 F.2d 1439, 1442-45 (9th Cir. 1987); *Austad Co. v. Pennie & Edmonds*, 823 F.2d 223 (8th Cir. 1987); *Paccar Int'l v. Commercial Bank of Kuwait, S.A.K.*, 757 F.2d 1058 (9th Cir. 1985).

became effective August 1, 1976, whereby Potain America, Inc., which was to be incorporated by H.B. Owsley & Sons, Inc., with assets purchased from Potain, Inc., would become the exclusive sales agent in the United States and Canada for all tower cranes, parts and accessories manufactured by Potain, SA. On July 20, 1976, Cerco Rentals, a leasing subsidiary of H.B. Owsley & Sons, Inc., leased the crane to Cassell Brothers, Inc., a Tennessee corporation, for use in the construction of a hospital in Kingsport, Tennessee. On August 1, 1976, H.B. Owsley & Sons, Inc., purchased the assets of Potain, Inc., and incorporated Potain America, Inc., under the laws of North Carolina, as a wholly-owned subsidiary of H.B. Owsley & Sons, Inc. The McCombs allege that on March 25, 1977, while in use at the hospital construction site in Kingsport, the crane malfunctioned causing them to suffer damages. There is no showing of any other connection between Potain, SA and the State of Tennessee. ...

[Because the Tennessee long-arm statute extends to the limits of the due process clause,] the only relevant inquiry here is whether the due process clause ... permits a Tennessee state court to exercise personal jurisdiction over a French manufacturer where its only connection with Tennessee is that one of its cranes entered this country through its wholly-owned subsidiary and was sold to an independent middleman which, while under contract to become the manufacturer's exclusive North American distributor, leased the crane to a Tennessee corporation for use in Tennessee, where damage occurred. ... Courts have held that where jurisdiction is sought upon the basis of a tort which occurred within the state, rather than merely upon the basis of a defendant doing unrelated business within the state, that it is not unreasonable nor unjust to hold the defendant answerable when the defendant has voluntarily placed its products into the channels of national commerce for ultimate use in another state and these channels have carried the product to Tennessee where it has caused damages. This holds true even where the product has entered the state through an independent middleman. *See Gray v. American Radiator & Standard Sanitary Corp.* ... The [due process clause's purposeful availment requirement] is satisfied by the defendant voluntarily injecting his product into the stream of interstate commerce, by which he should have reasonably foreseen that consequences could result in Tennessee. ...

[Potain] cites and relies upon the recent case of *World-Wide Volkswagen.* ... *World-Wide* is distinguishable from the case before us. In *World-Wide* the injury-producing product entered the state by the mere fortuity that a New York resident who purchased the automobile in New York drove it into Oklahoma. Here the crane entered Tennessee through a chain of distribution initiated by Potain, SA. This case is more analogous to *Gray v. American Radiator & Standard Sanitary Corp.*, which was contrasted with *World-Wide* in the quoted portion of the Supreme Court opinion. ...

In a well-reasoned opinion filed after *World-Wide*, the Fifth Circuit held in *Oswalt v. Scripto, Inc.*, 616 F.2d 191 (5th Cir. 1980), that a Japanese manufacturer of

cigarette lighters which were sold and delivered to Scripto in Japan and then marketed nationwide in the United States by Scripto pursuant to an exclusive distributor
agreement was subject to personal jurisdiction in a federal district court in Texas
wherein a lighter was purchased through a middlemen and allegedly caused injury,
although there was no evidence the manufacturer had any other contacts with Texas
or the United States. The Fifth Circuit held that the imposition of personal jurisdiction was (1) consistent with both the holding and dicta in *World-Wide*; and (2) reasonable and fair since the manufacturer delivered millions of lighters to Scripto with
the understanding Scripto would be the exclusive United States distributor and
would be selling them to national retail concerns, without the manufacturer in any
way attempting to limit the states in which they would be sold. The fact in our case
that only one product, of far greater value, entered Tennessee as opposed to the
many disposable lighters which presumably entered Texas does not distinguish the
case. The logic alluded to in the dicta in *World-Wide* and embraced in *Oswalt* is
equally applicable to the case before us. ...

Potain, SA exported its products to the United States for distribution throughout this country. The record reveals no evidence that Potain, SA either intended or
anticipated distribution to be limited to the State of North Carolina or to otherwise
exclude Tennessee, or made any efforts to so limit its distribution. Potain, SA could
reasonably anticipate being haled into a Tennessee court to answer to a product liability claim. Potain, SA indirectly availed itself of the laws of Tennessee by injecting
its product into the stream of national commerce through which it was eventually, in
the normal chain of distribution, leased to a Tennessee corporation for use in
Tennessee. The cause of action arises directly from the intended use of that product
in Tennessee, by which a Tennessee citizen was injured. The tort occurred in
Tennessee, presumably most of the prospective witnesses are in this State, and
Tennessee's substantive law is applicable. The exercise of personal jurisdiction is both
just and reasonable.

SANDERS, JUDGE, dissenting. ... Perhaps the principal basis for my disagreement with my colleagues is that I do not think the crane "entered Tennessee through
a chain of distribution initiated by Potain, SA" as stated in the majority opinion. In
my view, the crane entered Tennessee through a chain of circumstances unrelated to
any activity by Potain, SA or its distributor. ... Under the facts in the case at bar we
ask: How has [the purposeful contacts] criterion been met?

The majority opinion seems to answer this question by saying that Potain, SA
placed its product in the stream of commerce and it was foreseeable that the crane
might reach the State of Tennessee and cause the injury there. ... It will be observed
that the critical point of foreseeability is "the defendant's conduct or connection with
the forum state." What was the conduct or connection that Potain, SA had with the
State of Tennessee to bring it within the foreseeability rule? ... In my view, whatever
connection, if any, there is between Potain, SA and the State of Tennessee, it is an
isolated occurrence. Then we ask: What efforts are shown to have been made by

Potain, SA, or its distributor to market cranes in Tennessee? The majority opinion answers these questions by saying, "Here the crane entered Tennessee through a chain of distribution initiated by Potain, SA" I cannot agree that the record supports this conclusion. In my view, the holding in the majority opinion stands for the proposition that when the manufacturer of a product places it in the stream of commerce and it is foreseeable that it may go into other states and, due to a defective condition, a person is injured in Tennessee, Hawaii, Alaska, or any other state, that state can exercise *in personam* jurisdiction over the manufacturer even though there has been no other contact. ...

ASAHI METAL INDUSTRY CO. v. SUPERIOR COURT OF CALIFORNIA, SOLANO COUNTY

480 U.S. 102 (1987)

JUSTICE O'CONNOR announced the judgment of the Court and delivered the unanimous opinion of the Court with respect to Part I, the opinion of the Court with respect to Part II-B, in which THE CHIEF JUSTICE, JUSTICE BRENNAN, JUSTICE WHITE, JUSTICE MARSHALL, JUSTICE BLACKMUN, JUSTICE POWELL, and JUSTICE STEVENS join, and an opinion with respect to Part II-A and III, in which THE CHIEF JUSTICE, JUSTICE POWELL, and JUSTICE SCALIA join. This case presents the question whether the mere awareness on the part of a foreign defendant that the components it manufactured, sold, and delivered outside the United States would reach the forum state in the stream of commerce constitutes "minimum contacts" between the defendant and the forum state such that the exercise of jurisdiction "does not offend 'traditional notions of fair play and substantial justice.'"

I. On September 23, 1978, on Interstate Highway 80 in Solano County, California, Gary Zurcher lost control of his Honda motorcycle and collided with a tractor. Zurcher was severely injured, and his passenger and wife, Ruth Ann Moreno, was killed. In September 1979, Zurcher filed a product liability action in the Superior Court of the State of California in and for the County of Solano. Zurcher alleged that the 1978 accident was caused by a sudden loss of air and an explosion in the rear tire of the motorcycle, and alleged that the motorcycle tire, tube, and sealant were defective. Zurcher's complaint named, *inter alia*, Cheng Shin Rubber Industrial Co., Ltd. ("Cheng Shin"), the Taiwanese manufacturer of the tube. Cheng Shin in turn filed a cross-complaint seeking indemnification from its codefendants and from petitioner, Asahi Metal Industry Co., Ltd. ("Asahi"), the manufacturer of the tube's valve assembly. Zurcher's claims against Cheng Shin and the other defendants were eventually settled and dismissed, leaving only Cheng Shin's indemnity action against Asahi.

California's long-arm statute authorizes the exercise of jurisdiction "on any basis not inconsistent with the Constitution of this state or of the United States." Asahi moved to quash Cheng Shin's service of summons, arguing the State could not exert jurisdiction over it consistent with the Due Process Clause of the Fourteenth Amendment.

Asahi is a Japanese corporation. It manufactures tire valve assemblies in Japan and sells the assemblies to Cheng Shin, and to several other tire manufacturers, for use as components in finished tire tubes. Asahi's sales to Cheng Shin took place in Taiwan. The shipments from Asahi to Cheng Shin were sent from Japan to Taiwan. Cheng Shin bought and incorporated into its tire tubes 150,000 Asahi valve assemblies in 1978; 500,000 in 1979; 500,000 in 1980; 100,000 in 1981; and 100,000 in 1982. Sales to Cheng Shin accounted for 1.24 percent of Asahi's income in 1981 and 0.44 percent in 1982. Cheng Shin alleged that approximately 20 percent of its sales in the United States are in California. Cheng Shin purchases valve assemblies from other suppliers as well, and sells finished tubes throughout the world.

In 1983 an attorney for Cheng Shin conducted an informal examination of the valve stems of the tire tubes sold in one cyclery in Solano County. The attorney declared that of the approximately 115 tire tubes in the store, 97 were purportedly manufactured in Japan or Taiwan, and of those 97, 21 valve stems were marked with the circled letters "A," apparently Asahi's trademark. Of the 21 Asahi valve stems, 12 were incorporated into Cheng Shin tire tubes. The store contained 41 other Cheng Shin tubes that incorporated the valve assemblies of other manufacturers. An affidavit of a manager of Cheng Shin whose duties included the purchasing of component parts stated: "'In discussions with Asahi regarding the purchase of valve stem assemblies the fact that my Company sells tubes throughout the world and specifically the United States has been discussed. I am informed and believe that Asahi was fully aware that valve stem assemblies sold to my Company and to others would end up throughout the United States and in California.'" An affidavit of the president of Asahi, on the other hand, declared that Asahi, "'had never contemplated that its limited sales of tire valves to Cheng Shin in Taiwan would subject it to lawsuit in California.'"...

The Supreme Court of the State of California [held that Asahi was subject to the personal jurisdiction of the California courts]. The court considered Asahi's intentional act of placing its components into the stream of commerce — that is, by delivering the components to Cheng Shin in Taiwan — coupled with Asahi's awareness that some of the components would eventually find their way into California, sufficient to form the basis for state court jurisdiction under the Due Process Clause.

II A[151] Applying the principle that minimum contacts must be based on the act of the defendant, the Court in *World-Wide Volkswagen*, rejected the assertion that a *consumer's* unilateral act of bringing the defendant's product into the forum State was a sufficient constitutional basis for personal jurisdiction over the defendant. It had been argued in *World-Wide Volkswagen* that because an automobile retailer and its wholesale distributor sold a product mobile by design and purpose, they could foresee being haled into court in the distant States into which their customers might

---

151. [Part II-A of the *Asahi* opinion was joined only by Justices O'Connor, Rehnquist, Powell, and Scalia.]

drive. The Court rejected this concept of foreseeability as an insufficient basis for jurisdiction under the Due Process Clause. The Court disclaimed, however, the idea that "foreseeability is wholly irrelevant" to personal jurisdiction, concluding that "[t]he forum State does not exceed its powers under the Due Process Clause if it asserts personal jurisdiction over a corporation that delivers its products into the stream of commerce with the expectation that they will be purchased by consumers in the forum State." ...

Since *World-Wide Volkswagen*, lower courts have been confronted with cases in which the defendant acted by placing a product in the stream of commerce, and the stream eventually swept defendant's product into the forum State, but the defendant did nothing else to purposefully avail itself of the market in the forum state. Some courts have understood the Due Process Clause, as interpreted in *World-Wide Volkswagen*, to allow an exercise of personal jurisdiction to be based on no more than the defendant's act placing the product in the stream of commerce. Other courts have understood the Due Process Clause and the above-quoted language in *World-Wide Volkswagen* to require the action of the defendant to be more purposefully directed at the forum State than the mere act of placing a product in the stream of commerce.

The reasoning of the Supreme Court of California in the present case illustrates the former interpretation of *World-Wide Volkswagen*. The Supreme Court of California held that, because the stream of commerce eventually brought some valves Asahi sold Cheng Shin into California, Asahi's awareness that its valves would be sold in California was sufficient to permit California to exercise jurisdiction over Asahi consistent with the requirements of the Due Process Clause. The Supreme Court of California's position was consistent with those courts that have held that mere foreseeability or awareness was a constitutionally sufficient basis for personal jurisdiction if the defendant's product made its way into the forum State while still in the stream of commerce. ...

Other courts, however, have understood the Due Process Clause to require something more than that the defendant was aware of its product's entry into the forum State through the stream of commerce in order for the state to exert jurisdiction over the defendant. In the present case, for example, the State Court of Appeal did not read the Due Process Clause, as interpreted by *World-Wide Volkswagen*, to allow "mere foreseeability that the product will enter the forum state [to] be enough by itself to establish jurisdiction over the distributor and retailer." In *Humble v. Toyota Motor Co., Ltd.*, 727 F.2d 709 (CA8 1984), an injured passenger brought suit against Arakawa Auto Body Company, a Japanese corporation that manufactured car seats for Toyota. Arakawa did no business in the United States; it had no office, affiliate, subsidiary, or agent in the United States; it manufactured its component parts outside the United States and delivered them to Toyota Motor Company in Japan. The Court of Appeals, adopting the reasoning of the District Court in that case, noted that although it "does not doubt that Arakawa could have foreseen that its product would find its way into the United States," it would be "manifestly unjust" to require Arakawa to defend itself in the United States. ...

We now find this latter position to be consonant with the requirements of due process. The "substantial connection" between the defendant and the forum State necessary for a finding of minimum contacts must come about by *an action of the defendant purposefully directed toward the forum State.* The placement of a product into the stream of commerce, without more, is not an act of the defendant purposefully directed toward the forum State. Additional conduct of the defendant may indicate an intent or purpose to serve the market in the forum State, for example, designing the product for the market in the forum State, advertising in the forum State, establishing channels for providing regular advice to customers in the forum State, or marketing the product through a distributor who has agreed to serve as the sales agent in the forum State. But a defendant's awareness that the stream of commerce may or will sweep the product into the forum State does not convert the mere act of placing the product into the stream into an act purposefully directed toward the forum State.

Assuming, *arguendo*, that respondents have established Asahi's awareness that some of the valves sold to Cheng Shin would be incorporated into tire tubes sold in California, respondents have not demonstrated any action by Asahi to purposefully avail itself of the California market. Asahi does not do business in California. It has no office, agents, employees, or property in California. It does not advertise or otherwise solicit business in California. It did not create, control, or employ the distribution system that brought its valve to California. ... On the basis of these facts, the exertion of personal jurisdiction over Asahi by the Superior Court of California exceeds the limits of Due Process.

IIB. The strictures of the Due Process Clause forbid a state court from exercising personal jurisdiction over Asahi under circumstances that would offend "traditional notions of fair play and substantial justice." We have previously explained that the determination of the reasonableness of the exercise of jurisdiction in each case will depend on the evaluation of several factors. A court must consider the burden on the defendant, the interests of the forum state, and the plaintiff's interest in obtaining relief. It must also weigh in its determination "the interstate judicial system's interest in obtaining the most efficient resolution of controversies; and the shared interest of the several States in furthering fundamental substantive social policies." A consideration of these factors in the present case clearly reveals the unreasonableness of the assertion of jurisdiction over Asahi, even apart from the question of the placement of goods in the stream of commerce.

Certainly the burden on the defendant in this case is severe. Asahi has been commanded by the Superior Court of California not only to traverse the distance between Asahi's headquarters in Japan and the Superior Court of California in and for the County of Solano, but also to submit its dispute with Cheng Shin to a foreign nation's judicial system. The unique burdens placed upon one who must defend oneself in a foreign legal system should have significant weight in assessing the reasonableness of stretching the long arm of personal jurisdiction over national borders.

When minimum contacts have been established, often the interests of the plaintiff and the forum in the exercise of jurisdiction will justify even the serious burdens placed on the alien defendant. In the present case, however, the interests of the plaintiff and the forum in California's assertion of jurisdiction over Asahi are slight. All that remains is a claim for indemnification asserted by Cheng Shin, a Taiwanese corporation, against Asahi. The transaction on which the indemnification claim is based took place in Taiwan; Asahi's components were shipped from Japan to Taiwan. Cheng Shin has not demonstrated that it is more convenient for it to litigate its indemnification claim against Asahi in California rather than in Taiwan or Japan.

Because the plaintiff is not a California resident, California's legitimate interests in the dispute have considerably diminished. The Supreme Court of California argued that the State had an interest in "protecting its consumers by ensuring that foreign manufacturers comply with the state's safety standards." The State Supreme Court's definition of California's interest, however, was overly broad. The dispute between Cheng Shin and Asahi is primarily about indemnification rather than safety standards. Moreover, it is not at all clear at this point that California law should govern the question whether a Japanese corporation should indemnify a Taiwanese corporation on the basis of a sale made in Taiwan and a shipment of goods from Japan to Taiwan. ...

World-Wide Volkswagen also admonished courts to take into consideration the interests of the "several States," in addition to the forum state, in the efficient judicial resolution of the dispute and the advancement of substantive policies. In the present case, this advice calls for a court to consider the procedural and substantive policies of other *nations* whose interests are affected by the assertion of jurisdiction by the California court. The procedural and substantive interests of other nations in a state court's assertion of jurisdiction over an alien defendant will differ from case to case. In every case, however, those interests, as well as the Federal interest in its foreign relations policies, will be best served by a careful inquiry into the reasonableness of the assertion of jurisdiction in the particular case, and an unwillingness to find serious burdens on an alien defendant outweighed by minimal interests on the part of the plaintiff or the forum State. "Great care and reserve should be exercised when extending our notions of personal jurisdiction into the international field." *United States v. First National City Bank*, 379 U.S. 378, 404 (1965) (Harlan, J., dissenting). *See* Born, *Reflections on Judicial Jurisdiction in International Cases*, [17 Ga. J. Int'l & Comp. L. 1] (1987).

III. Considering the international context, the heavy burden on the alien defendant, and the slight interests of the plaintiff and the forum State, the exercise of personal jurisdiction by a California court over Asahi in this instance would be unreasonable and unfair.

JUSTICE BRENNAN, with whom JUSTICE WHITE, JUSTICE MARSHALL,

and JUSTICE BLACKMUN join, concurring in part and in the judgment. I do not agree with the plurality's interpretation of the stream-of-commerce theory, nor with its conclusion that Asahi did not "purposely avail itself of the California market." I do agree, however, with the Court's conclusion in Part II-B that the exercise of personal jurisdiction over Asahi in this case would not comport with "fair play and substantial justice." This is one of those rare cases in which "minimum requirements inherent in the concept of 'fair play and substantial justice' ... defeat the reasonableness of jurisdiction even [though] the defendant has purposefully engaged in forum activities." I therefore join Parts I and II-B of the Court's opinion, and write separately to explain my disagreement with Part II-A.

The plurality states that "a defendant's awareness that the stream of commerce may or will sweep the product into the forum State does not convert the mere act of placing the product into the stream into an act purposefully directed toward the forum State." The plurality would therefore require a plaintiff to show "[a]dditional conduct" directed toward the forum before finding the exercise of jurisdiction over the defendant to be consistent with the Due Process Clause. I see no need for such a showing, however. The stream of commerce refers not to unpredictable currents or eddies, but to the regular and anticipated flow of products from manufacture to distribution to retail sale. As long as a participant in this process is aware that the final product is being marketed in the same forum State, the possibility of a lawsuit there cannot come as a surprise. Nor will the litigation present a burden for which there is no corresponding benefit. A defendant who has placed goods in the stream of commerce benefits economically from the retail sale of the final product in the forum State, and indirectly benefits from the State's laws that regulate and facilitate commercial activity. These benefits accrue regardless of whether that participant directly conducts business in the forum State, or engages in additional conduct directed toward that State. Accordingly, most courts and commentators have found that jurisdiction premised on the placement of a product into the stream of commerce is consistent with the Due Process Clause, and have not required a showing of additional conduct. ...

In this case, the facts found by the California Supreme Court support its findings of minimum contacts. The Court found that "[a]lthough Asahi did not design or control the system of distribution that carried its valve assemblies into California, Asahi was aware of the distribution system's operation, and it knew that it would benefit economically from the sale in California of products incorporating its components." Accordingly, I cannot join the plurality's determination that Asahi's regular and extensive sales of component parts to a manufacturer it knew was making regular sales of the final product in California is insufficient to establish minimum contacts with California.

JUSTICE STEVENS, with whom JUSTICE WHITE and JUSTICE BLACKMUN join, concurring in part and concurring in the judgment. The judgment of the Supreme Court of California should be reversed for the reasons stated in Part II-B of the Court's opinion. While I join Parts I and II-B, I do not join Part II-A for two reasons. First, it is not necessary to the Court's decision. ... Part II-B establishes, after considering the factors set forth in *World-Wide Volkswagen Corp. v. Woodson*, that California's exercise of jurisdiction over Asahi in this case would be "unreasonable and unfair." This finding alone requires reversal. ...

Second, even assuming that [a "purposeful direction] test ought to be formulated here, Part II-A misapplies it to the facts of this case. The Court seems to assume that an unwavering line can be drawn between "mere awareness" that a component will find its way into the forum State and "purposeful availment" of the forum's market. Over the course of its dealings with Cheng Shin, Asahi has arguably engaged in a higher quantum of conduct than "[t]he placement of a product into the stream of commerce, without more. ..." Whether or not this conduct rises to the level of purposeful availment requires a constitutional determination that is affected by the volume, the value, and the hazardous character of the components. In most circumstances I would be inclined to conclude that a regular course of dealing that results in deliveries of over 100,000 units annually over a period of several years would constitute "purposeful availment" even though the item delivered to the forum State was a standard product marketed throughout the world.

GOULD v. P.T. KRAKATAU STEEL

957 F.2d 573 (8th Cir. 1992)

FLOYD R. GIBSON, SENIOR CIRCUIT JUDGE. ... P.T. Krakatau Steel ("Krakatau"), an Indonesian corporation with its principal place of business in Jakarta, Indonesia, manufactures steel products. Krakatau has no offices, agents or property located in the United States and all of its manufacturing and sales take place in Indonesia. In August of 1986, Krakatau placed an advertisement in the "Metal Bulletin," a steel industry journal published in the United Kingdom and distributed worldwide. In the advertisement Krakatau stated that its products complied with international standards, including the American Standards for Testing and Materials ("ASTM"). During 1987, Krakatau's general manager and marketing director met twice with representatives of Empire Steel Trading Company, Inc. ("Empire"), a New York corporation with its principal place of business in New York. The meetings took place in San Francisco, California and New York. On November 6, 1987, Krakatau and Empire entered into a contract for the sale of approximately 14,000 metric tons of Krakatau products, f.o.b. Indonesia. Empire accepted delivery of the products in Indonesia, transported the products to the United States and sent approximately 3,000 metric tons of the total shipment of cast wire rods [valued at approximately $900,000] to Forbes Steel in West Memphis, Arkansas. Leamon Gould, a Forbes employee, brought this products liability action against Krakatau for permanent injuries he received while unpacking the wire rods at the Forbes plant in August of 1988. The district court dismissed the complaint finding that Krakatau had insufficient contacts with the state of Arkansas to support in personam jurisdiction. Gould appeals. ...

[On appeal,] Gould argues that under the Arkansas "long-arm" statute, the district court may exercise personal jurisdiction over Krakatau. ... Because Arkansas' long-arm statute extends jurisdiction over nonresidents to the limits permitted by the due process clause of the United States constitution, our inquiry is limited to whether the district court's exercise of jurisdiction over Krakatau is consistent with due process. ...

Gould contends Krakatau had significant contact with the state of Arkansas by virtue of its advertising in a British trade journal circulated worldwide, the physical presence of Krakatau officers in the United States to solicit business, and the continual sales of Krakatau products to the United States. We disagree. In applying the principles set forth above, we conclude the exercise of personal jurisdiction over Krakatau would offend traditional notions of fair play and substantial justice. Although we recognize that Arkansas has a strong interest in providing a forum for an injured resident to bring a products liability action against a nonresident defendant, we find there are insufficient contacts between Krakatau and Arkansas to satisfy due process.

Krakatau is an Indonesian corporation; it is not licensed to do business in the state of Arkansas, nor does it have any office, agent, property, bank accounts or business operations in the state. Krakatau does not advertise or solicit any business in the state, nor does it specially design or tailor its products for use in Arkansas. We disagree with Gould's contention that Krakatau's advertisement in a British trade publication establishes minimum contacts with the state of Arkansas. Krakatau's advertisement, which states that it complies with international standards for steel products, is an insufficient contact with the forum state to satisfy due process. *See Soo Line Railroad v. Hawker Siddeley Canada Inc.*, 950 F.2d 526, 528 (8th Cir. 1991) (compliance with international railroad standards deemed insufficient contact with forum state).

Furthermore, Krakatau's placement of the wire rods into the stream of international commerce is not an act "purposefully directed" toward the state of Arkansas. Krakatau's contact with Arkansas consisted only of the "fortuitous" introduction of Krakatau products into Arkansas by Empire. Gould argues that Krakatau could have foreseen that its products would enter the state of Arkansas by virtue of its sales to Empire. We disagree. Although it is arguable that Krakatau could have foreseen that its products would enter the United States, it is highly unlikely that Krakatau could have reasonably anticipated being haled into an Arkansas court. *Humble v. Toyota Motor Co., Ltd.*, 727 F.2d 709, 710 (8th Cir. 1984). At most, Krakatau conducted a limited amount of business with Empire and it was solely at Empire's direction that the wire coils arrived in Arkansas. Standing alone, the fact that the Krakatau could foresee that its product might find its way to Arkansas is too attenuated to constitute purposeful availment of Arkansas' laws and protections. *See World-Wide Volkswagen*

Corp. v. Woodson, 444 U.S. 286, 297 (1980). It would be manifestly unjust to require Krakatau to defend itself in a foreign country based on these contacts between Krakatau and the state of Arkansas. ...

Notes on McCombs, Asahi Metal, and Krakatau

1. *Relevance of defendant's foreign identity to due process analysis in* Asahi. As described above, the Court gave no indication in *Benguet* or *Helicopteros* whether the same limitations on personal jurisdiction should apply to foreigners as are applied to U.S. citizens in domestic cases. How did *Asahi* resolve this issue?

(a) *Heightened restraint under reasonableness requirement in asserting jurisdiction over foreign defendants.* Among other things, in discussing the "reasonableness" prong of due process analysis, *Asahi* commented that "[t]he unique burdens placed upon one who must defend oneself in a foreign legal system should have significant weight in assessing the reasonableness of stretching the long arm of personal jurisdiction over national borders." In addition, the Court borrowed the following observation from Justice Harlan: "Great care and reserve should be exercised when extending our notions of personal jurisdiction into the international field." *United States v. First Nat'l City Bank*, 379 U.S. 378, 404 (1965) (Harlan, J., dissenting). What does it mean to give "significant weight" to burdens on foreign defendants, or to exercise "great care and reserve" in international cases? Is this heightened restraint relevant only to the reasonableness prong of due process analysis? Or does it also affect the quantity and quality of minimum contacts required under the "purposeful availment" prong? How did the defendant's foreign identity affect purposeful contacts analysis in *Asahi*?

(b) *Greater inconvenience as rationale for heightened restraint.* Why should U.S. courts exercise "great care and reserve" in asserting jurisdiction over foreigners? As noted above, one reason *Asahi* gave was the burdens imposed on foreign defendants litigating abroad:

> In many international cases one party will be required to follow procedural rules that differ markedly from those in its home jurisdiction. The most important differences involve broad discovery in the United States, greater reliance on the adversary system, trial by jury, different approaches to fee shifting and contingent fee arrangements, the relatively greater size of United States damage awards, and different choice-of-law rules. In addition, one litigant will generally be a significantly greater distance from the forum than in purely domestic cases, and time differences, language barriers, mail delays, transportation difficulties, and other logistical obstacles which impede efficient communications will create further hardships. Furthermore, while the United States is a relatively homogeneous legal, economic, cultural, social and political unit, the domestic institutions and attitudes within this country often differ markedly from those in foreign states. Born, *Reflections on Judicial Jurisdiction in International Cases*, 17 Ga. J. Int'l & Comp. L. 1, 24-25 n.102 (1987).

Are these persuasive reasons for restraining jurisdiction over foreigners? The burdens imposed on a foreign defendant in international litigation are not unique. U.S. plaintiffs will face the reverse difficulties that foreign defendants encounter in this country if jurisdiction is denied and they are required to litigate their claims abroad. How should this "symmetry" of burdens affect the treatment of foreign defendants? In apparent contrast to *Asahi*, consider the following: *Delong Equipment Co. v. Washington Mills Abrasive Co.*, 840 F.2d 843, 850, 854 ("[A]ny inconvenience caused to [defendants] by subjecting them to the jurisdiction of the Northern District of Georgia is overridden by the greater inconvenience of requiring a Georgia plaintiff, injured in Georgia by the defendants' purposeful activity in and directed at Georgia, to pursue its cause of action in a foreign forum.").

Note that personal jurisdiction analysis ordinarily focuses on the burdens that litigation in the forum imposes on the defendant, not the plaintiff. *See supra* p. 94; von Mehren & Trautman, *Jurisdiction to Adjudicate: A Suggested Analysis*, 79 Harv. L. Rev. 1121 (1966). Is this a sufficient response?

(c) *Foreign sovereignty as rationale for heightened restraint.* Asahi also reasoned that heightened restraint was necessary in evaluating reasonableness because assertions of jurisdiction over foreign defendants affect foreign policies, laws, and interests, as well as U.S. foreign relations. Before *Asahi* was decided, a number of lower courts had considered foreign sovereign interests and concluded that they required a greater showing of reasonableness to justify asserting jurisdiction over a foreign defendant than is required for domestic defendants. *E.g., Pacific Atlantic Trading Co. v. M/V Main Express*, 758 F.2d 1325, 1330 (9th Cir. 1985) ("sovereignty barrier is high"); *Rocke v. Canadian Auto. Sport Club*, 660 F.2d 395, 399 (9th Cir. 1981) ("Where the defendant is a resident of a foreign nation rather than a resident of another state within our federal system, the sovereignty barrier is 'higher.'"); *Bersch v. Drexel Firestone, Inc.*, 519 F.2d 974, 1000 (2d Cir.), *cert. denied*, 423 U.S. 1018 (1975) (when jurisdiction is based on foreign acts, court must proceed "with caution, particularly in an international context").

Was *Asahi* correct in indicating that foreign relations concerns should play a role in the due process analysis of U.S. courts? Or should these "political" concerns be cognizable only by Congress and the President in their conduct of the nation's foreign relations? Recall the U.S. government's *amicus curiae* brief in *Helicopteros* invoking U.S. export promotion efforts. *See supra* pp. 115-16. Suppose the defendants in *Asahi* had been tube and valve manufacturers that were incorporated and based in the United States (for example, Illinois). Would a California court's assertion of jurisdiction on these facts be any more or less reasonable than in the actual *Asahi* case? Why? Do the differences relate to the differing burdens on U.S. and foreign defendants? or to the different "sovereignty" concerns? *See Roth v. Garcia Marquez*, 942 F.2d 617, 623 (9th Cir. 1991) ("higher jurisdictional barrier" "in international cases is not dispositive because, if given controlling weight, it would always prevent suit against a foreign national in a United States Court"); *Saccamani v. Robert Reiser & Co.*, 348 F.Supp. 514 (W.D. Pa. 1972) ("Nor do we think it makes any difference that the manufacturer resides overseas. International trade is as commonplace as interstate trade in many products and the jet engine allows a German manufacturer to come here about as easily as one from California. We see no difference in requiring the [foreign defendant] to defend their products here and requiring some United States manufacturer to do the same so long as they both ship goods into Pennsylvania for sale.").

(d) *Effect of defendant's foreign identity on purposeful contacts analysis.* Did *Asahi* alter generally-applicable purposeful contacts standards because it was dealing with a foreign defendant? Did *McCombs* or *Krakatau*? Consider two possible modifications that might be made to purposeful contacts analysis in international cases: (i) a higher or lower showing of purposeful contacts must be made to obtain specific jurisdiction over a foreign defendant than over a domestic defendant; and (ii) the purposeful contacts inquiry should consider the defendant's contacts with the entire United States, not merely the particular forum state. Are these modifications permissible under the due process clause? Desirable?

2. *Passage of title abroad does not insulate foreign manufacturer from U.S. personal jurisdiction.* The sales in *Krakatau* were "f.o.b. Indonesia," generally meaning that title, risk of loss, and responsibility for shipping and insurance passed to the buyer in Indonesia. What role should this have in due process analysis? Does it matter whether jurisdiction is asserted in a tort suit by someone other than the buyer (as in *Krakatau*) or in a contract action by the buyer?

It is well-settled that a foreign manufacturer cannot insulate itself from the personal jurisdiction of a U.S. court by entering into agreements pursuant to which title to its products passes to a distributor outside the United States. *E.g., Renner v. Lanard Toys Ltd.*, 33 F.3d 277 (3d Cir. 1994) ("Nothing in Justice O'Connor's plurality opinion [in *Asahi*] suggests that the fact that a foreign manufacturer or seller rids itself of title by a sale F.O.B. a foreign port is enough to insulate that manufacturer or seller from jurisdiction ..."); *Oswalt v. Scripto, Inc.*, 616 F.2d 191, 197 n.8 (5th Cir. 1980) ("jurisdiction does not depend on the technicalities of when title passes"). Indeed, the fact that a foreign manufacturer consummates the sales of its products, and title passes, outside the United States, is often said to be irrelevant to jurisdictional analysis. *Vermeulen v. Renault, U.S.A. Inc.*, 965 F.2d 1014, 1025 (11th Cir. 1992) ("the fact that title to the [foreign defendant's] vehicles passed to [its U.S. distributor] in France in no way determines the degree of contacts"); *In re Connecticut Asbestos Litigation*, 677 F.Supp. 70 (D. Conn. 1986) ("The assertion that [the foreign defendant] always shipped its products F.O.B. Montreal is immaterial in determining whether there is personal jurisdiction over it."). Should this be true in contract as well as tort cases?

3. *Original stream of commerce doctrine.* As *Gray* and *McCombs* illustrate, some courts have held that due process permits jurisdiction whenever a manufacturer's products are carried by the "stream of commerce" into the forum. These decisions apparently did not consider whether the defendant either purposefully directed its products into the forum or knew or should have known that its products were sold or used in the forum; rather, the defendant need only purposefully "place its products in the stream of commerce." *See Hedrick v. Daiko Shoji Co.*, 715 F.2d 1355 (9th Cir. 1983); *Swanigan v. Amadeo Rossi, SA*, 617 F.Supp. 66 (E.D. Mich. 1985) ("Defendant Amadeo Rossi's handguns are sold in Michigan. This is a sufficient basis for the asserted personal jurisdiction."). What precedential value do these decisions have

after *World-Wide Volkswagen* and *Asahi*? Why shouldn't this minimalist stream of commerce analysis be adopted? If the defendant makes a product that allegedly malfunctions in the forum, why shouldn't that be an end of analysis? What interests are protected by requiring "purposeful" contacts with the forum? Does this requirement protect the defendant? or foreign sovereignty?

4. Stream of commerce doctrine in Asahi. In *Asahi*, the Court again divided sharply over the "stream of commerce" test.

(a) *Justice O'Connor's plurality opinion.* Four Justices concluded in *Asahi* that placing a product into the stream of commerce "without more" is not an act purposefully directed toward the forum State. That is true even where a defendant is "aware[] that the stream of commerce may or will sweep the product into the forum." Rather, the plurality required some additional evidence of "an intent or purpose to serve the market in the forum State," such as designing products for the forum's market, advertising in the forum, or marketing products through an agent who agreed to serve the forum market.

What does Justice O'Connor's opinion require to demonstrate "purposeful" contacts? One commentator has declared that Justice O'Connor's *Asahi* opinion "has made it virtually impossible for an injured plaintiff to sue a component parts manufacturer in any state or country other than its place of domicile or the state or country where delivery of the component part is made to a product assembler." Wiseman, *Reconstructing the Citadel: The Advent of Jurisdictional Privity*, 54 Ohio St. L. J. 403, 404 (1993). Is this correct? Consider the following judicial comment:

> The *Asahi-Volkswagen* approach is particularly pernicious in the advantage it gives to foreign producers whose goods enter the American common market. These firms can organize themselves to avoid jurisdiction in any state or federal court. Because jurisdictional due process allows many foreign manufacturers to circumvent American courts altogether, United States residents often will be unable to avail themselves of the strong protection of American tort law.

In re DES Cases, 789 F.Supp. 552, 575 (E.D.N.Y. 1992). Is this an accurate view of the law? *Compare Renner v. Lanard Toys Ltd.*, 33 F.3d 277 (3d Cir. 1994) ("the distinction between Justices O'Connor's view and Justice Stevens' may be a subtle one").

(b) *Justice Brennan's dissenting opinion.* Justice Brennan and three other Justices rejected the plurality's analysis in *Asahi*. They concluded that "[a]s long as *a participant* in [the distribution of products] *is aware* that the final product is being marketed in the forum State, the possibility of a lawsuit there cannot come as a surprise." These Justices would have held that "Asahi's regular and extensive sales of component parts to a manufacturer it knew was making regular sales of the final product in California" satisfied the due process clause. What is Justice Brennan's test? Is mere "awareness" enough to establish minimum contacts? Is this view consistent with *World-Wide Volkswagen*?

(c) *Justice Stevens' concurring opinion.* Justice Stevens did not join either Justice O'Connor's or Brennan's opinion in *Asahi*. He did, however, predict that "[i]n most circumstances I would be inclined to conclude that a regular course of dealing that results in deliveries of over 100,000 units annually over a period of several years would constitute 'purposeful availment.'" (Note that Justice Stevens' statistics were confused: the number of Asahi's valves that were sold each year in California by Cheng Shin appear to have been no more than 100,000 (in 1979 and 1980) and often only 20,000 — and then only by making the unlikely assumption that Cheng Shing sold *all* its tire tubes in the United States.)

(d) *Evaluating Asahi's stream of commerce opinions.* What are the differences between these three views of the stream of commerce analysis? Which is wiser? How would *McCombs* and *Krakatau* be decided under each of the *Asahi* opinions?

5. Lower court applications of stream of commerce doctrine after Asahi. Lower courts are badly divided over the effect of *Asahi*, and application of the stream of commerce test presently turns largely on the particular U.S. forum that considers the issue. As one lower court has observed: "The *Asahi* case left lower courts in a quandary, not knowing what principles they should apply in deciding the minimum contacts issue." *Lister v. Marangoni Meccanica SpA*, 728 F.Supp. 1524, 1527 (D. Utah 1990).

(a) *Lower courts holding that Asahi does not affect due process analysis. Krakatau* did not discuss *Asahi*'s stream of commerce analysis. A few other courts have taken much the same approach, reasoning that the Court's inability to produce a majority opinion in *Asahi* left the stream of commerce doctrine unchanged. In turn, that leaves litigants to contend with local, pre-*Asahi* interpretations of *World-Wide Volkswagen* and the stream of commerce test. *E.g., Beverly Hills Fan Co. v. Royal Sovereign Corp.*, 21 F.3d 1558, 1566 (Fed. Cir. 1994) (declining to adopt either Justice O'Connor or Justice Brennan's analysis);

Dehmlow v. Austin Fireworks, 963 F.2d 941, 946 (7th Cir. 1992) ("Because the Supreme Court established the stream of commerce theory, and a majority of the Court has not yet rejected it, we consider that theory to be determinative.").

(b) *Lower courts holding that Justice O'Connor's opinion in* Asahi *rejects the stream of commerce doctrine.* Some courts have held that Justice O'Connor's opinion indicates that the Court will reject the stream of commerce doctrine. *E.g., Jarre v. Heidelberger Druckmaschinen AG*, 19 F.3d 1430 (4th Cir. 1994); *Boit v. Gar-Tec Products, Inc.*, 967 F.2d 671, 683 (1st Cir. 1992) (plaintiff must show that foreign defendant "intended to serve the [forum's] market").

(c) *Lower courts holding that Justice Brennan's opinion in* Asahi *reaffirms stream of commerce doctrine.* Other lower courts have concluded that *Asahi*'s plurality opinion could not overrule *World-Wide Volkswagen* and other previous Supreme Court decisions purportedly adopting the stream of commerce doctrine; these courts have generally followed Justice Brennan's opinion. *E.g., Barone v. Rich Bros. Interstate Display Fireworks Co.*, 25 F.3d 610, 614 (8th Cir. 1994) ("five Justices agreed that continuous placement of a significant number of products into the stream of commerce with knowledge that the product would be distributed into the forum represents sufficient minimum contacts").

6. *Examples of purposeful availment in international stream of commerce cases.* What sorts of activities constitute purposeful availment in international product liability cases?

(a) *Designing products for forum market.* A common basis for purposeful availment is designing a product specifically for the forum market. *E.g., In re Perrier Bottled Water Litigation*, 754 F.Supp. 264, 268 (D. Conn. 1990) (holding that Perrier designed its product for U.S. market "which, of course, includes Connecticut and Pennsylvania," because bottles had ounce, rather than metric labels); *Lister v. Marangoui Meccanica SpA*, 728 F.Supp. 1524, 1527 (D. Utah) (upholding jurisdiction where a company in the forum provided the specifications for the custom-built product to the defendant). *Compare Soo Line RR Co. v. Hawker Siddeley Canada, Inc.*, 950 F.2d 526 (8th Cir. 1991) (refusing jurisdiction because "Hawker Siddeley did not design its railcars for use in Minnesota per se; it designed its railcars for use in most of North America").

(b) *Providing literature in or tailored for forum.* Lower courts have found purposeful availment based upon the defendant's supply of promotional or other literature tailored for forum users. *E.g., Weight v. Kawasaki Motors Corp., U.S.A.*, 604 F.Supp. 968 (E.D. Va. 1985) (foreign manufacturer subject to jurisdiction because, among other things, it provided English owner's manuals); *Van Eeuwen v. Heidelberg Eastern, Inc.*, 306 A.2d 79 (N.J. Super. 1973) (jurisdiction upheld where foreign manufacturer had $500,000 in annual sales to two unrelated U.S. distributors and provided promotional materials to distributors).

(c) *Sending employees or agents into forum.* Lower courts have cited foreign defendants' dispatch of employees or agents to the forum as evidence of purposeful availment. *E.g., Mason v. F. LLI Luigi and Franco Dal Maschio FU G.B.*, 832 F.2d 383 (7th Cir. 1987) (defendant "made the machine involved in the accident and similar machines especially [for the plaintiff's employer], and one of its employees visited [the employer] in [the forum] several times to show how to set up, operate and service the machines and to teach its personnel"); *Heins v. Wilhelm Loh Wetzlar Optical Machinery GmbH*, 522 N.E.2d 989 (Mass. App. 1988) (foreign manufacturer subject to specific jurisdiction where it was aware that its products were used in the forum, sent employees into forum to current and prospective clients, and provided advice to existing clients). *Compare Brabeau v. SMB Corp.*, 789 F.Supp. 873 (E.D. Mich. 1992) (no jurisdiction where defendant's "technician assist[ed] in the installation of a printing press" in the forum which caused injury to plaintiff).

(d) *Establishing distribution network in forum.* Significant factors in finding purposeful availment have been the defendant's establishment of a distribution system serving the forum and advertising in the forum. *E.g., Mott v. Schelling & Co.*, 966 F.2d 1453 (6th Cir. 1992) (defendant "actively cultivated its market here, and benefitted from numerous U.S. sales"); *Vermeulen v. Renault, U.S.A. Inc.*, 965 F.2d 1014, 1026 (11th Cir. 1992) (foreign defendant "created and controlled the distribution network that brought its products into the United States and Georgia").

(e) *Granting licenses for distribution in forum.* Lower courts have relied on a defendant's grant of a U.S. distribution license as evidence of purposeful availment. *E.g., Lister v. Marangoni Meccanica SpA*, 728 F.Supp. 1524, 1527 (D. Utah 1990) (upholding specific jurisdiction where, among other things, the "product was marketed through a distributor who agreed to serve this and other states"); *McDaniel v. Armstrong World Indus.*, 603 F.Supp. 1337 (D.D.C. 1985) (jurisdiction upheld over foreign manufacturer who granted sublicenses, expressly covering forum, to independent companies, which distributed product in forum). *Compare Maschinenfabrik Seydelmann v. Altman*, 468 So.2d 286 (Fla. App. 1985) (no jurisdiction where German defendant appointed exclusive U.S. distributor and, over 22-year period, sold 23 machines with total value of $750,000).

(f) *Substantial numbers of units sold.* A few lower courts have relied principally on large numbers of sales in the forum in inferring purposeful availment. *E.g., Oswalt v. Scripto, Inc.*, 616 F.2d 191 (5th Cir. 1980) (relying on 3-4 million units in annual sales); *McHugh v. Kenyon*, 547 So.2d 318 (D. Ct. App. Fla. 1989) ("A manufacturer that produces hundreds of thousands of product units [ladders] that are distributed over a five-year period in the United States, of which at least 6,000 were marketed in Florida, should reasonably anticipate being sued" there); *Allen v. Canadian General Electric Co.*, 410 N.Y.S.2d 707 (App. Div. 1978) (jurisdiction upheld over foreign manufacturer that derived only 1% of its revenues from shipments to forum; court rejected argument that 1% was de minimis, and focused on absolute value of shipments (which was $9 million annually)). *Compare* Justice Stevens' observations in *Asahi* as to the unit and dollar sales he thought sufficient for due process purposes, *supra* pp. 134-35, 139. Is it useful, or proper, to rely on the number or value of annual sales? How is this relevant to the territorial sovereignty of foreign states or the fairness to the defendant?

7. *Defining the territory of the forum — a preliminary view.* In *McCombs* and *Krakatau*, the foreign defendant knowingly sold its products to a U.S. company, located in the United States, for use in the United States. What importance should these contacts with the *entire United States* — as distinguished from the states of *Arkansas* or *Tennessee* — have for due process analysis? Do *McCombs* and *Krakatau* adopt a consistent approach to this issue?

Suppose in *Krakatau* that the steel had been sold directly to Mr. Gould's employer, following meetings in Arkansas with the defendant. Suppose that Empire Steel had been an Arkansas corporation doing business in Arkansas? On the actual facts of the case can Mr. Gould sue Krakatau in New York? As a practical matter, do you think Mr. Gould is going to sue Krakatau in Indonesia? In determining whether Krakatau has minimum contacts with Arkansas, what relevance does its contacts with New York and other U.S. states have? This question often appears highly relevant to a sensible analysis. Consider the discussion below of the national contacts test under the due process clause of the fifth amendment. *See infra* pp. 174-95.

Lower courts have generally not addressed the relevance of a foreign defendant's contacts with other U.S. states under the fourteenth amendment. Nevertheless, a number of lower courts have, without explanation, apparently attributed jurisdictional significance to a foreign defendant's contacts with the entire United States. *E.g., Vermeulen v. Renault, U.S.A. Inc.*, 965 F.2d 1014 (11th Cir. 1992) ("Although ... there is no evidence that [defendant] designed the LeCar specifically for the Georgia market, the fact that [defendant] designed its products for the United States generally as part of a nationwide marketing effort ..." satisfies *Asahi*); *Ensign-Bickford Co. v. ICI Explosives USA Inc.*, 817 F.Supp. 1018 (D. Conn. 1993) ("reasonable inference that the sale of a large number of devices to a firm with a nationwide distribution network will generally result in the sale ... of one of those devices in the state of Connecticut").

Other lower court decisions, like *Krakatau*, have apparently accorded no weight to a defendant's contacts with U.S. states other than the forum state. *E.g., Pawlnczyk v. Global Upholstery Co.*, 854 F.Supp. 364 (E.D. Pa. 1994) (rejecting argument that "the sale of [defendant's products] anywhere in the United States is sufficient to establish personal jurisdiction ... in Pennsylvania"); *Brabeau v. SMB Corp.* 789 F.Supp. 873, 878 n.2 (E.D. Mich. 1992) ("contacts with the state in which the district court sits are controlling, not contact with the United States as a whole"); *Sturgill v. Chema Nord Delakkemi Nobel Indus.*, 687 F.Supp. 351 (S.D. Ohio 1988) (annual U.S. sales over 10 year period of $200,000-$700,000, consisting of 10-30 shipments of 200-600 metric tons does not confer jurisdiction where no products were shipped directly into the forum state).

Which is the proper approach? Can it really be right for Mr. Gould to be forced to sue in Indonesia, because the defendant's contacts were with New York instead of Arkansas? Could Mr. Gould have invoked specific jurisdiction to sue in New York?

8. *Asahi's "reasonableness" test.* *Asahi* is also significant because of its detailed treatment of the "reasonableness" prong. Reconsider Part II-B of Justice O'Connor's opinion. Note that eight Justices agreed that, even if minimum contacts existed, reasonableness considerations would preclude jurisdiction.

Consider the factors cited in *Asahi's* reasonableness analysis. In addition to requiring "great care and reserve" in exercising personal jurisdiction over foreigners, the Court emphasized that "California's interests in the dispute have considerably diminished," because the case involved a fairly unusual indemnification dispute between two *foreign* companies. The Court also remarked that "[w]hen minimum contacts have been established, often the interests of the plaintiff and the forum in the exercise of jurisdiction will justify even the serious burdens placed on the alien defendant." It remains to be seen whether the unusual factual setting of *Asahi* will detract from the admonition to exercise "great care and reserve" in asserting jurisdiction over foreign defendants.

9. *Lower court applications of reasonableness requirement after* **Asahi**. A number of lower courts have applied *Asahi*'s reasonableness test in international cases.

(a) *General reluctance to decline jurisdiction where minimum contacts exist.* In general, lower courts have been reluctant to decline jurisdiction over foreign defendants that have minimum contacts with the forum because of reasonableness concerns. E.g., *Domtar. Inc. v. Niagra Fire Ins. Co.*, 518 N.W.2d 58 (Minn. App. 1994) ("Canadian General has not indicated any unique burdens imposed on it by having to enter a foreign legal system, nor ... any potential foreign policy concerns"). Nevertheless, a few post-*Asahi* decisions have denied jurisdiction on reasonableness grounds. E.g., *Core-Vent Corp. v. Nobel Industries AB*, 11 F.3d 1482 (9th Cir. 1993) (denying jurisdiction over Swedish defendants on reasonableness grounds where minimum contacts existed); *Falkirk Mining Co. v. Japan Steel Works Ltd.*, 906 F.2d 369 (8th Cir. 1990) (refusing jurisdiction over Japanese defendant in part because of burdens of international litigation).

(b) *Plaintiff's nationality or residence.* In *Asahi*, Justice O'Connor emphasized that "[b]ecause the plaintiff is not a California resident, California's legitimate interests in the dispute have considerably diminished." Suppose that the Court had been considering a Californian court's jurisdiction over Asahi (and Cheng Shin) in Mr. Zurcher's underlying suit. Would Justice O'Connor's reasonableness analysis have produced any different result? Note that Asahi would face the same burdens in defending the action, while California's "interest" in the suit would have been substantially greater. See *Irving v. Owens-Corning Fiberglas Corp.*, 864 F.2d 383, 384-85 (5th Cir. 1989) (unlike *Asahi*, "this asbestos litigation ... involves Texas plaintiffs using a local forum to pursue compensation for alleged injuries that occurred in Texas"); *Theunissen v. Matthews*, 935 F.2d 1454, 1462 (6th Cir. 1991) ("Michigan has interest in providing a forum for" Michigan citizens). Several lower courts have declined to assert jurisdiction in disputes between two non-U.S. parties. E.g., *Fields v. Sedgwick Assoc. Risks, Ltd.*, 796 F.2d 299, 300 (9th Cir. 1986) (no specific jurisdiction in dispute between two foreign parties); *Pacific Atlantic Trading Co. v. M/V Main Express*, 758 F.2d 1325, 1330 (9th Cir. 1985) (forum has only slight interest in dispute between two foreign parties).

In effect, under the reasonableness prong of the due process clause, it is easier for U.S. citizens than it is for foreign citizens to obtain personal jurisdiction over foreign defendants. Is this appropriate? Compare the importance of the plaintiff's nationality in the forum non conveniens and choice of law contexts, *infra* pp. 316-17 & 506-07. What if an injury to a forum domiciliary occurs outside the forum's territory? Is the plaintiff's nationality relevant to reasonableness analysis? to purposeful contacts analysis?

(c) *Situs of injuries.* Other courts have focused on a state's interest in redressing injuries that occur *on its territory* without regard to the nationality of the victim. E.g., *Keeton v. Hustler Magazine, Inc.*, 465 U.S. 770, 779 (1984) ("It is beyond dispute that New Hampshire has a significant interest in redressing injuries that actually occur within the State."). Which factor — the plaintiff's nationality/domicile or the situs of the tort — is more significant for due process analysis? Why? Consider the following:

> In both situations the state has an interest in discouraging negligent conduct within its borders. The deference due to a state's desire to protect its own residents needs no explanation. By discouraging negligent conduct within its borders not only nonresidents but residents too are afforded greater protection. In some ways, however, the interest of a state in the welfare of nonresidents injured within its borders is stronger. An injured resident can look to friends and relatives in the community to help him through the financial and emotional difficulties that accompany a physical injury. He may more readily obtain assistance in meeting medical bills and find a friendly home during the recuperative period. This is not so often the case when injury happens to a nonresident, particularly an alien. Not only is such a person less likely to have outside resources at his call, but barriers of language and custom may handicap him in getting a job to support himself and discharge financial obligations incurred within the state. The chances of his becoming a public charge and failing to pay his local creditors are increased. *Gkiafis v. SS Yiosonas*, 342 F.2d 546 (4th Cir. 1965).

Is that persuasive?

(d) *Strength of minimum contacts showing.* An important factor in reasonableness analysis is the strength of any showing of minimum contacts. *Asahi* involved what was at best a marginal minimum contacts showing, even in Justice Brennan's view. Lower courts have accorded considerable weight in reasonableness analysis to the quantum and quality of the defendant's minimum contacts. *E.g., Core-Vent Corp. v. Nobel Industries AB,* 11 F.3d 1482 (9th Cir. 1993) (reasonableness analysis considers "the extent of interjection" into the forum); *Felix v. Bomoro KG,* 241 Cal. Rptr. 670 (Calif. Ct. App. 1987) ("the degree to which a foreign corporation interjects itself into the forum state directly affects the fairness of subjecting it to jurisdiction. The smaller the element of purposeful interjection, the less is jurisdiction to be anticipated and the less reasonable is its exercise").

10. *International law limits on "stream of commerce" or "effects" doctrine.* Does (and should) international law limit assertions of jurisdiction based on a "stream of commerce" or "effects" doctrine? Consider §421(2)(j) ("the person ... carried on outside the state an activity having a substantial, direct and foreseeable effect within the state, but only in respect of such activity"). Note §421's requirement of "foreseeable" effects. How does that compare with *Asahi* and *World-Wide Volkswagen*?

11. *Brussels Convention jurisdiction in tort cases.* Article 5(3) of the Brussels Convention permits jurisdiction in tort actions in "the place where the harmful event occurred." In *Bier v. Mines de Potasse d'Alsace,* Case 21/76 [1976] E.C.R. 1735, the European Court of Justice held that Article 5(3) gives the plaintiff a choice of suing either (a) where tortious injury occurred, or (b) where tortious conduct occurred. The case involved claims that the dumping of pollutants in a river in one state caused injury in states to which the pollutants were carried. Assuming that the Court's reading of Article 5(3) extends beyond this context, is its interpretation consistent with §421 and international law? Does the rule in *Bier* suggest that *Asahi* and *World-Wode Volkswagen* impose unduly restrictive limits on stream of commerce jurisdiction?

2. Specific Jurisdiction in International Contract Disputes

International contract disputes have given rise to difficult issues of specific jurisdiction in U.S. courts. The general two-prong test articulated in *World-Wide Volkswagen* and *Asahi* again provides the foundation for due process analysis. In addition, the Supreme Court's 1985 decision in *Burger King Corp. v. Rudzewicz* provides more particular guidance in contract disputes.[152]

Burger King, a purely domestic case, discussed the circumstances in which a contract could support personal jurisdiction under the due process clause. The Court first held that the mere existence of a contract with a resident of the forum did not necessarily subject the defendant to jurisdiction there:

> [W]e note a continued division among lower courts respecting whether and to what extent a contract can constitute a "contact" for purposes of due process analysis. If the question is whether an individual's contract with an out-of-state party *alone* can automatically establish sufficient minimum contacts in the other party's home forum, we believe the answer clearly is that it cannot. The Court long ago rejected the notion that personal jurisdiction might turn on "mechanical" tests, or on "conceptualistic ... theories of the place of contracting or of performance."[153]

The Court went on to hold that the existence of a contract was nevertheless highly relevant to due process analysis:

---

152. 471 U.S. 462 (1985).
153. 471 U.S. at 478-79.

[W]e have emphasized the need for a "highly realistic" approach that recognizes that a "contract" is "ordinarily but an intermediate step serving to tie up prior business negotiations with future consequences which themselves are the real object of the business transaction." It is these factors — prior negotiations and contemplated future consequences, along with the terms of the contract and the parties' actual course of dealing — that must be evaluated in determining whether the defendant purposefully established minimum contacts within the forum.[154]

Applying this analysis, *Burger King* upheld a Florida district court's jurisdiction over an out-of-state franchisee of a Florida franchisor. The Court based its holding principally upon a long-term franchise agreement between the plaintiff and defendant. The Court emphasized the long-term character of the parties' agreement; the contract's "careful structure," "continuing wide-reaching" character, and "exacting regulation" of the franchisee's conduct; the fact that notices and payments were to be sent to an address within the forum state; and the defendants' dealing with plaintiff's representatives located within the forum state.[155] The decision excerpted below, in *Afram Export Corp. v. Metallurgiki Halyps, SA*, illustrates the application of *Burger King* and the due process clause to international contracts.

AFRAM EXPORT CORP. v. METALLURGIKI HALYPS, SA

772 F.2d 1358 (7th Cir. 1985)

POSNER, CIRCUIT JUDGE. Afram Export Corporation, the plaintiff, is a Wisconsin corporation that exports scrap metal. Metallurgiki Halyps, SA, the defendant, is a Greek corporation that makes steel. In 1979, after a series of trans-Atlantic telephone and telex communications, the parties made a contract through an exchange of telex messages for the purchase by Metallurgiki of 15,000 tons of clean shredded scrap, at $135 per ton, F.O.B. Milwaukee, delivery to be made by the end of April. ... Afram agreed to pay the expenses of an agent of Metallurgiki — Shields — to inspect the scrap for cleanliness before it was shipped. ... Shields arrived to inspect the scrap on April 12. He told Afram that the scrap was clean but that Metallurgiki would not accept it, because the price of the scrap had fallen. Sure enough, Metallurgiki refused to accept it. Afram brought this suit after selling the scrap to other buyers. Metallurgiki unsuccessfully challenged the court's jurisdiction over it, [and] the district judge gave judgment for Afram for $425,149. ...

Metallurgiki does not argue that international law or the due process clause of the Fifth Amendment places limitations on the district court's power to assert jurisdiction over Metallurgiki beyond those in the due process clause of the Fourteenth Amendment, while Afram does not argue that Metallurgiki, as an alien, has fewer

---

154. 471 U.S. at 479.
155. 471 U.S. at 476.

rights to challenge the long-arm statute than a nonresident American firm would have. Countless cases assume that foreign companies have all the rights of U.S. citizens to object to extraterritorial assertions of personal jurisdiction. *See, e.g., Helicopteros Nacionales; Securities Investor Protection Corp. v. Vigman,* 764 F.2d 1309, 1316 (9th Cir. 1985). The assumption has never to our knowledge actually been examined, but it probably is too solidly entrenched to be questioned at this late date, and in any event it has not been made an issue in this case.

In arguing against extraterritorial jurisdiction, Metallurgiki points out that it has no office, employees, or assets in Wisconsin and that all the dealings between the parties (apart from Shield's visit of inspection) were conducted by international telephone and telex communications and by face-to-face discussions in New York. Shields, the only representative of Metallurgiki who set foot in Wisconsin, although an agent and former employee of Metallurgiki, was in April 1979 an independent contractor, and he spent only five hours in Wisconsin on the inspection trip and only 20 to 40 minutes (the record is unclear which) in the actual inspection. It is also unclear who initiated the negotiations that led up to the making of the contract.

A state cannot force a nonresident to litigate in its courts unless there is "some act by which the defendant purposefully avails itself of the privilege of conducting activities within the forum State, thus invoking the benefits and protections of its laws." *Hanson v. Denckla,* 357 U.S. 235, 253 (1958). In other words, the defendant must derive some benefit from the state to balance the cost of exposure to suit in what is likely to be an inconvenient, perhaps even an unfriendly, forum. By this criterion, a contract between a resident of a state and a nonresident is not enough by itself to give the courts of the resident's state jurisdiction over the nonresident in the resident's suit for breach of the contract. *See Burger King Corp. v. Rudzewicz.* Imagine that a bank in Atlanta, in response to an advertisement in an Atlanta newspaper, ordered office equipment by mail from a company in California, and the seller arranged for the delivery of the equipment at the bank's office in Atlanta. The bank would be justifiably surprised to find that by doing this it has exposed itself to suit in California should a dispute arise over the sale. What benefit had California conferred on it? No doubt California provided some of the services that enabled the seller to produce and sell the office equipment, but the benefit thereby conferred on the distant buyer is too attenuated to require him to bear the expense of involuntarily litigating in so remote a forum. This would be even clearer if the buyer were an individual rather than a firm and the seller were trying to sue the buyer in a small-claims court in the seller's state, though these factors are not essential to the conclusion that the seller's effort to obtain extraterritorial jurisdiction over the buyer would fail.

Since the dispute must be litigated somewhere, there is perhaps implicit in the foregoing analysis the idea that the seller can sue more easily in the buyer's jurisdiction than the buyer can defend in the seller's. The seller in our example presumably sells office equipment all over the country and can without much difficulty arrange for local counsel wherever disputes with its buyers arise, while the buyer buys office equipment rarely and may be somewhat at a loss to arrange for an effective defense on the seller's home ground. This is one of several factors that distinguish our case from the hypothetical example. Putting aside the adventitious circumstance that Metallurgiki has an office in New York City and at oral argument (but not before then) expressed willingness to entertain the possibility of being suable in New York, the argument against extraterritorial jurisdiction here amounts to saying that if a foreign company negotiates by phone a large purchase of industrial raw materials from an American company for delivery in America, the American company still must go abroad in order to sue for breach of the contract. Since the buyer's role is not passive as in our mail-order hypothetical, since the buyer is not a one-time or infrequent purchaser of the product in question but a recurrent purchaser of what is a basic raw material used in his business, since performance is technically complete in the United States, and since the alternative forum may represent a substantial hardship to the seller, it is hard to see why it is more reasonable to make the seller go to the buyer's forum to sue (Georgia in our hypothetical example) than to make the buyer defend in the seller's forum. Most though not all courts probably would uphold extraterritorial jurisdiction in such a case. ...

We do not want to put too much weight on any single one of the distinguishing factors that we have mentioned. If the bank in our hypothetical example had sent its office manager to California to inspect the office equipment before it was shipped, we doubt whether this would be enough to subject the bank to the jurisdiction of the California courts in the event that the seller sued over the contract of sale. Neither would delivery in the seller's state be enough by itself. *Lakeside Bridge & Steel Co. v. Mountain State Construction Co.*, 597 F.2d 596 (7th Cir. 1979), a leading precedent for the rule that a single contract is not enough to confer personal jurisdiction over a nonresident buyer, refused to apply Wisconsin's long-arm statute in a case superficially much like this one: A Wisconsin seller had agreed to deliver the goods called for by the contract in Milwaukee, at the seller's rail siding, for shipment to the buyer, a company in West Virginia, and the contract had been negotiated in person outside of Wisconsin and over the telephone. ...

Our subsequent cases, however, treat *Lakeside* as standing at the outer limits of the principle that sale and delivery to the nonresident in the resident's state do not establish sufficient contacts with that state to give it jurisdiction over the nonresident in the resident's suit for breach of contract. These cases uphold jurisdiction if there are other contacts with the seller's state besides delivery. Here there is Shield's visit to Wisconsin to inspect the scrap — and thus inspection as well as delivery in the seller's state. The visit was brief, but Shields was the buyer's agent sent to the seller's state to carry out a vital function in the administration of the contract. We are not just mechanically counting contacts; Wisconsin not only provided police and fire protection and perhaps other services for the facilities at which the buyer took possession (as in *Lakeside*), but also provided protection for the visit of the buyer's agent to inspect the goods before shipment.

Another point distinguishes this case from *Lakeside.* The alternative forum for this litigation (for as we have said the suggestion that Afram might have sued Metallurgiki in New York comes too late) would have been Greece; and the fact that Metallurgiki has an office in the United States, but Afram (so far as appears) no office outside the United States, would seem to make the alternative forum more burdensome for Afram than Wisconsin was for Metallurgiki. Metallurgiki could not have been surprised to discover that if it ordered goods in America and went into America (through agents or directly) to inspect the goods and take delivery of them, it might be forced in the event of a contract dispute to litigate in America rather than being able to retreat to Greece.

Notes on Afram Export

1. *A contract does not necessarily sustain specific jurisdiction. Burger King* held that specific jurisdiction could not necessarily be based solely upon a defendant's contract with a forum resident. Like other lower courts, *Afram Export* repeats that proposition. Why doesn't entering into a contract with a forum resident ordinarily suffice for specific jurisdiction in the forum? Entering into a contract is usually a fairly clearly-defined act, universally understood as having binding legal consequences, that could provide reasonable notice that the courts of *either* of the contract parties might assert jurisdiction. Would not jurisdiction in such cases be more readily foreseen than jurisdiction based on the stream of commerce doctrine? Note that jurisdiction is routinely available in multiple forums under the due process clause; what harm would come from permitting the courts of the contracting parties' domiciles to decide disputes concerning their contract?

Consider the hypothetical in *Afram Export* concerning an Atlanta bank that purchases office equipment by mail from a California company. Would, in fact, the bank be "justifiably surprised" at being sued in California for failure to pay the purchase price? Why are the benefits that California provides to the buyer "too attenuated" for due process purposes? Are those benefits any different from those that Georgia provides to the seller? If somebody breaks a promise to pay money in the forum, why should not a forum resident be able to seek relief in the forum?

2. *Contract cases under the Brussels Convention.* How does the Brussels Convention deal with jurisdiction in contract cases? Consider Article 5(1) of the Convention, excerpted at p. 1075.) It provides for jurisdiction in "the place of performance of the obligation in question." How could this test be applied in *Afram Export*? Where was Metallurgiki obligated to accept and pay for the scrap metal? What if the contract had required Afram to deliver the steel to Metallurgiki in Greece? How would Article 5(1) resolve *Burger King* and the California bank hypothetical?

3. *Divergent treatment of foreign sellers and foreign purchasers.* As *Afram Export* suggests, U.S. courts have shown greater reluctance to assert specific jurisdiction over foreign purchasers than over foreign sellers. *See also* the discussion in *Helicopteros, supra* p. 116. What is the rationale underlying this distinction? Is it appropriate to deny a U.S. forum to U.S. companies who rely on mail, telex, or telephone orders placed by foreign companies, which then breach their promises?

4. *Purposeful contacts and reasonableness in contract cases.* Was *Afram Export*'s analysis directed to the purposeful contacts or the reasonableness prong of the due process clause? Does Judge Posner distinguish between these issues? Which of the additional factors cited by the court can be characterized as "contacts" and which are reasonableness considerations?

5. *Additional contacts necessary for specific jurisdiction over foreign purchaser. Afram Export* held that a sales contract with a foreign purchaser, even when delivery occurs or will occur in the seller's state, does not independently permit the seller's state to exercise personal jurisdiction over the purchaser. Instead, "other contacts with the seller's state besides delivery" are required — such as negotiations within the forum state, training courses for the purchaser's employees in the forum, and after-purchase requests for and provision of product assistance. Are any of these factors as significant as actually entering into the purchase contract specifying a place of performance? If service of process within the forum permits general jurisdiction, then why shouldn't agreement to purchase and take title to an item within the forum permit specific jurisdiction?

Was *Afram Export* correctly decided? If a sales contract, with delivery in the seller's state, does not provide the basis for jurisdiction, what additional factor in *Afram Export* permits a contrary result — Mr. Shields' inspection, Metallurgiki's New York office, Metallurgiki's role as a "recurrent purchaser" of scrap metal, or the "substantial hardship" that denying jurisdiction would have on Afram?

6. *Mail, telephone, and other international communications.* Contemporary international business is frequently conducted by international telephone, facsimile, and mail communications. In *Afram Export*, for example, the parties' contract was made by telex with no face-to-face meeting. That is not unusual: each day, thousands of international business transactions are negotiated and consummated in the same fashion. What importance should such international communications have in due process analysis? Note the apparently dispositive significance that *Afram Export* gives to the fact that "the buyer's agent was sent to the seller's state" where he received "police and fire protection." Is this emphasis on physical presence sensible, in the light of contemporary business practices? Does it remain necessary both as a consequence of territorial sovereignty (*see Burnham, supra* pp. 121-22), and as a good proxy for reasonable expectations (*see supra* p. 119 n. 135)?

Is it more sensible to give jurisdictional weight to the assurances made in international communications? Consider some of the following: *Burger King Corp. v. Rudzewicz*, 471 U.S. 462, 476 (1985) ("Although territorial presence frequently will enhance a potential defendant's affiliation with a State and reinforce the reasonable foreseeability of suit there, it is an inescapable fact of modern commercial life that a substantial amount of business is transacted solely by mail and wire communication across state lines, thus obviating the need for physical presence within a State in which business is conducted. So long as a commercial actor's efforts are 'purposefully directed' toward residents of another State, we have consistently rejected the notion that an absence of physical contacts can defeat personal jurisdiction there."); *Taylor v. Phelan*, 912 F.2d 429, 433 n.4 (10th Cir. 1990) ("so long as it creates a substantial connection, even a single telephone call into the forum state can support jurisdiction"), *cert. denied*, 111 S.Ct. 786 (1991); *American Greetings Corp. v. Cohn*, 839 F.2d 1164 (6th Cir. 1988) ("The use of interstate facilities such as the telephone and mail is a 'secondary or ancillary' factor and 'cannot alone provide the minimum contacts required by due process'").

7. *Effect of defendant's foreign residence.* Afram Export emphasized that Metallurgiki's foreign residence "would seem to make the alternative forum (*i.e.*, Greece) more burdensome for Afram than Wisconsin was for Metallurgiki." The basis for this conclusion was apparently the fact that Metallurgiki had a New York office, which presumably could oversee litigation in Wisconsin. Recall the similar analysis in *Amusement Equipment, supra* pp. 120 & 123. Why shouldn't the presence of a New York office have permitted Afram to sue in New York, thereby alleviating any alleged hardship of dismissing its Wisconsin suit? (What jurisdictional base would have permitted *Afram* to sue in New York?)

Suppose that Metallurgiki had not had a U.S. office. What effect should its foreign residence (and the foreign location of any alternative forum) have on personal jurisdiction analysis? *Compare Sea Lift, Inc. v. Refinadora Costarricense de Petroleo, SA*, 792 F.2d 989 (11th Cir. 1986) (nonexistence of alternative forum is relevant only to reasonableness inquiry, after a finding of purposeful availment).

8. *Relationship between choice of law and personal jurisdiction.* What role should choice of law considerations play in personal jurisdiction analysis? In particular, should due process analysis give controlling (or substantial) weight to the fact that the forum's substantive law will apply?

(a) *Applicability of forum's substantive law does not necessarily sustain jurisdiction.* The Supreme Court has consistently held that application of the forum's substantive law does not necessarily mean that due process permits personal jurisdiction. *See Burger King Corp. v. Rudzewicz*, 471 U.S. 462, 481 (1985) ("choice-of-law *analysis* — which focuses on all elements of a transaction, and not simply on the defendant's conduct — is distinct from minimum-contacts jurisdictional analysis — which focuses at the threshold solely on the defendant's purposeful connection to the forum"); *Shaffer v. Heitner*, 433 U.S. 186, 215 (1977) ("we have rejected the argument that if a State's law can properly be applied to a dispute, its courts necessarily have jurisdiction over the parties to that dispute").

On the other hand, various authorities have also accorded some weight, in due process analysis, to the fact that the forum's substantive laws would be applicable under conflict of laws rules. Justice Brennan wrote in dissent in *Shaffer v. Heitner*, 433 U.S. 186, 224-26 (1977):

> I would not compartmentalize thinking in this area quite so rigidly as it seems to me the Court does today, for both inquiries [*i.e.*, personal jurisdiction and choice of law] are often closely related. ... In either case an important linchpin is the extent of contacts between the controver-

sy, the parties, and the forum state. ... At a minimum, the decision that it is fair to bind a defendant by a State's laws and rules should prove to be highly relevant to the fairness of permitting that same State to accept jurisdiction for adjudicating the controversy.

What importance should choice of law have for personal jurisdiction analysis? If a state has a sufficient interest in a dispute to apply its own law, why shouldn't the due process clause permit it to exercise personal jurisdiction?

(b) *Jurisdictional significance of choice of law agreement.* Parties commonly include choice of law provisions in their contracts. *See infra* pp. 653-64. Lower courts have generally held that a choice of law clause does *not* constitute a submission to the jurisdiction of the courts of specified state. *E.g., Paccar Int'l, Inc. v. Commercial Bank of Kuwait, S.A.K.,* 757 F.2d 1058, 1063 n.6 (9th Cir. 1985) ("The fact that a contract is governed by the law of a particular state does not establish that the parties have purposefully availed themselves of the privilege of conducting business in that state. ... [c]hoice of law provisions ... are irrelevant to" purposeful availment). Other courts have held that a choice of law provision does have jurisdictional significance. *E.g., Sea Lift, Inc. v. Refinadora Costarricense de Petroleo, SA,* 792 F.2d 989, 992 n.2 (11th Cir. 1986) ("choice of English law to govern the agreement is in itself an indication that [defendant] did not avail itself of the benefits and protections of Florida law."); *Harper-Wyman Co. v. In-Bond Contract Mfg,* 1994 WL 22321 (N.D. Ill. 1994) ("it is not unfair to subject [the Mexican] defendants to a foreign legal system; they have already agreed that a foreign law will apply"). Is this general approach sensible?

9. *Scope of specific jurisdiction.* No dispute arose in *McCombs, Asahi, Krakatau,* or *Afram Export* regarding the scope of specific jurisdiction. All the defendant's contacts with the forum were clearly related to the plaintiff's claims: the only question was whether these contacts satisfied the due process clause's "purposeful availment" requirement. Other cases have raised questions as to whether the defendant's contacts with the forum were sufficiently related to the plaintiff's claims to count in assessing "purposeful contacts." What sort of connection should be required for the scope of specific jurisdiction?

(a) *Helicopteros' treatment of the scope of specific jurisdiction.* As discussed above, *Helicopteros* expressly refused to decide "what sort of tie between a cause of action and a defendant's contacts with a forum" will satisfy the specific jurisdiction requirement. Indeed, the Court declined either to choose between an "arising out of" and a "relating to" standard, or to indicate whether the two formulations differed materially. *See supra* pp. 107 n. 125 & 114-15. Similarly, a number of lower courts have applied the "arising out of" criteria without formulating any generally applicable standard. *Hirsch v. Blue Cross, Blue Shield,* 800 F.2d 1474 (9th Cir. 1986); *Afram Export Corp. v. Metallurgiki Halyps, SA,* 772 F.2d 1358 (7th Cir. 1985).

(b) *"But for" test for scope of specific jurisdiction.* Courts in several circuits have adopted broad "but for" tests for determining whether the plaintiff's claims arise out of the defendant's forum contacts. *Shute v. Carnival Cruise Lines,* 863 F.2d 1437 (9th Cir. 1990), is a leading example. *Shute* involved Carnival Cruise Lines, a Panamanian corporation with its principal place of business in Miami, which operated a cruise line. Plaintiff was a Washington state resident who purchased a cruise from California to Mexico on a Carnival Cruise vessel. The cruise was purchased through a Washington travel agent, and Carnival Cruise mailed the tickets purchased by plaintiff to the agent, who delivered them to the Shutes. Plaintiff travelled from Washington to California to embark on the cruise. While the vessel was off the coast of Mexico, plaintiff was injured in a slip-and-fall accident, and later filed suit against Carnival Cruise in Washington.

Aside from plaintiff's purchase of her ticket, through her travel agent, Carnival Cruise had few contacts with Washington. It advertised in national publications that were distributed (in limited numbers) in Washington and it had relationships with travel agents in Washington. Nonetheless, the Ninth Circuit held that Carnival Cruise was subject to specific jurisdiction in Washington. It adopted a "but for" test for jurisdiction, and held that but for Carnival's solicitations in Washington, and its mailing of the ticket to a Washington travel agent, plaintiff would not have taken the cruise or suffered her injury. *See also Theunissen v. Mathews,* 935 F.2d 1454 (6th Cir. 1991) (specific jurisdiction requires only that "the cause of action, of whatever type, have a substantial connection with the defendant's in-state activities"; "arising out of" requirement satisfied if plaintiff's cause of action is "made possible by," "lies in the wake of" or "relates to" the defendant's contacts with the forum); *Prejean v. Soratrach, Inc.,* 652 F.2d 1260 (5th Cir. 1981) (rejecting "view that a tort suit cannot arise from a contractual contact, and presumably vice versa." "In a case like this, the contractual contact is a 'but for' causative factor for the tort since it brought the parties within tortious 'striking distance' of each other.").

(c) *"Proximate cause" test for scope of specific jurisdiction.* In contrast, other circuits have adopted less expansive views of specific jurisdiction, sometimes referred to as "proximate cause" analysis. *E.g., Pizarro v. Hoteles Concorde Int'l CA,* 907 F.2d 1256 (1st Cir. 1990) (no specific jurisdiction over Aruba hotel because claim that hotel employee negligently injured plaintiff did not "arise out of" hotel's advertisements in forum); *City of Virginia Beach v. Roanoke River Basin Ass'n,* 776 F.2d 484, 489 (4th Cir. 1985) ("In order for a cause of action to arise from business transacted in Virginia, the activities that support the jurisdictional claim must coincide with those that form the basis of the plaintiff's substantive claim").

(d) *Appropriate scope of specific jurisdiction.* Which of these tests is more appropriate? Note that expanding the scope of specific jurisdiction benefits plaintiffs, by increasing their choice of forum.

D. Jurisdiction Based on Corporate Affiliations or Agency Relationships

It is common for companies engaged in international commerce to incorporate separate foreign subsidiaries; to engage agents, distributors, brokers, and other business partners; or to enter into joint ventures or strategic alliances. Corporate affiliations can take widely differing forms. At one extreme, a small, privately-held company in one country may engage an existing, unrelated business in another country to perform a specific task for it, such as distributing a product or supplying a service. At the other extreme, national tax regimes and other considerations drive some enterprises to establish corporate structures with complex tiers of 100%-owned subsidiaries and other affiliates — some engaging in little actual business, without separate management, and subject to day-to-day control by corporate affiliates.

Most visible are some of today's major multinational groups — like Exxon, IBM, Sony, Volkswagen, Mitsubishi, and Unilever. Such corporate enterprises typically include dozens (or hundreds) of separately-incorporated companies, many of which are 100%-owned by other corporate affiliates.[156] Ordinarily, the ultimate "parent" of the entire group is a publicly-traded company. In some cases, members of the corporate group will have one corporate name and logo (*e.g.*, Coca-Cola or Ford), and will deal in the same products or services. While each entity belonging to the corporate group will typically have its own board of directors and management, concerted efforts will be made to articulate a single corporate strategy. Moreover, different members of the corporate group will often engage in business dealings such as purchasing one another's products, providing financing, and supplying services.

For present purposes, these various types of arrangements are important because they can also have significant U.S. jurisdictional consequences. By acting through an agent, subsidiary, or other business partner, a foreign company can avoid direct contacts of its own with the United States: all U.S. contacts can be those of the agent, subsidiary, or distributor. This may permit a finding that the foreign company is not subject to U.S. judicial jurisdiction, because it lacks its own minimum contacts with the relevant U.S. forum under either the applicable long-arm statute or the due process clause.[157]

---

156. "[A]fter World War II ... the phenomenon of the multinational enterprise, as we now know it, became a major factor in the world scene. Since then tens of thousands of subsidiaries have been created or acquired by parent enterprises located in other countries. ... After the Second World War investment in the United States by foreign parent companies ... expanded tremendously. ... Total assets of foreign-owned affiliates in the United States in 1974 were $174.3 billion, of which more than one-fifth was Japanese-owned. These trends have accelerated. The vehicles of this modern international economic growth were and are the multinational enterprises. Their size is often awesome: the annual sales of General Motors exceeded the gross national products of Switzerland, Pakistan, or South Africa." *Bulova Watch Co. v. Hattori & Co.*, 508 F.Supp. 1322 (E.D.N.Y. 1981).

157. *See infra* pp. 153-56.

It is clear, however, that the use of an agent, subsidiary, or other business partner does not necessarily insulate a foreign corporation from U.S. jurisdiction.[158] In particular, lower U.S. courts have relied on two related theories in exercising jurisdiction over foreign companies by attributing to them their business partners' contacts with the U.S. forum. First, U.S. courts have asserted jurisdiction when a domestic company is merely the "alter ego" of a foreign parent. Second, personal jurisdiction may be exercised where a domestic subsidiary is the "agent" of its foreign parent.[159]

1. Personal Jurisdiction Based on Alter Ego Status

a. Law Governing Alter Ego Status

The starting point for analysis is the basic principle that corporations are distinct legal entities, with a separate identity from their shareholders and subsidiaries.[160] Thus, a foreign company's ownership of the shares of a corporation doing business within the forum state does not automatically confer liability on or personal jurisdiction over the parent corporation. In one authority's words, "[j]udicial jurisdiction over a subsidiary corporation does not of itself give a state judicial jurisdiction over the parent corporation. This is true even though the parent owns all of the subsidiary's stock."[161]

Despite this basic rule, there are circumstances in which a parent will be held to be the "alter ego" of its subsidiary, permitting the subsidiary's contacts to be attributed to the parent for purposes of jurisdiction. There is considerable disagreement over the content of "alter ego" standards. In Judge Cardozo's memorable phrase, the effect of parent-subsidiary relations is enveloped in "mists of metaphor."[162]

As in other jurisdictional contexts, two levels of alter ego analysis are necessary — statutory and constitutional. Only if both a legislative grant of jurisdiction exists, and the due process clause permits, may a U.S. court exercise jurisdiction on an alter ego basis.[163] Unfortunately, many decisions dealing with alter ego issues fail to dis-

---

158. We have already seen how a foreign manufacturer's use of independent U.S. distributors for its products may not preclude specific jurisdiction in U.S. product liability litigation on a stream of commerce theory. *See supra* pp. 124-43 & *infra* pp. 162-63.

159. U.S. courts may exercise personal jurisdiction over non-residents on several other less common theories, including conspiracy, ratification, and guaranty. *See* R. Casad, *Jurisdiction in Civil Actions* §4.03 (2d ed. 1991).

160. *E.g.*, *FMC Finance Corp. v. Murphree*, 632 F.2d 413 (5th Cir. 1980) ("A corporation is a legal entity existing separate and distinct from its shareholders, officers, and directors, who as a general rule are not liable for the corporation's debts and obligations.").

161. *Restatement (Second) Conflict of Laws* §52, comment b (1971). *See* C. Wright & A. Miller, *Federal Practice and Procedure* §1069 at 363-74 (2d ed. 1987).

162. *Berkey v. Third Ave. Ry. Co.*, 244 N.Y. 84 (1926) (Cardozo, J.).

163. *See Hargrave v. Fibreboard Corp.*, 710 F.2d 1154 (5th Cir. 1983); *Wells Fargo & Co. v. Wells Fargo Express Co.*, 556 F.2d 406 (9th Cir. 1977).

tinguish clearly between statutory and constitutional issues, further thickening the "mists" described by Justice Cardozo.

Virtually all state long-arm statutes are silent concerning the significance of alter ego relations, with state common law providing the only authority on the issue. Regardless of applicable law, state courts have often looked to due process precedents in formulating state alter ego doctrines.[164] Conversely, many due process discussions draw substantially on state common law principles. Given this, we focus on general principles of alter ego analysis, without always distinguishing between constitutional and statutory issues.

It is not settled what substantive law — apart from due process limits — governs whether one company is the alter ego of another. Possible choices of applicable law include the law of the subsidiary's state of incorporation, the law of the parent's state of incorporation, the forum's law, and the law of the state with the closest relationship to the transactions at issue. There is no clear consensus as to which approach should be followed.[165]

The conclusion that a foreign parent is subject to U.S. *jurisdiction* because of its U.S. subsidiary's activities does not necessarily mean that the foreign company will be *liable on the merits* because of its subsidiary's liability. It is often said that corporate veil-piercing standards for jurisdiction and liability differ significantly, and that jurisdiction can exist where liability does not.[166] Under most state laws, alter ego liability (as opposed to alter ego jurisdiction) requires that both: (i) corporate formalities were wholly disregarded by a pervasively controlling parent; and (ii) fraud or its equivalent was perpetrated on third parties.[167] As discussed below, contemporary decisions do not always impose similarly rigorous requirements on alter ego jurisdiction.

b. Cannon Manufacturing: The Importance of Corporate Formalities

Discussion of alter ego jurisdiction begins with *Cannon Manufacturing Company v. Cudahy Packing Company.*[168] In *Cannon*, a North Carolina corporation brought a breach of contract suit in North Carolina against a Maine corporation. Service was effected upon the North Carolina agent of an Alabama corporation, which was a

---

164. *E.g., Hargrave v. Fibreboard Corp.*, 710 F.2d 1154 (5th Cir. 1983); *Omni Exploration, Inc. v. Graham Engineering Corp.*, 562 F.Supp. 449 (E.D. Pa. 1983).

165. *E.g., Pauley Petroleum, Inc. v. Continental Oil Co.*, 231 A.2d 450, 457 (1967), *aff'd*, 239 A.2d 629 (1968) (applying Delaware law to question whether foreign subsidiary was alter ego of Delaware parent); *PowerUp of Southeast Louisiana Inc. v. PowerUp U.S.A., Inc.*, 1994 WL 54363 (E.D. La. 1994) (applying Louisiana conflicts issues to determine that law of Alberta should govern whether Canadian corporation is alter ego of two non-Louisiana companies); *Restatement (Second) Conflict of Laws* §302(2) (1971). Alter ego issues in cases involving foreign state-related entities are discussed below. *See infra* pp. 217-25.

166. *E.g., Dakota Indus., Inc. v. Ever Best Ltd.*, 28 F.3d 910, 915 (8th Cir. 1994) ("A determination to pierce the corporate veil does not necessarily answer the question of a court's jurisdiction over the individuals behind the veil.").

167. *See infra* pp. 160-61.

168. 267 U.S. 33 (1925).

wholly-owned subsidiary of the Maine corporate defendant. The plaintiff argued that service upon the Alabama subsidiary was effective as to its Maine parent, on the grounds that the two companies were in reality one. The Supreme Court affirmed dismissal of the suit on the grounds that service was invalid.

Cannon conceded that, "[t]hrough ownership of the entire capital stock and otherwise, the defendant dominates the Alabama corporation, immediately and completely," and "that the parent exerts its control both commercially and financially in substantially the same way, and mainly through the same individuals, as it does over those selling branches or departments of its business not separately incorporated."[169] Nevertheless, the Court concluded:

> The existence of the Alabama company as a distinct corporate entity is, however, in all respects observed. Its books are kept separate. All transactions between the two corporations are represented by appropriate entries in their respective books in the same way as if the two were wholly independent corporations.[170]

The Court later added that "[t]he corporate separation, though perhaps merely formal, was real. It was not pure fiction."[171]

Many lower courts have applied *Cannon*, reasoning that the decision permits jurisdiction on alter ego grounds only where a parent wholly disregards its subsidiary's "corporate formalities." This is true regardless whether the parent "controlled" or "dominated" the subsidiary.[172] In one lower court's words, "[t]he test under *Cannon* is not the degree of control over the subsidiary by the parent."[173]

c. Alternative Alter Ego Standards

Notwithstanding its importance, there is a lively debate regarding *Cannon's* original precedential significance. A number of courts and commentators have concluded that *Cannon* was not a due process holding, relying in part on a fairly cryptic comment in Justice Brandeis's opinion, that "[n]o question of the constitutional powers of the State, or of the federal Government, is directly presented."[174] Other courts have concluded that *Cannon* has been superseded by more recent due process

---

169. 267 U.S. at 335.

170. 267 U.S. at 335.

171. 267 U.S. at 337.

172. *E.g., Kramer Motors v. British Leyland*, 628 F.2d 1175 (9th Cir. 1980); *Quarles v. Fuqua Indus.*, 504 F.2d 1358 (10th Cir. 1974); *Farkas v. Texas Instruments*, 429 F.2d 849 (1st Cir. 1970), *cert. denied*, 401 U.S. 974 (1971); *Peters v. U-Haul Co.*, 409 F.2d 1174, 1182-83 (8th Cir. 1969); *Manville Boiler Co. v. Columbia Boiler Co.*, 269 F.2d 600 (4th Cir.), *cert. denied*, 361 U.S. 901 (1959) (no alter ego relationship where parent "extensively controlled" subsidiary but separate records were maintained); *Scalise v. Beech Aircraft Corp.*, 276 F.Supp. 58 (E.D. Pa. 1967) (following *Cannon*: "each subsidiary keeps separate records, files separate tax returns, owns its own property, conducts its own business and is responsible for its own activities and its own debts").

173. *Consolidated Engineering Co. v. Southern Steel Co.*, 88 F.R.D. 233, 237-38 (E.D. Va. 1980).

174. 267 U.S. at 336.

holdings.[175] Nevertheless, many authorities continue to apply *Cannon* in determining due process and common law restraints on the alter ego doctrine.[176]

A potentially significant departure from *Cannon* was the Supreme Court's decision in *United States v. Scophony Corp. of America*,[177] considering whether personal jurisdiction existed over a foreign defendant under §12 of the Clayton Act. *Scophony* held that both §12 and the due process clause permitted jurisdiction over a foreign company because its utilization of "complex working arrangements ... with [American subsidiaries that required] constant supervision and intervention beyond normal exercise of shareholders' rights by the [foreign parent]."[178] The *Scophony* alter ego standard is less stringent than the *Cannon* formula. It allows jurisdiction where a parent exercises a significant degree of direct operational control over the operations of its subsidiary, going beyond a controlling shareholder's "ordinary" rights. Jurisdiction can be asserted, on this version of the alter ego theory, even where corporate formalities are observed.[179] Some lower courts have concluded that *Scophony* implicitly overruled *Cannon*, at least in the antitrust context.[180] Other lower courts have disagreed, holding that *Cannon* remains good law.[181]

In recent years, a number of lower courts have expressly or impliedly modified *Cannon*'s focus on corporate formalities. In one court's words, "multitudinous decisions of state and federal courts ... [have] changed the older concept of jurisdiction and substantially eroded the stringent jurisdictional test applied in [*Cannon*]."[182] Although there have been many formulations of new alter ego standards, several general rules can be identified.

First, many lower courts now inquire into the extent and character of a parent corporation's "control" over its subsidiary.[183] A substantial number of lower courts have held that an alter ego relationship exists, for jurisdictional purposes, if one enti-

---

175. *E.g., Rollins v. Proctor & Schwartz*, 478 F.Supp. 1137, 1146 (D.S.C. 1979) ("the rule of *Cannon* ... exalts form over substance").

176. *See* note 172 *supra*; *Consolidated Engineering Co. v. Southern Steel Co.*, 88 F.R.D. 233, 237-38 (E.D. Va. 1980) ("This Court refuses to follow the lead of those courts which have attempted to modify or, in effect, overrule *Cannon* by the use of buzz words or phrases such as 'undue degree of control,' ... 'mere instrumentality or adjunct' and 'complete control.' Therefore the Court, under *Cannon*, is not concerned with the degree of control exerted by [the parent] over [its subsidiary] so long as corporate formalities are observed between the two.").

177. 333 U.S. 795 (1948).

178. 333 U.S. at 816.

179. 333 U.S. at 813-16.

180. *E.g., Omega Homes, Inc. v. Citicorp Acceptance Co.*, 656 F.Supp. 393, 397-98 (W.D. Va. 1987); *Chrysler Corp. v. General Motor Corp.*, 589 F.Supp. 1182 (D.D.C. 1984).

181. *E.g., Allen v. Toshiba Corp.*, 599 F.Supp. 381 (D.N. Mex. 1984); *Thompson Trading Ltd. v. Allied Lyons plc*, 123 F.R.D. 417 (D.R.I. 1989).

182. *Roorda v. Volkswagenwerk, AG*, 481 F.Supp. 868 (D.S.C. 1979).

183. *E.g., Velandra v. Regie Nationale des Usines Renault*, 336 F.2d 292, 296 (6th Cir. 1962) (whether "the parent has exercised an undue degree of control over the subsidiary"); *Clark v. Matsushita Elec. Indus. Co.*, 811 F.Supp. 1061, 1068 (M.D. Pa. 1993) ("actual day-to-day control ... required").

ty exercises sufficient "control" over another. Thus, according to the *Restatement (Second) Conflict of Laws* §52, comment b (1971):

> Judicial jurisdiction over a subsidiary corporation will ... give the state judicial jurisdiction over the parent corporation if the parent so controls and dominates the subsidiary as in effect to disregard the latter's independent corporate existence.

In one lower court's words, an alter ego relationship will be found if a parent corporation "exercises dominion and control over the subsidiary as demonstrated by its continual supervision of and intervention in the subsidiary's affairs."[184] Or, according to another lower court, an alter ego relationship exists where the parent "exercises day-to-day control over its [subsidiary] so complete as to render [it] a mere department of [the parent]."[185]

Second, other courts depart further from *Cannon*, finding alter ego status where a parent and its subsidiary are sufficiently "integrated."[186] For example, some lower courts have found alter ego relationships where a parent and subsidiary "function as an integrated whole" and "compete in a worldwide enterprise."[187]

Third, a few lower courts have adopted so-called "agency" tests for alter ego status, applicable where a subsidiary acts as its parent's "agent."[188] In reality, these standards appear to have little to do with common law agency principles (which we discuss in detail below).

Finally, some lower courts have held that alter ego status requires more than a showing that a parent controls its subsidiary, even if corporate formalities are disregarded. Relying principally on decisions concerning substantive alter ego liability, these courts have demanded proof that the subsidiary's separate incorporation was used to perpetrate a fraud on the plaintiff.[189] In one court's words, disregarding corporate identities "may be done only in the interest of justice, when such matters as fraud, contravention of law or contract, [or] public wrong ... are involved."[190]

---

184. *Omega Homes, Inc. v. Citicorp Acceptance Co.*, 656 F.Supp. 393, 397-98 (W.D. Va. 1987).

185. *Photo Promotions Assoc. v. Household Int'l Inc.*, 584 F.Supp. 227, 237 (D. Del. 1984).

186. *See Color Systems, Inc. v. Meteor Photo Reprographic Systems, Inc.*, 1987 WL 11085 (D.D.C. 1987) (purporting to conclude that *Cannon* is still "good law" but holding that an alter ego relationship exists because "the two corporations function as an integrated whole" and "compete in a worldwide enterprise"); *Finance Co. of Am. v. Bankamerica Corp.*, 493 F.Supp. 895 (D. Md. 1980) ("operations of the parent and subsidiary are sufficiently integrated to justify piercing the corporate veil").

187. *Color Systems, Inc. v. Meteor Photo Reprographic Systems, Inc.*, 1987 WL 11085 (D.D.C. 1987).

188. *E.g., Finance Co. of America v. Bankamerica Corp.*, 493 F.Supp. 895, 903-08 (D. Md. 1980); *Translation Systems, Inc. v. Applied Tech. Ventures*, 559 F.Supp. 566, 567 (D. Md. 1983) ("Under the agency theory a subsidiary will be attributed to its parent for personal jurisdiction purposes where the activities of the subsidiary are largely controlled by the parent.").

189. *E.g., Miller v. Honda Motor Co.*, 779 F.2d 769 (1st Cir. 1985) ("there is nothing fraudulent or against public policy in limiting one's liability by the appropriate use of corporate insulation"); *Luckett v. Bethlehem Steel Corp.*, 618 F.2d 1373, 1379 (10th Cir. 1980) ("fraud or illegal or inequitable conduct is the result of the use of the corporate structures").

190. *Pauley Petroleum Inc. v. Continental Oil Co.*, 239 A.2d 629, 633 (Del. 1968).

d. Selected Materials on the Application of Alter Ego Doctrine in International Cases

The decision in *Hargrave v. Fibreboard Corp.*, which is excerpted below, is a good example of an opinion that cites *Cannon* with approval, while looking more broadly to issues of "control." More recently, other courts have held that alter ego status exists even where corporate formalities are observed, provided that the parent is sufficiently integrated with its subsidiary's operations. The district court's opinion in *Bulova Watch Co. v. K. Hattori & Co.*, which is also briefly excerpted below, is a leading example of this approach.

HARGRAVE v. FIBREBOARD CORP.

710 F.2d 1154 (5th Cir. 1983)

GOLDBERG, CIRCUIT JUDGE. Three corporate entities — one now defunct — play the lead roles in this procedural sideshow: third-party plaintiff Nicolet, Inc. ("Nicolet"), third-party defendant T&N, and Keasbey & Mattison Co. ("K&M"), a former subsidiary of T&N. ... K&M was a Pennsylvania asbestos company founded in 1873; it was incorporated in 1892 and maintained its headquarters in Ambler, Pennsylvania. T&N is a publicly held English corporation formed in 1920 and headquartered in Manchester, England. T&N is involved in the asbestos, plastics, and electronics industries. In the mid-1930's T&N began acquiring the stock of K&M for investment purposes, until by 1938 it was K&M's sole shareholder. From 1938 until 1962, K&M operated as a wholly owned subsidiary of T&N. In 1962, as part of a plan of dissolution, K&M sold its manufacturing facilities and other assets to various companies. Nicolet was among the purchasers. Nicolet's acquisition from K&M included certain assets comprising K&M's asbestos insulation manufacturing facilities. K&M was formally dissolved in 1967 when the Pennsylvania Department of State issued a dissolution certificate.

[The case arose when numerous individual plaintiffs filed suits] alleged injury from exposure to asbestos-containing insulation products made by various defendants, including Nicolet. None of the plaintiffs made any claim against T&N. In each of these many [individual] actions Nicolet filed an identical third-party complaint against T&N. Each third-party complaint sought a declaratory judgment that T&N was liable for any and all injuries arising from the plaintiffs' exposure to asbestos products manufactured by K&M. Nicolet's third-party complaints urged a triumvirate of theories upon which T&N's liability might be based: (1) that T&N was liable as the "alter ego" of K&M; (2) that T&N was liable as the successor in interest to K&M; and (3) that T&N was liable for contribution or indemnity as K&M's supplier of asbestos fibre.

[Among other things, T&N moved to dismiss the third-party complaints against it for lack of personal jurisdiction. The district court denied T&N's motion, holding that T&N "exercised general guidance and retained the necessary authority" over

K&M to permit jurisdiction over T&N on an alter ego theory. T&N appealed.]
Nicolet asserts that personal jurisdiction existed over T&N through the torts of
K&M. In order to sustain jurisdiction under this ... theory, Nicolet is required to
show that K&M's activity in Texas would subject it to the reach of the Texas long-
arm statute and that K&M's activities may properly be imputed to T&N. For present
purposes, we will assume that K&M would be subject to jurisdiction in Texas and
focus upon the second prong of Nicolet's theory, the relationship between K&M and
T&N.

Generally, a foreign parent corporation is not subject to the jurisdiction of a
forum state merely because its subsidiary is present or doing business there; the mere
existence of a parent-subsidiary relationship is not sufficient to warrant the assertion
of jurisdiction over the foreign parent. It has long been recognized, however, that in
some circumstances a close relationship between a parent and its subsidiary may justify a finding that the parent "does business" in a jurisdiction through the local activities of its subsidiaries. The rationale for such an exercise of jurisdiction is that the
parent corporation exerts such domination and control over its subsidiary "that they
do not in reality constitute separate and distinct corporate entities but are one and
the same corporation for purposes of jurisdiction." 2 J. Moore & J. Lucas, [*Moore's
Federal Practice*] at 4-273. Problems arise, however, in articulating the type and
degree of control necessary to ascribe to a parent the activities of its subsidiary.

Cannon ... stands for the proposition that so long as a parent and subsidiary
maintain separate and distinct corporate entities, the presence of one in a forum state
may not be attributed to the other. Cases in this circuit appear to have followed the
Cannon rule in applying the Texas long-arm statute, although sometimes without
explicit citation. We have noted often that 100 percent stock ownership and com-
monality of officers and directors are not alone sufficient to establish an alter ego
relationship between two corporations. Generally, our cases demand proof of control
by the parent over the internal business operations and affairs of the subsidiary in
order to fuse the two for jurisdictional purposes. The degree of control exercised by
the parent must be greater than that normally associated with common ownership
and directorship. All the relevant facts and circumstances that surround the operations of the parent and subsidiary must be examined to determine whether two separate and distinct corporate entities exist.

In the instant case, T&N owned 100 percent of the stock of K&M from 1938 to
1962. During this entire period, T&N maintained its corporate headquarters in
Manchester, England, while K&M was headquartered in Ambler, Pennsylvania. The
two companies shared no common officers and at no time had more than one common director. The corporate formalities were scrupulously observed. T&N and K&M
maintained separate bank accounts, accounting and payroll systems, insurance contracts, budgets, and financial records; they also filed separate tax returns. No assets of
the corporations were commingled.

In terms of K&M's internal affairs, it appears that T&N had complete authority over general policy decisions at K&M, including such matters as selection of product lines, hiring and firing of K&M officers, and approval of sizeable capital investments. Day-to-day business and operational decisions, however, were made by K&M officers. K&M had sole responsibility for operation and management of its manufacturing facilities, research and development of new products, and marketing and sales strategies. Although T&N supplied the raw materials used to manufacture K&M products, K&M was in charge of determining its own supply requirements. ...

"To avoid precipitating too extensive an investigation of the merits at this stage of the litigation, only a prima facie showing is required on a jurisdiction motion." 4 C. Wright & A. Miller, [*Federal Practice and Procedure*] §1068, at 250. Even given the appropriateness of applying a less stringent standard for alter ego jurisdiction than for alter ego liability, however, we do not believe that Nicolet has demonstrated that T&N possessed and exercised the nature and degree of control over K&M necessary to fuse the two corporations for purposes of the Texas long-arm statute. T&N and K&M maintained a degree of corporate separation that was more than superficial; they were two separate corporations joined by the common bond of stock ownership. The policy making authority held and exercised by T&N was no more than that appropriate for a sole shareholder of a corporation, and certainly not enough to warrant the extraterritorial exercise of jurisdiction over that shareholder under the Texas statute. The Lone Star of Texas may shine brightly throughout the world, but its long arm is not judicially all encompassing. For the reasons stated above, we hold that Nicolet has failed to carry its burden of bringing T&N within the reach of the Texas long-arm statute; thus, we need not address the due process considerations ordinarily implicated by a motion to dismiss for lack of personal jurisdiction.

Notes on Hargrave v. Fibreboard Corp.

1. *Practical reasons for seeking jurisdiction over foreign parent.* If a foreign parent has incorporated a local subsidiary, why is it not sufficient for a U.S. plaintiff to sue that entity? Why should the U.S. plaintiff incur the expense of pursuing an additional, foreign defendant? Consider the following excerpt, involving an alleged alter ego relation between a German parent (BMW-Germany) and its U.S. subsidiary (BMW-U.S.):

[The] policies [relevant to "reasonableness" under the due process clause] favor the development of international trade to the benefit of American citizens no less than they require that manufacturers be responsible for their products. [BMW Germany] has acted responsibly by creating a "hostage" to the laws of the several states: [BMW-U.S.]. As to the former interests, the court believes that the policy of encouraging trade and economic well-being for American citizens is best served by not extending the "long-arm" of Texas jurisdiction to snare a foreign manufacturer when its domestic subsidiary is well within reach. ... In order to sell in the U.S., [BMW Germany] created an autonomous, albeit wholly-owned, subsidiary, [BMW-U.S.]. Organized under the laws of Delaware, [BMW-U.S.] maintains its offices and conducts the entirety of its business in the United States. [BMW-U.S.] exists to market in the U.S. the automobiles manufactured in Germany by [BMW-Germany]. As the distributor of [BMW-Germany] automobiles in the U.S., [BMW-U.S.] alone is the natural and logical defendant in this cause; its parent, [BMW-Germany], is not. Requiring the foreigner [BMW-Germany] to defend alongside the native [BMW-U.S.] serves neither legal nor economic purpose. To force the parent to defend itself for the alleged acts of its autonomous, solvent subsidiary has the unfortunate and unnecessary effect of increasing the costs of exporting to the U.S. this is harmful to the citizens and economy of the U.S. and, in this case, to defendant [BMW-Germany], as well. *Sammels v. BMW of North America, Inc.*, 554 F.Supp. 1191 (S.D. Tex. 1983).

Why is this reasoning not a compelling argument against alter ego jurisdiction in international cases? Why does a U.S. plaintiff have any legitimate need for drawing a foreign parent into expensive and inconvenient U.S. litigation?

2. *Lower standard for jurisdiction than liability.* As described above, alter ego standards for liability are generally more difficult to satisfy than those for jurisdiction. Is it appropriate to permit a reduced alter ego standard for jurisdiction? Note *Hargrave's* reliance on the rule that "only a prima facie showing is required on a jurisdiction motion." Is the reduced showing purportedly required for alter ego jurisdiction in fact an allocation of the burden of persuasion before discovery has occurred?

3. *Due process restraints on alter ego doctrine.* Even if the applicable state (or federal) long-arm statute authorizes jurisdiction based on an alter ego relation, due process must permit this exercise of jurisdiction. Despite its continuing influence, there is considerable question as to the precedential value of *Cannon* as a due process holding. *See supra* pp. 153-55. If *Cannon* was not a due process holding, then what constitutional limits *should* be imposed on the alter ego doctrine? Does the Constitution require states to provide for corporations with limited liability? Are states required to "recognize" corporations created as separate legal persons under the laws of sister states? What provision of the Constitution would require this? Would the obligation extend to foreign countries?

4. *The importance of corporate formalities under* Cannon. As *Hargrave* illustrates, *Cannon* continues to guide many courts in determining jurisdiction based on corporate affiliations. As described above, *Cannon* held that a parent corporation which "dominated" its subsidiary "immediately and completely" could nonetheless not be subjected to the forum state's personal jurisdiction because the existence of the subsidiary "as a distinct corporate entity [was] in all respects observed." 267 U.S. at 335. The *Cannon* alter ego theory requires showing that the subsidiary is a "pure fiction" and that its separate corporate existence is ignored, for example, by failing to maintain the "formal" trappings of corporate identity. Does *Cannon* adopt a sensible test? Should the due process clause really shield someone from jurisdiction so long as they complete routine corporate forms — such as board minutes, shareholders and board resolutions, tax filings, and annual reports? What weight does *Hargrave* attribute to the observance of corporate formalities?

5. *Control as a basis for alter ego jurisdiction.* Many courts cite *Cannon*, but apply less stringent tests for alter ego status. *Hargrave* is a good example: it discusses *Cannon* with approval but also inquires into the parent corporation's control over its subsidiary's operations, rather than merely examining "corporate formalities."

(a) *Control for alter ego purposes does not mean power to elect board of directors.* What is meant by the "control" required to establish an alter ego relationship? In one important sense, almost every parent corporation "controls" its majority-owned subsidiaries: by virtue of its stock ownership, the parent has the power to remove and elect its subsidiaries' boards of directors. (Indeed, as discussed below, U.S. courts have held in the context of U.S. extraterritorial discovery that a parent corporation "controls" its majority-owned subsidiaries, and can therefore be required to produce documents in the subsidiaries' possession, if it can replace their directors. *See infra* pp. 856-60.) Why is this standard not also applicable in defining alter ego relations? What standard of control does *Hargrave* apply?

(b) *Authorities holding that control requires showing of continual, day-to-day management.* Lower courts have generally said that alter ego status requires a showing that the parent exercises "intimate and complete" or "day-to-day" control of its subsidiary, or that the parent "continually supervises" and "intervenes in" its subsidiary's affairs. The parent's control must ignore the subsidiary's "separate existence," or treat it as a "mere instrumentality" or "pure fiction." *See supra* pp. 155-56.

(c) *Factors relevant to control.* These formulae do little to identify what types of conduct by a parent corporation constitute control for alter ego purposes. Instead, lower courts have typically relied on unreflective recitations of various "factors." These factors include the parent's percentage ownership, any overlap in directors and officers, adherence to corporate formalities, how the companies account and pay for goods provided to one another, the subsidiary's capitalization, and the interdependence of the parent and subsidiary's businesses. *See Volkswagenwerk AG v. Beech Aircraft*, 751 F.2d 117, 120-22 (2d Cir. 1984) (four factors: (1) common ownership; (2) financial dependency; (3) interference with subsidiary's selection of personnel and disregard for corporate formalities; and (4) control of subsidiary's marketing and operational policies); *Miles v. American Tel. & Tel. Co.*, 703 F.2d 193 (5th Cir. 1983).

(d) *What should constitute control for alter ego purposes?* What types of acts by a parent corporation should constitute sufficient "control" to create an alter ego relationship? One analysis was provided in *United States v. Scophony Corp. of America*, 333 U.S. 795, 816 (1948), where the Court required a showing of "constant supervision and intervention beyond *normal exercise of shareholders' rights.*" This formula contemplates that parent corporations will exercise control over subsidiaries in their capacity as shareholders. If they leave that role, and directly manage the subsidiary's business as its officers, then an alter ego relation may be found. Is this a sensible distinction? What is a "normal exercise of shareholders' rights"?

(e) *Relevance of company's cultural roots.* Is it appropriate for a U.S. court to consider the cultural milieu and character of a foreign parent corporation in determining whether the parent "controls" its U.S. subsidiary? The suggestion has been made that some cultures may be more disciplined, or authoritarian, and hence that "control" may more readily be presumed or found. Is this a legitimate line of reasoning? Consider the following excerpt from a lengthy opinion, upholding alter ego jurisdiction over a Japanese parent corporation, principally because of the acts of Japanese managers at the Japanese parent's U.S. subsidiary:

> Japanese subsidiaries in particular may be singularly responsive to the wishes of their parent companies. ... Significant in terms of cultural considerations that seem to affect real economic power relationships relevant to jurisdiction is the widely-noted hierarchical structure that joins the Japanese subsidiary to its parent, and the Japanese employee to his or her employer. In Japan subsidiaries are commonly referred to as ko-gaisha (child company) in relation to oya-gaisha (parent). "The use of the words 'parent' and 'child' suggests the existence of a familial relationship of control and dependency." K. Haitani, *The Japanese Economic System: An Institutional Overview* 126 (1976). Thus, quite apart from the matter of one hundred percent stock ownership, a Japanese parent may expect to exert control over any of its child companies. The sense of hierarchy is apparently to be found in typical employee-employer relations as well. An inferior in Japanese social organization is "conditioned to attribute authority to the wishes of his superior ... The subordinate is extremely conscious of his standing in the group." K. Haitani, *The Japanese Economic System: An Institutional Overview* 92 (1976). *Bulova Watch Co. v. K. Hattori & Co.*, 508 F.Supp. 1322, 1339 (S.D.N.Y. 1981).

Is it appropriate or helpful to use such stereotypes in analyzing whether one particular corporate management controlled another? On the other hand, can a court meaningfully evaluate control without understanding the expectations and behavior of foreign executives and employees?

6. *Economic integration as basis for alter ego jurisdiction.* As discussed above, a few lower court decisions have departed further from the *Cannon* analysis, instead considering whether a parent and its subsidiary are "economically integrated." *See supra* pp. 155-56. A leading example of this approach was *Bulova Watch Co. v. K. Hattori & Co.*, 508 F.Supp. 1322, 1327 (E.D.N.Y. 1981), where the court remarked:

> To any layman it would seem absurd that our courts could not obtain jurisdiction over a billion dollar multinational which is exploiting the critical New York and American markets to keep its home production going at a huge volume and profit. This perception must have a bearing on our evaluation of fairness. The law ignores the common sense of a situation at the peril of becoming irrelevant as an institution. ...

Most parents are economically integrated with their subsidiaries; they establish those subsidiaries to develop and expand their business into other territories. An economic integration standard would treat many such arrangements as alter ego relations. Is that appropriate? Should the strict *Cannon* standard remain the due process limit? Does the fairly frequent "economic integration" of numerous subsidiaries into a single unitary enterprise undermine the wisdom of *Cannon*'s formula?

7. *Specific jurisdiction based on alter ego status.* In *Hargrave*, the plaintiffs sought to subject T&N to specific jurisdiction in Texas, based upon the contacts of K&N (T&N's subsidiary) with Texas and on K&N's alleged status as T&N's alter ego. What facts should be relevant to the inquiry into an alter ego relationship between K&N and T&N? Are dealings of K&N and T&N *not* relating to asbestos (the subject of the claims in *Hargrave*) relevant? Are the dealings of K&N and T&N not relating to Texas relevant?

Suppose that the plaintiff in *Hargrave* made a compelling showing that T&N intimately and completely controlled K&N's allegedly tortious conduct. Does that establish an alter ego relationship? What if T&N demonstrates that in all other contexts — aside from the allegedly tortious conduct — K&N operated without the slightest control from T&N? Suppose the hypothetical is reversed: T&N exercised no control over K&N's tortious conduct in *Hargrave*, but in most other contexts T&N controlled K&N's actions.

8. *General jurisdiction based on alter ego status.* The alter ego doctrine provides that one company is in fact another company — that it is part, or a manifestation, of another company. If T&N's U.S. subsidiary *is in fact T&N itself*, then T&N would appear to be subject to general jurisdiction in all the places where the U.S. subsidiary is doing business. In *Hargrave*, suppose that an action were brought against T&N in Pennsylvania, where K&N was incorporated and based. As a result, K&N is clearly subject to general jurisdiction in Pennsylvania; if K&N is the alter ego of T&N, would T&N also be subject to general jurisdiction in Pennsylvania? For example, would T&N be subject to suit in Pennsylvania on claims arising out of its English operations? on a suit by its English bank to recover monies loaned in England to T&N? on a suit by an English worker injured in England? Is this not a ridiculous result? Ought not the due process clause require some connection between the plaintiff's claims and the defendant parent corporation's alter ego relationship with a domestic company?

9. *Specific jurisdiction based upon a foreign parent's own forum contacts related to its subsidiary's activities in forum.* Even if a U.S. subsidiary is not the alter ego of its foreign parent, the foreign parent's contacts with its subsidiary may still be relevant to establishing specific jurisdiction over it. Numerous courts have taken a foreign parent's dealings with its U.S. subsidiary into account in determining the parent's own forum contacts. *E.g., Laitram Corp. v. Oki Elec. Indus. Co.*, 1994 WL 24241 (E.D. La. 1994) (although foreign parent was not alter ego of U.S. subsidiary, parent's knowledge of subsidiary's marketing activities supported stream of commerce jurisdiction); *Brunswick Corp. v. Suzuki Co.*, 575 F.Supp. 1412 (E.D. Wis. 1983) ("Through their affiliated entities [defendants] have systematically injected themselves into the Wisconsin market place").

Consider the following explanation, drawn from a case where the plaintiff sought to establish personal jurisdiction in Georgia over a French car manufacturer, based upon its relations with its wholly-owned U.S. marketing subsidiary:

> Although we agree that (1) no "alter ego" relationship existed between [the U.S. subsidiary] and [the French parent], and that (2) to impute the actions of the former to the latter would therefore be improper, the fact that no alter ego relationship existed between the two entities does not mean that [the French parent] could not possess minimum contacts with Georgia as a result of its own independent role in the process that brought [the French parent]'s 1982 Renault LeCar to the United States. The question is not whether the contacts between [the U.S. subsidiary] and Georgia establish minimum contacts between Georgia and [the French parent], but rather whether [the French parent], by virtue of its relationship with [the U.S. subsidiary], purposefully availed itself of the privilege of conducting business in Georgia such that it could reasonably anticipate being haled into court there. That [the French parent] did not exercise sufficient control over [the U.S. subsidiary] to establish an alter ego relationship does not necessarily mean that it had insufficient contacts with Georgia as a result of its own actions and its participation in the decisions that resulted in [the U.S. subsidiary]'s presence and activity in Georgia. *Vermeulen v. Renault, U.S.A. Inc.*, 965 F.2d 1014 (11th Cir. 1992).

10. *Specific jurisdiction based upon a foreign parent causing a domestic subsidiary to engage in conduct in the forum.* If a parent corporation causes its subsidiary to engage in certain conduct, it may be subject to personal jurisdiction in the same manner that the subsidiary would be. According to one court, "[i]f the subsidiary corporation does an act, or causes effects, in the state at the direction of the parent corporation or in the course of the parent corporation's business, the state has judicial jurisdiction over the parent to the same extent that it would have had such jurisdiction if the parent had itself done the act or caused the effects." *Allen v. Toshiba Corp.*, 599 F. Supp. 381, 389 (D. N. Mex. 1984).

11. *Presence of "division" within the forum.* It is common for a single corporate entity to divide its operations among several unincorporated "divisions." This is done for both internal administrative and marketing purposes (as when a division does business under a different name than the company of which it is a part). It is well-settled that a company can be regarded as doing business in the places where its divisions are present. *E.g., Wells Fargo & Co. v. Wells Fargo Express Co.*, 556 F.2d 406, 425 (9th Cir. 1977) ("Clearly, a corporation may be 'present' in several jurisdictions by operating 'divisions' there so that it may not, in some instances, be unreasonable or unfair to subject the corporation to the general jurisdiction of any one of those forums regardless of where the cause of action arose or which of the corporation's

divisions' activities gave rise to it."). *See also supra* p. 113, discussing general jurisdiction based on presence of an office in the forum.

12. *Compelled submission of foreign subsidiary to U.S. jurisdiction.* What if a court orders a U.S. parent, which is subject to its personal jurisdiction, to use its control of one of its foreign subsidiaries to force the subsidiary to waive personal jurisdiction challenges and appear in the U.S. proceeding? *Compare* the treatment of parent-subsidiary relations in the discovery context, *infra* pp. 859-60.

2. Personal Jurisdiction Based on Agency Relationship

Closely related to the alter ego doctrine is personal jurisdiction based upon an "agency" relationship. It is well-settled that personal jurisdiction may be exercised over a foreign corporation by U.S. courts based upon its "agency" relationship with a U.S. corporation or other entity with U.S. contacts:

> Even in the absence of a stock relationship between a local and a foreign corporation, jurisdiction over the foreign corporation has sometimes been exercised on the basis of activities that the local corporation has conducted in the state as the agent of the foreign corporation.[191]

Numerous lower courts have exercised jurisdiction over foreign principals based upon their relations with local agents.[192]

a. Law Governing Agency Relationship for Jurisdictional Purposes

In order for jurisdiction to be exercised based upon an agency relationship, both statutory and due process requirements must be satisfied. As in the alter ego context, state and federal statutory jurisdictional grants seldom deal expressly with agency as a basis for jurisdiction. As a result, the circumstances in which jurisdiction may be asserted under state law as a result of an agency relationship are defined almost entirely by common law decisions. Lower courts seldom distinguish clearly between state common law requirements and due process limits, apparently assuming that state law extends to the limits of the Constitution.

b. Agency Standards for Jurisdictional Purposes

There is no clearly-articulated definition of "agency" for jurisdictional purposes under either most state laws or the due process clause. Courts often say that they have "focused on the realities of the relationship in question rather than the formalities of agency law."[193] As with the alter ego doctrine, courts have usually concluded that "a more informal" and "more lenient" definition of agency is appropriate for jurisdictional purposes, than for liability purposes.[194]

Following this rationale, the weight of lower court authority has held that an agency relationship exists if three requirements are satisfied: (a) the alleged agent

---

191. *Restatement (Second) Conflict of Laws* §52, comment b (1971).

192. *E.g., Ginten v. Swedish Match, AB,* 1990 U.S. Dist. Lexis 16579 (E.D.N.Y. 1990); *Brunswick Corp. v. Suzuki Motor Corp.,* 575 F.Supp. 1412 (E.D. Wis. 1983). Other courts have refused, on particular facts, to find any agency relationship. *E.g., Antares Aircraft, L.P. v. Total C.F.P.,* 1991 U.S. Dist. Lexis 1511 (S.D.N.Y. 1991); *Intersong-U.S.A. Inc. v. CBS Inc.,* 1990 U.S. Dist. Lexis 11645 (S.D.N.Y. 1990).

193. *CutCo Indus., Inc. v. Naughton,* 806 F.2d 361, 366 (2d Cir. 1986).

194. *Reiner v. Durand,* 602 F.Supp. 849, 851 (S.D.N.Y. 1985).

must have acted for the benefit of the alleged principal; (b) the principal must have had knowledge of, and must have consented to, the agent's actions on its behalf; and (c) the principal must have had sufficient control over the agent's actions.[195] Other courts have required only "the principal's express or implied authority to perform acts which give rise to submission to jurisdiction."[196] In order for its contacts to be attributed to its principal, an agent must have acted within the scope of its authority.[197]

There is no requirement that a principal have any ownership interest in, or other corporate affiliation with, its agent. Agency relations are routinely found between unaffiliated entities. Nevertheless, the existence of an ownership interest is not irrelevant to the existence of an agency relationship. Courts frequently say that the greater the degree of corporate affiliation, the more likely it is that jurisdiction will be exercised based on an agency relationship.[198]

Most courts have required that the alleged principal enjoyed a significant measure of "control" over its purported agent. The degree of control required to establish an agency relationship is unclear, with different courts requiring varying levels of control. Some opinions have said that "all that plaintiff need demonstrate is the degree of control required by common law agency rules."[199] Other cases say that "the parent must have actual, participatory and total control of the subsidiary."[200]

c. Selected Materials on Agency Relationship as a Basis for Personal Jurisdiction in International Cases

The two following decisions illustrate common applications of the agency doctrine in international cases. In *Frummer v. Hilton Hotels*, the New York Court of Appeals subjects the U.K. parent of a New York subsidiary to general jurisdiction because the subsidiary acted as its agent. The decision reflects an expansive, potentially exorbitant, jurisdictional doctrine. In *Cartwright v. Fokker Aircraft*, the district court relies on an agency relationship to subject a foreign aircraft manufacturer to specific jurisdiction.

FRUMMER v. HILTON HOTELS INTERNATIONAL

281 N.Y.S.2d 41 (1967)

FULD, CHIEF JUDGE. This appeal calls upon us to determine whether jurisdiction was validly acquired over one of the defendants, Hilton Hotels (U.K.) Ltd., a

---

195. *CutCo Indus., Inc. v. Naughton*, 806 F.2d 3261, 367 (2d Cir. 1986); *Grove Press, Inc. v. Angleton*, 649 F.2d 121, 122 (2d Cir. 1981).

196. *Boden Products, Inc. v. Novachem, Inc.*, 663 F.Supp. 226, 229 (N.D. Ill. 1987).

197. *E.g., Marshall Exports, Inc. v. Phillips*, 385 F.Supp. 1250, 1252 (E.D.N.C. 1974).

198. *E.g., Wells Fargo & Co. v. Wells Fargo Express Co.*, 556 F.2d 406, 419 (9th Cir. 1977); *H. Heller & Co. v. Novacor Chem. Ltd.*, 726 F.Supp. 49 (S.D.N.Y. 1988) ("corporate affiliation may, in light of the facts of a given case, give rise to a 'valid inference' of agency").

199. *Pennie & Edmonds v. Austad Co.*, 681 F.Supp. 1074, 1077 (S.D.N.Y. 1988).

200. *Akzona Inc. v. E.I. Du Pont de Nemours & Co.*, 607 F.Supp. 227, 237 (D. Del. 1984).

British corporation ["Hilton (U.K.)"]. The plaintiff alleges that in 1963 when he was on a visit to England he fell and was injured in his room at the London Hilton Hotel while attempting to take a shower in an "ovular," modernistic type bathtub. He seeks $150,000 in damages not only from the defendant Hilton (U.K.) but also from the defendants Hilton Hotels Corporation and Hilton Hotels International, both of which are Delaware corporations doing business in New York. The defendant Hilton (U.K.), which is the lessee and operator of the London Hilton Hotel, has moved for an order dismissing the complaint against it on the ground that the court lacks jurisdiction of the defendant's person. ...

The plaintiff does not allege that he had any dealings at all with the British corporate defendant or its agents in this State. Therefore, it may not be said that his cause of action arose from the British corporation's transaction of any business here, and he is not entitled to avail himself of C.P.L.R. §302(a)(1) in order to bring the defendant within the jurisdiction of our courts.

Jurisdiction was, however, properly acquired over Hilton (U.K.) because the record discloses that it was "doing business" here in the traditional sense. As we have frequently observed, a foreign corporation is amenable to suit in our courts if it is "engaged in such a continuous and systematic course of 'doing business' here as to warrant a finding of its presence in this jurisdiction." Although "mere solicitation" of business for an out-of-state concern is not enough to constitute doing business, due process requirements are satisfied if the defendant foreign corporation has "certain minimum contacts with [the State] such that the maintenance of the suit does not offend 'traditional notions of fair play and substantial justice.'"

In *Bryant v. Finnish Nat. Airline*, 15 N.Y.2d 426, 432, the court declared that the "test for 'doing business' ... should be a simple pragmatic one," and, applying that test, went on to hold that the requisite minimum contacts with New York were out when it appears that the defendant foreign corporation, an airline, "has a lease on a New York office ... employs several people and ... has a bank account here ... does public relations and publicity work for defendant here including maintaining contacts with other airlines and travel agencies ... transmits requests for space to defendant in Europe and helps to generate business."

In the case before us, these same services are provided for the defendant Hilton (U.K.) by the Hilton Reservation Service which has a New York office, as well as a New York bank account and telephone number. The Service advertises that it was "established to provide the closest possible liaison with Travel Agents across the country," that lodging "rates for certified wholesalers and/or tour operators [could] be obtained [from the Service] on request" and that it could "confirm availabilities immediately ... and without charge" at any Hilton hotel including the London Hilton. Thus, it does "public relations and publicity work" for the defendant Hilton (U.K.), including "maintaining contacts with ... travel agents" and tour directors; and it most certainly "helps to generate business" here for the London Hilton — which, indeed, was the very purpose for which it was established. Moreover, unlike the *Bryant* case, 15 N.Y.2d 426, where the defendant's New York office did not make reservations or sell tickets, the Hilton Reservation Service both accepts and confirms room reservations at the London Hilton. In short — and this is the significant and pivotal factor — the Service does all the business which Hilton (U.K.) could do were it here by its own officials.

The defendant's reliance on *Miller v. Surf Properties*, 4 N.Y.2d 475, is misplaced. In that case, we held that the activities of a "travel agency" were not sufficient to give our courts *in personam* jurisdiction over a Florida hotel when the agency's services "amounted to little more than rendering telephone service and mailing brochures" for the hotel and 30 other independent and unassociated Florida establishments. Indeed, in *Bryant*, we found it significant that in the *Miller* case the New York activities were carried on "not [by] an employee of the defendant [Florida hotel] but an independent travel agency representing defendant in New York City." Although, in the case before us, the Hilton Reservation Service is not the "employee" of Hilton (U.K.), the Service and that defendant are owned in common by the other defendants and the Service is concededly run on a "non-profit" basis for the benefit of the London Hilton and other Hilton hotels. ...

We are not unmindful that litigation in a foreign jurisdiction is a burdensome inconvenience for any company. However, it is part of the price which may properly be demanded of those who extensively engage in international trade. When their activities abroad, either directly or through an agent, become as widespread and energetic as the activities in New York conducted by Hilton (U.K.), they receive considerable benefits from such foreign business and may not be heard to complain about the burdens. Since, then, Hilton (U.K.) was "doing business" in New York in the traditional sense and was validly served with process in London, as provided by statute (CPLR §313), our courts acquired "personal jurisdiction over the corporation for any cause of action asserted against it, no matter where the events occurred which give rise to the cause of action.

BREITEL, JUDGE, dissenting. The occasion for disagreement in this case is the extension of personal jurisdiction over a foreign corporation simply because of its relationship with subsidiary or affiliated corporations of a parent corporation. Moreover, such jurisdiction is extended in the absence of fraud, misrepresentation, or intermingling of activities of separate corporations. Before considering the particular facts of this case it should be observed that important policy and commercial considerations are involved in preventing or allowing business enterprises to limit liability, suability, and exposure to governmental regulation, by the creation of truly separate corporate entities, with or without separate ownership structures, but especially where the ownership is not identical. These considerations are particularly important for a country engaged in worldwide trade and investment, often in the less developed countries of the world, because of the encouragement or discouragement to risk capital and the exposure to reciprocal treatment of jurisdictional bases in foreign countries. ...

There is no claim by plaintiff that the Hilton complex or any of its components is used to defraud, deceive, or mislead those who deal with it, or that there has been any failure in the operation and management of the several corporations to keep their internal affairs and management separate and distinct. It is contended and it is undisputed that the advertising and soliciting for business by the Hilton enterprises is done by offering the several respective services of the affiliated hotel corporations, reservations services, and credit card facilities, in common advertising.

The pivotal, but disputed, assertion upon which the present decision depends is that the Hilton Credit Corporation in handling reservations for the British corporation "does all the business which Hilton (U.K.) could do were it here by its own officials." ... As recognized, the solicitation or mere promotion of business for an out-of-State enterprise does not constitute the doing of business in the State. This is traditional law and there is no avowed intention to change it. On the other hand, the maintenance of localized activities in the State has, of course, been the basis for asserting personal jurisdiction. The majority bridges the gap between these two rules by finding that separate but affiliated corporations perform the localized services, albeit local services of the narrowest scope, on behalf of the foreign corporation and, therefore, the foreign corporation is performing the localized services here, thus subjecting it to personal jurisdiction. This, of course, is a *non sequitur*, unless there is no power or privilege on the part of business enterprises to limit and segregate their assets, liabilities, and suability, if done, in fact, and if done without fraud or deception, by the utilization of separate, adequately financed corporations, either subsidiary or affiliated. ...

On this analysis, the present case extends the "doing business" rule well beyond the existing principles or precedents. And the effect on the flexibility and promotion of world-wide business enterprises would be drastic and unhealthy. It is well established in this country that a foreign parent corporation will not be subjected to the judicial jurisdiction of a State merely because of its ownership of a subsidiary corporation doing business within the State, if the parent diligently maintains the formal separateness of the subsidiary entity (*e.g.*, *Cannon Mfg. Co. v. Cudahy Packing Co.*). Similarly, courts in the United Kingdom evidently will not assert jurisdiction over a foreign corporation merely because it maintains a subsidiary in [the forum]. In Civil Law and other code countries the recognized bases of personal jurisdiction over foreign corporations admits of the assertion of such jurisdiction only on the existence of a specially designated office, situs of headquarters, or what is described as "domicile" in a special sense. ...

While the circumstances in this case are not as serious in their effect in permitting personal jurisdiction, because plaintiff is indeed a New York resident, and the Hilton enterprises looked at in the large as a layman would view them are so much "present," the rules applied will not stay so limited. Under such grossly extended rules nonresidents would also be able to sue in New York, where tort verdicts are regarded as very high; and there are other categories in which jurisdiction might be invoked under circumstances much less appealing than here. Again, it is pointed out that this case does not involve a cause of action which arose here, but one that arose in another country across the seas.

CARTWRIGHT v. FOKKER AIRCRAFT U.S.A., INC.

713 F.Supp. 389 (N.D. Georgia 1988)

HORACE T. WARD, DISTRICT JUDGE. ... The complaint alleges that plaintiff, who was an airline baggage handler, was injured when he exited the baggage compartment of an airplane. It claims that the cargo compartment was negligently designed and defective and that its defects were the proximate cause of plaintiff's injuries. ... [I]n order for Fokker Aircraft BV to come within the coverage of the [Georgia long-arm] statute it must have, in person or through an agent, regularly done or solicited business in the state of Georgia, engaged in a persistent course of conduct with Georgia, or derived substantial revenue from sales in Georgia.

The complaint alleged that defendants Fokker Aircraft USA, Fokker Aircraft BV, and Fokker BV designed, manufactured, distributed, and sold the airplane which caused plaintiff's injuries. Plaintiff also submitted exhibits which indicate Fokker Aircraft USA is a wholly-owned subsidiary of Fokker Aircraft BV, Fokker Aircraft USA is licensed to do business in Georgia, and Fokker Aircraft USA provides Fokker Aircraft BV with marketing, sales and support of certain Fokker aircraft in the United States. Fokker Aircraft USA sold the airplane involved to Piedmont Airlines. The contract of sale indicates that Piedmont is obligated to pay certain taxes incurred by Fokker Aircraft BV; work done on the airplane pursuant to the contract is performed by or on behalf of Fokker Aircraft BV at Fokker Aircraft BV's plant; Fokker Aircraft BV provides field service representatives to advise Piedmont on aircraft maintenance and spare parts; and Fokker Aircraft BV provides training courses at its training facilities.

The parties agree that the airplane involved in this matter was manufactured by Fokker Aircraft BV and sold to Piedmont Airlines through Fokker Aircraft USA. The plane was sold by Fokker Aircraft BV to Fokker Aircraft USA in Amsterdam and then Fokker Aircraft USA resold the airplane to Piedmont Airlines. Defendant submitted an affidavit which states that Fokker Aircraft BV is a Dutch corporation, with its principal offices located in Amsterdam, The Netherlands; Fokker Aircraft BV holds title to certain inventory of spare parts which are located in a Georgia warehouse which is operated by Fokker Aircraft USA; all sales of aircraft by Fokker Aircraft BV are made in The Netherlands; Fokker Aircraft BV transacts no business within Georgia; Fokker Aircraft BV advertises in some national trade magazines but does not do or solicit business in Georgia; Fokker Aircraft BV does not derive any revenue from goods used or consumed or services rendered in Georgia; Fokker Aircraft BV does not own, use, or possess any real property situated within Georgia; Fokker Aircraft BV does not maintain an office in Georgia, nor does it have any employees or agents in Georgia; and Fokker Aircraft BV is not and never has been licensed to do business in Georgia. ...

[P]laintiff has made a prima facie showing that defendant Fokker Aircraft BV committed a tortious injury in this state which was caused by an act or omission outside the state. He has also made a prima facie showing that Fokker Aircraft BV, through its subsidiary Fokker Aircraft USA, engages in a persistent course of conduct with the state. Fokker Aircraft BV not only advertised in national trade publications and held title to certain spare parts kept in Georgia, it also utilized a subsidiary distributor who regularly does and solicits business in Georgia. The court finds that although Fokker Aircraft BV and Fokker Aircraft USA have separate corporate identities, it is appropriate in these circumstances to consider Fokker Aircraft USA the "agent" of Fokker Aircraft BV in the context of the Georgia long arm statute. ...

[As for due process,] defendant Fokker Aircraft BV has taken actions which were purposefully directed toward the forum state. It has advertised in national publications, some of whose audience is presumably in Georgia. More importantly, it markets its product through a distributor which services its products exclusively and is licensed to do business in Georgia. These facts establish the requisite "substantial connection" between defendant and the forum state which make the exercise over of jurisdiction over defendant consistent with "traditional notions of fair play and substantial justice."

Notes on Hilton Hotels and Fokker

1. *Jurisdiction where agent's responsibilities are ministerial.* An agent's responsibilities can range from the most trivial and limited to the most important and far-reaching. A defendant's reliance on agents to perform ministerial tasks — such as obtaining publicly filed document or acting as a travel agent — can quite properly have substantive consequences: these persons are the principal's agents and the two parties' substantive legal rights towards each other, and third parties, are governed by this agency relationship. But should such ministerial agency relations have any jurisdictional consequences? If so, are these consequences relevant only to specific jurisdiction? or do they extend more broadly?

2. *Agency relationship as a basis for specific jurisdiction.* Agency relationships can provide the basis for subjecting a foreign principal to specific jurisdiction. In such cases, the plaintiff's claims must arise out of the agent's actions in the forum in its capacity as the principal's agent. *Frummer* was not a specific jurisdiction case because "[t]he plaintiff does not allege that he had any dealings at all with the British corporate defendant or its agents in this case." Suppose that the plaintiff had contacted Hilton Reservation Service in New York and that it had reserved a room with Hilton (U.K.) for the plaintiff. Would specific jurisdiction have been proper?

Was *Fokker* a specific jurisdiction case? Note that Fokker BV manufactured the allegedly defective aircraft, which it sold to its alleged agent, Fokker USA. Note also that jurisdiction was based upon a provision of the Georgia long-arm statute applicable when "tortious injury" is caused within the state by an act committed outside the state. What if Fokker BV had manufactured the allegedly defective aircraft, but that it was *not* sold to or distributed by Fokker USA? Would jurisdiction still be permitted?

3. *General jurisdiction based on agency relationship.* *Hilton Hotels* exercised jurisdiction over Hilton U.K. based on the defendant's subsidiaries' activities within New York that were unrelated to the plaintiff's claims. Other courts have also relied on agency theories to assert general jurisdiction over foreign defendants. *E.g., Gottlieb v. Sandia Am. Corp.,* 452 F.2d 510 (3d Cir.), *cert. denied,* 404 U.S. 938 (1971). Is it appropriate to permit general jurisdiction based on an agency relationship? Was *Hilton Hotels* correctly decided? Suppose that the plaintiff was from Burma, had been injured in London, and had never had any contact with New York or Hilton U.K.'s New York agent. Would general jurisdiction really be appropri-

ate? Suppose an English supplier of Hilton U.K. sued in New York on unpaid invoices for goods purchased and delivered in London.

Would the agency relationship in *Fokker* sustain general jurisdiction? Could one of Fokker BV's Dutch suppliers (for example, of seatbelts) sue it in Georgia? Could a Chinese passenger, injured in a domestic Chinese flight on a Fokker aircraft sold to a Chinese airline, sue Fokker BV in Georgia? From the available facts, was the *Fokker* relationship any different from the *Hilton Hotel* relationship?

4. *What does "agency" mean for jurisdictional purposes?* At common law, "[a]gency is the fiduciary relation which results from the manifestation of consent by one person to another that the other shall act on his behalf and subject to his control, and consent by the other so to act." *Restatement (Second) Agency* §1 (1958). Neither *Frummer* nor *Fokker* devote much attention to the terms (or even existence) of an agency relationship between the defendant parties. Other lower courts have specifically disclaimed any obligation to consider the terms of agreements between an alleged principal and agent. E.g., *East New York Sav. Bank v. Republic Realty Mtg. Corp.*, 402 N.Y.S.2d 639, 641 (App. Div. 1978) (holding that jurisdiction based on agency relationship can be exercised, "regardless of whether the representative acted as an agent or an independent contractor"). These decisions suggest that, in the context of jurisdiction, agency means something less demanding than what it means for substantive purposes. *See supra* pp. 163-64. Is a "less stringent" agency standard appropriate? What exactly do *Frummer* and *Fokker* require to establish an agency relationship?

5. *"Control" required to establish agency relationship.* A critical element in establishing an agency relationship for jurisdictional purposes is the principal's "control" over the agent. *See supra* pp. 164-65. Recall that a parent almost always "controls" its subsidiary. Is that enough? What degree of control over the agent should be required?

6. *Scope of duties required for general agency relationship.* The character of control required for an agency relationship should vary depending on whether specific or general jurisdiction is involved. It is also clear that the existence of a general agency relationship depends on the breadth and character of the agent's duties. One standard for determining when a company is subject to the forum's general jurisdiction because of an agent's activities was suggested in *Gelfand v. Tanner Motors Tours*, 385 F.2d 116, 121 (2d Cir. 1967), *cert. denied*, 390 U.S. 996 (1968):

> [The defendant's] New York representative provides services beyond "mere solicitation" and these services are sufficiently important to the foreign corporation that if it did not have a representative to perform them, the corporation's own officials would undertake to perform substantially similar services.

Other decisions emphasize that the general agent must "have broad executive responsibilities and that his relationship [must] reflect a degree of continuity." *Gottlieb v. Sandia Am. Corp.*, 452 F.2d 510 (3d Cir.), *cert. denied*, 404 U.S. 938 (1971). That is apparently the focus of *Frummer's* comment that the U.S. subsidiary "does all the business which Hilton (U.K.) could do were it here by its own officials."

7. *Effect of parent-subsidiary relationship on existence of agency relationship.* The fact that an alleged principal is also the parent corporation of its purported agent is typically a significant consideration in agency analysis. *See supra* p. 164. Note that both *Frummer* and *Fokker* involved parent-subsidiary relations. Suppose that the Hilton Hotels reservation service in *Frummer* had been wholly-owned by local New York residents, not by Hilton U.K. Would *Frummer* still have found jurisdiction? Suppose that Fokker's U.S. distributors were independent companies. Would they still have been "agents" of Fokker BV?

8. *Wisdom of applying agency standard in international cases.* Consider Judge Brietel's dissent in *Frummer*. Is it wise to assert jurisdiction based on agency relations in international cases? Note that U.S. companies use such arrangements abroad with considerable regularity. Is it in the interest of U.S. (and international) commerce for U.S. courts to make expansive jurisdictional claims based upon agency relations? Note Judge Brietel's concern about the "important policy and commercial considerations" that attach to limited liability incorporation, particularly for a country, like the United States, "engaged in worldwide trade and investment." Are these relevant concerns for due process analysis?

E. Personal Jurisdiction in Federal Courts: Federal Rule of Civil Procedure 4 and the Due Process Clauses

1. Introduction

The personal jurisdiction of federal courts is subject to different rules than those applicable in state courts. Like a state court, a federal court cannot exercise personal jurisdiction unless two basic requirements are satisfied: (1) a legislative authorization to assert jurisdiction must exist; and (2) the Constitution must not prohibit the exercise of jurisdiction.[201] Unlike a state court, however, federal courts have no general federal long-arm statute on which to rely. Instead, federal courts are directed by Federal Rule of Civil Procedure 4 to "borrow" either specific federal long-arm statutes or local state long-arm statutes.[202] This approach produces complicated questions about the relationships between Rule 4, borrowed jurisdictional statutes, and the due process clauses of the fifth and fourteenth amendments. In important respects, the law is unsettled with divergent and confused lower court decisions.

a. Federal Rule of Civil Procedure 4: Amenability and Manner of Service Distinguished

The personal jurisdiction of federal courts is defined, in the first instance, by Federal Rule of Civil Procedure 4.[203] Rule 4 was recently the subject of comprehensive revisions, which went into effect in December 1993. The current text of Rule 4 is reproduced as Appendix C. Rule 4 deals with both a defendant's *amenability* to personal jurisdiction and the *manner* of effecting service of process on a defendant. These are separate requirements, which both must be satisfied to permit personal jurisdiction.[204]

Amenability refers to the circumstances in which the forum's courts may assert personal jurisdiction over the defendant.[205] Rule 4 does not itself directly define a foreign defendant's amenability to suit in federal court. Instead, new Rule 4(k) authorizes federal district courts to "borrow" other sources of jurisdictional power

---

201. *See infra* pp. 172-73 & 173-74. Other requirements exist before a federal court may hear a dispute, including the presence of subject matter jurisdiction, compliance with venue requirements, and valid service.

202. *See infra* pp. 171-72 & 174-95.

203. *Omni Capital Int'l v. Rudolf Wolff & Co.*, 484 U.S. 97, 104 (1987) ("service of process in a federal action is covered generally by Rule 4"). Special provisions concerning jurisdiction and service of process exist in a few fields, such as condemnation proceedings and admiralty. *See* C. Wright & A. Miller, *Federal Practice and Procedure* §1062 (1987 & 1994 Supp.).

204. *Omni Capital Int'l v. Rudolf Wolff & Co.*, 484 U.S. 97, 104-05 (1987).

205. C. Wright & A. Miller, *Federal Practice and Procedure* §1075 (1987); *Arrowsmith v. United Press Int'l*, 320 F.2d 219 (2d Cir. 1963).

— in particular, state and federal long-arm statutes — that themselves define amenability to personal jurisdiction.[206]

Rule 4 also prescribes rules regarding the manner of service. Service of process is the physical mechanism for giving notice to the defendant that an action has been commenced.[207] Most importantly for international litigants, Rule 4(f) provides detailed instructions regarding the modes of serving of process outside the United States (discussed in Chapter 10 below). These provisions deal only with the manner of serving process on foreign defendants and not with the circumstances in which they will be amenable to personal jurisdiction.

b. Rule 4(k)'s Jurisdictional Grants: An Overview

Rule 4's provisions dealing with amenability to jurisdiction are now contained in Rule 4(k). Rule 4(k) provides three principal jurisdictional authorizations:

(1) Rule 4(k)(1)(A) authorizes a district court to borrow the jurisdictional powers of state courts in the state where it is located;

(2) Rule 4(k)(1)(D) confirms the availability of any applicable federal statute granting personal jurisdiction; and

(3) Rule 4(k)(2) grants district courts personal jurisdiction to the limits of the due process clause in certain federal question cases.

Much of new Rule 4(k) is based on old Rule 4(e) of the Federal Rules of Civil Procedure.[208] Decisions under Rule 4(e) remain useful in interpreting the new Rule.

c. No Federal Personal Jurisdiction Without Legislative Authorization: Omni Capital

A federal court may not exercise personal jurisdiction without legislative authorization, generally provided by incorporation through Rule 4. That was most recently reaffirmed in *Omni Capital Int'l v. Rudolf Wolff & Co.*, where the Supreme Court specifically rejected the argument that federal courts should exercise a common law power to create their own bases of federal personal jurisdiction.[209]

Omni was a suit in federal district court asserting federal claims under the Commodity Exchange Act ("CEA")[210] and pendent state law claims. The defendants, who resided in England, moved to dismiss for lack of personal jurisdiction. The Court of Appeals held that neither the CEA nor the local state long-arm statute, which had been borrowed pursuant to old Federal Rule of Civil Procedure 4(e), con-

---

206. *See infra* pp. 174-75 & 183-84; *Omni Capital Int'l v. Rudolf Wolff & Co.*, 484 U.S. 97, 105 (1987). Rule 4(k)(2), which authorizes jurisdiction in certain federal question cases, is an exception to this general principle (although even it "borrows" the due process clause). *See infra* pp. 195-97.

207. *See infra* pp. 757-63.

208. *See Advisory Committee Notes, 28 U.S.C.A. Fed. R. Civ. Pro. 4*, 119; D. Siegel, *Supplementary Practice Commentaries*, 28 U.S.C.A. Fed. Rules Civ. Proc. Rule 4, C4-33 (1994 Supp.).

209. 484 U.S. 97 (1987). *See Insurance Corp. of Ireland v. Compagnie des Bauxites de Guinee*, 456 U.S. 694, 711 (1982) (Powell, J., concurring) ("As courts of limited jurisdiction, the federal courts possess no warrant to create jurisdictional law of their own.").

210. 7 U.S.C. §1 *et seq.*

ferred jurisdiction. Moreover, the court rejected the plaintiff's suggestion that a common law basis for federal personal jurisdiction be judicially fashioned.[211]

The Supreme Court affirmed. It first concluded that no federal or state long-arm statute, and no provision of old Rule 4(e), authorized jurisdiction over the foreign defendant. The Court then considered whether, "even if authorization for service of process ... cannot be found in a statute or rule, such authorization should be created by fashioning a remedy to fill a gap in the Federal Rules of Civil Procedure."[212] The Court flatly declined this invitation: "We reject the suggestion that we should create a common-law rule authorizing service of process, since we would consider that action unwise, even were it within our power."[213]

Although *Omni* was decided under old Rule 4(e), nothing in the text or drafting history of new Rule 4(k) suggests any different result under the revised Rule.[214] Moreover, *Omni* rested on a general reluctance by federal courts to fashion their own jurisdictional bases, rather than on a specific interpretation of Rule 4(e).[215] It is fairly clear, therefore, that the rule stated in *Omni* remains operative: a federal court generally cannot exercise jurisdiction over a defendant unless one of Rule 4(k)'s jurisdictional grants (or some other legislative authorization) permits it to do so.

d. Due Process Limits: "State" or "National" Contacts?

Even if personal jurisdiction in a federal court is authorized by Rule 4, the due process clause must also be satisfied. As discussed below, the application of due process standards to international cases in federal courts can raise additional layers of complex issues not present in state court actions.

A recurrent question concerns what territorial unit is relevant for due process purposes — an individual State or the entire United States. The issue arises most frequently in disputes whether a foreign defendant must have "state contacts" with the particular state where a federal court is located, or whether it is sufficient if the defendant has "national contacts" with the entire United States.[216] The same basic question can arise where jurisdiction is based on tag service in the United States, on U.S. nationality, or on other jurisdictional bases.[217]

---

211. *See Point Landing, Inc. v. Omni Capital Int'l, Ltd.*, 795 F.2d 415, 423 (5th Cir. 1986) (citing "the unmalleable principle of law that is unyielding to legal blandishments ... that federal courts ... must ground their personal jurisdiction on a federal statute or rule"). A dissenting opinion in the Court of Appeals reasoned that, even if no authorization for personal jurisdiction could be found in old Rule 4(e), the federal courts should act to fill the "interstices in the law inadvertently left by legislative enactment," by fashioning a common law basis for service and personal jurisdiction. 794 F.2d at 431-32.

212. 484 U.S. at 103.

213. 484 U.S. at 111.

214. The Advisory Committee Notes to new Federal Rule of Civil Procedure 4(k) cite *Omni* with approval, and, although they do not directly address the point, are generally supportive of the view that Rule 4(k)'s bases for personal jurisdiction are exclusive. *Advisory Committee Notes, 28 U.S.C.A. Fed. R. Civ. Pro. 4*, at 118.

215. *See* 484 U.S. at 104-5.

216. *See infra* pp. 178-81 & 190-94.

217. *See infra* pp. 182 & 196.

The distinction between national and state contacts can have considerable practical importance. As we have already seen, many foreign defendants have fairly significant contacts with the United States as a whole, but do not have substantial contacts with any particular U.S. state.[218] When this is the case, a national contacts test is of great practice significance, because it may provide the only means for *any* U.S. court to exercise jurisdiction over the foreign defendant.[219]

2. Federal Long-Arm Statutes Granting Jurisdiction Based Upon a Foreign Defendant's National Contacts

New Rule 4(k)(1)(D) of the Federal Rules of Civil Procedure provides that service of a summons (or filing a waiver of service) is "effective to establish jurisdiction over the person of a defendant ... (D) when authorized by a statute of the United States." New Rule 4(k)(1)(D) is revised version of old Rule 4(e), which also authorized the borrowing of federal jurisdictional statutes.

A number of federal statutes contain provisions explicitly addressing issues of personal jurisdiction and service of process. Some of the federal statutes that contain jurisdictional provisions expressly provide for personal jurisdiction based on the defendant's national contacts. The best example of this is the Foreign Sovereign Immunities Act of 1976 ("FSIA"), discussed in detail in Chapter 3 below.

Other federal statutes that address personal jurisdiction and service include the Clayton Act, the Securities Act of 1933, the Securities Exchange Act of 1934, RICO, and the Federal Interpleader Act.[220] Many of these federal statutes expressly permit "world-wide" service of process from any U.S. district court to any place that the defendant "transacts business" or "may be found."[221] Other federal statutes are limited to "nation-wide" service within the United States.[222]

Both "nation-wide" and "world-wide" service of process provisions have frequently been applied in purely domestic cases to allow personal jurisdiction in any U.S. district.[223] In addition, some lower courts have construed world-wide service provisions as legislatively authorizing both service abroad and the use of national contacts tests for purposes of asserting personal jurisdiction over foreign

---

218. Consider *McCombs v. Cerco Rentals,* 622 S.W.2d 822 (Tenn. Ct. App. 1981), and *Gould v. P.T. Krakatau Steel,* 957 F.2d 573 (8th Cir. 1992), excerpted above at pp. 126-37. *See* Born, *Reflections on Judicial Jurisdiction in International Cases,* 17 Ga. J. Int'l & Comp. L. 1 (1987).

219. *Advisory Committee Notes, 28 U.S.C.A. Fed. R. Civ. Pro. 4,* 119.

220. *See* 15 U.S.C. §22 (Clayton Act); 15 U.S.C. §77v (federal securities laws); 15 U.S.C. §78aa (federal securities laws); 18 U.S.C. §1965 (RICO); 28 U.S.C. §2361; 2 J. Moore, J. Lucas, H. Fink & C. Thompson, *Moore's Federal Practice* ¶4.33 (2d ed. 1988).

221. *See* 15 U.S.C. §22 (Clayton Act); 15 U.S.C. §§77v, 78aa (securities laws). *See infra* pp. 181-82.

222. *See* 18 U.S.C. §1965 (RICO). *See infra* p. 182.

223. *E.g., Mississippi Publishing Corp. v. Murphree,* 326 U.S. 438, 442 (1946); *Robertson v. Railroad Labor Bd.,* 268 U.S. 619, 622 (1925); *FTC v. Jim Walter Corp.,* 651 F.2d 251 (5th Cir. 1981).

defendants.[224] Lower courts have almost uniformly rejected due process challenges to the use of a national contacts test in these circumstances.[225] The following excerpt from *Go-Video, Inc. v. Akai Electric Company*, illustrates this interpretation of a world-wide service of process provision.

GO-VIDEO, INC. v. AKAI ELECTRIC COMPANY
885 F.2d 1406 (9th Cir. 1989)

REINHARDT, CIRCUIT JUDGE. The plaintiff in [this] action, Go-Video, Inc. ("Go-Video"), is a Delaware corporation with its principal place of business in Arizona. Since 1984, Go-Video has apparently been attempting to purchase parts from which it could assemble a "dual deck" video cassette recorder... . In its complaint Go-Video alleges that a number of foreign manufacturers of consumer electronics, a Japanese electronics trade association (collectively known as the "manufacturing defendants"), various domestic motion picture companies, and a motion picture trade association (the "motion picture defendants") conspired to prevent the marketing of dual deck VCR's in the United States and, pursuant to this allegedly illicit agreement, refused to deal with Go-Video. These actions, Go-Video claims, violated §1 of the Sherman Act, 15 U.S.C. §1. Go-Video served process on the manufacturing defendants through the long-arm provision of Section 12 of the Clayton Act, 15 U.S.C. §22, which provides:

> Any suit, action, or proceeding under the antitrust laws against a corporation may be brought not only in the judicial district whereof it is an inhabitant, but also in any district wherein it may be found or transacts business; and all process in such cases may be served in the district of which it is an inhabitant, or wherever it may be found.

As each of the manufacturing defendants was an alien corporation, Go-Video filed suit in the United States District Court for the District of Arizona, alleging venue to be proper under the terms of the Alien Venue Act: "§1391(d) An alien may be sued in any district."

The appellants here are the remaining manufacturing defendants, four Japanese and one Korean corporation[, which had] filed motions to dismiss Go-Video's complaint for lack of personal jurisdiction and improper venue, under Fed. R. Civ. P. 12(b)(2) and (3)... . The district court ruled in favor of Go-Video, determining venue to be proper in Arizona and the use of "national contacts" analysis consistent with ... [the due process clause and] *Securities Investor Protection Corp. v. Vigman*, 764 F.2d 1309 (9th Cir. 1985) ("*Vigman*").

---

224. *E.g., Securities Investor Protection Corp. v. Vigman*, 764 F.2d 1309, 1314-16 (9th Cir. 1985); *Fitzsimmons v. Barton*, 589 F.2d 330 (7th Cir. 1979); *International Controls Corp. v. Vesco*, 490 F.2d 1334 (2d Cir. 1974), *cert. denied*, 434 U.S. 1014 (1978); *Leasco Data Processing Equip. Corp. v. Maxwell*, 468 F.2d 1326, 1340 (2d Cir. 1972); *infra* pp. 179-80.

225. *See* cases cited in note 224 *supra*.

[The Court of Appeal first held that the Alien Venue Act is available in antitrust actions where process is served under 15 U.S.C. §22.] Having determined that venue lies in Arizona, we now address the related question whether personal jurisdiction could properly be exercised there. ... In this case, the district judge looked first to Clayton Act §12, a statute which ... authorizes worldwide service of process. Given the scope of permissible service of process, he concluded that §12 authorizes the exercise of personal jurisdiction over an alien corporation in any judicial district, so long as the corporation had sufficient minimum contacts with the United States at large, thus obviating the normal requirement that Go-Video demonstrate appellants' ties specific to the forum district. After choosing to apply this "national contacts" method of jurisdictional analysis, the judge considered whether Fifth Amendment considerations of fair play and substantial justice militated against the exercise of jurisdiction over the alien corporations. He concluded that such considerations were not offended by exercising jurisdiction over appellants and denied their motions to dismiss for want of personal jurisdiction. Appellants challenge both the proposition that the worldwide service of process provision of §12 confers jurisdiction over an alien defendant based solely on its national contacts, as well as the district court's conclusion that the Constitution is not offended by the exercise of personal jurisdiction based on national contacts analysis.[226]

The district court reasoned that, since process, under §12, could be served anywhere in the country (indeed anywhere in the world) and since venue, under §1391(d), was proper in any district, personal jurisdiction for an antitrust suit against an alien corporation could be obtained in any judicial district in the United States. Moreover, given the nationwide service provision of the Clayton Act, the court concluded that, in determining whether it could exercise personal jurisdiction over the alien defendants, it was proper to consider their national contacts. In the latter respect particularly, the court relied principally on our decision in *Vigman*, in which we held national contacts analysis to be appropriate in a suit in which process had been served on an alien corporation pursuant to §27 of the Securities Exchange Act. ... [W]e reasoned that a federal statute which permits the service of process beyond the boundaries of the forum state broadens the authorized scope of personal jurisdiction. Under such a statute, "'the question becomes whether the party has sufficient contacts with the United States, not any particular state.'" Accordingly, we held that "so long as a defendant has minimum contacts with the United States, §27 of the [Securities Exchange] Act confers personal jurisdiction over the defendant in any federal district court."

Appellants argue that *Vigman* does not control this case, inasmuch as it con-

---

226. Appellants apparently do not question the district court's conclusion that their contacts with the United States met the basic requirement imposed by *International Shoe* and its progeny — that a defendant maintain at least "minimum contacts" with the relevant forum. We thus assume that appellants' contacts are sufficient for the exercise of jurisdiction, as long as the Nation is the appropriate entity against which to assess them.

cerned a claim under the Securities Exchange Act, not the Clayton Act. There are two logical flaws in this argument. First, we believe that §27 of the Securities Exchange Act is a peculiarly apt statute from which to analogize to §12 of the Clayton Act; ... §27's provision ("... process may be served in any other district [i.e. districts other than the one in which suit is brought] of which the defendant is an inhabitant or wherever the defendant may be found") was modelled after §12 ("... process in such cases may be served in the district in which [the defendant] is an inhabitant, or wherever it may be found"). Second, the reasoning behind the *Vigman* holding is not essentially a function of the particular wording of a statute; rather, it flows from the fact that Congress has authorized service of process nationwide, in fact worldwide. As there is no dispute that §12 authorizes nationwide service, there is no principled reason not to apply *Vigman's* reasoning in this case. ... [W]e believe that the district judge was clearly correct in his view and that the worldwide service provision of §12 justifies its conclusion that personal jurisdiction may be established in any district, given the existence of sufficient national contacts. ...

[W]e turn to ... the constitutional aspects of the exercise of personal jurisdiction. ... [Appellants rely upon the following language from *Insurance Corp. of Ireland v. Compagnie des Bauxites de Guinee*, 456 U.S. 694 (1982):]

> The requirement that a court have personal jurisdiction flows not from Article III, but from the Due Process Clause. The personal jurisdiction requirement recognizes and protects an individual liberty interest. It represents a restriction on judicial power not as a matter of sovereignty, but as a matter of individual liberty. Thus, the test for personal jurisdiction requires that "the maintenance of the suit ... not offend 'traditional notions of fair play and substantial justice.'"

Appellants claim that this language rejects the notion that personal jurisdiction should be assessed by reference to the contacts with the Nation when the federal sovereign has provided for the cause of action. Furthermore, appellants contend, the federal cause of action theory is the only one that supports national contacts analysis. Their argument is fallacious, because it both reads too much into the *Bauxites* dictum and incorrectly describes the analytical basis for the national contacts approach. ...

Bauxites addressed questions only remotely relevant to those relating to the sufficiency of a defendants' contacts with a given forum; the case concerned the appropriateness of declaring certain jurisdictional facts admitted, or jurisdictional objections waived, when a party failed to comply with a district court's discovery orders. The quoted passage serves merely to introduce the discussion of the waivability of certain objections to personal jurisdiction. ... [A]ppellants' argument assumes that national contacts analysis is justified only by a particular notion of federal sovereignty in federal question cases. It is true that some courts have endorsed the national contacts approach based on the (not unarguable) proposition that, since the sovereign in federal question cases is the United States, the relevant contacts inquiry necessarily focuses on the Nation as a whole. Even so, as our decision here demonstrates, national contacts analysis more often finds its basis not in an abstract theory of sovereignty, but in the concrete language of a statute under which Congress has, as it is unquestionably empowered to, authorized nationwide service of process. Indeed, a recent Supreme Court decision implies that a national service provision is a necessary prerequisite for a court even to consider a national contacts approach. *See Omni Capital* (no need to address national contacts argument where no provision of statute authorized nationwide service).... . In light of our conclusion that there is no Supreme Court precedent to the contrary, we adhere to our decision in *Vigman* that, when a statute authorizes nationwide service of process, national contacts analysis is appropriate. In such cases, "due process demands [a showing of minimum contacts with the United States] with respect to foreign defendants" before a court can assert personal jurisdiction... .

[Appellants also] advert to the burden placed on an alien defendant who must litigate in Arizona and conclude that this burden, imposed by virtue of national contacts analysis, is inherently violative of the "fair play and substantial justice" elements of due process. We are not persuaded by appellants' somewhat skeletal argument on this point. As an initial matter, the concerns appellants raise are far more akin to a forum non conveniens argument than to a jurisdictional one. Considerations underlying a non-jurisdictional doctrine like forum non conveniens must be kept separate from the constitutional and jurisdictional analyses we conduct here. *See Fitzsimmons,* 589 F.2d at 334 (declining to "import [factors properly suited to forum non conveniens analysis] into determination of the constitutionality of exercise of personal jurisdiction"). Second, if there is something peculiarly oppressive about litigating in Arizona, appellants are free to avail themselves of the venue transfer statute (essentially the incorporation of common law forum non conveniens doctrine), 28 U.S.C. §1404(a), and seek to have the case transferred to another jurisdiction. ... [A]ppellants have not done so. ...

Notes on Go-Video

1. *International law limits on the use of national contacts test.* As we have seen, international law imposes limits on a U.S. court's jurisdiction over a foreign defendant who has no meaningful relationship to a particular forum. *See supra* pp. 86-91. Does international law restrict a U.S. court's power to base its judicial jurisdiction on a foreign defendant's national contacts with the entire United States, rather than its state contacts?

For purposes of international law, the individual States of the Union are generally irrelevant. In the Supreme Court's words, "[f]or local interests, the several States of the Union exist, but for national purposes, embracing our relations with foreign nations, we are but one people, one nation, one power." *Chae Chan Ping v. United States,* 130 U.S. 581, 606 (1889). *See United States v. Belmont,* 301 U.S. 324, 331 (1937) ("in respect of our foreign relations generally, state lines disappear. As to such purposes the State ... does not exist."); *Restatement (Third) Foreign Relations Law* §1 Reporters' Note (1987) ("A state of the United States is not a 'state' under international law. ... The United States alone, not any of its constituent states, enjoys international sovereignty and nationhood"). As a consequence, foreign states should have "no basis for complaint under international law when a United States court asserts jurisdiction over a national who has a reasonably close relationship to the United States, even if the foreign national has *no* connections with the state of the Union asserting jurisdiction." Born, *Reflections on Judicial Jurisdiction in International Cases,* 17 Ga. J. Int'l & Comp. L. 1, 37 (1987).

Is this conclusion entirely persuasive? What if different U.S. state courts (*e.g.*, Louisiana and Oregon) would apply significantly different substantive laws and procedural rules? What if this national contacts rule would subject foreign nationals to both great inconvenience and many potential forums from which plaintiffs could choose? Suppose that the EU nations that are party to the Brussels Convention adopted a "Community contacts" test, permitting a U.S. company that had contacts with England to be sued in Greece (notwithstanding its lack of Greek contacts).

2. *Supreme Court treatment of national contacts test.* The Supreme Court has expressly reserved decision on the question whether a national contacts test may constitutionally be applied by a federal court in a federal question case. Thus, in *Asahi Metal Indus. v. Superior Court,* the Court noted:

> We have no occasion here to determine whether Congress could, consistent with the Due Process Clause of the Fifth Amendment, authorize federal court personal jurisdiction over alien defendants based on the aggregate of *national* contacts, rather than on the contacts between the defendant and the State in which the federal court sits.

480 U.S. 102, 113 n.* (1987) (excerpted above). *See also Omni Capital Int'l v. Rudolf Wolff & Co.,* 484 U.S. 97, 103-04 n.5 (1987).

3. *Due process limits in federal question cases when a federal jurisdictional grant is relied on.* In considering due process limits on federal court jurisdiction, most authorities have distinguished (a) federal question from diversity cases, and (b) cases where federal long-arm statutes are invoked from those where state long-arm statutes are invoked. In *Go-Video*, a substantive federal statute provided the cause of action and a federal long-arm statute was the basis for personal jurisdiction.

(a) *Majority rule that due process permits national contacts test in federal question cases when a federal jurisdictional grant is relied on. Go-Video* held that the fifth amendment's due process clause permits consideration of a defendant's contacts with the entire United States where federal law claims are asserted and a federal jurisdictional statute is relied on. Virtually all other lower courts and commentators to consider the question have agreed. *See supra* pp. 174-75. Is this result persuasive? Why should issues of minimum contacts and fairness vary so significantly depending upon whether state or federal courts and claims are concerned? Are not the several states sufficiently important in U.S. legal and economic matters that judicial jurisdiction should depend on state contacts? Will not defendants be subject to identical inconvenience and surprise in both federal and state courts?

(b) *Congress's territorial sovereignty over entire United States.* The primary rationale supporting the constitutionality of a national contacts test in a federal court is that Congress and the President — which created the federal courts, federal substantive claims, and federal jurisdictional grants — possess sovereignty over the entire United States. That *national* territorial sovereignty is the equivalent of a *state's* territorial sovereignty under *Pennoyer, International Shoe,* and *Burnham.* Thus, just as the Constitution requires minimum contacts or other connections with a forum state before a state court can exercise judicial jurisdiction, so it should require minimum contacts or other connections *with the United States* before a federal court can assert federal question jurisdiction. Considerable authority supports this analysis. Several Supreme Court decisions expressly recognised Congress's power to authorize nationwide service of process from federal courts, at a time when such service was deemed sufficient without more to confer personal jurisdiction. For example, in *United States v. Union Pacific Railroad,* 98 U.S. 569, 603-04 (1878), the Supreme Court said that a federal statute permitted service in a federal action anywhere in the United States, not merely in the state where the federal court hearing the case was located: "[t]here is ... nothing in the Constitution which forbids Congress to enact that [any federal court] ... shall, by process served anywhere in the United States, have the power to bring before it all the parties necessary to its decision." *See Mississippi Publishing Corp. v. Murphee,* 326 U.S. 438, 442 (1946).

(c) *Role of fifth amendment's due process clause.* The foregoing analysis is almost always accompanied by observations that the jurisdiction of federal courts is limited by the fifth, rather than the fourteenth, amendment. *E.g., Trans-Asiatic Oil Ltd. SA v. Apex Oil Co.,* 743 F.2d 956 (1st Cir. 1984); *DeJames v. Magnificence Carriers,* 491 F. Supp. 1276, 1284 (D.N.J. 1980), *aff'd,* 654 F.2d 280 (3d Cir.), *cert. denied,* 454 U.S. 1085 (1981). Consider, for example, the following excerpt from the Advisory Committee Notes to the 1993 revision of Rule 4(k):

> constitutional limitations on the exercise of territorial jurisdiction by federal courts over persons outside the United States ... arise from the Fifth Amendment rather than from the Fourteenth Amendment ... The Fifth Amendment requires that any defendant have affiliating

contacts with the United States sufficient to justify the exercise of personal jurisdiction. 28 U.S.C.A. Fed. Rule Civ. Pro. 4, at 118.

It is also argued that the fifth amendment's due process clause imposes different limits than the fourteenth amendment:

> a Fifth Amendment analysis of due process is different from one undertaken under the Fourteenth Amendment. This is implicit in the Supreme Court's treatment of the Fourteenth Amendment analysis in *World-Wide Volkswagen*, [where] Justice White described two distinct but related functions performed by the Fourteenth Amendment: ["fairness" and protection of territorial sovereignty by ensuring] "that States, through their courts, do not reach out beyond the limits imposed on them by their status as coequal sovereigns in a federal system." Obviously, the second of these functions applies only to actions in state courts and diversity actions in federal courts. When a federal court is hearing and deciding a federal question case there are no problems of "coequal sovereigns." This is a Fourteenth Amendment concern which is not present in actions founded on federal substantive law. *Handley v. Indiana & Michigan Elec. Co.*, 732 F.2d 1265, 1271 (6th Cir. 1984).

(d) *Doubts about role of territorial sovereignty in due process analysis.* Does *Go-Video* accept the rationales discussed above for a national contacts test? As discussed above, there is an ongoing debate about the appropriate role of territorial sovereignty in jurisdictional analysis. *See supra* pp. 87-88. Note that the emphasis on territorial sovereignty is inconsistent with some Justices' focus on fairness and reasonableness. Is reliance on territorial sovereignty sufficient to justify a national contacts test?

As discussed above, *supra* pp. 87-88, dicta in *Compagnie des Bauxites de Guinee* and the due process analysis of Justice Brennan arguably abandon territorial sovereignty in due process analysis, in favor of more flexible notions of "reasonableness" and individual liberty. For courts adopting this conclusion, *see Wichita Federal S. & L. Ass'n v. Landmark Group, Inc.*, 657 F.Supp. 1182, 1194 (D. Kan. 1987) (*Bauxite's* "rejection of sovereignty as a basis for *in personam* jurisdiction means there is no compelling reason for a court to observe sovereign boundaries"); *Bamford v. Hobbs*, 569 F.Supp. 160, 164-65 (S.D. Tex. 1983) (*Bauxites* "appears to seriously undermine the rationale" of territorial sovereignty). Do the increasing ease of communication and transportation, the volume of international commerce, and expanding notions of jurisdiction under international law undermine the importance of territorial sovereignty? Should these factors argue that territorial sovereignty is *more*, not *less*, important? to provide predictability and order in a more fluid international environment?

(e) *Fairness considerations supporting national contacts test.* Territorial sovereignty is not the sole justification that has been advanced for a national contacts test under the due process clause in international cases. First, a national contacts test is sometimes the only way that U.S. jurisdiction can be asserted over a foreign defendant that has substantial U.S. contacts spread thinly over a number of individual states. *E.g.*, *Superior Coal Co. v. Ruhrkohle AG*, 83 F.R.D. 414, 418 n.3 (E.D. Pa. 1979) ("a foreign-based corporation may have substantial contacts diffused throughout the nation to the extent that in no one state do these contacts accumulate sufficiently to allow any state to assume jurisdiction"); *Engineered Sports Products v. Brunswick Corp.*, 362 F.Supp. 722, 728 (D. Utah 1973) (due process "should not immunize an alien defendant from suit in the United States simply because each state makes up only a fraction of the substantial nationwide market for the offending product"). *See Gould v. P.T. Krakatau Steel*, 957 F.2d 573 (8th Cir. 1992) (excerpted at *supra* pp. 135-37).

Second, foreign defendants will generally regard the United States as a single nation. It is their *U.S.* contacts, not their *state* contacts, that best reflect their reasonable expectations. And a foreign defendant usually will not face greater or lesser inconvenience by defending in one U.S. state instead of another. "[C]orporations ... headquartered in foreign lands will usually be no more inconvenienced by a trip to one state [of the Union] than another." *Centronics Data Computer Corp. v. Mannesmann AG*, 432 F.Supp. 659, 663 (D.N.H. 1977). *See Afram Export Corp. v. Metallurgiki Halyps, SA*, 772 F.2d 1358 (7th Cir. 1985) (excerpted at *supra* pp. 144-47).

Third, when a U.S. court exercises jurisdiction over a foreign defendant based on national (instead of state) contacts, it does not ordinarily intrude upon the sovereignty of other U.S. states. It may intrude on the sovereignty of foreign states, but international law does not appear to restrict application of a national contacts test. *See supra* pp. 178-79.

Are these generalizations necessarily accurate in all cases? Suppose that a Canadian defendant has significant contacts with Maine, but none at all with Louisiana. Should the due process clause permit personal jurisdiction based on national contacts in Louisiana? Recall the two-part due process analysis adopted in *World-Wide Volkswagen* and *Asahi*, which considered reasonableness and fairness to the defendant, as well as territorial sovereignty.

(f) *Minority position: "fairness" limits on national contacts test in federal courts.* Some lower courts have concluded that the fifth amendment imposes "fairness" limits on exercises of personal jurisdiction. *E.g., Horne v. Adolph Coors Co.*, 684 F.2d 255 (3d Cir. 1982); *Kinsey v. Nestor Exploration*, 604 F. Supp. 1365 (E.D. Wash. 1985); *GRM v. Esquire Inv. & Mgmt. Group*, 596 F. Supp. 307 (S.D. Tex. 1984). Under these decisions, a defendant's national contacts can be considered, but due process also requires that the location of the federal court hearing the dispute be "fair." Consider the following explanation of the fairness doctrine:

> [T]he U.S. Supreme Court [has] unequivocally rejected sovereignty as the basis for the Due Process Clause's minimum contacts requirement and corresponding limitations of personal jurisdiction. In *Compagnie des Bauxites de Guinee*, the Court stated that "[t]he personal jurisdiction requirement recognizes and protects an individual liberty interest. It represents a restriction on judicial power not as a matter of sovereignty, but as a matter of individual liberty." The minimum contacts requirement is therefore merely a method to establish whether or not the defendant's Due Process liberty interest in fundamental "fair play and substantial justice" is satisfied. There is no impelling reason to equate traditional fair play and substantial justice to minimum contacts with the nation as a whole. Nor, in light of modern communication and transportation and Congress's express authorization of nationwide service, can fair play and substantial justice turn simply upon whether the Andover defendants must cross a state border to get to the Southern District of Texas. For as another district court once observed, a Portland, Maine defendant forced to litigate in Raleigh, North Carolina must cross twelve state borders, yet travels no farther than an El Paso, Texas defendant forced to litigate in Beaumont, Texas. Since the bounds of fairness do not necessarily run along state borders, the Fifth Amendment's Due Process Clause does not go so far as to require that the Andover defendants have minimum contacts with the State of Texas.

GRM v. Equine Inv. & Mgt. Group, 596 F.Supp. 307, 314 (S.D. Tex. 1984). *Go-Video* flatly rejects any such argument, on the grounds that such considerations are only appropriate in a forum non conveniens analysis. Is this persuasive?

(g) *Effect of* Burnham *on national contacts test.* What effect, if any, does *Burnham, supra* p. 121, have on the argument that fairness restricts the importance of territorial sovereignty? Recall Justice Scalia's plurality opinion, concluding that reasonableness considerations are irrelevant if service is made in the forum's territory. Does *Burnham's* reaffirmation of territorial sovereignty support an unqualified national contacts test? Or is *Burnham* limited to tag service?

4. *Interpretation of jurisdictional reach of federal statutes.* Under new Rule 4(k)(1)(D), as with old Rule 4(e), federal courts can rely on federal jurisdictional grants. When a federal jurisdictional statute is used, it must be interpreted as a matter of federal law.

(a) *Antitrust and securities laws as statutory bases for national contacts test.* The Clayton Act, 15 U.S.C. §22, has been interpreted by a number of lower courts as authorizing both "world-wide" extraterritorial service and use of a national contacts test. *E.g., Go-Video, Inc. v. Akai Elec. Co.*, 885 F.2d 1406 (9th Cir. 1989); *Stabilisierungsfonds Fuer Wein v. Kaiser Stuhl Wine Distrib.*, 647 F.2d 200, 204 & n.6 (D.C. Cir. 1981). Lower federal courts have also held that the federal securities laws, 15 U.S.C. §§77v and 78aa, authorize a national contacts test in determining jurisdiction over foreigners. *E.g., Securities Investor Protection Corp. v. Vigman*, 764 F.2d 1309 (9th Cir. 1985); *Bersch v. Drexel Firestone*, 519 F.2d 974 (2d Cir.), *cert. denied*, 423 U.S. 1018 (1975); *Leasco Data Processing Equipment Corp. v. Maxwell*, 468 F.2d 1326 (2d Cir. 1972).

(b) *Interpretation of federal statutes containing world-wide service of process provisions to permit national contacts tests.* Go-Video relied on 15 U.S.C. §22 in concluding that it could consider the defendant's *national* contacts for personal jurisdiction purposes. Note that the relevant statutory provision of the Clayton Act merely authorizes service of process "wherever the defendant may be found." How is it that *Go-Video* interprets this language as permitting personal jurisdiction based on national contacts? Does §22's authorization for the service of process actually address the question of whether a foreign defendant's contacts with the United States as a whole should be considered in determining whether to assert personal jurisdiction? *See Leasco Data Processing Equipment Corp. v. Maxwell,* 468 F.2d 1326, 1340 (2d Cir. 1972) ("although the section does not deal specifically with *in personam* jurisdiction, it is reasonable to infer that Congress meant to assert personal jurisdiction over foreigners not present in the United States to but, of course, not beyond the bounds permitted by the due process clause of the fifth amendment."). Would it not be entirely possible to permit world-wide *service* of process without meaning to disturb the traditional state contacts approach to *jurisdiction*? Why would Congress want the enforcement of a federal statute, in federal court, to depend on state borders?`Would such borders provide a measure of predictability and be a reasonable proxy for convenience?

(c) *Interpretation of federal statutes containing nation-wide service provisions to permit national contacts test.* The service provisions of some federal statutes — including RICO — have been interpreted as *not* authorizing service of process outside the United States. *See Nordic Bank PLC v. Trend Group,* 619 F. Supp. 542 (S.D.N.Y. 1985) (RICO authorizes nation-wide but not extraterritorial service); *Soltex Polymer Corp. v. Fortex Indus.,* 590 F. Supp. 1453 (E.D.N.Y. 1984), *aff'd,* 832 F.2d 1325 (2d Cir. 1987) (same). *Compare Entek v. Southwest Pipe,* 683 F. Supp. 1092 (N.D. Tenn. 1988). Lower courts reaching this conclusion have relied on the fact that the statute in question only permits *nation-wide,* and not *world-wide,* service of process.

Suppose that a foreign defendant can be served within the United States under a federal statute (such as RICO) that authorizes only nation-wide service of process. Can a national contacts test be used in determining whether the district court has personal jurisdiction over the foreign defendant? What does *Go-Video* suggest? *See also Herbstein v. Bruetman,* 768 F.Supp. 79 (S.D.N.Y. 1991) (national contacts test applied in RICO action). RICO's "jurisdictional" grant obviously does not extend to the Constitution's limits, since it stops at U.S. borders. Does a statute need to "authorize" a national contacts test, or is it enough that it permit jurisdiction based on service which can then be justified by a national contacts test under the due process clause?

(d) *Interpretation of federal jurisdictional statutes to permit tag service.* Do the Clayton Act and securities laws authorize jurisdiction based upon tag service anywhere in the United States? If they extend to the limits of the due process clause, isn't the answer yes after *Burnham*?

5. *Use of national contacts test where federal statute does not address service.* Both the Supreme Court and a number of lower courts have refused to apply a national contacts test where the plaintiff's claim rested on a federal statute, but where the statute did not contain a nation-wide or world-wide service of process provision. *See Omni Capital Int'l v. Rudolf Wolff & Co.,* 484 U.S. 97 (1987) (Commodity Exchange Act contains no service or jurisdictional provision and therefore no national contacts test is authorized by federal law); *Chandler v. Barclays Bank plc,* 898 F.2d 1148 (6th Cir. 1990); *DeJames v. Magnificence Carriers,* 654 F.2d 280 (3d Cir.), *cert. denied,* 454 U.S. 1085 (1981). As discussed below, however, state long-arm statutes may provide a basis for application of a national contacts test, even if no federal statute does. *See infra* pp. 183-95.

6. *Availability of Alien Venue Act in cases where jurisdiction rests on particular federal long-arm statute.* Go-Video rejected the argument that a plaintiff in a Clayton Act suit that relies on the world-wide service and national contacts test of the Clayton Act, may establish venue only under the Clayton Act. The Ninth Circuit held that a Clayton Act plaintiff may invoke the Alien Venue Act, *see infra* pp. 367-69, which permits venue in any district in suits against aliens. It rejected the argument that the Clayton Act's service, jurisdiction, and venue provisions must be read as an "integrated whole." Is this sensible? What are the practical consequences of permitting use of the Alien Venue Act in cases brought under federal long-arm statutes?

7. *Transfers and forum non conveniens.* Many authorities adopting a national contacts test have also taken a more lenient view of transfers of venue under 28 U.S.C. §1404 and forum non conveniens. The purpose is to avoid significant inconvenience to foreign defendants subject to a national contacts jurisdictional test. *See Fitzsimmons v. Barton,* 589 F.2d 330, 334-35 (7th Cir. 1979). This is particularly important because, as *Go-Video* illustrates, the Alien Venue Act makes venue over a foreign defendant proper in any judicial district. Suppose that a Mexican defendant has minimum contacts with Arizona (and only Arizona), but that a U.S. plaintiff sues it in Maine, just to make defense difficult. Should the due process clause forbid this? Would the forum non conveniens doctrine or §1404 transfers provide sufficient protection? Note that district judges have broad discretion in both instances. *See infra* pp. 294-97 & 317.

3. Borrowed State Long-Arm Statutes Under New Rule 4(k)(1)(A) and the Due Process Clauses

a. New Rule 4(k)(1)(A)'s Borrowing Authority

State long-arm statutes play an important role in defining the jurisdiction of federal district courts, both in diversity and federal question cases. This is because of new Rule 4(k)(1)(A), which authorizes federal courts to borrow the jurisdictional powers of the state courts in the state where they are located. Rule 4(k)(1)(A) provides that:

> Service of a summons or filing of a waiver of service is effective to establish jurisdiction over the person of a defendant (A) who could be subjected to the jurisdiction of a court of general jurisdiction in the state in which the district court is located ...

New Rule 4(k)(1)(A) is the revised version of old Rule 4(e), which also permitted the "borrowing" of state long-arm statutes.[227]

Rule 4(k)(1)(A) permits the borrowing of state long-arm statutes in all cases — including diversity of citizenship, alienage, and federal question matters.[228] In federal question cases, a plaintiff may choose to borrow a state long-arm statute either because the applicable substantive federal statute contains no personal jurisdiction provision[229] or because its jurisdictional provisions do not reach the defendant.[230]

b. Selected Materials on Borrowed State Long-Arm Statutes Under Rule 4(k)(1)(A)

The two cases excerpted below illustrate the issues that arise in international disputes when federal courts "borrow" state long-arm statutes under Rule 4. *Wells Fargo & Co. v. Wells Fargo Express Co.*, which applied old Rule 4(e), refused to interpret a state long-arm statute as authorizing a national contacts test; as a result, the court declined to consider the defendant's alleged national contacts. Nevertheless, the

---

227. The predecessor to new Rule 4(k)(1)(A) was contained in the second sentence of old Rule 4(e), and authorized a federal court, in diversity of citizenship cases, to "borrow" the long-arm statute of the state in which it is located. Old Rule 4(e) provided that "service may ... be made under the circumstances and in the manner prescribed in [a] statute" of the state in which the district court is held. *See Point Landing, Inc. v. Omni Capital Int'l, Ltd.*, 795 F.2d 415 (5th Cir. 1986), *aff'd*, 484 U.S. 97 (1987); C. Wright & A. Miller, *Federal Practice and Procedure* §1075 (1987).

228. It was well-settled under old Rule 4(e) that state long-arm statutes could be borrowed in both federal question and diversity cases. *E.g., Omni Capital Int'l, Ltd. v. Rudolf Wolff & Co.*, 484 U.S. 97 (1987); C. Wright & A. Miller, *Federal Practice and Procedure*, §1075, at 495 (1987). Rule 4(k)(1)(A) produces the same result: nothing in the Rule draws any distinction between federal question and diversity actions, or suggests any change from old Rule 4(e). *See* D. Siegel, *Supplementary Practice Commentaries*, 28 U.S.C.A. Fed. Civ. Proc. Rule 4, C4-33 (1994 Supp.).

229. Many federal statutes that create private causes of action do not address the issue of personal jurisdiction. *See Omni Capital Int'l, Ltd. v. Rudolf Wolff & Co.*, 484 U.S. 97 (1987).

230. *See Delong Equip. Co. v. Washington Mills Abrasive Co.*, 840 F.2d 843 (11th Cir. 1988) (using federal nationwide service provisions of Clayton Act as to corporate defendants and state long-arm statute as to individual defendants (who were not covered by Clayton Act's jurisdictional grant)); *Karsten Mfg. Corp. v. United States Golf Ass'n*, 728 F.Supp. 1429 (D. Ariz. 1990) (same).

court suggested that the due process clause would not preclude a national contacts test if state law provided for such a test. In contrast, *United Rope Distributors, Inc. v. Seatriumph Marine* held that a state long-arm statute authorized personal jurisdiction, but that a state court could not constitutionally exercise such jurisdiction under the fourteenth amendment. The court went on to suggest, however, that a federal court might invoke a national contacts test under the *fifth* amendment in a federal question case to rely on the jurisdictional grant in a state long-arm statute (even if it could not be used in state court).

WELLS FARGO & CO. v. WELLS FARGO EXPRESS CO.

556 F.2d 406 (9th Cir. 1977)

CHOY, CIRCUIT JUDGE. ... Plaintiff Wells Fargo & Company, a California corporation ..., makes use of trade names, trademarks, and service marks which consist — in whole or in part — of the name "Wells Fargo," and which are registered in the United States under the Lanham Act. ... At the heart of plaintiffs' allegations is the claim that a group headed by Herman Heymann, a German national who resides in Gibraltar, has deliberately and wrongfully attempted to appropriate the "Wells Fargo" name both in Europe as well as in the United States. Defendant Wells Fargo Express Company, A.G. ("A.G."), a Liechtenstein corporation, was incorporated in 1967 by Heymann to engage in the business of loaning money and is the foreign defendant dismissed by the district court below. In the course of its activities, A.G. had acquired various European and American subsidiaries. ... [A]n American subsidiary, Wells Fargo Express Company ("Express"), is a named defendant.

Express was originally incorporated in Nevada in 1961 for the purpose of providing traveller's checks under the name "Wells Fargo" by K.F. Wilkinson, Sr., a business associate of Heymann. ... In 1968, the only capital stock of Express was issued to A.G. for a consideration of $50,000. ... Service was made on A.G. in Liechtenstein pursuant to Fed. R. Civ. P. 4(e) & 4(i)(1)(D), and the Nevada "long-arm" statute. A.G. received the summons as shown by the return of service required by Rules 4(g) & 4(i)(2). Through a letter from its Belgian counsel, however, A.G. notified the Nevada district court of its intention not to appear, maintaining that the court lacked jurisdiction over it and its activities. [The district court agreed and plaintiffs appealed.] ...

[A] court's exercise of *in personam* jurisdiction must, of course, be affirmatively authorized by the legislature. ... Under Rule 4(e)(1), "service may ... be made under the circumstances and in the manner prescribed in [a] statute [of the state in which the district court is held]." ... Thus, the federal district court of Nevada may ... service out-of-state defendants by availing itself of the *in personam* jurisdictional statutes of Nevada. ... This statute is in the broad, modern pattern of so-called "long-arm" statutes. Although there is not an extensive body of state law construing its reach, it is clear that the Nevada Supreme Court has read the statute liberally as affording jurisdiction to the fullest extent consonant with the due process limits of the United States Constitution. ...

[Plaintiffs first argue that A.G. independently possessed minimum contacts with Nevada.] First, plaintiffs point to a $10,000 loan to Express from A.G., which is in the business of making loans under the name Wells Fargo Express, A.G. They claim that the loan contract was negotiated and consummated by agents of A.G. who travelled to Nevada for that purpose, and that such in-state activity gives rise to one count of the instant causes of action. Such a purposeful single contact is clearly sufficient to satisfy the constitutional test for "minimum contacts" when the cause of action arises from that contact. Plaintiffs would seem to have a claim for trademark infringement and unfair competition growing out of this loan, and the activity of making the loan may, in this case, be characterized as either the transaction of business or the commission of a tortious act in Nevada for purposes of Nev. Rev. Stat. §14.065(2)(a) & (b). A single infringing or unfair act is sufficient to state a trademark or unfair competition cause of action.

Next, plaintiffs argue that where, as here, the court is to determine whether it has personal jurisdiction over an *alien* defendant who is being sued on a claim arising under *federal law*, it may appropriately consider not only the alien defendant's contacts with the forum state, but also the aggregate contacts of the alien with the United States as a whole. In this regard, plaintiffs point to two substantial loans made by A.G. in California. Although it is somewhat unclear, plaintiffs apparently hope to have the court consider these California transactions not only to buttress their argument that A.G. may be served from Nevada and sued there on the one Nevada loan, but also to establish their right to sue A.G. in Nevada for its two California loans as well. ...

It might very well be neither unfair nor unreasonable as a matter of due process to aggregate the nonforum contacts of an alien with his forum contacts or to require an alien to litigate in one state both those causes of action which originate in that forum state and those arising elsewhere in the United States.[231] Considering the relative distances between Liechtenstein and Nevada, on the one hand, and Nevada and California, on the other, due process may indeed not be a barrier to the adoption of plaintiffs' aggregation theory in the instant suit. What plaintiffs overlook, however, is that, not only must the requirements of due process be met before a court can properly assert *in personam* jurisdiction, but the exercise of jurisdiction must also be affir-

---

231. Alien defendants are, of course, entitled to due process. *See Galvan v. Press*, 347 U.S. 522, 530 (1954). Courts sometimes note that, where an alien defendant is involved, *see, e.g., Alco Standard Corp. v. Benalal*, 345 F. Supp. 14, 24-25 (E.D. Pa. 1972); *SEC v. Mayers*, 285 F. Supp. 743, 748-49 (D. Md. 1968), and possibly in all cases in which a federal question is at issue, *see, e.g., Honeywell, Inc. v. Metz Apparatewerke*, 509 F.2d 1137, 1143 (7th Cir. 1975), the due process clause of the fifth amendment rather than that of the fourteenth should be the focus of analysis. *See Volkswagen Interamericana, SA v. Rohlsen*, 360 F.2d 437, 440 n.3 (1st Cir. 1966). Since, however, no case seems to have interpreted these two provisions differently in the context of amenability to process, we need not comment on the distinction other than to note that, in any event, *International Shoe* and its progeny point the way.

matively authorized by the legislature. It is because of this factor that one case relied upon by the plaintiffs to support their aggregation theory, *Engineered Sports Prods. v. Brunswick Corp.*, 362 F. Supp. 722, 728 (D. Utah 1973), is distinguishable, while a second case cited by them, *Cryomedics, Inc. v. Spembly, Ltd.*, 397 F. Supp. 287, 290-92 (D. Conn. 1975), is of dubious validity.

In *Engineered Sports*, plaintiffs sued various European manufacturers of ski boots for patent infringement in the federal court in Utah. The court held that it could consider *all* United States contacts of defendants in determining whether to exercise *in personam* jurisdiction over them (apparently for all their American activities) under Utah's long-arm statute. Although the court's language is expansive, the rationale for its holding was not simply that defendants were aliens and that plaintiffs' cause of action was federal. Rather, the court relied on Utah Code Ann. §78-27-24(3) which confers long-arm jurisdiction over a defendant who caused "any injury within the state" when claims "arising from" that in-state injury were sued upon, to hold that plaintiffs, "whose business is relatively localized" in Utah, suffered injury there through defendants' worldwide activities.

The Nevada long-arm statute involved in the instant suit contains no such "causing of injury within the state" provision. Nev. Rev. Stat. §14.065 clearly contemplates that only causes of action "arising from" enumerated "acts" which took place "within" Nevada may be reached. There is no indication that any "acts" material to A.G.'s two California loans took place in Nevada. Moreover, even though a clause identical to Utah's commission of a "tortious act within the state" provision has been read to cover tortious conduct which results in economic injury in the forum state, there is no allegation here that the injury to either of the instant plaintiffs' profits is somehow uniquely located in the forum state as was that suffered by the plaintiffs in both *Engineered Sports* and *Honeywell*.

In *Cryomedics, Inc. v. Spembly, Ltd.*, the second case relied upon by plaintiffs for their aggregation theory, the district court of Connecticut held that all of the British defendants' American activities could be aggregated to establish *in personam* jurisdiction over them in Connecticut because that state's long-arm statute had been construed by state courts to extend to the limits of due process and the constitution did not forbid such aggregation. The court does not quote the provisions of the applicable Connecticut statute, but a reading of that act reveals that, like the Nevada statute at issue here, it too is limited to granting personal jurisdiction for causes of action "arising from" activities which took place "in" the forum state. The fact that courts have interpreted the words of the Connecticut statute liberally does not mean that the express legislative requirements themselves may be ignored in the course of that interpretation. And, unlike some state long-arm statutes, *see, e.g.*, Cal. Civ. Proc. Code §410-10, apparently neither the Connecticut nor the Nevada act contains a catch-all clause granting *in personam* jurisdiction in all instances which would not violate due process. ...

If policy considerations do indeed dictate that an alien defendant's contacts with the entire United States should be aggregated, and if the Constitution does not forbid such a practice — at least where the plaintiff is suing in federal court on a federal cause of action — the Federal Rules should be amended to authorize such a practice. Such a step is, however, not ours to take.

Finally, such aggregation of an alien's American contacts may already be proper when a federal statute authorizes world-wide service of process, *see, e.g.,* 15 U.S.C. §§22, 25, 77v, 78aa; 28 U.S.C. §1655, and, therefore, the only relevant constraint is fifth amendment due process rather than statutory authorization. But not all federal statutes which grant a federal right to recovery and provide for suit in federal court contain an additional provision granting such broad service of process powers. The Lanham Act, presently before us, apparently does not. *See* 15 U.S.C. §§1114-20 (remedies) & 1121 (subject matter jurisdiction).

Since the district court's power to exercise *in personam* jurisdiction is limited here to that provided by the Federal Rules of Civil Procedure and, through them, the laws of the state of Nevada, plaintiffs may not, absent defendants' "presence" in Nevada or a waiver of the objection by them, litigate in the Nevada district court their trademark infringement and unfair competition claims arising out of A.G.'s two California loans.

UNITED ROPE DISTRIBUTORS, INC. v. SEATRIUMPH MARINE CORP.

930 F.2d 532 (7th Cir. 1991)

EASTERBROOK, CIRCUIT JUDGE. [United Rope Distributors, a Minnesota corporation, bought 300,000 bales of baler twine from a Brazilian company, and arranged for Seatriumph Marine, a Liberian corporation with its principal place of business in Greece, to ship the twine from Brazil to Wisconsin on a vessel named the KATIA. Unfortunately, during the voyage, the KATIA sank in heavy weather off Nova Scotia, Canada. After various preliminary maneuvers United Rope filed suit against Seatriumph in Wisconsin.]

[The district court dismissed] the suit on the ground that Seatriumph has so few "contacts" with Wisconsin that the due process clause of the fifth amendment forbids the exercise of jurisdiction there. Seatriumph, a one-ship corporation, did no business in Wisconsin. The KATIA had never visited Wisconsin, coming no closer than Duluth, Minnesota, to which it delivered a cargo of beans in 1987. United Rope's only strand tying Seatriumph to Wisconsin is that the bills of lading called for delivery f.o.b. "Superior—U.S.A.". The KATIA was to land the twine in Superior, Wisconsin from which it would go overland to United Rope's customers, two of them located in Wisconsin. Duluth and Superior straddle the Minnesota-Wisconsin border, and some stevedores serve both ports, but Minnesota is not Wisconsin. So the standard bases of personal jurisdiction are missing. But Wis. Stat. §801.05(5)(e), part of its long-arm statute applicable by virtue of Fed. R. Civ. P. 4(e), establishes jurisdiction when the claim "[a]rises out of a promise, made anywhere to the plaintiff or to some 3rd party for the plaintiff's benefit, by the defendant to deliver ... within this state goods, documents or title, or other things of value." United contends, and Seatriumph does not deny, that the bills of lading that Seatriumph's agent signed in Brazil are promises to deliver goods in Wisconsin, and that these promises were made "for the plaintiff's benefit." This part of the Wisconsin code is unconstitutional, the district court held, as applied to a marine carrier whose ship never reaches Wisconsin.

United Rope stresses that Duluth is right across the border from Wisconsin, but close counts only in horseshoes. That two citizens of Wisconsin wanted to take delivery out of the shipment aboard the KATIA has nothing to do with Seatriumph. A consignee of a bill of lading cannot subject the vessel to an unknown forum by its contracts for resale. Seatriumph had no "contacts" at all with Wisconsin, having failed in its promise to acquire the first by putting the twine ashore there. The due process clause therefore would not allow the State of Wisconsin to exercise personal jurisdiction over Seatriumph.

Yet United Rope did not commence this suit in Wisconsin's courts. It filed in a federal court, invoking the protection of federal law — the law of admiralty and the Carriage of Goods by Sea Act, 46 U.S.C. App. §§1300-15, which governs the KATIA's journey according to the terms of the bills of lading. ... "[M]inimum contacts" cases such as *Helicopteros Nacionales* require only sufficient contacts between the defendant (or the defendant's transactions) and the forum. The question is whether the polity, whose power the court wields, possesses a legitimate claim to exercise force over the defendant. A state court may lack such an entitlement to coerce, when the defendant has transacted no business within the state and has not otherwise taken advantage of that sovereign's protection. ... A federal court in a federal question case is not implementing any state's policy; it exercises the power of the United States. When a national court applies national law, the due process clause requires only that the defendant possess sufficient contacts with the United States. Whether the forum within the United States is convenient for the defendant is a question of venue and discretionary doctrines allowing transfers; it has nothing to do with judicial power. *United States v. Union Pacific R.R.*, 98 U.S. 569, 603-04 (1878); *Fitzsimmons v. Barton*, 589 F.2d 330, 332-34 (7th Cir. 1979). Seatriumph has ample contacts with the United States. The KATIA made four voyages to seven different U.S. ports in 1986-87 and was bound for a fifth encounter, at an eighth port, when it sank. Seatriumph signed bills of lading submitting to the substantive law of the United States, as it submitted to U.S. law when borrowing in the United States the money to finance the KATIA's purchase. The United States is entitled to exercise sovereignty over vessels bound for its ports, even though they sink or are intercepted before reaching our territorial waters.

May United Rope take advantage of these national contacts to rope the case into federal courts in Wisconsin? The COGSA does not authorize service of process; neither does any other pertinent federal statute. United Rope asks us to establish a federal common law of personal jurisdiction for admiralty cases. ... *Omni Capital International, Ltd. v. Rudolf Wolff & Co.*, squelches any move along these lines, however. *Omni* holds that personal jurisdiction may be created only by statute or federal rule with the force of statute. The claim in *Omni* arose under a federal law that lacked a provision creating personal jurisdiction. State law did not create personal jurisdiction either. According to the Court, that was the end of the matter: no statute, no suit. ... Unless a federal or state law authorizes personal jurisdiction over the defendant, the court must dismiss the suit.

Logically, the next question is whether Wis. Stat. §801.05(5)(e), adopted by Fed. R. Civ. P. 4(e), is such a law. It creates personal jurisdiction over parties that contract to ship goods into the state, which describes this case. *Wisconsin* could not use this law, in its own courts, to exercise jurisdiction over Seatriumph, because that firm lacks "contacts" with Wisconsin. The shortcoming of a state statute of this kind carries over into diversity litigation in federal court because under *Erie*, a federal court acts as the state's agent in applying state law. The authority for the demands made on the defendant is state rather than national power. Federal courts accordingly absorb the "whole law" of the states including limitations on personal jurisdiction, except to the extent a national rule requires otherwise. State federal jurisdictional allocations would be thrown out of kilter if a federal court could give judgment in a diversity case that the state itself would have to dismiss. That rationale does not carry over to federal question cases. Whether Wisconsin may extract damages from a Liberian corporation with headquarters in Greece is irrelevant to the question whether the United States as a whole may do so.

May a state law, constitutionally insufficient to authorize jurisdiction in state court, supply the necessary basis of jurisdiction in federal court? The apparent oddity of a law being unconstitutional in the state forum and constitutional in the federal one need detain us only briefly. Courts often say that laws are constitutional in one application and unconstitutional in another. "Facial" unconstitutionality (to use the entrenched but maladroit metaphor) is the exception. No one doubts that §801.05(5)(e) may be applied to some defendants consistent with the Constitution, while the due process clause blocks its application to others. So too §801.05(5)(e) may be constitutional to the extent Fed. R. Civ. P. 4(e) absorbs its terms as the fulcrum of federal power, even though the state may not hale the party into its own courts.

Any obstacle to this result comes from Rule 4(e) itself, and not from either state law or the Constitution. The Rule specifies that service of process may be made "under the circumstances" prescribed by state law. Five courts of appeals believe that these words require lock-step treatment of personal jurisdiction in state courts under state law and federal courts under federal law, so that when assessing the constitutionality of an assertion of personal jurisdiction the federal court must pretend that it is a state court even when the issue arises under federal law. One has reached the contrary conclusion, *Handley v. Indiana & Michigan Electric Co.*, 732 F.2d 1265, 1268 (6th Cir. 1984).

Our sympathies lie with the minority view. "[U]nder the circumstances" is a slim thread on which to hang a conclusion that federal courts exercising national powers should pretend that they are state courts exercising state powers. The language was added to Rule 4(e) in 1963, and the Advisory Committee's notes do not discuss this subject. The language more naturally refers to the "circumstances" identified in the state statutes. Federal courts acquire personal jurisdiction only to the extent the state law authorizes service of process. When the state law authorizes this service (as Wisconsin's §801.05(5)(e) does here), the federal court has jurisdiction unless the Constitution bars the door. Whether it does depends on all of the circumstances of the case — not only the defendant's activities, but also the fact that the court is exercising national power. It is more anomalous to dismiss on "constitutional" grounds a suit that is within the constitutional power of the national judiciary than it is to say that a long-arm statue is unconstitutional as applied in state court but valid as applied in federal court. ...

Notes on Wells Fargo and United Rope

1. *Due process limits in federal question cases when a state long-arm statute is relied on.* Consider the territorial sovereignty rationale for a national contacts test articulated in the notes following *Go-Video*. Does this rationale apply because: (i) a federal *court* is asserting jurisdiction, *or* (ii) a federal *substantive claim* is involved, *or* (iii) a federal *jurisdictional statute* is used? Is any one of these factors sufficient?

(a) *Authorities concluding that due process clause permits national contacts to be considered in federal question cases where state long-arm statute is used.* In both *Wells Fargo* and *United Rope*, the courts considered whether the due process clause would permit a federal court to apply a national contacts test under the fifth amendment in a federal question case where personal jurisdiction is based upon a state long-arm statute. *United Rope* concluded, in dicta, that no due process obstacle existed, and *Wells Fargo* appeared to take the same approach. Most other lower courts have agreed. E.g., *Max Daetwyler Corp. v. R. Meyer*, 762 F.2d 290, 293-96 (3d Cir. 1985); *DeJames v. Magnificence Carriers, Inc.*, 654 F.2d 280, 283-84 (3d Cir. 1981) ("Because this suit arises under the district court's admiralty jurisdiction, the due process clause of the fifth amendment determines whether the district court has personal jurisdiction"). However, many of the courts that reached this result also concluded that old Rule 4(e) required "lock-step" federal jurisdiction and therefore did not permit a federal court to apply a national contacts test (even though the due process clause would). E.g., *DeJames v. Magnificence Carriers, Inc.*, 654 F.2d 280, 283-84 (3d Cir. 1981) (because "the state of New Jersey is limited by the due process constraints of the fourteenth amendment ... we believe that [the defendant's] amenability to suit in the District of New Jersey must be judged by fourteenth amendment standards").

(b) *Applicability of territorial sovereignty rationale when a federal court borrows a state long-arm statute.* Is the conclusion in *United Rope* and *Wells Fargo* — that the due process clause allows a national contacts test when a state long-arm statute is borrowed — correct? Consider the effect on the territorial sovereignty rationale when state law provides the federal court's basis for personal jurisdiction. Should the relevant territory for due process purposes in that case be the particular state?

Consider how the various rationales for a national contacts standard set forth below apply when a federal court bases jurisdiction on a state long-arm statute: *Stafford v. Briggs*, 444 U.S. 527, 554 (1980) (Stewart, J., dissenting) ("Due process requires only certain minimum contacts between the defendant and *the sovereign that has created the court*"); *Doll v. James Martin Associates (Holdings) Ltd.*, 600 F.Supp. 510, 516-17 (E.D. Mich. 1984) ("The principal constitutional limitation upon this court's exercise of personal jurisdiction over foreign defendants is of course the due process clauses of the fourteenth amendment (with respect to the pendent state law claims) and the fifth amendment (*with respect to the federal law claims*)."). Which rationale is most persuasive?

2. *Due process limits in diversity cases when a federal court borrows a state long-arm statute.* Would the due process clause permit a federal diversity court to consider national contacts where its jurisdiction

was based on a state long-arm statute? Putting aside possible limits imposed by Rule 4, *see infra* pp. 193-95, would this be consistent with due process?

Few lower federal courts have discussed the possibility of applying a national contacts test under the due process clause in diversity cases. Virtually all courts to consider the matter appear to conclude, however, that a national contacts test in a diversity action is substantially harder to justify than in a federal question case. *See United Rope Distributors, Inc. v. Seatriumph Marine Corp.*, 930 F.2d 532, 535-36 (7th Cir. 1991); *Dollar Savings Bank v. First Security Bank of Utah*, 746 F.2d 208, 211 (3d Cir. 1984) ("in this diversity case, the district court would have jurisdiction over the defendant only if a Pennsylvania state court would have that power"). Note that *United Rope* refuses to consider application of a national contacts test in a diversity case, on *Erie* grounds, even though it was prepared to apply a national contacts test in a federal question case. If a *federal* court hears a case, why should *due process* analysis be affected by the state law character of the underlying substantive rights or the long-arm statute? Consider again the quotation from *Stafford v. Briggs*.

3. *Due process limits on national contacts test in state courts.* Suppose a *state* court relied on a defendant's national contacts in a case involving substantive state law claims. Would the fourteenth amendment forbid this?

(a) *Authorities rejecting state court use of national contacts test.* No state court appears to have relied expressly on a national contacts test to justify personal jurisdiction over a foreign defendant, in either a federal question or a state law case. Indeed, *United Rope* appeared certain that the fourteenth amendment would forbid a Wisconsin court from considering the defendant's national contacts — even in a suit arising under federal law. *See also DeJames v. Magnificence Carriers, Inc.*, 654 F.2d 280, 283-84 (3d Cir. 1981) (because "the state of New Jersey is limited by the due process constraints of the fourteenth amendment ... we believe that [the defendant's] amenability to suit in the District of New Jersey must be judged by fourteenth amendment standards"). What is the basis for statements that a state court must apply a state contacts test? In *United Rope*, Judge Easterbrook reasoned, rightly enough, that "Minnesota is not Wisconsin," and, less clearly, that "close only counts in horseshoes." Is that an end of analysis? Where does the due process clause say that "close" doesn't count? Would Justices Brennan and Scalia answer this question differently?

(b) *Possible justifications for state court use of national contacts test.* Why is it that a state should not be able to take into account a foreigner's contacts with its sister states? Even if "Minnesota is not Wisconsin," it is the United States and it is inhabited by Americans. Cannot a powerful argument be made that these objections at most merely forbid consideration of national contacts in the "purposeful availment" prong of *World-Wide Volkswagen's* two-prong due process analysis? and not the "reasonableness" prong? Are not notions of territorial sovereignty relevant only to the minimum contacts prong of due process analysis? If the reasonableness prong permits inquiry into the interests of the "interstate system," can it not look to a defendant's contacts with other U.S. states?

Cannot a substantial argument be made that national contacts are also relevant to the minimum contacts prong? Consider the authorities quoted above declaring that international law would not affect a state's power to apply a national contacts test. Given that due process limits — including those reflecting territorial sovereignty — were first derived in *Pennoyer* from international law, should not the absence of any international law limit on a national contacts test be important?

(c) *Sub silentio applications of national contacts tests by state courts.* Although there are virtually no reported cases in which state courts have expressly applied a national contacts test, that conceals a more complex (and interesting) reality. Courts that apply the fourteenth amendment often appear to give at least some weight to the contacts of foreign defendants with other U.S. states. *E.g., Amusement Equip. v. Mordelt*, 779 F.2d 264 (5th Cir. 1985) (considering defendant's contacts with neighboring state); *Afram Export Corp. v. Metallurgiki Halyps, SA*, 772 F.2d 1358 (7th Cir. 1985) ("Metallurgiki could not have been surprised to discover that if it ordered goods in *America* and went into *America* (through agents or directly) to inspect the goods and take delivery of them, it might be forced in the event of a contract dispute to litigate in *America* rather than being able to retreat to Greece.") (emphasis added); *supra* p. 141. What justifies this?

(d) *Due process limits on state court use of national contacts test in federal question cases.* Many federal causes of action can be brought in either state or federal court. *See supra* pp. 11-12. Suppose that a federal claim is brought in state court and that a federal jurisdictional statute would permit jurisdiction based on a national contacts test. Could a state court constitutionally apply a national contacts test?

4. *Interpreting state long-arm statutes that are borrowed under Rule 4.* A federal court cannot exercise personal jurisdiction under Rule 4(k)(1)(A) unless the "borrowed" state long-arm statute authorizes an assertion of jurisdiction. That is clear from the language of Rule 4(k)(1)(A), and it was black letter-law under old Rule 4(e). *See Omni Capital Int'l v. Rudolf Wolff & Co.*, 484 U.S. 97 (1987); *supra* pp. 172-73.

   (a) *State court interpretations of state long-arm statutes binding on federal court.* In interpreting a borrowed state long-arm statute, federal courts are generally bound by the local state courts' statutory interpretations. *See supra* pp. 68-69. In the context of international litigation, however, that statement can conceal significant complexities. In particular, (i) as a matter of statutory interpretation, is a state long-arm statute meant to permit inquiry into a defendant's national contacts, and (ii) as a matter of fourteenth amendment due process analysis, can a state long-arm statute permit inquiry into national contacts?

   (b) *State long-arm statutes extending to the limits of the U.S. Constitution.* Some state long-arm statutes expressly grant jurisdiction to the full extent permitted by the U.S. Constitution. *See supra* p. 69; Gen. Laws. R.I. §9-5-33(a) ("every case not contrary to the provisions of the Constitution or laws of the United States."). Many other state long-arm statutes extend by implication to the limits of the U.S. Constitution. *See supra* p. 69.

   Should state long-arm statutes that extend expressly or impliedly to the U.S. Constitution's limits be interpreted as authorizing application of a national contacts test? For example, as described in *Wells Fargo*, the district court in *Cryomedics, Inc. v. Spembly, Ltd.*, 397 F. Supp. 287 (D. Conn. 1975), held that Connecticut's long-arm statute permitted use of a national contacts test. Although Connecticut's long-arm statute did not expressly permit a national contacts inquiry, the district court emphasized that the statute had been interpreted by Connecticut courts as authorizing jurisdiction to the fullest extent of the due process clause.

   Wells Fargo referred to a provision in California's long-arm statute, authorizing jurisdiction to the limits of the U.S. Constitution, as an example of a statute that would support application of a national contacts test. However, *Wells Fargo* also held that, in contrast to California's statute, the Nevada long-arm statute did not authorize the use of a national contacts test. The court reached this result even though Nevada courts had interpreted the Nevada long-arm statute as permitting jurisdiction to the limits of the due process clause. *Wells Fargo* specifically rejected *Cryomedics'* interpretation of the similar Connecticut statute.

   Which court's analysis of the local long-arm statute is more persuasive — *Cryomedics* or *Wells Fargo*? Why shouldn't the Nevada courts' interpretation of the Nevada long-arm statute as extending to the limits of due process indicate an intent to permit use of a national contacts test — or whatever other legal doctrine would sustain jurisdiction? Is it because the wording of the Nevada long-arm statute appeared inconsistent with a national contacts test in tort cases? or is it because a Nevada court, rather than a federal court, might not be permitted by the fourteenth amendment to apply a national contacts test?

   (c) *Fourteenth amendment limits on state long-arm statutes borrowed by federal courts.* Even if a state statute was specifically intended by a state legislature to extend to the U.S. Constitution's limits — or to authorize a national contacts test — *could* it be incorporated under Rule 4 by a federal court to its full extent? Or would the fourteenth amendment's limits on a state court's jurisdiction nonetheless limit the long-arm statute's purported reach, either as a matter of interpreting the statute or because of Rule 4(k)(1)(A)? Some lower courts have concluded that a borrowed state long-arm statute cannot reach beyond the fourteenth amendment's limits, apparently on the theory that state legislation is necessarily confined within such limits, even if it says it is not. *E.g.*, *DeJames v. Magnificence Carriers, Inc.*, 491 F.Supp. 1276, 1283 & n.3 (D.N.J. 1980) (refusing to permit national contacts based on state long-arm because "[t]he power of the State of New Jersey ... is still limited by the due process requirements of the fourteenth amendment"); *Amburn v. Harold Forster Indus. Ltd.*, 423 F.Supp. 1302, 1305 (E.D. Mich. 1976) ("It remains, however, a state statute and the power of the State of Michigan is limited by the due process requirements of the Fourteenth Amendment.").

   (d) *Authorities rejecting fourteenth amendment limits on state long-arm statute borrowed by federal courts.* Consider how *United Rope* dealt with the possibility that the fourteenth amendment imposed limits on the state long-arm statute that it borrowed:

   > May a state law, constitutionally insufficient to authorize jurisdiction in state court, supply the
   > necessary basis of jurisdiction in federal court? The apparent oddity of a law being unconstitu-

tional in the state forum and constitutional in the federal one need detain us only briefly. Courts often say that laws are constitutional in one application and unconstitutional in another. "Facial" unconstitutionality (to use the entrenched but maladroit metaphor) is the exception. No one doubts that [the local state long-arm statute] may be applied to some defendants consistent with the Constitution, while the due process clause blocks its application to others. So too [the long-arm statute] may be constitutional to the extent Fed. R. Civ. P. 4(e) absorbs its terms as the fulcrum of federal power, even though the state may not hale the party into its own courts.

Is that persuasive? A few other lower courts have also declined to impose fourteenth amendment limits on state long-arm statutes when applied in federal court. *E.g., Cryomedics, Inc. v. Spembly, Ltd.,* 397 F.Supp. 287, 290 (D. Conn. 1975) ("[w]hen a federal court is asked to exercise personal jurisdiction over an alien defendant sued on a *claim* arising out of a federal law, jurisdiction may appropriately be determined on the basis of the alien's aggregated contacts with the United States as a whole, regardless of whether the contacts with the state in which the district court sits would be sufficient if considered alone.").

(e) *Miscellaneous other state long-arm statutes.* Suppose that a state long-arm statute grants jurisdiction to the limits of the due process clause *of the fourteenth amendment. E.g.,* Utah Code Ann. §78-27-22 ("fullest extent permitted by the due process clause of the Fourteenth Amendment to the United States Constitution"). Does this formulation incorporate a possible fourteenth amendment requirement that a state contacts test be applied or other fourteenth amendment limits? Does it do so as a matter of state statutory interpretation, or federal constitutional law?

Suppose that a state long-arm statute grants jurisdiction to the limits of both the federal *and state* constitutions. *E.g.,* Calif. Civ. Pro. Code §410.10 ("A court of this state may exercise jurisdiction on any basis not inconsistent with the Constitution of this state or of the United States."); Ill. Rev. Stat. §2-209(c) ("A court may also exercise jurisdiction on any other basis now or hereafter permitted by the Illinois Constitution and the Constitution of the United States."). Do these formulations limit a federal court to application of a state contacts test?

5. *Old Rule 4(e)'s limits on personal jurisdiction of federal courts.* In addition to satisfying both the due process clause and the applicable jurisdictional statute, a federal court cannot exercise personal jurisdiction unless Rule 4 permits it to do so. As *United Rope* acknowledges, Rule 4 has been interpreted by some courts as precluding jurisdiction by a federal court where a state court could not, in identical circumstances, assert jurisdiction. In particular, some courts held that Rule 4(e) prevented federal courts from applying a national contacts test when a state court could not do so under the fourteenth amendment. *E.g., In re Damodar Bulk Carriers, Ltd.,* 903 F.2d 675, 679 n.5 (9th Cir. 1990); *Cable/Home Communications Corp. v. Network Productions, Inc.,* 902 F.2d 829, 855-56 & n.39 (11th Cir. 1990); *Point Landing, Inc. v. Omni Capital Int'l, Ltd.,* 795 F.2d 415, 427 (5th Cir. 1986), *aff'd,* 484 U.S. 97 (1987).

(a) *Authority of federal court under old Rule 4(e) to exercise jurisdiction based on national contacts.* Suppose that: (i) a state long-arm statute authorizes personal jurisdiction in a particular case, and (ii) a national contacts analysis (but *not* a state contacts analysis) would sustain the state long-arm statute's assertion of jurisdiction under the due process clause. This was the case in both *United Rope* and *Cryomedics.* Did old Rule 4(e) permit a federal court to exercise jurisdiction, under a borrowed state long-arm statute, where a national contacts test under the due process clause was required to sustain jurisdiction?

(b) *Minority view under old Rule 4(e): no "lock-step" approach in federal question cases.* In answering the preceding question, *United Rope* suggested an expansive jurisdictional doctrine. The court reasoned that, in a federal question case, a federal court could rely on a state long-arm statute to establish personal jurisdiction — even if application of the state statute by a state court in identical circumstances would be unconstitutional. The court then indicated it could rely on a national contacts test permitted by the fifth amendment's due process clause. The Seventh Circuit rejected the argument that old Rule 4(e) required federal courts to act in "lock-step" with state courts when asserting jurisdiction under a state long-arm statute. *See also Handley v. Indiana & Michigan Elec. Co.,* 732 F.2d 1265 (6th Cir. 1984); *Cryomedics, Inc. v. Spembly, Ltd.,* 397 F.Supp. 287 (D. Conn. 1975).

(c) *Majority view under old Rule 4(e): "lock-step" approach in federal question cases.* As *United Rope* indicates, however, most courts of appeals have taken the opposite view, holding that when a federal court asserts jurisdiction under a state long-arm statute, it must do so in precisely the same fashion that a state court would if it applied the statute. These decisions relied principally on the language of old Rule 4(e), interpreting it as limiting federal courts to asserting jurisdiction only "under the circumstances" that a state court could. Consider the precise language of old Rule 4(e): "service may be made under the circumstances and in the manner prescribed by [a] statute [of the state in which the district court is held.]" How does *United Rope* interpret Rule 4(e)'s phrase "under the circumstances" to authorize a federal court to assert jurisdiction that a state court could not assert under the fourteenth amendment? *Compare DeJames v. Magnificence Carriers Inc.*, 491 F.Supp. 1276, 1283 (D.N.J. 1980) ("intent of the draftsmen of Rule 4(e) to use state provisions for service in order to permit federal courts in a state to hear those cases that could be brought in the state's own courts"), *aff'd*, 654 F.2d 280 (3d Cir.), *cert. denied*, 454 U.S. 1085 (1981).

This "lock-step" approach of Rule 4 was criticized on the grounds that it was anomalous for the personal jurisdiction of federal courts to vary from state to state, and to be subject to state law limitations, particularly in federal question cases. *See* Born, *Reflections on Judicial Jurisdiction in International Cases*, 17 Ga. J. Int'l & Comp. L. 1, 36-42 (1987); Green, *Federal Jurisdiction In Personam of Corporations and Due Process*, 14 Vand. L. Rev. 967 (1961).

(d) *Unanimous view under old Rule 4(e): "lock-step" approach required in diversity actions.* Rejecting a lock-step approach under Rule 4 permits federal courts to exercise broader personal jurisdiction than state courts. In diversity actions, virtually all lower courts have concluded that it would be "anomalous" for a federal court "to utilize a state long-arm rule to authorize service of process in a manner that the state body enacting the rule could not constitutionally authorize." *DeJames v. Magnificence Carriers, Inc.*, 654 F.2d 280, 284 (3d Cir. 1981). Similarly, *United Rope* was not troubled by abandoning a lock-step approach in federal question cases, but it refused to do so in diversity actions:

> The shortcoming of a state statute ... carries over into diversity litigation in federal court because under *Erie*, a federal court acts as the state's agent in applying state law. The authority for the demands made on the defendant is state rather than national power. Federal courts accordingly absorb the "whole law" of the states including limitations on personal jurisdiction, except to the extent a national rule requires otherwise. State federal jurisdictional allocations would be thrown out of kilter if a federal court could give judgment in a diversity case that the state itself would have to dismiss. ... That rationale does not carry over to federal question cases. Whether Wisconsin may extract damages from a Liberian corporation with headquarters in Greece is irrelevant to the question whether the United States as a whole may do so.

Does this passage hang together? Are not "state jurisdictional allocations" equally unaffected in both diversity and federal question actions against foreign defendants? Does the final sentence — relying on the defendant's foreign nationality — have any logical relation to *United Rope's* distinction between diversity and federal question cases?

6. *Does new Rule 4(k)(1)(A) require a lock-step approach to state long-arm statutes?* As described above, old Rule 4(e) was replaced at the end of 1993 by new Rule 4(k)(1)(A). *See supra* pp. 69-70. Does this new Rule require a lock-step approach to state long-arm statutes?

(a) *New Rule 4(k)(1)(A).* New Rule 4(k)(1)(A) provides that a district court may exercise jurisdiction over a defendant "who could be subjected to the jurisdiction of a court of general jurisdiction in the state in which the district court is located." Is this language any clearer than that of old Rule 4(e)? Is the rationale of either *United Rope* or *Cryomedics* still sustainable under new Rule 4(k)(1)(A)? Can a federal court, whose jurisdiction rests on a borrowed state long-arm statute, rely on a national contacts test under Rule 4(k)(1)(A)? Does Rule 4(k)(1)(A) incorporate just a state's long-arm statute, as old Rule 4(e) did? or does it more broadly incorporate *all* of "the jurisdiction" of the local state court? If so, does the new Rule more clearly incorporate than its predecessor fourteenth amendment limits restricting a state court to consideration of state contacts?

(b) *Advisory Committee Notes to new Rule 4(k)(1)(A).* Nothing in the Advisory Committee Notes gives any meaningful guidance concerning the foregoing aspect of new Rule 4(k)(1)(A). On the one hand, the Notes suggest that Rule 4(k)(1) merely preserves current Rule 4(e): it "retains the substance of the former rule in explicitly authorizing the exercise of personal jurisdiction over persons who can be reached under state long-arm law." 28 U.S.C.A. Fed. Rule Civ. Pro. 4, at 118. On the other hand, the Notes also suggest both that Rule 4(e) incorporated the fourteenth amendment and that the new Rule omits that incorporation: the Notes say that constitutional limits on the exercise of personal jurisdiction by federal courts "arise from the Fifth Amendment rather than from the Fourteenth Amendment, which limits state-court reach, and which was incorporated into federal practice by the reference to state law in the text of the former subdivision (e) that is deleted by this revision." 28 U.S.C.A. Fed. Rule Civ. Pro. 4, at 118.

7. *Another look at* United Rope: *scope of specific jurisdiction.* *United Rope* appears to attach considerable importance to the fact that the KATIA delivered some beans to Duluth, Minnesota in 1987, but had never called upon Wisconsin. And, because "Minnesota is not Wisconsin," the Minnesota contacts were said to be irrelevant to Wisconsin jurisdiction. What if the KATIA *had* visited Wisconsin, not Minnesota? Would this visit have had any jurisdictional consequences for the present case? Can it plausibly be suggested either that (a) one visit allows general jurisdiction; or (b) that the 1988 dispute about carriage of baler twine "arose out of" or "related to" a 1987 shipment of beans? *See supra* pp. 114-15. More generally, what is the jurisdictional relevance of the KATIA's "four voyages to seven different ports [in the United States] in 1986-87"? Even assuming a national contacts test, or that all four voyages were to Wisconsin ports, these visits would not permit general jurisdiction. Would they sustain an assertion of specific jurisdiction? Does failure to satisfactorily complete a delivery to one U.S. port "relate to" successful earlier visits to different U.S. ports for different customers?

On the other hand, why wouldn't specific jurisdiction exist in Wisconsin based solely upon the KATIA's failure to arrive at the Wisconsin port to which it promised to deliver goods? How would Article 5 of the Brussels Convention answer this question?

4. Personal Jurisdiction Under New Rule 4(k)(2)

The 1993 revisions to Rule 4 made a fundamental change to the personal jurisdiction of federal district courts. As discussed above, prior to 1993, federal courts were generally subject to the same due process limits as state courts when personal jurisdiction was based on borrowed state long-arm statutes under Rule 4(e).[232] As a result, federal courts generally applied "state contacts" tests either under the applicable state long-arm statute or the fourteenth amendment's due process clause. Particularly in federal question cases and actions against foreign defendants, this "lock-step" approach was criticized.[233]

New Rule 4(k)(2) significantly extends the personal jurisdiction of federal courts in federal question cases. It authorizes federal district courts to exercise personal jurisdiction to the limits of the Constitution, in federal question cases, "over the person of any defendant who is not subject to the jurisdiction of the courts of general jurisdiction of any state." As discussed below, new Rule 4(k)(2) was specifically designed for international cases.

FEDERAL RULES OF CIVIL PROCEDURE RULE 4(k)(2)

If the exercise of jurisdiction is consistent with the Constitution and laws of the United States, serving a summons or filing a waiver of service is also effective, with respect to claims arising under federal law, to establish personal jurisdiction over the person of any defendant who is not subject to the jurisdiction of the courts of general jurisdiction of any state.

Notes on New Rule 4(k)(2)

1. *Application of new Rule 4(k)(2).* Consider how new Rule 4(k)(2) would have applied in *Wells Fargo, United Rope, Amusement Equipment, Krakatau Steel, Cryomedics, Asahi,* and *Afram Export.* In which

---

232. *See supra* pp. 193-94.
233. *See* authorities cited *supra* p. 194.

cases, if any, would Rule 4(k)(2) have permitted jurisdiction that was otherwise lacking? Suppose a federal claim had been involved in each case.

(a) *Specific jurisdiction based on national contacts under Rule 4(k)(2)*. Rule 4(k)(2)'s most obvious application will be to permit specific jurisdiction over foreign defendants who have "minimum contacts" with the entire United States. For example, the rule would be available in cases like *United Rope* to permit consideration of the defendant's national contacts. This was the purpose for which Rule 4(k)(2) was specifically intended. The Advisory Committee Notes explain that this provision was intended to "correct[ ] a gap in the enforcement of federal law":

> Under the former rule, a problem was presented when the defendant was a non-resident of the United States having contacts with the United States sufficient to justify the application of United States law and to satisfy federal standards of forum selection, but having insufficient contact with any single state to support jurisdiction under state long-arm legislation or meet the requirements of the Fourteenth Amendment limitation on state court territorial jurisdiction. 28 U.S.C.A. Fed. Rule Civ. Pro. 4, at 118.

(b) *Tag service under Rule 4(k)(2)*. New Rule 4(k)(2) also appears to have the unintended consequence of authorizing personal jurisdiction based solely on tag service. Rule 4(k)(2) grants federal courts the power to exercise personal jurisdiction whenever "consistent with the Constitution and laws of the United States." After *Burnham, supra* p. 121, tag service generally appears to be permitted under the fourteenth amendment. Assuming the same general rule under the fifth amendment, it seems likely that Congress could constitutionally authorize personal jurisdiction to any U.S. district based upon tag service anywhere in the United States. That is because the relevant territorial unit for purposes of federal jurisdictional grants is widely held to be the entire United States. *See supra* pp. 179-80; *United States v. Union Pacific Railroad*, 98 U.S. 569, 603-04 (1878). Because Rule 4(k)(2) authorizes jurisdiction to the Constitution's limits, it appears to incorporate this tag service. Is it wise to permit nation-wide tag service on foreign defendants? Would Rule 4(k)(2) be available to a district court in one state when tag service was made in a different state that permitted it as a jurisdictional base? Or would that run afoul of Rule 4(k)(2)'s requirement that jurisdiction not otherwise exist in "any state"?

(c) *Nationality, domicile, and incorporation under Rule 4(k)(2)*. The same rationale that supports jurisdiction based on tag service also presumably extends to jurisdiction based upon U.S. nationality, domicile, and incorporation. As described above, the due process clause permits the exercise of general jurisdiction based upon nationality, domicile, and incorporation within the forum. *See supra* pp. 95-100.

(d) *General jurisdiction under Rule 4(k)(2)*. Finally, Rule 4(k)(2) also may affect a federal court's exercise of general jurisdiction based upon "continuous and systematic" business contacts or "presence." Federal court jurisdiction has historically been required to satisfy local state standards for defining the level of "presence" or "continuous and systematic" necessary for general jurisdiction. *See supra* pp. 00; *Arrowsmith v. United Press Int'l*, 320 F.2d 219 (2d Cir. 1963); C. Wright & A. Miller, *Federal Practice and Procedure* §1075 (1987). That arguably continues to be the case under Rule 4(k)(1)(A). *See supra* pp. 183-95. Under Rule 4(k)(2), however, a federal court is now authorized to exercise personal jurisdiction in federal question cases to the limits of the due process clause. Thus, if a foreign corporation has sufficient contacts with New York (or any other State) to permit general jurisdiction under the due process clause, then a federal court in New York arguably may exercise general jurisdiction — provided of course that no state court may.

Indeed, Rule 4(k)(2) goes further. Under the new rule, all of the defendant's contacts with the entire United States can be considered in determining whether it is subject to general jurisdiction. "[F]inding a corporation present in any individual state, could permit the federal court to entertain any federal claim at all against the corporation, even if the claim itself does not arise out of the aggregate national activities of the defendant." D. Siegel, *Supplementary Practice Commentaries, 28 U.S.C.A. Fed. Rules Civ. Proc. Rule 4*, C4-36 (1994 Supp.). That is a significant change from the law under old Rule 4(e). *See supra* pp. 193-94. Again, however, this rationale only applies if no state forum would have jurisdiction over the defendant.

2. Requirement under Rule 4(k)(2) that defendant not be subject to U.S. jurisdiction elsewhere. Rule 4(k)(2) applies only if the defendant is subject to personal jurisdiction in no other U.S. state. The pertinent part of Rule 4(k)(2) provides that a defendant must not be "subject to the jurisdiction of the courts of general jurisdiction of any state."

What does it mean for a defendant to be "subject to the jurisdiction" of a state court? Several possibilities exist: (a) the defendant must be subject to jurisdiction in a state court on the claims at issue in the plaintiff's case; (b) the defendant need only be subject to jurisdiction in a state court on *some* claim; or (c) the defendant must be subject to general jurisdiction in a state court. The purpose underlying Rule 4(k)(2), as described in the Advisory Committee Notes, suggests that possibility (a) is the sensible alternative (although language in the Notes also points towards possibility (b)). Is inquiry under Rule 4(k)(2) confined to what state long-arm statutes provide? or are due process limits also relevant? What about state door-closing statutes and forum non conveniens rules?

Rule 4(k)(2) also raises unresolved burden of proof issues, and may lead to anomalous litigation positions. It is not clear whether a plaintiff is obliged under Rule 4(k)(2) to plead and prove that no state long-arm statute permits jurisdiction. Typically, a defendant is obliged to raise personal jurisdiction defenses, after which the plaintiff continues to have the burden of persuasion. *See Mellon Bank (East) PSFS, N.A. v. DiVeronica Bros., Inc.*, 983 F.2d 551 (3d Cir. 1993). But this approach fits awkwardly with Rule 4(k)(2), where a plaintiff would be required to prove a negative (i.e., no jurisdiction), under more than 50 different state and other long-arm statutes, as applied to facts that are generally within the defendant's possession. Conversely, defendants resisting jurisdiction under Rule 4(k)(2) will face a dilemma: if they cite a U.S. state as permitting jurisdiction, they may well be found later to have consented to jurisdiction there.

3. *"Claims arising under federal law" for Rule 4(k)(2) purposes.* Rule 4(k)(2) is only available "with respect to claims arising under federal law." In many cases, it is clear that particular claims arise under federal law — such as claims under the federal antitrust or securities laws. Other cases are less clear, including claims arising under international law and foreign law. There is substantial authority under 28 U.S.C. §1331 considering when a claim arises under federal law for purposes of federal subject matter jurisdiction. *See supra* pp. 55-56. That precedent is presumably of substantial guidance in interpreting Rule 4(k)(2). Among other things, it has been widely held that claims based on international law — including both U.S. treaties and customary international law — arise under "federal" law. *See supra* pp. 49-56.

4. *Proposed national contacts legislation.* What should the statutory and constitutional rules for U.S. personal jurisdiction over foreign defendants be? Consider the following excerpt from H.R. 3662, a bill introduced in the 100th Congress?

> (a) In any civil action for injury that was sustained in the United States by a citizen of the United States and that relates to the purchase or use of a product manufactured outside the United States by a citizen or subject of a foreign state, the district court for the district in which such injury occurred shall have jurisdiction over that citizen or foreign subject if that citizen or foreign subject knew or reasonably should have known that the product would be imported for sale or use in the United States.

> (b) Process in any action under subsection (a) may be served wherever such citizen or subject of a foreign state resides, is found, has an agent, or transacts business.

Is this proposed legislation constitutional? As applied in an action based on state product liability law? Is it wise?

3/Foreign Sovereign Immunity and Jurisdiction of U.S. Courts Over Foreign States[1]

In most nations, including the United States, foreign states and state-related entities enjoy important immunities from the judicial jurisdiction of national courts. Issues of "foreign sovereign immunity" arise with considerable frequency in contemporary international litigation. This is because of the extensive involvement of foreign governments and their agencies — including airlines, banks, shipping lines, and other "commercial" entities — in international trade and finance. This Chapter examines the circumstances in which foreign states are subject to the judicial jurisdiction of U.S. courts.

A. Introduction and Historical Background

1. Historical Background

Foreign sovereign immunity is a well-established feature of U.S. law.[2] An early statement of the doctrine in the United States was the Supreme Court's opinion in *The Schooner Exchange v. McFaddon*,[3] where the Court held a French naval vessel immune from the jurisdiction of U.S. courts. Although no statutory or constitutional provision granted jurisdictional immunity to foreign sovereigns,[4] Chief Justice

---

1. Commentary on foreign sovereign immunity includes, *e.g.*, J. Dellapenna, *Suing Foreign Governments and Their Corporations* (1988); Feldman, *The United States Foreign Sovereign Immunities Act of 1976 in Perspective: A Founder's View*, 35 Int'l & Comp. L.Q. 302 (1986); Lauterpacht, *The Problem of Jurisdictional Immunities of Foreign States*, 28 Brit. Y. B. Int'l L. 220 (1951); Singer, *Abandoning Restrictive Sovereign Immunity: An Analysis in Terms of Jurisdiction to Prescribe*, 26 Harv. Int'l L.J. 1 (1985); Kane, *Suing Foreign Sovereigns: A Procedural Compass*, 34 Stan. L. Rev. 385 (1982).

2. *See* E. Allen, *The Position of Foreign States Before National Courts* (1933); T. Guittari, *The American Law of Sovereign Immunity* 26-42 (1970).

3. 11 U.S. 116 (1812).

4. *Verlinden BV v. Central Bank of Nigeria*, 461 U.S. 480, 486 (1983) ("foreign sovereign immunity is a matter of grace and comity ... and not a restriction imposed by the Constitution").

Marshall relied on principles of international law and territorial sovereignty in concluding that U.S. courts lacked judicial jurisdiction over foreign sovereigns.[5] Among other things, Chief Justice Marshall's opinion for the Court reasoned:

> The jurisdiction of the nation within its own territory is necessarily exclusive and absolute. ... This full and absolute territorial jurisdiction being alike the attribute of every sovereign ... would not seem to contemplate foreign sovereigns nor their sovereign rights as its objects. ... This perfect equality and absolute independence of sovereigns, and this common interest impelling them to mutual intercourse, and an interchange of good offices with each other, have given rise to a class of cases in which every sovereign is understood to waive the exercise of a part of that complete exclusive territorial jurisdiction, which has been stated to be the attribute of every nation.[6]

The Court had no difficulty incorporating this international practice into U.S. law, and adopting a common law rule of sovereign immunity. In addition to relying on international law, *Schooner Exchange* also noted that the U.S. executive branch had appeared and argued that immunity would be appropriate.[7]

Schooner Exchange provided the basis for a common law doctrine of sovereign immunity which U.S. courts applied throughout the 19th century.[8] In general, U.S. courts applied the so-called absolute theory of foreign sovereign immunity, which granted foreign states immunity with respect to all their activities, both governmental and commercial.[9] For example, in *Berizzi Brothers Co. v. The Pesaro*,[10] the Court considered whether a foreign state-owned commercial vessel was subject to the jurisdiction of U.S. courts in a straightforward breach of contract case. The Court affirmed dismissal of the suit on sovereign immunity grounds:

> We think that the principles [of sovereign immunity stated in *Schooner Exchange*] are applicable alike to all ships held and used by a government for a public purpose, and that when, for the purpose of advancing the trade of its people or providing revenues for its Treasury, a government acquires, mans, and operates ships in the carrying of trade, they are public ships in the same sense that warships are.[11]

---

5. This analysis paralleled the Court's subsequent reliance on principles of international law to define U.S. judicial jurisdiction in cases like *Rose v. Himely* and *Pennoyer v. Neff. See supra* pp. 70-73 & 78-94.

6. 11 U.S. 116, 137 (1812).

7. 11 U.S. at 132-35.

8. *E.g., Berizzi Bros. Co. v. S.S. Pesaro*, 271 U.S. 562 (1926); *United States v. Diekelman*, 92 U.S. 520, 524 (1875). *See* T. Guittari, *The American Law of Sovereign Immunity* 26-42 (1970).

9. *E.g., Compania Espanola de Navegacion Maritima, SA v. The Navemar*, 303 U.S. 68 (1938). In this respect, U.S. law continued to parallel international practice, which saw widespread acceptance of absolute immunity. *See* Harvard Research in International Law, *Draft Convention and Comment on Competence of Courts in Regard to Foreign States*, 26 Am. J. Int'l L. 451, 527 (1932 Supp.).

10. 271 U.S. 562 (1926).

11. 271 U.S. at 574.

Pesaro rested entirely on the Supreme Court's understanding of prevailing international law principles. The Court did not consider the views of the Executive Branch regarding U.S. foreign relations.[12]

In subsequent years, however, the U.S. Department of State came to play a central role in the application of the doctrine of foreign sovereign immunity in the United States. In *Ex parte Peru*,[13] the Court held that a Peruvian state-owned commercial vessel was immune from U.S. jurisdiction even in a purely commercial case. In contrast to *Pesaro*, however, the Court placed central reliance on the views of the Department of State, which had formally recognized the Peruvian government's claim of immunity. According to *Ex parte Peru*, a State Department certificate of immunity "must be accepted by the courts as a conclusive determination by the political arm of the government that the continued retention of the vessel interferes with the proper conduct of our foreign relations."[14]

Two years later, in *Republic of Mexico v. Hoffman*,[15] the Supreme Court denied immunity to a Mexican state-owned commercial vessel. The Court justified its result (which, on the facts, appeared directly contrary to the results in *Pesaro* and *Ex Parte Peru*) by reference to the State Department's refusal to suggest immunity. According to Chief Justice Stone: "It is ... not for the courts to deny an immunity which our government has seen fit to allow, or to allow an immunity on new grounds which the government has not seen fit to recognize."[16]

After the Court's decisions in *Ex parte Peru* and *Republic of Mexico*, the State Department adopted a procedure by which it would make initial determinations of immunity based on submissions by foreign states wishing to claim immunity from U.S. jurisdiction. If the State Department concluded that a foreign state was entitled to immunity, it would make a "suggestion" of immunity to the court in which claims against the foreign state were pending. The courts, in turn, treated State Department suggestions as binding.[17]

During the early twentieth century, a number of foreign states abandoned the absolute theory of immunity in favor of the so-called "restrictive theory." Under the restrictive theory, states do not enjoy sovereign immunity with respect to their private or commercial activities *(jure gestionis)*, although immunity is retained for sov-

---

12. Indeed, in *Pesaro*, the U.S. Department of State had concluded that sovereign immunity should not be accorded, because of its view that the vessel was a commercial one (not a public one) and the dispute was purely commercial. The Department of Justice disagreed, however, and refused to submit the Department of State's views to the Court. *The Pesaro*, 277 F. 473, 479-80 n.3 (1921); 2 Hackworth, *Digest of International Law* 429-30, 438-39 (1941).

13. 318 U.S. 578 (1943).

14. 318 U.S. at 589.

15. 324 U.S. 30 (1945).

16. 324 U.S. at 35-6.

17. *See* T. Guittari, *The American Law of Sovereign Immunity* 111-121, 143-62, 174-87 (1970) (collecting commentary and cases).

ereign or public acts *(jure imperii).*[18] In 1952, the Department of State embraced the restrictive theory of immunity in a frequently-cited letter by Jack Tate, the State Department's Legal Adviser. The "Tate Letter" noted the growing international acceptance of the restrictive theory and the increasing involvement of state-owned enterprises in commercial dealings with private parties.[19] Relying on these developments, the Tate Letter declared that future suggestions of immunity would be made in accordance with the restrictive theory.[20] Subsequent State Department decisions sought to apply the letter's distinction between "sovereign" and "private" acts.[21]

2. Selected Historical Materials Concerning Foreign Sovereign Immunity

Excerpted below is the Supreme Court's opinion in *The Schooner Exchange v. McFaddon.* Consider the rationale adopted by the Court in denying U.S. jurisdiction, and compare the Court's reliance on international law to the reasoning in decisions like *Pennoyer v. Neff.* Also excerpted below are the Court's opinions in *Berizzi Bros. Co. v. S.S. Pesaro* and *Republic of Mexico v. Hoffman.* In reading these excerpts, recall the separation of powers considerations which were explored in the context of the Alien Tort Statute.[22] Finally, consider the Tate Letter and its impact on the doctrine of sovereign immunity.

THE SCHOONER EXCHANGE v. MCFADDON
11 U.S. 116 (1812)

MARSHALL, CHIEF JUSTICE. [Two U.S. nationals brought a libel against the vessel "the Schooner Exchange." The libellants claimed that the Schooner Exchange was theirs, and that they were entitled to possession of the vessel. They alleged that the vessel had been seized on the high seas in 1810 by French naval forces and that no prize court of competent jurisdiction had pronounced judgment against the vessel. No one appeared for the vessel to reply to the libellants' allegations. The United States Attorney for Pennsylvania appeared on behalf of the U.S. Government to request that the libel be dismissed. He stated that the United States and France were at peace, that a public ship (known as "the Balaou") of the Emperor of France had been forced by storms to enter the port of Philadelphia, and was prevented from leaving by the process of the court. The United States Attorney urged that, even if the

---

18. Dobrovir, *A Gloss on the Tate Letter's Restrictive Theory of Sovereign Immunity,* 54 Va. L. Rev. 1 (1968); Higgins, *The Death Throes of Absolute Immunity: The Government of Uganda Before the English Courts,* 73 Am. J. Int'l L. 465 (1979).

19. *See* Friedmann, *Changing Social Arrangements in State-Trading States and Their Effect on International Law,* 24 Law & Contemp. Probs. 350 (1959); Letter of Jack B. Tate, Acting Legal Adviser, to Acting Attorney General (1952) (hereinafter the "Tate Letter"), reprinted in Appendix 2 to *Alfred Dunhill of London v. Republic of Cuba,* 425 U.S. 682, 711 (1976).

20. Tate Letter, *reprinted in* 425 U.S. 682, 711 (1976).

21. *See* H.R. Rep. No. 1487, 94th Cong., 2d Sess. 8-9, *reprinted in* 1976 U.S. Code Cong. & Admin. News 6604, 6607; *Alfred Dunhill, Inc. v. Cuba,* 425 U.S. 682, 698-705 (1976).

22. *See supra* pp. 36-38 & 45-46.

vessel had in fact been wrongfully seized, ownership had passed to the Emperor of France. The District Court dismissed the libel, the Circuit Court reversed, and the United States Attorney appealed to the Supreme Court]. ...

The jurisdiction of the nation within its own territory is necessarily exclusive and absolute. It is susceptible of no limitation not imposed by itself. ... This full and absolute territorial jurisdiction being alike the attribute of every sovereign ... would not seem to contemplate foreign sovereigns nor their sovereign rights as its objects. One sovereign being in no respect amenable to another; and being bound by obligations of the highest character not to degrade the dignity of his nation, by placing himself or its sovereign rights within the jurisdiction of another, can be supposed to enter a foreign territory only under an express license, or in the confidence that the immunities belonging to his independent sovereign station, though not expressly stipulated, are reserved by implication, and will be extended to him.

This perfect equality and absolute independence of sovereigns, and this common interest impelling them to mutual intercourse, and an interchange of good offices with each other, have given rise to a class of cases in which every sovereign is understood to waive the exercise of a part of that complete exclusive territorial jurisdiction, which has been stated to be the attribute of every nation.

1st. One of these is admitted to be the exemption of the person of the sovereign from arrest or detention within a foreign territory ...

2d. A second case, standing on the same principles with the first, is the immunity which all civilized nations allow to foreign ministers ...

3d. A third case in which a sovereign is understood to cede a portion of his territorial jurisdiction is, where he allows the troops of a foreign prince to pass through his dominions.

[The Court reasoned that a state's permission for foreign armies to enter its territory must be express, and not merely implied, but that a different rule applied in the case of foreign ships.] ... If there be no prohibition, the ports of a friendly nation are considered as open to the public ships of all powers with whom it is at peace, and they are supposed to enter such ports and to remain in them while allowed to remain, under the protection of the government of the place. ...

When private individuals of one nation spread themselves through another as business or caprice may direct, mingling indiscriminately with the inhabitants of that other, or when merchant vessels enter for the purposes of trade, it would be obviously inconvenient and dangerous to society, and would subject the laws to continual infraction, and the government to degradation, if such individuals or merchants did not owe temporary and local allegiance, and were not amenable to the jurisdiction of the country. ... But in all respects different is the situation of a public armed ship. She constitutes a part of the military force of her nation; acts under the immediate and direct command of the sovereign; is employed by him in national objects. He has many and powerful motives for preventing those objects from being defeated by the interference of a foreign state. Such interference cannot take place without affecting his power and his dignity. The implied license therefore under which such vessel enters a friendly port, may reasonably be construed, and it seems to the Court, ought to be construed, as containing an exemption from the jurisdiction of the sovereign, within whose territory she claims the rights of hospitality. Upon these principles, by the unanimous consent of nations, a foreigner is amenable to the laws of the place; but certainly in practice, nations have not yet asserted their jurisdiction over the public armed ships of a foreign sovereign entering a port open for their reception.

Bynkershoek, a jurist of great reputation, has indeed maintained that the property of a foreign sovereign is not distinguishable by any legal exemption from the property of an ordinary individual, and has quoted several cases in which courts have exercised jurisdiction over causes in which a foreign sovereign was made a party defendant. Without indicating any opinion on this question, it may safely be affirmed, that there is a manifest distinction between the private property of the person who happens to be a prince, and that military force which supports the sovereign power, and maintains the dignity and the independence of a nation. A prince, by acquiring private property in a foreign country, may possibly be considered as subjecting that property to the territorial jurisdiction; he may be considered as so far laying down the prince, and assuming the character of a private individual; but this he cannot be presumed to do with respect to any portion of that armed force, which upholds his crown, and the nation he is entrusted to govern. ...

It seems then to the Court, to be a principle of public law, that national ships of war, entering the port of a friendly power open for their reception, are to be considered as exempted by the consent of that power from its jurisdiction. ... The arguments in favor of this opinion which have been drawn from the general inability of the judicial power to enforce its decisions in cases of this description, from the consideration, that the sovereign power of the nation is alone competent to avenge wrongs committed by a sovereign, that the questions to which such wrongs give birth are rather questions of policy than of law, that they are for diplomatic, rather than legal discussion, are of great weight, and merit serious attention. But the argument has already been drawn to a length, which forbids a particular examination of these points. ...

If the preceding reasoning be correct, the Exchange, being a public armed ship, in the service of a foreign sovereign, with whom the government of the United States is at peace, and having entered an American port open for her reception, on the terms on which ships of war are generally permitted to enter the ports of a friendly power, must be considered as having come into the American territory, under an implied promise, that while necessarily within it, and demeaning herself in a friendly manner, she should be exempt from the jurisdiction of the country.

BERIZZI BROS. CO. v. S.S. PESARO

271 U.S. 562 (1926)

VAN DEVANTER, JUSTICE. [The Pesaro was a merchant vessel owned and operated by Italy. It was engaged in carrying cargo and passengers on a purely commercial basis. A libel was brought against the Pesaro to enforce a claim for cargo damage. The case was considered on agreed facts showing, *inter alia*, that the vessel would not be immune from suit in Italy, and that merchant vessels owned by the United States would not be immune in Italian courts. The State Department declined to take a position on the vessel's immunity, but the ship's master objected on jurisdictional grounds. Judge Mack overruled the objections. *The Pesaro*, 277 Fed. 473 (S.D.N.Y. 1921). Among other things, he reasoned:

"To deprive parties injured in the ordinary course of trade of their common and well-established legal remedies would not only work great hardship on them, but in the long run it would operate to the disadvantage and detriment of those in whose favor the immunity might be granted. Shippers would hesitate to trade with government ships, and salvors would run few risks to save the property of friendly sovereigns, if they were denied recourse to our own courts and left to prosecute their claims in foreign tribunals in distant lands. ... The attachment of public trading vessels, in my judgment, is not incompatible with the public interest of any nation or with the respect and deference due a foreign power. ... [In] my opinion, a government ship should not be immune from seizure as such, but only by reason of the nature of the service in which she is engaged. And as the Pesaro was employed as an ordinary merchant vessel for commercial purposes at a time when no emergency existed or was declared, she should not be immune from arrest in admiralty, especially as no exemption has been claimed for her, by reason of her sovereign or political character, through the official channels of the United States.

[Even if that were error, the Pesaro would not be entitled to immunity.] I do not base this upon the fact that ships owned and operated for commercial purposes by the United States would not be exempt from ordinary process under Italian law, for retaliation and reprisal are for the executive branches of our government and not for the courts. ... But the fact that the steamship Pesaro itself is subject to the ordinary processes of the Italian court would seem to be vital and decisive. There is no reason of international comity or courtesy which requires that Italian property not deemed *extra commercium* in Italy should be treated as *res publica* and *extra commercium* in the United States. ..." Judge Mack was subsequently reversed, and the libellants appealed to the U.S. Supreme Court.] ...

The single question presented for decision by us is whether a ship owned and possessed by a foreign government, and operated by it in the carriage of merchandise for hire, is immune from arrest under process based on a libel in rem by a private suitor in a federal district court exercising admiralty jurisdiction. The precise question never had been considered by this Court before. ... The nearest approach to it in this Court's decisions is found in *The Exchange*. ... It will be perceived that the opinion ... contains no reference to merchant ships owned and operated by a government. But the omission is not of special significance, for in 1812, when the decision was given, merchant ships were operated only by private owners, and there was little thought of governments engaging in such operations. That came much later.

The decision in *The Exchange* therefore cannot be taken as excluding merchant ships held and used by a government from the principles there announced. On the contrary, if such ships come within those principles, they must be held to have the same immunity as war ships, in the absence of a treaty or statute of the United States evincing a different purpose. No such treaty or statute has been brought to our attention. We think the principles are applicable alike to all ships held and used by a government for a public purpose, and that when, for the purpose of advancing the trade of its people or providing revenue for its treasury, a government acquires, mans and operates ships in the carrying trade, they are public ships in the same sense that war ships are. We know of no international usage which regards the maintenance and advancement of the economic welfare of a people in time of peace as any less a public purpose than the maintenance and training of a naval force. ...

REPUBLIC OF MEXICO v. HOFFMAN (THE BAJA CALIFORNIA)
324 U.S. 30 (1945)

STONE, CHIEF JUSTICE. [The owner of a vessel damaged in a collision filed a libel against the *Baja California*, a Mexican Government-owned merchant vessel operated in freight service by a private Mexican company under a five-year contract. The contract provided for complete control of the vessel by the private company and for a sharing of profits with the state. The Mexican Ambassador filed a suggestion of immunity, and the U.S. District Attorney presented a communication from the U.S. Department of State calling attention to the claim of immunity and accepting as true its statement regarding Mexican Government ownership. The State Department expressed no opinion as to the immunity claimed by the Mexican state.] ...

It is therefore not for the courts to deny an immunity which our government has seen fit to allow, or to allow an immunity on new grounds which the government has not seen fit to recognize.[23] The judicial seizure of the property of a friendly state may be regarded as such an affront to its dignity and may so affect our relations with it, that it is an accepted rule of substantive law governing the exercise of the jurisdiction of the courts that they will accept and follow the executive determination that the vessel shall be treated as immune ... But recognition by the courts of an immunity upon principles which the political department of government has not sanctioned may be equally embarrassing to it in securing the protection of our national interests and their recognition by other nations.

---

23. This salutary practice was not followed in *Berizzi Bros. Co. v. The Pesaro*.

When such a seizure occurs the friendly foreign government may adopt the procedure of asking the State Department to allow it. But the foreign government may also present its claim of immunity by appearance in the suit and by way of defense to the libel. In such a case the court will inquire whether the ground of immunity is one which it is the established policy of the department to recognize . . . Such a policy, long and consistently recognized and often certified by the State Department and for that reason acted upon by the courts even when not so certified, is that of allowing the immunity from suit of a vessel in the possession and service of a foreign government . . .

The lower Federal courts have consistently refused to allow claims of immunity based on title of the claimant foreign government without possession . . . More important, and we think controlling in the present circumstances, is the fact that, despite numerous opportunities like the present to recognize immunity from suit of a vessel owned and not possessed by a foreign government, this government has failed to do so. We can only conclude that it is the national policy not to extend the immunity in the manner now suggested, and that it is the duty of the courts, in a matter so intimately associated with our foreign policy and which may profoundly affect it, not to enlarge an immunity to an extent which the government, although often asked, has not seen fit to recognize . . .

LETTER OF ACTING LEGAL ADVISER, JACK B. TATE, TO DEPARTMENT OF JUSTICE, MAY 19, 1952

26 Department of State Bulletin 984 (1952)

A study of the law of sovereign immunity reveals the existence of two conflicting concepts of sovereign immunity, each widely held and firmly established. According to the classical or absolute theory of sovereign immunity, a sovereign cannot, without his consent, be made a respondent in the courts of another sovereign. According to the newer or restrictive theory of sovereign immunity, the immunity of the sovereign is recognized with regard to sovereign or public acts (*jure imperii*) of a state, but not with respect to private acts (*jure gestionis*). There is agreement by proponents of both theories, supported by practice, that sovereign immunity should not be claimed or granted in actions with respect to real property (diplomatic and perhaps consular property excepted) or with respect to the disposition of the property of a deceased person even though a foreign sovereign is the beneficiary.

The classical or virtually absolute theory of sovereign immunity has generally been followed by the courts of the United States, the British Commonwealth, Czechoslovakia, Estonia, and probably Poland. The decisions of the courts of Brazil, Chile, China, Hungary, Japan, Luxembourg, Norway, and Portugal may be deemed to support the classical theory of immunity if one or at most two old decisions anterior to the development of the restrictive theory may be considered sufficient on which to base a conclusion. ...

A trend to the restrictive theory is already evident in the Netherlands where the lower courts have started to apply that theory following a Supreme Court decision to the effect that immunity would have been applicable in the case under consideration under either theory. The German courts, after a period of hesitation at the end of the nineteenth century have held to the classical theory, but it should be noted that the refusal of the Supreme Court in 1921 to yield to pressure by the lower courts for the newer theory was based on the view that that theory had not yet developed sufficiently to justify a change. In view of the growth of the restrictive theory since that time the German courts might take a different view today.

The newer or restrictive theory of sovereign immunity has always been supported by the courts of Belgium and Italy. It was adopted in turn by the courts of Egypt and Switzerland. In addition, the courts of France, Austria, and Greece, which were traditionally supporters of the classical theory, reversed their position in the 20's to embrace the restrictive theory. ...

Furthermore, it should be observed that in most of the countries still following the classical theory there is a school of influential writers favoring the restrictive theory and the views of writers, at least in civil law countries, are a major factor in the development of the law. Moreover, the leanings of the lower courts in civil law countries are more significant in shaping the law than they are in common law countries where the rule of precedent prevails and the trend in these lower courts is to the restrictive theory. ...

It is thus evident that with the possible exception of the United Kingdom little support has been found except on the part of the Soviet Union and its satellites for continued full acceptance of the absolute theory of sovereign immunity. There are evidences that British authorities are aware of its deficiencies and ready for a change. The reasons which obviously motivate state trading countries in adhering to the theory with perhaps increasing rigidity are most persuasive that the United States should change its policy. Furthermore, the granting of sovereign immunity to foreign governments in the courts of the United States is most inconsistent with the action of the Government of the United States in subjecting itself to suit in the same courts in both contract and tort and with its long established policy of not claiming immunity in foreign jurisdictions for its merchant vessels. Finally, the Department feels that the widespread and increasing practice on the part of governments of engaging in commercial activities makes necessary a practice which will enable persons doing business with them to have their rights determined in the courts. For these reasons it will hereafter be the Department's policy to follow the restrictive theory of sovereign immunity in the consideration of requests of foreign governments for a grant of sovereign immunity.

It is realized that a shift in policy by the executive cannot control the courts but it is felt that the courts are less likely to allow a plea of sovereign immunity where the executive has declined to do so. There have been indications that at least some Justices of the Supreme Court feel that in this matter courts should follow the branch of the Government charged with responsibility for the conduct of foreign relations.

Notes on Schooner Exchange, Pesaro, Republic of Mexico, and Tate Letter

1. *Sovereign immunity in* **Schooner Exchange.** In *Schooner Exchange*, the French vessel was located firmly within U.S. territory. Under prevailing territorial rules of judicial jurisdiction, the vessel was unambiguously subject to the jurisdiction of U.S. courts. *See supra* pp. 70-73. Nevertheless, Chief Justice Marshall held that the vessel was not subject to U.S. jurisdiction, adopting a rule that "national ships of war, entering the port of a friendly foreign power open for their reception, are to be considered as exempted by the consent of that power from its jurisdiction." What was the basis for this rule? What policies supported the rule?

2. *U.S. government's role in* **Schooner Exchange.** As noted above, a U.S. district attorney appeared and argued that the Schooner Exchange was immune from the jurisdiction of U.S. courts. What role did this play in the Court's analysis? Did *Schooner Exchange* reason that, since the Executive had taken a position in a matter involving foreign relations, U.S. courts should defer?

Consider the Court's brief reference, at the conclusion of its opinion, to the arguments concerning the "general inability of the judicial power to enforce its decisions in cases of this description," the fact that "the sovereign power of the nation is alone competent to avenge wrongs committed by a sovereign," the fact that "the questions to which such wrongs give birth are rather questions of policy than of law," and the fact that such questions "are for diplomatic, rather than legal discussion." The Court declines to pass upon these issues, beyond noting that they are of "great weight." Should the Court in fact simply have abstained in the case, on the grounds that dealing with a French warship was a matter for the Departments of State and War? Compare the political question and act of state doctrines. *See supra* pp. 45-48 & *infra* pp. 701-03.

3. *Relationship between international law and U.S. law.* Consider Chief Justice Marshall's reliance on "principles of public law," recognized by "the unanimous consent of nations." These are the same principles of international law that were invoked in *Rose v. Himely* and *Pennoyer* to justify territorial limitations on national jurisdiction. *See supra* pp. 70-73. Why did the Court, in *Schooner Exchange* and *Pennoyer*, look to international law in defining the jurisdiction of U.S. courts? In both cases, there were U.S. statutes that defined the jurisdiction of U.S. courts. What made international law relevant?

4. *Rationale for* **Schooner Exchange.** Recall how firmly entrenched the territoriality doctrine was in 19th century American law — permitting tag jurisdiction and forbidding the assertion of judicial jurisdiction over persons not served with process within the forum's territory. *See supra* pp. 70-73. Indeed, *Schooner Exchange* acknowledged that "[t]he jurisdiction of the nation within its own territory is necessarily exclusive and absolute," and that a nation's jurisdiction within its territory "is susceptible of no limitation not imposed by itself." What provision of law was sufficiently compelling to overcome this doctrine and deny jurisdiction over a ship in U.S. waters?

(a) *Judicial abstention. Schooner Exchange* might be regarded as a form of abstention; a judicial decision not to exercise jurisdiction granted by Congress because doing so would be contrary to international law and would interfere with U.S. foreign relations. Would it be legitimate for a court to refuse to exercise jurisdiction granted by a federal statute on these grounds? In other contexts, the Supreme Court has emphasized that U.S. federal courts are subject to a "virtually unflagging obligation" to exercise jurisdiction that Congress has granted to them. *Colorado River Water Conservation District v. United States*, 424 U.S. 800 (1976) ("virtually unflagging obligation of the federal courts to exercise the jurisdiction given to them"); *W.S. Kirkpatrick & Co. v. Environmental Tectonics Corp.*, 493 U.S. 400 ("The short of the matter is this: Courts in the United States have the power, and ordinarily the obligation, to decide cases and controversies properly presented to them."); *infra* pp. 462-63 & 712-18. Was *Schooner Exchange* a violation of the federal courts' duty to exercise jurisdiction conferred by Congress?

(b) *Due process clause and other constitutional limits.* In *Pennoyer*, the Supreme Court held that international law was incorporated or inherent in the Constitution, and hence operated directly upon the jurisdiction of state courts. *See supra* pp. 70-72. Could the same be said in *Schooner Exchange*? Were international law principles of foreign sovereign immunity incorporated within the fifth amendment's due process clause, and hence applicable to the federal courts' assertion of jurisdiction over foreign states? Did the Court suggest anything of the sort? *Compare Verlinden BV v. Central Bank of Nigeria*, 461 U.S. 480, 486 (1983) ("foreign sovereign immunity is a matter of grace and comity ... and not a restriction imposed by the Constitution"). Note the consequences of the foregoing constitutional analysis: Congress would likely be incapable of legislating in a manner inconsistent with prevailing principles of international law. Is that desirable?

(c) *Presumption that Congress intends to comply with international law.* Would it be appropriate to interpret the Court's opinion in *Schooner Exchange* as an exercise in statutory construction? In other contexts, the Court has applied the presumption that Congress does not intend to violate international law. Under this presumption, a federal statute will not be construed as violating international law unless Congress expressly requires this result. *See supra* p. 22; *infra* pp. 780-92 (service abroad); *infra* pp. 549-50 (extraterritorial application of U.S. law). How would this presumption apply to the generally worded jurisdictional statute in *Schooner Exchange?*

5. **Schooner Exchange** *and absolute immunity.* Was Chief Justice Marshall's opinion in *Schooner Exchange* a statement of the "absolute theory" of sovereign immunity? Consider the Court's discussion of the private property of a "prince." Is that consistent with the notion that all of a foreign state's property — commercial and non-commercial — enjoys sovereign immunity?

6. *Development of the absolute theory of immunity.* Whatever the intended scope of the rule of immunity in *Schooner Exchange*, the Court subsequently made it clear that foreign states *were* entitled to absolute immunity in U.S. courts. In *Berizzi Bros. Co. v. S.S. Pesaro*, 271 U.S. 562 (1926), the Court held that a vessel owned and operated by the Italian government, and used for carrying commercial cargo and passengers, was subject to the jurisdiction of U.S. courts. Is the principle of absolute immunity adopted in *Pesaro* sensible? What is the response to the district court's reasoning that it is both unjust to private parties and, in the long run, disadvantageous to foreign states, to immunize them from jurisdiction for their commercial acts?

7. *Considerations of reciprocity.* It was observed in *Pesaro* that "ships owned and operated for commercial purposes by the United States would not be exempt from ordinary process under Italian law." 277 F. 473, 482 (S.D.N.Y. 1921). The district court refused to draw any conclusion from this, noting that "retaliation and reprisal are for the executive branches of our government and not for the courts." Is this the right result? If Italy would not grant sovereign immunity to U.S. government commercial vessels, why should U.S. courts accord such immunity to Italian government vessels? Is this merely a matter of "retaliation and reprisal"? If it applies the cited rule, Italy presumably does not think international law forbids the exercise of judicial jurisdiction over foreign state-owned commercial vessels. Given that, how would U.S. application of the same rule violate Italy's rights under international law?

The district court did, however, consider the fact that Italian courts would also not accord immunity to the Pesaro in concluding that U.S. courts also should not grant immunity. Is this rationale persuasive? Might a nation be more willing to submit itself to its own courts than to foreign courts? Consider *Schooner Exchange's* basic rationale for sovereign immunity.

8. *The role of Executive Branch "suggestions" of immunity.* Contrast the rationale for immunity in *Republic of Mexico* with that in *Schooner Exchange*. Which rationale is more satisfactory? What are the difficulties with permitting the Executive Branch to make suggestions of immunity, that are binding on the courts? Is such an approach consistent with due process and the rule of law? Does it not permit a political branch of the government — relying on political considerations — to decide individual civil disputes? *See infra* pp. 729-32, discussing the *Bernstein* exception under the act of state doctrine.

9. *Restrictive theory and Tate Letter.* Consider the restrictive theory of sovereign immunity articulated in the Tate Letter. Are the justifications advanced for the theory persuasive? Note how the Tate Letter — like *Schooner Exchange* — relies primarily on state practice and evidence of contemporary international law, but reasons that international law had evolved significantly since 1812. Can any meaningful line be drawn between "commercial" or "private" activities, and "sovereign" or "public" ones? What, for example, is a foreign state's purchase of boots, which it intends to use to outfit its army? Is it a routine commercial transaction or a sovereign defense of national interests?

3. The Foreign Sovereign Immunities Act of 1976: Overview

Following release of the Tate Letter in 1952, the State Department routinely decided whether or not a foreign state's conduct or property was "sovereign," and hence entitled to immunity. Application of the restrictive theory by the Department of State encountered difficulties.[24] Although it is a political institution, the Tate Letter required the State Department to perform a judicial function. The Department lacked the capacity to take factual evidence or afford appellate review. Moreover, the State Department was subjected to diplomatic and political pressures in connection with immunity decisions. This produced unpredictable, sometimes unprincipled, results for private litigants and foreign states.[25]

Defects in executive branch application of the restrictive theory generated pressure for reform. After a lengthy legislative process, Congress enacted the Foreign Sovereign Immunities Act of 1976 (the "FSIA" or "Act"),[26] which is reproduced in Appendix E. The FSIA transferred responsibility for sovereign immunity decisions from the State Department to the judiciary.[27] The Act also provided a comprehensive statutory system governing issues of foreign state immunity, as well as procedural issues such as service of process, provisional relief, and the enforcement of judgments. In general, the FSIA implements the restrictive theory of immunity: it provides foreign states immunity for their "sovereign" acts and denies them immunity for their "commercial" or "private" acts.[28]

The FSIA was enacted to provide the "sole and exclusive standards to be used in resolving questions of sovereign immunity raised by foreign states before federal and state courts in the United States."[29] Under the Act, all "foreign states" are presumptively entitled to immunity, and thus cannot be subjected to the jurisdiction of U.S. courts (either state or federal).[30] However, the FSIA also contains important exceptions to this presumptive grant of immunity, which define circumstances in which foreign states will not enjoy immunity in U.S. courts.[31]

The FSIA is fundamentally a *jurisdictional* statute. As discussed elsewhere, where a foreign state does not enjoy immunity, 28 U.S.C. §1330 affirmatively grants federal courts both personal and subject matter jurisdiction involving claims against it.[32] The FSIA does *not* generally deal with issues of substantive liability: §1606 of the Act

---

24. *See* H.R. Rep. No. 1487, 94th Cong., 2d Sess. 12, *reprinted in* 1976 U.S. Code Cong. & Admin. News 6604, 6610-11.

25. *E.g.*, *Rich v. Naviera Vacuba SA*, 295 F.2d 24 (4th Cir. 1961) (per curiam) (State Department suggestion of immunity in a clearly commercial case, made as *quid pro quo* to gain release of hijacked airplane). *See* Cardozo, *Judicial Deference to State Department Suggestions*, 48 Corn. L.Q. 461 (1963); Jessup, *Has the Supreme Court Abdicated One of Its Functions?*, 40 Am. J. Int'l L. 168 (1946); H.R. Rep. No. 1487, 94th Cong., 2d Sess. 12, *reprinted in* 1976 U.S. Code Cong. & Admin. News at 6610-11.

26. 28 U.S.C. §§1330, 1602-1611 (1982).

27. 28 U.S.C. §1602 (1982).

28. *See* Verlinden BV v. Central Bank of Nigeria, 461 U.S. 480 (1983).

29. H.R. Rep. No. 1487, 94th Cong., 2d Sess. 12, *reprinted in* 1976 U.S. Code Cong. & Admin. News at 6610-11.

30. 28 U.S.C. §§1604, 1330(a) & (b).

31. 28 U.S.C. §1605.

32. *See supra* p. 66 & *infra* pp. 226-27.

provides that foreign states are liable "to the same extent as a private individual under like circumstances."[33]

Section §1330(a) limits the FSIA's grant of original jurisdiction to federal courts to "nonjury civil" actions. This provision is applicable only to federal court actions against foreign sovereigns, although it applies whether the action was initiated in federal court or removed from state to federal court.[34] Courts that have addressed the question have noted that §1330(a) was meant to prohibit use of juries when foreign sovereigns are sued even where there would otherwise be alternative grounds for subject matter jurisdiction (such as, alienage jurisdiction) that would permit use of a jury.[35] In addition, lower courts have concluded that §1330's provision for nonjury trials does not violate the Seventh Amendment.[36]

Finally, the FSIA contains a variety of provisions dealing with procedural and quasi-procedural issues. These include sections regarding service of process, time for answering, enforcement of judgments, and other matters.[37] These provisions are generally applicable in both federal and state courts.

---

33. *See First National City Bank v. Banco Para El Comercio Exterior de Cuba*, 462 U.S. 611, 620-21 (1983).

34. *See Arango v. Guzman Travel Advisors*, 761 F.2d 1527, 1532 (11th Cir.), *cert. denied*, 474 U.S. 995 (1985).

35. *See McKeel v. Islamic Republic of Iran*, 722 F.2d 582 (9th Cir. 1983), *cert. denied*, 469 U.S. 880 (1984); *Goar v. Compania Peruana de Vapores*, 688 F.2d 417 (5th Cir. 1982); *Rex v. Cia. Peruana de Vapores*, 660 F.2d 61 (3d Cir. 1981), *cert. denied*, 456 U.S. 926 (1982). *But see Icenogle v. Olympic Airways, SA*, 82 F.R.D. 36 (D.D.C. 1979).

36. *Bailey v. Grand Trunk Lines*, 805 F.2d 1097 (2d Cir. 1986); *Arango v. Guzman Travel Advisors Corp.*, 761 F.2d 1527 (11th Cir.), *cert. denied*, 474 U.S. 995 (1985); *Goar v. Compania Peruana de Vapores*, 688 F.2d 417 (5th Cir. 1982); *Rex v. Compania Peruana de Vapores*, 660 F.2d 61 (3d Cir. 1981), *cert. denied*, 456 U.S. 926 (1982); *Ruggiero v. Compania Peruana de Vapores*, 639 F.2d 872 (2d Cir. 1981).

37. *See infra* pp. 836-37 (service), p. 892 (discovery) & p. 951 (enforcement of judgments).

B. Entities Entitled to Immunity Under the FSIA

Only entities that satisfy the FSIA's definition of "foreign states" are entitled to §1604's presumptive grant of immunity. Conversely, only "foreign states" are subject to the FSIA's grants of personal and subject matter jurisdiction.

Section 1603 of the FSIA contains the basic statutory definition of "foreign state." The provision states, in §1603(a), that:

> A "foreign state," except as used in §1608 of this title, includes a political subdivision of a foreign state or an agency or instrumentality of a foreign state as defined in subsection (b).

Thus, §1603(a) defines "foreign state" to include each of three entities: (1) a *"foreign state,"* (2) "a *political subdivision* of a foreign state," and (3) "an *agency or instrumentality* of a foreign state." Section 1603(b) goes on to define an "agency or instrumentality" of a foreign state. The following sections examine each of these various categories.

1. Foreign States Proper

The first of the three categories of "foreign state" encompasses "foreign states proper" — that is, nation states such as the Federal Republic of Germany or the Kingdom of Saudi Arabia. For FSIA purposes, the definition of "foreign state" is generally understood as including any nation recognized by the United States in its diplomatic relations as an independent state. U.S. courts have routinely afforded the FSIA's protections to foreign countries, even when their relations with the United States are acrimonious, provided they enjoy U.S. diplomatic recognition.[38]

International law provides various definitions of "statehood."[39] For purposes of the FSIA, however, the application of these definitions has been left largely to the discretion of the U.S. Executive Branch. Most U.S. courts have said they will defer to the President's decisions regarding the recognition or nonrecognition of foreign states.[40] Nevertheless, atypical foreign entities, such as the Trust Territories and other quasi-national entities that are not recognized by the U.S. executive branch, have been held by some courts to qualify as foreign states because of their state-like characteristics.[41]

The FSIA generally treats "foreign states" in the same fashion as "agencies and

---

38. *E.g., Frolova v. USSR*, 761 F.2d 370 (7th Cir. 1985); *Berkovitz v. Islamic Republic of Iran*, 735 F.2d 329 (9th Cir.), *cert. denied*, 469 U.S. 1035 (1984); *Carey v. National Oil Co.*, 592 F.2d 673 (2d Cir. 1979) (Libya).

39. *E.g., Restatement (Third) Foreign Relations Law* §201 (1987) ("a 'state' is an entity which has a defined territory and permanent population, under the control of its own government, and which engages in, or has the capacity to engage in, formal relations with other such entities.").

40. *See Klinghoffer v. S.N.C. Achille Lauro*, 937 F.2d 44 (2d. Cir. 1991) (PLO is not a foreign state for FSIA purposes); *Transportes Aereos de Angola v. Ronair, Inc.*, 544 F. Supp. 858 (D. Del. 1982).

41. *Compare Morgan Guaranty Trust Co. v. Republic of Palau*, 639 F. Supp. 706 (S.D.N.Y. 1986) (notwithstanding status as Trust Territory, Palau is "foreign state" because of its de facto exercise of sovereign powers) with *Sablan Constr. Co. v. Government of Trust Territory of Pacific Islands*, 526 F. Supp. 135 (D.N. Mar. C. 1981) (Trust Territory is not a "foreign state").

instrumentalities." Nevertheless, it provides differing treatments in some important respects, including service of process, venue, punitive damages, and execution of judgments.[42] Difficulties have occasionally arisen in deciding how to classify, for these purposes, foreign entities that are related to what is concededly a "foreign state," but which also possess a measure of independence from the foreign government. Are such entities: (a) the "foreign state" itself or (b) an "agency" or "instrumentality" of the foreign state? In deciding whether particular foreign entities should be categorized as "foreign states" or "agencies or instrumentalities," courts have generally examined the degree to which the entity is integrated into the foreign government's political and administrative decision-making apparatus.[43] A recent appellate decision holds that the distinction turns on "whether the core functions of the foreign entity are predominantly governmental or commercial."[44]

2. Foreign State "Political Subdivisions"

The definition of foreign state in §1603(a) of the Act includes "political subdivisions" of foreign states.[45] According to the FSIA's legislative history, "[t]he term 'political subdivisions' includes all governmental units beneath the central government, including local governments."[46] Under this definition, the states, provinces, cantons, and other regional subdivisions of foreign nations qualify as "foreign states," while entities established and owned by these subdivisions can qualify as "agencies or instrumentalities of the foreign state."[47] It is not clear how foreign possessions or dependencies of foreign states would be treated under §1603(a).

3. Agencies and Instrumentalities of Foreign States

Foreign state-related entities that are not a foreign state proper or a foreign state's political subdivision nonetheless may qualify as a "foreign state" under §1603(a). To do so, they must fall within the FSIA's definition of "agency or instrumentality of a foreign state." Section 1603(b) of the Act defines an "agency or instrumentality" as an entity:

> (1) which is a separate legal person, corporate or otherwise, and (2) which is an organ of a foreign state or political subdivision thereof, or a majority of

---

42. In each of these contexts, foreign states proper receive different (usually more favorable) treatment than foreign state agencies or instrumentalities. *See* 28 U.S.C. §1608 (service); §1391(f) (venue); §1606 (punitive damages); §§1609-10 (enforcement).

43. *See Unidyne Corp. v. Aerolineas Argentinas*, 590 F. Supp. 398, 400 (E.D. Va. 1984) (Argentine Naval Commission "is part and parcel of the Argentine Navy thereby qualifying as a foreign state or a political subdivision of the Argentine government"); *Marlowe v. Argentine Naval Comm'n*, 604 F. Supp. 703 (D.D.C. 1985) (same).

44. *Transaero Inc. v. La Fuerza Aerea Bolivian*, 30 F.3d 148 (D.C. Cir. 1994).

45. 28 U.S.C. §1603(a) (1982).

46. H.R. Rep. No. 1487, 94th Cong., 2d Sess. 15, *reprinted in* 1976 U.S. Code Cong. & Admin. News at 6613.

47. *Restatement (Third) Foreign Relations Law* §452, comment b (1987). Cities and towns have traditionally not been accorded foreign sovereign immunity. *See Id.* Reporters' Note 1.

whose shares or other ownership interest is owned by a foreign state or political subdivision thereof, and (3) which is neither a citizen of a State of the United States ... nor created under the laws of any third country.

It is clear under §1603(b) that corporations incorporated and doing business within a foreign country and 100 percent owned by that foreign state are ordinarily regarded as foreign state "agenc[ies] or instrumentalit[ies]."[48] Similarly, a foreign company will be treated as a foreign state instrumentality even if it is less than wholly state-owned, provided that the foreign state holds more than 50 percent of the company's ownership interests.[49] The fact that a substantial percentage of the company's shares are publicly traded on a stock exchange, or that the company is engaged solely in ordinary commercial enterprise, does not preclude status as a foreign state agency or instrumentality.[50]

Lower courts appear to be divided about the date for determining whether a party is a foreign state for purposes of the FSIA. Several courts have held that the extent of foreign government ownership is determined as of the date an action is filed, rather than as of the date the claim arose.[51] Other decisions look to the status of the entity at the time the dispute arose.[52]

Lower courts have generally held that a foreign company may enjoy immunity even if its capital stock is held by an administrative agency of the foreign state,[53] or by another state-owned company,[54] rather than directly by the foreign state. Immunity is also available to foreign state companies under the FSIA even if those companies lack immunity under the law of the place where they are organized.[55]

A foreign state-related company is not entitled to immunity if it is less than 50

---

48. *E.g.*, *Alberti v. Empresa Nicaraguense de la Carne*, 705 F.2d 250 (7th Cir. 1983); *S&S Machinery Co. v. Masinenexportimport*, 706 F.2d 411 (2d Cir. 1983); *Arango v. Guzman Travel Advisors Corp.*, 621 F.2d 1371 (5th Cir. 1980); *Lopez del Valle v. Gobierno de la Capital*, 855 F.Supp. 34 (D.P.R. 1994); *Clemente v. Philippine Airlines*, 614 F. Supp. 1196 (S.D.N.Y. 1985).

49. *See* 28 U.S.C. §1603(b) (1982). *E.g.*, *Carey v. National Oil Co.*, 592 F.2d 673, 676 n.1 (2d Cir. 1979).

50. *Erickson v. Alitalia*, 1991 W.L. 117797 (D.N.J. June 5, 1991).

51. *E.g.*, *Cargill Int'l SA v. M/T Pavel Dybenko*, 1993 U.S. App. LEXIS 8433 (2d Cir. 1993); *General Electric Capital Corp. v. Grossman*, 1993 U.S. App. 7688 (8th Cir. 1993); *Callejo v. Bancomer, SA*, 764 F.2d 1101 (5th Cir. 1985).

52. *E.g.*, *Gould, Inc. v. Pechiney Ugine Kuhlmann*, 853 F.2d 445 (6th Cir. 1988); *Morgan Guaranty Trust Co. v. Republic of Palau*, 639 F. Supp. 706, 712 (S.D.N.Y. 1986).

53. *E.g.*, *O'Connell Mach. Co. v. M.V. Americana*, 734 F.2d 115, 116 (2d Cir. 1984) ("The fact that the Italian Government saw fit to double-tier its administrative agencies" does not preclude immunity); *Keller v. Transportes Aeros Militares Ecuadorianos*, 601 F. Supp. 787 (D.D.C. 1985).

54. *Cf. Canadian Overseas Ores v. Compania de Acero del Pacifico*, 528 F. Supp. 1337 (S.D.N.Y. 1982), *aff'd*, 727 F.2d 274 (2d Cir. 1984). *But see Gates v. Victor Fine Foods*, 1995 WL 293946 (9th Cir. 1995) (holding that foreign state proper must hold shares of an entitiy in order for it to qualify as foreign state "agency or instrumentality").

55. *Arriba Ltd. v. Petroleos Mexicanos*, 962 F.2d 528 (5th Cir. 1992) (foreign state-owned company's corporate charter permitted it to sue and be sued in local courts; "enabling legislation without more, is hardly a waiver of [the defendant's] sovereign immunity").

percent state-owned,[56] or if it is incorporated in a different state from that which owns it.[57] One court indicated a willingness to deny a foreign corporation status as an "agency or instrumentality of a foreign state" if the plaintiff could adduce facts showing that the foreign corporation's principal place of business was in the United States.[58] Where several foreign states jointly own a company, but no single state owns more than 50%, lower courts disagree whether §1603(b)'s definition is satisfied.[59]

Particular difficulties have arisen in applying the Act's definition of foreign state "agency or instrumentality" to foreign entities that are not organized along the lines of a stock corporation. The focus of §1603(b) is on the ownership of capital stock and, as one court has observed, this emphasis is "ill-suited to concepts which exist in socialist states," or other legal systems where stock companies are uncommon.[60] As a result, lower courts have reached divergent results in dealing with quasi-commercial entities, particularly in countries with non-Western legal systems. Thus, a Soviet press bureau was held to qualify as a foreign state agency or instrumentality even though the bureau was a separate legal entity that was not "owned" by the Soviet state and that possessed its own property, legal rights, and obligations. In granting immunity, the lower court relied on the fact that the bureau performed a "public function" and that the Soviet government supplied it certain "public" property free of charge.[61] Likewise, a "Committee of Receivers," established by government decree in Dubai, was held to be a foreign state agency or instrumentality because of its governmental charter and responsibilities.[62]

---

56. Thus, an Indonesian company was denied immunity because it failed to provide adequate evidence of its state ownership. *Outbound Maritime Corp. v. P.T. Indonesia Consortium*, 575 F. Supp. 1222 (S.D.N.Y. 1983). *Cf. Outbound Maritime Corp. v. P.T. Indonesian Consortium*, 582 F. Supp. 1136 (D. Md. 1984).

57. *See* 28 U.S.C. §1603(b) (1982).

58. *Bailey v. Grand Trunk Lines New England*, 609 F. Supp. 48 (D.Vt. 1984), *vacated in part*, 805 F.2d 1097 (2d Cir. 1986), *cert. denied*, 108 S.Ct. 96 (1987).

59. *Compare Mangattu v. M/V Ibn Hayyan*, 35 F.2d 205 (5th Cir. 1994) *with Linton v. Airbus Industrie*, 794 F.Supp. 650 (S.D. Tex. 1992).

60. *Yessenin-Volpin v. Novosti Press Agency*, 443 F. Supp. 849, 852 (S.D.N.Y. 1978).

61. 443 F. Supp. at 854 ("whether one relies on the fact that more than 63% of the property over which Novosti exercises the rights of possession and use is actually 'owned' by the state, or whether one looks to [its] essentially public nature the defendant is an 'agency or instrumentality' or an 'organ'"). *Cf. Gates v. Victor Fine Foods*, 1995 WL 293946 (9th Cir. 1995) (Canadian corporation, owned by private parties, held to be foreign state "organ" because of its role in governmental policy); *S&S Mach. Co. v. Masinenexportimport*, 706 F.2d 411 (2d Cir.), *cert. denied*, 464 U.S. 850 (1983); *Edlow Int'l Co. v. Nuklearna Elektrarna Krsko*, 441 F. Supp. 827 (D.D.C. 1977) (Yugoslav workers' cooperative at a nuclear power plant was found not to be an agency or instrumentality of a foreign state because there was no showing that the Yugoslav government actually owned the cooperative or that the cooperative performed "governmental" functions).

62. *Refco, Inc. v. Galadari*, 755 F.Supp. 79 (S.D.N.Y. 1991).

C. Attribution Of Liability Between Foreign Government Entities

Foreign states routinely establish a wide range of governmental, administrative, and corporate entities to perform various functions.[63] These entities possess varying degrees of functional and legal separation from the foreign state that creates them. Some foreign governmental entities are merely ad hoc administrative bodies, without separate legal identity under foreign law, that function as integral parts of the foreign government; other foreign governmental entities are separate juridical persons, with an independent legal status under foreign law. Examples of the latter include state-owned corporations such as airlines, banks, or shipping companies.

As discussed above, a foreign state agency or instrumentality that possesses separate legal status is treated as a foreign state "agency or instrumentality," as distinct from the "foreign state" proper, by the FSIA.[64] In general, U.S. courts will recognize the separate legal identity of such agencies and instrumentalities.[65] Nevertheless, there are circumstances in which the actions or liability of one foreign state instrumentality will be attributed to another agency, or to the foreign state itself. The issue can arise in a variety of circumstances, including cases attempting to enforce a judgment made as to one entity against a second entity, cases attempting to attribute one entity's jurisdictional contacts to a second entity, and cases asserting a claim or counterclaim based on the acts of one entity against a different entity. The Supreme Court addressed the question of the separate juridical status of a foreign state entity in *First National City Bank v. Banco Para El Comercio Exterior de Cuba ("Bancec")*.

FIRST NATIONAL CITY BANK v. BANCO PARA EL COMERCIO EXTERIOR DE CUBA
462 U.S. 611 (1983)

JUSTICE O'CONNOR. In 1960 the Government of the Republic of Cuba established respondent Banco Para El Comercio Exterior de Cuba ("Bancec") to serve as "[a]n official autonomous credit institution for foreign trade ... with full juridical capacity ... of its own. ..." Law No. 793, Art. 1 (1960). In September 1960 Bancec sought to collect on a letter of credit issued by petitioner First National City Bank (now Citibank) in its favor in support of a contract for delivery of Cuban sugar to a buyer in the United States. Within days after Citibank received the request for collection, all of its assets in Cuba were seized and nationalized by the Cuban Government.

---

63. *See* Hoffman, *The Separate Entity Rule in International Perspective: Should State Ownership of Corporate Shares Confer Sovereign Status for Immunity Purposes?*, 65 Tulane L. Rev. 535 (1991); Note, *Jurisdiction Over Foreign States for Acts of Their Instrumentalities: A Model for Attributing Liabilities*, 94 Yale L.J. 394 (1984).

64. *See supra* pp. 214-16.

65. *See First National City Bank v. Bancec*, 462 U.S. 611 (1983).

When Bancec brought suit on the letter of credit in U.S. District Court, Citibank counterclaimed, asserting a right to set off the value of its seized Cuban assets. The question before us is whether Citibank may obtain such a setoff, notwithstanding the fact that Bancec was established as a separate juridical entity. Applying principles of equity common to international law and federal common law, we conclude that Citibank may apply a setoff.

I. ... Bancec was established by Law No. 793, of April 25, 1960, as the legal successor to the Banco Cubano del Comercio Exterior ("Cuban Foreign Trade Bank"), a trading bank established by the Cuban Government in 1954 and jointly owned by the Government and private banks. ... Bancec's stated purpose was "to contribute to, and collaborate with the international trade policy of the Government and the application of the measures concerning foreign trade adopted by the 'Banco Nacional de Cuba,'" Cuba's central bank ("Banco Nacional"). Bancec was empowered to act as the Cuban Government's exclusive agent in foreign trade. The Government supplied all of its capital and owned all of its stock. The General Treasury of the Republic received all of Bancec's profits, after deduction of amounts for capital reserves. A Governing Board consisting of delegates from Cuban governmental ministries governed and managed Bancec. Its president was Ernesto Che Guevara, who also was Minister of State and president of Banco Nacional. A General Manager appointed by the Governing Board was charged with directing Bancec's day-to-day operations in a manner consistent with its enabling statute.

In contracts signed on August 12, 1960, Bancec agreed to purchase a quantity of sugar from [INRA], an instrumentality of the Cuban Government which owned and operated Cuba's nationalized sugar industry, and to sell it to the Cuban Canadian Sugar Company. The latter sale agreement was supported by an irrevocable letter of credit in favor of Bancec issued by Citibank on August 18, 1960, which Bancec assigned to Banco Nacional for collection. Meanwhile, in July 1960 the Cuban Government enacted Law No. 851, which provided for the nationalization of the Cuban properties of United States citizens. By Resolution No. 2 of September 17, 1960, the Government ordered that all of the Cuban property of three U.S. banks, including Citibank, be nationalized through forced expropriation. ...

On or about September 15, 1960, before the banks were nationalized, Bancec's draft was presented to Citibank for payment by Banco Nacional. The amount sought was $193,280.30 for sugar delivered at Pascagoula, Mississippi. On September 20, 1960, after its branches were nationalized, Citibank credited the requested amount to Banco Nacional's account and applied the balance in Banco Nacional's account as a setoff against the value of its Cuban branches.

On Februry 1, 1961, Bancec brought this diversity action to recover on the letter of credit in the U.S. District Court for the Southern District of New York. On February 23, 1961, by Law No. 930, Bancec was dissolved and its capital was split between Banco Nacional and "the foreign trade enterprises or houses of the Ministry of Foreign Trade," which was established by Law No. 934 the same day. All of

Bancec's rights, claims, and assets "peculiar to the banking business" were vested in Banco Nacional, which also succeeded to its banking obligations. All of Bancec's "trading functions" were to be assumed by "the foreign trade enterprise or houses of the Ministry of Foreign Trade." By Resolution No. 1, dated March 1, 1961, the Ministry of Foreign Trade created [Empresa, a state entity,] which was empowered to conduct all commercial export transactions formerly conducted by Bancec "remaining subrogated in the rights and obligations of said bank [Bancec] as regards the commercial export activities."

... Citibank's answer alleged that [Bancec's] suit was "brought by and for the benefit of the Republic of Cuba by and through its agent and wholly-owned instrumentality, [Bancec,] ... which is in fact and in law and in form and function an integral part of and indistinguishable from the Republic of Cuba." ... [T]he District Court granted judgment in favor of Citibank. The court rejected Bancec's contention that its separate juridical status shielded it from liability for the acts of the Cuban Government. [It reasoned:] "Under all of the relevant circumstances shown in this record, ... it is clear that Bancec lacked an independent existence, and was a mere arm of the Cuban Government, performing a purely governmental function. The control of Bancec was exclusively in the hands of the Government, and Bancec was established solely to further Governmental purposes. Moreover, Bancec was totally dependent on the Government for financing and required to remit all of its profits to the Government." ... [The] Second Circuit reversed. While expressing agreement with the District Court's "descriptions of Bancec's functions and its status as a wholly-owned instrumentality of the Cuban government," the court concluded that "Bancec was not an alter ego of the Cuban government for the purpose of [Citibank's] counterclaims."

IIA. As an initial matter, Bancec contends that the FSIA immunizes an instrumentality owned by a foreign government from suit on a counterclaim based on actions taken by that government. Bancec correctly concedes that, under 28 U.S.C. §1607(c), an instrumentality of a foreign state bringing suit in a United States court is not entitled to immunity "with respect to any counterclaim —... to the extent that the counterclaim does not seek relief exceeding in amount or differing in kind from that sought by the [instrumentality.]" It contends, however, that as a substantive matter the FSIA prohibits holding a foreign instrumentality owned and controlled by a foreign government responsible for actions taken by that government.

We disagree. The language and history of the FSIA clearly establish that the Act was not intended to affect the substantive law determining the liability of a foreign state or instrumentality, or the attribution of liability among instrumentalities of a foreign state. Section 1606 of the FSIA provides in relevant part that "[a]s to any claim for relief with respect to which a foreign state is not entitled to immunity ..., the foreign state shall be liable in the same manner and to the same extent as a private individual under like circumstances. ..." The House Report on the FSIA states: "The bill is not intended to affect the substantive law of liability. Nor is it intended to affect ... the attribution of responsibility between or among entities of a foreign state; for example, whether the proper entity of a foreign state has been sued, or whether an entity sued is liable in whole or in part for the claimed wrong." H.R. Rep. No. 94-1487, p. 12 (1976), U.S. Code Cong. & Admin. News 1976, pp. 6604, 6610. ...

B. We must next decide which body of law determines the effect to be given to Bancec's separate juridical status. Bancec contends that internationally recognized conflict-of-law principles require the application of the law of the state that establishes a government instrumentality — here Cuba — to determine whether the instrumentality may be held liable for actions taken by the sovereign.

We cannot agree. As a general matter, the law of the state of incorporation normally determines issues relating to the internal affairs of a corporation. Application of that body of law achieves the need for certainty and predictability of result while generally protecting the justified expectations of parties with interests in the corporation. Different conflicts principles apply, however, where the rights of third parties external to the corporation are at issue. See Restatement (Second) of Conflict of Laws §301 & §302, Comments a & e (1971). To give conclusive effect to the law of the chartering state in determining whether the separate juridical status of its instrumentality should be respected would permit the state to violate with impunity the rights of third parties under international law while effectively insulating itself from liability in foreign courts. We decline to permit such a result.[66]

Bancec contends in the alternative that international law must determine the resolution of the question presented. Citibank, on the other hand, suggests that federal common law governs. The expropriation claim against which Bancec seeks to interpose its separate juridical status arises under international law, which, as we have frequently reiterated, "is part of our law. ..." The Paquete Habana, 175 U.S. 677, 700 (1900). As we set forth below, the principles governing this case are common to both international law and federal common law, which in these circumstances is necessarily informed both by international law principles and by articulated congressional policies.

---

66. Pointing out that 28 U.S.C. §1606, contains language identical to the Federal Tort Claims Act ("FTCA"), 28 U.S.C. §2674, Bancec also contends alternatively that the FSIA, like the FTCA, requires application of the law of the forum state — here New York — including its conflicts principles. We disagree. Section 1606 provides that "[a]s to any claim for relief with respect to which a foreign state is not entitled to immunity ..., the foreign state shall be liable in the same manner and to the same extent as a private individual in like circumstances." Thus, where state law provides a rule of liability governing private individuals, the FSIA requires the application of that rule to foreign states in like circumstances. The statute is silent, however, concerning the rule governing the attribution of liability among entities of a foreign state. In Banco Nacional de Cuba v. Sabbatino, this Court declined to apply the State of New York's act of state doctrine in a diversity action between a United States national and an instrumentality of a foreign state, concluding that matters bearing on the nation's foreign relations "should not be left to divergent and perhaps parochial state interpretations." When it enacted the FSIA, Congress expressly acknowledged "the importance of developing a uniform body of law" concerning the amenability of a foreign sovereign to suit in United States courts. H.R. Rep. No. 94-1487, p. 32. In our view, these same considerations preclude the application of New York law here.

IIIA. ... Increasingly during this century, governments throughout the world have established separately constituted legal entities to perform a variety of tasks. The organization and control of these entities vary considerably, but many possess a number of common features. A typical government instrumentality, if one can be said to exist, is created by an enabling statute that prescribes the powers and duties of the instrumentality, and specifies that it is to be managed by a board selected by the government in a manner consistent with the enabling law. The instrumentality is typically established as a separate juridical entity, with the powers to hold and sell property and to sue and be sued. Except for appropriations to provide capital or to cover losses, the instrumentality is primarily responsible for its own finances. The instrumentality is run as a distinct economic enterprise; often it is not subject to the same budgetary and personnel requirements with which government agencies must comply. These distinctive features permit government instrumentalities to manage their operations on an enterprise basis while granting them a greater degree of flexibility and independence from close political control than is generally enjoyed by government agencies. These same features frequently prompt governments in developing countries to establish separate juridical entities as the vehicles through which to obtain the financial resources needed to make large-scale national investments. ...

Separate legal personality has been described as "an almost indispensable aspect of the public corporation." Provisions in the corporate charter stating that the instrumentality may sue and be sued have been construed to waive the sovereign immunity accorded to many governmental activities, thereby enabling third parties to deal with the instrumentality knowing that they may seek relief in the courts. Similarly, the instrumentality's assets and liabilities must be treated as distinct from those of its sovereign in order to facilitate credit transactions with third parties. Thus what the Court stated with respect to private corporations in *Anderson v. Abbott*, 321 U.S. 349 (1944), is true also for governmental corporations: "Limited liability is the rule, not the exception; and on that assumption large undertakings are rested, vast enterprises are launched, and huge sums of capital attracted."

Freely ignoring the separate status of government instrumentalities would result in substantial uncertainty over whether an instrumentality's assets would be diverted to satisfy a claim against the sovereign, and might thereby cause third parties to hesitate before extending credit to a government instrumentality without the government's guarantee. As a result, the efforts of sovereign nations to structure their governmental activities in a manner deemed necessary to promote economic development and efficient administration would surely be frustrated. Due respect for the actions taken by foreign sovereigns and for principles of comity between nations, *see Hilton v. Guyot*, 159 U.S. 113, 163-164 (1895), leads us to conclude — as the courts of Great Britain have concluded in other circumstances[67] — that government instru-

---

67. [The Court cited *C. Czarnikow, Ltd. v. Rolimpex*, [1979] A.C. 351, 364; *I Congreso del Partido*, [1983] A.C. 244, 271.]

mentalities established as juridical entities distinct and independent from their sovereign should normally be treated as such.

We find support for this conclusion in the legislative history of the FSIA. During its deliberations, Congress clearly expressed its intention that duly created instrumentalities of a foreign state are to be accorded a presumption of independent status. In its discussion of FSIA §1610(b), the provision dealing with the circumstances under which a judgment creditor may execute upon the assets of an instrumentality of a foreign government, the House Report states: "Section 1610(b) will not permit execution against the property of one agency or instrumentality to satisfy a judgment against another, unrelated agency or instrumentality. There are compelling reasons for this. If U.S. law did not respect the separate juridical identities of different agencies or instrumentalities, it might encourage foreign jurisdictions to disregard the juridical divisions between different U.S. corporations or between a U.S. corporation and its independent subsidiary. However, a court might find that property held by one agency is really the property of another." H.R. Rep. No. 94-1487, pp. 29-30, U.S. Code Cong. & Admin. News 1976, pp. 6628-6629. Thus, the presumption that a foreign government's determination that its instrumentality is to be accorded separate legal status is buttressed by this congressional determination. We next examine whether this presumption may be overcome in certain circumstances.

B. In discussing the legal status of private corporations, courts in the United States[68] and abroad,[69] have recognized that an incorporated entity ... is not to be regarded as legally separate from its owners in all circumstances. Thus, where a corporate entity is so extensively controlled by its owner that a relationship of principal and agent is created, we have held that one may be held liable for the actions of the other. *See NLRB v. Deena Artware, Inc.*, 361 U.S. 398, 402-404 (1960). In addition, our cases have long recognized "the broader equitable principle that the doctrine of corporate entity, recognized generally and for most purposes, will not be regarded when to do so would work fraud or injustice." *Taylor v. Standard Gas Co.*, 306 U.S. 307, 322 (1939). In particular, the Court has consistently refused to give effect to the corporate form where it is interposed to defeat legislative policies. And, in *Bangor Punta Operations, Inc. v. Bangor & Aroostook Railroad Co.*, 417 U.S. 703 (1974), we concluded:

---

68. *See* 1 W.M. Fletcher, *Cyclopedia of the Law of Private Corporations* §41 (Rev. Perm. Ed. 1974): "[A] corporation will be looked upon as a legal entity as a general rule, and until sufficient reason to the contrary appears; but, when the notion of legal entity is used to defeat public convenience, justify wrong, protect fraud, or defend crime, the law will regard the corporation as an association of persons."

69. In *Case Concerning The Barcelona Traction, Light & Power Co.*, 1970 I.C.J. 3, the International Court of Justice acknowledged that, as a matter of international law, the separate status of an incorporated entity may be disregarded in certain exceptional circumstances: "... It is in this context that the process of 'lifting the corporate veil' or 'disregarding the legal entity' has been found justified and equitable in certain circumstances or for certain purposes. The wealth of practice already accumulated on the subject in municipal law indicates that the veil is lifted, for instance, to prevent misuse of the privileges of legal personality, as in certain cases of fraud or malfeasance, to protect third persons such as a creditor or purchaser, or to prevent the evasion of legal requirements or of obligations." *Id.* at 38-39.

Although a corporation and its shareholders are deemed separate entities for most purposes, the corporate form may be disregarded in the interests of justice where it is used to defeat an overriding public policy. ... [W]here equity would preclude the shareholders from maintaining the action in their own right, the corporation would also be precluded. ... [T]he principal beneficiary of any recovery and itself estopped from complaining of petitioners' alleged wrongs, cannot avoid the command of equity through the guise of proceeding in the name of ... corporations which it owns and controls.

C. We conclude today that similar equitable principles must be applied here. In *National City Bank v. Republic of China*, 348 U.S. 356 (1955), the Court ruled that when a foreign sovereign asserts a claim in a U.S. court, "the consideration of fair dealing" bars the state from asserting a defense of sovereign immunity to defeat a setoff or counterclaim. *See* 28 U.S.C. §1607(c). As a general matter, therefore, the Cuban Government could not bring suit in a U.S. court without also subjecting itself to its adversary's counterclaim. Here there is apparently no dispute that, ... "the devolution of [Bancec's] claim, however viewed, brings it into the hands of the Ministry [of Foreign Trade], or Banco Nacional," each a party that may be held liable for the expropriation of Citibank's assets. Bancec was dissolved even before Citibank filed its answer in this case, apparently in order to effect "the consolidation and operation of the economic and social conquests of the Revolution" ... Thus, the Cuban Government and Banco Nacional, not any third parties that may have relied on Bancec's separate juridical identity, would be the only beneficiaries of any recovery. In our view, this situation is similar to that in the *Republic of China* case. "We have a foreign government invoking our law but resisting a claim against it which fairly would curtail its recovery. It wants our law, like any other litigant, but it wants our law free from the claims of justice."

Giving effect to Bancec's separate juridical status in these circumstances, even though it has long been dissolved, would permit the real beneficiary of such an action, the Government of the Republic of Cuba, to obtain relief in our courts that it could not obtain in its own right without waiving its sovereign immunity and answering for the seizure of Citibank's assets — a seizure previously held by the Court of Appeals to have violated international law. We decline to adhere blindly to the corporate form where doing so would cause such an injustice.

Respondent contends, however, that the transfer of Bancec's assets from the Ministry of Foreign Trade or Banco Nacional to Empresa and Cuba Zucar effectively insulates it from Citibank's counterclaim. We disagree. Having dissolved Bancec and transferred its assets to entities that may be held liable on Citibank's counterclaim, Cuba cannot escape liability for acts in violation of international law simply by retransferring the assets to separate juridical entities. To hold otherwise would permit governments to avoid the requirements of international law simply by creating juridical entities whenever the need arises. We therefore hold that Citibank may set off the value of its assets seized by the Cuban Government against the amount sought by Bancec.

IV. Our decision today announces no mechanical formula for determining the circumstances under which the normally separate juridical status of a government instrumentality is to be disregarded.[70] Instead, it is the product of the application of internationally recognized equitable principles to avoid the injustice that would result from permitting a foreign state to reap the benefits of our courts while avoiding the obligations of international law.

Notes on Bancec

1. *FSIA does not address substantive liability.* The FSIA is generally silent regarding a foreign state's substantive liability. Section 1606 of the FSIA provides that a foreign state will be liable "to the same extent as a private individual under like circumstances." Why was this approach adopted? What were the alternatives?

In one exception to this approach, §1606 forbids state or federal courts from awarding punitive damages against a foreign state. In contrast, §1606 expressly permits punitive damages to be awarded against foreign state agencies or instrumentalities. *E.g., Gibbons v. Ireland*, 532 F. Supp. 668 (D.D.C. 1982); *Letelier v. Republic of Chile*, 502 F.Supp. 259 (D.D.C. 1980); *Outboard Marine Corp. v. Pezetel*, 461 F. Supp. 384 (D. Del. 1978).

2. *Role of international law in* Bancec. Consider the role of international law in *Bancec.* Why does the Court consider international law in *Bancec?* Does the Court apply international law directly in the U.S. action; does it look to international law as persuasive, but not binding authority; does it leave open the question of the relationship between international and federal law; or does it do something else? Compare the role of international law in *Bancec* to that in *Pennoyer, Schooner Exchange*, and *Filartiga*.

3. *Federal common law rule in* Bancec. What was the basis for the rule of law adopted by *Bancec* with respect to the separate legal identity of foreign state entities? Does the FSIA address this issue? If not, then why don't ordinary state (or foreign) law rules on the subject apply? Why doesn't §1606 dictate that state law rules apply? What is the basis for adopting a rule of federal common law in *Bancec?* What makes the separate legal identity of Bancec any different from the separate legal identity of major companies like Citibank? Federal law does not generally govern this issue with respect to private entities; why should it do so with respect to foreign states?

Consider the standards set forth in *Boyle, supra* pp. 15-16, for the formation of rules of federal common law. Did the veil piercing issue in *Bancec* involve a "uniquely federal" area? Did the Court consider whether there was a "significant conflict" between federal policies under the FSIA and otherwise applicable law? What if state law provided for a very expansive alter ego theory based solely on "economic integration"? What if state law limited veil-piercing very narrowly?

4. *Presumption that foreign state's separate legal entity will be respected.* Is *Bancec* correct in concluding that a foreign state entity's separate legal status should presumptively be respected? Bancec was organized under Cuban law — not New York or other U.S. law. Why should a U.S. court give any effect to purported provisions of Cuban law that are said to grant Bancec a separate legal identity? What reasons does *Bancec* give for presumptively deferring to Cuban law?

Is it correct to analogize a foreign state-owned entity (like Bancec) to private companies? Does it matter that the relevant foreign law in *Bancec* was Cuban — the law of a state with a legal and political system which is fundamentally different from that of the United States? Would it be appropriate to distinguish between democracies with developed legal systems and other nations?

---

70. The District Court adopted, and both Citibank and the Solicitor General urge upon the Court, a standard in which the determination whether or not to give effect to the separate juridical status of a government instrumentality turns in part on whether the instrumentality in question performed a "governmental function." We decline to adopt such a standard in this case, as our decision is based on other grounds. We do observe that the concept of a "usual" or a "proper" governmental function changes over time and varies from nation to nation. ...

What would be the result if Cuban law had also provided that the Cuban state was ultimately responsible for the liabilities of Bancec? or that Bancec's shareholders were liable for its unsatisfied obligations? Should U.S. courts nevertheless respect its "separate" legal identity?

5. *Standards for ignoring the separate legal identity of a foreign state entity.* In what circumstances does *Bancec* permit a U.S. court to ignore the separate legal identity of a foreign state entity? Although the Court's opinion is not entirely clear, it appears to identify three conceivable bases for ignoring separate legal identity: (a) sufficiently extensive control; (b) to prevent fraud or injustice; and (c) public policy. In fashioning these standards, the Court relied principally on its own decisions in the context of private corporations in domestic U.S. cases. Is that an appropriate basis for rules governing foreign sovereign entities? In the context of state-owned entities, does the state not ultimately exercise greater control than in the context of private entities?

6. *Application of* Bancec *standards.* Why did *Bancec* conclude that Citibank could set off against Bancec's affirmative claims Cuba's liabilities to Citibank? What precisely led to the finding that Bancec's separate legal status could be ignored?

7. *Governmental functions test.* Consider the final footnote of the Court's opinion, describing an argument advanced by Citibank and the U.S. Department of Justice: "whether or not to give effect to the separate juridical status of a government instrumentality [should] turn[] in part on whether the instrumentality in question performed a governmental function." The Court expresses skepticism about this theory, and declines to adopt it (while also not rejecting it). Why would it be relevant to alter ego analysis to consider whether a state entity performs governmental functions? Note that the Court refused to accept the views of the U.S. government on a sensitive issue of international law and foreign relations. Is that appropriate?

8. *Lower court applications of* Bancec. It is unclear how significant a role *Bancec* will play in litigation against foreign states. In general, lower courts have been reluctant to disregard the separate legal structures of foreign state entities. Most courts have emphasized that foreign sovereign entities enjoy presumptively separate status and that the plaintiff bears a heavy burden in overcoming this presumption. *E.g.*, *NYSA-ILA Pension Trust Fund v. Garuda Indonesia*, 7 F.3d 35 (2d Cir. 1993); *Federal Ins. Co. v. Richard I. Rubin & Co.*, 1993 U.S. App. Lexis 33704 (3d Cir. 1993); *Hester Int'l Corp. v. Federal Republic of Nigeria*, 879 F.2d 170, 176-81 (5th Cir. 1989); *Hercaine Int'l, Inc. v. Argentina*, 821 F.2d 559 (11th Cir. 1987).

D. Bases for Judicial Jurisdiction Over Foreign States

The FSIA's general grant of jurisdictional immunity for "foreign states" is subject to important exceptions, set forth in §§1605 through 1607 of the Act.[71] These exceptions generally implement the restrictive theory of sovereign immunity, granting immunity for many "public" or "sovereign" acts and denying it for "private" or commercial activities. In outline, the Act denies sovereign immunity for eight statutory reasons: (1) waiver; (2) commercial activity with a U.S. nexus; (3) taking of property, located in the United States, in violation of international law; (4) rights to property in the United States that were acquired by succession or gift, or rights to immoveable property situated in the United States; (5) noncommercial torts in the United States; (6) arbitration-related matters; (7) certain admiralty matters; and (8) counterclaims. In addition, §1604 makes it clear that foreign state immunity is subject to variation by international agreement.

The plain language of the FSIA, as well as the Act's legislative history, makes it clear that these exceptions are the *exclusive* circumstances in which a foreign state will be denied immunity in U.S. courts.[72] The Supreme Court so held in *Argentine Republic v. Amerada Hess Shipping Corp.*, where it rejected the argument that the Alien Tort Statute provides an exception to the FSIA for violations of international law.[73]

As discussed above, the FSIA does not merely *deny* immunity when one of these exceptions applies to a foreign state's conduct. In addition, whenever an exception to immunity exists, the Act provides federal courts an *affirmative* grant of both personal and subject matter jurisdiction.[74] In short, the terse formulae of §1605's exceptions simultaneously serve three critical functions in litigation against foreign states: they grant personal jurisdiction, grant subject matter jurisdiction, and deny immunity.[75]

Some lower courts have been critical of both the FSIA's amalgamation of principles of immunity and jurisdiction and its sometimes cryptic language. In one court's view, the FSIA is "remarkably obtuse" and a "statutory labyrinth that, owing to the numerous interpretive questions engendered by its bizarre structure and its many deliberately vague provisions, has during its lifetime been a financial boon for the private bar but a constant bane of the federal judiciary."[76] Although these criticisms

---

71. 28 U.S.C. §1604 (1982). The general grant of foreign sovereign immunity from jurisdiction is also subject to any "existing international agreements to which the United States is a party at the time of enactment" of the FSIA. *Id.*

72. 28 U.S.C. §1602; H.R. Rep. No. 1487, 94th Cong., 2d Sess. 12, *reprinted in* 1976 U.S. Code Cong. & Admin. News at 6610.

73. 504 U.S. 607 (1989).

74. *See supra* pp. 66 & 211; 28 U.S.C. §§1330(a) & (b) (1982).

75. *See Verlinden BV v. Central Bank of Nigeria*, 461 U.S. 480, 488-90 (1983).

76. *Gibbons v. Udaras Na Gaeltachta*, 549 F. Supp. 1094, 1105-06 (S.D.N.Y. 1982). *See also Vencedora Oceanica Navigacion, SA v. Compagnie Nationale Algerienne de Navigation*, 730 F.2d 195 (5th Cir. 1984); *Texas Trading & Milling Corp. v. Federal Republic of Nigeria*, 647 F.2d 300 (2d Cir. 1981), *cert. denied*, 454 U.S. 1148 (1982).

may be somewhat overstated,[77] the Act's exceptions are complex and require careful attention. The following sections examine three of §1605's most significant exceptions to jurisdictional immunity — waiver, commercial activity with a nexus to the United States, and tortious conduct within the United States.

1. Waiver of Sovereign Immunity

The FSIA denies foreign states immunity where they have waived, or can be *Waiver* deemed to have waived, their immunity. Section 1605(a)(1) provides that a foreign state will not enjoy immunity if it "has waived its immunity either explicitly or by implication."[78] The Act provides no further guidance regarding what will constitute a waiver under §1605(a)(1), and the FSIA's legislative history is only slightly more illuminating:

> With respect to implicit waivers, the courts have found such waivers in cases where a foreign state has agreed to arbitration in another country or *Arbitration* where a foreign state has agreed that the law of a particular country should *Choice of Law* govern a contract. An implicit waiver would also include a situation where a foreign state has filed a responsive pleading in an action without raising the *Responsive* defense of foreign sovereign immunity.[79] *pleading*

Although the proposition that a foreign state should be held to a waiver of its sovereign immunity appears straightforward, lower courts have encountered difficulty applying §1605(a)(1). First, it has not always been clear whether particular foreign state acts or agreements constitute implied waivers of immunity under §1605(a)(1). In particular, choice of law and choice of forum clauses have presented thorny questions of interpretation.

Second, unlike §1605's other exceptions to immunity, neither §1605(a)(1) nor its legislative history appear to require any nexus between a foreign state's waiver and the United States.[80] Read literally, §1605(a)(1) would permit U.S. jurisdiction in all cases involving *any* "waiver" of immunity by a foreign state, even if a case has no connection to the United States and even if the foreign state's waiver was intended to apply only to proceedings in another country's courts. The case excerpted below — *Verlinden BV v. Central Bank of Nigeria* — illustrates both of these difficulties.

---

77. *See* Feldman, *The United States Foreign Sovereign Immunities Act of 1976 in Perspective: A Founder's View*, 35 Int'l & Comp. L.Q. 302 (1986).

78. 28 U.S.C. §1605(a)(1).

79. H.R. Rep. No. 1487, 94th Cong., 2d Sess. 18, *reprinted in* 1976 U.S. Code Cong. & Admin. News at 6617.

80. *Compare* 28 U.S.C. §1605(a)(2) ("commercial activity carried on *in the United States*") *and* §1605(a)(5) (noncommercial tort "occurring *in the United States*"). *See Verlinden BV v. Central Bank of Nigeria*, 461 U.S. 480, 490 n.15 (1983).

VERLINDEN BV v. CENTRAL BANK OF NIGERIA

488 F. Supp. 1284 (S.D.N.Y. 1980)

WEINFELD, DISTRICT JUDGE. Verlinden BV ("Verlinden") a Dutch corporation with its principal offices in Amsterdam, The Netherlands, commenced this action for anticipatory breach of an irrevocable documentary letter of credit established in its favor by the defendant Central Bank of Nigeria, and advised and payable by its correspondent bank, Morgan Guaranty Trust Company in New York. The defendant Central Bank of Nigeria ("Central Bank") is the central bank of the Federal Republic of Nigeria ("Nigeria") and is an "agency or instrumentality of a foreign state" within the meaning of the FSIA.

Although the instant action is based upon the alleged breach and repudiation by Central Bank of its obligations with respect to the irrevocable letter of credit, in order to put the matter into proper perspective, it is necessary to refer to events prior and subsequent to its issuance. On April 21, 1975, plaintiff entered into a contract whereby Nigeria agreed to buy from plaintiff, 240,000 metric tons of Portland Cement for the price of $60 per ton, or a total of $14,400,000.[81] The Nigerian government agreed to establish, within 21 days after the contract was signed, "an Irrevocable, Transferable abroad, Divisible and confirmed Letter of Credit in favor of the seller for the total purchase price through Slavenburg's Bank, Amsterdam, Netherlands."[82] ... The parties also agreed that the contract was to be governed by the Laws of the Netherlands and that disputes arising thereunder would be resolved by arbitration before the International Chamber of Commerce, Paris, France. ...

[O]n June 23, 1975 the defendant established its Documentary Credit No. CBN/BP/75/145 ("the letter of credit" or "the credit") in favor of plaintiff for the full contract price ($14,400,000); the credit included [as required by Nigeria's cement agreement with plaintiff] an open-ended amount for demurrage, to be paid at the rate of $3,500 per day per vessel. However, contrary to the terms of the cement agreement, the letter of credit was advised by and made payable through Morgan Guaranty Bank in New York, rather than plaintiff's bank (Slavenburg's) in the Netherlands [and, in addition, the credit varied from the terms of the cement agreement in other material respects]. ...

In August 1975, the ports of Nigeria became bottlenecked with hundreds of ships carrying cargoes of cement, sent by more than 68 other cement suppliers from whom Nigeria had purchased cement. As a result of the increasing congestion in these ports, Central Bank commencing in mid-September 1975 unilaterally directed its correspondent banks, including Morgan, to adopt a series of amendments to all irrevocable letters of credit issued in connection with the cement contracts. In

---

81. The contract was signed by the "Permanent Secretary, Ministry of Defense, Lagos ... on behalf of the Federal Military Government of the Federal Republic of Nigeria."

82. The letter of credit was to be governed by the Uniform Customs and Practice for Documentary Credits (The International Chamber of Commerce Brochure No. 222) (1962 Revision)... .

essence, the advising banks were directed to stop demurrage payments against documents unless those documents had been sent to and certified for payment by Central Bank. ... It can hardly be questioned — and the parties do not seriously dispute the fact — that these unilateral amendments to the irrevocable letter of credit constitute violations of the Uniform Customs and Practice for Documentary Credits the terms of which, by stipulation of the parties, are applicable.

Plaintiff alleges that, in reliance upon the issuance of an irrevocable letter of credit as agreed upon, it contracted with another European concern, Interbuco Anstalt, Vaduz, Liechtenstein ("Interbuco"), for the purchase of cement and thereby exposed itself to a potential liability in liquidated damages. It seeks to recover damages for payments already made or owing to Interbuco, as well as its own lost profits, counsel fees and expenses in the sum of $4,660,000 as compensatory damages and punitive damages in a like amount. Presently before the Court are the defendant's motion to dismiss the action for, [among other things,] lack of subject matter jurisdiction [and] lack of in personam jurisdiction over Central Bank based upon sovereign immunity. ...

Foreign states are not immune from the jurisdiction of the courts of the United States in any case "(1) in which the foreign state has waived its immunity either explicitly or by implication, ... notwithstanding any withdrawal of the waiver which the foreign state may purport to effect except in accordance with the terms of the waiver." ... There is no assertion in the case at bar that the defendant has explicitly waived its immunity; instead, plaintiff argues that Central Bank has implicitly waived its immunity in two related aspects. The cement contract signed by Nigeria and Verlinden contains the following provision:

> The construction, validity and performance of *this contract* shall be governed by the Laws of the Netherlands and all disputes of any nature whatsoever which may arise under, out of, in connection with, or in relation to *this contract* shall be submitted to the arbitration of the International Chamber of Commerce, Paris, France, in accordance with its Rules at the date thereof. (Emphasis supplied.)

Plaintiff contends that Nigeria's choice of a foreign forum for arbitration and of foreign law precludes it from asserting any immunity, on its own behalf or that of its instrumentalities, with respect to any issue connected with the Verlinden cement contract. Specifically, Verlinden contends that Nigeria's choice of Dutch law and a French tribunal constitutes a waiver of objection to American jurisdiction, and that this waiver is binding as well upon Central Bank, Nigeria's instrumentality charged with the task of making payments under the cement contract. Some support for this view appears in the cryptic language of the Congressional report, which noted:

> With respect to implicit waivers, the courts have found such waivers in cases where a foreign state has agreed to arbitration in another country or where a foreign state has agreed that the law of a particular country should govern a contract. An implicit waiver would also include a situation where a

foreign state has filed a responsive pleading in an action without raising the defense of sovereign immunity.

Moreover, at least one court has held, in one of the other cement contract cases, that Nigeria's choice of European laws and a European forum to resolve disputes constituted a waiver of its sovereign immunity in the American courts. Even if that case were correct on the law, it is inapplicable to the facts here.[83]

Here plaintiff, for reasons which are apparent, has decided not to sue upon its cement agreement with Nigeria. Instead it bases its claim upon the Verlinden letter of credit. But that instrument, unlike the contract, is devoid of any provision accepting foreign law for its interpretation, nor does it name any foreign tribunal for arbitration.

Plaintiff seeks to blur the distinctions between two separate obligations binding between different parties. The cement contract was signed by Nigeria's Minister of Defense on behalf of the Nigerian government; Central Bank is not a party to that agreement, which binds only Verlinden and Nigeria. By its very definition, the letter of credit is a separate and distinct obligation;[84] in this case, it bound only Central Bank, and not the Nigerian government. Nigeria's obligation under the contract was "*to establish*" the letter of credit in favor of Verlinden within a specified period of time. Central Bank's obligation under the letter of credit matured upon presentation of appropriate documents. Nigeria undertook no obligations under the letter of credit; nor did Central Bank, under the contract. This is not a hypertechnical distinction. The contract indicates that to whatever extent, if at all, Nigeria waived its immunity by reason of the arbitration provision, it did so only with respect to the contract, not the credit. Plaintiff can hardly have been unaware of these distinctions when it chose to pursue its remedies against Central Bank under the credit, rather than against Nigeria under the contract.

Even if Nigeria's waiver of immunity under one contract were held to bind its instrumentality under a different obligation, we would nevertheless find no implicit waiver, for Nigeria itself has never implicitly accepted the jurisdiction of American courts. The Congressional history cited by the plaintiff is not dispositive of this issue, indeed, it is at most ambiguous. The comment in the Congressional report, previously mentioned, that the courts had found an implicit waiver "where a foreign state has agreed to arbitration in another country or ... agreed that the law of a particular

---

83. *Ipitrade International, SA v. Federal Republic of Nigeria*, 465 F. Supp. 824 (D.D.C. 1978), did not require a decision on the issue of implicit waiver. The *Ipitrade* action was brought to enforce an arbitration award against Nigeria made by a French tribunal applying Swiss law. The District Court had subject matter jurisdiction of the enforcement action by virtue of a treaty to which the United States, France, Switzerland, and Nigeria all are parties. 9 U.S.C. §§201-208 (Supp. 1980). The treaty explicitly federalizes all such enforcement actions, *id.* §203, and sharply constricts the scope of review of arbitral awards. *Id.* §207. By signing the treaty Nigeria had explicitly waived its objection to such enforcement actions.

84. *See* Uniform Customs and Practice for Documentary Credits (1962 Rev.); General Provisions and Definitions §(c) ("Credits, by their nature, are separate transactions from the sales or other contracts on which they may be based and banks are in no way concerned with or bound by such contracts.").

country" would apply does not necessarily constitute an endorsement of that result.[85] More importantly, it is by no means clear that Congress intended, in referring to "another country" or "a particular country," to include a third-party country the adoption of whose law or forum by a foreign state as one of the contracting parties would operate as a waiver thereby subjecting the foreign state to jurisdiction in this country. It may be reasonable to suggest that a sovereign state which agrees to be governed by the laws of the United States — which is both "another country" and "a particular country" — has implicitly waived its ability to assert the defense of sovereign immunity when sued in an American court. But it is quite another matter to suggest, as did the Court in *Ipitrade*,[86] that a sovereign state which agrees to be governed by the laws of a third-party country — such as the Netherlands — is thereby precluded asserting its immunity in an American court.

Although both of these interpretations may be consistent with the literal language of the single paragraph of legislative history that addresses implicit waivers, there are strong reasons to reject the latter view. By its peculiar mixture of substantive and procedural provisions, the FSIA confers personal jurisdiction over all foreign states not entitled to immunity (assuming that valid service has been effectuated). Proof of an implicit waiver absolutely defeats the assertion of sovereign immunity. If the language of the Act is applied literally, the result is that a foreign sovereign which has waived its immunity can be subjected to the personal jurisdiction of United States courts regardless of the nature or quality of its contacts with this country.[87]

Plaintiff's view, if adopted, would presage a vast increase in the jurisdiction of federal courts in matters involving sensitive foreign relations: whenever a foreign sovereign had contracted with a private party anywhere in the world, and chose to be governed by the laws or answer in the forum of any country other than its own, it would expose itself to personal liability in the courts of the United States. Verlinden and Nigeria could scarcely have foreseen this untoward result when they signed the contract; and it is unlikely that Congress could have intended it.

Because the Act's waiver provision is written as broadly as it is, it is incumbent upon the Court to narrow that provision's scope. We need not now decide whether the Court would have personal jurisdiction over a foreign state whose only contact with this country occurs by virtue of a private agreement in which it adopts American law or an American forum. We only hold that when a foreign state agrees

---

85. [House Report No. 1487, 94th Cong., 2d Sess. 18, *reprinted in* 1976 U.S. Code Cong. & Admin. News at 6617.] There is no indication as to which cases the legislators were referring, or even whether they were cases decided under American law by American courts.

86. *Ipitrade International, SA v. Federal Republic of Nigeria*, 465 F. Supp. 824 (D.D.C. 1978).

87. There is reason to believe that Congress did not anticipate this problem at all. On the other hand, the legislative history indicates that Congress intended the courts to exercise personal jurisdiction only over foreign states having sufficient contacts with the United States. *See* [House Report No. 1487, 94th Cong., 2d Sess. 13-14, *reprinted in* 1976 U.S. Code Cong. & Admin. News at 6612.] On the other hand, the statute it wrote permits the assertion of jurisdiction either when there are sufficient contacts (*i.e.*, when one of the commercial activity exceptions has been met) *or* when there has been a waiver.

to submit its disputes with another, non-American private party to the laws of a third country, or to answer in the tribunals of such country, it does not implicitly waive its immunity to the jurisdiction of the courts of the United States. Because Nigeria has not waived the defense of sovereign immunity in the American courts, it necessarily follows that Central Bank has not either.

In sum, we find that none of the exceptions to the Act is applicable here. The motion of the defendant to dismiss the complaint for lack of personal jurisdiction under the FSIA is granted.

Notes on Verlinden

1. *Construction of implied waivers of sovereign immunity.* Lower courts have differed in their basic approach to implied waivers of sovereign immunity. Some courts have reasoned that waivers of immunity are disfavored and not lightly to be inferred. *E.g., Frolova v. USSR,* 761 F.2d 370, 377 (7th Cir. 1985) (courts "have been reluctant to stray beyond" examples of waivers in FSIA's legislative history and have "narrowly construed" purported waivers; *Castro v. Saudi Arabia,* 510 F. Supp. 309, 312 (W.D. Tex. 1980) ("There must be an intentional and knowing relinquishment of the legal right."). In contrast, other courts have expressly adopted expansive views of asserted waivers of sovereign immunity. *E.g., Proyecfin de Venezuela, SA v. Banco Industrial de Venezuela, SA,* 760 F.2d 390, 392 (2d Cir. 1985) ("broad reading of implicit waivers"). Which approach to the interpretation of purported waivers is more sensible? Is it necessary to adopt any general rule of construction?

2. *Verlinden — waivers and the "nexus" requirement.* Foreign states waive their immunity every day, for all sorts of purposes. They waive their immunity from the jurisdiction of different national courts (or arbitral tribunals) in particular contracts or legislation; they submit to the exclusive or non-exclusive jurisdiction of different courts or tribunals; and they agree to be bound by different national laws in various connections.

Read literally, §1605(a)(1) says that any "waiver" of immunity by a foreign state confers personal and subject matter jurisdiction on U.S. courts. *Verlinden* reasoned that, if the FSIA's waiver provision is "applied literally, the result is that a foreign sovereign which has waived its immunity can be subjected to the personal jurisdiction of United States courts regardless of the nature or quality of its contacts with this country." Consequently, the court reasoned, "it is incumbent upon the Court to narrow [§1605(a)(1)'s] scope." Is §1605(a)(1) in fact so open-ended? When it refers to "waivers" of immunity, what sorts of waivers of immunity must §1605(a)(1) have in mind — waivers of immunity from the jurisdiction of U.S. courts, or something else? If a foreign state impliedly waives its immunity by consenting to the jurisdiction of some foreign court (*e.g.,* Dutch), is that a waiver of immunity from the jurisdiction of U.S. courts?

Verlinden did not expressly provide a general formula for restricting the scope of §1605(a)(1). Its opinion suggests however, limiting waivers to those relating to activities by foreign states that would, putting aside the waiver, have "minimum contacts" with the United States for due process purposes. Is that persuasive? Why not simply consider whether a foreign state has waived its immunity from U.S. courts?

3. *Submission to jurisdiction of U.S. courts as waiver.* The fundamental question in most §1605(a)(1) cases is *what* the foreign state has waived; it will often be clear that a foreign state has waived its immunity with respect to some types of proceedings, but it will be less clear that the foreign state's waiver extends to an action on the merits in *U.S.* courts (as opposed to some foreign state's courts). The agreement of a foreign state to a forum selection clause designating U.S. courts as the contractual forum would appear to constitute a waiver of sovereign immunity in an action on the merits in U.S. courts for purposes of §1605(a)(1). Is this result inevitable? Could a party merely be undertaking to appear in U.S. courts for the purpose of asserting its sovereign immunity (which, after all, can be expressly waived)?

Verlinden suggested that personal jurisdiction might be lacking "over a foreign state whose only contact with this country occurs by virtue of a private agreement in which it adopts American law or an American forum." Is this correct? Note that Judge Weinfeld expressed doubt as to both choice of law and choice of forum clauses. Why should a foreign state's agreement submitting to U.S. courts' jurisdiction not constitute a valid waiver, even absent any other U.S. contacts? Judge Weinfeld's suggestion is squarely contrary to the rationale of *Marlowe v. Argentine Naval Commission*, 604 F.Supp. 703 (D.D.C. 1985), which found an effective waiver of immunity in a foreign sovereign's consent to a choice of U.S. law. The court reasoned that a waiver of immunity in U.S. courts constitutes a waiver even "in the absence of the normally required minimum contacts." 604 F. Supp. at 710.

Consider Judge Weinfeld's suggestion in *Verlinden*, that some additional showing of U.S. contacts is necessary for personal jurisdiction over a foreign state-related entity that expressly consents to U.S. jurisdiction. Is that view consistent with due process precedents, which generally treat such submissions to jurisdiction as establishing "minimum contacts" with the chosen forum. *National Equip. Rental, Ltd. v. Szukhent*, 375 U.S. 311, 324-30 (1964). *See supra* pp. 101-02. *See also Verlinden BV v. Central Bank of Nigeria*, 462 U.S. 480, 490 n.15 ("Section 1605(a)(1), which provides that sovereign immunity shall not apply if waived, may be seen as an exception to the normal pattern of the Act, which generally requires some form of contact with the United States. We need not decide whether, by waiving its immunity, a foreign state could consent to suit based on activities wholly unrelated to the United States.").

4. *Effect of submission to jurisdiction of foreign state's own courts.* A foreign state's agreement to submit contractual disputes to its own judicial system has not ordinarily been deemed a waiver of immunity in an action on the merits in U.S. courts. *Perez v. The Bahamas*, 482 F.Supp. 1208 (D.D.C. 1980), *aff'd*, 652 F.2d 186 (D.C. Cir.), *cert. denied*, 454 U.S. 865 (1981).

5. *Effect of submission to jurisdiction of a third state's courts.* The effect under §1605(a)(1) of a choice of forum clause selecting the courts of a third country is less clear. For example, suppose a Russian state-owned company and a U.S. company enter into a contract with a forum selection clause designating English courts. Several lower courts have indicated that agreement to such a clause will not constitute a waiver of immunity in an action on the merits in U.S. courts. *E.g., Ohntrup v. Firearms Center*, 516 F. Supp. 1281, 1285 (E.D. Pa. 1981), *aff'd*, 760 F.2d 259 (3d Cir. 1985) ("a waiver of immunity by a state as to one jurisdiction cannot be interpreted as a waiver as to all jurisdictions"); *Chicago Bridge & Iron Co. v. Islamic Republic of Iran*, 506 F.Supp. 981, 987 (N.D. Ill. 1980) ("the presence of third-party choice of law and forum clauses does not in any sense implicitly consent to jurisdiction" of U.S. courts). Note that an exclusive choice of forum clause selecting a non-U.S. forum would generally provide an independent basis for dismissing a U.S. action, although that would depend in part on applicable standards of enforceability. *See infra* pp. 374-78 & 378-94.

What does *Verlinden* say about the foregoing question? Are the above decisions the only plausible view of forum selection clauses that choose non-U.S. courts? There is a distinction, discussed *infra* pp. 371-72, between exclusive and nonexclusive forum selection clauses. Should a nonexclusive choice of forum clause permitting (but not requiring) suit in a designated third-country foreign forum constitute a general waiver of sovereign immunity, including immunity for purposes of U.S. litigation on the merits? Doesn't a foreign state's agreement to litigation in foreign courts (even if the chosen courts are not U.S. courts) indicate that the state is engaged in non-immune activities and that the private party expects judicial enforcement? What about an action in U.S. courts to enforce a foreign judgment resulting from foreign litigation pursuant to the forum selection clause?

What do you make of Judge Weinfeld's concern that this view of §1605(a)(1) would allow suits in U.S. courts against foreign parties "anywhere in the world" where the contract contained a forum selection clause? Assuming this is correct, wouldn't this concern be met by Judge Weinfeld's (and the due process clause's) requirement of a nexus between the defendant's cause of action and the United States?

6. *Choice of U.S. law as waiver.* Most U.S. courts have held that a foreign state's agreement to a choice of law clause selecting U.S. law constitutes a waiver of sovereign immunity in an action on the merits in U.S. courts. *E.g., Eckert Int'l, Inc. v. Government of Fiji*, 32 F.3d 77 (4th Cir. 1994); *Transamerican S.S. v. Somali Democratic Republic*, 767 F.2d 998, 1005 (D.C. Cir. 1985) (Wald, J., concurring); *Marlowe v. Argentine Naval Comm'n*, 604 F. Supp. 703 (D.D.C. 1985); *Ohntrup v. Firearms Center*, 516 F. Supp. 1281 (E.D. Pa. 1981), *aff'd*, 760 F.2d 259 (3d Cir. 1985). There is fairly strong support in the FSIA's legislative history for this view. H.R. Rep. No. 1487, 94th Cong., 2d Sess. 18, *reprinted in* 1976 U.S. Code Cong. & Admin. News at 6617.

Is it inevitable that a foreign sovereign's agreement to be bound by U.S. law is a submission to the jurisdiction of U.S. courts? One judge has argued that "[i]n the House Report, Congress declared that a foreign government may not assume duties generally under United States law, only to disclaim them by invoking immunity in United States court when a controversy arises." *Transamerican S.S. Corp. v. Somali*

Democratic Republic, 767 F.2d 998, 1006 (D.C. Cir. 1985) (Wald, J., concurring). Doesn't this confuse applicable law and jurisdiction: there is no reason to suppose that parties choosing one law to apply could not have intended the courts in another country to apply that law. *Cf. Burger King Corp. v. Rudzewicz,* 471 U.S. 462 (1985) (choice of forum's law is relevant to, but does not independently confer, personal jurisdiction); *supra* pp. 148-49. On the other hand, if U.S. law is selected, is it not fair to assume (absent contrary indication) that U.S. courts would also enjoy jurisdiction?

Recall that Judge Weinfeld expressed doubt in *Verlinden* that a U.S. choice of law clause would constitute a waiver in the absence of other U.S. contacts. Is that more plausible than his similar doubt about a U.S. choice of forum clause? Note that agreement to the application of a particular law is not the same as submission to the jurisdiction of the courts of that place. *See infra* p. 657. Is a "minimum contacts" test more appropriate in this context?

7. *Choice of foreign law as waiver.* Most U.S. courts have concluded, like *Verlinden,* that a foreign state's choice of its own law or the law of a third country does not constitute a waiver of sovereign immunity in an action on the merits in U.S. courts. *E.g., Eaglet Corp. v. Banco Central de Nicaragua,* 839 F.Supp. 232 (S.D.N.Y. 1993), *aff'd,* 23 F.3d 641 (2d Cir. 1994); *Maritime Int'l Nominees Establishment v. Republic of Guinea,* 693 F.2d 1094, 1102 n.13 (D.C. Cir. 1982), *cert. denied,* 464 U.S. 815 (1983); *Ohntrup v. Firearms Center,* 516 F.Supp. 1281, 1284 (E.D. Pa. 1981), *aff'd,* 760 F.2d 259 (3d Cir. 1985). *See also* H. Smit, N. Galston & S. Levitsky, *International Contracts* 259-60 (1981) ("a persuasive argument can be made that the choice of a particular law is at most a reference to the foreign sovereign immunity rules of the law chosen and does not constitute an absolute waiver of immunity. In any event ... the implied waiver should reasonably not be construed to be consent to the competence of a court other than that sitting in the State whose law has been chosen.").

Is the view set forth above persuasive? Why shouldn't any choice of law clause be regarded as a waiver of immunity (since it contemplates the application of objective standards, presumably by a neutral tribunal), thus leaving only the question whether the defendant had sufficient contacts with the United States to permit the exercise of personal jurisdiction by U.S. courts consistent with the due process clause? As *Verlinden* acknowledges, this is the approach suggested by the FSIA's legislative history. H.R. Rep. No. 1487, 94th Cong., 2d Sess. 18, *reprinted in* 1976 U.S. Code Cong. & Admin. News, at 6617.

8. *Agreement to arbitrate as waiver of immunity in action to enforce arbitral agreement or award —* §§1605(a)(6) *and* 1605(a)(1). In 1988, the FSIA was amended to deny foreign states immunity for actions to enforce certain arbitration agreements or confirm certain arbitral awards. Section 1605(a)(6) creates an exception to foreign sovereign immunity in cases brought to enforce either an arbitration agreement or an arbitral award.

Section 1605(a)(6) expressly preserves the fairly extensive body of case law which developed under §1605(a)(1)'s waiver provisions with respect to arbitration clauses. Under these decisions, it was relatively clear that a foreign state's agreement to arbitrate in the United States constitutes a waiver of immunity from actions in U.S. courts to compel arbitration or to confirm the resulting arbitral award. *E.g., Maritime Int'l Nominees Establishment v. Republic of Guinea,* 693 F.2d 1094 (D.C. Cir. 1982), *cert. denied,* 464 U.S. 815 (1983) (dicta); *Birch Shipping Corp. v. United Republic of Tanzania,* 507 F.Supp. 311 (D.D.C. 1980). Moreover, several lower court decisions have suggested that an open-ended agreement to arbitrate, without designation of a particular situs, constitutes a waiver of immunity in U.S. courts for actions to compel arbitration or confirm arbitral awards. *E.g., Birch Shipping Corp. v. United Republic of Tanzania,* 507 F. Supp. 311 (D.D.C. 1980); *Libyan American Oil Co. v. Socialist People's Libyan Arab Jamahirya,* 482 F. Supp. 1175 (D.D.C. 1980), *vacated,* 684 F.2d 1032 (D.C. Cir. 1981).

Finally, a few U.S. courts have ruled that an agreement to arbitrate outside the United States constitutes a waiver of a foreign state's immunity if, following the arbitration, the prevailing private parties seek to enforce the foreign arbitral award in the United States. *E.g., Ipitrade Int'l, SA v. Federal Republic of Nigeria,* 465 F. Supp. 824 (D.D.C. 1978) (court enforces arbitral award against foreign state). *Compare* H. Smit, N. Galston & S. Levitsky, *International Contracts* 259 (1981) ("[i]t may well not be an effective waiver ... when suit is brought on the arbitral award in a place other than that of the arbitration") *and Restatement (Third) Foreign Relations Law* §456(2)(b) (1987) (treating arbitration agreement for any fora as waiver for purposes of enforcement and compelling arbitration in U.S. courts).

9. *Defective waivers.* As discussed in Chapter 5 at *infra* pp. 395-430, U.S. law imposes a variety of restrictions on private parties' acceptance of forum selection clauses. *See The Bremen v. Zapata Off-Shore*

Co., 407 U.S. 1 (1972); *National Equip. Rental, Ltd. v. Szukhent*, 375 U.S. 311 (1964). These cases generally require submissions to jurisdiction to be "reasonable" and to be free of unconscionability. Are there circumstances in which a foreign state could avail itself of these requirements by arguing that its waiver of immunity was defective? *Cf.* Kahale & Vega, *Immunity and Jurisdiction: Toward a Uniform Body of Law in Actions Against Foreign States*, 18 Colum. J. Transnat'l L. 211, 231-35 (1979) (arguing that waiver agreed to by officials lacking authority under foreign law to bind foreign state is defective).

    10. *Waivers by related parties. Verlinden* held that the waiver of immunity by one party (the Federal Republic of Nigeria) would not be deemed a waiver of immunity by another party (the Central Bank of Nigeria). Several other lower courts have also held that waivers of sovereign immunity by one party will not bind another party, even if the two entities are related. *E.g., Zernicek v. Petroleos Mexicanos*, 614 F. Supp. 407 (D. Tex. 1985); *Paterson, Zochonis (U.K.), Ltd. v. Compania United Arrow*, 493 F. Supp. 621 (S.D.N.Y. 1980), *aff'd*, 826 F.2d 415 (5th Cir. 1987), *cert. denied*, 108 S.Ct 775 (1988). Is the result in *Verlinden* correct? If a state purports to waive immunity on behalf of its agencies and instrumentalities, why should that waiver not be binding on them?

2. Commercial Activity With a U.S. Nexus

[handwritten margin note: most important exception]

As noted earlier, the increase in the trading activities of foreign government entities was central to the development of the restrictive theory of sovereign immunity. The FSIA denies immunity to certain commercial activities of foreign states. This is the single most important exception to foreign sovereign immunity in the United States. The "commercial activity" exception is set forth in §1605(a)(2):

> (2) in which the action is based upon a commercial activity carried on in the United States by the foreign state; or upon an act performed in the United States in connection with a commercial activity of the foreign state elsewhere; or upon an act outside the territory of the United States in connection with a commercial activity of the foreign state elsewhere and that act causes a direct effect in the United States.

[handwritten margin note: commercial activity]

Three related issues of interpretation are critical to understanding §1605(a)(2). First, what types of governmental conduct constitute "commercial activity"? Second, when is an action "based upon" a commercial activity or an "act ... in connection with" a commercial activity? Third, what "nexus" is required between a foreign state's commercial activity and the United States?

a. Definition of "Commercial Activity"

The FSIA's definition of "commercial activity" raises difficult issues of interpretation. The general rationale for the commercial activity exception is that when a state enters into "commercial" contracts or engages in profit-making activity, it ceases to act in a "sovereign" capacity and should not enjoy immunity.[88] The difficulty, however, lies in determining what types of conduct are commercial, rather than sovereign. Some commentators have observed that there is no clear dividing line between commercial and public acts and that virtually all activities by states further

---

    88. *See supra* pp. 201-02 & 207-08; Tate Letter, *reprinted in* 425 U.S. 711 (1976); H.R. Rep. No. 1487, 94th Cong., 2d Sess. 16-17, *reprinted in* 1976 U.S. Code Cong. & Admin. News at 6614-15.

sovereign purposes.[89] Thus, according to a classic example, even the purchase of boots by a foreign state can serve sovereign objectives when, for example, the boots will be used to equip the purchaser's armed forces.

Against this background, §1603(d) defines "commercial activity" as "either a regular course of commercial conduct or a particular commercial transaction or act." In addition, §1603(d) provides that "[t]he commercial character of an activity shall be determined by reference to the nature of the course of conduct or particular transaction or act, rather than by reference to its purposes."[90] Many have remarked on the circularity of §1603(d), which fails to define the critical term "commercial."[91] In one authority's words, "[s]tart with 'activity,' proceed via 'conduct' or 'transaction' to 'character,' then refer to 'nature,' and then go back to 'commercial,' the term you started out to define in the first place."[92]

Nonetheless, §1603(d)'s emphasis on the "nature," rather than the "purpose," of a foreign state's activity places important limits on the scope of foreign sovereign immunity. The FSIA's legislative history explains that "the fact that goods or services to be procured [by a foreign state] through a contract are to be used for a public purpose is irrelevant; it is the *essentially commercial nature of an activity* or transaction that is critical."[93] By virtue of this gloss, the FSIA resolves the classic hypothetical of a foreign state's purchase of equipment for its armed forces: such purchases are commercial in nature, notwithstanding their public purpose.[94]

Legislative   The FSIA's legislative history also provides additional explanations of the
history   intended meaning of "commercial activity." Most importantly, the House Report on the Act provides:

> [S]ection 1603 defines the term "commercial activity" as including a broad spectrum of endeavor, from an individual commercial transaction or act to a regular course of commercial conduct. A "regular course of commercial conduct" includes the carrying on of a commercial enterprise such as a mineral extraction company, an airline or a state trading corporation. Certainly, if an activity is customarily carried on for profit, its commercial

---

89. *E.g.*, I. Brownlie, *Principles of Public International Law* 330 (1979) ("The short point is that there is a logical contradiction in seeking to distinguish the 'sovereign' and 'non-sovereign' acts of a state"); Sornarajah, *Problems in Applying the Restrictive Theory of Sovereign Immunity*, 31 Int'l & Comp. L.Q. 661 (1982).

90. 28 U.S.C. §1603(d).

91. *Republic of Argentina v. Weltover, Inc.*, 504 U.S. 607 (1992) (FSIA "leaves the term 'commercial' largely undefined"); *Texas Trading & Milling Corp. v. Federal Republic of Nigeria*, 647 F.2d 300, 308 (2d Cir. 1981), *cert. denied*, 454 U.S. 1148 (1982).

92. Lowenfeld, *Litigating a Sovereign Immunity Claim — The Haiti Case*, 49 N.Y.U. L. Rev. 377, 435 & n.244 (1974).

93. H.R. Rep. No. 1487, 94th Cong., 2d Sess. 16, *reprinted in* 1976 U.S. Code Cong. & Admin. News at 6615 (emphasis added). *See Restatement (Third) Foreign Relations Law* §453 & comment b (1987); *Republic of Argentina v. Weltover, Inc.*, 504 U.S. 607 (1992).

94. *Accord Texas Trading & Milling Corp. v. Federal Republic of Nigeria*, 647 F.2d 300 (2d Cir. 1981), *cert. denied*, 454 U.S. 1148 (1982).

nature could readily be assumed. At the other end of the spectrum, a single contract, if of the same character as a contract which might be made by a private person, could constitute a "particular transaction or act."

As the definition indicates, the fact that goods or services to be procured through a contract are to be used for a public purpose is irrelevant; it is the essentially commercial nature of an activity or transaction that is critical. Thus, a contract by a foreign government to buy provisions or equipment for its armed forces or to construct a government building constitutes a commercial activity. The same would be true of a contract to make repairs on an embassy building. Such contracts should be considered to be commercial contracts, even if their ultimate object is to further a public function. Activities such as a foreign government's sale of a service or a product, its leasing of property, its borrowing money, its employment or engagement of laborers, clerical staff or public relations or marketing agents, or its investment in a security of an American corporation, would be among those included within the definition.[95]

Despite this gloss, the Act's legislative history abjures any effort to define commercial activity comprehensively. Instead, Congress deliberately left the judiciary freedom to develop a definition on a case-by-case basis: "The courts would have a great deal of latitude in determining what is a 'commercial activity' for purposes of this bill. It has seemed unwise to attempt an excessively precise definition of this term, even if that were practicable."[96] Courts have been less confident about the wisdom of Congress's refusal to define "commercial activity."[97]

The Supreme Court considered the FSIA's definition of "commercial activity" at length in *Republic of Argentina v. Weltover, Inc.*, which is excerpted below. Although the Court's opinion provides guidance, the historic uncertainties that have surrounded the distinction between commercial and sovereign acts can be expected to persist. That is illustrated by *MOL, Inc. v. People's Republic of Bangladesh*, also excerpted below.

REPUBLIC OF ARGENTINA v. WELTOVER, INC.

504 U.S. 607 (1992) [also partially excerpted below at pp. 259-61]

JUSTICE SCALIA [for a unanimous Court]. This case requires us to decide whether the Republic of Argentina's default on certain bonds issued as part of a plan to stabilize its currency was an act taken "in connection with a commercial activity"

Summary

---

95. H.R. Rep. No. 1487, 94th Cong., 2d Sess. 16, *reprinted in* 1976 U.S. Code Cong. & Admin. News at 6614-15.

96. H.R. Rep. No. 1487, 94th Cong., 2d Sess. 16, *reprinted in* 1976 U.S. Code Cong. & Admin. News at 6615.

97. *See Republic of Argentina v. Weltover, Inc.*, 504 U.S. 607 (1992); *Gibbons v. Udaras na Gaeltachta*, 549 F.Supp. 1094, 1106 (S.D.N.Y. 1982).

that had a "direct effect in the United States" so as to subject Argentina to suit in an American court under [FSIA].

Since Argentina's currency is not one of the mediums of exchange acceptable on the international market, Argentine businesses engaging in foreign transactions must pay in U.S. dollars or some other internationally accepted currency. In the recent past, it was difficult for Argentine borrowers to obtain such funds, principally because of the instability of the Argentine currency. To address these problems, petitioners, the Republic of Argentina and its central bank, Banco Central (collectively Argentina), in 1981 instituted a foreign exchange insurance contract program ("FEIC"), under which Argentina effectively agreed to assume the risk of currency depreciation in cross-border transactions involving Argentine borrowers. This was accomplished by Argentina's agreeing to sell to domestic borrowers, in exchange for a contractually predetermined amount of local currency, the necessary U.S. dollars to repay their foreign debts when they matured, irrespective of intervening devaluations.

Unfortunately, Argentina did not possess sufficient reserves of U.S. dollars to cover the FEIC contracts as they became due in 1982. The Argentine government thereupon adopted certain emergency measures, including refinancing of the FEIC-backed debts by issuing to the creditors government bonds. These bonds, call "Bonods," provide for payment of interest and principal in U.S. dollars; payment may be made through transfer on the London, Frankfurt, Zurich, or New York market, at the election of the creditor. Under this refinancing program, the foreign creditor had the option of either accepting the Bonods in satisfaction of the initial debt, thereby substituting the Argentine government for the private debtor, or maintaining the debtor/creditor relationship with the private borrower and accepting the Argentine government as guarantor.

When the Bonods began to mature in May 1986, Argentina concluded that it lacked sufficient foreign exchange to retire them. Pursuant to a Presidential Decree, Argentina unilaterally extended the time for payment, and offered bondholders substitute instruments as a means of rescheduling the debts. Respondents, two Panamanian corporations and a Swiss bank who hold, collectively, $1.3 million of Bonods, refused to accept the rescheduling, and insisted on full payment, specifying New York as the place where payment should be made. Argentina did not pay, and respondents then brought this breach-of-contract action in the United States District Court for the Southern District of New York, relying on the [FSIA] as the basis for jurisdiction. Petitioners moved to dismiss for lack of subject-matter jurisdiction, lack of personal jurisdiction, and *forum non conveniens*. The District Court denied these motions and the Court of Appeals affirmed. ...

The [FSIA] establishes a comprehensive framework for determining whether a court in this country, state or federal, may exercise jurisdiction over a foreign state. Under the Act, a "foreign state *shall* be immune from the jurisdiction of the courts of the United States and of the States" unless one of several statutorily defined exceptions applies. §1604 (emphasis added). The FSIA thus provides the "sole basis" for obtaining jurisdiction over a foreign sovereign in the United States. *See Argentine Republic v. Amerada Hess Shipping Corp.* The most significant of the FSIA's exceptions — and the one at issue in this case — is the "commercial" exception of §1605(a)(2). ...

In the proceedings below, respondents relied only on the third clause of §1605(a)(2) to establish jurisdiction and our analysis is therefore limited to considering whether this lawsuit is (1) "based ... upon an act outside the territory of the United States"; (2) that was taken "in connection with a commercial activity" of Argentina outside this country; and (3) that "cause[d] a direct effect in the United States." The complaint in this case alleges only one cause of action on behalf of each of the respondents, viz., a breach-of-contract claim based on Argentina's attempt to refinance the Bonods rather than to pay them according to their terms. The fact that the cause of action is in compliance with the first of the three requirements — that it is "based upon an act outside the territory of the United States" (presumably Argentina's unilateral extension) — is uncontested. The dispute pertains to whether the unilateral refinancing of the Bonods was taken "in connection with a commercial activity" of Argentina, and whether it had a "direct effect in the United States." ...

Respondents and their *amicus*, the United States, contend that Argentina's issuance of, and continued liability under, the Bonods constitute a "commercial activity" and that the extension of the payment schedules was taken "in connection with" that activity. The latter point is obvious enough, and Argentina does not contest it; the key question is whether the activity is "commercial" under the FSIA.

[The FSIA's] definition [of commercial activity in §1603(d)] leaves the critical term "commercial" largely undefined: The first sentence simply establishes that the commercial nature of an activity does *not* depend upon whether it is a single act or a regular course of conduct, and the second sentence merely specifies what element of the conduct determines commerciality (*i.e.*, nature rather than purpose), but still without saying what "commercial" means. Fortunately, however, the FSIA was not written on a clean slate. As we have noted, *see Verlinden BV v. Central Bank of Nigeria*, the Act (and the commercial exception in particular) largely codifies the so-called "restrictive" theory of foreign sovereign immunity .... The meaning of "commercial" is the meaning generally attached to that term under the restrictive theory at the time the statute was enacted.

This Court did not have occasion to discuss the scope or validity of the restrictive theory of sovereign immunity until our 1976 decision in *Alfred Dunhill of London, Inc. v. Republic of Cuba*, 425 U.S. 682. Although the Court there was evenly divided on the question whether the "commercial" exception that applied in the foreign-sovereign-immunity context also limited the availability of an act-of-state defense, there was little disagreement over the general scope of the exception. The plurality noted that, after the State Department endorsed the restrictive theory of foreign sovereign immunity in 1952, the lower courts consistently held that foreign sovereigns were not immune from the jurisdiction of American courts in cases "arising out of purely commercial transactions." The plurality further recognized that the distinction between state sovereign acts, on the one hand, and state commercial and private acts, on the other, was not entirely novel to American law. The plurality stated that the restrictive theory of foreign sovereign immunity would not bar a suit based upon a foreign state's participation in the marketplace in the manner of a private citizen or corporation. A foreign state engaging in commercial activities "do[es] not exercise powers particular to sovereigns"; rather, it "exercise[s] only those powers that can also be exercised by private citizens." The dissenters did not disagree with this general description. Given that the FSIA was enacted less than six months after our decision in *Alfred Dunhill* was announced, we think the plurality's contemporaneous description of the then-prevailing restrictive theory of sovereign immunity is of significant assistance in construing the scope of the Act.

In accord with that description, we conclude that when a foreign government acts, not as regulator of a market, but in the manner of a private player within it, the foreign sovereign's actions are "commercial" within the meaning of the FSIA. Moreover, because the Act provides that the commercial character of an act is to be determined by reference to its "nature" rather than its "purpose," 28 U.S.C. §1603(d), the question is not whether the foreign government is acting with a profit motive or instead with the aim of fulfilling uniquely sovereign objectives. Rather, the issue is whether the particular actions that the foreign state performs (whatever the motive behind them) are the *type* of actions by which a private party engages in "trade and traffic or commerce." Thus, a foreign government's issuance of regulations limiting foreign currency exchange is a sovereign activity, because such authoritative control of commerce cannot be exercised by a private party; whereas a contract to buy army boots or even bullets is a "commercial" activity, because private companies can similarly use sales contracts to acquire goods.

The commercial character of the Bonods is confirmed by the fact that they are in almost all respects garden-variety debt instruments; they may be held by private parties; they are negotiable and may be traded on the international market (except in Argentina); and they promise a future stream of cash income. We recognize that, prior to the enactment of the FSIA, there was authority suggesting that the issuance of public debt instruments did not constitute a commercial activity. [*Victory Transport, Inc. v. Comisaria General*, 336 F.2d 354 (2d Cir. 1964), *cert. denied*, 381 U.S. 934 (1965).] There is, however, nothing distinctive about the state's assumption of debt (other than perhaps its purpose) that would cause it always to be classified as *jure imperii*, and in this regard it is significant that *Victory Transport* expressed confusion as to whether the "nature" or the "purpose" of a transaction was controlling in determining commerciality. Because the FSIA has now clearly established that the "nature" governs, we perceive no basis for concluding that the issuance of debt should be treated as categorically different from other activities of foreign states.

Argentina contends that, although the FSIA bars consideration of "purpose," a court must nonetheless fully consider the *context* of a transaction in order to determine whether it is "commercial." Accordingly, Argentina claims that the Court of Appeals erred by defining the relevant conduct in what Argentina considers an overly generalized, acontextual manner and by essentially adopting a *per se* rule that all "issuance of debt instruments" is "commercial." We have no occasion to consider such a *per se* rule, because it seems to us that even in full context, there is nothing about the issuance of these Bonods (except perhaps its purpose) that is not analogous to a private commercial transaction.

Argentina points to the fact that the transactions in which the Bonods were issued did not have the ordinary commercial consequence of raising capital or financing acquisitions. Assuming for the sake of argument that this is not an example of judging the commerciality of a transaction by its purpose, the ready answer is that private parties regularly issue bonds, not just to raise capital or to finance purchases, but also to refinance debt. That is what Argentina did here: by virtue of the earlier FEIC contracts, Argentina was *already* obligated to supply the U.S. dollars needed to retire the FEIC-insured debts; the Bonods simply allowed Argentina to restructure its existing obligations. Argentina further asserts (without proof or even elaboration) that it "received consideration [for the Bonods] in no way commensurate with [their] value." Assuming that to be true, it makes no difference. Engaging in a commercial act does not require the receipt of fair value, or even compliance with the common-law requirements of consideration.

Argentina argues that the Bonods differ from ordinary debt instruments in that they "were created by the Argentine Government to fulfill its obligations under a foreign exchange program designed to address a domestic credit crisis, and as a component of a program designed to control that nation's critical shortage of foreign exchange." In this regard, Argentina relies heavily on *De Sanchez v. Banco Central de Nicaragua,* 770 F.2d 1385 (5th Cir. 1985), in which the Fifth Circuit took the view that "[o]ften, the essence of an act is defined by its purpose"; that unless "we can inquire into the purposes of such acts, we cannot determine their nature"; and that, in light of its purpose to control its reserves of foreign currency, Nicaragua's refusal to honor a check it had issued to cover a private bank debt was a sovereign act entitled to immunity. Indeed, Argentina asserts that the line between "nature" and "purpose" rests upon a "formalistic distinction [that] simply is neither useful nor warranted." We think this line of argument is squarely foreclosed by the language of the FSIA. However difficult it may be in some cases to separate "purpose" (*i.e.*, the *reason* why the foreign state engages in the activity) from "nature" (*i.e.*, the outward form of the conduct that the foreign state performs or agrees to perform), the statute unmistakably commands that to be done. We agree with the Court of Appeals that it is irrelevant *why* Argentina participated in the bond market in the manner of a private actor; it matters only that it did so. We conclude that Argentina's issuance of the Bonods was a "commercial activity" under the FSIA. ...

MOL, INC. v. PEOPLE'S REPUBLIC OF BANGLADESH

(Oregon corp.)   *736 F.2d 1326 (9th Cir. 1984).*

WRIGHT, CIRCUIT JUDGE. MOL, Inc. sues Bangladesh for termination of a licensing agreement for the export of rhesus monkeys from Bangladesh. Because the granting and revocation of a license to export a natural resource are sovereign acts, we have no jurisdiction over this claim.

In 1977, a division of the Bangladesh Ministry of Agriculture granted MOL, Inc., an Oregon Corporation, a ten-year license to capture and export rhesus monkeys. The licensing agreement specified quantities and prices and required MOL to build in Bangladesh in 1978 a breeding farm for rhesus monkeys. By its terms, the agreement was granted "on the grounds and sole condition that the primates exported by [MOL] from Bangladesh shall be used exclusively for the purposes of medical and other scientific research by highly skilled and competent personnel for the general benefit of all peoples of the world." To enable Bangladesh to monitor uses of the monkeys, it required MOL to keep available records on each monkey and arrange for duplicate records in Bangladesh. The agreement provided for arbitration of disputes, each party selecting one arbitrator. Bangladesh reserved the right to terminate the agreement "without notice if [MOL] has failed to fulfill its obligations under this Agreement."

In November 1977, India banned the export of its rhesus monkeys. As India had been the major exporter of these animals, which are valuable for research because of their anatomical and behavioral similarity to humans, Bangladesh became an important supplier. Although world monkey prices rose while MOL's payments to Bangladesh remained fixed, Bangladesh complied with the licensing agreement through the spring of 1978. Bangladesh threatened to cancel the agreement in May 1978 because MOL had not built the breeding farm or exported agreed quantities. MOL denied any departure from the agreement. In September 1978, it delivered some Bangladesh monkeys to the United States armed services for radiobiological research.

Bangladesh announced on January 3, 1979, that it was terminating the agreement because MOL had not constructed the breeding farm in 1978 and had breached the requirement that the monkeys be used only for humanitarian purposes. It claimed that MOL sold the monkeys to the armed services for "neutron bomb radiation experiments." When MOL sought arbitration, Bangladesh refused, asserting its right to terminate for breach by MOL. Apparently MOL asked the State Department to intervene. Despite these efforts and MOL's reassurances that monkeys would not be used for radiation experiments, Bangladesh did not reinstate the licensing agreement. In 1982, MOL sued Bangladesh for $15 million. Bangladesh did not appear, and MOL moved for default. Amicus curiae, Attorneys for Animal Rights moved to dismiss for lack of jurisdiction under the FSIA. The district court denied the default judgment and dismissed the action, holding it barred [by] the FSIA. ... [We affirm.]

MOL argues that Bangladesh does not enjoy sovereign immunity because its acts fall under the commercial activity exception of the FSIA. That Act denies immunity in any case in which the action is based "upon an act outside the territory of the United States in connection with a commercial activity of the foreign state elsewhere and that act causes a direct effect in the United States." 28 U.S.C. §1605(a)(2). ... A crucial step in determining whether the basis of this suit was a commercial activity is defining the "act complained of here." *IAM v. OPEC*, 649 F.2d 1354, at 1357-58. The court must then decide whether that act is commercial or sovereign.

crucial step [handwritten margin note]

MOL asserts that the activity here relates to Bangladesh's contracting to sell monkeys. It admits that licensing the exploitation of natural resources is a sovereign activity. It argues, however, that this suit arises not from license revocation but from termination of a contract. In essence, Bangladesh lost its sovereign status when it contracted and then terminated pursuant to contract terms. The argument seems persuasive because, in breaking the agreement, Bangladesh itself spoke in commercial terms, basing its termination on MOL's alleged breaches. The true nature of the action, however, does not depend on terminology.

Bangladesh was terminating an agreement that only a sovereign could have made. This was not just a contract for trade of monkeys. It concerned Bangladesh's right to *regulate imports and exports*, a sovereign prerogative. It concerned Bangladesh's *right to regulate its natural resources*, also a uniquely sovereign function. *See IAM v. OPEC*, 477 F. Supp. 553, 567-68 (C.D. Cal. 1979), *aff'd on other grounds*, 649 F.2d 1354 (9th Cir. 1981). A private party could not have made such an agreement. MOL complains that this conclusion relies on the *purpose* of the agreement, in contradiction of the FSIA. *See* 28 U.S.C. §1603(d) (1982). But consideration of the special elements of export license and natural resource looks only to the *nature* of the agreement and does not require examination of the government's motives. In short, the licensing agreement was a sovereign act, not just a commercial transaction. Its revocation was sovereign by nature, not commercial. Bangladesh has sovereign immunity from this suit.

Right to regulate natural resources [handwritten margin note]

Notes on Weltover and MOL, Inc.

1. *"Commercial" and "sovereign" acts distinguished.* Is the restrictive theory's distinction between "commercial" and "sovereign" conduct either principled or workable? Isn't everything that a state does "sovereign"? Some critics have reasoned that "[t]he concept of acts *jure gestionis*, of commercial, non-sovereign, or less essential activity, requires value judgments which rest on political assumptions as to the proper sphere of state activity and of priorities in state policies." I. Brownlie, *Principles of Public International Law* 330 (3d ed. 1979). Even if this is true, does the restrictive theory rest only on notions of the "proper sphere of state activity"? or does it rest on fairness to private parties and on a desire to facilitate efficient, neutral international dispute resolution? Consider again the rationales for the restrictive theory in the Tate Letter and *Pesaro*. *See supra* pp. 201-02 & 205-10.

2. *"Nature" and "purpose" distinguished.* As noted above, the FSIA expressly requires that the commercial or noncommercial character of a foreign state's activity be determined by reference to the "nature" of the activity, rather than its "purpose." 28 U.S.C. §1603(d)(1982). What does this distinction mean? One commentator has remarked:

> the nature test ignores altogether the fact that one of the parties to the transaction is a sovereign State. Where a foreign sovereign State in pursuance of a newly formulated general policy

seeks to change its existing commercial obligations, a political element creeps into the situation and no amount of pretence will make it disappear.

Sornarajah, *Problems in Applying the Restrictive Theory of Sovereign Immunity*, 31 Int'l & Comp. L. Q. 661, 669 (1982). Is this criticism persuasive? Is the distinction between "nature" and "purpose" useful in deciding *Weltover*?

3. Weltover*'s historical approach to commercial activity definition. Consider *Weltover*'s analysis of §1603(d)'s definition of commercial activity. Note that Justice Scalia appears to adopt an historical approach to the issue: "The meaning of 'commercial' is the meaning generally attached to that term under the restrictive theory at the time the statute was enacted." (Compare Justice Scalia's similar historical approach to the due process clause in *Burnham, supra* p. 121.) Recall the significant recent evolution of foreign sovereign immunity from the absolute to the restrictive theory. Given this, is Justice Scalia's focus on the restrictive theory in 1976 an appropriate way to define "commercial activity"? Does this mean that post-1976 developments should be ignored? Is that consistent with Congress's instruction that the judiciary develop the definition of commercial activity on a case-by-case basis?

4. Weltover*'s reliance on* Dunhill *to define commercial activity. *Weltover* also relied in significant part on *Alfred Dunhill of London, Inc. v. Republic of Cuba*, 425 U.S. 682 (1976) (discussed below at pp. 733-38), to define the FSIA's commercial activity exception. In *Dunhill*, a plurality of the Court recognized a commercial exception to the act of state doctrine, but defined that exception in narrow terms: it applied only to "purely commercial transactions." *See infra* p. 737. Justice Scalia relied on *Dunhill* because it had just been decided when the FSIA was adopted. *Dunhill* was not, however, a sovereign immunity decision; it was an application of the act of state doctrine. It also was not a decision by the Court, which produced no majority opinion. *See infra* p. 733. Moreover, the FSIA's definition of "commercial activity" had been drafted before *Dunhill* was decided. Given these features of *Dunhill*, is *Weltover*'s reliance upon the plurality's analysis persuasive? In enacting the FSIA, is Congress likely to have thought about the plurality opinion in an act of state case decided after the FSIA had moved through the legislative process?

5. *Test for commercial activity after* Weltover. What definition does *Weltover* adopt for "commercial activity"? Consider the following: "when a foreign government acts, not as a regulator of a market, but in the manner of a private player within it, the foreign sovereign's actions are 'commercial' within the meaning of the FSIA." Is this a workable test? What does it mean to act "in the manner of a private player within [a market]"? Does the "market" have to be a private market — or does the market for sovereign debt (or jet fighters) also qualify? What exactly is the "manner of a private player"? How did Argentina act like a private player when it issued billions of dollars of public debt in close coordination with the International Monetary Fund, World Bank, and other public institutions? Is that what private people do? What precisely are the attributes of "private" conduct that led to a finding that the Court's "private player" test was satisfied? Is it because the Bonods are "in almost all respects garden-variety debt instruments"? What made them so ordinary?

6. *Application of the commercial activity definition in* Weltover. Was *Weltover* correct in concluding that the issuance of the Bonods was a commercial activity? What is the answer to Argentina's arguments that the debt was issued as part of a national economic recovery program, and that no private party could issue debt of this character? If you were advising a foreign government on the issuance of public debt, what suggestions would you make to ensure immunity?

7. *Profit-making enterprise as commercial activity.* The FSIA's legislative history indicates that an important factor in the "commercial activity" definition is whether the activity is carried on for profit: "Certainly, if an activity is customarily carried on for profit, its commercial nature could be readily assumed." *See* H.R. Rep. 1487, 94th Cong., 2d Sess. 16, *reprinted in* 1976 U.S. Code Cong. & Admin. News at 6615. Does this definition look to the actor's purpose (*i.e.*, earn a profit) in engaging in particular conduct? If so, is this consistent with the FSIA's distinction between nature and purpose?

The Bonods were not issued for purposes of earning a profit. Does that suggest that *Weltover* was wrongly decided? *Compare Cicippio v. Islamic Republic of Iran*, 30 F.3d 164 (D.C. Cir. 1994) (foreign state's efforts to lift U.S. freeze on its assets not commercial activity); *Aschenbrenner v. Conseil Regional de Haute Normandie*, 1994 WL 184666 (S.D.N.Y. 1994) (not-for-profit exhibition sponsored by governing body of Normandie held not "commercial"). Or is profit-making only one indicia of a "commercial" activity — as opposed to a requirement?

8. *Contractual relations as commercial activity.* The FSIA's legislative history also strongly suggests that when a foreign state enters into or breaches a contract, including a contract for the sale or purchase of goods or services, the state is engaged in a commercial activity. "[A] single contract, if of the same character as a contract which might be made by a private person, could constitute a "particular transaction or act" [and thus fall within the definition of commercial activity." *See* H.R. Rep. 1487, 94th Cong., 2d Sess. 16, *reprinted in* 1976 U.S. Code Cong. & Admin. News at 6615.

Even before *Weltover*, lower courts had concluded that a foreign state's breach of its contractual obligations falls within the commercial exception, even when the breach is motivated by political concerns or public objectives. *E.g.*, *McDonnell Douglas Corp. v. Islamic Republic of Iran*, 758 F.2d 341 (8th Cir.), *cert. denied*, 474 U.S. 948 (1985) (plaintiff's action was based on defendant's breach of contract regarding military aircraft, which was a commercial activity notwithstanding political motivations underlying breach); *Texas Trading & Milling Corp. v. Federal Republic of Nigeria*, 647 F.2d 300 (2d Cir. 1981), *cert. denied*, 454 U.S. 1148 (1982) (plaintiff's claim was based on defendant's breach of cement purchase contracts, which was commercial activity notwithstanding the fact that the cement was for public projects and the decision to breach was made at high levels of government).

Does this mean that *all* contracts of foreign states are "commercial activity"? Foreign states routinely enter into countless forms of agreements, both with private parties and other sovereigns. Are all of these agreements "commercial activities" within the meaning of the FSIA — including treaties and multilateral conventions? If only some contracts are "commercial" how does one tell the difference between those that are commercial and those that are not? Does the test adopted in *Weltover* enable one to do so?

9. **MOL, Inc.** *and the sovereign/commercial distinction.* Despite *Weltover*, *MOL, Inc.* illustrates how some U.S. lower courts have been reluctant to assert jurisdiction over foreign states, even when they are engaged in what appear to be commercial activities. What aspects of the MOL, Inc. contract with Bangladesh led the court to hold that it was "a sovereign act, not just a commercial transaction"? The fact that Bangladesh agreed to grant export licenses? That the agreement related to natural resources? Would either factor alone have led to a holding of immunity? Suppose the case had involved the export of handicrafts or consumer goods or automobiles pursuant to an agreement that obligated Bangladesh to grant export licenses? Suppose the case had involved Bangladesh's breach of an agreement to use MOL's services to raise rhesus monkeys in Bangladesh, without provisions regarding exports? What if the agreement called for the export of timber, coffee, or oil?

10. *Is* **MOL, Inc.** *correctly decided?* Was the result in *MOL, Inc.* consistent with the reasoning and holding in *Weltover*? Did Bangladesh act "in the manner of a private player"? How?

11. *The "based upon" requirement — an initial look.* The first clause of §1605(a)(2) requires that an action be "based upon" a commercial activity; the second and third clauses of §1605(a)(2) require that an action be "based upon" an act "in connection with" a commercial activity. *See infra* pp. 246-58 & 263-64. What "commercial activity" or "act" was the claim in *Mol, Inc.* "based upon"? Was the action based upon termination of the licensing agreement? or upon failure to grant export licenses? Does the distinction matter? *See infra* pp. 263-64.

12. *Relevance of acts concerning natural resources to commercial activity definition.* As *MOL, Inc.* illustrates, foreign states' activities relating to their natural resources appear to raise special concerns that have led some courts to refuse to assert jurisdiction under the FSIA. *E.g., In re SEDCO, Inc.*, 767 F.2d 1140 (5th Cir. 1985) (exploration for oil in Mexican waters is sovereign activity; emphasizing that activities occurred within Mexico's "patrimonial waters" and that "a very basic attribute of sovereignty is [a nation's] control over its mineral resources"); *IAM v. OPEC*, 477 F.Supp. 553, 569 (C.D. Calif. 1979), *aff'd on other grounds*, 649 F.2d 1354 (9th Cir. 1981), *cert. denied*, 454 U.S. 1163 (1982) (petroleum cartel not engaged in commercial activity); *Carey v. National Oil Corp.*, 453 F.Supp. 1097 (S.D.N.Y. 1978), *aff'd*, 592 F.2d 673 (2d Cir. 1979) (breach of oil supply contracts was sovereign act).

Are *MOL, Inc.* and other "natural resource" decisions correct in treating activities involving natural resources as uniquely deserving of immunity? Why are actions relating to natural resources afforded special treatment by some courts for sovereign immunity purposes? Is it because natural resources can be particularly important to national interests? Aren't other economic activities equally important, such as, for example, the national economic recovery program in *Weltover*? Even if natural resources are especially important, does the FSIA link sovereign immunity to the importance of a foreign state's national interests? As a policy matter, should foreign state actions that result from basic decisions about national policy be afforded immunity even if they are commercial? What effect would such a rule have upon private investment or trade with foreign states?

13. *Relevance of exercise of governmental authority to commercial activity.* In addition to suggesting

special treatment for activities relating to natural resources, *MOL, Inc.* and several other lower court decisions indicate that contracts are noncommercial if they include undertakings by foreign states or their agencies to exercise sovereign responsibilities (such as granting export licenses, tax benefits, or immigration waivers). *See Drexel Burnham Lambert Group, Inc. v. Committee of Receivers*, 12 F.3d 317, 329 (2d Cir. 1993); *Millen Industries, Inc. v. CCNAA*, 855 F.2d 879 (D.C. Cir. 1988); *Practical Concepts v. Republic of Bolivia*, 811 F.2d 1543 (D.C. Cir. 1987); *Jones v. Petty Ray Geophysical Geosource*, 722 F.Supp. 343 (S.D. Tex. 1989). *Compare Schoenberg v. Exportadora de Sal, SA*, 930 F.2d 777 (9th Cir. 1991) (state-owned company's transportation of Japanese university representatives, at request of Mexican government, held commercial activity). Is this aspect of *MOL, Inc.* persuasive? Why should a foreign state be permitted to make promises to do certain things — such as grant tax or tariff exemptions — and then breach these undertakings with impunity? Note that a U.S. court generally cannot compel a foreign state to perform a sovereign act — but that it could order damages for breach of an agreement to perform a sovereign act.

14. *Other problems in defining "commercial activities."* Lower courts have also encountered difficulties in classifying some quasi-commercial activities not concerning natural resources. In *Yessenin-Volpin v. Novosti Press Agency*, 443 F. Supp. 849 (S.D.N.Y. 1978), the court held that a Soviet press agency's publication and distribution of newspaper articles was sovereign propaganda, not commercial journalism. Similarly, the film making activities of a German state agency were held to be noncommercial diplomatic activity meant "to foster cultural relations and promote understanding between Germany and the United States." *Gittler v. German Information Center*, 408 N.Y.S.2d 600, 601 (1978). In contrast, the Soviet government's agreement to supply artists in connection with a cultural exchange has been held commercial. *United Euram Corp. v. USSR*, 461 F. Supp. 609 (S.D.N.Y. 1978). Does the FSIA's adoption of a "nature," rather than a "purpose," test cast doubt onto any of these results?

b. The "Based Upon" and "In Connection" Requirements

Section 1605(a)(2) lifts immunity only from suits that are "based upon" a commercial activity (§1605(a)(2)'s first clause) or that are "based upon" an act "in connection" with a commercial activity (§1605(a)(2)'s second and third clauses). The Act and its legislative history shed little light on the "based upon" or "in connection" requirements,[98] and lower courts have reached divergent results in applying them.[99]

Ascertaining the precise activity of a foreign state that an action is "based upon" has two important consequences.[100] First, this determination provides the basis for defining the conduct of a foreign state that must be examined to determine whether "commercial activity" (discussed immediately above) is involved. Second, it provides the basis for defining the conduct of the foreign defendant that must be examined for purposes of satisfying §1605(a)(2)'s "nexus" requirements (discussed immediately below). In both instances, the scope of the activity on which the plaintiff's claim is "based" can significantly affect the ultimate determination of immunity.

Following enactment of the FSIA, lower courts were not able to agree upon any precise definition of the "based upon" requirement. Two Courts of Appeals said that, in applying the "based upon" requirement, "we must isolate the specific conduct that underlies the suit," rather than looking generally to "the broad program or policy of

---

98. Lowenfeld, *Litigating a Sovereign Immunity Claim — The Haiti Case*, 49 N.Y.U.L. Rev. 377 (1974); Note, *Foreign Sovereign Immunity and Commercial Activity: A Conflicts Approach*, 83 Colum. L. Rev. 1440, 1488-91 (1983).

99. *See Vencedora Oceanica Navigacion v. Compagnie Nationale Algerienne de Navigation*, 730 F.2d 195 (5th Cir. 1984) (summarizing divergent lower court results).

100. *See Callejo v. Bancomer, SA*, 764 F.2d 1101, 1110 (5th Cir. 1985).

which the individual transaction is a part."[101] Other decisions took broader views, specifically rejecting a "niggardly construction" of the "based upon" requirement.[102] In *Saudi Arabia v. Nelson*,[103] the Supreme Court resolved this debate. It held that the "based upon" requirement called for a determination of "those elements of a claim that, if proven, would entitle a plaintiff to relief under his theory of the case."[104]

Relatively few cases have considered the meaning of the "in connection" requirement, as used in the second and third clauses of §1605(a)(2). In *Nelson*, the Court reasoned that the term must have a more expansive meaning than "based upon," but it did not say what that meaning was.[105] Lower courts have been cautious in reading the term broadly.[106]

SAUDI ARABIA v. NELSON

113 S.Ct. 1471 (1993)

JUSTICE SOUTER. The FSIA entitles foreign states to immunity from the jurisdiction of courts in the United States, subject to certain enumerated exceptions. One is that a foreign state shall not be immune in any case "in which the action is based upon a commercial activity carried on in the United States by the foreign state." [28 U.S.C. §1605(a)(2).] We hold that respondents' action alleging personal injury resulting from unlawful detention and torture by the Saudi Government is not "based upon a commercial activity" within the meaning of the Act, which consequently confers no jurisdiction over respondents' suit.

I. Because this case comes to us on a motion to dismiss the complaint, we assume that we have truthful factual allegations before us. ... Petitioner Kingdom of Saudi Arabia owns and operates petitioner King Faisal Specialist Hospital in Riyadh, as well as petitioner Royspec Purchasing Services, the Hospital's corporate purchasing agent in the United States. The Hospital Corporation of America, Ltd. ("HCA"), an independent corporation existing under the laws of the Cayman Islands, recruits Americans for employment at the Hospital under an agreement signed with Saudi Arabia in 1973.

In its recruitment effort, HCA placed an advertisement in a trade periodical seeking applications for a position as a monitoring systems engineer at the Hospital.

---

101. *Weltover, Inc. v. Republic of Argentina*, 941 F.2d 145, 150 (2d Cir. 1991) (quoting *Rush-Presbyterium St. Luke's Medical Center v. Hellenic Republic*, 877 F.2d 574, 580 (7th Cir. 1989), *aff'd*, 504 U.S. 607 (1992). *See also Baglab Ltd. v. Johnson Matthey Bankers Ltd.*, 665 F. Supp. 289, 294 (S.D.N.Y. 1987) (must "define with precision"); *Braka v. Bancomer, SA*, 589 F. Supp. 1465, 1469 (S.D.N.Y. 1984), *aff'd*, 762 F.2d 222 (2d Cir. 1985).

102. *Gemini Shipping, Inc. v. Foreign Trade Org.*, 647 F.2d 317, 319 (2d Cir. 1981). *See also Gilson v. Republic of Ireland*, 682 F.2d 1022, 1027 n.22 (D.C. Cir. 1982).

103. 113 S.Ct. 1471 (1993).

104. 113 S.Ct. at 1477.

105. 113 S.Ct. at 1477.

106. *See infra* pp. 263-64.

The advertisement drew the attention of respondent Scott Nelson in September 1983, while Nelson was in the United States. After interviewing for the position in Saudi Arabia, Nelson returned to the United States, where he signed an employment contract with the Hospital ... and attended an orientation session that HCA conducted for Hospital employees. ... HCA identified Royspec as the point of contact in the United States for family members who might wish to reach Nelson in an emergency.

In December 1983, Nelson went to Saudi Arabia and began work at the Hospital, monitoring all "facilities, equipment, utilities and maintenance systems to insure the safety of patients, hospital staff, and others." He did his job without significant incident until March 1984, when he discovered safety defects. ... Nelson repeatedly advised Hospital officials of the safety defects and reported the defects to a Saudi Government commission as well. Hospital officials instructed Nelson to ignore the problems. The Hospital's response to Nelson's reports changed, however, on September 27, 1984, when certain Hospital employees summoned him to the Hospital's security office where agents of the Saudi Government arrested him.[107] The agents transported Nelson to a jail cell, in which they "shackled, tortured and bea[t]" him, and kept him four days without food. Although Nelson did not understand Arabic, Government agents forced him to sign a statement written in that language. ... Two days later, Government agents transferred Nelson to the Al Sijan Prison "to await trial on unknown charges." At the Prison, Nelson was confined in an overcrowded cell area infested with rats, where he had to fight other prisoners for food and from which he was taken only once a week for fresh air and exercise. Although police interrogators repeatedly questioned him in Arabic, Nelson did not learn the nature of the charges, if any, against him. For several days, the Saudi Government failed to advise Nelson's family of his whereabouts, though a Saudi official eventually told Nelson's wife ... that he could arrange for her husband's release if she provided sexual favors.

Although officials from the United States Embassy visited Nelson twice during his detention, they concluded that his allegations of Saudi mistreatment were "not credible" and made no protest to Saudi authorities. It was only at the personal request of a United States Senator that the Saudi Government released Nelson, 39 days after his arrest, on November 5, 1984. Seven days later, after failing to convince him to return to work at the Hospital, the Saudi Government allowed Nelson to leave the country.

In 1988, Nelson and his wife filed this action against petitioners in the U.S. District Court for the Southern District of Florida seeking damages for personal injury. The Nelsons' complaint sets out 16 causes of action, which fall into three categories[: (i) various intentional torts, including battery, unlawful detainment,

---

107. Petitioners assert that the Saudi Government arrested Nelson because he had falsely represented to the Hospital that he had received a degree from the Massachusetts Institute of Technology and had provided the Hospital with a forged diploma to verify his claim. The Nelsons concede these misrepresentations, but dispute that they occasioned Scott Nelson's arrest.

wrongful arrest and imprisonment, false imprisonment; (ii) negligently failing to warn Nelson of otherwise undisclosed dangers of his employment, namely, that if he attempted to report safety hazards the Hospital would likely retaliate against him and the Saudi Government might detain and physically abuse him without legal cause; and (iii) claims that Vivian Nelson sustained derivative injury resulting from petitioners' actions.] Presumably because the employment contract provided that Saudi courts would have exclusive jurisdiction over claims for breach of contract, the Nelsons raised no such matters. ...

II. The [FSIA] "provides the sole basis for obtaining jurisdiction over a foreign state in the courts of this country." *Argentine Republic v. Amerada Hess Shipping Corp.*, 488 U.S. 428, 443 (1989). Under the Act, a foreign state is presumptively immune from the jurisdiction of United States courts; unless a specified exception applies, a federal court lacks subject-matter jurisdiction over a claim against a foreign state.

Only one such exception is said to apply here. The first clause of §1605(a)(2) of the Act provides that a foreign state shall not be immune from the jurisdiction of United States courts in any case "in which the action is based upon a commercial activity carried on in the United States by the foreign state." The Act defines such activity as "commercial activity carried on by such state and having substantial contact with the United States," §1603(e), and provides that a commercial activity may be "either a regular course of commercial conduct or a particular commercial transaction or act," the "commercial character of [which] shall be determined by reference to" its "nature," rather than its "purpose." §1603(d).

There is no dispute here that Saudi Arabia, the Hospital, and Royspec all qualify as "foreign state[s]" within the meaning of the Act. For there to be jurisdiction in this case, therefore, the Nelsons' action must be "based upon" some "commercial activity" by petitioners that had "substantial contact" with the United States within the meaning of the Act. Because we conclude that the suit is not based upon any commercial activity by petitioners, we need not reach the issue of substantial contact with the United States.

We begin our analysis by identifying the particular conduct on which the Nelsons' action is "based" for purposes of the Act. Although the Act contains no definition of the phrase "based upon," and the relatively sparse legislative history offers no assistance, guidance is hardly necessary. In denoting conduct that forms the "basis," or "foundation," for a claim, *see Black's Law Dictionary* 151 (6th ed. 1990) (defining "base"); *Webster's Third New International Dictionary* 180, 181 (1976) (defining "base" and "based"), the phrase is read most naturally to mean those elements of a claim that, if proven, would entitle a plaintiff to relief under his theory of the case. *See Callejo v. Bancomer, SA*, 764 F.2d 1101, 1109 (5th Cir. 1985) (focus should be on the "gravamen of the complaint"); *accord, Santos v. Compagnie Nationale Air France*, 934 F.2d 890, 893 (CA7 1991) ("An action is based upon the elements that prove the claim, no more and no less").

What the natural meaning of the phrase "based upon" suggests, the context confirms. [Section] 1605(a)(2) contains two clauses following the one at issue here. The second allows for jurisdiction where a suit "is based ... upon an act performed in the United States in connection with a commercial activity of the foreign state elsewhere," and the third speaks in like terms, allowing for jurisdiction where an action "is based ... upon an act outside the territory of the United States in connection with a commercial activity of the foreign state elsewhere and that act causes a direct effect in the United States." Distinctions among descriptions juxtaposed against each other are naturally understood to be significant, and Congress manifestly understood there to be a difference between a suit "based upon" commercial activity and one "based upon" acts performed "in connection with" such activity. The only reasonable reading of the former term calls for something more than a mere connection with, or relation to, commercial activity.[108]

In this case, the Nelsons have alleged that petitioners recruited Scott Nelson for work at the Hospital, signed an employment contract with him, and subsequently employed him. While these activities led to the conduct that eventually injured the Nelsons, they are not the basis for the Nelsons' suit. Even taking each of the Nelsons' allegations about Scott Nelson's recruitment and employment as true, those facts alone entitle the Nelsons to nothing under their theory of the case. The Nelsons have not, after all, alleged breach of contract, but personal injuries caused by petitioners' intentional wrongs and by petitioners' negligent failure to warn Scott Nelson that they might commit those wrongs. Those torts, and not the arguably commercial activities that preceded their commission, form the basis for the Nelsons' suit.

Petitioners' tortious conduct itself fails to qualify as "commercial activity" within the meaning of the Act, although the Act is too "'obtuse'" to be of much help in reaching that conclusion. *Callejo*, 764 F.2d at 1107. We have seen already that the Act defines "commercial activity" as "either a regular course of commercial conduct or a particular commercial transaction or act," and provides that "[t]he commercial character of an activity shall be determined by reference to the nature of the course of conduct or particular transaction or act, rather than by reference to its purpose." 28 U.S.C. §1603(d). If this is a definition, it is one distinguished only by its diffidence; as we observed in our most recent case on the subject, it "leaves the critical term 'commercial' largely undefined." *Republic of Argentina v. Weltover, Inc.*; Lowenfeld, *Litigating a Sovereign Immunity Claim — The Haiti Case*, 49 N.Y.U. L. Rev. 377, 435, n.244 (1974) ("Start with 'activity,' proceed via 'conduct' or 'transaction' to 'character,' then refer to 'nature,' and then go back to 'commercial,' the term you started out to define in the first place"); G. Born & D. Westin, *International Civil Litigation*

---

108. We do not mean to suggest that the first clause of §1605(a)(2) necessarily requires that each and every element of a claim be commercial activity by a foreign state, and we do not address the case where a claim consists of both commercial and sovereign elements. We do conclude, however, that where a claim rests entirely upon activities sovereign in character, as here, jurisdiction will not exist under that clause regardless of any connection the sovereign acts may have with commercial activity.

in United States Courts 479-480 (2d ed. 1992). We do not, however, have the option to throw up our hands. The term has to be given some interpretation, and congressional diffidence necessarily results in judicial responsibility to determine what a "commercial activity" is for purposes of the Act. ...

We explained in *Weltover* that a state engages in commercial activity under the restrictive theory where it exercises "'only those powers that can also be exercised by private citizens,'" as distinct from those "'powers peculiar to sovereigns.'" Put differently, a foreign state engages in commercial activity for purposes of the restrictive theory only where it acts "in the manner of a private player within" the market. ... Unlike Argentina's activities that we considered in *Weltover*, the intentional conduct alleged here (the Saudi Government's wrongful arrest, imprisonment, and torture of Nelson) could not qualify as commercial under the restrictive theory. The conduct boils down to abuse of the power of its police by the Saudi Government, and however monstrous such abuse undoubtedly may be, a foreign state's exercise of the power of its police has long been understood for purposes of the restrictive theory as peculiarly sovereign in nature. *See Victory Transport Inc. v. Comisaria General de Abastecimientos y Transportes*, 336 F.2d 354, 360 (2d Cir. 1964) (restrictive theory does extend immunity to a foreign state's "internal administrative acts"), *cert. denied*, 381 U.S. 934 (1965).[109] Exercise of the powers of police and penal officers is not the sort of action by which private parties can engage in commerce. ...

The Nelsons and their amici urge us to give significance to their assertion that the Saudi Government subjected Nelson to the abuse alleged as retaliation for his persistence in reporting Hospital safety violations, and argue that the character of the mistreatment was consequently commercial. ... But this argument does not alter the fact that the powers allegedly abused were those of police and penal officers. In any event, the argument is off the point, for it goes to purpose, the very fact the Act renders irrelevant to the question of an activity's commercial character. Whatever may have been the Saudi Government's motivation for its allegedly abusive treatment of Nelson, it remains the case that the Nelsons' action is based upon a sovereign activity. ...

In addition to the intentionally tortious conduct, the Nelsons claim a separate basis for recovery in petitioners' failure to warn Scott Nelson of the hidden dangers associated with his employment. The Nelsons allege that, at the time petitioners recruited Scott Nelson and thereafter, they failed to warn him of the possibility of severe retaliatory action if he attempted to disclose any safety hazards he might discover on the job. In other words, petitioners bore a duty to warn of their own propensity for tortious conduct. But this is merely a semantic ploy. For aught we can

---

109. The State Department's practice prior to the passage of the Act supports this understanding. Prior to the Act's passage, the State Department would determine in the first instance whether a foreign state was entitled to immunity and make an appropriate recommendation to the courts. A compilation of available materials demonstrates that the Department recognized immunity with respect to claims involving the exercise of the power of the police or military of a foreign state. ...

see, a plaintiff could recast virtually any claim of intentional tort committed by sovereign act as a claim of failure to warn, simply by charging the defendant with an obligation to announce its own tortious propensity before indulging it. To give jurisdictional significance to this feint of language would effectively thwart the Act's manifest purpose to codify the restrictive theory of foreign sovereign immunity.

HOLD

III. The Nelsons' action is not "based upon a commercial activity" within the meaning of the first clause of §1605(a)(2) of the Act, and the judgment of the Court of Appeals is accordingly reversed.

JUSTICE WHITE, with whom JUSTICE BLACKMUN joins, concurring in the judgment. ... The majority concludes that petitioners enjoy sovereign immunity because respondents' action is not "based upon a commercial activity." I disagree. I nonetheless concur in the judgment because in my view the commercial conduct upon which respondents base their complaint was not "carried on in the United States."

As the majority notes, the first step in the analysis is to identify the conduct on which the action is based. Respondents have pointed to two distinct possibilities. The first, seemingly pressed at trial and on appeal, consists of the recruiting and hiring activity in the United States. Although this conduct would undoubtedly qualify as "commercial," I agree with the majority that it is "not the basis for the Nelsons' suit," for it is unrelated to the elements of respondents' complaint.

In a partial change of course, respondents suggest to this Court both in their brief and at oral argument that we focus on the hospital's commercial activity in Saudi Arabia, its employment practices and disciplinary procedures. Under this view, the Court would then work its way back to the recruiting and hiring activity in order to establish that the commercial conduct in fact had "substantial contact" with the United States. The majority never reaches this second stage, finding instead that petitioners' conduct is not commercial because it "is not the sort of action by which private parties can engage in commerce." If by that the majority means that it is not the manner in which private parties ought to engage in commerce, I wholeheartedly agree. That, however, is not the relevant inquiry. Rather, the question we must ask is whether it is the manner in which private parties at times do engage in commerce.

To run and operate a hospital, even a public hospital, is to engage in a commercial enterprise. The majority never concedes this point, but it does not deny it either, and to my mind the matter is self-evident. By the same token, warning an employee when he blows the whistle and taking retaliatory action, such as harassment, involuntary transfer, discharge, or other tortious behavior, although not prototypical commercial acts, are certainly well within the bounds of commercial activity. The House and Senate Reports accompanying the legislation virtually compel this conclusion, explaining as they do that "a foreign government's ... employment or engagement of laborers, clerical staff or marketing agents ... would be among those included within" the definition of commercial activity. H.R. Rep. No. 94-1487, 16 (1976) (House Report); S.R. Rep. No. 94-1310, 16 (1976) (Senate Report), U.S. Code

Cong. & Admin. News 1976, pp. 6604, 6615. Nelson alleges that petitioners harmed him in the course of engaging in their commercial enterprise, as a direct result of their commercial acts. His claim, in other words, is "based upon commercial activity."

Indeed, I am somewhat at a loss as to what exactly the majority believes petitioners have done that a private employer could not. As countless cases attest, retaliation for whistleblowing is not a practice foreign to the marketplace. Congress passed a statute in response to such behavior, as have numerous States. On occasion, private employers also have been known to retaliate by enlisting the help of police officers to falsely arrest employees. More generally, private parties have been held liable for conspiring with public authorities to effectuate an arrest, and for using private security personnel for the same purposes.

Therefore, had the hospital retaliated against Nelson by hiring thugs to do the job, I assume the majority — no longer able to describe this conduct as "a foreign state's exercise of the power of its police," — would consent to calling it "commercial." For, in such circumstances, the state-run hospital would be operating as any private participant in the marketplace and respondents' action would be based on the operation by Saudi Arabia's agents of a commercial business.

At the heart of the majority's conclusion, in other words, is the fact that the hospital in this case chose to call in government security forces. I find this fixation on the intervention of police officers, and the ensuing characterization of the conduct as "peculiarly sovereign in nature," to be misguided. To begin, it fails to capture respondents' complaint in full. Far from being directed solely at the activities of the Saudi police, it alleges that agents of the hospital summoned Nelson to its security office because he reported safety concerns and that the hospital played a part in the subsequent beating and imprisonment. Without more, that type of behavior hardly qualifies as sovereign. Thus, even assuming for the sake of argument that the role of the official police somehow affected the nature of petitioners' conduct, the claim cannot be said to "rest[] entirely upon activities sovereign in character" [citing the majority opinion]. At the very least it "consists of both commercial and sovereign elements," thereby presenting the specific question the majority chooses to elude. ...

Reliance on the fact that Nelson's employer enlisted the help of public rather than private security personnel is also at odds with Congress' intent. The purpose of the commercial exception being to prevent foreign states from taking refuge behind their sovereignty when they act as market participants, it seems to me that this is precisely the type of distinction we should seek to avoid. Because both the hospital and the police are agents of the state, the case in my mind turns on whether the sovereign is acting in a commercial capacity, not on whether it resorts to thugs or government officers to carry on its business. That, when the hospital calls in security to get even with a whistleblower, it comes clothed in police apparel says more about the state-owned nature of the commercial enterprise than about the noncommercial nature of its tortious conduct. ...

C. Contrary to the majority's suggestion, this conclusion does not involve inquiring into the purpose of the conduct. Matters would be different, I suppose, if Nelson had been recruited to work in the Saudi police force and, having reported safety violations, suffered retributive punishment, for there the Saudi authorities would be engaged in distinctly sovereign activities. *Cf.* House Report, at 16 ("Also public or governmental and not commercial in nature, would be the employment of diplomatic, civil service, or military personnel"). The same would be true if Nelson was a mere tourist in Saudi Arabia and had been summarily expelled by order of immigration officials. In this instance, however, the state-owned hospital was engaged in ordinary commercial business and "[i]n their commercial capacities, foreign governments do not exercise powers peculiar to sovereigns. Instead, they exercise only those powers that can also be exercised by private citizens." *Alfred Dunhill v. Republic of Cuba*, 425 U.S. 682, 704 (plurality opinion). ...

II. Nevertheless, I reach the same conclusion as the majority because petitioners' commercial activity was not "carried on in the United States." The Act defines such conduct as "commercial activity ... having substantial contact with the United States." 28 U.S.C. §1603(e). Respondents point to the hospital's recruitment efforts in the United States, including advertising in the American media, and the signing of the employment contract in Miami. As I earlier noted, while these may very well qualify as commercial activity in the United States, they do not constitute the commercial activity upon which respondents' action is based. Conversely, petitioners' commercial conduct in Saudi Arabia, though constituting the basis of the Nelsons' suit, lacks a sufficient nexus to the United States. Neither the hospital's employment practices, nor its disciplinary procedures, has any apparent connection to this country. On that basis, I agree that the Act does not grant the Nelsons access to our courts. ...

JUSTICE KENNEDY, with whom JUSTICE BLACKMUN and JUSTICE STEVENS join as to Parts I-B and II, concurring in part and dissenting in part. I join all of the Court's opinion except the last paragraph of Part II, where, with almost no explanation, the Court rules that, like the intentional tort claim, the claims based on negligent failure to warn are outside the subject-matter jurisdiction of the federal courts. These claims stand on a much different footing from the intentional tort claims for purposes of the FSIA. In my view, they ought to be remanded to the District Court for further consideration.

I agree with the Court's holding that the Nelsons' claims of intentional wrongdoing by the Hospital and the Kingdom of Saudi Arabia are based on sovereign, not commercial, activity, and so fall outside the commercial activity exception to the grant of foreign sovereign immunity contained in 28 U.S.C. §1604. The intentional tort counts of the Nelsons' complaint recite the alleged unlawful arrest, imprisonment, and torture of Mr. Nelson by the Saudi police acting in their official capacities. These are not the sort of activities by which a private party conducts its business affairs; if we classified them as commercial, the commercial activity exception would in large measure swallow the rule of foreign sovereign immunity Congress enacted in the FSIA.

By the same token, however, the Nelsons' claims alleging that the Hospital, the Kingdom, and Royspec were negligent in failing during their recruitment of Nelson to warn him of foreseeable dangers are based upon commercial activity having substantial contact with the United States. As such, they are within the commercial activity exception and the jurisdiction of the federal courts. Unlike the intentional tort counts of the complaint, the failure to warn counts do not complain of a police beating in Saudi Arabia; rather, they complain of a negligent omission made during the recruiting of a hospital employee in the United States. To obtain relief, the Nelsons would be obliged to prove that the Hospital's recruiting agent did not tell Nelson about the foreseeable hazards of his prospective employment in Saudi Arabia. Under the Court's test, this omission is what the negligence counts are "based upon."

Omission of important information during employee recruiting is commercial activity as we have described it. It seems plain that recruiting employees is an activity undertaken by private hospitals in the normal course of business. Locating and hiring employees implicates no power unique to the sovereign. In explaining the terms and conditions of employment, including the risks and rewards of a particular job, a governmental entity acts in "the manner of a private player within" the commercial marketplace. ...

The recruiting activity alleged in the failure to warn counts of the complaint also satisfies the final requirement for invoking the commercial activity exception: that the claims be based upon commercial activity "having substantial contact with the United States." 28 U.S.C. §1603(e). Nelson's recruitment was performed by Hospital Corporation of America ("HCA"), a wholly owned subsidiary of a U.S. corporation, which, for a period of at least 16 years beginning in 1973, acted as the Kingdom of Saudi Arabia's exclusive agent for recruiting employees for the Hospital. HCA in the regular course of its business seeks employees for the Hospital in the American labor market. HCA advertised in an American magazine, seeking applicants for the position Nelson later filled. Nelson saw the ad in the United States and contacted HCA in Tennessee. After an interview in Saudi Arabia, Nelson returned to Florida, where he signed an employment contract and underwent personnel processing and application procedures. Before leaving to take his job at the Hospital, Nelson attended an orientation session conducted by HCA in Tennessee for new employees. These activities have more than substantial contact with the United States; most of them were "carried on in the United States." 28 U.S.C. §1605(a)(2). In alleging that the petitioners neglected during these activities to tell him what they were bound to under state law, Nelson meets all of the statutory requirements for invoking federal jurisdiction under the commercial activity exception.

Having met the jurisdictional prerequisites of the FSIA, the Nelsons' failure to warn claims should survive petitioners' motion under Federal Rule of Civil Procedure 12(b)(1) to dismiss for want of subject-matter jurisdiction. Yet instead of remanding these claims to the District Court for further proceedings, the majority dismisses them in a single short paragraph. ... The Court's summary treatment may stem from doubts about the underlying validity of the negligence cause of action. ... These doubts, however, are not relevant to the analytical task at hand. ...

JUSTICE STEVENS, dissenting. Under the [FSIA], a foreign state is subject to the jurisdiction of American courts if two conditions are met: The action must be "based upon a commercial activity" and that activity must have a "substantial contact with the United States." These two conditions should be separately analyzed because they serve two different purposes. The former excludes commercial activity from the scope of the foreign sovereign's immunity from suit; the second identifies the contacts with the United States that support the assertion of jurisdiction over the defendant.

In this case, as Justice White has demonstrated, petitioner's operation of the hospital and its employment practices and disciplinary procedures are "commercial activities" within the meaning of the statute, and respondent's claim that he was punished for acts performed in the course of his employment was unquestionably "based upon" those activities. Thus, the first statutory condition is satisfied; petitioner is not entitled to immunity from the claims asserted by respondent.

Unlike Justice White, however, I am also convinced that petitioner's commercial activities — whether defined as the regular course of conduct of operating a hospital or, more specifically, as the commercial transaction of engaging respondent "as an employee with specific responsibilities in that enterprise," — have sufficient contact with the United States to justify the exercise of federal jurisdiction. Petitioner Royspec maintains an office in Maryland and purchases hospital supplies and equipment in this country. For nearly two decades the Hospital's American agent has maintained an office in the United States and regularly engaged in the recruitment of personnel in this country. Respondent himself was recruited in the United States and entered into his employment contract with the hospital in the United States. Before traveling to Saudi Arabia to assume his position at the hospital, respondent attended an orientation program in Tennessee. The position for which respondent was recruited and ultimately hired was that of a monitoring systems manager, a troubleshooter, and ... it was precisely respondent's performance of those responsibilities that led to the hospital's retaliatory actions against him.

Whether the first clause of §1605(a)(2) broadly authorizes "general" jurisdiction over foreign entities that engage in substantial commercial activity in this country, or, more narrowly, authorizes only "specific" jurisdiction over particular commercial claims that have a substantial contact with the United States,[110] petitioners' contacts

---

110. Though this case does not require resolution of that question (because petitioners' contacts with the United States satisfy, in my view, the more narrow requirements of "specific" jurisdiction), I am inclined to agree with the view expressed by Judge Higginbotham in his separate opinion in *Vencedora Oceanica Navigacion, SA v. Compagnie Nationale Algerienne de Navigation*, 730 F.2d 195, 204-205 (1984) (concurring in part and dissenting in part), that the first clause of §1605(a)(2), interpreted in light of the relevant legislative history and the second and third clauses of the provision, does authorize "general" jurisdiction over foreign entities that engage in substantial commercial activities in the United States.

with the United States in this case are, in my view, plainly sufficient to subject petitioners to suit in this country on a claim arising out of its nonimmune commercial activity relating to respondent. If the same activities had been performed by a private business, I have no doubt jurisdiction would be upheld. And that, of course, should be a touchstone of our inquiry; for as Justice White explains, when a foreign nation sheds its uniquely sovereign status and seeks out the benefits of the private marketplace, it must, like any private party, bear the burdens and responsibilities imposed by that marketplace. ...

Notes on Nelson

1. *Significance of determining what activity an action is "based upon."* A critical issue in *Nelson* was whether the plaintiff's claims were "based upon" one set of activities (*i.e.*, employment relations at a commercial hospital) or another set of activities (*i.e.*, police and detention practices). As *Nelson* illustrates, determining what conduct the plaintiff's action is "based upon" is closely related to determining both whether particular conduct is "commercial activity" and whether that conduct has a sufficient U.S. nexus.

2. *Definition of "based upon" requirement.* Justice Souter's majority opinion in *Nelson* interpreted §1605(a)(2)'s "based upon" requirement as "denoting conduct that forms the 'basis,' or 'foundation,' for a claim." The Court continued: "[T]he phrase is read most naturally to mean those elements of a claim that, if proven, would entitle a plaintiff to relief under his theory of the case." None of the various dissents and concurrences in *Nelson* appear to disagree with this rule. Nevertheless, some lower courts had arrived at somewhat different interpretations of §1605's "based upon" requirement. In *Gilson v. Republic of Ireland*, 682 F.2d 1022, 1027 n.22 (D.C. Cir. 1982), the court rejected a "narrow construction" and held that "[s]ection 1605's 'based upon' standard is satisfied if plaintiff can show a direct causal connection between [the defendant's commercial activity in the United States] and the [acts] giving rise to his claims ... or if he can show that [the defendant's U.S. commercial activity] is an element of the cause of action under whatever law governs his claims." *Id.* at 1027 n.22.

Which view of the "based upon" standard is more persuasive? Are any of these tests workable? Are due process precedents defining the scope of specific jurisdiction relevant to the FSIA's "based upon" requirement?

3. *Application of "based upon" standard in* Nelson. Did Justice Souter correctly apply the "based upon" standard in *Nelson*? What conduct was the Nelsons' complaint based upon? Consider the following possibilities: (a) the arrest, detention, and mistreatment of Nelson; (b) the recruitment and hiring of Nelson; (c) the operation of the King Faisal Hospital.

(a) *Divergent views in* Nelson. What conduct did Justice Souter think the Nelsons' complaint was based upon? Justice White? Justice Kennedy? Did the various Justices apply different definitions of "based upon" in reaching their various different conclusions? What does this suggest about the value and reliability of the "based upon" standard? Which Justice reached the right conclusion in *Nelson* regarding the application of the "based upon" requirement?

(b) *Justice Souter's "based upon" analysis.* Is Justice Souter guilty of a "single-minded focus on the exercise of police power," as Justice White writes? Or was it the Nelsons' complaint that had a single-minded focus?

(c) *Justice White's "based upon" analysis.* Consider Justice White's argument that respondents suggested "to *this Court* both in their brief and at oral argument that we focus on the hospital's commercial activity in Saudi Arabia." Is that appropriate? Does not §1605(a)(2) of the FSIA (and sound judicial administration) require focussing on what is in plaintiff's complaint, not what it argues on appeal in the Supreme Court? Suppose that Nelson had complained that the Hospital had unlawfully procured his false arrest and subsequent poor treatment, in an effort to protect its shoddy operating practices. What activity would that claim be "based upon"?

(d) *Justice Kennedy's "based upon" analysis.* Consider Justice Kennedy's view that the Nelsons' intentional tort claims were "based upon" official police conduct, but that their negligent failure to warn claims were based upon the defendants' recruitment and hiring activities in the United States. How does Justice Souter deal with this point? Is Justice Kennedy correct in concluding, under the majority's own test, that the failure to warn claims were "based upon" recruitment in the United States? Or, were those claims ultimately "based upon" the same police practices as to which warnings should have been given?

4. *Mixed sovereign/commercial activities*. A plaintiff's complaint may be "based upon" both commercial and noncommercial activities. If this occurs, can §1605(a)(2) be satisfied? Or must "each and every element of a claim be commercial activity by a foreign state"? Justice Souter writes in a footnote that the Court does not "address the case where a claim consists of both commercial and sovereign elements." *See supra* pp. 250 n. 108. How should such cases be decided? Does it matter which clause of §1605(a)(2) is involved? Was the claim in *MOL, Inc.* based upon both sovereign and commercial activities?

As discussed above, some lower courts have held that promises to perform sovereign acts are not "commercial," even if they are contained in a "commercial" contract. A few of these courts have held that the contract must be dissected to distinguish between commercial and noncommercial obligations: the FSIA permits suits for the former, but not the latter. In the words of one court, considering whether a foreign state was immune from a suit based upon breach of its promise to exempt the plaintiff's products from duty:

> when a transaction partakes of both commercial and sovereign elements, jurisdiction under
> the FSIA will turn on which element the cause of action is based on ... [T]o the extent that the
> causes of action are based on promises, breaches of promises, and other allegedly actionable
> conduct involving extending duty-free status ... these would plainly be sovereign aspects of the
> transaction over which we lack jurisdiction. *Millen Industries, Inc. v. Coordination Council for
> North American Affairs*, 855 F.2d 879 (D.C. Cir. 1988)

Is this a sensible line of analysis? Is *Nelson* in fact a case that was based upon both commercial and sovereign acts?

5. *Application of "based upon" requirement under first clause of §1605(a)(2)*. Suppose that a foreign state engages in a sovereign act — such as issuing a decree or enacting a law — that cancels both its own commercial contracts and those of private parties. Is an action for breach of contract "based upon" the commercial contract or the sovereign decree? *See Jamini v. Kuwait University*, 1995 WL 19331 (D.C. Cir. 1995) (suit is based on contract's termination, not issuance of decree). What activities was the plaintiff's suit "based upon" in *Mol, Inc.* and *Weltover*?

c. The "Nexus" Requirements

Closely related to §1605(a)(2)'s "based upon" and "in connection" requirements are the section's so-called "nexus" requirements. Even if a plaintiff's action is "based upon" the indisputably "commercial activity" of a foreign state defendant, the defendant may still enjoy immunity from U.S. jurisdiction. In order to establish jurisdiction under §1605(a)(2), a plaintiff must also satisfy one of the section's three nexus requirements, which demand that the foreign state's commercial conduct have a sufficiently close relationship to the United States.

Section 1605(a)(2) enumerates three relationships between the defendant's conduct and the United States that will permit an exercise of U.S. jurisdiction:

1. The plaintiff's action is "based upon a commercial activity carried on in the United States by the foreign state";

2. The plaintiff's action is based upon an "act" in the United States "in connection with a commercial activity of the foreign state elsewhere"; or

3. The plaintiff's action is based "upon an act outside the territory of the United States in connection with a commercial activity of the foreign state elsewhere and that act causes a direct effect in the United States."

The Act and its legislative history shed little light on these three clauses. Section 1603(e) defines "a commercial activity carried on in the United States by a foreign state" as "commercial activity carried on by such state and having *substantial contact* with the United States."[111] The legislative history of the first clause of §1605(a)(2) adds that:

> [t]his definition includes cases based on commercial transactions performed in whole or in part in the United States, import-export transactions involving sales to, or purchases from, concerns in the United States, business torts occurring in the United States ... and an indebtedness incurred by a foreign state which negotiates or executes a loan agreement in the United States, or which receives financing from a private or public lending institution located in the United States.

The FSIA's legislative history also provides a gloss on the second clause of §1605(a)(2), which applies to acts within the United States in connection with commercial activities elsewhere. In the words of the House Report to the Act, the second clause "looks to conduct of the foreign state in the United States which relates either to a regular course of commercial conduct elsewhere or to a particular commercial transaction concluded or carried out in part elsewhere."[112] Examples provided by the legislative history include:

> a representation in the United States by an agent of a foreign state that leads to an action for restitution based on unjust enrichment; an act in the United States that violates U.S. securities laws or regulations; the wrongful discharge in the United States of an employee of the foreign state who has been employed in connection with a commercial activity carried on in some third country.[113]

The following cases illustrate how U.S. courts have applied the "U.S. nexus" requirements of §1605(a)(2). *Republic of Argentina v. Weltover, Inc.* applies the "direct effects" standard of the third clause of §1605(a)(2). *Saudi Arabia v. Nelson* examines the first clause of §1605(a)(2), as well as the "based upon" requirement.

REPUBLIC OF ARGENTINA v. WELTOVER, INC.

504 U.S. 607 (1992)
[also partially excerpted above at pp. 237-41]

JUSTICE SCALIA [for a unanimous Court]. [In a portion of the Court's opinion excerpted above, Justice Scalia held that Argentina's issuing of certain debt instrument, named "Bonods," constituted commercial activity within the meaning of §1605(a)(2). The remainder of the Court's opinion, excerpted below, concluded that

---

111. H.R. Rep. No. 1487, 94th Cong., 2d Sess. 17, *reprinted in* 1976 U.S. Code Cong. & Admin. News at 6615-16.

112. H.R. Rep. No. 1487, 94th Cong., 2d Sess. 17, *reprinted in* 1976 U.S. Code Cong. & Admin. News at 6615-16.

113. H.R. Rep. No. 1487, 94th Cong., 2d Sess. 17, *reprinted in* 1976 U.S. Code Cong. & Admin. News at 6615-16.

the rescheduling of the Bonods had a "direct effect" in the United States within the meaning of the third clause of §1605(a)(2).]

The remaining question is whether Argentina's unilateral rescheduling of the Bonods had a "direct effect" in the United States. In addressing this issue, the Court of Appeals rejected the suggestion in the legislative history of the FSIA that an effect is not "direct" unless it is both "substantial" and "foreseeable." That suggestion is found in the House Report, which states that conduct covered by the third clause of §1605(a)(2) would be subject to the jurisdiction of American courts "consistent with principles set forth in §18, *Restatement (Second) Foreign Relations Law* (1965)." H.R. Rep. No. 94-1487, p. 19 (1976). Section 18 states that American laws are not given extraterritorial application except with respect to conduct that has, as a "direct and foreseeable result," a "substantial" effect within the United States. Since this obviously deals with jurisdiction to *legislate* rather than jurisdiction to *adjudicate,* this passage of the House Report has been charitably described as "a bit of a *non sequitur,*" *Texas Trading & Milling Corp. v. Federal Republic of Nigeria,* 647 F.2d 300, 311 (2d Cir. 1981), *cert. denied,* 454 U.S. 1148 (1982). Of course the generally applicable principle *de minimis no curat lex* ensures that jurisdiction may not be predicated on purely trivial effects in the United States. But we reject the suggestion that §1605(a)(2) contains any unexpressed requirement of "substantiality" or "foreseeability." As the Court of Appeals recognized, an effect is "direct" if it follows "as an immediate consequence of the defendant's ... activity."

The Court of Appeals concluded that the rescheduling of the maturity dates obviously had a "direct effect" on respondents. It further concluded that that effect was sufficiently "in the United States" for purposes of the FSIA, in part because "Congress would have wanted an American court to entertain this action" in order to preserve New York City's status as "a preeminent commercial center." The question, however, is not what Congress "would have wanted" but what Congress enacted in the FSIA. Although we are happy to endorse the Second Circuit's recognition of "New York's status as a world financial leader," the effect of Argentina's rescheduling in diminishing that status (assuming it is not too speculative to be considered an effect at all) is too remote and attenuated to satisfy the "direct effect" requirement of the FSIA.

We nonetheless have little difficulty concluding that Argentina's unilateral rescheduling of the maturity dates on the Bonods had a "direct effect" in the United States. Respondents had designated their accounts in New York as the place of payment, and Argentina made some interest payments into those accounts before announcing that it was rescheduling the payments. Because New York was thus the place of performance for Argentina's ultimate contractual obligations, the rescheduling of those obligations necessarily had a "direct effect" in the United States; Money that was supposed to have been delivered to a New York bank for deposit was not forthcoming. We reject Argentina's suggestion that the "direct effect" requirement cannot be satisfied where the plaintiffs are all foreign corporations with no other connections to the United States. We expressly stated in *Verlinden* that the FSIA permits "a foreign plaintiff to sue a foreign sovereign in the courts of the United States, provided the substantive requirements of the Act are satisfied."

Finally, Argentina argues that a finding of jurisdiction in this case would violate the Due Process Clause of the Fifth Amendment, and that, in order to avoid this difficulty, we must construe the "direct effect" requirement as embodying the "minimum contacts" test of *International Shoe Co.*[114] Assuming, without deciding, that a foreign state is a "person" for purposes of the Due Process Clause, *cf. South Carolina v. Katzenbach*, 383 U.S. 301, 323-324 (1966) (States of the Union are not "persons" for purposes of the Due Process Clause), we find that Argentina possessed "minimum contacts" that would satisfy the constitutional test. By issuing negotiable debt instruments denominated in U.S. dollars and payable in New York and by appointing a financial agent in that city, Argentina "'purposefully avail[ed] itself of the privilege of conducting activities within the [United States],'" *Burger King Corp.*, quoting *Hanson*. ...

We conclude that Argentina's issuance of the Bonods was a "commercial activity" under the FSIA; that its rescheduling of the maturity dates on those instruments was taken in connection with that commercial activity and had a "direct effect" in the United States; and that the District Court therefore properly asserted jurisdiction, under the FSIA, over the breach-of-contract claim based on that rescheduling. Accordingly, the judgment of the Court of Appeals is affirmed.

SAUDI ARABIA v. NELSON

113 S.Ct. 1471 (1993)

[excerpted above at pp. 247-57]

Notes on Weltover and Nelson

1. *Section 1605(a)(2)'s three U.S. nexus requirements.* As discussed above, even if the plaintiff's claim is "based upon" a "commercial activity," each of §1605(a)(2)'s three clauses contains a "nexus" requirement: (a) the action must be "based upon a commercial activity carried on in the United States by the foreign state"; (b) the action must be "based ... upon an act performed in the United States in connection with a commercial activity of the foreign state elsewhere"; or (c) the action must be "based ... upon an act outside the territory of the United States in connection with a commercial activity of the foreign state elsewhere and that act causes a direct effect in the United States." Each of these three provisions requires a different type of U.S. nexus.

What purpose is served by these various U.S. nexus requirements? Note that the various provisions of §1605(a) — and particularly those of §1605(a)(2) — are all broadly similar to state long-arm statutes. Viewing §1605(a) as a federal long-arm statute over foreign states, does it serve the purposes of such jurisdictional grants? Could it be improved? Why didn't Congress merely rely on existing state and federal long-arm statutes (as Rule 4 of the Federal Rules of Civil Procedure does)? Alternatively, why didn't Congress merely authorize personal jurisdiction over foreign states to the limits of the due process clause?

2. *Section 1605(a)(2)'s first clause — commercial activity "carried on in the United States."* The first

---

114. Argentina concedes that this issue "is before the Court only as an aid in interpreting the direct effect requirement of the Act" and that "[w]hether there is a constitutional basis for personal jurisdiction over [Argentina] is not before the Court as an independent question." Brief for Petitioners 36 n.33.

clause of §1605(a)(2) grants jurisdiction over "commercial activity carried on in the United States by the foreign state." Section 1603(e) then defines "commercial activity carried on in the United States" as "commercial activity ... having substantial contact with the United States."

(a) *Justice Souter's application of first clause of §1605(a)(2).* Justice Souter did not reach the question whether the activity which the Nelsons' claim was "based upon" had a U.S. nexus. He did not need to, because he concluded that the only conduct that the Nelsons' suit was "based upon" was not "commercial activity," and therefore that the question of a U.S. nexus was moot.

(b) *Justice White's application of first clause of §1605(a)(2).* Justice White concluded that the operations of the King Faisal Hospital were "commercial activity," but then he held that the activity "lacks a sufficient nexus to the United States," because neither the "hospital's employment practices, nor its disciplinary procedures, has any apparent connection to this country." Is that persuasive? Once it is determined that the Nelsons' claim is "based upon" the Hospital's operations, why is it necessary to single out particular aspects of those operations — namely "employment practices" and "disciplinary procedures"? Why cannot analysis focus generally on the connections between the Hospital and the United States?

(c) *Justice Stevens' application of first clause of §1605(a)(2).* Justice Stevens agrees with Justice White that the Hospital's operations were "commercial activity," but goes on to conclude that those operations satisfy the U.S. nexus requirement of §1605(a)(2). Accepting Justice White's view that the Nelsons' complaint is "based upon" the Hospital's operations, which Justice is correct — Justice White or Justice Stevens — in his analysis of the nexus requirement?

(d) *Specific and general jurisdiction under the first clause of §1605(a)(2).* What rationale does Justice Stevens rely upon in finding a U.S. nexus? Note his willingness to rely on both specific and general jurisdiction in reaching this result. What do these due process standards have to do with the statutory language of §1605(a)(2)? Is it fair to assume that Congress meant to incorporate due process standards?

Would there be specific jurisdiction in a case like that brought by the Nelsons against the Hospital? What are the Hospital's minimum contacts with the United States? Does the Nelsons' claim arise from those comments? Would there be general jurisdiction, based upon the Hospital's purchasing of supplies? Recall the analysis in *Helicopteros.* (See also the discussion below regarding the availability of general jurisdiction, as a statutory matter, under the FSIA, *infra* pp. 262-63.)

A number of lower courts have considered whether §1605(a)(2) grants general jurisdiction — that is, jurisdiction over claims that do not have any nexus with the United States — over foreign sovereign entities with sufficiently close U.S. contacts. Most lower courts have refused to permit general jurisdiction. *Santos v. Companie Nationale Air France,* 934 F.2d 890 (7th Cir. 1991) (requiring an "identifiable nexus" between plaintiff's claim and defendant's commercial activity in the United States); *Barkanic v. CAAC,* 822 F.2d 11, 13 (2d Cir. 1987), *cert. denied,* 108 S.Ct 453 (1987) ("a nexus is required between the [defendant's] commercial activity in the United States and the [plaintiff's] cause of action"; tort action against Chinese airline for crash on Nanjing-Peking flight is within U.S. jurisdiction because ticket for flight was sold in U.S. by nonexclusive sales agent for Chinese airline); *Vencedora Oceanica Navigacion v. Compagnie National Algerienne de Navigation,* 730 F.2d 195 (5th Cir. 1984).

In contrast, some lower courts have held that §1605(a)(2)'s first clause is satisfied so long as the defendant is doing business in the United States, even if the plaintiff's cause of action does not arise directly from the defendant's activities in the United States. *E.g., In re Rio Grande Transp.,* 516 F.Supp. 1155, 1165 (S.D.N.Y. 1981) ("Congress apparently did not intend to require that the specific commercial transaction or act upon which an action is based have occurred in the United States or have had substantial contact with the United States; only the broad course of conduct must be so connected.").

(e) *Justice Stevens' view of general jurisdiction.* Consider Justice Stevens' brief analysis of the availability of general jurisdiction in *Nelson:* "I am inclined to agree ... that the first clause of §1605(a)(2), interpreted in light of the relevant legislative history and the second and third clauses of the provision, does authorize 'general' jurisdiction over foreign entities that engage in substantial commercial activities in the United States." Justice Stevens relied on a concurring opinion in *Vencedora Oceanica Navigacion, SA v. Compagnie Nationale Algerienne de Navigation,* 730 F.2d 195, 206-07 (5th Cir. 1984), which reasoned as follows:

When the relevant portions of §1603(d) and (e) are inserted into clause one of §1605(a)(2), we are left with the task of construing:

A foreign state shall not be immune from the jurisdiction of the courts of the United

States or of the States in any case in which the action is based upon a regular course of commercial conduct carried on by such state and having substantial contact with the United States.

Because this language cannot be interpreted literally, courts have been driven to substitutions for the words "based upon." The majority's substitution is "having a nexus with." ... I would expect a search for a nexus to be a search for an act or series of acts that will be part of the conduct of the business without constituting the entire conduct of the business. It follows that allowing only claims with a nexus to the "commercial activity" carried on in the United States would not exhaust the full range of clause one when "commercial activity" is defined as a "regular course of commercial conduct."

The "substantial contact" language of §1603(e) also supports my reading. This language appears to draw upon the "minimum contacts" test of *International Shoe.* That test marks off a "doing business" ground as involving "instances in which the continuous corporate operations within a state [are] thought so substantial and of such a nature as to justify suit against it on causes of action arising from dealings entirely distinct from these activities." The FSIA's "substantial contact" language thus does not signal a congressional intent to enact more stringent a test than the "minimum contacts" necessary for "doing business" jurisdiction. To the contrary, the phrase could be lifted straight from *International Shoe.*

Furthermore, reading clause one to embody a "doing business" jurisdictional ground gives a coherent organizational structure to the three clauses of the "commercial activities" exception. If "doing business" is allowed as a basis for jurisdiction under clause one, then the three clauses of §1605(a)(2) roughly correspond to three jurisdictional categories; personal jurisdiction exists where the defendant (1) does business in the United States, (2) commits an act within the United States but is not "doing business," and (3) does not commit a relevant act in the United States, but causes a direct effect in the United States. These categories reflect the development of jurisdictional principles, from *Pennoyer v. Neff* (doing business) [sic], through *International Shoe* (committing an act can constitute minimum contacts), *McGee v. International Life Insurance Co.,* (effects can constitute minimum contacts), and beyond. Given these three historical grounds, it seems reasonable to read clause one as embodying a "doing business" ground in addition to a "nexus" ground when the language can support this construction.

Does *Nelson* resolve the question whether general jurisdiction is available under §1605(a)(2)? How should the question be resolved? Is the foregoing excerpt from *Vencedora* persuasive?

3. *Relevance of "based upon" requirement to second and third clauses of §1605(a)(2).* How does *Nelsons'* statement of the "based upon" requirement apply to actions under the second and third clauses of §1605(a)(2)? Consider the specific language of each clause: what must the plaintiff's claim be "based upon" — an "act" or "commercial activity"? Suppose that a foreign state engaged in commercial activity outside the United States but performed a non-commercial act in the United States "in connection" with that commercial activity. Would the second clause of §1605(a)(2) apply? Suppose that a foreign state committed a non-commercial act outside the United States that concededly had a direct effect in the United States, and that the act was "in connection" with commercial activity. Would §1605(a)(2)'s third clause apply?

The "based upon" requirement is relevant to the second and third clauses of §1605(a)(2), but in a different way than under §1605(a)(2)'s first clause. The "based upon" requirement identifies an "act" which must: (a) have a particular U.S. nexus; and (b) have a "connection" to a course of "commercial activity."

4. *Section 1605(a)(2)'s "in connection" requirement.* What is the meaning of the "in connection" requirement of the second and third clauses of §1605(a)(2)? Note *Nelsons'* contrast between the more expansive "in connection" formulation and the less expansive "based upon" requirement. Justice Souter reasoned that the second two clauses referred to an action being "based upon" acts that were "in connection with" commercial activity; the Court reasoned that these provisions required only "a mere connection with, or relation to, commercial activity," and that the "based upon" requirement of the first clause "calls for something more." Just how expansive is the "in connection" standard? *See Drexel Burnham*

Lambert Group, Inc. v. Committee of Receivers, 12 F.3d 317, 329-30 (2d Cir. 1993) ("If the 'connection' language of §1605(a)(2) were read ... to include tangential commercial activities to which the 'acts' forming the basis of the claim have only an attenuated connection, the 'commercial activity' exception would effectively be rewritten to authorize the exercise of jurisdiction over acts that are essentially sovereign in nature").

5. *Second clause of §1605(a)(2) — U.S. acts*. The second clause of §1605(a)(2) grants jurisdiction where an action is based upon "an act performed in the United States in connection with a commercial activity of the foreign state elsewhere." Although not invoked in either *Nelson* or *Weltover*, the clause warrants exploration. What must the plaintiff's claim be "based upon" — the "act" or the "commercial activity"? Who must perform the "act" — the foreign state or someone else? Does the "act" have to be "commercial," or can it be sovereign? Does every element of the claim have to be provided by the "act"?

6. *Third clause of §1605(a)(2) — direct effects*. The third clause of §1605(a)(2) grants jurisdiction where an action is based upon an "act outside the territory of the United States in connection with a commercial activity of the foreign state elsewhere and that act causes a direct effect in the United States." This provision is potentially the most expansive of the three clauses of §1605(a)(2), and it has provoked considerable litigation, which is outlined below. Consider initially some of the interpretative issues arising under the third clause. As with the second clause, must the action be based entirely upon the "act," or can it be based more broadly on the "commercial activity"? Can the act be noncommercial? Must the foreign state commit the act? What is the meaning of the "in connection with" requirement?

7. *Relevance of legislative history to §1605(a)(2)'s "direct effects" requirement*. As *Weltover* observed, the FSIA's legislative history glosses §1605(a)(2)'s "direct effects" requirement by reference to §18 of the *Restatement (Second) Foreign Relations Law* (1965). H.R. Rep. No. 1487, 94th Cong., 2d Sess. 19, *reprinted in* 1976 U.S. Code Cong. & Admin. News at 6618. Section 18 permits the extraterritorial application of U.S. law to foreign conduct if the conduct has "substantial, direct and foreseeable" effects in the United States. *See infra* pp. 497-509. Prior to *Weltover*, most lower courts had looked to §18 for guidance. *E.g.*, *America West Airlines v. GPA Group, Ltd.*, 877 F.2d 793, 798 (9th Cir. 1989) ("most courts interpreting the 'direct effect' clause ... have concluded that Congress intended ... to reach only conduct causing an effect that is 'substantial' and 'direct and foreseeable'").

In *Weltover*, the Supreme Court characterized the legislative history's reference to §18 as a "non sequitur," because §1605(a)(2) deals with personal jurisdiction, while §18 concerns legislative jurisdiction (quoting *Texas Trading & Milling Corp. v. Federal Republic of Nigeria*, 647 F.2d 300, 312-13 (2d Cir. 1981), *cert. denied*, 454 U.S. 1148 (1982)). Because of this non sequitur, the Court also refused to give effect to the House Report's reference to §18, holding that only a "direct effect" — not a "substantial" or "foreseeable" effect — is required by §1605(a)(2). Isn't one of Congress's prerogatives the power to enact "non sequiturs"?

8. *Direct effects test adopted in* Weltover. What standard was adopted in *Weltover* for the direct effects test in §1605(a)(2)'s third prong? Note the Court's remark that "[b]ecause New York was thus the place of performance for Argentina's ultimate contractual obligations, the rescheduling of those obligations necessarily had a 'direct effect' in the United States; Money that was supposed to have been delivered to a New York bank for deposit was not forthcoming." What exactly is the "direct effects" test? Is it appropriate to rely in so conclusive a fashion on the contractual "place of performance"? Note that this will often mean that jurisdiction will turn upon fine details about payment, delivery, or place of performance in contracts. Is that appropriate? What other approaches might have been taken by the Court? What does the Court mean by "ultimate contractual obligations"?

For lower court applications of *Weltover's* direct effects test, *see National Bank of Kuwait v. Rafidain Bank*, 1994 WL 376037 (S.D.N.Y. 1994); *Reed Int'l Trading Corp. v. Donau Bank AG*, 866 F.Supp. 750 (S.D.N.Y. 1994).

9. *Application of direct effects test in* Weltover. Was the direct effects portion of *Weltover* correctly decided? *Weltover* relied on the fact that the plaintiff Bonod-holders "had designated their accounts in New York as the place of payment, and Argentina made some interest payments into those accounts. ..." Note that the Bonods did not independently require Argentina to pay money in the United States, and that it was only the Bonod-holders' designation of New York that imposed the obligation. Would the case have been decided differently if the Bonods had been repayable anywhere designated by the holders (as opposed to being repayable at any one of four cities, including New York, designated by the holders)? Note that the "funds" that were to be paid to the plaintiffs' in New York would likely have: (a) been paid

by electronic transfers between two U.S. banks (the parties' New York correspondents); and (b) remained in the plaintiffs' bank accounts only briefly (perhaps less than 24 hours) before being remitted to the plaintiffs' home country; and (c) all of these transfers would likely have been accomplished by book-keeping changes to the size of inter-bank accounts. Does this affect the *Weltover* "direct effects" conclusion?

What if the Bonods had no place of payment, but were governed by a substantive law, which required that (absent agreement) debts were payable at the lender's place of business? What if the Bonods contained no place of payment provision, but interest on the Bonods had historically been paid in New York? *See United World Trade, Inc. v. Mangyshakneft Oil Product Ass'n*, 33 F.3d 1232 (10th Cir. 1994) (fact that funds relating to European transaction were wired to New York, solely for currency conversion, and then transferred back to Europe held not to be a direct effect: "Congress did not intend to provide jurisdiction whenever the ripples caused by an overseas transaction manage eventually to reach the shores of the United States"); *Goodman Holdings v. Rafidain Bank*, 26 F.3d 1143 (D.C. Cir. 1994).

10. *"Direct effects" requirement in contract actions.* Prior to *Weltover*, several lower courts found the direct effects test satisfied where a foreign defendant has failed to make a payment that was contractually payable to a *U.S.* company within the United States. *E.g.*, *Gould, Inc. v. Pechiney Ugine Kuhlmann*, 853 F.2d 445 (6th Cir. 1988); *Texas Trading & Milling Corp. v. Federal Republic of Nigeria*, 647 F.2d 300 (2d Cir. 1981), *cert. denied*, 454 U.S. 1148 (1982) (foreign state breaches obligation payable within the U.S.); *Schmidt v. Polish People's Republic*, 579 F.Supp. 23 (S.D.N.Y.), *aff'd*, 742 F.2d 67 (2d Cir. 1984) (foreign state breaches obligation negotiated and payable within the United States). As *Weltover* illustrates, the result is the same where the defendant refuses to repay a *foreign* company at a contractually designated location in the United States.

Likewise, several lower courts have held that a foreign state's wrongful request for payment out of funds held by a U.S. company within the United States constitutes a "direct effect" in the United States. *E.g.*, *Transamerican Steamship Corp. v. Somali Democratic Republic*, 767 F.2d 998 (D.C. Cir. 1985) (foreign state wrongfully requires U.S. company to transfer funds to its U.S. bank account); *Harris Corp. v. National Iranian Radio & Television*, 691 F.2d 1344 (11th Cir. 1982) (wrongful call on letter of credit from U.S. bank).

11. *Relevance of plaintiff's nationality in* Weltover. Argentina argued in *Weltover* that the "'direct effect' requirement cannot be satisfied where the plaintiffs are all foreign corporations with no other connections to the United States." The Court rejected the argument. Was this correct? Why does an "effect" occur in the United States when a Swiss bank is not paid money by an Argentine debtor? Why doesn't the effect occur in Switzerland? Does the plaintiff's nationality have any relevance in direct effects analysis after *Weltover*? If so, what?

12. *Direct effects in* Nelson. Consider the possibility that the defendants in *Nelson* were subject to U.S. jurisdiction under §1605(a)(2)'s direct effects test. Mr. Nelson said he was tortured, by government officials who knew he was an American and that he would return to the United States. Did Mr. Nelson's ongoing pain and suffering when he returned to the United States constitute a direct effect there?

Suppose that Mr. Nelson had instead been a patient at the defendant hospital and that he was denied critical treatment because he was black. Suppose further that Mr. Nelson suffered devastating injuries because of the hospital's action and returned to the United States completely paralyzed. (*See Martin v. Republic of South Africa*, 836 F.2d 91 (2d Cir. 1987) for a case involving these facts). Why is that not a direct effect in the United States? Note that U.S. taxpayers would be required to support Mr. Nelson in this hypothetical for the remainder of his life. Note also that the defendants would have known that they were dealing with a U.S. national, and that their conduct could cause harm to him in the United States.

13. *Jurisdiction based upon the plaintiff's nationality.* Under the due process clause, is the *plaintiff's* U.S. nationality a basis for exercising U.S. jurisdiction over a foreign defendant that harms the plaintiff abroad? Recall the *Helicopteros* case, *supra* pp. 103-16. *Should* the fact that the plaintiff is a national of the forum provide jurisdiction over those who injure the plaintiff? Recall Article 14 of the French Civil Code, discussed above, *supra* p. 86. In the context of legislative jurisdiction, international law has long treated the "passive personality" doctrine as an illegitimate jurisdictional base. The passive personality principle would provide that a state can apply its laws to conduct outside its territory that harms its nationals. *See infra* pp. 507-08. Is this relevant to interpreting §1605(a)(2)?

14. *Direct effects and personal injuries abroad.* U.S. courts have been reluctant to assert "direct effects" jurisdiction in cases involving tort claims by U.S. plaintiffs for personal injuries or other damages suffered abroad. *E.g.*, *Martin v. Republic of South Africa*, 836 F.2d 91 (2d Cir. 1987) (refusal of state-owned

hospital to treat black American plaintiff lacked direct effect in U.S., although plaintiff's U.S. nationality was known); *Australian Gov't Aircraft Factories v. Lynn*, 743 F.2d 672 (9th Cir. 1984), *cert. denied*, 469 U.S. 1214 (1985) (crash in Indonesia of aircraft manufactured in Australia lacked direct effect in the U.S., even though not-for-profit organization located in United States owned, operated, and would be forced to replace the aircraft); *Zernicek v. Petroleos Mexicanos*, 614 F. Supp. 407 (S.D. Tex. 1985), *aff'd*, 826 F.2d 415 (5th Cir. 1987), *cert. denied*, 108 S.Ct. 775 (1988) (U.S. plaintiff exposed to radiation abroad by foreign state employer and suffers illness upon return to U.S.; court refuses jurisdiction on grounds that there was no "direct effect" in the United States).

When a U.S. citizen is injured or killed abroad, isn't it clear that substantial and "direct" economic effects will be felt in this country? Is this fact altered if the defendant is unaware of the nationality of the plaintiff, as appears generally to be true in these tort cases? Some commentators have contended that it is ironic that the financial losses of corporate plaintiffs appear to be treated more sympathetically than the personal injuries of individual plaintiffs. *See* Note, *Jurisdiction Over Foreign Governments: A Comprehensive Review of the Foreign Sovereign Immunities Act*, 19 Vand. J. Transnat'l L. 119, 146 (1986) ("This interpretation of the direct effects provisions has resulted in courts allowing corporations a chance to recover financial losses incurred as a result of extraterritorial commercial activity of a foreign sovereign. Individuals who have suffered physical, emotional, and financial effects, however, have been denied resolution of their claims against similar entities for equally grievous harms.").

15. *Nelson revisited.* Mr. Nelson alleged mistreatment was torture — a violation of international law. *See Filartiga v. Pena-Irala*, 630 F.2d 876 (2d Cir. 1980). Does that affect "direct effects" analysis? *See Argentine Republic v. Amerada Hess Shipping Corp.*, 488 U.S. 428 (1989); *infra* p. 273.

16. *Due process analysis under the FSIA after* **Weltover.** *Weltover* suggests that a "foreign state" may not be a "person" for purposes of the due process clause. Would this result be consistent with a conclusion that, for purposes of §1603(d), the foreign state had not acted in a sovereign capacity, but had instead acted "in the manner of a private player"? Would foreign state-owned companies also be deemed non-persons? Should Justice Scalia's suggestion be accepted? Note the Court's suggested analogy to cases holding that states of the Union are not persons for purposes of the due process clause. Are there any relevant differences between foreign states and states of the Union?

d. Due Process Limitations

Application of the commercial exception to the FSIA is complicated by the fifth amendment's potential due process limitations on assertions of personal jurisdiction authorized by the Act.[115] As noted above, *Weltover* refused to decide whether the due process clause applied to assertions of personal jurisdiction over foreign states. Indeed, the Court raised the possibility that foreign states are not "persons" within the meaning of the fifth amendment.[116]

Nevertheless, lower courts have uniformly concluded that exercises of personal jurisdiction under the FSIA must satisfy the due process clause's "minimum contacts" requirements, as well as the statutory nexus requirements of §1605(a)(2).[117] Most lower courts have held that §1605(a)(2) and the due process clause require separate inquiries. As a result, courts ordinarily examine whether the "nexus" requirements of §1605(a)(2) are satisfied, and then independently consider whether the var-

---

115. *See supra* pp. 173-74.

116. 504 U.S. at 619-20.

117. *E.g., Seetransport Wiking Trader v. Navimpex Centrala Navala*, 989 F.2d 572 (2d Cir. 1993); *Texas Trading & Milling Corp. v. Federal Republic of Nigeria*, 647 F.2d 300, 314 (2d Cir. 1981), *cert. denied*, 454 U.S. 1148 (1982); *Gilson v. Republic of Ireland*, 517 F. Supp. 477 (D.D.C. 1981), *aff'd in part and rev'd in part*, 682 F.2d 1022 (D.C. Cir. 1982); *Concord Reinsurance Co. v. Caja Nacional de Ahorro*, 1994 WL 259826 (S.D.N.Y. 1994).

ious "minimum contacts" formulae of the *International Shoe* line of cases are met.[118] The FSIA's legislative history confirms the need to satisfy the minimum contacts requirements of the due process clause, although it also indicates that the §1605 exceptions are generally consistent with these requirements.[119]

3. Noncommercial Torts Occurring Within the United States

The FSIA denies sovereign immunity in certain cases involving tortious injury occurring in the United States. Section 1605(a)(5) provides an exception to immunity where "money damages are sought against a foreign state for personal injury or death, or damage to or loss of property, occurring in the United States and caused by the tortious act or omission of that foreign state," or by the acts or omissions of the foreign state's employees acting within the scope of their employment.

The FSIA's legislative history explains that §1605(a)(5) is "directed primarily at the problem of traffic accidents" involving embassy automobiles and personnel.[120] Nonetheless, the provision is broadly drafted and has been held to reach a much wider range of tort claims.[121] Indeed, the House Report provides that "[a]s used in §1605(a)(5), the phrase 'tortious act or omission' is meant to include causes of action which are based on strict liability as well as on negligence."[122] Section 1605(a)(5) apparently permits recovery for all compensable injuries, intangible as well as tangible.[123]

Section 1605(a)(5) provides a potentially expansive and controversial exception to the sovereign immunity of foreign states. The provision contemplates the application of U.S. (or foreign) tort law principles in cases against foreign sovereigns, which is likely to require more judgmental, policy-laden assessments of foreign governmental conduct by U.S. courts than the application of commercial law in most cases under §1605(a)(2) demands. Section 1605(a)(5) is also a potential source of contro-

---

118. *E.g., Maritime Int'l Nominees Establishment v. Republic of Guinea,* 693 F.2d 1094, 1105-09 (D.C. Cir. 1982), *cert. denied,* 464 U.S. 815 (1983); *Texas Trading & Milling Corp. v. Federal Republic of Nigeria,* 647 F.2d 300 (2d Cir. 1981), *cert. denied,* 454 U.S. 1148 (1982).

119. H.R. Rep. No. 1487, 94th Cong., 2d Sess. 18, *reprinted in* 1976 U.S. Code Cong. & Admin. News at 6616.

120. H.R. Rep. No. 1487, 94th Cong., 2d Sess. 20-21, *reprinted in* 1976 U.S. Code Cong. & Admin. News at 6619.

121. *E.g., Risk v. Halvorsen,* 936 F.2d 393 (9th Cir. 1991) (conspiracy to violate California child custody order); *Liu v. Republic of China,* 892 F.2d 1419 (9th Cir. 1989), *cert. dismissed,* 111 S.Ct. 27 (1990) (homicide); *Joseph v. Office of Consulate General of Nigeria,* 830 F.2d 1018 (9th Cir. 1987), *cert. denied,* 485 U.S. 905 (1988) (destruction of property); *Gerritsen v. de la Madrid Hurtado,* 819 F.2d 1511 (9th Cir. 1987) (kidnap and assault); *Letelier v. Republic of Chile,* 488 F. Supp. 665, 673 (D.D.C. 1980) (murder).

122. H.R. Rep. No. 1487, 94th Cong., 2d Sess. 23-24, *reprinted in* 1976 U.S. Code Cong. & Admin. News at 6621.

123. *See De Sanchez v. Banco Central de Nicaragua,* 770 F.2d 1385, 1400 (5th Cir. 1985) (Rubin, J., concurring) (economic loss); *Persinger v. Republic of Iran,* 729 F.2d 835, 843-44 (D.C. Cir.) (Edwards, J., dissenting) (emotional distress), *cert. denied,* 469 U.S. 881 (1984). One commentator has suggested, however, that §1605(a)(5)'s phrase "damage to or loss of *property*" only permits recovery for tangible injury. G. Badr, *State Immunity: An Analytic and Prognostic View* 120-24 (1984).

versy because, at least in the view of those lower courts to consider the issue, it denies immunity to *all* tortious foreign state conduct — without regard to whether the conduct is "commercial," "private," or "sovereign."[124]

Perhaps in recognition of the sensitive inquiries required by §1605(a)(5), the FSIA's drafters provided several important exceptions to the provision. First, the section does not apply to claims based on malicious prosecution, libel, misrepresentation, or other similar torts.[125] Second, §1605(a)(5) applies only to actions based on torts causing damage "occurring in the United States." Finally, §1605(a)(5) is not applicable to claims based on the defendant's "discretionary functions."[126] As the following sections illustrate, disputes over these latter two exceptions have frequently arisen, with both provisions often being at issue in the same case.

a. Situs Requirement for Noncommercial Torts

Much as §1605(a)(2) imposes a nexus requirement for foreign state's commercial activity, §1605(a)(5) contains a "situs" requirement for noncommercial torts. In contrast to §1605(a)(2), however, §1605(a)(5)'s situs requirement is narrowly drafted and demands a much closer connection to the United States than is necessary in the commercial activity context. The two cases excerpted below — *SEDCO* and *Olsen ex rel. Sheldon* — illustrate two differing approaches that have emerged in applying the situs requirement.

IN RE SEDCO, INC.

543 F. Supp. 561 (S.D. Texas 1982)

O'CONNOR, DISTRICT JUDGE. The 1979 IXTOC I well disaster in the Bay of Campeche has produced a tangle of litigation. ... Petroleos Mexicanos (Pemex), which is both a direct defendant to certain private and public plaintiffs and a third party defendant to claims asserted by Sedco, has moved to be dismissed from all claims on the basis of the grant of sovereign immunity provided by the FSIA. By asserting this motion, Pemex alleges that this Court lacks jurisdiction to hear claims based upon acts purportedly done in its capacity as a foreign sovereign. ...

Petroleos Mexicanos was created in 1938 as a decentralized governmental agency charged with the exploration and development of Mexico's hydrocarbon resources. Unlike in the United States, the government of Mexico owns its country's natural resources, in particular, its hydrocarbon deposits. The Regulatory Law passed pursuant to the Mexican Constitution specifically creates a national oil company,

---

124. *E.g., MacArthur Area Citizens Assoc. v. Republic of Peru,* 809 F.2d 918 (D.C. Cir.), *vacated on other grounds,* 823 F.2d 606 (D.C. Cir. 1987); *Olson ex rel Sheldon v. Mexico,* 729 F.2d 641 (9th Cir. 1984); *Kline v. Republic of El Salvador,* 603 F. Supp. 1313 (D.D.C. 1985); *De Sanchez v. Banco Central de Nicaragua,* 515 F. Supp. 900, 914 (E.D. La. 1981), *aff'd on other grounds,* 770 F.2d 1385, 1399 n.19 (5th Cir. 1985); *Letelier v. Republic of Chile,* 488 F. Supp. 665, 673 (D.D.C. 1980). *But see Frolova v. USSR,* 558 F. Supp. 358, 362-63 (N.D. Ill. 1983), *aff'd on other grounds,* 761 F.2d 370 (7th Cir. 1985).

125. 28 U.S.C. §1605(a)(5)(B) (1982).

126. 28 U.S.C. §1605(a)(5)(A) (1982).

Pemex, to implement the National Development Plan for hydrocarbon resources. Pemex is not privately owned and is governed by a council (Consejo de Administracion) composed of Presidential appointees. Decisions made by the governing council are made in furtherance of Mexican National policy concerning its Petroleum resources. Beyond a doubt, Pemex is a "foreign state" as contemplated by §1603(a) of the FSIA. ...

[I]t is urged that this Court exercise jurisdiction over Pemex under the "noncommercial tort" exception to the FSIA, §1605(a)(5). Section 1605(a)(5) provides that a suit for damages based on an alleged noncommercial tort committed by a foreign state in the United States is actionable in federal court. For jurisdiction to exist, the following must be shown: (1) a noncommercial act by the foreign state; (2) causing personal injury or damages to, or loss of property; and (3) that the claim is not based upon the exercise of a discretionary function, or upon libel, slander, misrepresentation, or interference with contract rights.

Section 1605(a)(5) is silent with respect to where the noncommercial tort must occur for jurisdiction to exist. Plaintiffs argue the tort may occur, in whole or in part, in the United States, and that the tort occurs in the United States if the acts or omissions directly affect this country. This argument may be correct in other circumstances, *see Ohio v. Wyandotte Chemicals Corp.*, 401 U.S. 493 (1971); however, legislative history appears to reject this theory with respect to the FSIA. In describing the purpose of §1605(a)(5), the House Committee Report accompanying the House Bill, which ultimately became the FSIA, states: "[Section 1605(a)(5)] denies immunity as to claims for personal injury or death, or for damage to or loss of property caused by the tortious act or omission of a foreign state or its officials or employees, acting within the scope of their authority; *the tortious act or omission must occur within the jurisdiction of the United States.* ..." House Report, at p. 6619 (emphasis added). The primary purpose of this exception is to cover the problem of traffic accidents by embassy and governmental officials in this country. While the exception does extend generally to all noncommercial torts committed in this country, *see Letelier v. Republic of Chile*, 488 F. Supp. 665, 672 (D.D.C. 1980), this Court finds that the tort, in whole, must occur in the United States. The alleged acts or omissions made the basis of this lawsuit all took place in Mexico or its territorial waters in the Bay of Campeche, and §1605(a)(5) is, therefore, inapplicable.

Notwithstanding the fact that the tort did not occur wholly within the United States, the acts complained of were discretionary in nature, done in furtherance of Pemex' legal mandate to explore for Mexico's hydrocarbon deposits. Discretionary acts by a sovereign are specifically immunized from suit under the FSIA. 28 U.S.C. §1605(a)(5)(A). The language of this exemption and its legislative history demonstrate that it parallels the discretionary act exception to the Federal Tort Claims Act, 28 U.S.C. §2680(a). House Report, at p. 6620. The scope of this discretionary act exception has troubled courts for years. However, the facts of this case closely resemble those of *Dalehite v. United States*, 346 U.S. 15 (1953), still the leading case on the issue. In *Dalehite*, the Supreme Court found the government's actions in formulating and then directing the execution of a formal plan for a fertilizer export program could not form the basis of a suit under the Federal Tort Claims Act. Such actions were found to be discretionary under §2680(a), even though an alleged abuse of that discretion resulted in the 1947 Texas City disaster.

Pemex, in this case, was executing a national plan formulated at the highest levels of the Mexican government by exploring for Mexico's natural resources. Any act performed by a subordinate of Pemex in furtherance of this exploration plan was still discretionary in nature and immune from suit under the FSIA. To deny immunity to a foreign state for the implementation of its domestic economic policies would be to completely abrogate the doctrine of foreign sovereign immunity by allowing an exception to swallow the grant of immunity preserved by §1604.

OLSEN EX REL SHELDON v. GOVERNMENT OF MEXICO
729 F.2d 641 (9th Cir. 1984)

NELSON, CIRCUIT JUDGE. Erin Olsen and Ursula Sanchez appeal from the dismissal of their wrongful death claims for lack of personal jurisdiction. ... [T]he Government of Mexico ("Mexico") also challenges subject matter jurisdiction under the FSIA. We find that both subject matter jurisdiction and personal jurisdiction exist and therefore reverse.

Appellants Olsen and Sanchez, United States citizens domiciled in California, are minor children claiming the wrongful death of their parents. As prisoners of the Mexican government, the parents of appellants were to be transferred to authorities for incarceration in the United States pursuant to the Prisoner Exchange Treaty between the United States and Mexico. On the night of October 27, 1979, a twin-propeller plane owned and operated by the Mexican government carrying guards, pilots and appellants' parent, departed Monterrey, Mexico for Tijuana, where the transfer was to take place. En route, the pilots, employees of the Mexican Department of Justice, learned of thick fog and diminishing visibility at their destination. They requested an instrument landing which, at Tijuana Airport requires the airplane to enter United States airspace so it can approach the runway from the west. Following procedures established by a Letter of Agreement between aviation authorities of the United States and Mexico, Tijuana air control sought and received permission for the airplane to cross the border. ...

Because its radar and instrument landing navigational system were inoperative, Tijuana air control asked its counterpart in San Diego to radio direction headings, altitude and location data necessary for an instrument landing to the aircraft. ... [T]he San Diego air controllers relayed the information via the telephone "hotline" to Tijuana air control which radioed a translation to the pilots. ... With the continued use of navigational data from San Diego air control, the airplane re-entered United States airspace. The pilots aligned the aircraft with the proper compass heading and descended on course, but failed to maintain the proper altitude. After striking a telephone pole, the airplane crashed three-quarters of a mile inside the United States, killing all on board. ...

Mexico argues that §1605(a)(5) does not apply and it is therefore immune from suit. First, Mexico contends that Congress, in enacting the FSIA, adopted the restrictive theory of sovereign immunity and that Mexico's conduct was of the public nature held to be immune under that theory. Second, Mexico asserts that the §1605(a)(5) exception to immunity requires all the acts or omissions constituting the tort to occur within the United States. Finally, Mexico characterizes its activities which led to the crash as discretionary functions, thus falling within the exception to jurisdiction set forth in §1605(a)(5)(A). We consider these arguments in turn.

It is clear that the FSIA, for the most part, codifies the restrictive principle of sovereign immunity. Under this principle, the immunity of a foreign state is "restricted" to suits involving that state's public acts (*jure imperii*) and does not extend to suits based on its private or commercial acts (*jure gestionis*). Mexico argues that this public/private distinction applies not only to the FSIA generally, but specifically to §1605(a)(5), the noncommercial torts exception to immunity. According to Mexico's interpretation, foreign states would be immune from jurisdiction for those torts which otherwise come within the bounds of §1605(a)(5) but which are public in nature.

Section 1605(a)(5) cannot be read, however, other than in conjunction with §1605(a)(5)(A), which exempts from the reach of §1605(a)(5) those torts committed in a foreign state's discretionary capacity. Discretionary functions, as discussed below, include those acts or decisions made at the policy making or planning level of government. Those torts involving acts or omissions of a fundamentally governmental nature are not actionable. Thus, despite §1605(a)(5), a foreign state remains largely immunized from torts committed in its governmental capacity. Mexico's position, that governmental acts are automatically read out of §1605(a)(5), would render §1605(a)(5)(A) superfluous. Its argument is therefore untenable.

Section 1605(a)(5) requires the injury complained of to occur in the United States. The provision does not indicate that the conduct causing the tort must also take place in the United States. Ordinarily, this would end our inquiry and there would be no need to consider the location of the tortious conduct. Where, as in the instant case, the injuries occurred in the United States, and all other requirements of §1605(a)(5) are met, the foreign state would not be immune. However, the legislative history to §1605(a)(5) indicates that "the tortious act or omission must occur within the jurisdiction of the United States. ..." A careful reading of the record in this case suggests that many potentially tortious acts and omissions occurring both in Mexico and the United States caused the crash. Pilot error, the absence of operational radar and navigational aids at Tijuana airport, defective aircraft instruments, the decision to forego a visual landing at another airport, inaccurate data from San Diego air control, and other factors may have contributed causally to the accident.

Mexico, relying on *Matter of SEDCO*, 543 F. Supp. 1561, 1567 (S.D. Tex. 1982) (*SEDCO*), contends that §1605(a)(5) must be construed to require all of the tortious conduct to occur in the United States before a foreign state will be denied immunity. In *SEDCO*, an exploratory off-shore well operated by Pemex, the Mexican national oil company, exploded in Mexican waters. The resulting oil slick washed up on the shores of Texas. Citizens there sued Pemex and other parties under §1605(a)(5). Citing that section's legislative history requiring the tortious act or omission to occur within the United States, the court held that for the noncommercial tort exception to apply, "the tort, in whole, must occur in the United States." Thus, Mexico argues, because some allegedly tortious acts or omissions took place outside the United States — such as the maintenance of the aircraft and the inoperative radar at Tijuana airport — Mexico should be immune.

The instant case is distinguishable from *SEDCO* in one crucial respect. In *SEDCO*, *none* of the alleged acts or omissions, only the resultant injury, occurred in the United States. By requiring every aspect of the tortious conduct to occur in the United States, a rule such as in *SEDCO* would encourage foreign states to allege that some tortious conduct occurred outside the United States. The foreign state would thus be able to establish immunity and diminish the rights of injured persons seeking recovery. Such a result contradicts the purpose of FSIA, which is to "serve the interest of justice and ... protect the rights of both foreign states and litigants in United States courts." 28 U.S.C. §1602. ... Consequently, we hold that if plaintiffs allege at least one entire tort occurring in the United States, they may claim under §1605(a)(5). In this case, appellants allege conduct constituting a single tort of the negligent piloting of the aircraft — which occurred in the United States. We are satisfied that appellants have alleged sufficient conduct occurring in the United States to bring this case within the noncommercial torts exception. ...

Notes on SEDCO and Olsen ex rel Sheldon

1. *Rationale for noncommercial tort exception.* Why are noncommercial torts excepted from the FSIA's grant of immunity? Is this consistent with the restrictive theory of immunity? Under the FSIA, how would the following hypotheticals be resolved: (a) a Canadian Air Force plane, on military operations, crashes in the United States, killing persons on the ground; (b) an embassy guard at a foreign embassy in Washington D.C. shoots protesters; (c) a foreign state conspires with companies based in its territory to steal trade secrets located in the United States from a U.S. company and to drive the company out of business; (d) a Mexican factory releases toxic waste, which are carried into U.S. rivers and kill numerous U.S. citizens?

2. *Situs requirement for noncommercial torts.* SEDCO held that, in order for the FSIA's noncommercial tort exception to apply, the tortious act or omission of a foreign state must occur within U.S. territory. This result does not appear to be required by the language of §1605(a)(5), which is ambiguous, but which apparently lifts immunity in cases where *injury* is suffered in the United States from tortious conduct (regardless of where the *conduct* occurred). In the statute's words, the exception covers actions seeking damages "for personal injury or death, or for damage to or loss of property, occurring in the United States and caused by the tortious act or omission of that foreign state."

Both *SEDCO* and *Olson* placed particular emphasis on the Act's legislative history, which tersely comments that "the tortious act or omission must occur within the jurisdiction of the United States." H.R. Rep. No. 1487, 94th Cong., 2d Sess. 21, *reprinted in* 1976 U.S. Code Cong. & Admin. News at 6619. Does this language unambiguously require the result reached in *SEDCO* and *Olsen*? What is meant by "jurisdiction of the United States"? Is this something different from "territory" of the United States? If "jurisdiction" does not mean "territory," then what does it mean? Would principles developed in the judicial or legislative jurisdiction contexts provide guidance on this issue? *See supra* pp. 70-94 and *infra* pp. 493-509 (discussing territoriality presumption).

3. **Amerada Hess** *dicta.* The Supreme Court discussed §1605(a)(5)'s situs requirements in dicta in *Argentine Republic v. Amerada Hess Shipping Corp.*, 488 U.S. 428 (1989). *Amerada Hess* arose from an attack upon a vessel, in international waters, by the Argentine Air Force during the Falklands (Malvinas) War. The vessel was owned by Amerada Hess Shipping Corporation, a Liberian corporation (which was in turn ultimately owned by a U.S. company); after the attack, Amerada Hess filed suit against Argentina in the United States. Amerada Hess argued, and the Second Circuit agreed, that jurisdiction could be exercised under the Alien Tort Statute, 28 U.S.C. §1350, *see supra* pp. 36-49.

The Supreme Court reversed, holding that the FSIA was the exclusive basis for asserting jurisdiction over foreign states. The Court then considered whether the FSIA permitted jurisdiction, focussing on §1605(a)(5). In concluding that §1605(a)(5) did not permit jurisdiction, the Court reasoned:

> Section 1605(a)(5) is limited by its terms ... to those cases in which the damage to or loss of property occurs *in the United States*. ... In this case, the injury to respondent's ship occurred on the high seas some 5,000 miles off the nearest shores of the United States. The result in this case is not altered by the fact that petitioner's alleged tort may have had effects in the United States. ... Under the commercial activity exception to the FSIA, §1605(a)(2), a foreign state may be liable for its commercial activities 'outside the territory of the United States' having a 'direct effect' inside the United States. But the noncommercial tort exception ... makes no mention of 'territory outside the United States' or of 'direct effects' in the United States. Congress' decision to use explicit language in §1605(a)(2), and not to do so in §1605(a)(5), indicates that the §1605(a)(5) covers only torts occurring within the United States.

The result in *Amerada Hess* was both unexceptional and clearly right. Likewise, the Court's observation that §1605(a)(5) only applies when "damage to or loss of property occurs *in the United States*" is clearly correct. But the Court also said that §1605(a)(5) "covers only torts occurring within the United States"? Is this correct? Was it necessary to the Court's decision? Was the Court considering a case where damage to or loss of property occurred in the United States?

4. **SEDCO's** *situs requirement.* *SEDCO* held that §1605(a)(5) required that "the tort, *in whole*, must occur in the United States." That apparently means that every element of the tort must have occurred in the United States. Other courts have adopted the same test. *Polanco v. Dominican Republic*, 1991 W.L. 146306 (S.D.N.Y. July 22, 1991); *Kline v. Kaneko*, 685 F. Supp. 386, 391 (S.D.N.Y. 1988). Is this conclusion dictated by either the FSIA, the FSIA's legislative history or the *Amerada Hess* decision? Is it wise?

5. **Olsen's** *situs requirement.* *Olsen* apparently rejected the reading of the situs requirement adopted in *SEDCO*. What rule did *Olsen* ultimately adopt? Suppose two "entire torts" were alleged in *Olsen*: (1) pilot error wholly within the United States; and (2) negligent maintenance of the ill-fated aircraft wholly within Mexico. Under the *Olsen* rule, could the plaintiffs proceed on both counts, or only on the pilot error claim? As this hypothetical suggests, several possible views of §1605(a)(5)'s situs requirement emerge from *SEDCO* and *Olsen*: (1) only injury must occur within the United States; (2) all tortious conduct and injury must occur within the United States; (3) one "entire tort," including all elements of the tort and the injury, must occur within the United States; or (4) the center of gravity of the tort and injury must be within the United States. Which view is preferable?

6. *Third Restatement's situs requirement.* Section 454 of the ALI's *Restatement (Third) Foreign Relations Law* adopts a less restrictive situs requirement for noncommercial torts than that embraced in *SEDCO*. Comment e to §454 provides that "courts in the United States have jurisdiction over tort claims against a foreign state only if the injury took place in the United States, but the courts have jurisdiction even if the act or omission causing the injury took place elsewhere." *Restatement (Third) Foreign Relations Law* §454, comment e (1987).

7. *Cross-border torts.* Suppose an industrial accident occurs at a foreign state-owned pesticide factory located near the U.S. border. Toxic fumes escape and kill large numbers of Americans living in the United States. Would §1605(a)(5) provide a jurisdictional basis for claims against the foreign state? What result would *Amerada Hess* suggest? How is this hypothetical different from *SEDCO*? Would §1605(a)(2) apply to this hypothetical? What if the accident occurred at a military research facility? Suppose that decisions

are made in a foreign state in connection with tortious conduct by that nation in the United States. Does this decision-making activity constitute part of the tortious conduct, and if so, what effect does this have on the situs requirement? What law governs this question?

b. The Discretionary Function Exclusion for Noncommercial Torts

The noncommercial tort exception does not apply to actions arising out of a foreign state's performance of "discretionary functions."[127] Section 1605(a)(5)'s discretionary function exclusion was modelled on the Federal Tort Claims Act ("FTCA"), which sets forth the circumstances in which the U.S. government may be sued in tort.[128] The language of §1605(a)(5)(A) tracks that of 28 U.S.C. §2680(a), and the FSIA's legislative history refers courts to the FTCA.[129] Thus, lower courts have relied on FTCA precedents in §1605(a)(5) cases.[130]

The Supreme Court's decisions under the FTCA have provided only a measure of guidance. In *Dalehite v. United States*, the Court held that "discretion" meant:

> more than the initiation of programs and activities. It also includes determinations made by executives or administrators in establishing plans, specifications, or schedules or operations. Where there is a room for policy judgment and decision there is discretion.[131]

More recently, in *United States v. Varig Airlines*, the Court held that the United States could not be sued under the FTCA for the alleged negligence of the Federal Aviation Administration in administering air safety standards. The Court reasoned that the FTCA's discretionary function exception was designed to "prevent judicial 'second-guessing' of legislative and administrative decisions grounded in social, economic, and political policy through the medium of an action in tort."[132]

It is difficult to determine when the discretionary function exclusion from the noncommercial tort exception applies. Courts are required to decide whether a particular activity is sufficiently laden with policy-making, judgmental, and political factors to render it a "discretionary function." Some cases have taken a broad view of discretionary functions, apparently regarding all conduct "in furtherance" of an

---

127. 28 U.S.C. §1605(a)(5)(B).

128. *See Joseph v. Office of Consulate General of Nigeria*, 830 F.2d 1018, 1026 (9th Cir. 1987), *cert. denied*, 485 U.S. 905 (1988); *In re SEDCO*, 543 F. Supp. 561 (S.D. Texas 1982).

129. H.R. Rep. No. 1487, 94th Cong., 2d Sess. 21, *reprinted in* 1976 U.S. Code Cong. & Admin. News 6620.

130. *E.g., Risk v. Halvorsen*, 936 F.2d 393 (9th Cir. 1991); *Joseph v. Office of the Consulate General of Nigeria*, 830 F.2d 1018, 1026 (9th Cir. 1987), *cert. denied*, 485 U.S. 905 (1988); *In re SEDCO*, 543 F. Supp. 561 (S.D. Texas 1982).

131. 346 U.S. 15, 35-36 (1953).

132. 467 U.S. 797, 814 (1984).

important national policy as discretionary.[133] Other courts have taken narrower views of what constitutes a "discretionary function."[134]

The materials excerpted below explore the discretionary function exclusion. *SEDCO* considers whether a particular course of governmental conduct was "discretionary" or not. Also excerpted below is an opinion in *Letelier v. Republic of Chile*. Unlike *SEDCO*, it was clear in *Letelier* that the defendant's conduct involved high-level foreign policy-making. Nonetheless, *Letelier* invoked basic U.S. public policies in concluding that Chile was not entitled to immunity under the discretionary function exclusion.

IN RE SEDCO, INC.

543 F. Supp. 561 (S.D. Texas 1982) [excerpted above at pp. 268-70]

LETELIER v. REPUBLIC OF CHILE

488 F. Supp. 665 (D.D.C. 1980)

GREEN, DISTRICT JUDGE. [Orlando Letelier and Ronni Moffitt were active in an organization in the United States that was critical of the Republic of Chile. After the violent deaths of Letelier and Moffitt, their survivors filed suit against the Republic of Chile, its intelligence agency (Centro Nacional de Intelligencia or CNI), and various agents of CNI. The suit alleged that the defendants constructed, planted, and detonated a bomb that killed Letelier, the former Chilean foreign minister, and Moffitt. The plaintiffs sought damages under various tort-based causes of action.]

As is made clear both in the [FSIA] and in its legislative history, one of [the Act's] principal purposes was to reduce the foreign policy implications of sovereign immunity determinations and assure litigants that such crucial decisions are made on purely legal grounds, an aim that was to be accomplished by transferring responsibility for such a decision from the executive branch to the judiciary. In addition, the Act itself is designed to codify the restrictive principle of sovereign immunity that makes a foreign state amenable to suit for the consequences of its commercial or private, as opposed to public acts. ...

---

133. *E.g., In re SEDCO, Inc.*, 543 F.Supp. 561 (S.D. Tex. 1982). For recent decisions finding the discretionary function exception applicable, *see Risk v. Halvorsen*, 936 F.2d 393 (9th Cir. 1991) (consular officer's assistance to foreign national in leaving U.S. is discretionary function); *MacArthur Area Citizens Ass'n v. Peru*, 809 F.2d 918, 922 (D.C. Cir. 1987), *vacated on other grounds*, 823 F.2d 606 (1987); *Alicog v. Kingdom of Saudi Arabia*, 860 F.Supp. 379 (S.D. Tex. 1994) (confiscation of travel documents and forcible confinement held discretionary); *Travel Associates, Inc. v. Kingdom of Swaziland*, 1990 U.S. Dist. LEXIS 11455 (D.D.C. Aug. 30, 1990) (supervision of diplomat is discretionary function); *Anonymous v. Anonymous*, 1990 U.S. App. LEXIS 12353 (7th Cir. June 13, 1990) (military attack on Pearl Harbor was discretionary function).

134. *E.g., Olsen ex rel. Sheldon*, 729 F.2d 641 (9th Cir. 1984); *Joseph v. Office of Consulate General of Nigeria*, 830 F.2d 1018 (9th Cir. 1987), *cert denied*, 485 U.S. 905 (1988).

[R]elying on §1605(a)(5) ... plaintiffs have set forth several tortious causes of action arising under international law, the common law, the Constitution, and legislative enactments, all of which are alleged to spring from the deaths of Orlando Letelier and Ronni Moffitt. The Republic of Chile, while vigorously contending that it was in no way involved in the events that resulted in the two deaths, further asserts that, even if it were, the Court has no subject matter jurisdiction in that it is entitled to immunity under the Act, which does not cover political assassinations because of their public, governmental character. As supportive of its conclusion that political tortious acts of a government are to be excluded, the Republic of Chile makes reference to the reports of the House and Senate Judiciary Committees with regard to the Act, in which it was stated: "Section 1605(a)(5) is directed primarily at the problem of traffic accidents but is cast in general terms as applying to all tort actions for money damages." ... It is clear from these passages, the Chilean government asserts, that the intent of Congress was to include only private torts like automobile accidents within the exclusion from immunity embodied in §1605(a)(5).

Prominently absent from defendant's analysis, however, is the initial step in any endeavor at statutory interpretation: a consideration of the words of the statute. Subject to the exclusion of these [sic] discretionary acts defined in subsection (A) and the specific causes of action enumerated in subsection (B), neither of which have been invoked by the Republic of Chile, by the plain language of §1605(a)(5) a foreign state is not entitled to immunity from an action seeking damages "for personal injury or death ... caused by the tortious act or omission of that foreign state" or its officials or employees. Nowhere is there an indication that the tortious acts to which the Act makes reference are to only be those formerly classified as "private," thereby engrafting onto the statute ... the requirement that the character of a given tortious act be judicially analyzed to determine whether it was of the type heretofore denoted as *jure gestionis* or should be classified as *jure imperii*. Indeed, the other provisions of the Act mandate that the Court not do so, for it is made clear that the Act and the principles it sets forth in its specific provisions are henceforth to govern all claims of sovereign immunity by foreign states. 28 U.S.C. §§1602, 1604 (1976).

Although the unambiguous language of the Act makes inquiry almost unnecessary, further examination reveals nothing in its legislative history that contradicts or qualifies its plain meaning. The relative frequency of automobile accidents and their potentially grave financial impact may have placed that problem foremost in the minds of Congress, but the applicability of the Act was not so limited, for the committees made it quite clear that the Act "is cast in general terms as applying to all tort actions for money damages" so as to provide recompense for "the victim of a traffic accident or other noncommercial tort." ...

Examining then the specific terms of §1605(a)(5), despite the Chilean failure to have addressed the issue, the court is called upon to consider whether either of the exceptions to liability for tortious acts found in §1605(a)(5) applies in this instance. It is readily apparent, however, that the claims herein did not arise "out of malicious prosecution, abuse of process, libel, slander, misrepresentation, deceit, or interference with contract rights," 28 U.S.C. §1605(a)(5)(B) (1976), and therefore only the exemption for claims "based upon the exercise or performance or the failure to exercise or perform a discretionary function regardless of whether the discretion be abused," §1605(a)(5)(A), can be applicable.

As its language and the legislative history make apparent, the discretionary act exemption of subsection (A) corresponds to the discretionary act exception found in the Federal Tort Claims Act. As defined by the United States Supreme Court in interpreting the Federal Tort Claims Act, an Act that is discretionary is one in which "there is room for policy judgment and decision." *Dalehite v. United States*, 346 U.S. 15, 36 (1953). Applying this definition to the instant action, the question becomes, would the alleged determination of the Chilean Republic to set into motion and assist in the precipitation of those events that culminated in the deaths of Orlando Letelier and Ronni Moffitt be of the kind in which there is "room for policy judgment and decision."

While it seems apparent that a decision calculated to result in injury or death to a particular individual or individuals, made for whatever reason, would be one most assuredly involving policy judgment and decision and thus exempt as a discretionary act under §1605(a)(5)(A), that exception is not applicable to bar this suit. As it has been recognized, there is no discretion to commit, or to have one's officers or agents commit, an illegal act. *Cruikshank v. United States*, 431 F. Supp. 1355, 1359 (D. Hawaii 1977); *see Hatahley v. United States*, 351 U.S. 173, 181 (1956). Whatever policy options may exist for a foreign country, it has no "discretion" to perpetrate conduct designed to result in the assassination of an individual or individuals, action that is clearly contrary to the precepts of humanity as recognized in both national and international law. Accordingly there would be no "discretion" within the meaning of §1605(a)(5)(A) to order or to aid in an assassination and were it to be demonstrated that a foreign state has undertaken any such act in this country, that foreign state could not be accorded sovereign immunity under subsection (A) for any tort claims resulting from its conduct. As a consequence, the Republic of Chile cannot claim sovereign immunity under the Foreign Sovereign Immunities Act for its alleged involvement in the deaths of Orlando Letelier and Ronni Moffitt.

Notes on SEDCO and Letelier

1. *Public or sovereign torts.* Was §1605(a)(5) applicable at all in *Letelier?* Chile argued that its alleged torts arose from "public" or "governmental" acts and that the tort exception contained in §1605(a)(5) should be limited to "private" torts. Put differently, Chile argued that the restrictive theory lifts immunity with respect only to "private" acts and therefore that its tortious conduct had to be examined to determine whether it was "public" or "private." *Letelier* rejected the argument, on the grounds that it would render §1605(a)(5)(A)'s exceptions for discretionary acts superfluous. Is that persuasive? Recall that the FSIA was intended to codify the restrictive theory. Is there any way to interpret §1605(a)(5) as excluding "public" torts? Recall the presumption that Congress should not be interpreted as violating international law absent a clear statement to that effect. *See supra* p. 22.

2. *Definition of discretionary function.* Lower courts appear to have taken two principal factors into account in deciding whether particular conduct is discretionary: (a) whether there was discretion to act or

to choose appropriate conduct; and (b) whether the decisions were based upon social, economic or political policy. *Risk v. Halvorsen*, 936 F.2d 393, 395 (9th Cir. 1991); *MacArthur Area Citizens Ass'n v. Peru*, 809 F.2d 918, 922 (D.C. Cir. 1987), *vacated on other grounds*, 823 F.2d 606 (1987). What was the definition of discretionary function that was used in *SEDCO* and *Letelier*? Is this definition useful?

3. *Application of discretionary function test in* SEDCO. Did the court reach the correct result in *SEDCO*? Was the drilling of an oil well really a "discretionary" function? Is a malfunction on an oil rig not just an ordinary commercial and technical error, that has little to do with the broader programs and purposes of Pemex and Mexico's petroleum exploration program?

4. *"Discretionary functions" and illegal acts.* Although *Letelier* apparently conceded that the decision to execute a dissident involves "policy judgment and decision," it avoided applying §1605(a)(5)(A) by invoking the maxim that "there is no discretion to commit ... an illegal act." The Ninth Circuit reached much the same result in *Liu v. Republic of China*, 892 F.2d 1419 (9th Cir. 1990) (excerpted below), where it held that a foreign government official had no discretion to order the alleged murder of a dissident in the United States. Is this an appropriate line of analysis? Does the FSIA say anything about an "illegality" exception to the "discretionary function" exclusion? Particularly in sensitive areas like those in *Letelier* and *Liu*, is it desirable for U.S. courts to imply such limits on foreign states' immunity?

5. *Are all illegal acts non-discretionary?* What is the scope of *Letelier's* principle that there is no discretion to commit an illegal act? Must the defendant's action merely violate U.S. law before it ceases to be "discretionary"? Must such conduct also violate international law? Won't virtually all non-commercial tort actions involve alleged violations of U.S. tort law? Or did the *Letelier* court instead mean that some (but not all) illegal acts are so contrary to fundamental U.S. public policies that they will not enjoy immunity under the discretionary function exclusion? *Compare* the "public policy" exceptions that exist in the forum selection, antisuit injunction, choice of law, and enforcement of judgments contexts, *see infra* pp. 414-30, 486-87, 624-31, 661-62 & 974-86. *See also Berkovitz by Berkovitz v. United States*, 108 S.Ct 1954 (1988) ("The discretionary function exception applies only to conduct that involves the permissible exercise of policy judgment.").

In *Risk v. Halvorsen*, 936 F.2d 393 (9th Cir. 1991), a U.S. national brought suit under the FSIA against Norway and two Norwegian consular officers. The suit charged the officials, and Norway, with tortious interference with a California child custody order and with parent-child relations: the claims arose from assistance allegedly provided by the officials to the plaintiff's wife in removing the couple's children from California to Norway. California law apparently provided a substantial basis for treating the defendant's conduct as a felony. Cal. Penal Code §278.5 (West 1988) ("Intentional violation of a custody order, or of the rights of a parent under such an order, is a felony in California"). Citing *Liu* and *Letelier*, plaintiff argued that the defendants lacked "discretion" to commit felonies under California law, and thus that §1605(a)(5) was applicable. The Ninth Circuit distinguished *Letelier* and *Liu*, reasoning "[a]lthough these acts may constitute a crime under California law, it cannot be said that every conceivable illegal act is outside the scope of the discretionary function exception," apparently because both *Letelier* and *Liu* involved acts that were "clearly contrary to the precepts of humanity." 936 F.2d at 396 (*quoting Letelier*, 488 F. Supp. at 673). Is kidnapping a child less objectionable than murder?

c. The "Scope of Employment" Requirement

Unlike other parts of §1605, §1605(a)(5) contains specific language addressing the liability of foreign states for the tortious acts or omissions of their employees and agents. Thus, §1605(a)(5) denies foreign states immunity in cases where money damages are sought:

> for personal injury or death, or damage to or loss of property, occurring in the United States and caused by the tortious act or omission of that foreign state or *of any official or employee of that foreign state while acting within the scope of his office or employment.*

Only a few lower court decisions have considered the "scope of employment" requirement in any detail.[135] The following opinion, in *Liu v. Republic of China*, is one of these decisions.

LIU v. REPUBLIC OF CHINA
892 F.2d 1419 (9th Cir. 1989)

BOOCHEVER, CIRCUIT JUDGE. [The District Court and the Court of Appeals proceeded on the basis of factual findings reached in various Republic of China ("ROC") tribunals. In summary, these findings showed that one Henry Liu, a journalist and businessman living in California, was shot at his home by two gunmen. The gunmen were members of a criminal racketeering group in the ROC called the Bamboo Union Gang. The shootings occurred after leaders of the Bamboo Union Gang had met with one Vice-Admiral Wong — the Director of the ROC "Defense Intelligence Bureau" ("DIB"), a governmental agency within the ROC Ministry of Defense. Wong recruited the Bamboo Union Gang for various activities, including teaching Liu a "lesson" for his apparent hostility to Wong and his outspoken criticism of the ROC government. Wong arranged for the training of two gang members and supplied them with information concerning Liu. The gunmen travelled to the U.S., murdered Liu, and returned to the ROC where they reported to Wong.

Wong and the Gang members were later apprehended by the ROC police. They were tried and convicted for murder and conspiracy. They received sentences of life imprisonment. The ROC courts found that Wong had acted secretly, without the knowledge of his superiors, and in violation of ROC law and DIB regulations. These courts also found that Wong had a "personal grudge" against Liu.]

Liu's allegations were sufficient to bring this suit within the tortious activity exception of 28 U.S.C.A. §1605(a)(5). Liu sued for damages for the wrongful death of her husband which occurred within the United States. Section 1605(a)(5) removes immunity for torts committed either by a foreign state or its agents acting within the scope of their employment. Liu alleged both grounds: 1) that the ROC was involved in the conspiracy to kill Henry Liu; and 2) that Wong acted within the scope of his employment in ordering the assassination.

The district court eventually ruled that the act of state doctrine precluded inquiry into the alleged ROC involvement in the conspiracy and that Wong's act was not committed within the scope of his employment under California law. Consequently the court held that the ROC was not liable under the doctrine of respondeat superior for Liu's damages. This determination constituted a decision that the district court lacked subject matter jurisdiction because §1605(a)(5) requires that acts of agents of a foreign state be within the scope of their employment.

---

135. *E.g., Republic of China v. Liu*, 892 F.2d 1419 (9th Cir. 1989); *Joseph v. Office of Consulate General of Nigeria*, 830 F.2d 1018, 1025 (9th Cir. 1987), *cert. denied*, 485 U.S. 905 (1988); *Skeen v. Federative Republic of Brazil*, 566 F.Supp. 1414, 1417 (D.D.C. 1983).

"The 'scope of employment' provision of the tortious activity exception [of the FSIA] essentially requires a finding that the doctrine of respondeat superior applies to the tortious acts of individuals." *Joseph v. Office of Consulate General of Nigeria*, 830 F.2d 1018 1025 (9th Cir. 1987), *cert. denied*, 485 U.S. 905 (1988). In *Joseph*, we held that state law, not federal common law, governs whether an employee's action is within the scope of employment in determining the applicability of the FSIA.

Whether the ROC is liable under respondeat superior is crucial not only to the issue of the court's jurisdiction, but also to the merits of the appeal from the denial of Liu's motion for partial summary judgment on the wrongful death claim. Section 1606 of the FSIA provides:

> As to any claim for relief with respect to which a foreign state is not entitled to immunity under §1605 or 1607 of this chapter, the foreign state shall be liable in the same manner and to the same extent as a private individual under like circumstances; but a foreign state except for an agency or instrumentality thereof shall not be liable for punitive damages. ...

The FSIA does not create a federal rule of liability to be applied in an action involving a foreign state.

We have held that here are two choice of law questions that must be resolved prior to determining whether the ROC is liable under respondeat superior. First, we must decide the choice of law rule applicable to the respondeat superior issue determinative of jurisdiction under the FSIA. Second, assuming that we have jurisdiction under that Act, we must ascertain the law to be applied in determining whether the ROC is liable on the merits. ...

[F]ederal common law provides the choice of law rule applicable to deciding the merits of an action involving a foreign state. *See Harris v. Polskie Linie Lotnicze*, 820 F.2d 1000, 1003-1004 (9th Cir. 1987). In *Harris*, the parents of a passenger killed in an air plane crash in Poland sued the Polish airline in federal court in California. The FSIA applied to the suit because the Polish airline was an instrumentality of the state of Poland. The plaintiffs argued that California's choice of law rules should determine the substantive law of damages because the parties sued in California. We rejected this argument and held that federal common law provided the appropriate choice of law rule in cases arising under the FSIA. *Id.* at 1003. We adopted the *Restatement (Second) of Conflicts of Laws* (1969) approach, which creates a presumption that "the law of the place where the injury occurred applies" unless another state has a "more significant relationship to the [tort] and to the parties." In *Joseph*... [we] held that California's law of respondeat superior, not federal common law, applied to determine whether the tortious acts of Nigeria's employees were within the scope of employment for purposes of the tortious activity exception in the FSIA. ...

[W]e apply [a] federal choice of law rule to determine the applicable law of respondeat superior on the merits. If a different choice of law rule applied to determine the applicable respondeat superior law for jurisdictional purposes under the FSIA, it would be cumbersome, present grave practical difficulties, and could result in different substantive laws being applied in the same suit. We do not believe that Congress intended different choice of law rules to apply. We therefore hold that the federal choice of law rule controls the applicable law of respondeat superior both for jurisdiction under the FSIA and on the merits.

California is the place where injury occurred, and under the federal choice of law rule, its law will apply to the merits of the action unless the ROC has a more significant relationship to the tort and the parties. Although the ROC has some connection with the tort and the parties, we cannot say that it has the more significant relationship. California and the ROC have offsetting interests in the parties to this suit: Henry Liu was domiciled in California when he was killed, and the ROC and other ROC nationals are parties to the suit. California, however, has a significant interest in ensuring that its residents are compensated for torts committed against them, and in discouraging the commission of such torts within its borders. We conclude that California's relationship to the tort is at least as significant as the ROC's. ...

[Under California law,] an employer is vicariously liable for the torts of employees committed within the scope of their employment. *See, e.g., Alma W. v. Oakland Unified School Dist.*, 176 Cal.Rptr. 287, 289 (1981). "'This includes willful and malicious torts as well as negligence.'" California follows the "enterprise theory" of liability:

> California has adopted the rationale that the employer's liability should extend beyond his actual or possible control over the employees to include risks inherent in or created by the enterprise because he, rather than the innocent injured party, is best able to spread the risks through prices, rates or liability insurance.

Rodgers v. Kemper Constr. Co., 50 Cal.App.3d 608, 618 (1975). A country such as the ROC cannot spread risks like a private business by means of the prices it charges for a product. But by means of the public fisc, it similarly can spread risks which would otherwise fall on the individual harmed by the tortious conduct of the country's employees.

California has established a two-prong test to determine whether an employee is acting within the scope of employment. Generally, an employer will be liable for an employee's wrongful act if 1) the act was required or incident to the employee's duties or 2) the act was reasonably foreseeable to the employer. In this case, we find that Liu has established facts sufficient to meet the first prong of the test and therefore do not address the issue of foreseeability. ...

"In assessing whether an employee's wrongful act was required by or incidental to his duties, the law defines occupational duties broadly." "If an employee [, however,] substantially deviates from his duties for personal purposes, the employer is not vicariously liable for the employee's actions." The ROC contends that it is not liable for Wong's action because the ROC courts expressly found that Wong was motivated by a personal grudge to kill Henry Liu. The district court stated that:

The [ROC] courts found that Wong believed Liu was damaging the ROC by both words and deeds. The courts also found that Wong knew Liu was not satisfied with his performance as the Director of the DIB, that Liu has some materials that were not advantageous to him, and that Liu was going to initiate some action that would be detrimental to him.

The ROC contends that the courts actually found that Wong used this "ostensible nationalism" story only to persuade [the Bamboo Union] to murder Henry Liu, but did not actually believe this himself. The ROC courts, however, never stated that the "nationalism" story was merely a guise to lure [the Bamboo Union] into murdering Henry Liu. We agree with the district court's interpretation of these findings. Henry Liu was an historian and journalist who had criticized ROC leaders in the past. It is logical to assume that the action Henry Liu was going to take against Wong was another article criticizing another ROC leader, in this case Wong. Wong's response might be considered motivated by a personal grudge under the internal law of the ROC; however, under California law it is sufficiently job related to impose vicarious liability on the ROC.

The dispute between Liu and Wong arose out of Liu's dissatisfaction with Wong's performance as Director of the DIB. There is no evidence of any personal altercation unrelated to Wong's official duties. ... Even if we assume, despite the absence of evidence, that Wong acted partly out of a personal grudge "not engendered" by his employment as a high official in the ROC government, California courts have made clear that a "mixed motive" is sufficient to impose vicarious liability on the employer. The ROC courts' findings indicate that Wong acted in part to benefit the ROC. The courts stated that Wong believed that Henry Liu was damaging the ROC by his criticism of its government. Wong apparently believed that it would benefit the ROC to silence a known critic. We realize that the ROC incurred no benefit but rather suffered substantial detriment and embarrassment from Wong's act. Nevertheless, if Wong's complicity in the assassination had not been revealed, the ROC would have benefited from the silencing of a critic. If actual benefit, from the standpoint of hindsight, were required respondeat superior would practically be eliminated because damages usually offset any benefit.

California no longer requires that an act benefit the employer before vicarious liability will attach. It does not follow, however, that benefit to the employer "must be eliminated as a relevant factor determining whether conduct falls within the 'scope of employment'." Similarly, the employee's intent should also be a relevant factor in determining whether conduct is within the scope of employment. *See Restatement (Second) of Agency* §228 at 504 (1958) (listing as one factor whether "[conduct] is actuated, at least in part, by a purpose to serve the master"). We believe that California courts would recognize that the intent of the employee is a relevant factor in determining whether an employee's act was wholly personal or sufficiently connected with the employment to justify shifting the risk of loss to the enterprise.

The employee's intent is especially relevant when the act is an intentional tort which, if discovered, will rarely actually benefit the employer.

Another factor present in this case is that Wong used the ROC facilities entrusted to him to help [the Bamboo Union] prepare for the assassination. Wong sent [Bamboo Union members] to the DIB training school for four days, and provided them with a dossier on Liu prepared by the DIB. As the ROC correctly states, the mere use of facilities entrusted to the employee is insufficient to impose liability on the employer. Although Wong's use of facilities alone would be insufficient to impute liability to the ROC, this factor combined with Wong's use of his authority to accomplish a task, partly for the benefit of his employer, is sufficient to impose vicarious liability on the ROC. ...

In this case, we do not find that "the consequences of imposing liability are unacceptable." Imposition of vicarious liability would not undermine the overall effectiveness of a foreign government or its intelligence apparatus. Although a sexual assault by a teacher may be too attenuated to justify spreading the risk of loss to the beneficiaries of the enterprise, an employee's misuse of authority, done in part with the intent to benefit the employer, is within the risks broadly allocable to the enterprise. When an employee, such as Wong, uses governmental authority in a mistaken attempt to benefit his employer by silencing an outspoken critic of the government, there is nothing inequitable about spreading the loss among all the beneficiaries of the government.

Last, the ROC contends that it should not be liable for Wong's act because Wong violated ROC internal law prohibiting murder, and none of its other officials knew of or sanctioned his act. First, the mere fact than an employee violated an employer's express rules is not dispositive. If this were a complete defense, then "'few employers would ever be held liable'." Likewise, the fact that the ROC officials did not sanction Wong's act or were unaware of it is irrelevant because under respondeat superior an employer is held vicariously liable for the risks inherent in his enterprise irrespective of his own personal fault.

We can accept the ROC courts' findings that no other official was aware of or sanctioned Wong's wrongful act and still find that Liu has established as a matter of law that Wong's act was committed within the scope of his employment as Director of the DIB. Consequently, we reverse the district court's denial of Liu's motion for partial summary judgment and its decision that the ROC could not be vicariously liable for Henry Liu's death.

Because we conclude that the ROC is liable under respondeat superior, we also hold that there is subject matter jurisdiction under the FSIA, unless Wong's conduct falls within the discretionary function exception to that Act. 28 U.S.C. §1330 (a). [The court held that the exception was not satisfied.]

Notes on Liu v. Republic of China

1. *Federal common law choice of law rule under FSIA.* Issues of substantive liability are generally not governed by the FSIA. Under 28 U.S.C. §1606, a foreign state shall be "liable in the same manner and to

the same extent as a private individual under like circumstances." Thus, in determining the liability of a foreign state, a court must choose a body of substantive law. *Liu* held that choice of law questions under the FSIA were governed by federal common law: "federal common law provides the choice of law rule applicable to deciding the merits of an action involving a foreign state." The rationale of *Liu* is that the FSIA was intended to provide a uniform federal statutory framework for questions of jurisdiction over and immunity of foreign states, and that important federal foreign relations interests are served by such uniformity. Is this persuasive? Does not §1606 require application of the same choice of law rules that would apply in private litigation? Under *Klaxon v. Stentor Elec. Mfg. Co.*, this would be the local choice of law rules of the state in which the federal court was located. *See infra* pp. 681-84. Which approach to choice of law questions under the FSIA is wiser? How compelling is the need for uniform treatment of choice of law questions under the FSIA?

2. *Standard for determining scope of employment.* Applying a federal choice of law rule, *Liu* concluded that California state law governed the question whether Mr. Liu's killers had acted within their "scope of employment" by the Republic of China. Is it appropriate for the meaning of §1605(a)(5)'s jurisdictional provisions to be determined by state law?

Note that the phrase "scope of employment" occurs in a federal statute and thus that the meaning of this phrase would presumptively be a matter of federal law. *NLRB v. Hearst Publications, Inc.*, 322 U.S. 111, 123 (1944) ("it is not only proper but necessary for us to assume, 'in the absence of a plain indication to the contrary, that Congress ... is not making the application of [a] federal act dependant on state law.'") (*quoting Jerome v. United States*, 318 U.S. 101, 104 (1943)). Note also that the FSIA's drafters emphasized their intention of establishing uniform, federal standards governing the immunity of foreign states and the jurisdiction of U.S. courts over those states. 28 U.S.C. §1602; H.R. Rep. No. 1487, 94th Cong., 2d Sess., at 12, reprinted in 1976 U.S. Code Cong. & Admin. News 6604, 6610 (FSIA "sets forth the sole and exclusive standard to be used in resolving questions of sovereign immunity"); *Verlinden BV v. Central Bank of Nigeria*, 461 U.S. 480, 488, 493 (1983).

Even if §1605(a)(5) did not provide a specific federal statutory test for "scope of employment" jurisdiction, would this be an appropriate case for formulating a rule of federal common law? Note that in *First National City Bank v. Bancec*, 462 U.S. 611 (1983) (excerpted above at pp. 217-24), the Supreme Court adopted a rule of federal common law defining the circumstances in which U.S. courts could disregard the separate juridical identity of foreign state-owned companies, reasoning that:

> matters bearing on the Nation's foreign relations "should not be left to divergent and perhaps parochial state interpretations." When it enacted the FSIA, Congress expressly acknowledged the "importance of developing a uniform body of law" concerning the amenability of a foreign sovereign to suit in United States courts. [*Bancec*, 462 U.S. at 622 n.11 (quoting *Banco Nacional de Cuba v. Sabbatino*, and H.R. Rep. No. 1487, at 32).]

Does *Liu* provide an adequate response to these indications that federal law should govern §1605(a)(5)'s "scope of employment" standard? Note that the California standard of enterprise liability is significantly broader than that prevailing elsewhere. *See* 1 S. Speiser, C. Krause & A. Gans, *The American Law on Torts* §4.51 at 740 (1983) ("thus far used only in California"). Is it appropriate for individual states to define the immunity of foreign states through 50 divergent standards for defining "scope of employment"? What if a state broadens the scope of employment test significantly beyond that adopted by California? What if it adopts an especially broad (or narrow) test applicable only to foreign states?

3. *Content of scope of employment test.* What is the appropriate content of §1605(a)(5)'s scope of employment test? Note that the test adopted by *Liu* does not require any showing that the employer could have foreseen the employee's misconduct, and that it disregards both the fact that the employee committed an outrageous crime and that the employee had personal motivations. Section 228 of the *Restatement (Second) of Agency*, like the laws of most states, generally requires consideration of foreseeability, outrageousness of the employee's act, and personal motivations. Would this standard be more appropriate than California's theory of enterprise liability?

4. *Immunity of foreign heads of state and governmental officials.* Heads of foreign states and other governmental officials are not expressly accorded immunity under the FSIA. Nonetheless, lower courts have long recognized that foreign heads of state and other governmental officials enjoy a measure of immunity in U.S. courts. *See Restatement (Second) Foreign Relations Law* §65 (1965); *Republic of the Philippines v. Marcos*, 806 F.2d 344, 360-61 (2d Cir. 1986); *Chuidian v. Philippine Nat'l Bank*, 912 F.2d

1095, 1103 (9th Cir. 1990); *Lafontant v. Aristide*, 844 F.Supp. 128 (E.D.N.Y. 1994); *Herbage v. Meese*, 747 F. Supp. 60, 65-67 (D.D.C. 1990), *aff'd*, 1991 W.L. 180053 (D.C. Cir. 1991). The U.S. Government has on occasion submitted "suggestions" of immunity with respect to foreign heads of state or other senior government officials. *Kilroy v. Windsor*, 1978 Digest U.S. Prac. Int'l Law 641-3 (N.D. Ohio 1978); *Psirakis v. Marcos*, 1975 Digest U.S. Prac. Int'l Law 344-45 (N.D. Cal. 1975). The Executive Branch has taken the position that its suggestions are binding on courts.

Lower courts are divided over both the source and scope of head-of-state immunity. Some courts have held that the FSIA applies to foreign heads of state and other governmental officials. *Chuidian v. Philippine Nat'l Bank*, 912 F.2d 1095, 1103 (9th Cir. 1990); *Herbage v. Meese*, 747 F. Supp. 60, 65-67 (D.D.C. 1990), *aff'd*, 1991 W.L. 180053 (D.C. Circ. 1991) ("FSIA does extend to natural persons acting as agents of the sovereign"). Other courts have held that the FSIA does not extend to heads of state, but that federal common law supplies a roughly equivalent grant of immunity. *Republic of Philippines v. Marcos*, 806 F.2d 344, 360-61 (2d Cir. 1986); *In re Grand Jury Proceedings, Doc. No. 700*, 817 F.2d 1108, 1110-11 (4th Cir. 1987). In general, federal common law doctrines of head-of-state immunity draw heavily on the *Restatement (Second) Foreign Relations Law* §65 (1965).

Suppose Admiral Wong had been named a defendant in *Liu*, and that service was effected. Would he have been entitled to immunity?

5. *Situs requirement revisited*. Where did the tort allegedly committed by the ROC occur? in California, where the shooting occurred, or in the ROC, where it was allegedly ordered?

PART TWO:
CHOICE OF FORUM

As the materials set forth in Part One illustrate, many international disputes will be subject to the judicial jurisdiction of two or more different states. That is a consequence of the expansive character of contemporary rules of judicial jurisdiction.[1] Where two or more states may exercise judicial jurisdiction, choice of forum issues arise: which of the states that could adjudicate a particular dispute will do so? Will both states seek to do so? If so, will parallel litigations ensue, or are there means of confining the dispute to a single forum?

Under both U.S. federal and state law, several related devices permit litigants to influence the choice of which one of several competing forums with judicial jurisdiction should adjudicate a dispute. These devices are: (a) the forum non conveniens doctrine; (b) forum selection agreements; (c) *lis alibi pendens* stays; and (d) antisuit injunctions.

This Part considers the application of each of these choice of forum devices in U.S. international litigation. Chapter 4 examines the forum non conveniens doctrine, pursuant to which a U.S. court may dismiss an action (otherwise within its jurisdiction) in favor of a substantially more convenient and appropriate forum. Chapter 5 explores the enforceability of forum selection clauses, pursuant to which parties can permit or require litigation of disputes in a particular forum. Chapter 6 considers the *lis alibi pendens* doctrine, permitting U.S. courts to stay their own proceedings in deference to parallel foreign litigation; it also considers antisuit injunctions, which enjoin parties from participating in foreign parallel litigation.

As discussed above, selecting the forum where a dispute will be decided has critical practical importance in international disputes, particularly where one potential forum is the United States. The significant differences between substantive and procedural rules, decisionmakers, and damage awards produces dramatically different resolutions of the same dispute in different forums. Reread the discussion of these factors in Part One above.[2]

---

1. *See supra* pp. 73-77.
2. *See supra* pp. 3-5.

4/Forum Non Conveniens in International Litigation[1]

Forum non conveniens is a common law doctrine that permits a court to decline to exercise judicial jurisdiction if an alternative forum would be substantially more convenient or appropriate. Although it has no direct federal statutory or constitutional foundation, the forum non conveniens doctrine has been repeatedly applied by U.S. courts.[2] This Chapter examines the application of the forum non conveniens doctrine by U.S. courts in international cases.

A. Introduction and Background

1. Common Law Origins of the Forum Non Conveniens Doctrine

The historical origins of the forum non conveniens doctrine are fairly described as "obscure" and "murky."[3] The Supreme Court has said on several occasions that the "doctrine of forum non conveniens has a long history."[4] In fact, the forum non conveniens defense appears to be of relatively recent origin. Despite its Latin name, most commentators have said that there is no evidence in Roman law, or in conti-

---

1. Commentary on the forum non conveniens doctrine includes, *e.g.*, Barrett, *The Doctrine of Forum Non Conveniens*, 35 Calif. L. Rev. 380 (1947); Bickel, *The Doctrine of Forum Non Conveniens as Applied in the Federal Courts in Matters of Admiralty*, 35 Cornell L.Q. 12 (1949); Blair, *The Doctrine of Forum Non Conveniens in Anglo-American Law*, 29 Colum. L. Rev. 1 (1929); Braucher, *The Inconvenient Federal Forum*, 60 Harv. L. Rev. 908, 909 (1947); Stein, *Forum Non Conveniens and the Redundancy of Court-Access Doctrine*, 133 U. Pa. L. Rev. 781 (1985).

2. *E.g.*, *Piper Aircraft Co. v. Reyno*, 454 U.S. 235 (1981); *Gulf Oil Corp. v. Gilbert*, 330 U.S. 501 (1947); *Koster v. (American) Lumbermens Mutual Casualty Co.*, 330 U.S. 518 (1947).

3. Barrett, *The Doctrine of Forum Non Conveniens*, 35 Calif. L. Rev. 380, 386 (1947); *American Dredging Co. v. Miller*, 114 S.Ct. 981 (1994) ("origins of the doctrine in Anglo-American law are murky").

4. *Piper Aircraft Co. v. Reyno*, 454 U.S. 235, 248 n.13 (1981).

nental civil practice, of a forum non conveniens doctrine.[5] Instead, the doctrine is generally traced to Scottish common law decisions.[6]

Even in Scotland, it was not until the late 19th century that the phrase "forum non conveniens" was used. The term was apparently a neo-Latin translation of the English phrase "inconvenient forum." This term was coined to distinguish discretionary dismissals based upon convenience and comity from dismissals based upon a lack of judicial jurisdiction (which were termed "forum non competens").[7]

In the United States, the forum non conveniens doctrine was not adopted — at least under that name — until well into the 20th century.[8] It was long settled that neither foreign citizens nor foreign residents were barred from access to U.S. courts, including in actions arising abroad under foreign law. This rule rested on principles of international law, and was widely acknowledged by commentators.[9] Nevertheless, throughout the 19th century, U.S. courts dismissed actions based on reasoning that closely resembles the contemporary forum non conveniens doctrine. These courts relied upon a blend of notions of international law, comity, convenience, judicial administration, and relation to the forum, in dismissing actions that were concededly within their jurisdiction. The clearest examples were in federal admiralty actions.

Although the label "forum non conveniens" was not used, U.S. admiralty courts had dismissed actions within their jurisdiction from the beginning of the 19th century, citing justifications similar to those employed in the contemporary forum non conveniens doctrine.[10] As an 1801 decision explained:

> It has been my general rule not to take cognizance of disputes between the masters and crews of foreign ships. ... Reciprocal policy, and the justice due

---

5. Beale, *The Jurisdiction of Courts Over Foreigners*, 26 Harv. L. Rev. 193, 283 (1913); Pillet, *Jurisdiction in Actions Between Foreigners*, 18 Harv. L. Rev. 325 (1905). One commentator has suggested, however, that the Scottish courts must have borrowed the doctrine from continental sources before its appearance in Scotland in the mid-19th century. Dainow, *The Inappropriate Forum*, 29 Ill. L. Rev. 867, 881-86 (1935); Dicey & Morris, *The Conflict of Laws* 398 (12th ed. 1993).

6. *Piper Aircraft Co. v. Reyno*, 454 U.S. 235, 248 n.13 (1981); *Gulf Oil Corp. v. Gilbert*, 330 U.S. 501, 507 & n.6 (1947).

7. Braucher, *The Inconvenient Federal Forum*, 60 Harv. L. Rev. 908, 909 (1947). Two Scottish decisions — *Logan v. Bank of Scotland*, [1906] 1 K.B. 141, and *La Societe du Gaz v. La Societe Anonyme de Navigation 'Les Armateurs Francais'*, 1926 Sess. Cas. 13 — are frequently cited as the first modern statements of the forum non conveniens doctrine.

8. As discussed below, the Supreme Court first applied the forum non conveniens doctrine in diversity actions in *Gulf Oil Co. v. Gilbert*, 330 U.S. 501 (1947) and *Koster v. Lumbermens Mutual Casualty Co.*, 330 U.S. 518 (1947).

9. J. Story, *Commentaries on the Conflict of Laws* § 565 (2d ed. 1841); H. Wheaton, *Elements of International Law* § 140-1 (8th ed. 1866); Martens, *Law of Nations* 102 (Cobbett trans. 4th ed. 1829); Wilson, *Access-to-Court Provisions in United States Commercial Treaties*, 47 Am. J. Int'l L. 20 (1953); 3 G. Hackworth, *Digest of International Law* 562 (1941); 4 J. Moore, *Digest of International Law* 2 (1906).

10. *See* Bickel, *The Doctrine of Forum Non Conveniens as Applied in the Federal Courts in Matters of Admiralty*, 35 Cornell L.Q. 12, 13 (1949); A. Ehrenzweig, *The Conflict of Laws* 123 (1962) ("Admiralty courts have administered what in effect has been a doctrine of forum non conveniens much longer than land courts.").

from one friendly nation to another, calls for such conduct in the courts of either country.[11]

The Supreme Court repeatedly affirmed this discretionary power of admiralty courts to abstain from deciding sufficiently foreign matters.[12]

Early U.S. decisions also developed rules of abstention, similar to forum non conveniens, outside the admiralty context. This was most evident in cases involving the internal affairs of foreign corporations[13] and suits between aliens asserting foreign causes of action.[14] Although these rules were broadly similar to forum non conveniens, the doctrine was not invoked by that name.[15]

New York was the leading example of a jurisdiction that apparently permitted forum non conveniens dismissals under other names. As early as 1817, a New York court asserted the discretion to dismiss an action otherwise within its jurisdiction for reasons of convenience and comity.[16] Later in the 19th century, New York courts repeatedly declined jurisdiction in cases where one foreigner asserted tort claims against another foreigner based on acts committed outside of New York. In 1890, a New York court could declare:

> It is the well-settled rule of this state that, unless special reasons are shown to exist which make it necessary or proper to do so, the courts will not retain jurisdiction of and determine actions between parties residing in another state for personal injuries received in that state. ... The reason of the rule is obvious, — because the courts of this state should not be vexed with litigations between non-residents over causes of action arising outside of our own territorial limits. Our courts are not supported by the people for any such purpose.[17]

In contrast, New York courts did not recognize any discretionary power to decline

---

11. *Willendson v. Forsoket*, 29 F.Cas. 1283 (No. 17,682) (Pa. 1801).

12. *Mason v. Ship Blaireau*, 6 U.S. 240, 263 (1804) (referring to "the idea, that upon principles of general policy, this court ought not to take cognizance of a case entirely between foreigners," even absent "any positive incapacity to do so."); *The Maggie Hammond*, 76 U.S. 435, 457 (1870) (U.S. admiralty court may decline jurisdiction in case involving "the citizens or subjects of a foreign country, whose courts are not clothed with the power to give the same remedy in similar controversies to the citizens of the United States"); *The Belgenland*, 114 U.S. 355, 362-69 (1885).

13. *E.g., Williams v. Green Bay & W. R.R.*, 326 U.S. 549 (1946); *Rogers v. Guaranty Trust Co.*, 288 U.S. 123 (1933); *Burnrite Coal Briquette Co. v. Riggs*, 274 U.S. 208 (1927).

14. *E.g., Great Western Ry. Co. v. Miller*, 19 Mich. 305 (1869); *Gardner v. Thomas*, 14 Johns. 134 (N.Y. 1817); *Johnson v. Dalton*, 1 Cow. 543 (N.Y. 1923); *Avery v. Holland*, 2 Tenn. 71 (1806).

15. One commentator, urging adoption of the forum non conveniens doctrine in 1929, could cite only three or four precedents in the United States that had used the term. Blair, *The Doctrine of Forum Non Conveniens in Anglo-American Law*, 29 Colum. L. Rev. 1, 2 & n.4 (1929).

16. *Gardner v. Thomas*, 14 Johns. 134 (N.Y. 1817).

17. *Ferguson v. Neilson*, 11 N.Y.S. 524 (1890). *See also Hoes v. New York, N.H. & H.R.R. Co.*, 66 N.E. 119 (N.Y. 1903); *Collard v. Beach*, 81 N.Y.S. 619 (N.Y. 1903); *Gainer v. Donner*, 251 N.Y.S. 713 (1931).

contract and other commercial actions where only non-residents were involved as parties.[18]

With this 19th century background, U.S. commentators during the 1920s proposed adopting the Scottish forum non conveniens doctrine.[19] The author most widely credited with popularizing the doctrine in the United States was Paxton Blair — an associate at a New York law firm with an imperious writing style and brilliant timing.[20] In 1929, he published an article in the Columbia Law Review entitled *The Doctrine of Forum Non Conveniens in Anglo-American Law*. The article began with the observation that, of all the problems of the U.S. bar, "calendar congestion in the trial courts is easily foremost."[21] Blair then offered the following relief:

> in response to th[is] challenge we tender some observations directed toward the possibility of relieving court congestion by partially diverting at its source the flood of litigation by which our courts are being overwhelmed, it being our conviction that an additional effective method of dealing with the problem lies in the wider dissemination of the doctrine, and increased use of the plea, of forum non conveniens which deals with the discretionary power of a court to decline to exercise a possessed jurisdiction whenever it appears that the cause before it may be more appropriately tried elsewhere.[22]

Blair supported this argument with a measure of historical authority. He pointed to admiralty and other precedents (described above), which were characterized as having applied the forum non conveniens doctrine without realizing that this was what they were doing. In Blair's memorable metaphor, U.S. courts were like "Moliere's M. Jourdain, who found he had been speaking prose all his life without knowing it."[23]

---

18. *Wertheim v. Clergue*, 65 N.Y.S. 750 (App. Div. 1900) ("we know of no reason founded in public policy, and certainly nothing resting in precedent, which will close the courts of this State to non-resident suitors who invoke their aid against other non-residents sojourning within our borders for the enforcement of causes of action arising out of commercial transactions and affecting property or property rights. ... [We] certainly do not intend to establish a precedent which would shut our courts to great numbers of foreign merchants, non-residents of the State, who may find their non-resident debtors, fraudulent or honest, temporarily within our jurisdiction"); *Rodger v. Bliss*, 223 N.Y.S. 401 (1927).

That limitation was abandoned by New York courts during the early decades of the 20th century. *Wedemann v. United States Trust Co.*, 179 N.E. 712 (N.Y. 1932); *Bata v. Bata*, 105 N.E.2d 623, 625-26 (N.Y. 1952) ("it was thought, or held, at one time that only tort cases felt the doctrine's impact").

19. Blair, *The Doctrine of Forum Non Conveniens in Anglo-American Law*, 29 Colum. L. Rev. 1 (1929); Dainow, *The Inappropriate Forum*, 29 Ill. Rev. 867 (1935).

20. *See* Stein, *Forum Non Conveniens and the Redundancy of Court-Access Doctrine*, 133 U. Pa. L. Rev. 781, 811-12 (1985); *Alfaro v. Dow Chemical Co.*, 786 S.W.2d 674, 676 (Tex. 1990) (referring to forum non conveniens as the creation of a "Wall Street lawyer").

21. 29 Colum. L. Rev. 1, 1 (1929).

22. 29 Colum. L. Rev. 1, 1 (1929).

23. Blair, *The Doctrine of Forum Non Conveniens in Anglo-American Law*, 29 Colum. L. Rev. 1, 21-22 (1929). Blair's efforts to identify cases that applied a forum non conveniens doctrine sub silentio has been criticized. A. Ehrenzweig, *The Conflict of Laws* 125 (1962).

The next 20 years witnessed an extraordinary acceptance of the forum non conveniens doctrine by both state and federal courts in the United States. In 1932, the Supreme Court considered in *Canada Malting Co. v. Paterson S.S. Ltd.,*[24] whether a U.S. district court had the power to dismiss an admiralty action between two Canadian shipowners involved in a dispute occurring on the U.S. side of the international boundary line in Lake Superior. Writing for a unanimous Court, Justice Brandeis dismissed the argument that district judges had no discretion to decline jurisdiction that Congress had granted:

> Obviously, the proposition that a court having jurisdiction must exercise it, is not universally true; else the admiralty court could never decline jurisdiction on the ground that the litigation is between foreigners. Nor is it true of courts administering other systems of our law.[25]

The Court upheld dismissal of the suit, relying on the fact that both parties were Canadian, both vessels were Canadian-registered, all of the witnesses were in Canada, and both vessels were on voyages from one Canadian port to another.[26] The Court's opinion did not mention the phrase "forum non conveniens," except by way of citation to Paxton Blair's law review article on the subject.[27] Nevertheless, it went out of its way to indicate that courts enjoyed discretion to decline jurisdiction outside the admiralty context:

> Courts of equity and of law also occasionally decline, in the interest of justice, to exercise jurisdiction, where the suit is between aliens or nonresidents, or where for kindred reasons the litigation can more appropriately be conducted in a foreign tribunal.[28]

The Supreme Court soon thereafter went further, again in dicta, remarking that a state court "may in appropriate cases apply the doctrine of forum non conveniens."[29] With this background, Justice Frankfurter was comfortable referring in a 1941 dissent to "the familiar doctrine of forum non conveniens," which was "firmly imbedded in our law."[30] His comments elicited no objection from the remainder of the Court.

The Supreme Court did not, however, actually apply the forum non conveniens doctrine until two 1947 decisions in *Gulf Oil Corp. v. Gilbert*[31] and *Koster v.*

---

24. 285 U.S. 413 (1932).

25. 285 U.S. at 422.

26. 285 U.S. at 422-23.

27. 285 U.S. at 423 n.6 (citing Blair, *The Doctrine of Forum Non Conveniens in Anglo-American Law,* 29 Colum. L. Rev. 1 (1929)).

28. 285 U.S. at 423.

29. *Broderick v. Rosner,* 294 U.S. 629, 643 (1935). It has been observed, however, that "[n]ot until 1948 was the doctrine [of *forum non conveniens*] accepted for general application in the federal courts, and it received little or no attention in the state courts until after the federal adoption." Stein, *Forum Non Conveniens and the Redundancy of Court-Access Doctrine,* 133 U. Pa. L. Rev. 781, 796 (1985).

30. *Baltimore & Ohio R.R. v. Kepner,* 314 U.S. 44, 55-56 (1941) (Frankfurter, J., dissenting).

31. 330 U.S. 501 (1947).

Lumbermens Mutual Casualty Co.[32] In these cases, the Court for the first time expressly applied the "doctrine of forum non conveniens."[33] The principle has remained an important feature of U.S. civil procedure ever since.

In *Gulf Oil*, Justice Jackson asserted that the forum non conveniens doctrine "did not originate in federal but in state courts."[34] That does not appear to be correct. There is no evidence that U.S. state courts applied the forum non conveniens doctrine by name prior to 1947, save in a handful of 20th century decisions.[35] Indeed, one respected commentator could assert in 1947 that, at that time, the forum non conveniens doctrine "can be said to be in operation in barely half a dozen states."[36] In most U.S. states, the forum non conveniens doctrine was adopted only after *Gulf Oil* and *Koster*; in many cases, the Supreme Court's *Gulf Oil* and *Koster* decisions were the principal authority cited in support of the doctrine.[37]

2. Gulf Oil Co. v. Gilbert and Koster v. Lumbermens Mutual Casualty Co.

Gulf Oil was a diversity action brought in the U.S. District Court for the Southern District of New York. The plaintiff was a Virginian, resident in Virginia; the defendant was a Pennsylvania corporation registered to do business (and subject to personal jurisdiction) in both Virginia and New York. The plaintiff sought damages resulting from the defendant's alleged negligence, which allegedly caused a fire which damaged plaintiff's property. All of the relevant conduct and damage were in Virginia.

The district court dismissed the action on forum non conveniens grounds.[38] The Supreme Court affirmed.[39] Expressly relying on the forum non conveniens doctrine, the Court reasoned that, even where a district court has personal jurisdiction over the defendant, the court has discretion to decline jurisdiction:

> This Court, in one form of words or another, has repeatedly recognized the existence of the power to decline jurisdiction in exceptional circumstances...
> The principle of forum non conveniens is simply that a court may resist imposition upon its jurisdiction even when jurisdiction is authorized by the letter of a general venue statute.

Gulf Oil declined to "catalogue the circumstances" where a forum non conve-

---

32. 330 U.S. 518 (1947).

33. 330 U.S. at 506-509; 330 U.S. at 522, 525-26.

34. 330 U.S. at 505 n.4.

35. *See supra* pp. 291-92.

36. Barrett, *The Doctrine of Forum Non Conveniens*, 35 Calif. L. Rev. 380, 388-89 (1947). Barrett cited decisions from Florida, Louisiana, Massachusetts, New Hampshire, New Jersey, and New York. Id. at 389 n. 41.

37. *E.g., Bergquist v. Medtronic, Inc.*, 379 N.W.2d 508 (Minn. 1986); *Union Carbide Corp. v. Aetna Casualty and Surety Co.*, 562 A.2d 15 (Conn. 1989).

38. It cited the fact that all of the conduct giving rise to the litigation occurred in Virginia, the plaintiff's residence was in Virginia, the plaintiff and the defendant did business in Virginia, and most of the witnesses and evidence were in Virginia.

39. 330 U.S. 501 (1947).

niens dismissal would be proper. It instead identified two sets of factors bearing on the doctrine's application: "the private interest of the litigants" and "[f]actors of public interest."[40] The Court set forth a detailed list of these factors. The "private interest" factors include:

> the relative ease of access to sources of proof; availability of compulsory process for attendance of unwilling, and the cost of obtaining attendance of willing, witnesses; possibility of view of premises, if view would be appropriate to the action[;] ... all other practical problems ... [;] the enforceability of judgment ... [; and whether] the plaintiff [has sought to] vex, harass or oppress the defendant.[41]

The Court explained the "public interest" factors as follows:

> Administrative difficulties follow for courts when litigation is piled up in congested centers. ... Jury duty is a burden that ought not to be imposed upon the people of a community which has no relation to the litigation. In cases which touch the affairs of many persons, there is a reason for holding the trial in their view. ... There is a local interest in having localized controversies decided at home.[42]

The Court made clear that a strong showing of private and public inconvenience was necessary to justify a forum non conveniens dismissal: "unless the balance is strongly in favor of the defendant, the plaintiff's choice of forum should rarely be disturbed."[43] The Court also held, however, that the decision whether to grant a forum non conveniens dismissal rested largely with the trial judge's discretion: "[t]he doctrine leaves much to the discretion of the court to which the plaintiff resorts."[44]

Applying these standards, *Gulf Oil* upheld the district court's forum non conveniens dismissal of the action. It noted that the plaintiff resided in Virginia, and had advanced no plausible reason why New York was a convenient forum; similarly, it remarked that the evidence in the case was almost all in Virginia, and that Virginia law would likely govern the dispute. Hence, the Court was "convinced that the District Court did not exceed its powers or the bounds of its discretion in dismissing plaintiff's complaint."[45] The Court also made it clear that the doctrine applied only where an adequate alternative forum existed: "In all cases in which the doctrine of forum non conveniens comes into play, it presupposes at least two forums in which the defendant is amenable to process; the doctrine furnishes criteria for choice between them."[46]

Justice Black dissented in *Gulf Oil*. He concluded that, where Congress had

---

40. 330 U.S. at 508.
41. 330 U.S. at 508.
42. 330 U.S. at 508-09.
43. 330 U.S. at 508.
44. 330 U.S. at 508.
45. 330 U.S. at 512.
46. 330 U.S. at 506-07.

granted federal courts jurisdiction to decide a dispute, the courts had no discretion to decline to exercise that jurisdiction.[47] He invoked the principle that "'the courts of the United States are bound to proceed to judgment, and to afford redress to suitors before them, in every case to which their jurisdiction extends. They cannot abdicate their authority or duty in any case in favor of another jurisdiction.'"[48] Justice Black's dissent also warned that

> The broad and indefinite discretion left to federal courts to decide the question of convenience from the welter of factors which are relevant to such a judgment, will inevitably produce a complex of close and indistinguishable decisions from which accurate prediction of the proper forum will become difficult, if not impossible.[49]

Koster v. Lumbermens Mutual Casualty Co.[50] was a companion case to *Gulf Oil*. It involved a shareholders' derivative action, brought in the Eastern District of New York by a New York resident against three Illinois defendants. The Court reasoned:

> When there are only two parties to a dispute, there is a good reason why it should be tried in the plaintiff's home forum if that has been his choice. He should not be deprived of the presumed advantages of his home jurisdiction except upon a clear showing of facts which either (1) establish such oppressiveness and vexation to a defendant as to be out of all proportion to plaintiff's convenience, which may be shown to be slight or nonexistent, or (2) make trial in the chosen forum inappropriate because of considerations affecting the court's own administrative and legal problems.[51]

Like *Gulf Oil*, *Koster* upheld dismissal.[52]

3. Section 1404(a) — Domestic Forum Non Conveniens Statute

In 1948, Congress enacted 28 U.S.C. §1404(a), which codified the forum non conveniens doctrine for transfers among federal district courts. Section 1404(a) provides:

> For the convenience of parties and witnesses, in the interest of justice, a district court may transfer any civil action to any other district or division where it might have been brought.

---

47. 330 U.S. at 512 (Black, J., dissenting). *See* Redish, *Abstention, Separation of Powers, and the Limits of the Judicial Function*, 94 Yale L.J. 71 (1984); *W.S. Kirkpatrick & Co. v. Environmental Tectonics Corp.*, 493 U.S. 400 (1990) ("Courts in the United States have the power, and ordinarily the obligation, to decide cases and controversies properly presented to them.").

48. *Gulf Oil Corp.*, 330 U.S. at 513 (quoting *Hyde v. Stone*, 61 U.S. 170, 175 (1903)).

49. 330 U.S. at 516.

50. 330 U.S. at 518.

51. 330 U.S. at 524.

52. Lower courts have consistently held that *Gulf Oil* and *Koster* stated the same principles. *In re Air Crash Disaster Near New Orleans*, 821 F.2d 1147, 1163 n.24 (5th Cir. 1987); *Pain v. United Technologies Corp.*, 637 F.2d 775, 783 (D.C. Cir. 1980), *cert. denied*, 454 U.S. 1128 (1981); *Alcoa SS Co. v. M/V Nordic Regent*, 654 F.2d 147, 154-58 (2d Cir.), *cert. denied*, 449 U.S. 890 (1980).

The legislative history accompanying the section explained that it "was drafted in accordance with the doctrine of forum non conveniens, permitting transfer to a more convenient forum, even though the venue is proper."[53]

Section 1404(a) does not play a central role in international litigation, because it applies only to transfers between different federal courts. It does not apply to dismissals in favor of foreign forums, which continue to be governed by the common law doctrine of forum non conveniens.[54] In general, §1404(a) has been interpreted as requiring an analysis similar to that applicable under the forum non conveniens doctrine.[55]

---

53. 28 U.S.C. § 1404(a) annotation (1982) (Historical and Revision Notes). The legislative history's suggestion that §1404 codified a well-established common law doctrine of forum non conveniens was not entirely accurate. In fact, the provision had been proposed well before the Supreme Court's decisions in *Gulf Oil* and *Koster*.

54. *See infra* pp. 431-53.

55. *Van Dusen v. Barrack*, 376 U.S. 612 (1964). *See also infra* pp. 432-33.

B. The Modern Forum Non Conveniens Doctrine: Basic Principles

For 34 years following *Gulf Oil* and *Koster*, the Court did not revisit the subject of forum non conveniens. During the interim, the doctrine won substantial (but not universal) following in state courts,[56] and was the subject of considerable case law in the federal courts. In 1981, the Supreme Court decided *Piper Aircraft Co. v. Reyno*.[57] Its opinion is the leading contemporary statement of the forum non conveniens doctrine.

A substantial majority of U.S. states have adopted some variation of the forum non conveniens doctrine. A dozen or so states have statutorily codified the doctrine, generally in a form based upon the Uniform Interstate and International Procedure Act. Section 1.05 of the Act states the doctrine as follows:

> When the court finds that in the interest of substantial justice the action should be heard in another forum, the court may stay or dismiss the action in whole or in part on any conditions that may be just.

Another 30 or so states have, by common law decision, recognized the forum non conveniens doctrine is some fashion. These decisions have generally done so as a matter of state law — not in express deference to what they regard as federal common law.[58] Nevertheless, they have virtually unanimously cited *Gulf Oil* or *Piper Aircraft* as persuasive authority; in many cases, these decisions have been the only authorities relied upon in adopting forum non conveniens as a matter of state law.

Only a minority of states has either rejected the forum non conveniens doctrine or remained uncommitted. States that have declined to adopt the forum non conveniens doctrine include Georgia,[59] Louisiana,[60] Mississippi,[61] North Dakota,[62] and Texas.[63]

---

56. *See* Robertson & Speck, *Access to State Courts in Transnational Personal Injury Cases: Forum Non Conveniens and Antisuit Injunctions*, 68 Tex. L. Rev. 937, 948-53 (1990); Silberman, *Developments in Jurisdiction and Forum Non Conveniens in International Litigation: Thoughts on Reform and a Proposal for a Uniform Standard*, 28 Tex. Int'l L. J. 501, 518-25 (1993).

57. 454 U.S. 235 (1981) (excerpted below at pp. 299-305).

58. *E.g.*, *Satkowiak v. Chesapeake & Ohio Ry.*, 478 N.E.2d 370 (Ill. 1985); *Torrijas v. Midwest Steel Erection Co.*, 474 N.E.2d 1250 (Ill. App. 1984); *Blais v. Deyo*, 468 N.Y.S.2d 91 (1983); *Hamann v. American Motors Corp.*, 345 N.W.2d 699 (Mich. App. 1983); *McCracken v. Eli Lilly & Co.*, 494 N.E.2d 1289 (Ind. Ct. App. 1986) (in interpreting state forum non conveniens statute, relying on federal decisions because of "sufficient similarity of spirit of the state and federal rules as they relate to the doctrine of forum non conveniens in the context of international litigation").

59. *Smith v. Board of Regents*, 302 S.E.2d 124, 126 (Ga. App. 1983) (forum non conveniens has "never been expressly sanctioned in Georgia's courts").

60. *Fox v. Board of Supervisors*, 576 So.2d 978 (La. 1991) (relying on state statute); *Kassapas v. Arkon Shipping Agency, Inc.*, 485 So.2d 565 (La. Ct. App.), *writ denied*, 488 So.2d 208 (La.), *cert. denied*, 107 S.Ct. 422 (1986); *Trahan v. Phoenix Insurance Co.*, 200 So.2d 118, 122 (La. Ct. App.), *cert. denied*, 202 So.2d 657 (La. 1967) ("the doctrine of forum non conveniens is foreign to our jurisprudence and contrary to express legislative declaration").

61. *Vick v. Cochran*, 316 So.2d 242 (Miss. 1975).

62. *Kristensen v. Strinden*, 343 N.W.2d 67, 71 (N.D. 1983) ("Our Constitution does not permit State courts any discretion in determining whether or not to entertain actions properly brought before them.").

63. *Dow Chemical Company v. Castro Alfaro* 786 S.W.2d 674 (Tex. 1990), *cert. denied*, 111 S.Ct. 671 (1991) (excerpted below at pp. 305-13). The Texas legislature has since enacted legislation adopting the forum non conveniens doctrine in limited circumstances. Texas Civil Practice and Remedies Code §71.051 (1993).

Selected materials illustrating the basic principles of the forum non conveniens doctrine are excerpted below. The Supreme Court's opinion in *Piper Aircraft Co. v. Reyno*, excerpted below, remains the leading contemporary statement of the doctrine. The Texas Supreme Court's opinions in *Dow Chemical Co. v. Castro Alfaro* reflect the controversy that the forum non conveniens doctrine has generated.

PIPER AIRCRAFT CO. v. REYNO

454 U.S. 235 (1981)

JUSTICE MARSHALL. These cases arise out of an air crash that took place in Scotland. Respondent, acting as representative of the estates of several Scottish citizens killed in the accident, brought wrongful-death actions against petitioners. ... Petitioners moved to dismiss on the ground of *forum non conveniens*. After noting that an alternative forum existed in Scotland, the District Court granted their motions. The United States Court of Appeals for the Third Circuit reversed. The Court of Appeals based its decision, at least in part, on the ground that dismissal is automatically barred where the law of the alternative forum is less favorable to the plaintiff than the law of the forum chosen by the plaintiff. Because we conclude that the possibility of an unfavorable change in law should not, by itself, bar dismissal, and because we conclude that the District Court did not otherwise abuse its discretion, we reverse.

In July 1976, a small commercial aircraft crashed in the Scottish highlands during the course of a charter flight from Blackpool to Perth. The pilot and five passengers were killed instantly. The decedents were all Scottish subjects and residents, as are their heirs and next of kin. There were no eyewitnesses to the accident. At the time of the crash the plane was subject to Scottish air traffic control. The aircraft, a twin-engine Piper Aztec, was manufactured in Pennsylvania by petitioner Piper Aircraft Co. ("Piper"). The propellers were manufactured in Ohio by petitioner Hartzell Propeller, Inc. ("Hartzell"). At the time of the crash the aircraft was registered in Great Britain and was owned and maintained by Air Navigation and Trading Co., Ltd. ("Air Navigation"). It was operated by McDonald Aviation, Ltd. ("McDonald"), a Scottish air taxi service. Both Air Navigation and McDonald were organized in the United Kingdom. The wreckage of the plane is now in a hangar in Farnborough, England.

The British Department of Trade investigated the accident shortly after it occurred. A preliminary report found that the plane crashed after developing a spin, and suggested that mechanical failure in the plane or the propeller was responsible. At Hartzell's request, this report was reviewed by a three-member Review Board, which held a 9-day adversary hearing attended by all interested parties. The Review Board found no evidence of defective equipment and indicated that pilot error may have contributed to the accident. ...

In July 1977, a California probate court appointed respondent Gaynell Reyno administratrix of the estates of the five passengers. Reyno is not related to and does not know any of the decedents or other survivors; she was a legal secretary to the attorney who filed this lawsuit. Several days after her appointment, Reyno commenced separate wrongful-death actions against Piper and Hartzell in the Superior Court of California, claiming negligence and strict liability. ... Reyno candidly admits that the action against Piper and Hartzell was filed in the United States because its laws regarding liability, capacity to sue and damages are more favorable to her position than are those of Scotland. Scottish law does not recognize strict liability in tort. Moreover, it permits wrongful-death actions only when brought by a decedent's relatives. The relatives may sue only for "loss of support and society."

On petitioners' motion, the suit was removed to the United States District Court for the Central District of California, [and later transferred] to the United States District Court for the Middle District of Pennsylvania, pursuant to 28 U.S.C. §1404(a). ... [B]oth Hartzell and Piper moved to dismiss the action on the ground of *forum non conveniens*. The District Court granted these motions. ... It relied on the balancing test set forth by this Court in *Gulf Oil Corp. v. Gilbert*, and its companion case, *Koster v. Lumbermens Mut. Cas. Co.* In those decisions, the Court stated that a plaintiff's choice of forum should rarely be disturbed. However, when an alternative forum has jurisdiction to hear the case, and when trial in the chosen forum would "establish ... oppressiveness and vexation to a defendant ... out of all proportion to plaintiff's convenience," or when the "chosen forum [is] inappropriate because of considerations affecting the court's own administrative and legal problems" the court may, in the exercise of its sound discretion, dismiss the case. To guide trial court discretion, the Court provided a list of "private interest factors" affecting the convenience ... of the forum. ...

On the appeal, the United States Court of Appeals for the Third Circuit reversed and remanded for trial. The decision to reverse appears to be based on two alternative grounds. First, the Court held that the District Court abused its discretion in conducting the *Gilbert* analysis. Second, the Court held that dismissal is never appropriate where the law of the alternative forum is less favorable to the plaintiff. ...

The Court of Appeals erred in holding that plaintiffs may defeat a motion to dismiss on the ground of *forum non conveniens* merely by showing that the substantive law that would be applied in the alternative forum is less favorable to the plaintiffs than that of the present forum. The possibility of a change in substantive law should ordinarily not be given conclusive or even substantial weight in the *forum non conveniens* inquiry.

We expressly rejected the position adopted by the Court of Appeals in our decision in *Canada Malting Co. v. Paterson Steamships, Ltd.*, 285 U.S. 413 (1932). That case arose out of a collision between two vessels in American waters. The Canadian owners of cargo lost in the accident sued the Canadian owners of one of the vessels in Federal District Court. The cargo owners chose an American court in large part because the relevant American liability rules were more favorable than the Canadian rules. The District Court dismissed on grounds of *forum non conveniens.* The plaintiffs argued that dismissal was inappropriate because Canadian laws were less favorable to them. This Court nonetheless affirmed:

> We have no occasion to enquire by what law the rights of the parties are governed, as we are of the opinion that, under any view of that question, it lay within the discretion of the District Court to decline to assume jurisdiction over the controversy. ... "[T]he court will not take cognizance of the case if justice would be as well done by remitting the parties to their home forum." ...

It is true that *Canada Malting* was decided before *Gilbert,* and that the doctrine of *forum non conveniens* was not fully crystallized until our decision in that case.[64] However, *Gilbert* in no way affects the validity of *Canada Malting.* Indeed, by holding that the central focus of the *forum non conveniens* inquiry is convenience, *Gilbert* implicitly recognized that dismissal may not be barred solely because of the possibility of an unfavorable change in law. Under *Gilbert,* dismissal will ordinarily be appropriate where trial in the plaintiff's chosen forum imposes a heavy burden on the defendant or the court, and where the plaintiff is unable to offer any specific reasons of convenience supporting his choice.[65] If substantial weight were given to the possibility of an unfavorable change in law, however, dismissal might be barred even where trial in the chosen forum was plainly inconvenient.

The Court of Appeals' decision is inconsistent with this Court's earlier *forum non conveniens* decisions in another respect. Those decisions have repeatedly emphasized the need to retain flexibility. ... If central emphasis were placed on any one factor, the *forum non conveniens* doctrine would lose much of the very flexibility that makes it so valuable. In fact, if conclusive or substantial weight were given to the possibility of a change in law, the *forum non conveniens* doctrine would become virtually useless. Jurisdiction and venue requirements are often easily satisfied. As a result, many plaintiffs are able to choose from among several forums. Ordinarily, these plaintiffs will select that forum whose choice-of-law rules are most advantageous. Thus, if the possibility of an unfavorable change in substantive law is given substantial weight in the *forum non conveniens* inquiry, dismissal would rarely be proper. ...

---

64. The doctrine of *forum non conveniens* has a long history. It originated in Scotland, *see* Braucher, *The Inconvenient Federal Forum,* 60 Harv. L. Rev. 908, 909-911 (1947), and became part of the common law of many States, *see id.* at 911-912; Blair, *The Doctrine of Forum Non Conveniens in Anglo-American Law,* 29 Colum. L. Rev. 1 (1929). The doctrine was also frequently applied in federal admiralty actions. *See, e.g., Canada Malting Co. v. Paterson Steamships, Ltd.* ... In previous *forum non conveniens* decisions, the Court has left unresolved the question whether under *Erie R.R. v. Tompkins,* 304 U.S. 64 (1938), state or federal law of *forum non conveniens* applies in diversity cases. The Court did not decide this issue because the same result would have been reached in each case under federal or state law. The lower courts in these cases reached the same conclusion: Pennsylvania and California law on *forum non conveniens* dismissals are virtually identical to federal law. Thus, here also, we need not resolve the *Erie* question.

65. In other words, *Gilbert* held that dismissal may be warranted where a plaintiff chooses a particular forum, not because it is convenient, but solely in order to harass the defendant or take advantage of favorable law. This is precisely the situation in which the Court of Appeals' rule would bar dismissal.

The Court of Appeals' approach is not only inconsistent with the purpose of the *forum non conveniens* doctrine, but also poses substantial practical problems. If the possibility of a change in law were given substantial weight, deciding motions to dismiss on the ground of *forum non conveniens* would become quite difficult. Choice-of-law analysis would become extremely important, and the court would frequently be required to interpret the law of foreign jurisdictions. ... The doctrine of *forum non conveniens*, however, is designed in part to help courts avoid conducting complex exercises in comparative law. As we stated in *Gilbert*, the public interest factors point towards dismissal where the court would be required to "untangle problems in conflict of laws, and in law foreign to itself."

Upholding the decision of the Court of Appeals would result in other practical problems. At least where the foreign plaintiff named an American manufacturer as defendant,[66] a court could not dismiss the case on grounds of *forum non conveniens* where dismissal might lead to an unfavorable change in law. The American courts, which are already extremely attractive to foreign plaintiffs,[67] would become even more attractive. The flow of litigation into the United States would increase and further congest already crowded courts. ...

We do not hold that the possibility of an unfavorable change in law should *never* be a relevant consideration in a *forum non conveniens* inquiry. Of course, if the remedy provided by the alternative forum is so clearly inadequate or unsatisfactory that it is no remedy at all, the unfavorable change in law may be given substantial weight; the district court may conclude that dismissal would not be in the interest of jus-

---

66. In fact, the defendant might not even have to be American. A foreign plaintiff seeking damages for an accident [that] had occurred abroad might be able to obtain service of process on a foreign defendant who does business in the United States. Under the Court of Appeals' holding, dismissal would be barred if the law in the alternative forum were less favorable to the plaintiff — even though none of the parties are American, and even though there is absolutely no nexus between the subject matter of the litigation and the United States.

67. First, all but 6 of the 50 American States - Delaware, Massachusetts, Michigan, North Carolina, Virginia, and Wyoming - offer strict liability. 1 CCH Prod. Liability Rep. §4016 (1981). Rules roughly equivalent to American strict liability are effective in France, Belgium, and Luxembourg. West Germany and Japan have a strict liability statute for pharmaceuticals. However, strict liability remains primarily an American innovation. Second, the tort plaintiff may choose, at least potentially, from among 50 jurisdictions if he decides to file suit in the United States. Each of these jurisdictions applies its own set of malleable choice-of-law rules. Third, jury trials are almost always available in the United States, while they are never provided in civil law jurisdictions. G. Gloss, *Comparative Law* 12 (1979); J. Merryman, *The Civil Law Tradition* 121 (1969). Even in the United Kingdom, most civil actions are not tried before a jury. 1 G. Keeton, *The United Kingdom: The Development of its Laws and Constitutions* 309 (1955). Fourth, unlike most foreign jurisdictions, American courts allow contingent attorney's fees, and do not tax losing parties with their opponents' attorney's fees. R. Schlesinger, *Comparative Law: Cases, Text, Materials* 275-277 (3d ed. 1970): Orban, *Product Liability: A Comparative Legal Restatement - Foreign National Law and the EEC Directive*, 8 Ga. J. Int'l & Comp. L. 342, 393 (1978). Fifth, discovery is more extensive in American than in foreign courts. R. Schlesinger, *supra*, at 307, 310 and n. 33.

tice.[68] In these cases, however, the remedies that would be provided by the Scottish courts do not fall within this category. Although the relatives of the decedents may not be able to rely on a strict liability theory, and although their potential damages award may be smaller, there is no danger that they will be deprived of any remedy or treated unfairly.

No danger in Scottish courts

The Court of Appeals also erred in rejecting the District Court's *Gilbert* analysis. The Court of Appeals stated that more weight should have been given to the plaintiff's choice of forum, and criticized the District Court's analysis of the private and public interests. However, the District Court's decision regarding the deference due plaintiff's choice of forum was appropriate. Furthermore, we do not believe that the District Court abused its discretion in weighing the private and public interests.

The District Court acknowledged that there is ordinarily a strong presumption in favor of the plaintiff's choice of forum, which may be overcome only when the private and public interest factors clearly point towards trial in the alternative forum. It held, however, that the presumption applies with less force when the plaintiff or real parties in interest are foreign. The District Court's distinction between resident or citizen plaintiffs and foreign plaintiffs is fully justified. In *Koster*, the Court indicated that a plaintiff's choice of forum is entitled to greater deference when the plaintiff has chosen the home forum. 330 U.S. at 524.[69] When the home forum has been chosen, it is reasonable to assume that this choice is convenient. When the plaintiff is foreign, however, this assumption is much less reasonable. Because the central purpose of any *forum non conveniens* inquiry is to ensure that the trial is convenient, a foreign plaintiff's choice deserves less deference.

less force when P are foreign

The *forum non conveniens* determination is committed to the sound discretion of the trial court. It may be reversed only where there has been a clear abuse of discretion; where the court has considered all relevant public and private interest factors, and where its balancing of these factors is reasonable, its decision deserves substantial deference. Here, the Court of Appeals expressly acknowledged that the standard of

ONLY when clear abuse of discretion

---

68. At the outset of any *forum non conveniens* inquiry, the court must determine whether there exists an alternative forum. Ordinarily, this requirement will be satisfied when the defendant is "amenable to process" in the other jurisdiction. In rare circumstances, however, where the remedy offered by the other forum is clearly unsatisfactory, the other forum may not be an adequate alternative, and the initial requirements may not be satisfied. Thus, for example, dismissal would not be appropriate where the alternative forum does not permit litigation of the subject matter of the dispute. *Cf. Phoenix Canada Oil Co. Ltd. v. Texaco Inc.*, 78 F.R.D. 445 (Del. 1978) (court refuses to dismiss, where alternative forum is Ecuador, it is unclear whether Ecuadorean tribunal will hear the case, and there is no generally codified Ecuadorean legal remedy for the unjust enrichment and tort claims asserted).

69. In *Koster*, we stated that "[i]n any balancing of conveniences, a real showing of convenience by a plaintiff who had sued in his home forum will normally outweigh the inconvenience the defendant may have shown." 330 U.S. at 524. *See also Swift & Co. Packers v. Compania Colombiana del Caribe*, 339 U.S. 684, 697 (1950) ("suit by a United States citizen against a foreign respondent brings into force considerations very different from those in suits between foreigners"); *Canada Malting Co. v. Paterson Steamships, Ltd.*, 285 U.S. at 421 ("[t]he rule recognizing an unqualified discretion to decline jurisdiction in suits in admiralty between foreigners appears to be supported by an unbroken line of decisions in the lower federal courts"). ...

review was one of abuse of discretion. In examining the District Court's analysis of the public and private interests, however, the Court of Appeals seems to have lost sight of this rule, and substituted its own judgment for that of the District Court.

In analyzing the private interest factors, the District Court stated that the connections with Scotland are "overwhelming." This characterization may be somewhat exaggerated. Particularly with respect to the question of relative ease of access to sources of proof, the private interests point in both directions. As respondent emphasized, records concerning the design, manufacture, and testing of the propeller and plane are located in the United States. She would have greater access to sources of proof relevant to her strict liability and negligence theories if trial were held here.[70] However, the District Court did not act unreasonably in concluding that fewer evidentiary problems would be posed if the trial were held in Scotland. A large proportion of the relevant evidence is located in Great Britain.

The Court of Appeals found that the problems of proof could not be given any weight because Piper and Hartzell failed to describe with specificity the evidence they would not be able to obtain if trial were held in the United States. It suggested that defendants seeking *forum non conveniens* dismissal must submit affidavits identifying the witnesses they would call and the testimony these witnesses would provide if the trial were held in the alternative forum. Such detail is not necessary. Piper and Hartzell have moved for dismissal precisely because many crucial witnesses are located beyond the reach of compulsory process, and thus are difficult to identify or interview. Requiring extensive investigation would defeat the purpose of their motion. Of course, defendants must provide enough information to enable the District Court to balance the parties' interests. Our examination of the record convinces us that sufficient information was provided here. Both Piper and Hartzell submitted affidavits describing the evidentiary problems they would face if the trial were held in the United States.

The District Court correctly concluded that the problems posed by the inability to implead potential third-party defendants clearly supported holding the trial in Scotland. Joinder of the pilot's estate, Air Navigation, and McDonald is crucial to the presentation of petitioners' defense. If Piper and Hartzell can show that the accident was caused not by a design defect, but rather by the negligence of the pilot, the plane's owners, or the charter company, they will be relieved of all liability. It is true, of course, that if Hartzell and Piper were found liable after a trial in the United States, they could institute an action for indemnity or contribution against these parties in Scotland. It would be far more convenient, however, to resolve all claims in one trial. The Court of Appeals rejected this argument. Forcing petitioners to rely on actions for indemnity or contribution would be "burdensome" but not "unfair." Finding that trial in the plaintiff's chosen forum would be burdensome, however, is sufficient to support dismissal on grounds of *forum non conveniens.*

---

70. In the future, where similar problems are presented, district courts might dismiss subject to the condition that defendant corporations agree to provide the records relevant to the plaintiff's claims.

Public
interest
factors

The District Court's review of the factors relating to the public interest was also reasonable. On the basis of its choice-of-law analysis, it concluded that if the case were tried in the Middle District of Pennsylvania, Pennsylvania law would apply to Piper and Scottish law to Hartzell. It stated that a trial involving two sets of laws would be confusing to the jury. It also noted its own lack of familiarity with Scottish law. Consideration of these problems was clearly appropriate under *Gilbert*; in that case we explicitly held that the need to apply foreign law pointed towards dismissal.[71] The Court of Appeals found that the District Court's choice-of-law analysis was incorrect, and that American law would apply to both Hartzell and Piper. Thus, lack of familiarity with foreign law would not be a problem. Even if the Court of Appeals' conclusion is correct, however, all other public interest factors favored trial in Scotland.

Scotland has a very strong interest in this litigation. The accident occurred in its airspace. All of the decedents were Scottish. Apart from Piper and Hartzell, all potential plaintiffs and defendants are either Scottish or English. As we stated in *Gilbert*, there is "a local interest in having localized controversies decided at home." Respondent argues that American citizens have an interest in ensuring that American manufacturers are deterred from producing defective products, and that additional deterrence might be obtained if Piper and Hartzell were tried in the United States, where they could be sued on the basis of both negligence and strict liability. However, the incremental deterrence that would be gained if this trial were held in an American court is likely to be insignificant. The American interest in this accident is simply not sufficient to justify the enormous commitment of judicial time and resources that would inevitably be required if the case were to be tried here.

The Court of Appeals erred in holding that the possibility of an unfavorable change in law bars dismissal on the ground of *forum non conveniens*. It also erred in rejecting the District Court's *Gilbert* analysis. The District Court properly decided that the presumption in favor of the respondent's forum choice applied with less than maximum force because the real parties in interest are foreign. It did not act unreasonably in deciding that the private interests pointed towards trial in Scotland. Nor did it act unreasonably in deciding that the public interests favored trial in Scotland. Thus, the judgment of the Court of Appeals is reversed.

1) parties
foreign
2) privat
3) public

DOW CHEMICAL COMPANY v. CASTRO ALFARO

786 S.W.2d 674 (Supreme Court of Texas 1990)

RAY, JUSTICE. At issue in this cause is whether the statutory right to enforce a personal injury or wrongful death claim in the Texas courts precludes a trial court from dismissing the claim on the ground of forum non conveniens. ... [W]e conclude

---

71. Many *forum non conveniens* decisions have held that the need to apply foreign law favors dismissal. ... Of course, this factor alone is not sufficient to warrant dismissal when a balancing of all relevant factors shows that the plaintiff's chosen forum is appropriate. ...

that the legislature has statutorily abolished the doctrine of forum non conveniens in suits brought under §71.031 of the Texas Civil Practice and Remedies Code. ...

Domingo Castro Alfaro, a Costa Rican resident and employee of the Standard Fruit Company ("Standard Fruit"), and eighty-one other Costa Rican employees and their wives brought suit against Dow Chemical Company ("Dow") and Shell Oil Company ("Shell"). The employees claim that they suffered personal injuries as a result of exposure to dibromochloropropane ("DBCP"), a pesticide manufactured by Dow and Shell, which was allegedly furnished to Standard Fruit. [The Environmental Protection Agency issued ... an order suspending registrations of pesticides containing DBCP on November 3, 1977. Before and after the E.P.A.'s ban of DBCP in the United States, Shell and Dow allegedly shipped several hundred thousand gallons of the pesticide to Costa Rica for use by Standard Fruit.] The employees exposed to DBCP allegedly suffered several medical problems, including sterility.

Alfaro sued Dow and Shell in Harris County district court in April 1984. The amended petition alleged that the court had jurisdiction under article 4678 of the Revised Statutes. Following an unsuccessful attempt to remove the suit to federal court, Dow and Shell contested the jurisdiction of the trial court ... and contended in the alternative that the case should be dismissed under the doctrine of forum non conveniens. ... [T]he trial court dismissed the case on the ground of forum non conveniens.

Section 71.031 of the [Texas] Civil Practice and Remedies Code provides:

(a) An action for damages for the death or personal injury of a citizen of this state, of the United States, or of a foreign country may be enforced in the courts of this state, although the wrongful act, neglect, or default causing the death or injury takes place in a foreign state or country, if: (1) a law of the foreign state or country or of this state gives a right to maintain an action for damages for the death or injury; (2) the action is begun in this state within the time provided by the laws of this state for beginning the action; and (3) in the case of a citizen of a foreign country, the country has equal treaty rights with the United States on behalf of its citizens.[72] ... Tex. Civ. Prac. & Rem. Code Ann. §71.031 (Vernon 1986).

---

72. The United States and Costa Rica agreed to the following:

The citizens of the high contracting parties shall reciprocally receive and enjoy full and perfect protection for their persons and property, and shall have free and open access to the courts of justice in the said countries respectively, for the prosecution and defense of their just rights; and they shall be at liberty to employ, in all cases, the advocates, attorneys, or agents of whatever description, whom they may think proper, and they shall enjoy in this respect the same rights and privileges therein as native citizens. Treaty of Friendship, Commerce, and Navigation, July 10, 1851 United States-Costa Rica, Art. VII, para. 2, 10 Stat. 916, 920, T.S. No. 62.

Subsection (a)(3) requires the existence of similar treaty provisions before an action by a citizen of a foreign country may be maintained under §71.031.

At issue is whether the language "may be enforced in the courts of this state" of §71.031(a) permits a trial court to relinquish jurisdiction under the doctrine of forum non conveniens.

The statutory predecessors of §71.031 have existed since 1913. ... Texas courts applied the doctrine of forum non conveniens in several cases prior to the enactment of article 4678 in 1913. In 1890, this court in dicta recognized the power of a court to refuse to exercise jurisdiction on grounds essentially the same as those of forum non conveniens. *See Morris v. Missouri Pac. Ry.*, 14 S.W. 228, 230 (1890). In *Morris*, we stated:

> We do not think the facts alleged show the action to be transitory. But, if so, it has been held in such actions, where the parties were non-residents and the cause of action originated beyond the limits of the state, these facts would justify the court in refusing to entertain jurisdiction. Jurisdiction is entertained in such cases only upon principles of comity, and not as a matter of right. ...

We ... must determine whether the legislature in 1913 statutorily abolished the doctrine of forum non conveniens in suits brought under article 4678 [now §71.031]. Our interpretation of §71.031 is controlled by this court's refusal of writ of error in *Allen v. Bass*, 47 S.W.2d 426 (Tex. Civ. App. 1932). In *Allen* the Court of Civil Appeals held that old article 4678 conferred an absolute right to maintain a properly brought suit in Texas courts. The suit in *Allen* involved a New Mexico plaintiff and defendant arising out of an accident occurring in New Mexico. The court of appeals reversed a dismissal granted by the trial court on grounds similar to those of forum non conveniens, holding that "article 4678 opens the courts of this state to citizens of a neighboring state and gives to them an *absolute right* to maintain a transitory action of the present nature and to try their cases in the courts of this state." (emphasis added). ... [Like the court in *Allen*,] we conclude that the legislature has statutorily abolished the doctrine of forum non conveniens in suits brought under §71.031. ...

CONCUR

DOGGETT, JUSTICE, concurring. ... I write separately ... to respond to the dissenters. ... In their zeal to implement their own preferred social policy that Texas corporations not be held responsible at home for harm caused abroad, these dissenters refuse to be restrained by either express statutory language or the compelling precedent ... holding that forum non conveniens does not apply in Texas. To accomplish the desired social engineering, they must invoke yet another legal fiction with a fancy name to shield alleged wrongdoers, the so-called doctrine of forum non conveniens.

...

The dissenters are insistent that a jury of Texans be denied the opportunity to evaluate the conduct of a Texas corporation concerning decisions it made in Texas because the only ones allegedly hurt are foreigners. Fortunately Texans are not so provincial and narrow-minded as these dissenters presume. Our citizenry recognizes that a wrong does not fade away because its immediate consequences are first felt far away rather than close to home. Never have we been required to forfeit our membership in the human race in order to maintain our proud heritage as citizens of Texas.

The dissenters argue that it is inconvenient and unfair for farmworkers allegedly suffering permanent physical and mental injuries, including irreversible sterility, to seek redress by suing a multinational corporation in a court three blocks away from its world headquarters and another corporation, which operates in Texas this country's largest chemical plant. Because the "doctrine" they advocate has nothing to do with fairness and convenience and everything to do with immunizing multinational corporations from accountability for their alleged torts causing injury abroad, I write separately. ...

Shell is a multinational corporation with its world headquarters in Houston, Texas. Dow, though headquartered in Midland, Michigan, conducts extensive operations from its Dow Chemical USA building located in Houston. Dow operates this country's largest chemical manufacturing plant within 60 miles of Houston in Freeport, Texas. The district court where this lawsuit was filed is three blocks away from Shell's world headquarters, One Shell Plaza in downtown Houston. ...

[handwritten margin note: Dow Substantial contacts in TX]

The banana plantation workers allegedly injured by DBCP were employed by an American company on American-owned land and grew Dole bananas for export solely to American tables. The chemical allegedly rendering the workers sterile was researched, formulated, tested, manufactured, labeled and shipped by an American company in the United States to another American company. The decision to manufacture DBCP for distribution and use in the third world was made by these two American companies in their corporate offices in the United States. Yet now Shell and Dow argue that the one part of this equation that should not be American is the legal consequences of their actions.

... Both as a matter of law and of public policy, the doctrine of forum non conveniens is without justification. The proffered foundations for it are "considerations of fundamental fairness and sensible and effective judicial administration." In fact, the doctrine is favored by multinational defendants because a forum non conveniens dismissal is often outcome-determinative, effectively defeating the claim and denying the plaintiff recovery. ... A forum non conveniens dismissal is often, in reality, a complete victory for the defendant... . Empirical data available demonstrate that less than four percent of cases dismissed under the doctrine of forum non conveniens ever reach trial in a foreign court.[73] A forum non conveniens dismissal usually will end

---

73. Professor David Robertson of the University of Texas School of Law attempted to discover the subsequent history of each reported transnational case dismissed under forum non conveniens from *Gulf Oil v. Gilbert*, to the end of 1984. Data was received on 55 personal injury cases and 30 commercial cases. Of the 55 personal injury cases, only one was actually tried in a foreign court. Only two of the 30 commercial cases reached trial.

the litigation altogether, effectively excusing any liability of the defendant. The plaintiffs leave the courtroom without having had their case resolved on the merits.[74] ...

Advances in transportation and communications technology have rendered the
private [*Gulf Oil*] factors largely irrelevant: A forum is not necessarily inconvenient
because of its distance from pertinent parties or places if it is readily accessible in a
few hours of air travel. It will often be quicker and less expensive to transfer a witness
or a document than to transfer a lawsuit. Jet travel and satellite communications
have significantly altered the meaning of "non conveniens." ... In sum, the private
factors are no longer a predominant consideration — fairness and convenience to
the parties have been thrust out of the forum non conveniens equation. As the "doctrine" is now applied, the term "forum non conveniens" has clearly become a mis-
nomer. ...

[In addressing the public interest factors, the] dissenting members of the court
falsely attempt to paint a picture of Texas becoming an "irresistible forum for all
mass disaster lawsuits," and for "personal injury cases from around the world." They
suggest that our citizens will be forced to hear cases in which "[t]he interest of Texas
in these disputes is likely to be ... slight." Although these suppositions undoubtedly
will serve to stir public debate, they have little basis in fact. ... [A] state's power to
assert its jurisdiction is limited by the due process clause of the U.S. Constitution. ...
The personal jurisdiction-due process analysis will ensure that Texas has a sufficient
interest in each case entertained in our state's courts.[75]...

As stated previously, this suit has been filed against Shell, a corporation with its
world headquarters in Texas, doing extensive business in Texas and manufacturing
chemicals in Texas. The suit arose out of alleged acts occurring in Texas and alleged
decisions made in Texas. The suit also has been filed against Dow, a corporation with
its headquarters in Michigan, but apparently having substantial contacts with Texas.
Dow operates the country's largest chemical plant in Texas, manufacturing chemicals within sixty miles of the largest population center in Texas, where millions of

[margin annotation:] Constitution

---

74. Such a result in the name of "convenience" would undoubtedly follow a dismissal under forum
non conveniens in the case at bar. The plaintiffs, who earn approximately one dollar per hour working at
the banana plantation, clearly cannot compete financially with Shell and Dow in carrying on the litigation.
More importantly, the cost of just one trip to Houston to review the documents produced by Shell would
exceed the estimated maximum possible recovery in Costa Rica. In an unchallenged affidavit, a senior
Costa Rican labor judge stated that the maximum possible recovery in Costa Rica would approximate
100,000 colones, just over $1,080 at current exchange rates. ... Further, Costa Rica permits neither jury tri-
als nor depositions of nonparty witnesses. Attempting to depose a Dow representative concerning the
company's knowledge of DBCP hazards will prove to be an impossible task as Dow is not required to produce that person in Costa Rica. It is not unlikely that Shell and Dow seek a forum non conveniens dismissal not in pursuit of fairness and convenience, but rather as a shield against the litigation itself. If successful, Shell and Dow, like many American multinational corporations before them, would have secured
a largely impenetrable shield against meaningful lawsuits for their alleged torts causing injury abroad.

75. Justice Cook seems to suggest that it may violate due process for Shell to be sued in Houston. It is
an extremely novel holding, unprecedented in American constitutional law, that a corporation could be
denied due process by being sued in its hometown. ...

Texans reside. Shell and Dow cannot now seek to avoid the Texas civil justice system and a jury of Texans.

legal fiction

The next justification offered by the dissenters for invoking the legal fiction of "inconvenience" is that judges will be overworked. Not only will foreigners take our jobs, as we are told in the popular press; now they will have our courts. The xeno-

xenophobic

phobic suggestion that foreigners will take over our courts "forcing our residents to wait in the corridors of our courthouses while foreign causes of action are tried," is both misleading and false. It is the height of deception to suggest that docket back-logs in our state's urban centers are caused by so-called "foreign litigation."... Ten

NO docket congestion

states, including Texas, have not recognized the [forum non conveniens] doctrine. Within these states, there is no evidence that the docket congestion predicted by the dissenters has actually occurred. ...

Comity — deference shown to the interests of the foreign forum — is a consideration best achieved by rejecting forum non conveniens. Comity is not achieved when the United States allows its multinational corporations to adhere to a double standard when operating abroad and subsequently refuses to hold them accountable for those actions. As S. Jacob Scherr, Senior Project Attorney for the Natural Resources Defense Counsel, has noted "There is a sense of outrage on the part of many poor countries where citizens are the most vulnerable to exports of hazardous drugs, pesticides and food products." ... Comity is best achieved by "avoiding the possibility of 'incurring the wrath and distrust of the Third World as it increasingly recognizes that it is being used as the industrial world's garbage can.'" Note, *Hazardous Exports From A Human Rights Perspective*, 14 Sw. U. L. Rev. 81, 101 (1983).

The factors announced in *Gulf Oil* fail to achieve fairness and convenience. The public interest factors are designed to favor dismissal and do little to promote the efficient administration of justice. It is clear that the application of forum non conveniens would produce muddled and unpredictable case law, and would be used by defendants to terminate litigation before a consideration of the merits ever occurs.

The abolition of forum non conveniens will further important public policy considerations by providing a check on the conduct of multinational corporations. The misconduct of even a few multinational corporations can affect untold millions around the world. For example, after the United States imposed a domestic ban on the sale of cancer-producing TRIS-treated children's sleepwear, American companies exported approximately 2.4 million pieces to Africa, Asia and South America. A similar pattern occurred when a ban was proposed for baby pacifiers that had been linked to choking deaths in infants. These examples of indifference by some corporations towards children abroad are not unusual. ...

Some U.S. multinational corporations will undoubtedly continue to endanger human life and the environment with such activities until the economic consequences of these actions are such that it becomes unprofitable to operate in this manner. At present, the tort laws of many third world countries are not yet developed. Industrialization "is occurring faster than the development of domestic infrastructures necessary to deal with the problems associated with industry." When a court dismisses a case against a United States multinational corporation, it often removes the most effective restraint on corporate misconduct.

The doctrine of forum non conveniens is obsolete in a world in which markets are global and in which ecologists have documented the delicate balance of all life on this planet. The parochial perspective embodied in the doctrine of forum non conveniens enables corporations to evade legal control merely because they are transnational. This perspective ignores the reality that actions of our corporations affecting those abroad will also affect Texans. Although DBCP is banned from use within the United States, it and other similarly banned chemicals have been consumed by Texans eating foods imported from Costa Rica and elsewhere. In the absence of meaningful tort liability in the United States for their actions, some multinational corporations will continue to operate without adequate regard for the human and environmental costs of their actions. This result cannot be allowed to repeat itself for decades to come.

GONZALEZ, JUSTICE, dissenting. ... This decision makes us one of the few states in the Union without ... a procedural tool [like forum non conveniens], and if the legislature fails to reinstate this doctrine, Texas will become an irresistible forum for all mass disaster lawsuits. "Bhopal"-type litigation, with little or no connection to Texas will add to our already crowded dockets, forcing our residents to wait in the corridors of our courthouses while foreign causes of action are tried.[76] ...

COOK, JUSTICE, dissenting. Like turn-of-the-century wildcatters, the plaintiffs in this case searched all across the nation for a place to make their claims. Through three courts they moved, filing their lawsuits on one coast and then on the other. By each of those courts the plaintiffs were rejected, and so they continued their search for a more willing forum. Their efforts are finally rewarded. Today they hit pay dirt in Texas.

No reason exists, in law or in policy, to support their presence in this state. The legislature adopted within the statute the phrase "may be enforced" to permit plaintiffs to sue in Texas, irrespective of where they live or where the cause of action arose. The legislature did not adopt this statute, however, to remove from our courts all discretion to dismiss. To use the statute to sweep away, completely and finally, a common law doctrine painstakingly developed over the years is to infuse the statute with a power not contained in the words. Properly read, the statute is asymmetrical. Although it confers upon the plaintiffs an absolute right to bring claims in our

---

76. For example, in July 1988, there was an oil rig disaster in Scotland. A Texas lawyer went to Scotland, held a press conference, and wrote letters to victims or their families. He advised them that they had a good chance of trying their cases in Texas where awards would be much higher than elsewhere. Houston Post, July 18, 1988, at 13A, col. 1; The Times (London), July 18, 1988, at 20A, col. 1; Texas Lawyer, Sept. 26, 1988 at 3.

courts, it does not impose upon our courts an absolute responsibility to entertain those claims.

Even if the statute supported the court's interpretation, however, I would remain unwilling to join in the opinion. The decision places too great a burden on defendants who are citizens of our state because, by abolishing forum non conveniens, the decision exposes our citizens to the claims of any plaintiff, no matter how distant from Texas is that plaintiff's home or cause of action. The interest of Texas in these disputes is likely to be as slight as the relationship of the plaintiffs to Texas. The interest of other nations, on the other hand, is likely to be substantial. For these reasons, I fear the decision allows assertions of jurisdiction by Texas courts that are so unfair and unreasonable as to violate the due process clause of the federal constitution. ...

... [W]e are inviting into our courts disputes that may involve more substantial connections to foreign countries than to our own. Should we not stop to consider, as the *Asahi* court did, the possible effects of extending our laws beyond the shores of the United States? *See generally* Born, *Reflections on Judicial Jurisdiction in International Cases*, 17 Ga. J. Int'l & Comp. L. 1 (1987). ... There are in this case unresolved choice of law questions that, once resolved, may diminish the interest of this state in this litigation. ... There is a strong possibility that a choice of law analysis will result in the application of Costa Rican law. If so, what then is Texas' interest in adjudicating a foreign claim by foreign plaintiffs? ...

HECHT, JUSTICE, dissenting. Today the Court decrees that citizens of a foreign nation, Costa Rica, who claim to have been injured in their own country have an absolute right to sue for money damages in Texas courts. ... [This] inflicts a blow upon the people of Texas, its employers and taxpayers, that is contrary to sound policy.

The United States does not give aliens unlimited access to its courts. Indeed, one federal district court in California and two in Florida have already dismissed essentially this same lawsuit which the Court now welcomes to Texas. No state has ever given aliens such unlimited admission to its courts. The U.S. Supreme Court, the District of Columbia, and forty states have all recognized what has come to be called the rule of forum non conveniens. ... Until now, no state has ever rejected this rule. ...

The dearth of authority for the Court's unprecedented holding is disturbing. Far more disconcerting, however, is the Court's silence as to why the rule of forum non conveniens should be abolished in personal injury and death cases, either by the Legislature or by the Court. ... The benefit to the plaintiffs in suing in Texas should be obvious: more money, as counsel was candid enough to admit in oral argument.[77]

---

77. It is equally plain to me that defendants want to be sued in Costa Rica rather than Texas because they expect that their exposure will be less there than here. However, it also seems plain to me that the Legislature would want to protect the citizens of this state, its constituents, from greater exposure to liability than they would face in the country in which the alleged wrong was committed. This would be incentive for the Legislature not to abolish the rule of forum non conveniens.

... But what purpose beneficial to the people of Texas is served by clogging the already burdened dockets of the state's courts with cases which arose around the world and which have nothing to do with this state except that the defendant can be served with citation here? Why, most of all, should Texas be the only state in the country, perhaps the only jurisdiction on earth, possibly the only one in history, to offer to try personal injury cases from around the world? Do Texas taxpayers want to pay extra for judges and clerks and courthouses and personnel to handle foreign litigation? If they do not mind the expense, do they not care that these foreign cases will delay their own cases being heard? As the courthouse for the world, will Texas entice employers to move here, or people to do business here, or even anyone to visit? ... Who gains? A few lawyers, obviously. But who else? If the Court has good answers to these questions, why does it not say so in its opinion? If there are no good answers, then what the Court does today is very pernicious for the state.[78]

Notes on Piper and Castro Alfaro

1. *Judicial authority to adopt the forum non conveniens doctrine.* The district court in *Piper* was granted personal jurisdiction over the defendants by Rule 4 of the Federal Rules of Civil Procedure and a borrowed state long-arm statute. Similarly, statutory venue requirements were satisfied. Nonetheless, the Supreme Court held that the forum non conveniens doctrine permitted the trial court to decline jurisdiction on the grounds that it would have been an unduly "inconvenient" forum. *Piper* cited no statutory or constitutional basis for the forum non conveniens doctrine.

Is *Piper's* judicial abstention appropriate? Justice Black, dissenting in *Gulf Oil*, challenged what he characterized as an "abdication" of jurisdiction as violating the obligation of U.S. courts to exercise jurisdiction that Congress confers on them: "the courts of the United States are bound to proceed to judgment ... in every case to which their jurisdiction extends. They cannot abdicate their authority or duty in any case in favor of another jurisdiction." *Gulf Oil Corp. v. Gilbert*, 330 U.S. 501, 515 (1947) (citing *Hyde v. Stone*, 61 U.S. 170, 175 (1858)). The *Gulf Oil* majority responded that "[o]bviously, the proposition that a court having jurisdiction must exercise it, is not universally true; else the admiralty court could never decline jurisdiction on the ground that the litigation is between foreigners. ... Courts of equity and law also occasionally decline, in the interest of justice, to exercise jurisdiction, where the suit is between aliens or non-residents or where for kindred reasons the litigation can more appropriately be conducted in a foreign tribunal." 330 U.S. at 504 (quoting *Canada Malting Co. v. Paterson Steamships, Ltd.*, 285 U.S. 413, 422-23 (1932)).

---

78. Justice Doggett's concurring opinion undertakes to answer these questions that the Court ignores. It suggests that there are essentially two policy reasons to abolish the rule of forum non conveniens: to assure that injured plaintiffs can recover fully, and to assure that American corporations will be fully punished for their misdeeds abroad. Neither reason is sufficient. If the defendants in this case were Costa Rican corporations which plaintiffs could sue only in Costa Rica, plaintiffs would be limited to whatever recovery they could obtain in Costa Rican courts. The concurring opinion has not explained why Costa Rican plaintiffs who claim to have been injured by American corporations are unjustly treated if they are required to sue in their own country where they could only sue if they had been injured by Costa Rican corporations. In other words, why are Costa Ricans injured by an American defendant entitled to any greater recovery than Costa Ricans injured by a Costa Rican defendant, or a Libyan defendant, or an Iranian defendant? Moreover, the concurring opinion does not explain why the American justice system should undertake to punish American corporations more severely for their actions in a foreign country than that country does. If the alleged conduct of the defendants in this case is so egregious, why has Costa Rica not chosen to afford its own citizens the recovery they seek in Texas? One wonders how receptive Costa Rican courts would be to the pleas of American plaintiffs against Costa Rican citizens for recovery of all the damages that might be available in Texas, or anywhere else for that matter.

Is it appropriate for federal courts to abstain from exercising jurisdiction that Congress has granted them? From where is the authority to do so derived? Should federal courts have inherent power to control their dockets, notwithstanding Congress's jurisdictional statutes?

2. *Rationale for forum non conveniens doctrine.* What reasons are advanced in *Piper* to justify dismissal of a plaintiff's claims, wholly without legislative authorization? What values are served by the forum non conveniens doctrine?

(a) *Local judicial convenience.* Consider the following excerpt from an early decision foreshadowing the forum non conveniens doctrine:

> [I]f it appears upon the face of the pleadings that both of the litigant parties are foreigners and a foreign contract, we ought not to interpose. By the nature of all governments, courts were constituted to administer justice in relation to their own citizens; and not to do the business of citizens or subjects of other states. The judges of their own state are employed, and paid for that purpose. To encourage the resort of foreigners to our courts would be doing injustice to our own citizens who have business here to be attended to. *Avery v. Holland*, 2 Tenn. 71 (1806).

Similarly:

> To hold that two foreigners may import, bodily, a cause of action, and insist, as a matter of right, that taxpayers, citizens, and residents shall await the lagging steps of justice in the anteroom while the court hears and decides the foreign controversy, seems, on the face of it, to be unreasonable, if not absurd.

Disconto-Gesellschaft v. Umbreit, 106 N.W. 821, 823 (Wis. 1906), *aff'd*, 208 U.S. 570 (1908). Are these legitimate concerns, or mere xenophobia? Do not foreigners have a right of access to U.S. courts? *See supra* pp. 64-65. Even if they are legitimate concerns, are these adequate justifications for the forum non conveniens doctrine? What would Justice Doggett say?

(b) *Handling private litigation efficiently.* To what extent does the forum non conveniens doctrine concern issues of convenience and trial management? Note Justice Marshall's statement in *Piper* that "the central purpose of any forum non conveniens inquiry is to ensure that the trial is convenient." Consider the discussion in *Piper* of the "private interest" factors, such as the location of documents and witnesses, the availability of compulsory process, and the location of related litigation. Even if these factors indicate that the plaintiff's chosen forum is significantly less convenient than an alternative forum, is this a valid justification for a forum non conveniens dismissal? Note Justice Doggett's argument that modern communications and transport have made it easy and cheap to bring foreign evidence to the forum. Moreover, why should considerations of private convenience be permitted to override a plaintiff's substantive legal rights in a U.S. forum? Could a federal court, for example, decline to hear Title VII or antitrust claims on the grounds that the parties' disputes could be more expeditiously resolved in state court?

(c) *Foreign regulatory interests and comity.* Can the forum non conveniens doctrine be justified as a way to prevent U.S. courts from interfering with foreign states' sovereignty and regulatory regimes? Recall that 19th century admiralty courts invoked considerations of international comity and respect for foreign sovereignty in declining to decide certain types of disputes. *See supra* pp. 290-91. Consider *Piper's* discussion of the relative "public interests" of the United States and the United Kingdom. According to Justice Marshall, what were the respective U.S. and U.K. interests? Note Justice Doggett's views about the usefulness of the forum non conveniens doctrine in preventing interference with foreign sovereignty. Are his views persuasive? How do you think the U.K. government would have wanted *Piper* to have been decided? How would Costa Rica have wanted *Alfaro* decided? Recall *Sequihua v. Texaco, Inc.*, excerpted *supra* pp. 50-56. What was Ecuador's position there?

(d) *Treating U.S. defendants fairly.* Does the forum non conveniens doctrine reflect concerns over the unjustified imposition of tort liability on American companies that do business abroad? Consider the Court's concern in *Piper* that, if the Third Circuit's analysis had been accepted, "where the foreign plaintiff named an American manufacturer as defendant, a court could not dismiss the case on grounds of *forum non conveniens* where dismissal might lead to an unfavorable change in law." Justice Hecht's dissent in *Alfaro* is more direct: "[W]hy [should] the American justice system ... undertake to punish American corporations more severely for their actions in a foreign country than that country does?" "[W]hy are Costa Ricans injured by an American defendant entitled to any greater recovery than Costa Ricans injured by a Costa Rican defendant, or a Libyan defendant, or an Iranian defendant?" What are the answers? Can the forum non conveniens doctrine be justified as a device for fostering more equal treatment — from an international perspective — of like cases? Why should Mr. Alfaro (and his Texas lawyers) recover one hundred times more from Dow and Shell than Mr. Alfaro's neighbors could recover from a Costa Rican or Japanese company, guilty of exactly the same conduct as their U.S. counterparts? What would Justice Doggett say?

3. *Wisdom of forum non conveniens doctrine.* Was the Supreme Court wise in *Gulf Oil* and *Piper* to adopt the forum non conveniens doctrine? Consider the scathing remarks by Justice Doggett in *Alfaro*, and the equally vigorous comments by Justices Gonzalez and Hecht. Rhetoric aside, does the forum non conveniens doctrine serve useful objectives? What are they?

4. *Relationship between judicial jurisdiction and forum non conveniens.* The historical development of the forum non conveniens doctrine between 1925 and 1985 was closely related to the evolution of concepts of judicial jurisdiction. As described above, the due process clause was interpreted as imposing strict territorial restrictions on the judicial jurisdiction of U.S. courts during the 19th and early 20th centuries. *See supra* pp. 70-73; *Pennoyer v. Neff*, 95 U.S. 714 (1878). During this era, the forum non conveniens doctrine was primarily confined in the United States to admiralty cases — where the attachment of foreign vessels provided jurisdiction over foreign defendants and disputes that generally did not exist in non-admiralty cases. *See supra* pp. 289-91. Aside from anything else, the existence of strict territorial limits on judicial jurisdiction made principles of forum non conveniens largely irrelevant, because foreign defendants and disputes would generally not find their ways into local courts.

Pennoyer's territorial limits were gradually eroded during this century. *See supra* pp. 73-77. This culminated in the Supreme Court's 1945 formulation of the "minimum contacts" test in *International Shoe Co. See supra* pp. 73-74. Under *International Shoe*, plaintiffs enjoyed a new and substantially wider choice of courts in which to commence litigation. This was especially true as to general jurisdiction, which granted U.S. courts personal jurisdiction over defendants with respect to claims that had no connection with the forum. *See supra* pp. 77-78. Inevitably, the new jurisdictional regime meant that courts could adjudicate cases even if they were disproportionately burdensome to the defendant or would have very unusual or favorable choice of law and substantive rules. On occasion, plaintiffs would select a forum to commence litigation precisely because it had these attributes — engaging in "forum-shopping" for a court that would provide it with the maximum practical and legal advantages.

U.S. judicial acceptance of the doctrine of forum non conveniens occurred at precisely the same time that U.S. principles of judicial jurisdiction were being transformed. As *Pennoyer's* strict territoriality rules were eroded during the 1920's and 1930's, academic commentary suggested the forum non conveniens doctrine and other devices specifically to moderate newly-expanded jurisdictional powers. (Paxton Blair's article on forum non conveniens was published in 1929. Blair, *The Doctrine of Forum Non Conveniens in Anglo-American Law*, 29 Colum. L. Rev. 1 (1929). *See supra* pp. 292-93.) Likewise, *Gulf Oil* expressly adopted the forum non conveniens doctrine in 1946 — one year after the minimum contacts formula was articulated in *International Shoe*. And *Piper Aircraft* was decided in 1981, at the same time that *World-Wide Volkswagen* and similar decisions further expanded the reach of U.S. judicial jurisdiction. *See supra* pp. 73-77.

Is the forum non conveniens doctrine an appropriate means of moderating the expansion of contemporary judicial jurisdiction? Would it be wiser to articulate more precise jurisdictional rules?

5. *What does forum non conveniens really mean?* Perhaps because it is a catchy neo-Latin phrase, the forum non conveniens doctrine appears deceptively easy to comprehend. It is, surely, just a common sense question of determining whether the forum is inconvenient, isn't it? Consider:

> The general inference to be drawn from the Latin phrase is that jurisdiction should be declined when the forum is inconvenient. But inconvenient to whom? The court? The plaintiff? The defendant? Even if we have the answers to these questions, is it enough that the scale is weighted more heavily on the side of inconvenience to the defendant when the plaintiff has acted in good faith? In other words, must there be an element of abuse of court process before jurisdiction is declined? Perhaps, the search should be a broader one for that forum in which the ends of justice will best be served. Obviously, these questions must be answered before we know anything of the meaning of the doctrine of forum non conveniens.

Barrett, *The Doctrine of Forum Non Conveniens*, 35 Calif. L. Rev. 380, 404 (1947). In addition to these questions, which concern only issues of "convenience," the forum non conveniens doctrine also involves "public interest" factors and allocations of regulatory competence. *See supra* pp. 294-96. What precisely is the legal rule established by the forum non conveniens doctrine? What objectives does the doctrine really serve?

6. *Unexamined substantive assumptions of forum non conveniens doctrine.* Although it purports to concern "convenience," the forum non conveniens doctrine rests on unarticulated and unexamined substantive assumptions. Compare the excerpt from *Piper*, expressing concern about subjecting U.S. manufacturers to "liberal" U.S. substantive and procedural rules, with Justice Doggett's condemnation of perfidious multinationals engaged in world-wide depredations of the environment and developing nations. Who is correct — Justice Marshall or Justice Doggett? *Compare* the differing views in *Castro Alfaro* concerning international comity and foreign sovereignty. Is there any principled basis for a court to decide between these views without legislative guidance?

7. *Effect of unfavorable change in law on forum non conveniens analysis under* Piper. *Piper* held that the possibility of an unfavorable change in substantive law for the plaintiff is not to be "given conclusive or even substantial weight" in federal forum non conveniens analysis. Given the broad range of public and private interest factors that are relevant to forum non conveniens analysis, why should the vitally important question of substantive law changes be disregarded?

In answering this question, *Piper* emphasizes the central role of "convenience" in forum non conveniens analysis. Is this persuasive? The "public interest" factors relevant to forum non conveniens analysis have little to do with convenience. Moreover, defendants seldom seek forum non conveniens dismissals to obtain a more convenient forum; instead, they often want to avoid the substantive, procedural, and other characteristics of the original forum — for exactly the reasons that the plaintiff chose the forum. *See Bewers v. American Home Prods. Corp.*, 459 N.Y.S.2d 666, 668 (Sup. Ct. 1982) ("Plaintiff's choice of forum is being vigorously contested, probably not so much because defendants are unaccustomed to international travel, but because as both sides know, the outcome of this procedural motion may well be dispositive of plaintiffs' claims."). Given the strong substantive character of forum non conveniens analysis, is it appropriate to ignore changes in substantive law? In answering this question, what weight should be given to the fact that "changes" in substantive law result from the plaintiff's ability unilaterally to select the forum for its claims?

8. *Foreign forum that provides "no remedy at all."* Under *Piper*, are unfavorable changes of law entitled to *any* weight? *Piper* held that "the unfavorable change of law may be given substantial weight," if the "remedy provided by the alternative forum is so clearly inadequate or unsatisfactory that it is no remedy at all." Why must such drastic, all-or-nothing consequences be established before a trial court can take changes in substantive law into account? If it is appropriate for a U.S. court to consider the fact that a plaintiff may not be able to assert a $15,000 claim, why is it apparently inappropriate to consider the fact that a plaintiff's $15 million claim is reduced to $15,000? If other factors are not dispositive, can a court then give weight (including decisive weight) to unfavorable changes in law?

Note that even where a plaintiff would have "no remedy at all" abroad, *Piper* apparently suggests that a trial court "may" give this factor "substantial weight." "Must" the trial court do so? Even if it must, what other factors might counterbalance the "substantial weight" accorded to the unfavorable change in law? Notwithstanding the Court's language in *Piper*, lower courts generally have held that the lack of any adequate remedy abroad precludes forum non conveniens dismissal. *See infra* pp. 341-57.

9. *Presumptive validity of U.S. plaintiff's choice of U.S. forum. Piper* reaffirmed *Gulf Oil's* holding that a U.S. plaintiff's choice of forum should rarely be disturbed. The Court also said that U.S. citizens do not have any absolute right to protection from dismissal of their claims on forum non conveniens grounds. Given the wide range of forums that existing rules of personal jurisdiction allow plaintiffs — and the practical advantages this entails — should the forum selections of U.S. plaintiffs generally receive an automatic presumption of validity? What justifies this deference? Why should people be rewarded for suing first? Recall that, for purposes of due process limitations on judicial jurisdiction, the *plaintiff's* contacts with the forum are relatively unimportant. *Keeton v. Hustler Magazine, Inc.*, 465 U.S. 770, 779 (1984) ("[W]e have not to date required a plaintiff to have "minimum contacts" with the forum State before permitting that State to assert personal jurisdiction over a nonresident defendant. On the contrary, we have upheld the assertion of jurisdiction where such contacts were entirely lacking.").

10. *Reduced deference to a foreign plaintiff's choice of U.S. forum under* Piper. *Piper* also held that a *foreign* plaintiff's choice of a U.S. forum will not receive the "strong presumption" of validity that courts accord to a U.S. plaintiff's choice of a U.S. forum. As *Piper* noted, there are powerful reasons (such as favorable substantive laws, large jury verdicts, contingency fee arrangements, discovery opportunities, and the minimal chance of attorneys' fees being awarded against the losing side) that may entice foreign plaintiffs into U.S. courts without regard to convenience. *See supra* pp. 3-7. The Court justified differential treatment of U.S. and foreign plaintiffs on the grounds that it can be assumed that a U.S. plaintiff will choose a U.S. forum because it is convenient. The Court did not think that this assumption applied to a

foreign plaintiff's choice of a U.S. forum, reasoning that foreigners were likely attracted by U.S. damage awards. *Smith Kline & French Labs. v. Bloch* [1983] 2 All E.R. 72, 74 ("[a]s a moth is drawn to the light, so is a litigant drawn to the United States"). Is a plaintiff's U.S. nationality a reasonable proxy for the convenience of a U.S. forum? Does a party's nationality have any real relation to the convenience of different forums for a particular dispute? Won't many foreigners sue in U.S. courts because they are convenient?

11. *Degree of inconvenience required to warrant forum non conveniens dismissal.* *Piper* reaffirmed the demanding *Gulf Oil* standard for a forum non conveniens dismissals. If "trial in the chosen forum would 'establish ... oppressiveness and vexation to a defendant ... out of all proportion to plaintiff's convenience,' or when the 'chosen forum [is] inappropriate because of considerations affecting the court's own administrative and legal problems,'" then dismissal is permissible. Moreover, "dismissal will ordinarily be appropriate where trial in the plaintiff's chosen forum imposes a heavy burden on the defendant or the court, and where the plaintiff is unable to offer any specific reasons of convenience supporting his choice." Why is this the appropriate standard of proof? Why should it be necessary to show inconvenience to the defendant "out of all proportion" to the plaintiff's convenience? Why ought it not be enough to show "materially greater inconvenience" to the defendant? or simply that, on balance, another forum would permit a somewhat cheaper proceeding?

12. *Trial judge's discretion in applying forum non conveniens doctrine and standard of appellate review.* *Piper* reemphasized the role of the trial court's discretion in balancing private and public interests: "The *forum non conveniens* determination is committed to the sound discretion of the trial court. It may be reversed only when there has been a clear abuse of discretion." Why are trial court decisions in the forum non conveniens context accorded such deference? Is it because the weighing of multiple factors is an inherently fact-dependent exercise, poorly suited to appellate review? Note, however, that in *Piper* many of the facts relevant to the forum non conveniens decision were based on documentary evidence that appellate courts could readily review.

13. *Wisdom of* Piper *and Alfaro.* Was *Piper* correctly decided? Is it a desirable result? Compare the result in *Alfaro* to that in *Sequihua v. Texaco, Inc.*, 847 F.Supp. 61 (S.D. Tex. 1994) (excerpted above at pp. 51-52). Which result is wiser? Is the defendant's desire in *Sequihua* to be in federal court more comprehensible in the light of *Alfaro*?

14. *Unpredictability of forum non conveniens decisions.* Recall Justice Black's warning in *Gulf Oil* that the "broad and indefinite discretion" granted by the forum non conveniens doctrine "will inevitably produce a complex of close and indistinguishable decisions from which accurate prediction of the proper forum will become difficult, if not impossible." *See supra* pp. 295-96, 330 U.S. at 516. That may well be correct. *See infra* pp. 317-18. But suppose there were no forum non conveniens doctrine. Would it be any easier to make an "accurate prediction" of the "proper forum"? Wouldn't there be inevitable races to the courthouse and parallel proceedings in multiple forums? *See infra* pp. 459-60. Isn't the uncertainty that Justice Black derides a result of expansive rules of judicial jurisdiction, and not the forum non conveniens doctrine?

15. *Criticism of forum non conveniens standard of review.* Commentators have vigorously criticized *Piper's* deferential standard of review for forum non conveniens decisions. One writer has remarked that it has produced a "crazy quilt of ad hoc, capricious, and inconsistent decisions." Stein, *Forum Non Conveniens and the Redundancy of Court-Access Doctrine*, 133 U. Pa. L. Rev. 781, 785 (1985). Another has said that the forum non conveniens doctrine is "notoriously complex and uncertain," Currie, *Change of Venue and the Conflict of Laws*, 22 U. Chi. L. Rev. 405, 416 (1955), while a third has referred to the "chaos of forum non conveniens." A. Ehrenzweig, *The Conflict of Laws* 150 (1959). The late Judge Henry Friendly devoted an article — *Indiscretion About Discretion* — to criticizing *Piper's* reliance on trial courts' discretion. Friendly, *Indiscretion About Discretion*, 31 Emory L. J. 747 (1982).

The Supreme Court has not yet taken the opportunity to respond to such criticism. On the contrary, the Court has displayed little interest in the doctrine's practical effects on private litigation. Indeed, Justice Scalia made the following comments in *American Dredging Co. v. Miller*, purportedly to justify the Court's refusal to adopt a substantive federal common law rule of forum non conveniens in domestic admiralty cases:

> [T]o tell the truth, forum non conveniens cannot really be *relied* upon in making decisions about secondary conduct — in deciding, for example, where to sue or where one is subject to being sued. The discretionary nature of the doctrine, combined with the multifariousness of the factors relevant to its application ... make uniformity and predictability of outcome almost impossible. 114 S.Ct. at 989.

Is it unusual for the Supreme Court to say this about a common law doctrine that *it* created, wholly without statutory basis, for the purposes of facilitating the administration of justice?

16. *Appellate decisions seeking greater predictability in forum non conveniens decisions.* Several courts of appeals have shown greater attention to the predictability of forum non conveniens decisions than the Supreme Court. These courts have emphasized that a trial court's discretion in deciding forum non conveniens motions is not unlimited. Forum non conveniens determinations "represent exercises of structured discretion by trial judges appraising the practical inconveniences posed to the litigants and to the court should a particular action be litigated in one forum rather than another. *Pain v. United Technologies Corp.*, 637 F.2d 775, 781 (D.C. Cir. 1981). In order to permit meaningful analysis and appellate review, these courts have insisted that trial judges consider and evaluate each of the relevant *Gulf Oil* factors and articulate the basis for their decisions. *E.g., In re Air Crash Disaster Near New Orleans*, 821 F.2d 1147 (5th Cir. 1987) ("a district court abuses its discretion when it summarily denies or grants a motion to dismiss without either written or oral explanation ... [or] when it fails to address and balance the relevant principles and factors of the doctrine of forum non conveniens"); *Lacey v. Cessna Aircraft Co.*, 862 F.2d 38 (3d Cir. 1988). Is this wise? Is it consistent with *Piper?*

17. *Proposals for substantially broader power to dismiss on forum non conveniens grounds.* Some commentators have suggested that courts should radically reformulate the forum non conveniens doctrine and instead consider what forum would be the most convenient for litigation, without regard to the place that the plaintiff commenced litigation. *See* Redish, *Due Process, Federalism, and Personal Jurisdiction: A Theoretical Evaluation*, 75 Nw. U.L. Rev. 1112 (1981); Stein, *Forum Non Conveniens and the Redundancy of Court-Access Doctrine*, 133 U. Pa. L. Rev. 781, 844 (1985). In effect, trial courts (rather than plaintiffs) would be authorized to choose the most appropriate forum for litigating multi-jurisdictional disputes. What are the advantages of such an approach? What would authorize district courts to override the forum selections of plaintiffs?

18. *International law and due process limits on judicial competence.* As discussed above, international law arguably imposes limits on the competence of a nation's courts to adjudicate disputes having no connection to the forum — even when judicial jurisdiction exists and restrictions on legislative jurisdiction are observed. *See supra* pp. 32 & 49. Consider Justice Cook's dissent, arguing that due process imposes limits on a state court's power to adjudicate certain claims against "our citizens" — *e.g.*, Texas corporations or other entities ordinarily subject to general jurisdiction. In Justice Cook's view, the due process clause should not "expose[] our citizens to the claims of any plaintiff, no matter how distant from Texas is that plaintiff's home or cause of action." Is this view consistent with orthodox understandings of general jurisdiction? *See supra* pp. 95-123. Consider Justice Doggett's response to it. Why *shouldn't* international law and due process restrict a state court's power to hear claims that have *nothing* to do with it? Consider again the arguments advanced for general jurisdiction.

19. *Proposals to abolish forum non conveniens doctrine.* Justice Doggett's concurring opinion in *Castro Alfaro* characterizes the forum non conveniens doctrine as "a legal monstrosity" and argues strongly that it is unacceptable on policy grounds. Are Justice Doggett's arguments well-taken? Why?

20. *Effect of modern technology on forum non conveniens doctrine.* Modern communications and transportation have eliminated much of the "inconvenience" that the forum non conveniens doctrine sought to prevent. Documents can be faxed or couriered around the world in seconds; telephone and video conferences are easy and cheap; witnesses and lawyers can travel easily for hearings. In *Fitzgerald v. Texaco, Inc.*, 521 F.2d 448, 456 (2d Cir. 1975) (Oakes, J., dissenting), *cert. denied*, 423 U.S. 1052 (1976), Judge Oakes urged that "the entire doctrine of *forum non conveniens* should be reexamined in the light of the transportation revolution that has occurred" in the last 40 years and the "dispersion of corporate authority ... by the use of multinational subsidiaries to conduct international business." Judge Oakes went on to suggest abandoning the doctrine in favor of general acceptance of a plaintiff's choice of forum. Is this a sensible course to take? What effect do modern technological developments have on the forum non conveniens doctrine?

21. *Practical importance of forum non conveniens doctrine.* The passion that marks both Justice Doggett's and Justice Hecht's opinions reflects the underlying significance of a forum non conveniens dismissal to the litigants in many cases. This is because of the enormous differences between different national forums, and the likely judgments they will produce. In many cases, the forum non conveniens decision is dispositive, as a practical matter, of the parties' dispute. If the case is dismissed, the plaintiff will effectively capitulate, while the defendant will often settle on generous terms (by international standards) if the case is not dismissed.

C. The "Private and Public Interest" Factors

Central to *Piper* and other formulations of the forum non conveniens doctrine is a "weighing" of "private" and "public" interest factors. These factors were first detailed in *Gulf Oil*, and are repeated in *Piper* and subsequent authorities.[79]

Excerpted below are materials that illustrate application of the private and public interest factors referred to in *Gulf Oil* and *Piper*. The decisions in *Fiacco v. United Technologies Corp.* and *Howe v. Goldcorp Investment Ltd.* explore the role of the parties' nationalities, the location of evidence, and the other private interest factors in forum non conveniens analysis. Comment f to §84 of the *Restatement (Second) Conflict of Laws* describes the circumstances in which various forums will be regarded as "convenient." Finally, *Harrison v. Wyeth Laboratories* illustrates how some courts have applied *Gulf Oil*'s public interest factors.

FIACCO v. UNITED TECHNOLOGIES CORP.

524 F.Supp. 858 (S.D.N.Y. 1981)

VINCENT L. BRODERICK, DISTRICT JUDGE. This is an action arising out of a crash which occurred while a helicopter was transporting plaintiffs' decedents from Bergen, Norway to an oil drilling platform in the North Sea. Plaintiff Eleanor Fiacco, Administratrix of the Estate of Robert Fiacco, is a citizen and resident of the State of New York. Of the remaining eight plaintiffs, seven are Norwegian citizens, and one is a citizen of the United Kingdom. The defendant is a U.S. corporation organized and existing under the laws of Delaware with its principal place of business in Connecticut. Defendant is presumably "doing business" in New York for purposes of *P.J* personal jurisdiction, pursuant to N.Y. C.P.L.R. §301, and for purposes of venue, pursuant to 28 U.S.C. §1391(c) [the Alien Venue Statute]. The amended complaint alleges the following bases of jurisdiction: diversity of citizenship, the general maritime law, and the Death on the High Seas Act (46 U.S.C. §761 *et seq.*). The complaint sounds in strict liability in tort, negligence and breach of warranty.

Defendant asks this court to dismiss the action on the ground of forum non conveniens. Defendant asks alternatively that the action of plaintiff Fiacco be severed from the remaining actions, that the claims of the alien plaintiffs be dismissed on the ground of forum non conveniens, and that the Fiacco claim be transferred to Connecticut, pursuant to 28 U.S.C. §1404(a). Defendant has offered to concede liability and to submit itself to the jurisdiction of a competent Norwegian court, if this court will dismiss. Given these concessions, defendant argues, this court is required ... to dismiss the instant action. ... [D]efendant's motion is in all respects denied. ...

Defendant argues that since it is willing to concede liability and submit to in personam jurisdiction in the courts of Norway, the only proof needed will go to the

---

79. 454 U.S. at 241, 257-60; 330 U.S. at 508-09; *Restatement (Second) Conflict of Laws* §84 comment c (1971).

damages issue, and the bulk of the witnesses on this issue are located in Norway. While defendant concedes that the enforceability-of-judgment factor probably does not weigh in its favor, it urges that the remaining private, and most of the public interest, factors favor the defendant, given the concessions which it is willing to make.

This is essentially a products liability suit and the allegedly defective product was manufactured by a corporation whose principal place of business is in the United States. The site of the design and manufacture of the product, and all records relevant to such design and manufacture, are located in this country. With respect to design and manufacture, the potential witnesses are located in the United States. So far as the accident itself, and the investigations which ensued, the witnesses are in Europe. Witnesses and evidence with respect to damages as to plaintiff Fiacco are presumably to be found in the United States. With respect to damages as to the other plaintiffs, the witnesses and evidence are in Norway or the United Kingdom. It is not yet established what body of law will control this action, but it could quite conceivably be the law of Norway. This becomes a so-called "practical problem" which can interfere with the "easy, expeditious and inexpensive" trial of a case.

Public interest Turning to the factors of public interest, one of the primary functions of diversity jurisdiction is to give a plaintiff of a given state access to a federal court for purposes of vindicating claims as against citizens of other states. This much is apparent from the language of the diversity statute itself. This district has, to be sure, the paradigm of a congested docket. This is not, however, a case where a community which bears no relation to the litigation has the duties and expenses of jury trial imposed upon it. The community served by this court has a clear interest in providing a forum in which one of its citizens may seek to redress a wrong.

Absent the considerations delineated below, a balance of the *Gulf Oil Corp. v. Gilbert* factors would perhaps indicate that Norway rather than New York was a more appropriate forum. Given these considerations, however, I find that it would not be appropriate to dismiss on forum non conveniens grounds. The first is that the *P's choice* plaintiff Fiacco is a citizen of New York, and hence has a real and tangible interest in this forum.[80] This factor augments in this case the weight which normally should be given to the plaintiff's choice of forum.

The second consideration is a crucial one, which tips strongly in favor of retention of jurisdiction in this district. If plaintiffs had commenced this action against defendant in Norway, defendant could have resisted, probably successfully, on the

---

80. In attaching importance to the plaintiff's residence I am not unmindful of authority in this circuit and elsewhere which tends to deemphasize the significance of the plaintiff's citizenship or residence as a factor in determining the appropriate forum. *See Alcoa S.S. Co. v. M/V Nordic Regent*, 654 F.2d 147 (2d Cir. 1980) (en banc); *Farmanfarmaian v. Gulf Oil Corp.*, 588 F.2d 880 (2d Cir. 1978), and I do not accord to Mrs. Fiacco's citizenship a "talismanic significance." Perhaps Mrs. Fiacco's New York citizenship alone would not have been enough to persuade me to deny defendant's motion. I note that in *Pain v. United Technologies Corp.*, 637 F.2d 775, none of the plaintiffs resided in the District of Columbia. One plaintiff was an American citizen residing in New Hampshire.

basis that defendant was not subject to jurisdiction in Norway. On this view, not only Fiacco but also all of the other plaintiffs would necessarily have come to this court, or to another district in the United States which had jurisdiction over defendant, in order successfully to proceed against defendant. Thus, this is not a situation where plaintiffs could have proceeded against defendant in the Southern District of New York or in Norway and elected instead to proceed in this district. They could not have proceeded against defendant in Norway absent defendant's consent to submit to jurisdiction there. The fact is that defendant has consented to submit to jurisdiction in Norway, and has sweetened the offer by agreeing to concede liability if the action is transferred there. If there were not clear jurisdiction over defendant in this and other forums within the United States, however, query whether defendant would have been willing to submit to jurisdiction in Norway.

Obviously defendant wishes transfer of the action to Norway because it has made a value judgment that it will be advantageous for it to have damages assessed in Norwegian courts rather than in American courts. Perhaps where there are two forums, each with jurisdiction, the court in determining whether a transfer should be made on a forum non conveniens basis should not consider the question of the relative criteria used in the two jurisdictions for determining liability and assessing damages. *See, e.g., Fitzgerald v. Texaco, Inc.*, 521 F.2d 448, 453 (2d Cir. 1975), *cert. denied*, 423 U.S. 1052 (1976). Where of two possible forums one is possible only because the defendant consents to make it possible by submitting to its jurisdiction, it seems to me that the question of those relative criteria should weigh much more heavily. A plaintiff, who jurisdictionally has the right to proceed in one jurisdiction, should not, in my judgment, be required to proceed if at all only in another jurisdiction where jurisdiction will exist not as a matter of law but as a matter of conscious choice on the part of the party against whom he seeks recovery.

HOWE v. GOLDCORP INVESTMENTS, LTD.

946 F.2d 944 (1st Cir. 1991)   US citizen v. Canada corp.

BREYER, CHIEF JUDGE. ... The plaintiff in this case, Reginald Howe, an American shareholder of Goldcorp, claims that defendants Goldcorp, its officers, its investment advisors, and its lawyers, all of whom are Canadians, violated securities statutes, primarily by failing to disclose adequately their intentions, plans, objectives and other circumstances related to their efforts to take over two other Canadian companies called Dickenson and Kam-Kotia. He claims that, in these same circumstances, some of these defendants violated their fiduciary duties to Goldcorp or to its shareholders, and some, or all, of the defendants violated other statutes as well. The district court dismissed all of Mr. Howe's claims on grounds of forum non conveniens. [We affirm.] ...

The record indicates that Goldcorp's significant contacts with the United States are limited: First, Goldcorp is a Canadian corporation. Its shares trade on Canadian stock exchanges where anyone can buy them. Goldcorp sells its shares to residents of the United States only if they (or their agents) buy those shares in Canada. Goldcorp shares do not trade on stock exchanges (nor are they sold over the counter) in the United States. Second, Goldcorp sends annual reports, proxy statements and similar material to shareholders in whatever country they live [including the U.S.] ... as part of general, worldwide mailings. Third, Goldcorp sends regular dividends to share-holders in whatever country they live [including the U.S.] ... as part of a general dis-tribution to all shareholders. ... Fourth, Goldcorp employees have answered, by mail or by phone, specific questions addressed to them by Goldcorp's shareholders in the United States. Goldcorp employees have, from time to time, sent annual reports and similar written material to investment advisors or stock brokers in the United States, always at the request of those advisors or brokers, who themselves (or who have clients who) were already Goldcorp shareholders. ... Fifth, in 1989 Goldcorp acquired two Canadian companies (called Dickenson and Kam-Kotia) which owned some assets in the United States and had some American shareholders. In doing so, it had to comply — and did comply — with various U.S. Securities and Exchange Commission requirements. Sixth, Goldcorp's American shareholders, including Mr. Howe, own about one-third of Goldcorp's shares.

Mr. Howe's allegations grow out of the following events: 1. Before 1987 Goldcorp was a company that owned gold and held other diverse, gold-related investments. Its articles of incorporation forbid it to own more than 10 percent of the assets of any other single company or to invest more than 10 percent of its own assets in the shares of any other single company. Thus, investment in Goldcorp amounted to an investment approximately as safe as gold itself; for Goldcorp could itself own only (1) gold and (2) a small or diverse portfolio of other gold-related companies. 2. In 1987 Goldcorp asked its shareholders to approve changes in its arti-cles of incorporation that would permit it to own more than 10 percent of other individual companies and to invest more than 10 percent of its own assets in a single company's shares. The stockholders gave their approval. 3. In January 1989 a Canadian company called Corona tried to take over two other Canadian goldmining companies (Dickenson and Kam-Kotia). Goldcorp, appearing ... as a "white knight," thwarted Corona's bid by taking over these two companies itself. ... 4. As a result of the takeovers of Dickenson and Kam-Kotia, the value of Goldcorp's shares declined dramatically.

Mr. Howe's complaint claims that [these] facts ... reveal several kinds of unlaw-ful activity. First, he says that Goldcorp "defrauded" its shareholders, primarily by failing to explain adequately that the changes in its articles of incorporation meant a radical change in its investment policy. In particular, alleges Mr. Howe, Goldcorp failed to explain that the corporation would no longer invest its assets safely in gold and in a diversified portfolio, but, instead, would invest heavily in the shares of one or two companies, thereby greatly increasing the risks to investors in Goldcorp. This "misrepresentation" or "fraud," the complaint says, violates the federal securities laws, *see* 15 U.S.C. §§78j(b), 77q(a), Massachusetts consumer protection law, *see* Mass. Gen. L. ch. 93A, and the common law of fraud and misrepresentation. Second, the complaint claims another instance of "misrepresentation" or "fraud." It states that Goldcorp failed to disclose to the SEC (as part of its 1989 effort to buy shares of Dickenson and Kam-Kotia from United States shareholders) the existence of legal problems surrounding the 1987 amendment of its articles of incorporation. Third, the complaint says that officers of Goldcorp and Goldcorp's investment managers, when organizing the takeover of Dickenson and Kam-Kotia, tried to help themselves rather than to benefit Goldcorp. It says, for example, that, by improperly looking to their own financial gain, they violated fiduciary duties owed to the company — duties imposed by common law, Canadian law, securities statutes and the American Investment Company Act of 1940. Fourth, the complaint says that these same misrepresentations and violations of fiduciary duty violated various federal criminal statutes, such as the anti-racketeering laws. ... The district court ... dismissed Mr. Howe's complaint on grounds of forum non conveniens. Mr. Howe appeals this dismissal.

The doctrine of forum non conveniens ... permits a court to dismiss a case because the chosen forum (despite the presence of jurisdiction and venue) is so inconvenient that it would be unfair to conduct the litigation in that place. ... Appellant, first and most importantly, argues that ... special legal circumstances here deprive the district court of the legal power to employ the forum non conveniens doctrine at all. Supported by the SEC's amicus brief, he says that, no matter what the circumstances, no matter what the unfairness, a federal court (with jurisdiction and proper venue) lacks the power to invoke forum non conveniens if Congress has passed an applicable "special" venue statute, a statute that broadens the plaintiff's choice of forum beyond the choices that federal law's "general" venue statute otherwise would provide. [The federal securities laws contain such a "special" venue statute, 15 U.S.C. §78aa, as do the antitrust laws.

[I]n the international context one can ask, "What is so special about a special venue statute?" If a general venue statute opening federal court doors (say, in New York) is compatible with an international forum non conveniens transfer (say, to Italy), why does a special venue statute which simply opens another court's doors (say, in California) suddenly make the same international transfer unlawful? Both kinds of statutes open otherwise closed court doors. Neither kind of statute, explicitly or (absent some special legislative intent) implicitly, prohibits an international transfer. ...

[W]e can find no good policy reason for reading the special venue provisions as if someone in Congress really intended them to remove the courts' legal power to invoke the doctrine of forum non conveniens in an otherwise appropriate case. The growing interdependence of formerly separate national economies, the increased extent to which commerce is international, and the greater likelihood that an act performed in one country will affect citizens of another, all argue for expanded efforts to

help the world's legal systems work together, in harmony, rather than at cross purposes. To insist that American courts hear cases where the balance of convenience
and the interests of justice require that they be brought elsewhere will simply encourage an international forum-shopping that would increase the likelihood that decisions made in one country will cause (through lack of awareness or understanding)
adverse effects in another, eroding uniformity or thwarting the aims of law and policy. And, to deprive American courts of their transfer power when, but only when,
one of more than three hundred special venue statutes applies, would create a hodge-
podge, that would, or would not, bring about American adjudication of an essentially foreign controversy, depending upon the pure happenstance of whether Congress
— at some perhaps distant period and likely out of a desire to widen plaintiffs' venue
choices in typical domestic cases — enacted a "special venue" provision. Such a
result would seem thoroughly unsound.

We turn now to the appellant's second argument, also supported by the SEC —
that the district court misapplied the doctrine of forum non conveniens in the present case. We consider this argument in light of several well-established legal principles. First, forum non conveniens is a flexible, practical doctrine designed to avoid
trials in places so "inconvenient" that transfer is needed to avoid serious unfairness.
Second, although forum non conveniens is not "rigid," and "[e]ach case turns on its
facts," the Supreme Court has provided an illustrative list of relevant considerations.
Third, the "forum non conveniens determination is committed to the sound discretion of the trial court." ...

We can find no "clear abuse" of the district court's powers in this case. For one
thing, the balance of conveniences seems to favor, with unusual strength, the
Canadian defendants. The relevant events surrounding both plaintiff's "misrepresentation" and "breach of fiduciary duty" claims took place in Canada, not in the
United States. The Canadian directors of Goldcorp, its officers, its investment advisors, and its lawyers, meeting, speaking, planning, and acting in Canada, took (or
failed to take) the actions that allegedly amounted to a failure to remain properly
loyal to Goldcorp and its shareholders. Canadian individuals also decided, in
Canada, precisely what statements they or the corporation should make, or should
not make, in public descriptions of changes in Goldcorp's articles of incorporation,
of changes in Goldcorp's investment policies, and of circumstances surrounding the
takeover of Dickenson and Kam-Kotia. They presumably arranged to have printed in
Canada most of the documents embodying most of those statements (though they
then disseminated many of these documents to shareholders throughout the world).
Thus, the relevant actions, statements and omissions that underlie the plaintiff's
claims of "misrepresentation" or "fraud" originated in Canada. Most of the background facts that might show those statements or omissions to be materially false or
misleading occurred in Canada.

Given these facts, it is not surprising that most of the evidence is in Canada and
most of the witnesses are in Canada. Indeed, an undisputed affidavit by Goldcorp's

President says that, except for Mr. Howe, no resident of the United States "has knowledge relevant to the matters alleged in the amended complaint." And, only Canadian courts, not courts within the United States, have the legal power to compel the testimony of twelve Canadian potential witnesses who are not under the control of any party. ... Compulsory process would seem especially important where, as here, fraud and subjective intent are elements of the claim, making the live testimony of witnesses for the purposes of presenting demeanor evidence essential to a fair trial. ... At the same time, trial in Canada will not deprive the plaintiff of relevant legal advantages. Canadian courts will either apply American law, *see Restatement (Second) of Conflict of Laws* §6; or they will apply Canadian laws that offer shareholders somewhat similar protections by forbidding misrepresentation and fraud and imposing fiduciary obligations. We concede there may be some differences between Canadian and American law on these matters. Controlling precedent makes clear, however, that small differences in standards and procedural differences (such as greater difficulty in meeting class action requirements or less generous rules for recovering attorneys' fees) are beside the point. ...

Further, this case, except for the presence of an American shareholder, has little to do with Massachusetts or any other jurisdiction in the United States. Goldcorp's contacts with the United States consist of those listed earlier: (1) sending reports and statements to American shareholders among others, (2) answering questions sent by Americans about, how, for example, they might buy shares in Canada, (3) providing explanations of corporate policies and activities to American shareholders, such as Mr. Howe, who requested them, and (4) filing takeover information with the SEC so that Goldcorp could buy shares that Americans might hold in two Canadian companies (Dickenson and Kam-Kotia). In respect of Massachusetts, Goldcorp's activities apparently come down to keeping a mailing list of eight shareholders, sending those shareholders ordinary information, and answering requests for information from one firm of investment advisors (Shearson Lehman, to which Goldcorp sent ten annual, and ten interim, reports) and seven individuals.

Finally, this case has a great deal to do with Canada. The underlying circumstances involve actions of a Canadian corporation, its directors, officers and advisors. And the plaintiff's claims implicate duties the defendants owed to the corporation and its shareholders under Canadian law. Thus, at least some significant portion of the adjudication of Mr. Howe's case will involve tasks most easily and appropriately handled by a Canadian court: interpreting primarily Canadian law and applying it to matters principally of concern to Canada. ...

Of course, as we said, Goldcorp has a significant number of American shareholders; Mr. Howe claims to represent a class of 2,500 American shareholders; and federal securities laws are designed to protect American investors from misrepresentation and fraud. But, neither Mr. Howe nor the SEC has provided us with any reason to believe those laws seek so strongly to protect Americans who bought their shares abroad from misrepresentations (or violations of fiduciary duty) primarily taking place abroad that a court may not require an American shareholder to bring his case abroad in a nation that offers its shareholders roughly equivalent legal protections. To hold the contrary here would, in effect, remove the court's forum non conveniens power in securities cases, raising the practical concerns we mentioned earlier. That is to say, we believe that a holding barring transfer would increase the risk that national legal systems will work to frustrate one another and would hinder efforts to promote greater coordination and harmony among them.

In sum, in respect to Mr. Howe's basic claims involving misrepresentation and violations of fiduciary duties, these factors substantially outweigh Mr. Howe's suggestion in his affidavit that he would find it financially difficult to litigate in Canada. We cannot say that the district court was clearly wrong in finding that the balance of conveniences favors suit in Canada and that litigation in Mr. Howe's chosen forum would likely prove both unfair and oppressive.

HARRISON v. WYETH LABORATORIES DIVISION OF AMERICAN HOME PRODUCTS CORPORATION

510 F. Supp. 1 (E.D. Pa. 1980)

WEINER, DISTRICT JUDGE. Plaintiffs in these actions are all citizens and residents of the United Kingdom. They each allege that they purchased oral contraceptives within the United Kingdom, used them in accordance with the directions and instructions, and as a direct and proximate result of such usage suffered injury, damages, and/or death. ... Plaintiffs allege that defendant has its principal place of business in Pennsylvania, and is engaged in the development, testing, manufacture, production, sale, marketing, promotion and advertising of the oral contraceptives Ovram-30, Ovram and Ovranette. Plaintiffs allege that defendant caused the marketing, sale and distribution of the drugs in the United Kingdom and either actually produced and manufactured the drugs marketed in the United Kingdom themselves, or did so through others by agency, license, or otherwise. Plaintiffs allege that defendant was negligent in its conduct of these activities, and in its failure to give reasonable or adequate warning concerning the serious risk of which it had knowledge associated with the use of these drugs.

Defendant has submitted the affidavit of David Gibbens, the Secretary of John Wyeth & Brothers Limited ("JWB"), incorporated under the laws of the United Kingdom, a wholly owned subsidiary of American Home Products Corporation ("AHPC"). According to the affidavit, JWB is a sub-licensee of AHPC and pays royalties to AHPC for use of synthetic progestrogens, for which APHC holds the exclusive license, in the contraceptives it manufactures, including Ovram-30, Ovram and Ovranette. The affidavit states that all three of the drugs are manufactured, packaged and labelled in the United Kingdom by, or on behalf of, JWB for distribution in the United Kingdom and Ireland. The affidavit further states that JWB received product licenses under the laws of the United Kingdom authorizing distribution and marketing of the drugs. Defendant argues that the litigation could and should more conveniently and appropriately be brought in the United Kingdom, as that country is the domicile of the plaintiffs, and the situs of the licensing, manufacture, packaging, prescription, purchase, and ingestion of the drugs. Defendant contends that the activities complained of did not occur in Pennsylvania, and Pennsylvania has no legitimate interest in regulating the conduct of its citizens beyond its borders. Defendant reasons that the marketing decisions were made in light of British regulation and law, and should be judged by the standards of the community affected by the allegedly tortious activity. ...

Plaintiffs argue that while it may well be true that the particular drugs which caused the injury in these cases were actually manufactured and sold in the United Kingdom, such facts are not dispositive of its claim. Plaintiffs contend that the alleged tortious conduct consisted of marketing the drugs and placing them in the stream of commerce with knowledge that the warning accompanying the drugs was inadequate, thus creating an unreasonable risk of harm, irrespective of where the drugs were sold. Plaintiffs claim that the fundamental manufacturing and marketing decision, conceiving the formula for the drugs, the knowledge of the risk involved, the alleged withholding of adequate warning, and distribution of the drugs, all were made by defendant in Pennsylvania. Plaintiffs argue that the alleged tortious acts occurred in Pennsylvania, and that Pennsylvania has an interest in and direct concern with the safety of products which emanate from its borders and with conduct which occurs within Pennsylvania which may cause harm to others, regardless of where that harm may have occurred. ...

[acts in the U.S.]

The local interest in having this localized issue decided at home is strong. A Court versed in the law that must govern the case and familiar with the people and the community in which the law is to govern, is better able to establish the appropriate legal standards and apply them to the facts of the case. After careful consideration we have decided that these cases would be more conveniently and appropriately heard in the courts of the United Kingdom. Even assuming arguendo that all production and marketing decisions were made by defendant in Pennsylvania and not by JWB in the United Kingdom, Pennsylvania's interest in the regulation of the *conduct* of drug manufacturers and the safety of drugs produced and distributed *within* its borders does not extend so far as to include such regulation of conduct on drugs produced or distributed in foreign countries. Questions as to the *safety* of drugs marketed in a foreign country are properly the concern of that country; the courts of the United States are ill-equipped to set a standard of product safety for drugs sold in other countries. The issues raised here concern the knowledge, if any, of an allegedly unreasonable risk, and the sufficiency of the warning of that risk to users of the product. Both the British and the American governments have established requirements as to the standards of safety for drugs and the adequacy of any warnings to be given in connection with its use. Each government must weigh the merits of permitting the drug's use and the necessity of requiring a warning. Each makes its own determina-

[UK ✓]

tion as to the standards of degree of safety and duty of care. This balancing of the overall benefits to be derived from a product's use with the risk of harm associated with that use is peculiarly suited to a forum of the country in which the product is to be used. Each country has its own legitimate concerns and its own unique needs which must be factored into its process of weighing the drug's merits, and which will tip the balance for it one way or the other. The United States should not impose its own view of the safety, warning, and duty of care required of drugs sold in the United States upon a foreign country when those same drugs are sold in that country. Here, that foreign country is the United Kingdom, a society in some aspects similar to our own in a standard of living, beliefs, and values. At issue here is, among other things, the delivery of medical care and drugs, oral contraceptives, a category of drugs long considered controversial in the United States for reasons of health and morals. It is therefore tempting for us to believe that our standards of product safety and care, if more stringent than their own, ought to apply to the British in order to afford the British people a higher degree of protection from possibly harmful products.

The impropriety of such an approach would be even more clearly seen if the foreign country involved was, for example, India, a country with a vastly different standard of living, wealth, resources, level of health care and services, values, morals and beliefs than our own. Most significantly, our two societies must deal with entirely different and highly complex problems of population growth and control. Faced with different needs, problems and resources in our example India may, in balancing the pros and cons of a drug's use, give different weight to various factors than would our society, and more easily conclude that any risks associated with the use of a particular oral contraceptive are far outweighed by its overall benefits to India and its people. Should we impose our standards upon them in spite of such differences? We think not.

Furthermore, *fairness to the defendant* mandates that defendant's conduct be judged by the standards of the community affected by its actions. In addition, defendant claims to have complied by the dictates of the British government's requirements as to drug safety and warning standards. While it may be true in most states in this country that compliance with the minimum government requirements does not necessarily constitute compliance with the duty of care which a manufacturer owes users of its products, it is manifestly unfair to the defendant, as well as an inappropriate usurpation of a foreign court's proper authority to decide a matter of local interest, for a court in this country to set a higher standard of care than is required by the government of the country in which the product is sold and used.

Finally, under Pennsylvania choice of law rules, it is clear that the applicable law here is that of the United Kingdom. A federal court sitting in a diversity case must apply the choice of law rules of the forum state. *Klaxon Co. v. Stentor Electric Manufacturing Co.*, 313 U.S. 487 (1941) [discussed *infra* pp. 681-84]. Pennsylvania has adopted the "most significant relationship" test for determining which law to apply. This flexible approach permits analysis of the policies and interests underlying the particular issue before the court, and gives the place having the most interest in the problem paramount control over the legal issues arising out of a particular factual context and thereby allows the forum to apply the policy of the jurisdiction most intimately concerned with the outcome of the particular litigation. We have already shown that the United Kingdom, and not Pennsylvania, has the greater interest in the control of drugs distributed and consumed in the United Kingdom. Hence, it is the jurisdiction most intimately concerned with the outcome of this litigation and its law would be applied even if these cases were to be heard in this forum. ...

RESTATEMENT (SECOND) CONFLICT OF LAWS (1971)

§84 comment f

Whether a given forum will be held inappropriate depends upon the facts of the particular case and upon the discretion of the trial judge. ... [T]he plaintiff's choice of a forum will not be disturbed except for weighty reasons, and ... there will in the ordinary case be one or more forums available to the plaintiff which, in the great majority of situations will be appropriate. One of these is the state where the occurrence took place, which qualifies because its local law will usually govern the rights and liabilities of the parties, and because in the normal cases, at least, the majority of witnesses will reside there. A second forum is the state of the defendant's domicil or, in the case of a corporation, the state of its incorporation or principal place of business. These states will presumably be convenient places for the defendant to stand suit, and the defendant's relationship to them makes it appropriate for their courts to hear the case. A third forum is the state of the plaintiff's domicil. Suit in this state may involve hardship to the defendant, but the obvious convenience to the plaintiff in bringing suit there, together with the clear interest of this state in the plaintiff's welfare, will make this state an appropriate forum except in unusual circumstances.

Notes on Fiacco, Howe, Wyeth, and Restatement §84

1. *Foreign plaintiff's right of access to U.S. forum.* Why should foreign nationals ever be able to sue in United States courts? U.S. taxpayers pay for U.S. courts, and foreign taxpayers do not. Why let foreigners get a free ride by using U.S. courts, usually to pursue suits against U.S. defendants?

(a) *International law and comity.* As noted above, international law is widely understood as requiring states to grant foreigners access to their courts. *See supra* pp. 64-65. U.S. courts have generally not imposed any per se bar denying access to foreign plaintiffs. "Ordinarily, nonresidents are permitted to enter New York courts to litigate their disputes as a matter of comity." *Islamic Republic of Iran v. Pahlavi*, 62 N.Y.2d 474, 478 (1984). Is this a wise rule? Why not charge foreigners a special tax for access to the public justice system? What if a foreign state imposes such a tax on U.S. plaintiffs?

(b) *Treaties guaranteeing access to courts.* The United States has bilateral friendship, commerce, and navigation treaties with a number of countries. Among other things, these treaties usually contain provisions ensuring that citizens of each signatory state receive "national treatment with respect to ... access to the courts of justice" of the other signatory state. *E.g.*, Treaty of Friendship, Commerce and Navigation between the United States and Ireland, Art. VI, 1 U.S.T. 785, 790-91. Treaties of this character exist with Belgium, China, Denmark, Ethiopia, Egypt, Finland, France, Germany, Italy, Ireland, Uruguay, Colombia, Greece, Israel, Hungary, Switzerland, and the United Kingdom. *See Wilson, Access-to-Courts Provisions in U.S. Commercial Treaties*, 47 Am. J. Int'l L. 20 (1953).

(c) *Reciprocity.* Note that bilateral friendship, commerce, and navigation treaties involve a *reciprocal* arrangement in which nationals from each signatory state are granted access to the other signatory's courts on the same terms as its nationals. Compare the legislation at issue in *Dow Chemical Co. v. Alfaro*, which granted foreign nationals an absolute right of access to Texas courts, provided that their home state had entered into an access to courts treaty. Is the Texas statute constitutional? Does it interfere with the federal government's conduct of U.S. foreign relations? *Compare Zschernig v. Miller*, 389 U.S. 429 (1968) (discussed *infra* pp. 537-44) (holding that Oregon probate statute unconstitutionally interfered with federal foreign relations, *inter alia*, because it required reciprocity from foreign states). Is the Texas statute required by FCN treaties?

Would a reciprocity requirement be desirable under common law? Why should foreign nationals be afforded access to U.S. courts if their home state does not afford court access to U.S. citizens? Taking the argument further, why should U.S. courts provide remedies to foreign plaintiffs except when foreign courts provide equivalent remedies (in likely range of recovery) for U.S. plaintiffs? Consider: a U.S. admiralty court could decline jurisdiction in cases involving "the citizens or subjects of a foreign country, whose courts are not clothed with the power to give the same remedy in similar controversies to the citizens of the United States." *The Maggie Hammond*, 76 U.S. 435, 457 (1870).

2. *Application of friendship, commerce, and navigation treaties in forum non conveniens context.* Several lower courts have considered whether provisions in FCN treaties guaranteeing national treatment in access to courts affect forum non conveniens analysis. In particular, some U.S. courts have held that foreign plaintiffs must be treated as if they were U.S. citizens for purposes of forum non conveniens analysis if they are nationals of countries that have entered into such treaties. *See Blanco v. Banco Industrial de Venezuela, SA*, 997 F.2d 974, 981 (2d Cir. 1993); *Irish National Ins. Co. v. Aer Lingus Teoranta*, 739 F.2d 90 (2d Cir. 1984); *Alcoa Steamship Co. v. M/V Nordic Regent*, 654 F.2d 147, 152 (2d Cir. 1978) (en banc), *cert. denied*, 449 U.S. 890 (2d Cir. 1978).

Are these applications of "national treatment" provisions to forum non conveniens presumptions persuasive? *Piper* concluded that the plaintiff's citizenship was an accurate proxy for the convenience of a U.S. forum for litigation. Would foreign plaintiffs receive "national treatment" if U.S. courts considered the inconvenience of a U.S. forum for such plaintiffs on a case-by-case basis? Does the use of an apparently rebuttable presumption require a different conclusion?

3. *Should a U.S. plaintiff's action in a U.S. court ever be subject to dismissal on forum non conveniens grounds?* U.S. citizens pay for the operation of U.S. courts. The Constitution grants U.S. citizens broad rights of access to those courts. Why should the forum non conveniens doctrine *ever* permit a U.S. court to dismiss an action brought by a U.S. plaintiff?

(a) *Historic rule against forum non conveniens dismissals of U.S. plaintiff's claims in U.S. courts.* The law did not always allow U.S. courts to dismiss U.S. plaintiff's claims on forum non conveniens grounds. For example, in *United States Merchants' & Shippers' Ins. Co. v. A/S Den Norske Og Australi Line*, 65 F.2d 392, 392 (2d Cir. 1933), Judge Learned Hand wrote:

> the libellant is a [U.S.] citizen and asserts its absolute privilege of resort to its own courts, independently of any inconvenience to the respondent. ... Courts are maintained to give redress primarily to their own citizens; it is enough if these conform to the conditions set upon their jurisdiction.

Other authorities were to the same effect. *Mobil Tankers, Co. v. Mene Grande Oil Co.*, 363 F.2d 611 (3d Cir. 1966), *cert. denied*, 385 U.S. 945 (1966); *The Saudades*, 67 F.Supp. 820, 821 (E.D. Pa. 1946). Given the forum non conveniens doctrine's concern with imposing upon the forum's *courts*, should the doctrine not similarly reflect concern for imposing on the forum's *plaintiffs*?

(b) *Contemporary extension of forum non conveniens doctrine to U.S. plaintiff's claims.* Around the time of *Piper*, U.S. courts began to broaden the forum non conveniens doctrine to permit dismissal of U.S. plaintiffs' claims, provided there was a sufficient showing of inconvenience: "United States citizens do not have an absolute right to sue in American courts." *Allstate Life Ins. Co. v. Linter Group Limited*, 1992 U.S. Dist. Lexis 19617 (S.D.N.Y. 1992); *Overseas National Airways Inc. v. Cargolux Airlines International, SA*, 712 F.2d 11, 14 (2d Cir. 1983). This is a fundamentally different approach from the historic rule that U.S. plaintiffs had a basic right of access to U.S. courts. The shift was sometimes explained as a natural aspect of the "flexibility" of the forum non conveniens doctrine:

Although such residence [of the plaintiff in the forum] is, of course, an important factor to be considered, forum non conveniens relief should be granted when it plainly appears that New York is an inconvenient forum and that another is available which will best serve the ends of justice and the convenience of the parties. The great advantage of the doctrine — its flexibility based on the facts and circumstances of a particular case — is severely, if not completely, undercut when our courts are prevented from applying it solely because one of the parties is a New York resident or corporation. *Silver v. Great American Insurance Co.*, 328 N.Y.S.2d 356, 402-03 (N.Y. 1972).

Others reasoned that insulating U.S. plaintiffs from forum non conveniens dismissals was a "primitive rule," redolent of parochial xenophobia. N.Y. Civ. Pract. Law Rule 327 (McLaughlin, Practice Commentary) (McKinney 1979 Supp.). Consider:

The plaintiff falls back on its United States citizenship as the sole and only possible basis for suing these defendants in a court of the United States. This is not enough. In an era of increasing international commerce, parties who choose to engage in international transactions should know that when their foreign operations lead to litigation they cannot expect always to bring their foreign opponents into a U.S. forum when every reasonable consideration leads to the conclusion that the site of the litigation should be elsewhere.

Mizokami Bros. of Arizona v. Baychem Corp., 556 F.2d 975, 978 (9th Cir. 1977), *cert. denied*, 434 U.S. 1035 (1978). Relying on such reasoning, courts like that in *Howe* dismissed the claims of U.S. plaintiffs in many cases. *E.g., Alcoa Steamship Co. v. M/V Nordic Regent*, 654 F.2d 147 (2d Cir.), *cert. denied*, 449 U.S. 890 (1980) (dismissing suit by U.S. corporation; "American citizenship alone is not a barrier to dismissal on the ground of forum non conveniens"); *Sussman v. Bank of Israel*, 801 F.Supp. 1068 (S.D.N.Y. 1992) (same) ("plaintiff's American citizenship and residence do not constitute the powerful, near-decisive factors for which" he contends).

(c) *Wisdom of extending forum non conveniens doctrine to U.S. plaintiff's claims.* Which approach to the forum non conveniens doctrine is wiser — the historic guarantee of access for U.S. citizens or the "flexible" modern balancing test? Where a U.S. plaintiff seeks relief in his hometown courts, from a court paid for by his taxes, and where Congress or a state legislature has vested the court with jurisdiction to hear the plaintiff's claims, why should the court have "discretion" to dismiss those claims because of the "convenience" of local judges and jurors?

Is *Howe* correctly decided? Why should Mr. Howe, an American citizen who apparently never set foot in Canada, be forced to go there to litigate claims that are admittedly subject to the jurisdiction of U.S. courts? Particularly where a U.S. plaintiff asserts a claim under U.S. substantive law, should his claim ever be subject to dismissal on forum non conveniens grounds?

(d) *Considerations of reciprocity.* In deciding whether a U.S. plaintiff's claims against a foreign defendant should be subject to forum non conveniens dismissal, is it relevant to consider what the courts of the defendant's home nation would do? Suppose that the defendant is from France, and that French courts recognize an absolute right of access to French citizens in international disputes, without regard to issues of convenience. Should U.S. courts nonetheless order a U.S. plaintiff to France to litigate against its French adversary?

4. *Practical risk of forum non conveniens dismissal of U.S. plaintiff's claims.* Notwithstanding abandonment of the historic right of U.S. citizens of access to U.S. courts, it remains unusual for U.S. claimants to be subject to forum non conveniens dismissals. Consider the result and rationale in *Fiacco*, which is more representative of lower court decisions than *Howe*. This result rests upon *Piper's* requirement that substantial deference be accorded a U.S. plaintiff's choice of a U.S. forum. *See supra* pp. 316-17. Note that "[d]espite frequent statements that an American citizen has no constitutional right of access to American courts and that unusually extreme circumstances might bring about a dismissal on forum non conveniens grounds, the American plaintiff is almost assured that his case will be heard in this country notwithstanding the inconvenience to defendant. ... [I]n fact, this writer has found no case in which a bona fide American plaintiff has been sent abroad solely on forum non conveniens grounds." Note, *The Convenient Forum Abroad*, 20 Stan. L. Rev. 57, 67-68, 74 (1967). Although this is an overstatement, at least today, U.S. plaintiffs' claims are in practice seldom dismissed.

5. *How much deference should be afforded a U.S. plaintiff's choice of a U.S. forum?* *Piper* did not define with precision what level of deference was due a U.S. plaintiff's choice of a U.S. forum. It said gen-

erally that citizens deserve "somewhat more deference than foreign plaintiffs." How much "deference" should trial courts give to a U.S. plaintiff's choice of a U.S. forum?

How much deference did Mrs. Fiacco receive? Was *Fiacco* correctly decided? Suppose that in *Wyeth* the plaintiffs had included U.S. military personnel (or U.S. lawyers) working and living in Europe. Should their claims be dismissed, along with the English plaintiffs' claims? Suppose that in *Piper* the plaintiffs had been the survivors of U.S. tourists killed in Scotland. What deference did *Howe* give to Mr. Howe's decision to sue in his own home forum? Did the court discuss the level of deference? Is *Howe* correctly decided? Is its "internationalist" analysis, excerpted below, persuasive?

> The growing interdependence of formerly separate national economies, the increased extent to which commerce is international, and the greater likelihood that an act performed in one country will affect citizens of another, all argue for expanded efforts to help the world's legal systems work together, in harmony, rather than at cross purposes. To insist that American courts hear cases where the balance of convenience and the interests of justice require that they be brought elsewhere will simply encourage an international forum-shopping that would increase the likelihood that decisions made in one country will cause (through lack of awareness or understanding) adverse effects in another, eroding uniformity or thwarting the aims of law and policy.

When Howe sued at home, was he engaging in "international forum-shopping"? Any more so than when Goldcorp sought dismissal on forum non conveniens grounds? How does it "erod[e] uniformity" for a U.S. court to interpret the U.S. securities laws and their protections for U.S. investors?

6. **Foreign plaintiff's choice of U.S. forum is entitled to lesser degree of deference.** As discussed above, *Piper* held that a *non-U.S.* plaintiff's choice of a U.S. forum was not entitled to the same deference as a *U.S.* plaintiff's choice of a U.S. forum.

(a) *Reasons for lesser degree of deference for foreign plaintiff's choice of U.S. forum.* In explaining why a foreign plaintiff's choice of a U.S. forum was entitled to less deference than a U.S. plaintiff's choice, *Piper* reasoned: "When the plaintiff is foreign ... this assumption [that it has selected the forum for reasons of convenience] is much less reasonable. Because the central purpose of any *forum non conveniens* inquiry is to ensure that the trial is convenient, a foreign plaintiff's choice deserves less deference." Does this rationale make sense? First, is it in fact true that the "central purpose" of forum non conveniens is to ensure that "the trial is convenient"? If so, what are the "public interest" factors? Does *Wyeth* devote much attention to "convenience"? Considering only the *public* interest factors, would a distinction between U.S. and foreign plaintiffs be warranted?

Second, assuming that convenience *is* the true objective of the forum non conveniens analysis, then why adopt a presumption that sometimes may — and sometimes may not — have anything to do with convenience? U.S. plaintiffs can live or have their operations abroad; their documents and witnesses in a particular case can likewise be abroad; and they can select a particular U.S. forum solely to inconvenience and harass the defendant. Conversely, foreign plaintiffs can sue in the U.S. for reasons solely of convenience. Does the *Piper* distinction between U.S. and foreign plaintiffs in fact reflect considerations of convenience? or is it simply a gesture towards the historic rule that U.S. plaintiff's claims in U.S. courts were not subject to forum non conveniens dismissals?

(b) *Criticism of* Piper's *distinction between U.S. and foreign plaintiffs.* In the light of what we have seen about the forum non conveniens doctrine, is it appropriate for a foreign plaintiff's choice of a U.S. forum to be treated with less respect and deference than a U.S. plaintiff's choice? Some commentators have criticized the differential treatment of U.S. and foreign plaintiffs on the grounds that "citizenship [does not] serve as an adequate proxy for other factors that legitimately weigh against dismissal on grounds of *forum non conveniens*. In particular cases in which the plaintiff's American residence touches upon some other factors — the plaintiff's convenience, for example, or possible bias in the alternative forum — such factors can be dealt with adequately on their merits, case by case." Note, *Forum Non Conveniens and American Plaintiffs in the Federal Courts,* 47 U. Chi. L. Rev. 351, 373 (1980). Consider the following excerpt from an opinion of the Washington Supreme Court, refusing to adopt *Piper's* analysis:

> The Court's logic [in *Piper*] does not withstand scrutiny. The Court is comparing apples and oranges. Foreigners, by definition, can never choose the United States as their home forum. The Court purports to be giving lesser deference to the foreign plaintiffs' choice of forum when, in reality, it is giving lesser deference to *foreign plaintiffs,* based solely on their status as

foreigners. More importantly, it is not necessarily less reasonable to assume that a foreign plaintiff's choice of forum is convenient. Why is it less reasonable to assume that a plaintiff from British Columbia, who brings suit in Washington, has chosen a less convenient forum than a plaintiff from Florida bringing the same suit? To take it one step further, why is it less reasonable to assume that a plaintiff, who is a Japanese citizen residing in Wenatchee, who brings suit in Washington, has chosen a less convenient forum than a plaintiff from Florida bringing the same suit? The Court's reference to the attractiveness of United States courts to foreigners, combined with a holding that, in application, gives less deference to foreign plaintiffs based on their status as foreigners, raises concerns about xenophobia. This alone should put us on guard. *Myers v. Boeing Co.*, 794 P.2d 1272, 1281 (Wash.·1990).

Is that persuasive? For a hard-nosed reply, consider:

The Jehas [Saudi Arabian plaintiffs] have argued that it is un-American to deny them the world's best forum and American rights because they happen to be foreigners. ... We do not hold as an ideal or practice that America shall be obliged to furnish its public services to anyone in the world who may choose to prefer them to their own country's services. This case, to be candid, has nothing to do with America's commitment to justice or to the plaintiff's legal complaint; it is an attempt to convert America's fragile resource of public civil law into an open buffet for plaintiffs and their lawyers. Money, not justice, is the magnet for cases like this. *Jeha v. Arabian American Oil Co.*, 1990 U.S. Dist. Lexis 15680 (S.D. Tex. 1990).

Is that persuasive?

(c) *Alternative rationale for distinction between U.S. and foreign plaintiffs.* Is there a more fundamental logic to the lack of deference accorded foreign plaintiffs' choice of a U.S. forum? As described above, U.S. verdicts often exceed foreign damage awards by orders of magnitude. *See supra* pp. 3-7. This may be in part due to the absence, in the United States, of the social welfare guarantees that exist in some other countries, to differing costs of living, and to other similar factors. If that is correct, then permitting foreign plaintiffs to proceed in U.S. courts may produce unfair windfalls. Even if this is correct, is forum non conveniens an appropriate way to preclude such results? Why not take such factors into account in awarding damages?

(d) *Should a foreign plaintiff's choice of a U.S. forum receive more, less or the same deference as a U.S. plaintiff's choice of a U.S. forum?* *Piper* did not clearly state how much "less deference" a foreign plaintiff's choice of a U.S. forum should receive. It suggested in a footnote that "somewhat more deference" is applicable to U.S. plaintiffs' choices of U.S. forums, 454 U.S. at 256 n.23, and it remarked at the end of its opinion that the presumption in favor of a plaintiff's choice of forum applied "with less than maximum force" because the plaintiff was foreign.

Lower courts have usually concluded that it is error to accord *no* deference to a foreign plaintiff's choice of forum: "reduced deference 'is "not an invitation to accord a foreign plaintiff's selection of an American forum no deference since dismissal for forum non conveniens is the exception rather than the rule."'" *Lony v. E.I. Du Pont de Nemours*, 886 F.2d 628, 633 (3d Cir. 1991) (quoting *Lacey v. Cessna Aircraft Co.*, 862 F.2d 38, 45-46 (3d Cir. 1988) (quoting *In re Air Crash Disaster*, 821 F.2d 1147, 1164 n.26 (5th Cir. 1987))). Even these courts, however, have not provided any specific guidance as to just how much "deference" a foreign plaintiff's choice of a U.S. forum warrants. *Lacey v. Cessna Aircraft Co.*, 1990 U.S. Dist. Lexis 5489 (W.D. Pa. 1990) ("the Court of Appeals ... has indicated that, because [the foreign plaintiff] is forced to choose between two inconvenient foreign fora, his choice is due 'at least some weight.' Of course, this provides little direction and is impossible to quantify."). Most decisions merely say that a foreign plaintiff's choice of a U.S. forum is entitled to "some," "less," or "reduced" deference. What should lower courts and parties do with these various remarks? How much "less deference" should a foreign plaintiff's choice of forum be accorded?

(e) *Overcoming the reduced deference to a foreign plaintiff's choice of a U.S. forum.* There are, of course, many cases in which a foreign plaintiff brings suit in the United States for reasons of convenience. Whatever the specific standard of deference, most lower courts have permitted foreign plaintiffs to demonstrate that they selected the forum for reasons of convenience, and not to oppress the defendant; such a showing is sometimes held to invest their choice of a U.S. forum with the same deference to which U.S. plaintiffs are entitled. *E.g., Lony v. E.I. Du Pont de Nemours & Co.*, 886 F.2d 628, 634 (3d Cir. 1989) (foreign plaintiff on "the same footing as a domestic plaintiff"); *Banco Nominees Ltd. v. Iroquois Brands,*

Ltd., 1990 WL 161031 (D. Del. 1990) ("If a foreign plaintiff can make a strong showing that the forum is convenient, the foreign plaintiff should be accorded the same deference that a domestic plaintiff would receive.") The Third Circuit has explained:

> Because the reason for giving a foreign plaintiff's choice [of a U.S. forum] less deference is not xenophobia, but merely a reluctance to assume that the choice is a convenient one, that reluctance can readily be overcome by a strong showing of convenience. *Lony v. E.I. Du Pont de Nemours & Co.*, 886 F.2d 628, 634 (3d Cir. 1989).

7. *Availability of forum non conveniens doctrine where defendant resides in forum.* A number of courts have considered whether the forum non conveniens doctrine is available when the defendant resides, operates, or is incorporated in the forum. It has been argued that the doctrine should never apply in such circumstances, because it can be presumed that the forum has been chosen for reasons of convenience and because the forum will in fact be convenient (particularly to the defendant). Consider the remarks on this subject in comment f to §84 of the *Restatement (Second) Conflict of Laws* (1971).

Some state courts have held that the forum non conveniens doctrine simply does not apply where the defendant resides in the forum. *E.g., Murdoch v. A.P. Green Industries, Inc.*, 603 So.2d 655 (Fla. Dist. Ct. App. 1992) ("It is established Florida law that 'a case may be dismissed from the Florida courts in favor of a more convenient forum in another state only where none of the parties involved in the suit are residents of this state"); *Piper Aircraft Corp. v. Schwendemann*, 578 So.2d 319 (Fla. Dist. Ct. App. 1991). However, the trend is to abandon such absolute rules. *Silver v. Great American Ins. Co.*, 328 N.Y.S.2d 398 (N.Y. 1972) (overturning rule that no forum non conveniens dismissal is available if either party is New York resident).

Nevertheless, defendants who argue that it would be inconvenient for them to litigate in a court located only blocks away from their headquarters often encounter skeptical reactions: "It is, as Alice said, 'curiouser and curiouser.'" *Lony v. E.I. Du Pont de Nemours & Co.*, 886 F.2d 628, 641 (3d Cir. 1991) (noting that "Du Pont, which is headquartered in Wilmington, Delaware, and is the largest employer in that state, seeks to move the action against it to a forum more than 3,000 miles away"). Lower courts have thus generally concluded that a significant factor weighing against forum non conveniens dismissals is the defendant's domicile in the forum. As the Second Circuit has succinctly put it: "We begin by noting that plaintiff[, a Swiss attorney,] chose this forum and defendant resides here. This weighs heavily against dismissal." *Schertenleib v. Traum*, 589 F.2d 1156, 1164 (2d Cir. 1978).

8. *Representative fact patterns.* Can general rules based upon nationality be articulated to structure the forum non conveniens analysis? Suppose that there is evidence in both the United States and a foreign state, that the conduct principally occurred abroad with incidental U.S. activities, and that foreign law will probably govern. How should a forum non conveniens motion presumptively be handled if: (a) both parties are U.S. nationals; (b) the plaintiff is U.S., but the defendant is foreign; (c) the plaintiff is foreign, but the defendant is U.S.; (d) both parties are foreign nationals? Is this insufficient information to make a generalization? Would generalizations like those set forth above be useful?

9. *When is a plaintiff a "forum" resident?* Suppose that a Texas resident commences a suit in Massachusetts against a Mexican defendant, and a forum non conveniens motion to dismiss the suit to Mexico is made. Does the Texas plaintiff receive the deference accorded to a resident of the forum under *Piper*? Consider the following discussion by the First Circuit, after a district court held that New York and Florida plaintiffs who had sued in Massachusetts were not entitled to *Piper's* deference for forum residents:

> In the present case, the choice facing the district court was between two countries — the United States and Turkey. Seen in this light, the district court erred in concluding that the Merciers' non-Massachusetts citizenship and residence favored dismissing the case. Rather, the Merciers' United States citizenship and residence — plus Sheraton International's similar citizenship and residence — are factors that make this a controversy local to the United States, if not necessarily to Massachusetts. In turn, conducting the case in the United States would serve the substantial public interest of providing a convenient United States forum for an action in which all parties are United States citizens and residents.

Mercier v. Sheraton International, Inc., 935 F.2d 419 (1st Cir. 1991). Is this well-reasoned? Recall the similar issues in the context of personal jurisdiction and a "national contacts" test. *See supra* pp. 174-97. Does the *Mercier* reasoning depend on whether state or federal law governs the forum non conveniens doctrine?

What if a "foreign" party is the wholly-owned subsidiary of a U.S. company? Should this affect its nationality for purposes of forum non conveniens analysis?

   10. Piper's *"private interest" factors.* Consider again the "private interest" factors set out in *Piper*. On a quick reading, these factors seem sensible: they portray a meticulous assessment of the efficiencies of trial in the competing forums. But do the factors really make sense in today's world?

   (a) *Location of evidence.* A crucial factor in many forum non conveniens cases is the location of documents, witnesses, and other evidence. *See Piper*, 454 U.S. at 257-58 ("relative ease of access to sources of proof"); *Blanco v. Banco Industrial de Venezuela, SA*, 997 F.2d 974, 982-83 (2d Cir. 1993); *Lacey v. Cessna Aircraft Co.*, 932 F.2d 170 (3d Cir. 1991).

   Why does it matter where documents or witnesses are located? Can't both be put on a plane, fax, or telephone? How do these expenses compare to the costs of preparation for a new set of lawyers? Consider: "The time and expense of obtaining the presence or testimony of foreign witnesses is greatly reduced by commonplace modes of communication and travel." *Reid-Walen v. Hansen*, 933 F.2d 1390, 1396 (8th Cir. 1991). And, "[i]t will often be quicker and less expensive to transfer a witness or a document than to transfer a lawsuit." *Calavo Growers of California v. Belgium*, 632 F.2d 963, 969 (2d Cir. 1980) (Newman, J., concurring). In an age of Concordes, Internet, faxes, and FedEx, isn't this right?

   Further, as in *Piper*, evidence is often located in both of the competing jurisdictions (as well as other places). Then, either forum will impose some inconvenience on one party or the other:

> the inconveniences in this case run both ways. The fact that maintaining plaintiff's suit in this American forum will necessitate the production of Swedish documents and witnesses is entirely inconclusive; if the case were tried in defendant's preferred alternate forum, Sweden, witnesses and extensive amounts of evidence would have to be transported from the United States to Sweden. *Carlenstolpe v. Merck & Co.*, 638 F.Supp. 901, 907 (S.D.N.Y. 1986).

As one court aptly put it: in international disputes, "much of the 'inconvenience' is not local, but inherent in the situation out of which the lawsuit arises." *Bata v. Bata*, 105 N.E.2d 623, 626 (N.Y. 1952). That was the case in both *Fiacco* and *Wyeth*. What does this suggest about the utility of this factor in deciding forum non conveniens issues?

   (b) *Reach of compulsory process.* Non-party witnesses often have material evidence. *Piper* reasons that, where such witnesses are beyond one of the competing forum's compulsory process, this factor should play an important role in forum non conveniens analysis. Lower courts have routinely considered the availability of compulsory process. *Kempe v. Ocean Drilling & Exploration Co.*, 876 F.2d 1138, 1146 (5th Cir. 1989); *Schertenleib v. Traum*, 589 F.2d 1156, 1164 (2d Cir. 1978); *Fitzgerald v. Texaco, Inc.*, 521 F.2d 448, 451-52 (2d Cir. 1975), *cert. denied*, 423 U.S. 1052 (1976). But witnesses will often be willing to testify voluntarily (thus not requiring compulsory process); if they will not, parties often choose not to rely upon hostile witnesses. Moreover, as discussed below, the Hague Evidence Convention provides U.S. courts with a workable mechanisms for compelling the testimony of foreign non-party witnesses. *See infra* pp. 895-920. Even where the Convention is not available, customary letters rogatory provide a means that can often provide testimony. *See infra* pp. 893-94. *See R. Maganlal & Co. v. M.G. Chemical Co.*, 1991 WL 156389 (2d Cir. 1991); *Overseas Programming Companies, Ltd. v. Cinematographische Commerz-Anstalt*, 684 F.2d, 232, 235 (2d Cir. 1982). Given this, why should the reach of compulsory process be particularly important in forum non conveniens analysis?

   (c) *Plaintiff's motive in bringing suit in the forum.* As *Piper* remarked, "dismissal may be warranted where a plaintiff chooses a particular forum, not because it is convenient, but solely in order to harass the defendant or to take advantage of favorable law." Why is it relevant to consider the plaintiff's motive in choosing to sue in the forum? Few contemporary cases involve a plaintiff whose motive was held to be "oppressing" or "harassing" the defendant. Of course, there are sanctions for such conduct under U.S. law, as well as tactical arguments against it.

   Less clear is how courts will, and should, regard forum-selection based upon favorable substantive or procedural laws, rather than inflicting cost or inconvenience upon the defendant. Most contemporary cases involve a plaintiff whose motive was to obtain a favorable substantive or procedural regime. *Alfaro, Piper, Fiacco*, and *Howe* all illustrate this. And the reason that almost every defendant seeks forum non conveniens dismissal is to obtain the same advantages for itself in a foreign forum. Save in the most unusual cases, does it make sense to consider the plaintiff's desire to improve its chances of recovery?

   The Supreme Court has, in the personal jurisdiction context, held that the plaintiff's deliberate effort to obtain favorable substantive rules in both permissible and predictable. In *Keeton v. Hustler Magazine, Inc.*, 465 U.S. 770, 779 (1984), the Court rejected a due process challenge to a suit in New Hampshire, by a non-New Hampshire resident, where the sole reason for suing in New Hampshire was the fact that every other state's statute of limitations had already run: it noted the "litigation strategy of countless plaintiffs who seek a forum with favorable substantive or procedural rules or sympathetic local populations." On the other hand, *Piper* and other forum non conveniens decisions have discussed such efforts in terms that imply disapproval. In few cases, however, do the plaintiff's efforts to obtain favorable substantive or procedural rules appear to have played a significant role in forum non conveniens analysis.

(d) *Miscellaneous other private interest factors.* Many of *Piper's* other private interest factors are almost always extraneous. Few cases require a "view" of a physical location, and if they do, modern technology offers adequate alternatives. Translating documents or testimony can create problems, but they are almost never insurmountable. Judgments may need to be enforced abroad, but that is potentially true in all international cases.

11. *The irrelevant bottom line.* Lawsuits are about money. They get brought to recover money, and they get defended to save money. The one thing that the parties and their lawyers care about, in almost every case, is how much money they will win or lose. It hardly seems necessary to say all that. But consider the Court's analysis in *Piper*. It requires trial judges to tote up long lists of witnesses, evaluating where they live, how important they are to the case, what language they speak, how much their air fares to the forum for trial would cost, and the like; similarly, the trial court must consider whether its docket is more congested or less congested than some foreign court (that may not even have a docket). Yet, note the Court's refusal to pay any attention to the bottom line — the amount of money that the plaintiff would likely recover in the alternative forums.

Is this all not a little like college students on their first date, conscientiously talking about everything except what is on their minds? Why shouldn't courts try to assess the likely recovery of the plaintiff in the two alternative fora? What could a court do with this information? Suppose it is clear that the plaintiff would recover in both fora; that in the U.S. it would likely recover $600,000, while in the foreign court it would likely recover $300,000; that it would cost $400,000 in combined legal fees (split equally between the parties) to litigate in the United States, and only $50,000 to litigate in the foreign court. Suppose the likely U.S. recovery was $1.6 million or $16 million.

Can courts *really* ignore the bottom line; don't they just peek a bit at it in deciding forum non conveniens cases? Consider then Judge Breyer's remark in *Howe* that Canadian law offers shareholders "somewhat similar protection" and "roughly equivalent legal protections." Suppose that *Howe* had involved Liberian companies, or that the *Piper* crash occurred in Sudan, and the alternative forums were Liberia and Sudan. Conversely, note *Piper's* concern about subjecting U.S. companies to significant tort liability. Won't courts inevitably consider the likely outcome in such forums in deciding whether to dismiss on forum non conveniens grounds? How can courts really consider likely outcomes at the preliminary stage of a forum non conveniens motion?

12. *Do the private interest factors serve any meaningful purpose?* If *Piper's* private interest factors: (i) are mostly concerned with relatively minor logistical issues, which can be overcome by modern communications; and (ii) ignore the vastly more important effects that forum non conveniens dismissals have on the substantive outcome of a litigation, then what is the purpose of these factors? Consider cases like *Piper* and *Wyeth*, where U.S. defendants argue that it is more "convenient" to litigate 4,000 miles away, instead of in their hometowns, while foreigners insist that it makes perfect sense to sue an equal distance from where their accidents occurred. Do the private interest factors listed by *Piper* serve any meaningful purpose? Would other private interests — not identified in *Piper* — be more useful to forum non conveniens analysis? What about the defendant's interest in having a dispute decided by a court with a reasonable, predictable connection to the parties' conduct?

13. *Piper's "public interest" factors.* As discussed above, *Piper* also set forth a variety of "public interest" factors. Like the private interest factors, these initially seem unexceptionable. But again, a closer examination is useful.

(a) *Public "private interests."* Most of *Gulf Oil's* "public interest" factors bear upon the "convenience" of the forum court. This includes congestion in the forum, the need for a jury trial, the complexity and length of trial, and the need to apply foreign law. For the most part, these factors are simply the "public" side of private inconveniences, looking at the extent to which the local court and jury pool will be imposed upon by a trial.

It is unclear what significance factors such as docket congestion and the burden of jury duty should have. Considered only from the forum's perspective, both factors will always point towards forum non conveniens dismissal — because this will reduce docket congestion and the burdens of jury duty. *See Ernst v. Ernst*, 722 F.Supp. 61, 65 n.4 (S.D.N.Y. 1989); *Barrantes Cabalceta v. Standard Fruit Co.*, 667 F.Supp. 833, 838-39 (S.D. Fla. 1986); *Cuevas v. Reading & Bates Corp.*, 577 F.Supp. 462 (S.D. Tex. 1983) ("each Court of this District is presently taxed with the assignment of approximately 650 cases ... conservation of judicial resources is an extremely important objective"). Judge Newman accurately reflected appellate skepticism as to the weight of this factor when he wrote:

> There is an understandable temptation in a busy district like the Southern District of New York to transfer cases that can as appropriately be tried elsewhere. That temptation must be resisted. The plaintiff's choice of forum should normally be respected. *Calavo Growers of Calif. v. Generali Belgium*, 632 F.2d 963, 969 (2d Cir. 1980).

A few courts have said that the relative docket congestion in U.S. and foreign forums must be compared. *Lony v. E.I. Du Pont de Nemours & Co.*, 935 F.2d 604 (3d Cir. 1991); *Mercier v. Sheraton Int'l, Inc.*, 935 F.2d 419 (1st Cir. 1991). But comparing docket congestion and the costs of trial (including jury costs) in different countries is a difficult exercise. In general, the forum's docket has not played a decisive role in forum non conveniens analysis.

From another perspective, when foreigners come to the United States to litigate, they have to pay U.S. lawyers, reporting services, hotels, experts, and the like. In the context of international arbitration, nations around the world have aggressively sought to *attract* foreign companies to use their territory as an arbitral situs — in large part because of the benefits that accrue to the local legal community from such international business. *See* G. Born, *International Commercial Arbitration in the United States* 654-55 (1994). Should U.S. courts take into account the benefits to the local bar that accrue from such foreign cases? Was that a consideration in *Castro Alfaro*?

(b) *Need to apply foreign law.* Following *Piper*, a number of lower courts have accorded substantial weight to the fact that a U.S. court would be required to apply foreign law (and vice versa). *E.g., Blanco v. Blanco Industrial de Venezuela, SA*, 997 F.2d 974, 982-83 (2d Cir. 1993); *R. Maganlal & Co. v. M.G. Chemical Co.*, 942 F.2d 164 (2d Cir. 1991); *Sussman v. Bank of Israel*, 801 F.Supp. 1068 (S.D.N.Y. 1992). Nevertheless, other courts have made clear that this factor is not conclusive. *Piper*, 454 U.S. at 259-60; *Reid-Walen v. Hansen*, 933 F.2d 1390, 1396 (8th Cir. 1991); *Hoffman v. Goberman*, 420 F.2d 423, 427 (3d Cir. 1970) ("the mere fact that the court is called upon to determine and apply foreign law does not present a legal problem of the sort which would justify the dismissal of a case otherwise properly before the court.").

(c) *The central role of balancing governmental interests and substantive fairness.* The principal factor, in most lower court analyses of *Gulf Oil*'s "public interest" factors has been the two competing forums' "interests" in the dispute. That was true in *Piper*, where the private interest factors tipped at most only modestly towards dismissal; it was the Court's view that there was no "American interest" in the dispute, and that there was a strong Scottish interest, that justified the trial court's decision to dismiss. Similarly, the principal bases for the *Wyeth* decision were that: (a) a U.S. court "should not impose its own view of the safety, warning, and duty of care required of drugs sold in the United States upon a foreign country when those same drugs are sold in that country"; (b) "the United Kingdom, and not Pennsylvania, has the greater interest in the control of drugs distributed and consumed in the United Kingdom"; and (c) "fairness to the defendant mandates that defendant's conduct be judged by the standards of the community affected by its actions."

(d) *Defining national "interests" for forum non conveniens purposes.* In order to "balance" the public interests of competing forums, it is first necessary to define what those interests are. Where did *Piper* and *Wyeth* find the U.S. and U.K. interests that were decisive to their decisions? What federal (or state) statute supports the views, adopted in *Piper* and *Wyeth*, that (i) there is no (or only a minimal) U.S. interest in regulating the export of defective products from the United States; and (ii) there is a strong foreign interest in exclusively regulating the sales of defective U.S. products within the foreign state? Are these propositions so self-evident that they require no legal basis?

Not surprisingly, different judges have reached different conclusions in identifying U.S. and foreign interests in particular cases. Like *Wyeth*, some courts have considered the forum's interest in not burdening local manufacturers with "lawsuits involving extraterritorial injuries." *Doe v. Hyland Therapeutics*

Division, 807 F.Supp. 1117 (S.D.N.Y. 1992) (rejecting view that "[w]here the flow of defective products into the stream of world commerce springs from the United States, an American court is deemed aptly interested, and ably situated, to regulate the imprudent conduct ..."; "While imposing our presumably more stringent standards to deter tortious conduct within our borders could afford a higher degree of protection to the world community, such an approach would also ignore the unique significance of the foreign forum's interest in implementing its own risk-benefit analysis, informed by its knowledge of its community's competing needs, values and concerns"); *Jones v. Searles Laboratories,* 444 N.E.2d 157, 162 n.1 (Ill. 1982) (noting amicus briefs by Illinois Attorney General and Illinois corporations warning that "businesses [may be] hesitant to incorporate in this State if they are required to defend 'foreign suits'"). *Piper* noted this consideration, indicating concern about "American manufacturer[s]" facing suits by foreign plaintiffs seeking the benefits of U.S. laws that are "extremely attractive to foreign plaintiffs."

In contrast, other courts have found the mirror-image interest:

> An American forum has a significant or equal interest to that of a foreign forum in litigation involving foreign plaintiffs and defendant American pharmaceutical corporations ... where an allegedly defective drug has been developed, tested and manufactured in the United States, and is being distributed to, and presumably used by American citizens. *Carlenstolpe v. Merck,* 638 F.Supp. 901, 909 (S.D.N.Y. 1986).

Consider Justice Doggett's concurring opinion, excerpted above at *supra* pp. 307-11, in *Alfaro.* What does he think about the relevant public interests when a U.S. company manufactures products that cause injury abroad? Consider again:

> The doctrine of forum non conveniens is obsolete in a world in which markets are global and in which ecologists have documented the delicate balance of all life on this planet. The parochial perspective embodied in the doctrine of forum non conveniens enables corporations to evade legal control merely because they are transnational. This perspective ignores the reality that actions of our corporations affecting those abroad will also affect Texans. Although DBCP is banned from use within the United States, it and other similarly banned chemicals have been consumed by Texans eating foods imported from Costa Rica and elsewhere. In the absence of meaningful tort liability in the United States for their actions, some multinational corporations will continue to operate without adequate regard for the human and environmental costs of their actions. This result cannot be allowed to repeat itself for decades to come.

How does one decide whether Justice Doggett's views, or those of Judge Weiner in *Wyeth,* are correct? Are these interests defined by federal or state law? Note that neither judge cites any legal basis for his definition of "interests." What guides a judge in deciding which "interests" he should balance?

(e) *Irrelevance of "interest-balancing" to "convenience."* *Piper* said that "the central purpose of any *forum non conveniens* inquiry is to ensure that the trial is convenient." Does the balancing of governmental interests and consideration of substantive fairness to the defendant in *Piper* and *Wyeth* have anything to do with the *convenience* of a particular forum? Does Justice Doggett's vehement attack on the forum non conveniens doctrine have anything to do with convenience? In each case, haven't the judges adopted substantive principles regarding the allocation of territorial jurisdiction and regulatory competence? Don't these principles reflect questions of choice of law and identifying the sovereign state that should have the power to create and apply rules of law to particular disputes?

As discussed below, contemporary American choice of law rules are influenced significantly by "interest analysis," which attempts to identify the respective interests of all states having any connection to particular conduct. Consider the summary of interest analysis set forth below. *See infra* pp. 631-52. How does interest analysis in the choice of law context compare with interest analysis in the forum non conveniens context? Note the pro-forum bias of interest analysis in the choice of law context, reflected in rules protecting forum domiciliaries. *See infra* pp. 649-50. Does this suggest any basis for choosing between the interest analyses in *Wyeth* and *Castro Alfaro*?

(f) *Appropriateness of engaging in "interest-balancing" in forum non conveniens analysis.* Is it appropriate to use the forum non conveniens doctrine to balance competing national interests and determine what is substantively "fair" to defendants? Doesn't this convert a purportedly procedural, docket control device into a substantive interest-balancing doctrine similar to state choice of law rules?

(g) *Propriety of federal interest balancing rules under* Erie *doctrine.* What gives a federal court the power, in a diversity case, to adopt substantive rules regarding the appropriate scope of state regulation of local industries engaged in international commerce. As discussed below, *see infra* pp. 681-84, federal diversity courts are bound under the *Erie* doctrine to apply state choice of law rules, which define when state law can regulate conduct abroad. *Klaxon Co. v. Stentor Elec. Mfg. Co.*, 313 U.S. 487 (1941). Is it consistent with *Erie*, and its application in *Klaxon*, for federal diversity courts to determine when a U.S. state has enough of an "interest" in a dispute, as balanced against a foreign state's interest, to be able to litigate it? Recall that the federal diversity court that performs this analysis will be authorized by the U.S. state's long-arm statute to exercise jurisdiction. *See infra* pp. 358-66.

(h) *Relationship between choice of law issues and forum non conveniens.* Even if it is appropriate for a federal court to consider U.S. and foreign public interests, could the United Kingdom's supposedly superior interests in *Piper* and *Wyeth* have been accommodated if a U.S. court applied English law to the case? Note that many of the reasons that U.S. courts are favored by plaintiffs arise from procedural rules — contingent fees, jury trials, discovery, and punitive damages — that will almost always be governed by the forum's law. Do concerns about local autonomy and regulatory interests extend beyond what the law is, to who applies the law? Recall the discussion above regarding international law limits on the competence of courts to exercise subject matter jurisdiction over disputes having little connection to the form. *See supra* pp. 32 & 49.

14. *Balancing the private and public interest factors. Piper* requires the trial court to "balance" private and public interest factors to determine whether to dismiss the case. How is a trial court supposed to do this? And how are litigants supposed to have any idea how trial courts will decide such balancing exercises?

15. *Standard of proof required to justify forum non conveniens dismissal.* It is well-settled that the burden of proof in forum non conveniens analysis is on the party seeking dismissal. Less clear is the level of inconvenience needed to justify dismissal.

There is tension in Supreme Court pronouncements concerning this issue. Some remarks suggest that a fairly low showing of inconvenience is necessary: "[T]he ultimate inquiry is where trial will best serve the convenience of the parties and the ends of justice." *Koster v. Lumbermen's Mutual Casualty Co.*, 330 U.S. 518, 527 (1947). In general, however, the Court has indicated that a strong showing of substantial inconvenience and inappropriateness is necessary to sustain a forum non conveniens dismissal. *Piper* said that "dismissal will ordinarily be appropriate where trial in the plaintiff's chosen forum imposes a heavy burden on the defendant or the court, and where the plaintiff is unable to offer any specific reasons of convenience supporting his choice." Elsewhere, *Piper* remarked that "when trial in the chosen forum would 'establish ... oppressiveness and vexation to a defendant ... out of all proportion to plaintiff's convenience,' or when the chosen forum [is] inappropriate because of considerations affecting the court's own administrative and legal problems,' the court may, in the exercise of its sound discretion, dismiss the case." Most lower courts apply some variation of these standards. *E.g., Lony v. E.I. Du Pont de Nemours & Co.*, 886 F.2d 628, 635, 640 (3d Cir. 1989); *Howe v. Goldcorp Inv., Ltd.*, 946 F.2d 944 (1st Cir. 1991) ("the chosen forum ... is so inconvenient that it would be unfair to conduct the litigation in that place"); *R. Maganlal & Co. v. M.G. Chemical Co.*, 1991 WL 156389 (2d Cir. 1991) ("balance of convenience tilts strongly in favor of trial in the foreign forum").

How strongly should courts require that the public and private interest factors weigh in favor of dismissal in order to justify dismissal on forum non conveniens grounds? For whom ought the forum be inconvenient — the plaintiff or the defendant? How much inconvenience was there in *Piper, Alfaro, Fiacco*, and *Wyeth* — where the suits were in the U.S. defendant's hometown? to whom? How much inconvenience was there in *Howe*? to whom?

16. *Effect of international agreements, to which the United States is not party, on forum non conveniens.* As discussed above, a number of foreign states have concluded international agreements regulating the jurisdiction of national courts over nationals of other signatories. For example, the Brussels Convention specifies the national forums within the European Union that may exercise jurisdiction over EU domiciliaries. *See supra* pp. 90-92. Suppose that one EU domiciliary sues another EU domiciliary in U.S. courts. Does the Brussels Convention either prevent this or bear upon a forum non conveniens analysis? Consider:

> The defendant argues that plaintiff's choice of this forum violates the European Economic Community's Brussels Convention. ... Italy and France, the home countries of Carbotrade and

B.V., are signatories to the Brussels Convention, which provides that citizens of member countries shall be sued in their place of domicile or, in matters of tort, where the harmful event occurred. The United States is not, however, a signatory to this Convention. "An international agreement does not create either obligations or rights for a third state without its consent." *Restatement (Third) of the Foreign Relations Law of the United States* §324(1) (1987). The defendant has presented no authority for the proposition that a United States Court should give the Brussels Convention determinative weight in deciding a motion to dismiss based on forum non conveniens. *Carbotrade SpA v. Bureau Veritas*, 1992 U.S. Dist. Lexis 17689.

Is this persuasive? If the Brussels Convention were intended to forbid EU domiciliaries from suing in foreign courts in certain cases, shouldn't U.S. courts respect that prohibition? Does the Brussels Convention in fact prohibit suits outside the EU, or does it only allocate jurisdiction among courts within the EU.

D. The Adequate Alternative Forum Requirement and Public Policy Restrictions

1. Adequate Alternative Forum Requirement

A vital part of any forum non conveniens analysis is the so-called "adequate alternative forum" requirement. *Piper* said that "[a]t the outset of any *forum non conveniens* inquiry, the court must determine whether there exists an alternative forum."[81] Similarly, *Gulf Oil* held that the forum non conveniens doctrine "presupposes at least two forums in which the defendant is amenable to process."[82] Other authorities concur.[83]

There is no precise definition in *Piper*, or elsewhere, of an "inadequate" foreign forum. U.S. courts have considered a number of arguments that particular foreign courts would provide inadequate forums. In summary, these include cases where: (a) the foreign forum would lack jurisdiction over the subject matter of the dispute; (b) the plaintiff would not enjoy access to the foreign forum; (c) the defendant would not be subject to personal jurisdiction in the foreign forum; (d) the foreign forum would be biased or corrupt; or (e) the foreign forum would apply unfavorable substantive or procedural rules.

inadequate forums

Most U.S. courts have required that the party seeking a forum non conveniens dismissal bear the burden of proving that none of these circumstances renders the proposed alternative forum inadequate.[84] In general, U.S. courts are disinclined to hold that foreign courts are inadequate forums. *Piper* said "[o]rdinarily, th[e] adequate alternative forum requirement will be satisfied when the defendant is 'amenable to process' in the other jurisdiction."[85] Nevertheless, as discussed below, U.S. courts have denied forum non conveniens dismissals in a number of cases based upon failure to satisfy the adequate alternative forum requirement.

2. Public Policy as a Basis for Denying Forum Non Conveniens Dismissals

Related to the adequate alternative forum requirement is the less-common argument that the forum's public policy forbids forum non conveniens dismissal of certain claims. Neither *Piper* nor the *Restatement (Second) Conflict of Laws* alludes to the

---

81. 454 U.S. at 254 n.22.

82. 330 U.S. at 507.

83. *Restatement (Second) Conflict of Laws* §84 (1971); *Mercier v. Sheraton Int'l, Inc.*, 935 F.2d 419 (1st Cir. 1991); *In re Air Crash Disaster Near New Orleans*, 821 F.2d 1147, 1165 (5th Cir. 1987).

84. *Mercier v. Sheraton Int'l, Inc.*, 935 F.2d 419 (1st Cir. 1991) ("it remains the moving defendant's burden to establish that an adequate alternative forum exists"); *Baris v. Sulpicio Lines, Inc.*, 932 F.2d 1540, 1549-50 (5th Cir. 1991); *Contact Lumber Co. v. P.T. Moges Shipping Co.*, 918 F.2d 1146, 1149 (9th Cir. 1990); *Lacey v. Cessna Aircraft Co.*, 862 F.2d 38, 43-44 (3d Cir. 1988); *In re Air Crash Disaster Near New Orleans*, 821 F.2d 1147, 1164 (5th Cir. 1987); *Canadian Overseas Ores v. Compania de Acero del Pacifico, SA*, 528 F. Supp. 1337 (S.D.N.Y. 1982), *aff'd on other grounds*, 727 F.2d 1274 (2d Cir. 1984); *Cheng v. Boeing Co.*, 708 F.2d 1406 (9th Cir. 1983); *Schertenleib v. Traum*, 589 F.2d 1156, 1160 (2d Cir. 1978).

85. 454 U.S. at 254-55 n.22.

existence of a public policy defense to a forum non conveniens motion. It is clear, however, from both principle and lower court precedent that such a defense exists.

In most jurisdictions, the forum non conveniens doctrine is a common law principle of judicial abstention, or a generalized statutory codification of this principle.[86] Although seldom discussed in these terms, this general forum non conveniens principle must give way to specific forum public policies in particular cases. This result is analogous to public policy rules applicable to forum selection agreements, choice of law clauses, choice of law doctrine, and foreign judgments.[87]

As in other contexts, the public policy inquiry in the forum non conveniens context is an uncertain and unpredictable one.[88] The most clear-cut example is where a forum statute forbids forum non conveniens dismissals in particular kinds of cases, or requires that particular types of claims be litigated only in the forum.[89] In few cases, however, do U.S statutes expressly address the applicability of the forum non conveniens doctrine, and U.S. courts have rejected most arguments that particular statutes impliedly forbid forum non conveniens dismissals.[90]

Absent statutory guidance, the existence of a public policy precluding forum non conveniens dismissals must generally be implied from statutory and common law evidence that does not directly address the point. These arguments are most common where a plaintiff asserts claims under a regulatory statute in the forum state — such as antitrust, securities regulation, environmental, or employment laws. The basic argument is that in providing specific statutory protections, the legislature must have intended to override the common law forum non conveniens doctrine.

A few U.S. courts have refused to apply the forum non conveniens defense to particular U.S. statutory claims.[91] Most notably, lower courts have generally concluded that forum non conveniens is not available in federal antitrust actions.[92] In contrast, courts have almost always concluded that other federal statutory claims are subject to forum non conveniens dismissals. Claims under both the Carriage of Goods by Sea Act and the Jones Act have generally been held subject to forum non

---

86. *See supra* pp. 298-300.

87. *See infra* pp. 414-30, 486-88, 624-31, 655-56 & 974-86.

88. *See infra* pp. 354-56.

89. *E.g., Dow Chemical Co. v. Castro Alfaro*, 786 S.W.2d 674 (Tex. 1990) (relying on Tex. Civ. Prac. & Rem. Code §71.031).

90. *E.g., Howe v. Goldcorp Investments, Ltd.*, 946 F.2d 944 (1st Cir. 1991) (rejecting argument that "special venue" provision of federal securities laws forbids forum non conveniens dismissals).

91. *E.g., Zipfel v. Halliburton Co.*, 832 F.2d 1477, 1486 (9th Cir. 1987) (Jones Act); *Needham v. Phillips Petroleum Co. of Norway*, 719 F.2d 1481, 1483 (10th Cir. 1983) (Jones Act); *Szumlicz v. Norwegian American Line*, 698 F.2d 1192, 1195 (11th Cir. 1983) (Jones Act); *Lawford v. New York Life Ins. Co.*, 739 F.Supp. 906 (S.D.N.Y. 1990) (ERISA); *Galon v. M/V Hira II*, 1990 A.M.C. 342 (W.D. Wash. Oct. 27, 1989) (46 U.S.C. §10313); *First Pacific Corp. v. Sociedade de Empreendimentos e Construcoes, Ltda.*, 566 So.2d 3 (Fla. App. 1990) (Florida statutes).

92. *E.g., Industrial Inv. Dev. Corp. v. Mitsui & Co.*, 671 F.2d 876, 890 (5th Cir.), *vacated on other grounds*, 460 U.S. 1007 (1983); *Laker Airways v. Pan American World Airways*, 568 F. Supp. 811, 817-18 (D.D.C. 1983); *El Cid, Ltd. v. New Jersey Zinc Co.*, 444 F. Supp. 845, 846 n.1 (S.D.N.Y. 1977).

conveniens dismissal.[93] Similarly, lower courts have held that federal securities, RICO, and ERISA claims are subject to *forum non conveniens* dismissal.[94]

3. Conditions on Dismissals

Conditions are frequently imposed as a requirement for granting forum non conveniens dismissals.[95] These conditions are typically imposed in order to meet a plaintiff's contentions that a proffered foreign alternative forum would be inadequate. It is particularly common to condition forum non conveniens dismissal on: (1) the defendant's consent to suit and service of process in the alternative forum; (2) the defendant's agreement to produce documents or witnesses in the plaintiff's foreign action; (3) the defendant's waiver of any statute of limitation defense in the foreign action; and (4) the defendant's consent to pay any foreign judgment obtained by plaintiffs. If the defendant fails to abide by the U.S. court's conditions, the U.S. action may be restored to the trial court's docket.[96]

4. Selected Materials on Adequate Alternative Forums, Public Policy, and Conditions

Excerpted below are various materials on the alternative forum requirement and the imposition of conditions on forum non conveniens dismissals. The *Bhopal* decision considers the significance of differences in procedural rules. The opinions in *Howe* and *Laker* explore the role of public policy limits in application of the forum non conveniens doctrine. Finally, both the *Wyeth* and *Bhopal* decisions illustrate the role of conditions on forum non conveniens dismissals.

---

93. *E.g., Contact Lumber Co. v. P.T. Moges Shipping Co.,* 918 F.2d 1446 (9th Cir. 1990) (COGSA, with court indicating that foreign court might apply COGSA); *Ikospentakis v. Thalassic Steamship Agency,* 915 F.2d 176 (5th Cir. 1990) (Jones Act and maritime claims); *Monsanto Int'l Sales Co. v. Hanjin Container Lines, Ltd.,* 770 F. Supp. 832 (S.D.N.Y. 1991) (COGSA); *Gazis v. John S. Latsis, Inc.,* 729 F. Supp. 979 (S.D.N.Y. 1990) (Jones Act).

94. *E.g., Daley v. NHL,* 987 F.2d 172 (3d Cir. 1993) (ERISA); *Howe v. Goldcorp Inv., Ltd.,* 946 F.2d 944 (1st Cir. 1991); *Kempe v. Ocean Drilling and Exploration Co.,* 876 F.2d 1138 (5th Cir. 1989), *cert. denied,* 110 S.Ct. 279 (1989) (dismissing suit by foreign plaintiffs, where RICO claim was only one of numerous claims for relief; all parties conceded that alternative forum would not entertain RICO claim); *Transunion Corp. v. Pepsico,* 811 F.2d 127 (2d Cir. 1987) (RICO); *Schoenbaum v. Firstbrook,* 405 F.2d 200, *rev'd on other grounds,* 405 F.2d 215 (2d Cir. 1968) (en banc), *cert. denied,* 395 U.S. 906 (1969) (dicta suggesting forum non conveniens is available if foreign law also provides a cause of action); *The Scandinavia Co. v. Nordbanken Group,* 1992 U.S. Dist. Lexis 15330 (E.D. Pa. 1992) (forum non conveniens dismissal of RICO claims). *But see General Environmental Science Corp. v. Horsfall,* 753 F. Supp. 664 (N.D. Ohio 1990) (refusing to grant *forum non conveniens* dismissal of RICO claims); *Pioneer Properties, Inc. v. Martin,* 557 F. Supp. 1354, 1362 (D. Kan. 1983), *appeal dismissed,* 776 F.2d 888 (10th Cir. 1985).

95. *E.g., Ali v. Offshore Co.,* 753 F.2d 1327, 1334 n.16 (5th Cir. 1985); *Vaz Borralho v. Keydril Co.,* 696 F.2d 379 (5th Cir. 1983); *Calavo Growers v. Belgium,* 632 F.2d 963 (2d Cir. 1980), *cert. denied,* 449 U.S. 1084 (1981); *Fitzgerald v. Texaco,* 521 F.2d 448 (2d Cir. 1975), *cert. denied,* 423 U.S. 1052 (1976).

96. *Cesar v. United Technology,* 562 N.Y.S.2d 903 (S.Ct. 1990); *Sigalas v. Lido Maritime,* 776 F.2d 1512, 1516 (11th Cir. 1985) (if conditions are not fulfilled "the adverse party may return to the original forum and maintain his action"); *Chiazer v. Transworld Drilling Co.,* 648 F.2d 1015 (5th Cir. 1981).

IN RE UNION CARBIDE CORPORATION GAS PLANT DISASTER AT BHOPAL, INDIA IN DECEMBER, 1984

634 F. Supp. 842 (S.D.N.Y. 1986)
aff'd, 809 F.2d 195 (2d Cir.), cert. denied, 484 U.S. 871 (1987)

KEENAN, DISTRICT JUDGE. On the night of December 2-3, 1984 the most tragic industrial disaster in history occurred in the city of Bhopal, state of Madhya Pradesh, Union of India. Located there was a chemical plant owned and operated by Union Carbide India Limited ("UCIL"). ... UCIL manufactured the pesticides Sevin and Temik at the Bhopal plant at the request of, and with the approval of, the Government of India. UCIL was incorporated under Indian law in 1934, 50.9% of its stock is owned by the defendant, Union Carbide Corporation, a New York corporation. Methyl isocanate ("MIC"), a highly toxic gas, is an ingredient in the production of both Sevin and Temik. On the night of the tragedy MIC leaked from the plant in substantial quantities for reasons not yet determined. The prevailing winds ... blew the deadly gas into the overpopulated hutments adjacent to the plant and into the most densely occupied parts of the city. The results were horrendous. Estimates of deaths directly attributable to the leak range as high as 2,100. No one is sure exactly how many perished. Over 200,000 people suffered injuries ...

On December 7, 1984 the first lawsuit was filed by American lawyers in the United States on behalf of thousands of Indians. Since then 144 additional actions have been commenced in federal courts in the United States. ... The Indian Government on March 29, 1985 enacted legislation, the Bhopal Gas Leak Disaster (Processing of Claims) Act (21 of 1985) ("Bhopal Act"), providing that the Government of India has the exclusive right to represent Indian plaintiffs in India and elsewhere in connection with the tragedy. Pursuant to the Bhopal Act, the Union of India, on April 8, 1985, filed a complaint with this Court setting forth claims for relief similar to those in the consolidated complaint of June 28, 1985. By order of April 25, 1985 this Court established a Plaintiffs' Executive Committee, comprised of [lawyers], who represent individual plaintiffs and [lawyers who represent] the Union of India. ...

Before this Court is a motion by the defendant Union Carbide Corporation ("Union Carbide") to dismiss the consolidated action on the grounds of forum non conveniens. ... "At the outset of any forum non conveniens inquiry, the court must determine whether there exists an alternative forum." *Piper*, at 254, n.22. ... [T]he *Piper* Court delved into the relevance of the substantive and procedural difference in law which would be applied in the event a case was transferred on the grounds of forum non conveniens. The *Piper* Court determined that it was theoretically inconsistent with the underlying doctrine of forum non conveniens, as well as grossly impractical, to consider the impact of the putative transfer forum's law on the plaintiff in this decision on a forum non conveniens motion: "[I]f conclusive or substantial weight were given to the possibility of a change in law, the forum non conveniens doctrine would become virtually useless." ...

P's
argument

[T]he plaintiffs in this case argue that Indian courts do not offer an adequate forum for this litigation by virtue of the relative "procedural and discovery deficiencies [which] would thwart the victims' quest for" justice. ... Plaintiffs' preliminary concern, regarding defendant's amenability to process in the alternative forum, is more than sufficiently met in the instant case. Union Carbide has unequivocally acknowledged that it is subject to the jurisdiction of the courts of India. ...

Beyond this initial test, plaintiffs ... argue that the Indian legal system is inadequate to handle the Bhopal litigation. [Plaintiffs submitted expert witness testimony on the Indian legal system from a U.S. law professor, not admitted to practice in India; defendants submitted testimony from two senior members of the Indian bar] ... According to [plaintiff's expert], India's legal system "was imposed on it" during the period of colonial rule. [He] argues that "Indian legal institutions still reflect their colonial origins," in terms of the lack of broad based legislative activity, inaccessibility of legal information and legal services, burdensome court filing fees and limited innovativeness with reference to legal practice and education. ... Mr. Palkhivala responds with numerous examples of novel treatment of complex legal issues by the Indian Judiciary. ... The examples cited by defendant's experts suggest a developed and independent judiciary. ...

[Plaintiff's expert] discusses the problems of delay and backlog in Indian courts. Indeed, it appears that India has approximately one-tenth the number of judges, per citizen, as the United States and that postponements and high caseloads are widespread. [Plaintiff's expert] urges that the backlog is a result of Indian procedural law, which allows for adjournments in mid-hearing, and for multiple interlocutory and final appeals. ... This Court acknowledges that delays and backlog exist in Indian courts, but United States courts are subject to delays and backlog, too. ...

Plaintiffs contend that the Indian legal system lacks the wherewithal to allow it "to deal effectively and expeditiously" with the issues raised in this lawsuit. Plaintiffs urge that Indian practitioners emphasize oral skills rather than written briefs. They allegedly lack specialization, practical investigative techniques and coordination into partnership. These factors, it is argued, limit the Indian bar's ability to handle the Bhopal litigation. ... While Indian attorneys may not customarily join into large law firms, and as Mr. Palkhivala states, are limited by present Indian law to partnerships of no more than twenty, this ... does not establish the inadequacy of the Indian legal system. ... [T]his court is not convinced that the size of a law firm has that much to do with the quality of legal service provided. ... Many small firms in this country perform work at least on a par with the largest firms. Bigger is not necessarily better. ...

[Plaintiff's expert] asserts that India lacks codified tort law [and] has little reported case law in the tort field. ... Mr. Dadachanji responds that tort law is sparsely reported in India due to frequent settlement of such cases, lack of appeal to higher courts, and the publication of tort cases in specialized journals other than the All-India Reports. In addition, tort law has been codified in numerous Indian statutes. ...

Plaintiffs next assert that India lacks certain procedural devices which are essential to the adjudication of complex cases, the absence of which prevent India from providing an adequate alternative forum. They urge that Indian pre-trial discovery is inadequate and that therefore India is an inadequate alternative forum. [Plaintiff's expert] states that the only forms of discovery available in India are written interrogatories, inspection of documents, and requests for admissions. Parties alone are subject to discovery. Third-party witnesses need not submit to discovery. Discovery may be directed to admissible evidence only, not material likely to lead to relevant or admissible material, as in the courts of the United States. ... These limits on discovery are adopted from the British system. Similar discovery tools are used in Great Britain today. This Court finds that their application would perhaps, however, limit the victims' access to sources of proof. Therefore, pursuant to its equitable powers, the Court directs that the defendant consent to submit to the broad discovery afforded by the United States Federal Rules of Civil Procedure if or when an Indian court sits in judgment or presides over pretrial proceedings in the Bhopal litigation. ...

Final points regarding the asserted inadequacies of Indian procedure involve unavailability of juries or contingent fee arrangements in India. ... They are easily disposed of. The absence of juries in civil cases is a feature of many civil law jurisdictions, and of the United Kingdom. Furthermore, contingency fees are not found in most foreign jurisdictions. In any event, the lack of contingency fees is not an insurmountable barrier to filing claims in India, as demonstrated by the fact that more than 4,000 suits have been filed by victims of the Bhopal gas leak in India already. ...

Plaintiffs' final contention [is that they would have difficulty enforcing an Indian judgment.] The possibility of non-enforcement of a foreign judgment by courts of either country leads this Court to conclude that issue must be addressed at this time. Since it is defendant Union Carbide which, perhaps ironically, argues for the sophistication of the Indian legal system in seeking a dismissal on grounds of forum non conveniens, and plaintiffs, including the Indian Government, which state a strong preference for the American legal system, it would appear that both parties have indicated a willingness to abide by a judgment of the foreign nation whose forum each seeks to visit. Thus, this Court conditions the grant of a dismissal on forum non conveniens grounds on Union Carbide's agreement to be bound by the judgment of its preferred tribunal, located in India, and to satisfy any judgment rendered by the Indian court, and affirmed on appeal in India. ...

HOWE v. GOLDCORP INVESTMENTS, LTD.

946 F.2d 944 (1st Cir. 1991) [excerpted above at pp. 321-26]

LAKER AIRWAYS LIMITED v. PAN AMERICAN WORLD AIRWAYS

568 F.Supp. 811 (D.D.C. 1983)

HAROLD H. GREENE, DISTRICT JUDGE. ... [The plaintiff, Laker Airways Limited, was a budget air carrier based in the United Kingdom, that provided cheap transatlantic passenger air service between the United States and Europe (principally the United Kingdom). The defendants were Pan American World Airways and TWA (both U.S. air carriers), McDonnell Douglas Corporation, and British Airways, British Caledonia Airways, Lufthansa, Swissair, KLM, and Sabena (all European air carriers).] Briefly, the complaint alleges that the defendants, who in the main are American and foreign air carriers, engaged in a scheme to destroy plaintiff's low cost air service on the transatlantic routes between the United States and Europe. The scheme was allegedly perfected in part through the medium of the International Air Transport Association ("IATA"), including through IATA meetings in Florida and in Switzerland.

When a court considers the issue of forum non conveniens, the plaintiff's choice of forum is, of course, given significant weight and should rarely be disturbed.[97] In view of that general principle, the burden is on those who challenge plaintiff's choice to demonstrate that some other forum is more convenient. ... [T]he defendants contend that, since most of the defendants are airlines anchored in Europe,[98] it may be assumed that the convenience of the witnesses would be served and the documents would more easily be available if the Court were to defer to [an English court, before which was pending actions brought against Laker Airways by various of the defendants seeking antisuit injunctions to halt the U.S. action].

Defendants' argument based on the convenience of witnesses has little validity when advanced in the context of a lawsuit involving transatlantic air passenger carriers. The Court takes judicial notice of the fact that these carriers provide frequent flights between the continents; that the time involved and the expense of transporting witnesses would be minimal; and that all the defendants maintain extensive business establishments in the United States. ... Beyond that, there is the key fact of the configuration of the alleged conspiracy. If there was a conspiracy, the United States was its hub and the various countries in Europe were its spokes. Insofar as transatlantic traffic is concerned — the focus of the complaint — each of the non-American air carriers provides service between a particular European country and the United States. On that basis, a court in the United States is a far more logical forum than a tribunal elsewhere, for it is here that all the strands, or spokes, come together.[99]

---

97. Although that weight is somewhat less when the plaintiff is a foreign resident this does not mean, and the *Piper Aircraft* Court did not say in that case, that plaintiff's choice is not at least presumptively valid. It should also be noted that in *Piper Aircraft*, unlike here, the relationship of the action to the United States was minimal, and that the Supreme Court there did not overturn but upheld a district court's exercise of discretion.

98. Four defendants (Pan American, TWA, McDonnell Douglas Corporation, and McDonnell Douglas Finance Corporation) are American, two defendants (British Airways and British Caledonian Airways) are British, and four defendants (Swissair, Lufthansa, KLM, and Sabena) are incorporated on the European continent. ...

99. We are not concerned here with [air] service between Switzerland and Great Britain, or between Belgium and Germany, or between the Netherlands and Switzerland; we are concerned with [air] service between these countries, on the one hand, and the United States, on the other.

These considerations have direct applicability to the controversy regarding the appropriateness of this Court as a forum versus that of the British tribunal. In the final analysis, what reason is there to ascribe to a British court the responsibility to hear and decide this matter? Only two of the ten defendants are British. Two of the American defendants (the two McDonnell Douglas companies) are firmly located in the United States. The airlines anchored on the European continent (KLM, Sabena, Lufthansa, and Swissair) operate for purposes of this case between the United States and the Netherlands, Belgium, West Germany, and Switzerland, bypassing Great Britain. ...

For these reasons, absent specific and persuasive evidence to the contrary, a court in the United States must be deemed to be a more convenient forum than a British court or any tribunal in the individual "spoke" countries. To be sure, a trial here will require the movement of witnesses and documents, but certainly the "hub" of the alleged conspiracy is a far more logical place even in that respect, for wherever the trial will be held witnesses and documents will have to be transported. ... When, finally, to these considerations is added the fact that two of the air carrier defendants and the only two non-air carrier defendants are U.S. corporations based in the United States, the logic of a trial in this country, when compared to any other place that has been suggested, appears overwhelming. ...

Justice is blind; but courts nevertheless do see what there is clearly to be seen. What is apparent is that the defendants, secure in the knowledge that no liability attaches to their activities under the laws of Great Britain, are seeking to have the matter decided in the British tribunal rather than in an American court.[100] But a United States court, bound to enforce the Sherman Act with respect to those who are resident in or are doing business in the United States, would not be justified in regarding defendants' desire to litigate in Britain — because they expect there to be exonerated — as a search for a more convenient forum. That is not what the doctrine of forum non conveniens is all about. ...

In *Piper*, the Supreme Court ... reject[ed] the court of appeals' view that a plaintiff may defeat a motion to dismiss on forum non conveniens grounds merely by showing that the substantive law which would be applied in the alternative forum is less favorable to him than that of the present forum. Such a rule, said the Court, would render forum non conveniens decisions unduly difficult of application for they would require the courts to engage preliminarily in complex exercises in comparative law. The Court then went on to state, however, that "if the remedy provided by the alternative forum is so clearly inadequate or unsatisfactory that it is no remedy

---

100. Laker, too, may well have considered the effects of the American antitrust laws. It is nevertheless true that for perfectly neutral reasons the United States represents a more legitimate forum for the plaintiff than any other place, for it is doubtful that some of the participants in the alleged conspiracy could have been reached anywhere but in the United States. Moreover, had plaintiff not brought its action in the conspiracy's "hub," it would no doubt have been met with challenges to its choice far more serious and substantive than those which are being raised here.

at all, the unfavorable change in law may be given substantial weight; the district court may conclude that dismissal would not be in the interests of justice." ... [T]hat is precisely the situation in this case. British courts could not and would not[101] enforce the American antitrust laws. As for British substantive law, it fails entirely, for a number of reasons, to recognize liability for the acts which the defendants are alleged to have committed. That being so, this case is precisely within that group of cases which the Supreme Court in *Piper* said should not be dismissed.

It is difficult to see how it could be otherwise. It would be a cruel hoax on the plaintiff to oust it from a court where its allegations, if proved, would entitle it to recovery, and to relegate it instead, in the name of "convenience," to a tribunal which, on the facts alleged, would not be justified under its own laws in entering judgment in plaintiff's favor. Moreover, what is involved here in not an obscure, technical law in the enforcement of which the American courts could be said to have no significant interest. What is in jeopardy is the enforcement of the Sherman Act with respect to a market — travel between the United States and Europe — in which this nation has the highest interest.[102] The Sherman Act, as has often been observed, is our charter of economic liberty, comparable to the importance of the Bill of Rights with respect to personal freedom, and there is thus the highest kind of public interest in preventing the Act from being emasculated in this important area by use of an essentially logistical rule.[103]

In view of these considerations, it is not surprising that it has flatly been held that the doctrine of forum non conveniens does not apply to antitrust actions. *See Industrial Investment Development Corp. v. Mitsui Co.*, 671 F.2d 876 (5th Cir. 1982), where the Court of Appeals for the Fifth Circuit, confronted with an appeal from a decision that Indonesia was a more convenient forum, held that in view of the venue provisions of the antitrust laws (15 U.S.C. §22) and the fact that the Sherman Act is a quasi-penal statute, an antitrust action may never be dismissed on forum non conveniens grounds. ... The Court fully agrees with *Mitsui*.

Antitrust cases are unlike litigation involving contracts, torts, or other matters recognized in some form in every nation. A plaintiff who seeks relief by means of one of these types of actions may appropriately be sent to the courts of another nation where presumably he will be granted, at least approximately, what he is due. But the antitrust laws of the United States embody a specific congressional purpose to

---

101. *See, e.g., British Nylon Spinners Ltd. v. Imperial Chemical Industries, Inc.* [1953] 1 Ch. 19 (Court of Appeal 1952).

102. Although it is difficult to quantify such matters, it would appear that the United States has an economic and social interest in travel from this country to all of Europe outweighing the interest of any individual European nation in travel from it to the United States.

103. For that reason, too, it is hardly fair to condemn these United States courts which insist upon application of the Sherman Act to those doing business in this country as being engaged in "social jingoism" [citing Respondents' pleadings]. If the jingoism label is to be used at all, it would seem more appropriately to fit those who maintain that fair results may be achieved only under British procedure, and that American courts cannot be trusted, under American law, to do justice.

encourage the bringing of private claims in the American courts in order that the national policy against monopoly may be vindicated. To relegate a plaintiff to the courts of a nation which does not recognize the antitrust principles would be to defeat this congressional direction by means of a wholly inappropriate procedural device. That is an action which the Court cannot and will not take.

HARRISON v. WYETH LABORATORIES

510 F. Supp. 1 (E.D. Pa. 1980) [excerpted above at pp. 326-29]

WEINER, DISTRICT JUDGE. [As described in the excerpt of this opinion at *supra* pp. 326-29, United Kingdom residents who had used oral contraceptives in the United Kingdom brought suit against the defendant, the Wyeth Laboratories division of American Home Products Corporation ("AHPC"), a Pennsylvania corporation, in U.S. district court in Pennsylvania. The suit alleged negligence in connection with the production and marketing of the contraceptives, which were sold in the United Kingdom by John Wyeth & Brothers Limited ("JWB"), an English company that was wholly-owned by AHPC].

We turn now to consideration of the availability of an alternative forum, and to practical questions of process, expense, production of witnesses and evidence, and enforceability of judgment. Defendant argues that the alternative forum prerequisite is met by the availability of an action in the United Kingdom against AHPC's subsidiary, JWB, and that even if defendant is not subject to United Kingdom jurisdiction, the availability of JWB makes it unnecessary for plaintiffs to include defendant in any action against JWB. We do not agree. We are not sure if a suit against the subsidiary, JWB, is sufficient to constitute an adequate alternative forum for this suit, brought by plaintiffs against this defendant. As we have explained, this action is more appropriately heard and decided by a British court. But in dismissing this action as a matter of convenience, we should not insulate this defendant from judicial determination of its alleged liability and from the consequences of its actions by placing it beyond the reach of the plaintiffs and of the courts of this or any other jurisdiction. An action against JWB may or may not fully protect plaintiffs as regards their claims against defendant for the alleged tortious conduct of defendant.

Defendant itself recognizes the need for the availability of an alternative forum before there may be a dismissal on *forum non conveniens* grounds. Indeed, defendant advances the argument that an alleged lack of foreign jurisdiction over the defendant is not an obstacle to dismissal because courts may deal with the alternative forum prerequisite to a *forum non conveniens* dismissal by conditioning such dismissal upon the defendant's consent to foreign jurisdiction. ... Defendant has also brought to our attention the case of *Dahl v. United Technologies Corp.*, 472 F. Supp. 696 (D. Del. 1979). In dismissing on the ground of *forum non conveniens*, Chief Judge Latchum conditioned his order on: (1) Defendant's consent to suit and to accept process in a foreign jurisdiction (Norway) in any civil actions instituted by plaintiffs on their claims before the applicable statute of limitations; (2) Defendant's agreement to make available, at its own expense, any documents or witnesses within its control that are needed for fair adjudication of any action brought in Norway by the plaintiffs on their claims; (3) Defendant's consent to pay any judgment, if any, which may be rendered against it in Norway in any civil action brought by plaintiffs on their claims.

In order to preclude the possibility that defendant would be effectively insulated from plaintiff's claims if we dismiss this case on grounds of *forum non conveniens*, we will condition such dismissal on defendant's consent to similar requirements. As we have noted, defendant has itself raised the prospect of so conditioning our dismissal. Accordingly, defendant must agree to submit to the jurisdiction of the courts of the United Kingdom in any civil action timely instituted there against JWB on the claims alleged herein. In addition, important evidence, both documents and witnesses, may be located in Pennsylvania and under the control of defendant. This evidence must be available to plaintiffs and to the courts in any action brought on these claims in the United Kingdom if the courts of the United Kingdom are to constitute an alternative forum in which plaintiffs can receive a fair adjudication. Accordingly, defendant must agree to make available, at its own expense, any documents, witnesses or other evidence under its control that are needed for fair adjudication of any actions brought in the United Kingdom by plaintiffs on their claims. Finally, so that any judgment rendered against defendant in the United Kingdom on plaintiffs' claims will have effect, defendant must agree to pay any judgment so rendered.

Notes on Bhopal, Howe, Laker, and Wyeth.

1. ***The alternative forum requirement.*** *Piper* said that "[a]t the outset of any forum non conveniens inquiry, the court must determine whether there exists an alternative forum." Why is that the case? Recall that a forum non conveniens dismissal requires a compelling showing of oppression and inconvenience, coupled with a lack of any public interest in the forum. If the plaintiff's chosen forum is really so inappropriate, why does it matter whether another forum can be shown to exist?

2. ***Is an alternative forum required in all cases?*** Is the adequate alternative forum requirement really a "requirement," or is the existence of an alternative forum instead an important factor in the balance of public and private interest factors? A few lower courts have adopted the latter view, holding that in some cases a forum non conveniens dismissal may be granted even if no alternative forum exists. *See Veba-Chemie AG v. M/V Getafix,* 711 F.2d 1243, 1248 n.10 (5th Cir. 1983) ("[p]erhaps if the plaintiff's plight is of his own making — for instance, if the alternative forum was no longer available at the time of dismissal as a result of the deliberate choice of an inconvenient forum — the court would be permitted to disregard [the lack of alternative forum] and dismiss"); *Pietraroia v. New Jersey & Hudson River Ry. & Ferry,* 91 N.E. 120 (N.Y. 1910) (doctrine of unclean hands bars plaintiff from pleading lack of alternative forum if fraud or force was used to serve defendant).

The weight of authority is to the contrary, and imposes an absolute requirement that an adequate alternative forum exist. *E.g., In re Air Crash Disaster Near New Orleans,* 821 F.2d 1147, 1165-66 (5th Cir. 1987); *Restatement (Second) Conflict of Laws* §84, comment c (1971) ("the action will not be dismissed unless a suitable alternative forum is available to the plaintiff," and "the suit will be entertained, no matter how inappropriate the forum may be, if the defendant cannot be subjected to jurisdiction in other states").

Which of these two positions in wiser?

3. ***Factors relevant to existence of adequate alternative forum.*** There is no precise definition in *Piper* or elsewhere of an "inadequate" foreign forum. U.S. courts have identified a variety of circumstances in which a foreign forum will be regarded as an inadequate alternative.

(a) *Effect of foreign forum's lack of subject matter jurisdiction.* The one example cited by *Piper* of an inadequate alternative forum was "where the alternative forum does not permit litigation of the subject matter of the dispute." Does this exception apply only when foreign law precludes "litigation of the subject matter of the dispute," and not when it merely limits the types of legal claims that can be successfully asserted in connection with the subject matter of the parties' dispute (as with plaintiffs' strict liability claims in *Piper* and *Wyeth*)? Courts have frequently permitted forum non conveniens dismissals even where the proffered alternative forum would not permit litigation of certain of the plaintiff's legal claims. *E.g., Dowling v. Richardson-Merrell, Inc.,* 727 F.2d 608, 615 (6th Cir. 1984) (the fact that "certain theories of tort recovery are not recognized" in alternative forum does not make the "remedy provided by the alternative forum ... clearly inadequate or unsatisfactory"); *Mercier v. Sheraton International, Inc.,* 935 F.2d 419 (1st Cir. 1991) ("a meaningful cause of action available in the proposed alternative forum"). Is it clear that this requirement was satisfied in *Piper?* in *Howe?* in *Laker?*

(b) *Effect of plaintiff's lack of access to foreign forum.* Plaintiffs sometimes lack effective access to a putative alternative forum. Obstacles to access can include (i) visa or immigration restrictions that the plaintiff cannot satisfy, (ii) outstanding criminal investigations or prosecutions of the plaintiff, (iii) the risk of being subject to service of process in other, unrelated civil actions, and (iv) the costs of travel and foreign counsel. How should each of these asserted obstacles be weighed? *E.g., Mercier v. Sheraton Int'l Inc.,* 744 F.Supp. 380 (D. Mass. 1990) (U.S. plaintiff unable to enter Turkey because of pending criminal charges), *rev'd on other grounds,* 935 F.2d 419 (1st Cir. 1991); *Fiorenza v. U.S. Steel Int'l,* 311 F.Supp. 117 (S.D.N.Y. 1969) (plaintiff denied entry to Bahamas for purposes of pursuing his suit).

(c) *Effect of foreign forum's lack of jurisdiction over defendants.* As *Piper* noted, the alternative forum requirement will "ordinarily" be satisfied "when the defendant is 'amenable to process' in the other jurisdiction." If the defendant is not subject to the alternative forum's personal jurisdiction, it will not be an adequate alternative. In practice, this requirement is seldom important; defendants seeking a forum non conveniens dismissal will usually agree to submit to the jurisdiction of the alternative forum as a condition of obtaining dismissal (as in *Bhopal* and *Fiacco*). *See infra* p. 356. Suppose that the foreign jurisdiction arguably will not base personal jurisdiction upon consent. What should the U.S. court do if it believes that forum non conveniens dismissal is desirable? *See infra* p. 356.

(d) *Effect of foreign forum's bias.* Some U.S. courts have held that particular foreign courts would be inadequate forums because of bias, corruption, or incompetence. *E.g., Rasoulzadeh v. Associated Press,* 574 F.Supp. 854 (S.D.N.Y. 1983), *aff'd,* 767 F.2d 908 (2d Cir. 1985); *Canadian Overseas Ores Ltd. v. Compania de Acero del Pacifico, SA,* 528 F.Supp. 1337, 1342-43 (S.D.N.Y. 1982) (plaintiff "has raised serious questions about the independence of the Chilean judiciary vis a vis the military junta currently in power [and] ... a significant doubt remains whether [plaintiff] could be assured of a fair trial in the Chilean courts in view of the fact that [defendant] is a state owned corporation"), *aff'd on other grounds,* 727 F.2d 1274 (2d Cir. 1984). In one lower court's formulation, no dismissal will be granted if the plaintiff shows that "conditions in the foreign forum ... plainly demonstrate that the plaintiffs are highly unlikely to obtain basic justice therein." *Vaz Borralho v. Keydril Co.,* 696 F.2d 379, 393-94 (5th Cir. 1983). It is only in the rarest cases that such findings will be made, and in most instances claims of bias are rejected out-of-hand. *E.g., Sussman v. Bank of Israel,* 801 F.Supp. 1068 (S.D.N.Y. 1992) ("plaintiffs' preference for an American court cannot be indulged on the basis of an American judge's speculation that his Israeli colleagues would violate their oaths of office"); *Murty v. Aga Khan,* 92 F.R.D. 478, 482 (E.D.N.Y. 1981) ("comity as well as common knowledge preclude our characterizing the French judicial system as any less fair than our own.").

Query whether it is appropriate for U.S. courts to sit in judgment upon the adequacy of foreign judicial systems. "It is not the business of our courts to assume the responsibility for supervising the integrity of the judicial system of another sovereign nation." *Chesley v. Union Carbide Corp.,* 927 F.2d 60, 66 (2d Cir. 1991) (quoting *Jhirad v. Ferrandina,* 536 F.2d 478, 484-85 (2d Cir.), *cert. denied,* 429 U.S. 833 (1976)). How would India have reacted if U.S. courts had concluded that the *Bhopal* case was too complex or sensitive for the Indian judicial system? On the other hand, if a U.S. court is (without statutory basis) to decline to exercise its statutory jurisdiction, must it not ensure that the alternative forum will obey basic standards of fairness? Is this a due process requirement?

(e) *Effect of differences between U.S. and foreign procedures.* As discussed elsewhere, U.S. civil procedure differs dramatically from that in foreign legal systems. Aspects of American procedure such as jury trials, a robust adversary system, cross-examination, broad party-directed discovery, contingent fees, no fee-shifting, and pro-plaintiff substantive laws are unusual in the international context. *See supra* pp. 3-7. *Bhopal* notes a number of these differences (even with a common law jurisdiction such as India), but concludes that they did not render India an inadequate alternative forum. Was *Bhopal* correct? Is not a jury trial, with cross-examination, a constitutional right? Should a discretionary rule of abstention be able to deny plaintiffs their constitutional rights?

U.S. courts are generally reluctant to deny dismissal merely because foreign procedures differ from those in the United States. *E.g., Lockman Found. v. Evangelical Alliance Mission,* 930 F.2d 764, 768 (9th Cir. 1991) (lack of jury trial does not render Japan inadequate forum); *Macedo v. Boeing Co.,* 693 F.2d 683, 688 (7th Cir. 1982) (absence of jury trial and punitive damages, limited pretrial discovery, and filing fees do not render Portugal inadequate forum); *Peabody Holding Co. v. Costain Group plc,* 808 F.Supp. 1425 (E.D. Mo. 1992) (absence of jury trial, pretrial depositions, and broad discovery of documents does not render England inadequate forum).

Nevertheless, significant procedural differences are occasionally central factors in decisions holding foreign forums inadequate. *Mobil Tankers Co. v. Mene Grande Oil Co.,* 363 F.2d 611, 614 (3d Cir.), *cert. denied,* 385 U.S. 945 (1966) (limited discovery rules and restrictions on expert witness testimony render foreign forum inadequate); *Fiorenza v. United States Steel Int'l,* 311 F.Supp. 117, 120-21 (S.D.N.Y. 1969) (lack of contingent fee arrangements renders foreign forum inadequate); *Waterways Ltd. v. Barclays Bank plc,* 571 N.Y.S.2d 208 (App. Div. 1991) (burden imposed on financially distressed plaintiff of litigating in forum that did not permit contingent fees held to warrant denial of forum non conveniens motion).

(f) *Statutory limit on recovery in foreign forum.* Suppose that foreign law imposes a flat limit on the amount recoverable by the plaintiff, but that U.S. law does not. Does such a limit render the foreign forum inadequate? Does the answer depend on the amount of the limit? *See Wolf v. Boeing Co.,* 810 F.2d 943 (Wash. Ct. App. 1991) ($10,000 limit under Mexican law in wrongful death action does not render Mexico inadequate forum). Consider *Castro Alfaro,* excerpted *supra* pp. 305-13, and especially *supra* p. 309 n.74. Suppose that each plaintiff could recover no more than $1,080.00 in Costa Rican courts for serious long-term medical complaints allegedly caused by defendants' hazardous chemicals. Would Costa Rican courts satisfy the adequate alternative forum requirement?

(g) *Effect of foreign forum's highly unfavorable laws.* As discussed above, *Piper* held that adverse changes in applicable law were ordinarily irrelevant to forum non conveniens analysis. However, *Piper* also concluded that adverse changes in applicable laws *would* be significant "if the remedy provided by the alternative forum is so clearly inadequate or unsatisfactory that it is no remedy at all." When will an adverse change in applicable law be so substantial that the plaintiff will have "no remedy at all" in the foreign forum? Must the plaintiff's claims fall outside the foreign court's jurisdiction? What if the plaintiff's claims are not recognized, and no alternative claims are either? What if the plaintiff's claims are virtually certain to fail in the foreign court (although they would have good prospects of success in the U.S.)? What if the plaintiff's claims are substantially less likely to succeed? What if the likely amount of a recovery by the plaintiff is much less (say, 90%) than in the U.S. forum? Where on this spectrum of adverse changes in law does any "remedy at all" cease to exist?

Consider Judge Greene's opinion in *Laker Airways.* Is it faithful to *Piper's* rule that adverse changes in law must be ignored? Consider the following passage:

> As for British substantive law, it fails entirely, for a number of reasons, to recognize liability for the acts which the defendants are alleged to have committed. That being so, this case is precisely within that group of cases which the Supreme Court in *Piper Aircraft* said should not be dismissed. It is difficult to see how it could be otherwise. It would be a cruel hoax on the plaintiff to oust it from a court where its allegations, if proved, would entitle it to recovery, and to relegate it instead, in the name of "convenience," to a tribunal which, on the facts alleged, would not be justified under its own laws in entering judgment in plaintiff's favor.

Was it not, under this reasoning, also a "cruel hoax" to dismiss the claims in *Piper* and *Wyeth*? Is a foreign state an inadequate forum merely because the plaintiff is very likely to lose?

How should one go about evaluating whether a foreign forum is "so clearly inadequate or unsatisfactory that it is no remedy at all"? Does "no remedy at all" mean that the plaintiff must have 0% chances of recovery? If not, can a percentage likelihood of success be identified that constitutes "no remedy"? — say, 20%? 10%? Does it make sense to speak in black-and-white terms of "adequate alternative forums" and ignore "changes in substantive laws"? Is it more accurate to view a plaintiff as having greater or lesser probabilities of recovering greater or lesser amounts of money in two or more alternative forums? Should efforts be made to compare the plaintiff's likelihood of success or discounted recovery in its chosen forum and in the alternative forum? Would it not be sensible to do this, and then to compare those numbers with the estimated cost savings to each party from a forum non conveniens dismissal?

4. *Relevance of parties' nationality to adequate alternative forum analysis.* Suppose that in *Bhopal* the parties' positions on the forum non conveniens issue had been reversed. That is, suppose that Union Carbide had brought suit in the United States seeking a declaration that it was not liable for the disaster, and the Indian government (and Indian plaintiffs) had moved for forum non conveniens dismissal to India. Would the district court's analysis set forth above have been any less applicable? Would you be willing to force Union Carbide to litigate in India — given the limits described above on Indian discovery, jury trials, substantive law, and the like?

Is it not an ironic position, for a U.S. party to extol the benefits of a foreign legal system, while foreign plaintiffs attack it? Although not strictly applicable, does this not raise considerations of waiver and estoppel? Absent some specific bias directed at a foreign entity by its own courts, should it have standing to criticize the adequacy of those courts? Suppose that the plaintiffs in *Bhopal* had been U.S. nationals, working at the ill-fated plant, when the disaster struck. Suppose further that they sued Union Carbide in the United States. Would the same adequate alternative forum analysis apply to them? What would be the relevance of the Indian restrictions on discovery, jury trials, contingent fee arrangements, and the like?

5. *Public policy objections to forum non conveniens dismissals of statutory claims.* In many aspects of international litigation, general rules are subject to public policy exceptions. Examples include the enforceability of forum selection clauses (*infra* pp. 414-30); arbitration agreements (*infra* pp. 1016-29); choice of law (*infra* pp. 624-31 & 655-56); and foreign judgments (*infra* pp. 974-86). Should the forum non conveniens doctrine similarly be subject to a public policy exception, where compelling forum interests override generally applicable rules? Do you think that Congress intended for federal antitrust, securities, and RICO claims to be capable of dismissal to foreign courts on grounds of "convenience"? Would refusals to apply the forum non conveniens doctrine to statutory claims be consistent with *Piper's* holding that changes in substantive law are ordinarily irrelevant to forum non conveniens analysis?

6. *Refusal of courts to apply foreign "penal" and "revenue" laws — an initial view.* Note the remark in *Laker* that English courts "could not and would not enforce the American antitrust laws." As discussed in greater detail below, it has often been said that one nation's courts will not apply the penal or revenue laws of another nation. *See infra* pp. 629-30 & 955-60; *Holman v. Johnson,* 98 Eng. Rep. 1120, 1121 (1775) ("no country ever takes notice of the revenue laws of another"); *Banco Nacional de Cuba v. Sabbatino,* 376 U.S. 398, 413-14 (1964) ("a court need not give effect to the penal or revenue law of foreign countries"). Why is that? England, like the United States and most other countries, has choice of law rules, that frequently lead to the application of foreign law by English courts. Why wouldn't these rules require application of the U.S. antitrust laws?

7. *Applicability of forum non conveniens doctrine to federal antitrust claims.* Why is it, according to *Laker,* that antitrust claims cannot be subject to forum non conveniens dismissals? Note its characterization of the Sherman Act as "our charter of economic liberty," and its view that "[a]ntitrust cases are unlike litigation involving contracts, torts, and other matters recognized in some form in every nation."

(a) *Absence of any specific statutory prohibition on forum non conveniens.* Does anything in the text of the antitrust laws forbid forum non conveniens dismissals? Does *Laker* rely on any specific statutory provision to justify its result? Consider the argument that was unsuccessfully made in *Howe* — the "special venue" provisions in the federal securities laws indicate that Congress wished to guarantee plaintiffs the right to pursue their actions in particular "special" forums without risk of transfer or forum non conveniens dismissal. *Howe* rejects that argument. Does *Laker* rely on the venue provisions of the antitrust laws?

(b) *Relevance of U.S. legislation's "importance."* As noted above, *Laker* referred to the U.S. antitrust laws as a charter of economic liberty, comparable to the Bill of Rights. Does this mean that only claims under "extraordinary" congressional enactments will be immune from forum non conveniens dismissal? Is there any principled way to distinguish federal statutes in terms of importance? Can one distinguish between statutes in any way that is relevant to forum non conveniens analysis?

(c) *Relevance of parallel foreign remedies.* As noted above, *Laker* emphasized that English courts would not apply the antitrust laws, and that applicable English law would "fail" to grant the plaintiff a successful claim. Suppose the defendant in a U.S. antitrust action could show that the proffered foreign alternative forum would apply federal antitrust statutes. For example, suppose there was evidence in *Laker* that the English courts would have applied U.S. antitrust laws. Should Judge Greene still have refused to dismiss the suit? Suppose that English courts would not have applied U.S. antitrust laws, but they would have applied English or European laws that were broadly similar. Would the *Laker* analysis still apply? Note that this was the situation in *Howe* — Canadian courts would have applied Canadian law that was broadly similar to the federal securities laws. Is *Howe* correctly decided? Should not a U.S. court refuse to dismiss unless the foreign court will apply U.S. statutory law (and not some foreign imitation)?

(d) *Analogy to forum selection clauses.* Consider the analysis in *Mitsubishi Motors Corp. v. Soler Chrysler-Plymouth Inc.*, 473 U.S. 614 (1987), and in *Roby v. Corporation of Lloyds*, 996 F.2d 1353 (2d Cir. 1993), excerpted below at *infra* pp. 418-23. There, the courts held that arbitration agreements and forum selection clauses would be enforced as to federal statutory claims, *provided* that the claims (or a reasonable foreign analogue) would be considered abroad. *See infra* pp. 428-29. Is this a sensible way to approach public policy issues in the forum non conveniens context? Should it be easier or harder to get forum non conveniens dismissal of an antitrust claim than to enforce a foreign forum clause as to such claim? *See infra* pp. 414-30.

(e) *Relevance of choice of law analysis to public policy analysis.* Most of the disputed conduct in *Howe* occurred in Canada. Is it clear that the federal securities laws would have actually applied to that conduct? This is an issue that is examined in detail below. *See infra* pp. 607-15. For present purposes, it is enough to say that there would have been doubts that U.S. securities laws applied to the challenged conduct, because it lacked substantial contacts with the United States. Contrast *Laker,* where it was substantially clearer that the U.S. antitrust laws applied to the defendants' conduct (because it occurred in part in Florida and because it affected air service to and from the United States).

Are these choice of law considerations relevant to the forum non conveniens analysis? Although neither *Howe* nor *Laker* expressly considered them, note that both courts went to some lengths to describe where the disputed conduct occurred. Note also the discussion of U.S. and foreign interests in regulating the allegedly wrongful conduct. Both the location of the disputed conduct and the competing national interests are key considerations in contemporary U.S. choice of law standards. *See infra* pp. 631-51.

Suppose that, in *Howe,* the two target companies had been in the United States. Further, suppose that Goldcorp had conducted two meetings in New York with representatives of the U.S. shareholders to explain its acquisition plans, and that allegedly fraudulent statements were made at these meetings. That conduct would have provided a much more substantial basis for application of the federal securities laws. Under Judge (now Justice) Breyer's analysis, would the case have been decided any differently? Should it have? Suppose that, in *Laker,* Laker had flown on London-Mexico City routes, but not on routes to the United States, and that no allegedly wrongful conduct had occurred within the United States. Would that have affected Judge Greene's analysis? Should it have?

Suppose that U.S. choice of law rules would lead to the application of U.S. law to a U.S. plaintiff's claims against a foreign defendant. Suppose that foreign choice of law rules would lead to the application of foreign law, and that this law was less favorable to the U.S. plaintiff. In these circumstances, is the adverse change in applicable law relevant? What does *Piper* say? What if the foreign forum would apply its own law in circumstances that would violate U.S. due process limits on legislative jurisdiction? *See infra* pp. 512-44.

8. *Applicability of forum non conveniens to federal securities and RICO claims.* In contrast to *Laker's* treatment of antitrust claims, lower courts have unanimously held that federal securities and RICO claims are capable of dismissal on forum non conveniens grounds. *See supra* pp. 342-43. *Howe* is one example of such a decision. Why should the forum non conveniens doctrine apply in a different way to antitrust claims than to securities claims? Is it because, as *Howe* suggests, foreign courts are more likely to apply either federal securities laws or some closely-similar foreign law, than they are to apply the federal antitrust laws or some foreign analogue? If so, does this affect analysis? (Note that the court's generalization about antitrust and securities laws is not accurate: many foreign states (including the European Union, Germany, Japan, and England) have competition laws that are at least as well-developed as their securities law. Of course, these laws may not always produce the same results as the U.S. antitrust laws, but under *Piper* this should not matter.)

9. *Application of forum non conveniens doctrine when federal statutory claims are involved.* Even assuming that the doctrine of forum non conveniens did "apply" in antitrust cases, might not courts generally conclude that the public interest factors weighed against dismissal of such claims? How would a forum non conveniens analysis apply to federal statutory claims? How would public interest considera-

tions be dealt with? Does *Howe* afford special weight to federal statutory claims? Would it be better, under the "flexible" *Piper* analysis, to weigh the existence of federal statutory rights in the overall "public interest" inquiry? How would *Laker* have been decided if a forum non conveniens analysis had been applied?

10. *Conditions on forum non conveniens dismissals.* In both *Wyeth* and *Bhopal*, the courts conditioned their grants of forum non conveniens dismissals on the defendant's acceptance of certain "conditions." This is a common practice. See *supra* p. 343. It is designed to ensure that an adequate alternative forum exists, by removing obstacles such as lack of personal jurisdiction, statutes of limitations, and the like. Is the forum non conveniens analysis fairly conducted if a U.S. court in effect alters the legal standards that will apply in the foreign forum? Is it not comparing apples and oranges? Moreover, does the practice of imposing conditions interfere with the sovereignty of foreign states? Should plaintiffs be permitted to offer "conditions" on their U.S. trial tactics — such as limiting discovery, waiving punitive damages, and the like?

(a) *Requirement that defendants consent to personal jurisdiction in foreign forum.* *Wyeth* and *Bhopal* required that the defendants submit to the personal jurisdiction of the foreign forum at issue. In general, this requirement seems unobjectionable. The trial court must, of course, satisfy itself that the defendant's consent will be a sufficient basis for the proffered foreign court to assert jurisdiction, and should not dismiss if this is not the case. *Schertenleib v. Traum,* 589 F.2d 1156, 1163 (2d Cir. 1978) ("the district court should not dismiss ... unless it justifiably believes that the alternative forum will take jurisdiction, if the defendant consents"). A few courts have conditioned dismissal on the foreign forum actually taking jurisdiction over the plaintiff's substitute action, or provided mechanisms for the plaintiffs to refile in the U.S. forum if the foreign court does not assume jurisdiction. *Mercier v. Sheraton Int'l, Inc.,* 935 F.2d 419 (1st Cir. 1991); *Dowling v. Hyland Therapeutics Division,* 767 F.Supp. 57, 60 (S.D.N.Y. 1991). If a foreign court nonetheless declines jurisdiction, the plaintiff's U.S. action could be refiled. *Macedo v. Boeing Co.,* 693 F.2d 683, 687 (7th Cir. 1982) ("if there is any real possibility of a rejection of plaintiffs' case ... for lack of jurisdiction, plaintiffs are protected by reinstatement of their case here"). How would this affect statutory limitations periods?

(b) *Jurisdiction over U.S. parent.* In both *Bhopal* and *Wyeth*, plaintiffs sought to sue a U.S. parent company in a dispute occurring in a foreign nation that arose almost entirely from the acts of a foreign subsidiary of the U.S. parent. Is it appropriate for U.S. courts to require U.S. parent companies, in these circumstances, to submit themselves to a foreign nation's jurisdiction — where those foreign states might well not otherwise have judicial jurisdiction over the U.S. parent company? If a foreign state chooses to structure its regulatory and judicial systems in such a fashion that local subsidiaries are regulated and subject to civil actions — but their foreign shareholders are not — why should U.S. courts interfere? As long as the subsidiary is adequately capitalized, why should the plaintiff be provided with a claim against the U.S. parent? If the forum non conveniens doctrine permits a plaintiff to be denied some of its claims, why should it not also allow the plaintiff to be denied some of its defendants — especially where those which it cannot pursue are ones that U.S. law says it has no right to pursue?

(c) *Requirement that defendant waive statute of limitations defense.* As in *Wyeth* and *Bhopal,* courts have frequently required that defendants waive statute of limitations defenses in the alternative foreign forum. Is this an appropriate condition? The plaintiffs could have filed suit in what was clearly the convenient forum, but chose not to. Moreover, the plaintiffs generally could have made a protective filing in the alternative forum to safeguard their position, but did not. If it is appropriate to require waivers of statutes of limitations defenses, why shouldn't U.S. courts also require waivers of "reasonable care" defenses, so as to create a strict liability regime in the foreign forum? If this is inappropriate, how is a statute of limitations waiver different?

(d) *Requirement that defendant consent to U.S.-style discovery.* Following *Piper's* suggestion, *Wyeth* and *Bhopal* required that the defendant consent to providing the same documents and witnesses in the foreign litigation as would have been required in a U.S. litigation. See *De Melo v. Lederle Offshore Co.,* 753 F.2d 1058 (8th Cir. 1986); *Ali v. Offshore Co.,* 753 F.2d 1327 (5th Cir. 1985). Is this condition consistent with the rationale for the forum non conveniens doctrine? Is it consistent with the respect for foreign regulatory and judicial systems referred to in *Piper* and in *Wyeth?* Did the court in either case require the plaintiff also to give U.S.-style discovery to the defendant? Is it appropriate to have one-sided discovery? The district court's discovery condition was reversed by the Second Circuit in *Union Carbide,* 809 F.2d 195 (2d Cir. 1987), because of its one-sided character. See also *Doe v. Hyland Therapeutics Division,* 807 F.Supp. 1117 (S.D.N.Y. 1992).

There is also the risk that plaintiffs will file suit in inconvenient U.S. forums, in part with the expectation of obtaining a U.S.-style discovery condition even if their actions are dismissed on forum non conveniens grounds: as one court has observed, "we share defendants' concern that this District not become a way-station for plaintiffs world-wide, who choose to stop at Foley Square just long enough to obtain a grant of federal discovery with their forum non conveniens dismissal." *Doe v. Hyland Therapeutics Division*, 807 F.Supp. 1117 (S.D.N.Y. 1992). Note, however, that *Piper* appeared to bless U.S.-style discovery conditions. *See supra* p. 304 n.70.

(e) *Requirement that defendant pay any foreign judgment.* Both *Wyeth* and *Bhopal* required the defendant to agree to satisfy any foreign judgment that might be rendered in the alternative forum. Is it appropriate to condition a forum non conveniens dismissal on the defendant's commitment to pay any foreign judgment? Note that there are ample opportunities for enforcing foreign judgments in U.S. courts. *See* Chapter 12. What if the foreign proceedings turn out to be conducted in a way that is blatantly biased against the defendant? For example, press articles reported that the initial Indian trial judge in *Bhopal* had secretly filed a claim for damages against Union Carbide in the case over which he was presiding. A subsequent judge ordered Union Carbide to make a $190 million payment to Bhopal victims, before deciding whether Union Carbide was liable; the company condemned the action as "a judgment and decree without trial." *The Wall Street Journal*, May 18, 1988, at 33.

(f) *Miscellaneous other conditions.* Miscellaneous other conditions have been fashioned to meet the needs of particular cases. For example, conditions have been imposed requiring an undertaking from foreign governmental officials not to detain the plaintiff if he prosecuted his action in that nation, *Sussman v. Bank of Israel*, 990 F.2d 71, 71 (2d Cir. 1993); requiring that the foreign forum act within a specified time period on the plaintiff's request for provisional measures, *Borden, Inc. v. Meiji Milk Products Co.*, 919 F.2d 822, 829 (2d Cir. 1990), *cert. denied*, 500 U.S. 953 (1991); requiring acceptance of service of process, *Constructora Spilimerg, CA v. Mitsubishi Aircraft Co.*, 700 F.2d 225, 226 (5th Cir. 1983); and requiring that the defendant post security, *Great Prize, SA v. Mariner Shipping Pty.*, 1993 U.S. Dist. Lexis 1086 (E.D. La. 1993).

(g) *No conditions requiring foreign court to entertain particular claims.* U.S. courts have thus far *not* conditioned forum non conveniens dismissals on the alternative forum's willingness to entertain a particular cause of action. It would be possible, at least in principle, for a U.S. court to condition dismissal upon a foreign court's application of U.S. strict products liability standards or U.S. antitrust law. U.S. courts have imposed such conditions upon orders compelling parties to international arbitration. *E.g.*, *PPG Industries, Inc. v. Pilkington, plc*, 825 F.Supp. 1465 (D. Ariz. 1993) ("the Court directs that any damages determination, or arbitral award, made by the arbitrators shall be determined according to U.S. antitrust law irrespective of any conflict that may exist between those laws and the laws of England [the arbitral situs]"); G. Born, *International Commercial Arbitration in the United States* 375-82 (1994). Where foreign courts, rather than arbitral tribunals, are involved, U.S. penal legislation might well not be enforced. *See supra* p. 354 & *infra* pp. 629-31. Moreover, a U.S. court-ordered condition addressing the law applicable in a foreign court would be perceived as interference with the foreign court's functioning. Are these sufficient reasons not to protect a plaintiff's statutory rights?

11. *Forum non conveniens and the FSIA.* The Supreme Court has suggested (albeit in dictum) that the forum non conveniens doctrine remains applicable, under the FSIA. *Verlinden BV v. Central Bank of Nigeria*, 461 U.S. 480, 490 n.15 (1983) ("the [FSIA] does not appear to affect the traditional doctrine of *forum non conveniens*"). Lower courts have thus permitted defendants to raise the defense of *forum non conveniens* in actions against foreign states under the FSIA. *E.g.*, *Forsythe v. Saudi Arabian Airlines Corp.*, 885 F.2d 285 (5th Cir. 1989); *Gould, Inc. v. Pechiney Ugine Kuhlmann*, 853 F.2d 445 (6th Cir. 1988); *Proyecfin de Venezuela v. Banco Industrial de Venezuela*, 760 F.2d 390, 394 (2d Cir. 1985). Does the fact that the defendant is a foreign state entity affect forum non conveniens analysis? Does it affect the question whether an adequate alternative forum exists?

E. The Contemporary Forum Non Conveniens Doctrine: Applicable Law and the *Erie* Doctrine

As discussed elsewhere, the *Erie* doctrine generally requires federal courts sitting in diversity actions to apply the substantive law of the states where they sit, except where a valid federal statute, regulation, or other law applies.[104] No federal "forum non conveniens" statute exists,[105] and it is therefore at least arguable that forum non conveniens issues should be governed by state law in federal diversity actions (and in state courts). Even if no federal statute or regulation is applicable, the *Erie* doctrine permits federal courts to fashion federal law governing various "procedural" issues;[106] these rules are applicable only in federal courts, and not in state courts.[107] In limited circumstances, federal courts also have the power to fashion substantive federal common law, which preempts inconsistent state law; these rules are applicable in both federal and state courts.[108]

Applying these general principles, there are three basic possibilities for defining the character of the forum non conveniens doctrine under *Erie*: (1) state substantive law, applicable in both state and federal courts; (2) federal procedural law, applicable in federal courts, and state law, applicable in state courts; and (3) substantive federal common law, applicable in both federal and state courts. We explore each possibility below.[109]

The character of the forum non conveniens doctrine can have substantial practical significance. A number of states have adopted approaches to the forum non conveniens doctrine that differ from the *Piper* analysis.[110] In a few states, no forum non conveniens doctrine is recognized; in others, the doctrine is subject to different basic rules (such as the weight to be accorded a U.S. or foreign plaintiff's choice of forum).[111] Although application of the forum non conveniens doctrine involves substantial discretion, the differences between particular state versions of the doctrine and *Piper* can be outcome-determinative.

The Supreme Court has thus far avoided directly deciding the status of the forum non conveniens doctrine under the *Erie* doctrine, although it recently provided an arguable indication as to its likely conclusion. In both *Piper* and *Gilbert*, the Court specifically declined to decide whether state or federal law provided the applic-

---

104. *Erie R.R. Co. v. Tompkins*, 304 U.S. 64 (1938); *Stewart Organization, Inc. v. Ricoh Corp.*, 487 U.S. 22 (1988); *supra* pp. 13-14.

105. 28 U.S.C. §1404(a) applies only to transfers between federal districts (and not to dismissals in favor of foreign forums). *See infra* pp. 431-33.

106. *See supra* pp. 13-14; *Stewart Organization, Inc. v. Ricoh Corp.*, 487 U.S. 22 (1988).

107. *See supra* pp. 13-14;

108. *See supra* pp. 15-16; *Boyle v. United Technologies Corp.*, 487 U.S. 500, 504 (1988).

109. *See infra* pp. 359-66.

110. *See infra* pp. 365-66.

111. *See infra* pp. 365-66.

able forum non conveniens principles in a federal diversity case.[112] In each case, the Court concluded that the relevant state law was identical to the result that it reached as a matter of federal law.[113]

In 1994, however, the Court decided *American Dredging Company v. Miller*.[114] There, it arguably suggested that the forum non conveniens doctrine is a rule of federal procedural law, applicable in federal (but not state) courts. The Court's holding was directed at, and apparently limited to, domestic cases. Nevertheless, its rationale may apply in international cases.

In *American Dredging*, the Court considered whether a state court was bound to apply the federal doctrine of forum non conveniens in a domestic admiralty action. The Court acknowledged that in the admiralty context federal maritime law preempted state law in ways not true (after *Erie*) in diversity actions: general federal admiralty law preempts state laws that "work material prejudice to the characteristic features of the general maritime law or interferes with the proper harmony and uniformity of that law in its international and interstate relations."[115] The Court nevertheless concluded that there was no basis for fashioning a substantive federal doctrine of forum non conveniens in state court domestic admiralty actions, reasoning that forum non conveniens was not a peculiarly maritime doctrine and that there was no pressing need for domestic uniformity.[116]

American Dredging leaves state courts free to ignore federal forum non conveniens principles and apply state law in domestic admiralty actions. Moreover, the Court also suggested that federal courts were free to continue to apply a federal forum non conveniens doctrine; the rationale was that the doctrine was a "procedural" rule. In Justice Scalia's words: "[Forum non conveniens] is procedural rather than substantive."[117] He continued, reasoning that, "[a]t bottom, the doctrine of forum non conveniens is nothing more or less than a supervening venue provision, permitting displacement of the ordinary rules of venue when, in light of certain conditions, the trial court thinks that jurisdiction ought to be declined. But venue is a matter that goes to process rather than substantive rights — determining which among various competent courts will decide the case."[118]

In the last paragraph of its opinion, the Court observed that *American Dredging*

---

112. *See Piper Aircraft Co. v. Reyno*, 454 U.S. at 248 n.13; *Gulf Oil Corp. v. Gilbert*, 330 U.S. at 509. In one subsequent decision the Court also avoided passing directly on the subject. *Chick Kam Choo v. Exxon Corp.*, 486 U.S. 140 (1988).

113. In each case, the Court had to strain to find that the relevant state law was identical to federal law. Braucher, *The Inconvenient Federal Forum*, 60 Harv. L. Rev. 908, 928 (1947) (noting that lower courts in *Koster* had concluded that state law was different and that in *Gilbert* directly relevant state precedents were contrary).

114. 114 S.Ct. 981 (1994).

115. 114 S.Ct. at 985 (quoting *Southern Pacific Co. v. Jensen*, 244 U.S. 205, 216 (1917)).

116. 114 S.Ct. at 987-90.

117. 114 S.Ct. at 988.

118. 114 S.Ct. at 988.

only involved domestic entities, and that the proferred alternative forum was in the United States. Nevertheless, the Court declined the Solicitor General's request to limit its holding to cases involving domestic entities: "We think it unnecessary to do that. Since the parties to this suit are domestic entities it is quite impossible for our holding to be any broader."[119]

After *American Dredging*, it can be argued that the forum non conveniens doctrine will be regarded by the Court as a rule of federal procedural law in international cases. On the other hand, it is also arguable that federal interests in foreign commerce and foreign relations provide the basis for a substantive federal common law rule of forum non conveniens.[120] But, if federal interests in uniform domestic admiralty rules were an insufficient basis for rules of federal common law, reaching a different result in international cases will require attributing substantial weight to federal interests in foreign relations and foreign commerce.

Excerpted below is an early appellate decision in *Sibaja v. Dow Chemical Co.*, which presaged the *American Dredging* analysis. In reading the decision, keep in mind the vital importance of forum selection in international litigation. Also reread *Sequihua v. Texaco Oil, Inc.*, which is discussed above.

SIBAJA v. DOW CHEMICAL COMPANY

757 F.2d 1215 (11th Cir. 1985)

PER CURIAM. The district court dismissed this diversity case under the doctrine of forum non conveniens. The plaintiffs appeal, claiming that the *Erie* doctrine required the court to apply the state forum non conveniens rule which would have precluded the dismissal. We affirm.

The plaintiffs are fifty-eight Costa Rican agricultural workers. They claim to have been sterilized as a result of their exposure in Costa Rica to pesticides manufactured by either Dow Chemical Company or Shell Oil Company. In May 1983, they sued these companies in Florida state court, seeking damages under product liability theories of negligence, strict liability in tort and implied warranty. The Florida court had personal jurisdiction over the defendants because they were qualified to transact business in the State of Florida. Fla. Stat. §48.091 (1983).[121]

The defendants removed the case to the U.S. District Court for the Southern District of Florida, pursuant to 28 U.S.C. §1332(a)(2) (1982), and, thereafter, moved to dismiss the action on the ground of forum non conveniens. They argued that the plaintiffs should prosecute their claims in the courts of Costa Rica: the plaintiffs are Costa Rican citizens; they were injured in Costa Rica; and substantially all of the evi-

---

119. 114 S.Ct. at 990.

120. *See infra* pp. 365-66.

121. Dow Chemical Company and Shell Oil Company are major international corporations. They are subject to jurisdiction over their persons in the courts of every state and several foreign countries, including Costa Rica. The plaintiffs chose to sue them in Florida.

dence and witnesses are in Costa Rica. Furthermore, Florida's choice of law rule would require the district court to apply the substantive law of Costa Rica.

The plaintiffs, in response, argued that the *Erie* doctrine requires a federal district court, sitting in a diversity case, to apply the state forum non conveniens rule rather than the federal rule. Florida precludes the dismissal of an action under the doctrine, where one of the parties is a resident, *Waite v. Summit Leasing & Capital International Corp.*, 441 So.2d 185, 185 (Fla. Dist. Ct. App. 1983);[122] therefore, the plaintiffs continued, the district court transgressed the *Erie* rule in dismissing the action.

The district court, after weighing the traditional forum non conveniens factors, concluded that the convenience of the parties, the witnesses and the court, and the interests of justice, dictated that the case be dismissed, and it granted the defendants' motion. In appealing, the plaintiffs do not dispute the district court's interpretation of the doctrine, as it has been applied in the federal courts, and they do not dispute the court's weighing of the relevant factors. They also do not dispute that this case presents a paradigm for the invocation of the doctrine. Their argument is, purely, that *Erie* requires the application of the state rule because this is a diversity case.

The doctrine of forum non conveniens authorizes a trial court to decline to exercise its jurisdiction, even though the court has venue, where it appears that the convenience of the parties and the court, and the interests of justice indicate that the action should be tried in another forum. The doctrine derives from the court's inherent power, under article III of the Constitution, to control the administration of the litigation before it and to prevent its process from becoming an instrument of abuse, injustice and oppression. As the Supreme Court observed nearly 100 years ago, "the equitable powers of courts of law over their own process, to prevent abuses, oppression, and injustice, are inherent and equally extensive and efficient." *Gumbel v. Pitkin*, 124 U.S. 131, 144 (1888).

The doctrine of forum non conveniens is but one manifestation of that inherent power. The doctrine addresses "whether the actions brought are vexatious or oppressive or whether the interests of justice require that the trial be had in a more appropriate forum." *Koster v. Lumbermens Mutual Casualty Co.* Under the federal standard, "dismissal will ordinarily be appropriate where trial in the plaintiff's chosen forum imposes a heavy burden on the defendant or the court, and where the plaintiff is unable to offer any specific reasons of convenience supporting his choice." *Piper Aircraft Co.*

The court's inherent power to protect the integrity of its process through forum non conveniens is similar to the court's inherent power to punish contempt. Of the latter, the Supreme Court has written:

---

122. The other states of the Union would, apparently, apply the doctrine and dismiss the case under the circumstances presented here. *See, e.g., Alcoa Steamship Co. v. M/V Nordic Regent,* 654 F.2d 147, 155 n. 10 (2d Cir. 1980) ("[a]pparently the only state where the court of last resort has continued to reject the doctrine [of forum non conveniens] as a matter of law is Florida").

"It is essential to the administration of justice. The courts of the United States, when called into existence and vested with jurisdiction over any subject, at once become possessed of the power. So far as the inferior federal courts are concerned, however, it is not beyond the authority of Congress; but the attributes which inhere in that power and are inseparable from it can neither be abrogated nor rendered practically inoperative. That it may be regulated within limits not precisely defined may not be doubted."

We think this statement applies with equal force to the authority of a federal district court to dismiss an action for want of an appropriate forum.

The Court's interest in controlling its crowded docket also provides a basis for the Court's inherent power to dismiss on grounds of forum non conveniens. ... "Administrative difficulties follow for courts when litigation is piled up in congested centers instead of being handled at its origin. Jury duty is a burden that ought not to be imposed upon the people of a community which has no relation to the litigation." *Gulf Oil Corp. v. Gilbert.* ...

The plaintiffs acknowledge, as they must, the court's inherent power to dismiss a case for the purposes expressed in the doctrine. They insist, however, that *Erie* precludes a court from invoking this power if its invocation would control the "outcome" of the parties' controversy. The *Erie* rule holds that neither Congress nor the courts have the constitutional authority to promulgate the substantive rule of law that controls the controversy in a diversity case:

There is no federal general common law. Congress has no power to declare substantive rules of common law applicable in a state whether they be local in their nature or "general," be they commercial law or a part of the law of torts. And no clause in the Constitution purports to confer such a power upon the federal courts.

Erie Railroad v. Tompkins. It is obvious that the district court here, in deciding the merits of the defendants' motions to dismiss, did not explicitly promulgate a state common law rule. The question thus becomes whether the court did so by implication. We think not.

We recognize that the application of the federal, rather than the state, forum non conveniens rule alters the outcome of this case. Under Florida law, the plaintiffs would litigate their claims to a conclusion on the merits; under federal law, they are precluded from reaching the merits. They are, in effect, consigned to the Costa Rican courts for trial. This does not mean, however, that, in dismissing their case, the federal court fashioned a state substantive rule in violation of *Erie.*

The forum non conveniens doctrine is a rule of venue, not a rule of decision. The doctrine provides "simply that a court may resist imposition upon its jurisdiction even when jurisdiction is authorized by the letter of [the law]." *Gulf Oil Corp. v. Gilbert.* In contrast, "rules of decision" are the "substantive" law of the state, the "legal rules [which] determine the outcome of a litigation." *Guaranty Trust Co. v. York*, 326 U.S. 99, 109 (1945). It is true that a judge-made rule may qualify as a rule of decision if it substantially affects the "character or result of a litigation." *Hanna v. Plumer,* 380 U.S. 460, 467 (1965). But the trial court's decision, under the circumstances presented here, whether to exercise its jurisdiction and decide the case was not a decision going to the character and result of the controversy. Rather, it was a decision that occurred before, and completely apart from, any application of state substantive law. A trial court only reaches the state rule of decision, relating to the character and result of the litigation, once it has decided to try the case and determine whether the plaintiff has a valid claim for relief. We hold, accordingly, that the district court's application of the doctrine of forum non conveniens in this case did not operate as a state substantive rule of law and thus transgress *Erie*'s constitutional prohibition.[123]

SEQUIHUA v. TEXACO, INC.

847 F.Supp. 61 (S.D. Tex. 1994) [excerpted supra pp. 51-52]

Notes on Sibaja and Sequihua

1. *Forum non conveniens as a rule of substantive state law.* The plaintiffs in *Sibaja* argued that, under *Erie,* the forum non conveniens doctrine should be governed by state substantive law. A few federal court decisions (usually older ones) have adopted this view. *E.g., Weiss v. Routh,* 149 F.2d 193 (2d Cir. 1945) (L. Hand, J.); *Mizokami Bros. v. Mobay Chem. Corp.,* 483 F.Supp. 201 (W.D. Mo. 1980), *aff'd,* 660 F.2d 712 (8th Cir. 1981). Consider Learned Hand's argument for why state substantive law should govern forum non conveniens issues in federal court:

> It might well be argued that those considerations which will set a court in motion are peculiar and personal to itself, and that it does not follow that what is enough to move a state court to act, should be enough to move a federal; or vice versa. Such a doctrine would, however, imply that the decision to accept jurisdiction is not controlled by any principle and may be at the judge's whim; and that would certainly be too strong a statement. Here, as elsewhere, although judicial discretion does indeed imply that the limits are not rigidly fixed, it does not mean that there are none; and in dealing with the questions at bar, we are to remember the purpose of conformity in "diversity cases." It is that the accident of citizenship shall not change the outcome: a purpose which extends as much to determining whether the court shall act at all, as to how it shall decide, if it does. For this reason it seems to us that we should follow the New York decisions. *Weiss v. Routh,* 149 F.2d 193, 194-95 (2d Cir. 1945).

Is this persuasive? Given the vital bearing of the forum non conveniens doctrine on many international disputes, don't the objectives of the *Erie* doctrine require application of local state law?

2. *Forum non conveniens as a rule of federal procedural law.* Like the Eleventh Circuit in *Sibaja,* most courts have concluded that in federal courts the forum non conveniens doctrine is defined by federal procedural law. *See In re Air Crash Disaster Near New Orleans,* 821 F.2d 1147, 1154-59 (5th Cir. 1987) ("the interests of the federal forum in self-regulation, in administrative independence, and in self-management are more important than the disruption of uniformity created by applying federal forum non conveniens in diversity cases"), *reinstated in part,* 883 F.2d 17 (5th Cir. 1989); *Founding Church of Scientology v. Verlag,* 536 F.2d 429, 434 n.13 (D.C. Cir. 1976). Moreover, as noted above, the Supreme Court has suggested, in *American Dredging Co. v. Miller,* 114 S.Ct. 981 (1994), that forum non conveniens is a procedur-

---

123. The plaintiffs' claim that the district court's action violated the Rules of Decision Act, 28 U.S.C. §1652 (1982), is plainly foreclosed by the foregoing analysis. That act provides: "The laws of the several states, except where the Constitution or treaties of the United States or Acts of Congress otherwise require or provide, shall be regarded as rules of decision in civil actions in the courts of the United States, in cases where they apply."

al issue in domestic actions, governed in state courts by state law, and in federal courts by federal procedural law.

3. *Should forum non conveniens be regarded as a rule of federal procedural law?* Is the *Sibaja* analysis persuasive? Why is it, according to the Eleventh Circuit, that federal courts should apply a federal rule of forum non conveniens? Recall that issues of forum selection are often outcome-determinative; parties devote enormous resources to influencing forum selection and, in many cases, the forum in which a dispute is heard has a decisive effect on its resolution. *See supra* pp. 3-7. In at least some states, a local citizen enjoys a fundamental right of access to the local courts. *See supra* pp. 305-13. In these circumstances, is it persuasive to permit judge-made notions of judicial administration to override state law?

(a) *Argument in* American Dredging *that forum non conveniens is "procedural." American Dredging Co.* reasoned that:

> [Forum non conveniens] is procedural rather than substantive, and it is most unlikely to produce uniform results. ... At bottom, the doctrine of forum non conveniens is nothing more or less than a supervening venue provision, permitting displacement of the ordinary rules of venue when, in light of certain conditions, the trial court thinks that jurisdiction ought to be declined. But venue is a matter that goes to process rather than substantive rights — determining which among various competent courts will decide the case. ... [T]o tell the truth, forum non conveniens cannot really be *relied* upon in making decisions about secondary conduct — in deciding, for example, where to sue or where one is subject to being sued. The discretionary nature of the doctrine, combined with the multifariousness of the factors relevant to its application ... make uniformity and predictability of outcome almost impossible.

Is this persuasive? Does it explain satisfactorily why issues of forum non conveniens are to be decided differently in federal courts than in state courts? Does anything in *Sibaja* or *American Dredging* meet Learned Hand's argument, excerpted above? Consider the following:

> Matters of "substance" and matters of "procedure" are much talked about in the books as though they defined a great divide cutting across the domain of law. But, of course, "substance" and "procedure" are the same key-words to very different problems. ... [We should] put[] to one side abstractions regarding "substance" and "procedure." ... [The *Erie*] policy [is] so important to our federalism [that it] must be kept free from entanglements with analytical or terminological niceties. *Guaranty Trust Co. v. York*, 326 U.S. 99, 108-110 (1945) (Frankfurter, J.).

(b) *Erie's "twin aims" — state-federal forum shopping and inequitable administration of law.* The Supreme Court has in recent decades generally emphasized the "twin aims" of *Erie*: "discouragement of forum-shopping and avoidance of the inequitable administration of the laws." *Hanna v. Plumer*, 380 U.S. 460, 468 (1965); *supra* pp. 13-14. Consider how the analysis in *Sibaja* and *American Dredging* affect these twin objectives. Is it likely that plaintiffs will forum shop for state courts that do not have forum non conveniens doctrines? or that have different forum non conveniens doctrines than federal courts? The answer is unequivocally yes: state-federal forum shopping will occur with a vengeance. That is why the plaintiffs in *Sequihua, Alfaro,* and *Sibaja* all brought suit initially in state courts.

Is it likely that defendants will seek to remove actions brought in state court to federal court, where state forum non conveniens doctrines do not exist or are less favorable than *Piper*? Again, the answer is plainly yes. That is what happened in *Sibaja* (as well as in *Piper* and *Sequihua*). Where diversity, alienage, or federal question jurisdiction exists, removal will generally be possible. *See supra* p. 12. Consequently, identical cases will be decided differently depending upon a party's citizenship; compare *Alfaro* with *Sibaja* and *Sequihua*, where federal and state courts reached opposite results with respect to identical claims. Indeed, if one accepts the view that many claims dismissed on forum non conveniens grounds are simply dropped, *see supra* p. 308 n.73, some claims will never even be heard, while identical ones receive substantial U.S. jury awards.

(c) *Federal interests in federal judicial administration.* A good appellate analysis of the *Erie* issues raised by the forum non conveniens doctrine was *In re Air Crash Disaster Near New Orleans*, 821 F.2d 1147 (5th Cir. 1987), where the Court of Appeals concluded that the doctrine was governed by federal procedural law. The Court acknowledged that this result would produce "a tremendous disparity of result between the two court systems [i.e., state and federal]: One case will proceed to judgment and the other will be dismissed to a foreign land." 821 F.2d at 1157. Nevertheless, the Court reasoned that "the interests of the federal forum in self-regulation, in administrative independence, and in self-management are more important than the disruption of uniformity created by applying federal forum non conveniens in diversity cases." 821 F.2d at 1159. Is this reasoning satisfactory? Recall that the forum non conveniens doctrine is, in federal courts, a judge-made creature that involves a court's refusal to exercise jurisdiction that Congress has granted it. Is it proper that a party, upon whom Congress has conferred a right of action in federal court, be denied that right because of a judicial rule of "self-management"?

Recall also the forum non conveniens doctrine as enunciated in *Piper*. In particular, note that the doctrine contains specific rules regarding the deference owed to a U.S. plaintiff's choice of forum and the need to balance local versus foreign regulatory interests. *See supra* pp. 299-305. Are these really attributes of a rule of "self-management"? Are they in fact not rules of choice of law and jurisdictional competence?

(d) *State-state forum shopping.* Suppose that Judge Learned Hand's rationale, quoted above from *Weiss v. Routh*, is accepted and state substantive law is held to govern forum non conveniens issues in both state and federal actions. Will not forum shopping still occur? Will not plaintiffs seek out states like Texas and Louisiana that do not permit, or that only permit restrictive versions of, the forum non conveniens doctrine? Is this state-state forum shopping not an even greater evil than state-federal forum shopping? Even if that is correct, will not state-state forum shopping exist even under *Sibaja* and *American Dredging*, where plaintiffs expect to be able to avoid removal?

4. *Applicability of* American Dredging *in international cases.* As described above, *American Dredging* held that state courts were free to apply state forum non conveniens rules in domestic admiralty actions. The Court suggested that federal courts were similarly free to apply a federal forum non conveniens doctrine. The essential basis for the Court's holding was that the forum non conveniens doctrine is "procedural rather than substantive" and "nothing more or less than a supervening venue provision, permitting displacement of the ordinary rules of venue." Does this reasoning apply in international cases, where the putative alternative forum is not a U.S. court? Venue implies selecting the proper locality within a single national judicial system. It does *not* imply a nation's courts abstaining entirely from jurisdiction. Moreover, *see supra* pp. 336-39, in international cases, *Piper* requires consideration of national regulatory competence and interests — factors that do not exist in domestic cases. Given this, is *American Dredging* relevant to international cases like *Piper*? What do you think the Court will say?

5. *Substantive federal common law basis for forum non conveniens defense.* Should state courts be obliged to follow the *federal* rule of forum non conveniens in international cases? Is there any basis for federal courts to articulate a rule of substantive federal common law in international cases, requiring state courts to dismiss claims by foreign plaintiffs that impose undue inconvenience on U.S. courts and parties or that implicate sufficiently substantial foreign sovereign interests?

As discussed above, in order to sustain a federal common law rule, it would generally be necessary to demonstrate that forum non conveniens decisions arise in a "uniquely federal" field and that disregarding federal standards would significantly conflict with important federal policies. *See Boyle v. United Technologies Corp.*, 487 U.S. 500 (1988); *supra* pp. 15-16. Are these standards satisfied by the forum non conveniens doctrine in international cases? Consider the analysis in *Sequihua*. Does it support a general federal common law rule of forum non conveniens? or is its rationale limited to cases where unusual effects on foreign state interests are involved?

Recall *Piper's* concern that U.S. multinationals will become the targets of tort litigants from around the world, seeking application of U.S. legal standards and procedures to non-U.S. conduct. Does this sufficiently implicate federal interests in U.S. foreign commerce to warrant a federal forum non conveniens rule? Recall the governmental interest-balancing and concern for foreign regulatory structures reflected in *Wyeth*. Does this demonstrate that forum non conveniens decisions arise in a "uniquely federal" field of foreign relations?

Assuming that the forum non conveniens doctrine did arise in a uniquely federal field, would a state court's refusal to apply *Piper's* formulation of the doctrine "significantly conflict" with federal policies? Does the answer depend on the character of the divergence from *Piper*? Consider:

(a) Texas courts flatly refuse to apply *any* forum non conveniens defense in personal injury cases, *Dow Chemical Co. v. Castro Alfaro*, 786 S.W.2d 674 (Tex. Sup. Ct. 1990), *cert. denied*, 111 S.Ct. 671 (1991);

(b) Washington courts grant full deference to a foreign plaintiff's choice of a U.S. forum, *Myers v. Boeing Co.*, 794 P.2d 1272 (Wash. 1990);

(c) Florida courts refuse to apply a forum non conveniens defense to certain claims under Florida statutes, *First Pacific Corp. v. Sociedade de Empreendimentos e Construcoes, Ltda.*, 566 So.2d 3 (Fla. App. 1990); and

(d) some future state only allows forum non conveniens dismissals to courts in nations with stringent product liability laws.

In deciding, consider the following: (1) the policy of discouraging forum shopping within a state between state courts and federal courts; (2) the policy of permitting federal courts to control their own dockets; (3) the federal policy of deferring to foreign forums with greater interests in a dispute than U.S. forums; and (4) the federal government's dominant role in foreign relations and commerce.

F. Venue in International Litigation

U.S. courts will not adjudicate a case unless applicable U.S. venue requirements, specifying the proper location for the lawsuit, are satisfied. Venue and jurisdiction are often said to be distinguishable: jurisdiction refers to the power of a court to adjudicate a dispute, while venue refers to the place where jurisdiction may be exercised.[124] Venue provisions are designed principally to protect litigants, particularly defendants, from suits in inconvenient forums.[125]

The provisions of federal venue statutes specify the judicial district in which an action may be brought (assuming that personal and subject matter jurisdiction requirements are satisfied). Thus, in domestic diversity cases, U.S. citizens can be sued only in the district where all the plaintiffs or defendants reside or where the claim arose.[126] In non-diversity actions, U.S. citizens can ordinarily be sued only in the district where all the defendants reside or where the claim arose,[127] or as provided for in specialized venue provisions of particular federal statutes.[128]

Venue in suits against alien defendants is usually not a significant issue in international litigation in federal court. The so-called Alien Venue Statute provides that "[a]n alien may be sued in any district."[129] This enables a plaintiff to initiate an action against an alien in virtually any district in the United States that the plaintiff chooses. It is clear that the statute applies to corporate defendants, as well as to individual defendants.[130] It also appears that the Alien Venue Statute applies in cases involving both alien and U.S. defendants: The lower courts have suggested that, in these circumstances, the residence of the U.S. defendant is the sole relevant criteria for venue purposes.[131]

In general, the expansive Alien Venue Statute has been interpreted to override

---

124. Clermont, *Restating Territorial Jurisdiction and Venue for State and Federal Courts*, 66 Cornell L. Rev. 411 (1981); *Lindahl v. Office of Personnel Management*, 105 S.Ct. 1620, 1634 n.30 (1985).

125. *See Brunette Machine Works v. Kockum Indus., Inc.*, 406 U.S. 706 (1972); *Leroy v. Great Western United Corp.*, 443 U.S. 173 (1979) ("In most instances, the purpose of a statutorily specified venue is to protect the *defendant* against the risk that a plaintiff will select an unfair or inconvenient place of trial."); 15 C. Wright, A. Miller & E. Cooper, *Federal Practice and Procedure* §§3801-3829 (1986).

126. 28 U.S.C. §1391(a).

127. 28 U.S.C. §1391(b).

128. *E.g.*, 28 U.S.C. §1400(b) (patent); 15 U.S.C. §15 (antitrust); 15 U.S.C. §22 (antitrust); 28 U.S.C. §1400(a) (copyright).

129. 28 U.S.C. §1391(d). *See* Note, *The Alien Venue Statute: An Historical Analysis of Federal Venue Provisions and Alien Right*, 3 N.Y.U.J. Int'l & Comp. L. 307 (1982).

130. *Brunette Machine Works, Ltd. v. Kockum Indus., Inc.*, 406 U.S. 706 (1972); *Ohio Reinsurance Corp. v. British Nat'l Ins. Co.*, 587 F. Supp. 710 (S.D.N.Y. 1984); *Brunswick Corp. v. Suzuki Motor Co., Ltd.*, 575 F. Supp. 1412 (E.D. Wis. 1983); *Mowrey v. Johnson & Johnson*, 524 F. Supp. 771 (W.D. Pa. 1981); *Holt v. Klosters Rederi A/S*, 355 F. Supp. 354 (W.D. Mich. 1973).

131. *Mowrey v. Johnson & Johnson*, 524 F. Supp. 771 (W.D. Pa. 1981); *Japan Gas Lighters Ass'n v. Ronson Corp.*, 257 F. Supp. 219 (D.N.J. 1966); C. Wright, A. Miller & E. Cooper, *Federal Practice and Procedure* §3810 (1986).

the more restrictive venue provisions of specific federal statutes.[132] In the Supreme Court's words: "§1391(d) is properly regarded, not as a venue restriction at all, but rather as a declaration of the long-established rule that suits against aliens are wholly outside the operation of all the federal venue laws, general and special."[133] The rationale for this result is that many federal venue provisions rely on the defendants' residence. Because aliens usually lack any U.S. residence, affording them protection under ordinary venue statutes would often make venue in *any* U.S. district improper. Courts have understandably rejected such a result.[134]

One important exception to the general applicability of the Alien Venue Statute arises under the Foreign Sovereign Immunities Act ("FSIA").[135] The FSIA addressed the issue of venue with respect to foreign state defendants by adding a new subsection to the general federal venue statute. The provision states:

> (a) A civil action against a foreign state as defined in section 1603(a) of this title may be brought —
>
> (1) in any judicial district in which a substantial part of the events or omissions giving rise to the claim occurred, or a substantial part of property that is the subject of the action is situated;
>
> (2) in any judicial district in which the vessel or cargo of a foreign state is situated, if the claim is asserted under section 1605(b) of this title; or
>
> (3) in any judicial district in which the agency or instrumentality is licensed to do business or is doing business, if the action is brought against an agency or instrumentality of a foreign state as defined in section 1603(b) of this title; or
>
> (4) in the United States District Court for the District of Columbia if the action is brought against a foreign state or political subdivision thereof.

The legislative history of the FSIA makes it clear that Congress intended that the specific venue provisions applicable to foreign sovereigns should substitute for the Alien Venue Statute insofar as foreign sovereigns (including their agencies or instrumentalities) are involved.[136] Lower federal courts have routinely assumed that the

---

132. *Brunette Machine Works v. Kockum Indus., Inc.*, 406 U.S. 706 (1972) (Alien Venue Statute overrides venue provisions of patent statute). *See Go-Video, Inc. v. Akai Elec. Co.*, 885 F.2d 1406 (9th Cir. 1989); *General Electric Co. v. Bucyrus-Erie Co.*, 550 F.Supp. 1037 (S.D.N.Y. 1982); *General Aircraft Corp. v. Air America, Inc.*, 482 F. Supp. 3, 11 (D.D.C. 1979); *Centronics Data Computer Corp. v. Mannesmann, A.G.*, 432 F. Supp. 659 (D.N.H. 1977).

133. *Brunette Mach. Works, Ltd. v. Kockum Indus., Inc.*, 406 U.S. 706, 714 (1972).

134. One student commentator has suggested that the Alien Venue Statute unconstitutionally discriminates against aliens in violation of the Fifth Amendment. Note, *The Alien Venue Statute: An Historical Analysis of Federal Venue Provisions and Alien Rights*, 3 N.Y.U. Int'l & Comp. L. 307 (1982). No court appears to have adopted this suggestion.

135. The FSIA and the doctrine of foreign sovereign immunity are discussed in detail in Chapter 3 *supra.*

136. *See* H.R. Rep. No. 94-1487 at 31, *reprinted in* 1976 U.S. Code and Admin. News at 6630.

specific provisions of §1391(f), rather than the general provisions of §1391(d), apply when suits are brought against foreign sovereigns.[137]

Finally, alien *plaintiffs* in U.S. courts often encounter more significant venue obstacles than domestic plaintiffs. There is no federal venue statute, comparable to the Alien Venue Statute, dealing with venue for alien plaintiffs. As a result, alien plaintiffs must rely on generally applicable venue provisions. However, aliens typically have no U.S. residence and, as a result, alien plaintiffs usually cannot rely on venue provisions permitting suit at the plaintiff's residence.[138] Instead, alien plaintiffs can ordinarily bring suit only where all the defendants reside or where the plaintiff's claim arose.[139]

---

137. *See, e.g., Proyecfin de Venezuela, SA v. Banco Industrial de Venezuela, SA*, 760 F.2d 390, 395 n.4 (2d Cir. 1985); *Falcoal, Inc. v. Turkiye Komur Isletmeleri Kurumi*, 660 F. Supp. 1536 (S.D Tex. 1987); *Acosta v. Grammer*, 402 F. Supp. 736 (E.D. Mo. 1975).

138. *E.g.*, 28 U.S.C. §1391(a); *DuRoure v. Alvord*, 120 F. Supp. 166 (S.D.N.Y. 1954); *Prudencio v. Hanselmann*, 178 F. Supp. 887 (D. Minn. 1959).

139. *Fleifel v. Vessa*, 503 F. Supp. 129 (W.D. Va. 1980); *Akbar v. New York Magazine*, 490 F. Supp. 60 (D.D.C. 1980); *Acosta v. Grammer*, 402 F. Supp. 736 (E.D. Mo. 1975).

5/International Forum Selection Agreements[1]

In both domestic and international commercial matters, parties frequently "stipulate in advance to submit their controversies for resolution within a particular jurisdiction."[2] Contractual provisions selecting a particular judicial forum for the adjudication of disputes are typically referred to as "forum selection," "jurisdiction," or "choice of forum" clauses. This Chapter discusses forum selection agreements in international litigation. An important sub-set of forum clauses are arbitration provisions, which are examined in Chapter 13 below.

A. Introduction and Historical Background

1. Exclusive and Nonexclusive Forum Selection Agreements

There is a fundamental distinction between *exclusive* and *nonexclusive* forum selection agreements. An exclusive (or mandatory) forum clause requires that any litigation take place only in the specified forum, and nowhere else.[3] In contrast, a nonexclusive forum selection agreement permits litigation of disputes in a particular

---

1. Commentary on forum selection agreements includes, *e.g.*, Gilbert, *Choice of Forum Clauses in International and Interstate Contracts*, 65 Ky. L. J. 1 (1976); Gruson, *Forum-Selection Clauses in International and Interstate Commercial Agreements*, 1982 Ill. L. Rev. 133; Mullenix, *Another Choice of Forum, Another Choice of Law: Consensual Adjudicatory Procedure in Federal Courts*, 57 Fordham L. Rev. 291 (1988); Nadelmann, *Choice-of-Court Clauses in the United States: The Road to Zapata*, 21 Am. J. Comp. L. 124 (1973); Perillo, *Selected Forum Agreements in Western Europe*, 13 Am. J. Comp. L. 162 (1964); Sturley, *Strengthening the Presumption of Validity for Choice of Forum Clauses*, 23 J. Mar. L. & Comn. 131 (1992); *Restatement (Second) Conflict of Laws* §80 (1971 & 1986 Supp.); W. Park, *International Forum Selection* (Kluwer 1995).

2. *Burger King Corp. v. Rudzewicz*, 471 U.S. 462, 472 n.14 (1985).

3. Forum selection clauses may also be exclusive as to one party, while leaving the other party free to initiate litigation in courts other than the selected forum. *E.g.*, *Heller Financial, Inc. v. Midwhey Powder Co.*, 883 F.2d 1286 (7th Cir. 1989); *Product Components v. Regency Door & Hardware*, 568 F.Supp. 651, 652 (S.D. Ind. 1983) ("The parties agree that all controversies arising hereunder may, at Seller's option, be determined in Indiana and Buyer hereby expressly consents to the jurisdiction of Indiana courts."). *See infra* p. 413.

---

forum but does not preclude the parties from going forward in other courts if they also have jurisdiction.[4]

A nonexclusive forum selection clause (also called a "prorogation agreement" or a "permissive" forum clause) involves promises by both parties to submit to the jurisdiction of a specified court, without any undertaking to forego litigation elsewhere. In many cases, a nonexclusive forum clause will expressly submit each party to the personal jurisdiction of the contractual forum; where no express submission is present, such submission is virtually always implicit.[5] As discussed in Chapter 2, U.S. courts have typically enforced prorogation agreements, under applicable local law and the due process clause, absent proof of fraud or coercion.[6]

2. Reasons for Entering Into Forum Selection Agreements

Forum selection clauses can provide one or both parties to an agreement with important benefits. In some circumstances, bargaining power or negotiating ability may allow a party to select the forum it finds most convenient or advantageous. Parties to international agreements typically wish to have disputes resolved in the courts of their own "home" jurisdiction.[7] Doing so provides a party with a convenient, familiar forum where there may also be perceptions of a "home-court" advantage over foreign litigants.

Even if it is not possible to have disputes resolved in one party's home forum, selection of a neutral forum and avoidance of courts that are highly undesirable to one or both parties is also attractive. In those circumstances, a forum clause provides private parties with a measure of certainty and predictability. Particularly when coupled with a choice of law agreement,[8] a forum selection clause removes uncertainties about jurisdiction, procedural rules, and other matters. In the words of the Supreme Court, "[a] contractual provision specifying in advance the forum in which disputes shall be litigated and the law to be applied is ... an almost indispensable precondition to achievement of the orderliness and predictability essential to any international business transaction."[9]

Forum clauses can also reduce expense and delay in litigation. A forum selection agreement may reduce the likelihood of protracted disputes over jurisdiction, permitting the parties more promptly to focus on the merits of the case without expensive procedural distractions. Moreover, a forum selection agreement makes it more

---

4. *See infra* pp. 454-55.

5. *E.g., Northwestern Nat'l Life Ins. Co. v. Donovan*, 916 F.2d 372, 376-77 (7th Cir. 1990); *Luce v. Edelstein*, 802 F.2d 49, 57 (2d Cir. 1986); *Merrill Lynch, Pierce, Fenner & Smith Inc. v. Lecopulos*, 558 F.2d 842, 844 (2d Cir. 1977); *Paribas Corp. v. Shelton Ranch Corp.*, 742 F.Supp. 86, 90 (S.D.N.Y. 1990) ("Forum selection clauses are valid and enforceable consents to jurisdiction in the New York courts").

6. *See supra* pp. 101-02.

7. *The Bremen v. Zapata Off-Shore Co.*, 407 U.S. 1, 11-12 (1972) ("Not surprisingly, foreign businessmen prefer, as do we, to have disputes resolved in their own courts, but if that choice is not available, then in a neutral forum with expertise in the subject matter.").

8. Choice of law agreements are discussed at *infra* pp. 653-64.

9. *Scherk v. Alberto-Culver Co.*, 417 U.S. 506, 516 (1974).

likely that a given dispute will be resolved in a single forum, thus reducing the risk of costly parallel litigation in two or more courts.

3. Distinction Between Choice of Forum and Choice of Law Agreements

Under U.S. law, a choice of forum clause is not a choice of law clause, nor is a choice of law clause a forum selection clause. A number of lower courts have held that a choice of forum clause does not constitute the parties' agreement that the chosen forum's law should also govern their relations.[10] Conversely, an agreement as to governing law does not, under either state law or the due process clause, necessarily provide a submission to the jurisdiction of the courts of the chosen state.[11]

4. Historical Development of Enforceability of Forum Selection Clauses

The rules governing enforceability of forum clauses have evolved significantly over the past century. Moreover, depending upon applicable law, these rules continue to vary within the United States. Some states historically regarded, and a few continue to regard, forum selection clauses as *per se* unenforceable, while other states apply varying standards of enforceability. In addition, the enforceability of forum clauses in federal courts raises particularly complex questions under the *Erie* doctrine.

a. Historic Common Law Rule That Forum Selection Clauses Are Unenforceable

U.S. courts were historically hostile to forum clauses, both in international and domestic disputes.[12] Until fairly recently, both exclusive and nonexclusive forum selection agreements were almost uniformly held *per se* unenforceable in the United States.[13] This paralleled judicial hostility towards arbitration and choice of law agreements, which were also generally unenforceable.[14]

Until the middle of this century, the rule against enforcement of forum selection

---

10. Gruson, *Governing-Law Clauses in International and Interstate Loan Agreements — New York's Approach*, 1982 U. Ill. Rev. 207. As discussed below, however, a choice of forum agreement can provide evidence of an implied choice of law by the parties. *Scherk v. Alberto-Culver Co.*, 417 U.S. 506, 519 n.13 (1974) ("Under some circumstances, the designation of arbitration in a certain place might also be viewed as implicitly selecting the law of that place to apply to the transaction."); *Lummus Co. v. Commonwealth Oil Refining Co.*, 280 F.2d 915, 924 (1st Cir. 1960); *infra* p. 657.

11. *See supra* pp. 101-02. Agreement on a forum's governing law does, however, provide at least some evidence that litigation in that forum was foreseeable, for purposes of due process "minimum contacts" analysis. *Burger King Corp. v. Rudzewizc*, 471 U.S. 462, 472 (1985); *supra* pp. 148-49.

12. *See Bremen v. Zapata Off-Shore Co.*, 407 U.S. 1, 9 (1972) ("Forum-selection clauses have historically not been favored by American courts. Many courts, federal and state, have declined to enforce such clauses on the ground that they were 'contrary to public policy,' or that their effect was to 'oust the jurisdiction' of the court."); Gilbert, *Choice of Forum Clauses in International and Interstate Contracts*, 65 Ky. L. J. 1, 11-19 (1976); Reese, *The Contractual Forum: Situation in the United States*, 13 Am. J. Comp. L. 187 (1964).

13. An extensive compilation of decisions holding forum selection agreements unenforceable is found in Annotation, *Validity of Contractual Provision Limiting Place or Court in Which Action May be Brought*, 31 A.L.R.4th 404, 409-411; Annotation, 69 A.L.R.2d 1324 (1960 & Supp. 1978).

14. *See infra* pp. 653-55 & 993-94.

clauses was almost unanimously followed, by state and federal courts, in both domestic and international cases. Different courts remarked that "[n]othing is better settled than that agreements of this character are void,"[15] and cited the "universally accepted rule that agreements in advance of controversy whose object is to oust the jurisdiction of the courts are contrary to public policy and will not be enforced."[16] In writing his treatise on Contracts, Professor Corbin thought the subject sufficiently settled to dispose of it by rhetorically asking, "[h]ow can two individuals by private agreement limit or otherwise alter the 'jurisdiction' of the great courts of state or nation!"[17]

b. Rejection of Historic Rule That Forum Selection Agreements are Unenforceable

Starting in the late 1940's, U.S. courts began to abandon the traditional rule that forum selection agreements were per se unenforceable. Lower courts[18] and commentators[19] increasingly questioned the rationale of the rule. In 1955, *Wm. H. Muller & Co. v. Swedish American Line Ltd.*[20] expressly broke with the historic prohibition on forum clauses. In a case involving an exclusive forum selection agreement designating Swedish courts as the contractual forum, the Second Circuit held:

> In each case the enforceability of such an agreement depends upon its reasonableness. ... [I]f in the proper exercise of its jurisdiction ... the court finds that the agreement is not unreasonable in the setting of a particular case, it may properly decline jurisdiction and relegate a litigant to the forum to which he assented.

In the following years, a number of other lower federal courts refused to hold forum clauses per se unreasonable; such agreements could be enforced, in the trial court's

---

15. *Benson v. Eastern Bldg. & Loan Ass'n*, 174 N.Y. 83, 86 (1903).

16. *Carbon Black Export, Inc. v. The S.S. Monrosa*, 254 F.2d 297 (5th Cir.), *cert. dismissed*, 359 U.S. 180 (1959). *See also The Ciamo*, 58 F.Supp. 65 (E.D. Pa. 1944); *Mutual Reserve Fund Life Ass'n v. Cleveland Woolen Mills*, 82 F. 508, 510 (6th Cir. 1897); *Nashua River Paper Co. v. Hammermill Paper Co.*, 111 N.E. 678, 681 (Mass. 1916)("The same rule ... prevails generally in all states where the question has arisen.").

17. 6A A. Corbin, *Corbin on Contracts* §1431, at 381-82 (1962).

18. *See Krenger v. Pennsylvania R.R.*, 174 F.2d 556, 561 (2d Cir.) (L. Hand, J., concurring), *cert. denied*, 338 U.S. 866 (1949) ("be the original reasons good or bad, courts have for long looked with strong disfavor upon contracts by which a party surrenders resort to any forum which was lawfully open to him .... In truth, I do not believe that, today at least, there is an absolute taboo against such contracts at all; in the words of the Restatement, they are invalid only when unreasonable.... What remains of the doctrine is apparently no more than a general hostility, which can be overcome, but which nonetheless does persist"); *Gilbert v. Burnstine*, 174 N.E. 706 (N.Y. 1931); *Kelvin Engineering Co. v. Blanco*, 210 N.Y.S. 12 (Sup. Ct. 1925).

19. Nadelmann, *Choice-of-Court Clauses in the United States: The Road to Zapata*, 21 Am. J. Comp. L. 124, 127-34 (1973); Reese, *The Contractual Forum: Situation in the United States*, 13 Am. J. Comp. L. 187, 189 (1964); A. Ehrenzweig, *Conflict of Laws* 149 (1962)("Neither history nor rationale thus bear out the much-repeated axiom that parties may not 'oust' the courts from their jurisdiction.").

20. 224 F.2d 806 (2d Cir.), *cert. denied*, 350 U.S. 903 (1955), *overruled on other grounds, Indussa Corp. v. S.S. Ranborg*, 377 F.2d 200 (2d Cir. 1967).

discretion, if they were "reasonable."[21] Some state courts followed suit.[22] Observing this rapid erosion of the traditional rule against forum clauses, one commentator remarked that "[i]t is somewhat difficult to understand how that which was so well settled in 1930 could become unsettled in the space of nineteen years."[23]

The rule that forum selection clauses are unenforceable came increasingly to be identified with the indefensible adage that private parties cannot "oust" courts of their jurisdiction. According to one court, "[p]erhaps the true explanation [for the rule] is the power of the hypnotic phrase 'oust the jurisdiction.' Give a bad dogma a good name and its bite may become as bad as its bark."[24] Critics increasing branded this slogan a misleading mischaracterization: the real issue is not whether a court is deprived of its jurisdiction, but "whether, in a proper case, a court should refrain from exercising such jurisdiction as it admittedly possesses in order to give effect to the parties' intentions as expressed in a choice of forum clause."[25] The answer to this question came, almost invariably, to be in the affirmative.

In 1964, the U.S. Supreme Court took what came to be a significant step towards abandoning the traditional prohibition on forum selection agreements in *National Equipment Rental, Ltd. v. Szukhent.*[26] On its facts, *Szukhent* involved an interpretation of Rule 4 of the Federal Rules of Civil Procedure, and particularly the question whether Rule 4 permitted service on an agent designated in advance by contractual agreement.[27] In answering in the affirmative, however, the Court more broadly declared that "it is settled ... that parties to a contract may agree in advance to submit

---

21. *E.g., Furbee v. Vantage Press, Inc.,* 464 F.2d 835 (D.C. Cir. 1972); *Central Contracting Co. v. Maryland Cas. Co.,* 367 F.2d 341 (3d Cir. 1966); *Anastasiadis v. S.S. Little John,* 346 F.2d 281 (5th Cir. 1965), *cert. denied,* 384 U.S. 920 (1966). *See also* Bergman, *Contractual Restrictions on the Forum,* 48 Calif. L. Rev. 438, 438-47 (1960); Gilbert, *Choice of Forum Clauses in International and Interstate Contracts,* 65 Ky. L. J. 1, 11-20 (1976).

22. *E.g., Export Insurance Co. v. Mitsui S.S. Co.,* 274 N.Y.S.2d 977 (1st Dept. 1966); *Central Contracting Co. v. Youngdahl & Co.,* 209 A.2d 810, 816 (Pa. 1965); *Schwartz v. Zim Israel Navigation Co.,* 181 N.Y.S.2d 283 (Sup. Ct. 1958).

23. Bergman, *Contractual Restrictions on the Forum,* 48 Calif. L. Rev. 438, 440 (1960). Some courts resisted the trend towards enforcement of forum clauses. *E.g., Carbon Black Export v. The SS Monrosa,* 254 F.2d 297 (5th Cir. 1958); *United Fuel Gas Co. v. Columbian Fuel,* 165 F.2d 747, 749 (4th Cir. 1948).

24. *Kulukundis Shipping Co. v. Amtorg Trading Corp.,* 126 F.2d 978, 984 (2d Cir. 1942).

25. Reese, *The Supreme Court Supports Enforcement of Choice-of-Forum Clauses,* 7 Int'l Law. 530, 534 (1973). *See also* Aballi, *Comparative Developments in the Law of Choice of Forum,* 1 Int'l L. & Pol. 178, 179 (1968) ("When a party contracts that it will not bring any future disputes in courts other than that stipulated, it is surrendering a right to bring them before a court which the law has invested with jurisdiction to hear that controversy. The agreement as such does not 'oust' or 'confer' jurisdiction, but is legally effective because the courts will recognize it.").

26. 375 U.S. 311 (1964).

27. According to the Court, "the only question now before us is whether the person upon whom the summons and complaint was served was 'an agent authorized by appointment' to receive the same, so as to subject the respondents to the jurisdiction of the federal court in New York." 375 U.S. at 313.

to the jurisdiction of a given court, to permit notice to be served by the opposing party, or even to waive notice altogether."[28]

In 1968, the National Conference of Commissioners on Uniform State Laws approved the Model Choice of Forum Act (which is reproduced in Appendix F).[29] The Act provided for the enforceability of both submission to jurisdiction and exclusive forum selection clauses. Section 2 of the Act provided that written agreements "that an action on a controversy may be brought in this state," will be enforced if the contractual forum is "reasonably convenient" and if the agreement was not "obtained by misrepresentation, duress, the abuse of economic power, or other unconscionable means." Similarly, §3 provided that, if the parties enter into a written agreement that "an action on a controversy shall be brought only in another state," the forum court shall dismiss or stay the action, unless one of specified exceptions is satisfied.[30]

These developments were the basis in 1971 for a new provision in the *Restatement (Second) Conflict of Laws* (which has no parallel in the *First Restatement*). New §80 provided, for the first time, that forum selection clauses were enforceable, at least in some circumstances.[31] Section 80 of the Restatement provided:

> The parties' agreement as to the place of the action [cannot oust a state of judicial jurisdiction, but such an agreement] will be given effect unless it is unfair or unreasonable.[32]

Section 80 was subsequently amended, in 1986, to delete the language appearing in brackets above.

During the same period, traditional restrictions on parties' freedom to choose

---

28. 375 U.S. at 315-16. As discussed elsewhere, the Supreme Court had long permitted private parties to consent to a forum's personal jurisdiction *after* an action had been commenced there. *See supra* pp. 101-02; *Adam v. Saenger*, 303 U.S. 59 (1938).

29. The Act has been adopted, in varying forms, in the following state statutes: Neb. Rev. Stat. §25-415 (1989); N.H. Rev. Stat. Ann. §508-A (1983); N.Y. Gen. Oblig. Law §5-1402 (McKinney 1989 & Supp. 1994); N.D. Cent. Code §28-04.1 (1991); Ohio Rev. Code §2307.39 (Anderson Supp. 1992).

The Act was presaged by the draft Hague Convention on Choice of Court, adopted at the 10th Session of the Hague Conference on Private International Law in 1964. 4 Int'l Legal Mat. 348-49 (1965). The Convention was broadly similar to the Model Act. Only Israel ratified the Convention. Gilbert, *Choice of Forum Clauses in International and Interstate Contracts*, 65 Ky. L. J. 1, 29-30 (1976).

30. The exceptions are discussed in detail below. *See infra* pp. 395-430.

31. For a discussion of the process of adopting §80, *see* Nadelmann, *Choice-of-Court Clauses in the United States: The Road to Zapata*, 21 Am. J. Comp. L. 124, 130-33 (1973).

32. In a remarkably disingenuous exercise in selective citation, the Restatement's drafters acknowledged in the Reporter's Note to §80, that courts "have shown themselves reluctant" to dismiss actions brought in violation of forum selection clauses (without citation to any of the numerous decisions almost uniformly demonstrating not just "reluctance," but absolute refusal), but went on to assert that "actions have been dismissed, however, in situations where the contractual provision was deemed reasonable and serving the convenience of the parties" (citing all of the relatively few decisions then in existence which enforced forum selection agreements on any basis).

the law applicable to their contracts were eroded.[33] As discussed elsewhere, §1-105 of the Uniform Commercial Code and §187 of the *Restatement (Second) Conflict of Laws* were significant steps in this development, culminating in the recognition of a significant measure of party autonomy in the choice of law context.[34] The erosion of prohibitions against forum selection agreements was also facilitated by legislative and judicial acceptance of arbitration agreements. As discussed elsewhere, the Federal Arbitration Act was enacted in 1925, making certain arbitration agreements valid and enforceable; judicial enforcement of the Act was enthusiastic, and inevitably affected judicial attitudes towards forum selection clauses.[35]

One year after §80 was adopted, the Supreme Court decided what would become the leading contemporary U.S. case on the enforceability of forum clauses. In *The Bremen v. Zapata Off-Shore Co.*,[36] the Court held that, in federal admiralty suits, forum clauses "are prima facie valid and should be enforced unless enforcement is shown by the resisting party to be 'unreasonable' under the circumstances."[37] Following *Bremen*, most lower courts abandoned the historic prohibition against forum selection clauses in both domestic and international cases.[38] In 1986, §80 of the *Restatement (Second) Conflict of Laws* was amended to further emphasize the enforceability of such clauses.[39] And, most recently, the Supreme Court's 1991 decision in *Carnival Cruise Lines v. Shute,* strongly endorsed the enforceability of forum agreements and emphasized the narrow character of the exceptions to this general rule.[40] We explore these developments below.

---

33. Prebble, *Choice of Law to Determine the Validity and Effects of Contracts: A Comparison of the English and American Approaches to the Conflict of Laws,* 58 Cornell L. Rev. 433, 442-44 (1973); Gruson, *Governing Law Clauses in Commercial Agreements — New York's Approach,* 18 Colum. J. Trans. L. 323, 323 (1980).

34. *See infra* pp. 653-55.

35. *See infra* pp. 994-97; G. Born, *International Commercial Arbitration in the United States* 187-97 (1994).

36. 407 U.S. 1 (1972).

37. 407 U.S. at 10.

38. *See infra* pp. 379-81.

39. *See supra* pp. 376-77.

40. 499 U.S. 585 (1991).

B. Contemporary Approaches to the Enforceability of Forum Selection Clauses

Although *Bremen* and other authorities have abandoned the historic prohibition against forum selection clauses, this has produced surprisingly little certainty as to the new rules of enforceability. In part because of the discursive character of the *Bremen* opinion, and in part because of persisting unease with forum selection agreements, courts in different U.S. jurisdictions have adopted different approaches to the presumptive validity and weight to be accorded to forum clauses.

The enforceability of forum selection agreements is not as unsettled today as it was in 1964, when Willis Reese remarked: "One thing can be said with certainty. In the United States the effect of a choice of forum clause dealing with future controversies is uncertain."[41] But the standards for enforcement of a forum clause in the United States nevertheless continue to vary significantly in different jurisdictions. Five general approaches to the issue can be identified in contemporary decisions, ranging from historic *per se* unenforceability to virtually *per se* enforceability. Each approach is discussed below.

Despite the legal uncertainties arising from those multiple approaches, forum clauses are in practice very often enforced by U.S. courts. According to a recent commentator, "one is hard-pressed to find a recent case which refuses to enforce such clauses."[42] Although this is not entirely accurate,[43] it reflects the general predisposition of contemporary U.S. courts.

1. Forum Selection Clauses Per Se Unenforceable

Notwithstanding *Bremen* and the *Restatement (Second) Conflict of Laws*, a few U.S. jurisdictions continue to hold forum agreements unenforceable. Although counts vary, it appears that courts in at least four states — Alabama, Montana, Texas, and Idaho — hold that forum clauses choosing an out-of-state forum are per se unenforceable, at least in the domestic U.S. context.[44]

In Montana and Idaho local statutes render (or have been interpreted to render) forum selection clauses unenforceable.[45] In other states, courts have declared forum clauses unenforceable relying solely on historic, common law notions of public policy. Typical is the 1980 decision in *Redwing Carriers, Inc. v. Foster*, where the Supreme

---

41. Reese, *The Contractual Forum: Situation in the United States,* 13 Am. J. Comp. L. 187 (1964) (Proceedings).

42. Solimine, *Forum-Selection Clauses and the Privatization of Procedure,* 25 Cornell Int'l L. J. 51, 51 (1992).

43. *See infra* pp. 402-05, 410-14, & 426-30.

44. *White-Spunner Constr. v. Cliff,* 588 So.2d 865 (Ala. 1991); *Cerami-Kote, Inc. v. Energywave Corp.,* 773 P.2d 1143 (Idaho 1989) (relying on public policy expressed by Idaho Code §29-110); *Keelean v. Central Bank of the South,* 544 So.2d 153 (Ala. 1989); *Polaris Indus., Inc. v. District Court,* 695 P.2d 471 (Mont. 1985) (relying on public policy expressed by Montana §28-2-708); *Redwing Carriers, Inc. v. Foster,* 382 So.2d 554 (Ala. 1980); *Fidelity Union Life Ins. Co. v. Evans,* 477 S.W.2d 535 (Tex. 1972).

45. *See* Montana Code §28-2-708; Idaho Code §29-110.

Court of Alabama held that Alabama state public policy forbid enforcement of an exclusive forum clause, designating Florida courts, in a contract between an Alabama purchaser and a Florida seller.[46] The Court declared that "[w]e consider contract provisions which attempt to limit the jurisdiction of the courts of this state to be invalid and unenforceable as being contrary to public policy."[47]

A number of other states — including Arkansas, Connecticut, Florida, Georgia, Illinois, Maine, Massachusetts, North Carolina, Rhode Island, and West Virginia — appear not to have definitively resolved whether forum selection agreements are enforceable. In each state at least some local precedent suggests unenforceability, although in most instances more recent authority lends supports for a contrary result.[48]

2. Forum Non Conveniens Analysis

A number of lower courts treat forum clauses as merely one factor in a more generalized forum non conveniens analysis. Under this approach, a forum selection agreement is not enforced as a contract; rather, it is merely an indication of the parties' intentions at one time, which is to be weighed together with considerations of convenience, fairness, judicial economy and competence, and other factors.[49] As one lower court described it, a forum clause will be judged under "the totality of the circumstances measured in the interests of justice."[50] Some lower federal courts continue to follow this approach today,[51] as do a number of state courts (typically based upon domestic precedent).[52] Moreover, as discussed below, the Supreme Court has adopted a forum non conveniens analysis in those forum clause cases to which 28 U.S.C. §1404(a) is applicable.[53]

---

46. 383 So.2d 554 (Ala. 1980).

47. 383 So.2d at 556.

48. *See* W. Park, *International Forum Selection* 19-20 (1995).

49. *See* the cases compiled in Annotation, *Validity of Contractual Provision Limiting Place or Court in Which Action May be Brought*, 31 A.L.R.4th 404, 415-18; Lederman, *Viva Zapata!: Toward a Rational System of Forum-Selection Clause Enforcement in Diversity Cases*, 66 N.Y.U.L. Rev. 422, (1991) ("Perhaps the best way to understand forum-selection clauses is as a request that the court exercise its discretion to decline to hear the case where there is a more appropriate forum elsewhere, a request resembling the invocation of forum non conveniens.").

50. *D'Antuono v. CCH Computax Systems*, 570 F.Supp. 708, 712 (D. R.I. 1983) (setting forth 9 factors relevant to this inquiry).

51. *E.g.*, *Forsythe v. Saudi Arabian Airlines Corp.*, 885 F.2d 285 (5th Cir. 1989) (applying forum non conveniens doctrine without analysis even though "the parties had agreed in their contract to bring all disputes before" the Labor and Settlement of Disputes Committee in Saudi Arabia); *Furbee v. Vantage Press, Inc.*, 464 F.2d 835, 837 (D.C. Cir. 1972); *Neo Sack, Ltd. v. Vinmar Impex, Ltd.*, 1993 U.S. Dist. Lexis 377 (S.D. Tex. 1993). Some of these decisions fail to consider whether or not the forum selection agreement is an exclusive one.

52. *Exum v. Vantage Press, Inc.*, 563 P.2d 1314 (Wash. Ct. App. 1977) (holding, in domestic case, that trial court has discretion not to enforce forum clause); *Eads v. Woodmen of the World Life Ins. Society*, 785 P.2d 328 (Okla. Ct. App. 1989) ("a court in its discretion may refuse to exercise jurisdiction by necessarily respecting the intent of the contracting parties").

53. *See infra* pp. 432-33, 435-40.

3. Forum Selection Clause Enforced if "Reasonable"

A third general approach to the enforceability of forum selection clauses is reflected by *Bremen*, the *Restatement (Second) Conflict of Laws*, and the Uniform Law Commissioners' Model Choice of Forum Act. With some variations, all of these authorities treat forum clauses as presumptively valid contractual undertakings, provided that they are reasonable.

The rule adopted by all of these authorities accords significantly greater weight to forum selection agreements than a pure forum non conveniens analysis. Under this approach, a valid forum clause is not simply one of a number of relevant factors. It is presumptively enforceable, absent an affirmative showing that other factors make enforcement unreasonable.[54]

Nevertheless, the *Restatement* and Model Act analysis often falls short of requiring the enforcement of a choice of forum agreements in the same fashion that other contracts are enforced. The analysis can permit after-the-fact judicial inquiry into the "convenience," "reasonableness," and "fairness" of a particular forum provision — a degree of judicial scrutiny that most other contractual undertakings avoid. Some lower courts have followed this approach, occasionally declining to enforce forum agreements even absent substantial showings of inconvenience, unfairness, or unreasonableness.[55] Most courts, however, have scrutinized forum selection agreements for "reasonableness," but denied enforcement only in unusual circumstances.[56]

4. Forum Selection Agreements Enforced as Contracts

A fourth general approach has been to treat forum selection clauses as contractual obligations, like other contracts, and to enforce them in accordance with their terms. Emphasizing the significant interests in enforcing private agreements,[57] some lower courts have adopted this analysis. Decisions adopting this approach can be

---

54. *Hoes of America, Inc. v. Hoes*, 493 F.Supp. 1205, 1208 (C.D. Ill. 1979) (*Bremen* "rejected the application of the traditional forum non conveniens doctrine"). *But see* Gruson, *Forum-Selection Clauses in International and Interstate Commercial Agreements*, 1982 U. Ill. L. Rev. 133, 157 ("Some decisions make a distinction between passing on the reasonableness of a forum-selection clause and the exercise of discretion under the doctrine of forum non conveniens; however, the factors to be considered in deciding both motions are the same.").

55. *See infra* pp. 406-07.

56. *See infra* pp. 405-07.

57. *E.g.*, *Stewart Org. Inc. v. Ricoh Corp.*, 810 F.2d 1066, 1075 (11th Cir. 1987) (en banc) (Tjoflat, J., concurring) ("The law of contracts presumes that Ricoh has already compensated *Stewart*, through lowered costs or some other method, for any inconvenience that Stewart or its witnesses might suffer by trying the case in New York."), *rev'd on other grounds*, 487 U.S. 22 (1988); *Cerro De Pasco Copper Corp. v. Knut Knutsen, O.A.S.*, 187 F.2d 990 (2d Cir. 1951) (Clark, J., concurring) ("I prefer to place my concurrence upon the validity, under the circumstances here disclosed, of the contract requiring all claims to be settled in Norway. The apparently wider discretion granted in the opinion to the district judge to pass upon the appropriateness of the forum may, perhaps, raise more extensive questions which we need not now face.").

similar to those applying a deferential "reasonableness" analysis. The Supreme Court's decision in *Carnival Cruise Lines, Inc. v. Shute* is a leading example.[58]

5. New York General Obligation Law §5-1402

A fifth general approach is that taken to submissions to New York jurisdiction in §5-1402 of the New York General Obligations Law.[59] The section provides that "[a]ny person may maintain an action or proceeding against a foreign corporation" arising out of a contractual obligation for more than $1 million, where the parties' agreement "contains a provision ... whereby such foreign corporation ... agrees to submit to the jurisdiction of the courts of this state." The provision was expressly designed to eliminate uncertainty in the enforcement of forum selection agreements resulting from forum non conveniens and reasonableness analysis.[60]

6. Selected Materials on Approaches to the Enforceability of Forum Selection Agreements

Excerpted below are cases and statutory materials that illustrate various approaches to the enforceability of forum clauses. The Oregon Supreme Court's 1928 decision in *Kahn v. Tazwell*[61] refused to enforce an agreement designating Karlsruhe, Germany as the exclusive contractual forum, citing traditional public policy prohibitions. Reflecting the same attitude, §28-2-708 of the Montana Code invalidates contractual restraints on a plaintiff's choice of forum (both domestic or foreign). Also excerpted below are the Model Choice of Forum Act, and *Bremen v. Zapata Off-Shore Co.*, the Supreme Court's landmark decision recognizing the enforceability of forum clauses. Finally, the California Supreme Court's opinion, in *Smith, Valentino, & Smith, Inc. v. Superior Court*,[62] illustrates the forum non conveniens approach of some contemporary decisions to the enforceability of forum clauses.

KAHN v. TAZWELL

266 P. 238 (Oregon Supreme Court 1928)

BEAN, JUDGE. This is [a] proceeding ... to require the defendant, Hon. George Tazwell, judge of the circuit court for Multnomah County, to entertain jurisdiction of an action commenced by the relator, Adolf Kahn, against the New York Life Insurance Company, a New York corporation, on an insurance policy. ... The appli-

---

58. Solimine, *Forum Selection Clauses and the Privatization of Procedure*, 25 Cornell Int'l L. J. 51, 78 (1992) ("*Carnival* seems to lay to rest the notion that *The Bremen* authorized a free-wheeling balancing-of-interests test to govern the enforceability of choice-of-forum clauses.").

59. N.Y. Gen. Oblig. Law §5-1402 (McKinney 1989).

60. Friedler, *Party Autonomy Revisited: A Statutory Solution to a Choice of Law Problem*, 37 Kansas L. Rev. 471 (1989); Rashkover, *Title 14, New York Choice of Law Rule for Contractual Disputes: Avoiding the Unreasonable Results*, 71 Cornell L. Rev. 227 (1985).

61. 266 P. 238 (Ore. 1928).

62. 551 P.2d 1206 (Calif. 1976).

cation for the policy was made by the plaintiff in Germany, signed by the president and secretary of the New York Life Insurance Company at its main office, New York City, and was signed by the general secretary of the company for Europe at the [New York Life] office in Paris, France.

[New York Life] is authorized to conduct life insurance business anywhere. Prior to the declaration by the United States of war against Germany, this corporation was transacting life insurance business in Germany. This company, as one of the requirements essential to the right to transact its business in the state of Oregon, on February 16, 1923, executed and filed with the insurance commission, as required by §6327, Or. L., a power of attorney appointing R. A. Durham, a citizen of Oregon, residing at Portland, its attorney in fact, upon whom "lawful and valid service may be made of all writs, processes and summons in any case, suit or proceeding commenced by or against any such company or association in any court mentioned in this section and necessary to give such court complete jurisdiction thereof."

The action mentioned was commenced October 3, 1927, and summons and complaint was served by delivery to the said R. A. Durham, as such attorney in fact. The defendant appeared specially and filed a motion to quash the service of the summons, for the reason that the service was not authorized by law; and that the court could not obtain jurisdiction over the person of the defendant [New York Life] in that plaintiff was and is a resident and citizen of the republic, formerly empire, of Germany, and has not been a resident, inhabitant, or citizen of the state of Oregon, and was not at the time of the commencement of the action, and is not now, within the state of Oregon, as shown by affidavit. ... [The defendant also relied upon the following forum selection clause, contained in the insurance policy that it issued to Mr. Kahn:]

> For the fulfillment of this contract only the courts of Karlsruhe are competent; as the legal domicile of the company is agreed upon its office at Karlsruhe and for the insured or his legal successor the place mentioned in the application of insurance. ...

The further question arises whether the court has jurisdiction of a cause of action and of the parties. ... A corporation which goes into a foreign jurisdiction and there prosecutes its corporate affairs impliedly consents to be sued there. ... Under this theory, it has been held that process may be served on an actual agent or upon an agent designated by statute. ... The great weight of authority [holds that] the mere fact that the cause of action arose, or the transaction giving rise to it occurred, beyond the territorial limits of the state of suit, does not prevent effective service of process upon an actual agent of a foreign corporation, if the conditions of service are otherwise satisfied. [New York Life] qualified to do business in this state, and voluntarily, in a formal manner, appointed an agent upon whom service of process might be served in an action against the corporation. ... The court obtained jurisdiction of the corporation ... notwithstanding the fact that the contract of insurance was executed outside the state, and notwithstanding the fact that the plaintiff is a nonresident of the state of Oregon.

It is contended by the company that the clause in the policy, quoted above, in regard to domicile, restricts the jurisdiction, and limits the jurisdiction to enforce the conditions of the policy to the "courts of Karlsruhe." In *Sudbury v Ambi Verwaltung, etc.*, 210 N.Y.S. 164, 166, the court stated: "The federal rule is well settled that contracts by which parties attempt to confer exclusive jurisdiction upon a particular court, foreign or domestic, are contrary to public policy and void." The stipulation of the parties contained in the contract of insurance is contrary to public policy and void. The law prescribes the jurisdiction of our courts, and it cannot be diminished or increased by the convention of the parties. The stipulation is in effect a legal opinion of the parties that only "the courts of Karlsruhe" are competent for the fulfillment of the contracts. In *Kent v. Universal Film Manufacturing Co.*, 193 N.Y.S. 838, Mr. Justice Laughlin said: "The federal court regards contracts by which parties attempt to confer exclusive jurisdiction over a particular court, foreign or domestic, as contrary to public policy and void." ...

MONTANA CODE ANNOTATED

§28-2-708

Restraints upon legal proceedings void. Every stipulation or condition in a contract by which any party thereto is restricted from enforcing his rights under the contract by the usual proceedings in the ordinary tribunals or which limits the time within which he may thus enforce his rights is void.

THE BREMEN v. ZAPATA OFF-SHORE CO.

407 U.S. 1 (1972)

CHIEF JUSTICE BURGER. We granted certiorari to review a judgment of the United States Court of Appeals for the Fifth Circuit declining to enforce a forum-selection clause governing disputes arising under an international towage contract between petitioners and respondent. ... For the reasons stated hereafter, we vacate the judgment of the Court of Appeals.

In November 1967, respondent Zapata, a Houston-based American corporation, contracted with petitioner Unterweser, a German corporation, to tow Zapata's ocean-going, self-elevating drilling rig *Chaparral* from Louisiana to a point off Ravenna, Italy, in the Adriatic Sea, where Zapata had agreed to drill certain wells. ... The contract submitted by Unterweser contained the following provision, which is at issue in this case: "Any dispute arising must be treated before the London Court of Justice." In addition, the contract contained two clauses purporting to exculpate Unterweser from liability for damages to the towed barge.

After reviewing the contract and making several changes, but without any alteration in the forum-selection or exculpatory clauses, a Zapata vice president executed

the contract and forwarded it to Unterweser in Germany, where Unterweser accepted the changes, and the contract became effective. ... Unterweser's deep sea tug
Bremen departed Venice, Louisiana, with the *Chaparral* in tow bound for Italy. ...
[W]hile the flotilla was in international waters in the middle of the Gulf of Mexico, a
severe storm arose. The sharp roll of the *Chaparral* in Gulf waters caused its elevator
legs, which had been raised for the voyage, to break off and fall into the sea, seriously
damaging the *Chaparral*. In this emergency situation Zapata instructed the *Bremen*
to tow its damaged rig to Tampa, Florida, the nearest port of refuge.

On January 12, Zapata, ignoring its contract promise to litigate "any dispute
arising" in the English courts, commenced a suit in admiralty in the United States
District Court at Tampa, seeking $3,500,000 damages against Unterweser *in person-
am* and the *Bremen in rem*, alleging negligent towage and breach of contract.
Unterweser responded by invoking the forum clause of the towage contract, and
moved to dismiss for lack of jurisdiction or on *forum non conveniens* grounds, or in
the alternative to stay the action pending submission of the dispute to the "London
Court of Justice." Shortly thereafter, in February, before the District Court had ruled
on its motion to stay or dismiss the United States action, Unterweser commenced an
action against Zapata seeking damages for breach of the towage contract in the High
Court of Justice in London, as the contract provided. Zapata appeared in that court
to contest jurisdiction, but its challenge was rejected, the English courts holding that
the contractual forum provision conferred jurisdiction. ...

[T]he District Court denied Unterweser's January motion to dismiss or stay
Zapata's initial action ... reiterating the traditional view of many American courts
that "agreements in advance of controversy whose object is to oust the jurisdiction of
the courts are contrary to public policy and will not be enforced."... [T]he District
Court gave the forum-selection clause little, if any, weight. Instead, the court treated
the motion to dismiss under normal *forum non conveniens* doctrine applicable in the
absence of such a clause. ... Under that doctrine "unless the balance is strongly in
favor of the defendant, the plaintiff's choice of forum should rarely be disturbed." ...
The District Court concluded: "The balance of conveniences here is not strongly in
favor of [Unterweser] and [Zapata's] choice of forum should not be disturbed."

[The Court of Appeals affirmed.] It noted that (1) the flotilla never "escaped the
Fifth Circuit's mare nostrum, and the casualty occurred in close proximity to the district court"; (2) a considerable number of potential witnesses, including Zapata
crewmen, resided in the Gulf Coast area; (3) preparation for the voyage and inspection and repair work had been performed in the Gulf area; (4) the testimony of the
Bremen crew was available by way of deposition; (5) England had no interest in or
contact with the controversy other than the forum-selection clause. The Court of
Appeals majority further noted that Zapata was a United States citizen and "[t]he
discretion of the district court to remand the case to a foreign forum was consequently limited" — especially since it appeared likely that the English courts would
enforce the exculpatory clauses. In the Court of Appeals' view, enforcement of such

clauses would be contrary to public policy in American courts under *Bisso v. Inland Waterways Corp.*, 349 U.S. 85 (1955), and *Dixilyn Drilling Corp. v. Crescent Towing & Salvage Co.*, 372 U.S. 679 (1963). Therefore, "[t]he district court was entitled to consider that remanding Zapata to a foreign forum, with no practical contact with the controversy, could raise a bar to recovery by a United States citizen which its own convenient courts would not countenance."

We hold ... that far too little weight and effect were given to the forum clause in resolving this controversy. For at least two decades we have witnessed an expansion of overseas commercial activities by business enterprises based in the United States. The barrier of distance that once tended to confine a business concern to a modest territory no longer does so. Here we see an American company with special expertise contracting with a foreign company to tow a complex machine thousands of miles across seas and oceans. The expansion of American business and industry will hardly be encouraged if, notwithstanding solemn contracts, we insist on a parochial concept that all disputes must be resolved under our laws and in our courts. Absent a contract forum, the considerations relied on by the Court of Appeals would be persuasive reasons for holding an American forum convenient in the traditional sense, but in an era of expanding world trade and commerce, the absolute aspects of the doctrine [followed by the Court of Appeals] have little place and would be a heavy hand indeed on the future development of international commercial dealings by Americans. We cannot have trade and commerce in world markets and international waters exclusively on our terms, governed by our laws, and resolved in our courts.

Forum-selection clauses have historically not been favored by American courts. Many courts, federal and state, have declined to enforce such clauses on the ground that they were "contrary to public policy," or that their effect was to "oust the jurisdiction" of the court. Although this view apparently still has considerable acceptance, other courts are tending to adopt a more hospitable attitude toward forum-selection clauses. This view, advanced in the well-reasoned dissenting opinion in the instant case, is that such clauses are prima facie valid and should be enforced unless enforcement is shown by the resisting party to be "unreasonable" under the circumstances. We believe this is the correct doctrine to be followed by federal district courts sitting in admiralty. It is merely the other side of the proposition recognized by this Court in *National Equipment Rental, Ltd. v. Szukhent*, holding that in federal courts a party may validly consent to be sued in a jurisdiction where he cannot be found for service of process through contractual designation of an "agent" for receipt of process in that jurisdiction. In so holding, the Court stated: "[I]t is settled ... that parties to a contract may agree in advance to submit to the jurisdiction of a given court, to permit notice to be served by the opposing party, or even to waive notice altogether." ...

This approach is substantially that followed in other common-law countries including England. It is the view advanced by noted scholars and that adopted by the *Restatement [(Second)] Conflict of Laws*. It accords with ancient concepts of freedom of contract and reflects an appreciation of the expanding horizons of American con-

tractors who seek business in all parts of the world. Not surprisingly, foreign businessmen prefer, as do we, to have disputes resolved in their own courts, but if that choice is not available, then in a neutral forum with expertise in the subject matter. Plainly, the courts of England meet the standards of neutrality and long experience in admiralty litigation. The choice of that forum was made in an arm's-length negotiation by experienced and sophisticated businessmen, and absent some compelling and countervailing reason it should be honored by the parties and enforced by the courts.
...

There are compelling reasons why a freely negotiated private international agreement, unaffected by fraud, undue influence, or overweening bargaining power, such as that involved here, should be given full effect. In this case, for example, we are concerned with a far from routine transaction between companies of two different nations contemplating the tow of an extremely costly piece of equipment from Louisiana across the Gulf of Mexico and the Atlantic Ocean, through the Mediterranean Sea to its final destination in the Adriatic Sea. In the course of its voyage, it was to traverse the waters of many jurisdictions. The *Chaparral* could have been damaged at any point along the route, and there were countless possible ports of refuge. That the accident occurred in the Gulf of Mexico and the barge was towed to Tampa in an emergency were mere fortuities. It cannot be doubted for a moment that the parties sought to provide for a neutral forum for the resolution of any disputes arising during the tow. Manifestly much uncertainty and possibly great inconvenience to both parties could arise if a suit could be maintained in any jurisdiction in which an accident might occur or if jurisdiction were left to any place where the Bremen or Unterweser might happen to be found. The elimination of all such uncertainties by agreeing in advance on a forum acceptable to both parties is an indispensable element in international trade, commerce, and contracting. There is strong evidence that the forum clause was a vital part of the [Zapata/Unterweser] agreement, and it would be unrealistic to think that the parties did not conduct their negotiations, including fixing the monetary terms, with the consequences of the forum clause figuring prominently in their calculations. ...

Thus, in the light of present-day commercial realities and expanding international trade we conclude that the forum clause should control absent a strong showing that it should be set aside. Although their opinions are not altogether explicit, it seems reasonably clear that the District Court and the Court of Appeals placed the burden on Unterweser to show that London would be a more convenient forum than Tampa, although the contract expressly resolved that issue. The correct approach would have been to enforce the forum clause specifically unless Zapata could clearly show that enforcement would be unreasonable and unjust, or that the clause was invalid for such reasons as fraud or overreaching. Accordingly, the case must be remanded for reconsideration.

We note, however, that there is nothing in the record presently before us that would support a refusal to enforce the forum clause. [The Court discussed and rejected an argument that enforcement of the forum selection clause would violate a U.S. public policy against certain types of contractual exculpatory clauses.] Courts have ... suggested that a forum clause, even though it is freely bargained for and contravenes no important public policy of the forum, may nevertheless be "unreasonable" and unenforceable if the chosen forum is *seriously* inconvenient for the trial of the action. Of course, where it can be said with reasonable assurance that at the time they entered the contract, the parties to a freely negotiated private international commercial agreement contemplated the claimed inconvenience, it is difficult to see why any such claim of inconvenience should be heard to render the forum clause unenforceable. We are not here dealing with an agreement between two Americans to resolve their essentially local disputes in a remote alien forum. In such a case, the serious inconvenience of the contractual forum to one or both of the parties might carry greater weight in determining the reasonableness of the forum clause. The remoteness of the forum might suggest that the agreement was an adhesive one, or that the parties did not have the particular controversy in mind when they made their agreement; yet even there the party claiming should bear a heavy burden of proof.[63] Similarly, selection of a remote forum to apply differing foreign law to an essentially American controversy might contravene an important public policy of the forum. For example, so long as *Bisso* governs American courts with respect to the towage business in American waters, it would quite arguably be improper to permit an American tower to avoid that policy by providing a foreign forum for resolution of his disputes with an American towee.

This case, however, involves a freely negotiated international commercial transaction between a German and an American corporation for towage of a vessel from the Gulf of Mexico to the Adriatic Sea. As noted, selection of a London forum was clearly a reasonable effort to bring vital certainty to this international transaction and to provide a neutral forum experienced and capable in the resolution of admiralty litigation. Whatever "inconvenience" Zapata would suffer by being forced to litigate in the contractual forum as it agreed to do was clearly foreseeable at the time of contracting. In such circumstances it should be incumbent on the party seeking to escape his contract to show that trial in the contractual forum will be so gravely difficult and inconvenient that he will for all practical purposes be deprived of his day in court. Absent that, there is no basis for concluding that it would be unfair, unjust, or unreasonable to hold that party to his bargain.

In the course of its ruling on Unterweser's second motion to stay the proceedings in Tampa, the District Court did make a conclusory finding that the balance of

---

63. *See, e.g.,* Model Choice of Forum Act §3(3), comment: "On rare occasions, the state of the forum may be a substantially more convenient place for the trial of a particular controversy than the chosen state. If so, the present clause would permit the action to proceed. This result will presumably be in accord with the desires of the parties. It can be assumed that they did not have the particular controversy in mind when they made the choice-of-forum agreement since they would not consciously have agreed to have the action brought in an inconvenient place.

convenience was "strongly" in favor of litigation in Tampa. However, as previously noted, in making that finding the court erroneously placed the burden of proof on Unterweser to show that the balance of convenience was strongly in its favor. Moreover, the finding falls far short of a conclusion that Zapata would be effectively deprived of its day in court should it be forced to litigate in London. Indeed, it cannot even be assumed that it would be placed to the expense of transporting its witnesses to London. It is not unusual for important issues in international admiralty cases to be dealt with by deposition. Both the District Court and the Court of Appeals majority appeared satisfied that Unterweser could receive a fair hearing in Tampa by using deposition testimony of its witnesses from distant places, and there is no reason to conclude that Zapata could not use deposition testimony to equal advantage if forced to litigate in London as it bound itself to do. Nevertheless, to allow Zapata an opportunity to carry its heavy burden of showing not only that the balance of convenience is strongly in favor of trial in Tampa (that is, that it will be far more inconvenient for Zapata to litigate in London than it will be for Unterweser to litigate in Tampa), but also that a London trial will be so manifestly and gravely inconvenient to Zapata that it will be effectively deprived of a meaningful day in court, we remand for further proceedings.

MODEL CHOICE OF FORUM ACT

[excerpted in Appendix F]

SMITH, VALENTINO & SMITH, INC. v. SUPERIOR COURT

551 P.2d 1206 (Calif. 1976)

RICHARDSON, JUSTICE. ... [W]e consider the extent to which California courts in breach of contract actions may give effect to a contractual forum selection clause providing for trial of the action in another state. Relying on such a clause, the trial court herein found that the Pennsylvania forum specified in the contract was the proper forum for trial ... and consequently issued an order staying proceeding in this state. We conclude that the trial court acted within its discretion in doing so.

Petitioner Smith, Valentino & Smith, Inc. ("Smith") is a California corporation. Real party in interest Life Assurance Company of Pennsylvania ("Assurance") is a Pennsylvania corporation doing business in California. In March 1973, the two corporations entered into a contract by which Smith was appointed the "managing general agent" to represent Assurance in soliciting group insurance policies in California and other western states. The contract included a reciprocal forum selection clause whereunder Smith agreed to bring all actions arising out of the agency agreement only in Philadelphia, and Assurance in turn agreed to bring all such actions only in Los Angeles. Despite the provisions of this clause, in November 1974 Smith filed [suit] in the Los Angeles Superior Court against ... Assurance. Assurance moved for dismissal on the basis of the forum selection clause and Code of Civil Procedure §410.30(a), which provides:

When a court upon motion of a party or its own motion finds that in the interest of substantial justice an action should be heard in a forum outside this state, the court shall stay or dismiss the action in whole or in part on any conditions that may be just.

Smith opposed this motion on the basis that Smith's intended witnesses were all residents of California and that Smith was financially unable to bear the extra cost incident to the prosecution of the action in Philadelphia. The trial court denied Assurance's motion to dismiss but stayed all proceedings until further order, finding that the proper forum for trial ... was Philadelphia. Smith [appeals], contending that the forum selection clause is either void per se or unenforceable on the facts of this case. We disagree.

Preliminarily we note that the clause in question, in addition to designating the proper forum for litigation, also provides that Pennsylvania law is to govern disputes concerning the contract. Such choice of law provisions are usually respected by California courts. *Windsor Mills, Inc. v. Collins & Aikman Corp.*, 25 Cal.App.3d 987, 995 n.6 (1972); *Restatement (Second) Conflict of Laws* §187 [excerpted *infra* pp. 658-59] (1971). Assuming that Pennsylvania law applies, we observe that the courts of that state have held that forum selection clauses will be given effect unless the party assailing the clause establishes that its enforcement would be unreasonable, *i.e.*, that the forum selected would be unavailable or unable to accomplish substantial justice. *Central Contracting Co. v. C. E. Youngdahl & Co.*, 209 A.2d 810 (Pa. 1965). ...

Nonetheless, Smith contends that the subject clause is void and unenforceable as violative of California's declared public policy. In support, Smith cites *General Acceptance Corp. v. Robinson*, 277 P. 1039 (Calif. 1929) ... [and other decisions.] These cases do recite the general rule that the parties may not, by private agreement, "oust" the jurisdiction of the courts by preventing a court from hearing a cause otherwise within its jurisdiction. In the *General Acceptance* case, for example, the parties had attempted to specify the county in which contract disputes would be tried. We held the contractual provision void since it would contravene general statutory provisions which designate the proper counties in which actions may be tried. Forum selection clauses, in contrast, violate no such carefully conceived statutory patterns.

The assertion that forum selection clauses are void per se as constituting attempts to oust the courts of their jurisdiction has been challenged as "hardly more than a vestigial legal fiction" which "reflects something of a provincial attitude regarding the fairness of other tribunals." *The Bremen v. Zapata Off-Shore Co.* While it is true that the parties may not deprive courts of their jurisdiction over causes by private agreement *Restatement (Second) Conflict of Laws* §80, comment a (1971), it is readily apparent that courts possess discretion to decline to exercise jurisdiction in recognition of the parties' free and voluntary choice of a different forum although we have acknowledged a policy favoring access to California co dent plaintiffs, we likewise conclude that the policy is satisfied in those c as here, a plaintiff has freely and voluntarily negotiated away his right to a forum. In so holding we are in accord with the modern trend which favors enforce-ability of such forum selection clauses. ...

No satisfying reason of public policy has been suggested why enforcement should be denied a forum selection clause appearing in a contract entered into freely and voluntarily by parties who have negotiated at arm's length. For the foregoing reasons, we conclude that forum selection clauses are valid and may be given effect, in the court's discretion and in the absence of a showing that enforcement of such a clause would be unreasonable. While *General Acceptance Corp. v. Robinson*, 277 P. 1039, is factually distinguishable and, accordingly, may be said to rest upon policy considerations not involved in the present action, nevertheless to the extent that the rationale of *General Acceptance* is inconsistent with our opinion, we decline to follow it.

We turn to the question whether Smith has carried its burden of establishing that enforcement of the present clause would be unreasonable. Although Smith relies upon the factors of inconvenience and expense of a Pennsylvania forum, both Smith and Assurance reasonably can be held to have contemplated in negotiating their agreement the additional expense and inconvenience attendant on the litigation of their respective claims in a distant forum; such matters are inherent in a reciprocal clause of this type. As stated in *Central Contracting Co. v. C. E. Youngdahl & Co.*, "Mere inconvenience or additional expense is not the test of unreasonableness since it may be assumed that the plaintiff received under the contract consideration for these things." Moreover, although Smith's witnesses may reside in California, no rea-son appears why their testimony might not be obtained by deposition or at trial, at Smith's expense. Finally, since the trial court stayed the present action rather than dismissing it, the court has retained continuing jurisdiction over the cause. Should the Pennsylvania courts become unavailable for some unforeseeable reason, Smith may seek to reinstate its California action. ...

Finally, Smith contends that the clause is limited in its application to breach of contract actions and should not apply to the tort counts in Smith's complaint. These counts (unfair competition and intentional interference with advantageous business relationships) arose directly out of Smith's contractual relationship with Assurance and reasonably may be interpreted as falling within the clause which provides for a Pennsylvania forum to litigate "Any actions or proceedings instituted by . . . [Smith] under this Agreement with respect to any matters arising under *or growing out of this agreement*, ..." (Italics added.)

Dissent   MOSK, JUSTICE, dissenting. I dissent. Any analysis of this problem should begin with recognition of three basic precepts. First, while the private interests of liti-gants may be considered, the public interest is paramount. Second, unless a balance is strongly in favor of the defendant, the plaintiff's choice of forum should rarely be disturbed. Third, California has an overriding public policy favoring access to its courts by resident litigants.

Petitioner asserts the forum selection clause of the contract involved herein is void and unenforceable. Its contention is supported by ample authority. It is significant that the majority cite no California cases upholding this type of forum shopping by prearrangement. And without citation of authority from any source they attempt to carve a finely honed dichotomy between a court deprived of jurisdiction by agreement and a court declining to exercise jurisdiction because of an agreement. To a plaintiff denied an opportunity to be heard in the courts of his home state such a gossamer thin distinction is of dubious comfort.

The rule was well stated by the court in *Beirut Universal Bank [v. Superior Court*, 74 Cal. Rptr. 333 (Calif. 1969)], citing Corbin: "'It is a generally accepted rule in the United States that an express provision in a contract that no suit shall be maintained thereon, except in a particular court or in the courts of a particular county, state, or nation, is not effective to deprive any court of jurisdiction that it otherwise could have over litigation based on that contract.'" 6A *Corbin on Contracts* §1445, p. 477 (1962). ... The majority rely on *The Bremen v. Zapata Off-Shore Co.* But they overlook Chief Justice Burger's observation in that case that "[f]orum-selection clauses have historically not been favored by American courts." Nevertheless the Court concluded that such clauses are enforceable "by federal district courts sitting in *admiralty*." The Court did not direct that admiralty law is to be adapted to state courts in determining their jurisdiction. ...

Notes on Tazwell, Bremen, Smith, Montana Code, and Model Act

1. *Rationale for historic unenforceability of forum selection agreements.* What were the reasons for the historic unenforceability of forum selection agreements? What arguments are advanced in *Tazwell* and in Justice Mosk's dissent in *Smith*?

(a) *"Ousting" courts of jurisdiction.* Tazwell invoked the dogma that "agreements in advance to oust the courts of the jurisdiction conferred by law are illegal and void." *Insurance Co. v. Morse*, 87 U.S. 445, 451 (1874). The notion that private parties cannot "oust" courts of their jurisdiction paralleled the adage that "private parties cannot legislate," which was invoked by U.S. courts at the same time to invalidate choice of law agreements. 2 J. Beale, *Conflict of Laws* 1079 (1935). What does it mean to "oust" a court of jurisdiction? Does a forum clause really "oust" a court of its jurisdiction? Is that label necessary to the position that forum agreements should be unenforceable?

Would there be anything wrong with a forum clause requiring that all disputes be litigated before a specifically identified U.S. district judge? Why? What about a clause forbidding a specific judge — for example, Justice Doggett — from deciding the case? Why is either such provision different in principle from a standard exclusive forum selection clause? Do not both even further enhance certainty and predictability? Note the reliance (referred to in *Smith*) in *General Acceptance* on a state venue statute to invalidate a clause designating a specific California court in an intra-state dispute. How is this different from a forum selection clause?

(b) *Private agreements regarding public remedies.* Consider the remark in *Tazwell* that a forum clause should not be enforced because it is "in effect a legal opinion of the parties that only [specified courts] are competent." Compare the public policy reflected in §28-2-708 of the Montana Code Annotated. Is there anything disquieting about a private agreement, based ordinarily upon bargaining power, on an issue as open-ended and outcome determinative as the decision-maker that will settle all the parties' disputes? To what extent should it be permissible for private parties to barter over access to public courts and judicial relief?

(c) *Protecting local residents' access to justice.* Forum selection clauses were traditionally disfavored because they were held to burden a citizen's right of access to the courts:

Every citizen is entitled to resort to all the courts of the country, and to invoke the protection which all the laws or all those courts may afford him. A man may not barter away his life or his freedom, or his substantial rights. *Insurance Company v. Morse*, 87 U.S. 445, 451 (1874).

This rationale was most strongly advanced in cases where consumers or other individuals were involved, particularly when they sought access to their own local courts. Consider Justice Mosk's dissent in *Smith*, and particularly his conclusion that "California has an overriding public policy favoring access to its courts by resident litigants." Compare §28-2-708 of the Montana Code Annotated. Is this an improper legislative purpose? Is the welfare of local residents furthered by refusals to enforce forum selection clauses? How were local interests implicated in *Tazwell*? Who was the plaintiff? the defendant? Where did the cause of action arise? If ever there was a case for forum non conveniens dismissal, was it not *Tazwell*?

(d) *Protecting consumers and individuals.* Who was the party resisting the forum clause in *Tazwell*? in *Bremen* and *Smith*? What role did the negotiating power of the parties have in the cases? Is there any reason to treat forum clauses differently from other provisions in form contracts? Are forum selection agreements the same as most other contractual provisions, such as price, performance, liability, damages, and the like? To what extent is it likely that parties really know what the practical consequences of their agreement on a particular forum will mean when they enter into the agreement?

(e) *Judicial envy.* Some have suggested that common law judges were jealous of their jurisdiction, in part because they were compensated based upon their case-load. Cowen & Da Costa, *The Contractual Forum: Situation in England and the British Commonwealth*, 13 Am. J. Comp. L. 179, 189 (1964); Reese, *The Contractual Forum: Situation in the United States*, 13 Am. J. Comp. L. 187, 189 (1964). The same rationale has been advanced for judicial hostility towards arbitration agreements. G. Born, *International Commercial Arbitration in the United States* 187-88 (1994).

(f) *Skepticism regarding benefits of forum selection clauses.* Do the benefits of ensuring a "convenient" forum and preventing multiplicitous litigation really result from most forum agreements, and do these benefits outweigh their costs? What effects do forum clauses have on small businesses?

2. *Practical importance of forum selection clauses.* Recall the comments, cited above, regarding the practical importance of forum selection clauses. *See supra* pp. 372-73. A forum clause can oblige a party to litigate in a distant court (imposing expense and inconvenience), where its adversary is on "home ground," subject to unfavorable procedural and substantive law. Note the comparable practical consequences of the forum non conveniens doctrine. *See supra* pp. 3-7 & 318. Does justice permit private parties to bargain over such matters as their practical ability to litigate effectively and forum bias? Does it not compromise the judicial process to permit parties to agree, in effect, that one party shall be required to present its case less effectively because of distance, cost, and familiarity?

3. *Criticisms of historic rule against forum selection agreements.* How persuasive were the criticisms, launched in the 1950s, of the historic rule against forum clauses? Consider:

> The reasons stated by the courts for denying effect to choice of forum clauses are unconvincing. By and large, the courts have contented themselves with saying either (1) that the parties cannot by their agreement oust a court of jurisdiction, or (2) that to allow the parties to change the rules relating to the place where suit may be brought would 'disturb the symmetry of the law' and lead to inconvenience, or (3) simply that choice of forum provisions are against public policy. The last of these reasons does no more than state a conclusion without attempt at explanation. The second — that the parties should not be permitted to tamper with rules relating to the place of suit — also falls wide of the mark. There are in fact no rules, other than those concerned with jurisdiction, which determine whether suit should be brought in one state rather than in another. As to the first reason, it is, of course, true that the parties cannot by their agreement oust a court of jurisdiction. But a court is not always required to exercise such jurisdiction as it may possess. Courts often refuse to hear a case because of forum non conveniens considerations. Why cannot they likewise dismiss a suit on the ground that it was not brought in a forum selected by the parties? Reese, *The Contractual Forum*, 13 Am. J. Comp. L. 187, 188 (1964).

Professor Reese's views formed the intellectual justification for the *Second Restatement* (for which he was the Reporter) and *Bremen*. Does Reese really confront the fundamental objections to forum selection clauses? Does he explain why legislative rules conferring jurisdiction on a local court can be ignored? Does he address the concerns that forum clauses will deny local residents the protections of public court systems, for which they have paid, based solely on privately-negotiated contracts specifying where public justice may be obtained? Consider Justice Mosk's remark that "a finely honed dichotomy between a court deprived of jurisdiction ... and a court declining to exercise jurisdiction" would be regarded as a "gossamer thin distinction ... of dubious comfort," to most plaintiffs.

4. *Results in* Bremen *and* Smith. Was *Bremen* correctly decided? Should the Court have forced Zapata — an American employer, tax-payer, and company — to a far-off foreign court to enforce its tort claims? Why? Consider the facts in *Bremen*; is it not inconceivable that the law should prevent the parties from doing anything to limit the multitude of fora that were potentially available? On the other hand, if U.S. (and German) companies engage in business in many different countries, should they not accept that they will end up in court in those places? Why would that be such a "heavy hand" on international commerce?

Compare the result in *Bremen* with that in *Smith*. Was *Smith* correctly decided? What about Justice Mosk's dissenting views? Suppose that *Smith* had involved a German company and German contractual forum instead of a Pennsylvania party and forum clause. Should (and would) the California court reach the same result? Are the arguments for enforceability stronger or weaker in this hypothetical than in *Smith*?

5. *Rationales for general enforceability of forum selection agreements*. What are the rationales underlying the general approval of forum agreements in *Bremen*, the Model Choice of Forum Act, and the Restatement? Are these rationales persuasive?

(a) *"Ancient concepts of freedom of contract."* Is it plausible for the Court to cite "ancient freedoms" to contract in support of the *Bremen* rule? Recall the historic status of forum selection agreements at common law. *See supra* pp. 373-74.

(b) *"Heavy hand" on international commerce*. Will the wheels of international commerce grind to a halt if parties cannot enforce forum selection clauses? What happened before 1972? How exactly is it that forum selection clauses assist international businessmen (as opposed to international lawyers)?

(c) *"Elimination of all such uncertainties."* Do forum clauses really eliminate the uncertainties that are endemic in international litigation? How? Consider the numerous cases cited in this Chapter dealing with the enforceability of forum selection clauses. Would there not be greater certainty if forum selection clauses were *per se* unenforceable? In any event, why is "certainty" so important in commercial matters? Aren't countless uncertainties inherent in any contract?

6. *Different contemporary standards of enforceability of forum selection clauses*. Compare the standards of enforceability in *Restatement (Second) Conflict of Laws* §80 (1971), *Bremen*, and *Smith*. What are the differences in these approaches? Which approach is most likely to result in enforcement of a forum agreement?

(a) *Restatement (Second) Conflict of Laws §80*. What is the rule of enforceability set forth in §80? How is that rule influenced by comment a? How is enforcement of a forum selection clause under §80 different from a pure forum non conveniens analysis? How is enforcement of a forum selection agreement under §80 different from ordinary enforcement of a contract?

(b) Bremen. What is the rule of enforceability set forth in *Bremen*? Are forum selection clauses treated in precisely the same fashion as other contracts? Do courts ordinarily scrutinize privately-negotiated contracts for "reasonableness" and "fairness"? What, if anything, makes forum selection agreements different?

(c) Smith. What is the rule of enforceability set forth in *Smith*? How does the *Smith* rule differ from a pure forum non conveniens analysis? Are forum clauses entitled to any weight under *Smith*? If so, what weight? Recall the comment in *Bremen* that "it would be unrealistic to think that the parties did not conduct their negotiations, including fixing the monetary terms, with the consequences of the forum clause figuring prominently in their calculations." If that is correct, does the *Smith* approach deny one party the financial exchange it made to obtain a forum clause of its choosing?

7. *Appropriate approach to enforcing forum selection clauses*. Assuming that forum clauses are not *per se* unenforceable, which of the foregoing approaches is the *right* one? Is it more appropriate to (a) maintain a pure rule of forum non conveniens, in which a forum clause is one of numerous, equally-significant factors bearing on the ultimate question of selecting a convenient forum; or (b) enforce forum selection clauses in full accordance with their terms like other contracts; or (c) enforce forum clauses when they are "reasonable" and not "unfair"? Do the differences between forum clauses and other contracts require different rules of enforceability? If so, what rules? How would *Tazwell*, *Bremen*, and *Smith* be decided under each of the foregoing rules?

8. *Considerations of reciprocity.* Suppose a U.S. company enters into a contract with a company organized and operating in State A. The contract provides that State A's courts shall be the exclusive forum for resolving the parties' disputes. In deciding whether a U.S. court should enforce this agreement, is it relevant that State A refuses to enforce forum selection clauses selecting U.S. courts against its own residents? Why or why not? Concretely, would it have been relevant in *Tazwell* if German courts would not have enforced a clause requiring suit in the United States? Would it have been relevant in *Bremen* that German courts would have heard claims against Zapata without giving effect to the English forum clause?

9. *Forum selection clauses and long-arm jurisdiction.* The historic rule that forum selection clauses were unenforceable held sway in the time of *Pennoyer,* when judicial jurisdiction was subject to strict territorial limits. *See supra* pp. 70-73. Are the two historic rules related? Note that territorial restrictions on jurisdiction met their demise at roughly the same time that forum selection agreements became enforceable.

10. *Special need for forum selection clauses in international transactions.* Is there any greater need for forum agreements in international contracts than in domestic ones? What does *Bremen* suggest? Suppose that *Bremen* had involved a contract to be performed in a dozen different U.S. states, or that *Smith* had involved a contract with a Canadian company, selecting a Canadian forum. Would the need for a forum clause have been any different?

Consider the court's remarks in *General Engineering Corp. v. Martin Marietta Alumina, Inc.,* 783 F.2d 352, 358 n.6 (3d Cir. 1986), that "[in] a private international contract ... the question of forum selection is considerably more important than it would be in a purely domestic contract." *See In re Oil Spill by Amoco Cadiz,* 659 F.2d 789, 795 (7th Cir. 1981) ("special deference owed to forum-selection clauses in international contracts"). Do you agree with the suggestion that barriers to the enforcement of forum clauses should be particularly low in international disputes?

11. *Application of forum selection clauses to non-contractual claims.* Note that *Smith* involved a California plaintiff's tort claims. Should the standards of enforceability for forum clauses differ because tort, instead of contractual, claims were involved? Do tort claims implicate different, more "public" interests, than contract claims? Suppose *Smith* had involved claims based on California state or federal statutory protections. Should forum clauses be enforced in these circumstances? Should the same standards of enforceability apply? *See infra* pp. 426-30.

12. *Choice of law governing enforceability of forum selection clauses — an initial view.* What law governed the enforceability of the forum selection clauses in each of *Tazwell, Bremen,* and *Smith?* Did the courts apply the law of the contractual forums (*e.g.,* Germany, England) or the law of the enforcement forums (the United States)? If the law of the contractual forum would enforce the forum selection clause, does that end inquiry? Suppose that the parties have agreed that the law of the contractual forum will govern their relations. This was the case in both *Bremen* and *Smith.* What role, if any, did English and Pennsylvania law have in each case?

13. *Effect of forum selection clause on party's substantive claims.* Note that English courts would enforce the contractual exculpatory clauses at issue in *Bremen.* Suppose that a U.S. court would not, and that enforcement of the forum selection clause would deprive Zapata of its negligence and other tort claims. What impact should this have on the enforceability of the forum clause?

C. Grounds for Resisting Enforcement of Forum Selection Agreement

1. Introduction

As described above, *Bremen* announced that forum selection clauses are presumptively enforceable. *The Restatement (Second) Conflict of Laws*, the Model Act, and other authorities have adopted similar approaches. All of these authorities make it clear, however, that the presumptive enforceability of forum clauses is subject to exceptions. In summary, the following grounds are generally available in U.S. courts for resisting enforcement of forum agreements: (1) defects in the formation of the forum selection agreement, such as fraud, duress, unconscionability, and lack of assent; (2) unreasonableness; and (3) public policy.

(handwritten margin note: GROUNDS)

2. Defects in Formation as a Ground for Resisting Enforcement of Forum Selection Agreements

Like other agreement, the enforceability of a forum selection clause can be resisted by challenging the manner in which it has been entered into. These challenges are broadly similar to the defenses that are raised to the enforceability of arbitration agreements.[64]

Several specific defects in formation are invoked with particular frequency, all generally relating to unconscionability. *Bremen* said that a forum clause would not be enforced if it was procured by fraud, "undue influence," "overweening bargaining power," or "overreaching."[65] The same exceptions are contemplated by the Model Choice of Forum Act, and the comments to §80 of the *Restatement (Second) Conflict of Laws*.[66]

The *Colonial Leasing* case, excerpted below, illustrates a fairly expansive application of *Zapata's* exceptions for unconscionability, "overreaching" and "overweening bargaining power." After reading that decision, consider the excerpts, set forth thereafter, from the Supreme Court's recent decision in *Carnival Cruise Line, Inc. v. Shute*. *Carnival Cruise* adopts a narrow view of unconscionability and related exceptions.

---

64. *See infra* pp. 1012-16; G. Born, *International Commercial Arbitration in United States Courts* 183-458 (1994).

65. 407 U.S. at 12, 15. Conversely, the Court repeatedly observed that the parties' forum selection clause had been "freely negotiated" in an "arm's-length negotiation by experienced and sophisticated businessmen." 407 U.S. at 12, 17. The Court also emphasized that "it would be unrealistic to think that the parties did not conduct their negotiations ... with the consequences of the forum selection clause figuring prominently in their calculations." *Id.* at 14.

66. *Restatement (Second) Conflict of Laws* §80 comment a (1971 & 1986 Revisions) contemplates non-enforcement where a provision is the result of "overreaching" or "the unfair use of unequal bargaining power."

COLONIAL LEASING CO. OF NEW ENGLAND
v. PUGH BROTHERS GARAGE

735 F.2d 380 (9th Cir. 1984)

FERGUSON, CIRCUIT JUDGE. Colonial Leasing Company of New England, Inc. (Colonial) filed a complaint for breach of a leasing agreement against ... Pugh Brothers Garage. Colonial asserted personal jurisdiction over the defendant on the basis of a forum selection clause which was part of Colonial's standard form lease agreement. The district court dismissed for lack of personal jurisdiction on the ground that it would be unfair and unreasonable to enforce the forum selection clause. ... We affirm.

Colonial is a Massachusetts corporation having its principal place of business in Oregon. Colonial purchases equipment from manufacturers and vendors and leases it to businesses in Oregon and other states. The defendants Pugh Brothers Garage, Eugene Pugh and John Pugh (Pugh Bros.) are citizens of Georgia who operate an auto repair business in Georgia. In 1980, Pugh Bros. contacted Major Muffler, Inc., a New York corporation, through Major Muffler's Atlanta, Georgia representative, to obtain a pipe-bending machine and other equipment. At Major Muffler's request, Pugh Bros. filled out a financial statement which Major Muffler submitted to Colonial. Colonial approved the lease application, and agreed to purchase the equipment from Major Muffler and lease it to Pugh Bros. Major Muffler informed Pugh Bros. that the leasing company had approved the application. Major Muffler shipped the pipe-bending machine to Pugh Bros. from Alabama. Colonial then sent Pugh Bros. the lease agreement and began billing Pugh Bros. monthly from Oregon. Pugh Bros. thought that they were dealing with Major Muffler, a New York corporation, and had no idea Colonial was involved. The standard form lease which they signed included in small print on the back a clause which provided:

22. CHOICE OF LAW. ... This Lease shall be considered to have been made in the State of Oregon, and shall be interpreted, and the rights and liabilities of the parties hereto determined, in accordance with the constitution, statutes, judicial decisions, and administrative regulations of the State of Oregon. Lessees waive all right to a trial by jury in any litigation relating to any transaction under this agreement.

Lessee hereby designates as its agent for the purpose of accepting service of process within the State of Oregon and further agrees to arrange for any transmissions of notice of such service of process from said agent to Lessee as Lessee deems necessary or desirable. Lessee consents to Oregon jurisdiction in any action, suit or proceeding arising out of the Lease, and concedes that it, and each of them, transacted business in the State of Oregon in entry into this Lease. In the event of suit enforcing this Lease, Lessee agrees that venue may be laid in the country of Lessor's address below.

This clause was not negotiated nor discussed by the parties. No agent was designated for service of process. Pugh Bros. did not know that they could be sued in Oregon as a result of that clause. ... [T]he defendants eventually defaulted under the lease agreement. On March 24, 1982, Colonial filed a complaint against Pugh Bros. for breach of the equipment lease contract. Pugh Bros. moved to dismiss for lack of jurisdiction; the district court granted the motion. ...

Under Oregon law, a choice-of-forum clause will be given effect unless it would be unfair or unreasonable to do so. *The Bremen v. Zapata Off-Shore Co.* We agree with the district court's analysis that the standard of "unfair or unreasonable" is designed to invalidate clauses such as those in question here. The evidence disclosed in each case that there was in fact no bargaining on the clause in question. It was contained in a form contract in fine print at the bottom of a page. ... [T]his sort of take-it-or-leave-it clause will be disregarded.

CARNIVAL CRUISE LINES, INC. v. SHUTE

499 U.S. 585 (1991)

JUSTICE BLACKMUN. In this admiralty case we primarily consider whether the United States Court of Appeals for the Ninth Circuit correctly refused to enforce a forum-selection clause contained in tickets issued by petitioner Carnival Cruise Lines, Inc., to respondents Eulala and Russel Shute. The Shutes, through an Arlington, Washington, travel agent, purchased passage for a 7-day cruise on petitioner's ship, the TROPICALE. Respondents paid the fare to the agent who forwarded the payment to petitioner's headquarters in Miami, Florida. Petitioner then prepared the tickets and sent them to respondents [at their home] in the State of Washington. The face of each ticket, at its left-hand lower corner, contained this admonition:

SUBJECT TO CONDITIONS OF CONTRACT ON LAST PAGES IMPORTANT! PLEASE READ CONTRACT — ON LAST PAGES 1,2,3

The following appeared on "contract page 1" of each ticket:

TERMS AND CONDITIONS OF PASSAGE CONTRACT TICKET

3.(a) The acceptance of this ticket by the person or persons named hereon as passengers shall be deemed to be an acceptance and agreement by each of them of all of the terms and conditions of this Passage Contract Ticket.

8. It is agreed by and between the passenger and the Carrier that all disputes and matters whatsoever arising under, in connection with or incident to this Contract shall be litigated, if at all, in and before a Court located in the State of Florida, U.S.A., to the exclusion of the Courts of any other state or country. ...

Respondents boarded the TROPICALE in Los Angeles, California. The ship sailed to Puerto Vallarta, Mexico, and then returned to Los Angeles. While the ship was in international waters off the Mexican coast, respondent Eulala Shute was injured when she slipped on a deck mat during a guided tour of the ship's galley. Respondents filed suit against petitioner in the United States District Court for the Western District of Washington, claiming that Mrs. Shute's injuries had been caused by the negligence of Carnival Cruise Lines and its employees.

Petitioner moved for summary judgement, contending that the forum clause in respondents' tickets required the Shutes to bring their suit ... in the State of Florida. The District Court granted the motion. ... The Court of Appeals reversed. [T]he Court of Appeals acknowledged that a court concerned with the enforceability of such a clause must begin its analysis with *Bremen v. Zapata Off-Shore Co.*, [but] concluded that the forum clause should not be enforced because it "was not freely bargained for." As an "independent justification" for refusing to enforce the clause, the Court of Appeals noted that there was evidence in the record to indicate that "the Shutes are physically and financially incapable of pursuing this litigation in Florida" and that the enforcement of the clause would operate to deprive them of their day in court. ...

We begin by noting the boundaries of our inquiry. First, this is a case in admiralty, and federal law governs the enforceability of the forum-selection clause we scrutinize. Second, we do not address the question whether respondents had sufficient notice of the forum clause before entering the contract for passage. Respondents essentially have conceded that they had notice of the forum-selection provision. ... Within this context, respondents urge that the forum clause should not be enforced because, contrary to ... *Bremen*, the clause was not the product of negotiation, and enforcement effectively would deprive respondents of their day in court. ... Both petitioner and respondents argue vigorously that the Court's opinion in *Bremen* governs this case, and each side purports to find ample support for its position in that opinion's broad-ranging language. This seeming paradox derives in large part from key factual differences between this case and *Bremen*, differences that preclude an automatic and simple application of *Bremen's* general principles to the facts here. ...

[In *Bremen*, this Court held that, in general, "freely negotiated private international agreement[s]," should be given full effect, except where doing so would be "unreasonable."] The Court did not define precisely the circumstances that would make it unreasonable for a court to enforce a forum clause. Instead, the Court discussed a number of factors that made it reasonable to enforce the clause at issue in *Bremen* and that, presumably, would be pertinent in any determination whether to enforce a similar clause. ... In applying *Bremen*, the Court of Appeals in the present litigation took note of the foregoing "reasonableness" factors and rather automatically decided that the forum-selection clause was unenforceable because, unlike the parties in *Bremen*, respondents are not business persons and did not negotiate the terms of the clause with petitioner. Alternatively, the Court of Appeals ruled that the clause should not be enforced because enforcement effectively would deprive respondents of an opportunity to litigate their claim against petitioner.

Bremen concerned a "far from routine transaction between companies of two different nations contemplating the tow of an extremely costly piece of equipment from Louisiana across the Gulf of Mexico and the Atlantic Ocean, through the Mediterranean Sea to its final destination in the Adriatic Sea." These facts suggest that, even apart from the evidence of negotiation regarding the forum clause, it was entirely reasonable for the Court in *Bremen* to have expected Unterweser and Zapata to have negotiated with care in selecting a forum for the resolution of disputes arising from their special towing contract. In contrast, respondents' passage contract was purely routine and doubtless nearly identical to every commercial passage contract issued by petitioner and most other cruise lines. In this context, it would be entirely unreasonable for us to assume that respondents — or any other cruise passenger — would negotiate with petitioner the terms of a forum-selection clause in an ordinary commercial cruise ticket. Common sense dictates that a ticket of this kind will be a form contract the terms of which are not subject to negotiation, and that an individual purchasing the ticket will not have bargaining parity with the cruise line. But by ignoring the crucial differences in the business contexts in which the respective contracts were executed, the Court of Appeals' analysis seems to us to have distorted somewhat this Court's holding in *Bremen*.

In evaluating the reasonableness of the forum clause at issue in this case, we must refine the analysis of *Bremen* to account for the realities of form passage contracts. As an initial matter, we do not adopt the Court of Appeals' determination that a non-negotiated forum-selection clause in a form ticket contract is never enforceable simply because it is not the subject of bargaining. Including a reasonable forum clause in a form contract of this kind well may be permissible for several reasons: First, a cruise line has a special interest in limiting the fora in which it potentially could be subject to suit. Because a cruise ship typically carries passengers from many locales, it is not unlikely that a mishap on a cruise could subject the cruise line to litigation in several different fora. Additionally, a clause establishing *ex ante* the forum for dispute resolution has the salutary effect of dispelling any confusion about where suits arising from the contract must be brought and defended, sparing litigants the time and expense of pretrial motions to determine the correct forum, and conserving judicial resources that otherwise would be devoted to deciding those motions. Finally, it stands to reason that passengers who purchase tickets containing a forum clause like that at issue in this case benefit in the form of reduced fares reflecting the savings that the cruise line enjoys by limiting the fora in which it may be sued.

We also do not accept the Court of Appeals' "independent justification" for its conclusion that *Bremen* dictates that the clause should not be enforced because "[t]here is evidence in the record to indicate that the Shutes are physically and financially incapable of pursuing this litigation in Florida." We do not defer to the Court of Appeals' findings of fact. ... [T]he District Court made no finding regarding the physical and financial impediments to the Shutes' pursuing their case in Florida. The Court of Appeals' conclusory reference to the record provides no basis for this Court to validate the finding of inconvenience. Furthermore, the Court of Appeals did not place in proper context this Court's statement in *Bremen* that "the serious inconvenience of the contractual forum to one or both of the parties might carry greater weight in determining the reasonableness of the forum clause." The Court made this statement in evaluating a hypothetical "agreement between two Americans to resolve their essentially local disputes in a remote alien forum." In the present case, Florida is not a "remote alien forum," nor — given the fact that Mrs. Shute's accident occurred off the coast of Mexico — is this dispute an essentially local one inherently more suited to resolution in the State of Washington than in Florida. In light of these distinctions, and because respondents do not claim lack of notice of the forum clause, we conclude that they have not satisfied the "heavy burden of proof," required to set aside the clause on grounds of inconvenience.

It bears emphasis that forum-selection clauses contained in form passage contracts are subject to judicial scrutiny for fundamental fairness. In this case, there is no indication that petitioner set Florida as the forum in which disputes were to be resolved as a means of discouraging cruise passengers from pursuing legitimate claims. Any suggestion of such a bad-faith motive is belied by two facts: petitioner has its principal place of business in Florida, and many of its cruises depart from and return to Florida ports. Similarly, there is no evidence that petitioner obtained respondents' accession to the forum clause by fraud or overreaching. Finally, respondents have conceded that they were given notice of the forum provision and, therefore, presumably retained the option of rejecting the contract with impunity. In the case before us, therefore, we conclude that the Court of Appeals erred in refusing to enforce the forum-selection clause. ...

JUSTICE STEVENS, with whom JUSTICE MARSHALL joins, dissenting. ... I begin my dissent by noting that only the most meticulous passenger is likely to become aware of the forum selection provision. ... [Indeed, even a] careful reader [would] find the forum-selection clause [only] in the eighth of the twenty-five numbered paragraphs. Of course, many passengers, like the respondents in this case, will not have an opportunity to read paragraph 8 until they have actually purchased their tickets. By this point, the passengers will already have accepted the condition set forth in paragraph 16(a), which provides that "[t]he Carrier shall not be liable to make any refund to passengers in respect of ... tickets wholly or partly not used by a passenger." Not knowing whether or not that provision is legally enforceable, I assume that the average passenger would accept the risk of having to file suit in Florida in the event of an injury, rather than cancelling — without a refund — a planned vacation at the last minute. The fact that the cruise line can reduce its litigation costs, and therefore its liability insurance premiums, by forcing this choice on its passengers does not, in my opinion, suffice to render the provision reasonable. ...

Forum-selection clauses in passenger tickets involve the intersection of two strands of traditional contract law that qualify the general rule that courts will enforce the terms of a contract as written. Pursuant to the first strand, courts traditionally have reviewed with heightened scrutiny the terms of contracts of adhesion, form contracts offered on a take-it-of-leave basis by a party with stronger bargaining power to a party with weaker power. ... The second doctrinal principle implicated by forum-selection clauses is the traditional rule that "contractual provisions which seek to limit the place or court in which an action may ... be brought, are invalid as contrary to public policy." ... Although adherence to this general rule has declined in recent years, particularly following our decision in [*Bremen*], the prevailing rule is still that forum-selection clauses are not enforceable if they were not freely bargained for, create additional expense for one party, or deny one party a remedy. ...

Notes on Colonial Leasing and Carnival Cruise

1. *Separability of the forum selection agreement.* A preliminary issue is whether a forum selection agreement is "separable" from the underlying contract in which it is contained. In the related context of arbitration, governed by the Federal Arbitration Act, the Supreme Court has said that an arbitration agreement is generally a separate, independent agreement from the contract to which it relates. *Prima Paint Corp. v. Flood & Conklin Manufacturing Co.*, 388 U.S. 395 (1967); *infra* pp. 996-97. As a consequence, challenges to the validity, existence, and legality of the underlying contract do not necessarily call into question the "separate" arbitration agreement; this separate arbitration agreement is therefore capable of surviving defects in the underlying contract's formation or the contract's termination, invalidity, or illegality. *See infra* pp. 996-97 & 1013-16.

The separability doctrine should to be equally applicable to forum clauses. The Supreme Court has remarked that "an agreement to arbitrate before a specialized tribunal [is], in effect, a specialized kind of forum-selection clause." *Scherk v. Alberto-Culver Co.*, 417 U.S. 506, 519 (1974). The rationale for the separability doctrine — an exchange of promises to resolve disputes in a particular manner — thus applies to forum clauses with the same force as arbitration agreements. As noted below, most courts have adopted this analysis, although a few have apparently not.

2. *Wisdom of decision in* Carnival Cruise. Was *Carnival Cruise* correctly decided? Compare the opinions by Justice Blackmun and Justice Stevens. Which is a more persuasive reading of *Bremen*? Which result in *Carnival Cruise* is more persuasive from a policy perspective? Consider the following observation about *Carnival Cruise*: "the Supreme Court not only reaffirmed the presumption favoring enforcement but also narrowed the circumstances in which a choice of forum clause will be held unreasonable." Sturley, *Strengthening the Presumption of Validity for Choice of Forum Clauses*, 23 J. Mar. L. & Comm. 131 (1992). Is this accurate? If so, was the Court's action wise? Consider also:

> Carnival Cruise Lines was an easy case. It was based on the humblest, most uncomplicated, garden-variety slip-and-fall tort ever to grace the federal courts. It involved a pure, paradigmatic adhesive consumer contract, complete with non-negotiable, tiny, boilerplate print. Nonetheless, in spite of the utter simplicity of its facts, seven Justices managed to get *Carnival Cruise Lines* wrong. *Carnival Cruise Lines* made bad law. In holding that particular forum-selection clause enforceable, the Supreme Court gave its broad stamp of approval for forum-selection clauses generally as a method for establishing jurisdiction. However, in spite of their persistently touted virtues, forum-selection clauses can be unfair and insidious. The result in *Carnival Cruise Lines* was unfair because under existing precedent, and as a matter of pure contract law, courts should not enforce adhesive consumer forum-selection clauses. Yet, this is precisely what the Supreme Court did.

> Furthermore, at both the practical and theoretical levels, adhesive forum-selection clauses are anathema to long-standing jurisdictional principles that defer to a plaintiff's choice of forum balanced against a defendant's due process rights. As a practical matter, these clauses cause unwitting plaintiffs to forfeit legitimate legal claims due to the plaintiff's frequent inability to mount a case in a distant, inconvenient courtroom. As a theoretical matter, engrafting contract principles onto forum-access rules tips the procedural balance in favor of well-heeled, savvy defendants; thus, what repels us as a matter of contract law should repel us as a matter of jurisdictional theory.

Mullenix, *Another Easy Case, Some More Bad Law: Carnival Cruise Lines and Contractual Personal Jurisdiction*, 27 Tex. Int'l L. J. 323, 325-26 (1992). Is Professor Mullenix right?

3. *The* **Carnival Cruise** *forum selection clause.* What was the most troubling feature of the forum clause in *Carnival Cruise*? Consider the following remarks by Judge Richard Posner concerning the *Carnival Cruise* facts: the forum clause "plainly is neither intended nor likely to be read," and "[i]f ever there was a case for stretching the concept of fraud in the name of unconscionability, it was *Shute*, and perhaps no stretch was necessary." *National Insurance Co. v. Donovan*, 916 F.2d 372, 376 (7th Cir. 1990). Judge Posner is not often accused of paternalism or sentimentality. Is his characterization correct? Should, as Judge Posner suggests, the *Carnival Cruise* clause have been invalidated? On what ground? Is this a ground that was before the Supreme Court in *Carnival Cruise*? If the clause in *Carnival Cruise* is not enforceable, would *any* forum selection clause in a standardized form contract ever be enforceable? When?

4. *Fraud or duress as bases for resisting enforcement of forum selection agreements.* Bremen, Carnival Cruise, and other authorities recognize exceptions to the enforceability of forum selection clauses obtained by fraud, duress, or undue influence.

(a) *Lower court authorities finding fraud in formation of forum selection clause.* A few courts have found either fraud or duress in the procurement of a forum agreement. *Weidner Communications, Inc. v. Al Faisal*, 859 F.2d 1302 (7th Cir. 1988) (holding foreign forum selection clause unenforceable because of unequal bargaining power and physical intimidation of party's representative); *Farmland Industries, Inc. v. Frazier-Parrott Commodities, Inc.*, 806 F.2d 848 (8th Cir. 1986) ("in a situation where a fiduciary relationship ... is created by a contract tainted by fraud, the person defrauded cannot be held to the contractual forum selection clause"); *Crowson v. Sealaska Corp.*, 705 P.2d 905 (Alaska 1985) (bribery of contracting party's representatives would vitiate forum selection clause).

(b) *Most lower courts reject fraud challenges to forum selection agreements.* The fraud and duress exceptions have not, however, frequently been invoked. According to one commentator, "[s]ince outright fraud never forms the basis for a forum-selection clause, it is virtually impossible to challenge a clearly drafted provision." Mullenix, *Another Easy Case, Some More Bad Law: Carnival Cruise Lines and Contractual Personal Jurisdiction*, 27 Tex. Int'l L. J. 323, 363 (1992). Lower courts have almost uniformly rejected fraud and duress claims on their facts. *Frietsch v. Refco, Inc.*, 1994 WL 494945 (N.D. Ill. 1994); *Juels v. Deutsche Bank AG*, 1993 U.S. Dist. Lexis 1914 (N.D.N.Y. 1993); *Caldas & Sons, Inc. v. Willingham*, 791 F.Supp. 614 (N.D. Miss. 1992); *Envirolite Enterprises, Inc. v. Glastechnische Industrie Peter Lisec GmbH*, 53 B.R. 1007 (S.D.N.Y. 1985).

(c) *Application of separability doctrine to fraud defense.* If the separability doctrine is applied, only fraud or duress relating to the *inclusion of the forum selection clause itself* in the parties' agreement should be relevant. As the Supreme Court explained, in broad language, in a post-*Bremen* decision in the arbitration context:

> [The fraud exception] does not mean that anytime a dispute arising out of a transaction is based upon an allegation of fraud ... the "forum selection" clause is unenforceable. Rather, it means that ... [a] forum selection clause in a contract is not enforceable if the *inclusion of that clause in the contract* was the product of fraud or coercion.

Scherk v. Alberto-Culver Co., 417 U.S. 506, 519 n.14 (1974)(emphasis in original). *See AVC Nederland BV v. Atrium Inv. Partnership*, 740 F.2d 148, 158 (2d Cir. 1984). Despite this, some lower courts have held forum clauses unenforceable because the parties' underlying contract was procured by fraud or duress, without specifically considering whether the contract's forum clause was itself allegedly induced by fraud or similar misconduct. *E.g.*, *J.B. Hoffman v. Minuteman Press Int'l Inc.*, 747 F.Supp. 552 (W.D. Mo. 1990) (expressly refusing to apply separability doctrine in domestic context); *Gaskin v. Stumm Handel GmbH*, 390 F.Supp. 361 (S.D.N.Y. 1975). Nonetheless, most lower courts have adhered fairly closely to the rule that fraud in procuring the parties' underlying contract does not affect a forum clause within that agreement. *Envirolite Enterprises, Inc. v. Glastechnische Industrie Peter Lisec GmbH*, 53 B.R. 1007, 1012 (S.D.N.Y. 1985) (rejecting fraud claim because resisting party "does not claim that the forum selection clause, specifically, was induced by fraud"); *Frietsch v. Refco, Inc.*, 1994 WL 494945 (N.D. Ill. 1994) ("a claim for fraud is not sufficient to render a forum selection clause unenforceable unless the fraud is in the inclusion of the clause itself"). Suppose that Zapata Off-Shore had alleged in *Bremen* that Unterweser had fraudulently induced it into making the towage contract by deliberately misrepresenting its technical expertise and experience. Should such a claim provide a basis for ignoring the forum selection clause? Suppose that Zapata argues that the entire towage contract is void because of Unterweser's fraud.

5. *Unconscionability as basis for resisting enforcement of forum selection agreements.* Several related bases for challenging the formation of a forum clause are similar to the fraud exception; these are "overweening bargaining power," "the abuse of economic power," and "unconscionability." All of these grounds relate to the relative bargaining power of the parties, the extent and character of bargaining between them, and the exercise of undue commercial or other leverage.

(a) *Inequality in bargaining power as basis for nonenforcement of forum selection clause.* Challenges to the enforceability of forum selection clauses have frequently relied upon alleged inequalities in bargaining power between the parties. Even before *Carnival Cruise*, mere differences in economic strength would not, without more, require non-enforcement of forum selection clauses. Thus, the Restatement's comment to §80 referred to the "*unfair use* of unequal bargaining power," and §3(4) of the Model Act provided for non-enforcement where a forum selection agreement was obtained by "*the abuse* of economic power." Similarly, lower courts generally did not accord independent significance to disparities in bargaining power. *E.g.*, *Hodes v. S.N.C. Achille Lauro ed Altrigestione*, 858 F.2d 905, 913 (3d Cir. 1988) ("while the appellants certainly enjoyed a superior bargaining position, they did not take unfair advantage of that position to 'overween' the Hodes").

Does a disparity of bargaining power have any relevance to the enforceability of forum clauses after *Carnival Cruise*? Given the obvious disparities in bargaining power between Carnival Cruise and the Shutes, how can inequalities in bargaining power be an independent basis for resisting forum agreements in the future? Nevertheless, do inequalities in bargaining power have some relevance to the enforceability of forum selection clauses? If so, what? Note Justice Stevens' remark that "courts traditionally have reviewed with heightened scrutiny the terms of contracts of adhesion, form contracts offered on a take-it-or-leave basis by a party with stronger bargaining power to a party with weaker power."

(b) *Absence of bargaining as basis for nonenforcement of forum selection clause.* Bremen emphasized that the forum clause at issue was a "vital part" of the parties' agreement, which had been "freely negotiated" in an "arm's-length negotiation by experienced and sophisticated businessmen." *Colonial Leasing* refused to enforce the forum selection clause, largely on the grounds that "there was in fact no bargaining on the clause," which "was contained in a form contract in fine print at the bottom of a page."

Even before *Carnival Cruise*, however, most courts refused to accord significant weight to the absence of bargaining, with the vast majority of lower court decisions refusing to deny enforcement based on the absence of negotiations over the forum selection clause. *E.g.*, *Lien Ho Hsing Steel Enter. Co. v. Weihtag*, 738 F.2d 1455 (9th Cir. 1984); *Medoil Corp. v. Citicorp*, 729 F.Supp. 1456 (S.D.N.Y. 1990). Characteristic of these decisions was one lower court that declared that the "fact that a particular contractual provision may not have been specifically discussed does not preclude it from being enforceable." *Samson Plastic Conduit and Pipe Corp. v. Battenfeld Extrusionstechnik GmbH*, 718 F.Supp. 886 (M.D. Ala. 1989).

Nevertheless, a few courts refused to give effect to forum clauses based in part on the lack of negotiation or discussion of the provision. *Union Ins. Soc'y of Canton v. S.S. Elikon*, 642 F.2d 721 (4th Cir. 1981) (refusing enforcement in part because of lack of "hard bargaining"); *Corna v. American Hawaii Cruises, Inc.*, 794 F.Supp. 1005 (D. Haw. 1992); *Couch v. First Guaranty, Ltd.*, 578 F. Supp. 331 (N.D. Tex. 1984) ("not knowingly bargained for"; "obscure clause in a form contract").

Carnival Cruise makes it even less likely that the absence of bargaining will independently prevent enforcement of a forum clause. The Court held that the absence of negotiations over the forum clause was not of substantial weight: "Common sense dictates that a ticket of this kind will be a form contract the terms of which are not subject to negotiation, and that an individual purchasing the ticket will not have bargaining parity with the cruise line." Nonetheless, the Court upheld the forum clause, emphasizing the legitimate interests (of Carnival Cruise Lines and of the judicial system) in the certainty and efficiency provided by such clauses. Should the lack of actual negotiation over a forum clause result in nonenforcement? Should it even be relevant to nonenforcement? Did the facts in *Colonial Leasing* warrant nonenforcement under the *Bremen* standard? How would *Bremen* have been resolved if there had been no negotiation of the towage contract? Do decisions refusing to enforce forum selection clauses principally because they were not individually negotiated survive *Carnival Cruise*? How would *Colonial Leasing* be decided under *Carnival Cruise*?

Under general principles of contract law, there is no rule requiring that the parties either negotiate or read every term of their agreement. *See supra* p. 403. What rationale supported the apparent willingness of *Colonial Leasing* and other courts to impose particularly high standards of negotiation on forum clauses as compared to other contractual provisions — such as price or warranties? Is there some particular need to ensure that parties focus on and understand forum provisions? Is there a greater risk that this will not occur than with respect to other provisions?

6. *Lack of notice or assent as basis for resisting enforcement of forum selection clause.* In deciding whether to enforce forum selection clauses, a number of lower courts have considered whether both parties had adequate notice of them. Although *Carnival Cruise* did not consider whether the Shutes had received notice of the forum selection clause, the Court made it clear that inadequate notice would provide a basis for resisting enforcement of such an agreement. 499 U.S. at 590, 595.

It is well-settled that a party's failure to read a forum selection provision does not prevent that clause from forming part of the parties' agreement. Especially where businessmen are involved, courts have generally had little sympathy for claimed ignorance of a forum selection clause. In the words of one court, "no one deterred him from getting his glasses and reading the contract." *Hoffman v. National Equip. Rental,* 643 F.2d 987 (4th Cir. 1981). With this basic attitude, efforts to claim lack of notice or comprehension of a forum clause have generally failed. *Paribas Corp. v. Shelton Ranch Corp.,* 742 F.Supp. 86, 92 (S.D.N.Y. 1990) ("a sophisticated business person with practice in contractual negotiation cannot escape the effect of a forum selection clause by claiming lack of focus"); *Karlberg European Tanspa, Inc. v. JK-Josef Kratz Vertriebsgesellschaft mbh,* 618 F.Supp. 344, 347 (N.D. Ill. 1985) ("basic contract law establishes a duty to read the contract"). A few courts have even concluded that parties were obliged to read contracts in a language that they did not understand. *Gaskin v. Stumm Handel GmbH,* 390 F.Supp. 361, 365-67 (S.D.N.Y. 1975) (enforcing forum clause against U.S. party where contract was written in German); *Corna v. American Hawaii Cruises, Inc.,* 794 F.Supp. 1005 (D. Haw. 1992) (enforcing English language form forum clause against native Dutch speaker).

Nevertheless, courts have occasionally refused to enforce forum selection clauses that were buried in pages of finely printed boilerplate or on the back of form contracts — particularly in consumer cases. *Chasser v. Achille Lauro Lines,* 844 F.2d 50, 52 (2d Cir. 1988) ("in tiny type"), *aff'd,* 490 U.S. 495 (1989); *Couch v. First Guaranty Ltd.,* 578 F.Supp. 331, 333 (N.D. Tex. 1984) ("that the provision is knowingly inserted in the contract seems to be the underpinning of the *Bremen* decision"). Where a party can demonstrate that a forum clause was not communicated to it in a reasonable fashion, challenges to enforcement continue to be possible.

Should the plaintiffs' counsel in *Carnival Cruise* have conceded that the forum clause was "reasonably communicated" to the Shutes? What standards should be applied to determine whether a party did not receive notice of a forum clause? It cannot be dispositive, can it, that the plaintiff did not read the clause? If not, then what must be done to make it sufficiently easy for the plaintiff to read the clause? Would it be sensible to require, in every form contract, that the forum clause be in all capital letters? Note that some state statutes require that arbitration clauses must either be conspicuously printed, contained in a separate agreement, or noted on the first page of the contract. G. Born, *International Commercial Arbitration in the United States* 425-26 (1994). Should the law require this for forum clauses? Should courts fashion such a rule?

One way to reduce the risk of nonenforcement of a forum clause, based on lack of notice, is to require the clause to be initialled by both parties at closing. Another approach is to require the handwritten addition of the selected forum to the agreement (although, as *Colonial Leasing* illustrates, it is vital that the addition actually be made). Finally, forum selection provisions can be printed in large print or boldface, or placed immediately above the parties' signature lines. *See Baldwin v. Heinold Commodities,* 363 N.W.2d 191 (S.D. 1985).

7. *Lack of "fundamental fairness" as basis for nonenforcement of forum selection clause.* In *Carnival Cruise,* the Court said that it would not enforce a fundamentally unfair forum selection clause. What does this mean? The Court emphasized that Carnival Cruise Lines' forum clause did not designate "a remote alien forum," that there was no suggestion that Florida had been chosen to disadvantage or inconvenience consumers, and that a cruise line had legitimate interests in avoiding litigation in numerous different fora.

Suppose that the circumstances that attend cruise lines — passengers from multiple places on cruises to multiple destinations — are not present. Would the same deferential approach to forum clauses as that adopted in *Carnival Cruise* apply? What would render a forum clause "fundamentally unfair"? What if Carnival Cruise had chosen Panama as the contractual forum? What if Carnival Cruise was incorporated there? What if its vessels called there? What if Panama law drastically limited tort remedies generally? Consider:

> After bringing consumer form contracts within *The Bremen's* rule, and then lowering the applicable standard of reasonableness, *Carnival Cruise* proceeds to ensure that few forum-selection clauses will be voided on equitable grounds, ... [by] adopt[ing] a minimalist idea of what constitutes "fundamental fairness."

Purcell, *Geography as a Litigation Weapon: Consumers, Forum-Selection Clauses, and the Rehnquist Court,* 40 UCLA L. Rev. 423, 432-33 (1992). Is that accurate? Is it desirable?

What is relevant to determining the unconscionability of a forum clause? Suppose that the clause's drafter shows that, in other respects, the parties' underlying agreement was highly favorable to the other party? Suppose that a cruise line agreed to extremely discounted prices because of oversupply in the cruise market and slack consumer demand? What is the relevance of the separability doctrine?

8. *Termination of the underlying contract as a basis for nonenforcement of the forum selection clause.* A few courts have held that termination of a contract containing a forum clause also terminates the forum selection provision. *Certified Commodities Group, Inc. v. Roccaforte,* 441 So.2d 264 (La. Ct. App. 1983). *Compare Int'l Longshoremen's Ass'n v. West Gulf Maritime Ass'n,* 605 F.Supp. 723 (S.D.N.Y. 1985). This is inconsistent with the separability doctrine, which would treat the forum clause as a separate agreement, capable of surviving the underlying contract (at least with respect to disputes occurring during the term of the underlying contract). *See supra* p. 401. Suppose that the Shutes had *not* gone on their ill-fated voyage, and had instead terminated their contract with Carnival Cruise on the grounds that the *Tropicale* was allegedly unfit for human habitation. Would claims by the Shutes for return of their payments or deposits, and by Carnival Cruise for breach of contract, have been subject to the forum agreement?

9. *Relevance of distinction between exclusive and non-exclusive forum selection clauses.* Note that *Colonial Leasing* involved a non-exclusive, prorogation agreement, unlike the exclusive forum selection clause in *Bremen.* How should this affect the agreement's enforceability? Should it have been easier to enforce a submission to jurisdiction than it would be to enforce an exclusive forum selection clause? Why? *See infra* pp. 454-55.

3. Unreasonableness as a Ground for Resisting Enforcement of Forum Selection Agreements

a. Introduction

The enforcement of a forum selection agreement may be resisted on grounds of "unreasonableness" even if there is no basis for challenging the clause's formation on the basis of fraud, duress, unconscionability, lack of notice, and the like. This exception was recognized in *Bremen*,[67] where the Court said that forum selection agreements will not be enforced if doing so would be "unreasonable and unjust,"[68] or "unreasonable under the circumstances."[69] The unreasonableness defense was also at issue in *Carnival Cruise*, where the Court considered "the circumstances that would make it unreasonable for a court to enforce a forum clause."[70]

An unreasonableness defense to forum selection agreements is also reflected in the Model Act. The Act contains specific defenses to enforceability for several of the

---

67. 407 U.S. at 10 & 15.
68. 407 U.S. at 15.
69. 407 U.S. at 10.
70. 499 U.S. at 590-94.

factors identified in *Bremen* as bearing on unreasonableness, including (a) inability of plaintiff to obtain "effective relief" in the contractual forum; and (b) the fact that the contractual forum would be "a substantially less convenient place for the trial of the action."[71] In addition, the Act also contains a catch-all exception that applies where "it would for some other reason be unfair or unreasonable to enforce the agreement."[72]

Finally, the *Restatement (Second) Conflict of Laws* permits nonenforcement of forum clauses if they are "unfair or unreasonable."[73] Section 80 does not itself further define "unreasonableness," but the accompanying comments provide some explanation.[74] Among other things, comment c to §80 says that factors suggesting unreasonableness include the fact that: (a) the "courts of the chosen state would be closed"; and (b) "the chosen state would be so seriously an inconvenient forum" as to be "unjust."

Under almost all analyses, the unreasonableness defense is very difficult to satisfy. The Model Act makes it clear that the burden of proof is on the party resisting enforcement. *Bremen* emphasized that a party must "clearly show" unreasonableness and that it bears of "heavy burden" in so doing.[75] *Carnival Cruise* repeated this formulation, and relied upon it in upholding the parties' forum selection clause.[76] Lower courts have frequently invoked this burden of proof.[77]

b. Inconvenience of the Contractual Forum

A central concern the "reasonableness" analysis under most authorities is "convenience." Both *Bremen* and other sources hold that, if a forum selection clause designates a forum that is *sufficiently* inconvenient, enforcement may be denied.

It is difficult to establish that a foreign forum is sufficiently inconvenient to warrant non-enforcement of a forum selection clause. To be sure, a few lower court decisions have found the *Bremen* "inconvenience" standard satisfied.[78] Most courts, however, have enforced forum clauses in the face of inconvenience defenses. A num-

---

71. Model Choice of Forum Act §3(2) & 3(3).

72. Model Choice of Forum Act §3(5).

73. *Restatement (Second) Conflict of Laws* §80 (1971).

74. *Restatement (Second) Conflict of Laws* §80 comment c (1986 Revisions).

75. 407 U.S. at 17.

76. 499 U.S. at 594-95.

77. *E.g., Interamerican Trade Corp. v. Companhia Fabricadora de Pecas*, 973 F.2d 487 (6th Cir. 1992); *Diaz Contracting, Inc. v. Nanco Contracting Corp.*, 817 F.2d 1047 (3d Cir. 1987) ("heavy burden"); *General Engineering Corp. v. Martin Marietta Alumina, Inc.*, 783 F.2d 352, 356 (3d Cir. 1986) ("strict standard").

78. *E.g., Effron v. Sun Line Cruises, Inc.*, 158 F.R.D. 39 (S.D.N.Y. 1994); *Vignolo v. Chandris, Inc.*, 1989 W.L. 160986 (D. Mass. Jan. 3, 1990); *Kolendo v. Jerell, Inc.*, 489 F. Supp. 983 (S.D.W. Va. 1980); *Randolph Engineering Co. v. Fredenhagen KG*, 476 F. Supp. 1355 (W.D. Pa. 1979).

ber have done so notwithstanding evidence of considerable inconvenience, including when the resisting party is a U.S. national.[79]

c. No Effective Relief in Contractual Forum

Related to "inconvenience" as a ground for denying enforcement of a forum selection clause is the plaintiff's inability to obtain effective relief in the contractual forum. Section 3(2) of the Model Choice of Forum Act provides for nonenforcement where "the plaintiff cannot secure effective relief in the other state, for reasons other than delay in bringing the action." *Bremen* acknowledged, albeit in its discussion of "inconvenience," the possibility of nonenforcement where the plaintiff "will for all practical purposes be deprived of his day in court."[80]

Lower courts have almost always rejected claims that the parties' contractual forum cannot provide effective relief (just as they have usually rejected similar arguments under the forum non conveniens doctrine).[81] It is clear that something more is required than differences in substantive law that disadvantage the plaintiff. This is illustrated by *Bremen's* enforcement of the parties' forum selection clause even though it was clear that English courts would apply different substantive rules than American courts would.[82] Similarly, claims that foreign forums are unreasonable because of differences between U.S. and foreign procedural rules have also usually failed.[83]

In unusual cases, contractual forums may be found unreasonable because of the qualities of their courts. Where the courts in the contractual forum are biased or cor-

---

79. *E.g., Spradlin v. Lear Siegler Mgt. Serv. Co.*, 926 F.2d 865, 869 (9th Cir. 1990) ("Although we are troubled by Lear Siegler's standard inclusion of a Saudi Arabian forum selection clause in employment contracts when it is highly foreseeable that terminated American employees will be required to return to the United States and will thus face considerable obstacles in bringing wrongful termination actions, we cannot find that the district court abused its discretion in enforcing the forum selection clause based on the scant and conclusory information presented by Spradlin."); *In re Diaz Contracting, Inc.*, 817 F.2d 1047, 1051 (3d Cir. 1987) (enforcing forum selection clause notwithstanding district court's finding that bankrupt company would face "financial difficulty" litigating in selected forum).

80. 407 U.S. at 18. The comments to §80 of the Second Restatement explain: "A court will likewise entertain the action if it finds that for some reason the courts of the chosen state would be closed to the suit or would not handle it effectively or fairly." *Restatement (Second) Conflict of Laws* §80 comment c (1986 Revisions).

81. *See supra* pp. 351-54.

82. Lower courts have generally rejected challenges to forum selection clauses based solely on the fact that the foreign forum's laws were less favorable than U.S. laws. *E.g., Hugel v. Corporation of Lloyd's*, 999 F.2d 206 (7th Cir. 1993); *Medoil Corp. v. Citicorp*, 729 F.Supp. 1456 (S.D.N.Y. 1990); *Raskin SA v. Datasonic Corp.*, 1987 WL 8180 (N.D. Ill. 1987); *Karlsberg European Tanspa, Inc. v. JK-Josef Kratz Vertriebsgesellschaft mbh*, 618 F.Supp. 344 (N.D. Ill. 1985).

83. *E.g., Commerce Consultants International, Inc. v. Vetrerie Riunite, SpA*, 867 F.2d 697 (D.C. Cir. 1989) (in accepting Italian forum selection clause, party "also necessarily accepted the procedures that those courts follow, including different discovery procedures"); *Karlberg European Tanspa, Inc. v. JK-Josef Kratz Vertriebsgesellschaft mbh*, 618 F.Supp. 344, 348 (N.D. Ill. 1985) ("it is not this court's role to guarantee KETS the same probability of success on all its claims"); *Dukane Fabrics International, Inc. v. M.V. Hreljin*, 600 F.Supp. 202 (S.D.N.Y. 1985) (no showing that Italian courts would not provide adequate and fair forum).

rupt, enforcement may be denied.[84] Similarly, a forum clause will be found unreasonable "if jurisdiction would be lacking in the chosen state."[85] A forum selection agreement might also not be enforced "where the period of the statute of limitations applicable to the particular claim was unusually short [in the contractual forum] and had already expired."[86]

Finally, enforcement will ordinarily be denied "if no court of that state would be competent to hear the suit.[87] More difficult are cases in which the contractual forum will hear a suit, but will not permit assertion of particular causes of action. As discussed above, the fact that unfavorable substantive law will be applied in the contractual forum is generally not grounds for denying enforcement of a forum agreement.[88] The absence of any *viable* legal claim has generally not been considered by lower courts (except in the context of public policy, which is discussed below).[89]

d. Selected Materials Relating to Unreasonableness

The following decision, *Copperweld Steel Co. v. Demag-Mannesmann-Boehler*, considers the unreasonableness defense to enforcement of a forum selection clause.

COPPERWELD STEEL CO. v. DEMAG-MANNESMANN-BOEHLER
578 F.2d 953 (3d Cir. 1978)

ROSENN, CIRCUIT JUDGE. [The case arose from the sale by Demag-Mannesmann-Boehler (Demag), a German company, to Copperweld Steel Company (Copperweld), a U.S. company, of a "continuous casting machine." The machine failed to perform to Copperweld's requirements, and the U.S. company brought a diversity action in federal district court alleging: (1) breach of contract; (2) negligent design and manufacture; and (3) negligent and fraudulent misrepresentation. The district judge directed a verdict against Copperweld's fraud claim and, after a jury trial, entered judgment on the jury's verdict against Copperweld on its remaining claims. The district judge also denied Demag's motion, based on a forum selection clause, to dismiss the action. Copperweld appealed from the adverse verdict and Demag cross-appealed from the denial of its motion to dismiss, arguing that Copperweld's breach of an enforceable forum selection clause entitled Demag to damages. The Court of Appeals first affirmed the verdict on the merits against Copperweld and continued as follows.]

---

84. *Bremen v. Zapata Off-Shore Co.*, 407 U.S. 1, 12 (1972) (emphasizing neutrality and competence of English courts); Gruson, *Forum-Selection Clauses in International and Interstate Commercial Agreements*, 1982 U. Ill. L. Rev. 133, 167-69.

85. *Restatement (Second) Conflict of Laws* §80, comment c (1986 Revisions). This parallels the alternative forum requirement under the forum non conveniens doctrine, where lack of subject matter jurisdiction in the asserted alternative forum is grounds for denying dismissal. *See supra* p. 352.

86. *Restatement (Second) Conflict of Laws* §80, comment c (1986 Revisions).

87. *Restatement (Second) Conflict of Laws* §80, comment c (1986 Revisions).

88. *See supra* p. 407.

89. *See infra* pp. 428-29.

Demag has raised a single but interesting question in its cross-appeal — whether the district court erred in accepting jurisdiction in this case. Demag claims that the district court did err and that this error entitles it to a trial on the question of damages suffered because of the district court's failure to enforce the contract. We find no error in the retention of jurisdiction and therefore affirm the district court's disposition of Demag's claim.

During negotiations Demag sent Copperweld a standard form with its conditions for export contracts. Among these conditions was one requiring that "[a]ny disputes arising out of the terms of the contract" would have to be brought before a German court unless Demag chose to bring the action in the United States. This condition expressly applied to any *export contract* negotiated by Demag. Prior to the final agreement on the sale of the caster, however, Demag and Copperweld concluded that the machine, originally to be built in and exported from Germany, would be manufactured in the United States. From this Copperweld reasons that the agreement ceased to be an export contract, that Demag's forum selection clause did not become part of the new contract, and that therefore the district court correctly retained jurisdiction over the case.

The district court indicated some agreement with Copperweld's assertion, concluding that had the parties not amended their contract to provide for construction of the caster in the United States, it would have been inclined to enforce the forum clause. We need not decide whether the clause in fact became part of the contract, however, for there is an alternative reason that leads us to affirm the district court's assumption of jurisdiction over the case. The district court also reasoned and concluded that enforcement of the forum selection clause would be unreasonable. We see no error in that conclusion.

During pre-trial motions, the district court held that it had jurisdiction over Copperweld's complaint and that the forum selection clause did not deprive it of this jurisdiction. Judge McCune concluded that enforcement of the forum selection clause would be "unreasonable under the facts of this case" and refused to enforce the clause.[90]

Subsequent to this pre-trial decision, in *The Bremen v. Zapata Off-Shore Co.*, an

---

90. The district court gave the following reasons for its decisions not to enforce the forum selection clause: (1) that the facility which was the subject of the action was located in Warren, Ohio, and was likely to become the object of an intensive inspection during the trial; (2) that the facility was fabricated by Birdsboro Corporation, a Pennsylvania contractor, in this country; (3) that all of the records concerning operation of the plant were in this country; (4) that all of Copperweld's personnel who operated the plant were in this country; (5) that all of Copperweld's personnel who negotiated the contract were in this country; (6) that certain of Demag's personnel involved in the sale were in this country and that Demag was doing business in the United States and maintained offices in Pittsburgh, Pennsylvania; (7) that practically all of the activities undertaken in connection with the contract took place in the English language; (8) that almost all of the witnesses were English speaking; and (9) that conducting the litigation in Germany would have required translation with inherent inaccuracies. Furthermore, all of the plant's customers were in this country and if their testimony were necessary, the district court envisioned difficulties in compelling their attendance in a German forum.

admiralty case, the Supreme Court held that a forum selection clause in a contract between the parties is "prima facie valid and should be enforced unless enforcement is shown by the resisting party to be 'unreasonable' under the circumstances." The Court further stated that such a clause should not be set aside "absent a strong showing" such as that enforcement "would be unreasonable and unjust, or that the clause was invalid for such reasons as fraud or overreaching."

Demag contends that the district court's pre-trial decision that enforcement would be unreasonable must be reversed because it was based, at least in part, upon standards enunciated in the *Central Contracting Company* cases, [*Central Contracting Co. v. Maryland Casualty Co.*, 367 F.2d 341 (3d Cir. 1966)] ... decided prior to *The Bremen*. Demag also made this argument to Judge McCune, who in two separate opinions reiterated his initial reaction and held that the enforcement of the clause would be unreasonable. ... The district court's reliance on the *Central Contracting Company* case[] is not reversible error. Both cases held that a court should generally enforce a forum selection clause unless the enforcement would be unreasonable at the time of the litigation, and that mere inconvenience would not show unreasonability. *Id.* The courts instead suggested that the test is whether enforcement "will put one of the parties to an unreasonable disadvantage and thereby subvert the interests of justice." Although *Bremen* has language somewhat different than that relied upon by the district court, *compare Bremen*, 407 U.S. at 18 (deny enforcement of the clause if resisting party will be effectively denied his day in court) *with Maryland Casualty Co.* (deny enforcement if interest of justice is subverted), the district court captured the essence of the Supreme Court's opinion — the resisting party must prove unreasonability [sic] — and in fact held that Copperweld might well have been prevented from receiving "a fair and complete hearing" had the forum clause been enforced. We therefore find no material difference between the standards applied by the district court and those requested by Demag and affirm the district court's retention of jurisdiction.

Notes on Copperweld

1. *Structure of reasonableness analysis.* Is each of the various exceptions to enforceability set out in *Bremen* — such as fraud, unconscionability, inconvenience, forum bias, and the like — an independent and separate base for overcoming a forum selection clause? Alternatively, are all the factors collectively relevant to a single reasonableness inquiry that permits nonenforcement of "unreasonable" forum selection clauses?

A number of authorities have adopted the latter approach. *E.g., Restatement (Second) Conflict of Laws* §80 (1971); *Yoder v. Heinold Commodities*, 630 F.Supp. 765 (E.D. Va. 1986); *Couch v. First Guar.*, 578 F.Supp. 331 (N.D. Tex. 1984); *D'Antuono v. CCH Computax Sys.*, 570 F.Supp. 708 (D.R.I. 1983); *Kline v. Kawai Am. Corp.*, 498 F.Supp. 868 (D. Minn. 1980). Is this a sensible approach? Is it appropriate to mush the various *Bremen* factors together into an undisciplined reasonableness inquiry? How is this analysis different from forum non conveniens analysis?

2. *Inconvenience as a basis for denying enforcement of forum selection clause based upon inconvenience.* As *Bremen* and *Copperwell* illustrate, one basis for resisting enforcement of a forum selection clause is inconvenience.

(a) *Rigorous standard for inconvenience.* A compelling showing must be made to establish that the parties' chosen forum is so inconvenient that non-enforcement is warranted. *Bremen* adopted the following standard: A forum selection clause will be enforced unless the resisting party shows "that trial in the contractual forum will be so gravely difficult and inconvenient that he will for all practical purposes be deprived of his day in court." An inconvenient contractual forum would not be grounds for denying enforcement of a forum selection clause merely because "the balance of convenience is strongly in favor" of some place other than the contractual forum. The Court reiterated this in *Carnival Cruise*, where it reversed a Court of Appeals' decision that Miami was an inconvenient forum for two elderly Washington residents. According to the Court, "conclusory" findings of inconvenience do not satisfy the "heavy burden of proof" required to warrant non-enforcement. In the same fashion, the comments to Restatement §80 also declare:

> It should be emphasized that entertainment of the action in such a situation could not be justified on the simple ground that trial in the state of the forum would be more convenient than in the chosen state. Entertainment of the action could only be justified in the rare situation where the chosen state would be a seriously inconvenient place for the trial and the state of the forum would be far more convenient.

And, §3(3) of the Model Choice of Forum Act requires that the contractual forum be "substantially less convenient."

(b) *Copperweld's standard of inconvenience.* In *Copperweld*, why did the court rule that the forum selection clause was "unreasonable"? Is the *Copperweld* result correct? Is it consistent with *Bremen*? Consider how *Copperweld* compares the *Bremen* standard of inconvenience with that in *Central Contracting*.

(c) *Wisdom of* Bremen's *rigorous standard for inconvenience.* Why do *Bremen* and other authorities require such an extreme showing of inconvenience before they will deny enforcement? Why is it not enough, to demonstrate "unreasonableness," to show that it would be significantly more expensive for the plaintiff to litigate in the contractual forum? For example, why shouldn't unreasonableness have been found in *Carnival Cruise*? Recall that the elderly Shutes would have had to travel to Miami to attend relevant hearings.

What if the *overall* costs of litigating in the contractual forum would be higher, both for each party and for both parties together? Does it make sense to enforce a forum clause in these circumstances? How is anyone benefited? Why would it not be enough to show that one party would have its ability to litigate significantly impaired (for example, because of lack of compulsory process, limited discovery, and other procedural matters)? Is it "reasonable" to enforce forum selection agreements in these circumstances? Does it matter whether these impairments could have been foreseen at the time of contracting?

What sorts of showings should satisfy *Bremen's* requirement that the contractual forum will "for all practical purposes ... deprive [the party] of his day in court"? the fact that the contractual forum will not entertain the case? a statute of limitations will bar the action in the contractual forum? indispensable parties could not be joined in the contractual forum (*compare* Model Choice of Forum Act §3(2))? serious financial burden relative to the resisting party's resources? Did the inconvenience of a German forum in *Copperweld* rise to the level required by *Bremen*?

(d) *Relevance of post-contracting inconveniences.* It is not clear that inconveniences arising *after* the parties made their forum agreement would need to satisfy *Bremen's* elevated standard of proof. *Bremen* expressly linked the fact that particular inconveniences were "clearly foreseeable at the time of contracting" with the requirement that, "[i]n these circumstances," the plaintiff must show he will be "deprived of his day in court." Few cases have involved changed circumstances, but, as discussed below, it would appear sound to attach greater weight to unforeseen inconveniences than to others.

(e) *Relevance of inconvenience that existed, or could have been foreseen, at time of contracting.* In *Copperweld*, the parties presumably could have foreseen the foreign forum's inconvenience when they agreed to the forum selection clause. What relevance should this fact have? How would *Bremen* treat inconvenience that could have been foreseen at the time the contract was made? Which approach is more persuasive?

Most U.S. authorities have concluded that "inconvenience" is ordinarily relevant only if it arises from factors that became apparent *after* the forum selection agreement was entered into. Thus, *Bremen* suggested that inconveniences that were foreseeable at the time of contracting should play little, if any, role in deciding the enforceability of a forum selection clause: "Of course, where it can be said with reasonable assurance that at the time they entered into the contract, the parties to a freely negotiated private international commercial agreement contemplated the claimed inconvenience, it is difficult to see why any such claim of inconvenience should be heard." Applying this reasoning, lower courts have generally refused to accord substantial weight to factors that existed, or could have been foreseen, at the time the forum clause was entered into. *E.g., Interamerican Trade Corp. v. Companhia Fabricadora de Pecas*, 973 F.2d 487 (6th Cir. 1992) ("This is simply not a case in which a change of circumstances has occurred in Brazilian litigation that would justify a court in relieving ITC of its contractual commitment."); *Deolalikar v. Murlas Commodities, Inc.*, 602 F.Supp. 12, 15 (E.D. Pa. 1984)("'Mere inconvenience or additional expense is not the test of unreasonableness, since it may be assumed that the plaintiff received under the contract consideration for these things.'") (quoting *Central Contracting Co. v. Maryland Casualty Co.*, 367 F.2d 341, 344 (3d Cir. 1966)).

Are some levels of inconvenience so extreme that they will justify non-enforcement even if they were foreseeable at the time of contracting? For example, if inconveniences foreseeable at the time of contracting deny a party a meaningful opportunity to present its case, does *Bremen* say that those inconveniences should be ignored? Conversely, if inconveniences were *not* foreseeable at the time of contracting, should a forum selection clause be enforced if it imposes significant inconveniences on one party? As to unforeseen inconveniences, should a pure forum non conveniens analysis be adopted?

(f) *Effect of* Carnival Cruise *on "inconvenience" exception.* In *Carnival Cruise*, the Supreme Court rejected the Court of Appeals' conclusion that Florida was an unreasonable forum; the Supreme Court relied in part on the lack of evidence that Florida would have been inconvenient for the parties. Among other things, the Court flatly dismissed the Court of Appeals' unexplained assertion that "the Shutes are physically and financially incapable of pursuing" their suit in Florida. *See supra* pp. 399-400. Was this appropriate?

3. *Forum selection agreement's selection of biased or corrupt forum as basis for resisting enforcement.* The enforcement of a forum selection agreement can be resisted on several grounds that relate to the particular situs selected as the contractual forum. Bias or corruption are two such bases.

(a) *Biased or corrupt foreign tribunal as basis for nonenforcement of forum selection clause.* If a forum selection agreement chooses a forum that is biased or corrupt, U.S. courts will refuse to enforce the clause. The rule was frequently invoked in litigation during the 1980s involving Iranian entities. *E.g., McDonnell Douglas Corp. v. Islamic Republic of Iran*, 758 F.2d 341 (8th Cir.), *cert. denied*, 414 U.S. 948 (1985) (Iranian judicial system held inadequate); *Harris Corp. v. National Iranian Radio & Television*, 691 F.2d 1344, 1357 (11th Cir. 1982) ("effective access to Iranian courts unlikely"); *Rasoulzadeh v. Associated Press*, 574 F. Supp. 854, 861 (S.D.N.Y. 1983), *aff'd*, 767 F.2d 908 (2d Cir. 1985) ("courts administered by Iranian mullahs" held inadequate).

(b) *Standard for establishing bias or corruption.* As with the "unconscionability" exception, U.S. courts have been reluctant to deny enforcement based upon bias or corruption. Outside the Iranian context, U.S. courts have only rarely (and usually not explicitly) relied on the bias of a foreign forum to deny enforcement to a forum clause. *E.g., Skins Trading Corp. v. S.S. Punta del Este etc.*, 180 F.Supp. 609 (S.D.N.Y. 1960); *Sociedade Brasileira etc. v. S.S. Punta del Este*, 135 F.Supp. 394 (D.N.J. 1955).

In the vast majority of cases, U.S. courts have decisively rejected claims that a foreign forum will be biased. *E.g., Hodes v. S.N.C. Achille Lauro*, 858 F.2d 905 (3d Cir. 1988) ("The choice of Italian venue for disputes arising out of a cruise on an Italian vessel, departing from and returning to Italy was a sensible and fair choice."); *Hamakua Sugar Co. v. Fiji Sugar Corp.*, 778 F.Supp. 503 (D. Haw. 1991) ("possible community bias" arising from one party's status as major local employer not a "reason sufficient to ignore" the forum clause). This has been true even where the foreign party is a member of a dominant political elite in the foreign forum. *E.g., Forsythe v. Saudi Arabian Airlines Corp.*, 885 F.2d 285, 287-88 n.2 (5th Cir. 1989); *Weidner Communications Inc. v. Al Faisal*, 671 F.Supp. 531 (N.D. Ill. 1987) ("no showing here that the fact of defendants' association with the Saudi royal family will cause Saudi courts to treat plaintiff unfairly"), *rev'd on other grounds*, 859 F.2d 1302 (7th Cir. 1988).

(c) *Wisdom of current approach to foreign bias and corruption.* Is it appropriate for U.S. courts to sit in judgment on the fairness of foreign tribunals? Won't this have an adverse effect on U.S. foreign relations? Is there any alternative? Compare the treatment of similar issues in the forum non conveniens and enforcement of foreign judgments contexts, *see supra* pp. 352-53 & *infra* p. 985.

Why shouldn't a party that consents to what it can foresee will be an unfair forum be held to its bargain, at least absent coercion, fraud or the like? Courts in some countries cannot honestly be described as neutral, unbiased, and regular judicial bodies; sometimes the opposite is true. Is it not fundamentally unjust for a party to be forced to litigate in such a place — even if it has agreed? Does the due process clause permit a U.S. court to compel a party to proceed with its claims in a forum that — whether or not the party could have foreseen it — will be biased? Would it be acceptable to enforce a forum clause selecting an obviously biased and partial arbitrator to finally decide a dispute? Why should a biased foreign court be different?

(d) *Grounds for establishing that foreign forum is biased.* How can a party establish that a foreign forum is biased? Is it relevant that a foreign state-entity has selected its own home courts? Can the judges in such courts fairly decide cases involving the state that pays their salaries and decides on their career advancement (and other matters, as well)?

4. *Forum selection clause selecting one party's domicile as contractual forum.* Forum selection clauses very frequently designate one party's domicile; indeed, parties often seek to negotiate provisions designating their domicile as the contractual forum. As the Supreme Court remarked in *Bremen*, businessmen "prefer ... to have disputes resolved in their own courts." Should the fact that a forum selection clause chooses the courts of one party's home state be relevant in the *Bremen* analysis? If so, what weight should it have? should it be dispositive?

U.S. courts have almost always rejected enforceability challenges resting solely on the ground that one party, and not the other, is "at home" in the contractual forum. *Forsythe v. Saudi Arabian Airlines Corp*, 885 F.2d 285, 287-88 n.2 (5th Cir. 1989); *Crown Beverage Co. v. Cerveceria Moctezuma, SA*, 663 F.2d 886 (9th Cir. 1981); *Republic International Corp. v. Amco Eng'rs, Inc.*, 516 F.2d 161 (9th Cir. 1975); *Gaskin v. Stumm Handel GmbH*, 390 F.Supp. 361 (S.D.N.Y. 1975). Indeed, one of the affirmative justifications that Justice Blackmun advanced in *Carnival Cruise* for a non-negotiated forum selection clause was the fact that it designated the defendant's place of business as the contractual forum: "Any suggestion of ... a bad-faith motive is belied by [the fact that] petitioner has its principal place of business in Florida." Shouldn't the agreement's selection of one party's domicile be a cause for suspicion?

A few U.S. courts have commented (usually in passing) that selection of one party's domicile as the contractual forum is "suspect," and have considered it as a factor arguing for unenforceability. *Union Ins. Society of Canton, Ltd. v. S.S. Elikon*, 642 F.2d 721 (4th Cir. 1981) (choice of Bremen as forum "becomes more suspect in view of [the defendant's] headquarter in Bremen"); *Copperweld Steel Co. v. Demag-Mannesmann-Boehler*, 54 F.R.D. 539 (W.D. Pa. 1972), *aff'd*, 578 F.2d 953 (3d Cir. 1978).

5. *"One-sided" forum selection clauses.* Forum clauses can be "one-sided," requiring one party to sue in a particular place, while leaving the other party free to commence litigation in any forum that it chooses. The clause at issue in *Copperweld* gave Demag the option of suing in either Germany or the United States, while requiring Copperweld to sue in Germany. Does this sort of "one-sided" forum clause further the various policies that *Bremen* and *Carnival Cruise* held were advanced by forum agreements? What purpose(s) underlie such "one-sided" forum clauses? Should U.S. courts enforce such clauses? against U.S. parties? In practice, most lower U.S. courts have enforced such clauses. *E.g., Medoil Corp. v. Citicorp*, 729 F. Supp. 1456 (S.D.N.Y. 1990). *See also Sablosky v. Edward S. Gordon Co.*, 538 N.Y.S.2d 513, 516 (Ct. App. 1989) ("Mutuality of remedy is not required in arbitration contracts.").

6. *Forum selection clauses selecting the defendant's place of business.* Some forum selection clauses (like that in *Smith*) do not choose a particular geographic location, but instead require that disputes be resolved in the place where the defendant (whichever contracting party that may be) has its principal place of business. These clauses require that a party wishing to initiate litigation do so in the courts of its potential adversary. Most U.S. courts have been more than willing to presumptively enforce such clauses. *E.g., Warner & Swasey Co. v. Salvagnini Transferica SpA*, 633 F.Supp. 1209 (W.D.N.Y. 1986) (approving clause that was "clearly designed by the parties to place the burden of travel on the party who initiated the lawsuit"); *High Life Sales Co. v. Brown-Forman Corp.*, 823 S.W.2d 493 (Mo. 1992) ("Not only does the reciprocal nature of this clause favor its enforcement, but public policy also should favor such a clause because it discourages hasty litigation.").

7. *Forum's lack of connection to the parties' dispute as a basis for resisting enforcement of forum selection clause.* Suppose that the parties choose a forum that has no connection whatsoever to their contract or dispute. Does that render the forum clause "unreasonable"? Note, as discussed elsewhere, that a choice of law agreement may not be enforced if it lacks a "reasonable relationship" to the parties' dispute. *See infra* pp. 656-57. Should the same requirement be imposed on forum clauses?

What connection did England have to the parties and their dispute in *Bremen*? Note that *Bremen* emphasized that the parties' chosen forum should be respected precisely because it was "neutral": "[n]ot surprisingly, foreign businessmen prefer, as do we, to have disputes resolved in their own courts, but if that choice is not available then in a neutral forum with expertise in the subject matter." Is this sensible? Suppose the towage contract had only involved two territories — Mexico and the United States. Would the selection of a London forum still have been reasonable? What if it was a domestic U.S. contract?

Lower courts have generally rejected arguments that forum selection clauses are unenforceable simply because they designate a forum that has no factual connection to the parties or their dispute. *E.g., Interamerican Trade Corp. v. Companhia Fabricadora de Pecas*, 973 F.2d 487, 489 (6th Cir. 1992). Nevertheless, a forum's factual connection to the parties and their dispute can be relevant to its enforceability. *Bremen* emphasized:

> We are not here dealing with an agreement between two Americans to resolve their essentially local disputes in a remote alien forum. In such a case, the serious inconvenience of the contractual forum to one or both of the parties might carry greater weight in determining the reasonableness of the forum clause. The remoteness of the forum might suggest that the agreement was an adhesive one, or that the parties did not have the particular controversy in mind when they made their agreement; yet even there the party claiming should bear a heavy burden of proof.

If there is no indication that an unrelated forum was selected for its neutrality and expertise, nor that there was a need for a single contractual forum to dispel concerns about multiple possible fora, the selection of a "remote alien" forum to resolve "essentially local disputes" might well be unreasonable. *E.g., Berman v. Cunard Line*, 771 F.Supp. 1175 (S.D. Fla. 1991) (New York forum selection clause denied enforcement on grounds of lack of connection to dispute and inconvenience); *Tisdale v. Shell Oil Co.*, 723 F.Supp. 653 (M.D. Ala. 1987) ("agreement between two Americans to resolve their essentially local dispute in a remote forum ... would be highly suspect").

8. *Relevance of parties' nationality.* Should it matter, in deciding whether to send a dispute to an arguably biased, inconvenient, or otherwise unreasonable foreign forum, what the nationalities of the parties are? In particular, should U.S. courts exercise any special scrutiny when they are asked to send a U.S. plaintiff to a foreign forum? Recall the presumption, under the forum non conveniens doctrine, in favor of a U.S. (but not a foreign) plaintiff's choice of a U.S. forum. *See supra* pp. 330-33. Should the same rationale be applicable to forum clauses?

4. Public Policy as a Ground for Resisting Enforcement of Forum Selection Agreement

a. Introduction

A third general reason that U.S. courts refuse to enforce international forum clauses is "public policy." According to *Bremen*, "[a] contractual choice-of-forum clause should be held unenforceable if enforcement would contravene a strong public policy of the forum in which suit is brought, whether declared by statute or judicial decision."[91] Elsewhere, the Court remarked that "selection of a remote forum to apply differing foreign law to an essentially American controversy might contravene an important public policy of the forum."[92] Other authorities have also acknowledged a public policy defense.[93]

b. Sources of Public Policy

The public policy defense parallels related defenses to the enforcement of arbi-

---

91. 407 U.S. at 15.

92. 407 U.S. at 17.

93. Model Choice of Forum Act §3(1). *Cf. Restatement (Second) Conflict of Laws* §80, comments a-c (1986 Revisions) (not discussing public policy).

tration agreements, choice of law agreements, and foreign judgments.[94] It is settled under U.S. federal and state law that arbitration agreements, choice of law clauses, and foreign judgments need not be enforced if they are sufficiently contrary to the enforcing forum's law or public policy. Public policy defenses are notoriously difficult to define with precision, in these and any other context.[95] It is clear, however, that *Bremen's* public policy exception, like public policy rules in related contexts, is relatively narrow.[96]

First, the Court has said that public policies cannot be derived from "general considerations of supposed public interest," but must be based upon explicit and clearly-defined "laws and legal precedents."[97] The Court's observation in *Bremen* that public policy must be "declared by statute or judicial decision" suggests comparable limits.[98]

Second, the public policy exception requires something more than a showing that the substantive laws of the chosen forum and the U.S. forum are different.[99] As discussed below, this is illustrated by *Bremen* and confirmed by lower court authority.[100]

Going beyond these generalizations, however, and determining exactly when the public policy exception applies, is less clear. Judge Wisdom remarked:

> [i]n cases of bankruptcy, divorce, successions, real rights and regulation of public authorities, for example, courts cannot remit the dispute to a foreign forum lest a foreign court render a decree conflicting with our ordering of these affairs. And in cases where objectionable activity within our jurisdiction would be encouraged by the foreign court's decree, we would reach a similar result.[101]

The strongest case of a public policy forbidding enforcement of a forum selection clause is a statute in the forum expressly invalidating such agreements with respect to certain substantive causes of action. The Second Restatement,[102] the Model Choice of a Forum Act,[103] and other authorities[104] expressly recognize that statutory prohibitions of this character provide defenses to the enforcement of forum clauses.

In practice, however, few U.S. statutes (either federal or state) expressly address

---

94. *See infra* pp. 311-43, 486-88, 624-31, 655-56 & 974-86.

95. *See Id.*

96. Public policy exceptions are interpreted narrowly, in other circumstances, including recognition of foreign judgments, *see infra* pp. 974-86; choice of law agreements, *see infra* pp. 655-56; and enforcement of arbitration agreements and awards, *see infra* pp. 1011-12 & 1049-50.

97. *W.R. Grace & Co. v. Local 759, etc.*, 461 U.S. 757 (1983). *See also United Paperworkers Int'l Union v. Misco, Inc.*, 484 U.S. 29 (1987).

98. 407 U.S. at 17.

99. 407 U.S. at 14-16. *Compare Piper Aircraft Co. v. Reyno*, 454 U.S. 235 (1981) (change in substantive law not grounds for denying *forum non conveniens* dismissal); *supra* pp. 316 & 353-56.

100. *See infra* p. 430.

101. *In re Unterweser Reederei, GmbH*, 428 F.2d 888, 906 (5th Cir. 1970) (Wisdom, J., dissenting).

102. *Restatement (Second) Conflict of Laws* §80 comment b (1986 Revisions).

103. Model Choice of Forum Act §3(1).

104. *Bremen*, 407 U.S. at 15.

the enforceability of forum clauses. The Federal Employer's Liability Act is one example of a statutory prohibition against forum selection clauses. The Act permits actions under it to be brought "in the district of the residence of the defendant, or in which the cause of action arose, or in which the defendant shall be doing business," and invalidates any "contract" intended to "enable any common carrier to exempt itself from any liability created by this Act."[105] Another federal example is (or was) 46 U.S.C. App. §183c, which makes (or made) it unlawful for shipowners transporting passengers to or from any U.S. port to insert in any contract provisions purporting to "lessen, weaken, or avoid the right of any claimant to a trial by *any* court of competent jurisdiction on the question of liability" for loss.[106]

State statutory restrictions on the enforceability of forum selection clauses are also rare. Such prohibitions most frequently occur in legislation designed to protect particular classes — such as distributors[107] and franchisees.[108] These statutory restrictions are analogous to state statutes purporting to limit the enforceability of arbitration agreements in particular cases.[109]

Less explicit statutory statements of public policy are also invoked to justify nonenforcement of forum selection clauses. As discussed above, many federal and state statutes both establish substantive rules of law and specifically grant designated courts jurisdiction to adjudicate claims based on violations of these rules, but do not expressly exclude foreign courts (or arbitral tribunals) from adjudicating such claims. Statutes dealing with antitrust, securities, trademarks, patents, and RICO are leading examples of this on the federal level. Lower courts have occasionally held that particular federal or state statutory claims are not subject to foreign forum clauses.[110]

---

105. *Boyd v. Grand Trunk W. R.R.*, 338 U.S. 263 (1949) (applying 45 U.S.C. §45).

106. The word "any," italicized in text, was added to §183c in 1992 to overrule *Carnival Cruise's* holding that §183c did not invalidate foreign forum selection clauses. Pub. L. No. 102-587, 106 Stat. 5068. The word "any" was deleted, a year later, in 1993, Pub. L. No. 103-206, but legislative history accompanying the deletion purported to explain that it was not intended as a return to *Carnival Cruise.* 139 Cong. Rec. H10928, H10939 (daily ed. Nov. 22, 1993). Subsequent legislative history expressly disclaimed this explanation. 140 Cong. Rec. S1847 (daily ed. Feb. 24, 1994) (statement of Sen. Breaux) (1993 amendment "reinstates the Supreme Court decision in the *Shute* case as the applicable law for interpreting forum selection clauses."). Two lower courts have concluded that the various amendments have left *Carnival Cruise* intact. *Pant v. Princess Cruises, Inc.*, 1994 WL 539277 (S.D. Ohio 1994); *Compagno v. Commodore Cruise Line, Ltd.*, 1994 WL 462997 (E.D. La. 1994).

107. *See Caribbean Wholesales & Service Corp. v. U.S. JVC Corp.*, 855 F.Supp. 627 (S.D.N.Y. 1994) (Puerto Rico Law 75 prohibits enforcement of clauses in distribution agreements selecting foreign forums).

108. *See EEC Computer Centers, Inc. v. Entre Computer Centers, Inc.*, 597 F.Supp. 1182 (N.D. Ill. 1984) (Illinois Franchise Disclosure Act prohibits enforcement of clauses selecting forum outside Illinois).

109. *See infra* pp. 1010-11; G. Born, *International Commercial Arbitration in the United States*, 323-40 (1994).

110. *E.g., Karlberg European Tanspa, Inc. v. JK-Josef Kratz Vertriebsgesellschaft MbH*, 699 F.Supp. 669 (N.D. Ill. 1988); *Red Bull Assocs. v. Best Western Int'l*, 686 F.Supp. 447 (S.D.N.Y.), *aff'd*, 862 F.2d 963 (2d Cir. 1988); *Volkswagen Interamericana, SA v. Rohlsen*, 360 F.2d 437 (1st Cir.), *cert. denied*, 385 U.S. 919 (1966) (Automobile Dealers' Day in Court Act); *Cutter v. Scott & Fetzer Co.*, 510 F.Supp. 905 (E.D. Wis. 1981); *High Life Sales Co. v. Brown-Forman Corp.*, 823 S.W.2d 493 (Mo. 1992) (Missouri liquor law). *See also General Environmental Science Corp. v. Horsfall*, 753 F.Supp. 664 (N.D. Ohio 1990) (emphasizing importance of uniform application of RICO).

A number of lower courts have taken a different approach. Applying *Bremen*, these courts have dismissed federal and state statutory claims pursuant to forum selection agreements.[111] These decisions typically reject vigorous arguments that private forum clauses should not be permitted to undercut federal statutory guarantees and regulatory structures.[112]

Even more difficult to define are public policies based upon wholly common law rules. The public policy at issue in *Bremen* was in this category — a common law prohibition on contractual exculpation for negligent or reckless misconduct.[113] A limited additional number of such common law public policies exist, varying between jurisdictions. Representatives examples include restraints of trade, bribes and other corrupt agreements, usery, agreements to commit unlawful acts, and agreements to provide indemnification or exculpation for negligent or reckless misconduct.[114]

c. Selected Materials on Public Policy

Excerpted below are selected materials illustrating the application of public policy defenses to the enforcement of forum selection agreements. A concluding portion of *Bremen* is excerpted, illustrating the narrowness of the contemporary public policy exception, as well as the "choice of law" issues raised by public policies. The Second Circuit's decision in *Roby v. Corporation of Lloyd's* is also excerpted, illustrating how federal courts have been increasingly willing to enforce forum selection clauses when applied to federal statutory claims. Finally, *Triad Financial Establishment v. Tumpane Co.*, introduces some of the complex "choice of public policy" issues that can arise in the enforcement of forum agreements.

THE BREMEN v. ZAPATA OFF-SHORE CO.

407 U.S. 1 (1972) [excerpted above at pp. 383-88]

BURGER, CHIEF JUSTICE. [After concluding, as discussed and excerpted above, that the parties' forum selection clause was presumptively enforceable, the

---

111. *E.g., Omron Healthcare, Inc. v. Maclaren Exports Ltd.*, 28 F.3d 600 (7th Cir. 1994) (trademark infringement); *Royal Bed & Spring Co. v. Famossul Industria e Comercio de Moveis Ltda.*, 906 F.2d 45 (1st Cir. 1990) (Law 75 of Puerto Rico, protecting distributors); *AVC Nederland BV*, 740 F.2d 148 (federal securities laws); *Coastal Steel Corp. v. Tilghman Wheelabrator, Ltd.*, 709 F.2d 190, 202 (3d Cir.), cert. denied, 464 U.S. 938 (1983) (claims by debtor in bankruptcy); *Bense v. Interstate Battery Sys. of America, Inc.*, 683 F.2d 718 (2d Cir. 1982) (antitrust); *Medoil Corp. v. Citicorp*, 729 F. Supp. 1456 (S.D.N.Y. 1990) (RICO and federal securities laws).

112. *E.g., AVC Nederland BV*, 740 F.2d at 156-60 (private contractual expectations and foreign regulatory interests outweigh federal regulatory interests). *Cf. Mitsubishi Motors Corp. v. Soler Chrysler-Plymouth, Inc.*, 473 U.S. 614, 637 n.19 (1985) ("in the event [that] choice-of-forum and choice-of-law clauses operated in tandem as a prospective waiver of a party's right to pursue statutory remedies for antitrust violations, we would have little hesitation in condemning the agreement as against public policy.").

113. *See* 407 U.S. at 15-16; *Bisso v. Inland Waterways Corp.*, 349 U.S. 85 (1955).

114. *See* M. Rubino-Sammartano & C. Morse, *Public Policy in Transnational Relationships* USA Pt. (1991).

Court went on to consider whether enforcement should be denied on the grounds of some specific public policy. In particular, the Court considered the fact that the parties' agreement contained "two clauses purporting to exculpate Unterweser from liability for damages to the towed barge." The clauses provided: "[Unterweser], their masters and crews are not responsible for defaults and/or errors in the navigation of the tow" and "Damages suffered by the towed object are in any case for account of its Owners." 428 F.2d at 895 n.39. Zapata submitted uncontested expert testimony that English courts would enforce the exculpatory clause. Under U.S. admiralty law, however, contractual exculpations of liability of this character are unenforceable because of their perceived tendency to remove disincentives to negligent conduct and because of the likelihood that they are the product of unequal bargaining power. *Bisso v. Inland Waterways Corp.*, 349 U.S. 85 (1955).]

The Court of Appeals suggested that enforcement [of the parties' forum selection clause] would be contrary to the public policy of the forum under *Bisso*, because of the prospect that the English courts would enforce the clauses of the towage contract purporting to exculpate Unterweser from liability for damages to the *Chaparral.* A contractual choice-of-forum clause should be held unenforceable if enforcement would contravene a strong public policy of the forum in which suit is brought, whether declared by statute or by judicial decision. *See, e.g., Boyd v. Grand Trunk W.R. Co.*, 338 U.S. 263 (1949). It is clear, however, that whatever the proper scope of the policy expressed in *Bisso*, it does not reach this case. *Bisso* rested on considerations with respect to the towage business strictly in American waters, and those considerations are not controlling in an international commercial agreement. Speaking for the dissenting judges in the Court of Appeals, Judge Wisdom pointed out: " ... we should not invalidate the forum-selection clause here unless we are firmly convinced that we would thereby significantly encourage negligent conduct within the boundaries of the United States." ...

ROBY v. CORPORATION OF LLOYD'S

996 F.2d 1353 (2d Cir. 1993)

MESKILL, CHIEF JUDGE: Appellants, all American citizens or residents, are more than one hundred "Names" in the Corporation of Lloyd's ("Lloyd's"). Loosely speaking, Names are investors in Lloyd's syndicates, the entities that nominally underwrite insurance risk. ... Lloyd's is not a company; it is a market somewhat analogous to the New York Stock Exchange. Lloyd's governing bodies, the Council and Committee of Lloyd's, promulgate regulations and enforce compliance therewith. There are over 300 syndicates competing within Lloyd's for underwriting business, each managed by an entity called a Managing Agent. Each Managing Agent is responsible for its own syndicate's financial well-being; it tries to attract capital and underwriting business. Managing Agents owe a contractual duty to Names to manage their syndicates with reasonable care and skill. Capital comes from Names, who are represented in their dealings with Lloyd's by Members' Agents. ...

While eighty percent of Lloyd's 26,000 Names are English, about 2,500, representing more than $1 billion in capital, are American. The Roby Names were solicited in the United States by various Lloyd's entities and representatives. Except for a brief meeting in London — a mandatory formality — the entire process by which the Roby Names became Names took place in the United States. ... Upon becoming a Name, an individual selects from a list of syndicates ... and decides how much he wishes to invest in each one. In making these decisions, Names rely to a great extent on the advice of their Members' Agents. The profits that Names earn are in proportion to their capital contributions, and Names bear unlimited liability for their proportionate losses in each syndicate they join. ...

[Names are required to enter into a variety of agreements that define their relationships with Lloyd's, its governing bodies, the member agents, and the Managing Agents. Each agreement contained an English choice of law and either an English forum selection agreement or an English arbitration clause. For example, the "General Undertaking" contained a clause providing:

"Each party hereto irrevocably agrees that the courts of England shall have exclusive jurisdiction to settle any dispute and/or controversy of whatsoever nature arising out of relating to the [Name's] membership of and/or underwriting of insurance business at Lloyd's."]

In their consolidated complaint, the Roby Names allege violations of §§12(1) and 12(2) of the Securities Act, 15 U.S.C. §77l(1), (2), and §10(b) of the Securities Exchange Act, 15 U.S.C. §78j(b). In addition, they allege "controlling person" liability under §15 of the Securities Act, 15 U.S.C §77o, and §20 of the Securities Exchange Act, 15 U.S.C. §78t. Finally, using these securities law violations as predicate acts, the Roby Names allege several violations of RICO. Each cause of action names as defendants a different combination of the following parties: Lloyd's, Lloyd's governing bodies, certain Managing and Members' Agents, certain individual members of these entities (the Chairs), and certain syndicates. [The district judge] found that the interlocking set of agreements bound the Roby Names to arbitrate or litigate their disputes in London and dismissed. ...

The Roby Names argue [on appeal] that the public policy codified in the anti-waiver provisions of the securities laws renders unenforceable any agreement that effectively eliminates compliance with those laws. The Securities Act provides that "[a]ny ... stipulation ... binding any person acquiring any security to waive compliance with any provision of this subchapter ... shall be void." 15 U.S.C. §77n. Similarly, the Securities Exchange Act states, "[a]ny ... stipulation ... binding any person to waive compliance with any provision of this chapter or of any rule or regulation thereunder ... shall be void." 15 U.S.C. §78cc(a). According to the undisputed testimony of a British attorney[sic], neither an English court nor an English arbitrator would apply the U.S. securities laws, because English conflict of law rules do not permit recognition of foreign tort or statutory law. From this, Roby Names conclude that the contract clauses work to waive compliance with the securities laws and therefore are void.

We note at the outset that *Wilko v. Swan*, 346 U.S. 427 (1953), has been squarely overruled. See *Rodriguez de Quijas v. Shearson/American Express*, 490 U.S. 477, 484 (1989). *Wilko* held that an agreement to arbitrate future controversies was void under the antiwaiver provision of the Securities Act. We do not doubt that judicial hostility to arbitration has receded dramatically since 1953 and that the arbitral forum is perfectly competent to protect litigants' substantive rights. In the words of the *Mitsubishi* Court, quoted by both the *Rodriguez* and *McMahon* Courts, "[b]y agreeing to arbitrate a statutory claim, a party does not forgo the substantive rights afforded by the statute; it only submits to their resolution in an arbitral, rather than a judicial forum." 473 U.S. at 628. If the Roby Names objected merely to the choice of an arbitral rather than a judicial forum, we would reject their claim immediately, citing *Rodriguez* and *McMahon*. However, the Roby Names argue that they have been forced to forgo the substantive protections afforded by the securities laws, not simply the judicial forum. We therefore do not believe that *Rodriguez* and *McMahon* are controlling and must look elsewhere to determine whether parties may contract away their substantive rights under the securities laws.

The Tenth Circuit recently addressed this exact issue in a similar context in *Riley v. Kingsley Underwriting Agencies, Ltd.*, 969 F.2d 953 (10th Cir.), *cert. denied*, 113 S.Ct. 658 (1992). Relying primarily on four Supreme Court precedents, *Carnival Cruise Lines v. Shute; Mitsubishi*, 473 U.S. 614; *Scherk; Bremen*, the *Riley* Court concluded that "[w]hen an agreement is truly international, as here, and reflects numerous contacts with the foreign forum, the Supreme Court has quite clearly held that the parties' choice of law and forum selection provisions will be given effect." While we agree with the ultimate result in *Riley*, we are reluctant to interpret the Supreme Court's precedent quite so broadly.

The Supreme Court certainly has indicated that forum selection and choice of law clauses are presumptively valid where the underlying transaction is fundamentally international in character. *See, e.g., Bremen*.[115] In *Bremen*, the Court explained that American parochialism would hinder the expansion of American business and trade, and more generally, interfere with the smooth functioning and growth of global commerce. Forum selection and choice of law clauses eliminate uncertainty in international commerce and insure that the parties are not unexpectedly subjected to

---

115. The analysis is no different for the arbitration clauses. Indeed, an arbitration clause is merely a specialized type of forum selection clause. *See Scherk*, 417 U.S. at 519. We might have referred to the [New York] Convention reprinted in 9 U.S.C. §§201-08 ("the Treaty"), for further support with respect to the arbitration clauses; however, because we are not entirely persuaded that the Treaty applies in the securities context, we prefer to rest our decision on different grounds. Because we understand the Roby Names to complain primarily that the United States securities laws will not be applied and not that the arbitration forum is particularly inappropriate in their case, we do not believe a detailed analysis of the Treaty is necessary.

hostile forums and laws. Moreover, international comity dictates that American courts enforce these sorts of clauses out of respect for the integrity and competence of foreign tribunals. *See Mitsubishi.* In addition to these rationales for the presumptive validity of forum selection and choice of law clauses, the Court has noted that contracts entered into freely generally should be enforced because the financial effect of forum selection and choice of law clauses likely will be reflected in the value of the contract as a whole. *Carnival Cruise Lines.*

This presumption of validity may be overcome, however, by a clear showing that the clauses are "'unreasonable' under the circumstances." *Bremen*, 407 U.S. at 10. The Supreme Court has constructed this exception narrowly: forum selection and choice of law clauses are "unreasonable" (1) if their incorporation into the agreement was the result of fraud of overreaching, (2) if the complaining party "will for all practical purposes be deprived of his day in court," due to the grave inconvenience or unfairness of the selected forum, (3) if the fundamental unfairness of the chosen law may deprive the plaintiff of a remedy; or (4) if the clauses contravene a strong public policy of the forum state... .

[Turning to the fourth issue,] the Supreme Court in *Bremen* wrote, "[a] contractual choice-of-forum clause should be held unenforceable if enforcement would contravene a strong public policy of the forum in which suit is brought." By including antiwaiver provisions in the securities laws, Congress made clear its intention that the public policies incorporated into those laws should not be thwarted. ... [T]he securities laws are aimed at prospectively protecting American investors from injury by demanding "full and fair disclosure" from issuers. Private actions exist under the securities laws not because Congress had an overwhelming desire to shift losses after the fact, but rather because private actions provide a potent means of deterring the exploitation of American investors. We believe therefore that the public policies of the securities laws would be contravened if the applicable foreign law failed adequately to deter issuers from exploiting American investors.

In this sense, the securities laws somewhat resemble the antitrust laws at issue in *Mitsubishi. Mitsubishi* enforced a clause providing that all disputes arising under a contract between a Puerto Rican corporation and a Japanese corporation be submitted for arbitration by the Japan Commercial Arbitration Association. The Court recognized that private actions under the Sherman Act play a "central role" in promoting the national interest in a competitive economy. Like private actions in the securities context, private actions under the Sherman Act serve primarily a deterrent purpose. Nevertheless, *Mitsubishi* held that a Japanese arbitration panel, applying U.S. antitrust law, adequately would further the deterrent purpose of the Sherman Act, despite the panel's lack of allegiance to United States' interests. The Court indicated quite clearly in dicta, however, that "in the event the choice-of-forum and choice-of-law clauses operated in tandem as a prospective waiver of a party's right to pursue statutory remedies for antitrust violations, we would have little hesitation in condemning the agreement as against public policy."[116]

We are concerned in the present case that the Roby Names' contract clauses may operate "in tandem" as a prospective waiver of the statutory remedies for securities violations, thereby circumventing the strong and expansive public policy in deterring such violations. We are cognizant of the important reasons for enforcing such clauses in Lloyd's agreements. Lloyd's is a British concern which raises capital in over 80 nations. Its operations are clearly international in scope. There can be no doubt that the contract clauses mitigate the uncertainty regarding choice of law and forum inherent in the multinational affairs of Lloyd's. Comity also weighs in favor of enforcing the clauses. Yet we do not believe that a U.S. court can in good conscience enforce clauses that subvert a strong national policy, particularly one that for over fifty years has served as the foundation for the U.S. financial markets and business community. In this case, the victims of Lloyd's' alleged securities violations are hundreds of individual American investors, most of whom were actively solicited in the United States by Lloyd's representatives. We believe that if the Roby Names were able to show that available remedies in England are insufficient to deter British issuers from exploiting American investors through fraud, misinterpretation or inadequate disclosure, we would not hesitate to condemn the choice of law, forum selection and arbitration clauses as against public policy. For the reasons set forth ... below, however, we conclude that the Roby Names have failed to make such a showing.

We are satisfied not only that the Roby Names have several adequate remedies in England to vindicate their substantive rights, but also that in this case the policies of ensuring full and fair disclosure and deterring the exploitation if U.S. investors have not been subverted. ... English common law provides remedies for knowing or reckless deceit, negligent misrepresentation, and even innocent misrepresentation. Moreover, the Misrepresentation Act of 1967 provides some additional statutory remedies. While the Roby Names might have been able to sue "controlling persons" under the U.S. securities laws and establish liability without proving reliance, it certainly is not unfair for English law to require proof of actual misconduct and reliance. Furthermore we are skeptical that "controlling person" liability could be established against many of the defendants here. ...

---

116. *Scherk*, decided eleven years before *Mitsubishi*, is not to the contrary. *Scherk v. Alberto-Culver Co.* Although the *Scherk* Court enforced an arbitration clause which contained a choice of law provision (Illinois Law), the focus of the opinion is almost exclusively on the validity of the arbitration provision. Nowhere in the opinion is it suggested that a choice of law clause invariably trumps the public policies underlying the securities laws. In any event, Illinois law is certainly adequate to protect the substantive rights of Alberto-Culver, the American company that allegedly was defrauded in its purchase of Scherk, a German company. Indeed, viewed practically, the complaint was essentially a breach of contract action masquerading as a statutory misrepresentation claim. The Court could confidently rely on Illinois law to protect any public policy of the United States implicated in that action.

In any event, the available remedies are adequate and the potential recoveries substantial. This is particularly true given the low scienter requirements under English misrepresentation law (*e.g.*, negligence, "innocence"). Moreover, together with the contractual obligations imposing certain fiduciary and similar duties on Members' and Managing Agents, we believe that the available remedies and potential damages recoveries suffice to deter deception of American investors.

Finally, although ... §14 of the Lloyd's Act of 1982 exempts the Corporation of Lloyd's (and its officers and employees) from liability, no other entity within Lloyds's is exempt. Moreover, even the Corporation of Lloyd's is not exempt for acts "done in bad faith." Furthermore, as a self-regulation organization, we cannot say that Lloyd's' own bylaws will not insure the honesty and forthrightness that American investors deserve and expect. We conclude that the Roby Names have adequate remedies in England to vindicate their statutory fraud and misrepresentation claims. ... While we do not doubt that the U.S. securities laws would provide the Roby Names with a greater variety of defendants and a greater chance of success due to lighter scienter and causation requirements, we are convinced that there are ample and just remedies under English law. Moreover, we cannot say that the policies underlying our securities laws will be offended by the application of English law. ...

That RICO provides treble damages and seeks to deter persistent misconduct does not dissuade us from our view that the Roby Names' contract clauses must be enforced. As we have explained, the Roby Names have adequate potential remedies in England and there are significant disincentives to deter English issuers from unfairly exploiting American investors. Although the remedies and disincentives might be magnified by the application of RICO, we cannot say that application of English law would subvert the policies underlying that statute. ...

TRIAD FINANCIAL ESTABLISHMENT v. TUMPANE COMPANY
611 F.Supp. 157 (N.D.N.Y. 1985)

McCURN, DISTRICT JUDGE. Plaintiff, Triad Financial Establishment ("Triad") brings this breach of contract action against defendant, The Tumpane Company ("Tumco"), seeking more than $3.5 million in commissions allegedly owed to Triad under the contracts between the parties. ... Plaintiff Triad is a Liechtenstein entity controlled by Adnan Khashoggi, a well-known Saudi Arabian businessman. Triad describes itself as a "marketing and consulting organization" that "assists its clients in locating, identifying, and participating in international business ventures, particularly in Saudi Arabia." Defendant Tumco is a New York corporation with its principal place of business in Vancouver, Washington. Tumco is primarily engaged in providing support services such as housing, transportation, food services and health facilities for large military projects.

In 1971 the United States agreed to equip and modernize the Royal Saudi Air Force of the Kingdom of Saudi Arabia ("Saudi Arabia") through a long range, multi-billion dollar program called "Peace Hawk" ("Peace Hawk" or "program"). In accordance with the terms of the Foreign Military Sales ("F.M.S.") Contract, the Northrop Corporation ("Northrop") was designated the prime contractor for the entire program. Defendant Tumco was interested in being named as the sole-source subcontractor for support services on the Peace Hawk program. On December 1, 1971, Triad and Tumco entered into two agreements wherein Tumco appointed Triad as its marketing agent to assist Tumco in obtaining the Peace Hawk support services subcontract from Northrop. ... Tumco was awarded the support services subcontract for [certain] phases [of the project, commencing in April 1972 and ending in June 1979].

Triad contends that it has performed all of its obligations under the agreement and is entitled to commissions in excess of $3.5 million. Tumco contends that it does not owe Triad any commissions and has counterclaimed for the return of $1.7 million already paid to Triad under the agreements. ...

In the course of its efforts to obtain a subcontract on the Peace Hawk project, defendant Tumco entered into two agreements with Triad. The first, more general agreement is termed a "Marketing Agreement." It essentially provides that Triad will use its best efforts to develop specific projects to be delineated in more detailed "Product Agreements," and will be compensated at a rate provided for in the individual product agreements. The second, more specific agreement is captioned "Product Agreement # 1." This agreement specifically relates to the "Northrop F-5 Aircraft Maintenance and Training Program as sold by Tumco as a subcontractor to Northrop under a United States Government F.M.S. Contract," *i.e.* the Peace Hawk program. ...

[The court initially discussed motions for summary judgment by each party, alleging that the foregoing contracts plainly entitled it to relief (Triad seeking damages in the form of due, but unpaid, commissions; Tumco seeking return of funds paid and dismissal of Triad's claims).] [T]he Marketing Agreement between the parties contains a forum selection clause designating New York as the jurisdiction that would govern the interpretation of the contracts. New York courts will normally honor the parties' choice of forum provided the forum selected has a substantial relationship to the parties or the transaction and the application of the forum's law would not be contrary to a fundamental policy of a state with a materially greater interest than the forum state.[117] *Business Incentives Co. v. Sony Corporation of*

---

117. The parties agree that New York's policy with regard to this issue is based on the *Restatement (Second) of Conflict of Laws* §187 which reads in pertinent part: (2) The law of the state chosen by the parties to govern their contractual rights and duties will be applied, even if the particular issue is one which the parties could not have resolved by an explicit provision in their agreement directed to that issue, unless either (a) the chosen state has no substantial relationship to the parties or the transaction and there is no other reasonable basis for the parties' choice, or (b) application of the law of the chosen state would be contrary to a fundamental policy of a state which has a materially greater interest than the chosen state in the determination of the particular issue and which, under the rule of §188, would be the state of the applicable law in the absence of an effective choice of law by the parties. Tumco contends that this case falls squarely within §187(2)(b).

America, 397 F.Supp. 63, 67 (S.D.N.Y. 1975). Thus, New York courts do not consider themselves bound by a forum selection clause if its application would override the policies of a state with a materially greater interest in the controversy.

Tumco contends that Saudi Arabia has a far greater interest in this litigation than New York does and, consequently, Saudi law should apply notwithstanding the forum selection clause. Triad contends that Saudi Arabia has no interest in this controversy and accordingly, this court should honor the parties' choice of forum. In determining what law should apply, this court must weigh the relative interests of the states involved to determine which state has the greatest interest at stake in this litigation. The court must also consider which forum has the most significant relationship with the parties and transaction. Plaintiff Triad is a Liechtenstein entity. Defendant Tumco is incorporated in New York with its main office in Vancouver, Washington. At the height of the Peace Hawk program Tumco had only two employees in New York compared with 3750 in Saudi Arabia, 500 in Montana, 250 in California, 200 in Spain, and 100 in Washington. None of the relevant agreements were negotiated, executed, or performed in New York. It appears that New York's only significant contact with this litigation is via the forum selection clause contained in the Marketing Agreement.

In contrast, Saudi Arabia has a significant connection to this litigation and a compelling interest in the application of the law. Although Triad is a Liechtenstein entity, it has characterized itself as a "Saudi sales agent." Its reputation as an effective marketing agent is based almost entirely on Mr. Khashoggi's purported influence in Saudi Arabia. In addition, the Northrop-Tumco contracts, which are predicates to the Triad-Tumco contracts, were negotiated primarily in Saudi Arabia and call for performance entirely in Saudi Arabia. Moreover, Saudi Arabia has a compelling interest in having its law applied to this controversy. The Kingdom of Saudi Arabia prohibits the payment of agent's fees on contracts for arms and related services. The Saudi prohibition was formally expressed in Decree No. 1275 which was issued on September 17, 1975. The Decree prohibits the payment of any agent's fees in connection with the sale of armaments or related equipment:

> 1. No firm holding a contract with the Saudi Government for the supply of arms or equipment required by the Saudi Government may pay any sum as a commission to any intermediary, sales agent, representative, or broker. This prohibition shall apply regardless of the nationality of the firm or the nationality of the intermediary, sales agent, representative, or broker. It shall apply also whether the contract was concluded directly between the Saudi Government and the firm or through a third-party state. No recognition is accorded to any commission agreement previously concluded by any of such firm with any party, and such agreement shall have no validity vis-a-vis the Saudi Government.

> 2. If among the foreign firms mentioned in paragraph 1 above there are any that are obligated by commission agreements that they have made, they are

to stop payment of the commissions due after having been warned by this decision. ...

The Saudis enacted Decree No. 1275 in an attempt to root out corruption and bribery in military contracts. To allow a forum selection clause to circumvent this strong Saudi policy would render Decree No. 1275 meaningless. In contrast, New York has no policy at stake in this litigation. New York has little or no interest in upholding Triad's claim for fees. In view of the significant connection to Saudi Arabia, the fundamental Saudi policy against agent's fees in military contracts, and the negligible relation between this case and New York, the court finds that Saudi Arabian law should apply.

Under the concept of depacage, Saudi law will only be applied after September 17, 1975 as the Saudi interest in this action did not arise until Decree No. 1275 was issued.[118] There is no reason to displace the parties' choice of forum prior to the issuance of the Decree.

Notes on Bremen, Roby, and Triad Financial

1. *Public policy and non-contractual claims.* Why should forum selection agreements ever be enforceable as to non-contractual claims? Do not "ordinary" tort claims rest upon the forum's public policy determinations about what types of conduct is wrongful or economically undesirable? Should private parties be permitted to delegate these determinations to alien forums?

2. *Public policy as basis for nonenforcement of forum clauses.* As *Bremen* and *Roby* illustrate, enforcement of a forum agreement can be resisted on the grounds that it would violate the public policy of the forum.

(a) *Express statutory prohibition as source of public policy.* The most clearcut example of a public policy basis for resisting enforcement of a forum clause is a statute in the enforcing forum forbidding enforcement. Consider the provisions of the federal securities laws at issue in *Roby* — 15 U.S.C. §§77n and 78cc(a) — invalidating any contractual waiver of compliance with statutory requirements. Why don't these provisions forbid enforcement of any forum selection clause designating non-U.S. courts? *See Wilko v. Swan*, 346 U.S. 427 (1953) (holding that anti-waiver provision forbids enforcement of arbitration clause), *overruled Rodriquez de Quijas v. Shearson/American Express*, 490 U.S. 477, 484 (1989).

Consider *Roby*, which did not merely enforce a forum clause, but enforced a clause that would, in conjunction with an English choice of law clause, exclude *any* application of the U.S. securities laws. Is this result consistent with the anti-waiver provisions of §77n and §78cc(a)? Isn't it obvious that the Lloyd's choice of forum and choice of law clauses "waive compliance with" *every* provision of the U.S. securities laws?

(b) *Implied statutory prohibition as source of public policy.* Very few U.S. federal or state statutes expressly forbid enforcement of a forum selection clause. In these cases, what ought to qualify as "public policies"? Many federal and state statutes provide substantive rules of law and statutory protections, often coupled with jurisdictional grants and procedural rules. The federal antitrust, securities, trademark, patent, and employment discrimination laws are examples of this. Although these statutory regimes may not contain express prohibitions against forum clauses, it is often argued that such prohibitions should be implied, to ensure fulfillment of the regulatory objectives of the legislation.

Put aside the specific anti-waiver provisions of the federal securities laws, and consider whether the regulatory framework of the federal securities laws permits foreign forum clauses. Was *Roby* right to dismiss a U.S. plaintiff's U.S. securities law claims? *Roby* does "not doubt that the U.S. securities law would

---

118. Dépeçage has been defined as "applying the rules of different states to different issues." Reese, *Dépeçage: A Common Phenomenon in Choice of Law*, 73 Colum. L. Rev. 58 (1973). The court determines which law should apply with respect to each particular issue after weighing the appropriate choice-of-law factors.

provide the Roby Names with a greater variety of defendants and a greater chance of success due to lighter scienter and causation requirements," and that English law would not provide treble damages. Given these differences between a U.S. and an English forum, how can one say that enforcing the forum clause will not undercut the purposes of the federal securities laws?

In *Omron Healthcare Inc. v. MacLaren Exports Ltd.*, the Seventh Circuit considered the claim that U.S. public policy forbid enforcement of a forum clause in a case under federal trademark legislation. 28 F.3d 600 (7th Cir. 1994). The U.S. plaintiff

> tells us that the "policies" in question favor sending disputes to courts that have the expertise to resolve them, and ensuring that courts with the interest of Americans at heart interpret laws designed for the protection of American consumers. 28 F.3d at 603.

Judge Easterbrook summarily dismissed the argument. Observing that "neither of these policies has a secure footing in any statute," he held that foreign courts were capable of interpreting federal trademark statutes. 28 F.3d at 603. If a contrary view were accepted, "then *Scherk, Mitsubishi*, and many other cases are wrongly decided, for they depend on the belief that foreign tribunals will interpret U.S. law honestly, just as the federal courts of the United States routinely interpret the laws of the states and other nations." 28 F.3d at 603-04.

Is *Roby* correctly decided? Why or why not? Why do claims under the federal securities laws raise any questions of public policy? Are securities claims just like other causes of action — like contract and tort claims? Do not the antitrust and securities laws represent fundamentally important U.S. public policies, that will be undermined if foreign courts are permitted to decide statutory claims arising under those statutes? How can a foreign judge, untrained in U.S. law and unfamiliar with U.S. conditions, apply the Sherman Act? Is it appropriate, as most lower courts have held, to permit private parties to contract out of the substantive protections of fundamentally important federal regulatory statutes, like the antitrust and securities laws?

(c) *Common law as source of public policy.* What was the source of the public policy in *Bremen* that allegedly forbid enforcement of the parties' English forum clause? Note that there are a considerable variety of common law public policies that might arguably restrain enforcement of forum clauses; these include prohibitions against bribery, anti-competitive restrictions, usery, and the like. Is it appropriate for these public policies to preclude the enforcement of international forum clauses? Did *Bremen* accept that a U.S. public policy against exculpation for gross negligence might potentially preclude enforcement of a forum clause?

(d) *Hypothetical applications of U.S. public policy.* Consider whether U.S. "public policy" would preclude enforcement of a forum clause in the following hypotheticals:

> In *Bremen*, the accident had occurred within U.S. territorial waters, at the beginning of the oil rig's voyage to the Adriatic Sea.

> In a dispute arising out of a U.S. employer's termination of an employment contract, for alleged malfeasance by the employee, the employee brings claims for both wrongful termination and libel (based upon the employer's derogatory public statements alleging that the employee had engaged in wrongful conduct). The employment contract contains a provision selecting English courts as the contractual forum for both the wrongful termination and libel claims. English courts would permit recovery on the libel claim upon a significantly more liberal basis than the First Amendment would permit in the United States. The employer seeks to have the dispute resolved in U.S. courts, arguing that public policies derived from the First Amendment forbid enforcement of the forum selection agreement.

> In the foregoing dispute, the employee instead brings race discrimination claims under Title VII — the federal employment discrimination statute — in a U.S. court in violation of the forum clause. The employer seeks to dismiss the case in favor of the English contractual forum.

> In a dispute involving military technology, the export of which is prohibited by U.S. law absent an export license, the parties' agreement contains a forum clause specifying Russian courts. The parties are a U.S. seller of products based upon the military technology and a Russian purchaser. The U.S. party brings suit in the United States asserting that the forum clause violates U.S. public policy because it would require disclosure of the technology to unauthorized foreign parties.

3. Relevance of foreign courts' willingness to decide U.S. statutory or other claim. In deciding whether to enforce a forum selection clause as applied to U.S. statutory (or other) claims, is it relevant that a foreign court will or will not apply the U.S. statutory provisions and hear such claims? Where violations of the antitrust and securities law occur within U.S. territory, perpetrated against U.S. nationals, with adverse consequences for U.S. markets and third parties, should U.S. courts enforce a forum clause granting exclusive jurisdiction to the courts of the wrongdoer's home country? How does *Roby* resolve the foregoing questions? Is the content of English law relevant to the *Roby* outcome? If so, is this consistent with the basic premise, set forth in *Bremen*, that changes in substantive law are not relevant to the enforceability of forum clauses?

4. Prohibition against application of foreign penal and revenue laws — revisited. Recall the historic rule, discussed above, that one nation's courts will not apply the penal or revenue laws of another nation. *See supra* pp. 354-55 & *infra* pp. 629-30 & 955-60. Why was it that the English courts in *Roby* would not apply the U.S. federal securities laws? If English and U.S. law were in fact so similar, why should English courts refuse to apply U.S. law?

5. Is Roby consistent with Mitsubishi Motors? Consider the following excerpt from *Mitsubishi Motors Corp. v. Soler Chrysler-Plymouth, Inc.*, 473 U.S. 614 (1985), which held that federal antitrust claims could be arbitrated outside the United States:

> [C]ounsel for Mitsubishi conceded that American law applied to the antitrust claims and represented that the claims had been submitted to the arbitration panel in Japan on that basis. The record confirms that ... the arbitral panel had taken these claims under submission. We therefore have no occasion to speculate [on the tribunal's willingness to apply U.S. antitrust laws, rather than Swiss law as contemplated by the parties' choice of law agreement] at this stage in proceedings, when Mitsubishi seeks to enforce the agreement to arbitrate, not to enforce an award. Nor need we consider now the effect of an arbitral tribunal's failure to take cognizance of the statutory cause of action on the claimant's capacity to reinitiate suit in federal court. We merely note that in the event the choice-of-forum and choice-of-law clauses operated in tandem as a prospective waiver of a party's right to pursue statutory remedies for antitrust violations, we would have little hesitation in condemning the agreement as against public policy.

Does the foregoing language (cited in *Roby*) mean that a U.S. court would *not* compel arbitration of federal antitrust claims, pursuant to an otherwise valid arbitration agreement, if it was clear that the foreign arbitral tribunal would not apply the U.S. antitrust laws? If so, is there any meaningful distinction between an arbitration agreement and a forum clause? Is *Roby* consistent with the foregoing language from *Mitsubishi*?

6. Effect of parties' choice of law on U.S. public policy analysis. Why is the public policy of the forum where enforcement of a forum selection clause is sought the applicable public policy under *Bremen* and other authorities? If the parties have agreed that their contract is governed by a law other than that of the enforcement forum, why should not that foreign law be applied? Suppose, in each of the hypotheticals set forth above, that the parties' agreement contained a clause selecting the law of the contractual forum, and not U.S. law. Would that choice of law provision make U.S. public policies irrelevant? Would the parties' choice of law agreement be relevant to the U.S. public policy? Was it relevant in *Roby*? Suppose that the facts were identical, except that there were no English choice of law clauses, but English courts would nevertheless refuse to apply the U.S. securities laws.

7. Effect of U.S. state public policies on enforceability of forum selection clauses. The public policies at issue in *Bremen* and *Roby* were U.S. federal policies (derived respectively from federal admiralty and federal securities laws). What if a U.S. *state* public policy forbids enforcement of an international forum selection clause? Is there anything in federal law — constitutional, statutory, or common law — that forbids application of a state public policy to deny enforcement to an otherwise enforceable international forum clause?

For example, Law 75 in Puerto Rico forbids the enforcement of agreements selecting foreign forums in actions involving Puerto Rico distributors. Other states have comparable public policies that expressly or impliedly forbid enforcement of forum clauses in particular contexts. Examples include franchise agreements and automobile dealership agreements. *See supra* pp. 415-17. May a *state* public policy preclude enforcement of an international forum clause?

As discussed below, most lower courts have held that federal procedural law governs the enforceability of international forum selection clauses in federal courts. *See infra* pp. 449-51. Some courts have concluded, as a consequence, that state public policies are irrelevant to the enforceability of forum clauses in federal courts. *E.g.*, *Royal Bed and Spring Co. v. Famossul etc.*, 906 F.2d 45 (1st Cir. 1990) (holding that "there is no need to consider" Puerto Rico's law 75, forbidding forum clauses, because federal law governs enforceability of forum selection clauses in federal court). Other courts have taken the opposite view, permitting state public policies to deny enforcement to foreign forum selection agreements. *E.g.*, *Farmland Indus., Inc. v. Frazier-Parrott Commodities, Inc.*, 806 F.2d 848, 850-52 (8th Cir. 1986) ("Because of the close relationship between substance and procedure in this case we believe that consideration should have been given to the public policy of Missouri.").

Which is the correct approach? Should parochial state public policies be permitted to frustrate the enforcement of forum clauses in international cases? Wouldn't this have serious effects on U.S. foreign relations and commerce? *See infra* pp. 451-52. Is there any basis for arguing that these state public policies are preempted by federal law of some sort? State public policies regarding forum clauses generally do not contravene any particular federal statute (and if they do, they are preempted). Is there any basis for fashioning federal common law rules that would preempt state public policies rendering foreign forum clauses unenforceable? How would the enforcement of such clauses interfere with federal interests? Does it matter what the content of the state public policy is?

8. *Application of U.S. public policy when conduct occurs outside the United States.* Why did *Bremen* refuse to apply the public policy, set forth in *Bisso*, against exculpatory clauses?

(a) *Bremen's territoriality limitation.* What was the Court's justification for not giving effect to what was admittedly a strong U.S. public policy against exculpation for negligence? Is it fair to distill from *Bremen* a "territoriality" limitation on U.S. public policies? What would be the source of such a "territoriality" restriction on public policies? Note that U.S. courts have applied a "territoriality" presumption in other contexts, including service, *infra* pp. 780-94; extraterritorial application of national laws, *supra* pp. 546-52; and choice of law, *supra* pp. 616-24.

(b) *Wisdom of territoriality limitation.* Why is United States "territory" the correct definition of the limits of U.S. public policy? Recall that the injured plaintiff in *Bremen* was a U.S. company. Why did the relevant U.S. public policy against exculpation clauses not extend to the protection of U.S. citizens from negligence — wherever that negligence might occur? Alternatively, note that the parties' contract in *Bremen* was made in the United States and that the towage would occur at least partially in U.S. waters. Why did the relevant U.S. public policy not apply to performance of the entire contract, where it had this level of U.S. contacts?

(c) *Possible application of nationality principle.* Recall, as discussed above, that nationality is an accepted base for asserting general personal jurisdiction. *See supra* pp. 95-101. Is that relevant? *See infra* pp. 507-08, 584 & 649-50, for a discussion of the passive personality principle under international law and the treatment of the plaintiff's nationality under contemporary U.S. choice of law rules. Suppose that the defendant in *Bremen* had also been a U.S. company. Would the U.S. public policy against exculpatory clauses have extended to conduct — by a U.S. defendant directed against a U.S. plaintiff outside the United States — in these circumstances?

(d) *Possible application of effects doctrine.* What if substantial effects of Unterweser's alleged negligence were felt in the United States? For example, suppose that 1,000 U.S. workers lost their jobs when Zapata — bankrupted by the uncompensated loss of its rig — could not continue operations. Suppose that Unterweser's negligence in towing the rig through the Gulf of Mexico caused severe environmental damage that affected U.S. waters and shores. Suppose that the negligence posed a threat to shipping in the area — principally U.S. vessels with U.S. crews, passengers, and cargo. Why, in these circumstances, should U.S. public policies forbidding exculpation for negligence not be applicable?

Suppose that the conduct underlying a federal securities or antitrust claim occurred largely outside the United States, but had significant effects in the United States. In many circumstances, U.S. statutes apply extraterritorially to foreign conduct, *see infra* pp. 550-76, and would likely do so in this hypothetical. In these circumstances, why should the foreign situs of the parties' dispute affect the willingness of a U.S. court to enforce a forum clause applicable to claims arising from the dispute? Compare the public policy analysis under *Howe v. Goldcorp* and *Laker Airways*, *supra* pp. 346-57, in context of the forum non conveniens doctrine.

(e) *Conflict of laws analysis.* Is it desirable, as suggested in *Bremen*, to adopt rigid territorial limits governing the public policy exception? Or is it instead necessary to consider the situs of the conduct, the nationalities of the parties, and the precise character of the relevant U.S. and foreign regulatory interests before deciding public policy arguments? Would it be better for courts to apply a "conflict of public policies" analysis like that used in the choice of law context. *See infra* pp. 631-52.

9. *Application of foreign public policies.* If U.S. public policies may generally invalidate forum clauses in cases involving conduct in the United States, then what relevance do *foreign* public policies have in cases involving conduct in a *foreign* country. Suppose that two U.S. companies have entered into a contract, with a U.S. forum clause, involving actions occurring in Europe that implicate strong European public policies; should a U.S. court enforce the clause even if doing so would result in the application of U.S. substantive law and the violation of European public policies? Assuming that the case actually involves a forum clause, how does *Triad* resolve the foregoing issues? Is *Triad* correct? Why should a U.S. court ignore an otherwise valid contract based upon foreign public policies?

10. *Conflicts between national public policies.* Suppose that a foreign state's public policies are antithetical to U.S. public policies — for example, discriminating against U.S. nationals on the basis of race or religion. Should U.S. courts apply such foreign public policies in order to invalidate a U.S. forum selection clause? Suppose a U.S. court is asked to enforce a forum selection clause choosing Japanese courts, in a case where wrongful conduct occurred in Europe and where Japanese courts would disregard a fundamental European public policy. Note that in most such cases, European courts could be expected to vindicate their own local public policies and U.S. courts would ordinarily refuse to hear the case on the merits, *supra* pp. 289-97.

11. *Contractual forum's likely application of law of state not connected to parties' dispute.* As discussed elsewhere, the due process clause forbids U.S. courts from applying their substantive law to disputes which lack any reasonable connection to the forum state. *See infra* pp. 512-44. Suppose that a forum clause designates a contractual forum whose courts will apply a substantive law lacking any connection to the parties' dispute. Is this a basis for denying enforcement of the forum clause? Does the due process clause require a U.S. court to deny enforcement in such circumstances?

12. *Showing required to establish violation of public policy.* What must be shown to demonstrate that a foreign court's disposition of a case would be contrary to a U.S. public policy? It is commonly said that something more must be shown than the fact that foreign law provides a different result than U.S. law would. *See Tahan v. Hodgson,* 662 F.2d 862, 864 (D.C. Cir. 1981) (foreign judgment must be "repugnant to fundamental notions of what is decent and just" in the forum); *Loucks v. Standard Oil Co.,* 224 N.Y. 99, 110 (1918) ("We are not so provincial as to say that every solution of a problem is wrong because we deal with it otherwise at home"). Does this standard support the analysis in *Roby,* which emphasized the limited differences between U.S. and English law?

D. Enforceability of Forum Selection Clauses: Applicable Law

1. Introduction

As discussed above, there are significantly differing approaches in various U.S. jurisdictions to the enforceability of forum selection clauses. Foreign courts also take varying approaches to the issue. As a consequence, great practical importance attaches to the law applicable to enforceability of forum selection agreements. This section examines the different approaches that U.S. courts have taken to selecting the law governing the enforceability of forum clauses.

Several basic points are important at the outset. First, the law that governs the *validity and enforceability* of a forum agreement need not necessarily be the same as that governing the *interpretation* of the agreement. A number of courts have either expressly acknowledged this possibility, or assumed that two different laws can apply.[119] Other courts have disagreed, albeit without considered analysis.[120]

Second, the law that governs the validity and enforceability of a forum agreement is not necessarily the same as the law applicable to the underlying contract in which the forum selection clause appears. As discussed above, a forum clause is arguably "separable" from the underlying contract, therefore capable of being governed by a different applicable law.[121] Moreover, some U.S. courts have concluded or assumed that the validity and enforceability of forum clauses is governed by the law of the forum.[122]

Third, in U.S. courts the enforceability of forum clauses raises peculiarly complex questions under the *Erie* doctrine concerning the applicability of state or federal law.[123] In federal courts, judges must determine which of the following laws governs the enforceability of a forum selection agreement: (a) federal procedural law, based either on 28 U.S.C. §1404(a) or judge-made common law; (b) substantive federal common law, binding on both federal and state courts; (c) state substantive law, pro-

---

119. *E.g.*, *Northwestern Nat'l Ins. Co. v. Donovan*, 916 F.2d 372, 374 (7th Cir. 1990) ("Validity and interpretation are separate issues, and it can be argued that as the rest of the contract in which a forum selection clause is found will be interpreted under the principles of interpretation followed by the state whose law governs the contract, so should that clause.").

120. *E.g.*, *Manetti-Farrow, Inc. v. Gucci America, Inc.*, 858 F.2d 509, 513 (9th Cir. 1988) ("because enforcement of a forum clause necessarily entails interpretation of the clause before it can be enforced, federal law [which was held to govern enforcement] also applies to interpretation of forum selection clauses").

121. *See supra* p. 401.

122. *See infra* pp. 434-35.

123. *See* Mullenix, *Another Choice of Forum, Another Choice of Law: Consensual Adjudicatory Procedure in Federal Court*, 57 Fordham L. Rev. 291, 332 (1988) ("Beyond doubt, the most perplexing issue raised by forum-selection clauses for lower federal courts was the *Erie* issue presented by diversity jurisdiction."); Heiser, *Forum Selection Clauses in Federal Courts: Limitations on Enforcement After Stewart and Carnival Cruise*, 45 Fla. L. Rev. 553, 553 (1993) ("One of the ironies in the evolution of forum selection clauses is that their enforcement is now less certain in federal courts than in state courts").

vided by the forum; or (d) the substantive law applicable to the parties' contract under general choice of law rules. Similar choice of law questions arise in state courts, where the alternatives are generally: (a) state substantive law, provided by the forum; (b) the substantive law applicable to the parties' contract under general choice of law rules; or (c) substantive federal common law.

2. Available Approaches to Law Applicable to Enforceability of Forum Selection Agreements

a. Bremen: *A Federal Common Law Rule Governing the Enforceability of Forum Selection Clauses in Admiralty Cases*

The specific holding in *Bremen* concerned forum clauses in international *admiralty* contracts.[124] There is unanimity that federal courts have the power, under their admiralty jurisdiction, to establish rules of federal common law governing the enforceability of forum selection agreements in admiralty cases.[125] Lower federal courts have uniformly applied *Bremen*'s standards for the enforceability of forum selection clauses in admiralty actions.[126]

The Supreme Court has indicated that, by its own terms, *Bremen* applies only in admiralty actions.[127] Nevertheless, the Court has also said that *Bremen* is "instructive" in determining the enforceability of forum clauses even where it does not apply.[128] Moreover, as discussed below, many lower federal and state courts and commentators have extended the reasoning and rule in *Bremen* beyond the admiralty context, particularly in international cases. They have done so variously on the grounds that *Bremen* states a binding rule of federal law and on the grounds that its rationale is persuasive, even if not binding.

b. Section 1404(a) *Governs the Enforceability in Federal Courts of Forum Selection Clauses Selecting Other Federal Forums*

The domestic transfer of cases from one federal district court to another federal district court is generally governed by 28 U.S.C. §1404(a).[129] Section 1404(a) provides:

For the convenience of parties and witnesses, in the interest of justice, a dis-

---

124. 407 U.S. at 10.

125. *Offshore Logistics, Inc. v. Tallentire*, 477 U.S. 207, 222-23 (1986).

126. E.g., *Hodes v. S.N.C. Achille Lauro ed Altrigestione*, 858 F.2d 905 (3d Cir. 1988); *Marek v. Marpan Two, Inc.*, 817 F.2d 242 (3d Cir.), *cert. denied*, 484 U.S. 852 (1987); *Sun World Lines, Ltd. v. March Shipping Corp.*, 801 F.2d 1066 (8th Cir. 1986).

127. *Stewart Organization, Inc. v. Ricoh Corp.*, 487 U.S. 22, 28 n.7, 33 (1988); *Carnival Cruise Lines v. Shute*, 499 U.S. 585 (1991) ("this is a case in admiralty, and federal law governs the enforceability of the forum-selection clause").

128. *Stewart Organization, Inc. v. Ricoh Corp.*, 487 U.S. 22, 28 n.7, 33 (1988).

129. As discussed below, transfers between federal districts are also sometimes sought under 28 U.S.C. §1406(a), under Rule 12(b) of the Federal Rules of Civil Procedure, and under Rule 56 of the Federal Rules. *See infra* pp. 446 n.145 & 448.

trict court may transfer any civil action to any other district or division where it might have been brought.

Under §1404(a), federal district courts are granted broad discretion to decide motions to transfer. The trial court's exercise of discretion is guided by an open-ended list of considerations relating to convenience, fairness, and judicial economy; according to the Supreme Court, the discretion is exercised according to an "individualized, case-by-case consideration of convenience and fairness."[130]

By its terms, §1404(a) would appear to have nothing at all to do with the enforceability of forum selection agreements; it deals with non-contractual transfers where generalized considerations of convenience and judicial administration come into play. Nevertheless, the Supreme Court held in *Stewart Organization, Inc. v. Ricoh Corp.*[131] that §1404(a) provides a rule of federal law, both in federal question and diversity cases, that governs the enforceability in federal courts of forum selection clauses that designate a *U.S.* forum (other than a state court). As discussed below, *Ricoh's* analysis of §1404 treats a forum clause as one factor (but only one factor) in a generalized balance of convenience analysis.

Section 1404(a) clearly applies to purely domestic cases in federal courts. It is, for example, applicable where two U.S. parties have agreed to resolve their disputes in Kansas, but one party later brings suit in Nebraska federal district court: if the other party seeks to transfer the action to Kansas, §1404(a) and *Ricoh* govern. Conversely, §1404(a) does not by its terms apply to cases in which a foreign forum is specified in the parties' forum selection agreement. In such cases, no transfer to "any other district or division" of the federal judicial system is sought; rather, a dismissal or stay is sought so that a foreign court can hear the action.[132]

A more difficult category of cases arises in international contracts when a *foreign* party and a U.S. party agree that their disputes shall be resolved exclusively in a specific U.S. forum, and thereafter one party initiates litigation in a different U.S. district court (or seeks to transfer litigation to a different U.S. district court). In such cases, the literal terms of §1404(a) would appear to apply — since a transfer to another district is sought. But a substantial argument could be made that in international cases of this kind *Bremen's* rule of presumptive enforceability should apply, by virtue of a federal common law analysis. We consider this argument below.

---

130. 487 U.S. 22, 29 (*quoting Van Dusen v. Barrack*, 376 U.S. 612, 622 (1964)). *See supra* pp. 296-97

131. 487 U.S. 22 (1988).

132. *See Royal Bed & Spring Co. v. Famossul Indus.*, 906 F.2d 45, 51 (1st Cir. 1990); *Jones v. Weibrecht*, 901 F.2d 17, 19 (2d Cir. 1990); *Instrumentation Assocs., Inc. v. Madsen Electric (Canada), Inc.*, 859 F.2d 4, 6 n.4 (3d Cir. 1988) ("The forum selection clause before us calls for a Canadian forum which, by definition, is outside the limits of any 'district or division' to which ... §1404(a) permits transfer"); *Manetti-Farrow, Inc. v. Gucci America, Inc.*, 858 F.2d 509, 512 n.2 (9th Cir. 1988); *Crescent International v. Avatar Communities, Inc.*, 857 F.2d 943, 944 (2d Cir. 1988). *But see Ritchie v. Carvel Corp.*, 714 F.Supp. 700, 702 n.1 (S.D.N.Y. 1989); *Page Constr. Co. v. Perini Constr.*, 712 F.Supp. 9, 11-12 (D.R.I. 1989).

c. Erie Problems: Does State or Federal Law Govern the Enforceability of Forum Selection Clauses in Federal Diversity Actions?

The Supreme Court has not directly addressed the question whether federal or state law applies to the enforceability of international forum clauses in diversity cases (when §1404(a) does not govern). As in the forum non conveniens context, the question raises unsettled issues under the *Erie* doctrine. As discussed below, substantial arguments can be made for several possible conclusions, and lower courts have reached divergent results.

A number of lower courts have declined to decide whether federal or state law governs the enforceability of a forum clause, generally concluding or assuming that there is no substantial difference between the two.[133] When the issue has been expressly considered, lower federal diversity courts have reached divided results. As discussed below, some lower federal courts have applied state law.[134] More often, lower federal courts have applied federal law in diversity cases.[135]

d. Choice of Law Rules Apply to Select Law Governing the Enforceability of Forum Selection Clauses

The *Erie* issues that arise in connection with the enforceability of forum selection clauses are further complicated by the possible applicability of either the law chosen by the parties to govern their contract or the law applicable to their contract under choice of law rules. The logical possibilities that these lines of analysis pose have repelled most courts, who have simply ignored the issues. Indeed, one commentator has dismissed the possibility as "idle speculation [that] leads courts into predictable conflict-of-laws contortions."[136]

If a forum clause is contained in a contract that is, by operation of a choice of law clause, governed by the law of a foreign state, then U.S. courts arguably should

---

133. *E.g., General Electric Co. v. G. Siempelkamp GmbH & Co.*, 29 F.3d 1095, 1098 n.3 (6th Cir. 1994); *Lambert v. Kysar*, 983 F.2d 1110, 1116 (1st Cir. 1993); *Interamerican Trade Corp. v. Companhia Fabricadora de Pecas*, 973 F.2d 487 (6th Cir. 1992); *Weidner Communications, Inc. v. Al Faisal*, 859 F.2d 1302 (7th Cir. 1988); *Instrumentation Assoc., Inc. v. Madsen Elec. (Canada) Ltd.*, 859 F.2d 4, 7 (3d Cir. 1988); *Crescent Int'l, Inc. v. Avatar Communities, Inc.*, 857 F.2d 943 (3d Cir. 1988) (clause upheld under the law "in all three jurisdictions whose law might apply").

134. *E.g., Alexander Proudfoot Co. v. Tayer*, 877 F.2d 912 (11th Cir. 1989); *Diaz Contracting, Inc. v. Nanco Contracting Corp.*, 817 F.2d 1047, 1050 (3d Cir. 1987)

135. *E.g., Heller Financial, Inc. v. Midwhey Powder Co.*, 883 F.2d 1286 (7th Cir. 1989) (applying *Bremen* in domestic diversity case, without discussing possible applicability of state law); *Commerce Consultants Int'l, Inc. v. Vetrerie Riunite SpA*, 867 F.2d 697 (D.C. Cir. 1989) (applying *Bremen* without discussion in international diversity case); *Bryant Elec. Co. v. City of Fredericksburg*, 762 F.2d 1192 (4th Cir. 1985) (applying *Bremen* without analysis in domestic diversity case); *Bense v. Interstate Battery Sys. of Am.*, 683 F.2d 718, 721 (2d Cir. 1982); *In re Fireman's Fund Ins. Cos.*, 588 F.2d 93, 95 (5th Cir. 1979); *Crown Beverage Co. v. Cerveceria Moctezuma SA*, 663 F.2d 886, 888 (9th Cir. 1981) (applying Bremen without discussion in international case).

136. Mullenix, *Another Choice of Forum, Another Choice of Law: Consensual Adjudicatory Procedure in Federal Court*, 57 Fordham L. Rev. 291, 347 (1988).

apply the laws of that foreign state to the validity of a forum agreement.[137] This is apparently what the Supreme Court contemplated, albeit for only a narrow range of issues, with respect to arbitration agreements under the Federal Arbitration Act.[138] Under this analysis, foreign law would not, of course, override the enforcing forum's public policy,[139] but it would otherwise govern the validity of the forum agreement. Alternatively, a forum agreement could be required to satisfy *both* the parties' chosen law and the enforcing forum's law.[140]

3. Selected Materials on Law Applicable to Enforceability of Forum Selection Agreements

Excerpted below are cases that illustrate the approaches to choosing the law applicable to the enforceability of forum agreements. *Stewart Organization Inc. v. Ricoh Corp.* introduces basic issues raised by the *Erie* doctrine, and sets out current law on the enforceability of forum selection clauses under §1404(a). The First Circuit's opinion in *Royal Bed and Spring Co. v. Famossul Industria e Comercio de Moveis Ltda.*, illustrates the complex *Erie* questions that can arise in enforcing foreign forum clauses. The Third Circuit's opinion in *Instrumentation Assoc., Inc. v. Madsen Electronics (Canada) Ltd.*, provides an illustration of the choice of law issues that arise in disputes over the enforceability of forum agreements.

STEWART ORGANIZATION, INC. v. RICOH CORPORATION

487 U.S. 22 (1988)

JUSTICE MARSHALL. ... The dispute underlying this case grew out of a dealership agreement that obligated petitioner company, an Alabama corporation, to market copier products of respondent, a nationwide manufacturer with its principal place of business in New Jersey. The agreement contained a forum-selection clause providing that any dispute arising out of the contract could be brought only in a court located in Manhattan. ... In September 1984, petitioner brought a complaint in

---

137. *See Karlberg European Tanspa, Inc. v. JK-Josef Kratz Vertriebsgesellschaft mbh*, 618 F.Supp. 344 (N.D. Ill. 1985) (apparently required that forum selection clause satisfy both *Zapata* and German law (where parties agreed that German law governed their contract)); *Hoffman v. National Equipment Rental, Ltd.*, 643 F.2d 987 (4th Cir. 1981) (apparently requiring that forum selection clause satisfy New York law (where parties agreed that New York law governed their contract) and arguably federal law); *Wellmore Coal Corp. v. Gates Learjet Corp.*, 475 F.Supp. 1140 (W.D. Va. 1979) (apparently requiring that forum selection clause satisfy Arizona law (where forum's conflicts rules selected Arizona law) and federal law); *Hoes of America, Inc. v. Hoes*, 493 F.Supp. 1205 (C.D. Ill. 1979) (requiring that forum selection clause satisfy German law (where parties agreed that German law governed their contract)); *Goff v. Aamco Automatic Transmissions, Inc.*, 313 F.Supp. 667 (D. Md. 1970) (requiring that forum selection clause satisfy Pennsylvania law (where parties agreed that Pennsylvania law governed their contract)); *Cerami-Kote, Inc. v. Energywave Corp.*, 773 P.2d 1143, 1145 (Idaho 1989) (applying law chosen by choice of law clause in determining validity of forum selection clause).

138. *Volt Information Sciences, Inc. v. Board of Trustees*, 489 U.S. 468 (1989).

139. *See infra* pp. 655-56. *Restatement (Second) Conflict of Laws* §187 (1971).

140. *See* the cases cited in note 137 *supra*.

the United States District Court for the Northern District of Alabama. The core of the complaint was an allegation that respondent had breached the dealership agreement, but petitioner also included claims for breach of warranty, fraud, and antitrust violations.

Relying on the contractual forum-selection clause, respondent moved the District Court ... to transfer the case to the Southern District of New York under 28 U.S.C. §1404(a). ... The District Court denied the motion. It reasoned that the transfer motion was controlled by Alabama law and that Alabama looks unfavorably upon contractual forum-selection clauses. ... [On appeal, an en banc Eleventh Circuit eventually reversed. First,] citing Congress' enactment or approval of several rules to govern venue determinations in diversity actions, [it] determined that "[v]enue is a matter of federal procedure." The Court of Appeals then applied the standards articulated in the admiralty case of *The Bremen*, to conclude that "the choice of forum clause in this contract is in all respects enforceable generally as a matter of federal law. ..." We now affirm under somewhat different reasoning.

[The] Court of Appeals referred to the difficulties that often attend "the sticky question of which law, state or federal, will govern various aspects of the decisions of federal courts sitting in diversity." A district court's decision whether to apply a federal statute such as §1404(a) in a diversity action,[141] however, involves a considerably less intricate analysis than that which governs the "relatively unguided *Erie* choice." *Hanna v. Plumer*, 380 U.S. 460, 471 (1965) (referring to *Erie*). Our cases indicate that when the federal law sought to be applied is a congressional statute, the first and chief question for the district court's determination is whether the statute is "sufficiently broad to control the issue before the Court." *Walker v. Armco Steel Corp.*, 446 U.S. 740, 749-750 (1980). This question involves a straightforward exercise in statutory interpretation to determine if the statute covers the point in dispute.

If the district court determines that a federal statute covers the point in dispute, it proceeds to inquire whether the statute represents a valid exercise of Congress' authority under the Constitution. ... If Congress intended to reach the issue before the District Court, and if it enacted its intention into law in a manner that abides with the Constitution, that is the end of the matter; "[f]ederal courts are bound to apply rules enacted by Congress with respect to matters ... over which it has legislative power." *Prima Paint Corp. v. Flood & Conklin Mfg. Co.*, 388 U.S. 395, 406 (1967). ...

Applying the above analysis to this case persuades us that federal law, specifically 28 U.S.C. §1404(a), governs the parties' venue dispute. At the outset we underscore a methodological difference in our approach to the question from that taken by the

---

141. Respondent points out that jurisdiction in this case was alleged to rest both on the existence of an antitrust claim, *see* 28 U.S.C. §1337, and diversity of citizenship, *see* 28 U.S.C. §1332. ... Our conclusion that federal law governs transfer of this case, makes this issue academic for purposes of this case, because the presence of a federal-question could cut only in favor of the application of federal law. We therefore are not called on to decide, nor do we decide, whether the existence of federal-question as well as diversity jurisdiction necessarily alters a district court's analysis of applicable law.

Court of Appeals. ... The Court of Appeals [applied] the standards announced in our opinion in *The Bremen v. Zapata Off-Shore Co.*, to determine that the forum-selection clause in this case was enforceable. But the immediate issue before the District Court was whether to grant respondent's motion to transfer the action under §1404(a) and as Judge Tjoflat properly noted in his special concurrence below, the immediate issue before the Court of Appeals was whether the District Court's denial of the §1404(a) motion constituted an abuse of discretion. Although we agree with the Court of Appeals that the *Bremen* case may prove "instructive" in resolving the parties' dispute; *but cf. Texas Industries, Inc. v. Radcliff Materials, Inc.*, 451 U.S. 630, 641-642 (federal common law developed under admiralty jurisdiction not freely transferable to diversity setting), we disagree with the court's articulation of the relevant inquiry as "whether the forum selection clause in this case is unenforceable under the standards set forth in *The Bremen*." 810 F.2d at 1069. Rather, the first question for consideration should have been whether §1404(a) itself controls respondent's request to give effect to the parties' contractual choice of venue and transfer this case to a Manhattan court. For the reasons that follow, we hold that it does.

Section 1404(a) provides: "For the convenience of parties and witnesses, in the interest of justice, a district court may transfer any civil action to any other district or division where it might have been brought." Under the analysis outlined above, we first consider whether this provision is sufficiently broad to control the issue before the court. That issue is whether to transfer the case to a court in Manhattan in accordance with the forum-selection clause. We believe that the statute, fairly construed, does cover the point in dispute.

Section 1404(a) is intended to place discretion in the district court to adjudicate motions for transfer according to an "individualized, case-by-case consideration of convenience and fairness." *Van Dusen v. Barrack,* 376 U.S. 612, 622 (1964). A motion to transfer under §1404(a) thus calls on the district court to weigh in the balance a number of case-specific factors. The presence of a forum-selection clause such as the parties entered into in this case will be a significant factor that figures centrally in the district court's calculus. In its resolution of the §1404(a) motion in this case, for example, the District Court will be called on to address such issues as the convenience of a Manhattan forum given the parties' expressed preference for that venue, and the fairness of transfer in light of the forum-selection clause and the parties' relative bargaining power. The flexible and individualized analysis Congress prescribed in §1404(a) thus encompasses consideration of the parties' private expression of their venue preferences.

Section 1404(a) may not be the only potential source of guidance for the District Court to consult in weighing the parties' private designation of a suitable forum. The premise of the dispute between the parties is that Alabama law may refuse to enforce forum-selection clauses providing for out-of-state venues as a matter of state public policy.[142] If that is so, the District Court will have either to integrate the factor of the forum-selection clause into its weighing of considerations as prescribed by Congress, or else to apply, as it did in this case, Alabama's categorical policy disfavoring forum-selection clauses. Our cases make clear that, as between these two choices in a single "field of operation," *Burlington Northern R. Co. v. Woods*, 480 U.S. at 7, the instructions of Congress are supreme.

It is true that §1404(a) and Alabama's putative policy regarding forum-selection clauses are not perfectly coextensive. Section 1404(a) directs a district court to take account of factors other than those that bear solely on the parties' private ordering of their affairs. The district court also must weigh in the balance the convenience of the witnesses and those public-interest factors of systemic integrity and fairness that, in addition to private concerns, come under the heading of "the interest of justice." It is conceivable in a particular case, for example, that because of these factors a district court acting under §1404(a) would refuse to transfer a case notwithstanding the counterweight of a forum-selection clause, whereas the coordinate state rule might dictate the opposite result.[143] But this potential conflict in fact frames an additional argument for the supremacy of federal law. Congress has directed that multiple considerations govern transfer within the federal court system, and a state policy focusing on a single concern or a subset of the factors identified in §1404(a) would defeat that command. Its application would impoverish the flexible and multifaceted analysis that Congress intended to govern motions to transfer within the federal system. The forum-selection clause, which represents the parties' agreement as to the most proper forum, should receive neither dispositive consideration (as respondent might have it) nor no consideration (as Alabama law might have it), but rather the consideration for which Congress provided in §1404(a). This is thus not a case in which state and federal rules "can exist side by side ... each controlling its own intended sphere of coverage without conflict." *Walker v. Armco Steel Corp.*, 446 U.S. at 752.

Because §1404(a) controls the issue before the District Court, it must be applied if it represents a valid exercise of Congress' authority under the Constitution. The constitutional authority of Congress to enact §1404(a) is not subject to serious question. ... It ... falls comfortably within Congress' powers under Article III as augmented by the Necessary and Proper Clause.

---

142. In its application of the standards set forth in *The Bremen* to this case, the Court of Appeals concluded that the Alabama policy against the enforcement of forum-selection clauses is intended to apply only to protect the jurisdiction of the state courts of Alabama and therefore would not come into play in this case, in which case this dispute might be much ado about nothing. Our determination that §1404(a) governs the parties' dispute notwithstanding any contrary Alabama policy makes it unnecessary to address the contours of state law.

143. The dissent does not dispute this point, but rather argues that if the forum-selection clause would be unenforceable under state law, then the clause cannot be accorded any weight by a federal court. Not the least of the problems with the dissent's analysis is that it makes the applicability of a federal statute depend on the content of state law. If a State cannot preempt a district court's consideration of a forum-selection clause by holding that the clause is automatically enforceable, it makes no sense for it to be able to do so by holding the clause automatically void.

We hold that federal law, specifically 28 U.S.C. §1404(a), governs the District Court's decision whether to give effect to the parties' forum-selection clause and transfer this case to a court in Manhattan. We therefore affirm the Eleventh Circuit order reversing the District Court's application of Alabama law. The case is remanded so that the District Court may determine in the first instance the appropriate effect under federal law of the parties' forum-selection clause on respondent's §1404(a) motion.

JUSTICE KENNEDY, concurring. I concur in full. I write separately only to observe that enforcement of valid forum-selection clauses, bargained for by the parties, protects their legitimate expectations and furthers vital interests of the justice system. Although our opinion in *The Bremen* involved a Federal District Court sitting in admiralty, its reasoning applies with much force to federal courts sitting in diversity. The justifications we noted in *The Bremen* to counter the historical disfavor forum-selection clauses had received in American courts, should be understood to guide the District Court's analysis under §1404(a). ...

JUSTICE SCALIA, dissenting. ... When a litigant asserts that state law conflicts with a federal procedural statute or formal Rule of Procedure, a court's first task is to determine whether the disputed point in question in fact falls within the scope of the federal statute or Rule. In this case, the Court must determine whether the scope of §1404(a) is sufficiently broad to cause a direct collision with state law or implicitly to control the issue before the Court, *i.e.*, validity between the parties of the forum-selection clause, thereby leaving no room for the operation of state law. I conclude that it is not.

... [First,] the courts in applying §1404(a) have examined a variety of factors, each of which pertains to facts that currently exist or will exist: *e.g.*, the forum actually chosen by the plaintiff, the current convenience of the parties and witnesses, the current location of pertinent books and records, similar litigation pending elsewhere, current docket conditions, and familiarity of the potential courts with governing state law. [The Court casts] the issue [here] as how much weight a district court should give a forum-selection clause as against other factors when it makes its determination under 1404(a). ... But the Court's description of the issue begs the question: what law governs whether the forum-selection clause is a valid or invalid allocation of any inconvenience between the parties. If it is invalid, *i.e.*, should be voided, between the parties, it cannot be entitled to any weight in the §1404(a) determination. Since under Alabama law the forum-selection clause should be voided, *see Redwing Carriers, Inc. v. Foster*, 382 So.2d 554, 556 (Ala. 1980), in this case the question of what weight should be given the forum-selection clause can be reached only if as a preliminary matter federal law controls the issue of the validity of the clause between the parties.

Second, §1404(a) was enacted against the background that issues of contract, including a contract's validity, are nearly always governed by state law. It is simply contrary to the practice of our system that such an issue should be wrenched from state control in absence of a clear conflict with federal law or explicit statutory provision. ... Section 1404(a) is simply a venue provision that nowhere mentions contracts or agreements, much less that the validity of certain contracts or agreements will be matters of federal law. ...

Since no federal statute or Rule of Procedure governs the validity of a forum-selection clause, the remaining issue is whether federal courts may fashion a judge-made rule to govern the question. If they may not, the Rules of Decision Act, 28 U.S.C. §1652, mandates use of state law. In general, while interpreting and applying substantive law is the essence of the "judicial Power" created under Article III of the Constitution, that power does not encompass the making of substantive law. Whatever the scope of the federal courts' authority to create federal common law in other areas, it is plain that the mere fact that petitioner company here brought an antitrust claim, does not empower the federal courts to make common law on the question of the validity of the forum-selection clause.

In deciding what is substantive and what is procedural for these purposes, we have adhered to a functional test based on the "twin aims of the *Erie* rule: discouragement of forum-shopping and avoidance of inequitable administration of the laws." *Hanna*, 380 U.S. at 468. ... Under the twin-aims test, I believe state law controls the question of the validity of a forum-selection clause between the parties. The Eleventh Circuit's rule clearly encourages forum shopping. Venue is often a vitally important matter, as is shown by the frequency with which parties contractually provide for and litigate the issue. Suit might well not be pursued, or might not be as successful, in a significantly less convenient forum. Transfer to such a less desirable forum is, therefore, of sufficient import that plaintiffs will base their decisions on the likelihood of that eventuality when they are choosing whether to sue in state or federal court. With respect to forum-selection clauses, in a State with law unfavorable to validity, plaintiffs who seek to avoid the effect of a clause will be encouraged to sue in state court, and nonresident defendants will be encouraged to shop for more favorable law by removing to federal court. In the reverse situation — where a State has law favorable to enforcing such clauses — plaintiffs will be encouraged to sue in federal court. This significant encouragement to forum shopping is alone sufficient to warrant application of state law. ...

ROYAL BED AND SPRING CO. v.
FAMOSSUL INDUSTRIA E COMERCIO DE MOVEIS LTDA.

906 F.2d 45 (1st Cir. 1990)

RE, CHIEF JUDGE. In this diversity action, plaintiff-appellant, Royal Bed and Spring Co., Inc. ("Royal Bed"), sued defendant-appellee, Famossul Industria e Comercio de Moveis Ltda. ("Famossul"), in the United States District Court for the District of Puerto Rico for breach of contract in violation of the Puerto Rico Dealer's Contract Act. Royal Bed appeals from the judgment of the district court which granted Famossul's motion to dismiss on the grounds of forum non conveniens. ...

Royal Bed, a corporation organized and existing under the laws of Puerto Rico, distributes furniture products in Puerto Rico. Famossul, a Brazilian corporation, is a manufacturer of furniture products in Brazil. ... On January 26, 1984, Royal Bed and Famossul signed, in Brazil, an agreement entitled "Letter Of Exclusive Distributorship Appointment." This agreement, written in Portuguese, granted Royal Bed the exclusive distributorship of "products, both furniture and other products, which might be made or introduced into [Famossul's] manufacturing line, for the market in Puerto Rico and adjacent islands." The agreement contained a provision which designated "the judicial district of Curitiba, State of Parana, Brazil, as competent to settle any disputes or interpretations derived from this letter," and that the Brazilian Civil Code would apply "[i]n the case of any violation." ...

Royal Bed alleges that, during 1986, Famossul terminated the exclusive distributorship and suspended the shipment of goods without just cause[, and claimed damages exceeding $1 million. Famossul replied that Royal Bed had breached the contract. Royal Bed eventually filed a diversity suit in the U.S. District Court for the District of Puerto Rico.] Claiming that the court lacked jurisdiction, based on the doctrine[] of forum non conveniens ..., Famossul filed [a] motion[] to dismiss with the U.S. District Court. ... The district court acknowledged that, in adjudicating a motion for forum non conveniens, the court must conduct a case-by-case analysis of convenience and fairness. The court also recognized that Royal Bed had specifically asserted "that Puerto Rico law refuses to enforce forum-selection clauses providing for out-of-state or foreign venues as a matter of public policy." P.R. Laws Ann. Tit. 10, §278b-2 (Supp. 1987) ("Law 75"). The court noted that, given Law 75, the forum-selection clause in the parties' agreement must be integrated into the balancing of considerations. The court noted that the forum-selection clause "should not receive dispositive consideration ... but should rather be considered a significant factor that will figure centrally in our balancing of factors." The court concluded that "the convenience of a Brazil forum, given the parties' expressed preference for that venue, the fairness of transfer in light of the forum-selection clause and the parties' relative bargaining power, as well as their familiarity with the procedure and laws of that forum," made Brazil the most convenient forum.

In *Piper Aircraft Co. v. Reyno*, the United States Supreme Court stated that: "[t]he forum non conveniens determination is committed to the sound discretion of the trial court. It may be reversed only when there has been a clear abuse of discretion; where the court has considered all relevant public and private interest factors, and where its balancing of these factors is reasonable, its decision deserves substantial deference." ... In this circuit, we have stated that "[t]he doctrine of forum non conveniens presupposes at least two forums in which the defendant is amenable to process." *Tramp Oil and Marine, Ltd. v. M/V Mermaid I*, 743 F.2d 48, 50 (1st Cir. 1984) (*citing Gulf Oil*, 330 U.S. at 506-07). We have also noted that "[d]ismissal in one forum is only proper upon a supported finding that another adequate forum exists where the plaintiff can litigate essentially the same claim."

In this case, a forum-selection clause in the exclusive distributorship agreement of the parties clearly indicates the existence of an alternate forum to that of Puerto Rico. The agreement expressly provides that the judicial district of Curitiba in Brazil is the proper forum "to settle any disputes or interpretations derived from this [agreement]. ..." A specific question in this case is the effect that this court should give to the forum-selection clause contained in the agreement of the parties.

According to Royal Bed, since Puerto Rico "has the most significant contacts relating to the ... alleged termination without just cause of [the] contract[,]" the case should be tried in Puerto Rico under Puerto Rican law. Royal Bed asserts that, under the law of Puerto Rico, its rights and obligations under the agreement were protected by the Distributor's Law ("Law 75"). Pursuant to §278b-2 of this law, "[a]ny stipulation that obligates a dealer to ... litigate any controversy that comes up regarding his dealer's contract outside of Puerto Rico, or under foreign law or rule of law, shall be ... considered as violating ... public policy ... and is therefore null and void." P.R. Laws Ann. Tit. 10, §278b-2 (Supp. 1987). Hence, Royal Bed concludes that "any action that would imply mere intention of placing a dealers' contract outside the scope of this statute is null and void, as is the provision of this ... contract. ..."

Famossul contends that "Law 75 was never mentioned nor contemplated" in the agreement, and, if the forum-selection clause is rendered unenforceable by Law 75, "then ... all the rest of the contract might be unenforceable as well." Famossul states that it is not requesting that Law 75 be declared unconstitutional, "but rather tha[t] the parties be bound by their own acts."

In the seminal case of *The Bremen*, the Supreme Court upheld the validity of forum-selection clauses between parties of equal bargaining power. ... As a practical matter, therefore, it follows from the holding in *Bremen* that the burden is upon the party resisting the forum-selection clause to "show that enforcement [of the clause] would be unreasonable and unjust, or that the clause was invalid for such reasons as fraud or overreaching." It is also noteworthy that, according to the Supreme Court, a showing of inconvenience as to a foreign forum would not be enough to hold a forum-selection clause unenforceable, especially if that inconvenience was known or contemplated by the parties at the time of their agreement. ...

The question that has not been resolved, however, is whether the holding of *Bremen*, that is, "applying federal judge-made law to the issue of a forum selection clause's validity in admiralty cases, should be extended to diversity cases." *Instrumentation Assocs., Inc. v. Madsen Elecs. (Canada) Ltd.*, 859 F.2d 4, 7 n.5 (3d Cir. 1988). More than half a century ago, the Supreme Court established what is known as the *Erie* doctrine, pursuant to which the federal courts in diversity cases may not promulgate substantive rules of law that control the controversy. Nonetheless, it is also fundamental that "[f]ederal courts are able to create federal common law ... in those areas where Congress or the Constitution has given the courts the authority to develop substantive law ... or where strong federal interests are involved. ..." *General Eng'g Corp. v. Martin Marietta Alumina, Inc.*, 783 F.2d 352, 356 (3d Cir. 1986).

In *Bremen*, for example, federal law applied to the forum-selection clause because, since the case was in admiralty, the Constitution had vested original jurisdiction in the federal courts. Similarly, forum-selection clauses providing for mandatory arbitration in foreign countries have been upheld because "it is the congressional policy manifested in the Federal Arbitration Act [9 U.S.C. $1 *et seq.*] that requires courts liberally to construe the scope of arbitration agreements covered by that Act. ..." *Mitsubishi Motors Corp. v. Soler Chrysler-Plymouth, Inc.* In *Sun World Lines, Ltd. v. March Shipping Corp.*, 801 F.2d 1066 (8th Cir. 1986), the Court of Appeals for the Eighth Circuit held that in diversity cases, federal law controlled the enforceability of a forum-selection clause. The *Sun World Lines* case "held that the enforceability of a forum clause ... is clearly a federal procedural issue and that federal law controls." The court noted that, in deciding that enforceability of the clause "is a procedural matter, we support a policy of uniformity of venue rules within the federal system, as well as the policies underlying *The Bremen*."

It has been noted that forum non conveniens "is a rule of venue, not a rule of decision." *Sibaja*, 757 F.2d at 1219. The court in *Sibaja* explained that: "[t]he doctrine derives from the court's inherent power, under article III of the Constitution, to control the administration of the litigation before it and to prevent its process from becoming an instrument of abuse, injustice and oppression." ... It follows, therefore, that state forum non conveniens laws "ought not to be" binding on federal courts in diversity cases. Since we adopt this view, we decide this case on federal principles and considerations of forum non conveniens.

It would also seem clear that, had the transferee forum been a United States District Court, the applicable standard would be found in 28 U.S.C. $1404(a) (1988). ... In *Stewart Org., Inc. v. Ricoh Corp.*, the Supreme Court discussed the relevance of a forum-selection clause in light of $1404(a). ... [T]he Supreme Court reasoned that "[a] motion to transfer under $1404(a) ... calls on the District Court to weigh in the balance a number of case-specific factors. The presence of a forum-selection clause ... will be a significant factor that figures centrally in the District Court's calculus." ... As for the Alabama policy which did not favor forum-selection clauses, the Court noted that $1404(a) made "it unnecessary to address the contours of state law." The Court deemed that inquiry unnecessary since "Congress has directed that multiple considerations govern transfer within the federal court system, and a state policy focusing on a single concern or a subset of the factors identified in $1404(a) would defeat that command." ... *Stewart*, therefore, teaches that, after considering and balancing all of the private and public interest factors, a district court in a particular case may "in the interest of justice" still "refuse to transfer a case notwithstanding the counterweight of a forum-selection clause. ..."

In this case, since we are dealing with a forum-selection clause that refers to a forum outside of the United States, and not within the scope of the statute, $1404(a) does not apply. Nonetheless, even though a foreign jurisdiction was chosen by the parties, that fact should not preclude the application of the sound principles of

forum non conveniens enunciated in *Stewart* and similar cases. By their consideration and application, the forum-selection provision in the "Letter of Exclusive
Distributorship Appointment" is not given dispositive effect. Rather, it is simply one
of the factors that should be considered and balanced by the courts in the exercise of
sound discretion. Furthermore, in this case, there is no need to consider the constitutionality of Law 75. ... Hence, the application of Law 75 is not affected in the courts
of the Commonwealth of Puerto Rico. The total relevant factors analysis set forth in
Stewart permits a "flexible and individualized analysis" which considers "the parties'
private expression of their venue preferences" as well as "public-interest factors of
systemic integrity and fairness."

In *Piper Aircraft*, the Supreme Court stated "that there is ordinarily a strong presumption in favor of the plaintiff's choice of forum. ..." [T]he Supreme Court added
that the choice of a home forum "may be overcome only when the private and public
interest factors clearly point towards trial in the alternative forum." ... In this case,
Royal Bed states that "all the equipment sold by ... Royal Bed on behalf of ...
Famossul took place in Puerto Rico ... to Puerto Rican accounts and for use in
Puerto Rico. ..." Hence, Royal Bed contends that, since "Puerto Rico ... has the most
significant contacts[,]" the balance of private and public interest factors makes
Puerto Rico the applicable forum.

Although the district court acknowledged that Royal Bed's choice of a forum
was entitled to great deference since it chose a home forum, it nonetheless determined that "we must also take into consideration the convenience of a Brazil forum
given the parties' expressed preference for that venue. ..." Hence, the district court
also took into consideration that: "[the] contract [was] signed in Brazil[,] [and] ...
drafted in Portuguese. All the furniture provided by [Famossul] and sold by [Royal
Bed] in Puerto Rico was manufactured in Brazil. It also appears that [Royal Bed] is
no stranger to the judicial system of Brazil since it has previously litigated its disputes
in the courts of Brazil and obtained favorable results. Moreover, the contract ... contains a forum-selection clause providing that any legal action arising out of the contract would be brought in Brazil and Brazilian law would apply."

In giving effect to the validity of the forum-selection clause in *Bremen*, the
Supreme Court noted that there was strong evidence "that the forum clause was a
vital part of the agreement, and it would be unrealistic to think that the parties did
not conduct their negotiations, including fixing the monetary terms, with the consequences of the forum clause figuring prominently in their calculations." The holding
and ratio decidendi of that case place the burden squarely on the party seeking to
avoid the forum-selection clause to show that its enforcement "would be unreasonable and unjust, or that the clause was invalid for such reasons as fraud or overreaching." ... In this case, there is neither overreaching nor factors that would counsel
against the application of the forum selected by the parties in their agreement. ...
Since the district court considered and balanced all of the relevant factors and did
not abuse its discretion, its conclusion that Brazil is the most convenient forum

should not be disturbed. Therefore, the judgment of the district court granting Famossul's motion to dismiss on the grounds of forum non conveniens is affirmed.

INSTRUMENTATION ASSOCIATES, INC. v. MADSEN ELECTRIC
859 F.2d 4 (3d Cir. 1988)

HUTCHINSON, CIRCUIT JUDGE. Madsen Electronics (Canada) Ltd. ("Madsen") appeals from an order of the United States District Court for the Eastern District of Pennsylvania denying its motion to dismiss appellee Instrumentation Associates, Inc.'s ("Instrumentation's") action asserting wrongful termination of a distributorship agreement. Madsen's motion to dismiss was premised on a forum selection clause in the distributorship agreement. ... The enforceability of a forum selection clause is an issue of law, and our scope of review is plenary.[144] ...

Instrumentation is a Pennsylvania corporation with a place of business in Upper Darby, Pennsylvania. It is engaged in the business of selling audiological measuring devices. In August, 1984 it entered into a written agreement with Madsen, a Canadian audiological supply company with a place of business in Oakville, Ontario, Canada. The agreement gave Instrumentation an exclusive right to distribute Madsen products in Delaware, New Jersey, Pennsylvania and parts of New York and West Virginia. The agreement was for an initial one year term from August, 1984 until July, 1985 and provided for automatic annual renewal unless each party gave "at least three months written notice" of termination. On December 23, 1986 Madsen sent Instrumentation a written termination notice giving Instrumentation ninety days to settle outstanding accounts. On April 29, 1987, after unsuccessful attempts to resolve the dispute, Instrumentation filed this action for breach of the agreement in the district court. Madsen filed a motion to dismiss the case based on the agreement's forum selection clause, which provided: "Matters of dispute in connection with this Agreement shall be settled by a Canadian Court of Justice in accordance with the laws of Canada."

In denying Madsen's motion to dismiss, the district court reasoned that the forum selection clause's reference to the "laws of Canada" was too ambiguous to enforce because the "laws of Canada" varied widely from province to province. Madsen alleged in its submissions that the "general rule of Canada" required the forum selection clause to be enforced. However, because Madsen offered no evidence of a uniformly recognized "general rule of Canada," the district court held that the entire clause, including its choice of forum, was unenforceable. The agreement, however, purports not only to provide a choice of law, but also a choice of forum. The

---

144. Other courts of appeals review the district court's decision for abuse of discretion. *See, e.g., Pelleport Investors, Inc. v. Budco Quality Theatres, Inc.,* 741 F.2d 273, 280 n.4 (9th Cir. 1984). The difference is immaterial in this case. Under either standard the forum selection clause must be enforced on this record. As shown *infra,* no exceptional circumstance or strong policy against its enforcement is present in any jurisdiction whose law might apply. Accordingly, a refusal to enforce it would be an abuse of discretion.

district court should have resolved the preliminary issue of whether the parties' forum selection clause is enforceable before reaching the issue of whether the contract provision is ambiguous. This conflicts issue, in turn, requires a determination of what law is applicable.

In choosing what law to apply to the issue of whether the parties' forum selection clause is enforceable, a district court sitting in diversity must first determine whether the issue is encompassed by a federal statute or Rule. *See Stewart Organization, Inc. v. Ricoh Corp., supra.*[145] If there is no applicable federal statute or Rule, the district court must next determine whether to apply federal judge-made law or state law. In doing so, the district court must evaluate whether application of federal judge-made law would discourage forum shopping and avoid inequitable administration of the law.

This Court has not yet decided what law a district court sitting in diversity must apply in deciding whether a forum selection clause is enforceable. We have decided that such clauses are enforceable in other contexts. *See Diaz,* 817 F.2d at 1050 (bankruptcy); *Martin Marietta,* 783 F.2d at 357 (dispute between residents of Virgin Islands). Fortunately, we need not resolve this unanswered question of whether federal law, the law of the forum state, the law of Canada, or one of its provinces applies.[146] All of these jurisdictions look favorably on forum selection clauses. Thus, even assuming paragraph 21 of the contract is ambiguous as to choice of a particular

---

145. We are in agreement with the parties that *Ricoh* does not govern this case. Ricoh involved the application of a federal procedural statute, 28 U.S.C. §1404(a). In *Ricoh,* the Supreme Court held that §1404(a) governs a federal court's determination of whether to give effect to a forum selection clause and transfer a case to a different federal court. The Court did not address whether §1404(a) applies when a forum selection clause calls for a forum beyond the geographical scope of that statute. In our case, no §1404(a) application was filed and the motion to dismiss was premised on Fed. R. Civ. P. 12(b)(6). The forum selection clause before us calls for a Canadian forum which, by definition, is outside the limits of any "district or division" to which 28 U.S.C. §1404(a) permits transfer. The parties do not contend that any other federal statute controls, such as 28 U.S.C. §1406 permitting retention of venue in the court in which the action is pending in the "interest of justice," nor do they raise the common law doctrine of "forum non conveniens" to which §1404(a) is related, as a bar to a Canadian forum.

146. *Ricoh* leaves open the question of whether the holding in *The Bremen v. Zapata Off-Shore Co.,* 407 U.S. 1 (1972), applying federal judge-made law to the issue of a forum selection clause's validity in admiralty cases, should be extended to diversity cases. Justice Marshall, writing for the Court, states:

> Although we agree with the Court of Appeals that the *Bremen* case may prove "instructive" in resolving the parties' dispute, [*Stewart Organization v. Ricoh Corp.,*] 810 F.2d at 1069; ... we disagree with the court's articulation of the relevant inquiry as "whether the forum selection clause in this case is unenforceable under the standards set forth in *The Bremen.*" 810 F.2d, at 1069. Rather, the *first question* for consideration should have been whether §1404(a) itself controls.... *Ricoh,* 108 S.Ct. at 2243 (emphasis added).

Justice Scalia, dissenting, argues that the validity of a forum selection clause is a question of substantive law and accordingly the application of either §1404(a) or federal judge-made law conflicts with *Erie's* twin purposes of discouraging state-federal forum shopping and avoiding inequitable administration of the laws. In *Martin Marietta,* we rejected the idea that courts are bound as a matter of federal common law to apply *The Bremen* standard to forum selection clauses:

(continued on page 447)

jurisdiction, the judge-made law of all involved jurisdictions would honor the parties' choice of a Canadian forum for resolution of their disputes in connection with this distributorship agreement.

In this case, the choice narrows to Pennsylvania, Ontario and federal judge-made law.[147] In *Bremen*, the Supreme Court held that a forum selection clause is "prima facie valid and should be enforced" in the absence of a compelling countervailing reason making enforcement unreasonable. A Pennsylvania court would conclude that a forum selection clause is enforceable in the absence of a compelling, countervailing reason. *See, e.g., Central Contracting Co. v. C.E. Youngdahl & Co.*, 209 A.2d 810, 816 (1965) (Supreme Court of forum state, Pennsylvania, held contract's forum selection clause enforceable unless enforcement would "seriously impair plaintiff's ability to pursue his cause of action"). ... An Ontario court would also enforce the clause unless the forum selected could not possibly give any relief. In *Poly-Seal Corp. v. John Dale Ltd.*, [1958] O.W.N. 432 (Ont. H. C.), the Ontario High Court of Justice enforced forum selection clauses which chose the jurisdiction of English and Swedish courts, even though there was doubt about the ability of those courts to grant the injunctive relief which the American corporations sought. The Ontario High Court said "the Canadian Courts ought not to interfere, unless it was shown that the foreign Courts could not possibly give any relief to the parties." ...

We have determined that under Pennsylvania, Ontario and federal judge-made law, forum selection clauses are enforceable. Alternately, we could inquire whether those forums would honor the parties' choice of law as "the laws of Canada." *Klaxon*, 313 U.S. at 496. Arguably, they would not do so if the clause is ambiguous. However, it is not ... [T]he Supreme Court of Canada has held that the "proper law" of the contract is defined by considering the contract as a whole in light of all the surrounding circumstances and applying the law of the forum which has the closest and most substantial connection to the contract. ... In this regard a jurisdiction clause should be treated no differently from any other clause in the contract. Consequently, the issue of whether a jurisdiction clause is exclusive in nature should be determined by the proper law of the contract and not by [local law]. ...

Any jurisdiction whose law could properly apply to this case would enforce the

---

(continued from page 446)

The construction of contracts is usually a matter of state, not federal, common law. Federal courts are able to create federal common law only in those areas where Congress or the Constitution has given the courts the authority to develop substantive law, as in labor and admiralty, or where strong federal interests are involved, as in cases concerning the rights and obligations of the United States. ... As the Court in *Miree v. DeKalb County, Georgia*, 433 U.S. 25 (1977), observed, in a suit between private parties where federal common law is sought to be applied, "normally the guiding principle is that a *significant conflict between some federal policy or interest and the use of state law [exists]*."

Martin Marietta, 783 F.2d at 356 (emphasis added by *Miree* Court).

147. The contract was made and negotiated between a Pennsylvania corporation and an Ontario corporation, for performance in Pennsylvania and adjoining states.

parties' choice of a Canadian forum to settle their disputes "in connection" with this contract. We will therefore reverse the district court's order denying Madsen's motion to dismiss.

Notes on Ricoh, Royal Bed, and Madsen Electronics

1. *Section 1404(a) and* Ricoh. Was *Ricoh* correctly decided? Consider Justice Marshall's explanation for why §1404(a) governs the enforceability of forum selection agreements. Section 1404(a) provides that, "[f]or the convenience of parties and witnesses, in the interest of justice," district courts "may transfer" actions to other district courts. Is it even remotely possible that Congress meant to address the enforceability of private agreements regarding choice of forum when it enacted §1404(a)? Isn't Justice Scalia's dissent in *Ricoh* obviously correct? What response is there to Justice Scalia's observation that the Court's description of the issue begs the question: what law governs whether the forum selection clause is a valid or invalid allocation of any inconvenience between the parties?

2. *Application of §1404(a) to international forum selection agreements.* To what categories of forum selection agreements is the rule in *Ricoh* applicable? Consider the following: (a) a California resident and a French national enter into a forum selection agreement selecting Paris as the exclusive contractual forum, and the California party brings suit in California; and (b) a New York resident and a Mexican national enter into a forum selection agreement selecting New York as the exclusive contractual forum, and the Mexican party brings suit in Arizona.

Does §1404(a) apply to example (a) above if the French party invokes the forum clause? How did *Royal Bed* and *Madsen* resolve this question? Which result is correct? Does §1404(a) apply to example (b) above if the New York party invokes the forum agreement? What does the literal language of §1404(a) suggest? Should the rules governing the enforceability of forum clauses in examples (a) and (b) be different? Why?

Is *Ricoh*'s "interest of justice" standard limited to cases in which a party relies expressly on §1404 in a motion to transfer? Suppose, in example (b) in the preceding note, that the New York party does not seek a transfer under §1404, but instead moves to dismiss under Rule 12 of the Federal Rules of Civil Procedure?

3. *Authorities holding that state law should govern enforceability of international forum selection clauses where §1404 does not.* If §1404 is not applicable, state law would presumptively appear to govern the enforcement of forum agreements, both in federal diversity actions and state courts. No federal treaty or statute governs the enforceability of international forum clauses in diversity suits. A forum agreement is a contractual obligation, the enforceability of which ought presumptively to be subject to substantive rules of contract law. The enforceability of contractual obligations is generally governed by state law — because of the absence of any general federal contract law. Absent some basis for preempting state law with federal common law, *Erie* should therefore require the application of state law to the enforceability of forum clauses:

> We must correct the assumption that federal courts are bound as a matter of federal common law to apply *The Bremen* standard to forum selection clauses [in diversity cases]. The construction of contracts is usually a matter of state, not federal, common law. Federal courts are able to create federal common law only in those areas where Congress and the Constitution has given the courts the authority to develop substantive law, as in labor or admiralty, or where strong federal interests are involved, as in cases concerning the rights and obligations of the United States. ... The interpretation of forum selection clauses in commercial contracts is not an area of law that ordinarily requires federal courts to create substantive law. *General Eng'g Corp. v. Martin Marietta Alumina, Inc.*, 783 F.2d 352, 356-57 (3d Cir. 1986).

The Court has emphasized "twin aims of the *Erie* rule: discouragement of forum shopping [between state and federal courts] and avoidance of inequitable administration of the laws." *Hanna v. Plumer*, 380 U.S. 460, 468 (1965); *supra* pp. 13-15. Application of federal procedural law to the enforceability of forum clauses in federal courts, but not in state courts, would lead both to intra-state forum shopping and races to the courthouse. *Stewart Organization, Inc. v. Ricoh Corp.*, 487 U.S. 22, 34-35 (1988) (Scalia, J., dissenting). This would, in turn, produce inequitable administration of the laws, as identically situated parties were treated differently in state and federal court.

Applying the foregoing analysis, a number of federal courts have held that state substantive law governs the enforceability of forum clauses in diversity actions (albeit generally in domestic settings). *E.g.*, *Alexander Proudfoot Co. v. Tayer*, 877 F.2d 912 (11th Cir. 1989); *Diaz Contracting, Inc. v. Nanco Contracting Corp.*, 817 F.2d 1047, 1050 (3d Cir. 1987) ("the law of the state or other jurisdiction whose law governs the construction of the contract generally applies to the enforceability determination unless 'a significant conflict between some federal policy or interest and the use of state law [exists].'"); *Farmland Indus., Inc. v. Frazier-Parrott Commodities, Inc.*, 806 F.2d 848, 850-52 (8th Cir. 1986) ("Because of the close relationship between substance and procedure in this case we believe that consideration should have been given to the public policy of Missouri.").

Does *Ricoh* suggest that state substantive law should govern the enforceability of forum clauses in diversity cases? Does this include international forum agreements? State law generally applies to most "international" contract disputes. *See supra* pp. 8-9. Why should forum clauses be different from questions of contract validity, force majeure, performance, and damages.

4. *Authorities holding that federal law should govern the enforcement of international forum clauses when §1404(a) does not.* A number of lower federal courts have applied federal law to the enforceability of forum agreements in diversity cases without appearing to consider the basis for doing so. *E.g.*, *Heller Financial, Inc. v. Midwhey Powder Co.*, 883 F.2d 1286 (7th Cir. 1989) (applying *Bremen* in domestic diversity case, without discussing possible applicability of state law); *Commerce Consultants Int'l, Inc. v. Vetrerie Riunite SpA*, 867 F.2d 697 (D.C. Cir. 1989) (applying *Bremen* without discussion in international diversity case); *Pelleport Investors v. Budco Quality Theatres*, 741 F.2d 273, 279 (9th Cir. 1984) ("[w]e see no reason why the principles announced in *Bremen* are not equally applicable to the domestic context. Courts addressing the issue uniformly apply *Bremen* to cases involving domestic forum selection questions").

Two inconsistent rationales have been invoked to support the application of a federal rule of enforceability of forum clauses in federal courts (assuming that §1404(a) is not applicable). The first would regard this issue as one of federal "procedural" law, properly governed by judge-made federal rules applicable only in the forum (that is, in federal courts). The second rationale would treat the enforceability of forum clauses as a substantive federal common law issue, governed by judge-made federal rules that apply in both state and federal courts.

5. *Federal procedural law governs the enforceability of international forum clauses when §1404(a) does not.* The most common basis for applying federal law to the enforcement of forum clauses is that their enforcement implicates "procedure," "venue," and judicial docket control issues.

(a) *Lower courts applying federal procedural law to enforceability of forum clauses.* Like *Royal Bed*, most lower courts have held that the enforceability of forum selection clauses is a procedural issue subject to federal procedural law. In the words of one lower court, forum clauses are contracts, but "[i]n a larger sense ... this issue concerns the proper venue in the federal court system. Venue is clearly a matter of procedure, and, as such, governed by federal law." *Dick Proctor Imports, Inc. v. Sumitomo Corp.*, 486 F.Supp. 815, 818 (E.D. Mo. 1980). A representative judicial analysis is *Manetti-Farrow, Inc. v. Gucci America, Inc.*, 858 F.2d 509, 512-13 (9th Cir. 1988), which involved an Italian forum clause. The Ninth Circuit reasoned that "[t]he *Erie* choice is best accomplished by balancing the federal and state interests." The court thought "federal interests outweigh the state interests," because "[i]f venue were to be governed by the law of the state in which the forum court sat, the federal venue statute would be nugatory." *See also Royal Bed and Spring Co. v. Famossul Industria etc.*, 906 F.2d 45, 49 (1st Cir. 1990); *Jones v. Weibrecht*, 901 F.2d 17 (2d Cir. 1990) ("Questions of venue and the enforcement of forum selection clauses are essentially procedural, rather than substantive in nature."). The Supreme Court arguably adopted this view in *Stewart Organization v. Ricoh*, where it apparently treated the enforceability of forum selection clauses as a procedural matter. 487 U.S. at 32 ("Section 1404(a) is doubtless capable of classification as a procedural rule...").

(b) *Criticism of application of federal procedural law to enforceability of forum clauses.* The rule that the enforceability of forum clauses is subject to federal procedural law is subject to significant criticisms. It rests principally on labelling issues of forum selection as "venue" or "procedural," and does not address the equally clear "substantive" attributes of forum selection clauses, which are contractual undertakings that are bargained for and that significantly affect the parties' economic interests. Justice Scalia's dissent in *Stewart Organization, Inc. v. Ricoh Corp.*, 487 U.S. 22, 39-40 (1988), succinctly captured the extent to which the enforcement of forum clauses implicates "substantive" issues: "Venue is often a vitally important matter, as is shown by the frequency with which parties contractually provide for and litigate the issue. Suit might well not be pursued, or might not be as successful, in a significantly less convenient forum." *See also* Freer, *Erie's Mid-Life Crisis,* 63 Tulane L. Rev. 1087, 1109-10 (1989) ("Each of these characterizations — contract and venue — is partly correct.").

Is the issue of where an action is litigated a procedural question of venue, that ought to be subject to the forum's law? Consider the analysis in *Royal Bed.* Aren't the considerations of convenience, docket control, and "justice" that §1404 expresses equally applicable outside the section's scope? If this is correct, then is it not clear — as *Royal Bed* concluded — that federal procedural law should govern the enforceability of forum clauses in federal courts?

(c) *Inapplicability of federal procedural law in state courts.* Suppose that federal procedural law does govern the enforceability of forum selection clauses in federal courts. What law governs the same clauses in state courts? Under *Erie,* federal procedural law only applies in federal courts, and not in state courts. Would it be appropriate for different laws — state and federal — to apply to the same forum selection clause, depending upon whether the litigation was in state or federal court? Does *Erie* permit federal courts to fashion rules of federal procedural law governing the enforceability of forum clauses? How would Justice Scalia's dissenting opinion in *Ricoh* resolve this question? What considerations are relevant to the question? Recall the "twin aims of the *Erie* rule: discouragement of forum-shopping and avoidance of inequitable administration of the laws." *Hanna,* 380 U.S. at 468. How are these twin aims affected by the application of federal procedural law to the enforceability of forum selection clauses in federal courts? How would international commerce be affected? Under the analysis in *Royal Bed,* what law would govern the enforceability of forum selection clauses in Puerto Rico's courts? What effect does *Royal Bed* indicate would be given to Law 75 in Puerto Rico's courts? Why won't this lead to forum-shopping?

6. *Substantive federal common law governs the enforceability of international forum clauses where §1404 does not.* Some lower federal courts have said that *Bremen* states a rule of substantive federal common law that is applicable both in federal and state court actions. *E.g., General Eng'g Corp. v. Martin Marietta Alumina, Inc.,* 783 F.2d 352, 356-57 (3d Cir. 1986) (dicta that federal common law would apply in international cases); *Taylor v. Titan Midwest Constr. Corp.,* 474 F.Supp. 145, 147-48 (N.D. Tex. 1979) ("Resort to state law would balkanize venue rules when a uniform rule is patently preferable").

(a) *Authorities holding that substantive federal common law applies in domestic cases.* A few decisions appear to conclude that substantive federal common law rules apply even in entirely domestic diversity actions, involving state law claims. There is little reasoned justification for this view, which would presumably rest upon some sort of generalized federal interest in facilitating interstate commerce by ensuring enforceability of private choice of forum agreements. Heiser, *Forum Selection Clauses in Federal Courts: Limitations on Enforcement After Stewart and Carnival Cruise,* 45 Fla. L. Rev. 553, 559 (1993) ("Quite clearly, no uniquely federal interest exists when a federal court sitting in diversity determines the enforceability of a forum selection clause in a contract between private parties."). As discussed below, lower courts have applied federal law more frequently in actions involving substantive federal law claims, or in international cases. In both contexts, stronger arguments support the formulation of substantive federal common law rules regarding the enforceability of forum clauses than in simple domestic diversity actions.

(b) *Authorities applying federal common law to enforceability of forum clauses in international cases.* The Supreme Court has not considered whether there is any basis for substantive federal common law rules governing the enforceability of forum selection agreements in "international" cases. Some lower federal courts have resolved this question affirmatively, even in actions involving substantive state law claims. *E.g., TAAG Linhas Aereas v. Transamerica Airlines, Inc.,* 915 F.2d 1351 (9th Cir. 1990) (in international case under FSIA, "federal law governs the validity of a forum selection clause"); *Appell v. George Philip and Son, Ltd.,* 760 F.Supp. 167, 168 (D. Nev. 1991) ("With respect to international contracts containing forum selection clauses we are governed by" *Bremen*); *Tisdale v. Shell Oil Co.,* 723 F.Supp. 653 (M.D. Ala. 1987) ("particular importance of forum selection clauses in the context of international contracting"). Are these lower courts decisions consistent with *Erie*? Does *Erie* permit federal courts to fashion rules of federal common law governing the enforceability of forum selection agreements in either international cases or federal question cases? Recall the standards for judicially-fashioned rules of federal common law: Although *Erie* generally requires the application of state substantive law unless a federal statute preempts state law, there are "a few areas, involving 'uniquely federal interests' ... [which] are so committed by the Constitution and laws of the United States to federal control that state law is preempted and replaced, where necessary, by federal law of a content prescribed (absent explicit statutory directive) by the courts — so-called 'federal common law.'" In these uniquely federal fields, rules of federal common law will be fashioned when it is necessary to prevent "significant conflict" between state laws and federal policies or interests. *Boyle v. United Technologies Corp.*, 487 U.S. 500, 504 (1988); *supra* pp. 15-16.

(c) *Do international forum selection agreements arise in a "uniquely federal" field?* Is the enforceability of international forum selection clauses a subject involving "uniquely federal interests" that justifies formation of a rule of federal common law? As discussed elsewhere, the role of the individual states of the Union in matters involving foreign policy is narrowly limited, and federal foreign affairs powers are commensurately broad. *See supra* pp. 15-16. Federal authority over U.S. foreign commerce is also broad, and there are significant national interests in U.S. international trade. *See supra* pp. 15-16 & 541-44; *Japan Line v. County of Los Angeles*, 441 U.S. 434 (1979).

Broad federal powers over U.S. foreign affairs and commerce are said to sustain the formation of federal common law standards for the enforcement of forum clauses in international cases. The theory is that there is a substantial federal interest in the encouragement of international commerce, and that the effective enforcement of forum selection clauses in international cases is important to achieving this interest. In the words of the Supreme Court in *Bremen*, "[a] contractual provision specifying in advance the forum in which disputes shall be litigated and the law to be applied is ... an almost indispensable precondition to achievement of the orderliness and predictability essential to any international business transaction." Moreover, U.S. refusals to enforce forum selection clauses designating foreign forums would provoke foreign diplomatic responses and possible reciprocal refusals to enforce U.S. forum clauses; conversely, U.S. refusals to enforce forum clauses selecting U.S. forums would relegate U.S. citizens to foreign forums that they specifically bargained to avoid. In all these cases, parochial state law prohibitions on forum selection clauses would conflict with broader national interests in facilitating foreign commerce and structuring U.S. relations with foreign sovereigns.

Is this theory persuasive? Would U.S. foreign commerce really be hindered by parochial refusals by U.S. courts to enforce international forum clauses? *Cf. The Bremen v. Zapata Off-Shore Co.*, 407 U.S. 1, 9 (1972) (refusal to enforce forum selection clauses "would be a heavy hand indeed on the future development of international commercial dealings by Americans"). Is the following persuasive?

> It is clear from the opinion in *Zapata* that the validity of forum selection clauses in international contracts is viewed by the Supreme Court as a matter affecting important national interests. The federal interest in the effective conduct of foreign commerce is self-evident, and the perceptions of the importance of foreign commerce and the relationship of the forum-selection clause to the effectiveness of its conduct is a principal emphasis of the *Zapata* opinion.

Maier, *The Three Faces of Zapata: Maritime Law, Federal Common Law, Federal Courts Law*, 6 Vand. J. Trans. L. 387, 396 (1973).

Does the enforcement of forum clauses by U.S. courts really have an effect on U.S. foreign relations? Is the following remark persuasive? *AVC Nederland BV v. Atrium Inv. Partnership*, 740 F.2d 148, 156 n.13 (2d Cir. 1984) (quoting testimony of expert witness on Dutch law: "It would deeply offend Dutch notions of sovereignty for the courts of any other nation to assert jurisdiction" over a dispute between Dutch citizens which the parties agreed to submit to Dutch courts). How important is it that forum selection issues in international cases be resolved uniformly in different courts around the nation? *See supra* pp. 25-26 & 30-31 discussing the reasons that federal courts have been granted alienage jurisdiction.

(d) *Is there a "significant conflict" between state and federal rules governing enforceability of forum clauses?* Federal common law rules will ordinarily not be adopted unless there is a "significant conflict" between state (or foreign) law and asserted federal policies. *Boyle v. United Technologies Corp.*, 487 U.S. 500, 507 (1988). Suppose that a state law (or judicial decision) flatly denies *any* effect to forum selection clauses choosing out-of-state forums? This is what the rule in Alabama and a few other states is. *See supra* pp. 378-79. Suppose that state law denies any effect to clauses choosing any non-U.S. forum? to clauses choosing specific non-U.S. forums, such as non-market economy states, nondemocratic states, states with substantial trade surpluses with the United States (or an individual State), or states that use prison slave labor for commercial products? Are any of these types of state laws in significant conflict with federal policies?

Suppose that a state law imposes more rigorous limits on the enforceability of international forum clauses than does *Bremen*? for example, by reversing the burden of proof and requiring the proponent of the clause to establish the chosen forum's convenience or fairness? or by requiring the opponent of the clause to have received clear notice of the clause? or by adopting a forum non conveniens analysis in which a forum selection agreement is only one factor relevant to an overall "interest of justice" analysis? Which of these rules would significantly conflict with the federal policies reflected in *Zapata* (or elsewhere)?

(e) *Does federal common law govern the enforceability of forum clauses as applied to federal question claims?* *Ricoh* expressly declined to consider whether federal law should govern the enforceability of forum clauses in federal question cases: "Our conclusion that federal law governs the transfer of this case [under §1404(a)] ... makes this issue academic ... because the presence of a federal question could cut only in favor of the application of federal law. We therefore are not called on to decide, nor do we decide, whether the existence of federal question as well as diversity jurisdiction necessarily alters a District Court's analysis of applicable law." Almost always without analysis, a number of lower courts have applied federal law, derived from *Bremen*, in such cases. *Diaz Contracting, Inc. v. Nanco Contracting Corp.*, 817 F.2d 1047 (3d Cir. 1987) (bankruptcy); *AVC Nederland B.V. v. Atrium Inv. Partnership*, 740 F.2d 148 (2d Cir. 1984) (federal securities claims); *Bense v. Interstate Battery Sys. of America, Inc.*, 683 F.2d 718, 720-21 (2d Cir. 1982) (federal antitrust claims).

It is not clear what rationale supports these results. By creating substantive federal legal claims and granting the federal courts jurisdiction over these claims, Congress arguably also intended federal courts to apply federal rules to determine the enforceability of forum selection clauses that might waive or dilute these rights without adequate protections. This rationale would presumably preempt the application of state law that *enforced* forum clauses in circumstances not permitted by federal law. For example, federal law might forbid enforcement of forum selection clauses that provided insufficient notice or that would unduly dilute federal statutory protections. It is not clear, however, that state rules *denying* the enforceability of forum clauses as applied to federal statutory claims would interfere with either congressional intent or federal interests. Application of such state rules would merely enhance the options for plaintiffs seeking to vindicate federal rights, and thus presumably further federal interests. Solimine, *Forum Selection Clauses and the Privatization of Procedure*, 25 Cornell Int'l L.J. 51, 72-73 (1992).

7. **Bremen** *in state courts.* Where the federal courts enjoy authority to develop rules of substantive federal common law, the need to avoid forum-shopping between state and federal courts has had a "reverse-*Erie*" effect under which substantive federal common law preempts state law even in state court. See *Offshore Logistics, Inc. v. Tallentire*, 477 U.S. 207, 222-23 (1986); *Banco Nacional de Cuba v. Sabbatino*, 376 U.S. 398 (1964). If *Bremen* states a rule of federal common law applicable in federal courts in international cases otherwise governed by state law, should this rule be binding on state courts under the "reverse-*Erie*" doctrine? Wouldn't this prevent the intra-state forum shopping that *Erie* is concerned with?

8. *Effect of choice of law clause on forum selection clause.* Suppose a forum clause selects a foreign forum to resolve claims arising out of an international agreement that contains a choice of law provision selecting foreign law. These were the basic facts in *Madsen*. Should a U.S. court apply the U.S. standards set forth in *Bremen* to enforce the forum selection clause, or should it apply the parties' chosen law? In practice, most courts (including *Bremen*) have applied U.S. law, although there is some support for applying the parties' chosen law (or the law otherwise applicable to the agreement). See *supra* pp. 434-35. What was the approach of *Madsen*? What is the appropriate course?

9. *Intended effect of choice of law clause on forum selection agreement.* What is the scope of a choice of law clause in the underlying contract? Does such a clause, by its terms, purport to apply to the parties' choice of forum clause? Note that choice of law clauses are typically not construed to extend to "procedural" matters. See *infra* pp. 657-58. Is the enforceability of a forum selection clause within this procedural category? As discussed above, forum selection clauses are also often regarded as "separable" from the parties' underlying agreement. See *supra* p. 401. Does a choice of law clause in the parties' underlying agreement apply to the separable forum selection provision?

Consider the court's resolution of these issues in *Madsen*. In considering whether to enforce the forum clause, what weight did *Madsen* give to the parties' agreement that the "laws of Canada" applied? Reread *Smith*, excerpted above at *supra* pp. 388-91. What interpretation of the choice of law clause did *Smith* adopt?

10. *Need to satisfy enforcement standards of enforcing forum.* Even assuming that the parties' choice of law clause applies to their forum selection agreement, what consequences should that have for a U.S. court asked to dispatch a U.S. litigant to a foreign forum? Is it enough that the law of the foreign contractual forum be satisfied? Suppose that, under the standards of "unreasonableness" and "unfairness" articulated in *Bremen*, Restatement §80, and the Model Act, the clause in *Madsen* had been unenforceable —

but that under both Ontario and "Canadian" law, enforcement was required. Should the clause be enforced by a U.S. court under foreign law? What answer do you think *Madsen* would have reached? Consider again the analysis in *Smith, supra* pp. 388-91. Did the California court look solely to the law selected by the parties' choice of law clause, or did it also consider California law? What is the relevance of the enforcing forum's law in such cases?

A number of such courts appear to have required that a forum clause satisfy the requirements for enforceability of *both* the forum and the parties' chosen law. *See Karlberg European Tanspa, Inc. v. JK-Josef Kratz Vertriebsgesellschaft mbh*, 618 F.Supp. 344 (N.D. Ill. 1985) (apparently required that forum selection clause satisfy both *Zapata* and German law (where parties agreed that German law governed their contract)). Other courts have applied only the law selected by the parties to govern their contract. *In re Diaz Contracting, Inc.*, 817 F.2d 1047, 1050 (3d Cir. 1987) (applying New York law pursuant to choice-of-law clause); *General Eng'g Corp. v. Martin Marietta Alumina*, 783 F.2d 352, 357 (3d Cir. 1986) (applying Maryland law pursuant to choice-of-law clause: "In this case, the parties specified that the contract was to be governed by the law of Maryland. Therefore the enforceability of the forum selection clause in this case is governed by Maryland law."); *Hoes of Am., Inc. v. Hoes*, 493 F.Supp. 1205, 1207-08 (C.D. Ill. 1979) (applying German law pursuant to choice-of-law clause).

11. *Possible need to satisfy standards of law chosen by parties' choice of law clause.* Suppose that foreign law would not permit the forum selection clause to be enforced; for example, because foreign law has a per se rule against forum selection agreements (as was historically the case in the United States). Should the clause be denied enforcement by a U.S. court, even if the clause would be enforceable under U.S. standards? Suppose, for example, that "Canadian" law would have invalidated the forum selection clause in *Madsen*, but that *Bremen* required enforcement. What should the court do? Alternatively, suppose that foreign contract law requirements are not satisfied, and that the parties' forum clause is invalid under foreign law. Should a U.S. court enforce the clause?

12. *Erie issues raised by application of choice of law clause to choice of forum clause.* As *Madsen* suggests, complex *Erie* issues can arise when a choice of law clause applies to a forum selection agreement. One district court decision, in *Taylor v. Titan Midwest Construction Corp.*, 474 F.Supp. 145 (N.D. Tex. 1979), illustrates these difficulties. There, a U.S. district court in Texas considered the enforceability of a clause designating Missouri courts, where the parties' underlying contract also contained a choice of law clause selecting Missouri law. After indicating that federal law should apply, because the matter was procedural, the court went on to consider the possible effects of applying Texas state law:

> If this court were to apply state law, it would first apply the conflict of laws rules of Texas [under *Klaxon*], which would in all likelihood result in the application of Texas law to the question of venue, since venue is considered by Texas law as a matter of procedure to be determined by the law of the forum. ... Which state's law should apply [is] a problem, in view of the clause in the contract designating Missouri law as governing the contract. This court would have to determine whether under Texas conflicts law, this dispute is a matter of venue or a matter of contract law. If the former, Texas choice-of-law rules would dictate application of the law of the forum state, i.e., Texas. If under Texas conflicts law this were viewed as primarily a question of contract law, then arguably a Texas court would apply Missouri law to its resolution, in view of the contractual choice-of-law provision.

Is this persuasive? What should the forum court do?

E. Interpretation of Forum Selection Clauses

A forum selection clause is a contract: it is an exchange of promises about the situs (or situses) of future litigation. Like other contracts, a forum selection agreement must be interpreted to determine what obligations it imposes and what rights it confers. Disputes over the interpretation of forum selection agreements arise as frequently as disputes over enforceability.

1. Exclusive and Nonexclusive Forum Selection Agreements

As discussed above, forum clauses may be either exclusive or nonexclusive.[148] An exclusive forum selection agreement requires that claims be asserted *only* in the contractual forum, while a nonexclusive forum selection agreement permits claims in the contractual forum without precluding litigation elsewhere. Determining whether a forum clause is exclusive or nonexclusive is primarily an issue of interpretation, dependent largely on the wording of the provision.

Nevertheless, some generalizations are possible. Courts are usually reluctant to hold that a forum clause is exclusive, and often do so only if a provision includes language specifically excluding litigation in courts other than the chosen forum.[149] Thus, several lower courts have discerned the following "general rule": "When only jurisdiction is specified the clause will generally not be enforced without some further language indicating the parties' intent to make jurisdiction exclusive."[150] As Judge Weinfeld has explained, "the normal construction of the jurisdiction rules includes a presumption that, where jurisdiction exists, it cannot be ousted or waived absent a clear indication of such a purpose."[151]

Other lower courts have not demanded such unequivocal evidence of exclusivity. Thus, a number of decisions hold that various combinations of the terms "shall" and "any" are sufficient to render a forum selection agreement exclusive.[152] A few

---

148. *See supra* pp. 371-72.

149. A number of lower courts have held that particular forum selection clauses are nonexclusive. *E.g., McDonnell Douglas Corp. v. Islamic Republic of Iran*, 758 F.2d 341, 343 (8th Cir.), *cert. denied*, 474 U.S. 948 (1985) ("[a]ny difference ... should be settled through Iranian courts"); *Citro Florida v. Citrovale, SA*, 760 F.2d 1231, 1232 (11th Cir. 1985) ("[p]lace of jurisdiction is Sao Paulo/Brazil"); *Keaty v. Freeport Indonesia*, 503 F.2d 955, 956 (5th Cir. 1974) (per curiam) ("the parties submit to the jurisdiction of the courts of New York"); *Caldas & Sons, Inc. v. Willingham*, 791 F.Supp. 614 (N.D. Miss. 1992) ("the laws and courts of Zurich are applicable").

150. *John Boutari and Son, Wines and Spirits, SA v. Attiki Importers and Distributors Inc.*, 22 F.3d 51 (2d Cir. 1994) (quoting *Docksider, Ltd. Sea Technology, Ltd.*, 875 F.2d 762, 764 (9th Cir. 1987)).

151. *City of New York v. Pullman, Inc.*, 477 F.Supp. 438, 442 n.11 (S.D.N.Y. 1979). For a comparative perspective, *see* Lenhoff, *The Parties' Choice of Forum: 'Prorogation Agreements,'* 15 Rutgers L. Rev. 414 (1961).

152. *E.g., Seward v. Devine*, 888 F.2d 957, 962 (2d Cir. 1989) ("the New York State Supreme Court ... shall have jurisdiction over all litigation which shall arise out of any disputes..."); *Sterling Forest Assoc., Ltd. v. Barnett-Range Corp.*, 840 F.2d 249 (4th Cir. 1988) ("The parties agree that in any dispute jurisdiction and venue shall be in California" held exclusive; contrary district court interpretation reversed as "patently erroneous" and "evidence of a continuing hostility to forum selection clauses"); *Milk 'n' More, Inc. v. Beavert*, 963 F.2d 1342 (10th Cir. 1992) ("venue shall be proper under this agreement in Johnson County" held exclusive).

courts have been less demanding and construed forum clauses as exclusive even when no language clearly indicated this result.[153]

2. Scope of Forum Selection Clauses

A recurrent issue of interpretation is the definition of the classes of disputes that are covered by a particular forum clauses. This is largely a question of interpretation, turning on what categories of claims or disputes the parties intended to bring within the scope of their agreement.[154]

At one extreme, some forum selection clauses cover only specified and limited classes of disputes under an agreement, such as provisions regarding payment.[155] More broadly, forum clauses may cover all disputes arising under the contract, but may not also reach disputes under tort, antitrust, or similar noncontractual theories of recovery. At the other extreme are forum clauses that purport to cover any dispute relating to the parties' contractual relationship, regardless whether tort or other public law claims are involved.[156] Indeed, it is possible, at least as a drafting matter, for parties to agree to settle *all* their future disputes, regardless of connection to a particular agreement, in a designated forum.

There are few general rules that can be derived from decisions interpreting the scope of forum selection clauses. Some courts have, however, suggested that the interpretation of phrases in forum clauses — such as "arising from" — should be the same as interpretation of the same phrases in arbitration agreements.[157] Virtually all lower courts have held or assumed that forum clauses may be drafted to encompass both contract claims or disputes and non-contractual claims or disputes (such as tort or statutory claims).[158] This parallels the treatment of arbitration agreements, which

---

153. *E.g., General Electric Co. v. G. Siempelkamp GmbH*, 29 F.3d 1095 (6th Cir. 1994)("Place of jurisdiction for all disputes arising in connection with the contract shall be at the principal place of business of the supplier."); *Commerce Consultants Int'l, Inc. v. Vetrerie Riunite, SpA*, 867 F.2d 697 (D.C. Cir. 1989) ("The validity, enforceability and interpretation of this agreement shall be determined and governed by the appropriate court of Verona, Italy.").

154. *Manetti-Farrow, Inc. v. Gucci America, Inc.*, 858 F.2d 509, 514 (9th Cir. 1988).

155. *Cf. Mitsubishi Motors Corp. v. Soler Chrysler-Plymouth, Inc.*, 473 U.S. 614, 617 (1985) ("[a]ll disputes, controversies, or differences which may arise between [the parties] out of or in relation to Articles I-B through V of this Agreement or for the breach thereof, shall be finally settled by arbitration ...").

156. *E.g., Pascalities v. Irwin Yacht Sales North, Inc.*, 118 F.R.D. 298 (D.R.I. 1988); *Ronar, Inc. v. Wallace*, 649 F. Supp. 310 (S.D.N.Y. 1986); *Hoes of America, Inc. v. Hoes*, 493 F. Supp. 1205, 1208 (C.D. Ill. 1979) (clause extends to "business torts arising out of the relationship between the parties").

157. *Manetti-Farrow, Inc. v. Gucci America, Inc.*, 858 F.2d 509, 514 n.4 (9th Cir. 1988); *Omron Healthcare, Inc. v. MacLaren Exports Limited*, 28 F.3d 600, 603 (7th Cir. 1994) ("We cannot imagine why the scope of that phrase," *i.e.*, "arise out of" would be different for purposes of a forum selection clause than an arbitration agreement).

158. *Manetti-Farrow, Inc. v. Gucci America, Inc.*, 858 F.2d 509, 514 (9th Cir. 1988) ("forum selection clauses can be equally applicable to contractual and tort causes of action"); *Coastal Steel Corp. v. Tilghman Wheelabrator Ltd.*, 709 F.2d 190, 203 (3d Cir.), *cert. denied*, 464 U.S. 938 (1983); *Weidner Communications, Inc. v. Faisal*, 671 F.Supp. 531, 537 (N.D. Ill. 1987); *Clinton v. Janger*, 583 F.Supp. 284, 287-88 (N.D. Ill. 1984).

have uniformly been held capable of encompassing non-contractual claims and disputes.[159]

In interpreting the scope of arbitration clauses, U.S. courts have applied a strong "pro-arbitration" policy, resolving all ambiguities in favor of the inclusion of claims within the scope of the arbitration clause.[160] This presumption derives from the statutory provisions of the FAA and has not generally been applied to the interpretation of forum clauses. No similar statutory presumption applies to forum selection agreements. Nor have most courts fashioned any parallel rule of construction regarding the scope of forum clauses. Nevertheless, many lower courts have indicated reluctance to parse forum clauses finely in order to exclude claims.[161] They have generally done so on the grounds that hearing all disputes in a single forum "promotes a more orderly and efficient disposition of the case in accordance with the parties' intent."[162]

A recurrent issue is whether a forum clause encompasses non-contractual claims (as well as contractual ones). Most courts have reasoned that "pleading alternate non-contractual theories is not alone enough to avoid a forum selection clause if the claims asserted arise out of the contractual relation and implicate the contract's terms."[163] In contrast, a few courts appear to have taken the opposite view, reading forum clauses narrowly and refusing to apply them except where they encompass the parties' entire dispute.[164] It has been held that forum selection clauses will generally not be interpreted as applying to claims based upon intentional torts.[165]

Two common formulations for forum clauses are "all disputes arising under this Agreement" and "all disputes relating to this Agreement." Although these formulations appear similar, courts have sometimes concluded that the phrase "*arising under*

---

159. G. Born, *International Commercial Arbitration in the United States* 294-95, 323-81, 382-411 (1994).

160. *See infra* pp. 1029-39; G. Born, *International Commercial Arbitration in United States Courts* 382-411 (1994).

161. *Lambert v. Kysar*, 983 F.2d 1110, 1121 (1st Cir. 1993) ("contract-related tort claims involving the same operative facts as a parallel claim for breach of contract should be heard in the forum selected by the contracting parties"); *Interamerican Trade Corp. v. Companhia Fabricadora de Pecas*, 973 F.2d 487 (6th Cir. 1992); *Stewart Organization, Inc. v. Ricoh Corp.*, 810 F.2d 1066, 1070 (11th Cir. 1987), *aff'd on other grounds*, 487 U.S. 22 (1988); *Weidner Communications Inc. v. Al Faisal*, 671 F.Supp. 531 (N.D. Ill. 1987) ("the tort claims are too closely related to the contract to be treated as truly independent").

162. *Stewart Organization, Inc. v. Ricoh Corp.*, 810 F.2d 1066, 1070 (11th Cir. 1987).

163. *Hugel v. Corporation of Lloyd's*, 999 F.2d 206 (7th Cir. 1993); *Crescent International, Inc. v. Avatar Communities, Inc.*, 857 F.2d 943 (3d Cir. 1988). *See also Coastal Steel Corp. v. Tilghman*, 709 F.2d 190, 203 (3d Cir. 1983), *cert. denied*, 464 U.S. 938 (1983) ("public policy requires that [forum selection clauses] not be defeated by artful pleading of claims"); *Tisdale v. Shell Oil Co.*, 723 F.Supp. 653 (M.D. Ala. 1987); *Crescent Corp. v. Protor [sic] & Gamble Corp.*, 627 F.Supp. 745, 748 (N.D. Ill. 1986); *Envirolite Enterprises, Inc. v. Glastechnische Industrie Peter Lisec Gesellschaft MbH*, 53 B.R. 1007, 1010 (S.D.N.Y. 1985).

164. *Farmland Industries, Inc. v. Frazier-Parrott Commodities, Inc.*, 806 F.2d 848, 852 (8th Cir. 1986) ("we see no reason to require piecemeal resolution of this case"); *J.B. Hoffman v. Minuteman Press International Inc.*, 747 F.Supp. 552, 558 (W.D. Mo. 1990).

165. *Berrett v. Life Ins. Co. of the Southwest*, 623 F.Supp. 946 (D. Utah 1985).

this Agreement" is less expansive than the phrase "*relating to* this Agreement."[166] Thus, according to one court, a clause covering all actions "commenced under this agreement" did not include a suit for fraud in inducing the contract.[167] Most courts have not taken this approach.[168]

---

166. *See AVC Nederland BV v. Atrium Inv. Partnership*, 740 F.2d 148, 155-56 (2d Cir. 1984) ("arising under" is less inclusive than "relating to"); *In re Kinoshita & Co.*, 287 F.2d 951 (2d Cir. 1961); *General Environmental Science Corp. v. Horsfall*, 753 F. Supp. 664 (N.D. Ohio 1990) (court holds RICO and fraud claims not covered by following clause: "This Agreement shall be governed by the laws of Switzerland and the place of court is Rolle, Switzerland in case of claims by [plaintiff]."); *S.A. Mineracao Da Trinidade-Simitri v. Utah Int'l*, 576 F. Supp. 566, 570-73 (S.D.N.Y. 1983), *aff'd*, 745 F.2d 190 (2d Cir. 1984).

167. *Hodom v. Stearns*, 301 N.Y.S.2d 146 (1969). *See also J.B. Hoffman v. Minuteman Press International Inc.*, 747 F.Supp. 552 (W.D. Mo. 1990); *Fantis Foods, Inc. v. Standard Importing*, 406 N.Y.S.2d 763 (App. Div. 1978), rev'd on other grounds, 425 N.Y.S.2d 783 (1980).

168. *See Crowson v. Sealaska Corp.*, 705 P.2d 905 (Alaska 1985) ("arising under this lease" includes claim that lease was fraudulently induced).

6/International Parallel Proceedings: Lis Alibi Pendens and Antisuit Injunctions[1]

E xpansive contemporary principles of jurisdiction often make it possible for the courts of more than one nation to adjudicate the same international dispute. As discussed above, legal and other differences between available forums give private parties strong incentives to litigate in one country rather than another. In some cases, these incentives will lead parties to an international civil litigation to go forward simultaneously in the courts of two or more countries — with each party seeking resolution of the dispute in what it perceives to be the most favorable forum. This Chapter examines how U.S. courts have dealt with such parallel proceedings in international cases.

A. Introduction to Parallel Proceedings

There is no federal statutory or constitutional provision governing parallel proceedings in U.S. and foreign courts. Similarly, state legislation generally does not address the subject of parallel proceedings. In the absence of statutory direction, U.S. courts have fashioned several common law devices for dealing with parallel proceedings. These devices are often derived from approaches taken in domestic U.S. parallel proceedings, usually modified for international cases.

One mechanism for dealing with parallel proceedings is the forum non conveniens doctrine, considered in detail above, which permits a U.S. court to dismiss an

---

1. Commentary on antisuit injunctions and the *lis alibi pendens* doctrine includes, *e.g.,* Bermann, *The Use of Antisuit Injunctions in International Litigation*, 28 Colum. J. Trans. L. 589 (1990); Hartley, *Comity and the Use of Antisuit Injunctions in International Litigation*, 35 Am. J. Comp. L. 487 (1987); Teitz, *Taking Multiple Bites of the Apple: A Proposal to Resolve Conflicts of Jurisdiction and Multiple Proceedings*, 26 Int'l Law. 21 (1992); Note, *Antisuit Injunctions and International Comity*, 71 Va. L. Rev. 1039 (1985); Note, *Enjoining Suits in Foreign Jurisdictions*, 17 Colum. L. Rev. 328 (1917); Note, *Injunctions Against the Prosecution of Litigation Abroad: Towards a Transnational Approach*, 37 Stan. L. Rev. 155 (1984).

action in favor of a foreign forum.[2] Although the forum non conveniens doctrine often applies in the absence of any related foreign litigation, U.S. courts have occasionally applied the doctrine in cases involving parallel foreign litigation.[3]

A second mechanism for dealing with parallel proceedings is the *lis alibi pendens* doctrine.[4] The doctrine is related to the forum non conveniens doctrine, and permits a U.S. court to stay an action before it in deference to pending foreign litigation. It has been most extensively developed in domestic U.S. cases (involving both state-federal and federal-federal proceedings), but is also applicable in international cases.

A third mechanism for dealing with parallel proceedings is the antisuit injunction, which permits a U.S. court to enjoin a litigant from commencing or continuing litigation in a foreign forum.[5] U.S. lower courts have long asserted the power to issue antisuit injunctions, in a variety of circumstances, but the standards for issuing such injunctions remain unclear.

A fourth approach to parallel proceedings is simply to do nothing, and to allow the two (or more) actions to proceed at their own pace to judgment. The first final judgment is then available to be pleaded as res judicata in the second forum.[6] As discussed below, this is the generally preferred approach in many U.S. jurisdictions.

---

2. *See supra* pp. 289-369.

3. *E.g., Blanco v. Banco Industrial de Venezuela, SA*, 997 F.2d 974 (2d Cir. 1993); *Contact Lumber Co. v. P.T. Moges Shipping Co.*, 918 F.2d 1446 (9th Cir. 1990); *Brinco Mining Ltd. v. Federal Ins. Co.*, 552 F.Supp. 1233 (D.D.C. 1982).

4. *See infra* pp. 461-74.

5. *See infra* pp. 475-90.

6. *Laker Airways v. Sabena*, 731 F.2d 909, 928 (D.C. Cir. 1984); *Restatement (Second) Conflict of Laws* §86 (1971) ("A State may entertain an action even though an action on the same claim is pending in another state"); *infra* pp. 472-73 & 487-89.

B. The *Lis Alibi Pendens* Doctrine

1. Introduction

The *lis alibi pendens* doctrine allows a U.S. court to stay proceedings before it in favor of an action in another court that involves similar parties and matters. When a *lis alibi pendens* stay is issued, the foreign court is free to proceed to judgment. That judgment may then be pleaded in the U.S. forum, where it may be entitled to recognition under generally applicable rules for the enforcement of foreign judgments.[7] If the foreign litigation does not proceed, the U.S. action may be revived. The *lis alibi pendens* doctrine is closely related to the forum non conveniens doctrine, although it permits a stay of U.S. proceedings rather than outright dismissal.[8]

In federal and most state courts, *lis alibi pendens* is a common law rule not based upon any statutory or constitutional provision: "[T]he power to stay proceedings is incidental to the power inherent in every court to control the disposition of the causes on its docket with economy of time and effort for itself, for counsel, and for litigants."[9] Although it has occasionally been suggested that the *lis pendens* doctrine is not available in international cases,[10] the doctrine has frequently been invoked to stay domestic actions in favor of parallel proceedings in non-U.S. courts.[11]

There is no direct federal statutory or constitutional guidance for U.S. courts considering requests for stays in deference to foreign litigation, and virtually no state legislative direction.[12] The subject is governed almost entirely by common law prece-

---

7. These rules are discussed in Chapter 12 *infra*.

8. Some authorities treat the *lis alibi pendens* doctrine as a subset of the forum non conveniens doctrine, differing only with respect to relief. *Restatement (Second) Conflict of Laws* §84 comment e (1971).

9. *Landis v. North American Co.*, 299 U.S. 248, 254 (1936). *See I.J.A., Inc. v. Marine Holdings, Ltd.*, 524 F.Supp. 197, 198 (E.D. Penn. 1981).

10. *See* Bermann, *The Use of Antisuit Injunctions in International Litigation*, 28 Colum. J. Trans. L. 589, 610 & nn. 84-85 (1989) (doctrine not applicable in international context).

11. *E.g.*, *Turner Entertainment Co. v. Aegeto Film GmbH*, 25 F.3d 1512 (11th Cir. 1994) (staying U.S. action pending appeal of German parallel suit); *Saemann v. Everest & Jennings Int'l*, 343 F.Supp. 457, 461 (N.D. Ill. 1972) (staying domestic action pending outcome of parallel English court action where English case had been proceeding for more than three years before filing of U.S. action and hence parallel action would be "inequitable as well as wasteful of judicial resources."); *Barclays Bank, SA v. Tsakos*, 543 A.2d 802, 806-08 (D.C. App. 1988) (staying U.S. action, in lieu of granting *forum non conveniens* motion, pending outcome of parallel proceedings by French plaintiff against Greek debtor in courts of France and Switzerland); *Robinson v. Royal Bank of Canada*, 462 So.2d 101, 102 (Fla. Dist. Ct. App. 1985) (*per curiam*) (ordering stay of Florida action on grounds of comity pending outcome of Canadian action on similar claim); *Bentil v. Bentil*, 456 N.Y.S.2d 25, 26 (N.Y. Ct. App. 1982) (granting stay of New York divorce action in favor of previously filed action in Ghana). *See Laker Airways Ltd. v. Sabena*, 731 F.2d 909, 933-34 (D.C. Cir. 1984) ("a forum state may, but need not, stay its own proceedings in response to an antisuit injunction against a party before the court."); *Canadian Filters (Harwich) v. Lear-Siegler, Inc.*, 412 F.2d 577, 579 (1st Cir. 1969) (U.S. action may be stayed pending outcome of Canadian suit on same claims). *See Restatement (Second) Conflict of Laws* §84 comment e (1971).

12. The Uniform Interstate and International Procedure Act §1.05, provides that a court may "stay or dismiss" an action if "in the interest of substantial justice the action should be heard in another forum." Appendix B.

dent. Moreover, the Supreme Court has not considered the question in the international context, and there are few lower court decisions on the subject.[13] The content of U.S. law relating to the *lis pendens* doctrine is therefore often difficult to discern.

Lower courts have adopted two distinctly different approaches to motions for a stay of a U.S. action in deference to foreign proceedings. As outlined below, one line of authority emphasizes the obligation of U.S. courts to exercise legislatively-conferred jurisdiction, and narrowly limits the availability of *lis pendens* stays; the other line of precedent stresses the waste inherent in parallel proceedings, and permits much more liberal grants of *lis pendens* stays.[14] Most lower federal courts are agreed, under either approach, that the standards for issuing a *lis alibi pendens* stay are governed by federal law.[15] In contrast, state courts generally appear to apply state law to *lis pendens* issues.[16]

2. *Colorado River:* "Unflagging Obligation" to Exercise Jurisdiction

A substantial body of lower court decisions applying the *lis alibi pendens* doctrine in international cases have adopted the analysis contained in *Colorado River Water Conservation District v. United States.*[17] *Colorado River* was a domestic U.S. case involving a dispute over water rights to the Colorado River between two Indian tribes and a state instrumentality. The issue before the Supreme Court was whether a U.S. district court had properly abstained from considering the action because of a pending state court proceeding.[18] The Court reversed the trial judge, holding that the federal action should have proceeded notwithstanding the state court action.

---

13. *Advantage International Management, Inc. v. Martinez*, 1994 WL 482114 (S.D.N.Y. 1994) ("the Supreme Court has not addressed specifically the criteria that courts should consider when determining the propriety of staying or dismissing a federal action in deference to another lawsuit pending in a foreign jurisdiction...").

14. *See infra* pp. 462-63 & 464.

15. *Turner Entertainment Co. v. Degeto Film GmbH*, 25 F.3d 1512, 1518 (11th Cir. 1994); *Ingersoll Milling Machine Co. v. Granger*, 833 F.2d 680, 685 n.1 (7th Cir. 1987); *Faherty v. Fender*, 572 F.Supp. 142, 144 (S.D.N.Y. 1983).

16. *E.g., Hurst v. General Dynamics Corp.*, 583 A.2d 1334 (Del. Ca. 1990) (applying Delaware law to grant stay).

17. 424 U.S. 800 (1976). For cases following the *Colorado River* analysis, *see Neuchatel Swiss General Ins. Co. v. Lufthansa Airlines*, 925 F.2d 1193 (9th Cir. 1991); *Ingersoll Milling Machine Co. v. Granger*, 833 F.2d 680 (7th Cir. 1987) ("serve as a helpful guide in our evaluation"); *Advantage International Management, Inc. v. Martinez*, 1994 WL 482114 (S.D.N.Y. 1994) ("courts faced with this issue have articulated a standard premised, in part, on analogous Supreme Court precedent concerning the contemporaneous exercise of jurisdiction by federal courts, or by federal and state courts."); *Caspian Inv., Ltd. v. Vicom Holdings, Ltd.*, 770 F.Supp. 880, 884 (S.D.N.Y. 1991); *Brinco Mining Ltd. v. Federal Ins. Co.*, 552 F.Supp. 1233 (D.D.C. 1982). *See also Scheiner v. Wallace*, 832 F.Supp. 687, 693 (S.D.N.Y. 1993); *Biblical Archaeology Society v. Quimron*, 1993 WL 39572 (E.D. Pa. 1993); *Herbstein v. Bruetman*, 799 F.Supp. 1450, 1454 (S.D.N.Y. 1992) ("Generally, foreign and domestic courts should exercise jurisdiction concurrently"); *Eskofot A/S v. E.I. Du Pont de Nemours & Co.*, 872 F.Supp. 81 (S.D.N.Y. 1995) (refusing to stay U.S. antitrust action where English proceeding involving Article 86 EU competition claims was pending)

18. Although *Colorado River* is routinely applied in cases involving the *lis alibi pendens* doctrine, it in fact involved a district court's dismissal of the plaintiff's action, and not a stay of proceedings. 424 U.S. at 806.

Colorado River emphasized that federal courts are generally obliged to exercise jurisdiction that Congress has granted them. The Court referred to the "duty of a District Court to adjudicate a controversy properly before it,"[19] and the "virtually unflagging obligation of the federal courts to exercise the jurisdiction given to them."[20] The Court distinguished between parallel proceedings in two different federal courts, and those in a federal court and a state court. In the former, the "general principle is to avoid duplicative litigation," while in the latter "the pendency of an action in the state court is no bar to proceedings concerning the same matter in the Federal court having jurisdiction."[21]

Colorado River held that, in a case involving state-federal parallel proceedings, jurisdiction can be declined by a federal court only in "exceptional circumstances."[22] The Court identified a number of "general" principles that guide decision whether such exceptional circumstances are present:[23]

> In assessing the appropriateness of dismissal in the event of an exercise of concurrent jurisdiction, a federal court may ... consider such factors as the inconvenience of the federal forum, *cf. Gulf Oil Corp. v. Gilbert*; the desirability of avoiding piecemeal litigation; and the order in which jurisdiction was obtained by the concurrent forums, *Pacific Live Stock Co. v. Oregon Water Bd.*, 241 U.S. 440, 447 (1916). No one factor is necessarily determinative; a carefully considered judgment taking into account both the obligation to exercise jurisdiction and the combination of factors counselling against that exercise is required.

The Court emphasized that "[o]nly the clearest of justifications will warrant dismissal." It found no such exceptional circumstances in *Colorado River*, and reversed the district court's dismissal.

A number of lower federal courts have applied *Colorado River*'s analysis to cases involving foreign parallel proceedings. These courts have generally stressed the obligation of federal courts to exercise jurisdiction conferred upon them by Congress. They have also analogized foreign courts to U.S. state courts, holding that a foreign proceeding is entitled to no greater (and perhaps less) deference than a state court proceeding.[24]

---

19. 424 U.S. at 813 (quoting *County of Allegheny v. Frank Mashuda Co.*, 360 U.S. 185, 188-89 (1959)).

20. 424 U.S. at 817.

21. 424 U.S. at 817 (quoting *McClellan v. Carland*, 217 U.S. 268, 282 (1910)).

22. 424 U.S. at 818.

23. 424 U.S. at 817. The Court said that these principles "rest on considerations of '[w]ise judicial administration, giving regard to conservation of judicial resources and comprehensive disposition of litigation.'" *Id.*

24. *E.g.*, *Neuchatel Swiss General Ins. Co. v. Lufthansa Airlines*, 925 F.2d 1193, 1195 (9th Cir. 1991) ("the fact that the parallel proceedings are pending in a foreign jurisdiction is immaterial. We reject the notion that a federal court owes greater deference to foreign courts than to our own state courts."); *Ingersoll Milling Machine Co. v. Granger*, 833 F.2d 680 (7th Cir. 1987) ("Here, the alternate forum is not the tribunal of a state of the federal union to which, under our Constitution, we owe a special obligation of comity.").

3. *Landis:* Stays Within the District Court's "Sound Discretion"

A few courts have not followed the *Colorado River* analysis. Rather than analogizing parallel U.S.-foreign proceedings to the state-federal proceedings in *Colorado River*, these decisions have looked to *Landis v. North American Co.*,[25] a case involving parallel proceedings in two different federal courts. There, the Supreme Court upheld a stay on the grounds that it was within the district court's "discretion."[26] In marked contrast to *Colorado River*, *Landis* did not condition the grant of a stay on a showing of exceptional circumstances.

Following *Landis*, a second body of decisions have reasoned that, in international cases, "[a] court's ability to stay an action is 'incidental' to its 'inherent power.'"[27] This line of precedent has often concluded that requests to stay U.S. proceedings in deference to foreign proceedings are within the trial court's "discretion."[28] Relevant to the exercise of this discretion are a variety of factors:

> courts consider numerous factors, including principles of comity, the adequacy of relief available in the alternative forum, promotion of judicial efficiency, the identity of the parties and issues in the two actions, the likelihood of prompt disposition in the alternative forum, the convenience of the parties, counsel and witnesses, and the possibility of prejudice if the stay is granted.[29]

These factors are broadly similar to those identified in *Colorado River*, but with a lower burden of persuasion.

4. Selected Materials on *Lis Alibi Pendens*

Excerpted below are two federal court decisions considering requests for *lis alibi pendens* stays. The first, *Ingersoll Milling Machine Co. v. Granger*, follows *Colorado River:* it considers whether a U.S. action should be stayed in deference to a pending

---

25. 299 U.S. 248 (1936).

26. *E.g.*, *Ensign-Bickford Co. v. ICI Explosives USA, Inc.*, 817 F.Supp. 1018 (D. Conn. 1993); *Continental Time Corp. v. Swiss Credit Bank*, 543 F.Supp. 408 (S.D.N.Y. 1982); *I.J.A., Inc. v. Marine Holdings, Ltd.*, 524 F.Supp. 197 (E.D. Pa. 1981).

27. *See Itel Corp. v. M/S Victoria U*, 710 F.2d 199 (5th Cir. 1983); *Continental Time Corp. v. Swiss Credit Bank*, 543 F.Supp. 408, 410 (S.D.N.Y. 1982) ("inherent power to dismiss or stay this action in favor of the Swiss litigation presenting the same claims and issues"); *I.J.A., Inc. v. Marine Holdings, Ltd*, 524 F.Supp. 197 (E.D. Pa. 1981).

28. *Ensign-Bickford Co. v. ICI Explosives USA, Inc.*, 817 F.Supp. 1018 (D. Conn. 1993); *Ronar, Inc. v. Wallace*, 649 F.Supp. 310, 318-19 (S.D.N.Y. 1986); *Itel Corp. v. M/S Victoria U*, 710 F.2d 199 (5th Cir. 1983) ("abuse of discretion" standard); *I.J.A., Inc. v. Marine Holdings, Ltd*, 524 F.Supp. 197 (E.D. Pa. 1981).

29. *I.J.A., Inc. v. Marine Holdings, Ltd*, 524 F.Supp. 197 (E.D. Pa. 1981). *See also Ronar, Inc. v. Wallace*, 649 F.Supp. 310, 318 (S.D.N.Y. 1986) ("Numerous factors bear on the propriety of staying litigation while a foreign proceeding is pending. They include pragmatic concerns such as the promotion of judicial efficiency and the related issues of whether the two actions have parties and issues in common and whether the alternative forum is likely to render a prompt disposition. Also relevant are considerations of fairness to all parties or possible prejudice to any of them. A third group relates to comity between nations.").

foreign proceeding, both prior to and following the entry of a foreign judgment. The second, *Continental Time Corp. v. Swiss Credit Bank*, follows *Landis*, and dismisses a U.S. action in deference to pending foreign proceedings. Finally, the proposed "Conflict of Jurisdiction Model Act," which would codify means of dealing with parallel proceedings, is also excerpted below.

INGERSOLL MILLING MACHINE CO. v. GRANGER

833 F.2d 680 (7th Cir. 1987)

RIPPLE, CIRCUIT JUDGE. Appellant, Ingersoll Milling Machine Co. ("Ingersoll") appeals from a judgment enforcing a money judgment rendered by the Cour de Cassation of Belgium, that country's court of last resort, in favor of appellee, John P. Granger. Ingersoll argues [among other things, that the district court erred in staying a U.S. action that it had brought paralleling the Belgian proceedings]. ... [W]e affirm. ...

[Between 1963 and 1971, Mr. Granger worked for Ingersoll at its office in Rockford, Illinois. In 1971, Mr. Granger began working for an Ingersoll subsidiary, Ingersoll Manufacturing Consultants (the "Belgian Company"), in Brussels, Belgium. At the time of his transfer, Mr. Granger negotiated an agreement with Ingersoll governing his transfer. This agreement provided, among other things, for the payment of Mr. Granger's salary, insurance and expenses, and set forth how these matters would be affected by his move from Illinois to Belgium. In 1975, Mr. Granger was placed on the payroll of the Belgian Company and declared by the Belgian Company for tax purposes in Belgium. In 1977, Mr. Granger's employment with the Belgian Company was terminated.]

On April 27, 1978, Mr. Granger brought suit against Ingersoll and the Belgian Company in the Brussels' labor court. [He alleged] that, because he had been employed in Belgium from 1971 through 1977, he was entitled, under Belgian law, to certain compensation and termination benefits from both Ingersoll and the Belgian Company. Both defendants appeared and answered Mr. Granger's complaint. The Belgian Company claimed that Mr. Granger was an employee of Ingersoll only, and that, therefore, he could obtain no relief against the Belgian Company. Ingersoll claimed that, because of the agreement executed by Mr. Granger and Ingersoll prior to Mr. Granger's transfer to Brussels, the employment relationship was governed by Illinois law. ...

In August 1979, Ingersoll brought suit in the Winnebago County (Illinois) Circuit Court against Mr. Granger. Ingersoll sought a declaratory judgment that Mr. Granger was entitled to no further benefits from Ingersoll. Moreover, Ingersoll sought the return of funds advanced to Mr. Granger. Finally, Ingersoll sought to enjoin Mr. Granger from proceeding with the Belgian suit. Mr. Granger removed the Illinois suit to the U.S. District Court for the Northern District of Illinois. He also sought to dismiss the case on the ground that an action regarding the same dispute was then pending in Belgium and on the ground of forum non conveniens. The district court denied Mr. Granger's motion. The district court held that the pendency of the Belgian action did not deprive it of jurisdiction. Moreover, the court found that ... Illinois might be a more convenient forum that Belgium. ...

On March 20, 1980, the Belgian trial court found for Mr. Granger on his complaint for Ingersoll and the Belgian Company on the counterclaims. The award for Mr. Granger on his complaint was against Ingersoll and the Belgian Company jointly. ... On appeal, the Belgian Labour Court of Appeal affirmed the holding of the trial court. ... The Belgian Cour de Cassation affirmed the appellate court's decision on June 3, 1985. ...

After the Belgian trial court had rendered its judgment, Mr. Granger filed a second motion to dismiss Ingersoll's suit in the district court ... based on ... res judicata. Ingersoll opposed Mr. Granger's motion, filed a motion to compel discovery, and sought leave to add another count to its complaint seeking the return of certain funds advanced to Mr. Granger. ... The district court ... stayed further proceedings pending the outcome of the Belgian appellate process. After the Labour Court of Appeal issued its decision, Mr. Granger filed a counterclaim in the Illinois suit seeking enforcement of the Belgian judgment. Before the district court made any ruling, however, Ingersoll appealed the Belgian decision to the Cour de Cassation. On March 24, 1986, the district court ruled against Ingersoll on its complaint and granted summary judgment to Mr. Granger on his counterclaim. In so ruling, the court found that the Belgian judgment met the requirements of the Illinois Uniform Foreign Money-Judgments Recognition Act (the "Act" or the "Uniform Act")

On appeal, Ingersoll ... challenges ... the district court's March 24, 1986 order [on the grounds, inter alia,] that the court improperly stayed the action in the district court because of the pendency of the Belgian action. ... Relying on *Colorado River* and *Moses H. Cone Memorial Hosp. v. Mercury Constr. Corp.*, 460 U.S. 1, 16 (1983), Ingersoll argues that it was error for the district court to stay the proceedings simply on the basis that a parallel suit was proceeding in the Belgian courts.

In evaluating this argument, it is important, at the outset, to state the procedural posture of the case at the time a stay was granted with somewhat more precision than does Ingersoll. When Mr. Granger initially sought to dismiss or stay the action before the district court, the court denied Mr. Granger's motion because it recognized that it ought to exercise its jurisdiction over the subject matter concurrently with the Belgian courts. *See Laker Airways Ltd. v. Sabena*, 731 F.2d 909, 926-27 (D.C. Cir. 1984) (federal trial court should usually exercise jurisdiction concurrently with foreign trial court); *Colorado River*, (federal court has obligation to exercise concurrent jurisdiction with state court absent exceptional circumstances). It was only after the Belgian trial court had rendered its judgment that the district court decided to stay further proceedings pending the outcome of the Belgian appeal. Therefore, the precise issue before us is whether it was appropriate for the district court to stay its proceedings at this point in the parallel progression of the litigation in the United States and in Belgium.[30]

In *Colorado River* and *Moses H. Cone*, the Supreme Court enumerated the considerations that a federal district court should consider in determining whether it should exercise jurisdiction concurrently with state courts. In *Moses H. Cone*, 460 U.S. at 15-16, describing its earlier decision in *Colorado River*, the Court summarized those factors as follows:

> We declined to prescribe a hard-and-fast rule for dismissals of this type, but instead described some of the factors relevant to the decision.
>
> > "It has been held, for example, that the court first assuming jurisdiction over property may exercise that jurisdiction to the exclusion of other courts. ... In assessing the appropriateness of dismissal in the event of an exercise of concurrent jurisdiction, a federal court may also consider such factors as the inconvenience of the federal forum; the desirability of avoiding piecemeal litigation; and the order in which jurisdiction was obtained by the concurrent forums. No one factor is necessarily determinative; a carefully considered judgment taking into account both the obligation to exercise jurisdiction and the combination of factors counselling against that exercise is required. Only the clearest of justifications will warrant dismissal." [*Colorado River*, 424 U.S.] at 818-819.

Relying on the foregoing Supreme Court cases, this court recently has addressed the situation of a federal court staying its hand because of a parallel state court proceeding in *Lumen Constr., Inc. v. Brant Constr. Co.*, 780 F.2d 691 (7th Cir. 1985). The situation before us is somewhat different. Here the alternate forum is not the tribunal of a state of the federal union to which, under our Constitution, we owe a special obligation of comity. Nevertheless, the factors enunciated in those cases, when applied with this difference in mind, can serve as a helpful guide in our evaluation.

When the determination of the district court is reviewed in light of the *Colorado River-Moses H. Cone* factors, it is manifestly clear that the district court did not abuse its discretion in staying proceedings after the rendition of the Belgian trial court's judgement. First of all, there is no particularly strong federal interest in ensuring that this dispute be adjudicated in a federal district court or, indeed, in any American court. This case involves an employment relationship that spanned international boundaries. While the American interest can hardly be termed insubstantial, the Belgian interest also must be recognized as very significant. International judicial comity is an interest not only of Belgium but also of the United States. We certainly cannot fault the district court — informed that the Belgian trial court had rendered a verdict which, unless overturned on appeal, would resolve the dispute — for reject-

---

30. This question is a matter of federal law. *See Faherty v. Fender*, 572 F.Supp. 142, 144 (S.D.N.Y. 1983).

ing the "parochial concept that all disputes must be resolved under our laws and in our courts." *The Bremen v. Zapata Off-Shore Co.*

Moreover, considerations of judicial economy, especially the need to avoid piecemeal litigation, strongly favored staying the district court proceedings. The Belgian suit, which had begun before the American action was filed, had been brought to a conclusion in the trial court. Absent reversal on appeal, that judgment would adjudicate the rights of the parties. At that point, unless there was a barrier to the recognition of that judgment in the United States, and, as we discuss below, there was little chance of that contingency, there would be no need for further proceedings in the district court. Avoiding such duplication of effort and the possibility of piece-meal litigation is hardly an abuse of discretion. Attention to such "pragmatic concerns," *Ronar*, 649 F.Supp. at 318, is precisely the sort of "careful balancing of factors," *Moses H. Cone*, 460 U.S. at 16, that must be undertaken in such a situation.

Moreover, it is not insignificant — indeed, it is very significant — that the district court's action in this case was a decidedly measured one. The court did not dismiss the action; it simply stayed further proceedings until the Belgian appeals were concluded. This approach protects the substantial rights of the parties while permitting the district court to manage its time effectively. Such a common sense approach is clearly within the sound discretion of the trial court. *See Landis v. North American Co.*, 299 U.S. 248, 254 (1936). ...

CONTINENTAL TIME CORP. v. SWISS CREDIT BANK

543 F.Supp. 408 (S.D.N.Y. 1982)

LASKER, DISTRICT JUDGE. Continental Time Corp. ("Continental") sues to recover damages allegedly arising out of Credit Suisse's ("Suisse Credit") wrongful refusal to honor its obligations under an irrevocable letter of credit. The letter of credit was issued on January 10, 1980, in favor of Continental. On January 21, 1980, Continental assigned its entire interest in the letter of credit to S. Frederick & Company ("Frederick") and to Arlington Distributing Co., Inc. ("Arlington"). On January 29, 1980, Swiss Credit advised Merchants Bank, where Frederick held his account, that the air waybill did not conform to the requirements of the letter of credit. The expiration date on the letter of credit subsequently passed with no payment made. On May 28, 1980, Frederick and Arlington separately instituted suit in Switzerland for recovery of their assigned portions of the letter of credit. The Swiss court consolidated the actions and granted Swiss Credit's application to join Georges Bloch, the person who had originally requested the issuance of the letter of credit, in the action. The suit in Switzerland is currently pending.

Continental instituted this suit in 1981. Swiss Credit now moves to dismiss the complaint or stay the action on the grounds that Continental is not the real party in interest and that the precise issues are being litigated in the Swiss action. On March 18, 1982, Continental and Frederick settled related litigation between themselves. As part of the settlement, Frederick assigned back to Continental 75% of its interest in the letter of credit, agreed to attempt to intervene in this suit, and agreed to consent to a stay of the Swiss action. ...

Swiss Credit contends that, despite Frederick's reassignment of most of its interest in the letter of credit to Continental, the court should exercise its discretionary power to dismiss suits involving the same parties where, as is claimed here, the earlier initiated litigation will resolve the issues in the present suit. Swiss Credit argues that it would be prejudiced by the continuation of this suit through the assignment of claim from Frederick to Continental because it must continue to litigate the same issues in two fora, here and in Switzerland. In this regard, Swiss Credit notes that the assignment was only partial, that there has been no unconditional promise by Frederick to agree to a stay of the Swiss action, and that Frederick has yet to intervene here. Swiss Credit also maintains that Continental's maneuvers with Frederick amount to a method of forum shopping and that Continental has failed to join Arlington, a necessary party, in this suit. Swiss Credit contends that Switzerland is the appropriate forum for the litigation of the letter of credit claims because the Swiss action was filed first, Continental Time may "intervene" in the Swiss action, and all the relevant parties for the letter of credit claim are involved in the Swiss action.

Continental responds that Frederick's assignment to it renders Continental a real party in interest in this suit and that Arlington, as a minority assignee, is not an indispensable party under Fed. R. Civ. Pr. 19(b). Continental contends that this action should not be dismissed or stayed in favor of the Swiss action because the actions may proceed simultaneously, it is pressing claims against defendants other than Swiss Credit here, and Continental is not a party to the Swiss action. Continental emphasizes that this case, in contrast to the Swiss action, will involve all parties having an interest in the proceeds of the letter of credit. Continental also maintains that this action has proceeded to a further stage of litigation than the Swiss action, since discovery is nearly complete in this action and little activity has occurred in the Swiss action.

Swiss Credit's motion for dismissal of the claims against it is granted. The court has the inherent power to dismiss or stay this action in favor of the Swiss litigation presenting the same claims and issues. *See Landis v. North American Co.; I.J.A., Inc. v. Marine Holdings, Ltd.*, 524 F.Supp. 197 (E.D. Pa. 1981). The relevant factors in determining whether to grant a stay or a dismissal because of litigation pending in another forum include the adequacy of relief available in the alternative forum, the promotion of judicial efficiency, the identity of the parties and the issues in the two actions, the likelihood of prompt resolution in the alternative forum, the convenience of parties, counsel and witnesses, the possibility of prejudice to any party, and the temporal sequence of filing for each action. Weighing these factors in the present case, we conclude that this action should be dismissed. The suit was instituted some six months later than the Swiss action by a party who, at that time, had no cognizable interest in the letter of credit proceeds. Moreover, it appears that the Swiss action will proceed in any event since there is no indication that Arlington, to whom Continental assigned a significant share of its interest in the letter of credit, intends to join this action. In those circumstances, Swiss Credit would be faced with having to defend its actions in two fora with the attendant risk of inconsistent decisions. Moreover, Continental has not challenged Swiss Credit's assertion that Continental has the right to join the Swiss action. It thus appears that the Swiss suit has the potential of including all parties necessary for the resolution of the claims relating to the letter of credit transaction.

Finally, while, as Continental asserts, this action may be more convenient for various parties and witnesses, it is also true that it was the choice of Continental's predecessor in interest, Frederick, to sue in Switzerland rather than in the United States. In this regard, the fact that Continental and Frederick appear to have engaged in a type of forum-shopping as a by-product of the resolution of the claims between them militates in favor of Swiss Credit's position on this motion. Swiss Credit should not be required to defend against the letter of credit claims here when it is already engaged in litigation in Switzerland with parties who, at the time that litigation was commenced, represented the entire interests in the proceeds of the letter of credit. Frederick's decision to assign a portion of its interest back to Continental after it had already instituted litigation on the letter of credit should not be permitted to result in Swiss Credit's having to litigate the identical issue in two fora on either side of the Atlantic Ocean.

It is true that this action includes other parties and claims than those in the suit in Switzerland, relating to the purchase and sale of merchandise underlying the letter of credit transaction. However, this factor does not support Continental's contention that only this action can fully resolve the relevant issues, for it is settled that a letter of credit agreement constitutes an independent transaction between the issuer and the beneficiary, to be resolved without reference to underlying contracts or transactions. *Venizelos, SA v. Chase Manhattan Bank*, 425 F.2d 461 (2d Cir. 1970). Swiss Credit's motion to dismiss the action as to it is granted on condition that it not oppose Continental's becoming a party to the Swiss litigation.

CONFLICT OF JURISDICTION MODEL ACT

[reprinted in Appendix G]

Notes on Ingersoll, Continental Time, and Conflict of Jurisdiction Model Act

1. *Appropriate analysis for international lis pendens: analogies to* Colorado River *and* Landis. *Ingersoll* and *Continental Time* look to different Supreme Court precedents to establish the guidelines for *lis alibi pendens* analysis in international cases. *Ingersoll* relied principally on *Colorado River* — a case involving parallel proceedings in state and federal court — while *Continental Time* followed *Landis* — a case involving parallel proceedings in two different federal courts. Which analogy is more appropriate? If a federal court defers to a state court, then no federal court hears the action; the same is true when a federal court defers to a foreign court. Does this mean that *Colorado River* is the appropriate analogy?

When a federal court defers to a state court, it abstains from exercising jurisdiction unequivocally falling within its territorial jurisdiction and that does not intrude on the territorial jurisdiction of other co-equal sovereigns; the same is not necessarily true when a federal court defers to a foreign court. Do considerations of "international comity" counsel towards greater willingness of federal courts to defer to foreign courts than to state courts? *Neuchatel Swiss General Ins. Co. v. Lufthansa Airlines*, 925 F.2d 1193, 1195 (9th Cir. 1991) ("the fact that the parallel proceedings are pending in a foreign jurisdiction is immaterial. We reject the notion that a federal court owes greater deference to foreign courts than to our own state courts."). How does *Ingersoll* deal with the suggestion that foreign courts are entitled to greater deference than U.S. state courts? Does a federal court have a "virtually unflagging obligation" to exercise jurisdiction over international cases, when the courts of other nations can also resolve the dispute? Note the remark in *Ingersoll* which, while applying *Colorado River*, said: "there is no particularly strong federal interest in ensuring that this dispute be adjudicated in a federal district court or, indeed, in any American court." Is that correct? Does it matter what law — state or federal — governs the underlying substantive claims? Does it matter that both parties were U.S. nationals?

    2. *Standards governing* lis pendens *stays.* Compare the standards adopted by *Ingersoll* and *Continental Time* for the grant of a *lis pendens* stays. What are the differences between them? Should *lis pendens* stays be easy or hard to obtain in international cases?

    (a) *"Exceptional circumstances."* *Ingersoll* held that *lis pendens* stays would be granted only in "exceptional circumstances." This clearly did not include the mere expense of duplicative litigation, as illustrated by the U.S. trial court's refusal to stay its proceedings before any Belgian judgment had been rendered. The majority of other lower court decisions have adopted this view. E.g., *Neuchatel Swiss General Ins. Co. v. Lufthansa Airlines*, 925 F.2d 1193 (9th Cir. 1991); *Brinco Mining Ltd. v. Federal Ins. Co.*, 552 F.Supp. 1233 (D.D.C. 1982); *Advantage International Management, Inc. v. Martinez*, 1994 WL 482114 (S.D.N.Y. 1994); *supra* pp. 462-63. *See also Biblical Archaeology Society v. Quimron*, 1993 WL 39572 (E.D. Pa. 1993). Is this an appropriate standard? Why should U.S. proceedings be stayed only in extreme circumstances? Why should not the rule be that duplicative U.S. proceedings will be stayed when parallel foreign proceedings are pending, *absent* exceptional circumstances?

    What precisely does the "exceptional circumstances" test mean? The relevant factors are those identified in *Colorado River*, which in turn drew on the forum non conveniens analysis of *Gulf Oil*. Were there exceptional circumstances in *Continental Time*?

    There are two points in *Ingersoll* where a *lis pendens* stay was arguably appropriate: (i) immediately after filing of the U.S. action, and before any Belgian court decision; and (ii) after the Belgian trial court's decision. What did the U.S. trial judge do at each point? Were there *not* exceptional circumstances to support Mr. Granger's original request for a stay in *Ingersoll* (which the trial judge denied)? Should a stay have been granted before the Belgian decision was rendered? Were there exceptional circumstances supporting the trial court's grant of a stay in *Ingersoll* after the first Belgian decision? What were they? Were there exceptional circumstances for granting a stay in *Continental Time*? What were they?

    (b) *"Sound discretion."* *Continental Time* held that the grant of a *lis alibi pendens* stay was within the discretion of the trial court, applying the same factors as those used under *Colorado River* and the forum non conveniens doctrine. Is it appropriate to give a trial court "discretion" to make the fundamentally important, and often outcome-determinative, decision whether an action may proceed in the United States? Under the *Continental Time* analysis, would a stay have been granted in *Ingersoll*? before the Belgian judgment had been rendered? Should such a stay have been entered?

    (c) *Multi-factor balancing.* More recently, the Eleventh Circuit has adopted a multi-factor balancing approach to *lis pendens* stays. In *Turner Entertainment Co. v. Degeto Film GmbH*, 25 F.3d 1512, 1517-18 (11th Cir. 1994), the court granted a stay after applying the following standards:

> Courts have sought to fashion principles that will provide three readily identifiable goals in the area of concurrent international jurisdiction: (1) a proper level of respect for the acts of our fellow sovereign nations .. a rather vague concept referred to in American jurisprudence as international comity; (2) fairness to litigants; and (3) efficient use of scarce judicial resources.

Compare this standard with those in *Colorado River* and *Landis*. Does the Eleventh Circuit's standard provide meaningful guidance?

    (d) *Uncertainty regarding lis pendens standards.* *Ingersoll* relies on *Colorado River's* demanding "exceptional circumstances" standard — until the final paragraph of the opinion. There, the court appears to rely on *Landis'* "discretion" standard. Is this consistent? Is the fact that a Belgian judgment had already issued relevant?

3. *Majority view that parallel proceedings are not inherently improper.* The standards that should govern *lis pendens* stays are influenced significantly by one's attitude towards parallel proceedings. Are parallel proceedings an inherently undesirable occurrence? Or are they a natural feature of a multi-state environment, where the same dispute will often fall within the jurisdiction of two or more forums?

One court has reasoned that concurrent jurisdiction by two or more national courts is inevitable in international disputes, and that the "fundamental corollary" to concurrent jurisdiction is parallel proceedings: "parallel proceedings on the same in personam claim should ordinarily be allowed to proceed simultaneously, at least until a judgment is reached in one which can be pled as res judicata in the other." *Laker Airways Ltd. v. Sabena*, 731 F.2d at 909, 926-27 (D.C. Cir. 1984). Indeed, a number of U.S. lower courts have acknowledged a "rule permitting parallel proceedings in concurrent in personam actions," thus allowing both U.S. and foreign proceedings to go forward to judgment. *Laker Airways*, 731 F.2d at 928. *E.g., In the Matter of the Complaint of Maritima Aragua, SA*, 1990 U.S. Dist. Lexis 15235 (S.D.N.Y. 1990) (declining to enjoin parallel action where "there is no strong public policy of the United States that is threatened by the continuation of the action in Venezuela" but likewise refusing to grant Venezuelan plaintiffs' motion to dismiss U.S. action because "[n]o reason has been presented as to why claimants, having voluntarily subjected themselves to the jurisdiction of this Court, should not be required to remain in this proceeding while pursuing their claims in Venezuela."); *Black & Decker Corp. v. Sanyei America Corp.*, 650 F.Supp. 406, 408-10 (N.D. Ill. 1986) (refusing to enjoin parallel proceedings in Hong Kong court and declining to stay U.S. action, reflecting "courts' general policy of restraint in such cases"). Why is it a "fundamental corollary" of concurrent jurisdiction that parallel proceedings should be permitted to proceed? Why is it not that courts have a "virtually unflagging obligation" to mitigate the hardship that their assertions of concurrent jurisdiction can impose on private parties in international cases?

4. *Relevance of nationality of parties.* Are the parties' nationalities relevant to the grant of a *lis pendens* stay? Recall that the forum non conveniens doctrine, in most contemporary formulations, grants U.S. (but not foreign) plaintiffs a strong presumption in favor of their choice of a U.S. forum. *See supra* pp. 316-17 & 331-33. Should the same presumption shield a U.S. plaintiff from a stay of U.S. proceedings in deference to foreign litigation? Note that the plaintiffs in the U.S. proceedings in both *Ingersoll* and *Continental Time* were U.S. nationals.

5. *Relevance of enforceability of any foreign judgment.* Suppose that it is likely that the foreign proceedings will not produce a judgment that can be enforced in the United States, because U.S. standards for the recognition of foreign judgments will not be satisfied. *See infra* pp. 935-86. For example, suppose that the foreign court does not possess personal jurisdiction over the defendant under the due process clause; or that the foreign court is hearing claims that are contrary to U.S. public policy. Would it be appropriate — under either *Continental Time* or *Ingersoll* — to grant a stay in these circumstances?

6. *Relevance of first-filing of complaint.* Note that the *Colorado River* formula takes into account the sequence in which the actions were filed. A number of lower courts including *Continental Time*, have attributed significant weight to the sequence of filings. *E.g., Ronar, Inc. v. Wallace*, 649 F.Supp. 310, 318 (S.D.N.Y. 1986) ("When ... the foreign action is pending rather than decided, comity requires that priority generally goes to the suit first filed"; invoking "presumption" in favor of proceeding with first-filed U.S. suit). Is this appropriate? Why should it matter whether one party or the other won the race to the courthouse? On the other hand, should courts consider whether there are delays in the filing of the second suit — suggestive of an intention to complicate and delay matters?

7. *Relevance of first-filing of judgment.* In *Ingersoll*, the U.S. trial court refused to stay U.S. proceedings before a Belgian judgment was entered. Then, after a Belgian judgment was made, the U.S. court stayed its action. The U.S. appellate court affirmed. *See also Turner Entertainment Co. v. Degeto Film GmbH*, 25 F.3d 1512, 1521 (11th Cir. 1994) ("While courts regularly permit parallel proceedings in an American court and a foreign court, once a judgment on the merits is reached in one of the cases ... failure to defer to the judgment would have serious implications for the concerns of international comity. For example, the prospect of 'dueling courts,' conflicting judgments, and attempts to enforce conflicting judgments raise major concerns of international comity."); *Laker Airways*, 731 F.2d at 928 ("Parallel proceedings on the same in personam claim should ordinarily be allowed to proceed simultaneously, at least until a judgment is reached in one which can be pled as res judicata in the other.").

Is this an appropriate way to proceed? If the U.S. action had sufficient substance to warrant independent prosecution — and was within the U.S. court's jurisdiction — why should the fortuitous fact that the foreign court's docket moved more quickly be the basis for stopping the U.S. action? Does this not encourage races to judgment? More fundamentally, why grant decisive importance to the relative speed of two different judicial systems? It is often thought that fairer, more accurate results require various procedural safeguards — like discovery, cross-examination, and the like. These procedural devices take time. Why should proceedings that move more quickly, presumptively at the expense of procedural safeguards, be permitted to preempt slower, but presumptively more accurate, U.S. proceedings?

In many jurisdictions, a trial court's decision is subject to de novo review on appeal — often including the possibility of submitting new evidence. Should that affect the availability of a stay after a foreign trial court decision?

8. *Relevance of overlap between parties and issues in the parallel proceedings.* Continental Time considered whether two parallel proceedings were in fact all that "parallel" — by examining the identities of the parties to, and the similarity of the issues in, the two actions. Other lower courts have also considered the degree of similarity between pending foreign and U.S. proceedings. *Compare Itel Corp. v. M/S Victoria U*, 710 F.2d 199 (5th Cir. 1983) ("A stay pending adjudication in another tribunal should not be granted unless that tribunal has the power to render an effective judgment on issues that are necessary to the disposition of the stayed action") *with Herbstein v. Bruetman*, 743 F.Supp. 184 (S.D.N.Y. 1990)("comity requires that the parties and issues in both litigations are the same or sufficiently similar, such that the doctrine of res judicata can be asserted"). What degree of similarity or overlap is required before a stay can be granted? Is there a clear cut answer to this, or are there various gradations of overlap that strengthen or weaken the case for a stay? Is it sufficient that the foreign proceeding will decide *some* (but not all) of the claims in the U.S. suit? Some of the elements of the U.S. claims?

9. *Relevance of reciprocity.* In considering a request for a *lis pendens* stay, does it matter whether the foreign forum would grant a stay in favor of U.S. proceedings in reverse circumstances?

10. *Relevance of competing forum's jurisdictional claims.* In deciding whether to grant a *lis pendens* stay, should a court consider the respective "strength" of U.S. and foreign jurisdictional claims? If the foreign court lacks a jurisdictional base that would satisfy the due process clause, should a *lis pendens* stay ever be granted? Conversely, if the U.S. court has only a tenuous jurisdictional base, compared to a substantial foreign basis, would this argue for a *lis pendens* stay?

11. *Does federal law or state law govern* lis pendens *stays in federal court?* What law did *Ingersoll* apply to determine the applicable standards for granting a *lis pendens* stay in favor of foreign proceedings — state or federal? What law did *Continental Time* apply? Why should federal law govern whether a federal court should defer to foreign legal proceedings? In a diversity case, is this not a substantive matter that, under *Erie*, should be governed by state law? Or does the granting of a stay relate either to the jurisdiction of federal courts, or to the procedures and venue of such courts, and thus fall under federal procedural law? Should *lis pendens* stays in international cases be governed by substantive federal common law? Consider the related issues under the forum non conveniens doctrine and forum selection agreements. *See supra* pp. 358-66 & 431-53.

12. *Does federal law or state law govern the grant of a* lis pendens *stay in state court?* If *Ingersoll* had arisen in state court, what law would have provided the standards for granting a *lis pendens* stay in deference to foreign proceedings? If federal courts apply federal procedural law, then state courts would be free to apply state procedural law. *See supra* pp. 13-14. Suppose that a state court refuses *ever* to grant a stay in deference to foreign proceedings. What if *Ingersoll* had arisen in a U.S. state court, which refused to stay its proceedings even after the Belgian trial and appellate proceedings? Is there any rule of federal law that precludes such an approach by state courts? Do the federal interests in foreign relations and foreign commerce, discussed above, provide any basis for a federal common law rule? Note that the enforceability of foreign judgments in U.S. courts has generally been governed by state law. *See infra* pp. 960-62.

13. *Does a request for a stay pending parallel foreign proceedings mean that the case "arises under" federal law?* Consider again *Sequihua v. Texaco Oil Co.*, 847 F.Supp. 61 (S.D. Tex. 1994), *supra* pp. 50-56, where a federal district court held that a request for a dismissal on comity grounds arises under federal law for purposes of 28 U.S.C. §1331. Accepting that conclusion, does it also apply to cases where one party seeks a stay pending parallel foreign proceedings?

14. *Relation of lis pendens to forum non conveniens doctrine.* Continental Time dismissed a U.S. action in deference to a foreign proceeding. Why is the forum non conveniens doctrine not applicable when dismissal of an action is requested? How do the two standards applied in *Ingersoll* and *Continental Time* compare to the forum non conveniens doctrine articulated in *Piper Aircraft*? Under which of these standards is it easier to obtain a stay or dismissal?

15. *Conflict of Jurisdiction Model Act.* How would the Conflict of Jurisdiction Model Act handle the general problem of parallel proceedings? Is this a sensible way to deal with the issue? How would the Act resolve *Ingersoll* and *Continental Time?*

16. *Brussels Convention.* Consider Article 21 of the Brussels Convention, excerpted at Appendix D. Article 21 provides that whenever an action is filed in a European Union judicial forum that may properly exercise jurisdiction under the Convention, any subsequently-filed action in any other European Union state must be stayed, even if that state's court may assert jurisdiction under the Convention. Is this a wise approach for EU litigation? Would it be wise in domestic U.S. litigation? Should Article 21 provide a model for U.S. courts confronting parallel foreign litigation?

C. Antisuit Injunctions

1. Introduction

Lis pendens concerns a U.S. court's decision to stay its own proceedings, just as forum non conveniens concerns a U.S. court's decision to dismiss proceedings before it. It is also possible for courts to issue "antisuit injunctions" — orders forbidding a party from initiating or participating in judicial proceedings in foreign forums.[31] An antisuit injunction is sometimes an attractive option in international disputes: it can be sought from a local, convenient, and perhaps sympathetic tribunal as a means of foreclosing litigation in a potentially inconvenient or hostile foreign forum.

Antisuit injunctions are sought in several situations.[32] First, a party to proceedings in a U.S. forum can seek an injunction against litigation by its adversary of the same dispute in a pending or threatened action in a foreign forum.[33] Second, if related but not identical claims are pursued in two forums, an antisuit injunction may be sought to consolidate litigation in the moving party's preferred forum.[34] Third, the prevailing party in *completed* U.S. litigation can seek an injunction preventing the unsuccessful party from relitigating the parties' dispute in a foreign forum.[35] Finally, a court may issue a "counter-injunction," or "anti-antisuit injunction," designed to foreclose a party from obtaining an antisuit injunction in a foreign forum against litigation in the issuing court.[36]

2. Standards Governing Antisuit Injunctions in U.S. Courts

There is no statutory provision in federal law (nor in most state codes) granting federal courts the power to issue antisuit injunctions. Nevertheless, U.S. courts have long asserted the power to issue antisuit injunctions, regarding such orders as a corollary of a court's general equitable power over parties subject to its jurisdic-

---

31. Antisuit injunctions are one example of the power of courts to order persons subject to their personal jurisdiction to perform (or not to perform) specified acts outside of the forum. *E.g., United States v. First Nat'l City Bank*, 379 U.S. 378 (1965); *Restatement (Second) Conflict Of Laws* §53 (1971); Messner, *The Jurisdiction of a Court of Equity Over Persons to Compel the Doing of Acts Outside the Territorial Limits of the State*, 14 Minn. L. Rev. 494 (1930). *See also infra* pp. 856-60 (extraterritorial discovery orders).

32. It appears that antisuit injunctions were in use at common law at least as early as applications of the forum non conveniens doctrine. *See supra* pp. 289-91.

33. *E.g., Compagnie des Bauxites de Guinea v. Insurance Co. of N. Am.*, 651 F.2d 877 (3d Cir. 1981), *aff'd on other grounds*, 456 U.S. 644 (1982); *Timberland Co. v. Sanchez*, 129 F.R.D. 382 (D.D.C. 1990); *Cargill, Inc. v. Hartford Accident & Indem. Co.*, 531 F.Supp. 710 (D. Minn. 1982); *Medtronic Inc. v. Catalyst Research Corp.*, 518 F.Supp. 946 (D. Minn. 1981), *aff'd*, 664 F.2d 660 (8th Cir. 1981); *Western Elec. Co. v. Milgo Elec. Corp.*, 450 F.Supp. 835 (S.D. Fla. 1978).

34. *E.g., Seattle Totems Hockey Club v. National Hockey League*, 652 F.2d 852 (9th Cir. 1981), *cert. denied*, 457 U.S. 1105 (1982).

35. *E.g., Princess Lida of Thurn & Taxis v. Thompson*, 305 U.S. 456 (1939); *Wood v. Santa Barbara Chamber of Commerce*, 705 F.2d 1515 (9th Cir. 1983), *cert. denied*, 465 U.S. 1081 (1984); *Bethell v. Peace*, 441 U.S. 495 (5th Cir. 1971); *Scott v. Hunt Oil Co.*, 398 F.2d 810 (5th Cir. 1968).

36. *E.g., Owens-Illinois, Inc. v. Webb*, 809 S.W.2d 899 (Ct. App. Tex. 1991); *Laker Airways v. Sabena*, 731 F.2d 909 (D.C. Cir. 1984); *James v. Grand Trunk W. R.R.*, 152 N.E.2d 858 (Ill.), *cert. denied*, 358 U.S. 915 (1958).

tion.[37] Most federal courts also appear to agree (albeit without analysis) that the standards governing the issuance of an antisuit injunction in federal court are governed by federal law.[38]

There is, however, disagreement over the standards that should govern a U.S. court's grant of an antisuit injunction. Most U.S. courts express caution about the issuance of such orders.[39] This caution arises from the fact that, while antisuit injunctions are not issued directly against foreign tribunals, most courts acknowledge that such orders "effectively restrict the foreign court's ability to exercise its jurisdiction."[40] Nevertheless, while all lower courts have exercised "caution" in issuing antisuit injunctions, few lower courts have agreed on what standards this caution requires.

3. Decisions Applying Stringent Limits on Issuance of Antisuit Injunctions

Lower courts are divided over the standards that govern the issuance of antisuit injunctions. Several Courts of Appeals — including the District of Columbia, Second, and Sixth Circuits — have held that antisuit injunctions should virtually never be issued.[41] They have concluded that "duplication of parties and issues alone is not sufficient to justify issuance of an antisuit injunction."[42] Rather, an antisuit injunction generally may be issued only to: (a) protect a court's own legitimate jurisdiction (typically by issuing an anti-antisuit injunction); or (b) prevent "litigants' evasion of the forum's important public policies."[43]

---

37. *See* Messner, *The Jurisdiction of a Court of Equity Over Persons to Compel the Doing of Acts Outside the Territorial Limits of the State*, 14 Minn. L. Rev. 494, 495-96 (1930); *Restatement (Second) Conflict of Laws* §84 comment h (1971) ("On occasion, a court may enjoin a person over whom it has personal jurisdiction from bringing suit in what the court deems to be an inappropriate forum."); *Western Elec. Co. v. Milgo Elec. Corp.*, 450 F. Supp. 835, 837 (S.D. Fla. 1978) (a U.S. court "has the power to enjoin a party over whom it has personal jurisdiction from pursuing litigation before a foreign tribunal.").

38. *Gau Shan Co. v. Bankers Trust Co.*, 956 F.2d 1349 (6th Cir. 1992); *Sea Containers Ltd. v. Stena AB*, 890 F.2d 1205, 1214 (D.C. Cir. 1989); *China Trade & Dev. Corp. v. M.V. Choong Yong*, 837 F.2d 33 (2d Cir. 1987); *Laker Airways Ltd. v. Sabena*, 731 F.2d 909 (D.C. Cir. 1984).

39. *See Sea Containers Ltd. v. Stena AB*, 890 F.2d 1208 (D.C. Cir. 1989); *Laker Airways v. Sabena*, 731 F.2d 909, 927 (D.C. Cir. 1984) (antisuit injunctions are "rarely issued" and "only in the most compelling circumstances"); *Seattle Totems Hockey Club v. National Hockey League*, 652 F.2d 852, 855 (9th Cir. 1981), *cert. denied*, 457 U.S. 1105 (1982) (antisuit injunctions should be "'used sparingly'"); *Philip v. Macri*, 261 F.2d 945, 947 (9th Cir. 1958) (antisuit injunctions "should be used sparingly ... and 'is not to be lightly exercised'" (quoting *Williams v. Payne*, 94 P.2d 341, 343 (Kan. 1939)); *Chase Manhattan Bank v. Iran*, 484 F.Supp. 832 (S.D.N.Y. 1980); *Restatement (Second) Conflict of Laws* §84 comment h (1971) ("The factor which determined the award of [an antisuit injunction] are the same as those a court considers in deciding whether to dismiss a case on forum non conveniens grounds. Injunctions of this sort are only granted in extreme circumstances.").

40. *Laker Airways v. Sabena*, 731 F.2d 909, 927 (D.C. Cir. 1984). *See Donovan v. Dallas*, 377 U.S. 408, 413 (1964); *Peck v. Jenness*, 48 U.S. 612, 625 (1849); *China Trade and Dev. Corp. v. M.V. Choong Yong*, 837 F.2d 33, 35-36 (2d Cir. 1987).

41. *Laker Airways Ltd. v. Sabena*, 731 F.2d 909 (D.C. Cir. 1984); *Gau Shan Co. v. Bankers Trust Co.*, 956 F.2d 1349 (6th Cir. 1992); *China Trade & Dev. Corp. v. M.V. Choong Yong*, 837 F.2d 33 (2d Cir. 1987); *Sea Containers Ltd. v. Stena AB*, 890 F.2d 1205, 1214 (D.C. Cir. 1989).

42. *Laker Airways*, 731 F.2d at 928-29.

43. *Laker Airways*, 731 F.2d at 927-31; *Gau Shan Co. v. Bankers Trust Co.*, 956 F.2d 1349 (6th Cir. 1992); *Mutual Service Casualty Ins. Co. v. Frit Industries, Inc.*, 805 F.Supp. 919 (M.D. Ala. 1992).

The courts adopting this position have relied upon notions of international comity and analogies to domestic precedent. The leading authority is *Laker Airways*, which placed substantial weight on comity.[44] Other courts have agreed: "Comity dictates that foreign antisuit injunctions be issued sparingly and only in the rarest of cases."[45] *Laker Airways* and other lower courts have also relied upon domestic U.S. precedent, invoking the standards applicable to the issuance by federal courts of injunctions against *state* court proceedings. In particular, they have cited *Colorado River* for the proposition that parallel proceedings in state and federal courts should generally be permitted to proceed.[46]

4. Decisions Applying More Flexible Standards to Issuance of Antisuit Injunctions

Other lower courts have articulated less demanding standards governing antisuit injunctions. Both the Fifth and Ninth Circuits appear to "hold that a duplication of the parties and issues, alone, is generally sufficient to justify the issuance" of an antisuit injunction.[47] The Seventh Circuit also appears more readily to permit issuance of antisuit injunctions in international cases.[48] In one lower court's statement of this standard, an antisuit "injunction is in order when adjudication of the same issue in two separate actions will result in unnecessary delay, inconvenience, and expense to the parties and witnesses, and where separate adjudications could result in inconsistent rulings or a race to judgment."[49]

5. Selected Materials on Antisuit Injunctions

The following materials illustrate the differing approaches of U.S. courts to issuing antisuit injunctions in international cases. The decision in *Cargill, Inc. v. Hartford Accident & Indemnity Co.* applies one of the more flexible standards for issuing antisuit injunctions, while the decision in *China Trade & Development Corp. v. M.V. Choong Yong*, illustrates the trend towards more restrictive standards for such orders.

---

44. *Laker Airways*, 731 F.2d at 926-29.

45. *Gau Shan Co. v. Banker Trust Co.*, 956 F.2d 1349, 1354 (6th Cir. 1992).

46. *Laker Airways*, 731 F.2d at 926 (citing *Colorado River* and *Princess Lida of Thurn & Taxis v. Thompson*, 305 U.S. 456, 466 (1939)); *China Trade and Dev. Corp. v. M.V. Choong Yong*, 837 F.2d 33 (2d Cir. 1987) (citing *Colorado River* and *Donovan v. City of Dallas*, 377 U.S. 408, 412 (1964)). *See also Sea Containers Ltd. v. Stena AB*, 890 F.2d 1205, 1213 (D.C. Cir. 1989) (refusing to follow, in international case, the standards applicable to antisuit injunctions between "two Federal courts [that] entertained jurisdiction over claims arising out of essentially the same facts": "When a second action is brought in a foreign court, however, the possible waste of resources may be outweighed by another concern, international comity.").

47. *Gau Shan Co. v. Bankers Trust Co.*, 956 F.2d 1349, 1353 (6th Cir. 1992), citing *In re Unterweser Reederei GmbH*, 428 F.2d 888 (5th Cir. 1970), *aff'd en banc*, 446 F.2d 907 (5th Cir. 1971), *rev'd on other grounds*, *The Bremen v. Zapata Offshore Co.*, 407 U.S. 1 (1972); *Seattle Totems Hockey Club, Inc. v. National Hockey League*, 652 F.2d 852 (9th Cir. 1981). *See also Cargill, Inc. v. Hartford Accident & Indemnity Co.*, 531 F.Supp. 710, 715 (D. Minn. 1982).

48. *Allendale Mutual Ins. Co. v. Bull Data Systems, Inc.*, 10 F.3d 425 (7th Cir. 1993) (leaning towards Ninth Circuit's "laxer" test; also requiring "some indication that the issuance of an injunction really would throw a monkey wrench, however small, into the foreign relations of the United States").

49. *Cargill, Inc. v. Hartford Accident & Indemnity Co.*, 531 F.Supp. 710, 715 (D. Minn. 1982).

Finally, consider also the Conflict of Jurisdiction Model Act, which proposes more rigorous limits on parallel proceedings.

CARGILL, INC. v. HARTFORD ACCIDENT & INDEMNITY CO.

531 F.Supp. 710 (D. Minn. 1982)

MURPHY, DISTRICT JUDGE. Plaintiff Cargill, Incorporated ("Cargill") brings this action against defendants Hartford Accident and Indemnity Company ("Hartford") and Federal Insurance Company ("Federal") seeking recovery under two separate policies of insurance. Cargill alleges it is entitled to recovery under two separate policies of insurance. Cargill alleges it is entitled to recovery under both policies on the basis of losses incurred by Tradax Financial & Leasing, Ltd. ("TFL"), an English affiliate of Cargill, as a result of certain acts of Ronald Graham and Arthur Thompson, employees of TFL. Cargill seeks judgment of $5,000,000 under each of the policies. Jurisdiction is based on diversity of citizenship.

Federal has filed motions to ... dismiss the action on the ground of *forum non conveniens* ... [and/or] stay this action pending outcome of litigation against Cargill filed by Federal in England. ... Cargill has filed motions to (1) preliminarily enjoin Federal from proceeding with the English litigation against Cargill and (2) further enjoin Federal from instituting any other proceedings in any other court with regard to the issues which are the subject matter of the complaint.

The facts relevant for purposes of this motion appear to be as follows. At different times Cargill took out insurance policies with Hartford and Federal [against losses incurred through fraudulent or dishonest acts of Cargill employees.] ... Both policies were negotiated and agreed to by Cargill in Minnesota and were delivered to Cargill in Minnesota. Cargill alleges that TFL sustained losses due to employee dishonesty occurring primarily in England between 1973 and April, 1979, and has submitted claims to both Hartford and Federal. It appears that Cargill has a majority interest in TFL's stock. ... [Federal and Hartford denied liability on Cargill's policy and negotiations between the insurers and Cargill ensued. The negotiations were unsuccessful and] approximately five days before the contractual period to sue expired, the parties filed almost simultaneous lawsuits related to coverage under the Federal policy. Federal filed a declaratory judgment suit against Cargill and TFL in the High Court of Justice in London, England, on September 25, 1981. On the same day Cargill brought the action now before the court. There is evidence that Hartford is not subject to the jurisdiction of the English court.

In a ruling on a motion to dismiss for *forum non conveniens*, the court first must determine whether there is an alternative forum and, if so, whether the presumption in favor of plaintiff's choice of forum has been overcome by the private and public interest factors presented. In the situation before the court there exists another forum in which two of the parties here are present. However, since Hartford cannot be joined there, and it is important to Cargill to have a forum in which all parties can be joined... it could be argued that no adequate alternative forum exists. Whether these facts meet the test of those rare circumstances where the other forum is so inadequate as not to present an alternative need not be decided since an analysis of the private and public interest factors leads to the conclusion that the motion to dismiss must be denied. ...

Certain factors of private interest favor Federal, but not to the extent that Cargill's choice of forum should be disturbed. The relative ease of access to proof does not weigh heavily for either party. The contracts of insurance were negotiated and signed by Cargill in Minnesota and delivered here. Although Federal alleges that much documentary proof may remain in England, a great volume of Cargill's documents are located in the United States. It appears that Federal may not be able to produce TFL employees to testify before this court; however, at this stage it is unclear who will actually be called to testify. Moreover, English law provides a means similar to deposition for securing testimony. Federal has pointed to a large number of potential witnesses, many of whom reside in England, but has avoided stating to the court that it intends to rely on any particular testimony in presenting its case. It is not clear, in fact, whether Federal intends to base any substantial portion of its case on evidence of the events taking place in England. On the other hand, Cargill has designated six witnesses, five of whom reside in the United States. ...

There are a number of other factors indicating that the balance of convenience weighs in Cargill's favor. Cargill's American counsel has spent considerable time gaining familiarity with the case and could represent them here, but not in the English action. More importantly, it is only in this forum that Cargill's claims against both Hartford and Federal may be joined in one action. The claims against both companies are likely to have many of the same operative facts, including when Cargill discovered the alleged loss, and the coverage of each of the policies. It is clearly more convenient for Cargill to be able to present these facts once in this forum than both here and in England. Moreover, Cargill would face the risk of inconsistent results if it were required to present its claims against Federal in England and its claims against Hartford here. It is possible, for example, that the English court could find certain losses covered by Hartford and that Federal was not liable to the extent of Hartford's coverage. Such a decision would not be binding on Hartford because it is not subject to the jurisdiction of the English court; despite such a decision by the English court, the jury in this court could find Hartford not liable. The possibility of such an inconsistency would be highly prejudicial to Cargill.

The public interest factors do not balance in Federal's favor. Federal argues that because the acts of the employees at issue under its policy occurred in England, England has the closest relationship to the matter. As noted, however, Cargill, a Minnesota citizen, negotiated and agreed to the policy in Minnesota, and the policy was delivered to it here. The issues in this litigation deal with whether there is coverage under the respective insurance policies, and Minnesota has a very strong interest in the litigation. ...

It is not clear whether English law will apply to any issues in the case, [and] it has not been disputed that Minnesota law will apply to interpretation of the policies. At this stage it is unclear what issues Federal will actually raise or that English law would be used to define theft, for example. Judicial efficiency will be served by having the trial of this matter in this court where both defendant insurance companies can be joined since it appears that some of the proof in these matters will overlap. Discovery and trial of these issues can take place in this forum, rather than requiring two forums to litigate the same issues.

Cargill has filed a motion to preliminarily enjoin Federal from proceeding with the English action and to further enjoin Federal from instituting proceedings in any other court with regard to the issues which are the subject matter of the complaint in this action. A federal court may, in the exercise of its discretion, control its own proceedings by enjoining parties from bringing proceedings in other courts, including courts of foreign jurisdictions, although this power should be used sparingly. The threshold question is whether the parties are the same in both actions, the issues are the same, and resolution of the first action will be dispositive of the action to be enjoined. A foreign action should then be enjoined when it would (1) frustrate a policy of the forum issuing the injunction, (2) be vexatious or oppressive, (3) threaten the issuing court's in rem or quasi-in-rem jurisdiction, or (4) where the proceedings prejudice other equitable considerations. An injunction is in order when adjudication of the same issue in two separate actions will result in unnecessary delay, substantial inconvenience and expense to the parties and witnesses, and where separate adjudications could result in inconsistent rulings or a race to judgment.

The threshold considerations for enjoining Federal's English action have been met. Both Cargill and Federal are involved in that action, the issue in both is coverage under the policy, and disposition of this action will resolve the issue in that action. For the reasons stated in the discussion of *forum non conveniens*, the convenience of the parties, as well as the interest of judicial economy, weigh in favor of the issuance of the injunction. It would be vexatious to Cargill and a waste of judicial resources to require adjudication of Federal's liability in two separate forums. Separate adjudications could further prejudice Cargill by the risk of inconsistent results and a possible race to judgment. Accordingly, Federal should be enjoined from pursuing its English action.

CHINA TRADE AND DEVELOPMENT CORP. v. MV CHOONG YONG

837 F.2d 33 (2d Cir. 1987)

GEORGE C. PRATT, CIRCUIT JUDGE. Following oral argument this court reversed an order of the U.S. District Court for the Southern District of New York and vacated the injunction which had permanently enjoined Ssangyong Shipping Co., Ltd. ("Ssangyong") from proceeding in the courts of Korea with its action against China Trade & Development Corp., Chung Hua Trade & Development Corp. and Soybean Importers Joint Committee of the Republic of China (collectively, "China Trade").

The District Court had granted the injunction because it found that (1) the parties in the Korean action are the same as the parties in this action; (2) the issue of liability raised by Ssangyong in the Korean court is the same as the issue of liability raised here; (3) the Korean litigation would be vexatious to the plaintiffs in the United States action, which was commenced first; and (4) allowing the Korean litigation to proceed would result in a race to judgment. Because no important policy of the forum would be frustrated by allowing the Korean action to proceed, and because the Korean action poses no threat to the jurisdiction of the District Court, we conclude that the interests of comity are not overbalanced by equitable factors favoring an injunction, and we hold that the district court abused its discretion when it enjoined Ssangyong, a Korean corporation, from proceeding in the courts of Korea. ...

In 1984 China Trade sought to import 25,000 metric tons of soybeans into the Republic of China from the United States. Ssangyong, a Republic of Korea corporation, agreed to transport the soybeans on its ship the M.V. CHOONG YONG. The vessel ran aground, however, and as China Trade contends, the soybeans, contaminated by seawater, became virtually valueless. The litigation leading to this appeal began in 1985 when attorneys for China Trade attached the M.V. BOO YONG, another vessel owned by Ssangyong, which was then located in ... California. To release the vessel, the parties agreed that China Trade would lift the attachment and discontinue the California action and, in exchange, Ssangyong would provide security in the amount of $1,800,000, the approximate value of the attached vessel, and would appear in an action to be commenced by China Trade in the Southern District of New York and waive any right to dismissal of the new action on the ground of forum non conveniens.

China Trade then commenced this action in the Southern District seeking $7,500,000 in damages from Ssangyong for failure to deliver the soybeans. Both parties proceeded to prepare the case for trial through extensive discovery that has included both depositions and document production that required trips to Korea and to the Republic of China. Trial was scheduled to begin in September 1987. On April 22, 1987, while discovery was still progressing, Ssangyong's Korean attorneys filed a pleading in the District Court of Pusan, commencing an action, similar to our declaratory judgment action, which seeks confirmation that Ssangyong is not liable for China Trade's loss. Nearly two months later Ssangyong's New York counsel forwarded a copy of this pleading to counsel for China Trade. Immediately, and before taking any action in the district court of Pusan, China Trade moved by order to show cause in this action for an injunction against further prosecution of the Korean action.

To determine whether to enjoin the foreign litigation, the district court employed a test that has been adopted by some judges in the Southern District. In *American Home Assurance Corp. v. Insurance Corp. of Ireland, Ltd.*, 603 F.Supp. 636, 643 (S.D.N.Y. 1984), the court articulated two threshold requirements for such an injunction: (1) the parties must be the same in both matters, and (2) resolution of the case before the enjoining court must be dispositive of the action to be enjoined.

> When these threshold requirements are met, five factors are suggested in determining whether the forgoing action should be enjoined: (1) frustration of a policy in the enjoining forum; (2) the foreign action would be vexatious; (3) a threat to the issuing court's in rem or quasi in rem jurisdiction; (4) the proceedings in the other forum prejudice other equitable considerations; or (5) adjudication of the same issues in separate actions would result in delay, inconvenience, expense, inconsistency, or a race to judgment.

American Home Assurance, 603 F.Supp. at 643. Judge Motley found after a hearing that the two threshold requirements were met, since in both actions the parties and the issues of liability are the same. She then considered the additional five factors and found that the Korean litigation in this case would (1) be vexatious to the plaintiffs and (2) result in expense and a race to judgment. Considering these findings sufficient, the District Court permanently enjoined Ssangyong's prosecution of the Korean action. This appeal followed. ...

The power of federal courts to enjoin foreign suits by persons subject to their jurisdiction is well-established. The fact that the injunction operates only against the parties, and not directly against the foreign court, does not eliminate the need for due regard to principles of international comity, *Peck v. Jenness*, 48 U.S. 612, 625 (1849), because such an order effectively restricts the jurisdiction of the court of a foreign sovereign. Therefore, an anti-foreign-suit injunction should be "used sparingly," and should be granted "only with case and great restraint." *Canadian Filters (Harwich) v. Lear-Siegler*, 412 F.2d 577, 578 (1st Cir. 1969).

Concurrent jurisdiction in two courts does not necessarily result in a conflict. When two sovereigns have concurrent in personam jurisdiction one court will ordinarily not interfere with or try to restrain proceedings before the other. "[P]arallel proceedings on the same in personam claim should ordinarily be allowed to proceed simultaneously, at least until a judgment is reached in one which can be pled as res judicata in the other," *Laker*, 731 F.2d at 926-27, citing *Colorado River*, ... Since parallel proceedings are ordinarily tolerable, the initiation before a foreign court of a suit concerning the same parties and issues as a suit already pending in a U.S. court does not, without more, justify enjoining a party from proceeding in the foreign forum.

In general, we agree with the approach taken by Judge Motley. She began by inquiring (1) whether the parties to both suits are the same and (2) whether resolution of the case before the enjoining court would be dispositive of the enjoined action. She apparently found that both of these prerequisites were met here. While there is some question as to whether the Korean courts would recognize a judgment of the Southern District, it is not necessary to determine that question of Korean law because the injunction is deficient for another reason. Judge Motley found the necessary additional justification for this injunction in two of the five factors suggested in *American Home Assurance*: "vexatiousness" of the parallel proceeding to China Trade and a "race to judgment" causing additional expense. However, since these factors are likely to be present whenever parallel actions are proceeding concurrently, an antisuit injunction grounded on these additional factors alone would tend to undermine the policy that allows parallel proceedings to continue and disfavors anti-suit injunctions. Having due regard to the interest of comity, we think that in the circumstances of this case two of the other factors suggested in *American Home Assurance* take on much greater significance in determining whether Ssangyong should be enjoined from proceeding in its Korean action: (a) whether the foreign action threatens the jurisdiction of the enjoining forum, and (b) whether strong public policies of the enjoining forum are threatened by the foreign action.

A long-standing exception to the usual rule tolerating concurrent proceedings has been recognized for proceedings in rem or quasi in rem, because of the threat a second action poses to the first court's basis for jurisdiction. When a proceeding is in rem, and res judicata alone will not protect the jurisdiction of the first court, an antisuit injunction may be appropriate. Even in personam proceedings, if a foreign court is not merely proceeding in parallel but is attempting to carve out exclusive jurisdiction over the action, an injunction may also be necessary to protect the enjoining court's jurisdiction. In the *Laker* litigation, for example, when the English Court of Appeal enjoined Laker's litigation of its claims against British defendants in a U.S. court under U.S. law, the U.S. district court, in order to protect its own jurisdiction, enjoined other defendants in the *Laker* action from seeking similar injunctions from the English Court of Appeal. *Laker*, 731 F.2d at 917-21. In the present case, however, there does not appear to be any threat to the district court's jurisdiction. While the Korean court may determine the same liability issue as that before the Southern District, the Korean court has not attempted to enjoin the proceedings in New York. Neither the Korean court nor Ssangyong has sought to prevent the Southern District from exercising its jurisdiction over this case.

An antisuit injunction may also be appropriate when a party seeks to evade important policies of the forum by litigating before a foreign court. While an injunction may be appropriate when a party attempts to evade compliance with a statute of the forum that effectuates important public policies, an injunction is not appropriate merely to prevent a party from seeking "slight advantages in the substantive or procedural law to be applied in a foreign court," *Laker*, 731 F.2d at 931, n.73.

The possibility that a U.S. judgment might be unenforceable in Korea is no more than speculation about the race to judgment that may ensue whenever courts have concurrent jurisdiction. Moreover, we cannot determine at this point whether a judgment of the U.S. court in an amount exceeding the $1.8 million bond would be enforceable in Korea even if the Korean action were now enjoined. Should plaintiffs prevail, enforcement of any excess amount against Ssangyong in Korea may well require relitigation in the Korean courts of the issue of liability. In these circumstances, we are not persuaded that Ssangyong, the party seeking to litigate in the foreign tribunal, is attempting to evade any important policy of this forum.

The equitable factors relied upon by the District Court in granting the antisuit injunction are not sufficient to overcome the restraint and caution required by international comity. Because the Korean litigation poses no threat to the jurisdiction of the District Court or to any important public policy of this forum, we conclude that the District Court abused its discretion by issuing the injunction.

BRIGHT, SENIOR CIRCUIT JUDGE, DISSENTING. I dissent ... [The District Court found that:]

> [t]he defendant agreed to appear in this action in the Southern District of New York and post security in the amount of $1,800,000 in return for the release of the M.V. BOO YONG. Discovery for the case proceeded and was completed. Trial was scheduled by this court, without objection, for September 21, 1987. Ssangyong, however, some 2 1/2 years after [the accident and 1 1/2 years after] this action was begun, then proceeded to file a suit in Pusan Court of the Republic of Korea, naming the same parties to the action, as well as the same issues. Plaintiffs herein move to enjoin the defendant from proceeding with that action. The court finds as facts that the parties to the two actions are the same and that resolution of the action before this court would be dispositive of the Korean action. The court also finds that the Korean action would be vexatious to plaintiffs, and that the Korean action could potentially frustrate the proceedings before this court.

Those facts receive ample support from the record, and I accept them as true for the purposes of this appeal. ... It seems to me that in this day of exceedingly high costs of litigation, where no comity principles between nations are at stake in resolving a piece of commercial litigation, courts have an affirmative duty to prevent a litigant from hopping halfway around the world to a foreign court as a means of confusing, obfuscating and complicating litigation already pending for trial in a court in this country. This is especially true when that court has been processing the case for almost two years and has acquired personal jurisdiction over the parties and subject matter jurisdiction over the claim.

Notes on Cargill and China Trade

1. *Power to issue antisuit injunctions.* Neither *Cargill* nor *China Trade* betrayed any reservations about a U.S. court's *power* to enjoin a party from proceeding with an action in a foreign court: a U.S. court "has the power to enjoin a party over whom it has personal jurisdiction from pursuing litigation before a foreign tribunal." *Western Elec. Co. v. Milgo Elec. Corp.*, 450 F.Supp. 835, 837 (S.D. Fla. 1978).

Where does the power of a U.S. court to issue an antisuit injunction derive from? One of the few commentators to consider the issue has said: "[t]he theory upon which the courts act ... is that they have authority to control the persons within the territorial limits of the state, and, having jurisdiction of the parties, can render a decree that the parties are bound to respect and obey, even beyond the territorial limits of the state." Messner, *The Jurisdiction of a Court of Equity Over Persons to Compel the Doing of Acts Outside the Territorial Limits of the State*, 14 Minn. L. Rev. 494, 495-96 (1930). Is this persuasive? Is it self-evident that a U.S. court has the authority to order a foreign party, on foreign territory, to refrain from availing itself of avenues of justice provided by a foreign state?

2. **China Trade** — *stringent standards for issuing antisuit injunctions.* Consider the standards adopted by *China Trade* for the issuance of prejudgment antisuit injunctions. The court concluded that injunctions directed merely against duplicative, "vexatious" litigation are generally inconsistent with the rule permitting parallel proceedings in concurrent *in personam* actions: "Since parallel proceedings are ordinarily tolerable, the initiation before a foreign court of a suit concerning the same parties and issues as a suit already pending in a U.S. court does not, without more, justify enjoining a party from proceeding in the foreign forum." Under *China Trade*, antisuit injunctions are only appropriate to: (a) protect the issuing court's jurisdiction, or (b) prevent evasion of the forum's public policies. *See also Laker Airways*, 731 F.2d 909; *supra* pp. 476-77 for other lower court decisions narrowly limiting antisuit injunctions in international cases.

China Trade makes clear that the exceptions to the general rule against antisuit injunctions are narrow and do not permit injunctions to halt duplicative, wasteful litigation. Is the *China Trade* standard sensible? Consider the facts of *China Trade*. As Judge Bright's dissent notes, the case had been pending in U.S. courts for 2 years; the defendant had agreed to litigate in New York and had waived forum non conveniens defenses; discovery had been conducted and largely completed; the trial date scheduled with the parties' agreement was only months away; and the Korean lawsuit involved exactly the same issues as that in New York. The district judge, with a front-line perspective on the case, expressly found that the Korean action could be "vexatious." On these facts, does not justice cry out for resolving the dispute in the parties' chosen forum? If the *China Trade* standard forbids an antisuit injunction in these circumstances, is that standard not wrong?

What about the possibility, suggested by *China Trade*, that Korean courts would not recognize any U.S. judgment? Does that argue against the grant of an antitrust injunction? Suppose that the Korean actions rushes to judgment *before* the U.S. court's judgment. Must the Korean judgment be recognized?

3. *Rationale for stringent limits on antisuit injunctions.* What rationales would justify a rule permitting the result in *China Trade*?

(a) *Parallel proceedings.* Citing *Laker Airways, China Trade* held that concurrent jurisdiction was a frequent occurrence in contemporary international litigation, and that a "fundamental corollary to concurrent jurisdiction" is that "parallel proceedings on the same *in personam* claim should ordinarily be allowed to proceed simultaneously, at least until a judgment is reached in one which can be pled as res judicata in the other." Is this persuasive? Note that the same rationale is invoked to deny requests for *lis pendens* stays of U.S. proceedings in deference to foreign litigation. *See supra* p. 472. Does the fact that contemporary jurisdictional rules frequently permit concurrent jurisdiction compel the conclusion that courts are bound to allow parallel proceedings? Doesn't the argument cut the other way: because concurrent jurisdiction makes parallel proceedings so easy to start, courts should be vigilant in limiting the abuses of such proceedings? Recall the discussion above, demonstrating how the forum non conveniens doctrine developed to counterbalance the expansion of judicial jurisdiction. *See supra* p. 315.

(b) *International comity. China Trade* and other decisions have invoked "the need for due regard to principles of international comity" in explaining the standard for antisuit injunctions:

> Comity dictates that foreign antisuit injunctions be issued sparingly and only in the rarest of cases. The days of American hegemony over international economic affairs have long since passed. The United States cannot today impose its economic will on the rest of the world and expect meek compliance, if indeed it ever could. The modern era is one of world economic interdependence, and economic interdependence requires cooperation requires cooperation and comity between nations. ... Before taking [the] drastic step [of granting an antisuit injunction], this court must consider carefully the implications of such actions under principles of international comity.

Gau Shan Co. v. Bankers Trust Co., 956 F.2d 1349, 1354 (6th Cir. 1992); *Canadian Filters (Harwich) v. Lear-Siegler, Inc.*, 412 F.2d 577, 578 (1st Cir. 1969) ("[t]he issue is not one of jurisdiction, but one ... of comity"). Is this not patently silly? What do "American hegemony" and "world economic interdependence" have to do with a party's transparent effort to complicate and delay a case that is on the courthouse steps? Does economic interdependence mean that U.S. courts should forsake antisuit injunctions to protect the interests of U.S. litigants under U.S. law?

(c) *Domestic analogies.* Lower courts have also relied upon domestic U.S. precedent, involving the standards applicable to the issuance by federal courts of injunctions against state court proceedings. *See Laker Airways*, 731 F.2d at 926 (citing *Colorado River*); *China Trade*, 837 F.2d 33 (citing *Colorado River* and *Donovan v. City of Dallas*); *supra* pp. 482-83. In particular, they have cited *Colorado River*, which held that parallel proceedings in state and federal courts should generally be permitted to proceed. A similar trend exists in the *lis pendens* context. *See supra* pp. 462-63.

Why are the standards governing federal court injunctions against state court proceedings relevant to antisuit injunctions against foreign courts in the international context? Recall that state court proceedings are subject to Supreme Court review on federal constitutional and statutory grounds, that U.S. states share a largely homogeneous legal heritage, and that the full faith and credit clause requires recognition and enforcement of judgments among U.S. states. The same is not true in international cases. Is the analogy to federal-state antisuit disputes persuasive?

4. *Cargill — flexible standards for the issuance of antisuit injunction against "vexatious" or "oppressive" foreign proceedings.* Compare the standards for antisuit injunctions in *Cargill* to those in *China Trade*. Under *Cargill*, a party must satisfy two requirements to obtain an antisuit injunction: (a) there must be parallel foreign and U.S. proceedings involving the same parties and issues; and (b) the foreign proceeding must be vexatious, contrary to U.S. public policy, a threat to the U.S. court's jurisdiction, or otherwise inequitable.

5. *Meaning of "vexatious" or "oppressive" foreign proceedings.* What does the *Cargill* standard mean? There is no clear formula defining when a foreign proceeding is "vexatious" or "oppressive." The Supreme Court has remarked that an action is vexatious if it seeks to harass an opponent "by inflicting upon him expense or trouble not necessary to [one's] own right to pursue [one's] remedy." *Gulf Oil Corp. v. Gilbert*, 330 U.S. 501, 508 (1947). *See Paramount Pictures, Inc. v. Blumenthal*, 11 N.Y.S.2d 768 (App. Div. 1939) ("must be shown that [litigation was] instituted maliciously and without probable cause").

Cargill indicated that foreign proceedings would be vexatious if they involved unnecessary delay, substantial inconvenience, and potentially inconsistent rulings. Some other lower courts have taken the same approach. *E.g., Seattle Totem Hockey Club v. National Hockey League*, 652 F.2d 852 (9th Cir. 1981) ("Adjudicating this issue in two separate actions is likely to result in unnecessary delay and substantial inconvenience and expense to the parties and witnesses. Moreover, separate adjudications could result in inconsistent rulings or even a race to judgment."), *cert. denied*, 457 U.S. 1105 (1982); *In re Unterweser Reederei GmbH*, 428 F.2d 888 (5th Cir. 1970), *aff'd en banc*, 446 F.2d 907 (5th Cir. 1971), *rev'd on other grounds*, 407 U.S. 1 (1972).

Won't parallel proceedings almost *always* be less convenient than a single litigation, and therefore "vexatious" under the *Cargill* analysis? Note that *Cargill* relied heavily on forum non conveniens analysis in concluding that an English action would be vexatious. Did *Cargill* in effect hold that parallel proceedings will seldom be permitted and that U.S. courts should adjudicate the relative convenience of foreign and U.S. forums? If so, is this appropriate? How would *Cargill* have resolved *China Trade*? Conversely, how would *China Trade* have resolved *Cargill*?

6. *Cargill v. China Trade — what test should be applied for antisuit injunctions?* Compare the *China Trade* test for antisuit injunctions with that in *Cargill.* Which approach do you find wiser? Lower courts are divided in their use of the two approaches illustrated by *Cargill* and *China Trade*, with some decisions following each approach. *See supra* pp. 475-77. Is either approach adequate? Is there a middle ground that would be more desirable? Shouldn't, in fact, a rule be devised that would have permitted both of the two cases to be decided in the opposite ways — granting an antisuit injunction in *China Trade* and denying it in *Cargill*? Would it be wise to adopt a rule permitting an antisuit injunction to issued based on "vexatious" proceedings, but containing a requirement that extreme vexation (like that in *China Trade*) be demonstrated?

7. *Issuance of antisuit injunctions for protection of issuing court's jurisdiction. China Trade* held that one basis for issuing an antisuit injunction was to protect the issuing court's jurisdiction. This rule is typically invoked, as in *Laker Airways*, when a foreign court threatens to enjoin U.S. proceedings and the U.S. court issues an anti-antisuit injunction. *E.g., Owens-Illinois v. Webb*, 809 S.W.2d 899 (Tex. Ct. App. 1991) (issuing anti-antisuit injunction against antisuit injunction in Canada); *Mutual Service Casualty Ins. Co. v. Frit Industries, Inc.*, 805 F.Supp 919 (M.D. Ala. 1992). The exception for protecting U.S. courts' jurisdiction also arises when foreign proceedings undermine the integrity of U.S. proceedings. *E.g., Omnium Lyonnais D'Etancheite et Revetement Asphalte v. Dow Chem. Co.*, 441 F.Supp. 1385 (C.D. Cal. 1977)

(French proceeding enjoined because French plaintiff based its suit on evidence subject to U.S. confidentiality order). Why would an antisuit injunction in *China Trade* not have protected the jurisdiction of the district court — which had already devoted substantial effort to dealing with preliminary motions, overseeing discovery, and preparing for trial?

8. *Issuance of antisuit injunction to prevent frustration of U.S. public policy.* *China Trade* also held that an antisuit injunction could be issued to prevent the frustration of the forum's public policy. (Public policy exceptions are discussed in other contexts, *see supra* pp: 414-30 & *infra* pp. 624-31, 655-56, 974-86 & 1016-29.) Few antisuit injunction cases have relied on the public policy rationale. *E.g. United States v. Davis*, 767 F.2d 1025 (2d Cir. 1985) (enjoining U.S. national from pursuing Cayman Islands action to restrain production of evidence for use in U.S. proceeding.)

Does the public policy exception permit issuance of an antisuit injunction whenever a foreign court would apply foreign law, rather than U.S. law that is more favorable to the U.S. plaintiff? Note the remark in *China Trade* (quoting *Laker*) that an injunction "is not appropriate merely to prevent a party from seeking 'slight advantages in the substantive or procedural law to be applied in a foreign court.'" What if the advantages are not merely "slight"? Compare the *Piper Aircraft* rule that even significant changes in law are not entitled to "substantial" weight in forum non conveniens analysis. *See supra* pp. 316 & 351-56.

Suppose a U.S. libel plaintiff sues a U.S. publisher in a foreign court for damages sustained, principally in the United States, by virtue of misstatements that would not be actionable under the First Amendment. Would the foreign suit constitute an evasion of U.S. public policy? If so, would the public policy exception apply where a foreign court would apply significantly less favorable foreign substantive law to a contractual dispute arising in the United States? What if the libel plaintiff is not a U.S. national? What if the libel occurs principally abroad? Suppose that defendants in a U.S. antitrust action initiate parallel proceedings in a foreign forum seeking a declaration of no liability and favorable factual findings.

Suppose a U.S. and foreign company enter into a contract, out of which disputes arise. The foreign company sues the U.S. company abroad, where the foreign court will enforce contractual exculpatory provisions benefitting the foreign company. However, those provisions are contrary to U.S. public policy, and U.S. courts would not enforce them with respect to conduct in the United States. Would an antisuit injunction issue against the foreign action, in a case involving conduct in the United States? Note *China Trade's* emphasis on "the litigant's unconscionable evasion of the domestic laws," and its reliance on decisions where "the primary purpose of the foreign action is to avoid the regulatory effect of the domestic forum's statutes." *See also Sea Containers Ltd. v. Stena AB*, 890 F.2d 1208, 1214 (D.C. Cir. 1989) (litigant's decision to seek relief before "a foreign court with a lower standard for preliminary relief ... allows it to burden its adversary but it does not represent an 'evasion of forum law and policy' that justifies injunctive relief").

9. *Relevance of first filing of complaint.* Does *Cargill's* antisuit injunction analysis attach any weight to the identity of the forum where proceedings were first filed? Suppose the English proceedings had been filed several days (or months) before the U.S. proceedings. Does *China Trade* attach any importance to first filing? Should weight ever be attached to the situs of the parties' first filing? What advantages would a first-filed rule have? Is the following persuasive?

> No state is likely to permit the enforcement of its important public policies to rest upon the fortuities of winning the race to the courthouse. A 'first-filed' rule would also encourage preemptive resort to litigation.

Note, *Antisuit Injunctions and International Comity*, 71 Va. L. Rev. 1039, 1042 n.18 (1985). Note that even *Laker Airways v. Sabena*, 731 F.2d 909, 929 n.63 (D.C. Cir. 1984), which was one of the early decisions adopting stringent limits on antisuit injunctions, suggested a modified "first-filed" rule that would attach importance to first filing in cases involving lengthy delays between first and second filing.

10. *Relevance of changes in substantive law.* *Cargill* acknowledged that English law might apply to some issues in the case, and that English law might be more favorable to the U.S. defendants than U.S. law. Nonetheless, the court enjoined further proceedings in English courts. Although possible changes in substantive law are largely irrelevant in forum non conveniens analysis, *see Piper Aircraft Co. v. Reyno*, 454 U.S. 235 (1981), and *supra* pp. 316 & 351-56, should such changes be irrelevant in the antisuit injunction context? If not, what weight should they be given?

11. *Relevance of federal regulatory legislation.* Suppose a foreign court will not apply the U.S. antitrust laws to a dispute occurring in the United States and significantly affecting U.S. commerce. Does

this provide an adequate basis for issuing an antisuit injunction? *See Seattle Totems Hockey Club v. National Hockey League*, 652 F.2d 852 (9th Cir. 1981), *cert. denied*, 457 U.S. 1105 (1982) (enjoining foreign proceeding raising same issues as U.S. antitrust action); Hartley, *Comity and The Use of Antisuit Injunctions in International Litigation*, 35 Am. J. Comp. L. 487 (1987) (suggesting that refusal of foreign forum to apply issuing forum's law would provide basis for issuance of antisuit injunction). Recall that many lower courts have held that the forum non conveniens doctrine is not applicable in antitrust claims. *See supra* pp. 354-55.

What if the conduct in question occurred partly in the United States and partly abroad, and that the foreign forum will not apply U.S. law? What if, under U.S. choice of law rules, U.S. law would not apply to the claims?

12. *Relevance of nationality of the parties.* What role should nationality play in granting antisuit injunctions? Should a U.S. plaintiff be able to obtain an antisuit injunction more easily than a foreign plaintiff? Should a U.S. defendant be more readily subjected to an antisuit injunction than a foreign defendant? Consider the importance of nationality in the jurisdiction and forum non conveniens contexts. *See supra* pp. 95-101 & *infra* pp. 316-17 & 330-33.

Laker Airways considered these points in deciding whether to issue an anti-antisuit injunction against U.S. parties to prevent them from seeking antisuit injunctions in England against an English company. The court held that English courts had no special right to enjoin an English party from commencing U.S. proceedings: "Although a court has power to enjoin its nationals from suing in foreign jurisdictions, it does not follow that the United States courts must recognize an absolute right of the British government to regulate the remedies that the United States may wish to create for British nationals in the United States courts. United States courts must control the access to their forums. No foreign court can supersede the right and obligation of the United States courts to decide whether Congress has created a remedy for those injured by trade practices adversely affecting United States interests." 731 F.2d at 935-36. Is this persuasive? Why shouldn't a national of a country be subject to the orders issued by that country's courts, not to proceed with foreign litigation that violates the country's policies? Why shouldn't U.S. courts respect such orders?

In *China Trade*, suppose that the plaintiff had been a U.S. company (for example, a U.S. owner of the soybeans). Would this have been relevant to the court's refusal to enjoin the Korean proceeding?

13. *Relevance of foreign court's jurisdiction (or lack thereof).* Suppose that a parallel proceeding is litigated in a foreign court that lacks personal jurisdiction over the defendant (under U.S. and "international" standards). Should a U.S. court grant an antisuit injunction to prevent litigation abroad in a forum that could not "properly" exercise jurisdiction?

In *Midland Bank plc v. Laker Airways Ltd.* [1986] 1 All E.R. 526, the English Court of Appeal affirmed an English antisuit injunction against Laker Airways barring it from commencing U.S. litigation against Midland Bank, an English financial institution. Midland Bank sought the English antisuit injunction after Laker Airways had threatened to add the bank as a defendant in its U.S. antitrust action, based on Midland's alleged involvement in an airline conspiracy to drive Laker out of business. In granting Laker's request for an antisuit injunction, the English Court of Appeal relied on Midland's lack of any meaningful U.S. presence at the time of the conspiracy against Laker and on the fact that any allegedly unlawful activity by Midland occurred entirely in England. Given this, the court reasoned that the U.S. antitrust laws must be kept "within the territorial jurisdiction of the U.S. in accordance with accepted standards of international law," and that courts should respect the "general principle that 'everyone should be entitled to adjust his conduct to the law of the country in which he acts.'" *Compare Amchem Prods. Inc. v. Workers' Compensation Board*, 75 D.L.R.4th 1 (Can. S. Ct. 1990) (enjoining Texas class action in part because of "the tenuous jurisdiction of the Texas courts"). Is it appropriate for the courts of one nation to sit in judgment on a foreign court's exercise of jurisdiction? *Compare* the treatment of foreign jurisdiction in the enforcement of judgments context, *infra* pp. 968-74.

14. *Wisdom of considering "strength" of competing jurisdictional claims.* Should a U.S. court consider the strength of a foreign forum's jurisdictional claim in deciding whether a foreign proceeding is "vexatious" or "oppressive?" As described above, the reach of national judicial jurisdiction has expanded very substantially in the past century. *See supra* pp. 73-77. As a consequence, in many international cases, two or more states will enjoy concurrent jurisdiction over the same dispute. In such cases, why should courts treat both (or all) forums equally, following the *Laker Airways* "rule permitting parallel proceedings in concurrent in personam actions"? Instead, should courts consider the relative strengths of the competing

jurisdictional claims? Note, for example, that the *China Trade* dispute arose from a contract to transport soybeans from the United States to the Republic of China; there was no apparent connection to Korea, except that Ssangyong (the defendant in the U.S. action) was based there. What permitted Korean courts to assert personal jurisdiction over China Trade? Was that jurisdictional claim consistent with due process or international law limits? Even if China Trade was subject to Korean jurisdiction, what were the relative strengths of U.S. and Korean jurisdictional claims in relation to the parties' soybean dispute?

15. *Distinction between pre-judgment and post-judgment injunctions. Laker, Ingersoll,* and *China Trade* sharply distinguished between pre-judgment and post-judgment antisuit injunctions, setting forth a fairly liberal policy on enjoining foreign proceedings after a U.S. judgment has been reached, but generally denying injunctive relief before U.S. judgment: "The parallel proceeding rule applies only until one court reaches a judgment that may be pled as res judicata in the other."

Other lower courts have adopted the same rule. *See supra* pp. 472, 476-77 & 485. Is this consistent with the basic *Laker/China Trade* approach to antisuit injunctions? This approach is premised on the view that concurrent proceedings do not threaten either court's jurisdiction, and therefore should be permitted to proceed. *See supra* pp. 472 & 485. Is this correct? Imagine the following dialogue between the lawyer and chief executive of China Trade:

> Lawyer: "We did not succeed in enjoining the Korean action."
> Client: "Does that mean we must stop our U.S. suit?"
> Lawyer: "Oh no. The Korean suit does not affect the U.S. court's jurisdiction (and vice versa)."
> Client: "I see. So I don't need to worry about Ssangyong getting a favorable verdict from a friendly Korean judge. That wouldn't hurt my U.S. rights."
> Lawyer: "Well, not quite. You see, if the Korean suit finishes first, the U.S. court will probably stop the U.S. action and accept the Korean result."
> Client: I am confused. I thought you said that the Korean suit doesn't affect the U.S. court's jurisdiction."

How do you answer?

16. *Relevance of foreign court's willingness to recognize U.S. judgments.* As described above, the "parallel proceedings" rule rests on the assumption that a final judgment in one proceeding will be recognized in the second proceeding. Suppose that it is clear that a U.S. judgment will not actually be recognized in the foreign forum. Does this affect the appropriateness of the general presumption adopted in cases like *China Trade* against issuing antisuit injunctions against "vexatious" foreign proceedings? If so, how?

In assessing the distinction between pre- and post-judgment injunctions, note that some foreign courts refuse to recognize any U.S. judgments. Suppose that in *China Trade,* as the court suggests, the Korean courts will not recognize a U.S. judgment. Would that strengthen the case for an antisuit injunction? Two different lines of analysis are possible. First, the fact that foreign courts may not recognize U.S. judgments might argue for more liberal use of pre-judgment antisuit injunctions, to help ensure that the outcome of U.S. proceedings is not circumvented. Second, if U.S. judgments are not particularly likely to be recognized abroad, then why should the rendering of a U.S. judgment have such important consequences for antisuit injunctions? Put differently, if comity and respect for foreign regulatory authority preclude issuance of a pre-judgment antisuit injunction, don't these same concerns become even greater when a foreign court would invoke its public policy to deny enforcement to a U.S. judgment? Which of these analyses is more persuasive?

Japanese courts apparently refuse to enforce U.S. judgments that are inconsistent with subsequently-entered Japanese judgments. In *Marubeni-America Co. v. Kansai Iron Works,* Hanrei Tainuzu, No. 361, p. 127 (Osaka Dist. Ct. 1978), a U.S. employee of a U.S. company was injured by a power press manufactured by Kansai and sold in the United States by Marubeni. The employee sued Marubeni in U.S. courts, which sought indemnification from Kansai in the U.S. proceeding; eventually, both the employee and Marubeni obtained favorable U.S. judgments. One month after the U.S. judgments, however, Kansai obtained a judgment of non-liability from a Japanese court. When Marubeni sought to enforce its U.S. judgment in Japan it failed, on the grounds that "a foreign judgment that is inconsistent with a domestic judgment disturbs the order of our entire legal system" The Japanese court held that this was true "regardless of whether the [foreign action] was brought, held or finalized earlier" than the Japanese action.

Note that *China Trade* raised but did not pursue the possibility that Korean courts would not enforce a U.S. judgment. Shouldn't the court have sought to determine whether there were insuperable legal obstacles to enforcing the U.S. judgment in Korea? What if there were? Would that have changed the court's decision?

18. *Practical considerations.* Courts whose proceedings are the subject of an antisuit injunction may harbor resentment towards the issuing court and the litigant that requested the relief. *See Laker Airways v. Pan American World Airways*, 559 F.Supp. 1124, 1132 n.30, 1138 (D.D.C. 1983), *aff'd*, 731 F.2d 909 (D.C. Cir. 1984), where District Judge Greene declared "there is somewhat of an Alice-in-Wonderland flavor to the arguments made by defendants both in the British court and in this Court" and that the "proper remedy" for defendants "is not to assume the existence of a 'right' to go into the courts of a third country so as to circumvent American substantive and procedural law."

18. *Antisuit injunctions and* **Erie.** As noted above, federal law governs the issuance of antitrust injunctions in federal courts. *See supra* p. 476. Why is that? Are antisuit injunction issues in federal court governed by federal procedural law or by federal substantive common law? Recall the similar issues arising in the forum non conveniens and forum selection agreement contexts. *See supra* pp. 358-66 & 431-53. What law should govern the issuance of an antisuit injunctions in state court?

PART THREE:
LEGISLATIVE JURISDICTION AND CHOICE OF LAW

Courts adjudicating international civil disputes must decide what law governs the resolution of such disputes. This decision involves issues of (a) legislative jurisdiction; and (b) choice of law.

Legislative, or prescriptive, jurisdiction is the authority of a state to make its laws applicable to particular conduct, relationships, or status.[1] Put differently, legislative jurisdiction is the power of a state to prescribe substantive rules of conduct regulating private activities and other legal norms.

Restrictions on the legislative jurisdiction of U.S. courts can be imposed by either U.S. constitutional limitations or international law. The principal U.S. constitutional limitations in international matters are imposed by the foreign commerce clause and the due process clause of the U.S. Constitution.[2] International law also imposes limitations on the exercise of legislative jurisdiction, although these limits have seldom played a direct role in U.S. courts.[3]

Choice of law involves selection of the law of a particular state to govern a dispute, contract, tort, or issue that has connections to two or more states.[4] Unless a state possesses legislative jurisdiction over the issue in question, its law may not

---

1. *See Restatement (Third) Foreign Relations Law* §401 (1987) ("make its law applicable to the activities, relations, or status of persons, or the interests of persons in things, whether by legislation, by executive act or order, by administrative rule or regulation, or by determination of a court"); *Restatement (Second) Conflict of Laws* §9 & comment d (1971); Akehurst, *Jurisdiction in International Law*, 46 Brit. Y.B. Int'l L. 145, 179-212 (1978); Reese, *Legislative Jurisdiction*, 78 Colum. L. Rev. 1587 (1978).

2. *See infra* pp. 512-44.

3. *See infra* pp. 493-511.

4. *See Restatement (Second) Conflict of Laws* §2 & comment a (1971) ("Each state has rules to determine which law (its own local law or the local law of another state) shall be applied by it to determine the rights and liabilities of the parties resulting from an occurrence involving foreign elements."); *Restatement (Third) Foreign Relations Law* §101 comment c (1987).

properly be selected by choice of law analysis.[5] Even if a state can properly exercise legislative jurisdiction, it may choose not to do so: a state's substantive laws or choice of law rules may not call for application of its laws, even if they could properly be applied.

Choice of law issues are governed primarily by the choice of law rules of the forum state. Different states apply different choice of law rules and, in the United States, choice of law rules have evolved significantly over time. It is often said that the past four decades have witnessed an American "conflicts revolution."[6] This revolution has seen the displacement of traditional choice of law rules, based upon strict territorial principles, by more flexible analyses.

This Part examines U.S. rules governing both choice of law and legislative jurisdiction in international cases. Chapter 7 discusses restrictions on the legislative jurisdiction of U.S. courts, imposed both by the U.S. Constitution and international law. Chapter 8 examines choice of law rules used by U.S. courts. Chapter 9 discusses two specialized choice of law rules — the act of state doctrine and the foreign sovereign compulsion doctrine.

Issues of legislative jurisdiction and choice of law have substantial practical importance in international litigation. Different nations have profoundly different legal systems. The variations between different common law jurisdictions (*e.g.*, the United States, England, Canada, Australia) are often significant. These differences are slight, however, when compared with the divergences between common law and civil law, Islamic, or Asian legal systems.

The differences between U.S. substantive laws and the laws of other jurisdictions can often be particularly significant. Although basic U.S. rules of contract, agency, property, and the like are broadly similar to the rules prevailing in many foreign legal systems, other areas of the law are much different. U.S. approaches to issues of economic and market regulation, product liability, environmental matters, and tort law can be fundamentally different from the laws prevailing in foreign legal systems. Because of these differences, the same dispute can readily be resolved in dramatically different ways under different nations' laws. As a consequence, the outcome of choice of law analysis is often directly relevant to the outcome of the dispute.

---

5. *Restatement (Second) Conflict of Laws* §9, comment b (1971) ("At least two things are implied when the local law of a state is applied to create or affect local interests. The first is that the state has jurisdiction to apply its local law. The second may be either that the state is the state of the applicable law under choice-of-law principles or, when the applicability of a statute of the forum is the point in issue, that a proper construction of the statute leads to its application in the given case."); *Restatement (Third) Foreign Relations Law* §401(a) & comment (b) (1987).

6. *See infra* pp. 631-32.

7/Legislative Jurisdiction[1]

As described above, "legislative" or "prescriptive" jurisdiction involves the authority of a state to make its substantive laws applicable to conduct, relationships, or status. There are two principal constraints on the power of a U.S. legislature to enact laws applicable to international conduct, relationships, or status. First, international law has long been understood as restricting assertions of legislative jurisdiction by states, although the effects of such restrictions in U.S. and other national courts can be complex. Second, the U.S. Constitution limits the legislative jurisdiction of both Congress and state legislatures. This Chapter explores both sets of limits.

A. International Law Limits on Legislative Jurisdiction

This section examines historic and contemporary views of international law limits on legislative jurisdiction. It does not consider how those limits apply in U.S. courts, or their relationship to U.S. law. These subjects are examined in subsequent sections of this Chapter.

1. Introduction and Historical Background

During the 19th century, American courts, commentators, and other authorities understood international law as imposing strict territorial limits on national assertions of legislative jurisdiction. Here, as in other contexts,[2] Joseph Story's *Commentaries on the Conflict of Laws* dominated American thinking.

As recounted in greater detail elsewhere, Story's *Commentaries* built upon the work of Continental European jurists, particularly in the Netherlands and France,

---

1. Commentary on legislative jurisdiction includes, *e.g.*, Akehurst, *Jurisdiction in International Law*, 46 Brit. Y.B. Int'l L. 145 (1972); Born, *A Reappraisal of the Extraterritorial Reach of U.S. Law*, 24 Law & Pol'y Int'l Bus. 1 (1992); Gerber, *Beyond Balancing: International Law Restraints on the Reach of National Laws*, 10 Yale J. Int'l L. 185 (1984); Lowenfeld, *Public Law in the International Arena: Conflict of Laws, International Law, and Some Suggestions for Their Interaction*, 163 Recueil des Cours 311 (1979); Mann, *The Doctrine of Jurisdiction in International Law*, 111 Recueil des Cours 1 (1964); Mann, *The Doctrine of International Jurisdiction Revisited After Twenty Years*, 1986 Recueil des Cours 9 (1984); Reese, *Legislative Jurisdiction*, 78 Colum. L. Rev. 1587 (1978).

2. *See supra* pp. 70-73 and *infra* pp. 546-50.

who had argued that international law rested on principles of territorial sovereignty.[3] These commentators emphasized the generally exclusive jurisdiction of a state over events, persons, and property within its territory. Story relied in particular on Ulrich Huber, a seventeenth-century Dutch academic.[4] Huber is best known for his classic work, *De Conflictu Legum*, which articulated three basic principles of international law:

(1) Every state's laws apply within the state's territory, but not beyond.

(2) All persons within a state are subjects of the state.

(3) "Comity" calls on states to recognize and enforce rights created by other states, provided that such recognition does not prejudice the state or its subjects.[5]

Relying on Huber and other authorities, Joseph Story stated several "general maxims of international jurisprudence,"[6] which imposed territorial limits on national sovereignty.

Story began with the statement that "every nation possesses an exclusive sovereignty and jurisdiction within its own territory."[7] Second, he developed the corollary that nations could properly exercise legislative jurisdiction only within their own territory: "no state or nation can, by its laws, directly affect, or bind property out of its own territory, or bind persons not resident therein ... for it would be wholly incompatible with the equality and exclusiveness of the sovereignty of all nations, that any one nation should be at liberty to regulate either persons or things not within its own territory."[8]

Story's view of international law was highly influential in 19th century America. Other commentators concurred with his territorial vision of legislative jurisdiction.[9]

---

3. See Davies, *The Influence of Huber's De Conflictu Legum on English Private International Law*, 18 Brit. Y. B. Int'l L. 49 (1937); Nussbaum, *Rise and Decline of the Law-of-Nations Doctrine in the Conflict of Laws*, 42 Colum. L. Rev. 189 (1942); Lorenzen, *Territoriality, Public Policy and the Conflict of Laws*, 33 Yale L.J. 736 (1924); Yntema, *The Comity Doctrine*, 65 Mich. L. Rev. 9, 16-28 (1966).

4. See supra pp. 70-72; Lorenzen, *Huber's De Conflictu Legum*, in *Selected Articles on the Conflict of Laws* 136 (1947).

5. See Lorenzen, *Huber's De Conflictu Legum*, in *Selected Articles on the Conflict of Laws* 136 (1947). Of Huber's *De Conflictu Legum* it has been said: "In the whole history of law there are probably no five pages which have been so often quoted, and possibly so much read." F. Harrison, *On Jurisprudence and the Conflict of Laws* 116 (1919).

6. J. Story, *Commentaries on the Conflict of Laws*, 19 & Heading to Chapter II (2d ed. 1841).

7. J. Story, *Commentaries on the Conflict of Laws* 19, 21-22 (2d ed. 1841); Mann, *The Doctrine of Jurisdiction in International Law*, 111 Recueil des Cours 1, 33 (1964) ("Although Story's maxims, if properly understood, do have a bearing upon private international law no less than on law in general, they express principles of public international law").

8. J. Story, *Commentaries on the Conflict of Laws* 19, 21-22 (2d ed. 1841).

9. E.g., H. Wheaton, *Elements of International Law* §§77, 111-14, 134-51 (1855) ("Every independent State is entitled to the inclusive power of legislation, in respect to the personal rights and civil state and conditions of its citizens and in respect to all real and personal property situated within its territory, whether belonging to citizens or aliens."); J. Moore, *A Digest of International Law* 236 (1906) ("There is no principle better settled than that the penal laws of a country have no extraterritorial force."); D. Gardner, *Institutes of International Law* 100-01 (1860).

U.S. courts also agreed. *The Apollon*,[10] decided in 1824, illustrates prevailing U.S. judicial views of international law limits on legislative jurisdiction. The case required an interpretation of federal customs statutes to determine whether they extended to foreign vessels outside U.S. waters. Justice Story wrote that "[t]he laws of no nation can justly extend beyond its own territory, except so far as regards its own citizens. They can have no force to control the sovereignty or rights of any other nation, within its jurisdiction."[11] He also observed that the extraterritorial assertion of U.S. jurisdiction would be "at variance with the independence and sovereignty of foreign nations," and that such jurisdictional claims had "never yet been acknowledged by other nations, and would be resisted by none with more pertinacity than by the Americans."[12]

Relying on this territoriality principle, derived from what Story called the "law of nations," the Court invoked a presumption of territoriality: "however general and comprehensive the phrases used in our municipal laws may be, *they must always be restricted in construction, to places and persons, upon whom the legislature have authority and jurisdiction.*"[13] Story declined to interpret federal law as authorizing U.S. revenue authorities to seize vessels located in foreign water, concluding: "It would be monstrous to suppose, that our revenue officers were authorized to enter into foreign ports and territories, for the purpose of seizing vessels which had offended against our laws. It cannot be presumed, that Congress would voluntarily justify such a clear violation of the laws of nations."[14] Other early U.S. decisions took the same territorial view of international law.[15]

As Joseph Story's opinion in *The Apollon* suggested, the 19th century American understanding of international limits on legislative jurisdiction was related to the United States' resistance to efforts by other nations — particularly Great Britain and other European powers — to apply their criminal laws extraterritorially to conduct occurring on U.S. territory or vessels.[16] As early as 1793, Secretary of State Thomas Jefferson invoked principles of territorial sovereignty and the equality of states when resisting a claim by France of jurisdiction over vessels in U.S. waters:

---

10. 22 U.S. 362 (1824).

11. 22 U.S. at 370.

12. 22 U.S. at 370.

13. 22 U.S. at 370 (emphasis added).

14. 22 U.S. at 370. Similarly, in *United States v. Davis*, 25 Fed. Cas. 786 (C.C.D. Mass. 1837), Story (sitting as a Circuit Judge) concluded that federal criminal legislation did not apply to an American seaman who fired a shot from a U.S. vessel, anchored in non-U.S. waters, which struck and killed a man aboard a non-U.S. vessel. According to Story, "although the gun was fired from the U.S. Ship Rose, the shot took effect and the death happened on board of the Schooner; and the act was, in contemplation of law, done where the shot took effect." 25 Fed. Cas. at 787. "We decide the case wholly on the ground, that the Schooner was a foreign vessel, belonging to foreigners, and at the time under the acknowledged jurisdiction of a foreign government."

15. *E.g., Rose v. Himely*, 8 U.S. 241, 279 (1807); *Schooner Exchange v. McFaddon*, 11 U.S. 116, 135-36 (1812); *United States v. Palmer*, 16 U.S. 610, 631 (1818); *American Banana Co. v. United Fruit Co.*, 213 U.S. 347, 355 (1909); *United States v. Bowman*, 260 U.S. 93, 97-8 (1922).

16. *See* Dumbauld, *John Marshall and the Law of Nations*, 104 U. Pa. L. Rev. 38, 38-44 (1955).

Jeffers Every nation has, of natural right, entirely and exclusively, all the jurisdiction which may be rightfully exercised in the territory it occupies. If it cedes any portion of that jurisdiction to judges appointed by another nation, the limits of their power must depend on the instrument of cession.[17]

Similarly, in the *Cutting Case*, the United States vigorously protested through diplomatic channels against a Mexican judicial proceeding that appeared to apply Mexican libel law to newspaper articles published in El Paso, Texas.[18] Among other things, the United States urged that:

Cutting Case *Mexico*

> [t]he assumption of the Mexican tribunal, under the laws of Mexico, to punish a citizen of the United States for an offense wholly committed and consummated in his own country against its laws was an invasion of the independence of this Government. ... There is no principle better settled than that the penal laws of a country have no extraterritorial force. Each state may, it is true, provide for the punishment of its own citizens for acts committed by them outside of its territory. ... *To say, however, that the penal laws of a country can bind foreigners and regulate their conduct, either in their own or in any other foreign country, is to assert a jurisdiction over such countries and impair their independence.* ...[19]

Successive U.S. governments took similar positions on other occasions in the 19th century.[20]

The 19th century American view that international law imposed strict territorial limits on legislative jurisdiction paralleled similar restrictions on judicial jurisdiction.

---

17. American State Papers, Foreign Relations, I, pages 147-48, 167, 169 (Letter from Mr. Jefferson, Secretary of State, to Mr. Morris, Minister to France, dated August 16, 1793).

18. J. Moore, *Report on Extraterritorial Crime and the Cutting Case*, (1887), 1887 U.S. Foreign Relations 757. *See also* 1886 U.S. Foreign Relations viii (Annual Message to Congress by President Cleveland).

19. 1887 U.S. Foreign Relations 751 (emphasis added).

20. Between 1873 and 1875, when British courts entertained civil disputes arising on the high seas between sailors on U.S. vessels, the U.S. Department of State protested, on the grounds that Britain's extraterritorial assertions of both judicial and legislative jurisdiction violated "rules of comity between nations and the principles of international law." Letters from Secretary of State Fish to General Schenck, dated Nov. 8, 1873 and March 12, 1875, *reprinted in*, Foreign Relations of the United States 490 (1874) and *id.* 592, 633 (1875). *See also* Letter from Secretary of State Calhoun to Mr. Everett, dated August 7, 1844, *excerpted in*, II J. Moore, *A Digest of International Law* 225 (1906) ("Great Britain can not by her laws make an act committed within the jurisdiction of the United States criminal within her territories, however immoral of itself, and *vice versa.* The proposition is too clear to require illustration or to be contested."); Letter from Secretary of State Calhoun to Mr. Everett, dated Sept. 25, 1844, *excerpted in*, II J. Moore, *A Digest of International Law* 225 (1906) ("Standing on this well-established and unquestioned principle, we can not permit Great Britain or any other nation, be its object or motive what it may, to infringe our sovereignty and independence by extending its criminal jurisdiction to acts committed within the United States ..."); Letter from Secretary to State Cass to Mr. Dallas, dated February 23, 1859, *excerpted in*, II J. Moore, *A Digest of International Law* 226 (1906) ("By the law of nations every independent state possesses an exclusive right of police over all persons within its jurisdiction ..."). *See also Jacob Idler v. Venezuela* (1885), *reprinted in*, J. Moore, *International Arbitrations* 3491, 3511-12 (1898); *Island of Palmas Case (Netherlands v. United States)*, 2 U.S. Rep. of Int'l Arb. Awards 829, 839 (1928).

As discussed above, Story's *Commentaries* also viewed international law as imposing strict territorial limits on judicial jurisdiction.[21] Similarly, U.S. decisions like *Rose v. Himely* and *Pennoyer v. Neff* looked to international law as the basis for formulating territorial limitations on the judicial jurisdiction of U.S. courts.[22] International law principles of territorial sovereignty and sovereign equality also provided the basis for 19th century American treatment of foreign sovereign immunity.[23]

Even in the 19th century, however, the territoriality principle was never quite as absolute as the foregoing might suggest. There was general acknowledgment of "nationality" as a jurisdictional base, both in U.S. judicial opinions[24] and otherwise.[25] Nonetheless, there were very few actual assertions of legislative jurisdiction by the United States based on nationality during the 19th century.[26] A few early American state court decisions also embraced very limited versions of what would come to be known as the "effects doctrine," permitting states to exercise legislative jurisdiction over acts committed outside a state but causing effects within it, but such decisions appear to have been rare.[27]

2. Contemporary International Law Limits on Legislative Jurisdiction: The "Effects Test" and Erosion of Territorial Limits

During the early decades of this century, the United States and other states gradually began to depart from the view that international law imposed strict territorial limits on national assertions of legislative jurisdiction. They increasingly exercised

---

21. J. Story, *Commentaries on the Conflicts of Laws* §449-50 (2d ed. 1841). Story wrote:

"Considered in an international point of view, jurisdiction, to be rightfully exercised, must be founded either upon the person being within the territory or the thing being within the territory; for otherwise there can be no sovereignty exerted. ... [N]o sovereignty can extend its process beyond its own territorial limits to subject either persons or property to its judicial decisions."

22. *See supra* pp. 72-73.

23. *See supra* pp. 199-201; *Schooner Exchange v. McFaddon*, 11 U.S. 116 (1812).

24. *E.g., The Apollon*, 22 U.S. 362, 370-71 (1824) ("The laws of no nation can justly extend beyond its own territory, *except so far as regards its own citizens*"); *Rose v. Himely*, 8 U.S. 241, 279 (1807).

25. J. Story, *Commentaries on the Conflict of Laws* 21-22 (2d ed. 1841).

26. Harvard Research in International Law, *The Law of Nationality*, 23 Am. J. Int'l L. Supp. 11, 80-82 (1929); J. Moore, *Report on Extraterritorial Crime and the Cutting Case*, (1887), *excerpted in*, II J. Moore, *A Digest of International Law* 255 (1906); *Restatement (Third) Foreign Relations Law* §402 Reporters' Note 1 (1987).

27. *Commonwealth v. Smith*, 11 Allen 243; *Adams v. The People*, Comstock's Rep. (N.Y.) 173, 179; *The People v. Rathbun*, 21 Wend. 509 (N.Y.); *Barkhamsted v. Parsons*, 3 Conn. 1; *State v. Grady*, 34 Conn. 118. *But see People v. Merrill*, 2 Parker's Crim. Rep. 590 (N.Y.) ("It cannot be pretended or assumed that a State has jurisdiction over crimes committed beyond its territorial limits"; declining jurisdiction over non-New York resident for luring black man from New York and selling him as a slave outside New York in violation of New York law). In general, however, even those courts that applied the effects doctrine did so in a fairly narrow category of cases. As John Bassett Moore concluded in 1887, "in no case has an English or an American court assumed jurisdiction, even under statutes couched in the most general language, to try and sentence a foreigner for acts done by him abroad, unless they were brought, either by an immediate effect, or by direct and continuance [sic] causal relationship, within the territorial jurisdiction of the court." J. Moore, *Report on Extraterritorial Crime* (1887), *excerpted in*, II J. Moore, *A Digest of International Law* 255 (1906).

legislative jurisdiction based on the so-called "effects test," the nationality doctrine, and other bases.[28] This trend paralleled developments in other contexts. As discussed elsewhere, *Pennoyer*'s territorial limits on judicial jurisdiction gave way to more flexible rules, while the absolute theory of sovereign immunity was replaced by the restrictive theory during this same period.[29]

Near the turn of the century, John Bassett Moore, a leading U.S. commentator, authored a classic work — a *Report on Extraterritorial Crime* — which predicted that the effects doctrine would enjoy growing importance in the future.[30] In his words, "the methods which modern invention has furnished for the performance of criminal acts ... has made this principle one of constantly growing importance and increasing frequency of application."[31]

"Modern invention" also bred modern regulatory legislation, including antitrust, securities, shipping, employment, and other laws. The application of these statutes to international activities led to further erosion of territorial limits on legislative jurisdiction. In the antitrust field, the so-called "effects doctrine" was frequently invoked by U.S. regulatory authorities in the early 20th century to justify the extraterritorial application of the Sherman Act.[32] Likewise, various U.S. criminal laws were applied to conduct abroad that had U.S. effects.[33] Congress and other legislatures also began to enact regulatory statutes expressly applicable to foreign conduct by U.S. nationals, such as federal income tax legislation,[34] the Trading With the Enemy Act,[35] and the Walsh Act.[36]

Particularly significant to the development of international law was the 1927 decision of the Permanent Court of International Justice in *The S.S. Lotus (France v. Turkey)*.[37] The PCIJ held in *The Lotus* that international law did not forbid Turkey from applying its criminal laws to a French officer's actions on board a French vessel that had collided on the high seas with a Turkish vessel. Several sailors on the Turkish vessel died in the accident and criminal charges were brought against the French officer in Turkish court; France protested that Turkey could not properly exercise legislative jurisdiction, and the dispute was referred to the PCIJ.

---

28. *See infra* pp. 550-76 & 576-607.

29. *See supra* pp. 70-73 & pp. 199-201.

30. J. Moore, *Report on Extraterritorial Crime and the Cutting Case* (1887), *reprinted in*, II J. Moore, *A Digest of International Law* 244 (1906).

31. *Id.*

32. *United States v. Franz-Rintelen*, (S.D.N.Y. 1915); *United States v. Franz-Bopp*, (N.D. Cal. 1915); *United States v. Pacific and Arctic Railway and Navigation Co.*, 228 U.S. 87 (1913); *United States v. Aluminum Co. of America*, E.Q. 159 (W.D. Tenn. 1912).

33. *E.g., Ford v. United States*, 273 U.S. 593 (1927).

34. Internal Revenue Code §1 (imposing federal income tax on "all citizens of the United States, wherever resident"); *Cook v. Tait*, 265 U.S. 47 (1924).

35. 40 Stat. 415 (1917).

36. 28 U.S.C. §1783. The Walsh Act obliged U.S. nationals residing abroad to return to the United States to provide evidence in certain circumstances. *Blackmer v. United States*, 284 U.S. 421 (1932), upheld the Act against constitutional challenge. *See supra* pp. 95-100.

37. P.C.I.J., Ser. A, No. 10 (1927).

The PCIJ held that Turkey was not barred from exercising legislative jurisdiction over the French officer's conduct. The Court first rejected the argument that international law generally forbid the extraterritorial application of national laws.[38] According to the Court, national regulatory efforts are presumptively valid and states claiming that such efforts violate international law have the burden of persuasion:[39]

> Far from laying down a general prohibition to the effect that states may not extend the application of their laws and the jurisdiction of their courts to persons, property and acts outside their territory, [international law] leaves them in this respect a wide measure of discretion which is only limited in certain cases by prohibitive rules; as regards other cases every state remains free to adopt the principles which it regards as best and most suitable. ...
> The territoriality of criminal law, therefore, is not an absolute principle of international law and by no means coincides with territorial sovereignty.[40]

The PCIJ also rejected the argument that international law required states "only to have regard to the place where the author of the offense happens to be at the time of the offense."[41] On the contrary, "the courts of many countries, even of countries which have given their criminal legislation a strictly territorial character, interpret criminal law in the sense that offenses, the authors of which at the moment of commission are in the territory of another state, are nevertheless to be regarded as having been committed in the national territory, if one of the constituent elements of the offense, and more especially its effects, have taken place there."[42] The Court had little difficulty concluding that, under this standard, the defendant's negligence had sufficient effects on the Turkish vessel to sustain Turkish jurisdiction.

The *Lotus* decision aroused considerable controversy, and a variety of interpretations of the decision have been offered.[43] It is clear, however, that the PCIJ's opin-

---

38. P.C.I.J., Ser. A, No. 10, at 19 (1927).

39. *Accord* Akehurst, *Jurisdiction in International Law*, 46 Brit. Y.B. Int'l L. 145, 167 (1972); Mann, *The Doctrine of Jurisdiction in International Law*, 111 Recueil des Cours 1, 35 (1964); Berge, *The Case of the S.S. Lotus*, 26 Mich. L. Rev. 361, 377 (1928).

40. P.C.I.J., Ser. A, No. 10, at 19 (1927).

41. P.C.I.J., Ser. A, No. 10, at 23 (1927).

42. P.C.I.J., Ser. A, No. 10, at 23 (1927).

43. *E.g.*, Mann, *The Doctrine of Jurisdiction in International Law*, 111 Recueil des Cours 1, 35 (1964) (suggesting narrow reading of PCIJ's "obiter dictum," but concluding that even "such an approach would considerably undermine the Huber-Storyan canons"); A. Neale & M. Stephens, *International Business and National Jurisdiction* 19-20 (1988) (PCIJ only wished to "draw attention to the difficulty, even impossibility of specifying ex ante the precise extent to which the exercise of some sort of extraterritorial jurisdiction might be justified in particular cases"); Jennings, *Extraterritorial Jurisdiction and the U.S. Antitrust Laws*, [1957] Brit. Y.B. Int'l L. 152 (PCIJ shifts burden of proving "an ascertained prohibitive rule of international law", but international law forbids use of effects doctrine in criminal context unless a "constituent effect" is involved); Harvard Research in International Law, *Jurisdiction With Respect to Crime*, 29 Am. J. Int'l L. 435, 501 (1935) ("The decision in the *S.S. Lotus* clearly supports the conclusion that no principle of international law forbids the localization of an offense, consisting of unintended injury caused through negligence, at the place where the negligence takes effect. This conclusion is in harmony with tendencies clearly manifested in modern legislation.").

ion reflects a significant evolution in international law. The PCIJ rejected any strict territorial limit on national legislative jurisdiction and instead recognized an effects doctrine, or "objective territoriality" principle, of some (although disputed) breadth.

The *Lotus* decision's rejection of notions of strict territoriality was rapidly adopted elsewhere. In 1934, the *Restatement (First) Conflict of Laws* was released, adopting the territorial approach to choice of law problems championed by its Reporter, Professor Joseph Beale.[44] Nevertheless, the *First Restatement* contained provisions on legislative jurisdiction which were neither strictly territorial nor as rigid as traditional 19th century views. Section 55 of the Restatement stated the traditional territorial view of national jurisdiction: "A state has jurisdiction over all acts done or events occurring within the territory of a state." In addition, however, §65 expressly provided for an "effects doctrine": "If consequences of an act done in one state occur in another state, each state in which any event in the series of act and consequences occurs may exercise legislative jurisdiction," while §63 recognized the nationality principle.

Similarly, in 1935, the classic Harvard Research in International Law study on Jurisdiction With Respect to Crime was published. The study recognized a variety of significant exceptions to a principle of strict territoriality — including the nationality principle[45] and an effects test.[46] More generally, academic commentators began to recognize the effects doctrine and other extraterritorial jurisdictional bases.[47]

Twentieth century American courts also began to apply what amounted to an "effects doctrine." In 1911, Justice Holmes reasoned in *Strassheim v. Daily*,[48] a domestic criminal case, that "the usage of the civilized world would warrant Michigan in punishing [the defendant], although he never had set foot in the state until after the fraud was complete. Acts done outside the jurisdiction, but intended to produce and producing detrimental effects within it, justify a state in punishing the cause of the harm as if he had been present at the effect, if the state should succeed in getting him within its power." Other U.S. courts followed suit, with increasing frequency, as the 20th century progressed.[49]

---

44. *See infra* pp. 616-17.

45. 29 Am. J. Int'l L. Supp. 435, 519-39 (1935) ("A State has jurisdiction with respect to any crime committed outside its territory, (a) By a natural person who was a national of that State when the crime was committed or who is a national of that State when prosecuted or punished; or (b) By a corporation or other juristic person which had the national character of that State when the crime was committed.").

46. 29 Am. J. Int'l L. Supp. 435, 480-508 (1935). Article 3 of the draft Convention provided: "A State has jurisdiction with respect to any crime committed in whole or in part within its territory. This jurisdiction extends to (a) Any participation outside its territory in a crime committed in whole or in part within its territory; and (b) Any attempt outside its territory to commit a crime in whole or in part within its territory." *Id.* at 480. The commentary to Article 3 made clear that it adopted an effects test. *Id.* at 500-03.

47. *E.g.*, C. Hyde, *International Law* 805 (1945); L. Oppenheim, *International Law* 331-34 (7th ed. 1948) (strict territoriality "is not a view which, consistently with the practice of States and with common sense, can be rigidly adopted in all cases").

48. 221 U.S. 280, 284-85 (1911).

49. *E.g.*, *Ford v. United States*, 273 U.S. 593, 620-21 (1927); *Lamar v. United States*, 240 U.S. 60 (1916); *infra* pp. 550-76 & 576-607.

More recently, the United States and other countries have adopted increasingly expansive views of national legislative jurisdiction under international law.[50] Following 1945, the United States was often particularly robust in applying its laws extraterritorially, and took a commensurately broad view of international law. These views are reflected in the *Restatement (Second) Foreign Relations Law* and the *Restatement (Third) Foreign Relations Law*, excerpted and discussed below.[51] These assertions of U.S. legislative jurisdiction were not universally accepted and often aroused diplomatic protests and legal objections from foreign states, which are also examined below.[52]

3. Selected Materials Concerning Evolution of International Law Limits on Legislative Jurisdiction

Excerpted below are materials that illustrate the evolution of U.S. views regarding international law limitations on legislative jurisdiction. The materials begin with the strict territorial doctrine of Joseph Story's *Commentaries on the Conflict of Laws*. Next, consider the *Restatement (First) of Conflict of Laws*, published in 1934. Finally, examine the successive formulations of increasingly expansive views of legislative jurisdiction reflected in the *Restatement (Second) Foreign Relations Law* (1965), the *Restatement (Second) Conflict of Laws* (1971), and the *Restatement (Third) Foreign Relations Law* (1987).

J. STORY, COMMENTARIES ON THE CONFLICT OF LAWS
§§18, 20 & 23 (2d ed. 1841)

§18. The first and most general maxim or proposition is that ... every nation possesses an exclusive sovereignty and jurisdiction within its own territory. The direct consequence of this rule is, that the laws of every state affect, and bind directly all property, whether real or personal, within its territory; and all persons, who are resident within it, whether natural born subjects, or aliens; and also all contracts made, and acts done within it. A state may, therefore, regulate the manner and circumstances, under which property, whether real, or personal, or in action, within it, shall be held, transmitted, bequeathed, transferred, or enforced; the condition, capacity, and state, of all persons within it; the validity of contracts, and other acts, done within it; the resulting rights and duties growing out of these contracts and acts; and the remedies, and modes of administering justice ....

§20. Another maxim, or proposition, is, that no state or nation can, by its laws, directly affect, or bind property out of its own territory, or bind persons not resident therein, whether they are natural subjects of others. This is a natural consequence of the first proposition; for it would be wholly incompatible with the equality

---

50. *See Restatement (Third) Foreign Relations Law*, pt. IV, ch. 1, Intro. Note (1987); D. Lange & G. Born, *The Extraterritorial Application of National Laws* (1987).

51. *See infra* pp. 503-05.

52. *See infra* pp. 507 & 584-87.

and exclusiveness of the sovereignty of all nations, that any one nation should be at liberty to regulate either persons or things not within its own territory. It would be equivalent to a declaration, that the sovereignty over a territory was never exclusive in any nation, but only concurrent with that of all nations; that each could legislate for all, and none for itself; and that all might establish rules, which none were bound to obey. The absurd results of such a state of things need not be dwelt upon. ...

§23. From these two maxims or propositions, there flows a third, and that is, that whatever force and obligation the laws of one country have in another, depend solely upon the laws, and municipal regulations of the latter, that is to say, upon its own proper jurisprudence and polity, and upon its own express or tacit consent. A state may prohibit the operation of all foreign laws, and the rights growing out of them, within its own territories. It may prohibit some foreign laws, and it may admit the operation of others. It may recognise, and modify, and qualify some foreign laws; it may enlarge, or give universal effect to others. It may interdict the administration of some foreign laws; it may favor the introduction of others. When its own code speaks positively on the subject, it must be obeyed by all persons, who are within the reach of its sovereignty. When its customary, unwritten, or common law speaks directly on the subject, it is equally to be obeyed. ... When both are silent, then, and then only, can the question properly arise, what law is to govern in the absence of any clear declaration of the sovereign will. ...

RESTATEMENT (FIRST) CONFLICT OF LAWS (1934)

§§55, 63 & 65

§55. A state has jurisdiction over all acts done or events occurring within the territory of the state, and over all failures to act in cases where there is a legal duty to act within the state.

§63. A nation recognized as such in the law of nations has jurisdiction over its nationals wherever they may be to require or forbid them to do a act unless the exercise of this jurisdiction involves the violation of the law or public policy of the state where the national is.

§65. If consequences of an act done in one state occur in another state, each state in which any event in the series of act and consequences occurs may exercise legislative jurisdiction to create rights or other interests as a result thereof.

Comment b. *Creation of choice of law problem.* Under the rule stated in this Section, it may and frequently does happen that more than one state has legislative jurisdiction to attach rights or other interests to a series of events started by a person's act. In an action brought to enforce an obligation imposed by reason of such series of events ... the court at the forum must select the law of one of the several states thus having legislative jurisdiction, to govern the case. Thus when an act is done in state X which causes harm to a person in state Y, a court in state Z, if an action to recover is brought there, may choose the rule of either X or Y to govern the situation. ...

RESTATEMENT (SECOND) FOREIGN RELATIONS LAW OF THE UNITED STATES (1965)

§§17, 18, 30, 33, 39 & 40

§17. A state has jurisdiction to prescribe a rule of law (a) attaching legal consequences to conduct that occurs within its territory, whether or not such consequences are determined by the effects of the conduct outside the territory, and (b) relating to a thing located, or a status or other interest localized, in its territory.

§18. A state has jurisdiction to prescribe a rule of law attaching legal consequences to conduct that occurs outside its territory and causes an effect within its territory, if either (a) the conduct and its effects are generally recognized as constituent elements of a crime or tort under the law of states that have reasonably developed legal systems, or (b) (i) the conduct and its effects are constituent elements of activity to which the rule applies; (ii) the effect within the territory is substantial; (iii) it occurs as a direct and foreseeable result of the conduct outside the territory; and (iv) the rule is not inconsistent with the principles of justice generally recognized by states that have reasonably developed legal systems.

§30. (1) A state has jurisdiction to prescribe a rule of law (a) attaching legal consequences to conduct of a national of the state wherever the conduct occurs or (b) as to the status of a national or as to an interest of a national, wherever the thing or other subject matter to which the interest relates is located. (2) A state does not have jurisdiction to prescribe a rule of law attaching legal consequences to conduct of an alien outside of its territory merely on the ground that the conduct affects one of its nationals.

§33. (1) A state has jurisdiction to prescribe a rule of law attaching legal consequences to conduct outside its territory that threatens its security as a state or the operation of its governmental functions, provided the conduct is generally recognized as a crime under the law of states that have reasonably developed legal systems. (2) Conduct referred to in Subsection (1) includes in particular the counterfeiting of the state's seals and currency, and the falsification of its official documents.

§39 (1) A state having jurisdiction to prescribe or to enforce a rule of law is not precluded from exercising its jurisdiction solely because such exercise requires a person to engage in conduct subjecting him to liability under the law of another state having jurisdiction with respect to that conduct. (2) Factors to be considered in minimizing conflicts arising from the application of the rule stated in Subsection (1) with respect to enforcement jurisdiction are stated in §40.

§40. Where two states have jurisdiction to prescribe and enforce rules of law and the rules they may prescribe require inconsistent conduct upon the part of a person, each state is required by international law to consider, in good faith, moderating the exercise of its enforcement jurisdiction, in the light of such factors as

(a) vital national interests of each of the states,

(b) the extent and the nature of the hardship that inconsistent enforcement actions would impose upon the person,

(c) the extent to which the required conduct is to take place in the territory of the other state,

(d) the nationality of the person, and

(e) the extent to which enforcement by action of either state can reasonably be expected to achieve compliance with the rule proscribed by that state.

RESTATEMENT (SECOND) CONFLICT OF LAWS (1971)

§9

§9. A court may not apply the local law of its own state to determine a particular issue unless such application of this law would be reasonable in the light of the relationship of the state and of other states to the person, thing or occurrence involved.

RESTATEMENT (THIRD) FOREIGN RELATIONS LAW OF THE UNITED STATES (1987)

§§402, 403 & 441

§402. Subject to §403, a state has jurisdiction to prescribe law with respect to:

(1) (a) conduct that, wholly or in substantial part, takes place within its territory;

(b) the status of persons, or interests in things, present within its territory;

(c) conduct outside its territory that has or is intended to have substantial effect within its territory;

(2) the activities, interests, status, or relations of its nationals outside as well as within its territory; and

(3) certain conduct outside its territory by persons not its nationals that is directed against the security of the state or against a limited class of other state interests.

§403. (1) Even when one of the bases for jurisdiction under §402 is present, a state may not exercise jurisdiction to prescribe law with respect to a person or activity having connections with another state when the exercise of such jurisdiction is unreasonable.

(2) Whether exercise of jurisdiction over a person or activity is unreasonable is determined by evaluating all relevant factors, including, where appropriate:

(a) the link of the activity to the territory of the regulating state, *i.e.*, the extent to which the activity takes place within the territory, or has substantial, direct, and foreseeable effect upon or in the territory;

(b) the connections, such as nationality, residence, or economic activity, between the regulating state and the person principally responsible for the activity to be regulated, or between that state and those whom the regulation is designed to protect;

(c) the character of the activity to be regulated, the importance of regulation to the regulating state, the extent to which other states regulate such activities, and the degree to which the desirability of such regulation is generally accepted;

(d) the existence of justified expectations that might be protected or hurt by the regulation;

(e) the importance of the regulation to the international political, legal, or economic system;

(f) the extent to which the regulation is consistent with the traditions of the international system;

(g) the extent to which another state may have an interest in regulating the activity; and

(h) the likelihood of conflict with regulation by another state.

(3) When it would not be unreasonable for each of two states to exercise jurisdiction over a person or activity, but the prescriptions by the two states are in conflict, each state has an obligation to evaluate its own as well as the other state's interest in exercising jurisdiction, in light of all the relevant factors, Subsection (2); a state should defer to the other state if that state's interest is clearly greater.

§441 (1) In general, a state may not require a person

(a) to do an act in another state that is prohibited by the law of that state or by the law of the state of which he is a national; or

(b) to refrain from doing an act in another state that is required by the law of that state or by the law of the state of which he is a national.

(2) In general, a state may require a person of a foreign nationality

(a) to do an act in that state even if it is prohibited by the law of the state of which he is a national, or

(b) to refrain from doing an act in that state even if it is required by the law of the state of which he is a national.

Notes on Story's Commentaries and Restatements

1. *Nineteenth century limits on legislative jurisdiction.* Consider the territorial limits on legislative jurisdiction in Story's *Commentaries*. Compare them to the territorial limits imposed by 19th century international law on judicial jurisdiction. *See supra* pp. 70-73. What were the rationales for both sets of limits? What public and private interests are served by international limits on national legislative jurisdiction? Do such limits: (a) protect the sovereignty of other states; (b) protect individuals from unfair, arbitrary or unforeseeable applications of substantive law; (c) protect international commerce and the international system from unduly burdensome or conflicting national laws; or (d) achieve something else?

Some early U.S. authorities linked territorial limits on legislative jurisdiction to notions of the sovereign equality of States. *The Antelope*, 23 U.S. 66, 122 (1825) ("no principle of general law is more universally acknowledged, than the perfect equality of nations. Russia and Geneva have equal rights. It results from this equality, that no one can rightfully impose a rule on another."). Are territorial limits on jurisdiction a necessary consequence of sovereign equality? Can't equal states have equally valid powers to apply their laws extraterritorially?

2. *Evolution of U.S. view of international law limits on legislative jurisdiction — 1841-1934.* Contrast Story's territorial limits on legislative jurisdiction with the *Restatement (First) Conflict of Laws.* With the advent of global industries, mass transportation, and international capital and other markets, is there any question that the territorial views of Story, Jefferson, and other 19th century American authorities were simply unworkable by 1934? What are the principal differences between the American views of legislative jurisdiction in 1841 and 1934?

3. *Role of U.S. foreign policy in evolution of U.S. international law views.* Recall that Story and the Restatements reflect *American* conceptions of international law. Were there political, strategic, and commercial reasons for the United States to have different interests in the content of international law in the early 19th century — when it was a fledgling state, facing more powerful and expansive European nations — than in the mid-20th century — when it had emerged from the Second World War with military and commercial predominance? *See supra* pp. 495-96.

4. *Overview of bases for legislative jurisdiction under contemporary international law.* Contemporary international law recognizes several bases for legislative jurisdiction.

(a) *Territoriality.* The primary and least controversial jurisdictional base under international law remains the "territoriality principle," which derives from states' sovereignty over national territory. *See Restatement (Third) Foreign Relations Law* §402, comment c (1987) ("[t]he territorial principle is by far the most common basis for the exercise of jurisdiction to prescribe, and it has generally been free from controversy"); *Restatement (Second) Foreign Relations Law* §17 (1965); *Restatement (First) Conflict of Laws* §55 (1934); *Laker Airways v. Sabena,* 731 F.2d 909, 921 (D.C. Cir. 1984) ("the territoriality base of jurisdiction is universally recognized. It is the most pervasive and basic principle underlying the exercise by nations of prescriptive regulatory power."). The territoriality principle permits states to regulate transactions or conduct occurring within national borders, for example, by applying environmental laws to manufacturing activities within the state. In addition, the principle is now understood in the United States as permitting regulation of conduct or transactions occurring partially within and partially outside national territory. *See Restatement (Third) Foreign Relations Law* §402 (1987).

(b) *Nationality.* International law also recognizes the "nationality principle" as a legitimate base for legislative jurisdiction. The nationality principle permits a state to exercise legislative jurisdiction over its nationals and citizens, even when they are outside national territory. *See Skiriotes v. Florida,* 313 U.S. 69 (1941); *Restatement (Third) Foreign Relations Law* §402(2) & Reporter's Note 1 (1987); *Restatement (Second) Foreign Relations Law* §30 (1965); *Restatement (First) Conflict of Laws* §63 (1934). Under the nationality principle, for example, the United States can generally forbid U.S. citizens from trading with nations hostile to the United States, even if the trading occurs outside U.S. territory.

(c) *Effects doctrine.* The so-called "effects doctrine" is reflected in the *First Restatement* §65, the *Second Restatement* §18, and the *Third Restatement* §402. The effects doctrine is more controversial than either the territoriality or nationality principle. It permits a state to exercise legislative jurisdiction over conduct occurring outside the state, provided that the conduct has sufficient effects within the state's territory. *Restatement (Third) Foreign Relations Law* §402(1)(c) (1987); *United States v. Aluminum Co. of America,* 148 F.2d 416 (2d Cir. 1945); Harvard Research in International Law, *Jurisdiction with Respect to Crime,* 29 Am. J. Int'l L. Supp. 435, 484-88 (1935).

Unlike the territoriality and nationality principles, many formulations of the "effects doctrine" have been the subject of considerable controversy. *See infra* pp. 507 & 584-87. Some authorities still contend that the doctrine can be applied only in very limited categories of cases. Jennings, *Extraterritorial Jurisdiction and the United States Antitrust Laws,* 33 Brit. Y.B. Int'l L. 146 (1957); I. Brownlie, *Principles of Public International Law* 299-303 (4th ed. 1990). In particular, as discussed below, the extraterritorial application of U.S. antitrust laws based on the effects doctrine has provoked considerable controversy. *See infra* pp. 584-87.

(d) *Protective principle.* The "protective principle" permits the regulation of a narrow range of conduct that threatens national security (such as counterfeiting and espionage). *Restatement (Third) Foreign Relations Law* §402(3) (1987); *Restatement (Second) Foreign Relations Law* §33 (1965). This jurisdictional base is seldom invoked in civil litigation.

(e) *Universality principle.* The "universality principle," allowing extraterritorial jurisdiction over certain universally condemned crimes (such as piracy). See *Restatement (Third) Foreign Relations Law* §404 (1987). Like the protective principle, international commercial disputes seldom involve the universality principle (although it can be relevant to human rights litigation, *see supra* pp. 36-49).

5. *Evolution of U.S. views of international law limits on legislative jurisdiction — 1934-1971.* Consider the evolution of U.S. views of international law between 1934 and 1971.

(a) *Legislative jurisdiction distinguished from choice of law.* The *Restatement (First) Conflict of Laws* dealt with both legislative jurisdiction and choice of law, distinguishing carefully between the two subjects. In contrast, the *Restatement (Second) Conflict of Laws* concentrated on choice of law issues and did not deal with issues of legislative jurisdiction in a meaningful way. It instead merely referred readers to the

Restatement (Second) Foreign Relations Law. See Restatement (Second) Conflict of Laws §9, comment c (1971) ("As to limitations imposed by international law, see Chapters 1 and 2 of the Restatement of the Foreign Relations Law.").

(b) *Effects doctrine.* Compare the effects doctrine contained in §65 of the *Restatement (First) Conflict of Laws* with that in §18 of the *Restatement (Second) Foreign Relations Law.* Note that §65's effects doctrine is at least nominally more expansive than that in §18. What is the rationale for the limits in §18 of the *Second Restatement?* Consider the following hypotheticals:

> Foreign companies engage outside the United States in anticompetitive price-fixing directed at U.S. purchasers, and succeed in significantly raising the prices paid by U.S. consumers. The consumers sue in U.S. courts, which apply U.S. antitrust laws.

> U.S. newspapers print articles that are critical of foreign political and commercial figures, and copies of those newspapers are ultimately disseminated in those figures' home countries. They sue in their home courts, which apply local libel law to the U.S. defendants' U.S. conduct. Suppose the newspapers are distributed only in the United States, but the foreign individuals are damaged at home?

How would the *First Restatement* have resolved these hypotheticals? How would the *Restatement (Second) Conflict of Laws* and the *Restatement (Second) Foreign Relations Law* resolve them?

(c) *Nationality principle.* Compare the nationality principle contained in §63 of the *Restatement (First) Conflict of Laws* with that in §§30 and 40 of the *Restatement (Second) Foreign Relations Law.* Note the significant limitation contained in §63, forbidding use of the nationality principle to require conduct in violation of the law or public policy of the state where the conduct occurs. Is this approach preferable to that in §§30 and 40 of the *Restatement (Second) Foreign Relations Law?* What exactly is the latter approach? Compare the foreign sovereign compulsion doctrine and §441 of the *Third Restatement. See infra* pp. 508-09 & 745-52.

(d) *"Reasonableness" limits.* Consider the sole reference to limitations on legislative jurisdiction set forth in §9 of the *Restatement (Second) Conflict of Laws* — that the application of a state's law be "reasonable." Compare this limitation to the "reasonableness" standard articulated in the *Restatement (Third) Foreign Relations Law* §403 (1987); *supra* pp. 504-05. Would it be wise to replace traditional international law limits on legislative jurisdiction with a general "reasonableness" test? What would be the content, in a world of 160 sovereign states, of "reasonableness" limits? Would "reasonableness" have any meaningful limit on national assertions of legislative jurisdiction? Why is it important for such limits to exist?

6. *Foreign criticisms of U.S. effects doctrine.* Not all foreign states have agreed with *American* views of the jurisdictional limits of international law, and some have vigorously and repeatedly protested the extraterritorial applications of U.S. law. The target of much criticism has been the effects doctrine:

> [The effects doctrine, or objective territoriality principle,] is often said to apply where the offense "takes effect" or "produces its effects" in the territory. In relation to elementary cases of direct physical injury, such as homicide, this is unexceptionable, for here the "effect" which is meant is an essential ingredient of the crime. Once we move out of the sphere of direct physical consequences, however, to employ the formula of "effects" is to enter upon a very slippery slope; for here the effects within the territory may be no more than an element of alleged consequential damage which may be more or less remote .... [T]o extend the notion of effects, without qualification, from the simple cases of direct physical injury to cases such as defamation, sedition, and the like is to introduce a dangerous ambiguity into the basis of the doctrine. If indeed it were permissible to found objective territorial jurisdiction upon the territoriality of more or less remote repercussions of an act wholly performed in another territory, then there were virtually no limit to a State's territorial jurisdiction. Jennings, *Extraterritorial Jurisdiction and the United States Antitrust Laws*, [1957] Brit. Y.B. Int'l L. 146, 159.

Are such criticisms persuasive? In today's global economy, doesn't an "effects" doctrine permit almost limitless legislative jurisdiction. Compare the consequences of the effects doctrine on congressional power under the domestic "interstate commerce" clause. *See supra* pp. 8-9.

7. *Evolution of U.S. views of international law limits on legislative jurisdiction — 1971-1987.* Contrast the jurisdictional provisions of the *Restatement (Second) Foreign Relations Law* with those of the *Third Restatement,* published in 1987. Note that §402 broadens the "territorial" and "effects" bases for

jurisdiction, while substituting a general reasonableness limitation, set forth in §403. Is this desirable? Compare this evolution to that of restrictions on judicial jurisdiction. *See supra* pp. 70-77.

8. *No basis under international law for legislative jurisdiction based on passive personality.* Section 30(2) of the *Restatement (Second) Foreign Relations Law* provides that international law does not recognize the nationality of the victim of acts committed outside national territory as an independent basis for legislative jurisdiction. That is, if a U.S. national is harmed outside the United States, then the mere fact that the victim was a U.S. national does not permit the United States to apply its law to the harmful conduct. The *Third Restatement* affirms this rule, although only in a comment: "The passive personality principle asserts that a state may apply law — particularly criminal law — to an act committed outside its territory by a person not its national where the victim of the act was its national. The principle has not been generally accepted for ordinary torts or crimes, but it is increasingly accepted as applied to terrorism" and similar crimes. *Restatement (Third) Foreign Relations Law* §402, comment g (1987). Compare the relevance of the plaintiff's nationality to the existence of judicial jurisdiction. *See supra* pp. 95-100.

Is this a wise approach? Why should a nation be forbidden by international law from applying its laws extraterritorially to the misconduct of foreign persons who harm its nationals? In reality, don't nations have a strong and legitimate interest in safeguarding their nationals from mistreatment and injustice, wherever they may be? What is the harm of permitting this? In medieval times, laws were generally "personal," following individuals wherever they might go: "it often happens that five men, each under a different law, may be found walking or sitting together." Letter from St. Agobar, Archbishop of Lyon, to Louis the Pious, dated 817 (quoted in Juenger, *General Course on Private International Law,* 193 Recueil des Cours 119, 139 (1987)). Is this undesirable?

9. *Concurrent legislative jurisdiction.* Under contemporary international law, two or more states will frequently enjoy legislative jurisdiction over the same conduct. That is express in §40 of the *Restatement (Second) Foreign Relations Law* and §403 of the *Restatement (Third) Foreign Relations Law:* "[t]erritoriality and nationality are discrete and independent bases of jurisdiction; the same conduct or activity may provide a basis for exercise of jurisdiction both by the territorial state and by the state of nationality of the actor." *Restatement (Third) Foreign Relations Law* §402, comment b (1987).

Consider the difficulties that concurrent jurisdiction can produce. Most extreme, one state may require a private party to do something (*e.g.*, perform a contractual obligation), while a second state may forbid it from doing the required act (*e.g.*, not perform the contractual obligations). Conflicting legal obligations of this sort impose obvious unfairness on private parties, as well as chilling international commercial enterprise. Less extreme, if multiple states regulate or tax the same course of conduct, then there is an obvious risk of confiscatory or otherwise crippling results (*e.g.*, taxation in excess of 100% of income or property value). Should international law permit concurrent legislative jurisdiction? Is it not one thing to abandon territorial limits on national legislative jurisdiction, and another to say that two states can regulate the same conduct? Should international law provide, like physics, that two laws cannot occupy the same space?

10. *Moderation of consequences of concurrent jurisdiction.* Various efforts have been made to moderate the consequences of concurrent jurisdiction.

(a) *Section 63 of the First Restatement.* Conflicting legal requirements are imposed when one state requires what another state forbids. Note that conflicting legal requirements were less likely under the *Restatement (First) Conflict of Laws,* which did not permit use of §63's nationality principle to require conduct in violation of the laws of the place of the conduct. *See supra* p. 507. Is this a wise approach? Compare the approach that §65 took to the effects doctrine.

(b) *Section 40 of the Second Restatement.* Consider the "obligation" imposed by §40 on states that seek to exercise concurrent jurisdiction in conflicting ways. Does §40 provide a means for deciding which of two states' conflicting laws will apply in particular cases, or does it concern the enforcement of applicable law? Does §40 ever *require* a state to refrain from exercising concurrent jurisdiction? Consider the factors that §40 says are relevant to deciding whether a state should decline to enforce its prescriptive jurisdiction. Is it likely that these factors will be useful to courts or private parties?

(c) *Section 403 of the Third Restatement.* Compare §403 of the *Third Restatement* to §40 of the *Second Restatement.* Which rule is better? Does §403(1) address legislative or enforcement jurisdiction? Does §403 ever *require* a state not to assert jurisdiction? Does §403 forbid assertions of concurrent jurisdiction where conflicting obligations are imposed? If you were asked to design a superior rule, for cases of concurrent or conflicting jurisdiction, what would it be?

(d) *Foreign sovereign compulsion doctrine.* As discussed below, §441 of the *Restatement (Third) Foreign Relations Laws* provides that a state cannot compel acts in other states that are prohibited by the laws of the place of conduct or of the actor's nationality. Is this a sensible rule?

11. *Section 403's reasonableness test.* Consider §403's "reasonableness" analysis.

(a) *Limits of §403's reasonableness limitation.* It is entirely possible for the laws of two or more states to be "reasonable" under §403, even when both are applied to the same conduct. Moreover, §403 does not itself forbid a state from applying its laws extraterritorially, even if this results in the imposition of *conflicting* legal obligations. Instead, in cases involving conflicting legal requirements, §403(3) provides that a state is expected (but not necessarily required) to "defer to the other state if that state's interest is clearly greater." Recall, however, that §441 limits a state's power to compel acts in other states.

(b) *Utility of §403 factors.* Section 403(2) enumerates a nonexclusive list of "factors" to be considered in determining whether an extraterritorial assertion of prescriptive jurisdiction is reasonable. Do the factors listed in §403 provide meaningful guidance in deciding particular cases? Some critics have argued that §403's multifaceted balancing approach is unmanageable and unpredictable. For example, how is a U.S. judge to determine "the importance of the regulation to the international political, legal or economic system" or to resolve cases where §403's factors point in different directions? *See Laker Airways Ltd. v. Sabena,* 731 F.2d 909, 948-51 (D.C. Cir. 1984); *In re Uranium Contracts Litig.,* 617 F.2d 1248 (7th Cir. 1980). Could §403's rule of reason be clarified over time as courts build on a body of common law precedent?

(c) *Doubts about ability of national courts to assess national interests.* Some critics of §403's rule of reason have argued that U.S. courts lack the institutional capacities to assess the questions of national interests and foreign relations that the section raises. *See Laker Airways,* 731 F.2d at 949 ("[w]e are in no position to adjudicate the relative importance of antitrust regulation or nonregulation to the United States and the United Kingdom"). Is that correct?

(d) *Parochial bias of national courts.* Other critics of the rule of reason have argued that U.S. courts inevitably resolve interest-balancing tests in favor of U.S. interests. *Laker Airways Ltd.,* 731 F.2d at 948-54 ("courts inherently find it difficult neutrally to balance competing foreign interests"). Is there reason to think that parochialism would be less marked if an interest-balancing analysis were not applied in deciding jurisdictional issues? Does §403 cause parochial decisions? Several lower courts have relied upon a comity-based interest-balancing analysis to either dismiss complaints based on an extraterritorial application of the U.S. antitrust laws or to deny extraterritorial U.S. discovery. *See Timberlane Lumber Co. v. Bank of America N.T. & S.A.,* 749 F.2d 1378 (9th Cir. 1984); *Mannington Mills, Inc. v. Congoleum Corp.,* 595 F.2d 1287 (3d Cir. 1979); *Montreal Trading Ltd. v. Amax Inc.,* 661 F.2d 864 (10th Cir. 1981), *cert. denied,* 455 U.S. 1001 (1982); *Star-Kist Foods, Inc. v. P.J. Rhodes & Co.,* 769 F.2d 1393 (9th Cir. 1985); *O.N.E. Shipping Ltd. v. Flota Mercante Grancolombiana,* 830 F.2d 449 (2d Cir. 1987); *Zenger-Miller, Inc. v. Training Team GmbH,* 757 F. Supp. 1062 (N.D. Calif. 1991).

12. *Comparison between bases for legislative and judicial jurisdiction under international law.* Compare the bases under international law for judicial jurisdiction with those for legislative jurisdiction. Should the two sets of jurisdictional bases be the same, or at least similar? Compare the purposes served by each set of jurisdictional limits.

Recall that international law (and the due process clause) recognized various bases for "general" jurisdiction. General jurisdiction permits jurisdiction over all claims against a defendant, including claims with no connection to the forum state. Bases for general jurisdiction include nationality, domicile, incorporation, tag service, and systematic business presence. *See supra* pp. 95-123. In contrast, specific jurisdiction only permits adjudication of claims arising from the defendant's contacts with the forum. *See supra* pp. 77-78. The Restatements have not drawn any comparable distinction between "general" and "specific" legislative jurisdiction. Would such a distinction be useful in deciding questions of legislative jurisdiction? If a state may exercise judicial jurisdiction, should it therefore also be permitted to exercise legislative jurisdiction?

B. International Law Limits on Legislative Jurisdiction in U.S. Courts

International law limits on legislative jurisdiction have a complex relationship to U.S. law. As discussed above, these limits are almost entirely the product of customary international law, not international treaties. It is often said that customary "[i]nternational law is part of our law, and must be ascertained and administered by the courts of justice of appropriate jurisdiction, as often as questions of right depending on it are duly presented for their determination."[53] In fact, as we have seen, the relationship between U.S. and customary international law in U.S. courts is more complex.[54] That is as true in the context of limits on legislative jurisdiction as elsewhere.

1. U.S. Federal Law Prevails Over Inconsistent Jurisdictional Limits of Customary International Law in U.S. Courts

If Congress enacts legislation in violation of international law, it is well-settled that U.S. courts must disregard international law and apply the domestic statute.[55] This applies to federal statutes that exceed the limits of international law on legislative jurisdiction. Thus, the territorial reach of a federal statute is ultimately an issue of U.S. law — not of foreign or customary international law. "We are concerned only with whether Congress chose to attach liability to the conduct outside the United States... . [A]s a court of the United States, we cannot look beyond our own law."[56]

A different result would obtain if a federal statute were superseded by a subsequent self-executing U.S. treaty containing limits on U.S. legislative jurisdiction. That is because, when U.S. self-executing treaties and federal law conflict, U.S. courts will give effect to the "last in time."[57] As a practical matter, however, this is of little importance, because virtually no U.S. treaties affect U.S. legislative jurisdiction.

A different result would also obtain if a federal statute exceeded U.S. constitutional limits on legislative jurisdiction. We examine this possibility below.[58] A few courts have held that contemporary jurisdictional limits of international law are coextensive with constitutional limits on federal legislative jurisdiction.[59] In general,

---

53. *See supra* pp. 17-22 & 36-49; *The Paquete Habana,* 175 U.S. 677, 700 (1900); *Restatement (Third) Foreign Relations Law* §111(1) (1987).

54. *See supra* pp. 21-22.

55. *See supra* pp. 17-22 & *infra* pp. 780-81; *Restatement (Third) Foreign Relations Law* §115(1) & §403, comment g (1987); *Head Money Cases,* 112 U.S. 580, 598-99 (1884); *CFTC v. Nahas,* 738 F.2d 487 (D.C. Cir. 1984).

56. *United States v. Alcoa,* 148 F.2d 416, 443 (2d Cir. 1945).

57. *See supra* pp. 19-20.

58. *See infra* pp. 512-44.

59. *E.g., United States v. Javino,* 960 F.2d 1137 (2d Cir. 1992); *Tamari v. Bache & Co. (Lebanon),* 730 F.2d 1103, 1107 n.11 (7th Cir.), *cert. denied,* 469 U.S. 871 (1984); *United States v. Layton,* 509 F. Supp. 212 (N.D. Cal. 1981).

however, parties have seldom asserted international law objections to U.S. legislative jurisdiction.[60]

2. Presumptions That Congress Has Not Violated International Law and Has Not Extended U.S. Law Extraterritorially

As discussed above, Congress has the power to enact legislation that violates international law if that is what it wishes to do. Nevertheless, U.S. courts generally apply the *Charming Betsy* presumption that Congress does not wish to violate international law.[61] Only if a federal statute expressly and plainly requires a result inconsistent with international law will that interpretation be adopted.

Similarly, Congress has the power to enact legislation that applies to conduct outside U.S. territory.[62] However, U.S. courts have long relied upon the related "territoriality presumption": that presumption provides that federal legislation will not be interpreted to apply extraterritorially absent express language requiring this result.[63] In the words of the Supreme Court, "legislation of Congress, unless a contrary intent appears, is meant to apply only within the territorial jurisdiction of the United States."[64] The application of both presumptions is discussed in detail below.[65]

3. Relationship Between U.S. State Law and Jurisdictional Limits of Customary International Law

The relationship between U.S. state (as opposed to federal) law and customary international law is less clear. As discussed above, international law is regarded as federal law; under this view, it is supreme over state law.[66] Thus, at least according to some authorities, state law that is inconsistent with either prior or subsequent rules of customary international law is invalid.[67] There is little precedent reaching such a result.

---

60. *See* Brilmayer & Norchi, *Federal Extraterritoriality and Fifth Amendment Due Process*, 105 Harv. L. Rev. 1217 (1992).

61. *See supra* pp. 22 & *infra* pp. 549-50, 780-92; *Restatement (Third) Foreign Relations Law* §114 (1987); *Murray v. Schooner Charming Betsy*, 6 U.S. 64, 118 (1804).

62. In *EEOC v. Aramco*, 499 U.S. 244 (1991), the Court observed: "Both parties concede, as they must, that Congress has the authority to enforce [sic] its laws beyond the territorial boundaries of the United States." Of course, Congress has no power at all to "enforce its laws" — either inside or outside the United States. U.S. Const. Art. II. The Court meant to refer to Congress' "authority to enact laws applicable to conduct beyond the territorial boundaries of the United States."

63. *Foley Bros., Inc. v. Filardo*, 336 U.S. 281 (1949); *McCulloch v. Sociedad Nacional de Marineros de Honduras*, 372 U.S. 10, 21-22 (1968).

64. *Foley Bros., Inc. v. Filardo*, 336 U.S. 281, 285 (1949).

65. *See infra* pp. 545-607.

66. *See supra* pp. 17-22 & 49-56.

67. *See supra* pp. 21 & 53; *Restatement (Third) Foreign Relations Law* §115, comment e (1987).

C. Constitutional Limitations on Legislative Jurisdiction in U.S. Courts

The U.S. Constitution imposes limits on legislative jurisdiction (and, thus, the choice of law decisions) in U.S. courts. The principal textual bases for these limits are the full faith and credit clause and the due process clause.[68] The U.S. Supreme Court has for some time applied both provisions to limit state courts' application of local law to multistate events.[69] The full faith and credit clause is not applicable to Congress.[70] The due process clause is, but it has seldom been applied to limit the extraterritorial reach of federal legislation.[71]

1. Constitutional Limits on Federal Legislative Jurisdiction

Early Supreme Court decisions occasionally contained language suggesting that the Constitution forbid Congress from applying federal statutes outside U.S. territory.[72] No decision appears to have held, however, that Congress lacked the constitutional authority to enact extraterritorial legislation.

Nothing in the Constitution expressly or impliedly limits federal legislative power to conduct, persons or property located on U.S. territory. On the contrary, the Constitution specifically grants Congress broad power to regulate commerce with foreign nations.[73] A fairly natural component of this grant is the power to regulate conduct that occurs outside of U.S. territory. Likewise, the Constitution grants Congress other powers that inevitably call for the extraterritorial application of U.S. legislation.[74] Not surprisingly, early U.S. statutes sometimes reached conduct beyond the territorial boundaries of the United States, particularly activities on the high seas

---

68. The full faith and credit clause provides: "Full Faith and Credit shall be given in each State to the public Acts, Records and judicial Proceedings of every other State. And the Congress may by general Laws prescribe the Manner in which such Acts, Records and Proceedings shall be proved, and the effect thereof." U.S. Const. Art. IV, §1.

69. *See infra* pp. 518-37.

70. *See infra* pp. 534-35.

71. *See infra* pp. 512-18; Brilmayer & Norchi, *Federal Extraterritoriality and Fifth Amendment Due Process*, 105 Harv. L. Rev. 1217 (1992).

72. *E.g., Rose v. Himely*, 8 U.S. 241, 279 (1807) ("legislation of every country is territorial ... beyond its own territory, it can only affect its own subjects or citizens"); *United States v. Palmer*, 16 U.S. 610, 641 (1818) (Johnson, J.) ("Congress cannot make that piracy which is not piracy by the law of nations, in order to give jurisdiction to its own courts over such offenses"); *The Apollon*, 22 U.S. 362, 370 (1824) ("The laws of no nation can justly extend beyond its own territory, except so far as regards its own citizens.").

73. Art. I, §8. Indeed, the Framers intended Congress's power to regulate foreign commerce to be broader than its authority over interstate commerce. *See supra* pp. 8-9 & 15-16 & *infra* pp. 537-39.

74. Art. I, §8, cl. 9, 11 (granting Congress the power to define offenses on the high seas or against the law of nations and to grant letters of marque and reprisal).

or in so-called Indian territory.[75] As a result, it has long been accepted that federal legislation may constitutionally be applied to conduct outside the United States.[76]

For decades, in many contexts, the Supreme Court has summarily upheld the extraterritorial application of U.S. law against constitutional challenges.[77] The Court recently made it clear that the power of Congress to apply U.S. law extraterritorially was no longer open to debate: "Both parties concede, as they must, that Congress has the authority to enforce its laws beyond the territorial boundaries of the United States."[78]

As described above, it is equally well-settled that Congress possesses the power under the Constitution to exercise legislative jurisdiction in violation of international law. "Federal courts must give effect to a valid unambiguous congressional mandate, even if such effect would conflict with another nation's laws or violate international law."[79] In short, it is now settled that the Constitution does not categorically forbid Congress from enacting laws applicable to conduct and persons outside of U.S. territory, even where this violates international law.

Nonetheless, the Constitution may forbid the extraterritorial application of U.S. federal law in some circumstances. For example, the due process clause might preclude extension of federal law to conduct abroad that has only *de minimis* contact with or effect upon the United States or its nationals. Having said this, neither the due process clause nor other constitutional provisions have in fact imposed significant constraints on the extraterritorial reach of U.S. laws: no reported federal court decision has held an extraterritorial application of substantive federal law unconsti-

---

75. An Act for the Punishment of Certain Crimes Against the United States, 1 Stat. 112 (Act of April 30, 1790) (outlawing treason and other crimes on the high seas and other places); An Act More Effectually to Protect the Commerce and Coasts of the United States, 1 Stat. 561 (Act of May 28, 1798) (authorizing U.S. Navy to seize foreign vessels found "hovering on the coasts of the United States"); An Act to Regulate Trade and Intercourse With the Indian Tribes, 1 Stat. 329 (Act of March 1, 1793) (prohibiting various conduct in "Indian country"); An Act to Regulate Trade and Intercourse With the Indian Tribes, and to Preserve Peace on the Frontiers, 1 Stat. 743 (Act of March 3, 1799) (prohibiting various conduct within Indian territory). Nonetheless, there is virtually no early legislation expressly applicable to conduct occurring within the territory of another recognized sovereign state.

76. *EEOC v. Aramco*, 499 U.S. 24 (1991); Born, *A Reappraisal of the Extraterritorial Reach of U.S. Law*, 24 Law & Pol'y Int'l Bus. 1 (1992).

77. E.g., *Lauritzen v. Larsen*, 345 U.S. 571, 579 n.7 (1953); *Steele v. Bulova Watch Co.*, 344 U.S. 280, 282-86 (1952) (rejecting constitutional challenge to application of Lanham Act to conduct occurring in Mexico); *Vermilya-Brown Co. v. Connell*, 335 U.S. 377, 381 (1948) (Congress may "regulate the actions of our citizens outside the territorial jurisdiction of the United States whether or not the act punished occurred within the territory of a foreign nation."); *Blackmer v. United States*, 284 U.S. 421, 437 (1932) (rejecting Due Process challenge to subpoena issued to U.S. citizen residing in France); *United States v. Bowman*, 260 U.S. 94, 97 (1922) (rejecting Due Process challenge to extraterritorial application of legislation concerning fraud on U.S. government).

78. *EEOC v. Aramco*, 499 U.S. 24 (1991).

79. *CFTC v. Nahas*, 738 F.2d 487, 495 (D.C. Cir. 1984). Judge Learned Hand said in *United States v. Alcoa* that: "We are concerned only with *whether* Congress *chose* to attach liability to the conduct outside the United States ... [A]s a court of the United States, *we cannot look beyond our own law.*" *United States v. Alcoa*, 148 F.2d 416, 443 (2d Cir. 1945) (emphasis added).

tutional, and only a few lower courts have even alluded to the possibility of such a result.[80] One such decision is *United States v. Davis*, excerpted below.

UNITED STATES v. DAVIS

905 F.2d 245 (9th Cir. 1990)

Not U.S. citizen

WIGGINS, CIRCUIT JUDGE. Peter Malcolm Davis appeals his convictions for possession of, and conspiracy to possess, marijuana on a vessel subject to the juris-diction of the United States with intent to distribute in violation of the Maritime Drug Law Enforcement Act. The Coast Guard apprehended Davis on the high seas and he contests application of the Maritime Drug Law Enforcement Act to him ....

vessel

high seas

C.G.
Cape Romain
"the Myth"

[T]he Coast Guard cutter *Cape Romain* encountered the *Myth of Ecurie* ("*Myth*"), approximately 35 miles southwest of Point Reyes, California. The *Myth* is a sailing vessel approximately 58 feet in length. The *Myth* was headed in the direction of San Francisco. The *Cape Romain* approached the *Myth,* and Coast Guard person-nel by radio requested permission to board. Peter Davies, the captain of the *Myth*, denied the request. He stated that the Coast Guard had no authority to board his boat because it was of British registry and was sailing on the high seas having depart-ed from Hong Kong. Captain Davis announced his intention to alter his course for the Caribbean by the way of Mexico. The Coast Guard suspected the *Myth* of smug-gling contraband. Factors leading to that suspicion were that the El Paso Intelligence Centre had included the *Myth* on a list of vessels suspected of drug smuggling; the *Myth* was sailing in an area in which sailing vessels were infrequently found; and the *Myth* appeared to be carrying cargo.

The Myth

1981 Agmt w/U.K.

The Coast Guard then requested permission from the United Kingdom to board the *Myth* in accordance with procedures in a 1981 agreement between the United States and the United Kingdom. The Coast Guard informed the British officials of the circumstances which led the Coast Guard to believe the *Myth* contained contra-band material. By telex message, the United Kingdom gave the Coast Guard permis-

---

80. *E.g., United States v. Javino*, 960 F.2d 1137, 1142-43 (2d Cir. 1992) ("Even had Congress intended all foreign manufacturers of firearms to comply with the requirements set out in [26 U.S.C.] §5822, there is substantial question as to whether it could lawfully have done so. Though Congress may prescribe laws concerning conduct outside the territorial boundaries of the United States 'that has or is intended to have substantial effect' within the United States, *Restatement (Third) Foreign Relations Law* §402(1)(c) (1987) ..., it may not regulate such conduct 'when the exercise of ... jurisdiction is unreasonable'"); *United States v. Davis*, 905 F.2d 245 (9th Cir. 1990), *cert. denied*, 111 S. Ct. 753 (1991); *United States v. Peterson*, 812 F.2d 486 (9th Cir. 1987); *Tamari v. Bache & Co. (Lebanon)*, 730 F.2d 1103, 1107 n.11 (7th Cir.), *cert. denied*, 469 U.S. 871 (1984) ("Were Congress to enact a rule beyond the scope of [the] principles [contained in §§17-18 of the *Restatement (Second) Foreign Relations Law*], the statute could be challenged as violating the due process clause on the ground that Congress lacked the power to prescribe the rule"); *Chua Han Mow v. United States*, 730 F.2d 1308 (9th Cir. 1984); *United States v. Baker*, 609 F.2d 134 (5th Cir. 1980); *United States v. Conroy*, 589 F.2d 1258 (5th Cir.), *cert. denied*, 444 U.S. 831 (1979); *United States v. King*, 552 F.2d 833 (9th Cir. 1976); *Leasco Data Processing Equip. Corp. v. Maxwell*, 468 F.2d 1326, 1334 (2d Cir. 1972); *Gallagher v. United States*, 423 F.2d 1371 (Ct. Cl. 1970).

sion to board the *Myth* according to the terms of the 1981 Agreement .... Crew members from the *Cape Romain* boarded the *Myth*. By that time, the *Myth* had sailed to a location approximately 100 miles west of the California coast. The boarding officer smelled marijuana in the cabin of the *Myth*. Davis informed the boarding officer that he kept a shotgun below deck, and Davis and the boarding officer went below to obtain it. Below deck, the boarding officer saw numerous bales of material and smelled marijuana. Davis admitted that the bales were marijuana. The Coast Guard then arrested Davis and his crew and brought the *Myth* to the Coast Guard station on Yerba Buena Island in San Francisco. The Coast Guard there confiscated over 7,000 pounds of marijuana from the *Myth*. Davis is not a citizen of the United States. .... Davis filed a motion to dismiss for lack of jurisdiction .... The district court denied [the motion and later] found Davis guilty .... Davis timely appealed.

Davis contends that the provisions of the statute under which he was convicted, the Maritime Drug Law Enforcement Act, do not apply to persons on foreign vessels outside the territory of the United States. The question of whether the United States may punish Davis' conduct involves three issues: (1) whether Congress has constitutional authority to give extraterritorial effect to the Maritime Drug Law Enforcement Act; if so, (2) whether the Constitution prohibits the United States from punishing Davis' conduct in this instance; and, if not, (3) does the Maritime Drug Law Enforcement Act apply to Davis' conduct?

The Maritime Drug Law Enforcement Act, 46 U.S.C. App. §§1903(a) and (j) state:

> (a) It is unlawful for any person on board a vessel of the United States, or on board a vessel subject to the jurisdiction of the United States, to knowingly or intentionally manufacture or distribute, or to possess with intent to manufacture or distribute, a controlled substance.

> (j) Any person who attempts or conspires to commit any offense defined in this Act [46 U.S.C. App. §§1904] is punishable by imprisonment or fine, or both, which may not exceed the maximum punishment prescribed for the offense, the commission of which was the object of the attempt of the conspiracy.

The United States Congress sits as a legislature of enumerated and specific powers. *See Marbury v. Madison*, 5 U.S. 137, 176 (1803). The Constitution gives Congress the power to "define and punish piracies and felonies on the high seas..." U.S. Const. Art. 1 §8, cl. 10. The high seas lie seaward of the territorial sea, defined as the three mile belt of sea measured from the low water mark. *United States v. Rubies*, 612 F.2d 397, 402 n. 2 (9th Cir. 1979). We therefore find that the Constitution authorized Congress to give extraterritorial effect to the Act.

We next examine what limitations exist on the United States' power to exercise that authority. Contrary to Davis' assertions, compliance with international law does not determine whether the United States may supply the Act to his conduct.[81] Only two restrictions exist on giving extraterritorial effect to Congress' directives. We require Congress make clear its intent to give extraterritorial effect to its statutes. And secondly, as a matter of constitutional law, we require that application of the statute to the acts in question not violate the due process clause of the fifth amendment.

In this case, Congress explicitly stated that it intended the Maritime Drug Law Enforcement Act to apply extraterritorially. 46 U.S.C. App. §1903(h) (Supp. IV 1986) ("This section is intended to reach acts of possession, manufacture, or distribution outside the territorial jurisdiction of the United State"). Therefore, the only issue we must consider is whether application of the Maritime Drug Law Enforcement Act to Davis' conduct would violate due process. In order to apply extraterritorially a federal criminal statute to a defendant consistently with due process, there must be sufficient nexus between the defendant and the United States, *United States v. Peterson*, 812 F.2d 486, 493 (9th Cir. 1987), so that such application would not be arbitrary or fundamentally unfair.[82]

In the instant case, a sufficient nexus exists so that the application of the Maritime Drug Law Enforcement Act to Davis' extraterritorial conduct does not violate the due process clause. "Where an attempted transaction is aimed at causing criminal acts within the United States, there is a sufficient basis for the United States to exercise its jurisdiction." The facts found by the district court in denying Davis' motion to dismiss for lack of jurisdiction support the reasonable conclusion that Davis intended to smuggle contraband into United States territory. At the time of its first detection, the *Myth* was 35 miles away from, and headed for, San Francisco. As the Coast Guard approached, the *Myth* changed its course for the Caribbean by way of Mexico, although the *Myth* was many miles from the Great Circle route from Hong Kong to Acapulco. The *Myth* is on a list of boats suspected of drug smuggling.

---

81. International law principles, standing on their own, do not create substantive rights or affirmative defenses for litigants in United States courts. *United States v. Thomas*, 893 F.2d 1066, 1068-69 (9th Cir. 1990).

82. Some of our previous decisions have discussed international law jurisdictional principles simultaneously with the constitutionality of Congress' exercise of jurisdiction. *See Peterson*, 812 F.2d at 494 (extraterritorial application of statute is justified by protective principle and is constitutional); *Chua Han Mow v. United States*, 730 F.2d 1308, 1312 (9th Cir. 1984) (extraterritorial application of statute is justified by objective territorial and protective principle and is constitutional), *cert. denied*, 470 U.S. 1031 (1985); *United States v King*, 552 F.2d 833, 851-52 (9th Cir. 1976), *cert. denied*, 430 U.S. 966 (1977) (extraterritorial application of statute is justified by nationality and objective territorial principles and is constitutional); *United States v. Cotten*, 471 F.2d 744, 749 (9th Cir.), *cert. denied*, 411 U.S. 936 (1973) (extraterritorial application of statute justified by objective territorial principle); *Rocha v. United States*, 288 F.2d 545, 549 (9th Cir.), *cert. denied*, 366 U.S. 948 (1961) (extraterritorial application of statute is justified by protective principle). International law principles may be useful as a rough guide of whether a sufficient nexus exists between the defendant and the United States so that application of the statute in question would not violate due process. *See, e.g., Peterson*, 812 F.2d at 493. However, danger exists that emphasis on international law principles will cause us to lose sight of the ultimate question: would application of the statute to the defendant be arbitrary or fundamentally unfair?

It is unusual for a 58 foot sailing vessel to have sailed from the *Myth's* asserted point of departure, Hong Kong. The foregoing evidence is sufficient to establish a nexus between the *Myth* and the United States. We therefore find that the Constitution does not prohibit the application of the Marijuana Drug Law Enforcement Act to Davis ... [The court then held that the Act applied to Davis' conduct, noting that the United Kingdom had consented to U.S. agents boarding the *Myth*.]

Notes on United States v. Davis

1. *Affirmative constitutional basis for extraterritorial application of federal legislation.* As discussed above, the Framers granted Congress only limited legislative powers. *See supra* pp. 8-9. Given that, why is it so clear that Congress can enact legislation applicable outside U.S. territory? What provision of Article I grants Congress such power? Consider the court's analysis in *Davis.* What is it that sustains the Maritime Drug Enforcement Act? If the Framers specifically provided Congress with regulatory authority over piracies and felonies "on the high seas," what does that suggest about Congress' extraterritorial regulatory authority in matters not "on the high seas"? Recall the strength of the territoriality doctrine at the time that the Constitution was drafted. *See supra* pp. 493-97.

Does the foreign commerce clause grant Congress affirmative authority to extend federal legislation outside U.S. territory? Note that the clause grants Congress the power to "regulate commerce with foreign nations, and among the several states, and with Indian Tribes." Is it so clear that this confers power to regulate matters beyond U.S. territory? The Supreme Court and commentators have concluded that it is. *See supra* pp. 512-13.

2. *Due process limits on extraterritorial application of federal legislation.* Davis is one of the few U.S. decisions considering due process challenges to federal legislative jurisdiction. Is it correct, in principle, that the due process clause limits the legislative jurisdiction of Congress? Recall the discussion above of the fifth amendment's due process limits on federal court judicial jurisdiction. *See supra* pp. 179-80. What is the rationale for due process limits on federal legislative jurisdiction? What is the textual basis?

Would due process limits on legislative jurisdiction apply to protect foreign nationals outside the United States? Recall the Court's application of due process limits to judicial jurisdiction over non-U.S. defendants. *See supra* pp. 92 & 137-38.

3. *Content of due process limits on extraterritorial application of federal legislation.* Consider the standard adopted in *Davis* for due process limits on the extraterritorial reach of U.S. legislation. What does it mean to require a "sufficient nexus between the defendant and the United States that ... application [of U.S. law] would not be arbitrary or fundamentally unfair"? Was the outcome in *Davis* consistent with this standard? What factors are relevant to deciding whether extraterritorial application of U.S. law is "arbitrary or fundamentally unfair"? Are the factors articulated in the due process clause's "reasonableness" test for judicial jurisdiction relevant? What about the factors set forth in §403 of the *Restatement (Third) Foreign Relations Law*? Does *Davis* consider only the unfairness to private parties, or does it also (or instead) consider foreign nations' sovereignty?

4. *Authorities concluding that international law limits on legislative jurisdiction are irrelevant in U.S. courts.* Did extraterritorial application of federal law in *Davis* violate customary international law — as set out in the *Restatement (Third) Foreign Relations Law* §§402 & 403? Assume that it had. What relevance would this illegality have to the outcome of U.S. litigation?

Consider the comment in *Davis* that "[i]nternational law principles, standing on their own, do not create substantive rights or affirmative defenses for litigants in United States courts." Most lower courts have agreed, *see supra* pp. 513-14. The Supreme Court has evidenced no disagreement, although it has not confronted a case where it concluded that international law was inconsistent with U.S. legislation. What is the basis for *Davis's* statement that customary international law is not an independent basis for limits on U.S. legislative jurisdiction? Compare the Supreme Court's statement in *The Paquete Habana*, 175 U.S. 677, 700 (1900): "[i]nternational law is part of our law, and must be ascertained and administered by the courts of justice of appropriate jurisdiction." Under this rule, why don't international law limits on national legislative jurisdiction apply in U.S. courts? If such limits do apply, would a "last-in-time" rule also be applicable, as in the context of treaties?

5. *Authorities concluding that international law limits on legislative jurisdiction are incorporated by*

the due process clause. Recall that *Pennoyer* based due process limits on judicial jurisdiction on prevailing principles of international law, drawn principally from Joseph Story's *Commentaries. See supra* pp. 70-73. A broadly similar result applied in the context of legislative jurisdiction. *See supra* pp. 493-97 & *infra* pp. 546-52. Should the due process clause continue to incorporate *contemporary* international law limits on legislative jurisdiction? In contrast to *Davis*, a few courts have suggested that it does. *United States v. Javino*, 960 F.2d 1137, 1142-43 (2d Cir. 1992) ("Even had Congress intended all foreign manufacturers of firearms to comply with the requirements set out in [26 U.S.C.] §5822, there is substantial question as to whether it could lawfully have done so. Though Congress may prescribe laws concerning conduct outside the territorial boundaries of the United States 'that has or is intended to have substantial effect' within the United States, *Restatement (Third) Foreign Relations Law* §402(1)(c) (1987) ..., it may not regulate such conduct 'when the exercise of ... jurisdiction is unreasonable.'"); *Tamari v. Bache & Co. (Lebanon)*, 730 F.2d 1103, 1107 n.11 (7th Cir.), *cert. denied*, 469 U.S. 871 (1984) ("[w]ere Congress to enact a rule beyond the scope of [the] principles [contained in §§17-18 of the *Second Restatement*], the statute could be challenged as violating the due process clause"); *United States v. Layton*, 509 F. Supp. 212 (N.D. Cal. 1981). Is this an appropriate application of the due process clause?

6. *Authorities concluding that international law limits on legislative jurisdiction are not relevant to due process analysis.* Consider how *Davis* views the suggestion that international law is relevant to due process analysis: "International law principles may be useful as a rough guide of whether a sufficient nexus exists between the defendant and the United States so that application of the statute in question would not violate due process. However, danger exists that emphasis on international law principles will cause us to lose sight of the ultimate question: would application of the statute to the defendant be arbitrary or fundamentally unfair"? Is this a wise approach? Most courts have adopted the *Davis* approach, treating international law as nothing more than background material to what remains a question of U.S. fairness. *United States v. Peterson*, 812 F.2d 486 (9th Cir. 1987); *supra* pp. 512-13.

Which approach — that in *Davis* or that in decisions like *Javino* and *Tamari* — is wiser? Which is more consistent with the application of the due process clause to assertions of judicial jurisdiction?

7. *Relevance of foreign sovereignty to due process analysis.* Is a violation of a foreign state's sovereignty relevant to due process restrictions on U.S. legislative jurisdiction? The United Kingdom consented to the U.S. conduct in *Davis*. As a consequence, there was no basis for suggesting any infringement on U.K. sovereignty in violation of international law. Does this affect due process analysis? If the United Kingdom consents to the application of U.S. law, does this preclude any due process challenge to assertions of judicial jurisdiction? or are issues of fairness to private parties still relevant? Given the U.K. consent, is the court's focus on "fairness" more defensible?

Suppose that, in *Davis*, the United Kingdom had refused to consent to U.S. agents boarding the *Myth*, and that it had protested the extraterritorial application of U.S. law to Davis. Would those factors have been relevant to due process analysis? As discussed above, the due process clause has long been interpreted in the context of judicial jurisdiction as safeguarding the territorial sovereignty of co-equal states. *See supra* pp. 86-88. Recall also the concern in *Asahi Metal* over interference with U.S. foreign relations. *See supra* pp. 137-38. Are not such concerns even greater where legislative jurisdiction is concerned than where judicial jurisdiction is involved?

8. *Comparison between due process limits on federal legislation and due process limits on state choice of law.* How should due process limits on federal legislation, like those in *Davis*, compare to due process limits on state legislative jurisdiction, like those in *Dick* and *Allstate* (discussed below, *infra* pp. 518-44)? Should the due process clause impose more stringent limits on federal legislation than on state legislation? less stringent limits? or the same limits? Does the answer depend on whether you believe that foreign territorial sovereignty and federal foreign relations concerns are relevant? Suppose the only relevant concern to due process limits on legislative jurisdiction is fairness to individuals.

2. Constitutional Limits on State Legislative Jurisdiction

a. Historic Constitutional Limits on State Legislative Jurisdiction

In contrast to the general absence of constitutional limits on federal legislative jurisdiction, the Constitution has frequently been invoked as limiting the application of state law to conduct with interstate or international aspects.[83] A leading early decision concerning the Constitution's limits on state choice of law decisions was *New York Life Insurance Company v. Dodge*, decided in 1918.[84] The case arose from an application by Mr. Dodge, a Missouri resident, for life insurance from the New York Life Insurance Company. New York Life was a New York corporation, with its principal place of business in New York. The company accepted Mr. Dodge's application and issued a policy, which gave him the right to apply to its New York office for loans against the cash surrender value of the policy. Mr. Dodge duly borrowed money from New York Life, sending applications for loans from Missouri to New York, where they were accepted by New York Life.[85]

Disputes arose when Mr. Dodge missed a premium payment. As permitted by New York law, New York Life satisfied Mr. Dodge's outstanding indebtedness by drawing on the cash surrender value of Mr. Dodge's policy, thereby exhausting his funds. As a consequence, New York Life was also entitled to cancel Mr. Dodge's policy, which it did. He died shortly later, and his widow sued in Missouri on his insurance policy. She claimed that New York Life had no right, under Missouri law, to seize the value of Mr. Dodge's policy. The Missouri courts agreed.

The U.S. Supreme Court reversed in a 5-4 opinion by Justice McReynolds. The Court conceded that the life insurance policy was properly governed by Missouri law, because it has been issued in Missouri.[86] However, the Court held that the loans pursuant to the policy were "made" in New York, because that is where New York Life accepted Mr. Dodge's applications. Relying on its earlier decisions. Justice McReynolds reasoned that, for Missouri to apply its law to a New York contract

---

83. Indeed, a number of early U.S. state court decisions invoked strict territoriality principles, apparently based on the general common law, to conclude that state legislatures lacked the authority to extend state laws extraterritorially. *E.g.*, *State v. Knight*, 2 Hayw. (N.C.) 109 (1799) (North Carolina "cannot declare that an act done in Virginia by a citizen of Virginia shall be criminal and punishable in this state: our penal laws can only extend to the limits of this state, except as to our own citizens"); *People v. Merrill*, 2 Park. (N.Y.) 590 (1855) ("It cannot be pretended or assumed that a state has jurisdiction over crimes committed beyond its territorial limits"). *See* Beale, *The Jurisdiction of a Sovereign State*, 36 Harv. L. Rev. 241 (1923); George, *Extraterritorial Application of Penal Legislation*, 64 Mich. L. Rev. 609, 621 (1966).

84. 246 U.S. 357 (1918). *See also Western Union Telegraph Co. v. Brown*, 234 U.S. 542, 547 (1914) ("when a person recovers in one jurisdiction for a tort committed in another, he does so on the ground of an obligation incurred at the place of the tort that accompanies the person of the defendant elsewhere, and that is not only the ground but the measure of maximum recovery. The injustice of imposing a greater liability than that created by the law governing the conduct of the parties at the time of the act or omission complained of is obvious; and when a state attempts in this manner to affect conduct outside its jurisdiction, or the consequences of such conduct, and to infringe upon the power of the United States, it must fail.").

85. 246 U.S. at 365-66.

86. 246 U.S. at 371.

would "transcend[] the power of the state," in violation of the fourteenth amendment.[87]

Subsequent Supreme Court decisions departed from *Dodge*'s territorial reasoning. A 1943 decision in *Hoopeston Canning Company v. Cullen*[88] held that New York could regulate out-of-state reciprocal insurance companies covering New York risks, even where their contracts were made in other states. The territorial limits of *Dodge* and earlier decisions were replaced in *Hoopeston* by a flexible attention to "realistic considerations" and state regulatory interests:

> In determining the power of a state to apply its own regulatory laws to insurance business activities, the question in earlier cases became involved by conceptualistic discussion of theories of the place of contracting or of performance. More recently it has been recognized that a state may have substantial interests in the business of insurance of its people or property regardless of these isolated factors. This interest may be measured by highly realistic considerations such as the protection of the citizen insured or the protection of the state from the incidents of loss.[89]

Other decisions evidenced a similarly expansive view of the power of states to apply their own laws to multistate conduct.[90]

Nevertheless, in *Home Insurance Company v. Dick*,[91] a 1930 decision, the Supreme Court unanimously restated the continued importance of significant constitutional limits on state choice of law decisions. The Court's opinion in *Dick*, which is excerpted below, involved the application of Texas law to an insurance policy covering a vessel in Mexican waters. The Court ignored the potentially expansive rationale of *Hoopeston* and reaffirmed its historic territorial focus.

HOME INSURANCE CO. v. DICK
281 U.S. 397 (1930)

BRANDEIS, JUSTICE. Dick, a citizen of Texas, brought this action in a court of that State against Compania General Anglo-Mexicana de Seguros SA, a Mexican corporation, to recover on a policy of fire insurance for the total loss of a tug. ... This suit

---

87. 246 U.S. at 377. *Dodge* embraced a strictly territorial view of the due process clause, which appeared to constitutionalize prevailing territorial choice of law rules. The *Dodge* Court followed its earlier decision in *New York Life Ins. Co. v. Head*, 234 U.S. 149 (1914), where the Constitution was held to forbid Missouri from regulating a contract between New Mexico and New York residents: "It would be impossible to permit the statutes of Missouri to operate beyond the jurisdiction of that state and in the state of New York ... without throwing down the constitutional barrier by which all the states are restricted within the orbits of their lawful authority."

88. 318 U.S. 313 (1943).

89. 318 U.S. at 316.

90. *Watson v. Employers Liability Assurance Corp.*, 348 U.S. 66 (1954); *Pacific Employers Insurance Co. v. Industrial Accident Comm'n*, 306 U.S. 493 (1939).

91. 281 U.S. 397 (1930).

was not commenced till more than one year after the date of the loss. The policy provided: "It is understood and agreed that no judicial suit or demand shall be entered before any tribunal for the collection of any claim under this policy, unless such suits or demands are filed within one year counted as from the date on which such damage occurs." This provision was in accord with the Mexican law to which the policy was expressly made subject. It was issued by the Mexican company in Mexico to one Bonner, of Tampico, Mexico, and was there duly assigned to Dick prior to the loss. It covered the vessel only in certain Mexican waters. The premium was paid in Mexico; and the loss was "payable in the City of Mexico in current funds of the United States of Mexico, or their equivalent elsewhere." At the time the policy was issued, when it was assigned to him, and until after the loss, Dick actually resided in Mexico, although his permanent residence was in Texas. The contracts of reinsurance were effected by correspondence between the Mexican company in Mexico and the New York companies in New York. Nothing thereunder was to be done, or was in fact done, in Texas.

In the trial court, the garnishees contended that since the insurance contract was made and was to be performed in Mexico, and the one year provision was valid by its laws, Dick's failure to sue within one year after accrual of the alleged cause of action was a complete defense to the suit on the policy; that this failure also relieved the garnishees of any obligation as reinsurers. ... Dick demurred, on the ground that Article 5545 of the Texas Revised Civil Statutes provides: "No person, firm, corporation, association or combination of whatsoever kind shall enter into any stipulation, contract, or agreement, by reason whereof the time in which to sue thereon is limited to a shorter period than two years. And no stipulation, contract, or agreement for any such shorter limitation in which to sue shall ever be valid in this State."

The trial court sustained Dick's contention and entered judgment against the garnishees. On appeal, both [Texas] courts treated the policy provision as equivalent to a foreign statute of limitation; held that Article 5545 related to the remedy available in Texas courts; concluded that it was validly applicable to the case at bar; and affirmed the judgment of the trial court. The garnishees appealed to this Court on the ground that the statute, as construed and applied, violated their rights under the Federal Constitution. ...

The Texas statute as here construed and applied deprives the garnishees of property without due process of law. A State may, of course, prohibit and declare invalid the making of certain contracts within its borders. Ordinarily, it may prohibit performance within its borders, even of contracts validly made elsewhere, if they are required to be performed within the State and their performance would violate its laws. But, in the case at bar, nothing in any way relating to the policy sued on, or to the contracts of reinsurance, was ever done or required to be done in Texas. All acts relating to the making of the policy were done in Mexico. All in relation to the making of the contracts of reinsurance were done there or in New York. And, likewise, all things in regard to performance were to be done outside of Texas. Neither the Texas laws nor the Texas courts were invoked for any purpose, except by Dick in the bringing of this suit. The fact that Dick's permanent residence was in Texas is without significance. At all times here material, he was physically present and acting in Mexico. Texas was, therefore, without power to affect the terms of contracts so made. Its attempt to impose a greater obligation than that agreed upon and to seize property in payment of the imposed obligation violates the guaranty against deprivation of property without due process of law. ...

It is true ... that a State is not bound to provide remedies and procedure to suit the wishes of individual litigants. It may prescribe the kind of remedies to be available in its courts and dictate the practice and procedure to be followed in pursuing those remedies. Contractual provisions relating to these matters, even if valid where made, are often disregarded by the court of the forum, pursuant to statute or otherwise. But the Texas statute deals neither with the kind of remedy available nor with the mode in which it is to be pursued. It purports to create rights and obligations. It may not validly affect contracts which are neither made nor are to be performed in Texas. ... Dick urges that Article 5545 of the Texas law is a declaration of its public policy; and that a State may properly refuse to recognize foreign rights which violate its declared policy. ... [Texas] may not abrogate the rights of parties beyond its borders having no relation to anything done or to be done within them. ...

Finally, it is urged that the Federal Constitution does not require the States to recognize and protect rights derived from the laws of foreign countries — that as to them the full faith and credit clause has no application. ... The claims here asserted are not based upon the full faith and credit clause. ... They rest upon the Fourteenth Amendment. Its protection extends to aliens. ...

Notes on Dick

1. *Historic constitutional limitations on state legislative jurisdiction.* Early Supreme Court decisions applied relatively strict constitutional limitations on state legislative jurisdiction. *See New York Life Ins. Co., v. Dodge*, 246 U.S. 357 (1918); *Western Union Telegraph Co. v. Brown*, 234 U.S. 542 (1914); *New York Life Ins. Co. v. Head*, 234 U.S. 149 (1914). What is the Constitution's textual basis for limits on state legislative jurisdiction?

(a) *Full faith and credit clause.* Consider the language of the full faith and credit clause: "Full Faith and Credit shall be given in each State to the public Acts, Records and judicial Proceedings of every other State. And the Congress may by general Laws prescribe the Manner in which such Acts, Records and Proceedings shall be proved, and the effect thereof." U.S. Const. Art. IV, §1. Does this provision suggest constitutional limits on the power of a state to make its law applicable to particular conduct? How? Does the full faith and credit clause apply to the laws of foreign nations?

(b) *Due process clause.* Should the fourteenth amendment's due process clause be interpreted to limit the legislative jurisdiction of the several U.S. states? Consider the language of the due process clause: "No state shall ... deprive any person of life, liberty, or property, without due process of law." Does this suggest constitutional limits on state legislative jurisdiction? If so, would the fifth amendment's due process clause impose the same limits on federal legislation?

(c) *International law analogy.* Recall the strict territorial limits that the due process clause was said to impose on the judicial jurisdiction of state courts in *Rose v. Himely* and *Pennoyer v. Neff. See supra* pp. 70-73. The rationale for those limits was the Court's conclusion that the due process clause, and the federal structure of the Constitution more generally, made prevailing international law limitations on judicial jurisdiction applicable as between the several states. *See supra* pp. 70-73. Recall also the contemporary statement of this view in *World-Wide Volkswagen*, which looked to principles of federalism to limit state judicial jurisdiction:

[The due process clause] acts to ensure that the States, through their Courts, do not reach out beyond the limits imposed on them by their status as co-equal sovereigns in a federal system .... [T]he framers ... intended that the states retain many essential attributes of sovereignty, including in particular, the sovereign power to try causes in their court. The sovereignty of each state, in turn, implied a limitation on the sovereignty of all its sister states ... a limitation express or implicit in both the original scheme of the Constitution and the fourteenth amendment. 444 U.S. 286, 292 (1980).

See supra pp. 87-88. Is the same rationale also applicable to international law limitations on legislative jurisdiction?

What were prevailing international law limits on legislative jurisdiction in the 19th century? Consider the excerpts from Joseph Story's *Commentaries on the Conflict of Laws*, set forth above, *see supra* pp. 501-02. Consider also decisions like *The Apollon*, 22 U.S. 362 (1824), and *Schooner Exchange v. McFaddon*, 11 U.S. 116 (1812). As discussed above, these decisions reasoned that international law imposed strict territorial limits on national legislative jurisdiction. *See supra* pp. 494-97. Compare the effect of such international law limits on *Home Insurance Co. v. Dick* with the reliance on international law in *Pennoyer*.

(d) *Purposes of constitutional limits on state legislative jurisdiction.* What interests are served by imposing constitutional limits on state legislative jurisdiction? Do such limits: (a) protect the sovereignty of other states; (b) protect individuals from unfair arbitrary or unforeseeable applications of substantive laws; (c) protect interstate commerce and the interstate system from unduly burdensome or conflicting state regulation; or (d) accomplish something else? Compare the interests that are served by due process limits on judicial jurisdiction. *See supra* pp. 87-94.

3. *Constitutional limits on state legislative jurisdiction in* Dick. Consider the due process limits on state legislative jurisdiction in *Dick*. According to the Court, the Constitution denies a state the power to affect "the rights of parties beyond its borders having no relation to anything done or to be done within them." In *Dick*, "[a]ll acts relating to the making of the policy were done in Mexico. All in relation to the making of the contracts of reinsurance were done there or in New York. And, likewise, all things in regard to performance were to be done outside of Texas." Because Texas assertedly had no significant connection to Mr. Dick's claim, it was "without power to affect the terms of the contracts" he relied upon. The Court's language, at least, was reflective of territorial limits on state legislative jurisdiction, paralleling *Pennoyer*'s territorial limits on judicial jurisdiction. *See supra* pp. 70-73. Is the result in *Dick* appropriate? Should the due process clause, or other provisions of the Constitution, impose such territorial limits on state legislative jurisdiction?

4. *Dick's constitutional limits on state legislative jurisdiction.* What precisely is the test in *Dick* for when a state may not constitutionally exercise legislative jurisdiction? On its facts, was *Dick* indeed a case where Texas should have been constitutionally barred from applying its law? What is the relevance of the specific Texas law at issue — which dealt with statutes of limitations?

5. *Should the Constitution limit the application of state legislation to conduct or persons outside the United States.* In *Dick*, Texas courts applied Texas law to conduct in Mexico — and not to conduct in another U.S. state. Is that relevant to due process or full faith and credit analysis? If the focus of constitutional protections is on protecting the sovereignty of other U.S. states, is there any reason to restrict the application of U.S. state laws to conduct in other countries? Conversely, should state infringements of the sovereignty of foreign nations be regarded as more serious than infringement on the sovereignty of other U.S. states? Why?

(a) *Full faith and credit clause not applicable to foreign state's laws.* The full faith and credit clause only requires states to accord full faith and credit to the acts of other U.S. states. *Dick* expressly confirms this. Is there any way that the clause can apply in cases involving the laws or judgments of other nations?

(b) *Applicability of due process clause in international cases.* Does the due process clause have any limitation, like the full faith and credit clause, to domestic cases? What did the Court hold in *Dick* about the due process clause's applicability to state legislation purporting to extend to conduct in a foreign nation? As discussed above, one rationale for due process limits on state legislative jurisdiction is concern about infringing on the territorial sovereignty of other U.S. states. This rationale obviously did not apply in *Dick*. What does justify application of the due process clause in such cases? Is it the surprise and unfairness that private parties face when they are subjected to laws lacking any connection to their conduct? Is it the need to avoid infringing on foreign nations' sovereignty?

(c) *Content of due process limits in international cases.* If the Constitution does impose limits on the application of state legislation to conduct or persons outside the United States, what should those limits be? Is it appropriate to apply the same limits as those applicable to conduct or persons in other U.S. states? Is the sovereignty of foreign states a greater or lesser obstacle than the sovereignty of sister states to the application of U.S. state law to conduct abroad? Recall the similar issues that arise in the context of judicial jurisdiction. *See supra* pp. 92-93 & 137-38. In many cases, foreign law can be expected to be very different from any U.S. state law — while the variations between the substantive laws of different U.S. states are often slight. Does this affect the extent of constitutional limits on the application of U.S. state law to non-U.S. occurrences?

6. *Considerations of reciprocity.* Suppose that, in *Dick*, Mexican courts would readily have applied Mexican law to claims in the reverse circumstances (*i.e.*, cases involving events occurring wholly in Texas and lacking any Mexican nexus). Suppose that a particular foreign nation did not impose any limits at all upon the application of its law to conduct occurring in the United States. Should the Constitution forbid state courts from applying their laws to the conduct of foreign nationals in that country in an equally unrestrained fashion? If a foreign country takes the view that international law does not limit the extraterritorial application of *its* law, why should U.S. courts take a different view towards that state? Recall the similar issues that arise in the context of judicial jurisdiction. *See supra* p. 93. In *Dick*, one defendant was a U.S. company. Would reciprocity considerations apply to it?

7. *Applicability of due process protections to aliens.* One of the defendants in *Dick* was a Mexican company. Why does the due process clause protect non-U.S. parties? What does *Dick* say? Compare the discussion above of due process limits on judicial jurisdiction over non-U.S. defendants. *See supra* pp. 92-93 & 137-38.

8. *Texas's interest in protecting Texan domiciliaries.* Mr. Dick was a permanent resident of Texas. Did this not give Texas an interest in application of its law invalidating contract terms that unfairly treated Texas consumers? Does the Court assign any weight to Mr. Dick's Texas residence? Is that residence a sufficient basis for concluding that the Constitution should not bar application of Texan law? As discussed below, contemporary choice of law theory in the United States sometimes permits application of a state's law based solely on the fact that the injured plaintiff was a forum resident. *See infra* p. 649. Why wasn't a similar analysis followed in *Dick*?

As discussed above, international law does not generally permit legislative jurisdiction based on the "passive personality" principle. This principle would allow a state to apply its laws, outside its territory, to persons or conduct that harm its nationals. *See supra* pp. 507-08. Should due process analysis follow international law in rejecting the passive personality principle? In both domestic and international cases?

9. *Possibility of unfair surprise in* Dick. The Court did not mention it in *Dick*, but one could argue that the Mexican defendant (and the New York reinsurance defendants) would have been unfairly surprised by the application of Texas law to an insurance policy (expressly governed by Mexican law) that was issued in Mexico to a Mexican national, for a Mexican vessel, but only while the vessel was in Mexican waters. The policy was only later assigned to Mr. Dick, who happened to be a Texas resident. One might think, therefore, that the Mexican defendant would have been surprised to learn that Texas law was applicable to its dispute with Mr. Dick.

Some commentators have observed, however, that the insurance policy provided that any loss was "payable to the Texas Gulf Steamship Company of Galveston, Texas, and C.J. Dick, as their respective interests may appear." *Home Insurance Co. v. Dick*, Transcript of Record, at 38-39; 281 U.S. at 403 n.2. Moreover, the Mexican insurer had specifically consented to the assignment of the insurance policy to Mr. Dick. Arguably, therefore, the Mexican insurance company knew that it was dealing with a Texas resident (although there appears to have been nothing specifically identifying Mr. Dick as such). Perhaps it therefore should have foreseen the possibility that Texas law might apply to its dispute. *See* R. Weintraub, *Commentary on the Conflict of Laws* 522-23 (3d ed. 1986). Does the fact that a party enters into a contract with a national or resident of one country suggest that that country's laws will apply to the contract?

10. *Choice of law clause in* Dick. Buried in the *Dick* opinion is the passing observation that the parties had agreed that Mexican law would govern their contract. What is the relevance of the Mexican choice of law clause in Mr. Dick's insurance policy to due process analysis? Does it bear upon the Mexican insurer's likely expectations? Should the due process clause make it harder for a state to apply its law to override the parties' choice of law, than to apply its law in the absence of a choice of law agreement?

b. Contemporary Constitutional Limits on State Legislative Jurisdiction

As in other jurisdictional contexts, the strict territorial limits of *The Apollon*,

Dodge, and *Dick* did not survive for long.[92] The Court made it clear, in a number of decisions during the 1940's and thereafter, that both Congress and the states had the constitutional authority to exercise legislative jurisdiction over persons, property, and conduct beyond their borders.[93]

It is also now well-settled that "in many situations a state court may be free to apply one of several choices of law."[94] The Court and others have frequently said that the Constitution imposes only "modest restrictions on the application of forum law."[95] In international cases, these restrictions derived principally from: (i) the due process clause, and (ii) the foreign commerce clause and other affirmative grants of authority to the federal government in international matters.[96]

i. Due Process Limitations on State Choice of Law

Although the Court has not addressed the question with any frequency, it has apparently concluded that the due process and full faith and credit clauses impose substantially the same restrictions on state choice of law decisions.[97] As Justice Scalia put it recently, "[t]he nub of the ... controversy ... is the scope of constitutionally permissible legislative jurisdiction," and "it matters little whether that is discussed in the context of the Full Faith and Credit Clause ... or in the context of the Due Process Clause."[98] (In contrast, Justice Stevens, and some commentators, take the position that the two clauses impose different standards; they reason that the full faith and credit clause protects the "interests of other sovereign States," while the due process clause ensures "fairness of ... decision to the litigants."[99])

The basic standard applicable to legislative jurisdiction under the full faith and credit and the due process clauses is broadly similar in language to the Court's constitutional limits on judicial jurisdiction: "'for a State's substantive law to be selected in a constitutionally permissible manner, that State must have a significant contact or significant aggregation of contacts, creating state interests, such that choice of its law is neither arbitrary nor fundamentally unfair.'"[100] In contrast to the judicial jurisdiction context, however, the Court has seldom found state choice of law decisions to violate this standard. The plurality opinion in *Allstate Insurance Co. v. Hague*, excerpted below, is a good illustration of the modest effect of due process limits on state legislative jurisdiction.

---

92. *Compare supra* pp. 70-77.

93. *See infra* pp. 535-37.

94. *Phillips Petroleum Co. v. Shutts*, 472 U.S. 797, 823 (1985).

95. 472 U.S. at 818.

96. *See infra* pp. 525-44.

97. 472 U.S. at 818-19

98. *Sun Oil Co. v. Wortman*, 486 U.S. 717, 730 n.3 (1988). *See also Phillips Petroleum Co. v. Shutts*, 472 U.S. 797, 818 (1985).

99. *Phillips Petroleum Co. v. Shutts*, 472 U.S. 797, 824 (1985) (Stevens, J., concurring); *Allstate Ins. Co. v. Hague*, 449 U.S. 302, 320 (1981) (Stevens, J., concurring).

100. 472 U.S. at 818-19 (quoting *Allstate Ins. Co. v. Hague*, 449 U.S. 302, 312-13 (1981)).

ALLSTATE INSURANCE COMPANY v. HAGUE

449 U.S. 302 (1981)

JUSTICE BRENNAN announced the judgment of the Court and delivered an opinion, in which JUSTICE WHITE, JUSTICE MARSHALL, and JUSTICE BLACK-MUN joined. This Court granted certiorari to determine whether the Due Process Clause of the Fourteenth Amendment or the Full Faith and Credit Clause of Art. IV, §1, of the U.S. Constitution bars the Minnesota Supreme Court's choice of substantive Minnesota law to govern the effect of a provision in an insurance policy issued to respondent's decedent.

I. Respondent's late husband, Ralph Hague, died of injuries suffered when a motorcycle on which he was a passenger was struck from behind by an automobile. The accident occurred in Pierce County, Wisconsin, which is immediately across the Minnesota border from Red Wing, Minnesota. The operators of both vehicles were Wisconsin residents, as was the decedent, who, at the time of the accident, resided with respondent in Hager City, Wisconsin, which is one and one-half miles from Red Wing. Mr. Hague had been employed in Red Wing for the 15 years immediately preceding his death and had commuted daily from Wisconsin to his place of employment. Neither the operator of the motorcycle nor the operator of the automobile carried valid insurance. However, the decedent held a policy issued by petitioner Allstate Insurance Co. covering three automobiles owned by him and containing an uninsured motorist clause insuring him against loss incurred from accidents with uninsured motorists. The uninsured motorist coverage was limited to $15,000 for each automobile.[101]

After the accident, but prior to the initiation of this lawsuit, respondent moved to Red Wing. Subsequently, she married a Minnesota resident and established residence with her new husband in Savage, Minnesota ... [She later] brought this action in Minnesota District Court seeking a declaration under Minnesota law that the $15,000 uninsured motorist coverage on each of her late husband's three automobiles could be "stacked" to provide total coverage of $45,000. Petitioner defended on the ground that whether the three uninsured motorist coverages could be stacked should be determined by Wisconsin law, since the insurance policy was delivered in Wisconsin, the accident occurred in Wisconsin, and all persons involved were Wisconsin residents at the time of the accident. The Minnesota District Court disagreed. Interpreting Wisconsin law to disallow stacking, the court concluded that Minnesota's choice-of-law rules required the application of Minnesota law permitting stacking. The court refused to apply Wisconsin law as "inimical to the public policy of Minnesota" and granted summary judgment for respondent.

The Minnesota Supreme Court, sitting en banc, affirmed the District Court. The

---

101. Ralph Hague paid a separate premium for each automobile including an additional separate premium for each uninsured motorist coverage.

court, also interpreting Wisconsin law to prohibit stacking, applied Minnesota law after analyzing the relevant Minnesota contacts and interests within the analytical framework developed by Professor Leflar. *See* Leflar, *Choice-Influencing Considerations in Conflicts Law*, 41 N.Y.U. L. Rev. 267 (1966). The state court, therefore, examined the conflict-of-laws issue in terms of (1) predictability of result, (2) maintenance of interstate order, (3) simplification of the judicial task, (4) advancement of the forum's governmental interests, and (5) application of the better rule of law. Although stating that the Minnesota contacts might not be, "in themselves, sufficient to mandate application of [Minnesota] law," under the first four factors, the court concluded that the fifth factor — application of the better rule of law — favored selection of Minnesota law. The court emphasized that a majority of States allow stacking and that legal decisions allowing stacking "are fairly recent and well considered in light of current uses of automobiles." In addition, the court found the Minnesota rule superior to Wisconsin's "because it requires the cost of accidents with uninsured motorists to be spread more broadly through insurance premiums than does the Wisconsin rule." Finally, after rehearing en banc, the court buttressed its initial opinion by indicating "that contracts of insurance on motor vehicles are in a class by themselves" since an insurance company "knows the automobile is a movable item which will be driven from state to state." From this premise the court concluded that application of Minnesota law was "not so arbitrary and unreasonable as to violate due process."

II. It is not for this Court to say whether the choice-of-law analysis suggested by Professor Leflar is to be preferred or whether we would make the same choice-of-law decision if sitting as the Minnesota Supreme Court. Our sole function is to determine whether the Minnesota Supreme Court's choice of its own substantive law in this case exceeded federal constitutional limitations. Implicit in this inquiry is the recognition, long accepted by this Court, that a set of facts giving rise to a lawsuit, or a particular issue within a lawsuit, may justify, in constitutional terms, application of the law of more than one jurisdiction. *See generally Clay v. Sun Insurance Office, Ltd.*, 377 U.S. 179, 181-182 (1964) (hereinafter cited as *Clay II*). As a result, the forum State may have to select one law from among the laws of several jurisdictions having some contact with the controversy.

In deciding constitutional choice-of-law questions, whether under the Due Process Clause or the Full Faith and Credit Clause,[102] this Court has traditionally

---

102. This Court has taken a similar approach in deciding choice-of-law cases under both the Due Process Clause and the Full Faith and Credit Clause. In each instance, the Court has examined the relevant contacts and resulting interests of the State whose law was applied. *See, e.g., Nevada v. Hall*, 440 U.S. 410, 424 (1979). Although at one time the Court required a more exacting standard under the Full Faith and Credit Clause than under the Due Process Clause for evaluating the constitutionality of choice-of-law decisions, the Court has since abandoned the weighing-of-interests requirement. *Carroll v. Lanza*, 349 U.S. 408 (1955); *see Nevada v. Hall, supra*. Different considerations are of course at issue when full faith and credit is to be accorded to acts, records, and proceedings outside the choice-of-law area, such as in the case of sister state-court judgments.

examined the contacts of the State, whose law was applied, with the parties and with the occurrence or transaction giving rise to the litigation. In order to ensure that the choice of law is neither arbitrary nor fundamentally unfair, the Court has invalidated the choice of law of a State which has had no significant contact or significant aggregation of contacts, creating state interests, with the parties and the occurrence or transaction.[103]

Two instructive examples of such invalidation are *Home Ins. Co. v. Dick*, [excerpted above at pp. 520-22], and *John Hancock Mutual Life Ins. Co. v. Yates*, 299 U.S. 178 (1936). In both cases, the selection of forum law rested exclusively on the presence of one nonsignificant forum contact.... *Dick* and *Yates* stand for the proposition that if a State has only an insignificant contact with the parties and the occurrence or transaction, application of its law is unconstitutional. *Dick* concluded that nominal residence — standing alone — was inadequate; *Yates* held that a post-occurrence change of residence to the forum State — standing alone — was insufficient to justify application of forum law. Although instructive as extreme examples of selection of forum law, neither *Dick* nor *Yates* governs this case. For in contrast to those decisions, here the Minnesota contacts with the parties and the occurrence are obviously significant. Thus, this case is like *Alaska Packers Cardillo v. Liberty Mutual Ins. Co.*, 330 U.S. 469 (1947), and *Clay II* — cases where this Court sustained choice-of-law decisions based on the contacts of the State, whose law was applied, with the parties and occurrence.

In *Alaska Packers*, the Court upheld California's application of its Workmen's Compensation Act, where the most significant contact of the worker with California was his execution of an employment contract in California. The worker, a nonresident alien from Mexico, was hired in California for seasonal work in a salmon canning factory in Alaska. As part of the employment contract, the employer, who was doing business in California, agreed to transport the worker to Alaska and to return him to California when the work was completed. Even though the employee contracted to be bound by the Alaska Workmen's Compensation Law and was injured in Alaska, he sought an award under the California Workmen's Compensation Act. The Court held that the choice of California law was not "so arbitrary or unreasonable as to amount to a denial of due process," because "[w]ithout a remedy in California, [he] would be remediless," and because of California's interest that the worker not become a public charge. ...

Clay II upheld the constitutionality of the application of forum law. There, a policy of insurance had issued in Illinois to an Illinois resident. Subsequently the insured moved to Florida and suffered a property loss in Florida. Relying explicitly on the nationwide coverage of the policy and the presence of the insurance company

---

103. Prior to the advent of interest analysis in the state courts as the "dominant mode of analysis in modern choice of law theory," Silberman, *Shaffer v. Heitner: The End of an Era*, 53 N.Y.U.L. Rev. 33, 80 n.259 (1978), the prevailing choice-of-law methodology focused on the jurisdiction where a particular event occurred. *See, e.g., Restatement (First) Conflict of Laws* (1934). ...

in Florida and implicitly on the plaintiff's Florida residence and the occurrence of the property loss in Florida, the Court sustained the Florida court's choice of Florida law. The lesson from *Dick* and *Yates*, which found insufficient forum contacts to apply forum law, and from *Alaska Packers, Cardillo,* and *Clay II,* which found adequate contacts to sustain the choice of forum law,[104] is that for a State's substantive law to be selected in a constitutionally permissible manner, that State must have a signifi- cant contact or significant aggregation of contacts, creating state interests, such that choice of its law is neither arbitrary nor fundamentally unfair. ...

State must have significant contact or...

   III. Minnesota has three contacts with the parties and the occurrence giving rise to the litigation. In the aggregate, these contacts permit selection by the Minnesota Supreme Court of Minnesota law allowing the stacking of Mr. Hague's uninsured motorist coverages.

   First, and for our purposes a very important contact, Mr. Hague was a member of Minnesota's work force, having been employed by a Red Wing, Minn., enterprise for the 15 years preceding his death. While employment status may implicate a state interest less substantial than does resident status, that interest is nevertheless impor- tant. The State of employment has police power responsibilities towards the nonresi- dent employee that are analogous, if somewhat less profound, than towards resi- dents. Thus, such employees use state services and amenities and may call upon state facilities in appropriate circumstances.

   In addition, Mr. Hague commuted to work in Minnesota, a contact which was important in *Cardillo v. Liberty Mutual Ins. Co.,* 330 U.S. at 475-476 (daily commute between residence in District of Columbia and workplace in Virginia), and was pre- sumably covered by his uninsured motorist coverage during the commute. The State's interest in its commuting nonresident employees reflects a state concern for the safety and well-being of its work force and the concomitant effect on Minnesota employers.

   That Mr. Hague was not killed while commuting to work or while in Minnesota does not dictate a different result. To hold that the Minnesota Supreme Court's

---

104. The Court has upheld choice-of-law decisions challenged on constitutional grounds in numer- ous other decisions. *See Nevada v. Hall, supra* (upholding California's application of California law to automobile accident in California between two California residents and a Nevada official driving car owned by State of Nevada while engaged in official business in California); *Carroll v. Lanza,* 394 U.S. 408 (1955) (upholding Arkansas' choice of Arkansas law where Missouri employee executed employment con- tract with Missouri employer and as injured on job in Arkansas but was removed immediately to a Missouri hospital); *Watson v. Employers Liability Assurance Corp.,* 384 U.S. 66 (1954) (allowing application of Louisiana direct action statute by Louisiana resident against insurer even though policy was written and delivered in another State, where plaintiff was injured in Louisiana); *Pacific Employers Ins. Co. v. Industrial Accident Comm'n,* 306 U.S. 493 (1939) (holding Full Faith and Credit Clause not violated where California applied own Workmen's Compensation Act in case of injury suffered by Massachusetts employee tem- porarily in California in course of employment). Thus, *Nevada v. Hall,* and *Watson v. Employers Liability Assurance Corp.,* upheld application of forum law where the relevant contacts consisted of plaintiff's resi- dence and the place of the injury. *Pacific Employers Ins. Co. v. Industrial Accident Comm'n,* and *Carroll v. Lanza* relied on the place of the injury arising from the respective employee's temporary presence in the forum State in connection with his employment.

choice of Minnesota law violated the Constitution for that reason would require too narrow a view of Minnesota's relationship with the parties and the occurrence giving rise to the litigation. An automobile accident need not occur within a particular jurisdiction for that jurisdiction to be connected to the occurrence.[105] Similarly, the occurrence of a crash fatal to a Minnesota employee in another State is a Minnesota contact. If Mr. Hague had only been injured and missed work for a few weeks the effect on the Minnesota employer would have been palpable and Minnesota's interest in having its employee made whole would be evident. Mr. Hague's death affects Minnesota's interest still more acutely, even though Mr. Hague will not return to the Minnesota work force. Minnesota's work force is surely affected by the level of protection the State extends to it, either directly or indirectly. Vindication of the rights of the estate of a Minnesota employee, therefore, is an important state concern.

Mr. Hague's residence in Wisconsin does not — as Allstate seems to argue — constitutionally mandate application of Wisconsin law to the exclusion of forum law. If, in the instant case, the accident had occurred in Minnesota between Mr. Hague and an uninsured Minnesota motorist, if the insurance contract had been executed in Minnesota covering a Minnesota registered company automobile which Mr. Hague was permitted to drive, and if a Wisconsin court sought to apply Wisconsin law, certainly Mr. Hague's residence in Wisconsin, his commute between Wisconsin and Minnesota, and the insurer's presence in Wisconsin should be adequate to apply Wisconsin's law.[106] Employment status is not a sufficiently less important status than residence, when combined with Mr. Hague's daily commute across state lines and the other Minnesota contacts present, to prohibit the choice-of-law result in this case on constitutional grounds.

Second, Allstate was at all times present and doing business in Minnesota.[107] By

---

105. Numerous cases have applied the law of a jurisdiction other than the situs of the injury where there existed some other link between that jurisdiction and the occurrence. *See, e.g., Cardillo v. Liberty Mutual Ins. Co.; Alaska Packers Assn. v. Industrial Accident Comm'n; Babcock v. Jackson*, 12 N.Y.2d 473 (1963).

106. Of course Allstate could not be certain that Wisconsin law would necessarily govern any accident which occurred in Wisconsin, whether brought in the Wisconsin courts or elsewhere. Such an expectation would give controlling significance to the wooden *lex loci delicti* doctrine. While the place of the accident is a factor to be considered in choice-of-law analysis, to apply blindly the traditional, but now largely abandoned, doctrine would fail to distinguish between the relative importance of various legal issues involved in a lawsuit as well as the relationship of other jurisdictions to the parties and the occurrence or transaction. If, for example, Mr. Hague had been a Wisconsin resident and employee who was injured in Wisconsin and was then taken by ambulance to a hospital in Red Wing, Minn., where he languished for several weeks before dying, Minnesota's interest in ensuring that its medical creditors were paid would be obvious. ...

107. The Court has recognized that examination of a State's contacts may result in divergent conclusions for jurisdiction and choice-of-law purposes. *See Kulko v. California Superior Court*, 436 U.S. 84, 98 (1978) (no jurisdiction in California but California law "arguably might" apply); *Shaffer v. Heitner*, 433 U.S. at 215 (no jurisdiction in Delaware, although Delaware interest "may support the application of Delaware law"). Nevertheless, "both inquiries 'are often closely related and to a substantial degree depend upon similar considerations.'" *Shaffer*, 433 U.S. at 224-225 (Brennan, J., concurring in part and dissenting in part). Here, of course, jurisdiction in the Minnesota courts is unquestioned, a factor not without significance in assessing the constitutionality of Minnesota's choice of its own substantive law.

virtue of its presence, Allstate can hardly claim unfamiliarity with the laws of the host jurisdiction and surprise that the state courts might apply forum law to litigation in which the company is involved. "Particularly since the company was licensed to do business in [the forum], it must have known it might be sued there, and that [the forum] courts would feel bound by [forum] law." *Clay v. Sun Ins. Office Ltd.*, 363 U.S. 207, 221 (1960) (Black, J., dissenting).[108] Moreover, Allstate's presence in Minnesota gave Minnesota an interest in regulating the company's insurance obligations insofar as they affected both a Minnesota resident and court-appointed representative — respondent — and a longstanding member of Minnesota's work force — Mr. Hague.

Third, respondent became a Minnesota resident prior to institution of this litigation. The stipulated facts reveal that she first settled in Red Wing, Minn., the town in which her late husband had worked. She subsequently moved to Savage, Minn., after marrying a Minnesota resident who operated an automobile service station in Bloomington, Minn. Her move to Savage occurred "almost concurrently," 289 N.W.2d at 45, with the initiation of the instant case. There is no suggestion that Mrs. Hague moved to Minnesota in anticipation of this litigation or for the purpose of finding a legal climate especially hospitable to her claim.[109] The stipulated facts, sparse as they are, negate any such inference.

While *John Hancock Mutual Life Ins. Co. v. Yates*, 299 U.S. 178 (1936), held that a postoccurrence change of residence to the forum State was insufficient in and of itself to confer power on the forum State to choose its law, that case did not hold that such a change of residence was irrelevant. Here, of course, respondent's bona fide residence in Minnesota was not the sole contact Minnesota had with this litigation. And in connection with her residence in Minnesota, respondent was appointed personal representative of Mr. Hague's estate by the Registrar of Probate for the County of Goodhue, Minn. Respondent's residence and subsequent appointment in Minnesota as personal representative of her late husband's estate constitute a Minnesota contact which gives Minnesota an interest in respondent's recovery, an interest which the court below identified as full compensation for "resident accident victims" to keep them "off welfare rolls" and able "to meet financial obligations."

---

108. There is no element of unfair surprise or frustration of legitimate expectations as a result of Minnesota's choice of its law. Because Allstate was doing business in Minnesota and was undoubtedly aware that Mr. Hague was a Minnesota employee, it had to have anticipated that Minnesota law might apply to an accident in which Mr. Hague was involved. Indeed, Allstate specifically anticipated that Mr. Hague might suffer an accident either in Minnesota or elsewhere in the United States, outside of Wisconsin, since the policy it issued offered continental coverage. At the same time, Allstate did not seek to control construction of the contract since the policy contained no choice-of-law clause dictating application of Wisconsin law.

109. The dissent suggests that considering respondent's postoccurrence change of residence as one of the Minnesota contacts will encourage forum shopping. This overlooks the fact that her change of residence was bona fide and not motivated by litigation considerations.

aggregation of contacts

In sum, Minnesota had a significant aggregation[110] of contacts with the parties and the occurrence, creating state interests, such that application of its law was neither arbitrary nor fundamentally unfair. Accordingly, the choice of Minnesota law by the Minnesota Supreme Court did not violate the Due Process Clause or the Full Faith and Credit Clause.

STEVENS, JUSTICE, concurring. As I view this unusual case — in which neither precedent nor constitutional language provides sure guidance — two separate questions must be answered. First, does the Full Faith and Credit Clause require Minnesota, the forum State, to apply Wisconsin law? Second, does the Due Process Clause of the Fourteenth Amendment prevent Minnesota from applying its own law? The first inquiry implicates the federal interest in ensuring that Minnesota respect the sovereignty of the State of Wisconsin; the second implicates the litigants' interests in a fair adjudication of their rights. ...

I. The Full Faith and Credit Clause is one of several provisions in the Federal Constitution designed to transform the several States from independent sovereignties into a single, unified Nation. The Full Faith and Credit Clause implements this design by directing that a State, when acting as the forum for litigation having multistate aspects or implications, respect the legitimate interests of other States and avoid infringement upon their sovereignty. The Clause does not, however, rigidly require the forum State to apply foreign law whenever another State has a valid interest in the litigation. On the contrary, in view of the fact that the forum State is also a sovereign in its own right, in appropriate cases it may attach paramount importance to its own legitimate interests.[111] Accordingly, the fact that a choice-of-law decision may be unsound as a matter of conflicts law does not necessarily implicate the federal concerns embodied in the Full Faith and Credit Clause. Rather in my opinion, the Clause should not invalidate a state court's choice of forum law unless that choice threatens the federal interest in national unity by unjustifiably infringing upon the legitimate interests of another State.

In this case, I think the Minnesota courts' decision to apply Minnesota law was plainly unsound as a matter of normal conflicts law. Both the execution of the insurance contract and the accident giving rise to the litigation took place in Wisconsin. Moreover, when both of those events occurred the plaintiff, the decedent, and the operators of both vehicles were all residents of Wisconsin. Nevertheless, I do not believe that any threat to national unity or Wisconsin's sovereignty ensues from allowing the substantive question presented by this case to be determined by the law of another State. ...

II. It may be assumed that a choice-of-law decision would violate the Due

---

110. We express no view whether the first two contacts, either together or separately, would have sufficed to sustain the choice of Minnesota law made by the Minnesota Supreme Court.

111. For example, it is well established that "the Full Faith and Credit Clause does not require a State to apply another State's law in violation of its own legitimate public policy." *Nevada v. Hall*, 440 U.S. 410, 422 (1979).

Process Clause if it were totally arbitrary or if it were fundamentally unfair to either litigant. I question whether a judge's decision to apply the law of his own State could ever be described as wholly irrational. For judges are presumably familiar with their own state law and may find it difficult and time consuming to discover and apply correctly the law of another State. The forum State's interest in the fair and efficient administration of justice is therefore sufficient, in my judgment, to attach a presumption of validity to a forum State's decision to apply its own law to a dispute over which it has jurisdiction.

The forum State's interest in the efficient operation of its judicial system is clearly not sufficient, however, to justify the application of a rule of law that is fundamentally unfair to one of the litigants .... Concern about the fairness of the forum's choice of its own rule might arise if that rule favored residents over nonresidents,[112] if it represented a dramatic departure from the rule that obtains in most American jurisdictions, or if the rule itself was unfair on its face or as applied.

The application of an otherwise acceptable rule of law may result in unfairness to the litigants if, in engaging in the activity which is the subject of the litigation, they could not reasonably have anticipated that their actions would later be judged by this rule of law. A choice-of-law decision that frustrates the justifiable expectations of the parties can be fundamentally unfair. This desire to prevent unfair surprise to a litigant has been the central concern in this Court's review of choice-of-law decisions under the Due Process Clause.[113]

Neither the "stacking" rule itself, nor Minnesota's application of that rule to these litigants, raises any serious question of fairness. As the plurality observes, "[s]tacking was the rule in most States at the time the policy was issued." Moreover, the rule is consistent with the economics of a contractual relationship in which the policyholder paid three separate premiums for insurance coverage for three automobiles, including a separate premium for each uninsured motorist coverage. Nor am I persuaded that the decision of the Minnesota courts to apply the "stacking" rule in this case can be said to violate due process because that decision frustrates the reasonable expectations of the contracting parties.

Contracting parties can, of course, make their expectations explicit by providing in their contract either that the law of a particular jurisdiction shall govern questions of contract interpretation, or that a particular substantive rule, for instance "stacking," shall or shall not apply. In the absence of such express provisions, the contract

---

112. Discrimination against nonresidents would be constitutionally suspect even if the Due Process Clause were not a check upon a State's choice-of-law decisions. Moreover, both discriminatory and substantively unfair rules of law may be detected and remedied without any special choice-of-law analysis; familiar constitutional principles are available to deal with both varieties of unfairness.

113. Upon careful analysis most of the decisions of this Court that struck down on due process grounds a state court's choice of forum law can be explained as attempts to prevent a State with a minimal contact with the litigation from materially enlarging the contractual obligations of one of the parties where that party had no reason to anticipate the possibility of such enlargement.

nonetheless may implicitly reveal the expectations of the parties. For example, if a liability insurance policy issued by a resident of a particular State provides coverage only with respect to accidents within that State, it is reasonable to infer that the contracting parties expected that their obligations under the policy would be governed by that State's law.

In this case, no express indication of the parties' expectations is available. The insurance policy provided coverage for accidents throughout the United States; thus, at the time of contracting, the parties certainly could have anticipated that the law of States other than Wisconsin would govern particular claims arising under the policy. By virtue of doing business in Minnesota, Allstate was aware that it could be sued in the Minnesota courts; Allstate also presumably was aware that Minnesota law, as well as the law of most States, permitted "stacking." Nothing in the record requires that a different inference be drawn. Therefore, the decision of the Minnesota courts to apply the law of the forum in this case does not frustrate the reasonable expectations of the contracting parties, and I can find no fundamental unfairness in that decision requiring the attention of this Court.

In terms of fundamental fairness, it seems to me that two factors relied upon by the plurality — the plaintiff's postaccident move to Minnesota and the decedent's Minnesota employment — are either irrelevant to or possibly even tend to undermine the plurality's conclusion. When the expectations of the parties at the time of contracting are the central due process concern, as they are in this case, an unanticipated post-accident occurrence is clearly irrelevant for due process purposes. The fact that the plaintiff became a resident of the forum State after the accident surely cannot justify a ruling in her favor that would not be made if the plaintiff were a nonresident. Similarly, while the fact that the decedent regularly drove into Minnesota might be relevant to the expectations of the contracting parties, the fact that he did so because he was employed in Minnesota adds nothing to the due process analysis. The choice-of-law decision of the Minnesota courts is consistent with due process because it does not result in unfairness to either litigant, not because Minnesota now has an interest in the plaintiff as resident or formerly had an interest in the decedent as employee.

Notes on Allstate

1. *Possible differences between due process and full faith and credit clauses.* The Court has generally treated the full faith and credit and due process clauses as imposing substantially the same limits on choice of law decisions. *See supra* p. 525. Justice Stevens and others have rejected this approach. Consider:

[E]ach clause speaks to essentially different considerations. The Due Process Clause addresses issues of the territorial reach of state power and the fairness to individuals in the exercise of that power. Full Faith and Credit, on the other hand, balances conflicting state interests by commanding that the states respect the sovereignty of sister states in a federal context. E. Scoles & P. Hay, *Conflict of Laws* 80 (1982).

Compare Justice Steven's discussion of the difference between the two clauses. Is that persuasive? Consider the application of the due process clause to assertions of judicial jurisdiction. Does it only consider issues of fairness, or does it also consider state territorial sovereignty? As a practical matter, why does the distinction between the due process and the full faith and credit clauses matter? Could the due process

clause affirmatively require a state to apply a particular law (rather than merely forbidding it from applying its own law)?

2. *No constitutional bar to application of state law to conduct occurring outside state territory.* It is
now clear that there is no general prohibition in the Constitution against a state's application of its substantive laws to conduct occurring outside state territory. *Allstate* said that the "wooden *lex loci delicti* doctrine" had been "largely abandoned" and it emphasized that "[n]umerous cases have applied the law of a
jurisdiction other than the situs of the injury." See *Cardillo v. Liberty Mutual Ins. Co.*, 330 U.S. 469 (1947);
Alaska Packers Ass'n v. Industrial Accident Comm'n, 294 U.S. 532 (1935). See also *Skiriotes v. Florida*, 313
U.S. 69 (1941), discussed below.

3. *State legislative jurisdiction over citizens.* In *Skiriotes v. Florida*, 313 U.S. 69 (1941), the Supreme
Court rejected a constitutional challenge to the extraterritorial application of a Florida criminal statute.
The statute forbid the use of certain diving apparatus for the purpose of taking commercial sponges from
the Gulf of Mexico; a Florida resident was convicted under the statute outside the territorial waters of both
the United States and Florida. The Court held that "no question of international law, or of the extent of
the authority of the United States in its international relations is presented," because Mr. Skiriotes was a
Florida resident and U.S. national. The Court continued: "If the United States may control the conduct of
its citizens upon the high seas, we see no reason why the State of Florida may not likewise govern the conduct of its citizens upon the high seas with respect to matters in which the State has a legitimate interest
..." Is this persuasive? The Constitution limits the role of the states in international matters. See *supra* pp.
15-16 & *infra* pp. 537-44. Given this, is it persuasive to conclude that a state may exercise legislative jurisdiction simply because Congress may? Does the *Skiriotes* analysis apply where state law is sought to be
applied to conduct within the territory of a foreign country? What would be the basis for distinguishing
the two instances?

4. *Comparison between constitutional limits on judicial and legislative jurisdiction.* Compare the
minimum contacts test for judicial jurisdiction, *see supra* pp. 73-77, with the "significant contacts creating
state interests" test for legislative jurisdiction. Are the tests similar? Which language is more restrictive? In
practice, which test has imposed the more rigorous limits on state jurisdiction? Consider:

> [D]iffering treatment of contacts in the jurisdiction and choice-of-law cases turns things on
> their head. In the typical jurisdiction case, overreaching on the part of the forum state results at
> worst in inconvenience and greater expense for the defendant. In the typical conflicts case ... if
> the plaintiff has chosen his forum wisely, the defendant will lose a case he would otherwise
> have won, simply because the forum has asserted its legislative jurisdiction. ... [F]rom the
> defendant's perspective, it seems irrational to say that due process requires minimum contacts
> ... merely to hale him into the forum's courts, while allowing more tenuous contacts to upset
> the very outcome of the case. Martin, *Personal Jurisdiction and Choice of Law*, 78 Mich. L. Rev.
> 872, 879-80 (1980).

Is this persuasive? Should due process limits on state legislative jurisdiction be more stringent than *Allstate*
concluded? More stringent than limits on judicial jurisdiction? Is it true that "inconvenience" is the
"worst" that can result from exorbitant personal jurisdiction?

5. *Allstate plurality — due process standard for state choice of law decisions.* What due process limits
does the *Allstate* plurality impose on state choice of law decisions? What does the following test mean: "for
a State's substantive law to be selected in a constitutionally permissible manner, that State must have a significant contact or significant aggregation of contacts, creating state interests, such that choice of its law is
neither arbitrary nor fundamentally unfair"? How does a court determine whether a contact is "significant"? that it "creat[es] state interests"? that these contacts prevent a choice of law from being "arbitrary
[or] fundamentally unfair"?

(a) *Relation between the* Allstate *contacts.* Consider the application of the foregoing standard by the
Allstate plurality. The Court identified three "contacts" that permitted application of Minnesota law. What
is the relation between these contacts? Was it necessary that all three exist, to justify application of
Minnesota law?

(b) *Decedent's employment in forum.* What constitutional weight should be ascribed to the decedent's
employment in Minnesota for 15 years? Suppose that the decedent was a *resident* of Minnesota, killed in a
Wisconsin accident. Should that have given Minnesota a constitutionally sufficient interest to apply its
own law to the question of insurance-stacking? What different weight should be accorded to the fact that

the decedent was employed in Minnesota, rather than residing there? Note that Justice Stevens thought that the decedent's employment in Minnesota was "either irrelevant to or possibly even tend[ed] to undermine the plurality's conclusion."

(c) *Allstate's doing business in Minnesota.* What constitutional weight should be ascribed to the fact that Allstate did business in Minnesota? Suppose a company does business in every state in the Union — as many do. Does that mean that every state may apply its laws to any torts or contracts involving that company, regardless whether they have the slightest connection to the state? What about activities outside the United States?

(d) *Survivor's post-accident residence in Minnesota.* The *Allstate* plurality relied on the fact that the plaintiff moved to Minnesota after the accident occurred. Why was this relevant? Consider Justice Steven's criticism.

6. *Justice Stevens' concurrence in* **Allstate.** Compare Justice Stevens' concurring opinion in *Allstate* to the plurality's opinion. Justice Stevens distinguished between analysis under the full faith and credit clause and the due process clause. He thought that the former required states to "respect the legitimate interests of other states and to avoid infringement upon their sovereignty." Justice Stevens saw no threat to "national unity or Wisconsin's sovereignty" from Minnesota's application of its law to accidents in Wisconsin between Wisconsin residents. Is that correct? Suppose Minnesota courts *always* applied their law to accidents in Wisconsin, and that Minnesota law was significantly more favourable to plaintiffs. Would that affect primary behaviour in Wisconsin? Insurance costs? Why isn't that an infringement on Wisconsin's sovereignty?

Justice Stevens reasoned that the due process clause forbids state choice of law decisions that are "totally arbitrary" or "fundamentally unfair." He did not believe that this standard was violated in *Allstate.* Why not? Note Justice Stevens' suggestion that the due process clause would preclude application of laws that a party "could not reasonably have anticipated." Is sovereignty relevant at all to Justice Stevens' due process analysis? Since the full faith and credit clause does not apply in international cases, how would the due process clause be applied by Justice Stevens in such cases?

7. *Correctness of* Allstate *result.* Is *Allstate* correctly decided? Should the due process clause impose greater restrictions on state choice of law decisions? What would be the rationale for such limits? Do international cases, involving application of state law to foreign conduct, require different standards?

8. *Relevant connecting factors in due process analysis.* Allstate holds that if there is "no significant contact or significant aggregation of contacts, creating state interests," the due process clause forbids legislative jurisdiction. Under this analysis, what "contacts" are relevant, and how much do they "count" towards establishing a basis for jurisdiction?

(a) *Situs of wrongful conduct.* Suppose the underlying accident in *Allstate* occurred in Minnesota. Would that have been an independently sufficient basis to permit application of Minnesota law? What does *Dick* suggest? What does *Allstate* suggest?

(b) *Situs of injury.* Suppose that allegedly wrongful conduct occurs in one state, but causes injury in another state. Examples include the *Sedco* and *Olsen* cases, excerpted above, *supra* pp. 268-78, where negligent conduct allegedly occurred in Mexico, causing injury in the United States. There is little doubt that the due process clause would regard the situs of injury as a significant contact for due process purposes. Would either the due process clause or international law ever forbid the exercise of legislative jurisdiction by a state that was the situs of the injury?

(c) *Nationality or domicile of defendant.* Suppose that Allstate had been a Minnesota insurance company. Would its nationality or domicile have provided a significant contact, permitting application of Minnesota law? *See Skiriotes v. Florida,* 313 U.S. 69 (1941); *supra* p. 535. Would international law permit the exercise of legislative jurisdiction by a state over its nationals? Should the due process clause permit the application of *any* law to a national's conduct in other states? Presumably, local traffic regulations could not be applied extraterritorially? Why not? Note *Allstate's* requirement that a "significant contact" must "create state interests."

(d) *Defendant's "doing business."* One "contact" cited by *Allstate* was the fact that the defendant insurance company did business in Minnesota. Is this a legitimate basis for legislative jurisdiction? Recall that systematic business "presence" in a state provides a basis for general personal jurisdiction under the due process clause. *See supra* pp. 103-16. Should an analogous result follow in the context of legislative jurisdiction? Would contemporary international law permit legislative jurisdiction based on this factor?

(e) *Nationality or domicile of plaintiff.* Suppose that the decedent and his wife in *Allstate* had been domiciled in Minnesota at the time of the accident in Wisconsin, having moved there after purchasing his insurance policies in Wisconsin. Would the plaintiff's Minnesota domicile have permitted application of Minnesota law to: (a) tort claims against the Wisconsin drivers who caused plaintiff's injuries and (b) the "stacking" issue? *Allstate* made it clear that the plaintiff's domicile or residence is a significant contact for due process. Is that wise? Also recall that international law does not permit legislative jurisdiction based on the passive personality principle. *See supra* pp. 507-08. What does this suggest about *Allstate's* reliance on this factor?

(f) *Plaintiff's post-occurrence domicile or residence.* Consider: "The post-accident residence of the plaintiff-beneficiary is constitutionally irrelevant to the choice of law question." 449 U.S. at 337 (Powell, J., dissenting). Justice Stevens also rejected post-accident residence as a relevant connecting factor. Why is that? Why doesn't Minnesota have a significant "interest" in maximizing the recovery of its residents against non-Minnesota defendants? Or at least in insuring that its residents have the right to stack their insurance policies? If the plaintiff's domicile is a significant contact for due process purposes, then why does it matter whether domicile or residence commenced before or after the occurrences giving rise to the parties' dispute? What makes the plaintiff's residence/domicile "significant" for due process purposes? Is it anything more than the forum's interest in protecting its domiciliaries? Isn't that interest applicable regardless when the plaintiff became domiciled in the forum?

(g) *Parties' chosen law.* As discussed in detail below, *infra* pp. 653-64, commercial agreements frequently contain choice of law clauses specifying the law applicable to disputes between the parties. The due process clause would virtually always permit application of the parties' chosen law.

9. Comparison between due process limits on federal and state legislative jurisdiction. Compare the due process limits imposed on state laws in *Allstate* with those imposed on federal law in *Davis*. Which standard is more stringent? Should due process limits on state and federal legislative jurisdiction be identical? Neither decision (or line of decisions) acknowledges or cites the other. Is that sensible?

10. Relevance of foreign sovereignty to due process analysis. *Allstate* involved the exercise of legislative jurisdiction that arguably affected the sovereignty of another U.S. state, while *Davis* involved a jurisdictional assertion that affected foreign sovereignty. Suppose *Allstate* had involved an accident killing a Canadian resident on the Canadian side of the Canadian border, and the Canadian widow had subsequently moved to the United States. Would the application of U.S. state rules, permitting the stacking of three Canadian insurance policies, have been permitted — assuming that all of the other facts were identical to *Allstate*? Would international law permit application of U.S. law in this hypothetical? Note that *Dick* was an international choice of law case, while *Allstate* involved a purely domestic dispute. Is that relevant to differences in the due process standards?

11. Relevance of customary international law to limits on state legislative jurisdiction. Recall that *Davis* and most other judicial decisions hold that the jurisdictional limits of customary international law have no independent effect on the reach of federal legislation. *See supra* pp. 513-17. Recall that *Davis* also held that international law is not directly relevant to due process analysis. *See supra* p. 516. Are the same conclusions true with respect to the jurisdictional limits on *state* legislation? Note that customary international law has generally been categorized as federal law, which preempts state law. *See supra* pp. 21-22. Should contemporary jurisdictional limits (such as those in *Restatement (Third) Foreign Relations Law* §§402 & 403 (1987)) provide enforceable limits on state legislative jurisdiction? *See infra* p. 543.

ii. Foreign Commerce and Other Constitutional Limitations on State Legislative Jurisdiction

As discussed above, the Constitution grants Congress and the President broad powers over international matters. The foreign commerce clause grants Congress the power to regulate commerce "with foreign Nations,"[114] while other provisions of Article I grant Congress the power to define offenses against the law of nations, to define and punish piracies, and to declare war.[115] The President is vested with the power to make treaties (with the consent of two-thirds of the Senate), to act as

---

114. U.S. Const. Art. I, §8, cl. 3.

115. U.S. Const. Art. I, §8, cl. 10, 11.

ART. II

Commander in Chief, and to nominate ambassadors.[116] As discussed above, the Supreme Court has emphasized the breadth of federal powers over foreign commerce and relations.[117]

Broad federal authority over international matters is matched by limited state powers.[118] In particular, the Supreme Court has held that the Constitution imposes several types of restrictions on state legislative jurisdiction over international commercial matters. Most of these restrictions are based principally on federal common law, derived from the general predominance of federal power in international matters.

First, the foreign commerce clause has been held to restrict state taxation of international commerce and its instrumentalities. In *Japan Line Ltd. v. County of Los Angeles*,[119] the Court held that a local tax on containers used in foreign commerce violated the dormant foreign commerce clause. In reaching its conclusion, the Court reasoned that the foreign commerce clause imposed stricter scrutiny on state taxes than the interstate commerce clause.[120]

Similarly, in *Container Corporation of America v. Franchise Tax Board*,[121] the Court considered challenges to California's corporation franchise tax under the due process and foreign commerce clauses. Again emphasizing that taxes on foreign commerce were subject to more exacting scrutiny than interstate taxes,[122] the Court concluded that a state tax on international commerce must satisfy four requirements:[123] (a) the taxed activities must have a substantial nexus to the taxing state; (b) the tax must be fairly apportioned, such that there is a rational relationship between income or property attributed to the state and the intrastate values of the enterprise; (c) the tax must not discriminate against interstate or international commerce; and (d) there must be no substantial risk of international multiple taxation and no interference with the federal government's ability to "speak with one voice"[124] when regulating commercial relations with foreign governments. The Court found all four requirements satisfied on the *Container Corporation* facts.[125]

Second, a few Supreme Court decisions have held state laws unconstitutional on

---

116. U.S. Const. Art. II, §2, cl. 1, 2.

117. *See supra* pp. 15-16.

118. *See supra* pp. 15-16; U.S. Const. Art. I, §10 ("No State shall enter into any Treaty, Alliance, or Confederation"; "No State shall, without the Consent of Congress lay any Imports or Duties on Imports or Exports ... [or] enter into any Agreement or Contract with another State, or with a Foreign Power").

119. 441 U.S. 434 (1979).

120. 441 U.S. at 445-50. *See also Container Corp. v. Franchise Tax Board*, 463 U.S. 159 (1983) ("Given that [appellant's business] is international ... we must subject this case to the additional scrutiny required by the Foreign Commerce Clause"); *Mobil Oil Corp. v. Comm'r of Taxes*, 445 U.S. 425 (1980).

121. 463 U.S. 159 (1983).

122. 463 U.S. at 170, 184-85.

123. 463 U.S. at 169, 184-85.

124. *See Japan Line, Ltd. v. County of Los Angeles*, 441 U.S. 434 (1979); *Container Corp. v. Franchise Tax Board*, 463 U.S. 159 (1983).

125. 463 U.S. at 180-96.

the grounds that they unduly affect the federal government's exercise of its constitutional powers to conduct the Nation's foreign relations. The leading case is *Zschernig v. Miller*,[126] where the Court invalidated an Oregon probate statute on the ground that it "affects international relations in a persistent and subtle way," and must "give way [because it] impair[s] the effective exercise of the Nation's foreign policy."[127] The Oregon law conditioned the rights of foreign nationals to inherit property on their home countries' provision of reciprocal rights to U.S. nationals and the freedom of foreign nationals to receive the proceeds of Oregon estates "without confiscation." The Court's opinion in *Zschernig* was opaque, but it apparently rested on the view that Oregon (and other) state courts had engaged in detailed (and unflattering) analyses of foreign political and judicial systems.[128]

Justice Stewart filed a concurring opinion in *Zschernig* that was more coherent. He reasoned: "We deal here with the basic allocation of power between the States and the Nation. ... [T]he conduct of our foreign affairs is entrusted under the Constitution to the National Government, not to the probate courts of the several states."[129] According to Justice Stewart's concurrence, each of the conditions imposed by the Oregon probate statute was facially unconstitutional, because "[a]ny realistic attempt to apply any of the three criteria would necessarily involve the Oregon courts in an evaluation, either express or implied, of the administration of foreign law, the credibility of foreign diplomatic statements, and the policies of foreign governments."[130]

Third, the Court has fashioned rules of federal common law, derived from federal powers over foreign affairs and commerce, governing international matters which have the effect of limiting state choice of law decisions. The classic example is *Banco Nacional de Cuba v. Sabbatino*,[131] which held that U.S. courts could not consider the validity of certain foreign acts of state, notwithstanding contrary rules of U.S. state law.[132] As discussed elsewhere, the federal courts have fashioned other federal common law rules in international matters.[133]

State courts have only rarely considered these various federal limitations in international cases. Excerpted below is one exception, a New Mexico state court

---

126. 389 U.S. 429 (1968).

127. 389 U.S. at 440.

128. 389 U.S. at 434-36 ("they radiate some of the attitudes of the 'cold war,' where the search is for the 'democracy quotient' of a foreign regime").

129. 389 U.S. at 443.

130. 389 U.S. at 442. *See also United States v. Belmont*, 301 U.S. 324 (1937); *United States v. Pink*, 315 U.S. 203 (1942).

131. 376 U.S. 398 (1964) (excerpted at pp. 691-705 below).

132. 376 U.S. at 428 ("the Judicial Branch will not examine the validity of a taking of property within its own territory by a foreign sovereign government, extant and recognized by this country at the time of suit, in the absence of a treaty or other unambiguous agreement regarding controlling legal principles, even if the complaint alleges that the taking violates customary international law.").

133. *See supra* pp. 15-16; *First National City Bank v. Bancec*, 462 U.S. 611 (1983) (foreign state agency's corporate status).

opinion in *United Nuclear Corp. v. General Atomic Company*. The case was an action under New Mexico's state antitrust laws, and it involved allegations of a worldwide uranium price-fixing conspiracy. The defendants included major state-owned enterprises in Australia, Canada, France, and South Africa. The suit resulted in numerous foreign diplomatic protests to the United States, complaining that New Mexico's actions infringed upon their national sovereignty. The following excerpt rejects various arguments by the defendants that New Mexico law could not be applied to their conduct.

UNITED NUCLEAR CORPORATION v. GENERAL ATOMIC COMPANY

629 P.2d 231 (N.M. 1980)

PAYNE, JUSTICE. [United Nuclear Corporation ("United"), a major New Mexico uranium producer, filed suit in New Mexico state court against General Atomic Company ("GAC"). The complaint sought a declaration that two contracts obligating United to supply GAC with 27 million pounds of uranium at fixed prices were void and unenforceable. The complaint alleged that GAC and others had committed fraud and violated the New Mexico Antitrust Act (which parallels the U.S. antitrust laws). These claims were based on an alleged worldwide conspiracy among major uranium producers to raise the price of uranium and to allocate markets. The participants in this conspiracy allegedly included foreign companies, including state-owned companies, in Canada, South Africa, France and Australia. Among other things, the plaintiff sought far-reaching U.S.-style discovery of documents located in these countries.

The defendants raised various unsuccessful jurisdictional objections; they also objected vigorously (with support from their home states) to the plaintiff's discovery requests. The Court rejected both sets of objections and the complaint proceeded to trial. The trial judge subsequently terminated the trial, however, and entered a default judgment against GAG, for "the utmost bad faith in all stages of the discovery process." Appeals followed where, among other things, the defendants argued that the U.S. Constitution forbid the state courts from entertaining the plaintiff's claims under the New Mexico Antitrust Act.] ...

GAC claims that ... the principle of exclusive federal power over the conduct of foreign relations nevertheless precludes an American state court from conducting such an examination.[134] GAC relies on *Zschernig v. Miller*, in which the U.S. Supreme Court struck down an Oregon intestacy statute as it had been applied by

---

134. Although similar to the act of state doctrine, this ... principle is distinct in that the former looks to the power of American courts in general, whereas the latter is concerned with the power of an American state court. The act of state doctrine rests on the principle of separation of powers between branches of the federal government; the principle of exclusive federal power over the conduct of foreign relations is based on the concept of federalism.

the Oregon Supreme Court. The Oregon statute required that in order to take property belonging to an Oregon resident by succession or testamentary disposition a non-resident alien had to prove that (1) American residents had a reciprocal right to inherit in the alien's country; and (2) the non-resident alien would be able to receive "the benefit, use or control" of the proceeds of the Oregon estate "without confiscation" by his government.

In *Zschernig*, the Court held that, as applied, the statute constituted an impermissible intrusion by the state into foreign affairs, an area which the Court said was entrusted by the U.S. Constitution solely to the President and Congress. The Court said that the statute required local probate courts to launch "minute inquiries" into the nature of foreign governments, the quality of rights which those governments accorded to both American citizens and their own citizens, the credibility of the representations of officials of foreign governments, and the actual administration of foreign legal systems.

GAC contends that *Zschernig* precludes state courts from exercising jurisdiction over issues relating to the foreign cartel because of the Canadian Government's relationship to the cartel. GAC argues that because the trial court was without jurisdiction to consider the cartel-related issues, it could not enter discovery orders directing the production of cartel documents.

The *Zschernig* decision, which has not been applied by the U.S. Supreme Court outside of the limited context of the alien inheritance statutes at issue in that case, has nothing to do with this case. Unlike the statute at issue in *Zschernig*, the causes of action involved in this case are universally accepted by American jurisdictions — fraud, breach of fiduciary duty, commercial impracticability, economic coercion and antitrust. The effective enforcement of the antitrust laws is essential to the maintenance of free and fair business competition.[135] Unlike the alien inheritance statutes in *Zschernig*,[136] the causes of action in this case do not involve questionable attempts by states to directly affect the rights of citizens in foreign nations, nor are they related to the foreign policy attitudes of this or any other state court.

In this litigation the courts of this State have not undertaken the type of analysis that *Zschernig* prohibits. No pejorative criticism has been directed at Canada or any

---

135. "Antitrust laws in general, and the Sherman Act in particular, are the Magna Carta of free enterprise. They are as important to the preservation of economic freedom and our free-enterprise system as the Bill of Rights is to the protection of our fundamental personal freedoms." *United States v. Topco Associates*, 405 U.S. 596, 610 (1972). "So crucial are antitrust laws to the economy of the state that the New Mexico Constitution (Art. IV, §38) mandates the enactment of laws 'to prevent trusts, monopolies and combinations in restraint of trade.'" Wechsler, 9 N.M. L. Rev. at 22.

136. These statutes had largely been applied to communist countries. In the years following their passage, the statutes were subject to widespread criticism by legal scholars for being unsound legislation which had been both ineffective and prejudicially applied. In applying these statutes, state courts had on occasion criticized foreign governments in strong and intemperate language. Commentators were virtually unanimous in condemning these statutes and in applauding the *Zschernig* decision. One said: "[C]learly the state has no interests in inquiries of the sort which [*Zschernig*] condemned." 82 Harv. L. Rev. at 245.

other foreign government. No minute inquiry has been made into the actual administration of foreign law by a foreign government, or into the rights that such a government affords to its own citizens. The veracity of the representations of its diplomats has not been questioned. This case involves nothing more than an inquiry into what an American corporation has done in America, a situation which finds no appropriate analogy in *Zschernig* or its exceedingly limited progeny.

The states of this country have little interest in how a foreign government treats its own citizens, but they have every conceivable interest in anti-competitive conduct by American corporations occurring within their own borders. Likewise, foreign governments have a legitimate interest in the rights they choose to afford their own citizens; but they have no legitimate interest in whether a state court in this country will lend its judicial processes to the enforcement of contracts entered into in the United States by corporations based in this country for the supply of a resource to be mined and milled in the United States. Our courts have done no more than seek to enforce state laws which are consistent with federal laws, and with actions of the U.S. Congress[137] and U.S. Justice Department concerning Gulf's cartel activities. We therefore hold that ... *Zschernig* [does not] preclude[] the courts of New Mexico from litigating the cartel-related issues present in this case, or from seeking the production of documents which will facilitate the resolution of such litigation....

Notes on United Nuclear

1. *Zschernig* — *federal foreign affairs powers as a limit on state legislative jurisdiction.* As discussed above, *Zschernig* was an unusual case, involving an Oregon state probate statute which prohibited foreign nationals from inheriting their share of Oregon estates if the country of their nationality either: (a) denied U.S. citizens reciprocal rights to receive inheritances on the same terms as locals; (b) denied U.S. citizens the right to receive inherited sums in the United States; or (c) would confiscate the foreign nationals' inheritances.

(a) *Majority opinion in* Zschernig. The Court held the statute unconstitutional, on the grounds that it infringed upon federal foreign affairs powers. 389 U.S. 429 (1968). Justice Douglas thought that the law would "affect[] international relations in a persistent and subtle way," while Justice Stewart concluded that each of the three conditions in the statute would "launch the State upon a prohibited voyage into a domain of exclusively federal competence."

(b) *Justice Harlan's concurrence in* Zschernig. Justice Harlan concurred in the decision, but based his conclusion entirely on a treaty between the United States and Germany (so-called East Germany being the state whose national was adversely affected in the case). His concurrence went on, however, to reject the reasoning of Justices Douglas and Stewart. Justice Harlan observed that "the States may legislate in areas of their traditional competence even though their statutes may have an incidental effect on foreign relations." 389 U.S. at 459. He pointed out as well that there was no evidence — for example, by way of diplomatic protests — that the state statutes had in fact given offense to foreign governments, and that a U.S. government amicus brief expressly said that the United States did "not ... contend that the application of the Oregon escheat statute in the circumstances of this case unduly interferes with the United States' conduct of foreign relations." 389 U.S. at 460. Justice Harlan also observed that state courts routinely inquire into the content of foreign law — for example, when they consider the enforceability of foreign judgments or apply foreign law. He reasoned that, if the Oregon statute was unconstitutional, these state court actions would be as well.

---

137. It is worth noting that the Congressional subcommittee investigating the cartel held several of its hearings in unprecedented joint sessions with a committee of the New York State Assembly in order to assist that state's independent investigation of the cartel.

(c) *Correctness of* Zschernig *rationale.* Which of the views in *Zschernig* is more persuasive? Which of the three conditions in the Oregon statute is most troubling? Why is it unconstitutional for a state to require reciprocal treatment of its citizens? Note that many states will not enforce foreign judgments against U.S. nationals unless the foreign state's courts will enforce U.S. judgments against foreign nationals. *See infra* pp. 951-55. What part of the Constitution says that states cannot enact legislation that takes into account the laws of foreign governments? Do not numerous issues in international litigation (such as forum non conveniens, choice of law, and extraterritorial service and discovery) require exactly such inquiry?

(d) *Narrower rationale for* Zschernig. The Oregon statute would not permit a foreign national to inherit property if his or her home state would confiscate the property. Should a U.S. state be permitted to make legal rights depend on what a foreign government does on foreign territory with respect to its nationals after they inherit U.S. property? Is not the foreign state's conduct, on its own territory, towards its own citizens, a matter that U.S. states cannot properly regulate — both under international law and federal constitutional law? As discussed below, the act of state doctrine provides that federal common law forbids a U.S. court from considering the validity of a foreign state's taking of property within its own territory. *See infra* pp. 685-90 & 704. Is *Zschernig* merely an application of this rule?

2. *Foreign commerce and due process clause limits on state legislative jurisdiction.* Suppose that a U.S. state enacted a statute granting any of its residents the right to sue in state courts, under a state statute forbidding the unauthorized copying of intellectual property belonging to such residents; suppose further that the statute set forth the substantive elements of the offense of copying and was made expressly applicable to conduct anywhere in the world — so long as it injured a resident of the state. Alternatively, suppose a U.S. state statute granted a cause of action under state law for any state resident that was defrauded, in connection with a securities transaction, anywhere in the world. Or suppose a state statute permits any state resident or domiciliary to bring actions for defamatory statements, under local state law, made anywhere in the world. Would any of these statutes be constitutional? What provision of the Constitution would they violate? Recall the due process limitations, articulated in *Allstate*, on a state court's application of state law to conduct lacking significant contacts with the forum.

3. *Customary international law on state legislative jurisdiction.* Recall the customary international law limits contained in the *Restatement (Third) Foreign Relations Law* §402 and §403. As discussed above, customary international law arguably has the status of federal law and is directly applicable in state courts, notwithstanding inconsistent state law. *See supra* p. 21. Why shouldn't the jurisdictional limits imposed by customary international law have been enforceable in *United Nuclear*? Would they have affected the outcome of the case?

4. Japan Lines — *foreign commerce and due process limits on state taxing powers.* Does the fact that a state law is applied to foreign commerce — instead of interstate commerce — result in any stricter constitutional scrutiny? As noted above, the Court has held that the foreign commerce clause imposes stricter scrutiny on state taxes on international commerce than on interstate commerce. *See supra* pp. 538-40; *Container Corp. v. Franchise Tax Board*, 463 U.S. 159 (1983) ("Given that [appellant's business] is international ... we must subject this case to the additional scrutiny required by the Foreign Commerce Clause"). The Court explained the rationale for this in *Japan Lines, Ltd. v. County of Los Angeles*, 441 U.S. 434 (1979). It first observed that in domestic tax matters, it had the power to enforce due process limits on state taxation of interstate activities to ensure that each taxing state's tax was fairly apportioned to the value of the activity or property connected to that jurisdiction. But "neither this Court nor this Nation can ensure full apportionment when one of the taxing entities is a foreign sovereign. If an instrumentality of commerce is domiciled abroad, the country of domicile may have the right, consistently with the custom of nations, to impose a tax on its full value." 441 U.S. at 447. *Japan Line* also observed that state taxes on international commerce or its instrumentalies "may impair federal uniformity in an area where federal uniformity is essential. Foreign commerce is pre-eminently a matter of national concern. ... [T]he taxation of foreign commerce may necessitate a uniform national rule." State taxes on foreign commerce can give rise to "international disputes over reconciling apportionment formulae" and may provoke retaliation which "of necessity would be directed at American transportation equipment in general, not just that of the taxing State, so that the Nation as a whole would suffer." 441 U.S. at 450.

Do these rationales have application outside the tax context? Should state legislation applicable to foreign (*i.e.*, non-U.S.) commerce be subjected to stricter scrutiny under the due process clause than *Allstate* contemplates for domestic matters?

5. United Nuclear — *constitutional limits on state legislative jurisdiction. United Nuclear* involved allegations of a worldwide price-fixing cartel, where substantial conduct occurred within New Mexico, but much more occurred elsewhere (and particularly in foreign states). What was the *United Nuclear* rationale for rejecting constitutional challenges to the application of New Mexico law to the defendants' worldwide conduct? Is it conceivable that the foreign commerce clause might ever forbid a state from applying its law to conduct within its territory? Note that *Japan Line* held that the foreign commerce and due process clauses forbid California localities from applying ad valorem taxes on property located within California (containers used by international shipping companies, which were temporarily present in California). *See supra* p. 538.

Even if New Mexico could apply its law to the allegedly unlawful conduct occurring within its territory, does that mean that it should be constitutionally able to apply its law to the entire course of worldwide conduct engaged in by the various defendants? Suppose different U.S. states conducted parallel proceedings, each applying its own state antitrust law to the same international course of conduct. Is there anything wrong with that? Does anything in the Constitution forbid it? Consider the rationales of *Zschernig* and *Japan Line.* Do these decisions provide support for invalidating application of New Mexico's law to international commerce?

6. Sequihua v. Texaco *revisited.* Recall the district court's opinion in *Sequihua v. Texaco Oil, Inc.,* 847 F.Supp. 61 (S.D. Tex. 1994), holding that federal common law governed (and barred) a claim alleging massive environmental abuse in Ecuador by a U.S. company. *See supra* pp. 50-56. Compare the court's analysis in *Sequihua* with that in *United Nuclear.* Are the decisions consistent?

7. Filartiga *and* Tel-Oren *revisited.* Recall Judge Bork's opinion in *Tel-Oren v. Libyan Arab Republic,* 726 F.2d 774 (D.C. Cir. 1984), reasoning that separation of power considerations required limiting the scope of the Alien Tort Statute, because of concerns that sensitive claims of foreign officials' misconduct would interfere with the conduct of U.S. foreign relations by the President and Congress. *See supra* pp. 45-46. Judge Bork continued: "A state-court suit that involved a determination of international law would require consideration of much that it discussed here as well as the principle that foreign relations are constitutionally relegated to the federal government and not the states." 726 F.2d at 814 n.11. Contrast this with *United Nuclear.*

8/Choice of Law in International Litigation[1]

I nternational litigation inevitably presents choice of law issues, requiring courts to decide what law to apply in cases where two or more states could properly exercise legislative jurisdiction. In the United States, these questions have traditionally been considered under two largely distinct bodies of authority. First, U.S. courts have fashioned canons of construction for determining whether federal legislation applies to international activities, and particularly for determining whether U.S. legislation has extraterritorial reach. Second, U.S. courts have developed choice of law rules for deciding whether state law (both statutory and common law) applies to international activities. This Chapter examines both subjects.

A. Application of Federal Statutes in International Cases

1. Determining the Territorial Reach of Federal Legislation in International Cases: The Problem of Silent Statutes

This section examines the applicability of federal statutes in international cases, focusing particularly on the circumstances in which congressional legislation will be applied extraterritorially.[2] As discussed above, it is well-settled that if Congress enacts legislation in violation of international law, U.S. courts must disregard inter-

---

1. Leading contemporary works dealing with choice of law in the United States include, *e.g.*, L. Brilmayer, *Conflict of Laws: Foundations and Future Directions* (1991); B. Currie, *Selected Essays on the Conflict of Laws* (1963); A. Ehrenzweig, *A Treatise on the Conflict of Laws* (1962); A. Lowenfeld, *Conflict of Laws: Federal, State, and International Perspectives* (1986); J. Martin *Conflict of Laws: Cases and Materials* (2d ed. 1984); E. Scoles & P. Hay, *Conflict of Laws* (1982); R. Weintraub, *Commentary on the Conflict of Laws* (3rd ed. 1986).
2. Commentary on extraterritoriality includes, *e.g.*, J. Atwood & K. Brewster, *Antitrust And American Business Abroad* (2d ed. 1985 & Cum. Supp.); Born, *A Reappraisal of the Extraterritorial Reach of U.S. Law*, 24 Law & Pol'y Int'l Bus. 1 (1992); Brilmayer & Norchi, *Federal Extraterritoriality and Fifth Amendment Due Process*, 105 Harv. L. Rev. 1217 (1992); Gerber, *Beyond Balancing: International Law Restraints on the Reach of National Laws*, 10 Yale J. Int'l L. 185 (1984); Kramer, *Vestiges of Beale: Extraterritorial Application of American Law*, 1991 S.Ct. Rev. 111; Reese, *Legislative Jurisdiction*, 78 Colum. L. Rev. 1587 (1978). *See* Bibliography, 50 Law & Contemp. Probs. 303 (1987).

national law and apply the domestic statute.[3] Thus, the extraterritorial reach of federal statutes is ultimately an issue of U.S. law — not foreign or international law. "We are concerned only with whether Congress chose to attach liability to the conduct outside the United States. ... [A]s a court of the United States, we cannot look beyond our own law."[4]

In most cases, however, Congress's statutes are couched in general terms and provide no meaningful geographic limits.[5] Congress typically legislates by using words of "universal" application,[6] whose "literal catholicity"[7] would extend U.S. law to almost all conduct on the globe. As Justice Jackson said of the Jones Act in *Lauritzen v. Larsen*:

> Unless some [limit] is implied, Congress has extended our law and opened our courts to all alien seafaring men injured anywhere in the world in service of watercraft of every foreign nation — a hand on a Chinese junk, never outside Chinese waters, would not be beyond its literal wording.[8]

Rather than adopting this and other implausible results that would follow from a literal reading of most statutes, federal courts have turned to rules of statutory construction to establish the reach of federal law.

2. Historical Introduction: The Territoriality Presumption

The rules of construction applicable to contemporary federal legislation have their origins in the Middle Ages, when Continental European commentators developed choice of law rules.[9] These rules defined when local "statutes," enacted in vari-

---

3. *See supra* pp. 19-21; *Restatement (Third) Foreign Relations Law* §115(i) & §403, comment g (1987); *Head Money Cases*, 112 U.S. 580, 598-99 (1884); *Whitney v. Robertson*, 124 U.S. 190, 194 (1888); *CFTC v. Nahas*, 738 F.2d 487 (D.C. Cir. 1984).

4. *United States v. Alcoa*, 148 F.2d 416, 443 (2d Cir. 1945).

5. *E.g., Zoelsch v. Arthur Andersen & Co.*, 824 F.2d 27, 29-30 (D.C. Cir. 1987)(securities statutes "frame a broad grant of jurisdiction, but they furnish no specific indications of when American federal courts have jurisdiction over securities law violations arising from extraterritorial transactions"); *Bersch v. Drexel Firestone, Inc.*, 519 F.2d 974, 993 (2d Cir.), *cert. denied*, 423 U.S. 1018 (1975) ("We freely acknowledge that if we were asked to point to language in the statutes, or even in the legislative history, that compelled these conclusions [concerning the extraterritorial application of the federal securities laws], we would be unable to respond. ... Our conclusions rest on case law and commentary concerning the application of the securities laws and other statutes to situations with foreign elements and on our best judgment as to what Congress would have wished if these problems had occurred to it."); *Mannington Mills, Inc. v. Congoleum Corp.*, 595 F.2d 1287, 1291 (3d Cir. 1979) ("Neither the [Sherman] Act nor its legislative history gives any clear indication of the scope of the extraterritorial jurisdiction conferred, leaving such determination to the courts.").

6. *American Banana*, 213 U.S. at 357.

7. *Lauritzen*, 345 U.S. at 576-77.

8. *Lauritzen*, 345 U.S. at 577.

9. Choice of law theory has a long history, which has frequently been recounted. *See* De Nova, *Historical and Comparative Introduction to Conflict of Laws*, 118 Recueil des Cours 443 (1966); Juenger, *General Course on Private International Law*, 193 Recueil des Cours 119 (1983); Lipstein, *The General Principles of Private International Law*, 135 Recueil des Cours 96 (1972); Yntema, *The Historic Bases of Private International Law*, 2 Am. J. Comp. L. 296 (1953).

ous city-states or other jurisdictions, applied to conduct or persons having connections to multiple localities. Broadly speaking, the "statutists" divided statutes into categories, and applied different choice of laws rules to different categories. Some statutes were said to apply only within the territory of the jurisdiction that promulgated them (*e.g.*, "real" or "procedural" statutes); other categories were thought to apply elsewhere, typically based upon the nationality of the actor (*e.g.*, "personal" or "substantive" statutes). In order to determine whether a statute was applicable to particular multistate events, one simply determined what category it fell within.[10]

During the 16th and 17th centuries, some European writers, particularly in the Netherlands and France, abandoned the "statutist" approach, in part because of the arbitrary and unpredictable results it produced. Instead, they articulated choice of law (and other) rules based on principles of territorial sovereignty and international comity.[11] As discussed elsewhere, these analyses emphasized the generally exclusive jurisdiction of a state over events and persons within its territory.[12]

A leading proponent of the territoriality doctrine was Ulrich Huber,[13] whose *De Conflictu Legum* was a landmark in the development of choice of law theory. As described above, Huber stated three basic "maxims" of international law.[14] These maxims replaced the statutists' efforts to classify statutes with a strictly territorial approach that affirmed a state's absolute sovereignty within its territory, but no further. Huber's first maxim declared: "Every state's laws apply within the state's territory, but not beyond."[15]

Huber's territorial approach avoided the difficulties inherent in determining how to categorize particular statutes, but it left a difficulty in cases involving conduct or persons located outside the forum. If no law had extraterritorial reach, then the forum's law could not apply to foreign conduct. But the territoriality doctrine also appeared to prevent the forum court from applying foreign law — for this was thought to involve the extraterritorial application of that law.

Huber resolved this perceived dilemma by reference to international comity: "'Comity' calls on states to recognize and enforce rights created by other states, provided that such recognition does not prejudice the state or its subjects."[16] According

---

10. Juenger, *General Course on Private International Law*, 193 Recueil des Cours 119, 139-44 (1983).

11. *See* Juenger, *General Course on Private International Law*, 193 Recueil des Cours 119, 144-49 (1983); Lorenzen, *Territoriality, Public Policy and the Conflict of Laws*, 33 Yale L.J. 736 (1924); Yntema, *The Comity Doctrine*, 65 Mich. L. Rev. 9, 16-28 (1966).

12. *See supra* pp. 70-73 & 199-201.

13. *See supra* pp. 70-72; Davies, *The Influence of Huber's De Conflictu Legum on English Private International Law*, 18 Brit. Y. B. Int'l L. 49 (1937); Nussbaum, *Rise and Decline of the Law-of-Nations Doctrine in the Conflict of Laws*, 42 Colum. L. Rev. 189 (1942); Yntema, *The Comity Doctrine*, 65 Mich. L. Rev. 9 (1966).

14. *See supra* pp. 70-72.

15. *See* U. Huber, *De Conflictu Legum* (in E. Lorenzen, *Selected Articles on the Conflict of Laws* 136 (1947)).

16. *See* U. Huber, *De Conflictu Legum* (in E. Lorenzen, *Selected Articles on the Conflict of Laws* 136 (1947)).

to Huber, comity was not a precise, binding legal obligation capable of resolving specific cases, but a general principle governing the relations of sovereign states:

> the solution of the [choice of law] problem must be derived not exclusively from the civil law, but from convenience and the tacit consent of nations. Although the laws of one nation can have no force directly within another, yet nothing could be more inconvenient to commerce and to international usage than that transactions valid by the law of one place should be rendered of no effect elsewhere on account of a difference in the law.[17]

This general comity doctrine provided the foundation for more precise choice of law rules in specific contexts, which Huber developed, permitting courts to apply the laws of foreign jurisdictions.[18]

Huber's conception of international comity had a profound influence on American law.[19] Early American choice of law decisions routinely cited Huber's *De Conflictu Legum*, and the Supreme Court took the unusual step in *Emory v. Grenough*[20] of reprinting Huber's maxims in translation as a note to its opinion. But it was Joseph Story — first as a commentator and later as a Supreme Court Justice — who was the most important conduit for bringing Huber's ideas into American law. In particular, Story's monumental treatise — *Commentaries on the Conflict of Laws* — embraced Huber's maxims, and particularly the territoriality doctrine and the use of comity to moderate territorial limits on jurisdiction.[21]

As discussed elsewhere, Story's *Commentaries* began from the premise that "general maxims of international jurisprudence" guaranteed the territorial sovereignty of states.[22] Story's first maxim was that "every nation possesses an exclusive sovereignty and jurisdiction within its own territory."[23] Story went on to declare that nations could properly exercise legislative jurisdiction only within their own territory: his second maxim stated that "no state or nation can, by its laws, directly affect, or bind property out of its own territory, or persons not resident therein."[24]

---

17. U. Huber, *De Conflictu Legum* (in E. Lorenzen, *Selected Articles on the Conflict of Laws* 164-65 (1947)). In one commentator's words, Huber "made it clear beyond a doubt, that the recognition in each state of so-called foreign created rights was a mere concession which such state made on grounds of convenience and utility, and not as the result of a binding obligation or duty. ... Huber conceived of comity as a political concession which might be granted or withheld arbitrarily by the sovereign." E. Lorenzen, *Selected Articles on the Conflict of Laws* 138-39 (1947).

18. Yntema, *The Historic Bases of Private International Law*, 2 Am. J. Comp. L. 296 (1953); Juenger, *General Course on Private International Law*, 193 Recueil des Cours 119 (1983).

19. *See supra* pp. 70-73.

20. 3 U.S. 369 note a (1797).

21. *See* Lorenzen, *Story's Commentaries on the Conflict of Laws — One Hundred Years After*, 48 Harv. L. Rev. 15 (1934); Nadelmann, *Joseph Story's Contribution to American Conflicts Law: A Comment*, 5 Am. J. Legal Hist. 230 (1961).

22. Story adopted a territorial approach to issues of judicial jurisdiction, recognition of foreign judgments, and related issues. *See supra* pp. 70-73 and *infra* pp. 939-41.

23. J. Story, *Commentaries on the Conflict of Laws* 19 (2d ed. 1841).

24. J. Story, *Commentaries on the Conflict of Laws* 19, 21-22 (2d ed. 1841).

Finally, Story relied on the doctrine of comity to explain why states would apply foreign law and recognize foreign judgments. Citing Huber's third maxim, Story wrote that "the rules of every empire from comity admit, that the laws of every people, in force within its own limits, ought to have the same force everywhere, so far as they do not prejudice the powers or rights of other governments, or of their citizens."[25] Story, like Huber, saw comity as something less than a binding legal obligation, but more than an invitation to exercise unfettered discretion:

> The true foundation on which the administration of international law must rest is, that the rules which are to govern are those which arise from mutual interest and utility, from a sense of the inconveniences which would result from a contrary doctrine, and from a sort of moral necessity to do justice, in order that justice may be done to us in return.[26]

Relying on the comity doctrine, Story's *Commentaries* formulated a comprehensive set of rules concerning "private" international law topics, including judicial jurisdiction, choice of law, and recognition of foreign judgments.[27]

Story's territorial approach to international law had a significant influence on the application of federal legislation in international cases. As discussed elsewhere, U.S. courts have long presumed that Congress does not intend its enactments to violate international law.[28] Based in significant part on this *Charming Betsy* presumption, and Story's territorial views of international law, U.S. courts began in the early years of the Republic to apply a related presumption that Congress did not intend its legislation to apply extraterritorially.[29] As it was later formulated, this "territoriality presumption" provided that "legislation of Congress, unless a contrary intent appears, is meant to apply only within the territorial jurisdiction of the United States."[30]

An early application of the territoriality presumption was *The Apollon*, an 1824 decision discussed above.[31] The case required an interpretation of federal customs statutes to determine whether they extended to foreign vessels outside U.S. waters. Justice Story wrote that "[t]he laws of no nation can justly extend beyond its own

---

25. J. Story, *Commentaries on the Conflict of Laws* 30 (2d ed. 1841).

26. J. Story. *Commentaries on the Conflict of Laws* 32-35 (2d ed. 1841).

27. *See* Lorenzen, *Story's Commentaries on the Conflict of Laws — One Hundred Years After*, 48 Harv. L. Rev. 15 (1934); Nadelmann, *Joseph Story's Contribution to American Conflicts Law: A Comment*, 5 Am. J. Legal Hist. 230 (1961).

28. *See supra* pp. 22 & 494-96; *Restatement (Third) Foreign Relations Law* §114 (1987); *Murray v. Schooner Charming Betsy*, 6 U.S. 64, 118 (1804).

29. *Rose v. Himely*, 8 U.S. 241 (1807); *United States v. Palmer*, 16 U.S. 610 (1818); *The Apollon*, 22 U.S. 362 (1824).

30. *Foley Bros., Inc. v. Filardo*, 336 U.S. 281, 285 (1949). *See McCulloch v. Sociedad Nacional de Marineros de Honduras*, 372 U.S. 10, 21-22 (1968).

31. 22 U.S. 362 (1824); *supra* pp. 494-96. In 1807, Chief Justice Marshall acknowledged the territoriality presumption in *Rose v. Himely*, where he declared that "[i]t is conceded that the legislation of every country is territorial." 8 U.S. 241, 279 (1807).

territory, except so far as regards its own citizens."[32] He also observed that extraterritorial assertion of U.S. jurisdiction would be "at variance with the independence and sovereignty of foreign nations."[33] Relying on this view of the "law of nations," the Court invoked the following presumption: "however general and comprehensive the phrases used in our municipal laws may be, they must always be restricted in construction, to places and persons, upon whom the legislature have authority and jurisdiction."[34]

The territoriality presumption was invoked by U.S. courts throughout the 19th and into the 20th century.[35] The presumption was reaffirmed in uncompromising terms in the Supreme Court's 1909 decision in *American Banana Company v. United Fruit Company*,[36] excerpted below, which refused to apply the Sherman Act to a U.S. company's actions in Costa Rica. Citing both international law and conflict of laws authorities, Justice Holmes stated "[t]he general and almost universal rule . . . *that the character of an act as lawful or unlawful must be determined wholly by the law of the country where the act is done.*"[37] In the following two decades, the Supreme Court and other U.S. courts repeatedly applied the territoriality presumption.[38]

Despite their historic importance, the territoriality presumption and its rationale have been significantly eroded during this century.[39] In place of the territoriality doctrine, U.S. courts adopted an assortment of alternative approaches to determining the reach of federal legislation. A leading example is *Lauritzen v. Larsen*,[40] which is excerpted below. There, the Court considered whether the Jones Act applied to a personal injury claim by a Danish seaman, against a Danish shipowner, for injuries sustained on the defendant's ship while it was moored in Havana, Cuba.[41] Justice

---

32. 22 U.S. at 370.

33. 22 U.S. at 370.

34. 22 U.S. at 370.

35. *E.g., Rose v. Himely,* 8 U.S. 241, 279 (1807); *United States v. Palmer,* 16 U.S. 610, 631 (1818); *The Apollon,* 22 U.S. 362, 370-71 (1824); *American Banana Co. v. United Fruit Co.,* 213 U.S. 347 (1909); *United States v. Bowman,* 260 U.S. 94 (1922); *New York Central R. Co. v. Chisholm,* 268 U.S. 29 (1925); H. Black, *Handbook on the Construction and Interpretation of the Laws* 90-91 (1896); G. Endlich, *A Commentary on the Interpretation of Statutes* 239-43 (1888).

36. 213 U.S. 347 (1909).

37. 213 U.S. at 356 (emphasis added). The Court supported this formulation with citations to *Slater v. Mexican National R.R. Co.,* 194 U.S. 120, 126 (1904), and *Milliken v. Pratt,* 125 Mass. 374 (1878).

38. *MacLeod v. United States,* 229 U.S. 416, 434 (1913); *Sandberg v. McDonald,* 248 U.S. 185, 195 (1918) ("Legislation is presumptively territorial and confined to limits over which the lawmaking power has jurisdiction."); *United States v. Bowman,* 260 U.S. 94, 98 (1922); *New York Central R. Co. v. Chisholm,* 268 U.S. 29 (1925) (no extraterritorial application of statute that "contains no words which definitely disclose an intention to give it extraterritorial effect, nor do the circumstances require an inference of such purpose").

39. *E.g., Lauritzen v. Larsen,* 345 U.S. 571 (1953); *Romero v. International Terminal Operating Co.,* 358 U.S. 354 (1959); *Benz v. Compania Naveriera Hidalgo SA,* 353 U.S. 138 (1957); *McCulloch v. Sociedad Nacional de Marineros,* 372 U.S. 10 (1963); *United States v. Bowman,* 260 U.S. 94 (1922); *Ford v. United States,* 273 U.S. 593 (1927).

40. 345 U.S. 571 (1953).

41. 345 U.S. at 573.

Jackson noted the "literal catholicity of [the Jones Act's] terminology,"[42] and commented that the Act "makes no explicit requirement that either the seaman, the employment or the injury have the slightest connection with the United States."[43] The Court nevertheless refused to read the Jones Act as affording the plaintiff a cause of action — but in doing so, it rejected the territoriality presumption.

In determining whether the Jones Act applied to particular conduct, *Lauritzen* looked to "prevalent doctrines of international law,"[44] just as *The Apollon* and *American Banana* had. Instead of the historic territoriality doctrine,[45] however, the *Lauritzen* Court understood contemporary international law as requiring consideration of a variety of "connecting factors."[46] These factors included the place of the wrongful act, the law of the vessel, the plaintiff's nationality or domicile, the defendant's nationality, the place of the parties' contract, and the accessibility of foreign forums.[47] Applying these factors, *Lauritzen* held that the plaintiff's injury was more closely connected to Denmark than to the United States and that the Jones Act therefore did not apply.

Similarly, in 1959, *Romero v. International Terminal Operating Co.*[48] held that neither the Jones Act nor general maritime law provided a remedy for a foreign seaman, injured on a foreign vessel owned by a foreign shipowner, even though the plaintiff's injury occurred in U.S. territorial waters.[49] After rejecting a "mechanical" *lex loci delicti* test,[50] the Court reasoned:

> In the absence of a contrary congressional direction, we must apply those principles of choice of law that are consonant with the needs of a general federal maritime law and with due recognition of our self-regarding respect for the relevant interest of foreign nations in the regulation of maritime commerce as part of the legitimate concern of the international community.[51]

---

42. 345 U.S. at 573. The Jones Act creates a federal cause of action for seamen, for personal injury suffered in the course of employment. The Act provides: "Any seaman who shall suffer personal injury in the course of his employment may, at his election, maintain an action for damages at law, with the right of trial by jury, and in such action all statutes of the United States modifying or extending the common-law right or remedy in cases of personal injury to railway employees shall apply ..." 46 U.S.C. app. §688(a) (1988) (originally enacted as Act of Mar. 4, 1915, ch. 153, §20, 38 Stat. 1164, 1185). In 1982, Congress amended §688 to deny non-resident aliens any rights under §688(a) in most cases. Act of Dec. 29, 1982, Pub. L. No. 97-389, tit. V, §503, 96 Stat. 1954, 1955 (codified at 46 U.S.C. app. §688(b)).

43. 345 U.S. at 576-77.

44. 345 U.S. at 577. Citing *Charming Betsy*, the Court reasoned that international law principles have "the force of law, not from extraterritorial reach of national laws, nor from abdication of its sovereign powers by any nations, but from acceptance by common consent of civilized communities of rules designed to foster amicable and workable commercial relations." 345 U.S. at 581-82.

45. In addition to its non-application of the territoriality presumption, *Lauritzen* remarked that "the territorial standard is ... unfitted to an enterprise conducted many territorial rules."

46. 345 U.S. at 582.

47. 345 U.S. at 583-91.

48. 358 U.S. 354 (1959).

49. 358 U.S. at 384.

50. 358 U.S. at 383.

51. 358 U.S. at 382-83.

As in *Lauritzen, Romero* concluded that contemporary international maritime law called for a multi-factor analysis which included the place of the wrong, but only as one of many factors.[52]

Broadly similar results obtained in other cases involving international shipping. In *Benz v. Compania Naveriera Hidalgo, SA*,[53] and *McCulloch v. Sociedad Nacional de Marineros*,[54] the Court held that the Labor Management Relations Act and National Labor Relations Act did not apply to foreign sailors involved in labor disputes aboard foreign vessels, even when they were located within U.S. territorial waters. In each case, the Court cited the territoriality presumption, but then went on to instead consider contemporary international law rules governing jurisdiction over vessels.[55]

These and other developments suggested to many that the territoriality presumption was no longer viable in the mid-20th century.[56] Nevertheless, the presumption reawakened, with remarkable vitality, in recent years. This is illustrated by the Supreme Court's decision in *EEOC v. Arabian American Oil Company*, excerpted below. There, the Court reaffirmed the territoriality presumption, holding Title VII's employment discrimination provisions inapplicable to a dispute occurring outside the United States between two U.S. parties. Subsequent Supreme Court decisions have also forcefully restated the territoriality presumption.[57]

The materials excerpted below — *American Banana, Lauritzen*, and *Aramco* — illustrate the evolution of the territoriality presumption and the continuing debate over the geographic scope of federal legislation.

AMERICAN BANANA COMPANY v. UNITED FRUIT COMPANY

213 U.S. 347 (1909)

HOLMES, JUSTICE. This is an action brought to recover threefold damages under the act to protect trade against monopolies [the Sherman Act]. [Among other things, the Sherman Act forbids "[e]very contract, combination ... or conspiracy in restraint of trade or commerce ... with foreign nations."] ... The allegations of the complaint may be summed up as follows: The plaintiff is an Alabama corporation, organized in 1904. The defendant is a New Jersey corporation, organized in 1899. Long before the plaintiff was formed, the defendant, with intent to prevent competition and to control and monopolize the banana trade, bought the ... business of several of its previous competitors, with provision against their resuming the trade, made contracts with others ... [fixing the price of bananas]. For the same purpose it

---

52. 358 U.S. at 383-84.
53. 353 U.S. 138 (1957).
54. 372 U.S. 10 (1963).
55. *Benz*, 353 U.S. at 146-47; *McCulloch*, 372 U.S. at 21-22.
56. *See* Born, *A Reappraisal of the Extraterritorial Reach of U.S. Law*, 24 Law & Pol'y Int'l Bus. 1 (1992); *infra* pp. 497-502.
57. *Sale v. Haitian Centers Council*, 113 S.Ct. 2549 (1993); *Smith v. United States*, 113 S.Ct. 1178 (1993).

organized a selling company, of which it held the stock, that by agreement sold at fixed prices all the bananas of the combining parties. ... [O]ne McConnell, in 1903, started a banana plantation in Panama, then part of the United States of Columbia, and began to build a railway (which would afford his only means of export), both in accordance with the laws of the United States of Columbia. He was notified by the defendant that he must either combine or stop. Two months later, it is believed at the defendant's instigation, the governor of Panama recommended to his national government that Costa Rica be allowed to administer the territory through which the railroad was to run, and this although that territory had been awarded to Colombia under an arbitration agreed to by treaty. The defendant, and afterwards, in September, the government of Costa Rica, it is believed by the inducement of the defendant, interfered with McConnell. In November, 1903, Panama revolted and became an independent republic, declaring its boundary to be that settled by the award. In June, 1904, the plaintiff bought out McConnell and went on with the work, as it had a right to do under the laws of Panama. But in July, Costa Rican soldiers and officials, instigated by the defendant, seized a part of the plantation and a cargo of supplies and have held them ever since, and stopped the construction and operation of the plantation and railway. In August one Astua, by ex parte proceedings, got a judgment from a Costa Rican court, declaring the plantation to be his, although, it is alleged, the proceedings were not within the jurisdiction of Costa Rica, and were contrary to its laws and void. Agents of the defendant then bought the lands from Astua. The plaintiff has tried to induce the government of Costa Rica to withdraw its soldiers, and also has tried to persuade the United States to interfere, but has been thwarted in both by the defendant and has failed. The government of Costa Rica remained in possession down to the bringing of the suit.

As a result of the defendant's acts the plaintiff has been deprived of the use of the plantation, and the railway, the plantation, and supplies have been injured. The defendant also, by outbidding, has driven purchasers out of the market and has compelled producers to come to its terms, and it has prevented the plaintiff from buying for export and sale. This is the substantial damage alleged. ... It is contended, however, that, even if the main argument fails and the defendant is held not to be answerable for acts depending on the co-operation of the government of Costa Rica for their effect, a wrongful conspiracy resulting in driving the plaintiff out of business is to be gathered from the complaint, and that it was entitled to go to trial upon that.

It is obvious that, however stated, the plaintiff's case depends on several rather startling propositions. In the first place, the acts causing the damage were done, so far as appears, outside the jurisdiction of the United States, and within that of other states. It is surprising to hear it argued that they were governed by the act of Congress.

No doubt in regions subject to no sovereign, like the high seas, or to no law that civilized countries would recognize as adequate, such countries may treat some relations between their citizens as governed by their own law, and keep, to some extent, the old notion of personal sovereignty alive. *See The Hamilton*, 207 U.S. 398 (1907). They go further, at times, and declare that they will punish anyone, subject or not, who shall do certain things, if they can catch him, as in the case of pirates on the high seas. In cases immediately affecting national interests they may go further still and may make, and, if they get the chance, execute, similar threats as to acts done within another recognized jurisdiction. An illustration from our statutes is found with regard to criminal correspondence with foreign governments. Rev. Stat. §5335. ...

But the general and almost universal rule is that the character of an act as lawful or unlawful must be determined wholly by the law of the country where the act is done. *Slater v. Mexican Nat. R. Co.*, 194 U.S. 120, 126 (1904). This principle was carried to an extreme in *Milliken v. Pratt*, 125 Mass. 374 (1978) [excerpted below at pp. 666-69]. For another jurisdiction, if it should happen to lay hold of the actor, to treat him according to its own notions rather than those of the place where he did the acts, not only would be unjust, but would be an interference with the authority of another sovereign, contrary to the comity of nations, which the other state concerned justly might resent. *Phillips v. Eyre*, L.R. 4 Q.B. 225, 239; Dicey, [*Conflict of Laws*] 647 (2d ed.).

Law is a statement of the circumstances, in which the public force will be brought to bear upon men through the courts. But the word commonly is confined to such prophecies or threats when addressed to persons living within the power of the courts. A threat that depends upon the choice of the party affected to bring himself within that power hardly would be called law in the ordinary sense. We do not speak of blockade running by neutrals as unlawful. And the usages of speech correspond to the limit of the attempts of the lawmaker, except in extraordinary cases. It is true that domestic corporations remain always within the power of the domestic law; but, in the present case, at least, there is no ground for distinguishing between corporations and men.

The foregoing considerations would lead, in case of doubt, to a construction of any statute as intended to be confined in its operation and effect to the territorial limits over which the lawmaker has general and legitimate power. "All legislation is prima facie territorial." *Ex parte Blain*, L. R. 12 Ch. Div. 522, 528. Words having universal scope, such as "every contract in restraint of trade," "every person who shall monopolize," etc., will be taken, as a matter of course, to mean only everyone subject to such legislation, not all that the legislator subsequently may be able to catch. In the case of the present statute, the improbability of the United States attempting to make acts done in Panama or Costa Rica criminal is obvious, yet the law begins by making criminal the acts for which it gives a right to sue. We think it entirely plain that what the defendant did in Panama or Costa Rica is not within the scope of the statute so far as the present suit is concerned. ...

For again, not only were the acts of the defendant in Panama or Costa Rica not within the Sherman Act, but they were not torts by the law of the place, and therefore were not torts at all, however contrary to the ethical and economic postulates of that statute. The substance of the complaint is that, the plantation being within the de facto jurisdiction of Costa Rica, that state took and keeps possession of it by virtue of its sovereign power. But a seizure by a state is not a thing that can be complained of elsewhere in the courts. *Underhill v. Hernandez,* 168 U.S. 250 (1897). The fact, if it be one, that de jure the estate is in Panama, does not matter in the least; sovereignty is pure fact. The fact has been recognized by the United States, and, by the implications of the bill, is assented to by Panama.

The fundamental reason why persuading a sovereign power to do this or that cannot be a tort is not that the sovereign cannot be joined as a defendant or because it must be assumed to be acting lawfully. ... The fundamental reason is that it is a contradiction in terms to say that, within its jurisdiction, it is unlawful to persuade a sovereign power to bring about a result that it declares by its conduct to be desirable and proper. It does not, and foreign courts cannot, admit that the influences were improper or the results bad. It makes the persuasion lawful by its own act. The very meaning of sovereignty is that the decree of the sovereign makes law. In the case of private persons, it consistently may assert the freedom of the immediate parties to an injury and yet declare that certain persuasions addressed to them are wrong.

... The acts of the soldiers and officials of Costa Rica are not alleged to have been without the consent of the government, and must be taken to have been done by its order. It ratified them, at all events, and adopted and keeps the possession taken by them. The injuries to the plantation and supplies seem to have been the direct effect of the acts of the Costa Rican government, which is holding them under an adverse claim of right. The claim for them must fall with the claim for being deprived of the use and profits of the place. As to the buying at a high price, etc., it is enough to say that we have no ground for supposing that it was unlawful in the countries where the purchases were made. Giving to this complaint every reasonable latitude of interpretation we are of opinion that it alleges no case under the act of Congress, and discloses nothing that we can suppose to have been a tort where it was done. A conspiracy in this country to do acts in another jurisdiction does not draw to itself those acts and make them unlawful, if they are permitted by the local law.

LAURITZEN v. LARSEN

345 U.S. 571 (1953)

JUSTICE JACKSON. The key issue in this case is whether statutes of the United States should be applied to this claim of maritime tort. Larsen, a Danish seaman, while temporarily in New York joined the crew of the *Randa,* a ship of Danish flag and registry, owned by petitioner, a Danish citizen. Larsen signed ship's articles, written in Danish, providing that the rights of crew members would be governed by Danish law and by the employer's contract with the Danish Seamen's Union, of which Larsen was a member. He was negligently injured aboard the *Randa* in the course of employment, while in Havana harbor.

Respondent brought suit under the Jones Act[58] [in] the Southern District of New York and demanded a jury. Petitioner contended that Danish law was applicable and that, under it, respondent had received all of the compensation to which he was entitled. ... [T]he court ruled that American rather than Danish law applied, and the jury rendered a verdict of $4,267.50. The [Second Circuit] affirmed. ...

Denmark has enacted a comprehensive code to govern the relations of her shipowners to her seagoing labor which by its terms and intentions controls this claim. Though it is not for us to decide, it is plausibly contended that all obligations of the owner growing out of Danish law have been performed or tendered to this seaman. The shipowner, supported here by the Danish Government, asserts that the Danish law supplies the full measure of his obligation and that maritime usage and international law as accepted by the United States exclude the application of our incompatible statute.

That allowance of an additional remedy under our Jones Act would sharply conflict with the policy and letter of Danish law is plain from a general comparison of the two systems of dealing with shipboard accidents. Both assure the ill or injured seafaring worker the conventional maintenance and cure at the shipowner's cost, regardless of fault or negligence on the part of anyone. But, while we limit this to the period within which maximum possible cure can be effected, the Danish law limits it to a fixed period of twelve weeks, and the monetary measurement is different. The two systems are in sharpest conflict as to treatment of claims for disability, partial or complete, which are permanent, or which outlast the liability for maintenance and cure, to which class this claim belongs. Such injuries Danish law relieves under a state-operated plan similar to our workmen's compensation systems. Claims for such disability are not made against the owner but against the state's Directorate of Insurance Against the Consequences of Accidents. They may be presented directly or through any Danish Consulate. They are allowed by administrative action, not by litigation, and depend not upon fault or negligence but only on the fact of injury and the extent of disability. Our own law, apart from indemnity for injury caused by the ship's unseaworthiness, makes no such compensation for such disability in the absence of fault or negligence. But, when such fault or negligence is established by litigation, it allows recovery for elements such as pain and suffering not compensated under Danish law and lets the damages be fixed by jury. In this case, since negligence was found, United States law permits a larger recovery than Danish law. If the same injury were sustained but negligence was absent or not provable, the Danish law would appear to provide compensation where ours would not.

Respondent does not deny that Danish law is applicable to his case. The contention as stated in his brief is rather that "A claimant may select whatever forum he

---

58. "Any seaman who shall suffer personal injury in the course of his employment may, at his election, maintain an action for damages at law, with the right of trial by jury, and in such action all statutes of the United States modifying or extending the common-law right or remedy in cases of personal injury to railway employees shall apply. ..." 46 U.S.C. §688.

desires and receive the benefits resulting from such choice" and "A ship owner is liable under the laws of the forum where he does business as well as in his own country." This contention that the Jones Act provides an optional cumulative remedy is not based on any explicit terms of the Act, which makes no provision for cases in which remedies have been obtained or are obtainable under foreign law. Rather he relies upon the literal catholicity of its terminology. If read literally, Congress has conferred an American right of action which requires nothing more than that plaintiff be "any seaman who shall suffer personal injury in the course of his employment." It makes no explicit requirement that either the seaman, the employment or the injury have the slightest connection with the United States. Unless some relationship of one or more of these to our national interest is implied, Congress has extended our law and opened our courts to all alien seafaring men injured anywhere in the world in service of watercraft of every foreign nation — a hand on a Chinese junk, never outside Chinese waters, would not be beyond its literal wording.

But Congress in 1920 wrote these all-comprehending words, not on a clean slate, but as a postscript to a long series of enactments governing shipping. All were enacted with regard to a seasoned body of maritime law developed by the experience of American courts long accustomed to dealing with admiralty problems, in reconciling our own with foreign interests, and in accommodating the reach of our own laws to those of other maritime nations.

The shipping laws of the United States ... comprise a patchwork of separate enactments, some tracing far back in our history and many designed for particular emergencies. While some have been specific in application to foreign shipping and others in being confined to American shipping, many give no evidence that Congress addressed itself to their foreign application and are in general terms which leave their application to be judicially determined from context and circumstance. By usage as old as the Nation, such statutes have been construed to apply only to areas and transactions in which American law would be considered operative under prevalent doctrines of international law. Thus, in *United States v. Palmer*, 16 U.S. 610 (1818), this Court was called upon to interpret a statute of 1790, 1 Stat. 115, punishing certain acts when committed on the high seas by "any person or persons," terms which, as Mr. Chief Justice Marshall observed, are "broad enough to comprehend every human being." But the Court determined that the literal universality of the prohibition "must not only be limited to cases within the jurisdiction of the state, but also to those objects to which the legislature intended to apply them," and therefore would not reach a person performing the proscribed acts aboard the ship of a foreign state on the high seas.

This doctrine of construction is in accord with the long-heeded admonition of Mr. Chief Justice Marshall that "an Act of Congress ought never to be construed to violate the law of nations if any other possible construction remains." *The Charming Betsy*, 6 U.S. 64 (1804). *See The Nereide*, 9 Cranch 388, 389, 423; *MacLeod v. United States*, 229 U.S. 416, 434 (1913); *Sandberg v. McDonald*, 248 U.S. 185, 195 (1918).

And it has long been accepted in maritime jurisprudence that "if any construction otherwise be possible, an Act will not be construed as applying to foreigners in respect to acts done by them outside the dominions of the sovereign power enacting. That is a rule based on international law, by which one sovereign power is bound to respect the subjects and the rights of all other sovereign powers outside its own territory." *The Queen v. Jameson* (1896), 2 Q.B. 425, 430. This is not, as sometimes is implied, any impairment of our own sovereignty, or limitation of the power of Congress. "The law of the sea," we have had occasion to observe, "is in a peculiar sense an international law, but application of its specific rules depends upon acceptance by the United States." *Farrell v. United States*, 336 U.S. 511, 517 (1949). On the contrary, we are simply dealing with a problem of statutory construction rather commonplace in a federal system by which courts often have to decide whether "any" or "every" reaches to the limits of the enacting authority's usual scope or is to be applied to foreign events or transactions.

The history of the statute before us begins with the 1915 enactment of the comprehensive LaFollette Act, entitled, "An Act To promote the welfare of American seamen in the merchant marine of the United States; to abolish arrest and imprisonment as a penalty for desertion and to secure the abrogation of treaty provisions in relation thereto; and to promote safety at sea." 38 Stat. 1164. Many sections of this Act were in terms or by obvious implication restricted to American ships. Three sections were made specifically applicable to foreign vessels, and these provoked considerable doubt and debate. ... In 1920, Congress, under the title "An Act To provide for the promotion and maintenance of the American merchant marine ..." and other subjects not relevant, provided a plan to aid our mercantile fleet and included the revised provision for injured seamen now before us for construction. 41 Stat. 988, 1007. It did so by reference to the Federal Employers' Liability Act, 45 U.S.C.A. §51 *et seq.*, which we have held not applicable to an American citizen's injury sustained in Canada while in service of an American employer. *New York Central R. Co. v. Chisholm*, 268 U.S. 29 (1925).

Congress could not have been unaware of the necessity of construction imposed upon courts by such generality of language and was well warned that in the absence of more definite directions than are contained in the Jones Act it would be applied by the courts to foreign events, foreign ships and foreign seamen only in accordance with the usual doctrine and practices of maritime law.

Respondent places great stress upon the assertion that petitioner's commerce and contacts with the ports of the United States are frequent and regular, as the basis for applying our statutes to incidents aboard his ships. But the virtue and utility of sea-borne commerce lies in its frequent and important contacts with more than one country. If, to serve some immediate interest, the courts of each were to exploit every such contact to the limit of its power, it is not difficult to see that a multiplicity of conflicting and overlapping burdens would blight international carriage by sea. Hence, courts of this and other commercial nations have generally deferred to a non-national or international maritime law of impressive maturity and universality. It has the force of law, not from extraterritorial reach of national laws, nor from abdication of its sovereign powers by any nation, but from acceptance by common consent of civilized communities of rules designed to foster amicable and workable commercial relations.

International or maritime law in such matters as this does not seek uniformity and does not purport to restrict any nation from making and altering its laws to govern its own shipping and territory. However, it aims at stability and order through usages which considerations of comity, reciprocity and long-range interest have developed to define the domain which each nation will claim as its own. Maritime law, like our municipal law, has attempted to avoid or resolve conflicts between competing laws by ascertaining and valuing points of contact between the transaction and the states or governments whose competing laws are involved. The criteria, in general, appear to be arrived at from weighing of the significance of one or more connecting factors between the shipping transaction regulated and the national interest served by the assertion of authority. It would not be candid to claim that our courts have arrived at satisfactory standards or apply those that they profess with perfect consistency. But in dealing with international commerce we cannot be unmindful of the necessity for mutual forbearance if retaliations are to be avoided; nor should we forget that any contact which we hold sufficient to warrant application of our law to a foreign transaction will logically be as strong a warrant for a foreign country to apply its law to an American transaction.

In the case before us, two foreign nations can claim some connecting factor with this tort — Denmark, because, among other reasons, the ship and the seaman were Danish nationals; Cuba, because the tortious conduct occurred and caused injury in Cuban waters. The United States may also claim contacts because the seaman had been hired in and was returned to the United States, which also is the state of the forum. We therefore review the several factors which, alone or in combination, are generally conceded to influence choice of law to govern a tort claim, particularly a maritime tort claim, and the weight and significance accorded them.

1. *Place of the Wrongful Act.* — The solution most commonly accepted as to torts in our municipal and in international law is to apply the law of the place where the acts giving rise to the liability occurred, the *lex loci delicti commissi*.[59] This rule of locality, often applied to maritime torts, would indicate application of the law of Cuba, in whose domain the actionable wrong took place. The test of location of the wrongful act or omission, however sufficient for torts ashore, is of limited application to shipboard torts, because of the varieties of legal authority over waters she may navigate. ...

We have sometimes uncompromisingly asserted territorial rights, as when we

---

59. *See Slater v. Mexican National R. Co.*, 194 U.S. 120 (1904); *New York Central R. Co. v. Chisholm*, 268 U.S. 29 (1925); Rheinstein, *The Place of Wrong*, 19 Tul. L. Rev. 4, 165; *cf. Sandberg v. McDonald*, 248 U.S. 185, 195 (1918).

held that foreign ships voluntarily entering our waters become subject to our prohibition laws and other laws as well, except as we may in pursuance of our own policy forego or limit exertion of our power. *Cunard Steamship Co. v. Mellon*, 262 U.S. 100, 124 (1923). This doctrine would seem to indicate Cuban law for this case. But the territorial standard is so unfitted to an enterprise conducted under many territorial rules and under none that it usually is modified by the more constant law of the flag. This would appear to be consistent with the practice of Cuba, which applies a workmen's compensation system in principle not unlike that of Denmark to all accidents occurring aboard ships of Cuban registry. The locality test, for what it is worth, affords no support for the application of American law in this case and probably refers us to Danish in preference to Cuban law, though this point we need not decide, for neither party urges Cuban law as controlling.

2. *Law of the Flag.* — Perhaps the most venerable and universal rule of maritime law relevant to our problem is that which gives cardinal importance to the law of the flag. Each state under international law may determine for itself the conditions on which it will grant its nationality to a merchant ship, thereby accepting responsibility for it and acquiring authority over it. Nationality is evidenced to the world by the ship's papers and its flag. The United States has firmly and successfully maintained that the regularity and validity of a registration can be questioned only by the registering state.

This Court has said that the law of the flag supersedes the territorial principle, even for purposes of criminal jurisdiction of personnel of a merchant ship, because it "is deemed to be a part of the territory of that sovereignty (whose flag it flies), and not to lose that character when in navigable waters within the territorial limits of another sovereignty." On this principle, we concede a territorial government involved only concurrent jurisdiction of offenses aboard our ships. *United States v. Flores*, 289 U.S. 137, 155-59 (1933). ...

It is significant to us here that the weight given to the ensign overbears most other connecting events in determining applicable law. As this Court held in *United States v. Flores*, 289 U.S. at 158: "And so by comity it came to be generally understood among civilized nations that all matters of discipline, and all things done on board, which affected only the vessel, or those belonging to her, and did not involve the peace or dignity of the country, or the tranquillity of the port, should be left by the local government to be dealt with by the authorities of the nation to which the vessel belonged as the laws of that nation, or the interests of its commerce should require. ..." This was but a repetition of settled American doctrine.[60] These considerations are of such weight in favor of Danish and against American law in this case that it must prevail unless some heavy counterweight appears.

3. *Allegiance or Domicile of the Injured.* — Until recent times there was little occasion for conflict between the law of the flag and the law of the state of which the

---

60. *Wildenhus' Case*, 120 U.S. 1 (1887).

seafarer was a subject, for the long-standing rule, as pronounced by this Court after exhaustive review of authority, was that the nationality of the vessel for jurisdictional purposes was attributed to all her crew. *In re Ross*, 140 U.S. 453, 472. Surely during service under a foreign flag some duty of allegiance is due. But, also, each nation has a legitimate interest that its nationals and permanent inhabitants be not maimed or disabled from self-support. We need not, however, weigh the seaman's nationality against that of the ship, for here the two coincide without resort to fiction. ...

4. *Allegiance of the Defendant Shipowner.* — A state "is not debarred by any rule of international law from governing the conduct of its own citizens upon the high seas or even in foreign countries when the rights of other nations or their nationals are not infringed." *Skiriotes v. State of Florida*, 313 U.S. 69, 73 (1941). Until recent times this factor was not a frequent occasion of conflict, for the nationality of the ship was that of its owners. But it is common knowledge that in recent years a practice has grown, particularly among American shipowners, to avoid stringent shipping laws by seeking foreign registration eagerly offered by some countries. Confronted with such operations, our courts on occasion have pressed beyond the formalities of more or less nominal foreign registration to enforce against American shipowners the obligations which our law places upon them. But here again the utmost liberality in disregard of formality does not support the application of American law in this case, for it appears beyond doubt that this owner is a Dane by nationality and domicile.

5. *Place of Contract.* — Place of contract, which was New York, is the factor on which respondent chiefly relies to invoke American law. It is one which often has significance in choice of law in a contract action. But a Jones Act suit is for tort, in which respect it differs from one to enforce liability for maintenance and cure. ... But this action does not seek to recover anything due under the contract or damages for its breach.

The place of contracting in this instance, as is usual to such contracts, was fortuitous. A seaman takes his employment, like his fun, where he finds it; a ship takes on crew in any port where it needs them. The practical effect of making the *lex loci contractus* govern all tort claims during the service would be to subject a ship to a multitude of systems of law, to put some of the crew in a more advantageous position than others, and not unlikely in the long run to diminish hirings in ports of countries that take best care of their seamen.

But if contract law is nonetheless to be considered, we face the fact that this contract was explicit that the Danish law and the contract with the Danish union were to control. Except as forbidden by some public policy, the tendency of the law is to apply in contract matters the law which the parties intended to apply. We are aware of no public policy that would prevent the parties to this contract, which contemplates performance in a multitude of territorial jurisdictions and on the high seas, from so settling upon the law of the flag-state as their governing code. This arrangement is so natural and compatible with the policy of the law that even in the absence of an express provision it would probably have been implied. *The Belgenland*, 114

U.S. 355, 367. We think a quite different result would follow if the contract attempted to avoid applicable law, for example, so as to apply foreign law to an American
ship. ... We do not think the place of contract is a substantial influence in the choice
between competing laws to govern a maritime tort.

6. *Inaccessibility of Foreign Forum.* — It is argued ... that justice requires adjudication under American law to save seamen expense and loss of time in returning to a
foreign forum. This might be a persuasive argument for exercising a discretionary
jurisdiction to adjudge a controversy; but it is not persuasive as to the law by which it
shall be judged. ... [W]e do not find this seaman disadvantaged in obtaining his remedy under Danish law from being in New York instead of Denmark. The Danish
compensation system does not necessitate delayed, prolonged, expensive and uncertain litigation. It is stipulated in this case that claims may be made through the
Danish Consulate. There is not the slightest showing that to obtain any relief to
which he is entitled under Danish law would require his presence in Denmark or
necessitate his leaving New York. And, even if it were so, the record indicates that he
was offered and declined free transportation to Denmark by petitioner.

7. *The Law of the Forum.* — It is urged that, since an American forum has perfected its jurisdiction over the parties and defendant does more or less frequent and
regular business within the forum state, it should apply its own law to the controversy between them. The "doing business" which is enough to warrant service of process
may fall quite short of the considerations necessary to bring extraterritorial torts to
judgment under our law. Under respondent's contention, all that is necessary to
bring a foreign transaction between foreigners in foreign ports under American law
is to be able to serve American process on the defendant. We have held it a denial of
due process of law when a state of the Union attempts to draw into control of its law
otherwise foreign controversies, on slight connections, because it is a forum state.
Hartford Accident & Indemnity Co. v. Delta & Pine Land Co., 292 U.S. 143 (1934);
Home Insurance Co. v. Dick, 281 U.S. 397 (1930). The purpose of a conflict-of-laws
doctrine is to assure that a case will be treated in the same way under the appropriate
law regardless of the fortuitous circumstances which often determine the forum.
Jurisdiction of maritime cases in all countries is so wide and the nature of its subject
matter so far-flung that there would be no justification for altering the law of a controversy just because local jurisdiction of the parties is obtainable. ...

This review of the connecting factors which either maritime law or our municipal law of conflicts regards as significant in determining the law applicable to a claim
of actionable wrong shows an overwhelming preponderance in favor of Danish law.
The parties are both Danish subjects, the events took place on a Danish ship, not
within our territorial waters. Against these considerations is only the fact that the
defendant was served here with process and that the plaintiff signed on in New York,
where the defendant was engaged in our foreign commerce. The latter event is offset
by provision of his contract that the law of Denmark should govern. We do not
question the power of Congress to condition access to our ports by foreign-owned

vessels upon submission to any liabilities it may consider good American policy to exact. But we can find no justification for interpreting the Jones Act to intervene between foreigners and their own law because of acts on a foreign ship not in our waters.

In apparent recognition of the weakness of the legal argument, a candid and brash appeal is made by respondent and by amicus briefs to extend the law to this situation as a means of benefiting seamen and enhancing the costs of foreign ship operation for the competitive advantage of our own. We are not sure that the interest of this foreign seaman, who is able to prove negligence, is the interest of all seamen or that his interest is that of the United States. Nor do we stop to inquire which law does whom the greater or the lesser good. The argument is misaddressed. It would be within the proprieties if addressed to Congress. Counsel familiar with the traditional attitude of this Court in maritime matters could not have intended it for us. ...

EQUAL EMPLOYMENT OPPORTUNITY COMMISSION v. ARABIAN AMERICAN OIL COMPANY

499 U.S. 244 (1991)

CHIEF JUSTICE REHNQUIST. These cases present the issue whether Title VII applies extraterritorially to regulate the employment practices of United States employers who employ United States citizens abroad. The U.S. Court of Appeals for the Fifth Circuit held that it does not, and we agree. ...

Petitioner Boureslan is a naturalized United States citizen who was born in Lebanon. The respondents are two Delaware corporations, Arabian American Oil Company ("Aramco"), and its subsidiary, Aramco Service Company ("ASC"). Aramco's principal place of business is Dhahran, Saudi Arabia, and it is licensed to do business in Texas. ASC's principal place of business is Houston, Texas. In 1979, Boureslan was hired by ASC as a cost engineer in Houston. A year later he was transferred, at his request, to work for Aramco in Saudi Arabia. Boureslan remained with Aramco in Saudi Arabia until he was discharged in 1984. After filing a charge of discrimination with the Equal Employment Opportunity Commission ("EEOC"), he instituted this suit in the ... Southern District of Texas against Aramco and ASC. He sought relief under both state law and Title VII of the Civil Rights Act of 1964, 42 U.S.C. §§2000a-2000h-6, on the ground that he was harassed and ultimately discharged by respondents on account of his race, religion, and national origin.

Respondents filed a motion for summary judgment on the ground that the District Court lacked subject matter jurisdiction over Boureslan's claim because the protections of Title VII do not extend to United States citizens employed abroad by American employers. The District Court agreed, and dismissed Boureslan's Title VII claim; it also dismissed his state-law claims for lack of pendent jurisdiction, and entered final judgment in favor of respondents. [The Fifth Circuit affirmed.] ...

Both parties concede, as they must, that Congress has the authority to enforce its laws beyond the territorial boundaries of the United States. *Cf. Foley Bros., Inc. v. Filardo*, 336 U.S. 281, 284-285 (1949); *Benz v. Compania Naviera Hidalgo, SA*, 353 U.S. 138, 147 (1957). Whether Congress has in fact exercised that authority in this case is a matter of statutory construction. It is our task to determine whether Congress intended the protections of Title VII to apply to U.S. citizens employed by American employers outside of the United States.

It is a long-standing principle of American law "that legislation of Congress, unless a contrary intent appears, is meant to apply only within the territorial jurisdiction of the United States." *Foley Bros.*, 336 U.S. at 285. This "canon of construction ... is a valid approach whereby unexpressed congressional intent may be ascertained." It serves to protect against unintended clashes between our laws and those of other nations which could result in international discord. *See McCulloch v. Sociedad Nacional de Marineros de Honduras*, 372 U.S. 10, 20-22 (1963).

In applying this rule of construction, we look to see whether "language in the [relevant act] gives any indication of a congressional purpose to extend its coverage beyond places over which the United States has sovereignty or has some measure of legislative control." *Foley Bros.*, 336 U.S. at 285. We assume that Congress legislates against the backdrop of the presumption against extraterritoriality. Therefore, unless there is "the affirmative intention of the Congress clearly expressed," *Benz*, 353 U.S. at 147, we must presume it "is primarily concerned with domestic conditions." *Foley Bros.*, 336 U.S. at 285.

Boureslan and the EEOC contend that the language of Title VII evinces a clearly expressed intent on behalf of Congress to legislate extraterritorially. ... First, petitioners argue that the statute's definitions of the jurisdictional terms "employer" and "commerce" are sufficiently broad to include U.S. firms that employ American citizens overseas. Second, they maintain that the statute's "alien exemption" clause, 42 U.S.C. §2000e-1, necessarily implies that Congress intended to protect American citizens from employment discrimination abroad. ... We conclude that petitioners' evidence, while not totally lacking in probative value, falls short of demonstrating the affirmative congressional intent required to extend the protections of Title VII beyond our territorial borders.

Title VII prohibits various discriminatory employment practices based on an individual's race, color, religion, sex, or national origin. An employer is subject to Title VII if it has employed 15 or more employees for a specified period and is "engaged in an industry affecting commerce." An industry affecting commerce is "any activity, business, or industry in commerce or in which a labor dispute would hinder or obstruct commerce or the free flow of commerce and includes any activity or industry 'affecting commerce' within the meaning of the Labor-Management Reporting and Disclosure Act of 1959 [("LMRDA")] [29 U.S.C. §401 et seq.]." §2000e(h). "Commerce," in turn, is defined as "trade, traffic, commerce, transportation, transmission, or communication among the several States; or between a State and any place outside thereof; or within the District of Columbia, or a possession of the United States; or between points in the same State but through a point outside thereof." §2000e(g).

Petitioners argue that by its plain language, Title VII's "broad jurisdictional language" reveals Congress's intent to extend the statute's protections to employment discrimination anywhere in the world by a U.S. employer who affects trade "between a State and any place outside thereof." More precisely, they assert that since Title VII defines "States" to include States, the District of Columbia, and specified territories, the clause "between a State and any place outside thereof" must be referring to areas beyond the territorial limit of the United States.

Respondents offer several alternative explanations for the statute's expansive language. They contend that the "or between a State and any place outside thereof" clause "provide[s] the jurisdictional nexus required to regulate commerce that is not wholly within a single state, presumably as it affects both interstate and foreign commerce" but not to "regulate conduct exclusively within a foreign country." They also argue that since the definitions of the terms "employer," "commerce," and "industry affecting commerce," make no mention of "commerce with foreign nations," Congress cannot be said to have intended that the statute apply overseas. ...

We need not choose between these competing interpretations as we would be required to do in the absence of the presumption against extraterritorial application discussed above. Each is plausible, but no more persuasive than that. The language relied upon by petitioners — and it is they who must make the affirmative showing — is ambiguous, and does not speak directly to the question presented here. The intent of Congress as to the extraterritorial application of this statute must be deduced by inference from boilerplate language which can be found in any number of congressional acts, none of which have ever been held to apply overseas. *See, e.g.,* Consumer Product Safety Act, 15 U.S.C. §2052(a)(12); Federal Food, Drug, and Cosmetic Act, 21 U.S.C. §321(b); Transportation Safety Act of 1974, 49 U.S.C. App. §1802(1).

Petitioners' reliance on Title VII's jurisdictional provisions also finds no support in our case law; we have repeatedly held that even statutes that contain broad language in their definitions of "commerce" that expressly refer to "foreign commerce," do not apply abroad. For example, in *New York Central R. Co. v. Chisholm,* 268 U.S. 29 (1925), we addressed the extraterritorial application of the Federal Employers Liability Act ("FELA"), 45 U.S.C. §51 *et. seq.* FELA provides that common carriers by railroad while engaging in "interstate or foreign commerce" or commerce between "any of the States or territories and any foreign nation or nations" shall be liable in damages to its employees who suffer injuries resulting from their employment. 45 U.S.C. §51. Despite this broad jurisdictional language, we found that the Act "contains no words which definitely disclose an intention to give it extraterritorial effect," *Chisholm,* 268 U.S. at 31, and therefore there was no jurisdiction under FELA for a damages action by a U.S. citizen employed on a U.S. railroad who suffered fatal injuries at a point 30 miles north of the U.S. border into Canada.

Similarly, in *McCulloch v. Sociedad Nacional de Marineros de Honduras*, 372 U.S. 10 (1963), we addressed whether Congress intended the National Labor Relations Act ("NLRA"), 29 U.S.C. §§151-168, to apply overseas. Even though the NLRA contained broad language that referred by its terms to foreign commerce, 29 U.S.C. §152(6), this Court refused to find a congressional intent to apply the statute abroad because there was not "any specific language" in the Act reflecting congressional intent to do so. *McCulloch*, 372 U.S. at 19.

The EEOC places great weight on an assertedly similar "broad jurisdictional grant in the Lanham Act" that this Court held applied extraterritorially in *Steele v. Bulova Watch Co.*, 344 U.S. 280 (1952). ... The EEOC's attempt to analogize this case to *Steele* is unpersuasive. The Lanham Act by terms applies to "all commerce which may lawfully be regulated by Congress." The Constitution gives Congress the power "[t]o regulate Commerce with foreign Nations, and among the several States, and with the Indian Tribes." U.S. Const., Art. I, §8, cl. 3. Since the Act expressly stated that it applied to the extent of Congress's power over commerce, the Court in *Steele* concluded that Congress intended that the statute apply abroad. By contrast, Title VII's more limited, boilerplate "commerce" language does not support such an expansive construction of congressional intent. Moreover, unlike the language in the Lanham Act, Title VII's definition of "commerce" was derived expressly from the LMRDA, a statute that this Court had held, prior to the enactment of Title VII, did not apply abroad. *McCulloch*, 372 U.S. at 15.

Thus petitioner's argument based on the jurisdictional language of Title VII fails both as a matter of statutory language and of our previous case law. Many acts of Congress are based on the authority of that body to regulate commerce among the several States, and the parts of these acts setting forth the basis for legislative jurisdiction will obviously refer to such commerce in one way or another. If we were to permit possible, or even plausible interpretations of language such as that involved here to override the presumption against extraterritorial application, there would be little left of the presumption.

Petitioners argue that Title VII's "alien exemption provision," 42 U.S.C. §2000e-1, "clearly manifests an intention" by Congress to protect U.S. citizens with respect to their employment outside of the United States. The alien exemption provision says that the statute "shall not apply to an employer with respect to the employment of aliens outside any State." §2000e-1. Petitioners contend that from this language a negative inference should be drawn that Congress intended Title VII to cover United States citizens working abroad for United States employers. There is "[no] other plausible explanation [that] the alien exemption exists," they argue, because "[i]f Congress believed that the statute did not apply extraterritorially, it would have had no reason to include an exemption for a certain category of individuals employed outside the United States." Since "[t]he statute's jurisdictional provisions cannot possibly be read to confer coverage only upon aliens employed outside the United States," petitioners conclude that "Congress could not rationally have enacted an exemption for the employment of aliens abroad if it intended to foreclose all potential extraterritorial applications of the statute."

Respondents resist petitioners' interpretation of the alien-exemption provision and assert two alternative raisons d'etre for that language. First, they contend that since aliens are included in the statute's definition of employee, and the definition of commerce includes possessions as well as "States," the purpose of the exemption is to provide that employers of aliens in the possessions of the United States are not covered by the statute. Thus, the "outside any State" clause means outside any State, but within the control of the United States [such as leased military bases in foreign lands.] ...

Second, respondents assert that by negative implication, the exemption "confirm[s] the coverage of aliens in the United States." They contend that this interpretation is consistent with our conclusion in *Espinoza v. Farah Mfg. Co.*, 414 U.S. 86 (1973), that aliens within the United States are protected from discrimination both because Title VII uses the term "individual" rather than "citizen," and because of the alien-exemption provision.

If petitioners are correct that the alien-exemption clause means that the statute applies to employers overseas, we see no way of distinguishing in its application between United States employers and foreign employers. Thus, a French employer of a United States citizen in France would be subject to Title VII — a result at which even petitioners balk. The EEOC assures us that in its view the term "employer" means only "American employer," but there is no such distinction in this statute, and no indication that EEOC in the normal course of its administration had produced a reasoned basis for such a distinction. Without clearer evidence of congressional intent to do so than is contained in the alien-exemption clause, we are unwilling to ascribe to that body a policy which would raise difficult issues of international law by imposing this country's employment-discrimination regime upon foreign corporations operating in foreign commerce.

This conclusion is fortified by the other elements in the statute suggesting a purely domestic focus. The statute as a whole indicates a concern that it not unduly interfere with the sovereignty and laws of the States. *See, e.g.,* 42 U.S.C. §2000h-4 (stating that Title VII should not be construed to exclude the operation of state law or invalidate any state law unless inconsistent with the purposes of the act). ... While Title VII consistently speaks in terms of "States" and state proceedings, it fails even to mention foreign nations or foreign proceedings.

Similarly, Congress failed to provide any mechanisms for overseas enforcement of Title VII. For instance, the statute's venue provisions, §2000e-5(f)(3), are ill-suited for extraterritorial application as they provide for venue only in a judicial district in the state where certain matters related to the employer occurred or were located. And the limited investigative authority provided for the EEOC, permitting the Commission only to issue subpoenas for witnesses and documents from "any place in the United States or any Territory or possession thereof," §2000e-9, suggests that Congress did not intend for the statute to apply abroad.

It is also reasonable to conclude that had Congress intended Title VII to apply overseas, it would have addressed the subject of conflicts with foreign laws and procedures. In amending the Age Discrimination in Employment Act of 1967, 81 Stat. 602, as amended, 29 U.S.C. §621 et seq. ("ADEA"), to apply abroad, Congress specifically addressed potential conflicts with foreign law by providing that it is not unlawful for an employer to take any action prohibited by the ADEA "where such practices involve an employee in a workplace in a foreign country, and compliance with [the ADEA] would cause such employer ... to violate the laws of the country in which such workplace is located." 29 U.S.C. §623(f)(1). Title VII, by contrast, fails to address conflicts with the laws of other nations. ...

Our conclusion today is buttressed by the fact that "[w]hen it desires to do so, Congress knows how to place the high seas within the jurisdictional reach of a statute." *Argentine Republic v. Amerada Hess Shipping Corp.*, 488 U.S. 428, 440 (1989). Congress's awareness of the need to make a clear statement that a statute applies overseas is amply demonstrated by the numerous occasions on which it has expressly legislated the extraterritorial application of a statute. ... Congress, should it wish to do so, may similarly amend Title VII and in doing so will be able to calibrate its provisions in a way that we cannot.

Petitioners have failed to present sufficient affirmative evidence that Congress intended Title VII to apply abroad. Accordingly, the judgment of the Court of Appeals is affirmed.

Dissent

JUSTICE MARSHALL, with whom JUSTICE BLACKMUN and JUSTICE STEVENS join, dissenting. Like any issue of statutory construction, the question whether Title VII protects U.S. citizens from discrimination by U.S. employers abroad turns solely on congressional intent. As the majority recognizes, our inquiry into congressional intent in this setting is informed by the traditional "canon of construction which teaches that legislation of Congress, unless a contrary intent appears, is meant to apply only within the territorial jurisdiction of the United States." *Foley Bros., Inc. v. Filardo.* But contrary to what one would conclude from the majority's analysis, this canon is *not* a "clear statement" rule, the application of which relieves a court of the duty to give effect to all available indicia of the legislative will. Rather, as our case law applying the presumption against extraterritoriality well illustrates, a court may properly rely on this presumption only after exhausting all of the traditional tools "whereby unexpressed congressional intent may be ascertained." When these tools are brought to bear on the issue in this case, the conclusion is inescapable that Congress *did* intend Title VII to protect United States citizens from discrimination by United States employers operating overseas. Consequently, I dissent.

Because it supplies the driving force of the majority's analysis, I start with "[t]he canon ... that legislation of Congress, unless a contrary intent appears, is meant to apply only within the territorial jurisdiction of the United States." The majority recasts this principle as "the need to make a *clear statement* that a statute applies overseas." (Emphasis added.) ... In my view, the majority grossly distorts the effect of this rule of construction upon conventional techniques of statutory interpretation. ...

[For example, in *Foley Brothers*,] the Court ... engaged in extended analyses of the legislative history of the statute, and of pertinent administrative interpretations. The range of factors that the Court considered in *Foley Brothers* demonstrates that the presumption against extraterritoriality is not a "clear statement" rule. Clear-statement rules operate less to reveal *actual* congressional intent than to shield important values from an *insufficiently strong* legisiative intent to displace them. When they apply, such rules foreclose inquiry into extrinsic guides to interpretation, and even compel courts to select less plausible candidates from within the range of permissible constructions. The Court's analysis in *Foley Brothers* was by no means so narrowly constrained. Indeed, the Court considered the entire range of conventional sources "whereby *unexpressed* congressional intent may be ascertained," 336 U.S. at 285 (emphasis added), including legislative history, statutory structure, and administrative interpretations. Subsequent applications of the presumption against extraterritoriality confirm that we have not imposed the drastic clear-statement burden upon Congress before giving effect to its intention that a particular enactment apply beyond the national boundaries. *See, e.g., Steele v. Bulova Watch Co.* (relying on "broad jurisdictional grant" to find intention that Lanham Act applies abroad). ...

The majority also overstates the strength of the presumption by drawing on language from cases involving a wholly independent rule of construction: "that 'an act of congress ought never to be construed to violate the law of nations if any other possible construction remains.' ..." *McCulloch v. Sociedad Nacional,* quoting *The Charming Betsy*; *see Benz v. Compania Naviera Hidalgo, SA.* At issue in *Benz* was whether the Labor Management Relations Act of 1947 "applie[d] to a controversy involving damages resulting from the picketing of a foreign ship operated entirely by foreign seamen under foreign articles while the vessel is temporarily in an American port." Construing the statute to apply under such circumstances would have displaced labor regulations that were founded on the law of another nation and that were applicable solely to foreign nationals. In language quoted in the majority's opinion, the Court stated that "there must be present the affirmative intention of the Congress clearly expressed" before it would infer that Congress intended courts to enter "such a delicate field of international relations."

Far from equating *Benz* and *McCulloch's* clear-statement rule with *Foley's* presumption against extraterritoriality, the Court has until now recognized that *Benz* and *McCulloch* are reserved for settings in which the extraterritorial application of a statute would "implicat[e] sensitive issues of the authority of the Executive over relations with foreign nations." *NLRB v. Catholic Bishop of Chicago,* 440 U.S. 490, 500 (1979). The strictness of the *McCulloch* and *Benz* presumption permits the Court to avoid, if possible, the separation-of-powers and international-comity questions associated with construing a statute to displace the domestic law of another nation. Nothing nearly so dramatic is at stake when Congress merely seeks to regulate the conduct of U.S. nationals abroad.

Because petitioners advance a construction of Title VII that would extend its extraterritorial reach only to U.S. nationals, it is the weak presumption of *Foley Brothers*, not the strict clear-statement rule of *Benz* and *McCulloch*, that should govern our inquiry here. Under *Foley Brothers*, a court is not free to invoke the presumption against extraterritoriality until it has exhausted all available indicia of Congress' intent on this subject. Once these indicia are consulted and given effect in this case. I believe there can be no question that Congress intended Title VII to protect U.S. citizens from discrimination by U.S. employers abroad. ...

Confirmation that Congress did *in fact* expect Title VII's central prohibition to have an extraterritorial reach is supplied by the so-called "alien exemption" provision. The alien-exemption provision states that Title VII "shall not apply to an employer with respect to the employment of aliens *outside any State*." 42 U.S.C. §2000e-1 (emphasis added). Absent an intention that Title VII *apply* "outside any State," Congress would have had no reason to craft this extraterritorial exemption. And because only discrimination against aliens is exempted, employers remain accountable for discrimination against United States citizens abroad. ...

Finally, the majority overstates the importance of Congress' failure expressly to disclaim extraterritorial application of Title VII to foreign employers. As I have discussed, our cases recognize that application of U.S. law to U.S. nationals abroad ordinarily raises considerably less serious questions of international comity than does the application of U.S. law to foreign nationals abroad. *See Steele v. Bulova Watch Co.*; *Skiriotes v. Florida*. It is the latter situation that typically presents the foreign-policy and conflicts-of-law concerns that underlie the clear-statement rule of *McCulloch* and *Benz*. Because two different rules of construction apply depending on the national identity of the regulated parties, the same statute might be construed to apply extraterritorially to United States nationals but not to foreign nationals. *Compare Steele v. Bulova Watch Co.*, (applying Lanham Act to U.S. national for conduct abroad) with *Vanity Fair Mills, Inc. v. T. Eaton Co.*, 234 F.2d 633, 642-643 (2d Cir.) (declining to apply Lanham Act to foreign national for conduct abroad), *cert. denied*, 352 U.S. 871 (1956). ...

In the hands of the majority, the presumption against extraterritoriality is transformed from a "valid approach whereby unexpressed congressional intent may be ascertained," *Foley Bros.*, 336 U.S. at 285, into a barrier to any genuine inquiry into the sources that reveal Congress' actual intentions. Because the language, history, and administrative interpretations of the statute all support application of Title VII to U.S. companies employing U.S. citizens abroad, I dissent.

Notes on American Banana, Lauritzen, and Aramco

1. *The territoriality presumption. American Banana* and *Aramco* rest almost entirely on the so-called territoriality presumption. According to Justice Holmes in *American Banana*, "in case of doubt," a court should adopt a "construction of any statute as intended to be confined in its operation and effect to the territorial limits over which the lawmaker has general and legitimate power." Similarly, *Aramco* declared that "legislation of Congress, unless a contrary intent appears, is meant to apply only within the territorial jurisdiction of the United States."

(a) *Historical origins of territoriality presumption.* As discussed above the territoriality presumption had its origins in decisions during the early decades of the Republic. *See supra* pp. 546-50; *Rose v. Himely*,

8 U.S. 241, 279 (1807); *The Apollon*, 22 U.S. 362 (1824). It was vigorously restated in *American Banana* and was repeatedly applied during the early decades of the 20th century. *See supra* pp. 548-52; *Sandberg v. McDonald*, 248 U.S. 185, 195 (1918) ("Legislation is presumptively territorial and confined to limits over which the lawmaking power has jurisdiction."); *United States v. Bowman*, 260 U.S. 94, 98 (1922); *New York Central R. Co. v. Chisholm*, 268 U.S. 29 (1925) (no extraterritorial application of statute that "contains no words which definitely disclose an intention to give it extraterritorial effect, nor do the circumstances require an inference of such purpose").

(b) *Erosion of territoriality presumption.* As *Lauritzen* illustrates, the territoriality presumption was nearly abandoned during the middle decades of the 20th century. *See supra* pp. 550-52; *United States v. Aluminum Co. of America*, 148 F.2d 416 (2d Cir. 1945); *Romero v. International Terminal Operating Co.*, 358 U.S. 354 (1959); *Steele v. Bulova Watch Co.*, 344 U.S. 280 (1952).

(c) *Contemporary resurrection of territoriality presumption.* Notwithstanding *Lauritzen* and other decisions abandoning the territoriality presumption, recent Supreme Court precedent has reaffirmed the dominant role of territoriality in interpreting federal statutes. *Aramco* is a leading example of this resurrection of the territoriality presumption. Two more recent Supreme Court decisions have also applied the territoriality presumption. *See Smith v. United States*, 113 S.Ct. 1178 (1993); *Sale v. Haitian Centers Council, Inc.*, 113 S.Ct. 2549 (1993).

2. Rationale for territoriality presumption. What is the rationale for the territoriality presumption?

(a) *International law limits on legislative jurisdiction.* The territoriality presumption rests in part on international law limits on legislative jurisdiction, explored above. *See supra* pp. 546-48. As *American Banana* said:

> For another jurisdiction ... to treat [one] according to its own notions rather than those of the place where he did the acts ... would be an interference with the authority of another sovereign, contrary to the comity of nations, which the other state concerned justly might resent.

See also The Apollon, 22 U.S. 361, 370 (1824). Is this a persuasive basis for the territoriality presumption? If international law forbids extraterritorial applications of national law, isn't the territoriality presumption an inevitable corollary of the *Charming Betsy* rule that Congress will not be held to have violated international law unless its legislation expressly commands that result? *See supra* pp. 546-52.

(b) *Choice of law rules.* *American Banana* also cited contemporary choice of law rules, which provided that "the character of an act as lawful or unlawful must be determined wholly by the law of the country where the act is done" (citing *Slater v. Mexican National R.R. Co.*, 194 U.S. 120 (1904), and *Milliken v. Pratt*, 125 Mass. 374 (1878), discussed below, *infra* pp. 664-73)). Are choice of law rules relevant to determining the extraterritorial reach that Congress intended its statutes to have? On what theory?

Note that the antitrust laws, at issue in *American Banana*, are penal or public legislation which foreign states may not be willing to enforce under traditional choice of law rules. *See infra* pp. 630-31. Does this affect the relevance of choice of law principles to the reach of the antitrust laws? Did *Aramco* rely on choice of law analysis in deciding the reach of Title VII?

(c) *Minimizing conflicts between U.S. and foreign laws.* Both *American Banana* and *Aramco* reasoned that the territoriality presumption seeks to avoid conflicts between U.S. and foreign law. "It serves to protect against unintended clashes between our laws and those of other nations which could result in international discord." *See also McCulloch v. Sociedad Nacional de Marineros de Honduras*, 372 U.S. 10, 20-22 (1963). How does the territoriality presumption minimize conflicts with foreign law? The Supreme Court has held that the territoriality presumption is applicable even when there is little or no possibility of conflict with foreign law or international discord. *Sale v. Haitian Centers Council*, 113 S.Ct. 2549, 2560 (1993); *Smith v. United States*, 113 S.Ct. 1178, 1183 n.5 (1993) (even when no "clashes" between U.S. and foreign law exist, "the presumption is rooted in a number of considerations, not the least of which is the common-sense notion that Congress generally legislates with domestic concerns in mind").

(d) *Congress's concern with domestic concerns.* *Aramco* also reasoned that the territoriality presumption rests on the "assumption that Congress is primarily concerned with domestic conditions." *Foley Bros., Inc. v. Filardo*, 336 U.S. 281, 285 (1949). Is that persuasive? Just because Congress is "primarily concerned" with domestic matters, does that mean it does not also intend to address international matters? Recall the interdependence of global markets and the effects of foreign events on U.S. interests. *See supra* pp. 497-500.

(e) *Fairness to private parties.* *American Banana* reasoned that it would be "unjust" to judge a private party by the laws of a place other than where he acted. What is the cause of that unfairness? Is it in fact unfair to judge a private party by a law that is applied extraterritorially? Recall the due process limits on legislative jurisdiction in *Dick* and *Allstate*. *See supra* pp. 518-37.

3. Criticism of territoriality presumption. Do the foregoing justifications provide a persuasive basis for the territoriality presumption? What interests does the presumption further? What interests does it frustrate?

(a) *International law no longer forbids extraterritorial jurisdiction.* As discussed above, international law limits on legislative jurisdiction were one basis for the territoriality presumption. *See supra* pp. 546-50. Note, however, that early decisions, like *The Apollon*, did not in fact articulate a pure territoriality presumption. *See supra* pp. 549-50. Instead, the Court adopted an "international law" presumption that was not strictly territorial: "however general and comprehensive the phrases used in our municipal laws may be, *they must always be restricted in construction, to places and persons, upon whom the legislature have authority and jurisdiction.*" 22 U.S. at 370. Note also that international law recognized both a nationality principle and (less clearly) an effects doctrine in the early 20th century. *See supra* pp. 497-509. Consider the formulation of both principles in the *Restatement (First) Conflict of Laws, supra* p. 502. Would these principles have permitted application of the Sherman Act to the defendant's conduct in *American Banana*?

Moreover, this century has seen a substantial erosion of international law limits on legislative jurisdiction. *See supra* pp. 497-509. Thus, the nationality and effects principles are now widely recognized jurisdictional bases. *See supra* pp. 506-07; Kramer, *Vestiges of Beale: Extraterritorial Application of American Law*, 1992 S. Ct. Rev. 111. What effect does this evolution of international law have on the territoriality presumption?

(b) *American choice of law analysis no longer rests exclusively on the territoriality doctrine.* As discussed below, American conflict of laws underwent what is frequently called a "revolution" during the 1950s and 1960s. *See infra* pp. 631-32. The strict territorial analysis of the *Restatement (First) Conflict of Laws* was replaced by a variety of more flexible analyses. *See infra* pp. 632-36. This evolution is reflected, at least in part, in *Lauritzen*. None of the new analyses of the American conflicts revolution requires application of the law of the place of the tort; they instead look to a broader range of connecting factors and the likely legislative policies of conflicting national laws. These analyses frequently permit application of a state's law to events occurring outside the state's territory. *See infra* pp. 497-509. Should these developments lead to reconsideration of the territoriality presumption? Should contemporary choice of law rules be applied to determine the presumptive reach of federal legislation?

(c) *Congress's contemporary concern with international events.* Congress is frequently concerned intensely with events occurring outside the United States. Indeed, because of the interdependent character of the global economy, it is often difficult to regulate domestic matters meaningfully without taking into account matters abroad. Given that, is it wise to adopt a rule that presumes flatly that Congress cares only about domestic conditions? Why not look more carefully at the particular legislation at issue in a particular case — its language, legislative history, and purposes — to see what sort of territorial or extraterritorial reach Congress likely intended? How would *American Banana* and *Aramco* have been decided under such an approach?

(d) *Prevention of conflicts with foreign laws.* Is it in fact correct, as *Aramco* said, that the territoriality presumption prevents conflicts between U.S. and foreign law? If so, is that a sufficiently important goal to warrant ignoring other U.S. interests?

First, does the territoriality presumption not undervalue potential U.S. interests? For the reasons noted above, Congress frequently does wish to deal with events and actions outside U.S. territory, and its laws will therefore frequently come into conflict with foreign laws. Doesn't the territoriality presumption automatically resolve all such potential conflicts against U.S. interests?

Second, in many cases, an extraterritorial application of U.S. law will not conflict with foreign law. For example, in *American Banana*, application of the Sherman Act had been applied to the conduct of Costa Rica's courts and militia presumably would have conflicted with Costa Rican law. But would there have been a conflict if the Sherman Act had been applied to the defendant's private price-fixing agreements? In *Aramco*, for example, Saudi law was said to forbid discrimination on the basis of national origin, just as Title VII did. Does not the territoriality presumption sweep too broadly by preventing "false conflicts" between U.S. and foreign law in cases where both laws would require the same result? As *Lauritzen* suggests, a choice of law analysis could specifically inquire into the existence of a conflict between U.S. and foreign law.

Third, does a territoriality presumption perform well in preventing conflicts between U.S. and foreign law? Much modern commercial and other conduct has connections with multiple states, and a "territoriality" rule might permit each state effectively to regulate the entire course of conduct through one connection with its territory. *See Restatement (Third) Foreign Relations Law* §402(1)(a) (1987); *supra* pp. 504-05.

4. *Correctness of* American Banana. Was *American Banana* correctly decided? The Sherman Act was made applicable to "every contract ... in restraint of trade or commerce ... with foreign nations." 26 Stat. 209 (1890). Even accepting the territoriality presumption, doesn't this jurisdictional grant plainly apply to a conspiracy orchestrated from the United States and to contracts by which the defendant allegedly fixed prices of bananas exported to the United States? Doesn't the statutory reference to trade "with foreign nations" apply to sales of Costa Rican bananas to persons in the United States, or to persons intending to distribute the bananas in the United States? Further, why wouldn't the nationality principle or effects doctrine have provided a basis for applying the Sherman Act extraterritorially in *American Banana*?

What would the Sherman Act have had to say to satisfy Justice Holmes? What about: "Every contract, wherever in the world it is made or performed, in restraint of trade or commerce with foreign nations"?

Did Costa Rica have any "interest" in the outcome of the *American Banana* dispute? What might that interest have been? How would one go about identifying such an interest? Suppose that the dispute had not involved any acts by purported Costa Rican government authorities, but only private agreements and conduct. Would Costa Rica have had any interest in the case? What relevance did, and should, Costa Rican interests have to the interpretation of the Sherman Act?

5. *Correctness of* Aramco. Was *Aramco* correctly decided? In Chief Justice Rehnquist's view, Title VII did not contain sufficient evidence of Congress's intention to authorize extraterritorial application of U.S. law. Note that there is substantial evidence that Title VII *was* meant to apply extraterritorially. Consider Title VII's jurisdictional grant, which applied the Act to all racial discrimination by any employer "engaged in an industry" affecting commerce "among the several states ... or between a State and any place outside thereof." Did not Aramco plainly fall within this definition of "employer"? Moreover, the Act's "alien exclusion" provided that "[Title VII] shall not apply to an employer with respect to the employment of aliens outside any State," and the Act's legislative history (not addressed by the Court) explained that "the intent of [this] exemption is to remove conflicts of law which might otherwise exist between the United States and a foreign nation in the employment of aliens outside the United States by an American enterprise." H.R. Rep. No. 570, 88th Cong., 1st Sess. 4 (1963). Doesn't this plainly overcome *any* territoriality "presumption"?

6. *Meaning of territoriality presumption.* What exactly does the territoriality presumption mean? Compare the differing views adopted by the majority and dissenting opinions in *Aramco*. Is the territoriality presumption a "strong" or a "weak" presumption? Must a statute contain language that expressly extends its provisions to acts or persons outside U.S. territory? Must the statement be in statutory text, or will legislative history suffice? Does *Aramco* hold that a negative implication can never overcome the territoriality presumption? If there *is* to be a territoriality presumption, is Justice Rehnquist's or Justice Marshall's view of the presumption correct? *Compare Benz v. Compania Naviera Hidalgo, SA*, 353 U.S. 138, 147 (1957) ("affirmative intention of the Congress clearly expressed"); *New York Central R. Co. v. Chisholm*, 268 U.S. 29, 31 (1925) ("words which definitely disclose an intention to give [U.S. law] extraterritorial effect"); *Aramco, supra* ("a clear statement that a statute applies overseas").

7. *Relevance of statute's application to "foreign commerce."* As *Aramco* notes, Title VII and many other federal statutes apply to conduct in or affecting "foreign commerce." The Court has sometimes concluded that such statutory language permits the extraterritorial application of the relevant federal law. *E.g., Steele v. Bulova Watch Co.*, 344 U.S. 280 (1952). It has also concluded that such "boilerplate language" does not "speak directly" to the issue of extraterritorial application. *Aramco, supra. See New York R. Co. v. Chisholm*, 268 U.S. 29 (1925). When Congress makes federal law applicable to any conduct in, or affecting, U.S. foreign commerce, why *doesn't* this directly address the geographic reach of the legislation?

8. *Alternatives to the territoriality presumption.* Given the erosion of strict notions of territoriality in international law, is *Aramco*'s strict territoriality presumption warranted? Would it be more appropriate for the Court to adopt a principle of statutory construction that replicates contemporary international law limits on the extraterritorial application of U.S. law? For example, why could there not be an "international law" presumption, which would call for application of federal law in circumstances where §403 of the *Restatement (Third) Foreign Relations Law* would permit? Alternatively, why should there not be a "choice of law" presumption, that would permit application of federal law in cases where the "most significant relationship" test of the *Restatement (Second) Conflict of Laws* would permit? Or, why not adopt a "constitutional limits" presumption, that would interpret federal statutes as applicable to the limits permitted by the Constitution? Would these alternatives not better serve the asserted purposes of ascertaining congressional intent and fulfilling the goals of the territoriality doctrine? What interests would each presumption further? What interests would each hinder?

9. *Departures from the territoriality presumption* — Lauritzen's *"international law" presumption.* Consider the broad language of the Jones Act — its "literal catholicity." Why wasn't the Act applicable to the defendant's conduct in *Lauritzen*? Why shouldn't U.S. courts *always* apply federal law (unless Congress specifically provides otherwise)? Consider *Lauritzen's* explanation:

> If, to serve some immediate interest, the courts of each were to exploit every such contact to the limit of its power, it is not difficult to see that a multiplicity of conflicting and overlapping burdens would blight international carriage by sea. Hence, courts of this and other commercial nations have generally deferred to a non-national or international maritime law of impressive maturity and universality. It has the force of law, not from extraterritorial reach of national laws, nor from abdication of its sovereign powers by any nation, but from acceptance by common consent of civilized communities of rules designed to foster amicable and workable commercial relations.

Compare this to Joseph Story's explanations for international law limits on national legislative jurisdiction. *See supra* pp. 548-49. Are U.S. "interests" impaired by the Court's refusal to apply the Jones Act extraterritorially? Note that neither the plaintiff nor the defendant was a U.S. national. Do you think Congress cared about injuries to foreign seamen, at the hands of foreign shipowners, in foreign waters? Consider the final paragraph of the *Lauritzen* opinion. Does it suggest a U.S. interest?

What was the role of the territoriality presumption in *Lauritzen*? Why was the case not resolved simply on the traditional grounds — stated in *American Banana* — that the allegedly wrongful conduct occurred beyond U.S. territory and waters? Instead of applying the territoriality presumption, what canon of statutory construction did *Lauritzen* adopt? Consider the various factors identified by the Court as relevant to the applicability of the Jones Act. What authority made these factors relevant?

Like *American Banana*, *Lauritzen* looks to principles of international law in defining the reach of federal statutes. What explains the material differences between *American Banana's* territoriality presumption and *Lauritzen's* analysis?

10. *Departures from the territoriality presumption* — *the effects test*. As described below, *infra* pp. 577-607, the Court subsequently overruled *American Banana* and applied the antitrust laws to conduct occurring outside the United States. *E.g.*, *Continental Ore Co. v. Union Carbide & Carbon Corp.*, 370 U.S. 690, 705 (1962); *W.S. Kirkpatrick v. Environmental Tectonics Corp.*, 493 U.S. 400 (1990). Instead of the historic territoriality doctrine, the antitrust laws were interpreted in light of the "effects test" articulated in *United States v. Alcoa*, 148 F.2d 416 (2d Cir. 1945), excerpted below. Most recently, in *Hartford Fire Insurance Co. v. California*, 113 S.Ct. 2891 (1993), excerpted below, the Court did not apply a territoriality presumption to the federal antitrust laws — notwithstanding its decision only 2 years earlier in *Aramco*. Instead, the Court applied *Alcoa's* effects test, which permitted application of the antitrust laws to "foreign conduct that was meant to produce and did in fact produce some substantial effect in the United States." *See infra* pp. 594-607.

11. *Departures from the territoriality presumption* — *a nationality presumption*. Aramco was a U.S. corporation. Given the nationality principle, *see supra* p. 507, why wouldn't international law have quite comfortably permitted Title VII to apply to Aramco's conduct? Should U.S. courts assume, absent contrary evidence, that U.S. law applies extraterritorially to the conduct of U.S. nationals? As discussed above, §403 of the *Third Restatement* includes the parties' nationality as a factor relevant to the reach of national legislation. *See supra* p. 507. Similarly, lower U.S. courts have considered nationality as a factor in determining the extraterritorial reach of the federal antitrust and securities laws. *See infra* pp. 584 & 614.

Aramco appeared very troubled by the notion that any extraterritorial application of Title VII would extend equally to U.S. *and foreign* employers.

> We see no way of distinguishing in [Title VII's] application between United States employers and foreign employers. ... Without clearer evidence of congressional intent to do so than is contained in the alien-exemption clause, we are unwilling to ascribe to that body a policy which would raise difficult issues of international law by imposing this country's employment-discrimination regime upon foreign corporations operating in foreign commerce.

Is this assumption correct? Could the Court not apply a "nationality presumption," extending U.S. laws extraterritorially to U.S. parties' conduct?

Consider the consequences of a nationality presumption. U.S. companies operating outside the United States would be subject to two sets of laws — U.S. and foreign. Their foreign competitors would generally not be subject to U.S. law. Would this be a satisfactory state of affairs? Is it likely what Congress intended? Note that a nationality presumption would also lead inevitably to conflicts between U.S. law and the law of the foreign state where disputed conduct occurred. *See supra* p. 508. There are, however, provisions for resolving such conflicts. *See Restatement (Third) Foreign Relations Law* §§403 & 421; *supra* pp. 508-09.

12. *Departures from the territoriality presumption — a "constitutional limits" presumption.* Why shouldn't U.S. courts assume that Congress intends federal legislation to extend to the full limits permitted by the U.S. Constitution? (Those limits are discussed in detail above, *supra* pp. 512-44.) Recall that, in the personal jurisdiction context, many federal and state long-arm statutes have been interpreted as extending to the limits of the Constitution. *See supra* pp. 68-70. Shouldn't the same result extend to legislative jurisdiction? Note also that many federal grants of legislative jurisdiction expressly extend to "foreign commerce" — just as Article I, §8's grant of legislative power does.

Virtually no courts have adopted any such "constitutional limits" presumption. *But see Arnett v. Thompson*, 433 S.W.2d 109, 113 (Ky. 1968). Commentators have generally rejected the suggestion. Kramer, *Rethinking Choice of Law*, 90 Colum. L. Rev. 277, 295-96 (1990). What difficulties would arise from a "constitutional limits" presumption? Consider:

> [This approach] would extend U.S. law extraterritorially without regard to conflicts with foreign law or policies and would frequently place the United States in violation of contemporary principles of public international law. The diplomatic protests and other frictions resulting from existing U.S. practice would be multiplied, leading to just the "international complications" that even *Alcoa's* expansive effects doctrine sought to avoid. Moreover, in many cases no real U.S. interests would be served by the attempted regulation of distant activities only tenuously connected to this country.

Born, *A Reappraisal of the Extraterritorial Reach of U.S. Law*, 24 Law & Pol'y Int'l Bus. 1, 80 (1992). Is this persuasive?

13. *Choosing between various "presumptions" regarding the extraterritorial application of U.S. statutes.* The Court has not acknowledged that it has adopted the varying "presumptions" regarding the extraterritorial reach of different U.S. statutes in cases like *American Banana, Lauritzen,* and *Aramco.* That is, of course, unsatisfying. Future cases can be decided in significantly different ways, depending upon the presumption that the Court decides to apply, but no guidance is provided for deciding when one presumption, rather than another, should apply. The result is confusion for private parties and lower courts. *E.g., Kollias v. D & G Marine Maintenance*, 29 F.3d 67 (2d Cir. 1994) (considering and rejecting arguments that *Aramco's* presumption should not apply and that *Bowman* or *Lauritzen* presumption should); *Environmental Defense Fund, Inc. v. Massey*, 986 F.2d 528, 531 (D.C. Cir. 1993) (questioning applicability of *Aramco* where there are "adverse effects within the United States"); *Tamari v. Bache & Co. (Lebanon)*, 730 F.2d 1103, 1107 n.11 (7th Cir.), *cert. denied*, 469 U.S. 871 (1984) ("Reliance on this [territoriality] presumption is misplaced ... when the conduct under scrutiny has not occurred wholly outside the United States, or ... could otherwise affect domestic conditions.").

If the Court were to discuss the issue, which of the various presumptions discussed above is most appropriate in today's world? Does the approach taken in *Lauritzen* provide a better guide to Congress's likely intent than *Aramco's* strict territoriality presumption? Which presumption provides private parties with the greatest certainty?

Is there some way to reconcile the various presumptions used by the Court? Is the territoriality presumption used for certain types of statutes (*e.g.,* "local" ones), while an international presumption is used for other types? *See* Turley, *"When in Rome": Multinational Misconduct and the Presumption Against Extraterritoriality*, 84 Nw. U. L. Rev. 598 (1990). Is there a principled basis for distinguishing between statutes on such grounds?

As discussed below, modern American conflict of law theory focusses on the reasons that a particular statute was enacted. This inquiry requires ascertaining the domestic reasons for a legislature's enactment of a statute, and then determining whether those reasons would apply in a particular multi-state context.

See infra pp. 632-36, 636-39. Consider the "purposes" of the Sherman Act, the Jones Act, and Title VII. Do these purposes suggest differing extraterritorial reaches?

Are there material differences in the language used to define the jurisdictional reach of the various statutes considered by the Court? Compare the jurisdictional grants in the Sherman Act, Title VII, and the Jones Act.

14. **Lower court applications of** Aramco. Several lower courts have relied on *Aramco* in holding that particular federal statutes do not apply extraterritorially. *E.g., Kollias v. D & G Marine Maintenance*, 29 F.3d 67 (Longshore and Harbor Workers' Compensation Act); *Subafilms, Ltd. v. MGM-Pathe Communications Co.*, 24 F.3d 1088 (9th Cir. 1994) (Copyright Act); *Van Blaricom v. Burlington Northern RR Co.*, 17 F.3d 1224 (9th Cir. 1994) (Interstate Commence Act); *United States v. Javino*, 960 F.2d 1137 (2d Cir. 1992) (Firearms Act); *Smith v. United States*, 932 F.2d 791 (9th Cir. 1991) (Federal Tort Claims Act), *aff'd*, 113 S.Ct. 1178 (1993); *Cruz v. Chesapeake Shipping, Inc.*, 932 F.2d 218 (3d Cir. 1991) (Fair Labor Standards Act). *Compare United States v. Peralta*, 937 F.2d 604 (9th Cir. 1991) (applying federal criminal statute extraterritorially); *United States v. Felix-Gutierrez*, 940 F.2d 1200 (9th Cir. 1991) (same).

15. **Congressional overruling of** Aramco result. Congress promptly overturned the result in *Aramco*. The Civil Rights Act of 1991, 105 Stat. 1077, added a new §2000e(f), which provided: "With respect to employment in a foreign country, such term [*i.e.*, employee] includes an individual who is a citizen of the United States." In addition, Title VII was amended to include the following provisions:

> (b) It shall not be unlawful under §703 or 704 for an employer (or a corporation controlled by an employer) ... to take any action otherwise prohibited by such section, with respect to an employee in a workplace in a foreign country if compliance with such section would cause such employer (or such corporation) ... to violate the law of the foreign country in which such workplace is located.

> (c) (1) If an employer controls a corporation whose place of incorporation is a foreign country, any practice prohibited by §703 or 704 engaged in by such corporation shall be presumed to be engaged in by such employer.

> (2) Sections 703 and 704 shall not apply with respect to the foreign operations of an employer that is a foreign person not controlled by an American employer.

How do these amendments deal with situations where foreign law requires a U.S. company to discriminate in violation of Title VII? What effect do the amendments have on non-U.S. subsidiaries of U.S. companies?

3. Contemporary Approach to Extraterritorial Application of Federal Antitrust Statutes

U.S. courts have considered the extraterritorial reach of a wide range of federal legislation. The extraterritorial reach of the U.S. antitrust laws has received particular attention, both from U.S. courts and commentators.[61] It has also provoked numerous diplomatic disputes between the United States and foreign states. Because of its practical and academic significance, we examine the subject in detail below.

a. Overview of U.S. Antitrust Laws

Broadly speaking, the U.S. "antitrust laws" include a number of different federal and state laws regulating the methods by which business enterprises compete with one another and deal with their customers, suppliers, and others. These laws range from statutes limiting the circumstances in which sellers can charge different prices

---

61. *See, e.g.,* J. Atwood & K. Brewster, *Antitrust And American Business Abroad* (2d ed. 1985 & Cum. Supp.); 1 W. Fugate, *Foreign Commerce And The Antitrust Laws* (3d ed. 1982); Fox, *Extraterritoriality, Antitrust, and the New Restatement: Is Reasonableness the Answer?*, 19 N.Y.U. J. Int'l L. & Pol'y 565 (1987); ICC, *The Extraterritorial Application of National Laws* (D. Lange & G. Born eds. 1987).

for the same products[62] to provisions requiring advance notice to the federal government of certain mergers or acquisitions.[63]

The two most commonly invoked provisions of the U.S. antitrust laws are also the two provisions that arise most often in the international context. First, §1 of the Sherman Act declares illegal "[e]very contract, combination ... or conspiracy, in restraint of trade or commerce."[64] Second, §2 of the Sherman Act makes it a felony for any person "to monopolize, or combine or conspire ... to monopolize any part of the trade or commerce" among the several states or with foreign nations.[65] Section 4 of the Clayton Act authorizes private individuals to bring actions in federal court for treble damages for injuries suffered as a result of violations of Sherman Act §1 or §2,[66] while §16 of the Clayton Act permits private parties to seek injunctive relief.[67] Although provisions of the various antitrust statutes contain language making those laws applicable to foreign commerce,[68] the statutes are generally silent on the specific question of extraterritorial application.[69]

b. From American Banana's Territoriality Presumption to Alcoa's Effects/Intent Test

American Banana Company v. United Fruit Company[70] was the Supreme Court's first consideration of the Sherman Act in an international dispute. As described above, *American Banana* presented the question whether the Sherman Act reached allegedly anticompetitive acts performed in Central America by a U.S. company. The Act was, by its terms, applicable to all contracts in restraint of commerce "with foreign nations."[71] Nonetheless, Justice Holmes held that the antitrust laws did not reach beyond U.S. borders, declaring that "in case of doubt as to a construction of any statute [it should be construed] as intended to be confined in its operation and effect to the territorial limits over which the lawmaker has general and legitimate power."[72] Although the Sherman Act was couched in broad language, this did not overcome the territoriality presumption.[73]

---

62. Robinson-Patman Anti-Discrimination Act, ch. 592, §§1-4, 49 Stat. 1526 (1936) (*as codified at* 15 U.S.C. §13).

63. Hart-Scott-Rodino Antitrust Improvements Act, tit. II & III (1976), Pub. L. No. 94-435, 90 Stat. 1383 (*as codified at* 15 U.S.C. §§15c-15h, 18a, 66).

64. 15 U.S.C. §1.

65. 15 U.S.C. §2.

66. 15 U.S.C. §15(a).

67. 15 U.S.C. §26.

68. *See, e.g.,* 15 U.S.C. §1 ("[e]very contract, combination ... or conspiracy in restraint of trade or commerce ... *with foreign nations*") (emphasis added); 15 U.S.C. §2 ("[e]very person who shall monopolize, or attempt to monopolize ... any part of trade or commerce ... *with foreign nations*") (emphasis added).

69. The provision of the antitrust laws that most clearly addresses the subject of extraterritorial application is the Foreign Trade Antitrust Improvements Act, discussed *infra* p. 603.

70. 213 U.S. 347 (1909) (excerpted above at pp. 552-55).

71. 26 Stat. 209 (1890).

72. 213 U.S. at 357. The Court went on to say "'All legislation is prima facie territorial'" (quoting *Ex parte Blain*, 27 N.J. 499; *People v. Merrill*, 2 Parker, Crim. Rep. 590, 596.).

73. 213 U.S. at 357. "In the case of the present statute the improbability of the United States attempting to make acts done in Panama or Costa Rica criminal is obvious."

During the 1920s and 1930s, *American Banana* was eroded in a series of international antitrust decisions that adopted increasingly expansive views of the Sherman Act's jurisdictional reach.[74] This culminated in the 1945 decision in *United States v. Aluminum Co. of America ("Alcoa")*,[75] where Judge Learned Hand adopted a fundamentally new approach to the extraterritorial reach of the U.S. antitrust laws. In an opinion excerpted below, he rejected any notion of strict territoriality and instead adopted an expansive formulation of the "effects doctrine."[76]

Alcoa's effects test rapidly gained wide acceptance in the United States.[77] Relying on it, U.S. courts and governmental agencies frequently applied the U.S. antitrust laws to conduct occurring partially or entirely abroad.[78] Thus, major governmental actions involving the extraterritorial application of the U.S. antitrust laws were brought against the international oil, shipping, paper, synthetic fiber, watch-making, and dyestuff industries.[79]

Although subsequent decisions have reformulated *Alcoa*'s extraterritoriality standards, often very significantly, the decision's basic effects test remains the starting-point for contemporary analysis. *Industrial Investment Development Corp. v. Mitsui & Co.*, also excerpted below, illustrates how some U.S. courts have applied *Alcoa*'s effects test in recent years.

UNITED STATES v.
ALUMINUM COMPANY OF AMERICA

148 F.2d 416 (2d Cir. 1945)

LEARNED HAND, CIRCUIT JUDGE. [The U.S. government filed an antitrust complaint against Alcoa, a U.S. corporation, and Aluminium, Limited ("Limited"), a Canadian company that had acquired Alcoa's properties outside the United States. Limited had been a division of Alcoa in the past and, at the time of the government's

---

74. *United States v. Pacific & Arctic Railway & Navigation Co.*, 228 U.S. 87 (1913); *Thomsen v. Cayser*, 243 U.S. 66 (1917); *United States v. Sisal Sales Corp.*, 274 U.S. 268 (1927).

75. 148 F.2d 416 (2d Cir. 1945).

76. 148 F.2d at 443-44.

77. *Zenith Radio Corp. v. Hazeltine Research, Inc.*, 395 U.S. 100 (1969); *Continental Ore Co. v. Union Carbide & Carbon Corp.*, 370 U.S. 690 (1962); *Restatement (Second) Foreign Relations Law* §18 (1965) (relying on *Alcoa* to justify effects test as legitimate basis for legislative jurisdiction); U.S. Department of Justice, *Antitrust Guide For International Operations* 6-7 (1977).

78. *E.g.*, *United States v. General Dye-Stuff Corp.*, 57 F.Supp. 642 (S.D.N.Y. 1944); *United States v. American Bosch Corp.*, 1940-43 (CCH) Trade Cas. ¶ 56,253 (S.D.N.Y. 1942); *United States v. Alba Pharmaceutical Co., Inc.*, 1940-43 (CCH) Trade Cas. ¶ 56,150 (S.D.N.Y. 1941); *United States v. Bausch & Lomb Co.*, Crim. Dkt. No. 107-169 (S.D.N.Y. 1940).

79. *In re Grand Jury Investigation of the Shipping Indus.*, 186 F.Supp. 298 (D.D.C. 1960); *United States v. The Watchmakers of Switzerland Information Center*, 133 F.Supp. 40 (S.D.N.Y. 1955); *United States v. Imperial Chem. Indus.*, 105 F.Supp. 215 (S.D.N.Y. 1952); *In re Investigation of World Arrangements with Relation to the Prod., Ref., Transp. & Distrib. of Petroleum*, 13 F.R.D. 280 (D.D.C. 1952); *United States v. General Elec. Co.*, 80 F.Supp. 989 (S.D.N.Y. 1948); *In re Grand Jury Subpoenas Duces Tecum Addressed to Canadian Int'l Paper Co.*, 72 F.Supp. 1013 (S.D.N.Y. 1947).

suit, continued to be controlled by Alcoa's shareholders. The government's complaint alleged that Alcoa and Limited had unlawfully conspired to restrain both interstate and international production and sale of aluminum ingot. The government's suit sought to prohibit the participation of Alcoa and Limited in an international cartel involving several major European aluminum companies. The district court dismissed on jurisdictional grounds, and the Second Circuit was referred the case (because the Supreme Court could not muster a quorum). A principal issue on appeal was whether Limited's participation in an "alliance" with a number of foreign aluminum producers was a violation of §1 of the Sherman Act. The Second Circuit held that it was, reasoning as follows:]

Whether Limited itself violated [§1 of the Sherman Act] depends upon the character of the "Alliance." It was a Swiss corporation, created in pursuance of an agreement ... the signatories of which were a French corporation, two German, one Swiss, a British, and Limited. The original agreement, or "cartel," provided for the formation of a corporation in Switzerland which should issue shares, to be taken up by the signatories. This corporation was from time to time to fix a quota of production for each share, and each shareholder was to be limited to the quantity measured by the number of shares it held, but was free to sell at any price it chose. The corporation fixed a price every year at which it would take off any shareholder's hands any part of its quota which it did not sell. No shareholder was to "buy, borrow, fabricate, or sell" aluminum produced by anyone not a shareholder except with the consent of the board of governors, but that must not be "unreasonably withheld." ... [U]ntil 1936, when the new arrangement was made, imports into the United States were not included in the quota.

The agreement of 1936 abandoned the system of unconditional quotas, and substituted a system of royalties. Each shareholder was to have a fixed free quota for every share it held, but as its production exceeded the sum of its quotas, it was to pay a royalty, graduated progressively in proportion to the excess; and these royalties the "Alliance" divided among the shareholders in proportion to their shares. ... Although this agreement, like its predecessor, was silent as to imports into the United States, when that question arose during its preparation, as it did, all the shareholders agreed that such quotas should be included in the quotas. ...

Did either the agreement of 1931 or that of 1936 violate §1 of the Act? The answer does not depend upon whether we shall recognize as a source of liability a liability imposed by another state. On the contrary, we are concerned only with whether Congress chose to attach liability to the conduct outside the United States of persons not in allegiance to it. That being so, the only question open is whether Congress intended to impose the liability, and whether our own Constitution permitted it to do so: as a court of the United States, we cannot look beyond our own law. Nevertheless, it is quite true that we are not to read general words, such as those in this Act, without regard to the limitations customarily observed by nations upon the exercise of their powers; limitations which generally correspond to those fixed by the "Conflict of Laws." We should not impute to Congress an intent to punish all whom its courts can catch, for conduct which has no consequences within the United States. *American Banana Co. v. United Fruit Co.*, [excerpted above at pp. 552-55]; *United States v. Bowman*, 260 U.S. 94, 98 (1927); *Blackmer v. United States*, [excerpted above at pp. 95-100]. On the other hand, it is settled law — as Limited itself agrees — that any state may impose liabilities, even upon persons not within its allegiance, for conduct outside its borders that has consequences within its borders which the state reprehends; and these liabilities other states will ordinarily recognize. *Strassheim v. Daily*, 221 U.S. 280, 284 (1911); *Lamar v. United States*, 240 U.S. 60, 65 (1916); *Restatement (First) Conflict of Laws* §65 [excerpted above at p. 502; stating effects doctrine as basis for legislative jurisdiction]. It may be argued that this Act extends further. Two situations are possible. There may be agreements made beyond our borders not intended to affect imports, which do affect them, or which affect exports. Almost any limitation of the supply of goods in Europe, for example, or in South America, may have repercussions in the United States if there is trade between the two. Yet when one considers the international complications likely to arise from an effort in this country to treat such agreements as unlawful, it is safe to assume that Congress certainly did not intend the Act to cover them. Such agreements may on the other hand intend to include imports into the United States, and yet it may appear that they have had no effect upon them. That situation might be thought to fall within the doctrine that intent may be a substitute for performance in the case of a contract made within the United States; or it might be thought to fall within the doctrine that a statute should not be interpreted to cover acts abroad which have no consequence here. We shall not choose between these alternatives; but for argument we shall assume that the Act does not cover agreements, even though intended to affect imports or exports, unless its performance is shown actually to have had some effect upon them. Where both conditions are satisfied, the situation certainly falls within such decisions as *United States v. Pacific & Arctic R. & Nav. Co.*, 228 U.S. 87 (1913); *Thomsen v. Cayser*, 243 U.S. 66 (1917); and *United States v. Sisal Sales Corp.* 274 U.S. 268 (1927). ... It is true that in those cases the persons held liable had sent agents into the United States to perform part of the agreement; but an agent is merely an animate means of executing his principal's purposes, and, for the purposes of this case, he does not differ from an inanimate means; besides, only human agents can import and sell ingot.

Both agreements would clearly have been unlawful, had they been made within the United States; and it follows from what we have just said that both were unlawful, though made abroad, if they were intended to affect imports and did affect them. [The court held that the 1936 agreement was intended to affect U.S. imports and that, absent rebuttal by Limited, would be presumed to have had such an effect.]

INDUSTRIAL INVESTMENT DEVELOPMENT CORP. v. MITSUI & CO.

671 F.2d 876 (5th Cir. 1982)

REAVLEY, CIRCUIT JUDGE. This is an antitrust suit. [The district court granted summary judgment on the ground] that defendants' conduct is beyond the extraterritorial scope of the antitrust laws. ... [We reverse.]

The plaintiffs are an American corporation, Industrial Investment Development Corporation ("Industrial Investment"), and its two Hong Kong subsidiaries, Indonesia Industrial Investment Corporation, Ltd. ("Indonesia Industrial") and Forest Products Corporation, Ltd. ("FPC"). The defendants-appellees are a Japanese corporation, Mitsui & Co., Ltd. ("Mitsui-Japan") and its American subsidiary, Mitsui & Co. (U.S.A.), Inc. ("Mitsui-U.S.A."). A third defendant is an Indonesian corporation, P.T. Telaga Mas Kalimantan Company, Ltd. ("Telaga Mas"), which ... has not appeared. ...

Plaintiffs claim that the three defendants conspired to keep plaintiffs out of the business of harvesting trees in East Kalimantan (Borneo), Indonesia and exporting logs and lumber from Indonesia to the United States and other countries. Plaintiffs allege that defendants' conspiracy was intended to and did unreasonably restrain and monopolize the foreign commerce of the United States, in violation of §§1 and 2 of the Sherman Act, 15 U.S.C. §§1, 2. ... A restraint that directly or substantially affects the flow of commerce into or out of the United States is within the scope of the Sherman Act. *See Continental Ore Co. v. Union Carbide & Carbon Corp.; United States v. Aluminum Co. of America*, ("*Alcoa*"). A review of the summary judgment submissions and evidence convinces us that defendants have not demonstrated that there is no genuine issue concerning the existence of a direct or substantial effect on United States foreign commerce.

In their briefs prior to the first appeal, defendants' attack on the existence of an effect on United States commerce was only an attack on plaintiffs' pleadings. Defendants placed their own characterization on the complaint and declared that the case involved only the tree-cutting business in Indonesia; thus, they concluded, their conduct had no effect on United States commerce. Plaintiffs had alleged, however, that Mitsui-U.S.A., an American corporation which imports a sizeable amount of lumber or lumber products into the United States, had conspired to keep them out of the business of harvesting trees and exporting logs and lumber from Indonesia to the United States. There was ample evidence in the record to show that Mitsui-U.S.A. had appropriated much of the business that plaintiffs claim they would have derived from the forestry concession: Mitsui-U.S.A. was purchasing the bulk of the logs from the concession and selling them for export to Mitsui-Japan at a substantial profit.

The competition between two American importers to obtain a source of supply on foreign territory affects the foreign commerce of the United States. *Timberlane*

Lumber Co. v. Bank of America, 549 F.2d 597, 604-05, 615 (9th Cir. 1976). Mitsui-Japan was allegedly a co-conspirator in this attempt to restrain competition between two American competitors. Thus, defendants' attack on the pleadings did not make it "appear[] beyond doubt that the plaintiff [could] prove no set of facts in support of his claim which would entitle him to relief." *Conley v. Gibson*, 355 U.S. 41, 45-46 (1957) (motion to dismiss for failure to state a claim). ...

After we reversed the district court's first grant of summary judgment, the defendants shifted to a factual attack by arguing that the single, undisputed fact that Mitsui-Japan exported all of the lumber, purchased from Mitsui-U.S.A. in Indonesia, to Japan demonstrated that there was no genuine issue concerning an effect on United States commerce. Mitsui-Japan argued — and this is the argument it advances most strenuously in this court — that when a Japanese business competes with an American business in Indonesia and exports the fruits of that competition solely to Japan, any effect on United States commerce is purely incidental, indirect, and unintentional. Even if defendants' argument is correct — an issue we do not reach — it ignores the allegations in this case. Here, an American corporation with an interest in protection of its import business has allegedly conspired to eliminate a potential American competitor in both the business of purchasing logs in Indonesia and the business of importing lumber and lumber products into the United States. Defendants' showing did not demonstrate that there was no genuine fact issue for the simple reason that defendants' showing was not responsive to plaintiffs' allegations. That one co-conspirator — Mitsui-Japan — followed a course of business action that, in isolation, might not be considered a violation of the United States antitrust laws does not demonstrate either that the effect of the conspiracy as between the American competitors is not an effect on United States commerce or that the intent of the conspiracy was not to restrain competition between the American competitors. "[S]ummary procedures should be used sparingly in complex antitrust litigation where motive and intent play leading roles [and] the proof is largely in the hands of the alleged conspirators. ..." *Poller v. CBS*, 368 U.S. 464, 473 (1962). Summary judgment is even less appropriate here, where there is ample evidence of a conspiracy to keep plaintiffs from becoming a competitor, and plaintiffs have not had an opportunity to depose one of the conspirators on the effect and intent of their efforts.

Notes on Alcoa and Mitsui

1. *Alcoa's reliance on international law.* In important respects, *Alcoa's* analysis paralleled that in *American Banana.* In both cases, the courts concluded that the Sherman Act's language did not provide adequate guidance as to the statute's extraterritorial application. In both cases, the courts then looked to international law and choice of law principles — or, in Learned Hand's eclectic formulation, to "the limitation customarily observed by nations upon the exercise of their powers ... 'Conflict of Laws.'" This basic analysis parallels that in *Charming Betsy, Apollon, Blackmer,* and similar decisions.

2. *Content of international law in* Alcoa. Despite their similar approaches, the international law principles that *Alcoa* relied upon differed significantly from those invoked in *American Banana. American Banana* relied upon the "general and almost universal rule ... that the character of an act as lawful or unlawful must be determined wholly by the law of the country where the act is done." Three decades later,

however, *Alcoa* held that it was "settled law ... that any state may impose liabilities ... for conduct outside its borders that has consequences within its borders." Although *Alcoa* cited only *domestic* U.S. decisions, dealing with interstate matters, its holding reflected the development of international law limits on legislative jurisdiction, discussed above, *supra* pp. 493-509. It also paralleled the evolution in international law limits on personal jurisdiction, and similar developments in American choice of law rules. *See supra* pp. 70-77 & *infra* pp. 631-52.

In looking to the jurisdictional limits imposed by international law, should courts consider the law prevailing when a statute was enacted (1890, for the Sherman Act) or when the law is applied (1945, in *Alcoa*)?

3. **Wisdom of Alcoa's *effects test*.** Is *Alcoa's* effects test wise? What interests does it advance — and what interests does it hinder? Recall the reasoning in Joseph Story's *Commentaries* and *Lauritzen*, emphasizing the importance of mutual forbearance, uniform results in different forums, and reciprocal tolerance in conflict of laws decisions. *See supra* pp. 548-49 & 574. Is *Alcoa's* effects doctrine consistent with such reasoning?

4. **Alcoa's *intent/effects test*.** *Alcoa* held that conduct occurring outside the United States would be subject to the Sherman Act if two requirements were satisfied: (a) the conduct was intended to affect U.S. imports; and (b) the conduct actually had such an effect.

(a) *Alcoa's intent prong.* There has been disagreement among lower courts about the meaning of *Alcoa's* "intent" prong. Some courts simply omit the intent requirement, apparently adopting a pure effects test. *E.g., Sabre Shipping Corp. v. American President Lines*, 285 F.Supp. 949 (S.D.N.Y. 1968), *cert. denied*, 395 U.S. 922 (1969); *United States v. Imperial Chem. Indus.*, 100 F.Supp. 504 (S.D.N.Y. 1951). Other courts have required only proof of a general intent to affect U.S. commerce, *e.g., Zenith Radio Corp. v. Matsushita Elec. Indus. Co.*, 494 F.Supp. 1161 (E.D. Pa. 1980); *Fleishmann Distilling Corp. v. Distillers Co.*, 395 F.Supp. 221 (S.D.N.Y. 1975), while some courts apparently require a showing of specific intent, *e.g., United States v. General Elec. Co.*, 82 F.Supp. 753, 889-91 (D.N.J. 1949); *United States v. National Lead Co.*, 63 F.Supp. 513, 524-25 (S.D.N.Y. 1945), *aff'd*, 332 U.S. 319 (1947).

What is the purpose of *Alcoa's* "intent" requirement? How does *Alcoa's* intent prong compare to the due process clause's "purposeful availment" requirement for judicial jurisdiction? Which of these various "intent" formulations is most desirable?

(b) *Alcoa's effects prong — magnitude of effects.* Most lower courts agree that extraterritorial application of the antitrust laws is inappropriate when effects within the United States are merely "speculative." *Montreal Trading v. Amax, Inc.*, 661 F.2d 864, 870 (10th Cir. 1981), *cert. denied*, 455 U.S. 1001 (1982). Nonetheless, U.S. courts have over time applied a wide variety of formulations of the effects prong. *Compare Hartford Fire Insurance Co. v. California*, 113 S.Ct. 2891 (1993) ("some substantial effect in the United States"); *United States v. The Watchmakers of Switzerland Information Center*, 1963 Trade Cas. (CCH) ¶70,600 (S.D.N.Y. 1962) ("substantial and material") *with Dominicus American Bohio v. Gulf & Western Indus.*, 473 F.Supp. 680, 687 (S.D.N.Y. 1979) (any effect that is not "de minimis") *and National Bank of Canada v. Interbank Card Ass'n*, 666 F.2d 6, 9 (2d Cir. 1981) ("appreciable anticompetitive effects") *and United States v. Timken Roller Bearing Co.*, 83 F.Supp. 284, 309 (N.D. Ohio 1949) ("direct and influencing effect"). Do any of these various verbal formulae provide meaningful guidance?

(c) *Alcoa's effects test — character of effects.* Only a few lower court decisions have discussed what types of effects — as distinguished from the magnitude of effects — within the United States are necessary to permit extraterritorial application of the antitrust laws. One leading decision held that foreign conduct must have "appreciable *anticompetitive* effects on United States commerce." *National Bank of Canada v. Interbank Card Ass'n*, 666 F.2d 6, 9 (1981) (emphasis added). Several earlier decisions concluded that restricting imports into the United States, and thereby foreclosing potential competition within this country, sufficiently affected U.S. commerce to sustain antitrust jurisdiction. *See Occidental Petroleum Corp. v. Buttes Gas & Oil Co.*, 331 F.Supp. 92, 102-103 (C.D. Cal. 1971), *aff'd*, 461 F.2d 1261 (9th Cir.), *cert. denied*, 409 U.S. 950 (1972); *United States v. General Elec. Co.*, 82 F.Supp. 753, 891 (D.N.J. 1949).

5. **Effect of Aramco's *territoriality presumption* on *Sherman Act*.** Section 1 of the Sherman Act prohibits "[e]very contract, combination ... or conspiracy in restraint of trade or commerce ... with foreign nations." 15 U.S.C. §1 (1982). Does this language overcome the territoriality presumption articulated in *Aramco* and discussed above *supra* pp. 546-73. Does §1's reference to trade "with foreign nations" indicate a more focused congressional intention to extend the antitrust laws extraterritorially than was present in Title VII of the Civil Rights Act? Compare the two statutes' jurisdictional grants. In light of *Aramco*, were

Alcoa and *Mitsui* correctly decided? If *Aramco's* territoriality presumption is faithfully applied, isn't it clear that the Sherman Act cannot fairly be applied outside U.S. territory? Notwithstanding this, as discussed in greater detail below, the Supreme Court said in *Hartford Fire Insurance Co. v. California*, 113 S.Ct. 2891 (1993), that "it is well established by now that the Sherman Act applies to foreign conduct that was meant to produce and did in fact produce some substantial effect in the United States."

6. *Mitsui's application of* Alcoa's *effects test.* Although the allegedly illegal conduct in *Mitsui* occurred entirely outside the United States, the court nonetheless refused to grant summary judgment dismissing the plaintiff's claims on jurisdictional grounds. Instead, *Mitsui* held that the plaintiffs might succeed in showing that the defendants' foreign conduct had sufficiently substantial effects on U.S. commerce to permit application of the antitrust laws. Indeed, *Mitsui* apparently embraced a potentially far-reaching elaboration of the *Alcoa* effects test: "The competition between two American importers to obtain a source of supply on foreign territory affects the foreign commerce in the United States." How might U.S. commerce have actually been affected by the defendants' conduct in *Mitsui?*

7. *Foreign governmental "interests."* Did the Indonesian government have any "interest" in the outcome of *Mitsui?* If so, what might that interest be? Did such concerns play any role in interpreting the Sherman Act in *Mitsui?* Should they? What about Japanese governmental interests? Are Japanese interests entitled to greater or lesser weight than Indonesian interests? Why? Does *Alcoa* consider either Swiss, Canadian, or any other foreign governmental interests? Should it have?

8. *Wisdom of* Alcoa's *effects test.* Can *Alcoa's* "effects" test be predictably and neutrally applied? In an interdependent global economy, don't almost all significant international commercial activities have "effects" in the United States? Is the effects test improved by requiring "direct" or "substantial" effects? What do the adjectives mean? What interests does *Alcoa's* effects test further? What interests does it threaten?

9. *Relevance of parties' nationality to applicability of antitrust laws.* *Mitsui* went out of its way to identify the nationality of the plaintiffs and defendants; it emphasized that one of the parties suffering the alleged injury and one of the parties allegedly responsible for that injury were U.S. corporations. How are these facts relevant to U.S. antitrust jurisdiction?

(a) *Defendant's nationality.* As noted above, the actor's nationality provides an accepted basis under international law for the exercise of legislative jurisdiction. *See supra* p. 506. Moreover, the defendant's nationality plays an important role in the personal jurisdiction and choice of law contexts. *See supra* pp. 95-100 and *infra* p. 649. Is it appropriate to hold U.S. antitrust defendants to higher standards than foreign companies? Is it likely that Congress would have intended such a result? What role did the defendant's nationality play in *Aramco?*

(b) *Plaintiff's nationality.* *Mitsui* also emphasized that the plaintiff was a U.S. company. What relevance does this have? Recall that international law does not generally recognize the passive personality principle as a basis for legislative jurisdiction. *See supra* pp. 507-08. Is it appropriate for the antitrust laws to provide greater protection for Americans than for foreigners? Is it something Congress might have intended? As discussed below, many contemporary choice of law analyses accord substantial weight to the plaintiff's domicile or residence. *See infra* p. 649.

(c) *Difficulties in assigning nationality.* *Mitsui* also suggests the difficulty in assigning nationality to multinational corporations: in what sense can Mitsui-U.S.A. (one subsidiary of a major Japanese company with worldwide operations) be said to be a U.S. citizen? Does it matter how many U.S. employees it has? How much U.S. business it does? Consider the difficulties of defining nationality for purposes of personal jurisdiction. *See supra* pp. 95-101.

c. *Protests Against the Extraterritorial Application of the U.S. Antitrust Laws*[80]

The extraterritorial application of the U.S. antitrust laws became a frequent

---

80. Commentary on foreign protests to the extraterritorial application of the U.S. antitrust laws includes, *e.g.*, C. Olmstead, *Extraterritorial Application of Laws and Responses Thereto* (1984); A. Lowe, *Extraterritorial Jurisdiction* (1983); Henry, *The United States Antitrust Laws: A Canadian Viewpoint*, [1970] Can. Y.B. Int'l L. 249; Jacobs, *Extraterritorial Application of Competition Laws: An English View*, 13 Int'l Law. 645 (1979); Pengilley, *Extraterritorial Effects of United States Commercial and Antitrust Legislation: A View from "Down Under"*, 16 Vand. J. Transnat'l L. 833 (1983).

occurrence after *Alcoa* was decided.[81] This caused considerable friction between the United States and its trading partners, leading to diplomatic protests, foreign blocking statutes, antisuit injunctions, and other forms of reaction.

Foreign resistance to the extraterritorial application of the U.S. antitrust laws resulted in part from disagreement about the substantive regulatory policies reflected in the antitrust laws. Foreign economic and social regulatory policies often did not rely on competition in the same fashion as the United States, and foreign states sometimes saw such competition as a threat to their national economic interests.[82] This perception was complemented by the conviction that the regulation of economic affairs is a vital aspect of national sovereignty and that foreign law, not U.S. law, should govern economic activity occurring on a foreign state's territory. More recently, many foreign states have embraced principles of competition law similar to those embodied in the Sherman Act.[83] Nevertheless, they seldom regard American judges as the appropriate authorities to resolve disputes about international (or foreign) trading practices.

The following remarks, excerpted from debates in the U.K. Parliament, are illustrative of foreign objections to the extraterritorial application of substantive U.S antitrust policies:

> My objective in introducing this Bill is to reassert and reinforce the defenses of the United Kingdom against attempts by other countries to enforce their economic and commercial policies unilaterally on us. From our point of view, the most objectionable method by which this is done is by the extraterritorial application of domestic law. In theory, this is a general problem since many countries have policies which, given the occasion and the inclination, they might seek to enforce on persons located, or engaged in activities, beyond the normal bounds of national jurisdiction as recognized by international law. In effect, however, the practices to which successive United Kingdom Governments have taken exception have arisen in the case of the United States of America.
>
> I must emphasize that we do not dispute the right of the United States or any other nation to pass and enforce what economic laws it likes to govern businesses operating fully in its own country. Our objection arises only at the point when a country attempts to achieve the maximum beneficial reg-

---

81. *See supra* pp. 577-78.

82. J. Atwood & K. Brewster, *Antitrust and American Business Abroad* §§1.01-1.14 (2d ed. 1985 & Cum. Supp.). Foreign complaints often reflect a suspicion that the United States does not apply the antitrust laws with consistency, and that the enforcement of these laws often seeks to advance the commercial interests of U.S. companies. *E.g.*, *Id.* §3.24 ("the assertion is often made that America's less enthusiastic embrace of competition in shipping proves hypocrisy in its espousal of competition in other economic sectors").

83. During the last several decades many foreign states have adopted "competition laws" that are broadly similar to the U.S. antitrust laws. *See* J. Atwood & K. Brewster, *Antitrust and American Business Abroad* §3.01 *et seq.* (2d ed. 1985 & Cum. Supp.).

ulation of its own economic environment by ensuring that all those having any contact with it abide by its laws and legal principles. In other words, there is an attempt to export economic policy and law to persons domiciled in countries that may have different legal systems and priorities, without recognizing that those countries have the right to lay down the standards to be observed by those trading within their jurisdiction. ...[84]

Although foreign states' reactions to U.S. antitrust enforcement are often based on differences in substantive regulatory policies, foreign critics have also challenged the procedural framework in which the U.S. antitrust laws are enforced. These protests have focused in part on the provisions of the antitrust laws that permit private plaintiffs to bring actions for treble damages.[85] Even in those foreign nations that have enacted competition laws, enforcement has been largely in governmental hands, and there is resistance abroad to the notion that a private U.S. plaintiff can initiate litigation resulting in an extraterritorial application of the antitrust laws.[86] Moreover, the treble damages available under the U.S. antitrust laws are seen as a draconian penal measure that biases litigation against foreign defendants.[87] Finally, foreign protests about U.S. discovery procedures have special vigor in the antitrust context, where discovery is particularly onerous.[88]

Many foreign protests against the extraterritorial application of U.S. laws have taken the form of diplomatic notes.[89] Such notes typically assert that the extraterritorial application of U.S. law to conduct within the complaining state interferes with its sovereignty and is inconsistent with international law. During the 1970s and 1980s, diplomatic protests of this sort were commonplace:

> almost every bilateral or multilateral meeting between economic officials of the United States and Western Europe has included some objection from the European side to United States antitrust enforcement. It has become almost an automatic agenda item in diplomatic meetings with the Australians and Canadians.[90]

Some foreign states have taken more forceful action than diplomatic notes to resist the extraterritorial application of the U.S. antitrust laws. Most importantly, a number of states have enacted so-called blocking statutes designed to impede the

---

84. 973 Parl. Deb., H.C. (5th Ser.) cols. 1533-77 (1979).

85. *E.g.*, *Canadian Government Sponsors Bill to Address Extraterritoriality Issue*, 46 Antitrust & Trade Reg. Rep. (BNA) No. 1168, at 1106 (June 7, 1984) ("[i]t shouldn't be up to private individuals to determine foreign policy considerations for Canada [through U.S. antitrust suits]").

86. *See* Nijenhuis, *Antitrust Suits Involving Foreign Commerce: Suggestions for Procedural Reform*, 135 U. Pa. L. Rev. 1003, 1017-21 (1987).

87. Beckett, *Transnational Litigation — Part II: Perspectives from the U.S. and Abroad (United Kingdom)*, 18 Int'l Law. 773, 774 (1984).

88. *See infra* pp. 845 & 849-52.

89. 1 J. Atwood & K. Brewster, *Antitrust and American Business Abroad* §4.15 (2d ed. 1985 & Cum. Supp.).

90. 1 J. Atwood & K. Brewster, *Antitrust and American Business Abroad* §4.15 (2d ed. 1985).

application of U.S. antitrust laws to conduct within their territory. As discussed elsewhere, early blocking statutes forbade the production of evidence for use in U.S. antitrust proceedings.[91]

Later statutes sought more directly to prevent the extraterritorial application of the U.S. antitrust laws. The best-known foreign blocking statute is the United Kingdom's Protection of Trading Interests Act ("PTIA").[92] The PTIA deals directly with U.S. antitrust awards by preventing enforcement in the United Kingdom of awards of "multiple damages" and by providing parties in the United Kingdom with a "clawback" remedy by which they can recover in a separate English action two-thirds of any U.S. antitrust award from the U.S. plaintiff. These provisions apparently apply regardless whether the anticompetitive conduct giving rise to the U.S. antitrust award took place in the United Kingdom, in the United States, or in some third country and regardless whether the party seeking relief is a U.K. national.[93] Australia has also enacted a statute that forbids enforcement of U.S. antitrust judgments.[94]

d. Moderating the Extraterritorial Application of the U.S. Antitrust Laws: Timberlane *and Third Restatement §403*

Opposition to the extraterritorial application of the U.S. antitrust laws prompted various efforts to moderate U.S. jurisdictional claims. Early efforts focused on the enforcement of conflicting legal requirements against private parties. Section 40 of the *Restatement (Second) Foreign Relations Law*, excerpted above, was an example of this approach. It "balanced" conflicting U.S. and foreign interests in regulating particular conduct, contemplating that a state would decline to enforce its legislative jurisdiction in cases where its "interests" were clearly outweighed by foreign "interests."[95]

Later developments focused directly on the question whether national laws were applicable at all. A number of authorities sought to articulate a "jurisdictional rule of

---

91. *See infra* pp. 850-52.

92. *See supra* pp. 585-86 & *infra* p. 851. *See also* Toms, *The French Response to the Extraterritorial Application of United States Antitrust Laws*, 15 Int'l Law. 585 (1981)

93. Lowe, *Blocking Extraterritorial Jurisdiction: The British Protection of Trading Interests Act 1980*, 75 Am. J. Int'l L. 257 (1981); Lowenfeld, *Sovereignty, Jurisdiction and Reasonableness: A Reply to A.V. Lowe*, 75 Am. J. Int'l L. 629 (1981).

94. *See* Pettit & Styles, *The International Response to the Extraterritorial Application of United States Antitrust Laws*, 37 Bus. Law. 697 (1982).

With the exception of laws restricting the production of evidence located abroad, there has been relatively little practical experience to date with foreign blocking statutes. (The practical impact of this former class of statutes on U.S. litigation is discussed *infra* pp. 871-92.) Thus, for example, the PTIA's clawback remedy has never been invoked. If it were, its effect on a U.S. plaintiff who successfully obtained an antitrust judgment against an English company is unclear. It is unlikely that a U.S. court would enforce any such judgment and the attitude of other states towards enforcement is uncertain. In addition, it might be possible to obtain a U.S. antisuit injunction against resort to the PTIA. *See* Note, *Enjoining the Application of the British Protection of Trading Interests Act in Private American Antitrust Litigation*, 79 Mich. L. Rev. 1574 (1981).

95. *See supra* pp. 503-04.

reason" that would limit *Alcoa*'s expansive effects doctrine. The decision in *Timberlane Lumber Co. v. Bank of America*, excerpted below, is the classic statement of this new approach.[96] Other lower court decisions applied *Timberlane*'s approach, both in the antitrust and other contexts.[97]

Section 403 of the *Restatement (Third) Foreign Relations Law*, excerpted above, "codified" the jurisdictional rule of reason. Section 403's rule of reason is closely related to the analysis in *Timberlane*. Section 403 must be read in conjunction with §402 of the *Third Restatement*, which sets out the traditional bases under public international law for jurisdiction to prescribe. As discussed above, even when one of §402's jurisdictional bases is applicable, §403's rule of reason must nonetheless be satisfied.

RESTATEMENT (SECOND) FOREIGN RELATIONS LAW §40 (1965)

[excerpted above at pp. 503-04]

TIMBERLANE LUMBER CO. v. BANK OF AMERICA N.T. & S.A.

549 F.2d 597 (9th Cir. 1976)

CHOY, CIRCUIT JUDGE. ... [This action is] an antitrust suit alleging violations of §§1 and 2 of the Sherman Act. ... [Timberlane, the principal plaintiff, was a U.S. partnership that imported lumber into the United States from Central America. Bank of America was a U.S.-based bank that financed much of the lumber industry in Honduras. The dispute arose when a Honduran lumber company that the Bank had financed went bankrupt. The company's assets (including a lumber mill and tracts of forest land) passed to the company's creditors, who in turn sold the assets to Timberlane, which had recently decided to begin lumber operations in Honduras. After Timberlane commenced its Honduran lumber operations, the Bank of America allegedly conspired with several other Honduran lumber companies to drive Timberlane out of business. Among other things, the Bank allegedly joined a scheme in which a security interest it held in the property purchased by Timberlane was enforced in the Honduran courts, resulting in a judicial order forbidding Timberlane

---

96. *Timberlane Lumber Co. v. Bank of America*, 549 F.2d 597 (9th Cir. 1976), *on remand*, 574 F.Supp. 1453 (N.D. Cal. 1983), *aff'd*, 749 F.2d 1378 (9th Cir. 1984), *cert. denied*, 472 U.S. 1032 (1985). *See* Gill, *Two Cheers for Timberlane*, 10 Swiss Rev. Int'l & Comp. L. 3 (1980); Ongman, *"Be No Longer a Chaos"*: *Constructing a Normative Theory of the Sherman Act's Extraterritorial Jurisdictional Scope*, 71 Nw. U.L. Rev. 733 (1977).

97. *E.g.*, *O.N.E. Shipping Ltd. v. Flota Mercante Grancolombiana*, 830 F.2d 449 (2d Cir. 1987); *Montreal Trading Ltd. v. Amax Inc.*, 661 F.2d 864 (10th Cir. 1981), *cert. denied*, 455 U.S. 1001 (1982); *Mannington Mills, Inc. v. Congoleum Corp.*, 595 F.2d 1287 (3d Cir. 1979); *Transnor (Bermuda) Ltd. v. BP North America Petroleum*, 1990-1 Trade Cas. ¶68,997 (S.D.N.Y. April 18, 1990); *Dominicus Americana Bohio v. Gulf & Western Indus. Inc.*, 473 F.Supp. 680 (S.D.N.Y. 1979). *See also Star-Kist Foods, Inc. v. P.J. Rhodes & Co.*, 769 F.2d 1393 (9th Cir. 1985) (Lanham Act); *Zenger-Miller, Inc. v. Training Team, GmbH*, 757 F.Supp. 1062 (N.D. Ill. 1991) (same).

from using the property. The alleged purpose of the scheme was to drive Timberlane from the Honduran lumber business, so that other companies financed by Bank of America could continue to monopolize that market. The district court dismissed the complaint based on the act of state doctrine and a lack of any direct or substantial effect on U.S. foreign commerce.]

There is no doubt that American antitrust laws extend over some conduct in other nations. There was language in the first Supreme Court case in point, *American Banana,* casting doubt on the extension of the Sherman Act to acts outside United States territory. But subsequent cases have limited *American Banana* to its particular facts, and the Sherman Act — and with it other antitrust laws — has been applied to extraterritorial conduct. *See, e.g., Continental Ore Co. v. Union Carbide & Carbon Corp.; Alcoa.* ...

That American law covers some conduct beyond this nation's borders does not mean that it embraces all, however. Extraterritorial application is understandably a matter of concern for the other countries involved. Those nations have sometimes resented and protested, as excessive intrusions into their own spheres, broad assertions of authority by American courts. Our courts have recognized this concern and have, at times, responded to it, even if not always enough to satisfy all the foreign critics. In any event, it is evident that at some point the interests of the United States are too weak and the foreign harmony incentive for restraint too strong to justify an extraterritorial assertion of jurisdiction.

What that point is or how it is determined is not defined by international law. ... Nor does the Sherman Act limit itself. ... Courts have generally, and logically, fallen back on a narrower construction of congressional intent, such as expressed in Judge Learned Hand's oft-cited opinion in *Alcoa:*

> [I]t is settled law ... that any state may impose liabilities, even upon persons not within its allegiance, for conduct outside its borders that has consequences within its borders which the state reprehends; and these liabilities other states will ordinarily recognize.

Despite its description as "settled law," *Alcoa's* assertion has been roundly disputed by many foreign commentators as being in conflict with international law, comity, and good judgment. Nonetheless, American courts have firmly concluded that there is some extraterritorial jurisdiction under the Sherman Act. Even among American courts and commentators, however, there is no consensus on how far the jurisdiction should extend. ... In essence, as Dean Rahl observes, "[t]here is no agreed black-letter rule articulating the Sherman Act's commerce coverage" in the international context.

The effects test by itself is incomplete because it fails to consider other nations' interests. Nor does it expressly take into account the full nature of the relationship between the actors and this country. Whether the alleged offender is an American citizen, for instance, may make a big difference; applying American laws to American citizens raises fewer problems than application to foreigners. ... American courts have, in fact, often displayed a regard for comity and the prerogatives of other nations and considered their interests as well as other parts of the factual circumstances, even when professing to apply an effects test. To some degree, the requirement for a "substantial" effect may silently incorporate these additional considerations, with "substantial" as a flexible standard that varies with other factors. The intent requirement suggested by *Alcoa* is one example of an attempt to broaden the court's perspective, as is drawing a distinction between American citizens and noncitizens. The failure to articulate these other elements in addition to the standard effects analysis is costly, however, for it is more likely that they will be overlooked or slighted in interpreting past decisions and reaching new ones. Placing emphasis on the qualification that effects be "substantial" is also risky, for the term has a meaning in the interstate antitrust context which does not encompass all the factors relevant to the foreign trade case. ...

A tripartite analysis seems to be indicated. As acknowledged above, the antitrust laws require in the first instance that there be *some* effect — actual or intended — on American foreign commerce before the federal courts may legitimately exercise subject matter jurisdiction under those statutes. Second, a greater showing of burden or restraint may be necessary to demonstrate that the effect is sufficiently large to present a cognizable injury to the plaintiffs and, therefore, a civil *violation* of the antitrust laws. Third, there is the additional question which is unique to the international setting of whether the interests of, and links to, the United States — including the magnitude of the effect on American foreign commerce — are sufficiently strong, vis-à-vis those of other nations, to justify an assertion of extraterritorial authority. ...

The elements to be weighted [in applying this third factor] include the degree of conflict with foreign law or policy, the nationality or allegiance of the parties and the locations or principal places of business of corporations, the extent to which enforcement by either state can be expected to achieve compliance, the relative significance of effects on the United States as compared with those elsewhere, the extent to which there is explicit purpose to harm or affect American commerce, the foreseeability of such effect, and the relative importance to the violations charged of conduct within the United States as compared with conduct abroad. A court evaluating these factors should identify the potential degree of conflict if American authority is asserted. A difference in law or policy is one likely sore spot, though one which may not always be present.[98] Nationality is another; though foreign governments may have some concern for the treatment of American citizens and business residing there, they primarily care about their own nationals.[99] Having assessed the conflict, the court

---

98. Particularly in the field of trade regulation, American laws may not be duplicated by the other nation. That does not necessarily indicate a "conflict," however, since non-prohibition does not always mean affirmative approval. *See* P. Areeda, [*Antitrust Analysis* 127 (1974).]

99. Some argue that a defendant's American citizenship might be enough by itself to support jurisdiction. *See Restatement (Second) Foreign Relations Law* §30 (1965).

should then determine whether in the face of it the contacts and interests of the United States are sufficient to support the exercise of extraterritorial jurisdiction.

We conclude, then, that the problem should be approached in three parts: Does ① the alleged restraint affect, or was it intended to affect, the foreign commerce of the United States? Is it of such a type and magnitude so as to be cognizable as a violation ② of the Sherman Act? As a matter of international comity and fairness, should the ⑤ extraterritorial jurisdiction of the United States be asserted to cover it? The district court's judgment found only that the restraint involved in the instant suit did not produce a direct and substantial effect on American foreign commerce. That holding does not satisfy any of these inquiries. [The Court of Appeals remanded the case to the district court for application of the rule of reason. The district court applied the test and concluded that Timberlane's complaint should be dismissed. Timberlane appealed and the Court of Appeals affirmed. 749 F.2d 1378 (9th Cir. 1984).]

RESTATEMENT (THIRD) FOREIGN RELATIONS LAW OF THE UNITED STATES §§402 & 403 (1987)

[excerpted above at pp. 504-05]

Notes on Second Restatement, Timberlane, and Third Restatement

1. Timberlane*'s criticism of* Alcoa*'s effects test. Timberlane* concluded that *Alcoa*'s effects test was an inadequate formula for determining when the antitrust laws should be applied extraterritorially. In particular, Judge Choy reasoned that *Alcoa* failed to take into account the interests of other nations or the relationships between the litigants and the United States. Is *Timberlane's* criticism of the various formulations of the *Alcoa* "effects doctrine" persuasive? As an exercise in determining Congress's likely intent, which opinion is more persuasive?

2. Timberlane*'s reliance on international comity. Compare *Timberlane* with *American Banana* and *Alcoa.* Does Judge Chow look to international law in interpreting the Sherman Act? What sources does he consult in ascertaining limits on the extraterritorial reach of the antitrust laws? Note *Timberlane's* reliance on "comity and the prerogatives of other nations" and "international comity and fairness." What does *Timberlane* mean by "international comity"? Is it different from "international law"? What is the source of comity, and how does one ascertain what its limits are? Recall what Huber and Story meant by "comity." *See supra* pp. 546-50. Is "comity" a substitute for the *Charming Betsy* presumption and the territoriality presumption? Is it a wise substitute? Compare the reliance on international comity in other contexts, including forum non conveniens (*supra* p. 314); antisuit injunctions (*supra* p. 485); choice of law (*infra* p. 629); extraterritorial discovery (*infra* pp. 871-82 & 913); and recognition of foreign judgments (*infra* pp. 939-41).

3. Timberlane*'s effects test. The first two of the three prongs of the *Timberlane* analysis are derived from *Alcoa's* effects test. The first *Timberlane* prong requires only proof that the defendant's conduct had "*some effect* — actual or intended — on American foreign commerce." 549 F.2d at 613 (emphasis in original). Would any significant international economic activity fail to have "some effect" on U.S. commerce?

The second *Timberlane* prong also requires a showing of effects on U.S. commerce. A second Ninth Circuit opinion in *Timberlane* read this prong to require a "direct and substantial anticompetitive effect" on the foreign commerce of the United States. 749 F.2d 1378 (9th Cir. 1984). Nonetheless, the decision confirmed that the second *Timberlane* prong does not require a showing anywhere near as demanding as the traditional "direct, substantial and reasonably foreseeable" test. Some courts that have otherwise followed *Timberlane's* general approach have refused to adopt an "effects" requirement with the low threshold permitted in *Timberlane's* first and second prongs. *E.g., Mannington Mills, Inc. v. Congoleum Corp.*, 595 F.2d 1287, 1291-92 (3d Cir. 1979); *Conservation Council of Western Australia v. Aluminum Co. of Am.*,

518 F.Supp. 270 (W.D. Pa. 1981). *Cf. Zenith Radio Corp. v. Matsushita Elec. Indus. Co.*, 494 F.Supp. 1161, 1177 (E.D. Pa. 1980) (suggesting low threshold for jurisdictional inquiry into effects). *See also Hartford Fire Ins. Co. v. California*, 113 S.Ct. 2891, 2920 n.9 (1994) (Scalia, J., dissenting).

4. **Timberlane's *effects test and international law*.** Recall the contemporary statements of the effects test under international law. *See supra* p. 507. Is *Timberlane's* effects test consistent with contemporary international law?

5. **Timberlane's *"rule of reason."*** The central innovation of *Timberlane* is its third, "interest-balancing" prong: the extraterritorial application of the U.S. antitrust laws requires consideration of "the additional question which is unique to the international setting of whether the interests of, and links to, the United States — including the magnitude of the effect on American foreign commerce — are sufficiently strong, vis-à-vis those of other nations, to justify an assertion of extraterritorial authority." Compare the *Timberlane* interest-balancing test to contemporary rules governing forum non conveniens, *supra* pp. 319-40, choice of law, *infra* pp. 632-52, and extraterritorial discovery, *infra* pp. 871-92.

6. *Basis for* **Timberlane** *jurisdictional rule of reason*. *Timberlane* adopted a so-called "jurisdictional rule of reason" in international antitrust cases. However, Judge Choy was not clear about the source of this rule. In particular, the court does not specify whether it was inferring that Congress "intended" such a rule as an implicit limitation on the reach of the U.S. antitrust statutes, whether the rule was a canon of statutory construction, or whether the rule was instead a general principle of international law or international comity that courts may incorporate into U.S. law in the absence of contrary congressional intent.

Judge Adams' concurring opinion in *Mannington Mills, Inc. v. Congoleum Corp.*, 595 F.2d 1287, 1301-02 n.9 (3d Cir. 1979), argued that the "rule of reason" must be a jurisdictional requirement of the Sherman Act in order to be a legitimate basis for refusing to hear a plaintiff's claims. Recall the similar constitutional questions raised by judicial abstention in the *forum non conveniens* and act of state contexts, discussed *supra* pp. 313-14 and *infra* pp. 701-05. Other authorities have argued that the rule of reason was not intended by Congress and that it illegitimately circumscribes the antitrust laws. *See infra* pp. 592-93 & 604.

7. *Factors relevant to the rule of reason*. *Timberlane* lists a number of factors to be considered in applying the jurisdictional rule of reason, but gives little guidance regarding the weight to be given to any particular factor or the relevance of additional factors. Other authorities that have adopted the *Timberlane* rule of reason have suggested slightly different lists of factors. *See Mannington Mills, Inc. v. Congoleum Corp.*, 595 F.2d 1287 (3d Cir. 1979); *Restatement (Third) Foreign Relations Law* §403 (1987); U.S. Department of Justice, *Antitrust Enforcement Guidelines for International Operations* 94-97 (1988). Compare §403's factors to those set out in *Timberlane*. Is either list preferable?

How is a court to decide whether a balancing of the *Timberlane* factors indicates that "the contacts and interests of the United States are sufficient to support the exercise of extraterritorial jurisdiction"? What "weight" should be accorded each factor? What if different factors point strongly in different directions?

8. *Predictability of rule of reason*. Is the rule of reason adopted in *Timberlane* and §403 predictable? Does it not invite entirely subjective, unprincipled decisions? Could §403's rule of reason be clarified over time as courts build on a body of common law precedent? Is §403's interest-balancing any different from many approaches in the choice of laws context? *Cf. Restatement (Second) Conflict of Laws* §6 (1971), excerpted below at pp. 639-40.

9. *The* **Timberlane/Laker** *debate*. *Laker Airways Ltd. v. Sabena*, 731 F.2d 909, 948-51 (D.C. Cir. 1984), sharply criticized the *Timberlane* rule of reason:

> The suggestion has been made that this court should engage in some form of interest balancing, permitting only a "reasonable" assertion of prescriptive jurisdiction to be implemented. However, this approach is unsuitable when courts are forced to choose between a domestic law which is designed to protect domestic interests, and a foreign law which is calculated to thwart the implementation of the domestic law in order to protect foreign interests allegedly threatened by the objectives of the domestic law. Interest balancing in this context is hobbled by two primary problems: (1) there are substantial limitations on the court's ability to conduct a neutral balancing of the competing interests, and (2) the adoption of interest balancing is unlikely to achieve its goal of promoting international comity. ...
>
> Those contacts [relevant to the jurisdictional rule of reason] which do purport to provide a

basis for distinguishing between competing bases of jurisdiction, and which are thus crucial to the balancing process, generally incorporate purely political factors which the court is neither qualified to evaluate comparatively nor capable of properly balancing. One such proposed consideration is "the degree to which the *desirability of such regulation* [of restrictive practices] is *generally accepted.*" [Restatement (Revised) §403(a) (g), (h) (Tentative Draft No. 2)]. We doubt whether the legitimacy of an exercise of jurisdiction should be measured by the substantive content of the prescribed law. Moreover, although more and more states are following the United States in regulating restrictive practices, and even exercising jurisdiction based on effects within territory, *the differing English and American assessment of the desirability of antitrust law is at the core of the conflict. An English or American court cannot refuse to enforce law its political branches have already determined is desirable and necessary.* ...

The "importance of regulation to the state" is another factor on which the court cannot rely to choose between two competing mutually inconsistent legislative policies. We are in no position to adjudicate the relative importance of antitrust regulation or nonregulation to the United States and the United Kingdom. It is the crucial importance of these policies which has created the conflict. A proclamation by judicial fiat that one interest is less "important" than the other will not erase a real conflict.

Given the inherent limitations of the Judiciary, which must weigh these issues in the limited context of adversarial litigation, we seriously doubt whether we could adequately chart the competing problems and priorities that inevitably define the scope of any nation's interest in a legislated remedy. This court is ill-equipped to "balance the vital national interest of the United States and the [United Kingdom] to determine which interests predominate." [*In re Uranium Antitrust Litig.*, 480 F.Supp. 1138, 1148 (N.D. Ill. 1978).] When one state exercises its jurisdiction and another, in protection of its own interests, attempts to quash the first exercise of jurisdiction "it is simply impossible to judicially 'balance' these totally contradictory and mutually negating actions." *Id.* ...

We might be more willing to tackle the problems associated with the balancing of competing, mutually inconsistent national interests if we could be assured that our efforts would strengthen the bonds of international comity. However, the usefulness and wisdom of interest balancing to assess the most "reasonable" exercise of prescriptive jurisdiction has not been affirmatively demonstrated. This approach has not gained more than a temporary foothold in domestic law. Courts are increasingly refusing to adopt the approach. Scholarly criticism has intensified. Additionally, there is no evidence that interest balancing represents a rule of international law. Thus, there is no mandatory rule requiring its adoption here, since Congress cannot be said to have implicitly legislated subject to these international constraints.

If promotion of international comity is measured by the number of times U.S. jurisdiction has been declined under the "reasonableness" interest balancing approach, then it has been a failure. Implementation of this analysis has not resulted in a significant number of conflict resolutions favoring a foreign jurisdiction. A pragmatic assessment of those decisions adopting an interest balancing approach indicates *none where U.S. jurisdiction was declined* when there was more than a *de minimis* United States interest. Most cases in which use of the process was advocated arose before a direct conflict occurred when the balancing could be employed without impairing the court's jurisdiction to determine jurisdiction. When push comes to shove, the domestic forum is rarely unseated.

See also Zoelsch v. Arthur Andersen & Co., 824 F.2d 27 (D.C. Cir. 1987); *Reinsurance Co. of Am. v. ADAS*, 902 F.2d 1275 (7th Cir. 1990) (Easterbrook, J., dissenting) (excerpted *infra* pp. 882-92). Are *Laker's* criticisms of the rule of reason persuasive? Putting aside problems with applying the rule of reason, is the Court of Appeals correct in questioning the constitutional and statutory basis for the rule of reason?

9. *No need for conflict between U.S. and foreign law for application of §403(2).* Note that the rules of reason in *Timberlane* and §403(1) and (2) apply even if there is no conflict between U.S. and foreign law. Is this appropriate? If foreign law is not directly inconsistent with U.S. antitrust laws, should the Sherman Act not presumptively be applicable, or at least require only a de minimis connection to the United States? Recall that the rationale for the territoriality presumption was that the extraterritorial application of

national law interfered with the sovereignty of foreign states. *See supra* p. 571. If foreign law is not inconsistent with U.S. law, then how is foreign sovereignty interfered with by the application of U.S. law?

10. *Relevance of conflict between U.S. and foreign law under §403(2).* One of the factors listed for consideration by *Timberlane* and §403 is the degree of conflict between U.S. and Honduran laws. After a remand to the district court, the Ninth Circuit considered the application of its "rule of reason" in a second *Timberlane* case. 749 F.2d 1378 (9th Cir. 1984). There, the Court of Appeals found that a conflict between U.S. and Honduran law existed, even though the defendants could not identify any specific Honduran law requiring or even condoning the defendant's allegedly anticompetitive conduct. Instead, *Timberlane II* discerned a conflict between the U.S. antitrust laws and a general effort by the Honduran government to "foster a particular style of business climate." Under this sort of analysis, would there ever *not* be a conflict? *Compare Timberlane I*, 549 F.2d at 614 n.32 ("American laws may not be duplicated by the other nation. That does not necessarily indicate a 'conflict,' however, since non-prohibition does not always mean affirmative approval."). Suppose Honduras had its own antitrust laws, as many industrialized nations have. Would this reduce the conflict with U.S. laws or heighten it?

11. *Relevance of conflict between U.S. and foreign law under §403(3).* Section 403(3) is applicable where U.S. and foreign laws are in conflict. What does it mean for a "conflict" to exist between U.S. and foreign law? Does it require that U.S. law impose a legal obligation requiring a party to do something that foreign law forbids that party from doing? What if foreign law does not require particular conduct, but specifically declines to forbid it? What if foreign law deliberately chooses to leave particular conduct unregulated? The Supreme Court considered these questions in *Hartford Fire*, discussed below. *See infra* pp. 593-606.

12. *Nationality of parties. Timberlane's* reasonableness analysis accords a significant role to the nationality of the parties: "Whether the alleged offender is an American citizen ... may make a big difference." This approach rests in part on the nationality principle, which permits a state to regulate the conduct of its nationals abroad, *see supra* p. 506, and on the perception that foreign states will typically be more concerned with actions against their own citizens than with actions against U.S. nationals. *Cf. EEOC v. Aramco*, 499 U.S. 244 (1991).

13. *Applicability of rule of reason to government suits.* Should the rule of reason be available to dismiss antitrust suits brought by the Department of Justice or by other government agencies? The Justice Department's Antitrust Division has indicated its belief that actions it initiates should not be subject to dismissal on *Timberlane* grounds, on the theory that the Executive Branch takes comity concerns into account in deciding whether to bring suit. U.S. Department of Justice, *Antitrust Enforcement Guidelines for International Operations* 93 n.167 (1988). One lower court has agreed. *United States v. Baker, Hughes, Inc.*, 731 F.Supp. 3 (D.D.C. 1990). Is this an appropriate position? Is the Justice Department necessarily sensitive to the interests of foreign states? Note that discovery requests by U.S. government agencies are subject to interest-balancing analysis similar to that required by *Timberlane*. *See infra* p. 891. Does the position taken in the *Guidelines* undermine the authority of the federal courts to determine their own jurisdiction?

14. *Effect of choice of law clause on extraterritorial reach of U.S. statutes.* International commercial contracts frequently contain choice of law clauses. When such a clause selects the laws of a U.S. state, what effect does this have on the extraterritorial application of the U.S. antitrust laws or other federal statutes? In *Zenger-Miller, Inc. v. Training Team, GmbH*, 757 F.Supp. 1062 (N.D. Calif. 1991), the district court refused to apply the Lanham Act to conduct occurring in Europe, notwithstanding a California choice-of-law provision. The court reasoned that "defendants consented to the application of California, not federal law ... [and] subject matter jurisdiction, unlike personal jurisdiction 'cannot be consented to by the parties...'" Is this reasoning persuasive? Does such a choice-of-law provision have any relevance to extraterritoriality analysis?

e. *Contemporary Supreme Court Approach to Extraterritorial Application of U.S. Antitrust Laws:* Hartford Insurance

In 1993, the Supreme Court handed down a decision in *Hartford Fire Insurance Company v. California*[100] setting forth what appears to be its present view of the

---

100. 113 S.Ct. 2891 (1993).

extraterritorial reach of the U.S. antitrust laws. The decision came barely two years after *EEOC v. Aramco*'s reaffirmation of the territoriality presumption. Nevertheless, neither *Aramco* nor the territoriality presumption was alluded to in the Court's opinion. Instead, *Hartford Fire* embraced an effects test not much different from that in *Alcoa*, and apparently was willing to adopt §403's rule of reason to moderate the *Alcoa* standard.

As *Aramco* and *Hartford Fire* illustrate, the Court's recent approach to the extraterritorial reach of federal legislation leaves much to be desired. The Court has applied several fundamentally different rules of construction in international cases. One is the traditional *American Banana* rule, applied in *Aramco*, which imposes a strict territoriality presumption on federal legislation. A second is the *Hartford Fire* rule, which looks to the contemporary formulations of *Alcoa's* effects doctrine. A third is reflected in decisions such as *Lauritzen v. Larsen*[101] and *Steele v. Bulova Watch Co.*,[102] which adopt a multi-factor rule of reason approach similar to that in *Timberlane*. Unfortunately, the Court has neither acknowledged the existence of these different approaches, nor provided guidance as to when it will apply one, rather than another. The result is confusion for litigants and lower courts, and arbitrary, unpredictable results.

HARTFORD FIRE INSURANCE CO. v. CALIFORNIA

113 S.Ct. 2891 (1993)

JUSTICE SOUTER. ... The Sherman Act makes every contract, combination, or conspiracy in unreasonable restraint of interstate or foreign commerce illegal. 15 U.S.C. §1. These consolidated cases present questions about the application of that Act to the insurance industry ... abroad. The plaintiffs (respondents here) allege that both domestic and foreign defendants (petitioners here) violated the Sherman Act by engaging in various conspiracies to affect the American insurance market. ... [The] foreign defendants argue that the principle of international comity requires the District Court to refrain from exercising jurisdiction over certain claims against [them]. We hold that ... the principle of international comity does not preclude District Court jurisdiction over the foreign conduct alleged.

I. The two petitions before us stem from consolidated litigation comprising the complaints of 19 States and many private plaintiffs alleging that the defendants, members of the insurance industry, conspired in violation of §1 of the Sherman Act to restrict the terms of coverage of commercial general liability ("CGL") insurance available in the United States. ... According to the complaints, the object of the conspiracies was to force certain primary insurers (insurers who sell insurance directly to consumers) to change the terms of their standard CGL insurance policies to conform with the policies the defendant insurers wanted to sell. ... [The Fifth Claim for Relief

---

101. 345 U.S. 571 (1953); *supra* pp. 555-63.
102. 344 U.S. 280 (1952).

alleges a violation of §1 of the Sherman Act by certain London reinsurers who conspired to coerce primary insurers in the United States to offer CGL coverage on a claims-made basis, thereby making "occurrence CGL coverage ... unavailable in the State of California for many risks." The Sixth and Eighth Claims were similar.] ...

The District Court granted the motions to dismiss. It ... dismissed the three claims that named only certain London-based defendants, invoking international comity and applying the Ninth Circuit's decision in *Timberlane*. ... The Court of Appeals reversed. ... [A]s to the three claims brought solely against foreign defendants, the court applied its *Timberlane* analysis, but concluded that the principle of international comity was no bar to exercising Sherman Act jurisdiction. ...

III. At the outset, we note that the District Court undoubtedly had jurisdiction of these Sherman Act claims, as the London reinsurers apparently concede. *See* [Transcript of Oral Argument] 37 ("Our position is not that the Sherman Act does not apply in the sense that a minimal basis for the exercise of jurisdiction doesn't exist here. Our position is that there are certain circumstances, and that this is one of them, in which the interests of another State are sufficient that the exercise of that jurisdiction should be restrained."). Although the proposition was perhaps not always free from doubt, *see American Banana Co. v. United Fruit Co.*, it is well established by now that the Sherman Act applies to foreign conduct that was meant to produce and did in fact produce some substantial effect in the United States. *See Matsushita Elec. Industrial Co. v. Zenith Radio Corp.*, 475 U.S. 574, 582 n.6 (1986); *United States v. Alcoa*; *Restatement (Third) Foreign Relations Law* §415, and Reporters' Note 3 (1987); *cf. Steele v. Bulova Watch Co.*[103] Such is the conduct alleged here: that the London reinsurers engaged in unlawful conspiracies to affect the market for insurance in the United States and that their conduct in fact produced substantial effect.[104]

According to the London reinsurers, the District Court should have declined to

---

103. Justice Scalia believes that what is at issue in this case is prescriptive, as opposed to subject-matter, jurisdiction. The parties do not question prescriptive jurisdiction, however, and for good reason: it is well established that Congress has exercised such jurisdiction under the Sherman Act. *See* G. Born & D. Westin, *International Civil Litigation in United States Courts* 542, n.5 (2d ed. 1992) (Sherman Act is a "prime exampl[e] of the simultaneous exercise of prescriptive jurisdiction and grant of subject matter jurisdiction").

104. Under §402 of the Foreign Trade Antitrust Improvements Act of 1982 ("FTAIA"), 15 U.S.C. §6a, the Sherman Act does not apply to conduct involving foreign trade or commerce, other than import trade or import commerce, unless "such conduct has a direct, substantial, and reasonably foreseeable effect" on domestic or import commerce. 15 U.S.C. §6a(1)(A). The FTAIA was intended to exempt from the Sherman Act export transactions that did not injure the United States economy, *see* H.R. Rep. No. 97-686, pp. 2-3, 9-10 (1982), and it is unclear how it might apply to the conduct alleged here. Also unclear is whether the Act's "direct, substantial, and reasonably foreseeable effect" standard amends existing law or merely codifies it. We need not address these questions here. Assuming that the FTAIA's standard affects this case, and assuming further that that standard differs from the prior law, the conduct alleged plainly meets its requirements.

exercise such jurisdiction under the principle of international comity.[105] The Court of Appeals agreed that courts should look to that principle in deciding whether to exercise jurisdiction under the Sherman Act. This availed the London reinsurers nothing, however. To be sure, the Court of Appeals believed that "application of [American] antitrust laws to the London reinsurance market 'would lead to significant conflict with English law and policy,' "and that "[s]uch a conflict, unless outweighed by other factors, would by itself be reason to decline exercise of jurisdiction." But other factors, in the court's view, including the London reinsurers' express purpose to affect U.S. commerce and the substantial nature of the effect produced, outweighed the supposed conflict and required the exercise of jurisdiction in this case.

other factors outweigh

When it enacted the Foreign Trade Antitrust Improvements Act of 1982 ("FTAIA"), Congress expressed no view on the question whether a court with Sherman Act jurisdiction should ever decline to exercise such jurisdiction on grounds of international comity. *See* H.R. Rep. No. 97-686, p. 13 (1982) ("If a court determines that the requirements for subject matter jurisdiction are met, [the FTAIA] would have no effect on the court['s] ability to employ notions of comity ... or otherwise to take account of the international character of the transaction") (citing *Timberlane*). We need not decide that question here, however, for even assuming that in a proper case a court may decline to exercise Sherman Act jurisdiction over foreign conduct (or, as Justice Scalia would put it, may conclude by the employment of comity analysis in the first instance that there is no jurisdiction), international comity would not counsel against exercising jurisdiction in the circumstances alleged here.

The only substantial question in this case is whether "there is in fact a true conflict between domestic and foreign law." *Societe Nationale Industrielle Aerospatiale v. District Court*, 482 U.S. 522, 555 (1987) (Blackmun, J., concurring in part and dissenting in part). The London reinsurers contend that applying the Act to their conduct would conflict significantly with British law, and the British Government, appearing before us as amicus curiae, concurs. They assert that Parliament has established a comprehensive regulatory regime over the London reinsurance market and that the conduct alleged here was perfectly consistent with British law and policy. But

? Conflict?

---

105. Justice Scalia contends that comity concerns figure into the prior analysis whether jurisdiction exists under the Sherman Act. This contention is inconsistent with the general understanding that the Sherman Act covers foreign conduct producing a substantial intended effect in the United States, and that concerns of comity come into play, if at all, only after a court has determined that the acts complained of are subject to Sherman Act jurisdiction. *See United States v. Aluminum Co. of America*, 148 F.2d 416, 444 (2d Cir. 1945) ("it follows from what we have ... said that [the agreements at issue] were unlawful [under the Sherman Act], though made abroad, if they were intended to affect imports and did affect them"); *Mannington Mills, Inc. v. Congoleum Corp.*, 595 F.2d 1287, 1294 (3d Cir. 1979) (once court determines that jurisdiction exists under the Sherman Act, question remains whether comity precludes its exercise). *But cf. Timberlane Lumber Co.*; 1 J. Atwood & K. Brewster, *Antitrust and American Business Abroad* 166 (1981). In any event, the parties conceded jurisdiction at oral argument, and we see no need to address this contention here.

this is not to state a conflict. "[T]he fact that conduct is lawful in the state in which it took place will not, of itself, bar application of the United States antitrust laws," even where the foreign state has a strong policy to permit or encourage such conduct. *Restatement (Third) Foreign Relations Law* §415, Comment j. No conflict exists, for these purposes, "where a person subject to regulation by two states can comply with the laws of both." *Restatement (Third) Foreign Relations Law* §403, Comment e. Since the London reinsurers do not argue that British law requires them to act in some fashion prohibited by the law of the United States, or claim that their compliance with the laws of both countries is otherwise impossible, we see no conflict with British law. *See Restatement (Third) Foreign Relations Law* §403, Comment e, §415, Comment j. We have no need in this case to address other considerations that might inform a decision to refrain from the exercise of jurisdiction on grounds of international comity.

JUSTICE SCALIA delivered a dissenting opinion with respect to Part II, in which JUSTICE O'CONNOR, JUSTICE KENNEDY, and JUSTICE THOMAS have joined. ... The petitioners, various British corporations and other British subjects, argue that certain of the claims against them constitute an inappropriate extraterritorial application of the Sherman Act. It is important to distinguish two distinct questions raised by this petition: whether the District Court had jurisdiction, and whether the Sherman Act reaches the extraterritorial conduct alleged here. On the first question, I believe that the District Court had subject-matter jurisdiction over the Sherman Act claims against all the defendants (personal jurisdiction is not contested). The respondents asserted nonfrivolous claims under the Sherman Act, and 28 U.S.C. §1331 vests district courts with subject-matter jurisdiction over cases "arising under" federal statutes. As precedents such as *Lauritzen v. Larsen,* make clear, that is sufficient to establish the District Court's jurisdiction over these claims. *Lauritzen* involved a Jones Act claim brought by a foreign sailor against a foreign shipowner. The shipowner contested the District Court's jurisdiction, apparently on the grounds that the Jones Act did not govern the dispute between the foreign parties to the action. Though ultimately agreeing with the shipowner that the Jones Act did not apply, the Court held that the District Court had jurisdiction.

> As frequently happens, a contention that there is some barrier to granting plaintiff's claim is cast in terms of an exception to jurisdiction of subject matter. A cause of action under our law was asserted here, and the court had power to determine whether it was or was not founded in law and in fact. 345 U.S. at 575

The second question — the extraterritorial reach of the Sherman Act — has nothing to do with the jurisdiction of the courts. It is a question of substantive law turning on whether, in enacting the Sherman Act, Congress asserted regulatory power over the challenged conduct. *See EEOC v. Arabian American Oil Co.* ("*Aramco*") ("It is our task to determine whether Congress intended the protections of Title VII to apply to United States citizens employed by American employers outside of the United States"). If a plaintiff fails to prevail on this issue, the court does not dismiss the claim for want of subject-matter jurisdiction — want of power to adjudicate; rather, it decides the claim, ruling on the merits that the plaintiff has failed to state a cause of action under the relevant statute. ...

There is, however, a type of "jurisdiction" relevant to determining the extraterritorial reach of a statute; it is known as "legislative jurisdiction," *Aramco*, 499 U.S. at ——; *Restatement (First) Conflict of Laws* §60 (1934), or "jurisdiction to prescribe," *Restatement (Third) Foreign Relations Law* 235 (1987). This refers to "the authority of a state to make its law applicable to persons or activities," and is quite a separate matter from "jurisdiction to adjudicate," *see id.* at 231. There is no doubt, of course, that Congress possesses legislative jurisdiction over the acts alleged in this complaint: Congress has broad power under Article I, §8, cl. 3 "[t]o regulate Commerce with foreign Nations," and this Court has repeatedly upheld its power to make laws applicable to persons or activities beyond our territorial boundaries where United States interests are affected. *See Ford v. United States*, 273 U.S. 593, 621-23 (1927); *United States v. Bowman*, 260 U.S. 94, 98-99 (1922); *American Banana.* But the question in this case is whether, and to what extent, Congress has exercised that undoubted legislative jurisdiction in enacting the Sherman Act.

Two canons of statutory construction are relevant in this inquiry. The first is the "long-standing principle of American law 'that legislation of Congress, unless a contrary intent appears, is meant to apply only within the territorial jurisdiction of the United States.'" *Aramco* (quoting *Foley Bros., Inc. v. Filardo*). Applying that canon in *Aramco*, we held that the version of Title VII of the Civil Rights Act of 1964 then in force did not extend outside the territory of the United States even though the statute contained broad provisions extending its prohibitions to, for example, "'any activity, business, or industry in commerce.'" (quoting 42 U.S.C. §2000e(h)). We held such "boilerplate language" to be an insufficient indication to override the presumption against extraterritoriality. The Sherman Act contains similar "boilerplate language," and if the question were not governed by precedent, it would be worth considering whether that presumption controls the outcome here. We have, however, found the presumption to be overcome with respect to our antitrust laws; it is now well established that the Sherman Act applies extraterritorially. *See Matsushita Elec. Industrial Co. v. Zenith Radio Corp.; Continental Ore Co. v. Union Carbide & Carbon Corp.*

But if the presumption against extraterritoriality has been overcome or is otherwise inapplicable, a second canon of statutory construction becomes relevant: "[A]n act of Congress ought never to be construed to violate the law of nations if any other possible construction remains." *Murray v. The Charming Betsy*, 2 Cranch 64, 118 (1804) (Marshall, C.J.). This canon is "wholly independent" of the presumption against extraterritoriality. It is relevant to determining the substantive reach of a statute because "the law of nations," or customary international law, includes limitations on a nation's exercise of its jurisdiction to prescribe. Though it clearly has constitutional authority to do so, Congress is generally presumed not to have exceeded those customary international-law limits on jurisdiction to prescribe.

Consistent with that presumption, this and other courts have frequently recognized that, even where the presumption against extraterritoriality does not apply, statutes should not be interpreted to regulate foreign persons or conduct if that regulation would conflict with principles of international law. For example, in *Romero v. International Terminal Operating Co.*, the plaintiff, a Spanish sailor who had been injured while working aboard a Spanish-flag and Spanish-owned vessel, filed a Jones Act claim against his Spanish employer. The presumption against extraterritorial application of federal statutes was inapplicable to the case, as the actionable tort had occurred in American waters. The Court nonetheless stated that, "in the absence of contrary congressional direction," it would apply "principles of choice of law that are consonant with the needs of a general federal maritime law and with due recognition of our self-regarding respect for the relevant interests of foreign nations in the regulation of maritime commerce as part of the legitimate concern of the international community." "The controlling considerations" in this choice-of-law analysis were "the interacting interests of the United States and of foreign countries."

Romero referred to, and followed, the choice-of-law analysis set forth in *Lauritzen v. Larsen*. As previously mentioned, *Lauritzen* also involved a Jones Act claim brought by a foreign sailor against a foreign employer. The *Lauritzen* Court recognized the basic problem: "If [the Jones Act were] read literally, Congress has conferred an American right of action which requires nothing more than that plaintiff be 'any seaman who shall suffer personal injury in the course of his employment.'" The solution it adopted was to construe the statute "to apply only to areas and transactions in which American law would be considered operative under prevalent doctrines of international law." To support application of international law to limit the facial breadth of the statute, the Court relied upon — of course — Chief Justice Marshall's statement in *The Charming Betsy*. It then set forth "several factors which, alone or in combination, are generally conceded to influence choice of law to govern a tort claim." 345 U.S. at 583 (discussing factors).

Lauritzen, *Romero*, and *McCulloch* were maritime cases, but we have recognized the principle that the scope of generally worded statutes must be construed in light of international law in other areas as well. More specifically, the principle was expressed in *United States v. Alcoa*, the decision that established the extraterritorial reach of the Sherman Act. In his opinion for the court, Judge Learned Hand cautioned "we are not to read general words, such as those in [the Sherman] Act, without regard to the limitations customarily observed by nations upon the exercise of their powers; limitations which generally correspond to those fixed by the 'Conflict of Laws.'"

More recent lower court precedent has also tempered the extraterritorial application of the Sherman Act with considerations of "international comity." *See Timberlane Lumber Co.*; *Mannington Mills, Inc.*; *Montreal Trading Ltd.*; *Laker Airways* [sic]. The "comity" they refer to is not the comity of courts, whereby judges decline to exercise jurisdiction over matters more appropriately adjudged elsewhere, but rather what might be termed "prescriptive comity": the respect sovereign nations afford each other by limiting the reach of their laws. That comity is exercised by legislatures when they enact laws, and courts assume it has been exercised when they come to interpreting the scope of laws their legislatures have enacted. It is a traditional component of choice-of-law theory. *See* J. Story, *Commentaries on the Conflict of Laws* §38 (1834) (distinguishing between the "comity of the courts" and the "comity of nations," and defining the latter as "the true foundation and extent of the obligation of the laws of one nation within the territories of another"). Comity in this sense includes the choice-of-law principles that, "in the absence of contrary congressional direction," are assumed to be incorporated into our substantive laws having extraterritorial reach. *Romero*, 358 U.S. at 382-83; *Lauritzen*, 345 U.S. at 578-79; *Hilton v. Guyot*, 159 U.S. 113, 162-66 (1895). Considering comity in this way is just part of determining whether the Sherman Act prohibits the conduct at issue.[106]

In sum, the practice of using international law to limit the extraterritorial reach of statutes is firmly established in our jurisprudence. In proceeding to apply that practice to the present case, I shall rely on the *Restatement (Third) Foreign Relations Law* for the relevant principles of international law. Its standards appear fairly supported in the decisions of this Court construing international choice-of-law principles (*Lauritzen*, *Romero*, and *McCulloch*) and in the decisions of other federal courts, especially *Timberlane*. Whether the *Restatement* precisely reflects international law in every detail matters little here, as I believe this case would be resolved the same way under virtually any conceivable test that takes account of foreign regulatory interests.

Under the *Restatement*, a nation having some "basis" for jurisdiction to prescribe law should nonetheless refrain from exercising that jurisdiction "with respect to a person or activity having connections with another state when the exercise of such jurisdiction is unreasonable." *Restatement (Third)* §403(1). The [§403] "reasonableness" inquiry turns on a number of factors [which Justice Scalia quoted]. Rarely would these factors point more clearly against application of U.S. law. The activity relevant to the counts at issue here took place primarily in the United Kingdom, and the defendants in these counts are British corporations and British subjects having their principal place of business or residence outside the United States. Great Britain has established a comprehensive regulatory scheme governing the London reinsurance markets, and clearly has a heavy "interest in regulating the activity," §403(2)(g). ... Considering these factors, I think it unimaginable that an assertion of legislative

---

106. Some antitrust courts, including the Court of Appeals in the present case, have mistaken the comity at issue for the "comity of courts," which has led them to characterize the question presented as one of "abstention," that is, whether they should "exercise or decline jurisdiction." *Mannington Mills, Inc. v. Congoleum Corp.*, 595 F.2d 1287, 1294, 1296 (3rd Cir. 1979); *see also In re Insurance Antitrust Litigation*, 938 F.2d 919, 932 (9th Cir. 1991). As I shall discuss, that seems to be the error the Court has fallen into today. Because courts are generally reluctant to refuse the exercise of conferred jurisdiction, confusion on this seemingly theoretical point can have the very practical consequence of greatly expanding the extraterritorial reach of the Sherman Act.

jurisdiction by the United States would be considered reasonable, and therefore it is inappropriate to assume, in the absence of statutory indication to the contrary, that Congress has made such an assertion.

It is evident from what I have said that the Court's comity analysis, which proceeds as though the issue is whether the courts should "decline to exercise ... jurisdiction," rather than whether the Sherman Act covers this conduct, is simply misdirected. I do not at all agree, moreover, with the Court's conclusion that the issue of the substantive scope of the Sherman Act is not in the case. To be sure, the parties did not make a clear distinction between adjudicative jurisdiction and the scope of the statute. Parties often do not, as we have observed (and have declined to punish with procedural default) before. It is not realistic, and also not helpful, to pretend that the only really relevant issue in this case is not before us. In any event, if one erroneously chooses, as the Court does, to make adjudicative jurisdiction (or, more precisely, abstention) the vehicle for taking account of the needs of prescriptive comity, the Court still gets it wrong. It concludes that no "true conflict" counselling nonapplication of U.S. law (or rather, as it thinks, U.S. judicial jurisdiction) exists unless compliance with U.S. law would constitute a violation of another country's law. That breathtakingly broad proposition, which contradicts the many cases discussed earlier, will bring the Sherman Act and other laws into sharp and unnecessary conflict with the legitimate interests of other countries — particularly our closest trading partners.

In the sense in which the term "conflic[t]" was used in *Lauritzen*, 345 U.S. at 582, and is generally understood in the field of conflicts of laws, there is clearly a conflict in this case. The petitioners here, like the defendant in *Lauritzen*, were not compelled by any foreign law to take their allegedly wrongful actions, but that no more precludes a conflict-of-laws analysis here than it did there. ... Where applicable foreign and domestic law provide different substantive rules of decision to govern the parties' dispute, a conflict-of-laws analysis is necessary.

Literally the only support that the Court adduces for its position is §403 of the *Restatement (Third) Foreign Relations Law* — or more precisely Comment e to that provision, which states: "Subsection (3) [which says that a state should defer to another state if that state's interest is clearly greater] applies only when one state requires what another prohibits, or where compliance with the regulations of two states exercising jurisdiction consistently with this section is otherwise impossible. It does not apply where a person subject to regulation by two states can comply with the laws of both. ..." The Court has completely misinterpreted this provision. Subsection (3) of §403 (requiring one State to defer to another in the limited circumstances just described) comes into play only after subsection (1) of §403 has been complied with — *i.e.*, after it has been determined that the exercise of jurisdiction by both of the two states is not "unreasonable." That prior question is answered by applying the factors (*inter alia*) set forth in subsection (2) of §403, that is, precisely the factors that I have discussed in text and that the Court rejects.[107]

Notes on Hartford Fire

1. *Foreign Trade Antitrust Improvements Act.* In 1982, Congress enacted the Foreign Trade Antitrust Improvements Act, 15 U.S.C. §§6a, 45(a) (1982) ("FTAIA")). Among other things, the FTAIA addressed the jurisdictional requirements for the Sherman Act and the Federal Trade Commission Act. The FTAIA provides that both Acts:

> shall not apply to conduct involving trade or commerce (other than import trade or import commerce) with foreign nations unless —
>
> (1) such conduct has a direct, substantial, and reasonably foreseeable effect —
>
>> (A) on trade or commerce which is not trade or commerce with foreign nations, or on import trade or import commerce with foreign nations; or
>>
>> (B) on export trade or export commerce with foreign nations, of a person engaged in such trade or commerce in the United States; and
>
> (2) such effect gives rise to a claim under the provisions of sections 1 to 7 of this title other than this section. 15 U.S.C. §6a (1982).

Congress enacted the FTAIA in order to improve the competitiveness of U.S. firms in overseas markets, by freeing them from antitrust restraints on activities in "export trade." H.R. Rep. No. 686, 97th Cong., 2d Sess. 10 (1982).

2. *Scope of FTAIA.* The FTAIA does not apply to "import trade," which presumably would include the conduct and transactions at issue in, for example, *Mitsui* and *Alcoa.* Was the FTAIA applicable in *Hartford Fire*? Is the provision of reinsurance of U.S. insurance risks "import trade"? *Compare In re Insurance Antitrust Litigation*, 723 F.Supp. 464 (N.D. Cal. 1989) (case involved "import trade"), *aff'd*, 938 F.2d 919 (9th Cir. 1991). Does this suggest that the jurisdictional reach of the Sherman Act with respect to import trade is broader or narrower than the FTAIA's formula?

3. *Lower court applications of FTAIA.* A number of courts have relied on the FTAIA to dismiss antitrust actions. E.g., *McGlinchy v. Shell Chem. Co.*, 845 F.2d 802 (9th Cir. 1988); *McElderry v. Cathay Pacific Airways*, 678 F.Supp. 1071 (S.D.N.Y. 1988); *The 'In' Porters, SA v. Hanes Printables, Inc.*, 663 F.Supp. 494 (M.D.N.C. 1987); *Papst Motoren GmbH & Co. v. Kanematsu-Goshu (USA), Inc.*, 629 F.Supp. 864 (S.D.N.Y. 1986); *Liamuiga Tours v. Travel Impressions, Ltd.*, 617 F.Supp. 920 (E.D.N.Y. 1985); *Eurim-Pharm GmbH v. Pfizer, Inc.*, 593 F.Supp. 1102 (S.D.N.Y. 1984); *Power E., Ltd. v. Transamerica Deleval Inc.*, 558 F.Supp. 47 (S.D.N.Y.), *aff'd*, 742 F.2d 1439 (2d Cir. 1983).

4. *Effects test under FTAIA.* Lower courts have generally concluded that the FTAIA's effects test is more difficult to satisfy than *Alcoa*'s standard. *The 'In' Porters, SA v. Hanes Printables, Inc.*, 663 F.Supp. 494 (M.D.N.C. 1987); *Liamuiga Tours v. Travel Impressions, Ltd.*, 617 F.Supp. 920, 924 (E.D.N.Y. 1985). *But cf. Papst Motoren GmbH & Co. v. Kanematsu-Goshu (USA), Inc.*, 629 F.Supp. 864 (S.D.N.Y. 1986). *Hartford Fire* declined to consider whether the FTAIA set a different standard from the Sherman Act effects test.

5. *Why wasn't the territoriality presumption applied in* **Hartford Fire**? Two years before it decided *Hartford Fire*, the Supreme Court reaffirmed the territoriality presumption in *Aramco. See supra* pp. 563-76. Why wasn't *Aramco*'s territoriality presumption applicable in *Hartford Fire*? Consider the terms of the Sherman Act, applicable to contracts in restraint of trade "with foreign nations." Recall how *American Banana* interpreted that language in light of the territoriality presumption. How is it that the Court deals with the territoriality presumption in *Hartford Fire*? Note Justice Scalia's comment that "[t]he Sherman

---

107. The Court skips directly to subsection (3) of §403, apparently on the authority of Comment j to §415 of the *Restatement (Third)*. But the preceding commentary to §415 makes clear that "[a]ny exercise of [legislative] jurisdiction under this section is subject to the requirement of reasonableness" set forth in §403(2). *Restatement (Third)* §415, Comment a. Comment j refers back to the conflict analysis set forth in §403(3) which, as noted above, comes after the reasonableness analysis of §403(2).

Act contains similar 'boilerplate language' [to that in Title VII], and if the question were not governed by precedent, it would be worth considering whether that presumption controls the outcome here."

6. *Does the FTAIA affect application of the territoriality presumption?* How would the FTAIA be interpreted in light of the territoriality presumption? Can it be said that the FTAIA's language, quoted above, evidences an affirmative congressional intention to apply the Sherman Act extraterritorially? Is it not entirely clear, as a matter of common sense and legislative intent, that the drafters of the FTAIA understood and expected the Sherman Act to apply extraterritorially? Why else would Congress have set forth statutory limits on its extraterritorial application under an effects test? On the other hand, is the FTAIA any different from the alien exemption in Title VII, which *Aramco* found insufficient to overcome the territoriality presumption? With respect to import trade, not covered by the FTAIA, what effect does the territoriality presumption have?

7. *Defendants' concession in* **Hartford Fire** *that jurisdiction existed.* The defendants in *Hartford Fire* conceded that the Sherman Act applied to their conduct. *See supra* pp. 596-97. Should they have done that? In doing so, did the defendants miss the opportunity to argue that either the territoriality presumption or a *Lauritzen/Steele* presumption should apply? Note Justice Scalia's efforts to disregard this procedural misstep.

8. *Defendants' reliance in* **Hartford Fire** *on international comity.* Although they conceded jurisdiction, the defendants in *Hartford Fire* argued that "the exercise of that jurisdiction should be restrained." Citing *Timberlane* and §403, they relied on "the principle of international comity" to support that contention.

(a) *Justice Souter's view that comity is a separate basis for abstention apart from jurisdiction.* Justices Souter and Scalia disagreed over the relevance of international comity to the existence of jurisdiction under the Sherman Act. Justice Souter accepted the defendants' concession that jurisdiction existed, and then proceeded on the assumption that comity provided an additional, discretionary defense. Is this a legitimate mode of analysis? If Congress has applied the antitrust laws to particular conduct, can federal courts abstain from exercising jurisdiction in those cases? Justice Scalia, who usually is skeptical about abstention doctrines, *see W.S. Kirkpatrick & Co. v. Environmental Tectonics Corp.*, 493 U.S. 400 (1990), apparently would have permitted abstention in *Hartford Fire;* he did comment, however, in a footnote, that "courts are generally reluctant to refuse the exercise of conferred jurisdiction."

(b) *Propriety of comity or §403 analysis under the FTAIA and other antitrust legislation.* Does *Hartford Fire* hold that comity and/or §403 of the *Third Restatement* may be relied upon to decline jurisdiction under the Sherman Act or the FTAIA? Or does Justice Souter leave the question open? How should this question be answered? If Congress *has* granted jurisdiction, and made the antitrust laws applicable, in a particular case, what permits a U.S. court to decline to hear the case on grounds of comity? Consider again the *Timberlane/Laker* debate, *supra* pp. 592-93.

Recall Judge Adam's view in *Mannington Mills* that a court has no discretion to decline, on comity grounds, jurisdiction that Congress has conferred. *See supra* p. 592. Is that persuasive? Compare the role of comity in *Hartford Fire* with that in *Timberlane*. Compare also the debate over the legitimacy of the forum non conveniens doctrine. *See supra* pp. 313-14.

(c) *Justice Scalia's view that comity is relevant to the existence of jurisdiction.* Unlike Justice Souter, Justice Scalia thought that considerations of comity were relevant to the jurisdictional reach of the Sherman Act: "That comity is exercised by legislatures when they enact laws, and courts assume that it has been exercised when they come to interpreting the scope of laws that their legislatures have enacted." How does this analysis compare to the approach to interpreting the Sherman Act in *American Banana* and *Alcoa*? Note that, although Justice Scalia refers to "comity," he in fact adopts the "practice of using international *law* to limit the extraterritorial reach of statutes," citing the numerous decisions where the Court has done so (such as *Lauritzen, Romero,* and *McCulloch*).

9. *Justice Souter's §403 analysis in* **Hartford Fire.** Consider the Court's application of §403 in *Hartford Fire*. Why is it that the Court sees no need to engage in consideration of the various §403(2) factors?

(a) *No conflict with English law.* Justice Souter concludes that there was no conflict between the U.S. antitrust laws and the English legal regulatory structure for reinsurance. Why is that? Consider Justice Scalia's treatment of the same issue. Which view is correct?

(b) *Justice Souter's requirement of a direct conflict between U.S. and foreign law.* Justice Souter's opinion is unclear in its discussion of the lack of a conflict between U.S. and foreign law. That discussion arguably required a direct conflict between U.S. and English law, where inconsistent legal requirements are imposed, as a prerequisite to declining jurisdiction on grounds of comity. As Justice Scalia's dissent observes, if this is what Justice Souter meant, it is clearly a misreading of §403 and of *Timberlane.* As discussed above, *see supra* pp. 508-09, §403(2) lists a conflict between U.S. and foreign law as merely *one of many factors* relevant to the exercise of jurisdiction; the same is true of the *Timberlane* analysis, *see supra* pp. 593-94. The absence of a direct conflict — imposing inconsistent legal duties — does *not* make §403(1) and (2) inapplicable. *See also* Lowenfeld, *Conflict, Balancing of Interests, and the Exercise of Jurisdiction to Prescribe: Reflections on the Insurance Antitrust Case,* 89 Am. J. Int'l L. 42, 50 (1995) (comment by Reporter for *Restatement Third:* "it is clear to me that Justice Scalia understood, and Justice Souter misunderstood, the approach of the Restatement"). Moreover, although §403(3) *does* require a "conflict," this subsection is only applicable if §403(2) has first been satisfied.

Alternatively, Justice Souter might have been saying that, once jurisdiction was conceded, then only §403(3) — not §403(2) — is relevant. That would have been reading a great deal into the defendant's concession, although it is consistent with Justice Souter's opinion.

Finally, Justice Souter might have been saying (albeit opaquely) that a §403(2) comity analysis would only have permitted dismissal if there were a direct conflict. This is perhaps the most sensible position that the Court could have taken, but it is the least consistent with Justice Souter's opinion.

10. *Was* Hartford Fire *correctly decided?* How should *Hartford Fire* have been decided? Even if there was a conflict between U.S. and English law, was Justice Scalia right in concluding that the Sherman Act did not apply to the defendants' conduct? Note in particular Justice Scalia's statement that "this case would be resolved the same way under virtually any conceivable test that takes account of foreign regulatory interests." Consider the alleged magnitude of the U.S. effects of the defendants' conduct and the alleged intention of the defendants to affect U.S. conduct. Isn't Justice Scalia wrong about the ultimate outcome in *Hartford Fire?*

11. *Subject matter versus legislative jurisdiction.* Justices Souter and Scalia disagree over the question whether the jurisdictional issue in *Hartford Fire* was "subject matter" or "legislative" jurisdiction. Citing an earlier edition of this book, Justice Souter said that the case concerned subject matter jurisdiction, because the scope of federal subject matter and legislative jurisdiction was identical under the antitrust laws. G. Born & D. Westin, *International Civil Litigation in U.S. Courts* 542 n.5 (2d ed. 1992). Justice Scalia disagreed, saying that subject matter jurisdiction was broader, and he implied that subject matter jurisdiction might exist even where there was no prescriptive jurisdiction. In his view, the applicability of the Sherman Act to the defendants' conduct "has nothing to do with the jurisdiction of the courts."

In fact, earlier editions of this book merely said that the antitrust laws were a simultaneous exercise of prescriptive jurisdiction (*i.e.,* enacting the substantive standards of the Sherman Act) and grant of subject matter jurisdiction (*i.e.,* authorizing federal courts to hear such claims); it was not said that subject matter and prescriptive jurisdiction were co-extensive. G. Born & D. Westin, *International Civil Litigation in United States Courts* 542 & 616 (2d ed. 1991). Nevertheless, which view is correct — Justice Souter or Justice Scalia?

The answer to this question can have substantial practical importance. The extraterritorial application of the antitrust laws can be challenged either in a motion to dismiss for lack of subject matter jurisdiction, under Fed. R. Civ. P. 12(b)(1), or for failure to state a claim, under Fed. R. Civ. P. 12(b)(6). Under Rule 12(b)(6), all factual inferences favorable to plaintiff will be drawn and a motion to dismiss will not be granted if there is any genuine issue of material fact. In contrast, under Rule 12(b)(1) the trial judge has greater freedom to weigh the evidence and discount the weight of the plaintiff's allegations and evidence.

Prior to *Hartford Fire,* most lower courts had concluded (like Justice Souter) that challenges to the extraterritorial application of the antitrust laws should be treated as attacks on subject matter jurisdiction under Rule 12(b)(1). *E.g., Papst Motoren GmbH & Co. v. Kanematsu-Goshu (U.S.A.), Inc.,* 629 F.Supp. 864, 868 (S.D.N.Y. 1986); *Liamuiga Tours v. Travel Impressions, Ltd.,* 617 F.Supp. 920 (E.D.N.Y. 1985); *Zenith Radio Corp. v. Matsushita Elec. Indus. Co.,* 494 F.Supp. 1161, 1171-78 (E.D. Pa. 1980). *Cf. The 'In' Porters, SA v. Hanes Printables, Inc.,* 663 F.Supp. 494, 500 n.5 (M.D.N.C. 1987) ("[t]he better rule appears to be to treat such motions under 12(b)(1), unless the facts central to the merits ... are intertwined with the jurisdictional facts").

12. *Ascertaining and proving foreign interests.* As critics of §403 have pointed out, it is difficult for

U.S. courts to ascertain the character and intensity of foreign interests in particular cases. *See supra* pp. 592-93. This presents special challenges for counsel in international cases, who often must attempt to enlist foreign governmental assistance in articulating relevant foreign interests. *See Restatement (Third) Foreign Relations Law* §403, Reporters' Note 6 (1987) ("a court of the United States may take into account indications of national interest by the foreign government whether made through a diplomatic note, a brief amicus curiae, or a declaration by government officials in parliamentary debates, press conferences, or communiques"); *CFTC v. Nahas*, 738 F.2d 487, 490 n.5, 494 n.16 (D.C. Cir. 1984) (diplomatic note and protest letter from 35 members of Brazilian legislature). In addition, as occurred in *Timberlane*, counsel should attempt to provide expert witness testimony on any conflicts between U.S. and foreign law. Compare the similar issues that arise in the context of extraterritorial discovery. *See infra* pp. 855 & 881-82.

13. **Hartford's *effects test and international law*.** Recall the contemporary statements of the effect test under international law. *See supra* pp. 506-07. Is *Hartford's* effects test, and the effects test in the FTAIA, consistent with contemporary international law?

14. ***Extraterritorial application of antitrust laws based upon foreclosure of U.S. exports.*** Suppose that conduct in a foreign country makes it difficult for U.S. companies to export their products to that country. For example, suppose that Mitsui had involved efforts by Japanese companies to drive U.S. exporters of U.S. timber out of the Japanese market, by replacing U.S. exports with Indonesian exports. Does this have sufficient effects in the United States to sustain U.S. antitrust jurisdiction?

(a) *Historic approach.* How does Learned Hand answer the question whether the Sherman Act applies to foreign foreclosure of U.S. exports in *Alcoa*? The U.S. Department of Justice's *Antitrust Guide for International Operations* (1977) arguably would have permitted the antitrust laws to apply extraterritorially to the foreclosure of U.S. exports: "the U.S. antitrust laws should be applied to an overseas transaction when there is substantial and foreseeable effect on the United States commerce." Department of Justice, *Antitrust Guide for International Operations* at E-2 to E-3 (1977). In 1988, however, the Antitrust Division revised the Guide and suggested that it would enforce the antitrust laws only where U.S. *consumers* were harmed. Department of Justice, *Antitrust Guidelines for International Operations* at 30 n.159 (1988).

(b) *Recent developments.* In 1990 the Antitrust Division announced that it "will not tolerate violations of the U.S. antitrust laws where we have jurisdiction, that impair export opportunities for U.S. business." *See also* Department of Justice, Press Release (April 3, 1992); Ohara, *The New U.S. Policy on the Extraterritorial Application of Antitrust Laws and Japan's Response*, 17 World Comp. 49 (1994); Hawk, *The International Application of the Sherman Act in its Second Century*, 59 Antitrust L.J. 161, 163-64 (1990).

The Department of Justice has filed several cases relying on the new "export foreclosure" policy. In one matter it accused an English glass manufacturer of utilizing territorial and use restrictions in its patent and trade secret licenses to discourage exports of U.S.-made glass and U.S. glass-making technology. The English company denied the allegations but accepted a Consent Decree to avoid costly litigation. *United States v. Pilkington plc*, 7 Trade Reg. Rep. (CCH) ¶ 50,758 (D. Ariz. 1994).

In 1994, the Department of Justice filed an action against MCI Communications Corporation, alleging that the antitrust laws were violated by a proposal by British Telecom to purchase 20% of MCI's shares and form an MCI-British Telecom joint venture. The complaint alleged that the joint venture could reduce competition by obtaining unfair access to British Telecom's United Kingdom telecommunications network: "by creating the incentive to discriminate against competitors, in terms of conditions and access to British Telecom's local telephony monopoly in the UK, the venture could cause the price of international telephone calls and other telecommunications services to increase." The action was settled by a Consent Decree. *United States v. MCI Communications Corp.*, 7 Trade Reg. Rep. CCH) ¶ 50,761 (D.D.C. 1994). Among other things, the Consent Decree forbid the MCI-BT joint venture from providing certain international telecommunications services unless: (a) UK licenses were granted to certain U.S. competitors; and (b) the licensed U.S. competitors received standard, non-discriminatory opportunities to interconnect to British Telecom's domestic UK network.

(c) *Appropriate rule.* Which view regarding the legality of foreclosures of U.S. exports is the correct interpretation of the Sherman Act? What effect does international law have on these various interpretations?

Suppose Japanese or German automobile manufacturers conspire to exclude U.S. car makers from their home markets. Should the U.S. antitrust laws forbid such conduct? Suppose German and Japanese law permits such conduct. Is it more likely that Congress wanted to apply the Sherman Act to imports into America, than to exports from America? Why? Can one say categorically that effects on U.S. imports are more important to the U.S. economy than effects on U.S. exports? What about the effects on foreign economies of applying U.S. antitrust laws?

4. The Extraterritorial Application of Federal Securities Laws[108]

The federal securities laws contain broad prohibitions against fraudulent conduct in connection with the issuance and trading of securities.[109] These prohibitions have frequently been applied extraterritorially to fraudulent conduct occurring partially or entirely abroad.[110] It is instructive to compare the approach of U.S. courts to the extraterritorial application of the securities laws with the antitrust decisions in *Alcoa, Timberlane,* and *Hartford Fire.*

As in the antitrust context, U.S. courts have struggled to define the precise circumstances in which the federal securities laws will be applied extraterritorially. In some respects, the extraterritoriality guidelines that have been articulated in the securities law context are more developed and precise than those in antitrust decisions. The following decision, *Psimenos v. E.F. Hutton & Co.,* is representative.

PSIMENOS v. E. F. HUTTON & CO.

722 F.2d 1041 (2d Cir. 1983)

LUMBARD, CIRCUIT JUDGE. Plaintiff John Psimenos, a citizen and resident of Greece, brought this action under the anti-fraud provisions of the Commodities Exchange Act, 7 U.S.C. §1 et seq. (1982) ("CEA"),[111] as well as under common law

---

108. Commentary on the extraterritorial application of the U.S. securities laws includes, *e.g.,* Sachs, *The International Reach of Rule 10b-5: The Myth of Congressional Silence,* 28 Colum. J. Trans. L. 677 (1990); Thomas, *Extraterritoriality in an Era of Internationalization of the Securities Markets; The Need to Revisit Domestic Policies,* 35 Rutgers L. Rev. 453 (1983).

109. The three principal antifraud provisions of the federal securities laws are §10(b) of the Securities and Exchange Act of 1934, ch. 404, tit. I, §10, 48 Stat. 891, 15 U.S.C. §78j, and §§12(2) & 17(a) of the Securities Act of 1933, ch. 38, tit. I, §§7 & 12, 48 Stat. 78-84, 15 U.S.C. §§77g & 77l(2). In broad outline, all three provisions make it unlawful to engage in fraud in securities transactions.

110. *See, e.g., Itoba Ltd. v. Lep Group plc,* 54 F.3d 118 (2d Cir. 1995); *Alfadda v. Fenn,* 935 F.2d 475 (2d Cir. 1991); *Tamari v. Bache & Co. (Lebanon),* 730 F.2d 1103 (7th Cir.), *cert. denied,* 469 U.S. 871 (1984); *Grunenthal GmbH v. Hotz,* 712 F.2d 421, 425 (9th Cir. 1983); *SEC v. Kasser,* 548 F.2d 109 (3d Cir.), *cert. denied,* 431 U.S. 938 (1977); *Bersch v. Drexel Firestone, Inc.,* 519 F.2d 974 (2d Cir.), *cert. denied,* 423 U.S. 1018 (1975); *Leasco Data Processing Equipment Corp. v. Maxwell,* 468 F.2d 1326 (2d Cir. 1972); *Schoenbaum v. Firstbrook,* 405 F.2d 200 (2d Cir.), *rev'd on other grounds,* 405 F.2d 215 (2d Cir. 1968) (en banc), *cert. denied,* 395 U.S. 906 (1969).

111. Section 4b of the Act, 7 U.S.C. §6b (1982), declares it unlawful for members of a contracts market, or any of their associates, in connection with commodities contracts:

(A) to cheat or defraud or attempt to cheat or defraud such other person;

(B) wilfully to make or cause to be made to such other person any false report or statement thereof, or wilfully to enter or cause to be entered for such person any false record thereof;

(C) wilfully to deceive or attempt to deceive such other person by any means whatsoever in regard to any such order or contract or the disposition or execution of any such order or contract, or in regard to any act of agency performed with respect to such order or contract for such person; or

(D) to bucket such order, or to fill such order by offset against the order or orders of any other person, willingly or knowingly and without the prior consent of such person to become the buyer in respect to any selling order of such person, or become the seller in respect to any buying order of such person.

contract and agency principles, against E. F. Hutton & Company, a Delaware corporation having its principal place of business in New York, for damages resulting from Hutton's allegedly fraudulent procurement and management of his commodities trading account. Hutton moved ... to dismiss the federal claims for lack of subject matter jurisdiction ... Chief Judge Motley, holding that the alleged fraud was "predominantly foreign" and therefore outside the scope of the CEA, dismissed the federal claim for a lack of subject matter jurisdiction. We disagree with Judge Motley's reading of the jurisdictional limitations of the Act and, accordingly, reverse and remand for further proceeding.[112]

Since we are reviewing a motion to dismiss, we take the facts to be as stated in the plaintiff's amended complaint. In 1975, plaintiff became interested in investing in a commodities trading account with E. F. Hutton. Mathieu Mavridoglous, Hutton's agent and employee in Athens, told Psimenos "that his account would be managed in accordance with Hutton's standard procedures and with rules and regulations of the Commodities Futures Trading Commission." Psimenos was also informed by a flyer, printed by Hutton, of the quality and experience of Hutton's money managers. The flyer touted that Hutton's "experienced and qualified staff continually monitors the performance of each current Hutton approved manager ..." and that "Hutton's professionals thoroughly analyze and evaluate these managers in a manner beyond the resources of the ordinary investors." This flyer contained a tear-off post card to send to Hutton's New York office for more information.

Relying on these statements, Psimenos opened an account with Hutton's Athens office, executing blank forms that granted Hutton discretionary authority to trade in his account. Although Psimenos directed Mavridoglous to seek conservative investments, Hutton's agents often used money in Psimenos' account to participate in unresearched and highly speculative and leveraged transactions. ... Psimenos [ordered trading in his account stopped, but Mavridoglous later convinced him to resume.] Mavridogious told Psimenos that Hutton would recoup all his losses by assigning a new manager, Mario Michaelides, to the account. Michaelides was represented as a Hutton employee and qualified broker, though in fact he was not a Hutton employee, and was not nor had he ever been registered with the [CFTC] as a broker. Psimenos again told Mavridogiou that he wanted only low risk investments. He was told that Michaelides would trade on Psimenos' behalf only in United States Treasury Bill futures, which were represented as being risk-free. As a show of good faith, Michaelides said he would join Psimenos as a partner in his first trade, which turned out to be profitable. Later trades, however, resulted in large losses and Hutton

---

112. At our invitation, the Securities and Exchange Commission and the Commodities Futures Trading Commission each submitted a brief as *amicus curiae* urging us to find that the district court has subject matter jurisdiction to hear Psimenos' claim. The CFTC argues that trading on domestic commodities markets is sufficient to establish jurisdiction both because it involves substantial conduct in the United States and because it implicates the integrity of the United States markets.

began "churning" the account simply to generate commissions. Eventually, Psimenos lost in excess of $200,000.

In short, Psimenos alleges that, contrary to Hutton's representations, his account was not handled by qualified managers. In 1981, the manager assigned to Psimenos was neither a Hutton employee nor a registered broker. Several times, managers failed to close commodity purchase contracts by sale, with the result that Psimenos was forced to take possession of the commodity at an additional expense for which he was unprepared. Moreover, Hutton did not evaluate the performance of its managers, and did not monitor Psimenos' account as it had represented it would. Contrary to Psimenos' instructions, high risk trades were conducted in his account, resulting in significant losses.

Although most of the fraudulent misrepresentations alleged in the complaint occurred outside the United States, the trading contracts that consummated the transactions were often executed in New York. The issue on appeal is whether that trading in U.S. commodities markets is sufficient to confer subject matter jurisdiction on a federal district court to hear a claim for damages brought by an alien under the CEA.

We find that the district court has jurisdiction to hear Psimenos' claim. The trades Hutton executed on American markets constituted the final act in Hutton's alleged fraud on Psimenos, without which Hutton's employees could not have generated commissions for themselves. Coming as they did as the culminating acts of the fraudulent scheme, such trading could hardly be called "preparatory activity" not subject to review under the anti-fraud provisions of the CEA. *IIT v. Vencap, Ltd.*, 519 F.2d 1001, 1018 (2d Cir. 1975). On the contrary, Hutton's trades in the United States, involving domestic futures contracts, were material acts that directly caused Psimenos' claimed losses.

In construing the reach of jurisdiction under the CEA, courts have analogized to similar problems under the securities laws which have been more extensively litigated. *See, e.g., Mormels v. Girofinance, SA*, 544 F.Supp. 815, 817 n.8 (S.D.N.Y. 1982) ("[s]ecurities cases and principles are used as persuasive aids to interpretation of the CEA"). Several of our decisions have explored the limits of subject matter jurisdiction under the federal securities statutes. Our major consideration concerning transnational transactions is "whether Congress would have wished the precious resources of United States courts and law enforcement agencies to be devoted to them rather than leave the problem to foreign countries." *Bersch v. Drexel Firestone, Inc.*, 519 F.2d 974, 985 (2d Cir.), *cert. denied*, 423 U.S. 1018 (1975). Two tests have emerged, the "effects" test, as announced in *Schoenbaum v. Firstbrook*, 405 F.2d 215 (2d Cir. 1968) (en banc), *cert. denied*, 395 U.S. 906 (1969), and the "conduct" test. Since we find that there is jurisdiction under the latter, we do not need to reach the question whether the effects test provides an independent basis for jurisdiction.

The conduct test does not center its inquiry on whether domestic investors or markets are affected, but on the nature of conduct within the United States as it relates to carrying out the alleged fraudulent scheme, on the theory that Congress did not want "to allow the United States to be used as a base for manufacturing fraudulent security devices for export, even when these are peddled only to foreigners." *Vencap, supra,* 519 F.2d at 1017. This test was originally applied by us in *Leasco Data Processing Equipment Corp. v. Maxwell,* 468 F.2d 1326 (2d Cir. 1972). Plaintiffs, U.S. citizens, alleged fraud surrounding their purchase through British brokers on the London Stock Exchange of a British corporation whose stock was not registered or traded on U.S. exchanges. While we stated that "the adverse effect of the fraudulently induced purchases in England of securities of an English corporation, not traded in an organized American securities market, upon an American corporation," was insufficient to create jurisdiction under *Schoenbaum,* we nevertheless upheld jurisdiction because "substantial misrepresentations were made in the United States." Thus, domestic conduct alone was sufficient to trigger the applicability of the securities laws to a transaction occurring abroad.

We later clarified *Leasco* in *Bersch.* There, the named plaintiff was a citizen of the United States, but the class included thousands of purchasers, mostly foreign, of an international corporation organized under Canadian laws. While the prospectus stated that shares were not being offered in the United States, several U.S. citizens received prospectuses and purchased shares. Among other things, various meetings between the issuer, underwriters, accountants and SEC officials discussing the offering took place in the United States. The opinion linked the relative importance of the necessary conduct within the United States to the citizenship and residence of the purchasers of securities; it pointed out that the anti-fraud provisions of the federal securities laws:

(1) Apply to losses for sales of securities to Americans residing in the United States whether or not acts (or culpable failures to act) of material importance occurred in this country; and

(2) Apply to losses from sales of securities to Americans residing abroad if, but only if, acts of material importance in the United States have significantly contributed thereto; but

(3) Do not apply to losses from sales of securities to foreigners outside the United States unless acts (or culpable failures to act) within the United States directly caused such losses.

Since the acts occurring in the United States in *Bersch* were at most "preparatory," we held that the district court lacked subject matter jurisdiction to hear claims by foreign plaintiffs.

In *IIT v. Vencap,* 519 F.2d 1001 (2d Cir. 1975), decided the same day as *Bersch,* we reiterated our holding that foreign plaintiffs' suits under anti-fraud provisions of the securities laws would be heard only when substantial acts in furtherance of the fraud were committed within the United States:

Our ruling on this basis of jurisdiction is limited to the perpetration of fraudulent acts themselves and does not extend to mere preparatory activities or the failure to prevent fraudulent acts where the bulk of the activity was performed in foreign countries, as in *Bersch*. Admittedly, the distinction is a fine one. But the position we are taking here itself extends the application of the securities laws beyond prior decisions and the line has to be drawn somewhere if the securities laws are not to apply in every instance where something has happened in the United States, however large the gap between the something and a consummated fraud and however negligible the effect in the United States or on its citizens.

We find that under the conduct test, Hutton's activities in the United States in furtherance of the alleged fraud were substantial enough to establish subject matter jurisdiction. First, Hutton's pamphlet, promising continual supervision of highly qualified managers, emanated from Hutton's New York office. This may be considered substantial if, as Psimenos claims, it induced him to open and maintain an account with Hutton. That by itself, however, would not be enough to sustain jurisdiction. Far weightier is the fact that Hutton's agents completed the alleged fraud by trading domestic futures contracts on American commodities exchanges.

Judge Motley construed the language in *Vencap* limiting relevant conduct to "fraudulent acts themselves" to mean that since the trades which took place on U.S. markets were not fraudulent in that they were ordinary business transactions, they were not reviewable conduct. We disagree. *Bersch* reveals that our true concern was that we entertain suits by aliens only where conduct material to the completion of the fraud occurred in the United States. Mere preparatory activities, and conduct far removed from the consummation of the fraud, will not suffice to establish jurisdiction. Only where conduct "within the United States directly caused" the loss will a district court have over suits by foreigners who have lost money through sales abroad. Viewing the conduct test in this light, it is clear that the trading conducted by Hutton on U.S. exchanges should be weighed in determining this court's jurisdiction. Just as Congress did not want the United States to be used as a base for manufacturing fraudulent securities devices, irrespective of the nationality of the victim, *Bersch*, *supra*, neither did it want U.S. commodities markets to be used as a base to consummate schemes concocted abroad, particularly when the perpetrators are agents of American corporations.

Our decision in *ITT v. Cornfeld*, 619 F.2d 909 (2d Cir. 1980), supports our holding in this case. There, an international trust purchased the common stock of one U.S. company and the convertible note of another. We stated there that "we have no difficulty in finding subject matter jurisdiction. ... Apart from the fact these were securities of American corporations, the transactions were fully consummated within the United States." While we stressed that we were not holding that either of these factors was necessary or sufficient condition [sic] for finding jurisdiction, "the presence of both these factors points strongly toward applying the antifraud provisions of our securities laws."113

Both these factors are present in this case. The commodity futures contracts involved are domestic: they are created by domestic exchanges and may lawfully be traded only on those exchanges. CFTC Brief at 7; *see* U.S.C. §61 (1982). ... [T]he commodities futures contracts at issue here present at least as strong a factor in favor of finding jurisdiction as do securities of a U.S. corporation traded in the United States. Since, in this case, trading which consummated the alleged fraud occurred on United States markets, both of the factors that led us to find jurisdiction in *Cornfeld* are satisfied, and subject matter jurisdiction exists to hear suits by foreigners claiming the protection of the anti-fraud provisions of the CEA.

The fact that U.S. commodities markets were used to consummate the alleged fraud here distinguishes *Mormels v. Girofinance, SA,* upon which the district court relied. In that case, Mormels alleged that he and several others opened a commodities trading account in Costa Rica with Girofinance, a Costa Rican corporation that misrepresented itself as Hutton's agent. Plaintiffs claimed that Girofinance converted their funds in Costa Rica, and fled. Judge Weinfeld ruled that no subject matter jurisdiction existed since every fact necessary to complete the fraud, including misrepresentation, delivery of funds, and conversion of funds, occurred in Costa Rica. Thus, no act which directly caused Mormels' loss occurred in the United States; in contrast, in this case, the essential conduct needed to complete the fraudulent scheme, executing contracts on commodities markets, occurred in the United States.

Only one case has addressed the precise fact situation we face here. In *Tamari v. Bache & Co. (Lebanon) S.A.L.,* 547 F.Supp. 309 (N.D. Ill. 1982), [*aff'd,* 730 F.2d 1103 (7th Cir.), *cert. denied,* 469 U.S. 871 (1984)], plaintiffs, Lebanese investors, placed commodities futures orders in Lebanon which were executed in Chicago commodities markets. They alleged that Bache Lebanon114 misrepresented its expertise, gave false market advice, and mismanaged their accounts. They sued both under the CEA and principles of common law fraud. ... We agree with that portion of the Illinois district court's opinion that held that plaintiffs had established jurisdiction under the conduct test. Bache Lebanon's transmission of the plaintiff's order from Beirut to Chicago constituted conduct within the United States that was so important to the scheme as to satisfy *Bersch* and *Vencap.* The court concluded:

---

113. Other courts have gone further in finding subject matter jurisdiction. *See Grunenthal GmbH v. Hotz,* 712 F.2d 421, 425 (9th Cir. 1983) (subject matter jurisdiction found where execution of an agreement involving foreign citizens and foreign securities occurred in the United States); *Continental Grain (Australia) Pty. Ltd. v. Pacific Oilseeds, Inc.,* 592 F.2d 409, 420 (8th Cir. 1979) (jurisdiction upheld on transaction where sole victim was foreign corporation and securities were not traded on any American Exchange where conduct in the United States was "significant with respect to the alleged violation"); *SEC v. Kasser,* 548 F.2d 109 (3d Cir.), *cert. denied,* 431 U.S. 938 (1977) (same).

114. Bache Lebanon was a foreign corporation. Here, defendant is incorporated in the United States. Since our holding is based on the conduct on United States trading markets, the nationality of those executing trades is immaterial.

Bache Lebanon's wiring of the Tamaris' orders to Chicago and the execution of those orders on the Chicago exchanges were the final steps in the alleged scheme. And ... the "lawfulness" of Bache Delaware's execution of those orders ... does not cure any prior fraud in Bache Lebanon's solicitation from the Tamaris, nor does it prevent the execution of the orders from being a necessary and foreseeable step in a scheme to defraud, and thus substantial conduct within the United States. Hutton's conduct here was not only "substantial"; it also directly caused Psimenos' loss, thus satisfying *Bersch.*

Trading activities on U.S. commodities markets were significant acts without which Psimenos' losses could not have occurred, and are sufficient to establish jurisdiction. As the Ninth Circuit recently held in *Grunenthal GmbH v. Hotz*, 712 F.2d 421, 425 (9th Cir. 1983), "to hold otherwise could make it convenient for foreign citizens and corporations to use this country ... to further fraudulent securities schemes."

Notes on Psimenos

1. *No statutory language defining extraterritorial reach of securities laws.* The Commodities Exchange Act contains no statutory language expressly suggesting extraterritorial application. The same is true of the Securities Exchange Act of 1934, 15 U.S.C. §78j (1982), and the Securities Act of 1933, 15 U.S.C. §§77l(2) and 77g (1982). Moreover, most courts have fairly candidly admitted that Congress probably didn't think about the extraterritorial reach of the securities laws: "We freely acknowledge that if we were asked to point to language in the statutes, or even in the legislative history, that compelled these conclusions, we would be unable to respond." *Bersch v. Drexel Firestone, Inc.*, 519 F.2d 974, 993 (2d Cir. 1975) (Friendly, J.). *See also Zoelsch v. Arthur Andersen & Co.*, 824 F.2d 27, 29-30 (D.C. Cir. 1987) ("Fifty years ago, Congress did not consider how far American courts should have jurisdiction to decide cases involving predominantly foreign securities transactions with some link to the United States.") (Bork, J.). *But see* Sachs, *The International Reach of Rule 10b-5: The Myth of Congressional Silence*, 28 Colum. J. Trans. L. 677 (1990).

2. *Effect of* Aramco *on extraterritorial reach of federal securities laws.* As discussed above, it has frequently been held that U.S. courts will confine the application of federal statutes to conduct within U.S. territory unless Congress indicates otherwise. *See EEOC v. Aramco*, 499 U.S. 244 (1991); *supra* pp. 546-50, 563-70.

How can the statements, discussed above, that the federal securities laws simply do not address issues of geographic reach be squared with *Aramco's* territoriality presumption? If Congress did not clearly state that the securities law applied extraterritorially, then how can they be under *Aramco?* Consider the following excerpt from a recent Seventh Circuit decision involving the CEA:

> Finding nothing in the Act or its legislative history to indicate that Congress did not intend the CEA to apply to foreign agents, but recognizing there also is no direct evidence that Congress intended such application, we believe it is appropriate to rely on the "conduct" and "effects" tests in discerning whether subject matter jurisdiction exists over the dispute. As a matter of foreign relations law, the conduct and effects principles indicate whether the United States has jurisdiction to prescribe a rule that attaches legal consequences to conduct occurring in the United States, or to conduct occurring outside the United States that causes effects within the United States. *See Restatement (Second) Foreign Relations Law* §§17 and 18 (1965). ... When the question instead is whether Congress intended a statute to have extraterritorial application, the analysis of legislative intent becomes intertwined with these principles of foreign relations law. If extraterritorial application would have no impact on domestic conditions, it is presumed that Congress did not intend the statute to apply outside the territory, unless a contrary intent appears. *Foley Bros., Inc. v. Filardo.* Reliance on this presumption is misplaced, however, when

the conduct under scrutiny has not occurred wholly outside the United States, or ... could otherwise affect domestic conditions. In these cases, courts have looked to the nature of the conduct or effects in the United States to determine whether extraterritorial application would be consistent with the purposes underlying the statute.

Tamari v. Bache & Co. (Lebanon), 730 F.2d 1103, 1107 & n.11 (7th Cir.), *cert. denied*, 469 U.S. 871 (1984). Is this rationale consistent with *Aramco*? What do you make of the court's suggestion that reliance on the territoriality presumption is "misplaced" when foreign conduct could "affect domestic conditions"?

3. *Significance of parties' nationality.* As discussed previously, *supra* p. 584, U.S. courts frequently consider the parties' nationality in determining whether extraterritorial application of the antitrust laws is appropriate. What role should nationality play in securities cases?

(a) *Plaintiff's nationality.* Existing extraterritoriality standards in the securities law field place considerable weight on the *plaintiff's* nationality, affording greater U.S. securities law protections for U.S. citizens than for foreign citizens. *See Bersch v. Drexel Firestone, Inc.*, 519 F.2d 974 (2d Cir.), *cert. denied*, 423 U.S. 1018 (1975); *Restatement (Third) Foreign Relations Law* §416 (1987). This disparate treatment of U.S. and foreign plaintiffs is rationalized on the grounds of legislative intent: Congress presumably cared more about protecting Americans than foreigners.

Compare the role of the plaintiff's nationality in the antitrust context. In addition, recall the general rejection of the passive personality doctrine as a jurisdictional base under international law. *See supra* pp. 507-08. Should international law permit the plaintiff's U.S. nationality to play such a significant role in the extraterritorial reach of the securities laws?

(b) *Defendant's nationality.* There is less evidence of a distinction in extraterritoriality cases between U.S. and foreign securities law *defendants*. For example, what if *Psimenos* had involved actions by a *foreign* commodities trader that entered into contracts on a U.S. exchange? *See Psimenos*, 722 F.2d at 1047 n.7, indicating that U.S. jurisdiction would still exist. *Compare Psimenos*, 722 F.2d at 1046 ("particularly when the perpetrators are agents of American corporations"). What if the foreign trader had relied on an unaffiliated U.S. commodities trader to trade on U.S. exchanges? Would *Psimenos* or *Girofinance* control? Should U.S. companies be more readily subject to the extraterritorial application of U.S. securities laws than foreign companies? *See Restatement (Third) Foreign Relations Law* §416(2)(c) (1987).

4. *Fraud consummated in the United States. Psimenos* held that U.S. law was applicable extraterritorially because foreign transactions were consummated (albeit legally) on a U.S. exchange. Similarly, in *Zoelsch v. Arthur Andersen & Co.*, 824 F.2d 27, 33 n.4 (D.C. Cir. 1987), Judge Bork made it clear that the securities laws would apply "whenever any individual is defrauded in this country, regardless of whether the offer originates somewhere else, for the actual consummation of securities fraud in the United States in and of itself would constitute domestic conduct that satisfies all the elements of liability." *See also Alfadda v. Fenn*, 935 F.2d 475, 478 (2d Cir. 1991), *cert. denied*, 502 U.S. 1005 (1991).

5. *Substantial conduct in the United States.* Other cases have upheld application of the securities laws based on U.S. conduct related to trades on securities or commodities exchanges outside the United States. Lower courts have adopted differing formulae defining the showing for U.S. jurisdiction under the "conduct test." *E.g., Itoba Ltd. v. Lep Group plc*, 54 F.3d 118 (2d Cir. 1995) (suggesting that an "admixture" of the conduct and the effects test is appropriate); *Zoelsch v. Arthur Andersen & Co.*, 824 F.2d 27 (D.C. Cir. 1987) (fraudulent conduct in the U.S. must "directly cause" harm); *ITT v. Cornfeld*, 619 F.2d 909 (2d Cir. 1980); *Grunenthal GmbH v. Hotz*, 712 F.2d 421 (9th Cir. 1983); *SEC v. Kasser*, 548 F.2d 109 (3d Cir.) ("some activity designed to further a fraudulent scheme occurs in this country"), *cert. denied*, 431 U.S. 938 (1977).

6. *"Merely preparatory" conduct.* In evaluating the jurisdictional significance of U.S. conduct, courts have suggested that "merely preparatory" conduct within the United States will not support U.S. jurisdiction under the securities laws. *See Bersch v. Drexel Firestone, Inc.*, 519 F.2d 974 (2d Cir.), *cert. denied*, 423 U.S. 1018 (1975); *Fidenas AG v. Compagnie Internationale etc*, 606 F.2d 5 (2d Cir. 1979); *IIT v. Vencap, Ltd.*, 519 F.2d 1001 (2d Cir. 1975); *Kaufman v. Campeau Corp.*, 744 F.Supp. 808 (S.D. Ohio 1990) (complaint failed to allege that the United States was used as a "base" for fraud); *Department of Economic Development v. Arthur Andersen & Co.*, 683 F.Supp. 1463 (S.D.N.Y. 1988); *Koal Indus. Corp. v. Asland SA*, 808 F.Supp. 1143, 1153-55 (S.D.N.Y. 1992). Note that *Psimenos* concluded that E.F. Hutton's preparation of general advertising materials in the U.S. would not have constituted sufficient conduct to support jurisdiction.

7. *Effects test in the securities law context.* In addition to U.S. "conduct" as a basis for application of the federal securities laws, U.S. courts have also relied on an "effects" doctrine, similar to that in the antitrust context. For example, the Second Circuit has indicated that the securities laws would apply "if a defendant, even though acting solely abroad, had defrauded investors in the United States by mailing false prospectuses into this country." *Bersch v. Drexel Firestone, Inc.*, 519 F.2d 974, 989 (2d Cir.), *cert. denied*, 423 U.S. 1018 (1975). *See also Doll v. James Martin Assoc. (Holdings) Ltd.*, 600 F.Supp. 510, 518-20 (E.D. Mich. 1984). Similarly, where tender offer documents are provided by a foreign company to foreign nominees of U.S. shareholders, who are required by foreign law to transmit the documents to the shareholders, and in fact do so, then effects jurisdiction has been upheld. *Consolidated Gold Fields plc v. Minorco, SA*, 871 F.2d 252 (2d Cir. 1989). Greater controversy surrounds the import of more generalized economic effects, such as adversely affecting investor confidence in the United States. *Bersch*, 519 F.2d at 988. *See Itoba Ltd. v. Lep Group plc*, 54 F.3d 118 (2d Cir. 1995); *Kaufman v. Campeau*, 744 F.Supp. 808 (S.D. Ohio 1990).

8. *Differing jurisdictional reach of the federal securities laws' registration/reporting requirements and antifraud rules.* The federal securities laws contain two basic types of provisions: (a) registration or reporting obligations that require persons to file statements with U.S. regulatory agencies containing particular information; and (b) antifraud rules that prohibit certain mistatements relating to securities transaction. As a general matter, although the relevant jurisdictional grants are identical, it is well-established that the antifraud rules of the securities laws have greater extraterritorial reach than the registration requirements. *Consolidated Gold Fields plc v. Minorco, SA*, 871 F.2d 252 (2d Cir. 1989) ("the antifraud provisions of American securities laws have broader extraterritorial reach than American filing requirements"); *Bersch v. Drexel Firestone, Inc.*, 519 F.2d 974, 986 (2d Cir.), *cert. denied*, 423 U.S. 1018 (1975); *Restatement (Third) Foreign Relations Law* §416, comment a (1987). Why is that?

9. *Effect of U.S. plaintiff's efforts to avoid U.S. securities laws.* U.S. investors not infrequently take steps to ensure that the registration requirements of the U.S. securities law do not apply to their transactions. In these circumstances, should the antifraud provisions of the securities laws apply? Although the antifraud provisions of the securities law have broader extraterritorial reach than the registration requirements, in *MGC, Inc. v. Great Western Energy Corp.*, 896 F.2d 170 (5th Cir. 1990), the Court of Appeals held that a U.S. corporation that deliberately established a foreign subsidiary in order to purchase securities in an overseas offering that was closed to U.S. purchasers could not claim that the U.S. securities laws were violated in the offering.

10. *Low incidence of foreign objections to extraterritorial application of U.S. securities laws.* There have been relatively few cases of foreign governmental objections to the extraterritorial application of the U.S. securities laws. This is particularly true when compared with the vigorous protests in the antitrust context. What explains the differences between foreign reactions in the two contexts? It has been suggested that there are fewer substantive differences between U.S. and foreign antifraud protections than between U.S. and foreign competition laws, although this is a matter of degree.

11. *Greater predictability of rules governing extraterritorial application of U.S. securities law.* Compare the rules governing the extraterritorial application of the securities laws with *Hartford Fire* and *Timberlane*. Which rules are more precise and predictable?

B. Choice of Law Applicable to Torts

Largely distinct from rules of construction for federal statutes, U.S. courts and commentators have developed choice of law rules governing the application of state (and other) tort laws in multi-jurisdictional cases.[115] These rules have traditionally been considered in conflict of law treatises and courses,[116] and in the *First* and *Second Restatement of Conflict of Laws*. They have not been considered in the *Second* and *Third Restatements of Foreign Relations Law*.

The choice of law rules applicable to torts in the United States have undergone very substantial evolution during the past century. As described below, the outcome of that evolution remains uncertain, and different U.S. jurisdictions take significantly differing approaches to determining the law applicable to torts.[117] This section examines these various approaches. It focuses principally on state (as opposed to federal) choice of law rules.[118] Because of the uncertainty of prevailing contemporary choice of law rules, and because of the continuing vitality of traditional rules, this section devotes particular attention to historic doctrine and developments.

1. Traditional Approach: Territoriality and Vested Rights

a. The Territorial Rule: "Place of the Wrong"

During the 19th and early 20th centuries, the American approach to the choice of law applicable to torts was largely territorial, paralleling approaches to judicial jurisdiction and the extraterritorial application of federal laws.[119] Relying on principles of territorial sovereignty, 19th century American courts and commentators generally looked to the law of the place of the wrong (or *lex loci delicti commissi*).[120] This approach rested in substantial part on Joseph Story's territorial analysis of legislative jurisdiction, which is discussed above.[121]

In the early 20th century, Story's thinking provided the foundation for another highly-influential American choice of law treatise — Joseph Beale's *Treatise on the*

---

115. *See supra* p. 545 n.1.

116. Commentary on the choice of law applicable to torts includes, *e.g.*, R. Weintraub, *Commentary on the Conflict of Laws* 280-361 (3d ed. 1986); Juenger, *Choice of Law in Interstate Torts*, 118 U. Pa. L. Rev. 202 (1969); Kuhne, *Choice of Law in Product Liability*, 60 Calif. L. Rev. 1 (1972); Morris, *The Proper Law of a Tort*, 64 Harv. L. Rev. 881 (1951); Reese, *American Trends in Private International Law: Academic and Judicial Manipulation of Choice of Law Rules in Tort Cases*, 33 Vand. L. Rev. 717 (1980); Rheinstein, *The Place of Wrong: A Study in the Method of the Case Law*, 19 Tul. L. Rev. 4 (1944).

117. *See infra* pp. 631-52.

118. As discussed below, the *Erie* doctrine generally treats choice of law questions as "substantive" issues governed by state law. *See infra* pp. 681-84.

119. *See supra* pp. 70-73 & 546-50.

120. *E.g.*, H. Goodrich, *Conflict of Laws* 188 (1927) ("The general rule is that the law governing the creation and extent of tort liability is that of the place where the tort was committed."); *Restatement (First) Conflict of Laws* §377 (1934); *American Banana Co. v. United Fruit Co.*, 213 U.S. 347 (1909); *Slater v. Mexican National R. Co.*, 194 U.S. 120 (1904).

121. *See supra* pp. 493-97 & 546-50.

Conflict of Laws.[122] Beale championed the "vested rights" doctrine, according to which, "[a] right having been created by the appropriate law, the recognition of its existence should follow everywhere. Thus, an act valid where done cannot be called in question anywhere."[123] Beale served as the reporter for the *Restatement (First) Conflict of Laws*, which articulated his vested rights theory.[124] Published in 1934, the Restatement included numerous rules based on the traditional 19th century territoriality analysis, including the rule that torts were governed by the law of the "place of the wrong."[125]

The rationale for applying the law of the place of the wrong was based firmly on the territoriality doctrine. The "vested rights" theory rested on the premise that no state's laws could apply outside that state's territory, but that commission of a tort within one state gave rise to a "vested right," that other states would generally recognize.[126] Beale explained the doctrine as follows:

> It is impossible for a plaintiff to recover in tort unless he has been given by some law a cause of action in tort; and this cause of action can be given only by the law of the place where the tort was committed. ... That is the place where the injurious event occurs, and its law is the law therefore which applies to it.[127]

The *First Restatement*'s rules required determining the "place of the wrong," which Beale defined as the place where the last event necessary to make the tort-feasor liable occurred.[128] Until the second half of this century, most American courts followed the *First Restatement's* "place of the last event" rule in determining the "place of the wrong." Once selected, this law governed virtually all issues relating to a tort, including whether the defendant's conduct was tortious, causation, limitations upon the defendant's liability, vicarious liability, contribution, indemnity, and defenses to liability.[129]

b. Selected Materials on the Traditional "Place of Wrong" Rule

Excerpted below are materials that illustrate the traditional "place of wrong"

---

122. Beale developed the "vested rights" theory of conflict of laws, which rested on principles of territorial sovereignty. *See* J. Beale, *A Selection of Cases on The Conflict of Laws* (1902); J. Beale, *Treatise on the Conflict of Laws* 1289 (1935) ("The existence and nature of a cause of action ... is governed by the law of the place [of the] wrongful act or omission."); Beale, *The Jurisdiction of A Sovereign State*, 36 Harv. L. Rev. 241 (1923).

123. J. Beale, *Cases on the Conflict of Laws* 517 (1901).

124. *Restatement (First) Conflict of Laws* (1934).

125. *Restatement (First) Conflict of Laws* §§377 & 378 (1934).

126. *See* 3 J. Beale, *Treatise on the Conflict of Laws* 1964-65 (1935).

127. 3 J. Beale, *Treatise on the Conflict of Laws* 1964-65 (1935).

128. *Restatement (First) Conflict of Laws* §378 (1934); *Alabama Great Southern RR v. Carroll*, 11 So. 803 (Ala. 1892); H. Goodrich, *Conflict of Laws* 191 (1927) ("The tort, if any, [is] deemed to have been committed where the injury of which the plaintiff complains was inflicted, not where the defendant's acts were done."); Rheinstein, *The Place of Wrong: A Study in the Method of the Case Law*, 19 Tul. L. Rev. 4 (1944).

129. *Restatement (First) Conflict of Laws* §§377, 378, 379, 380, 383, 385, 387 & 388 (1934).

rule. Excerpts from Joseph Story's *Commentaries* state the territoriality doctrine that provided the basic foundation for traditional American choice of law rules; they also set forth the doctrine of international comity as the explanation for why one state will apply the tort laws of another state. The *First Restatement*, also excerpted below, provided a comprehensive set of choice of law rules based on these territorial principles. Finally, the Alabama Supreme Court's decision in *Alabama Great Southern Railroad Co. v. Carroll* is an example of application of the place of the wrong rule.

J. STORY, COMMENTARIES ON THE CONFLICT OF LAWS

[*§§18, 20 & 23, excerpted above at pp. 501-02*]
§§29, 32, 33, 35, 38 (2d ed. 1841)

§29. [Story repeated Huber's three maxims, including:] The third [maxim articulated by Huber] is, that the rules of every empire from comity admit, that the laws of every people, in force within its own limits, ought to have the same force every where, so far as they do not prejudice the powers or rights of other governments, or of their citizens. "From this," [Huber] adds, "it appears, that this matter is to be determined not simply by the civil laws, but by the convenience and tacit consent of different people ..."

§32. It is difficult to conceive, upon what ground a claim can be rested, to give to any municipal laws an extra-territorial effect, when those laws are prejudicial to the rights of other nations, or to those of their subjects. It would at once annihilate the sovereignty and equality of every nation, which should be called upon to recognize and enforce them; or compel it to desert its own proper interest and duty to its own subjects in favor of strangers, who were regardless of both. A claim, so naked of any principle or just authority to support it, is wholly inadmissible.

§33. It has been thought by some jurists, that the term "comity" is not sufficiently expressive of the obligation of nations to give effect to foreign laws, when they are not prejudicial to their own rights and interests. And it has been suggested, that the doctrine rests on a deeper foundation; that it is not so much a matter of comity, or courtesy, as a matter of paramount moral duty. Now, assuming, that such a moral duty does exist, it is clearly one of imperfect obligation, like that of beneficence, humanity, and charity. Every nation must be the final judge for itself, not only of the nature and extent of the duty, but of the occasions, on which its exercise may be justly demanded. And, certainly, there can be no pretence to say, that any foreign nation has a right to require the full recognition and execution of its own laws in other territories, when those laws are deemed oppressive or injurious to the rights or interests of the inhabitants of the latter, or when their moral character is questionable, or their provisions are impolitic or unjust. ...

§35. The true foundation, on which the administration of international law must rest, is, that the rules, which are to govern, are those, which arise from mutual interest and utility, from a sense of the inconveniences, which would result from a contrary doctrine, and from a sort of moral necessity to do justice, in order that justice may be done to us in return. ...

§38. There is, then, not only no impropriety in the use of the phrase, "comity of nations," but it is the most appropriate phrase to express the true foundation and extent of the obligation of the laws of one nation within the territories of another. It is derived altogether from the voluntary consent of the latter; and is inadmissible, when it is contrary to its own policy, or prejudicial to its interests. In the silence of any positive rule, affirming, or denying, or restraining the operation of foreign laws, courts of justice presume the tacit adoption of them by their own government, unless they are repugnant to its policy, or prejudicial to its interests. It is not the comity of the courts, but the comity of the nation, which is administered, and ascertained in the same way, and guided by the same reasoning, by which all other principles of municipal law are ascertained and guided. ...

RESTATEMENT (FIRST) CONFLICT OF LAWS (1934)

§§1, 6, 377 & 378

§1. (1) No state can make a law which by its own force is operative in another state; the only law in force in the sovereign state is its own law, but by the law of each state rights, or other interests in that state may, in certain cases, depend upon the law in force in some other state or states.

(2) That part of the law of each state which determines whether in dealing with a legal situation the law of some other state will be recognized, be given effect or be applied is called the Conflict of Laws.

§6. The rules of Conflict of Laws of a state are not affected by the attitude of another state toward rights or other interests created in the former state.

§377. The place of wrong is in the state where the last event necessary to make an actor liable for an alleged tort takes place.

§378. The law of the place of wrong determines whether a person has sustained a legal injury.

ALABAMA GREAT SOUTHERN RAILROAD CO. v. CARROLL

11 So. 803 (Ala. 1892)

McCLELLAN, JUSTICE. [The plaintiff was an Alabama domiciliary who was hired as a brakeman by the defendant, a railroad incorporated in Alabama. The employment contract was executed in Alabama. Negligence by other employees of the defendant in coupling cars in Alabama, on a train headed for Mississippi, caused the coupling to break. The accident occurred in Mississippi and injured the plaintiff. An Alabama employer's liability act, Alabama Code §2590 (1885), arguably made the defendant liable for the plaintiff's injury. It provided: "When a personal injury is received by a servant ... in the service ... of the master ... the master is liable to answer in damages ... as if he were a stranger ... [w]here the injury is caused by reason of the negligence of any person in the service of the master. ..." In Mississippi, a fellow-servant rule would exculpate the railroad from liability.] ...

[W]e do not understand appellee's counsel even to deny either the proposition or its application to this case, — that there can be no recovery in one state for injuries to the person sustained in another, unless the infliction of the injuries is actionable under the law of the state in which they were received. Certainly this is the well-established rule of law . ... The question is as to duty operating effectually at the place where its alleged failure caused harm to result. ... It is admitted, or at least cannot be denied, that negligence of duty unproductive of damnifying results will not authorize or support a recovery. Up to the time this train passed out of Alabama no injury had resulted. For all that occurred in Alabama, therefore, no cause of action whatever arose. The fact which created the right to sue, — the injury, — without which confessedly no action would lie anywhere, transpired in the state of Mississippi. It was in that state, therefore, necessarily that the cause of action, if any, arose; and whether a cause of action arose and existed at all, or not, must in all reason be determined by the law which obtained at the time and place when and where the fact which is relied on to justify a recovery transpired. Section 2590 of the Code of Alabama had no efficacy beyond the lines of Alabama. It cannot be allowed to operate upon facts occurring in another state, so as to evolve out of them rights and liabilities which do not exist under the law of that state, which is of course paramount in the premises. Where the facts occur in Alabama, and a liability becomes fixed in Alabama, it may be enforced in another state having like enactments, or whose policy is not opposed to the spirit of such enactments; but this is quite a different matter. This is but enforcing the statute upon facts to which it is applicable, all of which occurred within the territory for the government of which it was enacted. Section 2590 of the Code, in other words, is to be interpreted in light of universally recognized principles of private, international or interstate law, as if its operation had been expressly limited to this state, and as if its first line read as follows: "When a personal injury is received in Alabama by a servant or employee," etc. The negligent infliction of an injury here, under statutory circumstances, creates a right of action here, which, being transitory, may be enforced in any other state or country the comity of which admits of it; but for an injury inflicted elsewhere than in Alabama our statute gives no right of recovery, and the aggrieved party must look to the local law to ascertain what his rights are. Under that law this plaintiff had no cause of action. ... [A]n analogy ... is found in that well-established doctrine of criminal law that where the unlawful act is committed in one ... state, and takes effect ... in another ... state, the crime is deemed to have been committed and is punished in that ... state in which the result is manifested, and not where the act was committed. ...

[The plaintiff argued that he had entered into a contract in Alabama with the defendant railroad, providing for employment both in Alabama and elsewhere, and that this Alabama contract should be construed to incorporate the terms of the Alabama legislation, thereby enabling that legislation to be applied outside of

Alabama.] [T]he duties and liabilities incident to the relation between the plaintiff and the defendant, ... are not imposed by, and do not rest in or spring from, the contract between the parties. ... The whole argument is at fault. The only true doctrine is that each sovereignty, state or nation, has the exclusive power to finally determine and declare what act or omissions in the conduct of one to another ... shall impose a liability in damages for the consequent injury, and the courts of no other sovereignty can impute a damnifying quality to an act or omission which afforded no cause of action where it transpired. [The court quoted from *Whitford v. Railroad Co.*, 23 N.Y. 465, where a New York court refused to apply New York law to a deceased passenger's claim against a New York railroad, for an accident occurring in New Grenada:]

> Suppose the government of New Grenada to have enacted that the proprietors of a railroad company should not be responsible for the negligence of its servants, provided there was no want of due care in selecting them, it could not be pretended that its will could be set at naught by prosecuting the corporation in the courts of another state, where the law was different. ... The true theory is that no suit whatever respecting this injury could be sustained in the courts of this state, except pursuant to the law of international comity. By that law, foreign contracts and foreign transactions, out of which liabilities have arisen, may be prosecuted in our tribunals by the implied assent of the government of this state; but in all such cases we administer the foreign law as from the proofs we find it to be, or as without proofs we presume it to be. ...

For the error in refusing to instruct the jury to find for the defendant ... the judgment is reversed. ...

Notes on Story's Commentaries, First Restatement, and Carroll

1. *Choice of law rules subject to forum's legislation.* Section 2590 of the Alabama Code was silent about the territory in which conduct had to occur in order for the legislation to apply, and about the domicile or citizenship of persons entitled to claim protection under the law. Thus, courts were left to answer these questions, and *Carroll* interpreted §2590 as if it read: "When a personal injury is received in Alabama by a servant or employee. ..." Suppose that the actual language of the section had instead read: "When a personal injury is received, anywhere in the world, by a servant or employee of a railroad that does business in Alabama, which servant or employee is domiciled in Alabama and has signed a contract of employment in Alabama..." Putting aside constitutional considerations, would *Carroll* have required any lengthy analysis of choice of law precedents or international law? Would the decision have required considering anything beyond the plain language of §2590?

Note Story's caveat that choice of law "rules" apply in the "silence of any positive rule, affirming, or denying, or restraining the operation of foreign laws." J. Story, *Commentaries on the Conflict of Laws* §38 (2d ed. 1841). The same is true today. *Restatement (Second) Conflict of Laws* §6(1) (1971). Compare the interpretation of federal statutes. *See supra* pp. 510-11 & 570-76.

2. *Choice of law decisions as exercises in statutory construction.* What is the function of choice of law rules? Is it something more than an effort to ascertain unexpressed legislative intent (in the case of statutory claims) and the proper reach of judicial rules (in the case of common law rules)? Like many choice of law decisions, *Carroll* was ultimately a case concerning the interpretation of §2590. Note the court's statement that §2590 "must be interpreted in light of universally recognized principles of private, international or interstate law." Compare this choice of law approach with the role of the territoriality presumption (and other canons of construction like the international law presumption) in interpreting federal statutes.

See supra pp. 546-50, 570-76, 582-83 & 591-94. Is there any difference between the two efforts to decide when American law applies in international cases?

3. *Why should a court ever decline to apply "its" law?* Why should a U.S. court *ever* decline to apply U.S. law? Note Story's observation that it would "annihilate the sovereignty and equality" of states if they were compelled to apply foreign law. In *Carroll,* why shouldn't Alabama courts have applied Alabama law to the claim by Mr. Carroll? What purposes are served when a court refuses to apply the law that the local legislature has enacted? Recall the explanation in *Lauritzen* of international choice of law rules in the maritime context and Story's *Commentaries. See supra* pp. 546-50 & 574. When a U.S. court refuses to apply U.S. law, what law does it apply? What substantive law was applicable in *Carroll?*

4. *Reasons advanced for applying foreign law.* Different explanations have been advanced for why foreign law, instead of the forum's law, should be applied in certain international or interstate cases. These are reasons that courts may, as a general matter, presume to have motivated a legislature.

(a) *Territorial sovereignty and international law.* Consider the explanation advanced in *Carroll* for the court's refusal to apply the forum's laws. Citing "private international" law, *Carroll* relies on the "only true doctrine," that "each sovereignty, state or nation, has the exclusive power to finally determine and declare what act ... shall impose a liability in damages for the consequent injury, and the courts of no other sovereignty can impute a damnifying quality to an act or omission which afforded no cause of action where it transpired." Similarly, as described above, Story reasoned that "no state or nation can, by its laws, directly affect, or bind property out of its own territory, or bind persons not resident therein ... *it would be wholly incompatible with the equality and exclusiveness of the sovereignty of all nations, that any one nation should be at liberty to regulate either persons or things not within its own territory.*" J. Story, *Commentaries on the Conflict of Laws* §§18, 20 (2d ed. 1841) (emphasis added).

Is this a persuasive rationale? Consider Story's first and second maxims. Does the first maxim — territorial sovereignty — in fact dictate the second maxim — that no state's laws may apply within foreign territory? Developing the *Whitford* case, described in *Carroll,* how does it infringe New Grenada's sovereignty for U.S. law to be applied to conduct causing injury in New Grenada? Suppose that a Singapore court applies Singapore libel law to statements made in the New York Times, distributed in the United States. Does that infringe U.S. sovereignty?

(b) *International comity and reciprocity.* Why should U.S. courts care about the sovereignty of New Grenada? Is it not true that U.S. courts are established by the United States, to further U.S. policies for the benefit of U.S. citizens? Why should U.S. courts pay the slightest attention to foreign law or sovereignty? Consider the following observation by Waechter, a prominent 19th century Continental commentator:

> The judge's task is to give effect to the law in case of a dispute and of resistance. What law shall he effectuate? Certainly only the law laid down or otherwise recognized by the state. This comes from the nature of the positive law and from the relation of the judge to the positive laws whose mere instrument he should be. ... Waechter, *"On the Collision of Private Laws of Different States"*, 13 Am. J. Comp. L. 417, 421 (1964) (translation by Nadelmann).

One reason that U.S. courts should respect the sovereignty of foreign states, and international law, is to increase the prospects that foreign states will respect U.S. sovereignty. Simply put, U.S. courts should respect the territorial sovereignty of New Grenada, because it will encourage New Grenada courts to respect U.S. sovereignty. Note the reliance in §35 of Story's *Commentaries* on "mutual interest and utility" and the "moral necessity to do justice, in order that justice may be done to us in return." Compare also the rationale in *Lauritzen, supra* p. 574.

Should U.S. courts only respect the sovereignty of foreign states — and refrain from applying U.S. law to conduct within foreign states — that demonstrate that they will act reciprocally? Is that position not consistent with the rationale that Story articulates? *Compare Restatement (First) Conflict of Laws* §6 (1934).

(c) *Predictability.* Territorial approaches to choice of law issues are also justified as necessary to achieve predictability. Joseph Beale wrote: "International trade could not be carried on as has now become necessary unless the trader could be assured that he would not be placed absolutely at the mercy of the vagaries or unknown requirements of the local law, but would find a well-established body of law to protect his rights." 1 J. Beale, *Treatise on the Conflict of Laws* 4 (1935). Are the *First Restatement's* choice of law rules actually able to produce predictable results? Consider the outcome in *Carroll.* Why is predictability so important? Doesn't predictability depend upon all nations (and states) adopting identical choice of law rules? Would even that provide predictability? Suppose the same substantive rules are applied by a lay jury and a career judge.

(d) *Fairness.* Territorial choice of law rules were also justified on fairness grounds. Justice Holmes wrote in *American Banana:* "For [a] jurisdiction, if it should happen to lay hold of the actor, to treat him according to its own notions rather than those of the place where he did the acts ... would be unjust." 213 U.S. at 356. Compare the similar reasoning in due process decisions dealing with judicial and legislative jurisdiction. *See supra* pp. 517-18, 524 & 535-37.

If one lives and acts exclusively within one state, and if the consequences of one's acts are confined solely to residents of that state, within that state, it would be surprising to find that another state's laws applied. But few cases involve such hermetically-sealed conduct. Where multistate conduct is involved, do private parties expect that their acts will be subject only to the law of the place they act? Moreover, consider what law the railroad defendant in *Carroll* would have thought applicable to conduct by its employees in Alabama. Is the "last event" rule of *Carroll* and the *First Restatement* consistent with either *American Banana* or the goal of fairness? More fundamentally, aren't expectations merely a reflection of the law. If territorial choice of law rules prevail, then parties will expect to be judged according to the law of the place where they act; if other rules prevail, expectations will be different.

(e) *Vested rights.* The *First Restatement's* choice of law rules purported not to rely directly on international law limits on jurisdiction (which were specifically distinguished, *see infra* pp. 623) or on international comity (*see Restatement (First) Conflict of Laws* §6 (1934)). Rather the Restatement relied on a theory of "vested rights," which provided for the international recognition of rights that "vested" under the laws of particular sovereignties. In a classic explanation of the vested rights doctrine, Justice Holmes wrote:

> The theory of the foreign suit is that although the act complained of was subject to no law having force in the forum, it gave rise to an obligation, an *obligatio* which like other obligations follows the person, and may be enforced wherever the person may be found. But as the only source of this obligation is the law of the place of the act, it follows that that law determines not merely the existence of the obligation, but equally determines the extent.

Slater v. Mexican National RR Co., 194 U.S. 120, 126 (1904). Is this rationale persuasive? Does it make it easier or harder to defend territorial choice of law rules?

(f) *Uniformity.* The *First Restatement's* rules (like most other choice of law rules) seek to ensure that different jurisdictions will apply the same substantive law to the same dispute. This reduces the risk of "forum shopping," and accords with general fairness expectations. How can uniformity be achieved if different nations (and states) apply different choice of law rules?

5. *Distinction between international limits on legislative jurisdiction and national choice of law rules.* Read §§1 and 65 of the *First Restatement,* together with comment b to §65. *See supra* p. 502. There is a fundamental distinction between: (a) the limits that international law imposes on a nation's exercise of legislative jurisdiction; and (b) the decisions that a nation makes whether to make use of its rights under international law to assert legislative jurisdiction. As comment b to §65 makes clear, international law will frequently permit two (or more) states to assert legislative jurisdiction over the same conduct or transaction. *See supra* p. 508. In these circumstances, national choice of law rules determine whether a nation will apply its laws to conduct that it could properly regulate under international law.

6. *What does "territoriality" mean?* Does acceptance of Story's territorial view of national sovereignty, taken alone, solve anything except simple cases where all relevant conduct, effects, and parties are located within one state's territory? Or does accepting the territoriality doctrine merely present the question of what thing or "connecting factors" must be localized within a state's territory? Recall *American Banana,* where it was assumed that "territoriality" meant the application of the laws where the allegedly wrongful conduct occurred. *See supra* pp. 552-55. Compare *Pennoyer,* where territoriality meant the service of process within a state's borders. *See supra* pp. 70-73. What connecting factor does *Carroll* use? How are the purposes of the territoriality doctrine advanced by each of the connecting factors described above?

7. *The "place of the wrong" and the "last event" rules of the First Restatement.* Do the *First Restatement's* "place of the wrong" and "last event" rules provide constructive clarification of the territoriality doctrine?

(a) *The "last event" rule.* Section 377 of the *First Restatement* and *Carroll* provide for application of the tort law of the place where "the last event necessary to make an actor liable for an alleged tort takes place." Consider what this "last event" rule meant, in practical terms, in *Carroll.* Where did the negligent conduct that killed Mr. Carroll happen — Alabama or Tennessee? Why didn't Alabama law apply?

(b) *Does the "last event" rule protect territorial sovereignty.* Consider whether the "last event" rule furthers the policies — set forth above — supporting a territorial approach to choice of law issues. Does the application of Mississippi's law to Mr. Carroll's tort claims protect Mississippi's sovereignty? Does it impair Alabama's sovereignty? If one wanted to discourage negligent operation of railroads, without imposing undue costs upon railroad operators, would one seek to do that in the place where the railroad's allegedly culpable conduct occurs, or where the effects of that conduct occur, or in both places? Suppose that, in *Carroll*, the allegedly negligent conduct by Carroll's co-workers occurred in Mississippi, rather than in Alabama, but he had been killed in Alabama. Would the Alabama legislature have wanted Alabama law to apply to Mr. Carroll's tort claim in that case?

` (c). *Consistency of "last event" rule with international law. Carroll* and §377 arguably adopt what amounts to àn "effects test," granting regulatory authority to the state where harmful effects of conduct occur, rather than the place where the conduct itself occurred. Would this be appropriate? As discussed elsewhere, there is authority providing that it infringes upon a state's territorial sovereignty for a foreign state to regulate conduct occurring within that state based upon effects in the foreign state. *See supra* pp. 493-97 & 507; *American Banana, supra.*

(d) *Does the "last event" rule produce predictable results?* Is §377's "last event" test likely to produce predictable and uniform results? Suppose that the negligently coupled trains in *Carroll* had malfunctioned in Georgia, Tennessee, or Florida, instead of in Mississippi. Then what law would have applied? Suppose that Mr. Carroll had not died until he returned to Alabama. What law would have applied in a suit for wrongful death?

(e) *Is the "last event" rule derived from principles of territorial sovereignty?* Is there anything in international law or the doctrine of territorial sovereignty that requires a "last event" rule? Would a "wrongful conduct" rule be more consistent with principles of territorial sovereignty — permitting states to regulate conduct within their territory?

8. Nationality, citizenship, and domicile. Why do Story and the *First Restatement* focus exclusively on territoriality? Why should not Alabama apply §2590 to any tort claim by an Alabama citizen or domiciliary? That would have permitted Mr. Carroll to take advantage of §2590. Is that desirable? Is it likely to be what the Alabama legislature would have intended had it considered the facts in *Carroll*? Alternatively, why shouldn't §2590 apply to any tort claim against a railroad incorporated or headquartered in Alabama?

8. Domestic v. international choice of law rules. *Carroll* involved a domestic U.S. choice of law question: should Alabama courts apply Alabama or Mississippi law? Contrast both *Whitford* and *American Banana*, which required deciding whether a foreign nation's law should apply, rather than U.S. state or federal law. Should the same choice of law rules apply in both domestic and international cases? Why or why not? *See infra* pp. 650-51. Suppose the negligence in Tokyo of an employee of a Japanese trading house tortiously injured a Japanese employee — in New York. Would New York have any interest in regulating the conduct?

c. *Characterization, Escape Devices, and Procedural Laws*

Although the *First Restatement* was relentlessly territorial in its formal approach to torts, it also contained a number of significant provisions that called for application of laws other than those of the place of the wrong. These provisions, sometimes referred to as "escape devices," allowed for a forum court to apply its own law to certain issues, or to refuse to apply foreign law in particular circumstances.

First, the *Restatement* distinguished between "substantive" and "procedural" issues. Procedural issues were governed by the law of the forum, without regard to the law governing the substantive aspects of a dispute.[130] Procedural matters included many issues that would not appear capable of influencing the outcome of a dis-

---

130. *Restatement (First) Conflict of Laws* §585 (1934) ("All matters of procedure are governed by the law of the forum.").

pute, including the form of action, service, evidentiary issues, and mode of trial.[131] Additionally, however, "procedure" could include more "substantive" issues, such as statutes of limitations, contributory negligence, damages, and the like.[132]

Second, like most private international law systems, the *First Restatement* included exceptions to most of its basic rules for "public policy." As discussed elsewhere, tort claims were generally regarded in 19th century America as "transitory," except where they concerned damage to real property.[133] As a consequence, they could be asserted against the defendant — under the law of the place of the wrong — wherever he was subject to personal jurisdiction.[134] Foreign tort law would not be applied, however, where it was contrary to the forum's public policy.[135]

Third, a forum court was not obliged to enforce a foreign tort claim where a foreign penal or revenue claim was involved.[136] Similarly, the *First Restatement* did not require enforcement of foreign tort claims where the forum's legal system was sufficiently dissimilar from the foreign system as to make enforcement inappropriate.[137]

Fourth, the *First Restatement* also depended substantially on issues of "characterization." For example, in order to apply the Restatement's choice of law rules for torts, a court first had to determine that the case was in fact a tort case. If the court instead decided that a contract case was involved, different choice of law rules — producing different choices of law — were prescribed by the *First Restatement*.[138]

The materials excerpted below introduce these various rules. *Victor v. Sperry* illustrates the application of public policy exceptions, while excerpts from the *Restatement (First) Conflict of Laws* set forth the traditional rules regarding "procedure" and penal or public claims.

VICTOR v. SPERRY

329 P.2d 728 (Calif. Dist. Ct. App. 1958)

MUSSELL, JUSTICE. This is an action for personal injuries sustained by plaintiff in an automobile accident which occurred on the San Quintin highway, approximately 44 kilometers south of Tiajuana, Baja California, Republic of Mexico. At the time of the collision on July 3, 1955, defendant John C. Sperry, with the permission and consent of defendant John M. Sperry, was driving a Mercury automobile northerly on said highway when the Mercury collided with a Chevrolet automobile being driven in a southerly direction on said highway by Defendant Edward

---

131. *Restatement (First) Conflict of Laws* §§586-600 (1934).

132. *Restatement (First) Conflict of Laws* §§603-4, 601, & 606 (1934).

133. *See supra* pp. 39-44.

134. *See infra* pp. 628-29.

135. *Dennick v. RR Co.*, 103 U.S. 11 (1880); *infra* pp. 629-30.

136. *Restatement (First) Conflict of Laws* §§610 & 611 (1934); *Dale v. RR Co.*, 31 Minn. 11 (1883).

137. *Slater v. Mexican National RR Co.*, 194 U.S. 120 (1904); *Stewart v. Baltimore & O. RR Co.*, 168 U.S. 447 (1897).

138. *See infra* p. 628. *E.g.*, *Levy v. Daniels' U-Drive Auto Renting Co.*, 143 A. 163 (Conn. 1928).

Thornton. Plaintiff Rudolph Victor was an occupant of the Thornton vehicle and was severely injured in the collision. Plaintiff and the drivers of both cars were and now are residents and citizens of the State of California. The accident was the result of the negligence (and of the equivalent of negligence under Mexican law) of the drivers of both cars involved in the accident.

Article 1910 of the Civil Code of 1928 for the Federal District and Territories of Mexico, as amended, which had been adopted by the State of Baja California del Norte and which was in effect at the time of the accident, provided as follows: "A person who, acting illicitly or contrary to good customs, causes damages to another, is obligated to repair it, unless it is shown that the damage was produced as a consequence of the guilt or inexcusable negligence of the victim." Neither said code nor the general law of said state or of said Republic distinguished between guests and passengers in motor vehicles nor did they impose any restrictions upon the right of a guest to recover damages from the negligent operator of a motor vehicle in which he was riding.

Prior to the accident plaintiff had been employed as a house mover and his weekly wage was $99. He had not returned to work at the time of the trial and will not be able to engage in the same occupation or any occupation requiring a substantial amount of physical activity. The trial court found (and it is not disputed) that as a result of the accident plaintiff's spinal cord was damaged. He suffered a paralysis of the left upper and lower extremities and the disability in his left upper extremity is permanent and total. The disability in his lower extremity is permanent and partial. He is and will continue to be unable to walk without a limp or for protracted periods. The court further found that plaintiff suffered the following actual damages as a result of the accident:

Medical and hospital expenses	$ 2,962.05
Loss of earnings	7,500.00
Impairment of earning capacity	15,000.00
Pain, suffering and mental anguish	15,000.00
	$40,462.05

At the time of the accident the Mexican law in effect imposed restrictions on the recovery of damages for personal injuries regardless of their nature or extent. Under the Mexican law in effect at the time a victim of the negligent conduct of another could recover his medical and hospital expenses. For a temporary total disability he could recover only 75 per cent of his lost wages for a period not to exceed one year. Wages in excess of 25 pesos, or $2 per day, could not be taken into account in computing the amount allowed. If he suffered a permanent and total disability, he could recover lost earnings for only 918 days and, even though he earned more than 25 pesos per day, only that amount could be taken into account in computing the amount of the recovery. Where the disability was permanent but not total, the recovery was scaled down. For a permanent disability of an upper extremity the victim could recover only from 50 to 70 per cent of $2 per day for 918 days, the exact percentage depending upon age, the importance of the disability, and the extent to which the disability prevented the victim from engaging in his occupation. If the injured extremity was the "least useful," the indemnity was reduced by 15 per cent. In addition, "moral damages" up to a maximum of one third of the other recoverable damages might, in the discretion of the court, be awarded. "Moral damages" are defined as "damages suffered by a person in his honor, reputation, personal tranquillity or spiritual integrity of his life, and as damages which are not of a physical nature and not capable of exact monetary evaluation." The trial court concluded that enforcement of these restrictions on the recovery of damages is not contrary to the public policy of this State or to abstract justice or injurious to the welfare of the people of this State and that plaintiff was not entitled to recover his actual damages in the amount of $40,462.05. Judgment was thereupon rendered against defendants John C. Sperry and Edward Thornton in the amount of $6,135.96 The recovery was computed as follows:

Medical and hospital expenses	$ 2,962.05
Temporary total disability (75% of $2.00 for 365 days)	547.50
Permanent partial disability (70% of $2.00 for 918 days less 15%)	1,092.42
Sub-total	$ 4,601.97
Moral damages	1,533.00
Total	$ 6,135.96

Under Article 1913 of the Civil Code of 1928 for the Mexican Federal District and Territories, if a person has the use of mechanisms or instruments which are dangerous per se, by the speed they develop, or otherwise, he is obligated to answer for the damages he causes, even though he does not act illicitly, unless the damage is caused by the guilt or inexcusable negligence of the victim. The Mexican courts hold that an automobile is a dangerous mechanism or instrument within the meaning of this section and that a person injured by a motor vehicle is entitled to recover damages without regard to fault or negligence from both the owner and driver of the automobile. However, if liability exists only under Article 1913 "moral damages" are not recoverable. Since liability under Article 1910 was found to exist on the part of the drivers of both automobiles, it became immaterial whether liability under Article 1913 was found to exist as to them. Plaintiff, however, sought a judgment against John M. Sperry, owner of the [Mercury] automobile, for $4,601.97, under Article 1913. The trial court concluded that this article is contrary to the public policy of this State, is in substantial conflict with the law of this State, and should not be enforced. Judgment was entered in favor of defendant John M. Sperry.

Rudolph Victor appeals from the judgment (a) Insofar as it fails to award damages in excess of $6,135.96 as against defendants John C. Sperry and Edward Thornton; and (b) Insofar as it fails to award any damages against defendant John M. Sperry. ... [Victor appeals on the trial courts'] conclusions as to the enforceability of the Mexican law. ...

In the instant case, since the accident occurred in Mexico, plaintiff's cause of action arose there and the character and measure of his damages are governed by the laws of Mexico. The measure of damages in inseparably connected to the cause of action and cannot be severed therefrom. The limitation upon the amount of damages imposed by the laws of Mexico is not contrary to the public policy of the State of California or injurious to the welfare of the people thereof.

The trial court herein held that the application of Article 1913 of the Civil Code of 1928 for the Federal District and Territories of Mexico, which provides for liability without fault, was in opposition to the public policy of the State of California and refused to enforce that article against John M. Sperry, owner of one of the automobiles involved in the collision. We find no reversible error in this refusal. ... Since no right of action exists in California for damages for liability without fault under the circumstances set forth herein and in Article 1913 of the Civil Code of 1928 for the Mexican Federal District and Territories, the trial court herein properly concluded that this article should not be enforced as against John M. Sperry as owner of one of the automobiles involved.

RESTATEMENT (FIRST) CONFLICT OF LAWS (1934)
§§384, 585, 610, 611 & 612

§384. (1) If a cause of action in tort is created at the place of wrong, a cause of action will be recognized in other states.

(2) If no cause of action is created at the place of wrong, no recovery in tort can be had in any other state.

§585. All matters of procedure are governed by the law of the forum.

§610. No action can be maintained on a right created by the law of a foreign state as a method of furthering its own governmental interests.

§611. No action can be maintained to recover a penalty the right to which is given by the law of another state.

§612. No action can be maintained upon a cause of action created in another state the enforcement of which is contrary to the strong public policy of the forum.

Notes on Victor and First Restatement

1. *Characterization of choice of law issues.* As discussed below, the *First Restatement* provided that the law governing most contract issues was the law of the state where the contract was made. *See infra* pp. 664-73. In *Carroll*, Mr. Carroll's contract of employment was made in Alabama — which would have made Alabama law applicable if the case had been characterized as a contract dispute. Why should *Carroll* be viewed as a tort case, rather than a contract case? Does the distinction depend on how the plaintiff pleads the claim?

In time, courts and attorneys, found little difficulty in characterizing claims in whatever manner would achieve their view of justice in particular cases. *See* Cook, *Characterization in the Conflict of Laws*, 51 Yale L. J. 191 (1941); Lorenzen, *The Qualification, Classification and Characterization Problem in Conflict of Laws*, 50 Yale L. J. 743 (1941). The *First Restatement* provided no meaningful restrictions on such exercises in re-characterization. Whatever the merits of individual decisions, the manipulation of choice of law rules through characterization significantly detracted from the *First Restatement's* promise of predictability.

2. *Enforcement of foreign tort claims.* Principles of territorial sovereignty and the vested rights doc-

trine have both a negative and an affirmative aspect. First, as in *Carroll,* they forbid the application of the forum's law to foreign torts. Second, as in §384 of the *First Restatement,* they permit (indeed, require) a local forum court to apply foreign law to foreign torts.

Even if a state will not apply its law to events occurring outside its territory, why should its courts assist in the enforcement of foreign law by applying a foreign state's laws to foreign torts? Why should U.S. judicial resources be expended in the enforcement of foreign laws? Consider:

> A party legally liable in New Jersey cannot escape that liability by going to New York. If the liability to pay money was fixed by the law of the State where the transaction occurred, is it to be said it can be enforced nowhere else because it depended upon statute law and not upon common law? It would be a very dangerous doctrine to establish, that in all cases where the several States have substituted the statute for the common law, the liability can be enforced in no other State but that where the statute was enacted and the transaction occurred. *Dennick v. Railroad Co.,* 103 U.S. 11 (1880).

Why should U.S. courts not apply U.S. law to foreign torts? In general, why should not choice of law be determined by personal jurisdiction: if a state can hear a dispute, it should apply its own laws? Recall the reasons for the territoriality doctrine. *See supra* pp. 571-72.

3. *Role of comity in choice of law analysis.* What is the role of "comity" in choice of law analysis? Consider again the discussion of comity and reciprocity in Huber's *De Conflictu Legum* and Story's *Commentaries,* particularly §29 & 33. *See supra* pp. 546-50 & 617-24. What does "comity" mean? For other efforts to describe comity, *see Laker Airways,* 731 F.2d at 937 ("comity serves our international system like the mortar which cements together a brick house. No one would willingly permit the mortar to crumble or be chipped away for fear of compromising the entire structure"); *Republic of the Philippines v. Westinghouse Elec. Corp.,* 43 F.3d 65, 75 (3d Cir. 1995) ("Comity is essentially a version of the golden rule: a 'concept of doing to others as you would have them do to you.'") (quoting *Lafontant v. Aristide,* 844 F.Supp. 128, 132 (S.D.N.Y. 1994)).

4. *Public policy exception to application of foreign tort law.* Section 612 of the *First Restatement* provides that a U.S. court will not entertain a claim based upon foreign tort law "which is contrary to the strong public policy of the forum." Compare the similar recognition in §§33, 35, and 38 of Story's *Commentaries* that comity did not require a state to give effect to foreign laws that were contrary to the forum's public policies. What justifies this public policy exception?

5. *Meaning of public policy.* As discussed elsewhere, it is difficult to define the public policy exception. Consider:

> Our own scheme of legislation may be different [from that in a foreign nation.] We may even have no legislation on the subject. That is not enough to show that public policy forbids us to enforce the foreign right. A right of action is property. If a foreign statute gives the right, the mere fact that we do not give a like right is no reason for refusing to help the plaintiff in getting what belongs to him. ... The misleading word "comity" has been responsible for much of the trouble. It has been fertile in suggesting a discretion unregulated by general principles. ... The sovereign in its discretion may refuse its aid to the foreign right. From this it has been an easy step to the conclusion that a like freedom of choice has been confided to the courts. But that, of course, is a false view. The courts are not free to refuse to enforce a foreign right at the pleasure of judges, to suit the individual notion of expediency or fairness. They do not close their doors, unless help would violate some fundamental principle of justice, some prevalent conception of good morals, some deep-rooted tradition of the common weal. *Loucks v. Standard Oil Co.,* 224 N.Y. 99, 111 (1918).

Does this provide useful guidance?

6. *Sources of public policy.* What sources should a court consult in ascertaining the existence of a public policy? It is said that public policy is an unruly horse that may carry its rider to unanticipated destinations. Katzenbach, *Conflicts on an Unruly Horse: Reciprocal Claims and Tolerances in Interstate and International Law,* 65 Yale L.J. 1087 (1956). Partially in reaction to this, the Supreme Court has declared that public policy cannot be derived from "general considerations of supposed public interest," but must be based upon explicit and clearly defined "laws and legal precedents." *W. R. Grace & Co. v. Local 759, etc.,* 461 U.S. 757 (1983). *See supra* pp. 341-57 & 414-30.

7. *Application of public policy exception in* Victor. Consider the application of the public policy exception in *Victor*.

(a) *Mexican statutory damage limits.* Why wasn't the Mexican statutory limit on damages a violation of California public policy? Note that the Mexican statute limited the U.S. plaintiff to $2 per day, which was substantially less than prevailing U.S. wages. Note also that the U.S. plaintiff had returned to California, where his injuries would likely require public assistance. Should California public policy have overridden the Mexican limits? Try and state the California public policy.

Is it relevant to consider what insurance the defendants in *Victor* had? Note that standard automobile insurance policies issued in the United States at the time provided: "This policy applies only to accidents ... while the automobile is within the United States ... or Canada. ... It is agreed that the coverage provided by this policy is extended to apply when the automobile insured is being used for occasional trips into that part of the Republic of Mexico lying not more than 25 miles from the boundary line of the United States of American for a period not exceeding 10 days at any one time." *See* R. Weintraub, *Commentary on the Conflict of Laws* 297 (3d ed. 1986). Would the standard policy have covered the *Victor* defendants, whose accident occurred 27 miles south of the U.S.-Mexico border? Would Mexican insurance coverage have been based upon Mexican or U.S. damage awards? What about Mexican premiums?

What were the likely legislative policies of the Mexican statutory limits? Were those policies likely to be implicated in a suit between two California residents? Does Mexico have any interest in what damages are awarded for accidents occurring in Mexico? Why does it matter what Mexico's interests are?

(b) *Mexican no-fault liability. Victor* did apply the public policy exception to deny reliance upon a Mexican no-fault rule of liability for owners of "dangerous mechanisms," such as automobiles. Why was this rule contrary to California public policy? *Victor* did not mention that §402(a) of the California Code of 1935 provided that the owner of a vehicle was liable for the negligence of "any person using or operating the same with the permission, express or implied, of the owner." Because the defendant driver in *Victor* was negligent, §402(a) would have subjected the defendant owner to liability under California law. Is it sensible to refuse to apply a foreign rule of law, on the grounds that it violates public policy, when it produces the same result on the facts that the forum's law would?

8. *Actions based on foreign public rights and foreign penal actions.* Sections 610 and 611 of the *First Restatement* provide that a U.S. court will not entertain actions to enforce rights "created by the law of a foreign state as a method of furthering its own governmental interests" or to "recover a penalty" under foreign law. Why were these exceptions not applicable in *Victor*? Would they have been applicable if *American Banana* had involved an effort to persuade a U.S. court to apply a Costa Rican statute identical to the Sherman Act?

9. *Rationale for refusal to enforce foreign public rights.* Why won't courts enforce foreign penal or public rights? If the application of foreign law rests, in Story's words, on "mutual utility" and reciprocity, shouldn't foreign public claims be the *most* important ones to enforce? Consider:

> While the origin of the exception in the case of penal liabilities does not appear in the books, a sound basis for it exists, in my judgment, which includes liabilities for taxes as well. Even in the case of ordinary municipal liabilities, a court will not recognize those arising in a foreign state, if they run counter to the "settled public policy" of its own. Thus a scrutiny of the liability is necessarily always in reserve, and the possibility that it will be found not to accord with the policy of the domestic state. This is not a troublesome or delicate inquiry when the question arises between private persons, but it takes on quite another face when it concerns the relations between the foreign state and its own citizens or even those who may be temporarily within its borders. To pass upon the provisions for the public order of another state is, or at any rate should be, beyond the powers of a court; it involves the relations between the states themselves, with which courts are incompetent to deal, and which are intrusted to other authorities. It may commit the domestic state to a position which would seriously embarrass its neighbor. Revenue laws fall within the same reasoning; they affect a state in matters as vital to its existence as its criminal laws. No court ought to undertake an inquiry which it cannot prosecute without determining whether those laws are consonant with its own notions of what is proper.

Moore v. Mitchell, 30 F.2d 600, 604 (2d Cir. 1929) (L. Hand, J., concurring), *aff'd on other grounds,* 281 U.S. 18 (1930). Is this persuasive? Do not tort laws (and other legal rules) also involve the vital public policies of states? Why is it more "embarrassing" for revenue laws to be scrutinized on public policy grounds than for tort laws to be scrutinized? In any event, why should a state's "embarrassment" dictate the outcome of private litigation?

10. *A variation on* Victor — Hurtado v. Superior Court. *Hurtado v. Superior Court,* 522 P.2d 666 (Calif. 1974), involved the death of a Mexican resident in California as a result of the tortious acts of a California resident. The victim's survivors, also Mexican residents, filed a wrongful death action in California. Mexican law contained liability limits — like those in *Victor* — that restricted the amount the Mexican plaintiffs could recover. Should the Mexican limits apply in the California action? How would the case be decided under the *First Restatement?* What is the reason for the Mexican limits? What is the reason for the absence of any Californian limits?

11. *Distinction between substantive and procedure.* Consider §585, providing that "procedural" matters are governed by the law of the forum. The *First Restatement* defined procedure to include such matters as service of process, time of commencement of an action, form of pleadings, trial procedure, statutes of limitations, damages, and contributory negligence. *Restatement (First) Conflict of Laws* §§585-606 (1934). Why are "procedural" matters governed by the law of the forum? If a tort occurred in a foreign state, and that state's laws are held to govern disputes relating to the tort, why shouldn't that state's procedural rules also apply? Note that some "procedural" rules can have a significant impact on the outcome of the litigation.

12. *Statutes of limitations.* It was well-established at common law that statutes of limitations were generally governed by the law of the forum. Looking to international choice of law practice and commentary, early U.S. decisions uniformly held that the forum's statute of limitations applied to foreign claims (even when it was longer than the law of the state whose substantive law governed the merits of the dispute). *McElmoyle v. Cohen,* 13 Pet. 312 (1839); *Nash v. Tupper,* 1 Cai. 402, 412-13 (N.Y. 1803); *Pearsall v. Dwight,* 2 Mass. 84, 89-90 (1806); *Ruggles v. Keeler,* 3 Johns. 263, 267-68 (N.Y. 1808). The theory was that statutes of limitations merely affected "remedies," not substantive "rights." *Graves v. Graves's Executor,* 5 Ky. 207, 208-09 (1810) ("The statute of limitations ... does not destroy the right but withholds the remedy. It would seem to follow, therefore, that the *lex fori,* and not the *lex loci* was to prevail with respect to the time when the action should be commenced.").

2. Contemporary Approaches to Choice of Law Applicable to Torts

a. Criticism of Vested Rights Doctrine

Even as the *First Restatement* was released, criticism of its territorial rules began and progressively intensified. In the field of tort law, critics argued that Beale's territoriality doctrine produced arbitrary results, that it was unpredictable, and that the entire vested rights analysis rested on insupportable assumptions and question-begging.[139] Moreover, lower courts were thought to have frequently applied various of the *Restatement*'s provisions (such as those concerning public policy and procedure) as escape devices in order to avoid what were perceived to be unacceptable results of the vested rights analysis.[140] Other attacks demonstrated the increasing gulf between notions of territoriality and contemporary regulatory objectives and legislative intent.[141]

Academic commentators also increasingly challenged the propriety of "jurisdiction-selecting" choice of law rules, which specified which state's laws should apply

---

139. *E.g.,* Cook, *The Logical and Legal Bases of the Conflict of Laws,* 33 Yale L. J. 457 (1924); Lorenzen, *Territoriality, Public Policy and the Conflict of Laws,* 33 Yale L. J. 736 (1924); Yntema, *The Hornbook Method and the Conflict of Laws,* 37 Yale L. J. 468 (1928); D. Cavers, *A Critique of the Choice-of-Law Problem,* 47 Harv. L. Rev. 173 (1933).

140. *E.g., University of Chicago v. Dater,* 270 N.W. 175 (Mich. 1936); *Grant v. McAuliffe,* 264 P.2d 944 (Calif. 1953); *Kilberg v. Northeast Airlines, Inc.,* 211 N.Y.S.2d 133 (1961).

141. *See supra* note 139.

without regard to the content or policies of those laws. Rather, commentators suggested that attention be focused on the content and policies of purportedly conflicting laws. "The court is not idly choosing a law; it is determining a controversy. How can it choose wisely without considering how the choice will affect that controversy?"[142] Other commentators suggested that different torts required different choice of law rules.[143]

By the 1950's, criticisms of the *First Restatement* had prevailed, at least in academic circles: "the theory of 'vested rights' [was] brutally murdered."[144] Criticism of the *First Restatement* culminated in rejection of the vested rights analysis and the proliferation a variety of competing alternatives. In place of Beale's territorial vested rights system, an assortment of markedly different approaches to choice of law emerged in a process described as the American "conflicts revolution."

b. Contemporary Approaches: Interest Analysis

Among the first of the new choice of law approaches was Brainerd Currie's "interest analysis."[145] Under Currie's approach, the only real issue in multistate problems was whether the forum state had an "interest" in the outcome of a particular dispute; if it did, then a forum court had no choice but to apply the forum's law. Indeed, Currie thought that "[w]e would be better off without choice-of-law rules,"[146] because they seduce courts into the application of foreign law (thereby frustrating the forum's policies).[147]

The general approach under Currie's interest analysis was to start by "look[ing] to the law of the forum as the source of the rule of decision."[148] In particular, courts were to determine whether the relevant forum legislation or common law rules were applicable to the parties' dispute, by considering whether "the relationship of the forum state to the case ... is such as to bring the case within the scope of the state's governmental concern."[149] If so, then Currie would assign the forum state an "interest."

Attention then turned to any arguably interested foreign state, to determine whether those states also had an "interest." In most cases, Currie thought, states other than the forum would not have an interest. In Currie's words, this was a "false conflict," permitting application of the law of the forum.[150] In those cases where a

---

142. D. Cavers, *A Critique of the Choice-of-Law Problem*, 47 Harv. L. Rev. 173, 189 (1933).
143. Morris, *The Proper Law of a Tort*, 64 Harv. L. Rev. 881 (1951); Cheatam & Reese, *Choice of the Applicable Law*, 52 Colum. L. Rev. 959 (1952).
144. Katzenbach, *Conflicts on an Unruly Horse: Reciprocal Claims and Tolerances in Interstate and International Law*, 65 Yale L. J. 1087, 1087-88 (1956).
145. *See generally* B. Currie, *Selected Essays on the Conflict of Law* (1963).
146. B. Currie, *Selected Essays on the Conflict of Law* 183 (1963).
147. B. Currie, *Selected Essays on the Conflict of Law* 278 (1963) ("The traditional system of conflict of laws counsels the courts to sacrifice the interests of their own states mechanically and heedlessly, without consideration of the policies and interests involved.").
148. B. Currie, *Selected Essays on the Conflict of Laws* 188 (1963).
149. B. Currie, *Selected Essays on the Conflict of Laws* 188 (1963).
150. B. Currie, *Selected Essays on the Conflict of Laws* 189 (1963).

foreign state (as well as the forum state) did have an interest, an "apparent conflict" would exist. Currie's interest analysis then called for "restraint and enlightenment in the determination of what state policy is and where state interests lie."[151] If this moderation of each state's demands eliminated any conflict, analysis would end (with another "false conflict").

If a restrained interpretation does not produce a resolution, there would be a "true conflict," to which Currie would have applied the law of the forum. He reasoned that, if "conflict between the legitimate interests of the two states is unavoidable," then forum law must be applied.[152] Currie expressly said that a court was not to "weigh" the competing interests of its own polity and different states in the case of true conflicts.[153] The result of Currie's "interest analysis" was unreservedly pro-forum: "In contrast to the urbane neutrality of the *First Restatement*, Currie's approach is unabashedly parochial. ... [H]is governmental interest analysis amounts to little more than a complicated pretext for applying the *lex fori*."[154]

Following Currie, other academic commentators urged various alternative forms of interest analysis. Many of these approaches expressly required weighing competing state interests, even where the forum's interests were at issue.[155] Others required different inquiries, such as which legal rule was the "better law,"[156] or the comparative "impairment" of different state's interests.[157] In many observers' view, there came to be "almost as many approaches as there are legal writers,"[158] inhabiting a landscape littered with "stagnant pools of doctrine, each jealously guarded by its adherents."[159]

More generally, contemporary U.S. choice of law doctrines became increasingly arcane and complex, leaving practitioners and judges in confusion. The experience in New York is illustrative. In *Babcock v. Jackson*,[160] the New York Court of Appeals became one of the first U.S. courts to embrace interest analysis. The court considered what New York and Ontario interests were implicated in a tort action arising from an automobile accident in Ontario involving two New York domiciliaries. It expressly rejected the "place of the wrong" test, and instead gave "controlling effect to the

---

151. B. Currie, *Selected Essays on the Conflict of Laws* 186 (1963).

152. B. Currie, *Selected Essays on the Conflict of Law* 357 (1963).

153. B. Currie, *Selected Essays on the Conflict of Law* 182 (1963). Currie did permit a court to weigh the interests of two foreign states in cases where the forum had no interest. Currie, *The Disinterested Third State*, 28 Law & Contemp. Prob. 754 (1963).

154. Juenger, *General Course on Private International Law*, 193 Recueil des Cours 119, 218 (1982).

155. R. Weintraub, *Commentary on the Conflict of Laws* 266, 345-47 (2d ed. 1989); A. von Mehren & D. Trautman, *The Law of Multi-State Problems* 376-78 (1965); R. Leflar, *American Conflicts Law* 193-95 (3d ed. 1977).

156. Leflar, *Conflicts Law: More on Choice Influencing Considerations*, 54 Calif. L. Rev. 1584 (1966).

157. Baxter, *Choice of Law and the Federal System*, 16 Stan. L. Rev. 1 (1963).

158. Juenger, *General Course on Private International Law*, 193 Recueil des Cours 119, 219 (1983).

159. Kay, *The Use of Comparative Impairment to Resolve True Conflicts: An Evaluation of the California Experience*, 68 Calif. L. Rev. 577, 615 (1980) (quoted in Juenger, *General Course on Private International Law*, 193 Recueil des Cours 119, 219 (1983)).

160. 240 N.Y.S.2d 743 (1963).

law of the jurisdiction which, because of its relationship or contact with the occurrence or the parties has the greatest concern with the specific issues raised in the litigation."[161] Under this standard, the court concluded, New York law should apply to permit recovery, rather than Ontario law (whose guest statute would have denied recovery).

Over the next three decades, however, New York judicial decisions produced a confusing and inconsistent approach to choice of law in tort. New York courts enunciated a variety of differing analyses, emphasizing different factors and governmental interests, in a series of cases involving automobile accidents.[162] "The struggle of the Court with these cases has been awesome to behold — dissents, shifting doctrine, results not easily reconcilable. In short, a law professor's delight but a practitioner's and judge's nightmare."[163] Ultimately, in *Newmeier v. Kuehner*,[164] the Court of Appeals apparently abandoned orthodox interest analysis, and set forth a number of specific rules governing choice of law in automobile tort cases involving guest statutes.[165]

c. Contemporary Approaches: Second Restatement's "Most Significant Relationship" Standard

With this background, the 1971 *Restatement (Second) Conflict of Laws* expressly rejected the *First Restatement's* territorial "vested rights" doctrine. "Instead, the rights and liabilities of the parties in tort are said to be governed by the local law of the state which, with respect to the particular issue, has the most significant relationship to the occurrence and the parties."[166] The Restatement's drafters justified their rejection of territoriality principles in the same way that *Pennoyer's* limits on judicial jurisdiction were abandoned:

> These changes are partly a reflection of a change in our national life. State and national boundaries are of less significance today by reason of the increased mobility of our population and of the increasing tendency of men to conduct their affairs across boundary lines.[167]

Although there was academic consensus that the *First Restatement's* territoriality principles had to be abandoned, there was little agreement on what should replace them. The *Second Restatement* became an exercise in compromise, seeking to accom-

---

161. 240 N.Y.S.2d at 749.

162. *Dym v. Gordon*, 262 N.Y.S.2d 463 (N.Y. 1965); *Macey v. Rozbicki*, 274 N.Y.S.2d 591 (N.Y. 1965); *Tooker v. Lopez*, 301 N.Y.S.2d 519 (N.Y. 1969); *Neumeier v. Kuehner*, 335 N.Y.S.2d 64 (N.Y. 1972); *Towley v. King Arthur Rings, Inc.*, 386 N.Y.S.2d 80 (N.Y. 1976).

163. R. Weintraub, *Commentary on the Conflict of Laws* 327 (3d ed. 1986).

164. 335 N.Y.S.2d 64 (N.Y. 1972).

165. Other courts took the same view of the uncertainties and unpredictability of interest analysis. Presented with arguments that they should adopt interest analysis, these courts have refused on the grounds that it is an unadministratable and unpredictable standard. *Abendschein v. Farrell*, 170 N.W.2d 137 (Mich. 1969); *McMillan v. McMillan*, 253 S.E.2d 662 (Va. 1979). Nevertheless, as discussed below, the trend over recent decades has been away from traditional territoriality principles. *See infra* pp. 635-36.

166. *Restatement (Second) Conflict of Laws* 413 (1971).

167. *Restatement (Second) Conflict of Laws* 413 (1971).

modate all of the various factions of the American conflicts revolution. "As a result, the *Second Restatement* became a mixture of discordant approaches."[168]

Section 6 of the *Second Restatement* articulated the basic principles that were said to inform contemporary choice of law analysis. Where no legislative choice of law directive exists, §6 provides that "the factors relevant to the choice of the applicable rule of law" include: (a) the needs of the international system; (b) the relevant policies of the forum; (c) the relevant policies of other interested states; (d) justified expectations; (e) certainty, predictability, and uniformity; and (f) ease in determining the applicable law. Section 145 of the *Second Restatement* applied this basic analysis to tort claims, producing the following "rule":

> The rights and liabilities of the parties with respect to an issue in tort are determined by the local law of the state which, with respect to that issue, has the most significant relationship to the occurrence and the parties under the principles stated in §6.

Other provisions of the *Second Restatement* further refined the "most significant relationship" standard, setting forth specific rules governing particular torts (*e.g.*, personal injury or defamation)[169] and particular issues (*e.g.*, standard of care or defenses).[170]

d. Contemporary Lower Court Approaches to Choice of Law Applicable to Tort

Contemporary lower court decisions in the United States concerning the law applicable to torts are almost as diverse as the academic community.[171] A substantial number of states have refused to abandon the *First Restatement*'s "place of the wrong" rule; although this group is not an absolute majority, it appears to command the support of almost as many states as any other single position.[172] The single most substantial group of jurisdictions has adopted some version of the *Second Restatement*'s "most significant relationship" standard.[173] Other jurisdictions follow variations of interest analysis and other contemporary products of the American conflicts revolution.[174]

---

168. Juenger, *General Course on Private International Law*, 193 Recueil des Cours 119, 220 (1983).

169. *Restatement (Second) Conflict of Laws* §§146-55 (1971).

170. *Restatement (Second) Conflict of Laws* §§156-77 (1971).

171. *See* Westbrook, *A Survey and Evaluation of Competing Choice of Law Theories: The Case for Eclecticism*, 40 Mo. L. Rev. 407 (1972); Kozyris & Symeonides, *Choice of Law in the American Courts in 1989: An Overview*, 38 Am. J. Comp. L. 601 (1990); Symeonides, *Choice of Law in the United States*, 37 Am. J. Comp. L. 457 (1989).

172. Although estimates vary, approximately 13 states now appear to follow the *First Restatement*. Symeonides, *Choice of Law in American Courts in 1994: A View "from the Trenches,"* 43 Am. J. Comp. L. 1, 3 (1995); Symeonides, *Choice of Law in the American Courts in 1993 (and in the Six Previous Years)*, 42 Am. J. Comp. L. 599, 606 (1994); Smith, *Choice of Law in the United States*, 38 Hastings L. J. 1041 (1987).

173. Although estimates vary, approximately 22 states now appear to follow the *Second Restatement*. Symeonides, *Choice of Law in the American Courts in 1993 (and in the Six Previous Years)*, 42 Am. J. Comp. L. 599, 609 (1994); Smith, *Choice of Law in the United States*, 38 Hastings L. J. 1041 (1987).

174. It appears that about 15 states follow either traditional interest analysis, Leflar's doctrines, a "center of gravity" approach, or some hybrid. Symeonides, *Choice of Law in the American Courts in 1993 (and in the Six Previous Years)*, 42 Am. J. Comp. L. 599, 611-12 (1994).

In many states, courts have been inconsistent in their approach to choice of law:

> any systematic treatment of the cases will necessarily overstate the differences by making classifications and drawing distinctions when, in reality, the lines tend to be much more fluid. Few courts are entirely consistent in approaching choice of law problems. There are no *purely* "interest-analysis states" or "*Restatement (Second)* states."[175]

Moreover, in some states, courts have encountered serious difficulties in articulating any comprehensible choice of law analysis applicable to torts. As described above, New York's choice of law rules are said to be in "utter confusion" and "incoherent."[176]

Excerpted below are materials that chart the American conflicts revolution in the tort field. Consider the excerpt from Brainerd Currie's *Notes on Methods and Objectives in the Conflict of Laws*, which summarizes traditional interest analysis. Also consider the selected sections of the *Restatement (Second) Conflict of Laws*, setting forth the "most significant relationship" test. Finally, the decision in *Tramontana v. SA Empresa de Viacao Aerea Rio* illustrates a contemporary judicial effort to apply both Currie's interest analysis and the *Second Restatement's* most significant relationship test.

B. CURRIE, NOTES ON METHODS AND OBJECTIVES IN THE CONFLICT OF LAWS

[1959] Duke L. J. 171

The central problem of conflict of laws may be defined ... as that of determining the appropriate rule of decision when the interests of two or more states are in conflict — in other words, of determining which interest shall yield. The problem would not exist if this were one world, with an all-powerful central government. It would not exist (though other problems of "conflict of laws" would) if the independent sovereignties in the real world had identical laws. So long, however as we have a diversity of laws, we shall have conflicts of interest among states. Hence, unless something is done, the administration of private law where more than one state is concerned will be affected with disuniformity and uncertainty. To avoid this result by all reasonable means is certainly a laudable objective; but how? Not by establishing a single government; even if such a thing were remotely thinkable as a practical possibility, we attribute positive values to the principle of self determination for localities and groups. The attainment of uniformity of laws among diverse states is, to put it mildly, a long-range undertaking. ...

We do not, however, despair. We turn, instead, to the resources of jurisprudence, placing our faith primarily in the judges rather than the lawmakers. The judi-

---

175. E. Scoles & P. Hay, *Conflict of Laws* 551 (1982).

176. Juenger, *General Course on Private International Law*, 193 Recueil des Cours 119, 223 (1983).

cial function is not narrowly confined; we indulge the hope that it may even be equal to the ambitious task of bringing uniformity and certainty into a world whose conflicts political action has failed to resolve. At first, of course, the judges will not be so bold (or so frank) as to avow that they are assuming the high political function of passing upon the relative merits of the conflicting policies, or interests, of sovereign states. They will address themselves to metaphysical questions concerning the nature of law and its abstract operation in space — matters remote from mundane policies and conflicts of interest — and will evolve a set of rules for determining which state's law must, in the nature of things, control. If all states can be persuaded to adhere to these rules, the seemingly impossible will have been accomplished: there will be uniformity and certainty in the administration of private law from state to state. The fact that this goal will be achieved at the price of sacrificing state interests is not emphasized; rather, it is obscured by the metaphysical apparatus of the method.

The rules so evolved have not worked and cannot be made to work. In our times we have suffered particularly from the jurisprudential theory that has been compounded in order to explain and justify the assumption by the courts of so extraordinary a function. The territorialist conception has been directly responsible for indefensible results and, what is perhaps worse, has therefore driven some of our ablest scholars to consume their energies in purely defensive action against it. But the root of the trouble goes deeper. In attempting to use the rules we encounter difficulties that stem not from the fact that the particular rules are bad, nor from the fact that a particular theoretical explanation is unsound, but rather from the fact that we have such rules at all. ...

[D]espite the camouflage of discourse, the rules do operate to nullify state interests. The fact that this is often done capriciously, without reference to the merits of the respective policies and even without recognition of their existence, is only incidental. Trouble enough comes from the mere fact that interests are defeated. The courts simply will not remain always oblivious to the true operation of a system that, though speaking the language of metaphysics, strikes down the legitimate application of the policy of a state, especially when that state is the forum. Consequently, the system becomes complicated. It is loaded with escape devices: the concept of "local public policy" as a basis for not applying the "applicable" law; the concept of "fraud on the law"; the device of novel or disingenuous characterization; the device of manipulating the connecting factor; and, not least, the provision of sets of rules that are interchangeable at will. The tensions that are induced by imposing such a system on a setting of conflict introduce a very serious element of uncertainty and unpredictability, even if there is fairly general agreement on the rules themselves. A sensitive and ingenious court can detect an absurd result and avoid it; I am inclined to think that this has been done more often than not and that therein lies a major reason why the system has managed to survive. At the same time, we constantly run the risk that the court may lack sensitivity and ingenuity; we are handicapped in even presenting the issue in its true light; and instances of mechanical application of the rules to produce indefensible results are by no means rare. Whichever of these phenomena is the more common, it is a poor defense of the system to say that the unacceptable results that it will inevitably produce can be averted by disingenuousness if the courts are sufficiently alert. ...

[W]hen several states have different policies, and also legitimate interests in the application of their policies, a court is in no position to "weigh" the competing interests, or evaluate their relative merits, and choose between them accordingly. This is especially evident when we consider two co-ordinate states, with such decisions being made by the courts of one or the other. A court need never hold the interest of the foreign law inferior; it can simply apply its own law as such. But when the court, in a true conflict situation, holds the foreign law applicable, it is assuming a great deal: it is holding the policy, or interest, of its own state inferior and preferring the policy or interest for the foreign state. ...

But assessment of the respective values of the competing legitimate interests of two sovereign states, in order to determine which is to prevail, is a political function of a very high order. This is a function that should not be committed to courts in a democracy. It is a function that the courts cannot perform effectively, for they lack the necessary resources. Not even a very ponderous Brandeis brief could marshal the relevant considerations in choosing, for example, between the interest of the state of employment and that of the state of injury in matters concerning workmen's compensation. This is a job for a legislative committee, and determining the policy to be formulated on the basis of the information assembled is a job for a competent legislative body. ...

We would be better off without the choice-of-law rules. We would be better off if Congress were to give some attention to problems of private law, and were to legislate concerning the choice between conflicting state interests in some of the specific areas in which the need for solutions is serious. In the meantime, we would be better off if we would admit the teachings of sociological jurisprudence into the conceptualistic precincts of conflict of laws. This would imply a basic method along the following lines:

1. Normally, even in cases involving foreign elements, the court should be expected, as a matter of course, to apply the rule of decision found in the law of the forum.

2. When it is suggested that the law of a foreign state should furnish the rule of decision, the court should, first of all, determine the governmental policy expressed in the law of the forum. It should then inquire whether the relation of the forum to the case is such as to provide a legitimate basis for the assertion of an interest in the application of that policy. This process is essentially the familiar one of construction or interpretation. Just as we determine by that process how a statute applies in time, and how it applies to marginal domestic situations, so we may determine how it should be applied to cases involving foreign elements in order to effectuate the legislative purpose.

3. If necessary, the court should similarly determine the policy expressed by the foreign law, and whether the foreign state has an interest in the application of its policy.

4. If the court finds that the forum state has no interest in the application of its policy, but that the foreign state has, it should apply the foreign law.

5. If the court finds that the forum state has an interest in the application of its policy, it should apply the law of the forum, even though the foreign state also has an interest in the application of its contrary policy, and, a fortiori, it should apply the law of the forum if the foreign state has no such interest. ...

The suggested analysis does not imply the ruthless pursuit of self-interest by the states. ... There is no need to exclude the possibility of rational altruism: for example, when a state has determined upon the policy of placing upon local industry all the social costs of the enterprise, it may well decide to adhere to this policy regardless of where the harm occurs and who the victim is. There is also room for restraint and enlightenment in the determination of what state policy is and where state interests lie.

I have been told that I give insufficient recognition to governmental policies other than those that are expressed in specific statutes and rules: the policy of promoting a general legal order, that of fostering amicable relations with other states, that of vindicating reasonable expectations, and so on. If this is so, it is not, I hope, because of a provincial lack of appreciation of the worth of those ideals, but because of a felt necessity to emphasize the obstacles that the present system interposes to any intelligent approach to the problem. Let us first clear away the apparatus that creates false problems and obscures the nature of the real ones. Only then can we effectively set about ameliorating the ills that arise from a diversity of laws by bringing to bear all the resources of jurisprudence, politics, and humanism — each in its appropriate way.

RESTATEMENT (SECOND) CONFLICT OF LAWS (1971)

§§6, 10, 122, 145, 146, & 156

§6.(1) A court, subject to constitutional restrictions, will follow a statutory directive of its own state on choice of law.

(2) When there is no such directive, the factors relevant to the choice of the applicable rule of law include:

    (a) the needs of the interstate and international systems,

    (b) the relevant policies of the forum,

    (c) the relevant policies of other interested states and the relative interests of those states in the determination of the particular issue,

    (d) the protection of justified expectations,

    (e) the basic policies underlying the particular field of law,

    (f) certainty, predictability and uniformity of result, and

    (g) ease in the determination and application of the law to be applied.

§10. The rules in the Restatement of this Subject apply to cases with elements in one or more States of the United States and are generally applicable to cases with elements in one or more foreign nations. There may, however, be factors in a particular international case which call for a result different from that which would be reached in an interstate case.

§122. A court usually applies its own local law rules prescribing how litigation shall be conducted even when it applies the local law rules of another state to resolve other issues in the case.

§142. (1) An action will not be maintained if it is barred by the statute of limitations of the forum, including a provision borrowing the statute of limitations of another state.

(2) An action will be maintained if it is not barred by the statute of limitations of the forum, even though it would be barred by the statute of limitations of another state, except as stated in §143.

§143. An action will not be entertained in another state if it is barred in the state of the otherwise applicable law by a statute of limitations which bars the right and not merely the remedy.

§145. (1) The rights and liabilities of the parties with respect to an issue in tort are determined by the local law of the state which, with respect to that issue, has the most significant relationship to the occurrence and the parties under the principles stated in §6.

(2) Contacts to be taken into account in applying the principles of §6 to determine the law applicable to an issue include:

 (a) the place where the injury occurred,

 (b) the place where the conduct causing the injury occurred,

 (c) the domicil, residence, nationality, place of incorporation and business of the parties, and

 (d) the place where the relationship, if any, between the parties is centered.

These contacts are to be evaluated according to their relative importance with respect to the particular issue.

§146. In an action for a personal injury, the local law of the state where the injury occurred determines the rights and liabilities of the parties, unless, with respect to the particular issue, some other state has a more significant relationship under the principles stated in §6 to the occurrence and the parties, in which event the local law of the other state will be applied.

§156. (1) The law selected by application of the rule of §145 determines whether the actor's conduct was tortious.

(2) The applicable law will usually be the local law of the state where the injury occurred.

TRAMONTANA v. SA EMPRESA DE VIACAO AEREA RIO

350 F.2d 468 (D.C. Cir. 1964)

McGOWAN, CIRCUIT JUDGE. This appeal presents an international variant of a recurring domestic conflict of laws problem, namely, the applicability in the forum (the District of Columbia) of a monetary damage limitation contained in the wrongful death statute of the place of injury (Brazil). ...

Vincent Tramontana was killed on February 26, 1960, when the U.S. Navy airplane in which he was travelling on naval orders collided over Rio de Janeiro, Brazil, with an airplane owned and operated by a Brazilian airline. At the time of his death, Tramontant was a member of the U.S. Navy Band, which was on an official tour of Latin America. The record does not show his permanent duty station, but he resided with his wife, appellant here, in Hyattsville, Maryland. The Navy plane in which he was travelling when he was killed was en route from Buenos Aires in Argentina to Galeao, Brazil. Appellee Varig Airlines is a Brazilian corporation having its principal place of business in Brazil but carrying on its transportation activities in many parts of the world, including the United States. The Brazilian plane was on a regularly scheduled commercial flight from Campos, Brazil, to Rio de Janeiro when the accident occurred. ...

[A]ppellant instituted this action in the District Court against Varig and its predecessor, alleging that negligence in the operation of the Brazilian plane had caused her husband's death. She explicitly based her claim for recovery on certain provisions of the Brazilian Code of the Air which provide a cause of action for injury or death resulting from negligent operation of aircraft in Brazil. She claimed damages of $250,000. Service was made on Varig Airlines, which concededly is subject to suit in the District of Columbia. Varig ... moved for summary judgment dismissing the complaint or, in the alternative, for summary judgement in respect of so much of appellant's claim as exceeded the U.S. dollar equivalent of 100,000 Brazilian cruzeiros. Varig relied on Article 102 of the Brazilian Code, which limits liability for injury or death in aviation accidents to that amount. The District Court, with Varig's consent, entered judgment in favor of appellant in the amount of $170.00, the current dollar value of 100,000 cruzeiros. It awarded judgment in favor of Varig "for all of the plaintiff's claim which exceeds the sum of One Hundred Seventy Dollars ($170.00)." From this latter judgment Mrs. Tramontana appealed.[177]

The only question now before us is whether Brazil's limitation on the damages recoverable for death sustained in airplane accidents occurring there is to be applied in this suit in the District of Columbia. Appellant appears to concede that her cause

---

177. Seventeen other members of the Navy Band perished in the collision. They are represented in two other actions in the District Court, one involving eleven plaintiffs, the other, six. Appellee had summary judgment on the same terms in both suits. ... Of the seventeen other plaintiffs in these two suits, two, and perhaps three, were listed as residents of the District of Columbia, eight as residents of Maryland, and the remainder as residents of other states. ...

of action, if any, was created by, and arises under, a provision of Brazilian law enacted coincidentally and in conjunction with the damage limitation. She argues, however, that the forum law regarding damages for wrongful death occurring in the District of Columbia, *i.e.*, unlimited recovery, should govern that aspect of her claim. Initially, she accepts the applicability of the traditional conflict of law rule in personal injury cases that the *lex locus delicti*, the law of the place where the injury occurred, generally governs in a suit brought elsewhere, but she asserts that a court sitting in the District of Columbia should adopt the familiar exception to the effect that the forum will refuse to apply the otherwise applicable foreign law if it is contrary to some strong public policy of the forum. Appellant asserts the existence of a strong policy of the District of Columbia in favor of unlimited recovery for wrongful death, which she claims is evidenced by Congress' repeal in 1948 of the $10,000 maximum until then contained in the local wrongful death statute. She points also the fact that only thirteen states still limit recovery for wrongful death, and that none imposes a ceiling as low as that contained in the Brazilian Air Code. ... And, finally, she relies on the New York Court of Appeals decision in *Kilberg v. Northeast Airlines, Inc.*, 9 N.Y.2d 34 (1961), as a persuasive precedent for the position she urges us to adopt. ...

Appellant's essential effort throughout is to urge us to follow the "newer and more realistic judicial approach" to conflict of laws problems exemplified by *Kilberg* and *Babcock v. Jackson*, and more recent decisions of the Supreme Court, and to reject the assertedly outmoded and discredited teaching of *Slater v. Mexican Nat'l R.R.*, and kindred decisions. Under the test we are asked to employ, the choice of law to be applied to each legal issue presented is to be made in light of the "jurisdiction which has the strongest interest in the resolution of that issue," Appellant's Brief, p. 10. "Emphasis is [to be] placed ... upon the law of the place which has the most significant contacts with the matter in dispute." A cornerstone of this newer thinking, appellant contends, is the forum's reluctance to subordinate its policies to those of another state when its own interest in the case is real and substantial.

The Supreme Court ... has recognized the inadequacies of the theoretical underpinnings of *Slater* and its progeny. The latter cases have a highly attenuated precedential weight, both in authority and reason. Thus we are free to explore the question presented by this appeal in the light of the newer concepts of conflict laws. ...

The interest underlying the application of Brazilian law seems to us to outweigh any interest of the District of Columbia. Not only is Brazil the scene of the fatal collision, but Varig is a Brazilian corporation which, as a national airline, is an object of concern in terms of national policy. To Brazil, the success of this enterprise is a matter not only of pride and commercial well-being, but perhaps even of national security. The limitation on recovery against airlines operating in Brazil was enacted in the early days of commercial aviation, no doubt with a view toward protecting what was then, and still is, an infant industry of extraordinary public and national importance. The Brazilian limitation in terms applies only to airplane accidents, unlike the Massachusetts provision rejected in *Kilberg*, which was an across-the-board ceiling on recovery for wrongful death in that state. The focus of Brazilian concern could hardly be clearer.

We have seen nothing that would suggest that Brazil's concern for the financial integrity if her local airlines should be deemed to be less genuine now than when Article 102 was enacted, simply because of the depreciation of the cruzeiro. The failure to amend that provision may reflect a conscious desire to avoid enlarging the potential liability of local airlines during a period of general economic difficulty. It may represent an unwillingness to contribute to the inflationary spiral by adjusting "prices" fixed by statute which the government can control. ... [W]e are not persuaded that the fact of inflation itself ... should be deemed to render obsolete Brazil's legitimate interest in limiting recoveries against her airlines.

Appellant relies primarily on *Kilberg* as a precedent for the course she asks us to follow. A close analysis of that court's reasoning reveals that the relationships and interests, which it thought compelled the result reached, do not parallel those here. The decedent in *Kilberg* was both a resident and a domiciliary of New York. He was a paying passenger on the defendant airline, which relationship had originated in New York. As the Court of Appeals pointed out, once on board the plane the place of the injury was merely "fortuitous." New York's long-standing policy in favor of unlimited recovery in actions for wrongful death coalesced in this case with its real and immediate interest in providing full compensation for the death of one of its own citizens. And its interest would have been the same whether the defendant's aircraft had crashed in New York, in Long Island Sound, or, as it did, in Massachusetts.

In the case before us neither appellant, nor children, nor her husband were or are resident or domiciled in the District of Columbia. Vincent Tramontana was not a passenger on appellee's plane, and his "relationship" with appellee commenced and ended in Brazil in one shattering moment. The place of injury, under these circumstances, was clearly not fortuitous, although the accident was something of a freak. Vincent Tramontana could not have been killed by Varig's Campos-to-Rio Flight except in Brazil. To suggest that he might have been killed here in the District, or in Maryland, by one of Varig's international flights is to ignore the facts of this case.[178] It is one thing to say that airlines should not be the beneficiaries, nor their passengers the victims, of the vagaries of weather and faulty equipment that cause an aircraft to crash in one jurisdiction rather than another. It is quite another to say that an American traveller, who is injured in Brazil through the negligence of the operator of

---

178. The possible locations of Varig's wrongdoing, if such it was, are irrelevant to the determination of which law should measure appellant's recovery except insofar as they have some other connection with the parties or the accident, or some independent interest in the resolution of this issue. If the mere possibility, however remote, that Vincent Tramontana might have been killed through some negligence of appellee in the District of Columbia were thought to give the District some interest in the application of its law, whatever predictability remains in the conflict of laws of torts would disappear. Concededly, predictability is a depreciated coin in tort law, *see Babcock v. Jackson*, 240 N.Y.S.2d 743, 746-47 (1963), but it still retains some value. Varig's ability to predict and obtain the cost of insurance, for example, may depend to some extent on its ability to estimate its potential liability.

a local airline on which he was not a passenger and with which he had no previous connection, is entitled to the benefit of the law of a forum which is not his home, because its successor happens to do business there.[179] The District of Columbia's connection with the occurrence and with the parties and its interest in the resolution of the issue before us, are, if not wholly remote, certainly less than Brazil's. Neither appellant nor her decedent are or were residents of the District of Columbia. Varig Airlines is subject to suit here only because of the international operations in which it is engaged. Whatever negligence it may have been guilty of assuredly did not occur here, nor manifestly, did the decedent's death. If appellant and her children should ever become public charges, the burden will rest not on the District of Columbia but on the citizens of Maryland, where appellant resides.[180]

Although Maryland, the state of the decedent's and appellant's residence, might be thought to have a substantial interest in the amount recoverable for his death, no suggestion has been made that we should apply the law of Maryland to determine the issue before us. But this possibility inevitably suggests itself, and we therefore are inclined to say why we think that, even as between the law of Maryland and the law of Brazil, we are without warrant to look to the former. In striking this balance, the weight to be accorded the interests of Brazil remains unchanged. The question is whether Maryland has a significantly greater claim to the application of its law than the District of Columbia.

Maryland's only relationship with the parties or the transactions is that it is appellant's residence, and was that of the appellant's recovery is not insignificant, for it is on the citizens of Maryland that the burden of her support, if she is unable to support herself, is likely to fall in the first instance.[181] Yet it appears likely that a Maryland court could not have ignored the Brazilian limitation on recovery of this action had been brought there originally. ... The Maryland Court of Appeals has held that, where both accident and death occurred in another state, the defendant's liabili-

---

179. ... The case before us is much the same as if a resident of the State of Maryland, while on a summer vacation trip to Europe and while crossing the street in Amsterdam, were run over and killed by a beer truck making a local delivery. If Holland had a wrongful death act with a limitation on damages, and if the brewing company had a sales office in the District of Columbia, then a suit in the District by the Maryland widow would present us with a problem virtually identical with that we now have. The increasing international mobility of both ordinary citizens and business enterprises suggests that the issue is an important one already and is likely to become more so. There are obvious implications to be considered in respect of the degree of comity which should obtain between sovereign nations unrestrained by a full faith and credit clause in a world constitution.

180. The New York Court of Appeals' dominating concern in *Kilberg* was to ensure "protection for our own State's people against unfair and anachronistic treatment of the lawsuits which result from these [airline] disasters," 211 N.Y.S.2d at 135. The immediate objects of that concern were, of course, the victims and their dependents. The implicit assumption, however, was that if protection were not provided them, the cost of their support might have to be borne by the state and citizens of New York. The District of Columbia may have an altruistic interest in seeing that the survivors of residents of nearby states do not go uncompensated, but it faces no additional burden if compensation is not provided.

181. As noted above, this burden has, by reason of the action of Congress and the Court of Claims, been assumed to some degree by the citizens of the entire United States.

ty — and thus the plaintiff's right to recover — depends on the law of that state. It has not had an opportunity to consider whether the amount of damages recoverable is an element of that right, but it is speculative in the extreme for us to infer that it would hold it to be otherwise. The amount of damages recoverable for a tort is, in traditional theory, a matter of substantive law. The New York Court of Appeals, shortly after *Kilberg*, abandoned its position in that case that the measure of damages was governed by New York, and not Massachusetts, law because damage limitations are procedural in nature, and not substantive. ... And if a Maryland court would not disregard Brazilian law for the benefit of one of its own residents in a suit brought there, why should a court sitting in the District of Columbia do so at the expense of substantial and legitimate interests of Brazil? ...

Our decision is consistent as well with the most recent formulation of the *Restatement (Second) Conflict of Laws*. [The Court quoted a tentative draft of what would become *Restatement (Second) Conflict of Laws* §145 (1971).] This enumeration of significant relationships does not include that of *forum qua forum*.[182] The injury in the case before us occurred in Brazil, as did appellee's negligent conduct, if it was negligent at all. Vincent Tramontana was an American national, domiciled in Maryland, and so are his widow and children. Varig is a Brazilian corporation, which does business throughout the world. The "relationship" between the parties, if it can be called that, existed fleetingly — and in Brazil. By these criteria, the only state, other than Brazil, with a substantial claim to the application of its law is Maryland, which apparently would apply the Brazilian law in a case brought there. Thus it is that the only relationship of the District of Columbia to this claim is that it provides a forum with jurisdiction over appellee. That is hardly a reason for the forum to prefer its own notions of policy to those embodied in the Brazilian law which created the claim appellant is asserting. ...

A separate facet of appellant's public policy argument is that the Brazilian limitation on recovery for wrongful death should be disregarded entirely because of the recent marked decline in the dollar value of the Brazilian cruzeiro. Brazil's current economic problems are a matter of common knowledge, including the fact that inflation has depreciated the Brazilian currency by more than 600 per cent since the accident occurred in 1960. This development undoubtedly contributes to the appeal of appellant's argument, but it does not, in our view, warrant a result different from that we would reach had the value of the cruzeiro in terms of the dollar remained unchanged.

Brazil's interest in the protection of the financial integrity of its most important means of domestic transportation almost certainly has not been diminished by the decline in the value of its currency. ... A reluctance to reflect that decline in those prices that are subject to direct government control would be wholly understandable. Moreover, an unpredictable and virtually immeasurable factor would be imported

---

182. *Compare* Currie, *The Constitution and the Choice of Law: Government Interest and the Judicial Function*, 26 U. Chi. L. Rev. 9-10 (1958).

into the decision of international conflict of laws cases if the otherwise applicable law were subject to being displaced because of the recent history of the relative values of the currencies involved. Courts would be called upon in each case to determine at what point a declining rate of exchange of a foreign currency made application of the foreign law intolerable. Should Brazilian law be disregarded if the cruzeiro had depreciated only 300 per cent? Or 50 per cent? ...

Considerations of comity among sovereign nations certainly have relevance in this context. ... If the courts of one country make the applicability of the law of another turn on the way the exchange balance happens to be inclined at the moment, a speculative and highly artificial element would be intruded into those considerations normally recognized by civilized nations as germane in the choice of applicable law. And the forum so motivated, whether it knows it or not, wields a two-edged sword.

One further question remains, though it is one not raised by the parties.[183] The District Court converted the 100,000 cruzeiro ceiling in recovery into dollars at the rate of exchange prevailing on October 14, 1963, the date of the entry of its judgment. Although New York, alone among jurisdictions in this country, and England appear to follow a rule that recovery in tort is to be measured in terms of the rate of exchange on the date of the wrong, we think the District Court applied the sounder rule. This "day of judgment" rule has the support of the authors of the *Restatement (Second) Conflict of Laws* §612a (Tent. Draft No. 11, 1965), and is in accord with the Supreme Court's most recent decision on the point, *Die Deutsche Bank Filiale Nurnberg v. Humphrey*, 272 U.S. 517 (1926). ... The rule provides the plaintiff with the dollar equivalent of the amount he would recover if he had sued in the country whose law determines his right to recover, and it thereby ensures that he neither suffers nor benefits from the fact he chose another forum in which to litigate his claim.

Notes on Currie, Second Restatement, and Tramontana

1. *Currie's criticism of the First Restatement.* One of Currie's principal efforts was attacking the traditional approach of the *First Restatement.* "The courts simply will not remain always oblivious to the true operation of a system that, though speaking the language of metaphysics, strikes down the legitimate application of the policy of a state." B. Currie, *Selected Essays on the Conflict of Laws* 181 (1963). Is this correct? Consider how the "place of wrong" rule was applied in *American Banana, Carroll,* and *Victor.* Did the courts apply the rule without consideration of the legislative policies underlying the relevant Alabama and California laws? If so, is this an inevitable result of the *First Restatement's* rules?

2. *Interest analysis's nominal focus on legislative intent.* What is the rationale for either applying the *First Restatement* rules or engaging in interest analysis? If a court applied interest analysis to the Alabama statute at issue in *Carroll,* to the applicable rules in *Victor,* to the Sherman Act in *American Banana,* or to the Brazilian statute in *Tramontana,* what would justify it in doing so? Is interest analysis anything more than an elaborate way of trying to determine the intended scope of legislative or common law rules (and, if two or more rules overlap, the intended interaction)? Consider the following:

---

183. Appellant's argument has been that, because the judgment in dollars reflects a striking weakness if the cruzeiro vis-a-vis the dollar as of the day of its entry, the forum should disregard the Brazilian limitation entirely and apply its own law. It has not asked, even alternatively, that the conversion rate used in the judgment be that either of the date of the accident or of the initial enactment of the Brazilian Air Code.

[If a foreign law is argued, the forum court] should then inquire whether the relation of the forum to the case is such as to provide a legitimate basis for the assertion of an interest in the application of that policy. This process is essentially the familiar one of construction or interpretation. Just as we determine how a statute applies in time, and how it applies to marginal domestic situations, so we may determine how it should be applied to cases involving foreign elements in order to effectuate the legislative purpose. B. Currie, *Selected Essays on the Conflict of Laws* 183-84 (1963).

However, observing that legislative intent is important to choice of law analysis only begins debate. In most cases, the legislature will not have specified how statutes ought to apply in multistate cases. *See supra* pp. 545-46. As a consequence, judges must determine what the legislature intended in a particular multistate case. The basic purpose of choice of law rules is to provide structure and focus in answering this question. That is the purpose of both the *First* and *Second Restatements*, and Currie's choice of law analysis.

3. *Structure of Currie's interest analysis.* State concisely each step in Currie's interest analysis.

(a) *Determining a state's "interest" in having its law applicable.* How does a court determine whether a state has an "interest" in having its laws apply in a particular case? Why don't states always have *interests* in having their own law applied? What is relevant to deciding whether a state has an interest in applying its laws to certain multistate conduct?

(b) *Interest defined solely by substantive law.* Should a court look solely to the language, legislative history, and purposes of the relevant substantive legislation? That is what Currie suggests, when he argues that choice of law is merely a question of statutory construction and that "we would be better off without choice of law rules." The difficulty, however, is that most substantive statutes (and common law rules) are simply silent regarding their spatial or geographic reach, *see supra* pp. 545-46, and thus provide little guidance in defining a state's interests. What do the policies of the Sherman Act or §2590 of the Alabama Code say about the intended geographic reach of either?

(c) *Interest defined by choice of law rules.* If local legislation does not itself provide guidance regarding the legislature's interest in applying the law in multistate circumstances, where will a court find such guidance? Some commentators have argued that identifying an "interest" is a choice of law decision concerning the applicability of a particular domestic policy in particular multistate circumstances. Kay, *A Defense of Currie's Governmental Interest Analysis*, 215 Recueil des Cours 13 (1989). Does Currie's outline of interest analysis, excerpted above, provide any guidance for deciding when an interest exists or what choice of law rules to use?

(d) *Interests as escape devices.* As discussed above, a central criticism of the *First Restatement* was that it permitted judges to escape its rules through characterization and other escape devices. The same was later said of Currie's interest analysis. Consider:

Studying the vagaries of policy assessment and spatial delimitation, one becomes increasingly suspicious of the premises of interest analysis. As far as the guest statute [*e.g.*, legislation forbidding passengers riding in an automobile as guests from suing their hosts] is concerned, none of the propositions regarding its policies and spatial reach, I submit, can be proved (or disproved) with absolute certainty. An imaginative mind will have little difficulty in selecting and emphasizing the one guest statute rationale that justifies either application or displacement of the rule. de Boer, *Beyond Lex Loci Delicti: Conflicts Methodology and Multistate Torts in American Case Law* 439 (1987).

Is this risk not particularly great in international cases, where U.S. courts seek to determine the purposes of foreign laws, often relying on unfamiliar legislative history in an alien legal, economic and social environment?

4. *"False conflicts."* In certain cases, Currie's analysis would indicate that only one of two involved states would have an "interest" in application of its laws to a particular international issue. In these cases, a "false conflict" existed, and there was no need to consider application of any law other than that which was "interested" in the dispute. Compare the relevance of "conflicts" between U.S. and foreign law in determining the extraterritorial reach of federal legislation. *See supra* pp. 584-607.

Consider *Carroll, Victor,* and *American Banana.* Did any of these cases involve a "false conflict"? How does one go about trying to determine what the Mississippi, Mexican, and Costa Rican interests in each case are? How does one decide what the Alabama, California, and U.S. interests are in each case? Did *Tramontana* involve a false conflict?

5. *Currie's original forum bias in "true conflict" cases.* Currie initially concluded that the law of the forum should be applied whenever the forum had an "interest" in its application, notwithstanding the arguable applicability of foreign law and the existence of "stronger" foreign interests in the application of foreign law. *See supra* pp. 632-33. What justifies this preference for forum law? Is it a fair assumption that most legislatures would wish for local law to prevail over foreign law no matter how significant foreign interests might be or how trivial domestic interests might be? Would legislatures consider the international ramifications of such an attitude — including the possibility of reciprocal treatment by foreign states? Recall Story's explanation for the choice of law rules in his *Commentaries*: "The true foundation, on which the administration of international law must rest, is, that the rules, which are to govern, are those, which arise from mutual interest and utility, from a sense of the inconveniences, which would result from a contrary doctrine, and from a sort of moral necessity to do justice, in order that justice may be done to us in return." *See supra* pp. 546-50. Would not such considerations affect a legislature's application of its law internationally? How would Currie have decided *Tramontana*?

Compare Currie's forum bias with the "territoriality presumption." *See supra* pp. 546-52. How would Currie regard the territoriality presumption? Don't both the forum bias of Currie's interest analysis and the territoriality presumption purport to ascertain unexpressed legislative intent, albeit through extreme (and largely mirror-image) assumptions?

6. *Currie's refusal to balance competing "interests."* Currie expressly rejected any suggestion that the forum court should balance the interests of one forum against another:

> [A]ssessment of the respective values of the competing legitimate interests of two sovereign states, in order to determine which is to prevail, is a political function of a very high order. This is a function that should not be committed to courts in a democracy. B. Currie, *Selected Essays on the Conflict of Laws* 182 (1963).

Is this a satisfactory approach? Is it not likely that a rational legislature would have intended (even if without putting it into words) that its laws apply in international circumstances only where local interests outweighed foreign ones? Recall the balancing of national interests that occurs in forum non conveniens analysis, *supra* pp. 319-40, as well as in the context of extraterritorial discovery, pp. 871-92, and extraterritorial application of national laws, *infra* pp. 587-94. Recall in particular Justice Scalia's application of §403 of the *Third Restatement* in *Hartford Fire*. *See supra* pp. 604-05.

7. *Currie's "restrained" forum.* Currie also suggested at various times that, even where a true conflict was initially apparent, the forum should behave in a restrained and enlightened fashion, and interpret the competing laws with moderation and restraint. B. Currie, *Selected Essays on the Conflict of Laws* 592 (1963). What permits a court to interpret its own state's legislation in a "restrained" manner? Is it not the court's function to simply interpret the law — without special "restraint"? Does Currie's requirement for moderation call for the same sort of interest-balancing (under a different name) that he condemned? Note that, under Currie's analysis, the forum is to apply its own laws if a restrained interpretation indicates that the forum legislature still retains an interest in application.

8. *Balancing of "interests" in other choice of law contexts.* Other commentators and courts rejected Currie's refusal to balance competing interests of different jurisdictions.

(a) *Contemporary choice of law.* Some commentators advocate an explicit weighing of national interests. *E.g.*, R. Weintraub, *Commentary on the Conflict of Laws* 360-61 (3d ed. 1986); A. von Mehren & D. Trautman, *The Law of Multi-State Problems* 376-78 (1965); Baxter, *Choice of Law and the Federal System*, 16 Stan. L. Rev. 1 (1963). Consider §§6 and 145 of the *Restatement (Second) Conflict of Laws* (1971). Do they require the weighing of national interests?

Consider the opinion in *Tramontana*. Did the court balance the interests of the competing jurisdictions? Is it possible for a court to meaningfully balance the interests of two different sovereign states? What provides a court with rules for identifying or assessing the weight of different governmental interests? What permits a U.S. court to decide that foreign interests are more important than U.S. interests?

(b) *Extraterritorial reach of federal legislation.* As discussed elsewhere, "interest balancing" analyses have been adopted as a means of determining the extraterritorial reach of federal legislation. Examples include *Hartford Fire*, *Timberlane*, and §403 of the *Third Restatement*. These analyses explicitly weigh competing national interests. *See supra* pp. 587-607. Given these examples, what is your view of Currie's rejection of interest-balancing? Is he correct that courts will never be able to identify, or meaningfully compare, competing national interests? or that interest-balancing is a "political function of a very high order" that courts should not perform?

9. *Interest analysis as a guide to statutory interpretation.* At bottom, Currie's interest analysis purported to provide a means of construing statutes or common law rules in multistate contexts. According to Currie, determining the application of domestic law in international cases is nothing more than the "familiar one of construction or interpretation."

(a) *Utility of interest analysis as guide to statutory interpretation.* How useful is interest analysis as a guide to choice of law problems? Compare the guidance that interest analysis provides for statutory interpretation to that provided by the *First Restatement* or Story's *Commentaries*. What does interest analysis say should guide a court's construction of a silent statute in international cases? What role does territoriality play? What role do the parties' domiciles or nationality play? What role should other factors (such as place of conduct, place of effects, parties' chosen law, etc.) play in determining legislative intent? Does interest analysis provide any guidance at all in determining how to construe silent legislation?

(b) *Omissions of interest analysis.* Note that the "familiar" process of statutory construction makes no effort to take into account the basic institutional aspects of multistate and international problems. These features include the jurisdictional limits of international law; the existence of foreign legal systems with premises and interests that are profoundly different from one another; the possibility of retaliation, reciprocity, and cooperation among states; the desirability of uniform and predictable results; and the special burdens that private parties may encounter in international cases. The rules adopted by Story and the *First Restatement* sought to take these factors into account, as other choice of law theories have. Can interest analysis provide a useful guide to international choice of law problems without doing the same?

10. *Importance of domicile in interest analysis.* In addition to providing a general statement of interest analysis, Currie also gave examples of its application. Those examples turned significantly on the domiciles of the parties. For example, Currie devoted substantial attention to the classic case of *Milliken v. Pratt*, 125 Mass. 374 (1878) (excerpted below, *infra* pp. 666-69). As discussed below, *Milliken* involved a contract between a seller and a buyer, where the buyer's wife guaranteed his performance. Massachusetts, where the buyer and his wife lived, had a "married woman's contract" statute, that invalidated her guaranty. Maine, where the seller resided and where the contract was deemed made, would have given effect to the guarantee (because it did not have a married woman's contract statute). Currie considered how *Milliken* would have been decided under interest analysis:

> Massachusetts, in common with all other American states and many foreign countries, believes in freedom of contract. ... It also believes, however, that married women constitute a class requiring special protection. It has therefore subordinated its policy of security of transactions to its policy of protecting married women. More specifically, it has subordinated the interests of creditors to the interests of this particular, favored class of debtors ... married women. ... *What* married women? Why, those with whose welfare Massachusetts is concerned, of course — *i.e.*, Massachusetts married women. In 1866 Maine emancipated (its) married women. Is Massachusetts declaring that decision erroneous, attempting to alter its effect? Certainly not. ... Well, each to his own. Let Maine go feminist and modern; as for Massachusetts, it will stick to the old ways — for Massachusetts women. B. Currie, *Selected Essays on the Conflict of Law* 85 (1963).

That was the full extent of Currie's analysis. Is this reasoning persuasive? Why is it that Massachusetts is, "of course," concerned with "Massachusetts married women"? Why is it not concerned with *any* woman who makes a contract *in* Massachusetts? Why is Massachusetts concerned with what Massachusetts women may do when they go abroad? Consider the following remarks on Currie's analysis:

> As a general matter, where the laws of the parties' home states differ, each of these laws will either help the party who happens to be a local person or hurt the party who happens to be a local person. If it helps the local person, then the case is a true conflict. The reason is that if forum law helps the local, this means that foreign law hurts the local and therefore helps the foreigner. This gives rise to a forum interest in helping the local but also a foreign interest in helping the foreigner. If, in contrast, forum law hurts the local person, the case will be unprovided-for. The reason is that if forum law hurts the local, then the forum has no interest in

applying it. But if forum law hurts the local, then forum law helps the foreigner and foreign law hurts the foreigner. The foreign state therefore has no interest in having its law applied either.

Combining this set of assumptions about when interests exist with the proposed instructions about how to transform interests into case outcomes yields another interesting pattern. Either the law of the common domicile (if there is one) or forum law applies, and which one applies does not depend on the content of the state's laws. ... [O]ne can decide which law to apply even before one knows the content of the two competing rules. One need only know the domiciles of the parties, and (where the parties come from different states) whether the two states have identical rules or different ones. An interest analysis based on domiciliary-defined interests and a forum preference is, in other words, jurisdiction selecting like the *First Restatement*. ... Interest analysis is argued to better effectuate substantive policies than the *[First] Restatement* did because it does a more substantively sensible job of choosing the relevant jurisdiction selecting factors. Its suggested application of either the common domicile law (if there is one) or else forum law is argued to reflect substantive policies better than the vested rights regime did. L. Brilmayer, *Conflict of Laws: Foundations and Future Directions* 59-60 (1991).

Is this an accurate description of interest analysis? If it is, note that interest analysis in fact much like the *First Restatement*, substituting domicile and nationality for territoriality. Which party's (or parties') nationality is important in Currie's interest analysis?

11. *Interest analysis and international law.* Suppose that Professor Brilmayer is correct and that interest analysis does amount to applying the forum's law to protect forum residents that are injured abroad (where foreign law would limit their recovery) or forum residents that are sued for foreign actions (where foreign law would expand their liability). As discussed above, international law does not generally permit a state to apply its substantive laws to conduct occurring abroad based solely on the nationality or domicile of the plaintiff. *See supra* pp. 507-508. Is that relevant in assessing the wisdom of Currie's interest analysis? Is it relevant to the ability of interest analysis to accurately predict unexpressed legislative intent? Recall the *Charming Betsy* rule that Congress will not be presumed to violate international law. *See supra* pp. 22 & 510-11.

12. *Interest analysis in* Tramontana. Consider the application of interest analysis in *Tramontana*. Is the case correctly decided? Did the District of Columbia have *any* interest in the dispute in *Tramontana*? What does *Tramontana* say? Suppose that Mr. Tramontana and his widow had been residents of the District of Columbia at all relevant times. Would, in those circumstances, the District of Columbia have had an interest? How would *Tramontana* have assessed that interest? Would it have balanced the D.C. interest against the Brazilian interest? Or would it have concluded, as Currie would have, that the forum's interest prevailed?

Reconsider *Tramontana's* conclusion that the District of Columbia in fact had no significant interest. The court remarks that the Tramontanas resided in Maryland, and that Maryland (not D.C.) would bear the burden of Tramontana's indigency. Is that persuasive? in an international case? Don't *U.S.* taxpayers contribute to the cost of caring for public charges? In international matters, why should a state court not consider a plaintiff as a *U.S.* resident, rather than as a resident of some particular state of the United States? Recall the similar issue in the context of judicial jurisdiction and forum non conveniens. *See supra* pp. 171-97 & 334-35.

Is it in fact correct, as the court suggests in *Tramontana*, that the case was no different from a case involving a U.S. tourist killed in Amsterdam by a truck? What is the relevance of the fact that Mr. Tramontana was in a U.S. military aircraft on an official mission temporarily passing through Brazil in the course of his employment by the U.S. Navy? Does this affect the D.C. interest? the U.S. interest? What if Mr. Tramontana had been flying over Brazil, without stopping, on his way to Chile? What if the collision with Varig's plane had occurred over Chile, which had similar damage limits?

13. *Second Restatement's "most significant relationship" test.* Do §§6 and 145 of the *Second Restatement* adopt Currie's interest analysis? Do the two sections consider the underlying policies of the competing laws, or do they look to external jurisdiction-selecting factors like territoriality and domicile? Or do they try to do both?

How would §145 resolve: (a) *Carroll*; (b) *Victor*; (c) *Tramontana*; (d) *American Banana*; and (e) *Hartford Fire*? How certain would you be of the answer in each of these cases? How does §145 compare to

(a) the *First Restatement's* "place of the wrong" rule; and (b) Currie's interest analysis? Which analysis is preferable? Consider:

> [I]t hardly comes as news that the *Second Restatement* is flawed. But one needs to read a lot of opinions in a single sitting fully to appreciate just how badly the *Second Restatement* works in practice. ... One sees the *Second Restatement* at its worst in [cases applying §6's factors]. Judges try to make sense of the factors listed in §6, but the analysis is predictably question-begging and confusing. The drafters of the *Second Restatement* apparently hoped that courts would eventually sort through the considerations in §6 and construct a more systematic approach to choice of law. But §6 seems to have had exactly the opposite effect — encouraging courts to forego systematic analysis in favor of ad hoc intuition. Kramer, *Choice of Law in the American Courts in 1990: Trends and Developments*, 39 Am. J. Comp. L. 465, 486-87 (1991).

Compare §§145 and 146 of the *Second Restatement*. Is §146 an application of interest analysis? What is the rationale for §146's statement that the "law of the state where the injury occurred" generally is the applicable law in personal injury cases? How different is this from the *First Restatement*?

14. Contemporary choice of law theory and legislative purposes. Post-Currie American choice of law theory focuses on the legislative purposes of particular enactments:

> The key insight of the interest analysis ... was that it depends on the purpose of the law in question. The point is elegantly simple: if — in the interests of comity and mutual accommodation — we presume that a state's law is intended to apply only in cases that are connected to the state in some important way, the significant contacts ought to be those that implicate the reasons the law was enacted for wholly domestic cases. This has two advantages: first, it ensures that the state's laws apply in the cases that are likely to be of greatest concern to the state's law makers; second, it leaves room for the laws of other states in cases that are likely to be of especial concern to those states. Kramer, *Rethinking Choice of Law*, 90 Colum. L. Rev. 277, 298 (1990).

How is this observation applicable in the cases examined above — *Carroll, Victor, American Banana,* and *Tramontana*? What are the purposes of the tort laws at issue in *Carroll* and *American Banana*? Are they not designed to deter undesirable conduct and assist innocent victims to bear the cost of their injury by shifting costs to "wrongdoers"? If so, what classes of "undesirable conduct" and "innocent victims" are covered? Are there any clear (or other) answers to this question in the mere "legislative purpose" of a tort law?

What are the purposes of the liability limits in *Victor* and *Tramontana*? Does a legislative desire to protect defendants from "undue" liability provide any guidance in determining *what* defendants in *which* cases?

15. Baxter's principle of comparative impairment. Professor Baxter suggested resolving choice of law problems by considering what would happen if the legislatures of two states were to negotiate an interstate agreement dealing with the application of each state's laws in multistate cases. Baxter, *Choice of Law and the Federal System*, 16 Stan. L. Rev. 1, 9-10 (1963). Baxter predicted that each state "would cautiously give up what it wanted less to obtain what it wanted more, ... and the final agreement would approximate maximum utility to each." *Id.* at 7. He reasoned that courts could predict the outcome of such negotiations with a rule of "comparative impairment," that would apply the law of the state whose domestic policies would be most impaired by non-application. Is this a useful analysis? What results would one expect in cases like *American Banana, Carroll, Victor,* and *Tramontana*? What relevance would the preponderant economic and political power of the United States have in the negotiations contemplated by Baxter's analysis?

16. Domestic v. international choice of law rules. Consider §10 of the *Second Restatement*. Why might international choice of law rules differ from domestic ones? If the accident in *Tramontana* had occurred over Texas, would any different analysis be required? What if *Victor* had involved an accident in Arizona?

17. Public policy in contemporary choice of law applicable to torts. As discussed above, public policy remains a basis for a U.S. court to decline to apply foreign law, even under most contemporary choice of law principles. As in other contexts, however, defining "public policy" is an unpredictable undertaking. *See supra* pp. 341-43, 486-88, 624-31, 655-56 & 974-86.

Consider the application of the public policy doctrine in *Kilberg* and *Tramontana*. In *Kilberg*, the court held that a damage limitation of a sister state was invalid, as applied to a New York resident killed in the sister state on a flight originating in New York. Is the application of public policy in such cases appropriate? If so, what distinguishes *Kilberg* from *Tramontana*? Recall the discussions above of choice of public policy considerations. *See supra* pp. 428-30.

18. *Substance and procedure in contemporary choice of law analysis.* Although the *Second Restatement* abandoned many aspects of the *First Restatement's* approach to choice of law, it did not abandon the general principle that "procedural" matters are governed by the law of the forum. Why? Note, however, that §122 of the *Second Restatement* does not use the "procedural" label, and instead deals with "rules prescribing how litigation shall be conducted." Like its predecessor, the *Second Restatement* provides that the law of the forum governs matters such as form of action, service, rules of pleadings, and conduct of proceedings. *Restatement (Second) Conflict of Laws* §§124, 126 & 127 (1971). However, the *Second Restatement* treats other matters in less clearcut fashion, providing for example that questions of burden of proof, parties to an action, set-off, and sufficiency of evidence are generally governed by the forum's law, but may be displaced if the otherwise applicable substantive law indicates that such matters are relevant to a decision on the merits. *Restatement (Second) Conflict of Laws* §§125, 128, 133, 134 & 135 (1971).

19. *Statutes of limitations in contemporary U.S. choice of law analysis.* Sections 142 and 143 of the *Second Restatement*, which are excerpted above, change the *First Restatement's* rule regarding statutes of limitations. As §142 suggests, many U.S. states have enacted "borrowing statutes," which provide that an action cannot be maintained if the statute of limitations of another state, more closely connected to the dispute, would bar the action. Different borrowing statutes define the state whose limitations period is to be borrowed differently: some refer to the state where the plaintiff's cause of action "arose" or "accrued," while others refer to the state where the defendant was domiciled at the time of the events giving rise to the claim. *See, e.g.,* N.Y. C.P.L.R. §202 ("An action based upon a cause of action accruing without the state cannot be commenced after the expiration of the time limited by the laws of either the state or the place without the state where the cause of action accrued, except that where the cause of action accrued in favor of a resident of the state the time limited by the laws of the state shall apply.").

What does §143 mean? In what circumstances would it apply? In general, a statute of limitations will be held to bar the right, not merely the remedy, only when a statutory claim is involved and when the limitations provision is attached to the substantive right "so specifically as to warrant saying that it qualifie[s] the right." *Davis v. Mills,* 194 U.S. 451, 454 (1904). Is this a sensible distinction?

20. *Statutes of limitations in civil jurisdictions.* Many civil law states treat statutes of limitations as "substantive," and apply the law of the state whose law governs the merits of the parties' dispute. *See* McDonald, *Limitation of Acts — Conflict of Laws — Lex Fori or Lex Loci,* 35 Tex. L. Rev. 95 (1957). Is this wise?

C. Choice of Law Applicable to Contracts

Central features of all choice of law systems are rules governing the choice of law applicable to contracts. This was a principal focus of Huber's *De Conflictu Legum* and Story's *Commentaries on the Conflict of Laws*, as well as of the *First* and *Second Restatements*.[184] As with the law applicable to torts, U.S. choice of law rules concerning contracts have undergone substantial evolution in the past century, and remain subject to diverse approaches in different U.S. courts. Indeed, it is often said that the choice of law applicable to contracts is "the most complex and confused area of choice-of-law problems."[185] Because of the continuing relevance of traditional rules in many jurisdictions, this section devotes particular emphasis to historic rules and developments.

1. Party Autonomy and Choice of Law Clauses[186]

It is common for commercial contracts to include "choice of law" provisions that select the law that the parties agree should govern their disputes. Like forum selection clauses, private parties agree upon choice of law clauses in order to increase the predictability of their agreements, to avoid the costs of disputes over applicable law, and to obtain advantages by specifying a favorable body of substantive law.[187] Private parties will often prefer that the law of their own home jurisdiction govern their agreements (although this preference is generally unreflective, and may actually result in the application of unfavorable rules of substantive law). If this cannot be bargained for, international commercial agreements often specify the laws of a neutral, third country with a developed legal system (such as England, New York or Switzerland).

When a choice of law clause exists, three significant issues arise: (a) is the agreement enforceable; (b) if so, subject to what exceptions; and (c) how is the agreement to be interpreted? Different nations adopt significantly different approaches to all

---

184. *See* J. Story, *Commentaries on the Conflict of Laws* Chapter VIII (2d ed. 1841); *Restatement (First) Conflict of Laws* Chapter 8 (1834); *Restatement (Second) Conflict of Laws* Chapter 8 (1971).

185. R. Weintraub, *Commentary on the Conflict of Laws* 362 (3rd ed. 1986).

186. Commentary on party autonomy and choice of law agreements includes, *e.g.*, Covey & Morris, *The Enforceability of Agreements Providing for Forum and Choice of Law Selection*, 61 Denver L.J. 837 (1984); James, *Effects of the Autonomy of the Parties on the Conflicts of Law*, 36 Kent. L. Rev. 34 (1959); Prebble, *Choice-of-Law to Determine the Validity and Effect of Contracts: A Comparison of English and American Approaches to the Conflict of Laws*, 58 Cornell L. Rev. 433 (1973); Gruson, *Governing Law Clauses in Commercial Agreements — New York's Approach*, 18 Colum. J. Trans. L. 323 (1980); James, *Effects of the Autonomy of the Parties on Conflicts of Law*, 36 Chi. Kent. L. Rev. 34 (1959); Weinberger, *Party Autonomy and Choice of Law: The Restatement, Second, Interest Analysis and the Search for a Methodological Synthesis*, 4 Hofstra L. Rev. 605 (1976); Yntema, *Contract and the Conflict of Laws: "Autonomy" in the Choice of Law in the United States*, 1 N.Y.L. F. 46 (1955).

187. "A contractual provision specifying in advance the forum in which disputes shall be litigated and the law to be applied is ... an almost indispensable precondition to achievement of the orderliness and predictability essential to any international business transaction." *Scherk v. Alberto-Culver Co.*, 417 U.S. 506, 516 (1974). *See* Lowe, *Choice of Law Clauses in International Contracts: A Practical Approach*, 12 Harv. Int'l L. J. 1 (1971).

three of these questions; different approaches have prevailed in different historical periods; and different approaches presently prevail in different U.S. jurisdictions.

a. Traditional U.S. Approach: Choice of Law Clauses Are Not Enforceable

During the 19th and early 20th century, private choice of law agreements were sometimes said to be *per se* unenforceable (much like choice of forum and arbitration agreements).[188] The *Restatement (First) Conflict of Laws* contained no provisions regarding choice of law agreements, leaving the question to be governed by generally applicable choice of law rules for contracts (which accorded no weight to the parties' intended choice of law). Joseph Beale, the Reporter for the *First Restatement*, made it clear that he regarded choice of law clauses as unenforceable. Beale characterized the principle of party autonomy in choice of law as "absolutely anomalous," "theoretically indefensible," and "absolutely impracticable."[189] Beale reasoned that enforcement of a choice of law clause would mean that "at their will [private parties] can free themselves from the power of the law which would otherwise apply to their acts."[190]

Early U.S. judicial decisions were less doctrinaire and adopted divergent approaches to party autonomy in the choice of law. Some early decisions refused to recognize the concept of party autonomy.[191] But other decisions adopted a different approach, either enforcing express choice of law agreements,[192] or inquiring into the substantive law that the parties to a contract likely intended to govern their dealings.[193]

b. Contemporary U.S. Approach: Choice of Law Clauses Are Presumptively Enforceable

Historic skepticism about the enforceability of choice of law agreements has been substantially eroded in contemporary U.S. law. As detailed below, such clauses are now generally enforced by U.S. courts, subject to significant exceptions.[194] The *Restatement (Second) Conflict of Laws* states a widely accepted approach, providing in §187(1) that choice of law clauses will generally be enforced as to subjects that could have been resolved through an express provision in the parties' agreement (such as

---

188. *See supra* pp. 373-74 & 993-94.

189. 2 J. Beale, *A Treatise on the Conflict of Laws* 1080, 1083, & 1084 (1935).

190. 2 J. Beale, *A Treatise on the Conflict of Laws* 1080 (1935).

191. *E.g., E. Gerli and Co. v. Cunard S.S. Co.*, 48 F.2d 115, 117 (2d Cir. 1931).

192. *Dolan v. Mutual Reserve Fund Life Ass'n*, 53 N.E. 398 (Mass. 1899); *Griesemer v. Mutual Life Ins. Co. of New York*, 38 P. 1031 (Wash. 1894); *Fonseca v. Cunard SS Co.*, 27 N.E. 665 (Mass. 1891); *Kellogg v. Miller*, 13 Fed. 198 (D. Neb. 1881).

193. *Pritchard v. Norton*, 106 U.S. 124 (1882); *Wayman v. Southard*, 23 U.S. 1, 48 (1825); *Thompson v. Ketcham*, 8 Johns. 189 (N.Y. 1811).

194. *See Restatement (Second) Conflict of Laws* §187 (1971); Gruson, *Governing Law Clauses in Commercial Agreements - New York's Approach*, 18 Colum. J. Trans. L. 323, 324 n.3 (1979) (collecting authorities); Gruson, *Governing-Law Clauses in International and Interstate Loan Agreements — New York's Approach*, 1982 U. Ill. Rev. 207.

the time for performance).[195] Although it does not expressly say so, §187(1) contemplates non-enforcement of agreements in violation of forum public policy (because such agreements would not have been capable of resolution in the manner directed by foreign law even by an express agreement).

Section 187(2) permits enforcement of choice of law provisions as to issues that the parties could *not* have expressly dealt with, subject to exceptions.[196] Section 187(2) applies to matters such as capacity, substantive validity, and formalities. The general rule of enforceability is subject to exceptions where there is "no substantial relationship" between the chosen law and the parties or their transaction,[197] or where the chosen law would be contrary to the fundamental public policy of a state with a "materially greater interest."[198]

Most contemporary U.S. state and federal courts have adopted approaches that are broadly similar to §187.[199] The same is true of §1-105(1) of the Uniform Commercial Code.[200]

c. Public Policy

As in other contexts, there is no clear definition of what constitutes a public policy for purposes overriding a choice of law agreement,[201] nor of how "strong" a public policy must be before it will override the parties' chosen law.[202] Some courts have considered whether the asserted public policy is derived from statutory prohibitions, which are typically deemed to be more reflective of public policy than common law

---

195. The comments to §187 explain that §187(1) relates to "incorporation by reference and is not a rule of choice of law." In dealing with issues that the parties could have dealt with by explicit agreement, the section contemplates subjects that parties ordinarily "spell out ... in the contract." It extends to "most rules of contract law," which are generally "designed to fill gaps in a contract which the parties could themselves have filled with express provisions." The comment includes within this category "rules relating to construction, to conditions precedent and subsequent, to sufficiency of performance, and to excuse for nonperformance, including questions of frustration and impossibility." "As to all such matters, the forum will apply the provisions of the chosen law." *Restatement (Second) Conflict of Laws* §187 comment c (1971).

196. Section 187(2) applies "when it is sought to have the chosen law determine issues which the parties could not have determined by explicit agreement directed to the particular issue. Examples of such questions are those involving capacity, formalities and substantial validity. A person cannot vest himself with contractual capacity by stating in the contract that he has such capacity." *Restatement (Second) Conflict of Laws* §187 comment d (1971).

197. *Restatement (Second) Conflict of Laws* §187(2)(a) (1971).

198. *Restatement (Second) Conflict of Laws* §187(2)(b) (1971).

199. *See* Gruson, *Governing Law Clauses in Commercial Agreements — New York's Approach*, 18 Colum. J. Trans. L. 323 (1979); Reese, *Power of Parties to Choose Law Governing Their Contract*, 1960 Proc. Am. Soc. Int'l L. 49 (1960).

200. Uniform Commercial Code §1-105(1) provides: "when a transaction bears a reasonable relationship to this state and also to another state or nation the parties may agree that the law of either this state or of such other state or nation shall govern their rights and duties."

201. *See Restatement (Second) Conflict of Laws* §187 comment g (1971).

202. *Compare Restatement (Second) Conflict of Laws* §187(2)(b) (1971) ("fundamental policy") *with Intercontinental Hotels Corp. v. Golden*, 254 N.Y.S.2d 527 (1964) ("inherently vicious, wicked or immoral") *with Loucks v. Standard Oil Co.*, 224 N.Y. 99, 110 (1918) ("offend our sense of justice or menace the public welfare").

rules,[203] and if so, whether the statute in question is penal in nature or is specifically applicable in choice of law contexts.[204] Public policies that have been found capable of invalidating a choice of law clause have included usury restrictions,[205] labor relations rules (including covenants not to compete),[206] rules concerning governmental corruption,[207] rules concerning set-off,[208] rules protecting dealers or franchisees,[209] rules regarding indemnification,[210] and laws protecting insureds.[211]

As §187(2) indicates, a public policy will not override the parties' chosen law unless it is the public policy of a state (a) whose law would (but for the choice of law clause) apply to the parties' agreement; and (b) which has a "materially greater interest" than the state whose law has been chosen.[212] In general, the closer the relationship between the parties' transaction and the forum state, the more likely that local law will be deemed to constitute a substantial public policy.[213] As §187(2)(b) of the *Second Restatement* suggests, the public policy of states other than the forum may sometimes render the parties' choice of law clause unenforceable.[214]

d. Reasonable Relationship

Some courts refuse to enforce choice of law provisions that select the law of a state that lacks a "reasonable relation" to the parties' transaction. For example, §1-

---

203. *Restatement (Second) Conflict of Laws* §187 comment g (1971) (by implication).

204. *Reger v. National Assoc. of Bedding Mftrs.*, 372 N.Y.S.2d 97, 116 (1975); *Big Four Mills, Ltd. v. Commercial Credit Co.*, 211 S.W.2d 831, 836 (Ky. 1948); *MGM Grand Hotel, Inc. v. Imperial Glass Co.*, 65 F.R.D. 624, 632 (D. Nev. 1974), *rev'd on other grounds*, 533 F.2d 486 (9th Cir. 1976), *cert. denied*, 429 U.S. 887 (1976).

205. *E.g.*, *Whitaker v. Spiegel, Inc.*, 623 P.2d 1147 (Wash. 1981). The clear weight of authority is that usury restrictions are not sufficiently clear and fundamental to constitute fundamental public policies for choice-of-law purposes. *Seeman v. Philadelphia Warehouse Co.*, 274 U.S. 403 (1927); *Clarkson v. Finance Co.*, 328 F.2d 404 (4th Cir. 1964); *Gamer v. duPont Glore Forgan, Inc.*, 135 Cal. Rptr. 230 (1976).

206. *De Santis v. Wackenhut Corp.*, 793 S.W.2d 670 (Tex. 1990); *Cherry, Bekaert & Holland v. Brown*, 582 So.2d 502 (Ala. 1991); *Davis v. Jointless Fire Brick Co.*, 300 F.2d 1 (9th Cir. 1924); *Blalock v. Perfect Subscription Co.*, 458 F.Supp. 123 (S.D. Ala. 1978).

207. *Triad Financial Establishment v. Tumpane Co.*, 611 F.Supp. 157 (N.D.N.Y. 1985).

208. *Moore v. Subaru of America*, 891 F.2d 1445 (10th Cir. 1989).

209. *Modern Computer Systems, Inc. v. Modern Banking Systems, Inc.*, 858 F.2d 1339 (8th Cir. 1988); *Bush v. National School Studios, Inc.*, 407 N.W.2d 883 (Wis. 1987); *Rutter v. BX of Tri-Cities, Inc.*, 806 P.2d 1266 (Wash. Ct. App. 1991).

210. *Tucker v. R.A. Hanson Co.*, 956 F.2d 215 (10th Cir. 1992); *Donaldson v. Fluor Engineers, Inc.*, 523 N.E.2d 117 (Ill. App. 1st Dist. 1988); *Chrysler Corp. v. Skyline Indus. Services, Inc.*, 502 N.W.2d 715 (Mich. App. 1993) (refusal by Michigan court to enforce contractual indemnification provision that violated laws of Illinois, which was place of relevant conduct, notwithstanding Michigan choice of law clause).

211. *New York Life Ins. Co. v. Cravens*, 178 U.S. 389 (1900); *Nelson v. Aetna Life Ins. Co.*, 359 F.Supp. 271, 290-2 (W.D. Mo. 1973).

212. *Restatement (Second) Conflict of Laws* §187(2)(b) (1971).

213. *Restatement (Second) Conflict of Laws* §187 comment f (1971) ("The more closely the state of the chosen law is related to the contract and the parties, the more fundamental must be the policy of the state of the otherwise applicable law to justify denying effect to the choice-of-law provision").

214. *Connecticut General Life Ins. Co. v. Boseman*, 84 F.2d 701, 705 (5th Cir. 1936), *aff'd*, 301 U.S. 196 (1937); *Citizens National Bank v. Waugh*, 78 F.2d 325, 327 (4th Cir. 1935); *Fricke v. Isbrandtsen Co.*, 151 F.Supp. 465, 468 (S.D.N.Y. 1957).

105(1) of the Uniform Commercial Code provides that "when a transaction bears a reasonable relationship to this state and also to another state or nation the parties may agree that the law of either this state or of such other state or nation shall govern their rights and duties." Section 187(2)(a) is to the same effect.

The principal rationale for this requirement appears to be a concern that parties to purely local transactions, relating entirely to one state, not be able to circumvent local laws by choosing a foreign law.[215] Nonetheless, the reasonable relationship requirement is stated more broadly, suggesting that it is applicable to transactions involving relationships with two or more jurisdictions.[216]

e. Interpretation of Choice of Law Clauses

Like other contractual provisions, choice of law clauses must be interpreted. This usually turns primarily on the language that the parties used in their agreement. Nevertheless, there are recurrent issues of interpretation, as to which rules of construction have developed.

First, the parties' agreement to a choice-of-forum clause does not necessarily imply agreement that the chosen forum's law should also govern their relations.[217] Conversely, an agreement as to governing law does not, under due process precedents, necessarily provide a submission to the jurisdiction of the courts of the chosen state.[218]

Second, like choice of forum clauses, choice of law agreements often must be construed to determine their scope — the issues or claims that are subject to the parties' chosen law. As with forum selection agreements, this inquiry turns largely on the particular language of the parties' agreement. Some choice of law clauses state only that "[t]his agreement shall be construed in accordance with the laws of State A," which suggests that issues of capacity, contractual validity, formalities, excuses, and damages are not subject to the parties' chosen law. Other choice of law clauses

---

215. *Dolan v. Mutual Reserve Fund Life Ass'n*, 53 N.E. 398, 399 (Mass. 1899); *New England Mutual Life Ins. Co. v. Olin*, 114 F.2d 131, 136 (7th Cir. 1940).

216. *Restatement (Second) Conflict of Laws* §187(2)(a) (1971); Uniform Commercial Code §1-105 (1); *Seeman v. Philadelphia Warehouse Co.*, 274 U.S. 403 (1927); *Consolidated Jewellers, Inc. v. Standard Financial Corp.*, 325 F.2d 31, 34 (6th Cir. 1963); *Prows v. Pinpoint Retail Systems, Inc.*, 868 P.2d 809 (Utah 1993). For criticism of the reasonable relationship requirement, *see* A. Ehrenzweig, *Conflict of Laws* 469 (1962).

217. Gruson, *Governing-Law Clauses in International and Interstate Loan Agreements — New York's Approach*, 1982 U. Ill. Rev. 207. However, the parties' submission to the jurisdiction of a particular forum can be evidence of an implied selection of applicable law. *E.g., Restatement (Second) Conflict of Laws* §187 comment a (1971); *Lummus v. Commonwealth Oil Refining Co.*, 280 F.2d 915 (1st Cir. 1960), *cert. denied*, 364 U.S. 911 (1960); *Kress Corp. v. Levy Co.*, 430 N.E.2d 593 (Ill. 1981). *See also Paper Express Ltd. v. Pfankuch Maschinen GmbH*, 1990 WL 141424 (N.D. Ill. Sept. 24, 1990) (acceptance of rules of German trade association included acceptance of jurisdiction of German courts); *Walpex Trading Co. v. Yacimientos Petroliferos Fiscales Bolivianos*, 756 F.Supp. 136 (S.D.N.Y. 1991) (court rejects argument that Bolivian law would have required parties to include forum selection clause in contract, if it had been executed).

218. *See supra* pp. 101-02. It may, however, constitute a significant factor in minimum contacts analysis. *See supra* pp. 148-49.

state more broadly that "[t]his agreement shall be governed by the laws of State B," or "[t]his agreement and all disputes arising under it shall be subject to the laws of State C." Both formulations suggest that *all* issues of contract law are subject to the parties' chosen law, but that tort or other non-contractual claims that relate to the contract are not.[219] Finally, some choice of law clauses are drafted very broadly, attempting to include non-contractual claims (as well as contractual ones): "all disputes arising out of or relating to this agreement shall be governed exclusively by the laws of State D."

Third, choice of law clauses must be interpreted to determine which aspects of the parties' chosen law are applicable. In particular, does a reference to "the laws of State E" refer to the "whole law" of State E — including its choice of law rules — or does it refer only to the "local law" of State E? The *Second Restatement* provides that, absent contrary evidence of intent, the latter interpretation will prevail.[220]

Fourth, will a choice of law clause be interpreted to include issues relating to procedure, statutes of limitations, burdens of proof, excuses for non-performance, or damages?[221] The *Second Restatement* suggests that at least some of these issues will generally *not* be subject to the parties' chosen law, although evidence of contrary intent could produce a different construction.[222]

f. Selected Materials on Party Autonomy

Excerpted below are selected materials on choice of law agreements. First, consider §§187 and 204 of the *Restatement (Second) Conflict of Laws*, which adopt a general rule of enforceability for choice of law clauses as to specified issues. Then reread the excerpts from *The Bremen v. Zapata Off-Shore Co., Roby v. Corporation of Lloyds,* and *Triad Financial Establishment v. Tumpane Co.*

RESTATEMENT (SECOND) CONFLICT OF LAWS (1971)
§§187 & 204

§187. (1) The law of the state chosen by the parties to govern their contractual rights and duties will be applied if the particular issue is one which the parties could have resolved by an explicit provision in their agreement directed to that issue.

(2) The law of the state chosen by the parties to govern their contractual rights and duties will be applied, even if the particular issue is one which the parties could not have resolved by an explicit provision in their agreement directed to that issue, unless either

---

219. *E.g., T-Bill Option Club v. Brown & Co.,* 1994 WL 201104 (7th Cir. 1994); *Pollite v. McDonald's Corp.* 1994 U.S. App. Lexis 1506 (10th Cir. 1994); *Union Oil Co. v. John Brown E & C,* 1994 WL 535108 (N.D. Ill. 1994).

220. *Restatement (Second) Conflict of Laws* §187(3) (1971); *Siegelman v. Cunard White Star Ltd.,* 221 F.2d 189 (2d Cir. 1955); *Fuller Co. v. Compagnie des Bauxites de Guinee,* 421 F.Supp. 938, 946 (W.D. Pa. 1976); *infra* pp. 663-64.

221. *Restatement (Second) Conflict of Laws* §§122-43 (1971).

222. *See infra* pp. 663-64.

(a) the chosen state has no substantial relationship to the parties or the transaction and there is no other reasonable basis for the parties' choice, or

(b) application of the law of the chosen state would be contrary to a fundamental policy of a state which has a materially greater interest than the chosen state in the determination of the particular issue and which, under the [general choice-of-law] rule of §188, would be the state of the applicable law in the absence of an effective choice of law by the parties.

(3) In the absence of a contrary indication of intention, the reference is to the local law of the state of the chosen law.

§204. When the meaning which the parties intended to convey by words used in a contract cannot satisfactorily be ascertained, the words will be construed

(a) in accordance with the local law of the state chosen by the parties, or

(b) in the absence of such a choice, in accordance with the local law of the state selected by application of the rule of §188.

Comment a. Scope of section. The rule of this Section is applicable only in a limited number of situations. The forum will first seek to interpret the contract in the manner intended by the parties. It will consider the ordinary meaning of the words, the context in which they appear in the instrument, and any other evidence which casts light on the parties' intentions, including an intention, if any, to give a word the meaning given it in the local law of another state. The forum will apply its own rules in determining the relevancy of evidence, and it will use its own judgment in drawing conclusions from the facts. This process, which is called interpretation in the Restatement of this Subject (see §224), does not involve application by the forum of its choice-of-law rules. When the meaning which the parties intended to convey by words used in a contract cannot satisfactorily be ascertained, the forum must determine the meaning of these words by a process which in the Restatement of this Subject is called construction (see §224). This process involves the application of the rules of construction of a particular state. Consequently, a choice-of-law problem arises whenever a contract has a substantial relationship to two or more states with different rules of construction.

THE BREMEN v. ZAPATA OFF-SHORE COMPANY

407 U.S. 1 (1972) [excerpted above at pp. 383-88]

ROBY v. CORPORATION OF LLOYD'S

996 F.2d 1353 (2d Cir. 1993) [excerpted above at pp. 418-23]

TRIAD FINANCIAL ESTABLISHMENT v. TUMPANE CO.

611 F.Supp. 157 (N.D.N.Y. 1985) [excerpted above at pp. 423-26]

Notes on Second Restatement, Bremen, Roby, and Tumpane

1. *Distinction between interpretation, construction, and validity.* Comment a to §204 draws distinctions between: (a) interpreting a contract; (b) construing a contract; and (c) validity of a contract.

(a) *Interpretation of contract not subject to choice of law analysis.* When a court interprets a contract, it simply looks to the parties' likely intentions. According to the *Second Restatement*, this is not a process requiring the application of legal rules (other than evidentiary rules, which are provided by the forum's procedural law), or the application of choice of law rules. It is merely a process of attempting to ascertain what the parties intended.

(b) *Construction of contract subject to §§187 and 188.* Section 204 distinguishes rules of construction from mere interpretation. If a court cannot satisfactorily ascertain the meaning of a contract by interpreting it, then it must apply the rules of construction of a particular state. Section 204 requires application of the same basic choice of law rules as those provided for in §§187 and 188 for determining the rights and duties of parties to a contract. Is this a sensible approach? Aren't rules of construction merely ways of ascertaining the parties' intent? Why shouldn't the forum apply its own, familiar rules to this delicate task?

(c) *Validity of contract subject to §§187 and 188.* The validity of a contract, as well as issues relating to capacity, performance, and the existence and extent of contractual duties, are issues of law governed principally by §§187 and 188. There was once doubt that the parties could agree upon the law governing the issue of validity, *see Siegelman v. Cunard White Star Ltd.*, 221 F.2d 189 (2d Cir. 1955) ("much doubt"). This doubt has been largely dispelled. *A.S. Rampell, Inc. v. Hyster Co.*, 165 N.Y.S.2d 475 (1957); Weintraub, *Choice of Law in Contract*, 54 Iowa L. Rev. 399, 407 (1968); *supra* pp. 654-55.

2. *Basis for traditional rule that choice of law clauses are unenforceable.* Why is it that private parties should be permitted to select the law that governs their contractual relations? Consider the following remarks by Joseph Beale:

> The fundamental objection ... is that it involves permission to the parties to do a legislative act. It practically makes a legislative body of any two persons who choose to get together and contract. ... The meaning of the suggestion, in short, is that since the parties can adopt any foreign law at their pleasure to govern their act, that at their will they can free themselves from the power of the law which would otherwise apply to their acts. So extraordinary a power in the hands of any two individuals is absolutely anomalous. J. Beale, *Treatise on the Conflict of Laws* 1079-80 (1935).

Is that persuasive? Do parties really "legislate" when they agree on the law to govern certain of their relations with one another?

3. *Historic authorities permitting enforcement of choice of law clauses.* Beale did not express the only traditional view regarding the enforceability of choice of law agreements. In *Pritchard v. Norton*, 106 U.S. 124, 136 (1882), the Supreme Court applied Louisiana law to determine the validity of an indemnity bond that had been executed in New York. Under New York law, the bond would have been invalid, for lack of consideration, but under Louisiana law no consideration was required. The Court applied New York law, invoking the "principle that in every forum a contract is governed by the law with a view to which it is made." Other courts upheld express choice of law clauses. *See supra* pp. 654-55.

4. *Basis for rule that choice of law agreements are enforceable.* What is the rationale for enforcing choice of law agreements? Is Beale not correct in his observation that choice of law agreements are different from other contractual commitments? Consider the following explanation:

> Prime objectives of contract law are to protect the justified expectations of the parties and to make it possible for them to foretell with accuracy what will be their rights under the contract. These objectives may best be attained in multistate transactions by letting the parties choose the law to govern the validity of the contract and the rights created thereby. In this way, certainty and predictability of result are most likely to be secured. ... An objection sometimes made in the past was that to give the parties this power of choice would be tantamount to making legislators of them. ... This view is now obsolete and, in any event, falls wide of the mark. The forum in each case selects the applicable law by application of its own choice-of-law rules. There is nothing to prevent the forum from employing a choice-of-law rule which provides that, subject to stated exceptions, the law of the state chosen by the parties shall be applied to determine the validity of a contract and the rights created thereby. The law of the state chosen by the parties is applied, not because the parties themselves are legislators, but simply because

this is the result demanded by the choice-of-law rules of the forum. *Restatement (Second) Conflict of Laws* §187 comment e (1971).

Is this persuasive?

5. *Enforceability of choice of law clauses under interest analysis.* How do choice of law clauses fare under Currie's interest analysis? Consider: "[P]arty autonomy squares no better with interest analysis. If, as that methodology asserts, an important goal of choice of law is to assess the impact of competing choices on governmental duties such as paying welfare and regulating insurance rates within the state, it is doubtful that the parties' private expression of the preferences should be given much weight." Borchers, *Choice of Law in the American Courts in 1992: Observations and Reflections*, 42 Am. J. Comp. L. 125, 134 (1994). In fact, most states that have adopted Currie's interest analysis presumptively enforce choice of law clauses. *E.g., Nedlloyd Lines BV v. Superior Court*, 834 P.2d 1148 (Calif. 1992); *Comdisco Disaster Recovery Services, Inc. v. Money Mgt Systems, Inc.*, 789 F.Supp. 48 (D. Mass. 1992).

6. *Standards of enforceability of choice of law clauses.* What standard for the enforceability of choice of law clauses is set forth in §187? Other authorities have adopted less clear-cut rules, treating choice of law provisions as one factor in a general "center of gravity" or "grouping of contacts" analysis. *E.g., Haag v. Barnes*, 216 N.Y.S.2d 65 (1961). Compare this approach to some decisions concerning the enforceability of forum selection clauses, which hold that the existence of such a clause is merely one factor in a more generalized forum non conveniens or "reasonableness" analysis. *See supra* pp. 379-80. Which of these standards is wiser?

7. *Defects in formation of choice of law agreement.* Choice of law agreements, like other agreements, can be defective. Reasons include unconscionability, fraud, illegality, mistake, or lack of consideration. *Restatement (Second) Conflict of Laws* §187, comment b (1971) ("A choice-of-law provision, like any other contractual provision, will not be given effect if the consent of one of the parties to its inclusion in the contract was obtained by improper means, such as by misrepresentation, duress, or undue influence, or by mistake"); *Modern Computer Systems, Inc. v. Modern Banking Systems, Inc.*, 858 F.2d 1339 (8th Cir. 1988). What law should determine whether a choice of law clause is invalid? The *Second Restatement* provides that such issues "will be determined by the forum in accordance with its own legal principles." *Restatement (Second) Conflict of Laws* §187, comment b (1971). Why? Why not apply the parties' chosen law? Or the law of the state with the most significant relationship?

8. *Separability of choice of law agreement.* Should choice of law clauses be regarded as "separable," as with arbitration and forum selection agreements? *See supra* p. 401 & *infra* pp. 996-97 & 1013-16. What would be the consequences of such a result?

9. *Enforceability of contracts where the parties' chosen law invalidates the contract.* Suppose that the parties' choice of law clause selects a substantive law that invalidates the parties' basic contract. Should the parties' chosen law be applied to nullify the parties' contract? The *Second Restatement* answers in the negative:

> To do so would defeat the expectations of the parties which it is the purpose of the present rule to protect. The parties can be assumed to have intended that the provisions of the contract would be binding upon them. If the parties have chosen a law that would invalidate the contract, it can be assumed that they did so by mistake. If, however, the chosen law is that of the state of the otherwise applicable law under [generally applicable conflict of laws principles in §188], this law will be applied even when it invalidates the contract. *Restatement (Second) Conflict of Laws* §187 comment e (1971).

Is this persuasive? *See Pisacane v. Italia Societa Per Azione Di Navigazione*, 219 F.Supp. 424 (S.D.N.Y. 1963) (applying chosen Italian law, where Italy was also "center of gravity" of the contract, to invalidate provision in contract); *Atlas Subsidiaries, Inc. v. O & O, Inc.*, 166 So.2d 458 (Fla. Dist. Ct. App. 1964) (applying chosen law, where almost all contacts were with that state, to invalidate contractual interest provisions).

10. *Forum's public policy as ground for denying enforcement of choice of law agreement* — *Bremen.* Section 187(2)(b) provides that a choice of law clause will not be given effect if the chosen law "would be contrary to a fundamental policy of a state which has a materially greater interest than the chosen state." This exception parallels public policy exceptions in other contexts. *See supra* pp. 341-43, 486-88, 624-31 & 974-86. Compare the analysis in *Bremen*, where a forum selection clause was unsuccessfully challenged on the grounds that it would result in application of English substantive law that violated U.S. public policies. Suppose that *Bremen* had involved an English choice of law, rather than a choice of forum, clause. How

would the case have been decided by a U.S. court? under §187(2)? Would English law have been applied to determine the validity of the exculpatory clauses in the towage contract?

11. *Forum's public policy as ground for denying enforcement of choice of law agreement* — *Roby.* Consider the decision in *Roby*, which involved the enforcement of both forum selection and choice of law clauses. Is the court's decision — permitting the exclusion of U.S. securities laws by means of an English choice of law clause — correct?

Do claims under the securities laws raise questions of "public policy"? Why are they different from tort or contract claims? Would *Roby* have been decided the same way if it had only involved a choice of law clause (and not a choice of forum agreement)? Note the language excerpted above from *Mitsubishi Motors Corp. v. Soler Chrysler-Plymouth, Inc.*, 473 U.S. 614 (1985), indicating that the Court would not enforce "a prospective waiver of a party's right to pursue statutory remedies for antitrust violations." *See supra* pp. 421-22. *See also* pp. 1018-25.

12. *Forum's public policy as ground for denying enforcement of choice of law agreement* — *hypotheticals.* What sorts of forum public policies should be capable of rendering a choice of foreign law unenforceable? Consider:

In *Bremen*, the accident had occurred within U.S. territorial waters, at the beginning of the oil rig's voyage to the Adriatic Sea.

In an action in U.S. courts, arising out of a U.S. employer's termination of an employment contract, for alleged malfeasance by the employee, the employee brings claims for wrongful termination and libel (based upon the employer's public statements that the employee had engaged in wrongful conduct). The employment contract contains a choice of law clause selecting English law, which would permit recovery on libel claims on significantly more liberal basis than the First Amendment would permit. Assume that the employee works (a) solely in the U.S.; (b) solely in England; (c) partially in both the U.S. and England; and (d) solely in France.

In th~ foregoing employment dispute, the employee asserts race discrimination claims under Title VII — the federal employment discrimination statute. Assume the same workplaces.

A U.S. company licenses its technology to a French company, in an agreement that selects French law and imposes restrictive conditions on competition by the French company. The conditions violate New York state unfair competition laws and federal antitrust law. In an action in U.S. courts, the French company seeks to invalidate the restrictive conditions under New York and U.S. law. The license territory is: (a) the entire world; (b) Europe; (c) the U.S.; (d) France and New York.

13. *Federalism issues in enforcing choice of law clauses.* What law governs the enforceability of choice of law clauses? As discussed below, the Supreme Court has long held that choice of law rules are generally provided by state law (for *Erie* purposes). *See infra* pp. 681-84. Is there any reason that the enforceability of choice of law agreements would raise different issues? Recall the discussion of *Erie* issues in the context of forum selection agreements. *See supra* pp. 431-53. Is there any basis for a rule of federal common law governing the enforceability of choice of law agreements in international cases? Can choice of law clauses, like forum selection agreements, be regarded as issues of federal procedural law?

In applying the public policy exception, does it matter whether the "forum's" public policy is state or federal in origin? Recall the discussion, *supra* pp. 428-29, of the effect of state public policies on the enforceability of international forum selection agreements.

14. *Conspicuous notice requirements.* Some states require that choice of law provisions be "conspicuous." Consider:

If a contract to which this section applies contains a provision making the contract or any conflict arising under the contract subject to the laws of another state, to litigation in the courts of another state, or to arbitration in another state, the provision must be set out in boldfaced print. If the provision is not set out in boldfaced print, the provision is voidable by a party against whom it is sought to be enforced. Tex. Bus. & Comm. Code Ann. §35.53 (Vernon 1987).

Is this provision wise? Is it constitutional? Note that it only applies to the selection of non-Texas law. *See also Merriman v. Convergent Business Systems, Inc.*, 1993 U.S. Dist. Lexis 10528 (N.D. Fla. 1993) (refusing to apply Texas "conspicuous notice" requirement for choice of law clauses).

15. *Foreign public policy as ground for denying enforcement of choice of law agreement.* Consider the application of §187 in *Tumpane.* Was it appropriate for a U.S. court to decline to enforce the parties' "choice of law" clause? Would the parties not have been aware of the existence, or possible existence, of Saudi regulations, like that invoked by the defendant? Suppose that the parties agreed on New York law to govern their contract, specifically in order to avoid the effect of such Saudi regulations? Why should such choice of law agreements not be enforced?

16. *"Choice of public policy" problems.* Note that both *Bremen* and *Tumpane* involve choice of law analysis, but that the "laws" that are involved are public policies. Why is it, again, that the U.S. public policy against exculpatory clauses was not applied in *Bremen?* Note the Court's emphasis on the place where the accident occurred. Compare this rationale to (a) §145 of the *Second Restatement;* (b) Currie's interest analysis; and (c) §187(2)(b)'s choice of law rules. How should the *Bremen* "choice of public policy" analysis have been resolved under each of these more contemporary methods of choice of law analysis? *See Daniel Indus., Inc. v. Barber-Colman Co.*, 1993 U.S. App. Lexis 24248 (9th Cir. 1993) (refusing under §187 to apply California public policy (requiring reciprocity in contractual attorneys' fee provisions) to override parties' Texas choice of law agreement, on grounds that California did not have a "materially greater interest" in the issue).

17. *"Reasonable relationship" requirement as ground for denying enforcement of choice of law agreement.* Some contemporary authorities permit the enforcement of choice of law clauses only if they select a law that has some reasonable relationship to the parties or their transaction. For example, as discussed above, §1-105(1) of the Uniform Commercial Code requires a "reasonable relationship" between the parties' transaction and their chosen law. *See supra* pp. 656-57. Section 187(2)(a) of the *Second Restatement* is similar.

What is the purpose of this "reasonable relationship" requirement? Why should parties not be free to subject their agreement to whatever law they think best suits their purposes? Note that London was selected as the contractual forum in *Bremen* precisely because it was neutral — not associated with either party or any aspect of the transaction. Also as in *Bremen*, parties frequently agree to a similarly "neutral" governing law; they often choose a jurisdiction with developed commercial laws (like England, Switzerland, or New York). Should such choices be invalid because they lack a reasonable relationship to the parties' agreement? Consider:

> The parties to a multistate contract may have a reasonable basis for choosing a state with which the contract has no substantial relationship. For example, when contracting in countries whose legal systems are strange to them as well as relatively immature, the parties should be able to choose a law on the ground that they know it well and that it is sufficiently developed. For only in this way can they be sure of knowing accurately the extent of their rights and duties under the contract.

Restatement (Second) Conflict of Laws §187 comment f (1971). Is this persuasive? What choice of law clauses does this rationale protect? Suppose (a) U.S. and Mexican parties doing business in Mexico agree to English law; (b) New York and Florida parties doing business in the U.S. agree to Mexican law; (c) New York parties doing business in New York agree to Swiss law. *See Prows v. Pinpoint Retails Systems, Inc.*, 868 P.2d 809 (Utah 1994) (refusing to enforce New York choice of law clause under §187 because "Utah is the only state with an interest in the action").

18. *Interpreting choice of law clauses.* Like other contractual agreements, choice of law clauses must be interpreted. For the most part, this is a straightforward question of deciding what the parties meant when they used particular language. A few issues are recurrent, however, and courts appear to follow general approaches to construction.

(a) *Whole law v. substantive law.* Suppose that a choice of law clause chooses the "law of state X." Does that mean that the court should apply the substantive law of state X, or the whole law of state X (including its choice of law rules)? Consider §187(3), which provides that only the "local law" of the state of the chosen law should be applied, at least absent indication of contrary intention. Is that a likely statement of the parties' intent? *Restatement (Second) Conflict of Laws* §187, comment h (1971) ("To apply the 'law' of the chosen state would introduce the uncertainties of choice of law into the proceedings and would serve to defeat the basic objectives, namely those of certainty and predictability, which the choice-of-law provision was designed to achieve.").

(b) *Substantive v. procedural law.* Suppose that the parties choose the "law of state X" to govern all disputes arising from their contract. Does that mean that "procedural" or "judicial administration" issues, dealt with by *Second Restatement* §122, are also governed by the law of state X, even if the case is litigated in state Y? Note that §187 only applies to the law chosen by the parties "to govern their contractual rights and duties." Does this include procedural issues — such as burdens of proof, form of pleadings, evidentiary rules, mode of trial, and statutes of limitations? Lower courts have generally held that it does not. *E.g., Lago & Sons Dairy, Inc. v. H.P. Hood, Inc.*, 1994 WL 484306 (D.N.H. 1994) (choice of law clause does not reach statute of limitations); *Bridge Prods., v. Quantum Chem. Corp.*, 1990 U.S. Dist. Lexis 2202 (N.D. Ill. 1990) (same); *Financial Bancorp, Inc. v. Pingree and Dahle, Inc.*, 880 P.2d 14 (Utah Ct. App. 1994) (same, although express choice of law clause could reach statute of limitations); *Fisher v. Rice*, 1994 WL 673525 (S.D.N.Y. 1994); *JKL Components Corp. v. Insul-Reps, Inc.*, 596 N.E.2d 945, 950 (Ind. App. 1992) ("a contract provision that an agreement is to be governed by the law of another state operates only to import the substantive law of that state; the procedural law of the forum state applies to procedural issues"; waiver of arbitration held procedural); *Gambar Enterprises, Inc. v. Kelly Services Inc.*, 418 N.Y.S.2d 818 (1979); *Cardon v. Cotton Lane Holdings, Inc.*, 841 P.2d 198 (Ariz. 1992) (choice of law clauses generally do not reach procedural matters).

(c) *Applicability of choice of law clause to non-contractual claims.* Suppose that the parties agree to a choice of law clause that extends to "all claims relating to this contract," and that one party asserts a tort claim that is intertwined with the contract. Does the choice of law clause reach this claim? Lower courts have generally concluded that there is no *per se* public policy against application of choice of law clauses to noncontractual claims. *See Turtur v. Rothchild Registry Int'l, Inc.*, 26 F.3d 304 (2d Cir. 1994); *Roby v. Corporation of Lloyd's*, 996 F.2d 1353 (2d Cir. 1993). Whether or not a choice of law clause reaches a particular tort claim is a matter of interpretation. *Jiffy Lube Int'l, Inc. v. Jiffy Lube of Penn.*, 848 F.Supp. 569 (E.D. Pa. 1994) ("contractual choice of law provisions ... do not govern tort claims between contracting parties unless the fair import of the provision embraces all aspects of the legal relationship"); *Knieriemen v. Bache Halsey Stuart Shields*, 437 N.Y.S.2d 10 (1980) ("This contract shall be governed by the laws of ... New York" held not applicable to tort claims); *Fustok v. Conticommodity Services, Inc.*, 618 F.Supp. 1082 (S.D.N.Y. 1985) ("This agreement and its enforcement shall be governed by the laws of the State of Illinois" held not applicable to tort claims); *Merriman v. Convergent Business Systems, Inc.*, 1993 U.S. Dist. Lexis 10528 (N.D. Fla. 1993) ("choice of law provisions in contracts generally will not control the applicable law for tort claims between the contracting parties"). It is not clear whether the forum's rule of construction, or those of the parties' chosen law, should apply to construing the scope of a choice of law clause. *Nedlloyd Lines BV v. The Superior Court*, 834 P.2d 1148 (Calif. 1992).

2. Traditional Approach to Choice of Law Governing Contracts in the Absence of Choice of Law Agreement: Territoriality and Vested Rights

As with choice of law rules applicable to torts, traditional approaches to the law applicable to contracts rested on doctrines of territorial sovereignty. Joseph Story, following Huber, emphasized the importance of principles of international law in choosing the law applicable to contracts.[223] For Story, this meant a strict application of the law of the "place of contracting" to determine the validity of contracts, as well as a number of other contract-related issues. The *Restatement (First) Conflict of Laws* followed this approach, providing generally that the law of the place of contracting applied to most issues relating to the contract (while also providing a sub-rule that selected the law of the place of performance for certain performance-related issues).[224]

Nevertheless, to a much lesser extent than with torts, principles of territorial

---

223. *See* J. Story, *Commentaries on the Conflict of Laws* (2d ed. 1841).
224. *Restatement (First) Conflict of Laws* §332 (1934).

sovereignty did not consistently generate a single choice of law rule (such as the "place of the wrong"). Rather, a number of U.S. courts and other authorities adopted different choice of law rules. These variously looked to the law of the place of contracting,[225] the law of the place of performance,[226] and the law impliedly chosen by the parties.[227]

The materials excerpted below illustrate the historical approaches of U.S. courts to the choice of law applicable to contracts. Sections 332 and 358 of the *Restatement (First) Conflict of Laws* set forth the basic "place of contracting" and "place of performance" rules. The classic decision in *Milliken v. Pratt*, taught in most conflict of laws courses, applied the place of contracting test. The decision in *Louis-Dreyfus v. Paterson Steamship, Ltd.*, illustrates the "place of performance" test.

RESTATEMENT (FIRST) CONFLICT OF LAWS (1934)
§§332 & 358

§332. The law of the place of contracting determines the validity and effect of a promise with respect to

(a) capacity to make the contract;
(b) the necessary form, if any, in which the promise must be made;
(c) the mutual assent or consideration, if any, required to make a promise binding;
(d) any other requirements for making a promise binding;
(e) fraud, illegality, or any other circumstances which make a promise void or voidable;
(f) except as stated in §358, the nature and extent of the duty for the performance of which a party becomes bound;
(g) the time when and the place where the promise is by its terms to be performed;
(h) the absolute or conditional character of the promise.

§358. The duty for the performance of which a party to a contract is bound will be discharged by compliance with the law of the place of performance with respect to:

(a) the manner of performance;
(b) the time and locality of performance;
(c) the person or persons by whom or to whom performance shall be made or rendered;
(d) the sufficiency of performance;
(e) excuse for non-performance.

---

225. *Restatement (First) Conflict of Laws* §332 (1934) ("The law of the place of contracting determines the validity and effect of a promise. ...").
226. *Pritchard v. Norton*, 106 U.S. 124 (1882); *Restatement (First) Conflict of Laws* §358 (1934).
227. *Pritchard v. Norton*, 106 U.S. 124 (1882); *supra* pp. 653-55.

MILLIKEN v. PRATT

125 Mass. 374 (1878)

The plaintiffs are partners doing business in Portland, Maine, under the firm name of Deering, Milliken & Co. The defendant is and has been since 1850, the wife of Daniel Pratt, and both have always resided in Massachusetts. In 1870, Daniel, who was then doing business in Massachusetts, applied to the plaintiffs at Portland for credit, and they required of him, as a condition of granting the same, a guaranty from the defendant to the amount of five hundred dollars, and accordingly he procured from his wife the following instrument:

> Portland, January 29, 1870. In consideration of one dollar paid by Deering, Milliken & Co., receipt of which is here by acknowledged, I guarantee the payment to them by Daniel Pratt of the sum of five hundred dollars, from time to time as he may want — this to be continuing guaranty. Sarah A. Pratt.

This instrument was executed by the defendant two or three days after its date, at her home in Massachusetts, and there delivered by her to her husband, who sent it by mail from Massachusetts to the plaintiffs in Portland; and the plaintiffs received it from the post office in Portland early in February, 1870.

The plaintiffs subsequently sold and delivered goods to Daniel from time to time until October 7, 1871, and charged the same to him, and, if competent, it may be taken to be true, that in so doing they relied upon the guaranty. Between February, 1870, and September 1, 1871, they sold and delivered goods to him on credit to an amount largely exceeding $500, which were fully settled and paid for by him. This action is brought for goods sold from September 1, 1871, to October 7, 1871, inclusive, amounting to $860.12, upon which he paid $300, leaving a balance due of $560.12. The one dollar mentioned in the guaranty was not paid, and the only consideration moving to the defendant therefor was the giving of credit by the plaintiffs to her husband. Some of the goods were selected personally by Daniel at the plaintiff's store in Portland, others were ordered by letters mailed by Daniel from Massachusetts to the plaintiffs at Portland, and all were sent by the plaintiffs, by express from Portland to Daniel in Massachusetts, who paid all express charges. The parties were cognizant of the facts.

By a statute of Maine, duly enacted and approved in 1866, it is enacted that "the contracts of any married woman, made for any lawful purpose, shall be valid and binding, and may be enforced in the same manner as if she were sole." ... Payment was duly demanded of the defendant before the date of the writ, and was refused by her. The Superior Court ordered judgment for the defendant; and the plaintiffs appealed to this court.

GRAY, C. J. The general rule is that the validity of a contract is to be determined by the law of the state in which it is made; if it is valid there, it is deemed valid everywhere, and will sustain an action in the courts of a state whose laws do not permit such a contract. Even a contract expressly prohibited by the statutes of the state in which the suit is brought, if not in itself immoral, is not necessarily nor usually deemed so invalid that the comity of the state, as administered by its courts, will refuse to entertain an action on such a contract made by one of its own citizens abroad in a state the laws of which permit it.

If the contract is completed in another state, it makes no difference in principle whether the citizen of this state goes in person, or sends an agent, or writes a letter, across the boundary line between the two states. As was said by Lord Lyndhurst, "If I, residing in England, send down my agent to Scotland, and he makes contracts for me there, it is the same as if I myself went there and made them." *Pattison v. Mills*, 1 Dow & Cl. 342, 363. So if a person residing in this state signs and transmits, either by a messenger or through the post office, to a person in another state, a written contract, which requires no special forms or solemnities in its execution, and no signature of the person to whom it is addressed, and is assented to and acted on by him there, the contract is made there, just as if the writer personally took the executed contract into the other state, or wrote and signed it there; and it is no objection to the maintenance of an action thereon here, that such a contract is prohibited by the law of this Commonwealth.

The guaranty, bearing date of Portland, in the State of Maine, was executed by the defendant, a married woman, having her home in this Commonwealth, as collateral security for the liability of her husband for goods sold by the plaintiffs to him, and was sent by her through him by mail to the plaintiffs at Portland. The sales of the goods ordered by him from the plaintiffs at Portland, and there delivered by them to him in person, or to a carrier for him, were made in the State of Maine. The contract between the defendant and the plaintiffs was complete when the guaranty had been received and acted on by them at Portland, and not before. It must therefore be treated as made and to be performed in the State of Maine.

The law of Maine authorized a married woman to bind herself by any contract as if she were unmarried. The law of Massachusetts, as then existing, did not allow her to enter into a contract as surety or for the accommodation of her husband or of any third person. ... Since the making of the contract sued on, and before the bringing of this action, the law of this Commonwealth has been changed, so as to enable married women to make such contracts. The question therefore is, whether a contact made in another state by a married woman domiciled here, which a married woman was not at the time capable of making under the law of this Commonwealth, but was then allowed by the law of that state to make, and which she could not lawfully make in this Commonwealth, will sustain an action against her in our courts.

It has been often stated by commentators that the law of the domicil, regulating the capacity of a person, accompanies and governs the person everywhere. But this statement, in modern times at least, is subject to many qualifications; and the opinions of foreign jurists upon the subject the principal of which are collected in the treatises of Mr. Justice Story and of Dr. Francis Wharton on the Conflict of Laws, are too varying and contradictory to control the general current of the English and American authorities in favor of holding that a contract, which by the law of the place is recognized as lawfully made by a capable person, is valid everywhere, although the person would not, under the law of his domicil, be deemed capable of making it. ...

The principal reasons on which continental jurists have maintained that personal laws of the domicil, affecting the status and capacity of all inhabitants of a particular class, bind them wherever they go, appear to have been that each state has the rightful power of regulating the status and condition of its subjects, and, being best acquainted with the circumstances of climate, race, character, manners and customs, can best judge at what age young persons may begin to act for themselves, and whether and how far married women may act independently of their husbands; that laws limiting the capacity of infants or of married women are intended for their protection, and cannot therefore be dispensed with by their agreement; that all civilized states recognize the incapacity of infants and married women; and that a person, dealing with either, ordinarily has notice, by the apparent age or sex, that the person is likely to be of a class whom the laws protect, and is thus put upon inquiry how far, by the law of the domicil of the person, the protection extends.

On the other hand, it is only by the comity of other states that laws can operate beyond the limit of the state that makes them. In the great majority of cases, especially in this country, where it is so common to travel, or to transact business through agents, or to correspond by letter, from one state to another, it is more just, as well as more convenient, to have regard to the law of the place of the contract, as a uniform rule operating on all contracts of the same kind, and which the contracting parties may be presumed to have in contemplation when making their contracts, than to require them at their peril to know the domicil of those with whom they deal, and to ascertain the law of that domicil, however remote, which in many cases could not be done without such delay as would greatly cripple the power of contracting abroad at all. ...

It is possible also that in a state where the common law prevailed in full force, by which a married woman was deemed incapable of binding herself by any contract whatever, it might be inferred that such an utter incapacity, lasting throughout the joint lives of husband and wife, must be considered as so fixed by the settled policy of the state, for the protection of its own citizens, that it could not be held by the courts of that state to yield to the law of another state in which she might undertake to contact. But it is not true at the present day that all civilized states recognize the absolute incapacity of married women to make contracts. The tendency of modern legislation is to enlarge their capacity in this respect, and in many states they have nearly or quite the same powers as if unmarried. In Massachusetts, even at the time of the making of the contract in question, a married woman was vested by statute with a very extensive power to carry on business by herself, and to bind herself by contracts with regard to her own property, business and earnings, and, before the bringing of the present action, the power had been extended so as to include the making of all kinds of contracts, with any person but her husband, as if she were unmarried. There is therefore no reason of public policy which should prevent the maintenance of this action.

LOUIS-DREYFUS v. PATERSON STEAMSHIPS, LTD.

43 F.2d 824 (2d Cir. 1930)

L. HAND, CIRCUIT JUDGE. The libellants at Duluth shipped a parcel of wheat upon two ships of the respondent and received in exchange bills of lading, Duluth to Montreal, "with transshipment at Port Colbourne, Ontario." These contained an exception for "dangers of navigation, fire and collision," but nothing further which is here relevant. The respondent exercised its right of reshipment, unloaded the wheat at Port Colbourne, stored it in an elevator, and reloaded thirty-five thousand bushels in another ship, the Advance, belonging to one Webb, chartered by the respondent's agent, the Hall Shipping Company, for that purpose. This ship safely carried her cargo until she reached the entrance to the Cornwall Canal in the St. Lawrence River, where she took the ground, stove in her bottom and sank. The suit is for the resulting damage to the wheat.

The respondent defended on the ground that the strand, not being due to any fault in management, was a danger of navigation. Failing this, it relied upon the Harter Act (46 U.S.C. §§190-195) and the Canadian Water-Carriage of Goods Act (9-10 Edward VII, Chap. 81), which covers among other ships those "carrying goods from any port in Canada to any other port in Canada" (§3). It requires every bill of lading "relating to the carriage of goods from any place in Canada to any place out-side Canada" to recite that the shipment is subject to the act (§5), and, like §3 of the Harter Act (46 U.S.C. §192) provides that "if the owner of any ship transporting merchandise or property from any port in Canada exercises due diligence to make the ship in all respects seaworthy and properly manned, equipped and supplied, nei-ther the ship, nor the owner, agent or charterer" shall be liable "for faults or errors in navigation or in the management of the ship" (§6). The respondent tried to prove that the Advance was seaworthy, and was therefore within both statutes. ...

We shall assume arguendo that §3 of the Harter Act did not cover the case. ... We pass the point that the bills of lading did not incorporate that statute; §5 only requires such a recital in case of a shipment from a Canadian, to an outside, port, and apparently even in those cases it is only directory. Verbally at least §6 covered the situation; the Advance was "transporting goods" "from" a Canadian port, and the respondent was the charterer, as we have said.

The important question is whether we should look to Canadian law at all. Here is a contract of carriage, made in Minnesota without any relevant exceptions, to be performed partly in the United States and partly in Canada; the carrier fails in per-forming that part of it which is to take place in Canada; he does not safely transport the grain from the entrance of the canal to Montreal. The law of the place of that performance excuses him for those faults in navigation which have caused the loss. Does that law control? *Liverpool, etc., Co. v. Phoenix Ins. Co.*, 129 U.S. 397, decided that the validity of a provision in a contract of carriage, limiting the carrier's common-law duty, was to be determined by the law of the place where the contract was made, and this is well-settled law, [*Restatement (First) Conflict of Laws* §366 (Tent. Draft No. 4)], even when the parties expressly stipulate that all questions shall be decided according to some foreign law, which would require a different result. *Oceanic Steam Nav. Co. v. Corcoran*, 9 F.2d 724. It is of course only an instance of the usual rule that the law of the place where promises are made determines whether they create a contract (*Restatement (First) Conflict of Laws* §353 (Tent. Draft No. 4)); that law alone attaches any legal consequences to acts within its territory.

On the other hand, it is always said that as to matters of performance the law of the place of performance controls, *Andrews v. Pond*, 13 Pet. 65, 78; *Scudder v. Union National Bank*, 92 U.S. 408, though in application the boundaries of this doctrine are not easy to find, as the last two cases cited illustrate very well. An exchange of mutual promises, or whatever other acts may create a contract for future performance, do not put the obligor under any immediate constraint, except so far as the doctrine of anticipatory breach demands. A present obligation arises only in the sense that it is then determined that when the time for performance arrives, his conduct shall not be open to his choice. For the present nothing is required of him; he can commit no fault and incur no liability. When the time comes for him to perform, if he fails, the law requires him to give the equivalent of the neglected performance; that compulsion is the sanction imposed by the state and the measure of the obligation. The default must indeed be at the place of performance, but the promisor need not himself be there, nor may he there have any property to respond. In such cases it is impossible to say that any liability arises under the law of that place where the promisor chanced to be at the time of performance, especially if such a doctrine were extended to all places where he has any property. In the interest of certainty and uniformity there must be some definite place fixed whose law shall control, wherever the suit arises. Whether the place of performance is chosen because of the likelihood that the obligor will be there present at the time of performance, or — what is nearly the same thing — because the agreement presupposes that he shall be, is not important. All we need say here is that the same law which determines what liabilities shall arise upon nonperformance, must determine any excuses for nonperformance, which are no more than exceptions to those liabilities. ...

In the case at bar, the Canadian law says that performance of the contract of carriage, as respects navigation, shall be excused if the owner uses due care to examine his ship and make her fit for her voyage, to man and victual her and the like. The conduct so specified is thus made an excuse for his failure to carry the goods safely to their destination as he has promised to do. That is exactly like any other excuse for such failure; delay is as much a breach as default; payment not specified is no payment; delivery to another, no delivery.

It is indeed possible to say that any excuse for performance is a condition upon the undertaking, written into, and so a part of, the original promise. Courts which have insisted that the parties must be found in some way to have selected foreign law to control their rights, have so reasoned as to the law of the place of performance. We think that the imputation of any such intent is a fiction. It is quite true that civilized law will generally make part of their obligations whatever the parties choose to incorporate into their promises, foreign law like anything else. It is also true that if the parties have specified that performance shall be subject to certain excuses, the law of the place of performance will accept those excuses; that is no more than saying that the contract defined the performance. But the parties cannot select the law which shall control, except as it becomes a term in the agreement, like the by-laws of a private association. When they have said nothing, as here, the local law determines what shall excuse performance ex proprio vigore; the parties do nothing about it. An American contract carries with it none of the immunity of the sovereign which created it; Canadian law reaches it and Canadian contracts indifferently. ...

So far as written into the documents the [Harter] Act became a part of the contract, but no further. In no case did it appear that the default in performance took place in the United States, where alone §3 of the Harter Act (46 U.S.C. §192) was in force. Nor would it make any difference though we ourselves enforced the Act outside the United States in cases where it was not incorporated in the shipping documents. Whatever might be thought of that as law, if we did it, it would not affect the propriety of our recognizing the Canadian Act here. Were it not for §3 of our own Harter Act, we might indeed have to consider whether such an excuse for performance would so far answer our ideas of sound policy that we should accept the Canadian statute. But that statute was apparently drafted closely to conform to our own, and we can of course have no compunctions in taking it as the model of those liabilities which we will recognize. For this reason a provision in the bill of lading incorporating the Canadian Act by reference or at large, would not fall under the ban of *Liverpool, etc., Co. v. Phoenix Insurance Co.,* or *The Kensington,* 183 U.S. 263. On the other hand, the bill of lading might have expressly repudiated both the Harter Act and its Canadian progeny, and fixed the liability of the carrier as at common law or even as that of an unconditional insurer. We will not say that either statute would have prevented the enforcement of those stipulations, but this would be because under Canadian law the stipulated performance would then have been so modified that the statute did not excuse it, and because that result did not offend our local policy. When the parties have not so expressed themselves performance and excuses for nonperformance depend upon Canadian law. ...

Notes on First Restatement, Milliken, and Louis-Dreyfus

1. *Basis for place of contracting rule.* What was the rationale for §332's "place of contracting" rule? Consider the following excerpt from Story's *Commentaries*:

> Generally speaking, the validity of a contract is to be decided by the law of the place, where it is made. If valid there, it is by the general law of nations, *jure gentium,* held valid every where, by the tacit or implied consent of the parties. The rule is founded, not merely in the convenience,

but in the necessities, of nations; for otherwise, it would be impracticable for them to carry on an extensive intercourse and commerce with each other. The whole systems of agencies, of purchases and sales, of mutual credits, and of transfers of negotiable instruments, rests on this foundation; and the nation, which should refuse to acknowledge the common principles, would soon find its whole commercial intercourse reduced to a state, like that, in which it now exists among savage tribes, among the barbarous nations of Sumatra... J. Story, *Commentaries on the Conflict of Laws* §242 (2d ed. 1841).

For a more categorical justification of the "place of contracting" rule, *see* Beale, *What Law Governs the Validity of a Contract?*, 23 Harv. L. Rev. 260, 267 (1909) (to "make the law of the place of performance govern the act of contracting is an attempt to give that law extraterritorial effect").

2. *Does the "place of contracting" rule provide certainty and predictability?* Is it correct, as Story reasoned, that the "place of contracting" rule provides certainty?

(a) *Determining the "place of contracting."* The "place of contracting" rule initially requires identifying the state in which a contract was made — which in turn requires reference to the substantive contract law of the forum (or some other state). *Restatement (First) Conflict of Laws* §311, comment d (1934). Of course, different states will have different substantive rules of contract law; that means that the "place of contracting" rule will produce different results in different forums, because the same course of conduct will result in a contract being formed (or not formed) in different places when different substantive rules of contract law are applied. For example, where negotiations, communications, and conduct occurs in several different states, a contract can easily be found to have been made in each of the different states when different substantive rules of contract law are applied. *See* Cook, *"Contracts" and the Conflict of Laws*, 31 Ill. L. Rev. 143, 158-63 (1936).

What defines the "place of contracting"? Consider the definition contained in *First Restatement* §311, comment d, looking to "the place of the principal event, if any, which, under the general law of Contracts, would result in a contract." What definition is used in *Milliken*? Note the court's reliance on the place where the contract "was complete."

(b) *Distinguishing "performance" from "contracting."* The *First Restatement* also provided, in §358 that certain issues of contract would be governed by the place of performance, rather than the place of contracting. This is illustrated by *Louis-Dreyfus*. In particular, the manner, time, sufficiency, and other aspects of performance would generally be governed by the law of the place of performance. Why is this? Note that, whatever its explanation, the sub-rule introduced further uncertainty into the *First Restatement*'s approach to contract choice of law. Consider the following excerpt from comment c to *Restatement (First) Conflict of Laws* §332 (1934):

> A difficult problem is presented in deciding whether a question in a dispute concerning a contract is one involving the creation of an obligation or performance thereof. There is no distinction based on logic alone between determining the creation of the contract and the rights and duties thereunder on the one hand, and its performance on the other. ... The point at which initiation ceases and performance begins is not a point which can be fixed by any rule of law of universal application in all cases. Like all questions of degree, the solution must depend upon the circumstances of each case and must be governed by the exercise of judgment.

Did the issue in *Louis Dreyfus* concern performance (under §358) or the validity and effect of the parties' agreement (under §332)? Note §332(f).

3. **Milliken v. Pratt** — *application of place of contracting rule.* Where was the guaranty contract in *Milliken* signed? Where did *Milliken* say that the guaranty contract was made? Why? Suppose that the case had involved slightly different facts — for example, the seller delivered the goods itself to the buyer in Massachusetts, rather than handing them over to an "express" company. Would that have changed the place of contracting? If so, is the place of contracting rule likely to provide certainty or consistent results?

4. **Milliken v. Pratt** — *capacity and validity. Milliken* refused to apply Massachusetts law of capacity, instead applying Maine law of contractual validity. Why wasn't Massachusetts law applicable? Consider the Court's reply:

> It is more just, as well as more convenient, to have regard to the law of the place of the contract, as a uniform rule operating on all contracts of the same kind, and which the contracting parties may be presumed to have in contemplation when making their contracts than to

require them at their peril to know the domicile of those with whom they deal, and to ascertain the law of that domicile, however remote. ...

Is this persuasive? Is it easier to consult the law of a party's place of domicile, or to attempt to ascertain the law of the place of contracting?

Suppose that the laws in *Milliken* were reversed: suppose that Massachusetts law had granted Ms. Pratt the capacity to enter into the guarantee, but that Maine had denied her that power. How would *Milliken* have decided that case? What would a straightforward application of the "place of contracting" test suggest?

5. **Milliken v. Pratt — *interest analysis.*** How would *Milliken* have been decided under Currie's interest analysis? *See supra* p. 649. How would the hypothetical, discussed in the preceding note where Massachusetts and Maine laws were reversed, be decided?

6. ***Law governing capacity to contract.*** What law should govern a party's capacity to contract?

(a) *Traditional rule.* First Restatement §333 provided that "[t]he law of the place of contracting determines the capacity to enter into a contract."

(b) *Contemporary rule.* In contrast, as discussed below, contemporary choice of law rules generally subject issues of capacity to the contracting party's domicile: "The capacity of a party to contract will usually be upheld if he has such capacity under the local law of the state of his domicile." *Restatement (Second) Conflict of Laws* §198(2) (1971). What is the rationale for §198(2)?

7. ***The "place of performance" rule.*** First Restatement §358 and *Louis-Dreyfus* provide that a party's performance obligations are governed by the "law of the place of performance," rather than the place of contracting. What is the rationale for the rule that the place of performance governs issues relating to the performance of a contract? Is it based upon concerns about interfering with the territorial sovereignty of the place where performance occurred? Note that most issues relating to performance — such as timing, place, manner, and sufficiency — could readily be resolved by private agreement (and often are). Is a state's territorial sovereignty affected when foreign law fills in gaps of this sort in the parties' agreement? Is the place of performance rule based upon the parties' likely expectations?

8. **Louis Dreyfus — *choice of law clauses and place of performance rule.*** Consider the application of the place of performance rule in *Louis Dreyfus*. Consider how *Louis-Dreyfus* discusses the relationship between choice of law agreements and the "place of performance" rule. Suppose that the parties had agreed that "all questions shall be decided according to" the laws of some place other than Canada. According to *Louis-Dreyfus*, would the parties' chosen law have displaced Canadian law with respect to excuses for non-performance? How would *Second Restatement* §187 resolve the foregoing issue?

Was it likely that the parties expected their performance in Canada to be governed by Canadian law, when they entered into a contract in the United States? Suppose that, contrary to U.S. law, Canadian law had imposed the equivalent of strict liability on the vessel owner: reasonable care would not be a defense to non-performance. Would that affect analysis?

9. *Depecage.* The term depecage refers to the application of different laws to different issues arising with respect to a single contract or tort. *Restatement (Second) Conflict of Laws* §188, comment d (1971). Sections 332 and 358 of the *First Restatement* are a form of depecage. Is this a sensible way to deal with choice of law problems? Is it likely that the parties expect different laws to apply to different aspects of their contractual relations?

3. Contemporary Approach to Choice of Law Governing Contracts in the Absence of Choice of Law Agreement: "Most Significant Relationship"

The *First Restatement*'s rules regarding the choice of law applicable to contracts encountered the same sorts of criticism that traditional tort rules met. Indeed, Currie demonstrated the application of interest analysis by means of *Milliken v. Pratt* and hypotheticals derived from married women's contracts.[228]

A number of contemporary U.S. authorities have abandoned the "place of con-

---

228. Currie, *Married Women's Contracts*, 25 U. Chi. L. Rev. 227 (1958).

tracting" rule of the *First Restatement*.[229] A leading example of this trend is the *Second Restatement*, which applies the "most significant relationship" test to contracts. Section 188 of the *Restatement* provides that, in the absence of an effective choice of law by the parties, "the rights and duties of the parties with respect to an issue in contract are determined by the local law of the state which, with respect to that issue, has the *most significant relationship* to the transaction and the parties."

Although there has been considerable erosion of the *First Restatement*, there is little consistency or uniformity among contemporary U.S. choice of law decisions involving contracts. That is in part because of "the many different kinds of contracts and of issues involving contracts and ... the many relationships a single contract may have to two or more states."[230] In part, however, it is also because lower courts have simply not been able to agree upon any consistent approach to choice of law issues relating to contract.

A substantial number of lower U.S. courts — approximately 25 — have followed the "most significant relationship" analysis of §188 of the *Restatement Second*.[231] Another substantial number of state courts — approximately eleven states — have continued to follow the *First Restatement's* "place of contracting" and "place of performance" standards.[232] A few states have adopted some variation of interest analysis,[233] while other states appear to be undecided or eclectic in their approach.[234]

These analytical differences are sometimes said to conceal a more fundamental consistency of result. Several commentators have remarked that the trend among contemporary lower U.S. courts is to apply that law which will uphold the parties' agreement. "[T]here is a distinct tendency to apply a law that will uphold the contract provided the parties are not of widely disparate bargaining power and the state of the validating law has substantial contacts with the transaction."[235]

Consider the following materials, which illustrate some of the contemporary approaches to the choice of law applicable to contracts. The approach of the *Second*

---

229. See Symeonides, *Choice of Law in the American Courts in 1994: A View "From the Trenches,"* 43 Am. J. Comp. L. 1, 3 (1995) (only 11 states have not abandoned *First Restatement* in contract disputes); Symeonides, *Choice of Law in the American Courts in 1993 (and in the Six Previous Years),* 42 Am. J. Comp. l. 599, 606-10 (1994).

230. *Restatement (Second) Conflict of Laws* Chapter 8, Intro. Note (1971).

231. See Symeonides, *Choice of Law in American Courts in 1994: A View "From the Trenches,"* 43 Am. J. Comp. L. 1, 3 (1995) (listing 26 states as following *Restatement Second* in contracts cases).

232. Symeonides, *Choice of Law in American Courts in 1994: A View "From the Trenches,"* 43 Am. J. Comp. L. 1, 3 (1995) (11 states apply *First Restatement* in contracts cases); Symeonides, *Choice of Law in the American Courts in 1993 (and in the Six Previous Years),* 42 Am. J. Comp. L. 599, 608-10 (1994).

233. Symeonides, *Choice of Law in the American Courts in 1993 (and in the Six Previous Years),* 42 Am. J. Comp. L. 599, 608-10 (1994).

234. Symeonides, *Choice of Law in American Courts in 1994: A View "From the Trenches,"* 43 Am. J. Comp. I. 1, 3 (1995); Symeonides, *Choice of Law in the American Courts in 1993 (and in the Six Previous Years),* 42 Am. J. Comp. L. 599, 608-10 (1994).

235. Reese, *American Trends in Private International Law: Academic and Judicial Manipulation of Choice of Law Rules in Tort Cases,* 33 Vand. L. Rev. 717, 737 (1980).

Restatement is set forth in §188 and §206. Also consider *Lilienthal v. Kaufman*, which applies a version of interest analysis.

RESTATEMENT (SECOND) CONFLICT OF LAWS (1971)

§§188 & 206

§188. (1) The rights and duties of the parties with respect to an issue in contract are determined by the local law of the state which, with respect to that issue, has the most significant relationship to the transaction and the parties under the principles stated in §6.

(2) In the absence of an effective choice of law by the parties (*see* §187), the contacts to be taken into account in applying the principles of §6 to determine the law applicable to an issue include:

> (a) the place of contracting,
> (b) the place of negotiation of the contract,
> (c) the place of performance,
> (d) the location of the subject matter of the contract, and
> (e) the domicil, residence, nationality, place of incorporation and place of business of the parties.

These contacts are to be evaluated according to their relative importance with respect to the particular issue.

(3) If the place of negotiating the contract and the place of performance are in the same state, the local law of this state will usually be applied, except as otherwise provided in §§189-199 and 203.

§206. Issues relating to details of performance of a contract are determined by the local law of the place of performance.

LILIENTHAL v. KAUFMAN

395 P.2d 543 (Ore. 1964)

DENECKE, JUSTICE. This is an action to collect two promissory notes. The defense is that the defendant maker has previously been declared a spendthrift by an Oregon court and placed under a guardianship and that the guardian has declared the obligations void. The plaintiff's counter is that the notes were executed and delivered in California, that the law of California does not recognize the disability of a spendthrift and that the Oregon court is bound to apply the law of the place of the making of the contract. The trial court rejected plaintiff's argument and held for the defendant.

This same defendant spendthrift was the prevailing party in our recent decision in *Olshen v. Kaufman*, 385 P.2d 161 (Or. 1963). In that case the spendthrift and the plaintiff, an Oregon resident, had gone into a joint venture to purchase binoculars for resale. For this purpose plaintiff had advanced moneys to the spendthrift. The spendthrift had repaid plaintiff by his personal check for the amount advanced and for plaintiff's share of the profits of such venture. The check had not been paid because the spendthrift had had insufficient funds in his account. The action was for the unpaid balance of the check. The evidence in that case showed that the plaintiff had been unaware that Kaufman was under a spendthrift guardianship. The guardian testified that he knew Kaufman was engaging in some business and had bank accounts and that he had admonished him to cease these practices; but he could not control the spendthrift.

The statute applicable in that case and in this one is ORS 126.335:

> After the appointment of a guardian for the spendthrift, all contracts, except for necessaries, and all gifts, sales and transfers of real or personal estate made by such spendthrift thereafter and before the termination of the guardianship are voidable. ...

We held in that case that the voiding of the contract by the guardian precluded recovery by the plaintiff and that the spendthrift and the guardian were not estopped to deny the validity of plaintiff's claim. Plaintiff does not seek to overturn the principle of that decision but contends it has no application because the law of California governs, and under California law the plaintiff's claim is valid.

The facts here are identical to those in *Olshen v. Kaufman*, except for the Californian locale for portions of the transaction. The notes were for the repayment of advances to finance another joint venture to sell binoculars. The plaintiff was unaware that defendant had been declared a spendthrift and placed under guardianship. The guardian, upon demand for payment by the plaintiff declared the notes void. ...

Before entering the choice-of-law area of the general field of conflict of laws, we must determine whether the laws of the states having a connection with the controversy are in conflict. Defendant did not expressly concede that under the law of California the defendant's obligation would be enforceable, but his counsel did state that if this proceeding were in the courts of California, the plaintiff probably would recover. We agree. ...

Defendant contends that the law of California should not be applied in this case by the Oregon court because the invalidity of the contract is a matter of remedy, rather than one of substance. Matters of remedy, procedure, are governed by the law of the forum. What is a matter of substance and what is a matter of procedure are sometimes difficult questions to decide. Stumberg states the distinction as follows: "procedural rules should be classified as those which concern methods of presenting to a court the operative facts upon which legal relations depend; substantive rules, those which concern the legal effect of those facts after they have been established." Stumberg, *Principles of Conflict of Laws* 133 (3d ed.). Based upon this conventional statement of the distinction, it is obvious that we are not concerned with a procedural issue, but with a matter of substantive law.

Plaintiff contends that the substantive issue of whether or not an obligation is valid and binding is governed by the law of the place of making, California. This court has repeatedly stated that the law of the place of contract "must govern as to the validity, interpretation, and construction of the contract." *Jamieson v. Potts*, 105 P. 93, 95 (1910). *Restatement (First) Conflict of Laws* §332, so announced and specifically stated that "capacity to make the contract" was to be determined by the law of the place of contract.

This principle, that *lex loci contractus* must govern, however, has been under heavy attack for years. The strongest criticism has been that the place of making frequently is completely fortuitous and that on occasion the state of making has no interest in the parties to the contract or in the performance of the contract. ... As a result of this long and powerful assault, the principle is no longer a cornerstone of the law of conflicts. There is no need to decide that our previous statements that the law of the place of contract governs were in error. Our purpose is to state that this portion of our decision is not founded upon that principle because of our doubt that it is correct if the only connection of the state whose law would govern is that it was the place of making.

In this case California had more connection with the transaction than being merely the place where the contract was executed. The defendant went to San Francisco to ask the plaintiff, a California resident, for money for the defendant's venture. The money was loaned to defendant in San Francisco, and by terms of the note, it was to be repaid to plaintiff in San Francisco. On these facts, apart from *lex loci contractus*, other accepted principles of conflict of laws lead to the conclusion that the law of California should be applied. ...

There is another conflict principle calling for the application of California law — ... the application of the law which upholds the contract. Ehrenzweig calls it the "Rule of Validation." A. Ehrenzweig, *Conflict of Laws* 353 (1962). ... The "rule" is that, if the contract is valid under the law of any jurisdiction having significant connection with the contract, *i.e.*, place of making, place of performance, etc., the law of that jurisdiction validating the contract will be applied. This would also agree with the intention of the parties, if they had any intentions in this regard. They must have intended their agreement to be valid. ...

Thus far all signs have pointed to applying the law of California and holding the contract enforceable. There is, however, an obstacle to cross before this end can be logically reached. In *Olshen v. Kaufman*, we decided that the law of Oregon, at least as applied to persons applied domiciled in Oregon contracting in Oregon for performance in Oregon, is that spendthrifts' contracts are voidable. Are the choice-of-law principles of conflict of laws so superior that they overcome this principle of Oregon law?

To answer this question we must determine, upon some basis, whether the interests of Oregon are so basic and important that we should not apply California law despite its several intimate connections with the transaction. The traditional method used by this court and most others is framed in the terminology of "public policy." The court decides whether or not the public policy of the forum is so strong that the law of the forum must prevail although another jurisdiction, with different laws, has more and closer contacts with the transaction. Included in "public policy" we must consider the economic and social interests of Oregon. When these factors are included in a consideration of whether the law of the forum should be applied this traditional approach is very similar to that advocated by many legal scholars. Currie, *Selected Essays on the Conflict of Law* 64-72 (1963). ...

The difficulty in deciding what is the fundamental law forming a cornerstone of the forum's jurisprudence and what is not such fundamental law, thus allowing it to give way to foreign law, is caused by the lack of any even remotely objective standards. ... However, as previously stated, if we include in our search for the public policy of the forum a consideration of the various interests that the forum has in this litigation, we are guided by more definite criteria. In addition to the interests of the forum, we should consider the interests of the other jurisdictions which have some connection with the transaction.

Some of the interests of Oregon in this litigation are set forth in *Olshen v. Kaufman.* The spendthrift's family which is to be protected by the establishment of the guardianship is presumably an Oregon family. The public authority which may be charged with the expense of supporting the spendthrift or his family, if he is permitted to go unrestrained upon his wasteful way, will probably be an Oregon public authority. These, obviously, are interests of some substance. Oregon has other interests and policies regarding this matter which were not necessary to discuss in *Olshen*. As previously stated, Oregon, as well as all other states, has a strong policy favoring the validity and enforceability of contracts. This policy applies whether the contract is made and to be performed in Oregon or elsewhere. The defendant's conduct, — borrowing money with the belief that the repayments of such loan could be avoided — is a species of fraud. Oregon and all other states have a strong policy of protecting innocent persons from fraud. ... It is in Oregon's commercial interest to encourage citizens of other states to conduct business with Oregonians. If Oregonians acquire a reputation for not honoring their agreements, commercial intercourse with Oregonians will be discouraged. If there are Oregon laws, somewhat unique to Oregon, which permit an Oregonian to escape his otherwise binding obligations, persons may well avoid commercial dealing with Oregonians. The substance of these commercial considerations, however, is deflated by the recollection that the Oregon Legislature has determined, despite the weight of these consideration, that a spendthrift's contracts are voidable.

California's most direct interest in this transaction is having its citizen creditor paid. As previously noted, California's policy is that any creditor, in California or otherwise, should be paid even though the debtor is a spendthrift. California probably has another, although more intangible, interest involved. It is presumably to every state's benefit to have the reputation of being a jurisdiction in which contracts can be made and performance be promised with the certain knowledge that such contracts will be enforced. Both of these interests, particularly the former, are also of substance.

We have, then, two jurisdictions, each with several close connections with the transaction, and each with a substantial interest, which will be served or thwarted, depending upon which law is applied. The interests of neither jurisdiction are clearly more important than those of the other. We are of the opinion that in such a case the public policy of Oregon should prevail and the law of Oregon should be applied; we should apply that choice-of-law rule which will "advance the policies or interests of" Oregon. Courts are instruments of state policy. The Oregon Legislature has adopted a policy to avoid possible hardship to an Oregon family of a spendthrift and to avoid possible expenditure of Oregon public funds which might occur if the spendthrift is required to pay his obligations. In litigation Oregon courts are the appropriate instrument to enforce this policy. The mechanical application of choice-of-law rules would be the only apparent reason for an Oregon court advancing the interests of California over the equally valid interests of Oregon. The present principles of conflict of laws are not favorable to such mechanical application. We hold that the spendthrift law of Oregon is applicable and the plaintiff cannot recover.

GOODWIN, JUSTICE, DISSENTING. ... In the case before us, I believe that the policy of both states, Oregon and California, in favor of enforcing contracts, has been lost sight of in favor of a questionable policy in Oregon which gives special privileges to the rare spendthrift for whom a guardian has been appointed. The majority view in the case at bar strikes me as a step backward toward the balkanization of the law of contracts. *Olshen v. Kaufman* held that there was a policy in this state to help keep spendthrifts out of the almshouse. I can see nothing, however, in Oregon's policy toward spendthrifts that warrants its extension to permit the taking of captives from other states down the road to insolvency. I would enforce the contract.

Notes on Lilienthal and Second Restatement

1. *Criticism of traditional "place of contracting" rule.* *Lilienthal* rejected the *First Restatement*'s "place of contracting" test. Consider the criticisms of the traditional rule: it can be completely "fortuitous," it ignores the interests of states that are most affected by a transaction, and it gives effect to the law of states with "no interest" in the transaction. Are these persuasive criticisms? Doesn't the "place of contracting" test provide predictability and certainty, at least in most cases? Can't the real interests of other states be dealt with by the public policy exception?

2. *Rules of alternative reference or validation.* A number of contemporary (and some older) authorities have adopted rules of so-called "alternative reference." These rules permit a court to apply whichever of the laws that are potentially applicable to a contract that will uphold the validity of the parties' agreement. *E.g.,* A. Ehrenzweig, *A Treatise on the Conflict of Laws* 466 (1962) ("Parties entering into a contract upon equal terms intend their agreement to be binding, and the law of conflict of laws will give effect to their intent whenever it can do so under any proper law."); R. Weintraub, *Commentary on the Conflict of Laws* 397 (3d ed. 1986); *Cooper v. Cherokee Village Development Co.,* 364 S.W.2d 158 (Ark. 1963) (favors "applying the law of the state that will make the contract valid, rather than void"). *Lilienthal* also cited the "Rule of Validation," although ultimately refusing to apply it. Consider again the result in *Milliken.* Did it involve considerations of this sort? What is the rationale for a rule of validation?

3. *Legitimacy of rules of validation.* Are rules of alternative reference or validation acceptable in an international context? Virtually all nations now recognize private contracts and will enforce them. But most nations also provide basic limits on the validity and enforceability of contracts; those limits serve important public policies such as the protection of individuals from duress or overreaching, and the protection of the public from anticompetitive, corrupt, or otherwise undesirable agreements. Why is it that a U.S. court should refuse to give effect to such public policies — through the mechanism of applying rules of alternative reference? What if the contract in question clearly has closer connections to a foreign state?

Consider the *Triad* case. The New York court there refused to enforce a contract because it was invalid under Saudi law, notwithstanding the fact that it was valid under New York law. Rules of validation would have produced the opposite result. Should a U.S. court ignore Saudi public policy in order to "validate" as many agreements as it can?

4. *Second Restatement's "most significant relationship" test.* Consider the choice of law rule set forth in §188 of the *Second Restatement.* What does "most significant relationship" mean? In truly international transactions, having multiple contacts with several states, how does one select the "most significant" relationship? Note that §188 is an example of depecage, proceeding on an issue by issue basis.

A significant number of state courts have adopted some variation of a "most significant relationship" or "center of gravity" test. *See* Symeonides, *Choice of Law* in *American Courts in 1994: A View "From the Trenches,"* 43 Am. J. Comp. L. 1, 3 (1995) (listing 26 states as following *Restatement Second* in contracts cases); *supra* pp. 673-74.

5. Lilienthal — *public policy in choice of law governing contracts. Lilienthal* invoked Oregon public policy to prevent application of California law. The court acknowledged the "lack of any even remotely objective standards" for defining public policy. Consider the various Oregon public policies that *Lilienthal* identifies, and the court's ultimate conclusion that Oregon's legislature had incorporated these various policies into a spendthrift law. Is the Oregon spendthrift law appropriately characterized as stating public policy? Why is it that Oregon's public policies invalidating contracts by spendthrifts outweigh other *Oregon* public policies?

Consider *Lilienthal's* analysis of competing Oregon and California public policies. How can a court meaningfully weigh one state's policies or interests against those of another state? Is it inevitable that courts will be parochially biased in favor of local public policies? Compare the attention that *Lilienthal* devotes to Oregon's public policies to that devoted to California's policies. Note which policy ultimately prevails. Recall the doubts about parochial bias under §403's interest-balancing analysis. *See supra* 592-93.

Compare the *Lilienthal* result to that which would obtain under §332 of the *First Restatement. See supra* pp. 664-73.

6. Lilienthal — *application of interest analysis.* The final few paragraphs of *Lilienthal* adopt a form of interest analysis. Indeed, the court ultimately appears to rely on Currie's rule that the forum's interests are to be preferred over foreign interests. Consider the wisdom of *Lilienthal's* application of interest analysis. Compare the result in *Lilienthal* to that in *Milliken*; which case is the wiser result? Which case is more likely to promote a predictable and fair commercial environment? How would *Lilienthal* have been decided under the rules of alternative reference set forth above? How would *Lilienthal* have been decided under §188 of the *Second Restatement?* Recall §198(2) of the *Second Restatement* and its rules regarding capacity to contract. *See supra* p. 673.

How would Currie have decided *Lilienthal?* Does the case involve a "true conflict"? Would it be possible to adopt a restrained interpretation of Oregon's policies, so as to confine those policies to borrowing within Oregon, thereby revealing a false conflict and permitting application of California's law?

7. *Criticism of* Lilienthal*'s application of interest analysis.* Consider the dissent's remark in *Lilienthal* that the court's decision is "a step backward toward the balkanization of the law of contracts." What is meant by "balkanization"? How does the *Lilienthal* result affect California's interests? How would *Triad* be decided under the *Lilienthal* analysis?

8. *Does* Lilienthal *violate the Constitution?* Recall contemporary due process and full faith and credit limits on state choice of law decisions. Is the application of Oregon law in *Lilienthal* a violation of these constitutional limits? For an affirmative reply, *see* E. Scoles & P. Hay, *Conflict of Laws* 101 (2d ed. 1992). Recall also, however, the treatment of capacity under the *Second Restatement.*

9. *Procedure v. substance revisited.* The spendthrift's lawyer in *Lilienthal* argued that the validity of a contract was a matter of "remedy," and therefore a procedural issue subject to the law of the forum. *See supra* p. 676. *Lilienthal* dismissed that suggestion. Was it correct?

10. *Unpredictability in choice of law governing contracts.* Consider the various choice of law rules that are presently available to select the law governing contracts. Consider also the criticisms made of almost every rule, concerning its unpredictability, and the further uncertainties created by escape devices and characterization. All these factors make it extremely difficult, in any truly international case, to predict with confidence the likely law that a U.S. court will apply to a contract dispute. The possibility that foreign courts will apply different (and also unpredictable) choice of law rules makes matters even worse. Is this a satisfactory state of affairs for international businesses? What can be done to improve matters?

D. Erie and Choice of Law Rules in Federal Courts

Choice of law questions in federal court raise issues under the *Erie* doctrine.[236] In *Klaxon v. Stentor Electric Manufacturing Company*,[237] the Supreme Court held that a federal diversity court must apply the choice of law rules of the state in which it sits. The Court reasoned that application of state conflicts rules was necessary to ensure "equal administration of justice in coordinate state and federal courts sitting side by side."[238] *Klaxon* was extended (without discussion) to international cases in *Day & Zimmerman, Inc. v. Challoner*, which is excerpted below. The Court required a federal district court sitting in Texas to apply Texas choice of law rules (based on the *First Restatement*) to an accident occurring in Cambodia.

DAY & ZIMMERMAN, INC. v. CHALLONER
423 U.S. 3 (1975)

PER CURIAM. Respondents sued petitioner in the U.S. District Court for the Eastern District of Texas seeking to recover damages for death and personal injury resulting from the premature explosion of a 105-mm. howitzer round in Cambodia. Federal jurisdiction was based on diversity of citizenship. The District Court held that the Texas law of strict liability in tort governed and submitted the case to the jury on that theory. The Court of Appeals for the Fifth Circuit affirmed a judgment in favor of respondents.

The Court of Appeals stated that were it to apply Texas choice-of-law rules, the substantive law of Cambodia, the place of injury, would certainly control as to the wrongful death, and perhaps as to the claim for personal injury. It declined nevertheless to apply Texas choice-of-law rules, based in part on an earlier decision in *Lester v. Aetna Life Ins. Co.*, 433 F.2d 884 (5th Cir. 1970), *cert. denied*, 402 U.S. 909 (1971), which it summarized as holding that "[w]e refused to look to the Louisiana conflict of law rule, deciding that as a matter of federal choice of law, *we could not apply the law of a jurisdiction that had no interest in the case*, no policy at stake." 512 F.2d at 80 (emphasis in original). The Court of Appeals further supported its decision on the grounds that the rationale for applying the traditional conflicts rule applied by Texas "is not operative under the present facts"; and that it was "a Court of the United States, an instrumentality created to effectuate the laws and policies of the United States."

We believe that the Court of Appeals either misinterpreted our longstanding decision in *Klaxon*, or else determined for itself that it was no longer of controlling force in a case such as this. We are of the opinion that *Klaxon*, is by its terms applicable here and should have been adhered to by the Court of Appeals. In *Klaxon*, this

---

236. *See supra* pp. 13-14 for a discussion of *Erie* and its application in international cases.
237. 313 U.S. 487 (1941).
238. 313 U.S. at 496.

Court said: "The conflict of laws rules to be applied by the federal court in Delaware must conform to those prevailing in Delaware's state courts. Otherwise, the accident of diversity of citizenship would constantly disturb equal administration of justice in coordinate state and federal courts sitting side by side. *See Erie R. Co. v. Tompkins*, 304 U.S. 64, 74-77 (1938)."

By parity of reasoning, the conflict-of-laws rules to be applied by a federal court in Texas must conform to those prevailing in the Texas state courts. A federal court in a diversity case is not free to engraft onto those state rules exceptions or modifications which may commend themselves to the federal court, but which have not commended themselves to the State in which the federal court sits. The Court of Appeals in this case should identify and follow the Texas conflicts rule. What substantive law will govern when Texas' rule is applied is a matter to be determined by the Court of Appeals.

JUSTICE BLACKMUN, CONCURRING. ... [A]s I read the Court's per curiam opinion, the Court of Appeals on remand is to determine and flatly to apply the conflict of laws rules that govern the state courts of Texas. This means to me that the Court of Appeals is not foreclosed from concluding, if it finds it proper so to do under the circumstances of this case, that the Texas state courts themselves would apply the Texas rule of strict liability. If that proves to be the result, I would perceive no violation of any principle of *Klaxon*. I make this observation to assure the Court of Appeals that, at least in my view, today's per curiam opinion does not necessarily compel the determination that it is only the law of Cambodia that is applicable.

LIU v. REPUBLIC OF CHINA

892 F.2d 1419 (9th Cir. 1989) [excerpted above at pp. 278-85]

Notes on Day & Zimmerman and Liu

1. **Klaxon v. Stentor Electric.** *Klaxon* was an early application of *Erie*. It arose from an agreement, executed in New York, which provided for the transfer of a New York corporation's business to a Delaware corporation. Disputes later arose, and the New York seller sued the Delaware purchaser in federal district court in Delaware. After successfully winning a judgment, the plaintiff requested interest under a New York statute. The district court granted the request, without considering what a Delaware state court would have done. The Supreme Court reversed, holding that federal district courts were required to apply Delaware choice of law rules: "Otherwise, the accident of diversity of citizenship would constantly disturb equal administration of justice in coordinate state and federal courts, sitting side by side." 313 U.S. at 496.

2. **Is Klaxon *required by* Erie?** The Court's prevailing understanding of *Erie* focuses on the decision's "twin aims": "discouragement of forum-shopping and avoidance of inequitable administration of the laws." *Hanna v. Plummer*, 380 U.S. 460, 468 (1965); *supra* pp. 13-14. Are these twin aims applicable to choice of law rules? If federal courts apply one set of conflicts rules and state courts apply another, will parties engage in intrastate forum-shopping to obtain the most favorable applicable laws? On the other hand, interstate, as opposed to intrastate, forum-shopping will be exacerbated by *Klaxon*. Is that a sufficient reason to reject the *Erie* rule?

3. *Should choice of law questions in domestic cases be governed by federal common law?* One way to avoid intrastate forum shopping is to require federal courts to apply state law, as *Klaxon* and *Day & Zimmerman* do; another way is to permit federal courts to fashion substantive federal common law rules,

which state courts would be obliged to apply. The standards necessary to support federal common law rules are discussed in detail elsewhere. *See supra* pp. 15-16.

Would it be permissible for federal courts to fashion substantive federal common law rules governing choice of law in domestic cases? Do interstate choice of law issues arise in a "uniquely federal" field? For example, is there a federal interest in regulating the jurisdictional claims of the states with respect to interstate activities, thereby minimizing the infringement on state sovereignty by other states? Wolkin, *Conflict of Laws in the Federal Courts: The Erie Era*, 94 U. Pa. L. Rev. 293 (1956); Baxter, *Choice of Law and the Federal System*, 16 Stan. L. Rev. 1 (1963); Trautman, *Toward Federalizing Choice of Law*, 70 Tex. L. Rev. 1715 (1992). Consider:

> Choice-of-law questions arise out of the relations of persons or transactions to more than one state. They indisputably present problems that cannot be appropriately resolved under the choice-of-law rules of one of those states. Rather, they must be resolved under a single overriding or commonly agreed-upon choice-of-law rule. For interstate issues in the United States, the overriding rule would naturally be federal. Trautman, *Toward Federalizing Choice of Law*, 70 Tex. L. Rev. 1715 (1992).

Is this purpose already served by the full faith and credit and due process clauses? *See supra* pp. 518-37.

4. **Should choice of law questions in international cases be governed by federal common law?** Unlike *Klaxon, Day & Zimmerman* involved the question of what law a federal court should apply to an accident occurring on the territory of another nation (rather than another U.S. state), where one of the arguably applicable substantive laws was that of a foreign state. In these circumstances, are rules of federal common law appropriate? Did *Day & Zimmerman* suggest that any different *Erie* rule applied to international cases than to domestic ones?

Do questions of the law applicable to conduct outside the United States arise in a "uniquely federal" area? Do such questions sufficiently implicate federal interests in foreign commerce and foreign relations to conclude that they are "uniquely federal"? For an affirmative response, *see* Trautman, *Toward Federalizing Choice of Law*, 70 Tex. L. Rev. 1715, 1735-36 (1992).

Are there federal policies that are violated by the application of state choice of law rules in international cases? Can one argue that the United States as a whole has an interest — a federal interest — in the application of a uniform national set of choice of law rules that reflect U.S. understandings of international jurisdiction? Wouldn't this be a significant way to avoid parochial state court applications of local law to conduct affecting foreign interests and international commerce, but having no meaningful connection to the United States? Is it necessary to displace all state choice of law rules with such an approach, or do the due process and foreign commerce clauses accomplish the result? Suppose a state applied Currie's unreservedly pro-forum interest analysis in an international case (like *Tramontana*). *See supra* pp. 641-46. Would the due process clause forbid this? If not, should federal common law choice of law principles do so? Recall the general international law prohibition against the passive personality doctrine. *See supra* pp. 507-08.

Recall that issues of judicial jurisdiction are governed largely by the federal due process clause, and that the FSIA provides comprehensive federal jurisdictional and procedural rules governing actions against foreign states. *See supra* pp. 67-285. Moreover, as discussed below, the Hague Service Convention and Hague Evidence Convention provide federal rules for other procedural aspects of international disputes. *See infra* pp. 757-934. Finally, at least in federal courts, issues of forum non conveniens and forum selection are generally governed by federal law. *See supra* pp. 363-64 & 448-50. Does all this support the argument for federal common law choice of law rules?

5. **Federal common law choice of law rule under FSIA.** As described above, 28 U.S.C. §1606 requires a federal court with jurisdiction over a foreign state under the FSIA to apply the same rules of liability as those applicable in private actions. Thus, in determining the liability of a foreign state, a court must choose a body of substantive law. *Liu* held that choice of law questions under the FSIA were governed by federal common law: "federal common law provides the choice of law rule applicable to deciding the merits of an action involving a foreign state." As discussed above, other lower courts have reached the same conclusion. *See supra* pp. 283-84. These decisions reason that the FSIA provides a uniform federal statutory framework for immunity of foreign states, and that important federal foreign relations interests are served by such uniformity. Moreover, application of local choice of law rules would result in disparate substantive laws being applicable in different courts — contrary to the FSIA's goal of uniformity.

When are federal common law choice of law rules most needed? Is it to restrain parochial state choice of law rules that require application of forum law in cases having no connection to the forum? Is it to escape strict territorial limits required by traditional approaches?

6. *Rejection of federal common law choice of law rule under FSIA.* The Second Circuit has refused to apply a federal common law choice of law rule under the FSIA. In *Barkanic v. General Administration of Civil Aviation,* 923 F.2d 957 (2d Cir. 1991), the court held that §1606 requires application of the same choice of law rules that would apply in private litigation. Moreover, the court reasoned that, under *Klaxon,* this would be the local choice of law rules of the state in which the federal court was located. The court expressly rejected the argument that a uniform federal common law rule should govern choice of law questions under the FSIA.

7. *Appropriate approach to choice of law questions under the FSIA.* Which approach to choice of law questions under the FSIA is wiser? Does §1606 speak to choice of law questions? How compelling is the need for uniform treatment of choice of law questions under the FSIA? What relevance does the *Erie* doctrine have to choice of law issues under the FSIA?

8. *Federal common law choice of law rules in other federal question contexts.* Federal lower courts have also applied federal common law choice of law rules in other contexts where federal question jurisdiction exists (but where no express federal substantive statutory rules apply). For example, in actions arising under the Edge Act (dealing with international banking transactions), appellate courts have held that federal common law choice of law rules are applicable. *Corporacion Venezolana de Fomento v. Vintero Sales Corp.,* 629 F.2d 786 (2d Cir. 1980); *Aaron Ferer & Sons Limited v. Chase Manhattan Bank,* 731 F.2d 112 (2d Cir. 1984). These decisions have generally relied upon the existence of federal question jurisdiction, and federal interests in international matters, to justify this approach. *See also* A. von Mehren & D. Trautman, *The Law of Multistate Problems: Cases and Materials on Conflict of Laws* 1303-35 (1965).

9. *Content of federal common law choice of law rules.* The content of the federal common law choice of law rule has generally been determined by reference to the *Restatement (Second) Conflict of Laws* (1971). *See Harris v. Polskie Linie Lotnicze,* 820 F.2d 1000, 1003-04 (9th Cir. 1987) (applying situs/most significant relationship test of *Restatement (Second) Conflict of Laws* §175 (1971)); *Liu v. Republic of China,* 892 F.2d 1419 (9th Cir. 1989).

9/Act of State and Foreign Sovereign Compulsion Doctrines[1]

The act of state doctrine provides, in broad outline, that U.S. courts will not sit in judgment on the validity of the public acts of foreign sovereigns within their own territory.[2] It is related to the foreign sovereign compulsion doctrine, which provides that otherwise applicable U.S. law will not generally be applied to forbid conduct compelled by a foreign state within its own territory.[3] This Chapter examines both the act of state doctrine and the doctrine of foreign sovereign compulsion.

A. Act of State Doctrine: Introduction and Historical Background

The act of state doctrine has a long history.[4] It is useful to outline that history,

---

1. Commentary on the act of state doctrine includes, *e.g.*, Bazyler, *Abolishing the Act of State Doctrine*, 134 U. Pa. L. Rev. 325 (1986); Burley, *Law Among Liberal States: Liberal Internationalism and the Act of State Doctrine*, 92 Colum. L. Rev. 1907 (1992); Cane, *Prerogative Acts, Acts of State and Justiciability*, 29 Int'l & Comp. L.Q. 680 (1980); Chow, *Rethinking the Act of State Doctrine: An Analysis in Terms of Jurisdiction to Prescribe*, 62 Wash. L. Rev. 397 (1987); Dellapenna, *Deciphering the Act of State Doctrine*, 35 Vill. L. Rev. 1 (1990); Halberstam, *Sabbatino Resurrected: The Act of State Doctrine in the Revised Restatement of U.S. Foreign Relations Law*, 79 Am. J. Int'l L. 68 (1985); Henkin, *Act of State Today: Recollections in Tranquility*, 6 Colum. J. Trans. L. 175 (1967); Mathias, *Restructuring the Act of State Doctrine: A Blueprint for Legislative Reform*, 12 Law & Pol'y Int'l Bus. 369 (1980); Singer, *The Act of State Doctrine of the United Kingdom: An Analysis with Comparisons to United States Practice*, 75 Am. J. Int'l L. 283 (1981).

2. See infra pp. 685-90; *W.S. Kirkpatrick & Co. v. Environmental Tectonics Corp.*, 493 U.S. 400 (1990); *Banco Nacional de Cuba v. Sabbatino*, 376 U.S. 398, 416 (1964).

3. *See infra* pp. 745-52; *Interamerican Ref. Corp. v. Texaco Maracaibo*, 307 F.Supp. 1291, 1298 (D. Del. 1970) ("[W]hen a nation compels a trade practice, firms there have no choice but to obey").

4. See Singer, *The Act of State Doctrine of the United Kingdom: An Analysis, With Comparisons to United States Practice*, 75 Am. J. Int'l L. 283 (1981); E. Mooney, *Foreign Seizures* 7-10 (1967) (tracing doctrine to *Blad v. Bamfield*); A. Ehrenzweig, *A Treatise on the Conflict of Laws* §48 n.19 (1962) (tracing doctrine to 1364). A seventeenth-century English decision, *Blad v. Bamfield*, is sometimes cited as the doctrine's common law source. 36 Eng. Rep. 992 (Ch. 1674). *E.g., Banco Nacional de Cuba v. Sabbatino*, 376 U.S. 398, 416 (1964). In *Blad*, an English court refused to consider a challenge to the validity of a patent granted to a Danish trader by the king of Denmark.

focussing particularly on the divergent rationales that have been advanced for the doctrine.

The act of state doctrine is often traced to the 1848 decision of the House of Lords in *Duke of Brunswick v. King of Hanover.*[5] There, the former Duke of Brunswick (a German principality) sued the then Duke of Brunswick (who was also the King of Hanover), alleging that the defendant had wrongly seized certain funds in Brunswick belonging to the plaintiff. The House of Lords ruled for the defendant, reasoning "that a foreign sovereign ... cannot be made responsible [in an English court] for an act done in his sovereign character in his own country; ... the courts of this country cannot sit in judgment upon an act of a sovereign ... done in the exercise of his authority vested in him as sovereign."[6]

In the United States, the origin of the act of state doctrine is the Supreme Court's 1897 decision in *Underhill v. Hernandez.*[7] *Underhill* arose after a U.S. engineer filed suit in the United States seeking damages from a Venezuelan revolutionary commander for his wrongful imprisonment of the American during a coup in Venezuela. The Supreme Court affirmed dismissal of the claim, adopting (without citation) the *Duke of Brunswick's* reasoning:

> Every sovereign State is bound to respect the independence of every other sovereign State, *and the courts of one country will not sit in judgment on the acts of the government of another, done within its own territory.*[8]

The rationale in *Underhill* for this "classic American statement"[9] of the act of state doctrine was unclear. On the one hand, the Court suggested that the doctrine was compelled by international law, emphasizing the obligation of national courts "to respect the independence of every other sovereign State."[10] On the other hand, the Court did not clearly say this, and it cited nothing to support its formulation of the act of state doctrine. Moreover, it also referred to the "immunity of individuals from suits," suggesting that principles of sovereign immunity were relevant of the act of state doctrine.[11]

Other early U.S. decisions followed *Underhill* in dismissing suits on act of state grounds. The Court arguably applied the act of state doctrine in *American Banana*

---

5. (1848) 2 H.L. Cas. 1.

6. (1848) 2 H.L. Cas. at 17 (Lord Cottenham).

7. 168 U.S. 250 (1897).

8. 168 U.S. at 252 (emphasis added).

9. *Banco Nacional de Cuba v. Sabbatino*, 376 U.S. 398, 416 (1964).

10. 168 U.S. at 252.

11. 168 U.S. at 253-54. Like *Duke of Brunswick*, *Underhill* might have been resolved on grounds of sovereign immunity over foreign heads of state. *See also The Schooner Exchange v. McFaddon*, 11 U.S. 116, 146 (1812) (raising both act of state and foreign sovereign immunity concerns); *Hatch v. Baez*, 14 N.Y. Sup. Ct. 596 (App. Div. 1876). In *Hatch*, the lower court had held that "the courts of one country are bound to abstain from sitting in judgment on the acts of another government within its territory," citing "universal comity of nations and the established rules of international law." *Id.* at 599. The Appellate Division held that the defendant — the former President of San Domingo — was entitled to continuing sovereign immunity, citing *Schooner Exchange*.

Company v. United Fruit Company,[12] where the plaintiff challenged the Costa Rican government's seizure of his banana plantation (allegedly at the defendant's behest). Although dealing principally with the interpretation of the Sherman Act,[13] *American Banana* also cited *Underhill* for the proposition that "a seizure by a state is not a thing that can be complained of elsewhere in the courts."[14]

Unrest in Mexico during the early decades of the 20th century provided the background for further act of state rulings. In two 1918 cases — *Oetjen v. Central Leather Company* and *Ricaud v. American Metal Company* — U.S. citizens asserted claims against other private parties.[15] In each case, the claims were based upon the allegation that the plaintiff's property had been unlawfully seized by revolutionary forces in Mexico and subsequently transferred to the defendant. The plaintiffs sought return of "their" property, arguing that the defendant could not have obtained good title from the Mexican revolutionary regime, because its seizure of the property had been wrongful.[16] Relying on *Underhill*, both *Oetjen* and *Ricaud* applied the act of state doctrine, and refused to entertain the suits.

Again, however, the precise rationale for the act of state doctrine was unclear. Both *Oetjen* and *Ricaud* contained passages suggesting that the doctrine was derived from principles of international comity. According to *Oetjen*, the act of state doctrine "rests at last upon the highest considerations of international comity and expediency,"[17] reasoning that "[t]o permit the validity of the acts of one sovereign State to be reexamined and perhaps condemned by the courts of another would very certainly imperil the amicable relations between governments and vex the peace of nations."[18] Similarly, in *Ricaud*, the Court referred to the "political nature" of the parties' dispute.[19]

At the same time, however, both *Oetjen* and *Ricaud* also described the act of state doctrine as a choice of law rule, selecting the substantive law applicable to the challenged seizure:

> [T]itle to the property in this case must be determined by the result of the action taken by the military authorities of Mexico. ... [T]he act within its own boundaries of one sovereign State cannot become the subject of reexamination and modification in the courts of another. Such action, when

---

12. 213 U.S. 347 (1909).

13. *See supra* pp. 552-55.

14. 213 U.S. at 357-58. The Court also said that "[t]he very meaning of sovereignty is that the decree of the sovereign makes law." 213 U.S. at 358. Nevertheless, in *W.S. Kirkpatrick & Co. v. Environmental Tectonics Corp.*, 493 U.S. 400, 407-08 (1990), the Court said that "*American Banana* was not an act of state case."

15. *E.g.*, *Oetjen v. Central Leather Co.*, 246 U.S. 297 (1918); *Ricaud v. American Metal Co.*, 246 U.S. 304 (1918).

16. *Oetjen*, 246 U.S. at 299-301; *Ricaud*, 246 U.S. at 305-06.

17. 246 U.S. at 303-04.

18. 246 U.S. at 304.

19. 246 U.S. at 309.

shown to have been taken, becomes ... a rule of decision for the courts of this country.[20]

Under this view, application of the act of state doctrine was "not a surrender or abandonment of jurisdiction but ... an exercise of it."[21]

Although these early act of state decisions denied a U.S. judicial remedy, they did not contemplate leaving the plaintiffs with no remedy. Rather, the Court obliged the claimants to seek recovery by requesting the U.S. government to pursue their claims through diplomatic channels against the foreign state.[22] "The remedy of the former owner ... must be found in the courts of Mexico or through the diplomatic agencies of the political department of our Government."[23] The U.S. government frequently agreed to such requests, and the "espousal" of U.S. nationals' claims was a common (and often successful) occurrence in 19th century diplomatic relations.[24]

The Supreme Court's leading contemporary treatment of the act of state doctrine is *Banco Nacional de Cuba v. Sabbatino*.[25] *Sabbatino* arose from a suit by a Cuban state-owned bank seeking recovery of sugar that it had delivered to a U.S. purchaser, but for which it had not received repayment. The U.S. purchaser defended, among other things, on the grounds that Cuba had expropriated the sugar in violation of international law, and thus that the Cuban state-owned bank lacked title to the property in question. The bank replied by invoking the act of state doctrine, which, it urged, precluded U.S. judicial inquiry into the validity of Cuba's seizure of the sugar.

In a lengthy opinion, *Sabbatino* both reaffirmed the traditional act of state doctrine and expressed the doctrine's rationale in new terms. According to Justice Harlan, the doctrine has "'constitutional' underpinnings" that reflect "a basic choice regarding the competence and function of the Judiciary and the National Executive in ordering our relationships with other members of the international community."[26] More specifically, the act of state doctrine "expresses the strong sense of the Judicial Branch that its engagement in the task of passing on the validity of foreign acts of state may hinder rather than further this country's pursuit of goals both for itself and for the community of nations."[27] Thus, unlike earlier act of state decisions, which emphasized international law, comity, and choice of law principles, *Sabbatino* relied in significant part on domestic separation of powers considerations.

---

20. 246 U.S. at 309-10. *See also Oetjen*, 246 U.S. at 303.

21. *Oetjen*, 246 U.S. at 309.

22. *Underhill*, 168 U.S. at 252 ("Redress of grievances by reason of such acts must be obtained through the means open to be availed of by sovereign powers between themselves.").

23. *Oetjen*, 246 U.S. at 304.

24. *See Shapleigh v. Mier*, 299 U.S. 468, 469-71 (1937); *Dames & Moore v. Regan*, 453 U.S. 654, 679-84 (1981); *Ozanic v. United States*, 188 F.2d 228 (2d Cir. 1951); *Restatement (Third) Foreign Relations Law* §713, Reporters' Note 9 (1987).

25. 376 U.S. 398 (1964) (excerpted below).

26. 376 U.S. at 423, 425.

27. 376 U.S. at 423.

Following *Sabbatino*, lower courts frequently invoked the act of state doctrine to dismiss complaints involving foreign governmental activity.[28] The *Restatement (Third) Foreign Relations Law*, released in 1987, largely adopted the *Sabbatino* formulation.[29] The doctrine came to play a significant role in international litigation. Disagreement about the character and scope of the doctrine was endemic, however, leading to divergent and unpredictable results: "few doctrines in American law are in such a state of utter confusion as is the act of state doctrine."[30]

In 1990, the Supreme Court decided *W.S. Kirkpatrick & Co. v. Environmental Tectonics Corporation.*[31] The Court's opinion reformulated the act of state doctrine in potentially important respects and offered yet another rationale for the rule. The case arose from competing bids made by two U.S. companies for a Nigerian defense contract. After learning that its U.S. competitor had paid various "commissions" to Nigerian government officials in order to obtain the contract, the losing bidder filed a federal antitrust and RICO action against the successful bidder. The district court dismissed the suit, reasoning that it would require an adjudication of the official motivations for the Nigerian contract award, and that the act of state doctrine forbid such an inquiry.[32]

The Supreme Court rejected the trial court's reasoning and held that the act of state doctrine was simply not applicable. Justice Scalia, writing for a unanimous Court, declared that the act of state doctrine applied only to cases challenging the "validity" of foreign sovereign acts and that "nothing in the present suit required the court to declare invalid, and thus ineffective as 'rule of decision for the courts of this country,' the official act of a foreign sovereign."[33] Specifically overruling several expansive lower court interpretations of *Sabbatino*, the Court concluded that "[a]ct of state issues only arise when a court *must decide* — that is, when the outcome of the case turns upon — the effect of official action by a foreign sovereign."[34] Turning to the rationale for the act of state doctrine, Justice Scalia acknowledged that the doctrine's "jurisprudential foundation ... has undergone some evolution over the years."[35] Apparently rejecting both international law and comity, and separation of powers considerations, *Environmental Tectonics* treated the doctrine as a choice of law rule: "the act of state doctrine is not some vague doctrine of abstention but a '*principle of decision* binding on federal and state courts alike.'"[36]

The Supreme Court and other authorities have suggested a variety of significant

---

28. *See* Annotation, *Modern Status of the Act of State Doctrine*, 12 A.L.R. Fed. 707 (1972 & Supp. 1991).

29. *Restatement (Third) Foreign Relations Law* §443 (1987). *See infra* p. 700.

30. Dellapenna, *Deciphering the Act of State Doctrine*, 35 Vill. L. Rev. 1, 7 (1990).

31. 493 U.S. 400 (1990) (excerpted below).

32. 659 F.Supp. 1381 (D.N.J. 1987).

33. 493 U.S. at 405.

34. 493 U.S. at 406 (emphasis in original).

35. 493 U.S. at 404.

36. 493 U.S. at 406 (emphasis in original).

exceptions to the act of state doctrine. Unfortunately, the Court has been unable to produce a majority opinion dealing with any of these exceptions. In *Alfred Dunhill of London v. Republic of Cuba*, four members of the Court embraced an exception to the doctrine encompassing "commercial" acts of foreign states.[37] In *First National City Bank v. Banco Nacional de Cuba*, three members of a badly fractured Court adopted the so-called *"Bernstein"* exception, which provides that the act of state doctrine is inapplicable where the executive branch informs the judiciary that its adjudication of a case will not hinder the nation's foreign policy.[38] Additional exceptions to the act of state doctrine have been formulated by the lower courts[39] and by Congress.[40]

---

37. 425 U.S. 682, 695 (1976). Four other Justices rejected the commercial exception, while Justice Stevens did not expressly state a position. 425 U.S. at 715.

38. 406 U.S. 759, 768 (1972). Four Justices expressly rejected the *Bernstein* exception and two others expressed no clear view. 406 U.S. at 772 (Douglas, J., concurring); 406 U.S. at 775-76 (Powell, J., concurring).

39. *See First Nat'l City Bank v. Banco Nacional de Cuba*, 406 U.S. 759 (1972) (counterclaim exception); *Kalamazoo Spice Extraction Co. v. Provisional Military Gov't of Socialist Ethiopia*, 729 F.2d 422 (6th Cir. 1984) (treaty exception).

40. 22 U.S.C. §2370(e)(2) (1982) (Second Hickenlooper amendment) and 9 U.S.C. §15 (enforcement of certain arbitral awards). *See infra* p. 744.

B. Contemporary Formulations of the Act of State Doctrine

1. The *Sabbatino* Decision

Any consideration of the contemporary act of state doctrine must begin with *Banco Nacional de Cuba v. Sabbatino*, excerpted below. The opinion aroused considerable controversy,[41] and shortly after the Supreme Court's decision, Congress enacted legislation to overturn the specific *Sabbatino* holding.[42] Moreover, the Court's subsequent decisions in *Albert Dunhill*, *First National City Bank*, and *Environmental Tectonics* have eroded *Sabbatino's* statement of the act of state doctrine. Nonetheless, the Court's rationale remains significant, both in the act of state context and elsewhere.

BANCO NACIONAL DE CUBA v. SABBATINO
376 U.S. 398 (1964)

JUSTICE HARLAN. [In 1960, after Fidel Castro's seizure of power in Cuba, relations between the United States and Cuba grew increasingly strained. In July 1960, in response to a U.S. reduction of Cuba's quota for sugar imports into the United States, Cuba nationalized most property in Cuba belonging to U.S. nationals. In expropriating U.S. property, Castro declared that "Cuba must be a luminous and stimulating example for the sister nations of America and all the underdeveloped countries of the world to follow in their struggle to free themselves from the brutal claws of Imperialism." Among the companies whose property was nationalized was Compania Azucarera Vertientes ("CAV"), which had contracted to sell a shipload of sugar to Farr, Whitlock, a U.S. commodities broker. After nationalization of CAV's sugar, Farr, Whitlock entered into a second contract for the sugar with the Cuban government, which purported to be the new "owner" of the sugar. Farr, Whitlock then shipped the sugar and, after receiving payment from its customers, turned the proceeds over to the receiver for CAV ("Sabbatino"), rather than to Cuba. Banco Nacional de Cuba, which had been assigned the Cuban government's right to payment under Farr, Whitlock's second contract, then filed suit against Farr, Whitlock, and Sabbatino in U.S. courts. The defendants argued that the shipload of sugar never

---

41. *See, e.g.,* Cardozo, *Congress versus* Sabbatino: *Constitutional Consideration,* 4 Colum. J. Transnat'l L. 297 (1966); Henkin, *The Foreign Affairs Power of the Federal Courts:* Sabbatino, 64 Colum. L. Rev. 805 (1964); Jennings, *Comments,* in *The Aftermath of Sabbatino* 87 (Tondel ed. 1965); Kline, *An Examination of the Competence of National Courts to Prescribe and Apply International Law: The* Sabbatino *Case Revisited,* 1 U.S.F.L. Rev. 49 (1966); Mann, *The Legal Consequences of* Sabbatino, 51 Va. L. Rev. 604 (1965); McDougal, *Comments,* in *Panel: Enforcing International Law Against One Country Through Domestic Litigation in Others,* 58 ASIL Proc. 48 (1964); Metzger, *Act-of-State Doctrine Redefined: The* Sabbatino *Case,* 1964 Sup. Ct. Rev. 223.

42. Second Hickenlooper Amendment, 22 U.S.C. §2370 (e)(1)-(2); *infra* p. 744.

belonged to Cuba, because the Cuban seizure of the sugar violated international law.]

While acknowledging the continuing vitality of the act of state doctrine, the [trial] court believed it inapplicable when the questioned foreign act is in violation of international law. Proceeding on the basis that a taking invalid under international law does not convey good title, the District Court found the Cuban expropriation decree to violate such law in three separate respects: it was motivated by a retaliatory and not a public purpose; it discriminated against American nationals; and it failed to provide adequate compensation. Summary judgment against petitioner was accordingly granted. The Court of Appeals, affirming the decision on similar grounds, relied on two letters (not before the District Court) written by State Department officers which it took as evidence that the Executive Branch had no objection to a judicial testing of the Cuban decree's validity. ...

The classic American statement of the act of state doctrine ... is found in *Underhill v. Hernandez*, where Chief Justice Fuller said for a unanimous Court:

> Every sovereign State is bound to respect the independence of every other sovereign State, and the courts of one country will not sit in judgment on the acts of the government of another done within its own territory. Redress of grievances by reason of such acts must be obtained through the means open to be availed of by sovereign powers as between themselves.

Following this precept the Court in that case refused to inquire into acts of Hernandez, a revolutionary Venezuelan military commander whose government had been later recognized by the United States, which were made the basis of a damage action in this country by Underhill, an American citizen, who claimed that he had been unlawfully assaulted, coerced, and detained in Venezuela by Hernandez.

None of this Court's subsequent cases in which the act of state doctrine was directly or peripherally involved manifest any retreat from *Underhill. See American Banana Co. v. United Fruit Co.; Oetjen v. Central Leather Co.; Ricaud v. American Metal Co.*. On the contrary, in two of these cases, *Oetjen* and *Ricaud*, the doctrine as announced in *Underhill* was reaffirmed in unequivocal terms. ...

In deciding the present case the Court of Appeals relied in part upon an exception to the unqualified teachings of *Underhill*, *Oetjen*, and *Ricaud* which that court had earlier indicated. In *Bernstein v. Van Heyghen Freres Societe Anonyme*, 163 F.2d 246, suit was brought to recover from an assignee property allegedly taken, in effect, by the Nazi Government because plaintiff was Jewish. Recognizing the odious nature of this act of state, the court, through Judge Learned Hand, nonetheless refused to consider it invalid on that ground. Rather, it looked to see if the Executive had acted in any manner that would indicate that United States Courts should refuse to give effect to such a foreign decree. Finding no such evidence, the court sustained dismissal of the complaint. In a later case involving similar facts the same court again assumed examination of the German acts improper, *Bernstein v. N.V. Nederlandsche-Amerikaansche Stoomvaart-Maatschappij*, 173 F.2d 71, but, quite evidently following the implications of Judge Hand's opinion in the earlier case, amended its mandate to permit evidence of alleged invalidity, 210 F.2d 375, subsequent to receipt by plaintiff's attorney of a letter from the Acting Legal Adviser to the State Department written for the purpose of relieving the court from any constraint upon the exercise of its jurisdiction to pass on that question. This Court has never had occasion to pass upon the so-called *Bernstein* exception, nor need it do so now. For whatever ambiguity may be thought to exist in the two letters from State Department officials on which the Court of Appeals relied, is now removed by the position which the Executive has taken in this Court on the act of state claim; respondents do not indeed contest the view that these letters were intended to reflect no more than the Department's then wish not to make any statement bearing on this litigation.

[handwritten margin note: Bernstein exception]

The outcome of this case, therefore, turns upon whether any of the contentions urged by respondents against the application of the act of state doctrine in the premises is acceptable: (1) that the doctrine does not apply to acts of state which violate international law, as is claimed to be the case here; (2) that the doctrine is inapplicable unless the Executive specifically interposes it in a particular case; and (3) that, in any event, the doctrine may not be invoked by a foreign government plaintiff in our courts.

Preliminarily, we discuss the foundations on which we deem the act of state doctrine to rest, and more particularly the question of whether state or federal law governs its application in a federal diversity case. We do not believe that this doctrine is compelled either by the inherent nature of sovereign authority, as some of the earlier decisions seem to imply, *see Underhill, supra; American Banana, supra; Oetjen, supra,* or by some principle of international law. If a transaction takes place in one jurisdiction and the forum is in another, the forum does not by dismissing an action or by applying its own law purport to divest the first jurisdiction of its territorial sovereignty; it merely declines to adjudicate or makes applicable its own law to parties or property before it. The refusal of one country to enforce the penal laws of another is a typical example of an instance when a court will not entertain a cause of action arising in another jurisdiction. While historic notions of sovereign authority do bear upon the wisdom of employing the act of state doctrine, they do not dictate its existence.

That international law does not require application of the doctrine is evidenced by the practice of nations. Most of the countries rendering decisions on the subject fail to follow the rule rigidly. No international arbitral or judicial decision suggests that international law prescribes recognition of sovereign acts of governments, and apparently no claim has ever been raised before an international tribunal that failure to apply the act of state doctrine constitutes a breach of international obligation. If international law does not prescribe use of the doctrine, neither does it forbid application of the rule even if it is claimed that the act of state in question violated international law. The traditional view of international law is that it establishes substantive principles for determining whether one country has wronged another. Because of its peculiar nation-to-nation character the usual method for an individual to seek relief is to exhaust local remedies and then repair to the executive authorities of his own state to persuade them to champion his claim in diplomacy or before an international tribunal. *See United States v. Diekelman*, 92 U.S. 520, 524. Although it is, of course, true that the United States courts apply international law as part of our own in appropriate circumstances, *Ware v. Hylton*, 3 Dall. 199, 281 (1796); *The Paquete Habana*, 175 U.S. 677, 700 (1900), the public law of nations can hardly dictate to a country which is in theory wronged how to treat that wrong within its domestic borders.

Despite the broad statement in *Oetjen* that "The conduct of the foreign relations of our Government is committed by the Constitution to the Executive and Legislative ... Departments," 246 U.S. at 302, it cannot of course be thought that "every case or controversy which touches foreign relations lies beyond judicial cognizance." *Baker v. Carr*, 369 U.S. 186, 211 (1962). ... The text of the Constitution does not require the act of state doctrine; it does not irrevocably remove from the judiciary the capacity to review the validity of foreign acts of state.

The act of state doctrine does, however, have "constitutional" underpinnings. It arises out of the basic relationships between branches of government in a system of separation of powers. It concerns the competency of dissimilar institutions to make and implement particular kinds of decisions in the area of international relations. The doctrine as formulated in past decisions expresses the strong sense of the Judicial Branch that its engagement in the task of passing on the validity of foreign acts of state may hinder rather than further this country's pursuit of goals both for itself and for the community of nations as a whole in the international sphere. Many commentators disagree with this view; they have striven by means of distinguishing and limiting past decisions and by advancing various considerations of policy to stimulate a narrowing of the apparent scope of the rule. Whatever considerations are thought to predominate, it is plain that the problems involved are uniquely federal in nature. If federal authority, in this instance this Court, orders the field of judicial competence in this area for the federal courts, and the state courts are left free to formulate their own rules, the purposes behind the doctrine could be as effectively undermined as if there had been no federal pronouncement on the subject.

We could perhaps in this diversity action avoid the question of deciding whether federal or state law is applicable to this aspect of the litigation. New York has enunciated the act of state doctrine in terms that echo those of federal decisions decided during the reign of *Swift v. Tyson*, 41 U.S. 1 (1842). In *Hatch v. Baez*, 7 Hun. 596, 599 (N.Y. Sup. Ct.), *Underhill* was foreshadowed by the words, "the courts of one country are bound to abstain from sitting in judgment on the acts of another government done within its own territory." More recently, the Court of Appeals in *Salimoff & Co. v. Standard Oil Co.*, 262 N.Y. 220, 224, has declared, "The courts of one independent government will not sit in judgment upon the validity of the acts of another done within its own territory, even when such government seizes and sells the property of an American citizen within its own boundaries." Thus our conclusions might well be the same whether we dealt with this problem as one of state law, *see Erie R. Co. v. Tompkins*, or federal law.

However, we are constrained to make it clear that an issue concerned with a basic choice regarding the competence and function of the Judiciary and the National Executive in ordering our relationships with other members of the international community must be treated exclusively as an aspect of federal law.[43] It seems fair to assume that the Court did not have rules like the act of state doctrine in mind when it decided *Erie R. Co. v. Tompkins*. Soon thereafter, Professor Philip C. Jessup, now a judge of the International Court of Justice, recognized the potential dangers were *Erie* extended to legal problems affecting international relations.[44] He cautioned that the rules of international law should not be left to divergent and perhaps parochial state interpretations. His basic rationale is equally applicable to the act of state doctrine. ... We conclude that the scope of the act of state doctrine must be determined according to federal law.[45]

[margin handwritten: Federal law]

If the act of state doctrine is a principle of decision binding on federal and state courts alike but compelled by neither international law nor the Constitution, its continuing vitality depends on its capacity to reflect the proper distribution of functions between the judicial and political branches of the Government on matters bearing upon foreign affairs. It should be apparent that the greater the degree of codification or consensus concerning a particular area of international law, the more appropriate it is for the judiciary to render decisions regarding it, since the courts can then focus on the application of an agreed principle to circumstances of fact rather than on the sensitive task of establishing a principle not inconsistent with the national interest or with international justice. It is also evident that some aspects of international law touch much more sharply on national nerves than do others; the less important the implications of an issue are for our foreign relations, the weaker the justification for exclusivity in the political branches. The balance of relevant considerations may also be shifted if the government which perpetrated the challenged act of state is no longer in existence, as in the *Bernstein* case, for the political interest of this country may, as a result, be measurably altered. Therefore, rather than laying down or reaffirming an inflexible and all-encompassing rule in this case, we decide only that the Judicial Branch will not examine the validity of a taking of property within its own territory by a foreign sovereign government, extant and recognized by this country at

---

43. At least this is true when the Court limits the scope of judicial inquiry. We need not now consider whether a state court might, in certain circumstances, adhere to a more restrictive view concerning the scope of examination of foreign acts than that required by this Court.

44. Jessup, *The Doctrine of* Erie Railroad v. Tompkins *Applied to International Law*, 33 Am. J. Int'l L. 740 (1939).

45. Various constitutional and statutory provisions indirectly support this determination, *see* U.S. Const., Art. I, §8, cls. 3, 10; Art. II, §§2, 3; Art. III, §2; 28 U.S.C. §§1251 (a)(2), (b)(1), (b)(3), 1332 (a)(2), 1333, 1350-1351, by reflecting a concern for uniformity in this country's dealings with foreign nations and indicating a desire to give matters of international significance to the jurisdiction of federal institutions. ...

the time of suit, in the absence of a treaty or other unambiguous agreement regarding controlling legal principles, even if the complaint alleges that the taking violates customary international law.

There are few if any issues in international law today on which opinion seems to be so divided as the limitations on a state's power to expropriate the property of aliens. There is, of course, authority, in international judicial and arbitral decisions, in the expressions of national governments, and among commentators for the view that a taking is improper under international law if it is not for a public purpose, is discriminatory, or is without provision for prompt, adequate, and effective compensation. However, Communist countries, although they have in fact provided a degree of compensation after diplomatic efforts, commonly recognize no obligation on the part of the taking country. Certain representatives of the newly independent and underdeveloped countries have questioned whether rules of state responsibility toward aliens can bind nations that have not consented to them and it is argued that the traditionally articulated standards governing expropriation of property reflect "imperialist" interests and are inappropriate to the circumstances of emergent states.

The disagreement as to relevant international law standards reflects an even more basic divergence between the national interests of capital importing and capital exporting nations and between the social ideologies of those countries that favor state control of a considerable portion of the means of production and those that adhere to a free enterprise system. It is difficult to imagine the courts of this country embarking on adjudication in an area which touches more sensitively the practical and ideological goals of the various members of the community of nations.[46] ...

The possible adverse consequences of a conclusion [permitting U.S. courts to characterize foreign expropriations as violations of international law] are highlighted by contrasting the practices of the political branch with the limitations of the judicial process in matters of this kind. Following an expropriation of any significance, the Executive engages in diplomacy aimed to assure that United States citizens who are harmed are compensated fairly. Representing all claimants of this country, it will often be able, either by bilateral or multilateral talks, by submission to the United Nations, or by the employment of economic and political sanctions, to achieve some degree of general redress. Judicial determinations of invalidity of title can, on the other hand, have only an occasional impact, since they depend on the fortuitous circumstance of the property in question being brought into this country.[47] Such decisions would, if the acts involved were declared invalid, often be likely to give offense to the expropriating country; since the concept of territorial sovereignty is so deep seated, any state may resent the refusal of the courts of another sovereign to accord

---

46. There are, of course, areas of international law in which consensus as to standards is greater and which do not represent a battleground for conflicting ideologies. This decision in no way intimates that the courts of this country are broadly foreclosed from considering questions of international law.

47. It is, of course, true that such determinations might influence others not to bring expropriated property into the country, so their indirect impact might extend beyond the actual invalidations of title.

validity to acts within its territorial borders. Piecemeal dispositions of this sort involving the probability of affront to another state could seriously interfere with negotiations being carried on by the Executive Branch and might prevent or render less favorable the terms of an agreement that could otherwise be reached. Relations with third countries which have engaged in similar expropriations would not be immune from effect.

The dangers of such adjudication are present regardless of whether the State Department has, as it did in this case, asserted that the relevant act violated international law. If the Executive Branch has undertaken negotiations with an expropriating country, but has refrained from claims of violation of the law of nations, a determination to that effect by a court might be regarded as a serious insult, while a finding of compliance with international law, would greatly strengthen the bargaining hand of the other state with consequent detriment to American interests.

Even if the State Department has proclaimed the impropriety of the expropriation, the stamp of approval of its view by a judicial tribunal, however impartial, might increase any affront and the judicial decision might occur at a time, almost always well after the taking, when such an impact would be contrary to our national interest. Considerably more serious and far-reaching consequences would flow from a judicial finding that international law standards had been met if that determination flew in the face of a State Department proclamation to the contrary. When articulating principles of international law in its relations with other states, the Executive Branch speaks not only as an interpreter of generally accepted and traditional rules, as would the courts, but also as an advocate of standards it believes desirable for the community of nations and protective of national concerns. In short, whatever way the matter is cut, the possibility of conflict between the Judicial and Executive Branches could hardly be avoided. ...

Another serious consequence of the exception pressed by respondents would be to render uncertain titles in foreign commerce, with the possible consequence of altering the flow of international trade. If the attitude of the United States courts were unclear, one buying expropriated goods would not know if he could safely import them into this country. Even were takings known to be invalid, one would have difficulty determining after goods had changed hands several times whether the particular articles in question were the product of an ineffective state act.

Against the force of such considerations, we find respondents' countervailing arguments quite unpersuasive. Their basic contention is that United States courts could make a significant contribution to the growth of international law, a contribution whose importance, it is said, would be magnified by the relative paucity of decisional law by international bodies. But given the fluidity of present world conditions, the effectiveness of such a patchwork approach toward the formulation of an acceptable body of law concerning state responsibility for expropriations is, to say the least, highly conjectural. Moreover, it rests upon the sanguine presupposition that the decisions of the courts of the world's major capital exporting country and principal exponent of the free enterprise system would be accepted as disinterested expressions of sound legal principle by those adhering to widely different ideologies.

It is contended that regardless of the fortuitous circumstances necessary for United States jurisdiction over a case involving a foreign act of state and the resultant isolated application to any expropriation program taken as a whole, it is the function of the courts to justly decide individual disputes before them. Perhaps the most typical act of state case involves the original owner or his assignee suing one not in association with the expropriating state who has had "title" transferred to him. But it is difficult to regard the claim of the original owner, who otherwise may be recompensed through diplomatic channels, as more demanding of judicial cognizance than the claim of title by the innocent third party purchaser, who, if the property is taken from him, is without any remedy.

Respondents claim that the economic pressure resulting from the proposed exception to the act of state doctrine will materially add to the protection of United States investors. We are not convinced, even assuming the relevance of this contention. Expropriations take place for a variety of reasons, political and ideological as well as economic. When one considers the variety of means possessed by this country to make secure foreign investment, the persuasive or coercive effect of judicial invalidation of acts of expropriation dwindles in comparison. The newly independent states are in need of continuing foreign investment; the creation of a climate unfavorable to such investment by wholesale confiscations may well work to their long-run economic disadvantage. Foreign aid given to many of these countries provides a powerful lever in the hands of the political branches to ensure fair treatment of United States nationals. Ultimately the sanctions of economic embargo and the freezing of assets in this country may be employed. Any country willing to brave any or all of these consequences is unlikely to be deterred by sporadic judicial decisions directly affecting only property brought to our shores. If the political branches are unwilling to exercise their ample powers to effect compensation, this reflects a judgment of the national interest which the judiciary would be ill-advised to undermine indirectly.

It is suggested that if the act of state doctrine is applicable to violations of international law, it should only be so when the Executive Branch expressly stipulates that it does not wish the courts to pass on the question of validity. We should be slow to reject the representations of the Government that such a reversal of the *Bernstein* principle would work serious inroads on the maximum effectiveness of United States diplomacy. Often the State Department will wish to refrain from taking an official position, particularly at a moment that would be dictated by the development of private litigation but might be inopportune diplomatically. Adverse domestic consequences might flow from an official stand which could be assuaged, if at all, only by revealing matters best kept secret. Of course, a relevant consideration for the State Department would be the position contemplated in the court to hear the case. It is highly questionable whether the examination of validity by the judiciary should depend on an educated guess by the Executive as to probable result and, at any rate, should a prediction be wrong, the Executive might be embarrassed in its dealings with other countries. We do not now pass on the *Bernstein* exception, but even if it were deemed valid, its suggested extension is unwarranted.

However offensive to the public policy of this country and its constituent States an expropriation of this kind may be, we conclude that both the national interest and progress toward the goal of establishing the rule of law among nations are best served by maintaining intact the act of state doctrine in this realm of its application.

Finally, we must determine whether Cuba's status as a plaintiff in this case dictates a result at variance with the conclusions reached above. If the Court were to distinguish between suits brought by sovereign states and those of assignees, the rule would have little effect unless a careful examination were made in each case to determine if the private party suing had taken property in good faith. Such an inquiry would be exceptionally difficult, since the relevant transaction would almost invariably have occurred outside our borders. If such an investigation were deemed irrelevant, a state could always assign its claim. ... [Moreover,] the distinction proposed would sanction self-help remedies, something hardly conducive to a peaceful international order. ...

Respondents offer another theory for treating the case differently because of Cuba's participation. It is claimed that the forum should simply apply its own law to all the relevant transactions. An analogy is drawn to the area of sovereign immunity, *National City Bank v. Republic of China*, 348 U.S. 356, in which, if a foreign country seeks redress in our courts, counterclaims are permissible. But immunity relates to the prerogative right not to have sovereign property subject to suit; fairness has been thought to require that when the sovereign seeks recovery, it be subject to legitimate counterclaims against it. The act of state doctrine, however, although it shares with the immunity doctrine a respect for sovereign states, concerns the limits for determining the validity of an otherwise applicable rule of law. It is plain that if a recognized government sued on a contract with a United States citizen, concededly legitimate by the locus of its making, performance, and most significant contacts, the forum would not apply its own substantive law of contracts. Since the act of state doctrine reflects the desirability of presuming the relevant transaction valid, the same result follows; the forum may not apply its local law regarding foreign expropriations.

JUSTICE WHITE, dissenting. I am dismayed that the Court has, with one broad stroke, declared the ascertainment and application of international law beyond the competence of the Courts of the United States in a large and important category of cases. I am also disappointed in the Court's declaration that the acts of a sovereign state with regard to the property of aliens within its borders are beyond the reach of international law in the courts of this country. However clearly established that law may be, a sovereign may violate it with impunity, except insofar as the political branches of the government may provide a remedy. This backward-looking doctrine, never before declared in this Court, is carried a disconcerting step further: not only are the courts powerless to question acts of state proscribed by international upon a foreign law; they must render judgment and thereby validate the lawless act. Since the Court expressly extends its ruling to all acts of state expropriating property, however clearly inconsistent with the international community, all discriminatory expropriations of the property of aliens, as for example the taking of properties of persons belonging to certain races, religions or nationalities, are entitled to automatic validation in the courts of the United States. No other civilized country has found such a rigid rule necessary for the survival of the executive branch of its government; the executive of no other government seems to require such insulation from international law adjudications in its courts; and no other judiciary is apparently so incompetent to ascertain and apply international law.[48]

I do not believe that the act of state doctrine, as judicially fashioned in this Court, and the reasons underlying it, require American courts to decide cases in disregard of international law and the rights of litigants to a full determination on the merits. ...

Notes on Sabbatino

1. *Elements of act of state doctrine.* What elements must be proven for the act of state doctrine to apply? *Sabbatino* went to some lengths to state only a narrow holding, that U.S. courts "will not examine the validity of a taking of property within its own territory by a foreign sovereign government, extant and recognized by this country at the time of suit, in the absence of a treaty or other unambiguous agreement regarding controlling legal principles, even if the complaint alleges that the taking violates customary international law." The *Third Restatement* proposes the following formulation:

> In the absence of a treaty or other unambiguous agreement regarding controlling legal principles, courts in the United States will generally refrain from examining the validity of a taking by a foreign state of property within its own territory, or from sitting in judgment on other acts of a governmental character done by a foreign state within its own territory and applicable there.

Restatement (Third) Foreign Relations Law §443 (1987). The necessary elements of an act of state defense under §443 include: (1) a U.S. court sitting in judgment on, (2) a taking of property or other act of "governmental character," (3) by a "foreign state," (4) within its own territory, (5) that is not governed by any "controlling" statute or international agreement. Are the act of state rules adopted in *Sabbatino* and §443 identical?

2. *Comparison between act of state doctrine and rules governing recognition of foreign judgments.* As discussed below, U.S. courts have developed rules governing the circumstances in which the judgments of foreign courts will be entitled to recognition in the United States. These rules (which are generally a matter of state law, *see infra* pp. 960-62) provide that foreign judgments are presumptively enforceable, but subject to a number of important exceptions. Among other things, a foreign judgment will not be enforced if the foreign court lacked personal jurisdiction over the defendant under U.S. due process requirements, if the judgment is a "penal" or "revenue" judgment, or if the judgment violates the forum's public policy. Broadly analogous requirements exist for the recognition of foreign arbitral awards under the New York Convention. *See infra* pp. 1040-52.

Compare these requirements to the act of state doctrine. Under the act of state doctrine, foreign

---

48. The Court does not refer to any country which has applied the act of state doctrine in a case where a substantial international law issue is sought to be raised by an alien whose property has been expropriated. This country and this Court stand alone among the civilized nations of the world in ruling that such an issue is not cognizable in a court of law.

public acts are given effect (unlike foreign penal or public judgments), even where they violate local public policy or international law (unlike foreign money judgments). Why are foreign acts of state entitled to greater deference in U.S. courts than foreign judgments and arbitral awards? Isn't it anomalous for U.S. courts to accord binding effect to arbitrary foreign expropriations, but not to reasoned judgments following regular court proceedings? Why isn't a foreign court's judgment or a foreign arbitral award an act of state?

3. *Comparison between act of state doctrine and treatment of foreign public laws.* As described above, U.S. courts generally refuse to entertain claims based on foreign penal or revenue laws. *See supra* pp. 630-31; *Huntington v. Attrill*, 146 U.S. 657 (1892); *Menendez v. Saks & Co.*, 485 F.2d 1355 (2d Cir. 1973), *rev'd*, 425 U.S. 682 (1976). As, Justice White observed in dissent in *Sabbatino*, "our courts customarily refuse to enforce the revenue and penal laws of a foreign state, since no country has an obligation to further the governmental interests of a foreign sovereign." Is the act of state doctrine consistent with this rule?

4. *Application of the act of state doctrine to claims based on international law.* The U.S. parties in *Sabbatino* argued not just that Cuba's expropriation of their property violated U.S. law and public policy, but also that the expropriation violated international law. Under prevailing principles of international law, there was substantial support for this argument. *E.g., Restatement (Third) Foreign Relations Law* §712 (1987). Why wouldn't the Court in *Sabbatino* consider international law? Recall that "[i]nternational law is part of our law, and must be ascertained and administered by the courts of justice ... as often as questions of right depending upon it are duly presented for their determination." *The Paquete Habana*, 175 U.S. 677, 700 (1900); *supra* pp. 21 & 49-56. Shouldn't *Sabbatino* have applied international law rules prohibiting expropriations like those Cuba engaged in?

Note that most foreign courts will not apply the act of state doctrine to foreclose claims that international law has been violated. *See Sabbatino*, 376 U.S. at 440 (White, J., dissenting) ("No other civilized country has found such a rigid rule [as *Sabbatino's* refusal to permit application of international law] necessary for the survival of the executive branch of its government ... and no other judiciary is apparently so incompetent to ascertain and apply international law"). *See also* Stevenson, *Remarks*, in *The Aftermath of Sabbatino: Background Papers and Proceedings of the Seventh Hammarskjold Forum* 73, 74 (L. Tondel, Jr. ed. 1965) ("It has been our stated national policy to uphold and strengthen the role of international law. Yet the act of state doctrine cloaks even the most patently illegal international act in the protective veil of domestic legality.").

Sabbatino rejected this argument because of "disagreement as to relevant international law standards" regarding expropriation among different states. Why is the existence of disagreement about international law so important to the act of state doctrine? Don't the parties in most cases disagree about the applicable legal standards? Note that the Court also suggested that a "treaty or other unambiguous agreement regarding controlling legal principles" would permit adjudication by U.S. courts. *See infra* pp. 738-44. Why is an "unambiguous" agreement — rather than, for example, a "reasonably clear" agreement — needed to overcome the act of state doctrine? Why is an international "agreement," rather than customary international law, required? Under almost any standard of international law, the discriminatory, uncompensated seizure of privately-owned U.S. property by Cuba was wrongful. *See Restatement (Third) Foreign Relations Law* §712 (1987). Given this, why is it relevant that there might be disagreement about other cases involving less egregious misconduct?

5. *Sabbatino's rationale for act of state doctrine.* There has long been uncertainty about the rationale for the act of state doctrine. *See supra* pp. 685-90. In the words of one commentator, "the doctrine resembles the proverbial elephant described by a committee of the blind." Dellapenna, *Deciphering the Act of State Doctrine*, 35 Vill. L. Rev. 1, 7 (1990). Is sovereign immunity the basis for the doctrine? International law? Comity? Separation of powers? Choice of law rules? What does *Sabbatino* indicate?

(a) *Foreign sovereign immunity.* The common law act of state doctrine and U.S. statutory rules governing foreign sovereign immunity address closely related concerns. Broadly speaking, both sets of rules express deference to foreign laws and official acts and seek to minimize international frictions by insulating foreign sovereigns and their conduct from certain types of legal proceedings in U.S. courts.

Nonetheless, there are significant differences between the act of state and foreign sovereign immunity doctrines. First, the act of state doctrine is limited to a foreign government's conduct that is consummated within its own territory, *see infra* pp. 721-28, while foreign sovereign immunity can extend to conduct anywhere in the world. Second, the act of state doctrine can provide a substantive rule of decision that can be used offensively, as in *Sabbatino*, while foreign sovereign immunity merely provides a jurisdictional defense. Third, nongovernmental parties can sometimes avail themselves of protection under the act of state doctrine, *see infra* p. 720, while only "foreign states" and their "agencies or instrumentalities" can invoke foreign sovereign immunity, *see supra* pp. 213-16. Finally, the sources of the two sets of rules differ: the act of state doctrine is a common law rule with "constitutional underpinnings," while foreign sovereign immunity presently derives from comprehensive federal legislation. *See also Restatement (Third) Foreign Relations Law* §443, Reporters' Note 11 (1987).

(b) *Separation of powers concerns.* Many authorities have based the act of state doctrine on constitutional separation of powers concerns. *Sabbatino* declared:

> The act of state doctrine ... [has] "constitutional" underpinnings. It arises out of the basic relationships between branches of government in a system of separation of powers. It concerns the competency of dissimilar institutions to make and implement particular kinds of decisions in the area of international relations. The doctrine as formulated in past decisions expresses the strong sense of the Judicial Branch that its engagement in the task of passing on the validity of foreign acts of state may hinder rather than further this country's pursuit of goals both for itself and for the community of nations as a whole in the international sphere.

See also First Nat'l City Bank v. Banco Nacional de Cuba, 406 U.S. 759, 765 (1971) (Rehnquist, J., plurality) ("the act of state doctrine justifies its existence primarily on the basis that juridical review of acts of state of a foreign power could embarrass the conduct of foreign relations by the political branches of the government."); *Republic of Philippines v. Marcos*, 862 F.2d 1355, 1360-61 (9th Cir. 1988), *cert. denied*, 409 U.S. 1035 (1989) ("A court that passes on the validity of an 'act of state' intrudes into the domain of the political branches."). Is this concern about judicial interference in foreign policy justified? Haven't the political branches — Congress and the President — expressed their willingness for the courts to adjudicate international cases by vesting them with jurisdiction over those cases? Does *Sabbatino* provide any specific explanation as to how judicial decisions in expropriation cases might frustrate U.S. foreign policy? Consider *Sabbatino's* discussion of the Executive Branch's role in espousing expropriation claims against foreign states.

(c) *Political question doctrine.* Other authorities have concluded that the act of state doctrine is an application of the political question doctrine. The political question doctrine is a constitutional limitation on the judicial power of the federal courts, which bars the courts from resolving cases that raise issues more appropriately committed to other branches of government. *See supra* pp. 47-48; *Baker v. Carr*, 369 U.S. 186 (1962); *Goldwater v. Carter*, 444 U.S. 996 (1979). Among the factors relevant to determining whether a case presents a political question are a "textually demonstrable commitment" of an issue to the executive or legislative branches, the lack of "judicially discoverable and manageable standards" for resolving an issue, or the existence of prudential considerations counselling for judicial abstention. 444 U.S. at 997-98 (Powell, J., concurring). Several Justices have taken the position that the act of state doctrine is merely a particular application of the political question doctrine. *E.g., First National City Bank*, 406 U.S. at 785-90 (Brennan, J., dissenting) ("the validity of a foreign act of state in certain circumstances is a 'political question' not cognizable in our courts"); *Alfred Dunhill*, 425 U.S. at 726-28 (Marshall, J., dissenting).

Nonetheless, there are important distinctions between the act of state and the political question doctrines. The latter is a jurisdictional bar that requires abstention, which appears inconsistent with the offensive use of the act of state doctrine in cases like *Sabbatino*. Moreover, notwithstanding its "constitutional underpinnings," the act of state doctrine would appear to be subject to contrary congressional legislation, *see infra* p. 744; the political question doctrine, in contrast, is an Article III requirement, that is not directly subject to legislative revision.

(d) *Abstention.* Related to separation of powers concerns and the political question doctrine, other authorities explain the act of state doctrine as a principle of abstention. *Restatement (Third) Foreign Relations Law* §443, comment a (1987) ("doctrine was developed ... as a principle of judicial restraint, essentially to avoid disrespect for foreign states"). As discussed below, the U.S. Government argued in *Environmental Tectonics* that the act of state doctrine is an "unspecified" principle of abstention. *See infra* pp. 719-20. Given the concerns discussed in *Sabbatino* about judicial interference in U.S. foreign affairs and claims espousal, is abstention the appropriate way of viewing the doctrine? In *Environmental Tectonics*, however, the Court flatly rejected this characterization: "The act of state doctrine is not some vague doctrine of abstention but a 'principle of decision binding on federal and state courts alike.'" 493 U.S. at 405.

(e) *International law. Sabbatino* held that international law did not require the act of state doctrine. What if the substantive law that U.S. courts would apply to a foreign act of state was U.S. law (rather than international law, as in *Sabbatino*)? Would international law limit the power of a nation to apply its own substantive law to a foreign state's public acts within its own territory? Do any of the international law limits on legislative jurisdiction require the act of state doctrine?

(f) *International comity.* Recall the rationale most frequently cited in 19th century act of state decisions: "[t]o permit the validity of the acts of one sovereign State to be reexamined and perhaps condemned by the courts of another would very certainly imperil the amicable relations between governments and vex the peace of nations." *Oetjen*, 246 U.S. at 304. Is "comity" a persuasive basis for the act of state doctrine? What is the relationship between comity as a rationale and separation of powers concerns?

(g) *Choice of law rule.* Among other things, *Sabbatino* describes the act of state doctrine as a "principle of decision." This suggests that the doctrine is a choice of law rule (permitting a court to exercise jurisdiction, but dictating the applicable substantive law), and not a rule of abstention or an application of the political question doctrine (which would deny jurisdiction). Note also that *Sabbatino* gave affirmative effect to the Cuban government's seizure of sugar; it did *not* refuse to decide the dispute, but instead, in deciding the dispute, gave full effect to the validity of the Cuban government's seizure. A number of authorities have described the act of state doctrine as a choice of law rule. See *Alfred Dunhill*, 425 U.S. at 705 n.18 (act of state doctrine can be described in "choice of law terms"); *Ricaud*, 246 U.S. at 309 (act of state doctrine held to select applicable rule of decision, and not to constitute "a surrender or abandonment of jurisdiction but ... an exercise of it"); *Callejo v. Bancomer, SA*, 764 F.2d 1101, 1114 (5th Cir. 1985) ("super choice of law rule"); *Sharon v. Time, Inc.*, 599 F.Supp. 538, 546 (S.D.N.Y. 1984) ("act-of-state doctrine is, in its origins and essence, a federal rule mandating a choice of law by which to judge the validity of the official actions of sovereign states"); *Restatement (Third) Foreign Relations Law* §443, Reporters' Note 1 (1987) ("special rule of conflict of laws"); Henkin, *Act of State Today: Recollections in Tranquility*, 6 Colum. J. Trans. L. 175, 178 (1967). As discussed below, *Environmental Tectonics* appears to have embraced a choice of law explanation of the act of state doctrine. See *infra* p. 719.

If the act of state doctrine is a choice of law rule what would its precise content be? Would it provide, in effect, that the validity of acts of state are governed by the law of the state committing the act of state, without regard to the public policies (or other interests) of the forum or other states? *Restatement (Third) Foreign Relations Law* §443, Reporters' Note 1 (1987). *See also American Banana Co. v. United Fruit Co.*, 213 U.S. 347, 358 (1909) ("The very meaning of sovereignty is that the decree of the sovereign makes law").

Consistent with treating the act of state doctrine as a choice of law rule, *Sabbatino* applied the doctrine offensively to prevent a U.S. defendant from asserting a defense to a suit brought by a Cuban state-owned bank seeking to recover property that Cuba previously had seized. As a consequence, Cuba's claim of ownership went unchallenged and it obtained affirmative relief. Is this application of the act of state doctrine wise? Even though U.S. courts will not sit in judgment on foreign acts of state, does that mean they should also accept those acts as a basis for affirmatively ordering relief? Does this not make the United States complicit in the foreign state's misconduct? Does it not also inject U.S. courts into U.S. foreign relations — at a time selected by a hostile foreign state — in just the way that the act of state doctrine was meant to prevent? Is it consistent with the Court's asserted affirmation of the well-established principle that U.S. courts will not enforce foreign penal or revenue laws? See *supra* pp. 630-31.

(h) *Miscellaneous other explanations.* A variety of other explanations have been advanced from time to time for the act of state doctrine. *E.g.*, Dellapenna, *Deciphering the Act of State Doctrine*, 35 Vill. L. Rev. 1, 45-53 (1990) ("a rule of repose"); Chow, *Rethinking the Act of State Doctrine: An Analysis in Terms of Jurisdiction to Prescribe*, 62 Wash. L. Rev. 397, 400-03 (1987) (limit on legislative jurisdiction); Burley, *Law Among Liberal States: Liberal Internationalism and the Act of State Doctrine*, 92 Colum. L. Rev. 1907 (1992) (limit on rule of law in dealing with actions by "nonliberal" states). The act of state doctrine might also be explained as a choice of forum (or remedies) device, providing that certain types of claims must be resolved through diplomatic channels. Alternatively, it might be viewed as a mechanism for applying international law — which is "part of our law" — in U.S. courts, which includes consideration of whether private rights of action are provided by international law and consistent with U.S. policies. Other rationales can also be formulated.

(i) *Proper rationale for the act of state doctrine.* Which of the foregoing rationales is most persuasive? Which rationale best explains the outcome in *Sabbatino*?

6. *Foreign governmental acts protected by* Sabbatino — *what is an "act of state"?* *Sabbatino's* specific holding was limited to the taking of property. Does the act of state doctrine also apply to other governmental acts? Are all "public acts," provided that they occur on the foreign state's territory, entitled to protection under the act of state doctrine? How does §443 of the *Third Restatement* resolve this question?

Sabbatino suggests that governmental acts other than expropriations must be independently evaluated, and that relevant considerations to this determination include how sharply a particular issue "touch[es] on national nerves"; the "degree of codification or consensus concerning a particular area of international law"; and the "implications of an issue ... for our foreign policy." *Compare W.S. Kirkpatrick & Co. v. Environmental Tectonics Corp.*, 493 U.S. 400 (1990) (excerpted below at pp. 713-18 (questioning significance of *Sabbatino* factors)). *See infra* pp. 705-12 for discussion of foreign state actions covered by the act of state doctrine.

7. **Sabbatino** *as a rule of federal common law*. *Sabbatino* held that the act of state doctrine is a rule of federal common law, binding on state courts and federal courts in both federal question and diversity cases. The Court reasoned that *Erie R.R. Co. v. Tompkins*, 304 U.S. 64 (1938), did not require application of state law act of state rules because of the federal interest in the Nation's foreign affairs. The Court also indicated that state courts would be required to apply an act of state rule at least as deferential to foreign governmental acts as the federal act of state doctrine. Subsequent state court decisions have done so. *E.g.*, *Castro v. International Telegraph & Telephone Co.*, 1991 Del. Ch. Lexis 89 (Del. Ch. May 30, 1991); *Perez v. Chase Manhattan Bank*, 474 N.Y.S.2d 689 (N.Y.), *cert. denied*, 469 U.S. 966 (1984); *United Nuclear Corp. v. General Atomic Co.*, 629 P.2d 231 (N.M. 1980), *cert. denied*, 451 U.S. 901 (1981); *Hunt v. Coastal States Gas Producing Co.*, 589 S.W.2d 322 (Tex.), *cert. denied*, 444 U.S. 992 (1979).

8. *Federal common law basis for act of state doctrine*. What is the constitutional basis for requiring state courts to adopt the rule of federal common law enunciated in *Sabbatino*?

(a) *Federal common law rules in international litigation*. The act of state doctrine is a leading example of federal common law in the international context. Other possible examples of federal common law in international cases include foreign sovereign immunity, *supra* pp. 224-25; forum selection clauses, *supra* pp. 450-52; forum non conveniens, *supra* pp. 365-66; comity, *supra* pp. 49-56; extraterritoriality, *supra* pp. 541-44, and mandatory resort to the Hague Evidence Convention, *infra* pp. 913-14. The basis for the development of a federal common law rule in each of these contexts is the principle that "a few areas, involving 'uniquely federal interests,'... are so committed by the Constitution and laws of the United States to federal control that state law is preempted and replaced, where necessary, by federal law of a content prescribed (absent explicit statutory directive) by the courts — so-called 'federal common law.'" *Boyle v. United Technologies Corp.*, 487 U.S. 500 (1988); *supra* pp. 15-16.

(b) *Is a federal common law act of state doctrine appropriate?* Is *Sabbatino's* act of state doctrine an appropriate subject for substantive federal common law? *Sabbatino* declares that "an issue concerned with a basic choice regarding the competence and function of the Judiciary and National Executive in ordering our relationships with other members of the international community must be treated exclusively as an aspect of federal law," because of the federal interests that "the rules of international law should not be left to divergent and perhaps parochial [state court] interpretations" and in ensuring that U.S. judicial proceedings do not "hinder rather than further this country's pursuit of goals ... in the international sphere." Is this rationale persuasive? Is there a special need for uniform interpretation of international law by U.S. courts? What is it?

Even if there is a need for uniform interpretations of international law, the act of state doctrine can be (and usually is) invoked in cases not involving international law, but instead involving federal or state law. *E.g.*, *Grass v. Credito Mexicana, SA*, 797 F.2d 220 (5th Cir. 1986), *cert. denied*, 480 U.S. 934 (1987); *DeRoburt v. Gannett Co.*, 733 F.2d 701 (9th Cir. 1984) (U.S. libel law), *cert. denied*, 469 U.S. 1159 (1985); *IAM v. OPEC*, 649 F.2d 1354 (9th Cir. 1981) (U.S. antitrust law), *cert. denied*, 454 U.S. 1163 (1982); *Bandes v. Harlow & Jones, Inc.*, 570 F.Supp. 955 (S.D.N.Y. 1983). Is uniform treatment of any claims involving foreign governmental acts — regardless of applicable law — necessary? Recall that the FSIA dealt with the substantive law applicable to claims against foreign states by leaving the subject to otherwise applicable state (or federal) law. *See supra* pp. 211-12.

The second rationale suggested by *Sabbatino* for a federal act of state rule emphasized the potentially adverse effects on U.S. foreign relations of state court decisions passing upon the validity of foreign acts of state. Is this concern warranted? Will foreign nations really retaliate against the United States because a state court uses one version of the act of state doctrine rather than another? If the act of state doctrine is a choice of law rule, why doesn't *Klaxon* require application of state law? *See supra* pp. 681-84.

9. *Power of states to adopt a broader act of state doctrine.* What if a state court wished to adopt an act of state doctrine that was *more deferential* to foreign sovereign acts than the federal rule (*i.e.*, that recognized a broader act of state doctrine than that of the Supreme Court)? *Sabbatino* leaves this question open. *See supra* p. 695 n.43. Consider the following remark by the late Judge Friendly:

> It would be baffling if a foreign act of state intended to affect property in the United States were ignored on one side of the Hudson but respected on the other. ... The required uniformity can be secured only by recognizing the expansive reach of the principle ... that all questions relating to an act of state are questions of federal law. [*Republic of Iraq v. First National City Bank*, 353 F.2d 47, 50-51 (2d Cir. 1965), *cert. denied*, 382 U.S. 1027 (1966).]

Is Judge Friendly correct that it would be "baffling" for a foreign act of state to have different effects in different states? As suggested earlier, isn't this an inevitable consequence of a federal system where different states have different laws? What harm could arise from disparate treatment of foreign acts of state by different states?

10. *Criticism of* Sabbatino. Many commentators have sharply criticized the *Sabbatino* rule. *E.g.*, Bazyler, *Abolishing the Act of State Doctrine*, 134 U. Pa. L. Rev. 325 (1986); Mathias, *Restructuring the Act of State Doctrine: A Blueprint for Legislative Reform*, 12 Law & Pol'y Int'l Bus. 369 (1980). Among other things, critics charge that there is no constitutional basis for the act of state doctrine, that the doctrine is inherently ambiguous and unpredictable, that it undermines important national laws and policies, and that it has precluded the development of international law in U.S. courts:

> the act of state doctrine prompts automatic judicial reflexes that relegate all disputes involving foreign governments and international law to an unspecified — or nonexistent — forum outside the court room. Judicial circumspection ... as to ... matters touching on foreign affairs seem[s] to have become synonymous with unquestioning judicial abstention in cases alleging international law violations by foreign governments. Mathias, *Restructuring the Act of State Doctrine: A Blueprint for Legislative Reform*, 12 Law & Pol'y Int'l Bus. 369, 371 (1980).

Does *Sabbatino* provide adequate responses to these charges?

11. *Efforts to abolish act of state doctrine.* Critics of the act of state doctrine have proposed legislative reforms or abolition of the principle. The Second Hickenlooper Amendment was the first, and most successful, example of this trend. In 1980, Senator Mathias introduced legislation that would have abolished the act of state doctrine with respect to claims based on international law. *See* S. 2633, 96th Cong., 2d Sess., 126 Cong. Rec. 9453 (1980); S. 1434, 97th Cong., 1st Sess., 127 Cong. Rec. 13960 (1981). The proposed legislation died in the Senate Judiciary Committee. In 1984, the American Bar Association proposed legislation limiting application of the act of state doctrine in cases involving claims that an expropriation violates international law. S. 1071, 99th Cong., 1st Sess., 131 Cong. Rec. 5371 (1985). More recently, the ABA proposed additional legislation restricting or abolishing the doctrine. *See* H.R. 1888, 100th Cong., 1st Sess. (1987) (abolishing act of state doctrine in cases involving international law claims). Finally, in late 1988 Congress enacted legislation limiting application of the act of state doctrine in cases involving certain international arbitration agreements or awards. *See* 9 U.S.C. §15.

2. Elements of the Act of State Doctrine

Sabbatino left a number of uncertainties regarding the elements of the act of state doctrine, which have provoked confusion among both lower courts and in the Supreme Court.[49] In particular, courts grappled with the questions: (a) what constitutes an "act of state"; (b) when does a U.S. court "sit in judgment" on an act of state; and (c) where must an act of state occur? Each of these elements is examined below.

a. Definition of "Act of State"

Perennial difficulties have arisen in determining what foreign sovereign acts

---

49. *See* Dellapenna, *Deciphering the Act of State Doctrine*, 35 Vill. L. Rev. 1 (1990); Bazyler, *Abolishing the Act of State Doctrine*, 134 U. Pa. L. Rev. 325, 365-68 (1986).

constitute "acts of state." As discussed above, *Sabbatino* (as well as *Oetjen* and *Ricaud*) involved the expropriation of private property by a foreign state.[50] This is regarded as the quintessential "act of state." Less clear is whether other types of foreign governmental conduct constitute acts of state.

The classic Supreme Court precedent outside the expropriation context is *Underhill v. Hernandez*.[51] There, the Court invoked the act of state doctrine to dismiss a complaint against a foreign head of state arising from the allegedly illegal imprisonment and forced servitude of a U.S. citizen in a foreign country by the foreign revolutionary commander. *Underhill* had no difficulty treating the imprisonment as an act of state.[52]

Relying on *Underhill*, lower courts have frequently applied the act of state doctrine to governmental actions other than expropriations.[53] Nonetheless, some lower court decisions have found the doctrine inapplicable in particular cases to governmental acts other than takings of property.[54] Lower courts continue to struggle with the question whether a particular governmental act is an "act of state," qualifying for protection under the act of state doctrine.[55]

The only contemporary Supreme Court precedent considering what constitutes an "act of state" is *Alfred Dunhill of London, Inc. v. Republic of Cuba*,[56] which is excerpted below. *Dunhill* involved the Cuban government's refusal to pay certain invoices rendered to it by the plaintiff. Writing for the Court, Justice White held that the refusal to pay was not an act of state because "[n]o statute, decree, order, or resolution of the Cuban Government itself" was produced.[57]

ALFRED DUNHILL OF LONDON, INC. v. REPUBLIC OF CUBA

425 U.S. 682 (1976)

JUSTICE WHITE. The issue in this case is whether the failure of respondents to return to petitioner Alfred Dunhill of London, Inc. ("Dunhill"), funds mistakenly paid by Dunhill for cigars that had been sold to Dunhill by certain expropriated Cuban cigar businesses was an "act of state" by Cuba precluding an affirmative judgment against respondents.

---

50. *See supra* pp. 687-89.

51. 168 U.S. 250 (1897).

52. 168 U.S. at 252-54.

53. *E.g., O.N.E. Shipping v. Flota Mercante Grancolombiana*, 830 F.2d 449 (2d Cir. 1987); *DeRoburt v. Gannett Co.*, 733 F.2d 701 (9th Cir. 1984), *cert. denied*, 469 U.S. 1159 (1985) (allegedly illegal receipt of loan); *Clayco Petroleum Corp. v. Occidental Petroleum Corp.*, 712 F.2d 404 (9th Cir. 1983), *cert. denied*, 464 U.S. 1040 (1984) (bribery); *International Assoc. of Machinists, etc. v. OPEC*, 649 F.2d 1354 (9th Cir. 1981) (price-fixing), *cert. denied.*, 454 U.S. 1163 (1982).

54. *E.g., Mannington Mills, Inc. v. Congoleum Corp.*, 595 F.2d 1287 (3d Cir. 1979) (act of state doctrine not applicable to foreign patent issuance); *Timberlane Lumber Co. v. Bank of Am.*, 549 F.2d 597 (9th Cir. 1976) (act of state doctrine not applicable to alleged misuse of foreign judicial procedures).

55. *See infra* pp. 709-12.

56. 425 U.S. 682 (1976).

57. 425 U.S. at 695.

I. ... In 1960, the Cuban Government confiscated the business and assets of the five leading manufacturers of Havana cigars. These companies, three corporations and two partnerships, were organized under Cuban law. Virtually all of their owners were Cuban nationals. None were American. These companies sold large quantities of cigars to customers in other countries, including the United States, where the three principal importers were Dunhill, Saks & Co. ("Saks"), and Faber, Coe & Gregg, Inc. ("Faber"). The Cuban Government named "interventors" to take possession of and operate the business of the seized Cuban concerns. Interventors continued to ship cigars to foreign purchasers, including the United States importers.

This litigation began when the former owners of the Cuban companies, most of whom had fled to the United States, brought various actions against the three American importers for trademark infringement and for the purchase price of any cigars that had been shipped to importers from the seized Cuban plants and that bore United States trademarks claimed by the former owners to be their property. ... [T]he Cuban interventors and the Republic of Cuba were allowed to intervene in these actions, which were consolidated for trial. Both the former owners and the interventors had asserted their right to some $700,000 due from the three importers for postintervention shipments: Faber, $582,588.86; Dunhill $92,949.70; and Saks, $24,250. It also developed that as of the date of intervention, the three importers owed sums totaling $477,200 for cigars shipped prior to intervention: Faber, $322,000; Dunhill, $148,600; and Saks, $6,600. These latter sums the importers had paid to interventors subsequent to intervention on the assumption that interventors were entitled to collect the accounts receivable of the intervened businesses. The former owners claimed title to and demanded payment of these accounts.

Based on the "act of state" doctrine which had been reaffirmed in the District Court held ... that it was required to give full legal effect to the 1960 confiscation of the five cigar companies insofar as it purported to take the property of Cuban nationals located within Cuba. Interventors were accordingly entitled to collect from the importers all amounts due and unpaid with respect to shipments made after the date of intervention. The contrary conclusion was reached as to the accounts owing at the time of intervention: Because the United States courts will not give effect to foreign government confiscations without compensation of property located in the United States and because under *Republic of Iraq v. First Nat. City Bank*, 353 F.2d 47 (2d Cir. 1965), the situs of the accounts receivable was with the importer-debtors, the 1960 seizures did not reach the preintervention accounts, and the former owners, rather than the interventors, were entitled to collect them from the importers — even though the latter had already paid them to interventors in the mistaken belief that they were fully discharging trade debts in the ordinary course of their business.

This conclusion brought to the fore the importers' claim that their payment of the preintervention accounts had been made in error and that they were entitled to recover these payments from interventors by way of set-off and counterclaim. Although their position that the 1960 confiscation entitled them to the sums due for preintervention sales had been rejected and the District Court had ruled that they "had no right to receive or retain such payment," interventors claimed those payments on the additional ground that the obligation, if any, to repay was a quasi-contractual debt having a situs in Cuba and that their refusal to honor the obligation was an act of state not subject to question in our courts. The District Court rejected this position. ... The importers were accordingly held entitled to set off their mistaken payments to interventors for preintervention shipments against the amounts due from them for their post-intervention purchases. Faber and Saks, because they owed more than interventors were obligated to return to them, were satisfied completely by the right to setoff. But Dunhill — and at last we arrive at the issue in this case — was entitled to more from interventors — $148,000 — than it owed for postintervention shipments — $93,000 — and to be made whole, asked for and was granted judgment against interventors for the full amount of its claim, from which would be deducted the smaller judgment entered against it.

The Court of Appeals agreed that the former owners were entitled to recover from the importers the full amount of preintervention accounts receivable. It also held that the mistaken payments by importers to interventors gave rise to a quasi-contractual obligation to repay these sums. But, contrary to the District Court, the Court of Appeals was of the view that the obligation to repay had a situs in Cuba and had been repudiated in the course of litigation by conduct that was sufficiently official to be deemed an act of state: "[I]n the absence of evidence that the interventors were not acting within the scope of their authority as agents of the Cuban government, their repudiation was an act of state even though not embodied in a formal decree." Although the repudiation of the interventors' obligation was considered an act of state, the Court of Appeals went on to hold that *First Nat'l City Bank v. Banco Nacional de Cuba*, 406 U.S. 759 (1972), entitled importers to recover the sums due them from interventors by way of setoff against the amounts due from them for postintervention shipments. The act of state doctrine was said to bar the affirmative judgment awarded Dunhill to the extent that its claim exceeded its debt. The judgment of the District Court was reversed in this respect, and it is this action which was the subject of the petition for certiorari filed by Dunhill. ...

II. The Court of Appeals ... observed that interventors had "ignored" demands for the return of [money mistakenly paid on preintervention accounts receivable] and had "fail[ed] to honor the importers' demand (which was confirmed by the Cuban government's counsel at trial)." This conduct was considered to be "the Cuban government's repudiation of its obligation to return the funds" and to constitute an act of state not subject to question in our courts. We cannot agree. ...

In *The "Gul Djemal,"* 264 U.S. 90 (1924), a supplier libeled and caused the arrest of the *Gul Djemal*, a steamship owned and operated for commercial purposes by the Turkish government, in an effort to recover for supplies and services sold to and performed for the ship. The ship's master, "a duly commissioned officer of the Turkish Navy," appeared in court and asserted sovereign immunity, claiming that such an assertion defeated the court's jurisdiction. A direct appeal was taken to this Court, where it was held that the master's assertion of sovereign immunity was insufficient because his mere representation of his government as master of a commercial ship furnished no basis for assuming he was entitled to represent the sovereign in other capacities. Here there is no more reason to suppose that the interventors possess governmental, as opposed to commercial, authority than there was to suppose that the master of the *Gul Djemal* possessed such authority. The master of the *Gul Djemal* claimed the authority to assert sovereign immunity while the interventors' claim that they had the authority to commit an act of state, but the difference is unimportant. In both cases, a party claimed to have had the authority to exercise sovereign power. In both, the only authority shown is commercial authority.

We thus disagree with the Court of Appeals that the mere refusal of the interventors to repay funds followed by a failure to prove that interventors "were not acting within the scope of their authority as agents of the Cuban government" satisfied respondents' burden of establishing their act of state defense. Nor do we consider *Underhill v. Hernandez*, heavily relied upon by the Court of Appeals, to require a contrary conclusion. In that case ... it was apparently concluded that the facts were sufficient to demonstrate that the conduct in question was the public act of those with authority to exercise sovereign powers and was entitled to respect in our courts. We draw no such conclusion from the facts of the case before us now. As the District Court found, the only evidence of an <u>act of state</u> other than the act of nonpayment by interventors was "<u>a statement by counsel for the interventors, during trial, that</u> the Cuban Government and the interventors denied liability and had refused to make repayment." But this merely restated respondent's original legal position and adds little, if anything, to the <u>proof of an act of state</u>. No statute, decree, order, or resolution of the Cuban Government itself was offered in evidence indicating that <u>Cuba had repudiated its obligations in general or any class thereof or that it had as a sovereign matter determined to confiscate the amounts due three foreign importers.</u> ... [In a subsequent section of his opinion, excerpted below, Justice White considered whether the act of state doctrine was subject to a "commercial" exception.]

Notes on Alfred Dunhill

1. *Inquiring whether a foreign act of state exists.* As *Dunhill* illustrates, it is well-settled that "[t]he act of state doctrine <u>does not preclude an initial inquiry</u> as to whether a challenged act is in fact an act of state." *Restatement (Third) Foreign Relations Law* §443, comment i (1987). For an apparently contrary view, *see Texaco Maracaibo, infra* pp. 745-52.

2. **Burden of establishing an "act of state."** The burden of establishing an act of state is on the proponent of the doctrine's applicability. *Lamb v. Phillip Morris, Inc.*, 915 F.2d 1024, 1026 n.4 (6th Cir. 1990); *W.S. Kirkpatrick & Co. v. Environmental Tectonics Corp.*, 847 F.2d 1052, 1058 (3d Cir. 1988), *aff'd*, 493 U.S. 400 (1990). Did *Dunhill* consider who bore the burden of establishing the existence of an "act of state"? If so, what did it indicate?

3. *Definition of "act of state" in Dunhill.* What must be shown to establish an "act of state"? Note that *Dunhill* requires a "public" or "sovereign" act by persons with "authority to exercise sovereign powers." The Court held that this test was not satisfied in *Dunhill*, noting the absence of any "statute, decree, order or resolution of the Cuban Government ... indicating that Cuba had repudiated its obligations in general or any class thereof or that it had as a sovereign matter determined to confiscate the amounts

due." A dissenting opinion by Justice Marshall in *Dunhill* reasoned that "an act of state need not be formalized in any particular manner [and] it need not take the form of active, rather than passive, conduct." 425 U.S. at 719-20.

What if the Cuban government in *Dunhill* had promulgated a decree authorizing the interventors to repudiate certain classes of debts, including Dunhill's? How would the plurality in *Dunhill* have resolved the case? The remainder of the Court? How should the case then be resolved?

4. *Lower court definitions of act of state.* Lower courts have reached divergent results in deciding what constitutes an act of state.

(a) *"Sovereign" acts by senior officials.* Some lower courts have read *Dunhill* to require a fairly unambiguous showing that the case involves "sovereign" conduct by senior government officials. *E.g.*, *Remington Rand Corp. v. Business Sys.*, 830 F.2d 1260, 1265 (3d Cir. 1987) (acts of foreign debtor's trustees are not acts of foreign sovereign); *Filartiga v. Pena-Irala*, 630 F.2d 876, 889 (2d Cir. 1980) (torture by governmental officials is not an "act of state" because state did not authorize such conduct).

(b) *Expansive definitions.* Other lower courts have been more willing to apply the act of state doctrine even where the relevant conduct is not the formal, public action of a foreign state. *E.g.*, *DeRoburt v. Gannett Co.*, 733 F.2d 701 (9th Cir. 1984), *cert. denied*, 469 U.S. 1159 (1985) (act of state doctrine potentially applicable to allegedly illegal loan to foreign head of state); *Hunt v. Mobil Oil Corp.*, 550 F.2d 68, 72-75 (2d Cir.), *cert. denied*, 434 U.S. 984 (1977) (act of state doctrine applies to alleged conspiracy involving U.S. oil companies and Libya); *Bokkelen v. Grumman Aerospace Corp.*, 432 F.Supp. 329 (E.D.N.Y. 1977) (denial of export license is act of state); *General Aircraft Corp. v. Air America, Inc.*, 482 F.Supp. 3 (D.D.C. 1979) (military procurement decision is act of state).

(c) *"Ministerial" exception.* Several lower court decisions have recognized a so-called "ministerial exception" to the act of state doctrine, under which routine, ministerial functions (such as the issuance of a patent) are not the kind of governmental action contemplated by the act of state doctrine. *E.g.*, *Mannington Mills, Inc. v. Congoleum Corp.*, 595 F.2d 1287, 1293-94 (3d Cir. 1979) (issuance of a patent is not an act of state); *Sage Int'l Ltd. v. Cadillac Gage Co.*, 534 F.Supp. 896, 904 (E.D. Mich. 1981) (same); *Forbo-Giubiasco SA v. Congoleum Corp.*, 516 F.Supp. 1210 (S.D.N.Y. 1981) (same). *See Restatement (Third) Foreign Relations Law* §443, Reporters' Note 3 (1987).

5. *Is a foreign judgment or arbitral award an "act of state"?* Why isn't a foreign court's judgment or a foreign arbitral award an act of state? *Restatement (Third) Foreign Relations Law* §443, Reporters' Note 10 (1987) ("While the distinction between a foreign judgment and a foreign act of state is not always easy to draw, in general the public judgments doctrine is directed to judicial decisions, whereas the act of state doctrine is directed to acts of general application decided by the executive or legislative branches of the acting state, even if confirmed or applied by courts in that state"). *Compare Restatement (Second) Foreign Relations Law* §41, comment d (1965) ("A judgment of a court may be an act of state. Usually, it is not, because it involves the interests of private litigants or because court adjudication is not the usual way in which the state exercises its jurisdiction to give effect to its public interest."). Are these explanations persuasive?

6. *Is foreign legislation an "act of state"?* Is a foreign law an act of state? *Dunhill* emphasized that the existence of an "act of state" depended upon proof of a sovereign decision, as reflected in a "statute, decree, order, or resolution." *See also Restatement (Third) Foreign Relations Law* §443, comment i (1987) ("The act of state doctrine applies to acts such as constitutional amendments, statutes, decrees and proclamations.").

In *Ricaud* and *Oetjen*, suppose that Mexican authorities had never physically seized the plaintiffs' property, but had enacted a law purporting to transfer title. Would that law have been conclusive, in a subsequent U.S. action, as to ownership of the property? Suppose that the property had been moved out of Mexico to the United States only after enactment of the legislation. *Compare* Zander, *The Act of State Doctrine*, 53 Am. J. Int'l L. 826 (1959) (foreign "act of state" can include legislation); Falk, *Toward a Theory of the International Legal Order: A Critique of Banco Nacional de Cuba v. Sabbatino*, 16 Rutgers L. Rev. 1, 30 (1961) (act of state doctrine applies to "foreign legislation or executive acts"). Similarly, the *Third Restatement* suggests that the act of state doctrine applies to foreign legislation, even without executive implementation. *Restatement (Third) Foreign Relations Law* §443 comment i (1987) ("The act of state doctrine applies to acts such as constitutional amendments, statutes, decrees and proclamations, and in certain circumstances to physical acts, such as occupation of an estate by the state's armed forces in application of state policy").

Aren't the *Third Restatement*, and the other authorities cited above, wrong? A foreign law can authorize an act of state, but is generally not itself an act of state unless it is implemented. *See Restatement (Second) Foreign Relations Law* §41, comment d (1965) ("In determining whether an act is an act of state, the branch or agency of the government — executive, judicial, or legislative — that performed the act is not as important as is the nature of the action taken."). The unexecuted existence of foreign law presents a traditional choice of law issue, not an act of state case.

7. *Relevance of foreign law to acts of foreign government officials.* Many act of state decisions involve physical conduct by governmental authorities. When do such actions constitute acts of state? Most courts have concluded that foreign laws are the ultimate source of evidence as to whether particular conduct is a foreign act of state. *E.g., Galu v. Swiss Air Transport Co.*, 873 F.2d 650 (2d Cir. 1989); *Empresa Cubana v. Lamborn & Co.*, 652 F.2d 231, 237 (2d Cir. 1981); *Restatement (Third) Foreign Relations Law* §443, comment i (1987) ("An action or declaration by an official may qualify as an act of state, but only upon a showing (ordinarily by the party raising the issue) that the official had authority to act for and bind the state. ... An official pronouncement by a foreign government describing a certain act as governmental is ordinarily conclusive evidence of its official character.").

This approach is in considerable tension with the equally well-settled rule that U.S. courts may not inquire into the validity of a foreign state's officials under foreign law. *Sabbatino*, 376 U.S. at 415 n.17; *West v. Multibanco Comermex SA*, 807 F.2d 820, 828-29 (9th Cir.), *cert. denied*, 482 U.S. 906 (1987); *Banco de Espana v. Federal Reserve Board*, 114 F.2d 438, 444 (2d Cir. 1940); *French v. Banco Nacional de Cuba*, 295 N.Y.S.2d 433, 440-41 (1968).

In *Galu v. Swiss Air Transport Co.*, 873 F.2d 650 (2d Cir. 1989), the Second Circuit considered the significance of foreign law in considerable detail. *Galu* arose from the plaintiff's deportation from Switzerland by Swiss police, who forcibly placed her on a Swissair flight to New York. The plaintiff filed suit against Swissair, seeking damages in tort for Swissair's cooperation in her expulsion. On appeal, the Second Circuit held that, if the Swiss police officers had engaged in acts of state in forcibly expelling the plaintiff, then Swissair would also enjoy act of state protection for participating in those acts. The Court reasoned that conduct by relatively low-ranking officials would constitute an act of state if it was within the general scope of the officials' authority under local law:

> The issue is not whether the police officers may ... have slightly exceeded their authority in carrying out a decision of their government. The issue is whether the action taken against [the plaintiff] in removing her to the United States was an action that had been ordered in the exercise of the sovereign authority of Switzerland, or whether it was simply an ad hoc decision of local police officers. The burden is on defendant to establish foreign law to the extent necessary to demonstrate its entitlement to the act of state defense. Evidence of foreign law is required not to determine whether the forcible removal of [plaintiff] was lawful but whether it was in fact an act of state. 873 F.2d at 654.

Is this a sensible approach to the definition of acts of state? Does it involve courts in determining the lawfulness of a foreign official's acts under foreign law, one of the inquiries that the act of state doctrine ordinarily forbids? *See Banco de Espana v. Federal Reserve Bank*, 114 F.2d 438, 443 (2d Cir. 1940) ("the courts of this country will not examine the acts of a foreign sovereign within its own borders in order to determine whether or not those acts were legal under the municipal law of the foreign state"). If so, is that dispositive?

8. *"Private" acts of foreign officials.* A number of cases have raised the question whether misconduct of a foreign official, such as receipt of bribes or extortion, can constitute an act of state. In general, lower courts have concluded that a former government official cannot claim the protection of the act of state doctrine for private misconduct while in office. In this context, some lower courts appear to have defined the "public acts" necessary to trigger act of state protection fairly narrowly. *Republic of Philippines v. Marcos*, 862 F.2d 1355, 1361 (9th Cir. 1988); *DeRoburt v. Gannett Co.*, 733 F.2d 701 (9th Cir. 1984), *cert. denied*, 469 U.S. 1159 (1985); *Jimenez v. Aristeguieta*, 311 F.2d 547 (5th Cir. 1962) (financial crimes committed in violation of official position are "as far from being an act of state as rape"); *United States v. Noriega*, 1990 U.S. Dist. Lexis 7653 (S.D. Fla. June 8, 1990) (must show that acts "were taken on behalf of the state and not, as private acts, on behalf of the actor himself": "The Court fails to see how Noriega's alleged drug trafficking and protection of money launderers could conceivably constitute public action taken on behalf of the Panamanian State"); *Sharon v. Time, Inc.*, 599 F.Supp. 538, 544-45 (S.D.N.Y. 1984).

Other courts have defined "public acts" more broadly, apparently to include misuse of governmental authority for private purposes. *Republic of Philippines v. Marcos*, 818 F.2d 1473, 1484 (9th Cir. 1987) (defining public acts broadly to encompass appropriating public funds by government order), *vacated*, 862 F.2d 1355 (9th Cir. 1988) (en banc); *Banco de Espana v. Federal Reserve Bank*, 114 F.2d 438 (2d Cir. 1940).

Should the alleged abuse of official position for private gain constitute an act of state? According to one court, "gain[ing] access to public monies by statute, decree, resolution, order or some other 'governmental act' as president [would be an act of state]. It would greatly weaken the act of state doctrine if parties could put in question the validity of official government acts simply by attacking the motives of the government officials who undertake them." *Republic of Philippines v. Marcos*, 818 F.2d 1473, 1485 (9th Cir. 1987), *vacated*, 862 F.2d 1355 (9th Cir. 1989). Compare the dissenting opinion in the same case: "I cannot adhere to the position that the alleged acts of receiving bribes, plundering the treasury and extortion are (public acts]." 862 F.2d at 1493.

b. *"Sitting in Judgment" On An Act of State: Validity v. Motivations*

Lower courts have also reached divergent results in determining whether a particular U.S. litigation would require U.S. courts to "sit in judgment" on a foreign act of state so as to violate the act of state doctrine.[58] In the years after *Sabbatino* was decided, many courts applied the act of state doctrine where the plaintiff's claims would require factual inquiry into the "motivations" for a foreign state's act, as well as where the "validity" or "legality" of the foreign state's conduct was directly challenged.[59] Other courts refused to extend the doctrine to foreign governmental motivations.[60]

The Ninth Circuit's decision in *Clayco Petroleum Corporation v. Occidental Petroleum Corporation*[61] was a leading example of how some lower courts expansively applied the act of state doctrine. *Clayco* involved an antitrust action by one U.S. oil company against a second U.S. oil company. The suit charged the defendant with having made secret payments to an official of Umm Al Qaywayn (treated by all as a foreign state) to obtain an oil concession. The Ninth Circuit dismissed on act of state grounds:

> Appellants also argue that the examination of foreign governmental action which this case requires is not intrusive enough to warrant an act of state defense because the concern here is the motivation behind the sovereign's act, rather than its legal validity. ... In this case ... the very existence of plaintiffs' claim depends upon establishing that the motivation for the sovereign

---

58. The classic formulations of the act of state doctrine forbid foreign states from "sitting in judgment" on foreign acts of state. *Sabbatino*, 376 U.S. at 416; *Underhill*, 168 U.S. at 252; *Restatement (Third) Foreign Relations Law* §443 (1987).

59. *E.g.*, *O.N.E. Shipping v. Flota Mercante Grancolombiana*, 830 F.2d 449 (2d Cir. 1987); *IAM v. OPEC*, 649 F.2d 1354 (9th Cir. 1981), *cert. denied*, 454 U.S. 1163 (1982); *Hunt v. Mobil Oil Corp.*, 550 F.2d 68, 73 (2d Cir.), *cert. denied*, 434 U.S. 984 (1977); *General Aircraft Corp. v. Air America*, 482 F.Supp. 3, 6 (D.D.C. 1979); *Bokkelen v. Grumman Aerospace Corp.*, 432 F.Supp. 329, 333 (E.D.N.Y. 1977).

60. *E.g.*, *Industrial Inv. Dev. Corp. v. Mitsui & Co.*, 594 F.2d 48, 55 (5th Cir. 1979), *cert. denied*, 445 U.S. 903 (1980); *Williams v. Curtiss-Wright Corp.*, 694 F.2d 300, 304 n.5 (3d Cir. 1982); *Sharon v. Time, Inc.*, 599 F.Supp. 538, 548-53 (S.D.N.Y. 1984).

61. 712 F.2d 404 (9th Cir. 1983), *cert. denied*, 464 U.S. 1040 (1984).

act was bribery. Thus, embarrassment would result from adjudication. This circuit's decisions have similarly limited inquiry which would "impugn or question the nobility of a foreign nation's motivation." *Timberlane*, 549 F.2d at 607. In *Buttes*, the trial court, in an opinion adopted by this court, held judicial scrutiny of the motivation for foreign sovereign acts to be precluded by the act of state doctrine, noting that it has traditionally barred antitrust claims based on the defendant's alleged inducement of foreign sovereign action. ... Appellants thus cannot argue that inquiry into motivation in this case is unprotected.[62]

In *W.S. Kirkpatrick & Co. v. Environmental Tectonics Corporation*, however, the Supreme Court overruled *Clayco*, and rejected the suggestion that the act of state doctrine was applicable where a U.S. litigation would inquire only into the motivations behind an act of state. The Court instead held that the act of state doctrine applied only to cases where U.S. courts were required to decide the "validity" of foreign acts of state. *Environmental Tectonics* is excerpted below.

W.S. KIRKPATRICK & CO. v. ENVIRONMENTAL TECTONICS CORP.

493 U.S. 400 (1990)

JUSTICE SCALIA. In this case we must decide whether the act of state doctrine bars a court in the United States from entertaining a cause of action that does not rest upon the asserted invalidity of an official act of a foreign sovereign, but that does require imputing to foreign officials an unlawful motivation (the obtaining of bribes) in the performance of such an official act.

I. The facts as alleged in respondent's complaint are as follow: In 1981, Harry Carpenter, who was then Chairman of the Board and Chief Executive Officer of petitioner W.S. Kirkpatrick & Co., Inc. ("Kirkpatrick") learned that the Republic of Nigeria was interested in contracting for the construction and equipment of an aeromedical center at Kaduna Air Force Base in Nigeria. He made arrangements with Benson "Tunde" Akindele, a Nigerian citizen, whereby Akindele would endeavor to secure the contract for Kirkpatrick. It was agreed that, in the event the contract was awarded to Kirkpatrick, Kirkpatrick would pay to two Panamanian entities controlled by Akinele a "commission" equal to 20% of the contract price, which would in turn be given as a bribe to officials of the Nigerian Government. In accordance with this plan, the contract was awarded to petitioner W.S. Kirkpatrick & Co., International ("Kirkpatrick International"), a wholly owned subsidiary of Kirkpatrick; Kirkpatrick paid the promised "commission" to the appointed

---

62. 712 F.2d at 407-08. *See also Hunt v. Mobil Oil Corp.*, 550 F.2d 68, 71 (2d Cir.), *cert. denied*, 434 U.S. 984 (1977); *IAM v. OPEC*, 649 F.2d 1354, 1358-61 (9th Cir. 1981), *cert. denied*, 454 U.S. 1163 (1982) ("act of state doctrine is similar to the political question doctrine in domestic law").

Panamanian entities; and those funds were disbursed as bribes. All parties agree that Nigerian law prohibits both the payment and the receipt of bribes in connection with the award of a government contract.

Respondent Environmental Tectonics Corporation International, an unsuccessful bidder for the Kaduna contract, learned of the 20% "commission" and brought the matter to the attention of the Nigerian Air Force and the U.S. Embassy in Lagos. Following an investigation by the Federal Bureau of Investigation, the U.S. Attorney for the District of New Jersey brought charges against both Kirkpatrick and Carpenter for violations of the Foreign Corrupt Practices Act of 1977, 15 U.S.C. §78dd-1 *et seq.*, and both pleaded guilty.

Respondent then brought this civil action in the U.S. District Court for the District of New Jersey against Carpenter, Akindele, petitioners, and others, seeking damages under the Racketeer Influenced and Corrupt Organizations Act, the Robinson-Patman Act, and the New Jersey Anti-Racketeering Act. The defendants moved to dismiss the complaint under Rule 12(b)(6) of the Federal Rules of Civil Procedure on the ground that the action was barred by the act of state doctrine.

The District Court, having requested and received a letter expressing the views of the legal advisor to the U.S. Department of State as to the applicability of the act of state doctrine, treated the motion as one for summary judgment ... and granted the motion. The District Court concluded that the act of state doctrine applies "if the inquiry presented for judicial determination includes the motivation of a sovereign act which would result in embarrassment to the sovereign or constitute interference in the conduct of foreign policy of the United States" [citing *Clayco*]. Applying that principle to the facts at hand, the court held that respondent's suit had to be dismissed because in order to prevail respondents would have to show that "the defendants or certain of them intended to wrongfully influence the decision to award the Nigerian Contract by payment of a bribe, that the Government of Nigeria, its officials or other representatives knew of the offered consideration for awarding the Nigerian Contract to Kirkpatrick, that the bribe was actually received or anticipated and that 'but for' the payment or anticipation of the payment of the bribe, ETC would have been awarded the Nigerian Contract."

The Court of Appeals for the Third Circuit reversed. Although agreeing with the District Court that "the award of a military procurement contract can be, in certain circumstances, a sufficiently formal expression of a government's public interests to trigger application" of the act of state doctrine, it found application of the doctrine unwarranted on the facts of this case. The Court of Appeals found particularly persuasive the letter to the District Court from the legal advisor to the Department of State, which had stated that in the opinion of the Department judicial inquiry into the purpose behind the act of a foreign sovereign would not produce the "unique embarrassment, and the particular interference with the conduct of foreign affairs, that may result from the judicial determination that a foreign sovereign's acts are invalid." The Court of Appeals acknowledged that "the Department's legal conclusions as to the reach of the act of state doctrine are not controlling on the courts," but concluded that "the Department's factual assessment of whether fulfillment of its responsibilities will be prejudiced by the course of civil litigation is entitled to substantial respect." In light of the Department's view that the interests of the Executive Branch would not be harmed by prosecution of the action, the Court of Appeals held that Kirkpatrick had not met its burden of showing that the case should not go forward; accordingly, it reversed the judgment of the District Court and remanded the case for trial.

II. This Court's description of the jurisprudential foundation for the act of state doctrine has undergone some evolution over the years. We once viewed the doctrine as an expression of international law, resting upon "the highest considerations of international comity and expediency," *Oetjen v. Central Leather Co.*, 246 U.S. 297, 303-304 (1918). We have more recently described it, however, as a consequence of domestic separation of powers, reflecting "the strong sense of the Judicial Branch that its engagement in the task of passing on the validity of foreign acts of state may hinder" the conduct of foreign affairs, *Sabbatino*, 376 U.S. at 423. ... We find it unnecessary [to consider whether any exception to the act of state doctrine is applicable] since the factual predicate for application of the act of state doctrine does not exist. Nothing in the present suit requires the court to declare invalid, and thus ineffective as "a rule of decision for the courts of this country," *Ricaud v. American Metal Co.*, 246 U.S. 304, 310 (1918), the official act of a foreign sovereign.

In every case in which we have held the act of state doctrine applicable, the relief sought or the defense interposed would have required a court in the United States to declare invalid the official act of a foreign sovereign performed within its own territory. In *Underhill*, holding the defendant's detention of the plaintiff to be tortious would have required denying legal effect to "acts of a military commander representing the authority of the revolutionary party as government, which afterwards, succeeded and was recognized by the United States." In *Oetjen v. Central Leather Co.*, and in *Ricaud v. American Metal Co.*, denying title to the party who claimed through purchase from Mexico would have required declaring that government's prior seizure of the property, within its own territory, legally ineffective. In *Sabbatino*, upholding the defendant's claim to the funds would have required a holding that Cuba's expropriation of goods located in Havana was null and void. In the present case, by contrast, neither the claim nor any asserted defense requires a determination that Nigeria's contract with Kirkpatrick International was, or was not, effective.

Petitioners point out, however, that the facts necessary to establish respondent's claim will also establish that the contract was unlawful. Specifically, they note that in order to prevail respondent must prove that petitioner Kirkpatrick made, and Nigerian officials received, payments that violate Nigerian law, which would, they assert, support a finding that the contract is invalid under Nigerian law. Assuming that to be true, it still does not suffice. The act of state doctrine is not some vague doctrine of abstention but a "*principle of decision* binding on federal and state courts alike." *Sabbatino*, 376 U.S. at 427 (emphasis added). As we said in *Ricaud*, "the act within its own boundaries of one sovereign State ... becomes ... a rule of decision for the courts of this country." 246 U.S. at 310. Act of state issues only arise when a court *must decide* — that is, when the outcome of the case turns upon — the effect of official action by a foreign sovereign. When that question is not in the case, neither is the act of state doctrine. That is the situation here. Regardless of what the court's factual findings may suggest as to the legality of the Nigerian contract, its legality is simply not a question to be decided in the present suit, and there is thus no occasion to apply the rule of decision that the act of state doctrine requires. *Cf. Sharon v. Time, Inc.*, 599 F.Supp. 538, 546 (S.D.N.Y. 1984) ("The issue in this litigation is not whether [the alleged] acts are valid, but whether they occurred").

In support of their position that the act of state doctrine bars any factual findings that may cast doubt upon the validity of foreign sovereign acts, petitioners cite Justice Holmes' opinion for the Court in *American Banana Co.*. That was a suit under the United States antitrust laws, alleging that Costa Rica's seizure of the plaintiff's property had been induced by an unlawful conspiracy. In the course of a lengthy opinion Justice Holmes observed, citing *Underhill*, that "a seizure by a state is not a thing that can be complained of elsewhere in the courts." The statement is concededly puzzling. *Underhill* does indeed stand for the proposition that a seizure by a state cannot be complained of elsewhere — in the sense of being sought to be declared *ineffective* elsewhere. The plaintiff in *American Banana*, however, like the plaintiff here, was not trying to undo or disregard the governmental action, but only to obtain damages from private parties who had procured it. Arguably, then, the statement did imply that suit would not lie if a foreign state's actions would be, though not invalidated, impugned.

Whatever Justice Holmes may have had in mind, his statement lends inadequate support to petitioners' position here, for two reasons. First, it was a brief aside, entirely unnecessary to the decision. *American Banana* was squarely decided on the ground (later substantially overruled, *see Continental Ore Co. v. Union Carbide & Carbon Corp.*, 370 U.S. 690, 704-705 (1962)) that the antitrust laws had no extraterritorial application, so that "what the defendant did in Panama or Costa Rica is not within the scope of the statute." Second, whatever support the dictum might provide for petitioners' position is more than overcome by our later holding in *United States v. Sisal Sales Corp.*, 274 U.S. 268 (1927). There we held that, *American Banana* notwithstanding, the defendant's actions in obtaining Mexico's enactment of "discriminating legislation" could form part of the basis for suit under the United States antitrust laws. Simply put, *American Banana* was not an act of state case; and whatever it said by way of dictum that might be relevant to the present case has not survived *Sisal Sales*.

Petitioners insist, however, that the policies underlying our act of state cases —international comity, respect for the sovereignty of foreign nations on their own territory, and the avoidance of embarrassment to the Executive Branch in its conduct of foreign relations — are implicated in the present case because, as the District Court found, a determination that Nigerian officials demanded and accepted a bribe "would impugn or question the nobility of a foreign nation's motivations," and would "result in embarrassment to the sovereign or constitute interference in the conduct of foreign policy of the United States." The United States, as amicus curiae, favors the same approach to the act of state doctrine, though disagreeing with petitioners as to the outcome it produces in the present case. We should not, the United States urges, "attach dispositive significance to the fact that this suit involves only the 'motivation' for, rather than the 'validity' of, a foreign sovereign act," Brief for United States as Amicus Curiae 37, and should eschew "any rigid formula for the resolution of act of state cases generally." In some future case, perhaps, "litigation ... based on alleged corruption in the award of contracts or other commercially oriented activities of foreign governments could sufficiently touch on 'national nerves' that the act of state doctrine or related principles of abstention would appropriately be found to bar the suit," (quoting *Sabbatino*, 376 U.S. at 428), and we should therefore resolve this case on the narrowest possible ground, *viz.*, that the letter from the legal advisor to the District Court gives sufficient indication that, "in the setting of this case," the act of state doctrine poses no bar to adjudication.[63]

These urgings are deceptively similar to what we said in *Sabbatino*, where we observed that sometimes, even though the validity of the act of a foreign sovereign within its own territory is called into question, the policies underlying the act of state doctrine may not justify its application. We suggested that a sort of balancing approach could be applied — the balance shifting against application of the doctrine, for example, if the government that committed the "challenged act of state" is no longer in existence. But what is appropriate in order to avoid unquestioning judicial acceptance of the acts of foreign sovereigns is not similarly appropriate for the quite opposite purpose of expanding judicial incapacities where such acts are not directly (or even indirectly) involved. It is one thing to suggest, as we have, that the policies underlying the act of state doctrine should be considered in deciding whether, despite the doctrine's technical availability, it should nonetheless not be invoked; it is something quite different to suggest that those underlying policies are a doctrine unto themselves, justifying expansion of the act of state doctrine (or, as the United States puts it, unspecified "related principles of abstention") into new and uncharted fields.

The short of the matter is this: Courts in the United States have the power, and ordinarily the obligation, to decide cases and controversies properly presented to

---

63. Even if we agreed with the Government's fundamental approach, we would question its characterization of the legal advisor's letter as reflecting the absence of any policy objection to the adjudication. The letter, which is reprinted as an appendix to the opinion of the Court of Appeals, *see* 847 F.2d 1052, 1067-1069 (3rd Cir. 1988), did not purport to say whether the State Department would like the suit to proceed, but rather responded (correctly, as we hold today) to the question whether the act of state doctrine was applicable.

them. The act of state doctrine does not establish an exception for cases and controversies that may embarrass foreign governments, but merely requires that, in the process of deciding, the acts of foreign sovereigns taken within their own jurisdictions shall be deemed valid. That doctrine has no application to the present case because the validity of no foreign sovereign act is at issue.

Notes on Environmental Tectonics

1. ***Distinction between "validity" and "motivation."*** The classic formulation of the act of state doctrine forbids U.S. courts from "sitting in judgment" on foreign acts of state. *See supra* pp. 686-90 & 700. According to *Environmental Tectonics*, a U.S. court will not be required to "sit in judgment" on a foreign act of state merely because the plaintiff's claims "impugn or question the nobility of a foreign nation's motivations" or "may embarrass foreign governments." The Court held that the act of state doctrine does not apply unless "the validity of [a] foreign sovereign act is at issue." (Emphasis added.) What exactly does the Court's distinction between the "validity" of foreign acts of state and the "motivations" for those acts mean?

2. ***When does a claim challenge the "validity" or "effect" of a foreign act of state?*** The defendant urged that plaintiff's claims in *Environmental Tectonics* required proof of facts that would have established a violation of Nigerian law by Nigerian government officials. Nonetheless, the Court held that no challenge to the "validity" of Nigerian act of state was presented. The Court reasoned that "[a]ct of state issues only arise when a court must decide — that is, when the outcome of the case turns upon — the effect of official action by a foreign sovereign." And the Court concluded that "[r]egardless of what the court's factual findings may suggest as to the legality of the Nigerian contract, its legality is simply not a question to be decided in the present suit." Why *didn't Environmental Tectonics* require a decision on the "validity," "effect," or "legality" of the Nigerian contract?

When would a suit challenge the "validity" or "effect" of a foreign act of state? Would a suit by Environmental Tectonics against Nigeria or Nigerian government officials require decision on the validity on a foreign act of state? What if the action sought specific performance by Nigeria, awarding plaintiff the disputed contract? What if the action sought money damages from Nigeria for failure to award the contract? How would such an action differ from Mr. Underhill's suit? How does either suit differ from the actual suit filed by Environmental Tectonics against W.S. Kirkpatrick? How would either suit differ from *Sabbatino, Oetjen,* or *Ricaud*? Would either action involve any greater U.S. judicial inquiry into the "validity" of a foreign acts of state than the actual *Environmental Tectonics* lawsuit?

3. ***Possible distinction between "validity" and "legality."*** Does *Environmental Tectonics* distinguish between the "validity" of foreign acts of state and their "legality"? Note that in *Sabbatino, Ricaud,* and *Oetjen,* the act of state doctrine was applied in disputes between two U.S. citizens over the title to property — disputes easily characterized as involving the "validity" of one party's asserted ownership interest. In contrast, *Underhill* involved a tort action against a foreign official — a dispute arguably involving only the "legality" of official conduct, and not the "validity" of title derived from a foreign act of state. Did *Environmental Tectonics* hold that the act of state doctrine does not apply to suits challenging the "legality" of foreign acts of state?

When would a case require decision on the "legality" but not the "validity" of a foreign act of state? Suppose that the plaintiff in *Environmental Tectonics* had named either Nigeria or Nigerian officials as defendants? Would this suit have challenged the "legality" or "validity" of the Nigerian government's actions? Note that *Environmental Tectonics* clearly approved the decision in *Underhill,* where the act of state doctrine was held to bar a tort action against a foreign government official for his official acts. On the other hand, consider how Justice Scalia characterized *Underhill:* deciding the U.S. plaintiff's tort claim "would have required denying legal effect to acts of a [foreign state]." That characterization suggests that *Underhill* — like *Sabbatino, Ricaud,* and *Oetjen* — concerned the "validity" of the foreign defendant's acts. Recall, however, that *Underhill* involved a foreign military commander's imprisonment and forced servitude of a U.S. engineer. How would deciding Mr. Underhill's suit against the commander have "required denying legal effect" to foreign acts of state?

4. ***Rationale for "validity"/"motivation" distinction.*** Is it appropriate to distinguish between the "validity of" and the "motivation for" a foreign act of state? Given the policies underlying the act of state

doctrine, is there a more compelling case for judicial abstention in cases like *Ricaud* and *Oetjen* than in cases like *Environmental Tectonics* or *Underhill?* How does Justice Scalia resolve this question?

Consider the following excerpt from *Hunt v. Mobil Oil Corp.*, 550 F.2d 68, 77 (2d Cir.), *cert. denied*, 434 U.S. 984 (1977). The case arose from an antitrust action by Nelson Bunker Hunt against seven major oil companies, alleging that the defendants conspired to cut off Hunt's oil supplies from Libya by preventing him from reaching a satisfactory supply agreement with Libya. Barely beneath the surface of Hunt's claims was the fact that, allegedly because of defendants' conspiracy, Libya had nationalized his properties in Libya. The Second Circuit dismissed on act of state grounds, even though Libya was not named as a defendant:

> The United States has officially characterized the motivation of the Libyan government, the very issue which Hunt now seeks to adjudicate here. The attempted transmogrification of Libya from lion to lamb undertaken here [by plaintiff] does not succeed in evading the act of state doctrine because we cannot logically separate Libya's motivation from the validity of its seizure. The American judiciary is being asked to make inquiry into the subtle and delicate issue of the policy of a foreign sovereign, a Serbonian Bog, precluded by the act of state doctrine as well as by the realities of the fact finding competence of the court in an issue of far reaching national concern.

Is this persuasive? more persuasive than Justice Scalia's opinion in *Environmental Tectonics?*

5. *Rationale for act of state doctrine in* **Environmental Tectonics.** What rationale is advanced for the act of state doctrine in *Environmental Tectonics?* With varying degrees of emphasis, Justice Scalia rejected the suggestions that the act of state doctrine was a "vague doctrine of abstention," "an expression of international law," or a principle of "international comity." If this is what the act of state doctrine is *not*, then what *is* its rationale? *Environmental Tectonics* said at one point that the doctrine rested on separation of powers concerns. Elsewhere, however, Justice Scalia treated the act of state doctrine as a choice of law rule, quoting *Ricaud* for the proposition that, "the act within its own boundaries of one sovereign State ... becomes ... a rule of decision for the courts of this country." 246 U.S. at 310.

Does this resolve, more clearly than *Sabbatino*, the rationale of the act of state doctrine? Is the doctrine based on both choice of law and separation of powers considerations? Are these considerations consistent with one another? What do separation of powers considerations suggest about the correctness of Justice Scalia's distinction between validity and motivations?

6. *U.S. Government position in* **Environmental Tectonics.** As the Court's opinion indicates, the U.S. Government urged a different approach to the act of state doctrine from that adopted by Justice Scalia. Consider the following excerpt from the Government's *amicus curiae* brief:

> As synthesized in *Sabbatino*, the [act of state] doctrine has evolved from a rather rigid rule based on territorial sovereignty to a more flexible analysis based on international comity and the responsibility of the political Branches for the conduct of foreign relations. ... Although the Court's prior decisions have appeared to take a rather rigid view of the act of state doctrine, *Sabbatino* expressly declined to lay down or reaffirm any inflexible or all-encompassing rule for application of the doctrine in future cases. Consistent with *Sabbatino*, and in recognition of the widely divergent circumstances in which the issue may arise, we do not urge any rigid formula for the resolution of act of state cases generally. In particular, we do not urge the Court to choose among the expressions in judicial opinions and commentary that have variously sought to explain the act of state doctrine as a rule of judicial abstention, an aspect of the political question doctrine, a choice-of-law rule, a broader conflict-of-laws rule that incorporates both choice-of-forum and choice-of-law notions or a principle of repose that treats the act of a foreign sovereign as conclusively settling its legality in the courts of the United States. ... We ... rest our submission on the identification of a number of factors that, under principles of comity and separation of powers, indicate that application of the act of state doctrine is not required in the circumstances of this case. [In support of this conclusion, the Government's brief cited the facts that: (a) federal law was the basis of the U.S. suit, rather than international or state law; (b) no conflict with Nigerian law was involved; (c) no decision on the validity of the contract was required; (d) the contract was commercial; and (e) the State Department did not believe adjudication of the suit would affect U.S. foreign relations.] Brief for the United States as Amicus Curiae, at 6-10 (October 1989).

Is this a sensible view of the act of state doctrine? Is it more persuasive than that adopted in *Environmental Tectonics*? How does the Government's view differ from the Court's?

7. *Correctness of* Environmental Tectonics *result.* Was the result in *Environmental Tectonics* correct, under either the U.S. Government's rationale or that of Justice Scalia? Why should a U.S. court hear the kinds of claims at issue there? Suppose a German or Iranian court were to decide a dispute between two German or Iranian companies that required proof that a U.S. cabinet officer took bribes.

8. *Lower court applications of* Environmental Tectonics. Following *Environmental Tectonics*, lower courts have generally interpreted the act of state doctrine narrowly. *E.g., Grupo Protexa v. All American Marine Slip*, 20 F.3d 1224 (3d Cir. 1994) (refusing to apply act of state doctrine to foreclose inquiry into validity of Mexican government decree requiring removal of sunken vessel, in case where private party claimed reimbursement of removal costs from insurer); *Walter Fuller Aircraft Sales, Inc. v. Republic of Philippines*, 965 F.2d 1375 (5th Cir. 1992) (act of state doctrine does not bar contract claim against foreign state, because, even if challenged foreign acts of state were valid, they could breach parties' contract); *AMPAC Group Inc. v. Republic of Honduras*, 797 F.Supp. 973 (S.D. Fla. 1992) (holding that *Environmental Tectonics* restricted act of state doctrine, which would not preclude adjudication of contract claims).

9. *Foreign corruption suits after* Environmental Tectonics. One possible consequence of *Environmental Tectonics* is that lawsuits involving claims of foreign governmental corruption will more readily be maintained in U.S. courts. In *Lamb v. Phillip Morris, Inc.*, 915 F.2d 1024 (6th Cir. 1990), for example, the Court of Appeals held that the act of state doctrine did not bar an action by domestic tobacco growers against tobacco importers, alleging violations of the federal antitrust laws and the Foreign Corrupt Practices Act. The suit was based upon an alleged agreement between the defendants' subsidiaries and a Venezuelan charitable foundation (whose president was the wife of the then President of Venezuela); the agreement allegedly involved periodic contributions by the subsidiaries to the foundation in return for substantial economic benefits. The Court of Appeals held that the act of state doctrine did not bar the suit because "the antitrust claims ... merely call into question the contracting parties' motivations and the resulting anticompetitive effects of their agreement, not the validity of any foreign sovereign act."

Some pre-*Environmental Tectonics* decisions also permitted actions alleging foreign governmental corruption to go forward. *E.g., Gage Int'l v. Cadillac Gage Co.*, 534 F.Supp. 896, 905 (E.D. Mich. 1981); *Dominicus Americana Bohio v. Gulf & Western Indus.*, 473 F.Supp. 680, 690 (S.D.N.Y. 1979). *See* Note, *Act of State Doctrine: An Emerging Corruption Exception in Antitrust Cases*, 59 Notre Dame L. Rev. 455 (1984). Is it wise for U.S. courts to adjudicate sensitive allegations of foreign sovereign misconduct? Suppose a suit involves claims of corruption, or immoral conduct, by the head of state of a friendly foreign nation, or a hostile and potentially dangerous foreign nation. Note Judge Bork's discussion of separation of powers concerns under the Alien Tort Statute. *See supra* pp. 45-46. Why are these not equally applicable in the context of corruption actions?

Suits based upon foreign corruption have almost inevitably named U.S. companies as defendants. Is it appropriate for U.S. courts to impose a higher standard of business morality on U.S. companies' foreign operations than that prevailing abroad or imposed upon foreign companies?

10. *No requirement regarding presence of foreign state in litigation.* Environmental Tectonics considered whether to apply the act of state doctrine at the behest of a private litigant even though the Republic of Nigeria was not a party to the lawsuit. Like *Ricaud* and *Oetjen*, a number of lower court decisions have taken the same course. *E.g., Lamb v. Phillip Morris, Inc.*, 915 F.2d 1024, 1026 n.2 (6th Cir. 1990); *Galu v. Swiss Air Transport Co.*, 873 F.2d 650 (2d Cir. 1989); *O.N.E. Shipping v. Flota Mercanta Grancolombiana*, 830 F.2d 449 (2d Cir. 1987) ("such an inquiry is foreclosed ... regardless of whether the foreign government is named as a party to the suit ..."); *Occidental of Umm Al Qaywayn v. A Certain Cargo of Petroleum*, 577 F.2d 1196 (5th Cir. 1978), *cert. denied*, 442 U.S. 928 (1979); *Hunt v. Mobil Oil Corp.*, 550 F.2d 68 (2d Cir.), *cert. denied*, 434 U.S. 984 (1977). Are the purposes of the act of state doctrine implicated when the foreign state is not a party and has not urged application of the doctrine? To the same extent as when a foreign state is a party?

11. *Application of act of state doctrine in actions brought by the U.S. Government.* Should the act of state doctrine apply to actions brought by the U.S. Government, either against a foreign state itself or against a private party? On the one hand, the "offense" to foreign sovereigns caused by some governmental suits will be greater than that resulting from private suits, particularly where governmental proceedings involve quasi-criminal issues. (Government actions under the Foreign Corrupt Practices Act, 15 U.S.C.

§§78dd-1, 78dd-2 (1982), and the antitrust laws are good examples of such proceedings.) On the other hand, when the executive branch brings a suit that requires U.S. courts to pass judgment on foreign acts of state, it has presumably concluded that the action will not cause the judiciary to interfere in U.S. foreign relations. As a result, a principal rationale for the act of state doctrine is arguably inapplicable to government suits.

The few lower courts that have addressed this issue have generally concluded that the act of state doctrine does not apply to U.S. Government proceedings. *See Clayco Petroleum Corp. v. Occidental Petroleum Corp.*, 712 F.2d 404, 409 (9th Cir. 1983), *cert. denied*, 464 U.S. 1040 (1984) ("Executive bodies have discretion in bringing any action. ... Therefore, any governmental enforcement represents a judgment on the wisdom of bringing a proceeding, in light of the exigencies of foreign affairs. Act of state concerns are thus inapplicable since the purpose of the doctrine is to prevent the judiciary from interfering with the political branch's conduct of foreign policy."); *Jimenez v. Aristeguieta*, 311 F.2d 547, 558 (5th Cir. 1962); *United States v. Noriega*, 1990 U.S. Dist. Lexis 7653 (S.D. Fla. June 8, 1990). What if a U.S. state government brings a suit? What if a foreign state brings a suit?

12. Application of act of state doctrine to federal statutory claims. *Sabbatino* involved application of the act of state doctrine to state law and international law claims. A number of lower courts have held that the act of state doctrine also applies in cases based on federal statutory claims. *E.g., O.N.E. Shipping v. Flota Mercante Grancolombiana*, 830 F.2d 449 (2d Cir. 1987) (antitrust); *IAM v. OPEC*, 649 F.2d 1354 (9th Cir. 1981), *cert. denied*, 454 U.S. 1163 (1983) (antitrust); *Industrial Inv. Dev. Corp. v. Mitsui & Co.*, 594 F.2d 48 (5th Cir. 1979), *cert. denied*, 445 U.S. 903 (1980) (antitrust); *Hunt v. Mobil Oil Corp.*, 550 F.2d 68 (2d Cir.), *cert. denied*, 434 U.S. 984 (1977) (antitrust).

Environmental Tectonics involved federal statutory claims and the U.S. Government's *amicus curiae* brief urged the Court to apply the act of state doctrine less readily to bar such claims than claims based on state or foreign law:

> In *Sabbatino* and other cases, the act of the foreign state itself was challenged under the law of that state or international law. Respondent's suit, by contrast, is brought against private parties and arises under provisions of United States law (RICO, the Robinson-Patman Act, and New Jersey law) ... The interest of the United States in enforcing its laws weighs heavily in the comity analysis. Brief for the United States as Amicus Curiae, at 7.

Is it more difficult to justify application of the act of state doctrine when Congress has prescribed a substantive rule of law and vested the federal courts with jurisdiction over claims based on that rule? Doesn't this sort of federal legislative action embody a determination by the political branches that U.S. foreign policy interests are outweighed by U.S. regulatory interests? If a federal statute is applicable to conduct abroad (for example, under the antitrust laws because the jurisdictional requirements of *Hartford Fire, supra* pp. 595-603, are satisfied), what permits reliance on the common law "choice of law" rule referred to in the act of state doctrine to displace U.S. law?

c. The Situs Requirement

Sabbatino, like previous Supreme Court decisions,[64] was careful to confine the act of state doctrine to acts of a foreign state "within its own territory."[65] Subsequent lower court decisions have emphasized the importance of the "situs requirement," often denying act of state protection to conduct not occurring within the foreign state.[66]

---

64. *Oetjen*, 246 U.S. at 303-04; *Underhill*, 168 U.S. at 252 ("the courts of one country will not sit in judgment on the acts of the government of another done within its own territory").

65. *Sabbatino*, 376 U.S. at 414-45.

66. *F. & H.R. Farman-Farmaian Consulting Engineers Firm v. Harza Engineering Co.*, 882 F.2d 281 (7th Cir. 1989); *Bandes v. Harlow & Jones, Inc.*, 852 F.2d 661, 666-67 (2d Cir. 1988); *Drexel Burnham Lambert Group v. Galadari*, 777 F.2d 877 (2d Cir. 1985); *Maltina Corp. v. Cawy Bottling Co.*, 462 F.2d 1021, 1027 (5th Cir.), *cert. denied*, 409 U.S. 1060 (1972); *Republic of Iraq v. First Nat'l City Bank*, 353 F.2d 47 (2d Cir. 1965); *Boland v. Bank Sepah Iran*, 614 F.Supp. 1166 (S.D.N.Y. 1985).

The rationale underlying the situs requirement is not entirely clear. The requirement was first adopted in early act of state decisions that emphasized international law principles and respect for the territorial sovereignty of foreign nations.[67] The apparent erosion of the strict territoriality principle in various jurisdictional and choice of law contexts[68] and the emphasis on foreign relations concerns as the rationale for the act of state doctrine raises questions about the continued vitality of the situs requirement.[69] Nonetheless, lower courts continue to apply the requirement, saying that "[n]otions of territoriality run deep through the [act of state] doctrine."[70]

The situs requirement has frequently come into issue when foreign governments have attempted to seize property which is physically located outside their territory. U.S. courts have generally refused to afford act of state protection to such attempts.[71] Difficulties have arisen, however, in determining the situs of intangible property, such as debts. These difficulties are illustrated by *Braka v. Bancomer, S.N.C.*, excerpted below.

BRAKA v. BANCOMER, S.N.C.

762 F.2d 222 (2d Cir. 1985)

MESKILL, CIRCUIT JUDGE. This appeal represents our second opportunity in recent months to consider the effect of foreign finance decrees on the investments of United States entities. ... [W]e agree with the district court that plaintiffs' recovery is barred by the act of state doctrine. ...

In our previous excursion into the intricacies of the act of state doctrine, *Allied Bank International v. Banco Credito Agricola de Cartago*, 757 F.2d 516 (2d Cir. 1985) (on rehearing), we held that because the situs of the debt was in the United States, the act of state doctrine did not operate to prevent the creditors from recovering for their losses. In the case before us, however, the doctrine does bar relief because the situs of defendant's obligations was in Mexico.

Plaintiffs are a number of United States citizens who purchased peso- and dol-

---

67. *Underhill v. Hernandez*, 168 U.S. 250 (1987); *Oetjen v. Central Leather Co.*, 246 U.S. 297 (1918); Henkin, *The Foreign Affairs Power of the Federal Courts: Sabbatino*, 64 Colum. L. Rev. 805, 828 (1964); Note, *The Act of State Doctrine: Resolving Debt Situs Confusion*, 86 Colum. L. Rev. 594, 608-10 (1986).

68. *See supra* pp. 73-77 (judicial jurisdiction) & 497-501 (legislative jurisdiction).

69. Comment, *Act of State Doctrine Held Inapplicable to Foreign Seizures of Property When the Property at the Time of the Expropriation is Located Within the United States*, 9 N.Y.U. J. Int'l L. & Pol'y 515 (1977).

70. *Tchacosh Co. v. Rockwell Int'l Corp.*, 766 F.2d 1333, 1336 (9th Cir. 1985).

71. *See Allied Bank Int'l v. Banco Credito Agricola de Cartago*, 757 F.2d 516 (2d Cir.), *cert. dismissed*, 473 U.S. 934 (1985); *United Bank v. Cosmic Int'l*, 542 F.2d 868, 872 (2d Cir. 1976); *Republic of Iraq v. First Nat'l City Bank*, 353 F.2d 47 (2d Cir. 1965), *cert. denied*, 382 U.S. 1027 (1966) (foreign decree purporting to expropriate property in the United States); *Libra Bank v. Banco Nacional de Costa Rica*, 570 F.Supp. 870 (S.D.N.Y. 1983); *Compania Ron Bacardi v. Bank of Nova Scotia*, 193 F.Supp. 814 (S.D.N.Y. 1961). *See* Note, *The Territorial Exception to the Act of State Doctrine: Application to French Nationalization*, 6 Fordham Int'l L. J. 121 (1982); Zaitzeff & Kunz, *The Act of State Doctrine and the Allied Bank Case*, 40 Bus. Law. 449, 451-58 (1985).

lar-denominated certificates of deposit ("CDs") from defendant Bancomer, SA ("Bancomer"). When plaintiffs' purchases were made in 1981, Bancomer was a privately run Mexican bank. Plaintiffs arranged for their purchases by telephone with Bancomer's Mexico City office. The purchases were effected either through application of plaintiffs' funds that were on deposit in Mexico or through plaintiffs' delivery of checks drawn on their New York banks payable to Bancomer's New York agency. If the latter method was used, the agency, which was not authorized to accept deposits, transmitted the funds by interbank transfer to the Mexican office. The CDs indicated that Mexico was the place of deposit and the place of payment of principal and interest, although as a convenience such payments were sometimes transmitted to plaintiffs' New York banks. The total value of the CDs was $2,100,000. All of the CDs were scheduled to mature in February 1983, except one, which was to reach maturity in September 1982. The annual interest rates ranged from 14.3 percent to 23.25 percent.

In August 1982, shortly before the first certificate was to reach maturity, the Mexican Ministry of Treasury and Public Credit issued a decree requiring that all domestic obligations be performed by delivery of an equivalent amount in pesos at the prevailing exchange rate. This decree banned the use of foreign currency as legal tender. In September two more decrees were issued. The first nationalized Mexico's banks, including Bancomer. The second mandated a system of exchange controls that was carried out by the subsequent issuance of rules called "General Rules for Exchange Controls." As a result of these and later decrees, plaintiffs received Mexican pesos at the officially prescribed exchange rates, approximately 70-80 pesos per dollar, when they tendered their certificates on the maturity dates. Plaintiffs allege that because they did not receive the then actual market exchange rate of 135-150 pesos per dollar, they lost over $900,000.

Plaintiffs filed suit in federal district court in New York claiming damages for breach of contract and for violation of the federal securities laws. [The district] court held that Bancomer's issuance of CDs was a commercial rather than a sovereign act, and that it therefore fell within the commercial activity exception to the FSIA, 28 U.S.C. §1605(a)(2). ... However, the court went on to hold that the absence of immunity did not render plaintiffs' claims justiciable. Because the situs of plaintiffs' CDs was in Mexico, the court determined that act of state principles prevented judicial examination of the complaint. In addition ... the court held that Mexico's issuance of exchange controls was not a commercial activity. Therefore, the court rejected plaintiffs' claims as barred by the act of state doctrine. ...

[W]e must first determine the situs of the property that was taken by the Mexican exchange controls. As we noted in *Allied*, "the concept of the situs of a debt for act of state purposes differs from the ordinary concept." 757 F.2d at 521. The test we adopted in *Allied* was whether the purported taking was "able to come to complete fruition within the domination of the [Mexican] government." *Tabacalera Severiano Jorge, SA v. Standard Cigar Co.*, 392 F.2d 706, 715-16 (5th Cir.), *cert.*

denied, 393 U.S. 924 (1968). Here, unlike *Allied*, it is clear that Mexico's actions meet this test.

The property at issue was Bancomer's obligation to pay the contractually mandated return on plaintiffs' investment. Plaintiffs argue that the situs of this obligation was New York. They allege that because they made some purchases by giving checks to Bancomer's New York agency and received some interest payments in New York, they could demand that Bancomer fulfill its obligation by paying them in New York.

The CDs named Mexico City as the place of deposit and of payment of interest and principal. Although some of the CDs were dollar-denominated, Bancomer never agreed to pay them in any location other than Mexico. The fact that plaintiffs' deposits were occasionally accepted and transmitted to Mexico by Bancomer's New York agency does not alter the situs of Bancomer's obligation. It is clear that the accomplishment of interbank transfers, which was the extent of the New York agency's participation, does not change the contractually mandated situs of plaintiffs' property. The CDs were located in Mexico and were therefore subject to the effects of the exchange control regulations. The Mexican government "ha[d] the parties and the res before it and act[ed] in such a manner as to change the relationship between the parties touching the res." *Tabacalera*, 392 F.2d at 715. To intervene to contradict the result of the exchange controls would be an impermissible intrusion into the governmental activities of a foreign sovereign.

Plaintiffs' attempt to equate their case with *Garcia [v. Chase Manhattan Bank, NA*, 735 F.2d 645 (2d Cir. 1984),] is unavailing. In *Garcia* we held that the act of state doctrine did not bar recovery because the parties expressly provided for repayment at any Chase branch, anywhere in the world. Here, by contrast, no such wide-ranging agreement exists. Thus, we hold that the situs of defendant's obligation existed wholly within the boundaries of the foreign sovereign, and that the act of state doctrine therefore bars recovery. ... The act of state doctrine bars consideration of plaintiffs' complaint because the situs of defendant's obligations was in Mexico. ...

Notes on Bancomer

1. *The situs requirement*. *Sabbatino* emphasized that its decision was limited to acts of state committed by a foreign state within its own territory. 376 U.S. at 414-45. Lower courts have frequently applied this situs requirement. *E.g., Bandes v. Harlow & Jones, Inc.*, 852 F.2d 661, 666-67 (2d Cir. 1988); *Grass v. Credito Mexicano, SA*, 797 F.2d 220, 222 (5th Cir. 1986), *cert. denied*, 480 U.S. 934 (1987); *Randall v. Arabian Am. Oil Co.*, 778 F.2d 1146, 1153 (5th Cir. 1985); *Tchacosh Co. v. Rockwell Int'l Corp.*, 766 F.2d 1333, 1336 (9th Cir. 1988); *Republic of Iraq v. First National City Bank*, 353 F.2d 47, 51 (2d Cir. 1965), *cert. denied*, 382 U.S. 1027 (1966).

2. *Rationale for the situs requirement*. What is the rationale for the situs requirement's limitation of the act of state doctrine to a foreign state's acts within its own territory?

(a) *Territorial limits on national jurisdiction*. Territorial limits were included as part of the act of state doctrine by early decisions — like *Underhill* and *Ricaud* — that were decided at a time when legislative and judicial jurisdiction were also subject to strict territorial limits. *See supra* pp. 70-73 & 493-97. Thus, the situs requirement served as a means of limiting U.S. recognition of acts of state to those acts which a foreign state had jurisdiction to engage in under international law. *See* Chow, *Rethinking the Act of State Doctrine: An Analysis in Terms of Jurisdiction to Prescribe*, 62 Wash. L. Rev. 397, 448-50 (1987).

Chapters 7 and 8 above describe how contemporary international law has increasingly permitted states to extend their legislative jurisdiction extraterritorially in a significant range of cases, and how contemporary choice of law rules are no longer territorially-defined. Given this evolution in international jurisdictional limits, is a territorial situs requirement still appropriate? Does the answer vary depending on whether the act of state doctrine is a choice of law rule or a variation of the political question doctrine?

Was the act of state doctrine based upon a foreign state's exercise of either legislative or judicial jurisdiction? The former permits a state to prescribe laws (recognized by foreign nations pursuant to choice of law rules), while the latter permits a state to render judgments (recognized by foreign nations pursuant to rules regarding the enforcement of foreign judgments).

In fact, the act of state doctrine involves the exercise of enforcement jurisdiction — a foreign state's executive actions, fulfilling its legislative and judicial jurisdiction. Thus, acts of state include the seizure of property (*Ricaud* and *Oetjen*) or persons (*Underhill*), but generally do not include foreign judgments or legislative enactments. *See supra* pp. 700-01 & 710. International law traditionally limited a nation's exercise of enforcement jurisdiction to acts within its own territory. Moreover, contemporary international law generally continues to impose territorial limits on enforcement jurisdiction. *Restatement (Third) Foreign Relations Law* §432, comment b (1987). What does this suggest about the continued validity of territorial limits on the act of state doctrine?

(b) *Impact on U.S. foreign relations.* Is the territoriality requirement consistent with rationales for the act of state doctrine which emphasize the need to minimize judicial interference with U.S. foreign policy? Some authorities have reasoned that the situs requirement is based on the expectations of foreign states, which are said to contemplate international scrutiny of their extraterritorial acts, but not of their domestic conduct. Note, *The Act of State Doctrine: Resolving Debt Situs Confusion*, 86 Colum. L. Rev. 594, 608-09 (1986); *Tabacalera Severiano Jorge, SA v. Standard Cigar Co.*, 392 F.2d 706, 715 (5th Cir.), *cert. denied*, 393 U.S. 924 (1968).

(c) *Choice of law.* Is the territoriality requirement consistent with the view that the act of state doctrine is a choice of law rule? Recall the American "conflicts revolution" and the erosion of territoriality principles in contemporary choice of law thinking. *See supra* pp. 631-32.

3. *Acts of state in a third state's territory.* Suppose Mexico's exchange control regulations were, as a matter of Mexican law, applicable to a deposit whose situs was the Guatemalan branch of Bancomer. Would a U.S. court apply the act of state doctrine in a suit by the depositor? Should it? *See Drexel Burnham Lambert Group Inc. v. Galadari*, 777 F.2d 877, 881 (2d Cir. 1985). What if Guatemalan law was in conflict with Mexican exchange controls? Recall one of the early U.S. judicial explanations for the act of state doctrine: "The very meaning of sovereignty is that the decree of the sovereign makes law." *American Banana Co. v. United Fruit Co.*, 213 U.S. 347, 358 (1909). Is a state's conduct outside its territory entitled to this same presumption of absolute legality?

4. *Scope of the situs requirement.* Foreign governmental conduct will usually involve some actions — if only decision-making — within the foreign state's territory. Lower courts have struggled to articulate a general formula for determining when sufficient conduct has occurred outside a foreign state's territory to render the act of state doctrine inapplicable. The standard articulated in *Bancomer* is one of the better-accepted efforts in this context: it inquires "whether the purported taking was 'able to come to complete fruition within the [foreign state's] domination.'" 762 F.2d at 224 (quoting *Tabacalera Severiano Jorge, SA v. Standard Cigar Co.*, 392 F.2d 706, 715-16 (5th Cir.) (also holding that foreign sovereign must be "physically in a position to perform a fait accompli"), *cert. denied*, 393 U.S. 924 (1968)). Compare *F. & H.R. Farman-Farmaian Consulting Engineers Firm v. Harza Eng. Co.*, 882 F.2d 281 (7th Cir. 1989) (confiscation must be "complete within the foreign state in the sense that all of the firm's assets and operations were there and the victim is trying to get an American court to undo the confiscation"); *Restatement (Third) Foreign Relations Law* §443, Reporters' Note 4 (1987); *Restatement (Second) Foreign Relations Law* §43, comment a (1965) ("Act of state doctrine ... becomes applicable only when and if the act has been fully executed.").

5. *The situs of intangibles.* As *Bancomer* illustrates, the "situs" requirement has frequently been relevant in cases involving "intangibles," such as debts or causes of action. The situs requirement makes it necessary to determine where debts and other intangibles are "located," because a foreign state's seizure or refusal to pay a debt located within its borders can be deemed an act of state, while refusal to honor a foreign debt will not satisfy the situs requirement. *See* Lowenfeld, *In Search of the Intangible: A Comment on Shaffer v. Heitner*, 53 N.Y.U.L. Rev. 102 (1978); Note, *The Resolution of Act of State Disputes Involving Indefinitely Situated Property*, 25 Va. J. Int'l L. 901, 907-26 (1985).

6. *The situs of debts.* In cases involving the "location" of debts, most courts, like *Bancomer*, have concluded that the debt is located at the "contractually-mandated" situs for its repayment. Under this analysis, the act of state doctrine is applicable to the repudiation of debts that must be repaid within the foreign state, but not to debts payable only at other locations. *See Allied Bank Int'l v. Banco Credito Agricola de Cartago,* 757 F.2d 516 (2d Cir.), *cert. denied,* 473 U.S. 934 (1985); *Weston Banking Corp. v. Turkiye Garanti Bankasi, AS,* 456 N.Y.S.2d 684 (1982) (breach of promise to pay outside foreign state not covered by act of state doctrine); *Libra Bank v. Banco Nacional de Costa Rica, SA,* 570 F.Supp. 870 (S.D.N.Y. 1983) (same). Is this emphasis on private agreement consistent with the notions of territorial sovereignty underlying the situs requirement? Compare the emphasis on the "place of payment" with the historic focus on the "place of contracting" in the *Restatement (First) Conflict of Laws* (1934). *See supra* pp. 664-73. Would it be more appropriate to adopt some variation of the "most significant relation" standard of the *Restatement (Second) Conflict of Laws*?

Greater uncertainty surrounds the treatment of debts that are repayable both within the debtor state and elsewhere. Is a foreign state's repudiation of such obligations protected by the act of state doctrine (because the debt is sited, at least in part, in the foreign state) or is it unprotected (because the debt is sited, at least in part, outside the foreign state)? *Compare Garcia v. Chase Manhattan Bank, NA,* 735 F.2d 645 (2d Cir. 1984) (agreement to repay debt anywhere in the world renders act of state doctrine inapplicable) *with Perez v. Chase Manhattan Bank, NA,* 474 N.Y.S.2d 689 (App. Div.), *cert. denied,* 469 U.S. 966 (1984) (act of state doctrine applicable to promise to pay anywhere in the world, since promise could have been enforced in Cuba).

7. *Inferring the situs of intangibles.* If the parties have not agreed to a place for repayment of a debt, where is the debt's situs? Lower courts have not adopted a consistent approach.

(a) *Location of the debtor.* Some courts have looked to the location of the *debtor* in ascertaining the situs of a debt in the absence of clear contractual guidance. *See Harris v. Balk,* 198 U.S. 215, 222 (1904) ("The obligation of the debtor to pay his debt clings to and accompanies him wherever he goes."). Contemporary decisions have modified this analysis by reasoning that a debt is sited wherever the debtor is subject to personal jurisdiction. *See Menendez v. Saks and Co.,* 485 F.2d 1355, 1364-65 (2d Cir. 1973), *rev'd on other grounds,* 425 U.S. 682 (1976) ("a debt is not 'located' within a foreign state unless that state has the power to enforce or collect it. ... [T]he power to enforce payment of a debt ... generally depends on jurisdiction over the person of the debtor."); *United Bank Ltd. v. Cosmic Int'l, Inc.,* 542 F.2d 868 (2d Cir. 1976); *Republic of Iraq v. First Nat'l City Bank,* 353 F.2d 47 (2d Cir. 1965), *cert. denied,* 382 U.S. 1027 (1966); *Tabacalera Severiano Jorge, SA v. Standard Cigar Co.,* 392 F.2d 706, 715-16 (5th Cir.), *cert. denied,* 393 U.S. 924 (1968). As discussed above, contemporary principles of personal jurisdiction generally will permit numerous states to exercise personal jurisdiction over a debtor, and thus to enforce a debt. Does this mean that a debt is sited in numerous places? Would it be consistent with purposes and rationale of the act of state doctrine to treat judgments based on long-arm jurisdiction as acts of state?

(b) *Most significant relationship test.* Other courts have looked to a wider range of factors to determine whether the relationship between an intangible and the foreign state are "sufficiently close that we will antagonize the foreign government by not recognizing its acts." *Callejo v. Bancomer, SA,* 764 F.2d 1101 (5th Cir. 1985). *See also F. & H.R. Farman-Farmaian Consulting Engineers Firm v. Harza Engineering Co.,* 882 F.2d 281 (7th Cir. 1989); *Tchacosh Co. v. Rockwell Int'l Corp.,* 766 F.2d 1333 (9th Cir. 1985); *Libra Bank, Ltd. v. Banco Nacional de Costa Rica, SA,* 570 F.Supp. 870, 884 (S.D.N.Y. 1983). *Compare* the Third *Restatement's* view: "it might be preferable to approach the question of the applicability of the act of state doctrine to intangible assets not by searching for an imaginary situs for property that has no real situs, but by determining how the act of the foreign state in the particular circumstances fits within the reasons for the act of state doctrine and for the territorial limitation." *Restatement (Third) Foreign Relations Law* §443, Reporters' Note 4 (1987).

(c) *"Complete fruition" test.* Some courts have suggested that a debt or other intangible will be sited in a foreign state only if that state "has the parties and the res before it and acts in such a manner as to change the relationship of the parties touching the res." *Tabacalera Severiano Jorge, SA v. Standard Cigar Co.,* 392 F.2d 706, 715 (5th Cir.), *cert. denied,* 393 U.S. 924 (1968). *See also Ramirez de Arellano v. Weinberger,* 745 F.2d 1500, 1533-36 (D.C. Cir. 1984), *vacated,* 471 U.S. 1113 (1985) (presidential expropriation decree is not an "act of state" until property is actually seized); *Allied Bank Int'l v. Banco Credito Agricola de Cartago,* 757 F.2d 516, 521 (2d Cir.), *cert. denied,* 106 S. Ct. 30 (1985).

8. F. & H.R. Farman-Farmaian Consulting Engineers v. Harza Engineering Co. The Seventh Circuit's decision in *F. & H.R. Farman-Farmaian Consulting Engineers v. Harza Engineering Co.*, 882 F.2d 281 (7th Cir. 1989), illustrates the complexities of the situs requirement in cases involving intangibles. The case arose when the owners of an Iranian consulting firm ("Farman") brought suit in the United States to collect a debt that was owed to the consulting company by a former U.S. business partner ("Harza"). The debt arose from services rendered, entirely in Iran, by Farman to Harza. Harza had a lengthy history of business dealings with Farman and it had frequently paid invoices rendered to it, usually in Iranian currency. In 1979, however, Harza ceased business operations in Iran, because of the revolutionary unrest, and refused to pay some $2 million in outstanding invoices from Farman. Farman was subsequently dissolved by the new Iranian revolutionary regime; its owners received no compensation.

Some time later, Harza received an award from the Iran-U.S. Claims Tribunal for services rendered by Harza to the Iranian government before the revolution. Farman then claimed that it was entitled to payment of the invoices previously rendered by it, which related to the projects for which Harza had received compensation from the Claims Tribunal. Harza refused, and Farman filed suit in the United States. Harza defended, among other things, on act of state grounds: it reasoned that the Iranian government had confiscated Farman's claim against Harza. Farman replied that "the revolutionary government could not seize this claim because the debt giving rise to it was 'in Chicago' [where Harza's headquarters was located] rather than 'in Iran.'" The Seventh Circuit rejected the argument, reasoning that:

> [Farman] was an Iranian company all of whose assets and operations were in Iran; the revolutionary regime seized the firm and its assets; one of those assets was the firm's claim against Harza for payment for the services that the firm had rendered Harza in Iran. ... Granted, to describe [Farman's] claim for payment of Harza's debt to it as an asset located in Iran, as we have done, may be thought to beg the question. A debt (like a word, a number, an idea) has no space-time location; it is not a physical object and efforts to treat it as such ... seem bound to fail. This acknowledgement does not much help the plaintiffs, though, since they argue that the debt was "in" Chicago — a clearly untenable proposition. Harza's liability was [Farman's] asset, and it is strange to describe [Farman] as having an "American" asset by virtue merely of having a claim against an American company for services performed on that company's behalf in Iran. ...

> What is at issue in this case is not the rights or interests of an American company (Harza is American, but its only interest is in avoiding double payment, and is protected by applying the act of state doctrine to bar this lawsuit) but the propriety of dealings between the Iranian government and an Iranian corporation. With the American interest so attenuated, considerations of comity — that is, of sensitivity to the potential frictions between proud sovereigns — come to the fore; and it is those considerations, and the resulting concern with the judiciary's stepping on the State Department's toes, that inform the modern understanding of the act of state doctrine. For an American court to say to Iran, "We won't pay any attention to your seizure of [Farman] without compensation to the owners, because it's the sort of act that is abhorrent to Americans," would be a slap in the face of the Iranian regime. ... Granted, the slap would sting no less sharply if [Farman] had had assets in the United States or if its contract with Harza had contemplated transactions between the U.S. and Iran rather than wholly within Iran; and the considerations of territoriality may seem as anachronistic as they are elusive as a guide to the boundaries of the act of state doctrine. But the United States has an independent concern with protecting property and transactions ... within its borders; that is the interest which underlies the extraterritorial exception to the act of state doctrine. That interest is not present here.

Is the Seventh Circuit's analysis persuasive? What is the physical location of the actual invoices that Farman rendered? Where would the funds needed to pay those invoices come from? Where would Farman, whose owners are in the United States, receive those funds? The Court of Appeals largely discounted these issues and instead focussed primarily on Farman's close relations to Iran and the fact that Farman's services were rendered in Iran. In particular, the Court emphasized that "all" of Farman's assets were plainly "in Iran." But, although most of Farman's assets were plainly in Iran, surely the relevant question is whether the Harza receivable was "in" Iran. The fact that the work performed by Farman, which the invoices reflect, occurred in Iran does not dictate where the invoices are payable. Why isn't the receivable, represented by the invoice, "in Chicago"? Does the Seventh Circuit's opinion really depend on "where" the receivable/debt is "located" or does it engage in a broader balancing of U.S. and foreign interests? Is the opinion correct in ignoring traditional indicia of situs in favor of a broader inquiry into the likely effect of U.S. litigation on foreign sensibilities? Is this approach consistent with *Environmental Tectonics*? If Farman had owned a U.S. office building, would the act of state doctrine apply?

9. *Federal law governs determination of situs.* It has been held that federal law governs the determination of where particular property is located. *Tchacosh Co. v. Rockwell Int'l Corp.*, 766 F.2d 1333, 1337 (9th Cir. 1985); *Tabacalera Severiano Jorge, SA v. Standard Cigar Co.*, 392 F.2d 706, 715 (5th Cir.), *cert. denied*, 393 U.S. 924 (1968); *Republic of Iraq v. First Nat'l City Bank*, 353 F.2d 47, 51 (2d Cir. 1965), *cert. denied*, 382 U.S. 1027 (1966). Why is that the case? Is not the question of where a debt must be repaid an issue of contract interpretation, usually governed by state contract law?

10. *Application of comity doctrine where situs requirement is not satisfied.* What are the consequences of *not* satisfying the situs requirement? Lower courts have generally indicated that an action in U.S. courts may be dismissed on "comity" grounds even when a foreign act of state occurs outside the territory of the foreign state (or involves property located outside the foreign state). *Republic of Iraq v. First National City Bank*, 353 F.2d 47, 51 (2d Cir. 1965), *cert. denied*, 382 U.S. 1027 (1966) ("when property confiscated is within the United States at the time of attempted confiscation, our courts will give effect to acts of state only if they are consistent with the policy and law of the United States").

Some decisions require some special U.S. policy interest in overriding a foreign act of state notwithstanding the fact that the "situs" requirement is not satisfied. *Drexel Burnham Lambert Group Inc. v. Galadari*, 777 F.2d 877 (2d Cir. 1985); *Allied Bank Int'l v. Banco Credito Agricola de Cartago*, 757 F.2d 516 (2d Cir.), *cert. dismissed*, 473 U.S. 934 (1985). In most cases, however, the challenged act of state is an expropriation and uncompensated seizures have long been held "contrary to our public policy and shocking to our sense of justice and equity." *Vladikavkazsky Ry. v. New York Trust Co.*, 263 N.Y. 369, 378 (1934). *See Bandes v. Harlow & Jones, Inc.*, 852 F.2d 661, 667 (2d Cir. 1988); *Maltina Corp. v. Cawy Bottling Co.*, 462 F.2d 1021, 1027 (5th Cir.), *cert. denied*, 409 U.S. 1060 (1972); *Republic of Iraq v. First Nat'l City Bank*, 353 F.2d 47, 51 (2d Cir. 1965), *cert. denied*, 382 U.S. 1027 (1966); *Castro v. International Telegraph & Telephone Co.*, 1991 Del. Ch. Lexis 89 (Del. Ch. May 30, 1991).

C. Exceptions to the Act of State Doctrine

Various authorities have fashioned significant exceptions to the doctrine. These include the *Bernstein* exception, an exception for "commercial" acts, an "international law" or treaty exception, and the Second Hickenlooper amendment. The following sections examine each of these exceptions.

Like the basic act of state doctrine itself, considerable uncertainty surrounds most of these exceptions. This uncertainty is due in large part to two sharply divided decisions by the Supreme Court — *Alfred Dunhill* and *First National City Bank* — dealing with the act of state doctrine.[72] Because no Justice's opinion in either case was able to command a majority of the Court, the lower courts have been left largely without guidance in the field. Not surprisingly, their decisions are often inconsistent and sometimes confused.

1. The *Bernstein* Exception

A primary rationale advanced in *Sabbatino* for the act of state doctrine was avoiding judicial interference with the executive branch's conduct of foreign relations.[73] This concern appears to lose much of its force in cases where the executive branch states that a judicial decision will not harm U.S. foreign relations. As a result, courts have sometimes declined to apply the act of state doctrine when the executive branch formally advises that there is no need to do so. Judicial deference to executive branch views regarding the act of state doctrine has been justified under the so-called "*Bernstein* exception."

The term "*Bernstein* exception" derives from the Second Circuit's decisions in *Bernstein v. N.V. Nederlandsche-Amerikaansche Stoomvaart-Maatschappij.*[74] The case involved claims by a Jewish businessman to recover property seized during World War II by the Nazi regime. The Court of Appeals initially dismissed the plaintiff's claims on act of state grounds.[75] Subsequently, the Department of State submitted a letter to the court declaring that the "policy of the Executive ... is to relieve American courts from any restraint on the exercise of their jurisdiction to pass upon the validity of the acts of Nazi officials." In subsequent proceedings, the Second Circuit expressly relied on the Department of State's letter to reverse its earlier decision. The Court held that the act of state doctrine was inapplicable in the face of an express executive branch suggestion that U.S. courts exercise jurisdiction, thus giving rise to the so-called *Bernstein* exception.[76]

---

72. *See, e.g., Alfred Dunhill of London v. Republic of Cuba,* 425 U.S. 682 (1976); *First Nat'l City Bank v. Banco Nacional de Cuba,* 406 U.S. 759 (1972).

73. *See, e.g., First Nat'l City Bank,* 406 U.S. at 767 (plurality opinion); *Sabbatino,* 376 U.S. at 427-28. As discussed above, *Environmental Tectonics* repeated this separation of powers rationale, while also formulating the act of state doctrine as a choice of law rule. *See supra* p. 719.

74. 173 F.2d 71 (2d Cir. 1949) *and* 210 F.2d 375 (2d Cir. 1954).

75. 173 F.2d 71 (2d Cir. 1949).

76. 210 F.2d 375 (2d Cir. 1954).

The Supreme Court has thus far refused to accept the *Bernstein* exception. In *First National City Bank v. Banco Nacional de Cuba*, Justice Rehnquist delivered the judgment of the Court, and wrote a plurality opinion embracing the *Bernstein* exception.[77] Nevertheless, in the same case, at least five (and perhaps six) Justices rejected the doctrine.[78]

Lower courts have reacted to the Supreme Court's handling of the *Bernstein* exception with confusion. Some courts have applied the exception as it was originally framed in *Bernstein* — when the Executive Branch expressly states that adjudication of a matter will not impair U.S. foreign relations, these courts hold that the act of state doctrine is inapplicable.[79] Other courts have expressly rejected the *Bernstein* exception, and do not appear to give any weight to U.S. government statements.[80] The largest number of lower courts have adopted a variation of the original *Bernstein* exception, considering the existence of a *Bernstein* letter as a significant — but not dispositive — factor in act of state analysis.[81] In several decisions, the Second Circuit has given effect to *Bernstein* letters, but only where they relate to counterclaims, and where there is no showing that the litigation will interfere with U.S. foreign relations.[82]

W.S. KIRKPATRICK & CO. v. ENVIRONMENTAL TECTONICS CORP.

493 U.S. 400 (1990) [excerpted above at pp. 713-18]

Notes on Environmental Tectonics

1. *Application of the* Bernstein *exception in* First National City Bank. In *First National City Bank*, the Court was not able to agree on a majority opinion. Justice Rehnquist wrote a plurality opinion adopting the *Bernstein* exception, but it was only joined by two other Justices. Five (and perhaps six) of the Justices

---

77. 406 U.S. 759 (1972).

78. 406 U.S. at 770 (Douglas, J., concurring), 772 (Powell, J., concurring), 776 (Brennan, J., dissenting).

79. *See Williams v. Curtiss-Wright Corp.*, 694 F.2d 300, 303 (3d Cir. 1982) (dicta); *Occidental of Umm Al Qaywayn, Inc. v. A Certain Cargo of Petroleum*, 577 F.2d 1196, 1204 (5th Cir. 1978), *cert. denied*, 442 U.S. 928 (1979); *Beck v. Manufacturers Hanover Trust Co.*, 481 N.Y.S.2d 211 (Sup. Ct. 1984) (dicta).

80. *See Braniff Airways v. Civil Aeronautics Board*, 581 F.2d 846, 851 & n.18 (D.C. Cir. 1978) (dicta); *Hunt v. Coastal States Gas Producing Co.*, 570 S.W.2d 503, 507 (Tex. Civ. App. 1978), *aff'd*, 583 S.W.2d 322 (Tex.), *cert. denied*, 444 U.S. 992 (1979).

81. *See Environmental Tectonics Corp. v. W.S. Kirkpatrick, & Co.*, 847 F.2d 1052 (3d Cir. 1988), *aff'd on other grounds*, 493 U.S. 400 (1990); *Republic of Philippines v. Marcos*, 806 F.2d 344, 356-60 (2d Cir. 1986); *Allied Bank Int'l v. Banco Credito Agricola de Cartago*, 757 F.2d 516, 521 n.2 (2d Cir.), *cert. dismissed*, 473 U.S. 931 (1985) (act of state analysis "may be guided but not controlled by the position, if any, articulated by the executive as to the applicability *vel non* of the doctrine as to a particular set of facts. Whether to invoke the act of state doctrine is ultimately and always a judicial question."); *Sharon v. Time, Inc.*, 599 F.Supp. 538, 552 (S.D.N.Y. 1984); *Republic of Haiti v. Duvalier*, 1995 WL 279794 (N.Y. App. Div. 1995). This is also how the *Restatement (Third) Foreign Relations Law* §443 Reporters' Note 8 (1987), characterizes the consensus of the lower courts.

82. *E.g., Banco Nacional de Cuba v. Chase Manhattan Bank*, 658 F.2d 875, 884 (2d Cir. 1981).

then on the Court rejected the exception. Justice Rehnquist's plurality opinion offered the following justification for the *Bernstein* exception:

> The line of cases from this Court establishing the act of state doctrine justifies its existence primarily on the basis that juridical review of acts of state of a foreign power could embarrass the conduct of foreign relations by the political branches of the government. ... We think that [cases such as *Underhill* and *Oetjen* indicate] that this Court has recognized the primacy of the Executive in the conduct of foreign relations quite as emphatically as it has recognized the act of state doctrine. The Court in *Sabbatino* throughout its opinion emphasized the lead role of the Executive in foreign policy, particularly in seeking redress for American nationals who had been the victims of foreign expropriation, and concluded that any exception to the act of state doctrine based on a mere silence or neutrality on the part of the Executive might well lead to a conflict between the Executive and Judicial Branches. Here, however, the Executive Branch has expressly stated that an inflexible application of the act of state doctrine by this Court would not serve the interests of American foreign policy.
>
> The act of state doctrine is grounded on judicial concern that application of customary principles of law to judge the acts of a foreign sovereign might frustrate the conduct of foreign relations by the political branches of the government. We conclude that where the Executive Branch, charged as it is with primary responsibility for the conduct of foreign affairs, expressly represents to the Court that application of the act of state doctrine would not advance the interests of American foreign policy, that doctrine should not be applied by the courts. In so doing, we of course adopt and approve the so-called *Bernstein* exception to the act of state doctrine. We believe this to be no more than an application of the classical common-law maxim that "[t]he reason of the law ceasing, the law itself also ceases."

Is this persuasive? Note that it depends on Justice Rehnquist's view of the purposes of the act of state doctrine and his view that the President enjoys largely exclusive authority over U.S. foreign relations. Are his positions on these two subjects entirely accurate? *See supra* pp. 22-24.

2. *Criticism of the* **Bernstein** *exception.* Several concurring or dissenting opinions in *First National City Bank* criticized the *Bernstein* exception. Justice Brennan wrote that adopting the exception would "require us to abdicate our judicial responsibility to define the contours of the act of state doctrine so that the judiciary does not become embroiled in the politics of international relations to the damage not only of the courts and the Executive but of the rule of law." He reasoned:

> *Sabbatino* held that the validity of a foreign act of state in certain circumstances is a "political question" not cognizable in our courts. Only one — and not necessarily the most important — of those circumstances concerned the possible impairment of the Executive's conduct of foreign affairs. Even if this factor were absent in this case because of the Legal Adviser's statement of position, it would hardly follow that the act of state doctrine should not foreclose judicial review of the expropriation of petitioner's properties. To the contrary, the absence of consensus on the applicable international rules, the unavailability of standards from a treaty or other agreement, the existence and recognition of the Cuban government, the sensitivity of the issues to national concerns, and the power of the Executive alone to effect a fair remedy for all U.S. citizens who have been harmed all point toward the existence of a "political question." ... The Executive Branch, however extensive its powers in the area of foreign affairs, cannot by simple stipulation change a political question into a cognizable claim. ...
>
> The task of defining the contours of a political question such as the act of state doctrine is exclusively the function of this Court. The *"Bernstein"* exception relinquishes the function to the Executive by requiring blind adherence to its requests that foreign acts of state be reviewed. Conversely, it politicizes the judiciary. For the Executive's invitation to lift the act of state bar can only be accepted at the expense of supplanting the political branch in its role as a constituent of the international law-making community. The consequence of adopting the *"Bernstein"* approach would only be to bring the rule of law both here at home and in the relations of nations into disrespect. Indeed, the fate of the individual claimant would be subject to the political considerations of the Executive Branch. Since those considerations change as surely as administrations change, similarly situated litigants would not be likely to obtain even-handed treatment.

Justice Douglas also refused to accept the *Bernstein* exception. In his view, it would mean that "the Court [would] become[] a mere errand boy for the Executive Branch which may choose to pick some people's chestnuts from the fire, but not others.'"

Justice Rehnquist replied:

> Our holding is in no sense an abdication of the judicial function to the Executive Branch. The judicial power of the United States extends to this case, and the jurisdictional standards established by Congress for adjudication by the federal courts have been met by the parties. The only reason for not deciding the case by use of otherwise applicable legal principles would be the fear that legal interpretation by the judiciary of the act of a foreign sovereign within its own territory might frustrate the conduct of this country's foreign relations. But the branch of the government responsible for the conduct of those foreign relations has advised us that such a consequence need not be feared in this case. The judiciary is therefore free to decide the case without the limitations that would otherwise be imposed upon it by the judicially created act of state doctrine.

Which of these views is more persuasive? What is the basis for the act of state doctrine? If its basis is separation of powers concerns about judicial interference in U.S. foreign relations is the *Bernstein* exception sensible? If the basis for the act of state doctrine is choice of law considerations, or concerns based on international comity, is the answer different? Does the *Bernstein* exception leave the fate of claimants to the "political considerations of the Executive Branch"? Isn't this charge more accurately levelled against the act of state doctrine itself, which denies plaintiffs judicial relief in favor of executive branch espousal of their claims?

3. *Need for formal statement of executive branch policy to trigger* **Bernstein** *exception*. In *Environmental Tectonics*, the Legal Advisor of the U.S. State Department submitted a letter to the lower courts taking the position that the act of state doctrine was not applicable as a matter of law: We do "not believe the Act of State doctrine would bar the Court from adjudicating this dispute." *See* 847 F.2d at 1067-69 (reprinting Legal Advisor's letter). In their briefs to the Supreme Court, various parties argued that the Legal Advisor's letter did not fall within the *Bernstein* exception, because it merely opined about the legal applicability of the act of state doctrine, and did not formally state the executive branch's view that the doctrine should not be applied. Thereafter, the Legal Advisor submitted a new letter, attached to the U.S. Government's *amicus curiae* brief in the Supreme Court, specifically stating the executive branch's position that the act of state doctrine should not apply: "Cases could arise which present an unacceptable risk that adjudication would embarrass the Executive Branch in its conduct of U.S. foreign relations, leading the Executive to suggest the desirability of judicial abstention. We do not regard *Environmental Tectonics* as such a case, and we do not see any foreign relations obstacles to its adjudication on the merits."

In his opinion in *Environmental Tectonics*, however, Justice Scalia overlooked the second letter, mistakenly concluding that "we would question [the Government's] characterization of the legal advisor's letter as reflecting the absence of any policy objection to the adjudication. The letter ... did not purport to say whether the State Department would like to proceed, but rather responded (correctly, as we hold today) to the question whether the act of state doctrine was applicable." The Court then cited to the Legal Advisor's *first* letter, not to the *second* letter submitted to the Supreme Court. *See supra* p. 717 n.63. Putting aside the Court's unfortunate confusion about the U.S. Government's position, is the distinction between a legal opinion and a "policy objection" persuasive? What exactly does the *Environmental Tectonics* footnote require a *Bernstein* letter to say? Note also that the second letter submitted by the Legal Advisor in *Environmental Tectonics* went on to say: "We also believe that, in the absence of a representation to the contrary, the courts may properly assume that no unacceptable interference with U.S. foreign relations will occur on account of the adjudication of like cases."

4. *Practical impact of executive branch communications in act of state cases*. The Department of State reportedly receives two or three requests each year for *Bernstein* letters. *Bernstein* letters have been issued only rarely. Bazyler, *Abolishing the Act of State Doctrine*, 134 U. Pa. L. Rev. 325, 369-70 n.274 (1986) (listing cases). Although the legal foundation for the *Bernstein* exception is uncertain, an executive branch statement on act of state issues continues to be of considerable practical importance. *Compare Republic of Philippines v. Marcos*, 806 F.2d 344, 357 (2d Cir. 1986) *with Republic of Philippines v. Marcos*, 818 F.2d 1473 (9th Cir. 1987), *vacated*, 862 F.2d 1355 (9th Cir. 1988) (en banc) and *Allied Bank Int'l v. Banco Credito Agricola de Cartago*, 733 F.2d 23 (2d Cir. 1984), *rev'd*, 757 F.2d 516 (2d Cir. 1985).

2. The "Commercial" Exception[83]

The United States and most other nations do not grant foreign sovereign immunity to the "commercial" activities of foreign states.[84] As discussed above, this restrictive theory of sovereign immunity developed in part because the adjudication of claims involving a foreign state's commercial activity was thought less likely to infringe foreign sovereignty or public policy than litigation involving governmental or political acts.[85] In addition, most nations came to agree that it was unjust for a foreign state to enter into commercial relations with private parties and subsequently invoke its sovereignty against claims relating to that activity.[86]

The considerations that generated the commercial exception to foreign sovereign immunity have sometimes been thought applicable in the act of state context.[87] Nonetheless, a "commercial exception" to the act of state doctrine has been slow to develop. Before *Alfred Dunhill*, excerpted below, no lower court had adopted such an exception and, as the Supreme Court's splintered decision indicates, the commercial exception to the act of state doctrine has encountered more resistance than in the sovereign immunity context.

ALFRED DUNHILL OF LONDON, INC. v. REPUBLIC OF CUBA

425 U.S. 682 (1976) [also excerpted above at pp. 706-09]

JUSTICE WHITE.[88] [The facts of the case are excerpted above.]

III. If we assume with the Court of Appeals that the Cuban Government itself had purported to exercise sovereign power to confiscate the mistaken payments belonging to three foreign creditors and to repudiate interventors' adjudicated obligation to return those funds, we are nevertheless persuaded by the arguments of petitioner and by those of the United States that the concept of an act of state should not be extended to include the repudiation of a purely commercial obligation owed by a foreign sovereign or by one of its commercial instrumentalities. ... Distinguishing between the public and governmental acts of sovereign states on the one hand and their private and commercial acts on the other is not a novel approach [citing *Bank of the United States v. Planters' Bank of Georgia*, 9 Wheat. 904, 907 (1824).]

It is the position of the United States, stated in an amicus brief filed by the

---

83. For commentary on the commercial exception, *see* McCormick, *The Commercial Activity Exception to Foreign Sovereign Immunity and the Act of State Doctrine*, 16 Law & Pol'y Int'l Bus. 477 (1984); Zaitzeff & Kunz, *The Act of State Doctrine and the Allied Bank Case*, 40 Bus. Law. 449, 464-69 (1985); Comment, *The Act of State Doctrine: The Need for a Commercial Exception in Antitrust Litigation*, 18 San Diego L. Rev. 813 (1981).

84. *See supra* pp. 199-210 & 235-46.

85. *See supra* p. 210.

86. *See supra* p. 210.

87. *E.g., Alfred Dunhill of London, Inc. v. Republic of Cuba*, 425 U.S. 682 (1976).

88. The following excerpt, contained in Part III of the *Dunhill* opinion was joined only by the Chief Justice, Justice Powell, and Justice Rehnquist.

Solicitor General, that such a line should be drawn in defining the outer limits of the act of state concept and that repudiations by a foreign sovereign of its commercial debts should not be considered to be acts of state beyond legal question in our courts. Attached to the brief of the United States and to this opinion as Appendix I is the letter of November 26, 1975, in which the Department of State, speaking through its Legal Advisor agrees with the brief filed by the Solicitor General and, more specifically, declares that "we do not believe that the *Dunhill* case raises an act of state question because the case involves an act which is commercial, and not public, in nature."

The major underpinning of the act of state doctrine is the policy of foreclosing court adjudications involving the legality of acts of foreign states on their own soil that might embarrass the Executive Branch of our Government in the conduct of our foreign relations. But based on the presently expressed views of those who conduct our relations with foreign countries, we are in no sense compelled to recognize as an act of state the purely commercial conduct of foreign governments in order to avoid embarrassing conflicts with the Executive Branch. On the contrary, for the reasons to which we now turn, we fear that embarrassment and conflict would more likely ensue if we were to require that the repudiation of a foreign government's debts arising from its operation of a purely commercial business be recognized as an act of state and immunized from question in our courts.

Although it had other views in years gone by, in 1952, [in, the Tate Letter], the United States abandoned the absolute theory of sovereign immunity and embraced the restrictive view under which immunity in our courts should be granted only with respect to causes of action arising out of a foreign state's public or governmental actions and not with respect to those arising out of its commercial or proprietary actions. This has been the official policy of our Government since that time as the attached letter of November 26, 1975 confirms:

Moreover, since 1952, the Department of State has adhered to the position that the commercial and private activities of foreign states do not give rise to sovereign immunity. Implicit in this position is a determination that adjudications of commercial liability against foreign states do not impede the conduct of foreign relations, and that such adjudications are consistent with international law on sovereign immunity.

Repudiation of a commercial debt cannot, consistent with this restrictive approach to sovereign immunity, be treated as an act of state; for if it were, foreign governments, by merely repudiating the debt before or after its adjudication, would enjoy an immunity which our Government would not extend them under prevailing sovereign immunity principles in this country. This would undermine the policy supporting the restrictive view of immunity, which is to assure those engaging in commercial transactions with foreign sovereignties that their rights will be determined in the courts whenever possible. ...

Since [1952], the United States has adopted and adhered to the policy declining to extend sovereign immunity to the commercial dealings of foreign governments. It has based that policy in part on the fact that this approach has been accepted by a large and increasing number of foreign states in the international community; in part on the fact that the United States had already adopted a policy of consenting to be sued in foreign courts in connection with suits against its merchant vessels; and in part because the enormous increase in the extent to which foreign sovereigns had become involved in international trade made essential "a practice which will enable persons doing business with them to have their rights determined in the courts."

In the last 20 years, lower courts have ... declined to extend sovereign immunity to foreign sovereigns in cases arising out of purely commercial transactions. Indeed, it is fair to say that the "restrictive theory" of sovereign immunity appears to be generally accepted as the prevailing law in this country. *Restatement (Second) Foreign Relations Law* §69 (1965). Participation by foreign sovereigns in the international commercial market has increased substantially in recent years. The potential injury to private businessmen — and ultimately to international trade itself — from a system in which some of the participants in the international market are not subject to the rule of law has therefore increased correspondingly. As noted above, courts of other countries have also recently adopted the restrictive theory of sovereign immunity. Of equal importance is the fact that subjecting foreign governments to the rule of law in their commercial dealings presents a much smaller risk of affronting their sovereignty than would an attempt to pass on the legality of their governmental acts.[89] In their commercial capacities, foreign governments do not exercise powers peculiar to sovereigns. Instead, they exercise only those powers that can also be exercised by private citizens. Subjecting them in connection with such acts to the same rules of law that apply to private citizens is unlikely to touch very sharply on "national nerves." Moreover, as this Court has noted:

[T]he greater the degree of codification or consensus concerning a particular area of international law, the more appropriate it is for the judiciary to render decisions regarding it, since the courts can then focus on the application of an agreed principle to circumstances of fact rather than on the sensitive task of establishing a principle not inconsistent with the national interest or with international justice. [*Sabbatino*, 376 U.S. at 428.]

There may be little codification or consensus as to the rules of international law concerning exercises of governmental powers, including military powers and expropriations, within a sovereign state's borders affecting the property or persons of aliens. However, more discernible rules of international law have emerged with regard to the commercial dealings of private parties in the international market. The restrictive approach to sovereign immunity suggests that these established rules should be applied to the commercial transactions of sovereign states.

Of course, sovereign immunity has not been pleaded in this case; but it is

---

89. In *Sabbatino*, 376 U.S. at 428-29, the Court noted in the context of the act of state doctrine: "It is also evident that some aspects of international law touch much more sharply on national nerves than do others; the less important the implications of an issue are for our foreign relations, the weaker the justification for exclusivity in the political branches."

beyond cavil that part of the foreign relations law recognized by the United States is that the commercial obligations of a foreign government may be adjudicated in those courts otherwise having jurisdiction to enter such judgments. Nothing in our national policy calls on us to recognize as an act of state a repudiation by Cuba of an obligation adjudicated in our courts and arising out of the operation of a commercial business by one of its instrumentalities. For all the reasons which led the Executive Branch to adopt the restrictive theory of sovereign immunity, we hold that the mere assertion of sovereignty as a defense to a claim arising out of purely commercial acts by a foreign sovereign is no more effective if given the label "Act of State" than if it is given the label "sovereign immunity."[90]

In describing the act of state doctrine in the past we have said that it "precludes the courts of this country from inquiring into the validity of the *public* acts of a recognized foreign sovereign power committed within its own territory." *Sabbatino*, 376 U.S. at 401 (emphasis added), and that it applies to "acts done within their own States, in the exercise of *governmental* authority." *Underhill*, 168 U.S. at 252 (emphasis added). We decline to extend the act of state doctrine to acts committed by foreign sovereigns in the course of their purely commercial operations. Because the act relied on by respondents in this case was an act arising out of the conduct by Cuba's agents in the operation of cigar businesses for profit, the act was not an act of state.

Note on Dunhill

1. *Rationale for commercial exception.* What is Justice White's rationale for a "commercial exception" to the act of state doctrine? How does this rationale relate to the commercial exception to foreign sovereign immunity? Is Justice White's analysis persuasive? Does the wisdom of a commercial exception depend upon whether the act of state doctrine is regarded as an abstention doctrine or a choice of law rule?

2. *Lower courts' reaction to* Dunhill's *commercial exception.* The reaction of lower courts to *Dunhill's* "commercial exception" has been mixed. Several courts appear to have adopted some version of the exception. *E.g., Compania de Gas de Nuevo Laredo v. Entex, Inc.,* 686 F.2d 322, 326 (5th Cir. 1982), *cert. denied,* 460 U.S. 1041 (1983) (apparently recognizing commercial exception in dicta); *Empresa Cubana v. Lamborn & Co.,* 652 F.2d 231, 238 (2d Cir. 1981); *Arango v. Guzman Travel Advisors Corp.,* 621 F.2d 1371, 1380-81 (5th Cir. 1980); *Egyptian Nav. Co. v. Uiterwyk,* 1988 W.L. 70047 (M.D. Fla. Jan. 7, 1988); *Gage Int'l, Ltd. v. Cadillac Gage Co.,* 534 F.Supp. 896, 899-900 (E.D. Mich. 1981); *American Int'l Group v. Iran,* 493 F.Supp. 522, 525 (D.D.C. 1980), *rev'd on other grounds,* 657 F.2d 430 (D.C. Cir. 1981); *Dominicus Americana Bohio v. Gulf & Western Indus., Inc.,* 473 F.Supp. 680 (S.D.N.Y. 1979); *International Tin Council*

---

90. The dissent states that the doctrines of sovereign immunity and act of state are distinct — the former conferring on a sovereign "exemption from suit by virtue of its status" and the latter "merely [telling] a court what law to apply to a case." It may be true that the one doctrine has been described in jurisdictional terms and the other in choice-of-law terms; and it may be that the doctrines point to different results in certain cases. It cannot be gainsaid, however, that the proper application of each involves a balancing of the injury to our foreign policy, the conduct of which is committed primarily to the Executive Branch, through judicial affronts to sovereign powers, compare *Mexico v. Hoffman,* 324 U.S. at 35-36 (sovereign immunity), with *Sabbatino,* 376 U.S. at 423, 427-428 (act of state), against the injury to the private party, who is denied through judicial deference to a raw assertion of sovereignty, and a consequent injury to international trade. The State Department has concluded that in the commercial area the need for merchants "to have their rights determined in courts" outweighs any injury to foreign policy. This conclusion was reached in the context of the jurisdictional problem of sovereign immunity. We reach the same one in the choice-of-law context of the act of state doctrine.

v. Amalgamet, 524 N.Y.S.2d 971 (Sup. Ct. 1988). Other courts have questioned or rejected the commercial exception. *E.g., Kalamazoo Spice Extraction Co. v. Provisional Military Government of Socialist Ethiopia*, 729 F.2d 422, 425 n.3 (6th Cir. 1984); *Callejo v. Bancomer, SA*, 764 F.2d 1101, 1115 n.17 (5th Cir. 1985).

3. *Scope of commercial exception.* Assuming that a commercial exception to the act of state doctrine exists, what types of activity does it cover? The *Dunhill* plurality appeared to limit the exception to "purely" commercial obligations. This formulation appears significantly narrower than the commercial activity exception in the sovereign immunity context, *see supra* pp. 235-46. Assuming that the commercial exception is accepted, should the same standards be used for defining "commerciality" as apply in the sovereign immunity context?

As in the sovereign immunity context, *e.g., MOL, Inc. v. People's Republic of Bangladesh*, 736 F.2d 1326 (9th Cir.), *cert. denied*, 469 U.S. 1037 (1984), excerpted at *supra* pp. 242-43, the "commercial" exception to the act of state doctrine has been particularly difficult to apply to foreign governmental acts involving the exploitation of natural resources. For example, in *IAM v. OPEC*, 649 F.2d 1354 (9th Cir. 1981), *cert. denied*, 454 U.S. 1163 (1982), the Court of Appeals applied the act of state doctrine and dismissed an antitrust suit against OPEC's price-fixing of petroleum. The court reasoned that a U.S. decision against the OPEC member states would amount to "an order from a domestic court instructing a foreign sovereign to alter its chosen means of allocating and profiting from its own valuable natural resources." 649 F.2d at 1361. *See also Callejo v. Bancomer, SA*, 764 F.2d 1101, 1114-16 (5th Cir. 1985) (foreign state's acts are commercial for FSIA purposes, and non-commercial for act of state purposes).

For a narrow view of the commercial activity exception, *see Restatement (Third) Foreign Relations Law* §443, Reporters' Note 6 (1987) ("if state X cancels a long-term supply contract with a seller in the United States on the ground that the seller had supplied defective merchandise, a decision by a court in the United States in favor of the seller would probably not violate internationally shared expectations; in contrast, termination of the same contract because X had broken relations with the United States or had banned all 'capitalist enterprises' might well involve the kind of issue not appropriate for decision by the judiciary").

4. *Mixed commercial/sovereign conduct.* Foreign state's activities often contain both "sovereign" and "commercial" elements. In these cases, courts must determine whether the alleged acts of state are commercial or sovereign. In *Braka v. Bancomer SNC*, 762 F.2d 222 (2d Cir. 1985), for example, a state-owned Mexican bank failed to repay a certificate of deposit because Mexican foreign exchange controls prohibited repayment. When the certificate holders brought suit in the United States, the Mexican bank resisted on act of state grounds. The Second Circuit rejected the plaintiff's argument that *Dunhill's* commercial activity exception rendered the doctrine inapplicable:

> Even if we decided that the act of state doctrine is not applicable to commercial transactions of foreign governments, the result here would be the same. The activity that implicates act of state concerns here was the issuance by the Mexican government of exchange controls which prevented Bancomer from performing its contractual obligations. This action taken by the Mexican government for the purpose of saving its national economy from the brink of monetary disaster, surely represents the "exercise [of] powers peculiar to sovereigns." *Dunhill*, 425 U.S. at 704 (plurality opinion). Those sovereign powers, unlike acts that could be taken by a private citizen, trigger no commercial exception.

> Plaintiffs protest that they seek no intervention into Mexico's sovereign acts; they merely request that we order Bancomer to perform its commercial contractual commitments. However, Bancomer has already paid plaintiffs all that it may under Mexican law. Were we to issue the order they seek, we would find ourselves directing a state-owned entity to violate its own national law with respect to an obligation wholly controlled by Mexican law. This would clearly be an impermissible "inquiry into the legality, validity, and propriety of the acts and motivation of foreign sovereigns acting in their governmental roles within their own boundaries." *Arango v. Guzman Travel Advisors Corp.*, 621 F.2d 1371, 1380 (5th Cir. 1980). Therefore, the action at issue is sovereign rather than commercial. ...

Like *Dunhill*, *Braka* views the commercial exception to the act of state doctrine more narrowly than the FSIA's commercial exception. *See supra* pp. 244-46 & 258 for a discussion of mixed commercial/sovereign conduct in the FSIA context.

5. *Effects of FSIA.* What effect does the FSIA's commercial activities exception have on the act of

state doctrine? In general, courts have rejected the argument that the FSIA supersedes the doctrine as applied to commercial activities. *E.g., IAM v. OPEC,* 649 F.2d 1354, 1359 (9th Cir. 1981). *Compare Chisholm & Co. v. Bank of Jamaica,* 643 F.Supp. 1393, 1403 n.9 (S.D. Fla. 1986). Commentators are divided, with a substantial number contending that continued application of the act of state doctrine to non-immune activities would frustrate the FSIA. Bazyler, *Abolishing the Act of State Doctrine,* 134 U. Pa. L. Rev. 325, 377 (1986); Lengel, *The Duty of Federal Courts to Apply International Law: A Polemical Analysis of the Act of State Doctrine,* 1982 B.Y.U.L. Rev. 61, 62-63. *Compare* McCormick, *The Commercial Activity Exception to Foreign Sovereign Immunity and the Act of State Doctrine,* 16 Law & Pol'y Int'l Bus. 477, 519-24 (1984) and Dellapenna, *Deciphering the Act of State Doctrine,* 35 Vill. L. Rev. 1, 78-79 (1990).

6. *Waiver of act of state doctrine by foreign state.* If one of the bases for the act of state doctrine is a desire to avoid giving offense to foreign states, what is the status of the defense if the foreign state declares that it is willing for litigation to proceed? In general, U.S. courts have not been receptive to arguments that the act of state doctrine can be waived. *See Republic of Philippines v. Marcos,* 818 F.2d 1473, 1485-87 (9th Cir. 1987), *vacated,* 862 F.2d 1355 (9th Cir. 1988); *Compania de Gas de Nuevo Laredo, SA v. Entex, Inc.,* 686 F.2d 322, 326 (5th Cir. 1982) (declining to find waiver on the facts, and suggesting that even if waiver did exist, it would be only one of several factors relevant to act of state analysis); *Dayton v. Czechoslovak Socialist Republic,* 834 F.2d 203 (D.C. Cir. 1987) (failure to appear in U.S. litigation is not waiver of act of state defense).

One judge has reasoned that "[w]here the country's current government seeks an adjudication ... there is obviously less of a possibility that our pronouncements will embarrass our relations with that government," 818 F.2d at 1486, but that other factors nonetheless will often require abstention, including the fact that "a pronouncement by our courts ... would have a substantial effect on what may be a delicate political balance abroad" and the fact that "litigation proceeds at its own pace and the [U.S. court's] answer, whatever it may be, may well come at a time most inopportune from the point of view of our foreign policy." *Id.* Nonetheless, some authorities have taken the position that foreign states' waivers of the act of state doctrine are entitled to substantial deference: "insofar as the act of state doctrine is designed to reflect respect for foreign states, indications of consent to adjudication by the courts of another state are highly relevant, though they are not conclusive." *Restatement (Third) Foreign Relations Law* §443, comment e (1987).

What bearing, if any, does *Environmental Tectonics*'s characterization of the act of state doctrine as a "principle of law," rather than a species of abstention, have on the waiver of the doctrine?

7. *Use of the act of state doctrine against foreign state.* Should a private defendant be able to invoke the act of state doctrine in a suit by a representative of the foreign government whose act of state is allegedly involved? Lower courts have answered affirmatively. *DeRoburt v. Gannett Co.,* 733 F.2d 701 (9th Cir. 1984), *cert. denied,* 469 U.S. 1159 (1985); *Sharon v. Time, Inc.,* 599 F.Supp. 538 (S.D.N.Y. 1984). *See* Note, *Private Defendants May Assert the Act of State Defense Against a Resisting Sovereign,* 25 Va. J. Int'l L. 775 (1985). When a foreign state itself initiates suit in U.S. courts in a matter involving a foreign act of state, is the act of state doctrine necessary to prevent interference with U.S. foreign relations? to ensure fairness to private litigants?

3. The "Treaty" Exception[91]

The most widely-accepted exception to the act of state doctrine is the so-called "treaty" or "international law" exception. This exception is reflected in the Supreme Court's observation in *Sabbatino* that the act of state doctrine is applicable "in the absence of a treaty or other unambiguous agreement regarding controlling legal principles."[92] The apparent rationale for this suggestion is the fact that a treaty provides internationally accepted principles that are binding upon foreign states and

---

91. *See* Note, *Putting Meaning into the Treaty Exception to the Act of State Doctrine,* 17 Case W. Res. J. Int'l L. 107 (1985); Note, *A Treaty Exception to the Act of State Doctrine: A Framework for Judicial Application,* 4 B.U. Int'l L.J. 201 (1986).

92. 376 U.S. at 428.

that U.S. courts can apply without offending foreign sovereigns or resolving hotly disputed questions of international law. One of the few cases to apply the exception, *Kalamazoo Spice Extraction*, is excerpted below.

KALAMAZOO SPICE EXTRACTION CO. v. PROVISIONAL MILITARY GOVERNMENT OF SOCIALIST ETHIOPIA

729 F.2d 422 (6th Cir. 1984)

KEITH, CIRCUIT JUDGE. This is an appeal from a district court judgment, which dismissed appellant's counterclaim. The district court held that the act of state doctrine as interpreted by the Supreme Court in *Sabbatino*, precluded judicial inquiry into the validity of an expropriation by the Ethiopian government of shares in an Ethiopian business entity held by an American corporation.

Appellant, Kalamazoo Spice Extraction Company ("Kal-Spice") is an American corporation which, in a joint venture with Ethiopian citizens, established [in 1966] the Ethiopian Spice Extraction Company ("ESESCO"), ... an Ethiopian based corporation. Kal-Spice owned approximately 80% of the shares of ESESCO. Kal-Spice also contributed capital, built a production facility, and trained ESESCO's staff, which consisted of Ethiopian citizens. Production began in 1970. ... The Provisional Military Government of Socialist Ethiopia ("PMGSE") came to power in 1974. As part of its program to assure that Ethiopian industries would "be operated according to the philosophy of Ethiopian socialism," the PMGSE announced the seizure of "control of supervision and a majority shareholding" of a number of corporations, including ESESCO, in February 1975. As a result of the expropriation, Kal-Spice's ownership interest in ESESCO was reduced from 80% to approximately 39%.

In December 1975, the PMGSE established a Compensation Commission. The Commission's purpose was to compensate those claimants whose property had been expropriated. Kal-Spice claimed it was entitled to compensation of $11,000,000. In October 1981, the PMGSE offered Kal-Spice the equivalent of $450,000 in Ethiopian currency. Kal-Spice, however, has rejected the PMGSE's offer. The PMGSE contends that Kal-Spice should have accepted the offer because: 1) Kal-Spice retains an interest in ESESCO of approximately 40%; and 2) Kal-Spice carried expropriation insurance based on a total investment in ESESCO of less than $1,000,000.

A few months before the PMGSE's expropriation program, Kal-Spice, placed an order with ESESCO for the purchase of spices to be delivered to Kal-Spice in Michigan between November 1, 1974 and November 5, 1975. ESESCO shipped spices worth more than 1.9 million dollars to Kal-Spice. These shipments occurred in several installments, some before the February 3, 1975 seizure of ESESCO and some after that date. The post-expropriation shipments were drawn from inventories seized on the expropriation date. According to Kal-Spice, it continued to make payments for these shipments for a while after the expropriation until it realized that the PMGSE did not intend to compensate it for the expropriated property. ESESCO, now controlled by the PMGSE, filed a breach of contract action against Kal-Spice, demanding payment for goods received by Kal-Spice. Kal-Spice counter-claimed against ESESCO as the alter ego of the PMGSE, seeking, inter alia, damages for the expropriation of ESESCO. Once the suit reached the District Court of the Western District of Michigan, the court decided that the act of state doctrine precluded adjudication of the claims against the PMGSE based on the expropriation of Kal-Spice's interests. ...

The act of state doctrine is an exception to the general rule that a court of the United States, where appropriate jurisdictional standards are met, will decide cases before it by choosing the rules appropriate for decision from among various sources of law, including international law. ... [A]ppellant Kal-Spice, as well as the U.S. Departments of State, Treasury, Justice, and the American Bar Association, as amici curiae, request that this Court recognize a "treaty exception" to the act of state doctrine. According to appellant and amici, the following language in *Sabbatino* provides the basis for a treaty exception:

> [T]he Judicial Branch will not examine the validity of a taking of property within its own territory by a foreign sovereign government, extant and recognized by this country at the time of suit, *in the absence of a treaty or other unambiguous agreement regarding controlling legal principles,* even if the complaint alleges that the taking violates customary international law (emphasis added).

This language and the existence of a treaty between the United States and Ethiopia, asserts appellant and amici, require a "treaty" exception to the rule that a U.S. court will not exercise jurisdiction over a foreign sovereign for an act done by that sovereign within its borders. The treaty in existence between the United States and Ethiopia is the 1953 Treaty of Amity and Economic Relations ("Treaty of Amity"). Article VIII, paragraph two of that treaty provides:

> Property of nationals and companies of either High Contracting Party, including interests in property, shall receive the most constant protection and security within the territories of the other High Contracting Party. *Such property shall not be taken except for a public purpose, nor shall it be taken without prompt payment of just and effective compensation* (emphasis added).

Kal-Spice unsuccessfully argued before the district court that this treaty provision was the type referred to by the Supreme Court in *Sabbatino*, which would allow a court to exercise jurisdiction over a claim of expropriation of property by a foreign sovereign. Specifically, Kal-Spice alleged that the "prompt payment of just and effective compensation" provision of the Treaty of Amity set forth controlling legal principles which was [sic] referred to by the Supreme Court in *Sabbatino*.

The district court, however, did not agree with Kal-Spice's assertion. Instead, the district court agreed with the PMGSE's position that this provision of the treaty calling for the "prompt payment of just and effective compensation" was ambiguous. It found that this provision was "so inherently general, doubtful and susceptible to multiple interpretation that in the absence of an established body of law to clarify their meaning a court cannot reasonably be asked to apply them to a particular set of facts." The failure of the treaty to provide a controlling legal standard provided a possibility of conflict with the Executive Branch. It is this potential conflict, concluded the district court, that underlies the act of state doctrine.

We do not agree with the district court's decision that the provision of the treaty requiring payment of prompt, just and effective compensation fails to provide a controlling legal standard. To the contrary, we find that this is a controlling legal standard in the area of international law. As the appellant and amici correctly point out, the term "prompt, just, effective compensation" and similar terms are found in many treaties where the United States and other nations are parties. The Treaty of Amity is one of a series of treaties, also known as the FCN Treaties, between the United States and foreign nations negotiated after World War II. As the legislative history of these treaties indicates, they were adopted to protect American citizens and their interests abroad. Almost all of these treaties contain sections which provide for "prompt, adequate, and effective compensation," "just compensation," or similar language regarding compensation for expropriated property.

The U.S.-District Court for the District of Columbia used a treaty to find a "treaty exception" in *American International Group, Inc. v. Islamic Republic of Iran*, 493 F.Supp. 522 (D.D.C. 1980). There, several American insurance companies held investments in insurance companies doing business in Iran. After the Iranian revolution of 1979 the Iranian government nationalized the insurance industry, and did not compensate the American companies for their investments which had been expropriated. The American insurance companies subsequently brought suit seeking damages for the property that had been expropriated without compensation. The district court examined the 1957 Treaty of Amity between the United States and Iran, and concluded that the insurance companies were entitled to compensation. Specifically, the court examined Article IV, paragraph two, which stated:

> Property of nationals and companies of either High Contracting Party, including interests in property, shall receive the most constant protection and security within the territories of the other High Contracting Party, in no case less than that required by international law. *Such property shall not be taken except for a public purpose, nor shall it be taken without the prompt payment of just compensation.* Such compensation shall be in an effectively realizable form and shall represent the full equivalent of the property taken; and adequate provision shall have been made at or prior to the time of taking for the determination and payment thereof (emphasis added).

After examining the treaty the district court determined, *inter alia*, that the act of state doctrine did not preclude it from jurisdiction because the treaty was relevant, unambiguous, and set forth agreed-upon principles of international law, *i.e.*, a standard for compensation for the expropriated property.[93] Accordingly, the district court granted plaintiffs' motion for a partial summary judgment on the issue of liability as a result of the expropriation of their property without compensation by the Iranian government.

There is a striking similarity between the treaty in the present case and the one involved in *American International*. Both treaties contain similar provisions for compensation when property is expropriated by one of the nations that is a party to the treaty. Consequently, *American International* provides authoritative guidance to us on the use of the treaty exception, and illustrates the error of the district court's decision that the treaty in this case was too ambiguous to allow a court to exercise jurisdiction. ... Moreover, the Supreme Court's decision in *Sabbatino* ... requires a reversal of the district court decision ... :

> It should be apparent that the greater the degree of codification or consensus concerning a particular area of international law, the more appropriate it is for the judiciary to render decision regarding it, since the courts can then focus on the application of an *agreed principle* to circumstances of fact rather than on the sensitive task of establishing a principle not inconsistent with national interest or with international justice. [376 U.S. at 423.]

Numerous treaties employ the standard of compensation used in the 1953 Treaty of Amity between Ethiopia and the United States. Undoubtedly, the widespread use of this compensation standard is evidence that it is an agreed upon principle in international law. ... Additionally, there is a great national interest to be served in this case, *i.e.*, the recognition and execution of treaties that we enter into with foreign nations. Article VI of the Constitution provides that treaties made under the authority of the United States shall be the supreme law of the land. Accordingly, the Supreme Court has recognized that treaties, in certain circumstances, have the "force and effect of a legislative enactment." *See, e.g., Whitney v. Robertson*, 124 U.S. 190, 194 (1888). The failure of this court to recognize a properly executed treaty would indeed be an egregious error because of the position that treaties occupy in our body of laws.

Our decision that the 1953 Treaty of Amity makes the act of state doctrine inapplicable only begins this controversy. The district court must determine what rights, if any, the treaty confers upon Kal-Spice. We recognize that further proceedings will be an arduous task for all parties involved.

---

93. The district court also held that the act of state doctrine was inapplicable because the court was not deciding the validity of Iran's expropriation of the plaintiff's interest, but rather it was adjudicating the failure of Iran to provide compensation for the expropriated property in violation of international law. It was also decided that the act of state doctrine did not apply because of the commercial act exception of *Alfred Dunhill*. We decline, however, to reverse the district court on these additional grounds. Our decision to reverse the district court is based only upon the existence of a treaty between the United States and Ethiopia which may provide a basis for Kal-Spice to receive compensation.

Notes on Kalamazoo Spice

1. *Application of treaty exception.* Only a few lower court decisions have applied the treaty exception to the act of state doctrine. Some lower courts hold that existence of a treaty containing a controlling legal standard renders the act of state doctrine entirely inapplicable. *See Ramirez de Arellano v. Weinberger,* 745 F.2d 1500, 1540 (D.C. Cir. 1984), *vacated,* 471 U.S. 1113 (1985); *American Int'l Group v. Islamic Republic of Iran,* 493 F.Supp. 522, 525 (D.D.C. 1980), *vacated on other grounds,* 657 F.2d 430 (D.C. Cir. 1981); *Faysound Ltd. v. Walter Fuller Aircraft Sales, Inc.,* 1990 U.S. Dist. Lexis 14667 (E.D. Ark. 1990).

Other lower courts appear to consider the existence of an applicable treaty as only one factor relevant to a general balancing test to determine whether the act of state doctrine applies. *Callejo v. Bancomer, SA,* 764 F.2d 1101 (5th Cir. 1985); *IAM v. OPEC,* 649 F.2d 1354, 1358-59 (9th Cir. 1981), *cert. denied,* 454 U.S. 1163 (1982); *Sharon v. Time, Inc.,* 599 F.Supp. 538 (S.D.N.Y. 1984). Which approach is more consistent with *Sabbatino* and the policies underlying the act of state doctrine? Which approach is more consistent with *Environmental Tectonics* and the apparent status of the act of state doctrine as a choice of law rule?

2. *Scope of treaty exception. Kalamazoo Spice* holds that the treaty exception bars application of the act of state doctrine to at least some of Kal-Spice's claims. Does the court reach this conclusion simply because there was an applicable treaty provision providing a "controlling legal standard" or instead because there was an applicable treaty provision that contained an *unambiguous* legal standard? Note that the distinction is potentially critical. Was Article VIII(2) of the U.S.-Ethiopia Treaty of Amity "unambiguous"? Consider the final paragraph of the Court's opinion. Does it suggest that Article VIII is clearcut? One lower court has held that the treaty exception is applicable even if the agreement at issue is ambiguous. *Dayton v. Czechoslovak Socialist Republic,* 834 F.2d 203 (D.C. Cir. 1987). Is this consistent with *Sabbatino's* refusal to permit U.S. courts apply disputed issues of international law to foreign acts of state?

3. *Relevance of customary international law.* Could customary international law, rather than an "agreement," ever provide the basis for application of the "treaty" exception? Note that in *Sabbatino,* the Court required a "treaty or other unambiguous agreement regarding controlling legal principles." Although in some circumstances customary international law presumably could reflect an unambiguous agreement regarding international law principles, *Sabbatino* appears to have rejected any such possibility. If, as *Kalamazoo Spice* concludes, an ambiguous treaty provision may be applied, why can't an unambiguous rule of customary international law be applied?

4. *Human rights norms.* It has been suggested that certain customary international law principles are sufficiently well-established to warrant an exception to the act of the state doctrine. The best example of such suggestions occurs in the human rights context. Suppose foreign state officials brutally torture and murder a visiting U.S. citizen. The act of state doctrine articulated in *Sabbatino* would presumptively forbid U.S. courts from sitting in judgment on the foreign state's misconduct. Some authorities have argued, however, that customary international law forbids such human rights abuses, *see Restatement (Third) Foreign Relations Law* §§701-703 (1987), and that this provides an "unambiguous agreement" within the meaning of *Sabbatino.* Thus, comment c to §443 of the *Third Restatement* suggest that the act of state doctrine would not apply in the following circumstances: "A claim arising out of an alleged violation of fundamental human rights ... would ... probably not be defeated by the act of state doctrine, since the accepted international law of human rights is well established and contemplates external scrutiny of such acts." Recall, however, that international law restrictions on expropriation were both well-developed and clearly violated in *Sabbatino. See supra* p. 701.

If the treaty exception was *not* applicable where customary international law is involved, would there be any other way to avoid application of the act of state doctrine in cases involving human rights violations? *See Filartiga v. Pena-Irala,* 630 F.2d 876, 889 (2d Cir. 1980) (official torture not a public act of state).

5. *Rationale for distinction between treaties and customary international law.* Why are treaties and other international agreements treated so differently from customary international law under the act of state doctrine? Recall that "international law is part of our law." *The Paquete Habana,* 175 U.S. 677, 700 (1900). *See supra* p. 21. Why shouldn't U.S. courts therefore apply customary international law in the same way that they would apply a treaty?

6. *What agreements satisfy the treaty exception?* Could the "treaty" exception be triggered by a contract between a private party and a foreign state? Suppose that the contract incorporates international law prohibitions against expropriation? What if the contract contains choice of forum or arbitration clauses?

See Restatement (Third) Foreign Relations Law §443, comment e (1987) ("When a state has expressly subjected certain kinds of obligations to adjudication in the courts of another state, or to international arbitration ..., it may be said to have acknowledged that its acts with respect to those obligations ... are subject to international scrutiny; in such cases the justification for applying the act of state doctrine is significantly weaker. A dispute under a mining concession containing a clause calling for commercial arbitration in a neutral state would generally be considered to be arbitrable").

4. The Second Hickenlooper Amendment

The so-called Second Hickenlooper amendment[94] forbids any U.S. court from invoking "the federal act of state doctrine" in a case in which (1) "a claim of title or other right to property" (2) within the United States (3) is asserted on the basis of an act of state "in violation of the principles of international law." In addition, the amendment sets out specific principles of international law applicable in expropriation cases and provides that the act of state doctrine *should* apply if the president certifies to U.S. courts that application of the doctrine is required by U.S. foreign policy interests. Although the Hickenlooper amendment appears at first blush substantially to "overrule" *Sabbatino*, its effect has been otherwise.

Most U.S. courts have interpreted the Hickenlooper amendment narrowly and confined its application to a relatively limited class of cases. Courts have generally held that the amendment applies only if specific property directly involved in the allegedly unlawful foreign act of state is located in the United States.[95] Other courts have held that the amendment does not apply to the expropriation of "contract," as opposed to "property," rights.[96]

---

94. 22 U.S.C. §2370(e)(2) provides: "Notwithstanding any other provision of law, no court in the United States shall decline on the ground of the federal act of state doctrine to make a determination on the merits giving effect to the principles of international law in a case in which a claim of title or other right to property is asserted by any party including a foreign state (or party claiming through such state) based upon (or traced through) a confiscation or other taking after January 1, 1959, by an act of that state in violation of the principles of international law, including the principles of compensation and the other standards set out in this subsection: *Provided*, That this subparagraph shall not be applicable (1) in any case in which an act of a foreign state is not contrary to international law or with respect to a claim of title or other right to property acquired pursuant to an irrevocable letter of credit of not more than 180 days duration issued in good faith prior to the time of the confiscation or other taking, or (2) in any case with respect to which the president determines that application of the act of state doctrine is required in that particular case by the foreign policy interests of the United States and a suggestion to this effect is filed on his behalf in that case with the court."

95. *Banco Nacional de Cuba v. Chase Manhattan Bank*, 658 F.2d 875, 882 n.10 (2d Cir. 1981); *Compania de Gas de Nuevo Laredo v. Entex, Inc.*, 696 F.2d 322 (5th Cir. 1982), *cert. denied*, 460 U.S. 1041 (1983); *United Mexican States v. Ashley*, 556 S.W.2d 784 (Tex. 1977). *Compare Banco Nacional de Cuba v. First Nat'l City Bank*, 431 F.2d 394, 399-402 (2d Cir. 1970), *vacated*, 400 U.S. 1019 (1971) *and French v. Banco Nacional de Cuba*, 295 N.Y.S.2d 433 (1968); *Ramirez de Arellano v. Weinberger*, 745 F.2d 1500, 1541-42 n.180 (D.C. Cir. 1984), *vacated*, 471 U.S. 1113 (1985) ("It may be that a primary purpose of the statute was to prevent invocation of the act of state doctrine when property expropriated in a foreign country subsequently makes its way into the United States, but this was not the *sole* situation in which the amendment was to be activated.").

96. *Hunt v. Coastal States Gas Prod. Co.*, 583 SW.2d 322 (Tex.), *cert. denied*, 444 U.S. 992 (1979). *Compare West v. Multibanco Comermex, SA*, 807 F.2d 820 (9th Cir.), *cert. denied*, 482 U.S. 906 (1987); *Najarro de Sanchez v. Banco Central de Nicaragua*, 770 F.2d 1385 (5th Cir. 1985).

D. Foreign Sovereign Compulsion Doctrine

The so-called foreign sovereign compulsion doctrine provides, in broad terms, that State A generally may not require an individual or company to do an act on the territory of State B that would violate the laws of State B. Applying the doctrine, some U.S. courts have refused to interpret U.S. laws to apply extraterritorially to forbid conduct that was *required* by foreign states.[97]

Relatively few decisions have applied the foreign sovereign compulsion doctrine. One of the best known of these decisions is *Interamerican Refining Corp. v. Texaco Maracaibo, Inc.*, which is excerpted below. Also excerpted below are §441 of the *Restatement (Third) Foreign Relations Law* and §202 of the *Restatement (Second) Conflict of Laws.*

INTERAMERICAN REFINING CORP. v. TEXACO MARACAIBO, INC.

307 F.Supp. 1291 (D. Del. 1970)

WRIGHT, CHIEF JUDGE. This is an action arising under the United States antitrust laws, 15 U.S.C. §§1, 2, 15, commonly known as the Sherman and Clayton Acts. [Plaintiff Interamerican Refining Corp. ("Interamerican") is a company formed by prominent Venezuelan nationals apparently viewed with hostility by the Venezuelan government. Plaintiff sought to purchase crude oil from defendants Texaco Maracaibo, formerly the Superior Oil Co. of Venezuela ("Supven"), Monsanto Co. ("Monsanto"), Monsanto Venezuela ("Monven"), a wholly owned subsidiary of Monsanto, and Amoco Trading Corp. ("Amoco"), now survived by American International Oil Co. Plaintiff intended to export oil purchased from the defendants to the United States, where it was to be refined and reexported without incurring customs or other charges. After a few initial purchases, defendants allegedly refused to sell additional crude oil to plaintiff because the government of Venezuela prohibited such sales. When plaintiff was unable to escape from its lease agreement for a U.S. refinery to be used to process the Venezuelan crude oil, it brought this antitrust action against the defendants, alleging a concerted boycott in violation of the U.S. antitrust laws. The defendants sought summary judgment.]

Plaintiff insists that the evidence [raises] issues of fact requiring trial on the merits. If the evidence, when viewed in the light most favorable to plaintiff, discloses such issues, defendants' motion for summary judgment must be denied. *Continental Ore Co. v. Union Carbide & Carbon Corp.*, 370 U.S. 690 (1962). The Court concludes, however, for reasons hereinafter stated, that the undisputed facts demonstrate that

---

97. Several lower courts have apparently approved the doctrine of foreign sovereign compulsion as a defense in antitrust cases. *E.g., United States v. General Elec. Co.*, 115 F.Supp. 835, 878 (D.N.J. 1953); *United States v. Imperial Chem. Indus.*, 105 F.Supp. 215 (S.D.N.Y. 1952). *See* J. Atwood & K. Brewster, *Antitrust And American Business Abroad* §§8.14-8.23 (2d ed. 1985 & Cum. Supp.).

defendants were compelled by regulatory authorities in Venezuela to boycott plaintiff. It also holds that such compulsion is a complete defense to an action under the antitrust laws based on that boycott. ...

No party presents dispositive authority that such acts as occurred here do or do not immunize trade restraints otherwise illegal. The statement in *Sabre Shipping Corp. v. American President Lines, Ltd.*, 285 F.Supp. 949, 954 (S.D.N.Y. 1968), relied on by plaintiff, is not controlling. Judge Ryan's opinion, on a motion to dismiss, properly held that allegations that the unlawful activities were engaged in at the direction of the Japanese government were a matter for defense. His additional comment that if established such allegations might not immunize defendants, even if read literally, only reserves judgment on the conditions under which such direction might not be a defense.

Such conditions were present in *Continental Ore Co. v. Union Carbide and Carbon Corp.*, and *United States v. Sisal Sales Corp.*, 274 U.S. 268 (1927). In *Continental Ore*, Union Carbide's subsidiary, Electro Met of Canada, had been appointed by the Canadian government to be exclusive wartime purchasing agent for vanadium. That appointment did not immunize a conspiracy with the parent to monopolize vanadium production and sale. "Respondents are afforded no defense from the fact that Electro Met of Canada, in carrying out the bare act of purchasing vanadium from respondents rather than Continental, was acting in a manner permitted by Canadian law." In *Sisal Sales* defendants secured a monopoly through discriminatory legislation in Mexico and Yucatan. The Court held that inasmuch as the conspiracy was entered into and overt acts performed in this country, jurisdiction existed, and the legislation procured by the conspiracy was beside the point. "True, the conspirators were aided by discriminating legislation, but by their own deliberate acts, here and elsewhere, they brought about forbidden results within the United States."

Nothing in the materials before the Court indicates that defendants either procured the Venezuelan order or that they acted voluntarily pursuant to a delegation of authority to control the oil industry. The narrow question for decision is the availability of genuine compulsion by a foreign sovereign as a defense.

Defendants rely on dicta in *Continental Ore*,[98] and in *United States v. The Watchmakers of Switzerland Information Center, Inc.*, 1963 Trade Cas. 70,600 (S.D.N.Y.)[99] and on language in some consent decrees[100] to establish the defense. Without more, these would be scant authority. It requires no precedent, however, to

---

98. In *Continental Ore*, the Court pointed out that there was "no indication that the Controller or any other official directed that purchases from Continental be stopped." 370 U.S. at 706.

99. In *Watchmakers*, Judge Cashin held that a collective agreement could form a conspiracy notwithstanding that it was permitted by the laws of Switzerland. He added, "If, of course, the defendants' activities had been required by Swiss law, this Court could indeed do nothing." 1963 TRADE CAS. ¶70,600, at 77,456.

100. *See* the decrees in *United States v. Gulf Oil Corp.*, 1960 Trade Cas. ¶69,851 at 77,349 (S.D.N.Y.); *United States v. Standard Oil Co.*, 1960 Trade Cas. ¶69,849, at 77,340 (S.D.N.Y.).

acknowledge that sovereignty includes the right to regulate commerce within the nation. When a nation compels a trade practice, firms there have no choice but to obey. Acts of business become effectively acts of the sovereign. The Sherman Act does not confer jurisdiction on United States courts over acts of foreign sovereigns. By its terms, it forbids only anticompetitive practices of persons and corporations.[101] In his book, *Antitrust and American Business Abroad*, Professor (now President) Kingman Brewster states a proposition which should be self-evident. Anticompetitive practices compelled by foreign nations are not restraints of commerce, as commerce is understood in the Sherman Act, because refusal to comply would put an end to commerce. American business abroad does not carry with it the freedom and protection of competition it enjoys here, and our courts cannot impose them. Commerce may exist at the will of the government, and to impose liability for obedience to that will would eliminate for many companies the ability to transact business in foreign lands. Were compulsion not a defense, American firms abroad faced with a government order would have to choose one country or the other in which to do business. The Sherman Act does not go so far.

Plaintiff maintains that even if compulsion is a good defense, the acts of compulsion must be valid under Venezuelan laws. It urges the Court to consider the affidavit of a Venezuelan attorney to the effect that the Minister of Mines and Hydrocarbons had no authority to bar sales of crude oil to anyone and that no officer had authority to issue binding orders without putting them in writing and publishing them in the *Gazeta Official.* Since not legal, says plaintiff, the orders were not "compulsive."

This Court may not undertake such an inquiry. In *Sabbatino,* the Supreme Court held that it could not explore the validity under Cuban law of acts of expropriation by the Castro government. The act of state doctrine, based upon proper concepts of sovereignty and separation of powers, commands that conduct of foreign policy reside exclusively in the executive. For our courts to look behind the acts of a foreign government would impinge upon and perhaps impede the executive in that function. Whether or not Venezuelan officials acted within their authority and by legitimate procedures is therefore not relevant to the instant case. ...

Rule 56 of the Federal Rules of Civil Procedure provides that summary judgment may be rendered if the pleadings, depositions, answers to interrogatories and admissions on file, together with affidavits, if any, show that there is no genuine issue as to any material fact and that the moving party is entitled to judgment as a matter of law. [The Court examined the existing record and held that there was no genuine issue as to the Venezuelan government's requirement that sales to Interamerican be halted.] ...

---

101. This is analogous to the theory stated in *Parker v. Brown,* 317 U.S. 34 (1943), holding that compliance with a state regulatory program does not subject individuals to antitrust liability. The Sherman Act refers only to persons, not to states or nations, and both the Act and the Constitution would be badly misinterpreted to permit liability for acts of a sovereign.

The Court concluded earlier that for it to inquire into the validity of the acts of a foreign state would violate the act of state doctrine. Plaintiff now contends that whether or not action taken by the Ministry was "compulsive" is a question of fact. It urges that it be permitted to show at trial that the order was not binding because oral and without legal authority. For the same reasons as those announced above, whether the act was legal or "compulsive" under the laws of Venezuela is no more a proper inquiry for the jury than it is for the Court. Plaintiff correctly states that whether or not a foreign official "ordered" certain conduct is an evidentiary question. But the factual inquiry is limited to the existence of the officer and the order. Once governmental action is shown, further examination is neither necessary nor proper. ... The Court must conclude that the evidence relied on by plaintiff presents no issue of material fact and that trial is not necessary to resolve differing versions of the truth.

RESTATEMENT (THIRD) FOREIGN RELATIONS LAW (1987)

§441 *[excerpted at p. 505]*

RESTATEMENT (SECOND) CONFLICT OF LAWS (1971)

§202

§202.(1) The effect of illegality upon a contract is determined by the law selected by application of the rules of §§187-188.

(2) When performance is illegal in the place of performance, the contract will usually be denied enforcement.

Notes on Texaco Maracaibo and Restatements

1. *Foreign sovereign compulsion doctrine as canon of construction.* Is the foreign sovereign compulsion doctrine a rule of abstention, a constitutional limit on jurisdiction, or a canon for construing legislation? Suppose that the antitrust laws specifically provided: "The fact that conduct was compelled or required by a foreign state shall not be a defense under this section." If this provision had existed, would *Texaco Maracaibo* have been decided the same way? Is the foreign sovereign compulsion doctrine a rule of statutory construction, like the territoriality presumption?

2. *Foreign sovereign compulsion doctrine as rule of international law.* Is the foreign sovereign compulsion doctrine a rule of international law? The *Third Restatement* indicates that it is. *Restatement (Third) Foreign Relations Laws* 340 (1987) (citing U.S. authorities). If the foreign sovereign compulsion doctrine is a rule of international law, what effect does it have in state courts or on the application of state law? *See supra* pp. 21 & 541-44.

3. *Policies underlying foreign sovereign compulsion defense.* Several related policies underlie the foreign sovereign compulsion doctrine. First, the doctrine is rooted in notions that it is unfair to punish private entities that have been subjected to conflicting legal requirements. *Interamerican Ref. Corp. v. Texaco Maracaibo*, 307 F.Supp. 1291, 1298 (D. Del. 1970) ("[W]hen a nation compels a trade practice, firms there have no choice but to obey"); Competitive Impact Statement for Proposed Consent Judgment in *United States v. Bechtel Corp.*, 42 Fed. Reg. 3716, 3718 (Jan. 10, 1977); Wallace & Griffin, *The Restatement and Foreign Sovereign Compulsion: A Plea for Due Process*, 23 Int'l Law. 593 (1989) ("Due process should protect persons from punishment for conduct in which they were forced to engage").

Second, the foreign sovereign compulsion defense rests on principles of international comity akin to those underlying the act of state doctrine and the jurisdictional rule of reason. As one court has remarked,

U.S. courts have "no right to condemn the governmental activity of another sovereign nation." *Mannington Mills, Inc. v. Congoleum Corp.*, 595 F.2d 1287, 1292-94 (3d Cir. 1979). *See United States v. The Watchmakers of Switzerland Information Center*, 1963 Trade Cas. (CCH) ¶70,600, at 77,456 (S.D.N.Y. 1962) (if "defendant's activities had been required by Swiss law, this court could indeed do nothing. An American court would have under such circumstances no right to condemn the governmental activity of another sovereign nation"), *modified*, 1965 Trade Cas. (CCH) ¶71,352 (S.D.N.Y. 1965).

Third, where a foreign state compels conduct on its own territory, choice of law considerations argue for application of that state's law to the resulting conduct. *See supra* pp. 703 & 719.

Finally, the doctrine also rests on a practical perception that compliance with foreign governmental requirements is a condition to doing business abroad, and that the imposition of antitrust liability for such compliance would generally preclude U.S. companies from operating abroad. Competitive Impact Statement for Proposed Consent Judgment in *United States v. Bechtel Corp.*, 42 Fed. Reg. 3716, 3718 (Jan. 10, 1977); *Interamerican Ref. Corp. v. Texaco Maracaibo*, 307 F.Supp. 1291 (D. Del. 1970).

Why should violations of the antitrust laws or other important public legislation be immunized from liability merely because they were ordered by a foreign state? Aren't government-sponsored cartels or boycotts an even greater threat to the values of free competition protected by the Sherman Act than private cartels? Is this factor outweighed by concerns for fairness to private parties and respect for foreign sovereignty?

4. *Territorial limitations of foreign sovereign compulsion defense.* Suppose it was clear that the Venezuelan government had issued orders regarding petroleum sales or other conduct *within* the United States. Would foreign sovereign compulsion still be a valid defense? Most authorities answer in the negative. *See* U.S. Department of Justice, *Antitrust Enforcement Guidelines for International Operations* 97-102 (1988) (conduct must not have occurred "wholly or primarily" in U.S.); *Restatement (Third) Foreign Relations Law* §441 & comment b (1987); *Linseman v. World Hockey Ass'n*, 439 F.Supp. 1315, 1324-25 (D. Conn. 1977); *United Nuclear Corp. v. General Atomic Co.*, 629 P.2d 231, 263 (N.M. 1980), *cert. denied and appeal dismissed*, 451 U.S. 901 (1981). Note that in *Texaco Maracaibo* the defendant's conduct arguably occurred partially in the United States. The Department of Justice Antitrust Division has criticized the case on this ground. U.S. Department of Justice, *Antitrust Guide for International Operations* 51, 55 (1977).

What if State A compels a defendant to engage in anticompetitive conduct in State B? What if conduct compelled by State A within State A has direct and substantial effects on the United States? Should the doctrine of foreign sovereign compulsion apply? Compare the situs requirement of the act of state doctrine. *See supra* pp. 721-28.

5. *"Compulsion" requirement.* What sort of government action is required to trigger the foreign sovereign compulsion defense? It is clear that not all forms of government involvement with private conduct provide a basis for asserting the defense. A number of decisions have held that particular actions of foreign governments, such as approval of private conduct, did not amount to "compulsion." *See Continental Ore Co. v. Union Carbide & Carbon Corp.*, 370 U.S. 690 (1962) (Canadian government's award of exclusive franchise does not amount to compulsion to engage in other anticompetitive activities); *United States v. Sisal Sales Corp.*, 274 U.S. 268 (1927) (conspiracy in United States not immune merely because defendant succeeded in obtaining discriminatory Mexican tax and export legislation); *Williams v. Curtiss-Wright Corp.*, 694 F.2d 300, 303 (3d Cir. 1982); *Mannington Mills, Inc. v. Congoleum Corp.*, 595 F.2d 1287, 1293 (3d Cir. 1979) ("One asserting the defense must establish that the foreign decree was basic and fundamental to the alleged antitrust behavior and more than merely peripheral to the overall illegal course of conduct. ... Where governmental action rises no higher than mere approval, the compulsion defense will not be recognized. It is necessary that the foreign law must have coerced the defendant into violating American antitrust law. ... The defense is not available if the defendant could have legally refused to accede to the foreign power's wishes."); *Timberlane Lumber Co. v. Bank of America*, 549 F.2d 600 (9th Cir. 1976); *Outboard Marine Corp. v. Pezetel*, 461 F.Supp. 384, 398-99 n.29 (D. Del. 1978); *United States v. The Watchmakers of Switzerland Information Center*, 1963 Trade Cas. (CCH) ¶70,600, at 77,456-57 (S.D.N.Y. 1962) (Swiss government's approval of cartel not "compulsion").

Other authorities conclude that foreign sovereign compulsion requires the potential imposition of severe sanctions. *Restatement (Third) Foreign Relations Law* §441, comment c & Reporters' Note 4 (1987); U.S. Department of Justice, *Antitrust Enforcement Guidelines for International Operations* 97-102 (1988) (limiting defense to compulsion upon threat of "significant penalties" or loss of "substantial benefits," but recognizing possibility of comity-based defense in wider circumstances); *Texaco Maracaibo*, 307 F.Supp. at 1291.

Is it appropriate to draw this sharp distinction between conduct that is officially compelled and conduct that is merely approved or encouraged by a foreign government? Some commentators have rejected the distinction, on the grounds that nations often "implement important policies without compelling adherence to those policies by legal compulsion." *E.g.*, D. Rosenthal & W. Knighton, *National Laws and International Commerce* 28-29 (1982). In addition, U.S. concepts of governmental authority and compulsion may not accord with foreign cultural and economic realities, where governmental "suggestions" or "encouragement" may in fact be tantamount to binding orders.

The "state action" defense to liability under the domestic antitrust laws provides generally that private conduct will not be subject to antitrust liability if it was "authorized and actively supervised" by a U.S. state government. *Southern Motor Carriers Rate Conference, Inc. v. United States*, 471 U.S. 48, 64-65 (1985). Should the same degree of deference apply to conduct by foreign states? *See* Brief of the Governments of Australia, Canada, France, and the United Kingdom as Amici Curiae, *Matsushita Elec. Indus. Co. v. Zenith Radio Corp.*, 475 U.S. 574 (1986), *reprinted in*, 24 Int'l Leg. Mat. 1293 (1985).

6. *Legality of foreign compulsion under foreign law.* *Texaco Maracaibo* refused to consider whether the Venezuelan government's prohibition against sales to Interamerican was lawfully promulgated under Venezuelan law. For a contrary view, *see* U.S. Department of Justice, *Antitrust Guide for International Operations* 52, 54 (1977). Compare the treatment of the act of state doctrine, where U.S. courts inquire into the existence of an "act of state". *See supra* p. 709. Suppose alleged foreign sovereign compulsion is the result of action by a low-level official clearly without authority to speak for his government? *Compare* the discussion above of whether particular conduct by foreign government officials constitutes an act of state, *supra* pp. 710-12.

7. *Legality of foreign compulsion under international law.* What if it is argued that the foreign government's compulsion is a violation of international law? For example, suppose a foreign state requires private parties to engage in conduct that constitutes torture, genocide, or prohibited racial or religious discrimination. Does the foreign sovereign compulsion doctrine shield the private actors from liability in such cases?

8. *Legality of foreign sovereign compulsion under U.S. law.* Suppose that a foreign state's compulsive orders are not entitled to immunity under the FSIA — because they are commercial acts with a U.S. nexus. Suppose further that the foreign state's orders violate applicable substantive law. How does the foreign sovereign compulsion doctrine apply in such cases? Suppose that a foreign state compels conduct that violates fundamental U.S. public policies — for example, prohibitions against racial or religious discrimination. Consider the recent, post-*Aramco* amendments to Title VII, excerpted at *supra* p. 576.

9. *Foreign sovereign compulsion as an absolute defense.* *Texaco Maracaibo* apparently assumes that the foreign sovereign compulsion doctrine provides an absolute defense to an antitrust action, rather than merely being one factor that is relevant to antitrust jurisdiction and/or liability. As discussed *infra* pp. 871-94, foreign blocking statutes do not provide an absolute defense to failure to comply with U.S. discovery orders. Is there any basis for treating discovery and antitrust differently? Note that the jurisdictional rule of reason would presumably take into account the fact that a foreign government encouraged conduct alleged to violate the antitrust laws. *See supra* pp. 587-607.

10. *Application of foreign sovereign compulsion doctrine in suits by U.S. Government.* The U.S. Government has taken the position that the foreign sovereign compulsion defense does not apply to suits brought by the Government. *Brief of the United States as Amicus Curiae* at 23-24, *Matsushita Elec. Co. v. Zenith Radio Corp.*, No. 83-2004 (U.S. June 1985). What does this suggest about the Government's view of the policy reasons underlying the doctrine? What does the Government's position suggest about the status of the foreign sovereign compulsion doctrine as a rule of international law? Why shouldn't the foreign sovereign compulsion doctrine apply to Government suits?

11. *Comparison between foreign sovereign compulsion and extraterritorial discovery.* As discussed below, *infra* pp. 856-66, U.S. courts have long ordered parties subject to their personal jurisdiction to give discovery of materials located outside the United States. In some circumstances, foreign law, in the place where evidence is located, forbids compliance with U.S. extraterritorial discovery orders. Nevertheless, U.S. courts have frequently required parties to produce materials in violation of foreign law. Compare this to the foreign sovereign compulsion doctrine. Can the two approaches be reconciled?

12. *Inviting compulsion.* Suppose an antitrust defendant is shown to have requested a foreign gov-

ernment to compel it to take certain actions, in part to gain antitrust immunity. Although there is little direct precedent in the antitrust context, most authorities (including *Texaco Maracaibo*) suggest that the foreign sovereign compulsion defense would not be available in these circumstances. *United Nuclear Corp. v. General Atomic Co.*, 629 P.2d 231 (N.M. 1980), *cert. denied and appeal dismissed*, 451 U.S. 901 (1981); J. Atwood & K. Brewster, *Antitrust and American Business Abroad* §8.23 (2d ed. 1985 & Cum. Supp.). *Cf. Civil Aeronautics Bd. v. British Airways Bd.*, 433 F.Supp. 1379, 1387-88 (S.D.N.Y. 1977). Compare the significant sanctions that can result from efforts by litigants to procure foreign governmental prohibitions against disclosure of evidence for use in U.S. proceedings. *See infra* pp. 879-80.

13. *Historic approach to foreign sovereign compulsion.* Recall *Restatement (First) Conflict of Laws* §63 (1934), which permitted the extraterritorial assertion of legislative jurisdiction, based upon the nationality principle, but not if "the exercise of this jurisdiction involves the violation of the law or public policy of the state where the national is." Compare this rule with that in *Texaco Maracaibo*. Also compare *Restatement (Second) Foreign Relations Law* §40 (1965), which contemplated the existence of concurrent legislative jurisdiction, where two or more national laws "require inconsistent conduct upon the part of a person." Section 40 went on to require each state "to consider, in good faith, moderating the exercise of its enforcement jurisdiction," often balancing the competing national interests and other factors. *See supra* pp. 503-04 & 508-09. Compare this rule with that in *Texaco Maracaibo*.

14. *Applicability of foreign sovereign compulsion doctrine in state courts.* The leading judicial precedent directly relevant to the status applicability of the foreign sovereign compulsion doctrine in state courts is *United Nuclear Corp. v. General Atomic Co.*, 629 P.2d 231 (N.M. 1980), excerpted above, *supra* pp. 541-44. *United Nuclear* arose from a suit in New Mexico state court in which a U.S. company sought to be excused from its obligations to perform certain long-term uranium supply contracts on the grounds of fraud and violations of state antitrust laws. The plaintiff claimed that the defendants had participated in an international cartel to fix the prices of uranium on the world market and that this cartel violated New Mexico's unfair competition law. A central element of the defendant's response was that their conduct had been compelled by various foreign sovereigns, and that the act of state and foreign sovereign compulsion doctrines shielded them from liability.

The New Mexico Supreme Court rejected the defendants' claims. Acknowledging that the act of state doctrine "is a matter of federal law which is binding on state courts," the New Mexico court applied prevailing federal decisions and found the doctrine inapplicable. 629 P.2d at 257-59. *United Nuclear* also rejected the defendants' foreign sovereign compulsion argument; it did not specifically hold that the foreign sovereign compulsion defense is a rule of federal law, but it cited only to federal authorities, which it appeared to treat as binding precedents, 629 P.2d at 260-63, and its discussion of the subject was included as a part of its discussion of what it termed "the act of state doctrines." 629 P.2d at 266.

Moreover, *United Nuclear* later went on to consider the argument that "even if the act of state doctrines does not bar an American court from examining [the defendant's] cartel-related actions, the principle of exclusive federal power over the conduct of foreign relations nevertheless precludes an American *state* court from conducting such an examination." 629 P.2d at 266 (emphasis in original). The court rejected the argument that *Zschernig* precluded a state court from examining a private U.S. defendant's involvement in a cartel that had foreign sovereign involvement. But the court went out of its way to emphasize that it had "done no more than seek to enforce state laws which are consistent with federal laws" and the actions of the federal Executive and Legislative branches. *Id.*

Does the rationale underlying the foreign sovereign compulsion doctrine dictate its character as a rule of federal common law? The impact upon the Nation's foreign relations of disregarding foreign governmental orders relating to conduct within foreign territory is equally great whether a federal or a state court is involved. And the unfairness and disruption to U.S. foreign commerce is also unaffected by the status of the court that is involved. Do these reasons suffice to displace state law? *Compare supra* pp. 704-05. If the foreign sovereign compulsion doctrine is a rule of federal common law, is it merely a rule of statutory construction, or does it have a more binding effect on state law? Suppose that a state statute expressly penalizes or forbids conduct required by foreign law. Does a federal foreign sovereign compulsion doctrine forbid application of this state law?

Recall the discussion above of limits on state statutes that violate customary international law, on the grounds that international law is federal law that preempts state law. *See supra* pp. 21 & 541-44. Should the limits of §441 of the *Third Restatement* preempt state legislation that penalizes conduct required by foreign law?

15. *Extraterritorial application of the* Noerr-Pennington *doctrine.* Under domestic U.S. antitrust law, the so-called *Noerr-Pennington* doctrine generally shields companies from Sherman Act liability for competitive advantages obtained by lobbying or petitioning state or federal governments. *See United Mine Workers of America v. Pennington*, 381 U.S. 657 (1965); *Eastern R.R. Presidents Conf. v. Noerr Motor Freight*, 365 U.S. 127 (1961). The doctrine rests in part on first amendment concerns that might arise if the Sherman Act were applied to penalize lobbying efforts. The doctrine also reflects doubts that Congress meant for the antitrust laws to apply to lobbying activities, particularly since governmental acts are generally not subject to the antitrust laws.

Suppose a U.S. company gains a competitive advantage from a foreign government as a result of its foreign lobbying efforts. Does the *Noerr-Pennington* doctrine shield the company from antitrust liability? The U.S. Department of Justice has concluded that the doctrine should be applied extraterritorially. U.S. Department of Justice, *Antitrust Enforcement Guidelines for International Operations* 104 (1988). *See also Coastal States Marketing v. Hunt*, 694 F.2d 1358 (5th Cir. 1983). In contrast, several lower courts have held that the *Noerr-Pennington* doctrine does not apply to efforts to influence foreign governments. *See Bulkferts, Inc. v. Salatin, Inc.*, 574 F.Supp. 6 (S.D.N.Y. 1983); *Occidental Petroleum Corp. v. Buttes Gas & Oil Co.*, 331 F.Supp. 92, 107-08 (C.D. Cal. 1971), *aff'd*, 461 F.2d 1261 (9th Cir.), *cert. denied*, 409 U.S. 950 (1972). These decisions have reasoned that the first amendment does not apply to efforts to petition foreign governments, and therefore that a principal rationale for the *Noerr-Pennington* doctrine is absent in the international context. Is this a sufficient reason for refusing to apply the doctrine extraterritorially? *See also* Note, *The Noerr-Pennington Doctrine and the Petitioning of Foreign Governments*, 84 Colum. L. Rev. 1343 (1984); Comment, 58 St. John's L. Rev. 128 (1983).

16. *Illegality of contract.* Consider *Restatement (Second) Conflict of Laws* §202 (1971). What is the relation between the foreign sovereign compulsion doctrine and §202? When a U.S. court imposes damages on a party that has not performed its contractual obligations, because the foreign government at the place of performance forbid performance, does this implicate the foreign sovereign compulsion doctrine? Or is it just a question of which party bears the risk that the foreign government will take such action?

PART FOUR:
INTERNATIONAL JUDICIAL
ASSISTANCE[1]

International law prohibits a state from engaging in governmental activities within the territory of another state without that state's consent.[2] This principle applies to numerous aspects of international dispute resolution — including the service of process, the taking of evidence, and the enforcement of judgments. As a consequence, courts in one nation often cannot effectively proceed with an international litigation without the assistance of courts in other nations. The assistance that the courts of one state lend to courts or litigants of another state is referred to as "international judicial assistance."

International judicial assistance has long occurred even in the absence of treaties or other international agreements. Courts provided judicial assistance for reasons of what they termed comity:

> [The provision of international judicial assistance] appertains to the administration of justice in its best sense, and its exercise is now common and unquestioned among civilized nations. It is true that the duty may not be imposed by positive local law, but it rests on national comity, creating a that no state could refuse to fulfil without forfeiting its standing among the civilized states of the world.[3]

Thus, U.S. (and other) courts have long been willing to execute foreign "letters rogatory" seeking assistance in serving process or taking evidence, even in the absence of

---

1. Commentary on international judicial assistance includes, *e.g.*, B. Ristau, *International Judicial Assistance* (1990); Jones, *International Judicial Assistance: Procedural Chaos and a Program for Reform*, 62 Yale L.J. 515 (1953); Smit, *International Litigation Under the United States Code*, 65 Colum. L. Rev. 1015 (1965).

2. *Restatement (Third) Foreign Relations Law* 526 (1987).

3. *Oregon v. Bourne*, 27 P. 1048 (Or. 1891) (quoted in B. Ristau, *International Judicial Assistance* 3 (1990)).

treaty obligations to do so.[4] U.S. and other national courts have also long recognized and enforced the judgments of foreign courts, again without requiring any international agreement.[5]

Although international judicial assistance is possible without formal international agreements, the existence of such agreements generally improves cooperation among national courts. Thus, bilateral and multilateral treaties have been entered into by a number of states — including the United States — dealing with particular aspects of international judicial assistance. Most importantly for the United States, the Hague Service Convention and the Hague Evidence Convention deal with the service of process outside the United States and the taking of evidence located in foreign states.[6] Moreover, the United States is presently engaged in discussions in the Hague Conference on Private International Law[7] aimed at developing an international convention on the mutual recognition and enforcement of foreign judgments.[8] And the United States (and more than 100 other states) is already party to the New York Convention, providing for the recognition and enforcement of foreign arbitral awards.[9]

This Part examines the most significant aspects of international judicial assistance in U.S. civil litigation. Chapter 10 considers the service of process abroad in international disputes involving the United States. It examines the direct service of U.S. process on foreign defendants under Rule 4 of the Federal Rules of Civil Procedure and state counterparts, as well as the service of process abroad under the Hague Service Convention. It also discusses the use of customary letters rogatory as a means of serving process abroad with the assistance of foreign courts.

Chapter 11 examines the taking of evidence abroad and the discovery of materials located outside the United States.[10] It examines the direct discovery of materials located abroad under the Federal Rules of Civil Procedure, as well as the taking of evidence abroad under the Hague Evidence Convention. Chapter 11 also discusses the use of customary letters rogatory as a means of taking evidence abroad with the assistance of foreign courts.

Chapter 12 examines the recognition and enforcement of foreign judgments. This topic is not traditionally included within the category of "judicial assistance."[11]

---

4. *See infra* pp. 838-41 & 893-94.

5. *See infra* pp. 935-86.

6. *See infra* pp. 795-834 & 895-920.

7. *See infra* pp. 796-97, for a discussion of the Hague Conference.

8. *See infra* p. 938.

9. *See infra* pp. 990-91.

10. The "taking of evidence" often refers only to the formal reception of materials as evidence in a pending trial, while "discovery" is often defined more broadly to include "pre-trial" requests for information that may (and may not) be used as evidence at trial. Collins, *The Hague Evidence Convention and Discovery: A Serious Misunderstanding*, 35 Int'l & Comp. L. Q. 765 (1986).

11. *E.g.*, B. Ristau, *International Judicial Assistance* (1990) (not including recognition of foreign judgments); *Restatement (Third) Foreign Relations Law* Chapters 7 and 8 (1987) (treating international judicial assistance and recognition of foreign judgments as separate topics).

Nevertheless, the enforcement by one state of the judgment of the courts of another state fits squarely within the traditional rubric of international judicial assistance. Chapter 12 considers the standards under U.S. law for recognizing and enforcing judgments rendered by foreign courts.

Finally, Chapter 13 introduces international commercial arbitration, focusing particularly on the assistance that U.S. courts provide to the arbitral process. This topic is also not generally treated as a matter of international judicial assistance, but it can fairly be regarded as such. As Chapter 13 illustrates, U.S. courts often play a significant role in enforcing international arbitration agreements and international arbitral awards. In both respects, U.S. courts render judicial assistance to other tribunals — albeit private arbitral tribunals — engaged in international dispute resolution.

10/Service of U.S. Process on Foreign Persons[1]

U nder the laws of most nations, service of process must be effected upon the defendant in order either to commence a civil litigation or to take certain other significant procedural steps in a litigation. "Service of process" is the formal transmission of documents to a party involved in litigation, for the purpose of providing it with notice of claims, defenses, decisions, or other important matters.

In most domestic U.S. cases, the service of process is a fairly routine undertaking; it usually involves nothing more than the delivery of the plaintiff's complaint and summons to the defendant by a private process-server, or the mailing of these documents to the defendant by the plaintiff's lawyers. In contrast, the service of U.S. process in international cases can be difficult, slow, costly, and uncertain. The service of process abroad has been described as "a frequently lengthy, expensive and twisting process bordered on all sides with fatal pitfalls"[2] and "a tricky proposition."[3] This Chapter examines the service of process from U.S. courts on foreign persons.

A. Introduction and Historical Background

1. Choice of Law

Traditional U.S. choice of law rules provide that the manner for effecting service of process is governed by the law of the forum court.[4] Under this analysis, service of

---

1. Commentary on the service of process abroad includes, *e.g.*, 1 B. Ristau, *International Judicial Assistance* §§3-1 to 3-47 (1984 & Supp. 1990); Born & Vollmer, *The Effect of the Revised Federal Rules of Civil Procedure on Personal Jurisdiction, Service and Discovery in International Cases*, 150 F.R.D. 221 (1993); Committee on Federal Courts, N.Y. Bar Ass'n, *Service of Process Abroad: A Nuts and Bolts Guide*, 122 F.R.D. 63 (1989); Jones, *International Judicial Assistance: Procedural Chaos and a Program for Reform*, 62 Yale L. J. 515 (1953); Smit, *International Litigation Under the United States Code*, 65 Colum. L. Rev. 1015 (1965); Smit, *International Aspects of Federal Civil Procedure*, 61 Colum. L. Rev. 1031 (1961).

2. Horlick, *A Practical Guide to Service of United States Process Abroad*, 14 Int'l Law. 637, 638 (1980).

3. *Chowaniec v. Heyl Truck Lines*, 1991 U.S. Dist. Lexis 8138 (N.D. Ill. June 13, 1991).

4. *Restatement (Second) Conflict of Laws* §126 (1971) ("The local law of the forum determines the method of serving process and of giving notice of the proceeding to the defendant."); *Restatement (Third) Foreign Relations Law* §471(i) (1986); R. Leflar, L. McDougal & R. Felix, *American Conflicts Law* §§121-22 (4th ed. 1986).

757

process in federal courts is subject to Rules 4 and 4.1 of the Federal Rules of Civil Procedure. In particular, Rules 4(f) and 4(h)(2) of the Federal Rules provide a specialized regime governing the service of process outside U.S. territory.[5] In U.S. state courts, service of process must generally comply with local state law regarding service of process; state law occasionally contains special service mechanisms for service of process abroad, although often only generally applicable mechanisms are available.[6]

Although standard conflict of laws analysis asserts that the forum's law governs the service of process, other jurisdictions' laws are also relevant in international cases. First, where service of process must be made outside U.S. territory, the United States may be party to international agreements that supersede or supplement the Federal Rules of Civil Procedure and state service mechanisms. The Hague Service Convention and the Inter-American Convention on Letters Rogatory are the principal instances of such agreements. As discussed below, under these instruments, the laws of the state where service is effected can apply to the service of U.S. process abroad.[7]

Second, the laws of the place where service is effected can forbid particular service mechanisms, which may be permitted by the forum in which an action is pending. For example, as discussed below, many civil law jurisdictions impose strict limits on the service of foreign process.[8] These restrictions may make service in accordance with the forum's rules impossible as a practical matter. Violation of the laws of the place of service may also render service invalid (under the laws of the forum) or result in criminal or civil liability.[9]

Third, a foreign judgment will often not be recognized unless service on the defendant was made in accordance with the laws of the state where recognition is sought. Service in accordance with the laws of the forum may not be sufficient to satisfy those requirements.[10]

2. Service of Process in the United States: An Historical Overview

Service of process in the United States has undergone substantial evolution during this century. At common law, the service of civil process was accomplished by a writ of *capias ad respondendum*, which directed the local sheriff to locate the defendant and physically arrest him.[11] Doing so subjected the defendant to the local

---

5. *See infra* pp. 766-70.

6. *See infra* pp. 770-71.

7. *See infra* pp. 766-67 & 795-835.

8. *See infra* pp. 774-94.

9. *See infra* pp. 774-94.

10. The recognition and enforcement of foreign judgments in the United States is discussed below. *See infra* pp. 935-86.

11. *See* Miller, *Civil Procedure of the Trial Court in Historical Perspective* 76-78 (1952); Dodd, *Jurisdiction in Personal Actions*, 23 Ill. L. Rev. 427, 427-28 (1929); Levy, *Mesne Process in Personal Actions at Common Law and the Power Doctrine*, 78 Yale L. J. 52 (1968).

court's personal jurisdiction. In a very real sense, jurisdiction was based upon physical power.[12]

The use of physical arrest at English common law was gradually abandoned during the 18th century. Instead, the sheriff was authorized to "serve" the defendant with documents that "summoned" him to appear in court and defend against the plaintiff's claims.[13] Like physical arrest, personal service within the forum continued to be both necessary and sufficient to confer jurisdiction over the defendant.[14]

Courts in the 18th and 19th century United States adopted English common law approaches to service.[15] Service of process in the United States traditionally consisted of hand delivery to the defendant of the plaintiff's complaint, together with a summons. The summons was a document, usually issued by a court official, directing the defendant to answer the complaint.[16] Service on the defendant was generally effected by an official of the forum court, such as a sheriff or marshal.[17] Service of process within the forum's territory continued to be both sufficient and necessary to subject the defendant to personal jurisdiction.[18]

These traditional approaches to the service of process in the United States have significantly evolved in recent decades.[19] First, court officials have ceased to be primarily responsible for service of U.S. process. In 1983, the Federal Rules of Civil Procedure were amended to limit substantially the role of federal marshals in the service of process,[20] and to make the plaintiff responsible for serving its own complaint.[21] Under the Federal Rules, service today is often effected by the plaintiff's

---

12. *Cf. McDonald v. Mabee*, 243 U.S. 90, 91 (1917) ("the foundation of jurisdiction is physical power").

13. Dodd, *Jurisdiction in Personal Actions*, 23 Ill. L. Rev. 427, 427-28 (1929); Levy, *Mesne Process in Personal Actions at Common Law and the Power Doctrine*, 78 Yale L.J. 52 (1968).

14. For a more detailed discussion of the jurisdictional consequences of service during the 19th and early 20th centuries, and of the territorial limits on service, *see supra* pp. 70-73.

15. Kalo, *Jurisdiction as an Evolutionary Process: The Development of Quasi In Rem and In Personam Principles*, 1978 Duke L. J. 1147, 1150-53 & nn. 31-32; Miller, *Civil Procedure of the Trial Court in Historical Perspective* 76-78 (1952).

16. W. Alderson, *Law of Judicial Writs and Process* 225-26 (1895).

17. For example, until recently the Federal Rules of Civil Procedure provided for service of process from U.S. district courts to be made by federal marshals. *See* Sinclair, *Service of Process: Rethinking the Theory and Procedure of Serving Process Under Federal Rule 4(c)*, 73 Va. L. Rev. 1183, 1190-91 (1987).

18. *See supra* pp. 70-73; *Mississippi Publishing Corp. v. Murphree*, 326 U.S. 438, 44-45 (1946) ("Service of summons is the procedure by which a court having venue and jurisdiction of the subject matter of the suit asserts jurisdiction over the person of the party served.").

19. In addition to service by personal delivery to the defendant, other modes of service were also possible, including service by posting and publication. In general, such service would not be effective as to non-resident defendants located outside the forum's territory. *Pennoyer v. Neff*, 95 U.S. 714 (1878); *supra* pp. 70-73.

20. Sinclair, *Service of Process: Rethinking the Theory and Procedure of Serving Process Under Federal Rule 4(c)*, 73 Va. L. Rev. 1183, 1191 (1987).

21. The Federal Rules now expressly provide that service of the complaint and summons is the responsibility of plaintiff and not the court or any court official. Federal Rules of Civil Procedure, Rule 4(c)(1) ("The plaintiff is responsible for service of a summons and complaint. ...").

attorneys or by private firms specializing in the service of process — not by governmental officials.[22]

Second, service of process in the United States is no longer dominated by personal delivery to the defendant. The 1983 amendments to the Federal Rules of Civil Procedure permitted service by mail in certain cases. The new rules allowed the plaintiff, under some circumstances, to mail the defendant the complaint, summons, a notice of service and acknowledgement form, and a postage pre-paid envelope.[23] In order for mail service to be effective, the defendant was expected (but not required) to execute the acknowledgement form and return it to the plaintiff (or its counsel).

More recent amendments to the Federal Rules of Civil Procedure in 1993 further departed from the traditional service mechanism of personal delivery. The amendments established a "waiver of service" procedure, discussed below, which permits parties to dispense entirely with formal service of process. Plaintiffs enjoy broad freedom to select a method for transmitting requests for waiver of service of process, including by such mechanisms as mail, courier service, and telecopy transmission.[24]

Third, the jurisdictional consequences of service underwent substantial changes under U.S. law during the 20th century. As described in Chapter 2, personal service of process on the defendant within the forum's territory was both a necessary and sufficient requirement for personal jurisdiction in the United States for much of the 19th century. That is no longer the case. Because state long-arm statutes and the due process clause now permit personal jurisdiction over non-resident defendants based on their contacts with the forum state,[25] personal service within the forum has ceased to be a *necessary* requirement for personal jurisdiction.

Also as discussed in Chapter 2, effecting service of process has ceased to be a *sufficient* basis for personal jurisdiction. Thus, although service of process outside the forum's territory has become commonplace in 20th century U.S. litigation, it does not suffice to confer personal jurisdiction.[26] Indeed, even the efficacy of "tag" service *within* the forum's territory as an independently sufficient jurisdictional base has been challenged by some U.S. courts and commentators.[27]

---

22. Service may "be effected by any person who is not a party and who is at least 18 years of age." Federal Rules of Civil Procedure, Rule 4(c)(2).

23. Sinclair, *Service of Process: Rethinking the Theory and Procedure of Serving Process Under Federal Rule 4(c)*, 73 Va. L. Rev. 1183, 1191 (1987).

24. *See infra* pp. 769-70.

25. *See supra* pp. 73-77.

26. *See supra* pp. 73-77.

27. *See infra* pp. 121-22.

B. Contemporary U.S. Rules Governing Service of Process on Foreign Defendants

1. Service of Process in Federal Court Proceedings

a. Service of Complaint and Summons Under Rule 4 of the Federal Rules of Civil Procedure

In U.S. civil litigation, the principal classes of "process" that must be "served" are: (i) the summons and complaint, which commence an action;[28] (ii) the subpoena, which demands the giving of testimonial or documentary evidence,[29] and (iii) the notice, for example, of a deposition.[30] Different mechanisms may exist for the service of each of these classes of documents.[31]

At the outset of a civil litigation in U.S. district court, the defendant must ordinarily be served with a complaint and "summons." As discussed in Chapter 2, Federal Rule of Civil Procedure 4 provides that nonresident defendants will be "amenable" to service when applicable state or federal long-arm statutes authorize personal jurisdiction.[32] In addition, Rule 4 also plays a vital role in determining the "manner" or "mechanics" of service of a complaint on those foreign defendants who are amenable to a federal court's personal jurisdiction. Put differently, in addition to defining when a foreign defendant is subject to U.S. judicial jurisdiction, Rule 4 prescribes the mechanical process for notifying the defendant that an action against it has been commenced (*i.e.*, by requiring hand-delivery or sending by registered mail).[33]

Rules 4(a) and 4(b) of the Federal Rules of Civil Procedure prescribe the form and manner of issuance of the summons in federal court.[34] Under contemporary practice, the plaintiff's attorney prepares a summons that: (i) identifies the parties, the court, and the plaintiff's attorney; (ii) specifies the time that the defendant has to reply; and (iii) warns the defendant that, if it does not reply, a default judgment will result.[35] After the complaint in an action is filed, a summons in the action is presented to the clerk of the district court, for signature, and is sealed with the seal of the court.[36] Under Rule 4(c), both a copy of the complaint and the summons must be served upon the defendant (unless service is waived).[37]

---

28. *See* Federal Rules of Civil Procedure, Rule 4.

29. *See* Federal Rules of Civil Procedure, Rule 45.

30. *See* Federal Rules of Civil Procedure, Rules 5, 30(b).

31. *See* Federal Rules of Civil Procedure, Rules 4 and 4.1; D. Siegel, *Supplementary Practice Commentaries*, 28 U.S.C.A., Federal Rules of Civil Procedure, Rule 4, page C4-4 (1994).

32. *See supra* pp. 69-70 & 171-72.

33. *See supra* pp. 171-72 for a discussion of the distinction between "amenability" and "manner."

34. The contents of both documents, and the manner of service, is generally prescribed by the applicable procedural rules of the court in which the action is filed: in state courts, local rules of procedure generally apply. *See Restatement (Second) Conflict of Laws* §§126 & 127 (1971).

35. Federal Rules of Civil Procedure, Rule 4(a).

36. Federal Rules of Civil Procedure, Rules 4(a) and 4(b).

37. Federal Rules of Civil Procedure, Rule 4(c)(1).

b. Service of Summons and Complaint as a Jurisdictional Requirement Under the Federal Rules of Civil Procedure

As described above, service of process generally no longer provides a *sufficient* basis for personal jurisdiction, as it did at common law.[38] Nevertheless, service of process generally continues to be described as a jurisdictional *necessity*. Unless the defendant is properly served, or waives service, a U.S. court ordinarily cannot exercise personal jurisdiction over the defendant.[39] In the words of one court: "Personal jurisdiction is a composite notion of two separate ideas: amenability to jurisdiction ... and notice to the defendant through valid service of process."[40]

c. Service of Complaint and Summons as a Means of Notice Under the Federal Rules of Civil Procedure

The principal function of service under the contemporary Federal Rules of Civil Procedure is notification to the defendant. The traditional common law function of service — that is, conferring personal jurisdiction — now exists only in the relatively rare cases of tag service within the forum's territory.[41] In most contemporary cases, the function of service of the complaint is to inform the defendant of the commencement of an action against him and the nature of the plaintiff's claims.[42] "The purpose of the summons is to give notice to the defendant that it has been sued."[43] Likewise, service of the summons provides the defendant with an opportunity to respond to the plaintiff's claims before coercive judicial action is taken.

d. Service as Commencing an Action and Tolling Statutes of Limitations Under the Federal Rules of Civil Procedure

The date of service of process can have important timing consequences. First, it generally provides the basis for calculating the time in which the plaintiff has to answer the complaint.[44] Second, service can also have important consequences for statute of limitations purposes. In the words of one commentator on Federal Rule of Civil Procedure 4:

> [T]he rule is enmeshed, atomically fused, with the limitations' subject. Indeed, from a practical viewpoint the phenomenon, and perhaps the only

---

38. *See supra* pp. 73-77.

39. *Omni Cap. Int'l v. Rudolf Wolff & Co.*, 484 U.S. 97 (1987).

40. *Soltex Polymer Corp. v. Fortex Indus., Inc.*, 590 F.Supp. 1453, 1456 (E.D.N.Y. 1984).

41. *See supra* pp. 116-23.

42. *See Volkswagenwerk AG v. Schlunk*, 486 U.S. 694, 700 (1988) ("Service of process refers to a formal delivery of documents that is legally sufficient to charge the defendant with notice of a pending action."); *Mullane v. Central Hanover Bank & Tr. Co.*, 339 U.S. 306 (1950); *Milliken v. Meyer*, 311 U.S. 457 (1940).

43. *Grooms v. Greyhound Corp.*, 287 F.2d 95, 97-98 (6th Cir. 1961). As discussed below, the due process clause imposes constitutional requirements of reasonable notice, which service of process must fulfill. *See infra* pp. 771-73.

44. Federal Rules of Civil Procedure, Rule 12(a)(1)(A).

one, that gives moment to mistakes made under Rule 4 is the statute of limitations.[45]

Rule 3 of the Federal Rules of Civil Procedure provides: "A civil action is commenced by filing a complaint with a court." The Supreme Court has squarely held that, in federal question cases where a substantive federal claim is asserted, Rule 3 provides a federal rule tolling any applicable statute of limitations by the filing — not the service — of a complaint.[46]

Under the laws of some states, however, the filing of a complaint with a state court does not toll applicable statutes of limitations; in these jurisdictions, only the effective service of the complaint and summons upon the defendant tolls applicable limitation periods. The Supreme Court has held that, in diversity of citizenship cases, where state law claims are asserted and no federal statute of limitations exists, state statutes of limitations and tolling rules apply.[47] Accordingly, mere filing of a complaint in such diversity cases does not toll applicable statutes of limitations, unless that is what state law provides. "[I]f under forum state law the action is not deemed commenced until, for example, the summons is served on the defendant, the diversity plaintiff must be sure not only to file the complaint within the applicable statute of limitations, but also see to it that the summons is actually served on the defendant before the statute expires."[48]

2. Mechanisms for Serving Foreign Defendants With U.S. Process Within the United States

It is often possible to service a foreign defendant within the United States, rather than in its home jurisdiction. U.S. precedent has long permitted such service, without imposing any requirement that foreign defendants be served at their foreign residence or principal place of business.[49] This is as true under the Hague Service Convention as it is under the Federal Rules.[50] In order to serve a foreign defendant within the United States with process from a U.S. court, applicable U.S. law must provide a mechanism for service that can as a practical matter be used. Both the Federal Rules of Civil Procedure and state law offer a variety of potentially effective service mechanisms.

The most obvious circumstance in which service abroad can be avoided under U.S. law is when an individual foreign defendant is physically present within the

---

45. D. Siegel, *Supplementary Practice Commentaries,* 28 U.S.C.A., Federal Rules of Civil Procedure, at C4-45 (1994).

46. *West v. Conrail,* 481 U.S. 35 (1987).

47. *Walker v. Armco Steel Corp.,* 446 U.S. 740 (1980).

48. D. Siegel, at *Supplementary Practice Commentaries,* 28 U.S.C.A., Federal Rules of Civil Procedure, C4-40 (1994).

49. *E.g., Silvious v. Pharaon,* 54 F.3d 697 (11th Cir. 1995) (new Rule 4(f) does not require service on foreign defendant outside the United States).

50. *Volkswagenwerk AG v. Schlunk,* 486 U.S. 694 (1988); *infra* pp. 822-34.

forum and can be personally served there.[51] Service by personal delivery within the forum state is permitted under the laws of all the states,[52] and the Federal Rules.[53] It may also be possible, depending upon local law, to effect service upon foreign corporations or other legal persons by serving their officers or directors within the forum.[54]

The need for service of process abroad may also be avoided, at least under U.S. law, if a foreign defendant has appointed an agent to receive service of process within the forum. Rule 4(h)(1) of the Federal Rules of Civil Procedure permits service within the United States upon domestic and foreign corporations either: (a) as authorized by state law (in either the state where the district court is located or in the state where service is effected);[55] or (b) "by delivering a copy of the summons and of the complaint to an officer, a managing or general agent, or to any other agent authorized by appointment or by law to receive service of process..." Rule 4(e)(2) also permits service upon individuals within the United States by means of service upon their agents. There is substantial lower court precedent concerning the status of particular persons or entities as agents under Rule 4.[56]

Both federal law and the laws of most states permit service upon foreign (and other) defendants by means of service upon closely-affiliated persons or entities. The primary example of this type of service involves service upon a parent company by means of service upon its subsidiary.[57] Typically, such service requires proof of an alter ego or common law agency relationship between the parent and subsidiary.[58] Where such a relationship exists, applicable U.S. law will often permit service upon a foreign parent company by means of service on a local subsidiary.[59]

Individuals may sometimes retain their foreign nationality while acquiring U.S. residences. These individuals can occasionally be served by delivering process to their U.S. residence. Rule 4(e)(2) permits service upon individuals within the United

---

51. As discussed above, service within the forum may sometimes confer personal jurisdiction as well as avoid the need for service abroad. That is arguably true under new Rule 4(k)(2) of the Federal Rules of Civil Procedure, as well as under state law. *See supra* pp. 116-23 & 196.

52. R. Casad, *Jurisdiction in Civil Actions* §3.01[1] (2d ed. 1991).

53. Federal Rules of Civil Procedure, Rule 4(f).

54. *See infra* pp. 764-65 & 831-33.

55. Many state laws permit service of process on corporate and individual defendants by means of service upon agents authorized by appointment or by law. *See* R. Casad, *Jurisdiction in Civil Actions* - (2d ed. 1991)

56. *See* R. Casad, *Jurisdiction in Civil Actions* §3.01[2] (2d ed. 1991); C. Wright & A. Miller, *Federal Practice and Procedure* §§1102-03 (1987).

57. R. Casad, *Jurisdiction in Civil Actions* §3.02[2][6][ix] (2d ed. 1991); C. Wright & A. Miller, *Federal Practice and Procedure* §1069 (1987).

58. The standard that must be satisfied in order to establish an alter ego or agency relationship differs from state to state. *See supra* pp. 152-56 & 163-64. In addition, the due process clause imposes restrictions upon both the authority of a state to assert judicial jurisdiction based upon a parent-subsidiary or other corporate affiliation and the use of substituted service to provide the defendant with notice of an action. *See supra* pp. 160 & 163 and *infra* pp. 771-73.

59. *E.g., Volkswagenwerk AG v. Schlunk*, 486 U.S. 694 (1988).

States by "delivering copies [of the complaint and summons] at the individual's dwelling house or usual place of abode with some person of suitable age and discretion then residing therein." Determining whether a foreign defendant's residential property in the United States constitutes a "dwelling house" or "usual place of abode" can raise issues of interpretation.[60]

3. No Service of U.S. Process Abroad by U.S. Consuls

Before examining U.S. mechanisms for service outside U.S. territory, it is useful to note one conceivable avenue for service abroad that is *not* available. The U.S. Department of State and U.S. embassies virtually never serve process abroad on behalf of private litigants in U.S. courts. Indeed, current U.S. Consular Regulations explicitly prohibit foreign service officers from serving U.S. process abroad unless specifically authorized by the Department of State.[61] U.S. consular officers are precluded by these regulations from serving process even where local foreign law, or a bilateral U.S. treaty, would permit them to.[62]

4. Service of U.S. Process Abroad Under Old Rule 4(i) of the Federal Rules of Civil Procedure

Until recently, the service of process outside U.S. territory was governed in federal courts by Rule 4(i) of the Federal Rules of Civil Procedure. Old Rule 4(i) was added to the Federal Rules in 1963, as part of a comprehensive effort to improve federal law in international procedural matters.[63] The Rule was one of a series of proposals of the Commission on International Rules of Judicial Procedure, a body established by Congress in 1958 at the President's recommendation.[64] Concluding that "existing means for serving judicial documents abroad [are] cumbersome or insufficient,"[65] Congress directed the new Commission to study international judicial assistance and recommend improvements.[66]

The Commission recommended what became old Rule 4(i) as part of a general

---

60. *See National Development Co. v. Triad Holding Corp.*, 930 F.2d 253 (2d Cir. 1991).

61. 22 C.F.R. §92.85 provides that "The service of process and legal papers is not normally a Foreign Service function. Except when directed by the Department of State, officers of the Foreign Service are prohibited from serving process or legal papers or appointing other persons to do so." State Department authority is generally granted only in exceptional cases involving governmental litigation.

62. The United States is party to various treaties that would permit U.S. consuls from serving process abroad. *E.g.*, Hague Service Convention, Article 8; *infra* pp. 809-12. U.S. consular regulations do not permit use of the avenues permitted by treaty. *See infra* p. 809.

63. *See* Amram, *The Proposed International Convention on the Service of Documents Abroad*, 51 A.B.A.J. 650, 650-51 (1965); Kaplan, *Amendments of the Federal Rules of Civil Procedure, 1961-63 (I)*, 77 Harv. L. Rev. 633, 635 (1964).

64. *See* Act of Sept. 2, 1958, 72 Stat. 1743, 1744 (1958); S. Rep. No. 2392, 85th Cong., 2d Sess. at 3 (1958), *reprinted in*, 1958 U.S. Code Cong. & Admin. News at 5202; Jones, *Commission on International Rules of Judicial Procedure*, 8 Am. J. Comp. L. 341 (1959).

65. S. Rep. No. 2392, 85th Cong., 2d Sess. at 2, *reprinted in* 1958 U.S. Code, Cong. & Admin, News at 5202.

66. *Id.* at 1-2, *reprinted in* 1958 U.S. Code, Cong. & Admin. News at 5201.

effort to liberalize the rules governing the service of process in international cases.[67] Old Rule 4(i) did so by providing plaintiffs with five alternative mechanisms for service abroad:[68] (i) service as provided by local law; (ii) service by personal delivery; (iii) service by letter rogatory; (iv) service by mail, return-receipt requested; and (v) service as directed by court order. These mechanisms supplemented other service mechanisms that might have been available under Rule 4. Rule 4(i) left the plaintiff entirely free to choose whichever mechanism or combination of mechanisms it desired, without imposing any requirements or preferences for particular means of service and without requiring compliance with foreign law.[69]

5. Service of U.S. Process Abroad on Foreign Defendants Under New Rule 4(f) of the Federal Rules of Civil Procedure

Rule 4 of the Federal Rules of Civil Procedure was extensively revised in 1993.[70] Rule 4(i)'s provisions regarding service of process abroad were replaced by new Rule 4(f). As discussed in detail below, Rule 4(f) differs substantially from its pre-1993 counterpart.[71] New Rule 4(f) is reprinted in Appendix C.

a. Rule 4(f)(1): Service Abroad Pursuant to Hague Service Convention and Other "Internationally Agreed Means"

Rule 4(f)(1) begins by providing that service abroad may be made "by any internationally agreed means reasonably calculated to give notice, such as those means authorized by the Hague Convention on the Service Abroad of Judicial and Extrajudicial Documents." Rule 4(f)(1) had no counterpart in old Rule 4(i), which contained no reference to the Hague Service Convention or other international agreements. The drafters of new Rule 4(f)(1) intended the provision to "call[] attention to the important effect of the Hague Convention and other treaties bearing on service of documents in foreign countries."[72]

Rule 4(f)(1) applies to "international agreed means" of service. The provision specifically refers to the means authorized by the Hague Service Convention, which is reproduced in Appendix I and discussed below.[73] In addition, Rule 4(f)(1) refers more generally to internationally "agreed" means, while the Advisory Committee Notes explain that the provision applies to "an applicable treaty" or "international

---

67. Kaplan, *Amendments of the Federal Rules of Civil Procedure, 1961-1963 (I)*, 77 Harv. L. Rev. 633, 635 (1964).

68. Federal Rules of Civil Procedure, Rule 4(i), Advisory Committee Notes to the 1963 Amendments.

69. *See* G. Born & D. Westin, *International Civil Litigation in United States Courts* 163-68 & 171-79 (2d ed. 1992).

70. *See supra* pp. 69-70.

71. *See infra* pp. 766-70.

72. Federal Rules Civil Procedure, Rule 4, 28 U.S.C.A., Advisory Committee Notes, at 115.

73. *See infra* pp. 795-834.

agreement." This encompasses the Inter-American Convention on Letters Rogatory, but apparently no other international agreement.[74]

In certain cases, Rule 4(f) *requires* the use of "internationally agreed means" to effect service of process abroad. Rule 4(f)(2) provides that "*if* there is no internationally agreed means of service or the applicable international agreement allows other means of service," then specified other means may be used.[75] The Advisory Committee Notes to Rule 4 elaborate that internationally agreed means under Rule 4(f)(1) "*shall be* employed if available and if the treaty so requires."[76]

Under Rule 4, it appears that a plaintiff is required to use an "internationally agreed means" of service pursuant to Rule 4(f)(1) if two conditions are satisfied. First, in order for service to be required pursuant to "internationally agreed means" under Rule 4(f)(1), the relevant international method must be "available." That is, there must be an international method, to which both the United States and the relevant foreign country are parties, and which encompasses the plaintiff's action. Second, the relevant international agreement must prescribe the "exclusive" means of service; the agreement must forbid service in ways not specified by its terms.

Where service abroad is concerned, the Hague Service Convention satisfies these requirements. As described below, Article 1 of the Convention provides that the Convention "shall apply" in certain cases, and the Supreme Court has said that "compliance with the Convention is mandatory in all cases to which it applies."[77] Although the Convention allows the use of specified alternative service mechanisms, set forth in the Convention, it does not permit resort to other means not contemplated by the Convention.[78]

In contrast, the Inter-American Convention on Letters Rogatory is not exclusive, but merely available as one possible option for service abroad.[79] In such cases, Rule 4(f) does not require that the Inter-American Convention be used (although Rule 4(f)(1) authorizes its use as an option). No other international agreement of the United States appears to provide an exclusive mechanism for service.

b. Rule 4(f)(2): Alternative Mechanisms of Service Abroad

If no "internationally agreed means" of service is available under Rule 4(f)(1), or if such a means is non-exclusive, then Rule 4(f)(2) sets out additional alternatives

---

74. Unlike many nations, the United States has not concluded any bilateral service treaties. If it were to do so, Rule 4(f)(1) would appear to encompass them. It is not clear whether "internationally agreed means" include means set forth in contractual provisions in international commercial contracts relating to the service of process. Although a literal reading of Rule 4(f)(1) suggests it could extend to private agreements as well as treaties, there is no evidence in the Rule's legislative history that this was intended.

75. *See infra* pp. 767-68.

76. Federal Rules Civil Procedure, Rule 4, 28 U.S.C.A., Advisory Committee Notes, at 115 (emphasis added).

77. *Volkswagenwerk AG v. Schlunk*, 486 U.S. 694, 705 (1988); *infra* pp. 804-09.

78. *See infra* pp. 804-09.

79. *Pizzabiocche v. Vinelli*, 772 F.Supp. 1245 (M.D. Fla. 1991).

which may be used. There are several circumstances in which Rule 4(f)(2) will be applicable.

First, Rule 4(f)(2) applies if service is to be made in a nation that is not a signatory to the Hague Service Convention. This is true of a substantial majority of foreign states.

Second, Rule 4(f)(2) is applicable if service is to be made in a nation that is a signatory to the Inter-American Convention or another non-exclusive service agreement. That is because such international agreements "allow[] other means of service" than the mechanisms they establish.

Third, Rule 4(f)(2) is applicable in cases which fall outside the scope of the Hague Service Convention.[80] In these cases, there is no applicable "internationally agreed means," and service under Rule 4(f)(2) is permitted.

Fourth, Rule 4(f)(2) is arguably applicable to permit types of service that are not "authorized" by the Hague Service Convention, but that are "allowed" by it. This possibility is discussed below.[81]

Where it is applicable, Rule 4(f)(2) sets forth a number of options for service abroad. These are: (i) service in the manner permitted by foreign law; (ii) service as directed by a foreign authority; (iii) service by personal delivery to an individual (but not a corporation), unless prohibited by foreign law; and (iv) service by return-receipt mail, unless prohibited by foreign law. Rule 4(f)(2) imposes no preferences or hierarchy among these various mechanisms. Unlike old Rule 4(i), all of the options require compliance with foreign law in the place where the service is affected.[82]

c. Rule 4(f)(3): Service as Directed by District Court

New Rule 4(f)(3) permits service as ordered by the district court. This provision is similar to old Rule 4(i)(1)(E), except that the new rule expressly provides that the method of service may not be "prohibited by international agreement." Under new Rule 4(f)(3) a court may order any method "not explicitly authorized by international agreement if not prohibited by the agreement."[83]

The literal terms of Rule 4(f)(3) do not expressly forbid a district court from ordering service abroad in violation of foreign law. The Advisory Committee Notes also fairly clearly indicate an intention that courts may order service in violation of foreign law.[84] Rule 4(f)(3) does, however, appear to withhold from district courts the power to order service in violation of the Hague Service Convention.[85]

---

80. *See infra* pp. 800-01 for a discussion of the scope of the Hague Service Convention.
81. *See infra* pp. 808-09.
82. *See infra* pp. 791-94.
83. Federal Rules Civil Procedure, Rule 4, 28 U.S.C.A., Advisory Committee Notes, at 115.
84. Federal Rules Civil Procedure, Rule 4, 28 U.S.C.A., Advisory Committee Notes, at 115.
85. *See infra* pp. 808-09.

6. Waivers of Service Under New Rule 4(d)

Revised Rule 4(d) of the Federal Rules sets forth new "waiver of service" provisions, which were designed to reduce the expense and delay resulting from service of process. The new rule permits both domestic and foreign defendants to be asked to waive service. According to the Advisory Committee Notes: "The aims of the provision are to eliminate the costs of service of a summons on many parties and to foster cooperation among adversaries and counsel."[86]

Rule 4(d) allows a plaintiff to send a defendant by "first class mail or other reliable means" a complaint, a written request that the defendant waive formal service of process, and specified additional information.[87] Rule 4(d)(1) makes it clear that waiver of "service of a summons does not thereby waive any objection to the venue or to the jurisdiction of the court over the person of the defendant."

The new waiver of service procedure contains timing provisions intended to encourage defendants to waive service. Under new Rule 4(d)(2), a defendant has "a reasonable time to return the waiver, which shall be at least 30 days from the date on which the request is sent, or 60 days from that date if the defendant is addressed outside any judicial district of the United States."[88] A defendant who "timely" returns a waiver is allowed 60 days from the date on which the request for the waiver was sent in which to answer the complaint; defendants outside the United States are permitted 90 days from the dispatch of the waiver request.[89] In contrast, a defendant that refuses to waive formal service has only 20 days from service of the complaint.[90]

Revised Rule 4(d) creates a legal "duty to avoid unnecessary costs of serving the summons."[91] Rule 4(d)(2) authorizes district courts to impose sanctions for a defendant's refusal to waive service. The rule provides: "If a defendant located within the United States fails to comply with a request for waiver made by a plaintiff located in the United States, the court shall impose the costs subsequently incurred in effecting service on the defendant unless good cause for the failure be shown." Under new Rule 4(d)(5), legal fees are not part of recoverable costs except for the legal fees associated with a motion to collect the costs of service.[92]

Rule 4(d)'s waiver of service mechanism is available for use with foreign defen-

---

86. 146 F.R.D. 561.

87. Federal Rules of Civil Procedure, Rule 4(d)(2). New Rule 4(d)(2) provides: "To avoid costs, the plaintiff may notify [a defendant subject to service under Rule 4] of the commencement of the action and request that the defendant waive service of a summons." It goes on to prescribe the contents of requests for waivers of service, which are reflected in new Form 1A promulgated under Rule 84, and also requires that the request for waiver be "dispatched through first-class mail or other reliable means" and be accompanied by copies of the summons and the complaint. In addition, requests for waivers are to be accompanied by waiver forms (for example, as provided by new Form 1B).

88. Federal Rules of Civil Procedure, Rule 4(d)(2)(F).

89. Federal Rules of Civil Procedure, Rules 4(d)(3), 12(a)(1)(B).

90. Federal Rules of Civil Procedure, Rule 12(a)(1)(A).

91. Federal Rules of Civil Procedure, Rule 4(d)(2).

92. The Committee Notes allude to the same point. Federal Rules Civil Procedure, Rule 4, 28 U.S.C.A., Advisory Committee Notes, at 115.

dants. Waivers of service can be sought from any defendant that is subject to service under Rules 4(e), (f) or (h). This includes foreign individuals, corporations, and associations. Indeed, the Advisory Committee Notes encourage foreign defendants to agree to waive formal service of process.[93]

Previous proposed versions of Rule 4 did not limit Rule 4(d)'s cost-shifting provision to "defendant located within the United States"; they authorized the imposition of service costs on foreign as well as domestic defendants.[94] Foreign states objected to this, ultimately leading to the inclusion of limits in Rule 4(d). Although the final text of Rule 4 does not explicitly state that service costs may not be imposed on foreign defendants and although *all* defendants have a legal duty to avoid unnecessary costs of service, Rule 4(d)(2) clearly does not grant district courts discretion to impose service costs on a defendant outside of the United States.[95]

The cost-shifting provision applies only when *both* the plaintiff and the defendant are located within the United States. Thus, foreign plaintiffs may not benefit from Rule 4(d)(2)'s cost-shifting rule. If a Swedish plaintiff unsuccessfully requests a Californian defendant to waive service, Rule 4(d)(2)'s cost-shifting provision does not apply. The Committee Notes do not explain this limitation, although it is presumably a "sauce for the gander" reaction to foreign objections to shifting service costs.[96]

7. Service of Process on Foreign Defendants in Contemporary State Court Proceedings

Local state laws governing the service of process on a foreign defendant in a state court civil action vary from state to state. A number of states have adopted statutes or rules of court that are broadly similar to the pre-1993 version of Rule 4(i) of the Federal Rules of Civil Procedure.[97] A number of other states have adopted some version of §§2.01 and 2.02 of the Uniform Interstate and International Procedure Act, reproduced in Appendix B. Many other states require that service of process outside the jurisdiction be made "in the same manner as service is made within the state."[98]

In each case, applicable state law provides a variety of equally available options for service abroad, without imposing any express requirements or preference for any particular mechanism. These options generally include service by personal delivery,

---

93. *See* Born & Vollmer, *The Effect of the Revised Federal Rules of Civil Procedure on Personal Jurisdiction, Service and Discovery in International Cases*, 150 F.R.D. 221, 232-33 (1993).

94. Born & Vollmer, *The Effect of the Revised Federal Rules of Civil Procedure on Personal Jurisdiction, Service and Discovery in International Cases*, 150 F.R.D. 221, 231-35 (1993).

95. Born & Vollmer, *The Effect of the Revised Federal Rules of Civil Procedure on Personal Jurisdiction, Service and Discovery in International Cases*, 150 F.R.D. 221, 231-33 (1993).

96. The Committee Notes also do not discuss the validity of this provision under either U.S. Friendship, Commerce and Navigation treaties or the equal protection clause.

97. R. Casad, *Jurisdiction in Civil Actions* §4.06 (1991).

98. *E.g.*, N.Y.C.P.L.R. §313; Ill. Code Civ. Pro. §2-208(b).

service by registered mail, service by letter rogatory, service as permitted by foreign law, and service pursuant to court order.[99]

There are two significant exceptions to the general rule that the service of process in state courts is governed by state law. First, service on foreign states or state-owned entities in both federal and state courts is subject to the Foreign Sovereign Immunities Act ("FSIA").[100] Second, service in state court proceedings is subject to the Hague Service Convention if service abroad on a defendant located in another signatory state is required.[101] If either the FSIA or the Hague Service Convention is applicable, service of process must be made in accordance with its terms, even in state court. Service pursuant to inconsistent state law rules is preempted and invalid.[102]

8. Due Process Clause: Reasonable Notice Requirements

Service of process in both U.S. federal and state courts must comply with the due process clause of the fifth or fourteenth amendments to the U.S. Constitution, as well as with the service requirements imposed by the Federal Rules of Civil Procedure (or their state counterparts). The due process clause requires that service of process be reasonably likely to provide the defendant with notice of the proceedings against it. Specifically, due process demands "notice reasonably calculated under all the circumstances, to apprise interested parties of the pendency of the action and to afford them an opportunity to present their objections. ... The notice must be of such nature as reasonably to convey the required information."[103]

Personal service upon the defendant will virtually always satisfy the due process clause's "reasonable notice" requirement.[104] Similarly, service by a method of mail requiring some form of signed return receipt will generally satisfy the due process clause.[105] In contrast, service by publication will ordinarily be permitted only in the case of persons whose presence is unknown and cannot reasonably be ascertained.[106]

A Second Circuit decision illustrates the application of due process notice requirements in the international context, where locating and effecting service on defendants can be particularly difficult. In *SEC v. Tome*,[107] the Securities and

---

99. For a detailed discussion of old Rule 4(i), *see* G. Born & D. Westin, *International Civil Litigation in United States Courts* 161-66 (2d ed. 1992).

100. *See infra* pp. 836-37.

101. *See infra* pp. 804-09.

102. *See infra* pp. 807 & 836.

103. *Mullane v. Central Hanover Bank & Trust Co.*, 339 U.S. 306, 314 (1950); *SEC v. Tome*, 833 F.2d 1086 (2d Cir. 1987); *International Controls Corp. v. Vesco*, 593 F.2d 166 (2d Cir.), *cert. denied*, 442 U.S. 941 (1979).

104. *Milliken v. Meyer*, 311 U.S. 457 (1940); Federal Rules of Civil Procedure, Rule 4(i)(1)(C), Advisory Committee Note.

105. *Hess v. Pawloski*, 274 U.S. 352 (1927).

106. *Mullane v. Central Hanover Bank & Trust Co.*, 339 U.S. 306, 314-15 (1950); C. Wright & A. Miller, *Federal Practice and Procedure* §1074 (1987).

107. 833 F.2d 1086 (2d Cir. 1987).

Exchange Commission brought an insider trading action against a foreign bank and various unknown foreign individuals who had allegedly purchased U.S. securities using unlawfully obtained inside information. The SEC sought and obtained a district court order under Rule 4(i)(1)(E) of the old Federal Rules of Civil Procedure, authorizing service on the various unknown defendants by means of publication of notice of the suit in the "International Herald Tribune."[108]

The Second Circuit rejected the defendant's due process challenge to this method of service. Although there was no direct evidence that the defendants had read the published notices, the court concluded that "[p]ublication of the complaint and summons in the *International Herald Tribune* was 'reasonably calculated' to notify the unidentified purchasers ...[including the defendants] of the suit against them."[109] The court reasoned:

> Where the plaintiff can show that deliberate avoidance and obstruction by the defendants have made the giving of notice impossible, statutes and case law have allowed substitute notice by mail and by publication in media of general and wide circulation. Thus, as business dealings have become increasingly interstate and international, the means of giving notice have been extended to meet these situations, so that parties may be held accountable in our courts of justice. ...[110]

The court went on to observe that the defendants also were aware of the SEC's suit and that they were intended defendants, but that although they realized this, the SEC did not know their identities. In these circumstances, the court held, service by publication was proper.[111] The court indicated that the due process clause would *not* be satisfied if "a defendant's name and address are known or may be obtained with reasonable diligence. ..."[112]

In another recent insider trading action, the SEC obtained court-authorized service on foreign defendants by serving their U.S. securities brokers as agents for them.[113] The court reasoned that old Rules 4(e) and 4(i)(1)(E) authorized this form of court-ordered service and that the due process clause did not preclude such service because (i) the foreign defendants received actual notice; and (ii) the SEC had not known one defendant's identity and direct service on the other defendant would have been difficult.

An occasional issue in international cases involves the sufficiency of U.S. service of process upon foreign defendants who cannot read English. Although few decisions have addressed this question, the due process clause probably requires a plaintiff to

---

108. According to the Second Circuit, "[t]he *International Herald Tribune* is an English language paper which is widely read by the international financial community in Europe." 833 F.2d at 1091.

109. 833 F.2d at 1093.

110. 833 F.2d at 1092.

111. 833 F.2d at 1093.

112. 833 F.2d at 1094.

113. *SEC v. Foundation Hai*, Fed. Sec. L. Rep. (CCH) ¶94,961 (S.D.N.Y. 1990).

make reasonable efforts to provide notice of suit in a language that the defendant can comprehend.[114] It is unlikely, however, that U.S. courts will require U.S. process to be translated into the native language of a foreign defendant where the defendant is capable of reading English.[115] Similarly, the due process clause will probably be interpreted as requiring only a brief description of the plaintiff's action to be provided in the defendant's language — not a translation of the complaint and other documents.[116]

---

114. *Julen v. Larson*, 101 Cal. Rptr. 796 (App. Ct. 1972).

115. *Hunt v. Mobil Oil Corp.*, 410 F.Supp. 4 (S.D.N.Y. 1975); *Vasquez v. Sund Emba AB*, 548 N.Y.S.2d 728 (N.Y. App. Div. 1989); *Shoei Kako Co. v. Superior Court*, 109 Cal. Rptr. 402 (1973). *Compare Lyman Steel Corp. v. Ferrostaal Metals Corp.*, 747 F.Supp. 389 (N.D. Ohio 1990) (due process obstacle to service of untranslated pleadings on German defendants although recipients were known to be fluent in English) and *Julen v. Larson*, 101 Cal.Rptr. 796 (App. Ct. 1972) (not requiring translation of Swiss complaint against U.S. defendant, but requiring English summary of nature of action, date for any response and consequences of not responding).

116. *Lemme v. Wine of Japan Import, Inc.*, 631 F.Supp. 456 (E.D.N.Y. 1986). *Cf. Taylor v. Uniden Corp.*, 622 F.Supp. 1011 (E.D. Mo. 1985). *But see Teknekron Mgt., Inc. v. Quante Fernmeldetechnik*, 115 F.R.D. 175 (D. Neb. 1987).

C. Service of Process in Foreign Legal Systems

1. Rules Governing Service of Process in Foreign Courts[117]

The U.S. approach to the service of process in civil actions differs from that in many foreign nations. In many civil law jurisdictions, the service of process does not provide an independent basis for judicial jurisdiction. "Normally, regardless of the character of the action, service has a single function — that of providing notice."[118]

Nevertheless, particularly in civil law jurisdictions, the service of process is regarded as a "judicial" or "public" act, that may not be performed by private persons:

> Civil law states generally regard service of judicial process as a sovereign act that may be performed in their territory only by the state's own officials and in accordance with its own law.[119]

In many civil law states, service is effected by an official of the local court, or by specially designated officials subject to the court's control.[120] In France, for example, service is made by a "huissier" — a governmental official responsible for delivering process to the defendant.[121] In other states, service is effected by mail, dispatched by local court officials, return receipt requested.[122]

2. Restrictions on Service of Foreign Process Within National Territory

Many foreign nations, particularly civil law states, object to the service of process from foreign courts within national territory on local nationals, except where local

---

117. For descriptions of service of process rules in foreign states, *see* Jones, *International Judicial Assistance: Procedural Chaos and A Program for Reform*, 62 Yale L. J. 515 (1953); Smit, *International Aspects of Federal Civil Procedure*, 61 Colum. L. Rev. 1031 (1961); Miller, *International Cooperation in Litigation Between the United States and Switzerland: Unilateral Procedural Accommodation in a Test Tube*, 49 Minn. L. Rev. 1069 (1965); Schima & Hoyer, *Central European Countries*, and Kohl, *Romanist Legal Systems*, and Wengerek, *Socialist Countries*, XVI International Encyclopedia Of Comparative Law Chapter 6 (M. Cappelletti ed. 1984) [hereafter "Cappelletti"]; Ross, Ettinger, Moore-Bick, Gori-Montanelli, Botwinik & Heidenberger, *Service of Process in Austria, England, Italy and West Germany*, 9 Int'l Law. 689 (1975).

118. Ginsburg, *The Competent Court in Private International Law: Some Observations on Current Views in the United States*, 20 Rutgers L. Rev. 89, 90 (1965). *See* Grauper, *Some Recent Aspects of the Recognition and Enforcement of Foreign Judgments in Western Europe*, 12 Int'l & Comp. L. Q. 367, 377 (1963); Kaplan, von Mehren & Schaefer, *Phases of German Civil Procedure (I)*, 71 Harv. L. Rev. 1193, 1203-05 (1958).

119. *Restatement (Third) Foreign Relations Law* §471, comment b (1987). *See also* Miller, *International Cooperation in Litigation Between the United States and Switzerland: Unilateral Procedural Accommodation in a Test Tube*, 49 Minn. L. Rev. 1069, 1132 (1965); Jones, *International Judicial Assistance: Procedural Chaos and a Program for Reform*, 62 Yale L. J. 515, 537 (1953).

120. *See* Kohl, *Romanist Legal Systems* in XVI Cappelletti at Chapter 6, at 72 §92.

121. *See* Kohl, *Romanist Legal Systems* in XVI Cappelletti at Chapter 6, at 72 §92 (describing "huissier" in France); T. Hattori & D. Henderson, *Civil Procedure in Japan* §7.01[3] (1985).

122. Miller, *International Cooperation in Litigation Between the United States and Switzerland: Unilateral Procedural Accommodation in a Test Tube*, 49 Minn. L. Rev. 1069, 1083 (1965); T. Hattori & D. Henderson, *Civil Procedure in Japan* §7.01[3] (1985).

officials effect the service. As described below, local law makes it a criminal offense to serve or assist in serving foreign process on national territory in some countries.

For example, Switzerland has long adhered to the position that Swiss governmental authorities must serve judicial documents on persons residing in Switzerland. The Swiss Criminal Code forbids the service of foreign process within Switzerland except through Swiss governmental channels.[123] The Swiss Government has frequently protested to the United States[124] and other states[125] over the service of foreign process within Switzerland by either private or governmental litigants. These protests have declared that the "service of [judicial] documents by mail constitutes an infringement of Swiss sovereign powers."[126] France, Germany, and other countries have similar objections to the unauthorized service of foreign process within their territory.[127]

Several reasons are advanced for foreign objections to the service of U.S. process within their territory. Such objections rest in part on territorial conceptions of national sovereignty and on concerns about violations of local public policy.[128] In addition, foreign states may seek to ensure that service upon their nationals satisfies local requirements concerning fair notice — such as by requiring translations or summaries. Moreover, foreign states may wish to regulate the manner in which nationals are subjected to the compulsion that attaches to foreign service of process.[129] Finally, there may be a desire to insulate local nationals from liability in foreign proceedings, without regard to principle.[130]

3. Selected Materials on Foreign Service Restrictions

Excerpted below are selected materials illustrating foreign restrictions on the service of foreign process within national territory. First, consider Article 271 of the Swiss Penal Code, forbidding the performance on Swiss territory of certain governmental or administrative acts. That provision has been interpreted by Swiss courts to

---

123. Swiss Penal Code, Article 271; *infra* p. 776.

124. *See* 56 Am. J. Int'l L. 794 (1962) (aide-memoire).

125. 33 Annuaire Suisse de Droit International 203-205 (1977) (protest to European Communities Commission for mailing notification to Swiss company of commencement of legal proceedings).

126. 33 Annuaire Suisse de Droit International 203-205 (1977).

127. *Federal Trade Commission v. Compagnie de Saint-Gobain -Pont-a-Mousson*, 636 F.2d 1300, 1306 n.18 (D.C. Cir. 1980); (quoting French diplomatic note); Ettinger, *Service of Process in Austria*, 9 Int'l Law. 693, 694 (1975) (Austria); Heidenberg, *Service of Process and the Gathering of Information Relative to a Law Suit Brought in West Germany*, 9 Int'l Law. 725, 728-29 (1975) (Germany); Gori-Monanelli & Botwinik, *International Judicial Assistance -— Italy*, 9 Int'l Law. 717, 718 (1975) (Italy); Inter-American Juridical Committee, *Report on Uniformity of Legislation on International Cooperation in Judicial Procedures* 20 (1952).

128. Miller, *International Cooperation in Litigation Between the United States and Switzerland: Unilateral Procedural Accommodation in a Test Tube*, 49 Minn. L. Rev. 1069, 1076-77 (1965).

129. Miller, *International Cooperation in Litigation Between the United States and Switzerland: Unilateral Procedural Accommodation in a Test Tube*, 49 Minn. L. Rev. 1069, 1076-77 (1965).

130. Smit, *International Co-operation in Civil Litigation: Some Observations on the Roles of International Law and Reciprocity*, 9 Netherlands Int'l L. Rev. 137 (1962).

forbid the service of U.S. (and other) process in Switzerland.[131] Also excerpted below are two diplomatic notes, from the Republic of France and the Federal Republic of Germany, protesting the service of U.S. process on local territory without the intervention of local governmental authorities.[132]

SWISS PENAL CODE ARTICLE 271

271. Whoever, without authorization, executes acts on Swiss territory which are attributed to an administrative or government authority, on behalf of a foreign state, and whoever executes such acts on behalf of a foreign state, and whoever executes such acts on behalf of a foreign person or another foreign organization, and whoever encourages or otherwise participates in such acts, will be punished with prison, and in severe cases with penitentiary.

DIPLOMATIC NOTE OF JANUARY 10, 1980 FROM THE EMBASSY OF FRANCE TO THE U.S. DEPARTMENT OF STATE

636 F.2d 1300, 1306 n.18 (D.C. Cir. 1980)

The Embassy of France informs the Department of State that the transmittal by the [Federal Trade Commission] of a subpoena directly by mail to a French company (in this case Saint-Gobain Pont-a-Mousson) is inconsistent with the general principles of international law and constitutes a failure to recognize French sovereignty. Furthermore, the response to certain of the requests from the FTC could subject the directors of Saint-Gobain Pont-a-Mousson to civil and criminal liability and therefore expose them to judicial proceedings in France. Consequently, the Embassy of France would be grateful if the Department of State would make this position known to the various American authorities concerned by informing them that the French Government wishes such steps both in this matter and in any others which may subsequently arise, to be taken solely through diplomatic channels.

---

131. A leading Swiss judicial decision under Article 271 involved an investigation by German tax authorities of the tax affairs of Germans who owned shares in a Swiss company. The German tax authorities dispatched an accountant (apparently a private practitioner, not a governmental employee) to Switzerland to examine the books and records of the company. After he had done so, he was reported to Swiss police, and arrested. The Swiss Supreme Court held that the accountant had violated Article 271, and that it was irrelevant that he was not shown to be a foreign governmental official, because he had acted for German governmental officials. *Kaempfer v. Staatsanwaltschaft Zuerich, Bundesgericht*, March 6, 1939, 65(I), S.B.G. 39.

132. In addition to the protests excerpted above, *see Contemporary Practice of the United States Relating to International Law*, 56 Am. J. Int'l L. 793, 794 (1962) (Swiss diplomatic protest regarding service within Switzerland without use of letters rogatory); Committee on Federal Courts, N.Y. State Bar Ass'n, *Service of Process Abroad: A Nuts and Bolts Guide*, 122 F.R.D. 63, 67 n.22 (1989) (listing German diplomatic protests).

DIPLOMATIC NOTE DATED SEPTEMBER 27, 1979 FROM THE EMBASSY OF THE FEDERAL REPUBLIC OF GERMANY TO THE U.S. DEPARTMENT OF STATE

The Embassy of the Federal Republic of Germany presents its compliments to the Department of State and, referring to three recent cases in which German addressees were served judicial documents from the United States by mail, has the honor to inform the Department of State of the German view concerning service by mail of such documents by foreign countries:

Under German legal interpretation, German sovereignty is violated in cases where foreign judicial documents are served directly by mail within the Federal Republic of Germany. By such direct service, an act of sovereignty is conducted without any control by German authorities on the territory of the Federal Republic of Germany. This is not admissible under German laws. Under these laws, the German authorities must be in a position to examine whether the foreign request for service is in compliance with the legal provisions established for this purpose and whether it is in compliance with the ordre public of the Federal Republic of Germany. This is the reason why the Federal Republic of Germany has, when depositing the instrument of ratification to The Hague Convention of November 15, 1965 [the Hague Service Convention], concerning the service abroad of judicial and extrajudicial documents in civil or commercial matters objected in accordance with Article 21(2)(a) of the Convention to the application of the channels of transmission as stipulated in Article 10 of the Convention. ... Since the Hague [Service Convention] has gone into effect between the United States of America and the Federal Republic of Germany on June 26, 1979, the Federal Government would appreciate it if service of documents originating from American judicial proceedings to persons within the Federal Republic of Germany would be conducted in compliance with this convention only and if the courts and attorneys involved could be informed accordingly.

Notes on Article 271 and Diplomatic Notes

1. *Rationale for foreign restrictions on service of U.S. process within local territory.* Consider Article 271 of the Swiss Criminal Code and the French and German protests excerpted above. Note that the French protest relates to the service of a U.S. administrative agency's subpoena, while the German protest relates more broadly to any service of judicial documents (including both civil complaints and subpoenas). What is the rationale underlying the Swiss statute and the French and German protests? Consider:

> The need to examine the contents of foreign documents is ... defended as an integral element of Swiss sovereignty and essential to the national policies of neutrality and protection of commercial and industrial secrets. The theory appears to be that if requests for service were not channelled through and scrutinized by appropriate Swiss officials, there would be no effective way to insure that the service of the foreign documents was not contrary to Swiss public policy.

Miller, *International Cooperation in Litigation Between the United States and Switzerland: Unilateral Procedural Accommodation in a Test Tube*, 49 Minn. L. Rev. 1069, 1076-77 (1965). Is this a legitimate basis for a protest? Compare the reasons stated in the German Note. How are Swiss or German "public policy" impaired when a piece of paper is mailed to local residents, informing them that legal proceedings have been commenced abroad? What other reasons might a nation have for objecting to service of foreign process within its borders? Are such objections merely pretexts for protecting local companies from liability to foreign claimants, by erecting time-consuming procedural obstacles to foreign legal proceedings?

Suppose agents of a foreign state, with a fundamentalist religious regime, were dispatched to serve summonses or judgments of foreign religious tribunals on U.S. citizens?

2. *Criticism of foreign restrictions on the service of U.S. process within local territory.* Some observers have criticized foreign restrictions on the service of U.S. process within local territory:

> The absence of direct prohibitions under international law of service by ... private persons is highly desirable since it avoids the creation of unnecessary and improper obstacles to the smooth conduct of litigation with international aspects. ... Different countries take different views as to how service is to be made ... and international relations and justice are best served by letting each country conduct its litigation in the way it sees fit. Clearly, a mere local preference for domestic procedures cannot reasonably justify a refusal to let foreign litigants resort to procedures acceptable to foreign courts. It is difficult to ascertain how the domestic order can be disturbed by service by ... a private person; indeed, even when service is made by ... an official of the foreign government, the advantage of facilitating litigation with international aspects would ordinarily seem to outweigh by far the disadvantage of having a foreign official act within domestic borders. In a true family of nations, small favors should be readily granted for the benefit of the whole.

Smit, *International Co-operation in Civil Litigation: Some Observations on the Roles of International Law and Reciprocity*, 9 Netherlands Int'l L. Rev. 137 (1962). Is this correct? Are Switzerland, France, and Germany just parochially protectionistic in insisting that local officials be involved in serving foreign process on local citizens?

3. *International law restrictions on the service of U.S. process abroad.* Both the French and German diplomatic notes take the position that the direct service of U.S. process within their territory violates international law. Both notes take this position without reference to any specific local legislation — equivalent to Article 271 of the Swiss Penal Code. They rely merely on general principles of national sovereignty and international law. Section 471(i) of the *Restatement (Third) Foreign Relations Law* (1987) supports the view that international law forbids one state from effecting service within its territory without consent, even absent specific local legislation restricting foreign service:

> Under international law, a state may determine the conditions for service of process in its territory in aid of litigation in another state, but the state where the litigation is pending may determine the effect of such service.

See Id. at 526 ("A state may not conduct official activities in the territory of another state without that state's consent, express or implied. That principle is generally applied as well to the service of judicial documents."). Is the service of U.S. process on a person within a foreign state really the performance of governmental acts within that state? Suppose that the service is effected by a private process-server? or by ordinary mail?

4. *Doubts regarding international law restrictions on service of process abroad.* Not all authorities have agreed that international law forbids the service of process abroad without the consent of the destination state:

> In the absence of a treaty, international law does not oblige any country to render assistance in the making of service ... in connection with litigation conducted abroad. ... Furthermore, since each country is sovereign within its own territory, it may, without violating international law, enact laws forbidding or regulating the making of service ... within its territory. However, when internal laws are lacking, such acts are prohibited only if forbidden by international law. When service is made in one country by an official, such as a consul, of another country, the act of the official may be construed as the act of the foreign country. Since under international law one country may forbid another from acting within its borders, it might be argued that such service may be forbidden directly under international law even in the absence of domestic proscriptive legislation. ... However, this type of argumentation would seem wholly inappropriate when the service is made by ... a private person. ... There appears to be no authoritative source of international law specifically supporting the claim that the making of service by, ... a private person may be forbidden in the absence of prohibitions validly created by domestic law. Nor can the conduct of the private person who makes service ... possibly qualify as official conduct that may validly be forbidden by direct reference to rules of international law. The making of service by ... private persons do not in any way involve the exercise of judicial or other official

powers. ... In contradistinction to service by an official prescribed by the laws of many civil law countries, service by private persons under American rules can therefore not be construed to be other than a purely private act. ...

Smit, *International Co-operation in Civil Litigation: Some Observations on the Roles of International Law and Reciprocity*, 9 Netherlands Int'l L. Rev. 137 (1962).

Are these views persuasive? What is Professor Smit's position if local law expressly forbids foreign service? What is his position if local law is silent as to the permissibility of foreign service? Is it persuasive to say that only "internal law" may forbid foreign service? What if German executive officers take the position that, as a matter of German sovereignty and public policy, foreign service must be served through German governmental channels? Does international law require Germany to assert its sovereignty solely through statutory command? If Germany is silent regarding foreign service, is that consent to such service?

Note Professor Smit's assertion that service on foreign state territory by a "private" party does not necessarily violate international law, even if service by a consul or other government official would. Why exactly is it, in Professor Smit's view, that service by a private party of a judicial document is not a governmental act implicating international law? Compare this view with that expressed in the German diplomatic note and in the *Third Restatement*. Which is more persuasive?

5. *Relevance under international law of U.S. nationality of recipients of U.S. process served abroad.* When U.S. process is served abroad, is the nationality of the person on whom the U.S. process is served relevant, for purposes of international law or otherwise? Note that Article 271 of the Swiss Penal Code does not distinguish between Swiss nationals and others. Reread *Blackmer v. United States*, 284 U.S. 421 (1932), excerpted above at pp. 95-100. In *Blackmer*, a U.S. administrative subpoena was served by a U.S. consul upon a U.S. national residing in France, pursuant to what is now 28 U.S.C. §1783. The Court rejected the suggestion that service could not be effected upon a U.S. national abroad. It reasoned: "The mere giving of such a notice to the citizen in the foreign country of the requirement of his government that he shall return is in no sense an invasion of any right of the foreign government." Is that persuasive? Why is not the delivery to the U.S. national, on foreign territory, of governmental summons, by a U.S. government official "an invasion of [the] right of the foreign government" to control judicial acts on its own territory? Assuming that the foreign government does not consent, isn't the Supreme Court's statement flatly wrong?

Consider the following excerpt from *SEC v. Briggs*, 234 F.Supp. 618 (N.D. Ohio 1964), where the U.S. Securities and Exchange Commission had served process, allegedly in violation of Canadian law, upon a U.S. citizen residing in Canada:

> We seriously doubt that the defendant, admittedly a citizen of the United States, has standing to complain of an affront to a sovereign which is foreign to her. We need not reach that issue, however, because we perceive of no such invasion of Canada's sovereignty. In *Blackmer v. United States*, the Supreme Court stated: "The mere giving of such a notice to the citizen in the foreign country of the requirement of his government that he shall return is in no sense an invasion of any right of the foreign government." Therefore, we find no principle of comity between nations which precludes this Court from the exercise of jurisdiction over Mrs. Briggs.

What if Mrs. Briggs had been a Canadian? a French national? *Cf.* Hague Service Convention, Art. 8 (permitting receiving state to object to service by consular agents, except with respect to service on nationals of receiving state). What if Canada had protested service of U.S. process in Canada?

6. *Relevance under foreign laws of U.S. nationality of recipients of U.S. process served abroad.* Some states that generally forbid direct service of foreign process within their territory make an exception for service of process upon nationals of the state from which the process emanates. In Switzerland, for example, consular officials may serve process on their nationals, without the intervention of Swiss officials, provided that they do not use "compulsion." Miller, *International Cooperation in Litigation Between the United States and Switzerland: Unilateral Procedural Accommodation in a Test Tube*, 49 Minn. L. Rev. 1069, 1075-76 (1965). Similarly, as discussed below, Article 8 of the Hague Service Convention permits service upon the nationals of the state making service within the territory of other signatory states. Few states have objected to such service. *See infra* pp. 810-11. Compare this practice to nationality as a basis for judicial and legislative jurisdiction. *See supra* pp. 95-100 & 506-07. Are the results in *Blackmer* and *Briggs* explicable on the basis that, where service abroad is made on *U.S.* nationals, the foreign state's consent can be inferred in the absence of an express protest? Does state A have standing to protest unlawful service of state C's process on state B's national while located in state A?

D. A Closer Look at Service of U.S. Process Abroad: Selected Issues

1. Service of U.S. Process Abroad Under New Rule 4(f) and Other Legislative Grants Where Foreign Law Restricts U.S. Service

U.S. courts and legislative bodies have been obliged to respond to foreign restrictions on the extraterritorial service of U.S. process like those described above. In particular, U.S. courts and rulemakers have been required to consider whether and when the violation of foreign restrictions should invalidate U.S. service for purposes of U.S. law. U.S. reactions to this question have varied over time, as the following materials illustrate.

a. Congress May Authorize Service Abroad in Violation of International Law

A number of lower courts have held that, if Congress specifically authorizes service abroad in violation of foreign law, then that is conclusive for purposes of U.S. law: the fact that the congressionally-prescribed mechanism violates foreign law does not affect the mechanism's validity for U.S. purposes. Thus, in *Umbenhauer v. Woog*,[133] a decision (excerpted below) under old Rule 4 of the Federal Rules of Civil Procedure, the court held that service of a complaint and summons in Switzerland, in violation of Swiss law, was valid for purposes of the old Federal Rules.[134] Similarly, in *Commodity Futures Trading Commission v. Nahas*,[135] also excerpted below, the court starts from the premise that Congress may authorize service abroad in violation of both foreign and international law: "Federal courts must give effect to a valid, unambiguous congressional mandate, even if such effect would conflict with another nation's laws or violate international law."[136]

b. Presumption That Congress Does Not Intend to Authorize Service Abroad in Violation of International Law

Although Congress has the power to violate international law, this does not dispose of the further question whether U.S. service in violation of foreign or international law has in fact been authorized by Congress. In answering this question, U.S. courts have invoked the familiar presumption that Congress would not choose to violate international law.[137] Thus, *CFTC v. Nahas* holds that service in Brazil of a subpoena, in violation of Brazilian law, had not been authorized under the

---

133. 969 F.2d 25 (3d Cir. 1992).

134. Most other authorities agreed. *E.g.*, *SEC v. International Swiss Investments Corp.*, 895 F.2d 1272 (9th Cir. 1990) (SEC service on defendant residing in Mexico held valid notwithstanding violation of Mexican law); *Bersch v. Drexel Firestone*, 389 F.Supp. 446 (S.D.N.Y. 1974), *modified*, 519 F.2d 974 (2d Cir. 1975), *cert. denied*, 423 U.S. 1018 (1975); *Alco Standard Corp. v. Benalal*, 345 F.Supp. 14 (E.D. Pa. 1972); *Atlantic Steamers Supply Co. v. International Maritime Supplies Co.*, 268 F.Supp. 1009 (S.D.N.Y. 1967). *See also* Kaplan, *Amendments of the Federal Rules of Civil Procedure, 1961-63*, 77 Harv. L. Rev. 601, 637 (1964).

A few courts disagreed. *R.M.B. Electrostat v. Lectra Trading AG*, 1983 W.L. 1371 (E.D. 17, 1983); *Aries Ventures v. AXA Finance SA*, 729 F.Supp. 289 (S.D.N.Y. 1990).

135. 738 F.2d 487 (D.C. Cir. 1984).

136. 738 F.2d at 495.

137. *See supra* pp. 22 & 510-11 for a discussion of this presumption.

Commodities Future Trading Act.[138] In the absence of an express legislative mandate, the court declined to permit service abroad in violation of international law: "we are unwilling to infer enforcement jurisdiction absent a clearer indication of congressional intent."[139] Other lower courts have agreed.[140]

c. Old Rule 4(i)'s Treatment of Service Abroad in Violation of Foreign Law

Service of federal court process outside the United States was, until 1993, governed by old Rule 4(i) of the Federal Rules of Civil Procedure. Old Rule 4(i) was generally held to permit service abroad even if it was effected in a manner that violated foreign law.[141] The framers of Rule 4(i) were aware that this might jeopardize the enforcement of resulting U.S. judgments abroad, but thought it best to leave such risks to plaintiff's counsel's assessment: "if enforcement is to be sought in the country of service, the foreign law should be examined before a choice is made among the methods of service allowed by subdivision (i)."[142] This is illustrated by the decision in *Umbenhauer v. Woog*,[143] excerpted below.

d. New Rule 4(f)'s Limits on Service Abroad in Violation of Foreign Law

New Rule 4(f) of the Federal Rules of Civil Procedure is the principal mechanism for service of process abroad in federal civil actions. The provisions of Rule 4(f) significantly alter the approach to service abroad taken in old Rule 4(i) and *Umbenhauer*. As discussed below, the new Rule generally requires that service of U.S. process abroad comply with foreign law. Consider the wisdom and practical difficulties with this approach, and compare it to the earlier approach.

COMMODITY FUTURES TRADING COMMISSION v. NAHAS

738 F.2d 487 (D.C. Cir. 1984)

TAMM, CIRCUIT JUDGE. ... In March 1980, the [Commodity Futures Trading] Commission began investigating whether certain individuals had violated the Commodity Exchange Act ("Act"), 7 U.S.C. §§9, 13(b), 13b (1982), by manipulating the price of silver and silver futures contracts in 1979 and 1980. In the course of its investigation, the Commission discovered that [Naji Robert] Nahas, a Brazilian citizen and resident, had opened accounts in 1979 with several brokerage houses in the United States. Through these accounts, Nahas had purchased numerous silver futures contracts and approximately ten million ounces of silver bullion. ...

[T]he Commission issued a subpoena duces tecum pursuant to its investigative power under 7 U.S.C. §15. The subpoena, served by substituted service in Sao Paulo, Brazil, directed Nahas to appear ... at the Commission's offices in Washington, D.C.

---

138. 738 F.2d 487 (D.C. Cir. 1984); *infra* pp. 781-86.

139. 738 F.2d at 495.

140. *FTC v. Compagnie de Saint-Gobain-Pont-A-Mousson*, 636 F.2d 1300, 1327 (D.C. Cir. 1980).

141. *See supra* p. 780 n.134 & *infra* pp. 791-92.

142. Kaplan, *Amendments of the Federal Rules of Civil Procedure, 1961-63(I)*, 77 Harv. L. Rev. 633, 635 (1965).

143. 969 F.2d 25 (3rd Cir. 1992).

and to produce certain documents.[144] When Nahas failed to comply with the Commission's subpoena, the Commission petitioned the district court for an order directing Nahas to show cause why he should be relieved of compliance. ... Nahas ignored the show cause order [and the district court issued an order freezing his U.S. assets.]

On November 14, 1983, Nahas formally responded for the first time in this proceeding. ... Nahas contended that the Commission had exceeded its statutory authority in issuing an investigative subpoena to a foreign citizen in a foreign nation, and that the Commission's method of serving the subpoena was illegal.[145] In support of his contentions, Nahas submitted an affidavit prepared by Professor Irineu Strenger, a Brazilian attorney and a professor of law at the University of Sao Paulo, stating that the service of the Commission's subpoena violated Brazilian and international law. ... The district court rejected Nahas' arguments. ... [On appeal,] Nahas contends that 7 U.S.C. §15 does not empower a district court to enforce an administrative subpoena served on a foreign citizen in a foreign country. He claims the court therefore erred at the contempt proceeding in finding him in contempt and in imposing civil sanctions to compel his compliance. We agree. ...

A federal court's subject-matter jurisdiction, constitutionally limited by Article III, extends only so far as Congress provides by statute. When a federal court reaches beyond its statutory grant of subject-matter jurisdiction, its judgment is void. Similarly, when an enforcement order entered by default is beyond the jurisdictional grant of the issuing court, the order is void. In the instant case, the jurisdiction of the district court to enforce Commission subpoenas arises from 7 U.S.C. §15:

> For the purpose of securing effective enforcement ... and for the purpose of any investigation or proceeding ..., any member of the Commission ... may ... subpena [sic] witnesses ... and require the production of any ... records that the Commission deems relevant . ... *The attendance of witnesses and the production of any such records may be required from any place in the United States or any State* at any designated place of hearing. In case of ... refusal to obey a subpena [sic] ..., the Commission may invoke the aid of any court of the United States within the jurisdiction in which the investigation or proceeding is conducted . ... *Such court may issue an order requiring such person*

---

144. Prior to issuing the subpoena, the Commission consulted the U.S. Department of State concerning the proper method for serving an administrative subpoena on a Brazilian citizen in Brazil. The State Department advised that Brazilian law did not prohibit the service of an administrative subpoena by a Brazilian attorney upon a Brazilian citizen in Brazil. The State Department also provided the Commission with a list of Brazilian attorneys in Sao Paulo, where Nahas worked and resided, who could act as agents for the Commission in serving a subpoena. The Commission selected a Brazilian attorney from the list to serve the subpoena. The attorney delivered copies of the subpoena on June 14, 1983 to Nahas' office receptionist and to the doormen of Nahas' apartment building.

145. Nahas accompanied his cross-motion with an affidavit in which he averred he was a citizen of Brazil, had resided in Brazil since 1969, had never been a resident or citizen of the United States, had not conducted any business in the United States since May 6, 1983, and had not been personally served with the Commission's subpoena.

to appear before the Commission ... to produce records ... or to give testimony . ... Any failure to obey such order of the court may be punished by the court as a contempt thereof.

7 U.S.C. §15 (emphasis added). The district court thus has jurisdiction to enforce only those subpoenas issued to "such person[s]" as defined in §15. The plain language of the statute limits "such person[s]" to "witnesses ... from any place in the United States or any State . ...."

Although courts, in some instances, have construed similar language as authorizing enforcement of administrative subpoenas requiring the production of records from outside the United States, those subpoenas were served on individuals within the United States.[146] No court has expressly considered whether Congress intended 7 U.S.C. §15 to authorize judicial enforcement of an investigative subpoena served upon a foreign citizen in a foreign nation. Although the plain language of the statute does not confer such power, the district court in this case nevertheless inferred jurisdiction. Because this inference is not supported by legislative history or analogous precedent, we believe that sound rules of statutory construction compel a different conclusion.

An important canon of statutory construction teaches that "legislation of Congress, unless a contrary intent appears, is meant to apply only within the territorial jurisdiction of the United States . ...." *Foley Bros., Inc. v. Filardo*, 336 U.S. 281, 285 (1949). The text of 7 U.S.C. §15 does not empower the Commission to serve subpoenas on foreign nationals in foreign countries. Similarly, the legislative history does not indicate that Congress intended to clothe the Commission with the power to serve investigative subpoenas extraterritorially. We are not prepared, in the face of a silent statute and an uninstructive legislative history, to infer the existence of this power: "The service of an investigative subpoena on a foreign national in a foreign country ... [is] a sufficiently significant act as to require that Congress should speak to it clearly." *FTC v. Compagnie de Saint-Gobain-Pont-A-Mousson*, 636 F.2d 1300, 1327 (D.C. Cir. 1980) (McGowan, J., concurring).[147]

We are influenced as well by another canon of statutory construction that requires courts, wherever possible, to construe federal statutes to ensure their applica-

---

146. [*See infra* pp. 785-86 & 865.]

147. The Commission asserts that the court may infer from the language of §15 that Congress intended the Commission to have power to serve its subpoenas extraterritorially. The statute authorizes the Commission to subpoena witnesses and records from "*any* place in the United States or any State . ...." 7 U.S.C. §15 (emphasis added). In support of its assertion, the Commission invites our attention to 7 U.S.C. §3, which discusses transactions in interstate commerce and defines "State" as including foreign nations. The Commission ignores, however, that 7 U.S.C. §3 explicitly limits its definition of "State" to that section. We could as well be influenced by §13a-2, which discusses the jurisdiction of states and defines "State" as "any State of the United States, the District of Columbia, the Commonwealth of Puerto Rico, or any territory or possession of the United States." 7 U.S.C. §13a-2(6). Nevertheless, absent clear evidence of legislative intent, we are unwilling to extend to 7 U.S.C. §15 definitions intended exclusively for other sections. Instead, we are guided by established rules of statutory construction, and we presume that had Congress intended to authorize the Commission to serve subpoenas on foreign citizens in foreign nations, it would unambiguously have expressed that intent.

tion will not violate international law.[148] *Murray v. The Schooner Charming Betsy*, 6 U.S. 64 (1804). To construe 7 U.S.C. §15 as empowering the district court to enforce an investigative subpoena served on a foreign citizen in a foreign nation would seriously impinge on principles of international law. "When compulsory process is served [on a foreign citizen on foreign soil in the form of an investigative subpoena[149]], ... the act of service itself constitutes an exercise of one nation's sovereignty within the territory of another sovereign. Such an exercise [absent consent by the foreign nation] constitutes a violation of international law." *Saint-Gobain*, 636 F.2d 1313.

The extent of the intrusion on Brazil's sovereignty in this case is reflected in a letter of protest sent by the Brazilian government to the United States Secretary of State. Brazilian law requires that service of process by foreign nations be made pursuant to a letter rogatory or a letter of request transmitted through diplomatic channels. In its letter of protest, Brazil remonstrated that the Commission's method of serving the subpoena "[did] not conform to the [Brazilian laws] governing the handling of ... material [at the international level] . ..."[150] Letter from Brazilian Ministry

---

148. The Constitution commits to the Legislative and Executive Branches, not to the Judicial Branch, the conduct of foreign relations. *Oetjen v. Central Leather Co.*, 246 U.S. 297, 302 (1918). Our rules of statutory construction in the instant case embody concerns for preserving the relationships between the branches of government in a system of separation of powers. Hence, we hesitate to infer from 7 U.S.C. §15, absent clear congressional intent, enforcement jurisdiction that arouses foreign sensibilities and implicates international law concerns.

149. The distinction between service of compulsory process and service of notice is critical under principles of international law due to the difference in judicial enforcement power that accompanies each. When process in the form of a complaint is served extraterritorially, the informational nature of the process renders the act of service relatively benign in terms of infringement on the foreign nation's sovereignty. See *Saint-Gobain*. For example, when an agency serves a formal complaint on a foreign citizen in a foreign nation, the recipient simply receives information upon which he may decide whether to negotiate a consent order or proceed to litigation. The result of the litigation may always be appealed before a cease-and-desist order will issue. Not until the cease-and-desist order becomes final can the enforcement power of the courts be invoked. By contrast, when an agency serves compulsory process in the form of an investigative subpoena, it compels the recipient to act. Should the recipient refuse to comply with the subpoena, the enforcement power of the federal courts can be invoked immediately. See *Saint-Gobain*, 636 F.2d at 1311-13. In the instant case, service of the Commission's subpoena on Nahas in Brazil constituted an act of American sovereignty within Brazil, because the subpoena carried with it the full array of American judicial power. Such an intrusion on the sovereignty of another nation impinges on principles of international law and should be avoided unless expressly mandated by Congress.

150. Not only did the Commission fail to observe Brazilian law when serving the subpoena, it ignored guidance by this court in *Saint-Gobain* concerning methods of extraterritorial service that would minimize intrusion on another nation's sovereignty: "[W]herever possible, an agency attempting subpoena service on foreign citizens residing on foreign soil should make initial resort through established diplomatic channels or procedures authorized by international convention." 636 F.2d at 1323. In *Saint-Gobain*, this court discussed the significant international implications of an agency bypassing foreign authorities when serving an investigative subpoena abroad: "Given the compulsory nature of a subpoena, ... subpoena service by direct mail upon a foreign citizen on foreign soil, without warning to the officials of the local state and without initial request for or prior resort to established channels of international judicial assistance, is perhaps maximally intrusive. Not only does it represent a deliberate bypassing of the official authorities of the local state, it allows the full range of judicial sanctions for noncompliance with an agency subpoena to be triggered merely by a foreign citizen's unwillingness to comply with directives contained in an ordinary registered letter." ...

of Foreign Affairs to United States Embassy (Mar. 2, 1984). Brazil therefore admonished the United States to "ensure compliance, in future cases, with the formalities prescribed by Brazilian law for the execution of legal instruments required by foreign courts."[151] In light of this apparently significant intrusion on Brazilian sovereignty, inferring enforcement jurisdiction under 7 U.S.C. §15 would seriously impact on principles of international law. Because "an act of Congress ought never to be construed to violate the law of nations, if any other possible construction remains," *Charming Betsy*, 6 U.S. at 118, we are unwilling to infer enforcement jurisdiction absent a clearer indication of congressional intent.

We emphasize that this case does not pose a question about the authority of Congress; rather, it poses a question about the congressional intent embodied in 7 U.S.C. §15. Federal courts must give effect to a valid, unambiguous congressional mandate, even if such effect would conflict with another nation's laws or violate international law. A clear congressional mandate authorizing the Commission to serve investigative subpoenas on foreign citizens in foreign nations is lacking in 7 U.S.C. §15, and inferring such a mandate would run contrary to established canons of statutory construction. ...[152]

Finally, our conclusion that Congress did not intend in 7 U.S.C. §15 to empower federal courts to enforce investigative subpoenas served on foreign citizens in foreign nations comports with analogous cases in which courts have construed similar language. For example, in *SEC v. Minas de Artemisa, SA*, 150 F.2d 215 (9th Cir. 1945), the agency was statutorily authorized to subpoena witnesses and documents "from any place in the United States or any Territory . ..." The Ninth Circuit construed the agency's authority broadly to require the production of documents outside the United States, "provided only that the service of the subpoena is made within the territorial limits of the United States." In *Ludlow Corp. v. DeSmedt*, 249 F.Supp. 496 (S.D.N.Y.), *aff'd*, 366 F.2d 464 (2d Cir.), *cert. denied*, 385 U.S. 974 (1966), the agency was authorized to subpoena documents "from any place in the United States . ..."

---

151. The intrusion on Brazil's sovereignty is also indicated by a letter from 35 members of the Brazilian Chamber of Deputies, a House in Brazil's bicameral legislature, to the United States Ambassador in Brazil protesting "[t]he proceedings against a citizen not subject to territorial competence (jus loci) of American Justice . ... [The proceedings] affect personal and family honor of persons foreign to the Sovereignty and Competence of the Government of the United States. ... We are certain that Your Excellency, due to the international and national importance which the fact represents, will transmit to the honorable authorities of your Country this manifestation and protest."

152. The Commission correctly asserts that agencies generally are granted broad deference in determining the scope of their investigative authority. *CAB v. Deutsche Lufthansa AG*, 591 F.2d 951, 952 (D.C. Cir. 1979). Because the Commission has construed its jurisdiction under the Act as extending to all market participants regardless of nationality or location, it contends that any ambiguity in 7 U.S.C. §15 should be resolved in favor of promoting its investigative and regulative powers. The Commission fails to recognize, however, that judicial deference to an agency's interpretation of its investigative authority is not justified when the agency's action may have extraterritorial impact. *Saint-Gobain*, 636 F.2d at 1322. In light of the actual extraterritorial impact here and the absence of evidence indicating Congress intended to confer enforcement jurisdiction, we reject the Commission's argument and suggest that the argument more properly is directed to Congress.

The court there also construed broadly the agency's power to require the production of documents located outside the country, but it was careful to acknowledge "that the service of the subpoena [was] made within the territorial limits of the United States . ..." Finally, in *SEC v. Zanganeh*, 470 F.Supp. 1307 (D.D.C. 1978), the agency was authorized to subpoena witnesses "from any place in the United States or any State . ..." The court stated that where no individual service occurred and respondent was not in the United States, "the [agency] has no power to subpoena an alien non-resident to appear before it from a foreign land."

Our construction of 7 U.S.C. §15 is further strengthened by the existence of statutes in which Congress explicitly has authorized the extraterritorial service of investigative subpoenas on aliens. For example, Congress has authorized the Department of Justice in its antitrust investigations to serve civil investigative demands on foreign nationals "in such manner as the Federal Rules of Civil Procedure prescribe for service in a foreign country."[153] 15 U.S.C. §1312(d)(2) (1982). Congress also has empowered the Federal Trade Commission to serve its subpoenas on foreign nationals "in such manner as the Federal Rules of Civil Procedure prescribe for service in a foreign nation." *Id.* §57b-1(c)(6)(B). The existence of these statutes "indicates that when Congress intends to authorize extraterritorial service of investigative subpoenas, it will express that intent explicitly." *Saint-Gobain*, 636 F.2d at 1325 n.140. An explicit grant of power is conspicuously absent from 7 U.S.C. §15. Sound rules of statutory construction as well as analogous precedent therefore compel a construction of 7 U.S.C. §15 that does not authorize enforcement jurisdiction in the instant case. ...

FEDERAL RULES OF CIVIL PROCEDURE, RULE 4(i)
(AS IN EFFECT PRIOR TO 1993)

(i) *Manner.* When the federal or state law referred to in subdivision (e) of this rule authorizes service upon a party not an inhabitant of or found within the state in which the district court is held, and service is to be effected upon the party in a foreign country, it is also sufficient if service of the summons and complaint is made: (A) in the manner prescribed by the law of the foreign country for service in that country in an action in any of its courts of general jurisdiction; or (B) as directed by the foreign authority in response to a letter rogatory, when service in either case is reasonably calculated to give actual notice; or (C) upon an individual, by delivery to the individual personally, and upon a corporation or partnership or association, by delivery to an officer, a managing or general agent; or (D) by any form of mail, requiring a signed receipt, to be addressed and dispatched by the clerk of the court to the party to be served; or (E) as directed by order of the court. Service under (C) or

---

153. [Old] Federal Rule 4(i)(1) provide[d] five alternative methods for service upon a party in a foreign country: in the manner prescribed by the law of the foreign country; as directed by the foreign authority responding to a letter rogatory; by personal service; by any form of mail requiring a signed receipt; or as directed by order of the court where the action is brought.

(E) above may be made by any person who is not a party and is not less than 18 years of age or who is designated by order of the district court or by the foreign court. On request, the clerk shall deliver the summons to the plaintiff for transmission to the person or the foreign court or officer who will make the service.

UMBENHAUER v. WOOG

969 F.2d 25 (3d Cir. 1992)

GARTH, CIRCUIT JUDGE. ... On August 26, 1988, Xouth, Inc. ("Xouth") ... filed a voluntary petition in bankruptcy under Chapter 7 of the Bankruptcy Code. On August 24, 1990, Xouth's trustee in bankruptcy and several of Xouth's creditors ("plaintiffs") filed a complaint against Dr. Philippe-Guy Woog, who had served as Xouth's chairman, and against Les Produits Associes-Broxo, SA and M.I.H., SA, two foreign corporations that had been affiliated with Xouth. The plaintiffs alleged that the defendants had committed bankruptcy fraud, common law fraud, conspiracy to defraud, conversion, and breach of contract in connection with loans that the plaintiffs had made to Xouth.

On filing their complaint in the district court in the Eastern District of Pennsylvania, the plaintiffs attempted to serve process on Dr. Woog, a citizen of Switzerland, and Les Produits Associes-Broxo, SA, a Swiss corporation (hereinafter "Swiss defendants"). The plaintiffs initially attempted to serve process under [old] Federal Rules of Civil Procedure, Rule 4(i)(1)(D), which authorized service "by any form of mail, requiring a signed receipt, to be addressed and dispatched by the clerk of the court to the party to be served." However, the district court clerk informed the plaintiffs that, at the request of the U.S Department of State, the Administrative Office of the Courts had instructed its clerks not to serve process on Swiss citizens under that Rule.[154] The plaintiffs subsequently received from the Department of State a circular entitled "Judicial Assistance in Switzerland," which advised that service should be effected on Swiss defendants through letters rogatory; *i.e.*, letters from U.S. courts to corresponding foreign courts. The circular also advised that service could be effected on the Swiss defendants by international registered mail, but that a judgment resulting from such service may not be enforceable in Switzerland.

The plaintiffs next attempted to serve process on the Swiss defendants under [old] Federal Rules of Civil Procedure, Rule 4(c)(2)(C) by sending a copy of the summons, the complaint, and a federal acknowledgement of service form (Form 18-A) directly to the Swiss defendants on December 17, 1990. When the Swiss defendants failed to acknowledge service, the plaintiffs filed a motion in the district court for a judgment of default. The Swiss defendants countered with a motion under Federal Rules of Civil Procedure, Rule 12(b)(5) to dismiss the plaintiffs' complaint

---

154. Annexed to this opinion as "Exhibit A" is a copy of the memorandum issued by the Administrative Office of the United States Courts, entitled "Service of Process in Foreign Countries" and dated November 6, 1980.

for insufficiency of process because, under [old] Federal Rules of Civil Procedure, Rule 4(c)(2)(C)(ii), process is not considered served until it is acknowledged. The district court ... granted the Swiss defendants' motion to dismiss the plaintiffs' complaint.

[On appeal, the Court accepted the plaintiffs' argument that, even if their attempted service on the Swiss defendants was invalid, their complaint should not have been dismissed, but instead only service should have been quashed.] We turn, therefore, to a consideration of [old] Rule 4(i)(1)(D), which would permit service "by any form of mail, requiring a signed receipt, to be addressed and dispatched by the clerk of the court to the party to be serviced."

The record reveals that the plaintiffs initially endeavored to serve process on the Swiss defendants by requesting the district court clerk to address and dispatch the summons and complaint to the Swiss defendants. Nevertheless, and despite the clear language of [old] Rule 4(i)(1)(D), the district court clerk refused the plaintiffs' request. This refusal accorded with an articulated policy of the Administrative Office of the U.S. Courts. The Administrative Office, apparently at the behest of the U.S. Department of State, had instructed district court clerks not to serve Rule 4(i)(1)(D) process on defendants in countries which, like Switzerland, object to service of process on their citizens under that provision. We hold that the district court clerk improperly disregarded the dictates of Rule 4(i)(1)(D). Neither we, the Department of State, nor the Administrative Office of the U.S. Courts possess the authority to circumvent, ignore or deviate from the Federal Rules of Civil Procedure, which were approved by the Judicial Conference of the United States, the Supreme Court of the United States, and Congress. Whether or not the Rules should be amended to deal more adequately with the question of overseas service to countries which disapprove of Rule 4(i)(1)(D) is not for us to decide.

We note that the Standing Rules Committee of the Judicial Conference of the United States recently drafted relevant proposed revisions to Federal Rules of Civil Procedure, Rule 4. These proposed revisions, which will be submitted to the Judicial Conference in September 1992, would generally not authorize service by methods that violate the law of the country in which the defendant is located. Proposed Rule 4(f)(2)(C), which would replace current Rule 4(i)(1)(D), allows service on a foreign defendant:

> *unless prohibited by the law of the foreign country,* by (i) delivery to the individual personally of a copy of the summons and complaint; or (ii) any form of mail requiring a signed receipt, to be addressed and dispatched by the clerk of the court to the party to be served. (Emphasis added).

If proposed Rule 4(f)(2)(C) were in effect today, then contrary to our holding here, the new Rule would preclude a district court clerk from serving process by signed receipt mail on a defendant in a country whose laws forbid that method of service. Thus, the actions of the district court clerk in the present case in refusing to make service on the Swiss defendants would likely have been appropriate under the proposed Rule. However, the existing Rule, and not the proposed Rule, was in force when the district court clerk refused to allow service of process by signed receipt mail on the Swiss defendants. Consequently, the existing Rule must necessarily control the outcome in this case. While foreign objections to specific service methods may result in Congressional modifications to Rule 4, such objections cannot justify non-compliance with that Rule's current requirements at any time before the proposed revisions to Rule 4 are properly enacted. ...

We therefore disagree with the D.C. Circuit, which reasoned, albeit in dictum, that Rule 4(i)(1) provided five alternative methods of service so that the availability of an alternative method of service could render inoperative any methods to which objections had been raised by a foreign government. In so reasoning, the court stated that Rule 4(i)(1) "underlines rather than obviates the need for judicial sensitivity to foreign territorial sovereignty when scrutinizing particular methods of overseas service." *FTC v. Compagnie de Saint-Gobain-Pont-a-Mousson*, 636 F.2d 1300, 1314 (D.C. Cir. 1980) (holding the Federal Trade Commission's service by mail of an investigatory subpoena on a French corporation in France to be ineffective). We read no such message in the unambiguous language of Rule 4(i)(1). ... Rule 4(i)(1) neither explicitly nor implicitly requires any deference to foreign governments or to the U.S. Department of State in the manner by which service of process shall be made. We therefore hold that all five of that Rule's service methods must remain equally available to plaintiffs who, like the plaintiffs in the instant case, wish to serve process in foreign countries.

EXHIBIT A

Memorandum dated November 6, 1980 from the Administrative Office of the United States Court Clerks re Service of Process in Foreign Countries:

The Department of State has advised us that a number of foreign states have recently submitted diplomatic notes of protest objecting to service of process of international mail upon defendants residing within their territory. This memorandum is being distributed in an attempt to clarify the procedures to be followed in serving American judicial documents abroad.

Service upon defendants abroad in cases arising in federal district courts is governed generally by Rule 4(i) of the Federal Rules of Civil Procedure. Service by mail is dealt with in Rule 4(i)(1)(D). That Rule provides that the clerks of court shall be responsible for dispatching the summons and complaint into the international mails. When summonses and complaints are mailed abroad in accordance with Rule 4(i)(1)(D), this method of service, according to some foreign states, violates either the judicial sovereignty of those foreign states or international law. These governments protest that such service usurps the functions of duly designated officials of their country who are charged by the domestic laws of their country to perform service of process. Similarly, service by international mail in those countries which are a party of the [Hague Service] Convention, and which have made a reservation with respect to Article 10(a) of the Convention, whereby a state declares it objects to service by international mail, has also generated diplomatic notes of protest. In order to avoid this problem in the future, we are requesting clerks of court to refrain from sending summonses and complaints by international mail to foreign defendants in those countries which have protested service by international mail, namely Czechoslovakia, Switzerland, and the Union of Soviet Socialist Republics. In those countries, letters rogatory are the appropriate mechanism for service.

FEDERAL RULES OF CIVIL PROCEDURE, RULE 4(f)

[excerpted at pp. 1057-60, Appendix C]

Notes on Nahas, Old Rule 4(i), Umbenhauer, and New Rule 4(f)

1. *Appropriate U.S. response to foreign restrictions on the service abroad of U.S. process within local territory.* As a matter of policy, how *should* U.S. courts and legislatures respond when U.S. process is served abroad in violation of foreign law? Should such service be treated as valid under U.S. law? Or should U.S. courts hold that service which complies only with U.S. law is not effective?

2. *Federal statutes authorizing service of process abroad.* A number of federal statutes authorize the service of U.S. process abroad. One example is the Walsh Act, now codified at 28 U.S.C. §1783, which specifically authorizes service of subpoenas on U.S. citizens outside the United States. Section 1783 is reproduced in Appendix H, and provides:

> A court of the United States may order the issuance of a subpoena requiring the appearance as a witness before it, or before a person or body designated by it, of a national or resident of the United States who is in a foreign country, or requiring the production of a specified document or other thing by him, if the court finds that particular testimony or the production of the document or other thing by him is necessary in the interest of justice, and, in other than a criminal action or proceeding, if the court finds, in addition, that it is not possible to obtain his testimony in admissible form without his personal appearance or to obtain the production of the document or other thing in any other manner. ...

Other federal statutes, identified in *Nahas*, permit the service of investigative subpoenas abroad. *E.g.*, 15 U.S.C. §1312(d)(2); 15 U.S.C. §576-1(c)(6)(B). Indeed, after *Nahas* was decided, Congress amended 7 U.S.C. §15 to make it clear that the CFTC could serve subpoenas abroad.

3. *U.S. service abroad is valid under U.S. law, notwithstanding violation of foreign law, if federal law specifically permits such service.* If a valid federal statute specifically authorizes a mechanism of service abroad, federal courts generally do not have the power to forbid such service on the grounds that it violates foreign law. That is made clear by the comments in *Nahas* that "this case does not pose a question about the authority of Congress; rather, it poses a question about the congressional intent embodied in 7 U.S.C. §15." *Nahas* went on to make clear that "federal courts must give effect to a valid unambiguous congressional mandate, even if such effect would conflict with another nation's laws or violate international law." Or, as the Court says in *Umbenhauer*, "[n]either we, the Department of State, nor the Administrative Office of the United States Courts possess the authority to circumvent, ignore or deviate from the Federal Rules of Civil Procedure." This is, of course, similar to the role of customary international law in other U.S. contexts. *See supra* pp. 21-22 & 510-11.

4. *Interpretation of silent or ambiguous federal statutes or rules to determine whether service abroad in violation of foreign law is permitted.* Statutory authorizations for service do not always specifically address the question whether service abroad in violation of foreign law is permitted. In such cases, should U.S. courts interpret a silent or generally-worded statute to permit service abroad in violation of foreign law? Recall the *Charming Betsy* presumption that Congress does not intend to violate international law. *See supra* pp. 22 & 510-11.

Nahas held that the service of an administrative subpoena in Brazil, in violation of Brazilian law, was not authorized by 7 U.S.C. §15 — notwithstanding the provision's broad language. *Nahas* relied on the "canon of statutory construction that requires courts, wherever possible, to construe federal statutes to ensure their application will not violate international law." 738 F.2d at 493 (relying on *Charming Betsy*, 6 U.S. at 118). The same result was reached, with respect to a Federal Trade Commission subpoena served in France, in *Saint-Gobain*. 636 F.2d at 1323 & n.130.

5. *Propriety of presumption against service in violation of foreign law.* Is it appropriate for U.S. courts to adopt a presumption that federal law does not authorize service in violation of foreign, and therefore international, law? Recall the comments by Professor Smit concerning the legitimacy and wisdom of foreign prohibitions on U.S. service. *See supra* pp. 778-79. Is Congress more likely to be mindful of the sentiments underlying these comments, or of the *Schooner Betsy* adage against violations of international law? Recall also the debate whether service abroad by private means even involves government conduct or international law. *See supra* pp. 778-79.

Suppose that a foreign state simply refuses to permit service of foreign process. Suppose that it forbids service of various categories of complaints — such as antitrust actions, claims seeking punitive damages, or the like. Should Congress be presumed to defer to such prohibitions? If it voted on the question, what result do you think Congress would reach?

6. *Interpretation of Walsh Act and other federal service statutes.* Reread the Walsh Act and amended 7 U.S.C. §15. Does the text of any of these statutes expressly permit service abroad *in violation of foreign law?* Does an authorization for extraterritorial service necessarily constitute an authorization for service abroad contrary to foreign law? Must such an authorization be implied? Recall the application of the territoriality presumption in *Aramco*, requiring clear and affirmative language to extend U.S. legislation extraterritorially, *see supra* pp. 563-70 & 573. If an equivalent standard of proof if applied to the Walsh Act and 7 U.S.C. §15, is it satisfied? Under *Nahas*, is it permissible to imply such an authorization?

Under international law, a state may of course consent to the service of process on its territory; the United States and other nations do so. *See infra* pp. 838-41. Service of process in such states is not a violation of international law. Why, therefore, should it be presumed that Congress did not intend to permit *extraterritorial* service? Should not the relevant presumption be that Congress did not intend to permit extraterritorial service *in violation of foreign law, and hence, international law?* If so, would any of the above statutes, which merely authorize extraterritorial service, overcome this presumption?

7. *U.S. governmental responses to foreign diplomatic protests regarding extraterritorial service of U.S. process.* The U.S. Executive Branch has traditionally responded cooperatively to foreign diplomatic protests concerning U.S. service of process within local territory. After Swiss protests during the late 1950's to the service of U.S. administrative subpoenas within Swiss territory, the State Department responded in an aide-memoire expressing regret for the "inadvertent violation of applicable Swiss law" and stating that U.S. agencies would seek to "avoid any future transmittals of such documents in a manner inconsistent with Swiss law." *Contemporary Practice of the United States Relating to International Law*, 56 Am. J. Int'l L. 793, 794 (1962). Is this an appropriate attitude? What would Professor Smit say? What if a foreign state refuses to permit any service on its nationals?

8. *Administrative Office statement on extraterritorial service of administrative subpoenas.* During the 1970s, mail service abroad by private U.S. litigants led to renewed Swiss (and other) protests. In response, the Administrative Office of the United States Court Clerks issued a memorandum, dated November 6, 1980, directing that any service to be effected on Swiss soil be done pursuant to letter rogatory. The memorandum requested clerks of U.S. courts to "refrain from sending summonses and complaints by international mail to foreign defendants in those countries which have protested service by international mail." The memorandum is appended to the opinion in *Umbenhauer*, excerpted above. As discussed below, some courts relied on the Administrative Conference memorandum in requiring service of civil complaints in Switzerland by letters rogatory; other courts, like the Third Circuit in *Umbenhauer*, ignored the Administrative Office memorandum. Which position is wiser?

9. *Service abroad under pre-1993 Rule 4(i).* As described above, old Rule 4(i) set forth five mechanisms for service abroad; Rule 4(i) contained no express requirement that service be effected consistent with foreign law.

(a) *Lower courts holding that old Rule 4(i) permitted service of process abroad in violation of foreign law.* Applying the pre-1993 version of the Federal Rules of Civil Procedure, *Umbenhauer* and other courts flatly rejected the argument that service on the defendant in a foreign state in violation of local foreign law provided a basis for quashing service in U.S. courts. *Umbenhauer* held that service made as provided by the Federal Rules was valid under those Rules, and that violations of foreign law were simply irrelevant to the interpretation of the Federal Rules or to the validity of service under the Rules. *Umbenhauer* was consistent with the weight of lower court authority under old Rule 4. *See supra* p. 780. As the *Restatement (Third) Foreign Relations Law* §472, Reporters' Note 2 (1987), explains, "the prevailing view is that, absent a treaty obligation, courts in the United States will give effect to ... process" served abroad in violation of foreign law.

(b) *Lower courts holding that old Rule 4(i) did not permit service of process abroad in violation of foreign law.* A few U.S. courts refused to permit service of process abroad under old Rule 4 in violation of foreign law, on the theory that this was not specifically authorized by the Federal Rules. The court in *R.M.B. Electrostat v. Lectra Trading AG*, 1983 W.L. 1371 (E.D. Pa. Jan. 17, 1983), required use of letters rogatory when serving a civil complaint and summons in Switzerland. Citing the Administrative Office statement, *see supra* p. 791, the court apparently reasoned that the drafters of Federal Rule 4 did not intend to authorize service abroad in circumstances that would violate foreign and international law. *See also Aries Ventures v. AXA Finance SA*, 729 F.Supp. 289 (S.D.N.Y. 1990); *SEC v. Tome*, 833 F.2d 1086, 1091 (2d Cir. 1983) (amending order under Rule 4(i)(1)(e) to omit service by publication in Swiss newspaper, on grounds that such publication would violate Swiss law).

10. *Service of process abroad in violation of foreign law under new Rule 4(f).* As *Umbenhauer* discussed, new Rule 4(f) of the Federal Rules of Civil Procedure significantly transforms the service of U.S. process abroad.

(a) *Rule 4(f)(1).* Rule 4(f)(1) requires use of any mandatory "internationally agreed means" of service that is reasonably calculated to give notice. This category expressly includes the Hague Service Convention, discussed in detail below. *See infra* pp. 808-09. Only "if there is no internationally agreed means of service or the applicable international agreement allows other means of service," is Rule 4(f)(2) available. *See supra* pp. 766-68.

(b) *Rule 4(f)(2).* Rule 4(f)(2), which permits three alternative types of service, was drafted to require compliance with the laws of the place where service is effected. Thus, Rule 4(f)(2)(A) permits service in "the manner prescribed by the law of the foreign country for service in that country in an action in any of its courts of general jurisdiction." Rule 4(f)(2)(B) authorizes service as directed by a foreign authority "in response to a letter rogatory." And Rule 4(f)(2)(C) permits service by either personal delivery or return-receipt mail "unless prohibited by the law of the foreign country." The Advisory Committee Notes to Rule 4(f) explain that "[s]ervice by methods that would violate foreign law is not generally authorized."

(c) *Rule 4(f)(3).* Finally, Rule 4(f)(3) provides that service may be made "by other means [than those set forth above] not prohibited by international agreement as may be directed by the court." Thus, while the provisions of U.S. treaties cannot be violated, Rule 4(f)(3) does not specifically forbid courts from ordering means of service that violate foreign law. But, absent a court order, new Rule 4 generally forbids service abroad in violation of foreign law. This is a substantial change from old Rule 4(i).

11. *Wisdom of forbidding service abroad in violation of foreign law under new Rule 4(f).* Is the general approach of new Rule 4(f) sensible from a policy perspective? Should service in violation of foreign law be generally prohibited by the Federal Rules? Consider:

> Prohibiting U.S. methods of service that violate foreign law ... could lead to undesirable costs. ... The costs would stem from the anticipated distracting disputes over whether the method of service used by a plaintiff in a particular case conformed with or infringed foreign law. In the right circumstances, defendants can be expected to challenge service on exactly that ground, and such disputes will be especially burdensome because they will require a U.S. court to determine foreign law on a subject particularly sensitive to some foreign countries.

Born & Vollmer, *The Effect of the Revised Federal Rules of Civil Procedure on Personal Jurisdiction, Service and Discovery in International Cases*, 150 F.R.D. 221, 239-40 (1993). Are these costs important? Is it not more important to avoid giving offense to foreign states? What would Professor Smit, whose views were excerpted above, *supra* pp. 778-79, say? *See* Smit, *Recent Developments in International Litigation*, 35 S. Tex. L. Rev. 215, 224 (1994).

Why didn't old Rule 4(i) require U.S. service to comply with foreign law? Recall that old Rule 4(i) was adopted after a commission of experts comprehensively reviewed the subject of international service. *See supra* pp. 765-66. Consider the comments made at the time by proponents of Rule 4(i):

> The situations in which service in federal actions must be made abroad are diverse and so are the laws and conditions of the foreign countries. It therefore seemed wise to set up a number of

alternative permissible manners of service that would provide a fair amount of choice and flexibility while assuring that the foreign defendant would get good notice. Kaplan, *Amendments of the Federal Rules of Civil Procedure, 1961-1963 (I)*, 77 Harv. L. Rev. 633, 635 (1964).

Was it error to replace the flexible old Rule 4(i) with new Rule 4(f)?

12. *Validity of service in violation of foreign law under Rule 4(f)(3).* Recall the *Charming Betsy* presumption, invoked in *Nahas*, that Congress does not intend to violate international law. Is Rule 4(f)(3) sufficiently clear to permit the conclusion that U.S. courts may violate foreign and international law? Note that Rule 4(f)(3) merely authorizes court-ordered service that does not violate a U.S. treaty. Does this "silence" authorize service in violate of foreign law? *Compare EEOC v. Arabian American Oil Company*, 499 U.S. 244 (1991), excerpted and discussed above, holding that a negative implication is insufficient to overcome the presumption that federal statutes apply only to conduct within U.S. territory. *See infra* pp. 563-70 & 573.

Should new Rule 4(f)(3) have been drafted to permit U.S. courts to order service abroad in violation of foreign law? Is it not unacceptable for a U.S. court to deliberately order (or engage in) a violation of foreign law? Recall the rationales for the foreign sovereign compulsion doctrine. Are there circumstances in which such action would be justified?

13. *Validity under Rules Enabling Act of Federal Rules authorizing violations of foreign law.* The Federal Rules of Civil Procedure are made by the Supreme Court, pursuant to delegation from Congress by the Rules Enabling Act, 28 U.S.C. §2072. The Rules Enabling Act provides:

(a) The Supreme Court shall have the power to prescribe general rules of practice and procedure and rules of evidence for cases in the United States district courts (including proceedings before magistrates thereof) and courts of appeals.

(b) Such rules shall not abridge, enlarge or modify any substantive right. All laws in conflict with such rules shall be of no further force or effect after such rules have taken effect.

Nothing in the Rules Enabling Act contains any suggestion that the Federal Rules may violate international law. Can the Court nonetheless authorize such violations when it promulgates the Rules? *See* Burbank, *The World in Our Courts*, 89 Mich. L. Rev. 1456, 1481-4 (1991).

14. *New Rule 4(f)(2)(A)'s authorization for service as prescribed by foreign law.* New Rule 4(f)(2)(A) authorizes the service of process "in the manner prescribed by the law of the foreign country [where service is effected] for service in that country in an action in any of its courts of general jurisdiction." Rule 4(f)(2)(A) is an unhappily-drafted provision that can be expected to produce confusion. Suppose that a foreign state permits litigants in its local courts to effect service by ordinary mail, but requires that foreign service be made in some other fashion. Does Rule 4(f)(2)(A) authorize service by ordinary mail, notwithstanding the violation of foreign law regarding service from foreign courts? More generally, does Rule 4(f)(2)(A) permit service as permitted by local law for actions in local courts, or does it require reference to local law regarding service from foreign courts? This issue was considered, under similarly-worded language contained in old Rule 4(i)(A), in *Grand Entertainment Group, Ltd. v. Star Media Sales, Inc.*, 988 F.2d 476, 487-88 (3d Cir. 1993). The court concluded that compliance with local law regarding service of *foreign* process was required. The Rule's purpose:

would be frustrated, and it would be an affront to national sovereignty, if a U.S. court applied Spain's procedures for service in cases brought in a Spanish court against parties found in Spain if Spain has enacted special provisions governing service of process issued out of the courts of other nations on behalf of foreign plaintiffs against persons found in the receiving jurisdiction. It seems to us that Rule 4(i) permits a foreign jurisdiction to refuse to subject its residents or nationals to service of process issued by a foreign court in the same manner as it does for domestic plaintiffs suing in a Spanish court. Spain, or indeed any other foreign jurisdiction, could rationally decide to impose special burdens on foreign process because service of process issued by a foreign court may require residents of the receiving state to defend themselves in distant and inconvenient places against laws that impose duties that nationals or residents of the receiving state have not foreseen or are unaccustomed to taking into account. Thus, Spain may impose more onerous formalities on service of process issued by a foreign court than it would for service of domestic process. It could do so out of a desire to impress on its residents the need to take action, and not to ignore the foreign process simply because the court issuing it is remote, a kind of cavalier attitude that is less likely in the face of domestic process.

Is that persuasive? Doesn't the language of Rule 4(f)(2)(A) suggest that the relevant rules are those concerning service in *local* courts? *See also American Centennial Ins. Co. v. Seguros La Republica, SA,* 1991 WL 60378 (S.D.N.Y. 1991) (applying old Rule 4(i)(A) and requiring compliance with Mexican law regarding service from a foreign court); *Modern Computer Corp. v. Ma,* 862 F.Supp. 938 (E.D.N.Y. 1994).

15. *Distinction between service of a civil complaint and service of a subpoena. Nahas* drew a sharp distinction between service of a complaint -— which it characterized as merely giving "notice" -— and service of a subpoena -— which it characterized as exerting "compulsion." The court thought that "[w]hen process in the form of a complaint is served extraterritorially, the informational nature of the process renders the act of service relatively benign in terms of infringement on the foreign nation's sovereignty." *See also Saint-Gobain,* at 1323 & n.130.

Is the distinction between "notice" and "compulsory" process satisfying? Failure to comply with a subpoena may result in civil (or in some cases even criminal) penalties. For the most part, however, these will be fairly modest -— at least when compared with the potentially huge default judgments that can be triggered by proper service of mere "notice" pleadings such as civil complaints. Moreover, why should U.S. distinctions between a complaint and a subpoena determine the permissibility of service in a foreign nation that regards both types of service as equally unlawful? Does international law recognize a distinction between complaints and subpoenas?

If the notice/compulsion distinction is abandoned, is it possible to square *Nahas* with *Umbenhauer* — where the court apparently made no effort to reconcile the U.S. service provisions with either Swiss or international law? If U.S. service would violate foreign law, and international law, then shouldn't a specific authorization for such a result be required? Note that *Nahas* involved service of a document issued by a U.S. government agency. Is this relevant to the international law concerns underlying *Nahas*? Recall Professor Smit's efforts to distinguish "public" service from "private" service. *See supra* p. 778.

16. *Consequences of service abroad in violation of foreign law.* The plaintiff in *Umbenhauer* was permitted to proceed with its U.S. lawsuit, notwithstanding the fact that its service would be defective under Swiss law. Would you counsel a client to ignore the law of the defendant's home state in serving process in that country?

(a) *Liability resulting from service abroad in violation of foreign law.* One possible consequence of service abroad in violation of foreign law is criminal or civil sanctions against the process server. Recall the difficulties of the German accountant, noted above, who violated Article 271 of the Swiss Criminal Code. *See supra* p. 776 n.131. Several nations have imposed sanctions against U.S. process-servers for attempting to personally deliver U.S. complaints and summonses to foreign defendants. *See, e.g.,* U.S. Department of Justice Memorandum No. 386 at 20 (1977), *reprinted in* 16 Int'l Leg. Mat. 1331, 1338 (1977) (U.S. government attorneys sued for trespass for serving a subpoena in the Bahamas; U.S. government attorney indicted for serving subpoena in France). Civil liability is also a possibility.

(b) *Unenforceability of U.S. judgment based on service abroad in violation of foreign law.* Perhaps most importantly for private plaintiffs, service abroad in violation of foreign law can jeopardize the enforceability of any U.S. judgment that the plaintiff obtains. "The enforcement of a judgment in the foreign country in which the service was made may be embarrassed or prevented if the service did not comport with the law of that country." Federal Rules of Civil Procedure, Rule 4(i) Advisory Committee Notes. *See, e.g.,* Code of Civil Procedure (Federal Republic of Germany) §328 ("A judgment of a foreign court shall not be recognized ... if a defendant who has not entered an appearance on the merits was not properly served."); Westin, *Enforcing Foreign Commercial Judgments and Arbitral Awards in the United States, West Germany, and England,* 19 Law & Pol. Int'l Bus. 325 (1987); *Daiei K.K. v. Blagojevic,* 22 Japanese Annual of Int'l Law 160 (Tokyo Dist. Ct. 1978) (refusing to enforce French judgment because of defective mail service of untranslated complaint and summons). *See also infra* pp. 963-68.

2. Service of Process Abroad Pursuant to the Hague Service Convention[155]

The United States has ratified two multilateral conventions that institutionalize and improve the basic letter rogatory approach to service of process: the Hague Convention on Service Abroad of Judicial and Extrajudicial Documents in Civil and Commercial Matters (the Hague Service Convention)[156] and the Inter-American Convention on Letters Rogatory.[157] As described below, the Hague Service Convention and the Inter-American Convention adopt broadly similar approaches to the service of process abroad.[158]

a. The Hague Service Convention Is Not a Basis for Personal Jurisdiction

The Hague Service Convention does not provide a basis for personal jurisdiction in federal court. Rather, personal jurisdiction must be established through some substantive grant contained in Rule 4 of the Federal Rules of Civil Procedure, or the state and federal long-arm statutes that it incorporates.[159] This result is evident from the language and purposes of the Convention, which dealt only with the giving of notice, and not the granting of jurisdiction. In one court's words:

> We believe that the purpose and nature of the [Hague Service Convention] demonstrates that it does not provide independent authorization for service of process in a foreign country. The treaty merely provides a mechanism by which a plaintiff authorized to serve process under the laws of its country can effect service that will give appropriate notice to the party being served. ... We believe that the treaty merely serves as an important adjunct to state long-arm rules, and that it specifies a valid method of effecting service abroad only if the state long-arm rule authorizes service abroad. ... Nor do we read the treaty as the equivalent of a federal statute authorizing service in a foreign country. Instead, we believe that the treaty is similar to Rule 4(i) in

---

155. Commentary on the Hague Service Convention includes, *e.g.*, Committee on Federal Courts, N.Y. State Bar Ass'n, *Service of Process Abroad: A Nuts and Bolts Guide*, 122 F.R.D. 63 (1989); Amram, *The Convention on Service Abroad of Judicial and Extrajudicial Documents in Civil and Commercial Matters*, 59 Am. J. Int'l L. 90 (1965); Amram, *The Proposed International Convention on the Service of Documents Abroad*, 51 A.B.A.J. 650 (1965); Hamilton, *An Interpretation of the Hague Convention on the Service of Process Abroad of Judicial and Extrajudicial Documents Concerning Personal Service in Japan*, 6 Loy. L.A. Int'l & Comp. L.J. 143 (1983); Kim & Sisneros, *Comparative Overview of Service of Process: United States, Japan, and Attempts at International Unity*, 23 Vand. J. Trans. L. 299 (1990); Note, *The Interplay Between Domestic Rules Permitting Service Abroad by Mail and the Hague Convention on Service: Proposing an Amendment to the Federal Rules of Civil Procedure*, 22 Cornell Int'l L. J. 335 (1989); B. Ristau, *International Judicial Assistance* (1990 Rev.).

156. 20 U.S.T. 361-73, T.I.A.S. No. 6638, 658 U.N.T.S. 163. The Hague Service Convention is reprinted in Appendix I.

157. Inter-American Convention on Letters Rogatory, signed in Panama on January 30, 1975, *reprinted in* 14 Int'l Leg. Mat. 339 (1975) and Additional Protocol to the Inter-American Convention on Letters Rogatory, signed in Montevideo, Uruguay on May 8, 1979, *reprinted in* 18 Int'l Leg. Mat. 1238 (1979). For commentary on the Convention, *see* Low, *International Judicial Assistance among the American States - The Inter-American Conventions*, 18 Int'l Law. 705 (1984).

158. *See* Kearney, *Developments in Private International Law*, 81 Am. J. Int'l L. 724, 737 (1987).

159. *See supra* pp. 69-70 & 761-63.

that it provides a "manner" of service to be used by a litigant with the requisite authority to serve process. Were we to hold otherwise, we would attribute to the Senate that ratified the treaty the intent to authorize the equivalent of "world-wide" service of process in all federal-question, admiralty, and diversity cases while at the same time not authorizing nationwide service of process for those same claims.[160]

Other lower federal courts uniformly agree,[161] and the same result generally applies in state courts.[162]

b. Historical Background

The Hague Service Convention was drafted under the auspices of the Hague Conference on Private International Law.[163] The Convention was based upon, and intended to modernize, the Hague Convention on Civil Procedure of 1954 and the earlier 1905 Hague Convention on Civil Procedure.[164] Chapter I of both conventions dealt with service of process abroad.

Historically, the United States did not participate in the work of the Hague Conference, citing constitutional limitations arising from the U.S. federal system.[165] As U.S. international commerce expanded following 1945, however, U.S. interest in international judicial assistance increased. At the same time, U.S. federalism doctrines had evolved dramatically, and objections to federal involvement in interna-

---

160. *DeJames v. Magnificence Carriers, Inc.*, 654 F.2d 280, 288 (3d Cir. 1981). The Court of Appeals remarked that it did "not believe that the treaty in any way affect[ed] a state's chosen limits on the jurisdictional reach of its courts."

161. *See Richardson v. Volkswagenwerk AG*, 552 F.Supp. 73 (W.D. Mo. 1982); *Hantover, Inc. v. Omet, S.N.C.*, 688 F.Supp. 1377, 1384 n.10 (W.D. Mo. 1988); *Lana Mora, Inc. v. S.S. Woermann Ulanga*, 672 F.Supp. 125, 128 (S.D.N.Y. 1987). The Federal Rules of Civil Procedure are in accord. The language of new Rule 4(f) and 4(k), which specifically distinguish between the service of process and a basis for personal jurisdiction, also suggest that the Convention was not understood to provide a basis for personal jurisdiction in federal courts.

162. *Re v. Breezy Point Lumber Co.*, 460 N.Y.S.2d 264, 266 (Sup. Ct. 1983). Federal or state law could theoretically provide that service under the Hague Service Convention is an independently sufficient basis for personal jurisdiction. No state appears to have done so, however, and any such approach would encounter insurmountable due process problems in many cases.

163. The Hague Conference, organized in 1893, acts as an international forum for representatives of member states to discuss and propose multilateral accords for the unification and harmonization of private international law. *See* Pfund, *International Unification of Private Law: A Report on United States Participation*, 1985-86, 20 Int'l Law. 623 (1986); Pfund, *United States Participation in International Unification of Private Law*, 19 Int'l Law. 505 (1985); Comment, *The United States and the Hague Conferences on Private International Law*, 1 Am. J. Comp. L. 268 (1952); Amram, *Report on the Tenth Session of the Hague Conference on Private International Law*, 59 Am. J. Int'l L. 87 (1965); Graveson, *The Tenth Session of the Hague Conference of Private International Law*, 14 Int'l & Comp. L. Q. 528 (1965).

164. Amram, *Report on the Tenth Session of the Hague Conference on Private International Law*, 59 Am. J. Int'l L. 87 (1965); Graveson, *The Tenth Session of the Hague Conference of Private International Law*, 14 Int'l & Comp. L. Q. 528 (1965).

165. Nadelmann, *The United States Joins the Hague Conference on Private International Law (A History With Comments)*, 30 Law & Contemp. Probs. 291 (1965); Pfund, *United States Participation in International Unification of Private Law*, 19 Int'l Law. 505 (1985).

tional litigation reforms were muted. In 1956, the United States sent an observing delegation to the Hague Conference for the first time.[166]

In 1958, Congress established the Commission on International Rules of Judicial Procedure to study methods of international assistance and recommend improvements in federal law.[167] The Commission ultimately recommended a series of proposals, which significantly liberalized both the mechanisms for serving U.S. process abroad and assisting foreign courts in serving process in the United States.[168] On December 30, 1963, President Johnson signed a resolution authorizing U.S. participation in the Hague Conference,[169] and the United States attended the Tenth Session of the Hague Conference. Soon thereafter, the President signed into law the proposals of the Commission on International Rules of Judicial Procedure.[170] The new legislation was denominated as Public Law 88-619, later codified as 28 U.S.C. §§1696, 1781, 1782, and 1783.

The United States actively participated in the Tenth Session of the Hague Conference. The Tenth Session concerned a draft of the Hague Service Convention. Although the United States was not involved in the early drafting of the Convention, the proposed agreement complemented the parallel U.S. efforts to provide foreign nations with more extensive judicial assistance. The U.S. delegates urged that the Convention establish a liberal international regime for the transnational service of process. These delegates subsequently reported their perception that U.S. views were influential in shaping the Convention.[171]

The United States was an early signatory of the new Hague Service Convention in 1967.[172] It ratified the Convention in 1969. As of January 1, 1995, some thirty other nations had ratified or acceded to the Convention.[173] The Convention remains open for accession by any state.[174]

---

166. *See* Pfund, *United States Participation in International Unification of Private Law*, 19 Int'l Law. 505 (1985); Note, *The Effect of the Hague Convention on Service Abroad of Judicial and Extrajudicial Documents in Civil or Commercial Matters*, 2 Cornell Int'l L.J. 125, 126 (1969).

167. *See supra* pp. 765-66; S. Rep. No. 2392, 85th Cong., 2d Sess. 3 (1958).

168. Pub. L. 88-619, 78 Stat. 996 (1964). The Act's legislative history is at H.R. Rep. No. 1052, 88th Cong., 1st Sess. (1963); S. Rep. No. 1580, 88th Cong., 2d Sess. (1964). The proposals included what became Rule 4(i) of the Federal Rules of Civil Procedure, and statutory proposals that would be codified as 28 U.S.C. §§1696, 1781, 1782, and 1783.

169. Pub. L. No. 88-244, 77 Stat. 775 (1963).

170. Pub. L. No. 88-619, 78 Stat. 995 (1964).

171. Amram, *The Proposed International Convention on the Service of Documents Abroad*, 51 A.B.A.J. 650, 652 (1965).

172. *See* Note, *The Effect of the Hague Convention on Service Abroad of Judicial and Extrajudicial Documents in Civil or Commercial Matters*, 2 Cornell Int'l L.J. 125, 127-28 (1969).

173. As of October 1995, parties to the Hague Service Convention included Belgium, Canada, China, Cyprus, Czech Republic, Denmark, Egypt, Finland, France, Germany, Greece, Israel, Italy, Japan, Luxembourg, Netherlands, Norway, Pakistan, Portugal, Slovak Republic, Spain, Sweden, Switzerland, Turkey, the United Kingdom, and the United States. Complete lists of all parties to the Convention are included in the Martindale-Hubbell Law Directory and the United States Code Annotated sections following Federal Rules of Civil Procedure 4.

174. Hague Service Convention, Article 28.

3. Overview of the Hague Service Convention

The Hague Service Convention consists of 31 articles, which must be read in conjunction with the designations, declarations, and reservations made by individual member states in acceding to the Convention. The Convention is expressed in equally authoritative English and French versions.[175] The Convention's drafting history has been collected, and is useful in interpreting the agreement.[176]

The centerpiece of the Hague Service Convention is the "Central Authority" mechanism for service abroad, set forth in Articles 2 through 7. The Convention requires each contracting state to establish a Central Authority within its governmental administration.[177] In ratifying or acceding to the Convention, contracting states must identify their Central Authority.[178] The Central Authority is responsible for receiving foreign requests for service of process ("letters of request"); serving or arranging for the service of documents on local residents; and returning or arranging for return of proof of service to the requesting state.[179] This mechanism is available to litigants in virtually all civil or commercial cases where process is served from one contracting state into another contracting state.

The Convention establishes uniform requirements regarding the form and authentication of requests for service via the Central Authority mechanism.[180] A model letter of request is attached to the Convention,[181] as is a model certificate of proof of service.[182] These forms must be used. The Convention also establishes requirements concerning the languages to be used in letters of request and the translation of documents accompanying letters of request.[183]

With very limited exceptions, a Central Authority is obliged by the Convention to execute incoming requests for service from other signatory States; it has no discretion to decline to effect service. Only if a letter of request does not comply with the Convention's formal requirements[184] or if it infringes the receiving state's "sovereignty or security" may the request be denied.[185]

In addition to the Central Authority mechanism, the Convention also provides the possibility of service in alternative ways. In particular, Articles 8 and 9 of the Convention permit service through the requesting state's diplomatic or consular

---

175. Hague Service Convention, Final Clause.

176. Conference de la Haye de Droit International Privé, *Actes et Documents de la Dixième Session* (1964) (hereinafter "*Actes et Documents*"). Most of the significant documents prepared in connection with the drafting and negotiation of the Hague Service Convention, as well as transcripts of many proceedings, are compiled in the "*Actes et Documents.*"

177. Hague Service Convention, Article 2.

178. Hague Service Convention, Articles 2 & 21.

179. Hague Service Convention, Articles 5 & 6.

180. Hague Service Convention, Article 7.

181. Hague Service Convention, Article 3.

182. Hague Service Convention, Article 6.

183. Hague Service Convention, Articles 5 & 7.

184. Hague Service Convention, Article 4.

185. Hague Service Convention, Article 13.

agents; Article 10(b) and (c) permit service by "judicial officers or other competent persons"; Article 10(a) permits "sending" of documents by mail; and Article 19 permits service pursuant to the "internal law of a contracting State" where service is to be effected. Importantly, all of these alternative mechanisms are available only if the receiving state permits their use. In ratifying or acceding to the Convention, a state may declare which of these alternative mechanisms of service it will not permit.[186] As discussed below, many contracting states have objected to the use of one or more of these mechanisms.[187]

Finally, the Convention limits the circumstances in which default judgments can be made. Article 15 of the Convention provides that, where service abroad has been made under the Convention, a default judgment cannot be entered unless it is shown either that: (a) service was in accordance with local law in the place where service was effected, or (b) service was actually delivered to the defendant or his residence pursuant to a method permitted by the Convention.[188] The Convention also requires a showing that the defendant received service in sufficient time to respond.

4. Purposes of the Hague Service Convention

The Hague Service Convention was intended by its drafters to fulfill several related objectives. First, the Convention sought to provide a simple and expeditious procedure for service of process abroad.[189] The Convention's preamble states that its purpose is "to improve the organization of mutual judicial assistance ... by simplifying and expediting the procedure." The Convention attempts to accomplish this end primarily by means of the "Central Authority" mechanism and the introduction of mandatory forms of letters of request and proof of service. At the same time, the Convention also permits alternative forms of service — subject to objection by the state of destination — that are more flexible.

Second, the United States and other nations were concerned about service mechanisms in certain civil law states that did not afford defendants adequate notice.[190] The principal example was *"notification au parquet,"* whereby service was effected by depositing documents with a local government official.[191] The Convention sought to address concerns about service that failed to provide reason-

---

186. Hague Service Convention, Article 21.

187. *See infra* pp. 809-22.

188. *See infra* p. 834.

189. S. Rep. No. 2397, 85th Cong., 2d Sess. at 7 (1958), *reprinted in*, 1958 U.S. Code, Cong. & Admin. News at 5206; *Volkswagenwerk AG v. Schlunk*, 486 U.S. 694, 698 (1988).

190. S. Exec. Rep. No. 6, 90th Congress, 1st Sess. 6 (1967) ("Given the continually increasing volume of American travel abroad, especially in Europe, of international business transactions, of United States investment abroad, the subject of insuring that United States citizens who were sued in foreign courts received notice ... is a matter of substantial importance to this country."); Note, *Service Abroad Under the Hague Convention*, 71 Marq. L. Rev. 649, 650-57 (1988); *Volkswagenwerk AG v. Schlunk*, 486 U.S. 694, 702-05 (1988).

191. *See Volkswagenwerk AG v. Schlunk*, 486 U.S. 694 (1988).

able notice[192] by creating "appropriate means to ensure that judicial and extra-judicial documents to be served abroad shall be brought to the notice of the addressee in sufficient time."[193] The Convention does so by establishing service mechanisms likely to provide actual notice and by limiting default judgments in cases where proper notice was not given.[194]

Third, some civil law countries were concerned that reliance on "unofficial" means of service in the United States might interfere with their nationals' ability to effect "official" service, as required by foreign law, on U.S. residents in connection with civil law proceedings.[195] By establishing the Central Authority mechanism, the Convention provided a way that service could be effected in the United States (and other nations) by the actions of governmental agents.

Finally, the Convention was intended to remove obstacles to demonstrating that service had been effected abroad. Article 6 provide a uniform mechanism and form of certificate for attesting that service has been effected. This reduces difficulties in proving that service was actually made on a foreign defendant.

5. Scope of Hague Service Convention: "Civil or Commercial"

The Hague Service Convention applies in "all cases, in civil or commercial matters, where there is occasion to transmit a judicial or extrajudicial document for service abroad."[196] There is uncertainty as to the meaning of the phrase "civil or commercial matters." The phrase is not defined in the Convention, and there is little guidance in the Convention's negotiating history as to its intended meaning. Ironically, the drafters of the Convention concluded that the phrase "civil or commercial" should be used "to avoid any ambiguity," since earlier international judicial assistance agreements employed the phrase.[197] Unfortunately, neither the text of earlier conventions, nor their negotiating histories, clearly defines the term "civil or commercial."[198]

Disputes about the scope of the Hague Service Convention can arise for U.S. litigants that attempt to serve complaints asserting claims for multiple or punitive dam-

---

192. Amram, *The Proposed International Convention on the Service of Documents Abroad*, 51 A.B.A.J. 650, 652 (1965) (Convention said to move civil law countries towards "our concept of due process"); Hague Conference on Private International Law, Practical Handbook on the Operation of the Hague Convention of 15 November 1965 on the Service Abroad of Judicial and Extrajudicial Documents in Civil or Commercial Matters, at page 28 (1983) [hereafter "Practical Handbook"]; Report of the Senate Committee on Foreign Relations on the Convention on the Service Abroad of Judicial and Extrajudicial Documents, S. Exec. Rep. No. 6, 90th Cong., 1st Sess. 11-12 (Statement of Philip W. Amram) (1967).

193. Hague Service Convention, Preamble.

194. Hague Service Convention, Articles 15 and 16.

195. *See* Note, *The Effect of the Hague Convention on Service Abroad of Judicial and Extrajudicial Documents in Civil or Commercial Matters*, 2 Cornell Int'l L.J. 125, 128-29 (1969).

196. Hague Service Convention, Article 1.

197. III Conference de la Haye de Droit International Privé, *Actes et Documents de la Dixième Session* 79 (1964).

198. The "civil or commercial" phase was used in the 1905 and 1954 Hague Civil Procedure Conventions. *See* B. Ristau, *International Judicial Assistance* 107-11 (1990).

ages, or asserting claims based upon "public law" protections (like the antitrust laws). In Germany, the Central Authority for Bavaria refused to serve complaints in U.S. civil actions seeking punitive damages, on the theory that such complaints were penal in character.[199] The Court of Appeals for Munich later overturned the Bavarian Central Authority's action, holding that U.S. civil complaints seeking punitive damages can come within the scope of the Convention.[200] Appellate courts in Frankfurt and Duesseldorf reached the same conclusion, as has the Federal Supreme Court.[201] Other foreign authorities have suggested the possibility that they will refuse to serve U.S. complaints asserting antitrust claims and other actions that foreign states might regard as "public" or "penal."[202]

6. Service of Process by Central Authorities Under Article 5

Although other avenues for service exist under the Convention, the "Central Authority" mechanism is the centerpiece of the Convention. The Central Authority mechanism is set out in Articles 2 through 7.

Each state that becomes a party to the Hague Service Convention is *required* by Article 2 of the Convention to designate a "Central Authority" to "receive requests for service coming from other contracting States,"[203] and to serve or arrange for the service of complying documents.[204] Additionally, contracting states may, at their option, assign their Central Authorities the responsibility of sending requests for service to other contracting states. In the United States, the Central Authority is the Office of International Judicial Assistance (also called the Office of Foreign Litigation) of the Civil Division of the Department of Justice.[205] The Central Authority in each contracting state is set forth in the notifications of accession to the Convention, some of which are excerpted in Appendix J.

Service must be made by the receiving Central Authority under Article 5 in one of three ways: (1) under Article 5(a) in the manner used for service of process in domestic actions; (2) under Article 5(b) in any manner specified by the applicant

---

199. *See* Riesenfeld, *Service of United States Process Abroad: A Practical Guide to Service Under the Hague Service Convention and the Federal Rules of Civil Procedure*, 24 Int'l Law. 55 (1990) (recounting refusals to serve antitrust and RICO complaints seeking treble damages).

200. Decision of May 9, 1989, Docket No. VA 3/89, 29 Int'l Legal Materials 1571 (1989) and 10 Praxis des Internationalen Privat-und Verfahrensrechts [IPRax] 175 (1990); Decision of July 15, 1992, 13 Zeitschrift fuer Wirtschaftsrecht [ZIP] 1271 (1992).

201. Decision of March 21, 1991, 37 RIW 417 (Frankfurt Court of Appeals 1991); Decision of February 19, 1992, 38 RIW 846 (1992) (Duesseldorf Court of Appeal 1992).

202. *E.g., Westinghouse Elec. Corp. Uranium Contract Litig.* [1977] 1 All E.R. 434 (H.L.), *reprinted in,* 17 Int'l Leg. Mat. 38 (1978) (discussing application of Hague Evidence Convention to U.S. antitrust action).

203. Hague Service Convention, Article 2.

204. Hague Service Convention, Article 5.

205. The U.S. Central Authority's address is: Office of International Judicial Assistance, Civil Division, Department of Justice, Todd Building, Room 8102, 550 11th Street, NW, Washington DC 20530, U.S.A. Its telephone number is (202) 307-0983. The Office reports that it handles approximately 5,000 letters of request under the Convention each year.

(provided it is not incompatible with the laws of the receiving state); and (3) under the "second paragraph" of Article 5, the defendant may be permitted voluntarily to accept service.

a. Service Under Article 5(a) in the Manner Used For Service In Domestic Actions

Article 5(a) of the Convention provides for service through a Central Authority "by the method prescribed by its internal law for the service of documents in domestic actions upon persons who are within its territory." Unless the applicant requests a particular means of service under Article 5(b), Article 5(a) leaves it to the Central Authority of the receiving state to determine the mechanism of service to be used (at least where local law provides alternative means of service).

If Article 5(a) service is made through the Central Authority mechanism in the manner used in domestic actions, the receiving state may insist that the requesting party provide translations of the documents that are to be served into the official language of the receiving state.[206] The translation requirement does not expressly apply to the letter of request,[207] but it does apply to the complaint and summons.[208] One lower court has required translations of all documents to be served, including exhibits.[209] This can impose substantial expense on plaintiffs.

A number of foreign contracting states, including Germany and Japan, require that translations of all documents accompany any letter of request. The requirements of contracting states regarding translations can sometimes — but not always — be ascertained from the notifications of such foreign states of their instruments of ratification or accession to the Convention. In other cases, a *Practical Handbook on the Operation of the Hague Convention of 15 November 1965 on the Service Abroad of Judicial and Extrajudicial Documents in Civil or Commercial Matters*, published by the Hague Conference, lists the positions of contracting states regarding translations.

b. Service by Central Authority Pursuant to Article 5(b)

Article 5(b) permits the requesting party to ask that the receiving foreign Central Authority make service in a particular fashion. Article 5(b) was included in the Convention because of concerns that Article 5(a) service might not always permit a manner of service that would satisfy the due process and notice requirements of the requesting state.[210] Examples of service requested under Article 5(b) include service by hand delivery to a specific individual, service with a written receipt acknowledging delivery, and service where the process server attests that service was made on a per-

---

206. *See* Hague Service Convention, Article 5 ("If the document is to be served *under the first paragraph above*, the Central Authority may require the document to be written in, or translated into, the official language or one of the official languages of the State addressed.").

207. Hague Service Convention, Article 5 ("the Central Authority may require *the document* to be written in, or translated into, ...").

208. *Taylor v. Uniden Corp.*, 622 F.Supp. 1011, 1016 (E.D. Mo. 1985); *Teknekron Mgt, Inc. v. Quante Fernmeldetechnik GmbH*, 115 F.R.D. 175, 177 (D. Nev. 1987).

209. *Teknekron Mgt., Inc. v. Quante Fernmeldetechnik*, 15 F.R.D. 175 (D. Nev. 1987).

210. Amram, *Report on the Tenth Session of the Hague Conference on Private International Law*, 59 Am. J. Int'l L. 87, 90 (1957).

son shown in a photograph. Article 5(b) does not require a Central Authority to make service in a way that is incompatible with the internal law of the receiving state.

By its terms, Article 5(b) does not expressly give receiving states the right to demand translations if service is made by a method requested by the applicant. U.S. courts have generally not required translations where service is made via an alternative to Article 5(a),[211] although they have sometimes relied upon the absence of any foreign declaration requiring translations in these circumstances.[212] The U.S. Department of State advises, without explanation, that requests for service under Article 5(b) be accompanied by translations.[213] Similarly, some U.S. courts have suggested that translation of a summary of the complaint and a description of the proceedings is required.[214]

c. Service by the Central Authority Pursuant to Article 5's "Second Paragraph"

Article 5's "second paragraph" permits service of process on parties who voluntarily accept service (sometimes referred to in continental Europe as "remise simple"), provided that such service is consistent with local law. Voluntary service is not uncommon in Western Europe, notably France, Belgium, Netherlands, and Sweden. It typically involves delivery of documents to a local police station, which then requests the defendant to pick up the documents. The request is ordinarily accompanied by a statement that the defendant is free not to accept the documents.

No translations are expressly required by the Convention when service is made pursuant to Article 5's final paragraph. One U.S. court has held that, where a plaintiff's letter of request (not accompanied by translations), seeks service under Article 5 without specifying a sub-section, and the foreign Central Authority makes service notwithstanding its usual practice of requiring translations, then the service will be deemed "voluntary" under Article 5's final paragraph and the absence of translations will not affect its validity.[215]

It is not clear whether Article 5's final paragraph was intended to permit the "private" modes of service commonly used in the United States (*i.e.*, hand-delivery by a private attorney), or whether it only applies to service by a Central Authority.[216]

211. *Hunt v. Mobil Oil Corp.*, 410 F.Supp. 4 (S.D.N.Y. 1975); *Shoei Kako Co. v. Superior Court*, 33 Cal.App.3d 808 (1973).

212. *Vazquez v. Sund Emba AB*, 548 N.Y.S.2d 728 (App.Div. 1989) (where Sweden had not specifically declared that translation were required for alternatives to Article 5(a), no such requirement would be inferred; leaving open question whether Sweden could, consistent with the Convention, demand such translations).

213. U.S. Department of State Publication, Hague Convention on the Service Abroad of Judicial and Extra-Judicial Documents in Civil and Commercial Matters, at page 5 (undated).

214. *Julen v. Larson*, 25 Cal.App.3d 325 (1972); 1 B. Ristau, *International Judicial Assistance* §§3-14 to 3-17 (1984 & Supp. 1986). *Compare Hunt v. Mobil Oil Corp.*, 410 F.Supp. 4 (S.D.N.Y. 1975); *Shoei Kako Co. v. Superior Court*, 33 Cal.App.3d 808 (1973).

215. *Greenfield v. Suzuki Motor Co.*, 776 F.Supp. 698 (E.D.N.Y. 1991).

216. *See Tax Lease Underwriters v. Blackwell Green*, 106 F.R.D. 595 (E.D. Mo. 1985); *Tamari v. Bache & Co. (Lebanon)*, 431 F.Supp. 1226, 1229 (N.D. Ill. 1977); *Shoei Kako Co. v. Superior Court*, 411 (Cal. App. 1973); Report of U.S. Delegation, *reprinted in*, 17 Int'l Leg. Mat. 312, 316 (1978).

Given the structure of the Convention, and Article 5 in particular, the latter would appear to be the better view. Presumably, even if such private service is permitted, the defendant could refuse service and render it ineffective.

7. "Exclusivity" of the Hague Service Convention

It is important to define clearly the relationship between the Convention and other U.S. mechanisms for extraterritorial service within contracting states. Two issues must be distinguished. First, *must* the Convention's mechanisms be used even if U.S. law provides different mechanisms? Second, *can* the Convention's mechanisms be used even if domestic U.S. law does not authorize their use?

a. *The Hague Service Convention Preempts Service Mechanisms Under Local Law*

Most U.S. courts have concluded that, if service is to be made in the territory of a contracting state, and if the Hague Service Convention is available for such service, then the Convention *must* be complied with. According to these courts, traditional mechanisms for U.S. extraterritorial service — including Federal Rule of Civil Procedure 4 and its state counterparts — are preempted by the Convention when service must be made within a contracting state.[217]

In *Volkswagenwerk AG v. Schlunk*,[218] the Supreme Court endorsed this position, opining in dicta that the Hague Service Convention provides the exclusive means for service abroad in those cases where it applies: "By virtue of the Supremacy Clause, U.S. Const. Art. VI, the Convention pre-empts inconsistent methods of service prescribed by state law in all cases to which it applies."[219] This result applies without regard to whether state law makes any reference to the Convention. Even if state law specifically provided that service could be made in particular means *in addition* to the Convention mechanisms, *Schlunk* holds that such state rules are preempted.

The reasoning of those U.S. courts that have required resort to the Convention's service mechanisms is straightforward, at least on its face. Article 1 of the Convention provides that the Convention "*shall* apply in all cases, in civil or commercial matters, where there is occasion to transmit a judicial or extrajudicial document for service abroad." The use of apparently mandatory language — "shall" and "all cases" — has been interpreted to require use of the Convention for service abroad in preference to any other means of service provided for in federal or state

---

217. *E.g., Aspinall's Club Ltd. v. Aryeh*, 450 N.Y.S.2d 199, 202 (2d Dept. 1982); *Camp v. Sellers & Co.*, 281 S.E.2d 621, 623-24 (1981); *Cipolla v. Picard Porsche Audi*, 496 A.2d 130 (R.I. 1985); *Kadota v. Hosogai*, 608 P.2d 68 (Ariz. App. 1980) (excerpted below); *Sheets v. Yamaha Motors Corp., U.S.A.*, 891 F.2d 533, 536 (5th Cir. 1990).

A few lower courts reached contrary conclusions, but these decisions almost certainly do not survive *Volkswagenwerk AG v. Schlunk*, 486 U.S. 694 (1988). *See International Controls Corp. v. Vesco*, 593 F.2d 166, 179-80 (2d Cir.) (dictum), *cert. denied*, 442 U.S. 941 (1979); *Barefield v. Sund Emba, AB*, 1985 W.L. 4280 (E.D. Pa. Dec. 4, 1985) (dictum).

218. 486 U.S. 694 (1988).

219. 486 U.S. at 699.

law. This is illustrated by the Arizona Court of Appeals decisions in *Kadota v. Hosogai*,[220] excerpted below.

b. The Hague Service Convention Provides Service Mechanisms Supplementing Domestic Law

It is less clear whether the Convention's service mechanisms independently supplement the service mechanisms available under domestic U.S. law. If domestic law expressly or impliedly authorizes use of the Convention's mechanisms, then those mechanisms will be available. If domestic law does not expressly or impliedly authorize use of the Convention, then the question arises whether the Convention, of its own force, makes it mechanisms available to U.S. litigants. This issue is considered in the notes following *Kadota*.

KADOTA v. HOSOGAI

608 P.2d 68 (Ariz. App. 1980)

HAIRE, PRESIDING JUDGE. The sole issue on appeal is whether the trial court had personal jurisdiction over the appellant, Hiroshi Kadota, a resident of Japan. The appellant argues that appellee's various attempts to serve process on him were insufficient.... . This action is based upon an automobile accident that occurred in Arizona. As a result of the accident, appellee's husband, who was a passenger in the automobile driven by Mr. Kadota, died and appellant Kadota suffered severe brain damage. After a stay in a hospital in Arizona, the appellant returned to Japan to live with his family. The appellee, Michiko Hosogai, filed suit alleging that appellant's negligence had caused her husband's death.

The appellee has attempted to achieve valid service of process upon Mr. Kadota at least three times. On April 5, 1976, the appellee filed an affidavit of a private process server stating that he had served the superintendent of motor vehicles pursuant to the [Arizona] non-resident motorists statute.... . On May 5, 1976, appellee filed an affidavit of a Japanese attorney which stated that he was over 18 years old, not a party to the action and that he had personally served a copy of the summons with a Japanese translation on Mr. Kadota on April 25, 1976 in Japan.... . The third attempt to serve process upon the appellant involved service on appellant's guardian ad litem on July 7, 1976.... .

[After the trial court rejected appellant's objections to these methods of service,] the matter proceeded to trial and a jury verdict of $225,000 was awarded in favor of the appellee and against the appellant.... . On appeal, the appellant argues that all three methods of service were defective, thus depriving the trial court of jurisdiction over him. The three main contentions of the appellant are: (1) that the purported service pursuant to Rule 4(e)(6)(iii), Arizona Rules of Civil Procedure, by the Japanese attorney was invalid inasmuch as it was contrary to a treaty between the

---

220. 608 P.2d 68 (Ariz. App. 1980).

United States and Japan; (2) ... that compliance with [the non-resident motorists statute,] A.R.S. §§28-503A(2), was ineffective because that statute is contrary to the treaty between the United States and Japan; and (3) that service upon Mr. Kadota's guardian ad litem by itself was ineffective to confer jurisdiction upon the trial court... .

One method of service that appellee relied upon is the personal service by a Japanese attorney on the appellant in Japan. Appellee argues that this service was in compliance with Rule 4(e)(6)(iii), Arizona Rules of Civil Procedure. The appellant contends that, even if the appellee complied with the rule, a treaty between Japan and the United States [(the Hague Service Convention)] prohibits this type of service... . The appellant argues that the [Hague Service Convention] provides the exclusive means by which service may be accomplished in Japan, while the appellee contends that the treaty is merely a supplement to the existing methods of service of process provided for in the Arizona Rules of Civil Procedure... .

The second clause of Article VI of the United States Constitution provides that: ... "all Treaties made, or which shall be made, under the Authority of the United States, shall be the supreme Law of the Land ..." This provision of the Constitution has always been interpreted to mean that a treaty entered into by the United States shall be superior to and prevail over any conflicting laws of the individual states. *Ware v. Hylton*, 3 Dall. 199 (1796). Therefore, the State of Arizona cannot attempt to exercise jurisdiction under a rule promulgated by its courts if that rule would violate an international treaty. *United States v. Pink*, 315 U.S. 203 (1942) and *Hauenstein v. Lynham*, 100 U.S. 483 (1879).

Furthermore, Article I of the Treaty in this case expressly provides:

> The present Convention shall apply in all cases, in civil or commercial matters, where there is occasion to transmit a judicial or extrajudicial document for service abroad.

One law review writer has characterized the effect of the Convention this way: "The Convention, through the Supremacy Clause, supersedes all state and federal methods of service abroad, but specifically allows certain prior methods to remain in force." Downs, *The Effect of the Hague Convention on Service Abroad of Judicial and Extrajudicial Documents in Civil or Commercial Matters*, 2 Cornell Int'l L.J. 125, 131 (1969). Therefore, to the extent that the Convention is inconsistent with the Arizona Rules of Civil Procedure, the Convention controls. This being so, an inquiry into the relationship between the methods of service allowed by the Convention and those methods provided for in the Arizona Rules of Civil Procedure is necessary in order to determine to what extent, if any, the corresponding provisions are inconsistent. This analysis will provide an answer to the question of what methods of service are available for a plaintiff attempting to serve a defendant residing in Japan... .

[T]he key provision of the Convention in this case is Article 10 which states:

> Provided the State of destination does not object, the present Convention shall not interfere with —

(a) the freedom to send judicial documents, by postal channels, directly to persons abroad,

(b) the freedom of judicial officers, officials or other competent persons of the State of origin to effect service of judicial documents directly through the judicial officers, officials or other competent persons of the State of destination,

(c) the freedom of any person interested in a judicial proceeding to effect service of judicial documents directly through the judicial officers, officials or other competent persons of the State of destination.

Japan signed the Convention, but has objected to Article 10(b) and (c). The complete Convention (including Article 10(b) and (c)) appears to authorize all of the methods of service provided for in the Arizona Rules of Civil Procedure plus some additional methods. Article 19 and Rule 4(e)(6)(i) permit service in a manner prescribed by the law of the foreign country. Article 9 and Rule 4(e)(6)(ii) provide for service of letters rogatory. Rule 4(e)(6)(iii) and Article 10(b) and (c) allow for personal service by competent persons in the foreign country. Therefore, the Convention as a whole does not appear to contravene the Rules of Civil Procedure.

However, Japan has stated "It is declared that the Government of Japan objects to the use of the methods of service referred to in subparagraphs (b) and (c) of Article 10." As a result of this objection, the treaty between Japan and the United States is inconsistent with the Arizona Rules of Civil Procedure to the extent that personal service pursuant to Rule 4(e)(6)(iii) and Article 10(c) is objected to by Japan.

If the court were to agree with the appellee that the Convention was supplementary to the rules, Japan's objections would be meaningless in light of the inconsistency between Rule 4(e)(6)(iii) and Japan's objections to Article 10(b) and (c). Therefore, appellee's argument that her compliance with Rule 4(e)(6)(iii) was sufficient service of process on the appellant fails. The treaty between the United States and Japan specifically prohibits this method of service, although the Arizona rules allow for it. The law is clear that state statutes are abrogated to the extent that they are inconsistent with a treaty. Therefore, personal service by a Japanese attorney in Japan is ineffective service of process under the Convention.

Notes on Kadota

1. *Hague Service Convention supersedes state law and Federal Rules of Civil Procedure as to service abroad in contracting states. Kadota, Schlunk,* and other federal court decisions have almost unanimously held that the Convention supersedes state service of process rules and old Rule 4(i). *See supra* pp. 804-05. As a consequence, service mechanisms authorized by state law and old Rule 4(i) could not be used for service in a contracting state unless permitted by the Convention: the Convention was held to be mandatory and to preclude reliance on mechanisms of service other than those which it provided.

2. *Hague Service Convention is "self-executing."* Critical to the foregoing result is the conclusion that the Convention is "self-executing" — that is, it requires no implementing legislation in order for its terms to be enforced in U.S. courts. *United States v. Belmont,* 301 U.S. 324 (1937); *Restatement (Third) Foreign Relations Law* §111 (1987); *supra* pp. 19-20. Lower courts have uniformly concluded that the Hague

Service Convention is "self-executing." *E.g., Vorhees v. Fischer & Krecke*, 697 F.2d 574, 575 (4th Cir. 1983); *Pochop v. Toyota Motor Co.*, 111 F.R.D. 464, 465 (S.D. Miss. 1986). Is that correct?

3. *Are* Schlunk *and* Kadota *correctly decided?* Is the result in *Kadota*, which was later embraced in *Schlunk*, persuasive? Does the language of the Convention support the conclusion that it was meant independently to supersede all inconsistent state mechanisms for serving process abroad? Consider the precise language of Article 1. It says that the Convention "shall apply" when there is occasion to serve process abroad. Assuming that the Convention does "apply," what makes it exclusive? Note that there is no provision in the Convention that forbids a state from using service mechanisms not identified in the Convention. If the Convention "appl[ies]," does this imply that other service mechanisms do not also apply? Do the purposes of the Convention require holding that it is exclusive? Would the Convention's purposes not be achieved by merely recognizing the Central Authority mechanism as an available (but not exclusive) alternative? It has been said that "the American delegate to the Hague Conference ... had not even imagined that the Convention might be given exclusive effect." Smit, *Recent Developments in International Litigation*, 35 S. Tex. L. Rev. 215, 222-23 (1994).

4. *Hague Service Convention implemented by new Rule 4(f).* Unlike old Rule 4(i), new Rule 4(f) of the Federal Rules of Civil Procedure expressly incorporates the Hague Service Convention. Like pre-1993 precedent, Rule 4(f)(1) requires use of the means "authorized" by the Convention. *See supra* pp. 766-67. Thus, in federal courts, even if the Convention were not self-executing, it is made applicable in federal courts by new Rule 4(f).

5. *Service under Hague Service Convention pursuant to new Rule 4(f).* Unfortunately, the scope of new Rule 4(f)'s authorization for service of process pursuant to the Hague Service Convention is uncertain. The language of Rule 4(f)(1) is poorly drafted and must be examined carefully to determine what particular mechanisms of service are permitted.

(a) *What mechanisms of service are available under Rule 4(f)(1)?* Note that, under Rule 4(f)'s express terms, only mechanisms of service that are "agreed" or "authorized" by an applicable international convention may be invoked under Rule 4(f)(1). As described above, the Hague Service Convention contains a variety of provisions regarding the service of process abroad, including: (i) the Central Authority mechanism; (ii) service through diplomatic or consular agents; (iii) service through consular or diplomatic channels designated by the receiving state; (iv) sending of documents by postal channels; (v) service through the judicial officers or other competent persons of the receiving state; and (vi) Article 19's authorization to use any method of service permitted by the internal law of the country of destination. Which of the Convention's mechanisms are available under Rule 4(f)(1)?

(b) *Rule 4(f)(1) authorizes service by Central Authority mechanism.* At a minimum, it is clear that the Central Authority mechanism of the Convention is available under Rule 4(f)(1). This mechanism is plainly both "authorized" and "agreed" within the meaning of Rule 4(f)(1). Thus, a U.S. litigant seeking to serve a defendant located in a Convention signatory in a federal court action can effect service by using the Central Authority mechanism.

(c) *Does Rule 4(f)(1) authorize use of alternative mechanisms?* Are all of the Convention's alternative mechanisms for service outlined above also available under Rule 4(f)(1)? Put differently, are these alternative mechanisms for service either "internationally agreed means" or "authorized by the Hague [Service] Convention," and thus within the scope of Rule 4(f)(1)? An affirmative answer to the foregoing question would have an important consequence. It would mean that all of the alternative mechanisms available under the Convention may be used under Rule 4(f)(1), *without regard to whether or not a particular mechanism is also identified in Rule 4(f)(2).* These mechanisms could be used because they would be "agreed" in the Convention, and could therefore affirmatively incorporated by Rule 4(f)(1).

It is possible to read Rule 4(f)(1) more narrowly, as encompassing only service mechanisms that are specifically and affirmatively authorized under the Convention — that is, the Central Authority mechanism — and not as authorizing use of the alternative mechanisms under the Convention. Under this reading, the alternative mechanisms referred to above could only be used pursuant to Rule 4(f)(2). This interpretation would rest on the conclusion that the Convention does not affirmatively "authorize" use of alternative mechanisms, but merely leaves the availability of those mechanisms undisturbed. This view would also have important consequences. Under it, the mechanisms of service permitted under Rule 4(f)(2) would be available if they were also authorized by the Hague Service Convention. Importantly, however, other means of service permitted by the Convention, but not listed in Rule 4(f)(2), would not be available. What are some examples of such mechanisms? Which of the foregoing interpretations of Rule 4(f) is most consistent with the purposes of the Rule and the U.S. ratification of the Convention?

(d) *Must Rule 4(f)(1) authorize use of the Convention's alternative mechanisms?* Even if Rule 4(f)(1) only authorizes use of the Central Authority mechanism, and even if no other provision in Rule 4 permitted use of a particular service mechanism under the Convention, the Convention itself arguably provides an independent, self-executing means of serving process abroad. Some pre-1993 precedent held exactly this. *Ackermann v. Levine*, 788 F.2d 830, 840 (2d Cir. 1986) ("the Convention 'supplements' — and manifestly is not limited by — Rule 4"); *Loral Fairchild Corp. v. Matsushita Electric Industrial Co.*, 805 F.Supp. 3 (E.D.N.Y. 1992) ("service pursuant to the Hague Convention need not meet the requirements of Rule 4").

6. *Service under Hague Service Convention in manner not specifically authorized by U.S. state law.* Nothing in Arizona's Rules of Civil Procedure authorizes use of the Convention's Central Authority mechanism. Is the service nevertheless valid, on the grounds that the Convention's mechanisms automatically supplement state service mechanisms without the need for legislative implementation? State procedural rules generally do not specifically incorporate the Convention in the manner that Rule 4(f)(1) does. Does the Convention nonetheless permit a litigant in state court to ignore state procedural rules and serve process in a manner that the state's legislative body has refused to authorize? Most authorities have answered in the affirmative. "[B]y virtue of the Supremacy Clause, service made by a Central Authority pursuant to the Convention is valid in a state court even if, absent the Convention, the service would be defective." Committee on Federal Courts of the New York State Bar Association, *Service of Process Abroad: A Nuts and Bolts Guide*, 122 F.R.D. 63, 75 (1989); *Restatement (Third) Foreign Relations Law* §472, comment c & Reporters' Note 5 (1986); *MacIvor v. Volvo Penta of America, Inc.*, 471 So.2d 187 (Fla. Ct. App. 1985).

This conclusion does not appear to have been thoroughly analyzed. As we have seen, it appears that the Convention is "self-executing" under U.S. law. *See supra* p. 808. Thus, the Convention itself preempts inconsistent state service mechanisms, without the need for implementing legislation. *See supra* pp. 804-05. Suppose, however, that a U.S. state legislature wished to permit only specific service mechanisms in state courts, not all the mechanisms allowed by the Convention. Could a state forbid litigants in state courts from using particular Convention mechanisms? Although the Convention is the "supreme law of the land," and is "self-executing," does this necessarily mean that the Convention was intended to *require* states to use *all* of its alternatives. Is it inconsistent with the Convention for a state to decline to make use of one of the Convention's mechanisms?

The U.S. view of the Convention has long been that it was intended to liberalize service abroad. *See supra* pp. 796-800. The United States (as a whole) at least in theory gave various concessions to obtain the liberal service mechanisms permitted by the Convention. Would not these federal purposes be undercut if individual states could prevent U.S. nationals from making use of the Convention's mechanisms?

A similar issue arises with respect to federal restrictions on foreign service that pre-date the Convention. Recall that Articles 8 and 9 of the Convention permit service via consular channels. *See supra* pp. 798-99 & *infra* pp. 809-22. As described above, however, U.S. consular regulations have long forbid U.S. litigants from effecting service abroad through consular channels. *See supra* p. 765. Do the foregoing authorities suggest that the U.S. consular regulations are superseded by the Convention?

7. *Effect of Rule 4(d)'s waiver of service mechanism on Hague Service Convention.* As discussed above, *see supra* pp. 769-70, new Rule 4 includes a waiver of service mechanism. Plaintiffs are permitted to send a copy of their complaint to the defendant, together with a request that it waive formal service. Suppose this waiver provision is used as to defendants residing in signatories to the Hague Service Convention. Does Convention permit this? If not, would new Rule 4 override the previously-adopted Convention? *See* Burbank, *The World In Our Courts*, 89 Mich. L. Rev. 1456, 1485-89 (1991).

8. Alternative Mechanisms for Service Under Articles 8, 10, and 19

In addition to establishing the basic Central Authority mechanism for service under Article 5, the Hague Service Convention also permits other means of extraterritorial service. These alternatives are: (i) service through the requesting state's diplomatic or consular agents pursuant to Articles 8 and 9; (ii) service through the receiving state's "judicial officers or other competent persons" pursuant to Article 10(b) and (c); (iii) sending of documents by mail pursuant to Article 10(a); and (iv) service in accordance with the "internal law" of the receiving state pursuant to Article 19. One of the key purposes of the Convention was to ensure the flexibility that these various alternatives offered.[221]

The Convention generally only permits use of one of these alternative mechanisms where the receiving state has not objected to that mechanism.[222] Many of the Convention's contracting states have objected to some or all of the alternatives. Before attempting service under the Convention's alternatives, counsel must consult the declaration of the relevant member state.[223]

a. Direct Service by Consular and Diplomatic Channels Under Article 8

Article 8 provides that "[e]ach contracting State shall be free to effect service of judicial documents upon persons abroad, without application of any compulsion, directly through its diplomatic or consular agents." Service through consular agents is common in many jurisdictions. Given the general refusal of the State Department to assist in serving process abroad, however, Article 8 is of little practical importance to litigants in U.S. courts.[224]

b. Indirect Service by Consular and Diplomatic Channels Under Article 9

Article 9 provides that signatory states "shall be free ... to use consular channels to forward documents, for the purpose of service, to those authorities of another contracting State which are designated by the latter for this purpose." In "exceptional cases," diplomatic channels may be used for the same purpose. There is no specific provision in Article 9 permitting receiving states to object to such indirect service via consular or diplomatic channels, but service cannot be effected unless the receiving state has designated appropriate authorities for receipt of such service. Again, U.S. State Department regulations preclude effective use by U.S. litigants of this service mechanism.[225]

c. Alternative Service Mechanisms Under Article 10

Article 10 of the Convention provides for three alternative forms of service. Like service under Article 8, the Convention permits member states to object to alternative forms of service under Article 10. Service by an alternative means under Article 10 is permitted only if the receiving state has not objected.

i. Article 10(a): "Sending" Judicial Documents by Mail

Article 10(a) permits the "sending" of judicial documents by postal service directly to the defendant. It reads:

---

221. *See supra* pp. 796–800.

222. Under Article 8, contracting states are free (notwithstanding the objections of the receiving state) to effect service on the requesting state's own nationals through consular agents.

223. Selected declarations are excerpted in Appendix J. All such declarations are reproduced in the Martindale Hubbell Law Directory and United States Code Annotated for Federal Rule of Civil Procedure 4.

224. *See supra* p. 765.

225. *See supra* p. 765.

> Provided the State of destination does not object, the present Convention shall not interfere with — (a) the freedom to send judicial documents, by postal channels, directly to persons abroad ...

A number of foreign states — including China, Germany, Norway, Turkey, and Egypt — have objected to use of Article 10(a). Other nations — including the United States, Japan, France and the United Kingdom — have made no objection.

Article 10(a) has engendered more litigation in the United States than any other section of the Convention. The litigation has arisen because of attempts by U.S. plaintiffs to serve process on Japanese (and, to a lesser extent, other) defendants by mail under Article 10(a). U.S. lower courts are sharply divided over the validity of such "service."

A number of lower U.S. courts have held that Article 10(a) permits service by registered mail, addressed directly to the foreign defendant, provided that the country in which service is effected has not objected to the use of Article 10(a).[226] In contrast, a number of other lower courts have concluded that Article 10(a) only permits a plaintiff to "send" judicial documents, and not to "serve" them: these courts have held that "service" cannot be effected in a contracting state by mail under Article 10(a), even if that state has not objected to the use of Article 10(a).[227]

One reason that U.S. plaintiffs have sought to use Article 10(a) is its speed and efficiency. Postal service can be completed in a matter of days; Central Authority service takes two or more months. In addition, there is no express requirement that translations be provided if service can be made by mail under Article 10(a). Several of the U.S. lower courts that permit Article 10(a) mail service have affirmed this reading of the Convention's translation requirements.[228] Nonetheless, failure to provide translations could raise due process questions.[229]

ii. Articles 10(b) and 10(c): Service by "Competent Persons"

Articles 10(b) and 10(c) permit the sending of letters of request directly to the "judicial officers, officials or other competent persons" of the receiving state. There is uncertainty as to the identity of the "competent persons" who can be requested to make service abroad and as to the law for determining competency (*i.e.*, requesting state law or receiving state law). For example, applicable law might be said to recognize private process servers as "competent persons" for the service of process; if so,

---

226. *E.g.*, *Ackermann v. Levine*, 788 F.2d 830, 839-40 (2d Cir. 1986); *Patty v. Toyota Motor Corp.*, 1991 U.S. Dist. Lexis 16561 (N.D. Ga. 1991).

227. *E.g.*, *Sheets v. Yamaha Motor Corp., U.S.A.*, 891 F.2d 533 (5th Cir. 1990); *Bankston v. Toyota Motor Corp.*, 889 F.2d 172 (8th Cir. 1989); *Peabody Holding Co. v. Costain Group plc*, 808 F.Supp. 1425 (E.D. Mo. 1992).

228. *Lemme v. Wine of Japan Import, Inc.*, 631 F.Supp. 456, 464 (E.D.N.Y. 1986); *Weight v. Kawasaki Heavy Indus.*, 597 F.Supp. 1082, 1086 (E.D. Va. 1984); *Shoei Kako Co. v. Superior Court*, 33 Cal. App.3d 808 (1973).

229. *See supra* pp. 771-73; *Julen v. Larson*, 101 Cal. Rptr. 796 (App. Ct. 1972).

personal service abroad by a private foreign attorney might be permissible, absent an objection by the foreign state under Article 10(c).

d. Article 19's Savings Provision

Article 19 of the Convention indicates that neither the Central Authority mechanism, nor the Article 10 alternatives, override more liberal provisions of law in signatory nations concerning the service of foreign process within their territory. Article 19 provides:

> To the extent that the internal law of a contracting State permits methods of transmission, other than those provided for in the preceding Articles, of documents coming from abroad, for service in its territory, the present Convention shall not affect such provisions.

Article 19 was included in the Convention at the request of the United States to make clear that the Convention would not interfere with more liberal U.S. rules concerning service of process within the United States.[230] Several lower U.S. courts have held that service of process abroad in a Convention signatory state, in compliance with that state's internal law, is valid notwithstanding non-utilization of the procedures specifically identified in the Convention.[231]

It is not clear, under Article 19, when a foreign state's internal law permits use of a service mechanism. Article 19 could be narrowly construed as only allowing "use of alternative service methods which foreign law specifically authorizes" for service from abroad.[232] Alternatively, Article 19 could be interpreted as permitting the use of any service mechanism that foreign law does not expressly forbid.[233]

e. Selected Materials Concerning Alternative Service Mechanisms Under the Convention

A number of U.S. courts have considered when the alternative service mechanisms available under Articles 10 and 19 can be utilized. As described above, lower U.S. courts are divided in their interpretations of Article 10(a), with some permitting the service of process by mail in states that have not formally objected to Article 10(a), and others holding that Article 10(a) does not permit "service" by mail.[234] The decision in *Honda Motor Co. v. Superior Court*, excerpted below, adopts the latter view. In reading it, consider also the statements of position by the Japanese and U.S. governments concerning Article 10(a). Lower U.S. courts have also disagreed over

---

230. 113 Cong. Rec. 9404 (April 17, 1967).

231. *DeJames v. Magnificence Carriers, Inc.*, 654 F.2d 280, 288 (3d Cir. 1981); *Lemme v. Wine of Japan Import, Inc.*, 631 F.Supp. 456, 464 (E.D.N.Y. 1986); *Vasquez v. Sund Emba, AB*, 548 N.Y.S.2d 728 (N.Y. App. Div. 1989).

232. Comment, *Service of Process Abroad Under the Hague Convention*, 71 Marq. L. Rev. 649, 682 (1988) (emphasis in original). *See* Downs, *The Effect of the Hague Convention on Service Abroad of Judicial and Extrajudicial Documents in Civil or Commercial Matters*, 2 Cornell Int'l L. J. 125, 132 (1969).

233. These possibilities are discussed below. *See infra* pp. 820-22.

234. *See supra* pp. 810-11.

the availability of service mechanisms other than mail service under Article 10. Excerpted below is the decision in *Vasquez v. Sund Emba AB*, where the court considers the effect of Article 10(b) and (c) of the Convention on service by personal delivery in Sweden.

HONDA MOTOR CO. v. SUPERIOR COURT

12 Cal.Rptr.2d 861 (Calif. Court of Appeal 1992)

ELIA, ASSOCIATE JUSTICE. ... The issue presented, as to which the authorities conflict, is whether a California resident may obtain valid service on a Japanese national by a private mail service. We shall hold that such a service is invalid under the Hague Convention ...

The dispositive facts are not in controversy. Plaintiff Stephen G. Opperwall served defendant Honda Motor Co., Ltd. ("Honda") by sending the summons, complaint and other documents to Honda's office in Japan by certified mail, return receipt requested. The papers were unaccompanied by any Japanese translation. Honda admitted receipt of the papers. Honda's acknowledgement stamp of receipt on the documents was in English. The superior court denied Honda's motion to quash this service, and this petition followed.

The issue is one of statutory construction and depends on whether Article 10(a) of the Convention allows service of process upon a Japanese corporation by registered mail. ... The Convention provides specific procedures to accomplish service of process. Authorized modes of service are service through a central authority in each country; service through diplomatic channels; and service by any method permitted by the internal law of the country where the service is made. Each signatory nation may ratify, or object to, each of the articles of the Treaty. ... In addition to the specifically authorized modes of service, the Treaty also includes Article 10, the crucial provision which we must interpret here. ... Japan has objected to subparagraphs (b) and (c), but not to (a). It is on subparagraph (a) that plaintiff relies as permitting a mail service on a Japanese corporation.

There are two published California appellate decisions in point, which conflict. [*Compare Shoei Kako Co. v. Superior Court*, 33 Cal.App.3d 808 (Calif. Ct. App. 1973) *with Suzuki Motor Co. v. Superior Court*, 200 Cal.App.3d 1476 (Calif. Ct. App. 1988).] The Federal decisions also reach conflicting results, and also differ as to who has the weight of authority. [*Compare*] *Ackermann v. Levine*, 788 F.2d 830 (2d Cir. 1986) *with Bankston v. Toyota Motor Corp.*, 889 F.2d 172 (8th Cir. 1989). However, of the decisions since 1989 ... a clear majority have agreed with *Suzuki* that the mail service on a Japanese corporation violates the Treaty.

An important observation is that in Article 10 of the Treaty, the two subparagraphs which Japan has objected to — subparagraphs (b) and (c) — both refer to "service" of judicial documents, but subparagraph (a), which Japan has accepted, refers to the redom to "send" such documents. The cases which have invalidated a mail service on a Japanese corporation have relied heavily on this distinction. They have observed that the difference in wording is significant, not only because of the time honored statutory rule of construction that use of particular language in one part of a statute but not in another is deemed to be purposeful and meaningful, but also because it is not plausible to assume that Japan would reject the relatively formal methods of service provided in subparagraphs (b) and (c), yet would accept the less regulated and more informal method of subparagraph (a), a mail service by a private individual with no official involvement. It is more plausible to assume that Japan did not regard subparagraph (a) as authorizing any service. Rather, it is most likely that the drafters of the Convention intended, and that Japan understood them to intend, that subparagraph (a) merely authorized the mailing of judicial documents other than the summons, but that "service" required more rigorous control.

This interpretation is consistent with the fact that in Japan a private mail service is not authorized, and that service of process in that country cannot be effectuated by either attorneys or lay people, but only through the official action required by the court clerk and also by the mail carrier's implied-in-law acceptance of the role of a special officer of the court when he delivers the service which has been stamped by the clerk. It seems highly unlikely that Japan, which does not allow its own nationals to serve process by mail, would accept such a service by foreign nationals, and it is even more unlikely that Japan, having rejected mail service by its own nationals and also mail service under subparagraphs (b) and (c) of Article 10, of the Treaty would accept an informal mail service under subparagraph (a). Plainly the meaning of the word "send" was taken by that state to be something other than "service." ...

The authorities which have held otherwise have observed that interpreting Article 10(a) as not applying to service renders it superfluous, in that all it then provides is a "'freedom to send judicial documents'" which presumably has always existed, the mails being open to everyone. This point has some validity, although subparagraph (a) is not entirely superfluous even if it does not authorize original service, since it presumably does permit mailing of judicial documents other than process directly to litigants, a procedure which may not otherwise be available in a foreign state. But the persuasive value of the "superfluity" argument pales beside the reasons to adopt a contrary position, not only supported by canons of statutory construction, but also avoiding a glaring inconsistency with the internal procedural law of Japan. As the *Suzuki* court found, and later decisions have agreed, given that service of process by registered mail is not allowed in Japan, it is "extremely unlikely that Japan's failure to object to Article 10(a) was intended to authorize the use of registered mail as an effective mode of service of process, particularly in light of the fact that Japan specifically objected to the much more formal modes of service by Japanese officials which were available in Article 10(b) and (c)." *See Suzuki,* 200 Cal.App.3d at 1481.

Also of importance is that the opinion of the court in *Shoei Kako* is flawed by its misunderstanding of Japanese law. The decision noted that the record before the court did not demonstrate that service by mail with evidence of delivery was not a permissible method for service of documents in domestic Japanese actions. This mistake of Japanese law seriously undermines the persuasive value of *Shoei Kako.* ...

Plaintiff below ... emphasized here that there was actual service, the documents were received, and there was also evidence that the papers were understood, even though not translated into Japanese, because the acknowledgement of receipt was in English and the documents were quickly delivered to Honda's American attorneys. However, these arguments share a common fallacy; they assume that in California, actual notice of the documents or receipt of them will cure a defective service. That may be true in some jurisdictions, but California is a jurisdiction where the original service of process, which confers jurisdiction, must conform to statutory requirements or all that follows is void. Specifically, plaintiffs must comply with statutes prescribing the method of service on foreign corporations.

Plaintiff argues that it is ridiculous, wasteful and time consuming to reverse the trial court just to force plaintiff to go through the motions of a service under the Convention, when there is no question but that Honda has notice of the action, its attorneys stand ready to defend it, and no practical aim can be accomplished by quashing the service. However, plaintiff cites no authority permitting a California court to authorize an action to go forward upon an invalid service of process. ...

STATEMENT BY JAPANESE DELEGATION TO HAGUE CONFERENCE ON PRIVATE INTERNATIONAL LAW

28 Int'l Legal Mats. 1556, 1561 (1989)

Japan has not declared that it objects to the sending of judicial documents, by postal channels, directly to persons abroad. In this connection, Japan has made it clear that no objection to the use of postal channels for sending judicial documents to persons in Japan does not necessarily imply that the sending by such method is considered valid service in Japan; it merely indicates that Japan does not consider it as infringement of its sovereign power.

U.S. DEPARTMENT OF STATE, LEGAL ADVISOR'S OPINION

30 Int'l Legal Mats. 260 (1991)

I am writing with reference to the interpretation of United States treaty obligations in the recent [*Bankston v. Toyota Motor Corp.*, 889 F.2d 172 (8th Cir. 1989)] decision. As you are aware, while courts in the United States have final authority to interpret international treaties for the purposes of their application as law in the United States, they give great weight to treaty interpretations made by the Executive Branch.

The U.S. Government did not have an opportunity to express its views on the issues before the 8th Circuit Court in *Bankston.* The November 28 issue of the U.S. Law Week first brought the November 13, 1989 decision of the Court of Appeals in

Bankston to the attention of the Office of the Legal Advisor in the Department of State and the Office of Foreign Litigation in the Justice Department, which serves as the U.S. Central Authority under the Hague [Service] Convention. The Circuit Court in *Bankston*, examining Toyota's motion to dismiss for improper service on the defendant in Japan by registered mail rather than under procedures set out in the Hague Service Convention (to which both the United States and Japan are parties), concluded that service of summons and complaint by registered mail to a defendant in a foreign country (Japan) is not a method of service of process permitted by the Hague Convention.

We understand from appellant's/plaintiff's counsel that the time period for filing a petition for a rehearing in *Bankston* has elapsed. We understand further that neither the plaintiff nor the Court of Appeals was aware of a statement made by the delegate of Japan in April, 1989 at a meeting of representatives of countries that have joined the Hague Service Convention that appears to be relevant to the basic question addressed in the *Bankston* case. The Japanese statement in question was the result of efforts by the Departments of State and Justice to encourage the Government of Japan to clarify its position with regard to the service of process in Japan by mail from another country party to the Hague Service Convention. ...

We consider that the Japanese statement represents the official view of the Japanese Government that Japan does not consider service of process by mail in Japan to violate Japanese judicial sovereignty and that Japan does not claim that such service would be inconsistent with the obligations of any other country party to the Hague Service Convention vis-a-vis Japan. The Japanese statement suggests, however, that it is possible, and even likely, that service in Japan by mail, which may be considered valid service by courts in the United States, would *not* be considered valid service in Japan for the purposes of Japanese law. Thus, a judgment by a court in the United States based on service on the defendant in Japan by mail, while capable of recognition and enforcement throughout the United States, may well not be capable of recognition and enforcement in Japan by the courts of that country. We therefore believe that the decision of the Court of Appeals in *Bankston* is incorrect to the extent that it suggests that the Hague Convention does not permit as a method of service of process the sending of a copy of a summons and complaint by registered mail to a defendant in a foreign country. ...

VASQUEZ v. SUND EMBA AB

548 N.Y.S.2d 728 (New York Appellate Division 1989)

ROSENBLATT, JUSTICE. The case comes to us by virtue of the motion of the defendant Sund Emba AB ([a Swedish company,] hereinafter the appellant) to dismiss the complaint insofar as it is asserted against it for lack of in personam jurisdiction. The validity of the service of process and, hence, personal jurisdiction depends, for reasons which will follow, on whether service was effectuated in accordance with the Hague Convention. The Supreme Court denied the appellant's motion to dismiss, holding that pursuant to Article 10(c) of the Convention, the "plaintiff's personal service of the summons and complaint on appellant was sufficient service to give this court jurisdiction of the present dispute." We agree.

In his complaint, the plaintiff alleges that he was injured during the course of his employment in Farmingdale, New York, when his hand became caught in a corrugated box folding machine, allegedly manufactured by the appellant, a limited company organized under the laws of Sweden. The plaintiff's summons and complaint, written in English, was served by Anders Sandberg, a Swedish notary public, personally upon the appellant's managing director Erik Sjunnesson at the appellant's facility in Orebro, Sweden.

Suits involving parties in different countries present special problems relating to procedure under international law. The means by which a party may be subjected to the jurisdiction of the courts of another country goes to the very heart of national sovereignty and international political sensibilities. In this arena, one of the most vexing problems has involved the acquisition of jurisdiction, in the context of service or delivery of process, and the underlying issues of notice and fairness. ...

On February 10, 1969, the Hague Convention became effective with respect to the United States. For Sweden it became effective on October 1, 1969. ... It is noteworthy that while the member states contemplated a uniform procedure by conceiving of a Central Authority within each state, they also determined that the states should be free to consent to additional methods of service within their borders, consonant with their own laws (Articles 8 through 11, 19). ... In ratifying the Convention, most states, including Sweden, made various declarations reflective of their own sense of sovereignty,[235] in which they set forth objections or requirements with respect to certain methods of service.

Sweden signed the Convention with the following declaration:

(a) The Ministy of Foreign Affairs ... has been designated Central Authority.

(b) The Central Authority (the Ministry for Foreign Affairs) has been designated to receive documents transmitted through consular channels, pursuant to Art. 9. (c) *Swedish authorities are not obliged to assist in serving documents transmitted by using any of the methods referred to in sub-paragraphs (b) and (c) of Art. 10.* By virtue of the third paragraph of Art. 5 of the Convention the Central Authority requires that any document to be served under the first paragraph of the same article must be written in or translated into Swedish. (Emphasis supplied).

---

235. For example, the only form of service from abroad permitted by Switzerland is the use of letters rogatory. "The Swiss position is based on an extreme view of the nature of sovereignty, whereby any act touching Switzerland, including mailing of service *into* Switzerland from the United States, is viewed by Switzerland as a judicial act by the United States *within* Switzerland, thereby invading Swiss Sovereignty." Horlick, *A Practical Guide to Service of United States Process Abroad*, 14 Int'l Law. 637, 641 (1980) (emphasis in original).

The appellant argues that the method of service used by the plaintiff is incompatible with this declaration. Specifically, the appellant claims that Sweden's declaration italicized above must be interpreted as that State's objection to personal service of foreign documents except by the Central Authority. The appellant further contends that, in any event, service was improper because a Swedish translation of the summons and complaint was not provided.

Initially, the parties acknowledge, as do we, that compliance with the Convention is mandatory in all cases to which it applies, and that the law of the judicial forum (here, New York) determines whether or not service of process abroad is necessary. *Volkswagenwerk AG v. Schlunk.* ... Here, although the plaintiff alleged that the appellant was doing business in New York at all relevant times, neither party argues that service in this country was, or could have been, made. The parties therefore implicitly concede that service abroad, pursuant to the Convention, was the only proper means of service.

We hold that Sweden plainly contemplated service pursuant to the methods referred to in Article 10(b) and (c) (*i.e.*, personal service) and that the restrictive language in subdivision (c) of its declaration simply means that Swedish authorities are not constrained to aid in such service. Had Sweden been opposed to any method of service pursuant to Article 10, it could have, and we infer, would have expressly objected, as did, for example, Norway and Denmark, as well as Botswana, Germany, Japan, and Turkey.

This interpretation is consistent with Sweden's pre-Convention policies regarding service of foreign documents. Prior to the 1965 Convention, a Swedish decree based on the 1905 Hague Convention, to which Sweden was a signatory, permitted various modes of service ("delgivning"), including personal service of documents ("personlig delgivning") by authorized process servers ("stamningsmannadelgivning"), in response to requests by foreign authorities. Ginsburg, *Civil Procedure in Sweden*, 230, 231, 234 (1965). The decree, however, only regulated the assistance made available when Swedish authorities were involved, thereby leaving a party free to lawfully effectuate personal service, if possible, without the help of Swedish authorities. ...

The plaintiff draws our attention to a publication of the United States Department of State. It is a "general guideline" and advises that service of process in Sweden may be accomplished by sending the documents and appropriate forms to the Swedish Central Authority, but that such procedure "need not be used" and that "[a]ny private person may serve process in Sweden. An agent or a Swedish attorney could also be hired to do so." Although the State Department guideline lacks the force of law and is not controlling on this court, we recognize it to the extent that it reflects the State Department's advice to practitioners, based on an interpretation of Swedish law, furnished primarily by the Swedish Ministries of Foreign Affairs and Justice in 1981 to the American Embassy in Stockholm. As the appellant does not claim that Anders Sandberg, the Swedish notary public who served the summons and complaint upon it, was otherwise not qualified under Swedish law to make such service, we conclude that the summons and complaint were delivered personally to the appellant's agent in accordance with the Hague Convention and Sweden's declarations.

The appellant argues that even if the method of service used by the plaintiff was proper, the failure to translate the summons and complaint into Swedish violates Sweden's translation requirement under the Hague Convention. The appellant's contention with respect to Sweden's translation requirement is implausible. Initially, we note that translation is not a necessary element of all methods of service pursuant to the Convention. Article 5 states that "If the document is to be served under the first paragraph above [subparagraph (a)] the Central Authority may require the document to be written in, or translated into, the official language or one of the official languages of the State addressed." It therefore gives the Central Authorities of the signatory nations the right to require translations with respect to service pursuant to Article 5(a). As previously noted, Sweden, in its declaration stated:

> By virtue of the third paragraph of art. 5 of the Convention the Central
> Authority requires that any document to be served under the first para-
> graph of the same article must be written in or translated into Swedish.

However, the Convention provides no right to require translation of a document where service is made by the Central Authority "by a particular method requested by the applicant" pursuant to Article 5(b). Moreover, where, as here, the Central Authority is not involved in the service of a particular document, the translation requirement is not triggered at all.

Sweden's declaration clearly imposes no translation requirement where its Central Authority is not involved in the service. ...[236] Although we conclude that the requirements of service pursuant to the Convention are satisfied, one more point, while not raised by the appellant, is worth mentioning. Even though the Convention has been strictly followed, our own standards of due process require that the method of service be reasonably calculated, as a matter of fair play, to give actual notice to a prospective party abroad. Failure to provide a translation may, in some instances, constitute a denial of due process. However, in this case, in support of its motion to dismiss, the appellant submitted two affidavits of its Service Manager, Gosta Muhlbach. Those affidavits, which were on the appellant's letterhead containing preprinted English words, were written in English, and notarized in English. United States courts have refused to invalidate service where the defendant is a multinational corporation whose representatives have demonstrated an ability to deal in English, and the defendant is attempting to invalidate service on the grounds that the documents served should have been translated into the language of the country where served.

---

236. We need not and do not decide whether Sweden, compatibly with the Convention, could have required translation of documents served by means independent of the Central Authority, such as by personal service by notary public, as was effectuated here.

We conclude that the failure to serve the appellant with a Swedish translation of the summons and complaint violates neither Sweden's own declaration nor the intent of the Convention, and does not offend concepts of fairness in the service of process upon it.

Notes on Honda, U.S. and Japanese Statements, and Vasquez

1. *Division in U.S. authority over availability of Article 10(a) for "service."* Lower U.S. courts are divided over whether Article 10(a) permits "service" of process in states that have not objected to the section. Like *Honda*, a number of lower courts have parsed the language of Article 10(a) finely, noting that it refers only to the ability to "send" judicial documents rather than to the right to "effect service," as paragraphs (b) and (c) of Article 10 provide. From this, these courts have inferred that Article 10(a) was not meant to include service of a summons and complaint, but rather was limited to transmittal of more routine documents once litigation had begun. *See supra* pp. 810-11. Contrary to *Honda*, a number of other lower courts have held that Japan's failure to object to sending documents under Article 10(a) permits service of process by mail. *See supra* p. 811.

2. *How should Article 10(a) be interpreted?* Which view of the Convention is more persuasive? In almost all articles in the Convention, the word "serve" is used; only in Article 10(a) is the word "send" used. In the equally authoritative French language version of the Convention, the same pattern is followed: only in Article 10(a) is a different word used than in Articles 5, 8, 9, and 10(b) and (c). *See General Electro Music Corp. v. Samick Music Corp.*, 1991 U.S. Dist. Lexis 11905 (N.D. Ill. Aug. 23, 1991). That usage suggests that some distinction was intended when different words were used.

On the other hand, the negotiating history of the Convention strongly suggests that Article 10(a) was intended to permit "service" of process as well as "sending" of documents. III Conference de la Haye de Droit International Privé, *Actes et Documents de la Dixième Session* 90 (1964) ("The Commission did not accept the proposal that postal channels be limited to registered mail."). The Practical Handbook on the Convention, prepared by the Permanent Bureau of the Hague Conference on Private International Law contains the following:

> The majority of States do not oppose the forwarding of judicial documents originating in other Contracting States directly by mail to persons on their territory. For these States a distinction can be made between use of the postal channel as the sole method of service and service through the postal channel which is complementary to another means of effecting service. In this latter case, in the opinion of the experts who met in 1977, postal transmission of the judicial document should not be considered as being an infringement on the sovereignty of the State addressed: it should, therefore, be permitted notwithstanding an opposition made under Article 10(a). But of course it was desirable then to take into account only the date of the formal service, particularly where the operation of Article 15 was concerned. (III(B)).

Compare Id., at 15 ("Japan has not declared that it objects to service through postal channels."). Which view is more persuasive? Does the inapplicability of any translation requirement to documents "served" under Article 10(a) affect your analysis?

3. *Relevance of Japanese position to interpretation of Article 10(a).* What steps can Japan take if it disagrees with a reading of Article 10 that permits mail "service"? Consider the rationale in *Patty v. Toyota Motor Corp.*, 1991 U.S. Dist. Lexis 16561 (N.D. Ga. 1991):

> given the number of courts which have upheld service of process by direct mail, this Court must assume that the Japanese Government is aware of the interpretation given the Hague Convention in this country. The fact that no efforts to amend the Convention have been undertaken by the Japanese Government can only indicate tacit agreement.

Is that persuasive? *See Lyman Steel Corp. v. Ferrostaal Metals Corp.*, 747 F.Supp. 389 (N.D. Ohio 1990) (service on German defendant by registered mail quashed because of German objection to Article 10(a)). Consider the statement of the Japanese delegation concerning Article 10(a), which is excerpted above. Why does the U.S. Department of State think that it is important? What does the Department of State think the Japanese statement means?

4. *Relevance of Japanese domestic service rules.* The court remarks in *Honda* that Japanese law does

not provide for service by mail in domestic Japanese actions. Is that relevant to analyzing Article 10(a)? Would *Honda* have been decided differently if service by mail *were* permitted in domestic actions in Japanese courts? Neither *Honda* nor the Japanese government's statement says that Japanese law forbids mail service in Japan from foreign courts. If Japanese law *permitted* such service, then why isn't mail service available under Article 19 of the Convention?

Even if Japanese internal law *forbid* foreign service by mail, does the Japanese failure to object to Article 10(a) render such service effective under the Convention? If so, both U.S. and Japanese courts would be *required* by the Convention to give effect to mail service. If a Japanese court refused to enforce a U.S. judgment based upon the use of mail service, would the action violate the Convention?

5. *No "service" or "sending" of documents under Article 10(a) if foreign state has objected to Article 10(a).* Unlike Japan, a number of foreign states have objected to the use of Article 10(a) to transmit documents to their nationals. Examples include Germany, Norway, and Egypt. In these cases, no service by mail is permitted, even by those courts that permit Article 10(a) service in the absence of an objection. *Lyman Steel Corp. v. Ferrostaal Metals Corp.*, 747 F.Supp. 389 (N.D. Ohio 1990).

6. *Practical reasons not to attempt mail service under Article 10(a).* Even if a U.S. court will permit service by mail under Article 10(a), there are sound reasons for a U.S. plaintiff not to take this avenue.

(a) *Need for the defendant to return receipt attached to service by mail under Article 10(a).* First, if the foreign defendant does not return the receipt attached to the mail package containing the process, then service may be ineffective because the plaintiff may not be able to prove receipt. See *Lampe v. Xouth, Inc.*, 952 F.2d 697, 701 (3d Cir. 1991) (where plaintiff could not prove that return receipt was signed by defendant or its agent, no effective mail service); *Chowaniec v. Heyl Truck Lines*, 1991 U.S. Dist. Lexis 8138 (N.D. Ill. 1991) (where no receipt returned, court questioned efficacy of service).

(b) *Enforceability of judgments obtained following mail service under Article 10(a).* Even if a U.S. court upholds the validity of service under Article 10(a), a U.S. litigant may well encounter difficulty enforcing any subsequent judgment in the defendant's home jurisdiction. *Schlunk* and other authorities have emphasized this risk. *See infra* p. 834.

7. *Possibility of direct service by receiving state's "competent persons" under Article 10(b).* Article 10(b) preserves the "freedom" of a requesting state's "judicial officers, officials, or other competent persons" directly to request the "judicial officers, officials, or other competent persons" of the receiving state to serve process. Like Article 10(a), Article 10(b) can only be used if the receiving state has not objected. Many states have objected, making it important to consult the instrument of accession of a member state before attempting Article 10(b) service there. Moreover, Article 10(b) presents a choice of law question: is a person's "competence" under the section to serve process determined by the law of the requesting or the receiving state?

(a) *Authorities permitting direct service under Article 10(b) in accordance with foreign law.* Vasquez upholds service of process effected in Sweden by personal delivery from a Swedish attorney, relying on Article 10(b) and on its view of Swedish law. For other lower court decisions under Article 10(b) also permitting service in a foreign contracting state under foreign service rules, *see Tax Lease Underwriters, Inc. v. Blackwall Green, Ltd.*, 106 F.R.D. 595 (E.D. Mo. 1985) (upholding service effected in England by personal delivery to defendant by English solicitor; court holds that such service is permitted by Articles 10(b) and (c)); *Supreme Merchandising Co. v. Iwahori Kinzoku Co.*, 503 N.Y.S.2d 18, 19-20 (App. Div. 1986) ("record does not exclude the possibility that the personal service by a Japanese lawyer, presumably familiar with the requirements of his country's laws, was in pursuance of a procedure authorized by Japanese law, nor does it clearly demonstrate that Japan would not have recognized the service as lawful."); *Lemme v. Wine of Japan Import, Inc.*, 631 F.Supp. 456, 462-63 (E.D.N.Y. 1986) ("if authorized to serve abroad [by applicable jurisdictional provisions], a party may serve a document using any Rule 4(i) method, as long as the country receiving service has not objected to it in the Hague Convention or otherwise"). Compare the result in *Vasquez* (permitting personal service by a Swedish attorney) with that in *Kadota* (among other things, not permitting personal service of a Japanese attorney). What explains the different outcomes? Is the *Vasquez* analysis persuasive? Does it undercut the basic structure of the Convention to permit parties to make service in contracting states in whatever way local law allows?

(b) *Authorities apparently refusing to permit service under Article 10(b) pursuant to foreign law.* A few of lower courts have suggested, usually in passing, that only the specific mechanisms of service provided for in the Convention may be used. These decisions at least suggest that foreign service mechanisms, permitted in the contracting state where service is effected, cannot be used pursuant to Article 10(b) to supplement the Convention. *See Teknekron Mgt. v. Quante Fernmeldtechnik,* 115 F.R.D. 175, 176 (D. Nev. 1987) ("service must be effected strictly according to the procedures set forth in" Hague Service Convention).

8. *Service pursuant to the internal law of the receiving state under Article 19.* As discussed above, Article 19 permits use of the "internal law of a contracting state" to transmit documents. *See supra* p. 812.

(a) *Authorities concluding that Article 19 permits service abroad pursuant to the law of the receiving state.* Virtually no U.S. decisions have specifically considered whether Article 19 permits service abroad. However, a variety of commentators have concluded that Article 19 allows the service of process abroad pursuant to the internal laws of the contracting state where service is effected. *E.g.,* Committee on Federal Courts, N.Y. State Bar Ass'n, *Service of Process Abroad: A Nuts and Bolts Guide,* 122 F.R.D. 63, 76 (1989); Siegel, *Supplementary Practice Commentaries,* 28 U.S.C.A. Federal Rules of Civil Procedure, Rule 4, C-24.

(b) *If Article 19 permits service, when does internal law "permit" service?* Assuming that service abroad is authorized by Article 19, in what circumstances does it do so? Recall that Article 19 provides that, where "the internal law of a contracting State permits methods of transmission, other than those provided for in the preceding articles," the Convention does not affect those methods. Assuming that it permits service, two interpretations of this Article exist: (i) only if local law specifically authorizes a particular mechanism of service may it be used under Article 19; and (ii) so long as local law does not *forbid* a particular mechanism of service it may be used under Article 19.

(c) *Authorities concluding that Article 19 permits any service mechanism not forbidden by foreign law.* As outlined above, some authorities have concluded that service may be deemed proper under Article 19 as long as the receiving state's laws do not affirmatively prohibit the mechanism used; if foreign law is silent, then Article 19 allows such service:

> In short, although compliance with the Convention is "mandatory," that compliance encompasses not only methods of service that the Convention or the internal law of the foreign state expressly permit *but also those methods that neither the Convention nor the internal law of the foreign state prohibit.* Committee on Federal Courts, N.Y. State Bar Ass'n, *Service of Process Abroad: A Nuts and Bolts Guide,* 122 F.R.D. 63, 76 (1989) (emphasis added).

See also Siegel, Supplementary Practice Commentaries, 28 U.S.C.A. Federal Rules of Civil Procedure, Rule 4, C-24 ("We should be able to read the word 'permits' in Article 19 to mean 'does not prohibit.' In order to use one of the methods Rule 4(f) authorizes in paragraph (2), for example, one should not have to show that the method has a precise counterpart (and just how precise?) in the foreign nation's internal law. It should suffice that there is nothing in the foreign law, either explicitly or by compelling implication, to suggest that the method of service violates some deep-rooted policy of the nation involved.").

(d) *Authorities concluding that Article 19 only permits service mechanisms specifically authorized by foreign law.* Also as outlined above, Article 19 can also be interpreted to permit only "use of alternative service methods which foreign law *specifically authorizes.*" Comment, *Service of Process Abroad Under the Hague Convention,* 71 Marq. L. Rev. 649, 682 (1988) (emphasis in original). At least one lower court appears to have adopted this conclusion. *Hunt's Pier Associates v. Conklin,* 156 B.R. 464 (E.D. Pa. 1993) ("we conclude that Ontario, Canada, does indeed 'object' to the method of service utilized by the [plaintiff] here because it is not authorized under the rules of that jurisdiction").

(e) *How should Article 19 be interpreted?* Which of the foregoing interpretations of Article 19 is more sensible? What harm results from permitting service abroad in any manner specifically authorized by the receiving state's law? any manner not prohibited by the receiving state's law? If Swedish law ordinarily permits service by hand-delivery, outside the Convention, does the Convention forbid this?

What effect does the foreign state's position have on interpreting Article 19 in particular cases? If Sweden formally stated that it did not object to service under Article 19 in the manners permitted by Swedish law, does the Convention impose additional requirements? Conversely, if a receiving state does not like service to be made from abroad outside the Central Authority mechanism, why can't it say so?

9. Scope of the Convention: When is "Service Abroad" Required and When Can Service be Effected Within the United States on Foreign Defendants?

As we have seen, the Hague Service Convention provides a variety of mechanisms for use by U.S. litigants when service must be made "abroad" — that is within the territory of another Contracting state. U.S. courts have held, however, that service need not be made "abroad" when a foreign defendant can be found and served within the United States under U.S. law. As a result, these courts have concluded, the Convention simply has no application when process is served in accordance with U.S. procedural rules on a foreign defendant within the United States.[237]

The Supreme Court expressly endorsed this conclusion in *Volkswagenwerk AG v. Schlunk*, which is excerpted below.[238] It held that the question "whether there is service abroad must be determined by reference to the law of the forum state," because it is not addressed by the Convention itself.[239] Applying the *Schlunk* rationale, lower U.S. courts have considered numerous claims that local service within the United States on a foreign defendant or its U.S. representative obviated the need to serve process abroad under the Convention. This issue has frequently arisen when U.S. plaintiffs effect "indirect" or "substituted" service on foreign companies by serving their U.S. subsidiaries.[240] It also arises, as the notes following *Schlunk* illustrate, in other contexts, including service upon statutory agents and U.S. addresses of foreign defendants.

VOLKSWAGENWERK AG v. SCHLUNK

486 U.S. 694 (1988)

JUSTICE O'CONNOR. This case involves an attempt to serve process on a foreign corporation by serving its domestic subsidiary which, under state law, is the foreign corporation's involuntary agent for service of process. We must decide whether such service is compatible with the [Hague Service] Convention ... [The case was a product liability action, filed in Illinois state court, alleging that Volkswagen of America, Inc. ("VWoA") and Volkswagen Aktiengesellschaft ("VWAG") had designed and sold a defective automobile. VWAG, a German company with its principal place of business in Germany, wholly owns VWoA, a corporation registered to do business in Illinois. The plaintiff served VWAG by serving VWoA as its agent. The Illinois courts concluded that service on VWoA was effective service on VWAG, because "VWoA is a wholly owned subsidiary of VWAG, ... a majority of the mem-

---

237. *See Sheets v. Yamaha Motors Corp.*, 891 F.2d 533, 537 (5th Cir. 1990); *Gallagher v. Mazda Motor of America, Inc.*, 1992 U.S. Dist. Lexis 97 (E.D. Pa. Jan. 6, 1992); *Zisman v. Sieger*, 106 F.R.D. 194, 200 (N.D. Ill. 1985); *Ex Parte Volkswagenwerk AG*, 443 So.2d 880, 881 (Ala. 1983); *Luciano v. Garvey Volkswagen, Inc.*, 521 N.Y.S.2d 119, 120-21 (App. Div. 1987).

238. 486 U.S. 694 (1988).

239. *Schlunk*, 486 U.S. at 701.

240. *Acapalon Corp. v. Ralston Purina Co.*, 1991 Mo. App. Lexis 1322 (Mo. Ct. App. 1991) (service on U.S. parent effective as service on foreign subsidiary without need for recourse to Hague Service Convention). In some circumstances, both state and federal law permit the service of process on a foreign corporation by service upon an affiliated corporation within the United States. In general, indirect service of this character is permitted if the U.S. party can show a sufficiently close connection between the foreign parent and the domestic subsidiary to justify treating the subsidiary as the agent or alter ego of the parent. R. Casad, *Jurisdiction in Civil Actions* §3.02[2][b] & §4.03[5][a] (2d ed. 1991).

bers of the board of VWoA are members of the board of VWAG, and ... VWoA is by contract the exclusive importer and distributor of VWAG products sold in the United States."]...

The primary innovation of the Convention is that it requires each state to establish a central authority to receive requests for service of documents from other countries. ... Once a central authority receives a request in the proper form, it must serve the documents by a method prescribed by the internal law of the receiving state or by a method designated by the requester and compatible with that law. Article 5. The central authority must then provide a certificate of service that conforms to a specified model. Article 6. A state also may consent to methods of service within its boundaries other than a request to its central authority. Articles 8-11, 19. The remaining provisions of the Convention that are relevant here limit the circumstances in which a default judgment may be entered against a defendant who had to be served abroad and did not appear, and provide some means for relief from such a judgment. Articles 15, 16.

Article 1 defines the scope of the Convention, which is the subject of controversy in this case. It says: "The present Convention shall apply in all cases, in civil or commercial matters, where there is occasion to transmit a judicial or extrajudicial document for service abroad." The equally authentic French version says, "La presente Convention est applicable, en matiere civile ou commerciale, dans tous les cas ou un acte judiciaire ou extrajudiciaire doit etre transmis a l'etranger pour y etre signifie ou notifie." This language is mandatory, as we acknowledged last Term in *Societe Nationale Industrielle Aerospatiale v. United States District Court*, 482 U.S. 522, 534 n.15 (1987). By virtue of the Supremacy Clause, U.S. Const., Article VI, the Convention pre-empts inconsistent methods of service prescribed by state law in all cases to which it applies. Schlunk does not purport to have served his complaint on VWAG in accordance with the Convention. Therefore, if service of process in this case falls within Article 1 of the Convention, the trial court should have granted VWAG's motion to quash.

When interpreting a treaty, we "begin 'with the text of the treaty and the context in which the written words are used.'" *Societe Nationale*, 482 U.S. at 534 (quoting *Air France v. Saks*, 470 U.S. 392, 397 (1985)). Other general rules of construction may be brought to bear on difficult or ambiguous passages. "'Treaties are construed more liberally than private agreements, and to ascertain their meaning we may look beyond the written words to the history of the treaty, the negotiations, and the practical construction adopted by the parties.'"

The Convention does not specify the circumstances in which there is "occasion to transmit" a complaint "for service abroad." But at least the term "service of process" has a well-established technical meaning. Service of process refers to a formal delivery of documents that is legally sufficient to charge the defendant with notice of a pending action. The legal sufficiency of a formal delivery of documents must be measured against some standard. The Convention does not prescribe a standard, so we almost necessarily must refer to the internal law of the forum state. If the internal law of the forum state defines the applicable method of serving process as requiring the transmittal of documents abroad, then the Hague Service Convention applies.

The negotiating history supports our view that Article 1 refers to service of process in the technical sense. The committee that prepared the preliminary draft deliberately used a form of the term "notification" (formal notice), instead of the more neutral term "remise" (delivery), when it drafted Article 1. Then, in the course of the debates, the negotiators made the language even more exact. The preliminary draft of Article 1 said that the present Convention shall apply in all cases in which there are grounds to transmit or to give formal notice of a judicial or extrajudicial document in a civil or commercial matter to a person staying abroad. ... To be more precise, the delegates decided to add a form of the juridical term "signification" (service), which has a narrower meaning than "notification" in some countries, such as France, and the identical meaning in others, such as the United States. The delegates also criticized the language of the preliminary draft because it suggested that the Convention could apply to transmissions abroad that do not culminate in service. The final text of Article 1, eliminates this possibility and applies only to documents transmitted for service abroad. The final report (Rapport Explicatif) confirms that the Convention does not use more general terms, such as delivery or transmission, to define its scope because it applies only when there is both transmission of a document from the requesting state to the receiving state, and service upon the person for whom it is intended.

The negotiating history of the Convention also indicates that whether there is service abroad must be determined by reference to the law of the forum state. The preliminary draft said that the Convention would apply "where there are grounds" to transmit a judicial document to a person staying abroad. The committee that prepared the preliminary draft realized that this implied that the forum's internal law would govern whether service implicated the Convention. The reporter expressed regret about this solution because it would decrease the obligatory force of the Convention. Nevertheless, the delegates did not change the meaning of Article 1 in this respect.

VWAG protests that it is inconsistent with the purpose of the Convention to interpret it as applying only when the internal law of the forum requires service abroad. One of the two stated objectives of the Convention is "to create appropriate means to ensure that judicial and extrajudicial documents to be served abroad shall be brought to the notice of the addressee in sufficient time." The Convention cannot assure adequate notice, VWAG argues, if the forum's internal law determines whether it applies. VWAG warns that countries could circumvent the Convention by defining methods of service of process that do not require transmission of documents abroad. Indeed, VWAG contends that one such method of service already exists and that it troubled the Conference: notification au parquet.

Notification au parquet permits service of process on a foreign defendant by the deposit of documents with a designated local official. Although the official generally is supposed to transmit the documents abroad to the defendant, the statute of limitations begins to run from the time that the official receives the documents, and there allegedly is no sanction for failure to transmit them. At the time of the 10th Conference, France, the Netherlands, Greece, Belgium, and Italy utilized some type of notification au parquet.

There is no question but that the Conference wanted to eliminate notification au parquet. It included in the Convention two provisions that address the problem. Article 15 says that a judgment may not be entered unless a foreign defendant received adequate and timely notice of the lawsuit. Article 16 provides means whereby a defendant who did not receive such notice may seek relief from a judgment that has become final. Like Article 1, however, Articles 15 and 16 apply only when documents must be transmitted abroad for the purpose of service. VWAG argues that, if this determination is made according to the internal law of the forum state, the Convention will fail to eliminate variants of notification au parquet that do not expressly require transmittal of documents to foreign defendants. Yet such methods of service of process are the least likely to provide a defendant with actual notice.

The parties make conflicting representations about whether foreign laws authorizing notification au parquet command the transmittal of documents for service abroad within the meaning of the Convention. The final report is itself somewhat equivocal. It says that, although the strict language of Article 1 might raise a question as to whether the Convention regulates notification au parquet, the understanding of the drafting Commission, based on the debates, is that the Convention would apply. Although this statement might affect our decision as to whether the Convention applies to notification au parquet, an issue we do not resolve today, there is no comparable evidence in the negotiating history that the Convention was meant to apply to substituted service on a subsidiary like VWoA, which clearly does not require service abroad under the forum's internal law. Hence neither the language of the Convention nor the negotiating history contradicts our interpretation of the Convention, according to which the internal law of the forum is presumed to determine whether there is occasion for service abroad.

Nor are we persuaded that the general purposes of the Convention require a different conclusion. One important objective of the Convention is to provide means to facilitate service of process abroad. Thus the first stated purpose of the Convention is "to create" appropriate means for service abroad, and the second stated purpose is "to improve the organization of mutual judicial assistance for that purpose by simplifying and expediting the procedure." By requiring each state to establish a central authority to assist in the service of process, the Convention implements this enabling function. Nothing in our decision today interferes with this requirement.

VWAG correctly maintains that the Convention also aims to ensure that there will be adequate notice in cases in which there is occasion to serve process abroad. Thus compliance with the Convention is mandatory in all cases to which it applies, and Articles 15 and 16 provide an indirect sanction against those who ignore it. Our interpretation of the Convention does not necessarily advance this particular objective, inasmuch as it makes recourse to the Convention's means of service dependent on the forum's internal law. But we do not think that this country, or any other country, will draft its internal laws deliberately so as to circumvent the Convention in cases in which it would be appropriate to transmit judicial documents for service abroad. For example, there has been no question in this country of excepting foreign nationals from the protection of our Due Process Clause. Under that Clause, foreign nationals are assured of either personal service, which typically will require service abroad and trigger the Convention, or substituted service that provides "notice reasonably calculated, under all the circumstances, to apprise interested parties of the pendency of the action and afford them an opportunity to present their objections." *Mullane v. Central Hanover Bank & Trust Co.*, 339 U.S. 306, 314 (1950).[241]

Furthermore, nothing that we say today prevents compliance with the Convention even when the internal law of the forum does not so require. The Convention provides simple and certain means by which to serve process on a foreign national. Those who eschew its procedures risk discovering that the forum's internal law required transmittal of documents for service abroad, and that the Convention therefore provided the exclusive means of valid service. In addition, parties that comply with the Convention ultimately may find it easier to enforce their judgments abroad. See Westin, *Enforcing Foreign Commercial Judgments and Arbitral Awards in the United States, West Germany, and England*, 19 Law & Policy Int'l Bus. 325, 340-341 (1987). For these reasons, we anticipate that parties may resort to the Convention voluntarily, even in cases that fall outside the scope of its mandatory application.

In this case, the Illinois long-arm statute authorized Schlunk to serve VWAG by substituted service on VWoA, without sending documents to Germany. *See* Ill. Rev. Stat., ch. 110, §2-209(a)(1) (1985). VWAG has not petitioned for review of the Illinois Appellate Court's holding that service was proper as a matter of Illinois law. VWAG contends, however, that service on VWAG was not complete until VWoA

---

241. The concurrence believes that our interpretation does not adequately guarantee timely notice, which it denominates the "primary" purpose of the Convention, albeit without authority. The concurrence instead proposes to impute a substantive standard to the words, "service abroad." Evidently, a method of service would not be deemed to be "service abroad" within the meaning of Article 1 unless it provides notice to the recipient "in due time." This due process notion cannot be squared with the plain meaning of the words, "service abroad." The contours of the concurrence's substantive standard are not defined, and we note that it would create some uncertainty even on the facts of this case. If the substantive standard tracks the Due Process Clause of the Fourteenth Amendment, it is not self-evident that substituted service on a subsidiary is sufficient with respect to the parent. In the only cases in which it has considered the question, this Court held that the activities of a subsidiary are not necessarily enough to render a parent subject to a court's jurisdiction, for service of process or otherwise. *Cannon Mfg. Co. v. Cudahy Packing Co.*, 267 U.S. 333, 336-337 (1925); *Consolidated Textile Corp. v. Gregory*, 289 U.S. 85, 88 (1933). Although the particular relationship between VWAG and VWoA might have made substituted service valid in this case, a question that we do not decide, the factbound character of the necessary inquiry makes us doubt whether the standard suggested by the concurrence would in fact be "remarkably easy" to apply.

transmitted the complaint to VWAG in Germany. According to VWAG, this transmission constituted service abroad under the Hague Service Convention.

VWAG explains that, as a practical matter, VWoA was certain to transmit the complaint to Germany to notify VWAG of the litigation. Indeed, as a legal matter, the Due Process Clause requires every method of service to provide "notice reasonably calculated, under all the circumstances, to apprise interested parties of the pendency of the action and afford them an opportunity to present their objections." *Mullane v. Central Hanover Bank & Trust Co.* VWAG argues that, because of this notice requirement, every case involving service on a foreign national will present an "occasion to transmit a judicial ... document for service abroad" within the meaning of Article 1. VWAG emphasizes that in this case, the Appellate Court upheld service only after determining that "the relationship between VWAG and VWoA is so close that it is certain that VWAG 'was fully apprised of the pendency of the action' by delivery of the summons to VWoA."

We reject this argument. Where service on a domestic agent is valid and complete under both state law and the Due Process Clause, our inquiry ends and the Convention has no further implications. Whatever internal, private communications take place between the agent and a foreign principal are beyond the concerns of this case. The only transmittal to which the Convention applies is a transmittal abroad that is required as a necessary part of service. And, contrary to VWAG's assertion, the Due Process Clause does not require an official transmittal of documents abroad every time there is service on a foreign national. Applying this analysis, we conclude that this case does not present an occasion to transmit a judicial document for service abroad within the meaning of Article 1. Therefore the Hague Service Convention does not apply, and service was proper.

JUSTICE BRENNAN, concurring. We acknowledged last Term, and the Court reiterates today, that the terms of the [Hague Service] Convention are "mandatory," not "optional" with respect to any transmission that Article 1 covers. *Aerospatiale*, 482 U.S. at 534, and n. 15. Even so, the Court holds, and I agree, that a litigant may, consistent with the Convention, serve process on a foreign corporation by serving its wholly owned domestic subsidiary, because such process is not "service abroad" within the meaning of Article 1. The Court reaches that conclusion, however, by depriving the Convention of any mandatory effect, for in the Court's view the "forum's internal law" defines conclusively whether a particular process is "service abroad," which is covered by the Convention, or domestic service, which is not. I do not join the Court's opinion because I find it implausible that the Convention's framers intended to leave each contracting nation, and each of the 50 States within our Nation, free to decide for itself under what circumstances, if any, the Convention would control. Rather, in my view, the words "service abroad," read in light of the negotiating history, embody a substantive standard that limits a forum's latitude to deem service complete domestically.

The first of two objectives enumerated in the Convention's preamble is "to create appropriate means to ensure that judicial ... documents to be served abroad shall be brought to the notice of the addressee in sufficient time. ..." Until the Convention was implemented, the contracting nations followed widely divergent practices for serving judicial documents across international borders, some of which did not ensure any notice, much less timely notice, and therefore often produced unfair default judgments. Particularly controversial was a procedure, common among civil-law countries, called "notification au parquet," which permitted delivery of process to a local official who was then ordinarily supposed to transmit the document abroad through diplomatic or other channels. Typically, service was deemed complete upon delivery of the document to the official whether or not the official succeeded in transmitting it to the defendant and whether or not the defendant otherwise received notice of the pending lawsuit.[242]

The United States delegation to the Convention objected to notification au parquet as inconsistent with "the requirements of 'due process of law' under the Federal Constitution." The head of the delegation has derided its "'[i]njustice, extravagance, [and] absurdity. ...'" In its classic formulation, he observed, notification au parquet "'totally sacrificed all rights of the defense in favor of the plaintiff.'" The Convention's official reporter noted similar "'spirited criticisms of the system'... which we wish to see eliminated."

In response to this and other concerns, the Convention prescribes the exclusive means for service of process emanating from one contracting nation and culminating in another. As the Court observes, the Convention applies only when the document is to be "transmit[ted] ... for service abroad"; it covers not every transmission of judicial documents abroad, but only those transmissions abroad that constitute formal "service." It is common ground that the Convention governs when the procedure prescribed by the internal law of the forum nation or state provides that service is not complete until the document is transmitted abroad. That is not to say, however, as does the Court, that the forum nation may designate any type of service "domestic" and thereby avoid application of the Convention.

Admittedly, as the Court points out, the Convention's language does not pre-

---

242. The head of the United States delegation to the Convention described notification au parquet as follows: "This is a system which permits the entry of judgments in personam by default against a nonresident defendant without requiring adequate notice. There is also no real right to move to open the default judgment or to appeal, because the time to move to open judgment or to appeal, because the time to move to open judgment or to appeal will generally have expired before the defendant finds out about the judgment. "Under this system of service, the process-server simply delivers a copy of the writ to a public official's office. The time for answer begins to run immediately. Some effort is supposed to be made through the Foreign Office and through diplomatic channels to give the defendant notice, but failure to do this has no effect on the validity of the service. ... There are no ... limitations and protections [comparable to due process or personal jurisdiction] under the notification au parquet system. Here jurisdiction lies merely if the plaintiff is a local national; nothing more is needed." S. Exec. Rep. No. 6, at 11-12 (statement by Philip W. Amram). *See also* S. Exec. Doc. C, at 5 (letter of submittal from Secretary of State Rusk); Amram, *The Revolutionary Change in Service of Process Abroad in French Civil Procedure*, 2 Int'l Law. 650, 650-651 (1968) ("Amram").

scribe a precise standard to distinguish between "domestic" service and "service abroad." But the Court's solution leaves contracting nations free to ignore its terms entirely, converting its command into exhortation. Under the Court's analysis, for example, a forum nation could prescribe direct mail service to any foreigner and deem service effective upon deposit in the mailbox, or could arbitrarily designate a domestic agent for any foreign defendant and deem service complete upon receipt domestically by the agent even though there is little likelihood that service would ever reach the defendant. In fact, so far as I can tell, the Court's interpretation permits any contracting nation to revive notification au parquet so long as the nation's internal law deems service complete domestically, even though, as the Court concedes, "such methods of service are the least likely to provide a defendant with actual notice," and even though "[t]here is no question but that the Conference wanted to eliminate notification au parquet." ...

The negotiating history and the uniform interpretation announced by our own negotiators confirm that the Convention limits a forum's ability to deem service "domestic," thereby avoiding the Convention's terms. Admittedly, the Convention does not precisely define the contours. But that imprecision does not absolve us of our responsibility to apply the Convention mandatorily, any more than imprecision permits us to discard the words "due process of law." And however difficult it might be in some circumstances to discern the Convention's precise limits, it is remarkably easy to conclude that the Convention does not prohibit the type of service at issue here. Service on a wholly owned, closely controlled subsidiary is reasonably calculated to reach the parent "in due time" as the Convention requires. That is, in fact, what our own Due Process Clause requires, *see Mullane v. Central Hanover Bank & Trust Co.*, 339 U.S. 306, 314-315 (1950), and since long before the Convention's implementation our law has permitted such service, *see, e.g., Perkins v. Benguet Consolidated Mining Co.*, 342 U.S. 437, 444-445 (1952). This is significant because our own negotiators made clear to the Senate their understanding that the Convention would require no major changes in federal or state service-of-process rules. Thus, it is unsurprising that nothing in the negotiating history suggests that the contracting nations were dissatisfied with the practice at issue here, with which they were surely aware, much less that they intended to abolish it like they intended to abolish notification au parquet. And since notice served on a wholly owned domestic subsidiary is infinitely more likely to reach the foreign parent's attention than was notice served au parquet (or by any other procedure that the negotiators singled out for criticism) there is no reason to interpret the Convention to bar it.

My difference with the Court does not affect the outcome of this case, and, given that any process emanating from our courts must comply with due process, it may have little practical consequence in future cases that come before us. *But cf.* S. Exec. Rep. No. 6, at 15 (statement by Philip W. Amram suggesting that Convention may require "a minor change in the practice of some of our States in long-arm and automobile accident cases" where "service on the appropriate official need be accompanied only by a minimum effort to notify the defendant"). Our Constitution does not, however, bind other nations haling our citizens into their courts. Our citizens rely instead primarily on the forum nation's compliance with the Convention, which the Senate believed would "provide increased protection (due process) for American Citizens who are involved in litigation abroad." And while other nations are not bound by the Court's pronouncement that the Convention lacks obligatory force, after today's decision their courts will surely sympathize little with any United States national pleading that a judgment violates the Convention because (notwithstanding any local characterization) service was "abroad."

It is perhaps heartening to "think that [no] countr[y] will draft its internal laws deliberately so as to circumvent the Convention in cases in which it would be appropriate to transmit judicial documents for service abroad," although from the defendant's perspective "circumvention" (which, according to the Court, entails no more than exercising a prerogative not to be bound) is equally painful whether deliberate or not. The fact remains, however, that had we been content to rely on foreign notions of fair play and substantial justice, we would have found it unnecessary, in the first place, to participate in a Convention "to ensure that judicial ... documents to be served abroad [would] be brought to the notice of the addressee in sufficient time."

Notes on Volkswagenwerk v. Schlunk

1. *Service on a foreign defendant within the United States as an alternative to service "abroad" under the Convention.* Schlunk held that the Convention need not be used to serve process abroad if the law of the forum permits service on the defendant within the forum. The Court reasoned that the Convention only applies when, under Article 1 of the Convention, there is occasion to make "service abroad." If U.S. law provides that service is effected locally, within the United States, then the Convention simply does not apply.

2. *Was* Schlunk *correctly decided?* Is *Schlunk* correct? Consider the arguments advanced in Justice Brennan's concurrence. If a central objective of the Convention was to eliminate *notification au parquet* and other forms of service that failed to provide adequate notice, would contracting states have been left free to define when service "abroad" was necessary? Conversely, if the Convention meant to define when service abroad was necessary, would it not have said so expressly?

Note the Court's statement that, because the Convention does not directly address the issue, "we almost necessarily must" apply the forum's local laws to decide whether service must be made abroad. What other law might apply to determine the validity of domestic service upon a foreign corporation? Why could the Convention itself not set implied limits on domestic service? Are such limits not "almost necessarily" required to protect the integrity of the Convention and effectuate its basic purposes of ensuring that defendants in international disputes receive fair notice when sued abroad?

Consider VWAG's argument that service on *it* necessarily entailed VWOA's transmission of the complaint to Germany — in order to satisfy both the due process clause and state law — and that this transmission amounted to "service abroad" regulated by the Convention. How does the Court reply? Is that persuasive? How would Justice Brennan respond to this argument?

How difficult is it as a practical matter for plaintiffs to comply with the Convention? What unfairness will noncompliance cause foreign defendants if service is consistent with the due process clause? What effect will the Court's interpretation of the Convention have on U.S. defendants subject to suit in foreign countries that do not have a due process clause?

3. *Limits under* Schlunk *to use of domestic service mechanisms.* If the *Schlunk* conclusion is accepted, is there any limit to how the Convention might be circumvented by domestic laws permitting substituted service? Suppose a state law authorizes service on a foreign franchisor, by serving its entirely independent U.S. franchisee. Suppose that a state law authorizes service within the United States by service on *any* U.S.

subsidiary or affiliate of a foreign parent corporation. Suppose, in Justice Brennan's words, a state "pre-scribe[s] direct mail service to any foreigner and deem[s] service effective upon deposit in the mailbox." Are any of these service mechanisms consistent with the intent of the framers of the Convention? Are any of these mechanisms prohibited by the analysis in *Schlunk*? If the Convention does not expressly or implicitly forbid such service, is there any other source of law that might?

4. *Standards applicable to determining whether domestic service on defendant, or a representative, is permitted.* *Schlunk* holds that local law governs the question whether domestic service within the forum, rather than service "abroad" under the Convention, is permitted. In most cases, the applicable law will be state law, because service will be effected pursuant to state long-arm statutes. *See supra* 68-70. Where federal law provides the basis for jurisdiction, it will generally provide the applicable law. Under *Schlunk*, only the due process clause constrains the application of substituted service theories under state or federal law. The due process clause leaves the individual U.S. states broad discretion in serving process on non-resident defendants. *See supra* pp. 771-73.

5. *Possible "international comity" or federal common law limits on domestic service as a means of avoiding service abroad under the Convention.* What role, if any, could the principle of "international comity" have in providing a basis for requiring U.S. plaintiffs to utilize the Convention's procedures? As discussed in detail below, the Supreme Court held in *Société Nationale Industrielle Aerospatiale v. U.S. District Court*, 482 U.S. 522 (1987), that international comity requires use of the Hague Evidence Convention in certain circumstances in order to minimize infringements on the sovereignty of foreign nations that objected to direct U.S. discovery. *See infra* pp. 903-15. Although it was not argued in *Schlunk*, the same comity rationale would appear applicable to service under the Hague Service Convention, arguably requiring resort to the Convention in cases where foreign states object to substituted service.

6. *Service within the forum on domestic "alter ego" of foreign corporation.* *Schlunk* affirmed a lower court decision, applying Illinois law, that permitted service within Illinois on the local subsidiary of a foreign corporation. Like Illinois, most states permit indirect service on non-resident defendants through service within the state on either an "alter ego," an agent, or other representative of the foreign company. Federal law is similar. The applicable standards for alter ego, agency, and other relevant statuses vary from jurisdiction to jurisdiction. In general, indirect service on a domestic subsidiary is permitted only if the subsidiary is closely affiliated with its foreign parent. *See generally* R. Casad, *Jurisdiction in Civil Actions* §4.03[5] (2d ed. 1991).

A number of lower courts have reached the same result as *Schlunk*, also applying state law, to permit service on an alter ego of a foreign parent. *See Geick v. American Honda Motor Co.*, 117 F.R.D. 123, 124-25 (C.D. Ill. 1987). Other courts have acknowledged that service upon an alter ego of a foreign defendant can substitute for service abroad, but have concluded that applicable alter ego standards were not satisfied. *Fleming v. Yamaha Motor Corp., U.S.A.*, 774 F.Supp. 992 (W.D. Va. 1991); *Wasden v. Yamaha Motor Co.*, 131 F.R.D. 206 (M.D. Fla. 1990).

7. *Service within the forum on domestic "agent" of foreign corporation.* Under the analysis in *Schlunk*, service abroad can presumably be avoided by serving an agent of the defendant within the forum. Moreover, local law and the due process clause presumably provide the sole standards for determining when such service upon a U.S. agent is permitted. State law definitions of the types of agency relationships that will permit substituted service vary. *See* R. Casad, *Jurisdiction in Civil Actions* §3.01[2] (2d ed. 1991); *supra* pp. 763-65.

A number of lower court decisions have permitted service on foreign defendants, based in Convention signatory states, to be effected by serving their U.S. agents within the United States. *See Pittsburgh National Bank v. Kassir*, 153 F.R.D. 580 (W.D. Pa. 1994) (upholding service on German corporate defendant by means of serving contractually-designated U.S. agent, in accordance with Pennsylvania law); *King v. Perry and Sylva Machinery Co.*, 1991 U.S. Dist. Lexis 7901 (N.D. Ill. 1991); *New York Marine Managers, Inc. v. M.V. Topor-1*, 716 F.Supp. 783, 786 (S.D.N.Y. 1989). *Contra Trask v. Service Merchandise Co.*, 135 F.R.D. 17, 21 (D. Mass. 1991) (alternative holding, without reasoning, that domestic service upon foreign defendant's U.S. lawyers did not avoid need to serve abroad under Convention). Other lower courts have acknowledged that service within the forum on a domestic agent of a foreign corporation is not precluded by the Convention, but have found that local standards regarding agency relationships were not satisfied. *Sieng v. Muller GmbH Maschinenfabrik*, 1993 WL 337839 (E.D. Pa. 1993).

8. *Service within the forum on foreign corporation's address or mail box.* Some lower courts have suggested that, if a foreign corporation owns an office or a post office box, or operates at an address, within

the United States, service can be effected "on" that mail box or address without requiring resort to the Hague Service Convention. *Gallagher v. Mazda Motor of America, Inc.*, 1992 U.S. Dist. Lexis 97 (E.D. Pa. Jan. 6, 1992); *Jordan v. Global Natural Resources, Inc.*, 564 F.Supp. 59, 69-70 (S.D. Ohio 1983).

9. *Service on state officials and other statutory agents of foreign defendants.* Does the Court's holding in *Schlunk* extend to cases where a foreign company is served within the United States by delivery of service to a state official appointed by law to accept service?

(a) *Lower courts permitting service on statutory agents as substitute for service abroad under the Convention.* Relying on *Schlunk*, one court has upheld service upon the Rhode Island Secretary of State, appointed by law as statutory service agent for unregistered foreign companies doing business in Rhode Island. *Aelia v. Les Grands Cahais De France*, 1991 U.S. Dist. Lexis 817 (D.R.I. Jan. 14, 1991).

(b) *Lower courts forbidding service on statutory agents as substitute for service abroad under the Convention.* Other lower courts hav- held that *Schlunk* does not extend to domestic service upon statutorily-appointed agents, such as a state ecretary of State. *Shurtz v. Goldberg*, Civ. Action No. 94-907-A (E.D. Va. 1995) (service on Virginia Secretary of Commonwealth is not sufficient to avoid need for service abroad, because Virginia law required Secretary to transmit documents to defendant).

(c) *Authorities suggesting that local law regarding service on statutory agents is dispositive.* Some authorities have suggested that *Schlunk* permits local service on a statutory agent, rather than service abroad under the Convention, if local law deems service complete when the statutory agent receives process, but not if service is incomplete until the agent transmits the process abroad to the foreign defendant. Note, in this regard, *Schlunk's* comment that "[w]here service on a domestic agent is *valid and complete* under both state law and the Due Process Clause, our inquiry ends and the Convention has no further implications. ... The only transmittal to which the Convention applies is a transmittal abroad that is *required as a necessary part of service.*" (Emphasis added.) Consider the following analysis by the Committee on Federal Courts, N.Y. State Bar Ass'n, *Service of Process Abroad: A Nuts and Bolts Guide*, 122 F.R.D. 63, 73-74 (1989):

> Section 306 [New York B.C.L.] provides that one may serve New York corporations, and foreign corporations *licensed* to do business in New York, by delivering two copies of the process to the Secretary of State as agent for the corporation. "Service of process on such corporation shall be complete when the secretary of state is so served." [N.Y. B.C.L. §306(b)] The Secretary of State then sends one of the copies to the corporation. "The jurisdictional act is the delivery of the two copies to the Secretary. The latter's failure to forward one to the corporation does not void the service." A fortiori, if the Secretary transmits the process to the foreign corporation abroad in some manner that violates the Convention, personal jurisdiction over the defendant would still exist.
>
> Under N.Y. B.C.L. §307, one may serve *unlicensed* foreign corporations that are subject to jurisdiction in New York under article 3 of the C.P.L.R. by delivering one copy of the process to the Secretary of State as agent for the corporation and then personally delivering, or mailing, notice of that service, with a copy of the process, to the corporation. Failure to deliver or send a copy of the process to the foreign corporation is a fatal jurisdictional defect [under New York law]. Accordingly, as at least four New York courts have now held, jurisdiction is not obtained under B.C.L. §307 when a copy of the process is transmitted to the corporation abroad in a manner that violates the Convention.

See Vasquez v. Sund Emba AB, 548 N.Y.S.2d 728, 731 n.4 (App. Div. 1989). Is this a persuasive distinction? Is it what *Schlunk* envisaged? Could New York amend N.Y. B.C.L. §307 to make service complete upon delivery to the Secretary of State?

10. *Statutory agent must be authorized under local law to accept service in private actions.* Some state and federal statutes require foreign companies to appoint local agents for particular purposes. The National Traffic and Motor Vehicle Safety Act of 1966, is one example of such a statute. Most lower courts have held that service on an agent appointed for a limited statutory purpose is invalid for other, nonstatutory purposes such as a private civil law suit. In such cases, service on the statutory agent is not sufficient service on the defendant under local law. *E.g., Lamb v. Volkswagen*, 104 F.R.D. 95 (S.D. Fla. 1985); *Richardson v. Volkswagenwerk AG*, 552 F.Supp. 73, 77-79 (W.D. Mo. 1982).

11. *Service outside the forum state, but within the United States, on domestic "alter ego" of foreign corporation.* Some courts have extended *Schlunk* to permit service within the United States pursuant to a

state long-arm statute on the out-of-state U.S. subsidiary of a foreign parent located in a Hague Convention signatory state. *E.g., McHugh v. International Components Corp.*, 461 N.Y.S.2d 166 (Sup. Ct. 1983). Is this extension of *Schlunk* permitted by the Convention?

12. *Practical reasons for using the Convention's procedures, instead of effecting service within the United States.* Note that *Schlunk* merely *permits* U.S. plaintiffs to circumvent the Convention, by serving the U.S. agents of foreign defendants. The Court also commented, however, that this course of action may well make it difficult to enforce any resulting U.S. judgment abroad. Foreign courts may not follow *Schlunk's* interpretation of the Convention: as one lower court remarked, "this court cannot render an interpretation of the treaty which will bind the courts of [a foreign state] in the event plaintiff, if he obtains a judgment against [the foreign defendant], seeks to enforce it through the courts in that nation." *Shoei Kako Co. v. Superior Court*, 33 Cal.App.2d 808, 822 (1973). Unless practical reasons counsel otherwise, U.S. plaintiffs would generally be well-advised to comply with the Convention notwithstanding *Schlunk.*

13. *Does new Rule 4(f) overrule Schlunk?* It has been suggested that "there would appear to be a distinct danger that the relevant provisions [of new Rule 4(f)] will be construed to require service pursuant to the Hague Convention even when service can be made on an agent in the United States." Smit, *Recent Developments in International Litigation*, 35 S. Tex. L. Rev. 215, 224 (1994). Is this really a danger? What part of Rule 4(f) suggests such a result? Note that the Advisory Committee Rules cite *Schlunk* with approval:

> Use of the Convention procedures, when available, is mandatory if documents must be transmitted abroad to effect service. *See Volkswagenwerk AG v. Schlunk*, 486 U.S. 694 (1988) (noting that voluntary use of these procedures may be desirable even when service could constitutionally be effected in another manner).

10. Default Judgments Under Article 15

In addition to regulating the service of process abroad, the Hague Service Convention also imposes restrictions on the power of U.S. courts to enter default judgments on defendants that were served (or should have been served) pursuant to the Convention. The United States has availed itself of the opportunity, pursuant to the second paragraph of Article 15, to permit U.S. courts to enter default judgments if (i) process was actually transmitted pursuant to one of the Convention's mechanisms, (ii) no report has been made on the attempted service after a period (not less than six months), which the judge considers adequate, and (iii) the plaintiff has made "every reasonable effort" to secure a report on service or an Article 6 certificate.[243] A number of other contracting states have also issued similar declarations.[244]

Article 15 has not frequently been considered in U.S. litigation. One lower U.S. court has held that Article 15 would allow the issuance of a default judgment where a foreign Central Authority found the U.S. letter of request defective and so informed the plaintiff by letter; on receipt of the letter, the plaintiff did nothing, until, 9 months later, it moved for a default judgment. The court held that it had the power to issue a default judgment, because the six month period had passed, but it declined to exercise its discretion to do so under U.S. law.[245]

---

243. *See* 28 U.S.C.A. Federal Rules of Civil Procedure, Rule 4 (U.S. declaration); Appendix J.

244. *See* 28 U.S.C.A. Federal Rules of Civil Procedure, Rule 4 (Declarations of Canada, China, Germany, and the United Kingdom).

245. *Marschhauser v. Travelers Indemnity Co.*, 145 F.R.D. 605 (S.D. Fla. 1992). The court was obviously influenced, in concluding that it had the power to issue a default judgment, by the fact that it thought the foreign Central Authority's objections to the form of the U.S. letter of request were ill-founded.

E. Service of Process Abroad Pursuant to the Inter-American Convention on Letters Rogatory

The Inter-American Convention on Letters Rogatory grew out of the first Inter-American Specialized Conference on Private International Law, held in Panama City in 1975.[246] The United States subsequently proposed a Protocol to the Convention at the Second Inter-American Specialized Conference on Private International Law in Montevideo in 1979.[247] The Protocol was adopted with some amendments, thus largely conforming the Letters Rogatory Convention to the Hague Service Convention and leading to U.S. ratification in October 1986.[248]

Unlike the Hague Service Convention, the Inter-American Letters Rogatory Convention is not "exclusive."[249] The Convention's service mechanisms (which are broadly similar to those under the Hague Service Convention) are incorporated by Rule 4(f)(1) of the Federal Rules of Civil Procedure.[250] Where enforcement of a U.S. judgment abroad may be necessary, the Convention should generally be used. If the Convention is not used, then Rule 4(f)(2) and 4(f)(3) are available.

---

246. The Conference is a regional alternative to the Hague Conference on Private International Law. *See* Kearney, *Developments in Private International Law*, 81 Am. J. Int'l L. 724, 735 (1987).

247. *Id.* at 737.

248. Signatories to the Letters Rogatory Convention include Argentina, Chile, Ecuador, Guatemala, Mexico, Panama, Paraguay, Peru, the United States, Uruguay, and Venezuala.

249. *See supra* pp. 767-68.

250. *See supra* pp. 767-68.

F. Service of U.S. Process on Foreign States

The foregoing sections of this Chapter dealt with state and federal rules regarding service of process on *private* parties outside the United States. An entirely different set of rules apply to the service of U.S. process on foreign states and their agencies and instrumentalities.

1. FSIA's Specialized, Uniform Regime for Service on Foreign States

Service on foreign sovereigns and their agencies and instrumentalities is governed primarily by the Foreign Sovereign Immunities Act ("FSIA"), which establishes a distinct and specialized regime for the service of process.[251] Unlike most other service provisions, the FSIA's rules are uniform throughout all courts in the United States. The FSIA applies without regard to whether the action is in state or federal court and without regard to the character of the plaintiff's cause of action; the statute's service rules also apply both to service within and outside the United States. These aspects of the statute were adopted with the express purposes of promoting uniformity.[252]

The FSIA's general provisions on service of process are contained in §1608.[253] In federal courts, the FSIA's service provisions are incorporated by Rule 4(j)(1) of the Federal Rules of Civil Procedure. It provides that "[s]ervice upon a foreign state or a political subdivision, agency, or instrumentality thereof shall be effected pursuant to 28 U.S.C. §1608." In state courts, §1608 is directly applicable; it must be complied with, notwithstanding inconsistent state law rules.[254]

2. Alternative Mechanisms for Service Prescribed for "Foreign States Proper" and for Foreign State "Agencies and Instrumentalities"

Section 1608 sets out two separate lists of alternative means for service. The list contained in §1608(a) applies to service on the foreign state or its "political subdivisions"; §1608(b)'s list applies to service on "an agency or instrumentality" of the foreign state.[255] The alternatives listed in §1608(a) are different from those in §1608(b).

In effecting service on a foreign state-related entity, it is important to identify whether a proposed defendant is a "foreign state" or an "agency or instrumentality." That is because service that is appropriate for one category will not necessarily be

---

251. 28 U.S.C. §§1602-11 (1982). The FSIA is examined in detail in Chapter 3.

252. *See* H. R. Rep. No. 1487, 94th Cong., 2d Sess. 24-25, *reprinted in*, 1976 U.S. Code Cong. & Admin. News 6604, 6623. *See also Gibbons v. Republic of Ireland*, 532 F.Supp. 668 (D.D.C. 1982).

253. Rules governing service in certain admiralty proceedings are treated separately by 28 U.S.C. §1605(b).

254. *See* J. Dellapenna, *Suing Foreign Governments and Their Corporations* 110 (1988); *2 Tudor Place Assoc. v. Libya*, 470 N.Y.S.2d 301, 303-04 (Civ. Ct. 1983).

255. Section 1608(b) of the FSIA defines "agency or instrumentality of a foreign state" to be any "separate legal person, corporate or otherwise" that is not a citizen of the United States or created under the laws of any third country and that is either an "organ of a foreign state or political subdivision thereof, or a majority of whose shares or other ownership interest is owned by a foreign state or political subdivision thereof." *See infra* pp. 213-17.

adequate under the FSIA's provisions for the other.[256] It is also important to distinguish carefully between the foreign state and its agencies, and between different foreign state-related entities. Service upon the foreign state, or one of its agencies, will not necessarily constitute service upon other agencies or instrumentalities of the foreign state.[257]

Although their specific alternatives for service are different, §1608(a) and §1608(b) are similar in that their listings of alternatives are ranked in decreasing order of preference.[258] Plaintiffs are required to follow the statutory order of preference and may only attempt to serve process by less-preferred means if a more-preferred means is not available.[259]

---

256. *See Transaero, Inc. v. La Fuerza Aerea Boliviana*, 30 F.3d 148 (D.C. Cir. 1994); *Segni v. Commercial Office of Spain*, 650 F.Supp. 1040 (N.D. Ill. 1986), *aff'd*, 835 F.2d 160 (7th Cir. 1987); *Resource Dynamic Int'l v. General People's Committee*, 593 F.Supp. 572 (N.D. Ga. 1984); *Unidyne Corp. v. Aerolineas Argentinas*, 590 F.Supp. 398 (E.D. Va. 1984). The distinction between foreign states proper, and their agencies and instrumentalities, is discussed above. *See supra* pp. 213-17.

257. *Filus v. LOT Polish Airlines*, 819 F.Supp. 232 (E.D.N.Y. 1993).

258. *See* H.R. Rep. No. 1487, 94th Cong., 2d Sess. 24, *reprinted in*, 1976 U.S. Code Cong. & Admin. News 6604, 6623.

259. *Filus v. LOT Polish Airlines*, 819 F.Supp. 232 (E.D.N.Y. 1993); J. Dellapenna, *Suing Foreign Governments and Their Corporations* 19 (1988).

G. Service of Foreign Process in the United States

The preceding sections of this Chapter discussed the service of U.S. process on foreign defendants. International litigation also involves the service of foreign process on U.S. defendants in the United States.

1. No Direct U.S. Legal Restrictions on Service of Foreign Process in the United States

Unlike many foreign countries, the United States ordinarily imposes no significant direct restrictions on the service of foreign process on U.S. territory.[260] There is no federal law that forbids or criminalizes the service of process from foreign courts in the United States, nor that requires the participation of U.S. government officials in such service. In general, state laws simply do not address the service of process from foreign courts within state territory.

The result is that, subject to general tort and criminal laws, litigants in foreign courts are free to use whatever service mechanisms may be available under foreign law for serving process in the United States. This is acknowledged by the Official Commentary to §2.04 of the Uniform Interstate and Procedure Act, which describes the "existing freedom to make service within a state of the United States on behalf of litigation pending elsewhere as long as the particular manner employed does not constitute a disturbance of peace or other violation of law."[261]

Sections 1696(b) of Title 28 also reflects the general freedom of foreign litigants to serve process in the United States without the assistance of U.S. courts or governmental authorities. As discussed below, §1696(a) permits U.S. district courts to order the service of foreign process on persons within their districts. Section 1696(b) goes on to provide that "[t]his section does not preclude service of such a document without an order of the court." The section's legislative history remarks that the provision "reaffirms preexisting freedom in making service within the United States without the assistance of U.S. courts."[262]

---

260. *Restatement (Third) Foreign Relations Law* §472(2) (1987); Comment, *Revitalization of the International Judicial Assistance Procedures of the United States: Service of Documents and Taking of Testimony*, 62 Mich. L. Rev. 1375 (1964). As discussed above, many civil law states regard the service of process as a judicial act requiring local governmental participation. *See supra* pp. 774-79.

261. *See* 13 U.L.A. 484 (1980) & Appendix B; *Restatement (Third) Foreign Relations Law* §472(2) ("Service of any document issued in connection with a proceeding in a foreign court may be made in the United States (a) in any manner permitted by the law of the state of origin of the document; or (b) pursuant to the order of a United States district court in the district where the person to be served resides or is found."); McCusker, *Some United States Practices in International Judicial Assistance*, 37 Dep't of State Bull. 808 (1957). The Uniform Interstate and International Procedure Act, has been enacted in Arkansas, the District of Columbia, Massachusetts, Michigan, Oklahoma, and Pennsylvania.

262. H.R. Rep. No. 1052, 885th Cong., 1st Sess. (1963), *reprinted in* [1964] U.S. Code Cong. & Admin. News 3782, 3785-86.

2. Absence of Direct U.S. Legal Restrictions on Foreign Service of Process Mechanisms Does Not Imply That U.S. Courts Will Recognize Resulting Foreign Judgments

The absence of direct U.S. restrictions on the service of foreign process does *not* imply that U.S. courts will accept particular foreign service mechanisms in actions to enforce resulting foreign judgments in U.S. courts. U.S. requirements for the enforcement of foreign judgments are discussed in Chapter 12 below, and generally require that foreign service comply with the due process clause's notice requirements.[263] It is important to note that, merely because U.S. law does not forbid a particular form of service, does not mean that such service provides reasonable notice to the defendant.

The foregoing is made express in 28 U.S.C. §1696 and §2.04 of the Uniform Interstate and International Procedure Act. Section 1696 provides that "[s]ervice pursuant to this subsection does not, of itself, require the recognition or enforcement in the United States of a judgment, decree, or order rendered by a foreign or international tribunal." Similarly, §2.04(c) provides: "[s]ervice under this Section does not, of itself, require the recognition or enforcement of an order, judgment, or decree rendered outside this state."

3. U.S. Judicial Assistance in Serving Foreign Process in the United States

a. Section 1696

Foreign litigants sometimes seek the assistance of U.S. judicial authorities in serving process within the United States.[264] Both federal and state statutes contemplate such assistance. Section 1696 of Title 28 expressly authorizes federal district courts to honor foreign requests for judicial assistance in effecting service:

> The district court of the district in which a person resides or is found may order service upon him of any document issued in connection with a proceeding in a foreign or international tribunal. The order may be made pursuant to a letter rogatory issued, or request made, by a foreign or international tribunal or upon application of any interested person and shall direct the manner of service. Service pursuant to this subsection does not, of itself, require the recognition or enforcement in the United States of a judgment, decree, or order rendered by a foreign or international tribunal.

Section 1696 was enacted in 1964 for the purpose of permitting "desirable cooperation with foreign countries in the making of service within the United States."[265] It

---

263. *See infra* pp. 963-68.

264. In some foreign states, service of process abroad must be effected through official governmental channels in order to be valid under local law. *In re Letters Rogatory Out of First Civil Court of City of Mexico*, 261 F. 652 (S.D.N.Y. 1919); Jones, *International Judicial Assistance, Procedural Chaos and a Program for Reform*, 62 Yale L.J. 515, 543-45 (1953).

265. H.R. Rep. No. 1052, 88th Cong., 1st Sess. (1963), *reprinted in* [1964] U.S. Code, Cong. & Admin. News 3782, 3785-86.

was intended to overturn the reluctance that U.S. courts had traditionally displayed towards executing foreign letters rogatory issued by foreign courts.[266]

Section 1696 grants a district judge the power to order service of foreign process, but does not expressly require the judge to do so. Requests for service under §1696 can be made by either a "foreign or international tribunal" or by "any interested person." These categories would appear to permit district courts to execute requests by foreign judges, foreign clerks of court, litigants in foreign judicial proceedings (or their attorneys), and foreign consular officers or commissioners appointed by foreign courts.[267] As a practical matter, however, service of foreign process ordinarily should be made to the district court in the form of a petition by local U.S. counsel for the interested foreign litigant (or court). The final sentence of §1696 makes it clear that the execution of a letter rogatory by a U.S. court does not require U.S. recognition of any subsequent foreign judgment.[268]

b. Section 1781

In addition to direct presentation of requests for service to U.S. district courts under §1696, 28 U.S.C. §1781 authorizes the U.S. Department of State to receive requests for judicial assistance from foreign courts and to deliver such requests to the appropriate U.S. agency or court.[269] When the Department of State receives a request for service under §1781, its practice is to refer the request to the Department of Justice, which in turn ordinarily will transmit it to the U.S. Marshal's Service for service. The U.S. Marshal's Service will not serve foreign process that is directly transmitted to it by a foreign litigant or court.[270]

---

266. H.R. Rep. No. 1052, 88th Cong., 1st Sess. (1963), *reprinted in* [1964] U.S. Code, Cong. & Admin. News 3782, 3785-86. For example, in two frequently-cited decisions, both state and federal courts in New York refused to effect service as requested by foreign letters rogatory. *In re Letters Rogatory Out of First Civil Court of City of Mexico*, 261 F. 652 (S.D.N.Y. 1919); *In re Romero*, 107 N.Y.S. 621 (Sup. Ct. 1907). In both cases, the courts reasoned that:

> it is apparently possible through the aid of this court to render the person sought to be served subject to a personal judgment in Mexico, because the contract sued upon was to be performed there. Such a result is contrary to our system of jurisprudence, which treats the legal jurisdiction of a court as limited to persons within its territorial jurisdiction. ... I should hardly feel inclined to assume such a novel jurisdiction as is proposed without statutory authority. 261 F. at 653.

267. Some courts have suggested that foreign consular officials may transmit letters rogatory directly to a U.S. court. *In re Civil Rogatory Letters Filed By the Consulate of the United States of Mexico*, 640 F.Supp. 243 (S.D. Tex. 1986).

268. *Sprague & Rhodes Commodity Corp. v. Instituto Mexicana del Cafe*, 566 F.2d 861 (2d Cir. 1977); *In re Letters Rogatory From the City of Haugesund, Norway*, 497 F.2d 378 (9th Cir. 1978). Section 1696's legislative history goes further, stating that "judicial assistance under this subjection shall not, as a matter of Federal law, add any weight to the claim that the judgment, decree, or order rendered abroad is entitled to recognition in the United States." H.R. Rep. No. 1052, 88th Cong., 1st Sess. 6-7 (1963).

269. Section 1781 is reproduced in Appendix H.

270. 28 U.S.C. §569(b).

c. Section 2.04 of the Uniform Interstate and International Procedure Act

Section 2.04 of the Uniform Interstate and International Procedure Act parallels 28 U.S.C. §1696. It provides that a state court "may order service upon any person who is domiciled or can be found within this state of any document issued in connection with a proceeding in a tribunal outside this state." It also permits applications for service by interested persons or letters rogatory directly from foreign courts.

4. Ensuring That Foreign Process Is Served in a Manner That Will Permit U.S. Recognition of a Foreign Judgment

Foreign litigants will sometimes wish to ensure that any foreign judgment they obtain against a U.S. defendant will be enforceable in U.S. courts. If this is the case, it is vital for service of foreign process on the U.S. defendant to satisfy U.S. rules governing the recognition of foreign judgments. These rules are discussed in detail below.[271] As noted above, the fact that service has been effected with the assistance of a U.S. court under 28 U.S.C. §1696 does not require U.S. recognition of a resulting judgment.[272]

---

271. *See infra* pp. 693-98.
272. *See supra* p. 840.

11/Extraterritorial Discovery and Taking Evidence Abroad[1]

International litigation often requires access to materials or witnesses located out-side the forum state. In order to obtain evidence located abroad, U.S. litigants and courts usually have two basic alternatives. First, U.S. discovery rules can be unilaterally applied to obtain extraterritorial discovery. Second, U.S. courts can seek judicial assistance from foreign courts. This Chapter explores both alternatives.

A. Overview of U.S. Discovery of Materials Located Abroad

A basic premise of U.S. civil litigation is that fair, effective dispute resolution requires giving litigants the legal power to obtain largely unhindered access to all information that could be relevant to the resolution of their dispute. In the Supreme Court's words, "[m]odern instruments of discovery ... make a trial less a game of blind man's bluff and more a fair contest with the basic issues and the facts disclosed to the fullest practicable extent."[2] The purposes of broad U.S. pretrial discovery are variously described, but they include (a) narrowing disputed issues in order to focus trial on matters of real controversy; (b) permitting the parties wide access to information

---

1. Commentary on extraterritorial discovery and obtaining evidence from abroad includes, *e.g.*, Born & Hoing, *Comity and the Lower Courts: Post-Aerospatiale Applications of the Hague Evidence Convention*, 24 Int'l Law. 393 (1990); Collins, *The Hague Evidence Convention and Discovery: A Serious Misunderstanding?*, 35 Int'l & Comp. L.Q. 765 (1986); Gerber, *Beyond Balancing: International Law Restraints on the Reach of National Laws*, 10 Yale J. Int'l L. 185 (1984); Prescott & Alley, *Effective Evidence-Taking Under the Hague Convention*, 22 Int'l Law. 939 (1988); Lowenfeld, *Some Reflections on Transnational Discovery*, 8 J. Comp. Bus. & Cap. Mkt. L. 419 (1986); Maier, *Extraterritorial Discovery: Cooperation, Coercion and the Hague Evidence Convention*, 19 Vand. J. Transnat'l L. 239 (1986); Oxman, *The Choice Between Direct Discovery and Other Means of Obtaining Evidence Abroad: The Impact of the Hague Evidence Convention*, 37 U. Miami L. Rev. 733 (1983); B. Ristau, *International Judicial Assistance* (1990 Rev.); von Mehren, *Discovery Abroad: The Perspective of the U.S. Private Practitioner*, 16 N.Y.U. J. Int'l L. & Pol. 985 (1984); Weis, *The Federal Rules and the Hague Conventions: Concerns of Conformity and Comity*, 50 U. Pitt L. Rev. 903 (1989).

2. *United States v. Proctor & Gamble Co.*, 356 U.S. 677, 682-83 (1958).

---

that they may wish to use as evidence at trial; and (c) obtaining information that will lead to, or facilitate the introduction of, evidence at trial.[3]

Consistent with these premises, U.S. law grants litigants broad powers to obtain discovery from both other parties and non-parties. Thus, Rule 26 of the Federal Rules of Civil Procedure grants the parties to a civil action in federal court expansive authority to "obtain discovery regarding any matter, not privileged, which is relevant to the subject matter involved in the pending action."[4] Rule 26 underscores the broad scope of discoverable materials by further providing that "[it] is not ground for objection that the information sought will be inadmissible at the trial if the information sought appears reasonably calculated to lead to the discovery of admissible evidence."[5]

In addition to permitting discovery of a wide range of information, the Federal Rules provide U.S. litigants with numerous methods for obtaining discoverable materials. The most frequently used methods of discovery are depositions upon oral examination, requests for the production of documents, and written interrogatories to parties.[6] In addition, several other forms of discovery — including depositions on written interrogatories, requests for permission to enter and inspect land and other property, physical and mental examinations, and requests for admissions — are also available, although most of these methods are relatively infrequently used. Finally, amendments to the Federal Rules of Civil Procedure in 1993, adopted in some U.S. judicial districts, introduced "required disclosures" of matters without awaiting a discovery request.[7]

All forms of discovery provided for by the Federal Rules of Civil Procedure are available to obtain evidence from parties to an action. With respect to evidence from uncooperative non-parties, the court where the nonparty is found generally must issue a subpoena to obtain evidence by either oral deposition or production of documents. Written interrogatories, as well as some of the other less-frequently used forms of the U.S. discovery, are generally not available with respect to non-parties.[8]

---

3. *See Hickman v. Taylor*, 329 U.S. 495, 500 (1947) ("civil trials in the federal courts no longer need be carried on in the dark. Under the Federal Rules of Civil Procedure, the way is now clear, consistent with recognized privileges, for the parties to obtain the fullest possible knowledge of the issues and facts before trial.").

4. Fed. R. Civ. P. 26(b). Federal Rules of Civil Procedure 26, 30, 32, 34, and 45 are reprinted in Appendix C. *See* C. Wright, A. Miller, & R. Marcus, *Federal Practice and Procedure* §§2001-70 (1994); *Oppenheimer Fund v. Sanders*, 437 U.S. 340 (1978); *United States v. Procter & Gamble Co.*, 356 U.S. 677, 682 (1958); *Hickman v. Taylor*, 329 U.S. 495, 507 (1947) ("[n]o longer can the time-honored cry of 'fishing expedition' serve to preclude a party from inquiring into the facts underlying his opponent's case"). The discovery rules in many states are similar to the Federal Rules. Note, *Discovery Practice in States Adopting the Federal Rules of Civil Procedure*, 68 Harv. L. Rev. 673 (1955).

5. Fed. R. Civ. P. 26(b)(1).

6. *See* Fed. R. Civ. P. 28, 30 & 32 (depositions); 34 & 35 (documents requests and subpoenas); 33 (written interrogatories). *See* Appendix C.

7. Fed. R. Civ. P. 26(a).

8. Fed. R. Civ. P. 31, 34-36. *See* Appendix C.

U.S. discovery is initiated and largely conducted by the litigants themselves, with little direct judicial supervision.[9] Parties enjoy considerable freedom to make any combination of discovery requests without prior court approval.[10] In many cases, the extent of compliance with those requests is determined through private negotiations between the parties.[11] In the words of one commentator, "[m]odern discovery ... has removed most of the decisive play from the scrutiny of the court. Because so many civil cases are settled before trial and because the conduct of attorneys is subject only to fitful and superficial judicial review during the discovery stage, much of the decisive gamesmanship of modern litigation takes place in private settings."[12] Judicial intervention in the discovery process typically occurs only after negotiations have failed and the parties have filed either motions to compel or for protective orders against further discovery.[13]

The character of U.S. discovery is often affected by the underlying substantive claims for which discovery is sought. Trade regulation, patent, securities fraud, product liability, and other similar cases often result in sweeping demands for discovery, particularly of business records and other documents. Discovery in these cases can result in the production of tens of millions of documents relating to many aspects of a company's operations over a substantial period of time. These demands are fundamentally different from discovery in more straightforward U.S. cases involving routine contract or tort disputes.

Many U.S. judges, commentators, and practitioners have criticized the broad, party-directed character of U.S. pretrial discovery.[14] In particular, the expense and intrusion into personal and business secrets associated with broad pretrial discovery has generated significant concerns. In addition, others have argued that pretrial discovery in fact does not promote definition of disputed issues or early settlement:

---

9. Brazil, *The Adversary Character of Civil Discovery: A Critique and Proposal for Change*, 31 Vand. L. Rev. 1295 (1978); Carter, *Existing Rules and Procedures*, 13 Int'l Law. 5, 6-7 (1979).

10. Local rules of court in many jurisdictions impose restrictions on some aspects of discovery — such as limits on the number of interrogatories that may be propounded, or the number of witnesses that may be deposed, without prior court approval.

11. Brazil, *The Adversary Character of Civil Discovery: A Critique and Proposal for Change*, 31 Vand. L. Rev. 1295, 1304 (1978). In many jurisdictions, local rules of court affirmatively require litigants to attempt to resolve discovery disputes by negotiation before bringing the matter to the trial judge. In practice, litigants tend to make initial discovery requests containing sweeping demands for every conceivable bit of information — and then some — that might bear upon the parties' dispute. The party from whom discovery is sought invariably refuses to comply with substantial portions of such demands, citing various privileges, Rule 26(b)'s relevancy requirement, and particular practical obstacles. Negotiations then ensue between the parties to narrow their respective discovery requests and, in some cases, negotiated compromises are reached. When negotiations break down, resolution of remaining issues by the trial judge, a magistrate or a law clerk is required.

12. Brazil, *The Adversary Character of Civil Discovery: A Critique and Proposal for Change*, 31 Vand. L. Rev. 1295, 1304 (1978).

13. C. Wright, A. Miller & R. Marcus,, *Federal Practice And Procedure* §§2035-44 (1994).

14. 1980 Amendments to the Federal Rules of Civil Procedure, 85 F.R.D. 521 (1980) (Powell, J., dissenting); *Blue Chip Stamps v. Manor Drug Stores*, 421 U.S. 723, 741 (1975) (Rehnquist, J., dissenting); ABA Section of Litigation, *Second Report of the Special Committee for the Study of Discovery Abuse* (1980).

"instead of concluding [from discovery] that the adversary's position is just and strong, each side may think that it can gain victory from the new information. Consequently, trials do not seem to diminish in number, become more orderly, or become shorter."[15]

Finally, as discussed in detail below, U.S. courts are often willing to order the discovery of evidence located abroad unilaterally. Although U.S. courts can seek to obtain evidence located abroad by requesting the assistance of foreign judicial authorities,[16] the uncertainties and delays that were traditionally associated with such requests have led U.S. courts to prefer unilateral U.S. discovery efforts.[17] Thus, U.S. courts have frequently issued discovery orders under the Federal Rules of Civil Procedure (or state procedural rules) requiring both litigants and nonlitigants who are subject to U.S. jurisdiction to bring documents or persons located abroad to the United States for inspection or oral examination.[18] Failures to comply with extraterritorial U.S. discovery orders typically result in the imposition of sanctions under Federal Rule of Civil Procedure 37.[19]

Although compelled discovery is of fundamental importance, much discovery in U.S. litigation occurs voluntarily and court-ordered coercion is unnecessary. In these circumstances, if the foreign litigant or witness is willing to come to the United States, or send documents there, discovery may proceed in the same way that domestic U.S. discovery would. If the witness or litigant is not able to come to the United States, then discovery can generally be taken abroad, subject to local law restrictions.[20]

---

15. Glaser, *Pretrial Discovery And The Adversary System* 234 (1968).

16. Foreign judicial assistance was customarily sought by means of a letter rogatory, *see infra* pp. 893-94, although the Hague Evidence Convention now usually provides a preferable alternative where member states are concerned. *See infra* pp. 895-920.

17. *See infra* pp. 856-92.

18. *See infra* pp. 857-60 & 866-70; *Societe Nationale Industrielle Aerospatiale v. U.S. District Court*, 482 U.S. 522, 552-53 (1987) (Blackmun, J., concurring and dissenting).

19. As discussed below, sanctions range from monetary fines to dismissal of the plaintiffs' complaint to the assumption that facts alleged by the adverse party are true. *See infra* pp. 879-80.

20. *See infra* pp. 866-70.

B. Foreign Reactions to Unilateral Extraterritorial U.S. Discovery

1. Foreign "Discovery" Systems

The broad, party-controlled character of U.S. pretrial discovery contrasts sharply with methods for obtaining evidence in many foreign countries. First, the "discovery" of evidence in most civil law countries is controlled principally by the trial judge, rather than by the litigants.[21] As one commentator described the German "discovery" system, "the court rather than the parties' lawyers takes the main responsibility for gathering and sifting evidence, although the lawyers exercise a watchful eye over the court's work. ... It should be emphasized ... that neither plaintiff's nor defendant's lawyer will have conducted any significant search for witnesses or for other evidence unknown to his client. Digging for facts is primarily the work of the judge."[22]

Second, many nations do not permit "private" evidence-taking, in connection with either domestic or foreign judicial proceedings. Civil law nations generally regard the taking of evidence as a judicial function, requiring the supervision of local judges in order to safeguard nationals and others against undue coercion and to ensure the observance of relevant privileges. In these states, discovery without local judicial supervision is regarded as an infringement of national judicial sovereignty.[23]

Third, the scope of discovery in most foreign countries is much more limited than pretrial U.S. discovery, which most foreigners regard as permitting unrestrained "fishing expeditions." That is true, for example, in Germany,[24] France,[25]

---

21. *See, e.g.*, Lowenfeld, *Some Reflections on Transnational Discovery*, 8 J. Comp. Bus. & Cap. Mkt. L. 419, 422-23 (1986); Langbein, *The German Advantage in Civil Procedure*, 52 U. Chi. L. Rev. 823 (1985); Borel & Boyd, *Opportunities for and Obstacles to Obtaining Evidence in France for Use in Litigation in the United States*, 13 Int'l Law. 35 (1979).

22. Langbein, *The German Advantage in Civil Procedure*, 52 U. Chi. L. Rev. 823, 826-27 (1985).

23. Brief for the Federal Republic of Germany as Amicus Curiae at 6-7, *Anschuetz & Co., GmbH v. Mississippi River Bridge Authority*, 474 U.S. 812 (1985) (No. 85-98) ("The Federal Republic of Germany likewise considers it a violation of its sovereignty when a foreign court forces, under the threat of sanctions, a person under the jurisdiction of German courts to remove documents located in Germany to the United States for the purpose of pre-trial discovery, or orders a person, under the threat of sanctions, to leave the Federal Republic of Germany and travel to the United States to be available for oral depositions. The taking of evidence is a judicial function exclusively reserved to the courts of the Federal Republic of Germany."); Note of the Federal Republic of Germany to the U.S. Department of State (April 8, 1986), *Id.* at Exhibit A; Brief of Government of Switzerland as Amicus Curiae in Support of Petitioners at 3, 8 *Aérospatiale* (No. 85-1695) ("If a U.S. court unilaterally attempts to coerce the production of evidence located in Switzerland, without requesting governmental assistance, the U.S. court intrudes upon the judicial sovereignty of Switzerland."); Brief for the Republic of France as Amicus Curiae in Support of Petitioners at 12-15, *Aérospatiale* (No. 85-1695).

24. Gerber, *Extraterritorial Discovery and the Conflict of Procedural Systems: Germany and the United States*, 34 Am. J. Comp. L. 745 (1986); Kaplan et al., *Phases of German Civil Procedure*, 71 Harv. L. Rev. 1193 (1958); Langbein, *The German Advantage in Civil Procedure*, 52 U. Chi. L. Rev. 823 (1985).

25. Borel & Boyd, *Opportunities for and Obstacles to Obtaining Evidence in France for Use in Litigation in the United States*, 13 Int'l Law. 35 (1979); Herzog, *The 1980 French Law on Documents and Information*, 75 Am. J. Int'l L. 382 (1981); Toms, *The French Response to the Extraterritorial Application of United States Antitrust Laws*, 15 Int'l Law. 585 (1981).

England,[26] and Switzerland.[27] In one commentator's words, the broad "pretrial procedures presently permitted by many American courts is so completely alien to the
procedure in most other jurisdictions that an attitude of suspicion and hostility is
created, which sometimes causes discovery which would be considered proper, even
narrow, in this country to be regarded as a fishing expedition elsewhere."[28] The
restrictive scope of foreign discovery generally reflects foreign public policies, including protection against unreasonable intrusion into personal and business privacy.[29]

Fourth, most foreign countries are less willing than the United States to recognize the legitimacy of unilateral extraterritorial discovery under international law.
Civil law nations generally regard the discovery of evidence located within their territory as a formal, judicial act that must be conducted or approved by local officials.
Unilateral foreign discovery efforts, without the supervision of local authorities, are
regarded as a violation of national judicial sovereignty.[30] Indeed, even other common law nations often regard unilateral extraterritorial discovery by foreign courts of
evidence located within their territory as a violation of their sovereignty. In the
words of a 1965 report of the International Law Association:

> It is difficult to find any authority under international law for the issuance
> of orders compelling the production of documents from abroad. The docu-
> ments are admittedly located in the territory of another state. To assume
> jurisdiction over documents located abroad in advance of a finding of effect
> upon commerce raises the greatest doubts among non-Americans as to the
> validity of such order.[31]

For all these reasons, unilateral extraterritorial U.S. discovery orders have frequently
aroused substantial foreign opposition. In the words of the *Restatement (Third) of*

---

26. P. Matthews & H. Malek, *Discovery* 89-109 (1992); Collins, *Opportunities For and Obstacles to
Obtaining Evidence in England for Use in Litigation in the United States*, 13 Int'l Law. 27 (1979).

27. Comment, *The Supreme Court's Impact on Swiss Banking Secrecy: Société Nationale Industrielle
Aérospatiale v. U.S. District Court*, 37 Am. U. L. Rev. 827 (1988).

28. Carter, *Existing Rules and Procedures*, 13 Int'l Law. 5 (1979). *See* Lowenfeld, *Some Reflections on
Transnational Discovery*, 8 J. Comp. Bus. & Mkt. L. 419, 419-20 (1986) ("[t]he rest of the world ... thinks
U.S. lawyers, agencies and prosecutors start lawsuits or investigations on minimal bases, and rely on their
adversaries or targets to build their cases for them").

29. Heck, *Federal Republic of Germany and the EEC*, 18 Int'l Law. 793, 794 (1984). In addition, most
foreign states permit prevailing parties to recover their attorneys' fees, including any discovery costs, from
losing parties. The inability of foreign defendants to do so in U.S. litigation aggravates displeasure about
intrusive and expensive U.S.-style discovery.

30. *See* Brief for Anschuetz & Co. GmbH and Messerschmitt-Boelkow-Blohm GmbH as Amici
Curiae in Support of Petitioners, *Aerospatiale*, 482 U.S. 522 (1987); Brief of Amicus Curiae the Republic of
France in Support of Petitioners, *Aerospatiale*, 482 U.S. 522 (1987); Oxman, *The Choice Between Direct
Discovery and Other Means of Obtaining Evidence Abroad: The Impact of the Hague Evidence Convention*, 37
U. Miami L. Rev. 733 (1983).

31. International Law Association, Report Of The Fifty-First Conference 407 (1964). *See* Onkelinx,
*Conflict of International Jurisdiction: Ordering the Production of Documents in Violation of the Law of the
Situs*, 64 Nw. U.L. Rev. 487 (1969); April & Fried, *Compelling Discovery and Disclosure in Transnational
Criminal Litigation — A Canadian View*, 16 N.Y.U.J. Int'l & Pol. 961, 964-65 (1984).

Foreign Relations Law, "[n]o aspect of the extension of the American legal system beyond the territorial frontier of the United States has given rise to so much friction as the request for documents in investigation and litigation in the United States."[32]

2. Foreign Diplomatic Objections to U.S. Discovery

Unilateral U.S. discovery of materials located abroad has frequently provoked vigorous foreign resistance. The earliest manifestations of foreign resistance to U.S. discovery took the form of diplomatic notes from foreign nations to the United States protesting particular U.S. discovery orders.[33] There is a long history of such protests.

In 1874, for example, several German diplomatic notes protested the conduct of U.S. lawyers who sought to take sworn testimony within Germany from German nationals for use in U.S. judicial proceedings.[34] The United States replied that the evidence was taken by U.S. court-appointed commissioners, in accordance with U.S. procedural rules, and that all nations had an interest in facilitating transnational evidence-taking. Germany rejoined that where the U.S. "system for taking testimony is to be put in force in a foreign country ... then, according to international law, it can only take place with such limitations and under such restrictions ... as is provided by the existing law-forms of the respective foreign countries."[35] Germany assured the United States, however, that German courts would comply "very cheerfully" with a letter rogatory, which it characterized as "the proper means to harmonize with our institutions and laws any necessity of American courts ... for the taking of testimony in Germany."[36] The United States did not appear to press the point any further.

More recently, diplomatic notes involving discovery disputes have generally been reserved for cases of broad significance, usually concerning vital foreign industries or major foreign corporations. Thus, a flurry of foreign diplomatic notes was generated by each of the U.S. government's major antitrust investigations of interna-

---

32. *Restatement (Third) Foreign Relations Law* §442, Reporters' Note 1 (1987).

33. A diplomatic note is a formal communication from the government of one nation to that of another nation, and can deal with almost any conceivable issue of governmental concern. Diplomatic notes are drafted by the foreign ministry of the government lodging the protest and are typically transmitted through the foreign country's U.S. embassy to the U.S. Department of State.

34. Letter from Mr. von Bülow to George Bancroft (June 24, 1874), in *Papers Relating to the Foreign Relations of the United States* 446 (1874). One note described a visit by a U.S. vice-consul and an Assistant U.S. Attorney to a German company in Germany seeking sworn testimony; when this was refused, the U.S. officials threatened that U.S. compulsory process would be issued and that the German company's U.S. business would suffer. The German note described this as a "trespass irreconcilable with the lawful rights and duties of the German authorities." Letter from Nicholas Fish to Hamilton Fish (July 27, 1874) and Letter from Mr. von Bülow to Nicolas Fish (July 25, 1874), *in id.* at 453-54.

35. Letter from Mr. von Bülow to Mr. Schlözer (Oct. 12, 1874), *in id.* at 463.

36. Letter from Mr. von Bülow to Mr. Schlözer (Oct. 12, 1874), *in id.* at 463.

tional cartels during the 1950s and 1960s.[37] Foreign governmental protests have been less common in smaller-scale private disputes.

Despite the fairly limited circumstances in which diplomatic notes are ordinarily delivered, protests against extraterritorial U.S. discovery have been impressive both in number and vigor. According to one observer, "[t]he orders by American courts to oblige enterprises before the court to go abroad and gather documentary evidence have elicited so many protests from foreign governments that no one could seriously contend that such orders have been considered in conformity with international law by the majority of civilized countries."[38]

Foreign diplomatic notes protesting extraterritorial U.S. discovery typically follow the same general pattern. Foreign governments assert their sovereign right to control documents, witnesses, and other evidence located within their territory and characterize unilateral U.S. efforts to compel the production of such evidence in U.S. proceedings as infringements on their sovereign prerogatives and territorial integrity. These arguments are bolstered by references to local legislation forbidding foreign evidence-taking and by statements emphasizing the importance of the industry under investigation to the foreign economy.

3. Foreign Nondisclosure Statutes[39]

Despite their vigor, foreign diplomatic protests seldom persuade U.S. courts to abandon unilateral U.S. extraterritorial discovery efforts. As a result, some 15 foreign states have taken more vigorous steps to thwart U.S. discovery, at least in some cases, adopting so-called "blocking statutes." The basic effect of these statutes is to prohibit, as a matter of foreign law, compliance with U.S. discovery orders for the production of evidence located within the blocking state's territory. Foreign blocking statutes generally carry some sort of penal sanction for violations of prohibitions against disclosure.

Some nations have long-standing laws prohibiting the disclosure of particular types of information for any reason. Although these statutes prohibit compliance with foreign discovery orders, they were originally designed for other, broader purposes. A classic example of these older statutes is the Swiss bank secrecy law, enacted

---

37. *See* International Law Association, Report of the Fifty-First Conference 565-92 (1964) (excerpting protests concerning U.S. antitrust investigations of petroleum, shipping, paper, and electric lamp industries).

38. *Id.* at 403 (1964). *See Id.* at 565-92 (reproducing extracts of diplomatic notes and other communications protesting extraterritorial U.S. discovery orders); Note (No. 196) of British Embassy to United States Department of State, July 27, 1978, Brit. Y.B. Int'l L. 390; Copithorne, *Canadian Practice in International Law during 1978 as Reflected Mainly in Public Correspondence and Statements of the Department of External Affairs,* 17 Can. Y.B. Int'l L. 334, 336 (1979).

39. Commentary on foreign blocking statutes includes, *e.g.,* Cira, *The Challenge of Foreign Laws to Block American Antitrust Actions,* 18 Stan. J. Int'l L. 247 (1982); Lowe, *Blocking Extraterritorial Jurisdiction: The British Protection of Trading Interests Act,* 75 Am. J. Int'l L. 257 (1981); Pettit & Styles, *The International Response to the Extraterritorial Application of United States Antitrust Laws,* 37 Bus. Law. 697 (1982).

in 1934 to foreclose German and other government enquiries.[40] In general, however, most foreign nondisclosure statutes are comparatively recent enactments that were precipitated by unilateral U.S. extraterritorial discovery.

Recently enacted foreign blocking statutes fall into several general categories. First, some foreign blocking statutes prohibit any disclosure of documents or other information in connection with foreign discovery orders, unless the orders are passed through appropriate foreign governmental channels. Recently enacted French blocking legislation contains this sort of automatic, blanket prohibition against compliance with foreign discovery orders.[41]

Second, a number of foreign blocking statutes grant discretionary authority to particular governmental agencies to forbid compliance with specific foreign discovery orders. For example, the U.K. Protection of Trading Interests Act authorizes the Secretary of State to prohibit compliance with any foreign discovery order that would infringe the sovereignty or security of the United Kingdom.[42] Australia and Canada have adopted similar legislation.[43]

Finally, the largest number of foreign blocking statutes contain either automatic prohibitions against disclosure of information regarding particular industries, or grants of administrative discretion to prohibit such disclosures. Representative examples of this type of statute include bank secrecy laws,[44] statutes enacted to prohibit disclosure of information regarding uranium production,[45] and laws forbid-

---

40. Swiss Penal Code, Art. 273 (1971); Switzerland, Law on Banks and Savings Associations, Art. 47, dated Nov. 8, 1934. *See* Miller, *International Cooperation in Litigation Between the United States and Switzerland: Unilateral Accommodation in a Test-Tube*, 49 Minn. L. Rev. 1069 (1965); Note, *Obtaining Evidence in Switzerland for Use In Foreign Courts*, 3 Am. J. Comp. L. 412 (1954).

41. Law No. 80-538, [1980] Journal Officiel 1799, dated July 16, 1980. *See* Borel & Boyd, *Opportunities for and Obstacles to Obtaining Evidence in France for Use in Litigation in the United States*, 13 Int'l Law. 35 (1979); Toms, *The French Response to the Extraterritorial Application of the United States Antitrust Laws*, 15 Int'l Law. 585 (1981).

42. *See* Protection of Trading Interests Act, 1980, 27 Eliz. 2, ch. 11, *reprinted in* 21 Int'l Leg. Mat. 834 (1982); Lowe, *Blocking Extraterritorial Jurisdiction: The British Protection of Trading Interests Act*, 1980, 75 Am. J. Int'l L. 257 (1981); Lowenfeld, *Sovereignty, Jurisdiction, and Reasonableness: A Reply to A.V. Lowe*, 75 Am. J. Int'l L. 629 (1981).

43. Ontario Business Protection Act, R.S.O. chap. 56, §2(1)(1980); Foreign Extraterritorial Measures Act, *reprinted in*, 24 Int'l Leg. Mats. (1985) (granting attorney general of Canada authority to issue specific orders prohibiting disclosure of materials located within Canada); Foreign Proceedings (Prohibition of Certain Evidence) Act, 1976, Australian Acts No. 121, amended by Foreign Proceedings (Prohibition of Certain Evidence) Amendment Act, 1976, Australia Acts No. 202.

44. *See* Australia, 1979 Banking Statute of Australia §23; Bahamas, Banks and Trust Companies Regulation Act of 1965, §10, 1965 Bah. Act No. 64, as amended by the Banks and Trust Companies Regulation (Amendment) Act 1980, 1980 Bah. Act. No. 3; Bermuda, Evidence Act, 1905 §59; Cayman Islands, The Confidential Relationships (Preservation) (Amendment) Law, 1979; Liechtenstein, Banks and Savings Law of December 21, 1960; Panama, Banking Law of Panama, Rep. of Panama; Singapore, Banking Act, §42.

45. Canada, Uranium Information Security Regulations, Can. Stat. O. & Reg. 76-644 (P.C. 1976-2368, Sept. 21, 1976); South Africa, Atomic Energy Act, §30, 15 Stat. Repub. So. Afr. 1045 (1978).

ding disclosure of information concerning the shipping industry.[46] In almost all cases, these statutes were enacted in response to specific U.S. discovery efforts or investigations that were perceived abroad as threatening a particular foreign industry.[47]

4. Selected Materials on Foreign Diplomatic Notes and Blocking Statutes

The text of a representative diplomatic protest — a Canadian note protesting U.S. discovery orders in connection with uranium antitrust litigation in the 1970s — is excerpted below. Also excerpted below are several foreign blocking statutes: (a) a French statute, enacted during the 1980s, which forbids the taking of evidence in France for foreign judicial proceedings without French government approval; and (b) a Swiss statute, enacted in 1934 which forbids unauthorized disclosures to foreign government authorities.

DIPLOMATIC NOTE FROM THE SECRETARY OF STATE FOR EXTERNAL AFFAIRS OF CANADA TO THE AMBASSADOR OF THE UNITED STATES

17 Can. Y.B. Int'l L. 334, 336 (1979)

I have the honor to refer to civil proceedings relating to international uranium marketing arrangements, now before the courts in various jurisdictions within the United States. In certain of these proceedings U.S. courts have ordered the production of documents located in Canada or the disclosure of information contained in such documents. Persons or corporations to whom such orders have been directed, some of whom are Canadian nationals, have not produced some or all of the documents or information in question and have stated the reason for their inability to do so is that such documents or information are within the terms of the Uranium Information Security Regulations ... and their disclosure is prohibited by those Regulations. Because the documents and information in question have not been produced in response to the direction of the courts, the persons and corporations direct-

---

46. United Kingdom, Shipping Contracts and Commercial Documents Act 1964; Federal Republic of Germany, Law on the Responsibilities of the Federation in the Field of Shipping, dated May 24, 1965 [BGB 2, 835].

47. For example, the Ontario Business Records Protection Act, 1947 Ont. Rev. Stat. c.54, was adopted after U.S. courts ordered the production of documents stored in Canada for use in an antitrust grand jury investigation of the paper industry. Baker, *Antitrust Conflicts Between Friends: Canada and the United States in the Mid-1970's,* 11 Cornell Int'l L.J. 165 (1978). Similarly, blocking legislation applicable to the ocean shipping industry was enacted in the United Kingdom, the Federal Republic of Germany, France, and Norway after the U.S. Federal Maritime Commission ordered the production of evidence from a number of foreign states in connection with its investigation in the 1960s of anticompetitive practices in the shipping industry. *See* Batista, *Confronting Foreign "Blocking" Legislation: A Guide to Securing Disclosure from Non-Resident Parties to American Litigation,* 17 Int'l Law. 61 (1983); Pettit & Styles, *The International Response to the Extraterritorial Application of United States Antitrust Laws,* 37 Bus. Law. 697 (1982).

ed to produce them may face default judgements, negative inferences of fact, severe pecuniary liability and other sanctions.

A situation in which courts of the United States imposed sanctions for failure to produce documents or information located in Canada where such production would violate Canadian laws and regulations would be a matter of serious concern to the Government of Canada because it would subordinate to the procedures of U.S. courts the authority of the Government of Canada to prohibit the disclosure of certain information in Canada relating to the production and marketing of Canadian uranium. Such a failure on the part of courts in the United States to recognize the authority of the Canadian Government to prohibit such disclosure would be contrary to generally accepted principles of international law and would have an adverse impact on relations between the U.S.A. and Canada. ...

[T]he participation of all Canadian uranium producers in certain uranium marketing arrangements was a matter of Canadian Government policy. ... [T]he policy was adopted following action by the United States Government which effectively closed the large U.S. market to Canadian and other foreign uranium producers, with severe adverse consequences for the Canadian uranium mining industry. The Canadian Government ... was convinced that preservation of a viable uranium producing industry was essential to the Canadian national interest. ...

The Government of Canada wishes to state its serious objection to the imposition of any sanction by the judicial branch of the United States Government for failure to produce documents or to disclose information located in Canada where such production or disclosure would require a person or corporation in Canada to perform an act or omission in Canada which is prohibited by the Uranium Information Security Regulations or any other law of Canada. The threat or imposition of any such sanction would have the appearance of an attempt to induce the performance in Canada of acts which are prohibited in Canada and of attaching liability for acts performed in Canada in accordance with Canadian law and the publicly declared policy of the Canadian Government. Such procedure would be inconsistent with generally accepted principles of international law, with the manner in which the Governments of Canada and the United States carry on their mutual relations and with the spirit of those relations. I should be grateful if you would convey the foregoing to your Government with the request that these views and concerns be transmitted to those courts in the United States where trials related to this matter are in progress.

FRENCH PENAL CODE LAW NO. 80-538

ARTICLES 1A & 2

1A. Subject to treaties or international agreements and applicable laws and regulations, it is prohibited for any person to request, to investigate or to disclose, in writing, orally or by any other means, economic, commercial, industrial, financial or technical matters leading to the constitution of evidence with a view to foreign judicial or administrative proceedings or as a part of such proceedings. ...

2. The parties mentioned in [Article 1A] shall forthwith inform the competent minister if they receive any request concerning such disclosures.

SWISS PENAL CODE
ARTICLE 273

273. *Supply of economic information.* Anyone who obtains by investigation a secret relating to a manufacturing process or a business in order to render it accessible to an authority abroad, a foreign organisation or a private company or to one of its agents, anyone who renders a secret relating to a manufacturing process or a business accessible to an authority abroad, a foreign organisation or a private company or to one of its agents, shall be punished by imprisonment, in severe cases by penal servitude. The person receiving a custodial sentence may also be fined.

Notes on Objections to U.S. Discovery and Blocking Statutes

1. *Basis for foreign objections to U.S. discovery.* Why is it that foreign states object to unilateral extraterritorial U.S. discovery of evidence located on their territory? Is it simply because they want to protect local companies from liability to foreign plaintiffs? Or is there a principled basis for their objections? Is the concept of "judicial sovereignty" a legitimate one? Why should, for example, French courts or governmental authorities have a right to supervise a French national's disclosures of evidence to a foreign court that possesses personal jurisdiction over the French national?

2. *Challenges to the propriety of unilateral extraterritorial discovery under international law.* Are unilateral U.S. discovery orders, like that in *In re Uranium Antitrust Litigation, infra* pp. 856-60, consistent with principles of international law? Is it not clear that documents and other matters located within the territory of a foreign state are subject to its jurisdiction under international law? Consider the following excerpts from various amicus curiae briefs on behalf of foreign states in U.S. litigation:

> The Federal Republic of Germany likewise considers it a violation of its sovereignty when a foreign court forces, under the threat of sanctions, a person under the jurisdiction of German courts to remove documents located in Germany to the United States for the purpose of pretrial discovery, or orders a person, under the threat of sanctions, to leave the Federal Republic of Germany and travel to the United States to be available for oral depositions. The taking of evidence is a judicial function exclusively reserved to the courts of the Federal Republic of Germany. Brief for the Federal Republic of Germany as Amicus Curiae at 6-7, *Anschuetz & Co., GmbH v. Mississippi River Bridge Authority*, 474 U.S. 812 (1985).

> If a U.S. court unilaterally attempts to coerce the production of evidence located in Switzerland, without requesting governmental assistance, the U.S. court intrudes upon the judicial sovereignty of Switzerland. Brief of Government of Switzerland as Amicus Curiae in Support of Petitioners, at 3, 8, *Societe Nationale Industrielle Aerospatiale v. U.S. District Court.* 482 U.S. 522 (1987).

What is the answer to these assertions of territorial sovereignty? Why don't direct U.S. discovery orders violate international law?

One of the basic attributes of national sovereignty — discussed elsewhere in various contexts, *see supra* pp. 70-73 & 493-97 — is control over national territory and borders. When a U.S. court orders a foreign national to bring materials located in foreign territory to the United States, does it not infringe on the foreign state's territorial sovereignty? Is a state's sovereignty over documents located on its territory necessarily exclusive? How does ordering a foreign defendant to produce documents located abroad differ from ordering it to pay money?

3. *U.S. government defense of unilateral extraterritorial discovery under international law.* What is the legal basis under international law for unilateral extraterritorial discovery? Consider the following summary of the U.S. position:

Foreign parties have typically objected to American discovery methods on the ground that such devices violate their home country's "judicial sovereignty." But such assertions often have an abstract quality and do little, in and of themselves, to elucidate the substantive foreign interests at stake. ... [A]ssertions of "judicial sovereignty" often incorporate legitimate notions of territorial integrity — a reluctance to permit foreign litigants to invade one's borders, literally or figuratively, for the purpose of seizing evidence. ... [A]ssertions of "judicial sovereignty" [also] may reflect an understandable reluctance to forfeit the moderating effects of judicial supervision and to expose one's citizens to unpredictable and potentially abusive evidentiary demands. On the other hand, assertions of "judicial sovereignty" may simply illustrate a foreign nation's desire to protect its nationals from liability, or reflect a preference for its own mode of dispute resolution instead of ours.

In our view, assertions of foreign "judicial sovereignty" must be evaluated in light of the established American principle that a United States court may order a foreign national, properly subject to the court's jurisdiction, to produce evidence located abroad. As a general matter, it is not unreasonable in principle for this Nation's courts to subject foreign corporations doing business here to the same judicial procedures that are applied to domestic corporations. ... [A]n abstract claim of "judicial sovereignty" cannot equate to a right — indeed, it would be an extraordinary privilege — to have all of the benefits of access to American markets, yet to be free from the burdens that American judicial procedures generally impose. Brief for the United States and the Securities and Exchange Commission as Amici Curiae, at 22-23, *Societe Nationale Industrielle Aerospatiale v. U.S. District Court*, 482 U.S. 522 (1987).

What exactly is the U.S. rationale for unilateral extraterritorial discovery? Is this a satisfactory response to the objections set forth above?

4. *Importance of blocking statutes in international law analysis.* Suppose that one foreign state has enacted legislation forbidding compliance with foreign discovery efforts, while a second foreign state has not enacted such legislation. Is extraterritorial foreign discovery in these two states subject to different analyses under international law? Compare the discussion above concerning the service of foreign process. *See supra* pp. 777-79.

Suppose a foreign state imposes stricter limits on what its nationals may disclose abroad, as compared to what they must disclose in local court actions. Suppose the foreign state limits foreign discovery to the same scope as that which would be permitted in local proceedings. Are these foreign actions equally legitimate?

5. *Effect of foreign diplomatic notes in U.S. litigation.* It is difficult to assess the value of foreign diplomatic notes in U.S. litigation. On the one hand, U.S. courts frequently allude to the submission and contents of diplomatic notes and generally appear to take such submissions very seriously. *See Societe Nationale Industrielle Aerospatiale v. U.S. District Court*, 482 U.S. 522 (1987); *CFTC v. Nahas*, 738 F.2d 487 (D.C. Cir. 1984); *FTC v. Compagnie de Saint-Gobain-Pont-a-Mousson*, 636 F.2d 1300, 1306 (D.C. Cir. 1980); *Minpeco, SA v. Conticommodity Services, Inc.*, 116 F.R.D. 517, 524 (S.D.N.Y. 1987); *In re Grand Jury Investigation of the Shipping Indus.*, 186 F.Supp. 298, 318 (D.D.C. 1960). Moreover, the absence of a diplomatic note may sometimes lead U.S. courts to conclude that foreign governmental interests either do not exist or are unimportant. *E.g., United States v. First National City Bank*, 396 F.2d 898, 904 (2d Cir. 1968) ("[i]t is noteworthy that neither the Department of State nor the German Government has expressed any view on this case or indicated that, under the circumstances present here, enforcement of the subpoena would violate German public policy or embarrass German-American relations"); *United States v. Davis*, 767 F.2d 1025, 1035 (2d Cir. 1985) ("absence of any objection by the Cayman government ... is significant"); *SEC v. Banca Della Svizzera Italiana*, 92 F.R.D. 111 (S.D.N.Y. 1981).

6. *Practical guidance on use of diplomatic notes.* As noted above, U.S. courts generally take foreign diplomatic notes (or other government statements) seriously. Thus, in discovery disputes that may implicate foreign sovereign interests, counsel should carefully consider encouraging the relevant foreign states to evaluate the case and present their views to the United States authorities. Cost considerations will often make foreign governments unwilling to file *amicus curiae* briefs, save in the most important cases, and bureaucratic inertia may make it difficult to obtain even a diplomatic note. Nonetheless, the existence of a foreign governmental submission is often sufficiently important to justify efforts to explain to foreign states how a particular case implicates their interests.

C. Direct U.S. Discovery of Materials Located Abroad: Judicial Power

1. Direct Extraterritorial Discovery of Documents

Federal Rule of Civil Procedure 34 authorizes litigants in a civil action to request parties to the action to produce all documents within their "possession, custody, or control" that are relevant to the action, whether or not the documents are within the territorial jurisdiction of the court.[48] U.S. lawyers generally view the discovery of documents from adverse parties and witnesses as fundamental to a fair adjudication. "[T]he heart of any United States antitrust case is the discovery of business documents. Without them there is virtually no case."[49] The same is true in many other types of business litigation.

U.S. courts have long asserted and exercised the power under Rule 34 to order litigants to produce documents located abroad for use in U.S. proceedings — even though this obviously requires substantial activity on foreign territory.[50] A litigant's failure to comply with such discovery orders is punishable by the imposition of sanctions pursuant to Rule 37.[51] The decision in *In re Uranium Antitrust Litigation*,[52] which is excerpted below, illustrates how most U.S. courts have approached the question whether they have the power to order parties to produce documents located abroad for use in U.S. litigation. The following excerpt from *In re Uranium Antitrust Litigation* does not deal with the exercise of such power where U.S. discovery is inconsistent with foreign laws or public policies; that subject is examined later in this Chapter.[53]

---

48. *See* Fed. R. Civ. P. 34(a); C. Wright, A. Miller & R. Marcus,, *Federal Practice And Procedures* §2210 (1994). Similar procedures are often available with respect to non-parties under the subpoena provisions of Rule 45. *See infra* pp. 861-66.

49. *In re Uranium Antitrust Litigation*, 480 F.Supp. 1138, 1155 (N.D. Ill. 1979). *See also Laker Airways Ltd. v. Pan American World Airways*, 103 F.R.D. 42, 49 (D.D.C. 1983).

50. *E.g., Wyle v. R.J. Reynolds Indus.*, 709 F.2d 585 (9th Cir. 1983); *In re Marc Rich & Co.*, 707 F.2d 663 (2d Cir.), *cert. denied*, 463 U.S. 1215 (1983); *Arthur Andersen & Co. v. Finesilver*, 546 F.2d 338 (10th Cir. 1976), *cert. denied*, 429 U.S. 1096 (1977); *Lowrance v. Michael Weining, GmbH*, 107 F.R.D. 386 (W.D. Tenn. 1985); *International Society for Krisha Consciousness v. Lee*, 105 F.R.D. 435, 444 (S.D.N.Y. 1984); *Graco, Inc. v. Kremlin, Inc.*, 101 F.R.D. 503, 520-24 (N.D. Ill. 1984); *Restatement (Third) Foreign Relations Law* §442(1)(a) (1987) ("A court or agency in the United States, when authorized by statute or rule of court, may order a person subject to its jurisdiction to produce documents, objects, or other information relevant to an action or investigation, even if the information or the person in possession of the information is outside of the United States").

51. *See infra* pp. 878-80.

52. 480 F.Supp. 1138 (N.D. Ill. 1979).

53. *See infra* pp. 871-92.

IN RE URANIUM ANTITRUST LITIGATION

480 F.Supp. 1138 (N.D. Ill. 1979)

MARSHALL, DISTRICT JUDGE. [The *Uranium Antitrust Litigation* arose from long-term contracts between Westinghouse, on the one hand, and numerous electrical utilities, on the other. The contracts obligated Westinghouse to sell uranium to the utilities at fixed prices for specified terms. When world uranium prices dramatically escalated in the 1970s, Westinghouse refused to fulfill its agreements. In addition to claims that its obligations to the utilities were excused by commercial impracticability, Westinghouse filed an antitrust suit against a number of uranium producers, alleging that they had unlawfully conspired to monopolize the market for uranium. In order to support its claims, Westinghouse sought discovery of many documents in the possession of foreign uranium producers. Most foreign uranium producers refused to comply with Westinghouse's document requests, and Westinghouse then sought orders compelling production by the defendants.]

At the outset, we should identify the type of jurisdiction exercised by a court in issuing an order to produce foreign documents. In the field of foreign relations law, two types of jurisdiction have been defined. Prescriptive jurisdiction refers to the capacity of a state under international law to make a rule of law. It is exemplified by the enactment of the Federal Rules of Civil Procedure, *e.g.*, Rule 37. Enforcement jurisdiction, on the other hand, refers to the capacity of a state under international law to enforce a rule of law. When a court enters an order compelling production of documents under Rule 37, it exercises its enforcement jurisdiction. *Restatement (Second) Foreign Relations Law* §6 (1965); Onkelinx, *Conflict of International Jurisdiction: Ordering the Production of Documents in Violation of the Law of the Situs*, 64 Nw. L. Rev. 487, 495 (1969). The jurisdiction of American courts is unquestioned when they order their own nationals to produce documents located within this country. But jurisdiction is less certain when American courts order a defendant to produce documents located abroad, especially when the country in which the documents are situated prohibits their disclosure.

As a general rule, a court has the power to order a person subject to its jurisdiction to perform an act in another state. *Restatement (Second) Conflict of Laws* §53 (1971). There are two preconditions for the exercise of this power. First, the court must have personal jurisdiction over the person. Second, the person must have control over the documents. The location of the documents is irrelevant.

On the issue of control, there are certain corollary principles which apply to multinational corporations. The test for determining whether an American court can order an American parent corporation to produce the documents of its foreign subsidiary was stated in *In re Investigation of World Arrangements*, 13 F.R.D. 280, 285 (D.D.C. 1952):

> [I]f a corporation has power, either directly or indirectly, through another corporation or series of corporations, to elect a majority of the directors of

another corporation, such corporation may be deemed a parent corporation and in control of the corporation whose directors it has the power to
elect to officer.

Thus, for example, if the parent owns more than 50 percent of the foreign subsidiary's stock, it possesses the necessary control.

The test is less clear in situations where an order is directed to the American
subsidiary of a foreign corporation to produce documents from its head office located abroad. One court has held that a subpoena duces tecum was enforceable if it was
served on the subsidiary's offices in the United States, even though the corporation's
board of directors had passed a resolution prohibiting the removal of the requested
records from Canada and even though all the board members were residents of
Canada. *In Re Grand Jury Subpoenas Duces Tecum*, 72 F.Supp. at 1020. The court's
reasoning as to how the American officers had control over the withheld documents
seems to rest on the theory that it was sufficient that the documents were in possession of the corporation and that a subpoena had been served on some of its officers.
More helpful guidance can be drawn from *Societe Internationale v. McGranery*, 111
F.Supp. 435, 440-42 (D.D.C. 1953), in which the court held that plaintiff, a Swiss
corporation, had control over the papers of its Swiss-based bank, H. Sturzenegger &
Cie. The court attached significance to the fact that Sturzenegger was a director and
officer of plaintiff and was "perhaps" a dominant personality in plaintiff's affairs.
After an extensive examination of the corporate affiliations of the two partners, the
court concluded that "[t]hrough the interlocked web of corporate organization,
management and finance there runs the thread of a fundamental identity of individuals in the pattern of control." Thus, the issue of control is more a question of fact
than of law, and it rests on a determination of whether the defendant has practical
and actual managerial control over, or shares such control with, its affiliate, regardless of the formalities of corporate organization. Once personal jurisdiction over the
person and control over the documents by the person are present, a United States
court has power to order production of the documents. [The Court went on to consider and reject arguments for excusing discovery because of certain foreign blocking
statutes.]

Notes on Uranium Antitrust Litigation

1. *Control required to order document production.* Rule 34(a) permits discovery requests for any
documents in the "possession, custody or control" of other parties to a civil action. Corporations and
other business entities are presumed to "control" all corporate documents and business records. *See Elder-
Beerman Stores Corp. v. Federated Dept. Stores*, 45 F.R.D. 515 (S.D.N.Y. 1968); *In re Grand Jury Subpoenas
Duces Tecum Addressed to Canadian Int'l Paper Co.*, 72 F.Supp. 1013 (S.D.N.Y. 1947). Consider application of this rule in international cases. Are there any reasons to think that a company has less control over
documents that are located in foreign countries than those in the United States?

2. *Discovery under Rule 34 of documents located outside the United States.* The relevant documents
in *Uranium Antitrust* were located outside the United States. *Uranium Antitrust* conceded that U.S. "jurisdiction is less certain when American courts order a defendant to produce documents located abroad."
Why is that? Is it not clear that the defendant still "controls" the documents within the meaning of Rule
34(a)? Note the comment in *Uranium Antitrust* that, notwithstanding the court's doubts, "[t]he location
of the documents is irrelevant" to the court's power to order discovery. Why is this the case?

Does Rule 34(a) clearly extend to the discovery of documents located outside the United States, within the territory of another sovereign state? Recall the territoriality presumption, discussed above in the context of legislative jurisdiction. *See supra* pp. 510-11 & 546-50. Absent express language subjecting documents held abroad to U.S. discovery, should such authority be presumed? Consider also the reasoning in *Nahas* and the *Charming Betsy* presumption that Congress does not intend to violate international law. *See supra* pp. 22, 510-11 & 780-94. Is it relevant, in interpreting Rule 34, to consider whether international law permits U.S. courts to order extraterritorial discovery? Should *Uranium Antitrust* have done so?

3. *Discovery under Rule 34 of documents located abroad in violation of foreign law — an initial view.* *Uranium Antitrust* expressed particular concern about its jurisdiction to order discovery of documents located abroad when foreign law forbid law forbid disclosure. What is the relevance of the existence — or nonexistence — of foreign law prohibiting extraterritorial discovery? Compare the similar issues that arise in the context of service abroad. *See supra* pp. 777-79. Is the *absence* of a foreign law forbidding discovery equivalent to foreign consent to U.S. extraterritorial discovery? If a foreign law forbidding discovery does exist, should Rule 34(a) nonetheless be interpreted to require discovery? Consider again the *Nahas* rationale. *See supra* pp. 780-94.

4. *Lower court decisions ordering discovery from foreign subsidiary of U.S. litigant.* Difficulties in applying Rule 34's "control" test frequently arise where information is held by persons closely related to an entity over which the U.S. court has personal jurisdiction. A recurrent issue in international discovery disputes is whether a U.S. court may order a U.S. parent corporation to produce documents held by a foreign subsidiary that is not itself subject to the personal jurisdiction of the U.S. court. As *In re Uranium Antitrust Litigation* illustrates, lower courts have generally ordered the production of documents held by foreign subsidiaries of domestic corporate litigants, provided that the parent effectively controls the subsidiary. A typical formulation of the control standard was stated in *In Re Investigation of World Arrangements*, 13 F.R.D. 280, 285 (D.D.C. 1952), where the court held that "control" would be found if a corporation possesses the power "either directly or indirectly, through another corporation or series of corporations, to elect a majority of the directors of another corporation." Other lower courts have adopted similar tests. *E.g.*, *United States v. Vetco, Inc.*, 691 F.2d 1281 (9th Cir.), *cert. denied*, 454 U.S. 1098 (1981); *Garpeg Ltd. v. United States*, 583 F.Supp. 789 (S.D.N.Y. 1984); *In re Uranium Antitrust Litigation*, 480 F.Supp. 1138, 1144-45 (N.D. Ill. 1979).

5. *Wisdom of decisions ordering discovery from foreign subsidiaries of U.S. parents.* Are decisions ordering discovery from foreign subsidiaries of U.S. parents sound? As discussed above, *supra* pp. 152-53, it is a basic principle of corporate law in the United States and elsewhere that a corporation is a separate and distinct legal entity from both its parent and its subsidiaries. In general, a subsidiary is neither liable for its parent's obligations nor subject to personal jurisdiction because of its parent's contacts with the forum, even if the parent "controls" the subsidiary. Given this, why should the documents of a subsidiary be subject to discovery orders directed to the subsidiary's parent? Note that in such cases the subsidiary is not a party to the U.S. litigation, and may well not be subject to U.S. personal jurisdiction. Does it not violate basic principles of due process and corporate law to require one company to provide documents held by a different company, not subject to the forum court's jurisdiction?

On the other hand, assuming that "control" is the appropriate standard, is it realistic to focus only on parent company's formal power to elect its subsidiary's directors? In other contexts, control is defined more broadly. *E.g.*, Tariff Act of 1930, 19 U.S.C. §1677(13)(D) (treating exporter and importer as one for purposes of antidumping laws if third party owns or controls 20 percent of the stock of both).

6. *Discovery from foreign parent company of U.S. litigant.* Another recurrent issue is the power of U.S. courts to order a U.S. subsidiary to produce documents held abroad by its foreign parent. Although the U.S. subsidiary will ordinarily not control the selection of its parent's board of directors, there may nonetheless be circumstances in which an "upstream" control relationship will be found. For example, in *In re Electric & Musical Industries*, 155 F.Supp. 892, 895 (S.D.N.Y. 1957), *appeal dismissed*, 249 F.2d 308 (2d Cir. 1957), the court refused to quash an antitrust grand jury subpoena directed to the English parent of an American subsidiary that was subject to the issuing court's personal jurisdiction. The court relied on the fact that the English company, a multinational record manufacturer and distributor, and its American subsidiaries were "reciprocating partners" in a common enterprise.

The same analysis was applied in *Societe Internationale v. McGranery*, 111 F.Supp. 435 (D.D.C. 1953), where the court found that a company controlled a superficially unrelated bank because the same individuals held ownership and management power over both entities. *See also In re Marc Rich & Co. AG*,

707 F.2d 663 (2d Cir.), *cert. denied*, 462 U.S. 1215 (1983); *M.L.C. Inc. v. North Am. Philips Corp.*, 109 F.R.D. 134 (S.D.N.Y. 1986); *Cooper Industries, Inc. v. British Aerospace*, 102 F.R.D. 918 (S.D.N.Y. 1984); *In re Grand Jury Subpoenas Duces Tecum Addressed to Canadian Int'l Paper Co.*, 72 F.Supp. 1013 (S.D.N.Y. 1947). Findings of "control" in these types of cases typically turn on highly fact-specific circumstances and provide little basis for broad generalizations.

7. *Managing agents, officers, and employees.* In general, managing agents, directors, and officers of corporations are treated as part of the corporation itself, thus bringing any information in their possession within the effective control of the corporation. As a result, party discovery is frequently ordered of information held by managing agents, directors, and officers of corporate litigants who are not themselves otherwise subject to the U.S. court's personal jurisdiction. *See* C. Wright, A. Miller & R. Marcus,, *Federal Practice and Procedure* §2103 (1994).

In contrast, lower-level corporate employees are treated like unrelated third-party witnesses. Information held by present or former employees who are not managing agents or officers of the corporate party can be obtained only by a subpoena based on the court's personal jurisdiction over the individual holding the information. *E.g., Sykes Int'l v. Pilch's Poultry Breeding Farms, Inc.*, 55 F.R.D. 138 (D. Conn. 1972); *Haviland & Co. v. Montgomery Ward & Co.*, 31 F.R.D. 578 (S.D.N.Y. 1962); *Reliable Volkswagen Sales & Serv. Co. v. World-Wide Auto. Corp.*, 26 F.R.D. 592 (D.N.J. 1960).

8. *Jurisdictional discovery.* U.S. courts can unilaterally compel discovery only from persons subject to their personal jurisdiction. This is true for both litigants and nonparty witnesses. *E.g., In re Sealed Case*, 832 F.2d 1268 (D.C. Cir. 1987); *In re Marc Rich & Co. AG*, 707 F.2d 663 (2d Cir.), *cert. denied*, 463 U.S. 1215 (1983); *Ariel v. Jones*, 693 F.2d 1058, 1060-61 (11th Cir. 1982); *United States v. First National City Bank*, 396 F.2d 898 (2d Cir. 1968); *In re Grand Jury 81-2*, 550 F.Supp. 24 (W.D. Mich. 1982).

Although personal jurisdiction is a requirement for court-ordered discovery, it is also settled that "jurisdictional discovery" can be compelled from a foreign entity in order to determine whether it is subject to a U.S. court's jurisdiction. *See Insurance Corp. of Ireland, Ltd. v. Compagnie des Bauxites de Guinee*, 456 U.S. 694 (1982); *Oppenheimer Fund, Inc. v. Sanders*, 437 U.S. 340, 351 n.13 (1978)("where issues arise as to jurisdiction or venue, discovery is available to ascertain the facts bearing on such issues"); *United States v. United Mine Workers*, 330 U.S. 258, 292 n.57 (1947).

The decision whether or not to permit jurisdictional discovery lies in part within the discretion of the trial judge. *Data Disc Inc. v. Systems Tech. Assoc.*, 557 F.2d 1280, 1285 n.1 (9th Cir. 1977); *Wells Fargo & Co. v. Wells Fargo Express Co.*, 556 F.2d 406 (9th Cir. 1977). In order to obtain jurisdictional discovery, the moving party must ordinarily demonstrate "a reasonable probability that ultimately it will succeed in establishing the facts necessary for the exercise of jurisdiction." *In re Marc Rich & Co. AG*, 707 F.2d at 670; *In re Sealed Case*, 832 F.2d 1268, 1274 (D.C. Cir. 1987). *Compare Rich v. KIS California, Inc.*, 121 F.R.D. 254, 259 (M.D.N.C. 1988) *and Data Disc Inc. v. Systems Tech. Assoc.*, 557 F.2d 1280, 1285 n.1 (9th Cir. 1977) (jurisdictional discovery appropriate "where pertinent facts bearing on the question of jurisdiction are controverted or where a more satisfactory showing of the facts is necessary"). Courts will also consider whether jurisdictional facts are peculiarly within the control of the defendant, whether the defendant has presented competent evidence demonstrating an absence of jurisdiction, and other equitable factors. *Kamen v. American Tel. & Tel. Co.*, 791 F.2d 1006 (2d Cir. 1986); *John Briley, Trevone Prod., Inc. v. Blackford*, 1990 U.S. Dist. Lexis 10967 (S.D.N.Y. 1990). Jurisdictional discovery may be directed only to the issue of jurisdiction, not the merits of the parties' dispute. *Compagnie des Bauxites de Guinee v. L'Union*, 723 F.2d 357, 363 (3d Cir. 1983).

In international cases, is it appropriate to order jurisdictional discovery? What permits a U.S. court to order persons who may not be subject to U.S. jurisdiction to produce documents in the United States? Consider again the *Nahas* rationale.

9. *Interplay between opportunity for jurisdictional discovery and showing required to establish jurisdiction.* If the plaintiff is not permitted jurisdictional discovery, then it may be difficult as a practical matter to satisfy the minimum contacts test and other jurisdictional requirements. Consequently, most courts have applied a less demanding burden of proof on jurisdictional issues when no jurisdictional discovery has been available. According to some lower courts, if jurisdictional discovery and a hearing on jurisdiction are conducted, then the plaintiff must generally carry the burden of establishing jurisdiction by a preponderance of the evidence. R. Casad, *Jurisdiction in Civil Actions* §6.01[3] (1991). If jurisdictional discovery is not permitted, however, the plaintiff generally need only make a *"prima facie showing of jurisdictional facts."* *Data Disc, Inc. v. Systems Tech. Assoc.*, 557 F.2d 1280, 1285 (9th Cir. 1977).

2. Direct Extraterritorial Discovery of Documents from Nonparty Witnesses

The authority of U.S. courts to compel nonparties — persons not named in the lawsuit — to produce documents located abroad raises more complicated issues than party discovery. If a nonparty witness voluntarily complies with a request for information, then informal discovery can proceed without difficulty under U.S. law.[54] This frequently occurs and may obviate the need for a subpoena, formal discovery request, or court order.

Nonetheless, there are many circumstances in which witnesses will not cooperate voluntarily, and a subpoena must be issued. New Rule 45(a) permits the attorney for a party to issue subpoenas (and serve them) commanding either attendance at trial, attendance at a deposition, or production of documents or other evidence. In general, a nonparty can be compelled to produce nonprivileged documents and other materials — including materials located abroad — if it: (a) can be served with a subpoena duces tecum pursuant to the territorial limits of Federal Rule of Civil Procedure 45; (b) is subject to the personal jurisdiction of a U.S. court; and (c) prudential considerations do not lead to quashing of the subpoena.[55] Failure of a nonparty to comply with a subpoena is punishable by the imposition of sanctions pursuant to Rule 45(e) as a contempt of court.

The materials excerpted below illustrate the discovery of documents from nonparty witnesses. Rule 45 provides U.S. courts with the power, in certain circumstances, to order extraterritorial discovery from non-parties. *Laker Airways Ltd. v. Pan American World Airways* illustrates how U.S. courts have exercised this power. Also excerpted below is 28 U.S.C. §1783, which permits broad extraterritorial subpoena discovery from U.S. nationals.

FEDERAL RULES OF CIVIL PROCEDURE

Rule 45 [excerpted in Appendix C]

LAKER AIRWAYS LIMITED v. PAN AMERICAN WORLD AIRWAYS

607 F.Supp. 324 (S.D.N.Y. 1985)

BRIEANT, DISTRICT JUDGE. By separate motions argued together and fully submitted on March 12, 1985, Midland Bank plc ("Midland") and Samuel Montagu & Co. Ltd. ("Montagu") moved for orders pursuant to Rule 45(b) quashing deposition subpoenas duces tecum, which were served respectively in this district on the Midland Bank's New York branch office, and upon Montagu's New York

---

54. Foreign law may restrict the availability, scope, and manner of voluntary disclosure, particularly if discovery occurs on foreign territory. *See infra* pp. 893-94.

55. *In re Sealed Case*, 832 F.2d 1268 (D.C. Cir. 1987); *In re Westinghouse Elec. Corp. Uranium Contracts Litigation*, 563 F.2d 992 (10th Cir. 1977); *Laker Airways v. Pan American World Airways*, 607 F.Supp. 324 (S.D.N.Y. 1985); *In re Grand Jury 81-2*, 550 F.Supp. 24 (W.D. Mich. 1982).

Representative Office, or agency, ... by plaintiff. The subpoenas seek information and documents from movant non-party witnesses in the above entitled action, which is now pending in the U.S. District Court for the District of Columbia ...

We describe briefly the underlying action. It is a private civil action seeking treble damages for federal antitrust violations alleged to have resulted in injury to Laker Airways Limited ("Laker") at one time a well-known British passenger airline of which Sir Freddie Laker was the founder and chief executive officer. On February 5, 1982, Laker ceased doing business due to insolvency, and on February 17, 1982 an individual residing in the United Kingdom was appointed Liquidator. The action filed November 24, 1982 and thereafter consolidated with companion cases thereafter filed, alleges that plaintiff, described as a "foreign corporation in liquidation," exists under the laws of the Island of Jersey in the Channel Islands having its principal office in London, England. Plaintiff is represented to this Court to be insolvent allegedly as a result of the tortious and conspiratorial misconduct of various defendant American, British, Swiss, German, Dutch and Belgian airlines, the British Airways Board, an American aircraft manufacturer, and its finance subsidiary. The thrust of the two-pronged complaint is, first, that "the airline defendants agreed to a predatory scheme to destroy Trans Atlantic Charters and Laker's scheduled Skytrain [passenger] service by offering, among other things, high cost service, at prices below the costs of those services." After alleging other wrongful competition, which need not concern us here, the complaint also alleged as a second factual basis, that "Laker realized in May of 1981 that it might be unable to meet its aircraft loan repayment requirements in January 1982 and explained the situation to its lenders." ... [T]he Complaint alleges that "by Christmas Eve 1981 Laker was advised that all of the lenders had agreed to provide the necessary finance" to reschedule Laker's debts. It is then alleged that certain named airline defendants "pressured Laker's lenders" to deny Laker the necessary finance so as to force Laker out of business, that the lender defendants continued to mislead Laker into believing that the financing was being provided as agreed, that Laker relied on this misrepresentation to its detriment and did not seek other sources of financing. The non-party witnesses Midland and Montagu are not sued in the District of Columbia at this time. Implicit, however, is the suggestion that they are among the "lenders" believed by plaintiff to have colluded with Laker's competitors to deny financing to Laker.

... At present [Midland and Montagu] are no more than non-party witnesses, entitled to have their pending motion adjudicated in accordance with the present state of the litigation. Should either or both movants become parties defendant in the future, then any necessary pre-trial discovery may be obtained directly through the exercise of the powers of the district court in which the above entitled action is pending. ...

This Court concludes that the subpoenas must be vacated for a number of reasons. Foremost among them is the fact that all of Midland's activities in connection with this matter took place solely in the United Kingdom, and Midland's New York branch office had no involvement whatsoever with Laker. This point is not disputed at the hearing. The fact is that the New York branch of Midland did not open until April 1983, long after the alleged antitrust violations sued on in the District of Columbia. Similarly Montagu does not have a branch office in this District; it has a "representative office" which conducts no banking operations in New York. Here again there are no files or documents in the New York Representative Office of Montagu concerning Laker and no person at that office has any knowledge of the matters concerning Laker. That office also was not opened in New York until long after the events complained of by Laker in the District of Columbia action. Essentially then the deposition subpoenas duces tecum seek to require Midland and Montagu, by officers having custody in the United Kingdom to produce in New York for use in the District of Columbia litigation, documents and records regularly maintained at their home offices in London. This is inappropriate. *See generally Ings v. Ferguson*, 282 F.2d 149 (2d Cir. 1960); *First National City Bank of New York v. Internal Revenue Service*, 271 F.2d 616 (2d Cir. 1959); *Cates v. LTV Aerospace Corp.*, 480 F.2d 620 (5th Cir. 1973), which continue to reflect the law applicable to non-parties.

As a second reason to vacate, this Court finds that the service of the subpoenas in New York is a transparent attempt to circumvent the Hague Convention on the Taking of Evidence Abroad in Civil or Commercial Matters, codified at 28 U.S.C. §1781 (hereinafter the "Hague Convention"), which sets forth agreed international procedures for seeking evidence in this Court from non-parties abroad. The failure to use the Hague Convention is more than a mere technicality.

The extraterritorial jurisdiction asserted over foreign interests by the American antitrust laws has long been a sore point with many foreign government, including that of the United Kingdom. The English Protection of Trading Interests Act of 1980 ("PTIA") authorizes and empowers the Secretary of State for Trade and Industry to interpose the official power of the British Government so as to prevent persons conducting business in the United Kingdom from complying with foreign judicial or regulatory provisions designated by the Secretary of State as intrusive upon the sovereignty of that nation. With respect to the District of Columbia *Laker* action, the Secretary has already issued one directive that "no person or persons in the United Kingdom shall comply, or cause or permit compliance, whether by themselves, their officers, servants or agents, with any requirement to produce or furnish to the district court any commercial document in the United Kingdom or any commercial information ...." That the entire *Laker* litigation situation is a matter of sensitive international interest also is emphasized by the determination of the Department of Justice of the United States, announced November 20, 1984 to refrain from initiating civil or criminal antitrust action with respect to the refinancing aspect of the collapse of Laker, and the publicly announced determination on November 19, 1984 by the President that the grand jury investigating Laker antitrust violations in the District of Columbia since June 1983 should terminate its inquiry for "foreign policy reasons." ...

[T]he very real problems presented by the PTIA are cited to demonstrate that the attempt to effect the subpoena duces tecum in this District is in effect an end run, not only around the Hague Convention, but also an end run on the PTIA. In effect, this Court is being asked to aid the plaintiff in the District of Columbia in obtaining an order from this Court which would cause the Midland branch in New York and the Montagu agency to compel their principals in London to violate British law by disgorging in London and transferring to their New York offices, documents which plaintiff would like to see, none of which are now nor ever were located in New York. This is clearly an improper abuse of the subpoena power of this Court, and should not be permitted. ...

28 U.S.C. §1783

[excerpted in Appendix H]

Notes on Rule 45, Pan American World Airways, and §1783

1. *Territorial limits on service of subpoenas under Rule 45.* Rule 45 only permits a federal district court to issue a subpoena for service upon witnesses located within the judicial district of the court (or within 100 miles of the place of trial, deposition or production). *See* Fed. R. Civ. P. 45(b)(2) ("Subject to the provisions of clause (ii) of subparagraph (c)(3)(A) of this rule, a subpoena may be served at any place within the district of the court by which it is issued, or at any place without the district that is within 100 miles of the place of the deposition, hearing, trial, production, or inspection specified in the subpoena ..."). *See also* Wasserman, *The Subpoena Power: Pennoyer's Last Vestige*, 74 Minn. L. Rev. 37 (1989); Carlisle, *Nonparty Document Discovery from Corporations and Governmental Entities Under the Federal Rules of Civil Procedure*, 32 N.Y.L. S. L. Rev. 9 (1988).

Thus, a witness located in California cannot ordinarily be subjected to the subpoena power of the U.S. District Court for the Southern District of New York (unless the witness can be served in the Southern District). Instead, a litigant in an action in the Southern District is required by Rule 45(a)(2) to obtain service of a subpoena from a U.S. district court in the appropriate judicial district in California upon the Californian witness. Fed. R. Civ. P. 45(a)(2) ("A subpoena for attendance at a deposition shall issue from the court for the district designated by the notice of deposition as the district in which the deposition is to be taken."). Such subpoenas are routinely issued and discovery can usually proceed readily in domestic cases. The subpoena at issue in *Pan American* was issued from the Southern District of New York, even though the underlying litigation was pending in the U.S. District Court for the District of Columbia, because Midland and Montagu were located in New York, not the District of Columbia.

2. *Territorial limitations on service of subpoenas in international cases.* In the international context, these territorial limitations on the subpoena power make nonparty discovery substantially more difficult. When discovery is sought from a *foreign* nonparty witness, located in a foreign state, there is no local U.S. district court from which a litigant may obtain subpoena service. The limitation of subpoena service to the territorial jurisdiction of the district court can have important practical consequences. If foreign witnesses cannot be served in any U.S. judicial district, they will be beyond the reach of direct U.S. discovery. *E.g., In re Sealed Case*, 832 F.2d 1268 (D.C. Cir. 1987) (quashing subpoena because it was not served on witness, or acceptable representative, in the district); *Orlich v. Heim Brothers, Inc.*, 560 N.Y.S.2d 10 (N.Y. App. Div. 1990). Suppose, for example, that Midland Bank had never opened a New York office, and could not be served in New York. Would any question of Rule 45 subpoena discovery ever have arisen?

3. *Possibilities for serving subpoenas on foreign nonparty witnesses within U.S. territory.* Not all nonparty foreign companies and individuals will be beyond the service of a subpoena under Rule 45.

(a) *Rule 45 subpoena service on foreign party's U.S. branch.* If a foreign company has a branch office or other significant presence within the forum, then subpoena service on that office would be possible and might provide effective U.S. discovery. *E.g., In re Sealed Case*, 832 F.2d 1268 (D.C. Cir. 1987); *Minpeco, SA v. Conticommodities Serv.*, 116 F.R.D. 517 (S.D.N.Y. 1987). That was the case in *Laker*, where both Midland and Montagu had New York offices.

(b) *Rule 45 subpoena service on foreign party's officers or agents in U.S.* Some courts may permit sub-poena service upon a foreign company by means of service of the subpoena on an officer or agent of the company who is physically present within the forum. R. Casad, *Jurisdiction In Civil Actions* §3.07 (1991); C. Wright, A. Miller & R. Marcus,, *Federal Practice and Procedure* §§2454, 2460-62 (1994); *In re Marc Rich & Co., AG*, 707 F.2d 663 (2d Cir. 1983) (where minimum contacts existed, "service of a subpoena upon appel-lant's officers within the territorial boundaries of the United States would be sufficient to warrant judicial enforcement of the grand jury's subpoena"); *In re Sealed Case*, 832 F.2d 1268 (D.C. Cir. 1987); *Application of Johnson and Johnson*, 59 F.R.D. 174 (D. Del. 1973). Even if service is made upon the corporate agent of a witness, however, personal jurisdiction over the corporation must be established. *See infra* p. 865.

(c) *Rule 45 subpoena service on foreign individual temporarily present in U.S.* A Rule 45 subpoena can also be served upon a foreign non-party witness who is temporarily present in the United States.

4. *Personal jurisdiction over nonparty witness required to enforce Rule 45 subpoena.* Even if Rule 45's territorial limits on subpoena service are satisfied, a non-party witness can only be compelled to produce documents if it is subject to the court's personal jurisdiction. *See United States v. First National Bank of Chicago*, 699 F.2d 341 (7th Cir. 1983); *United States v. Bank of Nova Scotia*, 691 F.2d 1384 (11th Cir. 1982), *cert. denied*, 462 U.S. 1119 (1983); *In re Sealed Case*, 832 F.2d 1268, 1272-74 (D.C. Cir. 1987) ("service of a subpoena duces tecum on a corporate officer vacationing in the United States would not allow ... access to corporate records absent proof that a United States court had jurisdiction over the corporation itself"). Relatively few decisions have considered due process limits in this context in any detail. What role, if any, should the fact of service of the subpoena within the jurisdiction have? Recall the affirmation of tag service as a basis for general jurisdiction in *Burnham*. *See supra* pp. 116-23.

What level of contacts with the forum should be required in order to establish personal jurisdiction for purposes of compelling discovery? The consequences of a discovery order are generally less serious than those of litigation on the merits: the witness is required to provide information (subject to applicable privileges), while a civil defendant may be subjected to significant liability. On the other hand, witnesses often have no personal stake in the underlying litigation, and may suffer considerable harm from com-pelled disclosures. Lower courts have generally (although without discussion) applied the same due process standard for discovery from witnesses as those applicable to civil litigation. *E.g., In re Sealed Case*, 832 F.2d 1268 (D.C. Cir. 1987); *In re Marc Rich & Co., AG*, 707 F.2d 663 (2d Cir. 1983) (applying "mini-mum contacts" test based on national contacts). Is this appropriate? Are there reasons that the two stan-dards should differ? Consider the analysis in *Pan American*. Did the court rely on a lack of jurisdiction over Midland and Montagu? Could it have?

5. *Territorial limits on materials subject to subpoena power under Rule 45.* Even where Rule 45's ter-ritorial limits on the service of subpoenas are satisfied, and where personal jurisdiction over the witness exists, courts have shown reluctance to exercise subpoena power over foreign nonparty witnesses. For example, *Pan American* refused to order an English bank to produce records located in England even though the bank had a branch office in New York and therefore was presumably subject to the court's per-sonal jurisdiction. What was the principal basis for the court's decision? Was it that the materials sought were located outside the United States and the Southern District? If so, is this a sound basis for decision?

Does it matter that the materials sought by the subpoena in *Pan American* were not located within the territory of the Southern District? Does Rule 45 extend to materials located outside the district of the court from which the subpoena issues? Note Rule 45(a)(2) and the Advisory Committee Note accompa-nying the Rule:

> Paragraph (a)(2) makes clear that the persons subject to the subpoena is required to produce materials in that person's control *whether or not the materials are located within the district or within the territory within which the subpoena can be served*. The non-party witness is subject to the same scope of discovery under this rule as that person would be as a party to whom a request is addressed pursuant to Rule 34.

Doesn't this require rejecting at least part of the court's rationale in *Pan American*? Suppose that the docu-ments in *Pan American* had been located in Midland's Los Angeles office. Is there some reason to treat materials located outside the *United States* differently from the broader class of materials located outside the relevant *judicial district*? What would justify the different treatment of documents located outside the United States? Recall the territoriality presumption and the *Nahas* rationale, *see supra* pp. 22, 546-50 & 780-94. Would this affect the interpretation of Rule 45?

6. *Prudential limitations on Rule 45's subpoena power.* Putting aside the territorial limitation on Rule 45 apparently embraced in *Pan American,* the court still probably would not have enforced the subpoena. It cited "foreign policy" concerns, the arguable applicability of English legislation forbidding production of the requested materials, and the fact that Midland's New York office commenced operations after the *Pan American* dispute occurred. Are these legitimate considerations in deciding whether to enforce a Rule 45 subpoena? Suppose that (a) there had been no order under the PTIA forbidding discovery; or (b) Midland's New York office had existed well before the *Pan American* dispute began, but had no connection to the parties' conduct. Would either (or both) affect the result in *Pan American?*

7. *Alternatives for obtaining discovery if Rule 45 subpoena cannot issue.* If a nonparty cannot be served or is not subject to the personal jurisdiction of the forum court, then the court will lack the power to compel compliance with a subpoena under Rule 45. *See United States v. Bank of Nova Scotia,* 691 F.2d 1384 (11th Cir. 1982), *cert. denied,* 462 U.S. 1119 (1983); *United States v. First Nat'l City Bank,* 396 F.2d 897 (2d Cir. 1968). In this event, U.S. courts will ordinarily not issue or enforce a subpoena and instead will seek discovery by obtaining foreign judicial assistance. The two principal alternatives for obtaining foreign judicial assistance — customary letters rogatory and the Hague Evidence Convention — are discussed in detail below. Note that *Pan American* was of the view that the Rule 45 subpoena was in fact a backdoor effort to circumvent the Hague Evidence Convention. We return to this issue below. *See infra* pp. 895-920.

8. *Subpoenas ordering testimony by telecommunications links.* Several lower courts have ordered nonparty witnesses to testify via telecommunications links at trial. For example, in *In re San Juan Dupont Plaza Hotel Fire Litigation,* 1989 WL 164,148 (D.P.R. 1989), the district court ordered nonparty employees of several corporate defendants to testify via satellite television links from their residences (which were outside the trial court's judicial district). Although Rule 45(e)(1) only granted district courts the power to compel attendance of witnesses at trial who are within 100 miles of the place of trial, the court held that this did not "expressly prohibit" coerced testimony by telecommunications: according to the court, the Rule simply "restricts the reach of subpoenas to prevent inconvenience to witnesses, not to confer advantages on parties." Comparable arrangements were also used in a Wisconsin case to obtain trial testimony from witnesses in England who were unwilling to come to the United States. *The National Law Journal,* March 13, 1989, at 3.

Are these decisions correct? Are they consistent with the language of new Rule 45? If they are permitted, then what would prevent a court from ordering a foreign nonparty witness, subject to its jurisdiction but not to territorial service of a subpoena, to send documents by mail or courier to the United States? Would this be a desirable result?

9. *Subpoena service under 28 U.S.C. §1783 on U.S. citizens or residents located abroad.* Rule 45 also extends the subpoena power of the district courts to cases where evidence is sought from U.S. citizens or residents who are located abroad. Rule 45(b)(2) permits the issuance of subpoenas to persons in foreign countries pursuant to 28 U.S.C. §1783. Section 1783, in turn, authorizes U.S. courts to order the issuance of subpoenas to "a national or resident of the United States who is in a foreign country ... if the court finds that particular testimony or the production of [documents] ... is necessary in the interests of justice, and, in other than a criminal action or proceeding, if the court finds, in addition, that it is not possible to obtain his testimony ... in any other manner." The Supreme Court has upheld §1783 against due process and international law challenges. *See Blackmer v. United States,* 284 U.S. 421 (1932), excerpted above at *supra* pp. 96-97. Why are U.S. citizens or residents treated differently from foreign nationals by Rule 45 and §1783? Is this wise from a policy perspective? In *Pan American,* suppose that the relevant documents had been sought from a U.S. bank's London office, rather than from Midland's head office. Should U.S. banks be subject to different rules than Midland?

3. Direct Extraterritorial Discovery by Deposition Upon Oral Examination

As with the production of foreign documents, U.S. litigants can attempt to obtain depositions of foreign deponents either by a unilateral order of a U.S. court under the Federal Rules of Civil Procedure or by requesting assistance from a foreign court. Because of the uncertainties associated with judicial assistance, U.S. courts have preferred the former alternative.

In general, the same principles govern the power of U.S. courts to compel depositions as govern the production of documents. If the proposed deponent is a party, or is otherwise subject to the U.S. court's personal jurisdiction and to subpoena service, the court can require compliance with a deposition notice or subpoena on pain of sanctions under Rule 37 or Rule 45.[56] If, however, the proposed deponent is not subject to the U.S. court's personal jurisdiction, or (in the case of nonparties) to subpoena service, then there will ordinarily be no basis for directly compelling a deposition.[57] In that event, the assistance of a foreign court will be needed to obtain compulsory process.[58]

a. Standards for Ordering Deposition of Foreign Persons

If a proposed foreign deponent is a party subject to a U.S. court's personal jurisdiction, the method most attractive to U.S. litigants for obtaining the person's deposition is to arrange for the deponent to travel to the United States for examination. This obviates the need for compliance with foreign law in taking the deposition and eliminates a number of practical obstacles that frequently arise when depositions are conducted abroad.[59] If the proposed deponent is a party, a notice of deposition pursuant to Rule 30 is sufficient to require attendance.[60] If the deponent is a nonparty witness, attendance can be required only by subpoena pursuant to Rule 45 (subject to the territorial and other restrictions discussed above).[61] In order to resist a deposition that has been noticed or subpoenaed, the proposed deponent must obtain a protective order from the court.

If the parties are unable to agree upon a deposition situs for a foreign deponent, the trial court enjoys broad discretion in selecting a location that is convenient.[62]

---

56. *See* Fed. R. Civ. P. 37; C. Wright, A. Miller & R. Marcus, *Federal Practice And Procedure* §2083 (1994). Rules 37 and 45 are reproduced in Appendix C.

57. If the proposed deponent is a U.S. national, the U.S. court may have statutory authority to subpoena attendance at a deposition. *See* 28 U.S.C. §1783, discussed above at *supra* p. 866. This authority has not frequently been invoked.

58. The methods for obtaining such assistance are discussed below, *see infra* pp. 893-94 & 895-920.

59. These difficulties include scheduling difficulties and logistical problems such as obtaining a suitable court reporter and interpreter. *See* Light, *Discovery Abroad and the Consequences When Discovery is Not Possible*, 50 Antitrust L.J. 577 (1982); O'Kane, *Obtaining Evidence Abroad*, 17 Vand. J. Transnat'l L. 69 (1984).

60. C. Wright, A. Miller & R. Marcus, *Federal Practice and Procedure* §2112 (1994).

61. *Id.* §2107; *Cleveland v. Palmby*, 75 F.R.D. 654 (W.D. Okla. 1977). *See supra* pp. 861-66.

62. *Continental Bank & Trust Co. of Chicago v. Charles N. Wooten, Ltd.*, 890 F.2d 1312 (5th Cir. 1989); *Republic of the Philippines v. Marcos*, 888 F.2d 954 (2d Cir. 1989); *Asea, Inc. v. Southern Pac. Transp. Co.*, 669 F.2d 1242, 1248 (9th Cir. 1981). The Federal Rules have been interpreted as contemplating selection of a situs for depositions that is most convenient for the parties and the court. The Seventh Circuit, in one of the few appellate decisions on the situs of depositions of persons located abroad, affirmed the trial court's refusal to order a Greek deponent's deposition in Greece and its decision to order the deposition in the United States. *Afram Export Corp. v. Metallurgiki Halyps, SA*, 772 F.2d 1358, 1365-66 (7th Cir. 1985).

In addition to balancing the relative burdens to the litigants, the court reasoned, "[t]he absence of a federal judge or magistrate in Greece, which would make it difficult — though in an age of excellent international telephony not impossible — to rule on objections, was a factor tilting the balance of convenience." *See also Republic of the Philippines v. Marcos*, 888 F.2d 954 (2d Cir. 1989).

Despite the attractions of summoning foreign deponents to the United States, U.S. courts are understandably somewhat more hesitant to order persons physically to come to the United States than to require documents to be brought here. Nonetheless, a number of U.S. courts have required foreign litigants and nonparty witnesses subject to their personal jurisdiction to travel to the United States for depositions.[63] Lower courts have been particularly willing to require foreign plaintiffs to attend U.S. depositions.[64] Other courts have concluded that, in particular circumstances, requiring foreign deponents (especially defendants) to travel to the United States would be unreasonably burdensome.[65]

U.S. courts generally treat the officers, directors, and managing agents of foreign corporations as part of the corporation, thus permitting these individuals to be required to attend depositions upon notice.[66] In contrast, other corporate employees will usually be treated as third-party witnesses and their attendance at a deposition can be compelled only by subpoena or if a request for foreign judicial assistance is granted.[67] Depositions of corporate officers, directors, or managing agents are frequently ordered at the corporation's principal place of business or, in the case of corporate plaintiffs, in the forum state.[68]

There are many circumstances in which the deponent will be examined abroad.[69] As a general rule, however, depositions can be conducted abroad only if the law of the foreign situs permits the deposition. Many foreign countries prohibit or restrict U.S. depositions on their territory.[70] Where this is the case, foreign judicial assistance will generally be needed to conduct a deposition.[71] Alternatively, a cooper-

---

63. *See, e.g., Roberts v. Heim*, 1990 W.L. 32,553 (N.D. Calif. 1990); *Financial General Bankshares, Inc. v. Lance*, 80 F.R.D. 22 (D.D.C. 1978); *Seuthe v. Renwal Prods.*, 38 F.R.D. 323 (S.D.N.Y. 1965).

64. *E.g., Orrison v. Balcor Co.*, 132 F.R.D. 202 (N.D. Ill. 1990); *Clem v. Allied Van Lines Int'l Corp.*, 102 F.R.D. 938 (S.D.N.Y. 1984); *Sykes Int'l v. Pilch's Poultry Breeding Farm*, 55 F.R.D. 138 (D. Conn. 1972); *Grotrian, Helfferich, Schultz, Th. Steinweg Nachf. v. Steinway & Sons*, 54 F.R.D. 280 (S.D.N.Y. 1971).

65. For cases involving foreign defendants, *see Work v. Bier*, 107 F.R.D. 789 (D.D.C. 1985); *Huynh v. Desma Werke, GmbH*, 90 F.R.D. 447 (S.D. Ohio 1981); *River Plate Corp. v. Forestal Land, Timber & Ry.*, 185 F.Supp. 832 (S.D.N.Y. 1960); *Kurt M. Jachmann Co. v. Hartley, Cooper & Co.*, 16 F.R.D. 565 (S.D.N.Y. 1954). For cases involving foreign plaintiffs with unusual reasons precluding U.S. depositions, *see Hyam v. American Export Lines*, 213 F.2d 221 (2d Cir. 1954); *Haviland & Co. v. Montgomery Ward & Co.*, 31 F.R.D. 578 (S.D.N.Y. 1962); *Morrison Export Co. v. Goldstone*, 12 F.R.D. 258 (S.D.N.Y. 1952).

66. C. Wright, A. Miller & R. Marcus, *Federal Practice and Procedure* §2103 (1994).

67. *See Tietz v. Textron*, 94 F.R.D. 638 (E.D. Wis. 1982); *Sykes Int'l v. Pilch's Poultry Breeding Farms*, 55 F.R.D. 138 (D. Conn. 1972); *Haviland & Co. v. Montgomery Ward & Co.*, 31 F.R.D. 578, 580 (S.D.N.Y. 1962); *Reliable Volkswagen Sales & Serv. Co. v. World-Wide Auto. Corp.*, 26 F.R.D. 592, 594 (D.N.J. 1960).

68. C. Wright, A. Miller & R. Marcus, *Federal Practice and Procedure*, §2112 (1994).

69. *E.g., Asea, Inc. v. Southern Pac. Transp. Co.*, 669 F.2d 1242, 1248 (9th Cir. 1981) (nonparty witness).

70. *See* U.S. Department of State Circular, dated Apr. 13, 1987, on "Obtaining Evidence Abroad"; B. Ristau, *International Judicial Assistance* §§3-2-1 through 3-2-8 (1990 Rev.).

71. *See infra* pp. 893-94 & 895-920.

ative deponent can travel to a nearby country that does not restrict U.S. depositions,[72] or a telephone deposition may be possible.[73]   *telephone*

Importantly, even foreign states that usually allow depositions on their territory generally object to involuntary depositions.[74] In these circumstances, U.S. courts will generally not order the depositions of a recalcitrant deponent to be conducted abroad. In those foreign states that do not restrict the holding of voluntary U.S. depositions upon their territory,[75] U.S. litigants can proceed with depositions in much the same manner that would be followed domestically.

b. An Introduction to the Mechanics of Conducting Foreign Depositions   *Conducting foreign deposition*

If a deposition is to be conducted abroad, Rules 28(b) and 29 of the Federal Rules of Civil Procedure provide five alternative mechanisms for proceeding: (i) pursuant to any applicable treaty or convention; (ii) pursuant to a letter of request; (iii) by notice; (iv) by commission; and (v) by stipulation.[76]   *1)*

The first two alternatives for taking depositions abroad under Rule 28(b) are by   *letter*
letter of request (or letter rogatory) or pursuant to treaty. Letters rogatory are typi   *2)*
cally used when foreign law forbids other forms of deposition discovery or when the   *treaty*
deponent is uncooperative. The use of letters rogatory to obtain evidence located abroad is discussed below.[77] Also discussed below are treaty mechanisms for taking depositions abroad, including the Hague Evidence Convention.[78]

The three remaining alternatives for depositions under Rule 28(b) do not neces   *3) notice*
sarily require the assistance of foreign authorities. Depositions by notice or stipula   *4) commission*
tion can proceed in the same mechanical fashion (subject to foreign law, discussed below) as depositions in the United States.[79] Rule 28(b) also permits depositions by commission, which require an order from the district court designating a particular individual as a "commissioner."[80]

When a deposition is to be taken outside the United States, by notice, commission or stipulation under Rule 28(b), principles of U.S. law are overlaid by foreign law. Some foreign states regard the taking of depositions on their territory as judicial acts that infringe their judicial sovereignty if conducted without the supervision of local courts or officials.[81] Moreover, virtually all foreign states permit only "volun-

---

72. *E.g., The Signe,* 37 F.Supp. 819, 822 (E.D. La. 1941).

73. *But see Arrocha v. McAuliffe,* 109 F.R.D. 397 (D.D.C. 1986) (refusing to order telephone deposition).

74. *See* B. Ristau, *International Judicial Assistance* §3-2-3 (1990 Rev.).

75. *See* U.S. Department of State Circular, dated Apr. 13, 1987, on "Obtaining Evidence Abroad."

76. Rule 28(b), excerpted in Appendix C, sets forth the procedural alternatives for conducting depositions abroad.

77. *See infra* pp. 893-94.

78. *See infra* pp. 895-920.

79. *See* C. Wright, A. Miller & R. Marcus, *Federal Practice and Procedure* §§2131-33 (1994).

80. The commission will authorize its bearer to administer oaths and take testimony. *See* 3 J. Moore & L. Frumer, *Moore's Manual, Federal Practice Forms,* Forms Nos. 15:21, 15:22 (2d ed. 1988); Note, *Taking Evidence Outside of the United States,* 55 B.U.L. Rev. 368, 371 (1975).

81. *See supra* pp. 847-50.

tary" depositions on their territory, which excludes examinations compelled by U.S. courts. Conducting a deposition abroad in violation of foreign law may subject counsel to foreign criminal or civil penalties. Information about foreign restrictions on U.S. depositions before consular officers must be obtained on a country-by-country basis from the U.S. Department of State, the appropriate U.S. embassy abroad, or foreign local counsel.[82]

Some foreign states that forbid depositions before U.S. court officers or consular officers may permit depositions before foreign officials — an alternative that is specifically permitted by Rule 28(b)(3). As noted above, information about the possibility of depositions before a foreign official must be obtained on a country-by-country basis. If a foreign official is to preside over a deposition, it is important for U.S. counsel carefully to schedule the deposition and describe in advance the character of the deposition, the underlying action, and the officer's responsibilities.[83]

---

82. For a list of those countries that forbid depositions before U.S. consular officers, *see* U.S. Department of State Circular, dated Apr. 13, 1987, on "Obtaining Evidence Abroad." In addition, the Office of American Citizens' Services Room 4811, U.S. Department of State, Washington DC 20520-4818, provides country summaries for most foreign states, setting out basic rules regarding taking depositions in those countries. The telephone numbers are Africa (202-647-6060); East Asia and Pacific (202-647-6769); Eastern Europe (202-647-8088); Western Europe (202-647-6178); Latin America and Caribbean (202-647-5118); Near East and South Asia (202-647-7899).

83. It is generally preferable to have a U.S. consular official preside over U.S. depositions, rather than a foreign official. U.S. officials tend to be more familiar with U.S. practices and laws and can therefore be expected to ensure that the deposition proceeds more smoothly and expeditiously.

D. Direct U.S. Discovery of Materials Located Abroad: Resolving Conflicts Between U.S. Discovery Orders and Foreign Law

As described above, U.S. courts have traditionally favored direct discovery under the Federal Rules of Civil Procedure (or state equivalents) as a means of obtaining extraterritorial discovery. These direct U.S. discovery orders for evidence located abroad sometimes conflict with foreign nondisclosure laws. If U.S. courts order discovery in violation of foreign law, they may subject an innocent private party to either U.S. discovery sanctions or foreign criminal penalties. On the other hand, if U.S. courts defer to foreign blocking statutes, the scope of U.S. discovery is placed in the hands of foreign states. Neither alternative is particularly attractive.

1. Extraterritorial Discovery in Violation of Foreign Law: Historical Introduction and Judicial Power

a. Historical Introduction

Until fairly recently, U.S. courts generally declined to order discovery abroad in violation of the laws of the place where the evidence was located. The *Restatement (First) Conflict of Laws* required this result, providing that U.S. courts lacked the power to order acts abroad in violation of the law of the place where the acts would be performed.[84] The few lower court opinions to consider the issue generally declined to order discovery in violation of foreign law.[85] These decisions reasoned that "[u]pon fundamental principles of international comity, our courts dedicated to the enforcement of our laws should not take such action as may cause a violation of the laws of a friendly neighbor or, at the least, an unnecessary circumvention of its procedures."[86]

More recently, U.S. courts have abandoned traditional reluctance to order discovery abroad in violation of foreign law, and instead now generally follow a two-step analysis.[87] First, they begin from the premise that a court has the power to order discovery abroad, even where its order conflicts with foreign law, and then consider

---

84. *Restatement (First) Conflict of Laws* §94 (1934) (excerpted *infra* p. 874). Lower courts did, however, uphold their power to order discovery of materials outside the forum's territory where this would not entail violations of foreign law. *Securities and Exchange Comm'n v. Minas de Artemisa, SA*, 150 F.2d 215 (9th Cir. 1945).

85. *Ings v. Ferguson*, 282 F.2d 149 (2d Cir. 1960); *Securities and Exchange Comm'n v. Minas De Artemis, SA*, 150 F.2d 215 (9th Cir. 1945).

86. *Ings v. Ferguson*, 282 F.2d 149, 152 (2d Cir. 1960). *See Securities and Exchange Comm'n v. Minas de Artemisa, SA*, 150 F.2d 215 (9th Cir. 1945) (ordering discovery of documents located in Mexico after concluding that it would not violate Mexican law); *First Nat'l City Bank v. IRS*, 271 F.2d 616, 618 (2d Cir.), *cert. denied*, 361 U.S. 948 (1960).

87. *See Restatement (Third) Foreign Relations Law* §442, comment f (1987); *Societe Internationale v. Rogers*, 357 U.S. 197 (1958). *But see Securities and Exchange Comm'n v. Banca Della Svizzera Italiana*, 92 F.R.D. 111, 117 n.3 (S.D.N.Y. 1981) (suggesting that the Second Circuit, unlike other circuits, does not distinguish the analysis used for deciding to issue an order compelling discovery from that used for imposing sanctions).

2. whether or not to *exercise* this power.[88] Second, if discovery is ordered, but not provided, U.S. courts then consider what *sanctions* are appropriate for noncompliance. This two-step analysis derives from the Supreme Court's decision in *Societe Internationale pour Participations Industrielles et Commerciales v. Rogers*.[89]

b. Societe Internationale v. Rogers

Societe Internationale arose when a U.S. government agency — the "Alien Property Custodian" — seized assets during World War II pursuant to the Trading with the Enemy Act,[90] which authorized the confiscation of "enemy" assets. The basis for the seizure was the Custodian's conclusion that the assets (cash and shares in a Delaware corporation) were "owned by or held for the benefit of" I.G. Farbenindustrie, a German firm (and then an enemy national). After WWII concluded, a Swiss company named I.G. Chemie brought suit in the United States against the Alien Property Custodian's successors. The suit alleged that the confiscated property had belonged to I.G. Chemie — assertedly not an "enemy" national — rather than to I.G. Farbenindustrie.

The U.S. government defended by challenging I.G. Chemie's claim that it was a Swiss neutral, alleging that it was owned and dominated by I.G. Farbenindustrie. The government sought discovery under Rule 34 of the Federal Rules of Civil Procedure of "a large number of the banking records of Sturzenegger & Cie," a Swiss company allegedly controlled by I.G. Chemie.[91] The documents were said to be relevant to the government's defense. I.G. Chemie did not challenge the documents' relevance, but argued that producing them would violate Swiss penal law.[92] The district court ordered production, which I.G. Chemie partially made; after further proceedings, it supplemented its discovery, but still did not fully comply. At the government's request, the district court then sanctioned I.G. Chemie under Rule 37 by dismissing its complaint.[93]

On appeal, the Supreme Court adopted a two-step approach, upholding the district court's discovery order but reversing its dismissal of the plaintiff's claims. The Court first rejected the contention that "the interdictions of Swiss law bar a conclusion that petitioner had 'control' of these documents within the meaning of Rule 34."[94] The Court relied on three factors: (a) the policies underlying the Trading with the Enemy Act;[95] (b) the fact that the requested documents "might have a vital influ-

---

88. *See Societe Internationale v. Rogers*, 357 U.S. 197 (1958); *Restatement (Third) Foreign Relations Law* §442 (1987).

89. 357 U.S. 197 (1958).

90. 40 Stat. 415, 50 U.S.C. App. §5(b). The Act permitted the Custodian, during periods of war, to seize "any property or interest of any foreign country or national."

91. 357 U.S. at 200.

92. 357 U.S. at 200.

93. 357 U.S. at 200-02.

94. 357 U.S. at 204.

95. 357 U.S. at 204-05. The Court observed that the Act sought "to reach enemy interests which masqueraded under ... innocent fronts." *Clark v. Uebersee Finanz-Korp.*, 332 U.S. 480, 485 (1947).

ence upon this litigation;"[96] and (c) the fact that I.G. Farben "is in a most advantageous position to plead with its own sovereign for relaxation of penal laws."[97] The Court refused to issue any broad interpretation of Rule 34's application in international cases: "The propriety of the use to which [Rule 34] is put depends on the circumstances of a given case, and we hold only that accommodation of the Rule in this instance to the policies underlying the Trading with the Enemy Act justified" the district court's discovery order.[98]

Second, *Societe International* went on to reverse the district court's dismissal of I.G. Chemie's claims under Rule 37. The Court recited the district court's findings that "petitioner had not been in collusion with the Swiss authorities to block discovery, and had in good faith made diligent efforts to execute the production order."[99] The Court reasoned that "fear of criminal prosecution constitutes a weighty excuse for nonproduction, and this excuse is not weakened because the laws preventing compliance are those of a foreign sovereign."[100] With this background, the Court construed Rule 37 as not permitting dismissal of a complaint where failure to comply with a discovery order "has been due to inability, and not to willfulness, bad faith, or any fault of petitioner."[101] The Court also held, however, that the district court retained "wide discretion" to deal with I.G. Chemie's violation of its order, including by drawing adverse inferences or concluding that petitioner failed to meet its burden of proof.

Notwithstanding the narrow limits on the *Societe Internationale* holding, lower courts have adopted its basic two-step approach to extraterritorial discovery. Lower courts have struggled, however, to refine both prongs of *Societe Internationale's* analysis. The Second Circuit's opinion in *United States v. First National City Bank*,[102] which is excerpted below, is an early example of such efforts.

The *City Bank* decision also illustrates how U.S. courts have approached extraterritorial discovery that would require a party to violate foreign public policies or civil laws, rather than penal legislation. As discussed below, U.S. courts have acknowledged that penal blocking statutes are neither the only way of expressing a foreign state's interests in nondisclosure nor the only source of hardship for parties subject to extraterritorial U.S. discovery orders.[103] Moreover, lower courts have sometimes moderated extraterritorial U.S. discovery to accommodate the interests of foreign governments and private litigants even where no foreign blocking statute is involved.[104]

---

96. 357 U.S. at 205.
97. 357 U.S. at 205.
98. 357 U.S. at 206.
99. 357 U.S. at 208.
100. 357 U.S. at 211.
101. 357 U.S. at 212.
102. 396 F.2d 897 (2d Cir. 1968).
103. *See, e.g., Societe Nationale Industrielle Aerospatiale v. U.S. District Court*, 482 U.S. 522 (1987).
104. *See* cases cited *infra* pp. 878-80 & 890-92.

[handwritten margin note: how US courts have approached extraterritorial discovery that would require a party to violate foreign public policies]

RESTATEMENT (FIRST) CONFLICT OF LAWS (1934)

§94

§94. A state can exercise jurisdiction through its courts to make a decree directing a party subject to the jurisdiction of the court to do an act in another state, provided such act is not contrary to the law of the state in which it is to be performed.

RESTATEMENT (SECOND) FOREIGN RELATIONS LAW (1965)

§§39 & 40 [excerpted above at pp. 503-04]

UNITED STATES v. FIRST NATIONAL CITY BANK

396 F.2d 897 (2d Cir. 1968)

KAUFMAN, CIRCUIT JUDGE. [A federal antitrust grand jury served First National City Bank of New York ("Citibank") with a subpoena *duces tecum* requiring the production of documents held in Citibank's Frankfurt offices. The requested documents related to certain transactions involving two of the bank's customers, C.F. Boehringer & Soehne, GmbH and Boehringer Mannheim Corporation (collectively, "Boehringer"). After Citibank refused to supply the requested documents, the trial judge conducted a hearing concerning the validity of the order and the propriety of sanctions. *[margin note: German common law]* Citibank produced expert witnesses who testified that German common law created a bank secrecy privilege for bank customer's records and that breach of this privilege would subject Citibank to potential civil liability in a tort or contract action by Boehringer. The government produced an expert witness who testified that Citibank's production of the requested documents would not subject it to criminal liability and that the bank might well be able to raise valid defenses in any civil suit by Boehringer for breach of the bank secrecy privilege. The trial court found Citibank in civil contempt and fined it $2,000 per day until it produced the requested documents; the court also sentenced the Citibank officer responsible for the bank's noncompliance to up to sixty days' imprisonment. The defendants appealed.]

The basic legal question confronting us is not a total stranger to this Court. With the growing interdependence of world trade and the increased mobility of persons and companies, the need arises not infrequently, whether related to civil or criminal proceedings, for the production of evidence located in foreign jurisdictions. It is no longer open to doubt that a federal court has the power to require the production of documents located in foreign countries if the court has *in personam* jurisdiction of the person in possession or control of the material. *See, e.g., First National City Bank of New York v. Internal Revenue Service etc.,* 271 F.2d 616 (2d Cir. 1959), *cert. denied,* 361 U.S. 948 (1960). [Citibank does not contend that records located in its Frankfurt branch are not within the possession, custody, and control of the head office.] Thus, the task before us, as Citibank concedes, is not one of defining power but of developing rules governing the proper exercise of power. The difficulty arises, of course, when the country in which the documents are located has its own rules and policies dealing with the production and disclosure of business information — a circumstance not uncommon. This problem is particularly acute where the documents are sought by an arm of a foreign government. The complexities of the world being what they are, it is not surprising to discover nations having diametrically opposed positions with respect to the disclosure of a wide range of information. It is not too difficult, therefore, to empathize with the party or witness subject to the jurisdiction of two sovereigns and confronted with conflicting commands... .

In any event, under the principles of international law, "A state having jurisdiction to prescribe or enforce a rule of law is not precluded from exercising its jurisdiction *solely* because such exercise requires a person to engage in conduct subjecting him to liability under the law of another state having jurisdiction with respect to that conduct." *Restatement (Second) Foreign Relations Law* §39(1) (1965) (emphasis supplied). It is not asking too much, however, to expect that each nation should make an effort to minimize the potential conflict flowing from their joint concern with the prescribed behavior. *Id.* at §39(2). Where, as here, the burden of resolution ultimately falls upon the federal courts, the difficulties are manifold because the courts must take care not to impinge upon the prerogatives and responsibilities of the political branches of the government in the extremely sensitive and delicate area of foreign affairs. *See, e.g., Chicago & Southern Air Lines v. Waterman S.S. Corp.,* 333 U.S. 103, 111 (1948). Mechanical or overbroad rules of thumb are of little value; what is required is a careful balancing of the interests involved and a precise understanding of the facts and circumstances of the particular case.

With these principles in mind, we turn to the specific issues presented by this appeal. Citibank concedes, as it must, that compliance with the subpoena does not require the violation of the criminal law of a foreign power, as in *Societe Internationale etc. v. Rogers,* 357 U.S. 197 (1958) (discovery under the Federal Rules of Civil Procedure); *Ings v. Ferguson,* 282 F.2d 149, 152 (2d Cir. 1960), or risk the imposition of sanctions that are the substantial equivalent of criminal penalties, as in *Application of Chase Manhattan Bank,* 297 F.2d 611, 613 (2d Cir. 1962), or even conflict with the public policy of a foreign state as expressed in legislation. Instead, all that remains, as we see it, is a possible prospective civil liability flowing from an implied contractual obligation between Citibank and its customers that, we are informed, is considered implicit in the bank's license to do business in Germany.

But the government urges vigorously that to be excused from compliance with an order of a federal court, a witness, such as Citibank, must show that following compliance it will suffer criminal liability in the foreign country. We would be reluctant to hold, however, that the mere absence of criminal sanctions abroad necessarily mandates obedience to a subpoena. Such a rule would show scant respect for international comity; and, if this principle is valid, a court of one country should make an effort to minimize possible conflict between its orders and the law of a foreign state affected by its decision. The vital national interests of a foreign nation, especially in matters relating to economic affairs, can be expressed in ways other than through the criminal law. For example, it could not be questioned that, insofar as a court of the United States is concerned, a statement or directive by the Bundesbank (the central bank of Germany) or some other organ of government, expresses the public policy of Germany and should be given appropriate weight. Equally important is the fact that a sharp dichotomy between criminal and civil penalties is an imprecise means of measuring the hardship for requiring compliance with a subpoena.... .

In evaluating Citibank's contention that compliance should be excused because of the alleged conflict between the order of the court below and German law, we are aided materially by the rationale of the recent *Restatement (Second) Foreign Relations Law* §40 (1965) [excerpted above at pp. 503-04]. ... In the instant case, the obvious, albeit troublesome, requirement for us is to balance the national interests of the United States and Germany and to give appropriate weight to the hardship, if any, Citibank will suffer.

The important interest of the United States in the enforcement of the subpoena warrants little discussion. The federal Grand Jury before which Citibank was summoned is conducting a criminal investigation of alleged violations of the antitrust laws. These laws have long been considered cornerstones of this nation's economic policies, have been vigorously enforced and the subject of frequent interpretation by our Supreme Court. We would have great reluctance, therefore, to countenance any device that would place relevant information beyond the reach of this duly impaneled Grand Jury or impede or delay its proceedings. Judge Learned Hand put the issue in perspective many years ago: "The suppression of truth is a grievous necessity at best, more especially where as here the inquiry concerns the public interest; it can be justified at all only where the opposing private interest is supreme." *McMann v. S.E.C.*, 87 F.2d 377, 378 (2d Cir. 1937), *cert. denied*, 301 U.S. 684 (1937).

We examine the importance of bank secrecy within the framework of German public policy with full recognition that it is often a subtle and difficult undertaking to determine the nature and scope of the law of a foreign jurisdiction. There is little merit, however, in Citibank's suggestion that the mere existence of a bank secrecy doctrine requires us to accept on its face the bank's assertion that compliance with the subpoena would violate an important public policy of Germany. *See First National City Bank of New York [appellant herein] v. Internal Revenue Service etc.*, 271 F.2d 616, 619 (2d Cir. 1959), *cert. denied*, 361 U.S. 948 (1960) (analyzing, and rejecting, Citibank's contention that enforcement of a federal court order would require a violation of the law of Panama). While we certainly do not intend to deprecate the importance of bank secrecy in the German scheme of things neither can we blind ourselves to the doctrine's severe limitations as disclosed by the expert testimony. We have already made the assumption that the absence of criminal sanctions is not the whole answer to or finally determinative of the problem. But, it is surely of considerable significance that Germany considers bank secrecy simply a privilege that can be waived by the customer and is content to leave the matter of enforcement to the vagaries of private litigation. Indeed, bank secrecy is not even required by statute. *See Restatement (Second)* §40, comment c: "A state will be less likely to refrain from exercising its jurisdiction when the consequence of obedience to its order will be a civil liability abroad."

[Moreover,] it is not of little significance that a German court has noted, "The fact that bank secrecy has not been included in the penal protection of §300 of the Criminal Code must lead to the conclusion that the legislature did not value the public interest in bank secrecy as highly as it did the duty of secrecy of doctors and attorneys."... In addition, it is noteworthy that neither the Department of State nor the German Government has expressed any view on this case or indicated that, under the circumstances present here, enforcement of the subpoena would violate German public policy or embarrass German-American relations. The Supreme Court commented on this aspect in other litigation involving Citibank: "[If] the litigation might in time be embarrassing to United States diplomacy, the District Court remains open to the Executive Branch, which, it must be remembered, is the moving party in the present proceeding." *United States v. First National City Bank,* 379 U.S. 378, 384-385 (1965). We are fully aware that when foreign governments, including Germany, have considered their vital national interests threatened, they have not hesitated to make known their objections to the enforcement of a subpoena to the issuing court. So far as appears, both the United States and German governments have voiced no opposition to Citibank's production of the subpoenaed records.

We turn now to the nature and extent of the alleged hardships to which Citibank would be subjected if it complied with the subpoena. It advances two grounds on which it will suffer injury. First, it states that it will be subjected to economic reprisals by Boehringer and will lose foreign business that will harm it and the economic interests of the United States... . A partial answer is that the protection of the foreign economic interests of the United States must be left to the appropriate departments of our government, especially since the government is the moving litigant in these proceedings... Second, Citibank complains that it will be subject to civil liability in a suit by Boehringer... . Judge Pollack concluded that risk of civil damages was slight and speculative, and we agree.[105] The chance that Boehringer will suffer compensable damages is quite remote and Citibank appears to have a number of valid defenses if it is sued, both under the terms of the contract and principles of German civil law.

Notes on Restatements and City Bank

1. *Historic refusal of U.S. courts to order discovery in violation of foreign law.* U.S. courts historically

---

105. Judge Pollack based his finding of lack of good faith on the fact that Citibank, as noted above, had failed to even make a simple inquiry into the nature or extent of the records available at the Frankfurt branch. In addition, the expert testimony was clear that the bank secrecy doctrine applied only to material entrusted to a bank within the framework of any confidential relationship of bank and customer but not to records that were the bank's own work product. Citibank failed to produce any documents reflecting its own work product that were within the terms of the subpoena or to indicate that none existed.

showed greater deference than *Societe Internationale* to the laws of the place where discovery was to be ordered. That is reflected in *Restatement (First) Conflict of Laws* §94 (1934), which did not permit courts to order conduct abroad that was *"contrary to the law of the state in which it is to be performed."* U.S. courts adhered to this rule until surprisingly recently. *See Ings v. Ferguson*, 282 F.2d 149 (2d Cir. 1960) (refusing to order production of documents located in Canada because this would arguably violate Quebec law); *SEC v. Minas De Artemisa, SA*, 150 F.2d 215 (9th Cir. 1945) (indicating that the court would refuse to enforce subpoena for production of documents located in Mexico when this would violate Mexican law).

2. *Contemporary willingness of U.S. courts to order discovery in violation of foreign law.* Compare §§39 and 40 of the *Restatement (Second) Foreign Relations Law*, and the *City Bank* decision, with §94 of the *Restatement (First) Conflict of Laws*. Note the significant change in the treatment of orders requiring conduct outside the forum state in violation of the laws of the place of the conduct. The comments to §39 offer little explanation: "The rule stated in this Section is based upon the fact that international law, in most situations, does not provide for choosing among competing bases of jurisdiction to prescribe rules of conduct." *Restatement (Second) Foreign Relations Law* §39 comment b (1965). Is this a satisfactory explanation? What justifies a court in one country ordering a party to violate another country's laws on that state's own territory?

3. *Source of authority to order discovery of evidence located abroad in violation of foreign law.* As *Societe Internationale* indicates, U.S. courts have had little difficulty ordering production of documents located abroad, even if production would violate foreign law. What is the basis under U.S. law for a U.S. court's power to order such extraterritorial discovery? Does any provision of the Federal Rules of Civil Procedure grant such authority?

Consider the present language of Rules 34 and 45. Does anything in these Rules permit U.S. courts to order discovery in violation of foreign law? Recall *Schooner Exchange* and *Nahas*, and the presumption that Congress does not intend to violate international law. *See supra* pp. 22, 510-11 & 780-94. In the light of this presumption, and the historic refusal of U.S. courts to order discovery abroad in violation of foreign law, should Rule 34 and 45 be construed to permit extraterritorial discovery in violation of foreign law? Compare the broader deference currently afforded to foreign laws under the act of state doctrine, *see supra* pp. 685-705, and the doctrine of foreign sovereign compulsion, *see supra* pp. 745-52. Why should blocking statutes be treated differently? Should U.S. courts be permitted to order the discovery of evidence located abroad in violation of foreign law?

4. *Societe Internationale's two-step analysis in extraterritorial discovery disputes.* As discussed above, *Societe Internationale* distinguished between two issues: (1) the propriety of a order under Rule 34 for the production of foreign documents in violation of foreign law, and (2) the propriety of sanctions under Rule 37 for failure to comply with a discovery order. *City Bank* and most other lower courts have followed this basic two-step analysis in extraterritorial discovery disputes. *E.g., Ohio v. Arthur Andersen & Co.*, 570 F.2d 1370 (10th Cir.), *cert. denied*, 439 U.S. 833 (1978); *Trade Dev. Bank v. Continental Ins. Co.*, 469 F.2d 35 (2d Cir. 1972); *In re Uranium Antitrust Litig.*, 480 F.Supp. 1138 (N.D. Ill. 1979).

5. *Rationale for bifurcating decision to order discovery from imposition of sanctions.* One reason that U.S. courts bifurcate the decision to order discovery from the decision to sanction noncompliance is to place pressure upon the party from whom discovery is sought, who must take steps to comply (typically by obtaining a waiver of foreign blocking statutes) or face sanctions. Is it fair to hold private parties "hostage" to the decisions of foreign governments?

Using the threat of sanctions to coerce production reflects the often unstated suspicion of U.S. courts and litigants that foreign nondisclosure laws or policies are little more than efforts to assist foreign litigants in resisting discovery and that sanctions will never actually be imposed pursuant to foreign blocking statutes. *See Compagnie Francaise d'Assurance pour le Commerce Exterieur v. Phillips Petroleum Co.*, 105 F.R.D. 16, 30 (S.D.N.Y. 1984) ("never expected nor intended to be enforced against French subjects but was intended rather to provide them with tactical weapons and bargaining chips in foreign courts"); *Graco, Inc. v. Kremlin, Inc.*, 101 F.R.D. 503, 514 (N.D. Ill. 1984). This suspicion is reinforced by the legislative history of at least some foreign blocking statutes, which indicate that the laws were not intended actually to be enforced, but were instead designed to be used as bargaining chips by foreign companies to resist U.S. discovery. For example, the legislative history of the French blocking statutes says:

> [It] is necessary not to misunderstand the actual scope of these penalties, which does not clearly appear on the simple reading of the [statute].... [T]hese penalties are applied only on the

improvable assumption that the companies would refuse to make use of the protective provisions offered to them. In all other cases, those potential fines will assure foreign judges of the judicial basis for the legal excuse which the companies will not fail to make use of.

Report Made in the Name of the Commission of Production and Exchanges on the Law Project Adopted by the Senate Relating to the Communication of Documents and Information of Economic, Commercial or Technical Nature to Foreign Physical Persons or Companies, No. 1814, at 63-64 (quoted in Note, *Strict Enforcement of Extraterritorial Discovery*, 38 Stan. L. Rev. 841, 863-65 (1986)).

6. *Lower court applications of Societe Internationale's standard for ordering extraterritorial discovery in violation of foreign law.* Lower courts have reached divergent results in deciding whether to order discovery under *Societe Internationale.* This uncertainty is partially attributable to the limited reach of the holding in *Societe Internationale* and to the Court's refusal to articulate any generally applicable analytical approach. 357 U.S. at 205-06 ("depends upon the circumstances of a given case"; "[w]e do not say that this ruling would apply to every situation where a party is restricted by law from producing documents").

In approving the district court's discovery order, *Societe Internationale* considered three factors: (1) the policies underlying the Trading with the Enemy Act; (2) the "vital influence" that the requested materials might have on the lawsuit; and (3) the fact that Societe Internationale was a Swiss national and therefore was best-suited to seek relief from the Swiss blocking statute. Some courts have rigorously applied *Societe Internationale,* considering only the three factors specifically identified by the Supreme Court in deciding whether to order discovery. *E.g., Trade Dev. Bank v. Continental Ins. Co.,* 469 F.2d 35 (2d Cir. 1972); *In re Uranium Antitrust Litig.,* 480 F.Supp. 1138, 1148 (N.D. Ill. 1979).

Other lower courts have adopted an expanded version of *Societe Internationale's* three-factor test in deciding whether to order discovery. These courts have considered additional factors derived from *Restatement (Second) Foreign Relations Law* §40 (1965) — including a balancing of both U.S. and foreign national public policies and the hardships likely to be suffered by the private party. *E.g., United States v. First National Bank of Chicago,* 699 F.2d 341, 345 (7th Cir. 1983); *United States v. First Nat'l City Bank,* 396 F.2d 897, 902 (2d Cir. 1968). A few other lower courts have looked to an even broader range of factors than those contemplated by *Restatement* §40 in deciding whether to order discovery, considering in addition the good faith of the party from whom discovery would be ordered. *E.g., United States v. Vetco, Inc.,* 691 F.2d 1281, 1288 (9th Cir.), *cert. denied,* 454 U.S. 1098 (1981); *In re Westinghouse Elec. Corp. Uranium Contracts Litig.,* 563 F.2d 992, 998 (10th Cir. 1977). Finally, a few lower courts have interpreted *Societe Internationale* as reserving all questions relating to foreign blocking statutes and U.S. governmental interests to the sanctions stage. *E.g., Civil Aeronautics Board v. Deutsche Lufthansa AG,* 591 F.2d 951, 953 (D.C. Cir. 1979); *Arthur Andersen & Co. v. Finesilver,* 546 F.2d 338, 341 (10th Cir. 1976), *cert. denied,* 429 U.S. 1096 (1977) ("consideration of foreign law problems in a discovery context is required in dealing with sanctions ... and not in deciding whether the discovery order should issue").

Which of these various approaches to extraterritorial discovery is preferable? Does the existence of a foreign blocking statute have any relevance to the question whether a party "controls" documents? How did *Societe Internationale* answer this question?

7. *Dismissal as a sanction for failure to comply with U.S. discovery order.* Federal Rule of Civil Procedure 37, set forth in Appendix C, provides trial courts with broad discretion to impose sanctions upon a party for failure to produce discovery as ordered. *Societe Internationale* considered whether it was appropriate to impose the drastic sanction of dismissal under Rule 37 for failure to comply with the district court's discovery order. The Court relied principally on the fact that Societe Internationale's failure to comply was "due to inability, and not to willfulness, bad faith, or any fault of petitioner." Because Societe Internationale had not acted in bad faith the Court held that the sanction of dismissal was unduly severe. *See also National Hockey League v. Metropolitan Hockey Club, Inc.,* 427 U.S. 639, 643 (1976). Nonetheless, where bad faith or "conscious disregard" for the discovery process is present, even the extraordinary remedy of dismissal is permitted. *Republic of the Philippines v. Marco,* 888 F.2d 954 (2d Cir. 1989); *Founding Church of Scientology Inc. v. Webster,* 802 F.2d 1448, 1458 (D.C. Cir. 1986), *cert. denied,* 484 U.S. 871 (1987).

8. *Trial court's discretion to impose sanctions.* Even if the ultimate sanction of dismissal is not imposed, *Societe Internationale* and *City Bank* illustrate that U.S. courts retain significant discretion to sanction failure to comply with their extraterritorial discovery orders (including where the failure was required by foreign law). *Restatement (Third) Foreign Relations Law* §442(2)(c) (1987) (excerpted below at

pp. 883-84). Even if a litigant acts in good faith and avoids dismissal or other similar sanctions, it may nevertheless be subjected to evidentiary rulings (such as adverse inferences, or exclusion of particular evidence). Is it appropriate for a U.S. court to adopt adverse inferences against a party that acts in good faith but cannot lawfully disclose requested discovery materials?

Another possible type of sanction for violation of discovery orders or subpoenas is a monetary fine. Where nonparties refuse to produce requested information, fines may be the only means for punishing noncompliance (since evidentiary sanctions or default judgments will not concern a nonparty). *See United States v. Bank of Nova Scotia*, 740 F.2d 817 (11th Cir. 1984), *cert. denied*, 469 U.S. 1106 (1985) ($25,000 fine per day); *United States v. First Nat'l City Bank*, 396 F.2d 897 (2d Cir. 1968) ($2,000 fine per day plus 60 days imprisonment for bank vice president); *Vanguard Int'l Mfg. v. United States*, 588 F.Supp. 1229 (S.D.N.Y. 1984) ($10,000 fine per day). Although fines are also imposed outside the nonparty witness context, this is less common. *In re Marc Rich & Co. AG*, 707 F.2d 663 (2d Cir.), *cert. denied*, 463 U.S. 1215 (1983); *Remington Prods. v. North Am. Philips Corp. NV*, 107 F.R.D. 643 (D. Conn. 1985).

9. *Relevance of good faith to imposition of sanctions.* The likelihood that a foreign party will be subject to sanctions, and the severity of those sanctions, depends in significant part on the good faith efforts of the party to comply fully with the discovery process. *See, e.g., United States v. Bank of Nova Scotia*, 691 F.2d 1384 (11th Cir. 1982), *cert. denied*, 462 U.S. 1119 (1983) (failure to seek customer's waiver of nondisclosure law is bad faith); *Ohio v. Arthur Andersen & Co.*, 570 F.2d 1370 (10th Cir.), *cert. denied*, 439 U.S. 833 (1978) (failure to investigate effect of foreign nondisclosure law on defendant's documents is bad faith); *United States v. First Nat'l City Bank*, 396 F.2d 897 (2d Cir. 1968) (failure to ascertain precise effect of foreign nondisclosure law is bad faith).

It is settled that a party's actions "inviting" foreign prohibitions against U.S. discovery will be regarded as bad faith. *Restatement (Third) Foreign Relations Law* §442 comment b (1987) ("Evidence that parties or targets have actively sought a prohibition against disclosure, or that the information was deliberately moved to a state with blocking legislation, may be regarded as evidence of bad faith."). Is it appropriate for U.S. courts to punish foreign parties for petitioning their own government on matters of public concern? How would U.S. policy-makers react if a foreign court imposed sanctions on a U.S. national for petitioning U.S. officials for assistance in an international dispute?

In addition, some courts have concluded that actions taken well before U.S. litigation is initiated evidence bad faith. In *General Atomic Co. v. Exxon Nuclear Co.*, 90 F.R.D. 290 (S.D. Cal. 1981), for example, the court did not hesitate to find bad faith on the part of a Canadian company for taking various actions before the U.S. litigation began, including keeping particular documents in Canada, destroying copies of these documents in the United States, and postponing discovery in other litigation. *See also SEC v. Banca Della Svizzera Italiana*, 92 F.R.D. 111 (S.D.N.Y. 1981) (deliberately structuring a transaction so that it will fall within foreign nondisclosure law is bad faith). *Compare Restatement (Third) Foreign Relations Law* §442, comment h (1987) ("Merely notifying the authorities of another state or consulting with them about a request for discovery is not evidence of bad faith.").

In general, few U.S. courts have found that a party who failed to comply with a valid U.S. discovery order acted in sufficient good faith to escape sanctions. The leading post-*Societe Internationale* cases on the issue suggest that affirmative conduct by the party from whom discovery is sought — including vigorous efforts to secure a waiver from foreign authorities or customers — will be necessary to a finding of good faith. *See In re Westinghouse Elec. Corp. Uranium Contracts Litig.*, 563 F.2d 992 (10th Cir. 1977) (formal letter to Canadian government, coupled with other efforts, to obtain waiver of nondisclosure law constitute good faith). *Cf. United States v. Bank of Nova Scotia*, 691 F.2d 1384 (11th Cir. 1982), *cert. denied*, 462 U.S. 1119 (1983) (failure to seek waiver from customer is bad faith).

10. *Need to take U.S. discovery orders seriously.* U.S. courts typically have little patience with foreign companies that seek to justify noncompliance with discovery orders by reference to their unfamiliarity with the U.S. discovery process. For example, in *Phibro Energy v. Empresa de Polimeros*, 720 F.Supp. 312 (S.D.N.Y. 1989), the magistrate ordered a foreign defendant to pay attorneys' fees incurred by the plaintiff in connection with a discovery dispute. The magistrate rejected the argument that the defendant's "lack of familiarity with the American Litigation System" and its "good faith" justified an inadequate production of documents. It is important for U.S. counsel to work particularly closely with non-U.S. litigants in ensuring adequate compliance with discovery requests; failure to do so will often leave foreign employees with the difficult task of complying with unfamiliar requests. *See also King v. Perry and Sylvia Machinery*

Co., 1991 U.S. Dist. Lexis 7901 (N.D. Ill. June 11, 1991) (construing untranslated interrogatory answers in Japanese against Japanese litigant).

11. *Application of interest-balancing outside the blocking statute context. City Bank* determined whether or not to require extraterritorial discovery by balancing a variety of factors, including U.S. and German governmental interests and private hardships. This approach represents an extension of *Societe Internationale* from situations where foreign law *affirmatively prohibits* U.S. discovery to the many cases where foreign public policy merely *disfavors* U.S.-style discovery. Is this extension warranted? Why should U.S. courts concern themselves with foreign public policy in these circumstances? Is this a "false conflict," in choice of law terms? *See also infra* pp. 647-48.

12. *Effect of Hartford Fire on City Bank interest balancing.* Recall that *Hartford Fire Insurance v. California* held that the doctrine of international comity, and §403 of the *Restatement (Third) Foreign Relations Law,* did not apply except where U.S. and foreign substantive laws imposed conflicting obligations. *See supra* pp. 604-05. Does this holding undermine *City Bank's* application of §40's balancing analysis even in the absence of conflicting legal obligations?

13. *Balancing U.S. and foreign governmental interests.* A central feature of the *City Bank* and *Restatement* §40 analysis is the weighing of U.S. and foreign governmental interests. Application of this approach in deciding whether to order discovery is a departure from *Societe Internationale* which, as noted earlier, considered only U.S. interests, the importance of the requested documents, and the defendant's nationality in deciding whether to order discovery. A number of other lower courts have followed *City Bank* and §40 in balancing *both* U.S. and foreign governmental interests in deciding whether to order discovery. *See supra* p. 879.

Nonetheless, U.S. courts appear to be divided over the usefulness of attempting to balance U.S. interests against foreign interests in resolving extraterritorial discovery disputes. Unlike the decisions cited above, some courts have sharply criticized the *City Bank* interest-balancing approach. These decisions argue that U.S. judges are ill-equipped to balance competing national policies and, in any event, that U.S. judges invariably conclude that U.S. interests should prevail. *See Arthur Andersen & Co. v. Finesilver,* 546 F.2d 338 (10th Cir. 1976), *cert. denied,* 429 U.S. 1096 (1977); *In re Uranium Antitrust Litig.,* 480 F.Supp. 1138, 1148 (N.D. Ill. 1979) ("Aside from the fact that the judiciary has little expertise, or perhaps even authority, to evaluate the economic and social policies of a foreign country, such a balancing test is inherently unworkable in this case. The competing interests here display an irreconcilable conflict on precisely the same plane of national policy"). In addition, commentators have argued that balancing national interests is a political, not legal task, and is inconsistent with policies underlying the act of state and political question doctrines. *E.g.,* Gerber, *Beyond Balancing: International Law Restraints on the Reach of National Laws,* 10 Yale J. Int'l L. 185, 205 (1984). Compare the comparable arguments made in the choice of law context. *See supra* pp. 648-49.

Which approach is wiser? Should U.S. courts attempt to assess and "balance" conflicting U.S. and foreign governmental interests? Do *City Bank* and §40 actually require "evaluat[ing] economic and social policies of a foreign country"? Is there any realistic alternative to examining foreign laws and public policies, and seeking to reconcile those authorities with U.S. law?

14. *Is a foreign blocking statute or nondisclosure policy applicable? City Bank* considered the scope of the asserted German interest in bank secrecy, concluding that various exceptions limited the importance of the interest and made the possibility that German sanctions would be imposed speculative. Other courts have also examined particular foreign blocking statutes and concluded that they are not applicable to the facts of the proposed discovery and, thus, that foreign sovereign interests are not implicated. *E.g., Roberts v. Heim,* 1990 W.L. 32,553 (N.D. Calif. 1990). Can U.S. courts reliably determine the meaning of foreign blocking statutes? Is this any different from application of foreign law in other contexts by U.S. courts?

15. *Evaluating the "strength" of foreign governmental interests.* As noted earlier, *City Bank* relied on the German government's failure to express any concern about the requested U.S. discovery in concluding that German interests were not particularly great. *See supra* pp. 876-77. How does a court decide how "strong" a legislative policy is, particularly a policy of a foreign nation? Is it not just mumbo-jumbo to talk about the "strength" of particular foreign "interests"? Alternatively, could a court at least sensibly consider how a single legislature that enacted two conflicting laws would have wanted them to interact? Does that analysis work where the laws are broad discovery rules and blocking statutes?

In addition, in evaluating the "strength" of the German governmental interests opposed to U.S. discovery, *City Bank* considered the legal form in which the German interests were expressed, apparently envisaging a continuum of methods of expressing foreign public policy running from criminal statutes, to draconian civil sanctions, to public policy expressed in legislation, to public policy expressed in judicial decisions. Although the court emphasized that a nation need not enact criminal laws to express its public policies, the absence of such a law (or an equivalently severe civil sanction) appears to have caused *City Bank* to conclude that German sovereign interests were not particularly strong. Other authorities have also considered the legal form in which foreign interests are manifested in assessing the weight of those interests. *See Restatement (Third) Foreign Relations Law* §442 comment c (1987).

16. *Nationality and residence of person from whom discovery is sought.* What role does the nationality of the party from whom discovery is sought play in extraterritorial discovery analysis? *See Restatement (Second) Foreign Relations Law* §40(d) (1965) (listing nationality as relevant factor); *Societe Internationale v. Rogers*, 357 U.S. 197 (1958) (relying on Swiss nationality in ordering discovery since Swiss company was best situated to deal with Swiss government). *Compare Restatement (Third) Foreign Relations Law* §442(1)(c) (1987) (not specifically including nationality of party from whom discovery is sought as relevant factor). The party from whom discovery was sought in *City Bank* was, of course, a U.S. business. Should this be relevant to the outcome of the case?

In *United States v. Rubin*, 836 F.2d 1096 (8th Cir. 1988), a U.S. national appealed his conviction for securities fraud, arguing among other things that the district court had erred by quashing a subpoena duces tecum that sought allegedly exculpatory documents located in the Cayman Islands. The court of appeals held that the district court had properly quashed the defendant's subpoena. It observed initially that Cayman Islands bank secrecy laws forbid disclosure of the records in question. Moreover, the court emphasized, the defendant "is attempting to obtain records of Cayman Island residents who are neither the target of a United States criminal proceeding nor subject to the laws of the United States." *Id.* at 1002. *Rubin* contrasted this to cases in which "the government was seeking the bank records of United States citizens who are the target of a United State criminal proceeding" and in which U.S. courts concluded that "the Cayman interest in preserving the privacy of its banking customers is substantially diminished when the privacy interest is that of an American citizen (or entity) subject to American laws." *Id.* (citing *United States v. Field*, 532 F.2d. 404, 408-09 (5th Cir.), *cert. denied*, 429 U.S. 940 (1976)).

Is it appropriate for U.S. courts to order extraterritorial discovery more readily from U.S. companies than from foreign entities? Although extraterritorial discovery from U.S. nationals might not offend foreign states, is it wise to establish a double standard that treats U.S. companies less favorably than their foreign competitors?

2. Extraterritorial Discovery in Violation of Foreign Law: Contemporary Approaches

The *Restatement (Third) Foreign Relations Law* adopted a specific provision for moderating extraterritorial U.S. discovery, based on the <u>interest-balancing analysis</u> of *City Bank* and similar lower court decisions. The formulation, which is contained in §442 (excerpted below), was adopted only after considerable debate, and continues to be controversial.[106] Nonetheless, many courts have applied variations of §442's <u>interest balancing analysis</u>.[107] A leading example is the Seventh Circuit's opinion in

---

106. *E.g.*, Houck, *Restatement of the Foreign Relations Law of the United States (Revised): Issues and Resolutions*, 20 Int'l Law. 1361 (1986); Robinson, *Compelling Discovery and Evidence in International Litigation*, 18 Int'l Law. 533 (1984). In preliminary drafts, §442 was numbered as §437, and early judicial decisions refer to §437.

107. For some of the cases relying on §442, *see Societe National Industrielle Aerospatiale v. U.S. District Court*, 482 U.S. 522 (1987); *Reinsurance Co. of America, Inc. v. Administratia Asigurarilor De Stat*, 902 F.2d 1275 (7th Cir. 1990) ("new §442 provides a modified balancing test substantially similar to that of ... §40"); *United States v. First Nat'l Bank of Chicago*, 699 F.2d 341, 346 (7th Cir. 1983); *McKesson Corp. v. Islamic Republic of Iran*, 1991 U.S. Dist. Lexis 10226 (D.D.C. July 5, 1991). *Cf. United States v. Davis*, 767 F.2d 1025, 1034 n.16 (2d Cir. 1985) (noting existence of §437, but following Restatement (Second) §40); *Garpeg Ltd. v. United States*, 583 F. Supp. 789 (S.D.N.Y. 1984) (same).

Reinsurance Company of America, Inc. v. Administratia Asigurarilor de Stat, also excerpted below.

RESTATEMENT (THIRD) FOREIGN
RELATIONS LAW OF THE UNITED STATES §442 (1987)

§442(1) (a) A court or agency in the United States, when authorized by statute or rule of court, may order a person subject to its jurisdiction to produce documents, objects, or other information relevant to an action or investigation, even if the information or the person in possession of the information is outside the United States.

(b) Failure to comply with an order to produce information may subject the person to whom the order is directed to sanctions, including finding of contempt, dismissal of a claim or defense, or default judgment, or may lead to a determination that the facts to which the order was addressed are as asserted by the opposing party.

(c) In deciding whether to issue an order directing production of information located abroad, and in framing such an order, a court or agency in the United States should take into account the importance to the investigation or litigation of the documents or other information requested; the degree of specificity of the request; whether the information originated in the United States; the availability of alternative means of securing the information; and the extent to which noncompliance with the request would undermine important interests of the United States, or compliance with the request would undermine important interests of the state where the information is located.

(2) If disclosure of information located outside the United States is prohibited by a law, regulation, or order of a court or other authority of the state in which the information or prospective witness is located, or of the state of which a prospective witness is a national,

(a) a court or agency in the United States may require the person to whom the order is directed to make a good faith effort to secure permission from the foreign authorities to make the information available;

(b) a court or agency should not ordinarily impose sanctions of contempt, dismissal, or default on a party that has failed to comply with the order for production, except in cases of deliberate concealment or removal of information or of failure to make a good faith effort in accordance with paragraph (a);

(c) a court or agency may, in appropriate cases, make findings of fact adverse to a party that has failed to comply with the order for production, even if that party has made a good faith effort to secure permission from the foreign authorities to make the information available and that effort has been unsuccessful.

REINSURANCE COMPANY OF AMERICA, INC. v.
ADMINISTRATIA ASIGURARILOR de STAT

902 F.2d 1275 (7th Cir. 1990)

BAUER, CHIEF JUDGE. Plaintiff-appellee Reinsurance Company of America ("RCA"), an Illinois corporation engaged in the reinsurance business, [appeals] asserting that the district court's denial of its request for post-judgment interrogatories [directed to defendant-appellant Administratia Asigurarilor de Stat ("ADAS")], was ... an abuse of discretion. We find no abuse of discretion by the district court ... and therefore affirm. ...

Plaintiff and defendant entered into two Quota Share Retrocession Agreements, effective October 1, 1977, and January 1, 1980, respectively. Under the terms of the contract, ADAS agreed to participate as a retrocessionaire for risks which were reinsured by RCA. The contract was executed by representatives of RCA and CJV Associates ("CJV") which acted as agents for ADAS. On January 19, 1983, RCA sued ADAS for breach of these retrocession agreements. ADAS removed the case to federal court. ... [The district court eventually granted summary judgment against ADAS on liability and] awarded damages in the amount of $337,597.00. [RCA then sought to compel ADAS to answer certain post-judgment interrogatories designed to assist it in enforcing the judgment in its favor.] ADAS ... objected to RCA's inquiries as violating Rumanian law prohibiting disclosure of state secrets. RCA then sought a motion to compel responses. ... [T]he district court denied RCA's motion to compel indicating that the balance of the interests weighed in favor of Romania's laws protecting national secrecy.

RCA contends that the district court abused its discretion by denying its request for post-judgment interrogatories. RCA, in an effort to collect its damage award, filed a series of these interrogatories with the district court on October 27, 1986. ADAS refused to respond to three of these inquiries. Each of the interrogatories in controversy asked ADAS to provide information regarding insurance contracts with firms in the United States, Canada and the United Kingdom.[108] In explaining this

---

108. Specifically, ADAS objected to interrogatories 2, 6, and 9. These interrogatories provided:

2. For each and every person, partnership or corporation maintaining a residence or which is domiciled in the United States, which is insured or reinsured by ADAS and which has exposures in the United States, Canada and/or the United Kingdom, identify the following:
    (a) The name and address of the insured or reinsured;
    (b) The policy treaty or facultative certificates which provide the coverage; and
    (c) The policy limit for each coverage in U.S. dollars
6. State whether ADAS has in force any reinsurance agreements with any ceding companies located in the United States, Canada and/or the United Kingdom, pursuant to which funds held by such ceding companies earn interest which is ultimately payable to ADAS, and if so, identify for each:
    (a) The name of the ceding company;
    (b) The business address of the ceding company;
    (c) The date on which each agreement was entered into; and
    (d) The termination date, if any, for each agreement.

(continued page 885)

refusal to furnish a response, ADAS claimed that Rumanian law forbade disclosure of the requested information.[109]

When the laws of the United States and those of a foreign country are in conflict, as they are here, this circuit, along with several others, has employed a balancing *Restatement* test derived from §40, *Restatement (Second) Foreign Relations Law* (1965) ("§40"). *balancing test*

Applying [the §40] test, [the district court] determined that because Rumanian law considered the requested information a "service secret" and punished disclosure with criminal sanctions, and the law was apparently vigorously enforced, the balance favored ADAS's refusal to respond to the interrogatories over RCA's right to such responses. As the following discussion of the §40 factors demonstrates, [this] conclusion is correct.

Initially, we must balance the "vital national interests" of both the United States *1) vital national interests* and Romania. We approach this task with some misgivings. As Judge Marshall of the Northern District of Illinois noted, "the judiciary has little expertise, or perhaps even authority to evaluate the economic and social policies of a foreign country." *In re Uranium Antitrust Litigation*, 480 F.Supp. 1138 (N.D. Ill. 1979). Moreover, when allegedly considering only "vital national interests," we are left with the rather ridiculous assignment of determining which competing national interest is the more vital. Whatever the semantic difficulties of our test, the courts of the United States undoubtedly have a vital interest in providing a forum for the final resolution of dis-

---

(continued from page 884)

9. State whether ADAS has accepted reinsurance submissions from brokers or agents located in the United Kingdom who ADAS knows or believes receives business offerings from reinsurance brokers located in the United States and/or Canada, and if so, sate:

    (a) Whether the United Kingdom brokers or agents issue cover-notes or other formal evidence of coverage on behalf of ADAS;

    (b) Whether the United Kingdom brokers or agents collect premiums which are ultimately due to ADAS, and if so;

    (c) Identify the brokers, agents or companies located in the United States and Canada who remit such premiums, and provide their business addresses.

109. ADAS particularly raises two points of Rumanian law defining "state secrets" and "service secrets." A rough translation of the relevant law, as quoted by the district court, provides:

Art. 2. It is considered State secret according to the stipulations of the Penal Code, any information, data and documents which evidently show this character as well as those declared and qualified as such by a Council of Ministers decision.

The transmission or divulging of information data and documents which constitute State secrets, loss, detained outside Service duties, destruction [sic] alteration or taking away of documents with such character negligence which led to one of these facts or which enabled other persons to take possession of information data or documents which might endanger the economic, technical-scientific, military or political interests of the State as well as other infringement of the norms regarding the protection of the State secret, constitute unusually grave facts and are punished by penal law.

Art. 4. The information, data and documents which according to the present law do not constitute State secrets but are not destined to publicity are Service secrets and cannot be divulged.

Art. 251. The divulgement of the State secret, if this does not constitute infringement of art. 169, and also the divulgement of data or information which, although it does not constitute State secrets are not destined to publicity, if the act is of the nature to affect public interest, are punished by imprisonment from 6 months to 5 years.

putes and for enforcing these judgments. This rather general interest, however, is not as compelling as those interests implicated in other §40 cases cited by RCA. For instance, in *Graco, Inc. v. Kremlin, Inc.*, the court held that the United States had a compelling interest in ensuring that its patent laws were not undermined by a French blocking statute. Similarly, vital interests are involved when a commercial dispute implicates the integrity of American antitrust laws. *In re Uranium Antitrust Litigation, supra.* When the United States itself is a party in the litigation, the national interest involved may become compelling. Thus, enforcement of the tax laws, *United States v. Vetco, supra*, and the securities laws, *SEC v. Banca della Svizzera Italiana*, have been considered compelling national interest. In the case at hand, though, we are presented with a private dispute between two reinsurance corporations. The disputed materials are the subject of a post-judgment interrogatory request and not vital to the case-in-chief. While there is unquestionably a vital national interest in protecting the finality of judgments and meaningfully enforcing these decisions, this interest alone does not rise to the level of those found in these earlier cases.

Against this, we must weigh on the opposing side of the balance the Rumanian interest in protecting its state and so-called "service" secrets. Given the scope of its protective laws and the strict penalties it imposes for any violation, Romania places a high price on this secrecy. Unlike a blocking statue, Romania's law appears to be directed at domestic affairs rather than merely protecting Rumanian corporations from foreign discovery request. *Cf. Compagnie Francaise D'Assurance v. Phillips Petroleum Co.*, 105 F.R.D. 16, 30 (S.D.N.Y. 1984) (French blocking statute "never expected nor intended to be enforced against French subjects but was intended rather to provide them with tactical weapons and bargaining chips in foreign courts.") Given this choice between the relative interests of Romania in its national secrecy and the American interest in enforcing its judicial decisions, we have determined that Romania's, at least on the facts before us, appears to be the more immediate and compelling.[110]

The remaining factors are far less problematic. In evaluating the extent and nature of the hardship imposed upon ADAS by inconsistent enforcement actions, §40(b), our sole reference is the affidavit provided by Mr. Dumitriu, a Rumanian attorney. Mr. Dumitriu states that the officers of ADAS would face criminal sanctions for revealing "service" secrets as classified by the Rumanian government. Moreover, Dumitriu's affidavit states that the law protecting state and "service" secrets is vigorously enforced, thus, satisfying the factor under §40(e). RCA contends

---

110. We pause to note that between the argument of this case and this decision, there has been a profound and much celebrated change in the political structure of Romania. The high priority which national secrecy enjoyed under the old regime is presumably no longer in vogue. Neither plaintiff nor defendant, however, has brought supplemental information to this court regarding this matter. Thus we must decide this case on the facts before us. Should the parties believe that new facts have materially altered the foundation of our judgment, they are free to resubmit their claims. We note, however, that relevant changes in the law must be presented to the court rather than illusory changes in the political climate which provide little basis for re-evaluating this decision.

that §40(c), [which concerns] the extent to which the required conduct is to take place in the territory of the foreign state, was mismeasured by the district court. We disagree. All the information which plaintiff sought through these interrogatories is located within Romania. The offices of ADAS are located within Romania as well. Any responses to RCA's interrogatories would have to be prepared in Romania using this information. Obviously, ADAS could deliver this material to a site in the United States and prepare some of the responses there, as plaintiff contends. Yet, this does not affect the very real threat faced by officials at ADAS who would have to remove this information from Romania. Finally, it is undisputed that §40(d), the consideration of the nationality of the person in question, weighs in favor of ADAS. This is a Rumanian corporation whose offices are located only within that country. Those persons forced to comply with this discovery order would be Rumanian citizens subject to the criminal sanctions of the law protecting state secrets. Thus, considering all five factors provided under §40 — the competing national interests involved, the hardship to ADAS of compliance, the place of compliance, the nationality of ADAS and the likelihood of enforcement of the criminal sanctions — we conclude that on balance the district court correctly denied RCA's motion to compel responses to the interrogatories.

Complicating our determination, however, is the recent publication of the *Restatement (Third) Foreign Relations Law*. We noted in our decision in *United States v. First National Bank of Chicago*, 699 F.2d 341 (7th Cir. 1983), that a new draft was pending, and now we must review our precedent in light of this new standard. Section 442 of the *Third Restatement* considers the specific problem of conflicting jurisdiction over discovery. ... [T]he new §442 follows the path announced by this court in *First National Bank of Chicago* that "[t]he fact that foreign law may subject a person to criminal sanctions in the foreign country if he produces certain information does not automatically bar a domestic court from compelling production." 699 F.2d at 345. The new §442 provides a modified balancing test substantially similar to that of *First National Bank of Chicago* and §40. Although there are certain differences in emphasis, the factors to be considered remain largely synonymous and do not alter our determination that the district court's judgment was reasonable and correct.

Section 442, however, does make one significant change to the old standard by introducing an element of good faith to be included at the court's discretion. ... Similarly, in *United States v. First National Bank of Chicago*, this court remanded a case to the Northern District of Illinois in order to determine whether First Chicago must make a good faith effort to receive permission from the Greek authorities to produce bank information located in Greece but unavailable due to the bank secrecy provisions of Greek law. Here, the district court did not discuss the question of a good faith effort by ADAS to seek a waiver of Romania's secrecy laws. Given, our holding in *First National Bank of Chicago*, [w]e could remand this case for additional consideration of this issue. However, such a step is unnecessary. Our earlier case is easily distinguishable from the one at hand. In *First National Bank of Chicago*, the Greek law at issue appeared to provide a limited exception for furnishing certain information. Thus, it was unclear whether compliance would have resulted in criminal sanctions. Moreover, a treaty existed between the United States and Greece for the purposes of diplomatically resolving such banking disputes. Given this welter of uncertainty, there appeared at least the possibility of obtaining permission from the Greek authorities if First Chicago made a good faith effort.

[handwritten: Romanian law strictly applied]

By contrast, here the law is apparently strictly applied. There are no exceptions to Romania's secrecy law. There exists no treaty between these governments to diplomatically resolve such problems. Unlike ... *First National Bank of Chicago* ... there would be little purpose to requiring a good faith effort to comply with the discovery request. Therefore, the district court's decision not to impose a requirement of a

[handwritten: HELD]

good faith effort upon ADAS was reasonable. The denial of RCA's motion to compel responses was consistent with our prior holdings as well as the new standard under *Restatement (Third)* §442 and not an abuse of discretion.

EASTERBROOK, CIRCUIT JUDGE, concurring. Events have overtaken this case. Romania adopted a strict code of secrecy out of fear that sunlight would jeopardize the regime. Under Rumanian law, anything that is not a "State secret" is a "Service secret" - in other words, everything is a secret. The regime fell nonetheless, and not because of loose lips. Revolution in Romania means that yesterday's secrecy laws are of little moment. What the Securitate kept under covers its successors broadcast.

We have not heard from Romania's lawyer, perhaps because he has no idea who speaks for his client. I therefore join the court's opinion, which observes that the plaintiff may return to the district court for a fresh decision under contemporary law. The court applies a balancing approach that the parties agree is apt. Given this agreement, we have no occasion to decide whether to follow the *Restatement (Third) Foreign Relations Law* §442 (1987), to the extent we may create a federal common law of privileges.

If we were free of the parties' agreement, I would be most reluctant to accept an approach that calls on the district judge to throw a heap of factors on a table and then slice and dice to taste. Although it is easy to identify many relevant considerations, as the ALI's Restatement does, a court's job is to reach judgments on the basis of rules of law, rather than to use a different recipe for each meal.

Two sources of law dominate here. The first is Federal Rule of Evidence 501, which says that when state law supplies the rule of decision (as Illinois law does in this case), it also supplies the law with respect to privileges. Federal Rule of Civil Procedure 69, which governs this enforcement action, also directs the court to follow state law. Does (would?) Illinois follow the *Restatement (Third) Foreign Relations* in deciding whether documents held abroad are privileged? The parties do not discuss the question.

The other rules come from the Foreign Sovereign Immunities Act, 28 U.S.C.

§§1602-11. Defendant in this case ("AAS"), an arm of the Rumanian government, is open to suit under §1605(a)(2) because the claim is based on its commercial activity within the United States. With a default judgment in hand, plaintiff seeks to discover AAS's assets. AAS invokes Romania's secrecy laws, which forbid it to disclose any information in its hands, even information about assets located outside Romania. Their effect is that no judgment against Romania may be collected. I doubt that general interest-balancing principles of the sort discussed in the Restatement may countermand the decision of Congress that courts of the United States may impose liability. The FSIA provides that a prevailing party may execute against the foreign government's assets except to the extent the statute creates exceptions, see §§1609-11. This catalog of what is, and is not, available to satisfy a judgment eclipses any attempt by the foreign defendant to create its preferred list by using its domestic secrecy law. If we allow foreign states to exempt themselves after the fashion of (the old) Romania, we might as well forget about the FSIA.

Even the *Restatement* is no longer as favorable to foreign defendants as it once was. The catalog of relevant interests in §442(1)(c) of the *Third Restatement* is not to be used generally to assess demands for information. It is designed to inform the discretionary decision whether to impose one of the sanctions mentioned in Fed. R. Civ. P. 37 and §442(1)(b), such as contempt of court of a default judgment. As a rule, parties are entitled to seek information and, without regard to balancing national interests, the foreign party must make a good faith effort to secure its release, §442(2)(a) and (b). If release is not forthcoming, then

> a court or agency may, in appropriate cases, make findings of fact adverse to a party that has failed to comply with the order for production, even if that party has made a good faith effort to secure permission from the foreign authorities to make the information available and that effort has been unsuccessful.

Section 442(2)(c). In other words, the party seeking the information obtains its equivalent despite foreign secrecy rules. The balancing approach of §442(1)(c) in conjunction with the adverse inference under §442(2)(c) means that the party caught between inconsistent obligations to two nations with equal sovereign authority is not subject to extra penalty, such as imprisonment or fines exceeding the stakes of the case. A party may lose no more than the case — and then only if the law favors the adverse party once the facts have been deemed admitted under §442(2)(c). Such an approach is a careful accommodation of the legitimate interests of the parties and the nations alike, all without authorizing unconfined "balancing" of the "importance" of the nations' policies.

If I thought we had to do such balancing, I would be at sea. If I knew how to balance incommensurables, I would be hard pressed to agree with courts saying (as the district judge did) that a suit by the government is "more important" than private litigation. In a capitalist economy enforcement of contracts is a subject of the first magnitude. The gravity of the nation's interest is no less when it decides to enforce vital rules through private initiative. A court would need to know the "importance" of the substantive rule, which is not well correlated with the enforcement mechanism. (The antitrust laws are "more important" than the littering laws although the former are largely enforced by private suits and the latter by public prosecutions.)

Section 442(2)(c) breaks down in a case such as this one in which the judgment has been rendered and the prevailing party seeks to discover assets. This problem, which the Restatement does not discuss, is closer in principle to the rule of §442(2)(c) than to that of §442(1). Ascertaining assets under Rule 69 is not a "sanction" for misconduct. A prevailing party is entitled to relief; so much has been determined by the judgment. At this point resort to secrecy laws does nothing to nullify the rendering nation's substantive law. Because the FSIA does not contemplate such a step, foreign secrecy laws are not sufficient to block disclosures under Rule 69.

Notes on Restatement §442 and Reinsurance Company

1. *Section 442's heightened standard of materiality.* The comments to §442 state that extraterritorial discovery ordinarily should be ordered only of materials that are "necessary to the action — typically, evidence not otherwise readily obtainable — and directly relevant and material." *Id.* comment a. This standard is considerably more rigorous than the usually broad scope of discoverable material under domestic U.S. discovery rules. *See* Fed. R. Civ. P. 26(b)(1) ("any matter, not privileged, which is relevant to the subject matter involved in the pending action"); *Hickman v. Taylor*, 329 U.S. 495, 507 (1947); *supra* pp. 843-44. In applying an interest-balancing analysis, some lower courts appear to have adopted §442's heightened standard of materiality for extraterritorial discovery and to either have refused to order discovery of documents whose importance was not apparent or to have limited the scope of discovery. *See, e.g., Trade Dev. Bank v. Continental Ins. Co.*, 469 F.2d 35, 40-41 (2d Cir. 1972); *Minpeco, SA v. Conticommodity Services Inc.*, 116 F.R.D. 517 (S.D.N.Y. 1987); *Graco, Inc. v. Kremlin, Inc.*, 101 F.R.D. 503, 515-16 (N.D. Ill. 1984). Is this requirement of heightened materiality appropriate? Will a U.S. party, litigating against a foreign party, also be entitled to a heightened standard of materiality with respect to discovery of its U.S. materials? Is it appropriate to order discovery in an asymmetrical fashion?

2. *Section 442's interest-balancing analysis.* Section 442(1)(a)'s general rule permitting direct extraterritorial discovery is elaborated upon by subsection (1)(c), which calls on U.S. courts to take into account a variety of different factors. Several lower courts have adopted interest-balancing analyses that are similar to that proposed by §442(1)(c). *See Reinsurance Co. of America, Inc.*; *United States v. Davis*, 767 F.2d 1025 (2d Cir. 1985); *Minpeco, SA v. Conticommodity Serv.*, 116 F.R.D. 517 (S.D.N.Y. 1987); *Garpeg, Ltd. v. United States*, 583 F.Supp. 789 (S.D.N.Y. 1984). *See also Societe Nationale Industrielle Aerospatiale v. U.S. District Court*, 482 U.S. 522 (1987) (excerpted below at pp. 903-12).

3. *Continued application of* Societe Internationale's *two-step analysis under §442.* Section 442 continues to use the two-step approach to issuing discovery orders and imposing sanctions that the Supreme Court adopted in *Societe Internationale*. Does §442(2) alter the traditional rules governing the imposition of sanctions or the determination of good faith noncompliance with discovery orders?

4. *Comparison between discovery under §442 and foreign sovereign compulsion doctrine.* Section 442(2) grants a court power to order conduct abroad in violation of foreign law, just as *Societe Internationale* and *Restatement (Second) Foreign Relations Law* §§39 & 40 (1965), permitted. Compare §442(2) with the foreign sovereign compulsion doctrine, particularly as set out in §441 of the *Third Restatement* (excerpted above at pp. 505 & 748-52), which generally forbids states from requiring conduct abroad in violation of the law of the place of the conduct. What explains the different approaches? Consider:

> [Section] 441 is concerned with conflicts in substantive law between two or more states ... in situations where both states have jurisdiction to prescribe; [§442], in contrast, deals with the litigation process, and in particular with pretrial procedures, in situations where the forum state by definition has jurisdiction over the parties and the proceedings, and foreign substantive law

would not ordinarily be involved. Accordingly, somewhat less deference to the law of the other state may be called for. *Restatement (Third) Foreign Relations Law* §442 comment e (1987).

Is this persuasive? Are there better explanations for the different treatment?

5. *Power to impose sanctions under §442.* Note that §442(2)(c) preserves the authority of U.S. courts to make findings of fact adverse to a party who fails to provide requested discovery, even where the party has unsuccessfully made good faith efforts to obtain waivers of foreign blocking statutes. In addition, however, note that §442(2)(b) restricts the circumstances in which sanctions of contempt, dismissal or default are imposed.

6. *Distinction between private and governmental litigation.* Both *Societe Internationale* and *City Bank* were cases involving the U.S. government, while *Reinsurance Company* involved only a private U.S. plaintiff. What weight should the U.S. government's role in litigation have in the interest-balancing envisioned by §40 and *City Bank*? Note that *City Bank* relied on the U.S. government's involvement in emphasizing the strength of U.S. interests, while *Reinsurance Company* emphasized that only "private litigation" was involved. *See also United States v. Vetco, Inc.*, 691 F.2d 1281, 1288 (9th Cir.), *cert. denied*, 454 U.S. 1098 (1981) ("[T]he instant case turns upon an IRS summons issued pursuant to an investigation of potentially criminal conduct. Such summonses appear to serve a more pressing national function than civil discovery."); *United States v. Toyota Motor Corp.*, 569 F.Supp. 1158, 1162-63 (C.D. Cal. 1983) ("[T]he fact that this action was brought by the government, rather than a private litigant, weighs heavily towards finding a strong American interest in obtaining the information sought"). Note, however, Judge Easterbrook's criticism of this distinction between private and governmental litigation. Is his criticism persuasive?

7. *Federal common law character of §442 analysis.* Judge Easterbrook's concurrence suggests substantial doubt that "a federal common law of privilege" governs conflicts between extraterritorial U.S. discovery orders and foreign blocking statutes. Is this skepticism warranted? Consider the federal common law rules that have been recognized in other international litigation contexts. *See supra* pp. 224-25 (attribution of liability among foreign state entities); *supra* pp. 49-56 (comity as basis for dismissing suit); *supra* p. 490 (antisuit injunctions); *supra* pp. 704-05 (act of state); and *supra* pp. 541-44 (extraterritoriality). Does extraterritorial discovery in violation of foreign law implicate sufficiently weighty federal interests in foreign policy and commerce to justify a rule of federal common law?

8. *Futile foreign discovery. Reinsurance Company* interpreted §442 as generally requiring parties to make a good faith effort to obtain a waiver of foreign blocking statutes before quashing attempted discovery. The court nevertheless refused to require ADAS to make such an effort, reasoning that it would be futile because there "are no exceptions to Romania's secrecy law." Compare this approach to *Societe Internationale*, where the courts ordered discovery without regard to whether it could be procured.

9. *Basis for* **Reinsurance Company** *decision.* What were the critical considerations underlying the decision in *Reinsurance Company*? The supposedly "vigorous" enforcement of Romanian secrecy laws? The fact that these laws were neutrally applied in domestic affairs, not just in cases involving U.S. discovery? The nationality of ADAS? The supposedly attenuated U.S. interests? Which of these factors is most significant? Which could be ignored?

Did *Reinsurance Company* reach the correct result? What result would Judge Easterbrook have reached? What weight should be assigned to the fact that the requested information related principally to contracts involving U.S. companies?

10. *Criticism of §442's interest-balancing.* Judge Easterbrook's concurrence criticizes the §442 interest-balancing test: "If I thought we had to do such balancing, I would be at sea." Does §442 provide any meaningful guidance for courts and litigants? Do judicial decisions interpreting §442 (and its predecessors) do so? Compare the debate about interest-balancing in the context of legislative jurisdiction and choice of law, *supra* pp. 508-09, 592-93 & 648-49.

11. *Significance of foreign privileges in U.S. discovery.* Quite apart from "blocking statutes," most countries recognize various privileges against compelled disclosure of information. Examples include the attorney-client privilege and marital privileges. Suppose that a litigant in a U.S. proceeding seeks information that is protected under a foreign privilege, but would not be protected under a U.S. privilege. Should a U.S. court order discovery?

Relatively few decisions have considered how questions of privilege should be resolved. Traditionally, the forum's law governed procedural matters, which were generally understood as including questions of privilege. *See Restatement (Second) Conflict of Laws* §§122, 127 (1971); *Societe Internationale etc. v. Brownell*, 225 F.2d 532 (D.C. Cir. 1955), *rev'd on other grounds*, 357 U.S. 197 (1958). In general, lower courts appear not to rigidly apply the forum's law, and to view claims of privilege with substantially greater favor than claims based upon blocking statutes. *E.g.*, *Renfield Corp. v. Remy Martin SA*, 98 F.R.D. 442 (D. Del. 1982) (applying choice-of-law principles to determine that U.S., not French, attorney-client privilege should govern); *Duplan Corp. v. Deering Milliken, Inc.*, 397 F.Supp. 1146, 1169-71 (D.S.C. 1974) ("any communications touching base with the United States will be governed by the federal discovery rules while any communications related to matters solely involving France or Great Britain will be governed by the applicable foreign statute"). Why do foreign privileges appear to warrant different treatment than blocking statutes? Is there a principled basis for a distinction?

12. *Discovery from foreign sovereign entities.* Private parties often seek to take discovery from the foreign sovereign entities, just as they would do in the case of private litigants. In general, U.S. courts have been willing to order discovery from foreign sovereigns in actions under the FSIA. *E.g.*, *McKesson Corp. v. Islamic Republic of Iran*, 138 F.R.D. 1 (D.D.C. 1991); *United States v. Crawford Enterprises, Inc.*, 643 F.Supp. 370 (S.D. Tex. 1986); *Laker Airways v. Pan American World Airways*, 103 F.R.D. 42 (D.D.C. 1984). This willingness extends to "jurisdictional" discovery, as well as discovery on the merits. *E.g.*, *In re Bedford Computer Corp.*, 114 B.R. 2 (D.N.H. 1990); *Matter of SEDCO, Inc.*, 543 F.Supp. 561, 569 (S.D. Tex. 1982). Indeed, U.S. courts appear to be less receptive to efforts of foreign states to rely on their own blocking statutes than they are to the efforts of private litigants. *See Laker Airways v. Pan American World Airways*, 103 F.R.D. 42, 47 (D.D.C. 1984) ("the [defendant's] argument is really a claim that it should not have to comply with discovery because its owner — the German government — has decided ... not to comply with such discovery. Such a claim of de facto immunity is fallacious, and is rejected"); *Aerospatiale*, 482 U.S. at 544 n.29 ("It would be particularly incongruous to recognize such a preference [against direct U.S. discovery] for corporations that are wholly owned by the enacting nation.").

Nonetheless, some U.S. courts have also required careful consideration of foreign governmental interests before ordering discovery from foreign sovereign entities, and have suggested that discovery concerning the acts of foreign government officials raises especially sensitive issues. *E.g.*, *Environmental Tectonics v. W.S. Kirkpatrick, Inc.*, 847 F.2d 1052, 1062 n.11 (3d Cir. 1988), *rev'd on other grounds*, 484 U.S. 852 (1990).

A particularly extensive lower court opinion dealing with discovery from foreign sovereigns was issued in *McKesson Corp. v. Islamic Republic of Iran*, 138 F.R.D. 1 (D.D.C. 1991). The court observed that the FSIA does not itself prescribe rules governing discovery from foreign sovereigns, and that instead the Act's legislative history directs district courts to refer to domestic discovery law. In doing so, the court reasoned that the Supreme Court's decision in *Aerospatiale*, 482 U.S. 522 (excerpted below at pp. 903-12), concerning first-use of the Hague Evidence Convention, "offers considerable guidance in formulating the parameters of discovery in suits against foreign governments." The court went on to apply the *ad hoc* analysis set forth in *Aerospatiale* and in §442 of the *Third Restatement*; under this analysis, the court required Iran to comply with a number of document requests and interrogatories, but it refused to order compliance with particularly burdensome requests or requests that had only limited materiality.

13. *Discovery and the act of state doctrine.* As discussed *supra* pp. 685-90, the act of state doctrine precludes U.S. courts from reviewing the validity of certain actions of foreign nations. Most lower courts have rejected the argument that the act of state doctrine forbids ordering extraterritorial discovery that will violate foreign blocking statutes. These courts reason that their discovery orders do not require passing on the validity of the foreign statutes — they merely require foreign nationals to disregard those foreign statutes. *See United States v. Bank of Nova Scotia*, 740 F.2d 817, 831-2 (11th Cir. 1985), *cert. denied*, 469 U.S. 1106 (1985); *Associated Container Transp. (Australia) v. United States*, 705 F.2d 53, 60-62 (2d Cir. 1983); *In re Uranium Antitrust Litig.*, 480 F.Supp. 1138, 1149 (N.D. Ill. 1979).

E. Discovery Pursuant to Customary International Judicial Assistance

As described previously, U.S. courts have traditionally favored the use of direct discovery orders under the Federal Rules of Civil Procedure to obtain evidence located abroad. In many circumstances, however, persons who refuse to provide information voluntarily may not be subject to the personal jurisdiction or subpoena power of U.S. courts.[111] In these cases, U.S. courts are unable to order discovery directly and must seek the assistance of foreign courts.

The customary method of obtaining foreign judicial assistance in taking evidence abroad was by letter rogatory. As described previously, a letter rogatory is a formal request by the court of one nation to the courts of another country for assistance in performing judicial acts.[112] The Federal Rules clearly contemplate the use of letters rogatory and most federal courts have also concluded that they possess inherent authority to issue letters rogatory.[113] In the discovery context, a U.S. letter rogatory will typically request the foreign court receiving the letter to compel a person within the foreign court's jurisdiction to provide specified testimony or documents to the foreign court, which will in turn forward the evidence to the requesting court.

When letters rogatory are executed as requested, they can serve important purposes. Most obviously, if the person from whom discovery is sought is not subject to U.S. jurisdiction or subpoena power, then proceeding by letter rogatory may be the only avenue for compelling discovery from a recalcitrant foreign witness. Moreover, taking evidence abroad by letter rogatory will not offend foreign sovereignty, since the foreign state may decide whether to grant its assistance and a foreign judge will preside over the evidence-taking process.[114] Finally, in countries that forbid U.S. depositions within their borders, letters rogatory may provide the only method for obtaining evidence from cooperative witnesses who do not wish to travel to the United States.

Despite their potential importance, letters rogatory have historically had significant disadvantages as a means of obtaining extraterritorial discovery. First, foreign courts are under no obligation to execute letters rogatory. Foreign courts have frequently refused to execute U.S. letters of request — including because of poor diplo-

---

111. *See supra* pp. 861-66.

112. For cases where letters rogatory were used to obtain evidence located abroad, *see, e.g., United States v. Paraffin Wax, 2255 Bags*, 23 F.R.D. 289 (E.D.N.Y. 1959); *Danisch v. Guardian Life Ins. Co.*, 19 F.R.D. 235 (S.D.N.Y. 1956); *Branyan v. KLM*, 13 F.R.D. 425 (S.D.N.Y. 1953); *De Villeneuve v. Morning Journal Ass'n*, 206 F. 70 (S.D.N.Y. 1913); *Gross v. Palmer*, 105 F. 833 (C.C. Ill. 1900). A variety of forms exist for letters rogatory requesting assistance in the taking of evidence. *See, e.g.*, 22 C.F.R. §§92.54-92.66 (1987); 4 J. Moore, *Moore's Federal Practice* ¶28.05 (2d ed. 1987); 3 J. Moore & L. Frumer, *Moore's Manual, Federal Practice Forms*, Nos. 15:21, 15:22 (2d ed. 1988); B. Ristau, *International Judicial Assistance* §§3-3-1 through 3-3-5 (1990 Rev.).

113. *United States v. Reagan*, 453 F.2d 165, 171-73 (6th Cir. 1971), *cert. denied*, 406 U.S. 946 (1972); *Zassenhaus v. Evening Star Newspaper Co.*, 404 F.2d 1361 (D.C. Cir. 1968); *De Villeneuve v. Morning Journal Ass'n*, 206 F. 70 (S.D.N.Y. 1913); *Gross v. Palmer*, 105 F. 833 (C.C. Ill. 1900).

114. Note, *Taking Evidence Outside of the United States*, 55 B.U.L. Rev. 368, 374 (1975).

matic relations, because the underlying dispute involves claims that conflict with foreign public policy, or simply because of bureaucratic inertia.[115] Moreover, even when foreign courts agree to execute letters rogatory, they often prove to be unwilling to require the full extent of discovery sought by U.S. letters of request; the precise limits that foreign courts will place on U.S. discovery requests vary from country to country.[116] Finally, in at least some nations, courts object to (or misunderstand) "pretrial discovery" and will honor only requests for materials to be used as evidence at trial.[117]

When foreign courts provide judicial assistance to U.S. litigants, they ordinarily will do so according to their own judicial procedures and customs. In the case of oral testimony, this can often mean that no oath is administered to the deponent, no verbatim transcript is made, and all questioning is conducted by the judge (without participation by counsel).[118] Although U.S. procedural rules have been modified to ensure that evidence produced according to foreign procedures of this sort is admissible,[119] the value of the evidence-taking exercise may nonetheless be substantially diminished. Similarly, foreign courts will seldom enforce broad U.S.-style document requests to which U.S. lawyers are accustomed.[120]

Finally, letters rogatory must be transmitted to the appropriate foreign court through diplomatic channels.[121] This usually requires sending the letter to the U.S. Department of State, which will forward the letter to the receiving state's ministry of foreign affairs, which will in turn transmit the letter to the foreign court.[122] This process can be slow and unpredictable; it often requires a minimum of three months for completion and delays of more than a year are not uncommon.[123] Some countries permit direct transmittal of letters rogatory from the requesting U.S. court to the receiving foreign courts; where this alternative is available it should be used because it reduces somewhat the risk of bureaucratic delays.

---

115. *See, e.g.,* Jones, *International Judicial Assistance: Procedural Chaos and a Program for Reform,* 62 Yale L.J. 515, 529-34 (1953).

116. *E.g., Rio Tinto Zinc Corp. v. Westinghouse Elec. Corp.,* [1978] 1 All E.R. 434 (H.L. 1977); *Re Raychem Corp. v. Canusa Coating Sys., Inc.,* [1970] 14 D.L.R.3d 684; *Re Radio Corp. of America v. Rauland Corp.,* [1956] 5 D.L.R.2d 424.

117. *Cf.* Court of Appeals (Munich), Petition for Review of an Administrative Ruling under Secs. 23 et seq., EGGVG, Docket Nos. 9 VA 4/80, 9 VA 3/80, *reprinted in* 20 Int'l Leg. Mats. 1025 & 1049 (1981) (decision of West German appellate court under Hague Evidence Convention).

118. Jones, *International Judicial Assistance: Procedural Chaos and a Program for Reform,* 62 Yale L.J. 515, 529-32 (1953); Note, *Taking Evidence Outside of the United States,* 55 B.U.L. Rev. 368, 372-74 (1975).

119. Fed. R. Civ. P. 28(b) provides "Evidence obtained in response to a letter rogatory need not be excluded merely for the reason that it is not a verbatim transcript or that the testimony was not taken under oath or for any similar departure from the requirements of depositions taken within the United States under these rules."

120. *See supra* pp. 843-44.

121. *See* 22 C.F.R. §92.66 (1994); B. Ristau, *International Judicial Assistance* §3-3-3 (1990 Rev.).

122. 28 U.S.C. §1781(a)(2) authorizes the transmittal of letters rogatory to foreign authorities by the Department of State.

123. *See* U.S. Department of State Circular, dated Apr. 13, 1987, on "Obtaining Evidence Abroad"; Note, *Taking Evidence Outside of the United States,* 55 B.U.L. Rev. 368, 374 n.38 (1975).

F. Discovery Abroad Under The Hague Evidence Convention

1. Overview of Hague Evidence Convention

The difficulties that traditionally arose in the execution of U.S. letters rogatory led the United States to undertake efforts to facilitate the transnational taking of evidence. The principal U.S. initiative occurred in the Hague Conference on Private International Law.[124] At the urging of the United States, the Hague Conference negotiated and drafted the Hague Convention on the Taking of Evidence Abroad in Civil or Commercial Matters ("Hague Evidence Convention") between 1968 and 1970.[125] The United States became a party to the Convention in 1972. There are now nearly twenty parties to the Convention, including most Western European nations.[126]

The avowed objective of the Hague Evidence Convention was "to improve mutual judicial cooperation in civil or commercial matters."[127] This required drafting an agreement providing "methods to reconcile the differing legal philosophies of the Civil Law, Common Law, and other systems," as well as "methods to satisfy doctrines of judicial sovereignty."[128] In broad outline, the Convention's drafters sought to accomplish these goals by establishing a "Central Authority" mechanism.

States that ratify the Convention are obliged to designate a "Central Authority." When a court in one member state seeks access to evidence located in another member state, it sends a "letter of request" to the Central Authority for the second state. With limited exceptions, the receiving Central Authority is obliged by the Convention to execute the foreign letters of request that it receives. The receiving

---

124. The Hague Conference on Private International Law is described *supra* pp. 796-97.

125. Commentary on the Hague Evidence Convention includes, *e.g.*, Born & Hoing, *Comity and the Lower Courts: Post-Aerospatiale Applications of the Hague Evidence Convention*, 24 Int'l Law. 393 (1990); Collins, *The Hague Evidence Convention and Discovery: A Serious Misunderstanding?*, 35 Int'l & Comp. L.Q. 765 (1986); Oxman, *The Choice Between Direct Discovery and Other Means of Obtaining Evidence Abroad: The Impact of the Hague Evidence Convention*, 37 U. Miami L. Rev. 733 (1983); Prescott & Alley, *Effective Evidence-Taking Under the Hague Convention*, 22 Int'l Law. 939 (1988); Rogers, *On the Exclusivity of the Hague Evidence Convention*, 21 Tex. Int'l L.J. 441 (1986); B. Ristau, *International Judicial Assistance* §5-1-1 through 5-3-3 (1990 Rev.); Weis, *The Federal Rules and the Hague Conventions: Concerns of Conformity and Comity*, 50 U. Pitt L. Rev. 903 (1989).

126. Parties include Argentina, Barbados, Cyprus, Czechoslovakia, Denmark, Finland, France, Federal Republic of Germany, Israel, Italy, Luxembourg, Mexico, Monaco, Netherlands, Norway, Portugal, Singapore, Sweden, Switzerland, the United Kingdom, and the United States.

127. Hague Convention on the Taking of Evidence Abroad in Civil or Commercial Matters, Mar. 18, 1970; entered into force for the United States October 7, 1972, 23 U.S.T. 2555, T.I.A.S. No. 7444 [hereinafter Hague Evidence Convention]. The Hague Convention is reproduced in Appendix K.

128. Rapport de la Commission Speciale, 4 *Conference de La Haye de droit international prive: Actes et documents de la Onzieme session* 55 (1970) [hereinafter cited as Hague Evidence Convention Negotiating History]. The Hague Evidence Convention Negotiating History is a compilation of reports, questionnaires, drafts, and other communications regarding the Convention, as well as a transcript of certain negotiating sessions.

Central Authority forwards such letters to the appropriate local court for execution, including by coercive means, and the evidence obtained thereunder is then returned to the requesting court.

a. Scope of Convention

The Hague Evidence Convention is subject to a number of significant limitations. First, the Convention is applicable only to the taking of evidence in "civil or commercial" matters. As with the Hague Service Convention, this phrase is not defined in either the Convention or its negotiating history and member states have expressed differing views about the phrase's scope. Thus, the United States and United Kingdom exclude criminal matters from the Convention's coverage, but regard fiscal, administrative, and "public law" proceedings as "civil or commercial."[129] In contrast, most civil law states do not regard fiscal proceedings as within the Convention's scope, and probably have the same view with respect to administrative matters.[130] It is not yet clear how foreign countries will respond to letters of request in cases involving only treble damage claims under the antitrust laws.[131]

Second, the Hague Evidence Convention is limited to requests for assistance made by "judicial" authorities."[132] Some commentators have suggested that this formulation excludes administrative agencies and executive bodies, as well as requests by courts in aid of such entities.[133] The status of certain other proceedings, such as bankruptcy and arbitration, is unclear.[134]

Finally, the Convention is limited to requests "to obtain evidence" or to perform

---

129. Report of U.S. Delegation to the Special Commission on the Operation of the Convention of 18 March 1970 on the Taking of Evidence Abroad in Civil or Commercial Matters, The Hague, The Netherlands, 12-15 June, 1978, 17 Int'l Leg. Mat. 1417 (1978) [hereafter "U.S. Delegation Report"]; *In re the State of Norway*, 28 Int'l Leg. Mat. 693 (House of Lords 1989) (tax assessment proceeding is "civil" matter under both U.K. and Norwegian law); Report on the Work of the Special Commission of April 1989 on the Operation of the Hague Convention of 15 November 1965 on the Service Abroad of Judicial and Extrajudicial Documents in Civil or Commercial Matters and of 18 March 1970 on the Taking of Evidence Abroad in Civil or Commercial Matters [hereinafter "1989 Report on Hague Conventions"], 28 Int'l Leg. Mat. 1556, 1563-65 (1989).

130. *See* U.S. Delegation Report; 1989 Report on Hague Conventions. The 1989 Report on Hague Conventions observed that "a number of experts" would leave it to the requesting State to characterize actions as "civil or commercial." 1989 Report on Hague Conventions at 1559.

131. *See Court of Appeals (Munich) Petition for Review of an Administrative Ruling under Secs. 23 et seq., EGGVG*, Docket Nos. 9 VA 4/80, 9 VA 3180, *reprinted in,* 20 Int'l Leg. Mat. 1025 & 1049 (1981) (rejecting claim that antitrust suit is not "civil or commercial" because U.S. action involved other claims not seeking treble damages). *Compare* the reactions in the past of some foreign Central Authorities to U.S. requests under the Hague Service Convention in cases seeking punitive damages, *supra* pp. 800-01.

132. Hague Evidence Convention, Article 16.

133. B. Ristau, *International Judicial Assistance* §5-1-4 (1990 Rev.).

134. Report on the Second Meeting of the Special Commission on the Operation of the Hague Convention of 18 March 1970 on the Taking of Evidence Abroad in Civil or Commercial Matters, The Hague, The Netherlands July 1985, *reprinted in,* 24 Int'l Leg. Mat. 1668, 1676 (1985) [hereinafter cited as Second U.S. Delegation Report]. *See* 1989 Report on Hague Conventions, 28 Int'l Leg. Mat. 1556, 1563 (1989).

"other judicial act[s]."[135] These phrases are not defined, although the Convention's negotiating history makes it clear that they include oral depositions, the production of documents, and the inspection of property.[136] Moreover, Article 1 of the Convention makes it clear that the Convention applies to requests for assistance even with respect to proceedings that have not commenced.[137] The Convention's coverage of other quasi-judicial acts — such as appointing receivers or conducting conciliation — is unclear.[138]

b. Central Authority Mechanism

The principal means of taking evidence under the Convention is through the "letter of request" procedure provided by Articles 1 through 14. The Convention establishes the framework for this procedure by requiring each member state to designate a "Central Authority."[139] The purpose of the Central Authority is to receive letters of request from courts in other nations and to transmit the foreign requests to the appropriate domestic authorities for execution.[140] Unlike customary letters rogatory, member states are generally *required* by the Convention to execute properly completed letters of request.

Two features of the obligation to execute letters of request are important. First, member states are required to obtain requested evidence by applying the "appropriate measures of compulsion" available under internal law.[141] Thus, the Convention enables U.S. litigants to obtain evidence even if the foreign witness is uncooperative. Second, Article 9 of the Convention provides that letters of request "shall be executed expeditiously." At least in theory, the lengthy delays that letters rogatory encounter should be avoided.[142]

The general obligation of member states to execute letters of request under the Convention is subject to a number of important exceptions. Article 5 of the Convention allows Central Authorities to object to letters of request that do not "comply with the provisions" of the Convention. The objecting state is required to

---

135. Hague Evidence Convention, Article 17. It is clear, however, that the Convention does not apply to requests for the service of process or recognition of judgments, which are the subject of a specific exclusion in Article 1.

136. Hague Evidence Convention Negotiating History 57, 203.

137. Hague Evidence Convention, Article 1 ("judicial proceedings, *commenced or contemplated*") (emphasis added).

138. Hague Evidence Convention Negotiating History at 203.

139. Hague Evidence Convention, Article 2.

140. Article I of the Convention authorizes "a judicial authority of a Contracting State ... in accordance with the provisions of the law of that State" to request evidence-taking by means of a letter of request. After some uncertainty, foreign Central Authorities have generally accepted the proposition that U.S. law authorizes attorneys to act as "judicial authorities" in preparing letters of request.

141. Hague Evidence Convention, Article 10. The requested state is only obliged to apply the same degree of compulsion in responding to letters of request as is available in domestic actions. Thus, if compulsory process would not be available in purely domestic proceedings, then the receiving court need not use compulsion in attempting to execute a letter of request under the Convention.

142. Practical experience under the Convention suggests that between three and ten months are generally required for the execution of letters of request.

notify the requesting state promptly of its objections. Among the grounds for objection are failure of a letter of request to fall within the scope of Article 1 of the Convention or failure of a letter of request to satisfy the language or information requirements of Articles 3 and 4.[143]

Exception

Article 12 of the Convention permits a receiving state to refuse to execute requests seeking the performance of non-judicial functions or that the receiving state considers would prejudice its "sovereignty or security." Although other international agreements have used the "sovereignty or security" formula,[144] there has been little experience with the exception. The leading decision was in 1978, when the House of Lords concluded that the phrase could be properly invoked by the United Kingdom to refuse execution of a U.S. request for information in the Westinghouse uranium antitrust litigation. The House of Lords reasoned that "[i]t is axiomatic that in antitrust matters the policy of one state may be to defend what it is the policy of another state to attack."[145]

c. Article 23's Exception for Pretrial Document Requests

One of the Convention's exceptions to the obligation to execute letters of request is of special importance to U.S. litigants. Under Article 23, member states are given the option to declare that they "will not execute Letters of Request issued for the purpose of obtaining pretrial discovery of documents as known in Common Law countries." With the exception of Czechoslovakia, Israel, and the United States, all member states to the Convention have entered Article 23 declarations. A number of these declarations flatly provide that the declaring State will execute no letter of request seeking pretrial discovery.[146] Several other member states have made more limited Article 23 declarations, which refuse execution of requests for "pretrial discovery" except as to requests for specified documents or classes of documents.[147]

Article 23 severely limits the value of the Convention to U.S. litigants by permitting member states to refuse to execute a large category of U.S. requests for the pro-

---

143. "Any difficulties which may arise between Contracting States in connection with the operation of the Convention shall be settled through diplomatic channels." Hague Evidence Convention, Article 36.

144. *E.g.*, 1 Am. J. Comp. L. 282 (1952) (1954 Hague Civil Procedure Convention); Hague Service Convention; *supra* p. 798.

145. *Rio Tinto Zinc Corp. v. Westinghouse Elec. Corp.*, [1978] 1 All E.R. 434, 448. Several members of the House of Lords also emphasized that the U.S. antitrust investigation involved the extraterritorial application of U.S. law to conduct in the United Kingdom. Article 12 provides that execution cannot be refused solely because a receiving state does not recognize a particular cause of action or claims exclusive subject-matter jurisdiction over the subject matter of the action. The interplay of this provision with Article 12's "sovereignty or security" exception is not entirely clear, particularly in the light of the House of Lords' decision in *Westinghouse*.

146. These states currently include France, Germany, Luxembourg, Norway, and Portugal.

147. Nations with comparatively limited Article 23 declarations include the United Kingdom, Denmark, Finland, Sweden, and Singapore. The United Kingdom's Article 23 declaration provides that no letter of request seeking pretrial discovery will be executed if the request requires a person to (1) state what documents relevant to the foreign proceeding are in his control; or (2) produce any document other than particular documents specified in the letter of request.

duction of documents. The drafters of the Hague Evidence Convention included Article 23 at the United Kingdom's suggestion. Although the Convention's negotiating history contains relatively little discussion of the provision,[148] subsequent events indicate the reasoning underlying Article 23. In adopting Article 23, the United Kingdom and at least some other countries wished to ensure that they would not be obliged to assist U.S. "fishing expeditions" into the files of local companies. Moreover, it appears that civil law states, at least in part, misunderstood the purposes of U.S. discovery. Subsequent discussions among the Convention's member states suggested that most civil law states believed that U.S. pretrial discovery is permitted before initiation of any legal proceedings and can be used to build a case that subsequently may be filed. Clarifications of the role of pretrial discovery by U.S. authorities have alleviated some, but not all, civil law concerns. As a consequence, several foreign states have limited the scope of their Article 23 reservations.[149]

Article 23 allows refusals to execute letters of request only for "pretrial discovery of documents." Thus, Article 23 does not purport to affect methods of discovery other than requests for document production (*i.e.*, depositions or interrogatories) or the examination of documents for purposes other than pretrial discovery (*i.e.*, for production as evidence at trial). Nonetheless, as a practical matter, foreign law and practice determine the extent to which foreign courts will execute U.S. letters of request.[150] Because of the considerable differences between U.S. and civil law discovery, U.S. litigants not infrequently encounter foreign resistance to their letters of request.[151]

Even in England, where common law discovery rules are not dissimilar to U.S. procedures, Article 23 significantly restricts the value of the Hague Evidence Convention to U.S. litigants. In *In re Asbestos Insurance*[152], the House of Lords held that the United Kingdom's Article 23 reservation and the Evidence (Procedure in Other Jurisdictions) Act 1975 imposed strict limits on the assistance that English courts would provide under the Hague Evidence Convention. First, the House of Lords emphasized that "mere 'fishing' expeditions" would not be permitted.[153] Second, only "separately described" documents could be obtained: "an order for production of the respondent's 'monthly bank statements for the year 1984 relating to his current account' with a named bank would satisfy the requirements. ... But a general request for 'all the respondent's bank statements for 1984' would in my view

---

148. Hague Evidence Convention Negotiating History at 204.

149. *See Aerospatiale*, 482 U.S. at 536-37, 563-64.

150. Hague Evidence Convention, Article 9 (discussed *infra* at pp. 901-02).

151. *See Rio Tinto Zinc Corp. v. Westinghouse Elec. Corp.*, [1978] 1 All E.R. 434, (H.L. 1977), *reprinted in* 17 Int'l Leg. Mat. 38 (1978); Appeal of ITT (Opinion and Judgment of October 31, 1980, Docket No. 9 VA 3/80), *reprinted in* 20 Int'l Leg. Mat. 1049 (1981) (Germany); Appeal of Siemens Siecor and Individual Corporate Officers (Opinion and Judgment of November 27, 1980), *reprinted in,* 20 Int'l Leg. Mat. 1025 (1981) (Germany).

152. [1985] 1 W.L.R. 331 (House of Lords).

153. [1985] 1 W.L.R. at 337.

refer to a class of documents and would not be admissible."[154] Third, the documents requested "must be actual documents, about which there is evidence which has satisfied the judge that they exist, or at least that they did exist..."[155] Limitations on the scope of discovery in civil law states can be even more restrictive.[156]

d. Alternative Methods of Taking Evidence Pursuant to the Hague Evidence Convention

In drafting the Hague Evidence Convention, the United States was anxious to maximize the flexibility for taking evidence abroad. The Convention was drafted to include provisions permitting specified alternative methods of taking evidence which go beyond the basic Central Authority mechanism.[157] Unlike the Central Authority mechanism, however, these alternatives cannot be used without the approval (or acquiescence) of the receiving state and they do not ordinarily permit the use of compulsion to obtain evidence. In order to determine whether these alternatives are available in particular cases, counsel must consult the accessions of individual member states to the Convention.[158]

Article 15 authorizes consuls (*i.e.*, certain diplomatic representatives of one nation stationed in a second country) to take evidence from nationals of the consul's home state. This right is subject to three important limitations: (1) the consul cannot use compulsion to require the giving of evidence; (2) each member state may declare that consuls may take evidence only after obtaining permission to do so from the appropriate local authorities;[159] and (3) the consul may take evidence only for use in proceedings actually "commenced" (as opposed to merely "contemplated," *cf.* Article 1) in his or her home state.

Article 16 authorizes consuls to take evidence from nationals of the state where the consuls are stationed. Evidence-taking under Article 16 is subject to somewhat stricter limits than those under Article 15: (1) no compulsion may be used; (2) evidence can be taken only for proceedings that are actually commenced in the consul's home state; and (3) prior approval of the appropriate local authorities must be obtained in individual cases, unless the host state has affirmatively filed a declaration generally permitting Article 16 evidence-taking.[160]

Article 17 authorizes "commissioners" to take evidence within the receiving

---

154. [1985] 1 W.L.R. at 337-38.

155. [1985] 1 W.L.R. at 338.

156. *See supra* pp. 847-49.

157. Hague Evidence Convention, Articles 15-17.

158. Excerpted accessions of some Hague Evidence Convention parties are contained in Appendix L. The complete accessions of all Convention parties are contained at 28 U.S.C.A. §1781 (note) (1994).

159. Denmark, Norway, Portugal, and Sweden have filed declarations requiring foreign consuls to obtain prior approval of evidence-taking under Article 15.

160. Only the United States and Finland have permitted Article 16 evidence-taking without prior approval. The United Kingdom and Czechoslovakia permit evidence-taking under Article 16 without prior approval only on the basis of reciprocity.

state,[161] but only subject to limitations equivalent to those imposed by Article 16: (1) no compulsion may be used; (2) evidence may be taken only for use in proceedings actually commenced in the courts of a member state; and (3) prior approval of the appropriate local authorities must be obtained in individual cases, unless the host state has filed a declaration generally permitting Article 17 evidence-taking. Commissioners must be appointed by a judicial authority of the requesting state, and not by a private body or executive authority (*e.g.*, an arbitral institution or a consul).

Persons taking evidence under Article 15, 16, or 17 are specifically authorized to administer oaths and to take any form of evidence that is not "incompatible with the law of the State where the evidence is taken or contrary to any permission granted" to the person taking the evidence.[162] Article 21 also establishes various procedural requirements for evidence-taking under Articles 15, 16, and 17. These include a requirement that persons from whom evidence is taken (except for nationals of the requesting state) be provided with a request in the language of the host state and that the request inform the recipient that he or she is entitled to legal representation and is not under any compulsion to appear.[163] In addition, persons giving evidence under Articles 15 through 17 are entitled to invoke the same privileges and immunities as those authorized by Article 11 in connection with letters of request. The accessions of a number of signatories to the Convention provide important elaboration to these conditions.[164]

Although evidence-taking pursuant to Articles 15, 16, and 17 must ordinarily be conducted without compulsion, Article 18 permits member states to declare that foreign consuls and commissioners may seek coercive orders from local authorities to compel the giving of evidence.[165] Finally, any member state making a declaration under Article 15, 16, or 17, or granting a specific permission under these provisions, may attach whatever conditions it deems fit to the declaration or permission.[166]

e. Execution of Letters of Request

The execution of letters of request under the Convention ordinarily occurs according to the judicial procedures of the receiving state. Article 9 states this general principle: "The judicial authority which executes a Letter of Request shall apply its own law as to the methods and procedures to be followed." The use of local judicial

---

161. Commissioners are persons authorized by court order to preside over the taking of evidence in specified circumstances. The practice of appointing commissioners is a familiar procedure for taking depositions abroad under Fed. R. Civ. P. 28(b). *See supra* pp. 866-70. At least in common law countries, commissioners are ordinarily entitled to exercise compulsion to require the giving of discovery. Article 17 of the Convention precludes the use of compulsion by commissioners.

162. Hague Evidence Convention, Article 21(a).

163. Hague Evidence Convention, Article 21(b) & (c).

164. *See* Appendix L & *supra* note 158.

165. Only the United States has filed an unconditional declaration under Article 18, although the United Kingdom and Czechoslovakia have declared that they will permit requests for compulsion on a reciprocal basis.

166. Hague Evidence Convention, Article 19.

procedures in executing letters of request obviously has important practical consequences.

As described above, judicial procedures in civil law nations differ significantly
from those in the United States. In many states, the judge (and not counsel) conducts the examination of witnesses.[167] In some states, counsel may attend the examination and suggest questions; in others, examinations may be closed to counsel. In
addition, "counsel" in some countries refers only to local counsel; U.S. counsel may
be unable to participate in, or sometimes even attend, evidence-taking sessions.
Moreover, in many civil law countries the examination of witnesses is not under oath
and is recorded in a summary prepared by the judge rather than in a verbatim transcript.

Because of differences among methods of evidence-taking, Article 9 requires
receiving states to follow a "special method or procedure" for evidence-taking if
requested by the applicant. Under this provision, U.S. attorneys can request permission to take verbatim transcripts of witnesses' testimony, to participate in questioning, to allow cross-examination, and the like.[168] The requirement that "special"
methods be used is subject to two important exceptions: receiving states' judicial
authorities need not follow a procedure that (1) "is incompatible with the internal
law of the state of execution"; or (2) "is impossible of performance by reason of its
internal practice and procedure or by reason of practical difficulties." In practice,
foreign authorities appear generally to have accommodated most requests by U.S.
counsel.[169]

Article 10 governs the use of compulsion against witnesses who refuse to provide
evidence sought by a proper letter of request. As noted earlier, receiving states are
obligated in these circumstances to use coercive process to obtain the requested evidence. This obligation is subject to two limitations. First, any compulsion must be
"appropriate." Second, the receiving state is only required to use the type of compulsion (if any) that its domestic law provides for analogous internal proceedings.

2. "Exclusivity" of the Hague Evidence Convention: Aerospatiale

The Hague Evidence Convention has been the subject of frequent litigation in
the United States, most often over the extent to which U.S. litigants are required to
use the Convention's procedures exclusively instead of resorting to the more customary route of direct U.S. discovery of information located abroad. Lower courts
initially reached divergent conclusions as to the Convention's exclusivity.

---

167. *See supra* pp. 847-49.

168. For descriptions of how these provisions operate in practice, *see* Collins, *Opportunities for and
Obstacles to Obtaining Evidence in England for Use in Litigation in the United States*, 17 Int'l Law. 27 (1983);
Platto, *Taking Evidence Abroad for Use in Civil Cases in the United States — A Practical Guide*, 16 Int'l Law.
575 (1982).

169. 1989 Report on Hague Conventions, 28 Int'l Leg. Mat. 1562 (1989); Second U.S. Delegation
Report, 24 Int'l Leg. Mat. 1668, 1674-75 (1985); U.S. Delegation Report, 17 Int'l Leg. Mat. 1425, 1431
(1978).

Some courts concluded that Convention procedures had to be used in the first instance when a U.S. litigant sought to compel a party to produce documents, answer interrogatories, or make witnesses available from abroad.[170] Other courts ruled that the Convention was optional, at least where the U.S. court ordered that the formal production of the requested information take place on U.S. soil (*i.e.*, the deposition in the United States of a deponent who has traveled to this country or the production in the United States of documents transported here from abroad).[171] Finally, at least one court ruled that the Convention provided the exclusive means for obtaining evidence located in signatory countries; according to this decision, U.S. courts could not directly order discovery from signatory countries even if Convention procedures proved unavailing.[172] This conflict was resolved in *Aerospatiale*, excerpted below.

SOCIETE NATIONALE INDUSTRIELLE AEROSPATIALE v. U.S. DISTRICT COURT

482 U.S. 522 (1987)

JUSTICE STEVENS. The United States, the Republic of France, and 15 other Nations have acceded to the Hague [Evidence] Convention. This Convention ... prescribes certain procedures by which a judicial authority in one contracting State may request evidence located in another contracting State. The question presented in this case concerns the extent to which a Federal District Court must employ the procedures set forth in the Convention when litigants seek answers to interrogatories, the production of documents, and admissions from a French adversary over whom the court has personal jurisdiction.

The two petitioners are corporations owned by the Republic of France.[173] They are engaged in the business of designing, manufacturing, and marketing aircraft. One of their planes, the "Rallye," was allegedly advertised in American aviation publications as "the World's safest and most economical STOL plane." On August 19, 1980, a Rallye crashed in Iowa, injuring the pilot and a passenger. Dennis Jones, John George, and Rosa George brought separate suits based upon this accident in the United States District Court for the Southern District of Iowa, alleging that petition-

---

170. *See, e.g., Gebr. Eickhoff Maschinenfabrik und Eisengießerei Mott v. Starcher*, 328 S.E.2d 492 (W. Va. 1985); *Th. Goldschmidt AG v. Smith*, 676 S.W.2d 443 (Tex. Ct. App. 1984); *Vincent v. Ateliers de la Motobecane, SA*, 475 A.2d 686 (N.J. Super. 1984); *Pierburg GmbH & Co. KG v. Superior Court*, 186 Cal. Rptr. 876 (1982).

171. *See, e.g., In re Messerschmitt Bolkow Blohm, GmbH*, 757 F.2d 729 (5th Cir. 1985), *vacated*, 483 U.S. 1002 (1987); *In re Anschuetz & Co., GmbH*, 754 F.2d 602 (5th Cir. 1985), *vacated*, 483 U.S. 1002 (1987); *International Society for Krishna Consciousness v. Lee*, 105 F.R.D. 435 (S.D.N.Y. 1984); *Cooper Indus. v. British Aerospace*, 102 F.R.D. 918 (S.D.N.Y. 1984).

172. *See Cuisinarts v. Robot Coupe, SA*, No. CV 80 0050083C (Conn. Super. Ct. July 22, 1982).

173. Petitioner Societe Nationale Industrielle Aerospatiale is wholly owned by the Government of France. Petitioner Societe de Construction d'Avions de Tourisme is a wholly-owned subsidiary of Societe Nationale Industrielle Aerospatiale.

ers had manufactured and sold a defective plane and that they were guilty of negligence and breach of warranty. Petitioners answered the complaints, apparently without questioning the jurisdiction of the District Court... .

[After initially complying with plaintiffs' discovery requests, defendants subsequently resisted production. Among other things, defendants argued that the French "blocking statute"[174] forbade compliance with the U.S. discovery requests and that the Hague Evidence Convention provided the exclusive means of obtaining discovery of evidence located in France. The trial court rejected both arguments and defendants appealed. The Court of Appeals for the Eighth Circuit held that "when the district court has jurisdiction over a foreign litigant the Hague Convention does not apply to the production of evidence in that litigant's possession, even though the documents and information sought may physically be located within the territory of a foreign signatory to the Convention."]

Petitioners correctly assert that both the discovery rules set forth in the Federal Rules of Civil Procedure and the Hague Convention are the law of the United States. This observation, however, does not dispose of the question before us; we must analyze the interaction between these two bodies of federal law. Initially, we note that at least four different interpretations of the relationship between the federal discovery rules and the Hague Convention are possible. Two of these interpretations assume that the Hague Convention by its terms dictates the extent to which it supplants normal discovery rules. First, the Hague Convention might be read as requiring its use to the exclusion of any other discovery procedures whenever evidence located abroad is sought for use in an American court. Second, the Hague Convention might be interpreted to require first, but not exclusive, use of its procedures. Two other interpretations assume that international comity, rather than the obligations created by the treaty, should guide judicial resort to the Hague Convention. Third, then, the Convention might be viewed as establishing a supplemental set of discovery procedures, strictly optional under treaty law, to which concerns of comity nevertheless require first resort by American courts in all cases. Fourth, the treaty may be viewed as an undertaking among sovereigns to facilitate discovery to which an American court should resort when it deems that course of action appropriate, after considering the situations of the parties before it as well as the interests of the concerned foreign state.

In interpreting an international treaty, we are mindful that it is "in the nature of a contract between nations," *Trans World Airlines, Inc. v. Franklin Mint Corp.*, 466 U.S. 243, 253 (1984), to which "[g]eneral rules of construction apply." We therefore begin "with the text of the treaty and the context in which the written words are used." *Air France v. Saks*, 470 U.S. 392, 397 (1985). The treaty's history, "'the negotiations, and the practical construction adopted by the parties'" may also be relevant.

We reject the first two of the possible interpretations as inconsistent with the

---

174. [The French blocking statute is excerpted above at pp. 853-54.]

language and negotiating history of the Hague Convention. The Preamble of the Convention specifies its purpose "to facilitate the transmission and execution of Letters of Request" and to "improve mutual judicial cooperation in civil or commercial matters." The Preamble does not speak in mandatory terms which would purport to describe the procedures for all permissible transnational discovery and exclude all other existing practices.[175] The text of the Evidence Convention itself does not modify the law of any contracting State, require any contracting State to use the Convention procedures, either in requesting evidence or in responding to such requests, or compel any contracting State to change its own evidence-gathering procedures.

The Convention contains three chapters. Chapter I, entitled "Letters of Requests," and Chapter II, entitled "Taking of Evidence by Diplomatic Officers, Consular Agents and Commissioners," both use permissive rather than mandatory language. Thus, Article 1 provides that a judicial authority in one contracting State "may" forward a letter of request to the competent authority in another contracting State for the purpose of obtaining evidence. Similarly, Articles 15, 16, and 17 provide that diplomatic officers, consular agents, and commissioners "may ... without compulsion," take evidence under certain conditions. The absence of any command that a contracting State must use Convention procedures when they are not needed is conspicuous.

[In addition,] Article 23 expressly authorizes a contracting State to declare that it will not execute any letter of request in aid of pretrial discovery in a common law country. Surely, if the Convention had been intended to replace completely the broad discovery powers that the common law courts in the United States previously exercised over foreign litigants subject to their jurisdiction, it would have been most anomalous for the common law contracting Parties to agree to Article 23, which enables a contracting Party to revoke its consent to the treaty's procedures for pretrial discovery. In the absence of explicit textual support, we are unable to accept the hypothesis that the common law contracting States abjured recourse to all preexisting discovery procedures at the same time that they accepted the possibility that a contracting Party could unilaterally abrogate even the Convention's procedures. Moreover, Article 27 plainly states that the Convention does not prevent a contracting State from using more liberal methods of rendering evidence than those authorized by the Convention. Thus, the text of the Evidence Convention, as well as the history of its proposal and ratification by the United States, unambiguously supports the conclusion that it was intended to establish optional procedures that would facilitate the taking of evidence abroad... . We conclude accordingly that the Hague Convention did not deprive the District Court of the jurisdiction it otherwise pos-

---

175. The Hague Conference on Private International Law's omission of mandatory language in the preamble is particularly significant in light of the same body's use of mandatory language in the Preamble to the Hague Service Convention.

sessed to order a foreign national party before it to produce evidence physically located within a signatory nation.[176]

While the Hague Convention does not divest the District Court of jurisdiction to order discovery under the Federal Rules of Civil Procedure, the optional character of the Convention procedures sheds light on one aspect of the Court of Appeals' opinion that we consider erroneous. That court concluded that the Convention simply "does not apply" to discovery sought from a foreign litigant that is subject to the jurisdiction of an American court. Plaintiffs argue that this conclusion is supported by two considerations. First, the Federal Rules of Civil Procedure provide ample means for obtaining discovery from parties who are subject to the court's jurisdiction, while before the Convention was ratified it was often extremely difficult, if not impossible, to obtain evidence from nonparty witnesses abroad. Plaintiffs contend that it is appropriate to construe the Convention as applying only in the area in which improvement was badly needed. Second, when a litigant is subject to the jurisdiction of the District Court, arguably the evidence it is required to produce is not "abroad" within the meaning of the Convention, even though it is in fact located in a foreign country at the time of the discovery request and even though it will have to be gathered or otherwise prepared abroad.

Nevertheless, the text of the Convention draws no distinction between evidence obtained from third parties and that obtained from the litigants themselves; nor does it purport to draw any sharp line between evidence that is "abroad" and evidence that is within the control of a party subject to the jurisdiction of the requesting court. Thus, it appears clear to us that the optional Convention procedures are available whenever they will facilitate the gathering of evidence by the means authorized in the Convention. Although these procedures are not mandatory, the Hague Convention does "apply" to the production of evidence in a litigant's possession in the sense that it is one method of seeking evidence that a court may elect to employ.

---

176. The opposite conclusion of exclusivity would create three unacceptable asymmetries. First, within any lawsuit between a national of the United States and a national of another contracting Party, the foreign party could obtain discovery under the Federal Rules of Civil Procedure, while the domestic party would be required to resort first to the procedures of the Hague Convention. This imbalance would run counter to the fundamental maxim of discovery that "[m]utual knowledge of all the relevant facts gathered by both parties is essential to proper litigation." *Hickman v. Taylor*, 329 U.S. 495, 507 (1947).

Second, a rule of exclusivity would enable a company which is a citizen of another contracting State to compete with a domestic company on uneven terms, since the foreign company would be subject to less extensive discovery procedures in the event that both companies were sued in an American court. Petitioners made a voluntary decision to market their products in the United States. They are entitled to compete on equal terms with other companies operating in this market. But since the District Court unquestionably has personal jurisdiction over petitioners, they are subject to the same legal constraints, including the burdens associated with American juridical procedures, as their American competitors. A general rule according foreign nationals a preferred position in pretrial proceedings in our courts would conflict with the principle of equal opportunity that governs the market they elected to enter.

Third, since a rule of first use of the Hague Convention would apply to cases in which a foreign party is a national of a contracting State, but not to cases in which a foreign party is a national of any other foreign state, the rule would confer an unwarranted advantage on some domestic litigants over others similarly situated.

Petitioners contend that even if the Hague Convention's procedures are not mandatory, this Court should adopt a rule requiring that American litigants first resort to those procedures before initiating any discovery pursuant to the normal methods of the Federal Rules of Civil Procedure. The Court of Appeals rejected this argument because it was convinced that an American court's order ultimately requiring discovery that a foreign court had refused under Convention procedures would constitute "the greatest insult" to the sovereignty of that tribunal. We disagree with the Court of Appeals' view. It is well known that the scope of American discovery is often significantly broader than is permitted in other jurisdictions, and we are satisfied that foreign tribunals will recognize that the final decision on the evidence to be used in litigation conducted in American courts must be made by those courts. We therefore do not believe that an American court should refuse to make use of Convention procedures because of a concern that it may ultimately find it necessary to order the production of evidence that a foreign tribunal permitted a party to withhold.

Nevertheless, we cannot accept petitioners' invitation to announce a new rule of law that would require first resort to Convention procedures whenever discovery is sought from a foreign litigant. Assuming, without deciding, that we have the lawmaking power to do so, we are convinced that such a general rule would be unwise. In many situations the Letter of Request procedure authorized by the Convention would be unduly time consuming and expensive, as well as less certain to produce needed evidence than direct use of the Federal Rules.[177] A rule of first resort in all cases would therefore be inconsistent with the overriding interest in the "just, speedy, and inexpensive determination" of litigation in our courts. *See* Fed. Rule Civ. Proc. 1.

Petitioners argue that a rule of first resort is necessary to accord respect to the sovereignty of states in which evidence is located. It is true that the process of obtaining evidence in a civil law jurisdiction is normally conducted by a judicial officer rather than by private attorneys. Petitioners contend that if performed on French soil, for example, by an unauthorized person, such evidence-gathering might violate the "judicial sovereignty" of the host nation. Because it is only through the Convention that civil law nations have given their consent to evidence-gathering activities within their borders, petitioners argue, we have a duty to employ those procedures whenever they are available. We find that argument unpersuasive. If such a duty were to be inferred from the adoption of the Convention itself, we believe it would have been described in the text of that document. Moreover, the concept of

---

177. We observe, however, that in other instances a litigant's first use of the Hague Convention procedures can be expected to yield more evidence abroad more promptly than use of the normal procedures governing pretrial civil discovery. In those instances, the calculations of the litigant will naturally lead to a first-use strategy.

international comity[178] requires in this context a more particularized analysis of the respective interests of the foreign nation and the requesting nation than petitioners' proposed general rule would generate.[179] We therefore decline to hold as a blanket matter that comity requires resort to Hague Evidence Convention procedures without prior scrutiny in each case of the particular facts, sovereign interests, and likelihood that resort to those procedures will prove effective.[180]

Some discovery procedures are much more "intrusive" than others. In this case, for example, an interrogatory asking petitioners to identify the pilots who flew flight tests in the Rallye before it was certified for flight by the Federal Aviation Administration, or a request to admit that petitioners authorized certain advertising in a particular magazine, is certainly less intrusive than a request to produce all of the "design specifications, line drawings and engineering plans and all engineering change orders and plans and all drawings concerning the leading edge slats for the

---

178. Comity refers to the spirit of cooperation in which a domestic tribunal approaches the resolution of cases touching the laws and interests of over sovereign states. This Court referred to the doctrine of comity among nations in *Emory v. Grenough*, 3 Dall. 369, 370, n. (1797) (dismissing appeal from judgment for failure to plead diversity of citizenship, but setting forth an extract from a treatise by Ulrich Huber (1636-1694), a Dutch jurist):

> By the courtesy of nations, whatever laws are carried into execution, within the limits of any government, are considered as having the same effect everywhere, so far as they do not occasion a prejudice to the rights of the other governments, or their citizens ... [n]othing would be more inconvenient in the promiscuous intercourse and practice of mankind, than that what was valid by the laws of one place, should be rendered of no effect elsewhere, by a diversity of law.... . [*Id.*, at 370, n. (quoting 2 Huberus, B.I., Tit. 3, p. 26).]

See also Hilton v. Guyot, 159 U.S. 113, 163-164 (1895).... .

179. The nature of the concerns that guide a comity analysis are suggested by the *Restatement of Foreign Relations Law (Revised)* §437(1)(c) (Tent. Draft No. 7, 1986) (approved May 14, 1986). [This section is numbered §442 in the final draft of the Restatement.] While we recognize that §437 of the Restatement may not represent a consensus of international views on the scope of the District Court's power to order foreign discovery in the face of objections of foreign states, these factors are relevant to any comity analysis.... .

180. The French "blocking statute" does not alter our conclusion. It is well-settled that such statutes do not deprive an American court of the power to order a party subject to its jurisdiction to produce evidence even though the act of production may violate that statute. *See Societe Internationale Pour*, 357 U.S. at 204-06. Nor can the enactment of such a statute by a foreign nation require American courts to engraft a rule of first resort onto the Hague Convention, or otherwise to provide the nationals of such a country with a preferred status in our courts. It is clear that American courts are not required to adhere blindly to the directives of such a statute. Indeed, the language of the statute, if taken literally, would appear to represent an extraordinary exercise of legislative jurisdiction by the Republic of France over a United States District Judge, forbidding him or her from ordering any discovery from a party of French nationality, even simple requests for admissions or interrogatories that the party could respond to on the basis of personal knowledge. It would be particularly incongruous to recognize such a preference for corporations that are wholly owned by the enacting nation. Extraterritorial assertions of jurisdiction are not one-sided. While the District Court's discovery orders arguably have some impact in France, the French blocking statute asserts similar authority over acts to take place in this country. The lesson of comity is that neither the discovery order nor the blocking statute can have the same omnipresent effect that it would have in a world of only one sovereign. The blocking statute thus is relevant to the court's particularized comity analysis only to the extent that its terms and its enforcement identify the nature of the sovereign interests in nondisclosure of specific kinds of material.

Rallye type aircraft manufactured by the Defendants." Even if a court might be persuaded that a particular document request was too burdensome or too "intrusive" to be granted in full, with or without an appropriate protective order, it might well refuse to insist upon the use of Convention procedures before requiring responses to simple interrogatories or requests for admissions. The exact line between reasonableness and unreasonableness in each case must be drawn by the trial court, based on its knowledge of the case and of the claims and interests of the parties and the governments whose statutes and policies they invoke.

American courts, in supervising pretrial proceedings, should exercise special vigilance to protect foreign litigants from the danger that unnecessary, or unduly burdensome, discovery may place them in a disadvantageous position. Judicial supervision of discovery should always seek to minimize its costs and inconvenience and to prevent improper uses of discovery requests. When it is necessary to seek evidence abroad, however, the District Court must supervise pretrial proceedings particularly closely to prevent discovery abuses. For example, the additional cost of transportation of documents or witnesses to or from foreign locations may increase the danger that discovery may be sought for the improper purpose of motivating settlement, rather than finding relevant and probative evidence. Objections to "abusive" discovery that foreign litigants advance should therefore receive the most careful consideration. In addition, we have long recognized the demands of comity in suits involving foreign states, either as parties or as sovereigns with a coordinate interest in the litigation. See *Hilton v. Guyot*, 159 U.S. 113 (1895). American courts should therefore take care to demonstrate due respect for any special problem confronted by the foreign litigant on account of its nationality or the location of its operations, and for any sovereign interest expressed by a foreign state. We do not articulate specific rules to guide this delicate task of adjudication.

In the case before us, the Magistrate and the Court of Appeals correctly refused to grant the broad protective order that petitioners requested. The Court of Appeals erred, however, in stating that the Evidence Convention does not apply to the pending discovery demands. This holding may be read as indicating that the Convention procedures are not even an option that is open to the District Court. It must be recalled, however, that the Convention's specification of duties in executing States creates corresponding rights in requesting States; holding that the Convention does not apply in this situation would deprive domestic litigants of access to evidence through treaty procedures to which the contracting States have assented. Moreover, such a rule would deny the foreign litigant a full and fair opportunity to demonstrate appropriate reasons for employing Convention procedures in the first instance, for some aspects of discovery process.

Dissent

JUSTICE BLACKMUN, with whom JUSTICE BRENNAN, JUSTICE MARSHALL, and JUSTICE O'CONNOR join, concurring in part and dissenting in part. Some might well regard the Court's decision in this case as an affront to the nations that have joined the United States in ratifying the Hague Convention.... The Court ignores the importance of the Convention by relegating it to an "optional" status, without acknowledging the significant achievement in accommodating divergent interests that the Convention represents. Experience to date indicates that there is a large risk that the case-by-case comity analysis now to be permitted by the Court will be performed inadequately and that the somewhat unfamiliar procedures of the Convention will be invoked infrequently. I fear the Court's decision means that courts will resort unnecessarily to issuing discovery orders under the Federal Rules of Civil Procedure in a raw exercise of their jurisdictional power to the detriment of the United States' national and international interests. The Court's view of this country's international obligations is particularly unfortunate in a world in which regular commercial and legal channels loom ever more crucial.

I do agree with the Court's repudiation of the positions at both extremes of the spectrum with regard to the use of the Convention. Its rejection of the view that the Convention is not "applicable" at all to this case is surely correct: the Convention clearly applies to litigants as well as to third parties, and to requests for evidence located abroad, no matter where that evidence is actually "produced." The Court also correctly rejects the far opposite position that the Convention provides the *exclusive* means for discovery involving signatory countries. I dissent, however, because I cannot endorse the Court's case-by-case inquiry for determining whether to use Convention procedures and its failure to provide lower courts with any meaningful guidance for carrying out that inquiry. In my view, the Convention provides effective discovery procedures that largely eliminate the conflicts between United States and foreign law on evidence gathering. I therefore would apply a general presumption that, in most cases, courts should resort first to the Convention procedures. An individualized analysis of the circumstances of a particular case is appropriate only when it appears that it would be futile to employ the Convention or when its procedures prove to be unhelpful.... .

By viewing the Convention as merely optional and leaving the decision whether to apply it to the court in each individual case, the majority ignores the policies established by the political branches when they negotiated and ratified the treaty. The result will be a duplicative analysis for which courts are not well designed. The discovery process usually concerns discrete interests that a court is well equipped to accommodate — the interests of the parties before the court coupled with the interest of the judicial system in resolving the conflict on the basis of the best available information. When a lawsuit requires discovery of materials located in a foreign nation, however, foreign legal systems and foreign interests are implicated as well. The presence of these interests creates a tension between the broad discretion our courts normally exercise in managing pretrial discovery and the discretion usually allotted to the Executive in foreign matters....

Not only is the question of foreign discovery more appropriately considered by the Executive and Congress, but in addition, courts are generally ill equipped to assume the role of balancing the interests of foreign nations with that of our own.

Although transnational litigation is increasing, relatively few judges are experienced in the area and the procedures of foreign legal systems are often poorly understood. As this Court recently stated, it has "little competence in determining precisely when foreign nations will be offended by particular acts." *Container Corp. v. Franchise Tax Bd.*, 463 U.S. 159, 194 (1983). A pro-forum bias is likely to creep into the supposedly neutral balancing process and courts not surprisingly often will turn to the more familiar procedures established by their local rules. In addition, it simply is not reasonable to expect the Federal Government or the foreign state in which the discovery will take place to participate in every individual case in order to articulate the broader international and foreign interests that are relevant to the decision whether to use the Convention. ... Exacerbating these shortcomings is the limited appellate review of interlocutory discovery decisions, which prevents any effective case-by-case correction of erroneous discovery decisions.

The principle of comity leads to more definite rules than the ad hoc approach endorsed by the majority. ... Comity is not just a vague political concern favoring international cooperation when it is in our interest to do so. Rather it is a principle under which judicial decisions reflect the systemic value of reciprocal tolerance and goodwill. As in the choice-of-law analysis, which from the very beginning has been linked to international comity, the threshold question in a comity analysis is whether there is in fact a true conflict between domestic and foreign law. When there is a conflict, a court should seek a reasonable accommodation that reconciles the central concerns of both sets of laws. In doing so, it should perform a tripartite analysis that considers the foreign interests, the interests of the United States, and the mutual interests of all nations in a smoothly functioning international legal regime. [Under this analysis, U.S. courts should ordinarily require first use of the Convention.] ...

There are, however, some situations in which there is legitimate concern that certain documents cannot be made available under Convention procedures. Thirteen nations have made official declarations pursuant to Article 23 of the Convention, which permits a contracting state to limit its obligation to produce documents in response to a letter of request. These reservations may pose problems that would require a comity analysis in an individual case, but they are not so all-encompassing as the majority implies — they certainly do not mean that a "contracting Party could unilaterally abrogate the Convention's procedures." First, the reservations can apply only to *letters of request for documents*. Thus, an Article 23 reservation affects neither the most commonly used informal Convention procedures for taking of evidence by a consul or a commissioner nor formal requests for depositions or interrogatories. Second, although Article 23 refers broadly to "pretrial discovery," the intended meaning of the term appears to have been much narrower than, the normal United States usage. The contracting parties for the most part have modified the declarations made pursuant to Article 23 to limit their reach. Indeed, the emerging view of this exception to discovery is that it applies only to "requests that lack sufficient specificity or that have not been reviewed for relevancy by the requesting court." Thus, in practice, a reservation is not the significant obstacle to discovery under the Convention that the broad wording of Article 23 would suggest. ...

The second major United States interest is in fair and equal treatment of litigants. The Court cites several fairness concerns in support of its conclusion that the Convention is not exclusive and apparently fears that a broad endorsement of the use of the Convention would lead to the same "unacceptable asymmetries." Courts can protect against the first two concerns noted by the majority — that a foreign party to a lawsuit would have a discovery advantage over a domestic litigant because it could obtain the advantages of the Federal Rules of Civil Procedure, and that a foreign company would have an economic competitive advantage because it would be subject to less extensive discovery — by exercising their discretionary powers to control discovery in order to ensure fairness to both parties. A court may "make any order which justice requires" to limit discovery, including an order permitting discovery only on specified terms and conditions, by a particular discovery method, or with limitation in scope to certain matters. Fed. Rule Civ. Proc. 26(c). If, for instance, resort to the Convention procedures would put one party at a disadvantage, any possible unfairness could be prevented by postponing that party's obligation to respond to discovery requests until completion of the foreign discovery. Moreover, the Court's arguments focus on the nationality of the parties, while it is actually the locus of the evidence that is relevant to use of the Convention: a foreign litigant trying to secure evidence from a foreign branch of an American litigant might also be required to resort to the Convention.

When resort to the Convention would be futile, a court has no choice but to resort to a traditional comity analysis. But even then, an attempt to use the Convention will often be the best way to discover if it will be successful, particularly in the present state of general inexperience with the implementation of its procedures by the various contracting states. An attempt to use the Convention will open a dialogue with the authorities in the foreign state and in that way a United States court can obtain an authoritative answer as to the limits on what it can achieve with a discovery request in a particular contracting state.

Notes on Aerospatiale

1. *Mandatory use of the Convention for discovery conducted "on" foreign territory.* Suppose a U.S. litigant wishes to conduct the deposition of a foreign person within a member state's territory or to inspect a factory or other site at a foreign location? Must the Hague Evidence Convention be used? *Aerospatiale* did not address this question. Most authorities have concluded that the Convention must be used when the physical act of discovery formally occurs on foreign territory. *See Scotch Whiskey Ass'n v. Majestic Distilling Co.*, No. 88-808 (D. Md. Nov. 30, 1988); *Jenco v. Martech Int'l Inc.*, 1988 U.S. Dist. Lexis 4727 (E.D. La. May 20, 1988); *McLaughlin v. Fellows Gear Shaper Co.*, 102 F.R.D. 956 (E.D. Pa. 1984); *Graco, Inc. v. Kremlin, Inc.*, 101 F.R.D. 503, 524 (N.D. Ill. 1984).

Based on *Aerospatiale*'s reading of the Convention, could the Convention *itself* forbid direct U.S. discovery occurring abroad? If not, then what would permit U.S. courts to require resort to the Convention in such cases? How is discovery "in" foreign territory different from discovery "from" foreign territory? What differences could justify different treatment of the two types of discovery by U.S. courts? Recall the diplomatic protests that Germany made to the United States in the 19th century over the efforts by U.S. commissioners to take depositions on German territory. *See supra* pp. 849-52. Do such efforts constitute a greater infringement of foreign sovereignty than discovery "from" foreign territory? Recall the *Charming Betsy* presumption that Congress will not be assumed to have violated international law. *See supra* pp. 22 & 510-11.

2. *Optional use of the Convention for discovery conducted in the United States. Aerospatiale* squarely rejected the position of some lower courts that the Hague Evidence Convention simply had no application if the formal act of "producing" the requested information was to take place in the United States (*i.e.*, a deposition conducted in the United States or documents that are copied abroad and brought to the United States where they are then "produced"). *See, e.g., In re Anschuetz & Co.*, 754 F.2d 602 (5th Cir. 1985), *vacated*, 483 U.S. 1002 (1987). In this respect, the Court ruled that the Convention applied to taking evidence "from" a foreign country as well as to taking it "in" the foreign country.

Nonetheless, *Aerospatiale* emphasized that the Convention is not the *only* mechanism available for obtaining discovery from a foreign state. *Aerospatiale* held that the Convention does not by its terms supplant the use of direct discovery orders by U.S. courts: "the Hague Convention did not deprive the District Court of the jurisdiction it otherwise possessed to order a foreign national party before it to produce evidence physically located within a signatory nation."

3. *Aerospatiale's reliance on international comity.* According to *Aerospatiale*, when information is to be produced "from" (but not "in") a Convention signatory, by a party over whom the court has personal jurisdiction, two alternative discovery procedures are available: direct discovery under the Federal Rules of Civil Procedure or a letter of request through the Convention. *Aerospatiale* also holds that the U.S. court's choice between these two alternatives must be informed by principles of "international comity," rather than dictated by the Convention itself: "The concept of international comity requires in this context a more particularized analysis of the respective interests of the foreign nation and the requesting nation." Compare the use of the comity doctrine in other areas of U.S. litigation, including enforcement of foreign judgments (*see infra* pp. 939-41), choice of forum (*supra* pp. 49-56 & 314), act of state doctrine (*supra* pp. 701-02), antisuit injunctions (*supra* pp. 485-86), choice of law (*supra* pp. 547-52), and personal jurisdiction (*supra* pp. 86-94 & 137-38).

4. *Meaning of* Aerospatiale's *comity analysis.* Unfortunately, the application of comity in individual discovery cases is left unclear after *Aerospatiale*. At one point, the majority refers to the factors set out in §442 of the new *Restatement* (reproduced *supra* p. 883) as "relevant to any comity analysis." Nonetheless, at other points in its opinion, the Court sets forth other descriptions of the comity analysis, requiring "prior scrutiny in each case of the particular facts, sovereign interests, and likelihood that resort to those procedures will prove effective" and "more particularized analysis of the respective interests of the foreign nation and the requesting nation." Elsewhere, the Court said, the "exact line ... must be drawn by the trial court, based on its knowledge of the case and of the claims and interests of the parties and the governments whose statutes and policies they invoke." How is a district court to apply these various standards? Do they all mean the same thing?

5. *Source of authority to require resort to Hague Evidence Convention. Aerospatiale* held that the Hague Evidence Convention does not by its terms require use of the Convention's procedures rather than use of direct discovery under the Federal Rules. Nonetheless, the Court also held that in some cases international comity required litigants to resort to the Convention's procedures. From where is this "comity" requirement derived? What gives federal courts the power to deny litigants access to the discovery rights that Congress provided in the Federal Rules? *See supra* pp. 70-73, 493-97 & 546-52 discussing historical foundations of comity. What is the relation of comity to the Convention and to the Federal Rules of Civil Procedure? What is the relation of comity to the *Charming Betsy* presumption that Congress does not intend to violate international law? Why doesn't the *Aerospatiale* opinion discuss international law limits on extraterritorial discovery. *See supra* pp. 849-55. If these limits forbid compelled discovery "on" foreign territory, why should courts not also consider whether they forbid compelled discovery "from" foreign territory?

6. *Justice Blackmun's* Aerospatiale *opinion.* Justice Blackmun's concurring and dissenting opinion in *Aerospatiale* also applied a comity analysis but, unlike the majority, concluded that lower courts should follow a rule ordinarily requiring exhaustion of Hague Evidence Convention procedures before direct discovery under the Federal Rules of Civil Procedure is sought. What exactly are the differences between the approach of the four concurring and dissenting Justices and the majority? Which approach to use of the Convention is preferable?

7. *Appellate review and uniformity.* The lack of certainty in the majority's comity approach in

Aerospatiale may be exacerbated by the nature of the disputes to be reviewed. The essence of the majority's opinion is that judgments must be made in individual discovery cases based on a wide variety of factors. In the normal case this will call for deference to the trial court's discretion. *See In re Anschuetz & Co. GmbH*, 838 F.2d 1362, 1363 (5th Cir. 1988); *Sandsend Fin. Consultants, Ltd. v. Wood*, 743 S.W.2d 364 (Tex. App. 1988). Moreover, as noted above, discovery disputes involving parties generally are *not* reviewable at the interlocutory stage. (*Aerospatiale* itself reached the Supreme Court by way of an extraordinary writ of mandamus, something that is not to be anticipated except in unusual circumstances.) Moreover, any trial court's error is likely to be rendered moot by the time judgment is rendered on the merits. As a practical matter therefore, it seems unlikely that the courts of appeals will have much opportunity to review and ensure uniformity in the application of the *Aerospatiale* decision. Given the involvement of foreign governmental interests, is it appropriate to defer so extensively to single district judges?

8. *Possible parochial bias.* To what extent will trial courts — as opposed to courts of appeals or the Supreme Court — be likely to focus primarily on managing individual cases expeditiously and therefore tend to disregard "comity"? How likely is it that trial judges will be familiar with foreign public policies? Compare the similar concerns about parochial bias in the context of legislative jurisdiction and choice of law.

9. *Balancing U.S. and foreign interests.* The *Aerospatiale* majority did not hesitate to adopt a comity analysis requiring lower courts to "balance" U.S. and foreign interests. In contrast, Justice Blackmun cautioned that "courts are generally ill equipped to assume the role of balancing the interests of foreign nations with that of our own." Are Justice Blackmun's concerns justified? Compare the criticisms that have been made of ad hoc balancing analyses in other international civil litigation contexts. *See supra* pp. 317-18 (*forum non conveniens*) & *infra* pp. 508-09, 592-93 & 648-49 (extraterritoriality).

10. *Effect of foreign litigant's use of U.S. discovery rules.* Suppose that a foreign litigant avails itself of the benefits of full discovery from adverse parties under the Federal Rules of Civil Procedure. Should the foreign litigant be able to require that discovery from it be conducted only under the Convention? In *Aerospatiale*, both Justice Stevens and Justice Blackmun disapproved such a result. *See Great Lakes Dredge & Dock Co. v. Harnischfeger Corp.*, 1990 U.S. Dist. Lexis 12843 (N.D. Ill. Sept. 25, 1990) (refusing to permit German litigant to "have the best of all worlds").

11. *Application of* Aerospatiale *to state courts.* As noted above, *Aerospatiale* involved an interpretation of the Hague Evidence Convention itself. In particular, the Court decided that the Convention by its terms need not be used, but is available even where production of information is to take place on U.S. soil. As a treaty of the United States, the Convention is the supreme law of the land and therefore these interpretations by the Supreme Court bind the state courts, as well as lower federal courts. *See supra* pp. 912-13; U.S. Const. Art. VI, cl. 2; *Restatement (Third) Foreign Relations Law* §115(2) (1987); *Volkswagenwerk AG v. Schlunk*, 486 U.S. 694 (1988).

Aerospatiale also rested in part on international comity; the effect of this holding on state courts is less clear. Is *Aerospatiale*'s comity analysis a rule of *federal* law that state courts are obliged to follow? *See Sandsend Financial Consultants, Ltd. v. Wood*, 734 S.W.2d 364 (Tex. Ct. App. 1988) (applying *Aerospatiale* comity analysis: "this Court is duty-bound to follow Supreme Court precedent"); *Scarminach v. Goldwell GmbH*, 531 N.Y.S.2d 188, 190 (Sup. Ct. 1988). Recall the discussions above of the status of international law as federal law. *See supra* pp. 17-21 & 510-11.

On the one hand, state courts should arguably be bound to be at least as deferential to foreign sovereign interests as federal courts are. The Supreme Court's concerns about infringing foreign sovereignty apply as fully to state courts as to federal courts. On the other hand, from where would federal courts derive the authority to invoke international comity to regulate state court discovery practice? Similar issues arise with respect to the applicability of federal common law rules of *forum non conveniens*, forum selection, the act of state doctrine, the extraterritorial application of national laws and the enforcement of foreign judgments. *See supra* pp. 49-56, 224-25, 365-66, 450-52, 541-44 & 704-05 and *infra* pp. 960-62.

A related issue concerns the power of state courts to go *beyond* the minimum standard of deference to foreign interests established by *Aerospatiale*. For example, could a state court conclude that international comity requires first use of the Convention in all cases? Could this reading of comity harm U.S. interests? How? What if the state court based its first-use rule on concerns about local judicial administration? *See* Westin & Born, *Applying the Aerospatiale Decision to State Court Proceedings*, 26 Colum. J. Transnat'l L. 901 (1988).

12. *Effect of Article 23 reservations on Convention's efficacy.* One of the issues figuring in *Aerospatiale*

was the extent to which U.S. litigants could obtain meaningful discovery through Convention procedures. The large number of sweeping Article 23 declarations make this issue particularly important for U.S. litigants, and no doubt led to the Supreme Court's conclusion that "[i]n many situations the Letter of Request procedure authorized by the Convention would be unduly time-consuming and expensive, as well as less certain to produce needed evidence than direct use of the Federal Rules."

The effectiveness of the Convention continue to be an important issue in disputes about use of the Convention. This continued importance derives from the role played in the Court's comity analysis of the "likelihood that resort to [the Convention's] procedures will prove effective." 482 U.S. at 544. The French Government's *amicus curiae* brief in *Aerospatiale* pointed out that it had adopted procedures through which U.S. litigants could obtain documents through the Convention from France despite France's Article 23 reservation to the contrary. Brief of Republic of France as *Amicus Curiae, Aerospatiale*, 24-25.

13. *Application of* Aerospatiale *outside the Hague Evidence Convention context.* To what extent does *Aerospatiale's* conclusion that trial courts must consider carefully the scope of and need for U.S. extraterritorial discovery requests in light of foreign sovereign interests apply in ordering discovery from foreign countries that are not party to the Convention. Portions of the Court's opinion are apparently not apparently tied to the Convention itself, but apply equally to all transnational discovery. Indeed, the language the Court quotes from §442 of the *Third Restatement* does not pertain specifically to the Convention, but concerns extraterritorial U.S. discovery generally. If the *Aerospatiale* formula *is* generally applicable, how does this alter the analysis of decisions like *City Bank*, excerpted above? Does *Aerospatiale* suggest that there are circumstances in which "first-use" of customary letters rogatory could (or should) be required? *Compare supra* pp. 791-92 (discussion of lower court decisions requiring use of letters rogatory to serve process abroad).

14. *Applicability of Hague Evidence Convention to "discovery."* Aerospatiale *and virtually every other U.S. authority assumes that the Hague Evidence Convention applies to "discovery." Note, however, that the Convention applies to "taking of evidence." Does that mean that pre-trial discovery is not covered by the Convention? For an argument that the Convention was narrowly limited to taking "evidence," and does not apply to mere "discovery," *see* Collins, *The Hague Evidence Convention and Discovery: A Serious Misunderstanding?*, 35 Int'l & Comp. L.Q. 765 (1986). What does Article 23 suggest? What about Article 1, permitting the use of letters of request "to obtain evidence, or to perform some other judicial act," but not to "obtain evidence which is not intended for use in judicial proceedings, commenced or contemplated."

3. "Exclusivity" of the Hague Evidence Convention: Post-Aerospatiale Experience

Lower courts have had frequent occasion to apply *Aerospatiale*. Many district judges have found the *Aerospatiale* comity standard of dubious assistance. The following opinion in *Benton Graphics v. Uddeholm Corp.* is illustrative of trial court efforts to apply the *Aerospatiale* decision.

BENTON GRAPHICS v. UDDEHOLM CORP.

118 F.R.D. 386 (D.N.J. 1987)

FREDA L. WOLFSON, MAGISTRATE. This litigation involves allegations of fraud and breach of contract against several defendants, including two Swedish Companies, Uddeholms, A.B. and Uddeholm Strip Steel, A.B. The plaintiff, Benton Graphics, Inc., originally brought the instant motion on for an order compelling responses to interrogatories and the production of documents. The defendants opposed this motion claiming that the principles of comity required that discovery must first be sought under the applicable Hague Convention procedures. ...

In the instant motion, a major dispute is whether either party carries the burden in determining whether the Federal Rules or Convention procedures should be followed. ... [T]he plaintiff argues that parties seeking to invoke the Convention are required "to demonstrate appropriate reasons for employing the Convention" in lieu of the Federal Rules. On the other hand ... defendants argue that a party seeking discovery outside the Convention should be required to show by clear and convincing evidence that the Convention's procedures would be inefficient or unnecessarily burdensome. Anything less, according to the defendants, would derogate from the United States' obligations under the Convention and violate the judicial sovereignty of Sweden. ...

While the majority opinion is not crystal clear on the issue of who bears the burden of establishing which discovery procedure to utilize, I agree with the plaintiff that the party seeking to utilize Convention procedures must demonstrate appropriate reasons. *But see Hudson v. Hermann Pfauter GmbH & Co.*, 117 F.R.D. 33 (N.D.N.Y. 1987).[181] This is consistent with the policy expressed by the Court in *Aerospatiale* that foreign competitors voluntarily marketing their product in the United States should be subject to the same judicial burdens as their domestic counterparts. ... Therefore, foreign litigants attempting to supplant the federal rules with Convention procedures must demonstrate why the particular facts and sovereign interests support using the Convention. They must also demonstrate that resort to these procedures will prove effective. ...

Plaintiff, Benton Graphics, Inc., is a New Jersey corporation in the business of manufacturing and distributing doctor blades for use in the gravure printing industry. Defendant, Uddeholm Strip Steel, A.B. is a Swedish Corporation which manufactures and distributes steel products, including carbon steel for use in manufacturing doctor blades. Between 1979 and 1985, Benton Graphics entered into a series of contracts with defendants to purchase doctor blades. Prior to 1980, defendants manufactured and sold doctor blades under the designation UHB-20R steel. After 1980, defendants manufactured and sold to Benton a different grade carbon steel under the designation UHB-18-CR. Benton claims that defendant Knudsen represented on numerous occasions that the steel delivered to Benton since 1980 was UHB-20R. In February 1986, Benton brought this action against defendants alleging breach of contract, breach of

Claims

---

181. In *Hudson*, the court found that the burden should be placed on the party opposing the use of Convention procedures to demonstrate that those procedures would be ineffective. In reaching this decision the district court relied upon Justice Blackmun's concurring and dissenting opinion in *Aerospatiale*.

Justice Blackmun held that a court "should perform a tripartite analysis that considers the foreign interests, the interests of the United States, and the mutual interests of all nations in a smoothly functioning international legal regime," (Blackmun J., concurring in part and dissenting in part) when determining whether the Convention should be utilized in the first instance. In agreeing with Justice Blackmun, the court in *Hudson* also noted that international policy considerations transcend the interests of the individual litigants. I disagree with the *Hudson* court's analysis because it relies too heavily on the concurring and dissenting opinion of Justice Blackmun in *Aerospatiale*. While Justice Blackmun's opinion certainly is thoughtful and well reasoned, it is not the opinion of the majority of the members on the Supreme Court. In *Aerospatiale*, the majority did not elevate theoretical policy concerns over the effect Convention procedures would have upon particular litigants. Rather, the Court specifically directed district courts to analyze the interests of the parties and the intrusiveness of the discovery sought.

warranty, fraud and RICO violations based on the theory that defendants conspired to misrepresent the grade of steel sold to Benton between 1980 and 1985. Benton claims that there is a material difference between UHB-20R and UHB-18CR steel and that defendants intentionally withheld this information from Benton. ...

In the instant motion, defendants have made no attempt to relate the "particular facts" of this case to the discovery sought. Defendants only argue that the interrogatories and requests for documents are overbroad and burdensome. I note that the defendants have not identified the specific interrogatories or document requests that are overbroad or burdensome. They have not alleged that the discovery is unduly expensive or that the discovery is being sought for the "improper purpose of motivating settlement rather than finding relevant and probative evidence." Moreover, defendants have failed to allege any special problems because of their nationality or the location of their operations.

Because defendants have largely failed to specifically identify their objections it is impossible for me to determine which, if any, requests are overbroad and burdensome. However, having reviewed the interrogatories, I believe that a number of the requests are not "simple" and may require streamlining if we are to proceed under the federal rules. For example, a number of questions seek information held by "any employee of Uddeholm Strip Steel"; these appear too encompassing. I believe these questions can be limited to a defined group of individuals from Uddeholm who were involved in the manufacture of and the decision to sell UHR-18-CR grade steel in place of UHB-20R steel products. It is this that is important and not whether any employee had certain knowledge which may never have been communicated to any of the persons in control until the commencement of this litigation. Furthermore, these questions, as phrased, include even clerical employees. Identification of such persons, while being of little or no moment, would, however, involve substantial investigation by the foreign litigants. This type of expansive discovery without concomitant relevance is not what the Court envisioned when it handed down the *Aerospatiale* decision: "Some discovery procedures are much more 'intrusive' than others."

Thus, the parties shall have 10 days to confer in an effort to limit and resolve the scope of the discovery requests to ensure that they are reasonable and not overly burdensome, keeping in mind that discovery requests that are too "intrusive" may be limited by this court. After making such good faith effort to reach accommodation, I will permit the defendants to address any specific objections to interrogatories or document requests within ten days thereafter. Defendants are cautioned that they must explain *why* specific discovery sought is overbroad or burdensome. ...

Notwithstanding defendants' blanket objections to all discovery, I do not find that the "particular facts" of this case require resort to Convention procedures. The discovery sought in this case largely relates to the composition, qualities and testing of defendants' steel. Several of the defendants and all relevant tests are located in Sweden. This is conceded by defendants. It is essential that plaintiff and its experts have access to the tests if this litigation is to proceed to any semblance of a timely fashion. The foreign defendants have identified no special problem with responding to the requested discovery because of their nationality. Since discovery of these tests and other relevant information can be accomplished efficiently under the federal rules the "particular facts" of this case do not necessitate resort to the Convention.

2.   The second factor which must be analyzed before ordering use of the Convention is the sovereign interest involved. Defendants argue that "critical sovereign interests of Sweden" support utilizing Convention procedures. They have submitted the duly authenticated Declaration of Wanja Tornberg, Assistant Under-Secretary of the Swedish Ministry for Foreign Affairs, dated September 7, 1987 (the "Tornberg Declaration"). According to Tornberg, use of the Hague Convention serves a number of important Swedish interests including:

(a) It serves as an essential link and an effective mechanism for cooperation between different legal systems.

(b) It minimizes conflicts between the legal requirements of different states.

(c) It satisfies the urging of the United States for Sweden and other civil law nations to provide a means for complying with requests for pretrial discovery of documentary evidence in a manner which is consistent with the laws of Sweden.

(d) It discourages "fishing expedition" methods of obtaining unspecified evidence, which are regarded as unacceptable in Sweden and in other civil law nations.

(e) It effectively balances the divergent interests promoted by the United States' and Sweden's conflicting rules on who bears the costs associated with compliance. The rule in Sweden, as in most civil law countries, is that the losing party reimburses the winner for litigation expenses. Unlike the general rule in the United States, the Swedish rule forces plaintiffs to evaluate carefully the merits of a case before bringing it.

(f) It enables Swedish courts to limit discovery in sensitive and protected areas under Swedish law such as trade secrets and national security.

These "critical sovereign interests" are merely general reasons why Sweden prefers civil law discovery procedures to the more liberal discovery permitted under the federal rules. Defendants cite no reasons how the specific discovery sought by Benton implicates any specific sovereign interest of Sweden. Defendant claims that the Swedish government may have the right to protect some of the information requested. However, defendant does not explain which discovery is objectionable nor why it might have to be protected. No allegations are made that trade secrets are involved or that Benton is engaged in a "fishing expedition." In short, because defendant has not explained, and I do not see why Benton's discovery requests in their entirety or any particular request, violate any special sovereign interests of Sweden, resort to the Hague Convention is not required.

Lastly, I must consider whether Convention procedures in this case will prove effective. Here, I find that they will not. The Tornberg declaration states that the defendants' letter of request should be processed by the Swedish authorities in approximately two months. That is an approximation based upon past history; there are certainly no guarantees. This case has already endured numerous delays and discovery should proceed apace. Another delay while the Swedish authorities determine what discovery will be permitted and the further litigation undoubtedly spawned by their decision may bring actual discovery to a standstill. Therefore, in light of the lengthy history of discovery in this case and the potential for additional delays, I do not find that Convention procedures will prove effective. ...

Notes on Uddeholm

1. *Burden of proof.* What party had the burden of proof in *Uddeholm* on the question whether first-use of the Convention was required? Other lower courts have reached divergent results on this issue. *Compare Haynes v. Kleinwefers*, 119 F.R.D. 335 (E.D.N.Y. 1988) (party resisting discovery must demonstrate need to use Convention) with *Hudson v. Hermann Pfauter GmbH & Co.*, 117 F.R.D. 33 (N.D.N.Y. 1987) (contra). Which party *should* bear the burden of proof? Which party do you think the *Aerospatiale* majority intended to bear the burden of proof?

2. *Reluctance of trial courts to require first-use of Convention.* Justice Blackmun's opinion in *Aerospatiale* warned: "I fear the Court's decision means that courts will resort unnecessarily to issuing discovery orders under the Federal Rules of Civil Procedure in a raw exercise of their jurisdictional power." *Uddeholm* was unwilling to require first-use of the Convention. Most other lower courts have reached the same conclusion. See Born & Hoing, *Comity and the Lower Courts: Post-Aerospatiale Applications of the Hague Evidence Convention*, 24 Int'l Law 393 (1990); *Great Lakes Dredge & Dock Co. v. Harnischfeger Corp.*, 1990 U.S. Dist. Lexis 12843 (N.D. Ill. Sept. 25, 1990); *In re Bedford Computer Corp.*, 114 B.R. 2 (D.N.H. 1990). The principal exception to this trend was *Hermann Pfauter, supra*, where the trial judge flatly announced that he found Justice Blackmun's concurring and dissenting opinion in *Aerospatiale* more persuasive than the majority opinion. Is this trend desirable? consistent with the Convention?

3. *Jurisdictional discovery.* As described above, U.S. courts have frequently ordered litigants to make so-called jurisdictional discovery for the limited purpose of determining whether they are subject to personal jurisdiction. *See supra* pp. 860-61. If jurisdictional facts are located in a Hague Evidence Convention signatory state, is first-use or exclusive use of the Convention required? Note *Aerospatiale's* emphasis on the fact that the French defendants were concededly subject to the District Court's jurisdiction. Lower courts are divided on the question whether jurisdictional discovery must proceed under the Convention. *Compare Jenco v. Martech Int'l*, 1988 WL 106318 (E.D.La. 1988) (requiring use of Convention when foreign defendant disputes U.S. jurisdiction) with *Rich v. KIS California, Inc.*, 121 F.R.D. 254 (M.D.N.C. 1988) (contra) and *Manoir-Electroalloys Corp. v. Amalloy Corp.*, 711 F.Supp. 188 (D.N.J. 1989) *and in re Bedford Computer Corp.* 114 B.R. 2 (D.N.H. 1990). Even if use of the Convention is not *per se* required, does *Aerospatiale's* ad hoc comity analysis take into account the fact that jurisdiction has not yet been established? If so, what weight should this factor have?

4. *Foreign sovereign interests.* Note the court's discussion of the sovereign interests of Sweden in this case, and in particular its refusal to accord any weight to the "general" interests identified by the Swedish government. Other courts have taken the same approach. *Rich v. KIS Cal., Inc.*, 121 F.R.D. 254, 258 (M.D.N.C. 1988) (foreign sovereign interests are "overly broad and vague" and do not "warrant much deference); *Great Lakes Dredge & Dock Co. v. Harnischfeger Corp.*, 1990 U.S. Dist. Lexis 12843 (N.D. Ill. Sept. 25, 1990). See *Aerospatiale*, 482 U.S. at 544 n.29 ("identify the nature of the sovereign interests in the nondisclosure of specific types of material"). These courts have instead demanded a showing of some "specific" interest that protects the sought-after information. Parties seeking to require resort to the Convention must therefore apparently come forward with evidence of narrowly-tailored foreign nondisclosure laws aimed at particular subjects. *Compare* the general willingness of U.S. courts to recognize foreign privileges, *supra* pp. 891-92.

What weight should be given to the domestic applicability of blocking statutes? Put differently, should U.S. courts give effect to foreign laws that restrict only the discovery of U.S. (and other foreign) courts, or should they require that such laws also apply to the courts of the country in question?

5. *Tailoring discovery.* The magistrate in *Uddeholm* refused to fully enforce the plaintiff's discovery requests. Instead, relying on *Aerospatiale*, the court narrowed the scope of those requests. Other lower courts have taken much the same approach. *See Rich v. KIS Cal., Inc.*, 121 F.R.D. 254, 260 (M.D.N.C. 1988);

Scarminach v. Goldwell GmbH, 531 N.Y.S. 2d 188, 191 (S. Ct. 1988); *In re Bedford Computer Corp.*, 114 B.R. 2 (D.N.H. 1990). Is the general approach of these courts — foregoing first-use of the Convention but narrowing the breadth of direct U.S. discovery — a fair and sensible compromise? Consider the following:

> At least in principle, this analysis would provide a mechanism for compromising extraterritorial discovery disputes by carefully identifying what U.S. and foreign sovereign interests actually are at stake in particular cases and by carefully tailoring U.S.-style discovery to avoid compromising relevant foreign interests. In practical terms, the lower courts' heightened scrutiny of sovereign interests would mean that extraterritorial discovery would be conducted pursuant to U.S. procedural rules, but would be more limited than occurs in the purely domestic context; direct U.S. discovery would also apparently be subject to a requirement of first use of the Convention where specific and clearly articulated foreign nondisclosure laws exist. There is undeniably an attractive element of rough justice and reciprocity about this proposal.
>
> Ultimately, however, this approach is premised on a faulty view of foreign and U.S. sovereign interests. Specific foreign nondisclosure laws are generally relevant to the ultimate substantive question whether particular evidence can ever be produced, not to the procedures governing how such evidence can ever be produced. Foreign bank secrecy laws and privileges for confidential relationships do not reflect a desire that discovery into these matters occur pursuant to the Convention - instead, these laws generally reflect a prohibition against any discovery of protected materials. Similarly, in considering U.S. interests, the lower courts have typically inquired whether particular evidence is really needed by the U.S. litigant and how intrusive such discovery would be. Again, these questions are not relevant to the procedure for taking discovery into a particular matter, but instead go to the ultimate issue of whether particular materials should be discoverable at all.
>
> All of this suggests that the lower courts that have attempted conscientiously to apply the *Aerospatiale* comity analysis have considered the wrong types of sovereign interests. These courts should be examining the U.S. interest in obtaining broad discovery very promptly (rather than somewhat less broadly and less quickly pursuant to the Convention), not the more generalized question whether discovery of certain subjects is needed. Conversely, lower courts should inquire whether the foreign State has expressed a specific interest that particular types of inquiries be conducted pursuant to the Convention, not whether the foreign State has indicated that inquiries in a particular field are simply forbidden. Only by evaluating U.S. and foreign sovereign interests for and against use of the Convention can U.S. courts determine intelligently whether or not use of the Convention is required by comity. Evaluating other interests simply does not bear on the desirability of requiring resort to the Convention. Born & Hoing, *Comity and the Lower Courts: Post-Aerospatiale Applications of the Hague Evidence Convention*, 24 Int'l Law. 393, 404-05 (1990).

Is this persuasive?

6. *Efficacy of Hague Evidence Convention procedures.* As *Uddeholm* demonstrates, one very important factor in the *Aerospatiale* comity analysis is likely to be the perceived efficacy and speed of discovery under the Hague Evidence Convention. *See also Haynes v. Kleinwefers*, 119 F.R.D. 335, 339 (E.D.N.Y. 1988); *Scarminach v. Goldwell GmbH*, 531 N.Y.S.2d 188, 191 (S.Ct. 1988); *Manoir-Electroalloys Corp. v. Amalloy Corp.*, No. 88-4707 (D.N.J. July 24, 1989) (Transcript: "Court: Are you seriously suggesting that the Hague Convention is a speedy process?"). Parties wishing to require use of the Convention must, therefore, be prepared to provide evidence that the Convention has worked well in the past in a particular nation and that they will cooperate in ensuring full and expeditious discovery in the pending matter.

7. *Necessity of using Hague Evidence Convention to obtain discovery from nonparty witnesses.* *Aerospatiale* involved discovery from foreign litigants that were concededly subject to the U.S. court's personal jurisdiction. Discovery from nonparty witnesses, however, will often require obtaining materials from persons or entities that are not subject to U.S. personal jurisdiction or to effective subpoena service. *See supra* pp. 861-66. In these circumstances, direct U.S. discovery is not available and the Hague Evidence Convention must be used. *See Orlich v. Helm Bros., Inc.*, 560 N.Y.S.2d 10 (N.Y. App. Div. 1990) (discovery from German nonparty witness must proceed under Hague Evidence Convention: "When discovery is sought from a nonparty in a foreign jurisdiction, application of the Hague Evidence Convention ... is virtually compulsory").

G. Taking of Evidence in the United States in Aid of Foreign Proceedings

Litigants in foreign proceedings often require the taking of evidence located in the United States, just as U.S. litigants require evidence located abroad. This section examines the treatment of such evidence-taking under U.S. law.

1. Taking of Evidence in the United States Without Court Assistance

Unlike some civil law jurisdictions, the United States imposes no general prohibition against the taking of evidence on U.S. territory for use in foreign judicial proceedings.[182] The Uniform Interstate and International Procedure Act provides that "[a] person within this state may voluntarily give his testimony or statement or produce documents or other things for use in a proceeding before a tribunal outside this state in any manner acceptable to him."[183] Similarly, the legislative history to 28 U.S.C. §1782(b) refers to the "pre-existing freedom of persons within the United States voluntarily to give statements or produce tangible evidence in connection with foreign or international proceedings or investigations."[184] This general freedom is subject, of course, to restrictions such as export control laws, privileges, confidentiality duties, and the like.

2. Taking of Evidence in the United States With Court Assistance

U.S. courts will assist foreign courts and litigants in the taking of evidence located in the United States. As early as 1855, Congress enacted legislation authorizing federal courts to assist foreign courts in obtaining evidence.[185] Unfortunately, the statute was mis-catalogued, and apparently never used.[186] In 1863, Congress enacted another statute providing for U.S. judicial assistance, but only in a narrow range of

---

182. For a description of the limitations imposed in some civil law jurisdictions on discovery in aid of foreign litigation, *see supra* pp. 847-49.

183. Uniform Interstate and International Procedure Act §302(b), excerpted in Appendix B. The Commentary to this provision explains: "Sub-section (b) re-affirms the existing freedom of persons within the United States voluntarily to give testimony or produce evidence for use in proceedings or investigations elsewhere. The explicit reaffirmation is desirable in order to stress the large degree of freedom existing in this area." 13 U.L.A. 492 (1980).

184. S. Rep. No. 1580, 88th Cong., 1st Sess. (1963), *reprinted in*, [1964] U.S. Code Cong. & Admin. News 3782, 3789-90. Section 1782(a) is discussed below. *See infra* pp. 921-34. Section 1782(b) itself provides: "This chapter does not preclude a person within the United States from voluntarily giving his testimony or statement, or producing a document or other thing, for use in a proceeding in a foreign or international tribunal before any person and in any manner acceptable to him." 28 U.S.C. §1782.

185. 10 Stat. 630, ch. 140 §2 (March 2, 1855) ("Where letters rogatory shall have [been] addressed, from any court of a foreign country to any circuit court of the United States, and a United States commissioner designated by said circuit court to make the examination of witnesses in said letters mentioned, said commissioner shall be empowered to compel the witnesses to appear and depose in the same manner as to appear and testify in court."). The statute was enacted after the U.S. Department of State and Attorney General had concluded that a U.S. court lacked the power to execute a French letter rogatory. Jones, *International Judicial Assistance: Procedural Chaos and a Program for Reform*, 62 Yale L. J. 515, 540 (1953).

186. Jones, *International Judicial Assistance: Procedural Chaos and a Program for Reform*, 62 Yale L. J. 515, 540 n.77 (1953).

cases — specifically, where a foreign state itself, with which the United States was at peace, sought recovery of money or property.[187] Given the restrictive character of this authorization, it was seldom successfully invoked.[188]

Following 1945, Congress and the Executive Branch anticipated increased international commerce and litigation. As a consequence, the existing letter rogatory legislation was amended, in both 1948 and 1949.[189] Both amendments broadened the availability of U.S. judicial assistance, eliminating the requirement that a foreign state be a party to foreign proceedings and expanding the statute to assistance in aid of any pending foreign judicial proceeding.

As discussed above, the Commission and Advisory Committee on International Rules of Judicial Procedure was established in 1958 to study the general subject of international judicial assistance.[190] Among other things, the Commission recommended, and Congress adopted in 1964, amendments to the existing letter rogatory statute.[191] As amended, §1782 provides:

> The district court of the district in which a person resides or is found may order him to give his testimony or statement or to produce a document or other thing for use in a proceeding in a foreign or international tribunal. The order may be made pursuant to a letter rogatory issued, or request made, by a foreign or international tribunal or upon the application of any interested person....[192]

Section 1782 has been invoked with increasing frequency in international civil litigation. Parties to foreign judicial (and arbitral) proceedings have sought to take discovery under §1782 of U.S. materials. U.S. courts have been required to consider whether granting such requests would assist — or frustrate — the foreign proceedings. The decisions excerpted below in *In the Matter of the Application of Euromep SA*, illustrates the difficulties that such requests have created.

IN THE MATTER OF THE APPLICATION OF EUROMEP, SA

51 F.3d 1095 (2d Cir. 1995)

CALABRESI, CIRCUIT JUDGE. This case raises the question of the degree to which federal district courts, in deciding whether to order discovery under 28 U.S.C. §1782(a) in aid of a foreign litigation, should delve into the mysteries of foreign law.

---

187. 12 Stat. 769, 769-70, ch. 95 (March 3, 1863).

188. *Janssen v. Belding-Corticelli, Ltd.*, 84 F.2d 577 (3d Cir. 1936); *In re Letters Rogatory From Examining Magistrate of Tribunal of Versailles, France*, 26 F.Supp. 852 (D. Md. 1939); *In re Letters Rogatory From the First District Judge of Vera Cruz*, 36 F. 306 (S.D.N.Y. 1888).

189. Pub. L. No. 80-773, 62 Stat. 869, 949 (June 25, 1948); Pub. L. No. 81-72, 63 Stat. 89, 103 (May 24, 1949).

190. *See supra* pp. 765-66.

191. Pub. L. No. 88-619, 78 Stat. 995, 997 §9 (Oct. 3, 1964).

192. 28 U.S.C. §1782(a). *See* Appendix H.

Euromepa, SA, a French insurance brokerage firm, and Allied Insurance and Reinsurance Company, an affiliated underwriter of commercial risk coverage (hereinafter collectively referred to as "MEPA") appeal from the judgment of the U.S. District Court for the Southern District of New York, denying their petition for court-ordered discovery pursuant to §1782(a). MEPA requested that the district court direct Ralph Esmerian, Inc., a New York jewelry designer, to produce both witnesses for deposition and documents for use in a pending French litigation. The underlying dispute involves a claim that MEPA breached its duty as an insurance agent by failing to inform its insured, Esmerian's intermediary jewelry dealer, that a proposed gem courier was untrustworthy. MEPA's misrepresentations regarding the courier's honesty induced Esmerian's intermediary to cancel its employee "infidelity" coverage. Inevitably, the courier absconded with $26 million of Esmerian's gems.

After a trial, the Tribunal de Commerce de Nanterre, France found MEPA liable to Esmerian for $10,127,500. MEPA has appealed the judgment to the Cour d'Appel de Versailles (the "French Court of Appeal"), which will hear and consider new evidence — not introduced at trial — as part of the French appellate process. In aid of its French appeal, MEPA sought deposition and document discovery from Esmerian under §1782.

After reviewing the parties' conflicting submissions on French procedural law, the district court concluded that

> the elected representatives of France have, as a matter of policy, determined that pre-trial discovery and use of evidence is controlled by the court and not by the parties. ... Granting this petition would undeniably infringe on the power that the French legislature has bestowed on its courts. MEPA, instead of the French Court, would control the process by which any evidence was obtained and submitted. Such a decision would be contrary to the policy formulated and instituted by the French Legislature.

Exercising the discretion to withhold discovery assistance provided by §1782, *see* 28 U.S.C. §1782 (the district court "*may* order" discovery) (emphasis added), Judge Duffy denied MEPA's petition.

We review the district court's decision for abuse of discretion. *See In re Malev Hungarian Airlines*, 964 F.2d 97, 99 (2d Cir.), *cert. denied*, 113 S.Ct. 179 (1992). But to say that a district court may or may not, in its discretion, order discovery, does not mean that it is free to do so on inappropriate grounds. In this case, we conclude that the district court misapplied our guiding precedents, and misperceived the extent to which it should construe foreign law in deciding whether to order discovery. We therefore reverse the district court's judgment and remand the case for further consideration.

We have previously instructed the district courts in this Circuit to evaluate discovery requests under §1782 in light of the statute's "twin aims of providing efficient means of assistance to participants in international litigation in our federal courts and encouraging foreign countries by example to provide similar means of assistance to our courts." *Malev*, 964 F.2d at 100. We have also noted that Congress purposefully engineered §1782 as "'a one-way street. It grants wide assistance to others, but demands nothing in return.'" *Id.* at 101 (quoting Amram, *The Proposed International Convention on the Service of Documents Abroad*, 51 A.B.A.J. 650, 651 (1965)).

Relying on the plain language of the statute, this Court has also refused to engraft a "quasi-exhaustion requirement" onto §1782 that would force litigants to seek "information through the foreign or international tribunal" before requesting discovery from the district court. *Malev*, 964 F.2d at 100. By the same reasoning, we have also rejected "any implicit requirement that any evidence sought in the United States be discoverable under the laws of the foreign country." *In re Application of Aldunate*, 3 F.3d 54, 59 (2d Cir.) ("If Congress had intended to impose such a sweeping restriction on the district court's discretion, at a time when it was enacting liberalizing amendments to the statute, it would have included the statutory language to that effect."), *cert. denied*, 114 S.Ct. 443 (1993). Instead, we held that the discoverability of requested material under foreign law is simply one factor that a district judge may consider in the exercise of his or her discretion.

In this case, the district court denied MEPA's discovery request after conducting an analysis that runs counter to the principles set forth in *Malev, Aldunate*, and, we believe, in the statute itself. To start, the district judge noted that "a mechanism was available for MEPA to seek [specific] documents while in French courts," and then remarked disapprovingly that "MEPA failed to even attempt to use the mechanism provided by French procedure for obtaining documents." In essence, this criticism faults MEPA for having failed to exhaust its discovery options in France before seeking assistance in this country, and thus embodies the "extra-statutory barrier[] to obtaining discovery" that we explicitly rejected in *Malev*.

Recognizing *Malev*'s "non-exhaustion" rule, the district court sought to bypass it by linking MEPA's failure to exhaust its French discovery options to an additional factor that the court believed weighed against granting MEPA's request. Judge Duffy concluded that "MEPA's failure to seek production of documents and witnesses through the French courts cannot be disregarded when considering 'the nature and attitudes' of France toward discovery." (quoting S. Rep. No. 1580, 88th Cong., 2d Sess. (1964), *reprinted in* 1964 U.S.C.C.A.N. 3782, 3788 [hereinafter "Senate Report"]). On its face, this consideration seems to be just another way of examining whether the evidence that MEPA seeks in the United States is ultimately discoverable under French law. And linking an impermissible factor (lack of exhaustion) to a factor whose relevance we have held to be quite limited under the statute (lack of discoverability) cannot suffice to justify a denial of discovery.

The district court, however, sought to distinguish its inquiry into the "attitudes" of the French towards discovery from a discoverability analysis by stating that

> [w]hether the evidence MEPA seeks would be discoverable in France or not
> is unknown and irrelevant to me. My decision is based on the determina-

tion that granting this petition would be an unwarranted intrusion into France's system of evidence gathering.

We take this to mean that the court below was not so much concerned with whether comparable discovery exists under French law, but with whether France would in some sense be offended by our grant of discovery and, therefore, view it as an "unwarranted intrusion."

There is some support for this distinction. In *Aldunate*, we acknowledged "that in appropriate cases a determination of discoverability under the laws of the foreign jurisdiction is a useful tool in [a district judge's] exercise of discretion under §1782." That appeal involved a §1782 petition filed in aid of a Chilean incompetency hearing. The district court granted the petition, concluding that the requested discovery "would not be an affront to the Chilean court or the Chilean sovereignty" because "allowing the depositions to proceed would actually assist the Chilean court in its on-going proceedings." On review, we took note that "the district court did not make a finding as to the parties' ability to obtain pre-trial discovery under Chilean law," but we did not consider this problematic. Rather, we approved the discovery order because the district court "clearly made an inquiry into whether its grant of discovery under §1782 would circumvent Chilean restrictions on discovery and whether its grant of discovery would be an affront to the Chilean court or Chilean sovereignty."

The present case requires us to consider the appropriate scope of this "inquiry" into the likelihood that providing §1782 discovery assistance to foreign litigants will offend a foreign tribunal. We do not believe that an extensive examination of foreign law regarding the existence and extent of discovery in the forum country is desirable in order to ascertain the attitudes of foreign nations to outside discovery assistance. For, as a chief architect of §1782's current version recently stated:

> [the statute's] drafters realized that making the extension of American assistance dependant on foreign law would open a veritable Pandora's box. They definitely did not want to have a request for cooperation turn into an unduly expensive and time-consuming fight about foreign law. That would be quite contrary to what they sought to be achieved. They also realized that, although civil law countries do not have discovery rules similar to those of common law countries, they often do have quite different procedures for discovering information that could not properly be evaluated without a rather broad understanding of the subtleties of the applicable foreign system. It would, they judged, be wholly inappropriate for an American district court to try to obtain this understanding for the purpose of honoring a simple request for assistance. Hans Smit, *Recent Developments in International Litigation*, 35 S. Tex. L.J. 215, 235 (1994).

The Third Circuit has already tempered the need to engage in an extensive foreign law analysis under §1782. Addressing the reference in the statute's legislative history to the relevance of the "nature and attitudes of the Government of the country from which the [discovery] request emanates," the court read the drafters' statements as simply "authoriz[ing] district courts to scrutinize the underlying fairness of the foreign proceedings to insure they comply with notions of due process." *John Deere, Ltd.*, 754 F.2d at 136 n.3 (citing Senate Report at 3788). According to the court, it was "doubtful whether such language can be expanded to impose a requirement that district courts predict or construe the procedural or substantive law of the foreign jurisdiction." Thus, the Third Circuit concluded that "[t]o require that a district court undertake a more extensive inquiry into the laws of the foreign jurisdiction would seem to exceed the proper scope of §1782."

We agree with this interpretation and conclude that the district court's analytic approach promoted the very thing that §1782 was intended to avoid. The record reveals that this litigation became a battle-by-affidavit of international legal experts, and resulted in the district court's admittedly "superficial" ruling on French law. We think that it is unwise — as well as in tension with the aims of §1782 — for district judges to try to glean the accepted practices and attitudes of other nations from what are likely to be conflicting and, perhaps, biased interpretations of foreign law. Although "[a] grant of discovery that trenched upon the *clearly established* procedures of a foreign tribunal would not be within §1782," *John Deere, Ltd.*, 754 F.2d at 135 (emphasis added), we do not read the statute to condone speculative forays into legal territories unfamiliar to federal judges. Such a costly, time-consuming, and inherently unreliable method of deciding §1782 requests cannot possibly promote the "twin aims" of the statute.

Rather, we believe that a district court's inquiry into the discoverability of requested materials should consider only authoritative proof that a foreign tribunal would reject evidence obtained with the aid of §1782. Such proof, as embodied in a forum country's judicial, executive or legislative declarations that specifically address the use of evidence gathered under foreign procedures,[193] would provide helpful and

---

193. MEPA cites a useful example of the type of authoritative statement to which we refer. In *South Carolina Ins. Co. v. Assurantie Maatschappij "De Zeven Provincien" NV*, 3 W.L.R. 398 (Eng. 1986), a party to a British litigation sought third-party discovery under §1782 in the United States District Court for the District of Washington. Pre-trial discovery of this sort was not permitted under English procedures and the trial judge enjoined it on the grounds that "the English court should retain control of its own procedure and the proceedings that are before it." The intermediate appellate court affirmed the trial judge's order stating, "[o]nce the parties have chosen or accepted the court in which their dispute is to be tried they must abide by the procedure of that country and that court must be master of its own procedure. ... [I]f a party fighting a case in this country has to face the prospect of fighting procedural battles in whatever other jurisdiction his opponent may find a procedural advantage it may impose intolerable burdens, and encourage the worst and most oppressive form of procedural forum shopping. We should set our face against any such situation developing." On appeal, the House of Lords rejected the lower courts' reasoning and vacated the injunction. The Law Lords held that the contested discovery was not "conduct which is oppressive or vexatious or which interferes with the due process of the [British] court," and thus did not "amount to unconscionable conduct" warranting an injunction.

appropriate guidance to a district court in the exercise of its discretion.[194] Absent this type of clear directive, however, a district court's ruling should be informed by §1782's overarching interest in "providing equitable and efficacious procedures for the benefit of tribunals and litigants involved in litigation with international aspects." Senate Report at 3783.

In this case, the district court's denial of MEPA's discovery request was apparently most influenced by a cautious desire not to step on French toes. Since no authoritative declarations by French judicial, executive or legislative bodies objecting to foreign discovery assistance appear in the record, we are unable to accept the district court's conclusion that granting MEPA's discovery request will in fact offend the people of France.

We specifically disagree with the district court's finding that a grant of discovery under §1782 would allow "MEPA, instead of the French Court, [to] control the process by which any evidence was obtained and submitted." Whether or not American courts offer assistance to French litigants, we are confident that French courts will remain at all times the masters of their own domaine. As Judge Duffy recognized, once parties submit themselves to the jurisdiction of a French court, they "must comply with all orders of the French court or face punitive measures."

Because the French court can always enjoin MEPA from pursuing discovery in a manner that violates the judicial policies of France, or can simply refuse to consider any evidence that MEPA gathers by what might be — under French procedures — an unacceptable practice, we do not think that the district court's concern for trespassing upon the prerogatives of French sovereignty should have weighed so heavily in its decision. France can quite easily protect itself from the effects of any discovery order by the district court that inadvertently offended French practice.

Provided that a district court reasonably attempts to accommodate the evidence-gathering practices of other nations, it need not err on the side of completely withholding discovery assistance from international litigants. After all, a foreign tribunal's corrective response to a well-intentioned but unwelcome grant of discovery could bar the evidence gathered in the given case, and it could also constitute the kind of authoritative declaration mentioned earlier that would provide helpful instruction to American courts in handling future cases. *Cf. South Carolina Ins. Co. v. Assurantie Maatschappij "De Zeven Provincien" NV*, 3 W.L.R. 398 (Eng. 1986) (vacating lower court injunction restraining litigants in a British court from conducting §1782 pre-trial discovery in the United States). Since §1782 contemplates interna-

---

194. Even when such a foreign declaration exists, a district judge, in properly exercising discretion, would still have to compare the facts of the case then currently before the court to the foreign precedent cited by the party opposing the §1782 petition and determine whether the two contexts are sufficiently analogous to warrant a denial of discovery. Of course, any and all other limitations upon discovery that would be available under Fed. R. Civ. P. 26 (particularly subparagraphs (b) and (c)), pertaining both to privileged and trial preparation matters and to protective orders, are also available under §1782(a) as the district court may provide.

tional cooperation, and such cooperation presupposes an on-going dialogue between the adjudicative bodies of the world community, such a result would be far from undesirable.

There are, admittedly, many ways in which a blanket, "American-style" grant of discovery to one side in a foreign lawsuit may confuse or skew that litigation. But because "§1782 gives the court complete discretion in prescribing the procedure" for parties to follow in producing requested materials, Senate Report at 3789, we think that it is far preferable for a district court to reconcile whatever misgivings it may have about the impact of its participation in the foreign litigation by issuing a closely tailored discovery order rather than by simply denying relief outright. *See Malev*, 964 F.2d at 102 (noting that a district court has broad authority under §1782 and Fed. R. Civ. P. 26 to impose reasonable limitations and conditions upon discovery).

Here, the district judge was particularly concerned that by permitting the requested discovery he would allow MEPA to "examine documents that it may not wish to use in court" —something that French discovery rules may well bar. But this consideration certainly did not warrant the district court's extreme response. In order to "maintain[] the balance between litigants that each nation creates within its own judicial system," *Aldunate*, 3 F.3d at 60, the district court was free to insist that MEPA submit any evidence that it obtained in this country to the French Court of Appeal, regardless of whether the evidence helped or hindered MEPA's defense to Esmerian's claim.

Similarly, the district court may have been concerned — and if so, quite correctly — that MEPA could obtain discovery against Esmerian in the United States, while Esmerian would be unable to gain access to analogous MEPA documents or testimony in Europe. But if the district court wished to insure procedural parity between MEPA and Esmerian, it could have conditioned relief upon the parties' reciprocal exchange of information. *Cf. Malev*, 964 F.2d at 101-02 & n.4 (although a district court is "free to grant [a §1782] request without assuming responsibility for supervising" reciprocal discovery arrangements, a district court "can, of course, accept [a party's] offer to engage in reciprocal discovery").

On remand, the district court should consider these and other options in crafting an appropriate discovery order. ...

JACOBS, CIRCUIT JUDGE, dissenting. I respectfully dissent. The majority opinion asks to what degree federal district courts "should delve into the mysteries of foreign law" in deciding petitions for discovery under 28 U.S.C. §1782(a). I would reframe the question presented on this appeal to ask what inquiry concerning the foreign forum and its discovery mechanisms is appropriate where the petition under

§1782 seeks American-style discovery: whole categories of documents and multiple depositions.[195]

In its answer, the majority opinion alters law and precedent in three ways that are unnecessary and unwise. First, we have previously recognized that the discoverability abroad of material sought to be discovered here is a useful tool assisting district court discretion; the majority opinion rules that the relevance of that factor is "quite limited," and proceeds to disregard it. Second, we have previously counselled deference to attitudes of the foreign forum toward discovery; the majority opinion withdraws such deference except where there is "authoritative proof" that the foreign tribunal would "reject" our granting discovery assistance. Third, the majority opinion effectively limits the district court's statutory discretion to the crafting of "closely tailored discovery order[s] rather than [the denial of] relief outright."

I prefer the district court's approach. The district court evaluated the request for discovery assistance in light of the contesting parties (the plaintiff and defendant abroad), the nature of the material sought (extensive), the status of the foreign proceeding (on appeal), the overall scope and role of discovery in the foreign forum (curtailed), and its attitude toward American-style discovery (disfavor). After reviewing these factors, the district court concluded that "granting [MEPA's] petition would infringe on the French courts while not promoting the efficiency of the pending appeal in France." That approach is consonant with the purpose and design of the statute.[196]

A. *Discoverability.* Other circuits have read into §1782 the requirement that the discovery sought here be of a kind discoverable in the foreign forum. *See In re Application of Asta Medica, SA,* 981 F.2d 1, 7 (1st Cir. 1992); *Lo Ka Chun v. Lo To,* 858 F.2d 1564, 1566 (11th Cir. 1988). We have ruled that discoverability in the foreign jurisdiction is not a prerequisite to granting a §1782 request for assistance, but

---

195. The petitioner seeks the deposition of unspecified employees of Ralph Esmerian, Inc. and sixteen categories of documents relating to the jewelry that is the subject matter of the litigation in France, *e.g.*:

6. Documents, communications, memoranda, correspondence, contracts, invoices, sales agreements, or entrustments, between Esmerian and others relating to the Jewelry during the years 1988 to the present.

7. Documents, communications, memoranda, correspondence, contracts, invoices, or other written material among or between or reflecting communications among or between Esmerian, Wolfers, Wolfers Zug, Fakhreddin, Corvina, Guillaume, and George Chalhoub, MEPA and/or Allied.

10. All documents which substantiate the exact amount of loss that Esmerian allegedly suffered.

196. The Senate Report accompanying the 1964 amendments to §1782 state that "[§1782(a)] leaves the issuance of an appropriate order to the discretion of the court which, in proper cases, *may refuse to issue an order* or may impose conditions it deems desirable. In exercising its discretionary power, the court *may take into account the nature and attitudes of the government of the country from which the request emanates and the character of the proceedings in that country.*" S. Rep. No. 1580, 88th Cong., 2nd Sess. (1964), *reprinted in* 1964 U.S. Code Cong. & Admin. News 3782, 3788 (emphasis added).

that it is a "useful tool" for the district judge in exercising discretion. *See In re Application of Aldunate.* The district court expressly stated that it was not relying on whether the material sought by MEPA was discoverable under the laws of France, and proceeded to consider the issue in light of the "twin aims" of the statute: to "balance ... the policy of not infringing upon a foreign nation's procedural rules with the policy of promoting the efficient resolution of disputes in a foreign tribunal." In so doing, the district court observed that "MEPA failed to even attempt to use the mechanism provided by French procedure for obtaining documents." The majority opinion re-casts that observation as an impermissible requirement that MEPA exhaust its efforts to obtain this discovery in France before seeking §1782 assistance, and emphasizes that the relevance of discoverability is "quite limited." I think that it was appropriate for the district court to consider that American discovery is sought here — by one party against another party — as a substitute for discovery in France rather than as an aid and supplement to the procedures of a French tribunal. MEPA's petition was filed after the conclusion of the trial in France. Whatever pre-trial discovery is or is not permitted under French law, it is undisputed that MEPA took no step under French procedure for obtaining this discovery at issue prior to the entry of judgment. Now, MEPA seeks to conduct broad gauge, category by category, American-style discovery, citing a French appellate rule allowing additional documents to be submitted for the first time on appeal.

B. *Avoiding Offense to Foreign Tribunals.* We have emphasized that allowing §1782 petitions to be filed by "any interested person" represents an "effort to liberalize the assistance provided by American courts to foreign and international tribunals." *Malev,* 964 F.2d at 101.

The statute should not become an instrument of unilateral advantage as between the parties. It is therefore useful for the district court to inquire into the "nature and attitudes" of the foreign jurisdiction towards discovery. It seems undisputed that the French tolerate only the most circumscribed exchange of information: oral examination of witnesses only by a judge; and disclosure of specified documents rather than exploratory discovery and, even so, only with judicial intervention. The district court's brief review of the nature and attitudes of the French toward discovery bears upon an important discretionary value: whether the discovery sought here aids the proceedings abroad or whether it distorts the adversarial symmetry existing there. In my opinion, we should not "countenance the use of U.S. discovery procedures to evade the limitations placed on domestic pre-trial disclosure by foreign tribunals." *John Deere Ltd. v. Sperry Corp.,* 754 F.2d 132, 136 (3d Cir. 1985).

We have previously recognized that one policy consideration underlying §1782 is "maintaining the balance between litigants that each nation creates within its own judicial system, preventing circumvention of foreign restrictions on discovery and avoiding offense to foreign tribunals." *Aldunate,* 3 F.3d at 60. "Congress intended that these concerns be addressed by a district judge's exercise of discretion." Therefore, one important inquiry under *Aldunate* is whether the grant of §1782 discovery would circumvent the forum's procedures or be an affront to the foreign tribunal.

The majority opinion states: "We do not believe that an extensive examination of foreign law regarding the existence and extent of discovery in the forum country is desirable in order to ascertain the attitudes of foreign nations to outside discovery assistance."... With all due respect, I think this offers little guidance to the district court, and in effect displaces the discretion conferred on the district court by statute. ... The majority opinion chokes off any discretion on [inquiring into the "nature and attitudes" of the foreign forum] by limiting the district court's inquiry to "authoritative proof that a foreign tribunal would reject evidence obtained with the aid of §1782." And any such proof must be "embodied in a forum country's judicial, executive or legislative declarations that specifically address the use of evidence gathered under foreign procedures." This rigid formulation narrows useful discretion and invites friction with the courts of other countries, without avoiding the entanglement of American courts in the subtleties of foreign law: it is no easy task to determine what expressions by foreign courts or governments are "authoritative" and whether they authoritatively dispose of a particular petition for discovery. For example, the courts of France may well approve the discovery of a bill of lading from a nonparty in the United States without intending that the parties to French lawsuits be drawn into the coils of American discovery.

The majority opinion points out that a foreign court can always enjoin a party subject to its jurisdiction from pursuing discovery in the United States, and looks forward to "an on-going dialogue between the adjudicative bodies of the world community." On the whole, I think it may be unwise to stimulate declarations about the American system of discovery by foreign countries and tribunals. In any event, even if such a dialogue elicited categorical statements of position, I do not think that the statutory discretion of the district court should be narrowed on the theory that any resulting impairment of foreign procedures will elicit a corrective order or declaration from abroad.

C. *Permissible Limitations.* I agree with the majority that in many instances the misgivings of a district court in granting a petition under §1782 can be reconciled by a closely tailored discovery order. (Indeed, this may be the only substantial remaining area of discretion under the majority opinion.) The majority invites the district court to consider two provisos, neither of which seems to me practical or useful. The majority recognizes that French procedure discourages examination of documents that a party does not intend to offer in evidence, and that MEPA's document request casts a much broader net. The majority points out that the district court is free to require that all of the evidence gathered by MEPA in the United States be submitted to the French court, whether or not that material assists MEPA's cause. I think it makes little sense to contrive a hybrid Franco-American system by which mass discovery of inadmissible materials gathered under the American model is permitted to go forward on condition that the inadmissible material be submitted in bulk to the

French court. In this way, we both interfere with French discovery practice and clog the French appeals court with the random harvest of the American discovery.

The majority offers a second means of mitigating the effects of one-sided American discovery by conditioning the petitioner's discovery in American on an undertaking by the petitioner to furnish a reciprocal exchange of information in the United States. In this way, the entire discovery process is imported to the United States, and the procedures of the foreign forum are completely superseded, at least until such time as the foreign tribunal orders the petitioner to desist.

The majority does not advert to the only procedural device expressly approved by this court that may alleviate the effects of the majority opinion. The majority in *Malev* emphasizes that the district court may require a petitioner under §1782

> to prepare a discovery plan, make a showing that the discovery is "not obtainable from such other source that is more convenient, less burdensome, or less expensive," such as the [foreign] court, and then require [the petitioner] to take the discovery plan before the [foreign] court for a determination as to which requests are relevant before coming to the United States district court for actual discovery.

Malev, 964 F.2d at 102. Given the now narrowed scope of district court discretion in this circuit, this device may become the best instrument for avoiding the day when United States courts become "global 'Special Masters for Discovery.'" Id. at 103 (Feinberg, J., dissenting).

Notes on Euromep

1. *Parties entitled to utilize §1782.* Note who the requesting party was in *Euromep*. Was it a foreign court or other governmental official? *See* S. Rep. No. 1580, 88th Cong. 2d Sess. (1964), *reprinted in*, U.S. Code, Cong. & Admin. News 3782, 3789 ("interested person" includes "person designated by or under foreign law, or a party to the foreign or international litigation"); *In re Request for Assistance From Ministry of Legal Affairs of Trinidad and Tobago*, 848 F.2d 1151 (11th Cir. 1988), *cert. denied*, 488 U.S. 1005 (1989); *In re Application of Malev Hungarian Airlines*, 964 F.2d 97 (2d Cir.), *cert. denied*, 113 S.Ct. 179 (1992); *In re Application of Gianoli*, 3 F.3d 54 (2d Cir.), *cert. denied*, 114 S.Ct. 443 (1993).

What is the rationale for permitting "interested persons" in foreign litigation — including private parties — to obtain the assistance of U.S. courts directly, without first seeking the permission of the foreign court presiding over the foreign litigation? Note that this is a departure from traditional notions of international judicial assistance, which involved the aid of one court for another. Section 1782 involves U.S. judicial assistance for private litigants. Is this wise? What policies does it advance? What risks does it involve?

2. *Traditional reciprocity requirement for letters rogatory.* Although there is little formal precedent, the practice of executing foreign letters rogatory was predicated on notions of reciprocity. The traditional forms for letters rogatory promised reciprocal treatment. *See The Signe*, 37 F.Supp. 819, 821 (E.D. La. 1941); Stahr, *Discovery Under 28 U.S.C. §1782 For Foreign and International Proceedings*, 30 Va. J. Int'l L. 597 (1990).

3. *No reciprocity requirement under §1782.* As *Euromep* indicates, U.S. courts have repeatedly held that §1782 imposes no reciprocity requirement. That is, if a national of State A is litigating against a U.S. party in State A courts (or State B courts), §1782 permits the State A national to obtain U.S. style discovery from the U.S. party even if State A (or State B) would not provide similar assistance to a U.S. party. *In re Malev Hungarian Airlines*, 964 F.2d 97, 100-101 (2d Cir.), *cert. denied*, 113 S.Ct. 179 (1992); *John Deere Ltd. v. Sperry Corp.*, 754 F.2d 132, 135 (3d Cir. 1985) (s 1782 "does not require reciprocity as a predicate to the grant of a discovery order"); *In re Letter Rogatory From the Justice Court, District of Montreal, Canada,*

523 F.2d 562, 565 (6th Cir. 1975); *In re Request for Judicial Assistance From Seoul, Korea,* 428 F.Supp. 109, 112 (N.D. Calif. 1977), *aff'd,* 555 F.2d 720 (9th Cir. 1977).

Is this wise? Why should the United States provide assistance to foreign litigants, whose courts will not provide similar aid to U.S. courts and litigants? Who are the most likely parties to be harmed by the application of §1782 — U.S. parties or foreign parties? What parties are most likely to have evidence located in the United States? *Compare* the discussion of reciprocity in other contexts, *e.g.,* p. 93 (personal jurisdiction), pp. 393-94 (forum selection clauses), p. 473 (lis pendens), and pp. 951-55 (foreign judgments).

Consider the following rationale for §1782's lack of any reciprocity requirement:

> Enactment of the bill into law will constitute a major step in bringing the United States to the forefront of nations adjusting their procedures to those of sister nations and thereby providing equitable and efficacious procedures for the benefit of tribunals and litigants involved in litigation with international aspects. *It is hoped that the initiative taken by the United States in improving its procedures will invite foreign countries similarly to adjust their procedures.*

S. Rep. No. 1580, 88th Cong. 2d Sess. (1964), *reprinted in* U.S. Code, Cong., & Admin. News 3782, 3783. Is this a desirable goal? Is the enactment of §1782 a plausible basis for achieving the goal? Does it matter that, since 1964, no foreign state has granted reciprocal treatment?

   4. *No exhaustion requirement.* When a litigant in a foreign proceeding seeks discovery under §1782, is there any requirement that it first have attempted to obtain discovery in the foreign proceeding? Is there any such requirement in the statute's text? Should such a requirement be implied? U.S. courts have refused to impose any exhaustion requirement under §1782. *In re Malev Hungarian Airlines,* 964 F.2d 97, 100 (2d Cir.), *cert. denied,* 113 S.Ct. 179 (1992).

   5. *No admissibility requirement under §1782.* Lower U.S. courts have uniformly held that §1782 does not impose any requirement that the requested information be admissible as evidence under foreign law. *See John Deere Ltd. v. Sperry Corp.,* 754 F.2d 132, 132 (3d Cir. 1985); *In re Letter of Request From Supreme Court of Hong Kong,* 821 F.Supp. 204, 211 (S.D.N.Y. 1993).

   6. *Decisions holding that §1782 is only available to obtain materials that are "discoverable" in foreign proceedings.* Contrary to *Euromep,* a number of courts of appeals have held that discovery under §1782 is limited to information that would be discoverable under the laws of the foreign state in which the foreign proceeding is pending. *In re Application of Asta Medica, SA,* 981 F.2d 1, 7 (1st Cir. 1992); *In re Request From Crown Prosecution Service of United Kingdom,* 870 F.2d 686, 692-93 & n.7 (D.C. Cir. 1989); *Lo Ka Chun v. Lo To,* 858 F.2d 1564, 1566 (11th Cir. 1988); *In re Request for Assistance From Ministry of Legal Affairs of Trinidad and Tobago,* 848 F.2d 1151, 1156 (11th Cir. 1988), *cert. denied,* 488 U.S. 1005 (1989); *John Deere Ltd. v. Sperry Corp.,* 754 F.2d 132, 136 (3d Cir. 1985).

   These decisions have found a discoverability requirement to be "implicitly required by §1782, based upon its history, rationale, and ... policy considerations." *Asta Medica,* 981 F.2d at 7. These policies were (a) maintaining equality between the parties in respect of discovery opportunities; (b) preventing circumvention of foreign limitations on discovery in local judicial proceedings; and (c) avoiding offense to foreign courts. Consider:

> Under the [Second Circuit's] ruling, a U.S. party involved in litigation in a foreign country with limited pre-trial discovery will be placed at a substantial disadvantage vis-a-vis the foreign party. All the foreign party need do is file a request for assistance under §1782 and the floodgates are open for unlimited discovery while the U.S. party is confined to restricted discovery in the foreign jurisdiction. Congress did not amend §1782 to place U.S. litigants in a more detrimental position than their opponents when litigating abroad.... The [Second Circuit's] holding has another serious shortcoming; foreign litigants may use §1782 to circumvent foreign law and procedures. The information sought under §1782 may not be available in the foreign jurisdiction due to either procedural restrictions or the substantive law. ... Congress did not seek to place itself on a collision course with foreign tribunals and legislatures, which have carefully chosen the procedures and laws best suited for their concepts of litigation. 981 F.2d at 5-6.

Is this a persuasive basis for implying a discoverability requirement into §1782?

   7. *Decisions refusing to limit §1782 to materials that are discoverable under foreign law.* As *Euromep,* illustrates, the Second Circuit has refused to imply a discoverability limitation into §1782. It has acknowledged, at least in words, the significance of the policies cited in *Asta Medica* and elsewhere, but has reasoned that these are only relevant to the district court's exercise of its discretion:

> We agree that each of these is a legitimate policy consideration and that the legislative history indicates that these concerns were part of the motivation for the legislation. However, we disagree with the First Circuit's holding that, as a result of these concerns, Congress intended §1782 to have an implied discoverability requirement. Instead, we believe Congress intended that these concerns be addressed by a district court's exercise of discretion. *In re Application of Aldunate*, 3 F.3d at 60.

The Second Circuit has relied in particular on the following excerpt from the Senate Report accompanying §1782:

> [Section 1782(a)] leaves the issuance of an appropriate order to the discretion of the court which, in proper cases, may refuse to issue an order or may impose conditions it deems desirable. In exercising its discretionary power, the court may take into account the nature and attitudes of the government of the country from which the request emanates and the character of the proceedings in that country, or in the case of proceedings before an international tribunal, the nature of the tribunal and the character of the proceedings before it.

Which approach to §1782 — that in *Asta Medica* or that in *Aldunate* and *Euromep* — is more persuasive? Why can't issues of "discoverability" merely be a factor in exercising the district court's discretion? Doesn't this safeguard the policies identified in *Asta Medica*?

8. Application of Second Circuit's discretion standard in Euromep. Consider the application of the Second Circuit's "discretion" test in *Euromep*. What role do issues of discoverability play in a proper exercise of the trial court's discretion? Do they play any meaningful role? Is this a satisfactory interpretation of §1782?

Consider the dissenting opinion in *Euromep*. Is this not more persuasive than the majority opinion? What harm does it do to order discovery that is not permitted in foreign proceedings? Is it sufficient, as the *Euromep* analysis suggests, that a foreign court can always state expressly that discovery under §1782 (or similar mechanisms) is forbidden? or that it can affirmatively forbid such discovery?

9. What does the "discoverability" requirement mean? What must be established to show that the materials requested under §1782 are "discoverable" in the foreign jurisdiction? In *Asta Medica*, the First Circuit required a "showing that the information would be discoverable in the foreign jurisdiction if located there." 981 F.2d at 6. Why does the *Asta Medica* analysis "move" the sought after evidence to the foreign jurisdiction in considering whether it is "discoverable"? If evidence is not discoverable in a foreign proceeding, because it is located in the United States, why is that not an end of matters? Does not §1782 discovery of such evidence intrude upon the foreign jurisdiction's decision not to permit unilateral party-directed extraterritorial discovery? If the foreign court wants the evidence, can it not issue a letter rogatory?

10. Requiring mutual exchange of discovery. One criticism of the Second Circuit's approach to §1782 is that it gives one party an advantage — specifically, broad U.S.- style discovery — that the other party does not enjoy. Is this a legitimate concern? How does *Euromep* propose dealing with this problem? Consider the dissent's objections to mutual exchanges of discovery. Are these objections persuasive?

11. Requiring submission of all U.S. discovery to foreign court. The *Euromep* majority suggests that §1782 orders might require parties to submit all materials obtained in U.S. discovery to the foreign court. Is this a sensible suggestion? Consider the dissent's reply. Would such U.S. orders interfere with foreign judicial administration?

12/Recognition and Enforcement of Foreign Judgments[1]

International litigation, like domestic litigation, does not necessarily come to an end when one party succeeds in obtaining a favorable judgment. An unsuccessful defendant may refuse voluntarily to pay a judgment rendered against it, while a disappointed plaintiff may seek to relitigate its claim in a different forum. This Chapter deals with the principal mechanisms — the recognition and enforcement of foreign judgments — that prevailing parties in international litigation can use in U.S. courts to compel compliance with favorable foreign judgments that they have obtained.

A. Introduction

In most circumstances, the judgment of a national court has no independent force outside the forum's territory. Thus, most courts will (and can) enforce their own money judgments only against assets located within their territorial jurisdiction;[2] likewise, most courts will only infrequently attempt to preclude relitigation in foreign forums of claims already decided in a domestic proceeding.[3] As a general rule,

---

1. Commentary on recognizing and enforcing foreign judgments includes, *e.g.*, Bishop & Burnette, *United States Practice Concerning the Recognition of Foreign Judgments*, 16 Int'l Law. 425 (1982); Lutz, *Enforcement of Foreign Judgments, Part I: A Selected Bibliography on United States Enforcement of Judgments Rendered Abroad*, 27 Int'l Law. 471 (1993); Peterson, *Foreign Country Judgments and the Second Restatement of Conflict of Laws*, 72 Colum. L. Rev. 220 (1972); Reese, *The Status in this Country of Judgments Rendered Abroad*, 50 Colum. L. Rev. 783 (1950); Smit, *International Res Judicata and Collateral Estoppel in the United States*, 9 UCLA L. Rev. 44 (1962); von Mehren, *Recognition and Enforcement of Sister-State Judgments: Reflections on General Theory and Current Practice in the European Economic Community and the United States*, 81 Colum. L. Rev. 1044 (1981); von Mehren, *Enforcement of Foreign Judgments in the United States*, 17 Va. J. Int'l L. 401 (1977); von Mehren & Trautman, *Recognition of Foreign Adjudications: A Survey and a Suggested Approach*, 81 Harv. L. Rev. 1601 (1968); P. Weems, *Enforcement of Money Judgments Abroad* (1988); Westin, *Enforcing Foreign Commercial Judgments and Arbitral Awards in the United States, West Germany, and England*, 19 J. Law & Pol'y Int'l Bus. 325 (1987); Annotation, *Construction and Application of Uniform Foreign Money-Judgments Recognition Act*, 100 A.L.R.3d 792 (1980).

2. *E.g.*, *FTC v. Compagnie Saint-Gobain-Pont-a-Mousson*, 636 F.2d 1300, 1316 (D.C. Cir. 1980).

3. Although U.S. courts will sometimes issue antisuit injunctions seeking to preclude relitigation of disputes in foreign courts, this is not a common occurrence. *See supra* pp. 475-90.

therefore, a judgment will operate in foreign states only if the courts of those states are willing to provide assistance by recognizing or enforcing the judgment: "[a]s an act of government [a judgment's] effects are limited to the territory of the sovereign whose court rendered the judgment, unless some other state is bound by treaty to give the judgment effect in its territory, or unless some other state is willing, for reasons of its own, to give the judgment effect."[4]

1. Recognition and Enforcement Distinguished

"Recognition" and "enforcement" of foreign judgments are related but distinct concepts. The "recognition" of a foreign judgment occurs when a U.S. court relies upon a foreign judicial ruling to preclude litigation of a particular claim, or issue, on the ground that it has been previously litigated abroad.[5] Recognition is akin to the domestic U.S. doctrines of *res judicata* and collateral estoppel.[6] In contrast, the "enforcement" of a foreign judgment occurs when a court affirmatively uses its coercive powers to compel a defendant ("judgment debtor") to satisfy a judgment rendered abroad.[7] The enforcement of foreign judgments is typically sought by a plaintiff ("judgment creditor") who has obtained a money judgment in foreign proceedings that the judgment debtor refuses to satisfy.

2. Recognition and Enforcement of Sister State Judgments Under the U.S. Full Faith and Credit Clause

Before examining the recognition and enforcement of "foreign" judgments, it is useful to consider briefly the treatment of this issue in domestic U.S. litigation, where the judgments of one state's courts are routinely enforced in sister states.[8] As discussed above, Article IV, §1 of the U.S. Constitution requires that "Full Faith and Credit shall be given in each State to the public Acts, Records, and Judicial Proceedings of every other State."[9] The full faith and credit clause *requires* state

---

4. *Hilton v. Guyot,* 159 U.S. 113, 163 (1895).

5. *Restatement (Second) Conflict of Laws,* Chap. 5, Topic 2, Introductory Note & §§93-98 (1971); *Restatement (Third) Foreign Relations Law* §481, comments a & b (1987).

6. *Res judicata* (or "claim preclusion") prevents parties *or* their privies that have litigated the merits of a claim from relitigating the same claim against the parties to the prior proceeding. *Cromwell v. County of Sac,* 94 U.S. 351 (1877). Collateral estoppel (or "issue preclusion") extends the preclusive effect of a judgment to relitigation of issues that were decided in a prior action. *Restatement (Second) Judgments* §§18-19 (1980).

7. *Restatement (Second) Conflict of Laws,* Chap. 5, Topic 2, Introductory Note & §§99-102 (1971); *Restatement (Third) Foreign Relations Law* §481, comments a & b (1987).

8. Judgments rendered in a foreign nation are generally referred to as "foreign judgments" or "foreign country judgments." Judgments rendered in a different U.S. state than the state where recognition or enforcement is sought are referred to as "sister state judgments." Judgments rendered within the state where recognition or enforcement is sought are referred to as "domestic judgments."

9. Congress has implemented the full faith and credit clause by statutory enactment, providing that judicial proceedings "shall have the same full faith and credit in every court within the United States ... as they have by law or usage in the courts of such State ... from which they are taken." 28 U.S.C. §1738 (1982).

courts, as a matter of federal constitutional law, to recognize any valid final judgment rendered in another state of the Union.[10]

The general enforceability of state court judgments under the full faith and credit clause is subject to limited exceptions. These permit nonenforcement only where a state judgment was rendered by a court without personal or subject matter jurisdiction,[11] where the defendant did not receive adequate notice or an opportunity to be heard,[12] or where the state judgment was obtained by fraud.[13] Moreover, where the rendering court has considered and rejected defenses based on lack of jurisdiction or inadequate notice, the court where recognition or enforcement is sought is precluded from relitigating these issues.[14] Recognition or enforcement of a sister state judgment is required even where the underlying claim is contrary to the public policy of the state where enforcement is sought.[15]

The full faith and credit clause reflects fundamental national policies. The clause rests on the belief that national unity will be promoted by requiring individual states to give effect to the judicial decisions of other states:

> The very purpose of the full faith and credit clause was to alter the status of the several states as independent foreign sovereignties, each free to ignore obligations created under the laws or by the judicial proceedings of the others, and to make them integral parts of a single nation throughout which a remedy upon a just obligation might be demanded as of right irrespective of the state of its origin.[16]

The clause also reflects the public interest in judicial finality.[17] In the Supreme Court's words, "[t]o preclude parties from contesting matters that they have had a full and fair opportunity to litigate protects their adversaries from the expense and vexation attending multiple lawsuits, conserves judicial resources, and fosters reliance on judicial action by minimizing the possibility of inconsistent decision."[18]

---

10. *Restatement (Second) Conflict of Laws* §93 (1971).

11. *Restatement (Second) Conflict of Laws* §§104, 105 (1971); *Adam v. Saenger*, 303 U.S. 59 (1938).

12. *Mullane v. Central Hanover Bank & Trust Co.*, 339 U.S. 306 (1950); *Restatement (Second) Conflict of Laws* §104 (1971).

13. *Christopher v. Christopher*, 31 S.E.2d 818 (Ga. 1944); *Restatement (Second) Judgments* §70 (1972).

14. *American Surety Co. v. Baldwin*, 287 U.S. 156 (1932); *Baldwin v. Iowa State Traveling Men's Ass'n*, 283 U.S. 522 (1931); *Restatement (Second) Conflict of Laws* §§96-97 (1971).

15. *Fauntleroy v. Lum*, 210 U.S. 230 (1908); *Restatement (Second) Conflict of Laws* §117 (1971).

16. *Milwaukee County v.M. E. White Co.*, 296 U.S. 268, 276-77 (1935). *See also Industrial Comm'n v. McCartin*, 330 U.S. 622 (1947); *Magnolia Petroleum Co. v. Hunt*, 320 U.S. 430 (1943).

17. *See Allen v. McCurry*, 449 U.S. 90 (1980); *Restatement (Second) Conflict of Laws* §98, comment b (1971).

18. *Montana v. United States*, 440 U.S. 147, 153-54 (1979). *See also Baldwin v. Iowa State Traveling Men's Ass'n*, 283 U.S. 522, 525 (1931); *Hart Steel Co. v. Railroad Supply Co.*, 244 U.S. 294, 299 (1917).

B. Recognition and Enforcement of Foreign Judgments by U.S. Courts

1. No Express Federal Law Governing Recognition and Enforcement of Foreign Judgments

There is presently no federal standard governing the enforcement of judgments rendered by foreign courts in the United States.[19] Unlike sister state judgments, foreign judgments are not governed by the full faith and credit clause.[20] Nor is there any federal statute generally applicable to the enforcement of foreign court judgments in U.S. courts.

Unlike many foreign states, the United States is not a party to any international agreement regarding the mutual recognition of judgments.[21] In contrast, the United States is a party to the New York Convention, dealing among other things with the recognition and enforcement of foreign arbitral awards.[22] The United States has made few attempts to conclude treaties with other countries on the reciprocal recognition and enforcement of judgments, and those attempts have failed. In the 1970s, the United States and the United Kingdom unsuccessfully sought to conclude a bilateral agreement on mutual recognition of foreign judgments.[23] The United States is currently involved in discussions within the Hague Conference of Private International Law regarding a multilateral judgments convention.[24] It appears, however, that progress on any such convention will slow.

Thus, for the present and foreseeable future, there is no direct source of federal law governing the recognition of foreign judgments. Although it has been urged that federal common law standards may properly be developed to govern the recognition

---

19. This distinguishes the recognition and enforcement of foreign court judgments from the enforcement of international arbitral awards, where most issues are governed by federal statute (the Federal Arbitration Act) or by treaty (the New York Convention). *See infra* pp. 1040-42; G. Born, *International Commercial Arbitration in the United States* 459-64 (1994).

20. *Hilton v. Guyot*, 159 U.S. 113 (1895); *Restatement (Second) Conflict of Laws* §§98, 102, comment g (1971).

21. A few lower courts have interpreted standard friendship, commerce, and navigation treaties as covering the recognition and enforcement of foreign judgments, but this is a minority view. *See infra* p. 962.

22. *See infra* pp. 990-91; G. Born, *International Commercial Arbitration in the United States* 459-64 (1994).

23. The agreement was tentatively titled the United Kingdom-United States Convention on the Reciprocal Recognition and Enforcement of Judgments in Civil Matters. The proposed Convention is reprinted in 16 Int'l Leg. Mat. 71 (1977). *See* North, *The Draft U.K./U.S. Judgments Convention: A British Viewpoint*, 1 Nw. J. Int'l L. & Bus. 219 (1979). The agreement foundered on differences over the size and punitive nature of some U.S. civil judgments and the reach of U.S. judicial jurisdiction. Smit, *The Proposed United States-United Kingdom Convention on Recognition and Enforcement of Judgments: A Prototype for the Future?*, 17 Va. J. Int'l L. 443 (1977).

24. von Mehren, *Recognition and Enforcement of Foreign Judgments: A New Approach for the Hague Conference?*, 57 Law & Contemp. Probs. 271 (1994); Lowenfeld, *Thoughts About a Multinational Judgments Convention: A Reaction to the von Mehren Report*, 57 Law & Contemp. Probs. 289 (1994).

of foreign judgments, few courts have actually done so.[25] According to most authorities, the recognition and enforcement of foreign judgments in the United States is therefore governed by the laws of several states.[26]

2. Contemporary Approaches to Enforceability of Foreign Judgments in the United States

Although the United States lacks a uniform nationwide standard for enforcing foreign judgments, there are surprisingly few fundamental differences in the approaches taken by the various states. In more than 25 states, the recognition of foreign judgments is governed by state common law, derived from the Supreme Court's 1895 decision in *Hilton v. Guyot*.[27] Twenty-two other states have adopted the Uniform Foreign Money Judgments Recognition Act (the "UFMJRA"), which is modelled largely on *Hilton's* standards.[28]

a. Hilton v. Guyot: International Comity and the Presumptive Enforceability of Foreign Judgments

Most state courts have adopted the basic approach to foreign judgments taken almost a century ago in *Hilton v. Guyot*.[29] There, a French citizen sought to enforce in the United States a judgment of a French court against two New York residents arising out of the New Yorkers' business in France. The Supreme Court reviewed a New York federal court's enforcement of the judgment.

Writing for the Court, Justice Gray began by suggesting that the enforceability of a foreign judgment required looking to international law, citing the familiar *Paquete Habana* rule that international law "is part of our law, and must be ascertained and administered by the courts of justice, as often as such questions are presented in litigation between man and man."[30] With this explanation, Justice Gray turned to prevailing territorial limits on national jurisdiction as a ground for denying the French judgment any independent effect in the United States: "No law has any effect, of its own force, beyond the limits of the sovereignty from which its authority is derived."[31]

The Court went on to consider what rationale would justify a U.S. court in giving effect to a foreign court's judgment. It reasoned that international comity was the relevant source of authority:

---

25. *See infra* pp. 960-62.

26. *See infra* p. 961.

27. 159 U.S. 113 (1895).

28. *See infra* pp. 941-42.

29. 159 U.S. 113 (1895).

30. 159 U.S. at 163. He referred to "[i]nternational law in its widest and most comprehensive sense," which included "not only questions of right between nations, governed by what has appropriately called the law of nations," but also questions "concerning the rights of persons within the territory and dominion of one nation, by reason of acts, private or public, done within the dominions of another nation" — so-called "private international law, or the conflict of laws." 159 U.S. at 163.

31. 159 U.S. at 163.

The extent to which the law of one nation, as put in force within its territory, whether by executive order, by legislative act, or by judicial decree, shall be allowed to operate within the dominion of another nation, depends upon what our greatest jurists have been content to call "the comity of nations." Although the phrase has been often criticized, no satisfactory substitute has been suggested. "Comity," in the legal sense, is neither a matter of absolute obligation, on the one hand, nor of mere courtesy and good will, upon the other. But it is the recognition which one nation allows within its territory to the legislative, executive or judicial acts of another nation, having due regard both to international duty and convenience, and to the rights of its own citizens or of other persons who are under the protection of its laws.[32]

Based upon this principle of comity,[33] *Hilton* fashioned a rule of general common law governing when U.S. federal courts should enforce foreign judgments:

[W]here there has been opportunity for a full and fair trial abroad before a court of competent jurisdiction, conducting the trial upon regular proceedings, after due citation or voluntary appearance of the defendant, and under a system of jurisprudence likely to secure an impartial administration of justice between the citizens of its own country and those of other countries, and there is nothing to show either prejudice in the court, or in the system of laws under which it was sitting, or fraud in procuring the judgment, or any other special reason why the comity of this nation should not allow it full effect, the merits of the case should not, in an action brought in this country upon the judgment, be tried afresh, as on a new trial or an appeal, upon the mere assertion by the party that the judgment was erroneous in law or in fact.[34]

The Court rejected earlier U.S. (and other) authorities which had concluded that foreign judgments were only prima facie evidence of the defendant's liability and were subject to rebuttal in the court where recognition was sought.[35] On the facts in *Hilton*, the Court found that the French decree satisfied the above requirements, but nonetheless refused to enforce the judgment, citing a "reciprocity requirement." In a 5-4 decision, Justice Gray reasoned that international comity did not require

---

32. 159 U.S. at 163-64.

33. *See also* Casad, *Issue Preclusion and Foreign Country Judgments: Whose Law?*, 70 Iowa L. Rev. 53, 58 (1984); Peterson, *Foreign Country Judgments and the Second Restatement of Conflict of Laws*, 72 Colum. L. Rev. 220, 239-48 (1972); Barry, *Comity*, 12 Va. L. Rev. 353 (1926); Yntema, *The Enforcement of Foreign Judgments in Anglo-American Law*, 33 Mich. L. Rev. 1129, 1142 (1935).

34. 159 U.S. at 202-03.

35. *E.g., Williams v. Preston*, 3 J.J. Marsh. 600 (Ky. 1830); *Buttrick v. Allen*, 8 Mass. 273 (1811); *Smith v. Lewis*, 3 Johns. 157 (N.Y. 1808). *Compare Dunstan v. Higgins*, 138 N.Y. 70 (1893) (giving conclusive effect to foreign judgment); *Lazier v. Wescott*, 26 N.Y. 146 (1862) (same).

enforcement of the French judgment because French courts would not reciprocally enforce a U.S. judgment in reverse circumstances.[36]

Hilton's basic rule continued to be followed in the United States, with various modifications, for the next century. Over time, however, various rationales other than international comity were suggested to justify the presumptive enforceability of foreign judgments. Relying on Joseph Beale's more general "vested rights" doctrine, the *Restatement (First) Conflict of Laws* adopted the theory that a foreign judgment creates a "vested right" or "legal obligation" that is entitled to enforcement wherever the judgment debtor or his property can be found.[37]

The *Restatement (Second) Conflict of Laws* adopted the same basic rules regarding the enforceability of foreign judgments as those set forth in *Hilton* and the *First Restatement*.[38] In justifying this approach, the *Second Restatement* emphasized that the recognition of foreign judgments rests on the fact that "the public interest requires that there be an end of litigation."[39]

b. Statutory Mechanism for the Enforcement of Foreign Judgments: Uniform Foreign Money Judgments Recognition Act

Although a majority of states follow *Hilton's* common law approach, some twenty-two states have instead enacted statutes setting forth the circumstances in which their courts will enforce foreign money judgments.[40] Each of these states has adopted some form of the UFMJRA, which is based closely on *Hilton v. Guyot*.[41] The UFMJRA is excerpted in Appendix M.

For the most part, the UFMJRA codifies existing U.S. case law concerning recognition of foreign judgments. As with the common law, foreign judgments are presumptively entitled to recognition under the UFMJRA if they are "final and conclu-

---

36. 159 U.S. at 227-28. In *Ritchie v. McMullen*, 159 U.S. 235 (1895), decided the same day as *Hilton*, a Canadian judgment was recognized because Canadian courts gave conclusive effect to U.S. judgments.

37. *See Restatement (First) Conflict of Laws* §§429, 430 & 434 (1934); *Johnston v. Compagnie Generale Transatlantique*, 152 N.E. 121 (N.Y. 1926).

38. *See Restatement (Second) Conflict of Laws* §98 (1971); *infra* p. 948.

39. *Restatement (Second) Conflict of Laws* §98, comment b (1971). *See also* Reese, *The Status in This Country of Judgments Rendered Abroad*, 50 Colum. L. Rev. 783, 784 (1950); Smit, *International Res Judicata and Collateral Estoppel in the United States*, 9 UCLA L. Rev. 44 (1962).

40. Alaska, California, Colorado, Connecticut, Georgia, Idaho, Illinois, Iowa, Maryland, Massachusetts, Michigan, Minnesota, Missouri, New Mexico, New York, Ohio, Oklahoma, Oregon, Pennsylvania, Texas, Virginia and Washington. *See* 13 Unif. Laws Annot. 269-70 (1980 & 1991 Supp.).

41. The Uniform Act was developed in 1962 by the National Conference of Commissioners on Uniform State Laws and the American Bar Association. *See* 13 Unif. Laws Annot. 263 (1980 & 1991 Supp.). See *also* Bishop & Burnette, *United States Practice Concerning the Recognition of Foreign Judgments*, 16 Int'l Law. 425 (1982); Brand, *Enforcement of Foreign Money-Judgments in the United States: In Search of Uniformity and International Acceptance*, 67 Notre Dame L. Rev. 253 (1991); Kulzer, *Recognition of Foreign Country Judgments in New York: The Uniform Foreign Money-Judgments Recognition Act*, 18 Buffalo L. Rev. 1 (1968); Scoles & Aarnas, *The Recognition and Enforcement of Foreign Nation Judgments: California, Oregon, and Washington*, 57 Or. L. Rev. 377 (1978); Sorkowitz, *Enforcing Judgments under the Uniform Foreign Money-Judgments Recognition Act*, 37 Prac. Law. 57 (1991); Note, *The Uniform Foreign Money-Judgments Recognition Act: A Survey of the Case Law*, 14 Vand. J. Transnat'l L. 171 (1981).

sive and enforceable where rendered even though an appeal therefrom is pending or it is subject to an appeal."[42] If a foreign judgment does satisfy this standard, then it is "conclusive between the parties to the extent that it grants or denies recovery of a sum of money."[43] Again like *Hilton*, however, the Act sets forth a number of specific exceptions to the general enforceability of foreign money judgments.[44]

3. Foreign Approaches to the Enforceability of U.S. and Other Judgments

There is no uniform practice among foreign states regarding the recognition and enforcement of foreign judgments.[45] In many states (particularly civil law jurisdictions), the recognition of foreign judgments has been dealt with by bilateral or multilateral international agreements. Where no international agreement exists (as is the case where United States judgments are concerned), recognition of foreign judgments is often difficult.

In Germany, the recognition of foreign judgments is generally governed by §328 of the German Code of Civil Procedure. Section 328 provides:

Recognition of a judgment of a foreign court shall not be permitted:

1. if the courts of the relevant foreign state would not have jurisdiction pursuant to German law;
2. if the defendant, who did not appear in the proceeding and objects on that basis, was not properly served or served in sufficient time to allow him to defend himself;
3. if the judgment is inconsistent with a German judgment or with a prior foreign judgment whose recognition is sought or with a pending proceeding concerning the same facts;
4. if recognition of the judgment would manifestly lead to a result which is incompatible with fundamental principles of German law (ordre public), particularly, if recognition would be incompatible with constitutional principles;
5. if reciprocity is not assured....

In Japan, the recognition and enforcement of foreign judgments is, in the absence of an international agreement, generally subject to §200 of the Japanese Code of Civil Procedure. Section 200 provides:

A foreign judgment which has become final and conclusive shall be valid only upon the fulfillment of the following conditions:

(i) that the jurisdiction of the foreign court is consistent with Japanese laws or treaties;
(ii) that the unsuccessful defendant, if a Japanese national, received

---

42. Uniform Foreign Money-Judgments Recognition Act, §2.
43. Uniform Foreign Money-Judgments Recognition Act, §3.
44. *See infra* pp. 963-86.
45. *Restatement (Third) Foreign Relations Law* §481, Reporters' Note 6 (1987).

service of process necessary to commence the foreign proceedings by public notice or has appeared without receiving service;

(iii) that the judgment of the foreign court is not contrary to the public order or good morals of Japan;

(iv) that reciprocity is assured.

In England, the recognition and enforcement of foreign judgments is, in the absence of an international agreement, generally subject to common law standards. These standards can be summarized as follows:

> The basic rule under English law is that any foreign judgment for a debt or definite sum of money (not being a sum payable in respect of taxes, or other charges of a like nature, a fine or other penalty) which is final and conclusive on the merits, may be enforced at Common Law in the absence of fraud or some other overriding consideration of public policy provided that the foreign court had jurisdiction over the defendant in accordance with conflict of law principles.[46]

In cases involving default judgments, English law imposes strict jurisdictional limits. In particular, a foreign court will be found to have properly exercised jurisdiction only if the defendant was physically present in the foreign state at the time of the action,[47] or if the defendant voluntarily appeared in the action, or if the defendant contractually submitted to the jurisdiction of the foreign court.[48]

4. Selected Materials on the Presumptive Enforceability of Foreign Judgments

The following materials explore the basis for presumptively recognizing foreign judgments. Consider first the excerpts from *Hilton*. Then consider the excerpts from the *Restatement (Second) Conflict of Laws* and the UFMJRA. Finally, compare these approaches with that under the Brussels Convention.

HILTON v. GUYOT

159 U.S. 113 (1895)

JUSTICE GRAY. [Gustave Guyot was the French liquidator of a French firm named Charles Fortin & Co. Henry Hilton and William Libbey were U.S. nationals, residing in New York, who ran a business that operated in New York, Paris and elsewhere under the name A.T. Stewart & Co. Guyot apparently sued A.T. Stewart & Co., Hilton, and Libbey in French courts, for obligations they allegedly owed to

---

46. D. Campbell, *International Execution Against Judgment Debtors* Eng - 5 (1993).

47. *Adams v. Cape Industries plc,* [1990] Ch. 433 (suggesting that, in case of corporate defendant, English law would require the carrying on of the defendant's own business for more than a minimal time in the foreign state through agents or representatives at a fixed place of business); *State Bank of India v. Murjani,* (transcript of March 27, 1991) (dicta that principal residence of defendant in foreign state was sufficient even without physical presence at time of action).

48. *Emanuel v. Symon* [1908] 1 K.B. 302, 308-09.

Charles Fortin & Co. The defendants appeared and defended on the merits, but unsuccessfully. The French court of first instance entered a substantial judgment against Hilton and Libbey, who apparently appealed, but again unsuccessfully.

During the pendency of the French litigation, Hilton and Libbey removed their assets from France. When their French appeals were finally rejected, the U.S. defendants refused to pay the French judgment. Mr. Guyot then sought to enforce the judgment against them in the United States. A New York federal court permitted enforcement, and the Supreme Court reversed in the opinion excerpted below.] ...

International law in its widest and most comprehensive sense — including not only questions of right between nations, governed by what has been appropriately called the law of nations; but also questions arising under what is usually called private international law, or of persons within the territory and dominion of one nation, by reason of acts, private or public, done within the dominions of another nation — is part of our law, and must be ascertained and administered by the courts of justice, as often as such questions are presented in litigation between man and man, duly submitted to their determination.

The most certain guide, no doubt, for the decision of such questions is a treaty or a statute of this country. But when, as is the case here, there is no written law upon the subject, the duty still rests upon the judicial tribunals of ascertaining and declaring what the law is, whenever it becomes necessary to do so in order to determine the rights of parties to suits regularly brought before them. In doing this, the courts must obtain such aid as they can from judicial decisions, from the works of jurists and commentators, and from the acts and usages of civilized nations.

No law has any effect, of its own force, beyond the limits of the sovereignty from which its authority is derived. The extent to which the law of one nation, as put in force within its territory, whether by executive order, by legislative act, or by judicial decree, shall be allowed to operate within the dominion of another nation, depends upon what our greatest jurists have been content to call "the comity of nations." Although the phrase has been often criticized, no satisfactory substitute has been suggested.

"Comity," in the legal sense, is neither a matter of absolute obligation on the one hand, nor of mere courtesy and good will upon the other. But it is the recognition which one nation allows within its territory to the legislative, executive, or judicial acts of another nations, having due regard both to the international duty and convenience, and to the rights of its own citizens or of other persons who are under the protection of its laws. [The Court then quoted at length from Joseph Story's *Commentaries on the Conflict of Laws*, particularly §§23 through 28, excerpted *supra* pp. 501-02 & 618-19.] ...

Mr. Wheaton says: ... "No sovereign is bound, unless by special compact, to execute within his dominions a judgment rendered by the tribunals of another state; and if execution be sought by suit upon the judgment, or otherwise, the tribunal in which the suit is brought ... is on principle, at liberty to examine into the merits of such judgment, and to give effect to it or not, as may be found just and equitable. The general comity, utility, and convenience of nations have, however, established a usage among most civilized states, by which the final judgments of foreign courts of competent jurisdiction are reciprocally carried into execution, under certain regulations and restrictions, which differ in different countries." [H. Wheaton, *International Law* §147 (8th ed. 1866).] ...

A judgment *in rem*, adjudicating the title to a ship or other movable property within the custody of the court, is treated as valid everywhere. ... A judgment affecting the status of persons, such as a decree confirming or dissolving a marriage, is recognized as valid in every country, unless contrary to the policy of its own law. ... Other foreign judgments which have been held conclusive of the matter adjudged were judgments discharging obligations contracted in the foreign country between citizens or residents thereof. ...

The extraterritorial effect of judgments *in personam*, at law or in equity, may differ according to the parties to the cause. A judgment of that kind between two citizens or residents of the country, and thereby subject to the jurisdiction in which it is rendered, may be held conclusive as between them everywhere. So, if a foreigner invokes the jurisdiction by bringing an action against a citizen, both may be held bound by a judgment in favor of either. And if a citizen sues a foreigner, and judgment is rendered in favor of the latter, both may be held equally bound. The effect to which a judgment purely executory, rendered in favor of a citizen or resident of the country, in a suit there brought by him against a foreigner, may be entitled in an action thereon against the latter in his own country, — as is the case now before us, — presents a more difficult question, upon which there has been some diversity of opinion. ...

What was English law, being then our own law, before the Declaration of Independence? They demonstrate that by that law, ... a judgment recovered in a foreign country for a sum of money, when sued upon in England, was only prima facie evidence of the demand and was subject to be examined and impeached. ... It was because of that condition of the law as between the American colonies and states, that the United States, at the very beginning of their existence as a nation, ordained that full faith and credit should be given to the judgments of one of the states of the Union in the courts of another of those states. ... The decisions of this court have clearly recognized that judgments of a foreign state are prima facie evidence only, and that, but for these constitutional and legislative provisions, judgments of a state of the Union, when sued upon in another state, would have no greater effect. ... But [in no case] has this Court hitherto been called upon to determine how far foreign judgments may be reexamined upon their merits, or be impeached for fraud in obtaining them. In the courts of the several states, it was long recognized and assumed as undoubted and indisputable, that by our law, as by the law of England, foreign judgments for debts were not conclusive, but only prima facie, evidence of the matter adjudged. ...

[The Court quoted from Joseph Story's *Commentaries on the Conflict of Laws*:] "It is, indeed, very difficult to perceive what could be done ... [if a rule were adopted] to the full extent of opening all the evidence and merits of the cause anew on a suit upon the foreign judgment. Some of the witnesses may be since dead; some of the vouchers by be lost or destroyed. The merits of the cause, as formerly before the court upon the whole evidence, may have been decidedly in favor of the judgment; upon a partial possession of the original evidence, they may now appear otherwise. ... [T]he rule that the judgment is to be prima facie evidence for the plaintiff would be a mere delusion, if the defendant might still question it by opening all or any of the original merits on his side; for under such circumstances it would be equivalent to granting a new trial. ..." [*Id.* §607.] [The Court again quoted Story:] "It is difficult to ascertain what the prevailing rule is in regard to foreign judgments in some of the other nations of continental Europe; whether they are deemed conclusive evidence, or only prima facia evidence. Holland seems, at all times, upon the general principle of reciprocity, to have given great weight to foreign judgments, and in many cases, if not in all cases, to have given to them a weight equal to that given to domestic judgments, wherever the like rule of reciprocity with regard to Dutch judgments has been adopted by the foreign country whose judgment is brought under review. This is certainly a very reasonable rule, and may perhaps hereafter work itself firmly into the structure of international jurisprudence." [*Id.* §618.]...

[The Court then reviewed more recent English and U.S. authorities, and concluded:] In view of all the authorities upon the subject, and of the trend of judicial opinion in this country and in England following the lead of Kent and Story, we are satisfied that where there has been opportunity for a full and fair trial abroad before a court of competent jurisdiction, conducting the trial upon regular proceedings, after due citation or voluntary appearance of the defendant, and under a system of jurisprudence likely to secure an impartial administration of justice between the citizens of its own country and those of other countries, and there is nothing to show either prejudice in the court or in the system of laws under which it was sitting, or fraud in procuring the judgment, or any other special reason why the comity of this nation should not allow it full effect, the merits of the case should not, in an action brought in this country upon the judgment, be tried afresh, as on a new trial or an appeal, upon the mere assertion of the party that the judgment was erroneous in law or in fact. ...

[The Court then considered detailed evidence of foreign practice, leading it to conclude that:] It appears, therefore, that there is hardly a civilized nation on either continent, which, by its general law, allows conclusive effect to an executory foreign judgment for the recovery of money. In France and in a few smaller States ... the merits of the controversy are reviewed, as of course, allowing to the foreign judgment, at the most, no more effect than of being prima facie evidence of the justice of the claim. In the great majority of the countries on the continent of Europe ... and in a great part of South America, the judgment rendered in a foreign country is allowed the same effect only as the courts of that country allow to the judgments of the country in which the judgment in question is sought to be executed. The prediction of Mr. Justice Story (in §618 of his *Commentaries on the Conflict of Laws*, already cited) has thus been fulfilled, and the rule of reciprocity has worked itself firmly into the structure of international jurisprudence. The reasonable, if not the necessary conclusion appears to us to be that judgments rendered in France or in any other foreign country by the laws of which our own judgments are reviewable upon the merits, are not entitled to full credit and conclusive effect when sued upon in this country, but are prima facie evidence only of the justice of the plaintiff's claim. In holding such a judgment, for want of reciprocity, not to be conclusive evidence of the merits of the claim, we do not proceed upon any theory of retaliation upon one person by reason of injustice done to another, but upon the broad ground that international law is founded upon mutuality and reciprocity, and that by the principles of international law recognized in most civilized nations, and by the comity of our own country, which it is our judicial duty to know and to declare, the judgment is not entitled to be considered conclusive.

By our law at the time of the adoption of the Constitution, a foreign judgment was considered as prima facie evidence, and not conclusive. There is no statute of the United States, and no treaty of the United States with France or with any other nation, which has changed that law, or has made any provision upon the subject. It is not to be supposed that, if any statute or treaty had been or should be made, it would recognize as conclusive the judgments of any country which did not give like effect to our own judgments. In the absence of statute or treaty, it appears to us equally unwarrantable to assume that the comity of the United States requires anything more. ... [The Court therefore refused to enforce the French judgment.]

CHIEF JUSTICE FULLER, dissenting. ... [This case] I regard as one to be determined by the ordinary and settled rule in respect of allowing a party who has had an opportunity to prove his case in a competent court, to retry it on the merits; and it seems to me that the doctrine of *res judicata* applicable to domestic judgments should be applied to foreign judgments as well, and rests on the same general ground of public policy that there should be an end of litigation. This application of the doctrine is in accordance with our own jurisprudence, and it is not necessary that we should hold it to be required by some rule of international law. ...

[I]t is difficult to see why rights acquired under foreign judgments do not belong to the category of private rights acquired under foreign laws. Now the rule is universal in this country that private rights acquired under the laws of foreign states will be respected and enforced in our courts unless contrary to the policy or prejudicial to the interests of the state where this is sought to be done; and although the source of this rule may have been the comity characterizing the intercourse between nations, it prevails today by its own strength, and the right to the application of the law to which the particular transaction is subject to a juridical right. ...

I cannot yield my assent to the proposition that because by legislation and judicial decision in France [recognition] is not there given to judgments recovered in this country which, according to our jurisprudence, we think should be given to judgments wherever recovered, (subject, of course, to the recognized exception,) therefore we should pursue the same line of conduct as respects the judgments of French courts. The application of the doctrine of res judicata does not rest in discretion; and it is for the government, and not for its courts, to adopt the principle of retorsion, if deemed under any circumstances desirable or necessary. ...

RESTATEMENT (SECOND) CONFLICT OF LAWS (1971)
§§92 & 98

§92. A judgment is valid if

(a) the state in which it is rendered has jurisdiction to act judicially in the case; and

(b) a reasonable method of notification is employed and a reasonable opportunity to be heard is afforded to persons affected; and

(c) the judgment is rendered by a competent court; and

(d) there is compliance with such requirements of the state of rendition as are necessary for the valid exercise of power by the court.

§98. A valid judgment rendered in a foreign nation after a fair trial in a contested proceeding will be recognized in the United States so far as the immediate parties and the underlying claims are concérned.

UNIFORM FOREIGN MONEY JUDGMENTS RECOGNITION ACT
13 Uniform Laws Ann. 269 (1980) [excerpted as Appendix M]

BRUSSELS CONVENTION ON JURISDICTION AND THE ENFORCEMENT OF JUDGMENTS IN CIVIL MATTERS
[excerpted in Appendix D]

Notes on Hilton, Restatement Second, UFMJRA, and Brussels Convention

1. *Rationale for enforceability of foreign judgments in Hilton.* Consider the Court's rationale for presumptively enforcing foreign judgments in *Hilton.* Why is it that a U.S. court should ever give effect to the judgment of a foreign court?

(a) *Finality.* The *Second Restatement* reasoned that the recognition of foreign judgments rests on the fact that "the public interest requires that there be an end of litigation." *Restatement (Second) Conflict of Laws* §98, comment b (1971). *See also* Reese, *The Status in This Country of Judgments Rendered Abroad,* 50 Colum. L. Rev. 783, 784 (1950); Smit, *International Res Judicata and Collateral Estoppel in the United States,* 9 UCLA L. Rev. 44 (1962). Is this a satisfactory explanation for the *Hilton* and *Second Restatement* rules? What interests are served by finality? To the extent that finality is justified as conserving judicial resources, does this rationale apply to foreign judgments (where no prior U.S. judicial resources have been expended)? Does the finality rationale permit *any* refusals to recognize foreign judgments — for example, because the foreign court lacked personal jurisdiction, acted unfairly, or rendered a judgment in violation of U.S. public policy? Consider the discussion in Chief Justice Fuller's dissent in *Hilton* of the reasons for recognizing foreign judgments, and compare his reasoning to Justice Gray's. Is Chief Justice Fuller correct that *Hilton* can be decided without reference to international law, based simply on principles of res judicata? Is the identity and character of the foreign tribunal entirely irrelevant?

(b) *International law.* Does international law require U.S. courts to enforce foreign judgments, subject to the exceptions set forth in *Hilton*? Note the opening paragraphs of the Court's opinion, and its discussion of the practices of other states. Does *Hilton* conclude that state practice creates a rule of international law — sharing both public and private characteristics — that *requires* U.S. courts to recognize certain foreign judgments? Should international law impose any such obligation? What sources would support such a rule? Consider: "There is no uniformity of practice among foreign states in regard to recognition of judgments of other states." *Restatement (Third) Foreign Relations Law* §481 Reporters' Note 6 (1987). *See also* Golumb, *Recognition of Foreign Money Judgments: A Goal-Oriented Approach*, 43 St. John's L. Rev. 604, 610 (1969) ("Clearly, there is no internationally acknowledged customary rule of international law that a state must recognize any judgment."); Graupner, *Some Recent Aspects of the Recognition and Enforcement of Foreign Judgments in Western Europe*, 12 Int'l L. Comp. L. Q. 367, 374 (1963).

(c) *International comity.* Consider the role of international comity in *Hilton*. What precisely is international comity? How does it differ from international law? Why does "comity" argue for recognition of foreign judgments? Is it to ensure that private parties are treated fairly, to further the public policies of sovereign states, to strengthen the international legal system, or something else? What public policies does the recognition of foreign judgments further? Compare the role of international comity in *Hilton* with its role in other contexts, particularly choice of law (*supra* pp. 547-52), forum non conveniens (*supra* pp. 49-56 & 314), antisuit injunctions (*supra* pp. 485-86), and taking evidence abroad (*supra* pp. 913-14).

Does comity subsume concerns about international relationships among sovereign states — just as the full faith and credit clause reflects domestic policies concerning the relationships among sister states. *See supra* pp. 936-37. It has been suggested that international comity reflects the notion that standards governing the recognition of foreign judgments should reflect the "interest in fostering stability and unity in an international order in which many aspects of life are not confined to any single jurisdiction." von Mehren & Trautman, *Recognition of Foreign Adjudications: A Survey and a Suggested Approach*, 81 Harv. L. Rev. 1601, 1604 (1968). Put differently, liberal enforcement of foreign judgments facilitates international commercial and other relationships by making such relationships more stable and predictable. *See* Peterson, *Res Judicata and Foreign Country Judgments*, 24 Ohio St. L.J. 291, 307 & n.83 (1963). Is that persuasive? For criticism, *see* Smit, *International Res Judicata and Collateral Estoppel in the United States*, 9 UCLA L. Rev. 44, 54 (1962) (comity "says in fact only that recognition will be given when it will be given").

2. *Wisdom of recognizing foreign judgments.* Is the rule of presumptive enforceability recognized in *Hilton* and the UFMJRA wise? Why should U.S. courts ever recognize foreign judgments? Does the practice of doing so advance or hinder U.S. public policies and interests? In deciding whether U.S. courts should enforce foreign judgments, should U.S. public interests be considered? Should foreign public interests be considered? Should the private interests of the parties, and, if so, which parties, be considered? Is it relevant to know whether, as an empirical matter, U.S. companies are more likely to enforce U.S. judgments abroad, or have foreign judgments enforced against them in the United States? Is it relevant to know what the practice of foreign states is? *See supra* pp. 942-43.

3. *Comparison between Hilton and UFMJRA.* Compare the basic approach to the recognition of foreign judgments in *Hilton* with that in the UFMJRA. How does each source deal with the basic enforceability of foreign judgments? Consider §3 of the UFMJRA. What exceptions does each source recognize to the presumptive enforceability of foreign judgments? How are those exceptions implemented? Note the distinction between the exceptions in §4(a) and those in §4(b) of the UFMJRA.

4. *Comparison between Hilton and full faith and credit clause.* As *Hilton* notes, the full faith and credit clause of the U.S. Constitution requires U.S. state courts to recognize and enforce the judgments of other U.S. states, subject only to limited exceptions. *See supra* pp. 936-37. Compare the approach to foreign judgments in *Hilton* and the UFMJRA with that in the full faith and credit clause. Why should a different rule apply to the judgments of foreign nations' courts than that applicable to state court judgments? Why did the Framers confine the full faith and credit clause to U.S. state court judgments?

5. *Comparison between Hilton and Brussels Convention.* The member states of the European Union have entered into the Brussels Convention, regulating the jurisdiction of member state courts in civil matters. Those jurisdictional limits are set forth primarily in Articles 2, 3, and 5 of the Convention, and are discussed above. *See supra* pp. 90-93. In addition, the Brussels Convention also requires mutual recogni-

tion of the judgments of member state courts — much like the full faith and credit clause. The Convention begins from the premise that "[i]n no circumstances may a foreign judgment be reviewed as to its substance." Articles 29 & 34. In general "[a] judgment given in a Contracting State shall be recognized in the other Contracting States," Article 25, subject to exceptions, including for (a) public policy; (b) default judgments in the absence of proper service and opportunity to defend; (c) conflicts with earlier final judgments of the Contracting State where recognition is sought; (d) judgments involving status, marital status, capacity, or succession; and (e) judgments that are irreconcilable with an earlier, final judgment of a non-Contracting State, entitled to recognition in the enforcing forum. Brussels Convention, Articles 27 & 28.

Consider how the Brussels Convention deals with jurisdictional challenges. Also, compare the grounds for denying enforcement to foreign judgments under (a) the Brussels Convention; (b) the full faith and credit clause; and (c) the UFMJRA. Consider how each of these sources treats the following issues:

* presumptive enforceability of foreign judgments
* challenges to judicial jurisdiction of rendering court
* challenges based on violation of the public policy of the forum (or another state)
* challenges based on the fairness of the rendering court and its procedures
* challenges based on errors in foreign judgments
* challenges based on rendering court's choice of law decisions

6. *Requirement of "final" foreign judgment.* U.S. courts uniformly require that a foreign judgment be final and binding in the country where it was rendered before it will be recognized or enforced in the United States. *See* UFMJRA §2; *Restatement (Second) Conflict of Laws* §92, comment c, §98, comment a, & §107 (1971); Note, *The Finality of Judgments in the Conflict of Laws,* 41 Colum. L. Rev. 878 (1941); *Seetransport Wiking etc. v. Navimpex Centrala Navala,* 29 F.3d 79 (2d Cir. 1994). The fact that a foreign judgment is on appeal in the rendering forum does not prevent it from being "final." UFMJRA §2 ("This Act applies to any foreign judgment that is final and conclusive and enforceable where rendered even though an appeal therefrom is pending or it is subject to appeal."). Nevertheless, the U.S. court where enforcement is sought may stay its proceedings pending the foreign appeal. UFMJRA §6.

In determining whether a foreign judgment is final, the law of the country where the judgment was issued — not U.S. law — governs. *See Hunt v. BP Exploration Co. (Libya),* 492 F.Supp. 885, 903 (N.D. Tex. 1980); *Bata v. Bata,* 163 A.2d 493, 503 (Del. 1960), *cert. denied,* 366 U.S. 964 (1961); *Schoenbrod v. Siegler,* 283 N.Y.S.2d 881, 885 (1967); *Restatement (Third) Foreign Relations Law* §481, comment e (1987); UFMJRA §2; *Seetransport Wiking etc. v. Navimpex Centrala Navala,* 29 F.3d 79 (2d Cir. 1994). The possibility that an award may be modified by the foreign court in the future is not necessarily inconsistent with U.S. enforcement. *See Pilkington Bros. v. AFG Indus.,* 581 F.Supp. 1039, 1045 (D. Del. 1984); *Restatement (Third) Foreign Relations Law* §481, comment e (1987); *Restatement (Second) Conflict of Laws* §109, comment d (1971). For a U.S. decision refusing to reconsider a U.S. court's recognition of an English judgment, even though an English court had itself vacated the original English judgment, *see DSQ Property Co. v. DeLorean,* 745 F.Supp. 1234 (E.D. Mich. 1990).

7. *Default judgments.* The fact that a foreign judgment was issued by default does not mean that U.S. courts will not enforce it. *See Bank of Montreal v. Kough,* 612 F.2d 467 (9th Cir. 1980) (enforcing Canadian default judgment); *John Sanderson & Co. (Wool) v. Ludlow Jute Co.,* 569 F.2d 696 (1st Cir. 1978) (enforcing Australian default judgment); *Standard SS Owners' Protection and Indemnity Ass'n (Bermuda) Ltd. v. C & G Marine Services Inc.,* 1992 U.S. Dist. Lexis 7086 (E.D. La. May 13, 1992); *Fairchild, Arabatzis & Smith v. Prometco (Produce & Metals) Co.,* 470 F.Supp. 610 (S.D.N.Y. 1979); *Mercandino v. Devoe & Reynolds, Inc.,* 436 A.2d 942 (N.J. 1981); *Restatement (Third) Foreign Relations Law* §481, Reporters' Note 4 (1987).

Not all foreign states take a similar approach to foreign default judgments — even if they take an otherwise liberal approach to the enforcement of foreign judgments. In England, for example, foreign default judgments will not be recognized unless the defendant was present in the foreign forum at the time the litigation was initiated or submitted to the foreign court's jurisdiction by contract or appearance. *Soc. Cooperative Sidmetal v. Titan International, Ltd.* [1966] 1 Q.B. 828; Dicey & Morris, *The Conflict of Laws* 472-90 (12th ed. 1993 L. Collins ed.). Is this a more sensible approach than that in the United States? Why or why not?

8. *Effect of nonenforcement.* The refusal of a U.S. court to enforce a foreign court's judgment does not preclude the foreign judgment creditor from obtaining relief in U.S. courts. The judgment creditor can continue to pursue its claim on the merits in U.S. courts. *Restatement (Second) Conflict of Laws* §95, comment c(1) (1971). *But see* Peterson, *Foreign Country Judgments and the Second Restatement of Conflict of Laws*, 72 Colum. L. Rev. 220, 230-32 (1972). Indeed, in some circumstances, the foreign judgment creditor may be able to make some evidentiary use in its action on the merits of its foreign judgment.

9. *Relitigation of underlying claim by foreign judgment creditor.* Some authorities grant successful plaintiffs in foreign proceedings the option of seeking to enforce their foreign country judgment or of relitigating their underlying claim against the defendant. *E.g., Restatement (Second) Conflict of Laws* §95, comment c(l) (1971) ("a plaintiff who has not obtained complete satisfaction may maintain in the United States either an action on the original cause of action or an action to enforce the judgment"); A. Nussbaum, *Principles of Private International Law* 245-46 (1943). Is this appropriate? consistent with the rationales for recognizing foreign judgements? Why would a successful foreign plaintiff choose relitigation over enforcement? One reason may be that U.S. substantive law offers a larger recovery. Other reasons include perceived difficulties in establishing that the foreign judgment should be entitled to preclusive effect or the fact that the currency in which the foreign judgment was denominated has devalued against the U.S. dollar since judgment.

10. *Enforcement of foreign decrees.* The law concerning U.S. recognition of foreign decrees concerning status or ordering that specified action be taken by the foreign defendant is not well developed. *See Restatement (Second) Conflict of Laws* §102 (1971); *Wolff v. Wolff*, 389 A.2d 413 (Md. App. 1978), *aff'd mem.*, 401 A.2d 479 (Md. 1979) (per curiam) (enforcing English alimony decree based on comity); *Clarkson Co. v. Shaheen*, 544 F.2d 624 (2d Cir. 1976) (recognizing Canadian bankruptcy trustee's order concerning preservation of documents); *Pilkington Bros. v. AFG Indus.*, 518 F.Supp. 1039 (D. Del. 1984) (declining to issue preliminary injunction tracking language of English court preliminary injunction because enforcement could be inconsistent with comity); *Zanzonico v. Neeld*, 111 A.2d 772 (N.J. 1955) (recognition of an Italian adoption in proceeding where administratrix of estate of deceased appealed from assessment of a transfer inheritance tax); *Willson v. Willson*, 55 So.2d 905 (Fla. 1951) (recognition of Canadian divorce and child custody decree). *See* Note, *U.S. Recognition and Enforcement of Foreign Country Injunctive and Specific Performance Decrees*, 20 Cal. W. Int'l L. J. 91 (1990).

11. *Enforcement of judgments against foreign states.* The enforcement of foreign (and domestic) judgments against foreign states, and their agencies and instrumentalities, is comprehensively dealt with by the Foreign Sovereign Immunities Act, 28 U.S.C. §§1602-11 (1982). For a discussion of enforcement against foreign sovereigns, *see* J. Dellapenna, *Suing Foreign Governments and Their Corporations* 368-95 (1988).

5. The Reciprocity Requirement

As discussed above, *Hilton* enunciated a "reciprocity" requirement for the enforceability of foreign judgments. Justice Gray reasoned that, in most nations, "the judgment rendered in a foreign country is allowed the same effect only as the courts of that country allow to the judgments of the country in which the judgment in question is sought to be executed."[49] *Hilton* adopted this reciprocity requirement, applying it to deny recognition to the French judgment obtained by Mr. Guyot.

Many U.S. authorities have criticized the reciprocity requirement.[50] The UFMJRA did not include a specific reciprocity requirement, and a number of states have adopted versions of the UFMJRA that also omit the requirement.[51] Similarly, the *Restatement (Third) Foreign Relations Law* does not contain any reciprocity requirement.[52]

The materials excerpted below illustrate both the historic and contemporary

---

49. 159 U.S. at 227.
50. *See infra* pp. 954-55.
51. *See infra* p. 955.
52. *Restatement (Third) Foreign Relations Law* §481 & Reporters' Note 1 (1987).

U.S. approaches to the reciprocity requirement. *Hilton* adopts the reciprocity requirement, after concluding that it "has worked itself firmly into the structure of international jurisprudence."[53] In contrast, *Somportex, Ltd. v. Philadelphia Chewing Gum Corp.* abandons the requirement.

HILTON v. GUYOT

159 U.S. 113 (1895) [excerpted above at pp. 943-48]

SOMPORTEX, LTD. v. PHILADELPHIA CHEWING GUM CORP.

318 F.Supp. 161 (E.D. Pa. 1970)

LORD, CHIEF JUDGE. [Somportex, Ltd., an English company, obtained a default judgment from an English court against Philadelphia Chewing Gum Corp., a company doing business in Pennsylvania. Somportex then brought suit in the United States to enforce the judgment. After concluding that none of *Hilton's* specific exceptions were applicable, the district court considered the reciprocity requirement.] ...

[D]efendant argues that the English judgment should not be recognized and enforced by this Court because an English court would not enforce an American judgment under similar circumstances. The position that reciprocity is an essential element in determining whether or not to enforce a foreign judgment was first enunciated in 1895 by the Supreme Court in the *Hilton* case. In that case, the Court found all of the requisite conditions for enforcement of the French judgment had been met except that a French court, sitting *mutatis mutandis*, would not enforce the American judgment. Therefore the Court refused to give conclusive effect to the French judgment. However, we do not find the teaching of *Hilton* on reciprocity to be controlling in this case. The *Hilton* decision was a pre-*Erie R.R. Co. v. Tompkins* case and it has never been suggested that it was constitutionally dictated and therefore binding on the states. It is clear ... that the law governing the enforceability of foreign judgments by a federal court is the law of the state where the court is located. Therefore, the issue, as this Court perceives it, is whether the courts of Pennsylvania would hold that reciprocity is a necessary precondition to the enforcement of foreign judgments. The issue of the enforceability of foreign judgments has not frequently been litigated in Pennsylvania, and the Court has not been cited to ... any Pennsylvania cases which even intimate that a finding of reciprocity is an essential precondition to their enforcing a foreign judgment.

Since its beginning in *Hilton*, the concept of reciprocity has not found favor in the United States. It has often been the subject of criticism by commentators[54] and

---

53. 159 U.S. at 227.

54. *E.g.*, 2 J. Beale, *Conflict of Laws* 1385-89 (1935); Goodrich, *Conflict of Laws* 605-08 (3d ed. 1949); Reese, *The Status in This Country of Judgments Rendered Abroad*, 50 Colum. L. Rev. 783, 790-93 (1950).

most courts have refused to follow *Hilton* on this issue. The concept has been expressly rejected by the courts of New York,[55] and has been rejected by statute in California.[56] The courts and commentators have presented cogent reasons for their position that reciprocity should not be the determinative factor in a court's decision on the issue of recognition. The primary reason which has been advanced is that our legal system has adopted a policy that calls for an end to litigation. Whether or not a foreign court would recognize an American judgment is not relevant to this policy. However, it is in furtherance of that objective if litigation which was begun in a foreign court and which is presently before an American tribunal, is brought to an end. The Court find that the concept of reciprocity is a provincial one, one which fosters decisions that do violence to the legitimate goals of comity between foreign nations. Therefore, absent a positive showing that Pennsylvania would follow the *Hilton* decision with respect to reciprocity, this Court will not presume that [the Pennsylvania courts] would adhere to such an undermined concept. This Court finds that if presented with the issue, the Pennsylvania courts would follow its neighboring state of New York and expressly reject this concept. We find this to be particularly true since Pennsylvania, like New York, is one of the largest centers of both national and international commercial activities. ...

Notes on Hilton and Somportex

1. *The reciprocity requirement. Hilton* concluded that the judgment of a foreign court would not be recognized unless the foreign country would "give like effect to our own judgments." Simply put, if a U.S. court had rendered the judgment at issue in *Hilton* against a French citizen, would a French court enforce that judgment? If not, then a U.S. court would not enforce the French judgment.

The New York Court of Appeals has described Justice Gray's discussion of the reciprocity requirement as "magnificent dictum," on the theory that *Hilton* could in fact have been decided on one of Justice Gray's specific exceptions (*i.e.*, that for fraud). *Johnston v. Compagnie Generale Transatlantique*, 242 N.Y. 381 (Ct. App. 1926). Compare the more representative view of *Hilton* in *Somportex. See Cherun v. Frishman*, 236 F.Supp. 292, 294 (D.D.C. 1964); *Her Majesty etc. v. Gilbertson*, 597 F.2d 1161, 1165-66 (9th Cir. 1979).

2. *Scope of reciprocity requirement.* What exactly does the *Hilton* reciprocity requirement mean? Is it limited to suits where a foreign national obtains a judgment against a *U.S.* citizen in the foreign national's home country's courts? That is, suppose that Mr. Hilton had sued Mr. Guyot in France, and obtained a judgment, which he sought to enforce against assets of Mr. Guyot in the United States. Would the refusal of French courts to enforce U.S. judgments prevent the U.S. judgment creditor from enforcing the French judgment against a French defendant? Or is the reciprocity requirement available generally, without regard to the nationality of the parties?

Consider the discussion at the outset of the *Hilton* opinion, regarding the scope of the issue before the Court, which excludes from consideration suits between foreign parties, suits between U.S. parties, suits by U.S. nationals against foreign parties, and suits where a U.S. national prevails. On the other hand, consider the broader formulations at the conclusion of Justice Gray's opinion. Some authorities have concluded that the reciprocity exception will not apply in suits involving only foreign nationals, where a U.S. national seeks to enforce a foreign judgment against a foreign national, or where the rendering court is not in the foreign national's home state. *See Bata v. Bata*, 163 A.2d 493, 504 (Del. 1960), *cert. denied*, 366 U.S. 964 (1961) (reciprocity requirement "limited to cases in which it is invoked by an American citizen").

---

55. *Cowens v. Ticonderoga Pulp & Paper Co.*, 219 N.Y.S. 284, *aff'd*, 246 N.Y. 603 (1927); *Johnston v. Compagnie Generale Transatlantique*, 242 N.Y. 381 (Ct. App. 1926).

56. [Cal. Civil Code §1950.]

3. *Rationale of reciprocity requirement.* What is the rationale underlying the reciprocity rule? Is it that foreign courts and states will have no incentive to recognize U.S. judgments if U.S. courts indiscriminately recognize foreign judgments? Moore, *Federalism and Foreign Relations,* 1965 Duke L.J. 248, 254-55. Does the reciprocity requirement reflect a sense that it is unfair to enforce a foreign judgment against a U.S. litigant who could not have obtained enforcement of a U.S. judgment against its foreign adversary in its home country? If a U.S. litigant cannot effectively proceed in U.S. courts against a foreign defendant, doesn't enforcement of a foreign court's judgment by U.S. courts amount to acquiescence in a forum selection imposed by foreign law on the U.S. party?

What rationale does *Hilton* rely on for the reciprocity requirement? Consider the final two paragraphs of the Court's opinion, and particularly:

> It is not to be supposed that, if any statute or treaty had been or should be made, it would recognize as conclusive the judgments of any country which did not give like effect to our own judgments. In the absence of statute or treaty, it appears to us equally unwarrantable to assume that the comity of the United States requires anything more.

Is this persuasive? Note the Court's approach to attempting to determine what comity requires, by predicting what the terms of a U.S. treaty would be negotiated to provide.

4. *Comparison between Hilton and New York Convention.* As discussed elsewhere, the United States is a party to the New York Convention, providing for the recognition of foreign arbitral awards. *See infra* pp. 990-91 & 1040-42. Among other things, the Convention permits signatory states to declare that they will enforce foreign arbitral awards on the basis of reciprocity — only enforcing awards made in states that have ratified the New York Convention. G. Born, *International Commercial Arbitration in the United States* 290-91, 483-90 (1994). The United States has declared that it will enforce the Convention only on the basis of reciprocity. *Id.* What relevance does this have to determining the wisdom of *Hilton*'s reciprocity exception?

5. *Majority rule rejecting reciprocity requirement.* As *Somportex* illustrates, the majority U.S. rule presently disfavors looking to whether a foreign court would enforce a U.S. judgment in deciding whether a U.S. court will enforce a judgment of the foreign court. *See Bank of Montreal v. Kough,* 612 F.2d 467, 471 (9th Cir. 1980); *De La Mata v. American Life Insurance Co.,* 1991 U.S. Dist. Lexis 11274 (D. Del. Aug. 8, 1991); *Hunt v. BP Exploration Co. (Libya),* 492 F.Supp. 885, 898-99 (N.D. Tex. 1980); *Toronto-Dominion Bank v. Hall,* 367 F.Supp. 1009, 1012-13 (E.D. Ark. 1973); *Johnston v. Compagnie Generale Transatlantique,* 152 N.E. 121 (N.Y. 1926); *Restatement (Second) Conflict of Laws* §98, comment e (1971); *Restatement (Third) Foreign Relations Law* §481, comment d & Reporters' Note 1 (1987); Comment, *The Reciprocity Rule and Enforcement of Foreign Judgments,* 16 Colum. J. Transnat'l L. 327 (1977).

California was one of the first states to abandon the reciprocity requirement. In 1907, after German courts refused to recognize California judgments against a German insurer, Cal. Code Civil Procedure §1915 was enacted, which overturned the reciprocity requirement. The legislation's purpose was to improve the prospects of enforcing Californian judgments abroad (in foreign states following a reciprocity rule) by making it clear that foreign judgments would be recognized in California.

6. *Rationale for rejection of reciprocity requirement.* The rationale underlying rejection of the reciprocity rule urges that private rights in U.S. courts are not ordinarily dependent on the laws of foreign states, that it is unfair and arbitrary to penalize foreign judgment creditors for the positions of their home states (or, in some cases, other nations), and that the reciprocity rule cannot be predictably or efficiently applied. Comment, *The Reciprocity Rule and Enforcement of Foreign Judgments,* 16 Colum. J. Transnat'l L. 327, 346-48 (1977); Reese, *The Status in this Country of Judgments Rendered Abroad,* 50 Colum. L. Rev. 783, 793 (1950) ("the creditor is not to blame for the fact that the state of rendition does not accord conclusive effect to American judgments"). Moreover, some authorities have questioned whether U.S. *courts* should concern themselves with influencing the attitude of foreign states towards U.S. judgments. As the dissenting opinion in *Hilton v. Guyot* reasoned, "the doctrine of *res judicata* does not rest on discretion; and it is for the government, and not for its courts, to adopt the principle of retorsion, if deemed under any circumstances desirable or necessary." 159 U.S. at 234 (Fuller, C.J., dissenting). For representative judicial criticism, consider:

> *Hilton* has been severely and consistently criticized by commentators and courts. Three significant criticisms have been advanced. First, *Hilton* mandates a misplaced retaliation against judgment creditors for the acts of foreign states irrelevant to their case and over which they had no control. Second, judgments are enforced to bring an end to litigation so that the rights of

the parties might finally be determined and judicial energies might be conserved. These considerations are thwarted by the reciprocity requirement. The judgment of a foreign nation, when rendered in a proceeding in which the foreign court had jurisdiction and the issues were fully and fairly adjudicated, should be entitled to no less effect on policy grounds than a judgment of another state or federal court. ... Third, there is serious doubt that *Hilton* achieves either of its two probable goals: (1) protecting Americans abroad; and (2) encouraging foreign nations to enforce United States judgments. If protecting United States interests abroad was a goal of *Hilton*, it is clear that reciprocity does not achieve that goal because it does not look to the fairness or persuasiveness of the foreign judgments.

Nicol v. Tanner, 256 N.W.2d 796 (Minn. 1976). *See also* Golumb, *Recognition of Foreign Money Judgments: A Goal-Oriented Approach*, 43 St. John's L. Rev. 604, 616 (1969) ("Probably more damaging, however, to the fate of American judgments abroad is that foreign nations with reciprocity rules look at *Hilton* and conclude that the United States would not recognize one of their judgments. The *Hilton* rule then leads American courts to refuse recognition to judgments of those countries. This circularity does not further any of the relevant goals of judgment recognition policies. It would seem that a clear renunciation of the reciprocity doctrine by American courts might be a more effective method of obtaining recognition for American judgments in many other nations.").

7. *Wisdom of reciprocity requirement.* Is the reciprocity requirement a desirable rule in the recognition and enforcement context? If the United States does not demand reciprocity, what incentive is there for foreign countries to recognize U.S. judgments? In the international context, do private rights not frequently turn on the positions of foreign governments, reflected in treaties, laws, and other government acts? Compare *Hilton's* justifications for the reciprocity requirement with the criticisms by Chief Justice Fuller, *Somportex*, and the authorities cited above. Which view is more persuasive? Put concretely, is it wise for Mr. Guyot to be denied the right to enforce his judgment because French law provides that French courts will generally not enforce foreign judgments (including U.S. judgments)?

8. *Reciprocity under the UFMJRA.* The UFMJRA did not contemplate a reciprocity exception to the enforcement of foreign judgments. However, several states have included in the version of the Uniform Act that they have adopted provisions excusing their courts from enforcement of judgments of foreign courts that would not enforce U.S. judgments in similar circumstances. *See* Ga. Code Ann. §9-12-114(10) (1982) (reciprocity is mandatory condition of recognition); Idaho Code §10.1404(2)(g); Mass. Gen. Laws Ann. ch. 235, §23A (West 1966) (lack of reciprocity is basis for discretionary non-recognition); Ohio Rev. Code Ann. §2329.92 (Baldwin 1986) (same); Tex. Civ. Prac. & Rem. Code Ann. §36.005(b)(7) (Vernon 1986) (same); N.H. Rev. Stat. Ann. §524.11 (1974).

9. *Continued acceptance of reciprocity requirement.* It is often said that the *Hilton* reciprocity requirement "is no longer followed in the great majority of State and federal courts in the United States." *Restatement (Third) Foreign Relations Law* §481, comment d (1987). Nevertheless, a number of common law decisions have refused to abandon the reciprocity requirement. *Banque Libanaise pour Le Commerce v. Khreich*, 915 F.2d 1000, 1004-06 (5th Cir. 1990); *Corporacion Salvadorena de Calzado, SA v. Injection Footwear Corp.*, 533 F.Supp. 290 (S.D. Fla. 1982); *Atlantic Ship Supply v. M/V Lucy*, 392 F.Supp. 179, 183 (M.D. Fla. 1975), *aff'd*, 553 F.2d 1009 (5th Cir. 1977) (dicta); *Leo Feist, Inc. v. Debmar Publishing Co.*, 232 F.Supp. 623 (E.D. Pa. 1964); *Svenska Handelsbanken v. Carlson*, 258 F.Supp. 448 (D. Mass. 1966); *Medical Arts Bldg. v. Eralp*, 290 N.W.2d 241 (N.D. 1980); *Cannistraro v. Cannistraro*, 223 N.E.2d 629 (Mass. 1967); *Ogden v. Ogden*, 33 So.2d 870 (1947) (alternative holding).

A number of foreign states also continue to impose a reciprocity requirement on U.S. (and other) foreign judgments. *E.g.*, German Code of Civil Procedure Article 328; Graupner, *Some Recent Aspects of the Recognition and Enforcement of Foreign Judgments in Western Europe*, 12 Int'l & Comp. L. Q. 367, 369-79 (1963).

6. The Revenue Rule

Notwithstanding the general presumption of enforceability articulated in *Hilton*, U.S. courts have long refused to recognize foreign penal or revenue judgments.

Indeed, courts have generally held that foreign penal and revenue judgments are simply not enforceable in this country.[57]

As discussed below, this rule is grounded on concerns that U.S. enforcement of foreign judgments necessarily requires a degree of U.S. judicial scrutiny of foreign proceedings; where those proceedings involve sufficiently sensitive foreign governmental interests, U.S. judicial scrutiny could offend foreign states and jeopardize the nation's foreign relations.[58] To avoid this, foreign penal and revenue judgments have been denied enforcement. Although the revenue rule has frequently been criticized in recent years,[59] the following decision, *Her Majesty the Queen v. Gilbertson*, illustrates the continuing vitality of the doctrine.

HER MAJESTY THE QUEEN IN RIGHT OF THE PROVINCE OF BRITISH COLUMBIA v. GILBERTSON
597 F.2d 1161 (9th Cir. 1979)

J. BLAINE ANDERSON, CIRCUIT JUDGE. The plaintiff, the Canadian Province of British Columbia, filed this diversity action against the defendants ... in the U.S. District Court for the District of Oregon. ... The defendants are all citizens of Oregon who received income from logging operations in British Columbia. This income was apparently subject to taxation under the British Columbia Logging Tax Act. British Columbia originally assessed an amount of $210,600.00 for the logging tax against the defendants. ... British Columbia then served a "Notice of Intention to Enforce Payment" on the defendants in the United States, and filed a certificate of assessment in the Vancouver Registry of the Supreme Court of British Columbia. ... [U]nder the laws of British Columbia [the] filing [of the certificate] gave it the same effect as a judgment of the court. British Columbia then instituted the present action in the United States. It was dismissed because the court below concluded that the Oregon Courts would follow the "revenue rule." Stated simply, the revenue rule merely provides that the courts of one jurisdiction do not recognize the revenue laws of another jurisdiction. ...

In a diversity action, a federal district court applies the law of the forum state. *Erie Railroad Co. v. Tompkins*. Not only the substantive law, but also the conflicts of law rules of the forum are applied in diversity actions. *Klaxon Co. v. Stentor Electric Mfg. Co.* Normally, this would automatically limit our analysis to the law of Oregon since it is the forum state in the present case. However, the question presented here carries foreign relations overtones which may create an inference that this should not

---

57. *See Johansson v. United States*, 336 F.2d 809 (5th Cir. 1964); *In re Bliss' Trust*, 208 N.Y.S.2d 725 (1960); *Restatement (Second) Conflict of Laws* §120 (1971); Leflar, *Extrastate Enforcement of Penal and Governmental Claims*, 46 Harv. L. Rev. 193 (1932); Stoel, *The Enforcement of Non-Criminal Penal and Revenue Judgments in England and the United States*, 16 Int'l & Comp. L.Q. 663 (1967).

58. *Moore v. Mitchell* 30 F.2d 600 (2d Cir. 1929) (L. Hand, J., concurring); Leflar, *Extrastate Enforcement of Penal and Governmental Claims*, 46 Harv. L. Rev. 193 (1932); *infra* pp. 957 & 959.

59. *See infra* pp. 959-60.

be decided merely by reference to Oregon law. Nevertheless, we do not need to decide whether federal or state law should control, since the conclusion we reach would be the same under either Oregon or federal law.

Generally, judgments from a foreign country are recognized by the courts of this country when the general principles of comity are satisfied. Two often-stated exceptions to comity occur when the judgment is based on either the tax (the revenue rule) or penal laws of the foreign country. ... An analysis of ... the revenue rule ... supports our ultimate conclusion that British Columbia failed to state a claim upon which relief could be granted.

Lord Mansfield is generally credited as being the first to express the revenue rule. In 1775, while deciding a contract action, he said that "... no country ever takes notice of the revenue laws of another." *Holman v. Johnson*, 98 Eng. Rep. 1120, 1121 (1775). A few years later, Lord Mansfield had occasion to repeat the rule in another case where he said: "One nation does not take notice of the revenue laws of another." *Planche v. Fletcher*, 99 Eng. Rep. 164, 165 (1779). Although the rule may have only been dicta to these cases, since its inception it has become so well recognized that this appears to be the first time that a foreign nation has sought to enforce a tax judgment in the courts of the United States.

Judge Learned Hand best expressed the purpose behind the revenue rule:

> While the origin of the exception in the case of penal liabilities does not appear in the books, a sound basis for it exists, in my judgment, which includes liabilities for taxes as well. Even in the case of ordinary municipal liabilities, a court will not recognize those arising in a foreign state, if they run counter to the "settled public policy" of its own. Thus a scrutiny of the liability is necessarily always in reserve, and the possibility that it will be found not to accord with the policy of the domestic state. This is not a troublesome or delicate inquiry when the question arises between private persons, but it takes on quite another face when it concerns the relations between the foreign state and its own citizens or even those who may be temporarily within its borders. To pass upon the provisions for the public order of another state is, or at any rate should be, beyond the powers of a court; it involves the relations between the states themselves, with which courts are incompetent to deal, and which are entrusted to other authorities. It may commit the domestic state to a position which would seriously embarrass its neighbor. Revenue laws fall within the same reasoning; they affect a state in matters as vital to its existence as its criminal laws. No court ought to undertake an inquiry which it cannot prosecute without determining whether those laws are consonant with its own notions of what is proper.

Moore v. Mitchell, 30 F.2d 600, 604 (2d Cir. 1929) (L. Hand, J., concurring), *aff'd on other grounds*, 281 U.S. 18 (1930). While this reasoning no longer prevents a state from enforcing its tax judgment in the courts of a sister state because of the full faith and credit clause, this same rationale has continued validity in the international context. Additionally, if the court below was compelled to recognize the tax judgment from a foreign nation, it would have the effect of furthering the governmental interests of a foreign country, something which our courts customarily refuse to do.

Although the Supreme Court has never had occasion to address the question of whether the revenue rule would prevent a foreign country from enforcing its tax judgment in the courts of the United States, the indications are strong that the Court would reach the same result as we reach in the present case. Both the majority and the dissenting opinion in *Banco Nacional de Cuba v. Sabbatino*, discussed the rule in a spirit which indicates a continued recognition of the revenue rule in the international sphere.

There is no Oregon case law on point. The only inference which can be drawn from Oregon statutory law supports our conclusion. In 1977, Oregon adopted the Uniform Foreign Money Judgment Recognition Act. This provides that judgments from a foreign country for a sum of money which meet certain requirements are enforceable in the Oregon courts. However, the Act defines the judgments to which it applies as "(a)ny judgment of a foreign state granting or denying recovery to a sum of money, *other than a judgment for taxes*" (emphasis added) 1977 *Or. Laws*, S.B. 28 §1(2). The only conclusion which can be drawn from this specific exclusion is that the Oregon legislature continues to recognize the revenue rule.

The political branches of the U.S. Government have entered into two tax treaties with the Canadian Government. ... These treaties are quite extensive; they address various questions arising from situations where individuals or corporations as residents, or citizens of one country, own property or do business in the other country. One section provides for the exchange of information between the two countries for the purpose of preventing international tax evasion. This is as close as the treaties come to providing for enforcement powers. Even though the political branches of the two countries could have abolished the revenue rule between themselves at the time they entered into the treaties, they did not. ...

The revenue rule has been with us for centuries and as such has become firmly embedded in the law. There were sound reasons which supported its original adoption, and there remain sound reasons supporting its continued validity. When and if the rule is changed, it is a more proper function of the policy-making branches of our government to make such a change.

Notes on Her Majesty

1. *General refusal of U.S. courts to enforce tax and penal judgments.* As *Her Majesty* indicates, the general rule in the United States is that foreign tax and penal judgments will not be enforced by U.S. courts. *See supra* pp. 955-56. *Compare Restatement (Third) Foreign Relations Law* §483 (1987) ("Courts in the United States are not required to recognize or to enforce judgments for the collection of taxes, fines, or penalties rendered by the courts of other states."). What is the difference between the *Third Restatement* position and the historic revenue rule as articulated in *Her Majesty*?

2. *Treatment of revenue rule in UFMJRA.* As *Her Majesty* illustrates, the UFMJRA does not apply to foreign revenue or penal judgments. *See* UFMJRA §1(2) ("'foreign judgment' means any judgment of a foreign state granting or denying recovery of a sum of money, other than a judgment for taxes, a fine or other penalty ..."). What is the difference between the UFMJRA and the historic revenue rule? Would a foreign revenue or penal judgment be enforceable under common law in a UFMJRA state?

3. *Recent authorities questioning revenue rule.* More recently, a few lower courts have questioned the rule against enforcement of foreign tax and penal judgments. *E.g., Revenue Immobilien v. Silverstein*, 744 F. Supp. 429 (E.D.N.Y. 1990); *Bullen v. Her Majesty's Government of the United Kingdom*, 553 So.2d 1344 (Fla. Dist. Ct. App. 1990).

4. *Origins of revenue and penal exceptions.* The rationales for the revenue and penal exceptions are obscure. Both rules appear to date to a 1775 opinion on the King's Bench by Lord Mansfield, ruling that a French seller of tea could recover damages from an English purchaser notwithstanding the fact that the tea sale apparently violated English penal and revenue laws. In explaining that the French plaintiff's conduct in France was not unlawful, Lord Mansfield said broadly that "no country ever takes notice of the revenue laws of another." *Holman v. Johnson*, 98 Eng. Rep. 1120 (K.B. 1775). This dicta was subsequently invoked to justify the refusal of English (and U.S.) courts to enforce judgments of foreign courts based on tax or penal claims. *E.g., Government of India v. Taylor* [1955] A.C. 491 (H.L.(E.)); *Her Majesty the Queen v. Gilbertson*, 597 F.2d 1161 (9th Cir. 1979). This result is, of course, closely related to the choice of law rule that a state will not hear claims based on the penal or revenue laws of other nations. *Restatement (Second) Conflict of Laws* §89 (1971); *supra* pp. 630-31. It has been stated by one court as follows: "To pass upon the provisions for the public order of another state is, or at any rate should be, beyond the powers of the court." *Moore v. Mitchell*, 30 F.2d 600, 604 (2d Cir. 1929), *aff'd on other grounds*, 281 U.S. 18 (1930).

5. *Rationale for penal and revenue rule.* Why do courts generally refuse to enforce penal and revenue judgments? Consider Judge Learned Hand's explanation in *Moore v. Mitchell*, 30 F.2d 600, 601 (2d Cir. 1929), *aff'd on other grounds*, 281 U.S. 18 (1930), excerpted above at *supra* p. 957. Is this rationale persuasive?

How are revenue or penal judgments different from other judgments? Is it because they are based on proceedings by foreign governments against private litigants? Why should this be important? Suppose a foreign state agency recovers on an ordinary contract claim and seeks to enforce its judgment in U.S. courts.

Alternatively, are the revenue and penal rules based on the substantive content of the laws on which such judgments are based? If so, what would be the status of antitrust judgments, which are based on regulatory statutes reflecting broad public policy objectives? Suppose only single damages were awarded. Recall that some foreign nations have enacted legislation denying recognition or enforcement to U.S. antitrust judgments. *See supra* pp. 584-87. What would be the status of judgments based on product liability claims? Suppose punitive damages were awarded? *See SA Consortium General Textiles v. Sun & Sand Agencies* [1978] Q.B. 279, 299-300 ("there is nothing contrary to English public policy in enforcing a claim for exemplary damages"). *See also* Annotation, *Requirement of Full Faith and Credit to Foreign Judgment for Punitive Damages*, 44 A.L.R.3d 960 (1972) (collecting domestic U.S. decisions holding that sister state judgments based on punitive damages are entitled to full faith and credit).

It is also reasoned that, if U.S. courts were to hold out the possibility of recognizing foreign judgments, they would be obliged to consider all of the various requirements that *Hilton* prescribed for enforcement, and doing so might gravely offend foreign states. "The rule appears to reflect a reluctance of courts to subject foreign public law to judicial scrutiny." *Restatement (Third) Foreign Relations Law* §483, Reporters' Note 2 (1988). Why should greater offense result from such inquiries into judicial procedures in penal or revenue cases than in other types of cases? Why should a flat refusal to enforce a foreign judgment not create even more offense?

A second explanation for the revenue and penal exceptions may be "a reluctance to enforce laws that may conflict with the public policy of the forum state." *Restatement (Third) Foreign Relations Law* §483, Reporters' Note 2 (1988). This rationale may have had greater utility, as a general rule of thumb, in an age when penal and revenue laws differed markedly from state to state. Is this rationale still persuasive in today's world? Is there any reason to think that foreign revenue and penal laws are significantly more likely than other foreign laws to offend U.S. public policy? To the extent that foreign penal and revenue laws *do* violate U.S. public policy, would the generally-applicable public policy exception provide the appropriate response?

Note how the British Columbia "judgment" was obtained in *Her Majesty*. Does this suggest some of the pitfalls in recognizing foreign penal or revenue judgments?

6. *Criticism of revenue rule.* The historic revenue rule has been subjected to considerable criticism, although the penal exception has not. *See Restatement (Third) Foreign Relations Law* §483, Reporters' Note 2 (1987) (permitting, but not requiring, nonrecognition of foreign tax and penal judgments and expressing doubts as to continued wisdom of revenue rule); Note, *The Nonrecognition of Foreign Tax Judgments: International Tax Evasion*, 1981 U. Ill. L. Rev. 241. Consider:

> Although the rule as commonly stated treats tax and penal judgments alike, the considerations concerning foreign tax judgments are different from those for penal judgments. In an age when virtually all states impose and collect taxes and when instantaneous transfer of assets can be easily arranged, the rationale for not recognizing or enforcing tax judgments is largely obsolete. *Restatement (Third) Foreign Relations Law* §483 Reporters' Note 1 (1987).

Is that correct? If tax judgments are enforceable, why not penal judgments?

7. *What is a tax or penal judgment?* There is some uncertainty about what constitutes a penal or revenue judgment. In *Huntingdon v. Attrill*, 146 U.S. 657, 673-74 (1892), the Supreme Court said, "whether a statute of one State, which in some aspects may be called penal, is a penal law in the international sense, so that it cannot be enforced in the courts of another State, depends upon the question whether its purpose is to punish an offence against the public justice of the State, or to afford a private remedy to a person injured by the wrongful act." The *Third Restatement* suggests that a penal judgment is "a judgment in favor of a foreign state ... and primarily punitive rather than compensatory in character," *Restatement (Third) Foreign Relations Law* §483 comment b (1987), while a revenue judgment is "a judgment in favor of a foreign state ... based on a claim for an assessment of a tax, whether imposed in respect of income, property, transfer of wealth, or transactions in the taxing state." *Id.* comment c. *See Desjardins Ducharme v. Hunnewell*, 1992 Mass. Lexis 28 (1992) (award of attorney fees against unsuccessful plaintiff in foreign proceeding held not a fine, even where amount was based upon percentage of damages claimed in foreign case); *Chase Manhattan Bank, NA v. Hoffman*, 665 F.Supp. 73, 75-76 (D. Mass. 1987) ("the judgment was remedial ... [and] accrued in its particulars to the private party plaintiff").

7. Applicable Law and the Erie Doctrine

As in other international litigation contexts, the enforceability of foreign judgments in U.S. courts raises questions under the *Erie* doctrine. For the most part, U.S. lower courts have held that state substantive law governs the enforceability of foreign judgments.[60] Nevertheless, a few lower courts have suggested (typically in dicta) that federal common law rules may play a role in enforcing foreign judgments.[61] Reread *Somportex* and *Her Majesty*, excerpted above, which illustrate both approaches.

SOMPORTEX, LTD. v. PHILADELPHIA CHEWING GUM CORP.

318 F.Supp. 161 (E.D. Pa. 1970) [excerpted above at pp. 952-53]

HER MAJESTY THE QUEEN IN RIGHT OF THE PROVINCE OF BRITISH COLUMBIA v. GILBERTSON

597 F.2d 1161 (9th Cir. 1979)
[excerpted above at pp. 956-58]

Notes on Somportex and Her Majesty

1. *Source of law governing recognition and enforcement of foreign country judgments in diversity actions.* What law provided the rule in *Hilton* that foreign judgments are presumptively enforceable? Was it state, federal, or international? Reread the first few paragraphs of *Hilton* excerpted above. *See supra* pp. 943-44.

---

60. *See infra* p. 961.
61. *See infra* pp. 961-62.

2. *Application of state law to enforceability of foreign judgments.* What law did *Somportex* hold governed the enforceability of foreign judgments in the United States? Relying on *Erie* and *Klaxon Co. v. Stentor, supra* pp. 13-14 & 681-84, most lower federal courts have assumed or held that, in diversity actions, they are required to apply state law governing the recognition of judgments. *See, e.g., British Midland Airways v. International Travel,* 497 F.2d 869, 871 n.2 (9th Cir. 1974); *Bergman v. De Sieyes,* 170 F.2d 360 (2d Cir. 1948); *Fairchild, Arabatzis & Smith v. Prometco (Produce & Metals) Co.,* 470 F.Supp. 610, 614 (S.D.N.Y. 1979); *Mpiliris v. Hellenic Lines,* 323 F.Supp. 865 (S.D. Tex. 1969), *aff'd,* 440 F.2d 1163 (5th Cir. 1971); *Somportex, Ltd. v. Philadelphia Chewing Gum Corp.,* 318 F.Supp. 161 (E.D. Pa. 1970), *aff'd,* 453 F.2d 435 (3d Cir. 1971), *cert. denied,* 405 U.S. 1017 (1972); *Svenska Handelsbanken v. Carlson,* 258 F.Supp. 448 (D. Mass. 1966). *See* Note, *The Preclusive Effect of Foreign-Country Judgments in the United States and Federal Choice of Law,* 33 N.Y.L. S. L. Rev. 83 (1988).

State courts have also generally concluded that they are free to disregard *Hilton* and to develop their own local rules governing foreign judgments. *E.g., Johnston v. Compagnie Generale Transatlantique,* 152 N.E. 121 (N.Y. 1926); *Bonfils v. Gillespie,* 139 P. 1054 (Colo. 1914); *Restatement (Third) Foreign Relations Law* §481, comment a (1987) ("State courts, and federal courts applying State law, recognize and enforce foreign country judgments without reference to federal rules").

3. *Possible applicability of federal common law to enforceability of foreign judgments.* Is reliance on state law appropriate in enforcing *foreign country* judgments? Some commentators have suggested that the recognition of foreign judgments should be governed by a uniform federal rule. *E.g.,* Casad, *Issue Preclusion and Foreign Country Judgments: Whose Law?,* 70 Iowa L. Rev. 53, 77-80 (1984); Moore, *Federalism and Foreign Relations,* 1965 Duke L.J. 248, 261-68, 285-86; Scoles, *Interstate and International Distinctions in Conflict of Laws in the United States,* 54 Calif. L. Rev. 1599 (1966); Comment, *Judgments Rendered Abroad — State Law or Federal Law?,* 12 Vill. L. Rev. 618 (1967).

What national interests would be served by a uniform federal approach to the enforcement of foreign judgments? Note that some foreign nations refuse to enforce U.S. judgments. Could a uniform federal approach — for example, requiring reciprocity — help remedy this state of affairs? Does the existence of multiple state law rules governing enforcement confuse foreigners or give foreign courts a reason for refusing to enforce U.S. judgments? *See supra* p. 954. If so, is this sufficient grounds for adopting a uniform federal rule?

4. *Lower court authorities suggesting that federal common law affects enforceability of foreign judgments.* Contrary to the *Third Restatement,* several lower courts have suggested that state law is not the exclusive source for the rules governing the recognition and enforcement of foreign judgments. *See Her Majesty etc. v. Gilbertson,* 597 F.2d 1161 (9th Cir. 1979) (because of "foreign relations overtones" this matter "should not be decided merely by reference to Oregon law"); *John Sanderson & Co. v. Ludlow Jute Co.,* 569 F.2d 696, 697 (1st Cir. 1978); *Toronto-Dominion Bank v. Hall,* 367 F.Supp. 1009, 1011 (E.D. Ark. 1975) ("suits of this kind necessarily involve to some extent the relations between the United States and foreign governments and for that reason perhaps should be governed by a single uniform rule"); *Hunt v. BP Exploration Co. (Libya),* 492 F.Supp. 885 (N.D. Tex. 1980) (because of the unsettled nature of Texas law on recognition of foreign judgments, "coupled with the realization that recognition of foreign judgments is an element of United States foreign policy, the law of Texas is not the sole referent"). As yet, however, no lower court has actually formulated a rule of federal common law governing the enforcement of foreign judgments.

5. *Power of federal courts to apply federal common law to enforcement of foreign judgments.* Questions about the authority of federal courts to fashion federal common law arise in other international contexts. *See supra* pp. 224-25 (foreign sovereign immunity); pp. 450-52 (forum selection clauses); pp. 365-66 (*forum non conveniens*); pp. 914-15 (extraterritorial discovery); and pp. 704-05 (act of state doctrine). The same issue arises in the enforcement context: would federal courts have the authority to establish a rule of federal common law governing the recognition of foreign judgments?

As discussed elsewhere, development of a federal common law rule regarding the enforceability of foreign judgments would require demonstrating that this issue was "uniquely federal" and that state rules in the field undercut federal policies. *See supra* pp. 15-16. A rule of federal common law would presumably be derived from the federal government's extensive constitutional authority over foreign commerce and foreign relations, and from the "uniquely federal" character of this field. *See Banco Nacional de Cuba v. Sabbatino,* 376 U.S. 398 (1964); *Zschernig v. Miller,* 389 U.S. 429 (1968); *supra* pp. 15-16 & 541-44. On the other hand, there is substantial historical support for treating the recognition and enforcement of judgments as a matter of state law. *Cf. Zschernig v. Miller*, 389 U.S. 429, 443 (1968) (Harlan, J., concurring).

Assuming that the enforcement of foreign judgments is a uniquely federal issue, are any federal policies undercut by independent state policies? Consider the following:

> If *Hilton* was erroneously decided, then the solution is to change the federal rule, not to encourage a hodgepodge of independent state rules. In any event, the independent state positions regarding [the recognition and enforcement of foreign judgments], although perhaps more enlightened on the merits, have failed to achieve the foreign relations goal sought, namely the recognition of United States judgments abroad by reciprocity among nations. Thus, the lesson of *Hilton* reaffirms that the voice of foreign relations must be a federal voice. Moore, *Federalism and Foreign Relations*, 1965 Duke L.J. 248, 265.

Suppose that a state (a) refuses ever to recognize or enforce any foreign judgment; (b) refuses to recognize or enforce any foreign judgment against a U.S. national; (c) rejects the reciprocity requirement; (d) imposes much stricter scrutiny of foreign courts' jurisdiction than that contemplated by *Hilton* and the UFMJRA; or (e) only recognizes and enforces judgments of English-speaking countries. Would any of these state positions interfere with federal policies?

6. *Role of international law.* Recall *Hilton*'s treatment of the enforceability of foreign judgments as a subject governed by international law, *see supra* pp. 939-40 & 949, and the status of international law as federal law, *see supra* pp. 21 & 49-56. Compare the reasoning of the New York Court of Appeals:

> To what extent is this court bound by *Hilton v. Guyot*? It is argued with some force that questions of international relations and the comity of nations are to be determined by the Supreme Court of the United States. ... But the question is one of private rather than public international law, of private right rather than public relations, and our courts will recognize private rights acquired under foreign laws. ...

Johnston v. Compagnie Generale Transatlantique, 152 N.E. 121, 123 (N.Y. 1926).

7. *Comparison with act of state doctrine.* Recall that the act of state doctrine is a rule of substantive federal common law, requiring U.S. courts to give effect to foreign acts of states. Why does not the same rationale support federal common law rules governing the effect of foreign judgements?

8. *Comparison with New York Convention.* As discussed below, international arbitral awards are generally subject to enforcement under the New York Convention and Federal Arbitration Act. *See infra* pp. 1040-52. Does this have any relevance to the argument that federal common law rules should govern the enforceability of foreign judgments?

9. *Role of friendship, commerce, and navigation treaties in enforcing foreign judgments.* As described above, the United States is party to numerous friendship, commerce, and navigation ("FCN") treaties. These treaties typically include a so-called "national treatment" provision, along the following lines:

> Nationals and companies of either [nation] shall be accorded national treatment and most-favored-nation treatment with respect to access to the courts of justice and to administrative tribunals and agencies within the territories of the other [nation], in all degrees of jurisdiction, both in pursuit and in defense of their rights. Treaty of Friendship, Commerce, and Navigation Between the United States of America and the Republic of Korea, 8 U.S.T. 2217, Article V.

At least two lower courts have held that such "national treatment" provisions "elevat[e] a [foreign] judgment to 'the status of a sister state judgment.'" *Song v. Kim*, 1993 U.S. Dist. Lexis 17713 (D.N.J. 1993) (quoting *Vagenas v. Continental Gin Co.*, 988 F.2d 104, 106 (11th Cir. 1993)). In one court's words:

> the Court is precluded from applying comity principles established under New Jersey law, and must instead utilize those New Jersey standards that govern the enforcement of sister state judgments. In other words, the Friendship Treaty is effectively analogous to the Full Faith and Credit Clause because it obligates "the states to afford a [Korean] national the same treatment that any United States citizen would receive in an action to enforce a judgment." *Id.*

Is this correct? Suppose a U.S. national holds a foreign court judgment. What law ordinarily governs efforts to enforce the judgment in the United States? Suppose a foreign national holds a U.S. state court judgment. What law governs the foreign national's efforts to enforce the judgment in the United States?

C. Exceptions to the Presumptive Enforceability of Foreign Judgments in U.S. Courts

The presumptive enforceability of foreign judgments in U.S. courts under both common law standards and the UFMJRA is subject to important exceptions. As described below, there are many circumstances in which U.S. courts will *not* enforce foreign country judgments. In some circumstances, foreign judgments can be resisted on the same grounds as are available for challenging domestic judgments. In other cases, U.S. courts will not enforce a foreign judgment, even though they might enforce a comparable sister state judgment.

According to *Hilton*, a foreign judgment would not be enforced where:

1. There was no "due citation or voluntary appearance of the defendant" in the foreign judicial proceedings.
2. The foreign court lacked personal jurisdiction over the defendant.
3. The foreign court lacked subject matter jurisdiction over the dispute.
4. There was a showing of fraud or other irregularity in the foreign proceedings.
5. The foreign proceedings were biased or unfair.

The UFMJRA establishes broadly similar exceptions. Section 4 of the Act established two types of grounds for nonenforcement of foreign judgments. Section 4(a) sets forth three grounds — unfair foreign courts, lack of personal jurisdiction, and lack of subject matter jurisdiction — which *forbid* a U.S. court from enforcing a foreign judgment. Section 4(b) sets forth six other grounds that *permit*, but do not require, a U.S. court to deny recognition or enforcement. These grounds include lack of notice, fraud, public policy, existence of an inconsistent judgment, violation of forum selection clause, and inconvenient forum.[62]

1. Adequate Notice

One exception to the general principle favoring enforcement of foreign judgments is the requirement of adequate notice. According to *Hilton*, foreign judgments will not be recognized if they were not based upon "the due citation or voluntary appearance of the defendant."[63] Similarly, the UFMJRA permits non-recognition of a foreign judgment if "the defendant in the proceedings in the foreign court did not receive notice of the proceedings in sufficient time to enable him to defend."[64] Although these requirements appear straightforward, lower courts have frequently found them confusing. The following decision in *Ackermann v. Levine* illustrates this.

---

62. *Compare* the generally similar approach of the *Restatement (Third) Foreign Relations Law* §482 (1987).

63. 159 U.S. at 163.

64. UFMJRA §4(b)(1). *See also Restatement (Second) Conflict of Laws* §92(b) (1971) ("a reasonable method of notification is employed and a reasonable opportunity to be heard is afforded to persons affected"); *Restatement (Third) Foreign Relations Law* §482(2)(b) (1987) ("defendant did not receive notice of the proceedings in sufficient time to enable him to defend").

ACKERMANN v. LEVINE

788 F.2d 830 (2d Cir. 1986) [also excerpted below at pp. 975-78]

PIERCE, CIRCUIT JUDGE. [Mr. Ackermann, a German lawyer, sued Mr. Levine, a U.S. businessman, in German courts. Mr. Levine defaulted and Mr. Ackermann obtained a substantial judgment which he sought to enforce in the United States. Among other things, Mr. Levine challenged the judgment on the grounds that he had not received adequate notice.] ... We [next address] the question of whether service of the summons and complaint by registered mail provided Levine with adequate notice of the action.

Service of process must satisfy both the statute under which service is effectuated and constitutional due process.[65] The statutory prong is governed principally by the Hague Convention on the Service Abroad of Judicial and Extrajudicial Documents in Civil or Commercial Matters ("Hague Convention"). ... As a ratified treaty, the Convention is of course "the supreme law of the land." *See* U.S. Const. Art. VI, cl. 2. The service of process by registered mail did not violate the Hague Convention. Plaintiffs declined to follow the service route allowed under Article 5 of the Convention, which permits service via a "Central Authority" of the country in which service is to be made. Instead, plaintiffs chose to follow the equally acceptable route allowed under Articles 8 and 10. Article 8 permits each contracting state "to effect service of judicial documents upon persons abroad ... directly through its diplomatic or consular agents." The Regional Court of Berlin availed itself of this method by first sending the summons and complaint to the German Consulate in New York. As to the forwarding of those documents by registered mail from the Consulate to Levine's residence, the method of service was appropriate under Article 10(a), [which permits parties to "send judicial documents, by postal channels, directly to persons abroad."]

Since the United States has made no objection to the use of "postal channels" under Article 10(a), service of process by registered mail remains an appropriate method of service in this country under the Convention. ... *Shoei Kako*, 33 Cal.App.3d 808, 821-22. ...

Nor was service ineffective because it did not satisfy the Federal Rules of Civil Procedure. The old Federal Rule 4 was superseded by the Hague Convention and thus presumptively should not limit application of the Convention. ... The district court correctly notes that [old] Rule 4(c)(2)(C)(ii), permitting mail service conforming to certain technical requirements, did not exist when Ackermann's summons and complaint were served. In any event, whether Ackermann's service satisfied Rule 4 as it then existed or as it now exists is irrelevant because the United States has made no declaration or limitation to its ratification of the Convention regarding Federal Rule

---

65. Defendant-appellee also argues that service violated service of process laws of West Germany, [citing] *Appel v. Scheuler*, 78 Civ. 582 (E.D.N.Y. 1979) .... [T]his court, upon review [finds] that, under the evidence presented herein, service did not violate current German law.

4, or Article 10(a) of the Convention or otherwise regarding mail service under the Convention. ... Thus, the Convention "supplements" — and is manifestly *not* limited by — Rule 4.

The district court erred in holding that service under the Convention must satisfy both federal and state law. The court improperly cited *Aspinall's Club v. Aryeh*, 450 N.Y.S.2d 199 (App. Div. 1982), for the proposition. *Aspinall's Club* expressly held quite the opposite — that service of process under the Convention must satisfy federal *but not state* law. *See Aspinall's Club*, 450 N.Y.S.2d at 202 (service on an adult at defendant's residence must satisfy Federal Rule 4 but not the more stringent requirements under N.Y. C.P.L.R. §308(2)). Indeed, it seems to us that the only reason that service had to satisfy even Federal Rule 4 in *Aspinall's Club* was that the Convention is silent as to service on persons other than the defendant. Thus, some external law was needed to fill the interstices of the Convention, and the court in *Aspinall's Club*, though a state court, noted that "the Federal laws and treaties" are supreme to state law on this point, and that it would be "untenab[le]" to "promot[e] New York law over the Convention and the Federal Rule." In sum, where the Convention provides a rule of decision, that rule is dispositive, barring any contrary declaration by the United States; where the Convention is silent, federal law should govern where possible.

To construe the Convention otherwise would unduly burden foreign judgment holders with the procedural intricacies of fifty states. *Cf.* 18 C. Wright, A. Miller & E. Cooper, *Federal Practice and Procedure* §4473 at 743 (1981) ("It is intrinsically awkward to confront foreign judgments with the potentially divergent law of fifty states and federal courts, and recognition of foreign judgments at least touches concerns of foreign relations in which the national government has paramount interests."). While we could not similarly subordinate New York's interests in the *public policy* implications of the subject foreign judgment, as discussed *infra*, New York's rules regarding service are undoubtedly less compelling. *See Hanna v. Plumer*, 380 U.S. 460, 469 (1965) (state service rules not "substantial" enough to override federal rule). ...

It is of no moment that an employee of appellee Levine's apartment building received and signed for the service of process. First, as to this issue on which the Convention is silent, Federal Rule 4 requires merely that service be made on one of suitable age and discretion at the defendant's residence. *See Aspinall's Club*, 450 N.Y.S.2d at 202. Second, contrary to dicta in *Aspinall's Club* as to the more stringent requirements of the CPLR, even New York law may permit service upon one of suitable age and discretion who accepts process for residents of an apartment building.

Finally, service by registered mail does not violate constitutional due process. *See Mullane v. Central Hanover Bank & Trust Co.*, 339 U.S. 306, 314 (1950) (due process permits service of process by mail so long as such service provides "notice reasonably calculated ... to provide interested parties notice of the pendency of the action"). *See also FTC v. Compagnie de Saint-Gobain-Pont-A-Mousson*, 636 F.2d 1300, 1313 & n.4 (D.C. Cir. 1980). ...

Notes on Ackermann

1. *Adequate notice.* One of the *Hilton* requirements for the enforcement of foreign judgments is that of "proceedings following due citation or voluntary appearance of adversary parties." 159 U.S. at 202-03. Compare §4(b)(1) of the UFMJRA, *Restatement (Third) Foreign Relations Law* §482(2)(b) (1987) ("the defendant did not receive notice of the proceedings in sufficient time to enable him to defend"), and *Restatement (Second) Conflict of Laws* §92(b) (1971) ("a reasonable method of notification is employed and a reasonable opportunity to be heard is afforded to persons affected").

What does "adequate notice" or "due citation" require? What law answers this question? What role should service of process requirements play in the recognition and enforcement of foreign judgments? More specifically, should U.S. courts refuse to enforce foreign judgments if they involved service of foreign process within the United States in a manner that violates: (1) the due process clause; (2) the Hague Service Convention; (3) Federal Rule of Civil Procedure 4; (4) state rules regarding the service of process; or (5) foreign law regarding the service of process? How does *Ackermann* answer this question?

2. *Constitutional requirement of adequate notice.* As *Ackermann* illustrates, U.S. courts universally require that the judgment debtor have been given adequate notice and opportunity to appear in the foreign proceeding from which the judgment arose. The minimum standard for adequacy of notice is defined by the due process clause. Thus, in *Ackermann*, the Court of Appeals inquired whether the German court's use of registered mail for service satisfied the due process clause. *See Ma v. Continental Bank, NA*, 905 F.2d 1073, 1076 (7th Cir.), *cert. denied*, 498 U.S. 967 (1990); *Tahan v. Hodgson*, 662 F.2d 862, 864 (D.C. Cir. 1981); *Koster v. Automark Industries*, 640 F.2d 77, 81 n.3 (7th Cir. 1981); *Kohn v. American Metal Climax*, 458 F.2d 255, 303-04 (3d Cir.) (Adams, J., concurring and dissenting), *cert. denied*, 409 U.S. 874 (1972); *Somportex Ltd. v. Philadelphia Chewing Gum Corp.*, 453 F.2d 435, 443 (3d Cir. 1971), *cert. denied*, 405 U.S. 1017 (1972) ("The polestar is whether a reasonable method of notification is employed and reasonable opportunity to be heard is afforded to the person affected"); *De La Mata v. American Life Ins. Co.*, 771 F.Supp. 1375, 1386-88 (D. Del. 1991) (service upon former agent does not satisfy due process clause); *Bank of Montreal v. Kough*, 430 F.Supp. 1243, 1248 (N.D. Calif. 1977), *aff'd*, 612 F.2d 467 (9th Cir. 1980); *In re Estate of Klein*, 609 N.Y.S.2d 375 (N.Y. App. Div. 1994); *Rotary Club v. Chaprales Ramos de Pena*, 773 P.2d 467 (Ariz. App. 1989) (Mexican judgment based on substituted service not enforceable); *Julen v. Larson*, 25 Cal.App.3d 325 (1972) (service of process in German without U.S. translation did not provide U.S. defendant with adequate notice and resulting German judgment would therefore not be enforced); *Banco Minero v. Ross*, 172 S.W. 711, 714 (Tex. 1915); *Restatement (Second) Conflict of Laws* §98, comment c (1971); *Restatement (Third) Foreign Relations Law* §482(l)(a) (1987).

For decisions where foreign service was found inadequate under the due process clause, *see Thorteinsson v. M/V Brangur*, 891 F.2d 1547 (11th Cir. 1990); *Koster v. Automark Indus.*, 640 F.2d 77, 81 n.3 (7th Cir. 1981); *Victoria De La Mata v. American Life Insurance Co.*, 771 F.Supp. 1375 (D. Del. 1991); *Rotary Club v. Chaprales Ramos de Pena*, 773 P.2d 467 (Ariz. App. 1989). Note that the UFMJRA treats the lack of "notice" as a discretionary basis for nonrecognition under §4(b). Would a U.S. court be constitutionally permitted to enforce a foreign judgment based on service that did not satisfy the due process clause?

3. *Hague Service Convention. Ackermann* also required the German court's service of process on the judgment debtor to have satisfied what it called the "statute under which service is effectuated" — a requirement that the Court equated with the Hague Service Convention. *See also Aspinall's Club v. Aryeh*, 450 N.Y.S.2d 199 (1982) (requiring compliance with Hague Service Convention). Is this an appropriate requirement? Why shouldn't *only* the due process clause be relevant? *Cf. Volkswagenwerk AG v. Schlunk*, 486 U.S. 694 (1988) (suggesting that foreign courts will not honor U.S. judgments that are based on service that does not comply with the Hague Service Convention).

Suppose that foreign service of process satisfies the due process clause, but does not comply with the Hague Service Convention. Should a resulting foreign judgment be denied enforcement? Why or why not? Recall that the United States has long had a liberal policy regarding the service of foreign process within U.S. territory, and that the Hague Service Convention was not intended to limit this freedom. *See supra* pp. 795-800 & 838-41.

Note that in *Ackermann* the German plaintiff (or, more accurately, the German court) did not use Article 5's Central Authority mechanism. Recall also that the Hague Service Convention permits numerous alternative mechanisms of service, and that the United States has not objected to these alternatives. What theory justified the service in *Ackermann*? *See supra* pp. 809-22.

Suppose that the Central Authority mechanism *had* been used in *Ackermann*, and that the U.S. Central Authority had forwarded the documents to a U.S. Marshal who served them on a purported agent of Levine. Would Levine have been permitted to challenge compliance with the Hague Service Convention? Suppose that the "agent" that accepted the process was not in fact an agent permitted by Rule 4's formula ("an officer, a managing or general agent, or … any other agent authorized by appointment or by law to receive service of process") to receive service. Does this render notice inadequate? under *Ackermann's* analysis? under the UFMJRA?

Suppose that service is not consistent with the Hague Service Convention but the defendant nevertheless receives actual notice. *Compare Aspinall's Club v. Aryeh*, 450 N.Y.S.2d 199 (App. Div. 1982) (apparently requiring that Rule 4 be satisfied where service was made through Article 5 of Hague Service Convention and U.S. Marshal's Service: "The [receiving state's] Central Authority is to see that the papers in question are served 'by a method prescribed by its internal law for the service of documents in domestic actions upon persons who are within its territory.' The provisions of the Convention were duly observed in the instant matter. We thus conclude that the service on Aryeh met the standards of Rule 4 of the Federal Rules of Civil Procedure and thus satisfied the provisions of the Convention.").

4. Federal Rule of Civil Procedure 4. Citing *Aspinall's Club*, *Ackermann* arguably suggested that a foreign court's service of process on a U.S. defendant in the United States would be required to comply in at least some respects with the service provisions of the Federal Rules of Civil Procedure. The rationale for this requirement would apparently be that the Hague Service Convention does not always address particular aspects of service, and that where the Convention is silent, federal law should "fill the interstices of the Convention." Is compliance with the Federal Rules of Civil Procedure an appropriate requirement for the enforcement of foreign judgments? Why is not the due process clause alone an adequate safeguard? Read the final paragraphs of *Ackermann* carefully. Does the court require compliance with Rule 4, and, if so, when? Does the court adopt *Aspinall's* view of Rule 4, or does it merely require compliance with the Convention and the due process clause? Reconsider the hypothetical in the preceding note.

Ackermann did not require compliance with Rule 4's requirements concerning service by mail. Why not? Is it because Article 10 of the Convention permits specified types of mail service and the judgment creditor complied with these requirements?

Suppose that a foreign judgment is rendered by the court of a nation that is *not* a party to the Hague Service Convention. Would the foreign court's service on a defendant within the United States be required to satisfy the Federal Rules of Civil Procedure, as well as the due process clause? For one decision answering in the affirmative, *see Corporacion Salvadorena de Calzado, SA v. Injection Footwear Corp.*, 533 F.Supp. 290, 296-97 (S.D. Fla. 1982) ("service must nevertheless comport with Fed. R. Civ. P. 4. The relevant provisions of Rule 4 require that service on a corporation be made upon "an officer, a managing or general agent or any other agent authorized by appointment or by law to receive service of process," or alternatively, in accordance with subsection (i), Alternative Provisions for Service in a Foreign Country.") Is this wise? Did the drafters of Rule 4 have any intention that it should govern the service of process from foreign courts? *Compare Ma v. Continental Bank, NA*, 905 F.2d 1073, 1076 (7th Cir.), *cert. denied*, 498 U.S. 967 (1990) ("Although Hong Kong is not bound by our notions of due process, recognition of foreign judgments is a matter of comity, and as *Hilton* explains the United States will not enforce a judgment obtained without the bare minimum requirements of notice — although it does not insist on the additional niceties of domestic jurisprudence"); *Tahan v. Hodgson*, 662 F.2d 862, 864 (D.C. Cir. 1981) ("It would be unrealistic for the United States to require all foreign judicial systems to adhere to the Federal Rules of Civil Procedure"; case involved service outside the United States).

5. State service requirements. In addition to requiring compliance with the Federal Rules of Civil Procedure, *Ackermann* refused to require that foreign service of process satisfy *state* rules regarding the service of process. *See also Aspinall's Club v. Aryeh*, 450 N.Y.S.2d 199, 202 (1982) (same). *But see DSQ Property Co. v. Delorean*, 891 F.2d 128 (6th Cir. 1989) (apparently applying state service rules). What was the basis for this conclusion? the Hague Service Convention? or "concerns of foreign relations" referred to in the quotation from Wright and Miller?

Suppose the case had involved the judgment of a court in a country that is *not* party to the Hague Service Convention. Would state requirements regarding the service of process upon persons within the state be applicable? Having regard to the fact that state law generally govern the enforceability of foreign judgments, *supra* pp. 960-62, what would provide the basis for a federal law rule governing service?

6. *Significance of actual notice.* Suppose that the defendant receives actual notice of the foreign proceeding, in a manner that does not satisfy the due process clause. Some lower U.S. courts have suggested that the fact of actual notice is not sufficient, and that the failure to utilize service mechanisms that satisfy the due process clause results in non-recognition. *See Boivin v. Talcott*, 102 F.Supp. 979 (N.D. Ohio 1951). Other lower courts have apparently regarded the defendant's actual notice as sufficient evidence of service. *The Standard S.S. Owners' Protection and Indemnity Ass'n (Bermuda) Ltd. v. C & G Marine Services, Inc.*, 1992 WL 111186 (E.D. La. 1992); *Knothe v. Rose*, 392 S.E.2d 570, 573 (Ga. App. 1990).

7. *Service of foreign process outside the United States.* Many U.S. enforcement decisions involve U.S. judgment debtors who were, or should have been, served with foreign process in the United States. Some cases, however, involve non-U.S. defendants who were, or should have been, served with foreign process outside the United States. *E.g., Tahan v. Hodgson*, 662 F.2d 862 (D.C. Cir. 1981); *National Fire Ins. Co. v. People's Republic of Congo*, 727 F.Supp. 936 (S.D.N.Y. 1989). What standards should apply to such service of process? Suppose the service rules of both the foreign issuing court and the foreign defendant's state permit service that is inconsistent with the due process clause?

8. *Compliance with service requirements of issuing court.* Some U.S. courts have inquired whether service of process from a foreign court complied with the service of process rules of the foreign jurisdiction. *E.g., De La Mata v. American Life Ins. Co.*, 771 F.Supp. 1375, 1385-86 (D. Del. 1991) ("Analysis begins by examining the law governing service in Bolivia and determining whether the Bolivian court adhered to Bolivian laws"); *Royal Bank of Canada v. Trentham Corp.*, 491 F.Supp. 404 (S.D. Tex. 1980); *Bank of Montreal v. Kough*, 430 F.Supp. 1243, 1249-50 (N.D. Calif. 1977), *aff'd*, 612 F.2d 467 (9th Cir. 1980). Is this a sensible requirement? Is it consistent with the act of state doctrine? How does *Ackermann* deal with this issue?

9. *Preclusive effect of foreign courts' rulings on service.* Suppose that a party contests the adequacy of foreign service under the Hague Service Convention (or other U.S. law) in a foreign court, and the foreign court rejects the objection. Does this disposition have any preclusive effect in a U.S. enforcement action?

2. Personal and Subject Matter Jurisdiction

U.S. courts will not enforce a foreign judgment unless the court rendering the judgment possessed both personal and subject matter jurisdiction. *Hilton* required that a judgment be rendered by "a court of competent jurisdiction ... after due citation or voluntary appearance of the defendant."[66] Similarly, the UFMJRA deals at length with the subject of jurisdiction in §§4 and 5. The following case, *Mercandino v. Devoe & Raynolds, Inc.*, illustrates application of the jurisdiction requirement.

MERCANDINO v. DEVOE & RAYNOLDS, INC.

436 A.2d 942 (N.J. Super. 1981)

PER CURIAM. Plaintiff Franco Mercandino filed suit in the Hudson County District Court to enforce a default judgment which he had obtained against defendant Devoe and Raynolds, Inc., in Italy. Trial resulted in the entry of a judgment in plaintiff's favor, and defendant appeals, contending the Italian judgment should not have been enforced because ... the Italian court was without jurisdiction. ... We ... affirm.

A judgment issued by a court of a foreign nation will be recognized in the United States courts on the basis of comity, provided the court rendering the judgment had subject matter and personal jurisdiction over the defendant and provided

---

66. 159 U.S. at 163-64.

further that recognition will not offend the policies of the enforcing State. *Hilton v. Guyot*, 159 U.S. 113 (1895); *Fantony v. Fantony*, 122 A.2d 593 (1956).

It is well established that the issue of jurisdiction underlying such a judgment is always open to inquiry, provided that it has not been actually and fully litigated. In determining whether the Italian court had jurisdiction we deem it appropriate to apply the minimum contacts test. Under this test sufficient contacts are established when a nonresident seeking to avail himself of some benefit within a state affirmatively acts in a manner which he knows or should know will result in a significant impact within the forum state. Although this test was developed to determine whether a judgment of a sister state is entitled to full faith and credit, it is equally applicable where a court of a foreign nation has exercised long-arm jurisdiction. See *Bank of Montreal v. Kough*, 612 F.2d 467, 470-471 (9th Cir. 1980). In either instance, the minimum contacts standard provides assurance that the exercise of jurisdiction "does not offend traditional notions of fair play and substantial justice." *International Shoe Co. v. Washington.* ...

The record before us establishes that the defendant had a European representative, headquartered in Rotterdam, who went to Genoa and conducted talks with a representative of plaintiff. They reached an oral agreement, corroborated by correspondence, whereby plaintiff was to attempt to find marketing opportunities for defendant's products in Italy. Pursuant to that agreement plaintiff performed a variety of activities which, however, were unsuccessful. Plaintiff instituted this suit to recover for its expenditure of time and money on defendant's behalf. Though defendant had notice of this suit pending in Italy, it decided not to appear there but rather to take its chances fighting in the American courts. Plaintiff obtained a default judgment in Genoa which it seeks to enforce in this pending action.

It is clear that defendant acted in a manner which it knew or should have known would result in a significant impact within the jurisdiction of the Italian court, and the minimum contacts test is satisfied. ...

Notes on Mercandino

1. *Subject matter jurisdiction or competence.* It is well settled that U.S. courts will not enforce foreign judgments unless the foreign court possessed "competence" or subject matter jurisdiction under *foreign* law. *See Hilton*, 159 U.S. at 202 (foreign court must be one "of competent jurisdiction"); *Restatement (Second) Conflict of Laws* §92, comment i, §98, comment c, §105 (1971) (for a foreign judgment to be enforced, it must be "valid," which requires that the foreign court be competent to render judgment under local law); *Restatement (Third) Foreign Relations Law* §482(2)(a) (1987); *Hunt v. BP Exploration Co. (Libya)*, 492 F.Supp. 885 (N.D. Tex. 1980); UFMJRA §4(a)(3) (lack of subject matter jurisdiction is mandatory basis for non-recognition). Is it appropriate for U.S. courts to consider whether a foreign court properly exercised jurisdiction under foreign law? Is this consistent with the act of state doctrine? Should not foreign courts be presumed to have acted within their rightful subject matter jurisdiction under foreign law? *See The Standard S.S. Owners' Protection and Indemnity Ass'n (Bermuda) Ltd. v. C & G Marine Services, Inc.*, 1992 WL 111186 (E.D. La. 1992) ("Louisiana law presumes a rendering court has subject matter jurisdiction, and the burden rests with the judgment debtor to prove otherwise."); *Restatement (Third) Foreign Relations Law* §482 comment a (1987).

Does the subject matter jurisdiction requirement extend beyond the question whether *foreign* law granted jurisdiction? Suppose that foreign law grants a foreign court subject matter jurisdiction over a dispute that is entirely unrelated to the foreign state. Moreover, suppose that the foreign state prescribes a substantive rule of law that applies extraterritorially. If the foreign court grants a judgment in these circumstances, should the subject matter jurisdiction of the foreign court be open to challenge under U.S. (or international) standards? *Cf. Barry E. (Anonymous) v. Ingraham*, 400 N.Y.S.2d 772 (1977) (New York court refuses to recognize Mexican adoption where the child, the natural parents, and the adoptive parents were New York residents); *Restatement (Third) Foreign Relations Law* §482, comment d (1987) ("While jurisdiction of the foreign court over the subject matter of the action is normally presumed ... an order of a foreign court affecting rights in land in the United States or rights in a United States patent, trademark, or copyright is not entitled to that presumption.").

2. *Requirement that issuing court had personal jurisdiction.* As *Ackermann* illustrates, a basic prerequisite for the enforcement of a foreign judgment is that the foreign court issuing the judgment have possessed personal jurisdiction over the defendant. In one court's words, the rendering court must have had "in the international sense, jurisdiction over the defendant." *Somportex Limited v. Philadelphia Chewing Gum Corp.*, 318 F.Supp. 161, 165 (E.D. Pa. 1970), *aff'd*, 453 F.2d 435 (3d Cir. 1971), *cert. denied*, 405 U.S. 1017 (1982). *See also Restatement (Third) Foreign Relations Law* §482(l)(b) (1987); *Restatement (Second) Conflict of Laws* §104 (1971); UFMJRA §§4(a)(2) & 5.

A classic traditional illustration of the personal jurisdiction requirement was *Buchanan v. Rucker*, 9 East. 192 (K.B. 1808). There, a judgment made in Tobago against a foreign (non-Tobagoan) defendant was sought to be enforced in English courts. Enforcement was resisted on the grounds that service had been effected by nailing a notice to the courthouse door. The English courts denied recognition: "Can the island of Tobago pass a law to bind the rights of the whole world?" Recall also that the jurisdictional limits in *Pennoyer v. Neff, supra*, were developed in the context of an action to enforce a foreign judgment. *See supra* pp. 70-73 & 93.

3. *Applicable law for determining foreign court's jurisdiction.* What law should provide the standards for personal jurisdiction in this context — U.S. law, the rendering court's law, or international law?

(a) *U.S. authorities requiring that foreign court's jurisdiction satisfy due process clause.* Most U.S. courts have reviewed the personal jurisdiction of foreign courts according to U.S. jurisdictional standards, rather than by using the jurisdictional standards applicable under foreign law. *See Cunard S.S. Co. v. Salen Reefer Services, AB*, 773 F.2d 452, 457 (2d Cir. 1985) ("It is clearly established that in order to grant comity to a foreign court's award of a money judgment against a defendant, the foreign court must have valid personal jurisdiction over the defendant."); *Tahan v. Hodgson*, 662 F.2d 862, 864 (D.C. Cir. 1981); *Koster v. Automark Indus.*, 640 F.2d 77 (7th Cir. 1981); *Compagnie du Port de Rio de Janeiro v. Mead Morrison Mfg. Co.*, 19 F.2d 163, 166-67 (D. Me. 1927); *De La Mata v. American Life Ins. Co.*, 771 F.Supp. 1375, 1383-85 (D. Del. 1991); *South Carolina Nat'l Bank v. Westpac Banking Corp.*, 678 F.Supp. 596 (D.S.C. 1987); *Oman Int'l Finance, Ltd. v. Hoiyang Gems, Corp.*, 616 F.Supp. 351 (D.R.I. 1985); *Hunt v. BP Exploration Co. (Libya)*, 492 F.Supp. 885, 895 (N.D. Tex. 1980); *Royal Bank of Canada v. Trentham Corp.*, 491 F.Supp. 404, 406 (S.D. Tex. 1980), *rev'd on other grounds*, 665 F.2d 515 (5th Cir. 1981); *Fairchild, Arabatzis & Smith v. Prometco (Produce & Metals) Co.*, 470 F.Supp. 610 (S.D.N.Y. 1979); *Cherun v. Frishman*, 236 F.Supp. 292, 296 (D.D.C. 1964); *Mercandino v. Devoe & Raynolds, Inc.*, 436 A.2d 942 (Mass. 1981); *Davidson & Co. v. Allen*, 508 P.2d 6 (Nev. 1973). *See also* Reese, *The Status in This Country of Judgments Rendered Abroad*, 50 Colum. L. Rev. 783, 789 (1950).

What if a state's long-arm statute does not extend to the limits of the due process clause. Must a foreign court's judgment satisfy the more restrictive requirements of the state long-arm statute?

(b) *U.S. authorities suggesting that foreign court's jurisdiction need only satisfy foreign law.* A few U.S. courts have apparently considered only whether the foreign court had personal jurisdiction according to foreign law. *E.g., Hager v. Hager*, 274 N.E.2d 157, 160-61 (Ill. 1971).

(c) *U.S. authorities requiring that rendering court's jurisdiction satisfy both due process and foreign jurisdictional requirements.* Some authorities take the position that the rendering court must have had jurisdiction under *both* U.S. and foreign law. *E.g., Falcon Mfg. (Scarborough) v. Ames*, 278 N.Y.S.2d 684, 686 (1967). The *Restatement (Second) Conflict of Laws* §98 comment d (1971), suggests that a U.S. court may impose more rigorous personal jurisdiction requirements on foreign courts than apply to the U.S. court itself.

(d) *Authorities suggesting that rendering court's jurisdiction satisfy "international" standards.* The *Restatement (Third) Foreign Relations Law* §482(l)(b) (1987) provides that a foreign judgment may not be recognized if "the court that rendered the judgment did not have jurisdiction over the defendant in accordance with the law of the rendering state and with the rules set forth in §421." (Section 421, excerpted at *supra* p. 85, purports to state international law limitations on judicial jurisdiction.).

(e) *UFMJRA approach to personal jurisdiction.* The UFMJRA goes beyond existing common law in providing standards by which U.S. courts should judge the sufficiency of foreign courts' personal jurisdiction over judgment debtors. Under §5 of the Act, a foreign court's personal jurisdiction is to be upheld if it is based on personal service within the foreign state, voluntary appearance (other than to protect property or to contest jurisdiction), prior agreement to submit to the jurisdiction of the foreign court, domicile or principal place of business in the foreign country, business office in the foreign country (or the action arose out of business done through that office), or operation of a motor vehicle or airplane in the foreign country (if the action arose out of such operation). These sections of the Act, unlike some common law decisions, *see supra* p. 970, clearly contemplate application of U.S. standards of personal jurisdiction in deciding whether to enforce foreign judgments.

Note that the jurisdictional bases enumerated in the UFMJRA are fairly limited. Suppose a U.S. manufacturer aggressively markets its goods in a foreign country through a network of unrelated distributors. The goods malfunction, causing serious injuries to foreign purchasers, who successfully obtain personal jurisdiction over the nonresident U.S. manufacturer in foreign courts on theories analogous to those endorsed in *Asahi* and *International Shoe, see supra* pp. 73-77. Does the Act require enforcement of resulting foreign judgments? Why not?

Note that §5(b) of the Act permits, but does not require, U.S. courts to recognize bases of jurisdiction other than those enumerated in §5(a). What additional bases of personal jurisdiction should U.S. courts recognize? How should a U.S. court exercise its authority under §5(b) of the Act if confronted by the hypothetical in the previous paragraph?

(f) *Appropriate approach to rendering court's jurisdiction.* Which of the following approaches to the personal jurisdiction requirement is preferable? Should the due process clause provide the appropriate test for a rendering court's jurisdiction? What about applying international law instead, as the *Third Restatement* contemplates? What about applying the UFMJRA's narrower requirements?

4. *Judgment debtor's right to challenge jurisdiction in U.S. enforcement proceeding.* As discussed previously, if a judgment debtor did not appear to contest (and did not waive) the foreign court's personal and subject matter jurisdiction in the foreign proceedings, it can resist enforcement of the foreign judgment on jurisdictional grounds. *Ackermann v. Levine*, 788 F.2d 830 (2d Cir. 1986); *Covington Indus. v. Resintex, AG*, 629 F.2d 730 (2d Cir. 1980); *Somportex, Ltd. v. Philadelphia Chewing Gum Corp.*, 318 F.Supp. 161 (E.D. Pa. 1970); *Restatement (Third) Foreign Relations Law* §482 Reporters' Note 3 (1987) ("if jurisdiction of the foreign court was not contested or waived, the judgment debtor may challenge the jurisdiction of the rendering court in resisting enforcement in the United States").

5. *Effect of appearance in foreign proceeding on jurisdictional challenge in U.S. enforcement action.* A defendant may choose *not* to default in the foreign proceedings. As discussed below, the treatment of the jurisdiction requirement in cases where the judgment debtor did appear in foreign proceedings is difficult.

(a) *Litigation on the merits without challenging jurisdiction.* Most authorities indicate that a party that litigates in a foreign forum on the merits without raising a jurisdictional defense cannot subsequently challenge the jurisdiction of the foreign court. *Restatement (Third) Foreign Relations Law* §482, Reporters' Note 3 (1987) ("If the defendant ... defended on the merits without challenging the [foreign] court's jurisdiction, a ... challenge to jurisdiction of the rendering court is generally precluded"); *South Carolina National Bank v. Westpac Banking Corp.*, 678 F.Supp. 596, 598-99 (D.S.C. 1987) (defendant held to have waived right to challenge foreign court's jurisdiction because, after raising and losing jurisdiction in foreign trial court, defendant did not re-raise issue in foreign courts); *Norkan Lodge Co. v. Gillum*, 587 F.Supp. 1457 (N.D. Tex. 1984) (failure to raise jurisdiction in foreign proceedings, while resisting on merits, precludes argument in U.S. enforcement proceeding that foreign court lacked jurisdiction). As a noted English jurist has reasoned, the defendant "cannot be allowed, at one and the same time, to say that he will accept the decision on the merits if it is favorable to him and will not submit to it if it is unfavorable." *In re Dulles' Settlement* [1951] Ch. 842, 850, *quoted in*, von Mehren & Trautman, *Recognition of Foreign Adjudications: A Survey and Suggested Approach*, 81 Harv. L. Rev. 1601, 1669 (1968). Is this a sensible approach?

(b) *Litigation on the merits after unsuccessfully challenging jurisdiction.* Most U.S. courts also hold that a defendant who unsuccessfully litigates the issue of personal jurisdiction in a foreign court *and* subsequently defends on the merits has waived any right to challenge jurisdiction in the United States. *E.g.*,

Nippon Emo-Trans. Co. v. Emo-Trans. Co., 744 F.Supp. 1215 (E.D.N.Y. 1990); *Cherun v. Frishman*, 236 F.Supp. 292, 295-96 (D.D.C. 1964); *Restatement (Third) Foreign Relations Law* §482, Reporters' Note 3 (1987). *But see Hunt v. BP Exploration Co. (Libya)*, 492 F.Supp. 885, 895 (N.D. Tex. 1980) ("Litigating on the merits after loss on a jurisdictional challenge is thus not considered to be consent to jurisdiction."). This approach requires defendants to choose between having a U.S. court resolve jurisdictional challenges and having an opportunity to defend against the plaintiff's claims on the merits.

Query whether this approach is warranted. What if foreign standards governing personal jurisdiction differ materially from U.S. standards? Can it be correct that litigation in a foreign court about foreign jurisdictional rules, which do not satisfy the due process clause, can preclude a due process defense in the United States? Would the Constitution permit this?

(c) *Unsuccessfully challenging jurisdiction in the foreign proceeding.* It is unclear what preclusive effect follows from a defendant's unsuccessful challenge in a foreign proceeding to the foreign court's jurisdiction, followed by a default on the merits. Under the full faith and credit clause (and the Brussels Convention) the foreign court's jurisdictional ruling is preclusive. *Baldwin v. Iowa State Traveling Mens' Ass'n*, 283 U.S. 522 (1931). What result should follow in international cases? Suppose that foreign jurisdictional standards are different from — and more expansive than — U.S. ones.

Some authorities suggest that *res judicata* effect will generally be afforded to contested foreign jurisdictional holdings. *Somportex, Ltd. v. Philadelphia Chewing Gum Corp.*, 454 F.2d 435 (3d Cir. 1971), *cert. denied*, 405 U.S. 1017 (1972); *Sprague & Rhodes Commodity Corp. v. Instituto Mexicano del Cafe*, 566 F.2d 861, 863 (2d Cir. 1977).

In contrast, other U.S. courts have permitted personal jurisdiction challenges even though the judgment debtor litigated and lost the same issue in the foreign proceeding. *See, e.g., Hunt v. BP Exploration Co. (Libya)*, 492 F.Supp. 885, 895-96 (N.D. Tex. 1980); *Nippon Emo-Trans. Co. v. Emo-Trans. Co.*, 744 F.Supp. 1215 (E.D.N.Y. 1990) ("the determination of a foreign court as to jurisdiction is to be treated with circumspection"; even though jurisdictional theory relied upon by Japanese court was not consistent with U.S. due process clause, Japanese judgment will be enforced because facts found by Japanese court will be accepted and because they supported a jurisdictional predicate recognized in U.S.).

Consider the following excerpt from the *Restatement (Third) Foreign Relations Law* §482, comment c (1987):

> [A] court in the United States asked to recognize a foreign judgment should scrutinize the basis for asserting jurisdiction in the light of international concepts of jurisdiction to adjudicate. See §421. Since all the bases for jurisdiction to adjudicate listed in §421 satisfy the requirements of due process in the United States, any foreign judgment rendered on one of those bases will be entitled to recognition, provided the facts support the assertion of jurisdiction... .
> If the defendant appeared in the foreign court to challenge the jurisdiction of the court and failed to prevail it is not clear whether such determination will be considered res judicata by a court in the United States asked to recognize the resulting judgment. If the determination of jurisdiction depended on a finding of fact to support an otherwise unobjectionable basis of jurisdiction — for example, whether X was an agent through whom the defendant did business in the forum state — the determination after contest ordinarily will be respected. See §481, Reporters' Note 3. If the determination depended on a question of law or a mixed law/fact question — for example, whether a nonresident corporation is present in the forum state by virtue of having an "alter ego" subsidiary there — the court asked to recognize the resulting judgment will scrutinize the jurisdictional determination on its merits. See Reporters' Note 3. If the judgment of the foreign court is founded on a basis of jurisdiction not meeting the standards of §421 — for instance, the plaintiff's nationality under Article 14 of the French Civil Code — but another basis of jurisdiction would have supported the action — for instance, that the action grew out of an activity of the defendant conducted in the territory of the forum, §421(i) — a court in the United States may recognize and enforce the judgment.

Is this a sensible approach?

6. *Effect of default judgment on scrutiny of foreign court's jurisdiction.* As discussed above, U.S. courts will in principle enforce foreign default judgments. *See supra* p. 950. At the same time, as a practical matter, U.S. courts often take a particularly hard look at the foreign court's jurisdiction, procedural protections, and the like before enforcing a foreign default judgment. *Cf. Siedler v. Jacobson*, 383 N.Y.S.2d 833

(N.Y. 1976) (U.S. court holds that Austrian court lacks personal jurisdiction over U.S. tourist who spent one week in Vienna in suit by Austrian porcelain dealer for breach of contract entered into by U.S. tourist during his visit to Vienna); *Falcon Mfg. (Scarborough) v. Ames*, 278 N.Y.S.2d 684, 687 (1967) ("Since the judgment under consideration is a default judgment based upon personal service of the writ of summons outside of the jurisdiction of the rendering court it is *ipso facto* not as persuasive as it might have been were it rendered after a trial on the merits."); *Restatement (Second) Conflict of Laws* §98, comment e (1971).

7. *Inconvenient foreign forum under the UFMJRA.* Section 4(b)(6) of the UFMJRA permits U.S. courts to deny enforcement to foreign judgments rendered in forums that were seriously inconvenient to the judgment debtor, but only where the foreign court's jurisdiction was based solely on personal service. *Compare Restatement (Third) Foreign Relations Law* §482(2) (1987), which contains an inconvenient forum defense but omits the personal service limitation. What if a U.S. court permits personal jurisdiction based on an *Asahi* or *International Shoe* theory of minimum contacts with the forum, but the forum was seriously inconvenient to the nonresident defendant? Should an inconvenient forum defense to enforcement be permitted? *See Ingersoll Milling Machine Co. v. Granger*, 833 F.2d 680, 689 (7th Cir. 1987); *Bank of Montreal v. Kough*, 430 F.Supp. 1243 (N.D. Cal. 1980), *aff'd*, 612 F.2d 467 (9th Cir. 1980); *Southern Bell Tel. & Tel. Co. v. Woodstock, Inc.*, 339 N.E.2d 423 (Ill. 1975). What if the foreign court would have permitted assertion of a *forum non conveniens* defense? What if the foreign court considered and rejected the defendant's *forum non conveniens* defense?

8. *Violation of forum selection clause under the UFMJRA.* Section 4(b)(5) of the Act permits U.S. courts to deny recognition to foreign judgments that are entered in violation of a forum selection agreement. Recall the general rule, derived from the Supreme Court's decision in *The Bremen v. Zapata Off-Shore Co.*, 407 U.S. 1 (1972), that forum selection clauses in international contracts are enforceable except in limited circumstances. *See supra* pp. 378-81. The *Restatement (Third) Foreign Relations Law* §482(2)(f) & Reporters' Note 5 (1987) ("the proceeding in the foreign court was contrary to an agreement between the parties to submit the controversy on which the judgment is based to another forum"), adopts a rule that is similar to that in §4(b)(5). Suppose the foreign court considers the parties' forum selection clause, but concludes that it is unenforceable (for example, because of duress or lack of notice). Suppose that the foreign court concludes that the forum selection clause violates local public policy and should not be enforced. Should a U.S. court enforce a resulting foreign judgment? Does your answer depend upon the particular defense or public policy invoked by the foreign court? *See supra* pp. 426-30.

Suppose a defendant unsuccessfully resists the jurisdiction of a foreign court on the ground that a forum selection clause calls for litigation in U.S. courts, and then defends on the merits, again unsuccessfully. Can the judgment debtor resist enforcement by invoking the forum selection clause? *See Id.* comment h ("[p]arties may ... waive the forum selection clause, either expressly or by implication ... Subsection (2)(f) would ordinarily apply to default judgments, ... since participation by the judgment debtor in an action other than the one previously selected effectively waives the contractual choice of forum").

Conversely, a forum selection clause submitting to the jurisdiction of the rendering court will generally be regarded as a sufficient jurisdictional base. *See The Standard S.S. Owners' Protection and Indemnity Ass'n (Bermuda) Ltd. v. C & G Marine Services, Inc.*, 1992 WL 111186 (E.D. La. 1992).

9. *Personal jurisdiction of enforcing court.* Most personal jurisdiction questions in the enforcement of judgments context concern the jurisdiction of the foreign court that rendered the judgment. Fewer courts have addressed the different question of the requisite connection between the court enforcing the foreign judgment and the judgment debtor. The presence of the defendant within the enforcement forum, or the existence of "minimum contacts" between the defendant and the forum state, will ordinarily permit the exercise of jurisdiction for the purpose of enforcing a foreign judgment. *See Restatement (Third) Foreign Relations Law* §481, comment a (1987).

In addition, the presence of property belonging to the judgment debtor within the jurisdiction of a U.S. court ordinarily creates a sufficient nexus between the owner and the court to permit enforcement of a foreign judgment against that property. *See Shaffer v. Heitner*, 433 U.S. 186, 210-11 n.36 (1977); *Biel v. Boehm*, 406 N.Y.S.2d 231 (1978); *Restatement (Third) Foreign Relations Law* §481, comment h (1987) ("whereas under ... prevailing U.S. law ... a state has jurisdiction to adjudicate a claim on the basis of presence of property in the forum only where the property is reasonably connected with the claim, an action to enforce a judgment may usually be brought wherever property of the defendant is found, without any necessary connection between the underlying action and the property, or between the defendant and the forum"). For a decision where the U.S. enforcing court held that it lacked personal jurisdiction over the judgment debtor, *see Jiminez v. Mobil Oil Co.*, 1991 U.S. Dist. Lexis 4996 (S.D.N.Y. April 18, 1991).

3. Public Policy

It is well-established that a U.S. court need not recognize a foreign judgment that is contrary to the forum's "public policy." This exception to the presumptive enforceability of foreign judgments parallels analogous public policy rules in other international contexts.[67]

Although *Hilton* did not expressly adopt a public policy exception, the Court's opinion clearly provided the basis for one to develop. Justice Gray remarked that a foreign judgment was presumptively enforceable, except where "the comity of this nation should not allow it full effect."[68] Elsewhere, *Hilton* invoked Joseph Story's description of comity's limits:

> comity is, and ever must be, uncertain; ... it must necessarily depend on a variety of circumstances which cannot be reduced to any certain rule; ... *no nation will suffer the laws of another to interfere with her own to the injury of her citizens*; ... [and] whether they do or not must depend on the condition of the country in which the foreign law is sought to be enforced, the particular nature of her legislation, her policy, and the character of her institutions. ... [69]

Subsequent lower court decisions expressly recognized the public policy exception to *Hilton's* presumptive enforceability of foreign judgments.[70] The UFMJRA also recognizes a public policy exception, with §4(b) permitting, but not requiring, non-recognition of a foreign judgment if "the [cause of action] [claim for relief] on which the judgment is based is repugnant to the public policy of this state."[71]

As in other international contexts,[72] application of the public policy exception to foreign judgments has been difficult. The decisions excerpted below illustrate this. First, consider *Ackermann v. Levine*, where the court invokes the public policy exception to deny partial enforcement to a German judgment based on a statutory claim for attorneys' fees. Then consider *Bachchan v. India Abroad*, where the court denies enforcement to an English judgment for libel.

---

67. *Compare supra* pp. 414-30 (forum selection clauses); *supra* pp. 341-43 (forum non conveniens); *supra* pp. 624-31 & 655-56 (choice of law); and *infra* pp. 1011-12 & 1049-50 (arbitral awards).

68. 159 U.S. at 202-03 (emphasis added).

69. 159 U.S. at 164-65 (quoting J. Story, *Commentaries on the Conflict of Laws* §28 (no edition specified)).

70. *Neporany v. Kir*, 173 N.Y.S.2d 146 (App. Div. 1958); *Spann v. Compania Mexicana Radiodifusora Fromteriza*, 41 F.Supp. 907 (N.D. Tex. 1941), *aff'd*, 131 F.2d 609 (5th Cir. 1942).

71. *See also Restatement (Third) Foreign Relations Law* §482(2)(d) (1987) ("the cause of action on which the judgment was based, or the judgment itself, is repugnant to the public policy of the United States or of the State where recognition is sought"); *Restatement (Second) Conflict of Laws* §117, comment c (1971).

72. *See supra* p. 974 n.67.

ACKERMANN v. LEVINE

788 F.2d 830 (2d Cir. 1986) [also excerpted above at pp. 964-65]

PIERCE, CIRCUIT JUDGE. [Ackermann was a German lawyer and Levine was a U.S. real estate developer. In 1979, Levine visited Germany to interest local investors in participating in one of his developments. During his visit, Levine sought German legal advice and was referred to Ackermann. Ackermann and Levine met for a disputed period (between twenty and ninety minutes) to discuss Levine's proposed transactions. They did not discuss attorneys' fees. In a subsequent letter and telephone conversation, Levine authorized Ackermann to act on his behalf in connection with the transactions. Ackermann obtained a file of documents relating to the transaction from a mutual friend of both Ackermann and Levine; Levine stated that he did not know that Ackermann had received or reviewed the file. For various reasons, these transactions were never consummated. Ackermann subsequently claimed to have spent twenty days working full-time on Levine's project, although he was apparently unable to produce any written materials reflecting his efforts. In late 1979 Ackermann billed Levine for his services, computed pursuant to the German legal fee statute (Bundesrechtsanwaltsgebuehrenordnung or BRAGO), which totalled 190,827 Deutsche. Marks (approximately $100,000). The fee comprised two basic elements: (1) detailed discussions with prospective German investors and (2) study of Levine's proposed transaction. Levine did not respond to the bill and Ackermann filed suit in German court. Process was served on Levine by registered mail, but he ignored the suit. Ackermann obtained a default judgment and commenced enforcement proceedings in the U.S. District Court for the Southern District of New York. The lower court refused to enforce the German judgment because enforcement would violate a "New York public policy" that attorneys seeking recovery of fees "bear the burden of proving that a compensation arrangement is fair, reasonable and fully comprehended by the client." Ackermann appealed.] ...

We are confronted here with issues relating to the recognition and enforcement of a foreign judgment in a case involving attorney-client relations in an international business context. The district court appropriately framed the issues in accordance with the well-settled rule that a final judgment obtained through sound procedures in a foreign country is generally conclusive as to its merits *unless* (1) the foreign court lacked jurisdiction over the subject matter or the person of the defendant; (2) the judgment was fraudulently obtained; or (3) enforcement of the judgment would offend the public policy of the state in which enforcement is sought.... .

II. The district court held that, based on the undisputed fact that Ackermann never discussed fees with Levine, the German judgment was rendered unenforceable as violative of New York's public policy that "the attorney, not the client, must ensure the fairness, reasonableness and full comprehension by the client of their compensation agreement." On that basis, the district court declined enforcement of the entire award of approximately $100,000.

A judgment is unenforceable as against public policy to the extent that it is "repugnant to fundamental notions of what is decent and just in the State where enforcement is sought." *Tahan v. Hodgson*, 662 F.2d 862, 864 (D.C. Cir. 1981). ... The standard is high, and infrequently met. As one court wrote, "[o]nly in clear-cut cases ought it to avail defendant." *Tahan*, 662 F.2d at 866 n.17. ... In the classic formulation, a judgment that "tends clearly" to undermine the public interest, the public confidence in the administration of the law, or security for individual rights of personal liberty or of private property is against public policy.

The narrowness of the public policy exception to enforcement would seem to reflect an axiom fundamental to the goals of comity and res judicata that underlie the doctrine of recognition and enforcement of foreign judgments. As Judge Cardozo so lucidly observed: "We are not so provincial as to say that every solution of a problem is wrong because we deal with it otherwise at home." *Loucks v. Standard Oil Co.*, 120 N.E. 198 (N.Y. 1918). Further, the narrowness of the public policy exception indicates a jurisprudential compromise between two guiding but sometimes conflicting principles in the law of recognition and enforcement of foreign judgments: (1) res judicata and (2) ... fairness regarding the underlying transaction.

The question presented here involves the extent to which local public policy will permit recognition and enforcement of a foreign default judgment. Since a foreign default judgment is not more or less conclusive but *"as* conclusive an adjudication" as a contested judgment, *Somportex*, 453 F.2d at 442-43 & n.13 (emphasis added), the district court quite properly afforded Levine the same opportunity to contest the enforceability of the German judgment in light of the public policy issue. We disagree with dicta in *Tahan*, 662 F.2d at 867, suggesting that a defendant may not raise a public policy defense once he has defaulted in the foreign adjudication. By defaulting, a defendant ensures that a judgment will be entered against him, and assumes the risk that an irrevocable mistake of law or fact may underlie that judgment. ...

However, we believe that the district court erred in holding that the failure of German law regarding attorneys' fees to meet our more rigorous principles of fiduciary duties sufficiently offended local public policy as to justify nonenforcement of the entire judgment, and thus total vitiation of the values of comity and res judicata that enforcement would promote. ...

The narrow public policy exception to enforcement is not met merely because Ackermann did not inform Levine of the BRAGO billing statute. See *Compania Mexicana Rediodifusora Franteriza v. Spann*, 41 F.Supp. 907 (N.D. Tex. 1941), *aff'd*, 131 F.2d 609 (5th Cir. 1942) (exception not met where a foreign attorney had failed to apprise his American client of Mexico's rule that a losing plaintiff's liability for costs is proportionate to the amount of relief originally sought). Nor is the exception met in the event that Ackermann's bill should exceed the amount which American lawyers might reasonably have charged. See *Somportex*, 453 F.2d at 443 (exception not met where a British default judgment of $94,000 against an American defendant to a contract action included in substantial part damages for loss of good will and for attorneys' fees and other costs, none of which would be awarded by Pennsylvania, the state in which enforcement was granted). Certainly it is not enough merely that Germany provides a billing scheme by statute rather than by contractual arrangements subject to an attorney's fiduciary duties. We note that even New York policy permits statute-based billing systems in certain instances. ... Nor can we say that the German judgment is unenforceable because the attorney-client relationship herein was not structured commensurate with the New York policy favoring, though not requiring, written retainer agreements. It is not enough merely that a foreign judgment fails to fulfill domestic practice or policy. ...

Thus, we think that the district court erred in holding the judgment unenforceable as offensive to New York's public policy that lawyers discharge their fiduciary duty to ensure fair and reasonable fees, fully disclosed to and understood by their clients. However, that this broad, fiduciary-based public policy does not render the judgment unenforceable does not preclude the possibility that a narrower, evidentiary-based public policy might render the judgment unenforceable.

We hold that the applicable theory of public policy requires that recovery of attorneys' fees be predicated on evidence of, at a minimum, (1) the existence of some authorization by the client for the attorney to perform the work allegedly performed; and (2) the very existence of that work. These evidentiary predicates, we hold, constitute the *sine qua non* of a client's liability for legal fees. Without these predicates, there is a grave risk that American courts could become the means of enforcing unconscionable attorney fee awards, thereby endangering "public confidence" in the administration of the law and a "sense of security for individual rights ... of private property." *Somportex*, 453 F.2d at 443. Further, to forsake this fundamental public policy would impose upon American citizens doing business abroad an undue risk in dealing with foreign counsel — a result that, ironically, could undermine the very processes of transnational legal relations that the doctrines of comity and res judicata seek to promote. ...

In applying this evidentiary-based public policy, we note that courts are not limited to recognizing a judgment entirely or not at all. Where a foreign judgment contains discrete components, the enforcing court should endeavor to discern the appropriate "extent of recognition," *cf.* 18 C. Wright & A. Miller, *Federal Practice and Procedure* §4473, at 745 (1981), with reference to applicable public policy concerns.

Ackermann has laid the predicate in support of his bill for "detailed discussions with prospective buyers" and for the related travel and office expenses, but he has not done so for the "basic fee for the study of the project files, [and] discussion with client and his counsel." ... Recognition of the foreign judgment to this extent is consonant with the evidence that Levine engaged Ackermann's services and benefited therefrom. ... Levine clearly would have benefited from German law had his work with Ackermann proved fruitful. ... He thus "finds himself in the quite unenviable position of trying to take the good without the bad, the sweet without the bitter." As to the fifteen to twenty days of work that comprise the bulk of the "basic fee for study of the project files," the record reflects no evidence of an authorization to do such work or of the existence of any work product. The mere fact that Ackermann possessed the project files is inconsequential since Levine did not know that [a friend of Ackermann] had given those files to Ackermann. Nor do we find authorization in the office visit [between Levine and Ackermann], of late May or early June, since the district court found that visit had accomplished only the creation of a misunderstanding. Even if there had been an authorization, there was not a scintilla of evidence of work product. Ackermann offered no client memoranda, no memoranda to his files, no handwritten notes, no markings on the papers that [Ackermann's friend] had given him, and no other indicia of actual performance. ... We do not challenge the district court's finding as to Ackermann's character. However, we need not say that an attorney acted fraudulently or dishonestly to hold, as we do here, that the failure to adduce any evidence of work product requires disallowance of claimed legal fees. ...

This case involved an unfortunate disagreement between parties of different countries and legal cultures. As the district court found, both parties behaved honorably, and their dispute was born of mutual mistake. Although the defendant chose to default in a German action commenced by valid service of process, he did not thereby waive his right to contest the enforceability of the foreign judgment on grounds of public policy. The increasing internationalization of commerce requires "that American courts recognize and respect the judgments entered by foreign courts to the greatest extent consistent with 'our own ideals of justice and fair play." *Tahan*, 662 F.2d at 868. In light of that important imperative, we hold the Germany judgment to be enforceable in all respects except for the first item of DM 89.347,50 for the "[b]asic fee for the study of project files, discussion with client and his counsel," for which there was no evidence of authorization or of work product. ...

BACHCHAN v. INDIA ABROAD PUBLICATIONS INC.

585 N.Y.S.2d 661 (Sup. Ct. 1992)

SHIRLEY FINGERHOOD, JUSTICE. Although the cases interpreting constitutional limitations on libel actions are legion, this is apparently the first time that a New York court has been asked to apply those limitations to bar the enforcement of a foreign judgment. The judgment was granted in an action brought in the High Court of Justice in London, England by an Indian national against the New York operator of a news service which transmits reports only to a news service in India. The story held to be defamatory was written by a reporter in London, wired by defendant to the news service in India which sent it to newspapers there. It was reported in two Indian newspapers copies of which were distributed in the United Kingdom. The story was also reported in an issue of "India Abroad," defendant's New York newspaper. An edition of "India Abroad" was printed and distributed in the United Kingdom by defendant's English subsidiary, India Abroad (U.K.) and a claim based on that distribution was asserted in the lawsuit approximately a year after its commencement.

The wire service story transmitted by defendant on January 31, 1990 stated that *Dagens Nyjeter*, a Swedish daily newspaper (hereafter "DN") had reported that Swiss authorities had frozen an account belonging to plaintiff to which money was transferred from a coded account into which commissions paid by Bofars were deposited. Bofars is a Swedish arms company, which some time before had been charged with paying kickbacks to obtain a large munitions contract with the Indian Government. Plaintiff's name had previously been mentioned in connection with the scandal in a variety of Indian and other publications. On February 3, 1990, defendant's wire service transmitted plaintiff's denial that he was the holder of such a bank account or that he or any member of his family had any connection with the Bofars contract.

Plaintiff brought an action against DN in London at the same time as it sued India Abroad. DN settled the claim against it by paying a sum of money and issuing an apology saying that it had been misled by Indian government sources. India Abroad did not apologize but did report DN's settlement and apology.

The jury assessed 40,000 pounds in damages for the wire service story together with attorney's fees against India Abroad, Inc. and its reporter, Rahul Bedi. As authorized by Section 5303 of New York's Civil Practice Law and Rules ("CPLR") plaintiff seeks to enforce that judgment by motion for summary judgment in lieu of complaint. (A 40,000 pound judgment granted against India Abroad, U.K. for its distribution of the English edition of "India Abroad" is not directly at issue here.)

Entry of the judgment is opposed on the ground that it was imposed without the safeguards for freedom of speech and the press required by the First Amendment to the United States Constitution and Article 1, §8 of the Constitution of the State of New York. Defendant asks this court to reject the judgment as repugnant to public policy, a ground for nonrecognition of foreign judgments under CPLR §5304(b)(4).

CPLR §5304 is comprised of two parts: section (a) which is explicitly mandatory and precludes recognition of foreign judgments on certain constitutional grounds, *i.e.*, if the procedures pursuant to which a foreign judgment was rendered are not compatible with the requirements of due process of law or when the foreign court did not have personal jurisdiction over the defendant; and section (b) which provides that a foreign judgment "need not be recognized if," *inter alia*, "the cause of action on which the judgment is based is repugnant to the public policy of this state." (subsection 4)

It is plaintiff's position that the public policy exception to the rule that foreign judgments are afforded comity is narrow and inapplicable here. He asserts that this court should not reexamine the claim for which the judgment was awarded to determine whether it would be culpable under United States precedents. Pointing to CPLR §5304(b)(4)'s reference to "causes of action" rather than judgments, he argues that libel causes of action are cognizable in New York. If that subsection is deemed to refer to judgments as well as causes of action, plaintiff asks this court to exercise its discretion to recognize the judgment in view of the common antecedents of the law of Great Britain and that of the United States.

It is doubtful whether this court has discretion to enforce the judgment if the action in which it was rendered failed to comport with the constitutional standards for adjudicating libel claims. If, as claimed by defendant, the public policy to which the foreign judgment is repugnant is embodied in the First Amendment to the United States Constitution or the free speech guaranty of the Constitution of this state, the refusal to recognize the judgment should be, and it is deemed to be, "constitutionally mandatory." Accordingly, the libel law applied by the High Court of Justice in London in granting judgment to plaintiff will be reviewed to ascertain whether its provisions meet the safeguards for the press which have been enunciated by the courts of this country.

Both parties submitted descriptions of the defamation laws of England in affidavits and affirmations by English solicitors and barristers with copies of relevant statutes, rules and case laws. ... The instructions given to the jury by the presiding judge at the trial of plaintiff's claim, Mr. Justice Otten, have also been considered.

Under English law, any published statement which adversely affects a person's reputation, or the respect in which that person is held, is prima facie defamatory. Plaintiff's only burden is to establish that the words complained of refer to them, were published by the defendant, and bear a defamatory meaning. If, as in the present case, statements of fact are concerned, they are presumed to be false and the defendant must plead justification for the issue of truth to be brought before the jury. An unsuccessful defense of justification may result in the award of aggravated damages. For, in the language of Lord Hailsham of the House of Lords in *Broom v. Cassell & Co.* (1972) 1 All ER 1075 at 1081: "Quite obviously, the award must include factors for injury ... the absence of apology, or the reaffirmation of the truth of the matter complained of..."

English law does not distinguish between private persons and those who are public figures or are involved in matters of public concern. None are required to prove falsity of the libel or fault on the part of the defendant. No plaintiff is required to prove that a media defendant intentionally or negligently disregarded proper journalistic standards in order to prevail.

The defendant has the burden of proving not only truth but also of establishing entitlement to the qualified privilege for newspaper publications and broadcasters provided by the 1952 Defamation Act Section 7(3) where "the matter published is ... of public concern and ... its publication ... is ... for the public benefit." As stated by Mr. Gray, plaintiff's barrister, "[t]he difference between the American and English jurisdictions essentially comes down to where the burden of proof lies...."

Defendant argues that the defamation law of England fails to meet the constitutional standards required in the United States because plaintiff, a friend of the late prime minister of India Rajiv Gandhi and the brother and manager of a movie star and former member of Parliament, is a public figure. In *New York Times Co. v.*

Sullivan, 376 U.S. 254, 279-280 (1964), the Supreme Court of the United States ruled that in order to recover damages for defamation a public official must prove by clear and convincing evidence that the defendant published the allegedly defamatory statement with "'actual malice' — that is, with knowledge that it was false or with reckless disregard of whether it was false or not." That burden of proof was placed on public figures who sued media defendants in *Curtis Publishing Co. v. Butts*, 388 U.S. 130 (1967). However, it seems neither necessary nor appropriate to decide whether plaintiff, an Indian national residing in England or Switzerland, is a public figure. Instead, the procedures of the English Court will be compared to those which according to decisions of the United States Supreme Court are constitutionally mandated for suits by private persons complaining of press publications of public concern.

In *Gertz v. Robert Welch, Inc.*, 418 U.S. 323, 347 (1974), the Court held that a private figure could not recover damages for defamation without showing that a media defendant was at fault, leaving the individual States to "define for themselves the appropriate standard of liability for a publisher or broadcaster of defamatory falsehood injurious to a private individual." Reviewing the Supreme Court's decisions enunciating constitutional limitations on suits for defamation, Justice O'Connor stated in *Philadelphia Newspapers v. Hepps*, 475 U.S. 767, 775:

> One can discern in these decisions two forces that may reshape the common-law landscape to conform to the First Amendment. The first is whether the plaintiff is a public official or figure, or is instead a private figure. The second is whether the speech at issue is of public concern. When the speech is of public concern and the plaintiff is a public official or public figure, the Constitution clearly requires the plaintiff to surmount a much higher barrier before recovering damages from the media defendant than is raised by the common law. When the speech is of public concern but the plaintiff is a private figure, as in *Gertz*, the Constitution still supplants the standards of the common law, but the constitutional requirements are, in at least some of their range, less forbidding than when the plaintiff is a public figure and the speech is of public concern.

The issue in *Hepps* was the validity under the First Amendment of the common-law presumption that a defamatory statement is false, pursuant to which the burden of proving truth is on the defendant. Finding plaintiff to be a private figure and the subject of the newspaper articles in issue to be of public concern, the Court held that, "the common-law's rule on falsity — that the defendant must bear the burden of proving truth — must ... fall here to a constitutional requirement that the plaintiff bear the burden of showing falsity, as well as fault, before recovering damages." 475 U.S. at 776.

It is obvious that defendant's publication relates to a matter of public concern. The affidavits and documents submitted by both parties reveal that the wire service report was related to an international scandal which touched major players in Indian politics and was reported in India, Sweden, the United States, England and elsewhere in the world. Consider the revelation of Mr. Zaiwalla, who had the conduct of the action resulting in the English judgment, that it was given priority over other defamation actions waiting to be tried because "the Indian General Election was imminent and the Bofars affairs and the plaintiff's long-time family friendship with Mr. Rajiv Gandhi, the former prime minister of India ... and the leader of the main opposition party ... were being used as electoral weapons in India." ...

Placing the burden of proving truth upon media defendants who publish speech of public concern has been held unconstitutional because fear of liability may deter such speech.

> Because such a "chilling" effect would be antithetical to the First Amendment's protection of true speech on matters of public concern, we believe that a private-figure plaintiff must bear the burden of showing that the speech at issue is false before recovering damages for defamation from a media defendant. To do otherwise could "only result in a deterrence of speech which the Constitution makes free." *Philadelphia Newspapers, Inc. v. Hepps.*

The "chilling" effect is no different where liability results from enforcement in the United States of a foreign judgment obtained where the burden of proving truth is upon media defendants. Accordingly, the failure of Bachchan to prove falsity in the High Court of Justice in England makes his judgment unenforceable here.

There is, of course, another reason why enforcement of the English judgment would violate the First Amendment; in England, plaintiff was not required to and did not meet the "less forbidding" constitutional requirement that a private figure show that a media defendant was at fault.

New York's standard for liability in actions brought by private persons against the press is set forth in *Chapadeau v. Utica Observer-Dispatch*, 38 N.Y.2d 196, 199 (1975):

> [W]here the content of the article is arguably within the sphere of legitimate public concern, which is reasonably related to matters warranting public exposition, the party defamed may recover; however, to warrant such recovery he must establish, by a preponderance of the evidence, that the publisher acted in a grossly irresponsible manner without due consideration for the standards of information gathering and dissemination ordinarily followed by responsible parties.

As stated above, the English courts do not require plaintiff to prove that a press defendant was at fault in any degree. Bachchan certainly did not establish, as required by *Chapadeau*, that defendant was grossly irresponsible, a difficult task, where defendant disseminates another's new report. *See Rust Communication Group v. 70 State St. Travel Service*, 504 N.Y.S.2d 927 (4th Dept. 1986).

It is true that England and the United States share many common law principles of law. Nevertheless, a significant difference between the two jurisdictions lies in England's lack of an equivalent to the First Amendment to the United States Constitution. The protection of free speech and the press embodied in that amendment would be seriously jeopardized by the entry of foreign libel judgments granted pursuant to standards deemed appropriate in England but considered antithetical to the protections afforded the press by the U.S. Constitution.

Notes on Ackermann

1. *Rationale for public policy exception.* Unlike the enforcement of state judgments under the full faith and credit clause, U.S. courts will not recognize or enforce foreign judgments that violate important public policies of the forum where enforcement is sought. *See Overseas Inns SÀ v. United States,* 911 F.2d 1146 (5th Cir. 1990); *Toronto-Dominion Bank v. Hall,* 367 F.Supp. 1009, 1014-15 (E.D. Ark. 1973); *Restatement (Second) Conflict of Laws* §117, comment c (1971); *Restatement (Third) Foreign Relations Law* §482(2)(d) (1987); Note, *The Public Policy Exception to the Recognition of Foreign Judgments,* 22 Vand. J. Trans. L. 969 (1989).

Why is there a public policy exception to the enforcement of foreign, but not domestic, judgments? Note that, in contrast to the full faith and credit clause, the Brussels Convention provides for a public policy exception.

As discussed above, there are exceptions to the general enforcement requirement for foreign judgments for lack of jurisdiction, unfair foreign proceedings, fraud, lack of notice, and so forth. Given these exceptions, what purpose does the public policy exception serve? *Cf.* Scoles, *Interstate and International Distinctions in Conflict of Laws in the United States,* 54 Calif. L. Rev. 1599, 1606 n.33 (1966) ("in the great bulk of cases any reasonably cognizable defense of public policy can be accommodated under the [other] limitations" on the enforcement of foreign judgment); Paulsen & Sovern, *"Public Policy" in the Conflict of Laws,* 56 Colum. L. Rev. 969, 987 (1956); Peterson, *Foreign Country Judgments and the Second Restatement of Conflict of Laws,* 72 Colum. L. Rev. 220, 253 (1972) ("the policies involved [in the public policy exception] are potentially so numerous and variable, perhaps it is not feasible to provide the courts with ... specific guidance"). *See generally* Lorenzen, *Territoriality, Public Policy and Conflict of Laws,* 33 Yale L.J. 736 (1924); Simson, *The Public Policy Doctrine in Choice of Law: A Reconsideration of Older Themes,* 1974 Wash. U.L.Q. 391.

2. *Scope of public policy exception.* It is often said that the mere fact that the enforcing forum's law would not have permitted the foreign plaintiff to recover in an original action in that forum is not sufficient to warrant nonenforcement of a foreign judgment on public policy grounds. *See Ackermann v. Levine,* 788 F.2d 830 (2d Cir. 1986); *Pariente v. Scott Meredith Literary Agency,* 771 F.Supp. 609 (S.D.N.Y. 1991); *Hunt v. BP Exploration Co. (Libya),* 492 F.Supp. 885, 901 (N.D. Tex. 1980); *Toronto-Dominion Bank v. Hall,* 367 F.Supp. 1009 (E.D. Ark. 1973); *Knothe v. Rose,* 392 S.E.2d 570, 572-73 (Ga. App. 1990).

Rather, for the public policy exception to apply, the foreign judgment must run directly contrary to some fundamental policy of the forum where enforcement is sought. In the words of *Ackermann,* the public policy exception applies only where enforcement of a foreign judgment would "undermine the public interest, the public confidence in the administration of the law or security for individual rights." 788 F.2d at 844. For example, lower courts have found the public policy exception applicable where a foreign judgment undermines First Amendment protections for free speech *(see Bachchan v. India Abroad Pub., Inc.,* 585 N.Y.S.2d 661 (S.Ct. 1992); *Abdullah v. Sheridan Square Press, Inc.,* 1994 WL 419847 (S.D.N.Y. 1994); *Matusevitch v. Telnikoff,* 1995 WL 58741 (D.D.C. 1995)); state law protections for bail recovery agents *(see Jaffe v. Snow,* 610 So.2d 482 (5th Dist. Ct. App. Fla. 1992)); federal policy concerning priority of IRS claims in bankruptcy *(see Overseas Inns SA v. United States,* 911 F.2d 1146 (5th Cir. 1990)); federal policy favoring arbitration of international disputes *(see South Ionian Shipping Co. v. Hugo Neu & Sons Int'l Sales Corp.,* 545 F.Supp. 323 (S.D.N.Y. 1982)); state policy prohibiting the entry of judgments against deceased persons *(see In re Davis' Will,* 219 N.Y.S.2d 533 (1961), *aff'd mem.,* 227 N.Y.S.2d 894 (1962)); state policy relieving divorced husbands from alimony obligations subsequent to the divorced wife's remarriage *(see Pentz v. Kuppinger,* 107 Cal. Rptr. 540 (1973)); or state policies where two conflicting judgments (one U.S. and one foreign) existed *(Mangel v. Mangel,* 72 B.R. 516 (S.D. Fla. 1987)). *Compare* the similar difficulties that courts have encountered in defining and applying public policy exceptions in the forum selection clause (*supra* pp. 414-30) and choice of law (*supra* pp. 624-31 & 655-56) contexts.

3. *Application of public policy exception in* Ackermann. *Ackermann* held that the public policy exception was applicable, notwithstanding the court's assertions about the exception's narrow scope. The Court of Appeals discerned a "narrow[], evidentiary-based public policy" that required foreign attorneys to establish the client's authorization of their services and their actual performance of services before a judgment rendered abroad would be enforced. This requirement applies without regard to the existence of comparable requirements under foreign law. What was the basis in U.S. law for the public policy rule cited in *Ackermann*? Was the rule a product of federal law or New York law? Was this an appropriate rule to fashion?

Recall that a fundamental purpose of the recognition of foreign judgments is avoiding the need to relitigate the merits of disputes that have been fairly resolved abroad. *See supra* pp. 941 & 948-49. Did *Ackermann* apply the public policy exception in a manner that permitted it *sub silentio* to readjudicate the merits of the foreign plaintiff's underlying claim? If so, is this appropriate?

4. *Application of public policy exception in* Bachchan. *Bachchan* refused to enforce an English libel judgment because of differences between U.S. and English libel rules. Is this an appropriate application of the public policy exception?

5. *Source of public policy.* What was the basis in U.S. law for the public policy rule cited in *Bachchan*? Whose laws and policies should be consulted to establish a public policy defense to enforcement of a foreign judgment? Those of the United States, those of the individual state where enforcement is sought, or some international standard? As *Ackermann* suggests, state law is generally regarded as the source of public policies against enforcing foreign judgments. 788 F.2d at 840 ("we could not ... subordinate New York's interests in the *public policy* implications of the subject foreign judgment"). Would it be appropriate for U.S. courts to refuse to enforce foreign judgments based on parochial state policies disfavoring foreign tribunals? What if a state refused to enforce any foreign judgment from a totalitarian state? *Cf. Zschernig v. Miller*, 389 U.S. 429 (1968); *supra* pp. 541-44. Any foreign judgment from a state that practices unfair trading or commits human rights violations?

6. *Choice of law considerations.* Assume that U.S. (or U.S. state) law does contain each of the public policy rules cited in both *Ackermann* and *Bachchan*. Why were those public policies applicable in each case?

(a) *Ackermann.* Note that *all* of the relevant conduct in *Ackermann* occurred in Germany. Suppose that Mr. Levine had been a German businessman, who dealt with Mr. Ackermann solely in Berlin, and then later moved to the United States for unrelated reasons. Would the asserted New York public policy still apply to forbid enforcement of the German judgment? Recall the Supreme Court's treatment of U.S. public policy in *Bremen v. Zapata Off-Shore*, *supra* pp. 429-30. Why would New York public policy concern itself with dealings between two Germans in Germany in connection with a German real estate venture? If New York public policy would not apply to this hypothetical, what makes the actual *Ackermann* case any different? Is it relevant (and dispositive) that Mr. Ackermann was an American? Recall both the role of nationality (or domicile) in contemporary interest analysis and the general rejection of the passive personality principle under international law. *See supra* pp. 507-08 & 649.

(b) *Bachchan.* Where did the allegedly wrongful conduct in *Bachchan* occur? Where did the allegedly false publications circulate? Are these questions relevant to the application of the *Bachchan* public policy?

Suppose that *Bachchan* had involved an Indian news agency, with both U.S. and U.K. offices, and that the allegedly wrongful conduct had occurred in London. Suppose further that all allegedly false statements were circulated in India (not the United States). Would an English judgment be enforceable in U.S. courts? Why would the first amendment apply in this example? How is the actual *Bachchan* case different from this hypothetical? In determining whether the first amendment and its public policies are relevant, what is the importance of the situs of the defendant's conduct? The place of the allegedly wrongful statements? The place of the injury?

7. *Hypotheticals involving public policy exception to enforceability of foreign judgments.* When will the public policy exception apply in the following hypotheticals?

Suppose foreign laws that invidiously discriminate on religious, ethnic or racial grounds are fairly applied in foreign judicial proceedings, producing a judgment against a U.S. national. Does it matter that the parties' dispute — for example, employment — took place entirely outside the United States?

Following *Bremen, supra* pp. 417-18, suppose that an English court rendered a judgment against Zapata Off-Shore, giving effect to contractual exculpatory provisions, which excused Unterweser for grossly negligent conduct. Would it matter if the conduct occurred in U.S. waters?

Following *Triad Financial Establishment, supra* pp. 423-26, suppose that a European court had rendered a judgment in favor of Triad, against Tumpane, giving effect to the parties' contract, notwithstanding contrary Saudi law.

8. *Fairness of foreign judicial system.* As recounted in both *Hilton* and *Somportex,* one of the factors ostensibly examined by U.S. courts in deciding whether to enforce foreign judgments is whether the judicial system of the court issuing the judgment comports with U.S. notions of basic fairness and impartiality. In general, however, U.S. courts are loath to pass judgment on the fairness of other countries' judicial systems. *See Ingersoll Milling Machine Co. v. Granger,* 833 F.2d 680, 687-88 (7th Cir. 1987) ("the Uniform Act does *not* require that the procedures employed by the foreign tribunal be *identical* to those employed in American courts"); *British Midland Airways v. International Travel,* 497 F.2d 869, 871 (9th Cir. 1974) ("unless a foreign country's judgments are the result of outrageous departure"); *Pariente v. Scott Meredith Literary Agency, Inc.,* 771 F.Supp. 609, 616-17 (S.D.N.Y. 1991) ("it is well-established that mere divergence from American procedure does not render a foreign judgment unenforceable"); *Tonga Air Services Ltd. v. Fowler,* 826 P.2d 204 (Wash. 1992) (lack of verbatim transcript not violative of due process); *Panama Processes v. Cities Service Co.,* 796 P.2d 276, 285 (Okla. 1990) (differences between U.S. and foreign procedures not a basis for non-recognition even where "in Brazil (1) no witnesses of any party may be subpoenaed, (2) testimony of corporate employees is inadmissible, (3) there is no available process for requiring testimony of indispensable U.S. witnesses, (4) there is no right of cross-examination, and (5) the parties may neither conduct pre-trial discovery nor subpoena documents"); Peterson, *Foreign Country Judgments and the Second Restatement of Conflict of Laws,* 72 Colum. L. Rev. 220, 230-32 (1972).

How should the treatment of foreign tribunals' fairness in the enforcement context compare to the approaches by U.S. courts to the fairness of foreign legal systems in the context of forum selection clauses or forum non conveniens? *See supra* pp. 351-53 & 412-13.

Purely as a practical matter, U.S. courts appear far more willing to enforce Western European judgments (and particularly English judgments) than those of other nations. *Compare Somportex, Ltd. v. Philadelphia Chewing Gum Corp.,* 453 F.2d 435, 440 (3d Cir. 1971) (the English legal system "is the very fount from which our system has developed") *and Hunt v. BP Exploration Co. (Libya),* 492 F.Supp. 885, 906 (N.D. Tex. 1980) ("In sum, a litigant is entitled to no more than one clean bite of one clean apple — at least at the table of our British brethren.") *with Barry E. (Anonymous) v. Ingraham,* 400 N.Y.S.2d 772 (1977).

In *Hilton,* the French proceedings differed in material respects from U.S. proceedings:

> one of the plaintiffs was permitted to testify not under oath, and was not subjected to cross-examination by the opposite party, and ... the defendants were therefore deprived of the safeguards which are by our laws considered essential to secure honesty and to detect fraud in a witness, and ... documents and papers were admitted into evidence, with which the defendants had no connection, and which would not be admissible under our own system of jurisprudence. ... [However,] it having been shown ... that the practice followed and the method of examining witnesses were according to the laws of France, we are not prepared to hold that the fact that the procedure in these respects differed from that of our own courts is of itself a sufficient ground for impeaching the foreign judgment. 159 U.S. at 204-05.

9. *Fraud.* One of the issues frequently (and unsuccessfully) raised in resisting enforcement of a foreign judgment is that the judgment was obtained through fraud. *E.g., Bank of Montreal v. Kough,* 430 F.Supp. 1243 (N.D. Cal. 1977), *aff'd,* 612 F.2d 467 (9th Cir. 1980); *Harrison v. Triplex Gold Mines,* 33 F.2d 667 (1st Cir. 1929); *Norkan Lodge v. Gillum,* 587 F.Supp. 1457 (N.D. Tex. 1984); *In re Estate of Weil,* 609 N.Y.S.2d 375 (App. Div. 1994). Under U.S. law, fraud can be the basis for a collateral challenge to a foreign judgment if it was "extrinsic" to the foreign proceeding — that is, was fraud practiced on the judgment debtor to prevent it from presenting its case fully to the foreign court. "Intrinsic fraud" (*i.e.,* fraud committed on or in the presence of the foreign court, such as the use of perjured testimony) is generally not a basis for resisting enforcement of foreign judgments in U.S. courts. *See John Sanderson & Co. (Wool) v. Ludlow Jute Co.,* 569 F.2d 696, 697-98 (1978); *Scola v. Boat Frances R.,* 546 F.2d 459 (1st Cir. 1976);

Alleghany Corp. v. Kirby, 218 F.Supp. 164, 183 (S.D.N.Y. 1963), *aff'd*, 333 F.2d 327 (2d Cir. 1964), *cert. dismissed as improvidently granted*, 384 U.S. 28 (1966) (per curiam); *Christopher v. Christopher*, 31 S.E.2d 818 (Ga. 1944). Courts have recognized that the distinction between intrinsic and extrinsic fraud is seldom clearcut, *e.g.*, *Howard v. Scott*, 225 Mo. 685, 714, 125 S.W. 1158, 1166 (1980), and some authorities have rejected the distinction. *Restatement (Second) Judgments* §§68, 70 comment c (1980). Why should a distinction be drawn between the two types of fraud?

10. *Differing treatment of sister state and foreign country judgments.* The foregoing materials illustrate that the enforcement of foreign country judgments is a significantly more difficult undertaking than the enforcement of sister state judgments under the full faith and credit clause. The public policy defense, the treatment of jurisdictional requirements, and the reciprocity rule all contribute to this result. Why should it be more difficult to enforce foreign judgments than domestic judgments? Does this merely reflect parochialism or unspoken distrust of foreign legal systems? Or are there valid reasons for each of the various defenses to the enforcement of foreign country judgments?

Recall that foreign jurisdictional rules, service mechanisms, standards of procedural fairness, and substantive laws often differ substantially from their U.S. counterparts. *See* Casad, *Issue Preclusion and Foreign Country Judgments: Whose Law?*, 70 Iowa L. Rev. 53 (1984); Peterson, *Res Judicata and Foreign Country Judgments*, 24 Ohio St. L.J. 291 (1963); Scoles, *Interstate and International Distinctions in Conflict of Laws in the United States*, 54 Calif. L. Rev. 1599 (1966). Moreover, U.S. courts may be less concerned about the waste of judicial resources when an earlier litigation occurred abroad and thus did not involve U.S. judicial resources. Consider the following:

> Many of the reasons for recognition and enforcement of foreign country judgments are the same as for giving conclusive effect to domestic judgments: prevention of harassment of the successful party, elimination of duplicative judicial proceedings, and providing some measure of settled expectations to the parties. In a domestic context, the benefits of preclusion are palpable. In our Union, since courts in each state are subject to due process limitations, are subject to the same overlap of federal laws and the Constitution, are sharing to a large extent the same body of court precedents and socio-economic ideas and are presumptively fair and competent, the benefits of giving conclusive effect are not balanced by any recognizable costs. Giving an automatically conclusive effect — full faith and credit — to sister state judgments could be fully justified on the grounds of fairness to litigants and judicial economy; there is no reason for a second trial — the rendering forum had at least the constitutionally requisite contacts with the litigant, there is little possibility of an error in the rendering forum and the substantive policies given effect by that forum are likely fully acceptable in the recognizing forum.

> The benefit-cost calculation for giving an automatically conclusive effect to foreign country judgments is far less favorable. There is less expectation that the courts of a foreign country will follow procedures which would comport with our notions of due process and jurisdiction and that they will apply substantively tolerable laws. Moreover, especially if the loser in the initial litigation is American, there will be suspicions here of unfairness or fraud. The modern versions of the *Hilton v. Guyot* rule — neither pretending that the initial litigation never occurred, nor giving it an automatic conclusive effect — is a natural and tempered response to the tension between the benefits and costs of giving effect to foreign country judgments. By going to the halfway house, courts can deny effect to foreign country judgments when the rendering court has acted in ways intolerable by our country's then felt ideal of fundamental fairness.

Hunt v. BP Exploration Co. (Libya), 492 F.Supp. 885, 905-06 (N.D. Tex. 1980). Are you persuaded?

11. *Wisdom of current U.S. approach to recognition of foreign judgments.* Consider the current U.S. approach to the recognition of foreign judgments, and the results it produces. In general, U.S. courts are fairly willing to enforce foreign judgments, but "our judgments are treated shabbily in other nations." Golumb, *Recognition of Foreign Money Judgments: A Goal-Oriented Approach*, 43 St. John's L. Rev. 604, 635 (1969). *See also* Nadelman, *Reprisals Against American Judgments*, 65 Harv. L. Rev. 1184, 1186-87 (1952; von Mehren, *Recognition and Enforcement of Foreign Judgments: A New Approach for the Hague Conference?*, 57 Law & Contemp. Probs. 271 (1994). What is the cause of this imbalance? *See Id.* (suggesting lack of any federal standards, doubts about *Hilton*, and reciprocity rule).

13/International Commercial Arbitration and U.S. Courts: An Overview[1]

International arbitration is an increasingly common alternative to international litigation as a means of resolving multijurisdictional commercial disputes. This Chapter briefly describes the role of U.S. courts in the international arbitral process. It focuses in particular on the enforcement of international arbitration agreements and international arbitral awards by U.S. courts.

A. Overview of International Arbitration

1. Introduction

International arbitration, like domestic arbitration, is a means by which a dispute can be definitively resolved, pursuant to the parties' voluntary agreement, by a disinterested, non-governmental decision-maker. In the words of the U.S. Supreme Court, "an agreement to arbitrate before a specified tribunal [is], in effect, a specialized kind of forum-selection clause that posits not only the situs of suit but also the procedure to be used in resolving the dispute."[2]

Commercial arbitration has several defining characteristics. First, arbitration is *consensual* — the parties must agree to resolve their differences by arbitration.[3]

---

1. Commentary on international commercial arbitration includes, *e.g.*, G. Born, *International Commercial Arbitration in the United States* (Kluwer 1994); A. Redfern & M. Hunter, *International Commercial Arbitration* (2d ed. 1991); W. Craig, W. Park & J. Paulsson, *International Chamber of Commerce Arbitration* (2d ed. 1990).

2. *Scherk v. Alberto-Culver Co.*, 417 U.S. 506, 519 (1974). *See also* A. Redfern & M. Hunter, *International Commercial Arbitration* 3 (2d ed. 1991)("two or more parties, faced with a dispute which they cannot resolve for themselves, agreeing that some private individual will resolve it for them and if the arbitration runs its full course ... it will not be settled by a compromise, but by a decision.").

3. *E.g.*, *United Steelworkers of America v. Warrior and Gulf Navigation Co.*, 363 U.S. 574, 582 (1960) ("arbitration is a matter of contract and a party cannot be required to submit to arbitration any dispute which he has not agreed to so submit"); *infra* pp. 993-98. Most arbitration agreements are included as standard clauses in commercial contracts and provide for the arbitration of any dispute that may arise in the future between the parties within a defined category. It is also possible, although much less common, for parties to an *existing* dispute to agree to settle their disagreement through arbitration.

Second, arbitration produces a *definitive and binding award*, which is capable of enforcement through national courts. Third, arbitrations are resolved by *non-governmental decision-makers* — arbitrators do not act as governmental agents, but are private persons selected by the parties.

Although arbitration is common in purely domestic settings, it is particularly attractive in international matters. Parties to international transactions are often of different nationalities; they choose arbitration in order to obtain a neutral decision-maker (detached from the governmental institutions and cultural biases of either party) who will apply internationally neutral procedural rules (rather than a particular national legal regime). In addition, by designating a single dispute resolution mechanism for the parties' disagreements, arbitration is frequently regarded as a means of mitigating the peculiar uncertainties of international litigation — which, as discussed above, can include protracted jurisdictional and choice of law disputes and expensive parallel proceedings.[4] Moreover, international arbitration is often seen as a means of obtaining an award that is more readily enforceable than a national court judgment.

International arbitration can be either "institutional" or "*ad hoc.*" A number of organizations, located in different countries, provide institutional arbitration services. The best-known international arbitral institutions are the International Chamber of Commerce ("ICC"), the American Arbitration Association ("AAA"), and the London Court of International Arbitration ("LCIA").[5]

Many arbitral institutions have promulgated sets of procedural rules that apply where parties have agreed to arbitration pursuant to such rules.[6] Among other things, institutional rules set out the basic procedural framework and timetable for the arbitral process.[7] In addition, such rules typically authorize the host arbitral institution to select arbitrators in particular disputes, to resolve challenges to the neutrality of the arbitrators, to designate the place of arbitration, and (sometimes) to review the arbitrator's awards on formal grounds. Arbitral institutions themselves do *not*

---

4. *See supra* pp. 287 & 459-60.

5. For descriptions of these and other arbitral institutions, *see* G. Born, *International Commercial Arbitration in the United States* 11-16 (1994).

6. These include the ICC's Rules of Conciliation and Arbitration, the Rules of the LCIA, and numerous specialized rules of the AAA (such as the Commercial Arbitration Rules and the International Arbitration Rules).

7. The procedural timetable for arbitrations is broadly similar to that for a litigation. Arbitrations are typically commenced by a "notice of arbitration" or "request for arbitration," which identifies the parties to the proceeding and the claimant's claims. Ordinarily, the respondent then files a "reply" or "answer," within a specified time period, which sets forth its defenses (and any counterclaims). At the same time, the arbitrator(s) will be selected, either by agreement between the parties or by a contractually-designated "appointing authority." Most tribunals consist of either one or three arbitrators. Where there is a three-person tribunal, each party will typically nominate one "co-arbitrator," and the "presiding arbitrator" or "chairman" will be selected either by agreement between the co-arbitrators or by the arbitral institution.

Once a tribunal is in place, it will control the arbitral procedures, which will ordinarily include written submissions defining the parties' claims and defenses, a measure of discovery (often limited), evidentiary hearings, and issuance of a decision ("award"). *See* G. Born, *International Commercial Arbitration in the United States* 44-96 (1994).

arbitrate the merits of the parties' dispute. This is the responsibility of the particular individuals selected by the parties or by the institution as arbitrators.

Ad hoc arbitration is not conducted under the supervision of an arbitral institution. Instead, private parties simply select an arbitrator or arbitrators, who resolves the dispute without institutional support. The parties sometimes also select a preexisting set of procedural rules designed to govern *ad hoc* arbitrations. The United Nations Commission on International Trade Law ("UNCITRAL") has published a commonly used set of such rules.[8] Alternatively, the parties' arbitration agreement will set forth the relevant procedural rules or the arbitral panel will independently formulate a special set of procedural rules, tailored to the specific needs of the parties and their dispute. In either *ad hoc* or institutional arbitration, parties usually will (and certainly should) designate an "appointing authority,"[9] that will select the arbitrator(s) if the parties cannot agree.[10]

It is the procedural conduct of international arbitration proceedings, as much as any other factor, that leads parties to agree to arbitrate their disputes. National courts play little or no role in the arbitration proceedings themselves (at least in the United States and other major trading countries where arbitrations are commonly conducted).[11] Rather, the parties and the arbitral tribunal enjoy substantial autonomy to fashion an arbitral procedure tailored to their particular needs.

It goes without saying that arbitration proceedings are different from judicial proceedings. "As a speedy and informal alternative to litigation, arbitration resolves disputes without confinement to many of the procedural and evidentiary structures that protect the integrity of formal trials."[12] One of the reasons parties choose to arbitrate is their desire to obtain the comparative informality, flexibility, and occasional speed of arbitration. In theory, a party "trades the procedures and opportunity for review of the courtroom for the simplicity, informality, and expedition of arbitration."[13]

Nevertheless, particularly in major matters, the contrast between litigation and arbitration can be exaggerated and the procedures of an arbitration assume a fairly "judicial" cast. "Though litigation is compulsory and arbitration is consensual, both are judicial processes of an adversarial character."[14] Tribunals and parties often con-

---

8. For a discussion of the UNCITRAL Rules, *see* G. Born, *International Commercial Arbitration in the United States* 37-8 (1994).

9. Most leading arbitration institutions (including the ICC, the AAA, and the LCIA) will act as an appointing authority, for a fee, in ad hoc arbitrations.

10. If the parties fail to select an appointing authority, then the national arbitration statutes of many nations, including the United States, permit national courts to appoint arbitrators. *See* G. Born, *International Commercial Arbitration in the United States* 731-51 (1994).

11. These countries include England, Switzerland, France, Belgium, Netherlands, and Sweden. Elsewhere, and particularly in Latin America and the Middle East, local law often imposes restrictive conditions on international arbitrations and permits interference by local courts in the arbitral process. *See* G. Born, *International Commercial Arbitration in the United States* 35-7 (1994).

12. *Forsythe Int'l, SA v. Gibbs Oil Co.*, 915 F.2d 1017, 1022 (5th Cir. 1990).

13. *Mitsubishi Motors Corp. v. Soler Chrysler-Plymouth Inc.*, 473 U.S. 614, 628 (1985).

14. Nariman, *Standards of Behaviour of Arbitrators*, 4 Arb. Int'l 311 (1988).

clude that complex cases require considerable issue definition, scheduling, and the like, and it is common in international arbitration to encounter written pleadings, briefs, cross-examination, testimony under oath, verbatim transcripts, and a measure of discovery. Indeed, some argue that arbitration has lost the informality and expedition that once characterized it, and urge return to less judicial procedures.[15]

One of the most fundamental characteristics of international commercial arbitration is the parties' freedom to agree upon the arbitral procedure. Nevertheless, parties often do not agree in advance on detailed procedural rules for their arbitrations. At most, their arbitration agreement will provide for arbitration pursuant to a set of institutional rules, which supply only a broad procedural framework. Filling in the considerable gaps in this framework will be left to the subsequent agreement of the parties or, if they cannot agree, the arbitral tribunal.

Under U.S. and many other national laws, the arbitral tribunal has substantial discretion to establish the arbitral procedures.[16] A tribunal's use of this discretion will often be influenced significantly by the arbitrators' legal training, experience, and personal characteristics. In general, arbitrators with civil law backgrounds can be expected to adopt more "inquisitorial" procedures, with somewhat less scope for adversarial procedures — such as broad, party-initiated discovery, depositions, lengthy oral hearings, counsel-controlled cross-examination, and the like — than is familiar to U.S. lawyers.[17] Arbitrators from U.S. and other common law jurisdictions will be inclined to adopt "adversarial" procedures more broadly similar to those prevailing in U.S. litigation.

The parties' freedom to adopt arbitral procedures is generally subject to the mandatory requirements of applicable national law. Most developed jurisdictions only require that arbitral proceedings satisfy minimal standards of procedural fairness and equality, although local technical requirements, concerning subjects such as the number of arbitrators, the swearing of oaths, and the like, must also sometimes be complied with.

2. Overview of International Legal Framework for Arbitration

a. The New York Convention

Although international arbitration is a *consensual* means of dispute resolution, it has binding effect by virtue of a complex framework of national and international law. The United Nations Convention on Recognition and Enforcement of Foreign Arbitral Awards (the "New York Convention")[18] has been ratified by nearly 100 states, including virtually all significant trading states. The Convention, which is

---

15. H. Brown & A. Marriott, *ADR Principles and Practice* 83 (1993); Wetter, *The Present Status of the International Court of Arbitration of the ICC: An Appraisal,* 1 Am. Rev. Int'l Arb. 91, 101 (1990).

16. G. Born, *International Commercial Arbitration in the United States* 44-49 (1994).

17. Marriott, *Evidence in International Arbitration,* 5 Arb. Int'l 280, 283-86 (1989); ICC, *Taking Evidence in International Arbitral Proceedings* (1990).

18. *See* 9 U.S.C. §201.

reproduced in Appendix M, is by far the most significant contemporary international agreement relating to commercial arbitration.[19]

The Convention was designed to "encourage the recognition and enforcement of commercial arbitration agreements in international contracts and to unify the standards by which agreements to arbitrate are observed and arbitral awards are enforced in the signatory nations."[20] In broad outline, the Convention requires national courts to: (a) recognize and enforce foreign arbitral awards, subject to specified exceptions;[21] (b) recognize the validity of arbitration agreements, subject to specified exceptions;[22] and (c) to refer parties to arbitration when they have entered into a valid agreement to arbitrate that is subject to the Convention.[23]

b. U.S. Legislation Concerning International Commercial Arbitration

The basic source of U.S. law dealing with arbitration, in both the domestic and international contexts, is the Federal Arbitration Act ("FAA"). The Act was first enacted in 1925, but has been significantly expanded since then.[24] The FAA currently consists of three chapters: (a) the "domestic" FAA, 9 U.S.C. §§1-16, applicable to agreements and awards affecting either interstate or foreign commerce; (b) the New York Convention's implementing legislation, 9 U.S.C. §§201-210, applicable only to awards and agreements falling within the New York Convention; and (c) the Inter-American Arbitration Convention's implementing legislation, 9 U.S.C. §§301-07, applicable only to awards falling under the Inter-American Convention.[25]

The FAA applies to arbitration agreements and awards affecting either interstate or foreign commerce — a jurisdictional grant that U.S. courts have interpreted expansively.[26] The centerpiece of the FAA is §2, which provides that arbitration agreements involving interstate and foreign commerce "shall be valid, irrevocable, and enforceable, save upon such grounds as exist at law or in equity for the revocation of any contract."[27] Other sections of the FAA address different aspects of the arbitral

---

19. The Convention is widely regarded as "the most important Convention in the field of arbitration and ... the cornerstone of current international commercial arbitration." A. van den Berg, *The New York Arbitration Convention of 1958* 1 (1981). The Convention was signed in 1958 in New York after lengthy negotiations under U.N. auspices. *Id.* at 1-10.

20. *Scherk v. Alberto-Culver Co.*, 417 U.S. 506, 502 n.15 (1974).

21. New York Convention Articles III and V. *See infra* pp. 1040-52.

22. New York Convention Article II(1). *See infra* pp. 993-1016.

23. New York Convention Article II(3). *See infra* pp. 997-98.

24. Federal Arbitration Act, 43 Stat. 883 (1925), 61 Stat. 669 (1947) (as codified at 9 U.S.C. §§1-16).

25. In 1975, the United States and most South American nations negotiated the Inter-American Convention on International Commercial Arbitration, also known as the "Panama Convention." The Convention is reprinted at 9 U.S.C.A. §301. The United States ratified the Convention in 1990; other parties include Mexico, Venezuela, Columbia, Chile, Costa Rica, El Salvador, Guatemala, Honduras, Panama, Paraguay, and Uruguay. The Inter-American Convention is similar to the New York Convention in many respects. Among other things, it provides for the general enforceability of arbitration agreements and arbitral awards, subject to specified exceptions similar to those in the New York Convention.

26. 9 U.S.C. §1. The FAA's focus was principally domestic, although it also expressly applies to "foreign commerce." 9 U.S.C. §1.

27. 9 U.S.C. §2.

process. Section 5 grants district courts the power to appoint arbitrators if the parties have neither done so nor agreed upon an appointing authority.[28] Section 7 of the Act permits district courts to issue compulsory process to assist arbitral tribunals in taking evidence.[29] In turn, §§9, 10, and 11 of the FAA provide that, subject to limited exceptions, arbitration awards shall be enforceable; these sections also set forth procedures for confirming, vacating, or correcting arbitral awards subject to the Act.[30]

After U.S. ratification of the New York Convention in 1970, Congress enacted amendments to the FAA, in a second chapter to the Act, implementing the Convention.[31] Like the original domestic Act, the FAA's second chapter is remarkably brief. It provides that arbitration agreements and awards shall be enforceable, and contains various provisions assisting the international arbitration process.[32] In addition, the amendments expand federal subject matter jurisdiction, removal authority, and injunctive powers.[33]

The New York Convention and the FAA establish substantive federal law, generally ensuring the enforceability of international arbitration agreements and awards, that preempts inconsistent state and foreign law.[34] Nonetheless, state law can also be relevant to international arbitration issues in U.S. courts. The Supreme Court has held that the FAA does not "occupy the entire field" relating to arbitration.[35] As a result, state law is applicable to arbitration agreements and awards when — but only when — the Convention and FAA are inapplicable. That may be the case, for example, because the agreement or award does not affect interstate or foreign commerce. State law may also be applicable to ancillary issues bearing on international arbitration that federal statutory and common law do not directly or indirectly address. As discussed below, that appears to include generally-applicable contract law rules governing the formation and validity of arbitration agreements.[36]

---

28. 9 U.S.C. §5.

29. 9 U.S.C. §7; G. Born, *International Commercial Arbitration in the United States* 825-61 (1994).

30. 9 U.S.C. §9-11; G. Born, *International Commercial Arbitration in the United States* 459-687 (1994).

31. 9 U.S.C. §§201-210.

32. 9 U.S.C. §§206 & 207.

33. 9 U.S.C. §§203, 205, 206. *See* G. Born, *International Commercial Arbitration in the United States* 31-32, 429-34 (1994).

34. *Prima Paint Corp. v. Conklin Mfg. Co.*, 388 U.S. 395, 399-400 (1967); *Moses H. Cone Memorial Hospital v. Mercury Construction Corp.*, 460 U.S. 1, 24-25 (1983) (§2 of the FAA "create[s] a body of federal substantive law of arbitrability, applicable to any arbitration agreement within the coverage of the Act"); *Southland Corp. v. Keating*, 465 U.S. 1, 12 (1984)("federal substantive law requiring the parties to honor arbitration agreements").

These substantive provisions of federal law are applicable in state as well as federal court. *Southland Corp. v. Keating*, 465 U.S. 1, 12 (1984); *Volt Information Sciences, Inc. v. Board of Trustees*, 489 U.S. 468, 477 n.6 (1989).

35. *See Volt Information Sciences, Inc. v. Board of Trustees*, 489 U.S. 468, 477 (1989) ("The FAA contains no express pre-emptive provision, nor does it reflect a congressional intent to occupy the entire field of arbitration. But even when Congress has not completely displaced state regulation in an area, state law may nonetheless be preempted to the extent that it actually conflicts with federal law."); *Perry v. Thomas*, 482 U.S. 483 (1987).

36. *See infra* pp. 1010-11.

B. Enforceability of International Arbitration Agreements Under the New York Convention and the FAA

It is a fundamental principle of U.S. law that "[a]rbitration is a matter of contract and a party cannot be required to submit to arbitration any dispute which he has not agreed to so submit."[37] Arbitration agreements come in countless forms. As a model of brevity, if not prudence, European commentators cite a clause that provided "English law — arbitration, if any, London according ICC Rules."[38] At the opposite end of the spectrum are multi-paragraph arbitration clauses, recommended by assiduous practitioners for inclusion in commercial contracts.[39] Falling between these extremes are model clauses promulgated by the ICC, AAA, LCIA, and other international arbitration institutions.[40]

Under any arbitration agreement disputes can arise, typically when one party or the other decides that it no longer wishes to arbitrate. These disputes fall into three basic categories. First, the existence, validity, or enforceability of the arbitration agreement may be challenged. Second, one party may argue that particular claims are "non-arbitrable." Third, disputes arise over the interpretation of arbitration clauses — particularly over their scope or the classes of disputes that are subject to arbitration. As discussed below, U.S. (and other) courts are frequently called upon to resolve such disputes.

1. Introduction

a. Historical Background

Historically, U.S. courts would not enforce arbitration agreements.[41] Many courts held that agreements to arbitrate were revocable at will, because they "ousted" courts of jurisdiction contrary to public policy.[42] Even when such agreements were

---

37. *United Steelworkers of America v. Warrior and Gulf Navigation Co.*, 363 U.S. 574, 582 (1960). *See First Options of Chicago, Inc. v. Kaplan*, 115 S. Ct. 1920 (1995); *AT&T Technologies, Inc. v. Communications Workers of America*, 475 U.S. 643, 648-9 (1986).

38. *Arab African Energy Corp. Ltd. v. Olieprodukten Nederland BV* [1983] 2 Lloyd's Rep. 419.

39. *See*, for example, the clauses recommended in Ulmer, *Drafting the International Arbitration Clause*, 20 Int'l Law. 1335 (1986).

40. G. Born, *International Commercial Arbitration in the United States* 9-16 & 1001-1005 (1994). For example, the model ICC and AAA clauses provide:

Any disputes arising in connection with the present contract shall be finally settled under the Rules of [Conciliation and] Arbitration of the International Chamber of Commerce by one or more arbitrators appointed in accordance with the said Rules.

Any controversy or claim arising out of or relating to this contract shall be determined by arbitration in accordance with the International Arbitration Rules of the American Arbitration Association.

41. Jones, *Development of Commercial Arbitration*, 21 Minn. L. Rev. 240 (1927); F. Kellor, *American Arbitration: Its History, Functions and Achievement* (1948).

42. *Home Ins. Co. v. Morse*, 87 U.S. 445, 457-58 (1874) (agreement to arbitrate future disputes illegal and void); *Dickson Mfg. Co. v. American Locomotive Co.*, 119 F.Supp. 488 (M.D. Pa. 1902).

deemed valid and binding, a party could not obtain specific performance or equitable relief ordering its counter-party to arbitrate. Joseph Story made clear the common law hostility to arbitration:

> Now we all know that arbitrators, at the common law, possess no authority whatsoever, even to administer an oath, or to compel the attendance of witnesses. They cannot compel the production of documents and papers and books of account, or insist upon a discovery of facts from the parties under oath. They are not ordinarily well enough acquainted with the principles of law or equity, to administer either effectually, in complicated cases; and hence it has often been said, that the judgment of arbitrators is but *rusticum judicium.* Ought then a court of equity to compel a resort to such a tribunal, by which, however honest and intelligent, it can in no case be clear that the real legal or equitable rights of the parties can be fully ascertained or perfectly protected? ... [An arbitration agreement is not specifically enforceable because it] is essentially, in its very nature and character, an agreement which must rest in the good faith and honor of the parties, and like an agreement to paint a picture, to carve a statue, or to write a book ... must be left to the conscience of the parties, or to such remedy in damages for the breach thereof, as the law has provided.[43]

Throughout the 19th century, Story's attitude towards specific performance of arbitration agreements generally prevailed in U.S. courts.[44] At the same time, damages were seldom an effective means of enforcement, since proof of injury resulting from a refusal to arbitrate was difficult. Moreover, U.S. courts also refused to stay judicial proceedings where a valid arbitration agreement covered the parties' dispute. As a consequence, the utility of commercial arbitration was severely limited until well into this century.[45]

b. Overview of Enforceability of International Arbitration Agreements Under the FAA

In 1925, Congress enacted the FAA with the express purpose of making interstate and international arbitration agreements (and awards) enforceable.[46] At the heart of the FAA is §2's provision that a written arbitration provision in a contract involving interstate or foreign commerce shall be "valid, irrevocable, and enforceable," subject only to a savings clause permitting nonenforcement on "such grounds

---

43. *Tobey v. County of Bristol,* 23 Fed. Cas. 1313, 1321-1323 (C.C.D. Mass. 1845).

44. *See Kulukundis Shipping Co. v. Amtorg Trading Corp.,* 126 F.2d 978 (2d Cir. 1942), for a thorough review of the treatment of arbitration agreements at common law. *See also Red Cross Line v. Atlantic Fruit Co.,* 264 U.S. 109 (1924); *Rowe v. Williams,* 97 Mass. 163 (1887).

45. *See* H.R. Rep. 96, 68th Cong., 1st Sess. 1 (1924); Sayre, *Development of Commercial Arbitration Law,* 37 Yale L.J. 595 (1927).

46. 43 Stat. 883 (1925), *codified* 61 Stat. 669 (1947); G. Born, *International Commercial Arbitration in the United States* 188-90 (1994).

as exist at law or in equity for the revocation of any contract."[47] The section's avowed purpose was to "revers[e] centuries of judicial hostility to arbitration agreements ... by plac[ing] arbitration agreements 'upon the same footing as other contracts.'"[48]

As a result of the FAA, arbitration agreements are a significant exception to the general rule that state law governs the interpretation and enforcement of commercial contracts.[49] The Supreme Court has repeatedly held that §2 creates *substantive federal* law. That federal law is binding in both federal and state courts, and it preempts inconsistent state law.[50] Section 2 requires, as a matter of federal law, "courts to enforce privately negotiated agreements to arbitrate, like other contracts, in accordance with their terms."[51]

> Section 2 is a congressional declaration of a liberal federal policy favoring arbitration agreements, notwithstanding any state substantive or procedural policies to the contrary. The effect of the section is to create a *body of federal substantive law of arbitrability,* applicable to any arbitration agreement within the coverage of the Act.[52]

Although it is clear that §2 establishes a basic federal rule that arbitration agreements are enforceable, there has been debate over the precise role that federal law plays under §2's "savings clause." A few older lower court decisions held that federal law governs *all* issues of formation, validity, and interpretation of arbitration agreements.[53] Most other lower courts — and recent Supreme Court precedents — hold that the savings clause incorporates or preserves otherwise applicable state (or foreign) contract law, subject however to a federal prohibition against state laws that single out arbitration agreements for special disfavor.[54]

Notwithstanding §2's basic federal rule of enforceability, arbitration agreements will be unenforceable in some circumstances. Relying on §2's "savings clause," U.S. courts have refused to enforce arbitration agreements on generally-applicable con-

---

47. 9 U.S.C. §2.

48. *Shearson/American Express, Inc. v. McMahon,* 482 U.S. 220, 226 (1987) (quoting *Scherk v. Alberto-Culver Co.,* 417 U.S. 506, 510-11 (1974)).

49. In the United States, most contracts are interpreted according to, and are enforceable under, the laws of the several States. *See supra* pp. 13-16; *United States v. Little Lake Misere Land Co.,* 412 U.S. 580 (1973); *Clearfield Trust Co. v. United States,* 318 U.S. 363 (1943).

50. *Southland Corp. v. Keating,* 465 U.S. 1, 11, 15-16 n.9 (1984); *Mitsubishi Motors Corp. v. Soler Chrysler-Plymouth Inc.,* 473 U.S. 614 (1985); *Moses H. Cone Memorial Hospital v. Mercury Construction Corp.,* 460 U.S. 1, 24 (1983); *infra* pp. 1010-11 & 1035-39.

51. *Prima Paint Corp. v. Flood & Conklin Manufacturing Co.,* 388 U.S. 395, 404 n.12 (1967) (Congress intended to "make arbitration agreements as enforceable as other contracts, but not more so.").

52. *Moses H. Cone Memorial Hospital v. Mercury Construction Corp.,* 460 U.S. 1, 24 (1983) (emphasis added).

53. *See Lea Tai Textile Co. v. Manning Fabrics, Inc.,* 411 F.Supp. 1404 (S.D.N.Y. 1975); *Genesco, Inc. v. T. Kakiuchi & Co.,* 815 F.2d 840, 845 (2d Cir. 1987).

54. *See infra* pp. 1010-11; *Perry v. Thomas,* 482 U.S. 483 (1987); *Progressive Casualty Ins. Co. v. CA Reasequardora Nacional de Venezuela,* 991 F.2d 42 (2d Cir. 1993).

tract and quasi-contract grounds. These grounds include fraudulent inducement, fraud in the factum, non-existence of any agreement, illegality, unconscionability, and waiver.[55] In general, these defenses have been held by U.S. courts to be governed by generally-applicable state contract law.[56]

c. Separability of the Arbitration Agreement and "Kompetenz-Kompetenz"[57]

Analysis of the enforceability of international arbitration agreements requires considering the related doctrines of "separability" and Kompetenz-Kompetenz. Both doctrines establish fundamental principles regarding the respective roles of U.S. courts and arbitral tribunals in enforcing arbitration agreements.

It is frequently said that an arbitration clause is "separable" from the underlying contract within which it is found. The separability doctrine provides that an arbitration agreement, even though included in an underlying contract, is a separate and autonomous agreement. According to a leading U.S. decision, there is "a distinction between the *entire contract* between the parties on the one hand and the *arbitration clause* of the contract on the other."[58] Or, as the Supreme Court described the doctrine in *Prima Paint*, "*except where the parties otherwise intend ... arbitration clauses as a matter of federal law are 'separable' from the contracts in which they are embedded.*"[59]

The separability doctrine is generally regarded as having highly important consequences for the arbitral process: "Acceptance of [the] autonomy of the international arbitration clause is a conceptual cornerstone of international arbitration."[60] Among other things, the separability doctrine provides a basis for the survival of arbitration clauses notwithstanding the expiration, termination, or invalidity of the parties' underlying contract.[61]

Closely related to the separability doctrine is the allocation of authority between arbitrators and national courts to resolve disputes over the interpretation and enforceability of the parties' arbitration agreement. Many institutional arbitration rules, and some national laws, expressly provide that arbitral tribunals have jurisdiction to determine their own jurisdiction.[62] This principle is referred to in

---

55. *See infra* pp. 1012-15; G. Born, *International Commercial Arbitration in the United States* 231-84 (1994).

56. *See infra* pp. 1010-15.

57. For commentary on the separability doctrine, *see* A. Redfern & M. Hunter, *International Commercial Arbitration* 174-77 (2d ed. 1991); Nussbaum, *The Separability Doctrine in American and Foreign Arbitration*, 17 N.Y.U.L. Q. 609 (1940); S. Schwebel, *The Severability of the Arbitration Agreement*, in *International Arbitration: Three Salient Problems* 1 (1987).

58. *Robert Lawrence Co. v. Devonshire Fabrics, Inc.*, 271 F.2d 402, 409 (2d Cir. 1959) (emphasis added).

59. *Prima Paint Corp. v. Flood & Conklin Mfg. Co.*, 388 U.S. 395, 402 (1967) (emphasis in original).

60. *See* W. Craig, W. Park & J. Paulsson, *International Chamber of Commerce Arbitration* §5.04 (2d ed. 1990).

61. *See infra* pp. 1013-15.

62. *See* G. Born, *International Commercial Arbitration in the United States* 197-231 (1994).

Continental Europe as the doctrine of "Kompetenz-Kompetenz" or "competence-competence."[63]

The Kompetenz-Kompetenz doctrine can have significant effects on the judicial resolution of disputes over the interpretation and enforcement of arbitration clauses. At a minimum, the doctrine means that arbitrators *can* determine their own jurisdiction: if one party asserts that the arbitrators lack jurisdiction, the arbitrators may generally consider the challenge themselves (subject to eventual judicial review), and do not need to halt the arbitral proceedings pending a judicial decision. More broadly, the Kompetenz-Kompetenz doctrine could *require parties to initially submit their jurisdictional challenges to the arbitral tribunal*, subject to eventual judicial review, rather than seeking an immediate judicial determination. Most broadly, the doctrine might vest arbitrators with *sole jurisdiction to determine their own jurisdiction*, without the possibility of any meaningful judicial review. We consider below which of these alternatives U.S. courts have adopted.

d. Enforceability of International Arbitration Agreements in U.S. Courts Under the New York Convention

A primary objective of the New York Convention was to render international arbitration agreements enforceable.[64] The New York Convention contains a number of jurisdictional requirements, five of which warrant mention.[65] First, the Convention is applicable in U.S. courts only to differences arising out of "commercial" relationships. Second, the Convention is applicable in U.S. courts only on the basis of reciprocity (*i.e.*, vis-a-vis other nations that also have ratified the Convention). Third, the Convention only applies to agreements concerning "foreign" or "non-domestic" awards. Fourth, Article II(1) limits the Convention's coverage to "agreement[s] in writing." Fifth, the parties' agreement must provide for arbitration of "differences which have arisen or which may arise ... in respect of a defined legal relationship, whether contractual or not."[66]

If the New York Convention's jurisdictional requirements are satisfied, then Article II of the Convention imposes a general obligation on signatory states to "recognize" valid arbitration agreements[67] and "refer the parties to arbitration."[68] Article II sets forth the Convention's basic rule of enforceability, as well as limited exceptions to that rule:

1. Each Contracting State shall recognize an agreement in writing under which the parties undertake to submit to arbitration all or any differences

---

63. *See* S. Schwebel, *International Arbitration: Three Salient Problems* 1-60 (1987); Final Award in Case No. 5485 of 18 August 1987, XIV Y.B. Comm. Arb. 156, 159 (1989) ("in international commercial arbitration the arbitrators have the authority to determine their own jurisdiction").

64. *See supra* pp. 990-91.

65. G. Born, *International Commercial Arbitration in the United States* 285-96 (1994).

66. These jurisdictional requirements are discussed in greater detail elsewhere. *See* A. van den Berg, *The New York Convention of 1958* 11-55 (1981).

67. New York Convention Article II(1).

68. New York Convention Article II(3).

which have arisen or which may arise between them in respect of a defined relationship, whether contractual or not, concerning a subject matter capable of settlement by arbitration. ...

3. The court of a Contracting State, when seized of an action in a matter in respect of which the parties have made an agreement within the meaning of this article, shall, at the request of one of the parties, refer the parties to arbitration, unless it finds that the said agreement is null and void, inoperative or incapable of being performed.

U.S. courts have interpreted Article II in an avowedly "pro-enforcement" fashion:

> [t]he goal of the Convention, and the principal purpose underlying American adoption and implementation of it, was to encourage the recognition and enforcement of commercial arbitration agreements in international contracts and to unify the standards by which agreements to arbitrate are observed. ...[69]

U.S. courts have frequently said that the judicial role in determining whether to enforce an international arbitration agreement under the Convention is very limited. Assuming that jurisdiction, venue, and similar requirements are satisfied, lower U.S. courts have emphasized that Article II(3) requires simply that national courts "shall" refer parties to arbitration, save where the arbitration agreement is "null and void, inoperative or incapable of being performed."[70]

The FAA provides procedural mechanisms to implement the substantive provisions of §2 and Article II of the Convention. Sections 3 and 4 of the Act provide the principal mechanism for enforcing the general rule that arbitration agreements are valid: §3 requires "any court of the United States" to stay proceedings before it, if they involve issues that are "referable to arbitration," while §4 requires "United States district court[s]" to issue orders compelling arbitration of such issues.[71] Similarly, §206 of the FAA grants federal courts the power to compel arbitration in accordance with agreements that are subject to the New York Convention,[72] while §208 incorporates §3's stay provision.[73]

2. Selected Materials on Enforcement of International Arbitration Agreements in U.S. Courts

The materials excerpted below describe the role of U.S. courts in enforcing

---

69. *Scherk v. Alberto-Culver Co.*, 417 U.S. 506, 517 n.10 (1974). *See also infra* pp. 1011-12; *Mitsubishi Motors Corp. v. Soler Chrysler-Plymouth Inc.*, 473 U.S. 614, 626-27 (1985); *Rhone Mediterranee etc. v. Achille Lauro*, 712 F.2d 50 (3d Cir. 1983) ("Signatory nations have effectively declared a joint policy that presumes the enforceability of agreements to arbitrate").

70. *See McCreary Tire & Rubber Co. v. CEAT*, 501 F.2d 1032 (3d Cir. 1974); *Cooper v. Ateliers de la Motorbecane, SA*, 442 N.E.2d 1239 (N.Y. 1982).

71. 9 U.S.C. §§3 & 4.

72. 9 U.S.C. §206.

73. 9 U.S.C. §208.

international commercial arbitration agreements. *Ledee v. Ceramiche Ragno* and *Rhone Mediterranee* illustrate the approaches of U.S. courts to Article II(3). *Republic of Nicaragua v. Standard Fruit Co.* provides an example — albeit a controversial one — of a U.S. court's handling of a challenge to the existence of an arbitration agreement, and the Kompetenz-Kompetenz doctrine.

LEDEE v. CERAMICHE RAGNO

684 F.2d 184 (1st Cir. 1982)

COFFIN, CHIEF JUDGE. ... The defendants-appellees are Italian corporations that make and market ceramic tiles. The plaintiffs-appellants are two Puerto Rico corporations and an individual citizen of the Commonwealth. In 1964 the parties entered into a distributorship agreement giving the appellants exclusive rights to sell and distribute the appellees' ceramic tiles in the Antilles. The agreement ... contained the following paragraph 9:

> Any dispute related to the interpretation and application of this contract will be submitted to an Arbiter selected by the President of the Tribunal of Modena, [Italy,] who will judge as last resort and without procedural formalities.

In March, 1981, the appellants brought suit in the Superior Court of Puerto Rico, alleging that the appellees had breached the contract by unjustifiably terminating their distributorship. The complaint sought damages in accord with the provisions of the Puerto Rico Dealers Act, 10 L.P.R.A. §§278 *et seq.* The appellees removed the case to the United States District Court for the District of Puerto Rico. 9 U.S.C. §205; 28 U.S.C. §§1332(a)(2), 1441(a). The district court ordered arbitration in accord with paragraph 9 and dismissed the complaint. This appeal ensued.

Appellants contend first that, under the laws of the Commonwealth of Puerto Rico, paragraph 9 is void and unenforceable. They invoke the general principle that contracting parties may not agree to clauses or conditions "in contravention of law, morals, or public order." 31 L.P.R.A. §3372. And to show that paragraph 9 is contrary to the public order, they direct our attention to the Dealers Act, as amended. The Dealers Act was enacted to help protect Puerto Rico distributors from the allegedly exploitative practices of certain foreign suppliers.[74] Substantively, it prohibited termination of dealership contracts except "for just cause." 10 L.P.R.A. §278a.

---

74. The Act's statement of motives reads, in part:

"The Commonwealth of Puerto Rico cannot remain indifferent to the growing number of cases in which domestic and foreign enterprises, without just cause, eliminate their dealers, concessionaires or agents, as soon as these have created a favorable market and without taking into account their legitimate interests. The Legislative Assembly of Puerto Rico declares that the reasonable stability in the dealer's relationship in Puerto Rico is vital to the general economy of the country, to the public interest and to the general welfare, and in the exercise of its police power, it deems it necessary to regulate, insofar as pertinent the field of said relationship, so as to avoid the abuse caused by certain practices." Laws of Puerto Rico, 1964, p. 231.

Moreover, it declared that its provisions were of a public order and that the dealers' rights under it could not be waived. 10 L.P.R.A. §278c. ... [It] reads:

> "Any stipulation that obligates a dealer to adjust, arbitrate or litigate any controversy that comes up regarding his dealer's contract outside of Puerto Rico, or under foreign law or rule of law, shall be likewise considered as violating the public policy set forth by this chapter and is therefore null and void." 10 L.P.R.A. §278b-2.

Appellants continue their argument by suggesting that, given the arbitration clause's unenforceability under Puerto Rico Law, the federal district court could not enforce it. They observe that chapter one of the [FAA] is limited, in that it makes arbitration clauses enforceable "save upon such grounds as exist at law or in equity" for the revocation of paragraph 9. We need not, however, consider to what extent the phrase "grounds as exist at law or in equity" incorporates Commonwealth law. ... In particular, we need not consider whether the phrase incorporates the Dealers Act. The simple reason is that the district court did not purport to exercise authority under Chapter One of the [FAA]; rather, it acted under Chapter Two of the Act, 9 U.S.C. §201 *et seq.*, which implemented the [New York] Convention.

A court presented with a request to refer a dispute to arbitration pursuant to Chapter Two of the [FAA] performs a very limited inquiry. It must resolve four preliminary questions:

(1) Is there an agreement in writing to arbitrate the subject of the dispute? Convention, Article II(1), II(2).

(2) Does the agreement provide for arbitration in the territory of a signatory of the Convention? Convention, Articles I(1), I(3); 9 U.S.C. §206.

(3) Does the agreement arise out of a legal relationship, whether contractual or not, which is considered as commercial? Convention, Article I(3); 9 U.S.C. §202.

(4) Is a party to the agreement not an American citizen, or does the commercial relationship have some reasonable relation with one or more foreign states? 9 U.S.C. §202.

If the district court resolves those questions in the affirmative, as it properly did in this case, then it must order arbitration unless it finds the agreement "null and void, inoperative or incapable of being performed." Convention, Article II(3).

Appellants argue that the Dealers Act renders paragraph 9 of the contract "null and void, inoperative or incapable of being performed." They contend that the "null and void" clause was intended to incorporate the Dealers Act as an expression of Puerto Rico public policy. We disagree. Such an expansive interpretation of the clause would be antithetical to the goals of the Convention. In *Scherk v. Alberto-Culver Co.*, 417 U.S. 506, 517 n.10 (1974), the Supreme Court observed:

> The goal of the Convention, and the principal purpose underlying American adoption and implementation of it, was to encourage the recognition and enforcement of commercial arbitration agreements in interna-

tional contracts and to unify the standards by which agreements to arbitrate are observed and arbitral awards are enforced in the signatory countries.

The parochial interests of the Commonwealth, or of any state, cannot be the measure of how the "null and void" clause is interpreted. Indeed, by acceding to and implementing the treaty, the federal government has insisted that not even the parochial interests of the nation may be the measure of interpretation. Rather, the clause must be interpreted to encompass only those situations — such as fraud, mistake, duress, and waiver — that can be applied neutrally on an international scale. *I.T.A.D. Associates, Inc. v. Podar Brothers*, 636 F.2d 75 (4th Cir. 1981).[75] Nothing in the record suggests that the arbitration agreement was "null and void, inoperative or incapable of being performed" within the terms of Article II(3) of the Convention. ...

RHONE MEDITERRANEE COMPAGNIA FRANCESE DI ASSICURAZIONI E RIASSICURAZIONI v. ACHILLE LAURO

712 F.2d 50 (3d Cir. 1983)

GIBBONS, CIRCUIT JUDGE. Rhone Mediterranee Compagnia Francese di Assicurazioni E Riassicurazioni ("Rhone"), a casualty insurer, appeals from an order of the District Court of the Virgin Islands staying Rhone's action pending arbitration. The action results from a fire loss which occurred when the vessel Angelina Lauro burned at the dock of the East Indian Co. Ltd. in Charlotte Amalie, St. Thomas. At the time of the fire the vessel was under time charter to Costa Armatori SpA ("Costa"), an Italian Corporation. Rhone insured Costa, and reimbursed it for property and fuel losses totalling over one million dollars. Rhone, as subrogee of Costa, sued the owner of the vessel, Achille Lauro, ("Lauro") and its master, Antonio Scotto di Carlo, alleging breach of the Lauro-Costa time charter, unseaworthiness, and negligence of the crew. The district court granted defendants' motion for a stay of the action pending arbitration, and Rhone appeals.

As subrogee, Rhone stands in place of its insured, the time charterer Costa. In the time charter contract there is a clause:

"23. Arbitration. Any dispute arising under the Charter to be referred to arbitration in London (or such other place as may be agreed according to box 24) one arbitrator to be nominated by the Owners and the other by the Charterers, and in case the Arbitrators shall not agree then to the decision

---

75. Our conclusion accords with the general mode by which appellate courts have construed the Convention and Chapter Two of the [FAA]. *See Parsons & Whittemore Overseas Co., Inc. v. Societe Generale de l'Industrie du Paper (RAKTA)*, 508 F.2d 969, 973-74 (2d Cir. 1974) (construing narrowly the "public policy" defense to enforcement of awards under Article V(2)(b)); *McCreary Tire & Rubber Co. v. CEAT*, 501 F.2d 1032 (3rd Cir. 1974) (observing that there is "nothing discretionary" about Article II(3)). Similar considerations have influenced the construction of other domestic statutes in the context of international arbitration. *See Scherk, supra; Societe Generale de Surveillance, SA v. Raytheon European Management and Systems Co.*, 643 F.2d 863, 867 (1st Cir. 1981).

of an Umpire to be appointed by them, the award of the Arbitrators or the Umpire to be final and binding upon both parties. Box 24

Place of arbitration (only to be filled in if place other than London agreed (cl. 23) NAPOLI"

All the parties to the time charter agreement and the lawsuit are Italian. Italy and the United States are parties to the [New York] Convention. The [FAA,] 9 U.S.C. §§201-208 (1976), implements the United States' accession on September 1, 1970 to the Convention by providing that it "shall be enforced in United States courts in accordance with this chapter." 9 U.S.C. §201. [Rhone does not dispute that the Convention is applicable.]

What Rhone does contend is that under the terms of the Convention the arbitration clause in issue is unenforceable. Rhone's argument proceeds from a somewhat ambiguous provision in Article II(3) of the Convention:

"The court of a Contracting State, when seized of an action in a matter in respect of which the parties have made an agreement within the meaning of this article, shall, at the request of one of the parties, refer the parties to arbitration, unless it finds that the said agreement is null and void, inoperative or incapable of being performed."

Ambiguity occurs from the fact that no reference appears in II(3) to what law determines whether "said agreement ... is null and void, inoperative or incapable of being performed."

Rhone contends that when the arbitration clause refers to a place of arbitration, here Naples, Italy, the law of that place is determinative. It then relies on the affidavit of an expert on Italian law which states that in Italy an arbitration clause calling for an even number of arbitrators is null and void, even if, as in this case there is a provision for their designation of a tie breaker.

The ambiguity in Article II(3) of the Convention with respect to governing law contrasts with Article V, dealing with enforcement of awards. Article V(1)(a) permits refusal of recognition and enforcement of an award if the "agreement is not valid under the law to which the parties have subjected it or, failing any indication thereon, under the law of the country where the award was made." Article V(1)(e) permits refusal of recognition and enforcement if "[t]he award has not yet become binding on the parties, or has been set aside or suspended by a competent authority of the country in which, or under the law of which, that award was made." Article V(1)(d) permits refusal of enforcement if "[t]he composition of the arbitral authority or the arbitral procedure was not in accordance with the agreement of the parties, or, failing such agreement, was not in accordance with the law of the country where the arbitration took place." Thus Article V unambiguously refers the forum in which enforcement of an award is sought to the law chosen by the parties, or the law of the place of the award.

Rhone and the defendants suggest different conclusions that should be drawn from the differences between Article II and Article V. Rhone suggests that the choice of law rule of Article V should be read into Article II. The defendants urge that in the absence of a specific reference Article II should be read so as to permit the forum, when asked to refer a dispute to arbitration, to apply its own law respecting validity of the arbitration clause.

There is some treaty history suggesting that a proposal to incorporate in Article II choice of law language similar to that in Article V was rejected because delegates to the United Nations organization which drafted it were concerned that a forum might then have an obligation to enforce arbitration clauses regardless of its "local" law. G.W. Haight, *Convention on the Recognition and Enforcement of Foreign Arbitral Awards: Summary Analysis of Record of U.N. Conference*, May/June 1958 at 27-28. It thus appears that the ambiguity in Article II(3) is deliberate. How it should be resolved has been a matter of concern to commentators, who suggest, variously, that the forum state should look to its own law and policy, to the rules of conflicts of laws, or to the law of the place of execution of the agreement. Quigley, *Accession By The United States to the United Nations Convention on the Recognition and Enforcement of Foreign Arbitral Awards*, 70 Yale L. J. 1049, 1064 (§3 permits examination of forum law and policy).

None of the limited secondary literature sheds so clear a light as to suggest a certain answer. However, we conclude that the meaning of Article II(3) which is most consistent with the overall purposes of the Convention is that an agreement to arbitrate is "null and void" only (1) when it is subject to an internationally recognized defense such as duress, mistake, fraud, or waiver, *see Ledee v. Ceramiche Ragno*, 684 F.2d 184 (1st Cir. 1982); *I.T.A.D. Associates, Inc. v. Podar Brothers*, 636 F.2d 75 (4th Cir. 1981), or (2) when it contravenes fundamental policies of the forum state. The "null and void" language must be read narrowly, for the signatory nations have jointly declared a general policy of enforceability of agreements to arbitrate. ...

Signatory nations have effectively declared a joint policy that presumes the enforceability of agreements to arbitrate. Neither the parochial interests of the forum state, nor those of states having more significant relationships with the dispute, should be permitted to supersede that presumption. The policy of the Convention is best served by an approach which leads to upholding agreements to arbitrate. The rule of one state as to the required number of arbitrators does not implicate the fundamental concerns of either the international system or forum, and hence the agreement is not void.

Rhone urges that this rule may result in a Neapolitan arbitration award which, because of Italy's odd number of arbitrators rule, the Italian courts would not enforce. The defendants insist that even in Italy this procedural rule on arbitration is waivable and a resulting award will be enforced. Even if that is not the law of Italy, however, Rhone's objection does not compel the conclusion that we should read Article II(3) as it suggests. The parties did agree to a non-judicial dispute resolution mechanism, and the basic purpose of the Convention is to discourage signatory states from disregarding such agreements. Rhone is not faced with an Italian public policy disfavoring arbitration, but only with an Italian procedural rule of arbitration which may have been overlooked by the drafters of the time charter agreement. Certainly the parties are free to structure the arbitration so as to comply with the Italian procedural rule by having the designated arbitrators select a third member before rather than after impasse. Even if that is not accomplished an award may still result, which can be enforced outside Italy.

Rhone urges that Article V(1)(d) prohibits such enforcement outside Italy, because it refers a non-Italian forum to the law of Italy. We disagree. Section 1 says only that "enforcement of an award may be refused" on the basis of the law of the country where it was made. Where, as here, the law of such a country generally favors enforcement of arbitration awards, and the defect is at best one of a procedural nature, Article V(1) certainly permits another forum to disregard the defect and enforce. That is especially the case when defendants come before the court and, relying on Article II, seek a stay of the action in favor of arbitration. They will hardly be in a position to rely on Italy's odd number of arbitrators rule if Rhone seeks to enforce an award in the District Court of the Virgin Islands.[76]

The forum law implicitly referenced by Article II(3) is the law of the United States, not the local law of the Virgin Islands or of a state. That law favors enforcement of arbitration clauses. *Scherk v. Alberto-Culver Co.*, 417 U.S. 506 (1974); *Becker Autoradio U.S.A. Inc. v. Becker Autoradiowerk GmbH*, 585 F.2d 39 (3d Cir. 1978). Indeed, "[a]n action or proceeding falling under the Convention shall be deemed to arise under the laws and treaties of the United States." 9 U.S.C. §203. ... Since no federal law imposes an odd number of arbitrators rule — the only defect relied upon by Rhone — the district court did not err in staying the suit for breach of the time charter agreement pending arbitration. ...

REPUBLIC OF NICARAGUA v. STANDARD FRUIT CO.
937 F.2d 469 (9th Cir. 1991)

FERGUSON, JUDGE. The Republic of Nicaragua appeals from two orders of the district court which denied its motion to compel international arbitration of a contract dispute (Count I) and granted summary judgment to Standard Fruit Company ("SFC") and its two parent companies, Standard Fruit and Steamship Company ("Steamship") and Castle & Cooke, Inc. ("C&C"),[77] on Nicaragua's breach of contract claim (Count II). Nicaragua ... argues [on appeal] that the questions of whether a document entitled "Memorandum of Intent" was a valid contract

---

76. Had Rhone so requested it would have been proper for the district court to condition its stay order on the defendants' agreement to reform the arbitration clause so as to satisfy Italy's procedural requirement. Since no such request was made we do not consider whether, had it been made, we would remand for such a modification.

77. The three companies are herein referred to collectively as "Standard."

and whether Standard Fruit Company was bound by that contract should have been referred to arbitration in the first instance, not decided by the district court. Secondly, it contends that disputed issues of material fact exist on the question of whether the Memorandum of Intent was a binding contract for the purchase and sale of bananas, or merely an "agreement to agree" at some later date. ...

We hold that although it was the court's responsibility to determine the threshold question of arbitrability, the district court improperly looked to the validity of the contract as a whole and erroneously determined that the parties had not agreed to arbitrate this dispute. Instead, it should have considered only the validity and scope of the arbitration clause itself. In addition, the district court ignored strong evidence in the record that both parties intended to be bound by the arbitration clause. As all doubts over the scope of an arbitration clause must be resolved in favor of arbitration, and in light of the strong federal policy favoring arbitration in international commercial disputes, Nicaragua's motion to compel arbitration should have been granted. Whether the Memorandum was binding, whether it covered banana purchases, and whether Standard Fruit Company was bound by it are all questions properly left to the arbitrators. ...

Since 1970, defendant Standard Fruit Company has been involved in the production and purchase of bananas in western Nicaragua. ... In 1979, the Sandinistas overthrew the Somoza government in Nicaragua, forming a new "Government of National Reconstruction," led by a three-person junta. The Sandinistas wished to assume closer control over the banana industry, and eventually to transfer SFC's shares in [certain banana plantation] partnerships to the Nicaraguan government. ... [After unsuccessful negotiations,] Nicaragua promulgated "Decree No. 608," which declared that the banana industry was to become a state monopoly, that all plantation leases would be transferred to a new government agency, and that all preexisting lease, partnership, and fruit purchase contracts were nullified. SFC interpreted this decree as an expropriation of its business, and immediately ceased all operations in Nicaragua. Sousane and a few key employees left the country, and no more bananas were purchased. Both sides were surprised and upset by the issuance of the decree and the almost immediate withdrawal of SFC, with the bananas still ripe on the trees and ready to pick. As a result, Nicaragua requested a "summit meeting" at which SFC and its two parent companies, Steamship and C&C, could sort out their differences with the Sandinistas and come back to the country. ...

The meeting commenced in San Francisco on Friday, January 9, 1981, and continued for three days of intense negotiations, led by C&C Vice-President and General Counsel Robert Moore (principal draftsman of the Memorandum) and Norton Tennille, Nicaragua's legal counsel. On Sunday, January 11, a document entitled "Memorandum of Intent" was executed by two officers of C&C, two officers of Steamship, and two Ministers of Trade and a member of the ruling junta of Nicaragua. Sousane and other SFC representatives participated in the negotiations but did not sign the document.

The Memorandum, termed an "agreement in principle," contained an arbitration provision, and envisioned the renegotiation and replacement of four operating contracts between SFC and "the competent Nicaraguan national entity." These were to include a detailed fruit purchase contract, a technical assistance contract, the transfer of SFC's shares in the production societies, and Nicaragua's purchase of SFC's assets in the country. The Memorandum also established the essential elements of the fruit purchase contract: a price term ($4.30 per box, less specified deductions), the length of the contract (five years, although no dates were specified), and stated that it would cover all the first-quality bananas produced by the Nicaraguan growers. Additional provisions rescinded the terms of Decree 608 for five years, reinstated SFC's favored tax status, and clarified the financing arrangements for Nicaragua's banana industry.

Within a week after the Memorandum was signed, SFC returned to Nicaragua and resumed its operations there. In addition, it began negotiating with Nicaraguan officials regarding the technical assistance and fruit purchase contracts referred to in the Memorandum, as well as the share transfers and asset buy-outs. Many subsequent drafts of these four documents were exchanged, some similar to the Memorandum and some not, although none were ever finalized and executed. Throughout the negotiations and for the next 22 months, SFC complied with the terms of the Memorandum as though it were bound by it. For example, it began paying $4.30 per box of bananas. ... During this period, C&C and SFC produced and disseminated a number of documents which referred to the Memorandum as "a contract," a "commitment," or "a final agreement," several of which were signed and/or approved by Robert Moore. These included a C&C press release sent out the day after the Memorandum was signed, SEC reports, Annual Reports, letters, telexes, letters to the editor, and internal memoranda. Although SFC, Steamship, C&C, and Nicaragua all acted as though the Memorandum was binding for almost two years, the implementing contracts were never finalized, and SFC left Nicaragua for good on October 25, 1982.

The arbitration clause [contained in the Memorandum] states that:

> Any and all disputes arising under the arrangements contemplated hereunder ... will be referred to mutually agreed mechanisms or procedures of international arbitration, such as the rules of the London Arbitration Association.

Nicaragua admits that this clause is less than crystal clear and in fact refers to an association which does not exist. However, it introduced a letter written by Robert Moore, principal draftsman of the Memorandum, to explain the inconsistency. The letter, written to Nicaragua's representative only three weeks after the negotiations, described the "deep sense of urgency on both sides," the "exceedingly tight time schedule," and the "highly political nature of the agreement (from the Nicaraguan standpoint)." It explained that, during the negotiations themselves, neither side could remember the name of the arbitration body in London, and stated: "What resulted was an agreement for providing for arbitration but without finally fixing the forum or an automatic method of transmitting disputes." Moore suggested "we would be better off agreeing in advance that Paragraph IV was to be read and interpreted to provide for arbitration by [a certain] agency," and concluded "I am sure you will agree that it is best done in the infancy of *the agreement* and at a time that negotiations of the implementing agreements are being worked out." (Emphasis added).[78] Although this letter seems to suggest both that C&C intended the clause to be binding and that the parties intentionally left it vague because they could not remember the name of the London arbitration agency, the district court disregarded this evidence.

The district court applied a three-part test for arbitrability: "first, whether the parties entered into a contract; second, that the contract included an agreement to arbitrate disputes, and third, that the disputes covered by the arbitration agreement included those which are before the Court." It then proceeded to find that the Memorandum as a whole was not a binding contract, that the arbitration provision was not a present agreement to submit to arbitration, but merely "a provision declaring the expectations of the parties that contracts to be negotiated later would include agreements to arbitrate." ... The court [also] determined that the phrase "all arrangements contemplated hereunder" in Paragraph IV referred only to the "implementing agreements" subsequently to be negotiated, executed, and performed in Nicaragua, and not to the Memorandum itself. ...

Nicaragua contends that the district court erred in denying its motion to compel international arbitration of its breach of contract claim and to stay judicial proceedings pending arbitration. It claims that the court should have limited its inquiry to the narrow question of whether the parties had, in fact, agreed to submit the validity of the contract itself to arbitration. Instead, the district court first determined that no binding sales contract existed between the parties and then proceeded to conclude, based on a preponderance of the evidence standard, that there was also no agreement to arbitrate. In the alternative, the court also found that the scope of the arbitration clause did not cover the question of whether the Memorandum of Intent was a binding contract. ...

Both parties agree that federal substantive law governs the question of arbitrability. *See Moses H. Cone Memorial Hospital; Prima Paint.* ... Section 2 [of the FAA] ... embodies a clear federal policy of requiring arbitration unless the agreement to arbitrate is ... is revocable "upon such grounds as exist at law or in equity for the revocation of any contract." ... The standard for demonstrating arbitrability is not a high one; in fact, a district court has little discretion to deny an arbitration motion, since the Act is phrased in mandatory terms. The Supreme Court has emphasized that the Act leaves no place for the exercise of discretion by a district court, but instead mandates that district courts shall direct the parties to proceed to arbitration on issues as

---

78. Attached to the letter was a very explicit page-long "substitute arbitration clause," providing for arbitration in London pursuant to the Arbitration Act of Great Britain.

to which an arbitration agreement has been signed. *Dean Witter Reynolds Inc. v. Byrd*, 470 U.S. 213, 218 (1985). ... [T]his "'liberal federal policy favoring arbitration agreements' ... is at bottom a policy guaranteeing the enforcement of private contractual arrangements." *Mitsubishi Motors Corp. v. Soler Chrysler-Plymouth, Inc.*, 473 U.S. 614, 625 (1985) (quoting *Cone*, 460 U.S. at 24). "Thus, as with any other contract, the parties' intentions control, but those intentions are generously construed as to issues of arbitrability." *Id.* at 626. Therefore, the only issue properly before the district court was whether the parties had entered into a contract ... committing both sides to arbitrate the issue of the contract's validity. ...

Nicaragua's primary claim [or appeal] is that the three-part test applied to determine whether the parties had in fact agreed to arbitrate violates *Prima Paint*, which expressly held that courts may not consider challenges to a contract's validity or enforceability as defenses against arbitration. ... Relying on the "unmistakably clear congressional purpose that the arbitration procedure ... be speedy and not subject to delay and obstruction in the courts," *id.*, *Prima Paint* demands that arbitration clauses be treated as severable from the documents in which they appear unless there is clear intent to the contrary. An arbitration clause may thus be enforced even though the rest of the contract is later held invalid by the arbitrator.

[I]n *Prima Paint* the Supreme Court did not rule on whether the contract was valid or enforceable — just that it existed. The Court rejected *Prima Paint*'s argument that it could not be forced into arbitration because its entire contract (including the arbitration clause at issue) was fraudulently induced and therefore void. The Court held that because the fraud did not go to the making of the arbitration clause itself, the clause was severable and enforceable. It therefore ordered the parties to proceed to arbitration of all disputed issues, including the question of fraud in the inducement and the entire contract's validity.

In the instant case, the district court made a preliminary "Factual Conclusion" that the Memorandum "was not intended as a binding contract," in direct opposition to the *Prima Paint* rule.[79] ... [T]his conclusion is ... the basis for the [district court's] holdings that no agreement to arbitrate existed, and that the present dispute lay outside the scope of the clause. ... [This holding relied] chiefly on the trial testimony of Robert Moore, who drafted most of the Memorandum, and on what the court termed the "unambiguous" language of the document itself. However, as Nicaragua correctly points out, Moore's testimony directly conflicts with contemporary documents in the record, which should have precluded any summary judgment. As a matter of law, the key language in Paragraph IV seems highly ambiguous, since it refers to "the arrangements contemplated hereunder," and thus requires extensive inquiry into just what arrangements are being referred to. ...

---

79. The district court reasoned that an arbitrator can derive his or her power only from a contract, so that when there is a challenge to the existence of the contract itself, the court must first decide whether there is a valid contract between the parties. Although this appears logical, it goes beyond the requirements of the statute and violates the clear directive of *Prima* Paint, 388 U.S. at 404. *See* discussion below.

[We repeat] *Prima Paint's* clear directive that courts disregard surrounding contract language and "consider only issues relating to the making and performance of the agreement to arbitrate." 388 U.S. at 404. The correct analysis is set forth in *Sauer-Getriebe KG v. White Hydraulics, Inc.*, 715 F.2d 348, 350 (7th Cir. 1983), *cert. denied*, 464 U.S. 1070 (1984):

> "White argues that if there is no contract to buy and sell motors there is no agreement to arbitrate. The conclusion does not follow its premise. The agreement to arbitrate and the agreement to buy and sell motors are separate. Sauer's promise to arbitrate was given in exchange for White's promise to arbitrate and each promise was sufficient consideration for the other."

Id. There, the Seventh Circuit ordered arbitration despite the facts that the district court had found the contract "vague and ambiguous," and construed it against its drafter. *See also Teledyne, Inc. v. Kone Corp.*, 892 F.2d 1404, 1410 (9th Cir. 1990). Thus, in the absence of any evidence that Paragraph IV of the Memorandum was intended as non-severable, we must strictly enforce any agreement to arbitrate, regardless of where it is found. Under *Prima Paint* and *Teledyne*, we hold that the district court erred in considering the contract as a whole to determine the threshold question of whether Nicaragua may enforce the arbitration agreement contained in Paragraph IV. ...

The next question is whether Paragraph IV in fact constitutes an agreement to arbitrate, and whether it encompasses the dispute at hand. The district court stated that the parties had not made any present agreement to submit all disputes under the Memorandum to arbitration, but merely agreed to include such clauses in future contracts. ... It is unclear whether [this] statement[ ] [was] based on the language of the Memorandum itself, or on the evidence of the parties' intent developed during the evidentiary hearing. In any case, since "the issue of arbitrability 'is to be determined by the contract entered into by the parties,' the task before this court remains one of contractual interpretation."

However, because of the presumption of arbitrability established by the Supreme Court, courts must be careful not to overreach and decide the merits of an arbitrable claim. Our role is strictly limited to determining arbitrability and enforcing agreements to arbitrate, leaving the merits of the claim and any defenses to the arbitrator. Here, the district court disregarded "the emphatic federal policy in favor of arbitral dispute resolution [which] applies with special force in the field of international commerce." *Mitsubishi Motors Corp. v. Soler Chrysler-Plymouth, Inc.*, 473 U.S. 614, 631 (1985). ...

The district court also found that the clause's "lack of specificity" mitigated against its enforcement. However, the clear weight of authority holds that the most minimal indication of the parties' intent to arbitrate must be given full effect, especially in international disputes. *See, e.g., Bauhinia Corp. v. China Nat'l Machinery and Equip. Co.*, 819 F.2d 247 (9th Cir. 1987) (arbitration ordered where contract contained two incomplete and contradictory arbitration clauses); *Mediterranean*

Enterprises, Inc. v. Ssangyong Corp., 708 F.2d 1458, 1462-63 (9th Cir. 1983) (broadly construing scope of Korean arbitration clause under the Act). Under this analysis, Paragraph IV here was not too vague to be given effect, especially when considered in light of Robert Moore's letter explaining the ambiguity. ... Nicaragua's motion to compel arbitration is granted, and the case remanded to determine the appropriate arbitral agency.

Notes on Ledee, Rhone, and Standard Fruit Co.

1. *Historic development of enforceability of arbitration agreements.* Recall that arbitration agreements were unenforceable at common law. Compare this to the historic unenforceability of forum selection agreements at common law. *See supra* pp. 373-74 & pp. 993-94. Why were both types of agreements unenforceable? Was the historic approach wise? Compare the different ways in which the common law approach to each type of agreement was abandoned.

2. *Federal substantive law applies to the enforceability of international arbitration agreements.* As *Standard Fruit, Rhone,* and *Ledee* illustrate, parties frequently decide after disputes have arisen that they no longer wish to abide by their arbitration agreements. This often results in litigation, typically in one party's national courts. Sometimes, one party will seek to litigate the parties' dispute in a U.S. court, requiring the other party to seek a stay of litigation under §3 of the FAA. Alternatively, one party may seek an order under §§4 or 206 of the FAA compelling the other party to arbitration. Either action will often raise issues concerning the existence, validity, and legality of the parties' arbitration agreement.

What law will U.S. courts apply to determine the enforceability of an arbitration agreement when faced with actions under either §§3, 4 or 206? As discussed above, §2 of the FAA provides that arbitration agreements are valid and enforceable, "save upon such grounds as exist at law or in equity for the revocation of any contract." Section 2's rule of enforceability is incorporated into the second chapter of the FAA by §208. It is paralleled by Article II of the New York Convention, which requires recognition of arbitration agreements unless they are "null and vóid, inoperative or incapable of being performed." Thus, as *Standard Fruit, Rhone,* and *Ledee* illustrate, federal law plays a significant role in enforcing international arbitration agreements in U.S. courts.

Compare this approach to the law governing the enforceability of forum selection clauses. Recall that forum clauses have generally been held to be governed by federal procedural law in federal courts and by state law in state courts. *See supra* pp. 432-35. Which legal regime is more desirable — that governing international forum agreements or that governing international arbitration clauses?

3. *"Pro-enforcement" bias of Article II of the New York Convention. Ledee* and *Rhone* interpret Article II of the New York Convention as establishing a strong presumption favoring the enforceability of arbitration agreements. Other lower U.S. courts have endorsed the same "pro-enforcement" bias. *E.g., Riley v. Kingsley Underwriting Agencies, Ltd.*, 969 F.2d 953, 960 (10th Cir. 1992) ("'null and void' exception ... is to be narrowly construed"); *I.T.A.D. Associates, Inc. v. Podar Brothers*, 636 F.2d 75 (4th Cir. 1981); *Technetronics, Inc. v. Leybold-Geaeus GmbH*, 1993 U.S. Dist. Lexis 7683 (E.D. Pa. 1993). As *Ledee, Rhone,* and *Standard Fruit* suggest, there is precedent reasoning that "the liberal federal arbitration policy 'applies with special force in the field of international commerce.'" *David L. Threlkeld & Co. v. Metallgesellschaft Ltd.*, 923 F.2d 245, 248 (2d Cir. 1991) (quoting *Mitsubishi Motors*, 473 U.S. at 631).

Why should federal law actively encourage enforcement of international arbitration agreements? Enforcing an arbitration agreement usually means depriving parties of basic rights such as a jury trial, discovery, cross-examination, appellate review, and other procedural safeguards of the adversary system. *See infra* pp. 1027 & 1050. Is it wise to affirmatively encourage the enforcement of such agreements? Is this a different approach from that in *Bremen?*

4. *Scope of federal substantive law under §2.* What is the scope of federal substantive law under §2 of the FAA?

(a) *Section 2's "savings" clause.* Consider the language of §2: certain agreements to arbitrate "shall be valid, irrevocable and enforceable, save upon such grounds as exist at law or in equity for the revocation of any contract." What does the "savings clause" mean? Particularly given the savings clause, §2 could be read either as creating a general federal body of contract law or as merely referring to otherwise applicable substantive rules of contract law — which would typically be state law. Which reading should be adopted?

(b) *Preemption of state law by §2.* Most lower courts have held that §2 preempts state laws that single arbitration agreements out and impose particularly onerous standards for their validity or enforceability. Thus, U.S. courts have routinely struck down state statutes that limit the enforceability of arbitration agreements in particular ways not applicable to other contracts. *See Mastrobuono v. Shearson Lehman Hutton, Inc.,* 115 S.Ct. 1212 (1995) (FAA preempts state common law prohibition against arbitration of punitive damage claims); *Southland Co. v. Keating,* 465 U.S. 1 (1984) (FAA preempts state statutory prohibition against arbitration of franchise disputes); *Perry v. Thomas,* 482 U.S. 483 (1987) (FAA preempts California Labor Code prohibition against arbitration of employer-employee disputes over wage collection); *Securities Indus. Ass'n v. Connolly,* 883 F.2d 1114, 1123-24 (1st Cir. 1989) (FAA preempts state statutory requirement that arbitration clauses be "conspicuous").

(c) *Limits on preemptive effect of §2.* Although §2 establishes substantive federal law, there are significant limits on the section's preemptive effect. Most U.S. judicial decisions have not looked to federal law for basic contract law rules of validity, formation, consideration, capacity, and the like. Rather, they have applied generally applicable state contract law rules to these issues. *See Perry v. Thomas,* 482 U.S. 483 (1987) ("the text of §2 provides the touchstone for choosing between state law principles and the principles of federal common law envisioned by the passage of that statute: 'An agreement to arbitrate is valid, irrevocable, and enforceable, *as a matter of federal law*,' [citing *Moses H. Cone*], 'save upon such grounds as exist at law or in equity for the revocation of *any* contract.' Thus, state law, whether of legislative or judicial origin, is applicable *if* that law arose to govern issues concerning the validity, revocability, and enforceability of contracts generally. A state law principle that takes its meaning precisely from the fact that a contract to arbitrate is at issue does not comport with this requirement of §2."); *First Options of Chicago, Inc. v. Kaplan,* 115 S.Ct. 1920 (1995) ("in deciding whether the parties agreed to arbitrate a certain matter (including arbitrability), courts generally ... should apply ordinary state-law principles that govern the formation of contracts").

(d) *Broader views of preemptive effect of §2.* A few lower court decisions, usually older ones, have gone further and held that federal law provides the sole standards governing the formation, validity, legality, and interpretation of arbitration agreements. *E.g., Cohen v. Wedbush, Noble, Cooke, Inc.,* 841 F.2d 282, 285 (9th Cir. 1988) ("the availability and validity of defenses against arbitration are therefore to be governed by application of federal standards"); *Johnson Controls, Inc. v. City of Cedar Rapids,* 713 F.2d 370, 376 (8th Cir. 1983) ("federal substantive law preempts state law governing the enforceability of arbitration agreements in interstate contracts").

These decisions do not appear to survive *First Options, Perry v. Thomas,* and other more recent precedents. Are they nevertheless the better view? Compare again the applicable law governing international forum selection clauses and international arbitration agreements.

5. *Scope of federal law under Article II(3).* What is the scope of substantive federal law under Article II(3) of the Convention?

(a) *Article II(3)'s "null and void" exception.* Article II(3) contains an exception, similar to §2's savings clause, for arbitration agreements which are "null and void, inoperative or incapable of being performed." Like §2 of the FAA, Article II(3) does not itself set forth standards of nullity or voidness: instead, it looks to some national (or other) law to govern issues of nullity and validity. Sanders, *A Twenty Years' Review of the Convention on Foreign Arbitral Awards,* 33 So. Cal. L. Rev. 14, 16 (1959) (Article II(3) refers to conflict of laws); Contini, *International Commercial Arbitration,* 8 Am. J. Comp. L. 283, 296 (1959) (since Article II(3) is silent, courts may make determination on basis of forum law, including forum choice of law rules).

A variety of national laws are potentially applicable under Article II(3) to determine the validity of an arbitration agreement. These include: (a) the law which the parties have selected to govern their agreement; (b) the law of the forum (where judicial action is brought to enforce the arbitration agreement); (c) the law of the arbitral situs; or (d) the law of the place where an arbitral award would need to be enforced. Which law should be selected to govern the enforceability of international arbitration agreements under Article II(3)? What law should provide the choice of law rules that answer this question?

(b) *Article II(3) — "internationally neutral" defenses.* *Ledee* holds that Article II(3)'s exception for "null and void" agreements only applies to defenses that can be applied "neutrally on an international scale." The *Ledee* formulation appears to exclude state and foreign laws — like the Puerto Rican dealers' law — that single out arbitration agreements for special disfavor. *See also I.T.A.D. Associates, Inc. v. Podar Brothers,* 636 F.2d 75 (4th Cir. 1981); *Meadows Indemnity Co. v. Baccala & Shoop Ins. Serv., Inc.,* 760

F.Supp. 1036, 1043 (E.D.N.Y. 1991) (rejecting defense to action to compel arbitration where defendant argued that arbitration agreement was not enforceable in arbitral situs because claims were non-arbitrable; applying "emphatic federal policy" favoring arbitration).

What kinds of legal rules does *Ledee*'s "internationally neutral" requirement permit to be invoked to resist enforcement of an arbitration clause? Note the court's reference to defenses "such as fraud, mistake, duress, and waiver." What defines the content of "international neutral" defenses like fraud, mistake, duress, and waiver? Does *Ledee* contemplate some international standard of fraud or waiver, that each nation must apply? Alternatively, does *Ledee* regard the requirement of international neutrality as essentially negative, preempting various parochial defenses, but leaving it to national law (such as §2 of the FAA) to define the details of internationally neutral defenses? If so, what choice of law rules should be applied to select the appropriate national law?

Why was the Puerto Rican law in *Ledee* not "internationally neutral"? If both Italy and Puerto Rico (or the United States) forbid agreements to arbitrate franchise disputes, would that be an "internationally neutral" defense? What if most countries do so? Or does *Ledee* forbid *any* law that singles out arbitration agreements for special disfavor, no matter how widely accepted such a rule is? Recall the discussion of rules of alternative reference in the context of choice of law applicable to contracts. *See supra* p. 679.

(d) *Lower U.S. court decisions holding that Article II(3)'s "null and void" exception refers to forum's public policy.* In *Rhone*, the Third Circuit holds that an arbitration agreement is "null and void" if either: (i) like *Ledee*, it is null and void under an internationally neutral defense, *or* (ii) it is null and void because it contravenes a fundamental public policy of the forum. Compare this interpretation of Article II(3) with that in *Ledee*. Is it not clear that the Puerto Rican dealers' law in *Ledee* stated a fundamental public policy of the forum? Would that Puerto Rican public policy have rendered the parties' arbitration agreement null and void under *Rhone*'s analysis? Is the Puerto Rican public policy preempted, as a matter of U.S. law, by §2 of the FAA?

(e) *Lower U.S. court decisions refusing to apply foreign law to hold arbitration agreement "null and void" under Article II(3).* In *Rhone*, the court refused to apply Italian law, which appeared fairly clearly to render the parties' arbitration agreement invalid (because it called for an even number of arbitrators). Other U.S. courts have also refused to apply foreign law to determine the validity of arbitration agreements in actions under the New York Convention or FAA. *See I.T.A.D. Associates, Inc. v. Podar Brothers,* 636 F.2d 75 (4th Cir. 1981); *Ferrara SpA v. United Grain Growers, Ltd.,* 441 F.Supp. 778, 781 n.2 (S.D.N.Y. 1977) (reasoning in dicta that enforceability of arbitration agreement is governed by forum law). These decisions have reasoned:

> For example, consider the case where a contract containing an arbitration clause provides that the law of state X shall govern the agreement. Assume that the law of state X will not enforce, or gives very limited effect to arbitration clauses, such that under X law the dispute would not be submitted to arbitration. If one party sues on the contract in federal court, and the contract involves 'commerce,' the federal district court ... would look to federal law in determining the scope of the arbitration clause.

Becker Autoradio U.S.A., Inc. v. Becker Autoradiowerk GmbH, 585 F.2d 39, 44-44, 781 n.2 & n.8 (3d Cir. 1978). Compare again the rules of alternative reference discussed above.

Assume that the law of the parties' chosen arbitral situs rendered the arbitration agreement illegal or, at a minimum, incapable of performance. Why should a U.S. court order arbitration in those circumstances? What is the harm in doing so? What would be the harm in concluding incorrectly that foreign law prohibits arbitration and permitting U.S. litigation to go forward?

6. *Substantive grounds for challenging international arbitration agreements.* What grounds are available under both §2 of the FAA and Article II of the Convention for challenging the enforceability of an international arbitration agreement? As discussed above, both provisions refer one to other bodies of substantive law — either state or foreign — subject to the preemption of discriminatory legislation discussed above. In general terms, those bodies of law recognize generally-applicable contract law defenses similar to those under U.S. law: (a) lack of any agreement between the parties; (b) invalidity of an agreement for failure to obey formal requirements, or for lack of capacity; (c) illegality of the agreement, because it is contrary to mandatory national law (such as the antitrust or securities laws); (d) fraud in the factum (*e.g.,* forgery) or fraudulent inducement; (e) waiver; or (f) unconscionability. G. Born, *International Commercial Arbitration in the United States* 231-83 (1994).

7. *The separability doctrine — Prima Paint.* U.S. courts have generally held that an arbitration agreement is "separable" from the underlying contract in which it appears. The leading Supreme Court decision on the subject is *Prima Paint Corp. v. Flood & Conklin Mfg. Co.*, 388 U.S. 395 (1967), relied on in *Standard Fruit.* In *Prima Paint*, the Court considered whether the FAA required arbitration of a claim that a contract, containing an arbitration clause, had been fraudulently induced. Relying on §§2, 3, and 4 of the FAA, the Court held that the fraudulent inducement claim was arbitrable, and therefore that the FAA did not allow judicial consideration of the claim under §4 or otherwise. In particular, the Court relied on §4, which authorizes the issuance of orders compelling arbitration where "the making of *the agreement for arbitration* ... is not in issue":

> Under §4, with respect to a matter within the jurisdiction of the federal courts save for the existence of an arbitration clause, the federal court is instructed to order arbitration to proceed once it is satisfied that "the making of the agreement for arbitration or the failure to comply [with the arbitration agreement] is not in issue." Accordingly, *if the claim is fraud in the inducement of the arbitration clause itself — an issue which goes to the "making" of the agreement to arbitrate — the federal court may proceed to adjudicate it.* But the statutory language *does not permit the federal court to consider claims of fraud in the inducement of the contract generally.*

Concluding that "no claim has been advanced by [plaintiff] that [defendant] fraudulently induced it to enter into the agreement to arbitrate," the Court affirmed a stay of federal court proceedings pending arbitration.

8. *Rationale for separability doctrine.* What is the basis for the separability doctrine — parties' intent, national law, practical necessity, or something else?

One possible source for the separability doctrine is the parties' intent. Reliance on the parties' intent is least problematic where the arbitration agreement incorporates institutional rules — like the UNCITRAL, ICC, and AAA International Rules — which expressly embrace the separability doctrine. *See* G. Born, *International Commercial Arbitration in the United States* 215-16 (1994). The separability doctrine can also be justified on grounds of party intent even where the arbitration agreement does not expressly provide for such a result. It is often argued that: (a) parties to arbitration agreements generally "intend to require arbitration of *any* dispute not otherwise settled, including disputes over the validity of the contract"; and (b) without the separability doctrine, "it would always be open to a party to an agreement containing an arbitration clause to vitiate its arbitration obligation by the simple expedient of declaring the agreement void." S. Schwebel, *International Arbitration: Three Salient Problems* 3-6 (1987). Why would parties want their arbitration agreement to be separable? What effect would rejection of the separability doctrine have on the arbitral process? How far does reliance of the parties' intent carry one? Suppose that one party denies having made *any* agreement at all with the other party.

Second, some national laws provide expressly for separability and Kompetenz-Kompetenz. *E.g.*, UNCITRAL Model Law, Article 16(1) ("The arbitral tribunal may rule on its own jurisdiction, including any objections with respect to the existence or validity of the arbitration agreement. For that purpose, an arbitration clause which forms part of the contract shall be treated as an agreement independent of the other terms of the contract."). Consider §§2, 3, and 4 of the FAA. Do they adopt either of these doctrines? *Prima Paint* concluded that §4 mandated a separability doctrine, relying on the section's reference to "the making of the *agreement for arbitration.*" *See supra* p. 1013. Is that a correct reading of the section?

A commonsense reply to the foregoing explanations for the separability doctrine might run as follows:

> [I]f an agreement contains an obligation to arbitrate disputes arising under it, but the agreement is invalid or no longer in force, the obligation to arbitrate disappears with the agreement of which it is a part. If the agreement was never entered into at all, its arbitration clause never came into force. If the agreement was not validly entered into, then, *prima facie*, it is invalid as a whole, as must be all of its parts, including its arbitration clause.

S. Schwebel, *International Arbitration: Three Salient Problems* 1 (1987). Why is this not irrefutable logic? Surely, if the parties' alleged contract was never in fact agreed to, then none of it — arbitration clause included — is binding on the "parties," is it?

9. *Arbitrability of challenges to the parties' underlying agreement.* Lower U.S. courts are divided over the arbitrability of challenges to the parties' underlying agreement (rather than to the arbitration clause).

(a) *Fraudulent inducement of the underlying agreement.* Following *Prima Paint*, lower courts have almost always refused to hear claims that the underlying contract containing the parties' arbitration agreement was procured by fraud, instead requiring these arguments to be submitted to the arbitrators. *E.g., In re Oil Spill by Amoco Cadiz*, 659 F.2d 789 (7th Cir. 1981); *Al-Salamah Arabian Agencies Co. v. Reece*, 673 F.Supp. 748 (M.D.N.C. 1987); *Brener v. Becker Paribas, Inc.*, 628 F.Supp. 442, 446 (S.D.N.Y. 1985). Is this wise? If one party fraudulently induces another to enter into a contract with it, should the victim be required to forego judicial remedies and limit itself to "contractual" dispute resolution mechanisms? Is this likely what it intended when entering into the contract?

(b) *Non-existence of underlying agreement. Standard Fruit* holds that the arbitral tribunal — rather than a court — must initially decide whether the Memorandum (containing the alleged arbitration clause) is in fact a contract at all. As *Standard Fruit* illustrates, some U.S. courts have concluded that disputes about the *existence* of the parties' underlying agreement (as distinguished from the separable arbitration agreement) must be arbitrated. *See R.M. Perez & Assoc., Inc. v. Welch*, 960 F.2d 534 (5th Cir. 1992); *Teledyne, Inc. v. Kone Corp.*, 892 F.2d 1404, 1410 (9th Cir. 1990) (only issue for court is "whether there are grounds for an *independent* challenge to the arbitration clause, rather than a challenge to the arbitration clause which must rise or fall with a challenge to the contract as a whole"); *Hall v. Shearson Lehman Hutton, Inc.*, 708 F. Supp. 711 (D. Md. 1989) (arbitrator to resolve whether one party forged other party's signature on agreement containing arbitration clause).

In contrast, other courts have held that challenges to the very existence of any underlying agreement must be decided by the court. *E.g., Interocean Shipping Co. v. National Shipping & Trading Corp.*, 462 F.2d 673, 676 (2d Cir. 1972) ("There can be no doubt that the question of the very existence of the charter party which embodies the arbitration agreement" requires a trial under §4); *In re Kinoshita & Co.*, 287 F.2d 951, 953 (2d Cir. 1961) ("if it were claimed that ... there had at no time existed as between the parties any contractual relation whatever, ... a trial of this issue would be required"); *Donato v. Merrill Lynch, Pierce, Fenner & Smith, Inc.*, 663 F.Supp. 669 (N.D. Ill. 1987) (§4 trial on claim that signature on contract containing arbitration clause was forged).

Which approach is wiser? What considerations are relevant to deciding this issue? Consider the following observation of the House of Lords in *Heyman v. Darwins Ltd.* [1942] AC 356, 366 (Viscount Simon LC):

> If the dispute is whether the contract which contains the clause has ever been entered into at all, that issue cannot go to arbitration under the clause, for the party who denies that he has ever entered into the contract is thereby denying that he has ever joined in the submission [to arbitration]. Similarly, if one party to the alleged contract is contending that it is void ab initio (because, for example, the making of such a contract is illegal), the arbitration clause cannot operate, for, on this view, the clause itself is also void.

If the parties simply never entered into a contract, how can they be said to have agreed to arbitrate? Why is this not unanswerable? What would be the response of the author of *Standard Fruit*?

(c) *Invalidity or illegality of the underlying agreement.* Many lower U.S. courts have held that disputes about the validity or legality of the parties' underlying agreement must initially be arbitrated. *E.g., Sauer-Getriebe KG v. White Hydraulics, Inc.*, 715 F.2d 348, 350 (7th Cir. 1984) (arbitrators to "adjudicate the validity of [the] contract"); *Lawrence v. Comprehensive Business Services Co.*, 833 F.2d 1159 (5th Cir. 1987) (claim that underlying contract violated Texas Public Accountancy Act must be arbitrated); *Island Territory of Curacao v. Solitron Devices, Inc.*, 489 F.2d 1313 (2d Cir. 1973), *cert. denied*, 416 U.S. 989 (1974).

Other courts have held that courts must resolve claims that the parties' underlying agreement is illegal or invalid. *E.g., Continental Service Life and Health Ins. Co. v. A.G. Edwards & Sons*, 664 F.Supp. 997, 999 (M.D. La. 1987) ("Where the validity or the existence of a contract containing an alleged arbitration clause is put at issue, a trial on the merits is required before a party to a lawsuit can be ordered to arbitrate"); *Durst v. Abrash*, 253 N.Y.S.2d 351 (App. Div. 1964), *aff'd*, 266 N.Y.S.2d 806 (1966) ("If usurious agreements could be made enforceable by the simple device of employing arbitration clauses the courts would be surrendering their control over public policy."); *Kramer & Uchitelle, Inc. v. Eddington Fabrics Corp.*, 43 N.E.2d 493 (N.Y. 1942).

Which approach is wiser? What considerations are relevant to deciding this issue? Is it in fact defensible to require arbitration of claims that the parties' agreement is illegal? Suppose that an arbitration clause is included in a contract for payment of unlawful bribes or sale of unlawful weapons. Should a court require arbitration of claims arising from that unlawful agreement?

Suppose that the one party alleges that parties' underlying agreement is invalid because (a) it was not signed by authorized agents; or (b) it was not supported by consideration. Should a court require arbitration of jurisdictional objections where one party denies it has entered into a valid contract with the other party?

(d) *Parties' arbitration agreement requires judicial consideration of challenges to parties' underlying agreement.* In adopting the separability doctrine, *Prima Paint* observed that the parties' arbitration agreement was "easily broad enough to encompass Prima Paint's claim that ... the consulting agreement [was] procured by fraud." 388 U.S. at 405. The Court made it clear that nothing precludes the parties from agreeing to arbitration agreements that do *not* provide for arbitration of claims of fraudulent inducement or other invalidity of the underlying agreement. *See also Moseley v. Electronic & Missile Facilities, Inc.*, 374 U.S. 167 (1963).

A few lower courts have concluded, on particular facts, that the parties' arbitration agreement in fact did not grant the arbitrators power to consider challenges to the underlying agreement. *E.g., El Hoss Engineering & Transport Co. v. American Independent Oil Co.*, 289 F.2d 346 (2d Cir. 1961). However, most U.S. courts have concluded that the parties' arbitration agreement does reach challenges to the underlying agreement. *See* G. Born, *International Commercial Arbitration in the United States* 221-22, 241, 399-403 (1994).

10. *Arbitrability of challenges to the arbitration agreement.* In some cases, one party will not merely challenge the existence, validity or legality of the parties' underlying agreement, but will challenge the arbitration agreement itself. Should such disputes be resolved by the arbitrators, or, if one party insists, must a court consider them?

(a) *Relevance of parties' arbitration agreement.* The power of an arbitrator to decide at least some issues of arbitrability can depend on the parties' arbitration agreement. The Supreme Court recently held in *First Options of Chicago, Inc. v. Kaplan*, 115 S.Ct. 1920 (1995), that parties may grant an arbitrator jurisdiction to determine issues of arbitrability. The Court reasoned that "when deciding whether the parties agreed to arbitrate a certain matter (including arbitrability), courts generally ... should apply ordinary state-law principles that govern the formation of contracts." The Court then declared that courts "should not assume that the parties agreed to arbitrate arbitrability unless there is 'clea[r] and unmistakabl[e]' evidence that they did so."

How far does this reasoning extend? Suppose that one party challenges the scope of a concededly existing and valid arbitration agreement, or the validity or legality of an arbitration agreement that one party concededly executed. On the other hand, suppose that one party denies that it ever executed or otherwise committed itself to a purported arbitration agreement. Can the parties' arbitration agreement grant the arbitrators power to decide each of these types of disputes? Do all of the disputes involve the same issues?

(b) *Disputes about the existence, validity, or legality of the arbitration agreement.* As we have seen, §4 provides for orders compelling arbitration except where "the making of the agreement for arbitration ... is not in issue." Where the "making of the agreement for arbitration" *is* "in issue" then §4 apparently requires a trial on that question.

A number of lower courts have concluded that §4's language requires judicial resolution of claims that no arbitration agreement exists. *E.g., Moseley v. Electronic & Missile Facilities, Inc.*, 374 U.S. 167, 172 (1963) ("fraud in the procurement of an arbitration contract ... makes it void and unenforceable and ... this question of fraud is a judicial one, which must be determined by a court") (Black, J., concurring); *David L. Threlkeld & Co. v. Metallgesellschaft Ltd.*, 923 F.2d 245 (2d Cir. 1991); *Becker Autoradio v. Becker Autoradiowerk GmbH*, 585 F.2d 39, 44 & n.10 (3d Cir. 1978); *Interbras Cayman Co. v. Orient Victory Shipping Co.*, 663 F.2d 4, 7 (2d Cir. 1981) (ordering trial under §4 because of "genuine issue of fact" as to existence of arbitration agreement).

How can an arbitration agreement — no matter how broadly drafted — confer jurisdiction on arbitrators with respect to a party that denies that agreement's existence?

(c) *Disputes concerning interpretation of arbitration clause.* As discussed below, a number of lower courts have held that disputes about the *scope* of an arbitration agreement that concededly *exists* are presumptively for resolution by the arbitrators. *See infra* pp. 1035-37; *Apollo Computer, Inc. v. Berg*, 886 F.2d 469 (1st Cir. 1989); *Matter of Arbitration No. AAA13-161-0511-85*, 867 F.2d 130, 133 (2d Cir. 1989); *Societe Generale etc. v. Raytheon European Mgt. and Systems Co.*, 643 F.2d 863, 869 (1st Cir. 1981).

(d) *Parties' submission of dispute to arbitrators.* Even if the parties' arbitration agreement does not grant the arbitrators power to decide issues of arbitrability, the parties may through their subsequent conduct submit such issues to the arbitrators. *See First Options of Chicago, Inc. v. Kaplan,* 115 S.Ct. 1920 (1995).

11. *The Standard Fruit decision.* Is it sensible to conclude, as *Standard Fruit* does, that the parties' arbitration agreement is binding even if the underlying Memorandum of Intent is not? Suppose that Standard Fruit argued that the Memorandum of Intent was a forgery — that it had never discussed, much less signed, any such document. Would this really be irrelevant to Nicaragua's motion to compel arbitration? *See supra* pp. 1013-15. If the Memorandum is *not* a binding contract, then how can its arbitration provision be binding?

The standard answer to the foregoing, of course, is that the arbitration agreement is separable and therefore that it is supported by separate consideration (the exchange of promises to arbitrate) and separate evidence as to its existence. *See supra* pp. 1013-14. Is that answer persuasive in cases involving claims that *no* underlying agreement exists? If the very existence of *any* contract is challenged, is that not necessarily relevant to the existence of an agreement to arbitrate? In concrete terms, if Standard Fruit and Nicaragua had no intention to be bound by the Memorandum of Intent, would they have intended to be bound by the Memorandum's arbitration clause?

Even assuming that the binding character of the Memorandum is irrelevant, Standard Fruit *also* challenged the existence of the arbitration "agreement" itself. In particular, it argued that the arbitration clause was only a statement of intention to attempt to agree on an arbitration mechanism in the future. How did *Standard Fruit* resolve this? Consider the terms of the alleged arbitration "agreement." Was the provision relied upon by Nicaragua an agreement to arbitrate? Did the Ninth Circuit decide that it was? In deciding whether an arbitration agreement *exists,* is it satisfactory to rely on the federal policy favoring broad interpretation of arbitration agreements?

What are the limits of the *Standard Fruit* rationale? Suppose that the Memorandum of Intent had not been signed, but that Nicaragua argued it had been orally agreed to. Suppose the arbitration clause was contained in a draft prepared by Nicaragua, but not included in the unsigned Memorandum of Intent?

12. *Judicial review of arbitrator's jurisdictional rulings.* Suppose that a court requires the parties to arbitrate disputes concerning arbitrability. How will the arbitrator's jurisdictional ruling eventually be reviewed?

(a) *Interlocutory review of jurisdictional rulings.* Some foreign arbitration statutes permit interlocutory judicial review of arbitrators' jurisdictional rulings. UNCITRAL Model Law Article 16; G. Born, *International Commercial Arbitration in the United States* 217-18 (1994).

In contrast, U.S. courts have not frequently considered interlocutory appeals from arbitrators' jurisdictional rulings. If the tribunal does not make an interim award, then there generally will be no basis unaer the FAA for interlocutory judicial review. Even if an interim jurisdictional award *is* made by the tribunal, however, then interlocutory review probably is not available under the FAA. Under §§9 and 10 of the FAA, only "final" arbitral awards can be either confirmed or vacated, and U.S. courts have generally refused to consider interlocutory challenges to arbitral decisions. *See Id.* at pp. 218, 613-19. Although there are few reported decisions, these refusals have extended to interim jurisdictional awards. *Transportacion Maritima Mexicana, SA v. Companhia de Navegacao Lloyd Brasiliero,* 636 F.Supp. 474 (S.D.N.Y. 1983).

Is the U.S. approach a sensible one? Why shouldn't courts entertain challenges to interim jurisdictional awards? Consider the wasted resources if the tribunal incorrectly upholds its own jurisdiction. On the other hand, consider the delays that can result from preliminary litigation of arbitrability disputes.

(b) *Limited scope of judicial review of jurisdictional rulings under U.S. law.* As discussed in detail below, *infra* pp. 1048-49, judicial review of the merits of most arbitral rulings in U.S. courts is extremely limited. Should the same standard apply to jurisdictional rulings? For a discussion of the treatment of this issue by U.S. courts, *see infra* pp. 1051-52.

3. The Non-Arbitrability Doctrine in U.S. Courts

a. Introduction

Virtually all nations treat some categories of claims as incapable of resolution by arbitration. Claims are ordinarily deemed "non-arbitrable" because of their perceived public importance or a felt need for formal judicial procedures and protections. The types of claims that are non-arbitrable differ from nation to nation. Among other things, various nations refuse to permit arbitration of disputes concerning labor or employment grievances; intellectual property; competition (antitrust) claims; real estate; and franchise relations.[80]

Article II(1) of the New York Convention does not require arbitration of disputes that are not "capable of settlement by arbitration." Similarly, Article V(2)(a) provides that an arbitration award need not be recognized if "[t]he subject matter of the difference is not capable of settlement by arbitration under the law" of the country where recognition is sought. Together, these provisions permit the assertion of non-arbitrability defenses to the enforcement of arbitration agreements and awards.

Both U.S. federal law and state have, at various times, treated various claims as non-arbitrable.[81] Nevertheless, the FAA itself contains no provisions dealing expressly with the subject of non-arbitrability. Prohibitions on the arbitrability of claims under U.S. law are based, therefore, on other statutes or public policies. As discussed below, U.S. statutes have seldom dealt expressly with the subject of non-arbitrability, thus leaving development of the doctrine largely to the courts.

The Supreme Court's first modern treatment of the non-arbitrability doctrine was *Wilko v. Swan*.[82] There, an investor brought an action in federal district court against his brokers under the federal Securities Act of 1933, seeking damages for their alleged misrepresentations. The defendants sought to stay the plaintiff's action, relying on an arbitration provision in the parties' margin agreement.

The Supreme Court rejected the defendants' motion for a stay, reasoning that, while Congress wished to encourage arbitration generally, "it has enacted the Securities Act to protect the rights of investors and has forbidden a waiver of any of those rights."[83] The Court relied principally on §14 of the Securities Act, which provides:

> Any condition, stipulation, or provision binding any person acquiring any security to waive compliance with any provision of this subchapter or of the rules and regulations of the Commission shall be void.[84]

The Court concluded that "[r]ecognizing the advantages that prior agreements for arbitration may provide for the solution of commercial controversies, we decide that

---

80. *See* G. Born, *International Commercial Arbitration in the United States* 322-82 (1994).

81. *E.g., Wilko v. Swan*, 346 U.S. 427 (1953) (Securities Act of 1933); *Alexander v. Gardner-Denver Co.*, 415 U.S. 36 (1974) (Title VII); (Ark. Stat. Ann. §34-511 (Supp. 1985) (not permitting enforcement of arbitration agreements as to personal injury, tort, employer-employee, or insurance contract claims); Iowa Code §679A.1(2) (1985) (same as to adhesion contracts, employer-employee contracts, and tort claims (unless covered by a separate writing)).

82. 346 U.S. 427 (1953).

83. 396 U.S. at 438.

84. 15 U.S.C. §77n.

the intention of Congress concerning the sale of securities is better carried out by holding invalid such an agreement for arbitration of issues arising under the Act."[85]

Relying on *Wilko*, lower federal courts subsequently fashioned a variety of non-arbitrability exceptions designed to protect perceived public values or legislative objectives. Thus, patent, federal antitrust, Racketeer Influenced and Corrupt Organizations Act ("RICO"), and COGSA claims were held too important to be left to "private" arbitration.[86] At the same time, the Supreme Court concluded that other categories of federal statutory claims were also non-arbitrable under the FAA.[87]

During the 1980s, the Supreme Court brought the blossoming of the non-arbitrability doctrine to a fairly decisive end. Two landmark decisions concluded that federal securities and antitrust claims *could* be arbitrated, at least when they arose from "international" transactions. In *Scherk v. Alberto-Culver Co.*, the Supreme Court distinguished *Wilko* and held that a claim under the Securities Exchange Act of 1934 was arbitrable, provided that it arose from an "international" transaction.[88] And, in *Mitsubishi Motors Corp. v. Soler Chrysler-Plymouth, Inc.*, which is excerpted below, the Court held that federal antitrust claims were also arbitrable, again provided that they arose from an "international" transaction.[89]

More recently, the Supreme Court expressly overruled *Wilko v. Swan*, holding in two decisions that claims — both domestic and international — under RICO and the Securities Exchange Act are arbitrable.[90] In another decision, after remarking that "[i]t is by now clear that statutory claims may be the subject of an arbitration agreement," the Court held that claims under the Age Discrimination in Employment Act are arbitrable.[91]

b. Selected Materials on the Non-Arbitrability Doctrine

Excerpted below is the Supreme Court's opinion in *Mitsubishi Motors Corp. v. Soler Chrysler-Plymouth, Inc.* After considering *Mitsubishi*, reread both *Ledee v. Ceramiche Ragno* and *Roby v. Corporation of Lloyd's*.

MITSUBISHI MOTORS CORP. v. SOLER CHRYSLER-PLYMOUTH, INC.

473 U.S. 614 (1985) [also excerpted below at pp. 1032-35]

JUSTICE BLACKMUN. The principal question presented by these cases is the arbitrability, pursuant to the [FAA] and the [New York] Convention of claims aris-

---

85. 346 U.S. at 438.

86. *See* G. Born, *International Commercial Arbitration in the United States* 322-82 (1994).

87. *Alexander v. Gardner-Denver Co.*, 415 U.S. 36 (1974) (Title VII); *Barrentine v. Arkansas-Best Freight System, Inc.*, 450 U.S. 728 (1981) (Fair Labor Standards Act).

88. 417 U.S. 506 (1974).

89. 473 U.S. 614 (1985).

90. *Shearson/American Express, Inc. v. McMahon*, 482 U.S. 220 (1987); *Rodriguez de Quijas v. Shearson/American Express, Inc.*, 490 U.S. 477 (1989) (overruling *Wilko v. Swan*, 346 U.S. 427 (1953)).

91. *Gilmer v. Interstate/Johnson Lane Corp.*, 111 S.Ct. 1647, 1652 (1991).

ing under the Sherman Act, 15 U.S.C. §1 *et seq.*, and encompassed within a valid arbitration clause in an agreement embodying an international commercial transaction.

[Mitsubishi Motors Corporation ("Mitsubishi") is a Japanese corporation that manufactures automobiles in Tokyo, Japan. Mitsubishi is a joint venture between Chrysler International ("CISA"), a Swiss corporation owned by Chrysler Corporation, and Mitsubishi Heavy Industries, a Japanese corporation. Soler Chrysler-Plymouth, Inc. ("Soler"), is a Puerto Rico corporation. Soler entered into a distributor agreement with CISA that provided for the sale by Soler of Mitsubishi-manufactured vehicles within a designated area. At the same time, CISA, Soler, and Mitsubishi entered into a sales procedure agreement ("sales agreement") that provided for the direct sale of Mitsubishi products to Soler and governed the terms and conditions of such sales. Paragraph VI of the Sales Agreement, labeled Arbitration of Certain Matters, provides:

> All disputes, controversies or differences which may arise between [Mitsubishi] and [Soler] out of or in relation to Articles I-B through V of this Agreement or for the breach thereof, shall be finally settled by arbitration in Japan in accordance with the rules and regulations of the Japan Commercial Arbitration Association.

Soler failed to maintain the sales volume specified in its agreements and requested that Mitsubishi delay or cancel shipment of several orders. Mitsubishi and CISA refused, and Mitsubishi later brought an action against Soler in the District of Puerto Rico under the Federal Arbitration Act and the Convention. Mitsubishi sought an order, pursuant to 9 U.S.C. §4 and 206, to compel arbitration. Shortly after filing the complaint, Mitsubishi filed a request for arbitration before the Japan Commercial Arbitration Association seeking damages from Soler for breach of the parties' sales agreement. Soler denied the allegations and counterclaimed against both Mitsubishi and CISA under the Sherman Act; the Puerto Rico competition statute; and the Puerto Rico Dealers' Contract Act. In the counterclaim premised on the Sherman Act, Soler alleged that Mitsubishi and CISA had conspired to divide markets in restraint of trade. The Court of Appeals held that antitrust claims were "non-arbitrable" and permitted Soler's suit to proceed. The Supreme Court initially concluded that the parties' arbitration agreement was broadly enough drafted to encompass Soler's antitrust claims. *See infra* pp. 1032-35.]

We now turn to consider whether Soler's antitrust claims are non-arbitrable even though it has agreed to arbitrate them. In holding that they are not, the Court of Appeals followed the decision of the Second Circuit in *American Safety Equipment Corp. v. J.P. Maguire & Co.*, 391 F.2d 821 (1968). Notwithstanding the absence of any explicit support for such an exception in either the Sherman Act or the [FAA], the Second Circuit there reasoned that "the pervasive public interest in enforcement of the antitrust laws, and the nature of the claims that arise in such cases, combine to make ... antitrust claims ... inappropriate for arbitration." We find it unnecessary to assess the legitimacy of the *American Safety* doctrine as applied to agreements to arbitrate arising from domestic transactions. As in *Scherk v. Alberto-Culver Co.*, 417 U.S. 506 (1974), we conclude that concerns of international comity, respect for the capacities of foreign and transnational tribunals, and sensitivity to the need of the international commercial system for predictability in the resolution of disputes require that we enforce the parties' agreement, even assuming that a contrary result would be forthcoming in a domestic context.

Even before *Scherk*, this Court had recognized the utility of forum selection clauses in international transactions. [One example is the Court's decision in *The Bremen v. Zapata Off-Shore Co.*, 407 U.S. 1 (1972), which] clearly eschewed a provincial solicitude for the jurisdiction of domestic forums. ... *The Bremen* and *Scherk* establish a strong presumption in favor of enforcement of freely negotiated contractual choice-of-forum provisions. Here, as in *Scherk*, that presumption is reinforced by the emphatic federal policy in favor of arbitral dispute resolution. And at least since this Nation's accession in 1970 to the Convention ... that federal policy applies with special force in the field of international commerce. Thus, we must weigh the concerns of *American Safety* against a strong belief in the efficacy of arbitral procedures for the resolution of international commercial disputes and an equal commitment to the enforcement of freely negotiated choice-of-forum clauses.

At the outset, we confess to some skepticism of certain aspects of the *American Safety* doctrine. As distilled by the First Circuit, the doctrine comprises four ingredients [, all of which we find insufficient.] ... [First, the] mere appearance of an antitrust dispute does not alone warrant invalidation of the selected forum on the undemonstrated assumption that the arbitration clause is tainted. A party resisting arbitration of course may attack directly the validity of the agreement to arbitrate. Moreover, the party may attempt to make a showing that would warrant setting aside the forum-selection clause — that the agreement was "[a]ffected by fraud, undue influence, or overweening bargaining power"; that "enforcement would be unreasonable and unjust"; or that proceedings "in the contractual forum will be so gravely difficult and inconvenient that [the resisting party] will for all practical purposes be deprived of his day in court." *The Bremen*, 407 U.S. at 12, 15, 18. But absent such a showing — and none was attempted here — there is no basis for assuming the forum inadequate or its selection unfair.

[Second,] potential complexity should not suffice to ward off arbitration. We might well have some doubt that even the courts following *American Safety* subscribe fully to the view that antitrust matters are inherently insusceptible to resolution by arbitration, as these same courts have agreed that an undertaking to arbitrate antitrust claims entered into after the dispute arises is acceptable. ... [A]daptability and access to expertise are hallmarks of arbitration. The anticipated subject matter of the dispute may be taken into account when the arbitrators are appointed, and arbitral rules typically provide for the participation of experts either employed by the parties or appointed by the tribunal. ...

[Third,] for similar reasons, we also reject the proposition that an arbitration panel will pose too great a danger of innate hostility to the constraints on business conduct that antitrust law imposes. International arbitrators frequently are drawn from the legal as well as the business community; where the dispute has an important legal component, the parties and the arbitral body with whose assistance they have agreed to settle their dispute can be expected to select arbitrators accordingly.

We are left, then, with the core of the *American Safety* doctrine — the fundamental importance to American democratic capitalism of the regime of the antitrust laws. Without doubt, the private cause of action plays a central role in enforcing this regime. ... The treble-damages provision wielded by the private litigant is a chief tool in the antitrust enforcement scheme, posing a crucial deterrent to potential violators. The importance of the private damages remedy, however, does not compel the conclusion that it may not be sought outside an American court. Notwithstanding its important incidental policing function, the treble-damages cause of action conferred on private parties by §4 of the Clayton Act, and pursued by Soler here by way of its third counterclaim, seeks primarily to enable an injured competitor to gain compensation for that injury. "§4 ... is in essence a remedial provision." ...

There is no reason to assume at the outset of the dispute that international arbitration will not provide an adequate mechanism. To be sure, the international arbitral tribunal owes no prior allegiance to the legal norms of particular states; hence, it has no direct obligation to vindicate their statutory dictates. The tribunal, however, is bound to effectuate the intentions of the parties. Where the parties have agreed that the arbitral body is to decide a defined set of claims which includes, as in these cases, those arising from the application of American antitrust law, the tribunal therefore should be bound to decide that dispute in accord with the national law giving rise to the claim.[92] And so long as the prospective litigant effectively may vindicate its statu-

---

92. In addition to the clause providing for arbitration before the Japan Commercial Arbitration Association, the Sales Agreement includes a choice-of-law clause which reads: "This Agreement is made in, and will be governed by and construed in all respects according to the laws of the Swiss Confederation as if entirely performed therein." The United States raises the possibility that the arbitral panel will read this provision not simply to govern interpretation of the contract terms, but wholly to displace American law even where it otherwise would apply. The International Chamber of Commerce opines that it is "[c]onceivabl[e], although we believe it unlikely, [that] the arbitrators could consider Soler's affirmative claim of anticompetitive conduct by CISA and Mitsubishi to fall within the purview of this choice-of-law provision, with the result that it would be decided under Swiss law rather than the U.S. Sherman Act." At oral argument, however, counsel for Mitsubishi conceded that American law applied to the antitrust claims and represented that the claims had been submitted to the arbitration panel in Japan on that basis. The record confirms that before the decision of the Court of Appeals the arbitral panel had taken these claims under submission.

We therefore have no occasion to speculate on this matter at this stage in proceedings, when Mitsubishi seeks to enforce the agreement to arbitrate, not to enforce an award. Nor need we consider now the effect of an arbitral tribunal's failure to take cognizance of the statutory cause of action on the claimant's capacity to reinitiate suit in federal court. We merely note that in the event the choice-of-forum and choice-of-law clauses operated in tandem as a prospective waiver of a party's right to pursue statutory remedies for antitrust violations, we would have little hesitation in condemning the agreement as against public policy.

tory cause of action in the arbitral forum, the statute will continue to serve both its remedial and deterrent function.

Having permitted the arbitration to go forward, the national courts of the United States will have the opportunity at the award enforcement stage to ensure that the legitimate interest in the enforcement of the antitrust laws has been addressed. The Convention reserves to each signatory country the right to refuse enforcement of an award where the "recognition or enforcement of the award would be contrary to the public policy of that country." Article V(2)(b). While the efficacy of the arbitral process requires that substantive review at the award-enforcement stage remain minimal, it would not require intrusive inquiry to ascertain that the tribunal took cognizance of the antitrust claims and actually decided them.[93]

As international trade has expanded in recent decades, so too has the use of international arbitration to resolve disputes arising in the course of that trade. ... If [international arbitral institutions] are to take a central place in the international legal order, national courts will need to "shake off the old judicial hostility to arbitration," and also their customary and understandable unwillingness to cede jurisdiction of a claim arising under domestic law to a foreign or transnational tribunal. To this extent, at least, it will be necessary for national courts to subordinate domestic notions of arbitrability to the international policy favoring commercial arbitration.[94] Accordingly, we "require this representative of the American business community to honor its bargain," by holding this agreement to arbitrate "enforce[able] ... in accord with the explicit provisions of the Arbitration Act."

---

93. We note, for example that the rules of the Japan Commercial Arbitration Association provide for the taking of a "summary" of each hearing, Rule 28.1; for the stenographic recording of the proceedings where the tribunal so orders or a party requests one, Rule 28.2; and for a statement of reasons for the award unless the parties agree otherwise, Rule 36.1(4).

94. We do not quarrel with the Court of Appeals' conclusion that Article II(1) of the Convention, which requires the recognition of agreements to arbitrate that involve "subject matter capable of settlement by arbitration," contemplates exceptions to arbitrability grounded in domestic law. And it appears that before acceding to the Convention the Senate was advised by a State Department memorandum that the Convention provided for such exceptions.

In acceding to the Convention the Senate restricted its applicability to commercial matters, in accord with Article I(3). Yet in implementing the Convention by amendments to the Federal Arbitration Act, Congress did not specify any matters it intended to exclude from its scope. In *Scherk*, this Court recited Article II(1), including the language relied upon by the Court of Appeals, but paid heed to the Convention delegates' "frequent[ly voiced] concern that courts of signatory countries in which an agreement to arbitrate is sought to be enforced should not be permitted to decline enforcement of such agreements on the basis of parochial views of their desirability or in a manner that would diminish the mutually binding nature of the agreements." There, moreover, the Court dealt *arguendo* with an exception to arbitrability grounded in express congressional language; here, in contrast, we face a judicially implied exception. The utility of the Convention in promoting the process of international commercial arbitration depends upon the willingness of national courts to let go of matters they normally would think of as their own. Doubtless, Congress may specify categories of claims it wishes to reserve for decision by our own courts without contravening this Nation's obligations under the Convention. But we decline to subvert the spirit of the United States' accession to the Convention by recognizing subject-matter exceptions where Congress has not expressly directed the courts to do so.

JUSTICE STEVENS, dissenting. This Court's holding rests almost exclusively on the federal policy favoring arbitration of commercial disputes and vague notions of international comity arising from the fact that the automobiles involved here were manufactured in Japan. I respectfully dissent. ... [First, the parties' arbitration agreement does not encompass Soler's antitrust claims, *see infra* pp. 1032-35.] ...

[The] Court has repeatedly held that a decision by Congress to create a special statutory remedy renders a private agreement to arbitrate a federal statutory claim unenforceable. Thus, ... the express statutory remedy provided in the Ku Klux Act of 1871, the express statutory remedy in the Securities Act of 1933, the express statutory remedy in the Fair Labor Standards Act, and the express statutory remedy in Title VII of the Civil Rights Act of 1964, each provided the Court with convincing evidence that Congress did not intend the protections afforded by the statute to be administered by a private arbitrator. The reasons that motivated those decisions apply with special force to the federal policy that is protected by the antitrust laws. ... It was Chief Justice Hughes who characterized the Sherman Antitrust Act as "a charter of freedom" that may fairly be compared to a constitutional provision. *See Appalachian Coals, Inc. v. United States*, 228 U.S. 344, 359-360 (1933).

In view of the history of antitrust enforcement in the United States, it is not surprising that all of the federal courts that have considered the question have uniformly and unhesitatingly concluded that agreements to arbitrate federal antitrust issues are not enforceable. In a landmark opinion for the Court of Appeals for the Second Circuit, Judge Feinberg wrote:

> A claim under the antitrust laws is not merely a private matter. The Sherman Act is designed to promote the national interest in a competitive economy; thus, the plaintiff asserting his rights under the Act has been likened to a private attorney-general who protects the public's interest. ... Antitrust violations can affect hundreds of thousands — perhaps millions — of people and inflict staggering economic damage. ... We do not believe that Congress intended such claims to be resolved elsewhere than in the courts. ... [I]t is also proper to ask whether contracts of adhesion between alleged monopolists and their customers should determine the forum for trying antitrust violations. *American Safety Equipment Corp. v. J. P. Maguire & Co.*, 391 F.2d 821, 826-827 (1968) (footnote omitted).

This Court would be well advised to endorse the collective wisdom of the distinguished judges of the Courts of Appeals who have unanimously concluded that the statutory remedies fashioned by Congress for the enforcement of the antitrust laws render an agreement to arbitrate antitrust disputes unenforceable. Arbitration awards are only reviewable for manifest disregard of the law, 9 U.S.C. §§10, 207, and the rudimentary procedures which make arbitration so desirable in the context of a private dispute often mean that the record is so inadequate that the arbitrator's decision is virtually unreviewable.[95] Despotic decision making of this kind is fine for parties who are willing to agree in advance to settle for a best approximation of the correct result in order to resolve quickly and inexpensively any contractual dispute that may arise in an ongoing commercial relationship. Such informality, however, is simply unacceptable when every error may have devastating consequences for important businesses in our national economy and may undermine their ability to compete in world markets.[96] Instead of "muffling a grievance in the cloakroom of arbitration," the public interest in free competitive markets would be better served by having the issues resolved "in the light of impartial public court adjudication."[97]

The Court assumes for the purposes of its decision that the antitrust issues would not be arbitrable if this were a purely domestic dispute, but holds that the international character of the controversy makes it arbitrable. The holding rests on vague concerns for the international implications of its decision and a misguided application of *Scherk*. Before relying on its own notions of what international comity requires, it is surprising that the Court does not determine the specific commitments that the United States has made to enforce private agreements to arbitrate disputes arising under public law. As the Court acknowledges, the only treaty relevant here is the [New York Convention]. ... However, the United States, as *amicus curiae*, advises the Court that the Convention "clearly contemplates" that signatory nations will enforce domestic laws prohibiting the arbitration of certain subject matters. This interpretation is ... beyond doubt.

Article II(3) of the Convention ... [does not apply] (i) if the agreement "is null and void, inoperative or incapable of being performed," Article II(3), or (ii) if the dispute does not concern "a subject matter capable of settlement by arbitration," Article II(1). ... The latter clause plainly suggests the possibility that some subject matters are not capable of arbitration under the domestic laws of the signatory nations, and that agreements to arbitrate such disputes need not be enforced. ... [Moreover, if] an arbitration award is "contrary to the public policy of [a] country" called upon to enforce it, or if it concerns a subject matter which is "not capable of

---

95. The arbitration procedure in this case does not provide any right to evidentiary discovery or a written decision, and requires that all proceedings be closed to the public. Moreover, Japanese arbitrators do not have the power of compulsory process to secure witnesses and documents, nor do witnesses who are available testify under oath. *Cf.* 9 U.S.C. §7 (arbitrators may summon witnesses to attend proceedings and seek enforcement in a district court).

96. The great risk, of course, is that the arbitrator will condemn business practices under the antitrust laws that are efficient in a free competitive market. *Cf. Northwest Wholesale Stationers, Inc. v. Pacific Stationery & Printing Co.*, 472 U.S. 284 (1985), *rev'g*, 715 F.2d 1393 (9th Cir. 1983). In the absence of a reviewable record, a reviewing district court would not be able to undo the damage wrought. Even a Government suit or an action by a private party might not be available to set aside the award.

97. The Court notes that some courts which have held that agreements to arbitrate antitrust claims generally are unenforceable have nevertheless enforced arbitration agreements to settle an existing antitrust claim. These settlement agreements, made after the parties have had every opportunity to evaluate the strength of their position, are obviously less destructive of the private treble-damages remedy that Congress provided. Thus, it may well be that arbitration as a means of settling disputes is permissible.

settlement by arbitration under the law of that country," the Convention does not require that it be enforced. Articles V(2)(a) and (b). Thus, reading Articles II and V together, the Convention provides that agreements to arbitrate disputes which are non-arbitrable under domestic law need not be honored, nor awards rendered under them enforced.[98]

It is clear then that the international obligations of the United States permit us to honor Congress' commitment to the exclusive resolution of antitrust disputes in the federal courts. The Court today refuses to do so, offering only vague concerns for comity among nations. The courts of other nations, on the other hand, have applied the exception provided in the Convention, and refused to enforce agreements to arbitrate specific subject matters of concern to them.[99] It may be that the subject-matter exception to the Convention ought to be reserved — as a matter of domestic law — for matters of the greatest public interest which involve concerns that are shared by other nations. The Sherman Act's commitment to free competitive markets is among our most important civil policies. This commitment, shared by other nations which are signatory to the Convention, is hardly the sort of parochial concern that we should decline to enforce in the interest of international comity. ... [*Scherk v. Alberto-Culver Co.* is not relevant. In *Scherk*, the Court] based its decision on the [fact] that the outcome in *Wilko* was governed entirely by American law whereas in *Scherk* foreign rules of law would control and, if the arbitration clause were not enforced, a host of international conflict-of-laws problems would arise. ... That distinction fits this case precisely, since I consider it perfectly clear that the rules of American antitrust law must govern the claim of an American automobile dealer that he has been injured by an international conspiracy to restrain trade in the American automobile market. ... The merits of those claims are controlled entirely by American law. ... When Mitsubishi enters the American market and plans to engage in business in that market over a period of years, it must recognize its obligation to comply with American law and to be subject to the remedial provisions of American statutes. ...

LEDEE v. CERAMICHE RAGNO

684 F.2d 184 (1st Cir. 1982) [excerpted above at pp. 999-1001]

---

98. Indeed, it has been argued that a state may refuse to enforce an agreement to arbitrate subject matter which is non-arbitrable in domestic law under Article II(3) as well as under Article II(1). Since awards rendered under such agreements need not be enforced under Article V(2) the agreement is "incapable of being performed." Article II(3).

99. For example, the Cour de Cassation in Belgium has held that disputes arising under a Belgian statute limiting the unilateral termination of exclusive distributorships are not arbitrable under the Convention in that country, *Audi-NSU Auto Union A.G. v. SA Adelin Petit & Cie.* (1979), in 5 Yearbook Commercial Arbitration 257, 259 (1980), and the Corte di Cassazione in Italy has held that labor disputes are not arbitrable under the Convention in that country, *Compagnia Generale Construzioni v. Persanti*, [1980] Foro Italiano I 190, in 6 Yearbook Commercial Arbitration 229, 230 (1981).

ROBY v. CORPORATION OF LLOYD'S

996 F.2d 1353 (2d Cir. 1993) [excerpted above at pp. 418-23]

Notes on Mitsubishi, Ledee, and Roby

1. *New York Convention's exception for matters "not capable of settlement by arbitration."* Could the Supreme Court, consistently with the New York Convention, have held that federal antitrust claims are *not* arbitrable? In footnotes, *Mitsubishi* acknowledged that the Convention does not *require* enforcement of agreements to arbitrate a "subject matter [not] capable of settlement by arbitration." Moreover, the Court was of the view in *Mitsubishi* that the Convention would not have prohibited a holding that antitrust claims were non-arbitrable. Is that correct?

Consider the court's opinion in *Ledee*. What is its view of the Convention's limits on national "non-arbitrability" defenses? How would *Mitsubishi* have been decided under the *Ledee* rationale? Suppose that the antitrust laws specifically forbid arbitration of treble damages actions. Would *Ledee* give effect to those provisions?

2. *Law governing non-arbitrability under New York Convention.* What law governs the question of non-arbitrability when a U.S. court considers a claim that an international arbitration agreement, subject to the New York Convention, should not be enforced? What law did the Court look to in *Mitsubishi?* See A. van den Berg, *The New York Convention of 1958* 153 (1981) ("all courts [have] decided the question of arbitrability exclusively under their own law and [have] not take[n] account of the law of the country where the arbitration was to take place or was taking place").

Mitsubishi involved the arbitrability of *U.S.* statutory claims. What nation's standard would *Mitsubishi* have looked to if *foreign* statutory claims were at issue? Suppose, for example, that a U.S. court was asked to compel arbitration of competition law claims under European Union and German law. Would U.S. law apply? Or would EU and German rules of non-arbitrability apply?

Mitsubishi could have concluded that Article II itself contained or referred to some international standard of arbitrability. That was apparently the approach in *Ledee. See also Riley v. Kingsley Underwriting Agencies, Ltd.*, 969 F.2d 953 (10th Cir. 1992); *Meadows Indemnity Co. Ltd. v. Baccala & Shoop Ins. Serv., Inc.*, 1991 U.S. Dist. Lexis 4144 (E.D.N.Y. 1991) ("The determination of whether a type of claim is 'not capable of settlement by arbitration' under Article II(1) must be made on an international scale, with reference to the laws of the countries party to the Convention."). Reconsider the hypothetical above concerning EU and German competition law. What result would be reached under *Ledee's* analysis?

3. *Mitsubishi's rationale for non-arbitrability doctrine. Mitsubishi* concluded that particular federal statutory claims were arbitrable. If the Convention does not *require* arbitration of antitrust claims, should the Court have done so? Consider the following explanation from *Mitsubishi*:

> The utility of the Convention in promoting the process of international commercial arbitration depends upon the willingness of national courts to let go of matters they normally would think of as their own. ... [W]e decline to subvert the spirit of the United States' accession to the Convention by recognizing subject matter exceptions where Congress has not expressly directed the courts to do so.

Is that persuasive? Consider the reasons advanced for the *American Safety* doctrine. Do they not strongly support application of the non-arbitrability doctrine to antitrust claims? Recall the treatment of antitrust claims under forum selection clauses and the forum non conveniens doctrine. *See supra* pp. 341-57 & 414-30. Why should arbitration agreements be treated differently?

4. *International/domestic distinction. Mitsubishi* held that an arbitration clause contained in an international contract was enforceable, even as to federal antitrust claims. The Court expressly refused to decide whether the same result would apply in a purely domestic context, rather than in "an international commercial transaction." The Court based its decision to treat international and domestic transactions differently on the New York Convention's "spirit" and on "concerns of international comity, respect for the capacities of foreign and transnational tribunals, and sensitivity to the need of the international commercial system for predictability in the resolution of disputes." Is this a persuasive rationale?

After *Mitsubishi*, the characterization of a contract as "international," rather than domestic, may be of importance in determining the arbitrability of at least some types of statutory claims. However, recent

Supreme Court decisions indicate a readiness to enforce most arbitration agreements, even in the purely domestic context. *See Shearson American Express v. McMahon*, 482 U.S. 220 (1987) (Securities Exchange Act and RICO claims arbitrable, even in purely domestic context); *Rodriguez de Quijas v. Shearson/American Express, Inc.*, 490 U.S. 477 (1989) (Securities Act claims arbitrable).

5. *Criticism of* Mitsubishi. Although the Court's decision was applauded by the arbitration community, *Mitsubishi* also provoked criticism:

> if such fundamental issues as antitrust matters (and RICO claims) can be submitted to arbitration, what possible limits could there be to the reach of arbitrability in the international ... context? The confusing and potentially dangerous shift of domestic public law concerns to the enforcement stage is likely to be ineffectual, destined to act as the shadow of a safeguard rather than a genuine means of protection. ... The Court's rush to eradicate all national legal constraints not only compromises legitimate national concerns, but also threatens the integrity of international arbitral adjudication itself, frustrating its normal tendency to seek guidance and appropriate limits from external factors.

Carbonneau, *The Exuberant Pathway to Quixotic Internationalism: Assessing the Folly of Mitsubishi*, 19 Vand. J. Trans. L. 263, 297-98 (1986). Is this persuasive? Was *Mitsubishi* correctly decided?

6. *Procedural efficacy of arbitration of "public law" claims.* Does the arbitration process allow for adequate presentation and consideration of securities, antitrust, and other public law claims? Note the various aspects of arbitration (much valued by its proponents) which trouble the dissent in *Mitsubishi* — lack of appeal, confidentiality, lack of U.S.-style discovery, non-judicial decisionmaker, informal rules of evidence, and (frequently, in the United States) the absence of a reasoned award. Even if these features of arbitration do not amount to what Justice Stevens uncharitably terms "despotic decision-making" in *Mitsubishi*, do they render arbitration inadequate for resolving "public" law claims? If so, is it because arbitrators are more likely than judges to make mistakes in applying public law claims? Is this risk greater for public law claims than private law claims? What are the broader economic and social consequences of errors in each case? For the Supreme Court's current view of these issues, *see Shearson/American Express, Inc. v. McMahon*, 482 U.S. 220 (1987) ("the mistrust of arbitration that formed the basis for the *Wilko* opinion in 1953 is difficult to square with the assessment of arbitration that has prevailed since that time").

7. *Future v. existing disputes.* The majority in *Mitsubishi* reasons that, if arbitration can satisfactorily resolve an *existing* dispute, then there is no reason that arbitral procedures cannot suffice for *future* disputes. How does Justice Stevens reply to this? Is his answer persuasive?

8. *Showing required for non-arbitrability after* Mitsubishi. *Mitsubishi* acknowledged that "[d]oubtless, Congress may specify categories of claims it wishes to reserve for decision by our own Courts without contravening ... the Convention." Nonetheless, *Mitsubishi* formulated a high standard for holding a statutory claim non-arbitrable: "We must assume that if Congress intended the substantive protection afforded by a given statute to include protection against waiver of the right to a judicial forum, that intention will be deducible from text or legislative history." The Court also said that claims will be deemed arbitrable unless Congress "expressly directed" a contrary result. Why is such a high standard of proof required?

9. Mitsubishi's *treatment of choice-of-law clause excluding U.S. public policy or statutory claims.* How will a U.S. court asked to enforce an arbitral award dealing with U.S. antitrust claims react if the tribunal refuses to apply U.S. law? In a footnote, *Mitsubishi* strongly suggests that, where antitrust claims are concerned, such an arbitration agreement would not be enforced by U.S. courts: "in the event the choice-of-forum and choice-of-law clauses operated in tandem as a prospective waiver of a party's right to pursue statutory remedies for antitrust violations, we would have little hesitation in condemning the agreement as against public policy." Consider the parties' choice of law clause in *Mitsubishi*. Why did it not amount to a prospective waiver of U.S. antitrust claims? Compare the public policy exceptions to forum selection and choice of law agreements. *See supra* pp. 414-30 & pp. 662-63.

10. *Treatment of public policy and statutory claims under* Mitsubishi *and* Bremen — *a comparison.* Is *Mitsubishi's* treatment of "prospective waivers" of statutory claims consistent with the result in *Bremen v. Zapata Off-Shore Co.*, 407 U.S. 1 (1972)? In *Bremen*, the Court enforced a forum selection clause where the foreign forum would not apply U.S. law (which included important protections for the plaintiff that were imposed by U.S. public policy). Note, however, that *Bremen* emphasized that the case involved a dispute arising from activities conducted outside the United States. Note also that *Bremen* suggested, and

some lower courts have held, that, as to "essentially American" disputes, forum selection clauses that result in a waiver of substantive statutory rights are not enforceable. *See supra* pp. 429-30.

Suppose *Mitsubishi* had involved conduct having little or no relation to the United States — a distributorship termination in Canada or Mexico, for example. Would the Court still forbid forum selection/choice-of-law clauses that excluded the U.S. antitrust laws? Why should this hypothetical be treated differently from the actual facts in *Mitsubishi*? Suppose *Mitsubishi* had involved conduct with equally substantial connections to both the United States and Japan? How would *Bremen* have treated activities with this sort of U.S. nexus?

Should substantive statutory claims be "waivable" to the same extent in the context of arbitration as in the context of judicial forum selection clauses? How would a forum selection clause applicable to antitrust claims be enforced? Recall the treatment of antitrust claims in the forum non conveniens context. *See supra* pp. 354-55.

11. *Interpretation of choice-of-law clauses affecting public law claims.* Is it clear that the Swiss choice-of-law clause in *Mitsubishi* or the English choice-of-law clause in *Roby* was meant to exclude U.S. antitrust or securities law claims? Should a court ordinarily err on the side of extending ambiguous clauses to exclude, or leave standing, public law claims?

12. *The* Roby *decision.* Is the Second Circuit's decision in *Roby* consistent with *Mitsubishi*?

(a) *Prospective waivers of federal statutory rights.* How does the *Roby* decision comport with *Mitsubishi*'s treatment of "prospective waivers" of antitrust rights? Is it possible that securities law claims are simply entitled to less protection under U.S. law than antitrust claims? Note that although the securities laws contain provisions specifically forbidding waivers of their protections, *see Wilko v. Swan, supra,* no analogous provision exists under the antitrust laws.

(b) *Importance of comparable foreign remedies.* Under the *Roby* analysis, how is a U.S. court to conclude that foreign law and remedies are comparable to U.S. ones? Is it likely that Congress intended such a test for arbitrability? In *Scherk,* Justice Douglas wrote in dissent: "When a foreign corporation undertakes fraudulent action which subjects it to the jurisdiction of our federal securities laws, nothing justifies the conclusion that only a diluted version of those laws protects American investors." Does *Roby* permit such dilution?

(c) *Roby's analysis.* Note *Roby's* reliance on *Piper Aircraft,* a forum non conveniens decision involving state law claims. Is it persuasive to cite the "adequate alternative forum" requirement for diversity claims in cases involving federal law claims with specific anti-waiver provisions?

Roby also relies heavily on *Bremen,* which rejected an argument that enforcing a forum selection clause would result in the application of English law, which would enforce an exculpatory clause that was not enforceable, on public policy grounds, in the United States. As discussed above, however, *Bremen* emphasized that the case involved conduct occurring outside the United States and a public policy applicable only within the United States. In contrast, in *Roby* the defendants' allegedly unlawful conduct occurred within the United States and was, by hypothesis, plainly subject to the U.S. securities laws.

13. Mitsubishi *revisited in the light of* Roby. What does *Roby* imply about the treatment of antitrust claims in international arbitration? Suppose, for example, that two companies agree expressly to the application of Japanese (or European Union) competition laws to a course of conduct that takes place in, and affects, both the United States and either Japan or Europe? Would it matter what the content of those laws was, and how they compared with U.S. antitrust laws? What does *Roby* suggest about the enforceability of such clauses? Does *Roby's* holding extend to antitrust claims and other U.S. public law claims? Given the anti-waiver provisions of §29 of the 1934 Act, can any less stringent standard apply to the securities laws than to the antitrust laws?

14. *"Second look" doctrine — judicial review of arbitral panel's application of U.S. antitrust law.* In requiring arbitration of antitrust claims, *Mitsubishi* relies in significant part on the ability of U.S. courts to take a "second look" at the award: "Having permitted the arbitration to go forward, the national courts of the United States will have the opportunity at the award-enforcement stage to ensure that the legitimate interest in the enforcement of the antitrust laws has been addressed." Moreover, the Court indicated that nonrecognition of an award would be appropriate if the tribunal did not take "cognizance of the antitrust claims and actually decide[] them." *Mitsubishi* also indicated, however, that a U.S. court reviewing the arbitral panel's decision should engage in only "minimal" "substantive review." This is consistent with U.S. law regarding the enforcement of domestic arbitral awards, which at most only permits nonenforcement for a panel's "manifest disregard of law." *See infra* pp. 1048-49.

On the other hand, is it realistic to expect U.S. courts to defer almost entirely to decisions of private (often foreign) arbitrators on questions involving vital local public policies? *See* Craig, *Uses and Abuses of Appeal From Awards*, 4 Arb. Int'l 174, 215-16 (1988) ("However minimal, such second looks will happen because of the extreme sensitivity of the matters currently referred to private decisionmaking."); Park, *Private Adjudicators and the Public Interest: The Expanding Scope of International Arbitration*, 12 Brook. J. Int'l L. 629, 642 (1986) ("The 'second look' doctrine is a problematic safety valve for ensuring that public law issues receive proper consideration. If it calls for review on the merits, it disrupts the arbitral process. But if it calls only for a mechanical examination of the face of the award, it may not provide an effective check on an arbitrator who mentions the Sherman Act before he proceeds to ignore it.").

4. Interpretation of International Commercial Arbitration Agreements

Where a valid arbitration agreement concerning arbitrable disputes exists, determining whether particular claims or disputes are subject to arbitration is principally a matter of interpreting the relevant contractual provisions. "[T]he first task of a court asked to compel arbitration is to determine whether the parties agreed to arbitrate that dispute."[100]

Disputes frequently arise concerning the "scope" of the parties' arbitration agreement: that is, what category of disputes or claims have the parties agreed to submit to arbitration? Under the FAA, parties are generally free to provide for arbitration of no disputes, some contractual disputes, all contractual disputes, or virtually all disputes (contractual, tort, or otherwise) connected to their relationship.[101]

Questions concerning the scope of arbitration agreements raise choice of law issues — what national law governs the construction of the arbitration clause. In interpreting international arbitration agreements under the FAA, U.S. courts have generally applied a federal common law rule of contract interpretation that is expressly and vigorously "pro-arbitration." In the Supreme Court's words, "questions of arbitrability must be addressed with a healthy regard for the federal policy favoring arbitration [and] any doubts concerning the scope of arbitrable issues should be resolved in favor of arbitration."[102] Federal courts have generally applied this federal common law of contract interpretation, albeit without considered analysis, even when the parties' agreement selects a foreign or state governing law.[103]

U.S. courts have adopted divergent approaches to the respective roles of the arbitrators and national courts in interpreting arbitration agreements. Some U.S. courts appear to take the view, albeit not consistently or particularly clearly, that the interpretation of the scope of an arbitration agreement is, in the first instance, a matter for the arbitral tribunal, and only thereafter is judicial review appropriate.[104] In contrast, other U.S. courts have held that the resolution of disputes about arbitrability are for the courts, not for the arbitrators: "the question of arbitrability ... is unde-

---

100. *See Mitsubishi Motors Corp. v. Soler Chrysler- Plymouth, Inc.*, 473 U.S. 614, 626 (1985).

101. *See supra* pp. 994-98 & 1016-18.

102. *Moses H. Cone Mem. Hosp. v. Mercury Construction Corp.*, 460 U.S. 1, 24-25 (1983). *See Mitsubishi Motors Corp. v. Soler Chrysler-Plymouth Inc.*, 473 U.S. 614 (1985).

103. *See, e.g., Becker Autoradio U.S.A., Inc. v. Becker Autoradiowerk GmbH*, 585 F.2d 39, 43-44 & n.8 (3d Cir. 1978), discussed at *supra* p. 1012.

104. *See* cases cited *infra* pp. 1035-36.

niably an issue for judicial determination."[105] In both cases, the tribunal's jurisdictional decisions are ultimately subject to judicial review in actions to confirm, vacate or enforce the arbitrators' award, including for excess of authority under Article V(1)(c) of the New York Convention and §10(d) of the domestic FAA.[106]

Excerpted below are materials that illustrate prevailing U.S. judicial approaches to the interpretation of arbitration agreements. *Apollo Computer* is an example of judicial deference to jurisdictional rulings of an arbitral tribunal, while *Mitsubishi* suggests a greater judicial role.

APOLLO COMPUTER, INC. v. BERG

886 F.2d 469 (1st Cir. 1989)

TORRUELLA, CIRCUIT JUDGE. The plaintiff appeals from a district court order refusing its request for a permanent stay of arbitration proceedings. ... Apollo Computer, Inc. ("Apollo") and Dicoscan Distributed Computing Scandinavia AB ("Dico") entered into an agreement granting Dico, a Swedish company having its principal place of business in Stockholm, the right to distribute Apollo's computers in four Scandinavian countries. Helge Berg and Lars Arvid Skoog, the defendants in this action, signed the agreement on Dico's behalf in their respective capacities as its chairman and president. The agreement contained a clause stating that all disputes arising out of or in connection with the agreement would be settled in accordance with the Rules of Arbitration of the International Chamber of Commerce ("ICC"), and another clause that stated that the agreement was to be governed by Massachusetts law. The agreement also provided that it could not be assigned by Dico without the written consent of Apollo.

In September 1984, after disputes relating to the financing of Dico's purchases, Apollo notified Dico that it intended to terminate the agreement, effective immediately. Dico then filed for protection from its creditors under Swedish bankruptcy law and subsequently entered into liquidation, with its affairs being handled by its trustee in bankruptcy. The trustee assigned Dico's right to bring claims for damages against Apollo to the defendants. In May 1988, the defendants filed a complaint and a request for arbitration with the ICC.

On August 24, 1988, Apollo rejected arbitration, claiming that there was no agreement to arbitrate between it and the defendants, and that assignment of Dico's contractual right to arbitrate was precluded by the agreement's nonassignment clause. The ICC requested both parties to submit briefs on the issue. On December 15, 1988, the ICC's Court of Arbitration decided that pursuant to its rules, the arbitrator should resolve the issue of arbitrability, and directed the parties to commence arbitration proceedings to resolve that issue and, if necessary, the merits.

---

105. *AT&T Technologies, Inc. v. Communications Workers of America*, 475 U.S. 643, 649 (1986); *John Wiley & Sons, Inc. v. Livingston*, 376 U.S. 543, 546 (1964). *See infra* pp. 1035-36.

106. For discussion of judicial review of arbitrators' jurisdictional decisions, *see infra* pp. 1051-52.

On January 11, 1989, Apollo filed the instant action in federal district court under diversity of citizenship jurisdiction. It sought a permanent stay of the arbitration, pursuant to M.G.L. ch. 251, §2(b), on the grounds that there is no arbitration agreement between the parties. ... Apollo then moved for summary judgment. On May 11, 1989, the district court denied the request to stay arbitration and the motion for summary judgment...

The district court first decided that the parties had explicitly agreed to have the issue of arbitrability decided by the arbitrator. Notwithstanding this conclusion, the court then proceeded to analyze the issue of arbitrability itself. It determined that Dico would have the right to seek arbitration of the underlying claims if it had pursued them on its own behalf. The only remaining issue, the court reasoned, was whether the agreement's nonassignment clause prevented the defendants from asserting Dico's right to arbitrate. The court ruled that it did not because under Massachusetts law, a general nonassignment clause will be construed as barring only the delegation of duties, not the assignment of rights. ...

We ... find that the parties contracted to submit issues of arbitrability to the arbitrator. There is no question that this contract falls under the aegis of the [FAA]. Both parties agree that under the [FAA], the *general* rule is that the arbitrability of a dispute is to be determined by the court. Parties may, however, agree to allow the arbitrator to decide both whether a particular dispute is arbitrable as well as the merits of the dispute. *See Necchi*, 348 F.2d at 696.

In this case, the parties agreed that all disputes arising out of or in connection with their contract would be settled by binding arbitration "in accordance with the rules of arbitration of the International Chamber of Commerce." Article 8.3 of the ICC's Rules of Arbitration states:

> Should one of the parties raise one or more pleas concerning the existence or validity of the agreement to arbitrate, and should the [Court of Arbitration of the International Chamber of Commerce] be satisfied of the *prima facie* existence of such an agreement, the [Court of Arbitration of the International Chamber of Commerce] may, without prejudice to the admissibility or merits of the plea or pleas, decide that the arbitration shall proceed. In such a case, any decision as to the arbitrator's jurisdiction shall be taken by the arbitrator himself.

Article 8.4 of the ICC's Rules of Arbitration states:

> Unless otherwise provided, the arbitrator shall not cease to have jurisdiction by reason of any claim that the contract is null and void or allegation that it is inexistent provided that he upholds the validity of the agreement to arbitrate. He shall continue to have jurisdiction, even though the contract itself may be inexistent or null and void, to determine the respective rights of the parties and to adjudicate upon their claims and pleas.

The contract therefore delegates to the arbitrator decisions about the arbitrability of disputes involving the existence and validity of a *prima facie* agreement to arbitrate. Both the ICC's Court of Arbitration and the district court determined that a *prima facie* agreement to arbitrate existed. Therefore, they reasoned, Article 8.3 requires the arbitrator to determine the validity of the arbitration agreement in this specific instance — in other words, decide whether the arbitration agreement applies to disputes between Apollo and the assignees of Dico.

Apollo did not discuss this issue in its brief. At oral argument, it averred that Article 8.3 is inapplicable because no *prima facie* agreement to arbitrate exists between it and the defendants. We are unpersuaded by this argument. The relevant agreement here is the one between Apollo and Dico. The defendants claim that Dico's right to compel arbitration under that agreement has been assigned to them. We find that they have made the *prima facie* showing required by Article 8.3. Whether the right to compel arbitration survives the termination of the agreement, and if so, whether that right was validly assigned to the defendants and whether it can be enforced by them against Apollo are issues relating to the continued existence and validity of the agreement.

Ordinarily, Apollo would be entitled to have these issues resolved by a court. By contracting to have all disputes resolved according to the Rules of the ICC, however, Apollo agreed to be bound by Articles 8.3 and 8.4. These provisions clearly and unmistakably allow the arbitrator to determine her own jurisdiction when, as here, there exists a *prima facie* agreement to arbitrate whose continued existence and validity is being questioned. The arbitrator should decide whether a valid arbitration agreement exists between Apollo and the defendants under the terms of the contract between Apollo and Dico. Consequently, without expressing any opinion on the merits of the issues raised by Apollo, we affirm the district court's order denying a permanent stay of the arbitration proceedings.

MITSUBISHI MOTORS CORP. v. SOLER CHRYSLER-PLYMOUTH, INC.

473 U.S. 614 (1985) [also excerpted above at pp. 1018-25]

JUSTICE BLACKMUN. [The facts and arbitration clause are set forth above.][107] ... At the outset, we address the contention raised in Soler's cross-petition that the arbitration clause at issue may not be read to encompass the statutory counterclaims

---

107. The District Court found that the arbitration clause did not cover the fourth and six counterclaims, which sought damages for defamation, or the allegations in the seventh counterclaim concerning discriminatory treatment and the establishment of minimum-sales volumes. Accordingly, it retained jurisdiction over those portions of the litigation. In addition, because no arbitration agreement between Soler and CISA existed, the court retained jurisdiction, insofar as they sought relief from CISA, over the first, second, third and ninth counterclaims, which raised claims under the Puerto Rico Dealers' Contracts Act, the federal Automobile Dealers' Day in Court Act, the Sherman Act, and the Puerto Rico competition statute, respectively. These aspects of the District Court's ruling were not appealed and are not before this Court.

stated in its answer to the complaint. In making this argument, Soler does not question the Court of Appeals' application of Paragraph VI of the Sales Agreement to the disputes involved here as a matter of standard contract interpretation.[108] Instead, it argues that as a matter of law a court may not construe an arbitration agreement to encompass claims arising out of statutes designed to protect a class to which the party resisting arbitration belongs "unless [that party] has expressly agreed" to arbitrate those claims, by which Soler presumably means that the arbitration clause must specifically mention the statute giving rise to the claims that a party to the clause seeks to arbitrate. ...

We do not agree, for we find no warrant in the [FAA] for implying in every contract within its ken a presumption against arbitration of statutory claims. The Act's centerpiece provision makes a written agreement to arbitrate "in any maritime transaction or a contract evidencing a transaction involving commerce ... valid, irrevocable, and enforceable, save upon such grounds as exist at law or in equity for the revocation of any contract." 9 U.S.C. §2. The "liberal federal policy favoring arbitration agreements," *Moses H. Cone Memorial Hospital v. Mercury Construction Corp.*, 460 U.S. 1, 24 (1983), manifested by this provision and the Act as a whole, is at bottom a policy guaranteeing the enforcement of private contractual arrangements: the Act simply "creates a body of federal substantive law establishing and regulating the duty to honor an agreement to arbitrate." ...

Accordingly, the first task of a court asked to compel arbitration of a dispute is to determine whether the parties agreed to arbitrate that dispute. The court is to make this determination by applying the "federal substantive law of arbitrability, applicable to any arbitration agreement within the coverage of the Act." And that body of law counsels

> that questions of arbitrability must be addressed with a healthy regard for the federal policy favoring arbitration. ... The Arbitration Act establishes that, as a matter of federal law, any doubts concerning the scope of arbitrable issues should be resolved in favor of arbitration, whether the problem at hand is the construction of the contract language itself or an allegation of waiver, delay, or a like defense to arbitrability.

Thus, as with any other contract, the parties' intentions control, but those intentions are generously construed as to issues of arbitrability. There is no reason to depart from these guidelines where a party bound by an arbitration agreement raises claims

---

108. ... Soler does suggest that, because the title of the clause referred only to "certain matters," and the clause itself specifically referred only to "Articles I-B through V," it should be read narrowly to exclude the statutory claims. Soler ignores the inclusion within those "certain matters" of "[a]ll disputes, controversies or differences which may arise between [Mitsubishi] and [Soler] out of or in relation to [the specified provisions] or for the breach thereof." Contrary to Soler's suggestion, the exclusion of some areas of possible dispute from the scope of an arbitration clause does not serve to restrict the reach of an otherwise broad clause in the areas in which it was intended to operate. Thus, insofar as the allegations underlying the statutory claims touch matters covered by the enumerated articles, the Court of Appeals properly resolved any doubts in favor of arbitrability."

founded on statutory rights, [*Wilko v. Swan*, 346 U.S. 427 (1953), and] the Act itself provides no basis for disfavoring agreements to arbitrate statutory claims by skewing the otherwise hospitable inquiry into arbitrability.

That is not to say that all controversies implicating statutory rights are suitable for arbitration. There is no reason to distort the process of contract interpretation, however, in order to ferret out the inappropriate. Just as it is the congressional policy manifested in the [FAA] that requires courts liberally to construe the scope of arbitration agreements covered by that Act, it is the congressional intention expressed in some other statute on which the courts must rely to identify any category of claims as to which agreements to arbitrate will be held unenforceable. For that reason, Soler's concern for statutorily protected classes provides no reason to color the lens through which the arbitration clause is read. By agreeing to arbitrate a statutory claim, a party does not forgo the substantive rights afforded by the statute; it only submits to their resolution in an arbitral, rather than a judicial, forum. It trades the procedures and opportunity for review of the courtroom for the simplicity, informality, and expedition of arbitration. We must assume that if Congress intended the substantive protection afforded by a given statute to include protection against waiver of the right to a judicial forum, that intention will be deducible from text or legislative history. ...

JUSTICE STEVENS, dissenting. ... [First,] as a matter of ordinary contract interpretation, there are at least two reasons why that clause does not apply to Soler's antitrust claim against Chrysler and Mitsubishi. First, the clause only applies to two-party disputes between Soler and Mitsubishi. The antitrust violation alleged in Soler's counterclaim is a three-party dispute. Soler has joined both Chrysler and its associated company, Mitsubishi, as counterdefendants. ... Only by stretching the language of the arbitration clause far beyond its ordinary meaning could one possibly conclude that it encompasses this three-party dispute.

Second, the clause only applies to disputes "which may arise between MMC and BUYER out of or in relation to Articles I-B through V of this Agreement or the breach thereof. ..." Thus, disputes relating to only 5 out of a total of 15 Articles in the Sales Procedure Agreement are arbitrable. Those five Articles cover: (1) the terms and conditions of direct sales (matter such as the scheduling of orders, deliveries, and payment); (2) technical and engineering changes; (3) compliance by Mitsubishi with customs laws and regulations, and Soler's obligation to inform Mitsubishi of relevant local laws; (4) trademarks and patent rights; and (5) Mitsubishi's right to cease production of any products. It is immediately obvious that Soler's antitrust claim did not arise out of Articles I-B through V and it is not a claim "for the breach thereof." The question is whether it is a dispute "in relation to" those Articles. ...

The federal policy favoring arbitration cannot sustain the weight that the Court assigns to it. A clause requiring arbitration of all claims "relating to" a contract surely could not encompass a claim that the arbitration clause was itself part of a contract in restraint of trade. Nor in my judgment should it be read to encompass a claim that relies, not on a failure to perform the contract, but on an independent violation of federal law. The matters asserted by way of defense do not control the character, or the source, of the claim that Soler has asserted.[109] Accordingly, simply as a matter of ordinary contract interpretation, I would hold that Soler's antitrust claim is not arbitrable. ...

[Second,] until today all of our cases enforcing agreements to arbitrate under the [FAA] have involved contract claims. In one, the party claiming a breach of contractual warranties also claimed that the breach amounted to fraud actionable under §10(b) of the Securities Exchange Act of 1934. *Scherk v. Alberto-Culver Co.*, 417 U.S. 506 (1974).[110] But this is the first time the Court has considered the question whether a standard arbitration clause referring to claims arising out of or relating to a contract should be construed to cover statutory claims that have only an indirect relationship to the contract. In my opinion, neither the Congress that enacted the Arbitration Act in 1925, nor the many parties who have agreed to such standard clauses, could have anticipated the Court's answer to that question.

On several occasions we have drawn a distinction between statutory rights and contractual rights and refused to hold that an arbitration barred the assertion of a statutory right [citing *Alexander v. Gardner-Denver Co.*, 415 U.S. 36 (1974)]. ... In view of the Court's repeated recognition of the distinction between federal statutory rights and contractual rights, together with the undisputed historical fact that arbitration has functioned almost entirely in either the area of labor disputes or in "ordinary disputes between merchants as to questions of fact," it is reasonable to assume that most lawyers and executives would not expect the language in the standard arbitration clause to cover federal statutory claims. Thus, in my opinion, both a fair respect for the importance of the interests that Congress has identified as worthy of federal statutory protection, and a fair appraisal of the most likely understanding of the parties who sign agreements containing standard arbitration clauses, support a presumption that such clauses do not apply to federal statutory claims. ...

Notes on Apollo and Mitsubishi

1. *Applicability of the Kompetenz-Kompetenz doctrine in* Apollo *and* Mitsubishi. Compare the respective roles of the court and the arbitral tribunal in interpreting the scope of the arbitration agreement in *Mitsubishi* and *Apollo*. Is it the court or the arbitrator that decides the scope of the parties' arbitration clause in each case? Are the two decisions consistent? Note that *Mitsubishi* was prepared to hold that cer-

---

109. Even if Mitsubishi can prove that it did not violate any provision of the contract, such proof would not necessarily constitute a defense to the antitrust claim. In contrast, in *Prima Paint Corp. v. Flood & Conklin Mfg. Co.*, 388 U.S. 395 (1967), Prima Paint's claim of fraud in the inducement was asserted to rescind the contract, not as an independent basis of recovery.

110. "The dispute between these parties over the alleged shortage in defendant's inventory of European trademarks, a matter covered by contract warranties and subject to pre-closing verification, is the kind of commercial dispute for which arbitration is entirely appropriate. In my opinion, the fact that the 'fraud' language of Rule 10(b)(5) has been included in the complaint is far less significant than the desirability of having the Court of Arbitration of the International Chamber of Commerce in Paris, France, decide the various questions of foreign law which should determine the rights of these parties." *Alberto-Culver Co. v. Scherk*, 484 F.2d 611, 619-620 (7th Cir. 1973) (Stevens, J., dissenting), *rev'd*, 417 U.S. 506 (1974).

tain claims are outside the scope of the arbitration agreement and shall not be arbitrated. Would that result have been possible under the analysis in *Apollo*? Are there material differences between the arbitration agreements in the two cases which might explain the different approaches?

2. *Lower U.S. court decisions holding that disputes over the scope of an arbitration agreement are for judicial resolution.* The Supreme Court apparently held in *Mitsubishi* that disputes over the scope of an arbitration agreement are for judicial resolution. *See supra* p. 1033. Some lower courts have also held that such disputes are to be resolved by a court. *See Griffin v. Semperit of America, Inc.*, 414 F.Supp. 1384, 1389 (S.D. Tex. 1976); *Pollux Marine Agencies, Inc. v. Louis Dreyfus Corp.*, 455 F.Supp. 211 (S.D.N.Y. 1978) ("Absent an agreement to the contrary, arbitrability is clearly a question for the Court"). One lower court put the issue as follows:

> Imagine a contract for construction of a one room log cabin. The parties agreed that disputes over the glass used in the windows would be subject to arbitration. If the owner were to sue the builder on broad breach of contract and tort causes of action, alleging drafty walls, a leaky roof, and a complete lack of wooden flooring, it would defy logic to force the owner to submit the entire dispute to arbitration, when all he had agreed to arbitrate was disputes over window glass. *Mesquite Lake Associates v. Lurgi Corp.*, 754 F.Supp. 161 (N.D. Calif. 1991).

3. *Lower U.S. court decisions holding that disputes over the scope of an arbitration agreement are for the arbitrators.* Like *Apollo*, most U.S. lower courts have held that disputes over the scope of an arbitration agreement may be for resolution by the arbitral tribunal. *E.g., Nicaragua v. Standard Fruit Co.*, 937 F.2d 469 (9th Cir. 1991); *Teledyne v. Kone*, 892 F.2d 1404 (9th Cir. 1990); *Sauer-Getriebe KG v. White*, 715 F.2d 348 (7th Cir. 1983), *cert. denied*, 464 U.S. 1070 (1984). Is this approach more desirable than decisions like *Mitsubishi*? Which approach better accords with the parties' expectations?

4. *Applicability of Kompetenz-Kompetenz doctrine as a matter of contract construction.* The current state of U.S. law appears to be that disputes concerning the scope of an arbitration agreement can in principle be dispatched to the arbitrator for initial decision, but that whether or not this will be ordered depends upon what the parties' arbitration agreement was intended to mean. *See supra* p. 1032. Of course, arbitration agreements virtually never address this issue directly (although the ICC Rules at issue in *Apollo* did). Thus, deciding whether arbitrability is to be determined by a court or an arbitrator depends largely on presumptions as to the parties' likely intent.

Some courts have adopted a presumption that disputes concerning arbitrability are ordinarily for judicial resolution. *See Nordin v. Nutri/System, Inc.*, 897 F.2d 339, 344 (8th Cir. 1990); *I.S. Joseph Co. v. Michigan Sugar Co.*, 803 F.2d 396, 399 n.2 (8th Cir. 1986) ("It is conceivable that an arbitration agreement could be drafted so broadly as to give the arbitrator in the first instance the power to determine arbitrability. Such a broad commitment to the discretion of the arbitrator would be highly unusual, and the party asserting it would be bound to prove clearly the intent of the parties to do so.").

Other courts appear to have taken the opposite approach, and held that parties will be compelled to arbitrate disputes about the scope of an arbitration clause unless there is some affirmative showing that they meant to limit the scope of their arbitration agreement. *E.g., Matter of Arbitration No. AAA13-161-0511-85*, 867 F.2d 130, 133 (2d Cir. 1989); *Phillips Petroleum Co. v. Marathon Oil Co.*, 794 F.2d 1080, 1081 (5th Cir. 1986).

5. *First Options.* The Supreme Court recently held, in *First Options of Chicago, Inc. v. Kaplan*, 115 S. Ct. 1920 (1995), that there is a distinction between disputes over the existence of an arbitration agreement and disputes over the scope of an admittedly valid agreement. As to the former, *First Options* said that courts "should not assume that the parties agreed to arbitrate arbitrability unless there is 'clea[r] and unmistakabl[e]' evidence that they did so." 115 S. Ct. at 1924. As to the latter — whether a dispute is within the scope of a valid agreement — the opposite presumption applies: "Any doubts concerning the scope of arbitrable issues should be resolved in favor of arbitration." 115 S. Ct. at 1924. Is this a sensible approach to issues of Kompetenz-Kompetenz? What justifies the distinction?

6. *"Pro-arbitration" bias of interpretation under the FAA and New York Convention.* If a court does consider issues of arbitrability, *Mitsubishi* held that "any doubts concerning the scope of arbitrable issues should be resolved in favor of arbitration." Or, as the Court put it even more expansively in *United Steelworkers of America v. Warrior & Gulf Navigation Co.*, 363 U.S. 574, 582-83 (1960), arbitration must be compelled unless the court can say with "positive assurance that the arbitration clause is not susceptible to an interpretation that covers the asserted dispute."

Most lower U.S. courts have followed this vigorously pro-arbitration rule of interpretation of arbitration agreements. *E.g., Progressive Casualty Ins. Co. v. CA Reaseguradora Nacional de Venezuela*, 991 F.2d 42 (2d Cir. 1993) (Inter-American Convention); *Riley v. Kingsley Underwriting Agencies, Ltd.*, 969 F.2d 953 (10th Cir. 1992) (New York Convention); *David L. Threlkeld & Co. v. Metallgesellschaft Ltd.*, 923 F.2d 245, 250-51 (2d Cir. 1991); *Management & Technical Consultants SA v. Parsons-Jurden International Corp.*, 820 F.2d 1531, 1534-35 (9th Cir. 1987) ("An agreement to arbitrate 'any dispute' without strong limiting or excepting language immediately following it logically includes not only the dispute, but the consequences naturally flowing from it — here, the amount of additional compensation"); *Sedco, Inc. v. Petroleos Mexicanos Mexican National Oil Co.*, 767 F.2d 1140, 1145 (5th Cir. 1985); *SA Mineracao da Trindade-Samitri v. Utah International, Inc.*, 745 F.2d 190, 194 (2d Cir. 1984).

   7. *Rationale for pro-arbitration rule of interpretation.* Does the federal presumption in favor of arbitrability accord with the likely intent of private parties? Do either the FAA or the New York Convention contain provisions governing the interpretation of arbitration agreements? If not, then what authorizes federal courts to develop a federal common law governing the construction of international arbitration agreements? Are such rules necessary to safeguard the arbitral process?

   8. *Possible applicability of foreign law to the interpretation of international arbitration agreements.* In *Mitsubishi*, the parties' underlying agreement was subject to Swiss law. Why isn't the interpretation of the scope of the parties' arbitration agreement therefore a question of Swiss law? Note that the parties' arbitration agreement calls for arbitration in Japan under the rules of a Japanese arbitral institution. Arguably, therefore, Japanese law might govern the arbitration agreement, as well as the conduct of the arbitration proceedings. *See* G. Born, *International Commercial Arbitration in the United States*, ____ (1994).

   The foregoing suggests that either Swiss or Japanese law governed the parties' arbitration agreement in *Mitsubishi*. Why was U.S. law applied to the interpretation of the arbitration agreement? Should the Supreme Court have applied either Swiss or Japanese law to interpret the scope of the parties' arbitration agreement?

   U.S. courts have almost unanimously applied federal U.S. law to interpret the scope of arbitration agreements, even where a choice of law clause selected foreign law. In addition to *Mitsubishi, see Becker Autoradio U.S.A., Inc. v. Becker Autoradiowerk GmbH*, 585 F.2d 39, 43-44 & n.8 (3d Cir. 1978) ("[W]hether a particular dispute is within the class of those disputes governed by the arbitration and choice of law clause is a matter of federal law"); *Marchetto v. DeKalb Genetics Corp.*, 711 F.Supp. 936 (N.D. Ill. 1989) (refusing to apply Italian law to interpret agreement to arbitrate in Italy): *Pioneer Properties, Inc. v. Martin*, 557 F.Supp. 1354, 1365-66 & n.14 (D. Kan. 1983) (applying FAA to interpretation of arbitration clause after noting that agreements were subject to Ontario law); *Antco Shipping Co. v. Sidermar SpA*, 417 F.Supp. 207 (S.D.N.Y. 1976).

   There are a few lower court decisions that appear to apply, or lean towards applying, foreign law to the interpretation of the parties' arbitration agreement. *E.g., In re Oil Spill by Amoco Cadiz etc.*, 659 F.2d 789 (7th Cir. 1981) (apparently relying on English law to interpret scope of arbitration clause, but also relying on FAA's presumption of arbitrability); *SMG Swedish Machine Group, Inc. v. Swedish Machine Group, Inc.*, 1991 WL 10662 (N.D. Ill. Jan. 22, 1991) (applying Swedish law to determine whether an arbitration clause was mandatory); *Al-Salamah Arabian Agencies Co. v. Reese*, 673 F.Supp. 748, 750 (M.D.N.C. 1987) (assuming Saudi Arabian law applied, but, in absence of proof, looking to FAA). Is this approach wise?

   9. *Standard formulae in arbitration clauses.* There are a limited number of fairly standard formulae used in arbitration clauses to describe the scope of such provisions. The most common terms cover (a) "all" or "any"; (b) "disputes," "differences," "claims," or "controversies;" (c) "arising out of," "in connection with," or "relating to"; (d) the parties' agreement or relations.

   (a) *"Arising under" formula in arbitration clause.* Some courts have held that arbitration clauses using the formulation "arising under" are "narrow" and do not encompass various tort claims that do not directly involve application of the parties' contractual commitments. *See Mediterranean Enterprises, Inc. v. Ssangyong Corp.*, 708 F.2d 1458 (9th Cir. 1983); *In re Kinoshita & Co.*, 287 F.2d 951, 953 (2d Cir. 1961) (holding that "arising under" or "arising out of" does not encompass a claim of fraud in the inducement of the underlying contract); *Michele Amoruso e Figli v. Fisheries Dev. Corp.*, 499 F.Supp. 1074, 1080-81 (S.D.N.Y. 1980); *Sinva, Inc. v. Merrill, Lynch, Pierce, Fenner & Smith, Inc.*, 253 F.Supp. 359, 364 (S.D.N.Y. 1966).

(b) *"Relating to" formula in arbitration agreement.* A number of lower courts have concluded that the phrase "relating to" extends an arbitration clause to a broad range of disputes. *Swensen's Ice Cream Co. v. Corsair Corp.*, 942 F.2d 1307, 1309 (8th Cir. 1991); *In re Kinoshita & Co*, 287 F.2d 951, 953 (2d Cir. 1961); *McDonnell Douglas Corp. v. Kingdom of Denmark*, 607 F.Supp. 1016, 1019 (E.D. Mo. 1985) ("'relating to' is generally regarded as broad rather than narrow language").

(c) *"In connection with" formula in arbitration agreement.* Lower courts have generally accorded the phrase "in connection with" a broad interpretation. *See J.J. Ryan & Sons v. Rhone Poulenc Textile, SA*, 863 F.2d 315, 321-22 (4th Cir. 1988) (clause covering "'all disputes arising in connection with the present contract' must be construed to encompass a broad scope of arbitrable issues... It embraces every dispute between the parties having a significant relationship to the contract regardless of the label attached to the dispute").

(d) *Lower court decisions refusing to parse arbitration clauses' language finely.* Other courts have questioned efforts to distinguish between different linguistic formulations used in arbitration provisions. *See Peoples Security Life Ins. Co. v. Monumental Life Ins. Co.*, 867 F.2d 809 (4th Cir. 1989); *J.J. Ryan & Sons v. Rhone Poulenc Textile, SA*, 863 F.2d 315, 321 (4th Cir. 1988) (differences are "largely semantic"); *Genesco, Inc. v. T. Kakiuchi & Co.*, 815 F.2d 840, 848 & 854 (2d Cir. 1987).

Is it sensible to distinguish between formulations such as "arising under" and "in connection with" or "relating to"? Do you think that, in general, parties really intend different meanings to attach to these different terms? As a general rule, what presumption about the intended scope of an arbitration clause makes sense? that the parties wanted all disputes having some connection to their contractual relations and dealings to be arbitrated? Isn't this consistent with arbitration's promise of a single, efficient dispute resolution mechanism?

10. *Arbitrability of statutory claims.* *Mitsubishi* held that the parties had clearly intended to arbitrate the antitrust claims asserted by Soler. Is that persuasive? Should a "pro-arbitration" bias also apply to statutory claims? Consider Justice Stevens' dissent. Do parties ordinarily consider the existence and arbitrability of statutory claims — not based on the contract itself — when they include an arbitration provision in their agreement? If not, why is *Mitsubishi* willing to "distort the process of contract interpretation," 473 U.S. at 627, in this context? Consider Justice Stevens' dissent in *Mitsubishi*. Merely as a matter of contract interpretation, is it not persuasive?

U.S. courts have fairly consistently concluded that statutory claims are within the scope of the parties' arbitration agreement. *E.g., Roby v. Lloyd's Corporation*, 996 F.2d 1353 (2d Cir. 1993) (federal securities and RICO claims); *J.J. Ryan & Sons v. Rhone Poulenc Textile, SA*, 863 F.2d 315, 319-20 (4th Cir. 1988) (state unfair competition act claims); *Valero Refining, Inc. v. M/T Lauberhorn*, 813 F.2d 60, 62-63 (5th Cir. 1987) (RICO). *Compare Washburn v. Societe Commerciale de Reassurance*, 831 F.2d 149, 151 (7th Cir. 1987) (RICO claims not within arbitration agreement).

11. *Arbitrability of common law tort claims.* In a footnote, *Mitsubishi* observed that the district court had held that the parties' arbitration clause did not cover common law defamation claims asserted against Mitsubishi and CISA by Soler. It is common for disputes to arise in international arbitration over the arbitrability of common law tort claims. There is no general bar under federal law to inclusion of tort claims within the scope of an arbitration clause. *Fleck v. E.F. Hutton Group, Inc.*, 891 F.2d 1047, 1049-52 (2d Cir. 1989); *Pierson v. Dean Witter, Reynolds, Inc.*, 742 F.2d 334, 338 (7th Cir. 1984); *In re Oil Spill by Amoco Cadiz*, 659 F.2d 789, 794 (7th Cir. 1981); *Legg, Mason & Co. v. Mackall & Coe, Inc.*, 351 F.Supp. 1367 (D.D.C. 1972). *Compare Mar-Len of La., Inc. v. Parsons-Gilbane*, 773 F.2d 633, 637 (5th Cir. 1985) (arbitration agreement covering "any dispute arising under" the agreement or "with respect to the interpretation or performance of" the agreement held to cover duress claims) with *Armada Coal Export, Inc. v. Interbulk, Ltd.*, 726 F.2d 1566, 1568 (11th Cir. 1984) (tort claims based on foreign attachment held nonarbitrable where agreement covered "any dispute arising during the execution of the Charter Party") and *Michele Amoruso e Figli v. Fisheries Dev. Corp.*, 499 F.Supp. 1074 (S.D.N.Y. 1980) (holding that parties' arbitration clause did not reach claims of fraudulent inducement or illegality of underlying contract).

What is the appropriate approach to determining whether tort claims are arbitrable? If parties' arbitration clauses are generally silent, or if one questions the wisdom of fine distinctions between "arising under" and "relating to," what criteria can be used? *Compare Aspero v. Shearson American Express, Inc.*, 768 F.2d 106, 109 (6th Cir. 1985) (considering whether claim "goes to core" of parties' contractual relations); *Becker Autoradio U.S.A., Inc. v. Becker Autoradiowerk GmbH*, 585 F.2d 39, 47 (3d Cir. 1978) (considering whether claim "derive[s] from the [contractual] relationship"). How could the language of the parties' arbitration agreement in *Mitsubishi* have been improved, so as to cover defamation claims?

12. *Exclusivity of arbitration as a remedy.* One important issue of interpretation is whether arbitration is the parties' mandatory and exclusive remedy, or whether it is only a permissive remedy that leaves the parties free to resort to litigation in other forums. Although this is a matter of interpreting the parties' agreement, U.S. courts have generally held that the parties' inclusion of an arbitration clause indicates that arbitration is the exclusive forum for adjudication of substantive disputes. *E.g., Rogers, Burgun, Shahine, etc. v. Dongsan Construction Co. Ltd.*, 598 F.Supp. 754 (S.D.N.Y. 1984); *Eastern Europe, Inc. v. Transportmaschinen, Export-Import, Inc.*, 658 F.Supp. 612, 614 (S.D.N.Y. 1987); *Credit Alliance Corp. v. Crook*, 567 F.Supp. 1462 (S.D.N.Y. 1983). This is true even where the arbitration clause contains no express language regarding exclusivity. Contrast this approach with the treatment of forum selection clauses by U.S. courts, which have held that such a clause will be deemed non-exclusive unless it expressly provides to the contrary. *See* pp. 454-55.

C. Recognition and Enforcement of International Arbitral Awards

The arbitral process generally results in an award which, like the judgment of a national court, disposes of the parties' respective claims. Many awards do not require judicial enforcement, because they are voluntarily complied with.[111]

Nevertheless, the ultimate test of any arbitration proceeding is its ability to render an award which, if necessary, will be enforced in any relevant national court. An arbitral award is not a judgment of a court.[112] Instead, judicial confirmation and enforcement of an award must be sought in order to invoke coercive state enforcement mechanisms.[113] It is only if an arbitral award can successfully be enforced that a successful claimant can ensure that it will actually recover damages awarded to it.[114] And it is only if an award will be recognized that a successful respondent can ensure that new litigation on previously arbitrated claims is not commenced against it by a frustrated claimant.[115]

In marked contrast to foreign court judgments, whose enforcement in the United States is subject principally to state law,[116] the enforcement of international arbitral awards in the United States is governed primarily by federal law. Two sources of authority are particularly important — the New York Convention and the FAA.[117]

1. Enforceability of International Arbitral Awards Under The New York Convention

The New York Convention was designed in large measure to facilitate the enforcement of foreign arbitral awards.[118] Article III of the Convention imposes a

---

111. *See* Lalive, *Enforcing Awards,* in ICC, *60 Years of ICC Arbitration* 317, 319 (1984) (voluntary compliance with ICC awards exceeds 90%).

112. A foreign arbitral award "may not itself be treated as a foreign money judgment." *Fotochrome, Inc. v. Copal Co., Ltd.,* 517 F.2d 512 (2d Cir. 1975).

113. *Sentry Life Ins. Co. v. Board,* 759 F.2d 695, 698 (9th Cir. 1985); *Tamari v. Conrad,* 522 F.2d 778, 781 (7th Cir. 1977) ("An arbitrator's award is not self-executing.").

114. As with money judgments, the "enforcement" of an arbitral award refers to the implementation of coercive measures by national courts or other governmental authorities to effectuate the award. *See supra* p. 936.

115. Again like money judgments, the "recognition" or "confirmation" of an arbitral award refers to the decision of a national court (or comparable body) to give preclusive effect to the arbitrator's disposition of the parties' claim. *See supra* p. 936.

116. *See supra* pp. 938-39 & 960-62.

117. In a limited number of cases, other international agreements (such as the Inter-American Convention, bilateral treaties, and the ICSID Convention) are also potentially important. *See* G. Born, *International Commercial Arbitration in the United States* 20-24 (1994).

118. *See* A. van den Berg, *The New York Convention of 1958* 6-10, 264-74 (1981); *Bergesen v. Joseph Muller Corp.,* 710 F.2d 928, 932 (2d Cir. 1983) ("intended purpose" of Convention is "to encourage the recognition and enforcement of international arbitration awards"); *Parsons & Whittemore Overseas Co. v. Societe Generale De L'Industrie du Papier,* 508 F.2d 969, 973 (2d Cir. 1974) (Convention's "basic thrust was to liberalize procedures for enforcing foreign arbitral awards").

general requirement that signatory states recognize arbitral awards made in other countries:

> Each contracting state shall recognize arbitral awards as binding and enforce them in accordance with the rules of procedure of the territory where the award is relied upon, under the conditions laid down in the following articles. There shall not be imposed substantially more onerous conditions or higher fees or charges on the recognition or enforcement of arbitral awards to which the Convention applies than are imposed on the recognition or enforcement of domestic arbitral awards.

Several aspects of the Convention give special force to Article III's requirement and underscore its drafters' goal of facilitating transnational enforcement of arbitral awards. First, the Convention presumes the validity of awards and places the burden of proving invalidity on the party opposing enforcement.[119] Second, awards need not be confirmed in the arbitral situs before enforcement can be sought abroad.[120] Third, as Article III expressly provides, signatory states may not impose either conditions or procedural requirements that are more onerous than those applicable to domestic awards.[121]

Finally, Article V of the Convention sets forth a limited number of grounds for non-recognition of arbitral awards. Article V of the Convention is implemented by §207 of the FAA. Section 207 provides that a court "shall confirm" awards subject to the Convention "unless ... one of the grounds for refusal" specified in the Convention is present. U.S. courts have usually regarded Article V's exceptions as exclusive, and have emphasized the "general pro-enforcement bias informing the Convention."[122]

The presumption of enforceability, established in Article III of the New York Convention, and described above, is subject to eight exceptions, set forth in Articles V and VI. In summary, they are:

---

119. *See* A. van den Berg, *The New York Convention of 1958* 9 (1981) (Geneva Convention of 1927 required party enforcing award to prove its validity; New York Convention reversed burden of proof); *Parsons & Whittemore*, 508 F.2d at 973 ("While the Geneva Convention placed the burden of proof on the party seeking enforcement of a foreign arbitral award and did not circumscribe the range of available defenses to those enumerated in the Convention, the 1958 Convention clearly shifted the burden of proof to the party defending against enforcement and limited his defenses to seven set forth in Article V.").

120. G. Born, *International Commercial Arbitration in the United States* 464-65 (1994)

121. The Convention thus does not require either expeditious or efficient procedural mechanisms for enforcing awards; it merely requires signatory states to use procedures no more cumbersome than their domestic enforcement procedures. New York Convention Article III.

122. *Parsons & Whittemore*, 508 F.2d at 973. *See also Management & Technical Consultants SA v. Parson-Jurden Int'l Corp.*, 820 F.2d 1531, 1533 (9th Cir. 1987); *Biotronik etc. v. Medford Medical Instrument Co.*, 415 F.Supp. 133, 136-37 (D.N.J. 1976) ("basic thrust of the Convention was to liberalize the procedures for enforcing foreign arbitral awards"); *International Standard Elec. Corp. v. Bridas SA etc.*, 745 F.Supp. 172, 176 (S.D.N.Y. 1990) ("basic thrust of the Convention was to limit the broad attacks of foreign arbitral awards" available under Geneva Convention).

1. Article V(l)(a) — The award was rendered pursuant to an arbitration agreement that was invalid because, under the applicable law, the parties lacked capacity to make the agreement or the agreement was itself invalid.
2. Article V(l)(b) — The losing party "was not given proper notice of the appointment of the arbitrator or of the arbitration proceedings or was otherwise unable to present his case."
3. Article V(1)(c) — The arbitral award "deals with a difference not contemplated by or not falling within the terms of the submission to arbitrate."
4. Article V(l)(d) — The composition of the arbitral panel or the panel's procedures violated either the parties' agreement or the law of the arbitral forum.
5. Article V(l)(e) — The arbitral award is either not yet "binding" or has been set aside or suspended "by a competent authority of the country in which, or under the law of which, that award was made."
6. Article V(2)(a) — The subject matter of the parties' dispute is "not capable of settlement by arbitration" under the law of the enforcing nation.
7. Article V(2)(b) — Recognition or enforcement of the arbitral award would be contrary to the public policy of the enforcing nation.
8. Article VI — Where an application has been made to a court or other competent authority of the "country in which, or under the law of which, that award was made," then the court where enforcement is sought "may, if it considers it proper, adjourn the decision on the enforcement of the award. ..."

2. Selected Materials on the Enforceability of International Arbitral Awards

The cases excerpted below provide a brief introduction to the enforceability of international arbitral awards in U.S. courts. *Parsons & Whittemore* considers a number of separate challenges to the enforceability of an arbitral award under the FAA and New York Convention. *Northern Corp. v. Triad International Marketing SA* considers a public policy challenge to an award.

PARSONS & WHITTEMORE OVERSEAS CO. v. SOCIETE, GENERALE DE L'INDUSTRIE DU PAPIER

508 F.2d 969 (2d Cir. 1974)

J. JOSEPH SMITH, CIRCUIT JUDGE. Parsons & Whittemore Overseas Co., Inc., ("Overseas"), an American corporation, appeals from the entry of summary judgment ... on the counter-claim by Societe Generate de L'Industrie du Papier ("RAKTA"), an Egyptian corporation, to confirm a foreign arbitral award holding Overseas liable to RAKTA for breach of contract. ... Jurisdiction is based on 9 U.S.C. §203, which empowers federal district courts to hear cases to recognize and enforce foreign arbitral awards. ... We affirm the district court's confirmation of the foreign award.

In November 1962, Overseas consented by written agreement with RAKTA to construct, start up and, for one year, manage and supervise a paperboard mill in

Alexandria, Egypt. The Agency for International Development ("AID"), a branch of the United States State Department, would finance the project by supplying RAKTA with funds with which to purchase letters of credit in Overseas' favor. Among the contract's terms was an arbitration clause which provided a means to settle differences arising in the course of performance, and a "force majeure" clause, which excused delay in performance due to causes beyond Overseas' reasonable capacity to control.

Work proceeded as planned until May 1967. Then, with the Arab-Israeli Six Day War on the horizon, recurrent expressions of Egyptian hostility to Americans — nationals of the principal ally of the Israeli enemy — caused the majority of the Overseas work crew to leave Egypt. On June 6, the Egyptian government broke diplomatic ties with the United States and ordered all Americans expelled from Egypt except those who would apply and qualify for a special visa. Having abandoned the project for the present with the construction phase near completion, Overseas notified RAKTA that it regarded this postponement as excused by the force majeure clause. RAKTA disagreed and sought damages for breach of contract. Overseas refused to settle and RAKTA, already at work on completing the performance promised by Overseas, invoked the arbitration clause. Overseas responded by calling into play the clause's option to bring a dispute directly to a three-man arbitral board governed by the rules of the International Chamber of Commerce. [The tribunal issued a preliminary award, which recognized Overseas' force majeure defense as good only during the period from May 28 to June 30, 1967, and a final award in March, 1973: Overseas was held liable to RAKTA for $312,507.45 in damages for breach of contract and $30,000 for RAKTA's costs; additionally, the arbitrator's compensation was set at $49,000, with Overseas responsible for three-fourths of the sum.]

Subsequent to the final award, Overseas in the action here under review sought a declaratory judgment to prevent RAKTA from collecting the award out of a letter of credit issued in RAKTA's favor by Bank of America at Overseas' request. The letter was drawn to satisfy any "penalties" which an arbitral tribunal might assess against Overseas in the future for breach of contract. RAKTA contended that the arbitral award for damages met the letter's requirement of "penalties" and counter-claimed to confirm and enter judgment upon the foreign arbitral award. Overseas' defenses to this counterclaim, all rejected by the district court, form the principal issues for review on this appeal. ...

Article V(2)(b) of the Convention allows the court in which enforcement of a foreign arbitral award is sought to refuse enforcement, on the defendant's motion or *sua sponte*, if "enforcement of the award would be contrary to the public policy of [the forum] country." The legislative history of the provision offers no certain guidelines to its construction. Its precursors in the Geneva Convention and the 1958 Convention's *ad hoc* committee draft extended the public policy exception to, respectively, awards contrary to "principles of the law" and awards violative of "fundamental principles of the law." In one commentator's view, the Convention's failure to include similar language signifies a narrowing of the defense. Contini, [*International Commercial Arbitration,*] 8 Am. J. Comp. L. 283 at 304. ...

Perhaps more probative, however, are the inferences to be drawn from the history of the Convention as a whole. The general pro-enforcement bias informing the Convention ... points toward a narrow reading of the public policy defense. An expansive construction of this defense would vitiate the Convention's basic effort to remove preexisting obstacles to enforcement. ... Additionally, considerations of reciprocity — considerations given express recognition in the Convention itself — counsel courts to invoke the public policy defense with caution lest foreign courts frequently accept it as a defense to enforcement of arbitral awards rendered in the United States. We conclude, therefore, that the Convention's public policy defense should be construed narrowly. Enforcement of foreign arbitral awards may be denied on this basis only where enforcement would violate the forum state's most basic notions of morality and justice. *Cf.* 1 *Restatement (Second) Conflict of Laws* §117 comment c, at 340 (1971); *Loucks v. Standard Oil Co.*, 224 N.Y. 99, 111 (1918).

Under this view of the public policy provision in the Convention, Overseas' public policy defense may easily be dismissed. Overseas argues that various actions by United States officials subsequent to the severance of American-Egyptian relations — most particularly, AID's withdrawal of financial support for the Overseas-RAKTA contract — required Overseas, as a loyal American citizen, to abandon the project. Enforcement of an award predicated on the feasibility of Overseas' returning to work in defiance of these expressions of national policy would therefore allegedly contravene United States public policy. In equating "national" policy with United States "public" policy, the appellant quite plainly misses the mark. To read the public policy defense as a parochial device protective of national political interests would seriously undermine the Convention's utility. This provision was not meant to enshrine the vagaries of international politics under the rubric of "public policy." Rather, a circumscribed public policy doctrine was contemplated by the Convention's framers and every indication is that the United States, in acceding to the Convention, meant to subscribe to this supranational emphasis. *Cf. Scherk v. Alberto-Culver Co.*, 417 U.S. 506 (1974). To deny enforcement of this award largely because of the United States' failing out with Egypt in recent years would mean converting a defense intended to be of narrow scope into a major loophole in the Convention's mechanism for enforcement. We have little hesitation, therefore, in disallowing Overseas' proposed public policy defense.

Article V(2)(a) authorizes a court to deny enforcement, on a defendant's or its own motion, of a foreign arbitral award when "[t]he subject matter of the difference is not capable of settlement by arbitration under the law of that [the forum] country." ... Overseas' argument, that "United States foreign policy issues can hardly be placed at the mercy of foreign arbitrators 'who are charged with the execution of no public trust' and whose loyalties are to foreign interests," plainly fails to raise [a] substantial ... issue of arbitrability. The mere fact that an issue of national interest may incidentally figure into the resolution of a breach of contract claim does not make the dispute not arbitrable. Rather, certain *categories* of claims may be non-arbitrable because of the special national interest vested in their resolution. Furthermore, even were the test for non-arbitrability of an *ad hoc* nature, Overseas' situation would almost certainly not meet the standard, for Overseas grossly exaggerates the magnitude of the national interest involved in the resolution of its particular claim. Simply because acts of the United States are somehow implicated in a case one cannot conclude that the United States is vitally interested in its outcome. Finally, the Supreme Court's decision in favor of arbitrability in a case far more prominently displaying public features than the instant one, *Scherk v. Alberto-Culver Co.*, compels by analogy the conclusion that the foreign award against Overseas dealt with a subject of arbitrable under United States law. ...

Under Article V(I)(b) of the Convention, enforcement of a foreign arbitral award may be denied if the defendant can prove that he was "not given proper notice ... or was otherwise unable to present his case." This provision essentially sanctions the application of the forum state's standards of due process. Overseas seeks relief under this provision for the arbitration court's refusal to delay proceedings in order to accommodate the speaking schedule of one of Overseas' witnesses, David Nes, the United States Charge d'Affaires in Egypt at the time of the Six Day War. This attempt to state a due process claim fails for several reasons. First, inability to produce one's witnesses before an arbitral tribunal is a risk inherent in an agreement to submit to arbitration. By agreeing to submit disputes to arbitration, a party relinquishes his courtroom rights — including that to subpoena witnesses — in favor of arbitration "with all of its well known advantages and drawbacks." *Washington-Baltimore Newspaper Guild, Local 35 v. The Washington Post Co.*, 442 F.2d 1234, 1288 (1971). Secondly, the logistical problems of scheduling hearing dates convenient to parties, counsel and arbitrators scattered about the globe argues against deviating from an initially mutually agreeable time plan unless a scheduling change is truly unavoidable. In this instance, Overseas' allegedly key witness was kept from attending the hearing due to a prior commitment to lecture at an American university — hardly the type of obstacle to his presence which would require the arbitral tribunal to postpone the hearing as a matter of fundamental fairness to Overseas. Finally, Overseas cannot complain that the tribunal decided the case without considering evidence critical to its defense and within only Mr. Nes' ability to produce. In fact, the tribunal did have before it an affidavit by Mr. Nes in which he furnished, by his own account, "a good deal of the information to which I would have testified." ... The arbitration tribunal acted within its discretion in declining to reschedule a hearing for the convenience of an Overseas witness. Overseas' due process rights under American law, rights entitled to full force under the Convention as a defense to enforcement, were in no way infringed by the tribunal's decision.

... Both [Article V(1)(c) and FAA §10(d)] basically allow a party to attack an award predicated upon arbitration of a subject matter not within the agreement to submit to arbitration. This defense to enforcement of a foreign award, like the others already discussed, should be construed narrowly. Once again a narrow construction would comport with the enforcement-facilitating thrust of the Convention. In addition, the case law under the similar provision of the [FAA] strongly supports a strict reading.

In making this defense ... Overseas must therefore overcome a powerful presumption that the arbitral body acted within its powers. Overseas principally directs its challenge at ... $185,000 awarded for loss of production. Its jurisdictional claim focuses on the provision of the contract reciting that "[n]either party shall have any liability for loss of production." The tribunal cannot properly be charged, however, with simply ignoring this alleged limitation on the subject matter over which its decision-making powers extended. Rather, the arbitration court interpreted the provision not to preclude jurisdiction on this matter. As in *United Steelworkers of America v. Enterprise Wheel & Car Corp.*, 363 U.S. 593 (1960), the court may be satisfied that the arbitrator premised the award on a construction of the contract and that it is "not apparent," 363 U.S. at 598, that the scope of the submission to arbitration has been exceeded.

The appellant's attack on ... $60,000 awarded for start-up expenses ... cannot withstand the most cursory scrutiny. In characterizing the $60,000 as "consequential damages" (and thus proscribed by the arbitration agreement), Overseas is again attempting to secure a reconstruction in this court of the contract — an activity wholly inconsistent with the deference due arbitral decisions on law and fact. ...

Although the Convention recognizes that an award may not be enforced where predicated on a subject matter outside the arbitrator's jurisdiction, it does not sanction second-guessing the arbitrator's construction of the parties' agreement. The appellant's attempt to invoke this defense, however, calls upon the court to ignore this limitation on its decision-making powers and usurp the arbitrator's role. ...

Both the legislative history of Article V, and the statute enacted to implement the United States' accession to the Convention are strong authority for treating as exclusive the bases set forth in the Convention for vacating an award. On the other hand, the [FAA], specifically 9 U.S.C. §10, has been read to include an implied defense to enforcement where the award is in "manifest disregard" of the law. *Wilko v. Swan*, 346 U.S. 427, 436 (1953). This case does not require us to decide, however, whether this defense stemming from dictum in *Wilko*, *supra*, obtains in the international arbitration context. For even assuming that the "manifest disregard" defense applies under the Convention, we would have no difficulty rejecting the appellant's contention that such "manifest disregard" is in evidence here. Overseas in effect asks this court to read this defense as a license to review the record of arbitral proceedings for errors of fact or law — a role which we have emphatically declined to assume in the past and reject once again. "[E]xtensive judicial review frustrates the basic purpose of arbitration, which is to dispose of disputes quickly and avoid the expense and delay of extended court proceedings." *Saxis Steamship Co. [v. Multifacs Int'l Traders*, 375 F.2d 577, 582 (2d Cir. 1967).] Insofar as this defense to enforcement of awards in "manifest disregard" of law may be cognizable under the Convention, it, like the other defenses raised by the appellant, fails to provide a sound basis for vacating the foreign arbitral award. ...

NORTHROP CORP. v. TRIAD INTERNATIONAL MARKETING SA
811 F.2d 1265 (9th Cir. 1987)

BROWNING, JUDGE. In October 1970 Northrop and Triad entered into a 'Marketing Agreement,' under which Triad became Northrop's exclusive marketing representative [for certain armaments] in return for commissions on sales. Northrop made substantial sales to Saudi Arabia and paid Triad a substantial part of the commissions due under the Marketing Agreement. On September 17, 1975, the Council of Ministers of Saudi Arabia issued Decree No. 1275, prohibiting the payment of commissions in connection with armaments contracts. Northrop ceased paying commissions to Triad [which protested and then sought arbitration under AAA rules.]

[The Marketing Agreement contained a choice of law clause, which provided "The validity and construction of this Agreement shall be governed by the laws of the State of California." The arbitrators relied on the choice of law clause and rejected Northrop's argument that Saudi Decree No. 1275 rendered the Marketing Agreement unenforceable. Northrop pressed the argument on appeal, and the Ninth Circuit responded as follows.] Northrop also argues that if the Saudi Decree did not excuse performance of the Marketing Agreement under California [law], the choice-of-law clause in the Agreement should be set aside and the Saudi Decree should be applied directly to invalidate the Marketing Agreement under the principle announced in *Restatement (Second) Conflict of Laws* §187(2)(b) (1971). However, choice-of-law and choice-of-forum provisions in international commercial contracts ... should be enforced absent strong reasons to set them aside. ... We agree with the arbitrators that the general principle of conflicts Northrop cites is not sufficient standing alone to overcome the strong policy consideration announced in *Scherk* and *Bremen.* ...

Northrop's argument that the courts should decline to enforce the Marketing Agreement because it conflicts with the public policy Saudi Arabia announced in Decree No. 1275 flies in the face of the parties' agreement that the law of California, and not Saudi Arabia, would determine the validity and construction of the contract. Northrop has cited no California regulation, statute, or court decision demonstrating that enforcement of a contract to pay commissions to a marketing representative is contrary to the public policy of California, whether such commissions are illegal under the law of a foreign state or are not.

Northrop's most substantial argument is that the public policy reflected in

Decree No. 1275 was also the policy of the United States Department of Defense. In its opinion the district court said "it is clear [the Department of Defense] wished to conform its policy precisely to that announced by Saudi Arabia." ... To justify refusal to enforce an arbitration award on grounds of public policy, the policy "must be well defined and dominant." The Saudi Arabian policy the Department of Defense arguably adopted was neither. It is clear the Department wished to accommodate Saudi Arabian interests and sensibilities. It is also clear, however, that the Department was interested in encouraging sales to Saudi Arabia of American manufactured military equipment, and considered the efforts of Triad critical to that end. ... [The district court concluded that commissions on weapons were flatly prohibited,] but even if we were to agree, we could not say on this record the policy the Department adopted was "well-defined and dominant." The district court's refusal to enforce the arbitrators' decision on the ground that it conflicted with the policy of the Department of Defense was, therefore, unwarranted.

Notes on Parsons & Whittemore and Triad

1. *Exclusivity of defenses enumerated in New York Convention.* Parsons *&* Whittemore raises, but does not decide, the question whether the Convention's enumerated defenses are the exclusive grounds for resisting enforcement of a foreign arbitral award outside its country of origin. The language of the second chapter of the FAA suggests that *only* the Convention's defenses will be recognized. *See* 9 U.S.C. §207 ("The court *shall* confirm the award *unless* it finds one of the grounds for refusal or deferral of recognition or enforcement of the award specified in the [New York] Convention."). *See also Management & Technical Consultants SA v. Parsons-Jurden International Corp.*, 820 F.2d 1531, 1533 (9th Cir. 1987); *Fotochrome, Inc. v. Copal Co.*, 517 F.2d 512, 518 (2d Cir. 1975); *National Oil Corp. v. Libyan Sun Oil Co.*, 733 F.Supp. 800, 813 (D. Del. 1990).

Should U.S. courts recognize additional defenses to enforcement under the Convention — such as manifest disregard of law or an inconvenient arbitral forum? Could either of these defenses be fit within any of the Convention's enumerated defenses? Consider Articles III and V of the Convention, *supra* pp. 1041-42. Do they require that states recognize foreign arbitral awards subject to the specific exceptions in Articles V and VI of the Convention? Or does the Convention permit states to deny enforcement of foreign awards on the same grounds as those available under domestic law for domestic awards? Does §207 of the FAA permit awards to be denied recognition on grounds not specified in the Convention?

2. *Availability of manifest disregard defense under New York Convention.* It is not clear whether recognition of awards subject to the New York Convention can be withheld on "manifest disregard of law" grounds. The Convention's list of exceptions to enforceability in Article V does not include "manifest disregard."

Note that *Mitsubishi Motors*, 473 U.S. at 638, reasons that "substantive review at the award-enforcement stage [must] remain minimal," which suggests at least some sort of review of the substance of the arbitrators' ruling. For decisions apparently recognizing the manifest disregard exception under the Convention, *see, e.g., Office of Supply, Government of the Republic of Korea v. New York Navigation Co.*, 496 F.2d 377, 379-80 (2d Cir. 1972); *Jamaica Commodity Trading Co. v. Connell Rice & Sugar Co.*, 1991 U.S. Dist. Lexis 8976 (S.D.N.Y. 1991); *American Construction Machinery & Equipment Corp. v. Mechanised Construction of Pakistan Ltd.*, 659 F.Supp. 426 (S.D.N.Y. 1987).

Despite *Mitsubishi*, lower U.S. courts have generally concluded that the Convention would not permit non-recognition for manifest disregard of law. *E.g., Avraham v. Shigur Express Ltd.*, 1991 U.S. Dist. Lexis 12267 (S.D.N.Y. 1991); *International Standard Electric Corp. v. Bridas Sociedad Anonima Petrolera*, 745 F.Supp. 172, 181-82 (S.D.N.Y. 1990); *Brandeis Intsel Ltd. v. Calabrian Chem. Corp.*, 656 F.Supp. 160 (S.D.N.Y. 1987). Does *Whittemore* recognize the exception?

Which line of precedent is more persuasive? Should U.S. courts recognize and coercively enforce foreign arbitral awards that are not just plainly wrong, but that manifestly ignore applicable law and the facts?

Recall the treatment of foreign court judgments. *See supra* Chapter 12. Was there a manifest disregard exception to *Hilton* and the UFMJRA? Should there be?

3. *"Manifest disregard of law" not established by proof of erroneous decision.* When the defense is permitted, "manifest disregard of law" is universally held to require more than an erroneous statement of applicable law or an erroneous interpretation of the parties' agreement. *See Northrup Corp. v. Triad International Marketing, SA*, 811 F.2d 1265 (9th Cir.), *cert. denied*, 484 U.S. 914 (1987); *National Oil Corp. v. Libyan Sun Oil Co.*, 733 F.Supp. 800 (D. Del. 1990) ("A mere error of law would not, however, be sufficient grounds to refuse recognition of the award.").

Although it is easy to say what "manifest disregard" is not, it is harder to say what it is. Different courts have given a range of divergent interpretations to the manifest disregard exception. As one Court of Appeals said, "[t]his standard of judicial review has taken on various hues and colorations in its formulations ..." *Advest, Inc. v. McCarthy*, 914 F.2d 6, 9 (1st Cir. 1990). *Compare San Martine Compagnia de Navegacion v. Saguenay Terminals*, 293 F.2d 796, 801 (9th Cir. 1961) ("manifest disregard of the law must be something beyond and different from a mere error in the law or failure on the part of the arbitrators to understand or apply the law") *with Merrill Lynch, Pierce, Fenner & Smith v. Bobker*, 808 F.2d 930, 933 (2d Cir. 1986) (error on "well-defined, explicit, and clearly applicable" point of law "must have been obvious and capable of being readily and instantly perceived by the average person qualified to serve as an arbitrator") *with Carte Blanche (Singapore) Pte., Ltd. v. Carte Blanche International Ltd.*, 888 F.2d 260, 265 (2d Cir. 1989) (manifest disregard requires a showing either that the arbitrators simply ignored the applicable law, or were aware of the content of governing law, but refused to apply it).

4. *New York Convention's public policy exception.* Perhaps the most commonly invoked defense to the New York Convention's requirement for enforcement of arbitral awards involves Article V(2)(b)'s exception for cases where "the recognition or enforcement of the award would be contrary to the public policy of [the country asked to enforce the award]." The Convention's public policy exception derives in part from historic common law treatment of foreign judgments. *See supra* pp. 974-86.

Parsons & Whittemore and *Triad* construed Article V(2)(b)'s public policy exception narrowly to apply only where enforcement would violate the forum state's "most basic notions of morality and justice." 508 F.2d at 974. *See also Waterside Ocean Nav. Co. v. International Nav.*, 737 F.2d 150 (2d Cir. 1984) (public policy defense not implicated by claims of false testimony before arbitral tribunal); *Bergesen v. Joseph Muller Corp.*, 710 F.2d 928 (2d Cir. 1983).

Although the weight of authority reaches contrary results, a few U.S. decisions have invoked the public policy exception to deny recognition to a foreign arbitral award. *Laminoirs-Trefileries-Cableries de Lens, SA v. Southwire Co.*, 484 F.Supp. 1063 (N.D. Ga. 1980); *Victrix S.S. Co. v. Salen Dry Cargo AB*, 825 F.2d 709 (2d Cir. 1987). Should U.S. courts be more forceful in protecting U.S. interests and public policies under the Convention? Compare the treatment of the public policy defense in the context of the recognition and enforcement of foreign judgments. *See supra* pp. 974-86.

5. *Source of public policy standards under Article V (2) (b) — domestic or international?* From where are standards of public policy derived in cases under Article V(b)(2)? Do *Parsons & Whittemore* and *Triad* rely on the same sources of public policy?

(a) *"International" public policy.* A few U.S. courts appear to have looked at least in part to what they have called "international" public policy, as distinguished from U.S. "domestic" public policy. *See Parsons & Whittemore*, 508 F.2d at 974 (requiring "supranational emphasis" rather than reliance on "national political interests"); *Ledee*, 684 F.2d at 187; *National Oil Corp. v. Libyan Sun Oil Co.*, 733 F.Supp. 800, 819 (D. Del. 1990) ("'public policy' and 'foreign policy' are not synonymous"). How are U.S. courts to ascertain "international" public policy? What if international public policy permits actions that violate basic U.S. policies and laws, such as policies against racial or religious discrimination? *Cf. Antco Shipping Co. v. & Sidermar, SpA*, 417 F.Supp. 207, 215-17 (S.D.N.Y. 1976) (rejecting public policy defense to stay pending arbitration where parties' agreement contained provisions requiring boycott of Israel).

(b) *U.S. decisions adopting "national" public policy.* Notwithstanding the references to "international" public policy in *Parsons & Whittemore*, other U.S. courts have looked to *national* public policy. *See Victrix S.S. Co. v. Salen Dry Cargo AB*, 825 F.2d 709 (2d Cir. 1987); *Waterside Ocean Nav. Co. v. International Nav.*, 737 F.2d 150, 152 (2d Cir. 1984) ("public policy of the United States"); *McDonnell Douglas Corp. v. Kingdom of Denmark*, 607 F.Supp. 1016 (E.D. Mo. 1985); *La Societe Nationale etc. v. Shaheen Natural Resources Co.*, 585 F.Supp. 57, 63 (S.D.N.Y. 1983). Assuming that the public policy contemplated by

Article V(2) is national — not international — public policy, what is the source of that public policy in the United States? Is it state, or federal, public policy?

Recall the treatment of public policy in the context of recognizing foreign judgments, where courts generally look to *state* public policies. *See supra* pp. 984-85. In cases under the Convention, do federal interests in uniformity and undue interference with the arbitral process support preemption of state public policies?

6. *Effect of foreign public policies on enforceability of awards in U.S. courts.* To what extent should U.S. courts give effect to the public policies of *foreign* states in applying the Convention? Suppose, for example, that an arbitral award orders relief against European companies operating in Europe that violates European Union competition laws? or that requires or rewards conduct in a foreign state that is unlawful there? Should a U.S. court enforce the award? Would a U.S. court enforce a contract calling for such conduct?

How does *Triad* deal with Saudi Arabian public policy against bribery? Did it reach a sensible result? *Compare Triad Financial Establishment v. Tumpane Co.*, 611 F.Supp. 157 (N.D.N.Y. 1985) (applying Saudi law against broker fees on military sales to invalidate contract), which is excerpted above at pp. 423-26. What explains the difference in the cases?

As *Triad* suggests, even if foreign public policy were demonstrably in conflict with an arbitral award, and even if the concerned foreign jurisdiction has a reasonably close relationship to the parties' dispute, U.S. courts have been reluctant to vacate the award. *E.g.*, *American Construction Machinery & Equipment Corp. v. Mechanised Construction of Pakistan, Ltd.*, 659 F.Supp. 426, 429 (S.D.N.Y. 1987) (rejecting argument that "United States public policy would be offended by confirming an arbitral award in the face of a Pakistani judgment that the arbitration clause and proceeding were void," at least where Pakistan was not arbitral situs).

7. *Judicial review of arbitral awards involving federal statutory claims.* After an arbitral tribunal has disposed of federal antitrust, securities, or other statutory claims, what level of judicial scrutiny of such awards is applicable under U.S. law? As discussed above, *Mitsubishi* indicates that U.S. courts will have the opportunity to take a "second look" at arbitral dispositions of antitrust claims:

> Having permitted the arbitration to go forward, the national courts of the United States will have the opportunity at the award enforcement stage to ensure that the legitimate interest in the enforcement of the antitrust laws has been addressed. ... While the efficacy of the arbitral process requires that substantive review at the award-enforcement stage remain minimal, it would not require intrusive inquiry to ascertain that the tribunal took cognizance of the antitrust claims and actually decided them.

Does this mean that the manifest disregard standard will apply to review of public law disputes? something more searching? less searching?

8. *Procedural fairness and opportunity to present party's case.* The New York Convention's grounds for refusal of enforcement include cases where the "party against whom the award is invoked was not given proper notice of the appointment of the arbitrator or of the arbitration proceedings or was otherwise unable to present his case." Article V(1)(b). Broadly speaking, this exception permits challenges for grave procedural defects in the arbitral proceedings. As with other exceptions under Article V, U.S. courts have been reluctant to deny recognition of an award on the grounds of procedural irregularity. That reluctance is reflected, again, by *Parsons & Whittemore*. Consider the alleged procedural unfairness in *Parsons & Whittemore*. Was it sufficient to warrant non-recognition? What types of procedural unfairness should permit non-recognition?

9. *Applicable law under Article V(1)(b).* The New York Convention does not specify what nation's laws, or what international standards, apply in determining whether Article V(1)(b)'s procedural fairness exception is met. *Parsons & Whittemore* held that the law of the forum where enforcement is sought — there, the United States — should be applied to determine whether a party was given "proper" notice or was "unable" to present his case. Other lower U.S. courts have agreed. *Fotochrome, Inc. v. Copal Co.*, 517 F.2d 512 (2d Cir. 1975); *Compagnie des Bauxites de Guinee v. Hammermills, Inc.*, 1992 WL 122712 (D.D.C. 1992); *Biotronik etc. v. Medford Medical Instrument Co.*, 415 F.Supp. 133, 140 (D.N.J. 1976). Compare this use of U.S. due process standards to the treatment of adequate notice in the enforcement of foreign court judgments. *See supra* pp. 963-74.

When U.S. law applies under Article V(1)(b), what is the source of U.S. standards of procedural fairness? Is it the FAA, state law, or the U.S. Constitution? Lower U.S. courts have generally concluded that arbitral awards falling under the Convention are subject to scrutiny under the "due process" standards of the fifth and fourteenth amendments to the Constitution. *Iran Aircraft Industries v. Avco Corp.*, 980 F.2d 141 (2d Cir. 1992) ("'the fundamental requirement of due process is the opportunity to be heard 'at a meaningful time and in a meaningful manner.'"); *Fotochrome, Inc. v. Copal Co.*, 517 F.2d 512 (2d Cir. 1975); *Parsons & Whittemore*, 508 F.2d at 975. U.S. courts have not looked to state law procedural rules in applying Article V(1)(b). Is that appropriate? Should procedural rules applicable under state arbitration statutes apply under Article V(1)(b)? Why should the FAA or the Convention preempt such rules?

10. *Deference to special character of arbitral process under Article V(1)(b).* Decisions under Article V(1)(b) defer to the procedural informality and flexibility of arbitration. "Although arbitration hearings are of a quasi-judicial nature the prime virtue of arbitration is its informality, and it would be inappropriate for courts to mandate rigid compliance with procedural rules." *Transport Workers Union v. Philadelphia Transportation Co.*, 283 F.Supp. 597, 600 (E.D. Pa. 1968). *See also Legion Ins. Co. v. Insurance General Agency, Inc.*, 822 F.2d 541, 543 (5th Cir. 1987); *Bell Aerospace Co. v. Local 516*, 500 F.2d 921 (2d Cir. 1974).

Parsons & Whittemore and other authorities make it plain that the enforcing court will not sit in *de novo* review of procedural decisions of the arbitral panel. Rather, U.S. courts generally accord international arbitrators broad discretion in their conduct of proceedings. *See Parsons & Whittemore*, 508 F.2d at 975-76; *Compagnie des Bauxites de Guinee v. Hammermills, Inc.*, 1992 WL 122712 (D.D.C. 1992); *Laminoirs etc. v. Southwire Co.*, 484 F.Supp. 1063, 1066-67 (N.D. Ga. 1980) (curtailing cross-examination did not deny petitioner fair hearing). Is this appropriate? Recall Justice Stevens' concerns in *Mitsubishi* about "despotic decision-making," *see supra* pp. 1023-24.

11. *Excess of authority and no valid arbitration agreement.* As we have seen, international arbitration is consensual: unless the parties agreed to arbitrate a particular issue, the arbitral tribunal lacks authority to resolve it. A corollary of the consensual nature of arbitration is the unenforceability of awards that are not supported by a valid arbitration agreement.

The New York Convention contains three provisions relating to the arbitrators' obligation to act within the terms of a valid agreement to arbitrate. Article V(1)(a) permits non-recognition of an award if "the parties to the agreement referred to in Article II were, under the law applicable to them, under some incapacity, or the said agreement is not valid under the law to which the parties have subjected it or, failing any indication thereon, under the law of the country where the award was made." Article V(1)(a)'s requirement for a valid arbitration agreement is closely related to similar provisions in Articles II(1) and II(3). *See supra* p. 1042. Articles V(1)(c) and Article V(1)(d) also permit non-enforcement of awards that deal with matters not submitted to the arbitrators or where the procedural and other provisions of the parties' arbitration agreement were not followed.

Lower courts have interpreted the Convention's "excess of authority" exception under Article V(1)(c) narrowly, and seldom found it satisfied. *See Management & Tech. Consultants v. Parsons-Jurden Int'l Corp.*, 820 F.2d 1531 (9th Cir. 1987) ("we construe arbitral authority broadly to comport with the enforcement facilitating thrust of the Convention and the policy favoring arbitration"); *Andros Compania Maritima v. Marc Rich & Co.*, 579 F.2d 691 (2d Cir. 1978); *Avraham v. Shigur Express Ltd.*, 1991 U.S. Dist. Lexis 12267 (S.D.N.Y. 1991). Did *Parsons & Whittemore* involve a jurisdictional challenge, or a challenge to the arbitrators' procedural rulings? Or did it instead involve a claim that the arbitrators' substantive contract interpretation was incorrect?

12. *Excess of authority under Article V(1)(c) by exceeding scope of arbitration agreement.* When a case involves a *true* jurisdictional challenge — for example, to the existence, validity, or scope of an arbitration agreement — what deference should a court give to a ruling by the arbitrators on this issue? Suppose that the arbitrators reject one party's argument that it was not party to the purported arbitration agreement, or that the agreement is invalid. Suppose that the arbitrators reject the argument that the scope of the arbitration agreement does not extend to particular claims or disputes. Is the same deference applicable to each ruling?

In *First Options of Chicago, Inc. v. Kaplan*, 115 S.Ct. 1920 (1995), the Court considered whether an arbitral award had validly been made against two individual shareholders of a corporate defendant in an arbitration. The individuals had argued to the arbitrators that they were not party to the arbitration agreement, but the tribunal rejected their argument. The individuals moved to vacate the award, for excess of authority, and the Supreme Court held that independent de novo judicial review of the individuals' jurisdiction challenge was required.

First Options initially held that the question "who should have the primary power to decide" the arbitrability of a claim "turns upon what the parties agreed about that matter." If the parties had agreed to have the arbitrator decide arbitrability, then the court's standard for reviewing the arbitrator's decision about that matter should not differ from the highly deferential standard that court apply when they review any other matter the parties have agreed to arbitrate. On the other hand, if "the parties did not agree to submit the arbitrability question itself to arbitration, then the court should decide the question just as it would decide any other question that the parties did not submit to arbitration, namely independently."

The Court then considered whether the parties had agreed to arbitrate the question whether the individuals were personally bound to arbitrate. The Court reasoned that "when deciding whether the parties agreed to arbitrate a certain matter (including arbitrability), courts generally ... should apply ordinary state-law principles that govern the formation of contracts." The Court then declared that courts "should not assume that the parties agreed to arbitrate arbitrability unless there is 'clea[r] and unmistakabl[e]' evidence that they did so." The Court distinguished this presumption — about "who" decides arbitrability — from the reverse presumption about "whether" a particular dispute is within the scope of a concededly valid arbitration agreement: "Any doubts concerning the scope of arbitrable issues should be resolved in favor of arbitration." Applying this standard, the Court held that the individuals had not indicated a clear willingness to arbitrate the question whether they were bound by the arbitration agreement, and remanded to the lower courts for a de novo decision on that issue.

Is the *First Options* analysis persuasive? Why is there such a sharp distinction between the existence of an arbitration agreement and its scope?

Appendix A:
Selected State Long Arm Statutes

CALIFORNIA CIVIL PROCEDURE CODE (1973)

§410.10   Basis

A court of this state may exercise jurisdiction on any basis not consistent with the Constitution of this state or of the United States.

NEBRASKA REVISED STATUTES (1989)

§25-536   Jurisdiction Over a Person

A court may exercise personal jurisdiction over a person:

(1) Who acts directly or by an agent, as to cause of action arising from the person:

    (a) Transacting any business in this state;

    (b) Contracting to supply services or things in this state;

    (c) Causing tortious injury by an act or omission in this state;

    (d) Causing tortious injury in this state by an act or omission outside this state if the person regularly does or solicits business, engages in any other persistent course of conduct, or derives substantial revenue from goods used or consumed or services rendered, in this state;

    (e) Having an interest in, using, or possessing real property in this state; or

    (f) Contracting to insure any person, property, or risk located within this state at the time of contracting; or

(2) Who has any other contact with or maintains any other relation to this state to afford a basis for the exercise of personal jurisdiction consistent with the Constitution of the United States.

MAINE REVISED STATUTES ANNOTATED

Title 14

§704-A   Persons subject to jurisdiction

1. **Declaration of purpose.** It is declared, as a matter of legislative determination, that the public interest demands that the State provide its citizens with an effective means of redress against nonresident persons who, through certain significant minimal contacts with this State, incur obligations to citizens entitled to the state's protection. This legislative action is deemed necessary because of technological progress which has substantially increased the flow of commerce between the several states resulting in increased interaction between persons of this State and persons of other states.

This section, to insure maximum protection to citizens of this State, shall be applied so as to assert jurisdiction over nonresident defendants to the fullest extent permitted by the due process clause of the United States Constitution, 14th Amendment.

2. **Causes of action.** Any person, whether or not a citizen or resident of this State, who in person or through an agent does any of the acts hereinafter enumerated in this section, thereby submits such person, and, if an individual, his personal representative, to the jurisdiction of the courts of this State as to any cause of action arising from the doing of any of such acts:

    A. The transaction of any business within this State;

    B. Doing or causing a tortious act to be done, or causing the consequences of a tortious act to occur within this State;

    C. The ownership, use or possession of any real estate situated in this State;

    D. Contracting to insure any person, property or risk located within this State at the time of contracting;

    E. Conception resulting in paternity within the meaning of Title 19, chapter 5, subchapter III;

F. Contracting to supply services or things within this State;
G. Maintaining a domicile in this State while subject to a marital or family relationship out of which arises a claim for divorce, alimony, separate maintenance, property settlement, child support or child custody; or the commission in this State of any act giving rise to such a claim; or
H. Acting as a director, manager, trustee or other officer of a corporation incorporated under the laws of, or having its principal place of business within, this State.
I. Maintain any other relation to the State or to persons or property which affords a basis for the exercise of jurisdiction by the courts of this State consistent with the Constitution of the United States.

3. **Personal service.** Service of process upon any person who is subject to the jurisdiction of the courts of this State, as provided in this section, may be made by personally serving the summons upon the defendant outside this State, with the same force and effect as though summons had been personally served within this State.

4. **Jurisdiction based upon this section.** Only causes of action arising from acts enumerated herein may be asserted against a defendant in an action in which jurisdiction over him is based upon this section.

5. **Other service not affected.** Nothing contained in this section limits or affects the right to serve any process in any other manner now or hereinafter provided by law.

Appendix B:
Uniform Interstate and International Procedure Act

ARTICLE 1
BASES OF PERSONAL JURISDICTION OVER PERSONS OUTSIDE THIS STATE
§1.01   [Definition of Person]
        As used in this Article, "person" includes an individual, his executor, administrator, or other personal representative, or a corporation, partnership, association or any other legal or commercial entity, whether or not a citizen or domiciliary of this state and whether or not organized under the laws of this state.

§1.02   [Personal Jurisdiction Based upon Enduring Relationship]
        A court may exercise personal jurisdiction over a person domiciled in, organized under the laws of, or maintaining his or its principal place of business in, this state as to any [cause of action] [claim for relief].

§1.03   [Personal Jurisdiction Based upon Conduct]
        (a) A court may exercise personal jurisdiction over a person, who acts directly or by an agent, as to a [cause of action] [claim for relief] arising from the person's
            (1) transacting any business in this state;
            (2) contracting to supply services or things in this state;
            (3) causing tortious injury by an act or omission in this state;
            (4) causing tortious injury in this state by an act or omission outside this state if he regularly does or solicits business, or engages in any other persistent course of conduct, or derives substantial revenue from goods used or consumed or services rendered, in this state; [or]
            (5) having an interest in, using, or possessing real property in this state[; or
            (6) contracting to insure any person, property, or risk located within this state at the time of contracting].
        (b) When jurisdiction over a person is based solely upon this section, only a [cause of action] [claim for relief] arising from acts enumerated in this section may be asserted against him.

§1.04   [Service Outside the State]
        When the exercise of personal jurisdiction is authorized by this Article, service may be made outside this state.

§1.05   [Inconvenient Forum]
        When the court finds that in the interest of substantial justice the action should be heard in another forum, the court may stay or dismiss the action in whole or in part on any conditions that may be just.

§1.06   [Other Bases of Jurisdiction Unaffected]
        A court of this state may exercise jurisdiction on any other basis authorized by law.

ARTICLE II
SERVICE
§2.01   [Manner and Proof of Service]
    (a) When the law of this state authorizes service outside this state, the service, when reasonably calculated to give actual notice, may be made:
        (1) by personal delivery in the manner prescribed for service within this state;
        (2) in the manner prescribed by the law of the place in which the service is made for service in that place in an action in any of its courts of general jurisdiction;
        (3) by any form of mail addressed to the person to be served and requiring a signed receipt;
        (4) as directed by the foreign authority in response to a letter rogatory; or
        (5) as directed by the court.
    (b) Proof of service outside this state may be made by affidavit of the individual who made the service or in the manner prescribed by the law of this state, the order pursuant to which the service is made, or the law of the place in which the service is made for proof of service in an action in any of its courts of general jurisdiction. When service is made by mail, proof of service shall include a receipt signed by the addressee or other evidence of personal delivery to the addressee satisfactory to the court.

§2.02   [Individuals Eligible to Make Service]
    Service outside this state may be made by an individual permitted to make service of process under the law of this state or under the law of the place in which the service is made or who is designated by a court of this state.

§2.03   [Individuals to Be Serviced: Special Cases]
    When the law of this state requires that in order to effect service one or more designated individuals be served, service outside this state under this Article must be made upon the designated individual or individuals.

§2.04   [Assistance to Tribunals and Litigants Outside this State]
    (a) [A court] [The ... court] of this state may order service upon any person who is domiciled or can be found within this state of any document issued in connection with a proceeding in a tribunal outside this state. The order may be made upon application of any interested person or in response to a letter rogatory issued by a tribunal outside this state and shall direct the manner of service.
    (b) Service in connection with a proceeding in a tribunal outside this state may be made within this state without an order of court.
    (c) Service under this section does not, of itself, require the recognition or enforcement of an order, judgment, or decree rendered outside this state.

§2.05   [Other Provisions of Law Unaffected]
    This article does not repeal or modify any other law of this state permitting another procedure for service.

Appendix C:
Selected Provisions of Federal Rules of Civil Procedure

FEDERAL RULES OF CIVIL PROCEDURE
4, 26, 28, 29, 30, 34, 37, & 45

Rule 4. Summons

(a) **Form.**

The summons shall be signed by the clerk, bear the seal of the court, identify the court and the parties, be directed to the defendant, and state the name and address of the plaintiff's attorney or, if unrepresented, of the plaintiff. It shall also state the time within which the defendant must appear and defend, and notify the defendant that failure to do so will result in a judgment by default against the defendant for the relief demanded in the complaint. The court may allow a summons to be amended.

(b) **Issuance.**

Upon or after filing the complaint, the plaintiff may present a summons to the clerk for signature and seal. If the summons is in proper form, the clerk shall sign, seal, and issue it to the plaintiff for service on the defendant. A summons, or a copy of the summons if addressed to multiple defendants, shall be issued for each defendant to be served.

(c) **Service with Complaint; by Whom Made.**

(1) A summons shall be served together with a copy of the complaint. The plaintiff is responsible for service of a summons and complaint within the time allowed under subdivision (m) and shall furnish the person effecting service with the necessary copies of the summons and complaint.

(2) Service may be effected by any person who is not a party and who is at least 18 years of age. At the request of the plaintiff, however, the court may direct that service be effected by a United States marshal, deputy United States marshal, or other person or officer specially appointed by the court for that purpose. Such an appointment must be made when the plaintiff is authorized to proceed in forma pauperis pursuant to 28 U.S.C. §1915 or is authorized to proceed as a seaman under 28 U.S.C. §1916.

(d) **Waiver of Service; Duty to Save Costs of Service; Request to Waive.**

(1) A defendant who waives service of a summons does not thereby waive any objection to the venue or to the jurisdiction of the court over the person of the defendant.

(2) An individual, corporation, or association that is subject to service under subdivision (e), (f), or (h) and that receives notice of an action in the manner provided in this paragraph has a duty to avoid unnecessary costs of serving the summons. To avoid costs, the plaintiff may notify such a defendant of the commencement of the action and request that the defendant waive service of a summons. The notice and request

    (A) shall be in writing and shall be addressed directly to the defendant, if an individual, or else to an officer or managing or general agent (or other agent authorized by appointment or law to receive service of process) of a defendant subject to service under subdivision (h);

    (B) shall be dispatched through first-class mail or other reliable means;

(C) shall be accompanied by a copy of the complaint and shall identify the court in which it has been filed;

(D) shall inform the defendant, by means of a text prescribed in an official form promulgated pursuant to Rule 84, of the consequences of compliance and of a failure to comply with the request;

(E) shall set forth the date on which the request is sent;

(F) shall allow the defendant a reasonable time to return the waiver, which shall be at least 30 days from the date on which the request is sent, or 60 days from that date if the defendant is addressed outside any judicial district of the United States; and

(G) shall provide the defendant with an extra copy of the notice and request, as well as a prepaid means of compliance in writing.

If a defendant located within the United States fails to comply with a request for waiver made by a plaintiff located within the United States, the court shall impose the costs subsequently incurred in effecting service on the defendant unless good cause for the failure be shown.

(3) A defendant that, before being served with process, timely returns a waiver so requested is not required to serve an answer to the complaint until 60 days after the date on which the request for waiver of service was sent, or 90 days after that date if the defendant was addressed outside any judicial district of the United States.

(4) When the plaintiff files a waiver of service with the court, the action shall proceed, except as provided in paragraph (3), as if a summons and complaint had been served at the time of filing the waiver, and no proof of service shall be required.

(5) The costs to be imposed on a defendant under paragraph (2) for failure to comply with a request to waive service of a summons shall include the costs subsequently incurred in effecting service under sub-division (e), (f), or (h), together with the costs, including a reasonable attorney's fee, of any motion required to collect the costs of service.

(e) Service Upon Individuals Within a Judicial District of the United States.

Unless otherwise provided by federal law, service upon an individual from whom a waiver has not been obtained and filed, other than an infant or an incompetent person, may be effected in any judicial district of the United States:

(1) pursuant to the law of the state in which the district court is located, or in which service is effected, for the service of a summons upon the defendant in an action brought in the courts of general jurisdiction of the State; or

(2) by delivering a copy of the summons and of the complaint to the individual personally or by leaving copies thereof at the individual's dwelling house or usual place of abode with some person of suitable age and discretion then residing therein or by delivering a copy of the summons and of the complaint to an agent authorized by appointment or by law to receive service of process.

(f) Service Upon Individuals in a Foreign Country.

Unless otherwise provided by federal law, service upon an individual from whom a waiver has not been obtained and filed, other than an infant or an incompetent person, may be effected in a place not within any judicial district of the United States:

(1) by any internationally agreed means reasonably calculated to give notice, such as those means authorized by the Hague Convention on the Service Abroad of Judicial and Extrajudicial Documents; or

(2) if there is no internationally agreed means of service or the applicable international agreement allows other means of service, provided that service is reasonably calculated to give notice:

(A) in the manner prescribed by the law of the foreign country for service in that country in an action in any of its courts of general jurisdiction; or

(B) as directed by the foreign authority in response to a letter rogatory or letter of request; or

(C) unless prohibited by the law of the foreign country, by

(i) delivery to the individual personally of a copy of the summons and the complaint; or

(ii) any form of mail requiring a signed receipt, to be addressed and dispatched by the clerk of the court to the party to be served; or

(3) by other means not prohibited by international agreement as may be directed by the court.

(g) Service Upon Infants and Incompetent Persons.
Service upon an infant or an incompetent person in a judicial district of the United States shall be effected in the manner prescribed by the law of the state in which the service is made for the service of summons or other like process upon any such defendant in an action brought in the courts of general jurisdiction of that state. Service upon an infant or an incompetent person in a place not within any judicial district of the United States shall be effected in the manner prescribed by paragraph (2)(A) or (2)(B) of subdivision (f) or by such means as the court may direct.

(h) Service Upon Corporations and Associations.
Unless otherwise provided by federal law, service upon a domestic or foreign corporation or upon a partnership or other unincorporated association that is subject to suit under a common name, and from which a waiver of service has not been obtained and filed, shall be effected:
(1) in a judicial district of the United States in the manner prescribed for individuals by subdivision (e)(1), or by delivering a copy of the summons and of the complaint to an officer, a managing or general agent, or to any other agent authorized by appointment or by law to receive service of process and, if the agent is one authorized by statute to receive service and the statute so requires, by also mailing a copy to the defendant, or
(2) in a place not within any judicial district of the United States in any manner prescribed for individuals by subdivision (f) except personal delivery as provided in paragraph (2)(C)(i) thereof.

(i) Service Upon the United States, and Its Agencies, Corporations, or Officers.
(1) Service upon the United States shall be effected
   (A) by delivering a copy of the summons and of the complaint to the United States attorney for the district in which the action is brought or to an assistant United States attorney or clerical employee designated by the United States attorney in a writing filed with the clerk of the court or by sending a copy of the summons and of the complaint by registered or certified mail addressed to the civil process clerk at the office of the United States attorney and
   (B) by also sending a copy of the summons and of the complaint by registered or certified mail to the Attorney General of the United States at Washington, District of Columbia, and
   (C) in any action attacking the validity of an order of an officer or agency of the United States not made a party, by also sending a copy of the summons and of the complaint by registered or certified mail to the officer or agency.
(2) Service upon an officer, agency, or corporation of the United States shall be effected by serving the United States in the manner prescribed by paragraph (1) of this subdivision and by also sending a copy of the summons and of the complaint by registered or certified mail to the officer, agency, or corporation.
(3) The court shall allow a reasonable time for service of process under this subdivision for the purpose of curing the failure to serve multiple officers, agencies, or corporations of the United States if the plaintiff has effected service on either the United States attorney or the Attorney General of the United States.

(j) Service Upon Foreign, State, or Local Governments.
(1) Service upon a foreign state or a political sub-division, agency, or instrumentality thereof shall be effected pursuant to 28 U.S.C. §1608.
(2) Service upon a state, municipal corporation, or other governmental organization subject to suit shall be effected by delivering a copy of the summons and of the complaint to its chief executive officer or by serving the summons and complaint in the manner prescribed by the law of that state for the service of summons or other like process upon any such defendant.

(k) Territorial Limits of Effective Service.
(1) Service of a summons or filing a waiver of service is effective to establish jurisdiction over the person of a defendant

(A) who could be subjected to the jurisdiction of a court of general jurisdiction in the state in which the district court is located, or

(B) who is a party joined under Rule 14 or Rule 19 and is served at a place within a judicial district of the United States and not more than 100 miles from the place from which the summons issues, or

(C) who is subject to the federal interpleader jurisdiction under 28 U.S.C. §1335, or

(D) when authorized by a statute of the United States.

(2) If the exercise of jurisdiction is consistent with the Constitution and laws of the United States, serving a summons or filing a waiver of service is also effective, with respect to claims arising under federal law, to establish personal jurisdiction over the person of any defendant who is not subject to the jurisdiction of the courts of general jurisdiction of any state.

(l) **Proof of Service.**

If service is not waived, the person effecting service shall make proof thereof to the court. If service is made by a person other than a United States marshal or deputy United States marshal, the person shall make affidavit thereof. Proof of service in a place not within any judicial district of the United States shall, if effected under paragraph (1) of subdivision (f), be made pursuant to the applicable treaty or convention, and shall, if effected under paragraph (2) or (3) thereof, include a receipt signed by the addressee or other evidence of delivery to the addressee satisfactory to the court. Failure to make proof of service does not affect the validity of the service. The court may allow proof of service to be amended.

(m) **Time Limit for Service.**

If service of the summons and complaint is not made upon a defendant within 120 days after the filing of the complaint, the court, upon motion or on its own initiative after notice to the plaintiff, shall dismiss the action without prejudice as to that defendant or direct that service be effected within a specified time; provided that if the plaintiff shows good cause for the failure, the court shall extend the time for service for an appropriate period. This subdivision does not apply to service in a foreign country pursuant to subdivision (f) or (j)(1).

(n) **Seizure of Property; Service of Summons Not Feasible**

(1) If a statute of the United States so provides, the court may assert jurisdiction over property. Notice to claimants of the property shall then be sent in the manner provided by the statute or by service of a summons under this rule.

(2) Upon a showing that personal jurisdiction over a defendant cannot, in the district where the action is brought, be obtained with reasonable efforts by service of summons in any manner authorized by this rule, the court may assert jurisdiction over any of the defendant's assets found within the district by seizing the assets under the circumstances and in the manner provided by the law of the state in which the district court is located.

Rule 26. General Provisions Governing Discovery; Duty of Disclosure

(a) **Required Disclosures; Methods to Discover Additional Matter.**

(1) **Initial Disclosures.** Except to the extent otherwise stipulated or directed by order or local rule, a party shall, without awaiting a discovery request, provide to other parties:

(A) the name and, if known, the address and telephone number of each individual likely to have discoverable information relevant to disputed facts alleged with particularity in the pleadings, identifying the subjects of the information;

(B) a copy of, or a description by category and location of, all documents, data compilations, and tangible things in the possession, custody, or control of the party that are relevant to disputed facts alleged with particularity in the pleadings;

(C) a computation of any category of damages claimed by the disclosing party, making available for inspection and copying as under Rule 34 the documents or other evidentiary material, not privileged or protected from disclosure, on which such computation is based, including materials bearing on the nature and extent of injuries suffered; and

(D) for inspection and copying as under Rule 34 any insurance agreement under which any person carrying on an insurance business may be liable to satisfy part or all of a judgment which may be entered in the action or to indemnify or reimburse for payments made to satisfy the judgment.

Unless otherwise stipulated or directed by the court, these disclosures shall be made at or within 10 days after the meeting of the parties under subdivision (f). A party shall make its initial disclosures based on the information then reasonably available to it and is not excused from making its disclosures because it has not fully completed its investigation of the case or because it challenges the sufficiency of another party's disclosures or because another party has not made its disclosures.

(2) **Disclosure of Expert Testimony.**

(A) In addition to the disclosures required by paragraph (1), a party shall disclose to other parties the identity of any person who may be used at trial to present evidence under Rules 702, 703 or 705 of the Federal Rules of Evidence.

(B) Except as otherwise stipulated or directed by the court, this disclosure shall, with respect to a witness who is retained or specially employed to provide expert testimony in the case or whose duties as an employee of the party regularly involve giving expert testimony, be accompanied by a written report prepared and signed by the witness. The report shall contain a complete statement of all opinions to be expressed and the basis and reasons therefor, the data or other information considered by the witness in forming the opinions; any exhibits to be used as a summary of or support for the opinions; the qualifications of the witness, including a list of all publications authored by the witness within the preceding ten years; the compensation to be paid for the study and testimony; and a listing of any other cases in which the witness has testified as an expert at trial or by deposition within the preceding four years.

(C) These disclosures shall be made at the times and in the sequence directed by the court. In the absence of other directions from the court or stipulation by the parties, the disclosures shall be made at least 90 days before the trial date or the date the case is to be ready for trial or, if the evidence is intended solely to contradict or rebut evidence on the same subject matter identified by another party under paragraph (2)(B), within 30 days after the disclosure made by the other party. The parties shall supplement these disclosures when required under subdivision (e)(1).

(3) **Pretrial Disclosures.** In addition to the disclosures required in the preceding paragraphs, a party shall provide to other parties the following information regarding the evidence that it may present at trial other than solely for impeachment purposes:

(A) the name and, if not previously provided, the address and telephone number of each witness, separately identifying those whom the party expects to present and those whom the party may call if the need arises;

(B) the designation of those witnesses whose testimony is expected to be presented by means of a deposition and, if not taken stenographically, a transcript of the pertinent portions of the disposition testimony; and

(C) an appropriate identification of each document or other exhibit, including summaries of other evidence, separately identifying those which the party expects to offer and those which the party may offer if the need arises.

Unless otherwise directed by the court, these disclosures shall be made at least 30 days before trial. Within 14 days thereafter, unless a different time is specified by the court, a party may serve and file a list disclosing (i) any objections to the use under Rule 32(a) of a deposition designated by another party under subparagraph (B) and (ii) any objection, together with the grounds therefor, that may be made to the admissibility of materials identified under subparagraph (C). Objections not so disclosed, other than objections under Rules 402 and 403 of the Federal Rules of Evidence, shall be deemed waived unless excused by the court for good cause shown.

(4) **Form of Disclosures; Filing.** Unless otherwise directed by order or local rule, all disclosures under paragraphs (1) through (3) shall be made in writing, signed, served, and promptly filed with the court.

(5) **Methods to Discover Additional Matter.** Parties may obtain discovery by one or more of the following methods: depositions upon oral examination or written questions; written interrogatories; production of documents or things or permission to enter upon land or other property under Rule 34 or 45(a)(1)(C), for inspection and other purposes; physical and mental examinations; and requests for admission.

(b) **Discovery Scope and Limits.**

Unless otherwise limited by order of the court in accordance with these rules, the scope of discovery is as follows:

(1) **In General.** Parties may obtain discovery regarding any matter, not privileged, which is relevant to the subject matter involved in the pending action, whether it relates to the claim or defense of the party seeking discovery or to the claim or defense of any other party, including the existence, description, nature, custody, condition, and location of any books, documents, or other tangible things and the identity and location of persons having knowledge of any discoverable matter. The information sought need not be admissible at the trial if the information sought appears reasonably calculated to lead to the discovery of admissible evidence.

(2) **Limitations.** By order or by local rule, the court may alter the limits in these rules on the number of depositions and interrogatories and may also limit the length of depositions under Rule 30 and the number of requests under Rule 36. The frequency or extent of use of the discovery methods otherwise permitted under these rules and by any local rule shall be limited by the court if it determines that: (i) the discovery sought is unreasonably cumulative or duplicative, or is obtainable from some other source that is more convenient, less burdensome, or less expensive; (ii) the party seeking discovery has had ample opportunity by discovery in the action to obtain the information sought; or (iii) the burden of expense of the proposed discovery outweighs its likely benefit, taking into account the needs of the case, the amount in controversy, the parties' resources, the importance of the issues at stake in the litigation, and the importance of the proposed discovery in resolving the issues. The court may act upon its own initiative after reasonable notice or pursuant to a motion under subdivision (c).

(3) **Trial Preparation: Materials.** Subject to the provisions of subdivision (b)(4) of this rule, a party may obtain discovery of documents and tangible things otherwise discoverable under subdivision (b)(1) of this rule and prepared in anticipation of litigation or for trial by or for another party or by or for that other party's representative (including the other party's attorney, consultant, surety, indemnitor, insurer, or agent) only upon a showing that the party seeking discovery has substantial need of the materials in the preparation of the party's case and that the party is unable without undue hardship to obtain the substantial equivalent of the materials by other means. In ordering discovery of such materials when the required showing has been made, the court shall protect against disclosure of the mental impressions, conclusions, opinions, or legal theories of an attorney or other representative of a party concerning the litigation.

A party may obtain without the required showing a statement concerning the action or its subject matter previously made by that party. Upon request, a person not a party may obtain without the required showing a statement concerning the action or its subject matter previously made by that person. If the request is refused, the person may move for a court order. The provisions of Rule 37(a)(4) apply to the award of expenses incurred in relation to the motion. For purposes of this paragraph, a statement previously made is (A) a written statement signed or otherwise adopted or approved by the person making it, or (B) a stenographic, mechanical, electrical, or other recording, or a transcription thereof, which is a substantially verbatim recital of an oral statement by the person making it and contemporaneously recorded.

(4) **Trial Preparation: Experts.**

(A) A party may depose any person who has been identified as an expert whose opinions may be presented at trial. If a report from the expert is required under subdivision (a)(2)(B), the deposition shall not be conducted until after the report is provided.

(B) A party may, through interrogatories or by deposition, discover facts known or opinions held by an expert who has been retained or specially employed by another party in anticipation of litigation or preparation for trial and who is not expected to be called as a witness at trial, only as provided in Rule 35(b) or upon a showing of exceptional circumstances under which it is impracticable for the party seeking discovery to obtain facts or opinions on the same subject by other means.

(C) Unless manifest injustice would result, (i) the court shall require that the party seeking discovery pay the expert a reasonable fee for time spent in responding to discovery under this subdivision; and (ii) with respect to discovery obtained under subdivision (b)(4)(B) of this rule the court shall require the party seeking to pay the other party a fair portion of the fees and expenses reasonably incurred by the latter party in obtaining facts and opinions from the expert.

(5) **Claims of Privilege or Protection of Trial Preparation Materials.** When a party withholds information otherwise discoverable under these rules by claiming that it is privileged or subject to protection as trial preparation material, the party shall make the claim expressly and shall describe the nature of the documents, communications, or things not produced or disclosed in a manner that, without revealing information itself privileged or protected, will enable other parties to assess the applicability of the privilege or protection.

(c) Protective Orders.

Upon motion by a party or by the person from whom discovery is sought, accompanied by a certification that the movant has in good faith conferred or attempted to confer with other affected parties in an effort to resolve the dispute without court action, and for good cause shown, the court in which the action is pending or alternatively, on matters relating to a deposition, the court in the district where the deposition is to be taken may make any order which justice requires to protect a party or person from annoyance, embarrassment, oppression, or undue burden or expense, including one of more of the following:

(1) that the disclosure or discovery not be had:

(2) that the disclosure or discovery may be had only on specified terms and conditions, including a designation of the time or place;

(3) that the discovery may be had only by a method of discovery other than that selected by the party seeking discovery;

(4) that certain matters not be inquired into, or that the scope of the disclosure or discovery be limited to certain matters;

(5) that discovery be conducted with no one present except persons designated by the court;

(6) that a deposition, after being sealed, be opened only by order of the court;

(7) that a trade secret or other confidential research, development, or commercial information not be revealed or be revealed only in a designated way; and

(8) that the parties simultaneously file specified documents or information enclosed in sealed envelopes to be opened as directed by the court.

If the motion for a protective order is denied in whole or in part, the court may, on such terms and conditions as are just, order that any party or other person provide or permit discovery. The provisions of Rule 37(a)(4) apply to the award of expenses incurred in relation to the motion.

(d) Timing and Sequence of Discovery.

Except when authorised under these rules or by local rule, order, or agreement of the parties, a party may not seek discovery from any source before the parties have met and conferred as required by subdivision (f). Unless the court upon motion, for the convenience of parties and witnesses and in the interests of justice, orders otherwise, methods of discovery may be used in any sequence, and the fact that a party is conducting discovery, whether by deposition or otherwise, shall not operate to delay any other party's discovery.

(e) Supplementation of Disclosures and Responses.

A party who has made a disclosure under subdivision (a) or responded to a request for discovery with a disclosure or response is under a duty to supplement or correct the disclosure or response to include information thereafter acquired if ordered by the court or in the following circumstances:

(1) A party is under a duty to supplement at appropriate intervals its disclosures under subdivision (a) if the party learns that in some material respect the information disclosed is incomplete or incorrect and if the additional or corrective information has not otherwise been made known to the other parties during the discovery process or in writing. With respect to testimony of an

expert from whom a report is required under subdivision (a)(2)(B) the duty extends both to information contained in the report and to information provided through a deposition of the expert, and any additions or other changes to this information shall be disclosed by the time the party's disclosures under Rule 26(a)(3) are due.

(2) A party is under a duty seasonably to amend a prior response to an interrogatory, request for production, or request for admission if the party learns that the response is in some material respect incomplete or incorrect and if the additional or corrective information has not otherwise been made known to the other parties during the discovery process or in writing.

(f) Meeting of Parties: Planning for Discovery.

Except in actions exempted by local rule or when otherwise ordered, the parties shall, as soon as practicable and in any event at least 14 days before a scheduling conference is held or a scheduling order is due under Rule 16(b), meet to discuss the nature and basis of their claims and defenses and the possibilities for a prompt settlement or resolution of the case, to make or arrange for the disclosures required by subdivision (a)(1), and to develop a proposed discovery plan. The plan shall indicate the parties' views and proposals concerning:

(1) what changes should be made in the timing, form, or requirement for disclosures under subdivision (a) or local rule, including a statement as to when disclosures under subdivision (a)(1) were made or will be made;

(2) the subjects on which discovery may be needed, when discovery should be completed, and whether discovery should be conducted in phases or be limited to or focused upon particular issues;

(3) what changes should be made to the limitations on discovery imposed under these rules or by local rule, and what other limitations should be imposed; and

(4) any other orders that should be entered by the court under subdivision (c) or under Rule 16(b) and (c).

The attorneys of record and all unrepresented parties that have appeared in the case are jointly responsible for arranging and being present or represented at the meeting, for attempting in good faith to agree on the proposed discovery plan, and for submitting to the court within 10 days after the meeting a written report outlining the plan.

(g) Signing of Disclosures, Discovery Requests, Responses, and Objections.

(1) Every disclosure made pursuant to subdivision (a)(1) or subdivision (a)(3) shall be signed by at least one attorney of record in the attorney's individual name, whose address shall be stated. An unrepresented party shall sign the disclosure and state the party's address. The signature of the attorney or party constitutes a certification that to the best of the signer's knowledge, information, and belief, formed after a reasonable inquiry, the disclosure is complete and correct as of the time it is made.

(2) Every discovery request, response, or objection made by a party represented by an attorney shall be signed by at least one attorney of record in the attorney's individual name, whose address shall be stated. An unrepresented party shall sign the request, response, or objection and state the party's address. The signature of the attorney or party constitutes a certification that to the best of the signer's knowledge, information, and belief, formed after a reasonable inquiry, the request, response, or objection is:

(A) consistent with these rules and warranted by existing law or a good faith argument for the extension, modification, or reversal of existing law;

(B) not interposed for any improper purpose, such as to harass or to cause unnecessary delay or needless increase in the cost of litigation; and

(C) not unreasonable or unduly burdensome or expensive, given the needs of the case, the discovery already had in the case, the amount in controversy, and the importance of the issues at stake in the litigation.

If a request, response, or objection is not signed, it shall be stricken unless it is signed promptly after the omission is called to the attention of the party making the request, response, or objection, and a party shall not be obliged to take any action with respect to it until it is signed.

(3) If without substantial justification a certification is made in violation of the rule, the court, upon motion or upon its own initiative, shall impose upon the person who made the certification, the party on whose behalf the disclosure, request, response, or objection is made, or both, an appropriate sanction, which may include an order to pay the amount of the reasonable expenses incurred because of the violation, including a reasonable attorney's fee.

Rule 28. Persons Before Whom Depositions May be Taken

(a) Within the United States.

Within the United States or within a territory or insular possession subject to the jurisdiction of the United States, depositions shall be taken before an officer authorized to administer oaths by the laws of the United States or of the place where the examination is held, or before a person appointed by the court in which the action is pending. A person so appointed has power to administer oaths and take testimony. The term officer as used in Rules 30, 31 and 32 includes a person appointed by the court or designated by the parties under Rule 29.

(b) In Foreign Countries.

Depositions may be taken in a foreign country (1) pursuant to any applicable treaty or convention, or (2) pursuant to a letter of request (whether or not captioned a letter rogatory), or (3) on notice before a person authorized to administer oaths in the place where the examination is held, either by the law thereof or by the law of the United States, or (4) before a person commissioned by the court, and a person so commissioned shall have the power by virtue of the commission to administer any necessary oath and take testimony. A commission or a letter of request shall be issued on application and notice and on terms that are just and appropriate. It is not requisite to the issuance of a commission or a letter of request that the taking of the deposition in any other manner is impracticable or inconvenient; and both a commission and a letter of request may be issued in proper cases. A notice or commission may designate the person before whom the deposition is to be taken either by name or descriptive title. A letter of request may be addressed "To the Appropriate Authority in [here name the country]." When a letter of request or any other device is used pursuant to any applicable treaty or convention, it shall be captioned in the form prescribed by that treaty or convention. Evidence obtained in response to a letter of request need not be excluded merely because it is not a verbatim transcript, because the testimony was not taken under oath, or because of any similar departure from the requirements for depositions taken within the United States under these rules.

(c) Disqualification for Interest.

No deposition shall be taken before a person who is a relative or employee or attorney or counsel of any of the parties, or is a relative or employee of such attorney or counsel or is financially interested in the action.

Rule 29. Stipulations Regarding Discovery Procedure

Unless otherwise directed by the court, the parties may by written stipulation (1) provide that depositions may be taken before any person, at any time or place, upon any notice, and in any manner and when so taken may be used like other depositions, and (2) modify other procedures governing or limitations placed upon discovery, except that stipulations extending the time provided in Rules 33, 34, and 36 for responses to discovery may, if they would interfere with any time set for completion of discovery, for hearing of a motion, or for trial, be made only with the approval of the court.

Rule 30. Depositions Upon Oral Examination

(a) When Depositions May be Taken; When Leave Required.

(1) A party may take the testimony of any person, including a party, by deposition upon oral examination without leave of court except as provided in paragraph (2). The attendance of witnesses may be compelled by subpoena as provided in Rule 45.

(2) A party must obtain leave of court, which shall be granted to the extent consistent with the principles stated in Rule 26(b)(2), if the person to be examined is confined in prison or if, without the written stipulation of the parties.

(A) a proposed deposition would result in more than ten depositions being taken under this rule or Rule 31 by the plaintiffs, or by the defendants, or by third-party defendants;

(B) the person to be examined already has been deposed in the case; or

(C) a party seeks to take a deposition before the time specified in Rule 26(d) unless the notice contains a certification, with supporting facts, that the person to be examined is expected to leave the United States and be unavailable for examination in this country unless deposed before that time.

(b) Notice of Examination: General Requirements; Method of Recording; Production of Documents and Things; Deposition of Organization; Deposition by Telephone.

(1) A party desiring to take the deposition of any person upon oral examination shall give reasonable notice in writing to every other party to the action. The notice shall state the time and place for taking the deposition and the name and address of each person to be examined, if known, and, if the name is not known, a general description sufficient to identify the person or the particular class or group to which the person belongs. If a subpoena duces tecum is to be served on the person to be examined, the designation of the materials to be produced as set forth in the subpoena shall be attached to, or included in, the notice.

(2) The party taking the deposition shall state in the notice the method by which the testimony shall be recorded. Unless the court orders otherwise, it may be recorded by sound, sound-and-visual, or stenographic means, and the party taking the deposition shall bear the cost of the recording. Any party may arrange for a transcription to be made from the recording of a deposition taken by nonstenographic means.

(3) With prior notice to the deponent and other parties, any party may designate another method to record the deponent's testimony in addition to the method specified by the person taking the deposition. The additional record or transcript shall be made at that party's expense unless the court otherwise orders.

(4) Unless otherwise agreed by the parties, a deposition shall be conducted before an officer appointed or designated under Rule 28 and shall begin with a statement on the record by the officer that includes (A) the officer's name and business address; (B) the date, time, and place of the deposition; (C) the name of the deponent; (D) the administration of the oath or affirmation to the deponent; and (E) and identification of all persons present. If the deposition is recorded other than stenographically, the officer shall repeat items (A) through (C) at the beginning of each unit of recorded tape or other recording medium. The appearance or demeanor of deponents or attorneys shall not be distorted through camera or sound-recording techniques. At the end of the deposition, the officer shall state on the record that the deposition is complete and shall set forth any stipulations made by counsel concerning the custody of the transcript or recording and the exhibits, or concerning other pertinent matters.

(5) The notice to a party deponent may be accompanied by a request made in compliance with Rule 34 for the production of documents and tangible things at the taking of the deposition. The procedure of Rule 34 shall apply to the request.

(6) A party may in the party's notice and in a subpoena name as the deponent a public or private corporation or a partnership or association or governmental agency and describe with reasonable particularity the matters on which examination is requested. In that event, the organization so named shall designate one or more officers, directors, or managing agents, or other persons who consent to testify on its behalf, and may set forth, for each person designated, the matters on which the person will testify. A subpoena shall advise a non-party organization of its duty to make such a designation. The persons so designated shall testify as to matters known or reasonably available to the organization. This subdivision (b)(6) does not preclude taking a deposition by any other procedure authorized in these rules.

(7) The parties may stipulate in writing or the court may upon motion order that a deposition be taken by telephone or other remote electronic means. For the purposes of this rule and Rules 28(a), 37(a)(1), and 37(b)(1) a deposition taken by such means is taken in the district and at the place where the deponent is to answer questions.

(c) **Examination and Cross-Examination; Record of Examination; Oath; Objections.**

Examination and cross-examination of witnesses may proceed as permitted at the trial under the provisions of the Federal Rules of Evidence except Rules 103 and 615. The officer before whom the deposition is to be taken shall put the witness on oath or affirmation and shall personally, or by someone acting under the officer's direction and in the officer's presence, record the testimony of the witness. The testimony shall be taken stenographically or recorded by any other method authorized by subdivision (b)(2) of this rule. All objections made at the time of the examination to the qualifications of the officer taking the deposition, to the manner of taking it, to the evidence presented, to the conduct of any party, or to any other aspect of the proceedings shall be noted by the officer upon the record of the deposition; but the examination shall proceed, with the testimony being taken subject to the objections. In lieu of participating in the oral examination, parties may serve written questions in a sealed envelope on the party taking the deposition and the party taking the deposition shall transmit them to the officer, who shall propound them to the witness and record the answers verbatim.

(d) **Schedule and Duration; Motion to Terminate or Limit Examination.**

(1) Any objection to evidence during a deposition shall be stated concisely and in a non-argumentative and non-suggestive manner. A party may instruct a deponent not to answer only when necessary to preserve a privilege, to enforce a limitation on evidence directed by the court, or to present a motion under paragraph (3).

(2) By order or local rule, the court may limit the time permitted for the conduct of a deposition, but shall allow additional time consistent with Rule 26(b)(2) if needed for a fair examination of the deponent or if the deponent or another party impedes or delays the examination. If the court finds such an impediment, delay, or other conduct that has frustrated the fair examination of the deponent, it may impose upon the persons responsible an appropriate sanction, including the reasonable costs and attorney's fees incurred by any parties as a result thereof.

(3) At any time during a deposition, on motion of a party or of the deponent and upon a showing that the examination is being conducted in bad faith or in such manner as unreasonably to annoy, embarrass, or oppress the deponent or party, the court in which the action is pending or the court in the district where the deposition is being taken may order the officer conducting the examination to cease forthwith from taking the deposition, or may limit the scope and manner of the taking of the deposition as provided in Rule 26(c). If the order made terminates the examination, it shall be resumed thereafter only upon the order of the court in which the action is pending. Upon demand of the objecting party or deponent, the taking of the deposition shall be suspended for the time necessary to make a motion for an order. The provisions of Rule 37(a)(4) apply to the award of expenses incurred in relation to the motion.

(e) **Review by Witness; Changes; Signing.**

If requested by the deponent or a party before completion of the deposition, the deponent shall have 30 days after being notified by the officer that the transcript or recording is available in which to review the transcript or recording and, if there are changes in form or substance, to sign a statement reciting such changes and the reasons given by the deponent for making them. The officer shall indicate in the certificate prescribed by subdivision (f)(l) whether any review was requested and, if so, shall append any changes made by the deponent during the period allowed.

(f) **Certification and Filing by Officer; Exhibits; Copies; Notice of Filing.**

(1) The officer shall certify that the witness was duly sworn by the officer and that the deposition is a true record of the testimony given by the witness. This certificate shall be in writing and accompany the record of the deposition. Unless otherwise ordered by the court, the officer shall securely seal the deposition in an envelope or package indorsed with the title of the action and marked "Deposition of [here insert name of witness]" and shall promptly file it with the court in which the action is pending or send it to the attorney who arranged for the transcript or recording, who shall store it under conditions that will protect it against loss, destruction, tampering, or deterioration. Documents and things produced for inspection during the examination of the witness, shall, upon the request of a party, be marked for identification and annexed to the deposition and may be inspected and copied by any party, except that if the person producing the materials

desires to retain them the person may (A) offer copies to be marked for identification and annexed to the deposition and to serve thereafter as originals if the person affords to all parties fair opportunity to verify the copies by comparison with the originals, or (B) offer the originals to be marked for identification, after giving to each party an opportunity to inspect and copy them, in which event the materials may then be used in the same manner as if annexed to the deposition. Any party may move for an order that the original be annexed to and returned with the deposition to the court, pending final disposition of the case.

(2) Unless otherwise ordered by the court or agreed by the parties, the officer shall retain stenographic notes of any deposition taken stenographically or a copy of the recording of any deposition taken by another method. Upon payment of reasonable charges therefor, the officer shall furnish a copy of the transcript or other recording of the deposition to any party or to the deponent.

(3) The party taking the deposition shall give prompt notice of its filing to all other parties.

(g) **Failure to Attend or to Serve Subpoena; Expenses.**

(1) If the party giving the notice of the taking of a deposition fails to attend and proceed therewith and another party attends in person or by attorney pursuant to the notice, the court may order the party giving the notice to pay to such other party the reasonable expenses incurred by that party and that party's attorney in attending, including reasonable attorney's fees.

(2) If the party giving the notice of the taking of a deposition of a witness fails to serve a subpoena upon the witness and the witness because of such failure does not attend, and if another party attends in person or by attorney because that party expects the deposition of that witness to be taken, the court may order the party giving the notice to pay to such other party the reasonable expenses incurred by that party and that party's attorney in attending, including reasonable attorney's fees.

Rule 34. Production of Documents and Things and Entry Upon Land for Inspection and Other Purposes

(a) **Scope.**

Any party may serve on any other party a request (1) to produce and permit the party making the request, or someone acting on the requestor's behalf, to inspect and copy, any designated documents (including writings, drawings, graphs, charts, photographs, phonorecords, and other data compilations from which information can be obtained, translated, if necessary, by the respondent through detection devices into reasonably usable form), or to inspect and copy, test, or sample any tangible things which constitute or contain matters within the scope of Rule 26(b) and which are in the possession, custody or control of the party upon whom the request is served; or (2) to permit entry upon designated land or other property in the possession or control of the party upon whom the request is served for the purpose of inspection and measuring, surveying, photographing, testing, or sampling the property or any designated object or operation thereon, within the scope of Rule 26(b).

(b) **Procedure.**

The request shall set forth, either by individual item or by category, the items to be inspected, and, describe each with reasonable particularity. The request shall specify a reasonable time, place, and manner of making the inspection and performing the related acts. Without leave of court or written stipulation, a request may not be served before the time specified in Rule 26(d).

The party upon whom the request is served shall serve a written response within 30 days after the service of the request. A shorter or longer time may be directed by the court or, in the absence of such an order, agreed to in writing by the parties, subject to Rule 29. The response shall state, with respect to each item or category, that inspection and related activities will be permitted as requested, unless the request is objected to, in which event the reasons for the objection shall be stated. If objection is made to part of an item or category, the part shall be specified and inspection permitted of the remaining parts. The party submitting the request may move for an order under Rule 37(a) with respect to any objection to or other failure to respond to the request or any part thereof, or any failure to permit inspection as requested.

A party who produces documents for inspection shall produce them as they are kept in the usual course of business or shall organize and label them to correspond with the categories in the request.

(c) Persons Not Parties.

A person not a party to the action may be compelled to produce documents and things or to submit to an inspection as provided in Rule 45.

Rule 37. Failure to Make Disclosure or Cooperate in Discovery: Sanctions

(a) Motion For Order Compelling Disclosure or Discovery.

A party, upon reasonable notice to other parties and all persons affected thereby, may apply for an order compelling disclosure or discovery as follows:

(1) **Appropriate Court.** An application for an order to a party shall be made to the court in which the action is pending. An application for an order to a person who is not a party shall be made to the court in the district where the discovery is being, or is to be, taken.

(2) **Motion.**

    (A) If a party fails to make a disclosure required by Rule 26(a), any other party may move to compel disclosure and for appropriate sanctions. The motion must include a certification that the movant has in good faith conferred or attempted to confer with the party not making the disclosure in an effort to secure the disclosure without court action.

    (B) If a deponent fails to answer a question propounded or submitted under Rules 30 or 31, or a corporation or other entity fails to make a designation under Rule 30(b)(6) or 31(a), or a party fails to answer an interrogatory submitted under Rule 33, or if a party, in response to a request for inspection submitted under Rule 34, fails to respond that inspection will be permitted as requested or fails to permit inspection as requested, the discovering party may move for an order compelling an answer, or a designation, or an order compelling inspection in accordance with the request. The motion must include a certification that the movant has in good faith conferred or attempted to confer with the person or party failing to make the discovery in an effort to secure the information or material without court action. When taking a deposition on oral examination, the proponent of the question may complete or adjourn the examination before applying for an order.

(3) **Evasive or Incomplete Disclosure, Answer, or Response.** For purposes of this subdivision an evasive or incomplete disclosure, answer, or response is to be treated as a failure to disclose, answer, or respond.

(4) **Expenses and Sanctions.**

    (A) If the motion is granted or if the disclosure or requested discovery is provided after the motion was filed, the court shall, after affording an opportunity to be heard, require the party or deponent whose conduct necessitated the motion or the party or attorney advising such conduct or both of them to pay to the moving party the reasonable expenses incurred in making the motion, including attorney's fees, unless the court finds that the motion was filed without the movant's first making a good faith effort to obtain the disclosure or discovery without court action, or that the opposing party's nondisclosure, response, or objection was substantially justified, or that other circumstances make an award of expenses unjust.

    (B) If the motion is denied, the court may enter any protective order authorized under Rule 26(c) and shall, after affording an opportunity to be heard, require the moving party or the attorney filing the motion or both of them to pay to the party or deponent who opposed the motion the reasonable expenses incurred in opposing the motion, including attorney's fees, unless the court finds that the making of the motion was substantially justified or that other circumstances make an award of expenses unjust.

    (C) If the motion is granted in part and denied in part, the court may enter any protective order authorized under Rule 26(c) and may, after affording an opportunity to be heard, apportion the reasonable expenses incurred in relation to the motion among the parties and persons in a just manner.

(b) Failure to Comply with Order.

(1) **Sanctions by Court in District Where Deposition is Taken.** If a deponent fails to be sworn or to answer a question after being directed to do so by the court in the district in which the deposition is being taken, the failure may be considered a contempt of that court.

(2) **Sanctions by Court in Which Action is Pending.** If a party or an officer, director, or managing agent of a party or a person designated under Rule 30(b)(6) or 31(a) to testify on behalf of a party fails to obey an order to provide or permit discovery, including an order made under subdivision (a) of this rule or Rule 35, or if a party fails to obey an order entered under Rule 26(f), the court in which the action is pending may make such orders in regard to the failure are as just, and among others the following:

(A) An order that the matters regarding which the order was made or any other designated facts shall be taken to be established for the purposes of the action in accordance with the claim of the party obtaining the order:

(B) An order refusing to allow the disobedient party to support or oppose designated claims or defenses, or prohibiting that party from introducing designated matters in evidence;

(C) An order striking out pleadings or parts thereof, or staying further proceedings until the order is obeyed, or dismissing the action or proceeding or any part thereof, or rendering a judgment by default against the disobedient party;

(D) In lieu of any of the foregoing orders or in addition thereto, an order treating as a contempt of court the failure to obey any orders except an order to submit to a physical or mental examination;

(E) Where a party has failed to comply with an order under Rule 35(a) requiring that party to produce another for examination, such orders as are listed in paragraphs (A), (B), and (C) of this subdivision, unless the party failing to comply shows that that party is unable to produce such person for examination.

In lieu of any of the foregoing orders or in addition thereto, the court shall require the party failing to obey the order or the attorney advising that party or both to pay the reasonable expenses, including attorney's fees, caused by the failure, unless the court finds that the failure was substantially justified or that other circumstances make an award of expenses unjust.

(c) **Failure to Disclose; False or Misleading Disclosure; Refusal to Admit.**

(1) A party that without substantial justification fails to disclose information required by Rule 26(a) or 26(e)(1) shall not, unless such failure is harmless, be permitted to use as evidence at a trial, at a hearing, or on a motion any witness or information not so disclosed. In addition to or in lieu of this sanction, the court, on motion and after affording an opportunity to be heard, may impose other appropriate sanctions. In addition to requiring payment of reasonable expenses, including attorney's fees, caused by the failure, these sanctions may include any of the actions authorized under subparagraphs (A), (B), and (C) of subdivision (b)(2) of this rule and may include informing the jury of the failure to make the disclosure.

(2) If a party fails to admit the genuineness of any document or the truth of any matter as requested under Rule 36, and if the party requesting the admissions thereafter proves the genuineness of the document or the truth of the matter, the requesting party may apply to the court for an order requiring the other party to pay the reasonable expenses incurred in making that proof, including reasonable attorney's fees. The court shall make the order unless it finds that (A) the request was held objectionable pursuant to Rule 36(a), or (B) the admission sought was of no substantial importance, or (C) the party failing to admit had reasonable ground to believe that the party might prevail on the matter, or (D) there was other good reason for the failure to admit.

(d) **Failure of Party to Attend at Own Deposition or Serve Answers to Interrogatories or Respond to Request for Inspection.**

If a party or an officer, director, or managing agent of a party or a person designated under Rule 30(b)(6) or 31(a) to testify on behalf of a party fails (1) to appear before the officer who is to take the deposition, after being served with a proper notice, or (2) to serve answers or objections to interrogatories submitted under Rule 33, after proper service of the interrogatories, or (3) to serve a written response to a request for inspection submitted under Rule 34, after proper service of the request, the court in which the action is pending on motion may make such orders in regard to the failure as are just, and among others it may take any action authorized under subparagraphs (A), (B), and (C) of subdivision (b)(2) of this rule. Any motion specifying a failure under clause (2) or (3) of this subdivision shall include a certification that the movant has in good faith conferred or attempted to confer with the party failing to answer or respond in an effort to obtain such answer or response without court action. In lieu of any order or in addition thereto, the court shall require the party failing to act or the attorney advising that party or both to pay the reasonable expenses, including attorney's fees, caused by the failure unless the court finds that the failure was substantially justified or that other circumstances make an award of expenses unjust.

The failure to act described in this subdivision may not be excused on the ground that the discovery sought is objectionable unless the party failing to act has a pending motion for a protective order as provided by Rule 26(c).

(e) [Abrogated]

(f) [Repealed. Pub.L. 96-481, Title II, §205(a), Oct. 21, 1980, 94 Stat. 2330.]

(g) **Failure to Participate in the Framing of a Discovery Plan.**

If a party or a party's attorney fails to participate in good faith in the development and submission of a proposed discovery plan as required by Rule 26(f), the court may, after opportunity for hearing, require such party or attorney to pay to any other party the reasonable expenses, including attorney's fees, caused by the failure.

Rule 45. Subpoena

(a) **Form; Issuance.**

(1) Every subpoena shall
   (A) state the name of the court from which it is issued; and
   (B) state the title of the action, the name of the court in which it is pending, and its civil action number; and
   (C) command each person to whom it is directed to attend and give testimony or to produce and permit inspection and copying of designated books, documents or tangible things in the possession, custody or control of that person, or to permit inspection of premises, at a time and place therein specified; and
   (D) set forth the text of subdivisions (c) and (d) of this rule.
   A command to produce evidence or to permit inspection may be joined with a command to appear at trial or hearing or at deposition, or may be issued separately.

(2) A subpoena commanding attendance at a trial or hearing shall issue from the court for the district in which the hearing or trial is to be held. A subpoena for attendance at a deposition shall issue from the court for the district designated by the notice of deposition as the district in which the deposition is to be taken. If separate from a subpoena commanding the attendance of a person, a subpoena for production or inspection shall issue from the court for the district in which the production or inspection is to be made.

(3) The clerk shall issue a subpoena, signed but otherwise in blank, to a party requesting it, who shall complete it before service. An attorney as officer of the court may also issue and sign a subpoena on behalf of
   (A) a court in which the attorney is authorized to practice; or
   (B) a court for a district in which a deposition or production is compelled by the subpoena, if the deposition or production pertains to an action pending in a court in which the attorney is authorized to practice.

(b) **Service**

(1) A subpoena may be served by any person who is not a party and is not less than 18 years of age. Service of a subpoena upon a person named therein shall be made by delivering a copy thereof to such person and, if the person's attendance is commanded, by tendering to that person the fees for one day's attendance and the mileage allowed by law. When the subpoena is issued on behalf of the United States or an officer or agency thereof, fees and mileage need not be tendered. Prior notice of any commanded production of documents and things or inspection of premises before trial shall be served on each party in the manner prescribed by Rule 5(b).

(2) Subject to the provisions of clause (ii) of subparagraph (c)(3)(A) of this rule, a subpoena may be served at any place within the district of the court by which it is issued, or at any place without the district that is within 100 miles of the place of the deposition, hearing, trial, production, or inspection specified in the subpoena or at any place within the state where a state statute or rule of court permits service of a subpoena issued by a state court of general jurisdiction sitting in the place of the deposition, hearing, trial, production, or inspection specified in the subpoena. When a statute of the United States provides therefor, the court upon proper application and cause shown may authorize the service of a subpoena at any other place. A subpoena directed to a witness in a foreign country who is a national or resident of the United States shall issue under the circumstances and in the manner and be served as provided in Title 28, U.S.C. §1783.

(3) Proof of service when necessary shall be made by filing with the clerk of the court by which the subpoena is issued a statement of the date and manner of service and of the names of the persons served, certified by the person who made the service.

(c) **Protection of Persons Subject to Subpoenas.**

(1) A party or an attorney responsible for the issuance and service of a subpoena shall take reasonable steps to avoid imposing undue burden or expense on a person subject to that subpoena. The court on behalf of which the subpoena was issued shall enforce this duty and impose upon the party or attorney in breach of this duty an appropriate sanction, which may include, but is not limited to, lost earnings and a reasonable attorney's fee.

(2) (A) A person commanded to produce and permit inspection and copying of designated books, papers, documents or tangible things, or inspection of premises need not appear in person at the place of production or inspection unless commanded to appear for deposition, hearing or trial.

(B) Subject to paragraph (d)(2) of this rule, a person commanded to produce and permit inspection and copying may within 14 days after service of the subpoena or before the time specified for compliance if such time is less than 14 days after service, serve upon the party or attorney designated in the subpoena written objection to inspection or copying of any or all of the designated materials or of the premises. If objection is made, the party serving the subpoena shall not be entitled to inspect and copy the materials or inspect the premises except pursuant to an order of the court by which the subpoena was issued. If objection has been made, the party serving the subpoena may, upon notice to the person commanded to produce, move at any time for an order to compel the production. Such an order to compel production shall protect any person who is not a party or an officer of a party from significant expense resulting from the inspection and copying commanded.

(3) (A) On timely motion, the court by which a subpoena was issued shall quash or modify the subpoena if it
  (i) fails to allow reasonable time for compliance;
  (ii) requires a person who is not a party or an officer of a party to travel to a place more than 100 miles from the place where that person resides, is employed or regularly transacts business in person, except that, subject to the provisions of clause (c)(3)(B)(iii) of this rule, such a person may in order to attend trial be commanded to travel from any such place within the state in which the trial is held, or
  (iii) requires disclosure of privileged or other protected matter and no exception or waiver applies, or
  (iv) subjects a person to undue burden.

(B) If a subpoena
  (i) requires disclosure of a trade secret or other confidential research, development, or commercial information, or
  (ii) requires disclosure of an unretained expert's opinion or information not describing specific events or occurrences in dispute and resulting from the expert's study made not at the request of any party, or
  (iii) requires a person who is not a party or an officer of a party to incur substantial expense to travel more than 100 miles to attend trial, the court may, to protect a person subject to or affected by the subpoena, quash or modify the subpoena or, if the party in whose

behalf the subpoena is issued shows a substantial need for the testimony or material that cannot be otherwise met without undue hardship and assures that the person to whom the subpoena is addressed will be reasonably compensated, the court may order appearance or production only upon specified conditions.

(d) Duties in Responding to Subpoena.

(1) A person responding to a subpoena to produce documents shall produce them as they are kept in the usual course of business or shall organize and label them to correspond with the categories in the demand.

(2) When information subject to a subpoena is withheld on a claim that it is privileged or subject to protection as trial preparation materials, the claim shall be made expressly and shall be supported by a description of the nature of the documents, communications, or things not produced that is sufficient to enable the demanding party to contest the claim.

(e) Contempt.

Failure by any person without adequate excuse to obey a subpoena served upon that person may be deemed a contempt of the court from which the subpoena issued. An adequate cause for failure to obey exists when a subpoena purports to require a non-party to attend or produce at a place not within the limits provided by clause (ii) of subparagraph (c)(3)(A).

Appendix D:
Convention on Jurisdiction and Enforcement of Judgments in Civil and Commercial Matters ("Brussels Convention")

1. This Convention shall apply in civil and commercial matters whatever the nature of the court or tribunal. It shall not extend, in particular, to revenue, customs or administrative matters. The convention shall not apply to:-

1. The status or legal capacity of natural persons, rights in property arising out of a matrimonial relationship, wills and succession.
2. Bankruptcy, proceedings relating to the winding-up of insolvent companies or other legal persons, judicial arrangements, compositions and analogous proceedings.
3. Social security.
4. Arbitration.

2. Subject to the provisions of this Convention, persons domiciled in a Contracting State shall, whatever their nationality, be sued in the courts of that State. Persons who are not nationals of the State in which they are domiciled shall be governed by the rules of jurisdiction applicable to nationals of that State.

3. Persons domiciled in a Contracting State may be sued in the courts of another Contracting State only by virtue of the rules set out in Sections 2 to 6 of this Title. In particular the following provisions shall not be applicable as against them:

— in Belgium: Article 15 of the civil code (Code civil — Burgerlijk Wetboek) and Article 638 of the judicial code (Code judiciare — Gerechtelijk Wetboek);
— in Denmark: Article 246(2) and (3) of the law on civil procedure (lov om rettens pleje) and Chapter 3, Article 3 of the Greenland law on civil procedure (Lov for Gronland om rettens pleje);
— in the Federal Republic of Germany: Article 23 of the code of civil procedure (Zivilprozeßordnung);
— in Greece: Article 40 of the code of civil procedure ...;
— in France: Articles 14 and 15 of the civil code (Code civil);
— in Ireland: the rules which enable jurisdiction to be founded on the document instituting the proceedings having been served on the defendant during his temporary presence in Ireland;
— in Italy: Articles 2 and 4, Nos. 1 and 2 of the code of civil procedure (Codice di procedura civile);
— in Luxembourg: Articles 14 and 15 of the civil code (Code civil);
— in the Netherlands: Articles 126(3) and 127 of the code of civil procedure (Wetboek van Burgerlijke Rechtsvordering);
— in Portugal: Article 65(1)(c), Article 65(2) and Article 65A(c) of the code of civil procedure (Codigo de Processo Civil) and Article 11 of the code of labour procedure (Codigo de Processo de Trabalho);
— in the United Kingdom: the rules which enable jurisdiction to be founded on:
(a) the document instituting the proceedings having been served on the defendant during his temporary presence in the United Kingdom; or
(b) the presence within the United Kingdom of property belonging to the defendant; or
(c) the seizure by the plaintiff of property situated in the United Kingdom.

4. If the defendant is not domiciled in a Contracting State, the jurisdiction of the courts of each Contracting State shall, subject to the provisions of Article 16, be determined by the law of that State. As against such a defendant, any person domiciled in a Contracting State may, whatever his nationality, avail himself in that State of the rules of jurisdiction there in force, and in particular those specified in the second paragraph of Article 3, in the same way as the nationals of that State.

5. A person domiciled in a Contracting State may, in another Contracting State, be sued —

1. In matters relating to a contract, in the courts for the place of performance of the obligation in question; in matters relating to individual contracts of employment, this place is that where the employee habitually carries out his work, or if the employee does not habitually carry out his work in any one country, the employer may also be sued in the courts of the place where the business which engaged the employee was or is now situated.

2. In matters relating to maintenance, in the courts for the place where the maintenance creditor is domiciled or habitually resident or, if the matter is ancillary to proceedings concerning the status of a person, in the court which, according to its own law, has jurisdiction to entertain those proceedings, unless that jurisdiction is based solely on the nationality of one of the parties.

3. In matters relating to tort, delict or quasi-delict, in the courts for the place where the harmful event occurred.

4. As regards a civil claim for damages or restitution which is based on an act giving rise to criminal proceedings, in the court seised of those proceedings, to the extent that court has jurisdiction under its own law to entertain civil proceedings.

5. As regards a dispute arising out of the operations of a branch, agency or other establishment, in the courts for the place in which the branch, agency or other establishment is situated.

6. As settlor, trustee or beneficiary of a trust created by the operation of a statute, or by a written instrument, or created orally and evidenced in writing, in the courts of the Contracting State in which the trust is domiciled.

7. As regards a dispute concerning the payment of remuneration claimed in respect of the salvage of a cargo or freight, in the court under the authority of which the cargo or freight in question—
   (a) has been arrested to secure such payment, or
   (b) could have been so arrested, but bail or other security has been given; provided that this provision shall apply only if it is claimed that the defendant has an interest in the cargo or freight or had such an interest at the time of salvage.

6. A person domiciled in a Contracting State may also be sued-

1. Where he is one of a number of defendants, in the courts for the place where any one of them is domiciled;

2. As a third party in an action on a warranty or guarantee or in any other third party proceedings, in the court seised of the original proceedings, unless these were instituted solely with the object of removing him from the jurisdiction of the court which would be competent in his case;

3. On a counter-claim arising from the same contract or facts on which the original claim was based, in the court in which the original claim is pending;

4. In matters relating to a contract, if the action may be combined with an action against the same defendant in matters relating to rights in rem in immovable property, in the court of the Contracting State in which the property is situated.

6a. Where by virtue of this Convention a court of a Contracting State has jurisdiction in actions relating to liability from the use or operation of a ship, that court, or any other court substituted for this purpose by the internal law of that state, shall also have jurisdiction over claims for limitation of such liability.

7. In matters relating to insurance, jurisdiction shall be determined by this section [Articles 7-12A] without prejudice to the provisions of Articles 4 and 5 point 5.

8. An insurer domiciled in a Contracting State may be sued-

1. in the courts of the State where he is domiciled, or

2. in another Contracting State, in the courts for the place where the policy-holder is domiciled, or

3. if he is a co-insurer, in the courts of a Contracting State in which proceedings are brought against the leading insurer. An insurer who is not domiciled in a Contracting State but has a branch, agency or other establishment in one of the Contracting States shall, in disputes arising out of the operations of the branch, agency or establishment, be deemed to be domiciled in that State.

9. In respect of liability insurance or insurance of immovable property, the insurer may in addition be sued in the courts for the place where the harmful event occurred. The same applies if movable and immovable property are covered by the same insurance policy and both are adversely affected by the same contingency.

10. In respect of liability insurance, the insurer may also, if the law of the court permits it, be joined in proceedings which the injured party had brought against the insured. The provisions of Articles 7, 8 and 9 shall apply to actions brought by the injured party directly against the insurer, where such direct actions are permitted. If the law governing such direct actions provides that the policy-holder or the insured may be joined as a party to the action, the same court shall have jurisdiction over them.

11. Without prejudice to the provisions of the third paragraph of Article 10, an insurer may bring proceedings only in the courts of the Contracting State in which the defendant is domiciled, irrespective of whether he is the policy-holder, the insured or a beneficiary. The provisions of this Section shall not affect the right to bring a counterclaim in the court in which, in accordance with this Section, the original claim is pending.

12. The provisions of this Section may be departed from only by an agreement on jurisdiction—
1. Which is entered into after the dispute has arisen, or
2. which allows the policy-holder, the insured or a beneficiary to bring proceedings in courts other than those indicated in this Section, or
3. which is concluded between a policy-holder and an insurer, both of whom are domiciled in the same Contracting State, and which has the effect of conferring jurisdiction on the courts of that State even if the harmful event were to occur abroad, provided that such an agreement is not contrary to the law of that State, or
4. which is concluded with a policy-holder who is not domiciled in a Contracting State, except in so far as the insurance is compulsory or relates to immovable property in a Contracting State, or
5. which relates to a contract of insurance in so far as it covers one or more of the risks set out in Article 12a.

12a. The following are the risks referred to in point 5 of Article 12—
1. Any loss of or damage to—
   (a) sea-going ships, installations situated offshore or on the high seas, or aircraft, arising from perils which relate to their use for commercial purposes;
   (b) goods in transit other than passengers' baggage where the transit consists of or includes carriage by such ships or aircraft.
2. Any liability, other than for bodily injury to passengers or loss of or damage to their baggage—
   (a) arising out of the use or operation of ships, installations or aircraft as referred to in point 1 (a) above in so far as the law of the Contracting State in which such aircraft are registered does not prohibit agreements on jurisdiction regarding insurance of such risks;
   (b) for loss or damage caused by goods in transit as described in point 1 (b) above,
3. Any financial loss connected with the use or operation of ships, installations or aircraft as referred to in point 1 (a) above, in particular loss of freight or charter-hire.
4. Any risk or interest connected with any of those referred to in points 1 to 3 above.

13. In proceedings concerning a contract concluded by a person for a purpose which can be regarded as being outside his trade or profession, hereinafter called "the consumer," jurisdiction shall be determined by this Section, without prejudice to the provisions of Article 4 and point 5 of Article 5, if it is —
1. a contract for the sale of goods on instalment credit terms, or
2. a contract for a loan repayable by instalments, or for any other form of credit, made to finance the sale of goods, or

3. any other contract for the supply of goods or a contract for the supply of services, and
   (a) in the State of the consumer's domicile the conclusion of the contract was preceded by a specific invitation addressed to him or by advertising; and
   (b) the consumer took in that State the steps necessary for the conclusion of the contract.

Where a consumer enters into a contract with a party who is not domiciled in a Contracting State but has a branch, agency or other establishment in one of the Contracting States, that party shall, in disputes arising out of the operations of the branch, agency or establishment, be deemed to be domiciled in that State.

This section shall not apply to contracts of transport.

14. A consumer may bring proceedings against the other party to a contract either in the courts of the Contracting State in which that party is domiciled or in the courts of the Contracting State in which he is himself domiciled. Proceedings may be brought against a consumer by the other party to the contract only in the courts of the Contracting State in which the consumer is domiciled. These provisions shall not affect the right to bring a counter-claim in the court in which, in accordance with this Section, the original claim is pending.

15. The provisions of this Section [Articles 13-15] may be departed from only by an agreement—
1. which is entered into after the dispute has arisen, or
2. which allows the consumer to bring proceedings in courts other than those indicated in this Section or
3. which is entered into by the consumer and the other party to the contract, both of whom are at the time of conclusion of the contract domiciled or habitually resident in the same Contracting State, and which confers jurisdiction on the courts of that State, provided that such an agreement is not contrary to the law of that State.

16. The following courts shall have exclusive jurisdiction, regarding of domicile:
1. (a) in proceedings which have as their object rights in rem in immovable property or tenancies of immovable property, the courts of the Contracting State in which the property is situated;
   (b) however, in proceedings which have as their object tenancies of immovable property concluded for temporary private use for a maximum period of six consecutive months, the courts of the Contracting State in which the defendant is domiciled shall also have jurisdiction, provided that the landlord and the defendant are natural persons and are domiciled in the same Contracting State.
2. In proceedings which have as their object the validity of the constitution, the nullity or the dissolution of companies or other legal persons or associations of natural or legal persons, or the decisions of their organs, the courts of the Contracting State in which the company, legal person or association has its seat.
3. In proceedings which have as their object the validity of entries in public registers, the courts of the Contracting State in which the register is kept.
4. In proceedings concerned with the registration or validity of patents, trade marks, designs or other similar rights required to be deposited or registered, the courts of the Contracting State in which the deposit or registration has been applied for, has taken place or is under the terms of an international convention deemed to have taken place.
5. In proceedings concerned with the enforcement of judgments, the courts of the Contracting State in which the judgment has been or is to be enforced.

17. If the courts, one or more of whom is domiciled in a Contracting State, have agreed that a court or the courts of a Contracting State are to have jurisdiction to settle any disputes which have arisen or which may arise in connection with a particular legal relationship, that court or those courts shall have exclusive jurisdiction. Such an agreement conferring jurisdiction shall be either—
   (a) in writing or evidenced in writing, or
   (b) in a form which accords with practices which the parties established between themselves or
   (c) in international trade or commerce, in a form which accords with a usage of which the parties are or ought to have been aware and which in such trade or commerce is widely known to, and regularly observed by, parties to contracts of the type involved in the particular trade or commerce concerned.

Where such an agreement is concluded by parties, none of whom is domiciled in a Contracting State, the courts of other Contracting States shall have no jurisdiction over their disputes unless the court or courts chosen have declined jurisdiction.

The court or courts of a Contracting State on which a trust instrument has conferred jurisdiction shall have exclusive jurisdiction in any proceedings brought against a settlor, trustee or beneficiary, if relations between these persons or their rights or obligations under the trust are involved.

Agreements or provisions of a trust instrument conferring jurisdiction shall have no legal force if they are contrary to the provisions of Articles 12 or 15, or if the courts whose jurisdictions they purport to exclude have exclusive jurisdiction by virtue of Article 16.

If an agreement conferring jurisdiction was concluded for the benefit of only one of the parties, that party shall retain the right to bring proceedings in any other court which has jurisdiction by virtue of this Convention.

In matters relating to individual contracts of employment an agreement conferring jurisdiction shall have legal force only if it is entered into after the dispute has arisen or if the employee invokes it to seise courts other than those for the defendant's domicile or those specified in article 5(1).

18. Apart from jurisdiction derived from other provisions of this Convention, a court of a Contracting State before whom a defendant enters an appearance shall have jurisdiction. This rule shall not apply where appearance was entered solely to contest the jurisdiction, or where another court has exclusive jurisdiction by virtue of Article 16

19. Where a court of a Contracting State is seised of a claim which is principally concerned with a matter over which the courts of another Contracting State have exclusive jurisdiction by virtue of Article 16, it shall declare of its own motion that it has no jurisdiction.

20. Where a defendant domiciled in one Contracting State is sued in a court of another Contracting State and does not enter an appearance, the court shall declare of its own motion that it has no jurisdiction unless its jurisdiction is derived from the provisions of the Convention.

The court shall stay the proceedings so long as it is not shown that the defendant has been able to receive the document instituting the proceedings or an equivalent document in sufficient time to enable him to arrange for his defence, or that all necessary steps have been taken to this end.

The provisions of the foregoing paragraph shall be replaced by those of Article 15 of the Hague Convention of 15th November 1965 on the service abroad of judicial and extrajudicial documents in civil or commercial matters, if the document instituting the proceedings or notice thereof had to be transmitted abroad in accordance with that Convention.

21. Where proceedings involving the same cause of action and between the same parties are brought in the courts of different Contracting States, any court other than the court first seised shall of its own motion stay its proceedings until such time as the jurisdiction of the court first seised shall decline jurisdiction in favour of that court.

22. Where related actions are brought in the courts of different Contracting States, any court other than the court first seised may, while the actions are pending at first instance, stay its proceedings. A court other than the court first seised may also, on the application of one of the parties, decline jurisdiction if the law of that court permits the consolidation of related actions and the court first seised has jurisdiction over both actions.

For the purposes of this Article, actions are deemed to be related where they are so closely connected that it is expedient to hear and determine them together to avoid the risk of irreconcilable judgments resulting from separate proceedings.

23. Where actions come within the exclusive jurisdiction of several courts, any court other than the court first seised shall decline jurisdiction in favour of that court.

24. Application may be made to the courts of a Contracting State for such provisional, including protective, measures as may be available under the law of the State, even if, under this Convention, the courts of another contracting State have jurisdiction as to the substance of the matter.

25. For the purposes of this Convention "judgment" means any judgment given by a court or tribunal of a Contracting State, whatever the judgment may be called, including a decree, order, decision or writ of execution, as well as the determination of costs or expenses by an officer of the court.

26. A judgment given in a Contracting State shall be recognised in the other Contracting States without any special procedure being required. Any interested party who raises the recognition of a judgment as the principal issue in a dispute may, in accordance with the procedures provided for in sections 2 and 3 of this Title [Articles 5-12A], apply for a decision that the judgment be recognised. If the outcome of proceedings in a court of a Contracting State depends on the determination of an incidental question of recognition that court shall have jurisdiction over that question.

27. A judgment shall not be recognised:
1. If such recognition is contrary to public policy in the State in which recognition is sought;
2. where it was given in default of appearance, if the defendant was not duly served with the document which instituted the proceedings or with an equivalent document in sufficient time to enable him to arrange for his defence;
3. if the judgment is irreconcilable with a judgment given in a dispute between the same parties in the State in which recognition is sought;
4. if the court of the State of origin, in order to arrive at its judgment, has decided a property arising out of a matrimonial relationship, wills or succession in a way that conflicts with a rule of the private international law of the State in which the recognition is sought, unless the same result would have been reached by the application of the rules of private international law of that state;
5. if the judgment is irreconcilable with an earlier judgment given in a non-contracting state involving the same cause of action and between the same parties, provided that this latter judgment fulfils the conditions necessary for its recognition in the state addressed.

28. Moreover, a judgment shall not be recognised if it conflicts with the provisions of Sections 3, 4 or 5 of title II [Articles 7-16], or in a case provided for in Article 59.

In its examination of the grounds of jurisdiction referred to in the foregoing paragraph, the court or authority applied to shall bound by the findings of fact on which the court of the State of origin based its jurisdiction. Subject to the provisions of the first paragraph, the jurisdiction of the court of the State of origin may not be reviewed; the test of public policy referred to in point 1 of Article 27 may not be applied to the rules relating to jurisdiction.

29. Under no circumstances may a foreign judgment be reviewed as to its substance.

30. A court of a Contracting State in which recognition is sought of a judgment given in another Contracting State may stay the proceedings if an ordinary appeal against the judgment has been lodged. A court of a Contracting State in which recognition is sought of a judgment given in Ireland or the United Kingdom may stay the proceedings if enforcement is suspended in the State of origin, by reason of an appeal.

31. A judgment given in a Contracting State and enforceable in that State shall be enforced in another Contracting State when, on the application of any interested party, it has been declared enforceable there. However, in the United Kingdom, such a judgment shall be enforced in England and Wales, in Scotland, or in Northern Ireland when, on the application of any interested party, it has been registered for enforcement in that part of the United Kingdom.

32. The application shall be submitted [to specified courts in each Contracting State.]

The jurisdiction of local courts shall be determined by reference to the place of domicile of the party against whom enforcement is sought. If he is not domiciled in the State in which enforcement is sought, it shall be determined by reference to the place of enforcement.

33. The procedure for making the application shall be governed by the law of the state in which enforcement is sought.

The application must give an address for service of process within the area of jurisdiction of the court applied to. However, if the law of the State in which enforcement is sought does not provide for the furnishing of such an address, the applicant shall appoint a representative *ad litem*. The documents referred to in Article 46 and 47 shall be attached to the application.

34. The court applied to shall give its decision without delay; the party against whom enforcement is sought shall not at this stage of the proceedings be entitled to make any submission on the application. The application may be refused only for one of the reasons specified in Articles 27 and 28. Under no circumstances may the foreign judgment be reviewed as to its substance.

35. The appropriate officer of the court shall without delay bring the decision given on the application to the notice of the applicant in accordance with the procedure laid down by the law of the State in which enforcement is sought.

36. If enforcement is authorised, the party against whom enforcement is sought may appeal against the decision within one month of service thereof. If that party is domiciled in a Contracting State other than that in which the decision authorising enforcement was given, the time for appealing shall be two months and shall run from the date of service, either on him in person or at his residence. No extension of time may be granted on account of distance.

37. An appeal against the decision authorising enforcement shall be lodged in accordance with the rules governing procedure in contentious matters [in specified courts in each Contracting State.]

38. The court with which the appeal under Article 37(1) is lodged may, on the application of the appellant, stay the proceedings if an ordinary appeal has been lodged against the judgment in the State of origin or if the time for such an appeal has not yet expired; in the latter case, the court may specify the time within such an appeal is to be lodged. Where the judgment was given in Ireland or the United Kingdom, any form of appeal available in the State of origin shall be treated as an ordinary appeal for the purposes of the first paragraph. The court may also make enforcement conditional on the provision of such security as it shall determine.

39. During the time specified for an appeal pursuant to Article 36 and until any such appeal has been determined, no measures of enforcement may be taken other than protective measures taken against the property of the party against whom enforcement is sought. The decision authorising enforcement shall carry with it the power to proceed to any such protective measures.

40. 1. If the application for enforcement is refused, the applicant may appeal [to specified courts in each Contracting State.]
   2. The party against whom enforcement is sought shall be summoned to appear before the appellate court. If he fails to appear, the provisions of the second and third paragraphs of Article 20 shall apply even where he is not domiciled in any of the Contracting States.

41. A judgment given on an appeal provided for in Article 40 may be contested only [in specified manners in each Contracting State.]

42. Where a foreign judgment has been given in respect of several matters and enforcement cannot be authorised for all of them, the court shall authorise the enforcement for one or more of them. An applicant may request partial enforcement of a judgment.

43. A foreign judgment which orders a periodic payment by way of a penalty shall be enforceable in the State in which enforcement is sought only if the amount of the payment has been finally determined by the courts of the State of origin.

44. An applicant who, in the State of origin has benefited from complete or partial legal aid or exemption from costs or expenses, shall be entitled, in the procedures provided for in Articles 32 to 35, to benefit from the most favourable legal aid or the most extensive exemption from, costs or expenses provided for by the law of the State addressed. ...

45. No security, bond or deposit, however described, shall be required of a party who in one Contracting State applies for enforcement of a judgment given in another Contracting State on the ground that he is a foreign national or that the is not domiciled or resident in the State in which enforcement is sought.

46. A party seeking recognition or applying for enforcement of a judgment shall produce:
   1. a copy of the judgment which satisfies the conditions necessary to establish its authenticity;

2. in the case of a judgment given in default, the original or a certified true copy of the document which establishes that the party in default was served with the document instituting the proceedings or with an equivalent document.

47. A party applying for enforcement shall also produce;

1. documents which establish that, according to the law of the State of origin the judgment is enforceable and has been served;

2. where appropriate, a document showing that the applicant is in receipt of legal aid in the State of origin.

48. If the documents specified in point 2 of Articles 46 and 47 are not produced, the court may specify a time for their production, equivalent documents or, if it considers that it has sufficient information before it, dispense with their production. If the court so requires, a translation of the documents shall be produced; the translation shall be certified by a person qualified to do so in one of the Contracting States.

49. No legalisation or other similar formality shall be required in respect of the documents referred to in Articles 46 or 47 or the second paragraph of Article 48, or in respect of a document appointing a representative *ad litem.*

50. A document which has been formally drawn up or registered as an authentic instrument and is enforceable in one Contracting State shall, in another Contracting State, be declared enforceable there, on application made in accordance with the procedures provided for in Article 31 *et seq.* The application may be refused only if enforcement of the instrument is contrary to public policy in the State addressed. The instrument produced must satisfy the conditions necessary to establish its authenticity in the State of origin. The provisions of [Articles 46-49] shall apply as appropriate.

51. A settlement which has been approved by a court in the course of proceedings and is enforceable in the State in which it was concluded shall be enforceable in the State addressed under the same conditions as authentic instruments.

52. In order to determine whether a party is domiciled in the Contracting State whose courts are seised of a matter, the court shall apply its internal law. If a party is not domiciled in the State whose courts are seised of the matter, then, in order to determine whether the party is domiciled in another Contracting State, the court shall apply the law of that State.

53. For the purposes of this Convention, the seat of a company or other legal person or association of natural or legal persons shall be treated as its domicile. However, in order to determine that seat, the court shall apply its rules of private international law. In order to determine whether a trust is domiciled in the Contracting State whose courts are seised of the matter, the court shall apply its rules of private international law.

54. The provisions of the Convention shall apply only to legal proceedings instituted and to documents formally drawn up or registered as authentic instruments after its entry into force in the State of origin and, where recognition or enforcement of a judgment or authentic instruments is sought, in that state addressed. However, judgments given after the date of entry into force of this Convention between the State of origin and the State addressed in proceedings instituted before that date shall be recognised and enforced in accordance with the provisions of [Articles 25-49] if jurisdiction was founded upon rules which accorded with those provided for either in [Articles 2-24] of this Convention or in a convention concluded between the State of origin and the State addressed which was in force when the proceedings were instituted. If the parties to a dispute concerning a contract had agreed in writing before 1 June 1988 for Ireland or before 1 January 1987 for the United Kingdom shall retain the right to exercise jurisdiction in the dispute.

54a. For a period of three years from 1 November 1986 for Denmark and from 1 June 1988 for Ireland, jurisdiction in maritime matters shall be determined in these States not only in accordance with the provisions of Title II, but also in accordance with the provisions of paragraphs 1 to 6 following. However, upon the entry into force of the International Convention relating to the arrest of sea-going ships, signed at Brussels on 10 May 1952, for one of these States, these provisions shall cease to have effect for that State. ...

64. The Secretary General of the Council of the European Communities shall notify the signatory State of:

  (a) the deposit of each instrument of ratification;

  (b) the date of entry into force of this Convention

  (c) ...;

  (d) any declaration received pursuant to Article IV of the Protocol;

  (e) any communication made pursuant to Article VI of the Protocol.

65. The Protocol annexed to this Convention by common accord of the Contracting States shall form an integral part thereof.

66. This Convention is concluded for an unlimited period.

67. Any Contracting State may request the revision of this Convention. In this event, a revision Conference shall be convened by the President of the Council of the European Communities.

Appendix E:
Foreign Sovereign Immunities Act of 1976, 28 U.S.C. §§1330, 1602-11

§1330. Actions against foreign states

(a) The district courts shall have original jurisdiction without regard to amount in controversy of any nonjury civil action against a foreign state as defined in section 1603(a) of this title as to any claim for relief in personam with respect to which the foreign state is not entitled to immunity either under sections 1605-1607 of this title or under any applicable international agreement.

(b) Personal jurisdiction over a foreign state shall exist as to every claim for relief over which the district courts have jurisdiction under subsection (a) where service has been made under section 1608 of this title.

(c) For purposes of subsection (b), an appearance by a foreign state does not confer personal jurisdiction with respect to any claim for relief not arising out of any transaction or occurrence enumerated in sections 1605-1607 of this title.

§1602. Findings and declaration of purpose

The Congress finds that the determination by United States courts of the claims of foreign states to immunity from the jurisdiction of such courts would serve the interests of justice and would protect the rights of both foreign states and litigants in United States courts. Under international law, states are not immune from the jurisdiction of foreign courts insofar as their commercial activities are concerned, and their commercial property may be levied upon for the satisfaction of judgments rendered against them in connection with their commercial activities. Claims of foreign states to immunity should henceforth be decided by courts of the United States and of the States in conformity with the principles set forth in this chapter.

§1603. Definitions

For the purposes of this chapter -

(a) A "foreign state," except as used in section 1608 of this title, includes a political subdivision of a foreign state or an agency or instrumentality of a foreign state as defined in subsection (b).

(b) An "agency or instrumentality of a foreign state" means any entity -

    (1) which is a separate legal person, corporate or otherwise, and

    (2) which is an organ of a foreign state or political subdivision thereof, or a majority of whose shares or other ownership interest is owned by a foreign state or political subdivision thereof, and

    (3) which is neither a citizen of a State of the United States as defined in section 1332(c) and (d) of this title, nor created under the laws of any third country.

(c) The "United States" includes all territory and waters, continental or insular, subject to the jurisdiction of the United States.

(d) A "commercial activity" means either a regular course of commercial conduct or a particular commercial transaction or act. The commercial character of an activity shall be determined by reference to the nature of the course of conduct or particular transaction or act, rather than by reference to its purpose.

(e) A "commercial activity carried on in the United States by a foreign state" means commercial activity carried on by such state and having substantial contact with the United States.

§1604. Immunity of a foreign state from jurisdiction

Subject to existing international agreements to which the United States is a party at the time of enactment of this Act a foreign state shall be immune from the jurisdiction of the courts of the United States and of the States except as provided in sections 1605 to 1607 of this chapter.

§1605. General exceptions to the jurisdictional immunity of a foreign state

(a) A foreign state shall not be immune from the jurisdiction of courts of the United States or of the States in any case -

(1) in which the foreign state has waived its immunity either explicitly or by implication, notwithstanding any withdrawal of the waiver which the foreign state may purport to effect except in accordance with the terms of the waiver;

(2) in which the action is based upon a commercial activity carried on in the United States by the foreign state; or upon an act performed in the United States in connection with a commercial activity of the foreign state elsewhere; or upon an act outside the territory of the United Stares in connection with a commercial activity of the foreign. state elsewhere and that act causes a direct effect in the United States;

(3) in which rights in property taken in violation of international law are in issue and that property or any property exchanged for such property is present in the United States in connection with a commercial activity carried on in the United States by the foreign state; or that property or any property exchanged for such property is owned or operated by an agency or instrumentality of the foreign state and that agency or instrumentality is engaged in a commercial activity in the United States;

(4) in which rights in property in the United States acquired by succession or gift or rights in immovable property situated in the United States are in issue;

(5) not otherwise encompassed in paragraph (2) above, in which money damages are sought against a foreign state for personal injury or death, or damage to or loss of property, occurring in the United States and caused by the tortious act or omission of that foreign state or of any official or employee of that foreign state while acting within the scope of his office or employment; except this paragraph shall not apply to -

(A) any claim based upon the exercise or performance or the failure to exercise or perform a discretionary function regardless of whether the discretion be abused, or

(B) any claim arising out of malicious prosecution, abuse of process, libel, slander, misrepresentation, deceit, or interference with contract rights; or

(6) in which the action is brought, either to enforce an agreement made by the foreign State with or for the benefit of a private party to submit to arbitration all or any differences which have arisen or which may arise between the parties with respect to a defined legal relationship, whether contractual or not, concerning a subject matter capable of settlement by arbitration under the laws of the United States, or to confirm an award made pursuant to such an agreement to arbitrate, if (A) the arbitration takes place or is intended to take place in the United States, (B) the agreement or award is or may be governed by a treaty or other international agreement in force for the United States calling for recognition and enforcement of arbitral awards, (C) the underlying claim, save for the agreement to arbitrate, could have been brought in a United States court under this section or section 1607, or (D) paragraph (1) of this subsection is otherwise applicable.

(b) A foreign state shall not be immune from the jurisdiction of the courts of the United States in any case in which a suit in admiralty is brought to enforce a maritime lien against a vessel or cargo of the foreign state, which maritime lien is based upon a commercial activity of the foreign state; Provided, That -

(1) notice of the suit is given by delivery of a copy of the summons and of the complaint to the person, or his agent, having possession of the vessel or cargo against which the maritime lien is asserted; and if the vessel or cargo is arrested pursuant to process obtained on behalf of the party bringing the suit, the service of process of arrest shall be deemed to constitute valid delivery of such notice, but the party bringing the suit shall be liable for any damages sustained by the foreign state as a result of the arrest if the party bringing the suit had actual or constructive knowledge that the vessel or cargo of a foreign state was involved; and

(2) notice to the foreign state of the commencement of suit as provided in section 1608 of this title is initiated within ten days either of the delivery of notice as provided in paragraph (1)

of this subsection or, in the case of a party who was unaware that the vessel or cargo of a foreign state was involved, of the date such party determined the existence of the foreign state's interest.

(c) Whenever notice is delivered under subsection (b)(1), the suit to enforce a maritime lien shall thereafter proceed and shall be heard and determined according to the principles of law and rules of practice of suits in rem whenever it appears that, had the vessel been privately owned and possessed, a suit in rem might have been maintained. A decree against the foreign state may include costs of the suit and, if the decree is for a money judgment, interest as ordered by the court, except that the court may not award judgment against the foreign state in an amount greater than the value of the vessel or cargo upon which the maritime lien arose. Such value shall be determined as of the time notice is served under subsection (b)(1). Decrees shall be subject to appeal and revision as provided in other cases of admiralty and maritime jurisdiction. Nothing shall preclude the plaintiff in any proper case from seeking relief in personam in the same action brought to enforce a maritime lien as provided in this section.

(d) A foreign state shall not be immune from the jurisdiction of the courts of the United States in any action brought to foreclose a preferred mortgage, as defined in the Ship Mortgage Act, 1920 (46 U.S.C. 911 and following). Such action shall be brought, heard, and determined in accordance with the provisions of that Act and in accordance with the principles of law and rules of practice of suits in rem, whenever it appears that had the vessel been privately owned and possessed a suit in rem might have been maintained.

§1606. Extent of liability

As to any claim for relief with respect to which a foreign state is not entitled to immunity under section 1605 or 1607 of this chapter, the foreign state shall be liable in the same manner and to the same extent as a private individual under like circumstances; but a foreign state except for an agency or instrumentality thereof shall not be liable for punitive damages; if, however, in any case wherein death was caused, the law of the place where the action or omission occurred provides, or has been construed to provide, for damages only punitive in nature, the foreign state shall be liable for actual or compensatory damages measured by the pecuniary injuries resulting from such death which were incurred by the persons for whose benefit the action was brought.

§1607. Counterclaims

In any action brought by a foreign state, or in which a foreign state intervenes, in a court of the United States or of a State, the foreign state shall not be accorded immunity with respect to any counterclaim.

(a) for which a foreign state would not be entitled to immunity under section 1605 of this chapter had such claim been brought in a separate action against the foreign state; or

(b) arising out of the transaction or occurrence that is the subject matter of the claim of the foreign state; or

(c) to the extent that the counterclaim does not seek relief exceeding in amount or differing in kind from that sought by the foreign state.

§1608. Service; time to answer; default

(a) Service in the courts of the United States and of the States shall be made upon a foreign state or political subdivision of a foreign state:

(1) by delivery of a copy of the summons and complaint in accordance with any special arrangements for service between the plaintiff and the foreign state or political subdivision; or

(2) if no special arrangement exists, by delivery of a copy of the summons and complaint in accordance with an applicable international convention on service of judicial documents; or

(3) if service cannot be made under paragraphs (1) or (2), by sending a copy of the summons and complaint and a notice of suit, together with a translation of each into the official language of the foreign state, by any form of mail requiring a signed receipt, to be addressed and dispatched by the clerk of the court to the head of the ministry of foreign affairs of the foreign state concerned, or

(4) if service cannot be made within 30 days under paragraph (3), by sending two copies of the summons and complaint and a notice of suit, together with a translation of each into the official language of the foreign state, by any form of mail requiring a signed receipt, to be addressed and dispatched by the clerk of the court to the Secretary of State in Washington,

District of Columbia, to the attention of the Director of Special Consular Services - and the Secretary shall transmit one copy of the papers through diplomatic channels to the foreign state and shall send to the clerk of the court a certified copy of the diplomatic note indicating when the papers were transmitted.

As used in this subsection, a "notice of suit" shall mean a notice addressed to a foreign state and in a form prescribed by the Secretary of State by regulation.

(b) Service in the courts of the United States and of the States shall be made upon an agency or instrumentality of a foreign state:

(1) by delivery of a copy of the summons and complaint in accordance with any special arrangement for service between the plaintiff and the agency or instrumentality; or

(2) if no special arrangement exists, by delivery of a copy of the summons and complaint either to an officer, a managing or general agent, or to any other agent authorized by appointment or by law to receive service of process in the United States; or in accordance with an applicable international convention on service of judicial documents; or

(3) if service cannot be made under paragraphs (1) or (2), and if reasonably calculated to give actual notice, by delivery of a copy of the summons and complaint, together with a translation of each into the official language of the foreign state —

(A) as directed by an authority of the foreign state or political subdivision in response to a letter rogatory or request, or

(B) by any form of mail requiring a signed receipt, to be addressed and dispatched by the clerk of the court to the agency or instrumentality to be served, or

(C) as directed by order of the court consistent with the law of the place where service is to be made.

(c) Service shall be deemed to have been made —

(1) in the case of service under subsection (a)(4), as of the date of transmittal indicated in the certified copy of the diplomatic note; and

(2) in any other case under this section, as of the date of receipt indicated in the certification, signed and returned postal receipt, or other proof of service applicable to the method of service employed.

(d) In any action brought in a court of the United States or of a State, a foreign state, a political subdivision thereof, or an agency or instrumentality of a foreign state shall serve an answer or other responsive pleading to the complaint within sixty days after service has been made under this section.

(e) No judgment by default shall be entered by a court of the United States or of a State against a foreign state, a political subdivision thereof, or an agency or instrumentality of a foreign state, unless the claimant establishes his claim or right to relief by evidence satisfactory to the court. A copy of any such default judgment shall be sent to the foreign state or political subdivision in the manner prescribed for service in this section.

§1609. Immunity from attachment and execution of property of a foreign state

Subject to existing international agreements to which the United States is a party at the time of enactment of this Act the property in the United States of a foreign state shall be immune from attachment, arrest and execution except as provided in sections 1610 and 1611 of this chapter.

§1610. Exceptions to the immunity from attachment or execution

(a) The property in the United States of a foreign state, as defined in section 1603(a) of this chapter, used for a commercial activity in the United States, shall not be immune from attachment in aid of execution, or from execution, upon a judgment entered by a court of the United States or of a State after the effective date of this Act, if —

(1) the foreign state has waived its immunity from attachment in aid of execution or from execution either explicitly or by implication, notwithstanding any withdrawal of the waiver the foreign state may purport to effect except in accordance with the terms of the waiver, or

(2) the property is or was used for the commercial activity upon which the claim is based, or

(3) the execution relates to a judgment establishing rights in property which has been taken in violation of international law or which has been exchanged for property taken in violation of international law, or

(4) the execution relates to a judgment establishing rights in property —
    (A) which is acquired by succession or gift, or
    (B) which is immovable and situated in the United States: Provided, That such property is not used for purposes of maintaining a diplomatic or consular mission or the residence of the Chief of such mission, or

(5) the property consists of any contractual obligation or any proceeds from such a contractual obligation to indemnify or hold harmless the foreign state or its employees under a policy of automobile or other liability or casualty insurance covering the claim which merged into the judgment, or

(6) the judgment is based on an order confirming an arbitral award rendered against the foreign State, provided that attachment in aid of execution, or execution, would not be inconsistent with any provision in the arbitral agreement.

(b) In addition to subsection (a), any property in the United States of an agency or instrumentality of a foreign state engaged in commercial activity in the United States shall not be immune from attachment in aid of execution, or from execution, upon a judgment entered by a court of the United States or of a State after the effective date of this Act, if —

(1) the agency or instrumentality has waived its immunity from attachment in aid of execution or from execution either explicitly or implicitly, notwithstanding any withdrawal of the waiver the agency or instrumentality may purport to effect except in accordance with the terms of the waiver, or

(2) the judgment relates to a claim for which the agency or instrumentality is not immune by virtue of section 1605(a)(2),(3) or (5), or 1605(b) of this chapter, regardless of whether the property is or was used for the activity upon which the claim is based.

(c) No attachment or execution referred to in subsections (a) and (b) of this section shall be permitted until the court has ordered such attachment and execution after having determined that a reasonable period of time has elapsed following the entry of judgment and the giving of any notice required under section 1608(e) of this chapter.

(d) The property of a foreign state, as defined in section 1603(a) of this chapter, used for a commercial activity in the United States, shall not be immune from attachment prior to the entry of judgment in any action brought in a court of the United States or of a State, or prior to the elapse of the period of time provided in subsection (c) of the section, if —

(1) the foreign state has explicitly waived its immunity from attachment prior to judgment, notwithstanding any withdrawal of the waiver the foreign state may purport to effect except in accordance with the terms of the waiver, and

(2) the purpose of the attachment is to secure satisfaction of a judgment that has been or may ultimately be entered against the foreign state, and not to obtain jurisdiction.

(e) The vessels of a foreign State shall not be immune from arrest in rem, interlocutory sale, and execution in actions brought to foreclose a preferred mortgage as provided in section 1605(d).

§1611. Certain types of property immune from execution

(a) Notwithstanding the provisions of section 1610 of this chapter, the property of those organizations designated by the President as being entitled to enjoy the privileges, exemptions, and immunities provided by the International Organizations Immunities Act shall not be subject to attachment or any other judicial process impeding the disbursement of funds to, or on the order of, a foreign state as the result of an action brought in the courts of the United States or of the States.

(b) Notwithstanding the provisions of section 1610 of this chapter, the property of a foreign state shall be immune from attachment and from execution, if —

(1) the property is that of a foreign central bank or monetary authority held for its own account, unless such bank or authority, or its parent foreign government, has explicitly waived its immunity from attachment in aid of execution, of from execution, notwithstanding any withdrawal of the waiver which the bank, authority or government may purport to effect except in accordance with the terms of the waiver; or

(2) the property is, or is intended to be, used in connection with a military activity and
    (A) is of a military character, or
    (B) is under the control of a military authority or defense agency.

Appendix F:
Uniform Law Commissioners' Model Choice of Forum Act

§1. [Definitions.] As used in this Act, "state" means any foreign nation, and any state, district, commonwealth, territory or insular possession of the United States.

§2. [Action in This State by Agreement.]

(a) If the parties have agreed in writing that an action on a controversy may be brought in this state and the agreement provides the only basis for the exercise of jurisdiction, a court of this state will entertain the action if

    (1) the court has power under the law of this state to entertain the action;

    (2) this state is a reasonably convenient place for the trial of the action;

    (3) the agreement as to the place of the action was not obtained by misrepresentation, duress, the abuse of economic power, or other unconscionable means; and

    (4) the defendant, if within the state, was served as required by the law of this state in the case of persons within the state or, if without the state, was served either personally or by registered [or certified] mail directed to his last known address.

(b) This section does not apply [to cognovit clauses] [to arbitration clauses or] to the appointment of an agent for the service of process pursuant to statute or court order.

§3. [Action in Another Place by Agreement.] If the parties have agreed in writing that an action on a controversy shall be brought only in another state and it is brought in a court of this state, the court will dismiss or stay the action, as appropriate, unless

    (1) the court is required by statute to entertain the action;

    (2) the plaintiff cannot secure effective relief in the other state, for reasons other than delay in bringing the action;

    (3) the other state would be a substantially less convenient place for the trial of the action than this state;

    (4) the agreement as to the place of the action was obtained by misrepresentation, duress, the abuse of economic power, or other unconscionable means; or

    (5) it would for some other reason be unfair or unreasonable to enforce the agreement.

§4. [Uniformity of Interpretation.] This Act shall be so construed as to effectuate its general purpose to make uniform the law of those states which enact it.

§5. [Severability.] If any provision of this Act or the application thereof to any person or circumstance is held invalid, the invalidity does not affect other provisions or applications of the Act which can be given effect without the invalid provision or application, and to this end the provisions of this Act are severable.

Appendix G:
The Conflict of Jurisdiction Model Act

§1. Declaration of Public Policy.

It is an important public policy of this State to encourage the early determination of the adjudicating forum for transnational civil disputes, to discourage vexatious litigation and to enforce only those foreign judgments which were not obtained in connection with vexatious litigation, parallel proceedings or litigation in inconvenient forums.

§2. Discretion to Enforce Judgments.

a. In cases where two or more proceedings arising out of the same transaction or occurrence were pending, the courts of this State shall enforce the judgments of any of such courts only if application for designation of an adjudicating forum was timely made to the first known court of competent jurisdiction where such a proceeding was commenced, or to the adjudicating forum after its selection, or to any court of competent jurisdiction if the foregoing courts were not courts of competent jurisdiction.

b. An application for designation of an adjudicating forum is timely if made within six months of reasonable notice of two such proceedings, or of reasonable notice of the selection of an adjudicating forum.

c. The determination of the adjudicating forum is binding for the purpose of enforcement of judgments in this State upon any person served with notice of an application to designate. The courts of this State shall enforce the judgments of the designated adjudicating forum pursuant to the ordinary rules for enforcement of judgments. The selection of the adjudication forum shall be accorded presumptive validity in this State if the written decision determining the adjudicating forum evaluated the substance of the factors set forth in the following section.

d. Where no conclusive determination has been made by another court as provided above, the proper adjudicating forum shall be determined in accordance with the following sections by the courts of this State requested to enforce the judgment.

§3. Factors in Selection of Adjudicating Forum.

A determination of the adjudicating forum shall be made in consideration of the following factors:

a. the interests of justice among the parties and of worldwide justice;

b. the public policies of the countries having jurisdiction of the dispute, including the interest of the affected courts in having proceedings take place in their respective forums;

c. the place of occurrence, and of any effects, of the transaction or occurrence, and of any effects, of the transaction or occurrence out of which the dispute arose;

d. the nationality of the parties;

e. substantive law likely to be applicable and the relative familiarity of the affected courts with that law;

f. the availability of a remedy and the forum most likely to render the most complete relief;

g. the impact of the litigation on the judicial systems of the courts involved, and the likelihood of prompt adjudication in the court selected;

h. location of witnesses and availability of compulsory process;

i. location of documents and other evidence and ease or difficulty associated with obtaining, reviewing or transporting such evidence;

j. place of first filing and connection of such place to the dispute;

k. the ability of the designated forum to obtain jurisdiction over the persons and property that are the subject of the proceeding;

l. whether designation of an adjudicating forum is a superior method to parallel proceedings in adjudicating the dispute;

m. the nature and extent of litigation that has proceeded over the dispute and whether a designation of an adjudicating forum will unduly delay or prejudice the adjudication of the rights of the original parties; and

n. a realigned plaintiff's choice of forum should rarely be disturbed.

§4. Evidence.

The court may consider any evidence admissible in the adjudicating forum or other court of competent jurisdiction, including but not limited to:

a. affidavits or declarations;

b. treaties to which the state of either forum is a party;

c. principles of customary international law;

d. testimony of fact or expert witnesses;

e. diplomatic notes or amicus submissions from the state of the adjudicating forum or other court of competent jurisdiction; and

f. statements of public policy by the state of the adjudicating forum or other court of competent jurisdiction set forth in legislation, executive or administrative action, learned treatises, or participation in intergovernmental organizations.

Reasonable written notice shall be given by any party seeking to raise an issue concerning the law of a forum of competent jurisdiction other than the adjudicating forum. In deciding questions of the law of another forum, the court may consider any relevant material or source, including testimony, whether or not admissible.

Appendix H:
Selected Provisions of 28 United States Code

§1331. Federal question

The district courts shall have original jurisdiction of all civil actions arising under the Constitution, laws, or treaties of the United States.

§1332. Diversity of citizenship; amount in controversy; costs

(a) The district courts shall have original jurisdiction of all civil actions where the matter in controversy exceeds the sum or value of $50,000, exclusive of interest and costs, and is between—

    (1) citizens of different States;

    (2) citizens of a State and citizens or subjects of a foreign state;

    (3) citizens of different States and in which citizens or subjects of a foreign state are additional parties; and

    (4) a foreign state, defined in section 1603(a) of this title, as plaintiff and citizens of a State or of different States.

For the purposes of this section, section 1335, and section 1441, an alien admitted to the United States for permanent residence shall be deemed a citizen of the State in which such alien is domiciled.

(b) Except when express provision therefor is otherwise made in a statute of the United States, where the plaintiff who files the case originally in the Federal courts is finally adjudged to be entitled to recover less than the sum or value of $50,000, computed without regard to any setoff or counterclaim to which the defendant may be adjudged to be entitled, and exclusive of interest and costs, the district court may deny costs to the plaintiff and, in addition, may impose costs on the plaintiff.

(c) For the purposes of this section and section 1441 of this title—

    (1) a corporation shall be deemed to be a citizen of any State by which it has been incorporated and of the State where it has its principal place of business, except that in any direct action against the insurer of a policy or contract of liability insurance, whether incorporated or unincorporated, to which action the insured is not joined as a party-defendant, such insurer shall be deemed a citizen of the State of which the insured is a citizen, as well as of any State by which the insurer has been incorporated and of the State where it has its principal place of business; and

    (2) the legal representative of the estate of a decedent shall be deemed to be a citizen only of the same State as the decedent, and the legal representative of an infant or incompetent shall be deemed to be a citizen only of the same State as the infant or incompetent.

(d) The word "States", as used in this section, includes the Territories, the District of Columbia, and the Commonwealth of Puerto Rico.

§1350. Alien's action for tort

The district courts shall have original jurisdiction of any civil action by an alien for a tort only, committed in violation of the law of nations or a treaty of the United States.

§1391. Venue generally

(a) A civil action wherein jurisdiction is founded only on diversity of citizenship may, except as otherwise provided by law, be brought only in (1) a judicial district where any defendant resides, if all defendants reside in the same State, (2) a judicial district in which a substantial part of the events or omissions giving rise to the claim occurred, or a substantial part of property that is the subject of the action is situated, or (3) a judicial district in which the defendants are subject to personal jurisdiction at the time the action is commenced, if there is no district in which the action may otherwise be brought.

(b) A civil action wherein jurisdiction is not founded solely on diversity of citizenship may, except as otherwise provided by law, be brought only in (1) a judicial district where any defendant resides, if all defendants reside in the same State, (2) a judicial district in which a substantial part of the events or omissions giving rise to the claim occurred, or a substantial part of property that is the subject of the action is situated, or (3) a judicial district in which any defendant may be found, if there is no district in which the action may otherwise be brought.

(c) For purposes of venue under this chapter, a defendant that is a corporation shall be deemed to reside in any judicial district in which it is subject to personal jurisdiction at the time the action is commenced. In a State which has more than one judicial district and in which a defendant that is a corporation is subject to personal jurisdiction at the time an action is commenced, such corporation, shall be deemed to reside in any district in that State within which its contacts would be sufficient to subject it to personal jurisdiction if that district were a separate State, and, if there is no such district, the corporation shall be deemed to reside in the district within which it has the most significant contacts.

(d) An alien may be sued in any district.

(e) A civil action in which a defendant is an officer or employee of the United States or any agency thereof acting in his official capacity or under color of legal authority, or an agency of the United States, or the United States, may, except as otherwise provided by law, be brought in any judicial district in which (1) a defendant in the action resides, (2) a substantial part of the events or omissions giving rise to the claim occurred, or a substantial part of property that is the subject of the action is situated, or (3) the plaintiff resides if no real property is involved in the action. Additional persons may be joined as parties to any such action in accordance with the Federal Rules of Civil Procedures and with such other venue requirements as would be applicable if the United States or one of its officers, employees, or agencies were not a party. The summons and complaint in such an action shall be served as provided by the Federal Rules of Civil Procedure except that the delivery of the summons and complaint to the officer or agency as required by the rules may be made by certified mail beyond the territorial limits of the district in which the action is brought.

(f) A civil action against a foreign state as defined in section 1603(a) of this title may be brought—
  (1) in any judicial district in which a substantial part of the events or omissions giving rise to the claim occurred, or a substantial part of property that is the subject of the action is situated;
  (2) in any judicial district in which the vessel or cargo of a foreign state is situated, if the claim is asserted under section 1605(b) of this title;
  (3) in any judicial district in which the agency or instrumentality is licensed to do business or is doing business, if the action is brought against an agency or instrumentality of a foreign state as defined in section 1603(b) of this title; or
  (4) in the United States District Court for the District of Columbia if the action is brought against a foreign state or political subdivision thereof.

§1441. Actions removable generally

(a) Except as otherwise expressly provided by Act of Congress, any civil action brought in a State court of which the district courts of the United States have original jurisdiction, may be removed by the defendant or the defendants, to the district court of the United States for the district and division embracing the place where such action is pending. For purposes of removal under this chapter, the citizenship of defendants sued under fictitious names shall be disregarded.

(b) Any civil action of which the district courts have original jurisdiction founded on a claim or right arising under the Constitution, treaties or laws of the United States shall be removable without regard to the citizenship or residence of the parties. Any other such action shall be removable only if none of the parties in interest properly joined and served as defendants is a citizen of the State in which such action is brought.

(c) Whenever a separate and independent claim or cause of action within the jurisdiction conferred by section 1331 of this title is joined with one or more otherwise non-removable claims or causes of action, the entire case may be removed and the district court may determine all issues therein, or, in its discretion, may remand all matters in which State law predominates.

(d) Any civil action brought in a State court against a foreign state as defined in section 1603(a) of this title may be removed by the foreign state to the district court of the United States for the district and division embracing the place where such action is pending. Upon removal the action shall be tried by the court without jury. Where removal is based upon this subsection, the time limitations of section 1446(b) of this chapter may be enlarged at any time for cause shown.

(e) The court to which such civil action is removed is not precluded from hearing and determining any claim in such civil action because the State court from which such civil action is removed did not have jurisdiction over that claim.

§1781. Transmittal of letter rogatory or request

(a) The Department of State has power, directly, or through suitable channels—

    (1) to receive a letter rogatory issued, or request made, by a foreign or international tribunal, to transmit it to the tribunal, officer, or agency in the United States to whom it is addressed and to receive and return it after execution; and

    (2) to receive a letter rogatory issued, or request made, by a tribunal in the United States, to transmit it to the foreign or international tribunal, officer, or agency to whom it is addressed, and to receive and return it after execution.

(b) This section does not preclude—

    (1) the transmittal of a letter rogatory or request directly from a foreign or international tribunal to the tribunal, officer, or agency in the United States to whom it is addressed and its return in the same manner; or

    (2) the transmittal of a letter rogatory or request directly from a tribunal in the United States to the foreign or international tribunal, officer, or agency to whom it is addressed and its return in the same manner

§1782. Assistance to foreign and international tribunals and to litigants before such tribunals

(a) The district court of the district in which a person resides or is found may order him to give his testimony or statement or to produce a document or other thing for use in a proceeding in a foreign or international tribunal. The order may be made pursuant to a letter rogatory issued, or request made, by a foreign or international tribunal or upon the application of any interested person and may direct that the testimony or statement be given, or the document or other thing be produced, before a person appointed by the court. By virtue of his appointment, the person appointed has power to administer any necessary oath and take the testimony or statement. The order may prescribe the practice and procedure, which may be in whole or part the practice and procedure of the foreign country or the international tribunal, for taking the testimony or statement or producing the document or other thing. To the extent that the order does not prescribe otherwise, the testimony or statement shall be taken, and the document or other thing produced, in accordance with the Federal Rules of Civil Procedure.

A person may not be compelled to give his testimony or statement or to produce a document or other thing in violation of any legally applicable privilege.

(b) This chapter does not preclude a person within the United States from voluntarily giving his testimony or statement, or producing a document or other thing, for use in a proceeding in a foreign or international tribunal before any person and in any manner acceptable to him.

§1783. Subpoena of person in foreign country

(a) A court of the United States may order the issuance of a subpoena requiring the appearance as a witness before it, or before a person or body designated by it, of a national or resident of the United States who is in a foreign country, or requiring the production of a specified document or other thing by him, if the court finds that particular testimony or the production of the document or other thing by him is necessary in the interest of justice, and, in other than a criminal action or proceeding, if the court finds, in addition, that it is not possible to obtain his testimony in admissible form without his personal appearance or to obtain the production of the document or other thing in any other manner.

(b) The subpoena shall designate the time and place for the appearance or for the production of the document or other thing. Service of the subpoena and any order to show cause, rule, judgment, or decree authorized by this section or by section 1784 of this title shall be effected in accordance with the provisions of the Federal Rules of Civil Procedure relating to service of process on a person in a foreign country. The person serving the subpoena shall tender to the person to whom the subpoena is addressed his estimated necessary travel and attendance expenses, the amount of which shall be determined by the court and stated in the order directing the issuance of the subpoena.

Appendix I:
Convention on Service Abroad of Judicial and Extrajudicial Documents in Civil or Commercial Matters ("Hague Service Convention")

The States signatory to the present Convention,

Desiring to create appropriate means to ensure that judicial and extrajudicial documents to be served abroad shall be brought to the notice of the addressee in sufficient time,

Desiring to improve the organisation of mutual judicial assistance for that purpose by simplifying and expediting the procedure,

Have resolved to conclude a Convention to this effect and have agreed upon the following provisions:

Article 1

The present Convention shall apply in all cases, in civil or commercial matters, where there is occasion to transmit a judicial or extrajudicial document for service abroad.

This Convention shall not apply where the address of the person to be served with the document is not known.

CHAPTER I - JUDICIAL DOCUMENTS

Article 2

Each contracting State shall designate a Central Authority which will undertake to receive requests for service coming from other contracting States and to proceed in conformity with the provisions of articles 3 to 6.

Each State shall organize the Central Authority in conformity with its own law.

Article 3

The authority or judicial officer competent under the law of the State in which the documents originate shall forward to the Central Authority of the State addressed a request conforming to the model annexed to the present Convention, without any requirement of legalisation or other equivalent formality.

The document to be served or a copy thereof shall be annexed to the request. The request and the document shall both be furnished in duplicate.

Article 4

If the Central Authority considers that the request does not comply with the provisions of the present Convention it shall promptly inform the applicant and specify its objections to the request.

Article 5

The Central Authority of the State addressed shall itself serve the document or shall arrange to have it served by an appropriate agency, either —

(a) by a method prescribed by its internal law for the service of documents in domestic actions upon persons who are within its territory, or

(b) by a particular method requested by the applicant, unless such a method is incompatible with the law of the State addressed.

Subject to sub-paragraph (b) of the first paragraph of this article, the document may always be served by delivery to an addressee who accepts it voluntarily.

If the document is to be served under the first paragraph above, the Central Authority may require the document to be written in, or translated into, the official language or one of the official languages of the State addressed.

That part of the request, in the form attached to the present Convention, which contains a summary of the document to be served, shall be served with the document.

Article 6

The Central Authority of the State addressed or any authority which it may have designated for that purpose, shall complete a certificate in the form of the model annexed to the present Convention.

The certificate shall state that the document has been served and shall include the method, the place and the date of service and the person to whom the document was delivered. If the document had not been served, the certificate shall set out the reasons which have prevented service.

The applicant may require that a certificate not completed by a Central Authority or by a judicial authority shall be countersigned by one of these authorities.

The certificate shall be forwarded directly to the applicant.

Article 7

The standard terms in the model annexed to the present Convention shall in all cases be written either in French or in English. They may also be written in the official language, or in one of the official languages, of the State in which the documents originate.

The corresponding blanks shall be completed either in the language of the State addressed or in French or in English.

Article 8

Each contracting State shall be free to effect service of judicial documents upon persons abroad, without application of any compulsion, directly through its diplomatic or consular agents.

Any State may declare that it is opposed to such service within its territory, unless the document is to be served upon a national of the State in which the documents originate.

Article 9

Each contracting State shall be free, in addition, to use consular channels to forward documents, for the purpose of service, to those authorities of another contracting State which are designated by the latter for this purpose.

Each contracting State may, if exceptional circumstances so require, use diplomatic channels for the same purpose.

Article 10

Provided the State of destination does not object, the present Convention shall not interfere with —
  (a) the freedom to send judicial documents, by postal channels, directly to persons abroad,
  (b) the freedom of judicial officers, officials or other competent persons of the State of origin to effect service of judicial documents directly through the judicial officers, officials or other competent persons of the State of destination,
  (c) the freedom of any person interested in a judicial proceeding to effect service of judicial documents directly through the judicial officers, officials or other competent persons of the State of destination.

Article 11

The present Convention shall not prevent two or more contracting States from agreeing to permit, for the purpose of service of judicial documents, channels of transmission other than those provided for in the preceding articles and, in particular, direct communication between their respective authorities.

Article 12

The service of judicial documents coming from a contracting State shall not give rise to any payment or reimbursement of taxes or costs for the services rendered by the State addressed.

The applicant shall pay or reimburse the costs occasioned by —
  (a) the employment of a judicial officer or of a person competent under the law of the State of destination,

(b) the use of a particular method of service.

Article 13

Where a request for service complies with the terms of the present Convention, the State addressed may refuse to comply therewith only if it deems that compliance would infringe its sovereignty or security.

It may not refuse to comply solely on the ground that, under its internal law, it claims exclusive jurisdiction over the subject-matter of the action or that its internal law would not permit the action upon which the application is based.

The Central Authority shall, in case of refusal, promptly inform the applicant and state the reasons for the refusal.

Article 14

Difficulties which may arise in connection with the transmission of judicial documents for service shall be settled through diplomatic channels.

Article 15

Where a writ of summons or an equivalent document had to be transmitted abroad for the purpose of service, under the provisions of the present Convention, and the defendant has not appeared, judgment shall not be given until it is established that —
  (a) the document was served by a method prescribed by the internal law of the State addressed for the service of documents in domestic actions upon persons who are within its territory, or
  (b) the document was actually delivered to the defendant or to his residence by another method provided for by this Convention, and that in either of these cases the service or the delivery was effected in sufficient time to enable the defendant to defend.

Each contracting State shall be free to declare that the judge, notwithstanding the provisions of the first paragraph of this article, may give judgment even if no certificate of service or delivery has been received, if all the following conditions are fulfilled —
  (a) the document was transmitted by one of the methods provided for in this Convention,
  (b) a period of time of not less than six months, considered adequate by the judge in the particular case, has elapsed since the date of the transmission of the document,
  (c) no certificate of any kind has been received, even though every reasonable effort has been made to obtain it through the competent authorities of the State addressed.

Notwithstanding the provisions of the preceding paragraphs the judge may order, in case of urgency, any provisional or protective measures.

Article 16

When a writ of summons or an equivalent document had to be transmitted abroad for the purpose of service, under the provisions of the present Convention, and a judgment has been entered against a defendant who has not appeared, the judge shall have the power to relieve the defendant from the effects of the expiration of the time for appeal from the judgment if the following conditions are fulfilled —
  (a) the defendant, without any fault in his part, did not have knowledge of the document in sufficient time to defend, or knowledge of the judgment in sufficient time to appeal, and
  (b) the defendant has disclosed a *prima facie* defence to the action on the merits.

An application for relief may be filed within a reasonable time after the defendant has knowledge of the judgement.

Each contracting State may declare that the application will not be entertained if it is filed after the expiration of a time to be stated in the declaration, but which shall in no case be less than one year following the date of the judgment.

This article shall not apply to judgments concerning status or capacity of persons.

CHAPTER II - EXTRAJUDICIAL DOCUMENTS

Article 17

Extrajudicial documents emanating from authorities and judicial officers of a contracting State may be transmitted for the purpose of service in another contracting State by the methods and under the provisions of the present Convention.

CHAPTER III- GENERAL CLAUSES

Article 18

Each contracting State may designate other authorities in addition to the Central Authority and shall determine the extent of their competence.

The applicant shall, however, in all cases, have the right to address a request directly to the Central Authority.

Federal States shall be free to designate more than one Central Authority.

Article 19

To the extent that the internal law of a contracting State permits methods of transmission, other than those provided for in the preceding articles, of documents coming from abroad, for service within its territory, the present Convention shall not affect such provisions.

Article 20

The present Convention shall not prevent an agreement between any two or more contracting States to dispense with —

- (a) the necessity for duplicate copies of transmitted documents as required by the second paragraph of article 3,
- (b) the language requirements of the third paragraph of article 5 and article 7,
- (c) the provisions of the fourth paragraph of article 5,
- (d) the provisions of the second paragraph of article 12.

Article 21

Each contracting State shall, at the time of the deposit of its instrument of ratification or accession, or at a later date, inform the Ministry of Foreign Affairs of the Netherlands of the following —

- (a) the designation of authorities, pursuant to articles 2 and 18,
- (b) the designation of the authority competent to complete the certificate pursuant to article 6,
- (c) the designation of the authority competent to receive documents transmitted by consular channels, pursuant to article 9.

Each contracting State shall similarly inform the Ministry, where appropriate, of —

- (a) opposition to the use of methods of transmission pursuant to articles 8 and 10,
- (b) declarations pursuant to the second paragraph of article 15 and the third paragraph of article 16,
- (c) all modifications of the above designations, oppositions and declarations.

Article 22

Where Parties to the present Convention are also Parties to one or both of the Conventions on civil procedure signed at The Hague on 17th July 1905, and on 1st March 1954, this Convention shall replace as between them articles 1 to 7 of the earlier Conventions.

Article 23

The present Convention shall not affect the application of article 23 of the Convention on civil procedure signed at The Hague on 17th July 1905, or article 24 of the Convention on civil procedure signed at The Hague on 1st March 1954.

These articles shall however, apply only if methods of communication, identical to those provided for in these Conventions, are used.

Article 24

Supplementary agreements between parties to the Conventions of 1905 and 1954 shall be considered as equally applicable to the present Convention, unless the Parties have otherwise agreed.

Article 25

Without prejudice to the provisions of articles 22 and 24, the present Convention shall not derogate from conventions containing provisions on the matters governed by this Convention to which the contracting States are, or shall become, Parties.

Article 26

The present Convention shall be open for signature by the States represented at the Tenth Session of the Hague Conference on Private International Law.

It shall be ratified, and the instruments of ratification shall be deposited with the Ministry of Foreign Affairs of the Netherlands.

Article 27

The present Convention shall enter into force on the sixtieth day after the deposit of the third instrument of ratification referred to in the second paragraph of article 26.

The Convention shall enter into force for each signatory State which ratifies subsequently on the sixtieth day after the deposit of its instruments of ratification.

Article 28

Any State not represented at the Tenth Session of the Hague Conference on Private International Law may accede to the present Convention after it has entered into force in accordance with the first paragraph of article 27. The instrument of accession shall be deposited with the Ministry of Foreign Affairs of the Netherlands.

The Convention shall enter into force for such a State in the absence of any objection from a State, which has ratified the Convention before such deposit, notified to the Ministry of Foreign Affairs of the Netherlands within a period of six months after the date on which the said Ministry has notified it of such accession.

In the absence of any such objection, the Convention shall enter into force for the acceding State on the first day of the month following the expiration of the last of the periods referred to in the preceding paragraph.

Article 29

Any State may, at the time of signature, ratification or accession, declare that the present Convention shall extend to all the territories for the international relations of which it is responsible, or to one or more of them. Such a declaration shall take effect on the date of entry into force of the Convention for the State concerned.

At any time thereafter, such extensions shall be notified to the Ministry of Foreign Affairs of the Netherlands.

The Convention shall enter into force for the territories mentioned in such an extension on the Sixtieth day after the notification referred to in the preceding paragraph.

Article 30

The present Convention shall remain in force for five years from the date of its entry into force in accordance with the first paragraph of article 27, even for States which have ratified it or acceded to it subsequently.

If there has been no denunciation, it shall be renewed tacitly every five years.

Any denunciation shall be notified to the Ministry of Foreign Affairs of the Netherlands at least six months before the end of the five year period.

It may be limited to certain of the territories of which the Convention applies.

The denunciation shall have effect only as regards the State which has notified it. The Convention shall remain in force for the other contracting States.

Article 31

The Ministry of Foreign Affairs of the Netherlands shall give notice to the States referred to in article 26, and to the States which have acceded in accordance with article 28, of the following —

(a) the signatures and ratifications referred to in article 26;

(b) the date on which the present Convention enters into force in accordance with the first paragraph of article 27;

(c) the accessions referred to in article 28 and the dates on which they take effect;

(d) the extensions referred to in article 29 and the dates on which they take effect;

(e) the designations, oppositions and declarations referred to in article 21;

(f) the denunciations referred to in the third paragraph of article 30.

IN WITNESS WHEREOF the undersigned, being duly authorised thereto, have signed the present Convention.

DONE at The Hague, on the 15th day of November, 1965, in the English and French languages, both texts being equally authentic, in a single copy which shall be deposited in the archives of the Government of the Netherlands, and of which a certified copy shall be sent, through the diplomatic channel, to each of the States represented at the Tenth Session of the Hague Conference on Private International Law.

Appendix J:
Declarations Concerning Hague Service Convention

Belgium

1. In conformity with the first paragraph of Article 2 of the Convention, the Ministry of Justice, Administration de la Legislation, Place Poelaert, 4, 1000 Brussels is designated as the Central Authority;

2. The Ministry of Justice is also designated as the competent authority to receive documents forwarded by the channels provided for in the first paragraph of Article 9 of the Convention;

3. The Belgian Government is opposed to use being made within its territory of the freedom to effect service provided for in the first paragraph of Article 8;

4. The Belgian Government declares that it will avail itself of the provision contained in the second paragraph of Article 15;

5. In conformity with the third paragraph of Article 16, the Belgian Government declares that the applications mentioned in the second paragraph of Article 16 will not be entertained if they are filed after the expiration of a period of one year following the date of the judgment;

6. The Belgian Government believes it should draw attention to the fact that any request for the service of documents made under sections a) or b) of the first paragraph of Article 5 requires the agency of a process-server (huissier de justice) and that the resulting costs should be reimbursed in conformity with Article 12 of the Convention.

Denmark

With respect to Articles 2 and 18

The Ministry of Justice is designated as the Central Authority.

With respect to Article 6

The Danish court of law that has asked for the service to be made is designated as competent to complete the certificate in accordance with Article 6.

With respect to Article 9

The local judge of first instance — though, as regards the court of first instance at Copenhagen and the court of first instance of the city and of the canton of Arhus, the president of the court — is designated as competent to receive documents forwarded through consular channels in accordance with Article 9.

With respect to Article 10

Denmark is unable to recognize the method of effecting service set out in Article 10, para. c.

With respect to Article 15

Denmark avails itself of the power, provided for in Article 15, second paragraph, to declare that the judge may give judgment in a matter even if the provisions of Article 15, first paragraph, are not fulfilled.

With respect to Article 16

Denmark avails itself of the power, provided for in Article 16, third paragraph, to declare that an application will not be entertained if it is made after the expiration of a period of one year following the date of judgment. The question of the re-hearing of a matter in which a person has been judged by default shall be decided in accordance with the rules of the code of procedure, Article 373 and Article 374, cf. Article 434. According to these rules, any person against whom judgment is given by default in an action, in first instance may apply for a re-hearing of the matter if he can prove that the default cannot be imputed to him. The application for a re-hearing should be filed as soon as possible and may not be submitted after the expiration of a period of one year following the date of judgment.

France

1. In conformity with Articles 2 and 18 of the Convention, the Ministry of Justice, Civil Division of International Judicial Assistance (Ministere de la Justice, Service Civil de l'Entraide judiciaire internationale), 13 Place Vendome, Paris (1er), is designated as the Central Authority to the exclusion of all other authorities.

2. The authority competent to complete the certificate referred to in Article 6 is the Public Prosecutor of the Republic (Procureur de la Republique) in whose district the addressee of the document to be served resides.

3. The Public Prosecutor of the Republic (Procureur de la Republique) is likewise authorized to receive documents forwarded through consular channels in accordance with Article 9.

4. The Government of the French Republic declares that it is opposed, as has been provided for in Article 8, to the direct service, through diplomatic and consular agents of the contracting States, of documents upon person who are not nationals of those States.

5. The Government of the French Republic declares that the provisions of the second paragraph of Article 15 have its approval. It furthermore declares, with reference of Article 16, paragraph 3, that an application for relief from the effects of the expiration of the time for appeal from a judgment will not be entertained if it is filed more than twelve months following the date of the judgment.

Federal Republic of Germany

(1) Requests for service shall be addressed to the Central Authority of the Land where the request is to be complied with. The Central Authority pursuant to Article 2 and paragraph 3 of Article 18 of the Convention shall be for

Baden-Württemberg	das Justizministerium (The Ministry of Justice of Baden-Württemberg), D 7000 Stuttgart
Bavaria	das Bayerische Staats-ministerium der Justiz (The Bavarian State Ministry of Justice), D 8000 München
Berlin	Der Senator für Justiz (The Senator of Justice), D 1000 Berlin
Bremen	der Präsident des Landgerichts Bremen (The President of the Regional Court of Bremen), D 2800 Bremen
Hamburg	der Präsident des Amtsgerichts Hamburg (The President of the Local Court of Hamburg), D 2000 Hamburg
Hesse	der Hessische Minister der Justiz (The Hessian Minister of Justice), D 6200 Wiesbaden

Lower Saxony	der Niedersächsische Minister der Justiz (The Minister of Justice of Lower Saxony), D 3000 Hannover
North Rhine-Westphalia	der Justizminister des Landes Nordrhein-Westfalen (The Minister of Justice of North Rhine-Westphalia), D 4000 Düsseldorf
Rhineland-Palatinate	das Ministerium der Justiz (The Ministry of Justice), D 6500 Mainz
Saarland	der Minister für Rechtspflege (The Minister of Justice), D 6600 Saarbrücken
Schleswig-Holstein	der Justizminister des Landes Schleswig-Holstein (The Minister of Justice of the Land Schleswig-Holstein), D 2300 Kiel

The Central Authorities are empowered to have requests for service complied with directly by postal channels if the conditions for service in accordance with paragraph 1(a) of Article 5 of the Convention have been fulfilled. In that case the competent Central Authority will hand over the document to the postal authorities for service. In all other cases the local court (Amtsgericht) in whose district the documents are to be served shall be competent to comply with requests for service. Service shall be effected by the registry of the local court.

Formal service (paragraph 1 of Article 5 of the Convention) shall be permissible only if the document to be served is written in or translated into, the German language.

(2) The Central Authority shall complete the certificate (paragraphs 1 and 2 of Article 6 of the Convention) if it has itself arranged for the request for service to be complied with directly by postal channels; in all other cases this shall be done by the registry of the local court.

(3) The Central Authority of the Land where the documents are to be served and the authorities competent under Section 1 of the Act of 18th December 1958 implementing the Convention on Civil Procedure, signed at The Hague on 1st March 1954, to receive requests from consuls of foreign States, shall be competent to receive requests for service transmitted by a foreign consul within the Federal Republic of Germany (paragraph 1 of Article 9 of the Convention). Under that Act the president of the regional court (Landgericht) in whose district the documents are to be served shall be competent; in his place the president of the local court shall be competent if the request for service is to be complied with in the district of the local court which is subject to his administrative supervision.

(4) In accordance with paragraph 2(a) of Article 21 of the Convention, the Government of the Federal Republic of Germany objects to the use of methods of transmission pursuant to Articles 8 and 10. Service through diplomatic or consular agents (Article 8 of the Convention) is therefore only permissible if the document is to be served upon a national of the State sending the document. Service pursuant to Article 10 of the Convention shall not be effected.

The Convention shall also apply to Land Berlin.

Japan

(1) The Minister for Foreign Affairs is designated as the Central Authority which receives requests for service from other contracting States, pursuant to the first paragraph of Article 2.

(2) The District Court which has rendered judicial aid with respect to the service is designated as the authority competent to complete the certificate in the form of the model annexed to the Convention, pursuant to the first paragraph of Article 6.

(3) The Minister for Foreign Affairs is designated as the authority competent to receive documents transmitted through consular channels, pursuant to the first paragraph of Article 9.

(4) It is declared that the Government of Japan objects to the use of the methods of service referred to in subparagraphs (b) and (c) of Article 10.

(5) It is declared that Japanese courts may give judgment if all the conditions specified in the second paragraph of Article 15 are fulfilled.

United Kingdom

(1)(a) In accordance with the provisions of Articles 2 and 18 of the Convention, her Majesty's Principal Secretary of State for Foreign Affairs is designated as the Central Authority; and the Senior Master of the Supreme Court, Royal Courts of Justice, Strand, London, WC2, the Crown Agent for Scotland, Lord Advocate's Department, Crown Office, 9 Parliament Square, Edinburgh 1, and the Master (Queen's Bench and Appeals), Royal Courts of Justice, Belfast 1, are designated as additional authorities for England and Wales, Scotland, and Northern Ireland respectively.

(b) The authorities competent under Article 6 of the Convention to complete the Certificate of Service are the authorities designated under Articles 2 and 18.

(c) In accordance with the provisions of Article 9 of the Convention, the United Kingdom designates as receivers of process through consular channels the same authorities as those designated under Articles 2 and 18.

(d) With reference to the provisions of paragraphs (b) and (c) of Article 10 of the Convention, documents for service through official channels will be accepted in the United Kingdom only by the central or additional authorities and only from judicial, consular or diplomatic officers of other Contracting States.

(e) The United Kingdom declares its acceptance of the provisions of the second paragraph of Article 15 of the Convention.

(f) In accordance with the provisions of the third paragraph of Article 16 of the Convention, the United Kingdom declares, in relation to Scotland only, that applications for setting aside judgments on the grounds that the defendant did not have knowledge of the proceedings in sufficient time to defend the action will not be entertained if filed more than one year after the date of judgment.

The authorities designated by the United Kingdom will require all documents forwarded to them for service under the provisions of the Convention to be in duplicate and, pursuant to the third paragraph of Article 5 of the Convention, will require the documents to be written in, or translated into, the English language.

A notification under the second and third paragraphs of Article 29 regarding the extension of the Convention to the territories for the international relations of which the United Kingdom is responsible will be addressed to the Royal Netherlands Government in due course.

(2)(a) In accordance with Article 18 of the Convention the Colonial Secretary of Hong Kong is designated as the Authority competent to receive requests for service in accordance with Article 2 of the Convention.

(b) The authority competent under Article 6 of the Convention to complete the Certificate of Service is the Registrar of the Supreme Court of Hong Kong.

(c) In accordance with the provisions of Article 9 of the Convention the Registrar of the Supreme Court of Hong Kong is designated as the receiver of process sent through consular channels.

(d) With reference to the provisions of paragraphs (b) and (c) of Article 10 of the Convention, documents sent for service through official channels will be accepted in Hong Kong only by the central or additional authority and only from judicial, consular or diplomatic officers of other Contracting States.

(e) The acceptance by the United Kingdom of the provisions of the second paragraph of Article 15 of the Convention shall equally apply to Hong Kong.

The authorities designated above will require all documents forwarded to them for service under the provisions of the Convention to be in duplicate and, pursuant to the third paragraph of Article 5 of the Convention, will require the documents to be written in, or translated into, the English language.

3(a) In accordance with Article 18 of the Convention the authority shown against the name of each territory in the Annex (hereinafter severally called "the designated authority") is designated as the authority in that territory competent to receive requests for service in accordance with Article 2 of the Convention.

(b) The authority in each territory competent under Article 6 of the Convention to complete the Certificate of Service is the designated authority.

(c) In accordance with the provisions of Article 9 of the Convention, the designated Authority shall receive process sent through consular channels.

(d) With reference to the provisions of paragraphs and (b) and (c) of Article 10 of the Convention, documents sent for service through official channels will be accepted in a territory listed in the Annex by the designated authority and only from judicial, consular or diplomatic officers of other Contracting States.

(e) The acceptance by the United Kingdom of the provisions of the second paragraph of Article 15 of the Convention shall equally apply to the territories named in the Annex.

The authorities designated in the Annex will require all documents forwarded to them for service under the provisions of the Convention to be in duplicate and, pursuant to the third paragraph of Article 5 of the Convention, will require the documents to be written in, or translated into, the English language.

...

United States

1. In accordance with Article 2, the United States Department of Justice is designated as the Central Authority to receive requests for service from other Contracting States and to proceed in conformity with Articles 3 to 6.

2. In accordance with Article 6, in addition to the United States Department of Justice, the United States Marshal or Deputy Marshal for the judicial district in which service is made are designated for the purpose of completing the certificate in the form annexed to the Convention.

3. In accordance with the second paragraph of Article 15, it is declared that the judge may, notwithstanding the provisions of the first paragraph of Article 15, give judgment even if no certificate of service or delivery has been received, if all the conditions specified in subdivisions (a), (b) and (c) of the second paragraph of Article 15 are fulfilled.

4. In accordance with the third paragraph of Article 16, it is declared that an application under Article 16 will not be entertained if it is filed (a) after the expiration of the period within which the same may be filed under the procedural regulations of the court in which the judgment has been entered, or (b) after the expiration of one year following the date of the judgment, whichever is later.

5. In accordance with Article 29, it is declared that the Convention shall extend to all the States of the United States, the District of Columbia, Guam, Puerto Rico, and the Virgin Islands.

United States Marshals will charge a standard fee of $15.00 for their services under the Convention. Therefore, each request for service should be accompanied by an international money order made payable to the 'Treasurer of the United States' in the sum of $15.00.

The United States Marshals only have access to persons who are physically present within their areas of jurisdiction. Therefore, it will not be possible for them to effect service on United States citizens or residents of the United States who are temporarily outside of the country either by reason of service with the Armed Forces of the United States, employment with the United States Government, or in some other capacity.

The requirement that each request for service be accompanied by an international money order made payable to the 'Treasurer of the United States' in the sum of $15.00 was not intended to include international postal money orders. The use of postal money orders is not feasible because the negotiable instrument does not physically accompany the request and is extremely difficult to correlate with a particular request for service. The appropriate means to remit prepayment of the Marshal's fee is an international money order or check — preferably a bank or certified check — which can accompany the request until service is made.

As of June 28, 1978, the United States will not charge a fee for service of judicial documents which it receives from any State party to the Convention which does not impose a charge for the service of documents sent from the United States for service under the Convention.

Appendix K:
Convention on the Taking of Evidence Abroad in Civil or Commercial Matters ("Hague Evidence Convention")

The States signatory to the present Convention,

Desiring to facilitate the transmission and execution of Letters of Request and to further the accommodation of the different methods which they use for this purpose,

Desiring to improve mutual judicial co-operation in civil or commercial matters,

Have resolved to conclude a Convention to this effect and have agreed upon the following provisions —

CHAPTER I - LETTERS OF REQUEST

Article 1

In civil or commercial matters a judicial authority of a Contracting State may, in accordance with the provisions of the law of that State, request the competent authority of another Contracting State, by means of a Letter of Request, to obtain evidence, or to perform some other judicial act.

A Letter shall not be used to obtain evidence which is not intended for use in judicial proceedings, commenced or contemplated.

The expression 'other judicial act' does not cover the service of judicial documents or the issuance of any process by which judgments or orders are executed or enforced, or orders for provisional or protective measures.

Article 2

A Contracting State shall designate a Central Authority which will undertake to receive Letters of Request coming from a judicial authority of another Contracting State and to transmit them to the authority competent to execute them. Each State shall organize the Central Authority in accordance with its own law.

Letters shall be sent to the Central Authority of the State of execution without being transmitted through any other authority of that State.

Article 3

A Letter of Request shall specify —

(a) the authority requesting its execution and the authority requested to execute it, if known to the requesting authority;
(b) the names and addresses of the parties to the proceedings and their representatives, if any;
(c) the nature of the proceedings for which the evidence is required, giving all necessary information in regard thereto;
(d) the evidence to be obtained or other judicial act to be performed.

Where appropriate, the Letter shall specify, inter alia —

(e) the names and addresses of the persons to be examined;
(f) the questions to be put to the persons to be examined or a statement of the subject-matter about which they are to be examined;
(g) the documents or other property, real or personal, to be inspected;
(h) any requirement that the evidence is to be given on oath or affirmation, and any special form to be used;

(i) any special method or procedure to be followed under Article 9.

A Letter may also mention any information necessary for the application of Article 11.

No legalization or other like formality may be required.

Article 4

A Letter of Request shall be in the language of the authority requested to execute it or be accompanied by a translation into that language.

Nevertheless, a Contracting State shall accept a Letter in either English or French, or a translation into one of these languages, unless it has made the reservation authorized by Article 33.

A Contracting State which has more than one official language and cannot, for reasons of internal law, accept Letters in one of these languages for the whole of its territory, shall, by declaration, specify the language in which the Letter or translation thereof shall be expressed for execution in the specified parts of its territory. In case of failure to comply with this declaration, without justifiable excuse, the costs of translation into the required language shall be borne by the State of origin.

A Contracting State may, by declaration, specify the language or languages other than those referred to in the preceding paragraphs, in which a Letter may be sent to its Central Authority.

Any translation accompanying a Letter shall be certified as correct, either by a diplomatic officer or consular agent or by a sworn translator or by any other person so authorized in either State.

Article 5

If the Central Authority considers that the request does not comply with the provisions of the present Convention, it shall promptly inform the authority of the State of origin which transmitted the Letter of Request, specifying the objections to the Letter.

Article 6

If the authority to whom a Letter of Request has been transmitted is not competent to execute it, the Letter shall be sent forthwith to the authority in the same State which is competent to execute it in accordance with the provisions of its own law.

Article 7

The requesting authority shall, if it so desires, be informed of the time when, and the place where, the proceedings will take place, in order that the parties concerned, and their representatives, if any, may be present. This information shall be sent directly to the parties or their representatives when the authority of the State of origin so requests.

Article 8

A contracting State may declare that members of the judicial personnel of the requesting authority of another Contracting State may be present at the execution of a Letter of Request. Prior authorization by the competent authority designated by the declaring State may be required.

Article 9

The judicial authority which executes a Letter of Request shall apply its own law as to the methods and procedures to be followed.

However, it will follow a request of the requesting authority that a special method or procedure be followed, unless this is incompatible with the internal law of the State of execution or is impossible of performance by reason of its internal practice and procedure or by reason of practical difficulties.

A Letter of Request shall be executed expeditiously.

Article 10

In executing a Letter of Request the requested authority shall apply the appropriate measures of compulsion in the instances and to the same extent as are provided by its internal law for the execution of orders issued by the authorities of its own country or of requests made by parties in internal proceedings.

Article 11

In the execution of a Letter of Request the person concerned may refuse to give evidence in so far as he has a privilege or duty to refuse to give the evidence —

(a) under the law of the State of execution; or

(b) under the law of the State of origin, and the privilege or duty has been specified in the Letter, or, at the instance of the requested authority, had been otherwise confirmed to that authority by the requesting authority.

A Contracting State may declare that, in addition, it will respect privileges and duties existing under the law of States other than the State of origin and the State of execution, to the extent specified in that declaration.

Article 12

The execution of a Letter of Request may be refused only to the extent that —

(a) in the State of execution the execution of the Letter does not fall within the functions of the judiciary; or

(b) the State addressed considers that its sovereignty or security would be prejudiced thereby.

Execution may not be refused solely on the ground that under its internal law the State of execution claims exclusive jurisdiction over the subject-matter of the action or that its internal law would not admit a right of action on it.

Article 13

The documents establishing the execution of the Letter of Request shall be sent by the requested authority to the requesting authority by the same channel which was used by the latter.

In every instance where the Letter is not executed in whole or in part, the requesting authority shall be informed immediately through the same channel and advised of the reasons.

Article 14

The execution of the Letter of Request shall not give rise to any reimbursement of taxes or costs of any nature.

Nevertheless, the State of execution has the right to require the State of origin to reimburse the fees paid to experts and interpreters and the costs occasioned by the use of a special procedure requested by the State of origin under Article 9, paragraph 2.

The requested authority whose law obliges the parties themselves to secure evidence, and which is not able itself to execute the Letter, may, after having obtained the consent of the requesting authority, appoint a suitable person to do so. When seeking this consent the requested authority shall indicate the approximate costs which would result from this procedure. If the requesting authority gives its consent it shall reimburse any costs incurred; without such consent the requesting authority shall not be liable for the costs.

CHAPTER II-TAKING OF EVIDENCE BY DIPLOMATIC OFFICERS, CONSULAR AGENTS AND COMMISSIONERS

Article 15

In a civil or commercial matter, a diplomatic officer or consular agent of a Contracting State may, in the territory of another Contracting State and within the area where he exercises his functions, take the evidence without compulsion of nationals of a State which he represents in aid of proceedings commenced in the courts of a State which he represents.

A Contracting State may declare that evidence may be taken by a diplomatic officer or consular agent only if permission to that effect is given upon application made by him or on his behalf to the appropriate authority designated by the declaring State.

Article 16

A diplomatic officer or consular agent of a Contracting State may, in the territory of another Contracting State and within the area where he exercises his junctions, also take the evidence, without compulsion, of nationals of the State in which he exercises his functions or of a third State, in aid of proceedings commenced in the courts of a State which he represents, if —

(a) a competent authority designated by the State in which he exercises his functions has given its permission either generally or in the particular case, and

(b) he complies with the conditions which the competent authority has specified in the permission.

A contracting State may declare that evidence may be taken under this Article without its prior permission.

Article 17

In a civil or commercial matter, a person duly appointed as a commissioner for the purpose may, without compulsion, take evidence in the territory of a Contracting State in aid of proceedings commenced in the courts of another Contracting State if —

    (a) a competent authority designated by the State where the evidence is to be taken has given its permission either generally or in the particular case; and

    (b) he complies with the conditions which the competent authority has specified in the permission.

A Contracting State may declare that evidence may be taken under this Article without its prior permission.

Article 18

A Contracting State may declare that a diplomatic officer, consular agent or commissioner authorized to take evidence under Articles 15, 16 or 17, may apply to the competent authority designated by the declaring State for appropriate assistance to obtain the evidence by compulsion. The declaration may contain such conditions as the declaring State may see fit to impose.

If the authority grants the application it shall apply any measures of compulsion which are appropriate and are prescribed by its law for use in internal proceedings.

Article 19

The competent authority, in giving the permission referred to in Articles 15, 16 or 17, or in granting the application referred to in Article 18, may lay down such conditions as it deems fit, *inter alia,* as to the time and place of the taking of the evidence. Similarly it may require that it be given reasonable advance notice of the time, date and place of the taking of the evidence; in such a case a representative of the authority shall be entitled to be present at the taking of the evidence.

Article 20

In the taking of evidence under any Article of this Chapter persons concerned may be legally represented.

Article 21

Where a diplomatic officer, consular agent or commissioner is authorized under Articles 15, 16 or 17 to take evidence

    (a) he may take all kinds of evidence which are not incompatible with the law of the State where the evidence is taken or contrary to any permission granted pursuant to the above Articles, and shall have power within such limits to administer an oath or take an affirmation;

    (b) a request to a person to appear or to give evidence shall, unless the recipient is a national of the State where the action is pending, be drawn up in the language of the place where the evidence is taken or be accompanied by a translation into such language;

    (c) the request shall inform the person that he may be legally represented and, in any State that has not filed a declaration under Article 18, shall also inform him that he is not compelled to appear or to give evidence;

    (d) the evidence may be taken in the manner provided by the law applicable to the court in which the action is pending provided that such manner is not forbidden by the law of the State where the evidence is taken;

    (e) a person requested to give evidence may invoke the privileges and duties to refuse to give the evidence contained in Article 11.

Article 22

The fact that an attempt to take evidence under the procedure laid down in this Chapter has failed, owing to the refusal of a person to give evidence, shall not prevent an application being subsequently made to take the evidence in accordance with Chapter I.

CHAPTER III-GENERAL CLAUSES

Article 23

A Contracting State may at the time of signature, ratification or accession, declare that it will not execute Letters of Request issued for the purpose of obtaining pre-trial discovery of documents as known in Common Law countries.

Article 24

A Contracting State may designate other authorities in addition to the Central Authority and shall determine the extent of their competence. However, Letters of Request may in all cases be sent to the Central Authority.

Federal States shall be free to designate more than one Central Authority.

Article 25

A Contracting State which has more than one legal system may designate the authorities of one of such systems, which shall have exclusive competence to execute Letters of Request pursuant to this Convention.

Article 26

A Contracting State, if required to do so because of constitutional limitations, may request the reimbursement by the State of origin of fees and costs, in connection with the execution of Letters of Request, for the service of process necessary to compel the appearance of a person to give evidence, the costs of attendance of such persons, and the cost of any transcript of the evidence.

Where a State has made a request pursuant to the above paragraph, any other Contracting State may request from that State the reimbursement of similar fees and costs.

Article 27

The provisions of the present Convention shall not prevent a Contracting State from —

(a) declaring that Letters of Request may be transmitted to its judicial authorities through channels other than those provided for in Article 2;

(b) permitting, by internal law or practice, any act provided for in this Convention to be performed upon less restrictive conditions;

(c) permitting, by internal law or practice, methods of taking evidence other than those provided for in this Convention.

Article 28

The present Convention shall not prevent an agreement between any two or more Contracting States to derogate from

(a) the provisions of Article 2 with respect to methods of transmitting Letters of Request;

(b) the provisions of Article 4 with respect to the languages which may be used;

(c) the provisions of Article 8 with respect to the presence of judicial personnel at the execution of Letters;

(d) the provisions of Article 11 with respect to the privileges and duties of witnesses to refuse to give evidence;

(e) the provisions of Article 13 with respect to the methods of returning executed Letters to the requesting authority;

(f) the provisions of Article 14 with respect to fees and costs;

(g) the provisions of Chapter II.

Article 29

Between Parties to the present Convention who are also Parties to one or both of the Conventions on Civil Procedure signed at the Hague on the 17th July 1905 and the 1st of March 1954, this Convention shall replace Articles 8-16 of the earlier Conventions.

Article 30

The present Convention shall not affect the application of Article 23 of the Convention of 1905, or of Article 24 of the Convention of 1954.

Article 31

Supplementary Agreements between Parties to the Conventions of 1905 and 1954 shall be considered as equally applicable to the present Convention unless the Parties have otherwise agreed.

Article 32

Without prejudice to the provisions of Article 29 and 31, the present Convention shall not derogate from conventions containing provisions on the matters covered by this Convention to which the Contracting States are, or shall become Parties.

Article 33

A State may, at the time of signature, ratification or accession exclude, in whole or in part, the application of the provisions of paragraph 2 of Article 4 and of Chapter II. No other reservation shall be permitted.

Each Contracting State may at any time withdraw a reservation it has made; the reservation shall cease to have effect on the sixtieth day after notification of the withdrawal.

When a State has made a reservation, any other State affected thereby may apply the same rule against the reserving State.

Article 34

A State may at any time withdraw or modify a declaration.

Article 35

A Contracting State shall, at the time of the deposit of its instrument of ratification or accession, or at a later date, inform the Ministry of Foreign Affairs of the Netherlands of the designation of authorities, pursuant to Articles 2, 8, 24 and 25.

A Contracting State shall likewise inform the Ministry, where appropriate, of the following —

(a) the designation of the authorities to whom notice must be given, whose permission may be required, and whose assistance may be invoked in the taking of evidence by diplomatic officers and consular agents, pursuant to Articles 15, 16, and 18 respectively;

(b) the designation of the authorities whose permission may be required in the taking of evidence by commissioners pursuant to Article 17 and of those who may grant the assistance provided for in Article 18;

(c) declarations pursuant to Articles 4, 8, 11, 15, 16, 17, 18, 23 and 27;

(d) any withdrawal or modification of the above designations and declarations;

(e) the withdrawal of any reservation.

Article 36

Any difficulties which may arise between Contracting States in connection with the operation of this Convention shall be settled through diplomatic channels.

Article 37

The present Convention shall be open for signature by the States represented at the Eleventh Session of the Hague Conference on Private International Law.

It shall be ratified, and the instruments of ratification shall be deposited with the Ministry of Foreign Affairs of the Netherlands.

Article 38

The present Convention shall enter into force on the sixtieth day after the deposit of the third instrument of ratification referred to in the second paragraph of Article 37.

The convention shall enter into force for each signatory State which ratifies subsequently on the sixtieth day after the deposit of its instrument of ratification.

Article 39

Any State not represented at the Eleventh Session of the Hague Conference on Private International Law which is a Member of this Conference or of the United Nations or of a specialized agency of that Organization, or a Party to the Statute of the International Court of Justice may accede to the present Convention after it has entered into force in accordance with the first paragraph of Article 38.

The instrument of accession shall be deposited with the Ministry of Foreign Affairs of the Netherlands.

The Convention shall enter into force for a State acceding to it on the sixtieth day after the deposit of its instrument of accession.

The accession will have effect only as regards the relations between the acceding State and such Contracting States as will have declared their acceptance of the accession. Such declaration shall be deposited at the Ministry of Foreign Affairs of the Netherlands; this Ministry shall forward, through diplomatic channels, a certified copy to each of the Contracting States.

The Convention will enter into force as between the acceding State and the State that has declared its acceptance of the accession on the sixtieth day after the deposit of the declaration of acceptance.

Article 40

Any State may, at the time of signature, ratification or accession, declare that the present Convention shall extend to all the territories for the international relations of which it is responsible, or to one or more of them. Such a declaration shall take effect on the date of entry into force of the Convention for the State concerned.

At any time thereafter, such extensions shall be notified to the Ministry of Foreign Affairs of the Netherlands.

The Convention shall enter into force for the territories mentioned in such an extension on the sixtieth day after the notification indicated in the preceding paragraph.

Article 41

The present Convention shall remain in force for five years from the date of its entry into force in accordance with the first paragraph of Article 38, even for States which have ratified it or acceded to it subsequently.

If there has been no denunciation, it shall be renewed tacitly every five years.

Any denunciation shall be notified to the Ministry of Foreign Affairs of the Netherlands at least six months before the end of the five year period.

It may be limited to certain of the territories to which the Convention applies.

The denunciation shall have effect only as regards the State which has notified it. The Convention shall remain in force for the other Contracting States.

The Minister of Foreign Affairs of the Netherlands shall give notice to the States referred to in Article 37; and to the States which have acceded in accordance with Article 39, of the following —

    (a) the signatures and ratifications referred to in Article 37,

    (b) the date on which the present Convention enters into force in accordance with the first paragraph of Article 38;

    (c) the accessions referred to in Article 39 and the dates on which they take effect;

    (d) the extensions referred to in Article 40 and the dates on which they take effect;

    (e) the designations, reservations and declarations referred to in Articles 33 and 35;

    (f) the denunciations referred to in the third paragraph of Article 41.

In WITNESS WHEREOF the undersigned, being duly authorised thereto, have signed the present Convention.

DONE at The Hague, on the 18th day of March 1970, in the English and French languages, both texts being equally authentic, in a single copy which shall be deposited in the archives of the Government of the Netherlands, and of which a certified copy shall be sent, through the diplomatic channel, to each of the States represented at the Eleventh Session of the Hague Conference on Private International Law.

Appendix L:
Declarations Concerning Hague Evidence Convention

Argentina

The Argentine Republic totally excludes the application of the provisions of paragraph 2 of Article 4, as well as those of Chapter II.

The Argentine Republic will not execute Letters of Request issued for the purpose of obtaining pre-trial discovery of documents as known in the Common Law Countries.

The Argentine Republic excludes the extension of the application of the Convention to the Malvinas, South Georgia, and South Sandwich Islands, which was notified by the United Kingdom of Great Britain and Northern Ireland to the Ministry of Foreign Affairs of the Kingdom of the Netherlands on November 23, 1979, and reaffirms its rights of sovereignty over the Malvinas, South Georgia and South Sandwich Islands, which form an integral part of its national territory.

The Argentine Republic excludes the June 19, 1986 approval formulated by the United Kingdom of Great Britain and Northern Ireland for the Malvinas, South Georgia and South Sandwich Islands with respect to the accession of the Principality of Monaco to the aforementioned Convention.

Denmark

1) Availing itself of the provisions laid down in Article 33, the Danish Government hereby declares, in accordance with Article 4, that Denmark will not accept Letters of Request which are sent in French.

2) Availing itself of the provisions laid down in Article 33, the Danish Government hereby declares, in accordance with Article 17, that Denmark will not accept the taking of evidence by commissioners.

Article 2

The Ministry of Justice is hereby designated as Central Authority.

Article 4

Letters of Request may be sent in Norwegian and Swedish, and Denmark accepts no obligation to return evidence taken in other languages than Danish.

Article 8

Members of the judicial personnel of the requesting authority of another contracting State may be present at the execution of a Letter of Request if they have obtained prior authorization from the competent Danish authority.

Article 15

A diplomatic officer or consular agent may take evidence if he has been authorized to do so by the Ministry of Justice.

Article 16

The Ministry of Justice will issue authorizations to take evidence.

Article 23

Letters of Request issued for the purpose of obtaining pre-trial discovery of documents may not be executed in Denmark.

Article 27a

As has been the case hitherto, Letters of Request may be transmitted directly to the competent Danish court by the consular agents of foreign States.

Additional declaration of July 23, 1980:

The declaration made by the Kingdom of Denmark in accordance with article 23 concerning 'Letters of Request issued for the purpose of obtaining pre-trial discovery of documents' shall apply to any Letter of Request which requires a person:

a) to state what documents relevant to the proceedings to which the Letter of Request relates are, or have been in his possession, other than particular documents specified in the Letter of Request; or

b) to produce any documents other than particular documents which are specified in the Letter of Request, and which are likely to be in his possession.

France

With respect to the first paragraph of Article 40 of the Convention, France declares that the Convention shall apply to all the Territory of the French Republic.

In conformity with Article 33, the French Government declares:

That, in application of the second paragraph of Article 4, it will execute only Letters in French or accompanied by a translation in French.

That, pursuant to Article 23, it will not execute Letters of Request issued for the purpose of obtaining pre-trial discovery of documents as known in Common Law countries;

In conformity with Article 2, the Ministry of Justice, Civil Division of International Judicial Assistance, 13 Place Vendome, Paris (ler), is designated as the Central Authority to the exclusion of any other authority.

In conformity with Article 16, the Ministry of Justice, Civil Division of International Judicial Assistance, 13 Place Vendome, Paris (ler), is designated as the competent authority to give permission to diplomatic officers or consular agents of a Contracting State to take the evidence, without compulsion, of persons other than nationals of that State in aid of proceedings commenced in the courts of a State which they represent.

That permission, which shall be given for each specific case and shall be accompanied by special conditions when appropriate, shall be granted under the following general conditions:

1. Evidence shall be taken only within the confines of the Embassies or Consulates;

2. The date and time of taking the evidence shall be notified in due time to the Civil Division of International Judicial Assistance so that it may have the opportunity to be represented at the proceedings;

3. Evidence shall be taken in premises accessible to the public;

4. Persons requested to give evidence shall be served with an official instrument in French or accompanied by a translation into French, and that instrument shall mention:

a. That evidence is being taken in conformity with the provisions of the Convention and relates to legal proceedings pending before a jurisdiction specifically designated by a Contracting State;

b. That appearance is voluntary and failure to appear will not give rise to criminal proceedings in the State of origin;

c. That the parties of the trial are consenting or, if not, the grounds of their objections;

d. That in the taking of evidence the person concerned may be legally represented;

e. That a person requested to give evidence may invoke a privilege or duty to refuse to give evidence. A copy of these requests shall be transmitted to the Ministry of Justice.

5. The Civil Division of International Judicial Assistance shall be kept informed of any difficulties.

In conformity with Article 17, the Ministry of Justice, Civil Division of International Judicial Assistance, 13 Place Vendome, Paris (ler), is appointed as the competent authority to give permission to persons duly appointed as commissioners to proceed, without compulsion, to take any evidence in aid of proceedings commenced in the courts of a Contracting State.

This permission, which shall be given for each specific case and shall be accompanied by special conditions when appropriate, shall be granted under the following general conditions:

1. Evidence shall be taken only within the Embassy confines of the Embassies of Consulates:

2. The date and time of taking the evidence shall be notified in due time to the Civil Division of International Judicial Assistance so that it may have the opportunity to be represented at the proceedings;

3. Evidence shall be taken in premises accessible to the public;

4. Persons requested to give evidence shall be served with an official instrument in French or accompanied by a translation into French, and that instrument shall mention:

a. That evidence is being taken in conformity with the provisions of the Convention and relates to legal proceedings pending before a jurisdiction specifically designated by a Contracting State;

b. That appearance is voluntary and failure to appear will not give rise to criminal proceedings in the State of origin;

c. That the parties to the trial are consenting or, if not, the grounds of their objections;

d. That in the taking of evidence the person concerned may be legally represented;

e. That a person requested to give evidence may invoke the privilege and duty to refuse to give evidence.

A copy of these requests shall be transmitted to the Ministry of Justice.

5. The Civil Division of International Judicial Assistance shall be kept informed of any difficulty.

The request for permission transmitted by the requesting authority to the Ministry of Justice shall specify:

1. The motives that led to choosing this method of taking evidence in preference to that of a Letter of Request, considering the judiciary costs incurred;

2. The criteria for appointing commissioners when the person appointed does not reside in France.

The French Government declares that, in the application of Article 8, members of the judicial personnel of the requesting authority of a Contracting State may be present at the execution of a Letter of Request.

United Kingdom

...In accordance with the provisions of Article 33 the United Kingdom will not accept a Letter of Request in French.

1. In accordance with Article 8 Her Majesty's Government declare that members of the judicial personnel of the requesting authority may be present at the execution of a Letter of Request.

2. In accordance with Article 18 Her Majesty's Government declare that a diplomatic officer, consular agent or commissioner authorised to take evidence under Articles 15, 16 and 17 may apply to the competent authority designated hereinbefore for appropriate assistance to obtain such evidence by compulsion provided that the Contracting State whose diplomatic officer, consular agent or commissioner makes the application has made a declaration affording reciprocal facilities under Article 18.

3. In accordance with Article 23 Her Majesty's Government declare that the United Kingdom will not execute Letters of Request issued for the purpose of obtaining pre-trial discovery of documents. Her Majesty's Government further declare that Her Majesty's Government understand 'Letters of Request issued for the purpose of obtaining pre-trial discovery of documents' for the purposes of the foregoing Declaration as including any Letter of Request which requires a person:

a. to state what documents relevant to the proceedings to which the Letter of Request relates are, or have been, in his possession, custody, or power; or

b. to produce any documents other than particular documents specified in the Letter of Request as being documents appearing to the requesting court to be, or to be likely to be, in his possession, custody or power.

4. In accordance with Article 27 Her Majesty's Government declare that by the law and practice of the United Kingdom the prior permission referred to in Articles 16 and 17 is not required in respect of diplomatic officers, consular agents or commissioners of a Contracting State which does not require permission to be obtained for the purposes of taking evidence under Articles 16 and 17.

In accordance with Article 35 of the Convention, the Government of the United Kingdom made the following designations:

1. Under Article 2: the Foreign and Commonwealth Office.

2. Under Article 16: the Foreign and Commonwealth Office.

3. Under Article 17: The Foreign and Commonwealth Office.

4. Under Article 18: the Senior Master of the Supreme Court (Queen's Bench Division) for England and Wales; the Crown Agent for Scotland, for Scotland; the Registrar of the Supreme Court of Northern Ireland, for Northern Ireland.

5. Under Article 24: the Senior Master of the Supreme Court (Queen's Bench Division) for England and Wales; the Crown Agent for Scotland, for Scotland; the Registrar of the Supreme Court of Northern Ireland in Northern Ireland.

c) Under Article 24 of the Convention, His Excellency the Governor is designated as an additional authority competent to receive Letters of Request for execution in the Cayman Islands.

1. In accordance with Article 8, members of the judicial personnel of the requesting authority may be present at the execution of a Letter of Request in the Cayman Islands.

2. In accordance with Article 18, a diplomatic officer, consular agent or commissioner authorized to take evidence under Article 15, 16 and 17 of the Convention may apply to the competent authority in the Cayman Islands designated hereinbefore for appropriate assistance to obtain such evidence by compulsion provided that the Contracting State whose diplomatic officer, consular agent or commissioner makes the application has made a declaration affording reciprocal facilities under Article 18.

3. In accordance with Article 23, the Cayman Islands will not execute Letters of Request issued for the purpose of obtaining pre-trial discovery of documents. The Government of the Cayman Islands understand "Letters of Request issued for the purpose of obtaining pre-trial discovery of documents" for the purposes of the foregoing declaration as including any Letter of Request which requires a person:

a) to state what documents relevant to the proceedings to which the Letter of Request relates are, or have been, in his possession, custody or power; or

b) to produce any documents other than particular documents specified in the Letter of Request as being documents appearing to the requested court to be, or likely to be, in his possession, custody or power.

4. In accordance with Article 27, by the law and practice of the Cayman Islands the prior permission referred to in Articles 16 and 17 of the Convention is not required in respect of diplomatic officers, consular agents or commissioners of a Contracting State which does not require permission to be obtained for the purposes of taking evidence under Article 16 or 17.

United States of America

The United States Department of Justice, Washington, D.C., 20530, is designated as the Central Authority referred to in Article 2 of the Convention.

Under paragraph 2 of Article 4 of the Convention the United States have agreed to accept a Letter of Request in or translated into French. The United States wishes to point out that owing to the necessity of translating such documents into English it will take the Central Authority longer to comply with a Letter of Request in or translated into French than with a similar request received in English.

In accordance with paragraph 3 of Article 4 the United States declares that it will also accept Letters of Request in Spanish for execution in the Commonwealth of Puerto Rico.

In accordance with Article 8 the United States declares that subject to prior authorization members of the judicial personnel of the requesting authority of another Contracting State may be present at the execution of a Letter of Request. The Department of Justice is the competent authority for the purposes of this Article.

The United States declares that evidence may be taken in the United States under Articles 16 and 17 without its prior permission.

In accordance with Article 18 the United States declares that a diplomatic or consular officer or a commissioner authorized to take evidence under Articles 15, 16 or 17 may apply for appropriate assistance to obtain the evidence by compulsion. The competent authority for the purposes of Article 18 is the United States district court of the district in which a person resides or is found. Such court may order him to give his testimony or statement or to produce a document or thing for use in a proceeding in a foreign tribunal. The order may direct that the testimony or statement be given, or the document or other thing be produced, before a person appointed by the court.

In accordance with Article 40 the United States declares that the Convention shall extend to Guam, Puerto Rico and the Virgin Islands.

Appendix M:
Uniform Foreign Money-Judgments
Recognition Act—1962

§1. Definitions. As used in this Act:

(1) *"foreign state"* means any governmental unit other than the United States, or any state, district, commonwealth, territory, insular possession thereof, or the Panama Canal zone, the Trust Territory of the Pacific Islands, or the Ryukyu Islands;

(2) "foreign judgment" means any judgment of a foreign state granting or denying recovery of a sum of money, other than a judgment for taxes, a fine or other penalty, or a judgment for support in matrimonial or family matters.

§2. Applicability. This Act applies to any foreign judgment that is final and conclusive and enforceable where rendered even though an appeal therefrom is pending or it is subject to appeal.

§3. Recognition and Enforcement. Except as provided in section 4, a foreign judgment meeting the requirements of section 2 is conclusive between the parties to the extent that it grants or denies recovery of a sum of money. The foreign judgment is enforceable in the same manner as the judgment of a sister state which is entitled to full faith and credit.

§4. Grounds for Non-recognition. (a) A foreign judgment is not conclusive if

(1) the judgment was rendered under a system which does not provide impartial tribunals or procedures compatible with the requirements of due process of law;

(2) the foreign court did not have personal jurisdiction over the defendant; or

(3) the foreign court did not have jurisdiction over the subject matter.

(b) A foreign judgment need not be recognized if

(1) the defendant in the proceedings in the foreign court did not receive notice of the proceedings in sufficient time to enable him to defend;

(2) the judgment was obtained by fraud;

(3) the [cause of action] [claim for relief] on which the judgment is based is repugnant to the public policy of this state;

(4) the judgment conflicts with another final and conclusive judgment;

(5) the proceeding in the foreign court was contrary to an agreement between the parties under which the dispute in question was to be settled otherwise than by proceedings in that court; or

(6) in the case of jurisdiction based only on personal service, the foreign court was a seriously inconvenient forum for the trial of the action.

§5. Personal Jurisdiction. (a) The foreign judgment shall not be refused recognition for lack of personal jurisdiction if

(1) the defendant was served personally in the foreign state;

(2) the defendant voluntarily appeared in the proceedings, other than for the purpose of protecting property seized or threatened with seizure in the proceedings or of contesting the jurisdiction of the court over him;

(3) the defendant prior to the commencement of the proceedings had agreed to submit to the jurisdiction of the foreign court with respect to the subject matter involved;

(4) the defendant was domiciled in the foreign state when the proceedings were instituted, or, being a body corporate had its principal place of business, was incorporated, or had otherwise acquired corporate status, in the foreign state;

(5) the defendant had a business office in the foreign state and the proceedings in the foreign court involved a [cause of action] [claim for relief] arising out of business done by the defendant through that office in the foreign state; or

(6) the defendant operated a motor vehicle or airplane in the foreign state and the proceedings involved a [cause of action] [claim for relief] arising out of such operation.

(b) The courts of this state may recognize other bases of jurisdiction.

§6. Stay in Case of Appeal. If the defendant satisfies the court either that an appeal is pending or that he is entitled and intends to appeal from the foreign judgment, the court may stay the proceedings until the appeal has been determined or until the expiration of a period of time sufficient to enable the defendant to prosecute the appeal.

§7. Saving Clause. This Act does not prevent the recognition of a foreign judgment in situations not covered by this Act.

§8. Uniformity of Interpretation. This Act shall be so construed as to effectuate its general purpose to make uniform the law of those states which enact it.

§9. Short Title. This Act may be cited as the Uniform Foreign Money-Judgments Recognition Act.

Appendix N:
United Nations Convention on Recognition and Enforcement of Foreign Arbitral Awards

Article I

1. This Convention shall apply to the recognition and enforcement of arbitral awards made in the territory of a State other than the State where the recognition and enforcement of such awards are sought, and arising out of differences between persons, whether physical or legal. It shall also apply to arbitral awards not considered as domestic awards in the State where their recognition and enforcement are sought.

2. The term "arbitral awards" shall include not only awards made by arbitrators appointed for each case but also those made by permanent arbitral bodies to which the parties have submitted.

3. When signing, ratifying or acceding to this Convention, or notifying extension under Article X hereof, any State may on the basis of reciprocity declare that it will apply the Convention to the recognition and enforcement of awards made only in the territory of another Contracting State. It may also declare that it will apply the Convention only to differences arising out of legal relationships, whether contractual or not, which are considered as commercial under the national law of the State making such declaration.

Article II

1. Each Contracting State shall recognize an agreement in writing under which the parties undertake to submit to arbitration all or any differences which have arisen or which may arise between them in respect of a defined legal relationship, whether contractual or not, concerning a subject matter capable of settlement by arbitration.

2. The term "agreement in writing" shall include an arbitral clause in a contract or an arbitration agreement, signed by the parties or contained in an exchange of letters or telegrams.

3. The court of a Contracting State, when seized of an action in a matter in respect of which the parties have made an agreement within the meaning of this article, shall, at the request of one of the parties, refer the parties to arbitration, unless it finds that the said agreement is null and void, inoperative or incapable of being performed.

Article III

Each Contracting State shall recognize arbitral awards as binding and enforce them in accordance with the rules of procedure of the territory where the award is relied upon, under the conditions laid down in the following articles. There shall not be imposed substantially more onerous conditions or higher fees or charges on the recognition or enforcement of arbitral awards to which this Convention applies than are imposed on the recognition or enforcement of domestic arbitral awards.

Article IV

1. To obtain the recognition and enforcement mentioned in the preceding article, the party applying for recognition and enforcement shall, at the time of application, supply:

    (a) The duly authenticated original award or a duly certified copy thereof;

    (b) The original agreement referred to in Article II or a duly certified copy thereof.

2. If the said award or agreement is not made in an official language of the country in which the award is relied upon, the party applying for recognition and enforcement of the award shall produce a translation of these documents into such language. The translation shall be certified by an official or sworn translator or by a diplomatic or consular agent.

Article V

1. Recognition and enforcement of the award may be refused, at the request of the party against whom it is invoked, only if that party furnishes to the competent authority where the recognition and enforcement is sought, proof that:

(a) The parties to the agreement referred to in Article II were, under the law applicable to them, under some incapacity, or the said agreement is not valid under the law to which the parties have subjected it or, failing any indication thereon, under the law of the country where the award was made; or

(b) the party against whom the award is invoked was not given proper notice of the appointment of the arbitrator or of the arbitration proceedings or was otherwise unable to present his case; or

(c) The award deals with a difference not contemplated by or not falling within the terms of the submission to arbitration, or it contains decisions on matters beyond the scope of the submission to arbitration, provided that, if the decisions on matters submitted to arbitration can be separated from those not so submitted, that part of the award which contains decisions on matters submitted to arbitration may be recognized and enforced; or

(d) The composition of the arbitral authority or the arbitral procedure was not in accordance with the agreement of the parties, or, failing such agreement, was not in accordance with the law of the country where the arbitration took place; or

(e) The award has not yet become binding on the parties or has been set aside or suspended by a competent authority of the country in which, or under the law of which, that award was made.

3. Recognition and enforcement of an arbitral award may also be refused if the competent authority in the country where recognition and enforcement is sought finds that:

(a) The subject matter of the difference is not capable of settlement by arbitration under the law of that country; or

(b) The recognition or enforcement of the award would be contrary to the public policy of that country.

Article VI

If an application for the setting aside or suspension of the award has been made to a competent authority referred to in Article V(1)(e), the authority before which the award is sought to be relied upon may, if it considers it proper, adjourn the decision on the enforcement of the award and may also, on the application of the party claiming enforcement of the award, order the other party to give suitable security.

Article VII

1. The provisions of the present Convention shall not affect the validity of multilateral or bilateral agreements concerning the recognition and enforcement of arbitral awards entered into by the Contracting States nor deprive any interested party of any right he may have to avail himself of an arbitral award in the manner and to the extent allowed by the law or the treaties of the country where such award is sought to be relied upon.

2. The Geneva Protocol on Arbitration Clauses of 1923 and the Geneva Convention on the Execution of Foreign Arbitral Awards of 1927 shall cease to have effect between Contracting States on their becoming bound and to the extent that they become bound, by this Convention.

Article VIII

1. This Convention shall be open until 31 December 1958 for signature on behalf of any Member of the United Nations and also on behalf of any other State which is or hereafter becomes a member of any specialized agency of the United Nations, or which is or hereafter becomes a party to the Statute of the International Court of Justice, or any other State to which an invitation has been addressed by the General Assembly of the United Nations.

2. This Convention shall be ratified and the instrument of ratification shall be deposited with the Secretary-General of the United Nations.

Article IX

1. This Convention shall be open for accession to all States referred to in Article VIII.

2. Accession shall be effected by the deposit of an instrument of accession with the Secretary-General of the United Nations.

Article X

1. Any State may, at the time of signature, ratification or accession, declare that this Convention shall extend to all or any of the territories for the international relations of which it is responsible. Such a declaration shall take effect when the Convention enters into force for the State concerned.

2. At any time thereafter any such extension shall be made by notification addressed to the Secretary-General of the United Nations and shall take effect as from the ninetieth day after the day of receipt by the Secretary-General of the United Nations of this notification, or as from the date of entry into force of the Convention of State concerned, whichever is the later.

3. With respect to those territories to which this Convention is not extended at the time of signature, ratification or accession, each State concerned shall consider the possibility of taking the necessary steps in order to extend the application of this Convention to such territories, subject, where necessary for constitutional reasons, to the consent of the Governments of such territories.

Article XI

In the case of a federal or non-unitary State, the following provisions shall apply:

(a) With respect to those articles of this Convention that come within the legislative jurisdiction of the federal authority, the obligations of the federal Government shall to this extent be the same as those of Contracting States which are not federal States;

(b) With respect to those articles of this Convention that come within the legislative jurisdiction of constituent states or provinces which are not, under the constitutional system of the federation, bound to take legislative action, the federal Government shall bring such articles with a favourable recommendation to the notice of the appropriate authorities of constituent states or provinces at the earliest possible moment;

(c) A federal State Party to this Convention shall, at the request of any other Contracting State transmitted through the Secretary-General of the United Nations, supply a statement of the law and practice of the federation and its constituent units in regard to any particular provision of this Convention, showing the extent to which effect has been given to that provision by legislative or other action.

Article XII

1. This Convention shall come into force on the ninetieth day following the date of deposit of the third instrument of ratification or accession.

2. For each State ratifying or acceding to this Convention after the deposit of the third instrument of ratification or accession, this Convention shall enter into force on the ninetieth day after deposit by such State of its instrument of ratification or accession.

Article XIII

1. Any Contracting State may denounce this Convention by a written notification to the Secretary-General of the United Nations. Denunciation shall take effect one year after the date of receipt of the notification by the Secretary-General.

2. Any State which has made a declaration or notification under Article X may, at any time thereafter, by notification to the Secretary-General of the United Nations, declare that this Convention shall cease to extend to the territory concerned one year after the date of the receipt of the notification by the Secretary-General.

3. This Convention shall continue to be applicable to arbitral awards in respect of which recognition or enforcement proceedings have been instituted before the denunciation takes effect.

Article XIV

A Contracting State shall not be entitled to avail itself of the present Convention against other Contracting States except to the extent that it is itself bound to apply the Convention.

Article XV

The Secretary-General of the United Nations shall notify the States contemplated in Article VIII of the following:

(a) Signatures and ratifications in accordance with Article VIII;

(b) Accessions in accordance with Article IX;

(c) Declarations and notifications under Articles I, X, and XI;

(d) The date upon which this Convention enters into force in accordance with Article XII;

(e) Denunciations and notifications in accordance with Article XIII.

Article XVI

1. This Convention, of which the Chinese, English, French, Russian and Spanish texts shall be equally authentic, shall be deposited in the archives of the United Nations.

2. The Secretary-General of the United Nations shall transmit a certified copy of this Convention to the States contemplated in Article VIII.

INDEX

ALIENS
(*see CITIZENSHIP, DOMICILE, NATIONALITY, and RESIDENCE*)

COMITY

CONFLICT OF JURISDICTION MODEL ACT

CURRIE, BRAINERD

DOMICILE

EFFECTS DOCTRINE

(*see LEGISLATIVE JURISDICTION and CHOICE OF LAW*)

ENFORCEMENT OF FOREIGN JUDGMENTS

FEDERAL QUESTION JURISDICTION 33-66

FOREIGN GOVERNMENTS

FOREIGN JUDGMENTS

FOREIGN SOVEREIGN COMPULSION DOCTRINE 745-52

FOREIGN SOVEREIGN IMMUNITY

FOREIGN TRADE ANTITRUST IMPROVEMENTS ACT

FORUM NON CONVENIENS

INTERNATIONAL AGREEMENTS

INTERNATIONAL LAW

POLITICAL QUESTION DOCTRINE 45-46, 702

PUBLIC LAWS 354, 629-30, 955-60

PROTECTION OF TRADING INTERESTS ACT (U.K.)...................587

PUBLIC POLICY

REVENUE RULE 354, 629-30, 955-60

SECURITIES ACTIONS

SEPARABILITY

SERVICE OF PROCESS

TREATIES

UNIFORM FOREIGN MONEY JUDGMENTS RECOGNITION ACT......941-42

VENUE 367-69

WAIVER